THE COLLECTED LETTERS OF C. S. LEWIS

VOLUME II

Books, Broadcasts, and the War, 1931–1949

EDITED BY WALTER HOOPER

HarperSanFrancisco

A Division of HarperCollins*Publishers*

On the cover: Background C. S. Lewis handwriting image supplied by the Marion E. Wade Center, Wheaton College, Wheaton, IL.

HarperCollins books may be purchased for educational, business, or sales promotional use. For information please write: Special Markets Department, HarperCollins Publishers, 10 East 53rd Street, New York, NY 10022.

HarperCollins Web site: http://www.harpercollins.com

HarperCollins®, ®, and HarperSanFrancisco™ are trademarks of HarperCollins Publishers.

PREVIOUSLY PUBLISHED AS A HARDCOVER EDITION IN 2004

Library of Congress Cataloging-in-Publication Data is available.

ISBN-13: 978–0–06–088332–4
ISBN-10: 0–06–088332–4

05 06 07 08 09 RRD(H) 10 9 8 7 6 5 4 3 2 1

THE COLLECTED LETTERS OF
C. S. LEWIS

VOLUME II

BOOKS BY C. S. LEWIS

AVAILABLE FROM HARPERSANFRANCISCO

Mere Christianity

Mere Christianity Journal

The Screwtape Letters (with "Screwtape Proposes a Toast")

Miracles

The Abolition of Man

The Great Divorce

The Problem of Pain

The Weight of Glory

A Grief Observed

George MacDonald: An Anthology

A Year With C. S. Lewis

The Collected Letters of C. S. Lewis Volume I

ALSO AVAILABLE FROM HARPERCOLLINS

The Chronicles of Narnia:

The Magician's Nephew

The Lion, the Witch and the Wardrobe

The Horse and His Boy

Prince Caspian

The Voyage of the Dawn Treader

The Silver Chair

The Last Battle

CONTENTS

Preface vii
Abbreviations xix

Letters:
1931 1
1932 33
1933 94
1934 131
1935 153
1936 176
1937 209
1938 221
1939 238
1940 316
1941 458
1942 506
1943 545
1944 600
1945 635
1946 696
1947 752
1948 826
1949 902

Biographical Appendix 1015
Index 1087

PREFACE

'I have just passed on from believing in God to definitely believing in Christ – in Christianity.'[1] C. S. Lewis had been an atheist for twenty years, and this was news his boyhood friend Arthur Greeves longed to hear. Arthur pressed him for details, and in the letter of 18 October 1931 with which Volume I of the *Collected Letters of C. S. Lewis* closed, Lewis described his momentous evening on 19 September when J. R. R. Tolkien and Hugo Dyson dined with him at Magdalen. They strolled through Addison's Walk and then sat in Lewis's rooms until 4 a.m. talking about Christianity and its relation to myth. 'The story of Christ,' Lewis concluded, 'is simply a *true myth*: a myth working on us in the same way as the others, but with this tremendous difference that it *really happened*.'[2]

This second volume of letters begins at that point, and the reader soon discovers what a 'tremendous difference' conversion to Christianity made in Lewis. In the *Family Letters* Lewis was struggling to find his voice as a poet; in the letters included in this volume he had, it seems, found many voices. He writes on such a wide range of subjects that some readers will wonder if, perhaps, there was more than one C. S. Lewis.

Owen Barfield,[3] the intimate friend whose letters from Lewis run through all three volumes, suggested that there was indeed more than one Lewis. In a piece entitled 'The Five C. S. Lewises' Barfield wrote:

> *A fairly unsophisticated person who had never had any personal contract with Lewis, but who . . . had read the whole or most of what has been written about him, might be pardoned for wondering if it were not one writer, but three, with whom he was*

1 *CL* I, letter to Arthur Greeves of 1 October 1931, p. 974.
2 ibid., letter to Arthur Greeves of 18 October 1931, p. 977.
3 See Owen Barfield in the **Biographical Appendix** to *CL* I, pp. 979–82.

> *becoming acquainted: three men who just happened to have the same name and the same peculiar vigor of thought and utterance. Such a reader (I will venture to put myself in his shoes) might, to avoid confusion, adopt the nomenclature L1, L2, and L3, L1 being a distinguished and original literary critic, L2 a highly successful author of fiction, and L3 the writer and broadcaster of popular Christian apologetics.*[4]

Barfield went on to point out that one of the first things the 'unsophisticated person' would notice is that, while admirers of Lewis the Original Literary Critic usually have little interest in the Lewis the Christian Apologist, readers of both Lewis the Original Literary Critic and Lewis the Christian Apologist *are* interested in Lewis the Writer of Fiction. Another thing such a person would notice, said Barfield, is that Lewis the Original Literary Critic has received much less attention than the other two Lewises, and that it would hardly be too much to say that the Literary Critic has been 'swamped' by the Apologist and the Writer of Fiction.

The other two Lewises mentioned by Owen Barfield are 'the one before and the other after his conversion'.[5] Given that Lewis was now a Christian, how were these four remaining Lewises related? Again I turn to Owen Barfield who knew them longer and probably thought more about them than anyone:

> *The unity* of all these Lewises is to my feeling as impressive, or even more impressive, than their diversity. Others, of course, have drawn attention to it, but I am not sure that anyone has succeeded in locating it. Some have pointed to his 'style,' but it goes deeper than that. 'Consistency?' Noticeable enough in spite of an occasional inconsistency here or there. His unswerving 'sincerity' then? That comes much nearer, but still does not satisfy me. Many other writers are sincere – but they are not Lewis. No. There was something in the whole quality and structure of his thinking, something for which the best label I

4 'The Five C. S. Lewises', Owen Barfield on C. S. Lewis, ed. G. B. Tennyson (Middletown, Connecticut: Wesleyan University Press, 1989), pp. 120–1.

5 ibid., p. 121.

> can find is 'presence of mind.' If I were asked to expand on that, I could say only that somehow what he thought about everything was secretly present in what he said about anything.[6]

While all but the last three letters in Volume I were written by the unconverted Lewis, those in Volume II were written by the convert.

As it turns out, the neglected Original Literary Critic is the first C. S. Lewis to appear in this volume. Lewis would have considered it unconscionable to use his tutorials, lectures and letters as a pulpit for his Christian beliefs, but his conversion to the Faith certainly made a difference, not least to the book he began writing in 1928 and which was published in 1936 as *The Allegory of Love: A Study of Medieval Tradition*. 'A believed idea,' he said, '*feels* different from an idea that is not believed.'[7] Or, as he observed in 29 January 1941 to Mary Neylan, once his pupil, 'One of the minor rewards of conversion is to be able to see at last the real point of all the old literature which we are brought up to read with the point left out!'[8]

Shortly before *The Allegory of Love* was published, Oxford University Press had announced that it was undertaking the production of The Oxford History of English Literature in twelve volumes, each the work of a single author. Lewis was persuaded to write the volume on the sixteenth century and although *English Literature in the Sixteenth Century, Excluding Drama* would not be published until 1954, he was labouring over this magisterial work during most of the years the letters in this volume were being written. 'When they asked me to do that,' he told one of his students, 'I was tremendously flattered. It's like a girl committing herself to marrying an elderly millionaire who's also a duke. In the end she finally has to settle down with the chap, and it's a hellish long time before he dies.'[9]

The next Lewis to appear is Barfield's Highly Successful Author of Fiction. This volume contains many letters Lewis wrote in response to the wide appeal of his interplanetary trilogy, *Out of the Silent Planet*

---

6 ibid., pp. 121–2.

7 'Is Theology Poetry?' *Screwtape Proposes a Toast and Other Pieces* (London: 1965; Fount, 1998), p. 37.

8 Letter to Mary Neylan, 29 January 1941, in this volume.

9 Charles Wrong, 'A Chance Meeting', *C. S. Lewis at the Breakfast Table and Other Reminiscences*, ed. James T. Como (1979; new edn, 1992), pp. 109–10.

(1938), *Perelandra* (1943) and *That Hideous Strength* (1945). But just when the tone of the letters suggests that Lewis had written all the fiction he would write, the book concludes with an unexpected 'twist'.

To understand the unexpectedness of the 'twist' it is necessary to summarize Lewis's relationship to Mrs Janie King Moore up to the end of this book.[10] Lewis met Mrs Moore in 1917, shortly after she arrived in Oxford with her eleven-year-old daughter, Maureen.[11] Mrs Moore was in Oxford because her son, Edward 'Paddy' Moore, was a member of the Officers' Training Corps billeted in Keble College.[12] Lewis began his training with the Officers' Training Corps at the same time, and he and Paddy shared a room in Keble. Lewis came to know Paddy's family, and the young men promised each other that if either of them survived the war he would look after Lewis's father and Paddy's mother. When their training ended Paddy was sent to France with the Rifle Brigade, and Lewis soon followed with the Somerset Light Infantry. Paddy was killed at Pargny on 24 March 1918, and Lewis was wounded weeks later in the Battle of Arras.

When Lewis returned to Oxford in 1919 to continue his studies at University College, he was joined by Mrs Moore and Maureen who took accommodation in Headington. Mrs Moore, forty-seven at this time, had been separated from her husband since 1908. Thereafter, the 'family', as Lewis began to refer to himself and the Moores, lived in numerous rented properties until, in 1930, they bought The Kilns in Headington Quarry.

Roger Lancelyn Green and I pointed out in our biography of Lewis that while his relationship with Mrs Moore 'may have started with that incomprehensible passion which middle-aged women seem occasionally able to inspire in susceptible youths . . . it soon turned from the desire for a mistress into the creation of a mother-substitute.'[13] Indeed we come across what may be the first reference to Mrs Moore as 'mother' in a letter to Sister Penelope of 9 November 1941, in which Lewis asked her to 'Pray for *Jane* . . . She is the old lady I call my mother and live

---

10 See **Janie King Moore** in the Biographical Appendix to *CL* I.

11 See **Dame Maureen Dunbar of Hempriggs** in the Biographical Appendix to *CL* I.

12 See **Edward Francis Courtenay 'Paddy' Moore** in the Biographical Appendix to *CL* I.

13 Roger Lancelyn Green and Walter Hooper, *C. S. Lewis: A Biography* (London: Bles, 1974; rev. edn, 2002), ch. 2, p. 46.

with (she is really the mother of a friend) – an unbeliever, ill, old, frightened, full of charity in the sense of alms, but full of uncharity in several other senses. And I can do so little for her.'[14]

By the middle of the 1940s Mrs Moore, in her late seventies, was crippled, often in great pain, and in need of constant care. Lewis divided his time between his duties at Magdalen College and nursing his old friend. 'My mother is old & infirm, we have little and uncertain help, and I never know when I can, even for a day, get away from my duties as a nurse and a domestic servant',[15] Lewis wrote to Lord Salisbury on 9 March 1947. It was not in Lewis's nature to abandon anyone and by the spring of 1949 the situation was worse. Mrs Moore could hardly be left alone for a minute and Lewis was worn out.

But just when he feared that old age had crept up on him and that his literary impulses were drying up, he began dreaming of lions. Suddenly Aslan, the great royal beast of Narnia, bounded in. 'Apart from that,' Lewis said, 'I don't know where the Lion came from or why he came. But once He was there He pulled the whole story together, and soon He pulled the six other Narnian stories in after him.'[16] This volume ends with Lewis writing to Owen Barfield and the illustrator of Narnia, Pauline Baynes, about one of the best-loved books in the world, *The Lion, the Witch and the Wardrobe.*

There is still another C. S. Lewis – 'the writer and broadcaster of popular Christian apologetics'. Following the publication of *The Problem of Pain* (1940) the BBC's Director of Religious Broadcasting, the Reverend James W. Welch, wrote to Lewis on 7 February 1941 asking if he would be willing to give a series of radio talks 'on something like "The Christian Faith As I See It"'. From this came the four series of talks eventually published as *Mere Christianity.* There has never been anything like them. Of the many reasons for their success, one must be simply that Lewis believed the Gospel to be *true.* And because true, therefore important. 'Christianity is a statement,' said Lewis, 'which, if false, is of *no* importance, and, if true, of infinite importance. The one thing it cannot be is moderately important.'[17]

14 see p. 496.

15 See p. 766.

16 'It All began with a Picture . . .', *Of This and Other Worlds*, ed. Walter Hooper (London: Collins, 1984; Fount, 2000), p. 64.

17 'Christian Apologetics', *EC*, p. 158.

Everything the three 'Lewises' wrote is immensely readable, but the BBC broadcasts taught him to translate complicated truths into the vernacular. 'Any fool can write *learned* language,' Lewis once observed, 'The vernacular is the real test. If you can't turn your faith into it, then either you don't understand it or you don't believe it.'[18] But Lewis knew that no vernacular lasts forever, and one of the most valuable letters in this book is his reply to Canon John Beddow of 7 October 1945. Beddow, struck by the success of Lewis's radio broadcasts, asked him to 'translate' some writings for the Christian Workers' Union. 'People praise me as a "translator"', Lewis replied, 'but what I want is to be the founder of a school of "translation". I am nearly forty-seven. Where are my successors?'[19]

Where indeed? While we wait in hope for them to appear, we rejoice in Lewis's theological legacy. It is breathtaking that during the war, when he had so much else to do, Lewis provided the Western world with its primary body of modern Christian apologetics – *The Problem of Pain* (1940), *The Screwtape Letters* (1942), *The Abolition of Man* (1943), *Mere Christianity* (1942–4), *The Great Divorce* (1946) and *Miracles* (finished in 1945, published in 1947).

We may now add to this list Lewis's theological letters, most of which appear here for the first time, or at least for the first time in their entirety. Lewis was annoyed when he saw how many letters he received as a result of his first radio talks. On 25 February 1942 he complained to Eric Fenn, the director of his broadcasts, 'I wrote 35 letters yesterday . . . It "gets one down" – not to mention postage.' This fretfulness ended as quickly as it began: Lewis realized that if you publish a book you are responsible for its consequences. As more and more people turned to him for help he saw it as a clear duty to help them, and letter-writing thus became a valuable aspect of his apostolate. Thereafter Lewis answered nearly all letters by return of post. When one considers what a large part of the letters in this volume are replies to those who wrote to him about his books it must seem that Lewis spent more time replying to their letters than writing the books themselves.

---

18 'Version Vernacular', *The Christian Century*, Vol. LXXV (31 December 1958), p. 515. Reprinted in *EC*, p. 779.

19 Letter to Canon John Beddow of 7 October 1945, p. 674.

In this he was given great help by his devoted brother, Warnie Lewis. Warnie had acquired a portable Royal typewriter many years before and, while he never advanced beyond the hunt-and-peck system with two fingers, he did it well. He came to the job of being his brother's secretary well qualified; between 1933 and 1935 he had typed the 3,000-odd pages that make up the unpublished 'Memoirs of the Lewis Family: 1850–1930', or the 'Lewis Papers' as they are known. While we cannot be certain when Warnie began helping his brother, the first of his typed letters to appear in the *Collected Letters* is that to Eric Fenn of 30 November 1942.

C. S. Lewis – Jack – did not dictate his letters to Warnie, but using a kind of shorthand the brothers both knew – 'cd' for 'could', 'wd' for 'would', 'shd' for 'should' etc. – he scribbled his reply on to whatever letter he was answering, after which Warnie typed it. Lewis used the same abbreviations in many of the letters written in his own hand, but with the difference that he could do it faster if Warnie was his only reader. In Lewis's correspondence with Dorothy L. Sayers, for instance, a number of his replies are written on her letters. As an example, the typed letter to Sayers of 14 December 1945 is exactly as Lewis wrote it for Warnie to copy. Because Warnie looked after the posting of his brother's letters, Jack could rely on him to add technical information. On 4 January 1946 Dorothy L. Sayers asked Lewis to return the copy of an essay she had sent him. In his draft reply of 7 February Lewis began, 'I enclose the MS . . .', which words Warnie altered to read: 'I forward the MS as a registered packet by this post'. The remainder of the letter is exactly as Lewis dashed it off on the letter from Sayers. The typed letters to Sayers of 7 August 1946, 5 June 1947, and 1 January 1949 are exactly as Lewis scribbled them.

Warnie was especially useful in replying to some of the many people who sent parcels of food during and after the war. These generous folk had a special place in Warnie's heart, not least because he and the other Inklings shared that food. Some of Jack's replies to them, if not written entirely by Warnie, contained passages by him. A number of instances appear in the letters to Edward A. Allen and his mother of Westfield, Massachusetts. This passage in the letter to Mr Allen of 10 August 1948 was almost certainly written by Warnie; as Jack did not read newspapers it is unlikely he would have known that Paul Gray Hoffman was the administrator of the Marshall Plan:

> I quite agree with you that Mr. Hoffman has a man size job in front of him; he has so far as I can judge, made a good impression so far, which is a big start. And I feel that the task is being tackled in the right way, i.e. insistance on Europe helping *itself*, not merely standing by to collect American money . . .[20]

This did not mean that Jack did not care what went into these letters, but his brother was able to make the replies more interesting and informative. After replying to people like the Allens over a period of years, C. S. Lewis let it be known that the letters were a joint production. On a few occasions Warnie even signed his brother's name for him, although Jack himself signed all the letters to Edward A. Allen in this volume. Mr Allen was one of the American friends to whom Warnie continued to write after Jack died.

In 1944, Warnie began evolving a 'system' for dealing with the correspondence, although its workings are not easy to follow and it appears to have changed form more than once over the years. Beginning with the letter to J. S. A. Ensor of 26 February 1944, he gave most letters a reference number, 'REF. 55/44'. The number probably means this was the 55th letter Warnie typed in 1944, and we later find that '55' has become Mr Ensor's reference number, one that appears on all correspondence to him. But this did not hold true for all Lewis's correspondents. His first letters to Dorothy L. Sayers bear the reference number '231', but thereafter the number changed every year.

The Lewis brothers were not good spellers. Warnie – who kept a diary for fifty years – joked that he was never sure whether he kept a 'diary' or a 'dairy'. I should mention that his most characteristic error concerned contractions. He spelled, for instance, 'can't' as 'ca'nt' and 'couldn't' as 'could'nt', although at least he was consistent. His spelling, and that of his brother, has been retained throughout.

I mentioned in the Preface to Volume I that, following his brother's death, Warnie set out to write a biography of Jack to be called 'C. S. Lewis: 1898–1963'. However, instead of an account of his brother's life containing occasional quotations from his letters, the book was mostly quotation. The publishers objected, and in the end most of Warnie's

---

20 See p. 869.

narrative was gathered into a 'Memoir' attached to what became *Letters of C. S. Lewis* (1966; revised and enlarged edition, 1988). Warnie was very hurt, not least because the publishers failed to include the dedication – 'To Those Overseas Friends Who Helped Him In the Lean Years' – which *was* added to the edition of 1988.

Shortly after I came to know Warnie in January 1964 I began helping him copy the letters from his brother which people were sending back to him as he prepared his biography. If there was a method of photocopying in Oxford neither of us knew about it, and so we could not make exact copies. Since I feared we might never see the letters again, I copied every word of the letters Warnie assigned me. But because Warnie believed himself to be writing a biography of his brother, he typed only the parts he intended to include in his book, after which he returned the letters to their recipients.

It is impossible to imagine a more courteous man than Warnie, and when some female correspondents asked him to keep their identities secret, he more than complied. He provided them with fictitious names which even now, years after their deaths, cannot be penetrated. And with their identities went their addresses. The identities of a few of these correspondents have since been revealed: Mary Neylan let it be known that she was the recipient of some of the letters addressed 'To a Lady' in the *Letters* of 1966, and it has come to light that the late Mrs Mary Van Deusen was 'Mrs Arnold' of the 1966 *Letters*. But we still do not know who 'Mrs Ashton' is and cannot discover if her letters from Lewis have survived. The result is that in a few instances the only copy of a letter (or part of a letter) we have is the one found in *Letters of C. S. Lewis* or in Warnie's typescript of 'C. S. Lewis: 1898–1963'. When this happens the location of the original letter is given as given as '*L*' – *Letters of C. S. Lewis* – or 'WHL' – the unpublished typescript of 'C. S. Lewis: 1898–1963', copies of which are held in the Bodleian Library, Oxford, and the Wade Center, Wheaton College, Wheaton, Illinois.

As with Volume I of the *Collected Letters*, I have provided the name of the person to whom a letter is addressed followed by the place where the reader can consult the original. The list of abbreviations reveals that 'Bod' means the Bodleian Library, 'W' the Wade Center, and so on. The Bodleian and the Wade Center have a reciprocal arrangement which means that each receives copies of what the other acquires. It was my intention to include in this volume all Lewis's existing letters from the period 1931–49, but – inevitably – I learned of a few when it was too late for them to go in. However, HarperCollins are making provision for Volume III to include a supplement containing letters omitted from the first two volumes.

The letters in Volume I were addressed primarily to family members or close friends, and because most were very important in Lewis's life I felt I should provide substantial biographies of them in a Biographical Appendix. During the period covered by Volume II Lewis was writing to a greatly enlarged circle of correspondents, and I have included substantial biographies of close friends, such as Sister Penelope, as well as shorter biographies of associates and various prominent or otherwise interesting people whose details were too long to be included merely as footnotes.

During the forty years I have been editing the writings of C. S. Lewis I have rarely needed so much help as I have with this volume. It is one thing to edit a single 'C. S. Lewis', quite another to edit *three*! I make the claim Lewis made in *The Allegory of Love* – that of standing on the shoulders of giants. The first is Dr Francis Warner who was Lewis's last pupil, and whom Lewis described as 'the best mannered man of his generation I have ever met'.[21] Nothing could be truer, and no one has given me as much encouragement as he. Other giants are Professor Emrys Jones and Dr Barbara Everett who are responsible for identifying most of Lewis's quotations from English literature.

Lewis's friends often asked him to criticize their work, and this volume includes a number of his replies. It is astonishing how generous he was with his time. I was unsure whether to include such letters, especially if, as in the case of that to J. A. Chapman of 6 July 1949, the composition in question was never published. Dr Warner and the others thought I should. Dr Everett opened my eyes to an aspect of Lewis's generosity I had not considered before. Regarding Lewis's letter to J. A. Chapman, she wrote in April 2003:[22]

---

21 Letter to Nancy Warner of 26 October 1963 quoted in Green and Hooper, *C. S. Lewis: A Biography*, p. 415.

22 Letter to Walter Hooper of 5 April 2003.

> *What is remarkable about the letter is his gentlemanly kindness, something more than courtesy, and the fact that he is telling the exact truth. You couldn't have a better 'report' in the sense that it is terribly truthful and terribly gentle with it . . . This is a sort of model . . . of how to write nicely about a book which the reader knows is unpublishable, not to say unreadable. You must publish it!*

Another on whose shoulders I often stand is Dr A. T. Reyes, the Classics scholar, whom I have relied on for helping with Lewis's Greek and Latin quotations since I began work on the *Collected Letters*.

My debts are very great, and I owe good words to those who have helped in numerous and valuable ways. They include Miss Priscilla Tolkien, Raphaela Schmid, Professor James Como, Professor G. B. Tennyson, Dr John Walsh, Dr Richard Mullen, Dr James Munson, and Dr Robin Darwall-Smith, archivist of Magdalen College and University College, who provided copies of the Lewis letters in Magdalen College Library. Mrs Valerie Eliot graciously supplied me with copies of Lewis's letters to her husband, while Dr Edwin W. Brown donated copies of the letters to Mary Neylan and others. Laurence Harwood, Lewis's godson, gave valuable help with the letters to the Harwood family. I am indebted to Mrs Anne Al-Shahi for helping with the biography of her grandfather, E. R. Eddison. Thanks to Madame Eliane Tixier and Dr René Tixier, to Dr David L. Neuhouser and Taylor University, Upland, Indiana, for providing copies of letters to Lady Freud and her mother, and my warmest thanks to Lady Freud for annotating those letters. Mrs Jacquie Kavanagh of the Written Archives Centre of the BBC provided copies of Lewis's letters to the BBC, Princeton University Library donated copies of the letters to Paul Elmer More, and Professor Brian Murdoch drew my attention to the letters to Eliza Marian Butler in the London University Germanic Institute. I am grateful to Mrs Madeleine F. Stebbins for giving the Bodleian Library the letter to her husband H. Lyman Stebbins, the late Dorothy Robinson who gave the Bodleian the letter to her father, Canon John Beddow, and Lewis's former pupil, Harry Blamires, for help with Lewis's letters to him. Thanks to Dr Christopher Mitchell of the Wade Center for providing copies of the Charles Williams letters, and Tracy Fleischman and the University of Texas at Austin for copies of the letters to Herbert

Palmer. Dr Andrew Cuneo helped me type the letters in this volume.

There seems no end to my debts – which include thanks to William Griffin, Aidan Mackey, Dr C. M. Bajetta, Dr Don W. King, George J. Houlé, Father Robert Byrne of the Oxford Oratory, Dr David Downing, with particular thanks to my friends Michael Ward, Richard Jeffery and Scott Johnson for proof-reading this volume. Dr Judith Priestman and Colin Harris of the Bodleian Library know how many reasons I have to be grateful to them. There would have been no volume of letters without the encouragement of David Brawn of HarperCollins*Publishers*, and my copy-editor, Steve Gove, who is responsible for much of the care that has gone into the editing of this second volume of Lewis's *Collected Letters*. The best thing of all was getting to know well so many people who share my admiration for the author of this book.

Walter Hooper
22 November 2003
Oxford

ABBREVIATIONS

AMR = *All My Road Before Me: The Diary of C. S. Lewis 1922–1927*, edited by Walter Hooper (1991)

BBC = Written Archive Centre, British Broadcasting Corporation

BF = *Brothers and Friends: The Diaries of Major Warren Hamilton Lewis*, edited by Clyde S. Kilby and Marjorie Lamp Mead (1982)

Bod = Bodleian Library, Oxford University

CG = Walter Hooper, *C. S. Lewis: A Companion and Guide* (1996)

CL I = C. S. Lewis, *Collected Letters*. Vol. I: *Family Letters 1905–1931*, edited by Walter Hooper (2000)

CP = C. S. Lewis, *Collected Poems*, edited by Walter Hooper (1994)

EC = C. S. Lewis, *Essay Collection and Other Short Pieces*, edited by Lesley Walmsley (2000)

L = *Letters of C. S. Lewis*, edited with a Memoir by W. H. Lewis (1966); revised and enlarged edition edited by Walter Hooper (1988)

Lambeth Palace = Lambeth Palace Library, Lambeth Palace, London

LU = London University Germanic Institute

M = Magdalen College, Oxford

OUP = Oxford University Press, Oxford

P = Private collection

Prin = Princeton University Library, Princeton, New Jersey

SBJ = C. S. Lewis, *Surprised by Joy: The Shape of My Early Life* (1955)

SLE = C. S. Lewis, *Selected Literary Essays*, edited by Walter Hooper (1969)

T = Taylor University, Upland, Indiana

Tex = University of Texas at Austin

UC North Wales = University College of North Wales, Bangor

V = Congregation of the Poor Servants of Divine Providence, Verona, Italy

Vic = University of Victoria, British Columbia, Canada

W = Marion E. Wade Center, Wheaton College, Wheaton, Illinois

WHL = W. H. Lewis's unpublished biography of his brother, 'C. S. Lewis: 1898–1963'. The greater part of the narrative was brought together as a 'Memoir' and it was published with most of the letters as *Letters to C. S. Lewis*, edited with a Memoir by W. H. Lewis (1966). There are two typescripts of 'C. S. Lewis: 1898–1963', one in the Bodleian Library, and one in the Wade Center

1931

Volume I of the Collected Letters *ended with a letter of 18 October 1931 in which Lewis described to his friend, Arthur Greeves, what happened on the night of 19 September when J. R. R. Tolkien and Hugo Dyson dined with him at Magdalen College. The three of them were up until 4 a.m. discussing Christianity and its relation to myth. Lewis wrote:*

> *What Dyson and Tolkien showed me was this: that if I met the idea of sacrifice in a Pagan story I didn't mind it at all: again, that if I met the idea of a god sacrificing himself to himself . . . I liked it very much and was mysteriously moved by it: again, that the idea of the dying and reviving god (Balder, Adonis, Bacchus) similarly moved me provided I met it anywhere* except *in the Gospels. The reason was that in Pagan stories I was prepared to feel the myth as profound and suggestive of meanings beyond my grasp . . . Now the story of Christ is simply a true myth: a myth working on us in the same way as the others, but with this tremendous difference that* it really happened.

Volume II opens with a letter to Warnie who had left on 9 October for a second tour of China with the Royal Army Service Corps. He would not reach Shanghai until 17 November. Meanwhile, at Magdalen, Lewis was giving a series of lectures on Textual Criticism and writing The Allegory of Love. *He, Mrs Moore and Maureen Moore had been in their new home, The Kilns, for a year.*

TO HIS BROTHER (W):

[Magdalen College]
Oct. 24th 1931

My dear W –

Your letter from Gibraltar has arrived and my reading aloud of as much as was suitable to the female capacity had something of the air of an event in the household. As you say it seems long ago to our day at Whipsnade and so many things have since followed it into the past that I must write history and get you up to date before I can talk.

By a stroke of bad luck for you Mr. Thomas rang up and invited you and me to tea the day after you had left.[1] His wife was there at the meal but he took me into his study afterwards and we had quite a long talk. He is, I think, a little shy, or at any rate in a first meeting seemed to be feeling his way with me. He is a moderate conservative, an enemy of the wireless, has travelled a good deal, encourages us 'not to stand any nonsense' from the fox-hunters, was bred in Surrey, approves strongly of our afforestation programme,[2] and knows his Foord Kelsie.[3]

I ventured to remark that I noticed how a sermon preached in his Church had reached the honours of print in the Oxford Times. 'The old rascal!' said Thomas, bursting into laughter. 'Do you know the history of that? The Wednesday after he preached it, he met me and asked me if there had been a reporter in the Church, for somehow or the other they had got hold of his sermon. So I taxed him with it. "*You*

---

1 The Rev. Wilfrid Savage Thomas (1879–1959) took a BA from Pembroke College, Cambridge, in 1900. Ordained in 1903 after a year at Wells Theological College, he was Curate of Great Marlow until 1906 and spent the next two years in Australia as Domestic Chaplain to the Bishop of Adelaide. He returned to Great Marlow, 1909–11, and was assigned Banbury with Grimsbury, 1911–13. After a further spell in Australia in 1915 as priest-in-charge of Mallala Mission, he was Curate of Amersham, 1916–18, Vicar of Holy Trinity, Lambeth, and Chaplain of St Thomas's Hospital, London, 1918–23. Thomas became Vicar of Holy Trinity, Headington Quarry, in 1924 and remained there until 1935. He was subsequently Vicar of Adderbury with Milton, 1935–9.

2 The grounds of The Kilns covered nine acres, and the Lewis brothers began planting trees and clearing pathways immediately after moving there.

3 The Rev. Edward Foord-Kelcey (1859–1934) matriculated at Pembroke College, Oxford, in 1884. He read Theology at Cuddesdon College and was ordained in 1888. He was Curate of St Saviour, Leicester, 1887–92, Vicar of Quorn (or Quorndon), Leicestershire, 1892–1909, and Rector of Great Kimble, Buckinghamshire, 1909–26. He officiated in the Diocese of Oxford from 1927 until his death. His wife died shortly before the First World War. In a short biography of Foord-Kelcey (LP XI: 24–5), Lewis wrote: 'A common love of Scott and Johnson was the ground on which we met . . . These, with Shakespeare and Carlyle, were the constant themes of his talk. . . . As a man of letters his range was not very wide – of poetry, for example, he knew little – nor was his judgement above the ordinary: but he was always worth listening to for the intensity of his gusto, and his chuckles and ecstatic repetition.'

sent it to the papers," I said; and then he owned up. The old rascal – the old rascal!'

He also gave me the final stages of the footpath quarrel, in which we have practically got our point: at least a route v. nearly the same as the original path has been conceded.[4] Apparently old Snow ended, as he had begun, by being the hero of the story. Thomas asked for written statements from as many parishioners as he could get hold of, and Snow produced one the length of your arm – a marvellous and highly autobiographical document which Thomas forwarded to the committee of the Town Council as likely to move anyone who had a sense of humour. But it was embarrassing when the case came into court and Thomas, going down to give evidence, found that old Snow had prepared the second and much longer statement which he proposed to read to the Magistrates from the spectators gallery during the hearing of the case: and since the old man thought that he could give a good account of himself if the police attacked him, Thomas had great difficulty in persuading him that he would be removed if he spoke or that the probability of removal was any reason for not at any rate beginning to read his statement. By the bye, the doury old man who made the speech about women and children turns out to be our local member of the Town Council, in fact one of the enemy: so that Snow's instinct ('I want him stopped') guided him very well.

The next important event since you left is that Maureen has been offered and accepted a residential job in a school at Monmouth[5] – a choice of time in which again you might have been more fortunate. I didn't know whether to approve or disapprove. Minto[6] was in favour of it, and I only held back by the greater solitude she would be exposed to. Now that it is all settled, Minto, as I foresaw, fears the loneliness and is a little depressed about the whole thing. One must hope that

4 There had been a footpath running across a field from Headington to Headington Quarry since 1804. The Oxford City Corporation wished to divert it, but many people who had been using the footpath for the whole of their lives, including Mr J. Snow, managed to have the City's plan altered. See the letter from Mr Thomas, 'Closing the Quarry Field Footpath' in the *Oxford Times* (7 August 1931), p. 10.

5 Maureen Moore, the daughter of Janie King Moore, taught music at the Monmouth School for Girls, Monmouthshire, 1930–3. See **Dame Maureen Dunbar of Hempriggs** (1906–97) in the Biographical Appendix to *CL* I.

6 The nickname of Mrs **Janie King Moore** (1872–1951). See the Biographical Appendix to *CL* I.

the actual freedom from the innumerable extra jobs and endless bickerings wh. Maureen's presence occasions will make up *in fact* for any feeling of 'missing' her.

In public works I have made tolerable headway. As soon as I began to choose a site for my first tree in this autumn's programme, it occurred to me that even if uprooting of all the elders were impracticable, still, there was no reason why each tree should not replace an elder instead of merely supplementing it. The job of digging out a complete elder root proved much easier than I had expected, and does not take much longer than digging an ordinary hole – the extra time you spend on extraction being compensated for by the fact that when once you have got the root out you find little solid digging left to be done. Unfortunately some of the places I chose as sites for the trees did not contain elder stumps, and many elders are in spots where one could hardly hope to make a new tree grow. However of the four tree holes which I have dug *in* the wood three are *vicê* elders cashiered. When I came to the problem of afforestation *outside* the wood I was held up by the necessity of doing a good deal of mowing. I have now scythed a wide open space round the western clump (i.e. the clump containing the ill fated beech) and a more or less continuous strip along past the Wasps nest to where I rejoined my summer's mowing. General October has proved a complete failure and last week while I was at work near the enemy lines vedettes seemed to be out and as twilight drew on riders or working parties were constantly passing me on their homeward journey.

Talking of beeches, Snow (you remember, the Magdalen botanist)[7] tells me that beeches will never grow well on a soil of clay and sand: chalk is what they want. I am inclined (if you agree) after one more trial to give up the effort to grow beeches, as Snow certainly knows his stuff: and you remember Johnson 'Nay Sir, never grow things simply to show that you cannot grow them.'[8]

And this, in turn, raising the idea of books, I hasten to tell you of a stroke of good luck for us both – I now have the 15 volume Jeremy

7 George Robert Sabine Snow (1897–1969) was a Fellow of Magdalen College, 1922–60.

8 James Boswell, *The Life of Samuel Johnson*, ed. George Birkbeck Hill, 6 vols. (1934), 18 April 1783, vol. IV, p. 205, slightly misquoted.

Taylor, in *perfect* condition, and have paid the same price of 20/-.[9] My old pupil Griffiths[10] spent a night with me last Monday and told me that Saunders[11] the bookseller, who is a friend of his, had a copy. He went round next day, got the book reserved and arranged the price: so we have done much better than if Galloway and Porters had had it. It is not indeed the nicest type of book – nineteenth century half leather of the granular and nearly black type, giving the volumes a legal or even commercial appearance. Still the Cambridge copy would probably have been the same *plus* its admitted dilapidations.

On the same visit Griffiths presented me with a poorly bound but otherwise delightful copy (1742) of Law's An Appeal/To all that doubt, or disbelieve/The Truths of the Gospel/Whether they be *Deists*, *Arians/ Socinians* or *Nominal* Christians/. It bears the book plate of Lord Rivers. I like it much better than the same author's *Serious Call*,[12] and indeed like it as well as any religious work I have ever read. The *prose* of the *Serious Call* has here all been melted away, and the book is saturated with delight, and the sense of wonder: one of those rare works which make you say of Christianity 'Here is the very thing you like in poetry and the romances, only this time it's true.'

I had nearly forgotten about the Parkin dinner.[13] I think it was a success: at any rate he sat with me till 12.30. We didn't get much beyond puns, bawdy, and politics, but there is a real friendliness (and

---

9 Jeremy Taylor, *The Whole Works . . . With a Life of the Author, and a Critical Examination of His Writings, by Reginald Heber*, 15 vols. (1822).

10 See **Dom Bede Griffiths** in the Biographical Appendix. Alan Richard Griffiths became a Catholic on Christmas Eve 1932. He spent much of the following year at Prinknash, the Benedictine priory near Gloucester, testing his vocation as a monk. On 20 December 1933 he was clothed as a novice and took the name Dom Bede Griffiths.

11 For the biography of Frank Sanders see note 28 to the letter of 22 March 1941.

12 William Law, *A Serious Call to a Devout and Holy Life* (1728).

13 Major Herbert Denis Parkin (1886–1958) joined the army in 1908 and the Army Service Corps (later Royal Army Service Corps) in 1911. He became captain in 1915 and major in 1918. He served in France during the First World War, in India during 1922, and Egypt, 1927–8. Major Parkin was Warnie's commanding officer in Shanghai, 1928–9 and they became lifelong friends, but this was the first time Jack had met him. On learning of Parkin's death, Warnie wrote in his diary of 13 November 1958: 'He was a friend of almost thirty years standing, and one whose place no one can fill . . . We shared a stock of memories which were very precious to both of us, and he had a humour that was entirely his own . . . I shall miss him to the end – the only real friend I ever made in the army' (*BF*, p. 246).

an almost embarrassing modesty) about him which makes even ordinary ante-room talk worth while. By a stroke of luck he had Christie next to him at dinner who is one of the few fellows of Magdalen who keeps up the quaint old tradition of being polite to guests.[14] He told me your sunset at Southampton had been richly illuminated: you had departed, as Browne would doubtless say, like that unparalleled piece of nature the Phoenix.

I am glad you like Browne as far as you got when your letter was written.[15] Your query 'Was there anything he didn't love?' hits the nail on the head. It seems to me that his peculiar strength lies in liking everything *both* in the serious sense (Christian charity and so forth) *and* in the Lambian[16] sense of natural gusto: he is thus at once sane and whimsical, and sweet and pungent in the same sentence – as indeed Lamb often is. I imagine that I get a sort of double pleasure out of Thomas Browne, one from the author himself and one reflected from Lamb. I always feel Lamb, as it were, reading the book over my shoulder. A lot of nonsense is talked about the society of books, but 'there's more in it than you boys think' in a case of this sort: it *is* almost like getting into a club.

The discomforts of your train journey must have added the finishing touch to that unpleasant evening. Your departure affected Mr. Papworth so much that he retired to his basket as soon as you and I had left the house and refused to take any notice of anyone till the following morning.[17] I am glad the book on the literature of the Grand Siecle proved a success. I owe it one little debt myself, for I have been repeating at odd moments ever since the La Fontaine quatrain – 'j'aime le jeu, l'amour, les livres, la musique'.[18]

---

14 John Traill Christie (1899–1980) was Fellow and Classical Tutor at Magdalen College, 1928–32, Headmaster of Repton School, 1932–7, Headmaster of Westminster School, 1937–49, and Principal of Jesus College, Oxford, 1950–67.

15 Sir Thomas Browne (1605–82), natural historian, antiquary, and moralist, best known for his *Religio Medici* (1642).

16 i.e. like Charles Lamb.

17 Mr Papworth, or Baron Papworth as he was also known, was Lewis's and Mrs Moore's dog. Of the many pets they had over the years, he was their favourite. He died in 1937.

18 'I love games, love, books, music.' From Jean de La Fontaine, *Les Amours de Psyché et de Cupidon* (1669), quoted in *The Oxford Book of French Verse*, ed. St John Lucas (1920), p. 182.

Yes indeed: how many essays I have heard read to me on Descartes' proofs (there are more than one) of the existence of God.[19] (It was a remark of Harwood's first suggested to me that God might be defined as 'a Being who spends his time having his existence proved and disproved'.)[20] The particular one you quote ('I have the idea of a perfect being')[21] seems to me to be valid or invalid according to the meaning you give the words 'have an idea of'. I used to work it out by the analogy of a machine. If I have the idea of a machine which I, being unmechanical, couldn't have invented on my own, does this prove that I have received the idea from some really mechanical source – e.g. a talk with the real inventor? To which I answer 'Yes, if you mean a really detailed idea': but of course there is another sense in which e.g. a lady novelist 'has an idea' of a new airship invented by her hero – in the sense that she attached *some* vague meaning to her words, which proves nothing of the sort. So that if anyone asks me whether the idea of God in human minds proves His existence, I can only ask 'Whose idea?' The Thistle-Bird's[22] idea, for instance, clearly not, for it contains nothing whereof his own pride, fear, and malevolence could not easily provide the materials (cf. McAndrew's Hymn 'Yer mother's God's a grasping deil, the image of yourself').[23]

On the other hand it is arguable that the 'idea of God' in *some* minds does contain, not a mere abstract definition, but a real imaginative perception of goodness and beauty, beyond their own resources: and this not only in minds which already believe in God. It certainly seems to me that the 'vague something' which has been suggested to ones mind as desirable, all ones life, in experiences of nature and music and poetry, even in such ostensibly irreligious forms as 'The land East of

---

19 René Descartes (1596–1650) was the chief architect of the seventeenth-century intellectual revolution. His philosophical masterpiece, *Meditations on First Philosophy* (1641) contains many of his proofs of the existence of God.

20 See **Alfred Cecil Harwood** (1898–1975) in the Biographical Appendix to *CL* I. After taking his BA from Oxford in 1921 he became a teacher at Michael Hall School in London.

21 In the third of his *Meditations on First Philosophy* Descartes's argument for the existence of God runs: 'I have the idea of a perfect being. Whatever caused this idea must have all the perfections that are represented in the idea.'

22 By the 'Thistle-Bird' Lewis probably meant the Rev. Henry Edward Bird who, after serving in various London parishes, was Vicar of St Andrew's, Headington, 1924–46. He sometimes preached at Holy Trinity, Headington Quarry.

23 Rudyard Kipling, *The Seven Seas* (1896), 'McAndrew's Hymn', slightly misquoted.

the Sun and West of the Moon' in Morris,[24] and which rouses desires that no finite object even pretends to satisfy, can be argued *not* to be any product of our own minds. Of course I am not suggesting that these vague ideas of something we want and haven't got, wh. occur in the Pagan period of individuals and of races (hence mythology) are anything more than the first and most rudimentary forms of the 'idea of God'.

This subject has drawn me into a longer digression (if indeed *digression* is possible in my type of letter!) than I had intended. I do wish you could see the Kilns now. We have had very cold weather (the last few mornings have been white with frost) and little wind: most of the leaves have become yellow and red without dropping from their branch, and those that have fallen lie in smooth circular carpets at the foot of their tree. The firs in the top wood are getting slowly barer, and working these afternoons in the high countries I begin to get the real autumn beauties.

Meanwhile you have been having very different beauties. I was intrigued by your account of the Portugal coast, which sounds both scenically and socially an admirable place: well worthy to be added (it costs nothing) to the lengthening list of places the Pigibudda[25] must visit some day. I resent more and more these impertinent three years which still divide us from the beginning of a joint rational life.

I am at present writing this on a Sunday afternoon in the Common Room, having begun it yesterday in College. Maureen has her usual week end guest, a harmless girl whom we carried to [the] sermon this morning. Our pew felt a little awkward when Thomas, before the text, said 'We shall be glad if members of the congregation who are absolutely unable to stay for the whole service, will go out during the hymn: but it is very much to be preferred that they should wait till the service is over.' We went out during the hymn according to our usual practice.

---

24 'The Land East of the Sun and West of the Moon' is a story in William Morris, *The Earthly Paradise* (1868–70).

25 One of Jack and Warnie's nicknames for each other. When they were small children their nurse sometimes threatened to smack their 'pigieboties' or 'piggiebottoms'. Over time the brothers decided that Warnie was 'Archpiggiebotham' or 'APB' and Jack 'Smallpiggiebotham' or 'SPB', and thereafter they frequently addressed each other by these names or variations of them. In his letter to Warnie of 2 August 1928 (*CL* I, p. 768), Jack discusses the nature of 'pigiebotism' – the manners and ideas of young men like Warnie and Jack.

I think myself he is a little unfair to try and make it a rule that you must communicate if you want to hear a sermon. Of these (since you mention them among items of news) I have heard two, having skipped on the first Sunday after you left in order to correct my collection papers. This morning's was on the 'armour of God'[26] and not one of his best.

Last week's was on St Luke's day,[27] from which I learned that St Luke was a painter as well as a doctor and that there is at Rome a painting of the Good Shepherd traditionally attributed to him. The attribution is probably wrong, said Thomas, but the tradition of his being a painter was interesting if we considered the specially *artistic* character of the 3rd gospel, as against the purely *facty* nature of the other two synoptics, or the mystical nature of the 4th.[28] I have so many different departments of news, what with sermons and swans, that I could well adopt the different datings of the Tatler 'fashion from White's coffee house, politics from Wills' etc.

This is a great feather in my cap, specially as next year is the first exam held under the syllabus which my party and I have forced upon the junto after much hard fighting: so that if I get a good colleague we shall be able to some extent to mould the new tradition. In fact, in English School politics, the anti-junto is in the ascendant – perhaps, from a prejudiced point of view, might be said to have become the junto. How long will it take us to become corrupt in our turn?[29]

---

26 Ephesians 6:13.

27 18 October.

28 John is the 'mystical' fourth Gospel. The other three Gospels – Matthew, Mark and Luke – are remarkably similar in workings and structure; scholars call these three Gospels *synoptic* (from the Greek for 'seeing together or at the same time', a name derived from the practice of tabulating their similarities in parallel columns for comparison). It is generally believed that Mark was used as a source by Matthew and Luke.

29 The English School was divided between those who upheld the primacy of the study of English literature and those advocating the importance of language. Lewis had complained when Professor J. R. R. Tolkien wanted more linguistic courses, these to be based on Old or Middle English literature, but by 1931 he had come to see the merit of Tolkien's proposals and thereafter gave him his full support. Soon the curriculum of the English School required that students learn the English language of all periods, while the literature syllabus began with *Beowulf* and ended with the Romantics in 1830. There were murmurings of dissent from the other side about the monopoly of philology and the absence from the curriculum of any modern literary criticism.

The General Election takes place on Tuesday next, and the results will be stale long before this reaches you. I had a wonderful conversation about it last Sunday with a Dr Lees whom Kathleen Whitty[30] brought here (or rather he drove her) to tea in the course of a motor drive from Bristol. I said 'Politics have really become unintelligible to the amateur now. In the old days when it was about votes for women or home rule for Ireland one could have an opinion: now I feel one's opinion, and therefore one's vote, is quite worthless' – He replied with emotion 'I'm so glad to hear you say that, because that is *exactly how I feel.* What is the good of all these ignorant opinions? That is why we must leave it to the government who really understand, and that is why it is so all important to vote against Labour.' I tried again. 'One is rather sickened to see the way the papers are buttering up Macdonald[31] and Snowden[32] now, while a month ago they couldn't find anything bad enough to say for them' – 'Yes, indeed. Very sickened' – 'And it is such nonsense all this about Macdonald having "done the big thing"' – 'Ah well *there* I don't agree with you. You see no man likes to desert his old friends, but this chap, when he saw the good of the country demanded it etc' – then followed verbatim the whole of the Daily Mail stuff about the big thing. All this from an old blether in a black city coat and streaked trousers and spats introduced by Kathleen as 'the cleverest doctor in Bristol'. Alas, this description may well be perfectly true! An essay on the conception of 'cleverness' would be worth writing.

I finished the Wodehouse the day after you left. It is not the best (I think) of his that I have read, but *very* well worth reading indeed. I also re-read Northanger Abbey[33] about the same time. Christie well describes it as 'Jane Austen in high spirits'. It is much nearer farce (or burlesque) than the others, but none the worse on that account.

I enclose a formal letter to you on the mortgage. If you will write one to me, the same except for the necessary changes, and return *both* with your next letter, I will send them to be taken care of by Barfield.[34]

30 Miss Kathleen Whitty had been Maureen's music teacher when the Moores lived in Bristol, and she often visited them in Oxford.

31 Ramsay MacDonald (1866–1937), Labour Prime Minister, 1924, 1929–35.

32 Philip, Viscount Snowden (1864–1937), Chancellor of the Exchequer, 1924, 1929–31.

33 Jane Austen, *Northanger Abbey* (1818).

34 See **Owen Barfield** (1898–1997) in the Biographical Appendix to *CL* I. Barfield, one of Lewis's closest friends, joined the family law firm in London, Barfield and

He has not been to see me yet so your will has not yet been regularised. Minto was – to use a trite phrase in its genuine sense – 'overcome' by your kind provision for Maureen.

As I look up (3.30) I see those obscene birds advancing across the lawn, turning their infernal conning towers this way and that.[35] They are unfed, Tykes unwalked, and I must go out. I suppose this will cross your next letter and so produce a mal-adjustment of question and answer which we shall not right for the whole three years. Meanwhile one quarter of first term of the nine Non-APB terms is gone.

Yours
Jack

TO ARTHUR GREEVES (W):

[The Kilns]
Nov 8, 1931

My dear Arthur,

I was sorry to hear of your cold and of your musical disappointment, though I must confess that your beginning your letter with an (unfavourable) account of a concert was pleasantly remeniscent of old times.

It is delightful to hear of your reading *Endymion*.[36] Funnily enough I had been re-dipping into it the last week end too. I don't think you can say that either it or Hyperion[37] is the better for they are different in kind. The one is a sweet, the other a dry, flavour. It is like comparing Spenser & Milton, or Wagner (at his richest) with Bach (at his most classical). People will tell you that Hyperion is more Greek, but I doubt if that is a good description. As to *why* the goddess takes on the form of a mortal at the end, he may mean that the mystical love does not complete itself until it has appeared as a human love also, and that the soul, when this happens, may dread as an infidelity to the spiritual what is really its completion. But I am inclined to think that when

---

Barfield, in 1929. After taking a degree of Bachelor of Civil Law from Oxford in 1930, he began preparing for law exams in London. During his many years with Barfield and Barfield he acted as Lewis's solicitor.

35 Lewis had been given a pair of swans by the Provost of Worcester College. See Fred W. Paxford, 'He Should Have Been a Parson' in *We Remember C.S. Lewis*, ed. David Graham (2001), p. 122.

36 John Keats, *Endymion* (1818).

37 John Keats, *Hyperion* (1820).

Keats wrote Endymion he was not v. certain of his own intention: that he faltered between the myth as his imagination set it before him (full of meaning, but not meaning necessarily decipherable by Keats' intellect) and between various ideas of conscious meanings of his own invention, wh., considering his age and education, were possibly confused and even shallow. There is thus some confusion throughout: and this, along with another fault, prevents it from being a perfect poem.

The other fault is the lack of spiritual experience. He knows about the hunting for 'it'[38] and longing and wandering: but he has, as yet, no real idea of what it wd. be if you found it. Hence while Endymion's description to Peona of his unrest, and Endymion's journeying under earth and sea, are wonderful, his actual meetings with Cynthia are (to me) failures: not because they are erotic but because they are erotic in a rather commonplace way – all gasps and exclamations and a sort of suburban flirtatious air. It is horrible to use such words of Keats, but I think he would be the first to agree.

My memories of the *Phaedrus*[39] are vague – mainly of the beautiful scene in which the discussion takes place and of the procession of the gods round the sky. You must be enjoying yourself no end. I don't know any greater pleasure than returning to a world of the imagination which one has long forsaken and feeling 'After all this is my own.' Be careful of Reid.[40] I am sure he is in danger of stopping at the purely sensuous side of the Greek stories and of encouraging you to do the same. You, on the other hand, if you are in for a new Greek period, will be able to do him some good.

I, like you, am worried by the fact that the *spontaneous* appeal of the Christian story is so much less to me than that of Paganism. Both the things you suggest (unfavourable associations from early upbringing and the corruption of one's nature) probably are causes: but I have a sort of feeling that *the* cause must be elsewhere, and I have not yet discovered it. I think the thrill of the Pagan stories and of romance may be due to the fact that they are mere beginnings – the first, faint

---

38 'It' was Lewis's original name for the inconsolable longing he called 'Joy' in *SBJ*.

39 This, one of Plato's dialogues, is about Persuasion and Eros and their part in our perception of the eternal Forms.

40 Arthur's friend, the novelist Forrest Reid (1875–1947), was living in Belfast at this time. Reid told his story in two autobiographies, *Apostate* (1926) and *Private Road* (1940). His novel, *Uncle Stephen*, was published in October 1931.

whisper of the wind from beyond the world – while Christianity is the thing itself: and no thing, when you have really started on it, can have for you then and there just the same thrill as the first hint. For example, the experience of being married and bringing up a family, cannot have the old bittersweet of first falling in love. But it is futile (and, I think, wicked) to go on trying to get the old thrill again: you must go forward and not backward. Any *real* advance will in its turn be ushered in by a new thrill, different from the old: doomed in its turn to disappear and to become in its turn a temptation to retrogression. Delight is a bell that rings as you set your foot on the first step of a new flight of stairs leading upwards. Once you have started climbing you will notice only the hard work: it is when you have reached the landing and catch sight of the new stair that you may expect the bell again. This is only an idea, and may be all rot: but it seems to fit in pretty well with the general law (thrills also must die to live) of autumn & spring, sleep and waking, death and resurrection, and 'Whosoever loseth his life, shall save it.'[41]

On the other hand, it may be simply part of our probation – one needs the sweetness to *start* one on the spiritual life but, once started, one must learn to obey God for his own sake, not for the pleasure. Perhaps we are in the stage Endymion went through on the bottom of the sea.

I saw a most attractive review of *Uncle Stephen* in the T.L.S.[42] I am glad he stuck to that name after all, though surprised, for I thought he had definitely turned it down.

Did I tell you I had bought the complete works of Jeremy Taylor in 15 volumes – half leather (not v. nice – the rather pimply, nearly black, office-looking type of leather but excellent paper and print) for 20/-. I have also been presented by an old pupil with what I think must be a frst editn of Law's Appeal: much better than the *Serious Call*, but it will need a letter to itself.

I wish you could see the Kilns at present in the autumn colours

Yours
Jack

P.S. Minto says I must have left a suit of pyjamas at Bernagh, and I seem to remember your saying something about it (wh. I didn't heed)

---

41 Luke 9:24.

42 *The Times Literary Supplement* (29 October 1931), p. 838.

in a previous letter. If so 'woooo-d' you please send them. Really Arthur, I am awfully sorry, honestly, really Yrs J.

P.P.S. I chust wanted to say, Arthur, how very sorry I am.

On 17 November 1931, Warnie arrived in Shanghai where he was to serve as the officer commanding the Royal Army Service Corps. He had been here in 1927–9 as officer in command of the Supply Depot. He wrote in his diary on 23 November:

> *I almost feel as I had never left Shanghai, a feeling accentuated by the fact that I have bought back from Bill Wilson the identical pieces of furniture which I sold him when I went home. I am writing this at the same old desk, and in front of me are my own old curtains and mosquito windows . . . Now that I have got my pictures up, and bought a $30 Japanese rush carpet, unpacked all my books and the gramophone, I feel I can sit back and breathe.*[43]

TO HIS BROTHER (W):

[The Kilns]
Nov. 22nd 1931

My dear W,

I really think your recent editorial difficulties have impressed upon me the habit of dating my letters![44] And talking of the Lewis papers, I looked into the editorial drawer the other day and made a correction, by adding to your note 'Grace by A.J.L.' the words 'On the contrary, traditional Latin Grace translated by C.S.L.' Such are the traps into which even a careful editor falls.

I am sorry I have not been able to write for some weeks. During the week it is out of the question. My ordinary day is as follows. Called

---

43 *BF*, p. 89.

44 Before he left for Gibraltar Warnie had begun editing the enormous number of family diaries, letters and other memorabilia amassed by Albert Lewis. When he finished in 1933, the 'Memoirs of the Lewis Family: 1850–1930' consisted of eleven volumes of papers with numerous notes by the Lewis brothers. The original of the unpublished 'Lewis Papers', as the 'Memoirs' are known, is in the Marion E. Wade Center, Wheaton College, Wheaton, Illinois, with microfilm in the Bodleian Library, Oxford, and the Southern Historical Collection, the University of North Carolina at Chapel Hill.

(with tea) 7.15. After bath and shave I usually have time for a dozen paces or so in Addison's walk[45] (at this time of year my stroll exactly hits the sunrise) before chapel at 8. 'Dean's Prayers' – which I have before described to you – lasts about quarter of an hour. I then breakfast in common room with the Dean's Prayers party (i.e. Adam Fox,[46] the chaplain, Benecke[47] and Christie) which is joined punctually by J. A. Smith[48] at about 8.25. I have usually left the room at about 8.40, and then saunter, go to the stool, answer notes etc till 9. From 9 till 1 is all pupils – an unconscionable long stretch for a man to act the gramaphone in. At one Lyddiatt[49] or Maureen is waiting for me with the car and I am carried home.

My afternoons you know. Almost every afternoon as I set out hillwards with my spade, this place gives me all the thrill of novelty. The scurry of the waterfowl as you pass the pond, and the rich smell of autumnal litter as you leave the drive and strike into the little path, are always just as good as new. At 4.45 I am usually driven into College again, to be a gramaphone for two more hours, 5 till 7. At 7.15 comes dinner.

On Tuesday, which is my really shocking day, pupils come to me to

---

45 This was the favourite walk of the essayist and poet Joseph Addison (1672–1719). When a Fellow of Magdalen he lived in New Buildings and greatly enjoyed the walk which runs northward from the college buildings. Since the nineteenth century it has been known as 'Addison's Walk'. On the centenary of Lewis's birth in 1998 a memorial stone was placed along the walk inscribed with Lewis's poem 'What the Bird Said Early in the Year' in which he mentions Addison's Walk.

46 See **Adam Fox** in the Biographical Appendix.

47 Paul Victor Mendelssohn Benecke (1868–1944), great-grandson of the composer Felix Mendelssohn, was Classics Tutor at Magdalen College, 1893–1925. He was Lewis's history tutor when he was an undergraduate at University College. See Lewis's letter to Albert Lewis of 21 January 1921.

48 John Alexander Smith (1893–1939), philosopher and classical scholar, was Waynflete Professor of Moral and Metaphysical Philosophy and Fellow of Magdalen, 1910–36. Born at Dingwall in Cromarty, he came up to Balliol College from Edinburgh University in 1884. After taking a First in Classics in 1887 he was Fellow in Philosophy at Balliol, 1891–1910, before moving to Magdalen. A distinguished scholar of Aristotle, for many years he exercised great influence in the Oxford Aristotelian Society. His translation of *De Anima* appeared in 1931. He maintained the Idealist tradition of T. H. Green and Edward Caird. A chapter is devoted to him in James Patrick, *The Magdalen Metaphysicals: Idealism and Orthodoxy at Oxford, 1901–1945* (Macon, Georgia: Mercer University Press, 1985).

49 Frederick David Lyddiatt, who lived at 52 Wharton Road, Headington, helped out at The Kilns, sometimes acting as chauffeur.

read Beowulf at 8.30 and usually stay till about 11, so that when they have gone and I have glanced round the empty glasses and coffee cups and the chairs in the wrong places, I am glad enough to crawl to bed. Other standing engagements are on Thursday when a man called Horwood[50] (another English don) comes and reads Dante with me, every second Monday when the College literary society meets. When you have thrown in the usual irregular dinner engagements you will see that I am lucky when I have two evenings free after dinner.

The only exception to this programme (except of course Saturday when I have no pupils after tea) is Monday when I have no pupils at all. I have to employ a good deal of it in correcting transcripts done by B. Litt. pupils, and other odd jobs. It has also become a regular custom that Tolkien[51] should drop in on me of a Monday morning and drink a glass. This is one of the pleasantest spots in the week. Sometimes we talk English school politics: sometimes we criticise one another's poems: other days we drift into theology or 'the state of the nation': rarely we fly no higher than bawdy and 'puns'.

What began as an excuse for not writing has developed into a typical diary or hebdomadal compendium. As to the last two week ends, they have both been occupied. The one before last I went to spend a night at Reading with a man called Hugo Dyson[52] – now that I come to think of it, you heard all about him before you left. We had a grand evening. Rare luck to stay with a friend whose wife is so nice that one *almost* (I can't say quite) *almost* regrets the change when he takes you up to his study for serious smoking and for the real midnight talking. You would enjoy Dyson very much for his special period is the late 17th century: he was much intrigued by your library when he was last in

50 Chesney Horwood (1904–90) came up to Oxford in 1922 as an exhibitioner of the Non-Collegiate Society. After graduating he spent two years as Lektor in English Literature at the University of Freiburg-im-Breisgau. On returning to Oxford in 1928 he became Fellow of English and Dean at the Non-Collegiate Society which in 1930 was refounded as St Catherine's Society, and which in 1962 became St Catherine's College. Apart from 1940–6, when he served in the Intelligence Service, Horwood spent his entire working life in the service of the society.

51 See **J. R. R. Tolkien** (1892–1973) in the Biographical Appendix to *CL* I. Tolkien and Lewis were just beginning their regular meetings which led to the founding of the Inklings.

52 See **Henry Victor Dyson 'Hugo' Dyson** (1896–1975) in the Biographical Appendix to *CL* I. He was a lecturer and tutor in English in the University of Reading, 1921–45, and Fellow and Tutor in English at Merton College, Oxford, 1945–63.

our room. He is a most fastidious bookman and made me (that same occasion) take out one of the big folios from the bottom shelf of the Leeboro bookcase because they were too tightly packed. He disapproved strongly of the method (wh. I confess I had always followed) of taking books out of the shelf by putting a finger at the top so – and adopts a different one: which you will find described in 'Portrait of a Scholar' in that book of essays you took away with you.[53]

At the same time he is as far from being a dilettante as anyone can be: a burly man, both in mind and body, with the stamp of the war on him, which begins to be a pleasing rarity, at any rate in civilian life. Lest anything should be lacking, he is a Christian and a lover of cats. The Dyson cat is called Mirralls, and is a Viscount. That accounts for one week end.

Last Saturday Barfield came down. He arrived unexpectedly for lunch in College – Saturday being my day for a rotatory lunch with Keir[54] and Lawson.[55] As it happened, Keir didn't turn up, and the bore Lawson was neither here nor there. Barfield remarked afterwards that he went away feeling that Lawson had contributed most valuably to the conversation, though when he came to think it over he could not remember his having made a single rational remark. You know the type – the man who has an *air* of saying something interesting, which often carries you away.

Barfield and I then motored to the Kilns, took our packs (or rather your pack and mine) and set out to walk to the Barley Mow.[56] We failed to get any four o'clock [tea] at Marsh Baldon, but being both tired of work, and badly in need of a jaunt, we were too delighted to find ourselves on the road again and in each other's company, to be dampened even by that. It was dark before we reached the B.M., and after a noble supper of ham and eggs and a little yawning at the fire in that panelled room (shared with the same couple whom you and I

---

53 R. W. Chapman, *The Portrait of a Scholar & Other Essays Written in Macedonia, 1916–1918* (1922).

54 David Lindsay Keir (1895–1973) was a Fellow of New College, Oxford, 1921–39, President and Vice-Chancellor of Queen's College, Belfast, 1939–49, and Master of Balliol College, 1949–65.

55 Frederick Henry Lawson (1897–1983) was Fellow and Tutor in Law at Merton College, Oxford, 1930–48, and Professor of Comparative Law and a Fellow of Brasenose College, 1948–64.

56 The Barley Mow pub at Blewbury, Oxfordshire.

saw there) we went to bed. We lay in one room, mighty snug, and had a good deal of talk before it drifted off into prodigious yawns. We didn't stir till about 9 the Sunday morning, he being delighted with the unaccustomed absence of a restless child (how do married men live?) and I glad enough not to have chapel at 8.

That day we walked up Didcot Clumps (Sinodun Hills? Wittenham Clumps?) and crossed the Thames, not at Shillingford but at a ferry *near* Shillingford. As we reached the bank a torrent of dogs and one cat burst from the ferryman's house on the far shore and got as near as they could on the bows of a barge: and when finally we were ferried across they all (cat included) leaped aboard us before we were well alongside with the frantic haste of porters or customs officials. The ferryman's only explanation was the cryptic sentence 'Brought us all together' which he repeated about four times.

The rest of the day was spent tramping along the route Warborough – Stadhampton–Denton–Cuddesdon–Wheatley–Kilns. It was a colourless autumn day – about a quarter of the leaves still hanging on the trees: you know – just a yellow freckle on the black timber. We had tea at Wheatley, Barfield denouncing birth control. I could not help thinking, though I hardly cared to say, that a man married to an obviously barren woman was in this matter an arm chair critic. We were both home for supper, both feeling enormously the better for our jaunt. It is curious how the actual length of a holiday and the *feeling* of length are almost in inverse ratio. We had the sensation of having been away from our routine for an almost endless time.

Looking back on our own last trip I feel the same. I can believe that we were only a day and two nights at Larne: as for Castlerock, we seem we have been there for weeks, in all kinds of weather and at different seasons of the year. Did we really walk only *twice* to the tunnel? In retrospect, by the bye, the thing that wears best of all in my mind is the narrow gauge journey: the journey back, of course, is – like a lane by a brickyard on a hot day. Before Barfield went to bed that night (in your room) I gave him your will and he is doubtless now re-writing it in unintelligible language.

Which reminds me – I have had a letter from Condlin[57] about the

57 J. W. A. Condlin was Albert Lewis's managing clerk from 1917 until Albert's death in 1929.

Templeton family: but *what* he is saying about them, or whether he has found them, I can't for the life of me make out. Did I tell you that his acknowledgment of the £100 tip was not very enthusiastic? I don't say it was definitely chilly – nor, by the way, do I know how far Condlin's epistolary style is adapted for registering surprise or pleasure – or, for the matter of that, anything whatever on any subject.

I have also heard from the Tower of Glass[58] to say that they have at last got the Bishop's authority (*he* doesn't kill himself with work, does he? Prissy prelatical dog!) and also – which pleased me less, that the Rev. Chevasse[59] had suggested that *St Mark's Tower* should be included somewhere in the window.[60]

Clearly the proper [answer] is 'Ah such nonsense.' I actually replied by telling them to consult the artist, and to ask him to consider the proposal on *purely aesthetic* grounds. Unless the artist is a fool, that ought to safeguard us pretty well, and if he *is* – why then there is no help for us in any case.

It just occurs to me as I write, that Chevasse in this matter is probably the unwilling mouthpiece of the Select Vestry: I daresay even that the monstrous regiment of women,[61] incarnated in Lily Ewart,[62] is really at the bottom of it. Zounds! – I'd like a few minutes at the bottom of

---

58 'The Tower of Glass' was the Rev. Ernest William Carlisle Hayes (1896–1950). Hayes took his BA from Sidney Sussex College, Cambridge, in 1889, and was ordained in the Church of Ireland in 1893. After serving in a number of parishes, he was Rector of St Mark's, Dundela, 1925–35. The Lewis brothers gave him this nickname after the firm of stained-glass artists (see note 60) because he was in charge of installing the window dedicated to their parents.

59 The Rev. Claude Lionel Chavasse (1897–1983), of an Anglo-Irish family, took his BA from Exeter College, Oxford, in 1922. He was trained at St Stephen's House, Oxford, and ordained in the Church of Ireland in 1929. He was Curate of St Mark's, Dundela, 1928–31, after which he served in a number of parishes in County Cork. He was Vicar of Kidlington, Oxfordshire, 1947–57.

60 Jack and Warnie planned to give a stained-glass window to St Mark's in honour of their parents. The window, erected in 1935, was designed by Michael Healy (1873–1941). He was a member of The Tower of Glass, a group of stained-glass window artists of the time. For information about the window see David Bleakley, *C. S. Lewis – At Home in Ireland* (Belfast: Strandtown Press, 1998), pp. 182–3.

61 John Knox, *The First Blast of the Trumpet Against the Monstrous Regiment of Women* (1558).

62 Mary Elizabeth 'Lily' Ewart (1888–1976) was the sister of Arthur Greeves, and the wife of Charles Gordon Ewart (1885–1936).

her! No 'thought infirm' would there 'stain my cheek':[63] a firm hand rather would stain both hers. I also sent them the (revised by Christie) inscription. That, I think, is all the business news.

As regards books – what time have I to read? Tutorial necessities have spurred me into reading another Carlyle 'Past and Present'[64] which I recommend: specially the central part about Abbot Samson. Like all Carlyle it gets a little wearisome before the end – as all listening to these *shouting* authors does. But the pungency and humour and frequent sublimity is tip-top. It is very amusing to read the 19th century editor's preface (in our Leeborough edition),[65] obviously by a P'daita:[66] pointing out that, of course, the matter of the book is out of date, but it 'lives by its style'. 'We can afford to smile at the pessimism with which the sage approached problems that have since vanished like a dream before the onward march etc. etc.' Actually the book is an indictment of the industrial revolution pointing out precisely the problems we have *not* solved and prophesying most of the things that *have* happened since.

I get rather annoyed at this endless talk about books 'living by the style'. Jeremy Taylor 'lives by the style in spite of his obsolete theology'; Thos. Browne does the same, in spite of 'the obsolete cast of his mind': Ruskin and Carlyle do the same in spite of their 'obsolete social and political philosophy'. To read histories of literature one would suppose that the great authors of the past were a sort of chorus of melodious idiots who said, in beautifully cadenced language that black was white and that two and two made five. When one turns to the books themselves – well I, at any rate, find nothing obsolete. The silly things these

63 John Milton, *Paradise Lost* (1667), V, 384–5: 'no thought infirm/Altered her cheek'.

64 Thomas Carlyle, *Past and Present* (1843).

65 'Leeborough' or 'Leeboro' was Jack and Warnie's private name for their family home, Little Lea. A 'Leeborough edition' is a book from Little Lea.

66 Since they were boys Jack and Warnie had been amused by their father's 'low' Irish pronunciation of 'potatoes' as 'p'daytas'. As a result, Mr Lewis was nicknamed 'The P'dayta' or 'The P'daytabird'. The term came to be applied to anyone displaying the characteristics of their father, in particular an ignorant dogmatism. Jack eventually discovered this characteristic in himself: 'I'm afraid I must be a P'dayta,' he wrote to Warnie on 2 August 1928, 'for I made a P'daytism the other day: I began talking about the world and how it was well explored by now and, said I "We know there are no undiscovered islands." It was left for Maureen to point out the absurdity' (*CL* I, p. 777).

great men say, were as silly then as they are now: the wise ones are as wise now as they were then.

At this stage in my letter I begin to be haunted by the idea of having read and experienced many interesting things which I meant to tell you but cannot now bring to mind. One *un*-interesting thing was being preached to in 'mine own church' by little 'Clarkie' (the m-yes man).[67] He is the sort of preacher who calls God 'gudd', and soars off into great emotion cadenzas. The matter was good enough, the manner detestable. This morning was the commemoration of the dedication of the church, and why they saw fit to let (or even *get*) Clark to preach I don't know: Bathtowel and Thomas being both there.

I had to set a paper for School Certificate the other day on the Clarendon Press selections from Cowper – a ridiculous book for schoolboys.[68] It includes a large chunk of Bagehot's Essay on Cowper which makes me think I must read all Bagehot. We have him, haven't we? Not that I 'hold with him', he is too much of a pudaita by half: but he has great fun. 'Boy – the small pomivorous animal so called.'

How delicious Cowper himself is – the letters even more than the poetry. Under every disadvantage – presented to me as raw material for a paper and filling with a job an evening wh. I had hoped to have free – even so he charmed me. He is the very essence of what Arthur calls 'the homely' which is Arthur's favourite genre. All these cucumbers, books, parcels, tea-parties, parish affairs. It is wonderful what he makes of them.

I suppose we may expect a Colombo letter from you soon. I will vary the usual 'must stop now' by saying 'I am going to stop now'. I am writing in the common room (Kilns) at 8.30 of a Sunday evening: a moon shining through a fog outside and a bitter cold night.

Yours
Jack

67 The Rev. Alured George Clarke was Vicar of All Saints, Highfield, Oxford, 1920–35.

68 William Cowper, *Poetry & Prose, With Essays by Hazlitt & Bagehot*, introduction and notes by Humphrey S. Milford (Oxford: Clarendon Press, 1921).

TO ARTHUR GREEVES (W):

[The Kilns]
Dec 6th 1931

My dear Arthur,

Hurrah! I was beginning to feel the want of a word from you. I envy you your stay at Ballycastle, or rather I wish I had been there: I feel I can do so without selfishness because I should have enjoyed the storms better than Reid who doubtless lost through them most of the pleasure he expected to get out of his jaunt.

That is a thing you and I have to be thankful for – the fact that we do not only don't dislike but positively enjoy almost every kind of weather. We had about three days of dense fog here lately. That was enough to tax even my powers of doing without the sun, but though it became oppressive in the end I felt that it was a cheap price to pay [for] its beauties. There was one evening of mist about three feet deep lying on the fields under the moon – like the mist in the first chapter of Phantastes.[69] There was a morning (up in the top wood) of mist pouring *along the ground* through the fir trees, so thick and visible that it looked tangible as treacle. Then there were afternoons of fairly thin, but universal fog, blotting out colour but leaving shapes distinct enough to become generalised – silhouettes revealing (owing to the suppression of detail) all sorts of beauties of grouping that one does not notice on a coloured day. Finally there were days of *real* fog: days of chaos come again: specially fine at the pond, when the water was only a darker tinge in the fog and the wood on the far side only the ghostliest suggestion: and to *hear* the skurry of the waterfowl but not to see them. Not only was it an exciting time in itself but by the contrast has made to day even more beautiful than it would have been – a clear, stinging, winter sunshine.

As to Lucius[70] about the atonement not being in the Gospels, I think he is very probably right. But then nearly everyone seems to think that the Gospels are much later than the Epistles, written for people who had already accepted the *doctrines* and naturally wanted the *story*. I certainly don't think it is historical to regard the Gospels as the *original*

---

69 George MacDonald, *Phantastes: A Faerie Romance* (1858).

70 Mr (later Sir) Frederick Lucius O'Brien (1896–1974), a Quaker, was Arthur's cousin on his mother's side. During his life he held many civil and governmental positions in Belfast. He and Arthur often travelled together.

and the rest of the New Testament as later elaboration or accretion – though I constantly find myself doing so. But really I feel more and more of a child in the whole matter.

I begin to see how much Puritanism counts in your make up – that both the revulsion from it and the attraction back to it are strong elements. I hardly feel either myself and perhaps am apt to forget in talking to you how different your experience and therefore your feeling is. All I feel that I can say with absolute certainty is this: that if you ever feel that the *whole spirit and system* in which you were brought up was, after all, right and good, then you may be quite sure that that feeling is a mistake (tho' of course it might, at a given moment – say, of temptation, be present as the alternative to some far bigger mistake).

My reasons for this are *1.* That the system denied pleasures *to others* as well as to the votaries themselves: whatever the merits of *self*-denial, this is unpardonable interference. *2.* It inconsistently kept *some* worldly pleasures, and always selected the worst ones – gluttony, avarice, etc. *3.* It was ignorant. It could give no '*reason* for the faith that was in it'.[71] Your relations have been found very ill grounded in the Bible itself and as ignorant as savages of the historical and theological reading needed to make the Bible more than a superstition. *4.* 'By their fruits ye shall know them.'[72] Have they the *marks* of peace, love, wisdom and humility[73] on their faces or in their conversation? Really, you need not *bother* about that kind of Puritanism. It is simply the form which the *memory* of Christianity takes just before it finally dies away altogether, in a commercial community: just as extreme emotional ritualism is the form it takes on just before it dies in a fashionable community.

Like you I can get very little out of the *Imitation*.[74] Since last writing I have read Carlyle's *Past and Present*. One gets rather tired of a certain monotonous stridency, as in *Sartor*[75] but more so, but it is tremendously exciting (often wrong-headed) and very well worth reading, specially the mediaeval part in the middle.

---

71 1 Peter 3:15.

72 Matthew 7:20.

73 Galatians 5:22–3: 'But the fruit of the Spirit is love, joy, peace, patience, kindness, goodness, faithfulness, gentleness, self-control.' (RSV)

74 *The Imitation of Christ*, a manual of spiritual devotion first put into circulation in 1418 and traditionally ascribed to Thomas à Kempis (c. 1380–1471).

75 Thomas Carlyle, *Sartor Resartus* (1836).

I also read the *Dream of John Ball*, perhaps the most serious of W. Morris's works, except *Love is Enough* and the fullest exposition of his whole philosophy of life and *The Wood Beyond the World* wh. is neither better nor worse than any other of the prose romances.[76] What an achievement his treatment of love is: so undisguisedly physical and yet so perfectly sane and healthy – *real* paganism at its best, which is the next best thing to Christianity, and so utterly different from the nonsense that passes under the name of paganism in, say, Swinburne or Aldous Huxley.

I wish you knew my two pupils, Lings[77] and Paterson.[78] Both are poets (quite promising I think) and fast friends of each other. They are just in the state you and I remember so well – the whole world of beauty opening upon them – and as they share the same digs they must have a glorious time. One or other of them often accompanies me on my afternoon walk. Paterson is the wild, and Lings the steady one. Paterson looks very southern, almost an Italian face, and is all moods, and a little effeminate, and is at present in the throes of a terrific quarrel with his father which he poured into my sympathetic ear the other day. Lings is about five feet nothing, very ugly, very dark, and looks a hundred years old, and moves and sits as stiffly as an old man. Paterson truly says that Lings hurrying noiselessly along the cloisters is like nothing so much as a furtive mouse. This doesn't sound like a poet, does it? But he is the better poet and the better man of the two. What times you and I could have had if we had been up here together as undergraduates! Neither of them knows many other people in College and they only discovered each other after they had been up some time. Paterson spent most of his first two terms sitting in his rooms listening to the feet of people on the staircase, always hoping that it was someone coming to call on him, but it never was.

You can imagine how I enjoy them both. Indeed this is the best part of my job. In every given year the pupils I really like are in a minority;

---

76 William Morris, *A Dream of John Ball* (1888); *Love is Enough* (1872); *The Wood Beyond the World* (1894).

77 See **Martin Lings** in the Biographical Appendix.

78 Adrian Hugh Paterson (1909–40) took his BA from Magdalen in 1934. He lectured on English in the University of Hong Kong, 1934–8, and was a lecturer on English at Cairo University from 1938 until 1940 when he died as a result of an accident that occurred while he and Martin Lings were riding together in the desert.

but there is hardly a year in which I do not make some real friend. I am glad to find that people become more and more one of the sources of pleasure as I grow older.

Not that I agree for a moment about books & music being 'vanity and vexation'. Really imaginative (or intellectual) pleasure is neither the one or the other: the *bad* element is the miserly pleasure of *possession*, the delight in this book because it is *mine*.

Of course it was entirely my own fault about the pyjamas – I only hope that your mother was not worried when you asked about them. Give her my love and if her mind needs setting at rest on the subject – why Sir, set it.

Try to write soon again.

Yours
Jack

TO HIS BROTHER (W):

[The Kilns]
Christmas Day 1931

My dear W –

I believe that for the first time I shall be really gravelled for matter in this letter to you, simply because what with examining and lecture writing I have done, read, and heard nothing for a long time that could possibly interest you. Minto has had a letter from you dated from your 'improved' hotel in Shanghai, and we were surprised that you found none of ours awaiting you. No doubt you have had several by this [time].

The afforestation programme 1931 has been carried out, successfully, but not according to plan. What I am more pleased to record is that *in* the wood four new trees have *replaced* (instead of being added to) four elder stumps. I think I told you before that the uprooting of these is practicable, and I shall make it a rule never to plant a new tree without getting rid of a stump. I hope also, if I am energetic enough, to be able to do a little buckshee uprooting during the rest of the year. What interfered with the design of my afforestation was water. I dug one hole far on the Eastern frontier ('in the parts over against Phillipsland') and found it half full of water next day. This I attributed to rain and set to with gum boots and bucket to bail it out. Next morning, although there had been no rain it was fuller than before, so I concluded

I had struck a spring. I shifted my ground and dug another a little to the West. This time was even worse. It was not a question of water 'collecting' – water leaped round my spade as if I had struck a pipe. I hastily filled in what I had dug and tried again. This time my excavation remained dry for a day or so and then began to fill with water. The upshot of it all is that the afforestation this year has been entirely lop sided. I have only managed to plant two at the east end, and the West is overweighted. Next autumn, if we have had a drier summer, the eastern frontier may be practicable again and I shall then restore the balance. If, on the other hand, these springs are permanent, we shall just be unable to plant that side ('there won't *be* any wood there'). After all, regularity is not our aim, and an irregularity, not devised for ornament, but dictated by the nature of the ground, is an honest sort of beauty.

Except for the afforestation there have naturally been no public works so far this Vac. An examiner can hardly be expected to occupy his scanty hours off in such a vigorous way. I hope to do a little now that I am free and shall begin this afternoon by finishing off with the sickle the evacuated (at least I hope it is evacuated) strongpoint of the wasps and the piece of nettle and briar which we left – I can't think why – along the Philipian boundary.

The only social diversion I have had lately was the binge of the English 'Cave' – the anti-junto which, as I said in an earlier letter, is in danger of becoming simply the regular junto.[79] I mention this because I heard recited there a bawdy ballad which was quite new to me, and which seems to me in its conclusion so ludicrous that I can't resist handing it on. Perhaps you know it already. (The rimes seem to have degenerated during the process of oral tradition and now are mere assonances – if that). The early stanzas don't matter: we will begin with the one that ends –

---

79 'The Cave' was a group of English dons who met regularly for talks about literary subjects or to discuss matters in the English School. It was named after the Cave of Adullam in which David organized the conspiracy against Saul (1 Samuel 22:1: 'David . . . escaped to the cave Adullam: and when his brethren and all his father's house heard it, they went down thither to him'). The membership, which included Lewis, Tolkien, Nevill Coghill, Hugo Dyson, Leonard Rice-Oxley, H. F. B. Brett-Smith and Maurice Ridley, were opponents of what had been, until 1931, the reigning faction in the School of English. See also note 29 to the letter to Warnie of 24 October 1931.

Never a word the damsel said
But roared with laughter when the fun was over.
(Rum-ti-iddle-ey etc)

Then comes the good part:

Hark! I hear a step on the stair!
Sounds to me like an angry father,
With a pistol in either hand,
Looking for the man who screwed his daughter
(Rum-ti-iddle-ey etc)

I have seized him by the hair of his head
And shoved it into a bucket of water,
And I screwed his pistol up his arse
A dam sight harder than I screwed his daughter
(Rum-ti-iddle-ey etc)

With the rôle of the heavy father properly cast – stumping up the stairs with a desperate expression and his two pistols – this anticlimax, this adding of injury to insult, seems to me irresistible.

I also heard at the same binge a very interesting piece of literary history from an unexceptionable source – that the hackneyed 'A German officer crossed the Rhine' was being sung at undergraduate blinds[80] in 1912. What do you make of that? Can it date from the Franco Prussian war? Or is it a German student song made in anticipation of *Der Tag* about 1910? The latter would be an interesting fact for the historian. I never heard the ballad as a whole, but think it is poor – in fact, nasty. Bawdy ought to be outrageous and extravagant like the piece quoted. It can, of course, be funny through sheer indefensible insolence, like the following (to the tune of 'Here we go gathering nuts in May')

The Dean of Balliol sleeps with men
Sleeps with men, sleeps with men,
The Dean of Balliol sleeps with men
Till three o'clock in the morning.

80 Drinking parties.

But any parts I have ever heard of the 'German Officer' relate quite possible happenings that have really nothing funny about them. Again, bawdy must have nothing cruel about it, like 'Old Mother Riley': it must not approach anywhere near the pornographic like the poem in which every line begins 'A little'. Within these limits I think it is a good and wholesome *genre*: though I can't help feeling sorry that it should be the *only* living folk-art left to us. If our English binge had been held in a mediaeval university we should have had, mixed with the bawdy songs, tragical and even devotional pieces, equally authorless and handed on from mouth to mouth in the same way, with the same individual variations.

I go to Cambridge on New Years Eve for a couple of day's awarding, not this time to be lodged in Queen's but in the University Arms: with – would you believe it – the same carte blanche. So, at least, I gather from Hugh-Jones of Keble,[81] who stayed there on the same job some years ago and wondered till the last night, when he discovered (almost but not quite too late) the explanation – wondered at the lavish orders of his colleagues and concluded them all to be rich men.

This same Hugh-Jones has been one of my disappointments. I met him in Cambridge at the Award last year: we discovered a common enthusiasm for Shaw and Chesterton and just an interesting amount of disagreement on the subjects they led on to: sat till after midnight: and parted with a strong desire to continue the acquaintance. A few weeks ago he asked me to dine, not in Keble but at his house. That was the first shock – *married*! I arrived and got the second shock – not only a wife present, but a sister in law – an *Anglo-Indian* sister in law. Still I consoled myself with the expectation that he would carry me off to his study after dinner for some talk. Not a bit of it. Not even a temporary separation from the ladies over our wine. He had asked me, apparently, to sit solidly with his wife and sister in law till ten o'clock when I could endure it no longer and went.

The sister in law was the sort of woman who, when the talk drifted

---

81 Edward Maurice Hugh-Jones (1903–97) read History at New College, Oxford, in 1924, after which he read Philosophy, Politics and Economics (PPE) and took a BA in 1925. He was a lecturer at Keble College, 1926–7, and Tutor in Economics, 1927–59. He was Professor of Economics at Keele University, 1959–68. His works include (with E. A. Radice) *An American Experiment* (1936) and *Woodrow Wilson and American Liberalism* (1947).

towards education, remarked that it was astonishing how badly children were taught now a days: she had met a boy of fourteen who didn't know the principal export of Burma. 'He thought it was *fruit*' she said, and laid down her needles and gazed at me. In fact I was like Lamb, left alone with his sensible, well-informed man. (I could have told her the chief export of Anglo-India all right). The wife was not so bad, and I had seen her a few days before acting the part of the maid in *Tartuffe* (in English)[82] given by the Magdalen dramatic society. She had 'done very well' wh. is surprising, for my pupil Lings (I think you met him) who was producer, as well as playing Organ, had given me an amusing account of her behaviour at rehearsals. In his scene with her he had a speech ending 'His only care is religion,'[83] which he inadvertently altered to 'Religion is his only care.' After a long pause she said dreamily 'Are you waiting for me? I haven't got to say my speech until you get to "is religion", you know.'

Tartuffe was really excellently done. I had neither read nor seen it before and enjoyed it thoroughly. To a reader I daresay the savagery is the most striking thing, but on the stage it made me laugh 'consumedly'. The final scene between Organ and his wife is as funny as anything I know ('But I tell you, Mother, I saw him with my own eyes. I saw the rascal embracing my wife' – 'Ah, my son, beware of tale-bearers. Without doubt the worthy man has been slandered' – 'I shall go mad! I saw it *myself*' – 'Ah tongues *will* wag, to be sure' etc.) A most maddening type of female P'dayta. By the way doesn't *Tartuffe*, specially in the opening scenes, bring out very strongly that Latin dominance of the *familia* which you have often spoken of? – except that in Tartuffe's household it is not so much *patria* potestas as *materna* potestas: which possibly is very French too.

It is now after tea and I have put in a very tolerable afternoon's walk on the nettles and brambles. A civil gamekeepery kind of man walked up on the Philips side of the boundary – I think he lives in the other house on Philips land – and had a chat about trees.[84] He knows the place very well having originally *ploughed up* what is now the grass platform before the top wood when Mrs Goodman got rid of the

82 Molière, *Le Tartuffe* (1664).

83 Molière, *Tartuffe, or The Hypocrite*, trans. Curtis Hidden Page (1912) Line 58.

84 This was probably William Taylor, who lived at Shotover Cottage, Old Road, Headington Quarry.

hawthorns. I regretted the loss of the hawthorns less when this man told me that before he ploughed it that part was a mass of undergrowth so that you couldn't walk through it. I was not so pleased to learn that our new holly is, after all our instructions to Suttons, the bush type and not the tree. He promised to find out for me the real name of the tree kind, which he will be able to do as one of his employers is a Forestry tutor. He also remarked that elder and bramble are the two strongest growing things there are and that, left a free field, each will defeat everything except the other.

It was a foggy afternoon, but very warm: really springlike early this morning as I went to 'the early celebbbrrration'.[85] We had a poorish discourse from Thomas at Matins, but otherwise he has been keeping his end up very well. In one sermon on foreign missions lately he gave an ingenious turn to an old objection. 'Many of us' he said 'have friends who used to live abroad, and had a native Christian as a cook who was unsatisfactory. Well, after all there are a great many unsatisfactory Christians in England too. In fact I'm one myself.' Another interesting point (in a different sermon) was that we should be glad that the early Christians expected the second coming and the end of the world quite soon: for if they had known that they were founding an organisation for centuries they would certainly have organised it to death: believing that they were merely making provisional arrangements for a year or so, they left it free to live.

---

85 The 8 a.m. 'early celebration' of Holy Communion at Holy Trinity Church, Headington Quarry. This was an important turning point in Lewis's life. For some time he had been attending matins and evensong in his college chapel and at Holy Trinity, but in participating in the sacrament, Lewis was doing something he knew would be blasphemous unless he was a believer. Jack knew his brother would understand the seriousness of his action.

Warnie, too, went to Holy Communion on Christmas Day 1931. He wrote in his diary that day: 'I attended the service with very mixed feeling, gladness predominating at once again finding myself a full member of the Church after so many years of indifference or worse . . . I came away feeling profoundly thankful that I have once again become a communicant, and intend (D.V.) [Deo Volente – "God Willing"] to go regularly at least four times a year in future' (*BF*). On receiving the present letter from his brother, Warnie wrote on 17 January 1932: 'A letter from J today containing the news that he too has once more started to go to Communion, at which I am delighted. Had he not done so, I, with my altered views would have found – hardly a bar between us, but a lack of a complete identity of interest which I should have regretted' (ibid.).

How odd it is to turn from Thomas to F.K.[86] He really surpassed himself the other day when he said that he objected to the early chapters of St Luke (the Annunciation particularly) on the ground that they were – *indelicate*. This leaves one gasping. One goes on reacting against the conventional modern reaction against nineteenth century prudery, and then suddenly one is held up by a thing like this, and almost pardons all the followers of Lytton Strachey. If you turn up the passage in St Luke the thing becomes even more grotesque. The Middle Ages had a different way with these things. Did I tell you that in one of the Miracle Plays, Joseph is introduced as a typical comic jealous husband, and enters saying 'This is what comes of marrying a young woman.'

F.K., however, gave me a treat last week by showing a treasure which I never would have guessed that he had – a letter in Johnson's own hand to Mrs Thrale. He talks of giving it to Pembroke but as he has had it for many years I guess that he will never part with it.[87]

Minto has probably told you that we are at present revelling in the unaccustomed luxury of a good maid. (What an ambiguous sentence!) You will hardly imagine the Kilns under the rêgime of a maid who not only can cook (that is odd enough) but who is actually *allowed* to cook by Minto – a state of affairs I had long since given up hoping for. Esto perpetua!

As I said at the outset I have been able to read very little: and nothing in your line. The *Somnium Scipionis*[88] is worth mentioning only because the handiest edition I could get was a school edition, & it was rather delightful to renew ones acquaintance with that highly specialised form of composition – a preface to a school text. You know. 'Plato, the celebrated Gk. philosopher (500–400 B.C.) thought –' and then a clear, dogmatic, and misleading sentence. No half lights.

Wuthering Heights[89] which I re-read the other day is, I believe, one

---

86 i.e. the Rev. Edward Foord-Kelcey.

87 Foord-Kelcey would no doubt have thought of donating his letter from Dr Johnson to Mrs Hester Thrale (1741–1821) to Pembroke College, Oxford, because this was the college of both Johnson and Foord-Kelcey himself. When he died in 1934, Foord-Kelcey left the letter to C. S. Lewis, who kept it for the rest of his life. Upon his death in 1963, Warnie gave it to Pembroke College.

88 The *Somnium Scipionis* ('Dream of Scipio') is the fable with which Cicero ends his *De Republica*.

89 Emily Brontë, *Wuthering Heights* (1847).

of your *biblia abiblia*.[90] I should not like to make it my constant fare, but I still like it very much. R. Macaulay's *Mystery at Geneva*[91] I also re-read recently: much the poorest she has written, and a mere repetition of all her favourite tricks. I feel P'daytesque and ask 'Will she *live*?'

I have bought *The Brothers Karamazov*[92] but not yet read it with the exception of some special detachable pieces (of which there are many). Thus read, it is certainly a great religious and poetical work: whether, as a whole, it will turn out a good, or even a tolerable novel I don't know. I have not forgotten your admirable Russian novel 'Alexey Poldorovna lived on a hill. He cried a great deal.'

It is pleasant to reflect that one of the nine terms of your exile is now over.

Yrs
Jack

---

90 'one of those books which are not books'. Charles Lamb, *Last Essays of Elia* (1833), 'Detatched Thoughts on Books and Reading': 'I can read anything which I call a book. There are things in that shape which I cannot allow for such. In this catalogue of books which are not books – *Biblia A-Biblia* – I reckon . . . all those volumes which "no gentleman's library should be without."'

91 Rose Macaulay, *Mystery at Geneva* (1922).

92 Fyodor Mikhailovich Dostoevsky, *The Brothers Karamazov* (1880).

1932

TO ARTHUR GREEVES (W):

[The Kilns]
Jan 10th 1932

My dear Arthur,

I was glad to hear from you again, and sorry you are so dull. Perhaps you are suffering from too much turkey and 'plumb' pudding – or too many late nights and dances! How did you manage to get your mother's consent to the introduction of a dog – I thought she was the insuperable difficulty?

I quite understand the *mood* in wh. you fall back upon detective stories, though I have never been able to understand how that mood could lead to detective stories. I mean, I know well from experience that state of mind in which one wants immediate and certain pleasure from a book, for nothing – i.e. without paying the price of that slight persistence, that almost imperceptible tendency *not* to go on, which, to be honest, nearly always accompanies the reading of [a] good book. Not only accompanies by the way, but (do you agree) actually makes part of the pleasure. A *little* sense of labour is necessary to all perfect pleasures I think: just as (to my palate at least) there is no really delicious taste without a touch of astringency – the 'bite' in alcoholic drinks, the resistance to the teeth in nuts or meat, the tartness of fruit, the bitterness of mint sauce. The apple must not be *too* sweet, the cheese must not be *too* mild. Still, I know the other mood, when one wants a book of sheer pleasure.

In fact I have been going through such a mood lately. I have had to work v. hard all day this Vac. and in the evenings I have wanted relaxation. I have accordingly read *The Wood Beyond the World*, Rider Haggard's *The People of the Mist*,[1] and am now at Kingsley's *Hereward*

---

1 Henry Rider Haggard, *The People of the Mist* (1894).

the Wake.[2] In fact when I am in that state of mind I want not so much a grown-up 'light' book (to me usually the hardest of all kinds of reading) as a boy's book; – distant lands, strange adventures, mysteries not of the American but of the Egyptian kind. Of course what makes detective stories appeal to you is that they were one of your first loves in the days when you used to come round and borrow *Sherlock Holmes* from my father, and therefore in reading them now you have the sense of *return*, you step back as into an old easy shoe – and that certainly is one of the essentials for this kind of reading. One would never read a new *type* of book for pure relaxation: and perhaps *re-reading* of an old friend – a Scott with much skipping – is the best of all. I don't think you re-read enough – I know I do it too much. Is it since I last wrote to you that I re-read *Wuthering House*?[3] I thought it very great. Isn't it (despite the improbability) an excellent stroke of art to tell it all through the mouth of a very homely, prosaic old servant, whose sanity and mother-wit thus provides a cooling medium through which the wild, horrible story becomes tolerable? I have also re-read Burke's *Reflections on the French Revolution*[4] and find that I had forgotten it nearly all. It is, in the famous words, 'too long drawn out' and becomes mere scolding in the end.

What wd. perhaps interest you more is Pater's *Marius the Epicurean*[5] which I had twice before tried to read without success but have this time reached the end of – and reached it before my desire to punch Marius' head had become *quite* unbearable. Do you know it? It is very well worth reading. You must give up all idea of reading a *story* and treat it simply as a vaguely narrative essay. It interests me as showing just how far the purely aesthetic attitude to life can go, in the hands of a master, and it certainly goes a good deal further than one would suppose from reading the inferior aesthetes like Oscar Wilde and George Moore. In Pater it seems almost to *include* the rest of the spiritual life: he has to bring in chastity, he nearly has to bring in Christianity, because they are so beautiful. And yet somehow there is a faint flavour of decay over it all. Perhaps it is his *patronage* of great things which is so offensive – condescending to *add* the Christian religion to his nosegay

---

2 Charles Kingsley, *Hereward the Wake* (1866).

3 i.e. *Wuthering Heights*. See the letter to Warnie of Christmas Day 1931, pp. 31–2.

4 Edmund Burke, *Reflections on the Revolution in France* (1790).

5 Walter Pater, *Marius the Epicurean* (1885).

of spiritual flowers because it has a colour or a scent that he thinks would just give a finishing touch to the rest. It is all balls anyway – because one sees at a glance that if he *really* added it it would break up the whole nosegay view of life. In fact that is the refutation of aestheticism: for perfect beauty you need to include things which will at once show that mere beauty is not the sole end of life. If you don't include them, you *have* given up aestheticism: if you do, you *must* give it up Q.E.D. But Pater is valuable just because, being a perfectly honest aesthete, he really tries to follow its theory to the bitter end, and therefore betrays its weakness. I didn't mean to make this letter a mere catalogue of books read, but one thing has led on to another.

About Lucius' argument that the evangelists would have put the doctrine of the atonement into the Gospel if they had had the slightest excuse, and, since they didn't, therefore Our Lord didn't teach it: surely, since we know from the Epistles that the Apostles (who had actually known him) *did* teach this doctrine in his name *immediately* after his death, it is clear that he *did* teach it: or else, that they allowed themselves a very free hand. But if people shortly after his death were so very free in interpreting his doctrine, why should people who wrote much later (when such freedom wd. be more excusable from lapse of memory in an honest writer, and more likely to escape detection in a dishonest one) become so very much more accurate? The accounts of a thing don't usually get more and more accurate as time goes on. Anyway, if you take the sacrificial idea out of Christianity you deprive both Judaism and Paganism of all significance. Can one believe that there was just *nothing* in that persistent *motif* of blood, death, and resurrection, which runs like a black and scarlet cord through all the greater myths – thro' Balder & Dionysus & Adonis and the Graal too? Surely the history of the human mind hangs together better if you suppose that all this was the first shadowy approach of something whose reality came with Christ – even if we can't at present fully understand that something.

Try and write soon.

Yrs

Jack

TO HIS BROTHER (W):

[Magdalen College]
Jan 17th 1932.

My dear W –

Term began yesterday (Saturday) and I am seated this fine Sunday morning in our room in College having finished my collection papers and now about to allow myself an hour's letter writing before setting out home where I shall be to night.

Through the window on my left I see a most beautiful, almost a springlike, sunshine on the pinnacles of the Tower and the delicious sound of Sunday morning bells has just stopped. On an ordinary Sunday morning I should of course be out at the house, or rather at Church, but as you know the first week end of term is sacred to collections, and having finished them rather earlier than I expected – here we are. I am so seldom in College on a Sunday morning that to be there and at leisure in the unaccustomed sounds and silences of Lord's Day among all the pleasant Leeburiana[6] is quite a holiday.

Your welcome letter of Dec 8th arrived a few days ago, and is so full of conversational openings that I shall hardly find room to inaugurate any subject of my own.

First, as to the Chinese. As to their language, it is pretty certain that its extreme simplicity is that of *second* childhood – the simplicity of a fossil and not of a seed. The essence of it is monosyllabic words each expressing an extremely general idea and given its particular meaning by the context and the position – in fact words approaching the function of the Arabic numerals, where it all depends whether you say 201, 102, 120 or 210. How far European language has already advanced towards this fossil condition you can well see if you compare Latin *Amavisset* with English *He would have loved*: though even *amavisset* is well away. A really primitive tongue would have special words for about twenty special kinds of love (sexual, gastronomic, parental, and what not) and no word for the more abstract 'love': as French, a stage nearer Chinese than we are, has now only one word for our 'love' and 'like'. In fact I look upon Chinese as upon the Moon – a death's head or *memento mori* to nations as the moon is to worlds.

---

6 The books and papers they had brought over from Little Lea, their family home in Belfast.

It is one of the 'painful mysteries' of history that all languages progress from being very particular to being very general. In the first stage they are bursting with meaning, but very cryptic because they are not general enough to show the common element in different things: e.g. you can talk (and therefore think) about all the different kinds of trees but not about *Trees.* In fact you can't really reason at all. In their final stage they are admirably clear but are so far away from real things that they really say nothing. As we learn to talk we forget what we have to say. Humanity, from this point of view, is rather like a man coming gradually awake and trying to describe his dreams: as soon as his mind is sufficiently awake for clear description, the thing which was to be described is gone. You see the origin of journalese and of the style in which you write army letters.

Religion and poetry are about the only languages in modern Europe – if you can regard them as 'languages' which still have traces of the dream in them, still having something to say. Compare 'Our Father which art in Heaven' with 'The supreme being transcends space and time'. The first goes to pieces if you begin to apply the literal meaning to it. How can anything but a sexual animal really be a father? How can it be in the sky? The second falls into no such traps. On the other hand the first really *means* something, really represents a concrete experience in the minds of those who use it: the second is mere dexterous playing with counters, and once a man has learned the rules he can go on that way for two volumes without really using the words to refer to any concrete *fact* at all. But perhaps I have let the subject run away with me. Your point about children always finding their nurses language the easiest is, I take it, a complete answer to your author on that score.

I suppose Minto has already told you of the outrage in the topwood – the two new Scotch firs planted nearest the lane both stolen, and the rascals have neatly levelled in the holes where they were. Clearly to plant two saplings so eminently suitable for Christmas trees so near the road at that time of the year was asking for trouble. But one somehow does not (or did not) think of *trees* as things in danger of theft. You who have not put your sweat into the actual planting of them can hardly imagine my fury: though there is a funny side to it. I smile when I remember myself moving along towards the top gate – then pausing to contemplate my latest achievement – then thinking I was looking in the wrong place – then wondering if I was bewitched – finally the *very* gradual dawn of the truth. We must really get on with some wiring as soon as possible.

I suppose you heard that Mrs. Kreyer[7] has now planted a few shrubs on *our* side of the frontier? And further – most exasperating of all – during the Christmas holiday I hardly ever went in or out by our stile on that side without meeting one or both of her whelps in the very article of trespass, and acknowledging the situation no more than to throw me a patronising 'good afternoon'. What should one do at such a rencontre?

But perhaps the offence itself hardly annoys me more than F.K.'s reaction which consists in chuckling and saying, 'Ah you Irish! I love to listen to dear Mrs. Moore – wouldn't be happy without a grievance. Its really most remarkable'. He is, I think, in every *mental* characteristic (not *moral*, for of course he is no pessimist) the most complete P'daita that ever walked: in some respects he surpasses his original. What a magnificent conversation they could have had, say, in politics!

I was out with him this afternoon and he was quite grieved to hear your unfavourable verdict on Tristram Shandy[8] re-read. I certainly did not get very far with my re-reading of it, but that was due to other causes. I still have hopes that I may enjoy it again *in toto*; and I rather fancy that a long immersion in English Literature has made me more tolerant of that kind of humour by now than you. Oddly enough Barfield has just made your experiment with exactly your result: he agrees with you in excepting Uncle Toby, but thinks most of the book, specially the Wadman parts, revolting.

And talking of the revolting, you will hardly believe the following. The junior parrot (you remember) has just got engaged. As soon as the news was out, his friends and owners, in other words the rest of the junto, all made a raid on his rooms – placed copies of 'Married Love' and 'Lasting Passion' under every cushion – put a large nude india rubber doll in his bed – plastered his walls with lewd good wishes – finished his whisky and beer – and retired. Such is his senility that it was left to him to spread this story as an excellent joke with his own mouth. I should like to be able to argue 'If the fellows of a college

---

7 Lieutenant-Colonel and Mrs J. A. C. Kreyer were the Lewises' closest neighbours. They lived in Tewsfield, a house adjoining the north-west side of The Kilns property.

8 Foord-Kelcey's favourite book was Laurence Sterne's *Tristram Shandy* (1759–67).

behave like this, how much more will the rest of the world', but I'm afraid things are so topsy-turvey – or 'arsie-versy' as the Elizabethans say – that it is the other way round, and for sheer blockheaded vulgarity our common room is just the place to look. Would a jeu d'esprit of this sort be tolerated in barracks?

The reservoir to the West of the top wood is finished. It has been covered with earth so that the total effect is now that of a big plateau jutting out from the hillside, at present of brown mud, but soon, I hope, of smooth bright grass; and there is a little tile-roofed building on it – I suppose protecting a man hole into the interior. The silhouette which I see every evening against the sunset is therefore roughly as drawn, and on the whole I think it is agreeable. It often gives me an odd sensation as I progress homewards to tea along the cliff edge to look at this very distinctive shape in all its novelty and to reflect that, if God pleases, it will someday be as immemorially familiar to you and me as the contour of the Cave Hill. On such occasions you must picture me equipped with both axe and spade for the standard public work at present is 'the extraction of roots' – I admit I have been making slow progress, but that is not because the work is turning out impracticable, but because of many interruptions.

Thus every Monday there is F.K. Last Saturday (by the way this is now Jan 24th – in fact the following Sunday) I was out for a walk with Lings. I have also missed some afternoons when the state of my health would not support the exertion. But I have little doubt that we shall have every single elder out of it before we have done. Another of my interruptions was a miniature walking tour with Barfield and Harwood just before term – so miniature indeed that it should be called a strolling tour: we just dithered along to Abingdon one day, and then Harwood and I alone (Barfield having had to leave us by bus) sauntered to Oxford all the way by river bank. The jaunt is worth mentioning because you and I have hitherto entirely underrated Abingdon. Their [sic] is a church standing in a quadrangle of almshouses right down on one of those little fresh water wharves on the river wh. is excellent. Also, on our saunter back to Oxford, we saw so many 'abandoned lashers' and silver falls that a man who followed the same route in July could 'make one long bathing of a summer day'.[9] And talking about Wordsworth, pray

9 William Wordsworth, *The Prelude: or, Growth of a Poet's Mind* (1850), I, i, 290.

Sir, did you ever read the *White Doe of Rylstone*?[10] I read the first canto last night and recommend it strongly.

I don't remember what I said about Law's *Serious Call.* It is not a book which I would advise anyone to read with great urgency. There is a severity, even a grimness about it which strikes me as excessive. I must also go far to revise the favourable account I gave of *The Appeal.*[11] It did not fulfill the promise of its first passages. An XVIIIth century critic would have complained that it was 'infected with Enthusiasm', and would have been right in this sense that the ideas – *very* valuable ones – which it contains are held by the author with a rather feverish insistence to the exclusion of many other sides of religion. There is a great deal of repetition, and neither the good will which the author won from me at the outset, nor the charm of a delightful edition, nor the literary beauty of many passages (for Law can be really eloquent) prevented me from feeling in the end a sort of discomfort and desire for escape into the open air – as if I had been in a small hot room with a man of genius and piety who was not *absolutely* sane. It is the same quality that moved Johnson to say of Boehme – Law's master in these later books – 'If Jacob had seen the unutterable, Jacob should not have tried to utter it'.[12]

Most of my recent reading, before term, has been of rather a simple and boyish kind. I re-read *The People of the Mist* – a tip-top yarn of the sort. If someone would start re-issuing all Rider Haggard at 1/- a volume I would get them all, as a permanent fall-back for purely recreational reading. Then I read *The Wood Beyond the World* – with some regret that this leaves me no more Wm Morris prose romances to read (except *Child Christopher*[13] wh. is an adaptation of a mediaeval poem already known to me and therefore hardly counts). I wish he had written a hundred of them! I should like to have the knowledge of a new romance always waiting for me the next time I am sick or sorry and want a real treat.

---

10 William Wordsworth, *The White Doe of Rylstone* (1815).

11 In his letter of 24 October 1931, p. 5.

12 Boswell, *The Life of Samuel Johnson*, 1770, vol. II, p. 123. 'Law, (said he,) fell latterly into the reveries of Jacob Boehme, whom Law alleged to have been somewhat in the same state with St. Paul, and to have seen *unutterable things.* Were it even so, (said Johnson,) Jacob would have resembled St. Paul still more, by not attempting to utter them.'

13 William Morris, *Child Christopher and Goldilind the Fair* (1893).

Then I read Kingsley's *Hereward the Wake*, largely for a naif reason – that I had been wondering all my life who Hereward was and had a special reason in my work for wanting to know. The distinguishing feature of Kingsley's novel is that the 'manners and sentiments' are nowhere near so glaringly anachronistic as they are in most novels of the kind – even in Scott whenever he goes further back than the '45. It has, however, the opposite fault of sticking too close to history and therefore giving us (what is unpardonable in a tale of adventure) an unhappy ending. The hero betrays the heroine, deserts his followers, and dies miserably. You would want to vet it as you vetted the *Life and Death of Jason*,[14] and for the same reason.

While at Cambridge (staying, as I foretold you in a posh hotel, at the expense of the Board. Four of us had to hold an examiners meeting one evening, and accordingly, just like the heroes of a romance, called for fire, lights, and a bottle of claret in a private room. All that was lacking was to have prefaced the order by tweaking the landlord's nose with a 'Hark'ee, rascal!' This was in the University Arms which perhaps you know) – while in Cambridge or rather on my long, slow, solitary, first class journey there and back through fields white with frost – I read Pater's *Marius the Epicurean*. This is the best specimen extant of the Epicurean-aesthetic business: which one wrongs by reading it in its inferior practitioners such as George Moore and Oscar Wilde. As you probably know it is a novel – or, since the story is so slight, a faintly narrative *causerie* – laid in the reign of Marcus Aurelius. The interesting thing is, that being a really consistent aesthete, he has to bring in the early Christians favourably because the *flavour* of the early Church – the new music, the humility, the chastity, the sense of order and quiet decorum – appeal to him aesthetically. It is doubtful if he sees that he can only have it in by blowing to bits the whole Epicurean basis of his outlook – so that aestheticism, honestly followed, refutes itself by leading him to something that will put aestheticism in its place – and Pater's position is therefore, in the long run, all nonsense. But it is [a] very beautiful book – much enriched by a full prose translation of the *Cupid and Psyche* story from Apuleius who first told it and who is one of the minor characters. I should try it if it is in your library. Gad! – how it

14 William Morris, *The Life and Death of Jason* (1867).

would have bowled one over if one had read it at eighteen. One would be only just beginning to recover now.

But all these books fade into insignificance beside my really great discovery, Barbour's *Bruce*[15] (XIVth century). This is 'The' modern epic: all that Scott's poems try to recover: chivalrous sentiment, pawky humour, smell of heather, and all the rest of it – only all *real*, all done while that world was still there, not a 'revival'. I am afraid the language is just beyond that thin unmistakable line which divides the readable from the unreadable for those who haven't learned 'Middle English' as a school language. A very little 'modernising' would make it alright. I wonder could I persuade Dents to let me modernise it for an Everyman. You would think Scotch patriotism would give it a sale: till quite modern times every 'cottar' had a copy of it. (Do Scotch patriots *buy* books?). It contains, among other things, an account of Bruce landing at Rathlin which suggests that the bathing would *not* be good there. There seems to be some terrific current

> *'Like the straight of Morrak in Spaine'*

– if that conveys anything to you, which it doesn't to me. (From Rathlin, Bruce went on to Carrick Fergus).

If your idea of reading Descartes holds, begin with the *Discourse on Method*.[16] This is in biographical form and is on the border-land between philosophy proper and what might be called the 'history of intellectual manners'. But I'm not at all sure that a man so steeped in the XVIIth century as you would not find his natural starting point in Boethius – I suppose 'Boece' is as common in France at that time as he was in England? As he was translated about once a century into every civilised language, you would have no difficulty in finding a well flavoured version. In England he had the remarkable adventure of being rendered successively by K. Alfred, Chaucer, and Q. Elizabeth.

As to Thomas' rap over the knuckles about going out during the hymn – my case is this. Complete neglect of communicating is not tolerated by any Church nor practised by me. But is it within his rights to make it impossible for you to hear a sermon without communicating?

15 John Barbour, *The Bruce* (1376).
16 René Descartes, *Discourse on Method* (1637).

Has anyone laid down the exact *proportion* of the intellectual and ritual elements – roughly symbolised by sermons and sacraments – which is necessary to membership of the Church of England. That is my 'case' as a controversialist: but I bear no malice.

By the bye, what are your views, now, on the question of sacraments? To me that is the most puzzling side of the whole thing. I need hardly say I feel none of the materialistic difficulties: but I feel strongly just the opposite ones – i.e. I see (or think I see) so well a sense in which *all* wine is the blood of God – or all *matter*, even, the body of God, that I stumble at the apparently *special* sense in which this is claimed for the Host when consecrated. George Macdonald observes that the good man should aim at reaching the state of mind in which all meals are sacraments. Now that is the sort of thing I can understand: but I find no connection between it and the explicit 'sacrament' proprement dit. The Presbyterian method of sitting at tables munching actual *slices* of bread is clearly absurd under ordinary conditions: but one can conceive a state of society in which a *real* meal might be shared by a congregation in such a way as to be a sacrament without ceasing to be also their actual dinner for that day. Possibly this was so in the very early Church. Don't bother about this if you are not inclined to discuss the question. I trotted it out because it seemed artificial to mention it at all without saying what I was thinking.

How ones range of interests grows! Do you find a sort of double process going on with relation to books – that while the number of subjects one wants to read is increasing, the number of books on each which you find worth reading steadily decreases. Already in your own corner of French history you have reached the point at which you know that most of the books published will be merely re-hashes, but in revenge you are reading Vaughan and thinking of reading Taylor. Ten years ago you would have read eight books on your period (getting only what the *one* book behind those eight would have given you) and left Vaughan and Taylor out of account. In the same way, on the subject of sacraments, a few years ago I should not have wanted any information, but *if I had*, shd. have read book after book about it. Now – one knows [in] advance that here in Oxford there are probably 4000 books dealing exclusively with that subject, and that at least 3990 of them would advance your understanding of it precisely nothing. Once the world was full of books that seemed boring because they gave answers to questions one hadn't asked: every day I find one of these boring books to be really boring for the opposite reason – for failing to answer some question I have asked. Even in things like Anglo Saxon Grammar! 'Why Sir, the quantity to be known is larger than I supposed; but the quantity of knowledge is less than I had conceived possible.'

Your Cathedral sounds mildly good – architecturally. Now that Maureen is away my week is quite differently arranged in order to give Minto as few solitary nights as possible. I lie here on Sunday and Wednesday: Maureen on Friday and Saturday. I still have the schoolboy's pleasure in any change of routine and particularly relish the *division* of my two out nights. I suppose I told you that we have a good maid who really cooks? She doesn't cook as well as Minto, but that is a bagatelle. What is more serious is the steady reduction in the *quantity* of meals which she seems to be effecting. If it goes on at the present rate, when you come back it will be a case of 'I suppose there's some sort of pot-house in this village where a man could get a biscuit, huh?'[17] (This had better *not* be mentioned in your next letter to Minto. I daresay we shall pull through). I have fewer tutorials this term – the Junto is quiet – my lecture is well attended – and all shapes for a much pleasanter term than usual: the *second* of the nine, as it is pleasing to note. Why don't you write that paper on Thomas Browne yourself? I've no time for it.

yours
Jack.

P.S. Minto tells me to tell you I like Troddles the puppy because she says if I don't mention him you'll think I don't like him but I say that is not the masculine way of reading letters nor of writing them but she is not quite convinced so here goes; – I like Troddles. So does Papworth. Cham can't abide him and cuffs him whenever they meet.

Jack was very afraid that Warnie, who had been in Shanghai since 17 November 1931, was in danger from a Japanese attack on the Chinese part of that city. On 18 September 1931, in violation of its treaty obligations, Japan occupied Manchuria. On 21 September China appealed to the Council of the League of Nations, and on 30 September the Council

---

17 Lewis was giving Warnie an imitation of their father.

adopted unanimously a resolution taking note of the Japanese representative's statement that his Government would continue as rapidly as possible the withdrawal of its troops.

The Japanese Government failed to carry out the assurances given the Council, but adopted the attitude that a preliminary agreement, binding China to recognize Japan's treaty rights in Manchuria, was an essential element of security and must be a condition precedent to evacuation. After being rebuffed by the League of Nations, Japan announced its withdrawal from the League to take effect in 1935. To consolidate its gains, Japan landed troops in Shanghai on 28 January 1932 to quell an effective Chinese boycott of Japanese goods. By 5 February the whole of the three provinces of Manchuria were occupied. China was unable to resist the superior Japanese forces and in May 1933 it recognized the Japanese conquest by signing a truce.

Writing about it later, Warnie said the Army Service Corps was 'not involved, but there was thought to be a grave risk that the Japanese, in an endeavour to outflank the Chinese, might violate the International Settlement. Consequently the Settlement garrison had been put on an active service basis, with manned trenches, strong points etc, round our perimeter'.[18]

TO HIS BROTHER (W):

Feb 15th 1932
The Kilns

My dear Warnie –

This will be a shortish letter, partly because I am still a convalescent from flu – this being not my first day but my first afternoon up – partly because we don't really care to bank on the security of any letter reaching you in the present state of Shanghai.

Anxiety is of all troubles the one that lends itself least to description. Of course we have been and are infernally bothered about you – probably not more than you have been bothered about yourself! I suppose that about as often as I have stopped myself from repeating the infuriating question '*Why* was he such a fool' etc, you have abstained from the parallel '*Why* was I such a fool as ever to come out here'. I will refrain from asking you any particular questions because I remember

18 WHL, p. 200.

from war experiences that questions from home are always based on a misunderstanding of the whole situation.

It will be more useful as a guide to your reply to tell you that we have (from the *Times*) a map of Shanghai large enough to mark *Gt. Western Road*, so we should be able to follow your news in some detail. As for the printed news, it is plainly nonsense: the almost daily story being that fierce fighting raged all day in Chapei and the Japanese had one man killed and three wounded. In other parts of the paper the 'fierce fighting', I admit, usually turns out to be a heavy Japanese barrage replied to by two trench mortars. You will see at any rate that it is impossible from here to form any idea of the only aspect of the thing that concerns me: *viz*: the actual and probable distance between the A.P.B. and the firing. It is true that I have to my hand the axiom that the distance will be as great as the A.P.B. has been able to contrive – but that carries me only a very little way. The result is that my fancy plays me every kind of trick. At one time I feel as if the danger was very slight and begin reckoning when your first account of the troubles will reach us: at another I am – exceedingly depressed. All the news is of the sort that one re-interprets over and over again with new results in each new mood. A beastly state of affairs.

The last letter we had from you was the one you wrote to Minto immediately after your flu'. I had written to you a few days before that arrived. Since then I don't know that much to record has happened. I was going on steadily with the 'extraction of roots' in the wood: but you'd hardly believe how the doubt about your situation takes the relish out of public works.

My term was continuing in a pretty good course. Segar[19] has been specially attentive in inquiries about you and in his characteristic half comical attempts to put the situation in as favourable a light as possible.

19 Robert Segar (1879–1961) was a barrister until, at the age of forty, he went to Magdalen College and read Law. He was Lecturer in Jurisprudence at Wadham College and Tutor in Law at Magdalen College, 1919–21, and Fellow of Magdalen, 1921–35. See Lewis's portrait of him in the Magdalen College Appendix to *AMR*, in which he says of Segar: 'He brings about him the air of a bar parlour: to sit with him is to be snug and jolly and knowing and not unkindly, and to forget that there are green fields or art galleries in the world. All this is the side he shows us day by day: but there is more behind, for he is a war wreck and spends his nights mostly awake.'

I must say I am a little surprised that he is the only person in College who has done so.

I have now been in my room for precisely a week. It has been an ideal illness. My little east room, as you know, gives one two views – one over to Philips an t'other up to the top wood – and the grate does not smoke. Most of the week there has been snow falling during some part of the day – wh. is just the finishing touch to a comfortable day's reading in bed. I have re-read three Scotts. *1. The Monastery*[20] wh. I had read in the very old days – pre-Wynyard[21] and quite forgotten. I think it the poorest Scott I have yet read, tho worth reading. What really gave me most pleasure was to meet your quotation (in the Capt. Clutterbuck epistle) about the paradise of half-pay and the purgatory of duty. Lord – I wish you were out of the latter this moment. *2. The Abbot* – originally read at the same time. This is much better, and I should put it fairly high among the pre-17th century novels, wh. as a whole I find inferior to the others. Still, it shares with *Rob Roy* the rare advantage of having a natural and even pleasant heroine. Finally *The Antiquary* for about the fifth time, wh. I have almost fixed on as *the* Scott novel.[22] I have read it so often that I do not remember at which reading I ceased to regard Mr. Oldbuck as 'a character' and began to think him (as I now do) simply the one sensible man in the book, living as any rational man would live if he were given peace.

I wonder, supposing that the P.O. is working when this reaches you, would you mind letting me have a cable to say that you're alright? Unless, of course everything is quiet by the end of the next fortnight. It would really cheer us up immensely.

I shall resume proper letter writing with the rest of my regular routine as soon as I get back to work. For the moment this is the best I can do. With best wishes, brother, for a speedy removal of your person to some quieter area.

Yours
Jack.

---

20 Sir Walter Scott, *The Monastery* (1820).

21 Wynyard School in Watford, Hertfordshire, was the boys' preparatory school attended by the Lewis brothers, who both hated their time there. Warnie was a pupil 1905–9, and Jack, who was there 1907–9, referred to it as 'Belsen' in *SBJ*, ch. 2.

22 Sir Walter Scott, *The Abbot* (1820); *Rob Roy* (1817); *The Antiquary* (1816).

P.S. Your pictures have come. I think *hanging* them is the safest method of storing them and I shall do so as soon as I am about again: till then I have refused to have them unpacked.

TO HIS BROTHER (W):

[The Kilns]
Feb 21st 1932

My dear W –

Since I last wrote to you, four or five days ago, we had two communications from you. *First*, a message by Bibby Wireless which took exactly a fortnight to reach us. As this is much too short a time for anything but telegraphy, and much too long for any telegraph (wireless *or* wiry) I don't know what to make of it: but I'm inclined to think that you expected it to reach us sooner and that its actual date of arrival *does* shew some dislocation of services. Thanks for sending it. The re-assuring view of the crisis is quite obviously untrue by *now*, whatever it may have been when you sent it; but thanks all the same.

Secondly, I have had your cheering letter of Jan 14th – 'cheering' for giving one some conversation with you, though of course it bears not at all on the source of anxiety. I must confess I have imbibed enough of that rather specially shabby superstition which cries 'Touch wood' etc, to shudder when I read your proposals about walks in Ulster etc. In fact I have two unpleasantly contrasted pictures in my mind. One 'features' the two Pigibudda with packs and sticks de-training into the sudden stillness of the moors at Parkmore:[23] the other is of you progressing from the Bund to Gt. Western Rd. with an eye cocked skyward, just in the old French manner, curse it, and ducking at the old *Who-o-o-o-p – Bang*! Like Boswell, on that perilous crossing in the Hebrides, I 'at last took refuge in piety: but was much embarrassed by the various objections which have been raised against the doctrine of special providences'.[24] Unfortunately I have not at hand the work of Dr. Ogden in

---

23 In Co. Antrim.

24 Boswell, *The Life of Samuel Johnson*, 3 October 1773, vol. V, p. 282. 'I upbraided myself, as not having a sufficient cause for putting myself in such danger. Piety afforded me comfort; yet I was disturbed by the objections that have been made against a particular providence, and by the arguments of those who maintain that it is in vain to hope that the petitions of an individual, or even of congregations, can have any influence with the Deity.'

which Boswell found this difficulty solved.[25] I suppose the solution lies in pointing out that the efficacy of prayer is, at any rate *no more* of a problem then the efficacy of *all* human acts. i.e. if you say 'It is useless to pray because Providence already knows what is best and will certainly do it,' then why is it not equally useless (and for the same reason) to try to alter the course of events in any way whatever – to ask for the salt or book your seat in a train?

However, in spite of this discomfort, I cannot help joining you in your day-dream of a Parkmore walk. That is partly because I am now back in bed (nothing serious, just a slight re-rise of temperature owing to having tried to get up too soon). Do you find, during the endless afternoons of a week in bed, that one's imagination is constantly haunted with pictures of seacoasts and cliffs and such like? Mine has been specially busy with the walk you suggest. I think it would be better to go down to the coast by the *second* of the two glens to Cushendun (not Cushendall) after a glance down the first, which is better as a *view* than as a *route*. The impressive simplicity – one huge fold of land – which makes it so good a view would make it a little monotonous for footing: the other is a perfect paradise of ups and downs and brawling streams, little woods, stone walls, and ruined cottages. The next days walk – on North with Rathlin in view – I did an hour of with Arthur last summer, and it is even better than you can possibly imagine if you haven't done it. The lunch problem is a pity: but one can never be utterly stranded in a country full of streams – spring water being not only better than nothing with which to wash down a man's victuals but better than anything except beer or tea. It is the dry dollop of unmitigated sandwich on top of a waterless chalk down in Berkshire that really spoils a day's walk. But perhaps this is enough of the day dream – the other picture begins to bother me.

By the way, if you get through this damned battle next door to you, it will have had one incidental advantage – that of having made me very familiar with Shanghai. I could now draw quite a good map from memory: certainly could get in Chapei Station, Gt. Western Rd, Trinity Cathedral, Cathay Hotel, the Creek, Hongkew fairly correctly.

I thoroughly agree with your revised proposals for the Lewis papers. If you remember, I was always to this extent opposed to your first

25 Dr Samuel Ogden, *Sermons on the Efficacy of Prayers and Intercession* (1770).

scheme, that I wanted *all* letters put in together in their chronological order so as to secure the *va-et-vient*[26] of actual intercourse, whereas you wanted A's letters in a block, then B's letters in a block. But your new idea is better than either. How far will you extend it? It seems to me that all good traditional information (e.g. 'I thought your father would have gone wild') now can and ought to go in: and I am not at all sure that the contents of *P'daita Pie*[27] should not find their place in the main narrative. Many pages of Boswell are just such 'pie' mosaiced into the biography. You see how impossible it is *not* to be always counting on the future and then being always pulled up by recollection of those shells and made to feel that any such counting is a positive tempting of fate. However, what is one to do.

I shall make this a short letter and try to send you another short one soon, because whatever you say, it is quite obvious that mails are not safe. How can they be when any boat coming up that river may stop a Chinese shell? I was much taken by the photos of the model railway – though his wall-painting scenery seems to have left some problems of perspective unsolved. I doubt if I should care for a toy of that kind now: toy *country* would be my fancy – i.e. where you wd. have country as a background to a railway, I should have railway as a feature of the country. Perhaps some such complementary difference was already present in our own humbler attic system. But a man could have great fun, you will allow, landscape-building on that same scale. Indeed I fancy you could produce something of which the photos would really deceive.

I wonder how I shd. enjoy a performance of *The Count of Luxembourg*?[28] I hum over to myself *Rootsie-Tootsie* and *As they pass the gay cafes* and of course remember, in a way, all the same things as you: but probably with quite different emotions. I see now that my enjoyment of musical comedy in the old days, though quite *real*, was largely 'caught'

---

26 'to-ing and fro-ing'.

27 Over the years Jack and Warnie preserved 100 of their father's characteristic sayings which they copied into a notebook entitled 'Pudaita Pie'. This was the source of many of the sayings of Albert found in *SBJ*. In the end, they decided against including the document in the Lewis Papers. The manuscript of 'Pudaita Pie' is found in the Wade Center at Wheaton College.

28 *The Count of Luxembourg* is a musical play by Basil Hood, with music by F. Lehar, first performed on 20 May 1911.

from you – or rather from the fashionable world of 1912–14 of which you were in my case the conductor: and it has all passed without going deep enough to make the *real* remeniscent feeling as they do in you. The sound that I get in our room in college when I pull the study curtains (that unique rumble) releases memories that 'come home to my business and bosoms' as the musical comedy tunes do not. Contrariwise, *my* old Wagner favourites, which are still startlingly evocative for me, wd. probably now not be so for you.

This, by the bye, shows the absurdity of the statement often made 'Well at least a man knows when he's enjoying himself'. I *thought* I liked the musical comedy tune in my musical comedy period just as much as I *thought* I liked the Wagner tune in my next period. Memory shows that I was mistaken. And why should I remember with such delight sitting with you near that fountain on the high Holywood Road that summer evening during the great Row – and remember with such complete coldness going to *The Arcadians*.[29] The first seemed at the time a most miserable, the second a most pleasurable evening: but the first has 'kept' (as they say of meat) and the second has not. Still, I wd. willingly go with you to one of the old musical comedies if the chance came our way.

It is a springlike evening here – all the birds twittering – and I am beginning to be tired of bed. I am certainly tired of novels and must get something nutritious fetched from college to morrow. I'm not at all sure that I shan't, after your remarks, have a cut at the *Georgics*.[30] I need not urge you to look after yourself as well as you can. I suppose you are wearing tin-hats – alack the day! All send their love

Yrs
Jack.

TO ARTHUR GREEVES (W):

[The Kilns]
Feb 1932

My dear Arthur,

I have been laid up with flu' for over a fortnight or I shd. have

---

29 *The Arcadians* is a musical play by Mark Ambient, with music by Lionel Monkton and Howard Talbot, first performed on 28 April 1909.

30 A didactic poem in four books of hexameters by Virgil on the various forms of rural industry. It was written between 37 and 30 BC.

answered you before. As you preferred my last letter to my previous ones, and also took longer to answer it than ever, I suppose if I want a speedy answer to this I had better write a letter you *don't* like! Let me see – I must first select all the subjects which are least likely to interest you, and then consider how to treat them in the most unattractive manner. I have half a mind to do it – but on second thoughts it would be almost as big a bore for me to write it as for you to read it. How exasperating to think of you being at Ballycastle with an unappreciative companion, in bad weather, and a lethargic mood: it seems such a waste.

I thought we had talked about Naomi Mitchison before. I have only read one (*Black Sparta*)[31] and I certainly agree that it 'holds' one: indeed I don't know any historical fiction that is so astonishingly vivid and, on the whole, so true. I also thought it astonishing how, despite the grimness, she got such an air of beauty – almost dazzling beauty – into it. As to the cruelties, I think her obvious relish is morally wicked, but hardly an *artistic* fault for she cd. hardly get some of her effects without it. But it is, in *Black Sparta*, a historical falsehood: not that the things she describes did not probably happen in Greece, but that they were not typical – the Greeks being, no doubt, cruel by modern standards, but, by the standards of that age, extremely humane. She gives you the impression that the cruelty was essentially Greek, whereas it was precisely the opposite. That is, she is unfair as I should be unfair if I wrote a book about some man whose chief characteristic was that he was the tallest of the pigmies, and kept on reminding the reader that he was very short. I should be telling the truth (for of course he would be short by our standards) but missing the real point about the man – *viz*: that he was, by the standards of his own race, a giant. Still, she is a wonderful writer and I fully intend to read more of her when I have a chance.

I am so glad to hear you have started Froissart.[32] If I had the book

---

31 Naomi Mitchison, *Black Sparta* (1928).

32 Jean Froissart's *Chroniques* (c. 1373–1400) is a lively, though sometimes inaccurate, record of Europe in the fourteenth century with particular emphasis on the first half of the Hundred Years' War between France and England. The best-known translation is that by Lord Berners, published 1923–5. Lewis was using the Globe Edition of *The Chronicles of Froissart*, trans. John Bouchier, Lord Berners, ed. and reduced into one volume by G. M. Macaulay (1924).

here (I am out at the Kilns – only got up yesterday) we could compare passages. What I chiefly remember from the first part is the Scotch wars and the odd way in which just a very few words gave me the impression of the scenery – the long wet valleys and the moors. How interesting too, to find how much of the chivalry in the romances was really practised in the wars of the period – e.g. the scene where Sir Thing-um-a-bob (you see you are not the only one who forgets things) espouses the cause of the lady of Hainault. Or again, at the siege of Hennebont (?) where you actually have a lady-knight fighting, just like Britomart in the *Faerie Queene*.

To enjoy a book like that thoroughly I find I have to treat it as a sort of hobby and set about it seriously. I begin by making a map on one of the end leafs: then I put in a genealogical tree or two. Then I put a running headline at the top of each page: finally I index at the end all the passages I have for any reason underlined. I often wonder – considering how people enjoy themselves developing photos or making scrap-books – why so few people make a hobby of their reading in this way. Many an otherwise dull book which I had to read have I enjoyed in this way, with a fine-nibbed pen in my hand: one is *making* something all the time and a book so read acquires the charm of a toy without losing that of a book.

By the way, when you ask me to 'pray for you' (in connection with Froissart) I don't know if you are serious, but, the answer is, I do. It may not do you any good, but it does me a lot, for I cannot ask for any change to be made in you without finding that the very same needs to be made in me; which pulls me up and also by putting us all in the same boat checks any tendency to priggishness.

While I have been in bed I have had an orgy of Scott – *The Monastery*, *The Abbot*, *The Antiquary* and the *Heart of Midlothian*[33] which I am at present in the middle of. The *Monastery* and *Abbot* I have read only once before – long, long ago, long before you and I were friends – so that they were the same as new ground to me. Neither of them is Scott at his best – the *Monastery* indeed is about the worst I have yet read – but both are worth reading. *The Antiquary* I have read over and over again, and old Oldbuck is almost as familiar to me as Johnson. What a *relish* there is about him and his folios and his tapestry room and his

33 Sir Walter Scott, *The Heart of Midlothian* (1818).

paper on Castrametation and his 'never taking supper: but trusting that a mouthful of ale with a toast and haddock, to close the orifice of the stomach, does not come under that denomination'[34] (How like my father and his 'little drop of the whiskey').

I think re-reading old favourites is one of the things we differ on, isn't it, and you do it very rarely. I probably do it too much. It is one of my greatest pleasures: indeed I can't imagine a man really enjoying a book and reading it only once. *Do* try one of the old Scotts again. It will do admirably as a rest in the intervals of something that needs working at, like Froissart.

There has been a good deal of snow during my illness. Where I lay in bed I could see it through two windows, and a bit of the wooded hill gradually whitening in the distance. What could be snugger or nicer? Indeed my flu' this year would have been delightful if I hadn't been worried about Warnie, who is in Shanghai. When there is something like this wh. forces one to read the papers, how one loathes their flippancy and their sensational exploitation of things that mean life and death. I wish to goodness he had never gone out there.

Do try and let me know when you are coming to London and when there is a chance of your coming here. Otherwise you know what it will be: you will turn up unexpectedly on some day when I have 15 hours' work to do, and I shall be angry with you and you will be angry with me, and we shall meet for a comfortless half hour in a teashop and snap and sulk at each other and part both feeling miserable. Surely it is worth while trying to avoid this. Give my love to your mother and to the dog. I hope we shall have some famous walks with him

Yours

Jack

---

34 Scott, *The Antiquary*, ch. 35. After remarking that he never tastes anything 'after sun-set', Mr Oldbuck says to Lord Glenallan: 'A broiled bone, or a smoked haddock, or an oyster, or a slice of bacon of our own curing, with a toast and a tankard or something or other of that sort, to close the orifice of the stomach before going to bed, does not fall under my restriction, nor, I hope, under your Lordship's.'

TO OWEN BARFIELD (W):

The Kilns,
Headington Quarry,
Oxford.
March 16th/32

My dear Barfield

Death and damnation! This will never do. Look here – when you walk I walk. If you are finally forced to take your holiday earlier, make that the walk and Griffiths and I will come with you. A walk with the new Anthroposophical[35] member and without you is not good enough. But I trust you will be able to stick to the original arrangement.

Somehow *prurient* doesn't seem to be the right word for Spenser. *Delicatus* – relaxed in will – of course he is.

You must have been having a horrible time alternating between bed and exams.[36] Condolences! I have written about 100 lines of a long poem in my type of Alexandrine. It is going to make the *Prelude* (let alone the *Tower*)[37] look silly.

Yours
C. S. Lewis

---

35 Anthroposophy is a religious system founded by Rudolf Steiner (1861–1925). Steiner's aim was to develop the faculty of spirit cognition inherent in ordinary people and to put them in touch with the spiritual world from which materialism had caused them to be estranged. Owen Barfield and Cecil Harwood became Anthroposophists in 1923. Lewis was later to write in *SBJ*, ch. 13, p. 161: 'Barfield's conversion to Anthroposophy marked the beginning of what I can only describe as the Great War between him and me . . . it was an almost incessant disputation, sometimes by letter and sometimes face to face, which lasted for years.' Perhaps the most important of the 'Great War' documents is Lewis's unpublished *Metaphysices contra Anthroposophos* – better known as the *Summa* after its model by St Thomas Aquinas. For an account of the 'Great War' see Lionel Adey, *C. S. Lewis's Great War with Owen Barfield* (British Columbia, University of Victoria, ELS Monograph Series no. 14, 1978; new edn, Rosley, Ink Books, 2002). Lewis eventually got over his disagreement with Barfield and Harwood.

36 Barfield was taking the examinations required for practice as a solicitor.

37 'The Tower' is a long poem by Owen Barfield, much admired by Lewis. It has never been published.

TO OWEN BARFIELD (W):

The Kilns,
Headington Quarry,
Oxford.
March 19th 1932

My dear Barfield –

Rê Walk: (1) I could certainly come earlier, but very strongly deprecate a date too near Easter on account of crowded hotels etc. (2) I would reluctantly agree to changing the terrain to Sussex: but if the date is put near Easter, this reluctance increased to *just not being* absolute recalcitrance. *That* country at *that* time will be a stream of hikers talking about yaffles. Is it, by the way, to any one's interest besides yours to walk in Sussex.

(3) I enclose Griffiths' letter, to which I have replied telling him all I know (it isn't much) about dates. It is an alarming and disappointing letter. I am afraid Anthroposophy is his only chance now. He seems to be heading for unmitigated egoism. I wrote him rather a breezy letter trying to give him the feeling, without saying it, that the idea of *his* being a 'burden' on our walk (damn his impudence) was unutterably ridiculous. I'd like to see anyone try? This walk is his last chance. Either we'll cure him or make an enemy of him for life!

Thanks for the *Note on Pain*. 'I kan not bult it to the bran'[38] at all. When you say that the redeemed self can feel no pain, does this mean that the actual sense-data would be different, or only that the self's attitude to them would be i.e. it would feel *what we call* pain but would not 'mind it' – have λύπη[39] but not λυπεῖν.[40] Again, is 'being aware of something as good' equal to 'feeling something as pleasurable'. If pain disappears as soon as we find it good, then can't we be said to find pain good? You see I am all muddled. I will try to get clear and write about it later on: but I think the 'note' very important.

I am still pleased with my new poem. What Wordsworth didn't see was that the subjective epic can learn a lot from the structure of the

38 Geoffrey Chaucer, *Canterbury Tales*, The Nun's Priest's Tale, 474: 'But I ne kan nat bulte it to the bren': 'But I cannot sift the chaff from the grain.'

39 'pain'.

40 'vexation'.

old epic. There need be no flats if you use the equivalent of *inlet* narrative and hastening *in media res.*

Have you passed your exam?

Yours

C. S. Lewis

TO HIS BROTHER (W):

[The Kilns]
March 20th 1932

My dear Warnie –

We had a few days ago your letter of Jan. 28th and the first written by you during the troubles. The papers had of course relieved our minds some time before we got it: and I have now passed from anxiety to that sulky state in which I feel that you have given us all a great deal of unnecessary trouble. I feel as the P'daitabird did when he replied to a Cherbourg letter of mine, telling him how I had had a nasty fall in a puddle, 'Please try *for my sake* to avoid such drenchings in the future.' I hope you will be equally considerate. By the way, as regards one point in your letter, – there is no question of building a fence *instead* of building the two rooms. Indeed, considering the comparative cost of the two works, this would be rather like buying a new pair of braces *instead* of a Rolles-Royce.

Next to the good news from China, the best thing that has happened to me lately is to have assisted at such a scene in the Magdalen smoking room as rarely falls one's way. The Senior Parrot – that perfectly ape-faced man whom I have probably pointed out to you – was seated on the padded fender with his back to the fire, bending down to read a paper, and thus leaving a tunnel shaped aperture between his collar and the nape of his neck [designated P in a drawing of the man]. A few yards in front of him stood MacFarlane.[41] Let MacFarlane now light a cigarette and wave the match to and fro in the air to extinguish it. And let the match be either not wholly extinguished or so recently extinguished that no fall of temperature in the wood has occurred. Let M. then fling the match towards the fire in such a way that it follows the dotted line and enters the aperture at P with the most unerring

41 Kenneth Bruce McFarlane (1903–66) took a BA from Exeter College, Oxford, in 1925 and was Tutor in Modern History at Magdalen College, 1927–66.

accuracy. For a space of time which must have been infinitesimal, but which seemed long to us as we watched in the perfect silence which this very interesting experiment so naturally demanded, the Senior Parrot, alone ignorant of his fate, continued absorbed in the football results. His body then rose in a vertical line from the fender, without apparent muscular effort, as though propelled by a powerful spring under his bottom. Re-alighting on his feet he betook himself to a rapid movement of the hands with the apparent intention of applying them to every part of his back and buttock in the quickest possible succession: accompanying this exercise with the distention of the cheeks and a blowing noise. After which, exclaiming (to me) in a very heightened voice 'It isn't so bloody funny' he darted from the room. The learned Dr Hope (that little dark, mentally dull, but very decent demi-butty who breakfasted with you and me)[42] who alone had watched the experiment with perfect gravity, at this stage, remarked placidly to the company in general, 'Well, well, the match will have gone out by now', and returned to his periodical – But the luck of it! How many shots would a man have taken before he succeeded in throwing a match into that tiny aperture if he had been trying?

You asked Minto in a recent letter about this Kenchew man.[43] As a suitor he shows deplorable tendency to hang fire, and I fancy the whole thing will come to nothing. (Ah there won't *be* any proposal): as a character, however, he is worth describing, or seems so to me because I had to go for a walk with him. He is a ladylike little man of about fifty, and is to-a-tee that 'sensible, well-informed man' with whom Lamb dreaded to be left alone. My troubles began at once. It seemed good to him to take a bus to the Station and start our walk along a sort of scrubby path between a factory and a greasy strip of water – a walk, in fact, which was as good a reproduction as Oxford could afford

42 Edward Hope (1866–1953) took a Sc.D. from Manchester and in 1919 was elected Fellow and Tutor in Natural Science at Magdalen and Lecturer in Chemistry. Lewis provides a portrait of him in the Magdalen College Appendix to *AMR*: 'This is one of those men in whom knowledge and intellect have taken up their abode without making any difference: they are added on to a decent drab nonentity of character, and the character has not been transformed. If you wiped out his technical knowledge there would be nothing left to distinguish him from any respectable shopkeeper in Tottenham Court Road . . .'

43 Nothing is known of Mr Kenchew except that he was a teacher of geography who failed to win Maureen's affections.

of our old Sunday morning 'around the river bank'. I blundered at once by referring to the water as a canal. 'Oh – could it be possible that I didn't know it was the Thames? I must be joking. Perhaps I was not a walker?' I foolishly said that I was. He gave me an account of his favourite walks; with a liberal use of the word 'picturesque'. He then called my attention to the fact that the river was unusually low (how the devil did he know that?) and would like to know how *I* explained it. I scored a complete Plough, and was told how *he* explained it.

By this time we were out in Port Meadow, and a wide prospect opened before him. A number of hills and church spires required to be identified, together with their 'picturesque', mineral, or chronological details. A good many problems arose, and again I did very badly. As his map, though constantly brought out, was a *geological* map, it did not help us much. A conversation on weather followed, and seemed to offer an escape from unmitigated fact. The escape, however, was quite illusory, and my claim to be rather fond of nearly all sorts of weather was received with the stunning information that psychologists detected the same trait in children and lunatics.

Anxious to turn my attention from this unpleasing fact, he begged my opinion of various changes which had recently been made in the river: indeed every single lock, bridge, and stile for three mortal miles had apparently been radically altered in the last few months. As I had never seen *any* of the places before ('But I thought you said you were a walker . . .') this bowled me middle stump again. The removal of a weir gave us particular trouble. He could not conceive how it had been done. What did I think? And then, just as I was recovering from this fresh disgrace, and hoping that the infernal weir was done with, I found that the problem of *how* it had been removed was being raised only as the preliminary to the still more intricate problem of *why* it had been removed. (My feelings were those expressed by Macfarlane at dinner one night last term, in an answer to someone's question. 'Yes. He is studying the rhythms of mediaeval Latin prose, and it is a very curious and interesting subject, but it doesn't interest me.')

For a mile or so after the weir we got on famously, for Kenchew began 'I was once passing this very spot or, no, let me see – perhaps it was a little further on – no! It was exactly here – I remember that very tree – when a very remarkable experience, really remarkable in a small way, happened to me.' The experience remarkable in a small way, with the aid of a judicious question or two on my part, was bidding fair to last out the length of the walk, when we had the horrible misfortune of passing a paper mill (You see, by the bye, what a jolly walk it was even apart from the company!). Not only *a* paper mill but *the* paper mill of the Clarendon Press. 'Of course I had been over it. No? Really etc.' (The great attraction was that you could get an electric shock.)

But I must stop my account of this deplorable walk somewhere. It was the same all through – sheer information. Time after time I attempted to get away from the torrent of isolated, particular facts: but anything tending to opinion, or discussion, to fancy, to ideas, even to putting some of his infernal facts together and making something out of them – anything like that was received in blank silence. Once, while he was telling me the legendary foundation of a church, I had a faint hope that we might get onto history: but it turned out that his knowledge was derived from an Edwardian Oxford *pageant*. Need I add that he is a scientist? A geographer, to be exact. And now that I come to think of it he is exactly what one would have expected a geographer to be. But I mustn't give you too black an impression of him. He is kind, and *really* courteous (you know the rare quality I mean) and a gentleman. I imagine he is what women call '*Such* an interesting man. And *so* clever.'

One day in College lately I had a long browse over Lockhart,[44] using your pencilled index as a guide. It had almost the effect of having a conversation with you. What a good book it is, isn't it? I must gradually browse through it all. Some baggage called Dame Una Pope-Henessy has just brought out (for the centenary) a real petty, chatty, Strachey-esque Life of Scott which begins by expressing a desire to 'rescue' Scott from 'the solemn nine-volume tomb' of Lockhart.[45] This kind of thing is insufferable. Christie reviewed it for the Oxford Magazine and, very happily in my opinion, ended up with the view that this chatty, impudent life was 'bound to come' and it was a good thing to have it over.[46]

---

44 John Gibson Lockhart, *Memoirs of the Life of Scott*, 10 vols. (1839).

45 Una Pope-Hennessy, *The Laird of Abbotsford; an Informal Presentation of Sir Walter Scott* (1932).

46 John Christie, *The Oxford Magazine*, L (10 March 1932), pp. 570–1: 'In truth Dame Una seems less interested in the author of *Waverley* than, to use her own phrase, in "spicy gossip" . . . It was bound to come, this bright, inquisitive, anything but intimate portrait of Sir Walter, with his foibles, his snobbery, and his subterfuges touched in with loving care, and most of the deeper traits left out.'

Talking about Scott, I finished the *Heart of Midlothian* shortly after I last wrote to you. It seems to me on the whole one of the best. *Dumbiedikes* is one of the great lairds – almost as good as Ellangowans, though not quite. I suppose every one has already remarked how wonderfully Jennie escapes the common dulness of perfectly good characters in fiction. Do you think that the fact of her being uneducated helps? Is it that the reader wants to feel some superiority over the characters he reads about, and that a social or intellectual one will give him a sop and induce him to believe in the purely *moral* superiority? But this sounds rather too 'modern' and knowing to be true; I for one not beleiving that we are all such ticks as is at present supposed. I did *not* read the *Georgics* after all, but did read the Aeneid.

The other day Foord-Kelsie succeeded in carrying out a project that he has been hammering away at for a long time, that of taking me over to see his old village of Kimble where he was rector. I mention it in order to say that you and I have unduly neglected the Chilterns. Of course you have been there, and noticed how completely different they are from the Cotswolds, but one forgets the beauty. We drove for hours through the finest old beech woods – a real forest country where the villages are only clearings. The local industry is chair making, and as beech, apparently, can be worked green, the old method of actually working in the wood, turning the newly felled timber with a primitive lathe, still goes on. At least F.-K. – come, I see for the first time that it won't do on paper – Foord-Kelsie says so. Perhaps this is no more reliable than the consolations which he offered me when you were in danger at Shanghai, when he pointed out that the combatants were firing at each other not at the Settlement. I replied that shells, once fired, didn't discriminate on whom they fell. To which he answered 'Oh but you know modern artillery is a wonderful thing. They can place their shells with the greatest possible nicety.' This from him to me, considering our relative experience, is worthy of the P'daitabird at his best.

By the way, talking of shells, we had a conversation about the next war in College the other night, and the Senior Parrot (the hero of the match episode) who flies in the reserve was treating us to the usual business – modern weapons – capital cities wiped out in an hour – non-combatants decimated – whole thing over in a month. It suddenly occurred to me that after all, these statements are simply the *advertisement* of various *new machines*: and the next war will be precisely as like this as the real running of a new car is like the account of it in the catalogue. We had all, of course, – at least people of your and my way of thinking – been skeptical, but I never saw the 'rationale' of it before.

To return to Foord-Kelsie. I had one magnificent score off him that drive. All the way along, whenever we passed a rash of bungalows or a clutch of petrol pumps, he was at his usual game. 'How ridiculous to pretend that these things spoiled the beauty of the countryside etc.' Late in the day, and now in his own country, he waved his hand towards a fine hillside and remarked 'My old friend Lee – a most remarkable man – bought all that and presented it to the nation to save it from being covered with bungalows.' He saw the pit he had fallen into a moment too late.

His old rectory at Kimble is one of the very best places I have ever seen. It is a huge garden sloping down one side and up the other of a little ravine: beyond that divided only by a fence from the almost miniature-mountain scenery of Chekkers park. In this little ravine is a good specimen of a kind of beauty we shall never, I fear, have at the Kilns – that of *uneven* ground *evenly* shaved by lawn-mowers. You know the effect (one sometimes gets it on golf links) – rather like the curves on a closely clipped race-horse: an almost sensuous beauty – one wants to stroke the hillside. If you add a few finely clipped yews you will have the picture complete.

I have done little reading other than work since the Aeneid, except, of course, the inevitable snippet of Boswell. I began the first epistle to the Corinthians but didn't make much of it. Lately I have been skimming *The Way of All Flesh*.[47] I thought I should probably not like it on a re-reading, but it wears well. Its crudities of satire are so honest and hilarious that one can't resist them.

Elder-rooting in the top wood has begun again, and this afternoon, thanks to a night and morning of delicious soft rain which had softened the earth after a long continued drought, I got up four of them. I wished you were with me. The wood, and, even more, the path to it, smelled deliciously. There were still drops on every branch, and a magnificent chorus of birds. It was one of those days when, in the old phrase, you can almost hear things growing. The catkins (half way up

47 Samuel Butler, *The Way of All Flesh* (1903).

to the topwood) are all out, and the first purple look on the birches is just beginning. There is something unusually pleasant about public works when one is just getting really strong again after being ill: it is nice to sweat again.

Thanks for two copies of the *North China News*. You were really a good deal nearer the front than I supposed.

Yours
Jack

TO OWEN BARFIELD (W):

The Kilns,
Hdngtn Quarry
March 22nd [1932]

Dear old chap

(Is this a sufficiently untruculent opening?) I have received your incoherent and exasperating letter. You asked me for *opinions* ('a short essay' were your words) on the time and place you proposed for a walk, and I volunteered 'em. There is no question in my mind of going for a walk with Griffiths and Beckett (preposterous conjunction) without you. *When you walk, I walk.* I think Sussex a bad place to walk in but shall of course go there if you can't go anywhere else. And at any time you choose. Now, is that clear? Got it, old bean.

Now for another bibfull. Please tell me *which* Thursday night we are assembling on at Eastbourne (Sorry, I see you have. March 31st) Right, I'll do that. Where, in Eastbourne? Will you tell Griffiths or shall I?

Kent is a perfectly stinking place. Let us go west rather than go there.

Bridges[48] – what the devil would I imitate Bridges for? I'd as soon think of imitating Tupper.[49]

If you can't see the joke about Griffiths being a burden – it's all one. Plague o' these pickled herrings.

Nobody ever said the note on Pain was nonsense. But if you *insist*, I am prepared to call *anything* you say nonsense.

Well: 31st of March at Eastbourne: at a place to be later arranged. I

---

48 Robert Bridges (1844–1930), Poet Laureate from 1913. Lewis had enjoyed his poetry when he was younger.

49 Martin Tupper (1810–89), whose four series of *Proverbial Philosophy* (1838–76), maxims and reflections couched in rhythmical form, were the favourite of many who knew nothing about poetry.

shan't tell Griffiths unless ordered to, for I cannot make out from your letter what, whether, and when you have written to him. Ta-ta, old boy

Yours
C. S. Lewis

P.S. Please acknowledge this and confirm details in your next moment of calm.

P.P.S. Harwood wants not 'his bottom kicked' but, more idiomatically 'his bottom kicking'.

TO ARTHUR GREEVES (W):

[The Kilns]
Easter Sunday [27 March] 1932

My dear Arthur,

We are about 'quits' this time in lateness of answering. I had to get off a letter to Warnie before I wrote to you, as he had been longer in my debt, and that of course had to be a long one. (By the bye the trouble in China seems to be over, I am glad to see.) And now I find that your last letter is in College, while I am out here at the Kilns, so that I shan't be able to *answer* it very definitely.

Almost the only thing I remember about it is that you are writing a detective story. After I have spent so much of my life in writing things of the kind that don't appeal to you, I suppose I should not be surprised at you writing in one of the kinds that doesn't appeal to me – gradually more of your letter begins to come back to me. You have given up Naomi Mitchison because you find the characters unreal. I *didn't* feel that myself. Of course one does not feel the same intimacy in detail with characters from the far past as with those in a novel of contemporary life. I don't think I mind that. Hamlet or, say, the Baron of Bradwardine – of course one doesn't in *one* way know them as well as Soames Forsyte or Kipps:[50] in another way I feel I know them better. In fact 'in one way it is, in another way it isn't'. But then, I think one of the differences between us [is] that you appreciate much more than I do the 'close-up' detail – superficial detail I often think – of modern character drawing.

50 The Baron of Bradwardine is a character in Sir Walter Scott's *Waverley* (1814); Soames Forsyte is a character in John Galsworthy's *Forsyte Saga* (1922); Arthur Kipps is a character in H. G. Wells's *Kipps* (1905).

There I go in my usual way – expressing an opinion on modern fiction when the real state of the case is that I have read so little of it, and that so carelessly, that I ought to have no opinion on it at all. I must rely mainly on you. Perhaps as time goes on you will drift more to the present and I more to the past and we shall be useful to each other in that way. Fortunately, there is a solid something, neither of the present or of the past, which we shall always have in common.

Talking of the past, I had a really delightful experience some weeks ago. An old pupil of mine, one Wood,[51] came to spend a night with me. When I was his tutor he had been a curiously naïf, almost neurotic youth, who was always in love and other troubles, and so childish that he once asked me (as if I were his father!) whether one fell in love less often as one grew older, because he hoped so. Altogether an appealing, but somewhat ridiculous young man. When he went down he was compelled against his will to go into his father's business: and for a year [or] so I got letters from him, and accounts of him from common friends, which seemed to show that he was settling down into a permanent state of self-pity.

You can imagine how pleased I was to find that he had got over this: but above all – that is why I am telling the story – to find that his whole support is romantic reading in those precious evening hours 'after business' which you remember so well. He quoted bits of Middle English poems which he had read with me for the exam. They were mere drudgery to him at the time, but now, in memory, they delight him. He has just re-read the whole of Malory with more delight than ever, and has bought, but not yet begun, *The High History of the Holy Graal*. He also writes a bit – in those same precious evenings, and Saturday afternoons.

In fact as I sat talking to him, hearing his not very articulate, but unmistakable, attempts to express his pleasure, I really felt as if I were

---

51 Arthur Denis Blackford Wood (1907–92), after taking his BA in 1929, joined the family firm of William Wood & Son Ltd., landscape gardeners, Taplow. He served with the RAF, 1941–5. Later he published a number of books on gardening: *Terrace and Courtyard Gardens for Modern Homes* (1965), (with Kate Crosby) *Grow it and Cook It* (1975), and *Practical Garden Design* (1976). Mr Wood, on being shown this letter, said he was 'engaged in *one*, continuing, happy love-affair' as an undergraduate, and that he thinks Lewis may have confused him with someone else.

meeting *our* former selves. He is just in the stage that we were in when you worked with Tom and I was at Bookham.[52] Of course there was an element of vanity on my side – one liked to feel that one had been the means of starting him on things that now are standing him in such good stead. There was also a less contemptible, and, so to speak, professional, pleasure in thus seeing a proof that the English School here does really do some good. But in the main the pleasure was a spiritual one – a kind of love. It is difficult, without being sentimental, to say how extraordinarily *beautiful* – ravishing – I found the sight of some one just at that point which you and I remember so well. I suppose it is this pleasure which fathers always are hoping to get, and very seldom do get, from their sons.

Do you think a good deal of parental cruelty results from the disappointment of this hope? I mean, it takes a man of some tolerance to resign himself to the fact that his sons are *not* going to follow the paths that he followed and *not* going to give him this pleasure. What it all comes to, anyway, is that this pleasure, like everything else worth having, must not be reckoned on, or demanded as a right. If I had thought of it for a moment in the old days when I was teaching Wood, this pleasant evening would probably never have happened.

By the way he left a book with me, as a result of which I have lately read, or partially read, *one* modern novel – *The Fountain*, by Charles Morgan.[53] It is about a mystic, or would-be mystic, who was interned in Holland. I thought I was going to like it very much, but soon got disappointed. I was just going to say 'it soon degenerates into an ordinary novel', but realised only just in time that this wd. show an absurd point of view – as if one blamed an egg for degenerating into a chicken, forgetting that nature intended it for precisely that purpose. Still the fact remains that I personally enjoy a novel only in so far as it fails to be a novel pure and simple and escapes from the eternal love business into some philosophical, religious, fantastic, or farcical region.

By the way how did the Macdonald historical novel turn out? I shd. imagine it might suit him better than his modern ones.

I had meant to tell you all about my work in the wood these days,

52 Arthur worked for his brother Thomas Jackson Greeves (1886–1974), a linen merchant, 1915–17.

53 Charles Morgan, *The Fountain* (1932).

and how nice it looked and smelled and sounded: but I am suffering from a disease, rare with me, but deserving your sympathy – namely an extreme reluctance to write, even to my oldest friend about the things I like best. You see I have struggled with this reluctance for three pages. It is your turn now to reply soon and wake me from my lethargy as I have often tried to do you

Yrs
Jack

P.S. I think being up very late last night and up for the early 'celebrrr-ation' this morning may be the cause of my dulness.

TO HIS BROTHER (W):

[The Kilns]
April 8th 1932

My dear W –

I have your excellent letter of Feb. 14th. You are right in supposing that this Sino-Japanese war provides us at last with a political subject in which we are on the same side: but in suggesting that it is the law of chances which thus brings me into the line of archipigibotian orthodoxy, you are surely forgetting that, if that is true, you can claim no credit for predicting the fact, since if the phenomenon (my opinion) is purely irrational, there can be no rational prediction of it – you can foretell it only by luck. Indeed your hitting it would, by the rule of chances, be so unlikely, that it is clear there is no chance in the business at all. The truth being that *you*, having at last, and indeed by chance, found your own prejudices coincident with the dictates of justice and humanity – and feeling something unusual, not to say distressing, in this situation – you foresaw that *this time* I would be on the same side.

To be serious, my main feeling, and yours too, I expect, is an uneasy balance between indignation and the restraining knowledge that we English have of all people most deprived ourself, by our own imperial history, of the right to be indignant. But I don't know why I have let the whole dam thing waste even this much of my letter.

I wonder can you imagine how reassuring your bit about Spenser is to me who spend my time trying to get unwilling hobble-de-hoys to read poetry at all? One begins to wonder whether literature is not, after all, a failure. Then comes your account of the *Faerie Queene* on your office table, and one remembers that all the professed 'students of literature' don't matter a rap, and that the whole thing goes on, unconcerned by the fluctuations of the kind of 'taste' that gets itself printed, living from generation to generation in the minds of the few disinterested people who sit down alone and read what they like and find that it turns out to be just the things that every one has liked since they were written. I agree with all you say about it, except about the distinctions of character. The next time I dip in it I shall keep my weather eye on them. It would be quite in accord with all ones experience to find out one day that the usual critical view (i.e. that Spenser had no characters) was all nonsense.

I notice that great men are overshadowed by their own qualities: because Johnson talked so well, it gets about that his writings are poor: because Cowper is 'homely' it is assumed that he cannot be anything else. The doctrines of Crabbe's unbroken gloom, of Jane Austen's pure comedy, of Tennyson's 'sweetness' etc etc belong to the same illusion. So very likely it is the same with Spenser. By the way, I most fully agree with you about 'the lips being invited to share the banquet' in poetry, and always 'mouth' it while I read, though not in a way that would be audible to other people in the room. (Hence the excellent habit which I once formed, but have since lost, of not smoking while reading a poem). I look upon this 'mouthing' as an infallible mark of those who really like poetry. Depend upon it, the man who reads verses in any other way, is after 'noble thoughts' or 'philosophy' (in the revolting sense given to that word by Browning societies and Aunt Lily)[54] or social history, or something of the kind, not poetry.

To go back to Spenser – the battles *are* a bore. I thought I could trace a difference in that point between him and Tasso.[55] Tasso's battles – specially the single combats – always sounded real to me, and I had the feeling that if one knew anything about sword-technique one would be able to follow them in detail. Talking of that, if we had money to

54 Their mother's sister, Mrs Lilian 'Lily' Suffern (1860–1934), the eldest daughter of the Rev. Thomas Hamilton. An ardent suffragette, she quarrelled with everyone in her family. Following the death of her husband, William, in 1913 she was constantly on the move, but wherever she lived she bombarded Jack with books and a pseudo-metaphysical correspondence. After her widowhood the poetry of Robert Browning became her chief intellectual solace.

55 Torquato Tasso, *Gerusalemme Liberata* (1581).

spare on whims, I should like to have a fencing-master when you come home. Wouldn't it be a very fine occupation on wet days for the two pigibudda to 'take their exercise' in the barn? It would also make many passages in literature, which at present are mere words, start into light. But now that I come to think of it, I suppose 'singlestick' is the exercise proper to our humble rank.[56] (You know the hearty passages about it in books 'Ralph made his stave ring and rebound again on the bald head of his opponent'). And singlestick would be intolerable – except the sort we used to play with copies of – was it the *Spectator* or the *Law Journal Report*?

The novel you mention – *The Good Earth*[57] – I think I saw reviewed, and will certainly read if it is in the Union. As for *The Countryman* (by the way my Malaprop friend was Robson not Robertson-Scott),[58] I have not received [a] specimen copy, but I did happen to see a copy in the Barley Mow during the week end walk I recorded. I thought it a rather praiseworthy undertaking, but was rather disappointed at a later copy I saw on the spring walk last week (of which more anon) in which there was such an increase of advertisement that the text seemed in danger of vanishing altogether.

The whole puzzle about Christianity in non-European countries is very difficult. To the statement that only the riff-raff are converted, I suppose the enthusiastic missionary would reply that if you had lived under the Roman empire, at the period of the first conversions of all, you would have said exactly the same. (He could quote St Paul, [1] Cor. 1:26 'Not many clever people in the ordinary sense, nor many in important positions, nor many people of quality'). This is a very cold, uncomfortable reflection! I take it we could answer it by saying that, at all events, the same *kind* of riff-raff which now lives on the missions could not have been attracted by a poor and persecuted Church: so that *that* explanation is ruled out.

---

56 Singlestick was a method of fighting or fencing with a wooden stick provided with a large basket-handle and requiring only one hand. It was used by young boys and people of 'inferior quality' or social standing. A good description of it is found in Thomas Hughes, *Tom Brown's Schooldays* (1857).

57 Pearl Buck, *The Good Earth* (1931).

58 William Douglas Robson-Scott (1900–80) was at University College, Oxford, at the same time as Lewis. He took his BA in 1923, and went on to teach German Language and Literature at Birkbeck College, University of London. Lewis mentions his malapropisms in his letter to Warnie of 18 April 1927 (*CL* I, p. 694).

Of course one sees, from all history and from ones own circle, that the people who already have a high intellectual and moral tradition of their own, are, of all people, the least likely to embrace Christianity. Fancy converting a man like J. S. Mill! Or again, the really good Stoic emperors of Rome were the most anti-Christian. Even in the Gospels – does one suppose that the Pharisees, the 'High Church party' of Judaism, did not contain most of the refined, educated, enlightened population of Palestine – people, by ordinary standards very much nicer than the women of the town and little tax-farmers (that is modern English for 'publicans and sinners') who seem to have made up the background of Our Lord's circle. Still, we would reply that *some* Pharisees (e.g. Joseph of Arimathea and Nicodemus) did come in: and, on the other hand, none of the riff-raff came in for money, because there 'was *no* money in the thing'.

So that for this absolute cleavage in the East (if it really is so absolute as you say) we still need an explanation. Sometimes, relying on his remark, 'Other sheep I have that are not of this fold'[59] I have played with the idea that Christianity was never intended for Asia – even that Buddha is the form in which Christ appears to the Eastern mind. But I don't think this will really work. When I have tried to rule out all my prejudices I still can't help thinking that the Christian world is (partially) 'saved' in a sense in which the East is not. We may be hypocrites, but there is a sort of unashamed and *reigning* iniquity of temple prostitution and infanticide and torture and political corruption and obscene imagination in the East, which really does suggest that they are off the rails – that some necessary part of the human machine, restored to us, is still missing with them. (My friend's story about the I.C.S.[60] regulation 'No pornographic books or pictures shall be imported except for *bona fide* religious purposes' is relevant here).

On the whole, my present conclusion is that the difficulty about the Oriental *present* is really the same as the difficulty about the years B.C. For some reason that we cannot find out they are still living in the B.C. period (as there are African tribes still living in the stone-age) and it is apparently not intended that they should yet emerge from it. I admit that I have myself fallen into an Orientalism, and am giving

59 John 10:16.
60 Indian Civil Service.

instead of an explanation, the true eastern platitude 'God is great'. In fact, like Nettleship, 'I don't know, you know, I don't know, you know.' (Mind you, there is this to be said for my view, that you wd. hardly expect *time* to be quite as important to God as it is to us.)

Since last writing I have had my usual Easter walk. It was in every way an abnormal one. First of all, Harwood was to bring a new Anthroposophical member (not v. happily phrased!) and I was bringing a new Christian one to balance him, in the person of my ex-pupil Griffiths. Then Harwood and his satellite ratted, and the walk finally consisted of Beckett,[61] Barfield, Griffiths, and me. As Harwood never missed before, and Beckett seldom comes, and Griffiths was new, the atmosphere I usually look for on these jaunts was lacking. At least that is how I explain a sort of disappointment I have been feeling ever since. Then, owing to some affairs of Barfield's, we had to alter at the last minute our idea of going to Wales, and start (of all places!) from Eastbourne instead. All the same, I wd. not have you think it was a *bad* walk: it was rather like Hodge who, though nowhere in a competition of Johnsonian cats, was, you will remember, 'a very fine cat, a very fine cat indeed.'[62]

The first day we made Lewes, walking over the bare chalky South Downs all day. The country, except for an occasional gleam of the distant sea – we were avoiding the coast for fear of hikers – is almost exactly the same as the Berkshire downs or the higher parts of Salisbury Plain. The descent into Lewes offered a view of the kind I had hitherto seen only on posters – rounded hill with woods on the top, and one side quarried into a chalk cliff: sticking up dark and heavy against this a little town climbing up to a central Norman castle. We had a very

---

61 (Sir) Eric Beckett (1896–1966), who sometimes walked with Lewis and the others, was a particular friend of Barfield. He was educated at Wadham College, where he took a First in Jurisprudence in 1921. He was a Fellow of All Souls, Oxford, 1921–8. He was called to the Bar in 1922 and was Assistant Legal Adviser to the Foreign Office, 1925–45, and Legal Adviser, 1955–8.

62 Boswell, *The Life of Samuel Johnson*, 1783, vol. IV, p. 197: 'I shall never forget the indulgence with which he treated Hodge, his cat . . . I recollect him one day scrambling up Dr. Johnson's breast, apparently with much satisfaction, while my friend smiling and half-whistling, rubbed down his back, and pulled him by the tail; and when I observed he was a fine cat, saying, "why yes, Sir, but I have had cats whom I liked better than this;" and then as if perceiving Hodge to be out of countenance, adding, "but he is a very fine cat, a very fine cat indeed."'

poor inn here, but I was fortunate in sharing a room with Griffiths who carried his asceticism so far as to fling off his eiderdown – greatly to my comfort.

Next day we had a delicious morning – just such a day as downs are made for, with endless round green slopes in the sunshine, crossed by cloud shadows. The landscape was less like the Plain now. The sides of the hill – we were on a ridgeway – were steep and wooded, giving rather the same effect as the narrower parts of Malvern hills beyond the Wych. We had a fine outlook over variegated blue country to the North Downs. After we had dropped into a village for lunch and climbed onto the ridge again for the afternoon, our troubles began.

The sun disappeared: an icy wind took us in the flank: and soon there came a torrent of the sort of rain that feels as if ones face were being tattooed and turns the mackintosh on the weather side into a sort of wet suit of tights. At the same time Griffiths began to show his teeth (as I learned afterwards) having engaged Barfield in a metaphysico-religious conversation of such appalling severity and egotism that it included the speaker's life history and a statement that most of us were infallibly damned. As Beckett and I, half a mile ahead, looked back over that rain beaten ridgeway we could always see the figures in close discussion. Griffiths *very* tall, thin, high-shouldered, stickless, with enormous pack: arrayed in perfectly cylindrical knickerbockers, very tight in the crutch. Barfield, as you know, with that peculiarly blowsy air, and an ever more expressive droop and shuffle.

For two mortal hours we walked nearly blind in the rain, our shoes full of water, and finally limped into the ill omened village of Bramber. Here, as we crowded to the fire in our inn, I tried to make room for us by shoving back a little miniature billiard table which stood in our way. I was in that state of mind in which I discovered without the least surprise, a moment too late, that it was only a board supported on trestles. The trestles, of course, collapsed, and the board crashed to the ground. Slate broken right across. I haven't had the bill yet, but I suppose it will equal the whole expences of the tour. Griffiths gave me a surprise equal to that which the Quakers gave Lamb in another inn[63]

63 Charles and Mary Lamb, *Letters 1796–1820*, vol. I (1912), letter from Charles Lamb to Samuel T. Coleridge of 13 February 1797: 'I have had thoughts of turning Quaker . . . Unluckily I went to [a meeting] and saw a man under all the agitations and workings of a fanatic, who believed himself under the influence of some

– indeed the two stories are closely parallel – by refusing to see that there was any claim against me at all for the damage.

From Bramber we ascended again in a lovely evening after rain, through lovely scenes – the downs here assuming rather the character of moors. But it very soon began to drizzle again, and an error in map reading involved us in hours of stumbling and circling up there in the twilight. We lay at Findon. Griffiths was quite intolerable after dinner. Don't mistake me. I don't mean that he was rude. But he displayed a perversity and disingenuousness in argument and a cold blooded brutality – religious brutality is the worst kind – which quite revolted us. To expound his position wd. carry us too far: but you would be getting near it if you imagined a Calvinist Jesuit with strong leanings to the doctrine that the elect cannot sin, who had borrowed from metaphysics the view that 'love' cannot be predicated of God, and from economics the doctrine that it is no real charity to give anything to the poor. In fact if you mix together all the harshest aspects of every form of religion and irreligion which you know and imagine them delivered with the dryness of a scientist and the intolerance of a verminous monk of the fourth century, you have the recipe. Barfield and I slept in one room and consoled ourselves with chaff and chat in our old manner, recalling happier walking tours. We were very footsore.

The next day made amends. We had good weather all day long. Griffiths improved surprisingly. In fact we have all forgiven him, and shall ask him again. His exhibition of the previous day was really, I believe, only the reaction of a solitary on finding himself suddenly at bay among people all older than himself and all disagreeing with him. We refused to let conversation become serious. We laughed away his monstrous positions. Before lunchtime we had him laughing himself and making jokes, even bawdy jokes.

We were in quite a different kind of country today: still the Sussex downs, but not like any 'downs' you or I have known, being heavily wooded. It is very pleasant to combine the damp, mysterious delights of a forest walk with the hill-feeling which is called up every now and then by a few open fields revealing the real contours.

"inevitable presence." This cured me of Quakerism . . . I detest the vanity of a man thinking he speaks by the Spirit, when what he says an ordinary man might say without all that quaking and trembling' (p. 97).

We got to Arundel for tea, where Beckett left us by train. Coddling ourselves after the hardships of the previous day, we went no further. Arundel impressed me as much as any place I have ever seen. The castle[64] has been greatly added to in the XIXth century so that the original Norman kernel is hardly visible: but, provided a castle is big enough and set high enough above the town, it can hardly help being impressive. But it is the surroundings that are the chief beauty, and specially the park. The Magdalen stags are dwarfs compared with the Arundel stags. It contains some of the finest beeches I have ever seen, and hill and dale for miles, and a sheet of water echoing with exotic birds. (There were also some swans to remind me that 'the rich have their own troubles') We passed a very pleasant evening here, a great contrast to the night before. Next day we walked to Midhurst, and having slept there, broke up the party after breakfast.

I find that the account I have written gives quite an exaggerated idea of the less pleasant aspects of this jaunt (*Memo*: to read all collections of letters in the light of the fact that a letter writer tends to pick out what is piquant, or unusual. He may tell no lies: but his life is never as odd, either for good or ill, as it sounds in the letters.) We had at least some of the rare fine days of this spring while walking. As you know, I do not hold with the undue importance now attached to weather: but I confess that spring – 'being a thing so comfortable and necessary' can still disappoint me when day after day is ushered in with driving rain or black east winds, and the primroses are battered into the mud as soon as they show their faces. There are signs of budding on all (I think) the new trees, but of course one cannot say what they will come to.

About Miracle Plays – I agree with you. Is it not all part of the perverse modern attempt to behave as if we were younger, simpler, and more ignorant than we really are? It was natural for the populace in the middle ages to accept a man in a gilt mask appearing as God the Father – who sends Gabriel to the Virgin, who tells her to hurry up and agree to the scheme 'For they (i.e. the Trinity) think long till I come again.' It is equally natural, I think, for us, reading the old plays, to find this naiveté touching and delightful – as a grown man likes to watch, or to remember childhood. But a grown man getting into pina-

64 Arundel Castle, the chief seat of the Duke of Norfolk.

fores and going off to play red Indians in the shrubbery is intolerable. Nor will he *in that way* really recover the pleasures of childhood half so well as he can by reminiscence: nor is there any way in which he can be more utterly unlike a real child. For a child surely *wants* to be as grown up and sophisticated as it can manage: the enjoyment of naiveté for its own sake is the most hopelessly adult enjoyment there is. I suppose the don reading Edgar Wallace, and the civilised man dancing negro dances, are examples of the same thing. I have read very little but middle english texts since I last wrote: specially the *Owl and the Nightingale* which you must read in Tolkien's translation some day.

I asked old Mr. Taylor (the aged deaf man who once played croquet with us at Hillsborough)[65] up to supper one night, and went there in return. This, you know, I reckon almost among charities, as he is old, poor, friendless, and surrounded by a beastly family. I mention him here in order to record a super P'daitism, when after an hour or so of talk about life on the other planets, education, Einstein, and other oddments, he suddenly explained 'Ah, I see you know all about this universe business.' Further than that one can't possibly go in that particular kind of P'daitism.

I have been reading Tylor's *Anthropology*[66] over my morning tea lately having bought it to read in the train. Kirk's[67] old friends the Rationalist Press Association are bringing out a series at a 1/- each of works which they conceive to be anti-religious, and which are to be found on every station bookstall. One has no sympathy with the design – nor does one like to read books in an edition called *The Thinker's Library* with a picture on the jacket of a male nude sitting thinking. (The whole thing reminds me of Butler's remark that a priest is a man who disseminates little lies in defence of a great truth, and a scientist is a man who disseminates little truths in defence of a great lie.) Still it is rather nice to be able to pick up on a railway journey a real classic of medium-popular

65 Hillsboro – not 'Hillsborough' – is the house at 14 Holyoake Road, Headington, where Lewis and the Moores lived most of the time from April 1923 until they moved into The Kilns in October 1930.

66 Sir Edward Burnett Tylor, *Anthropology: An Introduction to the Study of Man and Civilization* (1881; Thinker's Library, 1930).

67 See **W. T. Kirkpatrick** (1848–1921) in the Biographical Appendix to *CL* I. Kirkpatrick, 'the Great Knock', was a friend of the Lewis family and prepared Jack for Oxford. He is the subject of *SBJ*, ch. 9.

science. I find I am enjoying the Tylor very much: the chapters on Language and Writing particularly. Still no news of the Henry instalment from Condlin. I confess I am worried about it. Isn't the Everyman Molière[68] one of the very small print Everyman's?

Yours
J.

P.S. Old Brightman is dead – a great loss.[69] When shall we see such a figure again?

This reminds me of a conversation I had lately when a very courtly old man was condoling with a certain professor on the death of his brother 'A charming man your poor brother was – such a dear *modest* fellow – no speech making or anything of that kind about him – in fact I never remember his saying anything.' A beautiful epitaph. HIC JACET/N OR M/WHO NEVER SAID ANYTHING./I SAID I WILL TAKE HEED TO MY TONGUE/.

Just to fill up the page I add J.A.'s latest; –

To all the fowls that wing the air
The Goose is much preferred;
There is so much of nourishment
On that sagacious bird.

TO OWEN BARFIELD (W):

[The Kilns]
May 6 1932

My dear Barfield

'Very facetious to be sure.' I have not answered your previous letter (I know of only one) because I have been very busy. I didn't know I had been asked to stay with you until I got this one – not very long ago: and beyond a single night for the opera I can't manage it very well. Can't you come for a night to me?

---

68 Molière, *Comedies*, trans. Henry Baker and J. Miller, with an introduction by Frederick C. Green, Everyman's Library (1929).

69 The Reverend Frank Edward Brightman FBA (1856–1932), who died on 31 March 1932, was a distinguished liturgiologist and a Fellow of Magdalen College since 1902. His publications include *The English Rite*, 2 vols. (1915). For more on Brightman see note 5 to the letter of 5 January 1926 (*CL* I, p. 658).

As to operas I should like May 16th (*Siegfried*).[70] Monday and Saturday are the only days possible, which rules out the Rheingold. Would this suit you? What wd. be best of all wd. be if you could get off work on Tuesday 17th and we could come back here together during the morning and be here Tuesday night. Do try.

I am very sorry (seriously) if I have been rude: but getting the term started immediately after flu' (did you know I had another bout in the last week of the Vac.) has pretty well boxed my compass.

Yours
C.S.L.

P.S. I send (P.T.O.) the opening of the poem. I am not satisfied with any part I have yet written and the design is ludicrously ambitious. But I feel it will be several years anyway before I give it up.

I feel it wd show ill temper if I didn't use the stamped envelope.

I will write down the portion that I understand
Of twenty years wherein I went from land to land.
At many bays and harbours I put in with joy
Hoping that there I should have built my second Troy
And stayed. But either stealing harpies drove me thence,
Or the trees bled, or oracles, whose airy sense
I could not understand, yet must obey, once more
Sent me to sea to follow the retreating shore
Of this land which I call at last my home, where most
I feared to come; attempting not to find whose coast
I ranged half round the world, with vain design to shun
The last fear whence the last security is won.
Oh perfect life, unquivering, self-enkindled flame
From which my fading candle first was lit, oh name
Too lightly spoken, therefore left unspoken here,
Terror of burning, nobleness of light, most dear
And comfortable warmth of the world's beating side,
Feed from thy unconsumed what wastes in me, and guide

70 In *SBJ*, ch. 5, Lewis recalls the moment he came across a reference to Richard Wagner's *Ring des Nibelungen*. Lewis came to love the entire *Ring* cycle on gramophone records, but it was not until this occasion (Monday 16 May 1932) that he saw *Siegfried* performed on stage.

My soul into the silent places till I make
A good end of this book for after-travellers' sake.
In times whose faded chronicle lies in the room
That memory cannot turn the key of, they to whom
I owe this mortal body and terrestrial years,
Uttered the Christian story to my dreaming ears.
And I lived then in Paradise, and what I heard
Ran off me like the water from the water-bird;
And what my mortal mother told me in the day
At night my elder mother nature wiped away;
And when I heard them telling of my soul, I turned
Aside to read a different lecture when I learned
What was to me the stranger and more urgent news,
That I had blood and body now, my own, to use
For tasting and for touching the young world, for leaping
And climbing, running, wearying out the day, and sleeping . . .[71]

TO OWEN BARFIELD (W):

Magdalen College,
Oxford.
[?] 6th May 1932

My dear Barfield

I *am* sorry to hear that you can't manage *Siegfried*. I am going to be selfish. I find that my desire – born 'in painful side' since 1913 – has been so inflated that I would rather not give up the hope. Will you v. kindly at once book me the cheapest bookable seat for *Siegfried* May 16th. I will go to 20/- if need be, or a bit over. If you don't put me up in the 'enormous room' for that night perhaps you could advise me about a bed elsewhere. Would you accept a seat (*Siegfried*, not a seat in your own flat!) from me? Schools this summer make me affluent. You will do me a real kindness if you will.

For a visit – any week night this term except Mondays I shall be delighted if you will come. If that is impossible make it a week end, but I shd. prefer the former.

It really takes a load off my mind to hear that you like the poem. Couplets, however dangerous are needed if one is to try to give to

71 This is the only surviving portion of the autobiographical poem Lewis wrote.

the subjective poem some of the swing and narrative zest of the old epic.

Yrs
C. S. Lewis

P.S. I shall be as anxious as a child till I hear that you have got two seats for Siegfried.

TO OWEN BARFIELD (W):

Magdalen College,
Oxford.
Thursday [12 May 1932]

Dear Barfield

I am in horrors and raptures – if only you wd. have come it wd. be raptures alone. I *would* like the bed at Swiss Cottage on Monday night if it is convenient – in sending me directions please give me the exact address. (A letter posted by return ought to reach me before Monday morning).

If you reconsider your decision and *can* get an extra seat my offer of course still holds – you would be cheap at the price. I can't refund you the 15/- by this post, as I am in College. A thousand thanks: I didn't know till now that I had so much boyish appetite for a show left.

Yours
C.S.L.

P.S. If there is anyway of getting my existing ticket (Amphitheatre Stall 191) changed for *two* of the 28/- ones and you cd. come. I honestly can afford it this year and it wd. make good better.[72]

TO HIS BROTHER (W):

[Magdalen College]
June 14th 1932

Dear W –

I have just read your letter of May 15th, but not as you suppose

72 In the end Lewis went to *Siegfried* alone on 16 May 1932. The cast included Lauritz Melchior as Siegfried, Eduard Habich as Alberich, Frida Leider as Brunhild and Friedrich Schorr as Wotan. An account of the performance was given in *The Times* (17 May 1932) p. 8.

in College. 'Schools' has arrived and I am invigilating[73] and although your letter arrived before lunch I deliberately brought it here unopened so that the reading it might occupy at least part of the arid waste of talk-less, smoke-less, exercise-less time between 2 p.m. and 5 p.m.

Theoretically of course there ought to be no greater blessing than three hours absolutely safe from interruption and free for reading: but somehow or other – everyone has made the discovery – reading is impossible in the Schools. There is a sort of atmosphere at once restless and soporific which always ends in that stage which (for me) is a signal to stop reading – the stage I mean at which you blink and ask yourself 'Now what *was* the last page about.' Whether it will turn out that writing under schools conditions is more possible than reading, the fate of this letter will decide. At any rate thank heaven for grandfather's black alpacca coat: with this I feel as if I were in bathing things (at any rate from the waist up) while most of my colleagues are sweating in their best blue or brown suitings.

You will gather from this that summer has arrived: in fact last Sunday (it is Tuesday to day) I had my first bathe. You will be displeased to hear that in spite of my constant warnings the draining of the swamp has *not* been carried out without a fall in the level of the pond. I repeatedly told both Lydiatt (who began the job) and Knight (usually a very reliable man, who finished it) that the depth of water in the pond was sacrosanct: that nothing which might have even the remotest tendency to interfere with *that* must be attempted: that I would rather have the swamp as swampy as ever than lose an inch of pond. But of course I might have known that it is quite vain ever to get anything you want carried out: and the pond *is* lower. However, don't be too alarmed. I don't think it can get any lower than it is now.

I don't know how much of the draining operations Minto has described to you nor whether you understood them. In fact, remembering what a mechanical process described by Minto is like I may assume that the more she has said the less you know about it. The scheme was a series of deep holes filled with rubble and covered over with earth. Into each of these a number of trenches drain: and from

73 When students were taking their final examinations or 'Schools' in the Examination Schools building in the High Street, dons took turns 'invigilating', that is, keeping watch over the students.

each of these pipes lead into the main pipe now occupying the old ditch between the garden and the swamp, which in its turn, by pipes under the lawn, drains into the ditch beside the avenue.

It was however useless to do all this as long as the overflow outlet from the pond (you know – the tiny runnel with the tiny bridge over near the Philips end of the pond) was meandering – as it did – over all the lower parts of the swampy bit. Nor was it possible to stop this up and deny the pond any outlet, as it would then have been stagnant and stinking in summer, and overflowing in winter. It was therefore decided to substitute a *pipe* outlet for the mere *channel* outlet – wh. pipe could carry the overflow from the pond, *through* the swampy bit without wetting it, to the rest of the drainage system. When they first laid this pipe I said that its mouth (i.e. at the pond end) was too low and that it would therefore carry off more water than the old channel and so lower the pond. The workmen shortly denied this but I stuck to my point and actually made them raise it. Even after they had raised it I was still not sure that it wasn't taking off more water than the old channel did: so I have now had a stopper made which is in the mouth of the pipe at this moment. I have also given the spring-tap up beyond the small pond a night turned on, and I trust that by thus controlling in-flow and outflow of water I can soon nurse the pond back to its old level.

At any rate I don't see how it can sink as long as its escape is bunged up. As to the degree of loss at present, as there are no perpendicular banks anywhere it is hard to gauge. I should think that the most pessimistic episode could hardly be more than ¾ of a foot: i.e. a difference one is unconscious of in bathing. Still I grudge every inch. By the way, it has just occurred to me that the sinking may not be due to the draining at all: for the old 'channel' escape, when I looked at it just before the operations began, had certainly widened itself extremely from what I first remembered, and must have been letting out more than it ought. In that case the new pipe may have arrested rather than created a wastage.

I have been infernally busy getting ready for Schools and have therefore little to tell you (By the bye Percy Tweedlepippin[74] is my colleague

74 This was Lewis's nickname for Percy Simpson (1865–1962) who with his wife, Evelyn M. Simpson, and C. H. Herford, edited the eleven volumes of Ben Jonson's *Works* (1925–52). He was the librarian of the new English faculty library, and a lecturer on textual criticism.

and his principles as an examiner are perhaps worth recording. In answer to a suggested question of mine he retorted 'Its no good setting that. They'd *know* that!')

I have read, or rather re-read, one novel namely *Pendennis*.[75] How pleased the Pdaitabird would have been – why hadn't I the grace to read it a few years ago. Why I re-read it now I don't quite know – I suppose some vague idea that it was time I gave Thackeray another trial. The experiment, on the whole, has been a failure. I can just see, mind you, why they use words like 'great' and 'genius' in talking of him which we don't use of Trollope. There are indications, or breakings in, all the time of something beyond Trollope's range. The scenery for one thing (tho' to be sure there is only one scene in Thackeray – always summer evening – English-garden – rooks crowing) has a sort of depth (I mean in the painting sense) wh. Trollope hasn't got. Still more there are the sudden 'depths' in a very different sense in Thackeray. There is one v. subordinate scene in *Pendennis* where you meet the Marquis of Steyne and a few of his led captains and pimps in a box at a theatre. It only lasts a page or so – but the sort of rank, salt, urinous stench from the nether pit nearly knocks you down and clearly has a kind of power that is quite out of Trollope's range. I don't think these bits really improve Thackeray's books: they do, I suppose, indicate whatever we mean by 'genius'. And if you are the kind of reader who values genius you rate Thackeray highly.

My own secret is – let rude ears be absent – that to tell you the truth, brother, *I don't like genius*. I like enormously some *things* that only genius can do: such as *Paradise Lost* and the *Divine Comedy*.[76] But it is the results I like. What I don't care twopence about is the sense (apparently dear to so many) of being in the hands of 'a great man' – you know; his dazzling personality, his lightening energy, the strange force of his mind – and all that. So that I quite definitely prefer Trollope – or rather this re-reading of *Pen.* confirms my long standing preference. No doubt Thackeray was the genius: but Trollope wrote the better books.

All the old things I objected to in Thackeray I object to still. Do you

75 William Makepeace Thackeray, *Pendennis* (1848–50).

76 Dante Alighieri (1265–1321), *The Divine Comedy* (comprising *Inferno*, *Purgatorio*, *Paradiso*).

remember saying of Thomas Browne in one of your letters 'Was there anything he didn't love?' One can ask just the opposite of Thackeray. He is wrongly accused of making his virtuous women too virtuous: the truth is he does not make them virtuous enough. If he makes a character what he wd. call 'good' he always gets his own back by making her (its always a female character) a bigot and a blockhead. Do you think, Sir, pray, that there are many slum parishes which could not produce half a dozen old women quite as chaste and affectionate as Helen Pendennis and ten times more charitable and more sensible? Still – the Major deserves his place in ones memory. So does Foker – surely the most *balanced* picture of the kindly vulgar young fop that there is. I'm not sure about Costigan. There's a good deal too much of Thackeray's habit of laughing at things like poverty and mispronunciation in the Costigan parts. Then, of course there's 'the style' – Who the deuce wd. begin talking about the style in a novel till all else was given up.

I have had another visit to Whipsnade[77] – Foord Kelsie motored Arthur and me over on a fine Monday when Arthur was staying here. This was not the best company in the world with whom to revisit Whipsnade as F.K. combines extreme speed of tongue with a very slow walk, which is reduced to a stop when he has a good thing to say. However, after lunch he very wisely went and sat down and left Arthur and me on our own. Arthur was like a child: painfully divided between a desire 'not to tire himself' and a desire to see everything. When I tried to construct a harmony between these two aims by suggesting a route which would not make a very long walk and yet not really miss much, he was perfectly intractable because everything, to left, or to right, distracted him and he never cd. be made to believe that it was something we either had seen already or were just going to see. In fact it was a sad contrast to [the] sauntering unanimity of our last trip to the same place.

Perhaps however it was just as well that A. drew me out of my course, for the place has been so increased and altered that I should

77 Lewis was remembering the visit he and Warnie took to Whipsnade Zoo in Warnie's motorbike and sidecar on 28 September 1931. The part that visit played in Lewis's conversion is recounted in the last chapter of *SBJ*. See *CL* I, p. 972.

have missed a good deal. The novelties include lions, tigers, polar bears, beavers etc. Bultitude was still in his old place. Wallaby wood, owing to the different season, was improved by masses of bluebells: the graceful faun-like creatures hopping out of one pool of sunshine into another over English wildflowers – and so much tamer now than when you saw them that it is really no difficulty to stroke them – and English wildbirds singing deafeningly all round, came nearer to ones idea of the world before the Fall than anything I ever hoped to see.

One other important experience, as experiences go in a retired life, was my first visit to Covent Garden. It suddenly occurred to me this spring that my desire to hear *Siegfried* dated from 1912, and that 20 years was quite long enough to have waited. So I stood myself 15/- worth of 'Amphitheatre Stalls'. I mention it here not in order to describe *Siegfried* (wh. I enjoyed quâ music and drama enormously) but to record my complete disillusionment as regards the Covent Garden level of performance. It was in fact exactly like any other performance of an opera: i.e. one's inner criticism ran on the familiar lines 'Ah this is a lovely bit coming now . . . what a pity that girl hasn't a really good voice' – in fact I was on the point of saying to myself 'By Jove its a splendid thing – what wouldn't I give to hear it done properly at Covent Garden.' When I say it was just like any other performance of an opera I mean that out of the eight characters *two* were magnificent, *one* 'had been a very fine singer in his young days,' two were quite adequate but had no v. great passages to sing, and two were frankly bad. The odd thing was that the *acting* was a great deal better than I had dared to expect. I had always supposed that these 'head bummers' were even insolently negligent of it: as a matter of fact they were distinctly good.

The Lamb's letters must surely be a new Everyman – and a very good one too.[78] Confound those Tower of Glass people – I will write to them. I have dozens of things to reply to in this letter and your last, but it is now 4.30 and finished papers are beginning to dribble in. Also I am nearly asleep. I shall not be able to write to you again till examining is over – i.e. in August. I don't think the passage in S. James is really

78 Charles Lamb, *Letters*, ed. William Macdonald, with notes and illustrations. Introduction by Ernest Rhys (Everyman's Library, 1909).

the same as the 'Touch Wood' business. I shall try to get down to Ardglass for a day at least when I'm over.[79]

Yours

Jack.

P.S. I had nearly forgotten to acknowledge the philosophical instrument wh. you so unexpectedly sent. After one or two experiments I am getting a gadget made for fastening it onto my belt as I can find no pocket which will keep it perpendicular. Thanks very much. It is a thing I have been vaguely wanting to possess for many years.

I am afraid it will be a long time before I can resume proper letter writing – examining will hold me up till mid August.

During Warnie's first tour of duty in China in 1927–9 he thought of retiring from the army. In a letter to Jack of 5 December 1929 he said: 'I have had just about enough of the army, which becomes more tedious with every year that passes' (LP X: 208). He calculated that by December 1932 he would be entitled to a pension of £200, and so he set his retirement for the end of 1932. In July 1932 he applied for retirement from the Royal Army Service Corps, and it was soon decided that he would sail for home on 22 October.

TO ARTHUR GREEVES (W):

The Kilns,
Headington Quarry,
Oxford
July 29th 1932

My dear Arthur,

Thank heavens – *at last* I have finished examining. I am much too tired to write a letter: and also hungry to get to a morning's reading – my first since the beginning of last term 18 weeks ago. This is merely to ask whether it will suit you if I come from Aug. 15th to 29th? I am looking forward to it immensely. Thanks for your letter of June 12th.

Yrs

Jack

79 Lewis was planning a trip to Ireland in August, and he hoped to visit the village of Ardglass in Co. Down known for its interesting lighthouse.

TO ARTHUR GREEVES (W):

The Kilns,
Headington Quarry,
Oxford.
Aug 11th 1932

My dear Arthur,

I have written to book a berth[80] for the night of Monday the 15th (which, by the bye, they have not yet acknowledged) and am at present in a fever of pleasing anticipation. I am so tired that our old rôles will be reversed: you will be the one who wants to walk further and sit up later and talk more. The latter probably sounds too good to be true!

Yours
Jack

TO ARTHUR GREEVES (W):

2 Princess Villas,
Bayview Park,
Kilkeel.
[Co. Down
30 August 1932][81]

My dear Arthur,

I am very sorry you did not come down but I quite see your point of view. I don't think the idea of a meeting half way would be much good. I can't drive: it would have to be a party of three at least – perhaps a mass meeting – and what should we all do when we had met? There would certainly be no opportunity for walk or talk on our own. Dotty sends profuse thanks for your exertions about her luggage, which has since turned up. I hope your cold will soon be better. I am alright now and have done some good mountain climbs.

I quite understand about the cheque – it was quite absurd suggesting

---

80 A berth on a cross-channel boat. As planned, Lewis crossed over to Ireland on 15 August and was there as Arthur's guest at Bernagh, Circular Road, Belfast, until 29 August.

81 This letter is undated, but if Lewis's mention of 'Thursday Sept. 1st' is correct it was almost certainly written in 1932. Lewis and the Moores normally had a holiday together in Ireland, and Lewis probably met Mrs Moore, Maureen and their friend Dorothea 'Dotty' Vaughan (a close friend of the family who had been at Headington School with Maureen Moore) for a few days in Kilkeel before returning to England.

such a roundabout method. We shall be crossing (D.V.) on Thursday Sept. 1st. and I shall tell you my train later.

I don't think the meeting half way *would* be any good: do you?

Yours

Jack

TO OWEN BARFIELD (W):

Magdalen College,
Oxford.
Oct 29th 1932

My dear Barfield

Thanks. I was in some anxiety for your letter; – the whole thing (thanks to the long preparation by failure in the prose 'It' and the autobiographical poem) spurted out so suddenly that I have still very little objective judgement of it.

Friday is my best day as I have no afternoon pupil. Say next Friday (Nov 4th), and try to arrive in College about 5 p.m.

Yrs

C. S. Lewis

TO OWEN BARFIELD (W):

Magdalen College,
Oxford.
Nov 2nd 1932

My dear Barfield

I was already a good deal bothered as to whether the crossing of the Main Road ought not to have been recorded: and it says much for your sagacity that you have guessed it quite right. The map is [Lewis here drew that part of the Mappa Mundi which appears on the end leaves of almost all copies of *The Pilgrim's Regress*: to the north of the Grand Canyon is Eschropolis and Claptrap and in the south is Wisdom.]

Nov 18th it is – I wish it were sooner.

Yours

C.S.L.

TO OWEN BARFIELD (W):

Magdalen College,
Oxford.
Nov 7th 1932

My dear B.

(1.) You are the pilgrims, rot you, as you go always a little further. Let it be Friday the 25th if 't suits you so – but please don't make it 1933.

(2.) No – you must keep your dental affair till Saturday morning, since that morning I spend piddling in Pinkery pond.

(3.) Show the MS. to any one you please provided you bring it with you when you do at last come

Yours
C.S.L.

TO ARTHUR GREEVES (W):

[The Kilns]
Dec 4th 1932

My dear Arthur,

Thank you very much for your list of suggestions. I am really grateful for the trouble and interest you have taken. As for the future, I think I cannot ask you to sweat through the rest of the book[82] in quite such detail. What I had in mind was not so much criticisms on *style* (in the narrower sense) as on things like confusion, bad taste, unsuccessful jokes, contradictions etc., and for a few of these I should be very much obliged. These would be less trouble to you than minute verbal points: and also, if anything, *more* useful to me. I have not had a free day yet to work through your notes, but from a cursory glance I anticipate that on the purely *language* side of writing our aims and ideals are very far apart – too far apart for either of us to be of very much help to the other. I think I see, from your criticisms, that you

82 For some time Lewis had been trying to write the story of his conversion, and especially of the part 'Joy' played in it. While he probably had no intention of attempting this on his holiday, *The Pilgrim's Regress: An Allegorical Apology for Christianity, Reason and Romanticism* (1933) came quite unexpectedly and was written during the fortnight spent at Bernagh. The manuscript had been sent to Arthur for criticism. For details of his earlier attempts to tell the story of his conversion see the treatment of *The Pilgrim's Regress* in *CG*.

like a much more correct, classical, and elaborate manner than I. I aim chiefly at being idiomatic and racy, basing myself on Malory, Bunyan, and Morris, tho' without archaisms: and would usually prefer to use ten words, provided they are honest native words and idiomatically ordered, than one 'literary word'. To put the thing in a nutshell you want 'The man of whom I told you' and I want 'The man I told you of'. But, no doubt, there are many sentences in the P.R.[83] which are bad by *any* theory of style.

I have just finished the 2nd volume of Lockhart and it fully justifies all the recommendations both of you and of Warnie. After Boswell it is much the best biography I have read: and the subject is in some ways, or at least in some moods, more attractive. Didn't you enjoy the account of his ballad-hunting journey in Liddesdale?[84] It will send me back to the Dandie Dinmont parts of *Guy Mannering*[85] with renewed appetite.

It is a very consoling fact that so many books about real lives – biographies, autobiographies, letters etc. – give one such an impression of *happiness*, in spite of the tragedies they all contain. What could be more tragic than the main outlines of Lamb's or Cowper's lives?[86] But as soon as you open the letters of either, and see what they were writing from day to day and what a relish they got out of it, you almost begin to envy them. Perhaps the tragedies of real life contain more consolation and fun and gusto than the comedies of literature?

I wish you could see this place at present. The birch wood is a black bristly mass with here and there a last red leaf. The lake is cold, cold lead colour. The new moon comes out over the fir trees at the top and a glorious wail of wind comes down from them. I certainly like my garden better at winter than any other time.

I hope I shall soon have a letter from you. This, by the bye, is not a letter, but a note of acknowledgement. And I hope you will not think me any less grateful for your criticisms because of what I have said. I *do* appreciate your pains most deeply.

---

83 i.e. *The Pilgrim's Regress*.

84 Lockhart, *Memoirs of the Life of Scott*, vol. II, ch. 10.

85 Sir Walter Scott, *Guy Mannering* (1815).

86 Charles Lamb (1775–1834) and William Cowper (1731–1800).

Do you ever take a run down to your cottage in winter. It would be 'rather lovely'.

Yours
Jack

TO HIS BROTHER (W):

The Kilns
Dec 12th 1932

My dear W –

A thousand welcomes to Havre (of hated memory.) We have had so many alarms about you that I shall hardly believe it till I see you with my own eyes. But on that score, and on all your last six month's adventures there is so much to be said that it is absurd to begin. You would be amused to hear the various hypotheses that were entertained during your long summer silence – that you had been captured by bandits – were in jail – had gone mad – had married – had married a Chinese woman. My own view of course was 'Indeed he's such a fellow etc,' but I found it hard to maintain this against the riot of rival theories.

I think you will find us all pretty ship shape here. The only two things to complain of are, the presence of Vera,[87] and the threatened arrival of Lings to pay me a visit – both, of course, arranged before we had any hopes of seeing you this year: indeed, when we were beginning to wonder if we should see you at all or not. However, Lings is not going to be allowed to interfere with any jaunt of yours and mine, having made himself such a friend of the family that I can be away even while he is here. (He shows a tendency to play duets with Maureen which Minto thinks ought to be encouraged.) But how differently all such interruptions will henceforth appear to you – like church going to the Superannuated man – no longer hewing great cantels out of tiny leaves, but punctuating a leisure *sine die*. It all seems too good to be true! I can hardly believe that when you take your shoes off a week or so hence, please God, you will be able to say 'This will do for me – for life.'

---

87 Vera Henry, Mrs Moore's goddaughter, ran a holiday resort at Annagasan, a few miles from Drogheda, where Jack and Warnie sometimes spent holidays. From time to time Vera acted as housekeeper at The Kilns, but inevitably Jack had to act as peacemaker when she and Mrs Moore quarrelled.

I have not had any opportunity to reply till now to your questions about money. We shall do very well on what your percentage comes to: the only request I have to make on the bursarial side is that you must *wash less* (I mean your clothes, not your person) – your present standard of *shifting* being the one item in which you live beyond our scale. Minto says I ought not to mention this, but I expect you would prefer to know. (Of course if you like to wash any number of clothes *yourself*, no one will object!)

I have just planted a holly tree – the one we got last season being, despite our order, a bush, not a tree. I have also successfully resisted an attempt made by old Jacks to abbotsford[88] us (I owe this delightful verb to you) into going shares with him in buying, if you please, the whole of Phillips' (deceased – did you hear?) property, on the ground that gypsies wd. otherwise buy it. A ramp, I think.

Talking of abbotsfording I am now reading Lockhart through, and am just at the Shetland and Orkney diary:[89] which you will constantly have been reminded of if you have read *The Pirate*.[90] It is a capital book.

I am examining at the moment, but lightly as you can see from the fact that I manage about an hour's Lockhart *per diem*. I hope to finish my papers on the 21st: but the Award is not till the day after Boxing Day, so that it looks like Jan. 1st for our walk, 'from which I promise myself more satisfaction, perhaps, than is possible.' The date will be a good omen. I am so stiff from carrying that infernal tree up that I hardly know what to do with myself.

The only thing that can really dash your home coming will be the cold: you will have to 'cokker' yourself like anything for the first few weeks, unless this frost breaks. Well – and now to Chaucer's papers. But even they can hardly depress me at such a moment as this

Yours
Jack.

---

88 Abbotsford is the name of Sir Walter Scott's house near Melrose on the Tweed in Scotland.

89 Lockhart, *Memoirs of the Life of Scott*, vol. IV, chs 28–32.

90 Sir Walter Scott, *The Pirate* (1821).

TO ARTHUR GREEVES (W):

[The Kilns
17 December 1932]

My dear Arthur,

You really must forgive me for being a slack correspondent in term time. I think we have talked of this before! However, I was much to blame for not at least letting you have a line about W. who, thank God, turned out to be well though he *had* been ill, and had had a worreying summer in various ways. He had also warned us, he said, (wh. was quite true, though we all forgot it) that he might not keep up his regular correspondence during the hot weather. We were all greatly relieved.

I am sorry to hear about the flu' – one of the few ailments of which I can speak with as large an experience as your own. We have both talked of it and agreed often enough about its pleasures and pains. I hope you are quite set up by now. It was, in any case, almost worth having for its throwing you back on the old favourites. I will make a point of telling Foord-Kelsie – how pleased he will be. I wish I had your early associations with Pickwick:[91] and yet I often feel as if I had. So many scenes come to me with the *feel* of a long since familiar atmosphere returning after absence – I suppose because even without having read it as a boy one has drunk in so much of the Dickensy world indirectly through quotation and talk and other orders. Certainly what I enjoy is *not* the jokes simply as jokes – indeed the earlier and more farcical parts like the military review and Mrs Leo Hunter's party are rather unpleasant to me – but something festive and friendly about D's whole world. A great deal of it (in a way how different from Macdonald's!) the charm of goodness – the goodness of Pickwick himself, and Wardle, and both Wellers.

Thanks for your criticisms on P.R. The detailed criticisms (the 'passages where one word less wd. make all the difference') are what I should like best and could profit by most. Perhaps when you sent the MS back (there is no special hurry) you wd. mark on the blank opposite pages any bits that you think specially in need of improvement and add a note or two in pencil – but don't let it be a bother to you. As to your major criticisms

91 Charles Dickens, *The Pickwick Papers* (1836–7).

1. Quotations. I hadn't realised that they were so numerous as you apparently found them. Mr Sensible, as you rightly saw, is in a separate position: the shower of quotations is part of the character and it wd. be a waste of time to translate them, since the dialogue (I hope) makes it clear that his quotations were always silly and he always missed the point of the authors he quoted. The other ones may be too numerous, and perhaps can be reduced & translated. But not beyond a certain point: for one of the contentions of the book is that the decay of our old classical learning is a contributary cause of atheism (see the chapter on Ignorantia). The quotations at the beginnings of the Books are of course never looked at at all by most readers, so I don't think they matter much.

2. Simplicity. I expect your dissatisfaction on this score points to some real, perhaps v. deep seated, fault: but I am sure it cannot be remedied – least of all in a book of controversy. Also there may be some real difference of conception between you and me. You remember we discussed last summer how much more sympathy you had than I with the Puritan simplicity. I doubt if I interpret Our Lord's words[92] quite in the same way as you. I think they mean that the *spirit* of man must become humble and trustful like a child and, like a child, *simple in motive*, i.e. disinterested, not scheming and 'on the look out'. I don't think He meant that adult Christians must *think* like children: still less that the processes of thought by wh. people *become* Christians must be childish processes. At any rate the *intellectual* side of my conversion was *not* simple and I can describe only what I know. Of course it is only too likely that much of the thought in P.R. offends against simplicity simply by being confused or clumsy! And where so, I wd. gladly emend it if I knew how.

We have had a most glorious autumn here – still, windless days, red sunsets, and all the yellow leaves still on the trees. I wish you could have seen it. This is a Saturday evening after a hard week, so you will excuse me if I close. I will *try* and write again soon but can't promise. It was *very* nice to see your hand again. Your peculier spellinge is indeerd bi long associashuns!*

* I had to make them violent mistakes for feer you wldn't notis them

Yours,
Jack

92 Matthew 18:3–4; Mark 10:15; Luke 18:16–17.

1933

TO GUY POCOCK (W):[1]

Magdalen College,
Oxford.
Jan 17th 1933

Dear Pocock

I have written a new book and should like to know whether it is worth my while sending it to you. After our experiences over *Dymer* I can hardly suppose that you will be very eager! The new one, however, is in prose. It is called *The Pilgrim's Regress: an allegorical apology for Christianity, Reason, and Romanticism*, and is a kind of Bunyan up to date. It is serious in intention but has a good many more comic passages than I originally intended, and also a fair controversial interest (the things chiefly ridiculed are Anglo Catholicism, Materialism, Sitwellism, Psycho-analysis, and T. S. Elliot.) If published, it would be under my own name.

Perhaps you could let me know whether, if I sent it, I could rely on its having a fair and moderately early consideration.

yours sincerely
C. S. Lewis

On 19 January Pocock answered: 'Yes, indeed . . . the Firm would be glad to have an opportunity of considering your new book for publication.'[2] *After reading the manuscript Pocock wrote again on 2 February:*

> *I am writing now to say that we shall be very pleased to publish it for you . . . I look upon it as an important and penetrating book. Now there are one or two important points we want to*

1 See **Guy Noel Pocock** in the Biographical Appendix. Pocock was the editor for J. M. Dent of *The Pilgrim's Regress.*

2 Bodleian Library, MS. Facs. d. 297, fol. 27.

discuss with you. First, we all feel that it is a little long for complete success . . . Secondly, something would have to be done about the Latin in the text. Will you make a suggestion, or shall we? Thirdly, we feel that the book ought to be illustrated. I suggest landscape and figures in the Nash style. Mr Dent has in mind woodcut figures. What are your views? Lastly, we feel that the present title won't do. 'Pilgrim' or 'Pilgrimage' by all means, but not the other part.[3]

TO ARTHUR GREEVES (W):

The Kilns.
Feb 4th 1933

My dear Arthur,

I am really penitent for having left you so long without a letter. The reasons are the usual ones – term and its demands, coupled this time with a good deal of laziness for I have been rather less busy than usual and have been in excellent health and form.

Warnie has been home since before Christmas and is now *retired* (Read Lamb's Essay on The Superannuated Man).[4] He has become a permanent member of our household and I hope we shall pass the rest of our lives together. He has settled down as easily as a man settles into a chair, and what between his reading and working in the garden finds himself busy from morning till night. He and I are making a path through the lower wood – first along the shore of the pond and then turning away from it up through the birch trees and rejoining at the top the ordinary track up the hill. It is very odd and delightful to be engaged on this sort of thing together: the last time we tried to make a path together was in the field at Little Lea when he was at Malvern and I was at Cherbourg. We both have a feeling that 'the wheel has come full circuit', that the period of wanderings is over, and that everything which has happened between 1914 and 1932 was an interruption: tho' not without a consciousness that it is dangerous for mere mortals to expect anything of the future with confidence. We make a very contented family together.

3 ibid., fol. 28. Lewis's original title, which appeared on the proofs, was *The Pilgrim's Regress*, or Pseudo-Bunyan's *Periplus: An Allegorical Apology for Christianity, Reason and Romanticism.*

4 In Charles Lamb, *Essays of Elia* (1823). 'Elia' was a name Lamb adopted for himself.

I have had some fine solitary moments too when we have been working in different parts of the wood. You know how intensely silent it is in a thicket on a warm winter afternoon: and how if you are digging sooner or later a robin comes up and hops about for worms – both his eye and his breast looking unnaturally bright among the prevailing greys and greyish greens. I say *warm* days, for the warm weather has just arrived with a rush: but we had the frost alright. The pond was frozen and we had two days skating. You can imagine how lovely the smooth flow of ice looked as the sun came down onto it through the steep little wood.

In the way of reading Lockhart kept me going through the whole vac. and I am still only at Vol. 8. What an *excellent* book it is, isn't it? – and what a nice addition. I think Scott is the one of all my favourite authors whom I admire most as a man – though of course there is a side of him that you and I would not have got on with, the rather insolent Tory country-gentleman side with the coursing, hard riding and hard drinking. Also perhaps as a father he was a little heavy – how sententious (and how unlike all his other letters) the letters to young Walter are.

Since term began I have had a delightful time reading a children's story which Tolkien has just written.[5] I have told of him before: the one man absolutely fitted, if fate had allowed, to be a third in our friendship in the old days, for he also grew up on W. Morris and George Macdonald. Reading his fairy tale has been uncanny – it is so exactly like what we wd. both have longed to write (or read) in 1916: so that one feels he is not making it up but merely describing the same world into which all three of us have the entry. Whether it is really *good* (I think it is until the end) is of course another question: still more, whether it will succeed with modern children.

And, talking of this sort of thing, would you believe it – I am actually officially supervising a young woman who is writing a thesis on G. Macdonald.[6] It is very odd – and curiously difficult – to approach as work something so old and intimate. The girl is, unfortunately, quite

5 This was J. R. R. Tolkien's *The Hobbit: or There and Back Again*, parts of which were probably rewritten before it was published in 1937.

6 Mary McQueen McEldowney, 'The Fairy Tales and Fantasies of George MacDonald' (1934). A copy is in the Bodleian Library, MSS B.Litt. d. 257.

unworthy of her subject: apart from everything else, she is an American.

Dent's has accepted the *Pilgrim's Regress* with a number of conditions – shortening, alteration of title etc – which I intend to make some resistance to.[7] I have no right to expect a letter after my long silence, but of course I shd. like one. How does the detective story go? It will soon be getting suitable weather for your cottage again: although, as you see, I am having a good time, the memory of the Mournes is still very poignant. Give my love to Mrs Greeves, and to the McNeills[8] (all *three* – the one on the hill included) if you see them.

Yours,
Jack

Warnie sends you his greetings and hopes we shall see you this year.

TO GUY POCOCK (W):

Magdalen College,
Oxford.
Tuesday [14 February 1933]

Dear Pocock

I am sending you to-morrow the revised MS. The quotations are translated (I am glad you thought of that – it was great fun) and all the cuts that I can make. I should like you to glance at Bk I. chap. 4 (pp. 15–17). I have cut practically the whole chapter because it is such an easy cut: on the other hand some people like it and the gain in space is not great. I don't much care myself whether it stays or goes, so I leave you to do what you please with it. I have scored it only in pencil, so that you can remove the scorings if you think fit. After that, the book has had all done to it that I can do and may go straight to the printer as soon as we have signed an agreement.

I am still strongly in favour of publication in June if it is still possible, but of course the final decision on that, and on price, rests with you.

7 The title was shortened to *The Pilgrim's Regress: An Allegorical Apology for Christianity, Reason and Romanticism*.

8 James Adams McNeill (1853–1907), who had been Lewis's mother's teacher at the Methodist College, Belfast, was Headmaster of Campbell College, 1890–1907. He and his wife, Margaret Cunningham McNeill, lived in Strandtown with their daughter Jane ('Tchainie') McNeill, a close friend of Lewis and Arthur Greeves.

I have enclosed a *map* with the MS. A surprising number of people independently asked for one. Ought there to be one? – certainly not, in my view, if it is expensive. (Of course the one I enclose would not do anyway – but with help I could concoct a better one)

yours sincerely
C. S. Lewis

TO GUY POCOCK (W):

The Kilns,
Headington Quarry,
Oxford.
Feb. 27th 1933

Dear Pocock

It is most unfortunate at this moment that I should be laid up with flu' and practically an idiot. However, some points won't wait.

1. Could you get the Firm to agree to some wording of the 'next book' clause which will leave me free to offer to the Clarendon Press a work now in hand on *Allegory from Prudentius to Spenser*.[9] This is a purely academic work wh. I don't think you would consider – at least I don't remember your producing anything of the kind – and it seems rather the duty of a young scholar to give his own university press the first refusal of his first scholarly work. If they will agree (Dents, I mean) they probably have a suitable form of words, or can invent one more easily than I. ('Next novel, poem, play, or other imaginative work' or 'Next work of a popular character') I don't much mind, but I fancy they will make no objection.

2. I enclose two alternative 'blurbs' for the catalogue as asked. I am so ill that they are probably both hopeless. Hash up anything you can out of the two: if neither any use you'll have to get a new one done in the office – I can no more at the moment.

3. No objection to picture on jacket – you know, from correspondence about the *Dymer* decoration what kind of drawing I *don't* like!

4. Yes – end leaves a good place for map. I take it no one wd. be

9 Lewis is referring to the book eventually published as *The Allegory of Love: A Study in Medieval Tradition* (1936).

such a fool as to work out literally the *distances* on that map I sent you – they are probably all wrong.

5. Just occurs to me – in the revised MS chapter numberings have not all been corrected since omissions. I suppose printers look after that sort of thing for themselves. By the bye – I suppose these very short chapters will not be given a fresh page each: it wd. be very bothering to the eye apart from waste of paper. If not, what about headings in the margin as in Temple Classics?

Very glad to hear you will run down. Let me know in time to collect Coghill[10] and we'll make a feast of it.

I hope this is not so incoherent as it feels to me

yours
C. S. Lewis

P.S. The above address for the next few days

PP.S. The blurbs shd. have gone to Department C.

TO GUY POCOCK (W):

The Kilns,
Headington Quarry,
Oxford.
March 23rd 1933

Dear Pocock

The map has just arrived and is excellent. There is one correction – for TALE MEN read PALE MEN. Am I to send it back (I rather distrust my powers of putting up such an odd parcel) or will you convey this single correction to the cartographer – with my congratulations.

I hope you have not abandoned the idea of paying me a visit,

yours sincerely
C. S. Lewis

10 See **Nevill Coghill** (1899–1980) in the Biographical Appendix to *CL* I. Coghill, a member of the Inklings, was Fellow of English at Exeter College, Oxford, 1924–57, and Merton Professor of English Literature, 1957–66.

TO J. M. DENT PUBLISHERS (W):

Dept. B
Pilgrim's Regress

The Kilns
Headington Quarry,
Oxford
March 24th 1933

Dear Sir

I enclose one correction for Map and suggestion for title etc. on a separate sheet,

yours faithfully
C. S. Lewis

P.S. I am at this address till May 1st.

TO J. M. DENT PUBLISHERS (W):

Department B.
Correction
For TALE MEN read PALE MEN.

If a title is wanted I wd. suggest MAPPA MUNDI or MIDDLE-EARTH (The artist may decide between these on decorative grounds). If you merely want something to fill up the corner a [compass drawn in, basically a cross with N, E, S and W around clockwise from the top] might do.

C. S. Lewis

TO J. M. DENT PUBLISHERS (W):

Dept B
(Pilgrim's Regress)

The Kilns,
Headington Quarry,
Oxford.
March 25th 1933

Dear Sir

I have your letter of the 24th about stippling the sea parts of the map. After the very strong and pleasing contour lines with wh. the artist has emphasised the coast line, stippling is certainly not needed *for clarity*. Whether it would be an improvement *decoratively* is a question I would leave to the artist. Does it not partly depend on factors which are not before me: e.g. the type of paper, the colour of the cover (of which a rim will probably show) and the size?

yours faithfully

C. S. Lewis

TO ARTHUR GREEVES (W):

The Kilns,
Headington Quarry,
Oxford.
March 25th. 1933.

My dear Arthur,

I wonder how you have been getting on this many a day. I am certain I was the last to write, but whoever began it we have both been wrong to keep such a silence. We ought to be ashamed when we remember the weekly letters of the Bookham period. Fortunately each feels sure that the cause of this decline, whatever else it may be, is no diminution of the friendship. I think you pointed out to me once that it was natural we should write more easily in the old days, when everything was new and our correspondence was really like two explorers signalling to one another in a new country. Also – neither of us had any other outlet: we still thought that we were the only two people in the world who were interested in the right kind of things in the right kind of way.

I think I mentioned the skating in my last letter. Since then life has gone on in a pretty smooth way. Warnie sinks deeper and deeper into the family life: it is hard to believe he was not always here. What a mercy that the change in his views (I mean as regards religion) should have happened in time to meet mine – it would be awkward if one of us were still in the old state of mind. He has an excellent gramophone and is building up a complete set of the Beethoven symphonies, one of which (complete) he often plays us on a Sunday evening. I have quite foresworn the old method of hearing one's favourite bits played separately, and I am sure one gains enormously by always hearing one symphony as a whole and nothing else. By the way which is the one that contains the beautiful slow movement you played me – the one whose quality you defined as 'compassion'? I have been waiting for it eagerly but so far W. has not produced it. I am getting back more of my old pleasure in music all the time.

I saw Bryson last night.[11] We were having a little supper for some of the English tutors, at the 'Golden Cross', which Bryson ought to have attended and as we knew he was in Oxford we went round to his digs to root him out. We found him sitting nursing a terrific black eye (the result of a very mild motor accident – better not mention this at home) and refusing to join us. I suspect that these little suppers are not really much to his taste: the fare is fried fish, ham and eggs, bread and cheese, and beer, and the whole thing is too homely, too rowdy, and too unluxurious for Bryson. This sounds like malice, but it isn't. Between ourselves, Bryson's beautiful clothes and general daintiness are a perfectly friendly and well established joke among some of his colleagues. There must be some real good in him; for though many laugh at his foppery and grumble at his laziness, I have never met any one, even in this hotbed of squabbles, who seriously dislikes him.

I had to abandon Lockhart at the beginning of last term and have not yet resumed it. It is most annoying when the last few volumes of a long book have to be left over like that. One somehow feels a disinclination to begin them again and to find how many names and facts one has forgotten: yet it is uncomfortable not to polish the book off. You will have the laugh of me this time.

While having a few days in bed recently I tried, at W's earnest recommendation, to read the *Three Musketeers*,[12] but not only got tired of it but also found it disgusting. All these swaggering bullies, living on the money of their mistresses – faugh! One never knows how good Scott is till one tries to read Dumas. Have you noticed how completely Dumas lacks any background? In Scott, behind the adventures of the hero, you have the whole society of the age, with all the interplay of town and country, Puritan and Cavalier, Saxon and Norman, or what not, and all the racy humour of the minor characters: and behind that again you have the eternal things – the actual countryside, the mountains, the weather, the very *feel* of travelling. In Dumas, if you try to look even an inch behind the immediate intrigue, you find just nothing

11 John Norman Bryson (1896–1976) was born in Portadown, Co. Armagh, and educated at the Queen's University, Belfast, and at Merton College, Oxford, taking his BA from Oxford in 1922. He was a lecturer in English at Balliol, Merton and Oriel College, 1923–1940, and Fellow and Tutor in English Literature at Balliol College, 1940–63.

12 Alexandre Dumas, *The Three Musketeers* (1844).

at all. You are in an abstract world of gallantry and adventure which has no *roots* – no connection with human nature or mother earth. When the scene shifts from Paris to London there is no sense that you have reached a new country, no change of atmosphere. And I don't think there is a single passage to show that Dumas had ever seen a cloud, a road, or a tree. In a word, if you were asked to explain what you and I meant by 'the homely' in literature, you could almost reply, 'It means the opposite of *The Three Musketeers.*' But perhaps I am being too hard on what after all was written only for amusement. I suppose there must be a merit in the speed and verve of the plot, even if I don't like that kind of thing.

I was talking about this to Tolkien who, you know, grew up on Morris and Macdonald and shares my taste in literature to a fault. We remarked how odd it was that the word *romance* should be used to cover things so different as Morris on the one hand and Dumas or Rafael Sabatini on the other – things not only different but so different that it is hard to imagine the same person liking both. We agreed that for what *we* meant by romance there must be at least the hint of another world – one must 'hear the horns of elfland'.[13]

For fear you shd. think I am going too much off the deep end, let me add that I have just read a real modern thriller (Buchan's *Three Hostages*)[14] and enjoyed it thoroughly. So perhaps I shall be able to enjoy yours. Is it finished, by the way, and am I to see it? I have also read a war book (*Landlocked Lake* by Hanbury Sparrow)[15] – but that was because Barfield is introducing him as a new member of our Easter walking party. A 'regular' colonel seems an odd fish to come on a walk with my friends and me – I wonder if I shall quarrel with him!

Do try to write me a long letter soon. You are constantly in my mind even when I don't write, and to lose touch with you would be like losing a limb.

Dents say they will have *Pilgrim's Regress* out by the end of May. I have successfully resisted a foolish idea they had of an illustrated edition – whose price wd. of course have killed any sale it might hope for. But it is going to be decorated by a map on the end leaf which I had great

13 Alfred, Lord Tennyson, *The Princess* (1847), part 4, song (added 1850): 'The horns of elfland faintly blowing!'

14 John Buchan, *The Three Hostages* [1924].

15 Arthur Alan Hanbury-Sparrow, *The Land-Locked Lake* [1932].

fun in drawing the sketch for. I suppose you have no objection to my dedicating the book to you? It is yours by every right – written in your house, read to you as it was written, and celebrating (at least in the most important parts) an experience which I have more in common with you than anyone else. By the bye, you will be interested to hear that in finally revising the MS I did adopt many of your corrections, or at least made alterations where you objected. So if the book is a ghastly failure I shall always say 'Ah it's this Arthur business'[16]

Do write. W. in bed with flu' (mild) but otherwise all well here

Yours

Jack

Give my love to your mother: I hope she is well.

TO OWEN BARFIELD (W):

[The Kilns],
March 28th 1933

My dear Barfield –

Thanks for sending me the book.[17] Any war-book that is any good at all stirs up my θρεπτική[18] so much that I find it difficult – through the din – to discover what it is really like. But this is, of course, much more than a war book. My chief complaint is that it stops too soon, without pulling the threads (the philosophical ones) together. Is it, by any chance, the first of a trilogy? As *that*, it would be capital. There are, as it stands, several things I want to know more about. e.g.

1. Courage used to be less conscious, more in the blood: that is why our ancestors did not have to exhaust on keeping brave all the conscious energy needed for the fighting. Good! But does the author's solution by discipline mean that nature was simply wrong in transferring courage from the blood to the mind? For this discipline (sharply distinguished from regimental spirit etc) is just a method of putting the courage-problem *back* on the unconscious: i.e. he says to nature 'I don't want this freedom. All you have done is to put me to the trouble of inventing

16 He is imagining a comment his father might make.

17 He is referring to Hanbury-Sparrow's *The Land-Locked Lake*, mentioned in the letter to Arthur Greeves of 25 March 1933.

18 There is no true English equivalent. Essentially Lewis meant 'sympathy for the living' (more literally θρεπτική is a desire to encourage growth or nourishment).

an elaborate machinery for making myself again un-free in this matter – freedom in this matter having turned out to be such a job that if I attend to it I have no time to attend to anything else.' Is this what H-S's position comes to? And does he know that it does?

2. One wants emphatically to know more about those Australians and Canadians. We are told that they were braver than the English. If, as I surmise, they were not subjected to the martinettery, then they cast doubt on the whole thesis. If they were, then still, since it did not produce the same effect on them and on the English, why then, (by the 'method of difference') discipline can't be the whole secret.

3. How much weight does he give to the discovery made at the end of the book that martinettery can be applied by anyone who has learned the trick i.e. it depends on no spiritual quality in the applier?[19] Wd. he admit that this is the same as saying it is *mechanical.* When I got to the end, where this discovery is made, I at once connected it with the early passage 'Spirit wept . . .' (that bit is splendid)[20] and saw discipline related to courage precisely as the mechanical battle of heavy guns is related (by H-S) to 'the noble end of war.'

In fact, all my three points come to one – an uncertainty how far the author has faced his own growing discovery of the bad element in discipline and how far he has seen the resulting problem. For the position he leaves us in is this. Discipline is the only way of making it at all probable that your men will win battles: and therefore without discipline the cause of freedom and virtue, so far as it lies with you, will be lost. On the other hand, discipline is unfree, can be applied mechanically like a trick, there is no warrant that it will fall justly etc etc: so that it looks as if discipline itself may be just as fatal to the cause as defeat. This is where one would like the next book to take up the problem. (It is the old damnable fix – efficiency at the cost of the values for whose sake only you wish to be effective, *or* justice, liberty, and

19 Hanbury-Sparrow, *The Land-Locked Lake*, Part I, ch. 3, p. 287: 'Sometimes it frightened you, this terrific power that discipline held over modern men. We'd get our drafts of reluctant but sensible conscripts, and of returned wounded undergoing God alone knew what agonies of fear, and in a few weeks we'd turn them into troops as brave, if not as skilful, as any the battalion had ever had. Once an officer knew the trick of it, it was all so terribly easy.'

20 ibid., Part I, ch. 5, p. 60: 'Spirit wept, for it knew that the reign of materialism, of metal against flesh, would henceforth have to rule.'

equality preserved only to be knocked on the head by your efficient neighbour. All this bears acutely on the problem of the college junto – of wh. we must discuss).

There were places in the book where one felt the old hatred. Gr-r-r- – θεοῖσιν ἐχθρός ταξιαρχός.[21] Still, he seems to share them himself. On the purely literary side, I think it good: vivid without the journalese that usually accompanies these vivid war books. Some of the battles are not v. easy to visualise, but that is almost unavoidable: they are certainly easier than Blunden's.[22] One really glorious bit is the description of the gusto he feels even for the filthy air and Stygian landscape of the front when expecting death: the preciousness of *matter* as such. I don't think that's been done before.

I am a good deal worried by my inability to understand some of your article on Coleridge.[23] It is all *exciting*, but I can't really find much to correspond with the diagrams, except the first. Things I *do* get are *a*. The explanation of C's apparent incoherence.[24] *b*. The privileged position of the vb. to be[25] (By the bye, Sadism and Masochism are both over-emphases of the *Difference* element, but the first as verb and the second as Noun. Will that do?)[26] *c*. The insect as externalised consciousness.[27] All the rest you must explain on the walk.

---

21 'a commander hateful to the gods'. Aristophanes *Peace*, line 1172.

22 Edmund Blunden, *Undertones of War* (1928).

23 Owen Barfield, 'The Philosophy of Samuel Taylor Coleridge', *Anthroposophy*, 7 (Christmas 1932), pp. 385–404. Reprinted in Owen Barfield, *Romanticism Comes of Age* (1944).

24 Barfield, *Romanticism Comes of Age*, p. 149: 'His extraordinarily unifying mind was too painfully aware that you cannot really say one thing correctly without saying everything. He was rightly afraid that there would not be time to say everything before going on to say the next thing, or that he would forget to do so afterwards. His incoherence of expression arose from the coherence of what he wanted to express. It was a sort of intellectual stammer.'

25 ibid., pp. 155–6. In his *Treatise on Logic*, says Barfield, Coleridge 'points out how the world of grammar subsists between the two poles of verb and noun, the one expressing activity and the other passivity, the one an action and the other a state. . . . We may think of grammar as a sort of world revolving about an axis. Only in the axis itself do the two poles coincide. And what is this axis? It is the verb "*to be*" itself.'

26 ibid., p. 57: 'Sameness and Difference are the positive and negative aspects – of what? Of *Likeness*.'

27 ibid., p. 162: 'Coleridge points out the startling metamorphosis of outward form which characterizes nature's transition to the next stage of animal existence. The exuberant complexity of structure typical of the insect disappears altogether from the surface, having been withdrawn to the interior parts of the body . . . Nature

Both poems improve on re-reading, but the first one still remains the better, for the reasons given before. The *selection* of imagery in it is almost perfect and the effect all one like a taste.

HAVE YOU BOOKED THOSE SEATS FOR THE RHEINGOLD?

Have the venue where you like: but with such a large party – and in Easter week – some room-booking shd. be done at once

Yours

C. S. Lewis

Last Saturday was the anniversary of the Creation of the World!

TO DAPHNE HARWOOD (BOD):[28]

Magdalen College,
Oxford.
March 28th 1933

Dear Mrs. Harwood,

I hope it was not only literary vanity that made me enjoy so much your very kind and very discriminating letter. Thank you very much indeed.

I was much interested in the account of your journey. I was never myself up against anything quite so bad as I take Ogden to be, but I can quite imagine him on the St. Theresa theme.[29]

I am glad you never read my *Summa*,[30] for all that is dead as mutton to me now: and the points chiefly at issue between the Anthroposophists and me then were *precisely* the points on which anthroposophy is certainly right – i.e. the claim that it is possible for man, here and now, in the phenomenal world, to have commerce with the world beyond – which is what I was denying. The present difference between us is quite

sinks back exhausted from the line which she has hitherto been following and in her repose gathers strength for her newest creation – consciousness.'

28 See **Daphne Harwood** in the Biographical Appendix.

29 This was Charles Kay Ogden (1889–1957), whose works include (with I. A. Richards) *The Meaning of Meaning* (1923), *Basic English* (1930) and *The Basic Words* (1932). Lewis disliked *The Meaning of Meaning* for reasons given in his essay 'Bluspels and Flalansferes' in *SLE.*

30 Lewis is referring to his 'Great War' with Owen Barfield over Anthroposophy, and the document into which Lewis put many of his arguments, known as the '*Summa*'. See footnote 35 to the letter to Barfield of 16 March 1932.

other. The only thing that I now wd. object eagerly to [in] anthroposophy is that I don't think it can say 'I believe in one God the Father Almighty.' My feeling is that even if there are a thousand orders of beneficent being above us, still, the universe is a cheat unless at the back of them all there is the one God of Christianity. But I did not mean to raise controversial points: there is certainly quite a lot for us to agree on as against nearly the whole contemporary world! I would quite agree, for instance, with your discovery that it is *Will* wh. lets the cat out of the bag – and also with your refusal to rest in Croce.[31] His is the kind of idealism that for all practical purposes is indistinguishable from materialism. What a ghastly pun that his name should mean 'Blessed Cross'!

I don't understand the part about the eternal feminine (and masculine) in your letter, and look forward to hearing more about it when next we meet. Cecil was looking grand when he came down to us – he is the most-un-ageing of my friends.

We are all disappointed that your father has abandoned the idea of buying Tewsfield.[32] With very many thanks,

Yours sincerely,
C. S. Lewis

TO GUY POCOCK (W):

The Kilns
Headington Quarry,
Oxford
March 31st 1933

Dear Pocock

This is unfortunate! Since I last wrote family arrangements have been maturing which will take me out of Oxford from the 6th onwards – so that Monday, Tuesday and Wednesday of next week are the only days (until the 23rd and after). I don't want to be a nuisance: on the

31 Benedetto Croce (1866–1952), Italian philosopher and critic, whose aesthetics were profoundly influential in Italy before the Second World War. Lewis was probably referring to Croce's most important work, *Aesthetics as the Science of Expression and General Linguistics* (1902).

32 Daphne Harwood's father had thought of buying the house, Tewsfield, which almost adjoined The Kilns. The house was bought shortly after this by Mrs Alice Griggs. See note 123 to the letter to Warnie of 2 October 1939.

other hand I should very much like to see you. So just do as you would like. If you want to get me at short notice my Telephone number is 6963 Oxford – preferably after dinner. So sorry.

yours

C. S. Lewis

TO J. M. DENT PUBLISHERS (W):

Department B

Flint Hall
Hambledon,
Bucks
April 12th 1933

Dear Sir

I return corrected proof of the *Pilgrim's Regress*. Would you kindly direct the special attention of the printer to the following points

1. Greek quotations pp 101–107. Make quite sure of the correction in several places: i.e. read Δ (= 'Delta,' 4th letter of the Gk. alphabet) for ó.

2. On p. 228 my note may not be perfectly clear. I want the poem to be spaced like this: [series of eight lines close together, the final one separated by a line or two]

3. Quotations on pp 11, 31 etc. Ought these to have stops after them? And if so, ought the dashes to be removed? I have put in the stops and not removed the dashes, but am ready to be guided by the printer's decision as to what is usual in such cases.

yours faithfully

C. S. Lewis

Address after Monday next,
Magdalen College,
Oxford.

TO GUY POCOCK (W):

Magdalen College.
Oxford.
May 4th 1933

Dear Pocock

Yes – I heartily approve Derrick's jacket: but should prefer to see the legend 'Reason set . . . up' omitted. Photo will be sent as soon as taken.

In haste,

Yours

C. S. Lewis

It really *is* good: quite beyond my hopes. The legend under it however *must* be omitted, because nothing less like a *spurring* rider could well be imagined. Anyway it is not needed.

The Pilgrim's Regress: An Allegorical Apology for Christianity, Reason and Romanticism *was published by J. M. Dent on 25 May 1933.*

TO GUY POCOCK (W):

MAGDALEN COLLEGE.
OXFORD.
June 9th 1933

Dear Pocock

Could you let me have 4 more copies of P. R. and tell me what I owe you for them?

I recommend the underlined passage in the enclosed for advertisement use as soon as we get anything on the other side to set beside it,

yours

C. S. Lewis

TO ARTHUR GREEVES (W):

Magdalen College,
Oxford.
June 13th. 1933

My dear Arthur,

You ought to have had a copy of *Pilgrim's Regress* from me before now and a letter long before. My six complementary copies turned out to have so many unexpected claimants that I had exhausted them before I knew where I was: some new ones are now on order and I will send you one as soon as they arrive.

As for letters, they have been rather out of the question. I have never had a busier term – 9 to 1 and 5 to 7 every week day and two Sundays completely filled with extra work in the middle of the term: not to mention exams which have now set in and which will keep my nose to the grindstone till the end of July. However I have kept very well and have therefore nothing to complain of – except that I am rather hungry for reading and don't know when I shall get a few uninterrupted hours again.

'Invigilating' in exams last week I did manage to read one novel (I find that anything harder than novels is too much for me in the Schools) which I can recommend – *Tom's a-cold* by John Collier.[33] The theme is one not uncommon now-a-days: that of a barbaric 'heroic' society growing up on the ruins of the present civilisation. But it has two great advantages over most such books. *1.* It doesn't waste time telling you how civilisation collapsed but starts a 100 years on. *2.* It lays the scene in the South of England and is very topographical, so that you can actually see the Berkshire downs and Savernake Forest turning into the fortresses, the greenwoods, and the valley communities of a world at about the same stage of development as that in *The Roots of the Mountains*.[34] One gets v. well the idea of how much *larger* England would seem under those conditions.

I must announce with regret that I shall not be paying you a visit this summer (Perhaps this is premature as I have not yet been asked!) I have come to the decision with considerable doubt, but I think on the whole I am right. Warnie and I want to go and see the Scotch uncles[35] and as they are getting on it ought to be done this year. This will sound an odd programme to you. It is not all 'duty' – curiosity, desire to revive childish memories, and the anticipation of an amused yet affectionate pleasure in seeing our father in them, all come in to it. We shall then go back from Glasgow by the Clyde Shipping Company boat – and I admit I shall be such a rag by the time exams are over that I rather look forward to some lazy days at sea as the best, if not the only, holiday I shall be capable of. I am sorry to disappoint you (if I may flatter myself

---

33 John Collier, *Tom's A-Cold: A Tale* (1933).

34 William Morris, *The Roots of the Mountains* (1890).

35 The 'Scotch uncles' were the two brothers of Albert Lewis, William Lewis (1859–1946) and Richard Lewis (b. 1861). After William lost his job with the Belfast Ropeworks, in 1883 he and his brother went to Glasgow where they entered into partnership as W. & R. Lewis, Rope and Twine Manufacturers. The two brothers lived close together in the coastal town of Helensburgh, north-west of Glasgow. See **The Lewis Family** in the Biographical Appendix to *CL* I.

that it is a disappointment). At any rate don't think that this is a precedent or that it means the end of my appearances at Belfast!

I was up to London for the *Rheingold*, which I enjoyed less than *Siegfried* – chiefly I think because we had very bad seats (*We* is Barfield and I).[36] MacFarlane – who has had a nervous breakdown since, poor chap – says he saw you* at one of the other operas: what a pity we hadn't known and gone together.

I had an extremely kind letter from Reid about the book. I think it is going to be at least as big a failure as *Dymer*, and am consequently trying to take to heart all the things I wrote you when you were bowled over by Reid's decision on your first novel – not entirely without success. How goes the detective story?

I hardly deserve a letter, but hope you will treat me better than my deserts

Yours
Jack

* Sounds as if this were the cause of the breakdown!

TO T. R. HENN (P):[37]

Magdalen College,
Oxford.
July 2nd 1933.

Dear Henn

If you like this,[38] accept it as a peace offering. If you think it worth disliking heartily, then have at me in print or private – dismount your tuck, be yare in your preparing.[39] If it is simply a bore, then pass it on to your second hand bookseller.

Yours
C. S. Lewis

---

36 They saw Wagner's *Das Rheingold* at Covent Garden on 2 May. There is an account of the performance in *The Times* (3 May 1933), p. 12.

37 Thomas Rice Henn (1901–74) was educated at St Catharine's College, Cambridge, where he took a BA in 1922. He was Fellow of English at St Catharine's College, 1926–69 and Reader in Anglo-Irish Literature. His books include *Longinus and English Criticism* (1934) and *The Bible as Literature* (1970).

38 A copy of *The Pilgrim's Regress*. Professor Henn kept this letter inside the cover of that book.

39 William Shakespeare, *Twelfth Night* (1623), III, iv, 247–9: 'Dismount thy tuck, be yare in thy preparation, for thy assailant is quick, skilful, and deadly.'

TO MARY SHELLEY (T):[40]

Magdalen
July 21st [1933]

Dear Miss Shelley,

If you are not, at the moment, too sick of me and all my kind to read further, it may be worth saying that you must not run away with the idea that you are a Fourth Class mind. What really ruined you was an NS and a Δ on language, which would of course have spoiled even very good work elsewhere.[41] In the Lit. your highest mark was β+ (XIXth century).

Why your literature papers were not better I do not understand. I blame myself for not having exhorted more essays from you – but I doubt if that was the whole cause. You were very *short* and *general.* But I am quite clear in my own mind that you have not done yourself justice and that your real quality is far beyond the work you did in Schools.

This is cold comfort to you with the world to face! – but at least it is said quite sincerely and not merely for the sake of consoling you.

Try to forgive me both as an examiner and as a tutor. If there should at any time be any way in which I can be of use to you, let me know at once. Till then, good-bye and good luck.

Yours very sincerely
C. S. Lewis

TO ARTHUR GREEVES (W):

The Kilns,
Headington Quarry,
Oxford.
Aug. 17th. 1933.

My dear Arthur,

I have been silent for a terribly long time, I know, but it has not really been my fault. I had a solid month's examining after term ended,

---

40 See **Mary Neylan** in the Biographical Appendix. Lewis was her tutor in English although Mary Shelley was a member of St Hugh's College. This letter of 21 July 1933 was written after she had taken a Fourth in English.

41 The language paper was on Anglo-Saxon which was marked with an 'NS' ('*non satis*' meaning 'not satisfactory' and a Δ (D) which is the lowest grade that can be given. Clearly, Anglo-Saxon was her undoing.

and then I went away for my sea holiday. I had pictured myself writing to you on the boat, but this turned out to be practically impossible: so that I am really writing if not on the first possible day, at any rate on the second or third. Before I go on to anything else I must answer one point in your last letter: – you comment on my saying nothing about your having come so near me without visiting me. The fact is I deliberately said nothing about it because I feared that, if I did, it might seem that *my* intention of not visiting *you* this year was a kind of tit-for-tat – that I was offended and was thus taking my revenge, or, at least, was excusing my intention by your action. I would have liked you to come and see me, of course: but I never thought that England ought to be forbidden ground to you if you were not seeing me for any reason. I have no wish to reduce you to stealing past Oxford with a false beard on – like you and me stealing past Leeborough from Bernagh in the old days.

I did not enjoy the *Rheingold* this year *nearly* as much as I enjoyed *Siegfried* last year – neither at the time nor in memory. Oddly enough the hammer passage which you mention I actually disliked. I had enjoyed it on your gramophone, but at Covent Garden it seemed to me so much cruder and, before it ended (and I thought it would never end) nearly ridiculous. You must not think that my loyalty to the *Ring* is wavering. The main causes of my disliking the *Rheingold* were (a) Our having very bad seats (b) My not liking the man who sang Alberich.[42] I admit that Alberich must sometimes shout instead of singing – but that man seemed to shout unnecessarily. Next year I hope to go to the *Valkyrie*.

While I am on these things, I might add that I have actually been to the films to-day! – to see *Cavalcade*!![43] This is one of the most disgraceful confessions I have ever made to you. I thought it would be interesting historically, and so I suppose it was: and certainly very clever. But there is not an idea in the whole thing from beginning to end: it is a mere brutal assault on one's emotions, using material which one can't help feeling intensely. It appeals entirely to that part of you which

---

42 Eduard Habich.

43 The stage play, *Cavalcade*, about contemporary British history, was written by Noël Coward and first performed in 1932. It was made into a film by Frank Lloyd in 1933, and was so popular that a command performance was given at Windsor Castle before King George V and Queen Mary on 2 May 1933.

lives in the throat and chest, leaving the spirit untouched. I have come away feeling as if I had been at a debauch.

The sea holiday was a success. We went first by train to Arrochar where we slept a night[44] and had one glorious day's walking on the shores of Loch Long and Loch Lomond and across the mountains between them. I forget if you have been in those parts. They seemed to me to excell all other mountains in one respect – the curiously fantastic, yet heavy shapes of rock into which the summits are formed. They realise one's idea of mountains as the fastnesses of the giants. The actual *beach* of Loch Lomond also pleased me very much – an ordinary pebbly beach such as you might find at the sea with the unusual addition that it had trees on it and that you could drink the water. Up in the mountains we had a glorious hour at a stream – a golden brown stream, with cataracts and deep pools. We spread out all our clothes (sweat-sodden) to dry on the flat stones, and lay down in a pool just under a little waterfall, and let the foam come down the back of our heads and round our necks. Then when we were cool, we came out and sat naked to eat our sandwiches, with our feet still in the rushing water. Why have you and I never done this? (Answer – because we never came to a suitable stream at a suitable time)

This glorious day was followed by a very tiring and trying, but extremely interesting, week end *chez l'oncle* at Helensburgh. It was uncannily like being at home again – specially when Uncle Bill announced on the Sunday evening 'I won't be going into town tomorrow', and we with well-feigned enthusiasm replied 'Good!'. But to describe the whole thing would take a book. On the Monday afternoon[45] we sailed from Glasgow. The journey down the Clyde was beautiful, despite some rain, and tho' there were more passengers on board than I would have chosen, there was usually a quiet corner to read in. I liked – you would probably not – the homely feeling on these boats, with dinner at 1 and 'High Tea' at 6. It was very strange coming into Belfast next morning.

I had made up my mind that it was no good trying to arrange a meeting with you. The time – we were sailing again at one o'clock – was much too long for a three-handed talk of you and W. and me,

---

44 4 August.

45 7 August.

and too short for sending *him* off anywhere so that I could have you tete-à-tete. Our programme was simple. We trammed to Campbell and thence walked up the hills round the Shepherd's hut. The sight of all those woods and fields made me regret very much that I was not having an Irish holiday with you: and the new house (near Kelsie's new house) made me wonder how much more might be altered by next year. We walked down by the ordinary, poignantly familiar, route, stopped to look at Leeborough – how the trees are growing! – and then went down the Circular Rd. to St Marks to see the window which W. had never yet seen.[46] He was delighted with it. Here we had a conversation with the verger – who referred to Gordon[47] as 'Gordon'! Then, after a drink in the reformed pub at Gelson's corner, we got back into town.

The rest of the tour I shall not describe in detail. The bit I should most like to have shared with you was the departure from Waterford. The sail down the river, peppered with v. early Norman castles, was good, but what was better was the next three hours out to sea. Imagine a flat French grey sea, and a sky of almost the same colour: between these a long fish-shaped streak of pure crimson, about 20 miles long, and lasting, unchanged or changing imperceptibly, for hours. Then add three or four perfectly transparent mountains, so extraordinarily spiritualised that they absolutely realised the old idea of Ireland as the 'isle of the saints'. Like this – I do not remember that I have ever seen anything more calm and spacious and celestial. Not but what we had some wonderful sunsets at other times in the voyage. You with your dislike of the sea will hardly admit it, but from a boat out of sight of land one does get effects hardly to be got elsewhere. For one thing the sky is so huge and the horizon is uninterrupted in every direction, so that the mere *scale* of the sky-scenery is beyond anything you get ashore:

---

46 The stained-glass window designed for St Mark's, Dundela, which Jack and Warnie had erected in memory of their parents. See note 60 to the letter to Warnie of 22 November 1931.

47 i.e. Charles Gordon Ewart (1885–1936) who married Lily Greeves, sister of Arthur Greeves. He was the second son of Lewis's mother's cousins, Sir William Quartus Ewart (1844–1919) and Lady Ewart (1849–1929) who lived near Little Lea in a house named Glenmachan. They are referred to in *SBJ*, ch. 3 and elsewhere as 'Cousin Quartus' and 'Lady E'. They had four other children: Robert Heard 'Bob' Ewart (1879–1939); Hope Ewart (1882–1934); Kelso 'Kelsie' Ewart (1886–1966); and Gundreda 'Gunny' Ewart (1888–1978). See **The Ewart Family** in the Biographical Appendix to *CL* I.

and for another, the extreme simplicity of the design – flat disk and arched dome and nothing else – produces a kind of concentration. And then again to turn suddenly from these huge sublimities as one passes a staircase head and hear the sound of plates being laid or the laugh of a boy coming up on the warmer air from below, gives that delicious contrast of the homely and familiar in the midst of the remote, which is the master-stroke of the whole thing.

I am re-reading Malory, and am astonished to find how much more connected, more of a unity, it is than we used to see. I no longer lose myself in the 'brasting'. There is still too much of it, to be sure, but I am sustained by the beauty of the sentiment, and also the actual turns of phrase. How could one miss 'He commanded his trumpets to blow that all the earth trembled and *dindled* of the sound.'[48] Clearly one must read every good book at least once every ten years. It now seems to me that my Bookham reading of Malory was almost worthless. Did you ever realise that it is full of *pathos*? I never did until a pupil pointed it out to me a few months ago – wh. is what set me re-reading it.

I hope I shall be able to be a fairly regular correspondent again for the rest of the summer. Bad luck about the book!

Yours,
Jack

TO ARTHUR GREEVES (W):

[The Kilns]
Sept 1st. 1933

My dear Arthur,

I have no right to complain that I have not yet heard from you. Nor have I much to say on my own account: but I think I will write a little just to feel that we are keeping the channel open.

W. and I are heartily sick of the summer, the others not. The pond is sinking lower and lower and all sorts of stones and roots that ought to be covered are projecting – it seems almost an indecency. The water is getting dirtier and warmer and bathing has been abandoned. Flowers and vegetables are withering and the ground is so hard that a short walk leaves you footsore as if you had been walking on pavements. This morning we woke to coolness and thick mist and spangled cobwebs. I

48 Sir Thomas Malory, *Le Morte D'Arthur*, book V, 'Arthur's War with Lucius'.

thought it was the first day of autumn and felt the old excitement. But it was all a cheat and by the time we came out of church it was another blazing day – pitiless blue sky, sun hammering bleached white grass, wasps buzzing, dragon flies darting, and Mr Papworth panting in the shade with his tongue out.

Which reminds me – I am so sorry to hear about your Paddy. I couldn't lay my hands on your letter when I was writing last – I knew there was something in it I hadn't dealt with but couldn't remember what. How heartless you must have thought me. I now have your letter and can fully sympathise. It is always hard luck when you feel that other people have hidden facts from you till it is too late. I don't now agree – how heartily I once would have – with any idea of 'trying to forget' things and people we have lost, or indeed with trying always and on principle to exclude any kind of distressing thought from one's mind. I don't mean one ought to sentimentalize a sorrow, or (often) scratch a shame till it is raw. But I had better not go on with the subject as I find my ideas are all in disorder. I know I feel very strongly that when in a wakeful night some idea which one 'can't stand' – some painful memory or mean act of ones own or vivid image of physical pain – thrusts itself upon you, that you ought not to thrust it away but look it squarely in the face for some appreciable time: giving it of course an explicitly devotional context. But I don't fully know why and am not prepared to work the thing out. Anyway, this only very faintly arises out of what you said – and it won't bring the poor beast back to life!

I have just re-read *Lilith*[49] and am much clearer about the meaning. The first thing to get out of the way is all Greville Macdonald's nonsense about 'dimensions' and 'elements' – if you have his preface in your edition.[50] That is just the sort of *mechanical* 'mysticism' which is worlds away from Geo. Macdonald. The main lesson of the book is against secular philanthropy – against the belief that you can effectively obey the 2nd command about loving your neighbour without first trying to love God.

The story runs like this. The human soul exploring its own house

49 George MacDonald, *Lilith: A Romance* (1895).

50 MacDonald, *Lilith: A Romance*, with introductory key, a paraphrase of an earlier manuscript version, and explanation of notes by Greville MacDonald (1924).

(the Mind) finds itself on the verge of unexpected worlds which at first dismay it (Chap. I–V). The first utterance of these worlds is an unconditional demand for absolute surrender of the Soul to the will of God, or, if you like, for Death (Chap. VI). To this demand the soul cannot at first face up (VI). But attempting to return to normal consciousness finds by education that its experiences are not abnormal or trivial but are vouched for by all the great poets and philosophers (VII *My Father's MS*). It repents and tries to face the demand, but its original refusal has now rendered real submission temporarily impossible (IX). It has to face instead the impulses of the subconscious (X) and the slightly spurious loyalties to purely human 'causes' – political, theological etc (XI). It now becomes conscious of its fellow men: and finds them divided into 'Lovers' (= 'Hearts' in our old classification) and 'Bags' or 'Giants' (= 'Spades'). But because it is an unconverted soul, has not yet died, it cannot really help the Lovers and becomes the slave of the Bags. In other words the young man, however amiably disposed towards the sweet and simple people of the world, gets a job or draws a dividend, and becomes in fact the servant of the economic machine (XII–XIII). But he is too good to go on like this, and so becomes a 'Reformer', a 'friend of humanity' – a Shelley, Ruskin, Lenin (XIV). Here follows a digression on Purgatory (XV–XVII).

With the next section we enter on the deepest part of the book which I still only v. dimly understand. Why do so many purely secular reformers and philanthropists fail and in the end leave men more wretched and wicked than they found them? Apparently the unconverted soul, doing its very best for the Lovers, only succeeds first in *waking* (at the price of its own blood) and then in becoming the tool of, *Lilith*. Lilith is still quite beyond me. One can trace in her specially the Will to Power – which here fits in quite well – but there is a great deal more than that. She is also the real ideal somehow spoiled: she is not primarily a sexual symbol, but includes the characteristic *female* abuse of sex, which is love of Power, as the characteristic male abuse is sensuality (XVIII–XXIX). After a long and stormy attempt to do God's work in Lilith's way or Lilith's work in God's way, the soul comes to itself again, realises that its previous proceedings are 'cracked absolutely' and in fact has a sort of half-conversion. But the new powers of will and imagination which even this half conversion inspires (symbolised in the horse) are so exhilarating that the soul thinks *these* will do instead of 'death' and again shoots off on its own. This passage is v. true and important. Macdonald is aware how *religion itself* supplies new temptations (XXX–XXXI). This again leads to another attempt to help the Lovers in his own way, with consequent partial disaster in the death of Lona (XXXII–XXXVII). He finds himself the *jailer* of Lilith: i.e. he is now living in the state of tension with the evil thing inside him only just held down, and at a terrible cost – until he (or Lilith – the Lilith-part of him) at last repents (Mara) and consents to die (XXXVIII–end)

I hope this has not bored you. I am so excited about it myself that for the moment I can hardly imagine anyone else being bored: but probably I have done it so badly that in the result nothing survives to be excited about. For one thing, I have emphasised the external side too much. Correct everything above by remembering that it is not only helping the Lovers outside against the Bags, but equally the Lover in himself against the Bag in himself.

You will be surprised to hear that I have been at the Cinema again! Don't be alarmed, it will not become a habit. I was persuaded into going to *King Kong*[51] because it sounded the sort of Rider Haggardish thing that has always exercised a spell over me. What else I have done I hardly know. Read Plato's *Gorgias*, and am reading a long *Histoire de la Science Politique* (!!) by Janet[52] – surprisingly interesting. Almost everything is, I find, as one goes on.

You say nothing about Harrogate – was it nice? I have missed our annual meeting a good deal. I remember you at least once a day whatever happens and often in between, and wish we could see more of one another. I wonder if the time will ever come when we shall? And would it work if we did? I often feel that you are the one who has changed. This seems absurd when I have changed from atheism to Christianity and from *The Crock of Gold*[53] to, say, the history of political science! But I feel all my changes to be natural developments of the original thing we had in common, and forget that of course they seem natural to me because they are mine, while yours, doubtless equally natural, can never seem so to me

51 *King Kong* (1933), in which a film producer goes on safari and brings back a giant ape which causes terror to New York.

52 Paul-Alexandre Janet, *Histoire de la Science Politique dans ses Rapports avec la Morale* (1872).

53 James Stephens, *The Crock of Gold* (1912).

to the same extent. I don't know how I come to be writing about this and writing it so badly. I had better stop.

Any news of your MS yet? I have tried to keep myself this time from getting too wrapped up in my own book's success and think I have partially succeeded – just as well, too!

Yours
Jack

TO ARTHUR GREEVES (W):

Hotel Victoria,
Milford-on-Sea,
Hants.
Sept 12 1933

My dear Arthur,

It was a delightful surprise to get your long and interesting letter: certainly the longest and one of the most interesting letters I have ever had from you.

I have been thinking all morning over your question about God and evil which is very far from being 'elementary' to me – or for that matter, I suppose, to the angels. If I understand you rightly you are not *primarily* concerned with the sort of logical problem as to how the All-Good can produce evil, or produce a world in which there is evil, but with a more personal, practical, and intimate problem as to how far God can sympathise with our evil will as well as with our good – or, to draw it milder, *whether* he does.

I should begin, I think, by objecting to an expression you use: 'God must have a potentiality of His opposite – evil.' For this I would substitute the idea which someone had in the Middle Ages who defined God as '*That which has no opposite*' i.e. we live in a world of clashes, good and evil, true and false, pleasant and painful, body and spirit, time and eternity etc, but God is not simply (so to speak) *one* of the two clashes but the ultimate thing beyond them all – just as in our constitution the King is neither the Prime Minister nor the Leader of the Opposition, but the thing behind them which alone enables these to be a lawful government and an opposition – or just as space is neither bigness or smallness but that in which the distinctions of big and small arise. This then is my first point. That Evil is not something outside and '*over against*' God, but *in some way* included under Him.

My second point seems to be in direct contradiction to this first one, and is (in scriptural language) as follows: that God 'is the Father of Lights and in Him is *no darkness at all*'.[54] *In some way* there is no evil whatever in God. He is pure Light. All the *heat* that in us is lust or anger in Him is cool light – eternal morning, eternal freshness, eternal springtime: never disturbed, never strained. Go out on any perfect morning in early summer before the world is awake and see, not the thing itself, but the material symbol of it.

Well, these are our two starting points. *In one way* (our old phrase!) God includes evil, in another way he does not. What are we to do next? My beginning of the 'next' will be to deny another remark of yours – where you say 'no good without evil'. This on my view is absolutely untrue: but the opposite 'no evil without good' is absolutely true. I will try to explain what I mean by an analogy.

Supposing you are taking a dog on a lead through a turnstile or past a post. You know what happens (apart from his usual ceremonies in passing a post!). He tries to go the wrong side and gets his lead looped round the post. *You* see that he can't do it, and therefore pull him back. You pull him *back* because you want to enable him to go *forward*. He wants exactly the same thing – namely to go *forward*: for that very reason he resists your pull *back*, or, if he is an obedient dog, yields to it reluctantly as a matter of duty which seems to him to be quite in opposition to his own will: tho' *in fact* it is only by yielding to you that he will ever succeed in getting where he wants.

Now if the dog were a theologian he would regard his own will as a *sin* to which he was tempted, and therefore an *evil*: and he might go on to ask whether you understand and 'contained' his evil. If he did you cd. only reply 'My dear dog, if by your will you mean what you really want to do, viz. to get forward along the road, I not only understand this desire but *share* it. Forward is exactly where I want you to go. If by your will, on the other hand, you mean your will to pull against the collar and try to force yourself forward in a direction which is no use – why I *understand* it of course: but just because I understand it (and the whole situation, which you *don't* understand) I cannot possibly share it. In fact the more I sympathise with your *real* wish – that is, the wish to get on – the less can I sympathise (in the sense of 'share'

54 John 1:5.

or 'agree with') your resistance to the collar: for I see that this is actually rendering the attainment of your real wish impossible.'

I don't know if you will agree at once that this is a parallel to the situation between God and man: but I will work it out on the assumption that you do. Let us go back to the original question – whether and, if so in what sense God contains, say, my evil will – or 'understands' it. The answer is God not only understands but *shares* the desire which is at the root of all my evil – the desire for complete and ecstatic happiness. He made me for no other purpose than to enjoy it. But He knows, and I do not, how it can be really and permanently attained. He knows that most of *my* personal attempts to reach it are actually putting it further and further out of my reach. With these therefore He cannot sympathise or 'agree': His sympathy with my *real* will makes that impossible. (He may *pity* my misdirected struggles, but that is another matter.) The practical results seem to be two.

1. I may always feel looking back on any past sin that in the very heart of my evil passion there was something that God approves and wants me to feel not less but more. Take a sin of Lust. The overwhelming thirst for *rapture* was good and even divine: it has not got to be unsaid (so to speak) and recanted. But it will never be quenched as I tried to quench it. If I refrain – if I submit to the collar and come round the right side of the lamp-post – God will be guiding me as quickly as He can to where I shall get what I really wanted all the time. It will not be very like what I now think I want: but it will be more like it than some suppose. In any case it will be the real thing, not a consolation prize or substitute. If I had it I should not need to fight against sensuality as something impure: rather I should spontaneously turn away from it as something dull, cold, abstract, and artificial. This, I think, is how the doctrine applies to past sins.

2. On the other hand, when we are thinking of a sin in the future, i.e. when we are tempted, we must remember that *just because* God wants for us what we really want and knows the only way to get it, therefore He must, in a sense, be quite ruthless towards sin. He is not like a human authority who can be begged off or caught in an indulgent mood. The more He loves you the more determined He must be to pull you back from your way which leads nowhere into His way which leads where you want to go. Hence Macdonald's words 'The *all-punishing, all-pardoning* Father'. You may go the wrong way again, and

again He may forgive you: as the dog's master may extricate the dog after he has tied the whole lead round the lamp-post. But there is no hope *in the end* of getting where you want to go except by going God's way. And what does '*in the end*' mean? This is a terrible question. If endless time will really help us to go the right way, I believe we shall be given endless time. But perhaps God knows that time makes no difference. Perhaps He knows that if you can't learn the way in 60 or 70 years on this planet (a place probably constructed by Divine skill for the very purpose of teaching you) then you will never learn it anywhere. There may be nothing left for Him but to destroy you (the kindest thing): *if He can.*

I think one may be quite rid of the old haunting suspicion – which raises its head in every temptation – that there is something else than God – some other country (Mary Rose . . . Mary Rose)[55] into which He forbids us to trespass – some kind of delight wh. He 'doesn't appreciate' or just chooses to forbid, but which wd. be real delight if only we were allowed to get it. The thing *just isn't there.* Whatever we desire is either what God is trying to give us as quickly as He can, or else a false picture of what He is trying to give us – a false picture wh. would not attract us for a moment if we saw the real thing. Therefore God does really in a sense contain evil – i.e. contains what is the real motive power behind all our evil desires. He knows what we want, even in our vilest acts: He is longing to give it to us. He is not looking on from the outside at some new 'taste' or 'separate desire of our own'. Only because he has laid up *real* goods for us to desire are we able to go wrong by snatching at them in greedy, misdirected ways. The truth is that evil is not a real *thing* at all, like God. It is simply good *spoiled.* That is why I say there can be good without evil, but no evil without good. You know what the biologists mean by a parasite – an animal that lives on another animal. Evil is a *parasite.* It is there only because good is there for it to spoil and confuse.

Thus you may well feel that God understands our temptations – understands them a great deal more than we do. But don't forget Macdonald again – '*Only God understands evil and hates it.*'[56] Only the

---

55 In J. M. Barrie's play, *Mary Rose* (1920), Mary Rose while visiting the Hebrides is spirited away by Elvish voices calling her name, although angel voices try to counteract them.

56 MacDonald, *Lilith*, ch. 39.

dog's master knows how useless it is to try to get on with the lead knotted round the lamp-post. This is why we must be prepared to find God implacably and immovably forbidding what may seem to us very small and trivial things. But He knows whether they are really small and trivial. How small some of the things that doctors forbid would seem to an ignoramus.

I expect I have said all these things before: if so, I hope they have not wasted a letter. Alas! they are so (comparatively) easy to say: so hard, so *all but* impossible to go on *feeling* when the strain comes.

I have not time left for the rest of your letter. It was bad luck getting ill at the cottage: an illness at home has its pleasures, but on a holiday it is – well 'disconsolate' is the word that best fits my feeling about it. We have had a spate of unwanted and mostly uninvited visitors all summer and have (all four of us) come down here to give Minto a rest. It is opposite the Isle of Wight, and quite pleasant. We went to Beaulieu Abbey this afternoon – which would well deserve a letter in itself. I have since I came down read Voltaire's *Candide*,[57] and Gore's *Jesus of Nazareth* (Home University Library)[58] which I most strongly advise you to get at once. It is perhaps the best book about religion I have yet read – I mean of the theological kind – not counting books like *Lilith*. I am particularly pleased at having at last found out what Sadducees and Pharisees really were: tho' it is an alarming bit of knowledge because most of the religious people I know are either one or the other. (Warnie is a bit of a Sadducee, and I am a good bit of a Pharisee.) I am now going to tackle a John Buchan.

When I suggested that you had changed, I didn't mean that you had changed towards me. I meant that I thought the centre of your *interests* might have shifted more than mine. This leads on to what you say about being a mere mirror for other people on which each friend can cast his reflection in turn. That certainly is what you *might* become, just as a hardened bigot shouting every one down till he had no friends left is what I am in danger of becoming. In other words *sympathy* is your strong point, as *stability* is mine – if I have a strong point at all, which is doubtful: or *weakness* is your danger, as *Pride* is mine. (You have no idea how much of my time I spend just *hating* people whom

57 Voltaire, *Candide* (1759).
58 Charles Gore, *Jesus of Nazareth*, Home University Library (1929).

I disagree with – tho' I know them only from their books – and inventing conversations in which I score off them.) In other words, we all have our own burdens, and must do the best we can. I do not know which is the worse, nor do we need to: if each of us could imitate the other.

The woods are just beginning to turn here – the drive was exquisite this afternoon. Love from all.

Yours,
Jack

TO GUY POCOCK (W):

The Kilns,
Headington Quarry,
Oxford
Sept. 18th 1933.

Dear Pocock

Would you kindly tell the right department to send a copy of the *Regress* to A. Griffiths, Prinknash Priory, Gloucester, and debit me accordingly,

yours
C. S. Lewis

TO J. M. DENT PUBLISHERS (W):

Magdalen College,
Oxford.
Oct. 16th 1933

Dear Sir

Please forward a copy of my *Pilgrim's Regress* to Miss Whitty, 7 Cherlsey Rd, Bristol 6. I enclose cheque for 8/2 to cover this and previous copies.

yours faithfully
C. S. Lewis

TO ARTHUR GREEVES (W):

[The Kilns]
Nov 5th 1933

My dear Arthur,

I was glad to see your hand again. In spite of the remarks at the beginning of your letter, which tempt me to further discussion I must try to prevent this also from becoming an essay in amateur Theology.

I am glad to hear that Tchainie[59] is once more sufficiently my friend to ask about my mediaeval book.[60] You can tell her that it is not finished yet, though it might have been if I had not been made English Examiner which has devoured a good deal of my last two long Vacs. As one holds the job only for two years I am now free again and hope to get on with it. By the way has she read the *Regress* – I don't mean '*Ask her* if she has read the *Regress*'!

To answer the next point in your letter, MacFarlane is back at work again and seems alright: but that perhaps does not count for much as he seemed alright to me up to the moment when he went sick. I have no eye for health. 'How much better he is looking' – 'How ill he is looking' people say to me as a visitor leaves the room, and I have never noticed any difference. I hope mere selfishness is not the cause.

The news of your learning to ride was surprising, amusing (as you foresaw!) and on the whole good. Perhaps you will be a 'huntin' man' when I next meet you, slapping your leggings with a crop, and drinking whiskies with the county families' fast daughters and hard-riding sons. What a fine sight it would be to see Bob, Janie, and you, altogether and all in full hunting kit (Janie wd. look fine in a tall hat and breeches) taking a fence together. What would attract me most about riding, viz. the unity of man and beast, is, I suppose, largely spoiled by having to use hired horses. But if you find you like it I suppose you could easily afford a horse of your own, if Lea knows anything about the care of a horse. Certainly I should enjoy very much strolling round with you to visit it in its stable.

I haven't read the new De La Mare,[61] but probably shall. Galsworthy, though I fully acknowledge his merits, I somehow never feel any desire to return to. Warnie feels quite differently and the original *Saga*[62] is one of his old favourites which he can always read again. I forget

59 Jane ('Janie' or 'Tchainie') McNeill (1889–1959), the daughter of James and Margaret McNeill, would have liked to go to university, but remained at home to look after her widowed mother. See the biography of Jane McNeill in *CG*.

60 Lewis had been working on *The Allegory of Love* since 1928. See the letter to Albert Lewis of 10 July 1928 (*CL* I, pp. 766–7).

61 Walter de la Mare, *The Fleeting, and Other Poems* (1933).

62 John Galsworthy, *The Forsyte Saga* (1922).

whether I mentioned to you Collier's *Poor Tom's A-cold*[63] as the new book I have enjoyed most for a long time.

Did I (also) tell you that Warnie has complete sets of all the Beethoven symphonies, and that we have a whole symphony each Sunday evening? This is one of the best hours of the week. Maureen who is (to be frank) the difficult one of the household has by then returned to Monmouth from her week end at home: the rush and crowd of visitors and continual flurry of the week end subsides and after a quiet supper Minto, Warnie, Mr Papworth and myself sit down in the study and have our music. In this way we have worked through the first Seven, and it was my recollections of the Seventh (last Sunday) which made me mention the matter – just to let you know that I had once more been enjoying what I still think the best slow movement there is, and, of course, enjoying it all the more because of the associations. I don't however think the Seventh quite satisfactory as a whole: the final movement is by no means one of the best, and still less is it fit to follow the other. So far I think the Fifth quite easily the best, thus agreeing with the orthodox view: tho' I differ from it in finding the Eroica the poorest of the lot.[64] The Eroica (the connection is Napoleon) leads me to what you say about Germany.

I might agree that the Allies are partly to blame, but nothing can fully excuse the iniquity of Hitler's persecution of the Jews, or the absurdity of his theoretical position. Did you see that he said 'The Jews have *made no contribution to human culture* and in crushing them I am doing *the will of the Lord*.' Now as the whole idea of the 'Will of the Lord' is precisely what the world owes to the Jews, the blaspheming tyrant has just fixed his absurdity for all to see in a single sentence, and shown that he is as contemptible for his stupidity as he is detestable for his cruelty. For the German people as a whole we ought to have charity: but for dictators, 'Nordic' tyrants and so on – well, read the chapter about Mr Savage in the *Regress*[65] and you have my views.

I wish you didn't always choose summer for your visits here. The place is to day at its best: the pond a smooth almost black sheet, sprinkled, or rather *paved* with bright leaves: the little birch wood

63 i.e. Collier, *Tom's A-Cold*.

64 Of the nine symphonies of Ludwig van Beethoven (1770–1827), the 'Eroica', composed to celebrate the memory of Napoleon, is No. 3.

65 *The Pilgrim's Regress*, book VI, ch. 6.

flaming on the far side, and the hill and fir wood beyond fading into mist. Yes – the weather is alright *now* and I am getting all those fine feelings of revival – beginning to take longer walks again, remembering how much mere branch and sky and hedge ought to mean to one, and noticing suddenly for how long one has been only half awake.

Write again soon. Love to Mrs Greeves.

Yours,
Jack

TO DAPHNE HARWOOD (BOD):

Magdalen College,
Oxford.
Dec 28th 1933

Dear Mrs Harwood

I don't know when I have been so rude to anyone as I have been to you after my long silence since I stayed with you. The truth is that if Cecil had not lent me Popelbaum's book,[66] I should have behaved better. I followed the *ignis fatuus*[67] of postponing my letter until I could include some remarks on reading the book – then the time for reading the book didnt come as soon as I expected – and so here we are.

I have now read it and am very much impressed. A good deal of it, of course, is difficult to one so ignorant of science as I am, but it is all interesting and, I expect, deserves most serious consideration. Has any notice been taken of it in 'orthodox' scientific circles? What particularly stuck in my mind – more as a tragedy than as a theorem – is the illustrated 'rake's progress' of the Chimpanzee. What a subject for a poem! By the bye I have met a young philosophical tutor at New College (Crossland)[68] who seems – which is rare at Oxford – to be well informed

66 Hermann Poppelbaum, *Man and Animal: Their Essential Difference*, trans. Edith Rigby and Owen Barfield (1931).

67 'will-o'-the-wisp', lit. 'the foolish fire'.

68 Richard Howard Stafford Crossman (1907–74), who took a double First in Classics at New College, Oxford, was Fellow and Tutor of Philosophy at New College, 1930–7. He became the assistant editor of the *New Statesman and Nation* in 1938 but in 1940 was drafted into the Ministry of Economic Warfare to organize the British propaganda effort against Hitler's Germany. He was elected MP for Coventry East in 1945, holding the seat until 1974, and was appointed Minister for Housing and Local Government by Harold Wilson in 1964. His three-volume *Diaries of a Cabinet Minister* (1975–7), the first of which was published shortly

about Anthroposophy, and sympathetic tho' not converted. I think that is really more important for you than an out and out convert would be: it is a great point gained when a movement begins to be treated with respect by those who are not members of it. Incidentally, he is in several ways the most intelligent new acquaintance I have made for several years.

I hope you have not misinterpreted my long silence. I have the most grateful memories of my last week end with you and value the novel honour of my *God-sibbe*[69] very much. How is my godson? I hope his laughing all through the service does not mean that he is going to grow up an *esprit fort*: but as soon as he is old enough I shall try to collaborate with you in preventing this.

How is Stein? – a man I would like to meet again. And how is yourself and the *guideman*[70] and the children? We are all pretty well, though Mrs. Moore is almost worn out with the Christmas charities, which 'an autumn 'twas that grew the more by reaping.'[71] We would all very much like to see you at the Kilns again when you can manage it. I have been disgustingly busy for a long long time: each year jobs seem to increase on one – as no doubt you find. Please give Cecil my love and accept all our best wishes for the new year.

Yours (penitent)
C. S. Lewis

---

after his death, were followed by *The Backbench Diaries of Richard Crossman* (1981).

69 His position as godfather to the Harwoods' son, Laurence. See **Laurence Hardy Harwood** in the Biographical Appendix.

70 The 'guideman', 'gudeman' or 'goodman' means husband or head of the house.

71 William Shakespeare, *Antony and Cleopatra* (1606–7), V, ii, 87–8.

1934

Maureen Moore had acquired a car and in April 1934 she took Lewis and her mother on a motor tour of parts of England and Ireland, stopping to visit Arthur Greeves in Belfast.

TO HIS BROTHER (W):

[2 Princess Villas,
Bayview Park,
Kilkeel, Co. Down]
April 3rd 1934

My dear W.,

This is turning out a great success. Even the journey was pleasant as far as Chester. There Maureen discovered that she still had far too much petrol, and time, so we used up both by going round through Warrington and Runcorn – the most hideous Morlockheim[1] you can imagine. Lime Street Hotel, where we had hoped to lounge for a few hours, is now shut up, all except the Grill: another landmark gone.

On the way to Bernagh next morning I noticed a new big house half way up the hill, in the field by the Glenmachan quarry. I had an excellent morning with Arthur, who at last has something wrong with him: an internal narrowing, poor man, almost amounting to a stoppage. His mother does not know about it, I think: and, paradoxically, tho' not unprecedently, he is taking it with fortitude. Lunch, for which Minto and Maureen arrived, was enlivened by Minto upsetting a tumbler, but was not otherwise so amusing as I had anticipated – tho' Maureen dropped a brick at the outset by saying that 'Of course, Co. Down isn't *real* Ireland.'

The drive down from town was a pure joy. I took them by Comber,

1 The Morlocks are the subterranean workers in H. G. Wells's *The Time Machine* (1895).

Downpatrick, Dundrum, and Newcastle. Maureen rather affected to sniff at the countryside for the first few miles, but the Mournes knocked all that out of her. Kilkeel itself is, I think, among the two or three most beautiful places I have ever been. It is on a point or flat tongue which spreads out almost eight miles from the foot hills of the mountains. This distance is a positive advantage as it saves you from the darkness and obtrusiveness of mountains too near and also gives you a huge panorama of blue and jagged shapes which you couldn't have closer. The *coup d'oeil*[2] suggests the Tyrol rather than anything else: if it were not for the middle distance of white cottages, fir clumps, stone walls & flax ponds – and the foreground of Fakerty's Spirit Grocery, Orange Hall etc – I should hardly believe I was in Ulster.

In a word, for varied pleasure (the scale runs from a mountain like a castle ten miles off to a silent harbour full of apparently dead schooners and one puffer half a mile off) this is just the best place I have struck for years. I very much wish we were not moving to Rostrevor to-morrow. I am strongly upholding this house as a place for a family holiday in August. It is a dingy, faded place with the indescribable smell of all Irish lodging houses, but all the *important* things are right, i.e. light that you can really read by, comfortable chairs, *very good beds*, hot baths, and a capital chapter house round the corner. The landlady was rather too talkative at the beginning but we see less of her now. (Memo – Canon Hayes was rector of Kilkeel before he went to St Marks 'He was a very queer man. He did awfully crazy things')

You were wrong in supposing that I would be attending the Easter celebration at the same time as you: they have it at 8.*30* instead of 8, which is an excellent idea. We had quite a good congregation. At the 11.30 service we had a very large one. I had quite forgotten the most unpleasant feature of an Irish service – the large number of people present who have obviously no interest in the thing, who are merely 'good prodestants'. You know what one is supposed to find – 'the spirit of worship which burns all the brighter in the stark simplicity of the service etc.'[3] In fact, one finds something that to my present eyes looks like studied indifference. I am sure the English practice of not going

---

2 'quick survey'.

3 Lewis was here mimicking evangelical clergymen such as his maternal grandfather, the Rev. Thomas Robert Hamilton (1826–1905), Rector of St Mark's, Dundela, 1874–1900. See **The Hamilton Family** in the Biographical Appendix to *CL* I.

unless you believe is a much better one. The Rector, 'the Reverend Belton' is a poor creature.[4]

I saw a lovely thing done yesterday on the lines of 'Give me a bottle of soda water.'[5] An elderly labourer had been standing for several minutes with his back to the bar on which rested his empty tumbler. Without moving, or even turning his eyes from the window, he whispered reflectively 'Anither pint.' The barman instantly filled his glass with porter *and added a large tot from a bottle of spirits*. The customer never looked round during the whole transaction.

Minto is frightfully sorry about Vera. It is not a practical joke nor was it intended.

Yours
Jack

P.S. Leeboro' garden is a paradise of daffodils: it has never looked so well before, I must confess

TO DOM BEDE GRIFFITHS (W):

Rostrevor,
Co. Down
[4 April 1934]

My dear Griffiths,

A wet day – and a cold – and this delightful sea and mountain village where I have been spending my holiday, seems a good occasion for answering your most welcome letter.

I think our positions about Pantheism are exactly the same: for we both, in places, travelled the same road to Christianity, and the result of the arrival is certainly not any ingratitude or contempt to the various signposts or hostelries that helped on the journey. On the contrary, it is only since I have become a Christian that I have learned really to value the elements of truth in Paganism and Idealism. I *wished* to value

4 The Rev. John Thomas Belton (1899–1966) took his BA from Trinity College, Dublin, in 1917 and was ordained in the Church of Ireland in 1920. He was Curate of Aghalee, Co. Down, 1919–20, Vicar of Shankill, 1921–5, and Rector of Kilkeel, 1925–57.

5 He is referring to their father's way of ordering whisky. When he wrote to Warnie on 7 August 1921 about a family holiday in England, Jack said their father told the waitress: 'I'll have a bottle of soda water . . . and if you'd just put a little Scotch whiskey in it' (*CL* I, p. 573).

them in the old days; now I really do. Don't suppose that I ever thought myself that certain elements of pantheism were incompatible with Christianity or with Catholicism.

What I did think – and still do think – was that an influential school of thought both in your church and mine – were very antagonistic to Idealism,[6] and in fact were availing themselves of a general secular reaction against 19th century thought, to run something which they call Neo-Scholasticism[7] as the cure for all our evils. The people I mean are led by Maritain[8] on your side and by T. S. Eliot on ours. Perhaps I over-rate their importance. I hope I do, for I confess there is no section of religious opinion with which I feel less sympathy. Indeed I consider that it is no overstatement to say that your Church and mine are, at the moment, closest to each other where each is at its worst. God forgive me if I do them wrong, but there are some of this set who seem to me to be anxious to make of the Christian faith itself one more of their high brow fads. Then their ignorance! As if there

---

6 Idealism in this context is a metaphysical theory about the nature of reality, maintaining that matter does not exist in its own right but is related to the contents of our minds. Thus, all objects, even the world, are mental creations. In *SBJ*, ch. 13, Lewis explained the place of Idealism in his conversion, describing how he reached the point where he accepted Idealism and admitted 'that the whole universe was, in the last resort, mental; that our logic was participation in a cosmic *Logos*'.

7 Scholasticism was originally a teaching device developed in the schools and universities of Western Europe from the end of the eleventh century and largely associated with the methods of three major philosophers of the thirteenth and fourteenth centuries – St Thomas Aquinas, Duns Scotus and William of Ockham. It proceeded by questioning ancient and authoritative texts. A favoured method was to draw up lists of contradictory statements in the texts, applying to them the rules of logic in order to reveal their underlying agreement. Its purpose was to get to the inner truth of things to which the texts bore witness. The method flourished until the sixteenth century when it came under attack from humanist scholars.

An attempt to restore scholasticism began in Rome about 1830. The most important of several theologians who wanted to extend this 'neo-Scholasticism' to the universal Church was Pope Leo XIII; in his encyclical *Aeterni Patris* (1879), he recommended that scholasticism be the only philosophy and theology used in Catholic seminaries. The Pope enjoined the study of St Thomas Aquinas on all theology students as a clear, systematic philosophy capable of defending Christian tradition from contemporary attack.

8 Jacques Maritain (1882–1973), French philosopher. Following his conversion to Roman Catholicism in 1906 he turned to the study of St Thomas Aquinas whose philosophy he sought to relate to modern culture. He held professorial chairs at the Institut Catholique in Paris, 1914–33, the Institute for Medieval Studies in Toronto, 1933–45, and Princeton University, 1948–52.

ever was any such thing as 'scholasticism' as a doctrine! But enough of this.

The question of 'generality' in prayer is not so simple. The doctrine held by your own Church about the position of the virtuous heretic or pagan – I need hardly say that I use both the word *virtuous* and the word *heretic positionis causa* – is, you will find, far from crude. Is it not held that many who have lived and died outside the visible Church are finally saved, because Divine Grace has guided them to concentrate solely on the true elements in their own religions?[9] And if so, must one not admit that it was the mysterious will of God that these persons should be saved in that peculiar way? I use this argument to point out that even such a comparatively general prayer as that for a man's conversion, may yet be too particular.

And while I am on the subject, I had better say once and for all that I do not intend to discuss with you in future, if I can help it, any of the questions at issue between our respective churches. It would have the same unreality as those absurd conversations in which we are invited to speak frankly to a woman about some indelicate matter – wh. means that she can say what she likes and we can't. I could not, now that you are a monk, use that freedom in attacking your position which you undoubtedly would use in attacking mine. I do not think there is any thing distressing for either of us in agreeing to be silent on this matter:

---

9 The salvation of the virtuous infidel was to become an increasingly important issue to Lewis. He was familiar with the fact that in *The Divine Comedy* Dante put the Emperor Trajan in Paradise (see *Purgatorio* X, 74–93; *Paradiso* XX, 44–5) because of the legend that Pope Gregory the Great, through his prayers, brought Trajan back from Hell and baptized him to salvation. Of greater importance was Aquinas's teaching on 'baptism by desire', e.g. *Summa Theologica*, Part III, Question 68: 'when a man wishes to be baptized, but by some ill-chance he is forestalled by death before receiving Baptism . . . such a man can obtain salvation without being actually baptized, on account of his desire for Baptism, which desire is the outcome of faith that worketh by charity . . .'

Lewis came to believe that virtuous heretics or pagans could be saved through Christ. 'I think that every prayer which is sincerely made even to a false god or to a very imperfectly conceived true God,' he wrote to Mrs Ashton on 8 November 1952, 'is accepted by the true God and that Christ saves many who do not think they know Him' (WHL, p, 428). He provided an illustration of this in *The Last Battle* (1956), ch. 15. On meeting Aslan in the heavenly Narnia, Emeth the Calormene explains that he had been seeking Tash all his life. 'Beloved,' said Aslan, 'unless thy desire had been for *me* thou wouldst not have sought so long and so truly. For all find what they truly seek.'

I have had a Catholic among my most intimate friends for many years[10] and a great deal of our conversation has been religious. When all is said (and truly said) about the divisions of Christendom, there remains, by God's mercy, an enormous common ground. It is abstaining from one tree in the whole garden.

I should rather like to attend your Greek class, for it is a perpetual puzzle to me how New Testament Greek got the reputation of being easy. St Luke I find particularly difficult. As regards matter – leaving the question of language – you will be glad to hear that I am at last beginning to get some small understanding of St Paul: hitherto an author quite opaque to me. I am speaking now, of course, of the general drift of whole epistles: short passages, treated devotionally, are of course another matter. And yet the distinction is not, for me, quite a happy one. Devotion is best raised when we intend something else. At least that is my experience. Sit down to meditate devotionally on a single verse, and nothing happens. Hammer your way through a continued argument, just as you would in a profane writer, and the heart will sometimes sing unbidden.

I think I agree with you that 'historical research' as now understood, is no work for a monk, nor for a man either. To all that side of my own work I attach less and less importance: yet I become each year more contented in the actual teaching and lecturing. I have very little doubt now that the work is worth doing. It is true that neither the terms of my appointment nor my own stature allow me to teach the most important things: but on the lower level there is honest work to be done in eradicating false habits of mind and teaching the elements of reason herself, and English Literature is as good a subject as any other. I should be in a bad way by now if I had been allowed to follow my own desire and be a research fellow with no pupils. As it is, nearly every generation leaves me one permanent friend.

Please accept my thanks, and convey them to the Prior, for your offered hospitality. Some week end in the long Vacation would suit me best, and I should like to come.

Yours
C. S. Lewis

---

10 i.e. J. R. R. Tolkien.

P.S. This has some relevance both to the questions of Prayer and Idealism. I wrote it over a year ago.

They tell me, Lord, that when I seem
To be in speech with You,
Since You make no replies, it's all a dream
– One talker aping two.

And so it is, but not as they
Falsely believe. For I
Seek in myself the things I meant to say,
And lo!, the wells are dry.

Then, seeing me empty, You forsake
The listener's part, and through
My dumb lips breathe and into utterance wake
The thoughts I never knew.

Therefore You neither need reply
Nor can: for while we seem
Two talking, Thou art one forever; and I
No dreamer, but Thy dream.[11]

For months Jack, Warnie, Tolkien, Barfield and Harwood had been planning to attend a festival of Wagner's Ring of the Nibelung *at Covent Garden in London. Cecil Harwood was appointed to book tickets for the party, and in preparation Jack and Warnie were meeting regularly with Tolkien to read the operas in German. The opportunity of seeing the whole* Ring *cycle meant so much to Lewis that he reminded Harwood of the important commission placed upon him:*

11 Lewis published this 'anonymously' with slight variations in *Letters to Malcolm: Chiefly on Prayer* (1964). It is included under the title 'Prayer' in *CP*, pp. 136–7.

TO CECIL HARWOOD (BOD):

Magdalen College
Oxford
[April 1934]

Dear Harwood

It is vain to conceal from you the solicitude we feel for our seats at Co. Garden. Pray, pray, Sir, exert yourself. Reflect that no small part of the satisfaction of five persons depends upon your conduct: that the object of their desires is rational and innocent: and that their desires are fervent and of long standing. Omit no manly degree of importunity and complaisance that may achieve our object, and thus, my dear Sir, give me one more reason to subscribe myself

your most obliged
most obedient servant
C. S. Lewis

For some reason Harwood failed to book seats for the Ring of the Nibelung. *On learning of this Lewis sent him the following letter:*

TO CECIL HARWOOD (BOD):

Magdalen College
Oxford
May 7th 1934

Sir,

I have read your pathetical letter with such sentiments as it naturally suggests and write to assure you that you need expect from me no ungenerous reproach. It would be cruel, if it were possible, and impossible, if it were attempted, to add to the mortification which you must now be supposed to suffer. Where I cannot console, it is far from my purpose to aggravate: for it is part of the complicated misery of your state that while I pity your sufferings, I cannot innocently wish them lighter. He would be no friend to your reason or your virtue who would wish you to pass over so great a miscarriage in heartless frivolity or brutal insensibility. As the loss is irretrievable, so your remorse will be lasting. As those whom you have betrayed are your friends, so your conduct admits of no exculpation. As you were once virtuous, so now you must be forever miserable. Far be it from me that ferocious virtue which would remind you that the trust was originally transferred from Barfield to you in the hope of better things, and that thus both our honours were engaged. I will not paint to you the consequences of your conduct which are doubtless daily and nightly before your eyes. Believe, my dear Sir, that I forgive you.

As soon as you can, pray let me know through some respectable acquaintance what plans you have formed for the future. In what quarter of the globe do you intend to sustain that irrevocable exile, hopeless penury, and perpetual disgrace to which you have condemned yourself? Do not give in to the sin of Despair: learn from this example the fatal consequences of error and hope, in some humbler station and some distant land, that you may yet become useful to your species.

Yours etc
C. S. Lewis

TO CECIL HARWOOD (BOD):

[Magdalen College]
May 16th 1934

Sir

Your resolution of seeing me and receiving my forgiveness face to face before you forever quit these shores does not displease me. As you have rightly judged, to admit you to my house would now be an offence against the grand Principle of Subordination, but you will be welcome to the grounds – flumina ames silvasque *inglorius*.[12]

You will please to observe the strictest propriety of behaviour while you remain there, and to be guided in everything by the directions of Mr. Barfield.

Under his protection I doubt not that you will be able to achieve the journey without any great disaster or indecency. Do not hold any communication with your fellow travellers in the steam-train without his approval: where you bait,[13] you had best abstain from all use of fermented liquours. Many things lawful in themselves are to be denied to one who dare not risk a further miscarriage. Above all, do not attempt to save your guinea by travelling under the seat, nor to shorten

12 'May you *humbly* love the rivers and woods', adapting Virgil, *Georgics* 2. 486.
13 i.e. stop to obtain food or drink.

your journey by any approaches to familiarity with your female fellow passages. Do not bring with you any musical instrument.

Your obedient servant
C. S. Lewis

TO SISTER MADELEVA (W):[14]

Magdalen College,
Oxford.
June 6th [1934]

Dear Madam,

This is just to let you know that I have your letter and will answer it in the course of the next few days. But I should warn you that what you apparently expect to lie behind the lecture is both more and other than is really there. In lecturing to students who know nothing about the middle ages I have had to be clear and brief, therefore dogmatic: and I have probably – tho' I hope this was not my intention – appeared much more learned than I am.

Yours sincerely,
C. S. Lewis

TO SISTER MADELEVA (W):

Magdalen College,
Oxford,
June 7th 1934

Dear Madam,

In answer to your first question, there are probably such printed bibliographies as you mention but I have no knowledge of them. The

---

14 Sister M. Madeleva CSC (1887–1964), a member of the Congregation of Sisters of the Holy Cross, was a teacher of English at St Mary's College, Notre Dame, Indiana. While staying in Oxford during Trinity Term 1934 she attended Lewis's lectures on medieval poetry, and had a particular interest in the lecture devoted to Boethius. Besides lending Sister Madeleva his notebooks giving details of the works mentioned in his lectures, Lewis invited her to visit him in Magdalen. On her return to Notre Dame in 1934, Sister Madeleva was made President of St Mary's College, a post she held until her retirement in 1961. Her numerous books include *Knights Errant and other Poems* (1923), *Chaucer's Nun and Other Essays* (1925), *Pearl: A Study in Spiritual Dryness* (1925), *Penelope and Other Poems* (1927), *Selected Poems* (1939), *A Lost Language* (1951), *The Four Last Things* (1959) and an autobiography, *My First Seventy Years* (1959). See Gail Porter Mandell, *Madeleva: A Biography* (1997).

history of my lecture is this. After having worked for some years on my own subject (which is the medieval allegory), I found that I had accumulated a certain amount of general information which, tho far from being very recondite, was more than the ordinary student in the school could gather for himself. I then conceived the idea of my 'prolegomena'.[15]

There were however several gaps in the general knowledge which I had accidentally got. To fill these up I adopted the simple method of going through Skeat's notes on Chaucer and Langland,[16] and other similar things, and followed these up to their sources when they touched on matters that seemed to me important. This led me sometimes to books I already knew, often to new ones. This process explains why I inevitably appear more learned than I am. E.g. my quotations from Vincent of Beauvais[17] don't mean that I turned from a long reading of Beauvais to illustrate Chaucer, but that I turned from Chaucer to find explanations in Vincent. In fine, the process is inductive for the most part of my lecture: tho' on allegory, courtly love, and (sometimes) in philosophy, it is deductive – i.e. I *start* from the authors I quote. I elaborate this point because, if you are thinking of doing the same kind of thing (i.e. telling people what they ought to know as the *prius* of a study of medieval vernacular poets) I think you would be wise to work in the same way – starting *from* the texts you want to explain. You will soon find of course that you are working the other way at the same time, that you can correct current explanations, or see things to explain

15 During the Trinity Term of 1934 (22 April–16 June) Lewis gave a series of lectures entitled 'Prolegomena to the Study of Medieval Poetry', later adapted into *The Discarded Image: An Introduction to Medieval and Renaissance Literature* (1964). For a detailed list of Lewis's lectures see Walter Hooper, 'The Lectures of C. S. Lewis in the Universities of Oxford and Cambridge', *Christian Scholar's Review*, XXVII, no. 4 (Summer 1998), pp. 436–53.

16 Walter William Skeat, *The Chaucer Canon* (1900). William Langland (c. 1330–c. 1386) is the author of *Piers Plowman*, which Lewis discussed in *The Allegory of Love*, ch. 4, pp. 158–61.

17 One 'Prolegomena' lecture had discussed the connection between Vincent of Beauvais (fl. 1250) and Chaucer's ballad, *Fortune*. In *The Discarded Image* Lewis wrote (p. 84): 'Adversity has the merit of opening our eyes by showing which of our friends are true and which are feigned. Combine this with Vincent of Beauvais' statement that hyena's gall restores the sight (*Speculum Naturale*, xix, 62), and you have the key to Chaucer's cryptic line "Thee nedeth nat the gall of noon hyene" (*Fortune*, 35).'

where the ordinary editors see nothing. I suppose I need not remind you to cultivate the wisdom of the serpent: there will be misquotations, and misunderstood quotations in the best books, and you must always hunt up all quotations for yourself and find what they are really *in situ*.

But of course, I do not know what it is you propose to do. I have therefore mentioned all the more important 'sources' in my note-book without any attempt at selection. You will see at once that this is the bibliography of a man who was following a particular subject (the love-allegory), and this doubtless renders the list much less useful to you, who are hardly likely to be after the same quarry. In the second part, texts, I have been more selective, and have omitted a certain amount of low or lowish Latin love poetry which is useful only for my own special purpose.

You will observe that I begin with classical authors. This is a point I would press on anyone dealing with the middle ages, that the first essential is to read the relevant classics over and over: the key to everything – allegory, courtly love etc – is there. After that the two things to know really well are the Divine Comedy and the Romance of the Rose.[18] The student who has really digested these,* with good commentaries, and who also knows the Classics and the Bible (including the *apocryphal* New Testament) has the game in his hands, and can defeat over and over again those who have simply burrowed in obscure parts of the actual middle ages.

Of scholastic philosophy and theology you probably know much more than I do. If by any chance you don't, stick to Gilson[19] as a guide and beware of the people (Maritain in your Church, and T. S. Eliot of mine) who are at present running what they call 'neo-scholasticism' as a fad.

Of Periodicals you will find *Romania*, *Speculum* and *Medium Aevum* useful.

* I don't claim to be such a person myself!

---

18 *The Romance of the Rose* is a thirteenth-century French allegorical romance by Guillaume de Lorris and Jean de Meun. It is discussed in chapter 3 of *The Allegory of Love.*

19 Etienne Gilson (1884–1978), French authority on medieval philosophy, is the author of *La Philosophie au Moyen Age* (1922), *Moral Values and the Moral Life: The System of St Thomas Aquinas*, trans. Leo Richard Ward (1931), and many other works.

Remember (this has been all important to me) that what you want to know about the Middle Ages will often not be in a book on the Middle Ages, but in the early chapters of some history of general philosophy or science. The accounts of your period in such books will, of course, usually be patronizing and ill-informed, but it will mention dates and authors whom you can follow up and thus put you in the way of writing a *true* account for yourself.

If there is any way in which I can assist you, or if you would care to call and discuss anything with me, do not hesitate to let me know.

Yours sincerely,

C. S. Lewis

TO SISTER MADELEVA (W):

Magdalen College,
Oxford.
June 11th [1934]

Dear Madam,

Thanks for your letter. You make too much of a very trifling service. If I am ever in those parts (which is unlikely) I will certainly brave the 'terrors of convents' and accept your kind hospitality.

Yours sincerely

C. S. Lewis

TO ARTHUR GREEVES (W):

[The Kilns]
Oct 1st. 1934

My dear Arthur,

I am sending you back Pope Hadrian.[20] Warnie and I have both read it with a good deal of amusement and enjoyment. The latter is due, I suppose, entirely to the subject – for everyone likes to imagine what a man could do if he were a dictator, or Pope, or Caliph –; the amusement is mainly at the author's expence. The style is one of the most preposterous I have ever read, and I doubt if I ever saw so much pedantry combined with so much ignorance. Almost every one of his numerous and unnecessary Greek quotations contains some mistake: and in English he seems to think that *euphuism* means *euphemism* and

20 Frederick Rolfe ('Baron Corvo'), *Hadrian the Seventh* (1904).

that *verisimilar* means *very similar*. He is a queer fish – a man with a grievance, obviously: a sincere Catholic who hates almost everything and everybody with which Catholicism is associated: specially France and Ireland. He must have been a most disagreeable man.

We had a most interesting journey back. We drove from Heysham across the back of England to Lincoln. A great deal of this route was spoiled by big industrial towns, but the first stages were lovely: very big, pale hills with many cliffs of that silvery-white rock – it is limestone. It is very different when you get down into Lincolnshire, which is as flat as a pancake. Lincoln itself is quite the best cathedral city I have ever seen. The centre of the town, where the cathedral stands, is on the only hill for miles, and the cathedral consequently dominates the whole countryside. The surroundings of the cathedral are magnificent – a beautiful close, a castle, and a Roman wall. What would specially have appealed to you was that after dinner as we strolled round it, we had the accompaniment of a little summer lightning and very distant *gentle* thunder. Do you know the kind of thunder which has almost a tinkle in it, like a musical sound?

I don't know that much has happened since we got back. My reading has been of a most miscellaneous order – Rider Haggard, Thomas Aquinas, Trollope, the Old Testament. Do you remember the passage in the latter where Moses sends spies into Canaan and they come back and say 'We have seen the giants, the sons of Anak; and we were in our own eyes as grasshoppers.'[21] Isn't that perfect? It brings out the monstrosity of the giants so well, because one thinks of the grasshopper as being not only small, but fragile, light and even flimsy. 'Beetles', for example, would not have done nearly so well.

Summer still drags on – far outstaying its welcome with me – and the pond shows no sign of rising to its normal level, though we have had a fairish amount of rain. Everyone is well – that is to say, we have all recovered from our holiday and are nearly as fit as if we had never been away. Of how few holidays can this be said!

Give my love to your mother, and – write soon.

Yours,
Jack

---

21 Numbers 13:33.

TO PAUL ELMER MORE (PRIN):[22]

Magdalen College,
Oxford.
Oct 25th 1934

Dear Mr. More

It is a long time since I have got so much out of any book as I have got out of your *Sceptical Approach*.[23] The sixth chapter especially will entitle you to a place in an American *Patrologia* if such a collection is ever made.

What is of most importance to me as an individual is that you have made me understand for the first time why most of the representatives of the present Christian renaissance so hate Idealism – perhaps you will have made *them* understand too. To you it may be a matter of surprise that I could ever have found this hatred unintelligible: but you would not wonder if you had travelled the same route as I, which was from materialism to idealism, from idealism to Pantheism, from pantheism to theism, and from theism to Christianity.

Our different views are natural enough. A field which seems a high place to one ascending the mountain, seems almost part of the valley to one descending. Idealism is suspect to you as a door *out of* Christianity: for me it was the door *in*. Clearly a door, *ex vi termini*,[24] has this double aspect. I do not think I should be disrespectful in urging to you remember the 'door *in*' aspect – to remember that in shutting the door to keep the faithful in, as you do so very firmly, you are inevitably, by the same act, shutting out those who might return.

I am bold to do this because my whole case rests on mere experience – this is the door by which, as a mere matter of fact, I entered and it will always be dear to me on that account. Contrariwise I most freely

---

22 Paul Elmer More (1864–1937), American critic and philosopher, was born in St Louis, Missouri. He taught Sanskrit at Harvard, 1894–5, and Bryn Mawr, 1895–7, and was a newspaper editor for twelve years. During 1919 he lectured on Plato at Princeton University. More was associated with Irving Babbitt, champion of humanism and founder of the modern humanistic movement. His major works are the *Shelburne Essays* (11 vols., 1904–21), *The Greek Tradition* (5 vols., 1921–31), and the *New Shelburne Essays* (3 vols., 1928–36). Princeton University Library has in its Department of Rare Books and Special Collections the three letters from Lewis to More published in this volume, and also copies (in Lewis's hand) of three letters from More to Lewis.

23 Paul Elmer More, *The Sceptical Approach to Religion* (1934).

24 'by the force of the term'.

acknowledge that your whole treatment of the subject has reminded me of the 'door *out*' aspect, which I had certainly unduly neglected hitherto. And now I am wondering just how far I can go with you. Not the whole way, I think. Fully realising the danger of the 'Illusion of Reason' (so much I owe to your book), I still find it not so much a philosophical as a religious impossibility quite to relinquish the Absolutist view of God.

For one thing I am not quite clear how far your 'teleology' will go. Does it imply that God can be better, more blessed, wiser, to-morrow than He is from of old? Does it involve that He may fail, that the ἀναγκη[25] (I dare put no accents, writing to you!) might win – a Twilight of the Gods? If so, I am afraid it would be as great a blow to my 'intuitions' as materialism itself. My 'wish-belief' demands the eternal, even, in a sense, the necessary: while also not wanting the immobile, the unanswering. In fine, I want to have it both ways: and this would be the flimsiest self indulgence, but for the huge historic fact of the doctrine of the Trinity. For surely that doctrine is just the doctrine that we are to give up *neither* of those conceptions of God of which you accept one and (most convincingly, yet in the long run dismayingly) reject the other. Is the traditional Christian belief not precisely this; that the same being which is eternally perfect, *purus actus*,[26] already at the End etc etc, yet also, in some incomprehensible way, is a purposing, feeling, and finally crucified Man in a particular place and time? So that somehow or other, we have it both ways?

I wish you could visit England more often. My spiritual fathers are many and scattered, but I left you, on the two occasions we met, with the sensation of having been with a *spiritual uncle* – and appropriately enough, in your avuncular character, you have sent me a spiritual *tip*. Very many thanks for the book. There is a lot more to say about it, but that would reach the scale of an article rather than a letter. I have an obituary of Irving Babbitt also to thank you for.

With my kindest regards and thanks,

Yours sincerely

C. S. Lewis

---

25 'necessity'. The reference here is to the old proverb: 'Against necessity not even the gods may fight.'

26 'a pure act', in the sense of the pure actuality of God. The phrase is standard in some later Latin literature (St Bonaventure uses it, as does Aquinas to describe 'the Divine Being').

TO JANET SPENS (BOD):[27]

Magdalen College,
Oxford.
Nov. 16th 1934.

Dear Miss Spens

I had envisaged this as a letter of discussion, but I am finding so few disagreements with you that I have less to discuss, and more to re-echo, than I had supposed.

The only thing I almost regret in your book[28] is the inevitable prominence of the thesis developed in Chap 1: not because I dissent from it (indeed without a careful re-reading of the whole F.Q.[29] I hardly could) but because I foresee that it will draw off attention from succeeding chapters which seem to me very much more important, and that the question 'What do you think of Miss Spens' book?' will come among careless people to mean simply and solely 'Do you agree with this theory about the composition of the F.Q.?' However, there is no help for this.

As regards the thesis itself I certainly think you have made a good *prima facie* case; the part about Orgoglio's castle (pp. 24, 25) seems to me very strong – so strong that here at any rate the *onus probandi*[30] now almost rests on the supporters of the traditional view. But chap 2 really interests me more, and I have learned a good deal from your analysis of the Mutability cantos. Can you tell me something more about Professor Nygren's *Eros and Agape*?[31] I haven't heard of it.

But chap 3 is the best of all. It was the second paragraph on p. 55 that delivered me from an old error: incredible as it now seems to me I had never before realised that the figures were to the Elizabethans

27 Dr Janet Spens (1876–1963) was born in Lanarkshire and educated at Glasgow University. She was joint founder and co-headmistress of Laurel Bank School, Glasgow, 1903–8, then returned to Glasgow University as Lecturer and Tutor, 1908–11. She was afterwards Fellow and Tutor in English at Lady Margaret Hall, Oxford, 1911–36. Her books include *Spenser's Faerie Queene: An Interpretation* (1934), *Two Periods of Disillusion* (1909), *An Essay on Shakespeare's Relation to Tradition* (1916) and *Elizabethan Drama* (1922).

28 Spens, *Spenser's Faerie Queene.*

29 i.e. *The Faerie Queene.*

30 'burden of proof'.

31 Anders Nygren, *Agape and Eros: A Study of the Christian Idea of Love*, authorized trans. A. G. Hebert (London: SPCK, 1932–9).

what the landscape was to the 19th century.[32] For this and for the four pages that follow I cannot thank you enough: they open doors, and your treatment of Una and Superstition (pp. 58, 59) is that rare sort of criticism which, as I believe, does truly and substantially create new qualities in the poem criticised. (Whom are you quoting at the bottom of p. 61?) The explanation of the importance of the clothes of Spenser's figures (62, ad fin.) must, I think, be right, and ought to silence a deal of misguided censure.

Addisonian on p. 68 is delicious: the one right epithet out of a score of possibles.[33] And I'm glad you have inserted a cooling card for the 'new poet' business on p. 71. Personally I find the whole of Renwick's treatment curiously antipathetic.[34]

Chap 5, I think, stands next in importance. The main contention that the predominance of the love theme is mainly due to the allegory – i.e. that it is ever-present in the symbols precisely because it is *not* the thing symbolised – convinced me at once: and this again opens doors, gives me the feeling of being more *free* within the world of the F.Q. than I was.

I am not at all sure where, in detail, your interpretation of Busyrane is right, but of course I must wait till I have re-read the poem.[35] But

---

32 Spens, *Spenser's Faerie Queene*, p. 55: 'Spenser is essentially an Elizabethan, and the Elizabethans tended to utter their more intense emotions through the imagery of human figures; the men of the nineteenth century had been trained to accept the expression of theirs through the imagery of inanimate nature.'

33 ibid., p. 68: 'The description here [Edmund Spenser, *The Faerie Queene* (1590, 1596), I, xii, 10, line 9] is almost Addisonian in its delineation of the mixture of superficiality and pose with naïve self-revelation and vacant wonder characteristic of an English crowd. It gives the dragon concrete reality as nothing else could do.'

34 William Lindsay Renwick, *Complaints: Edmund Spenser* (1928).

35 In *Spenser's Faerie Queene* Dr Spens stated of Busyrane (or Busirane): 'There has been some discussion of the meaning of Amoret's experience, but there can, I think, be little doubt. Her tortures at the hands of Busyrane in the House of Cupid represent the mental sufferings of the young wife in consequence of the too lustful element in Sir Scudamour's passion for her' (p. 105). Cf., however, *The Allegory of Love*, ch. 12: 'To find the real foe of Chastity, the real portrait of false love, we must turn to Malecasta and Busirane. The moment we do so we find that Malecasta and Busirane are nothing else than the main subject of this study – Courtly Love; and that Courtly Love is in Spenser's view the chief opponent of Chastity. But Chastity for him means Britomart, married love. The story he tells is therefore part of my story: the final struggle between the romance of marriage and the romance of adultery.'

ought not the conflicts to be mainly those of the Soul herself rather than those of one soul against another in particular human relationships?

By the bye I disagree with you about 'an unconvincing attempt' to distinguish the two people called Genius (top of p. 22). Although Lewis & Short[36] do not distinguish, I am pretty certain that Genius always did mean two quite distinct people:

A. *Genius* (still retaining his connection with *gigno*) the spirit of Reproduction or Generation (cf. 'torus *genialis*' etc). This is the 'Genius' of Alanus *De Planctu*,[37] the *Rom. of the Rose*, the *Confessio Amantis*,[38] and the Garden of Adonis.[39]

B. *Genius* (as translation of Gk. δαιμων), guardian spirit of a place or person > guardian angel > higher self > 'genius' of a poet. This is the 'genius' of Shakespeare's *Troil.* IV.iv.50 etc,[40] and of the bower of bliss.[41]

On p. 65 at the top, might one add Deut. XXXIII 2,[42] as a common influence on both?

But it is time I stopped. I have no other points even of trivial disagreement, and if I continued I should only pile up praises in a way you might reasonably dislike. I will only say that you have left me longing to re-read the F.Q. – and all previous books on Spenser have produced just the opposite effect.

I suppose you got my second note agreeing to take one pair of gaseous but intelligent scholars?

Yours sincerely

C. S. Lewis

---

36 *A Latin Dictionary founded on Andrews' edition of Freund's Latin Dictionary*, rev. and enlarged edn by C. T. Lewis and C. Short (1879).

37 Alanus ab Insulis (c. 1128–1203) mentions 'Genius' in *De Planctu Naturae*, Prosa V, 40ff. See *The Allegory of Love*, p. 106.

38 John Gower (?1330–1408) wrote about 'Genius' in *Confessio Amantis*, Prologue, 881ff.

39 The Garden of Adonis is described in Spenser, *The Faerie Queene*, II, vi, 34ff.

40 William Shakespeare, *Troilus and Cressida* (1609), IV, iv, 50: 'Some say the Genius so/Cries "Come" to him that instantly must die.'

41 In Spenser, *The Faerie Queene*, II, xii.

42 Deuteronomy 33:2: 'The Lord came from Sinai, and rose up from Seir unto them; he shined forth from mount Paran, and he came with ten thousands of saints: from his right hand went a fiery law for them.'

TO DOM BEDE GRIFFITHS (W):

[The Kilns]
26th Dec. 1934

My dear Griffiths

There was nothing to apologise for. My friendship with you began in disagreement and matured in argument, and is beyond the reach of any dangers of that kind.

If I object at all to what you said, I object not as a friend or as a guest, but as a logician. If you are going to argue with me on the points at issue between our churches, it is obvious that you must argue *to* the truth of your position, not *from* it. The opposite procedure only wastes your time and leaves me to reply, moved solely by embarrassment, *tu sei santo ma tu non sei filosofo*![43] But I still think it more profitable to adhere to our former agreement and to keep off the question.

But I enjoyed my visit very much and so, I hope, did de Peyer – *anima candida*,[44] a man whom I prize more every time I see him.[45]

Please thank the Prior for his hospitality and accept my best wishes (my prayers you may be sure you have) for every success both spiritual and natural.

Yours
C. S. Lewis

TO ARTHUR GREEVES (W):

[The Kilns]
Dec. 26th. 1934

My dear Arthur,

I have carried your letter about in a pocket all this term with the intention of answering it, and here goes at last! I wonder how much of its news is still up to date. For example, if I had replied when the

---

43 'You are a holy one, but you are no philosopher!' It is not known why Lewis wrote this in Italian.

44 '(speaking) in a sincere spirit'.

45 This was probably Charles Hubert Sebastian de Peyer (1905–83), one of three brothers who went to Magdalen College. He was educated at Cheltenham School, after which he read PPE at Magdalen and took his BA in 1929. He was a civil servant with the Ministry of Power and a member of the UK Delegation to the High Authority in the European Coal and Steel Community, with rank of minister in the Labour Party, 1953–7. He served as borough councillor for West Hertfordshire, 1964–75.

letter came I should have said 'I am so glad to hear that you have settled down in a comfortable routine' – but I can't do so now because you may have got unsettled since!

I wish you had told me a little more about Voyage to Arcturus.[46] Even if you can't describe it, you could at least give me some idea what it is about: at least whether it is about a voyage to Arcturus or not. I haven't come across the book yet, but will certainly read it if I do.

Which reminds me have you read 'Gape Row' by Agnes Romilly White?[47] Gape Row is the name of a village which turns out with absolute certainty to be Dundonald, if you work out all the geographical indications. It is not a very good novel – indeed I am not sure it isn't a definitely bad novel (tho' several reviewers seem to have thought otherwise), but fancy reading of characters in a book looking down on the Lough from above Holywood Barracks, or, again, nearer Dundonald, looking over to the Castlereagh Hills! The scenery is quite well described, and it is probably the only chance you and I will ever have of seeing that landscape described in fiction – except our own fiction, of course! The characters [are] all of the cottage class, and the dialect is well done – not that that kind of thing interests me after a few pages. If you want a New Year's Gift for any one like Gundrede[48] or Janie (I mean like them in love of dialect) this would do admirably. Now I come to think of it, is Janie the author? (Don't let this raise false expectations in your mind. I don't mean what you mean.)

We had this term a concert which I enjoyed more than any I have ever heard.[49] Beecham conducted and the bill of fare was Beethoven's Fifth Symphony,[50] a Debussy suite, Sibelius' *Tapiola* (forest-god of the Finns)[51] and Elgar's Enigma Variations.[52] For one thing, I have hardly ever before been at a concert where I liked all the items. The Elgar (do

---

46 David Lindsay, *A Voyage to Arcturus* (London: Methuen, 1920). This book was to have an important influence on Lewis's science fiction novels; see the letters to Charles A. Brady of 29 October 1944 and to Ruth Pitter of 4 January 1947.

47 Agnes Romilly White, *Gape Row* [1934].

48 i.e. Gundreda Ewart. See **The Ewart Family** in the Biographical Appendix to *CL* I.

49 The concert by the London Philharmonic Orchestra, under the direction of Sir Thomas Beecham, was performed in the Sheldonian Theatre on 15 November 1934.

50 Ludwig van Beethoven, Symphony No. 5, first performed in 1808.

51 Jean Sibelius, *Tapiola*, a symphonic poem first performed in 1926.

52 Edward Elgar, *Enigma Variations*, first performed in 1899.

you know it?) I had never heard before and did not fully understand, but I understood enough to admire it greatly. For another thing, the playing was marvellous. I thought I knew the symphony from Warnie's records, but Beecham brought things out of it that I'd never dreamed of.

Apart from this, very little has happened to me. I have addressed societies at Manchester and Birmingham and am doing one at Cambridge next term, which, I suppose, is a step in one's career. I have had lunch and spent the afternoon at a monastery in the Cotswolds, where a former pupil of mine is a monk.[53] Funny to have a silent lunch (except that a book is read aloud) amidst rows of white robed figures and then to file out behind them – chanting – down the long, dark corridor. One of them was a fine old man with a white beard, which just added the last touch. Don't be alarmed: the effect on me was purely aesthetic, not religious, and during the afternoon my host talked nonsense enough to put me off the conventual life for ever and a day. Give my love to your mother and let me have a letter when you can.

Yours
Jack

---

53 i.e. Dom Bede Griffiths.

1935

TO JANET SPENS (BOD):

The Kilns,
Headington Quarry.
Jan 8th 1935

Dear Miss Spens

You will have begun to wonder if your *Agape & Eros*[1] was lost forever! It is an intensely interesting book. I am inclined to think I disagree with him. His central contrast – that Agape is selfless and Eros self-regarding – seems at first unanswerable: but I wonder if he is not trying to force on the conception of love an antithesis which it is the precise nature of love, in all its forms, to overcome.

Then again, is the contrast between Agape (God active coming to man passive) and Eros (man by desire ascending to God quâ passive object of desire) really so sharp? He might accuse me of a mere play upon words if I pointed out that in Aristotle's 'He moves as the beloved' (κινεῖ ὡς ερωμενον) there is, after all, an active verb, κινεῖ.[2] But is this merely a grammatical accident – is it not perhaps the real answer? Can the thing really be conceived in one way *or* the other? In real life it feels like both, and both, I suspect, are the same. Even on the human level does any one feel that the passive voice of the word *beloved* is really exclusive – that *to attract* is a – what do you call it – the opposite

1 Nygren, *Agape and Eros*.

2 Aristotle, *Metaphysics*, 1072b. κινεῖ means 'moves'. In *The Discarded Image* (1964), Lewis mentioned Aristotle's teachings about God as Unmoved Mover: 'We must not imagine Him moving things by any positive action, for that would be to attribute some kind of motion to Himself and we should then not have reached an utterly unmoving Mover. How then does He move things? Aristotle answers, κινεῖ ὡς ἐρώμενον, "He moves as beloved". He moves other things, that is, as an object of desire moves those who desire it' (ch. 5, p. 113).

of a deponent? However, I must tackle him again. He has shaken me up extremely.[3]

I was one of a party of four some weeks ago who discussed your parallel between those passages from F.Q. and the *Prelude*,[4] and divided – two agreeing with you in finding an important similarity-in-dissimilarity between them, and the other two failing to find any reason why you had brought them together at all. Now for the interesting point. We all gave analyses of the effect which both passages had on us, which disclosed the fact that the opposition were attending exclusively to the *things mentioned in* the passages, and had apparently no sensation of the immediate all pervading imaginative *flavour* – and no idea that they ought to look for it, or that there was such a thing. I was astonished and was led on to wonder whether many people read poetry in the same way. If so, no wonder we hear such odd judgements.

Yes – the passage about Genius in the Bower of Blisse[5] is more difficult than I had remembered. I will tell you sometime how I was trying to take it (I haven't the book handy) – but I now think my way involves almost impossible syntax. And what on earth does he mean by 'good Agdistes'[6] – the only Agdistes story I can find is a long nightmare of meaningless cruelties and obscenities. Why 'good'? I shall have to work at this rather hard. My own work is a book on medieval allegory which will end with a chapter on Spenser, and it is towards that that you have helped me so much. By the bye, one of my party of four (the one who sided with us) maintains that Spenser's great fault is his prosaic style, but that his *stories* are so good that they save him. This is not such nonsense as it sounds!

Yours sincerely
C. S. Lewis

3 Lewis went on considering the relation of Agape and Eros for years, and in *The Four Loves* (London, 1960; Fount, 1998) he discusses them under the names 'gift-love' and 'need-love' (using 'Eros' to mean sexual love).

4 In Spens, *Spenser's Faerie Queene*, pp. 57–9.

5 Spenser, *The Faerie Queene*, II, xii, 46–9.

6 ibid., II, xii, 48.

TO CECIL HARWOOD (BOD):

Magdalen College,
Oxford.
Feb 5th 1935.

My dear Harwood,

The poem is *very good* – perfect except for the rather clumsy end of stanza one.

I note your position about the walk: you and Beckett are about equally problematical, but for different dates. A pretty tangle!

Yours
C.S.L.

TO OWEN BARFIELD (W):

Magdalen College,
Oxford.
[March 1935]

My dear Barfield

What a glorious relief – I thought I was done for. No, I don't transfer non philosophical letters straight to the W.P.B.:[7] contrariwise, as soon as [I] see that they deal with contingent, empirical matter of fact, I transfer them to my *pocket* to note and deal with later: but sometimes (specially if I change my coat) the second part of the plan does not get carried out. I know I am a guiter.[8]

Yes – I would love to go with Beckett & you on the Tuesday and return on Sunday night. Where is the Venue?

---

7 i.e. the waste paper basket.

8 Barfield, Harwood and Lewis planned a walking-tour for April 1936, but at the last minute Lewis was unable to go. As a joke Barfield and Harwood decided Lewis must sit for a re-examination – based on the old School Certificate – before he could be readmitted to their 'College of Cretaceous Perambulators'. The questions and answers were published as Owen Barfield and C. S. Lewis, *A Cretaceous Perambulator (The Re-examination of)* ed. Walter Hooper (Oxford: The Oxford University C. S. Lewis Society, 1983, limited to 100 copies). One of the questions was 'Give the (long) semantic history of the word "Guiting".' Lewis did not attempt this question, but the editor supplied the following explanation (p. 14): 'The semantic history of the word "Guiting" is, that it became for the perambulators a convenient expletive for anything they didn't like. A "guiter" was, for instance, a bad person. It may have been suggested by the inconveniences caused them on the 1928 walk when they passed the villages of Temple Guiting and Guiting Power in Gloucestershire.'

I don't think I can come and stay this Vac. If I find I can I shall just ask myself and you can refuse me *if*.

The Christmas poem is a complete success. The other is perfectly satisfactory stuff but too uncoloured to stand alone: in a *context* it would come out alright.

Why don't you send *Tertium Quid*[9] to a publisher? Now that P.R.[10] has gone through so easily, I am sure T.Q. would – and they'd make a pretty pair.

I have done about 200 lines of the Aeneid into riming alexandrines: it goes like fun into that metre, and you can reproduce the effect of the hexameter, getting nearly a prose rhythm in the middle and pulling itself together at the end.

Harwood was down for the week end. He gets better and better – not to talk to, you know (in that respect he gets worse) but just better.

Apparently Sparrow is a great man in military circles.[11] My brother is quite impressed at our venturing to walk with him. We are devils of fellows aren't we?

Did you ever read Jeckyll & Hyde?[12] It is a καθαρσις[13]

Yours

C. S. Lewis

TO PAUL ELMER MORE (PRIN):

The Kilns,
Headington Quarry,
Oxford.
April 5th 1935

My dear Mr. More

Your letter gave me a great deal of pleasure. I had thought of sending you that essay as some return for the books you have sent me: but then again I thought that what was kind from you to me would be merely 'pushing' from me to you.[14] But I always regretted my decision

---

9 This was probably one of Barfield's poems. It has not been published.

10 *The Pilgrim's Regress.*

11 i.e. Lieutenant-Colonel Arthur Alan Hanbury-Sparrow, author of *The Land-Locked Lake.*

12 Robert Louis Stevenson, *The Strange Case of Dr Jekyll and Mr Hyde* (1886).

13 'catharsis'.

14 Lewis was probably referring to his essay 'The Personal Heresy in Criticism' in which he argued that the 'concealed major premise' in E. M. W. Tillyard's *Milton*

for I really wanted to know whether we were of one mind on this subject. I am 'continuing the work' as best I can. The *Criterion* (the only likely periodical on other grounds) is closed to me,[15] so I am coming back to the lecture for its original purpose, i.e. a method of publication, I give two or three a year on this kind of subject and get a very good audience – sometimes am even applauded, wh. is rare here.

I mention this, partly no doubt from vanity, but partly because it proves that there is a demand for some literary theory not based, like the prevailing ones, on materialism. (You rightly fixed on that as the real point). In a few years I hope to collect these and publish them: I shall call it a 'Realistic' theory of literature, explaining of course that I mean the word in the sense of Plato not of Zola. I wish I knew how many of us there are. Sometimes I suspect that we are more numerous than each of [us] supposes, and that if we can only get together we may blow the whole composite fog (French Symbolism *cum* Croce *cum* Eliot with, oddly enough Karl Marx and Neo-Scholasticism somewhere in the background) away by 1950.

I am not ready yet to say anything about your book on Plato's religion.[16] The immediate reaction is an irrelevant one – a groan at discovering how much less Plato I remember than I thought I did. The main point at issue doubtless is this: are we to continue the Bosanquet[17] and Archer Hind[18] tradition of subtilising the Ancients, or embrace

---

(1930) was 'plainly the proposition that all poetry is *about* the poet's state of mind'. 'The Personal Heresy in Criticism' was eventually published in *Essays and Studies by Members of the English Association*, XIX (1934). It then became the first chapter of a joint work between Lewis and Tillyard, *The Personal Heresy: A Controversy*, published in 1939.

15 In November 1930 Lewis sent 'The Personal Heresy in Criticism' to *The Criterion*, an influential literary periodical edited by T. S. Eliot. Six months later, in May 1931, Eliot turned it down. Lewis wrote to Eliot again on 2 June 1931 with the proposal that Eliot publish not only 'The Personal Heresy in Criticism' but four other essays. It is proposed to publish that important letter, not included in *CL* I, in the Addendum to *CL* III. See **Thomas Stearns Eliot** in the Biographical Appendix.

16 Paul Elmer More, *Platonism* (1931).

17 Bernard Bosanquet (1848–1923), Fellow of Philosophy at University College, Oxford, 1870–81, whose works include *Knowledge and Reality* (1885) and *A History of Aesthetic* (1892).

18 Richard Dacre Archer-Hind (1849–1910), Greek scholar and Platonist, who was a Fellow of Trinity College, Cambridge. He published editions of Plato's *Phaedo* (1883) and *Timaeus* (1888).

your view that the great thing is to leave uncontaminated their 'invaluable naïvety'. On the whole I am with you: at least I'm with you as *against* Archer Hind. But I'm dreadfully muddled, just as I am about the 'Absolute' kind of God and your kind. I remain like Boethius in the song 'stupens de hac lite'.[19] The view I am *not* holding for the moment always seems unanswerable. Have you read Nygren's *Eros and Agape*? It is a closely related problem and leaves me equally puzzled. With many thanks,

Yours sincerely
C. S. Lewis

TO OWEN BARFIELD (W):

[The Kilns]
April 5th 1935

I hope to arrive at Rudyard (wh. on nearer acquaintance with guidebooks turns out to be Rudyard Lake) at 3.13 on Monday.[20]

Where reservoys ripple
And sun-shadows stipple
The beard of the corn,
We'll meet and we'll kipple
We'll camp and then kipple
At Rudyard we'll kipple
From evening to morn.

And then we'll set off, yes!,
Discussing your Orpheus[21]
His meaning and myth,
Till fettered by Morpheus,
The leaden maced Morpheus,
Inaccurate Morpheus
At Chapel-en-le Frith.

19 '*Assidet Boetius stupens de hac lite*' – 'Boethius sits nearby bewildered by this dispute.'
20 In the end Lewis and Barfield, who met at Rudyard, Derbyshire, were the only ones on this Easter walk which began on 8 April.
21 This suggests that Barfield, even if he had not written any part of his poetic drama, *Orpheus*, was thinking and talking about it. See Lewis's criticism of the finished work in his letter to Barfield of 28 March 1938.

Good about Field. Find out in Manchester how to pronounce Chapel-en-le Frith *and* Edale. I have got all necessary maps. I shall be in fine form for yr poem as I am just examining the Newdigate![22]

Can it really come off?

Yrs

C. S. Lewis

TO ARTHUR GREEVES (W):

The Kilns,
Headington Quarry,
Oxford.
April 23d 1935

My dear Arthur

It is a weary time since I heard from you and I ought to have answered you before: but though I am in your debt I doubt if my silences are longer than yours. The immediate object of this letter is to ask if I can come and stay a week with you this summer, please. As at present advised any date between July 1st and Oct. 5th will suit me. Now if you could within the next few weeks fix on any date between these two (preferably quand tu seras seul!)[23] it would be a great advantage: for though all that period is at present free I do not know when engagements may begin to creep in. Of course it may not be convenient to have me at all, but I am assuming you would have no scruple about telling me if that were so. I am only anxious that if you are able and willing to have me we shd. not let the thing slip through our fingers as we did last year. If you can't arrange so far ahead, of course you can't (what it is to have a brain!) and there we are: but no doubt you see the advantage of so doing if it is possible.

I had seen the reviews of the Powys book[24] and also heard (by an accident) what you hint about its contents: therefore I shall not read it. I do not always win even when the enemy attack me in my own lines,[25]

---

22 Lewis was one of the examiners for the Newdigate Prize. This annual prize for English verse, founded in 1806 by Sir Roger Newdigate, is the most widely known of university prizes.

23 'when you are alone'.

24 Llewelyn Powys, *Damnable Opinions* (1935).

25 Powys did not mention Lewis by name in *Damnable Opinions*, but he attacked orthodox Christianity, especially as practised and written about at Oxford. On p. 5 he said: 'True religion is simple – it is to worship life, to bow down before life, beating our heads upon the grass in jubilant acquiescence.'

but the one thing I can do is to make sure that at least I never go out of my way to seek him. What an extraordinary profile Powys has – I suppose you saw the pictures in several papers. I take it he is almost a lunatic? The most interesting story I have read recently is *Land Under England* by one O'Neill:[26] you should try it.

I am just back from my Easter walking tour with Barfield and co., this year in Derbyshire.[27] Have you been there? It is appreciably more like my ideal country than any I have yet been [to]. It is limestone mountains: which means, from the practical point of view, that it has the jagg'd sky lines and deep vallies of ordinary mountainous country, but with this important difference, that owing to the paleness of the rock and the extreme clarity of the rivers, it is *light* instead of sombre – sublime yet smiling – like the delectable mountains.[28] It gives you something the same sensation as Blake's songs.[29]

This place is being ruined by building and what was Kiln Lane is turning into a street of council houses.[30] Where will it end? If we live

---

26 Joseph O'Neill, *Land Under England* (1935).

27 After retracing the walk with Owen Barfield, Walter Hooper gave the following account in *Through Joy and Beyond: A Pictorial Biography of C. S. Lewis* (1982), pp. 76–7: 'They entered [Derbyshire] from Staffordshire by Rudyard Lake. Then after lunch down the Goyt Valley to Chapel-en-le-Frith and so next day to Kinder Downfall, where the shallow river Kinder plunges off the edge of the peaty moor. Here on windy days when the sun warms the moorside the water is blown into myriad droplets of rainbowed light. Crossing the Kinder Scout and down Grindsbrook they came to Edale and at last stopped the night in Castleton. Next day they walked up the Winnat Pass and across Tideswell Moor to Wardlow and Monsal Dale. It's just a short way now to Ashford in the Water and Bakewell and on again the fourth day to Ashbourne and Dovedale.'

28 John Bunyan, *The Pilgrim's Progress from this World to That which is to Come*, ed. James Blanton Wharey, 2nd edn rev. Roger Sharrock (Oxford: Clarendon Press, 1960), First Part, p. 119: 'They went then, till they came to the delectable Mountains, which Mountains belong to the Lord of that Hill . . . so they went up to the Mountains, to behold the Gardens, and Orchards, the Vineyards, and Fountains of water, where also they drank, and washed themselves, and did freely eat of the Vineyards.'

29 William Blake, *Songs of Innocence* (1789).

30 This was due to the expansion of Morris Motors Ltd. In 1912 William Richard Morris (1877–1963), created 1st Baron Nuffield in 1934 and 1st Viscount Nuffield in 1938, opened his first car factory at Cowley, halfway between Oxford and Headington Quarry. In 1926 he started the Pressed Steel Company, employing more than 10,000 people, alongside the car factory. Morris Motors is only about a mile from The Kilns, and by 1935 it had expanded so much that, whereas The Kilns had been one of only a few houses for miles around, a rash of small houses now almost surrounded it.

to be old there will hardly be any real country left in the South of England.

Give my love to your mother and any other of my friends whom you may meet: and let me have an answer as soon as possible to my question.

Yours
Jack

TO LEO BAKER (BOD):[31]

Magdalen College,
Oxford.
April 28th 1935

My dear Baker

I was very distressed on meeting Barfield this year for a walk (a ghost of its old self for he and I were the only participants) to hear of your illness. It stimulated an impulse that has been hovering in my mind for some time to write to you and to try and pick up some of the old links. That they were ever dropped was, I imagine, chiefly my fault – at least even self-love on my part cannot find any substantial respect in which it could have been yours. Will you forgive me? I think I have learned a little since those days and can promise not to serve you so again.

You must not bother yourself with letter writing while you are unwell, nor need you: for I trust that any news of your state will trickle to me in the end by one channel or another. The last I heard from Barfield was a little more encouraging. Beyond wishing you well, I cannot enlarge on the subject: almost anything said from a well man to a sick man seems an impertinence.

My father is dead and my brother has retired from the army and now lives with us. I have deep regrets about all my relations with my father (but thank God they were best at the end). I am going bald. I am a Christian. Professionally I am chiefly a medievalist. I think that is all my news up to date.

I suppose you have heard from, or at least of, the others fairly

31 See **Leo Baker** in the Biographical Appendix to *CL* I. Leo Baker was for a long time in an Austrian clinic with suspected cancer. It later proved to be a false alarm.

regularly. I don't know if you met the new addition to our party before you left – namely Hanbury Sparrow, a Lt. Colonel and all that. Barfield picked him up somewhere on the continent: he has written a good book called 'The Landlocked Gate' and a bad one called 'Gilt-Edged Insecurity'.[32] I mention him to boast of our power of assimilation, for tho' an Anthroposophist and an author he remains very much a colonel and a man of the world – so that when on the last walk but one we heard him and Beckett agreeing that 'you could now get quite a decent suit for fifteen guineas', the rest of us felt this element in the firm was at last adequately represented.

Beckett, by the way, I am a little nervous about: he is becoming a real bureaucrat – but I trust his very delightful family (whom I recently met for the first time) will save him. But you can imagine the whole scene of him and Sparrow together: and how that bursts on the unconscious pin-point of Field or passes unobserved over the rustic, almost parochial, solidity of Cecil.

Barfield is writing a play – or a masque or a ballet rather – on Orpheus and Eurydice. You shd. get him to send it to you if you are well enough to care for such things. It is excellent and ultra poetical in matter (poetry itself), plain to baldness in style. A funny change from the Barfield of the *Tower*. But how archaic that sounds now! I hardly write anything these days except things proper to a don. I suppose we have all lived to discover that we are not great men, and not to mind: there are better things than that in the world, and out of it.

All this may be silly chat – as letters from home so often were to a man in the front line, which, I know, is where you are at present. We have so spoiled language that I cannot even say God bless you without pausing to try and explain that I mean the words in their literal sense.

Don't attempt to reply unless some day you feel quite up to it and apt for it.

Yours,
C. S. Lewis

32 Arthur Alan Hanbury-Sparrow, *Gilt-Edged Insecurity* (1934).

TO PAUL ELMER MORE (PRIN):

Magdalen College,
Oxford.
May 23rd 1935

Dear Mr. More

Very many thanks for the *American Review*.[33] It contains only one of the articles you mention, the other, I suppose, having been postponed. I am pretty sure I should agree with you about Joyce if I had read him, but I never have, and would as soon choose a treadmill for my recreation.

There may be many reasons why you do not share my dislike of Eliot, but I hardly know why you should be surprised at it. On p. 154 of the article on Joyce you yourself refer to him as 'a great genius expending itself on the propagation of irresponsibility'. To me the 'great genius' is not apparent: the other thing is. Surely it is natural that I should regard Eliot's work as a very great evil. He is the very spear head of that attack on πέρας[34] which you deplore. His constant profession of humanism and his claim to be a 'classicist' may not be consciously insincere, but they are erroneous. The plea that his poems of disintegration are all satiric, are intended as awful warnings, is the common plea of all these literary traitors to humanity. So Juvenal, Wycherley, Byron excuse their pornography: so Eliot himself excuses Joyce. His intention only God knows. I must be content to judge his work by its fruits, and I contend that no man is fortified against chaos by reading the *Waste Land*,[35] but that most men are by it infected with chaos.

The opposite plea rests on a very elementary confusion between poetry that represents disintegration and disintegrated poetry. The *Inferno* is not infernal poetry: the *Waste Land* is. His criticism tells the

---

33 In his letter to Lewis of 26 April 1935 More wrote: 'I have directed the publisher of the *American Review* to send you a copy of the May issue, which contains an article of mine on James Joyce. I hope and believe, that you will approve of my treatment of that gentleman, though you may perhaps think I have credited him with too much native genius. In the June issue I shall have an article on the modernist movement in French poetry'.

34 'limit'. More had been arguing for a return to Christian humanism as exemplified by limit and order – an idea which Eliot's *Waste Land* explodes by its repeated emphasis on chaos.

35 T. S. Eliot, *The Waste Land* (1922). This complex poem, praised for its sense of depression and futility, was the epitome of what Lewis hated in modern poetry.

same tale. He may say he is a classicist, but his sympathy with depraved poets (Marlowe, Jonson, Webster) is apparent: but he shows no real love of any disciplined, and magnanimous writer save Dante. Of Homer, Sophocles, Virgil, Milton, Racine he has nothing to say. Assuredly he is one of the enemy: and all the more dangerous because he is sometimes disguised as a friend.

And this offence is aggravated by attendant circumstances, such as his arrogance. And (you will forgive me) it is further aggravated for an Englishman by the recollection that Eliot stole upon us, a foreigner and a neutral, while we were at war – obtained, I have my wonders how, a job in the Bank of England – and became (am I wrong) the advance guard of the invasion since carried out by his natural friends and allies, the Steins and Pounds and *hoc genus omne*,[36] the Parisian riff-raff of denationalised Irishmen and Americans who have perhaps given Western Europe her death wound.

Enough. You see my views; and may answer them as bluntly as I have put them. Of the man himself I know nothing and will do my best to believe any good that I may hear from you or other authorised sources.

As for your story – it is an amusing comment on human vanity that other peoples' conversation about oneself always pleases if it is not directly insulting: and so did this.[37]

---

36 'and all that sort'. Horace, *Satires*, I, ii, 2.

37 In his letter of 26 April 1935 More wrote: 'Eliot is a dear friend of mine, and on the whole I do not like to see him placed among the enemies. He started out wrong, under the influence of the French notion of "pure art", but he has been . . . moving away from that nasty heresy. Naming him, I am tempted to tell you a story – I hope not committing an indiscretion. It was after I had first met you and had read *The Pilgrim's Regress*. Eliot was visiting me at Oxford, and [John Wolfenden (1906–85), Magdalen's Tutor in Philosophy] invited us to luncheon at Magdalen. I asked W. about you, and particularly what you meant by return to "Mother Kirk", whether you had turned Roman Catholic, or Anglo Catholic, or Scotch Presbyterian, or what. W. avowed that he didn't know, but was pretty sure you had not become R.C. And then he added: "The other day several of us were together when X (I don't recall the name) burst into the room in a state of great excitement. 'Do you know,' he shouted, 'what that man Lewis is up to? Y (another forgotten name) says he saw him in the College chapel, and that on inquiry he finds the fellow has been going to chapel for weeks unbeknownst to any of us. What's it all mean?' " So Wolfenden. And then Eliot with that sly smile of his: "Why, it's quite evident that if a man wishes to escape detection at Oxford, the one place for him to go is the college chapel" ' (Princeton University Library).

Of Nygrens, another time. I don't fully agree – Protestant is not for me a dyslogistic term.[38]

A Mr. Shafer has sent me a long book,[39] nominally about you but actually *de omnibus rebus*,[40] which I am enjoying.

Yours very sincerely
C. S. Lewis

TO ARTHUR GREEVES (W):

Magdalen College,
Oxford.
June 17th. 1935

My dear Arthur,

'Will you come Sunday or Monday?' says the host. 'No, I'll come Saturday,' says the guest. 'Oh Lord,' says the host (as it might be my father) or '*Why* do you do these things?' (as it might be another). On second thoughts I am booking a berth for Monday night, July 1st by Liverpool – leaving you Mon 8th.

There is just one cloud on the horizon. Minto's sister is seriously ill (in Dublin) and if Minto has to go over for a funeral she may want me to stay and run the house. Let us hope this won't happen. If it does, I suppose we shall be able to fix on a week that will suit both you and me later. In the meantime I thought it better to let the arrangement stand, and hope for the best – I hate putting off anything so nice.

Give my love to your mother and many, many thanks.

Yours,
Jack

---

38 ibid.: 'Yes, I have read *Agape and Eros*, and I don't like it at all, indeed I very heartily dislike it. It seems to me the last word of the most abominable form of Protestantism in a straight line from Luther through Barth.'

39 Robert Shafer, *Paul Elmer More and American Criticism* (1935).

40 'about all matters'.

TO EUGÈNE VINAVER (W):[41]

Magdalen College,
Oxford.
Sept 19th. 1935

Dear Vinaver

Thank you very much for the copy of your lecture.[42] Ever since I heard it at the Arthurian[43] I have wished for more of it than memory could carry – as it is now a *sine quâ non* for any reading of Malory.

About *holes* in VI vi, it may interest you to note that my own MS. note on the passage gives 'Hole = fenestra' (*Catholicon Anglicum* 1483)[44] – a reference I probably got from the N. E. D.[45] But can you throw any light on 'hole of the tree' in VI ii? Your knowledge of 'F' will enable you to say at once whether this is merely an error for 'bole', or whether we must consider further. (Tolkien showed me O. E. *Healh = angulus* > fork (of a tree) but this is difficult phonologically.)

Thanks also for your very kind reference in a footnote to my somewhat pert review.[46]

---

41 Professor Eugène Vinaver (1899–1979) was born in St Petersburg, and was educated in Paris and Oxford. He was a lecturer in French Language and Literature at Lincoln College, Oxford, 1924–8, and lecturer in French, 1928–31. He was appointed a Reader in French Language and Literature at Oxford in 1931, and was Professor of French Language and Literature at the University of Manchester, 1933–66. His many works include *Malory* (1929), *The Works of Sir Thomas Malory*, 3 vols. (1947), *The Tale of the Death of King Arthur* (1955) and *The Rise of Romance* (1971).

42 Eugène Vinaver, 'Malory's *Morte d'Arthur* in the Light of a Recent Discovery' (1935). The 'discovery' referred to here is that of a manuscript of Malory's Arthurian romances roughly contemporary with Caxton's edition and independent of it, found in Winchester College in 1934. See the passage from Lewis's review of Professor Vinaver's edition of the *Works of Sir Thomas Malory* (1947) that follows the letter to Ruth Pitter of 6 June 1947.

43 The Arthurian Society.

44 *Catholicon Anglicum: An English–Latin Wordbook, dated 1483*, introduction and notes by Sidney J. H. Herrtage (Early English Text Society, 1881).

45 *The New English Dictionary.*

46 In his review of E. K. Chambers' *Sir Thomas Wyatt and Some Collected Studies* (1933) in *Medium Aevum*, III, No. 3 (October 1934), pp. 237–40, Lewis criticized Vinaver for the importance he attached to 'sources'. 'It is possible for our reading of an author to become what we may call 'source-ridden', so that we no longer see his book as it is in itself, but only as it contrasts with its sources. This is clearly an injustice to the author, for we are preserving in their original form elements which he has transmuted, and even elements which he rejected. It is as though we ate all the ingredients of a pudding along with the pudding itself: such an eating is emphatically not the pudding's proof' (p. 238).

I do wish you could see your way to give us a commentary as well as a text when you bring out the W. MS. – it is badly needed for all aspects of the work and whose business is it if not yours?

With many thanks.

Yours

C. S. Lewis

In the winter of 1935 the Delegates of the Oxford University Press conceived the idea of the Oxford History of English Literature, and in March 1935 they appointed as general editors the distinguished scholars, F. P. Wilson[47] *and Bonamy Dobrée.*[48] *They were to work in close co-operation with Kenneth Sisam (1887–1971), who was assistant secretary to the Delegates of the Oxford University Press at this time.*

In October 1935 the Press announced that it had undertaken the production of this daunting task, which was to consist of twelve volumes, each volume the work of a single author. While each volume would, in the main, begin and end at a definite date, there would have to be a certain degree of dovetailing, and authors were expected to consult with those writing the volumes on either side of them so as to avoid overlapping.

Shortly before making this announcement, F. P. Wilson wrote to Lewis,

---

In note 1 of 'Malory's *Morte d'Arthur* in the Light of a Recent Discovery', Vinaver responded: 'I do not feel with Mr Lewis that those who see too much of Malory's sources are apt to overlook the book "as it is in itself". We must obviously avoid eating "all the raw ingredients of a pudding along with the pudding itself" for "such eating is emphatically not the pudding's proof" . . . but literature is one of the few things to which the metaphor of the pudding does not apply. Knowledge of the recipe may spoil the taste of a pudding but it need not distort our immediate impression from a literary work. It is of course possible to read Malory "as if we knew nothing about his sources", but our understanding of him will be deepened, not spoilt, by the knowledge of what is peculiar and unique in his work.'

47 Frank Percy Wilson (1889–1963), who had been Lewis's tutor in English, took a B.Litt. from Lincoln College, Oxford. After serving in the First World War, he returned to Oxford as a university lecturer. He was Professor of English at the University of Leeds, 1929–36, and Merton Professor of English at Oxford, 1947–57. Wilson contributed the volume on *English Drama 1485–1585* (1969), ed. G. K. Hunter, to the Oxford History of English Literature.

48 Bonamy Dobrée (1891–1974), distinguished scholar and lecturer, went to Christ's College, Cambridge, after serving in the First World War. In 1936 he was appointed to the Chair of English Literature at the University of Leeds, a post he held until his retirement in 1955. His books include the volume on *The Early Eighteenth Century* (1959) in the Oxford History of English Literature.

explaining who had been invited to write which volume, and asking if he would write the one on the sixteenth century.[49] *There followed this reply from Lewis:*

TO FRANK PERCY WILSON (OUP):

Magdalen College,
Sept. 23rd 1935

My dear Wilson

Really, really! In other words you have missed the chance of Tolkien on O.E.[50] and R. W. Chambers[51] on the XVIth century. For heaven's sake, if it is still possible, do that, and either check me out or give me the XVth.

The Allegory book is done and I am now in communication with Sisam about it.

But, really –

Yours ever
C. S. Lewis

No answer, forsooth! Marry, come up![52]

The planning of the Oxford History of English Literature – 'O Hell!' as Lewis called it – continued. The task of writing a volume in this series was so onerous that a number of those who originally agreed to write for the series either opted out of the programme or died before the work was done. F. P. Wilson continued firm in his belief that the sixteenth-century volume was right for Lewis, and Lewis agreed to write it. However, Lewis did not want to include drama in his work, and Wilson agreed to write a separate volume entitled English Drama 1485–1585 *(1969).*

---

49 See the 'Background' *to English Literature in the Sixteenth Century* in *CG*, pp. 474–82.

50 J. R. R. Tolkien had too many other commitments to write a volume on Old English literature, and in the end the series began with Middle English literature.

51 Raymond Wilson Chambers (1874–1942) graduated in English from University College, London, in 1894 and spent his entire professional life at University College. He became a Fellow of English in 1900, Assistant Professor in 1904, and Professor of English, 1922–41. His works include *Beowulf* (1914) and *Thomas More* (1935).

52 William Shakespeare, *Romeo and Juliet* (1597), II, v, 64: 'Are you so hot? Marry, come up, I trow.'

TO ARTHUR GREEVES (W):

[The Kilns]
Dec 7th 1935

My dear Arthur,

I am sorry you have had to haul this letter out of me by the scruff of its neck. It's not that I have nothing to say to you and don't want to hear what you have to say. I believe I could still make a fair attempt at a *regular* correspondence, but you yourself vetoed that, and odd letters, like odd bills, I do find it hard to meet when I'm busy.

Minto told you about our present bother. The guests are still here, and will be, so far as I can see, until the end of January.[53] Oh Arthur, what a snag it is that the people who are *pitiable* are not necessarily likeable. Molly Askins is emphatically one of those people of whom old Foord-Kelsie said 'We must learn to love those whom we can't like.' She's what you would call an encroaching person – do you know the type of small, dark woman with big gentle eyes and soft voice, who just gently and softly and even pathetically gets her own way in everything and really treats the house as a hotel? However, the thing's a duty and there's an end of it: tho', by the bye, as W. and I were saying the other day, the New Testament tells us to *visit* the widows, not to let them visit us![54]

I have finished my book, which is called *The Allegorical Love Poem*, and is dedicated to Barfield. The Clarendon Press have accepted it and hope to have it out by May.[55] As I am to get 12 free copies (Dents only give one 6) you and Tchanie shall each have one and save your silver: and whatever you think of the matter, I hope, from experience of the Clarendon Press, that binding, paper etc will be – in our old formula – excellent, exquisite, and admirable. In other words, if you can't read it, you will enjoy looking at it, smelling it, and stroking it. If not a good book, it will be a good pet! It will be about 400 pp, they say. (It

53 The guests were Molly Askins and her son Michael. Molly was the widowed daughter-in-law of Mrs Moore's brother, Dr Robert Askins (1880–1935) who, while practising medicine in Southern Rhodesia died at sea on 1 September 1935.

54 James 1:27: 'Pure religion and undefiled before God and the Father is this, To visit the fatherless and widows in their affliction, and to keep himself unspotted from the world.'

55 In the end Lewis was persuaded to call his book *The Allegory of Love: A Study in Medieval Tradition*.

will be very funny, after this, if they do it in double columns and a paper cover.)

My other bit of literary news is that Sheed and Ward have bought the *Regress* from Dent. I didn't much like having a book of mine, and specially a religious book, brought out by a Papist publisher: but as they seemed to think they could sell it, and Dents clearly couldn't, I gave in. I have been well punished: for Sheed, without any authority from me, has put a blurb on the inside of the jacket which says 'This story begins in Puritania (Mr Lewis was brought up in Ulster)' – thus implying that the book is an attack on my own country and my own religion.[56] If you ever come across any one who might be interested, explain as loudly as you can that I was not consulted & that the blurb is a damnable lie told to try and make Dublin riff-raff buy the book. I didn't mean to spend so much of this letter on egoism.

I have tried in vain to buy *Voyage to Arcturus* but it is out of print. For reading, lately, I have re-read the *Faerie Queene* with enormous enjoyment. It must be a really great book because one can read it as a boy in one way, and then re-read it in middle life and get something very different out of it – and that to my mind is one of the best tests. I am at present engaged with Sir Thomas More's English works[57] (i.e. everything except the Utopia)[58] which are necessary to a job I'm doing. They are quite interesting, and sometimes really helpful in religious aspects, but not so good as they have lately been made out to be.

The worst of these letters at long intervals is that I can never remember how much has happened since I wrote last. e.g. did I tell you how much I was moved by seeing *A Winter's Tale*?[59] I can't have told you about the magnificent philharmonic performance of the Ninth Symphony we were at a few weeks ago.[60] You know I used to dislike the

---

56 Sheed and Ward of London published their edition of *The Pilgrim's Regress* in October 1935. Lewis had been worried about obscurity in the work, and this edition differs from the first in having a short 'Argument' at the beginning of each of the ten books.

57 *The Workes of Sir Thomas More Knyght, sometyme Lorde Chauncellour of England, wrytten by him in the Englysh tonge*, ed. William Rastell (1557).

58 *Utopia* (1516), in Latin, is the principal literary work of Sir Thomas More.

59 William Shakespeare, *The Winter's Tale* (1623).

60 This concert, conducted by Malcolm Sargent, was given by the London Philharmonic Orchestra in the Sheldonian Theatre on 28 November 1935. For details see *The Oxford Magazine*, LIV (5 December 1935), pp. 244, 246.

choral part of it. I was completely converted and have seldom enjoyed anything more. How *tonic* Beethoven is, and how festal – one has the feeling of having taken part in the revelry of giants. By the way, the Siegfried Idyll,[61] which we had in the same programme seems to me the dullest thing Wagner ever wrote: do you agree? The only successor to Wagner (since we've got onto that subject), the only man who has exercised the same enchantment over me since the old days, is Sibelius. This bent to 'Northern' things is quite real and one can't get over it – not that I ever thought of trying!

You would like this day. Behind the hill there is yellow early morning light and small clouds racing. Then, the bit of wood, bare and brown, and furiously agitated. Then, the pond half skinned with ice – the swans both ashore. And round the house a terrific wind is roaring – 'Arthur O'Bower has broken his band.'[62] In fact I have enjoyed the whole of this winter – especially after the really tropical summers.

The only member of the visiting family whose society we like is the boy, Michael, about 5. You will be interested to hear that W. gets on with him much better than I do. That is, I theoretically hold that one ought to like children, but am shy with them in practice: he theoretically dislikes them, but is actually the best of friends. (So many new sides to his character have appeared in the last few years.)

Minto reads him the Peter Rabbit books every evening, and it is a lovely sight. She reads very slowly and he gazes up into her eyes which look enormous through her spectacles – what a pity she has no grandchildren. Would you believe it, that child had never been read to nor told a story by his mother in his life? Not that he is neglected. He has a whole time Nurse (an insufferable semi-lady scientific woman with a diploma from some Tom-fool nursing college), a hundred patent foods, is spoiled, and far too expensively dressed: but his poor imagination has been left without any natural food at all. I often wonder what the present generation of children will grow up like (how many middle aged men in all generations have said this). They have been treated with so much indulgence yet so little affection, with so much science and so little mother-wit. Not a fairy tale nor a nursery rhyme.

---

61 Richard Wagner, *Siegfried Idyll*, first performed in 1870.

62 Beatrix Potter, *Squirrel Nutkin* (1903): 'Arthur O'Bower has broken his band,/He comes roaring up the land.'

Please thank your mother for her kind and forgiving letter; I was very rude to her. I should like to be at home in these gales. I am sure there are waves in the Lough, and the firs are lifting the earth in our old wood. I must stop now and do a little work. A happy Christmas to you all, and from all.

Yours,
Jack

TO OWEN BARFIELD (W):

Magdalen College,
Oxford.
[9? December 1935]

In the crescendo of horror at the end of the myth you have done what v. few people could now do.[63] About the greatness and truth of that part I have no doubts. In the earlier parts of the myth I had not been prepared for so large a satiric element and therefore had to make rapid re-adjustments: but of course the ordinary reader will not be in that position. There are lovely things all about the place – the honest Caliban, Ariel, Bottom, the luring voice that all old civilisations hear. (By the bye, you have been re-imbursing yourself pretty freely for 'sheep dotted downs'! – or else Dymer and English People have a common source).[64]

The Diary of an Old Soul is magnificent.[65] You placed the moment of giving it to me admirably. I remember with horror the absurdity of my last criticism of it, and with shame the vulgarity of the form in which I expressed it. He knows all about the interplay between the religious and metaphysical aspects of the One. I see now (since I began this letter) that these two are opposite only with the fruitful opposition of male & female (how deep the old erotic metaphor of the *proelia veneris* is) and what they beget is the solution.

Incidentally, since I have begun to pray, I find my extreme view of

---

63 Barfield had sent Lewis a copy of a verse-drama he had written, and which remains unpublished.

64 The words 'sheep-dotted downs' are found in Canto V, stanza 32 of Lewis's poem, *Dymer* (1926), and he discovered them in Barfield's unpublished novel, 'English People'.

65 Barfield gave Lewis a copy of George MacDonald's *The Diary of an Old Soul* (1885).

personality changing. My own empirical self is becoming more important and this is exactly the opposite of self love. You don't teach a seed how to die into treehood by throwing it into the fire: and it has to become a good seed before its worth burying.

As to my own book – the question whether notes shd. come at the end of the chapter or the bottom of the page is partly for publisher & printer.[66] Personally I loathe a book where they come at the end – and I am writing mainly for people who will want to know where they must look to verify my facts. Your other criticism about the two classes of readers whom I conflate, I don't understand. I meant this to be only a note.

Yours
C. S. Lewis

TO OWEN BARFIELD (W):

[Magdalen College
12? December 1935]

My dear Barfield

What a drivelling letter I wrote you a few days ago. A day in bed has given me the chance to re-read Pt IV and my opinions are revised. In every way the merits are *far* greater than I had seen, specially the myth of wh. the 'crescendo of horror' tho' perfectly adequate is, as I now perceive, the least excellence. You have done what you wanted – how you could get so much good tenderness & so much good sensuousness into prose is a mystery. There is of course a lot I don't follow – has the extraordinary jumble of Hindu with Mohameddan accessories any significance? But the whole thing is a real evocation.

Yrs
CSL

P.S. The 'Ah woe . . . kiss . . . ah woe' is astonishing. It's not like a *passage in a book* at all: it's a *thing*.

---

66 As Lewis mentions in the letter to Arthur Greeves of 29 December 1935, he was correcting the proofs of *The Allegory of Love*.

TO ARTHUR GREEVES (W):

[The Kilns]
29th. Dec. 1935

My dear Arthur,

I am staying at home from Church this morning with a cold on the chest, so it seems a good occasion to answer your letter.

As regards your news – sympathy and congratulations. Sympathy on the wrench of parting and the gap it will leave: congratulations on having done the right thing and made a sacrifice. The chief consolation at such times, I think, is that the result, however unpleasant, must be a kind of relief after the period of saying 'Shall I really have to – no I won't – and yet perhaps I'd better.' There is always some peace in having submitted to the right. Don't spoil it by worrying about the *result*s, if you can help it. It is not your business to succeed (no one can be sure of that) but to do right: when you have done so, the rest lies with God – and Will!

I don't think you exaggerate at all in your account of how it feels. After all – tho' our novels now ignore it – friendship is the greatest of worldly goods. Certainly to me it is the chief happiness of life. If I had to give a piece of advice to a young man about a place to live, I think I shd. say, 'sacrifice almost everything to live where you can be near your friends.' I know I am v. fortunate in that respect, and you much less so. But even for me, it wd. make a great difference if you (and one or two others) lived in Oxford.

I am correcting the first bunch of proofs for my book and am (as we wd. have said in the old days) tearing my hair because it doesn't look at all the size of page I expected. It will not be as *tall* a book as I had pictured – and what is the good of a scholarly work if it does not rise like a tower at the end of a shelf?! I fear it may even be thickish and stumpy. Mon Dieu! quel douleur, o rage, o desespoir! (What on earth would we have done if either of us had succeeded in publishing a book in the old days – I imagine we might have gone literally out of our minds with horrors and ecstasies.)

I'm sorry you didn't have our weather. We had about a week of snow with frost on top of it – and then rime coming out of the air and making thick *woolly* formations on every branch. The little wood was indescribably beautiful. I used to go and crunch about on the crusted snow in it every evening – for the snow kept it light long after sunset. It was a labyrinth of white – the smallest twigs looking thick as seaweed and building up a kind of cathedral vault overhead. One thing the snow showed me was the amazingly high population of rabbits – usually concealed among the greens and greys. On the snow one cd. see them scuttling. W. and I have been much puzzled by some of the footprints. There seem to be a great many more and larger animals than we had supposed. Bears, Arthur, bears – at least it looks like it. I wish you cd. have had a couple of strolls with me round this place in the snow: it would have charmed away all your sorrows.

No, no, I never meant that Sibelius had the *tonic* quality of Beethoven. Do you remember our once talking about B. and Wagner & agreeing that B. was Olympian, W. titanic – B spiritual, W. natural? Well Sibelius is definitely like W. not like B. in that respect. He is not *noble* like Beethoven: he is inarticulate, intimate, enthralling, and close to one, like Nature itself. Very, very *Northern*: he makes me think of birch forests & moss and salt-marshes and cranes and gulls. I mean the symphonies. You needn't be busied for music while you have a gramophone. Set aside a portion of your money for buying big works (symphonies etc): never play them except in their entirety – but perhaps I've given you all this good advice before.

I never finished *Gape Row*. But the descriptions of our own walks & hills were v. interesting. I thinkk yourr neww methodd of sspellingg bby ddoubbllingg alll cconnssonnannts ssavvess a ggreatt ddeall off ttroubbllle!

Please give my love to Mrs Greeves and remember me to all our friends.

Yours,
Jack

When I said you had vetoed the idea of regular correspondence, I meant that you had vetoed the idea of *your* taking part in it. I didn't mean you had actually *forbidden* me to write to you!!

1936

TO DOM BEDE GRIFFITHS (W):

The Kilns,
Headington Quarry,
Oxford.
Jan 8th 1936

My dear Griffiths,

Thank you for your kind and interesting letter. It must be nice to know some Aristotle, and it is a relief to hear that kind of philosophy praised by you who have a right to judge: for in the Oxford world 'Neo-Scholasticism' has become such a fashion among ignorant undergrads. that I am sick of the sound of it. A man who was an atheist two terms ago, and admitted into your Church last term, and who had never read a word of philosophy, comes to me urging me to read the *Summa*[1] and offering to lend me a copy!

By the way, I hope that the great religious revival now going on will not get itself too mixed up with Scholasticism, for I am sure that the revival of the latter, however salutary, must be as temporary as any other movement in philosophy. Of things on the natural level, now one, now another, is the ally or the enemy of Faith. The scientists have got us in such a muddle that at present rationalism is on our side, and enthusiasm is an enemy: the opposite was true in the 19th century and will be true again. I mean, we have no abiding city even in philosophy: all passes, except the Word.

I should be interested to see your Review of my little book.[2] I am afraid it will have misled you into thinking my position more catholic than it really is, and that not for a spiritual reason but a merely literary

1 The *Summa Theologica*, the chief dogmatic work of St Thomas Aquinas. See also note 7 to the letter to Griffiths of 4 April 1934.

2 Dom Bede's review of *The Pilgrim's Regress* is found in *Pax: The Monthly Review of the Benedictines of Prinknash, Glos.*, no. 172 (February 1936), pp. 262–3.

one. I did not want to keep introducing the Lord Himself, and 'Christianity' is not a plausible name for a character. Hence the name, and some of the functions, of my Mother Kirk – adopted clumsily for convenience, without my realising till I began to read my reviewers, that I had given a much more ecclesiastical bent to the whole thing than I had intended. You may say 'All the better'; but I tell you the facts to defend my honesty.[3] And by the same token, I fear Mr. Sheed is a rascal. That blurb on his jacket, insinuating that the book contains an attack on my own religious upbringing, was printed without my knowledge or authority, and he must have known it was a *suggestio falsi*: at least he took good care not to know!

Thank you for your prayers: you know mine too, little worth as they are. Have you found, or is it peculiar to me, that it is much easier to pray for *others* than for oneself. Doubtless because every return to ones own situation involves action: or to speak more plainly, obedience. That appears to me more and more the whole business of life, the only road to love and peace – the cross and the crown in one. Did you ever notice a beautiful touch in the Faerie Queene

> '*a groom them laid at rest in easie bedd,*
> *His name was meek Obedience.*'[4]

What indeed can we imagine Heaven to be but unimpeded obedience. I think this is one of the causes of our love of inanimate nature, that in it we see things which unswervingly carry out the will of their Creator, and are therefore wholly beautiful: and though their *kind* of obedience is infinitely lower than ours, yet the degree is so much more perfect that a Christian can see the reason that the Romantics had in feeling a certain holiness in the wood and water. The Pantheistic conclusions

---

3 Lewis did not know it at the time but Dom Bede criticized his use of 'Mother Kirk' in his review: 'unhappily his Mother Kirk is not in fact the true Mother Church. If we may be allowed to adopt his own allegory we would say that his Mother Kirk is an elder daughter of the old Mother Kirk, who ran away from her mother and eloped with one of the sons of Mammon nearly 400 years ago now, and though she fortunately retained many things with her which she took from Mother Kirk's household, and has since shown many signs of repentance and some desire to return, yet she still remains unreconciled and in bondage to the Spirit of the Age' (ibid.).

4 Spenser, *The Faerie Queene*, I, x, 17, adapted from lines 6–9.

they sometimes drew are false: but their feeling was just and we can safely allow it in ourselves now that we know the real reason.

Remember me to the Prior. Did I tell you that I have met both Waterman[5] & Skinner[6] and liked them v. much.

Yours
C. S. Lewis

TO DOM BEDE GRIFFITHS (W):

Magdalen College,
Oxford.
Feb 20th 1936

Dear Griffiths

Thanks very much for the copy of *Pax* and the too kind review of my little book.

One sentence in your letter has kept me chuckling ever since: 'you have no reason to fear that anything you say can have any serious effect on me'. The underlying assumption that anyone who knew you would feel such a fear is not only funny but excruciatingly funny . . . ask the Prior if he sees the joke: I rather think he will.

As to the main issue I can only repeat what I have said before. One of the most important differences between us is our estimate of the importance of the differences. You, in your charity, are anxious to convert me: but I am not in the least anxious to convert you. You think my specifically Protestant beliefs a tissue of damnable errors: I think your specifically Catholic beliefs a mass of comparatively harmless human tradition which may be fatal to certain souls under special conditions, but which I think suitable for you. I therefore feel no *duty* to attack you: and I certainly feel no *inclination* to add to my other works an epistolary controversy with one of the toughest dialecticians of my acquaintance, to which he can devote as much time and reading as he likes and I can devote very little. As well – who wants to debate with a man who begins by saying that no argument can possibly move

5 Hugh Waterman (1906–), who had been to Marlborough, matriculated at Magdalen in 1925 and, with Martyn Skinner, was Griffiths's closest friend at Oxford. After taking his BA in 1928 he spent his life as a farmer. For more about this charming man see Dom Bede Griffiths, *The Golden String* (1954).

6 Martyn Skinner (1906–93) and Lewis were to become friends a few years later. See Lewis's letter to Skinner of 23 April 1942.

him? Talk sense, man! With other Catholics I find no difficulty in deriving much edification from religious talk on the common ground: but you refuse to show any interest except in differences.

It was a great shock to learn that Thomism is now *de fide* for your Church – if that is what you mean. But is that really so? I should welcome a letter clearing the matter up – I don't mean clearing up the content of Thomism but the degree to which it has been made necessary to salvation.[7]

With continued good wishes.

Yours

C. S. Lewis

TO ARTHUR GREEVES (W):

Magdalen College,
Oxford.
Feb 26th 1936

My dear Arthur,

I see to my consternation that it is over a month since your letter came. It certainly deserved an earlier answer but you must forgive me.

I was very sorry indeed to hear about 'Tommy'. I am particularly sorry for John.[8] You know I crossed with the pair of them last time I left home: and I should like to say as impressively as I can – and you to take note – that I was very much impressed by seeing them together and by the fine, almost the spiritual atmosphere of their whole world

---

7 Lewis had misunderstood. In Catholic theology a proposition is said to be *de fide* ('of faith') if it has been expressly declared and defined by the Church to be true; there are, however, different degrees of certainty in Catholic theology. The highest order of certainty, *de fide catholica*, appertains to those truths, such as the inerrancy of the Bible, that are revealed by God and taught by the Church. When such a truth is solemnly defined by the pope or by a council it may also take the notation *de fide definita*, an example of this being the doctrine of the Immaculate Conception. Lewis had in mind Pope Leo XIII's encyclical *Aeterni Patris* (1879). However, one cannot apply '*de fide*' certainty to every word contained in the writings of St Thomas Aquinas; rather, it was the *wisdom* of St Thomas that Leo XIII wished to restore, as he said in *Aeterni Patris*, paragraph 31: 'We exhort you, venerable brethren, in all earnestness to restore the golden wisdom of St. Thomas . . . The wisdom of St. Thomas, We say; for if anything is taken up with too great subtlety by the Scholastic doctors, or too carelessly stated – if there be anything that ill agrees with the discoveries of a later age, or, in a word, improbable in whatever way – it does not enter Our mind to propose that for imitation to Our age.'

8 Tommy and John were Arthur's dogs.

of mountain climbing. It gave me a new and most favourable sidelight on John: and I am afraid it is most unlikely that he will find any one to take Tommy's place. I am very sorry for him. Try to be as nice to him as you can – but I have no doubt you are doing that already.

For yourself I expect days are pretty dim at present. Do you hear good news of the boy? As I said before, I am sure you have done the right thing, and I'm afraid that is all the comfort I can offer.

I quite understand what you say about the comfort derived from all a dog's 'little affairs', and enjoyed reading that passage as much as any in your letter. They are a *busy* folk. And talking of dogs, poor old Mr Papworth has been gathered to his fathers. He had been ailing for some time and finally got a bad ulcer on his chin. He was given a strong sleeping draught. When I went to bed he was asleep in his basket and breathing as gently as a child: in the morning he was dead. Minto has been very badly upset – almost as if for a human being. I don't feel it as badly as that myself and would discourage the feeling (I think) if I had it. But it is a parting, and one sometimes remembers his old happy days, especially his puppyhood, with an ache.

I have just read what I think a really great book, 'The Place of the Lion' by Charles Williams.[9] It is based on the Platonic theory of the other world in which the archtypes of all earthly qualities exist: and in the novel, owing to a bit of machinery which doesn't matter, these archtypes start sucking our world back. The lion of strength appears in the world & the strength starts going out of houses and things into him. The archtypal butterfly (enormous) appears and all the butterflies of the world fly back into him. But man contains and ought to be able to rule all these forces: and there is one man in the book who does, and the story ends with him as a second Adam 'naming the beasts' and establishing dominion over them.

It is not only a most exciting fantasy, but a deeply religious and (unobtrusively) a profoundly learned book. The reading of it has been a good preparation for Lent as far as I am concerned: for it shows me (through the heroine) the special sin of abuse of intellect to which all my profession are liable, more clearly than I ever saw it before. I have learned more than I ever knew yet about humility. In fact it has been a big experience. Do get it, and don't mind if you don't understand

9 Charles Williams, *The Place of the Lion* (1931).

everything the first time. It deserves reading over and over again. It isn't often now-a-days you get a *Christian* fantasy.

My own book will be 15/-, so if you can sell it it will be 15/- clear! I am sick of proof correcting which has had to go on concurrently with all my other work this whole term.[10]

Our visitors, thank God, are gone. They have left Minto very worn out but not, so far as I can see, actually ill.

We have had such a severe winter that even I, with all my polar bear instincts am tired of it. But the snow drops are up now and we have had one or two of those very early fine days which excite me more than the real spring. You know – that thin, tingling, virginal weather.

Most of Sibelius' symphonies are recorded and are glorious. I agree with you about the *Old Curiosity Shop*[11] – one of the most homely and friendly of all Dickens. With love to you all.

Yours
Jack

Since the early 1930s a group of Christian friends had been meeting in Lewis's Magdalen College rooms every Thursday evening to talk and usually to read aloud whatever they might be writing. The group had its origins in J. R. R. Tolkien's weekly visits to Lewis's rooms in 1929 where he read aloud his stories of Middle-Earth. Shortly afterwards, Edward Tangye Lean (1911–74),[12] *a brilliant young student and one of Lewis's pupils, founded a society of undergraduates and dons who met in his rooms to read unpublished manuscripts aloud, after which there would be comments and criticism. Lewis and Tolkien both became members. Lean christened the group 'The Inklings' – suggesting someone who dabbles in ink. The club founded by Lean died when he took his degree and left Oxford. But, wrote Professor Tolkien,*

> *Its name was transferred (by C.S.L.) to the undetermined and unelected circle of friends who gathered about C.S.L., and met in his rooms in Magdalen. Although our habit was to read aloud compositions of various kinds (and lengths!), this association and*

10 Lewis's 'own book' was *The Allegory of Love.*

11 Charles Dickens, *The Old Curiosity Shop* (1841).

12 See the biography of Edward Tangye Lean in *CG*.

> *its habit would in fact have come into being at this time, whether the original short-lived club had ever existed or not. C.S.L. had a passion for hearing things read aloud, a power of memory for things received in that way, and also a facility in extempore criticism, none of which were shared (especially not the last) in anything like the same degree by his friends.*[13]

By 1936 this informal group included Lewis, Tolkien, Warnie Lewis, Owen Barfield, Hugo Dyson, Nevill Coghill, Lord David Cecil,[14] *Dr Robert E. Havard*[15] *and Charles Wrenn.*[16] *Besides the Thursday meetings in Lewis's rooms in Magdalen, they met on Tuesday mornings at the Eagle and Child ('Bird and Baby') pub. Lewis's next letter was to a man he was keen to introduce to these friends.*

---

13 *The Letters of J. R. R. Tolkien*, ed. Humphrey Carpenter (1981), letter to William Luther White of 11 September 1967, p. 388.

14 Lord David Cecil (1902–86), second son of the fourth Marquess of Salisbury, taught Modern History and English Literature at Wadham College, 1924–30, leaving Oxford in 1930 to pursue literary work in London. He returned in 1939 to become Fellow of English at New College, a position he held until he became Goldsmith's Professor of English Literature in 1949. His numerous writings include a biography of William Cowper, *The Stricken Deer* (1929), as well as biographies of Lord Melbourne and Jane Austen. See his biography in *CG*.

15 Dr Robert Emlyn Havard (1901–85) took a First in Chemistry at Keble College in 1921. He became a Catholic shortly afterwards, and because of Keble's ban on Catholics, moved to Queen's College, Oxford, where he received a degree of Bachelor of Medicine. He practised at London Hospital and the Radcliffe Infirmary, Oxford, and then taught in the Biochemistry Department of Leeds University. He returned to Oxford in 1934 to take over a surgery in Headington and St Giles. Lewis became his patient in 1934 and soon afterwards Havard joined the Inklings. Lewis gave him the nickname 'Humphrey' after the doctor in *Perelandra*. See his biography in *CG*.

16 Charles Leslie Wrenn (1895–1969) became a lecturer in English Language at Oxford in 1930, where he helped J. R. R. Tolkien with the teaching of Anglo-Saxon. In 1939 he was appointed Professor of English Language and Literature at the University of London, where he remained until 1946. When Tolkien became Merton Professor of English Language and Literature, Wrenn returned to Oxford to replace him as Rawlinson and Bosworth Professor of Anglo-Saxon, a post he held until his retirement in 1963. His writings include an edition of *Beowulf* (1940), *The Poetry of Caedmon* (1947) and *A Study of Old English Literature* (1967). See his biography in *CG*.

TO CHARLES WILLIAMS (W):[17]

[Magdalen College]
March 11th 1936

[Dear Mr Williams,]

I never know about writing to an author. If you are older than I, I don't want to seem impertinent: if you are younger, I don't want to seem patronizing. But I feel I must risk it.

A book sometimes crosses ones path which is so like the sound of ones native language in a strange country that it feels almost uncivil not to wave some kind of flag in answer. I have just read your *Place of the Lion* and it is to me one of the major literary events of my life – comparable to my first discovery of George Macdonald, G. K. Chesterton, or Wm. Morris. There are layers and layers – first the pleasure that any good fantasy gives me: then, what is rarely (tho' not so very rarely) combined with this, the pleasure of a real philosophical and theological stimulus: thirdly, characters: fourthly, what I neither expected nor desired, substantial edification.

I mean the latter with perfect seriousness. I know Damaris very well: in fact I was in course of becoming Damaris (but you have pulled me up). That pterodactyl . . . I know all about him: and wanting not Peace, but (faugh!) 'peace for my work'. Not only is your diagnosis good: but the very way in which you force one to look at the matter is itself the beginning of a cure. Honestly, I didn't think there was anyone now alive in England who could do it.

Coghill of Exeter put me on to the book: I have put on Tolkien (the Professor of Anglo Saxon and a papist) and my brother. So there are three dons and one soldier all buzzing with excited admiration. We have a sort of informal club called the Inklings: the qualifications (as they have informally evolved) are a tendency to write, and Christianity. Can you come down some day next term (preferably *not* Sat. or Sunday), spend the night as my guest in College, eat with us at a chop

17 See **Charles Williams** in the Biographical Appendix. Williams, the author of seven 'supernatural thrillers' and numerous other works, was an employee of the Oxford University Press in London. All Lewis's letters to Charles Williams, with the exception of the one dated 22 February 1939, are transcripts believed to have been made by Williams from the originals, which are lost. These transcripts, as well as Williams's letter to Lewis of 12 March 1936, appear to have been typed on the same typewriter.

house, and talk with us till the small hours. Meantime, a thousand thanks.

[C. S. Lewis]

On 12 March Charles Williams wrote to Lewis from Oxford University Press, Amen House, London:

> *My dear Mr Lewis, If you had delayed writing another 24 hours our letters would have crossed. It has never before happened to me to be admiring an author of a book while he at the same time was admiring me. My admiration for the staff work of the Omnipotence rises every day.*
>
> *To be exact, I finished on Saturday looking – too hastily – at proofs of your* Allegorical Love Poem. *I had been asked to write something about it for travellers and booksellers and people so I read it first . . . I admit that I fell for the* Allegorical Love Poem *so heavily because it is an aspect of the subject with which my mind has always been playing; indeed I once wrote a little book called* An Essay in Romantic Theology, *which the Bishop of Oxford (between ourselves) shook his head over. So Amen House did not publish it, and I quite agree now that it was a good thing. For it was very young and rhetorical. But I still toy with the notion of doing something on the subject, and I regard your book as practically the only one that I have ever come across, since Dante, that shows the slightest understanding of what this very peculiar identity of love and religion means. I know there is Coventry Patmore, but he rather left the identity to be deduced.*
>
> *After vacillating a good deal I permit myself to believe in your letter and in the interests of the subject so far as to send you a copy of one of my early books of verse,*[18] *because the Poems from page 42 – page 81 may interest you. . . .*
>
> *You must be in London sometimes. Do let me know and come and have lunch or dinner . . . I should like very much to come to Oxford as you suggest; the only thing is that I am a little uncertain about next term because I may be at Canterbury off*

18 Charles Williams, *Poems of Conformity* (1917).

> *and on to see the rehearsals of the Play*[19] *I have written for the Friends of the Cathedral to do in June . . . You will conceive Cranmer as coming under a similar danger to that from which Damaris was saved by the Mercy. Do forgive this too long letter, but after all to write about your* Love Poem *and my* Lion *and both our Romantic Theology in one letter takes some paragraphs . . . P.S.2. And I am 49 – so you can decide whether that is too old or too young.*[20]

TO CHARLES WILLIAMS (W):

[Magdalen College]
March 23rd 1936

[Dear Williams,]

This is going to be a complicated matter. To make a clean breast of it, that particular species of romanticism which you found in my book and which is expressed in the poems[21] you send me, is not my kind at all. I see quite clearly why you think it is – the subject of the book, the at any rate respectful treatment of the sentiment, the apparently tell-tale familiarity with Coventry Patmore – it all fits in perfectly and must seem to you almost like a trap: while it shows me for the first time how paradoxical it is that I, of all men, should have elected, or been elected, to treat such a subject. I trust, however, that there has been no writing with (horror of horrors!) my tongue in my cheek. I think you will find that I nowhere commit myself to a definite approval of this blend of erotic and religious feeling. I treat it with respect: I display: I don't venture very far. And this is perhaps what one ought to expect from a man who is native in a quite distinct, though neighbouring, province of the Romantic country, and who willingly believes well of all her provinces, for love of the country herself, though he dare not affirm except about his own.

I hope you will find that where I talk of the value of the gods and, above all, of their death and resurrection, I speak much more confidently than I ever do of the Celestial and Terrestrial Cupids: there I am on my own ground. That's where I live.

---

19 Charles Williams, *Thomas Cranmer of Canterbury*, acting edn (Canterbury: H. J. Goulden, 1936).

20 Bodleian Library, MS. Eng. c. 6825, fols. 48–9.

21 i.e. Williams's *Poems of Conformity*.

I don't know how far I am making myself clear . . . the matter, at this stage in our knowledge of each other, is not easy. Put briefly, there is a romanticism which finds its revelation in love, which is yours, and another which finds it in mythology (and nature mythically apprehended) which is mine. Ladies, in the one: gods in the other – the bridal chamber, or the wood beyond the world – a service incensed with rich erotic perfume, a service smelling of heather, salt water etc.

But this distinction is a little complicated by two facts. 1. While writing about Courtly Love I have been so long a student of *your* province that I think, in a humble way, I am nearly naturalised. 2. In the book I am sending you (don't read it unless it interests) you will find lots about the frontier between sexual and religious experience.[22] But look to your feet, here. It really has nothing to do with your province: it is simply about desire, longing, the impersonal thing: which oddly enough can be diverted from the wood beyond the world (are you still following me?) into lust just as quickly as 'love' can. We shall have a great deal to talk about when we meet.

After this you will not be surprised to learn that I found your poems excessively *difficult*. I think I have followed *Ascension*.[23] I take it this deals with the death of passion into matrimonial routine and the discovery that this death is also a birth – the birth of something which is to passion as the Church is to the earthly life of Our Lord. Am I right? If so it is because we touch here: the death and re-birth motive being of the very essence of my kind of romanticism. If so, it is a good poem, specially stanzas 2 and 7. The *Christian Year*[24] I take to be on the same theme, but there are a lot of gaps in my understanding. What I liked best was the bit about the Shepherds at the top of page 73. This may quite possibly be even a great poem – I'll tell you in a year or so, if I find out. (And talking of years, I'm 37.) *Churches* I didn't like, except *that dear duplicity of love and Love* – which I suppose is the thing we're talking about. *Presentation* I liked, and the bit in *Gratia Plena* about the provincial dialect. *Orthodoxy* and *Ecclesia Docens* I definitely disliked. (I embrace the opportunity of establishing the precedent of brutal frankness, without which our acquaintance begun like this would easily

22 It was probably *The Pilgrim's Regress*.

23 Williams, *Poems of Conformity*, p. 78.

24 ibid.

be a mere butter bath!) But the thing I liked best of all came outside the 'pages prescribed for special study' – notably *Endings*, *The Clerk*, and *Ballade of a Street Door* (tho' I can't *construe* line 2).

I have read *Many Dimensions*[25] with an enormous enjoyment – not that it's as good as the *Lion*, but then in a sense it hardly means to be. By Jove, it is an experience when this time-travelling business is done by a man who really thinks it out. I believe all your conclusions do really follow – and I never thought of being caught in that perpetual to-and-fro. The effect which that first idea of a really possible hell has on Lord Thingummy is excellent.

I shouldn't dream of coming to London without visiting you, but I can and do dream of not being in London for a long time. But Canterbury can't claim you all the time, and there are others besides me who want to meet you. The fourth week of next term (May 18th–May 22nd) would be a good time. Could we nail you *now* for a week day night between those dates? Of course, I realise that this letter, for more than one cause, may have quenched all wish for a meeting: but acting on the pleasanter hypothesis –

[C. S. Lewis]

P.S. Thanks for the very kind and intelligent *blurb*[26] – a relief, after the nonsensical one put out from Walton Street! But not a word, he[27] may have been doing his best.

TO DOM BEDE GRIFFITHS (W):

[Magdalen College]
April 24th [1936]

My dear Griffiths –

I was more than usually glad to hear from you this time because I had been feeling that my last letter was somewhat ill tempered. If so, forgive me. The truth is that I have a constant temptation to over asperity as soon as I get a pen in my hand, even when there is no subjective anger to prompt me: it comes, I think, simply from the pleasure of using the English language forcibly – i.e. is not a species of

25 Charles Williams, *Many Dimensions* (1931).

26 On the cover of *The Allegory of Love*.

27 Sir Humphrey Milford.

Ira but of *Sapientia*.[28] This problem of the pleasure in what Aristotle called an 'unimpeded activity' is one that exercises me very much – not of course in an instance like the one I have just been discussing where it is plainly abused, but when the work done is a duty, or at least innocent.

On the one hand, Nature, whether we will or know [not], attaches pleasure to doing as well as we can something we can do fairly well: and as it is a clear duty to practise all virtuous activities until we can do them well – possess the Habit of doing them – it is a sort of duty to increase such pleasures. On the other hand, they are pleasures of a particularly urgent, absorbing sort, very apt to become idols, and very closely allied to Pride. I heard it recently said in a Lenten sermon that even self-denial can become a kind of hobby – and in a way it is true.

Put in another form, the question is how you decide whether an ability and strong propensity for some activity is a temptation or a vocation. You will answer that it all depends whether we can and do offer it to God. But frankly – and I want your answer very much – have you made any approaches to a state in which the conscious offering to God can be maintained *concurrently* with the actual donkey work of doing the job? I find that I can do those things (even) which I believe that God wills me to do (such as writing this letter) by forgetting God while I do them. I don't mean forgetting intellectually (which wd. be absurd in the present instance) but turning away – not offering. Is this due to sin or to the very nature of human consciousness?

About the Scholastics, I must have expressed myself very badly if you thought I held that one system of philosophy was as good as another or that pure reason was mutable. All I meant was that no philosophy is perfect: nor can be, since, whatever is true of Reason herself, in the human process of reasoning there is always error and even what is right, in solving one problem, always poses another. I therefore reject the idea of any real *philosophia perennis*.[29] The dominance (and revival) of particular philosophy does seem to me to have historical causes. In any age, foolish men want that philosophy whose truths they

---

28 *Ira* is the Latin word for anger or wrath, one of the seven deadly sins; *Sapientia* is the Latin word for wisdom.

29 'enduring' or 'perennial philosophy'. The expression comes from the sixteenth-century theologian, Augustine Steuch (1497–1548), and was popularized by the German philosopher, Gottfried Wilhelm Leibniz (1646–1716).

least need and whose errors are most dangerous to them: and wise men want the opposite. In the next age neither fools nor wise want the same.

My original point was that Scholasticism could hardly have had its present prestige in an age like the 19th century when hard thinking seemed to be on the side of materialism: then the business of Christian philosophy was to remind people that there is something which escapes discursive thought. For the moment, the collapse of scientific dogmatism and the growth of a kind of spurious mysticism among anti-Christian thinkers (Heavens! *you* ought to know all about it) has reversed the situation. But don't think this state of affairs will be more permanent than any other. Reason, no doubt, is always on the side of Christianity: but that amount and kind of human reasoning which gives an age its dominant intellectual tone, is surely sometimes on one side and sometimes on the other.

Again, we must believe that there is no real conflict between the Rational and the Mystical: but in a given period now one, now the other, will be what the world actually needs to be most reminded of – I mean the unbelieving world: and one *or* the other will usually be the bridge to faith. Thus you and I came to it chiefly by Reason (I don't mean, of course, that any one comes at all but by God's grace – I am talking about the route not the motive power) but dozens of other converts, beginning with St. Paul, did not.

I have often wished I had time to learn Hebrew, but I think it would be for me more an indulgence than a duty. I should like to hear more about your doctrine of sophistication: I am inclined to think you may be right, but one would have to define 'sophistication' carefully. I certainly suppose (but this may be ignorance) that the Hebrew scriptures are the *only* document of religion carried to the very highest sub-Christian height, while remaining as anthropomorphic as primitive polytheism . . . What a bugbear 'anthropomorphism' used to be! How long it repelled me from the truth! Yet now that one has submitted to it how easy is the burden, how light the yoke.[30] Odd too, that the very things we thought proofs of our humility while we were philosophers, now turn out to be forms of pride.

30 Matthew 11:29–30: 'Take my yoke upon you, and learn of me; for I am meek and lowly in heart: and ye shall find rest for your souls. For my yoke is easy, and my burden is light.'

Sayer – pray for Sayer.[31] He is just what I was at a slightly earlier age than his: at the mercy of something which is innocent in itself (the desire to be liked) but which, unresisted, leads to ludicrous vanity, pretentiousness, and direct, pitiful lying. Yet he is likable because of the one redeeming trait that he really knows himself to be (at present) rather a little tick: oh, and the good side of his ruling passion, which is a peculiar accessibility to shame. All this, of course, is very much in confidence.

I re-read St. Augustine's *Confessions* during Lent, and found it better than I remember, tho' still it is the explicitly devotional parts that edify me least. I'll see if I can let you have a copy of my book if you want it. But the main subject is the rise of a romantic conception of sexual love and the transition from adultery to marriage as the normal channel for it: i.e. it would be an odd book to find in a monastery.

Write again. Write at the end of every term when I shall have a bright new Vac. to answer in.

Yours,
C.S.L.

TO ARTHUR GREEVES (W):

Magdalen College,
Oxford.
May 1st 1936

My dear Arthur,

I must confess it would not have been a good time for you to turn up. *Why* will you insist on coming to England in vacations and summers? If you would only come in the Autumn term (Oct 11th–Dec. 5th) I would try to make you comfortable in college: and I don't need to breakfast so early now. About the Kilns, I am sorry: I know that for many reasons it can never be a comfortable house for you to stay in.

I shall be free on and after June 27th and would come any time you suggested. I look forward to it with enormous pleasure – tho' rather

31 George Sayer (1914–) read English with Lewis, and took his BA from Magdalen in 1938. He served in the Army during the Second World War, and in 1949 became the senior English master at Malvern College. He retired in 1974. Over the years he became a close friend of Lewis, and is the author of *Jack: C. S. Lewis and his Times* (1988). See his biography in *CG*.

ashamed that I can make so little return. I trust you won't be packing all the time I'm with you!

Oddly enough I read *Aerial*[32] too, and in the same edition a few weeks ago – good fun. I don't know how far it is reliable.

No time to write now. Please let me have a line saying which dates after the 27th wd. suit you. Is the enclosed good? – I can't help hoping not. I shall be sending you my book in a week or so. Love to all

Yours,
Jack

The Allegory of Love: A Study in Medieval Tradition *was published by the Clarendon Press of Oxford on 21 May 1936.*

TO DOM BEDE GRIFFITHS (W):

[Magdalen College]
May 23rd 1936

Dear Griffiths

I am very surprised that your old anti-intellectualism should be so active – and yet perhaps I should not be since it is often said that conversion alters only the direction not the character of our minds. (This, by the bye, is very important and explains how personal and affectional relations between human souls can recognisably survive even in the full blaze of the beatific vision: and that if we are both saved I shall find you to all eternity in one sense still the same old Griffiths – indeed *more* the same than ever).

I don't agree. In the first place, I question your account of Our Lord, when you say 'He is essentially a poet and not at all a philosopher.' Surely the 'type of mind' represented in the human nature of Christ (and in virtue of His humanity we may, I suppose, neither irreverently nor absurdly speak of it as a 'type of mind') stands at just about the same distance from the poetic as from the philosopher. The overwhelming majority of His utterances are in fact addressed neither to thought nor to the imagination, but to the 'heart' – i.e. to the will and the affections: that is, the type is that of the φρονιμος[33] (as opposed to the σοφος),[34]

32 John H. Bone, *The Aerial: A Comedy in One Act* (1932).

33 'prudent'.

34 'clever'.

the hortatory and advisory practical moralist. I shudder to use so bleak a word as 'moralist', but I think it less untrue than 'poet' or 'philosopher'.

You will say that it approaches the poetic in the parables. But this is only an approach: it would (on my view) be an entirely misdirected reverence that would on that basis call him a poet. The parables approach poetry just about as much [as] His argumentative utterances approach philosophy. And it is easy to make too little of these latter. After all, how full of argument, of repartee, even of irony, He is. The passage about the denarius ('whose image and superscription');[35] the dilemma about John's baptism;[36] the argument against the Sadducees from the words 'I am the God of Jacob etc';[37] the terrible, yet almost humorous, trap laid for his Pharisaic host ('Simon, I have something to say to you');[38] the repeated use of the *â fortiori* ('If . . . , how much more');[39] and the appeals to our reason ('Why do not ye of yourselves judge what is right?')[40] – surely in all these we recognise as the human and natural vehicle of the Word's incarnation a mental complexion in which a keen-eyed peasant *shrewdness* is just as noticeable as an imaginative quality – something in other words quite as close (on the natural level) to Socrates as to Aeschylus.

Even about the parables I want to make a point. It is a commonplace that Our Lord, in them, often paradoxically chooses to illustrate the ways of God by the acts not of good men, but of bad men. But surely this means that the mode in which the fable represents its truth is intellectual rather than imaginative – like a philosopher's *illustration* rather than a poet's *simile*. The unjust judge,[41] to the imagination, presents no likeness of God – carries into the story no divine flavour or colour (as the Father of the Prodigal Son,[42] for instance, does). His likeness to God is purely for the intellect. It is a kind of proportion sum – A:B::C:D.

---

35 Matthew 22:20.

36 ibid., 21:25: 'The baptism of John, whence was it? from heaven, or of men?'

37 ibid., 22:32.

38 Luke 7:40.

39 Matthew 6:30, Luke 12:28.

40 Luke 12:56–7: 'Ye hypocrites, ye can discern the face of the sky and of the earth; but how is it that ye do not discern this time? Yea, and why even of yourselves judge ye not what is right?'

41 ibid., 18:2–6.

42 ibid., 15:11–32.

I therefore on the whole reject any divine authority which your anti-intellectualism seems to draw from the person of Our Lord. I also deny that the ordinary man, with his mind full of images and poor in concepts, is really any nearer to the poet than to the philosopher. For the poet uses images as such, because they are images: the ordinary man (that is, all of us from most of our waking hours) uses them *faute de mieux*[43] to attain knowledge, i.e. his end is the same as the philosopher's. What is functional in the poet is merely an accidental imperfection in the plain man. Surely the process of mistaking an image for a concept is quite different from that of using images for their proper purposes: processes are distinguished teleologically. Should I be a surgeon because, lacking a knife, I one day used a lancet to cut up my dinner? To be a surgeon means to use a surgeon's tools not anyhow but surgically – you can find all this in Aristotle.

Nor does any sane man, however 'plain', use images for thought quite as much as you suggest. His thought is accompanied by images but he is quite well aware that it is not *about* them he thinks – e.g. he knows perfectly well that the things he believes about London are not true of his image of London, which may be a mere huddle of roofs.

Again, if you are suggesting that the Hebrew consciousness was just right and the Greek just wrong, this seems to me to be quite foreign to the tenor of St. Paul's teaching. He seems to hold quite definitely (a) That Our Lord has 'broken down the middle wall of partition and made one Man',[44] wh. is quite different from simply bringing errant Hellenism back to Hebraic rectitude (b) That the 'reasonings' of the Pagans (see *Romans*) are related to the new Faith much as the Jewish Law is.[45] In *Galatians* he even seems to equate the Pagan bondage to the στοιχεια with Jewish bondage to the Law.[46]

I know they dispute what στοιχεια means, whether elemental powers (gods, angels) or 'rudiments' in the educational sense: but surely it is clear that it means both, that St. Paul is using a *double entendre*. For the 'rudiments' meaning is demanded by III 25, IV 1–3: and the other by IV 3 (τοῦ κοσμου) and 8. In fact the whole relation between

43 'for want of any better alternative'.

44 Ephesians 2:14–15.

45 Romans 2.

46 Galatians 4.

Paganism and Judaism wh. I hinted [at] in my *Regress* is quite Pauline – more so than I really knew at the time.[47] The great thing is to stick to the 'one Man'. That is why I have a great objection to any theory that would set parts of us at loggerheads with one another. It is a kind of προσωποληψία.[48] The Pagans, by their lights, may wisely have constructed a hierarchical scheme of Man, Reason ruling Passion politically and Soul ruling body despotically. But in Christ there is neither male nor female, bond nor free.[49] If the whole man is offered to God, all disputes about the value of this or that faculty are, as it were, henceforward out of date.

You said in your letter (going further than some would go) that every natural desire *per se* shd. be regarded as an attraction of grace. But if so, how much more every natural faculty!

This view of yours about desire is, I suppose, Augustinian. *Habe caritatem et fac quod vis.*[50] This is certainly sound, but not perhaps very practical: for it implies *Donec caritatem habens, noli facere quod vis.*[51] I wholly agree with what you say about escaping from the circle of morality into the love of God: in fact you have written an excellent commentary on St. Paul's view of the 'Law'. But in the meantime?

---

47 *The Pilgrim's Regress* (1933; Fount, 1998), book 8, ch. 8, pp. 191–2. 'The Pagans couldn't read . . . but they had pictures . . . And then the Pagans made mistakes. They would keep on trying to get the same picture again: and if it didn't come, they would make copies of it for themselves . . . They went on making up more and more stories for themselves about the pictures, and then pretending the stories were true . . . The Shepherds could read: that is the thing to remember about them. And because they could read, they had from the Landlord, not pictures but Rules.'

48 'respect of persons'.

49 Galatians 3:28.

50 'Have charity, and do as you will.' St Augustine nowhere uses this sentence in precisely these words. The words *Habe caritatem* are taken from his *Sermon 78*, ch. 6. The phrase *et fac quod vis* seems to be a conflation taken from Augustine's *Commentary on the First Letter of John*, Book 10, ch. 8, where he writes, '*dilige et quod vis fac*' – 'Cherish, and do as you will.' The conflation of these two components is probably the product of St Thomas Aquinas's faulty memory, since he says precisely what Lewis quotes and attributes this to Augustine in his sermon on the Beatitudes. Lewis may have been remembering a quotation from St Thomas, who, in turn, had misquoted Augustine.

51 'Until you have charity, do not do as you will.' This is Lewis's gloss and expansion of the Augustinian phrase.

This letter is getting too long: the subject has endless ramifications, but I will wait for your next. Rejoice with me – timidly, for it is only the first streak of dawn and may be false dawn – there are faint signs of a movement away from Anthroposophy in Barfield.

Yours
C. S. Lewis

TO LEO BAKER (BOD):

Magdalen College
June 24th /36

My dear Baker

I should have hesitated to send you the book[52] if I had known that it would find you in pain and by the need to acknowledge it lay a new burden on you. The book itself, I fear, is more than a grasshopper – as I find from this dialogue between myself and the Merton Professor of English[53] – more or less my 'chief' as they would say in the disciplined professions.

> *P. Well, Lewis, you've certainly gone beyond the whole English school with your new book.*
> *L. (Blushing at the supposed extremity of the compliment) Oh, really –*
> *P. Oh clearly.* Much *the longest book any of us has written.*
> *L. (With ghastly laughter) Oh surely not. I can understand it* seeming *the longest.*
> *P. No, no, there's no seeming about it. It is a very long book. (Pause) A very long book indeed.*
> *L. Come, it's not as long as X.*
> *P. X? It's half as long again. Far longer than X.* Far *longer.*
>
> (And so on)

---

52 Lewis had sent Baker a copy of *The Allegory of Love.*

53 David Nichol Smith (1875–1962) was educated at the University of Edinburgh. He was appointed to a readership at Oxford in 1908 where he gave valuable help in organizing the English School. In 1921 he became a Fellow of Merton College and was Merton Professor of English Literature, 1929–46. Much of his work was turned towards the eighteenth century, and included *Shakespeare in the Eighteenth Century* (1928) and *Some Observations on Eighteenth Century Poetry* (1937).

I am greatly distressed to hear that you are still suffering. Is it possible that the doctors can have a man so long in their hands and find out so little about him. It is indeed a comfort that the number of serious diseases which you know you have *not* got must be higher – far higher than anything the ordinary person in health could boast of. I take it, if the arthritis diagnosis is correct, the pain is the main thing i.e. that it hurts out of all proportion to the harm it will do. Am I right?

I must confess I have not myself yet got beyond the stage of feeling physical pain as the worst of evils. I am the worst person in the world to help anyone else to support it. I don't mean that it presents quite the intellectual difficulties it used to, but that my nerves even in imagination refuse to move with my philosophy. In my own limited experience the sufferer himself nearly always towers above those around him: in fact, nothing confirms the Christian view of this world so much as the treasures of patience and unselfishness one sees elicited from quite commonplace people when the trial really comes. Age, too – nearly everyone improves as he gets old, if this is a 'vale of soul making',[54] it seems to, by round and by large, to be working pretty well. Of course I can't hazard a guess why you should be picked out for this prolonged suffering.

I am told that the great thing is to *surrender* to physical pain – I mean not to do what's commonly called 'standing' it, above all not to brace the soul (which usually braces the muscles as well) not to try to ignore it: to be like earth being ploughed not like marble being cut. But I have no right to discuss such things on the basis of my very limited experience.

You were talking about Peele[55] when you last wrote. Personally I find Renaissance poetry on the whole less and less attractive as time goes on. When it succeeds ('His thunder is entangled in my hair' – 'Take but thy lute and make the mountains dance')[56] it has a wonderful gloss

---

54 John Keats, *Letters*, ed. Maurice Buxton Forman (1931; 4th edn 1952), Letter 123 to George and Georgiana Keats, 14 February–3 May 1819, pp. 334–5: 'Call the world if you Please "The vale of Soul-making". Then you will find out the use of the world . . . There may be intelligences or sparks of divinity in millions – but they are not souls till they acquire identities, till each one is personally itself.'

55 George Peele (1556–96) of London was educated at Christ Church, Oxford. He wrote pageants, plays and verse. His *Life and Works* were edited by C. T. Prouty (3 vols., 1952–70).

56 George Peele, *David and Bethsabe* (1599), 1169, 1648.

on; but even then I prefer the dull finish – something either *humbler* or *harder*. When it fails –! Did you notice how Peele allows Venus to describe Helen in the *Arraignement of Paris*? If not look on p. 319 of my book (the very long one).[57]

I think probably the greatest influence on my purely literary taste since the old days has been old Germanic poetry, which, as a friend says, sometimes makes everything else seem a little thin and half hearted. There is a metre in Icelandic called the *Drapa* which goes like this:

Wildest brunt of winter
Woke amidst the oak-wood

(This isn't meant to make sense) First you have the three alliterations (wild – wint – woke). Then you have the half-rhyme (consonantal but not vocalic) of -unt and -int. Then you have the full rhyme woke–oak. All these features are required to make a couplet. And note well – the beats must be *long in quantity* as well as accented: i.e.

Wildest broth of weather

would be unmetrical. This sounds mere puzzle poetry. In fact it works up a storm of sound which, when combined, as it usually is, with a tragic theme, and contrasting its rock-like form with the vain liquidity of sorrow, produces an almost unbearable tension of stoical pathos – 'iron tears down Pluto's cheek.'[58] W. H. Auden (one of the few good young poets) has caught something of it in places. You might try hammering one out some night when sleep is denied: but the thing is so difficult to our metrical habits, that you won't finish it by morning.

But I don't know why I have digressed into Icelandic prosody. More to the points – read any of Charles Williams' novels (Gollancz) which you can get hold of – specially *The Place of the Lion* and *Many*

57 *The Allegory of Love*, pp. 318–19: '[Spenser] wrote in an age when English poetry had reached its stylistic nadir, the age of "hunting the letter", of violent over-emphasis and exquisitely bad taste, the age in which that most ignoble metre, the Poulter's measure, was popular. . . . It was an age in which even Peele could make Venus speak thus to Paris in description of Helen: "A gallant girl, a lusty minion trull,/That can give sport to thee thy bellyful." '

58 John Milton, *Il Penseroso* (1645), 105.

Dimensions. In the rare genre of 'theological shocker' which Chesterton (I think) invented, these are superb. On the first level they are exciting stories: beyond that, the philosophical implications are extremely interesting: finally he has the power (absolutely unknown in our generation) of painting *virtue.* His morally best characters are his artistically best. The fact that Gollancz publishes them (in lurid covers) suggests that all this substantial edification – for it is nothing less – must be reaching the ordinary thriller-reader. If so, I may be telling you about a historical event of the first moment.

I think it is hospitality heroical on your own part and that of your wife to ask guests to a sick-house. Do accept my real (not conventional) thanks for this very great kindness. But I can't well come. I am busy this vac. with work undertaken at haste and now to be repented – not heaven knows, at leisure, but at length: and such breaks as I shall take have to be concerted with a good many other people's plans. But I hope some lawful occasion will take me your way sooner or later. Till then, better health,

Yours truly,
C. S. Lewis

TO OWEN BARFIELD (W):

[The Kilns]
June 28th 1936

My dear Barfield

1. I lent *The Silver Trumpet*[59] to Tolkien and hear that it is the greatest success among his children that they have ever known. His own fairy-tales, which are excellent, have now no market: and its first reading – children are so practical! – led to a universal wail 'You're not going to give it back to Mr. Lewis, are you?'

All the things which the wiseacres on child psychology in our circle said when you wrote it turn out to be nonsense. 'They liked the sad parts', said Tolkien 'because they were sad and the puzzling parts because they were puzzling, as children always do.' The youngest boy liked Gamboy because 'she was clever and the bad people in books usually aren't.' The tags of the Podger have become so popular as to be almost a nuisance in the house. In fine, you have scored a direct hit.

59 Owen Barfield's fairy tale, *The Silver Trumpet*, was published in 1925.

2. After the sugar, the rhubarb. Can you *repeat* the poem on the dedication you sent me? I liked it immensely, not only, I hope, for the intimacy, but for the *felicity* (not hitherto the commonest excellence in your work or mine): but after keeping it on my table for about ten days with the intention of copying it onto the fly leaf of the book, I cannot find it high or low. I am very, very sorry.

3. I wish I could Christianise the *Summa*[60] for you – but I dunno, I dunno! When a truth has ceased to be a mistress for pleasure and become a wife for fruit it is almost unnatural to go back to the dialectic ardours of the wooing. There may come a moment – one of those recoveries of virginity, or to speak more suitably to the subject, one of those Nth deaths, and then I'll try

4. We must exchange week end visits this Vac: I am ready to begin discussing dates.

5. Cecil now has *The Place of the Lion*: get it out of him before he returns it to me. And read *The Castle* by Kafka[61] (Secker).

Yours
The Alligator of Love[62]

TO CECIL HARWOOD (BOD):

Magdalen College
Oxford
[? July 1936]

My dear Harwood

How nice to get poems again! It was a bit of a shock to find you writing vers libre just as if you were beardless and modern, but that poem is the best of the three all the same: specially the second stanza ('there is no rainbow'[63] 'light like fine sand'[64] are lovely[)]. The first doesn't work with me because I never have resisting lids nor close them

60 i.e. Lewis's unpublished 'Great War' document. See note 35 to the letter to Barfield of 16 March 1932.

61 Franz Kafka, *The Castle* (London: Secker and Warburg, 1926).

62 Playing on the title of *The Allegory of Love*, which is dedicated to Barfield, this signature is accompanied by the drawing of an alligator serenading a young lady in a castle. The word-play is based on the malapropism 'allegories in the Nile'.

63 *The Voice of Cecil Harwood: A Miscellany*, ed. Owen Barfield (London: Rudolf Steiner Press, 1979), 'Day and Night', stanza 2, 2.

64 ibid., 6.

consciously and my eyes at bedtime are hungry for darkness not light.[65]

The *Hero* etc is also good. The third one is not quite a success to my mind. *Makes his room* for *makes his room here* or *makes this his room* creaks rather, and the rest has the opposite fault – too facile. It is a good subject of course.

There was a young person of Streatham
Who said to his friends when he met 'em
'Old Lewis is dyin'
For The Place of the Lion
But I keep *people's books once I get 'em.'*

Have a heart!
Yours
C. S. Lewis

Ubi est leonis locus?
Caecilii lar et focus![66]

TO DOM BEDE GRIFFITHS (W):

[Magdalen College
28 July 1936]

My dear Griffiths

First, about the PS in your letter. I think both your old attitude to poetry (when you looked for religion in it) and your present one (in which you reject it as a bridge you have now finally crossed) are equally based on an error common to all modern critics – that of taking poetry as a substantive thing like chemistry or agriculture.

Surely the truth is that poetry is simply a special kind of speech, a way of saying things, and one can no more talk about poetry in the abstract than about 'saying'. When what the poet is saying is religious, poetry is simply a part of religion. When what he says is simply entertaining, poetry is a form of entertainment. When what he says is wicked, poetry is simply a form of sin. Whenever one is talking, if one begins

65 ibid., stanza 1, 4–6: 'I shut consciously the lids of my eyes,/I spiritually close the gates of the sense of hearing,/I forget all touch and taste and the intake of breath and I wait.'

66 'Where is "The Place of the Lion"?/The home and hearth of Cecil!'

to utilize rhythm, metaphor, association etc, one is beginning to use 'poetry': but the whole place of that poetry in the scheme of things depends on what you are talking about. In fact, in a sense there is no such thing as poetry. It is not an element but a *mode*. Of course poetry falls out of sight in the highest levels of devotion; but only in the same way in which other forms of expression (work, gestures etc) also fall out of sight. Most people who talk about Poetry in the abstract are, I think, οὐδὲν λέγοντες.[67]

I have not made up my mind about Mysticism. Two things give me pause. *1.* That the similarity between Christian and non Christian mysticism is so strong. I by no means conclude from this that it is un-Christian in the sense of being incompatible with Christianity: but I am inclined to think that it is not *specifically* Christian – that it is simply one of those neutral things which the Spirit utilises in a given man when it happens to be there. I.e. it may be a given man's vocation to approach God mystically because he has the mystical faculty, but only in the same way as it is another man's duty to serve God by driving a plough because he is a good ploughman. And if any one tried to impose mysticism as the *norm* of Christian life I suspect he would be making the same mistake as one who said we ought all to be fishermen because some of the apostles were.

2. I am struck by the absence of much mysticism from the New Testament. I am not, I hope, forgetting which is the first and great commandment – but you would probably agree that the mystic's way of obeying it is not the only way.

I quite agree with you that the *change* which even the greatest saint must undergo (how much more, we) in being redeemed is beyond all imagination: I take καινη κτίσις[68] in as serious sense as I am able. But *1.* the new man must still be in some sense the same, or else salvation has no meaning. The very ideas of *conversion* and *regeneration* are essentially different from the idea of substitution. Also, don't we actually see it beginning in this life – I mean the turning round of the very same aptitudes which previously determined the kind of sin.

2. I object to your saying 'What is of real value in us is that which is hidden from each other and *even from ourselves*'. I would have said

67 'saying nothing'. The phrase is a catch-phrase in Plato, as in *Apology* 18, b, 2.
68 'a new foundation'. The reference is to 2 Corinthians 5:17 and Galatians 6:15.

'From ourselves and *even from each other*'. That is, I think that when A loves B, tho' A's picture of B is doubtless very unlike the redeemed B, I suppose it to be much less unlike than B's picture of himself. For we have often agreed, haven't we, that one can love nothing but good – sin consisting in the love of the inferior good at the expense of the superior. And if so, what we really love in our friend (in so far as we do love *him*, not the pleasure he gives us) must be the good in him. Would it not follow that the redeemed B will differ from B as we now know him not by being simply strange but by being that of which we should say 'Ah – he is himself at last'?

By the way (tho' it is a little irrelevant), I am astonished at the reward in *knowledge* given here and now to even very feeble attempts at obedience. I have found once or twice lately that whenever I succeed in beating down my selfish point of view and make an approach to charity, the motives and feelings of all the other people concerned become transparent: and things about them which one didn't know a moment before, stare one in the face. Is this self deception? If not, I would put it this way. *Tout comprendre c'est tout pardonner* is a false maxim with a strong tendency to promote the wrong kind of forgiveness: the really true and fruitful maxim is the converse – *tout pardonner c'est tout comprendre.*[69]

I can't go into your questions about prayer. I don't find that thinking about prayer (I mean in that introspective way) helps me to pray. Of course philosophical thought about it with a view to answering the common objections is another matter. On the whole, you know, I feel that self-examination should be confined to examining one's *conduct*. One's *state* in general I don't think one knows much about. But this is all very tentative.

Yours
C. S. Lewis

---

69 In his letter to Arthur Greeves of 14 February 1920 (*CL* I, p. 475), Lewis wrote: 'When a thing is explained it loses half its nastiness, "tout comprende [sic] c'est tout pardonner."' The expression comes from Madame de Staël (1766–1817), who said in *Corinne* (1807), book 18, ch. 5, 'Tout comprendre rend très indulgen' ('To understand everything makes one very indulgent'). The first expression used by Lewis, 'tout comprendre c'est tout pardonner' ('to understand everything is to forgive everything') is also attributed to Madame de Staël, while 'tout pardonner c'est tout comprendre' means 'to forgive everything is to understand everything'.

P.S. I had a long talk with Barfield who admits that his views are in 'a very liquid condition'. Perhaps our wish is going to be granted.

TO R. W. CHAPMAN (T):[70]

[The Kilns]
Aug 20th 1936

My dear Chapman

Thanks for both letters. After wondering whether the best reply to the 'pinpricks' would not be 'Ah yes – that's the worst of depending on these *local printers*!', I accept them all except *sheows*[71] which is Spenser's own spelling. I will also add two more, worse,

p 96 quotation l 5. for *ye* read *He*.

p 331 5 lines before the first quotation for *pictures* read *pictured*.

Yes – Cissie and Flossie do appear in Tasso and I trust it doesn't matter though I'd just as soon they didn't.[72] But I don't mind about the lovely lay – it is just the sort of enervating Omar Khyyam stuff you ought to find there.

'Puryfying complexities' – the next time you come across a real commercial pornogram in a French bookshop read a page or two and note how it all depends on isolating *one* nerve in a way quite impossible in real life – in fact is just as conventional (tho' for a worse purpose) as roaring farce.

Smoky rain is alright seasoned with sufficient usquebaugh – see *Waverley*![73]

Yours
C. S. Lewis

---

70 Robert William Chapman (1881–1960), secretary to the delegates of Oxford University Press, 1920–42, was the editor of *The Allegory of Love*. He took a First in *Literae Humaniores* from Oriel College, Oxford, in 1906, after which he began working for the Clarendon Press. He was the editor of Jane Austen's novels and letters, and his many distinguished books include *Jane Austen – A Critical Bibliography* (1953) and an edition of *The Letters of Samuel Johnson with Mrs Thrale's Genuine Letters to Him*, 3 vols. (1952).

71 *The Allegory of Love*, p. 336. The reference is to Spenser, *The Faerie Queene*, III, vii, 29.

72 ibid., p. 331: 'Acrasia's two young women (their names are obviously Cissie and Flossie) are ducking and giggling in a bathing-pool for the benefit of a passer-by: one does not need to go to fairy land to meet them.'

73 Scott, *Waverley*, ch. 6: 'The laird was only rejoiced that his worthy friend, Sir Everard Waverley of Waverley-Honour, was reimbursed of the expenditure which he had outlaid on account of the house of Bradwardine . . . A yearly intercourse took place, of a short letter and a hamper or a cask or two, between Waverley-Honour and Tully-Veolan, the English exports consisting of mighty cheeses and

Congratulations to the 'local printer' on giving us a translation of Otto's *Das Heilige* at 3/6 – very nice.[74]

TO DOM BEDE GRIFFITHS (W):

[Magdalen College]
Postmark: 14 September 1936

My dear Griffiths –

Excuse me for having left your letter so long unanswered. One thing that delayed it was the more imperative task of answering an other ex-pupil (much junior to you) who is trying to convert me to Hindooism, or at least has sent me three long books by a Frenchman called Guénon[75] – as obvious a quack as ever I smelled out. My wretched man, mark you, is embarking on this without having given the least attention to Christianity or even to secular European philosophy: consequently to write to him is a double battle against the man and against my own impatience. However, since he was up till this a person of exclusively literary interests, I daresay even Hindooism is a step upwards (at least if it is better to worship false gods than not even to care whether gods exist or not) and – who knows – by some long way round he may be led home in the end. The more one sees the confusion in which young men's minds grow up now-a-days, the more cause we have to be thankful on our own part. Now for *our* affair –

1. I am sorry we should have been fogged by what is really a purely linguistic difficulty about rationalism and intellectualism. Surely I drew your attention in the old days, to the fact that these two words have swapped meanings, so that 'intellect' in mod. English means the lower faculty (*ratio*) and 'reason' the higher (*intellectus*). An exactly similar change has effected *fancy* and *imagination*: and both are due to Coleridge.[76] Don't let us allow this to confuse us again.

---

mightier ale, pheasants, and venison, and the Scottish returns being vested in grouse, white hares, pickled salmon, and usquebaugh.'

74 Rudolf Otto, *The Idea of the Holy*, trans. John W. Harvey (London: Oxford University Press, 1923; 7th impression, 1936).

75 René Guénon (1886–1950), Sufi and founder of the Traditionalist School. The 'ex-pupil' was Martin Lings, a member of Guénon's household in Egypt and a convert to Traditionalism. See **Martin Lings** in the Biographical Appendix, and Lings' essay, 'René Guénon', *Sophia: The Journal of the Traditional Studies*, I, no. 1 (Summer 1995).

76 Samuel Taylor Coleridge, *Aids to Reflection* (1825), Aphorism VIIIb: 'Understanding is discursive; Reason is fixed. The Understanding in all its judgments refers to some other faculty as its ultimate authority; The Reason in all

2. I never meant to give you the idea that I would rule a book out because it was scholastic. I denied your view that scholasticism is the *philosophia perennis* and I expressed distrust of many moderns who call themselves scholastics: quite a different thing.

2. [sic] Before going on to consider the higher mode of knowledge in the Thomist system, I want to ask you does Aquinas himself connect it with *poetry*? Is there any reason to suppose that he would have allowed us to do so? Does the word *poetria*[77] occur anywhere in the *Summa*?[78] I ask this because one of my objections to some 'neo-scholastics' is that they often pick out Thomist texts and string them together with little regard to their real position in Aquinas' thought, thus producing an account of 'Thomist aesthetics', 'St. Thomas on representative government' etc etc which really corresponds to nothing their master ever thought or could have thought. If you could give me a few *references* (I now have both *Summae*) I could look up the passages *in situ*: but till then I cannot judge their real significance. I have a strong suspicion that if I did look them up I should find they had nothing to do with

---

its decisions appeals to itself as the ground and *substance* of their truth. Understanding is the faculty of reflection; Reason [the faculty] of contemplation.'

Samuel Taylor Coleridge, *Biographia Literaria* (1817), ch. 13: 'The primary imagination I hold to be the living power and prime Agent of all human perception, and as a repetition in the finite mind of the eternal act of creation in the infinite I AM. The secondary imagination I consider as an echo of the former, co-existing with the conscious will, yet still as identical with the primary in the *kind* of its agency, and differing only in *degree*, and in the *mode* of its operation . . . Fancy, on the contrary, has no other counters to play with but fixities and definites. The fancy is indeed no other than a mode of memory emancipated from the order of time and space; and blended with, and modified by that empirical phenomenon of the will which we express by the word *choice*.'

77 The medieval term for 'poetry'.

78 Aquinas, *Summa Theologica*, Part I, Question 1, Article 9, 'Whether Holy Scripture Should Use Metaphors': Objection 1. 'It seems that Holy Scripture should not use metaphors. For that which is proper to the lowest science seems not to befit this science, which holds the highest place of all. But to proceed by the aid of various similitudes and figures is proper to poetry, the least of all the sciences. Therefore it is not fitting that this science should make use of such similitudes.' Reply: 'Poetry makes use of metaphors to produce a representation, for it is natural to man to be pleased with representations. But sacred doctrine makes use of metaphors as both necessary and useful.'

ibid., Part I, Question 115, Article 5: 'We know by experience that many things are done by demons, for which the power of heavenly bodies would in no way suffice: for instance, that a man in a state of delirium should speak an unknown tongue, recite poetry and authors of whom he has no previous knowledge.'

poetry, and we could then be clear *which* we were discussing – the nature of intellectus or the nature of poetry. If one had asked the Doctor to define *poetria*, do you suppose he wd. have said any more than *p. est ars dictandi in versibus. Quaest I. Utrum rhythmus sit versus modus*[79] – or something of that sort.

3. Prior to all discussion about the form of knowledge you describe, I must make a logical point. Since this knowledge is admittedly prayer and love, and could be shown, from what you say, to be also painting and music, I do not see what is gained by calling it poetry or 'poetic experience': for it clearly covers two things *higher* than poetry, and two things different. At best it would be *one of the pre-conditions* of poetry. And other conditions which you have left out (e.g. one of *language*) are surely the *differentia* of poetry?

4. The various things said about this higher knowledge rather puzzle me. Thus the criteria since *discursu, per contactum, quasi ex habitu*[80] seem to me to apply to a great many experiences of what I would call *sensuous acquaintance* (by acquaintance I mean the French *connaitre* as opp. to *savoir*) – e.g. my 'knowledge' of toothache or cheese. On this level I would agree that all the arts depend on turning *savoir* into *connaitre* as far as possible. But the same criteria also apply to something quite different – knowledge of axioms. As to *per viam voluntatis*[81] – when you say 'The will (in mystical prayer) goes out beyond all abstract and conceptual knowledge', would the proposition remain equally true, or not, if for 'mystical prayer' we substituted (a) prayer. (b) every attempt however rudimentary to do the will of God (c) every action of whatever kind (d) every moment of consciousness (e) error.

I am afraid this will sound like carping, but do you see my real difficulty? I can't feel sure from your account whether we are dealing with a special kind of experience or with one aspect of nearly all experience – in fact of all except thought made *deliberately* abstract for scientific purposes. All day long my experience is going outside *ratio* in directions wh. cd. quite well be described in the words you quote. And,

---

79 'poetry is the art of speaking in verses. Question 1: Whether rhythm is a type of verse.'

80 'by its activity, through contact, as from its appearance'. These are the criteria St Thomas Aquinas uses in the *Summa Theologica*, Part I, Question 75, Article 1 to discuss whether the soul has a body.

81 'through the path of the will'. This was a standard concern of the Church Fathers.

of course, poetry is nearly always based on that normal experience rather than on the specially and artificially purified moments of *ratio*. But that is a very different thing from a special 'poetic experience'. It is rather that there is a special *un*poetic experience.

5. When we come to the religious life it seems that we are still, up to a point, in the realm of this normal (and if you will 'poetic', but only in the sense 'not antipoetic') experience. Thus the soul is not 'content with an external and superficial knowledge or attachment'. True: but the soul is equally discontent with these in its sensual and affectional life. So far, have we not merely the *normal* experience, exercised on a much higher object? 'Love takes up where knowledge leaves off'[82] – is not this true of my knowledge of a friend, an animal, a garden – nay even of a sensual pleasure. E.g. surely my *liking* for sleep goes far beyond my knowledge of it.

At this point it suddenly occurs to me that perhaps we are really in agreement: that while you are saying 'As above, so below' I am replying 'As below, so above'. And if you say that the former is to be preferred since the higher explains the lower and not *vice-versa*, I agree with you. The points I want to make clear are

a. That I don't wish to deny (how could I) that really *supernatural* experience can be and is conferred on the soul – some souls – by God even in this life. But,

b. That most of the descriptions you give seem to me to refer to an essentially normal experience, which is not *specifically* religious or poetic or anything but concrete and human.

6. I hope the discussion about primitive man will go on though I cannot do more than make a few comments here – or ask a few questions.

a. By primitive do you mean *unfallen* man or early fallen man?

b. If he was 'unable to distinguish between God and Nature and himself' he was a Pantheist. Therefore fallen? You can't mean God created Adam heretical? For God and Nature and Man are *distincts* (as you and I believe), and not to feel the distinction is a defect. Mind you, I don't say they are necessarily distinct to just the degree and in just the way the modern mind instinctively assumes.

c. Surely the mystic's *inability* to recall or distinguish is not *per se*

82 Aquinas, *Summa Theologica*, Part II, Question 27, Article 5.

good. It may be a price well worth paying for supernatural experiences: but it is the defect of the patient not the excellence of the grace that produces the unconsciousness etc. It would be better still to have these experiences and not to lose the power of distinguishing etc. That is, if there are distinctions in the Object. If not, of course, our distinguishing would be disease. But we believe that the real is full of distinctions. To begin with it is not the blank One of Pantheists, but One in Three – distinction straight away. To go on with it *is* not, but *creates* nature – a nature not consubstantial with itself. We are not even allowed to say that human souls are naturally sons of God, but 'to as many as believe He gave *power to become* sons of God'.[83]

But I can't go on: I have a headache and am tired. I will try another time.

Yours
C. S. Lewis

As usual, discussion obliterates the elements of agreement. I should have agreed with nearly all you say if you hadn't brought in Poetry. What you call Poetry I call simply 'life' or 'concrete experience'. In fact I think you give poetry too high a place, in a sense.

83 John 1:12.

1937

TO JOAN BENNETT (*L*):[1]

[Magdalen College]
13 January 1937

A foul copy of an essay (which now that I re-read it doesn't seem as good as I had hoped) is a poor return for the delightful, the champagne holiday you gave me. But you asked for it and here it is.[2]

What splendid talk goes on in your house! – and what a wonderful thing . . . your English Faculty is. If only we and you could combine into a single teaching body (leaving out your freaks and nonentities) we could make 'English' into an education that would not have to fear any rivalries. In the meantime we have lots to exchange. I am sure you practise more 'judgement'; I suspect we have more 'blood'. What we want is to be well commingled.

The Lucas book proves disappointing as you go on.[3] His attack on Richards[4] for splitting up poetic effects which we receive as a unity, is silly; that is what analysis *means* and R. never suggested that the products

1 Joan Bennett (1896–1986) was born in London, the daughter of novelist Arthur Frankau who wrote under the pseudonym Frank Danby. In 1920 she married Stanley Bennett (1889–1972), Librarian of Emmanuel College, Cambridge. Mrs Bennett was a Fellow of Girton College, Cambridge, and a lecturer in English at Cambridge University, 1936–64. Her books include *Sir Thomas Browne* (1962) and *Five Metaphysical Poets: Donne, Herbert, Vaughan, Crashaw, Marvell* (1965). Lewis was a frequent visitor to the home of Stanley and Joan Bennett, and his *Studies in Words* (1960) was dedicated to them. The original letters to Bennett have disappeared, and the only copies that survive are found in *L*.

2 Bennett was helping to edit a *Festschrift* – a collection of writings – entitled *Seventeenth Century Studies Presented to Sir Herbert Grierson* (1937), to which Lewis contributed 'Donne and Love Poetry in the Seventeenth Century'.

3 Frank Laurence Lucas, *The Decline and Fall of the Romantic Ideal* (1936).

4 I. A. Richards (1893–1979), literary critic, and Fellow of Magdalene College, Cambridge. His works include *Principles of Literary Criticism* (1925) and *Practical Criticism* (1929). It was the former of these that Lucas was criticizing.

of analysis were the same as the living unity. Again, he doesn't seem to see that Richards is on his side in bringing poetry to an ethical test in the long run; and his own ethical standard is so half-hearted – he's so afraid of being thought a moralist that he tries to blunt it by gas about 'health' and 'survival'. As if survival can have any value apart from the prior value of what survives. To me especially it is an annoying book; he attacks *my* enemies in the wrong way . . . and a good deal of mere 'superiority' too . . .

TO JOAN BENNETT (*L*):

[Magdalen College
February 1937]

I also have been having 'flu or you should have heard from me sooner. I enclose the article: pray make whatever use you please of it[5] . . . It is a question (for your sake and that of the *Festschrift*, not mine) whether a general pro-Donne paper called *Donne and his critics* – a glance at Dryden and Johnson and then some contemporaries including me – wouldn't be better than a direct answer. C.S.L. as professional controversialist and itinerant prize-fighter is, I suspect, becoming already rather a bore to our small public, and might in that way infect you.[6] Also, if you really refute me, you raise for the editor the awkward question, 'Then why print the other article?' However, do just as you like . . . and good luck with it whatever you do.

I've had a grand week in bed – *Northanger Abbey*, *The Moonstone*,[7] *The Vision of Judgement*,[8] *Modern Painters* (Vol. 3),[9] *Our Mutual Friend*,[10] and *The Egoist*.[11] Of the latter I decided this time that it's a rare instance of the conception being so good that even the fantastic faults can't kill it. There's a good deal of the ass about Meredith – that dreadful first chapter – Carlyle in icing sugar. And isn't the supposedly witty conversation much poorer than much we have heard in real life?

5 i.e. 'Donne and Love Poetry in the Seventeenth Century'.
6 He and E. M. W. Tillyard were halfway through their debate over 'The Personal Heresy'. Lewis's most recent contribution, an 'Open Letter to Dr Tillyard', was published in *Essays and Studies by Members of the English Association*, XXI (1936).
7 Wilkie Collins, *The Moonstone* (1868).
8 George Gordon, Lord Byron, *The Vision of Judgement* (1822).
9 John Ruskin, *Modern Painters*, vol. III (1856).
10 Charles Dickens, *Our Mutual Friend* (1864–5).
11 George Meredith, *The Egoist* (1879).

Mrs Mounstuart is a greater bore than Miss Bates[12] – only he didn't mean her to be. The Byron was not so good as I remembered: the Ruskin, despite much nonsense, glorious.

TO MARY NEYLAN (T):[13]

Magdalen College
Oxford
March 8th 1937

Dear Mrs. Neylan

What a nice letter! To be read is nice enough: but to have led anyone back to the poets themselves is more what critics dream of than what usually happens.

I ought to be able to reward you with a good list of books, as desired, but you know bibliographies are my Waterloo: in my own reading I always sacrifice critics to the poets, which is unkind to my own trade. However, let's try.

I haven't yet got Grierson's new book *Milton and Wordsworth*,[14] but I'm going to: it ought to kill two of your birds with one stone. Have you read F. L. Lucas' *Decline and Fall of the Romantic Ideal*? Hideously over-written in parts, but well worth reading: he has grasped what seems to be a hard idea to modern minds, that a certain degree of a thing might be good and a further degree of the same thing bad. Elementary, you will say – yet a realisation of it would have forbidden the writing of many books. These are new.

A few years old – but you may not have read it – is E. K. Chambers' *Sir Thomas Wyatt and other studies*.[15] Some of the essays are medieval, but most of it is 16th century. I can't think of anything much on 'general tendencies of the 17th century' since one you almost certainly read when you were up, Grierson's *Cross Currents of XVIIth c. Lit*,[16] very good indeed. By the bye a festschrift to Grierson shortly appearing (Tillyard, Nichol Smith, Joan Bennett and myself are among the

12 A character in Jane Austen, *Emma* (1816).

13 i.e. the former Mary Shelley, who had married Daniel Neylan in 1934. See **Mary Neylan** in the Biographical Appendix.

14 Sir Herbert Grierson, *Milton and Wordsworth, Poets and Prophets: A Study of the Reactions to Political Events* (1937).

15 E. K. Chambers, *Sir Thomas Wyatt and Some Collected Studies* (1933).

16 Sir Herbert Grierson, *Cross Currents in English Literature of the XVIIth Century: or, The World, the Flesh and the Spirit, Their Actions and Reactions* (1929).

contributors) might contain something of what you want. The book on the 17th c. by Willy[17] (I have forgotten the title) is more on the thought background than the poets, rather doing for that century what my Prolegomena tried to do for the middle ages. I don't know of anything general on the 18th century. Sherburn's Early Life of Pope[18] tho' good is hardly what you want.

You don't say how you or your husband are: I hope all is well.

Yours sincerely
C. S. Lewis

TO ARTHUR GREEVES (W):

The Kilns
Easter Sunday
[28 March] 1937

My dear Arthur,

I have been meaning to write to you for some time, and had partly excused myself because I was waiting to send you a story of Tolkien's which is to be published soon and which I think you may like:[19] but Uncle Gussie[20] turned up on Thursday (the coolest and most characteristic visit – merely a wire to announce his arrival!) and jogged my conscience with a message from you.

Thanks for your letter. I suppose I shall hear more from you about America when we meet. Am I right in concluding from your mere list of towns that on the aesthetic side – as regards mountains, rivers and woods etc. – it made no impression?[21] I am glad to hear that you think

---

17 Basil Willey, *The Seventeenth Century Background: Studies in the Thought of the Age in Relation to Poetry and Religion* (1934).

18 George Sherburn, *The Early Career of Alexander Pope* (1934).

19 J. R. R. Tolkien's *The Hobbit* was published on 21 September 1937.

20 Lewis's mother's brother, Augustus Warren 'Gus' Hamilton (1886–1945). See **The Hamilton Family** in the Biographical Appendix to *CL* I.

21 Arthur's trip to the United States was at the invitation of William Moncrief McClurg (1907–) of Belfast. The two young men met in the 1920s and, though unlike in many ways, they delighted in one another's company and took a number of trips together. Arthur's visit to America, presumably in the summer of 1936, was described by Dr McClurg in a letter to Walter Hooper of 25 April 1978: 'We drove up to the Adirondack Mountains in New York state and stayed in Hurricane Lodge, a delightful place – chalets with balcony and main building and dining room: the air was so fresh after the City . . . We drove through Vermont state and visited some friends there, then we started on our trip to Cape Cod . . . There is

of risking another visit to us and will do my best to make you less uncomfortable than you usually are. I suppose it *must* be in the summer term? I have often told you that this is an injudicious (lovely adjective!) time to choose, but I know you are not entirely free. By the bye, I should warn you that you will find the Kilns changed much for the worse – which you might have thought impossible – by a horrible rash of small houses which has sprung up all round us. All thanks to Lord Nuffield, I suppose: it would take a good deal more than a million pounds to undo the harm he has done to Oxford.[22]

We have had rather an unfortunate spring. First of all a maid got flu' just before she was leaving and had to be kept on as a patient for several weeks. Then I got flu'. Then as I was getting better Paxford (that is our indespensable fac-totum, like your Lea, you know) got flu'.[23] Then I had a grand week end doing as much as I could of his work and the maid's until I got flu' again. Then Minto's varicose ankles broke down. Then Warnie got flu' and was rather bad. However, we have come through it all and seem pretty cheery now. The 'dreadful weather' I have been rather enjoying: I quite like seeing the primroses one day and the snow the next.

I have not read anything you would be likely to care for lately except a *Vie de Jésus* by a Frenchman called Mauriac,[24] which I strongly recommend: it is papist, of course, and contains what English and Protestant taste would call lapses, but it is very good in spite of them. I suppose you noticed about Christmas time that someone has republished the complete *Adventures of Tim Pippin* by Roland Quiz.[25] I half

---

quite an artists colony there and of interest to Arthur to see some paintings by local artists.'

22 He was referring to William Richard Morris, later Lord Nuffield, who had built Morris Motors about a mile from The Kilns. See note 30 to the letter to Arthur Greeves of 23 April 1935.

23 Frederick William Calcutt Paxford (1898–1979), gardener and handyman at The Kilns. Mrs Moore hired him shortly after they moved into The Kilns and he remained there until after Lewis's death in 1963. Over the years he became an indispensable member of the family, tending the nine acres of ground, growing vegetables, managing an orchard, driving a car and often serving as cook. He never married. This inwardly optimistic, outwardly pessimistic man became the model for Puddleglum in *The Silver Chair* (1953). See his biography in *CG.*

24 François Mauriac, *Vie de Jésus* (1936).

25 Richard M. H. Quittenton, 'Roland Quiz' (1833–1914), *Giant-land: or the Wonderful Adventures of Tim Pippin* (London: [1874]; new edn, 1936).

thought of getting it, but have satisfied myself with assuming that you have done so. I hope you have not satisfied yourself with a similar assumption about me!

I have been progressing all this lent through the first volume of a v. nice edition of St Augustine's *City of God* only to find that the other volume has been so wrongly bound that it begins and ends in the middle of sentences. What a tragedy this would once have been!

We have got (*vice* Mr. Papworth, now gathered to his fathers) a golden retriever puppy who is about the size of a calf and as strong as a horse: has the appetite of a lion, the manners of a hurricane, the morals of a gangster, and an over salivated mouth.

Please give my love to your mother, and remember me to Reid. I saw Bryson about a fortnight ago and I think he said he was going home this Vac. Will you be able to have me this summer? It is a very bright spot in the year, but don't hesitate to say if it is inconvenient.

Yours
Jack

TO DANIEL NEYLAN (T):[26]

Magdalen College,
Oxford.
May 5th 1937

Dear Neylan,

I am sorry your wife has been ill – give her my sympathy. Your offer is attractive to the hot-gospeller in me, but after a lot of thought I feel I must refuse. I have no notion how to handle such an audience nor what to say to them: but many thanks.

I am in the middle of a scholarship exam. or I shd. write more.

Yours
C. S. Lewis

---

26 Daniel Neylan (1905–69) was the husband of Lewis's former pupil, Mary (Shelley) Neylan.

TO JOAN BENNETT (WHL):

Magdalen College,
Oxford.
May 7th 1937.

Dear Mrs Bennett

Will this do?[27] Don't hesitate to let me know if there is an expression in it which you think unfortunate or obscure, or any emphasis in dangerous directions.

About the imaginary chronology (by which I mean the sorting out of the love poems into cynical and idealistic periods), I find it nearly so embedded in everyone's mind that I am haunted by the fear that there may be some real evidence for it which I don't know; my jibe was made in the hope of eliciting this.

All I meant about the book was that it is not nearly so *exciting* as a book by you ought to be. Of course I disagree with the phonetic criticism, but very respectable people agree with you . . .

TO ARTHUR GREEVES (W):

Magdalen College.
Oxford.
June 10th 1937

My dear Arthur,

In my diary I have down 'cross to Arthur' for July 12th not July 5th and as I have arranged everything on this basis I trust it will be alright.

Your suspicion that I was fuming with wrath during the lunch is a sad commentary on my previous character, and coming from one who knows me so well, it must (I fear) be correct. This time, however, tho' of course I would have preferred to see you alone, I quite liked it.

Stamps . . . I can't understand the attraction: but I send all I have.*

Yours
Jack

* Of course there are many more in number, but only duplicating what I enclose

---

27 Mrs Bennett had applied for a lectureship in Cambridge University and Lewis was supplying a letter of reference. The rest of the letter refers to her book, *Four Metaphysical Poets: Donne, Herbert, Vaughan, Crashaw* (1934).

TO CECIL HARWOOD (BOD):

Magdalen College
Oxford
June 19th 1937

My dear Harwood

I had a quite unexpected windfall the other day as a result of which I am able to make Lawrence a present. My idea is that you should lodge it in a deposit account and let the trifle of interest accumulate, the whole to be used for or by him when he reaches the costly age (18–20). But you probably understand such matters better than I – at least a professional Bursar ought to – so dispose it for Godson's future use as you think best.

Is there any chance of seeing you this summer? Give my love to Daphne.

Yours
C. S. Lewis

TO DOM BEDE GRIFFITHS (W):

Magdalen College,
Oxford.
[27] June 1937

Dear Griffiths

Your reply about the body leaves all my questions unanswered. I'd better tell you how it arose. I was talking the other day to an intelligent infidel who said that he pinned all his hopes for any significance in the universe on the chance that the human race by adapting itself to changed conditions and first planet jumping, then star jumping, finally nebula jumping, could really last forever and subject matter wholly to mind.

When I said that it was overwhelmingly improbable, he said Yes, but one had to believe even in the 1000th chance or life was mockery. I of course asked why, feeling like that, he did not prefer to believe in the other and traditional 'chance' of a spiritual immortality. To that he replied – obviously not for effect but producing something that had long been in his mind – 'Oh I never can believe that: for if *that* were true our having a physical existence wd. be so pointless.' He's a nice, honest chap, and I have no doubt at all that this is one of the things standing between him and Christianity.

Your remarks seem to me to leave the question much where they found it. Whatever you hold about the blessed in the state of separation, the resurrection either makes some change in it or none. If none, why does it occur? If change, then either for the worse or for the better. For the worse? – *nefas credere.*[28] If for the better . . . well there the question stands.

As to the rest of your letter – the question of Divine Presence was introduced rather for example: but, of course, I have no wish to discuss with you anything you don't want to discuss with me. I received your statement that you do not think I am acting 'in bad faith' with some puzzlement: as if, in a conversation that had no apparent connection with money, you suddenly remarked 'I am not saying you are bribed'. One is of course glad to be acquitted: but quite in the dark as to how one came to be on trial.

I also am doing a lot of rustic work at present but more with a scythe than a spade.

Yours
C. S. Lewis

TO OWEN BARFIELD (W):

The Kilns,
Headington Quarry,
Oxford.
Sept 2nd 1937

Instrument approved with the exception of 'were reduced to' which hardly seems the right style

Malory – Morris – are you preparing a chapter on *Quellen* for a book about me.

'Curiously comfortless stuff in the background' is the criticism of a sensible man just emerging from the popular errors about Morris. Not so curiously, nor quite in the background – that particular *discomfort* is the main theme of all his best work, the thing he was born to say. The formula is 'Returning to what seems an ideal world to find yourself all the more face to face with gravest reality without ever drawing a pessimistic conclusion but fully maintaining that heroic action in, or amelioration of, a temporal life is an absolute duty though the disease of temporality is incurable.'[29]

---

28 'It is forbidden to believe this.'
29 These thoughts echo those found in Lewis's essay 'William Morris' in *SLE*.

Not quite what you expected, but just what the essential Morris is. 'Defeat and victory are the same in the sense that victory will open your eyes only to a deeper defeat: so fight on.'[30] In fact he is the final statement of *good* Paganism: a faithful account of what things are and always must be to the *natural* man. Cf. what are in comparison the ravings of Hardy on the one hand and optimistic Communists on t'other. But the Earthly Paradise after that first story is inferior work. Try Jason, House of the Wolfings, Roots of the Mts, Well at the World's End.[31]

The thriller is finished and called 'Out of the Silent Planet.'

Yes, another next term, certainly.

Yrs
C.S.L.

If you want my sonnets, I've a very good one beginning 'The Bible says Sennacherib's campaign was spoiled.'[32]

TO CHARLES WILLIAMS (W):

[Magdalen College]
Sept. 23rd, 1937

[Dear Williams]

Many thanks for the book;[33] fortunately I had seen it announced and ordered a copy before it arrived, so that both of us have it both ways. I think this is much the best book you have given us yet.

In the first place I find the form of evil that you are dealing with much more real than the Evil (with a big E) that appears in the other books and which, though I enjoy it, (like pantomime red fire) in a story, I do not believe in. But your Gomorrah is the real thing, and Wentworth a truly tragic study. Of course he can't in the nature of things be as good *fun* as Sir Giles Tumulty,[34] but he's more important. And Mrs Sammile is excellent too.

---

30 *Bhagavad-Gita*, ch. 2.

31 William Morris, *The Earthly Paradise* (1868–70); *The House of the Wolfings* (1889); *The Well at the World's End* (1896).

32 This poem, entitled 'Sonnet', was published in *The Oxford Magazine*, vol. LIV (14 May 1936) under the pseudonym, 'Nat Whilk'. It is reprinted in *Poems* and *CP*.

33 Charles Williams's new supernatural thriller, *Descent into Hell* (1937).

34 A character in one of Williams's other supernatural thrillers, *War in Heaven* (1930).

In the second place I'm glad to have got off the amulet or 'sacred object' theme.

Thirdly – I hope this doesn't sound patronising – in sheer writing I think you have gone up, as we examiners say, a whole class. Chapter II is in my opinion your high water mark so far. Your have completely overcome a certain flamboyance which I always thought your chief danger: this is crisp as grape nuts, hard as a hammer, clear as glass. I am a little worried in the Wentworth part by the tendency to Gertrude Steinisms (eaves eves, guard card, etc.).[35] I agree, of course, that if there is any place for this kind of writing, the descent into Hell is the place.

But I believe this representative style, this literary programme music in which the writer writes as if *he* were in the predicament he describes, to be a false trail. I would rather see you becoming or remaining rigidly sober and classic as you describe chaos, your limit emphasizing nearly all good, except in the conversations between Stanhope and Pauline.

I fancy the rift between us is here pretty wide. I know *you* would talk that way when most serious and most sincere: but most people wouldn't. I'm afraid that the interchange of formulae like 'Under the Mercy'[36] may sound like a game to people who don't know you. The L.C.M.[37] between Dante and P. G. Wodehouse is a difficult thing to hit and I'm not sure if it's a good thing to aim at. The worst of trying to explain one's minor objections to a book one has very much liked is that they don't sound minor enough when the inevitably lengthy explanation has been made.

This is a thundering good book and a real purgation to read. I shall come back to it again and again. A thousand thanks for writing it – without prejudice to thanks on a different level for the presentation copy.

I want you to be at the next Inklings probably on 20 or 27 October. Can you keep yourself fairly free about the time? This sounds a large order, but the others are not get-at-able yet. I have written a thriller

---

35 Gertrude Stein (1874–1946), American author who lived in Paris and turned her home into a salon for the avant-garde. Lewis disliked her idiosyncratic poems such as *Tender Buttons* (1914) which carried fragmentation and abstraction to the point of idiocy.

36 'Under the Mercy' was perhaps Williams's favourite formula. It appeared in ch. 10 of *Descent into Hell*, at the end of many of his letters, and even on his gravestone.

37 i.e. lowest common multiple.

about a journey to Mars on which I urgently want your opinion: also you'd be able to take your revenge!

[C. S. Lewis]

TO E. F. CARRITT (P):[38]

Magdalen College,
Oxford.
Oct. 29th [1937]

Dear Carritt

Alas – I *have* no Saturdays now! The B. Litt work which I do involves correcting of transcripts which can be done only when Bodley is open, so that Saturday afternoon has become one of my busiest times.[39] I should have loved to come.

If any time in the Vac. you feel you have a free afternoon and a permit for Wytham eating their heads off, I'm your man.

Where are the walks? Where are the woods? Where is Wytham gone?
Leisure and literature are lost under
The night's helmet as tho never they had been![40]

Yrs
C.S.L.

---

38 Edgar Frederick Carritt (1876–1964), Lewis's tutor in Philosophy, was Fellow of Philosophy at University College, 1898–1941. See his biography attached to the letter to Albert Lewis of 1 May 1920 (*CL* I, pp. 485–6).

39 During this time the Bodleian Library was open every day from 9 a.m. to 7 p.m., but on 1 July 1938 it began closing at 1 p.m. on Saturdays and all day Sunday.

40 Lewis was imitating lines 92 and 95–6 of the Anglo-Saxon poem, *The Wanderer*, which may be translated:

Where went the horse, where went the hero? Where went the hoard-giver?
. . . . . . How the time has gone,
Has darkened under night's helmet as if never had been!

1938

As mentioned earlier, the editors of the Oxford History of English Literature, F. P. Wilson and Bonamy Dobrée, knew that the individual volumes of this history would require some dovetailing, and it was up to them to see that there was no overlapping of periods. The American scholar, Douglas Bush,[1] *agreed to write to 'The Early Seventeenth Century, From c. 1600 to c. 1660' and in January 1938 Wilson informed Lewis of this, asking if he wanted to include William Dunbar and Gavin Douglas in his sixteenth-century volume.*

TO FRANK PERCY WILSON (OUP):

Magdalen College
Oxford
Jan 25th 1938

My dear Wilson

No, I don't want Dunbar: and I don't cleave to Douglas even, if anyone wants him. And at the other end of the principle is a simple one – the sooner Bush can begin and I leave off, the better I shall be pleased. The O HELL lies like a nightmare on my chest ever since I got your specimen bibliography: I shan't try to desert – anyway, I suppose the exit is thronged with dreadful faces and fiery arms[2] – but I have a growing doubt if I ought to be doing this.

---

1 Professor Douglas Bush (1896–1983), born in Morrisburg, Ontario, Canada, was educated at the University of Toronto and Harvard University. An instructor in English at Harvard, 1924–7, he taught in the Department of English at the University of Minnesota, 1927–36. In 1936 he returned to Harvard as Professor of English, a position he held until his retirement in 1966. He and Lewis were both writing volumes for the Oxford History of English Literature, Bush's contribution being *English Literature in the Earlier Seventeenth Century* (1945). His other books include *Classical Influences in Renaissance Literature* (1952), *John Milton* (1964) and *Pagan Myth and Christian Tradition in English Poetry* (1968).

2 Milton, *Paradise Lost*, XII, 641–4: 'They, looking back, all the eastern side beheld/Of Paradise, so late their happy seat,/Waved over by that flaming brand, the gate/With dreadful faces thronged and fiery arms.'

Mind you, I'd sooner have Dunbar than Donne: sooner, in general, come early on the scene than linger late. Let the others choose.

I hoped we should all meet at the Aldwych and set out to find it with Tillyard who proved to know no more about London than I do. We got to a thing called Bush House in the end where we lunched in a barber's shop, served by tailors, off sponges. I was sorry not to see you again.

Do you think there's any chance of the world ending before the O HELL appears?

Yours, in deep depression,
C. S. Lewis

TO OWEN BARFIELD (W):

[The Kilns]
March 28th 1938

My dear Barfield –

Thanks for letter: I have written to Tolkien. 'Omit no manly degree of importunity'[3] towards Harwood. I begin to realise how much the quidity of the walks depended on him. I love your part in him as Lamb said. Can nothing be done about it. I am ready for feudal arrangements if they are any good. Also, I must warn you that something seems to be wrong with my left foot. I shall come, of course, D.V.,[4] but how much I'll be able to walk, I don't know. (Memo: I can't drive a car) and H.J.[5] said 'I hope you are not the sort of people who walk 12 or 15 miles a day.' (That's where the Sadism will come in!) So there'll be much more tour than walking. I suppose you know Bournemouth is about 20 miles long.

Orpheus goes back to-morrow.[6] I can't pretend to have anything like

3 Boswell, *The Life of Samuel Johnson*, vol. I, 1759, letter to Joseph Simpson, p. 347: 'Omit no decent nor manly degree of importunity.'

4 *Deo volente* – 'God willing'.

5 This was probably his friend of undergraduate days, Alfred Kenneth Hamilton Jenkin. See note 3 to the letter to Hamilton Jenkin of 11 January 1939.

6 Barfield had finally completed his poetic drama, *Orpheus*, which is first mentioned in the poem Lewis included in his letter to Barfield of 5 April 1935. The play was performed on stage in 1948 and was eventually published as *Orpheus: A Poetic Drama*, ed., with an afterword by John C. Ulreich, Jr (West Stockbridge, Massachusetts, Lindisfarne Press, 1983). In the foreword to the published work Barfield wrote: 'I had casually mentioned to my friend C. S. Lewis that I seemed to be feeling an impulse to write a play in verse and was wondering about a subject

taken it in yet: think what one would make of the *Ring* under similar conditions – and this presents difficulties of the same kind. I like the matter of I i as much as I always did and am more reconciled to the style. I ii is excellent, though I'd like more (and better) variations in the Hiawatha metre. I iii I'm still not quite sure about: I expect it wd. act well. Act II is simply superb. It brought tears to my eyes. III i also very good – until the scene with Persephone which I don't understand. IV i Aristaeus's opening speech does not get me at all. The 'thing' may be good. I begin to see my way a little more in the scene between O. and the satyr, but this needs more re-reading. IV ii very good: Cyrene's ritual goes off admirably. IV iii – I don't know. Mostly above my head. The lyrical part at the end: that is very unlike you. A sort of Swinburne-Morris-Kipling style (I deemed that I had good hunting . . . Have I used well, Demeter, the man's good gift of his breath – the high gods etc). Is there some point in this that I'm missing? This is rotten criticism: but it's not an easy poem.

Yours
C.S.L.

TO JANET SPENS (BOD):

The Kilns,
Headington Quarry,
Oxford.
April 18th 1938

Dear Miss Spens

Thanks for your kind and interesting letter. You are right of course about the silliness of dragging in Mason: that was merely (as sillinesses so often are) the intrusion of a favourite hobby horse of mine in a place where it was not wanted – my belief, namely, that the continuity between the Romantics and the XVIIIth c. needs to be stressed more than it usually is.

Yes, the *Dynasts* is very queer: the invention of a whole pantheon to symbolise the non existence of God. I think it is not uncommon to

. . . He said in effect: "Why not take one of the myths and simply do your best with it – Orpheus for instance?" . . . Apart from the actual writing, the "getting down to it" consisted almost exclusively of a careful re-reading, with a classical dictionary beside me, of Virgil's presentation of the myth in the fourth *Georgic.*'

find atheists perpetually angry with God for not being there. Perhaps it is a laudable trait!

I hadn't noticed the parallel between Urania and Cymoent.[7] But I still think there is an important difference. Marinell is, in the story, Cymoent's literal son, and Cymoent is a character not a personification only. But Adonais and the Muse are 'a poet' and 'the spirit of poetry' and I don't count the latter to break down like a bereaved human being. Shelley seems to be taking his symbols too seriously in one way and not seriously enough in another. It is like making the sun weep because a candle has gone out. I must re-read *The Witch*.[8]

The chief reason why I can't read Godwin is that I have never got hold of a copy of *Political Justice*;[9] but I intend to 'one of these days'. I shall be very interested to hear what you think of him. My own growing suspicion is that he can't be so bad as our critical tradition (a very flippant, elegant, belle-lettristic tradition) makes out. If Shelley likes an author[10] and the Saintsburies and Raleighs and Garrods sneer at him – well, it makes one wonder. I hope you will find time to let me know how he struck you.

With many thanks.

Yours sincerely

C. S. Lewis

TO DOM BEDE GRIFFITHS (W):

Magdalen College,
Oxford.
29th April 1938

Dear Griffiths

It was nice to hear from you again and of course I read the articles with interest.[11] I think at the top of p. 8 in the first you might have expressed more clearly the actually antimoral side of romanticism you

7 A character in Spenser, *The Faerie Queene*, III, iv.

8 Percy Bysshe Shelley, *The Witch of Atlas* (1824).

9 William Godwin, *Enquiry Concerning Political Justice* (1793).

10 Percy Bysshe Shelley married Godwin's daughter, Mary.

11 Griffiths published the two-part story of his conversion to Catholicism in the Benedictine periodical, *Pax*, nos. 198 and 199 (April/May 1938).

were in when we first met.[12] Have you forgotten that in our fiercest arguments you were actually defending cruelty and lechery. On p. 9 – is it your considered view that Berkeleyian idealism is to be found in the *Confessions*? I shd. doubt it.[13] 'Strange as it may seem' a few lines lower is ambiguous. I take it you mean it was strange that this shd. have been a discovery.[14] In next para. I shd. have liked an explicit statement of the view you then expressed to me, in words that I have never forgotten 'The choice in the long run is between Christianity and Hinduism'.

In the second article your account of the night of prayer (p. 31)[15] omits a v. interesting fact you told me shortly after it – that what started you off was the consciousness of sin in some religious writer you were reading which you could not share tho' you were satisfied on objective grounds that you were more sinful than the writer. They are nice, plain articles and very clear.

I have been in considerable trouble over the present danger of war. Twice in one life – and then to find how little I have grown in fortitude despite my conversion. It has done me a lot of good by making me realise how much of my happiness secretly depended on the tacit assumption of at least tolerable conditions for the body: and I see more clearly, I think, the necessity (if one may so put it) which God is under

---

12 *Pax*, no. 198, p. 8: '[At Oxford] I found friends who were of a like mind with myself, and the love of nature and poetry became the ruling passion of our lives. We sought out the solitude of the hills and the sea, whenever it was possible, and passed whole days, and weeks in the vacation, in reading and walking, in silent communion with nature. All our philosophy was to live according to nature, and all our religion was the worship of nature.'

13 ibid., p. 9: 'I . . . found in them [St Augustine's *Confessions*] the idealism of Berkeley taken up into a magnificent system of Christian philosophy, and the "intellectual love" of Spinoza transformed into a deep passion of religious love.'

14 ibid.: 'The discovery, strange as it may seem, that another [Lewis] had been led to the Christian faith by the path of philosophy which I was pursuing, and had found the fulfilment of his philosophy in his faith, was an inspiration which was destined never to fade.'

15 *Pax*, no. 199, p. 31: 'I decided that Anglicanism represented as pure a form of Christianity as I could find . . . But nothing could bring me any peace . . . I went up into a chapel at the top of the mission house, in which I was staying, one evening to pray, and there the thought came to me that I must make an effort to break with this world, which was destroying the peace of my soul. I formed a resolution that I would not go to bed that night, but would spend the whole night in prayer. It is difficult to describe the agony which I endured.'

of allowing us to be afflicted – so few of us will *really* rest all on Him if He leaves us any other support.

About our differences: I feel that whenever two members of different communions succeed in sharing the spiritual life so far as they can now share it, and are thus forced to regard each other as Christians, they are really helping on re-union by producing the conditions without which official reunion would be quite barren. I feel sure that this is the layman's chief contribution to the task, and some of us here are being enabled to perform it. You, who are a priest and a theologian, are a different story: and on the purely natural & temperamental level there is, and always has been, a sort of tension between us two which prevents our doing much mutual good. We shall both be nicer, please God, in a better place. Meanwhile you have my daily prayer and good wishes.

Yours
C. S. Lewis

TO JOHN BETJEMAN (VIC):[16]

Magdalen College,
Oxford.
May 28th 1938

Dear Betjeman

Mea culpa! I don't like to think how long these two books of yours have been on my shelves and my conscience. Not that I've been reading them – I'm afraid the mere reluctance to let books go – and a still greater reluctance to put up a parcel – has been the main factor. Your pardon.

Why do you never drop in and see me?

Yours
C. S. Lewis

16 See **Sir John Betjeman** in the Biographical Appendix.

TO JOHN BETJEMAN (VIC):

Magdalen College,
Oxford.
June 3rd 1938

Dear Betjeman

Sorry, I couldn't manage Whit Monday, but very many thanks. Pay my respects to that very great man Dawkins.[17]

yours
C. S. Lewis

TO CHARLES WILLIAMS (W):

[Magdalen College]
June 7th 1938.

[Dear Williams]

Though I have not yet finished it I feel I must write and congratulate you on producing a really great book in your *He Came Down from Heaven*.[18] It is thickly inlaid with patins of bright gold – 'He does not exist primarily for us' (p. 3) – 'All that could be said would be that they had not *yet* happened' (p. 6).[19] (This is really overwhelming. I honestly think it quite likely that when we are in our graves this may become one of the sentences that straddle across ages like the great dicta of Plato, Augustine, or Pascal) – on Bible-worship of the odious new 'literary' sort (7, 8.)[20] – and every word on

17 While at Oxford Betjeman had become friends with Professor Richard MacGillivray Dawkins (1871–1955), Director of the British School of Archaeology, Athens, 1906–14, and Bywater and Southby Professor of Byzantine and Modern Greek Language and Literature at Oxford, 1922–39. Lewis and Dawkins had been members of Tolkien's Icelandic Society.

18 Charles Williams, *He Came Down From Heaven* (London: Heinemann, 1938).

19 ibid., ch. 1, pp. 5–6: 'it might be said that the Bible, up to and including the Acts of the Apostles, is concerned rather with *what happened*, the Rituals with *what is happening*. The Epistles belong to both. It is true that all that did happen is a presentation of what is happening; all the historical events, especially of this category, are a pageant of the events of the human soul. But it is true also that Christendom has always held that the two are indissolubly connected; that the events in the human soul could not exist unless the historical events had existed. If, *per impossibile*, it could be divinely certain that the historical events upon which Christendom reposes had not yet happened, all that could be said would be that they had not *yet* happened.'

20 ibid., pp. 7–8: 'It is the habit nowadays to talk of the Bible as great literature; the Bible-worship of our forefathers has been succeeded by a more misguided and more offensive solemnity of conditioned respect, as accidentally uncritical as

p. 25.[21] And it's so *clear*, which at one time I should never have expected a book of yours to be.

Damn you, you go on getting steadily better ever since you first crossed my path: how do you do it? I begin to suspect that we are living in the 'age of Williams' and our friendship with you will be our only passport to fame. I've a good mind to punch your head when we next meet.

[C. S. Lewis]

TO OWEN BARFIELD (W):

Magdalen College,
Oxford.
June 10th 1938

My dear Barfield

What frightfully bad luck. (This would have been really an ideal week end as, in addition to having papers to correct so that I couldn't talk, I have run a needle into my foot so that I can't walk: you could have concentrated on *Orpheus* with almost no interruption). I hope the measles will soon go over, and it'll go hard but we'll fix up another time in the long vac. I'm afraid the lyric is not very appropriate, now!

Think not the doom of man reversed for thee. Apropos of Johnson, isn't this good, from the Rambler, from a man who decided not to marry a blue-stocking on finding her an atheist and a determinist. 'It was not difficult to discover the danger of committing myself forever to one who might at any time mistake the dictates of passion, or the calls of appetite, for the decree of fate; or consider cuckoldom as necessary to

---

deliberately irreligious. Uncritical, because too often that literary respect is oddly conditioned by an ignoring of the book's main theme.'

21 ibid., ch. 2, p. 25: 'The distinction between necessary belief and unnecessary credulity is as necessary as belief; it is the heightening and purifying of belief. There is nothing that matters of which it is not sometimes desirable to feel: "this does not matter." "This also is Thou; neither is this Thou." But it may be admitted also that this is part of the technique of belief in our present state; not even Isaiah or Aquinas have pursued to its revelation the mystery of self-scepticism in the divine. The nearest, perhaps, we can get to that is in the incredulous joy of great romantic moments – in love or poetry or what else: "this cannot possibly be, and it is". Usually the way must be made ready for heaven, and then it will come by some other; the sacrifice must be made ready, and the fire will strike on another altar.'

the general system, as a link in the everlasting chain of successive causes.'[22]

And, in another way, isn't this splendid 'Whenever, after the shortest relaxation of vigilance, reason and caution return to their charge, they find hope again in possession.'[23]

What is the betting I forget to put that lyric in after all? – They keep sheep in Magdalen grove now and I hear the fleecy care bleating all day long; I am shocked to find that none of my pupils, though they are all acquainted with pastoral poetry, regards them as anything but a nuisance: and one of my colleagues has been heard to ask why sheep have their wool cut off. (Fact)

It frightens me almost. And so it did the other night when I heard two undergrads. giving a list of pleasures which were (a) Nazi. (b) Leading to homosexuality. They were, feeling the wind in your hair, walking with bare feet in the grass, and bathing in the rain. Think it over: it gets worse the longer you look at it. More cheering is the true report from Cambridge of a conversation

A. *What is this Ablaut* that K. keeps on talking about in his lectures?
B. Oh don't you know, he was in love with Eloise.

I must fix my Irish visit before I can make a new date with you, but we'll manage one before or after your holidays. When are you going away? You note that hope is once again in possession.

Yours
C. S. Lewis

TO OWEN BARFIELD (W):

Sept 6th 1938

My dear B.

(1.) As at present advised I can come on 23rd, but no date is so

22 *The Rambler* was a twice-weekly periodical in 208 numbers issued by Dr Samuel Johnson between 20 March 1750 and 14 March 1752. The quotation comes from no. 113 (16 April 1751), 'The History of Hymenaeus's Courtship' (*The Rambler*, ed. W. J. Bate and Albrecht B. Strauss, Yale Edition of the Works of Samuel Johnson, vol. IV (1969), p. 239).

23 ibid, no. 123 (21 May 1751), 'The Young Trader Turned Gentleman', p. 291.

safe as the 30th. I am sure Cecil said he could not come before the end of Sept. but α I may be wrong and β the fixture between you and me was prior and he is merely appenditical and agglutinative. All the same I'd much prefer the 30th if you can possibly do it.

(2.)

Some believe the slumber
Of trees is in December
When timber's naked under star
And the squirrel keeps his chamber.

But I believe their fibre
Awakes to life and labour
When turbulence comes roaring up
The land in loud October,

And charges, and enlarges
The beach, and long besieges,
And scourges trees till, like the bones
Of thought, their shape emerges.

Form is soul. In warmer
Seductive days, disarming
Its firmer will, the wood grows soft
And spreads its dreams to murmur;

Into earnest winter,
Like souls awaked, it enters.
The hunter frost and the cold light
Have quelled the green enchanter.[24]

(3.) Isn't Jupiter splendid these nights?

C.S.L.

Lewis had already mentioned in his letter to Griffiths of 29 April the

24 This poem was published with slight variations as 'Experiment' in *The Spectator*, CLXI (9 December 1939), p. 998. It was further revised, and retitled 'Pattern', before it appeared in *Poems* and *CP*.

impending danger of war; in the next two he explores his increasing and justified concern. For this was the time of the Munich crisis. In March 1938 Germany had invaded Austria. By the end of May, encouraged by the lack of reaction to the invasion on the part of Britain and France, Hitler began to threaten Czechoslovakia, and especially the Sudetenland – a tiny section of the Czech Republic that lay on the border of Germany.

In June 1938 Neville Chamberlain, the British Prime Minister, said 'off the record' that Britain favoured turning over the Sudetenland to Germany 'in the interest of peace'. He sent a representative to Czechoslovakia to mediate between that country and the Sudeten Germans. Finally, on 5 September, the Czech president agreed to accept the German demands. That was not at all what Hitler wanted, and he used his own propaganda machine to cause outbreaks of fighting in the Sudetenland. This, in turn, led Czechoslovakia to declare martial law.

Britain and its allies were very keen to avoid war, and on 29 September 1938 representatives from Germany, England, France and Italy met in Munich to decide Czechoslovakia's fate. An agreement was signed stating that Germany would take over the Sudetenland. On 1 October German troops began occupying the region. After that similar settlements were made over Hungary and Poland. Hitler had succeeded and by 15 March 1939 he was to occupy the whole of Czechoslovakia.

TO OWEN BARFIELD (W):

Magdalen College
Oxford
Sept 12th 1938

My dear Barfield

What awful quantities of this sort of thing seem necessary to break us in, or, more correctly, to break us off. One thinks one has made some progress towards detachment, some μελετή θανάτου,[25] and begin[s] to realise, and to acquiesce in, the rightly precarious hold we have on all our natural loves, interests, and comforts: then when they are really shaken, at the very first breath of that wind, it turns out to have been all a sham, a field-day, blank cartridges.

This is how I was thinking that night, about the war danger. I had so often told myself that my friends and books and even brains were

25 'awareness of death'. Plato, *Phaedo*, 81a.

not given me to keep: that I must teach myself at bottom to care for something else more (and also of course to care for them more but in a different way) and I was horrified to find how *cold* the idea of really losing them struck. An awful symptom is that part of oneself still regards troubles as 'interruptions' as if (ludicrous idea) the happy bustle of ones personal interests was our real ἔϱγον,[26] instead of the opposite.

I did in the end see (I dare not say 'feel') that since nothing but these forcible shakings will cure us of our worldliness, we have at bottom reason to be thankful for them. We *force* God to surgical treatment: we won't (mentally) diet.

This morning comes your letter, and I know you at least (I cd. hardly depend on any one else for so much) will not think me heartless for connecting it in this way with what I was already thinking, for the subjects really flowed together – indeed they are the same subject.

Well, well: you know all I am thinking about at least as well as I do. As you said in that essay of yours one cannot in the Simon of Cyrene moment see the cross from the Joseph of Arimathea point of view, but one can remember that the other side is real: hence that apparently naked will, stripped of its emotional motives, which, on your view, is alone free.

I have a lot more to say on this (I've just read the *Theologia Germanica*)[27] when we meet. That is, if we meet, for of course our whole joint world may be blown up before the end of the week. I can't feel in my bones that it will, but my bones know dam' all about it. If we are separated, God bless you, and thanks for a hundred good things I owe to you, more than I can count or weigh. In some ways we've had a corking time these 20 years.

Be thankful you have nothing to reproach yourself about in your relations with your father (I had lots) and that it is not some disease.

---

26 'task' or 'work'.

27 The *Theologia Germanica* is an anonymous fourteenth-century German spiritual treatise counselling radical poverty of spirit and renunciation of self as a way of union with God. Martin Luther published an incomplete text in 1516 and the full text in 1518, giving it the title *Deutsch Theologia*. The edition Lewis used was *Theologia Germanica*, trans. from the German by Susanna Winkworth, with a preface by the Rev. Charles Kingsley and a letter to the translator by the Chevalier Bunsen (London: Macmillan, 1907).

The horror of a stroke must be felt almost entirely by the spectators.[28]

I'll fix with Cecil.

Yours

C. S. Lewis

Out of the Silent Planet *was published by John Lane, the Bodley Head on 23 September 1938.*

TO DOM BEDE GRIFFITHS (W):

Magdalen College
Oxford
Oct 5th 1938

Dear Dom Bede

I am afraid I have forgotten most of the things I said in my last letter. The opinion of my friend about the end of life was not, I should suppose, quoted with any approval of mine. As to whether reason can rigorously prove God and immortality, what is one to say? I do not remember to have seen a proof that appeared to me absolutely compelling, but that may be only *my* reason or the writer's reason: At any rate it is obvious that pure reason, in human beings, is very often in fact not convinced. I shd. suppose that the truths imbedded in Paganism owe at least as much to tradition and divine guidance as to ratiocination.

About war – I have always believed that it is lawful for a Christian to bear arms in war when commanded by constituted authority unless he has very good reason (which a private person rarely has) for believing the war to be unjust. I base this 1. On the fact that Our Lord does not appear to have regarded the Roman soldiers as *ex officio* sinners. 2. On the fact that the Baptist told soldiers not to leave the army, but to be *good* soldiers.[29] 3. On the opinion of St Augustine (somewhere in *De Civitate*).[30] 4. On the general agreement of all Christian communities

28 Owen's father, Arthur Edward Barfield, died at his home, Red Roofs, Burtons Lane, Chalfont St Giles, on 15 September 1938, aged seventy-four.

29 Luke 3:14.

30 St Augustine, *The City of God* (*De Civitate Dei*), trans. John Healey (London: Everyman's Library, 1945), book XIX, ch. 12: 'War's aim is nothing but glorious peace. For what is victory but a suppression of resistants, which being done, peace follows? And so peace is war's purpose, the scope of all military discipline, and the limit at which all just contentions aim. All men seek peace by war, but none seek war by peace.' The same idea is expressed in some of his other writings.

except a few sects – who generally combine pacifism with other odd opinions. I take the dicta in the Sermon on the Mount to be prohibitions of revenge, not as a counsel of perfection but as absolutely binding on all Christians.[31] But I do not think punishment inflicted by lawful authorities for the right motives is revenge: still less, violent action in the defence of innocent people. I cannot believe the knight errant idea to be sinful. Even in the very act of fighting I think charity (to the enemy) is not *more* endangered than in many necessary acts wh. we all admit to be lawful.[32]

On reunion I have no contribution to make: it is a matter quite above my sphere.[33]

I was terrified to find how terrified I was by the crisis. Pray for me for courage.

Yours
C. S. Lewis

TO MRS STUART MOORE (EVELYN UNDERHILL) (M):[34]

As from Magdalen College,
Oxford.
Oct 29th 1938

Dear Madam

Your letter is one of the most surprising and, in a way, alarming

---

31 Matthew 5:39: 'But I say unto you, that ye resist not evil: but whosoever shall smite thee on thy right cheek, turn to him the other also.'

32 In 1940 Lewis addressed an Oxford pacifist society on 'Why I Am Not a Pacifist', which is published in *Timeless at Heart* (1987) and *EC*.

33 Lewis was eventually persuaded to devote a short paper to 'Christian Reunion'. It was published in *Christian Reunion and Other Essays* (1990) and is reprinted in *EC*.

34 Evelyn Underhill (1875–1941), who was married to Hubert Stuart Moore, was famous for her works on mysticism. She converted to Christianity in 1907, and to Anglicanism in 1921. Profoundly influenced by Friedrich von Hügel, she devoted herself to giving spiritual direction, retreats, and writing. Her books include *Mysticism* (1911), *The Life of the Spirit and the Life of To-day* (1922) and *Worship* (1936). Lewis was replying to Underhill's letter of 26 October 1938: 'May I thank you for the very great pleasure which your remarkable book "Out of the Silent Planet" has given me? It is so seldom that one comes across a writer of sufficient imaginative power to give one a new slant on reality: & this is just what you seem to me to have achieved. And what is more, you have not done it in a solemn & oppressive way but with a delightful combination of beauty, humour & deep seriousness. I enjoyed every bit of it, in spite of starting with a decided prejudice against "voyages to Mars". I wish you had felt able to report the conversation in which Ransom explained the Christian mysteries to the eldil, but I suppose

honours I have ever had. I have not been for very long a believer and have hitherto regarded the great mystical writers as a man in the foothills regards the glaciers and precipices: to find myself noticed from regions which I scarcely feel qualified to notice is really quite overwhelming. In trying to thank you, I find myself regretting that we have given such an ugly meaning to the word 'Condescension' which ought to have remained a beautiful name for a beautiful action.

I am glad you mentioned the substitution of heaven for space as that is my favourite idea in the book.[35] Unhappily I have since learned that it is also the idea which most betrays my scientific ignorance: I have since learned that the rays in interplanetary space, so far from being beneficial, would be mortal to us. However, that, no doubt, is true of Heaven in other senses as well!

Again thanking you very much,

Yours very truly,

C. S. Lewis

During the course of 1938 the Delegates of the Oxford University Press asked F. P. Wilson to prepare a 'progress report' on the Oxford History of English Literature. In his Report to the Delegates, dated 20 December 1938, Wilson said that C. S. Lewis had written to him thus:

> *I go on reading and write on each subject while it is fresh in mind. Out of these scattered sheets, perhaps after much correction, I hope to build up a book. The subjects so treated already are Platonism, Douglas, Lyndsay, Tottel, Mulcaster's Elementarie, Sir Thomas More, Prayer-book, Sidney, Marlowe (non-dramatic),*

---

that would be too much to ask. We should be content with the fact that you have turned "empty space" into heaven!' (Bodleian Library, MS. Eng. c. 6825, fol. 68).

35 In ch. 5 of *Out of the Silent Planet* (London: 1938; HarperCollins, 2000), Ransom is in the spaceship on the way to Mars: 'He had read of "Space": at the back of his thinking for years had lurked the dismal fancy of the black, cold vacuity, the utter deadness, which was supposed to separate the worlds . . . now . . . the very name "Space" seemed a blasphemous libel for the empyrean ocean of radiance in which they swam . . . it was the womb of worlds, whose blazing and innumerable offspring looked down nightly even from the earth with so many eyes – and here, with how many more! No: Space was the wrong name. Older thinkers had been wiser when they named it simply the heavens' (p. 29).

Nashe, Watson, Barclay, Googe, Raleigh (poems), Shakespeare (poems), Webbe; and among other sources Petrarch and Machiavelli.

I am at present hard at work not directly on the book but on a lecture entitled 'Prolegomena to Renaissance Poetry': a similar Prolegomena to Medieval Poetry which I have and still give proved to be a useful buttress to the other book.[36]

I can give no indication of when it will be done. I find the work to be got through is enormous and would be delighted for an honourable pretext to withdraw: excessive pressure from the delegates might come to constitute an honourable pretext.[37]

TO ROGER LANCELYN GREEN (BOD):[38]

[The Kilns]
Dec. 28th 1938

Thanks for kind letter. I don't think letters to authors in praise of their works really require apology for they always give pleasure.

You are obviously much better informed than I about this type of literature and the only one I can add to your list is *Voyage to Arcturus* by David Lyndsay (Methuen) wh. is out of print but a good bookseller will prob. get you a copy for about 5 to 6 shillings. It is entirely on the imaginative and not at all on the scientific wing.

What immediately spurred me to write was Olaf Stapledon's *Last and First Men* (Penguin Libr.)[39] and an essay in J. B. S. Haldane's *Possible Worlds*[40] both of wh. seemed to take the idea of such travel seriously and to have the desperately immoral outlook wh. I try to pillory in Weston. I like the whole interplanetary idea as a *mythology*

---

36 i.e. *The Allegory of Love.*

37 *CG*, p. 477.

38 See **Roger Lancelyn Green** in the Biographical Appendix. Green was reading English Literature and had been attending Lewis's 'Prolegomena' lectures. He had written to thank Lewis for *Out of the Silent Planet.*

39 Olaf Stapledon, *Last and First Men* (1930; Penguin, 1937).

40 J. B. S. Haldane, 'Last Judgement', *Possible Worlds and Other Essays* (1927). John Burdon Sanderson Haldane (1892–1964), geneticist, was Professor of Genetics at University College, London, 1933–57. For most of his life he was a disillusioned Marxist. Haldane hated Lewis's science fiction novels and attacked them in his essay 'Auld Hornie, F.R.S.' in the *Modern Quarterly* (Autumn 1946). Lewis's 'Reply to Professor Haldane' is published in *Of This and Other Worlds*, ed. Walter Hooper (London: Collins, 1982; Fount, 2000).

and simply wished to conquer for my own (Christian) pt. of view what has always hitherto been used by the opposite side. I think Wells' *1st Men in the Moon*[41] the best of the sort I have read. I once tried a Burroughs[42] in a magazine and disliked it. The more astronomy we know the less likely it seems that other planets are inhabited: even Mars has practically no oxygen.

I guessed who you were as soon as you mentioned the lecture. I did mention in it, I think, Kircher's *Iter Celestre*,[43] but there is no translation, and it is not v. interesting. There's also Voltaire's *Micromégas*[44] but purely satiric.

Yrs.
C. S. Lewis

41 H. G. Wells, *The First Men in the Moon* (1901).

42 Edgar Rice Burroughs (1875–1950), American novelist remembered principally for his Tarzan stories and who wrote a number of stories set on other planets.

43 Athanasius Kircher (1602–1680), *Iter Exstaticum Coelestre* (1656).

44 Voltaire, *Micromégas* (1753).

1939

TO DAPHNE HARWOOD (BOD):

The Kilns,
Headington Quarry,
Oxford.
Jan. 6th 1939.

Dear Daphne

Thanks very much for your nice long letter – I hope I have not thereby stolen time which ought to have been employed in the best of all occupations, and by you, perforce, the most neglected – doing nothing.

As a bachelor who has seldom even talked to children I should be very foolish if I gave any advice as to books for Lawrence: if I felt qualified to choose books I should send books – not tokens.

But John is right about rum. It *has* a romantic interest. It is one of those things which give us a sensuous and an imaginative pleasure at once. And the only reason why I am going to refuse your very tempting offer of a bottle (or was it a keg? do say it was a keg – or a noggin) of rum is that it is your positive wifely duty to see that Cecil drinks it all. If he turns coy and altruistic and says (as men will say anything) that he doesn't care for rum, you may reply lightly in the Latin tongue *Hoc est omnis meus oculus*, or *Nonne narrabis ista marinis equestribus*?[1] He has not forgotten dancing through the streets of Caerleon with the bottle of white rum in one hand and his cutlass in the other. Of course for domestic purposes the question shd. not be put in a nakedly convivial form: some proper pretext about wet feet, overwork, or the like will do gentle violence to his coyness. But ye maun ablains give it to the guideman, ma'am.[2]

---

1 'That is all my eye!'; 'Tell that to the marines!'

2 An imitation of Scottish dialect: 'Anyway you must give it to your husband, ma'am.'

I don't remember anything you said that day which could possibly offend anyone.

All here sent their loves, and best wishes for the New Year. I hope it will be less exciting than the last but not with much confidence: one is reduced to the last form of hope now (I mean as regards this world) which consists in remembering that creaking gates hang long and things expected never happen. However, the prospect of leaving* this planet gets daily less terrible. Tell Cecil to write to me some time.

Yours
Jack Lewis

* I should say 'of having left'. The modes of leaving do not much improve perhaps.

TO A. K. HAMILTON JENKIN (BOD):[3]

The Kilns,
Headington Quarry,
Oxford.
Jan 11th 1939

My dear Jenkin –

I had hoped to be dining somewhere in London to-night with you and Barfield and Harwood (who had, by the way, announced that he was bringing a bottle of Jamaica rum), but I heard yesterday that the arrangement was breaking down as far as they were concerned and to day the much worse news that you were smitten with a fell disease. Very bad luck! – and I suppose you have, in addition, hated every minute of this fine old English winter: unless, at least, your tastes in weather have changed very much since the old days.

I who profess the predilections of a polar bear tried to make believe that I was enjoying it, but the week before Christmas wore the pretence pretty thin: it wasn't so much the snow underfoot that depressed me as the vast clot of lentil soup which had replaced the sky.

The second fall in the first week of the New Year spoiled my annual

3 Alfred Kenneth Hamilton Jenkin (1900–80), a friend from undergraduate days, was a journalist and broadcaster in Cornwall. See his biography in the Biographical Appendix to *CL* I.

January walking tour with my brother. We had one glorious day crossing Wenlock Edge (our course was from Church Stretton to Ludlow)[4] with new snow on the ground and cloudless sunshine from end to end of the skies – beautiful shadows. And out in the country snow is a great betrayer. Rabbits and squirrels became as easy to see as bushes. The *tracks* are rather exciting, too, aren't they? To climb up some unearthly lane to a hill crest far from any house, still early in the morning, and find from the innumerable paw-prints how long ago the animals' day has begun. But on the second day we had to give it up before noon and make the rest of the way by train.

Which, by the way, on those remote railways took us nearly as long as it would have done on foot and was rather fun. We had pleasant hours sitting by roaring fires with the combined station-master, porter, and ticket clerk of tiny stations: and one specially good talk with a little Welsh porter about four feet tall (probably a leprechaun disguised as a porter) who praised Balfour's *Foundations of Belief*.[5] What things any twenty square miles of country contains if a man can only find them. Still, I confess that even I am tired of this winter.

The truth is I am tired of so many things – of weather, of work, of reading, of writing, above all of News. In other words I have a cold: to complain of which to you in your present state is rather carrying colds to Newcastle. As to News and 'the state of the nation' what worries me sometimes more than the dangers is our reaction to them, beginning, of course, with my own reaction. To be faced with wars and ruins is I suppose the normal state of humanity: did any people before lie shivering under it as we do? Just after the September crisis I sat next to old Powick[6] the professor of history and asked him how it had compared with what people felt in 1914: he said at once 'The difference is that this time one missed the note of exaltation that one felt then.' Exaltation begad! Yes: I know they were ignorant of some things we

---

4 This was Jack's and Warnie's eighth and final walking tour. It took place between 2 and 6 January during which they covered forty-two miles on and around Wenlock Edge in Shropshire, leaving the walk at one point to visit Malvern.

5 Arthur James Balfour, *The Foundations of Belief* (1895).

6 Sir Maurice Powicke (1879–1963), historian, was Professor of Modern History at Queen's University, Belfast, 1909–19, Professor of Medieval History at the University of Manchester, 1919–28, and Professor of Modern History at Oxford, 1928–47.

have learned, but I can't believe that is the only difference. Something has slipped.

This is a grand cheery letter to write to a sick man, isn't it? The mention of snow, I now realise, was a fatal blunder, for you once told me that when you woke up cold and ill in the middle of the night one of your main troubles was that you couldn't even imagine warm and pleasant places – that nothing would arise before your inner eye except cold rocks with rain falling on them and ice-fringed ponds. Something of the same kind occasionally happens to me.

But talking of places, has Barfield yet suggested to you that you should try to join us on our Easter walk this year? I know he wanted you to be asked. You needn't be afraid of the distances. There is often a car in attendance and, failing that, by judicious bus-hopping you can always manage to have all the fun and little of the fatigue. We will make you billeting officer and send you on ahead by wheels to book rooms. So you will be sitting with a pipe and a pint in some cheery bar, with a stuffed pike in a glass case on one wall and a tradesman's calendar on the other, and a loud-ticking clock, and a board for shove-halfpenny, and through the window you'll see us wearily limping up to the door – and you'll come out fresh as a new pin and say 'Wherever have you been? I expected you two hours ago.' At least that is what you'll feel like saying but after a glance at our faces you will change it to 'What will you have?'

We'll make it a southern walk, Dorset perhaps. Somewhere, at any rate, where the spring will be surprisingly far on, the woods almost green, and great cushiony clumps of primroses, and a view of the sea: and we'll have glorious mid-morning halts lying in barns or on the sunny side of hills. Make a note of it. (You'll probably be the only atheist present, by the way, but we will respect your susceptibilities – 'Leave thou thy sister when she fails to pray/Her simple unbelief, for that's her way.'* (Give the context of and add any explanatory note that seems necessary)).[7]

* Some MSS 'Leave thou thy sister when she prays/Her knickers, but remove her stays.'

---

7 These lines are based on a line in Alfred, Lord Tennyson, *In Memoriam A.H.H.* (1850), XXXIII, ii, 1–2: 'Leave thou thy sister when she prays,/Her early Heaven, her happy views.'

What did you think of *Snowwhite and the vii Dwarfs*?[8] I saw it at Malvern last week on that holiday. And talking of Malvern, what an exquisite, unchanging place that is. Hardly a sound in the streets after eight o'clock: such nice, warm, quiet, carpeted immemorial hotels: such comfort, such bright, quiet cheerfulness with no silly luxury or novelty. 'I design to end my days' in Malvern. Let me especially recommend the Tudor Hotel for a bottle of really excellent burgundy. They also have a splendid idea that 'gentlemen', being noisy, tobacco-smelling animals, should be segregated, which means that as soon as you arrive a fire is lit in a little, dark, warm, cushioned smoking-room miles away from anywhere, and it's as good as a private sitting room.

But about Snow-White. Leaving out the tiresome question of whether it is suitable for children (which I don't know and don't care) I thought it almost inconceivably good and bad – I mean, I didn't know one human being could be so good and bad. The worst thing of all was the vulgarity of the winking dove at the beginning, and the next worst the faces of the dwarfs. Dwarfs ought to be ugly of course, but not in that way. And the dwarfs' jazz party was pretty bad. I suppose it never occurred to the poor boob that you *could* give them any other kind of music. But all the terrifying bits were good, and the animals really most moving: and the use of shadows (of dwarfs and vultures) was real genius. What might not have come of it if this man had been educated – or even brought up in a decent society?

If you'd care for a copy of my story (a journey to Mars) let me know and I'll send you one. But I rather think it is not a genre you care for: and I know that if people don't like stories of that kind they usually dislike them very much indeed. These sharp *frontiers* of taste are a very interesting literary fact which I've never seen discussed by any critic, and which are far more important in dividing readers than any of the *formal* divisions, even that of verse and prose. 'Do you like stories about other planets – or hunting stories – or stories of the supernatural – or historical novels?' – surely these are questions which elicit an unalterable Yes or No from the very depth of a reader's heart: but Aristotle, Johnson, and Coleridge have nothing to say about them.[9]

---

8 Walt Disney's first full-length cartoon film, *Snow White and the Seven Dwarfs* (1937).

9 Years later Lewis devoted an essay to this subject. See *Of This and Other Worlds*, 'On Science Fiction'.

(By the way, why is North's Plutarch[10] such very dull reading?)

I hope you'll be mending by the time you get this. If you are unable to write, then,** as soon as you conveniently can, let me have word through someone else, how you are getting on and whether there is anything of any kind I can do for you.

Yours
C. S. Lewis

** *Then* here means 'in that event' not 'at that time.' Not one of our best sentences.

TO ALEC VIDLER (BOD):[11]

Magdalen College,
Oxford
Jan 17th 1939

Dear Mr. Vidler

I fear I am a very bad salesman, but I enclose the names of those people who might be induced to take *Theology*.[12]

On the question of reviewing – would it be a good thing sometimes to review books which had *not* been sent for review? I am thinking chiefly of infamous and ill informed books. Review copies of what you specially want to refute are not likely to be sent you, and that is one of the ways in which nonsense circulates uncontradicted. The reviewer wd. presumably, in such cases, pay for his own copy. (I have no particular book in view at the moment).

Yours sincerely,
C. S. Lewis

---

10 Plutarch, *Lives of the Noble Grecians and Romans, Englished by Sir Thomas North anno 1579*, introduction by George Wyndham (1895–6).

11 See **The Rev. Dr Alexander Roper Vidler** in the Biographical Appendix. Vidler was editor of the monthly journal *Theology*.

12 Before becoming editor of *Theology*, Vidler had asked Lewis to write a piece on Charles Williams for the periodical, and he now wanted to know if he would serve as a 'literary collaborator' with it.

TO A. K. HAMILTON JENKIN (BOD):

[The Kilns]
Jan 22nd 1939.

My dear Jenkin –

I was delighted to hear from Barfield that you are quite markedly better though not yet well enough for writing. I have, thank God, no experience of your ailment so I don't know what the recovery is like – whether as after fever you suddenly wake up after the first good night feeling ravenous with hunger (oh those first slices of bread and butter: angel's food!) – or itch as after chickenpox – or (I hope not) whether you pass into a state of melancholy as after flu.

On the assumption of melancholy, let me cheer you up. I don't think it is likely we shall enjoy that walk much as we shall be so hard up after the capital levy in February (you heard about that I suppose): even if we do go you will have seen in the papers that a spring of unprecedented rains and sleet is prophesied. Still we must make a push for it. I shouldn't get maps and plan out a tour: those ordinance survey maps are so unreliable that its not much use. I'm told Prohibition will probably be brought in as soon as Parliament meets. Never mind: we must drink the pure element, Adam's wine (tho' by the bye you will have noticed warnings lately against drinking any water south and west of a line drawn from London to Carlisle). Milk, of course, there will be none. And whatever happens don't worry about your *feet* on a first walk – newcomers are nearly always quite alright again by Xmas. So you see, dear friend, how our little troubles melt away if only they are faced in the right spirit. Ripeness is all.[13]

You would (seriously) like it here to day. The Cherwell is up almost to a level of Addison's walk and running (so Salters[14] told my brother yesterday) 10 miles an hour, the speed being very visible by the endless procession of big mats or flakes of froth that go shooting by. The meadow enclosed within Addison's walk (you remember?) is flooded

13 William Shakespeare, *King Lear* (1608), V, ii, 9–11: 'Men must endure/Their going hence, even as their coming hither:/Ripeness is all.'

14 Salters Boatyard, established in 1858 by John and Stephen Salter, is located on the River Cherwell at Folly Bridge just south of Christ Church. The company built and maintained Warnie's river cruiser, the *Bosphorus*. They also built and rented out punts and other boats, and at one time ran passenger steamers along the Thames. Today the company still rents out boats and berths.

and under a greyish, fine, morning sky gives pleasant reflections of trees and upward lights in unexpected places. Several birds are singing. There is always a specially fresh and poignant quality about them at this time of the year – like voices in a big empty ball-room the day before the ball – perhaps because they are few, or perhaps only because ones ears have grown unused to them in the winter.

Which reminds me, I heard an explanation the other day of why the stars look so unnaturally bright if one wakes up at night from really deep sleep and looks out: viz. because one's eyes are rested and completely on top of their job.

Talking of jobs, did you see that D. L. Keir of Univ. has been made Principal of Queen's University Belfast. A little galling to me because he will now become such a great man in *my* home town that whenever I go there I shall find people regarding it as the very peak of my career to have known him.

I have just been writing a review of Charles Williams' new poem *Taliessin through Logres,*[15] and wonder if you have read his novels. The two I recommend most strongly are *The Place of the Lion* and *Descent into Hell.*[16] They are 'shockers' in a sense, but of a peculiar sort. The first is of special interest to chaps like you (a B. Litt.!) and me (a don) because it is about a perfect bitch of a female researcher called Damaris who is writing a doctorate thesis on the relation between 'ideas' in Plato and Angels in Abelard, without the slightest idea that it ever really meant anything, and all the time treating Plato and Aristotle and Dionysius and Abelard like 'the top form of a school in which she was an inspector.' Then, suddenly, owing to a piece of supernatural machinery which needn't be described, she wakes up to find that the things she is studying are really there – one such primal energy looking in at her study window in the form of a gigantic pterodactyl. The novels are also interesting as the only modern ones I know which contain convincing 'good' characters.

I have a theory why the 'good' characters in literature are so often dull. To make an interesting character you have to see him from the inside, all agree. Now to imagine from within a person morally inferior to yourself you don't need to do anything, you only need to *stop* doing something – to take the brake off and give all your usually suppressed

15 Charles Williams, *Taliessin Through Logres* (1938).
16 Charles Williams, *Descent into Hell* (1937).

vanity, or greed, or cruelty, or envy a delightful holiday. But how to make one *better* than yourself? Well, you can make him a little better by making him actually do what you only try to do, or do often what you only do seldom. That is, you can give him the sort of virtue in full which you have in some degree yourself. But for anything beyond that you simply haven't got the material. Not only do you not actually behave as a hero would, you don't even know what he feels like. Hence in most literature ideally good characters have to be made 'from outside' and accordingly look like puppets.[17]

From which silly readers draw the conclusion that good people are dull in real life – as if there were anything particularly delectable in the society of bullies, cheats, egoists and drug-addicts, or as if the same qualities which made a man an egoist did not normally make him a bore. Moral – beware of putting 'good' characters into a book for that's where you give yourself away, as Richardson (to my mind) is given away by Pamela.[18] I said 'to my mind' not only because of my habitual modesty and temperance (you will remember that of old) but because Dr. Johnson thought differently.[19]

I go to Cambridge to lecture once a week this term, so if you have any commissions in Bletchley now is your time. Did I tell you I have discovered the Renaissance never occurred – that is what I'm lecturing on.[20] Do you think it is reasonable to call the lecture 'The Renaissance' under the circumstances? 'Absence of the Renaissance' sounds so odd, and 'What was happening while the Renaissance was not taking place'

---

17 This idea was developed in the chapter on 'Satan' in *A Preface to 'Paradise Lost'* (1942), p. 98: 'Satan is the best drawn of Milton's characters. The reason is not hard to find. Of the major characters whom Milton attempted he is incomparably the easiest to draw . . . In all but a few writers the "good" characters are the least successful, and every one who has ever tried to make even the humblest story ought to know why. To make a character worse than oneself it is only necessary to release imaginatively from control some of the bad passions which, in real life, are always straining at the leash . . . But if you try to draw a character better than yourself, all you can do is to take the best moments you have had and to imagine them prolonged and more consistently embodied in action.'

18 Samuel Richardson, *Pamela, or Virtue Rewarded* (1740–1).

19 Samuel Johnson, *Lives of the English Poets*, ed. George Birkbeck Hill (1905), vol. III, Life of William Shenstone, p. 354.

20 Lewis gave weekly lectures on the 'Prolegomena to Renaissance Literature' every Tuesday during Lent Term at Cambridge (11 January–16 March 1939). They later formed part of *English Literature in the Sixteenth Century, Excluding Drama* (1954).

is inaccurate because, of course, if the Renaissance *never* occurred, then all times were times at which it did not occur, and therefore everything that ever happened happened 'while the Renaissance was not taking place'. Alas, as Wordsworth said, 'I fear/That I am trifling.'[21]

So, I hope, are you by now. Don't bother writing for ages yet: I look to hear good news of you from Owen Barfield from time to time. I forget whether I told you last time that all of us here were very concerned to hear of your illness and Mrs. Moore particularly. But you'd have guessed that.

Yours
C. S. Lewis

TO ALEC VIDLER (BOD):

Magdalen College
Oxford
Feb 1st 1939

Dear Mr Vidler

I enclose MS.[22] It has in the end worked out to less than 4000 words but I dare say you will be glad of the extra room. If not Williams or Mr. Eliot might give you a poem of the right length. In the unlikely event of your being stuck, I cd. let you have about 1500 words on Christianity and War in continuation of the discussion begun in the last number. I thought it all good – except perhaps Mr. Roberts on poetry.[23]

Yours
C. S. Lewis

TO OWEN BARFIELD (W):

[The Kilns]
Feb 8th [1939]

My dear Barfield –

I am recovering (at least they tell me I am recovering) from an unusually bad attack of flu'. Two weekends of Feb. fall in term: the

---

21 Wordsworth, *The Prelude*, VIII, 555–6.

22 This was Lewis's review of Charles Williams's *Taliessin Through Logres*, entitled 'A Sacred Poem', published in *Theology*, XXXVIII, no. 226 (April 1939), pp. 268–76.

23 He was referring to Michael Roberts' review of J. Middleton Murry, *Studies in Keats: New and Old* (1939) in *Theology*, XXXVIII, no. 227 (May 1939), pp. 392–3.

5th–8th and the 12–15th. If you choose the former you will be able to hear Tillyard and me finishing our controversy *viva voce*,[24] but as I have to give him a bed perhaps the 12th wd. be better. No doubt I shall be defeated in the controversy.[25]

I don't know if Plato *did* write the Phaedo: the canon of those ancient writers, under the surface, is still quite chaotic. It is also a very corrupt text. Bring it along by all means, but don't pitch your hopes too high. We are both getting so rusty that we shall make very little of it – and my distrust of all lexicons and translations is increasing. Also of Plato – and of the human mind. I suppose for the sake of the others we must do something about arranging a walk. Those maps are so unreliable by now that it is rather a farce – but still 'Try lad, try! No harm in trying.'[26] Of course hardly any districts in England are unspoiled enough to make walking worth while: and with two new members – I have very little doubt it will be a ghastly failure. I haven't seen C.W.'s play: it is not likely to be at all good.[27] As for Orpheus – again it's no harm trying. If you can't write it console yourself by reflecting that if you did you wd. have been v. unlikely to get a publisher.[28] I am more and more convinced that there is no future for poetry. Nearly everyone has been ill here: I try to prevent them all croaking and grumbling but it is hard being the only optimist. Let me know which week end: whichever you choose something will doubtless prevent it. I hear the income-tax is going up again. The weather is bad and looks like getting worse. I suppose war is certain now. I don't believe language is a

24 See **E. M. W. Tillyard** in the Biographical Appendix. His book *Milton* (1930) had drawn Lewis's fire, leading to their controversy. At the time of their meeting on 7 February 1939 each man had contributed three essays to *The Personal Heresy: A Controversy* (1939) and their debate in Magdalen College was the conclusion to the controversy.

25 This was certainly not what happened. Lewis's pupil, John Lawlor (1918–99), who was present for the debate, recalled in *C. S. Lewis: Memories and Reflections* (1998), p. 4: 'There was a memorable occasion when in the Hall at Magdalen Dr Tillyard met him to round off in debate the controversy begun with the publication of Lewis's indictment of "The Personal Heresy". I am afraid there was no debate. Lewis made rings round Tillyard; in, out, up, down, around, back again – like some piratical Plymouth bark against a high-built galleon of Spain.'

26 A. E. Housman, *A Shropshire Lad* (1896), no. XVII: 'Try I will: no harm in trying.'

27 Charles Williams, *Judgement at Chelmsford* (1939).

28 See Lewis's criticism of Barfield's *Orpheus* in his letter of 28 March 1938.

perpetual Orphic song. The Cheedle reader is dead, I suppose you saw.[29]

Yours
C.S.L.

P.S. Even my braces are in a frightful condition. 'Damn braces' said Blake.[30]

TO CHARLES WILLIAMS (W):

(as from) Magdalen
Feb 22nd 1939.

Dear Williams,

I don't press my criticisms. I thought we'd done with dummies and when they turned up (I was in bed with flu') and I found I'd got to send one back and one to Tillyard, I took the line 'If they insist on having opinions, opinions by gum (blessed be he) they shall have!' I still think that

Re
habilit-
ations[31]

wd. be tolerable, but I'm not making a stand: so whatever happens *don't* send me any more dummies but fire ahead and get the book out. (You see, in this house one is never allowed to *buy* large envelopes because 'There are lots in that drawer': so that returning a dummy means a domestic crisis and the dinner is spoiled and the cats' tails are trodden and charity is imperilled).

I've finished the review.[32] My opinion of the poem, except for The Coming of Galahad wh. I think mannered, went up and up. A great work, full of glory. I also re-read the *Place of the Lion* and *Many D.* while I was ill, with undiminished enjoyment. But hurry up and write another for I shall soon know them all too well. I also tried to read

29 The reference to 'Cheedle' seems to be part of the private language between Lewis and Barfield. Cf. 'Gurton in Cheedle' in the letter to Barfield of?May 1949, p. 938.

30 William Blake, *The Marriage of Heaven and Hell* (c. 1790–3), 'Proverbs of Hell', stanza 3, 18.

31 Williams was seeing Lewis's new book, *Rehabilitations and Other Essays* (1939) through the press.

32 Of Williams's *Taliessin Through Logres*.

Don Quixote[33] and failed: it seems to me a wretched affair. I suppose I must be wrong.

Yours
C. S. Lewis

TO THE EDITOR OF *THEOLOGY* (*EC*):[34]

Magdalen College,
Oxford.
February 27, 1939.

Sir,

In your January number Mr Mascall mentions six conditions for a just war which have been laid down by 'theologians.' I have one question to ask, and a number of problems to raise, about those rules.

The question is merely historical. Who are these theologians, and what kind or degree of authority can they claim over members of the Church of England?

The problems are more difficult. Condition 4 lays down that 'it must be morally certain that the losses, to the belligerents, the world, and religion, will not outweigh the advantages of winning'; and 6, that 'there must be a considerable probability of winning.' It is plain that equally sincere people can differ to any extent and argue for ever as to whether a proposed war fulfils these conditions or not. The practical question, therefore, which faces us is one of authority. Who has the duty of deciding when the conditions are fulfilled, and the right of enforcing his decision? Modern discussions tend to assume without argument that the answer is 'The private conscience of the individual,' and that any other answer is immoral and totalitarian.

Now it is certain, in some sense, that 'no duty of obedience can justify a sin,' as Mr Mascall says. Granted that capital punishment is compatible with Christianity, a Christian may lawfully be a hangman; but he must not hang a man whom he knows to be innocent. But will anyone interpret this to mean that the hangman has the *same* duty of investigating the prisoner's guilt which the judge has? If so, no executive

33 Miguel de Cervantes, *Don Quixote de la Mancha* (1605, 1615).

34 This letter was published in *Theology*, XXXVIII, no. 227 (May 1939), pp. 373–4, under the title 'The Conditions for a Just War'. It is a reply to the Rev. E. L. Mascall's letter on 'The Christian and the New War' published in *Theology*, XXXVIII, no. 222 (January 1939), pp. 53–8.

can work and no Christian state is possible; which is absurd. I conclude that the hangman has done his duty if he has done his share of the general duty, resting upon all citizens alike, to ensure, so far as in him lies, that we have an honest judicial system; if, in spite of this, and unknowingly, he hangs an innocent man, then a sin has been committed, but not by him.

This analogy suggests to me that it must be absurd to give to the private citizen the *same* right and duty of deciding the justice of a given war which rests on governments; and I submit that the rules for determining what wars are just[35] were originally rules for the guidance of princes, not subjects. This does not mean that private persons must obey governments commanding them to do what they know is sin; but perhaps it does mean (I write it with some reluctance) that the ultimate decision as to what the situation at a given moment is in the highly complex field of international affairs is one which must be delegated.

No doubt we must make every effort which the constitution allows to ensure a good government and to influence public opinion; but in the long run, the nation, as a nation, must act, and it can act only through its government. (It must be remembered that there are risks in both directions: if war is ever lawful, then peace is sometimes sinful.) What is the alternative? That individuals ignorant of history and strategy should decide for themselves whether condition 6 ('a considerable probability of winning') is, or is not, fulfilled? – or that every citizen, neglecting his own vocation and not weighing his capacity, is to become an expert on all the relevant, and often technical, problems?

Decisions by the private conscience of each Christian in the light of Mr Mascall's six rules would divide Christians from each other and result in no clear Christian witness to the pagan world around us. But a clear Christian witness might be attained in a different way. If all Christians consented to bear arms at the command of the magistrate, and if all, after that, refused to obey anti-Christian orders, should we not get a clear issue? A man is much more certain that he ought not to murder prisoners or bomb civilians than he ever can be about the justice of a war. It is perhaps here that 'conscientious objection' ought to begin. I feel certain that one Christian airman shot for refusing to

35 Aquinas, *Summa Theologica*, Part II, Question 40, Article 2.

bomb enemy civilians would be a more effective martyr (in the etymological sense of the word) than a hundred Christians in jail for refusing to join the army.

Christendom has made two efforts to deal with the evil of war – chivalry and pacifism. Neither succeeded. But I doubt whether chivalry has such an unbroken record of failure as pacifism.

The question is a very dark one. I should welcome about equally refutation, or development, of what I have said.

I am, sir,

Your obedient servant,

C. S. Lewis

For some years Lewis had been concerned about what he regarded as the 'inordinate esteem of culture'[36] *by such unbelieving literary critics as Matthew Arnold, Benedetto Croce, I. A. Richards and F. R. Leavis. The latter wanted to see culture made the basis of a humane society, and to this end he founded* Scrutiny. *The editors of this periodical, which ran from 1932 to 1953, expressed a belief in 'a necessary relationship between the quality of the individual's response to art and his general fitness for a humane existence'.*[37]

Lewis was appalled to find this 'inordinate esteem' expressed in the pages of Theology. *In an essay entitled 'The Necessity of* Scrutiny*', published in the issue of March 1939, the Anglican monk Brother George Every SSM,*[38] *after paying tribute to the literary beliefs of Leavis, D. H. Lawrence and T. S. Eliot, asked: 'What are Mr Eliot's admirers to think of a church where those who seem to be theologically equipped prefer the late Professor Housman, Mr Charles Morgan, and Miss Dorothy Sayers, to Lawrence, Joyce and Mr E. M. Forster?' This essay would eventually lead Lewis to write one of his most valuable works of literary criticism, 'Christianity and Culture'.*

---

36 'Christianity and Culture', *Christian Reflections* (London: 1967; Fount, 1998), p. 15.

37 'Scrutiny: A Manifesto', *Scrutiny*, I, no. 1 (May 1932), p. 5.

38 See **Brother George Every SSM** in the Biographical Appendix.

TO ALEC VIDLER (BOD):

Magdalen College
Oxford
March 11th 1939

Dear Mr. Vidler

I enclose (1) Corrected proof of article on *Taliessin.* (2) A letter about Christianity and war for your consideration.[39] If you think it worth printing (and I am not sure that it is) I believe the MS. will be clear enough for the printer: but if not, get it typed and tell me how much I owe you for the job.

I have been ill or I would before now have answered your letter suggesting an early meeting of the 'literary collaborators'. I should have great pleasure in attending this if it takes place. At the same time I ought to warn you that each number makes it clear to me that my only use to you in literary matters can be that of permanent opposition, for I find myself in sharp disagreement with Mr Roberts and Brother Every. It will be for you to decide when the limits of useful disagreement have been passed – if you eject me I shall not feel in the least ill used. The hint in Brother Every's paper that good taste is essential to salvation seemed to me precisely one of our greatest enemies in this age of intellectual converts – there is a danger of making Christianity itself appear as one more highbrow fad.

Don't bother answering this at present. I write it only because I don't want you to buy a pig in a poke.

Yours sincerely
C. S. Lewis

Dr Vidler nevertheless replied to Lewis on 14 March:

> *I am grateful for your warning . . . There seems a danger that* Theology *may be falling into the hands of a certain literary clique, but I am determined to avoid that, if possible. It so happens that George Every was one of the first to urge upon me the importance of giving attention in* Theology *to literary matters, and he made many suggestions . . . While I wish Every and his friends to have an opportunity of saying what they want to say, I do not intend*

39 i.e. the letter to the editor of *Theology* of 27 February reproduced above.

that Theology *shall be an exclusive organ for their views, and I shall welcome any opportunity of making this clear. The best way no doubt will be to publish articles from other points of view.*

TO ALEC VIDLER (BOD):

Magdalen College
Oxford
March 16th 1939

Dear Mr Vidler

Sorry to have imposed such a long letter on you: this one will need no answer. As long as I can occasionally contribute an article on the opposite side, I am quite content.

Yours sincerely
C. S. Lewis

TO MARY NEYLAN (T):

The Kilns,
Headington Quarry,
Oxford.
March 21st 1939.

Dear Mrs Neylan

Miss Moore and I are both very much obliged to you: she looks forward with great pleasure to seeing the school under such privileged conditions.[40]

Congratulations on your daughter[41] – it makes the production of mere books seem rather silly, for at the very best they can never say or do any more than you put into them.

I can't understand Dyson's not writing to you. You know the address has changed to 30 Alexandra Rd.? I am sure there is some innocent reason for the silence. My own idea, remembering his handwriting, is that he did write but you thought it was a letter *from* someone else *about* something else.

Please tell my youthful critics that tho' Weston is a caricature, Weston*ism* is v. nearly as silly as I have made out. The crowning idiocy

40 Maureen Moore was interested in seeing Dartington Hall School with a view towards teaching there.

41 Mary Neylan's daughter, Sarah, was born in 1938. For more information see **Mary Neylan** in the Biographical Appendix.

on p. 224 ('It is enough for me that there is a Beyond') is the last words of Lilith in Shaw's *Back to Methuselah*.[42] Most of the other nonsense derives from the last essay in J. B. S. Haldane's 'Possible Worlds'. With best wishes.

Yours sincerely
C. S. Lewis

TO ALEC VIDLER (BOD):

Magdalen College
Oxford
March 23rd 1939

Dear Mr Vidler

Never trouble yourself again about who reviews things of mine – open lists and 'the rigour of the game'[43] is what I want, and offer. But thanks for writing.

Yours
C. S. Lewis

Rehabilitations and Other Essays *was published by Oxford University Press on 23 March 1939.*

TO JOAN BENNETT (*L*):[44]

[Magdalen College
5 April 1939]

I'm sorry about the Athanasian Creed[45] – the passage illustrates how important it is in writing to say what you mean and not to say

42 George Bernard Shaw, *Back to Methuselah* (1921), Part V: 'Of Life only is there no end; and though of its million starry mansions many are empty and many are still unbuilt, and though its vast domain is as yet unbearably desert, my seed will one day fill it and master its matter to its uttermost confines. And for what may be beyond, the eyesight of Lilith is too short. It is enough that there is a beyond.'

43 Lamb, *Essays of Elia*, 'Mrs. Battle's Opinions on Whist': 'A clear fire, a clean hearth, and the rigour of the game.'

44 It appears that Mrs Bennett had read *The Pilgrim's Regress* and objected to the chapter entitled 'Limbo'.

45 The Athanasian Creed, found in the *Book of Common Prayer*, is a profession of faith used in Western Christendom, also known for its opening words '*Quicunque vult*' ('Whoever will be [saved]'). It differs from the Apostles' and Nicene Creeds in various ways, as well as embodying anathemas, one of which is 'Which Faith except every one do keep whole and undefiled: without doubt he shall perish everlastingly.'

anything you don't mean. As the context suggests, I was thinking purely of the Trinitarian doctrine and had quite forgotten the damnatory clauses. There are however several palliatives. Residence in Limbo I am told is compatible with 'perishing everlastingly' and you'll find it quite jolly, for whereas Heaven is an acquired taste, Limbo is a place of 'perfect *natural* happiness'.[46]

In fact you may be able to realise your wish 'of attending with one's whole mind to the history of the human spirit'. There are grand libraries in Limbo, endless discussions, and no colds. There will be a faint melancholy because you'll all know that you have missed the bus, but that will provide a subject for poetry. The scenery is pleasant though tame. The climate endless autumn.

Seriously, I don't pretend to have any information on the fate of the virtuous unbeliever. I don't suppose this question provided the solitary exception to the principle that actions on a false hypothesis lead to some less satisfactory result than actions on a true. That's as far as I would go – beyond feeling that the believer is playing for higher stakes and incurring danger of something really nasty.

The Personal Heresy: A Controversy *by Lewis and E. M. W. Tillyard was published by Oxford University Press on 27 April 1939.*

TO DOM BEDE GRIFFITHS OSB (W):

[Magdalen College]
May 8th 1939

My dear D.B. –

It was nice to hear from you again. I think I said before that I have no contribution to make about re-union. It was never more needed. A united Christendom should be the answer to the new Paganism. But how reconciliation of the Churches, as opposed to conversions of individuals from a church to another, is to come about, I confess I cannot

46 In Catholic theology, Limbo designates the place or condition of those who have died without the conditions necessary for entrance into Heaven, but also without the guilt necessary for condemnation to Hell. In *The Pilgrim's Regress*, book 10, ch. 3, p. 226, the Guide speaks of Limbo as 'the twilight porches of the black hole', the place of those 'who have kept alive and pure the deep desire of the soul but through some fatal flaw, of pride or sloth or, it may be, timidity, have refused till the end the only means to its fulfilment; taken huge pains, often, to prove to themselves that the fulfilment is impossible.'

see. I am inclined to think that the immediate task is vigorous co-operation on the basis of what even now is common – combined, of course, with full admission of the differences. An *experienced* unity on some things might then prove the prelude to a confessional unity on all things. Nothing wd. give such strong support to the Papal claims as the spectacle of a Pope actually functioning as head of Christendom. But it is not, I feel sure, my vocation to discuss reunion.

Yes, I do like George Eliot. *Romola*[47] is a most purgative work on the *facilis descensus*,[48] because the final state of the character is so different from his original state and yet all the transitions are so dreadfully natural. Mind you, I think George Eliot *labours* her morality a bit: it has something of the ungraceful ponderousness of all heathen ethics. (I recently read all Seneca's epistles and think I like the Stoics better than George Eliot). The best of all her books as far as I have read is *Middlemarch*.[49] It shows such an extraordinary understanding of different kinds of life – different classes, ages, and sexes. Her humour is nearly always admirable.

I thought we had talked of Patmore. I think him really great within his own limited sphere. To be sure he pushes the parallel between Divine and human love as far as it can sanely or decently go, and perhaps at times a little further. One can imagine his work being most pernicious to a devout person who read it at the wrong age. But a superb poet. Do you remember the comparison of the naturally virtuous person who receives grace at conversion to a man walking along and suddenly hearing a band playing, and then 'His step unchanged, he steps in time.'[50] Or on the poignancy of Spring, 'With it the blackbird breaks the young day's heart.'[51] Or the lightening during a storm at sea which reveals 'The deep/*Standing* about in stony heaps.'[52] That is sheer genius. And the *tightness* (if you know what I mean) of all his work. The prose one (*Rod, Root & Flower*)[53] contains much you might like.

---

47 George Eliot, *Romola* (1863).

48 Virgil, *Aeneid*, VI, 126: '*facilis descensus Averno*': 'easy is the descent to the underworld.'

49 George Eliot, *Middlemarch, A Study of Provincial Life* (1871–2).

50 Coventry Patmore, *The Victories of Love* (1862), book II, 'The Wedding Sermon', stanza 6, 7.

51 Coventry Patmore, *The Unknown Eros* (1877), book I, no. 1, 'Saint Valentine's Day', 21.

52 Patmore, *The Victories of Love*, book I, 'From Frederick', stanza 1, 9–10: The deep/ Standing about in stony heaps.'

53 Coventry Patmore, *The Rod, The Root and The Flower* (1895).

No, I haven't joined the Territorials.[54] I am too old. It wd. be hypocrisy to say that I regret this. My memories of the last war haunted my dreams for years. Military service, to be plain, includes the threat of *every* temporal evil: pain and death wh. is what we fear from sickness: isolation from those we love wh. is what we fear from exile: toil under arbitrary masters, injustice and humiliation, wh. is what we fear from slavery: hunger, thirst, cold and exposure wh. is what we fear from poverty. I'm not a pacifist. If its got to be, its got to be. But the flesh is weak and selfish and I think death wd. be much better than to live through another war.

Thank God, He has not allowed my *faith* to be greatly tempted by the present horrors. I do not doubt that whatever misery He permits will be for our ultimate good unless, by rebellious will, we convert it to evil. But I get no further than Gethsemane: and am daily thankful that that scene, of all others in Our Lord's life, did not go unrecorded. But what state of affairs in this world can we view with satisfaction? If we are unhappy, then we are unhappy. If we are happy, then we remember that the crown is not promised without the cross and tremble. In fact, one comes to realise, what one always admitted theoretically, that there is nothing here that will do us good: the sooner we are safely out of this world the better. But 'would it were evening, Hal, and all well.'[55] I have even, I'm afraid, caught myself wishing that I had never been born, wh. is sinful. Also, meaningless if you try to think it out.

The process of living seems to consist in coming to realise truths so ancient and simple that, if stated, they sound like barren platitudes. They cannot sound otherwise to those who have not had the relevant experience: that is why there is no real teaching of such truths possible and every generation starts from scratch.

I hope you keep well. I have advanced from having flu' once a year to having it once a term!

Yours
C. S. Lewis

---

54 With war looming over Britain in 1939, the government had decided to double the size of its Territorial Army (amateur and part-time soldiers employed to supplement the regular army in defence of the realm). On 1 September 1939 all Territorial units lost their independent status and became part of the regular army for the duration of the war.

55 William Shakespeare, *Henry IV Part 1* (1623), V, i, 125: 'I would it were bed-time, Hal, and all well.'

TO ALEC VIDLER (BOD):

Magdalen College,
Oxford.
May 10th 1939.

Dear Mr Vidler

It's a great bore that June 10th shd. be the date as I shall be engaged that night (I nearly always am on Saturdays). If it suits you to be in Oxford early enough for lunch (wh. need not be till 1.30) and you cared to lunch with me here I should be somewhat consoled for losing the evening.

I don't think you need bother sending me Mascall's reply as I shall see it in print. I suppose he doesn't feel hurt at being answered by me just after he had reviewed me so kindly? As I said, I don't sympathise with that sort of feeling myself. But if you think a line from me to him about it is desirable, let me know.

Yours sincerely
C. S. Lewis

P.S. I liked MacKinnon's *Vexilla Regis.*[56]

TO OWEN BARFIELD (W):

[Magdalen College]
June 1st 1939

My dear Barfield

I find the chapters intensely interesting – read them, so to speak, with my spectacles poised half way to my nose – and think this was not due to knowing the author. Go on with it by all means: I am eager for the next instalment.

I have often wondered what it is makes a good 'anthology poem' like *Toll for the brave*[57] or *Casa Bianca.*[58] We must talk of this.

I wish I could come and see you. Mrs Moore is painfully, tho' I hope not seriously, ill with a varicose ulcer and I am examining from next week till mid July. On Aug. 31st and Sept 1st I am lecturing in Stratford.

---

56 D. M. MacKinnon, '*Vexilla Regis*: Some Reflections for Passiontide, 1939', *Theology*, XXXVIII, no. 226 (April 1939), pp. 254–9.

57 William Cowper, 'On the Loss of the *Royal George*' ('Toll for the Brave'), first published in William Hayley, *The Life, and Posthumous Writings, of William Cowper, Esqr*, 3 vols (1803–4).

58 Felicia Hemans, *The Forest Sanctuary* (1829), 'Casabianca'.

Shall we *both* go, and see a play or so? – you needn't attend the lectures. Do try: it will make a bore into a beatitude.

Yours
C. S. Lewis

TO OWEN BARFIELD (W):

The Kilns,
Headington Quarry,
Oxford.
July 23rd 1939.

My dear Barfield

In order to begin as pleasantly as possible let me say that your enclose was a great disappointment: when I saw the large envelope I thought it was going to be another chapter of the *Dichtung und Wahrheit*[59] (on the Wahrheit aspect, the candid Mr Harwood assures me that you have omitted to mention that it was only *after* he left that you began to win prizes). When I'd forgiven the Diction & Fiction for not being what it wasn't, I liked it very well. No criticisms occurred to me at a first reading. The two illustrations from Christina Rossetti and de la Mare seemed to me very good ones.

There's *no* 'anti-great-men' part of my Weltanschauung.[60] I'm all for great men and for imitating them ᾗ μεγάλους.[61] What I object to is imitating them ᾗ οὔκ[62] – e.g. imitating the life or personality of one who is great only as a poet. You can imitate whatever is imitable in his poetry ad lib.

I quite agree that the Personal Heresy is not important – *now*! But it was rapidly becoming so. I was just in the nick of time – 'This Lewis bore not . . .'

I quite agree that Stratford wd. be intolerable at the end of August. Some neighbouring village was my idea. But Stratford or no we must meet this summer if there's no war.

I was wondering the other day how many of my friends I shd. continue to love if the common intellectual interests were taken away

59 'Poetry and Truth'; this is a reference to the autobiography of Johann Wolfgang von Goethe, *Dichtung und Wahrheit* (1811–32).

60 'world-view'.

61 'in respect to their greatness'.

62 'not, in fact, with respect to what makes them great'.

(which perhaps do not survive death) and Harwood and you were the only two I felt much confidence about. So little do the years add.

Mrs. Moore is much better, thanks.

No – I don't 'feel quite at ease' in Christianity. Do you?

Gosh!

One of my lectures at Stratford has to be on *The Taming of the Shrew*.[63] Can you supply me with any ideas? It is difficult to make that tedious farce the peg to hang anything on – unless one raises the whole problem – I mean the one we discussed among the gooseberry bushes at Streatham.

If not Stratford we must have a week end elsewhere: if all is well, at the Kilns, if not at some pub

Yours
C. S. Lewis

TO SISTER PENELOPE CSMV (BOD):[64]

Magdalen College,
Oxford.
July [August][65] 9th 1939

Dear Madam –

Thank you very much for the book and for your kind letter.[66]

The letter raises for me rather an acute problem – do I become more proud in trying to resist or in frankly revelling in, the pleasure it gives me? One hopes there will come a day when one can enjoy nice things said about one's self just in the same innocent way as one enjoys nice things about anyone else – perfect humility will need no modesty. In the meantime, it is not so.

The letter at the end is pure fiction and the 'circumstances wh. put the book out of date'[67] are merely a way of preparing for a sequel. But

63 William Shakespeare, *The Taming of the Shrew* (1623).

64 See the biography of **Sister Penelope CSMV** in the Biographical Appendix. Sister Penelope, an Anglican nun of the Community of St Mary the Virgin in Wantage, had written to compliment Lewis on *Out of the Silent Planet* and to ask if he planned to write a sequel.

65 Lewis gave this letter the wrong date for it answers Sister Penelope's letter of 5 August 1939.

66 Sister Penelope had sent him a copy of her book, *God Persists: A Short Survey of World History in the Light of Christian Faith* (1939).

67 *Out of the Silent Planet* (1938; HarperCollins, 2000), ch. 22, p. 160: 'What neither of us foresaw was the rapid march of events which was to render the book out of date before it was published.'

the danger of 'Westonism' I mean to be real. What set me about writing the book was the discovery that a pupil of mine took all that dream of interplanetary colonisation quite seriously, and the realisation that thousands of people, in one form or another depend on some hope of perpetuating and improving the human species for the whole meaning of the universe – that a 'scientific' hope of defeating death is a real rival to Christianity.

At present, of course, the prospect of a war has rather damped them: which shows that whatever evil Satan sets on foot God will always do some good or other by it. I don't think, even 'for believers only' I could 'describe' Ransom's revelation to Oyarsa: the fact that you want me to really proves how well advised I was merely to *suggest* it.[68]

You will be both grieved and amused to learn that out of about 60 reviews, only 2 showed any knowledge that my idea of a fall of the Bent One was anything but a private invention of my own? But if only there were someone with a richer talent and more leisure, I believe this great ignorance might be a help to the evangelisation of England: any amount of theology can now be smuggled into people's minds under cover of romance without their knowing it.

I have given your *God Persists* a first reading with great pleasure. I value it particularly for its frank emphasis on those elements in the faith which too many modern apologists try to keep out of sight for fear they will be called mythical. I am sure this weakens our case. I like very much your treatment of Heathenism[69] (my own debts to it are enormous – it was through *almost* believing in the gods that I came to believe in God) on p. 31. Also p. 33 on the seedlings for special culture and the danger of

---

68 In her letter Sister Penelope said, 'Could you not, for believers only, perhaps as a *Theology* article, write the scene where Ransom tells Oyarsa about the Incarnation? Do you mean to write a sequel?'

69 A Member of CSMV [Sister Penelope], *God Persists*, ch. 4, p. 31: 'We want to clear our minds here of any narrow preconceptions in regard to "heathenism." In even its lowest forms there is a flame of truth and sincerity, and that flame God cherishes. Respecting man's twofold constitution, He leads him to Himself through nature: so there is nothing wrong *per se* in the fact that these people worshipped the heavenly bodies, and offered animal sacrifices in order, not to destroy life, but to set it free to return to the Giver and then flow back on them. There was, of course, much that was crude and even evil in such worship; but God looked for the best.'

reverting to 'common' weed.[70] Can you tell me anything more about the 'crossing' of the nomadic and agricultural religions on p. 36?[71] On p. 43 'God sat again for his portrait' is a most successful audacity.[72]

I think your task of finding suitable fiction for the convalescents must be interesting. Do you know George Macdonald's fantasies for grown-ups (his tales for children you probably know already). *Phantastes* & *Lilith* I found endlessly attractive, and full of what I felt to be holiness before I really knew that it was. One of his novels, *Sir Gibbie* (Everyman),[73] though often, like all his novels, amateurish, is worth reading. And do you know the works of Charles Williams? Rather wild, but full of love and excelling in the creation of convincing *good* characters. (The reason these are rare in fiction is that to imagine a man worse than yourself you've only got to stop doing something, while to imagine one better you've got to do something).

Thanks, again, for p. 67. I never knew the meaning of Israel before[74] and the gloss on *glory* is most important:[75] it can be so easily misunderstood in a sense which makes God a being hungry (what an absurdity!) for admiration.

Though I'm forty years old as a man I'm only about twelve as a

---

70 ibid., ch. 5, p. 33: 'Hitherto [God] had been like a gardener growing all his seedlings in one box; now the time had come to take the best of them and put it in a pot for special culture, so that it might at last bear perfect fruit . . . the Enemy is trying all the time to reverse God's work and make the plant revert to common weed.'

71 ibid., p. 36: 'When Israel enters Canaan, her promised land, we see God employing with His precious plant the methods of a selective breeder. The religion of the wandering shepherds must be crossed with that of the settled farmers, whose way of life they now adopt; and it is a dangerous process, because the Enemy is trying all the time to achieve opposite results by the same method, and there is plenty in the native worship of the Canaanites that serves his purpose.'

72 ibid., ch. 6, p. 43: 'In His Mother creation reached its climax; in Himself it began again, for in the humanity of Jesus God sat again for His portrait, and this time it was a perfect likeness.'

73 George MacDonald, *Sir Gibbie* (1879; Everyman [1914]).

74 A Member of CSMV, *God Persists*, Postscript, p. 63: 'The name Israel . . . is properly *yisra-'Ēl, 'Ēl* meaning God, and *yisra*, [He] persists; though, as in the case of the name of *Yahweh* referred to on page 35, the verb really covers past and future time as well as present. God persisted, He persists, He will persist; there could indeed be no better summary of the message of revelation.'

75 ibid.: 'I may add that *glory* really means *revealed beauty*, and the verb *to glorify* is the same as *to clarify* or *make clear*. A doxology, such as the last of these verses or the familiar *Gloria Patri*, is therefore a prayer for the complete fulfilment of God's purpose in creation.'

Christian, so it would be a maternal act if you found time sometimes to mention me in your prayers.

Yours sincerely

C. S. Lewis

TO SISTER PENELOPE CSMV (BOD):

The Kilns,
Headington Quarry,
Oxford.
Aug 24th 1939.

Dear Madam

Thank you very much for your most interesting letter and for *Leaves*.[76] I hardly dare to say that you are right in 'scenting' a philologist – in a milieu where an 'amateur' is one who knows 'a modicum of Hebrew' (see p. xi) I shall cut a poor figure. I know just as much as a man wd. know who had been brought up a classic, then had to teach Anglo Saxon and now enjoys the friendship of a real philologist – J. R. Tolkien (By the bye, if you want a good fairy story by a Christian for a 12-year old, try his *The Hobbit*.)

Hross[77] is taken from the root wh. appears in wal*russ*, *rosmarine* (in Spenser)[78] and (possibly) *horshwæl* in K. Aelfred's version of Orosius.[79] *Har* for mountain – and *sorn-séroni* going like the 'broken' declension in Arabic, and *handramit* resembling the *hadramaut* in Arabia – are all accidents which I knew nothing of, not having a word of Semitic. It only shows how hard it is to invent something which wasn't there already.

Your book raises a whole host of points that interest me. I have often thought of the parallel between the dog-man and the man-God relation and agree with all you say. I have found it helpful, too, in trying to understand Grace – wh. I suppose comes in on top of our humanity as the many quasi-human qualities wh. the dog learns from living with us come in on

76 A Member of CSMV [Sister Penelope], *Leaves from the Trees* (1937).

77 The *Hrossa* are one of the three species that inhabit Malacandra in *Out of the Silent Planet.*

78 Spenser, *The Faerie Queene*, II, xii, 24, 9: 'And greedy *Rosmarines* with visages deforme.'

79 *Horschwaelum* = walrus. See *King Alfred's Orosius*, ed. Henry Sweet (London: Early English Text Society, 1883), I, i, p. 17, 36.

top of his caninity.[80] I had never thought before of the point you make in the other book about Our Lord being prenatally incarnate in sub-human forms by palingenesis.[81] And did the divine humility really descend so far? . . . I suppose so. And I very earnestly hope that you are right on p. 76 about tails wagging as well as trumpets sounding: *not* (as the anti-sentimental do vainly talk!) through sentiment, but because animal suffering raises quite terrifying problems about divine justice.[82] Yet it is difficult to me to accept your suggestion, partly because the whole Christian tradition is so silent on the subject (or is that my ignorance?) and partly – well, what about all the wasps? – remembering, as you well remind us elsewhere, that the living members of any species are such a small minority. Perhaps the real answer is beyond human understanding: we know so little about Time and Individuality.

If I can get one out of my publisher – who is a difficult man – I will send you a copy of *Pilgrim's Regress*. Under what name does your book on the Psalms appear?[83]

I expect it'll be beyond me, but I'll have a look and see. And can

---

80 In ch. 1 of *Leaves from the Trees*, entitled 'Consider the Dog: A Study in Right Relationship', Sister Penelope wrote: 'The object of this essay is to consider, not the frequent failure of men in their stewardship, but what we ourselves may learn from the humanized animal, to whom we are as God, about the relationship that ought to exist between God and us' (p. 1). This chapter almost certainly served as the inspiration for Lewis's similar treatment of the subject in *The Problem of Pain* (1940).

81 A Member of CSMV, *God Persists*, ch. 6, pp. 42–3: 'He recapitulated in the nine months within His Mother's womb the whole evolutionary process. That was the beginning: He assumed at its simplest the life that He Himself had called to be, and carried it right through. He is one with the whole created series, blood-brother to all that lives, like us in that He traces His ancestry to the first man and the primaeval cell: yet new because His created nature is wholly pure, the work of God unflawed. In His Mother creation reached its climax; in Himself it began again, for in the humanity of Jesus God sat again for his portrait, and this time it was a perfect likeness.'

82 A Member of CSMV, *Leaves from the Trees*, ch. 7, p. 76: 'S. Paul did not know anything about evolution, but he expresses the same truth when he says that "the whole creation groaneth and travaileth in pain together until now" – that is, until the advent of the Redeemer brought to birth the new creation out of the old. Now notice that this is not just the expression of the hope so many of us cherish that there may be tails to wag as well as trumpets to sound for us on the other side; still less is it the gushing sentimentality of the lady who is sure her darling Toto will go to Heaven. S. Paul shows little interest in nature in his writings and probably cared nothing for individual animals. What he does care about is the solidity of the universe and the universality of its redemption.'

83 A Member of CSMV [Sister Penelope], *Scenes from the Psalms, arranged for use in Schools* (1939).

you tell me of a good essay on the meaning of that momentous little word ἐν in N.T. Greek (ἐν Χριστω[84] etc) and whether[85] the usages of any corresponding Hebrew or Aramaic word.

I hope your eyes don't trouble you now.

Yours sincerely

C. S. Lewis

TO OWEN BARFIELD (W):

[The Kilns
?August 1939][86]

My dear B –

As regards our argument about Gethsemane, I quite see that it sounds odd to attribute to perfect man a fear which imperfect men have often overcome. But one must beware of interpreting 'perfect man' in a sense which would nullify the temptation in the wilderness:[87] a scene on which, at first, one would be tempted to comment (a) As regards the stone and bread[88] 'Imperfect men have voluntarily starved' (b) As regards Satan's demand for worship[89] 'Most men have never sunk so low as to feel this temptation at all.'

If we are to accept the Gospels however, we must interpret Christ's perfection in a sense which admits of his feeling *both* the commonest and most animal temptations (hunger and the fear of death) and those temptations which usually occur only to the worst of men (devil worship for the sake of power). I am assuming that the stones and bread represent hunger: but if you prefer to regard it as primarily a temptation

84 'in Christ' as in Romans 9:1: 'I say the truth in Christ.'

85 Lewis probably meant 'what are'.

86 It is very difficult to assign this letter a date. However, in arranging his letters from Lewis, Barfield placed it in between the letter of 23 July 1939 and that of 2 June 1940.

87 Matthew 4:1–11.

88 ibid., 4:3–4: 'And when the tempter came to him, he said, If thou be the Son of God, command that these stones be made bread. But he answered and said, It is written, Man shall not live by bread alone, but by every word that proceedeth out of the mouth of God.'

89 ibid., 4:8–10: 'Again, the devil taketh him up into an exceeding high mountain, and sheweth him all the kingdoms of the world, and the glory of them; And saith unto him, All these things will I give thee, if thou wilt fall down and worship me. Then saith Jesus unto him, Get thee hence, Satan: for it is written, Thou shalt worship the Lord thy God, and him only shalt thou serve.'

to *thaumaturgy*[90] ('If thou be the Son of God, command these stones') then it falls into my second class.

The consideration of this second class at once raises the question 'Are there no temptations proper to the very best and the very worst, which the middle sort of men do not feel?': or, again, 'Do not common temptations attack most fiercely the best and the worst?' I should answer Yes, and say that fear of death was one of these: and in respect of that fear I wd. divide men into three classes.

A. The very bad to whom death represents the final defeat of the systematic self-regarding caution and egoism which has been the sole occupation of life. (False freedom defeated)

B. The virtuous. These in fact do not conquer fear of death without the support of any or all of the following

α Pride (αἰδέομαι τρώιας και τρώαδας ελκεσπέπλους)[91]

β Fear (Charge, charge, 'tis too late to retreat!)[92]

γ Taedium vitae[93] (My baby at my breast, that lulls the nurse asleep.)[94]

δ Abandonment of the exhausting attempt at real freedom wh. makes the Necessary appear as a *relief* (The ship glides under the green arch of peace)

C. The Perfect. He cannot resort to any of the aids wh. class B. have, for they all depend on defect. His position is thus closely parallel to class A: death for Him also is the final defeat, but this time of *real* Freedom (I am taking it for granted that the spiritual essence of death is 'the opposite of Freedom': hence the most mortal images are rigidity, suffocation etc)

No doubt, He also knows the answer – that voluntary death (really voluntary, not the anodynes and dutch courages) makes unfreedom itself the assertion of freedom. But voluntary submission does not mean that there is nothing to submit to.

What is it to an ordinary man to die, if once he can set his teeth to

---

90 i.e. the working of miracles.

91 'I feel shame before the Trojans and the Trojan-wives with their trailing robes.' The quotation is from Homer, *Iliad*, Book 22, 105, in which Hector reproaches himself for his failure to bring victory to Troy.

92 John Dryden, *A Song for St Cecilia's Day* (1687), III, 8.

93 'the weariness of life'.

94 Shakespeare, *Antony and Cleopatra*, V, ii, 310–11: 'Dost thou not see my baby at my breast,/That sucks the nurse asleep?'

bear the merely animal fear? To give in – he has been doing that nine times out of ten all his life. To see the lower in him conquer the higher, his animal body turning into lower animals and these finally into the mineral – he has been letting this happen since he was born. To relinquish control – easy for him as slipping on a well worn shoe.

But in Gethsemane it is essential Freedom that is asked to be bound, unwearied control to throw up the sponge. Life itself to die. Ordinary men have not been so much in love with life as is usually supposed: small as their share of it is they have found it too much to bear without reducing a large portion of it as nearly to non-life as they can: we love drugs, sleep, irresponsibility, amusement, are more than half in love with easeful death[95] – if only we could be sure it wouldn't hurt! Only He who really lived a human life (and I presume that only one did) can fully taste the horror of death.

I am sure that if the thing were presented to you in a myth you wd. be the first to cry out upon the prosaic critic who complained that the Sun was discredited because it fled from the Wolves.

Your idea of Christ as *suffering* from the mere fact of being in the body, and therefore tempted, if at all, to hasten rather than postpone his death, seems to imply that he was not (as the Christian mystery runs) 'perfect God and perfect man'[96] but a kind of composite being, a δαιμον or archangel imprisoned in a vehicle unsuitable to it (like Ariel in the oak)[97] and in constant revolt against that vehicle. This is mythological in the bad sense. The Son was certainly not incarnated in such a sense as not also to remain God (if He had been, the universe wd. have disappeared). I don't pretend to have an explanation: but I take it that the precise *differentia* of the Christian doctrine is that 'Something wh. eternally *is* in the Noumenal world (and is impassible, blessed, omniscient, omnipotent etc) nevertheless once *was* in the phenomenal world (and was suffering etc).' You can't regard the earthly life of Jesus as an episode in the eternal life of the

95 John Keats, 'Ode to a Nightingale' (1820), VI, 2: 'many a time/I have been half in love with easeful Death.'

96 The Athanasian Creed: 'Perfect God and Perfect Man: of a reasonable soul and human flesh subsisting.'

97 William Shakespeare, *The Tempest* (1611), I, ii. Ariel was in fact imprisoned by Sycorax in a pine (I, ii, 274–7); Lewis was perhaps confusing this with Prospero's threat (ll. 294–6) to imprison him in an oak.

Son: as the slavery to Admetus was an episode in the immortal life of Apollo.[98]

I need not say that on my view, the doctrine (do you hold it) that what was incarnated was 'One of the hierarchies' (or 'one of' the 'anythings') appears to me quite incompatible with the position given to Christ by his own words and by his followers.*

Give my love to all

Yours

C. S. Lewis

* *Aut deus aut malus angelus* is as true as the old *aut deus aut malus homo.*[99]

The long-threatened war was now inevitable and life was to be seriously affected for years to come. As Sir Martin Gilbert wrote,

> *The Second World War was among the most destructive conflicts in human history; more than forty-six million soldiers and civilians perished, many in circumstances of prolonged and horrifying cruelty. During the 2,174 days of war between the German attack on Poland in September 1939 and the surrender of Japan in August 1945, by far the largest number of those killed, whether in battle or behind the lines, were unknown by name or face except to those few who knew or loved them; yet in many cases, perhaps also numbering in the million, even those who might in later years have remembered a victim were themselves wiped out. Not only forty-six million lives, but the vibrant life and livelihood which they had inherited, and might have left to their descendants, were blotted out: a heritage of work and joy, of struggle and*

98 When Zeus killed Asclepius for restoring Hippolytus to life, Apollo, father of Asclepius, took vengeance on the Cyclopes, who had forged Zeus' thunderbolt, and slew them. To expiate this crime Apollo was made for a year the serf of Admetus. For a treatment of this story see Euripides' *Alcestis*.

99 '"Either God or a bad angel" is as true as the old "Either God or a bad man".' Lewis may have been recalling Pope Innocent III's treatise *On the Misery of the Human Condition*, ch. 36, in which the king encounters a philosopher who says: 'Aut deus es aut homo: si deus es, debui te adorari; si homo, potui iuxta te sedere. You are either a god or a man: if you are a god, I ought to worship you; if a man, I should be able to sit beside you.' Lewis's treatment of the argument as to whether Christ was God or a good man first appeared in his BBC talk, 'The Shocking Alternative', published in *Mere Christianity*, book II, ch. 3 (1952).

> *creativity, of learning, hopes and happiness, which no one would ever inherit or pass on.*[100]

The Lewis brothers had followed the events leading up to war, and as Warnie was in the Army Reserve, he was not surprised at being called back into service. The Germans advanced into Poland on 1 September 1939, and the same day Warnie left Oxford for Catterick in Yorkshire. The next morning four schoolgirls from London were evacuated to The Kilns.

TO HIS BROTHER (W):

Magdalen College
Oxford
Sep 2nd 1939

My dear APB

Apparently I arrived at Oxford station yesterday very shortly before you left from it – however, this is perhaps a good thing for though a farewell tankard can just be carried off, a farewell cup of camp coffee is almost unbearable.

Our schoolgirls have arrived and all seem to me – and, what's more important, to Minto – to be very nice, unaffected creatures and all most flatteringly delighted with their new surroundings.[101] They're fond of animals which is a good thing (for them as well as for us).

I redeemed your Elsan[102] from the Bosphorus this morning.[103] The tall melancholy workman with the grey moustache constrained me to look

---

100 Sir Martin Gilbert, *The Second World War* (1989; new edn, 2000), p. 1.

101 During the Second World War a number of children from schools near the blitzed areas of London were evacuated to Oxford and other parts of the country. All the evacuees accepted by Mrs Moore and Lewis were girls. There were usually three children there at a time, most of whom stayed for several months. Margaret Leyland, one of the evacuees at The Kilns between January and June 1940, recorded her experiences in *The Lamp-Post of the Southern California C. S. Lewis Society*, I, no. 3 (July 1977), pp. 1–2.

102 A type of lavatory in which chemicals, such as carbolic acid, are used for cleaning.

103 In 1936 Warnie had acquired a twenty-foot motor boat named the *Bosphorus*, which he named after a similar boat in the Boxen stories (*Boxen: The Imaginary World of the Young C. S. Lewis* (1985), 'Boxen or Scenes from Boxonian City Life', ch. 1, p. 63) and which he kept moored at Salters' Boatyard. A small two-berth cabin cruiser which he had specially built, it was intended for inland cruising only, and he used it on various canals and rivers near Oxford. Whenever Warnie felt a need to get away from the tensions of The Kilns the *Bosphorus* provided a means of escape. See *BF*, p. 174.

into it and then to board another launch where the corresponding apparatus after three weeks' use was as clean as a new pin because carbolic had been used. Even after the receipt of a florin tip he continued in the same strain and said that your Elsan was the dirtiest job he had to do.

My second lecture at Stratford was cancelled and my first went down very well. It was fully reported (the irony!) in the Times yesterday.[104] I had a pretty ghastly time – a smart, nearly empty hotel in a strange town with a wireless blaring away all the time and hours and hours to get through without work compose perhaps the worst possible background to a crisis. And I didn't much like my colleagues – and the two plays I saw (free) were two I'd seen before, *Richard III* & *Much Ado*[105] – the latter really v. good.

The brightest spot was *Right-Ho Jeeves*[106] which, in opposition to you, I think one of the funniest books I've ever read. Fink-Nottle's speech at the speech-day made me laugh aloud in an empty lounge.

I've just been to see the President[107] who laughs to scorn the alarms raised in my breast by the announcement of liability to service up to 41. I hope he's right. Tell Parkin they mustn't reach the 40 class till after Nov. 29th.

Did you see that the enemy planes retreated from Warsaw (?) before Polish fighters & went to bomb a holiday resort in the neighbourhood instead!

God save you, brother.

Yours

Jack

---

104 'The Renaissance and Shakespeare: Imaginary Influences', *The Times* (1 September 1939), p. 8: 'A person who wished to parody the lecture might, Mr Lewis said, give it its true title "How the Renaissance didn't happen and why Shakespeare was not affected by it!" . . . *Renascentia* had originally meant the revival of classical studies; it had then been extended to cover contemporary developments in music, painting, and vernacular literature, with a tacit assumption that these were due to the *Renascentia*; and, finally, to cover Copernican astronomy, the discovery of America, and even the Reformation. The Renaissance could be defined as "an imaginary entity responsible for everything we happen to like in the fifteenth and sixteenth centuries".'

105 William Shakespeare, *King Richard III* (1597); *Much Ado About Nothing* (1600).

106 P. G. Wodehouse, *Right Ho Jeeves* (1922).

107 George Stuart Gordon (1881–1942) became the first Fellow of English in Magdalen College in 1907. He left Oxford to become Professor of English at Leeds University, 1915–22, but returned in 1932 to become Merton Professor of English. He was President of Magdalen College, 1928–42.

TO HIS BROTHER (W):

[The Kilns]
Sept 10th 1939

My dear APB –

One of the most reminiscent features of the last war has already appeared – i.e. the information which always comes too late to prevent you doing an unnecessary job. We have just been informed that New Building will not be used by Govt. and that fellows' rooms in particular will be inviolable: also that we *are* going to have a term and quite a lot of undergraduates up. So you see – I had pictured myself either never seeing those books again or else, with you, and in great joy, unearthing them after the war. To-morrow, I suppose, I must start on the never envisaged task of bringing them up single-handed during a war. I daresay it's the sort of thing you'd think funny!

Another quite unexpected blow is Bleiben's[108] announcement this morning that though 'some of us would know' he had been intending to leave the Parish, 'in the present circumstances he feels it his duty' to stay on. A *non sequitur* in my opinion. In the Litany this morning we had some extra petitions, one of which was 'Prosper, oh Lord, our righteous cause'. Assuming that it was the work of the Bishop or some-one higher up, when I met Bleiben in the porch, I ventured to protest against the audacity of informing God that our cause was righteous – a point on which He may have His own view.* But it turned out to be Bleiben's own. However, he took the criticism very well.

Along with these not very pleasant indirect results of the war, there is one pure gift – the London branch of the University Press has moved to Oxford so that Charles Williams is living here.[109] I lunched with him on Thursday and hope to do so again on Monday.

* I hope it's quite like ours, of course: but you never know with Him.

---

108 The Rev. Thomas Eric 'Peter' Bleiben (1903–47) succeeded the Rev. Wilfred Savage Thomas as Vicar of Holy Trinity, Headington Quarry. Bleiben received his BA from New College, Oxford, in 1924, after which he went to Wells Theological College. Following his ordination in 1928 he was Curate of St Michel's, Oxford, 1927–35, and Vicar of Holy Trinity, Headington Quarry, 1935–47. During these years he was also Assistant Master at Magdalen College School, 1931–7, and Chaplain of New College, 1929–47. See the chapter devoted to him in *Holy Trinity, Headington Quarry, Oxford, 1849–1999* [1999], pp. 71–5. While Mr Thomas had been exactly right for the Anglo-Catholic church in this parish, Lewis found Bleiben too much of a liberal.

109 On 7 September 1939 Charles Williams moved into 9 South Parks Road, Oxford.

Life at the Kilns is going on at least as well as I expected. We had our first air raid warning at 7.45 the other morning when I expect you had yours too. Everyone got to the dug-out quite quickly and I must say they all behaved well, and though v. hungry and thirsty before the all clear went, we quite enjoyed the most perfect late summer morning I have ever seen. The main trouble of life at present is the blacking out which is done (as you may imagine) with a most complicated Arthur Rackham system of odd rags – quite effectively but at the cost of much labour. Luckily I do most of the rooms myself, so it doesn't take me nearly so long as if I were assisted.

Another thing which wd. amuse you is the daily bathe – I've never known the pond so clean at this time of year – which is in two shifts because they have not enough bathing suits to go round, and each shift interminable because of the insatiable appetite of children. In fact we had the whole Dunbar technique – me bawling 'Time to come out' and a head disappearing and then emerging ten yards further away to say 'What?', and then twenty yards further away still to say 'I can't hear what you say.'

Your father had a great deal more patience than we boys thought. But Lord!, what a thing youth is. Last Sunday when I came back from Church – the children had been but gone out after sermon – they met me on the avenue, jumping with joy, to tell me 'War has been declared' – and one added 'Perhaps there'll be an air raid *to-night*!!' The nicest of the three is a Rose Macaulay child – pure boy in everything except anatomy, a reader of Henty.[110] Quite a new phenomenon to me.

I have hardly ever ceased sweating since I last saw you, and have practically no time to read. In the very little time I have I am starting *The Prelude* again, with great appreciation. Here's a funny thing I found out yesterday: that Tolkien is descended from one of the Saxon nobility to whom Frederick the Great gave the alternative of exile or submission when he took Saxony; and the old *graf* chose exile and came over to England and became a clock maker. T. is the very last of my friends whom I shd. have suspected of being *geboren*. Dyson, whom I saw yesterday, commended himself to you with even more than usual affection.

Yours

J.

---

110 George Alfred Henty (1832–1902), who wrote many stories for boys.

TO ARTHUR GREEVES (W):

The Kilns,
Headington Quarry,
Oxford.
Sept. 15th 1939

My dear Arthur,

My position is that I am 41 on Nov. 29th so that till then I am within the ages liable to military service 'if and when called up'. Unless things go *very* ill with the allies I don't think I am very likely to be required, the less so as they want some dons to teach the people between 18 and 20 (they're not calling up boys under 20 at present) and others in govt. departments. We are having a university term and I shall probably, for a bit, continue in my own job.

In fact so far this household has nothing to complain of. Warnie has, of course, had to rejoin, being on the reserve, and is pretty miserable, tho' safe & physically comfortable, at Catterick. We have three evacuated children in the house, but all really nice girls. Minto is bearing up wonderfully. We have had *one* air raid warning but it was a false alarm. So we mustn't cry out before we're hurt.

I'm very sorry to hear you have been ill and very sorry too that we are not to meet this year. You are very often in my mind.

The next few years will be ghastly, but though my *nerves* are often staggered, my faith and reason are alright. I have no doubt that all this suffering will be for our ultimate good if we use it rightly . . . but I can't help wishing one could *hibernate* till it's all over! As W. said in his last letter what makes it worse is the ghostly feeling that it has all happened before – that one fell asleep during the last war and had a delightful dream and has now waked up again.

I daresay for me, personally, it has come in the nick of time: I was just beginning to get too well settled in my profession, too successful, and probably self complacent.

Write when you can. Give my love to your mother and to F. Reid.

Yours
Jack

TO HIS BROTHER (W):

[The Kilns]
Sept. 18th 1939.

My dear W –

Thanks for your letter of the 10th and for a shorter one yesterday proposing a meeting at Darlington.[111] As regards this, the Newcastle lecture has been cancelled so that the particular occasion you mention does not arise: but if it is at all possible I will certainly spend a week end with you at that pub this winter – a kind of *ersatz* for the peace-time January walk.

And now about my own position. Men between 18 and 41 are liable 'if and when called up'. No one seems to think it likely that they will want men of 40 this year, so that if it means 'under 41 at the time of being called up' it is not likely to concern me. But does it mean 'under 41 at the date of the passing of the act'? I don't know. For the moment dons are a reserved occupation: and as long as they stick to their present plans of not calling up boys between 18 and 20 there will, of course, be a full generation of freshmen each year who must do something between leaving school and joining the army.

A propos of our suggestion about the A.E.C.,[112] I had a talk with Gentleman George[113] about my suitability for a kindred line: i.e. instructor of cadets. This is certainly the military job for which I shd. be most suited, having been engaged for 15 years in teaching adolescents of the potential officer class. (Perhaps, if it becomes necessary, Parkin could some day make this obvious point in the right quarter). But Smoothboots[114] laughed at me and said I should be 'wasted' in such a post and he wanted to get me into the Ministry of Information. I said I didn't want to find myself suddenly in the ranks as a result of shilly-shallying. He said this was fantastic, and if it happened he would protest. That's how things stand at present.

I am about two-thirds of the way through the job of restoring the books to the shelves. Your bookcase by the window is now almost full again and looks, to my unskilled eye, very nearly its old self, though *you*

111 Darlington in Co. Durham.

112 Army Educational Corps.

113 i.e. George Gordon, President of Magdalen.

114 Another of Gordon's nicknames.

will doubtless perceive a most perverse disorder, suggesting a positive determination to separate natural neighbours.

I was surprised to find how war-weary our library looked after even this short stay in the cellar – several were stuck to one another and (what I had not anticipated) there were a lot of flakes of plaster mixed in with them. The unpacking job differed from the packing (1) By the solitude, which was irksome and at times poignant (2) By the obvious fact, which nevertheless I had not thought of, that one was going *down* light and coming *up* heavy instead of *vice-versa* (3) By using a tray borrowed from Hatton[115] instead of clasping piles to ones chest – a great improvement (4) By the invincible fact that putting books on shelves is a nice, constructive activity whereas packing them away in boxes is not. As shelf after shelf reassumes its cheerful, familiar face it is impossible not to *feel*, however irrationally, that one of the minor horrors of war is over. In reality, of course, one has no idea how often Government may change its mind about Magdalen – no doubt we shall hear next week that New Building is to be used for mentally deficient German prisoners.

I will carry out your charitable message to Victor Drew.[116] The nicest of our evacuated girls (the Rose Macaulay one) has been taken away by a peripatetic lip-sticked mother who has changed her mind, and been replaced by an Austrian Jewess (aged about 16) whom the school warned us against as difficult: but so far neither Minto nor Maureen nor I can find any fault in her. The house has shaken down into its 'war-economy' quite well, and indeed the children are incomparably less of a nuisance than the various Askins and Irwins with whom we have often been afflicted in peacetime. To-day is a bad day because we have just heard the news about Russia and poor Minto, for the moment, regards this as sealing the fate of the allies – and even talked of buying a revolver! This sort of atmosphere is very trying: but if one abstains from too much contradiction it does not usually last long.

115 William Kembrey Hatton (1900–43) who joined the staff of Magdalen College in 1923. He became a 'scout' or college servant in January 1926, and now performed that duty for Lewis.

116 Victor Drew, Lewis's barber, ran the little barber's shop now called High St Barbers in 38 High Street, Oxford. Lewis referred to Victor Drew in 'The Efficacy of Prayer': 'My barber at that time was a fellow-Christian and a man of many troubles whom my brother and I had sometimes been able to help' (*EC*, p. 237).

I am much interested in what you tell me about the change in subalterns' quarters (the very idea!) and privates' handwriting. Yes, there's no doubt that with all their beastliness the [last] twenty years have witnessed a good many improvements. On Shotover Plain the other day I was passed by a big column of guns, armoured cars etc, and nearly every driver nodded to me or said 'Good evening': surely last time if any notice had been taken of one it would have been some 'ludicrous and disgusting image'. Another change, by the way, has come like lightening. I met Hewitt[117] yesterday, who used to be one of the strongest pacifists among my pupils, on his way from the central recruiting office – thanking God that some slight weakness of his heart was *not* sufficient to keep him at home – so much so that I had to re-adjust my own tone; I had been talking the 1918 language to a 1914 man. Of course one must not forget that the outbreak of war is presumably producing similar transformations all over Germany too. Everyone seems much better here since it began: and I do so agree with you about the relief of no longer hanging on the wireless and the infernal speeches.

I have said that the children are 'nice', and so they are. But modern children are poor creatures. They keep on coming to Maureen and asking 'What shall we do now?' She tells them to play tennis, or mend their stockings, or write home: and when that is done they come and ask again. Shades of our own childhood! Even Joey knew better than that. The Rose Macaulay one was different, and usually 'missing' in the wood or on the pond.

One unexpected feature of life at present is that its quite hard to get a seat in church – every local family, apparently taking the view that whether they go or not, at any rate their evacuees *shall.* But I don't like to be surrounded by a writhing mass of bored urchins who obviously have no idea what's going on or why.

We had a really excellent discourse from Blanchette[118] this morning.

117 Richard Thornton Hewitt (1917–) read English at Magdalen College and took his BA in 1939. He saw war service in the Cheshire Regiment and Special Forces, and was promoted to lieutenant-colonel. Following the war he was assistant to the Regius Professor of Medicine at Oxford, and secretary of the Medical Society, 1947–52. In 1952 he became the Executive Director of the Royal Society of Medicine.

118 The Rev. Arthur William Blanchett (1909–86) was brought up in Oxford. After taking a BA from Keble College in 1931, he read theology at Ridley Hall,

I have been in correspondence with Bleiben about his offending petition, and, as the announcer says, 'the talks have been cordial'. Williams is forwarding to the Bishop of Chichester,[119] who knows, or knows of, all our set, Cranmer's prayer during the Scotch war which I have ferreted out for him, and asking whether something like it cannot now be enforced.[120] I see no hope for the Church of England if it allows itself to become just an echo to the press.

I have a new Imperial Policy Bulletin which I will send on in a few days. Knowing the tone of that publication you will be interested to hear their opinion that 'no power or coalition of powers could conceivably defeat the British Empire'. I quite agree that one of the worst features of this war is the spectral feeling of all having happened before. As Dyson said 'When you read the headlines (French advance – British steamship sunk) you feel as if you'd had a delightful dream during the last war and woken up to find it still going on.' But perhaps the better view is the Frenchman's 'Well, that was a good armistice!' If one could only hibernate. More and more sleep seems to me the best thing – short of waking up and finding yourself safely dead and not quite damned.

Cambridge. He was ordained in 1933 and was Curate of Holy Trinity, Headington Quarry, 1935–40. After serving at Charlbury with Chadlington and Shorthampton, 1940–6, he was Vicar of Steeple Barton, 1946–57, Rector of Islip, 1951–7, and Curate-in-Charge of Woodeaton, 1956–69.

119 George Kennedy Allen Bell (1883–1957) was educated at Winchester and Christ Church, Oxford. Following his ordination in 1908 he served in many posts, including Dean of Canterbury, 1924–9, and Bishop of Chichester, 1929–58. He instituted dramatic performances in cathedrals and did much to encourage the arts. His writings include *Christianity and World Order* (1940).

120 The prayer composed by Archbishop Thomas Cranmer and ordered to be used by King Edward VI for peace between England and Scotland in 1548 encapsulated Lewis's beliefs about war between nations: 'Give to all of us desire of peace, unity, and quietness, and a speedy wearisomeness of all war, hostility, and enmity to all them that be our enemies; that we and they may, in one heart and charitable agreement, praise thy most holy name, and reform our lives to thy godly commandments. . . . Put away from us all war and hostility, and if we be driven thereto, hold thy holy and strong power and defence over us: be our garrison, our shield, and buckler. And seeing we seek but a perpetual amity and concord, and performance of quietness promised in thy name, pursue the same with us, and send thy holy angels to be our aiders, that either none at all, or else so little loss and effusion of Christian blood as can, be made thereby.' It is found in *The Remains of Thomas Cranmer*, collected and arranged by the Rev. Henry Jenkyns (4 vols, 1933), vol. II, p. 186.

Thank goodness the hot weather is gone anyway. Wd. you like [me] to tell your newsagent to forward your various periodicals to you direct?

Yours

J.

In October Warnie was posted to No. 3 Base Supply Depot at Le Havre.

TO HIS BROTHER (W):

[The Kilns]
Oct 2nd 1939

My dear W –

I write chiefly to enclose the rarity of a letter from Uncle Gussie.[121] You had probably seen before that the baronetcy now falls to Tad.[122]

You were asked for kindly at the bottom of the church by that nice choirman whose name I never can remember, and also by Dyson who had lunch and tea with me to day in Oxford. You may hear in your next letter from Minto that the children are being 'troublesome': my version is that they have discovered that Maureen is ragable! Blanchette has become a lodger at the Griggs's,[123] which seems a funny arrangement.

The proclamation calling up men between 20 and 22 will affect

---

121 'Uncle Gussie' was their mother's brother, Augustus Warren Hamilton (1866–1945), Albert Lewis's best friend. See **The Hamilton Family** in the Biographical Appendix to *CL* I. He wrote to Jack from the Ulster Club, Belfast, on 28 September 1939: 'We have been wondering what you and Warren are doing. Has Warren been called upon for service? And are the Colleges closing for the duration? I hope none of them will be bombed. We are busy with Admiralty and other war work. I suppose you heard of Bob Ewart's death, now his cousin, who succeeded to the title is also dead, the title goes to an American cousin, who probably won't use it. Glenmachan goes to Kelsie & Gundred – Kelsie would like Gunny to live in it, but I don't think she will. With the best good wishes for you all and a safe deliverance from the war. Your aff Uncle Gussie.'

122 'Tad' was Sir Ivan Ewart, who had ultimately succeeded to the baronetcy after the death of Sir Robert 'Bob' Ewart on 12 August 1939. While the title moved out of Sir Robert's immediate family, Glenmachan itself was inherited by his sister, Gundred Forrest, who lived there until her death in 1978. For information on **The Ewart Family** see note 47 to the letter to Arthur Greeves of 17 August 1933, and the Biographical Appendix to *CL* I.

123 See **Alice Griggs** in the Biographical Appendix. Mrs Griggs was now Lewis's neighbour at Tewsfield, the house once occupied by Lieutenant-Colonel and Mrs Kreyer (see letter to Warnie of 17 January 1932).

Tolkien's eldest boy, in his seminary at Birmingham – bad luck, for if it had come a few weeks later he'd have been over the age, and if a few months later, in deacon's orders.[124]

Of course, it is only one of countless such tragedies.

I am re-reading Barchester Towers[125] with great satisfaction and discover that one of the secrets of Trollope's charm is that there is so much non-narrative work in his novels – like the chapter headed 'The Stanhope family' or the six page description of Ullathorn.

I've lost my university lectureship – i.e. been mulcted £200 a year. As it would have expired next year anyway, I suppose one must not grumble – they are all being stopped for the duration (Strange the difference between saying when I got it 'Aha! £200 more for doing the same work' and saying now 'Humph! Lose £200 and still have to give the lectures').

If only we could both enjoy it in some pleasant place, this is one of the most perfect autumns I ever remember. By the bye, did I tell you I'd found in the Anglo-Saxon chronicle the perfect summing up of my personal war-aims – 'During all this evil time Abbot Martin retained his abbacy'?[126] Alas, I have already lost part.

Yours
Jack.

TO HIS BROTHER (W):

[The Kilns]
5th Nov. 1939.

My dear W. –

Thanks for your letter. The newspaper cutting did not arrive, not, I think, for the usual reason that you never enclosed it, but because the censor removed it; at any rate the letter had been opened and re-addressed. This, in all the circumstances is as good as any of the anecdotes about the censorship at present in circulation.

I was glad to hear that your journey had proved so much pleasanter than we both expected. The account of the moonlight ride in [the] black-out train was, for some reason, curiously vivid and I almost have

124 See **Father John Francis Reuel Tolkien** in the Biographical Appendix.
125 Anthony Trollope, *Barchester Towers* (1857).
126 *The Anglo-Saxon Chronicle*, 1137.

the sense of having done it myself. I suppose I shall hear a definite address from you soon. And by the way, what percentage of your post do you want sent on? I mean, do you want Blackwell's catalogues, and Rip van Winkles'[127] etc? Would you like it *all* to avoid the risks of giving me a discretionary power? At present it is all on the table in our North room.

Old Mrs Moore died on Thursday evening.[128] She had complained of being 'uncomfortable' and feeling 'only middling' for about 24 hours before, but on the whole her last days seem to have been painless and only partially conscious – in fact she was, in most senses of the word, dead for the last week or so. Miss Griggs,[129] whose behaviour I can't praise enough has relieved Minto of a lot of the work and slept in the bungalow for the last night or so of the old lady's life. We are all thankful that she had before her death quite recovered from the brain storm of a few months ago, and died, as far as one can judge, in charity with all – I was going to say 'mankind', but no doubt she would have excluded the Pope up till the end. I hope she is gone where everyone, including Popes, will only regard this as a matter for laughter.

We have had all the usual bother that follows a death, of course. The registrar lives at Thame of all places and is usually out: and Dr Radford[130] made a mistake in the death certificate which meant that Maureen has had to make a second journey to Thame – or would have had to if she had not to-day retired to bed with a cold. As you may imagine this gave her an opportunity for a few comments on Dr Radford (referred to as 'Radford' *tout court*).

The funeral is to morrow (Monday), any earlier day having proved for various reasons impossible. Lee the sexton excelled himself in conversation with me on this point, when, having pointed out that the

127 Blackwell's Bookshop, 50 Broad Street, Oxford, was founded in 1879 and has grown to become one of the largest and best-known bookshops in the world. It was already in 1939 Oxford's best known shop. 'Rip Van Winkle's' is probably Lewis's name for an Oxford bookshop specializing in second-hand books.

128 Mrs Alice Hamilton Moore (1853–1939) was not related to Janie King Moore, but was a friend from Ireland whom Janie King Moore allowed to live in a small bungalow on land belonging to The Kilns. When Janie King Moore died in 1951 she was buried in the same grave as Alice Hamilton Moore.

129 i.e. Rhoda Griggs.

130 Dr Mary Cowper Radford was a doctor in Headington.

burial could not be till Monday, he added brightly 'But, of course, you can get the good lady screwed down right away.'

The children are all fortunately away this week end for a half term visit home. And Annamarie is leaving for good: but being replaced.

I heard as good a story as I know this week about old Phelps the Provost of Oriel[131] – you probably remember him, with the beard and the black straw hat. Jenner was a fellow of Jesus, a high-minded dissenter and fanatical tee-totaller. He was dining at Oriel and the Provost asked him to take wine with him:

> *Jenner*: Sir, I would rather commit adultery than drink a glass of *that*.
> *Provost*: (in a low, stern voice) So would we all, Jenner; but not at the table, if you please.

On Friday Stevens[132] and I made our way up through blacked-out North Oxford – and a very pleasant, quiet, way it was – to call on J.A.[133] Two bits of the conversation are worth mentioning. One was that J.A.'s mother died in 1914, and her brother had died 110 years earlier. I suppose this is possible if the brother died in infancy and the sister was born when her mother was middle aged. The other is a variant, and a daring one, on 'It's a funny thing the way the human mind works.' It consists in saying, not in a furtive parenthesis but with the weight of a lecturer, 'I shall not trouble you with the intervening steps that lead from the subject we have been discussing to what I am now going to say.'

Benecke has been ill, and Fox also, but both are better. I was a little alarmed last Sunday evening to hear from old Taylor on the telephone that one of the fellows was dead, fearing it might be Benecke, but it

---

131 Lancelot Ridley Phelps (1853–1936), Provost of Oriel College, Oxford, 1914–29, was an authority on poor law administration and chairman of the Departmental Committee on Relief of Casual Poor, 1929–30.

132 Courtney Edward 'Tom Brown' Stevens (1905–76), a member of the Inklings, was elected a Fellow of Magdalen in 1933, leaving in 1940 to join the Foreign Office where he worked as an intelligence officer with Radio Atlantic. He returned to Magdalen in 1946 as an Official Fellow and Tutor in Ancient History and made his debut as an Inkling in 1947. A great Oxford character, he is remembered as one of the best tutors in the university. See his biography in *CG*.

133 John Alexander Smith, mentioned in the letter of 22 November 1931.

turned out to be the very aged Poole[134] (medieval historian) who has never been in college since you knew the place.

Owing to the absence of B. and F. I found myself compelled last Friday at Dean's prayers (where, and in many other places, I will do as you suggest) to read the Litany to a congregation consisting of Mackay: and having an uncorrected prayer book got to the petitions for the royal family just in time to realise I had forgotten all the names! So I had to say merely 'And the queen, and the Princess.' I forgot the Queen Mother altogether – but, as Fox says, she is the best able to look after herself.

I had a pleasant evening on Thursday with Williams, Tolkien, and Wrenn, during which Wrenn *almost* seriously expressed a strong wish to burn Williams, or at least maintained that conversation with Williams enabled him to understand how inquisitors had felt it right to burn people. Tolkien and I agreed afterwards that we *just* knew what he meant: that as some people at school, coll. punts, are eminently kickable, so Williams is eminently combustible.

The occasion was a discussion of the most distressing text in the Bible ('narrow is the way and few they be that find it')[135] and whether one really could believe in a universe where the majority were damned and also in the goodness of God. Wrenn, of course, took the view that it mattered precisely nothing whether it conformed to your ideas of goodness or not, and it was at that stage that the combustible possibilities of Williams revealed themselves to him in an attractive light. The general sense of the meeting was in favour of a view on the lines taken in *Pastor Pastorum* – that Our Lord's replies are never straight answers and never gratify curiosity, and that whatever this one meant its purpose was certainly not statistical.[136]

---

134 Reginald Lane Poole (1857–1939) was educated at Balliol and Wadham Colleges. He was Lecturer in Modern History at Jesus College, Oxford, 1886–1910, and Fellow of Magdalen College, 1898–1933. Dr Poole was the editor of the *English Historical Review*, 1885–1920, and his books include *Illustrations of the History of Medieval Thought* (1884) and *Benedict IX and Gregory VI* (1917).

135 Matthew 7:14.

136 Henry Latham, *Pastor Pastorum: or the Schooling of the Apostles by Our Lord* (1890), ch. 1: 'The truths which He revealed and the commandments He gave were to be accepted by different nations, and in various states of society: they belonged therefore to what is primary in the nature of man. It is in this that Christ's doctrine differs from all systems. It does not belong to one age or one nationality but to all. . . . I only say that the substance of Christ's teaching is suitable for men in different conditions; that the form in which it is put makes

Is it kind or unkind to tell you how lovely the place is looking at present? Real autumn colouring has now arrived, often accompanied with rocking winds and showers of leaves. This morning particularly, which began with mist, but gave way to gleams of exquisitely gentle sunshine as I watched it from my room window while 'doing the washing' just before going to Church – where we learned that someone's proposed bride was 'on the electoral roll' of her parish. In such weather I find the woody snugness of the Ridings particularly attractive – tho' you'll be sorry to hear that in the fields between the two woods to the South of it some extensive building operations are going on.

I haven't read much except a book called *Blind Guides* sent to me by one Paton, the author,[137] whom I met at Swanwick. It's an attack on modern universities (as opposed to the 'ancient' ones like us and Cambridge) and contains a good deal of bilge. He complains that statistics of the Unions, Dramatic Societies, etc, etc, at these places show that only a minority of the students are getting the 'social benefits' of university life. Isn't that typical of a man who has spent his life 'organising'? Doesn't he know that the real 'social benefits' will never appear by such a test, because they are going on by twos or threes in bed-sitting rooms and public houses among people who have something better to do than join the big official societies? Also, while being very democratic, he yet complains that dons aren't 'leaders'. He seems, too, to have an idea that you go to a university to study university life – as if you went to the doctor to study medicine or to the rears to study sewage, or wore spectacles to study optics. I can't make out the modern young man and what he is in such an everlasting fidget about.

I was interested in your account of the staterooms for a two hour daylight passage – and can think of only one purpose for which they'd be useful. But who, however libidinous or however rich, would choose a cross-channel boat for that?

Yours
J.

All send their love. Do you want 1 khaki shirt and 1 khaki collar sent to you?

---

this teaching easy for the ignorant to retain; and that the circumstances which accompanied it were singularly conducive to its spread.'

137 David M. Paton, *Blind Guides? A Student Looks at the University* (1939).

TO SISTER PENELOPE CSMV (BOD):

Magdalen College,
Oxford.
Nov 8th 1939.

Dear Madam

Thank you very much for your parcel and letter.[138] Your account of those psalms was quite a new light to me for I had only the vaguest idea of how they were, so to speak, 'performed.' But how very much more they mean now than they did then!

I was interested in your account of the haunted island of your childhood – a good example of what Otto would call the lowest grade of the 'Numinous'.[139] The idea that water cuts off pursuing spirits is quite common in folk-lore, is it not?, and it is interesting that you reached it independently. I suppose the anthropologists wd. say it was derived from the fact that it spoils the scent for a pursuing beast.

The Tableland represents *all* high and dry states of mind, of which High Anglicanism then seemed to me to be one – most of the representatives of it whom I had then met being v. harsh people who called themselves scholastics and appeared to be inspired more by hatred of their father's religion than anything else.[140] I wd. modify that view now: but I'm still not what you'd call high. To me the real distinction is not between high and low but between religion with a real supernaturalism & salvationism on the one hand and all watered-down and modernist versions on the other. I think St Paul has really told us what to do about the divisions within the Ch. of England: i.e. I don't myself care twopence what I eat on Friday but when I am at table with High Anglicans I abstain in order not 'to offend my weak brother'.[141]

I return *The Divine Journey*[142] which I read with interest. My theological interest in the conceptions was perhaps greater than my enjoyment of the poetry as such, but I daresay the author would not resent that.

My brother, who is a regular, has been sent to France: a sad business

---

138 Sister Penelope sent him a copy of her new book, *Scenes from the Psalms.*

139 Rudolf Otto, *The Idea of the Holy.*

140 The reference is to *The Pilgrim's Regress*, book VI, ch. 2.

141 1 Corinthians 8:9–13.

142 James George Gillman, *The Divine Journey* (1934).

for us both, since he was retired and we had both hoped these partings were over. With many thanks.

Yours sincerely
C. S. Lewis

TO HIS BROTHER (W):

[The Kilns]
Nov 11th [1939]

My dear W –

Your letter of Oct 30th arrived about two days ago – yes, in fact on Friday morning I remember for Dyson was with me and was much interested in it. He made a note of your address, so you will probably receive one of his illegible letters.

Well! – no smoking, early to bed and early to rise, sea air: you seem to have been incarcerated in a sort of 'Westward Ho!'. The not smoking at work has my sympathy. No doubt it will become alright in time if you are in your present billet long enough, just as one does not feel the want at Church or at a lecture, but it must be very trying for the moment. French breakfast would not worry you or me who have so long lived on it. (By the way it infuriated me, who regard a meat or fish breakfast as an occasional treat, to learn that hefty great brute Morris – you know, the enormous silent Nordic-looking lawyer[143] – said at dinner the other night in a vicious tone 'I suppose, when this rationing really begins one will have to learn to eat kedgeree for breakfast!'. The very idea.) Indeed I think French *dinners*, after delighting one for the first week or so, would in the end pall on me much more – I get so sick of the oil.

And talking of gastronomy, we had last night what never occurred at the Kilns before, a haunch of venison. They had thinned the deer in College and Lee[144] (who is now Home Bursar, Opie[145] having wangled

143 John Humphrey Carlile Morris (1910–84) took a First in Law from Christ Church, Oxford, in 1931. He qualified as a barrister-at-law in 1934, and was Fellow and Tutor of Law at Magdalen College, 1936–77. He served as Clerk to Magdalen College, 1946–50, and was University Reader in Conflict of Law, 1951–77.

144 Stephen Grosvenor Lee (1889–1962) read History at Magdalen College as an undergraduate. He was a lecturer at Magdalen, 1913–14, and after serving in the First World War he returned to Magdalen as Fellow and Tutor in Modern History, 1920–47. See Lewis's biographical sketch in the Magdalen College Appendix to *AMR*.

145 Redvers Opie (1900–84) was educated in the United States, and was Lecturer in Economics at the University of Durham, 1919–23. He taught at Wellesley College

a job in America) sent round a notice saying any one who applied could have a joint: so in view of the general difficulty of feeding our enormous household I indented, tho' not having very pleasant memories of venison. I began to regret my decision at about 6 p.m. last night when, on leaving the study, I discovered that the cooking of the haunch had filled the whole house with the most intolerable stench. When we came to eat it, however, we all (including Minto) found it excellent: the College kitchen had supplied a bottle of dark, thick winy gravy and the total effect was rather the consistency of mutton and the flavour of jugged hare. As with cheeses, kippers, and other malodorous dainties, the smell disappeared while you were eating – but I must confess it re-asserted itself as soon as appetite was satisfied and the dining room became a room to leave at the first possible moment.

This has been on the whole a crowded week. On Monday afternoon we had the old lady's funeral. The brother (old Captain (?) Kennet) and his wife arrived rather too early and the undertakers rather too late, so that there was an intolerable interval of conversation – with one eye on the clock – in the common room. I had not met him before, though I think you had: a fine type of old sailor, I thought. The ceremony was conducted by Blanchett, in a cape and biretta which I am afraid the principal would not have approved of. I find – and I think I remember you saying the same – that since one's conversion one has lost, in a great measure, one's old morbid feeling about funerals: and what a satisfaction it is to find that the new outlook has, in even one direction, worked down as far as the level of the instinctive feelings. Would that it were so in *all* directions. What I still find almost untouched is the speech habits – I mean that in the full tide of conversation one still finds oneself saying automatically things that are uncharitable, profane, or even untrue.

I went straight from the churchyard through Quarry to sit on the bench by the telephone box near the Workhouse and await a bus into town: for I have to tea in College every Monday to take part, along with Fox, in a 'discussion group' of pious undergraduates – nice fellows,

(USA), 1923–4, and at Harvard University, 1924–30. He was a Fellow of Magdalen College, 1931–45, and served as Home Bursar, 1930–9. After serving in the Second World War he was senior staff member of the Brookings Institution, Washington DC, 1947–52. He became the Director of Business International in New York in 1954.

but with an ignorance of theology which, I suppose, would have astonished even an 'infidel' in the 18th century. That evening I did my weekly chunk of Dante with Hardie.[146] We have decided, as a war economy, to drink tea instead of Madeira at this function in future.

Tuesday was a tiring day – old Taylor in the afternoon and, in the evening, a sort of *conversazione* at the Gordons to meet the freshmen. They are very bad hosts (or, rather, Mrs. and Janet are very bad hostesses – Smoothboots is alright) and it was very hot and crowded, with nothing on earth to do, and not very much to eat or drink. As Hunt broke a glass in the hall, and a freshman trod on Mrs Gordon's train, I don't suppose the evening was specially successful from their points of view either! (Is the destruction of the hostess's dress a regular feature of a *conversazione*, do you suppose, or am I too hastily generalising from two instances?) Luckily, in view both of the black-out and the fog they had left open the door from the Lodgings into cloisters, so that fellows could get in and out that way, so I slipped silently away at an early hour.

Wednesday I lunched in College and attended a College Meeting, which was over by about 3.30 – after that the rare pleasure of a dogless stroll & tea in our own rooms,[147] glancing through Mammy's old copy of the *Water Babies*,[148] and after dinner the unusual pleasure of an evening to myself.

On Thursday we had a meeting of the Inklings – you and Coghill both absented unfortunately. We dined at the Eastgate.[149] I have never in my life seen Dyson so exuberant – 'a roaring cataract of nonsense'. The bill of fare afterwards consisted of a section of the new Hobbit

---

146 Colin Hardie (1906–98), Fellow and Classical Tutor at Magdalen College, 1936–73, was a Dante and Virgil scholar of rare distinction, and Public Orator of the University, 1967–73. In 1940 he married Christian Lucas. Lewis and Hardie were members of the Oxford Dante Society, and after the Second World War Hardie became a member of the Inklings. See his biography in *CG*.

147 i.e. he did not return to The Kilns to take their dog out for a stroll, but spent the afternoon in his college rooms, two of which he had been sharing with Warnie since 1930.

148 Charles Kingsley, *The Water-Babies: A Fairy Tale for a Land-Baby* (1863).

149 The Eastgate Hotel, 73 High Street, is across the road from Magdalen College. It was one of Lewis's favourite places, and he entertained there many of those who came to see him. The Eastgate occupies the site of a seventeenth-century inn known as the Crosse Sword. It was demolished in 1772 to be replaced by another inn, The Flying Horse, which was in turn replaced in 1900 by the Eastgate Hotel.

book[150] from Tolkien, a nativity play from Williams (unusually intelligible for him, and approved by all)[151] and a chapter out of the book on the Problem of Pain from me.[152] It so happened – it would take too long to explain why – that the subject matter of the three readings formed almost a logical sequence, and produced a really first rate evening's talk of the usual wide-ranging kind –'from grave to gay, from lively to severe'. I wished very much we could have had you with us.

The only interesting thing on Friday was an interview with my American D. Phil. Pupil, Battles of Exeter.[153] It is rather fine to meet a neutral who has not even dreamed of leaving the country and who frankly decides to *ignore* the war altogether. He said that 'if America came in' he would do so-and-so. I asked him if he thought there were any chance of her coming in: he replied at once 'Yes, if Hitler invades Holland, every chance.' I had heard this opinion before, but not from an American.

The house is very much pleasanter since Annamarie left. We have in her place a girl who has just got a scholarship from an elementary school to the High School – almost as quiet as a mouse, very shy, and, unlike the others, a reader.

The garden and country are now in the last stage of autumn dilapidation – leaves so thick on the ground, and trees having such a magpie appearance that the whole place looks as if it had been 'sacked' rather than as if it were merely undergoing a natural process – you know the stage I mean.

I was awake for some time coughing in the night and woke with a

---

150 The 'new Hobbit' then being written is *The Lord of the Rings* (1954, 1955).

151 This was *The House by the Stable*, published in Williams's *Seed of Adam and Other Plays*, ed. Anne Ridler (1948).

152 This is the first reference to Lewis's first theological work, *The Problem of Pain*, which he began shortly before this meeting of the Inklings. The book was written at the request of Ashley Sampson, founder of the Centenary Press, for his 'Christian Challenge' series which was intended to introduce the Christian faith to people outside the Church.

153 Ford Lewis Battles (1915–79) was unable to remain in England to complete a dissertation. He returned to the United States, taking his doctorate from Hartford Seminary. He was Professor of Church History at Hartford Seminary, 1950–7, and Professor of Church History and Doctrine at Pittsburgh Theological Seminary, 1967–78. An authority on the writings of John Calvin, his publications include his translation of *Calvin: Institutes of the Christian Religion*, Library of Christian Classics, vols. XX and XXI, ed. John T. McNeill (1960), and *Calvin Catechism 1538* (1976).

baddish cold, so have not gone to Church this morning, but after 'washing' and reading morning prayer to myself have been writing this with the table pulled well into the room to get the benefit of the fire. That I have not been reading much this week will appear from the rest of the letter.

Yes – I too enjoyed our short time together in College enormously, until the shadow of the end began to fall over it: not that one has lost the art (our boyhood was well trained in it) of dealing with such shadows, but that one so *resents* having to start putting it into practice again after so many years. Pox on the whole business.

Yours
Jack.

TO HIS BROTHER (W):

[The Kilns]
Nov 19th 1939

My dear W –

A bitter though bright morning to day so that I was only just warm enough walking to church in my lined mack. As all four children, and Maureen, went with me, and in two's (Maureen and I at the rear of the column) we presented a real crocodile which I felt for some reason to be ridiculous. So did most of the people we passed on the way.

It was the anniversary of the Dedication of the church to-day, a festival I find it hard to be moved by, with very dreary hymns, a sermon from Blanchett not at all at his best, and a long list of notices. Two more young women have attained to matrimony as a result of being on the electoral rolls of their respective parishes.

I am now warming up again over the study fire and the sabbatical cup of coffee. We had an hour extra in bed thanks to putting back the clocks. It didn't do Minto much good, as she was kept awake most of the night by the storm – of which I was quite unconscious and which does not seem to have done much damage in the wood. By one of those coincidences (at least, I suppose they are nothing more) which confirm superstition, her mind was vividly carried to those at sea and how awful it wd. be to be torpedoed on such a night, and this morning we hear of the loss of the Dutch liner.[154]

154 'Nazi War on Neutrals: Dutch Liner Mined', *The Times* (20 November 1939), p. 6: 'The Dutch liner *Simon Bolivar* . . . outward bound from Holland to the West Indies, with about 400 people on board, including many women and children,

By the bye, I hope this bit of news is not contraband – nor Dyson's wh. I forgot to mention in my last letter, that Unity Mitford wired her father Lord Redesdale 'Don't worry about Hitler's secret weapon . . . know from personal inspection that it is N.B.G.'[155] But perhaps this is already stale. (Have just got up in exasperation to pull back the curtain which Mollie has left respectably drawn half way across the windows. The black-out apparatus enables this trick to be played even more effectively than usual).

This week I have re-read *Jane Eyre*.[156] It is quite prodigiously better than the other Bronte books. I know you have never gone back to it, but I think if one omits (as I did this time) the early chapters about the school days – a senseless recording of miseries which have no effect upon the main story – it is very well worth reading. Part of the interest lies in seeing in the most (apparently) preposterous male characters how quite ordinary people look through the eyes of a shy, naïve, inflexibly upright, intelligent little woman of the mouse-like governessy type. It opens vistas – how you or I look to Maureen's friend 'Fuller'[157] or how we may all have looked to Smudge[158] (except that she was hardly 'intelligent'). Particularly delicious is her idea of conjugal bliss when she says almost on the last page 'We talk, I believe, all day.'[159] Poor husband!

---

struck a German mine and sank . . . Some survivors expressed the view that the liner had been torpedoed. In official circles in London yesterday it was stated that there was no doubt that the vessel had been struck by a German mine.'

155 'no bloody good'. Unity Valkyrie Mitford (1914–48) was the fourth of the remarkable daughters of Lord Redesdale. Unity became fascinated with the British Union of Fascists led by Sir Oswald Mosley (1896–1980), who married her sister Diana (1914–2003). In Germany she was star-struck by the Nazis, and after charming Hitler she made her way into the inmost circle of his life. Faced, however, with the outbreak of war between England and Germany, her adopted country, she attempted to shoot herself, whereupon she was ordered home by Hitler himself. See David Pryce-Jones, *Unity Mitford: A Quest* (1976).

156 Charlotte Brontë, *Jane Eyre* (1847).

157 Fuller was possibly a school friend of Maureen Moore.

158 Vida Mary 'Smudge' Wiblin (1895–1937), an Oxford girl often mentioned in *AMR*, was a friend of Lewis and the Moores in the 1920s. After taking a degree in music from St Anne's College in 1924, she read Latin and Greek. She was musical director at Magdalen College School, 1926–37. See her biography in the Biographical Appendix to *AMR*.

159 Charlotte Brontë, *Jane Eyre*, vol. III, ch. 12.

On Monday evening I called on the Becks[160] (you remember, he married Joachim's daughter)[161] by arrangement to discuss a theological problem. Hardie, with whom I usually read Dante on Monday evenings, accepted my excuse for not doing so, but, to my great annoyance, accompanied me to the Becks and took part in the discussion, complaining towards the end of the 'assumptions' we were making – i.e. complaining that two Christians, met on purpose to discuss a problem that only arrives on Christian presuppositions, did not begin by inquiring whether Christianity were true! It is the sort of stupidity that you and I have often commented on.

On Tuesday a meeting to nominate a 'pass moderator' kept me in Oxford in the afternoon. I met Kingdom[162] and walked beside him in Parks Road, thence, having got free, round to Magdalen by the back way – those quiet roads full of dead leaves have a particular charm for me on a still autumn afternoon, quite different from the country. I think it is connected with memories of seeing such roads on ones way back to Wynyard from games or a walk, and liking them as part of the free, adult outside world and envying every messenger-boy or nursemaid: and the present pleasure consists in feeling – with one's grave middle-aged stride and air of tranquil preoccupation – that one is now part of that envied world. It would be interesting to know how many of our pleasures are indirectly due to Oldie![163]

---

160 Leslie John Beck (1908–78) received degrees from Oxford and the Sorbonne, and was a lecturer in Philosophy at Magdalen College, 1937–9. He was Director of French Intelligence in the Political Intelligence Department of the Foreign Office, 1940–5. On his return to Oxford he lectured in Philosophy at Merton College, 1946–57.

161 Harold Henry Joachim (1868–1938), philosopher, was educated at Harrow and Balliol College, Oxford, where he took a BA in Classics in 1890. He was Fellow of Philosophy at Merton College, 1897–1919, and Wykeham Professor of Logic in the University of Oxford, 1919–35. The name of his daughter is unknown.

162 The Rev. Henry Paul Kingdom (1907–89) took his BA from Corpus Christi College, Oxford, in 1930, and was ordained in 1934. He was Chaplain of Exeter College, Oxford, 1934–45; Lecturer in Theology at King Alfred's College, Winchester, 1951–61; Lecturer at Wells Theological College, 1956–8; and Vicar of Chewton Mendip, 1956–64.

163 'Oldie' is the nickname of the Rev. Robert Capron (1851–1911), the cruel headmaster of Wynyard School in Watford, Hertfordshire, attended by both Lewis brothers. Lewis described Capron in *SBJ*, ch. 2, and there is a biography of him in *CG*.

Wednesday, from 11, when I end my lecture, till lunch time, is normally my free time, but was all occupied this week, as it will be next, with work for Mr Battles and his thesis: I loathe taking people for research degrees, above all other work incident to my job.

Forgot to say that on Tuesday evening I went to the J.C.R.[164] of St Hugh's to hear Williams read a paper – or rather not 'read' but 'spout' – i.e. deliver without a single note a perfectly coherent and impassioned meditation, variegated with quotations in his incantatory manner. A most wonderful performance and impressed his audience, specially the young women, very much. And it really *is* remarkable how that ugly, almost simian, face, becomes transfigured. It was at this function, oddly enough, that I got rid of my cold: sitting for three hours in a densely crowded and hermetically blacked out room with an atmosphere like the black hole of Calcutta did the trick, thus refuting most modern medical opinion and confirming the old doctrine of the 'sweating house'.

On Wednesday my 6 o'clock pupil arrived late and explained that he'd been playing in a football match against Malvern: odd, till you remember that Malvern is at Blenheim. They tell him that tho' they have been ejected, no one has yet moved into the Coll. buildings or houses at Malvern. The Coll. lost the football match.[165]

On Thursday at 3 p.m. I attended a lecture by Fox in his capacity of Professor of Poetry – the first time in my life I have ever heard any professor of Poetry lecture, and so the first time I've ever been in the old Divinity School.[166] This is simply the most beautiful room in Oxford or perhaps in England – all stone, perpendicular, with a most choice roof – all very white set off with almost black unpolished oak for railings and benches. The lecture was 'good but not capital'.

---

164 Junior Common Room.

165 In October 1939, Malvern College removed to Blenheim Palace, Woodstock, ready for the Admiralty to move into its buildings in order to avoid the anticipated bombing of London. Before this could happen, underground shelters were built in London to house the Admiralty, enabling the college to return to Malvern in September 1940. Malvern College was forced to evacuate a second time when the Telecommunications Research Establishment, with its vital radar equipment, moved into some of the college buildings. See Ralph Blumenau, *A History of Malvern College 1865 to 1965* (1965).

166 The Divinity School, which forms part of the Bodleian Library, is regarded as one of the wonders of Oxford. It was begun about 1420 and completed in 1483.

That evening Williams, Hopkins (his colleague and nephew of the poet),[167] Wrenn and I met and, falling into the mention of it by chance, read about half of *Irene Iddesleigh* right through. When you do it like that, instead of picking out the plums, it turns out, as we all agreed, to have a kind of nightmare reality – indeed the characters au fond are such primitive savages that it would be quite sinister if the absurdity of the presentation were not always resolving the whole thing into laughter.[168]

I hope these letters are reaching you. If, by any chance, this should be the first to do so, I may record that I have been writing every week. Minto has been very busy sorting out the 'effects' of the old lady, and distributing them to various deserving people, but once that is over the burden of the household ought to be noticeably diminished. Did I tell you of the great domestic revolution – that we have ceased to take the *Sunday Pictorial*. Write when you can. I hope the pleasant surroundings mentioned in your last letter continue.

Yours

J.

TO HIS BROTHER (W):

[The Kilns]
Nov 24th 1939

My dear W. –

I got your letter of the 16th on Friday. I am very sorry to hear you are not sleeping. If it goes on, I recommend *Veganin* which – you'll see why later – I used last Monday night and which not only gave me unbroken sleep but woke me up next morning feeling as fit as possible and not the least like a drugged man.

---

167 Gerard Walter Sturgis Hopkins (1892–1961), nephew of Gerard Manley Hopkins (1844–89), was a translator and critic. He worked for Oxford University Press, 1920–47, first as publicity manager and later as editorial assistant. During the war, Hopkins, like Charles Williams, had rooms in 9 South Parks Road, Oxford.

168 Amanda McKittrick Ros (1860–1939), known as 'The World's Worst Writer', was a Belfast client of Albert Lewis, and through him the Lewis brothers discovered the lady's appalling novel, *Irene Iddesleigh* (1897), and her *Poems of Puncture* (1915). It was to become a customary feature of Inkling meetings to bet that no one could read a passage from her colourful writings with a straight face.

I am almost ashamed to describe my leisurely days to one leading such a gruelling life as you – by the way, there is a curious irony about your present job, because, thirty years ago, bustling about between ships and trains would have seemed to you *the* ideal occupation. Do you remember what a triumph a bit of 'unforced traffic' was in the attic days? Well, my son, you have it now! No, I hadn't thought of it's being a crime to keep an engine waiting, though it's fairly obvious when you come to think of it: I *had* known already, I suppose from notices half consciously read in goods stations that 'an engine in steam' is a venerable object, almost like a mare in foal.

A few hours ago while waiting for the bus outside Magdalen I saw a sight I bet you've never seen – an undergraduate whom I know approaching with what I took to be a dead pheasant in his hand but what turned out to be a live falcon on his wrist. It was hooded with a little leather hood and is quite a gaily coloured bird, provided on the lower leg with natural spats of a kind of yellow varnish. Blessings on the man who while waiting to be called up for a first class European war is exclusively intent on restoring the ancient sport of hawking. He is a very small, pudding-faced, youth of the type that sometimes looks twelve and sometimes sixty years old. His name is Routh and he is the great nephew of old President Routh, whom he rather resembles.[169] I met him at the Discussion Group which I think I have mentioned before.

And that reminds me, your words about prompt arrival of letters smote my conscience, for I took my last letter in in my case on Monday morning to post in College and never discovered it again till Friday. Many regrets! I will try to avoid such delays in future.

This week began badly in another way. While standing up drying in my bath (out here at the Kilns) I reached out for my pyjama jacket

---

169 Martin Hugh Routh (1923–) came up to Oxford in 1939 to read Natural Science. He spent the years 1940–6 in the Royal Navy, returning to Magdalen College in 1948. On taking his BA in 1950 he joined the Food and Agriculture Organization and was their representative in Haiti, 1950–60, and in Tunisia, 1960–1. His great-uncle, Martin Joseph Routh (1755–1854), was elected to a Fellowship at Magdalen College in 1775; he became in succession college librarian, Dean of Arts, Senior Proctor and, at the age of thirty-five, President of Magdalen, holding that position until his death in his hundredth year. He is buried in the College Chapel.

hanging on the door, and my feet suddenly went from under me bringing me down slightly twisted with my back and side on the edge of the bath. I was quite relieved to find I could even get up again but by that evening I was wondering if a rib had gone bust. When I got into bed and tried to turn round I discovered sensations very like those I remember having in the C.C.S.[170] last war – which I suppose shows that the wound itself was hardly painful at all – all the pain coming from bruises and twists. It was then that the Veganin came in useful. It is very nearly quite better now and I am agreeably surprised that any pain so bad should go off so quickly. While it lasted even to utter a man's wind was no light matter – and as for a cough (of which I had many) it is a thing 'not to be thought of'.

Thank heaven the clocks have gone back! Like you I rather welcome early darkness in the afternoon, but I do like it to be light as I go across to chapel. The weather later in the day has been mostly drab and wet and bedraggled but I have got some most lovely pearly dawns seen through the gate into Adders.[171]

The Discussion Group has moved from Monday afternoon to Tuesday evenings, a great improvement from my point of view. We were assisted this time by the Wounded Buffalo.[172] Such was the extreme vagueness of the undergraduate's theology that he and I oddly found ourselves back to back in defence of orthodoxy – he, I suppose, thinking of me as I thought of him 'He's not nearly so ignorant as one might suppose.'

The change of time has produced one funny little result – as I sat listening to an essay between 12 and 1 the other morning (I am living in your room exclusively now because the grate takes less coal) I was surprised to find my head in sunlight and wondered how this should never [have] happened in that chair (the left-hand one) before: and then realised of course that at the hour when the sun gets round there I am usually at home – and so, watching the mild sunlight of winter

---

170 Casualty Clearing Station.

171 i.e. Addison's Walk.

172 'The Wounded Buffalo' and 'The Wounded Bison' were Lewis's nicknames for Henry Michael Denne Parker (1894–1972), Fellow and Tutor in Ancient History at Magdalen College, 1926–45. He was a single man whose rooms in New Buildings were directly above Lewis's. See Lewis's portrait of him in the Magdalen College Appendix to *AMR*.

on the brass candlesticks and all the other Leeburiana, which I very much wish you were here to share, I awoke with a bump to realise that I hadn't taken in the last few sentences of the essay. But I daresay they may be deemed to have been of standard quality.

On Thursday night the usual party met. Tolkien is in trouble again, poor fellow, his wife having to have an operation, and some trouble with evacuees wh. I didn't quite understand. I notice that his trials, besides being frequent and severe, are usually of such a complicated nature as to be impenetrable. Did it ever occur to you that there is a real similarity between his way of communicating a fact and Phippy's?[173]

And talking of the human mind, what do you think of this? I read out your letter to Minto at lunch and when I came to your suggestions about dates on old Mrs Moore's tomb (and many thanks for the offer) and their desirability *although* 'history was hardly likely to interest itself' etc she interrupted me to say very earnestly 'Dates will live.' I've been turning it over in my mind but I make nothing of it.[174]

We finished *Irene Iddesleigh* on Thursday with great enjoyment and some instruction. The latter part of the week was mucked up by examining in B6 – 'Pass' English. This had to be done in the Taylorian, Schools being now in the hands of swaggering R.A.M.C.[175] My colleague Bone[176] asked me to lunch with him at St John's prior to an afternoon's invigilation. I've known him quite good company: on this occasion, however, he spoke in almost a whisper and very seldom, and while other people

---

173 'Phippy' was the nickname of Mrs Harry Joseph Phipps who lived at 151 Windmill Road, Headington. She was Mrs Moore's charlady and friend during the 1920s when they lived at Hillsboro, 14 Holyoake Road, Headington. Lewis first mentions her in his diary entry for 25–30 June 1924. See *AMR*, p. 340.

174 The epitaph on the joint tombstone of the two Mrs Moores is: 'In memory of/ ALICE HAMILTON, Widow of Dr ROBERT MOORE, of Bush Hills Ireland/Born Nov. 20th 1853/Died 2nd Nov. 1939/Sleep, after toil, port after stormy seas/Also of/JANIE KING MOORE/Died Jan. 12th 1951.'

175 Royal Army Medical Corps. Various parts of the army were commandeering some of the university buildings for the war.

176 Gavin David Bone (1902–42) took a First in English from St John's College, Oxford, in 1928. He was a lecturer in English at St John's College, 1929–31, and Fellow and Tutor of St John's College, 1931–42. His works include *Anglo-Saxon Poetry* (1943) and *Beowulf in Modern Verse* (1945). Some of his drawings are found in B. J. Brooke, *The Wild Orchids of Britain* (1950).

were eating all round us (this was in John's Common Room) nothing arrived for us till I was 'nearly sick' with hunger and embarrassment. When at last we'd had some chicken another pause ensued, during which, almost in desperation for something to say, I asked him for the cheese, only to be told in sepulchral tones that there was a sweet coming. It came. Another pause. Desperate for my coffee, I said presently that I supposed I'd better be getting along: my host, after pondering this for a minute or two, replied yes, he supposed I had. On our way out he stopped at the other end of the table and introduced me to a jolly old man as his father Sir Muirhead Bone.[177] Now can it be that the mere paternal presence explains the whole business? One can imagine such things! Anyway I went off to my 3 hours' invigilating without any coffee.

I suppose a French novel is the very last thing you want to read at present, but I can't refrain from telling you that in the French library (where the exam was held) I picked up Balzac's *Curé de Tours* quite carelessly and was immediately enchanted – just as I was by his *Père Goriot* in 1917.[178] It is so very *unlike* most French things – the Cure and the whole cathedral surroundings in Tours are almost Trollopian: so provincial, loveable, prosaic, unobtrusive.

On Friday night I left my rooms at about 11 p.m. to see a guest out into Longwall and saw, I think, the most beautiful night I've ever seen – full moon, and Jupiter, not, as when you were here, over Adders but over the tower and under the moon: dew or frost on all the grass: the branches of that huge plane tree visible to the top – and such silence. I slept badly (and so, by the way, did Parker: at least the noise from overhead suggested 'attempted bedroom scene with a virtuous elephant') so went over to Common Room about 1.45 to get 'a little drop of the whiskey'. It was still just the same then, perhaps a shade brighter, almost ghastly bright, and colder – hours and hours of it apparently.

To day is wet – an outside world of dripping branches and hens in the mud and cold which I am glad to have shut out (tea is just

177 Sir Muirhead Bone (1876–1953) was a watercolour painter and etcher. He was the first official war artist, and published *The Western Front*, 2 vols. (1917) with text by C. F. Montague.

178 Honoré de Balzac, *Le Curé de Tours* (1832); *Le Père Goriot* (1834).

finished) but which, no doubt, is very much pleasanter than your sugar-floored sheds. How nasty the sugar cottage in Hansel and Grettel must have been in wet weather. I gave your greetings to those of the Inklings who were present on Thursday, which were received with gratification.

Yours

J.

TO HIS BROTHER (W):

[The Kilns]
Dec 3rd 1939

My dear W –

I have just returned from Church where I had the novel experience of hearing you prayed for by name, along with numerous Coppocks and Tolleys as one of those serving from this parish. The compilation of this list, which is inserted in the prayer for the Church Militant, was of course the subject of typically Bleibenian notices. It includes Davenport's name but whether this means that the son is old enough or that the old chap has been found young enough, I don't know. None of them were in Church.

This has been a beautiful week. It began to clear up last Sunday (you remember my letter was written on Saturday) and that afternoon I had the first really enjoyable walk I've had this many a day, round by the grove and the ploughed field – an afternoon of very pale, lucid* skies revealed between dark blue-grey horizons and scurrying black clouds which covered the higher part of the heaven.

Later, I had the odd experience of leaving home for college at about 6, as Harwood had announced his intention of coming for the night. The journey in by bus was delightful because it was now bright moonlight and the lights inside the bus were so dimmed as to make no difference, so that I had the quite unusual experience of seeing Magdalen bridge and tower by moonlight from the height and speed of a bus-top: a *short* thing compared with the train journey you described, but of course the elevation gave it an advantage. Harwood, owing to train difficulties, didn't turn up till about 10.30, but we sat up lateish and had a good talk.

* Not lurid!

I may have mentioned to you that he has evacuated to Minehead – nicely placed for country but with bad prospects financially, as the splitting up of their pupils' London homes has led to their losing a good many. His son John[179] is not with them but billeted in the neighbourhood – with the local M.F.H.![180] and already has acquired a new language and says that his father ought to get his hair cut! I hardly know which to pity more – a father like Harwood who watches his son being thus 'translated' or a son in process of such translation who has the embarrassment of a father like Harwood. I think, the son: for as some author whom I've forgotten says the anxiety that parents have about children 'being a credit to them' is a mere milk and water affair beside the anxiety of children that their parents should not be an absolute disgrace. Certainly it wd. not be pleasant to have to explain to a M.F.H. that one's father was an Anthroposophist – except that the only impression left on the M.F.H.'s mind wd probably be that your father was some kind of chemist. (If the M.F.H. was a P'daita it might, of course, lead to almost anything – 'Sort of fellow who comes to the door offering to feel your bumps').

Tuesday I was in Addison's walk for a few more minutes than usual before going to chapel, and enjoyed v. much the effects of a clear still morning (sky of pigeon-grey, pearl-grey, and, eastward, pale butter colour verging on cream) on a state of partial flood. The meadow was full of pools – the grass reduced to a complicated system of archipelagos – and the pools full of reflected trees: the Cherwell swollen and gravel-coloured with an endless series of rafts of foam running by at about 12 miles an hour, and long V-shaped ripples wherever an overhanging branch touched the water.

After years of estrangement I found myself this week going back to

---

179 John Olivier Harwood (1926–), the eldest son of the Harwoods, was educated at Michael Hall School, Minehead, after which he served two years in the Royal Navy. He went up to Oxford in 1947 and read English with Lewis, taking his BA in 1950. Following an executive training course he began working with Dunlop Rubber Co. In due course he became an overseas executive, working first in East Africa, then in the Middle East, prior to appointments in Ceylon, 1950–63, and Sweden, 1964–8. In 1968 he joined BTR Industries as assistant to the managing director, becoming Overseas General Manager and finally President of BTR Canada. He left BTR in 1973 to start his own consultancy company, retiring (more or less) in 1995.

180 Master of Foxhounds.

Horace, who has at least this advantage that a single ode makes just the right length of reading for the odd five minutes before a pupil appears, or between the last pupil and dinner. I suppose the first lines would still wake in you as they do in me a flood of reminiscence – Solvitur acris hiems[181] – O fons Bandusiae[182] – Vides ut alta stet nive candidum:[183] and even the first lines of odes one never read at school such as Cum tu Lydia Telphi.[184]

And talking of books, I have been looking rapidly through St François de Sales this week end to find a passage I wanted to quote, and have derived much 'social pleasure' from your pencillings: as I have experienced before, to read a book marked by you in your absence is almost the nearest thing to a conversation. When I read that hares turn white in winter because they eat nothing but snow (used as an argument for frequent communion)[185] and see your mark it is almost as if one of us was pointing the passage out to the other here in the study.

On Wednesday evening, being my birthday, I entertained a few pupils to wine and coffee after dinner: one of them, Monteith, lives in the Antrim Road. And was educated at the Inst. I think he's a credit to us too, as far as brains and knowledge go, though, to be sure, he doesn't excel in sensibility.[186]

---

181 Horace, *Odes*, Book 1, poem 4: 'Winter relaxes its grip'.

182 ibid., Book 3, poem 13: 'O fons Bandusiae splendidior vitro/dulci digne mero non sine floribus': 'Spring of Bandusia, whose crystalline/Glitter deserves our garlands and best wine'.

183 ibid., Book 1, poem 9: 'Vides ut alta stet nive candidum/Soracte': 'Look how the snow lies deeply on glittering/Soracte'.

184 ibid., Book 1, poem 13, 1–2: 'Cum tu, Lydia, Telephi/Cervicem roseam, cerea Telephi': 'O Lydia, when you praise the nape/Of Telephus's rosy neck, the smooth waxen skin'.

185 St François de Sales, *Introduction to the Devout Life*, trans. Michael Day (1619; Everyman's Library, 1961), Book II, ch. 21, 'Receiving Communion', p. 86: 'As mountain hares become white in winter because they neither see nor eat anything but snow, so by adoring and feeding on beauty, purity and goodness in the Eucharist you will become altogether beautiful, pure, and good.'

186 Charles Montgomery Monteith (1921–95) was from Belfast and was educated at the Royal Belfast Academical Institution. He came up to Magdalen College in 1939 to read Law, but left after a year to serve on the General Staff of the Royal Inniskillen Fusiliers in India and Burma, 1940–5. He returned to Magdalen after the war and in 1947 took a First in Law. He was called to the Bar in 1949 and was a member of Grays Inn. Monteith was a Fellow of All Souls College, Oxford, 1948–88. He joined the publishers Faber & Faber in 1953, becoming a director in 1954. He was vice-chairman, 1974–6, chairman, 1977–80, and senior editorial consultant, 1981–6.

The usual Thursday evening party did not meet as Williams & Hopkins were both away, so I went up to Tolkien's – the house safely visitable because his wife is in the Acland (an operation, poor woman, but she's doing alright). I was much struck by the difference between the black-out in the town proper and in even such a very faint approach to country as North Oxford. In Longwall and Holywell I had to walk almost as one does in a dark room: but when I had got as far as Keble and houses began to be further apart and trees became visible against the grey sky (no stars, or moon) I strode along nearly as well as in an ordinary country walk after nightfall. We had a very pleasant evening drinking gin and limejuice (wh. sounds chilly, but I was quite in a sweat by the time I got to Northmoor Rd.) and reading our recent chapters to each other – his from the new Hobbit and mine from the 'Problem of Pain'. (N.B. If you are writing a book about pain and then get some actual pain as I did from my rib, it does *not* either, as the cynic wd. expect, blow the doctrine to bits, nor, as a Christian wd. hope, turn into practice, but remains quite unconnected and irrelevant, just as any other bit of actual life does when you are reading or writing). On my way back at about 12 I found the moon risen. I let myself in through the little door into the Grove near the corner of Longwall and found the Grove v. pale, luminous, and solemn.

On Friday night I had a more difficult expedition going to some plays Coghill has got up, in the Clarendon Press Institute, Walton St. Perhaps you remember our efforts, even without a black-out to find the Observatory in that trackless region. I got to the Clarendon Press proper with great difficulty and was told by a Porter 'Ah, you want to go *back* 150 yards and you'll find the institute on the other side.' Went back about 300 yds. And met a dark figure. Did he know where it was? Yes, he thought he did: it was much further *on* and he was going there too. About turn & five minutes or so walking. Guide became doubtful. We asked another pedestrian 'The Institute? Ah, you've come too far. You got to go *back* about 500 yds.' So on, I don't know how many times. But I question whether the black-out had much to do with it, being in a 'queer country'.

The plays were worth seeing: one, by Yeats, his last one, was really powerful: conversation between a tramp and his son outside the ruins of a great house and then the ghost of its last mistress at the window, re-enacting her past life – she being the one who had finally let the whole thing down, marrying a horse-dealer . . . all the usual tragedy of the Irish aristocracy. Not quite true, of course, because probably most of the preceding generations had been pretty good wasters too: but an effective play.[187]

Minto thanks you for a letter. The Imperial News Bulletin asks me to renew my subscription. I think I shall not. What's the use of paying 2/- a month to be tormented by prophecies wh. if false are needless misery and if true can't be averted by us? After next week letters may be suspended for a fortnight by School Certificate examining: my first real war time budget measure. Ugh! – but I suppose you'd say *you're* working every week!

Yours
J.

TO HIS BROTHER (W):

[The Kilns]
Dec. 18th 1939

My dear W –

Thanks for your letter of the 8th. I immediately looked up Charlotte M. Young[188] in Oliver Elton.[189] I found the *non* cloak-and-rapier ones praised for their 'simple Anglican piety and their unobtrusive skill in description of countryside and wealth'. I sent Blackwell a list of titles – three or so in order of rough preference, but told them to send any, failing the ones mentioned. One of those I gave was a sequel to another – but the first of those two seems to be either for, or about, children. If it is not too childish (a different thing from the other two possibilities) it might be the ideal form of saga – *really* to begin at the beginning and grow up with the characters.

I am rather gratified at your estimate of the 'Varsity officer – though, I suppose, in fairness one shd remember that he is probably older than the Sandhurst product you remember. Tell your Worcester man that the

---

187 W. B. Yeats, *Purgatory* in *Last Poems and Two Plays* (1939).

188 Charlotte M. Yonge (1823–1901) lived all her life in the Hampshire village of Otterbourne. In 1838 she came under the influence of the Reverend John Keble (1792–1866), the Tractarian clergyman who was one of the founders of the Oxford Movement. As a result Tractarian religious views coloured all her writings. She excelled as a novelist in depicting large families and village life. Her most famous novel is *The Heir of Redclyffe* (1853).

189 Oliver Elton, *Essays and Addresses* (1939), p. 120.

Wilk[190] has blossomed into full glory in connection with the O.T.C.[191]

For the last fortnight I have been having a taste of what must be your daily experience – over School Certificate – i.e. the nausea of taking upon long disused limbs a harness laid aside, one supposed forever, many years ago. All the old features appeared – the aching limbs, the threat of toothache, and the nightmare continuation of the work even in ones sleep. It has during this period been as cold and dark as I have ever known it and I have had the light on in the study nearly all day.

That is, it has been what all the others call vile weather: I, in my shortened walks found it rather nice. The prospect from the top of Dug-out Mound has been specially good – a preternaturally smooth and clean pond which, in the foreground at Stinkhaven reveals the bottom with a pleasant mixture of colours and, at the far end, mirrors perfectly every limb of the birch trees and the now almost faded bracken. I have had one or two very bracing views of the 'ploughed field' too: seen from the end where, owing to the slight swell in the ground, only the gables of our soaking-machine[192] and the haystack appear. Above these a sky in which no 'blue' appears but the clouds themselves are blue as if with cold – and across this the inestimable midwinter cloud of birds performing their evolutions. In the examining I was struck – tho' this may be an illusion – with the great deterioration of the work: 'it is wonderful with what speed we advance to dissolution'. Which reminds me of what you say about Johnson.

Yes, I know well what you mean by the *materialistic* gains of being a Christian. It more often presents itself to me the other way round – how on earth did we manage to enjoy all these books so much as we did in the days when we had really no conception of what was at the centre of them? Sir, he who embraces the Christian revelation rejoins

---

190 Cyril Hackett Wilkinson (1888–1960), Vice-Provost of Worcester College, Oxford, 1920–47, was the Oxford Secretary to the Oxford and Cambridge Schools Examinations Board and the man to whom Lewis was answerable regarding School Certificates.

191 Officers' Training Corps.

192 Lewis defined 'soaking-machine' in his letter to Arthur Greeves of 11 May 1915 (*CL* I, p. 119): 'The word Soaking-Machine can hardly be styled "slang", being, as it is, coined by myself for private circulation . . . The word "soak" means to sit idly or sleepily doing nothing, and a S'ing machine is [a] place for this operation, i.e. a comfortable seat.'

the main tide of human existence! And I quite agree about Johnson. If one had not experienced it, it wd. be hard to understand how a dead man out of a book can be almost a member of one's family circle – still harder to realise, even now, that you and I have a chance of someday really meeting him.

I was very amused last night on going to the little Leeborough writing table in the study to find some sealing wax, to notice how all its drawers except the central one which you have occupied – though cleared from the move from Leeboro' and given a new start in life, have by now completely recovered the character they always had – old pipes, rulers, string, prehistoric documents. Can a piece of furniture have a life of its own and impose its character on successive owners? You can't say it is simply me – because other bits of Leeburian furniture, even under my hands, have not similarly reverted to type. And you will notice it has also re-asserted its old character of being a writing table that is hardly ever written at. And why did we bring it? Or did Minto insist on its being brought because it was 'a dear little table'? – and did Mammy rescue it from Tigh-Essa[193] on the same ground? At any rate it is a concrete lump of destiny if ever there was one.

I am glad to learn that the pressure of work has eased for you, if only a little. I daresay you would sooner have had shorter hours at equal pressure, but I believe the other is wholesomer and less 'devitalising'. But I don't like that German broadcast at all, Pigibuddie. Still, we live in such a mass of lies that perhaps one should take no notice of anything. This battle off Montevideo has been an odd experience, hasn't it?[194] I suppose there has never been a war till now in which people at home were getting news of distant naval actions only a few minutes after the event. At the Kilns where, Heaven knows, there is no danger of excessive

193 "Tigh-Essa" is Lewis's phonetic spelling of the Welsh name Ty-Isa, the home of Lewis's grandfather, Richard Lewis (1832–1908) from 1870 until his death in 1908. It is in Sydenham, Belfast, and there is a photograph of it in Bleakley, *C. S. Lewis – At Home in Ireland*, p. 103.

194 The first naval battle of the Second World War had taken place after three Royal Navy cruisers, *HMS Exeter*, *HMS Ajax* and *HMS Achilles*, were ordered on 12 December 1939 to intercept the German battleship *Graf Spee*. The following day the British vessels engaged the *Graf Spee* east of the River Plate, continuing their pursuit while she headed towards the Uruguayan port of Montevideo. The battle ended when, about midnight on 13 December, the *Graf Spee* successfully docked in Montevideo harbour.

cheerfulness, it is alright: but I can imagine it being disgusting in a bar full of fine eating elderly civilians – a suggestion of the *arena* about it.

The cock swan was found dead and disembowelled in the swamp this week, presumably the fox's doing (That's the same construction as 'Let us do a Helen-killing – a great grief to Menelaus'!) I am sorry for the widow (if swans are sensible of bereavement) and can't help wishing Dan Russell had finished the job while he was about it. From the purely aesthetic point of view, you have no idea how lop-sided and unfinished it looks to see always *one* swan, never two.

We had a very pleasant Cave in Balliol last Wednesday. Everyone remarked that it was more frolic and youthful than any we have had for years – quite one of the old caves in fact – a curious result, if it is a result, of war conditions. During the evening Ridley[195] read to us a Swinburne ballad and, immediately after it, that ballad of Kipling's which ends up 'You've finished with the flesh, my Lord'.[196]

Nobody except me knew who the second one was by, and everyone agreed that it just *killed* the Swinburne as a real thing kills a sham. I then made him read 'Iron, cold iron' with the same result and later he drifted into McAndrew's Hymn. Surely Kipling must come back? When people have had time to forget 'If' and the inferior Barrack Room Ballads, all this other stuff must come into its own. I know hardly any poet who can deliver such a *hammer stroke*. The stories, of course, are another matter and are, I suppose, even now admitted to be good by all except a handful of Left idiots.

Bleiben rang me up last night to ask your address and also to invite me to the Vicarage on Boxing day. It is a sad business to be going alone to that annual function which we have usually both enjoyed.

The *Spirit of Man*,[197] by the way, has no particular claim on our attention. The principle on which it is compiled, as the title indicates, is sub-Christian and rather woolly: it is just an ordinary good anthology

---

195 Maurice Roy Ridley (1890–1969), who had been an undergraduate at Balliol College, was a Fellow and Tutor in English Literature at Balliol, 1920–45. From there he went on to become a lecturer at Bedford College, University of London, 1948–67.

196 Rudyard Kipling, *The Light that Failed* (1890), 'Heriot's Ford', stanza 8, 4.

197 Robert Bridges, *The Spirit of Man: An Anthology in English and French From the Philosophers & Poets made by the Poet Laureate in 1915 & Dedicated by gracious permission to His Majesty the King* (1916).

– and personally I don't think much of anthologies except for lyric poetry. Aren't bits of prose taken out of their contest – 'beauties' – rather boys' reading?

Some of my S.C. papers revealed a lot of facts about the modern schoolboy under the evacuation scheme. We (the City of London school) are evacuated to Marlborough and use their buildings, Box and Cox i.e. play games in the morning and work in the afternoon. Pubs are out of bounds and 'the prefects are continually raiding them' but I know one or two that are nearly safe. We (cheek of the d—d cockney) don't think much of the Marlborough chaps. In order to go safely to a cinema you must get over to Swindon. You can smoke in billets provided your 'hosts' don't object. Preparation in most billets is difficult because the hosts keep the wireless on – but one boy sensibly adds to 'Preparation' the clause 'supposing you want to do it'.

I must go and get a warm now: this is one of those days on which spells at the table have to be punctuated by frequent returns to the fireside.

Yours
Jack

TO HIS BROTHER (W):

[The Kilns]
Dec 24th 1939

My dear W –

I have been thinking much this week on the absurdity of Christmas customs in an infidel society, specially the Christmas *card*. Waiving the great absurdity of celebrating the nativity at all if you don't believe in the incarnation, what in heaven's name is the idea of everyone sending every one else pictures of stage-coaches, fairies, foxes, dogs, butterflies, kittens, flowers etc? We can just trace the connection between some of these pictures and the original festival, but have you ever thought how it would appear to a person who met it for the first time?

The parallel would be if you had visited a Chinese and found him at a table covered with small pictures, and, on asking what he would be at, received the reply 'Well, personally I very much question whether to-morrow *is* the anniversary of Buddha's being protected by the dragons, or even whether it ever happened. But I'm keeping up the old custom. No – there aren't any pictures of Buddha or of the dragons here. I don't care for that sort of goody-goody business. But here's one of a traction engine for Hu Flung Dung, and I'm sending this study of a napkin-ring to Lo Hung Pit, and these jolly ones of bluebottles are for the children.' You can't find anything more preposterous in Gulliver.[198]

I've had a good week, having at last got back to the book on pain. I don't know anything more teasing than to be kept back, first by one job and then by another, from getting on with a scheme which one has started and which is buzzing in your head all the time. That is one of the reasons why I feel that you deserve more sympathy than most of your colleagues because you really have things you want to do at home; whereas to many of the other dug-outs (and by the way, did you ever imagine during the last war that *you* would one day be a dug-out?) the recall to the colours may have come almost as a relief to boredom. Or at least if they dislike their present jobs they dislike them simply for what they are and not *also* as a maddening interruption of real life. Another man I am very sorry for is the chap at the end of our drive whose rock garden was just all but complete when he was called up. However, I dare say he has much solace in adding continued finishing touches in his imagining.

I started in the evenings this week to read a book Maureen has out of her library, Clemence Dane's *White Ben*.[199] I think you read the reviews of it – it's the one about the scarecrow that comes to life. I couldn't go on with it because of the allusiveness of the style and the way in which she keeps jumping on to the time after the end of the book ('Joyce has made a good deal of this first meeting since')[200] I am sure this, take all quirks and kinks, is quite wrong for a *fantastic* story: plain matter-of-fact narrative on the model of Swift or Defoe is what you want. But I mention the book for one really splendid touch. The scarecrow, having just uprooted himself, is stumping down a country road by night when he comes to a sign-post and 'he did not care for this sign post. It made him self conscious, like a man in the presence of a monkey.'[201]

---

198 Lewis was later to devote an essay to the commercialization of Christmas entitled 'Xmas and Christmas: A Lost Chapter from Herodotus'. First published in 1954, it is reprinted in *EC*.

199 Clemence Dane, *The Arrogant History of White Ben* (1939).

200 ibid., ch. 11, p. 129: 'Years later [Angela] described to her grandson the experiences she had seen.'

201 ibid., ch. 6, p. 67: 'The sign-post embarrassed him, much as a monkey embarrasses a self-conscious human being.'

I have also had a good week out of doors. The pond began to get a thin skin of ice about four o'clock on Wednesday. Since then we have had both kinds of frozen days – those with bright yellow suns, turning at sunset to red cannon balls, and those with damp dark-grey fog through which the ridges of the grass loom up white. This morning, during my ante-prandial garden walk with Bruce, was a particularly beautiful example of the former – the sun just rising behind the top wood as I emerged onto the edge of the 'cliff': and the flat, golden-yellow of the sunrise behind the perfectly distinct branches giving a sort of Chinese screen effect.

Few things are more to be pitied in your present situation than your incarceration in a town. Even the small readjustments which the war has so far thrown up at the Kilns lead to curious discoveries. For instance the presence of the revolving bookcase in the study has just introduced me to a book of Minto's mother's[202] which is well worth studying. It is called Gems of Literature/Elegant, rare, and Suggestive/ Edinburgh:/William P. Nimmo – no date.[203] A most extraordinary rag-bag in which first-class bits from Johnson, Addison, Keats, Milton etc jostle Robert Montgomery,[204] David Smith (whoever he is)[205] Hemans,[206] and many forgotten names. The engravings are of a sort you can probably imagine – damsels with those peculiar comic-section or peg-top legs and eyes raised to heaven and old men with what can only be

202 Mrs Moore's mother, Jane King Askins (1846–90), was the daughter of the Venerable Francis King (1817–91) and his wife Jane Jelly (d. 1899). Jane's father, Archdeacon King, was educated at Trinity College, Dublin, and following his ordination in 1844 he was Curate of Abbeyleix, 1843–9, Curate of Oswestry, 1849–53, Principal Curate of St Patrick's, Newry, 1853–70, Rector of St Patrick's, 1870–91, and Archdeacon of Dromore. On 8 June 1869 Jane King married the Rev. William James Askins (1842–95), at that time Principal Curate of Altedesert, 1869–71. They had three sons and three daughters. It was while her husband was Vicar of Dunleer that she died on 22 December 1890. She is buried with her husband at Dunleer.

203 *Gems of Literature, Elegant, Rare, and Suggestive* [1866].

204 Robert Montgomery (1807–55), author of *The Omnipresence of the Deity* (1828), *Oxford: A Poem* (1831) and *The Poetical Works of Robert Montgomery*, collected and revised by the author (1854).

205 This was a mistake for Horace Smith (1779–1849), author of *Rejected Addresses: or Theatrum Poetarum* (1812) and *The Tin Trumpet: or, Head and Tails, for the Wise and Waggish* (1836).

206 None of the works of the poet, Felicia Dorothea Hemans (1793–1853) is found in *Gems of Literature.*

called *Biblical* beards. But Sydney Smith is an author neither you nor I know, and apparently ought to. Isn't this (from a *Gem* entitled *Man's Superiority*) good? 'There is a very strong anthropical party who view all eulogiums on the brute creation with a very considerable degree of suspicion, and look upon every compliment which is paid to the ape as high treason to the dignity of man. There may, perhaps, be more of rashness and ill-fated security in my opinion than of magnanimity or liberality; but I confess I feel myself so much at my ease about the superiority of mankind – I have such a marked and decided contempt for the understanding of every baboon I have yet met[207] – I feel so sure that the blue ape without a tail will never rival us in poetry, painting, and music – that I see no reason whatever why justice may not be done to the few fragments of soul and tatters of understanding which they may really possess.'[208] Isn't it, by the way, an interesting point in style that the fact of saying you have a *contempt* for the baboon's understanding really has the opposite effect of what you'd anticipate and seems, for the moment, to put the baboon on a level with you? – on which most of the whimsicality of the passage turns.

The study stove is smoking abominably while I write, and as Paxford is away on his Xmas holiday I suppose there is no chance of having anything done about it for days. It's at that stage now when I don't notice it (visually) as long as I keep my eyes on the paper, but if I look up at the bookcase I perceive that I am sitting in the middle of a fog. It is also giving out practically no heat. So you see 'we also have our crosses'.

Have any of those Charlotte Yonges arrived yet? I hope the *Malvernian* which I re-addressed yesterday will reach you alright, for it looks a really interesting one, giving you the whole epic of the move to Blenheim. You will also soon get, or have got, a letter from *either* Limpopo *or* Uncle Dick (I don't know which):[209] if you are too busy to answer it, send it back to me and I'll do so.

Well, Brother, (as the troops say) it's a sad business not to have you with me to-morrow morning – and not to have the January walk ahead.

---

207 A misquote – Smith actually wrote 'seen'.

208 *Gems of Literature*, p. 34. The quotation was from Sydney Smith's lecture, 'On the Faculties of Animals, as Compared with Those of Men,' from his *Elementary Sketches of Moral Philosophy* (1854), p. 232.

209 i.e. the 'Scotch uncles', William and Richard Lewis. 'Limpopo' was the nickname of William Lewis. See note 35 to the letter to Arthur Greeves of 13 June 1933.

The most cheerful thing at present (oddly enough) is the News. Russia's attempt to do to Finland what Germany did to Poland[210] reminds me of your father's story of the 'great bosthoon' whom his athletic friend took out for the run and who tried to imitate him in jumping the flax-pond – one of those of his wheezes whose point lay wholly in *his* telling.

I shall be asphyxiated in a few minutes. I can hardly see out of the window by now.

Yours
Jack

TO HIS BROTHER (W):

[The Kilns]
Dec 31st 1939.

My dear W –

I forgot to mention in my last week's letter (but I fancy Minto has told you since) that we have lost J.A.[211] He was not only so very much a part of my earlier Magdalen life but also (for some reason) a person in whom your father took such an interest that I feel a big link gone. The choir, on some suspicion of scarlet fever, had been dispersed this year instead of being kept up for Christmas, so there was a purely *prose* service in Chapel of an appropriately Scotch character. The old chap was not, of course, a believer: but I've never heard anything recorded of him that was not wholly good – and he did once, in print describe all philosophy as 'the groping for a far-off trans-experiential unity': so let's hope he has reached it.

You will remember that while I was writing to you last Sunday I was being nearly smoked out of the study. Until the chimney could be cleaned Minto had the fire lit in the bungalow and that became my study for about half of last week. It is not really, as at present furnished, quite as comfortable as the study, and the constant putting on and off of gum-boots becomes a bore: but it's very snug and quiet and has a

210 On 30 November 1939 the Red Army launched a massive assault across the Soviet-Finnish border. Soviet divisions, numbering 465,000 men, threw themselves against nine Finnish divisions, totalling 130,000 men. As Hitler's aircraft had attacked Warsaw, so now Stalin's bombed Helsinki. The carnage was terrible, and was to continue. On 2 December 1939 the Soviet news agency Tass announced the establishment of a People's Government of Finland.

211 J. A. Smith died in Oxford on 19 December 1939. See his obituary in *The Oxford Magazine*, vol. LVIII (18 January 1940), p. 140.

kind of little-end-room remoteness which you would appreciate. Its aesthetic advantages are great. Stepping out of it to empty my bladder at about 6 one evening I thought I had never seen this place more beautiful. Just behind me a moon, the colour of a harvest moon, was rising: the sky was blazing 'with few, but with how splendid stars',[212] Jupiter among them: the grass was frosty: into the dimness ahead stretched the white concrete slabs of the path leading the eye on to the dark gable-end of the Kilns proper. An absolute enchantment – which led me to define a beautiful place as 'one, which after years of familiarity, still looks as if *anything* might happen there'. But the opposite wd. be equally plausible 'A place which, even at the first glance, proclaims that *nothing* can ever happen there'. I prefer the second on the whole. Too much happens, Brother, far too much.

Over there on Christmas Day I read Stevenson's *Lay Morals*[213] in a little cheap edition which has been about the house for some years. I can't remember if you know it: if not, shall I send that copy out to you? It seems to me not only the best (non-fiction) book of his, but one of the best books by anyone, I've ever read.

We didn't make much Christmas cheer. It was a sad business setting out for the early service without you (and still sadder going to the Bleiben's the following night, because the evening journey to a party is a thing so datelessly associated with you! I think if ever we *are* old men and still have any money and are still even asked out together, we ought to do the thing properly by always going in a horse-drawn four wheeler). I drank a bottle of your Bosphorus *vin rouge* and thought it not at all bad.

The Bleiben party was not nearly as good as we were having at the beginning of the holiday. Margaret Meyer[214] is a new and unwelcome addition. She asked me 'Where is Maureen?' *Self* 'Oh she's at home at present. *M.M.* Then why isn't she here? *Self* Will you have one of those sandwiches? *M.M.* 'Wasn't she invited?' I didn't repeat this at home as I thought it would not tend to the increase of charity! But what is one to do in such a situation? However, we had one great consolation, in the game where selected couples come in and enact a historical scene, when

212 James Elroy Flecker, *A Ship, an Isle, a Sickle Moon* (1913), 2.

213 Robert Louis Stevenson, *Lay Morals, and Other Papers* (1911).

214 Margaret Meyer remains to be identified.

Mrs Davenport, as Robert Bruce, sat brooding while Bleiben made a number of jumps at the wall in the character of the spider – the joke being that what with his blackness, his ugliness, & his smallness, he looked so very much *more* like a spider than he probably intended or supposed.

This was Boxing Day. Minto has probably told you of the 'ludicrous episode' on the Wednesday in which Havard had to come up with a hack-saw and saw my ring off my finger. To you, I expect, the most interesting feature of this event will be the extreme P'dayta-ishness of my act in forcing the damned thing into such a position originally: it being a marked trait in the character of a P'dayta that tho' being physically rather feeble for any useful purpose such as cranking a car or lifting a log, he is subject to fits of demoniac strength when it is a question of jamming, twisting, bursting or crushing anything into ruin – e.g. a lobster or a door. Havard performed his operation with great skill and delicacy, beguiling the time with interesting and edifying conversation.

I couldn't help contrasting him with B. E. C. Davies, a professor of London,[215] whom I went on to see in Old Headington the same morning. Here is a man of my own age, who knew Barfield when he was up: of my own profession, who has written on Spenser. You'd have thought these were all the materials for a good meeting. But no. One got through all the preliminary stuff about how his London she-students were getting on in Oxford, thinking that the real conversation would then begin. But every single time I tried to turn it to books, or life, or friends (as such) I was completely frustrated. i.e. about friends, he'd talk of their jobs, marriages, houses, incomes, arrangements, but not of them. Books – oh yes, editions, prices, suitability for exams – not their contents. In fact hardly since the days of 'How are things at the yard, Gussie?'[216]

215 Bernard Eustace Cuthbert Davis (1898–1973) joined the Royal Naval Volunteer Reserve in September 1917, but soon transferred to the newly formed Royal Air Force as a lieutenant, serving in Italy. He went up to Wadham College, Oxford, in 1919 as an exhibitioner and read English. While there he was secretary of the Diagnostic Society (debates), and in 1921 he gained a distinction in the shortened course for war veterans. After taking his BA, he became a lecturer in English at East London College (now Queen Mary College). In 1926 he was appointed Reader and Head of English at Westfield College, London University, the first man to join the full-time staff. He is the author of *Edmund Spenser: A Critical Study* (1933). He and his wife Elizabeth Davis edited *Poets of the Early Seventeenth Century* (1967).

216 Their father's proverbial greeting to his brother-in-law, Augustus Hamilton.

have I had to endure so much irredeemably 'grown-up conversation'. Unless I misjudge him, he is one of those dreadful fellows who never refers to literature except during the hours he's paid for talking about it. Just as one meets clergymen – indeed we are told the Archdeacon was one of them – who resent the intrusion of Christianity into the conversation.[217] How small a nucleus there is in each liberal profession of people who care about the thing they are supposed to be doing: yet I suppose the percentage of garage-hands and motor-touts who are really interested in motoring is about 95!

I have had cards from Westdene and Holywood and have written to Uncles Dick & Gussie.

I am at present reading Locke's *Treatises of Civil Government*[218] which, as you probably know, is the classic refutation of Filmer's *Patriarcha*.[219] Locke makes great play with an objection to which I confess I don't know what the orthodox answer was – that this theory, so far from supporting, would subvert either every existing monarchy or else every existing monarchy except one: for whichever of the possible rules of inheritance you adopt, there cannot now be more than one heir to Adam – one eldest son of an eldest son all the way back. It is a very richly and racily written book like all Locke, and I'm enjoying it.

My ex-pupil Mrs Neylan dragged me into College to meet her and give her tea yesterday, over half frozen snow (it snowed all day on Thursday – I think it was) but with some reward for I think it was 'to profit'. You remember her, she teaches at Dartington Hall, co-education, no punishments and no obedience expected unless the *reason* for the order can be made clear to the child. She now has a child of her own and finds it all won't work and is beginning to doubt the whole Dartington system, and what with that and the general stress of things, is just beginning to throw out a tentative feeler in the direction of Christianity (she is a gratifyingly constant *re*-reader of the *Regress*)

A very much edited account of the conversation which I gave to Minto on returning (partly to explain why I was so late) produced the

---

217 Lewis was referring to Archdeacon Grantly, one of the chief characters in Anthony Trollope's *The Warden* (1855) and *Barchester Towers*. His impatience with those who prattle about religion is evident throughout the books in which he appears.

218 John Locke, *Two Treatises of Government* (1690).

219 Robert Filmer, *Patriarcha; or, The Natural Power of Kings* (1680).

characteristic and now immovable conviction that 'that fool of a woman wanted you, of all people, to tell her how to bring up a baby'. Maureen is away in London for the week end. I got to Minehead on Friday to spend a few days with Harwood. Your message to Magnus Pike[220] has been handed on and Dotty says in her last letter that it will be attended to. Vera (I know this will annoy you, but I'm afraid she'll ask me at supper time whether I've done so) asks to be remembered to you.

Is there any point in wishing each other a happy New Year? Well, yes, I suppose there is – a hell of a point! I await with interest your verdict on Charlotte Yonge.

Yours
Jack

---

220 Magnus Pike remains to be identified.

1940

TO HIS BROTHER (W):

[The Kilns]
Jan 9th 1940

My dear W. –

It seems almost brutal to describe a January walk taken without you in a letter *to* you, but I suppose 'concealment is in vain'. But before plunging into it I must mention a little scene which I have regularly intended to mention in every letter for about 3 weeks and regularly forgotten. I was coming home from a walk and had just reached the Bourdillon's hedge[1] when I saw Bruce standing across the path with his head erect and his tail wagging furiously. There is a very slight bend to the right in that path just after the Bourdillon's, so that I could not see what he was looking at. Presently a cloud of steam in the frosty air appeared to descend towards him – to be followed by the long grave face of the mushroom-white horse who lives in that field. Dog continued looking up and horse's head leaned down till their noses almost touched: then they withdrew with every mark of mutual esteem. Now that I have at last written it down it hardly seems worth much: but it was an odd sight at the time.

It was on Friday morning I set out for my jaunt. Maureen was going the same day to her godmother so she motored me as far as Bath. I was very doubtful about the wisdom of accepting this offer, but I'm glad I did for it turned out one of the most beautiful drives I've ever had. I don't know if you've ever seen the Cotswolds in snow – but you

---

1 Their neighbour Francis Bernard Bourdillon (1883–1970) and his wife Mary Dorothea Bourdillon lived in The Oaks on Shotover Hill. Mr Bourdillon was a lecturer in German at University College, Reading, 1908–14, a lecturer in Modern Language at Balliol College, 1913–15, and Secretary of the Royal Institute of International Affairs, 1926–9. He worked in the Research Department of the Foreign Office, 1943–9.

can imagine how well it sets off those bushy copses and long 'eyebrows' of elms, and the grey stone walls, and how the silence and muffling effect of it emphasises the sense of remoteness and forgottenness which one always gets in that country. When we stopped for a few moments at Bibury the noise and life of the water gave it almost the air of an oasis. Maureen dropped me at Bath station where, after a glass of sherry, a pork-pie, and a cup of coffee, I had about an hour to wait – and discovered a most unexpected beauty.

When you walk to one end of the platform you find yourself looking down from the parapet of a bridge. The view consists of the usual Bath arrangements – semi circular terraces of Regency houses descending like the tiers of a theatre: but the lowest, in this case, instead of opening on a street opens on a quay, and the quay flanks the canal – of which the water, on that particular day, was almost a bright green. The quay was quite deserted except for a black cat. The whole thing with its marriage of Jane Austenish propriety and Wapping nauticality made up a very pleasing medley.

As usual on the first day of a holiday things began to deteriorate after this – a crowded train to Bristol, and from Bristol to Taunton the sort of train where you try three coaches before you can fight your way into one, and then, after standing wedged tightly in a 1st class corridor for ten minutes, are turned out because 'plenty of 3rd class carriages' have been added on at the back. I finally got a seat and was somewhat consoled till Taunton by a conversation between a sailor and a man in plain clothes who claimed also to be a sailor and whom the other regarded as a spy. It was during this stage – having set out from arctic Oxford wearing great coat, gauntlets and muffler and carrying my lined mack for walking purposes – that I became aware of a not entirely welcome change in the climate. When I reached Taunton it was definitely a warm evening.

God send us to be soon together again, for here came that moment in a holiday which you would so have appreciated and wh. cannot be fully enjoyed alone – the moment when, at the last of the big stations, you find, far from the other traffic, in a remote silent bay, the little, dark, non-corridor train of two coaches – usually, for some reason, exuding steam from all the compartments – which is going to jerk and bump you to your real destination. And then those stops at unheard-of halts with wooden platforms, and the gleam of an oil lantern in a porter's hand. It wd. have been partly spoiled for you, however, by the presence of a young man of undergraduate type and age who turned out to be a student training to be a mining engineer, and who, having tackled me on politics, the English character, propaganda, improvements in the Everyman series, Hindu theology and so forth, exclaimed 'You must be a man of very wide interests!' – and, do you know, I never realised before the naïvete with which we all *think* this, even if we do not say it, in such circumstances – i.e. the bland inference 'By gum! His interests are as wide as *mine*!'

This brought me to Minehead, at about 6.30. I dined that evening with the Harwoods, and being 'carried' back to my hotel by him at about 10.30 had the very unpleasant surprise of finding it locked up and silent as the grave. It was about 10 minutes' work of banging and shouting and ringing before I was let in – and during the time I had, as you may suppose, some 'very uneasy sensations'.

Next morning, leaving my greatcoat and suitcase at this hotel, and retaining rucksack and mack, I climbed the steep hill to Harwood's billet and collected him. His children are now so numerous that one ceases to notice them individually, any more than a scuffle of piglets in a field or a waddle of ducks. A few platoons of them accompanied us for about the first mile of the walk, but returned, like tugs, when we were out of harbour.

The idea had been to cross Dunkery Beacon and lie at Exford, but the day was so misty that we decided to hug the valleys where one wd. have those near-at-hand beauties which mist rather enhances than destroys. It wouldn't be much good trying to describe the route without a map – but it consisted in reaching Porlock by a very wide detour up one valley and down another. I was 'very angry' with Harwood when, though professing to know the country, he brought us at 1 o'clock to a village without a pub! (Luccombe). We succeeded (a sort of success, by the bye, which *never* happens to you and me when we are on our own) in finding a cottage that gave us tea and bread and cheese and jam – in one of those slippery, oil-clothy, frosty best parlours, with an oil stove that created an intolerable stench and a small library of *reference* works – you know, *Plain Man's Encyclopaedia, Inquire within about everything* – monuments, doubtless, to the success of those advertisements which promise you a rise in salary and endless occupation for the long winter evenings if you will buy such works. One that specially intrigued us was 'Every Man his own Lawyer – *Illustrated*'.[2] We looked in vain however for a portrait of a tort or a south aspect of Habeas Corpus – the pictures consisting entirely of photos of court-houses and famous judges. Can you imagine anything more infuriating than, on turning to such a book to try to extricate yourself from an income tax muddle or an injudicious betrothal (and for what other purpose wd. you ever open it?) to be met by the bland features of Lord Darling?[3]

Well, we went on. We passed a 'shoot', and I can truly say like Johnson, that the accuracy either of fowling pieces or of the people who fire them seemed less than one wd. have supposed possible. Nor had I realised at what extremely short range it is done – a miserable business: not much more fun, to the outsider, than walking into the hen run and wringing a fowl's neck.

The valley of the Horner (suspiciously near Codsend Moor) in which most of our afternoon was spent is a most beautiful place: very deep, almost a gorge, with a path crossing and re-crossing the river. The trees are covered with ferns and it is odd to see them sprouting out of branches far above your head. The chief drawback for me was that my lined mack proved much too hot and heavy and the lining soon became so damp that to sit on it at a soak was not much drier than sitting on the ground. But it was a grand afternoon all the same and I arrived at Porlock without a touch of walker's anus. I presume you and I lunched at Porlock before ascending the hill on the march that ended at Brendon but I can't now remember any of that day *before* the hill.[4] Marry, the hill itself, and the exquisite relief of getting off it into that bracken country, and drinking our whisky – all that is fresh enough.

After hot baths we repaired to tea in the lounge which we shared with one other guest who presently found means to insinuate himself into our conversation but 'displayed such a fund of literature and fertility of illustration' that we did not regret it – in fact *his* interests were as wide as ours! He turned out to be a master at Charterhouse. It was certainly very odd to find oneself discussing fine points out of

2 T. Williams, *Every Man His Own Lawyer: or, A Complete Law Library* (1812).

3 Charles John Darling, first Baron Darling (1849–1936), a judge, who had been called to the bar in 1874. He presided over many important cases, his judgements characterized by close reasoning.

4 This was probably their sixth annual walking tour, 5–9 January 1937, mentioned by Warnie in *BF*, p. 174.

Herodotus with 'the other man in the hotel'. In true 18th century style we begged the favour of his society at dinner. That evening, the young man having gone out to a darts match at Porlock Weir, Harwood and I read to each other from Jane Austen's *The Watsons*[5] with almost continual chuckles. I slept badly, as you and I also do on these occasions.

Next day there was delicious winter sunshine struggling through milky mist. We sauntered rather than walked to the point where the range dividing us from Minehead comes down to the coast. All was dreamlike – church bells ringing. We had a long and satisfying soak at one of the pleasantest places nature provides – under a tree on a grassy slope but within sight and sound of waves breaking on a pebbled beach. All Porlock bay lay before us: on the far side one saw wooded headland after wooded headland basking in a light that was very luminous without being at all clear – and somewhere among them, no doubt, that magnificent hotel miles from anywhere in which you and I once had lunch. But sterner stuff awaited us . . .

He led me up the sea-ward side of the hill by a path which seemed to end in a coastguard station. Seeing a man behind a telescope in the O.P.[6] window I asked him 'Does the path end here?' He replied (rot him) 'Oh no, it goes on a long way and then up into the hills.' So we rounded the coastguard station and went on. As soon as we had passed that promontory I began to dislike it. The path was narrow and what Harwood affected to regard as the 'hillside' appeared to me every minute more like precipices. I'd had some nasty visions of precipices in the night too. Then came a sudden bend to the right into a wide re-entrant on the other side of which I could see no path at all. Harwood pointed it out to me in the end – an almost imperceptible thread across one of those abominable slides of shingle wh. I believe are called 'screes'. I had to admit frankly that I funked it, and the only alternative was to go up the re-entrant, which was all boulders. I didn't like the look of the re-entrant either and have seldom spent an unpleasanter 10 minutes. We were both completely blown – and then needless to say the top turned out not really to be the top. However, after a fairish tramp along the real top – indescribable beauties to the inland side – we were rewarded.

5 Jane Austen, *The Watsons* (1871).
6 Observation Post.

We found a little stone building with a seat in each of the four alcoves of which it consisted. One alcove contained verses by Keble[7] (fairly good) and the opposite one verses by Heber[8] (bad). The one between bore a delightful inscription: (from memory, but certainly accurate at the end) 'In memory/of/Sir Robert Acland/who/on these hills/in Sunday walks/trained his children and grandchildren/in the love of Nature/and of Christian poetry.'

'In Sunday walks'! Not even the knowledge that Sir Robert's mischievous activity was mainly responsible for the 'dry' condition of many surrounding villages could steel our hearts against this winning picture. Happy age – pleasant, comfortable, pious people! How thankful I am that we saw in Cousin Quartus the last gleam of all that. '*Trained* his grandchildren.'

We descended – exercising the love of nature and of Christian poetry – into Selworthy for lunch where there is an abominable temperance hotel which will give you 'the full lunch' (3/6) but refuses bread and cheese on the ground (honest Indian!) that 'they haven't the service'. The Lunch began with 'oeufs surprice' but we were consoled by seeing cold pigeon on the menu. It consisted, however, of no more than wd. *literally* (not à la P'dayta)[9] make a mouthful. As Harwood said, in such a place one pays for the 'good taste', for it certainly was a beautifully furnished house. We sat in the drawing room till about 3 o'clock, both very tired – Harwood actually went to sleep.

The concluding march back into Minehead was v. beautiful. I returned to my original hotel and had a stand easy in an arm chair before a good fire with a tea-trap and Gore's *Philosophy of the Good Life* (Everyman)[10] wh. is good, though by no means outstanding.

I entertained both Harwood and Field[11] that night to a hotel dinner

---

7 John Keble (1792–1866) was one of the leaders of the Oxford Movement, and the author of *The Christian Year* (1827).

8 Reginald Heber (1783–1826), educated at Oxford, became Bishop of Calcutta in 1822. Among his publications was an edition of the *Whole Works* of Jeremy Taylor mentioned in the letter to Warnie of 24 October 1931. Bishop Heber is the author of a number of hymns including 'Brightest and best of the sons of the morning', and several volumes of poems.

9 Not, that is, the substantial amount which their father presumably referred to as 'a mouthful'.

10 Charles Gore, *The Philosophy of the Good Life* (1930; Everyman's Library, 1935).

11 i.e. Walter Ogilvie 'Woff' Field. See note 98 to the letter of 10 May 1943.

embellished with 2 bottles of Pommard and we were very merry. The following morning I spent alone looking for the house in wh. Dyson had told me he was staying with his in-laws. He had given me an insufficient address and I never found it, but it led me up over the hill behind Minehead into admirable fir-woods with views out over the channel in beautiful sunshine – and the pleasure of walking without a coat or pack was very great. I also strolled along the 'Front' to that pleasant point where a seaside resort turns into a real harbour – you can picture the whole scene, the little jetty, the grounded collier, and the solitary crane. I lunched in a pub off a 7d pork pie and a pint of cider – the latter really first class and only 4d, so it was about the cheapest satisfactory meal I've ever had. I dined at the Harwoods that night and came away – on Tuesday morning – as you said in your last letter 'thanking the Giver' which, by the way, is the *completion* of a pleasure.[12] One of the things about being an unbeliever is that the steam or 'spirit' (in the chymical sense) given off by experiences has nowhere to go to.

This morning (Wed) we again have a frost here: the whole place is *grey*. Term begins on Saturday.

Bruce has apparently had a damaged tail while I was away and Vera told Minto a story about a dog in Tounley Foolface's care who had broken his tail so that it had to be kept in plaster of Paris and lifted up for him when he went to stool! Fortunately Bruce's is alright!

Yours
Jack

TO HIS BROTHER (W):

[The Kilns]
Jan 14th 1940

My dear W –

This will probably be a short letter for I feel I've only just finished writing my last and little has happened to me since then. We all look forward to hearing from you fairly soon, but realise your situation and

12 This anticipates an observation Lewis later made in *Reflections on the Psalms* (1958; Fount, 1998), ch. 9, p. 81: 'We delight to praise what we enjoy because the praise not merely expresses but completes the enjoyment: it is its appointed consummation.'

have no intention of pestering you for letters. By the way, Parkin[13] rang up some days ago (I think from Camberley) to hear news of you: I invited him to dine & lie in College the next time he was in these parts.

My return from Minehead brought me back to Arctic conditions. They have been skating on the pond all the week. There is no snow, I'm (on the whole) glad to say, but very thick rime on bushes and trees and the paths and roads are in that curious state when they are perfectly dry but yet the foot has a tendency to *stick* to them at each step: also iron-hard and probably not much kinder to the feet than your *pavé*.[14] My favourite walks at present are in the Nuffield wood, where there is always pale yellow sunlight these afternoons and comparative (*very* comparative) warmth and a pleasant mixture of black, white, grey and pale green.

In College, where I slept for the first time last night, Hatton has had a brain wave of putting the electric heater in my bedroom, to be turned on when he brings the morning tea: so you can think of me at 7.15 shaving by it.

Hone from Marlborough is up and dined with me last night.[15] He told me one thing that surprised me very much. He is staying at Worcester and there met a German Rhodes Scholar. This fellow's father spotted that war was coming, told the young man 'You go back to Oxford and mind you keep in England till the war is over' and packed him off. I am very glad to say that after some trouble with the Warden of Rhodes House, who kept on 'warning' him of the danger of war and 'offering him facilities' to leave the country, he is being left quite unmolested: largely, Hone tells me, through the good offices of Wilkinson. He then went on to say that he had found out that of all

---

13 i.e. Major Herbert Denis Parkin. See note 13 to the letter to Warnie of 24 October 1931.

14 'cobblestone'.

15 Sir Brian William Hone (1907–78), cricketer and educator knighted in 1970, was born in Adelaide and educated at Prince Alfred College and Adelaide University. He won a Rhodes scholarship to New College, Oxford, in 1931 and came to know C. S. Lewis while reading English. After taking his BA in 1932 Hone was assistant master at Marlborough College, Wiltshire, 1933–40. Returning to Australia in 1940, he was headmaster of Cranbrook School, Sydney, 1940–50, and headmaster of Melbourne Church of England Grammar School, 1950–70. He was Chairman of Headmasters' Conference of Independent Schools of Australia, 1954–71 and Chairman of the Commonwealth Secondary Schools Libraries Committee, 1971–5. He published *Cricket Practice and Tactics* (1937).

the German Rhodes Scholars since his own day (and there are four Germans a year) only *one* was now actually in Germany, the rest being all distributed in England and America. He also told me a remark of Wilkinson's wh. is delightful to hear when so many people are talking of the collapse of all civilisation. Hone had said something about a new building at Marlborough being too expensive. 'Well,' said the Wilk, 'What I feel is that when you are adding to a school or college you are building for eternity and ought to do the thing properly.' That's the stuff!

He stayed rather too late (Hone, I mean) and became a little boring at times. I wonder does an extreme optimism result from being a schoolmaster – because you are always 'turning out' promising boys and never living among what they actually become when it's all over.

I have just had to get out the keys of your wardrobe to put away Phippy's Christmas box to you – the usual handkerchiefs: so if you have not yet done so, you'd better say something about them when you next write. I finished Gore's book[16] on the journey back with considerable enjoyment, but perhaps a faint feeling that it was rather thin.

Since the first part of this letter I have been, for my first time, to 3 o'clock evensong, having spent the morning on the 'washing', reading (my 'Sunday book' is Niebuhr's *Interpretation of Christian Ethics*[17] a very disagreeable but not unprofitable book) & writing to you. This afternoon Church is a very pleasant institution and I think I shall make it my usual one in future. The Church is really warm by that time and looks even warmer with the sunset glowing in through the West window. It would also give one a Sunday *morning* walk, a thing which from early associations has always an attraction whereas a Sunday *afternoon* walk is always to me the most insipid of the week. It wd. also give one an appetite for lunch. In fact I believe it wd. realise the long-sought desideratum of a pious Sunday without the P'dayta atmosphere. But I forget that to you in your present unfortunate position the P'dayta-est of Sundays would be like a slice of heaven: nor, I suppose, is it any consolation to you [to] reflect that however hard you may be working you'll have to work very hard indeed to bring yourself up to the average as regards your life's total.

16 i.e. *The Philosophy of the Good Life*.
17 Reinhold Niebuhr, *An Interpretation of Christian Ethics* (1936).

Do you know, so far – but of course the future may be very different – my experience of a war seen from this end makes me even more indignant than I used to be, at the absolute balls talked by civilians last time. Not, of course, that all civilian professions are having as good a time as mine. One thing that infuriates me is the continual letters to the papers by all sorts of busybodies suggesting what we should 'do with' young men between the school leaving age and their enlistment – how to keep them happy, interested, and useful. No one seems to think of leaving the poor young devils alone. But as Hone pointed out there is a real problem about supporting them, as employers naturally don't want to give jobs to men who will be called up in a year or so. Still, I can't help feeling there is a different 'urge' behind most of the letters.

I've been reading a book you hate in the evenings of this week – *Pickwick.*[18] I still see what you dislike about it and dislike it myself though in a less degree. Perhaps what I really enjoy is the illusion of having a chat with F.K. I have never ceased to miss that old man. I liked the gusto – a bad joke with him was better than a good joke with other people.

Havard has been up skating this afternoon. A visit from Maureen's friend Blake[19] (or as Minto says 'that little black bounder') is threatened in the near future. As if rationing were not enough, we have a domestic restriction: the best hens are being kept alive to be killed when you come on leave! Now I maintain that in respect of good eating you are the fortunate one and that this is unbalanced.

Yours
Jack

TO DOM BEDE GRIFFITHS OSB (W):

[Magdalen College]
Jan 17th 1940

My dear Dom Bede –

Thanks for letter and article. I believe I found myself in agreement with every point you made in the latter. The Platonic and neo-Platonic

18 i.e. Dickens, *The Pickwick Papers.*

19 See **Leonard James Blake** in the Biographical Appendix. Blake married Maureen Moore on 27 August 1940.

stuff has, no doubt, been reinforced (a) By the fact that people not very morally sensitive or instructed but trying to do their best recognise temptations of appetite as temptations but easily mistake all the spiritual (and worse) sins for harmless or even virtuous states of mind: hence the illusion that the 'bad part' of oneself is the body. (b) By a misunderstanding of the Pauline use of σάρξ,[20] wh. in reality cannot mean the body (since envy, witchcraft, and other spiritual sins are attributed to it) but, I suppose, means the unregenerate manhood as a whole. (You have no doubt noticed that σωμα[21] is nearly always used by St Paul in a good sense.)

(c) By equating 'matter' in the ordinary sense with ὕλη[22] or *materia* in the scholastic and Aristotelian sense, i.e. equating the concrete corporeality of flesh, grass, earth or water with 'pure potentiality'. The latter, being nearest to not-being and furthest from the Prime Reality can, I suppose, be called the 'least good' of things. But I fear Plato thought the concrete flesh and grass bad, and have no doubt he was wrong. (Besides these two senses of 'matter' there is also a third – the thing studied in physics. But who would dare to vilify such a miracle of unceasing energy as *that*? – it's more like pure form than pure potentiality.)

Yes, I've read the *Scale of Perfection*[23] with much admiration. I think of sending the anonymous translator a list of passages that he might reconsider for the next edition. I've also read the work of R. W. Chambers which you mention.[24] It is first class as an essay on the continuity of the devotional tradition, but not, what it professes, the continuity of prose style. At least I think some of the passages he quotes as similar in style are really similar only in matter. I doubt if he recognises that More's style is greatly inferior to Hilton's. But Chambers is a very good man. If you have his *Man's Unconquerable Mind*,[25] read the essay on *Measure*

20 'flesh'.

21 'body'.

22 'matter' or 'the material', the stuff of which something is made.

23 The edition Lewis used was *The Scale of Perfection by Walter Hilton, Augustinian canon of Thurgarton Priory, Nottinghamshire*, modernized from the first printed edition of Wynkyn de Worde, London, 1494, by an oblate of Solesmes; with an introduction from the French of Dom M. Noetinger (London: Burns, Oates and Washbourne Ltd [1927]).

24 R. W. Chambers, *On the Continuity of English Prose from Alfred to More and his School* (1932).

25 R. W. Chambers, *Man's Unconquerable Mind: Studies of English Writers, from Bede to A. E. Housman and W. P. Ker* (1939).

for Measure.[26] He simply treats it as an ordinary Christian story and all the old stuff about 'Shakespeare's dark period' vanishes into thin air.

I see what you mean by calling G. Eliot's Dorothea[27] a saint *manquée*: nothing is more pathetic than the potential holiness in [the] quality of the devotion which actually wrecks itself on Casaubon. If you like such leisurely novels, let me recommend John Galt: specially the *Entail.*[28]

About active service – I think my account was true in what it said, but false in what it excluded. I quite agree that the obedience and comradeship are very good things: and I have no sympathy with the modern view that killing or being killed is *simpliciter* a great evil. But perhaps these truths are rather odious on the lips of a civilian, unless some pastoral or civil office absolutely obliges him to utter them.

Fascism and Communism, like all other evils, are potent because of the good they contain or imitate. *Diabolus simius Dei.*[29] And, of course, their occasion is the failure of those who left humanity starved of that particular good. This does not for me alter the conviction that they are very bad indeed. One of the things we must guard against is the penetration of both into Christianity – availing themselves of that very truth you have suggested and I have admitted. Mark my words: you will presently see both a Leftist and a Rightist pseudo-theology developing – the abomination will stand where it ought not.

I forgot what I said in my last letter, but probably *dolor locutus est.*[30] I agree with you very strongly about the necessity of trying as hard as we can to obey the apostolic 'Rejoice always':[31] and I think we sin by needless neglect of this as often as by anything else. The attempt to obey it is at present one of my three morning resolutions each day. I had not realised its importance till recently. There may be objections to saying the End is happiness *tout court*, but I agree, I think, with all you really mean.

Yours
C. S. Lewis

---

26 William Shakespeare, *Measure for Measure* (1623).

27 In Eliot's *Middlemarch.*

28 John Galt, *The Entail* (1823).

29 'The devil is the ape of God.' Tertullian, *De Exhortatione Castitatis* (On Exhortation to Chastity), section 928c.

30 'My grief spoke.' Lewis may have had Job 16:6 in mind.

31 Philippians 4:4.

TO HIS BROTHER (W):

[The Kilns]
Jan 21st 1940

My dear W –

We were all relieved to hear from you again – or rather, all pleased, but Minto specially 'relieved' because of her usual inability to imagine any causes for silence except major disasters. I take it (though you don't very emphatically say so yourself) that the illness has been on the whole 'a Good Thing' and that the horizontal position and leisure more than outweigh the tinned rabbits – or is it only now, in retrospect, that they begin to do so? I admit, on second thoughts, that good (or fairly good) eating is part of ones picture of a comfortable day in bed.

I was much interested in what your room mate told you about Anglo-Indian society, and I got it confirmed by Chang (you remember my diminutive Buddhist 'Quashee'?) who says that Mohammedans have very largely abandoned their tee-totalism. What a blow this would be to your poor father! I'm not sure myself that I take quite as rose a view of it as you. When you speak of the 'colour and creed nonsense' I want to distinguish. They have surely on both sides got over the creed nonsense by getting over the creed? It is presumably not an unusually charitable Christian and an unusually charitable Mussulman[32] whom one sees drinking together, but simply two men who have both abandoned their creeds and cultures and are now two ordinary standardised, urban, cinema-fed, materialistic, denationalised wops? I am very glad they should get over the colour bar, of course, and I'd be glad if they got *over* the creed bar leaving the creed intact.

Perhaps I've got the wrong picture; what do you think? For instance when their wives meet, are the white ones learning chastity and wifely obedience from the Indiennes, or are they teaching them to be b—s and Mrs Hawksbees?[33] Of course one might be tempted to say that even if all this is so, the political and humanitarian gains are very great. But will they be in the long run? I mean, won't these standardised wops (the chamber 'empty, swept, and garnished')[34] be just as open as Europe to the

---

32 i.e. Muslim.

33 Mrs Hauksbee is a character in Rudyard Kipling's *Plain Tales from the Hills* (1888).

34 Matthew 12:44.

inroads of Fascism or Communism or any other devil that comes along?

Chang went on to add another thing about India, which is quite outside the picture you and I have been discussing: that one of the great missionary appeals both of Islam and of Buddhism when they started in India was the fact that both offered an escape from the Hindu caste system but that both, by now, in imitation of Hinduism, and (presumably) quite inconsistently with their own tenets, have introduced something that almost amounts to caste in their own ranks. So impossible is it, apparently, to exorcise the *local* demon. It almost makes one think that the Parkinian and ancient idea of the indigenous gods or devils, is right!

I enclose (or *intend* to enclose, for who dare absolutely predict it?) a letter from Mary Cullen.[35] I will reply to Uncle Dick, though, as I told you, I wrote to him about three weeks ago. By an odd concatenation of circumstances I never had time between reading your letter and leaving College at 1 o'clock yesterday to look up the relevant walk in your diary. I got as far, on Saturday morning, as opening that bookcase and trying one volume, before the next pupil came. But I hope to be able to report next week.

While it comes into my head, I saw yesterday in *The New Statesman* a wonderful example of something we have often discussed – the extreme badness of nearly all attempts at Johnsonian pastiche. They had set a competition in which you had to invent Johnsonian remarks on a variety of given subjects: and one which they actually quoted with approval, on Psychoanalysis, began 'Behind the flamboyant façade of its incomprehensible terminology'.[36] Can you see *anything* like Johnson in that? I don't believe *flamboyant* existed at the time. I am sure *façade* except as 'a cant term of architecture' did not. And I'll bet my shirt J. would not have regarded the terminology as 'incomprehensible'. Neither the candidate nor the judge can be a reader of Boswell at all. Much better was another entry – on Wireless Talks. 'Sir, you cannot have

35 Mary Cullen, usually referred to as 'the Witch of Endor', was the cook-housekeeper at Little Lea from 1917 until its break-up in 1930. She was so called because of a certain breathless manner in speaking. After leaving Little Lea she became a cook in a public kitchen and lived rent free in a house which had belonged to Albert Lewis.

36 *The New Statesman and Nation*, XIX (20 January 1940), p. 86. The subject was not psychoanalysis, but the *New English Dictionary*.

good talk without give and take. Now the wireless is all take and no give.'[37] That certainly would have been his basic objection to it *in fact*, whether he had said it in that way or not.

I expect that you, like me, are growing sick of Weather. On Tuesday night (I think it was) I woke up about four unable to sleep again for cold, though I was wearing a pullover and had an enormous pile of blankets. I keep no spirits in the rooms now and the journey to the smoking room was 'not to be thought of'. In the end I got up and made myself cocoa – added the Leeboro' sofa blanket (a really portentous thing) to the bed, and returned to bed wearing over my pyjamas two pullovers and a pair of pants! Even so, I was only just warm enough. It is quite a noticeable minor inconvenience not to be able to get a sip of water in the night by simply stretching out your hand. (Slowly licking the surface of the ice in your tumbler would, I suppose, quench your thirst after twenty minutes or so, but, as we say, it's 'hardly the same thing'.)

On Friday I did not go home, having time for only a short walk between the ending of a T.B.[38] meeting at 3 o'clock and the assembly of our pious study group[39] (see letters of last term) at 4.

A stroll through Mesopotamia[40] and Adders[41] yielded some very striking observations in natural philosophy. The Cher[42] still had a free channel under Magdalen Bridge, but a few yards higher it was frozen right across. The weir (beside that little house just after you have left the fellows' garden and entered Mesopotamia proper) was a very fine spectacle. The water came down between walls of ice into a big pool, dark and shuddering. At the other side of this pool i.e. about 20 feet below the weir, the ice began again, but fringed with what I've never seen before – very thin pancakes of that rather unpleasant froth, like

37 ibid., p. 88. The subject was the BBC, and the winning answer was: 'Why no, Sir! I cannot thank this Corporation. A man cannot hold conversation with a *valve*. It is all take and no give; and we are told that the giving is the more blessed part.'

38 i.e. Tutorial Board.

39 The 'Discussion Group' first mentioned in the letter to Warnie of 11 November 1939, pp. 287–8.

40 'Mesopotamia' is a narrow strip of land north of Magdalen College lying between the River Cherwell on one side and a branch of the river on the other. Running along the shady bank of the Cherwell is a path about three-quarters of a mile long.

41 i.e. Addison's Walk.

42 i.e. The River Cherwell.

the froth of a guinneass (realise the spelling is quite beyond me. Read STOUT!), all of them detached and riding up and down on the ripple. At the bridge by Parson's Pleasure[43] the river was frozen across below the bridge, but above it still had a narrow fairway: on the shelves of ice to either side of it a number of the actual Oxford oriental ducks were squatting and preening themselves with no sign of discomfort. The warm, vivid colours of the drakes, in such a landscape, were almost fantastic.

I got as far as the Parks. Up there the river was completely frozen and I saw people skating. Perhaps even better than this was my walk 'round the bottom of Shotover' yesterday afternoon – red sunset reflected from the ice of lonely pools about which one 'would need Colours and words that are unknown to man to paint the visionary dreariness'.[44]

This morning, before breakfast, I had a pleasant glimpse of rabbits lolloping across the pond. The centre has been brushed for skating but where the rabbits were was level snow, and they looked so distinct & hairy that they seemed like rabbits in a modern woodcut. And talking of the frozen pond, here is a superb example of the stock phrase defeating itself. The ice is much better and smoother this time than in the earlier frost and Minto warned one of Maureen's guests 'You want to be careful. You have no conception how slippery it is. It's simply *like ice*.' That swan has *not* been killed. My opinion of foxes goes down. They start a thing but won't carry it through. They have good ideas but no staying power.

To-day I am again carrying out the afternoon evensong plan, i.e. I have had a delightful walk this morning (over Shotover, down the Pullen's Gap path, round Nuffield wood & home by the same route) came back in time for coffee, began this letter, enjoyed my Sunday roast, and am now finishing this off in the odd 20 minutes before it is time to start for Church. It is certainly a much better scheme – slightly impaired by the fact that Paxford and 'Nobby' have been passing through the study rather too often and working a blow lamp in your

43 Inside Mesopotamia, where the two branches of the Cherwell come together, was a bathing place for men. Until it was turned into a park in recent years men had been using this since the seventeenth century to swim and sunbathe in the nude.

44 William Wordsworth, *The Prelude*, XII, 255–6.

room where there is a burst pipe. I have the writing desk at right angles to the fire with the light from the window above the Leeboro table coming in on my left. One of my feet is roasting and the other freezing. One seldom has all parts of the body warm at present, except in bed or in a bath.

Well, I wish you a good (i.e. a safe but slow) recovery. Uncle Dick's letter is sad reading. How everything falls to bits. I see leave has started again.

Yours
Jack

TO ALEC VIDLER (BOD):

Magdalen College,
Oxford.
Jan 25th 1940

Dear Vidler

I enclose the article. I hope that by cutting it down a bit (as I have done) I have not brought it to the awkward size which is too long for one number and not long enough for two.

Since the last number I go labouring under a new temptation: that of murdering MacKinnon!

Yours
C. S. Lewis

Lewis had sent Dr Vidler his reply to Brother George Every's article on 'The Necessity of Scrutiny' published in Theology *(March 1939). In his article, entitled 'Christianity and Culture' and published in* Theology *in March 1940, Lewis concluded,*

> *My general case may be stated in Ricardian terms – that culture is a storehouse of the best (sub-Christian) values. These values are in themselves of the soul, not the spirit. But God created the soul. Its values may be expected, therefore, to contain some reflection or antepast of the spiritual values. They will save no man. They resemble the regenerate life only as affection resembles charity, or honour resembles virtue, or the moon the sun. But though 'like is not the same', it is better than unlike. Imitation may pass into initiation. For some it is a good beginning. For*

others it is not; culture is not everyone's road into Jerusalem, and for some it is a road out.[45]

TO HIS BROTHER (W):

[The Kilns]
Jan 28th 1940

My dear W –

Damn! I have just realised that I forgot to look up your diary for our Exmoor walk, though I had promised myself a great deal of pleasure from reading it and from discussing it in this letter. That's the worst of the life on two bases which we lead in the Kilns–Magdalen axis: a moment's forgetfulness in the week may mean a wasted week end.

We have in a sense heard from you since you last wrote, for Kathleen forwarded to Minto a letter you had written her, which seems to have given great satisfaction. We here felt some of the expressions to be slightly hyperbolical! – e.g. your great hope of finding her at the Kilns when you came on leave. But perhaps this is one innocent *double entendre* – you really hope *for her sake* that she'll get a holiday. We also hear that you have written to Phippy, though we have not yet seen the letter. In fact you seem to have devoted your convalescence (which I hope is not yet over) to good works. I trust it has proved a time worthy to be added to your rich store of blessed periods in sick rooms, 'san's,[46] and hospitals – pleasant backwaters whence one drowsily hears the roar of the main stream going past. They are certainly among the nicest recollections I have of school and army.

One such I spent at Le Tréport with the now probably abolished complaint of 'Trench Fever' very early in 1918;[47] of specially blessed memory since it was there I first began to conceive that beer was not an utterly unpleasant drink. As my experiments were being made with bottled Bass, it is a little odd that such a result was reached. I remember too nice solitary walks on the 'front' of that empty watering place: which, mixed with recollections of the Olderfleet[48] in winter and the

45 'Christianity and Culture', *Theology*, XL (March 1940), p. 177, and reprinted in *Christian Reflections*, pp. 28–9.

46 i.e. sanatoria, such as that at Malvern College.

47 See *CL* I, pp. 352ff. All the letters of February 1918 are written from No. 10 British Red Cross Hospital, Le Tréport, France.

48 Olderfleet Castle is close to Larne Harbour in Co. Antrim.

not disagreeable feebleness of a convalescent's first walks, increase the general 'backwater' feeling.

Another very good one was at the San. at Malvern in a snowy winter where I began, but did not finish, my first Trollope – *Framley Parsonage.*[49] A very nice Scotch woman was in charge of the San.[50] – perhaps you remember her. Re-reading *Framley Parsonage* not long ago, I was vividly reminded of how much more antique the society depicted in it seemed to me as a boy than it does now: in fact I think what put me off as a boy was disappointment that anything so definitely in the class of 'historical novels' should not be more romantic. I seem to remember that *Crime & Punishment*[51] was another of the books in the San. If so, what an odd collection to put there for schoolboys! But I suppose it was merely the chance sediment left behind by masters and visitors in any of the houses.

This week I have been reading an Elizabethan, Hall's *Satires*[52] (as dull as ditchwater) and Cicero's *De Legibus.* The latter you might suppose to be rather a bromide, but it is perfectly delightful. It's in dialogue form, held out of doors. Isn't this nice? – 'Now we have reached the island. I don't know a more charming spot. Look how the stream divides as if round the bow of a ship.'[53] And again 'But I've another reason for liking this place which can't affect you in the same way. My brother and I are "on our native heath" here. We come of an old family hereabouts: all round here you find our sacred places, our own people, and all the relics of our forebears. You see the house as it now is, rebuilt by the care of my father, who was an invalid and spent pretty well all his life here among his books. But in this very spot, in my grandfather's time, there was a little house in the old style – like the one Curius has down in the Sabine country – and in it I was born.'[54]

All very ordinary and obvious, of course, but, like Boswell, so full of sense and leisure and happiness. Does it occur to you that people have written of that sort of thing in almost all ages but our own? I begin to suspect that the world is divided not only into the happy and the

---

49 Anthony Trollope, *Framley Parsonage* (1861).

50 See the letters written from the sanatorium at Malvern College in *CL* I, pp. 39–43.

51 Fyodor Dostoevsky, *Crime and Punishment* (1866).

52 Joseph Hall, *Virgidemiarum: First Three Bookes, of Toothless Satyrs* (1597).

53 Cicero, *De Legibus*, II, 6.

54 ibid., II, 3.

unhappy, but into those who *like* happiness and those who, odd as it may seem, really don't.

Perhaps I am a little jaundiced by two religious parties I've attended this week in which I was struck by the extreme harshness and violence of all the young men. They seem to want everything to be as beastly as possible. Part of the agenda for the second one was a 'report' or 'memorandum' by the undergraduate members (they love reports and memoranda) in which, among other things, they expressed the hope that senior members wd. avoid the danger of 'looking on the war as an unpleasant interlude, cherishing the hope of a return to normal, and concentrating on "keeping things going"'.

By the way, there's only one number of the *Gramophone* in College, which I will send on to Kathleen: ought there to be more? After my boosting my new Sunday regime to you in my last letter (I think I dwelled specially on the superior warmth of Church in the afternoon) I went to the 3 o'clock service and had feet like blocks of ice all through it. Bleiben preached a too-relevant sermon on the decay of *family* religion – one saw sometimes the older, sometimes the younger, members of a household in church, but seldom both together.

I returned to College after breakfast on Monday morning, which is my free morning this term when Tolkien comes to see me. It won't by the way be free in the same sense to-morrow for Charles Williams begins a course of lectures on Milton which T. and I have promised to attend. It was my idea to smuggle him onto the Oxford lecture list, so that we might have some advantage from the great man's accidental presence in Oxford. (A-propos of this the vulgarest of my pupils asked me, with an air, if Williams had a degree. The whelp!)

Thursday and Friday of this week, owing to meetings, were passed wholly in College. Part of Thursday afternoon I spent with unusual pleasure in the dark, pleasantly smelling, warmth of the old library with a slow dampish snow falling outside – flakes the size of matchboxes. I had gone in to look for something quite different, but became intrigued by the works of Dr Dee, a mysterious magician and astrologer of Queen Elizabeth's time.[55] The interesting thing about this was the fact that it was so uninteresting: I mean that the spirit conversations displayed, so

55 Dr John Dee (1527–1608), mathematician and astrologer, was a Fellow of Trinity College, Cambridge.

far as I could see from turning over a few pages, just exactly the same fatuity wh. one observes in those recorded by modern spiritualists. What can be the explanation of this? I suppose that both are hallucinations resulting from the same kind of mental weakness which, at all periods, produces the same rubbish. One can't help, however, toying with the hypothesis that there are all real spirits in the case, and that we tap either a ghostly college of buffoons or a ghostly home for imbeciles.

The usual party assembled on Thursday night, heard a chapter of the new Hobbit, drank rum and hot water, and talked. Parker attends our Friday afternoon meetings of the S.C.M.[56] study group and behaves with great decorum tho' sometimes, obviously, at a cost. College gets pleasanter and pleasanter so much does the removal of one or two disturbers rectify the whole mass.[57]

Out here, things are perhaps a little dreary to-day – the ladies snapping at one another a good deal. Vera we have not seen for a long time: *she* says she's ill and Minto says she's 'sulking' – but I'm blessed if I can remember what about.

Your friend Mr Laski has written a book, I see, entitled *The Danger of being a Gentleman*,[58] reviewed to day by Desmond McCarthy.[59] A good many people seem to exaggerate the risk. Someone called Trevor-Roper has produced a new book on Laud,[60] reviewed by Charles Williams, in which a case is made out for him as friend of the poor and a champion against encroaching landlords, one of whom had trouble

56 Student Christian Movement.

57 He is referring in particular to two dons who had just left to serve with the armed forces. Thomas Dewar Weldon (1896–1958) was Fellow and Tutor in Philosophy at Magdalen College, 1923–58. On leaving school Weldon served with the Royal Field Artillery, 1915–18. He went up to Magdalen in 1919, and after taking his BA in 1921 he was a lecturer at Magdalen, 1922–3. He served with the Air Ministry, 1940–2. See Lewis's portrait of him in the Magdalen College Appendix to *AMR*.

William James Millar Mackenzie (1909–96) was educated at Balliol College and Edinburgh University, and was Fellow of Politics at Magdalen College, 1933–48. During 1939–44 he served as a civil servant with the Air Ministry. After the war he was Professor of Government at Manchester University, 1949–66. His books include *British Government Since 1919* (1950), *Free Elections* (1958) and *Power, Violence, Decision* (1975).

58 Harold Joseph Laski, *The Danger of Being a Gentleman, and Other Essays* (1939).

59 *The Sunday Times* (28 January 1940), p. 5.

60 Hugh Redwald Trevor-Roper, *Archbishop Laud* (1940).

with him about what he (the landlord) delightfully described as 'a very humane enclosure'.[61] It is one of the minor evils of your absence that you are not here to buy and read this and tell me the guts of it.

I am afraid this is a scrappy and dull letter. The truth is, Brother, I'm dry to day, very dry. Did you see that the Finns, like the British at Mons, have been seeing angels?[62]

Yours
Jack

TO HIS BROTHER (W):

[The Kilns]
Feb 3rd 1940

My dear W –

Do you ever spend an hour on Boswell without finding something new? Here is one I should certainly have read out to you if you had been in the room, so I produce it now instead; the account of Tom Tyers who 'was bred to the law but . . . could not confine himself to the regularity of practice. He therefore ran about the world with a pleasant carelessness, amusing everybody by his desultory conversation.'[63] A beautiful character sketch.

Well, I've found our Exmoor trip in your diary.[64] It took me most of a solitary evening yesterday because I began on the simple idea that if I looked at every January I should be bound to come to it. But I hadn't realised that the most recent volume consisted almost entirely of Januaries – and chancing to light on the wrong one of *those*, and therefore rejecting that volume, I was at sea for over an hour. In fact

---

61 'a most benign and charitable enclosure', *The Sunday Times* (28 January 1940), p. 6.

62 As the British troops were retreating during the aftermath of the Battle of Mons on the Western Front during August 1914 many soldiers claimed to have seen visions in the sky of St George surrounded by angels, horsemen and cavalry. On 25 January 1940 *The Daily Mail* ran a front-page story entitled 'Battle Weary Finns See Angels': 'Instead of guns and bombs and tanks, the principal news from Finland to-day is of "angels." Battle-weary Finnish troops say they have seen them north of Lake Ladoga. They speak of gigantic white figures with arms stretched out in the sky as if to protect them from the repeated attacks launched from the Russian lines . . . They are as convinced as the thousands of British and French troops who "saw" and believed in the "Angels of Mons" during the last war.'

63 Boswell, *The Life of Samuel Johnson*, vol. III, 17 April 1778, p. 308.

64 This, their seventh walking tour, was in January 1938. See *BF*, p. 175.

I spent an evening browsing over them: which would have been a very pleasant occupation if you were only away for a short holiday, but which in the present circumstances produced a great depression of spirits.

And have you ever noticed what a fine line, crossed in a split second, separates the snugness of privacy from the vacuity of loneliness? You glance round the room – all the same, but all changed. I know only one place in literature where this is expressed. All through the earlier parts of Paradise Lost the rural beauty of Eden is kept before your mind: then suddenly, in Bk X (910) you see it all different when Adam says 'How can I live without thee, how forego Thy sweet converse and love so dearly joined To live again in *these wild woods* forlorn.'[65] Isn't that real imagination?

Still, I got a lot out of the account of the tour. I wonder how much you remember? We saw Athelney from the train across flooded country. At Dulverton station we idly speculated on the possibility that the hotel might be *at* the station instead of 2 miles on, thus putting 2 miles onto the next day's march – and it was. You had a bedroom hung with prints of types of Napoleon's army 'and very appropriately over the bed was one of the *Train des Equipages Militaires*'.[66] Next day, according to you, the country to Dunster was dull. (It wasn't really but, as I well remember, you were so disgusted with the headwind that you damned the whole thing!) Then came the Frenchwoman with the two boys (I could have sworn it was only one) who partially spoiled the evening in the Luttrell Arms. I question if you are right in putting the castle at the *Southern* end of that street. On two mornings during this tour you record v. beautiful sickle moons seen from your bedroom window when you were called.

We set off from Dunster 'in great spirits in the cold keen sunshine'. Our first soak was Woot[t]on Courtney, with a dug-out chest in the church. Luccome (MS. Emend Luccombe) – wh. I think is where Harwood and I failed to get lunch you describe with an enthusiasm wh., I suspect, wd. never have appeared in the diary if your arrival there had been at 1 o'clock. 'One of the most beautiful villages I have ever seen: as we began to go down the hill we saw below us the churchyard

65 Milton, *Paradise Lost*, IX, 908–10.
66 'train of military equipment'.

very green and smooth in the brilliant light . . . the tower rising from behind a belt of yews "conventionalised" in the modern poster fashion by the violent light and shade.'

I see exactly what you mean – as I usually do in all your descriptions – but have quite forgotten it: not so what you next describe and what came back very vividly as I read – the soak with a tot of whiskey under the lee of a garage by Horner Water, attended by a volunteer collie. It must have been much higher up the Horner valley than this that Harwood and I did most of our walk last month. You are quite wrong about Porlock: so far from not getting cider there you got 'the best cider I ever drank, a *dry* draft cider'.

The account of getting up Porlock Hill almost made my legs ache in retrospect. The soak and the long walk down to Brendon you probably remember. Next day was white frost down in the valley where we were 'whilst in the heights the sun shone richer and warmer looking than yesterday making the wooded slopes exquisitely *alive*'. I made a balls of the course and got us up from water level, and we had to come down again with some difficulty. It [was] at Lynmouth, our mid morning soak, that the episode about the cider really happened. You describe the hill wh. we then scaled to find Padré Parkin as being worse than Porlock – but it must be much shorter.

Then came the Valley of Rocks and the superb Lee Abbey Hotel for lunch. It was no mean day's march that, Pigibuddie. All sorts of things happened to us after lunch – down into Woody Bay, and up those very steep wooded lanes, trouble with a flock of sheep, and finally (as I very well remember) some of the negus, lying absolutely dead beat on a heap of roadmetal just outside Combe Martin. Here, next morning, you 'had a v. rare pleasure: without lifting your head from the pillow you cd. see a steep sunny hillside.' Of Ilfracombe you felicitously observe 'It seems to cater for all classes, wh. produces a nastier looking town than either opulent Folkstone or trippery Clacton', and also that Devonshire seems to be 'a good air for dogs'. I had quite forgotten, till I read it in you, the Ilfracombe station perched on the highest peak of the town.

This has been an interesting week in some ways. On Monday Williams began his lectures in the beautiful carved Divinity School. A good audience. I attended with Tolkien and Hopkins and afterwards repaired to the Mitre Bar, joined by Williams, to drink sherry. I think he will retain most of his audience.

That afternoon I had the coldest dawdle round the estate with old Taylor that I have yet had. In spite of the bitter wind we had to stop to examine every track and speculate what kind of animal it was – but indeed I am rather ashamed that a man of over 70 should have so much more gust for natural philosophy and so much less shrinking from the wind than I. (Between ourselves, too, I have a sort of faint hope that what I can put in with such as F. K. and old Taylor may be accepted as a kind of penance for my many sins against the P'daitabird: the blackest chapter in my life).

He decided that there were really surprisingly few rabbits in our wood. One interesting thing was the number of branches which were enclosed by the frost in what seemed perfect glass cases, so that they rattled like a milk cart when a gust caught the tree.

By the bye, I suppose *now* the weather censor will not object to my describing an admirable practical joke wh. nature devised here during the cold. It first produced a chandelier of icicles just over the front door – about 30 of them, varying from 1 or 2 feet in length and shaped like parsnips. Then, by a most ingenious device, there began a thaw while the ground remained at freezing, so that you had a brisk shower bath from above and a continually increasing patch of ice below, and anyone casually looking out of the door wd. first receive a cold douche down the back of his neck and, if he started at this, had a very good chance of sitting down hard on the ice. I say 'had a chance' because you will learn with regret that this gravity dispelling episode never actually occurred.

On Monday evening I went to St Peter's in New Inn Hall Street which they have hired for the duration to Westfield (a she-college from London university)[67] to dine and read a paper. That record bore B.E.C. Davies (see an earlier letter) who is their professor of English had asked me. I took a taxi, and tried to find the S.C.R. 'opposite the hall' as I had been told. Could find nothing, so passed across the snowy street in the dark to the Lodge. Was there met by a rather pretty girl and conducted back across the street to the S.C.R. Had just time to pull off my coat and swallow a glass of sherry à la P'dayta[68] when I was told

67 Westfield College, London University, was founded in 1882 and was the first residential college for women in London. In September 1939 the college moved into the buildings of St Peter's College, Oxford.

68 i.e. in large amounts, as their father liked.

to struggle into my coat again and cross the street for the third time, and lead across several intricate quadrangles to some kind of ante-room.

Here I met among others a woman of about my own age with a face of such unanswerable and insurmountable ugliness (like Mrs Conrady)[69] and with so downright looking, diligent, prosaic and respectably vulgar, that I was hardly surprised when she claimed me as a fellow countryman. She was the Anglo-Saxon tutor, a Miss Galway of Dundonald, and an intimate friend of Sal Stokes[70] – who, by the way, would look like a Gainsborough beside her. She says Sal is better off in the money way than she used to be and has a house of her own in Sydenham Avenue, though she is pretty well an invalid. At dinner in Hall I was put next to the Principal whom I afterwards discovered to be Mrs Stocks,[71] author of that rather vile play *Hail Nero*.[72]

She had committed no such widowish errors about wine as made Dr Middelton an upholder of second marriages,[73] for indeed fair cold water, soup, hot boiled ham and fruit salad was our regale. What a typically female choice for a snowy evening – fruit salad! It wd. be cruel to ask for splendour in a poor society, but why not an honest rice pudding?

As soon as this was over it was coats and hats again and another pitch black walk through snow to a room where we drank coffee till it was time to get on our coats again and set off for the room where the

---

69 Mrs Conrady was probably someone the Lewis brothers had known when growing up in Strandtown.

70 Mrs Sally Stokes, a family friend, from the neighbourhood of Strandtown.

71 Mary Danvers Brinton Stocks (1891–1975), later Baroness Stocks, economist and writer, grew up in London where she was educated at St Paul's Girls' School and the London School of Economics. She was a lecturer in the London School of Economics, 1916–19 and at King's College for Women, 1918–19. In 1913 she married John Leofric Stocks (1882–1937), then a Fellow of St John's College, Oxford. In 1924 the couple left Oxford on his election to the Chair of Philosophy at Manchester University, where she was a lecturer in extra-mural studies, 1924–37. Following her husband's death, Mrs Stocks was Principal of Westfield College, 1939–1951. She became a life peer in 1966 and was very active in government projects. Her books include *Fifty Years in Every Street* (1945), *History of the Workers' Educational Association* (1953) and an autobiography, *My Commonplace Book* (1970).

72 Mary Danvers Brinton Stocks, *Hail Nero! A Reinterpretation of History in Three Acts* (1934).

73 Dr Middleton is a character in George Meredith's *The Egoist*, who insists in ch. 32 that 'Widows should marry!'

paper was to be read. I was talking about Psychoanalysis and Criticism[74] – a warning against the errors of the former wh., of course presupposed – and in Oxford had already found – an audience deeply infected by those errors and ripe for deliverance. Alas! – as far as I could gather, the Westfield girls had hardly heard of it and if they understood it at all (which I doubt) had the thrill of being introduced to a number of new vices.

This was particularly annoying since when I had discussed the matter originally with that ass Davies he had given me the impression that his students were very hard boiled eggs indeed, and I had consequently retained in my paper a number of scientific obscenities which I should otherwise have spared before a female audience. (Davies was the only other man present.)

So I came away at last with the mortifying consciousness that in return for my chilly dinner and many walks in the snow I had done just what the stupid vicar does when he upsets the faith of the congregation by answering difficulties they have never heard of before and will never again forget. Davies told me afterwards it had 'done them good', which was the last straw. The Principal too, I fear, will have liked it. But for all the Mrs Jennings's[75] I suppose I shall live forever as that dreadful man who came and tried to put all those horrid ideas into the girls' heads. Not least disagreeable is the certainty that through the Galway–Stokes axis the story has probably reached Lisnadene[76] by now: and I – one of the few people left in the world who really admire innocence and modesty – will be subjected to the most dreadfully arch approval. 'I suppose' as Mr Bultitude said 'This is the kind of thing you'd think funny.'[77]

One of the first things Phippy did with the money you sent her was to present us with a duck which we had for dinner last night (Saturday – in fact I broke off to eat it just at about the top of p. 4). I am now writing between coffee-time and lunch.

---

74 The lecture was published as 'Psycho-analysis and Literary Criticism' in *Essays and Studies by Members of the English Association*, XXVII (1942), pp. 7–21, and is reprinted in *SLE* and *EC*.

75 A character in Jane Austen's *Sense and Sensibility* (1811).

76 The home of his friend Jane McNeill in Strandtown.

77 F. Anstey, *Vice Versa: A Lesson to Fathers* (1882), in which Mr Bultitude is magically transformed into his son and vice versa. Lewis named the bear, Mr Bultitude, in *That Hideous Strength* after Anstey's character and described this tale in *SBJ*, ch. 2, p. 31, as 'the only truthful school story in existence'.

To day, unhappily, will be my last Sunday with evensong at 3, as they are then moving to the normal time: no doubt rightly, for they certainly have much poorer congregations at 3 than they used to have whenever you and I went to evensong in peacetime. We hear from the Griggs's that Blanchette has gone all to pieces since he got engaged and does practically no visiting.

We had the usual pleasant party on Thursday evening in college with the welcome addition of Havard, who has been bidden all along but has hitherto been prevented from attending by various accidents. He read us a short paper on his clinical experience of the effects of pain, wh. he had written in order that I might use all or part of it as an appendix to my book.[78] We had an evening almost equally compounded of merriment, piety, and literature. Rum this time again. The Inklings is now really v. well provided, with Fox as chaplain, you as army, Barfield as lawyer, Havard as doctor – almost all the estates! – except, of course, anyone who could actually produce a single necessity of life, a loaf, a boot, or a hut.

I see they have started leave again.

Yours
Jack

P.S. Just to check the postal arrangements let me know in your next letter whether you have received a letter a week from me since you went out, except for the School Certificate period.

TO HIS BROTHER (W):

[The Kilns]
Feb 11th 1940.

My dear APB –

I am spending a Sunday in doors and have such a hundred horse power cold that I don't know whether I shall be able to retain my coherence through a letter of my usual length.

We have your letter (with note enclosed for me) telling us that you are again in hospital. It is impossible, on your hint that you might be sent home, not to wish that this may happen, though I see your point of view about it too. But surely if you keep on returning to bed with

78 Dr R. E. Havard's paper on pain was published as the Appendix to *The Problem of Pain*.

these high temperatures even the invincible army must decide in the end that keeping you in France *at all* is too costly? Anyone who knows your medical history for the last ten years must realise that active service even at the base is for you 'an impossible pleasure'. Let us, while you are ill, have short notes at pretty frequent intervals, will you?

Nellie has been in bed most of the week with a feverish cold but is now up again. Havard rang up on Thursday night to say that he couldn't come as he was just retiring to bed from flu'.

On Friday, at the Gibbon Club, we had a paper from Cyril Bailey[79] on his experiences in his present job as a member of the tribunal for investigating conscientious objections. It introduced one anew to that simply fantastic side of English life which has always impressed foreigners but which *we* are apt to forget – tho' occasionally reminded of it by such things as our friend of the Interplanetary Society or the Leprechaun philosophical porter at the Welsh Station.

One story comes straight out of Dickens. The candidate was a 'Waste Products Merchant' which is much what mortals call a rag and bone man. He appeared for his interview at 2 o'clock in the afternoon in a dinner jacket and black bow tie. Asked for details of his occupation, he explained that he collected scraps of wood. What for? To sell to the manufacturers of mungo and shoddy (uncomfortable silence on the part of the tribunal). Asked for his Objection, explained that it was derived from the study of Moral Philosophy, and lectured the Tribunal at considerable length on the nature of this subject. As evidence produced his mother. The old body, being asked whether she could testify to the candidate's account of his studies, looked hard at the chairman for about a minute and then replied with much feeling 'Well, Sir – he reads *them* books. And then he says *them* things.'

I was interested and relieved to hear from Bailey that in his opinion the vast majority of the objectors are perfectly sincere, and often want to be put on dangerous non combatant works such as mine sweeping: and also that the communists and intellectuals are a minority – most of them are Jehovah's Witnesses, Seventh Day Adventists etc. Often

79 Cyril Bailey (1871–1957), Fellow and Classics Tutor at Balliol College, 1902–39, was a well-known teacher of classics and a notable Oxford personality. He edited the text of Lucretius (1898) and his other works include *The Legacy of Rome* (1923), *The Greek Atomists and Epicurus* (1928), *Phases in the Religion of Ancient Rome* (1932) and *Religion in Virgil* (1935).

yokels, almost inarticulate. The Adventists, oddly enough, do not object to *all* war: on the contrary, at the Second Coming, which they expect daily, they will all take part in the Battle of Armageddon, but they don't think this is it, and are not allowed to fight in *carnal* (not *camel*) campaigns. Another sect, on the contrary, takes the view that the world *has* already ended. Whether they draw from this the conclusion that the present state of affairs is simply a hallucination, I did not gather.

The business of the Tribunal is, of course, not to find out whether the man's conscience is rational but whether his objection is conscientious: a very different matter. The sincerity is in some cases proved by the fact that famished creatures on the dole have before the war began, refused jobs indirectly connected with armaments and forfeited the dole by doing so. It is v. interesting, too, that Bailey received two quite independent letters from former pupils who had no objections themselves and were either in, or about to enter, the army, but who said they were glad he was on the job, because 'that sort of thing is part of what we are fighting for'.

This is a great change from the attitude you wd. have found among soldiers in 1914. The truth is the one really contemptible figure in the whole business is the typical intellectual Oxford communist undergraduate, living on an allowance from a father (perhaps in the army) or, if you please, on a *state* scholarship, who was never observed to run such a costly luxury as a conscience about anything until this issue cropped up. The proper question (I have already tried it on one, and got no answer) is 'Would you mind drawing up a list of the *other* abstinences your conscience imposes on you?' For of course the poor Adventists and Witnesses from remote Welsh pits or Northumbrian farms could presumably draw you up a list the length of your arm – which they have really kept to.

On Monday C.W.[80] lectured nominally on *Comus* but really on Chastity. Simply as criticism it was superb – because here was a man who really started from the same point of view as Milton and really cared with every fibre of his being about 'the sage and serious doctrine of virginity'[81] which it would never occur to the ordinary modern critic to take seriously. But it was more important still as a sermon. It was

80 i.e. Charles Williams.
81 John Milton, *Comus* (1637), 786–7.

a beautiful sight to see a whole room full of modern young men and women sitting in that absolute silence which can *not* be faked, very puzzled, but spell-bound: perhaps with something of the same feeling which a lecture on *un*chastity might have evoked in their grandparents – the forbidden subject broached at last. He forced them to lap it up and I think many, by the end, liked the taste more than they expected to. It was 'borne in upon me' that that beautiful carved room had probably not witnessed anything so important since some of the great medieval or Reformation lectures. I have at last, if only for once, seen a university doing what it was founded to do: teaching Wisdom. And what a wonderful power there is in the direct appeal which disregards the temporary climate of opinion – I wonder is it the case that the man who has the audacity to get up in any corrupt society and squarely preach justice or valour or the like *always* wins? After all, the Nazis largely got into power by simply talking the old straight stuff about heroism in a country full of cynics and buggers.

While I think of it, will you remember when you next write to let me know whether I'm putting the right things into these letters – I mean is there anything you want to hear more or less of – or (worse still) anything you hear a lot of and don't want to hear *at all*? Not that such a life as mine admits of a very wide selection, but a certain amount could be done. I have been sparing lately of anything about the countryside because I gather from the papers that the weather (what balls it all is) is part of the hush-hush[82] material: not that I doubt for one moment that it is perfectly well known both to you and the enemy, but I don't want half my letter to be scored out before it reaches you.

I began Lent on Wednesday by going to 'the early celebration' where I knelt beside the Wounded Buffalo. I see a lot more of him now-a-days because we both go to that study circle.[83] Do you know, he improves steadily? I don't mean he 'improves on acquaintance', but that he really gets better. Christianity does have an effect. Incidentally, I am feeling specially humble about him since I found out that (tho' he's not doing it this time) he has before now completely given up smoking in Lent. A nasty shock, because, you know, you and I could no more do that than we could fly to the moon. But also the *fact* of its being a shock

---

82 i.e. the rules of postal censorship during the Second World War.
83 i.e. the meetings of the Student Christian Movement.

is itself a shock because it shows how completely one had assumed one's own superiority to the Buffalo – the violence of the bump demonstrates the height of the perch one has been knocked off.

Benecke, after a very long period in hospital, is back among us, very cheerful and talkative. The fire of sea-coals in the common room has been replaced by the worst kind of electric heater – the sort that has real heat above but, below, an elaborate stage-set of 'properly' glowing coals which give out no heat. Opie's infallible hotwater system, in favour of wh. he officiously abolished the scouts' gas rings, is showing its fallibility more and more. I have a great number of 'shaves luke'.

We were wondering if we can persuade Lee[84] to re-install the gas-rings while the busybody is away. At College meeting on Wed. we had a wonderful scene when Stevens denounced some action of Opie's as 'gross negligence'. As Stevens hardly ever speaks, and sounds so odd when he does, it created a mild sensation, and some thought he was joking. But not a bit. His face was white with moral passion, and he repeated 'I see no use in mincing words, Sir. I regard it as gross negligence.'

Yours
Jack

TO HIS BROTHER (W):

[The Kilns]
Feb 18th 1940

My dear W –

Thanks for your very interesting note from hospital: which comes in oddly with a letter of mine you will have had describing when and where I first graduated as a beer drinker.

A pleasant spot: a place where, in happier times, you and I might well do a week or a week's-end soak. Did you gather any interesting facts about the blood specialist? I trust your eagerness to get out of hospital – which is certainly paradoxical – will not prove imprudent.

I suppose I'm not allowed to write to you about the weather in England – beyond saying that I endorse Mr Badger's view and am more thoroughly sick of all weather and all news every day.[85]

---

84 Stephen Grosvenor Lee, Tutor in Modern History, who was serving as Domestic-Bursar.

85 In Kenneth Grahame's *The Wind in the Willows* (1908), ch. 4, Mr Badger says: 'There's no security, or peace and tranquillity, except underground. And then, if

One thing can hardly come under the Hush Hush – I mean the beautiful planetary conjunction about last Tuesday. Did you happen to see the moon (first quarter), Jupiter and Venus, all in a line and not more than 'three fingers' apart? I saw them on a clear evening, emerging from the cloister of New Building to go to dinner, and understood what is at the back of all astrology i.e. the difficulty of believing that anything so splendid is without significance. They were so bright that they looked *heavy* – if you know the impression I mean.[86]

By the way, our little friend Knight of Walsall,[87] is coming to lunch on Saturday. Now that I come to think of it, it can't have been Tuesday when I saw the conjunction for that was an impenetrably black night, as I well remember for I had to plod my way to Trinity for the Dante Society: almost repaid by the pleasure of passing suddenly from absolute dark and bitter cold into the light and warmth of one of their common rooms, with a roaring fire reflected from panels and silver. I was the reader on this occasion. I had had to write it entirely against the grain last Vac. when I wanted to be getting on with the book on pain, so it was very dull; probably the worst performance I have given for a long time.[88]

At dinner I sat next to Dawkins[89] who told me lot about Amanda McCitrock Ros's *other* novel.[90] The great thing in it, apparently, is the trial scene, where the heroine and her rival are placed in the dock together, not on a *joint* charge of murder, but on the charge that one *or* other of them has committed it: a conveniently Boxonian arrangement

---

your ideas get larger and you wanted to expand – why, a dig and a scrape and there you are! If you feel your house is a bit too big, you stop up a hole or two and there you are again! No builders, no tradesmen, no remarks passed on you by fellows looking over your wall, and, above all, no *weather*.'

86 Cf the passage in *That Hideous Strength* (1945; HarperCollins, 2000) when the planetary intelligences come down to inhabit the body of Merlin: 'Saturn, whose name in the heavens is Lurga, stood in the Blue Room. His spirit lay upon the house, or even on the whole Earth, with a cold pressure such as might flatten the very orb of Tellus to a wafer. Matched against the lead-like burden of his antiquity the other gods themselves perhaps felt young and ephemeral' (ch. 15, part I, pp. 361–2).

87 It has not been possible to identify this friend.

88 The paper Lewis read to the Dante Society on 13 February was 'Dante's Similes' which is published in *Studies in Medieval and Renaissance Literature*, ed. Walter Hooper (1966).

89 Richard MacGillivray Dawkins who is identified on p. 227.

90 Amanda McKittrick Ros, *Delina Delaney* [1898].

whereby the counsel for the defence of one automatically becomes counsel for the prosecution of the other. Foligno[91] was also present, but I expect I mentioned that he returned to Oxford from Italy months ago: one wonders whether it gave any indication of her foreign policy, or at least of his views about it.

I believe I forgot to mention in my last week's letter the really excellent performance of a *Midsummer Nights Dream*[92] which Tolkien and I saw at the Playhouse[93] – a Miss Griffiths (a tiny little co-religionist of his who teaches at Cherwell Edge)[94] remarked, it is such a rare pleasure to be able to see the play *not* out of doors! No: Lamb was right. Literature and nature shd. not be mixed. Out of doors is a place for walking, bathing, or soaking, and when he has finished there a sensible man comes in, takes off his shoes, and sits down in a chair, and stays in it till he wants to do one of those three things again.[95] But, like the Well Meaning Woman, I have lost the thread.[96]

I meant to tell you how this production created a new character by a very simple and perfectly legitimate device. You may almost have forgotten the eunuch Philostrate who comes in at the play scene at the end to tell Theseus of the various entertainments that are available, thus leading up to Pyramus & Thisbe.[97] Usually he is the merest walking gentleman. The Playhouse however, by taking the eunuch idea seriously

---

91 Cesare Carolo Foligno (1878–1963) was the Taylorian Professor in Italian in Oxford University, 1909–15, and Serena Professor of Italian and Fellow of Magdalen, 1919–40. He became Professor of English at the University of Naples in 1940 where he remained until his retirement in 1953.

92 William Shakespeare, *A Midsummer Night's Dream* (1600).

93 For a review of *A Midsummer Night's Dream* produced by Willard Stoker see *The Oxford Magazine*, LVIII (1 February 1940), p. 175.

94 Elaine Griffiths (1909–96) matriculated at the Society of Home-Students (later St Anne's College) in 1928. After taking a BA in English in 1931, she began research in Anglo-Saxon studies with Professor Tolkien. In the course of this she began teaching at Cherwell Edge, a Catholic hostel attached to the Society of Home-Students. She returned to her old college as Fellow and Tutor in 1938, and besides being an exceptional and much-loved teacher, was its faithful servant for forty years. She retired in 1976. For obituary and photograph see *The Times* (13 December 1996), p. 21.

95 Charles Lamb, *Last Essays of Elia* (1833), 'Detached Thoughts on Books and Reading': 'I am not much a friend to out-of-doors reading. I cannot settle my spirits to it.'

96 Stephen McKenna, *The Confessions of a Well-Meaning Woman* (1922), ch. 1, p. 6.

97 Shakespeare, *A Midsummer Night's Dream*, V, i.

and making him an enormously fat Negro with a little pointed grey beard who talked in a richly unctuous voice (rather, I imagine, like Edward the Bookmaker) turned him into one of the major laughs of the evening.

Barfield has been up to spend an evening with me: rather unfortunately it was Thursday, for, though he knows most of that set and harmonises with them very well, I should have preferred to have him to myself. He is going to take a part time job in – of all disgusting things – the Inland Revenue.

He is very much depressed having a greater faculty than you or I for feeling the miseries of the world in general – which led to a good deal of argument, how far, as a man and a Christian, one *ought* to be vividly and continuously aware of, say, what it's like on the Mannerheim line at this moment.[98]

I took the line that the present rapidity of communication etc. imposed a burden on sympathy for which sympathy was never made: that the natural thing was to be distressed about what was happening to the poor Jones's in *your own village* and that the modern situation, in which journalism brings the Chinese, Russians, Finns, Poles and Turks to your notice each morning really *could not* be met in the same way. Of course I know the more obvious reply, that you can't do them any good by being miserable, but that is hardly the point, for in the case of the Jones's next door we should think ill of the man who felt nothing whether his feeling did them good or not. I am afraid the truth is in this, as in nearly everything else I think about at present, that the world, as it is now becoming and has partly become, is simply *too much for* people of the old square-rigged type like you and me. I don't understand its economics, or its politics, or any dam' thing about it.

Even its theology – for that is a most distressing discovery I have been making these last two terms as I have been getting to know more and more of the Christian element in Oxford. Did you fondly believe – I did – that where you got among Christians, there, at least, you would escape (as behind a wall from a keen wind) from the horrible ferocity and grimness of modern thought? Not a bit of it. I blundered

---

98 The Soviet army was attempting to set up a longer coastline on the Gulf of Finland for the purpose of protecting Leningrad. On 1 February the Soviets launched a large-scale offensive against the principal Finnish defences, one of which was known as the Mannerheim Line. By 16 February the Finnish troops were almost exhausted, and they were soon defeated.

into it all, imagining that I was the upholder of the old, stern doctrines against modern quasi-Christian slush: only to find that *my* 'sternness' was *their* 'slush'. They've all been reading a dreadful man called Karl Barth,[99] who seems the right opposite number to Karl Marx. 'Under judgement' is their great expression. They all talk like Covenanters or Old Testament prophets. They don't think human reason or human conscience of any value at all: they maintain, as stoutly as Calvin, that there's no reason why God's dealings should appear just (let alone, merciful) to us: and they maintain the doctrine that *all* our righteousness is filthy rags[100] with a fierceness and sincerity which is like a blow in the face.

Sometimes the results are refreshing: as when Canon Raven[101] (whom you and Dyson and I sat under at Ely) is sharply told in a review in *Theology* that 'it is high time persons of this sort learned that the enjoyment of a chair of theology at Cambridge does not carry with it a right to criticise the Word of God'[102] – that's the kind of rap on the knuckles which has not been delivered for a hundred years!

But the total effect is withering. Of two things I am now persuaded. (1) That a real red-hot Christian revival, with iron dogma, stern discipline, and ruthless asceticism, is very much more possible than I had supposed. (2) That if it comes, people like us will not find it nearly so

---

99 Karl Barth (1886–1968), Protestant theologian from Switzerland who, in his *Commentary on Romans* (1918), revived Pauline and Reformation themes which had become muted in liberal theology. A professor at Bonn when Hitler came to power, he was deprived of his chair because he attacked Nazism. In 1935 he became Professor of Theology at Basle, where he remained until his retirement. In his works he attempted to lead theology away from what he believed to be the erroneous nineteenth-century synthesis between theology and culture. He believed that human reason had no power to attain to the knowledge of God, which is given only in God's revelation in Christ.

100 Isaiah 64:6: 'But we are all as an unclean thing, and all our righteousnesses are as filthy rags.'

101 The Rev. Charles Earle Raven (1885–1964) was educated at Gonville and Caius College, Cambridge, and was Fellow of Theology at Emmanuel College, Cambridge, 1909–20, Canon of Liverpool, 1924–32, Regius Professor of Divinity and Master of Christ's College, Cambridge, 1932–50.

102 Reviewing Raven's *The Gospel and the Church: A Study of the Distortion and its Remedy* (1940) in *Theology*, LX (February 1940), p. 156, Geoffrey Bryant Bentley wrote: 'It is high time it was realized that a Chair at the University does not entitle a man to judge the word of God . . . It is clear that the distortion which Professor Raven discerns in the Church is largely a projection from his own defective theology.'

agreeable as we had expected. 'Why have they desired the Day of the Lord? It is darkness not light.'[103] I have no doubt the young gentlemen are substantially right: this is the goods. We ought to have expected that if the real thing came it would make one sit up (you remember Chesterton 'Never invoke gods unless you really want them to appear. It annoys them very much').[104]

But, in a private letter, one may, for a moment, bewail happier days – the old world when Politics meant Tariff Reform, and war, war with Zulus, and even religion meant (beautiful word) Piety. 'The *decent* church that crowns the neighbouring hill'[105] – Sir Roger at Church[106] – 'Mr Arabin sent the farmers home to their baked mutton very well satisfied'.[107]

Since beginning this letter I have been to Church, where we had a novelty, 'Pastor Kramm', a refugee, preaching on the German Church. He wore the black gown and white bands which I have never seen before except on the stage. If he had preached on the suffering of German Christians he would have found, no doubt, a sympathetic audience: but he touched on that only once, to quote an admirable passage from a letter written by Niemöller[108] in prison to his wife, wh.

---

103 Amos 5:18.

104 G. K. Chesterton, *All Things Considered* (1908), 'Spiritualism': 'Praise [the gods]; or leave them alone; but do not look for them unless you know they are there. Do not look for them unless you want them. It annoys them very much.'

105 Oliver Goldsmith, *The Deserted Village* (1770), 12: 'The decent church that topt the neighbouring hill.'

106 'Sir Roger at Church', *The Spectator*, no. 112 (9 July 1711). Sir Roger de Coverley, a character described in various issues of *The Spectator*, was probably invented by Sir Richard Steele (1672–1729) who described him in *The Spectator*, no. 2 (2 March 1711) as 'a gentleman of Worcestershire, of ancient descent, a baronet. His great-grandfather was inventor of that famous country-dance which is called after him. He is a gentleman that is very singular in his behaviour, but his singularities proceed from his good sense . . . It is said he keeps himself a batchelor, by reason he was crossed in love by a perverse beautiful widow of the next county to him.'

107 Trollope, *Barchester Towers*, ch. 22: 'Mr Arabin . . . after twenty minutes succeeded in sending his new friends home to their baked mutton and pudding well pleased.'

108 Martin Niemöller (1892–1984), a German Lutheran pastor who served as a submarine commander during the First World War, was imprisoned in 1937 for his anti-Nazi religious activities. He became the symbolic figure of Protestant opposition to National Socialism, and after the Second World War he was head of the Foreign Relations Department of the Evangelical Church in Germany. See

united the confessor and the U-Boat captain in the following passage on *inner* peace 'However rough the weather may be on the surface, it is always calm twenty fathom down.'[109] For the rest, it was a very brief account of Lutheranism in general, probably quite unintelligible to every one save Bleiben and me, and for what purpose it should be preached to an Anglican congregation I don't know. (A propos, I saw quoted the other day from H. G. Wells an amusing description of *Black Beauty*[110] as 'a book about the adventures of a strictly Anglican horse').

One interesting bit of information was that the Lutherans have bishops in Scandinavia, including Finland, but not in most parts of Germany – just according as the existing bishops accepted Lutheranism or not at the time of the Reformation. But perhaps you knew this already.

Any more talk about Leave? I enclose a letter from Uncle Dick; poor Eileen![111] Did I tell you that someone wants to include that St Mary's sermon of mine in a collection of (save the mark) *Famous Sermons*? I am divided between gratification and a fear that I shall be merely made a fool of by appearing in the same book as Bede, Latimer, Donne, Taylor etc. However, let's hope that I shall be divided from them by some good 19th century duds! – but I grow impious.[112]

Yours
S.P.B.

From U-boat to Concentration Camp: the Autobiography of Martin Niemöller (1939).

109 *Exile in the Fatherland: Martin Niemöller's Letters from Moabit Prison*, trans. Ernst Kaemke, Kathy Elias and Jacklyn Wilferd, ed. Hubert G. Locke (1986). In his letter of 18 August 1937 to Mrs Else Niemöller, her husband said: 'You don't have to worry about me; I live my day and it's never long, and should there be occasional rough weather and storms on the surface, at a diving depth of twenty meters there is total calm.'

110 Anna Sewell, *Black Beauty* (1877).

111 Eileen was the daughter of Albert Lewis's brother Richard Lewis and his wife Agnes. Richard – 'Uncle Dick' – reveals in his letter of 14 February 1940 that he and his wife are laid low with influenza, and that Eileen is looking after them. See **The Lewis Family** in the Biographical Appendix to *CL* I.

112 The sermon Lewis preached at St Mary the Virgin, Oxford, on 22 October 1939 was published as a pamphlet by the Student Christian Movement under the title *The Christian in Danger* (1939). Now the publisher, Ashley Sampson, who had asked Lewis to write *The Problem of Pain*, wanted to include it in an anthology he was editing, *Famous English Sermons* (London: Thomas Nelson, 1940). When Lewis included the sermon in *Transposition and Other Addresses* (1949) he changed its title to 'Learning in War-Time'.

TO HIS BROTHER (W):

[The Kilns]
Feb 25th 1940

My dear W –

Plague on this nonsense of putting back the clock which has docked me of an hour's sleep and which for the next few weeks will give me darkness at shaving and dressing time when I want light and light after tea when it is an impertinence: and which also, by abolishing 3.30 Evensong has sent me back to mattins and the old morning rush.

I am just back from it now. The change was aggravated by the fact that, as Bleiben announced, 'we are now approaching that time of year in which the Church revises her Electoral Roll'. We had the whole bag of tricks of course, followed by a full exposition of the Free Will Offering scheme.

He preached a very good sermon, however, on Joseph, as the type of man who has an almost unique series of excuses for being 'embittered', 'disillusioned' and all the usual bunk but doesn't take them. Reflection on the story raised in my mind a problem I never happen to have thought of before: why was Joseph imprisoned, and not killed, by Potiphar?[113] Surely it seems extraordinarily mild treatment for attempted rape of a great lady by a slave? Or must one assume that Potiphar, tho' ignorant of the lady's intention to make him a cuckold, was aware in general (like Bishop Proudie and many other husbands) that her stories about the servants were to be taken with a grain of salt – that his real view was 'I don't suppose for a moment that Joseph did anything of the sort, but I foresee there'll be no peace till I get him out of the house'? One is tempted to begin to imagine the whole life of the Potiphar family: e.g. how often had he heard similar stories from her before?

I think I have mentioned before how pleasant it is to have our Leftists such a diminished element in College. We had a delightful scene one night at dinner this week when Austin[114] foolishly attempted to argue with Morris (you remember Morris, that huge, perfectly silent, yellow haired lawyer) on the point of international law about the Alt-

113 The story of Joseph and Potiphar's wife is found in Genesis 39:1–20.

114 John Langshaw Austin (1911–60), who had been an undergraduate at Balliol College, was Fellow of Philosophy at Magdalen College, 1935–52, and White's Professor of Moral Philosophy and Fellow of Corpus Christi, Oxford, 1952–60.

mark.[115] Morris has the immovable face of a poker player, and like every lawyer is a Condlin at heart. So that one kept on getting some position which seemed unanswerable from Austin 'You mean then that there is some sense in continuing to talk about Law and yet making ourselves the sole judges of it?' and from Morris some such answer as '*We've* got nothing to do with it. It depends on the decisions of prize courts' or 'Do you mean international law or the law of international relations.' It went on all through dinner and Austin's advance was still zero at the end. Talking of the Altmark, did our ship really and truly 'grapple' her as the papers said? And if so, how have grappling irons survived all these years – perhaps simply to give the matelots something to clean? Or does it simply mean they threw a hook on a rope and worked themselves alongside with the winch?

I do wish the P'daytabird had seen the photo of the man who led the boarding party: he seemed to correspond exactly to the 'lar-di-dar' fellow in his story, the man 'who could hardly see over his collar'[116] but afterwards went and sorted the mutinous Lascars.

The whole story is full of problems. How did an armed German crew allow themselves to be overpowered by such a very small party and so quickly that our men describe it as being 'like a rat-hunt'. No one ever accused the German navy of cowardice.

Another pleasing thing that happened this week was the confirmation of our little party's good judgement in making Fox professor of poetry. The defeated rival, run by our orthodox elders, Sir Edmund Chambers, delivered the Sidney Lee lecture on Wednesday, and was so portentously dull that I think even his own supporters must have been ashamed of him.[117] And the cream of the joke was that Fox went up to ask him a

115 See *The Times* (19 February 1940), p. 6, 'H.M.S. Cossack's Daring Exploit'. On 16 February in Jösing Fjord, south of Egersund in Norway, sailors from the British destroyer HMS *Cossack* violated Norwegian neutrality when they boarded the German naval auxiliary ship, *Altmark*, and released 299 British sailors and merchant seamen held prisoner below deck. Despite the fact that the *Altmark* was armed with two pom-poms and four machine guns, Germany's official news described it as 'an unarmed German merchant ship'. This led to a dispute about whether or not the British Admiralty had violated international law.

116 This was Bradwell Talbot Turner, who was pictured in *The Times* (20 February 1940), p. 10.

117 Sir Edmund Chambers's lecture was published as *The Timelessness of Poetry* (1940).

question, and, through sheer humility and nothing else, wishing to explain who he was and to justify himself for trespassing on the great man's time, began 'Good evening Excuse me – I'm the Professor of Poetry.' The lecture was unbelievable – delivered at great speed, with his eyes half closed, on 'contributions to Shakespearian scholarship in the last decade' wh., if there had been the least suspicion of a twinkle in his eye, I shd. have taken for a parody – you know 'Professor Hodo of Chicago has discovered that the Sir Richard Squid of Uffington who in 1630 was bound over to keep the peace is probably not the R. Squid who is known to have married Shakespeare's niece, but his first cousin.'

I have contributed four poems to an anthology which the Cambridge University Press is bringing out on a most original plan: i.e. no author's names at all. It will be very interesting to see what reviewers make of it. At first one would suppose that they will be so afraid of backing the wrong horses that they will ignore it completely: but then that might prove equally dangerous.[118]

On Monday night I was in Univ. chapel (a weekly Lenten business) for the first time for I don't know how many years, and was astonished both at its beauty and its discomfort. The latter, no doubt, a v. proper penance for the irreligious spirit in which I must often have sat there in bygone days. I saw a Magdalen undergrad. called Dobson sitting opposite me, a man who has spent his time ploughing in Pass Mods ever since he came up.[119] He is very fat and has a freckled pudding-like face with tow coloured hair, and wears bright green corduroys like a North-of-Ireland railway porter in the old days. As the address was on 'Failure' I hoped the poor chap was deriving comfort from it. But Fox told me later that Dobson had disapproved of it and said one ought to have a proper pride. 'Pride about what?', asked Fox. 'Oh, well,'

---

118 The work is entitled *Fear No More: A Book of Poems for the Present Time by living English Poets* (Cambridge University Press, 1940). For record purposes six copies were sent to the National Libraries containing a bound sheet giving the authors' names. The poems Lewis contributed to *Fear No More* are 'Essence', 'Break, Sun, my crusted earth' (a version of 'A Pageant Played in Vain'), 'The World in Round' ('Poem for Psychologists and/or Theologians'), 'Arise my Body' ('After Prayers, Lie Cold'). The four poems, the last three of which were revised and given different titles, are found in *CP*.

119 Quentin Burrington Dobson (1921–66) matriculated in 1939 and read English under Lewis, taking his BA in 1943.

said Dobson after several minutes reflection 'Well, you know, in *ones appearance*'

This has been a beautiful week out of doors. On Friday, coming back to College at about 10.30, I was moved by the beautiful wild freshness to take a turn in Adders. There was brilliant moonlight and a gentle wind: and the river, almost up to the level of the path, was going past, with heavy mats of foam and drift, at about ten miles an hour. It gave just a touch of wildness to the peaceful scene. Another day on my way back from my afternoon walk I emerged from the top wood onto the open platform just as the sun came out. All the birds, which one doesn't seem to have heard for ages, were singing. I walked over to that bit of shorter grass where the unsuccessful holly bush grows and enjoyed the pleasant effect of the red and gray roofs down below.

Will *nothing* overcome the illusions of a fine day early in the year? Not even a European war can rid one of the feeling of the good time ahead. You may reply perhaps that a war seen from France might prove more potent in that way than one seen from III New Building; but I think I had the same feeling in spring 1918. Edith Sitwell's line hits it off to a nicety 'The mirage/Of an eternal beauty that is not'[120] – but thank God, one now adds 'is not here' and accepts the annual promise as being true in another sense.

I enclose a letter from Janie McNeill, containing very good news about Glenmachan. The proposed alterations are regrettable, but nothing to what might have happened. And how appropriate it will be if in years to come we find Glenmachan the *one* thing that has not disappeared – an inertia that even fate thinks twice about tackling.[121]

I'm still re-reading and re-noting Paradise Lost for tutorial reasons and find the books about the war in heaven very much better than I thought them at the last reading. This is partly due to Williams' really superb lectures.

---

120 Edith Sitwell, *The Sleeping Beauty* (1924), No. 11, 20–5: 'But age has dimmed our innocent paradise/With a faith shadow, shaken dust within our eyes – /And we are one now with the lonely wise,/Knowing the spring is only the clear mirage/Of an eternal beauty that is not.'

121 Following the death in 1939 of Sir Robert Heard Ewart, the family home, Glenmachan, had gone to his sister Gundreda Ewart Forrest who returned there to live. In her letter to Lewis of 15 February 1940 Jane McNeill described the alterations Gundreda planned to make to the house.

At our Thursday meeting we had a furious argument about cremation. I had never realised the violence of the Papist dislike of the practice, which they forbid. Neither Tolkien nor Havard, to my mind, produced a real argument against it, but only said 'you'd find in fact' that it was always supported by atheists; and that a human corpse was the temple of the Holy Ghost. I said 'but a vacated temple' and said it wd. be reasonable to blow up a Church to prevent it being defiled by Communists. They denied this, and said if you destroyed a chalice to prevent it being used for Black Mass you wd. be mortally guilty: for it was *your* business to reverence it and what the magicians did to it afterwards was theirs. I was surprised at the degree of passion the subject awoke in us all.

The week after term (9th–16th) will be mainly b'–d up with scholarship exams, but I hope to write as usual. We shall be glad to hear from you again.

Yours
Jack

TO HIS BROTHER (W):

[The Kilns]
March 3rd 1940

My dear W –

Delighted to get your letter of the 28th which arrived on Friday. You don't repeat your instructions to write to the Hospital but as you don't cancel them I shall send this to that address. The action of the previous hospital fills me with dismay not only about your own chances as a patient but about larger issues. Yes, I know that curious vividness of impression – tho' its apt suddenly to switch over to no impression at all or to a sinister dazzle.

What a rich harvest you must be reaping all the time from your studies: I don't suppose there are half a dozen officers in France to whom the country offers so many points of interest. I can't construe *Prince je le daigne*. Does *daigner* mean '*dis*dain' or does it mean 'I wouldn't *mind* being a prince' – if so, it rather weakens the third sense. You certainly fell on your feet as regards that room-mate. What people there are in the world! He must feel almost the same, specially as he didn't *hear* you play the piano.

I don't understand the last sentence of your letter about the barbarian tide crashing on the civilised shores of the S.E. of Europe. Are you referring to the Italian invasion of Albania – or has Russia invaded the Balkans and the news been suppressed in England? But you have often complained of my faculty for not understanding what you say. I hope you won't fall between two stools: but surely, surely, if you go on going in and out of hospital like this, they must decide that you are too costly a luxury to keep in France – 'Some were for laying honest David by/ On principles of sheer good husbandry'. Your letter, and the knowledge that you are for the moment favourably placed, is the only bright spot this morning.

Although there is no one particular thing to be alarmed about, the papers this morning have filled me with a vague uneasiness: you know that sudden clouding over of one's interior sky which has no definite cause but which is almost irresistible.

In addition, a long domestic groundswell has culminated in my being greeted on my return from Church ten minutes ago with the news that Nellie has given notice – and so the longest and incomparably the best ministry we have ever had has fallen. Maureen I gather (but doubtless one needs to hear the other side) has responded by the not very helpful reaction of fury. It's a small trouble, no doubt, in the midst of a European war: but troubles differ from sins in this that the relative proportions of the mote in *ones own* eye and the beam in the neighbour's[122] are reversed.

Finally, I have what feels like an incipient toothache! That's partly due to the weather which is of the kind you frankly detest and I rather like: i.e. weather that looks from in-doors like a 'glorious spring day' – indeed so bright that you can hardly keep both eyes open – but which is really kept almost at freezing point by a parching east wind carrying clouds of dust. Bare earth (in flower beds etc) is a very pale *powder*. But the light, after so many days of darkness, almost makes amends for all.

One pleasant thing which happened this week was a visit from Dyson on Thursday which produced a meeting of all Inklings except yourself and Barfield. Fox read us his latest 'Paradisal' on Blenheim Park in winter. The only line I can quote (wh. seems to me very good) is 'Beeches have figures; oaks, anatomies'. It was in the *Troilus* stanza and

122 Matthew 7:3–5.

full of his own 'cool, mellow flavour' as the tobacconists say. He has really in some respects a considerable similarity to Miss Sackville West. Dyson, according to Tolkien (you know how bad an observer of such things I am) was looking changed and ill, but he was in his usual form and, on being told of Williams' Milton lectures on 'the sage And serious doctrine of virginity', replied 'The fellow's becoming a common chastitute.'

By the way, as an example of wonderful self-ignorance, Williams in his last lecture, having refuted the study about Milton making his daughters read Homer to him without knowing Greek, went on to show us what it would have sounded like, in a misunderstanding and cockney voice – but prefaced it with the caution 'Of course I can't do the cockney very well.'!! It is painful to reflect that each of us is presumably if not under the same, yet under an equal, delusion about the sound of his own voice!

Last Monday my former pupil Turner spent an evening with me, on leave between several months as a private and joining the S.W. Borderers (needless to say, he has no connections with Wales) as a 2nd Lieut. He never stated, nor disguised, the general unhappiness of his life in the army but I gather they are treating them reasonably well – the beastliness being mainly in the nature of things.[123] But the mere mention of rows about 'filthy hat badges' etc (by the way how odd it is to use the word *filthy* of an object because it is not polished?) of orderly rooms and canteens brought it back to me very vividly. What a world we are living in, in which the life of a British Tommy would be absolute heaven to some millions of people in central Europe.

I have spent a good deal of this week end reading in proof a book of Dyson's.[124] It is, as one would expect, almost too bright, but some of the sparks are admirable. 'A pot is not the less black because it is

---

123 John Symonds Turner (1914–92) read English and Theology at Magdalen College. After taking a BA in 1936 he was assistant master at Giggleswick School, 1938. In 1940 he received a commission with the South Wales Borderers, becoming a major in 1946. He was a lecturer at the YMCA College for Adults at Broadstairs, 1946, a lecturer at St Paul's College, Calcutta University, 1947–9, Principal of La Martinière College, Calcutta, 1949–50, Reader in English, Dacca University, 1950–3, Professor of English at Dacca University, 1954–8, Senior Lecturer in Divinity, Avery Hill Training College, 1960–9, and then was a lecturer at Emerson College, 1970–1.

124 Hugo Dyson and John Butt, *Augustans and Romantics 1689–1839* (1940).

the kettle that calls it so'[125] seems a maxim which needs quoting very frequently in political and domestic arguments. Of Byron's amours he says 'He was terrified of not being found out.'[126] Of the comparative acquiescence of the people in the regime before the Industrial Revolution 'The English have always had a *weakness* for squires.'[127] Smollett 'never quite outgrows the medical student.'[128] 'Almost any poet could have written Gray's *Elegy* provided only that he were good enough.'[129] 'Governesses make bad governors.'[130] The following about Wordsworth is interesting, tho' I am not yet sure whether it is true or false. 'He is an earth poet. Not the green earth of the pastoral poetry of Pope and Gray and Philips, but the ancient, bitter earth from which men wrest a living.'[131] Anyway, as you see, it is going to be a very lively work.

You will be sorry to hear that the Musical Club is in great difficulties. I forget whether it was before or after your departure that it found itself obliged by declining membership to amalgamate with the Ladies Musical. Even this has not served and what between the continued decline and the perpetual leakage from its library it is now faced with extinction. Maureen says the decline is *not* due to the War, but to the rivalry of college musical societies. I suspect myself that it is primarily due to the increasing absorption of the young persons in their infernal political activities. If the musical club goes out, one is faced with the question to wh. no one in this house knows the answer – who owns the Holywell Musical Room? It wd. be the last straw if it belonged to the Club and has to be sold and is turned into a Cinema. I wonder if any event that you or I *like* will ever happen again?

By the bye, 'tell me' as your poor father used to say: how does one in practice (I don't say, intellectually) – in the actual practice of prayer – combine the attitude 'Thy will be done'[132] with obedience to the exhortation that we should ask 'believing that we shall receive'?[133] It

---

125 ibid., p. 97: 'The kettle is not the less black because it is a pot that calls it so.'
126 ibid., p. 96: 'He was terrified lest he should not be found out.'
127 ibid., p. 22: 'Englishmen have always had a weakness for squires.'
128 ibid., p. 64.
129 ibid., p. 72.
130 ibid., p. 95.
131 ibid., pp. 90–1.
132 Matthew 6:10.
133 ibid., 21:22: 'All things, whatsoever ye shall ask in prayer, believing, ye shall receive.'

seems to me almost impossible. One can choose the first: but surely in the very act of doing so one *ipso facto* abandons all confidence that one's prayer is likely to have any causal efficacy in bringing about the event prayed for? I have never seen the question discussed anywhere nor got an answer from anyone whom I asked.[134] Last Sunday evening I re-read some of Lubbock's *Earlham*[135] and was again struck with its great beauty.

Since writing the above I have been out for my afternoon walk 'round the railway line'. The day has altered so much that I have come back bathed in perspiration. I had a long halt at the gate on the left of the Wheatley Rd. where one looks across that up and down of plough to Capability Brown's avenue. It was looking specially fine to day, with very soft blue distances down beyond Wheatley.

On my way back I overheard a curious conversation between two small boys. One of them had said something about Bruce which I didn't catch. 'No, he ain't,' replied the second 'He's only an ordinary dog.' 'All dogs are ordinary dogs' returned the first. Have I heard the first riposte of a future Johnson? The brevity and logicality seemed to me quite astonishing from any educated person, let alone a child.

By the way, I had occasion to differ strongly from Parker at a committee this week, and, do you know, he came and said he was sorry he had had to disagree with me. That he should think this necessary shows the misconception: but that he should *do* it is a great sign of Grace.

I can't see that the enclosed is of importance but send it just on the off chance that it may be. Minto was genuinely pleased, even touched, at your consideration for her possible anxiety when I read her out your letter. So long, Brother, and a *gentle* recovery: there's no good hurrying the thing –

Yours
Jack

134 Lewis read a paper on this subject entitled 'Petitionary Prayer: A Problem Without an Answer' to the Oxford Clerical Society on 8 December 1953. It is published in *Christian Reflections*.

135 Percy Lubbock, *Earlham* (1922).

TO HIS BROTHER (W):

[The Kilns]
Palm Sunday March 17th 1940

My dear W –

I was delighted to get your letter describing your pleasant existence at the Base near the hospital – and what luck to have picked up your talented gunner again.

I am disappointed to hear that your last letter from me was a month old when you wrote. You have had one (sent, I mean) each week, tho' only a note last week because of the Scholarship exam., so there must be about four following you round France or rotting in some empty office. It's a nuisance: it gives me the sensation of conversing with a deaf man!

This is a day of steady downpour. I am starting my letter before Church because the ceremony of the *lavage*[136] has been postponed so that Minto and Maureen can set off as soon as possible to Gloucester on a maid-hunting expedition. It is one of those days when the night has left one dazed. I had two unpleasant dreams – one in which I was a Tommy acting as batman to Bleiben, and another in which I was puzzled by a terror spreading through a large crowd of which I was a member until, in the very moment of waking, I realised that it was 'the Last Day!' I suppose the second dream is an appropriate prelude to Holy Week.

I am much amused at the idea of your archaic French conversation. As you say, it would be very odd to meet a Frenchman who talked about the Lord's Day and complained that something 'did make me mad'. But I envy you being able on any terms to converse in a foreign language, and am always ashamed that I can't.

I am in the rather unusual situation of having been lent a book by Benecke, a novel called *He and His* by one Carter.[137] Benecke got it because the man was an old friend. The blurb said it was a wonderful reconstruction of an older and more tranquil civilisation and compared it to Trollope. Benecke said it wasn't a wonderful reconstruction at all, because Carter was a contemporary of his and was merely writing what he remembered. If you have seen the blurb and been attracted by it,

136 'washing'.

137 Reginald Carter, *He and His* (1940).

my advice is *not* to get it. It is a dull story with a theatrical plot and I can see no single Trollopian feature. One or two historical facts about the 90's are interesting: e.g. that young 'swells' used literally to *manure* their whiskers – I mean, with manure.[138] But I doubt this: surely, if it were so, this of all things would have been known to the P'daytabird and frequently mentioned. Indeed it wd have been permanently on tap whenever the subject of your moustache came up.

Another thing I have been reading is Sylvester's translation of Du Bartas' *Divine Weeks and Works*[139] – a book which seems to have escaped Lamb but wh might have been written for him. One meets all one's old friends: 'the wise Beaver that pursu'd by foes/Tears off his codlings[140] and amongst them throws'[141] – the 'Carry-castle'[142] or elephant 'With's crooked trumpet he doth sometimes write'.[143] While Arion was singing 'Lobstars floated fearless all the while',[144] and Arion, on the dolphin's back, still singing, 'Paies his deer Pylot his delightful fare'.[145] One rejoices to meet 'the' adulterous Sargus'[146] in its proper context: and to learn that 'A firmer league of friendship is not seen/Than is the Pearl-fish and the Prawn between'.[147] But this one is quite new to me: after commenting on the odd way in which lightenings will harm a man's clothes but not the man, or *vice versa*, he adds the interesting example 'My younger eyes have often seen a Dame/To whom the flash of heaven's fantastic flame/Did else no harm, save (in a moment's space)/ With windy razor shave a secret place'.[148] He is not always merely ridiculous: the description of snowy mountains as 'mealie' seems

138 ibid., ch. 14, p. 195: 'Starting from the axiom that a whisker is a vegetable they reached the conclusion that it must be treated like other desirable vegetables – it must be manured. Here was one of the heroisms of a youthful life – one more illustration of the sad truth that one must suffer in order to be beautiful.'

139 *The Divine Weeks and Works of Guillaume de Salluste, Sieur du Bartas*, 2 vols, trans. Josiah Sylvester, ed. with introduction and commentary by Susan Snyder (Oxford: Clarendon Press, 1979).

140 'gonads'.

141 Saluste, *Divine Weeks and Works*, vol. I, Sixth Day of the First Week, 139–40.

142 ibid., 54.

143 ibid., 40.

144 ibid., Fifth Day of the First Week, 507.

145 ibid., 532.

146 ibid., 195.

147 ibid., 353–4.

148 ibid., Second Day of the First Week, 741–5.

to me rather good – and by the way anticipates a line of R. L. Stevenson.

Term ended a week ago. We had our Cave on Wednesday, at the Golden Cross. Drinking sherry with Dyson in the bar before it I saw that sinister man Eric Stone[149] but managed not to catch his eye. Poor devil, he has since then, as Vera tells us, gone completely blotto – D.T.[150] I think. How misleading fiction is in its presentation of the waster, by always making him a *merry* roisterer! Just as common in real life, and more terrible, is the gloomy feckless.

Everyone had promised to come to the Cave but only Tolkien, R.O.,[151] Bretters,[152] Dyson and I really turned up. At this, as at the Inklings, Coghill is a rarer and rarer attendant, and Dyson and I confessed to one another that, at least at the Inklings, we 'got on better without him'. His Leftism, and his 'Producing'[153] and his, I fear, unsoundness in religion, are producing a rift. Not that it much matters whether there is a rift or not in the case of [a] man who always says 'Yes' to *any* engagement and seldom keeps it.

Dyson staid the following night here in order that we might both keep an engagement to dine with the Havards – not unpleasant, but of course a meeting with a real friend like Havard *en famille* is always partly a meeting wasted.

I am now back from Church which was full, but I had the pleasure (now unusual) of sitting in our own pew – and of reading *your* notice about the Easter offering. Being driven back from my walk with Bruce by rain yesterday I did a little public works sweeping the path. A job

149 Eric Stone (1924–95) came up to read History at Magdalen College in 1941, but left to serve in the Royal Armoured Corps, 1943–5, before taking a BA in 1947. A lecturer in History at Manchester University, 1948–54, he was Fellow and Tutor in Medieval History, Keble College, Oxford, 1955–90. He is the author of *Oxfordshire Hundred Rolls of 1279* (1968).

150 delirium tremens.

151 i.e. Leonard Rice-Oxley (1892–1960) who read History at Keble College, Oxford, and took his BA in 1915. He served as a captain in the 18th Battalion of the London Irish Rifles in the First World War. On his return he spent the rest of his career at Keble College, as a lecturer in Modern History in 1921, and then as Fellow and Tutor in English Language and Literature, 1921–60. Lewis and Rice-Oxley met when both were training with the Officers' Training Corps at Keble College in 1917.

152 Herbert Francis Brett-Smith (1884–1951) who took his BA from Corpus Christi College, Oxford, in 1907. He was afterwards a lecturer in English Literature in several Oxford colleges, and Goldsmith's Reader in English.

153 Nevill Coghill produced many plays for the Oxford University Dramatic Society.

I didn't know how to tackle is the punt, which got frozen in early in the winter and in the thaw has drifted to the far side, waterlogged and not easily reached from the land. I noticed the first primrose to day – in the gulley by Las Pelotas. The crocuses on the little back lawn – the one I see from where I sit at this moment at the study table – have been up for about a week. I was quite excited by your description of the country in your neighbourhood, and wondered whether fate would ever allow us to explore it together . . .

Ahh! I have come back from my walk and just ordered tea: you remember the rare pleasure of being able to have tea at a reasonable hour in this house.

After lunch I looked through the first instalment of John Buchan's memoirs in the Sunday Times.[154] I find to my surprise that he had a hedge-school education in a Scots village, never saw the inside of a public-school, and had no interest in games. I should have supposed just the opposite. He was a very enthusiastic lover of the classics which he learned at Glasgow university under the then young Gilbert Murray.

My walk was not unpleasant; it was in the non-raining period of what remains a rainy day, with a great deal of bird music, diamonds from every branch, and the catkins out. 'Not but what' I was in a gentle perspiration when I came back.

I wonder did you get my last letter in wh. I suggested that *if* you had any control over the dates of your leave you should try to avoid April 4th to 16th as that might be the walk period? But it is now uncertain, and in any case you probably can't choose. Only let me know as far ahead as you can, for I shdn't like to be away when you arrived and to waste perhaps a day in getting back to you. Brother, brother, what a miserable thing it is to be back in these shifts and contrivances again (Ah, there's the gong)

Damn! I went up to the dining room counting on a leisurely and solitary tea – my book in my hand – to find Vera! Your exquisite sensibility will enable you to paint my emotions.

The Wounded Buffalo met Lord Halifax[155] when he was down here

---

154 *The Sunday Times* (17 March 1940), p. 10. The other instalments of John Buchan's memoirs, *Memory Hold-the-Door* (1940) appeared in *The Sunday Times* on 24 and 31 March, and 7, 14 and 21 April 1940.

155 Edward Frederick Lindley Wood, First Earl of Halifax (1881–1959), had a long and distinguished career as a statesman. He was Conservative MP for Ripon,

some weeks ago, was told by him that Hitler was within an ace of carrying out a big air raid on England last March! If this is true (and we are much nearer the horse's mouth than one usually is for such stories) the odd result is that here in England we are safer at war than we were, had we only known it, when at peace. Lord H. didn't know what prevented him, in the end, from carrying out the scheme.

An article of mine has appeared in *The Guardian*,[156] wh. I suppose is a milestone on one's ecclesiastical career. I'm sure they take the *Guardian* at Glenmachan.

Yours
J.

TO HIS BROTHER (W):

[Magdalen College]
Maundy Thursday 40 [21 March 1940]

My dear W –

You really did miss your vocation. You were born to be a commentator explaining what every reader understands and keeping silence about difficulty. Now, let's understand one another. I was *not* puzzled as [to] how *daigner* cd. mean *deign*, but as to how *je le daigne* cd. mean *je ne le daigne pas*.[157] Got it, blockhead?

Similarly, I was not puzzled as to how you could ask for something while being ready to abide loyally by an adverse decision: but as to how you cd. consider the possibility of an adverse decision while 'believing that you will receive' what you ask for.[158] However, don't let us have any unpleasantness about it.

You will gather from this exordium that I have just got your letter of the 15th announcing the very regrettable fact that you will be returning to work – but also, I hope, soon coming on leave. I am not sure that I can quite imagine the *relief* you speak of: at least I can

---

1910–25, and Foreign Secretary, 1938–41. In his memoirs, *Fullness of Days* (1957) Lord Halifax wrote of Hitler's rise to power and his position towards him.

156 *The Guardian* was a weekly Anglican newspaper founded in 1846 by R. W. Church to uphold High Church Tractarian principles. Lewis's 'Dangers of National Repentance' was published in *The Guardian* (15 March 1940), p. 127, and is reprinted in *EC*.

157 He was referring to the comments he made about *daigner* in the letter to Warnie of 3 March 1940.

158 This refers to his questions about prayer in the letter of 3 March 1940.

understand very much better the charm of a *secret* restaurant – the charm which kept you and me and others faithful to the Eastgate long after its prices had become exorbitant and its food bad. To have the secrecy along with good gastronomic value is almost too much. What pleasant hours you and the learned gunner must have spent there, and how I should like to have been present.

About Spain – after, first, Hitler's, and, now, Mussolini's, abandonment of anti-Communism I am prepared for almost anything. There are people in Europe quite depraved enough to stage that whole ceremony without having the slightest belief in Christianity or the slightest intention of treating it as anything more than a bait. Let us hope – and indeed pray – that Franco is not one of them. Even if he is not, he might be sincere in a sense which bodes very ill for us. I mean, his Christendom might be, on the Papist side, what Ulster Orangeism is on the Protestant side. One can imagine Condlin, if he were a Dictator, whipping up a kind of Protestant revival which wd. be in a sense sincere, but which would be quite ready to ally itself with Germany or Russia or both for the destruction of Italy and Spain. I can never forget Tolkien's Spanish friend who, after having several colleges pointed out to him by name from the roof of the Radder,[159] observed with surprise 'So this was once a Christian country?'

Mind you, I think the Pope[160] is sound. Something might be done through him to persuade France to put the Christian-Totalitarian issue first, at any rate for the present, and the Papist-Protestant second. Of course I absolutely agree with you that Papistry even of the most obscurantist and persecuting kind would be better (I mean in terms of this world) than the great rebellion of the other force not only against Grace but against Nature.

Why should quiet ruminants as you and I have been born in such a ghastly age? Let me palliate the apparent selfishness of this complaint by asserting that there *are* people who, while not, of course, liking actual suffering when it falls to their own share, *do* really like the 'stir', the 'sense of great issues'. Lord!, how I loathe great issues. How I wish they were all adjourned *sine die*.[161] 'Dynamic' I think is one of the words

159 The Radcliffe Camera, part of the Bodleian Library.

160 Pope Pius XII (1876–1958) who held office 1939–58.

161 'indefinitely'.

invented by this age which sums up what it likes and I abominate. Could one start a Stagnation party – which at General Elections would boast that during its term of office *no* event of the least importance had taken place.

I was much interested in the opinions of the 'bearer of a famous name' – and, by the bye, I see one of the uses of the fact that we all have different hobbies: for I get quite a vicarious thrill in recognising how *you* must enjoy such a meeting – such as you would perhaps feel if I told you I had met a great philosopher. Thus one savours through ones friends dishes which would not please one's own palate.

I have been reading this week the 'Revelations' of Mother Julian of Norwich (14th century); not always so profitable as I had expected, but well worth reading. This is a curious vision 'Also He showed me a little thing, the bigness of a hazel-nut, in my hand. I thought, What may this be? And it was answered, it is all that is made. I marvelled how it might last, for methought it might suddenly have fallen to naught for littleness.'[162] Now that is a good turn given to the monkish (or indeed Christian) view of the whole created universe: for to say that it is bad, as some are inclined to do, is blasphemous and Manichean – but to say that it is *small* (with the very odd dream twist 'so small it might fall to bits'), that seems just right. Very odd too is her doctrine of 'the Grand Deed'. Christ tells her again and again 'All shall be well, and all shall be well, and all manner of thing shall be well.'[163] She asks how it can be well, since some are damned. He replied that all that is true, but the secret grand deed will make even that 'very well'. 'With you this is impossible, but not with Me.'[164]

My mood changes about this. Sometimes it seems mere drivel – to invent a necessarily inconceivable grand deed which makes everything quite different while leaving it exactly the same. But then at other times it has the unanswerable, illogical convincingness of things heard in a dream and appeals to what is one of my deepest convictions, viz. that

---

162 Lewis's edition was *Revelations of Divine Love Recorded by Julian, Anchoress at Norwich Anno Domini 1373, A Version from the MS. in the British Museum*, ed. Grace Warrack (London: Methuen, 1901). First Revelation, ch. 5, p. 10. See the photographs of Lewis's annotations to his copy of this book in Lawlor, *C. S. Lewis: Memories and Reflections*.

163 ibid., Thirteenth Revelation, ch. 27, p. 56.

164 ibid., ch. 32, p. 67.

reality always escapes prediction by taking a line which was simply not in your thought at all. Imagine oneself as a flat earther questioning whether the Earth was endless or not. If you were told 'It is finite but never comes to an end', one wd. seem to be up against nonsense. Yet the escape (by being a sphere) is so easy – once you know it. At any rate, this book excites me.

And talking of books *did* you take away the Everyman volume of Shakespeare's Comedies[165] from the study? Not that I want it, but I wonder where it is. To-day I attended in Weldon's rooms the last of many meetings about that annual pest the 'Modern Subjects Scholarship'. He (and Mackenzie) had both managed to get leave from whatever absurd office they are now in – I suppose 'To see that ass Lewis doesn't fill the place up with duds while we are away.' However it passed off most amicable. I mentioned your friend Sankey[166] to him and he 'made a countenance' to remember him, but I think it was only politeness: he hadn't the look of a man who is remembering a *real* person.

From there I went on (it was a beautiful blue windy day) to see Hodges – professor of Pastoral Theology – about business arising out of our S.C.M. activities. He is a Canon of the House and lives in Tom Quad.[167] The house is furnished with two amiable cats and, what is rare now-a-days, a genuine pug. His wife, whom I met for tea after our talk, is an Archer, of Moy, Co Tyrone, so we had some quite pleasant 'crack'. A very pleasant spot, Tom Quad on a sunny evening in spring or autumn: on a summer's afternoon it ranks with 'the lane by the brickyard'.

Saturday afternoon. I have just had tea. On my afternoon walk I noticed great activity among the rabbits, specially as I crossed the bridge

---

165 *Shakespeare's Comedies*, biographical introduction by Oliphant Smeaton, prefatory notes of D. C. Browning, Everyman's Library (1906).

166 Sankey remains to be identified.

167 Lewis was confused about the name. His visit was to the Reverend Leonard Hodgson (1889–1969). After reading Greats and Theology at Hertford College, Oxford, Hodgson was Principal of St Edmund Hall, Oxford, 1914–19, Dean of Divinity at Magdalen College, 1919–25, and Professor of Christian Apologetics at the General Theological Seminary, New York, 1925–31. He returned to England as Canon of Winchester Cathedral, 1931–8, after which he was Regius Professor of Moral and Pastoral Theology at Oxford, 1938–44, and Regius Professor of Divinity, 1944–58. In 1920 he married Ethel Margaret du Plat, the daughter of the Rev. Charles Frederick Archer, late Rector of Moy, Co. Tyrone. Ethel Hodgson died in 1960.

onto your embankment at the East end of the pond. Here, as you know, our neighbour's ground is higher than ours, so that one of the pretty fools[168] started up not only a few inches from, but on a *level* with, my face! Bruce put up two Scouts (one of them our friend the nice scout-master) in the top wood. I walked round the ploughed field, halting for a longish soak in the pine-grove above Horspath. A beautiful after-noon with a sky of what I call *spring* gray – long level clouds of white, silver, pearl, and dove-colour. To be distinguished from winter gray – ragged and pleated clouds of iron colour: or from the hot summer gray or celestial damp blotting paper.

After my walk I did a little sweeping. On Dug-out plateau I took the path (i.e. swept and added a few touches of the spade) round in a curve away from our neighbour and towards the pond, so as to get the 'sea-view' and so that by constantly walking near the descent we may prevent the nettles and brambles growing up between the path and the pond. During my absence the Scouts (there were only two of them) had spontaneously bailed the punt and now, at my suggestion (they were 'looking for a job' – rum creatures) they took it across to its proper place and beached it.

I hope you will find some letters from me awaiting you at No 3 B.S.D. I trust you will be more fortunate for the Easter communion than you were for Christmas: at any rate you will be in my mind to-morrow morning. A happy Easter, Brother.

Yours
J.

TO MARY NEYLAN (T):

The Kilns,
Headington Quarry,
Oxford.
March 26th 1940.

Dear Mrs Neylan,

(1) About obedience. Nearly everyone will find himself in the course of his life in positions where he ought to command and in positions where he ought to obey. Which he ought to be doing in any given situation, or whether he ought to be doing either, of course will

168 Presumably one of the rabbits.

always admit of dispute, but that doesn't invalidate the principle – any more than the general rule 'I oughtn't to overeat' is invalidated by the difficulty of saying whether one bun here and now constitutes overeating. Still less is it invalidated by the fact that some people are too fond of ruling and others too fond of obeying: sooner or later each of them may be a duty for everyone.

Now each of them requires a certain training or habituation if it is to be done well: and indeed the habit of command, or of obedience, may often be more necessary than the most enlightened view as to the ultimate moral grounds for doing either; and certainly, where there is no training, the enlightened views will either be ineffective, or effective at the cost of great nervous tension. You can't begin training a child to command until it has reason and age enough to command someone or something without absurdity. You can at once begin training it to obey: that is, teaching it the act of obedience *as such* – without prejudice to the views it will later hold as to who should obey whom, or when, or how much. Just as you try to train it in *courage*, without in the least prejudging the question as to which challenges in adult life ought to be faced and which ought to be declined.

Of course I personally think (a) That there is in existence a Being so intrinsically authoritative that obedience is the essential business of a human being in a way in which command (tho' unfortunately humans must sometimes assume it) is not. (b) That humility is in itself good. But you would NOT have to agree with these two purely theological views if you agreed that children ought to learn obedience as such, since it is perfectly obvious that every human being is going to have to spend a great deal of his life in obeying parents, schoolmasters, employers, magistrates etc. Nor of course am I making any *political* statement. The question whether *persons to be obeyed* should be democratically elected or otherwise (I personally am a democrat) leaves where it was the truth that in any human society there will have to be a lot of obeying.

(2) Psychoanalysis. In talking to me you must beware, because I am conscious of a partly pathological hostility to what is fashionable, of which I think I could give the causes if it were necessary. I may therefore have been betrayed into statements (or, at least, what is perhaps more insidious, a *tone*) on this subject wh. I am not prepared to defend. No doubt, like every young science, it is full of errors, but so long as it remains a science and doesn't set up to be a philosophy I have no

quarrel with it – i.e. as long as people judge whatever it reveals by the best human logic and scheme of values they've got and don't try to derive logic and values from it. In practice, no doubt, as you say, the patient is always influenced by the analyst's own values.

Further, in so far as it attempts to *heal*, i.e. to make *better*, every treatment involves a value judgement. This could be avoided if the analyst said 'Tell me what kind of chap you want to be and I'll see how near that I can make you': but of course he really has his own idea of what goodness and happiness consist in and works to that. And his idea is derived not from his science (it couldn't be) but from his age, sex, class, culture, religion & heredity, and is just as much in need of criticism as the patient's. In fact if you suspect *your* values come from the nursemaid, you may console yourself by reflecting that so do *his*! For no amount of knowledge about how states of mind are produced could of itself teach you which states to prefer: for that, he must be falling back on whatever general philosophy of life he has.

In reality, of course, neither his values nor yours are invalidated by the fact that they have a history in which nursemaids play a part – any more than reason collapses when you realise that you learned most of it from your elders.

Another way in which *any* therapeutic art may have bad philosophical results is this. It must, for the sake of method, take perfection as the Norm and treat every departure from it as disease: hence there is always a danger that those who practise it may come to treat a perfectly ideal perfection as 'normal' in the popular sense and consequently waste their lives in crying for the moon.

When Dr. Sprenger says Sarah is 'nervous' he probably is right *in the sense that* she is not, and never will be, perfectly wise, good, and happy. God-a-mercy! Fancy equating 'happiness' and 'normality'! Worm's meat, neighbour: Adam's sons, Eve's daughters: 'life will not bear refining on'[169] – 'think not the doom of man reversed for thee'.[170]

I see no reason why a Christian shd. not be an analyst. Psychoanalysis after all merely defines what was always admitted, that the moral choices of the human soul operate inside a complex non-moral situation. Even

---

169 Boswell, *The Life of Samuel Johnson*, vol. III, 19 September 1777, p. 169: 'Life will not bear refinement: you must do as other people do.'

170 Samuel Johnson, *The Vanity of Human Wishes* (1749), 155–6: 'Yet hope not life from grief or danger free,/Nor think the doom of man reversed for thee'.

Hamlet knew that 'the devil' was 'very potent' with men of the melancholy complexion – i.e. men with certain complexes, which really gives the whole thing in a nutshell.[171]

The Christian view would be that every psychological situation, just like every degree of wealth or poverty, talent or stupidity etc, had its own peculiar temptations and peculiar advantages, that the worst could always be turned to a good use and the best cd. always be abused to one's spiritual ruin. In fact 'all fortune is good' as Boethius said.[172]

This doesn't mean that it wd. be wrong to try to cure a complex any more than a stiff leg: but it does mean that if you can't, then, so far from the game being up, life with a complex, or with a stiff leg, is precisely the game you have been set. To the person whom you imagine who says 'I'm a neurotic and can't afford to be analysed and so can't do anything about it', I suppose a Christian wd. give just the same advice as to a person who needed a holiday and couldn't get it – advice you doubtless heard long ago from that obviously excellent nursemaid. Even a Stoic wd. not listen to the plea you imagine. We must play the parts we find ourselves given. The despair at not being able to be analysed is really a revolt against the conditions of existence. Once make the medical Norm our ideal of the 'normal' and we shall never lack an excuse for throwing up the sponge. But these are all illegitimate abuses of analysis. The real thing has obviously done you nearly pure good – you've learned from it some of the most valuable lessons, and they needn't be *un*-learned.

(3) *Christianity*. My own experience in reading the Gospels was at one stage even more depressing than yours. Everyone told me that I should find there a figure whom I couldn't help loving. Well, I could! They told me I would find moral perfection – but one sees so very little of Him in ordinary situations that I couldn't make much of that either. Indeed some of His behaviour seemed to me open to criticism, e.g. accepting an invitation to dine with a Pharisee and then loading him with torrents of abuse.

Now the truth is, I think, that the sweetly-attractive-human-Jesus is a product of 19th century scepticism, produced by people who were

171 William Shakespeare, *Hamlet* (1623), II, ii, 636–40: 'The devil hath power/To assume a pleasing shape; yea, and perhaps/Out of my weakness and my melancholy – /As he is very potent with such spirits – /Abuses me to damn me.'

172 Boethius, *The Consolation of Philosophy*, book IV, prosa 7.

ceasing to believe in His divinity but wanted to keep as much of Christianity as they could. It is not what an unbeliever coming to the records with an open mind will (at first) find there. The first thing you really find is that we are simply not *invited*, so to speak, to pass any moral judgement on Him, however favourable: it is only too clear *He* is going to do whatever judging there is: it is we who are *being* judged, sometimes tenderly, sometimes with stunning severity, but always *de haut en bas*.[173] (Have you noticed that you can hardly free your imagination to picture Him as shorter than yourself?) The first real work of the Gospels on a fresh reader is, and ought to be, to raise v. acutely the question, 'Who – or What – is This?' For there is a good deal in the character which, *unless* He really is what He says He is – is not lovable nor even tolerable. If He *is*, then of course it's another matter: nor will it then be surprising if much remains puzzling to the end. For if there is anything in Christianity we are now approaching something which will never be fully comprehensible.

On this whole aspect of the subject I should go on (since you've read his Orthodoxy) to Chesterton's *The Everlasting Man*.[174] You might also find Mauriac's *Vie de Jésus* useful. (Unless you are very up to date with the most modern French, Julie Kernan's translation – Hodder & Stoughton 7/6 – may be better: at least I found it almost unintelligibly idiomatic).[175] By the way, if childish associations are too intrusive in reading the New Testament, it's a good idea to try it in some other language, or in Moffatt's modern translation.[176]

As for theology proper: a good many misunderstandings are cleared away by Edwyn Bevan's *Symbolism and Belief*.[177] A book of composite authorship and of varying merits, but on the whole good is *Essays Catholic and Critical* ed. E. G. Selwyn S.P.C.K.[178] Gore's *The Philosophy of the Good Life* (Everyman) is rather wordy but taught me a lot. If you can stand serious faults of style (and if you can get them, they are long

173 'From high to low'.

174 G. K. Chesterton, *Orthodoxy* (1909); *The Everlasting Man* (1925).

175 François Mauriac, *Life of Jesus*, trans. Julie Kernan (London: Hodder & Stoughton, 1937).

176 James Moffatt, *The New Testament: A New Translation* (1913; 2nd edn 1936); *The Old Testament: A New Translation* (1924); *A New Translation of the Bible: Containing the Old and New Testaments* (1925; rev. edn 1935).

177 Edwyn Bevan, *Symbolism and Belief* (1938).

178 *Essays Catholic and Critical*, ed. E. G. Selwyn (London: SPCK, 1926).

out of print) Geo. Macdonald's 3 vols. of *Unspoken Sermons*[179] go to the very heart of the matter. I think you wd. also find it most illuminating to re-read now many things you once read in 'Eng. Lit' without knowing their real importance – Herbert, Traherne, *Religio Medici*.

As for a person 'with whom to discuss', choice is more ticklish. L. W. Grensted is very interested in Psychoanalysis and wrote a book on its relations to Christianity:[180] would that be an advantage or the reverse? O. C. Quick[181] is a man whom I know and like. Milford,[182] the present rector of St Mary's, some like and some don't. Let me know what, or what sort, you want and I'll see what can be done.

I like v. much what you say about 'not having it both ways' and something that can't be 'indefinitely avoided'. If it was really psychoanalysis that taught you that, more power to its elbow: but I suspect it is your own. Propaganda, my books? Tut! Only the two that almost profess to be (*Regress* and *Silent Planet*). Come and see me when you're better and bring the gudeman. Very good wishes to all.

Yours sincerely
C. S. Lewis

TO HIS BROTHER (W):

[The Kilns]
March 29th 1940

My dear W –

The Walk is now arranged, after many alterations, to be from the

179 George MacDonald, *Unspoken Sermons* (1867, 1885, 1889).

180 L. W. Grensted, *Psychology and God: A Study of the Implications of Recent Psychology for Religious Belief and Practice* (1930).

181 Canon Oliver Chase Quick, Regius Professor of Divinity at Oxford, 1939–43. See note 3 to the letter of 18 January 1941.

182 The Reverend Theodore Richard Milford (1895–1987) volunteered for service in the First World War and served with the 19th Royal Fusiliers. He went up to Magdalen College in 1919 where he read Classics. His connection with the Student Christian Movement led him to India where he taught for three years. He served two years in Liverpool as local SCM secretary, 1924–6, after which he spent a year at Westcott House, Cambridge, 1930–1, training for ordination. He was ordained in India in 1934. On returning to England he worked for the SCM. He was Vicar of St Mary the Virgin, the Oxford University church, 1938–47. In 1942 he took part in the founding of the Oxford Committee for Famine Relief, later known as Oxfam, and he was its first chairman. In 1947 he became chancellor of Lincoln Cathedral, and in 1958–68 he was Master of the Temple. His writings include *Foolishness to the Greeks* (1953).

5th April to the 8th – i.e. returning to the Kilns on the 9th.[183] I hope to goodness fate is not going to send you on leave before the 9th. While away, I shall try to ring up home as often as possible in case there should be news of you and will, of course, return at once if there is. I think the risk has to be taken, as the only perfectly safe alternative would be never to leave the Kilns for the duration.

On Easter morning we had the biggest crowd at 8 o'clock that I've ever seen – I was one of *four* in our pew; trying to rejoice in spirit that there should be so many communicants but very far from comfortable in the flesh – my hip being tightly wedged against the pillar and my bottom resting on the *angle* at the end of the bench.[184] Also slightly *twisted*, as one usually is in a crowd.

I had arrived early in true P'daita style and had a stroll in the churchyard (in that beautiful before breakfast luminosity so common on this occasion which makes the Resurrection seem almost *natural*) and had a look at Mrs Moore's tombstone.[185] It's a poor colour (like greyish-blue cardboard) and not at all what I thought it wd. look like from the catalogue. In fact I'm very much afraid it looks *cheap*: the last thing an Ulster widow of the bourgeoisie would wish her tomb to look. The beautiful morning had changed into cold mist on my way home again. There was a good congregation at the 11 o'clock service too.

I celebrated Easter by drinking another bottle of your claret, but foolishly made it my 'six o'clock'. No, Brother: Bosphorus claret may be very well as a table drink, but taken alone it is mere physic. I read a little more Lady Julian of Norwich. Monday was a beautiful day. I took Bruce for his walk in the morning, and after lunch bussed into Oxford to meet Tolkien at College preparatory to a committee.

He turned up but told me the committee was postponed till Thursday, so we spent a pleasant aimless afternoon together, walking through Adders and Mesopotamia. The crocuses are full out now, their leaves opened and their flame-shape lost – I prefer them in their earlier stage.

---

183 He was referring to a planned walking tour on Exmoor with Cecil Harwood and Owen Barfield.

184 The 'Lewis Pew', now designated by a plaque, is a few feet of bench divided from the main part of the pew by a stone pillar.

185 i.e. Mrs Alice Hamilton Moore (1853–1939). See note 124 to the letter to Warnie of 5 November 1939.

I was glad to see in the Fellows' Garden (what at first puzzled me) a thing like a C.O.'s latrine or sentry-box with a door, and a seat inside it: obviously a 'sulky' to be used in bad weather by that little mouse-like stiff jointed man (you remember him?) who defends the garden from landing parties. I suppose it is the fruit of Lee's excellent and humane home-bursarship – Opie would 'never have tolerated it' (By the way, did I tell you the v. happy pun – the undergraduate on his way to a tutorial with Opie who was heard to remark 'I'm off for my weekly Opiate'?) Tolkien gathers, I think from his son in Rome,[186] that the grand desire of every Italian is to avoid anything that might possibly bring them into the war.

Tuesday was also a broken day because poor Houghton[187] came up in the afternoon. He was not to come up till tea-time if it looked like rain. Well it did look like rain after lunch so I decided to take Bruce out for a short walk before it came down: but it cleared up and when I got back, after going round the ploughed field, I found Houghton waiting for me in the study and pointing out that we could still get quite a nice breather before tea. So out again – why are two short walks so much more tiring than one long walk?

St Peter's has almost ceased to exist during the war and he wanted me to write him a testimonial for a chair at Aberystwyth (of blessed memory! Don't it conjure up that very Welsh-faced war memorial, and the Fliedermaus film, the ghastly pair of accordionists on whom our pity turned out to be so wasted?) I of course agreed, but it is uncomfortable as I can say v. little, not really thinking him worth the job. But I am very sorry for a man who, at my age, has to go back to the odious business of job-hunting.

This week I received a letter from my former pupil Mrs Neylan (the Dartington Hall mistress) who is trembling on the verge of Christianity – admits that the issue 'can no longer be avoided' – and asks what to read and (more difficult still) who to see. I felt almost overwhelmed

186 John Tolkien was at this time studying for the priesthood in the English College in Rome. See **Father John Francis Reuel Tolkien** in the Biographical Appendix.

187 The Rev. Ralph Edward Cunliffe Houghton (1896–1990) took his BA from Christ Church in 1921. After teaching at Westminster School, he was ordained in 1925 and was Librarian and Fellow of English at St Peter's College, Oxford, 1928–63. He is the author of *The Influence of the Classics on the Poetry of Matthew Arnold* (1923) and has edited many of the plays of Shakespeare.

by the responsibility of my reply, and naturally the more because the two other people whose conversion had something to do with me became Papists![188]

After writing at great length I fortunately re-read her letter and discovered that, owing to her omission of inverted commas, I had wholly misunderstood one of her points (will anyone teach women to punctuate) so I had to do nearly the whole job over again. The letter's gone now. I suppose if God intends to have Mrs Neylan it won't make much difference what I've written! – yet that is a dangerous argument wh. wd. lead to its not mattering what you did in any circumstances.

The other thing I've been busy on this week is a book called *L'Amour et l'Occident* by one Denis de Rougemont,[189] apparently a French Protestant, wh. I have to review.[190] It contains a thoroughly bad historical thesis about medieval love, and an absolutely first class *moral* thesis about the utter incompatibility of *l'amour passion* with Christian marriage, happiness, or even enjoyable physical sexuality. He's a corker of a man, tho' with some bogus elements in him: I've written to him to-day. If, as I suspect, he is now a *poilu*,[191] my letter may give a moments happiness.

On Thursday I went in for the postponed committee. It was a windy and sunny afternoon and I walked through Merton St. and Ch. Church

---

188 i.e. Dom Bede Griffiths and George Sayer.

189 Denis de Rougemont, *Passion and Society* [*L'Amour et l'Occident*], trans. Montgomery Belgion (London: Faber & Faber, 1940). A revised, augmented version of Belgion's translation was published as *Love in the Western World* (New York: Pantheon, [1956]). Denis de Rougemont (1906–85), a Catholic born in French Switzerland, was the publisher of a literary review in Paris, 1933–5, after which he lectured at the University of Frankfurt, 1935–6. Serving with the Swiss army early in the Second World War he co-founded the 'Ligue de Gothard', designed to strength Swiss resistance against Nazism. A conference and lecture-visit to the United States in 1941 was turned into a four-year sojourn by America's entry into the war, and he became the chief editor of the 'Voice of America' French services. On his return to Geneva he promoted the idea of a united Europe based on Switzerland's federal structure. In 1950 he founded the European Cultural Centre, which he directed until 1967. He was the author of numerous books and essays, many of which expounded his belief that European civilization must reassert itself.

190 Lewis's review of de Rougemont's *Passion and Society* and Claude Chavasse's *The Bride of Christ* was published in *Theology*, XL (June 1940), pp. 459–61.

191 'soldier'.

to Pembroke, the rendez-vous, thinking I had never seen Oxford look more beautiful. Tolkien had promised us tea at the committee but the kitchen at Pembroke was shut and we had to do the best we could with sherry – a wretched substitute for tea at 4 o'clock: not that I refrained on that account from sullenly swallowing as much of it as I could get.

On Friday I had old Taylor in the afternoon. To-day (Saturday) has been one of those rare and blessed days when Maureen and Fuller took Bruce out, so that I was able to do a little public works. I removed several sack-fulls of leaves, the result of my other day's sweeping, and started sweeping the coast section of the path. Its odd – when we made it I imagine we both thought of that as the essential path and the rest as branch lines, but in fact is less used than any other. I didn't get very far, for the snows had left the tree to the West of the slanting bridge so hopelessly bowed across the path (completion of a process begun by a previous winter, as you remember) that I had to cut nearly all of it away, which took me nearly till tea time.

I had my mid afternoon halt sitting on one of the rocks with my back against the flat stone we excavated near the bottom of the *grand escalier*.[192] Very pleasant: the first misty green just coming over the wood, the daffodils with the flower not yet out but visible in its sheath, the pond visible below, and the moss very rich and cushiony. This time, for me, physical exercise did what it is popularly supposed to do; i.e. I had a headache when I began and it was gone when I ended. You and I are more familiar with the reverse process. My right hand and arm are aching from the broom, followed by the pen, but otherwise I have the well being that comes after a 'good perspiration'. Now I must go and read my portions of scripture,[193] and may perhaps make a start on my review of de Rougemont before dinner. So long, Pigibuddie,

Yours
Jack

---

192 The name given to the path, to the right of Lewis's pond, leading to Shotover Hill.

193 When Lewis did not attend morning or evening prayer in his College chapel or a church, he usually read the Old Testament and New Testament lessons appointed for the day in the Prayer Book lectionary.

TO HIS BROTHER (W):

[The Kilns]
April 11th 1940

My dear W –

The other cat's name was Origen, called after the heretical father of that name who, taking literally the text about some who are eunuchs for the King's sake, cut off his stones.[194]

And à propos of stones, Barfield made a good pun during the walk. I had been talking of the Castor's habit of biting off its stones when pursued and someone, not knowing the word, said 'I thought that was the Beaver.' SELF: 'Castor is the Latin for Beaver.' BARFIELD: 'Hence the association of Castor and Bollox.'[195] From this you will see that I have got your letter and had my walk.

I was on tenter hooks for fear your leave should come before I got back and did the best I could by ringing up home every evening to see if they had any news of you. If the war lasts long you will find a certain monotony in the account of these walks, for as long as Harwood is at Minehead they will always begin and end there to save him expense.

I left home by the 12.45, having lunched at the station, on Friday 8th.[196] I had with me a book by Chavasse (did you meet him when he was curate of St Mark's? – an Exeter man and a friend of Coghills – it was he who in the army riding school, for sitting all hunched up, was told 'If you swallowed a poker you'd sh-t a corkscrew) wh. had been sent me to review for *Theology*, called *The Bride of Christ*.[197] Its thesis is that the idea of the Church as Bride was disastrously transmuted into that of the individual believer as Bride (see some of your quietists etc) and then into that of the Blessed Virgin, but recovered in its purity by 'the Anglican reformation'.

From Reading on I had a crowded train. The first part of the journey

---

194 Origen (c. AD 185–c. 254), Alexandrian biblical critic and theologian, who at one point began to lead a strictly ascetic life. Misinterpreting Matthew 19:12 ('There are some eunuchs, which were so born from their mother's womb: and there are some eunuchs, which were made eunuchs of men: and there be eunuchs which have made themselves eunuchs for the kingdom of heaven's sake'), Origen mutilated himself.

195 In Greek mythology Castor and Pollux were the twin sons of Zeus and Leda who were worshipped as deities and protectors of sailors.

190 He meant Friday 5 April.

197 See note 190 to the letter of 29 March 1940.

I passed sitting on my pack in the corridor, till told by a ticket collector that I had 'no excuse' for doing that. Excuse indeed! It's almost Paxfordian. However, in obedience to his exhortations I went further down the train and got a seat – not much of an improvement really, since I had a blistering sun beating on my head and a small child walking in and out of the compartment saying 'A-a-a' *continuously* for about two hours. I had the grace even at the time to think myself rather a sullen creature in disliking two such very symbols of life as solar radiation and a child: but there's no denying I was glad to make Taunton.

Here I had the rather pleasant experience of finding bathed in evening light that same little local train which I described to you as dark and smoking on the winter walk. From then on all was delightful, specially that first glimpse of waves and wet beach at Watchet – and then ones final emergence from the station at Minehead into all the freshness (even ordinary *sounds* sound different) of a town one doesn't live in.

I reached the Plume of Feathers at about 6.10 and, after a wash, was just seated in the bar consuming a glass of sherry when, to my delight, I was visited by Dyson, who is staying down there with his in-laws, and had got into touch with Harwood only the day before. Characteristically, he knew a better tap across the road and carried me there to drink draught Bass.

On our return we met both the Harwoods (there had been no possibility of excluding Mrs from the evening: Mrs Dyson cd. not come, having measles) with Field. We were a little damped to hear that Barfield had wired to say he cd. not join us till the following day. It was arranged, for his sake, that H. and I would do for our first day some walk that would bring us back to Minehead in the evening. We had a pleasant night. Somewhat to my surprise, Field and Dyson took to one another amazingly, and that despite the fact that Field unloaded the whole Douglas scheme on him.[198] It was a novelty to hear Dyson reduced to comparative silence. Whenever he attempted to speak, Field, though having held the floor ever since we finished dinner, interrupted him with some such expression as 'If I might just put *one* word in'. All the same he seemed to like it.

198 'The Douglas Scheme' is named after Clifford Douglas (1879–1952), originator of the theory of Social Credit. He advocated subsidies to liberate prices from cost of production. See his *Social Credit* (1924).

The whole party had just left me when Barfield rang up to say that he was at Taunton and would arrive for breakfast in the morning. I had, as is part of the ritual on holidays, a bad night, but all the taste of it vanished as I walked down to the sea-front to meet Barfield in a fine crisp sunshiny morning, and returned with him to a really good breakfast (you have not had Kilns bacon for so long now that you will hardly realise the inwardness of this).

The arrangement for returning to Minehead that night was now no longer necessary, but we decided to let it stand so as to have the advantage of Dyson's company (who had naturally no idea of walking) and of Field's (who had not enough petrol to follow us far by car). When Harwood turned up, we decided to spend the day in the ascent of Dunkery Beacon.

And now comes one of the curious black-outs of the human mind. I see from the map that we must have lunched at Woot[t]on Courtney after crossing a wooded ridge, but the whole of that morning – landscape, weather, conversation etc – has absolutely gone. Sorry! And I can't explain it. Memory begins at the coming down into Woot[t]on Courtney a little too early for lunch and going in to inspect the Church, where the others asked me (according to our old custom) to 'read a chapter'. I chose the second Psalm – wh. led to a series of enquiries and hypotheses from Harwood on the meaning of 'Kiss the Son lest He be angry'[199] of which I could make neither head nor tail until we discovered that he was mistaking SON for SUN, which naturally made the text rather hard.

Oh the heathen ignorance of these Anthroposophists – and you may add, of these Congregationalists, for I think he was of that sect by birth and a minister's son.[200] I had always supposed him (and indeed found him) a man of 'too much literature' for such an absurdity.

By the way, you will gather from the fact that we had to fill in time at this village before lunch, that we were there before 12 o'clock, and hence that the morning stretch had been very short – perhaps that is why I can't remember it. We now turned to a very A.A.-looking hotel

---

199 Psalm 2:12: 'Kiss the Son, lest he be angry, and so ye perish from the right way: if his wrath be kindled, (yea, but a little) blessed are all they that put their trust in him.'

200 Cecil Harwood's father, the Rev. William Hardy Harwood, was a Congregationalist minister.

which was the only hostelry the place afforded and approached it up a drive lined with stables – a long equine head regarding us scornfully from almost each half-door, for this [is] almost as horsy a place as Newbury. It turned out, however, to have a bar, and there we got good beer, bread and cheese, and tea.

Emerging we saw our work before us – a green descent of lanes and fields sloping down for about half a mile, and beyond that an almost interminable upward slope of heather – rather like a roller (*not* a breaker) when you turn round and see it behind you in a rough bathe. It soon became the sort of walk in which you straggle far apart and do not converse. Presently we had a soak – you know how good heather is for that purpose! I have the clearest picture of the view – Woot[t]on Courtney below us and above it a steep green hill with bare flanks and wooded top which we had descended in the morning: and funnily enough I remember tracing from there the whole route we had come through. I cannot remember traversing it.

We went on. The prospect – hills on hills on hills to the end of the world – was magnificent but the slow ascent, with no sign of a top, never steeper and never less steep, began to lose its charm. Presently one began to get to the *false tops*; and so at long last to the stone cairn and the real top with (as usual) a change of weather for the worse, sunless sky and cold wind. We stayed no longer than it took Barfield to recite a sonnet, and then began descending the N.W. side which is much steeper than the one we had come up by and sinks into delightfully winding woods and combes.

We got to a farm called Cloutsham for tea, where we unfortunately had to share the room with an odd family. The father was a man rather like a fat edition of Condlin (can you imagine it) who sprang to his feet without any warning to examine a print on the wall, read out very slowly and gravely the legend underneath it (about thirty words – of no conceivable interest) and sat down without any comment. I had to bite my lip to keep a straight face.

After tea we proceeded, in the tracks of the January walk, down the decaying, mossy-tread valley of the Horner and debouched onto the Porlock–Minehead Rd, where we awaited a bus home in the unusual convenience of a proper bus-stop with roof and bench – true, it was the narrowest bench I have ever sat on, but better than 'hanging about'.

We had a splendid evening 'telling a story' – an old diversion on these walks in which each player invents a chunk in turn: the natural tendency of each to introduce new characters and complications and then to 'hand the baby' to the next man, produces the fun. Dyson proved specially good at it, and two young officers who were sitting in the room followed him with every sign of appreciation – up to his final shot, when the whole thing was over. 'Next week – *The man with the magic truss.*'

I remarked, after the two officers had left, that the subalterns of this war looked both more manly and more military than what I remembered of those in the last: but Barfield says it is unfair to compare the 1918 ones with those who really correspond to the 1914 vintage. (This reminds me of another point he and I discussed on the journey home, â propos of the boarding of the *Altmark* and one or two similar episodes – how wonderful it is after twenty years of cocktails and cynicism to find such a supply of 'the Kipling virtues' still existing – almost beyond our desert.)

On Sunday morning Barfield, Harwood, and I set off on the only real 'tour' of this holiday – i.e. the only day that involved lying at a different place. It was a fine, but not bright, morning. We began by walking to Dunster – then along that beautiful town and out at its S.E. end, across several foot bridges, and slowly up steep paths into fir woods with a short soak on that *tinder*-like reddish brown surface which makes the floor of such places. A troup of glossy horses ridden by glossy young women went creaking and jingling by with their leathery and fleshy smell.

Harwood described to us all the new insights he had gained (as master of a billeted school) into the hierarchy of a small town – town councillors, municipal Condlins etc. We continued on our path for a long way and had our next soak in a clearing at the foot of a steep ascent: much bothered by an aeroplane which kept on circling round and coming v. low each time as it reached us – I took it the more unkindly since Harwood told me it was almost the first he'd seen since he'd come to Minehead. (Horrid thought – have the Little People[201] developed an air-arm?)

The ascent after this wd. have been quite tolerable but that last winter's snow had felled so many trees that the path presently became

201 i.e. the faerie folk.

impracticable and we were forced right out of the wood onto a much steeper path along its eaves – one of those bits on a walk at the end of which – whatever the time and however recent the last soak – all with one accord fling themselves flat on their backs and for many minutes speech is 'not to be thought of'. When we recovered we had a delightful view of Minehead and the hill behind it and the channel. Sounds I don't like could be heard in the offing.

We strolled on again – it always feels like *strolling* on the first bit of level after a steep pull, doesn't it? – for a bit over open hill country, soon to descend again into woods, and presently to find that we were lost. We got involved in an interminable steep glen with low mossy trees only a couple of yards apart – not a breath of air – and I, at least, was dripping before we reached the top of Croydon Hill.

We walked down fine broad breezy rides cut in the woods, into the village of Luxborough – to find that the inn marked on the map no longer existed 'but' (it was now about 1.40!) 'there's one a mile down the road'. I had done the first ten yards of that mile almost before the words were out of the informant's mouth. I plugged along well ahead of the others for about half of it, when I was overtaken by Barfield who had broken into a trot. We *just* made it. The landlady at first took up the astonishing position that of course [we] cd. have beer, but she 'didn't know about the bread and cheese as it was really after two'! – however, she overcame this scruple in the end.

Our luck was still out, for a fine rain began to fall while we were at lunch. The others had found 'an admirable short cut' for the first bit of the afternoon march but seeing from the map that it consisted of intricate paths through woods and feeling I had had quite enough of that sort of thing for one day, I stuck to my guns and said I would go 'round by the road' and meet them where their path emerged.

So, buttoned up to the chin in my mack, I fought my way up a long winding hill, to be rewarded at the top with a sudden burst of sunshine and a fine wind in which to get dry. I had little difficulty in finding the rendez-vous, but as I had taken a goodish time I was surprised to find it empty. I took my seat on a felled tree, spread out my dripping mack and admired as fine a prospect as I had yet seen – endless domed hills picked out in a brilliant variety of colours both by the varieties of cloud-shadow and sunlight and also by their own alterations of plough and pasture and different kinds of wood – dusky forest-trees, black fir, and larch almost arsenically green. I had time to smoke two cigarettes before two weary figures came in sight.

Barfield tried to put a good face on their boasted short cut, but Harwood admitted to me (aside) that they had had 'a perfectly bloody walk'. As usually happens at a soak which is also a reunion I was rested and beginning to get chilly when they were still getting through their groans. (I wonder what you were doing at that moment? Ordering tea in the office, I shouldn't wonder!)

The rest of this not very satisfactory day made some amends. It was *down-hill*: no nonsense about scenery, you understand! It led us to tea at Bridgetown, and thence on through evening sunlight on that best possible kind of road which, keeping more or less level, follows the windings of a green, narrow valley, with a river on one side and a low cliff of rocks on the other. We came at about 7 to Winsford where we found a delightful hotel within sound of the water in a village so small and quiet that you could dawdle about in the street listening to that sound. We had to sleep in the 'Annexe' not the hotel proper, which turned out to be rather an advantage, for the annexe had a sitting room of its own with a 'cosy stove' lit in it and we had it to ourselves.

By a perversity I have often noticed this ideal opportunity for a really good evening's talk glided away unused – Harwood going to bed early, being tired, and Barfield and I falling into a few rather gloomy 'comparisons of notes' on – well, on the whole damn business. I slept excellently.

Monday morning brought a cold wind so we picked out a route to avoid the bleak moorland heights. Nothing could have worked better. The first half of the morning was spent in one of those delightful little lanes with high banks (primroses) and hedges (still retaining last year's beech leaves) on both sides, and plenty of straw underfoot from carts, so that one has almost the sense of being indoors.

The second half was quite different but quite as good. We struck one of the longest and best fieldpaths I have ever met, which carried us effortlessly over miles of soft turf – all in little valleys with barns and sheepcotes and rivers. Perfect Pilgrims Progress country 'Where streams of living water flow My ransomed soul He leadeth.'[202]

Catcombe, our lunch halt, was itself a rather unpleasant village, but

202 From the second verse of the hymn 'The King of love my Shepherd is' by Henry William Baker.

the approach to it was delightfully appropriate; the fieldpath brought you slap up to a building bearing on its wall the legend 'Rest and be Thankful', and then, noticing the stile and looking more closely, you saw that this was your pub and that was its name. It was during lunch here that B. produced his *mot* about Castor and Bollux. Less fortunately, Harwood's 'tiredness' of the previous night was now unmistakably a bad chill of the inwards which hot rum and water failed to shift. From here to Timberscombe along the valley of the Exe the mainroad was most fortunately duplicated by a little third class road on the opposite side of the water, so we accomplished this stage in great ease.

At Timberscombe H. was so poorly that we decided to get Field to come out and meet him by car. Barfield volunteered to leave the cold, glossy, horsehair-sofa'd little room where we were having tea and work the local telephone kiosk. He returned to say he cd. get no answer: but as it was found on cross examination that he had rung up the wrong number, I sallied forth, and succeeded. (Why does one so *loathe* using a call box?) Things began to mend. We were met by Field earlier than we expected, H. got into the car, and Field walked home with us.

The little-road-parallel-with-the-mainroad which we were still following now revealed itself as a road along which Minto and I had cycled in the reverse direction, from Dunster, when we were staying at Old Cleeve in 1920.[203] A few feet of very comfortable vegetation (it turned out to be garlic! but it's good for sitting on) between the road and the river gave us an admirable soak. To crown all, in Dunster itself we found that pubs were opened at 5.30, and stopped for that 'uncovenanted mercy'[204] – the unexpected drink. Mine was a mug of cider. The tramp from Dunster to Minehead was a little boring but it had been a good day, and, but for the absence of H., we had a good evening.

On Monday[205] I travelled with Barfield as far as Reading, lunching with him in the train. It was only as I was going down the High on my bus (at about 2.45) that I saw from the placards what had happened

203 See the letters from Old Cleeve of 2, 4 and 11 April and 14 August 1920 (*CL* I, pp. 477–85, 503–6).

204 The expression Lewis probably came across in Rudyard Kipling's story 'The Uncovenanted Mercies', found in *Limits and Renewals* (1932).

205 He meant Tuesday.

in Scandinavia.[206] I'll give up going away. This is the second time a holiday has played me the scary trick of ending with a public shock.

When I go on to say that we have been maidless all week till yesterday (Friday), that there is a bitterly cold wind, that Maureen and Minto have been v. much at loggerheads – when I ask you to close your eyes and imagine that peculiar sound of a crisis announcer on the wireless heard from the common room, or (worse still) the ghastly music that precedes the news – why, then I very much hope that your present situation is not so uncomfortable as to make you wish *in all respects* that you cd. change places with me.

I am unable to take up your comments on the *Guardian* as I lent my copy to Williams and have not read the articles (Also – it's a dreadful confession – I find that to have an article in a periodical produces a mysterious disinclination to read the rest of that number. Only Limpopo,[207] if he were a writer, could do full justice to the feeling 'Grr-grr – it's like looking at the frame – huh? – instead of the picture – huh?')

I was much amused at the picture your French colonel must have of 'English bourgeois life' if he believes the Brontës to be realistic. The real formula is 'Solitary young woman's half erotic, half melodramatic fantasies of *high* life (see *Peg's Paper*)[208] redeemed by flashes of high poetic, almost mythopoeic, imagination' – in *both* ways as far from realism as anything cd. be.

But I'm not surprised about Kipling. Sir, you must distinguish. The *objects* to wh. Kipling attaches his sentiments are indeed very English, the sentiments themselves are not. Could *statesmen* in the Lakes be a corruption of *steadsmen*?[209]

Alas, Brother, I was anxious your leave should not come while I was away: where has it receded to now? A black world. I used to think the

---

206 In the early hours of Tuesday, 9 April, German troops invaded Denmark. King Christian X, knowing his army was in no condition to resist, ordered an immediate ceasefire. Denmark thus followed Poland, becoming Hitler's second military conquest.

207 Their uncle, William 'Limpopo' Lewis, ended almost everything he said with 'huh?'

208 An English literary periodical which ran from 1919 to 1930.

209 Rudyard Kipling did not write a poem entitled 'Lakes'. Lewis probably had in mind Kipling's 'The Rupaiyat of Omar Kal'vin' in *Departmental Ditties and Other Verses* (1886), stanza 6: 'Let Scribes spit Blood and Sulphur as they please,/Or Statesmen call me foolish – Heed not you.'

prayer in the burial service hypocritical ('That it may please thee shortly to accomplish the number of thine elect')[210] I don't know. If one had Grandfather Hamilton's[211] assurance of salvation, one cd. really be hungry for the end. I like to think there may be a moment in eternity from wh. we shall look back on all this as you and I have often looked back on Wynyard.

By the way, when you say it makes you 'heartsick' you mean belly-sick, don't you? It does me. I've never felt sensations bout the *heart* from *any* emotion. Well, good bye Pigibuddie. Write when you can.

Yours
Jack

TO DOM BEDE GRIFFITHS OSB (W):

[Magdalen College]
April 16th 1940

My dear Dom Bede –

Congratulations (if that is the right word) on becoming a Priest,[212] and thanks for the pleasing woodcut. Yes: Melchisedech is a figure who might have been intended (nay, was intended, since God provides not for an abstraction called Man but for individual souls) for people who were being led to the truth by the peculiar route that you and I know.[213]

I do most thoroughly agree with what you say about Art and Literature. To my mind they are only healthy when they are either (a) Definitely the handmaids of religious, or at least moral, truth – or (b)

---

210 *Book of Common Prayer*, The Order for the Burial of the Dead: 'We give thee hearty thanks, for that it had pleased thee to deliver this our brother out of the miseries of this sinful world; beseeching thee that it may please thee, of thy gracious goodness, shortly to accomplish the number of thine elect, and to hasten thy kingdom; that we, with all those that are departed in the true faith of thy holy Name, may have our perfect consummation and bliss, both in body and soul, in thy eternal and everlasting glory . . .'

211 i.e. the Rev. Thomas Robert Hamilton. See **The Hamilton Family** in the Biographical Appendix to *CL* I.

212 Griffiths was ordained a priest on 9 March 1940.

213 According to Genesis 14:18 Melchisedech was 'King of Salem' and 'priest of the most high God' who offered Abraham bread and wine as he was returning from his defeat of the four kings. The only other mention of him in the Old Testament occurs in Psalm 110:4 where the King addressed is styled 'a priest for ever after the order of Melchisedech'. These passages are used in the Epistle to the Hebrews to prove the superiority of the priesthood of Christ, prefigured by Melchisedech, over that of Aaron and the Levites.

Admittedly aiming at nothing but innocent recreation or entertainment. Dante's alright, and *Pickwick* is alright. But the great *serious irreligious* art – art for art's sake – is all balderdash; and, incidentally, never exists when art is really flourishing. In fact one can say of Art as an author I recently read says of Love (sensual love, I mean) 'It ceases to be a devil when it ceases to be a god'.[214] Isn't that well put? So many things – nay, every real *thing* – is good if only it will be humble and ordinate.

One thing we want to do is to kill the word 'spiritual' in the sense in which it is used by writers like Arnold and Croce. Last term I had to make the following remark to a room full of Christian undergraduates 'A man who is eating or lying with his wife or preparing to go to sleep, in humility, thankfulness, and temperance, is, by Christian standards, in an infinitely *higher* state than one who is listening to Bach or reading Plato in a state of pride' – obvious to you, but I could see it was quite a new light to them.

I don't know what to think about the present state of the world. The sins on the side of the democracies are very great. I suppose they differ from those on the other side by being less deliberately blasphemous, fulfilling less the condition of a *perfectly* mortal sin. Anyway, the question 'Who is in the right' (in a given quarrel) is quite distinct from the question 'Who is righteous?' – for the worse of two disputants may always be in the right on one particular issue. It is therefore *not* self righteous to claim that we are in the right now. But I am chary of doing what my emotions prompt me to do every hour; i.e. identifying the enemy with the forces of evil. Surely one of the things we learn from history is that God never allows a human conflict to become unambiguously one between simple good and simple evil?

The practical problem about charity (in our prayers) is very hard work, isn't it? When you pray for Hitler & Stalin, how do you actually teach yourself to make the prayer real? The two things that help me are (a) A continual grasp of the idea that one is only joining one's feeble little voice to the perpetual intercession of Christ, who died for those very men (b) A recollection, as firm as one can make it, of all one's own cruelty wh. might have blossomed, under different conditions, into something terrible. You and I are not, at bottom, so different from these ghastly creatures.

214 De Rougemont, *Passion and Society*, book VII, ch. 5, p. 321.

I have been reading Lady Julian of Norwich. What do you make of her? A dangerous book, clearly, and I'm glad I didn't read it much earlier. (Have you noticed how God so often sends us books at just the right time?) One thing in her pleased me immensely. *Contemptus mundi* is dangerous and may lead to Manicheeism. Love of the creature is also dangerous. How the good of each is won, and the danger rejected, in her vision of 'all that is made'[215] as a little thing like a hazel nut 'so small I thought it could hardly endure'.[216] Not bad, you see: just very, very small.

I'm enclosing a book in which you might like the last essay. I've been busy this winter on a book called *The Problem of Pain* wh. I was asked to write for a thing called The Christian Challenge Series. I have hopes you may like it.

A woman, an ex-pupil of mine called Mary Neylan, seems in her last letter to be hovering on the brink of conversion to Christianity – a proper subject for your prayers.

Yours
C. S. Lewis

TO MARY NEYLAN (T):

[Magdalen College]
April 18th 1940

Dear Mrs Neylan

(1) On the marriage service. The three 'reasons' for marrying, in modern English are (a) To have children. (b) Because you are very unlikely to succeed in leading a life of total sexual abstinence, and marriage is the only innocent outlet, (c) To be in a partnership.[217] What is there to object to in the order in which they are put?

The modern tradition is that the proper reason for marrying is the state described as 'being in love'. Now I have nothing to say against 'being in love': but the idea that this is or ought to be the exclusive

---

215 Julian of Norwich, *Revelations of Divine Love*, First Revelation, ch. V, p. 10.

216 ibid.

217 Lewis is citing the service for the 'Solemnization of Matrimony' in the *Book of Common Prayer*: 'First, It was ordained for the procreation of children . . . Secondly, It was ordained for a remedy against sin, and to avoid fornication . . . Thirdly, It was ordained for the mutual society, help, and comfort, that the one ought to have of the other.'

reason or that it can ever be by itself an *adequate* basis seems to me simply moonshine.

In the first place, many ages, many cultures, and many individuals don't experience it – and Christianity is for all men, not simply for modern Western Europeans. Secondly, it often unites most unsuitable people. Thirdly, is it not usually transitory? Doesn't the modern emphasis on 'love' lead people either into divorce or into misery, because when that emotion dies down they conclude that their marriage is a 'failure', tho' in fact they have just reached the point at wh. *real* marriage begins. Fourthly, it wd. be undesirable, even if it were possible, for people to be 'in love' all their lives. What a world it wd. be if most of the people we met were perpetually in this trance!

The Prayer Book therefore begins with something universal and solid – the biological aspect. No one is going to deny that the *biological* end of the sexual functions is offspring. And this is, on any sane view, of more importance than the *feelings* of the parents. Your descendants may be alive a million years hence and may number tens of thousands. In this regard marriages are the fountains of *History*. Surely to put the mere emotional aspects first would be sheer sentimentalism. Then the second reason. Forgive me: but it is simply no good trying to explain this to a woman. The *emotional* temptations may be worse for women than for men: but the pressure of mere *appetite* on the male, they simply don't understand. In this second reason, the Prayer Book is saying 'If you can't be chaste (and most of you can't) the alternative is marriage.' This may be brutal sense, but, to a man, it is *sense*, and that's that. The third reason gives the thing that matters far more than 'being in love' and will last and increase, between good people, long after 'love' in the popular sense is only as a memory of childhood – the partnership, the loyalty to 'the firm', the composite creature. (Remember it is not a *cynic* but a devoted husband and inconsolable widower, Dr Johnson, who said that a man who has been happy with one woman cd. have been equally happy with any one of 'tens of thousands' of other women.[218] i.e. the original attraction will turn out in the end to have been almost accidental: it is what is built up on that,

---

218 Boswell, *The Life of Samuel Johnson*, vol. II, 22 March 1776, p. 461: 'Boswell. "Pray, Sir, do you not suppose that there are fifty women in the world, with any one of whom a man may be as happy, as with any one woman in particular." Johnson. "Ay, Sir, fifty thousand." '

or any other, basis wh. may have brought the people together that matters.)

Now the second reason involves the whole Christian view of sex. It is all contained in Christ's saying that two shall be 'one flesh'.[219] He says nothing about two 'who married for love': the mere fact of marriage *at all* – however it came about – sets up the 'one flesh'. There is a terrible comment on this in I *Cor* VI 16 'he that is joined to a harlot is one flesh'.[220] You see? Apparently, if Christianity is true, the mere fact of sexual intercourse sets up between human beings a relation wh. has, so to speak, transcendental repercussions – some *eternal* relation is established whether they like it or not.

This sounds very odd. But is it? After all, if there *is* an eternal world and if our world is its manifestation, then you would expect bits of it to 'stick through' into ours. We are like children pulling the levers of a vast machine of which *most* is concealed. We see a few little wheels that buzz round on *this* side when we start it up – but what glorious or frightful processes we are initiating *in there*, we don't know. That's why it is so important to do what we're told (cf. – what does the Holy Communion imply about the real significance of *eating*?)

From this all the rest flows. (1) The seriousness of sexual sin and the importance of marriage as 'a remedy against sin' (I don't mean, of course, that sins of that sort will not, like others, be forgiven if they are repented, nor that the 'eternal relations' wh. they have set up will not be redeemed. We believe that God will use all repented evil as fuel for fresh good in the end.) (2) The *permanence* of marriage wh. means that the intention of fidelity matters more than 'being in love'. (3) The *Headship* of the Man.

I'm sorry about this – and I feel that my defence of it wd. be more convincing if I were a woman. You see, of course, that if marriage is a permanent relation, intended to produce a kind of new organism ('the one flesh') there must be a Head. It's only so long as you make it a temporary arrangement dependent on 'being in love' and changeable by frequent divorce, that it can be strictly democratic – for, on that view, when they really differ, they part. But if they are not to part, if the thing is like a nation not a club, like an organism not a heap of

---

219 Matthew 19:5.

220 1 Corinthians 6:16.

stones, then, in the long run, one party or other must have the casting vote.

That being so, do you really *want* the Head to be the woman? In a particular instance, no doubt you may. But do you really want a matriarchal world? Do you really like women in authority? When you seek authority yourself, do you naturally seek it in a woman?

Your phrase about the 'slave-wife' is mere rhetoric, because it assumes servile subordination to be the only kind of subordination. Aristotle cd. have taught you better. 'The householder governs his slaves despotically. He governs his wife and children as being both *free* – but he governs the children as a constitutional monarch, and the wife politically'[221] (i.e. as a democratic magistrate governs a democratic citizen).

My own feeling is that the Headship of the husband is necessary to protect the outer world against the family. The female has a strong instinct to fight for its cubs. What do nine women out of ten care about justice to the outer world when the health, or career, or happiness of their own children is at stake? That is why I want a 'foreign policy' of the family, so to speak, to be determined by the man: I expect more mercy from him!

Yet this fierce maternal instinct must be preserved, otherwise the enormous sacrifices involved in motherhood wd. never be borne. The Christian scheme, therefore, does not suppress it but protects us defenceless bachelors from its worst ravages! This, however, is only my own idea.

The Headship doctrine is that of Christianity. I take it to be chiefly about man *as* man and woman *as* woman, and therefore about husbands and wives, since it is only in marriage that they meet *as* epitomes of their sex. Notice that in I Cor XI just after the bit about the man being the Head, St Paul goes on to add the baffling reservation (v. 11) that the sexes 'in the Lord' don't have any separate existence. I have no idea what this means: but I take it it must imply that the existence of a man or woman is not exhausted by the fact of being male or female, but that they exist in many other modes. I mean, you may be a citizen, a musician, a teacher etc as well as a woman, and you needn't transfer to all these personalities everything that is said about you as wife *quâ* wife.

---

221 Aristotle, *Politics*, 1252a.

I think that is the answer to your view that the Headship doctrine wd. prevent women going in for education. St Paul is not a *system* maker, you know. As a Jew, he must, for instance, have believed that a man ought to honour and obey his Mother: but he doesn't stop and put that in when talking about the man being Head in marriage.

As for Martha & Mary, either Christ and St Paul are inconsistent here, or they are not. If they're not, then, whether you can see how or not, St Paul's doctrine can't have the sense you give it. If they *are* inconsistent, then the authority of Christ of course completely overrides that of St Paul. In either event, you needn't bother.

I very strongly agree that it's no use trying to create a 'feeling'. But what feeling do you want to have? Isn't your problem one of thought, not feeling? The question is 'Is Christianity true – or even, is there some truth mixed up in it?' The thing in reading Macdonald is not to try to have the feelings he has, but to notice whether the whole thing does or does not agree with such *perceptions* (I mean, about good & evil etc) as you already have – and, where it doesn't, whether it or you are right.

Term begins on Saturday next. If you and the gudeman cd. come and lunch with me on the following Saturday (27th) it wd. suit admirably. Let me know (address to College).

Thank you for taking my mind off the war for an hour or so!

Yours sincerely
C. S. Lewis

P.S. I don't think the Marriage Service is ascetic, and I think your real objection to it may be that it's not *prudish* enough! The service is *not* a place for celebrating the flesh, but for making a solemn *agreement* in the presence of God and of society – an agreement which involves a good many other things besides the flesh.

Distinguish the Church from the bedroom and don't be silly! Wd. you really think it suitable for erotic excitement to be expressed by the young couple while visiting the family solicitor, while asking their parents' blessing, while bidding good-bye to the old home? If not, then why when asking God's blessing? Do you think a grace before meals should be so written as actually to make the mouth water? If we began holidays with a religious service, wd. you take your bathing suit to Church, and practice a few golf strokes in the choir?

'Sober and godly matrons'[222] may be a stickler, if you haven't read the English School: but *you* ought to know that all the associations you are putting into it are modern and accidental. It *means* 'Married women (matrons) who are religious (godly) and have something better and happier to think about than jazz and lipstick (sober).' But you must know that as well as I do!

TO HIS BROTHER (W):

[The Kilns]
April 21st 1940

My dear W –

Minto has had your letter occasioned by finding a note in a parcel of socks (that wd. be a good title for a minor Wordsworthian poem) and describing the ravages of disease on the Archpigibotian frame. The *corrugations* where the chins used to be must look very ludicrous and disgusting. It reminds me of the sentence in Thomas Nashe of 'the old wife, in these late heats, who wiped all her chins away with one stroke of a napkin'.[223]

This has been a beautiful week. As you reach the top of the grand escalier and come out among the sycamores you are conscious of a change – just a suggestion of *shade*, and you notice the leaves a little further out each day. A little further on, where one turns right over two sleepers onto the mossy bit of path (the best bit of the whole place to my mind) you see chestnut buds all sticky in the trees that grow in the wet hollow and the thorn ahead of you (at the next turn to the left) is almost in full green. Further on, in the sunken stretch between the grand viaduct and las Pelotas, there are several primroses, and yesterday in the lane between the top gates and the Bourdillons I saw that the blackthorns are fully out. This morning, before I was called, I heard the cuckoo: and every night Venus grows more spectacular. It is true *Chaucerian* weather! How impossible not to believe, after so many disappointments, that it *means* what it says.

---

222 In one of the prayers of the Marriage Service the minister prays 'that this woman may be loving and amiable, faithful and obedient to her husband; and in all quietness, sobriety, and peace, be a follower of holy and godly matrons.'

223 *The Unfortunate Traveller, The Works of Thomas Nashe*, ed. Ronald B. McKerrow, rev. F. P. Wilson (Oxford, 1966), vol. 2, p. 229: 'I haue seene an old woman at that season, hauing three chins, wipe them all away one after another, as they melted to water, and left hir selfe nothing of a mouth but an vpper chap.'

I have been reading two interesting books this week. One is European Balladry by Entwhistle,[224] which really gives one the illusion of having travelled over Europe – such enormous differences, but all shading into each other. The Serbian ballads are apparently the most lofty and heroic of all in Europe, and so much alive that the Serbian army in the last war, on crossing the plain of Kosovo wh. is the site of all their stories, did what I thought no one did in real life – fell down and kissed the turf. Opposite – and not v. good news – is the *complete* absence of the heroic from Rumanian balladry which is all nature, and shepherdesses and shepherds' tombs. A pity that it should be a pity, if you see what I mean.

The other is *Beyond Politics* by Christopher Dawson.[225] The main argument is too complex to describe, but what interested me was the clarity with wh. he distinguished between the ideal of 'Freedom' and the ideal of 'Democracy'. He points out that strict Democracy as envisaged by Rousseau and to some extent embodied in the French republic, is the assertion of the 'general will' or the community life against all individual aberrations: the ideal of Freedom, in the English sense, asserts individual conscience, honour and idiosyncrasy against the claims of the community, and its real parents are English Nonconformity and English Aristocracy. He draws the conclusion that modern Democracy in the strict sense *and* modern Dictatorship are the twin children of the Revolution – both asserting the *community*.

It all seems to fit in quite well, doesn't it? That's why there is no exemption for conscientious objectors or even priests in France, while there is in England. Or again, the Whig alliance between great aristocrats and dissenting tradespeople was not quite such a *mariage de convenance* as one used to suppose. It also explains why people like us can feel so keenly about 'freedom' (making the world safe for 'humourists'!) and much less so about Democracy.

On Wednesday I dined in College with Coghill as my guest, later joined by Rice-Oxley, to compare draft papers for Schools. Poor Coghill – his daughter is in Sweden! And would you believe it, he is worried not only about her safety but about her support, for it appears that tho' his wife has remarried, he and his mother are still keeping her and

224 William James Entwhistle, *European Balladry* (1939).
225 Christopher Dawson, *Beyond Politics* (1939).

the child – the second husband being apparently one of those amiable modern gentlemen without job or income.[226] To *pay* for ones own horns is really a bit steep.

I can't tell you how much more remote the war seems in Magdalen than it does at the Kilns: partly, of course, the luxury, the shaded candles, the wine, the saddle of mutton, and the conversations about routine matters: but more, I suspect, because of the really enormous superiority of any male society over any household in respect of phlegm.

On Thursday I dined at the Carlyles.[227] The old man was in great form. He highly praised Churchill's *Marlborough*,[228] which is praise worth having since he is both a great historian and an extreme liberal. He expatiated on Marlborough's first campaign in Belgium, which you doubtless know all about, but wh. is news to me. Is it true that he managed to chivvy every French soldier out of the country without fighting a single battle – by pure 'war of positions'?

He also talked of the talents of Lloyd George[229] – how he had gone up, early in his career, to deal with a committee of railway magnates at Glasgow, who were all asking themselves 'Why do they send this wretched little attorney to talk about things we have studied all our lives and he knows nothing about?' – but before the meeting was over he was correcting them left and right on their own subject. I wonder if this is so? It is a very different picture from Clemenceau's. But perhaps not incompatible: I suppose the advocate's ability to make up a subject

---

226 In 1927 Nevill Coghill married Elspeth Nora Harley and they had one daughter, Carol. Their marriage was dissolved in 1933, after which Mrs Coghill married again.

227 The Rev. Edgar Frederick Carlyle (1876–1964), political philosopher, ecclesiastical historian and social reformer, was ordained in 1888, and became Fellow and Chaplain of University College, Oxford, in 1893. He was required to give up the fellowship when he married in 1895, but he continued to serve the College as a lecturer in Politics and Economics and as chaplain. He was the mainstay of the Christian Social Union. His works include the influential *History of Medieval Political Theory in the West* (6 vols., 1903–36), which he wrote with his brother, Sir Robert Warrand Carlyle. Lewis and Dr Carlyle were fellow members of the Martlets Society, and Lewis was often invited to visit Dr Carlyle and his family at their home in Holywell Street.

228 Winston Churchill, *Marlborough: His Life and Times*, 4 vols. (1933–8). Warnie owned a copy of this book.

229 David Lloyd George (1863–1945), statesman, was elected a Liberal MP in 1890 and was Prime Minister, 1916–22. During his long political career he proved a patient negotiator, especially in settling strikes.

intensively for an emergency and retain it for forty-eight hours, is quite compatible with extreme ignorance of the sort of knowledge required for international politics. In fact that wd. be just the point – he thought that things which had been growing for centuries and which have to be learned by long *steeping* of the mind in history could be 'made up' like a railway dispute.

Term began on Saturday. In the middle of the usual kerfuffle-ish morning (how well you remember those 'first Saturdays') I was pleasantly surprised by a visit from an ex-pupil whom you may remember – Hewitt, once a pacifist, now a cadet: white hatband and all. I dined with him and two of his friends at the Golden Cross. I don't know why I've mentioned this because I now realise that none of the interesting things he said can be retailed or the Censor wd. object to them. You never mentioned whether you got a letter from me enclosing one from Janie McNeil.

And I never told you a curious thing – I have meant to include it in several letters – wh. provides a new instance of the malignity of the Little People. I was going into town one day and had got as far as the gate when I realised that I had odd shoes on, and one of them clean and the other dirty. There was no time to go back. As it was impossible to clean the dirty one, I decided that the only way of making myself look less ridiculous was to *dirty* the clean one. Now wd. you have believed that this is an impossible operation? You can of course get some mud on it – but it remains obviously a clean shoe that has had an accident and won't look in the least like a shoe that you have been for a walk in. One discovers new catches and snags in life every day.

For instance, did you ever think (I only thought yesterday) of the peculiar horror of a summer campaign in Norway? – *No* darkness: 24 hours' war out of 24! What an achievement the transporting our army has been. The papers keep on complaining that we don't advertise enough, that the enemy has us beaten in propaganda: but don't you think that as the war goes on, this reticence of ours is bound to become impressive till in the end our most pessimistic communiqués are thought to hide victories, while the enemy's method must become subject to a law of diminishing returns?

I wish you cd. see the view from the dining room window as it is to day. As Minto remarked, whenever you look away and look back at it, it seems to have got greener in the interval. But I've had a very 'exhausting' walk,

Yours,
Jack

TO HIS BROTHER (W):

[The Kilns]
April 28th 1940

My dear W –

I am very annoyed with Carritt and with the editor of *Theology* (our friend the librarian of St Deiniol's, Hawarden, you will remember).[230] Carritt has written, and they have accepted, an answer by him to an article of mine. As he is not a Christian and his attack is really against the fundamentals – which I thought it safe to assume in a theological magazine – I can't see why they printed it, nor how I am to reply – and the things that first come to my mind wd. hardly be suitable to one's old tutor.[231] It is as if you had contributed (unlikely supposition) an article to a military journal on some technical Q point and found yourself being answered not by a rival Q-ologist but by a Pacifist! One feels something of the same irritation and bewilderment which are produced by a really good P'daitaism.

---

230 i.e. Dr Alec Vidler.

231 S. L. Bethell and E. F. Carritt criticized 'Christianity and Culture' in a two-part article entitled 'Christianity and Culture: Replies to Mr Lewis', *Theology*, XL (May 1940), pp. 356–66. Carritt's contribution is found on pp. 362–6. He was annoyed with Lewis's criticism of Matthew Arnold and the assertion that 'Culture is a storehouse of the best sub-Christian values', but most of all with the suggestion that aesthetics – his speciality – was not of great importance. Carritt concluded: 'I think that by "values of the soul" Mr Lewis really must mean what has also been called "the only unconditionally good thing, the good will" – what I have called conscientiousness. That is to say, I can best, and indeed only, glorify God by doing my duty, which would include, if that is possible, helping others to do theirs. And among my duties may be the production of whatever is good; for, if it is really good, it is good in God's sight. And is not aesthetic experience good? What on earth is the "contradiction in terms to attempt a sinless Literature of sinful man"? What else is the Old Testament? To know the human heart, even to sympathize with all its ecstasies and temptations and weaknesses and agonies and rebellions, may, like "the religious life" itself, have its dangers. It is certainly not self-indulgence. Conduct is not, as Arnold said, three-fourths of life, but the whole. But then, art is part of conduct. Is that the whole of Mr Lewis's quarrel with him?' Lewis's reply to some of Carritt's criticisms is found in 'Peace Proposals for Brother Every and Mr Bethell', *Christian Reflections*, pp. 34–45.

Perhaps this is rather an odd beginning to a letter from home to France in the middle of a war: but I always start simply with what happens to come uppermost in my mind just as I would if you were in the study. I only wish the choice of subject *did* mean the complete calm on my part wh. it suggests.

Every week of *this* war fills me with more astonishment at my total indifference to the last, both at Bookham, and after I was in the army. I remember asking vaguely in the C.C.S.[232] what the news was and being told cheerily by an orderly 'We're still *running*, Sir!', and being quite unaffected by it. I suppose it was partly youth, but partly, too, the mere fact of being in the army. I had no idea before how v. much windier the civilian world is during a war. I don't mean, of course, that a little real danger – one minute of machine-gun fire – would not make this home wind-up seem quite mild by comparison: I mean the sort of fights about the main issue which one might have felt out of the line in France, but never did.

However, I didn't mean to talk war to you, and will stop after asking whether you saw (it's too good to miss, if you didn't) the story of the three Norwegian bus drivers. They had been pressed as drivers of German troops. All three got their full cargo of Bosches on board – started up – stepped on the gas – and drove over a precipice.

I have now had my first week of term. Monday and Tuesday were quiet days, with evenings to myself which I spent in finding out what Thomas Aquinas had to say on the Law of Nature, in re-reading *Rasselas*[233] and in beginning Johnson's *Life of the King of Prussia.*[234] It turns out to be one of his very best performances – extremely balanced, quite devastating on the various iniquities wh. Carlyle praises, as you wd. expect, but also allowing some good qualities. Is it Johnson, or is it fact, when the Queen replies to Frederic, after his occupation of Silesia and his offer of a bribe, that 'she had never known a prince take up arms to compel another to accept money'? What a rascal that man was, and how true to type the Germans keep.

---

232 Casualty Clearing Station.

233 Samuel Johnson, *The History of Rasselas, Prince of Abyssinia* (1759).

234 Samuel Johnson, *Memoirs of Charles Frederick, King of Prussia. With notes, and a continuation to the time of his death. Also a geographical description of his dominions. To which are added, translations of select poems, written by the king of Prussia* (1786).

On Wednesday I dined with Coghill to complete the examiner's meeting wh. R.O.'s dilatoriness prevented us from finishing last Wednesday. Exeter common room was rather empty. The Rector[235] (le grant-bailly et justicier de Sark)[236] was exuberant and foolish, which amused me, but irritated Dawkins to the verge of hysterics. Coghill tells me they are worried about Dawkins who looks like progressing to a nervous breakdown.

I told Coghill the story of the Norwegian bus-drivers and was interested to see that he crossed himself, I suppose in prayer for their souls, and pleased because his faith seems to be a very variable thing, and I had sometimes lately wondered whether he had cut the painter altogether.

The dinner was not so good as we get at Magdalen (where the slight restriction on butcher's meat has produced an increasing use of 'offal' i.e. of all the forms you and I like best). R.O., though asked for dinner, had rung up to put it off, and didn't join us till 9 o'clock, even then with his work insufficiently done. Knowing his ill-health, I shd. feel only pity but for the fact that he has sulked for some five years about never being allowed to examine and moved heaven and earth to get the job. As a result of all this we had a v. gruelling evening's work wh. lasted till midnight: then bed for R.O. and me, but not for Coghill who had been called on half way through the job by one of his ghastly undergraduate friends (a long-haired man in a cloak – sort of blend of Austen and Philips)[237] and had made an appointment with him *for midnight*! Coghill had started teaching at 9 a.m.!

I suppose he must *like* this way of life. The truth is, he is an Irishman.

---

235 Robert Ranulph Marett (1866–1943), philosopher and anthropologist, was Rector of Exeter College, Oxford, 1928–43. He was born in Jersey where his father was Attorney-General and later Bailiff and President of the legislative assembly of the island. He took a first class degree in *Literae Humaniores* from Balliol College, Oxford, in 1888, after which he studied Philosophy at Berlin University. He became a Fellow of Exeter College in 1891 and Tutor in Philosophy in 1893, and was Sub-rector, 1893–8. His publications include *Faith, Hope and Charity in Primitive Religion* (1932) and *Sacraments of Simple Folk* (1933).

236 'the head-bailiff and judge of Sark'.

237 i.e. John Langshaw Austin (see note 114 to the letter to Warnie of 25 February 1940) and Eric George Phillips (1909–85) who read Mathematics at Christ Church, Oxford, taking his BA in 1930. After taking a D.Phil. in Mathematics from Magdalen College in 1932, Phillips was a Fellow of Magdalen, 1933–9, and University Lecturer in Mathematics, 1950–62, becoming Fellow and Tutor in Mathematics at Keble College, 1962–72. He is the author of the *Advanced Mathematics Course* (1964, 1966).

In spite of the overwhelming differences of breeding and intelligence there is something in common between him and the Rev. the Buffoon;[238] each detail of the comfortless kafuffle in wh. they live sounds necessary – even kind – but it is hard not to feel that the aggregate is somehow the expression of their character and wd. not be altered.

Thursday was a good day. I lectured in the morning and had no pupils: instead, a visit from Hone who has got a headmastership in Australia. I suppose under the modern system where everyone is told what is demanded of them, it *is* alright a great athletic man in the early prime availing himself of his reserved occupation and his Australian citizenship just to decamp to the end of the world in the middle of the war – or isn't it? I can't *feel* that it's 'quite the thing'. Query – is this feeling pure anachronism – a relic from the days of the voluntary system? Anyway, no business of mine. I am definitely sorry to see the last of him.

Out at home in the afternoon we had a visit from Sheila Morrison, the nicest of our old lot of evacuees, and her mother – disappointing, because (a) the mother proved to be a terrible bore and (b) one of the things we had looked forward to was Sheila's meeting with Bruce as each had been the other's inseparable playmate. But the stupid creature had either forgotten her or lost interest in her and with desperate animal sincerity took no notice of her at all!

In the evening we had the first weekly Inklings. (By the way, Williams brought back the *Guardian* and I have read the article you mentioned on Karl Barth.[239] Yes, that certainly *might* be what's coming.[240] (But as Mr. Bennett said 'Do not give way to gloomy thoughts, my dear. Let us hope better things. Let us flatter ourselves that I may be the survivor.')[241] Even without being as apocalyptic as Barth one cd. imagine

---

238 Lewis was probably referring to the Rev. Claude Chavasse, another Irishman.

239 'Dr Karl Barth and The War, A Letter to a French Pastor', *The Guardian* (15 March 1940), p. 133.

240 He is referring to the following passage in Barth's letter: 'we as Christians have to remind ourselves that there are such things as "miracles of the antichrist" . . . We do not know whether Hitlerism is not capable of such a miracle – there is much in its development hitherto which tends in this direction . . . Perhaps the nations of Europe may be destined to resist this enemy in vain, and finally to live a life of dishonour under the rule of undisguised Lie, a life comparable to that of men and Christians in Germany to-day.'

241 Jane Austen, *Pride and Prejudice* (1813), ch. 23: 'My dear, do not give way to such gloomy thoughts. Let us hope for better things. Let us flatter ourselves that I may be the survivor.'

the enemy being allowed to win for the ultimate good of Europe – I mean a German revolution following a German victory – their system could hardly last in peace – and the net result a united Europe. Not much fun for us in the meantime! (But I find it hard to believe in any of these grandiose World-Dominion people succeeding, except in my very gloomiest early-morning moments.)

Havard read us an account of a mountain climb he had taken part in – a straight account in plain language, which made our hair stand on end. Tolkien told us, from his boy in Rome, that the students in the English college are simply pestered with Italians wanting to know what the English papers say. (A-propos of them, I heard an addition to the various Gamelin-on-the Italian stories, the other day. 'But, General, what forces have you on the Italian frontier?' – 'Il y a la douane!'[242])

Friday was a beastly day: dullish pupils both morning and afternoon, the news bad, Minto suffering from rheumatism, the new maid not a success, thundery heat, only consolation that, having Nichol Smith to dinner in the evening, I felt justified in standing us a bottle of claret.

He lent me a very interesting book on Swift by one Jackson of T.C.D.,[243] now a rector in Co. Tiperary. It is called *Swift: Dean and Pastor*[244] and makes the v. obvious point that *most* of his life was spent doing his job, not writing, nor visiting Pope. It answers Johnson's taunt about 'turned richman for life' by pointing out that most persons of the period wd. simply have lived at Bath and drawn the decanal stipend. He has ferreted out all the records of Swift's actual reign as Dean of S. Patrick's and I must say he comes out of it very well and was almost up to modern standards in his care for the cathedral, and for the music, wh. is specially to his credit seeing that he did not know one note from another himself. His great charities one knew about before. V. unexpected that he was accused of Popish leanings for bowing to the communion table.[245] On the whole, the book is an important new light.

This week end – or rather this Saturday night – we have had Maureen's ugly little friend Blake staying with us – but glory be, he's already gone. She produced a real good one at lunch to-day. They had

242 'There's the customs house!' Maurice Gamelin (1872–1958) was a French general of the time who was known to have scant regard for the Italian armed forces.

243 i.e. Trinity College, Dublin.

244 Robert Wyse Jackson, *Jonathan Swift, Dean and Pastor* (1939).

245 ibid., p. 98.

been describing some unusual poultry they had seen, and she wound up by asking 'Do they lay eggs?' – in fact Johnson and 'Is a cat oviparous?' the other way round.[246]

It is now nearly tea time: a gray dark day with lots of rain in the air and all the birds singing, and I have the pleasant sensation that comes when you have got into a good perspiration and come in and changed and sat down.

Is the invasion of Norway going to be made the pretext for permanently stopping *your* leave from *France*, and, if so, why? Oh, the absurdity of the whole damn affair. I told you, did I, our little Mr Knight's comment on the war? 'Less than what it costs per day wd. furnish a first class rocket to the moon.' So true is it (in Johnson's words) that 'No man forgets his original trade: the rights of nations, and of kings, sink into questions of grammar, if grammarians discuss them.'[247] So long, Pigibuddie.

Yours
Jack

TO HIS BROTHER (W):

[The Kilns]
May 4th 1940

My dear W –

Thanks for your extremely interesting letter of the 25th. In trying to give any opinion on your physicist one starts ignorant of several relevant facts: e.g. is he a good physicist? Does he ever mention these views among scientists, or are they just such a private whimsy as any

---

246 *Thraliana: The Diary of Mrs Hester Lynch Thrale (Later Mrs. Piozzi) 1776–1809*, ed. Katharine C. Balderston, 2 vols. (1951), vol. I, *Anecdotes of Johnson*, p. 100: 'A young Gentleman whom [Johnson] had never seen called one day at his House and after some introductory civilities informed him that his Father was lately fallen into unexpected Fortune . . . and that he now wished to procure himself some *Learning* . . . Mr Johnson . . . engaged Scott of University College to be his Tutor – Scott however in a short Time found his Pupil so ignorant of common things . . . that he grew weary of explaining to him Things perfectly familiar to every one else, for Example . . . the Tutor observed that some Animals were Oviparous, some Viviparous, expounding the Terms at the same Time – The Cat for example says Scott – Ay Sir She is *oviparous* – no no replies the other – She brings her Young alive you know – does She returns the Pupil – I thought She had laid Eggs.'

247 Johnson, *Lives of the English Poets*, vol. I, Life of Milton, p. 113.

man, being a 'humourist' may loosely and after dinner draw from his own subject? On the other hand, it is important to remember that two admittedly great physicists (Jeans and Eddington)[248] have both arrived at a spiritual view of the universe and that Haldane, though a Left in politics and very 'hard-boiled' inclines in that direction.

Perhaps one might assume that your friend was an extremist instance of a tendency which is definitely present in modern physics: and even that is very well worth considering. (Mind you, you probably got him at an *extremist* moment. You must have noticed yourself that when, being quite away from your own intellectual circle, you make a conversational report on it to a complete outsider, you are inclined to 'let yourself go' and opinions which you wd. express v. tentatively to your colleagues tend to become certainties. e.g. I am sure you have expressed certain military and historical views at the Kilns more absolutely than you would have done at the Staff College or in conversation with professional historians. Of course, this cuts both ways: if this licence encourages some errors it may also give some timid truths courage to appear.)

The thing that really knocked me over was that bit about the number of the plusses and minuses differing with each man but the total always coming out + 1. That is (a) so unlike what anyone could invent or imagine. (b) So v. like what we already know of reality – the sort of 'sell' it's always giving you. (c) So v. like what we must believe as Christians, viz: that souls are quite unequal and also quite equal.

The relapse into gibberish at 12 miles high, on the other hand, did not impress me at all. I am almost sure Haldane says that is just what happens if you put a man in a sealed chamber and exhaust the oxygen – and, if I remember aright, he gives a most amusing account of the progressive deterioration of his own notes under these conditions[249] (Try this on your physicist).

By the way, how wd. one distinguish 'a sentient somebody restricting our discoveries' from a mere insentient obstacle? I mean, all obstacles

248 Sir James Jeans (1877–1946) developed an interest in mathematics, physics and astronomy at Cambridge University, and over time became an authority on specific heats of gases and the mechanism of radiation. Sir Arthur Stanley Eddington (1882–1944), like Jeans, was educated at Cambridge and was for many years Plumian Professor of Astronomy at Cambridge, and an early exponent of relativity.

249 Lewis is referring to the essay on 'Oxygen Want' in Haldane, *Possible Worlds and Other Essays*.

feel at times as if they were animate ('The figures *won't* come right to-day' – 'This is the worst-tempered car I've ever driven'). But I very much hope, for both our sakes, that you'll see more of this man – and for his. You may succeed in turning his attention to Christianity.

Your other question about loving our enemies has been very much in my mind lately, and it must be faced, every time we say the Lord's Prayer. No exemption seems to be allowed – of Johnson's *Rambler* 185 (for Xmas Eve 1751) wh. ends thus: 'Of him that hopes to be forgiven, it is indispensably required that he forgive. On this great duty eternity is suspended: and to him that refuses to practise it, the throne of mercy is inaccessible, and the Saviour of the world has been born in vain.'[250] It sounds impossible. I pray every night for the people I am most tempted to hate or despise (the present list is Stalin, Hitler, Mussolini, Mackenzie, Austen & Opie)* and in the effort to make this real I have had to do a good deal of thinking.

(1) There were three words in Gk. which covered most kinds of love (Eros = sexual love, Storge = family affection, Philia = friendship)[251] but the N.T. word for 'love' or 'charity' is Agapë, wh. has hardly any use in classical Gk – i.e. it is a new word for a new thing. It is obvious that it cannot mean 'an involuntary sentiment'. We all *say* that God is wise, and habitually argue as if He were a fool! How cd. He be commanding the involuntary? Agapë, is best seen, I think, in the words 'love your neighbour as yourself'.[252] i.e. by an act of will, aim at your neighbour's good in the same way as you aim at your own.

Now you don't 'love' yourself because of your own 'lovable qualities'. You may, in moments of vanity, attribute lovable qualities to yourself, but that is not the *cause* of your self-love but one of the *results* of it. At other moments, when you dislike yourself, you still wish for your own happiness. This attitude to ones own self is dictated by nature: towards other selves it has to be acquired.[253]

*N.B. I don't mean that I'm tempted to hate them equally, of course!

---

250 *The Rambler*, no. 185 (24 December 1751), vol. III, p. 210.

251 This anticipates much of what became the subject of Lewis's *The Four Loves* (1960).

252 Matthew 22:39.

253 Lewis devoted several paragraphs to this in his BBC talk on 'Forgiveness', published first in *Christian Behaviour* (1943) and then in *Mere Christianity* (1952; Fount, 1977), book III, ch. 7, p. 96: 'I have not exactly got a feeling of fondness or affection for myself, and I do not even always enjoy my own society. So

I take it, it has nothing in the world to do with trying to pretend that the enemy is 'not so bad after all' or that his sins 'don't matter', or that he is really lovable. Not a bit. It's the old business about 'loving the sinner and hating the sin' wh. becomes alive to me when I realise that this is what I do to myself all the time. In fact I provisionally define Agapë as 'steadily remembering that inside the Gestapo-man there is a thing wh. says I and Me just as you do, which has just the same grounds (neither more nor less) as your "Me" for being distinguished from all its sins however numerous, which, like you, was made by God for eternal happiness – remembering, and always acting for the real interests of that thing as far as you can.'

(2) If one takes seriously your suggestion that they are literally possessed, really it only makes this point of view easier? Suppose your eyes were opened and you cd. see the Gestapo man visibly fiend-ridden – a twisted and stunted human form, covered with blood and filth, with a sort of cross between a mandrill and a giant centipede *fastened* onto it? Surely you, and the human remains, become almost allies against the horror which is tormenting you both, him directly and you through him?

(3) Of course there is a further stage. We are not asked to love the damned. When the fiend's victim has wholly ceased to be human, when his will is no longer merely dominated by but unrecoverably identified with, his rider, charity is no longer commanded. But we are not allowed to assume that this has taken place in any man still alive, and obviously we don't know enough. But I think the *possibility* is a positive help to charity. These 'swine', as you rightly call them, are to be regarded as people in whom the human self (made for happiness, like you) is still alive, and steadily moving towards that final identification with its fiend – but still capable (we must assume) of being rescued. From this point of view I do not find it impossible to desire, and pray, that that rescue may occur. (Remember, you are not asked to wish that, *remaining what they now are*, they shd. be happy: far from it.)[254]

---

apparently "Love your neighbour" does not mean "feel fond of him" or "find him attractive".... Do I think well of myself, think myself a nice chap? Well, I am afraid I sometimes do . . . but that is not why I love myself. In fact it is the other way round: my self-love makes me think myself nice, but thinking myself nice is not why I love myself. So loving my enemies does not apparently mean thinking them nice either.'

254 Lewis had just finished writing *The Problem of Pain* (London: Geoffrey Bles, 1940; HarperCollins Signature Classics, 2002), and he had in mind a passage about the

(4) Of course the parable of the servant who wouldn't forgive his fellow servant[255] comes in. You and I take a high line about Nazi cruelties. You and I, of all people. Think it over.

(5) We are told that God desires the salvation of all men.[256] One is to picture Christ perpetually interceding for these swine; when we pray for them we are merely joining our infantile prayer to His. One can put it almost comically 'I don't fancy that man myself, Sir, but of course, if you make a point of it . . .' Of course His intercession for them is not because of any value they have; but so is His intercession for us. My own tendency to give a free rein to hatred and to regard it as virtuous or natural is much cooled by noticing that hatred comes as often from wind-up as from anything else.

I must give *Sir Nigel*[257] another try if only for the sake of Baddlesmere: but oddly enough it is about the only one of my early favourites to which I have never felt even an inclination to return. In fact I don't like Doyle. Where his short stories deal with themes I like they usually leave me reflecting how much better almost any other writer wd. have done it. (Surely the real Baddlesmere was not a fraudulent promoter but a lunatic inventor? The fact that he was a kidnapper – of Benjamin – hardly adds to the character, for nearly everyone was that.[258]) I dined at Univ. on Monday and had a long and rather annoying talk with Carritt.

We had an unusually good Inklings on Thursday at wh. Charles Williams read us a Whitsun play,[259] a mixture of very good stuff and some deplorable errors in taste.

---

person who rejects God: 'Supposing he *will* not be converted, what destiny in the eternal world can you regard as proper for him? Can you really desire that such a man, *remaining what he is* (and he must be able to do that if he has free will) should be confirmed forever in his present happiness – should continue, for all eternity, to be perfectly convinced that the laugh is on his side?' (ch. 8, pp. 122–3).

255 Matthew 18:23–35.

256 I Timothy 2:3–4: 'For this is good and acceptable in the sight of God our Saviour; Who will have all men to be saved.'

257 Sir Arthur Conan Doyle, *Sir Nigel* (1906).

258 When they wrote the Boxen stories as children, they borrowed the name of a young archer, Hugh Baddlesmere, from Conan Doyle's *Sir Nigel* and gave it to the lunatic inventor and chief enemy of King Benjamin VII of Animal-Land. See *SBJ*, p. 62.

259 Charles Williams, *Terror of Light*, performed May 1940, published in *Collected Plays by Charles Williams*, ed. John Heath-Stubbs (1963).

That morning, being Ascension Day, I had made my communion and had the (for me) v. unusual experience of hearing the Magdalen choir. One is of course sorry that there shd. be so few communicants: but there is something rather gorgeous in hearing a full male choir singing an anthem that would blow the roof off for the benefit of a congregation of six – or rather, to the glory of God: for I am falling into the amusing error told me the other day to illustrate the dangers of extempore prayer, of an American dissenter who congratulated a minister by saying 'Well, Sir, your prayer this morning was the finest ever *addressed to* a Chicago congregation'!

I have a bad cold most of this week wh. is now about at its climax: if you will combine that internal fact with the external one of the first really hot day (colours of flowers and flowering trees looking unnatural, they are so bright and so sudden) you will get a good idea of my experience at the moment – a certain unreality.

I had a visit one night last week from Pirie-Gordon[260] back from leave from Palestine, where (and in Egypt and Turkey) he says everything is 'as good as gold'. The last riot was quelled by the cavalry regiment in wh. Rivière serves[261] – you remember the very tall, raw-boned, poet and sportsman from Norwich who sent us a pheasant. In fact as P.G. said 'I raised the riot and Rivière quelled it.' He asked particularly after you (confirming, by the way, the report that you are known among the young gentlemen as 'the General') and asked to be remembered to you.

I enjoyed your picture of the room and the basin full of yachts

---

260 Christopher Martin Pirie-Gordon of Buthlaw (1911–80) read History at Magdalen College, taking his BA in 1937. He served with the colonial administration of Palestine in 1935, after which he was First Secretary and Consul with the British Legation in Amman, 1946. He entered the Foreign Service in 1951 and was Assistant Political Agent in Kuwait, 1952, and Political Agent in Dubai, 1953. Thereafter he was with the Eastern Department of the Persian Gulf, 1955–8, becoming Chargé d'Affaires for the Yemen, 1958–60. He was appointed Consul in Innsbruck, 1960–3, Consul in Florence and Consul-General in San Marino, 1964–70. Following his retirement in 1970 he lived in Florence.

261 Michael Valentine Briton Rivière (1919–) came up to Magdalen College in 1937 but left to serve with the Sherwood Rangers, 1939–46. He was Chairman of the Centre of East Anglian Studies, East Anglia University, 1970– . His published poems include *The Poetical Works of Michael Rivière* (1956), *Late in the Day* (1982) and *Selected Poems* (1984).

and the 'blue Nelsons' v. much. 'Would it were evening, Hal, and all well!'[262]

Yours
Jack

A few days after this last letter was written Warnie was evacuated with his unit from France. Thereafter he spent several days with Jack, this being the 'leave' that Lewis mentions in his letter to Arthur Greeves of 9 May. After his few days in Oxford, Warnie joined his unit at Wenvoe Camp, Cardiff, Wales.

TO ALEC VIDLER (BOD):

Magdalen College
Oxford
May 8th 1940

Dear Vidler

Is this letter too late to go in?[263] If not, I hope it is clear enough for the printer without typing. Carritt's letter raises a problem. If articles in *Theology* are all to be armed *cap à pie*[264] against criticism from unbelievers, it will both swell the size and alter the character of the magazine.

Yours
C. S. Lewis

TO ARTHUR GREEVES (W):

Magdalen College,
Oxford.
May 9th 1940

My dear Arthur,

It was very nice to hear from you. I also missed our annual meeting last year very much.

---

262 Shakespeare, *Henry IV Part 1*, v, I, 125. See also note 55 to the letter to Dom Bede Griffiths of 8 May 1939.

263 This was Lewis's response to Bethell and Carritt's 'Christianity and Culture: Replies to Mr Lewis'. It was was published as 'Christianity and Culture' in *Theology*, XL (June 1940), pp. 475–7, and is reprinted in *Christian Reflections*, pp. 31–4.

264 'from head to foot'.

At present, tho' part of my income has disappeared for the duration, I have as little to complain of as anyone in England. My job still exists and is in one way even nicer for some of those whom I liked least in college have gone away to work in Govt. departments and one to America.[265] Two of the things that worry most civilians – lack of petrol and the blackout – to me (as, I expect, to you) are no grievance at all, rather the reverse. Indeed the blackout has given me so many beautiful sights of Oxford in moonlight that, for purely selfish reasons, I shouldn't mind if it continued for ever.

Warnie is on leave at the moment: his first since he went out. He is so wholly confident about the war and so different from the people here in that respect that his presence is like a breath of fresh air.

Don't you find it quite extraordinarily different from last time? When you were in Tom's office and I was at Bookham I can't remember that either of us gave a fig for the whole business or even felt the slightest anxiety about the ultimate issue: and certainly, after I was in the army, I never thought about the war in general at all. Is it just the difference between a man in the 20's and a man in the 40's – or am I forgetting what we really did think & feel in those days?

The other Mrs Moore died:[266] I think your aunts will have heard this by now. I'm sorry to hear you have been ill. I got through last winter (a magnificent winter it was – the pond frozen for about 12 weeks on end) without flu'. Minto has a touch of rheumatism, but not too bad.

I'm interested in what you tell me about Marjorie Bowen.[267] (Is that the same one who writes historical romances?) Did you read my tale about Mars 'Out of the Silent Planet': if not, shall I send you a copy? But I can make a v. good guess what your criticism wd. be.

Give my love to your Mother and to both the McNeills. I don't think I shall be able to get over this summer, much as I should like to.

Why doesn't the world end?

Yours
Jack

---

265 i.e. Redvers Opie, who was in the United States at this time.

266 i.e. Mrs Alice Hamilton Moore.

267 Marjorie Bowen (1886–1952) was a prolific writer of historical novels and children's stories.

TO HIS BROTHER (W):

[The Kilns]
May 18th 1940

My dear APB –

If this letter is illegible that will be because I have been swinging a scythe all afternoon and it has left my arms all of a tremble. Wednesday was a vile day. It would never have recovered from the twofold disadvantage of your departure and the Dutch news[268] in any case, but a continual thunder heat and a college meeting just put the cap on it.

I hope you were enjoying the sea air. It is the *length* of such days that is intolerable – as you remarked to me on board the *S.S. Pladda* on that morning before we made the Land's End, having preferred not to breakfast. Tea in the smoking room was a brightish spot because of the perennial fortitude of Onions[269] (by the way, I was very glad to hear from him last night that his son, judging by a recent letter, is not in the show). After dinner I went to an evening's sherry (at least the invitation said it was sherry, but it turned out to be port) with Monteith, my pupil from the Inst.[270]

Some other of the young gentlemen, all but one my pupils, were there. Not a bright lot, and the conversation never got much above the anecdotal level. One anecdote is worth repeating. Cooper is the name of the undergraduate with the drawling, monotonous voice wh. you overheard and commented on.[271] Apparently they persuaded him to

---

268 On 13 May 1940 the German army had begun marching towards Holland. Warned that she might be kidnapped by the Germans, the Dutch queen, Wilhelmina, fled to England. The next day the Germans confronted a stronger Dutch defence than they expected, especially as British troops were landing in support. However, the Germans prevailed and by the evening of 15 May the Dutch had capitulated.

269 Charles Talbut Onions (1873–1965), distinguished lexicographer and grammarian. After taking a BA from the University of Birmingham in 1892 he published *An Advanced English Syntax* (1904). In 1895 James Murray invited him to join the staff of the Oxford Dictionary at Oxford, and Onions remained in Oxford for the rest of his life. He became a Fellow of Magdalen in 1923. Besides his work on the Dictionary, he was a lecturer in English, 1920–7, and Reader in English Philology, 1927–49.

270 i.e. the Royal Belfast Academical Institution.

271 John Phillip Cooper (1920–78) matriculated at Magdalen College in 1938 but left in 1940 to serve in the Army, 1940–5. He returned to Oxford in 1945, and he took a First in History in 1947. He was a Fellow of All Souls College, 1948–50, and a Fellow and Lecturer in History at Trinity College, Oxford, 1952–78. His

act a small part (a gypsy) in the College melodrama. One night he made, and corrected, a small error in his lines. To get the effect you must imagine his speaking as follows in an absolutely level drawl with no change of expression: YONDER-THE-MOON-IS-RISING-OH-BUGGER-SETTING-I MEAN.

This dullish party was the best thing that could have happened to me. I would hardly have been 'in spirits' for intelligent conversation, but the innocent gambolling of these youths and their liking for one another and (apparently) for me had a soothing charm, almost, of animal society.

Thursday was rather better. Williams attended my lecture and we drank a pint together in the buttery after: during which a young man invited me to go to the English Club next Tuesday where an attack on me is being delivered by a man called Bateson.[272] He was a junior contemporary of mine and I remember arguing with him in the presence of Robson Scott (who was under the painful illusion that *salacious* meant *salubrious*, you remember) on the very subject wh. he will deal with on Tuesday. I never remember continuing a conversation after quite such a long hiatus as that comes to – some seventeen years.

I caught a Green Road bus and went home. Minto in pretty poor form, as one wd. expect. My walk was leisurely – to a spot under three oak trees in Pullen's Gap, where one is in deep shadow and the smell of all the hawthorn comes up to one. Milton is quite right about 'vernal delights able to charm all sadness but despair'.[273] A sufficiently prolonged attention to the bees, bluebells, and clouds, does in fact leave you feeling the world to [be] much more tolerable.

After tea had Mr Leyser (pronounced LICE-AIR) a German Jewish

---

publications include (ed. with Joan Thirsk) *Seventeenth-Century Economic Documents* (1972) and (ed.) *Wentworth Papers, 1597–1628* (1973).

272 Frederick Wilse Bateson (1901–78) was educated at Charterhouse and Trinity College, Oxford. He was a Commonwealth Fellow of Harvard University, 1927–9, lecturer in the Workers' Educational Association, 1935–40, and Fellow of English at Corpus Christi College, Oxford, 1946–69. He was the editor of the *Cambridge Bibliography of English Literature* (1930–40) and founder and editor of *Essays in Criticism* (1951–74). His works include *English Comic Drama, 1700–1750* (1929) and *English Poetry and the English Language* (1934).

273 Milton, *Paradise Lost*, IV, 155–6: 'Vernal delight and joy, able to drive/All sadness but despair.'

pupil: naturally in no great spirits, poor devil, as his parents are in Holland.[274] Everyone is talking, by the way, of the new round-up of aliens, and it is being asked (at home) 'What about Welles?'[275] and (in college) 'What about Barbarossa Koeppler?'[276]

I regret the necessity very much. I was talking to Dixon[277] about it at dinner on Thursday, and pointing out how enemy aliens used to live at large in England thro' the old civilised wars. But as we both agreed that was because in those days people were gentlemen first and nationals second, and now 'ideology' has put an end to all that. Continuing on ideologies in general he observed with no passion: 'Yes, and so many of one's younger colleagues: one quite likes them but one sees they ought to be destroyed.'

I went back and sat in our North room looking out on the hawthorn in the grove and waiting for the Inklings to arrive and much regretting that you had passed from the status of a sense-object to that of a mental picture. Humphrey came first, then Williams, then Tolkien. I noticed going into the South Room with them what I never noticed during your leave – the exquisite smell of the wisteria pervading the whole room. Wrenn turned up later and we went round the walks. All asked

---

274 Karl Joseph Leyser (1920–92) was born in Germany and educated at the Hindenburg Gymnasium in Düsseldorf. He matriculated at Magdalen College in 1939, but left to serve with the Black Watch during the Second World War. He took a First in History in 1948. He was Fellow in History at Magdalen College, 1948–84, and Chichele Professor of Medieval History and Fellow of All Souls College, Oxford, 1984–8. His books include *Rule and Conflict in an Early Medieval Society: Ottonian Saxony* (1979) and *Medieval Germany and its Neighbours* (1982).

275 Maureen Moore, who was teaching music at Oxford High School, was an admirer of Egon Joseph Wellesz (1885–1974), a composer and musicologist of international reputation. Wellesz was born in Vienna and was Professor of Music at the University of Vienna, 1929–38. Although a Catholic, he was Jewish, and he fled to Oxford at the beginning of the war. He was a Fellow of Lincoln College, Oxford, 1939–62, and Reader in Byzantine Music, 1948–56.

276 Heinrich Koeppler (1912–) was educated in Berlin and Heidelberg. He matriculated at Magdalen College in 1933, receiving his D.Phil. in 1936. He was a lecturer in History at Oxford, 1938–40, and during the war he served with the Political Intelligence Department of the Foreign Office. He was Warden of Wilton Park, 1946– . His publications include (with Maxwell Garnett) *A Lasting Peace* (1940).

277 Arthur Lee Dixon (1867–1955) was a Fellow of Merton College, 1891–1922, and Fellow of Magdalen and Waynflete Professor of Pure Mathematics, 1922–45. See Lewis's portrait of him in the Magdalen College Appendix to *AMR*.

whether you had been recalled before the end of your leave and were glad you had survived. –

(Continuing on Sunday after church) Bleiben excelled himself to-day in giving out the notice of a service to be held next Sunday in the town-hall. 'Those of you who intend to go are requested to take your own hymn books. The hymns will be *Oh God our help in ages past*, *Lead us heavenly Father*, and *Onward Christian soldiers*, all of which will be found in Hymns Ancient [and] Modern[278] or in the English Hymnal.'[279] (Damn it – now that I've written it down, I see that it's not so absurd as I thought. In fact I think I've been committing a P'daytism)

Blanchette's bans were read out. In spite of this he preached a very good sermon for Trinity Sunday, taking a text from the Athanasian Creed with his usual hardihood. He said some people after reading that Creed were inclined to ask 'Did our Lord really teach all that?' His answer was that you can take in the beauty of a garden by looking at it, but if you want to grow things you need a text book on gardening. The life of Our Lord corresponded to the garden, the creeds to the text book. Not bad for a man who can never get through any exam. Indeed his success in these things (you and I have often remarked on it) makes me doubt whether he can really have gone to pieces as the Griggsian accounts lead me to believe – or, at least, gives good hope that it will be very temporary.

I am as stiff as a poker to day, having fallen yesterday in a most gravity dispelling fashion while emerging from the clerical privy (the one near the lodge) and got such a bruise on my left hip that last night I couldn't easily lie on that side; and also scything yesterday. That was not so much public works proper as *corvée:*[280] the nettles by the hen run and the grass and weeds in the neighbouring plantation. This afternoon I hope to start on the paths again. While not questioning

278 The famous hymnal *Hymns Ancient and Modern*, ed. Henry Williams Baker (1861), was a product of the Oxford Movement. It drew on ancient, medieval and modern sources and contained many of the traditional Office hymns. A completely new edition, *Hymns Ancient and Modern: Revised*, was published in 1950.

279 *The English Hymnal*, published in 1906, was the result of an attempt by a group, mainly of Anglo-Catholic sympathies, to raise the quality of English hymnody. Various supplements have been added over the years to this widely used hymnal.

280 'forced labour'.

our well proved opinion that physical exercise is an unhealthy thing for the body, I am more convinced (as we learned at the time of the Munich crisis) that it is sovran for the mind. After tea yesterday I reached a greater degree of peace of mind than I had known for many a day.

After beginning this letter to you I took the learned Poggio[281] for a walk on Shotover at about 6 o'clock. It was a most beautiful moonlit night and I slept with my door open for the first time. By the bye, I wrote to Limpopo the day you left and found this family duty rather comfortable than irksome. I am wondering very much whether the present shindy has altered your hours, and generally mucked up your job.

Moby[282] treats me with renewed respect since you left – presumably your tip exceeded his expectations. It was a grand time as far as I'm concerned – in quality: marry, the quantity was an impertinence. Your departure has had a lowering effect on everyone's *morale*.

Yours
Jack

TO OWEN BARFIELD (W):

[The Kilns]
June 2nd 1940

My dear Barfield –

Mrs Moore told me yesterday about your loss of your mother.[283] I cannot imagine myself, in similar circumstances, not feeling very strongly *felix opportunitate mortis*,[284] but I daresay, when it comes to the point, that is very far from being the predominant emotion; I have always remembered what you told me of the dream in which you were condemned to death and of the part your mother played in it.

I am very sorry you should have this particular desolation added to the general one in which we all are. It is like the first act of *Prometheus* 'Peace is in the grave, the grave hides all things beautiful and good.'[285]

281 One of Lewis's dogs.

282 'Moby' was possibly a waiter at the Roebuck Restaurant, 8 Market Street, one of Warnie's favourite eating places.

283 Owen's mother, Mrs Elizabeth Barfield, died at her home, Redroofs, Burtons Lane, Chalfont St Giles, on 28 May 1940, aged seventy-nine.

284 Tacitus, *Agricola*, ch. 45, section 3: 'lucky in the timeliness of death'.

285 Percy Bysshe Shelley, *Prometheus Unbound* (1820), I, 638–9.

He was near, however, to his release when he said that, and I accept the omen – that you and I and our friends will soon be past the worst, if not in one way, then in the other. For I am very thankful to say that while my θρεπτική[286] often plays tricks I am ashamed of, I retain my faith, as I have no doubt you do yours.

'All shall be well, and all shall be well, and all manner of thing shall be well' – This is from Lady Julian of Norwich whom I have been reading lately and who seems, in the Fifteenth century, to have rivalled Thomas Aquinas' reconciliation of Aristotle and Christianity by nearly reconciling Christianity with Kant. The real difficulty is, isn't it, to adapt ones steady beliefs about tribulation to this *particular* tribulation; for the particular, when it arrives, always *seems* so peculiarly intolerable. I find it helpful to keep it very particular – to stop thinking about the ruin of the world etc, for no one is going to experience *that*, and to see it as each individual's personal sufferings, which never can be more than those of one man, or more than one man, if he were very unlucky, might have suffered in peacetime. Do you get sudden lucid intervals? islands of profound peace? I do: and though they don't last, I think one brings something away from them.

I wish we could meet more, but I can hardly reckon on any one evening at present. But make no mistake: if you ever feel inclined to doubt whether (to talk in our old style!) language really *is* a P.O.S.,[287] you needn't. All is well still – except ones stomach. And oddly enough, I notice that since things got really bad, everyone I meet is less dismayed. Macdonald observes somewhere that 'the approach of any fate is usually also the preparation for it'.[288] I begin to hope he is right. Even at this present moment I don't feel nearly so bad as I should have done if anyone had prophesied it to me eighteen months ago.

But I am merely doling out what you know as well as I and are better qualified to say to me than I to you. Blessings on you for everything in our common life these twenty years.

Yours
C. S. Lewis

---

286 'ability to heal'.
287 This is an example of the private language used between Lewis and Barfield.
288 George MacDonald, *Wilfred Cumbermede* (1872), ch. 17.

Lewis's reason for writing the following piece 'exonerating' his three Anthropoposophical friends, Owen Barfield, Cecil and Daphne Harwood, is not known. It may have been intended to mark the end of his dispute with Anthroposophy, and as a mark of respect for the three friends. The document was found among the letters addressed to Owen Barfield, and the date of July 1940 is suggested because Cecil Harwood's The Way of a Child *was published in July 1940.*

TO OWEN BARFIELD (W):

Magdalen College,
Oxford.
[?July 1940]

Though I reject (in so far as I understand them) the philosophy and theology of Dr. Rudolph Steiner and the Anthroposophical Movement, I have been intimately acquainted with some who adhere to it for over seventeen years.

One of them is the man of all my acquaintance whose character both moral and intellectual I should put highest, or very nearly so.

Another has written a work on education entitled *The Way of a Child*[289] which seems to me full of good sense.

Another (perhaps the most enthusiastic Anthroposophical of the three)[290] has continued throughout the time of our acquaintance to be an excellent mother of five children. The eldest son, who is now old enough for a judgement to be formed about the matter, appears to me to be an alert, healthy, civil and manly boy who reflects nothing but credit to his up-bringing.

Believing the doctrines of Dr. Steiner to be erroneous (though not more so than those of many philosophers who are more widely influential than he in modern England) and being frequently engaged in controversy with my Anthroposophical friends on this subject, I believe I should have been very quick to notice any evidence that adherence to the system was producing either intellectual or moral deterioration. Of such evidence I have found not a shred. The friends of whom I speak are all highly educated people and I have not found anything to diminish my respect either for their characters or their capacities.

289 A. C. Harwood, *The Way of a Child: An Introduction to the Work of Rudolf Steiner for Children* (London: Anthroposophical Publishing Company, 1940).

290 i.e. Daphne Harwood.

I should perhaps add that the works of Dr. Steiner are extremely difficult reading: unassisted popular opinion on them is likely to be no more reliable than the same opinion on Kant or Whitehead.

TO HIS BROTHER (W):

[The Kilns]
July 12th 1940

My dear W –

Thanks for your letter of the 9th. I was much amused by the account of your journey with the bore and was inclined at first to think you less than charitable in shipping the poor boob off to Paddington. But it occurred to me afterwards that a man with his notions of cosmography wd. have felt no particular surprise or disappointment on reaching it, but would merely ask for the Cardiff train and be put into it, even the length of the total journey wd. provoke no more than 'Humph! I never realised Cardiff was so far *beyond* London.'

I've been up for some days now, still feeling rather weak, and shall be embroiled in examiners' meetings all the week end. Before the illness was over I read your copy of Southey's letters[291] from end to end with great enjoyment: – a bad poet, but a delightful man. I also found things in it that were very consoling; as (a) The daily fear of invasion.[292] (b) The haunting fear of traitors on the home front.[293] (c) The repeated statement that 'even now' we might pull through if only we had a decent government. (d) The settled conviction that 'even if' we defeated Buonaparte we should still have to face revolution at home. God send it's a true omen.

Other impressions were (a) How much *nicer people*, tho' worse writers, the Tory romantics were than the other crew – the Shelleys and L. Hunts and even Keats (b) What a happy life he had on the whole, and yet what a grim business even a happy human life is when you read it rapidly though to the inevitable end.

I've had a letter from Limpopo enclosing an old letter to him from the P'daytabird, wh. is too much of a relic to send to you. Not very good though – an O.T. parody, not in his happiest manner. Indeed I

291 Robert Southey, *Letters. A Selection*, ed., with introduction and notes, by Maurice H. Fitzgerald (Oxford: Oxford University Press, World's Classics, 1912).

292 ibid., letter to Grosvenor C. Bedford, 11 September 1816, p. 267.

293 ibid.

don't know any humourist whose *written* productions do him so little justice.

I developed during my flu' a habit of reading the morning and evening psalms each day:[294] capital war time reading they make. The odd thing is that when I turn to Moffatt[295] for the explanation of something unintelligible I find his version more poetical than the Prayer Book.

Thanks for cutting from the *Guardian* wh. I heartily agree with.

Yours
C. S. Lewis

TO DOM BEDE GRIFFITHS OSB (W):

[Magdalen College]
July 16th 1940

Dear Dom Bede –

A lot of work and an illness have kept me from answering your letter, but I have been intending ever since I got it to let you know that I think your criticisms on my Aristotelian idea of leisure are largely right. I wouldn't write that essay now.[296] In fact I have recently come to the conclusion that a besetting sin of mine all my life has been one which I never suspected – laziness – and that a good deal of the high sounding doctrine of leisure is only a defence of *that*.

The Greek error was a punishment for their sin in owning slaves and their consequent contempt for labour. There was a good element in it – the recognition, badly needed by modern commercialism, that the economic activities are not the *end* of man: beyond that, they were probably wrong. If I still wanted to defend my old view I shd. ask you

294 The *Book of Common Prayer* contains Miles Coverdale's translation of the Psalms divided into thirty days for use in morning prayer and evening prayer.

295 James Moffatt, *Old Testament*, 1924; *Complete Bible*, revised, 1935.

296 Griffiths had probably criticized the essay 'Our English Syllabus' in *Rehabilitations and Other Essays*, in which Lewis stated: 'The purpose of education has been described by Milton as that of fitting a man "to perform justly, skilfully, and magnanimously all the offices both private and public, of peace and war".... Aristotle would substantially agree with this, but would add the conception that it should also be a preparation for leisure, which according to him is the end of all human activity ... Human life means to me the life of beings for whom the leisured activities of thought, art, literature, conversation are the end, and the preservation and propagation of life merely the means' (pp. 81–3).

why *toil* appears in Genesis not as one of the things God originally created and pronounced 'very good',[297] but as a punishment for sin, like death.[298] I suppose one wd. point out in reply that Adam was a gardener before he was a sinner, and that we must distinguish two degrees and kinds of work – the one wholly good and necessary to the animal side of the *animal rationale*, the other a punitive deterioration of the former due to the Fall.

My enjoyment of the Psalms has been greatly increased lately. The point has been made before, but let me make it again: what an admirable thing it is in the Divine economy that the sacred literature of the world shd. have been entrusted to a people whose poetry, depending largely on parallelism, shd. remain poetry in any language you translate it into.

Well: we are on the very brink of the abyss now. Perhaps we shan't be meeting again in this world. In case we don't, good bye and God bless you.*

Yours
C. S. Lewis

* Now that it's written down I realise with shame that there was a sort of melodramatic impulse behind these words – shall we ever be cured of being play-actors? But mind you, the modern fear of play acting, when allowed to inhibit every expression of piety or affection, may become worse than the disease it intended to cure.

TO HIS BROTHER (W):

Magdalen College
Oxford
July 19th [1940]

My dear APB –

I found only *one* policy, dated from June 29th 1939 to June 28th 1940. I presume this is what you meant by the current one, and have sent it to Matthew 6 St. Aldate's.

297 Genesis 1:31: 'And God saw every thing that he had made, and behold, it was very good.'

298 ibid., 3:17: 'Cursed is the ground for thy sake'; 3:19: 'In the sweat of thy face shalt thou eat bread' and 'unto dust shalt thou return.'

Is there no bookseller in Cardiff to save you from Miss Mannin?[299]

Yours

Jack

TO HIS BROTHER (W):

[The Kilns]

July 20th 1940

My dear W –

You would never guess the present I have received by this afternoon's post: one of a privately printed edition of Revolution Thompson's autobiography in verse, in fact his *Prelude*.[300] I see already that it is to be largely an account (rather complacent) of his passage from 'Victorian' Christianity to Edwardian agnosticism: but the couplets are really very neat and I think there is something delightfully unexpected about his spending his retirement in such a way. He disclaims poetry but is really quite poetical: in fact, as I shall say to him in acknowledging it, 'poetry' with the Eliots and Audens has become such a horror that the real thing now mainly survives in verse not intended to be fully serious – e.g. there is more real poetry in *Punch* now than in the high brow periodicals.[301]

Last week end I had two visitors from Cardiff, both from the university. One was D. G. James, author of a book I admired and wrote to him about[302] – I had the usual irrational shock at finding a reputable printed author not (as one always pictures them) older than myself, but unmistakably younger. The other was Llewellyn, their professor, our colleague in the English exam.[303] The whole week-end was taken up with examiners' meetings, involving many meals at the Golden Cross and pints in the courtyard, often joined by Dyson who is up for his

299 Ethel Mannin (1900–84), the author of numerous novels and other books, was prominent among the London bohemians of the 1920s. She was a passionate supporter of free love, feminism and birth control.

300 James Matthew Thompson, *My Apologia/By J.M.T.* (Oxford: The Alden Press, for private circulation only, 1940). See note 322 to the letter to Thompson of 25 July 1940.

301 Beginning in 1946 Lewis published a number of poems in *Punch* under the pseudonym 'Nat Whilk' or 'N.W.'

302 David Gwilym James (1905–68), *Scepticism and Poetry: An Essay on the Poetic Imagination* (1937).

303 Evan Clifford Llewellyn (1898–1989) was born in Llantrisant, Glamorganshire. After taking a BA from University College, Cardiff, he went up to Jesus College,

usual summer bout of School Certificate. All very pleasant, but it left me rather knocked up, as I am still sweating at nights and merely convalescent. Llewellyn told me about the destruction of Wenvoe pub: that must be a sore inconvenience to many an honest fellow.

Dyson is in very poor form these days. On the whole I should say that Fox and he are the two among my acquaintance who are bearing up least well. Dyson I should have expected it of, for he's obviously all on wires at any time, but I'm surprised at Fox. The truth is he was *too* tranquil before, with a tranquillity born of inexperience: the shock has reached him late and he is still absorbing it. No doubt, when that process is complete, he'll be among the best.

Humphrey came up to see me last night (not in his medical capacity) and we listened to Hitler's speech together.[304] I don't know if I'm weaker than other people: but it is a positive revelation to me how *while the speech lasts* it is impossible not to waver just a little.[305] I should be useless as a schoolmaster or a policeman. Statements which I *know* to be untrue all but convince me, at any rate for the moment, if only the man says them unflinchingly. The same weakness is why I am a slow examiner: if a candidate with a bold, mature handwriting attributed *Paradise Lost* to Wordsworth, I shd. feel a tendency to go and look it up for fear he might be right after all.

I should have resumed my L.D.V. duties[306] next Tuesday but as I am

---

Oxford, as a senior affiliated student in 1922. He took a first in English in 1924, taking his BA in 1925, his MA in 1928 and a B.Litt. in March 1931. He subsequently became Assistant Professor of English at University College of South Wales, Cardiff. By the time Lewis knew him he had become a Professor of English at University College. He is the author of *The Influence of Low Dutch on the English Vocabulary* (1936).

304 During Hitler's speech from the Reichstag in Berlin at 6 p.m. the BBC gave a running translation so that it was possible to hear both the original utterance and an English rendering.

305 In his speech, published in *The Times* (20 July 1940), p. 4, Hitler made a 'final appeal to common sense', which concluded: 'It never has been my intention to wage war, but rather to build up a State with a new social order and the finest possible standard of culture. Every year that this war drags on is keeping me away from this work, and the causes of this are nothing but ridiculous nonentities . . . Mr Churchill ought, perhaps, for once to believe me, when I prophesy that a great empire will be destroyed – an empire which it was never my intention to destroy or even to harm . . .'

306 On 14 May 1940 the Secretary of State for War, Anthony Eden, broadcast an appeal to all men between the ages of seventeen and sixty-five to enrol in an organization to be known as the Local Defense Volunteers. Their main purpose

still incapable of keeping on my feet for more than half an hour I have got it postponed till Tuesday week. I shall be in the same unit as the Wounded Buffalo who is dissatisfied with our commander and told me a much funnier story than he knew. 'Of course when I saw the way things were going I offered to go down to —— and straighten it out but he said I was to go back to my platoon. I tried to point out so-and-so and so-and-so to him but he merely replied "Well I order you back to your platoon."' Shades of Tassel[307] and the brass-hat: or of Boswell and the rope.[308] Provided always that we don't meet any Germans I anticipate some considerable enjoyment from this brotherhood in arms. –

I resume at coffee-time on Sunday morning.[309] I have been to Church for the first time for many weeks owing to the illness, and considered myself invalid enough to make a mid-day communion. I am pleased to find (though one must not mistake the effects of habit for those of grace) that if this duty has to be omitted for several weeks I do now feel the lack of it – if only in a very low way as one feels uncomfortable if one has postponed cutting ones nails or visiting the barber too long. Blanchette preached, not very profitably.

Before the service was over – one cd. wish these things came more seasonably – I was struck by an idea for a book wh. I think might be both useful and entertaining. It wd. be called *As one Devil to Another* and would consist of letters from an elderly retired devil to a young devil who has just started work on his first 'patient'.[310] The idea wd. be

---

was to deal with the threat of German parachutists, and within a month the new force numbered nearly a million and a half. Lewis joined the LDV (which was shortly afterwards renamed the Home Guard) in the summer of 1940. The organization, which was very effective during the war, received its 'stand down' on 3 December 1944.

307 Douglas Spencer Montague Tassell (1872–1956), a teacher at Malvern College, was in charge of the Malvern contingent of the Officers' Training Corps during the First World War. See note 18 to the letter to Albert Lewis of 28 September 1913 (*CL* I, p. 30).

308 Boswell, *The Life of Samuel Johnson*, vol. V, *The Tour to the Hebrides*, 3 October 1773, p. 282. While Boswell and Dr Johnson were sailing for Mull, a storm broke out which caused Boswell such fright that the captain gave him a rope which was fixed to the mast. 'Thus,' said Boswell, 'did I stand firm to my post, while the wind and rain beat upon me, always expecting a call to pull my rope.'

309 21 July.

310 These ideas formed the conception of *The Screwtape Letters*, which Lewis wrote over the next few months. The work was published in thirty-one instalments in *The Guardian* between May and November 1941, and as a book in 1942.

to give all the psychology of temptation from the other point of view. e.g. 'About undermining his faith in prayer, I don't think you need have any difficulty with his intellect, provided you never say the wrong thing at the wrong moment. After all, the Enemy will either answer his prayers or not. If he does *not*, then that's simple – it shows prayers are no good. If He *does* – I've always found that, oddly enough, this can be just as easily utilised. It needs only a word from you to make him believe that the very fact of feeling more patient after he's prayed for patience will be taken as a proof that prayer is a kind of self hypnosis. Or if it is answered by some external event, then since that event will have causes which you can point to, he can be persuaded that it would have happened anyway. You see the idea? Prayer can always be discredited either because it works or because it doesn't.'[311]

Or again 'In attacking faith, I should be chary of argument. Arguments only provoke answers. What you want to work away at is the mere unreasoning *feeling* that "that sort of thing can't really be true".'[312]

I've nearly finished Thompy's poem. Did you know (what I learn from it) that the last Louis kept a hunting diary, and, having killed nothing, wrote the single word *Rien* as his sole entry on the day when the Bastille was taken?[313] And close to this is a reference to his own diaries kept at school – all cricket scores etc – and their contrast with what he remembers of his actual feelings at the time, with the comment 'So from its hard outside you'd never tell/How the soft creature shivered in its shell.'[314] Another good couplet gives advice to the historian 'Let him frequent the What and How, not pry/Into the undiscoverable

---

311 These ideas on prayer found their way into Letter 27 of *The Screwtape Letters* (1942; Fount, 1998), p. 106: 'Don't forget to use the "heads I win, tails you lose" argument. If the thing he prays for doesn't happen, then that is one more proof that petitionary prayers don't work; if it does happen, he will, of course, be able to see some of the physical causes which led up to it, and "therefore it would have happened anyway", and thus a granted prayer becomes just as good a proof as a denied one that prayers are ineffective.'

312 This idea is expanded in *The Screwtape Letters*, Letter 1, p. 2: 'By the very act of arguing, you awake the patient's reason; and once it is awake, who can foresee the result? Even if a particular train of thought can be twisted so as to end in our favour, you will find that you have been strengthening in your patient the fatal habit of attending to universal issues and withdrawing his attention from the stream of immediate sense experiences.'

313 Thompson, *My Apologia*, p. 23.

314 ibid.

Why'[315] – or this delightful ending to his portrait of Brightman 'The only subject that he felt some shame on/Was that in early life he'd been a layman'[316] – an almost Elian whimsicality.[317] One more, of the change that Nuffield has made in Oxford – 'neither Board, Commission, nor Report/Has altered Oxford's *acta* and *agenda*/So much as one successful cycle-mender.'[318]

If you have seen today's Observer you will have read an article by McCarthy giving just the view that you have always taken of Carlyle and saying that if he were alive today he would be a Fifth Columnist.[319]

We have had plenty of good wind and driving rain which is a great relief to me – and, I trust, very unpleasant weather for being in the channel in a flat-bottomed boat loaded with tanks.

Yours
SPB

TO JAMES MATTHEW THOMPSON (W):[320]

The Kilns,
Headington Quarry,
Oxford.
July 25th 1940

My dear Tompy,

Thank you very much indeed for the *Apologia*. I read it at once and my brother, who happens to be here on leave, has just finished it this morning: both of us with great enjoyment.

---

315 ibid., p. 105.

316 ibid., p. 70.

317 That is, sharing the tone of Charles Lamb's *Essays of Elia*.

318 Thompson, *My Apologia*, p. 73.

319 He is referring to Desmond McCarthy's review of Sir Herbert Grierson's *Essays and Addresses* (1940) in *The Sunday Times* (21 July 1940), p. 4. McCarthy said of Grierson's essay on 'Carlyle and Hitler': 'As far as Carlyle's own ethics are concerned, I cannot see a pin to choose between them and those of Nazism. Sir Herbert, partly, I surmise, from a sense of personal debt to Carlyle, and partly because Carlyle's assault on *laissez-faire* economics was so thoroughly justified, is reluctant to admit that if Carlyle were alive to-day he would be, if he were consistent, a most formidable "fifth-columnist".'

320 James Matthew Thompson (1878–1956) was educated at the Dragon School in Oxford, and at Christ Church, Oxford, where he took a first class degree in *Literae Humaniores* in 1901. He was ordained in the Church of England in 1904, and the same year he was appointed Fellow of Modern History in Magdalen College. He remained there as a Fellow until his retirement in 1935. Thompson

The modest pretence of merely comic verse, kept up by the Hudibrastic rhymes, does not conceal the fact that there is plenty of good serious poetry in it – poetry of what, with you and Fox, we may begin to call the Magdalen School. I would instance specially the contrast between schoolboy diaries and schoolboy reality on p. 25, the most of p. 27, the bit beginning 'The Rectory child' on p. 50, and many more. Still, the assumption of 'light verse' is almost necessary now that the Eliots and Audens have made such a podder of 'poetry' and the Muses perform their original function of solacing wretched mortals hardly anywhere except in *Punch.* (The moderns have confused them with the Furies)

Elsewhere I admired a great many pungent 'good things', sometimes almost as neat as Pope, such as 'Let him frequent . . . undiscoverable Why' or 'His taste in facts is like his taste in rock' – and the admirably whimsical couplet on Brightman's one subject of shame. My great regret is that you excluded the living and so were prevented from giving us a portrait of Benecke. Perhaps you have one – in MS.?[321]

The mental journey described is almost the opposite of my own: which gives me great hope that since I have now reached the stage of being

A moralist and preacher, prig and spike[322]

I may end up in something like the late Victorian childhood which you describe as your start – exciting tons of envy and not an ounce of ridicule from one reader!

Well, very many thanks. It came just when I needed a pick-me-up.

Yours
C. S. Lewis

was also a university lecturer in French History, 1931–8, and editor of *The Oxford Magazine*, 1945–7. His publications include *An Annotated Psalter* (1907), *Jesus According to St Mark* (1909), *Through Facts to Faith* (1912), *Leaders of the French Revolution* (1929), *Robespierre* (1935) and *Napoleon Bonaparte: His Rise and Fall* (1951).

321 Thompson included in his *Collected Verse 1939–1946* (1947) a poem in honour of Benecke entitled 'The Senior Fellow (P.V.M.B., 1891–1946)'.

322 Thompson, *My Apologia*, p. 74.

TO HIS BROTHER (W):

[The Kilns]
Aug 3rd 1940

My dear W. –

I am alone in the house on Saturday afternoon, Maureen having dragged Minto off most unwillingly to help her to buy clothes this morning and lunch in town. I took the opportunity of having my own lunch in the dining room and proved it to be quite untrue that 'the wasps are really just as bad in-doors'. And oh the relief of the table's broad acreage and solidity, and a comfortable chair: and, paradoxically enough, the sense of spaciousness.

Bruce is shut up in Minto's room but has at last stopped expressing his feelings out loud. Talking of Bruce, I met the bulldog again yesterday on my after tea walk. It was up at the East corner of the top plateau – near the little holly-tree and the grave of the lamented Baron Papworth – and his owners were on their own side of the hedge but he had come through on individual reconnaissance. I at once slipped the crook of my stick through Poggio's collar and shouted to them to call the bulldog off. He didn't answer them very quickly, but to my great relief did not fly at Poggio but contented himself with approaching to within a few feet. His expression was ambiguous, possibly even friendly. But it is going to be a great nuisance. One can't write a letter telling them sharply to keep their dog their side of the hedge, for the excellent reason that we are quite unable to keep Bruce on our side.

Leonard has departed, after excelling himself by contributing to a conversation on lip-stick, in wh. someone had asked how women can endure the discomfort of perpetually greasy lips, the amazing statement 'Oh I don't know. I always *vaseline* my own lips twice a day.' (He had succeeded that morning in saluting Minto despite her efforts to the contrary).

The pond has cleared up in the recent gentle but steady wind and I have bathed twice since you left.

I had had a letter from the Professor[323] in answer to my report on [Yang][324] in which he says 'I must confess I found him almost impossible

323 i.e. Professor Evan Clifford Llewellyn, Lewis's fellow examiner in the English school.

324 The name here is impossible to be sure about. However, it seems likely that the student whose examination papers Lewis and Professor Llewellyn found difficult

to read. I could not make out what precise point he was making or what he conceived himself exactly to have said.' This is a great relief for in reading, under compulsion, what seems to be tripe, I am always haunted by the feeling 'It can't really be so bad as it looks.'

That's about all my news. It is *very* warm and I am struggling with somnolence. You, at the moment, have probably abandoned the struggle. The young couple[325] are most deeply impressed with your present.

Yours
Jack

TO HIS BROTHER (W):

[The Kilns]
Aug 11th [1940]

My dear W –

Thanks for your letter. I am very glad indeed to hear that your little affair is 'in train'. I dealt with the news as you advise – partly in order to prevent myself from building false hopes on it, for whatever one says one cannot help being a little infected by an assumption on the part of those one lives with.

What you say about Jeans surprises me. In the book I have (*This Mysterious Universe*)[326] he certainly holds that there is a mind behind the universe. That is at least Theism, though not yet Christianity. A propos of the 'smallness of the Earth' argument, was it the night you were with us that Tolkien said that the Earth might owe its importance in the eyes of God solely to the principle of the one lost sheep as against

to read and understand, was the Chinese student, Hsien-yi Yang (1917–). Yang was born in China on 12 January 1917, and after attending the Anglo-Chinese College in Tsientsin, he became a student at Merton College, Oxford. After taking a Third in Classical Moderations in 1938, he went on to read English, taking a fourth class degree in 1940. While at Oxford he met Gladys Tayler (1919–99) who was born in Beijing of English missionaries in China. Gladys read Chinese at Somerville College, Oxford, and after she and Hsien-yi married they returned to China in 1941. Over the years they translated Chinese classics into English, continuing to work despite China's Cultural Revolution during which they were imprisoned. Some of their many translations include Moruo Guo, *Chu-Yuan: A Play in Five Acts* (1953) and Tsao Hsueth-Chin and Kao Ngo, *A Dream of Red Mansions* (1986).

325 i.e. Maureen Moore and Leonard Blake.

326 Sir James Jeans, *The Mysterious Universe* (1930).

the ninety nine. ('A beautiful application. Pray, Sir, have you ever thought of it' as Boswell said of the fair Quakeress's remark about St. John).[327]

I agree with you that an alliance between Bruce and the bulldog would be the best thing and would gladly act as a mediator. The trouble is that dogs are not much more reliable than dictators when it comes to treaty obligations.

Talking of dictators, Bleiben preached on forgiving our enemies this morning, which I admired him for doing. He made the right points but, in my opinion, muffed his argument a bit. And he omitted to make clear –which I think the laity need very much to have clarified – the point you and I discussed that 'Love' in the N.T. does not mean primarily, if at all, a state of emotion.

Maureen accompanied me to Church, as a result of which we got caught by the Meyers. The daughter said she wanted to congratulate Maureen by word of mouth 'to save her answering one more letter'. I said with a grin that that was very thoughtful of her and showed great imagination, receiving the paralysing reply 'Oh I don't think I've often been lacking in *that*.'

I have commenced my L.D.V. Duties with the 1.30 a.m. patrol on what they call Saturday morning and mortals call Friday night. As it seemed no use going to bed to be raked out at 12.45 I asked Dyson and Humphrey to dine and the others to join us afterwards so as to make a 'wake' of it in the original sense.

On getting into the smoking room I got the unexpected and splendid news that Onions has had a card from the missing boy who is unwounded and a prisoner. Dinner, as a dinner, proved disappointing: College has gone down to three courses and made Friday a meatless day. One had enough – but the idea of Magdalen, of all places, doing that is the most genuinely alarming piece of war news I have heard since the surrender of France. Let us hope it is one of those 'unnecessary economies' wh. Tubby Turner[328] so bitterly remembered from the Benecke regime last time.

---

327 Boswell, *The Life of Samuel Johnson*, vol. III, 15 April 1778, pp. 289–90.

328 Sir Eric Gardner Turner (1911–83) came up to Magdalen College in 1930, taking a First in Classical Moderations in 1932 and a First in *Literae Humaniores* in 1934. He was a lecturer in Classics at Aberdeen University, 1938–48, Reader in Papyrology at the University of London, 1948–50, and Professor of Papyrology at

By the way it appears that those stalled rabbits we saw in the grove are for the table – the last thing I would have expected from their small size and decorative appearance.

We had a very good Inklings breaking up about ten to one, when the others went home and I set out for my rendez-vous at Lake St. – eating my sandwiches on the way, as I didn't feel I cd. provide sandwiches for the whole party and hadn't the face to eat my own in their presence.

I was with two men much younger than myself, one a bluecoat and the other, I think, a burley – both very nice and intelligent and neither too talkative nor too silent. One is allowed to smoke and I was pleased to find that our tour of duty included a quite prolonged soak on the veranda of a college pavilion – a pleasant spot, looking out over broad playing fields in a mild but windy night of sufficient starlight and some light clouds – with the occasional interest of a train trundling past. Unfortunately our watch was not so well arranged as Dogberry's ('All sit in the church porch till two, and then every man to bed');[329] still, the three hours passed surprisingly quickly and if it hadn't been for the bother of lugging a rifle about all the time I should have said that pleasure distinctly predominated. I had quite forgotten the weight of a 'tripe'.[330] We broke off at 4.30 and after a really beautiful walk back through an empty and twilight Oxford I was in bed by 5.

I had started a Tolstoi novel wh. one never hears of called *Resurrection*[331] wh. I think is going to be at least as good (tho' not so long) as *War and Peace*.[332] Don't you think the following really excellent. The hero is surprised to find that an old flame of his who has since become a prostitute is not in the least ashamed of her profession. The author continues 'People who are put in a condition, form such a view of life in general that their position appears to them good and respectable. In order to support such a view, they instinctively cling to that circle in which it is accepted. Máslova had formed such a conception. It consisted

University College, London, 1950–78. 'Tubby' Turner is mentioned in Thompson, *Apologia*, p. 70.

329 William Shakespeare, *Much Ado About Nothing* (1600), III, 3, 94: 'Let us go sit here upon the church-bench till two.'

330 i.e. a rifle.

331 Leo Tolstoy, *Resurrection* (1899).

332 Leo Tolstoy, *War and Peace* (1863–9).

in the view that the chief good of all men without exception lay in sexual intercourse. For ten years she had seen that all men needed her: she neither saw nor noticed those men who did not. She valued this conception of life more than anything in the world, because if she changed it she wd. lose the importance it gave her.'[333]

Needless to say, Tolstoi goes on to point out that the trait is not peculiar to prostitutes. But doesn't it throw a flood of light on the conversation of nearly everyone? I never understood before the *passion* with wh. a man like Weldon maintains universal selfishness or a fox hunter defends hunting. Even your foot-drill fan is now explicable. I seem to get more passages of this sort of penetration in Tolstoi than in any other author – certainly any other novelist.

If you buy next week's *Time and Tide* you will see an article by me in it.[334]

The pond continues clean but it has really been too chilly for bathing the last two days – great winds. That new punt must be leaking badly: I have to bale whenever I bathe.

Yours
Jack

TO HIS BROTHER (W):

[The Kilns]
Aug 17th/40.

My dear W. –

I actually have a uniform now and say 'as I look in the glass, it's one to a million that any civilian will look such an absolute ass.' I suppose you had a batman to put it all together for you and explain its intricacies. I had great difficulty in finding out the meaning of all the gadgets. But now that I come to think of it your complaint that the blouse slips up shows that you haven't yet discovered what the two port and starboard buttons on the inside of the trousers are for.

This has been a cheery week. On Monday I had a whole day visit from Barfield, looking, as Minto and Maureen said, extremely well – the dog might be ten years my junior to judge by his face. He is

333 Tolstoy, *Resurrection*, book I, ch. 37.
334 'Notes on the Way', *Time and Tide*, XXI (17 August 1940), p. 841. Reprinted as 'The Necessity of Chivalry' in *Present Concerns* (1991) and *EC*.

nevertheless in rather a bad way as his partner in the office is of an age to be called up. We thought, though we didn't tell him, that his unusually healthy appearance was due to the fact that he is living with his sisters most of the week and not in his own ménage.

I have also got in touch with some of my old awarding friends who are up doing certificate work in St. Catherine's. While drinking beer with them in the Checkers, High St. – do you know it? down one of the little alleys on the South side of the High and a v. pleasant pub – I saw there a very primitive but good pun wh. was new to me. 'Careless Talk cost thousands of lives in the last War. N.B. Don't talk in your sleep; there may be a Jerry under your bed.'

Stanley Bennett from Emmanuel[335] was one of them and I had him to dine in College on Wed. night. Apparently the rumour wh. we have all believed for some months about Cambridge 'liquidating itself' is wholly false – in fact he described it as a specimen of 'Oxford's wishful thinking'!

Colin Hardie is to be married – to a papist – by which there hangs a tale showing that the old Roman fashion is not extinct. He and the girl went through the promises wh. have to be made when a Papist marries an outsider. The last one was in Latin, tho' all the others were in English.

'What's this?' said Hardie, tho' he had already seen that it contained a promise on the Papist side to do all in his or her power to convert the other. 'Oh *that*,' said the Father Condlin, 'That's a mere formality,' then – I suppose, noting Hardie's expression – 'Er – you don't read Latin, do you?'

The bride at this point remarked that they both read Latin. 'Ah,' said the Condlin, gliding away from the subject 'Now that's really very interesting. In my young days a lady who admitted to knowing Latin would have been thought a bluestocking – etc, etc.'[336]

---

335 Henry Stanley Bennett (1889–1972) served during the First World War in the 22nd London Regiment in France, during which he lost his right foot. On leaving the army in 1918 he entered Emmanuel College, Cambridge, where he read English. He was elected a Fellow of Emmanuel in 1933 and he served the College as Librarian for twenty-five years. His many scholarly works include *Life on the English Manor* (1937), *English Books and Readers 1475–1557* (1952) and *Six Medieval Men and Women* (1955).

336 Colin Hardie and his bride, Christian Lucas, were married in St Andrew's Chapel, Westminster Cathedral, London, on 10 September 1940.

On Friday none of the others could turn up and Tolkien was compelled to be at home. I dined in College and then Humphrey called for me by car and motored me up to Tolkien's where we stayed till about 12:45 – quite pleasant, but as Tolkien himself has often said it never feels quite the real thing outside 3 New Building. Humphrey then dropped me at College where I made myself a pot of tea, ate my sandwiches and an apple, changed into my uniform, said my prayers, had a smoke and a rest with my shoes off – rather enjoying the whole thing – and emerged again at about ten to one.

It was one of the most brilliant moonlight nights I have ever been out in, and the High, seen in coolness and emptiness was exquisite. I was going to say the 'deserted' High, but that wd. have been untrue: for it's a very odd thing in my experience that at whatever hour you go out you always pass at least one mysterious and solitary person about every three minutes.

One excellent thing about this job is that it gives you, once a week, the chance of a walk at the only time in the 24 hours when it is really pleasant for walking in summer. Indeed 'pleasant' is too weak a word for the actual patrol – which with owls and bats and night smells and moonlight reflected from water, and the sort of dreamlike receptivity one gets from being rather tired – it was ravishing.

On Thursday while I was in College dining Minto was playing 'the spirited old lady'. Hearing footsteps in the garden she instantaneously decided they were parachutists and sallied forth to meet them. They turned out to be two Tommies trespassing – a fact which was completely lost sight of when she discovered that they came from Newry.[337] The adventure concluded of course with bottles of stout in the kitchen – need I add that their old world courtesy led them to return the hospitality by calling on her the following evening?

I have finished *Resurrection* which rather tails off at the end but is well worth reading. I am now on Peacock's three whimsical novels wh. Nelson's have just published in one volume at 2/-, an amazingly good bargain.[338]

I am also working on a book sent me to review, *Le Mystere de la*

337 In Co. Down.

338 Thomas Love Peacock, *Three Novels: Headlong Hall, Nightmare Abbey, Crotchet Castle*, introduction by John Mair (London: Thomas Nelson, 1940).

Poesie by a professor at Dijon,[339] of which my feeling is 'If this is typical of modern France, nothing that has happened in the last three months surprises me' – such a mess of Dadaists, Surrealists, nonsense, blasphemy and decadence, as I could hardly have conceived possible. But one ought to have known for, now that I come to think of it, all the beastliest traits of our intelligentsia have come to them from France.

I hope you are keeping your hand on that wine of yours.

Yours
Jack

Warnie was transferred to the Reserve of Officers and he arrived at The Kilns immediately after receiving his brother's letter of 17 August. He was now officially retired from the Army, and he began serving as a private soldier with the 6th Oxford City Home Guard Battalion. During the summer months he served as part of the 'floating' Home Guard from his boat, the Bosphorus.

TO ELIZA MARIAN BUTLER (LU):[340]

As from Magdalen College,
Oxford.
Aug 18th 1940

Dear Professor Butler

Thank you for all the kind things you say about my book.[341] There are parts of that book which I don't feel too happy about now and the

---

339 This work cannot be traced.

340 Professor Eliza Marian Butler (1885–1959), distinguished German scholar, was born in Bardsea, Lancashire, the daughter of Theobald Fitzwalter Butler and Catherine Elizabeth Barradouth Butler. She was first educated in Hanover, which laid the foundation for a lifelong interest in German literature. From there she went to Cheltenham College and Newnham College, Cambridge, where she graduated in 1911. After teaching for a year at St Felix School, she attended Bonn University. She was then a lecturer at Newnham College, 1914–17. During 1917–18 she served in Dr Elsie Inglis's Scottish Women's Hospitals units in Russia and Macedonia. After a year at Avery Hill Training College, 1919–20, she returned to Newnham College where she taught German and carried out research, 1922–36. In 1936 she was elected Henry Simon Professor of German Language and Literature at the University of Manchester, and she was Schröder Professor of German at the University of Cambridge, 1945–51.

341 i.e. *The Allegory of Love.*

passage on symbolism and allegory is one of them.[342] I would still stick to the point that a symbolical view of the material universe is, in the sense I suggested, the opposite of allegory: but it was unfortunate to use the word *Symbolism* wh. we want, as I now find, to describe a *literary* procedure, distinct from allegory but liable to overlap with it. If I had it now to do again I shd. make the following distinction:

1. *Allegory* Each symbol, in isolation, has a meaning and the total meaning is built up out of these, e.g. you first know who Bialacoil[343] is and what the Rose [means] then see what Bialacoil-guarding-the Rose means.

2. *Symbolical narrative or myth.* What has a meaning is the total story, and the separate characters or 'properties' are mere products of analysis. i.e. 'rescuing-Eurydice-from-Hell-and-losing-her-by-looking-back' has a meaning that neither Eurydice in isolation, nor Hell in isolation has – or, if it has, you get it by analysis out of the total meaning and don't build up the total meaning out of them. Also in a symbolical narrative the meaning usually cannot be stated in conceptual terms: it lives only in the story.

But an odd thing follows. The same story may be mythical or symbolical to one person and allegorical to another. This I have tested in experience. When I read George Macdonald's stories as a boy I was overwhelmed with a sense of significance, but couldn't have identified any one thing in them with any idea, nor got the significance of the

342 *The Allegory of Love*, ch. 2: 'On the one hand you can start with an immaterial fact, such as the passions which you actually experience, and can then invent *visibilia* to express them. If you are hesitating between an angry retort and a soft answer, you can express your state of mind by inventing a person called *Ira* with a torch and letting her contend with another invented person called *Patientia*. This is allegory, and it is with this alone that we have to deal.

'But there is another way of using the equivalence . . . If our passions, being immaterial, can be copied by material inventions, then it is possible that our material world in its turn is the copy of an invisible world. As the god Amor and his figurative garden are to the actual passions of men, so perhaps we ourselves and our "real" world are to something else. The attempt to read that something else through its sensible imitations, to see the archtype in the copy, is what I mean by symbolism or sacramentalism.'

343 The allegorical figure of the friendly behaviour of the Lady in Guillaume de Lorris and Jean de Meun, *Le Roman de la Rose*. In *The Allegory of Love* Lewis used *Le Roman de la Rose*, ed. Ernest Langlois (Paris: Société des Anciens Textes Français, 1914).

whole conceptually apart from the story. Now, when I re-read them, they are almost pure allegory to me – because, in the interval, I have discovered what they are 'about' by quite a different route.

Kafka's stories – I have read (in English) his *Castle*[344] and *Trial*[345] – are to me at present purely symbolical or mythical. I feel a profound significance but it emanates from the whole story and is not built up by understanding the parts, nor could I state it except by re-telling the story. But it is quite a different question whether Kafka was in the same state. For all I know it may have been allegory to him.

I imagine a person totally ignorant of any religion reading *The Pilgrim's Progress.* He wd. feel 'this journey is very like something – it suggests something in the actual *quality* of my experience or of all my experiences.' But he would not be able to say *what* the burden on Christian's back was or *who* Giant Despair was. And he wd. waste his time if he tried, by fixing 'meanings' on these, to work out the total meaning like a puzzle: whereas by asking no questions and just submitting to the imaginative effect of the whole he wd. get a very good deal. But then Bunyan's position was quite different from his!

I probably don't make it v. clear, because I am far from clear myself on the whole subject.

It will not escape you that the *pleasure* is greatest while a story is mythical or symbolical, and tends to grow less when that same story becomes allegorical to us. But this is a familiar law. Love is pleasanter than childbirth and looking at *Stories from Homer*[346] in the nursery is pleasanter than learning Greek Grammar at school!

Of course, the two things are not absolutely separable. Whoever tries to write allegory will become symbolical in places because he always has an imaginative knowledge of his matter which transcends his conceptual knowledge – something more than he consciously meant will keep creeping in.

I find little that is of any help written on this subject. The most helpful comes in O. Barfield *Poetic Diction.*[347] Maud Bodkin's *Archtypal*

---

344 Franz Kafka, *The Castle, a Novel*, trans. Willa and Edwin Muir (1930).

345 Franz Kafka, *The Trial*, trans. Willa and Edwin Muir (1937; rev. edn Professor E. M. Butler, with additional chapters and notes, 1956).

346 Alfred John Church, *Stories from Homer* (1878).

347 Owen Barfield, *Poetic Diction: A Study in Meaning* (London: Faber and Gwyer, 1928; 3rd edn, Middletown, CO: Wesleyan UP, 1973).

Patterns in Poetry[348] and Jung (whom she is following)[349] are relevant but don't really get us much further. The truth is that the few people who care about this sort of thing care so much that they get excited and really *contribute* to the class of 'unanalysably suggestive writing' instead of helping us to understand it.

I agree with you that Kafka is a wonderful writer. If you don't know David Lindsay's *Voyage to Arcturus* (Methuen. Out of print, but not hard to get) you might find it very interesting. It is mere 'popular' fiction, but this kind of writing (like religion on the one hand and pornography on the other) cuts across the ordinary stratifications.

I hope you won't be disappointed with the *Roman*. I hope I admitted that the second part has its *longueurs*![350]

Have you any views on the inset story in *Heinrich von Ofterdingen* – the one about the *Schreiber* and Arcturus etc?[351]

With thanks.

Yours sincerely
C. S. Lewis

P.S. The reason why a certain kind of analysis might be right for the *Roman* and wrong for the *Castle* is that in one case you start knowing the whole system of ideas the author is talking about while in the other you start from zero. Detailed interpretation in the second condition is likely, in my experience, to find 'mares' nests'.

P.S. You are, no doubt, aware that they all tell us now that the key to Kafka is in Kierkegaarde.[352]

---

348 Maud Bodkin, *Archetypal Patterns in Poetry: Psychological Studies of Imagination* (1934).

349 As indicated by the title of her book, Bodkin was indebted to Carl Jung's theory of archetypes in his major work, translated by R. F. C. Hull as *The Archetypes and the Collective Unconscious* (1959).

350 *The Allegory of Love*, ch. 3, part iv, pp. 137–8: 'It is as well to make it clear at the outset that Jean's work is only in a very superficial sense a continuation of Guillaume's. It is not the allegorical narrative which swells it to its prodigious length; it is the digressions.'

351 Friedrich Leopold von Hardenberg (or Novalis), *Heinrich von Ofterdingen* (1802). Lewis mentioned this to Arthur Greeves in his letter of 13 August 1930 (*CL* I, p. 922): 'As you know, "Heinrich Von Ofterdingen" wh. I am reading is a very Macdonaldy book – indeed Novalis is perhaps the greatest single influence on Macdonald – full of "holiness", gloriously German-romantic.'

352 Søren Aabye Kierkegaard (1813–55), Danish philosopher.

TO ELIZA MARIAN BUTLER (LU):

The Kilns,
Headington Quarry,
Oxford.
Aug 23rd 1940

Dear Miss Butler

My experience is the same as yours in that I enjoy the things most while they remain baffling: but I add the rider that any attempt to prolong this initial thrill after the point at which further understanding offers itself, is, like all attempts to prolong initial thrills, a failure and subject to the law of diminishing returns.

Yes – I find Goethe's *Märchen*[353] unreadable. Not so the Novalis. Is it possible that your dislike of the latter came from trying to find an allegorical, separable *significacio* instead of just swallowing the story?

Yes, I should be interested to see the essay provided always that what you send me is *not* the unique MS. Since once losing the only text of a friend's short story, I have made an iron rule never to receive unique MSS.

Yours sincerely
C. S. Lewis

TO ELIZA MARIAN BUTLER (LU):

The Kilns,
Headington Quarry,
Oxford.
Sept 12th 1940

Dear Miss Butler

I have read the essay with great interest. What I liked best was the distinction between the direct and indirect methods, and the recognition (often missed) that Ibsen at his best is predominantly direct. The case of Shaw's misunderstanding of Ibsen I believe to be more complicated than you wd. suggest. His love for Ibsen, Bunyan, Wagner and *The Magic Flute*[354] indicate a real love for the direct wh. I think he experiences; but he has no notion what is happening to him and tries to explain it all on rationalistic, Fabian grounds.

---

353 Johann Wolfgang von Goethe, *Das Märchen* (1795).

354 Mozart's opera, *Die Zauberflöte* (*The Magic Flute*) was first performed on 30 September 1791.

I think your discussion of the two methods only needs, to make it complete, a recognition that what now has to be read as *direct* was sometimes *indirect* to contemporaries: e.g. Shakespeare's witches and ghosts (p. 14) were almost taken by him and his audience to be representations of fact, and Dante's geography *d'outre-tombe*[355] had, when it was written, in addition to its present interest the same kind of interest people now get from Wells' *First Men in the Moon* – an account of places believed to exist in the material universe, but inaccessible.

As to the wider position behind your whole essay, I am in disagreement. But what matters more to you, I am in some doubt what you really mean. 'There is a spirit of poetry.' This may mean 3 things.

1. There is an actual concrete spirit (a god, daemon, Muse, or what not.)

2. There is an abstract universal, a 'common quality' wh. cd. be defined if we knew enough.

3. There is a 'spirit' in the sense of a temper or psychological tone, common to all men in their poetic moments.

It makes a good deal of difference how you come to think that 'poetry generates life' (p. 8) and that in poets 'the human element is strongly crossed with the Divine' (p. 31). But then, if we are to take this position seriously, you are in fact offering us a theology or at least a pneumatology for which we demand evidence. If, on the other hand, you only mean *2.* or *3.* many of the claims you make for poetry seem rather excessive. I find a similar ambiguity when you describe what poetry does. On p. 8 it creates 'illusions.' On p. 21 it 'reveals the nature of the spiritual world' (cf p. 28 'a genuine source of revelation'). Now which do you mean?

And what is 'the spiritual world.' Does this mean (a) The psychological world. If so, you wd., I suppose, mean simply that 'Poetry expresses how people feel' – a much tamer, but perhaps clearer, statement than the one in the text. (b) The 'metaphysical world' on pp. 2 and 7. And what is this 'metaphysical world'? Does it mean a supersensual *reality*, existing whether we think about it or not? Or does it only mean something in men's minds?

All this worries me, because I think you may be (I know that I have often been) in danger of a tendency which more jejune critics like

355 'beyond the grave'.

Richards or Eliot rightly expose – the danger of talking for 'emotive' purposes *as if* we had a theology or at least a metaphysic up our sleeves when in fact we haven't. One must in the long run, mustn't one, decide what one really believes. Speaking with the hand on the heart, 'sad brow, true maid',[356] what do *you* mean when you talk about 'the divine.' Because there's no middle way. You either mean a great deal, or just nothing.

That is why I think you are much harder on the theologians than you are entitled to be. *C'est facile aux speculatifs d'estre severes*![357] You see, they were really trying to say what they believed to be true. As long as you never come down to brass-tacks it is easy enough to avoid becoming dry & rationalistic etc. – just as it is easy to avoid getting dirty hands if one never does any work!

But in revenge an element of fundamental frivolity creeps into ones work (look at Mackail!) and those moments at which ones style sounds most serious become the moments when one is saying a little more than one means. And what you say about Eliot's 'collapse into Anglo-Catholicism' instead of 'newer and stranger things' (p. 34) is profoundly disquieting. You don't seem even to consider the hypothesis that he might have embraced this belief because he thought it *true* – that he might be looking for the true, not the 'new and strange' (of course the two might turn out to coincide, but we've no right to assume that *â priori*, and the seeking of the former is a quite different activity from seeking the latter).

If you cared to look into a book by Tillyard and me called *The Personal Heresy*, you will see my view on this at the end of the first essay. The kernel is 'Don't attribute superhuman qualities to poetry unless you really believe in a superhuman subjects[358] to support them.'[359]

---

356 William Shakespeare, *As You Like It* (1623), III, ii, 228: 'speak, sad brow and true maid.'

357 'It is easy for theoreticians to be severe!'

358 Lewis wrote 'superhuman subjects', after which he inserted an 'a' over a caret before 'superhuman' but did not remove the plural.

359 Tillyard and Lewis, *The Personal Heresy* (London: Oxford University Press, 1939), ch. 1, p. 27: 'The objects . . . we contemplate in reading poetry are not the private furniture of the poet's mind . . . A mind which habitually saw as synthetically – which saw each single object with so vast a context – as we are made to see for moments by poetry, would be as far removed from us as we are from the brutes. It would not, indeed, be the Divine Mind . . . but it would be a mind, none the less, greatly beyond the human. The ancients called it the Muse. That she exists is

I'm sure that to neglect this is to embark on a sea of half-voluntary illusions.

I hope all this is not rude. I enjoyed the essay and you see it has proved a powerful irritant!

Yours sincerely
C. S. Lewis

TO ELIZA MARIAN BUTLER (LU):

The Kilns,
Headington Quarry,
Oxford.
Sept 25th 1940

Dear Miss Butler –

I feel ashamed of having troubled you with controversial correspondence at such an inopportune moment. If I am now troubling you again it is on the strict understanding that in dropping this letter into the waste paper basket unread and unanswered you will have my full approval. To put it more plainly, I don't know whether you want to continue the subject or not, and there is no earthly reason why you should if you don't want to: by continuing it on my side I am merely offering you the alternative of doing so or not. If you don't answer this I shall assume that you don't, and be perfectly content.

I also am an Irishman and a congenital rhetorician: that is why I assume in speaking to you the melancholy privileges of a fellow-patient!

A *pure* agnostic is a fine thing. I have known only one and he was the man who taught me to think.[360] What I am worried about is the purity of your agnosticism: for one of the most dangerous things about the modern world seems to me the fact that most of those who call themselves agnostics have not really got rid of religion but merely exchanged civilised religion for barbarous religion – worship of sex, or the State, or the *élan vital*, or the dead, or Mystery as such.

And I still think you are not quite out of this danger. Nearly everything you say in your letter can be read in a double sense: and I think

a needless hypothesis, though, for all I know, not an absurd one. At all events, only in her will personal critics find the haven they seek. Much criticism is faced with this dilemma. It asserts of poetry superhuman attributes: it believes in no superhuman subjects to support them.'

360 i.e. W. T. Kirkpatrick ('The Great Knock').

the best way of making my point is to write out the two quite different letters concealed in your one letter.

A. All mythologies & religions are products of imagination in the sense that their content is *imaginary*, i.e. false. The more *imaginary* ones are 'nearer the mark' in the sense that they come nearer to admitting their falsity. Poetry 'creates life' in the sense of producing life-like fictions, and the world of fictions I call the 'spiritual world' (i.e. a department of the psychological world – what goes on in our minds when, with the help of Dickens, we *pretend* there was a man called Pickwick). Poets 'proclaim the mystery' in the sense that they remind us we don't know what the real universe is like: for it is a 'mystery' like anything else we happen not to know – like the mystery 'who killed Jones' in a detective story. Oddly enough they also produce the illusion of penetrating the mystery: i.e. besides reminding us that we don't know they sometimes make us think (falsely) that we do. Poetry is a dynamic power (i.e. a powerful or great power) – in the sense of producing strong emotions in the reader.

B. Mythologies and religions are products of imagination in the sense that their content is *imaginative*. The more *imaginative* ones are 'nearer the mark' in the sense that they communicate more Reality to us. Poetry 'creates life' in the sense that its products are something more than fictions occurring in human minds, mere psychological phenomena, and can therefore be described as inhabiting a 'spiritual world.' Poets 'proclaim the mystery' in the sense that they somehow convey to us an inkling of supersensual and super-intellectual Reality: which is a Mystery in the sense of *mysterium tremendum*, something not merely wh. we happen not to know but which transcends our common modes of perception. They produce the illusion of penetrating it in the sense that they make us feel we have *understood* when we have really been refreshed by contact of quite a different kind with Reality. Poetry is a great power in the sense of actually enriching our deepest life by such contacts.

'You pays your money and you takes your choice.' What you mustn't do is to sit on the fence and use the language of both while paying for neither. If you embrace A you mustn't talk about 'proclaiming the mystery' (words steeped in religious associations) when you only mean 'telling us we are ignorant of many things.' If you embrace B you mustn't use 'products of our imagination' to imply 'containing only fictions.' Because, you see, there is something to *pay*.

A is clear, and comfortable and gives you the assurance that what you enjoy in poetry and mythology will never interfere with your liberty: but the price you pay for it is to abandon the excitingness of B. B is exciting and alluring; but the price you pay for it is the disquieting recognition that this Reality with a big R might interfere with you and that the whole thing may go further than you wished or intended.

I cd make this letter sound less like an uncle writing to a niece or a *directeur* to a penitent only by dint of making it much longer: so pray pardon the tone. Anyway, you are quite free to ignore it.

Of course you 'meant it all quite honestly.' So did I, for years. But it can't go on indefinitely!

With apologies for the great liberties I'm taking.

Yours sincerely
C. S. Lewis

P.S. The letter cd. have been shorter after all! The whole contradiction comes in one sentence of yours. 'Revelation . . . of the superhuman powers, if any.' If you don't know whether there are any such powers, why call the literature that suggests them 'Revelation'? If you know that poetry is 'Revelation' why add 'if any'?

Brother George Every SSM, who had started the 'Christianity and Culture' debate with his essay on 'The Necessity of Scrutiny*', returned to the debate with 'In Defence of Criticism', published in* Theology *in September 1940.*[361] *Lewis then fired the last shot in the debate with 'Peace Proposals for Brother Every and Mr Bethell' which appeared in the December issue of* Theology.[362]

TO BR GEORGE EVERY SSM (BOD):[363]

[The Kilns]
Oct 12th 1940

My dear Every –

With one exception I think we can now agree. Most of the differ-

361 Br George Every, 'In Defence of Criticism', *Theology*, XLI (September 1940), pp. 159–65.

362 'Peace Proposals for Brother Every and Mr Bethell', *Theology*, XLI (December 1940), pp. 339–48, reprinted in *Christian Reflections*.

363 See **Brother George Every SSM** in the Biographical Appendix. While corresponding with Lewis, Every was an Anglican lay brother of the Society of the Sacred Mission.

ences belong, as you say, to the realm of policy rather than that of principle. The reason for restricting moral judgements to a few v. 'clear and trenchant' ones is humility and the wish not to mislead. We can say 'this book prompts to lechery' because we *know* that lechery is evil. To condemn because it 'implies the baroque standards which descend from North's Plutarch' (this is a purely imaginary, laboratory example) is dangerous because the standards mentioned are not *known* by you and me to be bad – at most they are merely suspected. And I don't feel happy about 'leaving the moral implications to speak for themselves' – unless the critic is a v. great & good man; for surely that is just the method by which every little anti-clerical guttersnipe in the *New Statesman* manages to insinuate into the mind of the readers (without their knowledge) all sorts of positions wh. he wd. be quite incapable of defending if he were forced to come out into the open.

Let us exchange confessions: surely I have a habit of using 'fashionable', and you have a habit of using 'liberal', to 'put it across' our readers – i.e. by the unpopular associations of the very words to *imply* that something is bad wh., if we attempted to *prove* it bad *en regle*, we should be very much less – well, impressive! But it is a question of method, I admit. I think a method of which all modern critics (and specially myself) are guilty contains a v. dangerous element.

The real difference is all this business about Calvinism, and Grace & Nature. I sincerely believe this to be a *pure* red herring. You & Bethell are quite mistaken in thinking I have a Calvinistic background: indeed for the first 20 years of my life I was too ill instructed to be in any such danger. The difference I am drawing between moral and non-moral good comes rather from secular ethics. And to ask whether the chasm between a *good* horse or *good* meal and *good* man is wider or narrower than that between a *good* man and a *holy* or *spiritual* man seems to me meaningless – the chasms are of such different kinds.

The answer wd. be 'Chasm A is wider in one sense and chasm B is wider in another.' Natural and theological virtue both stand together *quâ* things that make the possessor good and are divided by an immense chasm from goods like health or beauty. But also, health and natural virtue both stand together *quâ* parts of the natural order, divided by an immense chasm from the theological virtues wh. are of grace. And all that seems to me to have nothing to do with our present problem. I think the truth is that the Grace-Nature antithesis was v. much in your mind, and hardly at all in mine, & you have read it into my articles. (I certainly think with you that the natural virtues are sustained, even in unbelievers, by Divine aid – tho' it may be more scriptural to attribute this office to Christ rather than the Holy Ghost). But my aim here is not to meet you on the Grace-Nature issue but to get it of out the way, because I think it is side-tracking us.

In the small hours of this morning I succeeded in making my L.D.V. fellow sentry realise for the first time in his life that 'nature' can't have 'purposes' unless it is a rational substance, and if it is you'd much better call it God, or the gods, or a god, or the devil. The fact that he'd never seen this before is, I suppose, an example of just what you mean about style – the great fog of nonsense spread over all nations. Though, by the bye, it began probably in this case from something that was *not* bad – legitimate personifications of 'Nature' by real poets (and Stoics too) who knew what they were doing. Trusting you'll come and see me soon,

Yours
C. S. Lewis

TO ELIZA MARIAN BUTLER (LU):

Magdalen, Oxford.
Oct 14th 1940

Dear Miss Butler –

I was writing carelessly when I condemned 'sitting on the fence.' Where one cannot find sufficient evidence for either alternative (I mean *probable* evidence, since mathematical certainty is not to be hoped for) suspense of judgement is the only honest and rational course. What I ought to have objected to was something quite different from sitting *on* the fence: namely, talking (also thinking, and feeling) as if one could be on both sides of the fence, i.e. as if *both* the alternatives could be true.

What makes me specially sensitive to this danger is that I believe I fell a victim to it myself for many years, during which I professed indeed to be in mental suspense but really talked, felt, and behaved sometimes as if one answer were right and sometimes as if the other were right, choosing whichever happened to suit the rhetorical or emotional needs of the moment – with the result that the *total* effect of my talk, feeling, and behaviour was compatible with *no* conceivable universe. For the one thing we do know is that both can't be true.

And I now feel that there was a certain dishonesty in this. I had the pleasures of every theory and paid the price for none. I embraced the excitement of polytheism or demonology when I happened to want it, but became a materialist if some old nursery fears, in darkness and solitude, threatened to make that sort of stuff a little *more* exciting than I wanted. I was nearly religious when that mood offered comfort, and sternly sceptical if it threatened to impose any obligation. I would 'rather have believed' in the Norse gods than in Christianity, and I now know why – because I secretly knew perfectly well that neither I nor anyone else could now *really* believe in Asgard as hundreds of people *really* believe in Christ – I knew, in fact that my bluff wd. never be called, that my flirtation cd. never commit me to marriage.

So all I have been doing is to hold myself up to you as a horrid warning – for I am sure you wouldn't like to become what I was!

Yours sincerely
C. S. Lewis

P.S. You naturally feel 'thinner' because you are now living on the food really supplied by the mental country you inhabit. I have cut off the *smuggled* provisions which have been trickling across the frontier from richer adjacent countries.

Sister Penelope wrote to Lewis on 22 October 1940 – one of only two letters she sent him that have survived (the other being that of 5 August 1939):

> *I was beside myself with flatteration at receiving a copy of your book;*[364] *but my gratitude to you for giving me the book, great though it is, is small compared to my gratitude to God for having given it to you to write it; & that, I think, is as you would wish it. I expected to enjoy myself reading it, & I have done so even beyond my hope. It made me bolt my dinner to get more time for it – we read to ourselves at dinner, such a good plan, & incidentally one which gives many of us almost our only chance of reading history, travel etc.; & now that I have finished it,*

364 *The Problem of Pain.*

reading every word, & a good many bits twice over, I am longing to read it again. That, I think, is a peculiar quality of your writing: I am aching to re-read both Pilgrim's Regress *&* Out of the Silent Planet, *tho' I have already read the latter twice, once aloud; but this book outstrips even those, & I cannot be sufficiently thankful for it. It is lovely to meet 'Nippy' on the Fall*[365] *in, so to speak, a ready-digested form; & I wonder very much whether he lies behind* The Silent Planet *also, or whether you read him only after writing that . . .*'[366]

TO SISTER PENELOPE CSMV (BOD):

Magdalen College,
Oxford.
Oct 24th 1940

Dear Madam –

Thanks for your very kind letter. No, I only read Nippy after the *Silent Planet*, and to tell you the truth didn't find him very helpful. The man who can dismiss 'sinned *in* Adam' as an 'idiom' and identify virtue with the herd instinct is no use to me, despite his very great learning.

About angels' bodies: as far as I have seen incorporeality is the normal medieval view (appearances being explained by the temporary manufacture of a body of air), while real embodiment is the view of the Christian Platonists of the Renaissance (hence, by the bye, much of the corporeality of angels in *Paradise Lost* wh. we easily mistake for mere poetical machinery is probably up-to-date pneumatology believed by Milton).[367]

About Hell: how do we get over Mt. VII 13,14?[368] But I agree we *must* get over that one somehow or go mad. And leaving that one out,

---

365 By 'Nippy' she meant Norman Powell Williams, *The Ideas of the Fall and of Original Sin* (1927), a book Lewis mentions in the chapter in *The Problem of Pain* on 'The Fall of Man'.

366 Bodleian Library, MS. Eng. c. 6825, fol. 61.

367 Lewis dealt with this issue in detail in the chapter 'The Mistake about Milton's Angels' in *A Preface to Paradise Lost*.

368 Matthew 7:13–14: 'Enter ye in at the strait gate: for wide is the gate, and broad is the way, that leadeth to destruction, and many there be which go in thereat: Because strait is the gate, and narrow is the way, which leadeth unto life, and few there be that find it.'

perhaps we can accept your argument that tho' Hell exists we are not absolutely forced to hold that anyone will reach it. But wouldn't the same, in logic, on the same grounds, hold of Heaven? And was Origen not condemned?[369]

I have never read Irenaeus,[370] and got the idea of the knot from the otherwise rather dull med. Latin poem *Architrenius* – wh. may of course in its turn be indebted to Irenaeus. On *archtypal* or *archetypal*, note as the first principle of textual criticism in dealing with me that *all* odd spellings [have no] more interesting explanation than ignorance – now I can't spell! *Waking* for *walking* is such a charming misprint that I can hardly regret it.

I read Gilson's book on St. Bernard in the French edtn. of 1934.[371] I have just turned up your review[372] and am pleased to see you fighting, as usual, for the O.T. The Romans so often need to be reminded of it.

Thanks – my brother is not only safe from France but, better still, back on the retired list and living at home: so that what with that and a house full of really delightful refugee children (I am a bachelor and never appreciated children till the war brought them to me) I have very much to be thankful for. I will try to remember Vincent Taylor[373] – dare I hope that my frequent quotations from Geo. Macdonald will lead you to read him? He deserves to be much better known.

The only sermon I ever preached (and therefore presumably the one you have seen) is coming out in a collection of sermons by various hands shortly, I believe.[374]

---

369 Origen reacted strongly against the literal interpretation of the Scriptures, and according to his theory of Apocatastasis the punishments of the damned come to an end and they are saved. It was condemned by the Church in AD 543.

370 St Irenaeus (c. AD 130–c. 200), Bishop of Lyons, was the first great Catholic theologian. His principal work, *Adversus Omnes Haereses*, is an attack on Gnosticism. The strength of his attack lay in emphasizing the traditional elements in the Church, the Episcopate, Scripture, and religious and theological tradition. Sister Penelope valued St Irenaeus principally for his emphasis on the reality of the Incarnation.

371 Etienne Gilson, *La Théologie Mystique de Saint Bernard* (1934).

372 Sister Penelope's review of Gilson, *The Mystical Theology of St Bernard*, trans. A. H. Downes (1940) is found in *Theology*, XLI (July 1940), pp. 59–61.

373 Vincent Taylor (1887–1968) was the author of *The Atonement in New Testament Teaching* (1940) and other works.

374 Sister Penelope had seen a copy of Lewis's sermon 'None Other Gods: Culture in War Time' which had been published as *The Christian in Danger*.

I am going to make my first confession next week, wh. will seem odd to you, but I wasn't brought up to that kind of thing. It's an odd experience. The *decision* to do so was one of the hardest I have ever made: but now that I am committed (by dint of posting the letter before I had time to change my mind) I begin to be afraid of the opposite extreme – afraid that I am merely indulging in an orgy of egoism. However, *quod ubique quod ab omnibus*![375] It *will* be terrifying to face the A.T.S.[376] but it is a wonderful opportunity. Remember that resistance at the time means v. little. Those who resist most violently in words are often those who go away and think it over most fruitfully. Good wishes,

Yours sincerely,

C. S. Lewis

TO DOUGLAS BUSH (W):

Magdalen College,
Oxford.
Nov. 1st 1940

Dear Professor Bush

Now did I, or did I not, answer your last kind letter? If not, let the smallness and unimportance of my share in this book be excused by the peculiar nature of the offering. I had hoped, if times were happier, that we might have met before now and talked of many things including the O.H.E.L., but that must wait.

We're doing very nicely here and the way these young freshmen with only two or three terms before they join the army manage to take an interest in their work is really astonishing. They're a nicer lot, I think, than my own war generation was 20 years ago.

Yours sincerely,

C. S. Lewis

---

375 '*quod ubique, quod ab omnibus*' is an abbreviated form of the following quotation from St Vincent of Lerins, *Commonitorium*, ch. 4, section 3: '*Id teneamus, quod ubique, quod semper, quod ab omnibus creditum est*', 'Let us hold on to that which has been believed everywhere, always, by everyone.'

376 Auxiliary Territorial Service, founded in 1938. Sister Penelope said in her letter of 22 October: 'I am now a Licensed Teacher in Theology. . .There is a chance I may be asked to go & address A.T.S. girls, mostly quite heathen. It wd. be thrilling to get a chance to try to help them but I shd. be terribly frightened' (Bodleian Library, MS. Eng. c. 6825, fol. 61).

TO SISTER PENELOPE CSMV (BOD):

Magdalen College,
Oxford.
Nov 4th 1940

Dear Sister Penelope

Well – we have come through the wall of fire and find ourselves (somewhat to our surprise) still alive and even well.[377] The suggestion about an orgy of egoism turns out, like all the enemy propaganda, to have just a grain of truth in it, but I have no doubt that the proper method of dealing with that is to continue the practice, as I intend to do. For after all everything – even virtue, even prayer – has its dangers and if one heeds the grain of truth in the enemy propaganda one can never do anything at all.

Don't bother sending Irenaeus as he is certainly in the college library and if I find him nutritious I shall buy him. I think, about Heaven and Hell, your strongest point is that about free will, wh. forbids any destiny to be absolutely assigned to any soul whatsoever. Yet Luke xiii 24 gives a plain future indicative, ουκ ισχύσουσιν.[378] I don't really think belief in perdition depends much on a Pharisaical desire to contemplate the damnation of others.

Thanks for the little book which is very good and wise as far as I have gone.

I was told that *Madam* was the proper way of addressing a nun, and the fact that it suggests a shop shows how we have degraded the language: I regard it simply as the Fem. of *Sir* and v. nearly the English for Voc. γύναι.[379] But I gladly accept the other mode.

Isn't *Phantastes* good? It did a lot for me years before I became a Christian, when I had no idea what was behind it. This has always made it easier for me to understand how the better elements in mythology can be a real *praeparatio evangelica*[380] for people who do not yet know whither they are being led.

---

377 Beginning this week Lewis made regular confessions to Father Walter Adams, a member of the religious community the Society of St John the Evangelist. See **Father Walter Adams SSJE** in the Biographical Appendix.

378 '[they] shall not be able'.

379 This is often used in Greek as a term of respect, usually given as 'mistress' or 'lady' in older translations of a more courtly age, but 'woman' in the King James Bible.

380 'preparation for the Gospel'.

Thank you for your prayers and all other kindnesses – I seem to be surrounded with kindness from all sorts of people at present,

Yours sincerely
Clive S. Lewis

TO BR GEORGE EVERY SSM (BOD):

As from Magdalen
Dec 11th [1940]

My dear Every –

Thanks very much for the book[381] wh. I read at a sitting, always with interest and nearly always with the pleasure of unexpected agreement. I accept the main position almost entirely i.e. for 99% of what we shd. call Taste – tho' I still think there is something left over, wh. we might call 'pure' or 'mere' taste – I mean that even under perfect conditions some people wd. be inferior to others in, say, sense of colour or design, just as they are in 'ear'.

I agree v. strongly with pp. 3 et seq, having myself already formulated the rule '*ceteris paribus*[382] the wish-fulfilment element in a book is in a direct ratio to its apparent realism'[383] (see pp. 7 and 9, on Wells especially). Pp. 15 et seq are important, obviating a silly primitivism wh. some easily fall into at this stage of the argument.[384] P 20 – thanks! I'm glad to see someone attacking the Keatsian heresy about verification

381 George Every, *Christian Discrimination* (1940).

382 'other things being equal'.

383 Every, *Christian Discrimination*, ch. 1, p. 3: 'In a satisfactory long novel with which we must live, or in a satisfying house which we can desire to bequeath to our children, all the parts must be in their place. But in the romance which we read to relieve our feelings by identifying ourselves with the hero or heroine it is essential that certain things should not be in their place, that certain obstructions to the fulfilment of our desires which are always there in ordinary life should disappear and be overcome, or that they should become so overwhelming as to destroy our substitute in a magnificent and exciting way.'

384 ibid., ch. 2, p. 16: 'All art is fiction, and in fiction nothing is true or untrue, nothing is right or not right. . . . You will get to the end of the book and wake up, or you can shut the book, or leave the theatre, when art presents you with something which you do not like. Fundamentally this is the philosophy of latter-day Hellenism in the Roman empire, the theory that all religions, world-views, imaginative visions, are equally true and equally false. They are all dreams. But in earlier and later ages . . . there was a belief in a real world beyond the world of plain matter-of-fact, a world that was actually organized, and works of art were believed to be right or wrong by the laws of that world.'

on the pulses.[385] Cap 3: I wonder do you not rather idealise the old Rhetoric (it's pretty ghastly!) and underestimate the *vocational* element in it?[386] P. 31 on Arnold, I agree.[387]

P. 32, 'Centred around' – am I pedantic in objecting to this metaphor (I mean, things can circle round a centre, but how do they centre round?).[388] P. 33 at bottom. I agree entirely. The whole thesis system is an abomination: imported into humane studies, where it has *no* value, from the empirical sciences where it has some.[389]

P. 38 (end of xix). Pardon me. There is a quite different possible defence of democracy.[390] I am a democrat *because* I believe in the Fall and therefore think men too wicked to be trusted with more than the minimum power over other men. P. 42 good on Crabbe.[391] P. 52 on that hymn – you get it exactly right 'good in themselves but not to be

---

385 ibid., pp. 19–20: D. H. Lawrence 'spent all his life looking for a way to understand what he called "the dark gods" in terms of physical experience, and then in terms borrowed from the old natural religions . . . But . . . he never altogether escaped from the presupposition inbred in him by an individualist background that all truth must be verified upon his own pulses and with his own eyes.'

386 ibid., ch. 3, p. 25: 'The purpose of the trivium, grammar, rhetoric, and dialectic, and of the quadrivium, arithmetic, geometry, astronomy, and music, was to help us to understand the modes in which human thought find precise expression, in the spoken and written word, in number and line, and in rhythm and tone. It was not primarily to give information about any subject except the mysteries of astronomy . . .'

387 ibid., p. 31: Matthew Arnold's 'semi-theological writings must be judged to be, on the whole, a failure. Sometimes his critical skill did help him to throw real light on a passage in St Paul, but much of his talk of "something not ourselves that makes for righteousness" was a mere fencing with the problem of belief in God.'

388 ibid., p. 32: 'In so far as the secondary school curriculum is a unity at all, it is centred not around literature, but around natural science.'

389 ibid., pp. 33–4: 'Now the great majority of degrees are in physical science, or in history treated as a science . . . Even the study of language and literature conforms more and more to this scheme, as the most interesting subjects for theses are worked out, and students have to proceed in search of the rarer Icelandic roots and the washing-bills of the Elizabethan poets.'

390 ibid., ch. 4, p. 38: 'The assumption of democratic politics is that the individual citizen's judgement of political issues is so far valid that a majority of votes ought, at least in the last resort, to determine the right course of action.'

391 ibid., p. 42: George Crabbe 'could still write stories in verse at the beginning of the nineteenth century, like any other country parson talking to his own flock whom he knows and likes, and he assumes that they share with him a common belief in God and in redemption which, if not very fervent, brings with it a rather deeper insight into human weakness and strength than was common in the

confused'. That is good thinking: no exaggeration, but all accounted for.[392] P. 57 'when the unbelievers come to Church' v. good.[393] P. 66 Sword in the Stone.[394] I strongly disagree. One of the most deeply vulgar books I've ever read. Its humour is exactly on the level of an urchin with a lead pencil drawing a moustache on the lip of a classical statue. What can be cheaper than his Palomides? It is the work of a sad, shabby little mind. P. 64 'The Church is in danger' – yes, I shd. just think so.[395]

One thing needs going into, wh. you haven't had time to touch – i.e. the difficulty of deciding what a work means to different people, wh. increases as we go down the scale. Prob. most are agreed as to what the *Antigone* 'means' – i.e. all who enjoy it enjoy it more or less in the same way. But two boys enjoying Wells' *First Men in the Moon* may be getting almost unrecognisably different things out of it. I know this from a rather shocking experience. Such things are always pure fairy-tale to me and it makes no difference whether the machinery is 'scientific' or frankly 'magical'. But when I published a story of that type myself I received letters from the queerest societies who take it all as *real* i.e. 'possible in this world'. And you bet there were contemporaries of Homer who took the *Odyssey* that way. In other words the proposition 'The break between fantasy & reality has been blurred' is often as much about the reader as about the book: just as to some people any picture of the nude is pornography. Trollope is a funny

---

eighteenth century, and makes Crabbe on the whole a more interesting poet, more human and less topical, than his master Pope'.

392 ibid., ch. 5, p. 52: The original editors of *Hymns Ancient and Modern* did not include such hymns as 'Dear Lord and Father of Mankind' which has the verse 'O Sabbath rest by Galilee!' where 'an appeal is made to our Sunday morning feelings about Nature and sunshine, good feelings in themselves, but not to be confused with the apprehension of the eternal'.

393 ibid., p. 57: 'When the unbeliever comes to church, he does not come to be argued with and met half-way in the meeting-place of believers and unbelievers. He comes to see what it is like to be a believer.'

394 T. H. White, *The Sword in the Stone* (1938).

395 Every, *Christian Discrimination*, ch. 6, p. 64: 'the longest and strongest resistance to any attempt to impose a new explicitly formulated materialist philosophy upon society will come not from individual sceptical personalities but from the Christian Church. At the same time . . . the Church is in danger of confounding those who are also opposed to the main enemy of the moment with her true friends, as the French Catholics did when they clung too hard to the old régime, and the Spanish and Italian Catholics when, out of hatred of Liberalism and fear of Communism, they embraced the Fascists.'

case. His *Autobiography* makes it clear that the *root* of all his work was wish-fulfilment: but this has largely disappeared in the completed product, and what survives of it (the love interest) is just the part we now skip. One wants a dist.[inction] between wish-fulfilment as end and W.F. as a means of getting 'weigh' on to steer by.

Many thanks.

Yours

C. S. Lewis

1941

Lewis began the year by responding to two distinguished Christians, Evelyn Underhill and Canon Oliver Chase Quick, whose praise for The Problem of Pain *had been tempered by criticism of certain passages. Underhill, who had written to Lewis in 1938 commending* Out of the Silent Planet, *objected to the chapter on 'Animal Pain', in which he stated:*

> *Man was appointed by God to have dominion over the beasts, and everything a man does to an animal is either a lawful exercise, or a sacrilegious abuse, of an authority by Divine Right. The tame animal is therefore, in the deepest sense, the only 'natural' animal – the only one we see occupying the place it was made to occupy, and it is on the tame animal that we must base all our doctrine of beasts. Now it will be seen that, in so far as the tame animal has a real self or personality, it owes this almost entirely to its master. If a good sheepdog seems 'almost human' that is because a good shepherd has made it so . . . You must not think of a beast by itself, and call that a personality and then inquire whether God will raise and bless* that. *You must take the whole context* in *which the beast acquires its selfhood – namely 'The-goodman-and-the-goodwife-ruling-their-children-and-their-beasts-in-the-good-homestead' . . . In this way it seems to me possible that certain animals may have an immortality, not in themselves, but in the immortality of their masters.*[1]

Underhill responded to this argument in her letter of 13 January 1941:

> *I find it impossible to follow you in your chapter on animals. 'The tame animal is in the deepest sense the only natural animal*

1 *The Problem of Pain* (London: Bles, 1940; HarperCollins, 2002), ch. 9, pp. 142–4.

> *. . . the beasts are to be understood only in their relation to man & through man to God.' This seems to me frankly an intolerable doctrine & a frightful exaggeration of what is involved in the primacy of man. Is the cow which we have turned into a milk machine or the hen we have turned into an egg machine really nearer the mind of God than its wild ancestors? This seems like saying that the black slave is the only natural negro. You surely* can't *mean that, or think that the robin red breast in a cage doesn't put heaven in a rage but is regarded as an excellent arrangement. Your own example of the good-man, good-wife, & good-dog in the good homestead is a bit smug & utilitarian don't you think over against the wild beauty of God's creative action in the jungle & deep sea? And if we ever get a sideways glimpse of the animal-in-itself, the animal existing for God's glory & pleasure & lit by His light . . . we don't owe it to the Pekinese, the Persian cat or the canary, but to some wild free creature living in completeness of adjustment to Nature a life that is utterly independent of man. And this, thank Heaven, is the situation of all but the handful of creatures we have enslaved.*[2]

TO MRS STUART MOORE (EVELYN UNDERHILL) (M):

Magdalen College,
Oxford.
Jan 16th 1941

Dear Mrs. Stuart Moore

Your kind letter about the *Silent Planet* has not been forgotten and is not likely to be. It was one of the high lights of my literary life.

Now about these animals. I don't admit that my position is 'like saying that the black slave is the only natural negro'. It *would* be like it only if the Negro differed from the white man as much, and in the same way, as beast from man: i.e. if he were irrational. And if this were true (but it is not), I then should say that the well-treated slave was the only natural Negro. But of course I might have to add that most white men had shown themselves unfit to exercise the authority which (if black men were really sub-human) wd. be theirs by nature.

2 Bodleian Library, MS. Eng. c. 6825, fols. 70–1. The letter is given almost in its entirety in *The Letters of Evelyn Underhill*, ed. with an introduction by Charles Williams (London: Religious Book Club, 1945).

And this point partly supplies my answer about the animals. I said that everything a man does to a beast is *either* a lawful exercise *or* a sacrilegious abuse of an authority by divine right. I didn't say which of the things we now see men doing to beasts fall into which class. The robin in a cage and the over-fed Peke are both, to me, instances of the *abuse* of man's authority, tho' in different ways. I never denied that the *abuse* was common: that is why we have to make laws (and ought to make a good many more) for the protection of animals.

I *do* know what you mean by the sudden ravishing glimpse of animal life in itself, its wildness – to meet a squirrel in a wood or even a hedgehog in the garden makes me happy. But that is because it is, being *partly* exempt from the Fall, a symbol and reminder of the unfallen world we long for. That wildness wd. not be lost by the kind of dominion Adam had. It wd. be nicer, not less nice, if that squirrel wd. come and make friends with me at my whistle – still more if he wd. obey me when I told him not to kill the red squirrel in the next tree. I don't envisage the taming of all beasts as involving domestication of all – only perhaps the dog and a few others. In a Paradisal state if you wanted a horse to ride you would walk up to the nearest herd and ask for volunteers – and the one you chose wd. be regarded as the lucky one.

I'm not so happy as you about what my cat does when she goes off on her own. She has nasty ways with her disabled, but living, prey. I don't think she'd lose any real beauty by being obedient.

I suspect we are not in great disagreement. With very many thanks.

Yours sincerely

C. S. Lewis

TO CANON OLIVER CHASE QUICK (P):[3]

As from Magdalen

Jan 18th 1941

My dear Canon Quick –

Thank you very much indeed for your kind letter, all the more

3 Canon Oliver Chase Quick (1885–1944) was educated at Harrow and Corpus Christi College, Oxford. Following his ordination in 1912 he served at Newcastle, 1920–3, Carlisle, 1923–40, and St Paul's, London, 1930–4. He was Professor of Divinity at the University of Durham, 1934–9, and Regius Professor of Divinity at Oxford, 1939–43. His books include *The Christian Sacraments* (1927), *The Ground of Faith and the Chaos of Thought* (1931) and *Doctrines of the Creed* (1938).

acceptable because of its criticisms:[4] for praise without criticism is rather like an egg without salt.

1.[5] I fully agree that our fallibility as reasoners leads not only to the consequences 'some things may be possible which we think contradictory' but equally to 'some things may be contradictory wh. we think possible'. So far from wishing to suppress the second, I had a good deal to say about it wh. I only omitted for brevity. I wanted to draw the conclusion 'And therefore it wd. not be surprising if about 40% of the petitionary prayers addressed to God shd. turn out to conceal impossibilities' – clearly, if sound, a view in our favour.

I don't see how the admission of both consequences takes the point out of the doctrine. Does it not leave us in the position in wh. we already are about fellow creatures who know more than we. ('I'm pretty sure this can (or can't) be done but it's just possible that the Secretary of Faculties will find a way (or an obstacle).') A refusal to claim infallibility does not reduce us on this, or any other subject, to sheer nescience. The fact that we *may*, after all, have made a mistake does not justify us in expecting of God things wh. our best thinking pronounces to be impossible. Or have I missed your whole point?

---

4 Canon Quick began his letter: 'I have been so much impressed by your *Problem of Pain* that I hope you will not mind my sending you a few critical comments' (Bodleian Library). He was quoting from the original edition of *The Problem of Pain* (Bles, 1940), but the page numbers of the current edition (HarperCollins, 2002) are given here.

5 Quick wrote: 'The Thomist approach to the doctrine of omnipotence (which you follow) seems to me radically unsatisfactory, for a reason which you actually mention, without apparently feeling its force. "We may think things (intrinsically) possible which are really impossible." (p. 16) Exactly. Then what good does the Thomist doctrine of omnipotence do us? God may be omnipotent, and yet all the ultimate triumph of good which we look to God to achieve may, for all we know, be an impossibility. Apart then from the Christian revelation, the doctrine of divine omnipotence, however true, becomes quite insignificant. But this is not what St Thomas meant, nor anyone else who has believed in divine omnipotence. The doctrine does not mean that God can do everything not impossible (where the element of impossibility remains an X); it means that God can & will achieve His will in all things. From the sentence I have quoted (p. 16) you draw the conclusion, "We ought to use great caution in defining those intrinsic impossibilities which even Omnipotence can perform." But logically you might just as well infer "We ought to use great caution in defining those possibilities which even Omnipotence can perform – they may be very much smaller than most of us think." Surely there is something wrong with this doctrine of omnipotence?'

2.[6] I suspect I have got myself into a real difficulty here, and your question forces me to realise that I had no clear definition of the word *species* in my mind. And I am pretty ignorant of the theology of the incarnation. Can I, without heresy, get out of it as follows: 'incarnate in fallen manhood'. *Distinguo.*[7] If this means with original perversion of the will, *nego.*[8] If it means without the powers, as a man, of Adam before the fall, who had 'members' wh. did not even attempt to disobey, *concedo.*[9] i.e. can I say 'Our Lord had a perfect will even in the weakened and anarchical psycho-physical organism inherited from fallen human ancestors.' And if not, how cd. He be 'tempted as we'? I shd. then explain 'Perfect Man' as meaning *both* (a) Completely a member of the species *homo* as it has been since the Fall, *and* (b) Making a perfect response to the problem (temptation etc.) wh. membership of that species poses to the will. Is this possible?

3.[10] I agree about the self-forgetfulness in certain pleasures, or all pleasures (I think *all* pleasure simply good: what we call bad pleasures are pleasures produced by actions, or inactions, wh. break the moral

6 Lewis stated in the chapter on 'The Fall of Man' in *The Problem of Pain*, p. 79: '[The Fall] was transmitted by heredity to all generations, for it was the emergence of a new kind of man – a new species, never made by God, had sinned itself into existence.' On this point Quick responded: 'You say, p. 71, that the Fall resulted in the emergence of a new kind of man, a new species. What then of the Incarnation? Either the Son of God was incarnate in a species of manhood different from ours, or else He was incarnate in fallen manhood. I cannot reconcile either alternative with the orthodox doctrine or true gospel of the Incarnation. It was precisely the notion that our species of manhood is inherently sinful that led Apollinarius into heresy.'

7 'I make a distinction'.

8 'I deny this'.

9 'I agree with this'.

10 Quick's third point was as follows: 'I never have been able to understand . . . how an act of self-surrender to God can be an act in itself without some further & other content. I must surrender myself to God in doing *something* . . . and I cannot see why that thing must always necessarily be unpleasant. "A joyful & pleasant thing it is to be thankful" – may not a Christian do something he enjoys as part of a thank offering of himself to God? I have often thought that we need a more radical examination of the Christian concept of self-denial. Since I'm trying to put the *opposite* side of the truth to you, I would even agree that there can be a self-denial in joyful experience (i.e. a true self-forgetfulness) which is impossible in the doing of unpleasant duties even for God's sake. For pain naturally makes one intensely conscious of oneself, whereas pleasure, at any rate of certain kinds, prevents one thinking of oneself, because one is "absorbed" in the other.'

law, and it is those actions or inactions wh. are bad, not the pleasures). But I doubt whether any pleasure *is* (tho' many accompany) an act of will. But self-surrender is an act of will. In a pleasant act of obedience then we must distinguish the obedient movement of the will from the pleasure. Appetite and will are here moving in unison.

Now I do feel a real difficulty not only in being sure which is the main mover but in the reality of the will when the unison is complete – like the impossibility of steering a ship unless it is going faster than the current. And the *less* the agreement of will and appetite, the *greater* the *esse*[11] of the will at that moment. Of course the least perceptible difference of speed between the current and the ship allows *some* steering, so that there is a degree of will higher than zero in lots of acts we shd. call predominantly pleasant. All I say is that self-surrender can be willed 'to the height' only when the will is not being supported by appetite at all. Mind, I don't say that pleasures and pleasant actions have no value, only that they have not this particular value of self surrender.

I wasn't writing on the Problem of Pleasure! If I had been you might find my views *too* hedonistic. I wd. say that every pleasure (even the lowest) is a likeness to, even, in its restricted mode, a foretaste of, the end for wh. we exist, the fruition of God. But is it not also, here & now, the *road* to that fruition for fallen creatures. I daresay this is all full of fallacies: but I've got into them in the effort to follow what I conceive to be the normal value judgement of all unsophisticated people. That judgement seems to hold two positions quite equally strongly, one or other of which philosophers are always neglecting. A. That pleasure is simply good and is what the good deserve (whatever that means) B. That an act decreases in moral worth in proportion as the agent enjoys doing it.

You may ask, do I then think that moral value will have no place in the state of perfection? Well it sounds a dreadful thing to say, but I'm almost inclined to answer No. It is never presented in Scripture in terms of service is it? – always in terms suggesting fruition – a supper, a marriage, a drink. 'I will give him the morning star.'[12] May not that be one of the divine jokes – to see people like Marcus Aurelius and

11 'nature'.
12 Revelation 2:28.

Arnold & Mill at last submitting to the fact that they can give up being *good** and start *receiving* good instead.

But I'm writing at the end of a rather hectic day and I daresay I have only increased confusion. I shall be delighted to hear more of *your* views on these subjects whenever you feel disposed. With very many thanks,

Yours very sincerely
C. S. Lewis

* I don't mean, of course, 'can begin being bad', but that when the *beata necessitas non peccandi*[13] is attained, the will – the perilous bridge by wh. we get home – will cease to be the important thing or to exist, as we now know it, at all. The sword will be beaten into a ploughshare. The supreme volition of self-surrender is thus a *good suicide* of will: we will thus once, in order to will no more.

P.S.

4.[14] The point of the metaphor 'full speed astern' is that when you do this you change a ship's direction, and don't try to turn the ship into a railway engine. I was distinguishing the Christian view that all the Affections have to be re-directed from the egocentric to the theocentric, from Stoicism or Buddhism in wh. they have to be annihilated. (Do you know Donne's *Litany*, where he prays 'That our Affections kill us not, nor die'?)[15]

I tended to use 'movement full speed astern' and 'dying' as more or less synonymous, and have made a blunder in using 'death' in a different way on p. 92. I'm not [at] all sure that you and I really disagree about point 4.[16] Don't we both mean that *nulla natura mali*

---

13 'the blessed necessity of not sinning'. Lewis was quoting St Anselm (c. 1033–1109), *Cur Deus Homo*, ch. 10; here Anselm refers to *beata necessitas non posse peccare*, which means the same.

14 *The Problem of Pain*, p. 100: 'The supreme cancelling of Adam's fall, the movement "full speed astern" by which we retrace our long journey from Paradise, the untying of the old, hard knot, must be when the creature, with no desire to aid it, stripped naked to the bare willing of obedience, embraces what is contrary to its nature, and does that for which only one motive is possible.' Quick responded to this: 'I do not [see] how a movement of "full speed astern" could be required in the *strict* application of those words, unless the nature were *totally* depraved.'

15 John Donne, *Poems* (1633), 'The Litanie', XXVII, 242.

16 *The Problem of Pain*, ch. 6, p. 104: 'Where other systems expose our total nature to death (as in Buddhist renunciation) Christianity demands only that we set right a

est,[17] that our (good) nature is depraved, and that a turning round or conversion (rhetorically describable as death or going astern) is necessary. i.e. the *notes* are alright but need to be re-arranged into a new tune.

5.[18] If *eternal* = possession of limitless life, as in Boethius,[19] it cannot be attributed to the lost. But cd. there not be a negative eternity i.e. the merely timeless – existence no richer in reality than one moment

---

misdirection of our nature, and has no quarrel, like Plato, with the body as such, nor with the psychical elements in our make-up.' To this Quick replied: 'I find myself questioning your assertion that Christianity does not expose our total nature to death. I think it *does*, for the simple reason that what has not died cannot rise again . . . I do not think I am or ever was totally depraved – nor can I make real to myself the notion of a movement "full speed astern", which would take me nearer God. But I'm quite sure that I shall have to die altogether and thoroughly, if I'm ever to be fit for heaven.'

17 'There is no such thing as the nature of evil.' Lewis was suggesting that evil is in fact goodness depraved, and therefore redeemable.

18 *The Problem of Pain*, ch. 8, pp. 127–8: 'People often talk as if the "annihilation" of a soul were intrinsically possible. In all our experience, however, the destruction of one thing means the emergence of something else. Burn a log, and you have gases, heat and ash. To *have been* a log means now being those three things. If souls can be destroyed, must there not be a state of *having been* a human soul? And is not that, perhaps, the state which is equally well described as torment, destruction, and privation? You will remember that in the parable, the saved go to a place prepared for *them*, while the damned go to a place never made for men at all. To enter heaven is to become more human than you ever succeeded in being on earth; to enter hell, is to be banished from humanity. What is cast (or casts itself) into hell is not a man: it is "remains".'

Quick replied to this: 'Surely it is inconceivable that *eternal* life in this sense should be given to the lost or damned. It is by its very nature enrichment and enlargement of earthly-temporal life. And it seems to me inconsistent to suppose that the lost can have this sort of eternal life and yet that their being must become a sort of shadowy existence, approximating rather to nonentity, as you go on to suggest later. Moreover, it seems to me unsatisfactory to argue that the lost must be immortal, because not even a log can be annihilated. All that those who deny immortality to the lost need allege is that a lost soul is finally dissolved: and why not? To me it seems inevitable that *if* a lost soul is immortal, its life must be everlasting and unending in time, and *not* eternal. Now I do not believe that an everlasting life in this sense is *objectively* possible. But I do not see why (as Berdyaev points out) it should not be *subjectively possible*, i.e. the life of the lost soul might appear to itself to be unending and everlasting, if only because it could not possibly experience its own annihilation or dissolution.'

19 Boethius, *The Consolation of Philosophy*, Book V, prosa 6: 'What we should rightly call eternal is that which grasps and possesses wholly and simultaneously the fulness of unending life.'

of temporal life but, unlike temporal life, *not* compensating for this by extension into a series of moments? Such existence might perhaps be the opposite of what you and Berdyaev (whom I haven't read) suggest[20] – the true eternals, looking at it from the outside, would perceive that that mere point or minimum of being never passed away to make room for another, but the 'punctual' creature inside it wd. experience something like an *instantaneous* horror. (Are we at all sure that our present moments are not really like that? I mean, may we not find that, seen from eternity, they are all there still?)

But I am on the borders of the meaningless – perhaps have crossed them!

C.S.L.

TO BROTHER GEORGE EVERY SSM (BOD):

Magdalen
Jan 28. 1941

My dear Every

Thanks for the carbon. It is possible I am under the influence of Kant: but I wonder are you dealing efficiently with the authorities I quoted in my first article? They can't *all* have been Kantians you know! As for the *philosophia perennis*, Aquinas does distinguish the *peccatum* of an artist as such from his *peccatum* as a man (*Hoc peccatum non est proprium artificis in quantum artifex sed in quantum homo est* etc. I. II. Quaest xxi. Act 2).[21] Of course it is wrong to divide will, reason, & taste too rigidly: but I accuse you of being in danger of the opposite fallacy – using the fact that [day & night] or vegetable & animal merge

20 Quick appears to have been thinking of Nicolas Berdyaev's *Freedom and the Spirit* (1935), ch. 9, p. 324: 'The idea of hell does not receive its justification from the judgement of God nor the punishments which He awards, nor yet from the idea of justice, but rather from human freedom . . . Man is free to choose torment without God rather than happiness in God; he has a right to hell, as it were.'

21 Aquinas, *Summa Theologica*, Part I–II, Question 21, Article 2: 'But this sin is not proper to the artist as such, but as man.' The paragraph begins: 'Sin may occur in two ways, in a production of art. First, by a departure from the particular end intended by the artist: and this sin will be proper to the art; for instance, if an artist produce a bad thing, while intending something good, or produce something good, while intending to produce something bad. Secondly, by a departure from the general end of human life: and then he will be said to sin, if he intend to produce a bad work, and does so in effect, so that another is taken in thereby.'

into one another by imperceptible degrees to belittle the real differences between them.

I've just written a review of Pearsall Smiths *Milton & His Modern Critics*[22] for the *Cambridge Review.*[23] What a perfectly ghastly book! I hope you understand that if I thought Smith's case for Milton the real and best one, I shd. join Leavis at once. Against all that bilge Leavis & Milton and I almost stand together: and Milton wd. resent *this* defence more than the attack.

Yours
C. S. Lewis

If a man's diligence were perfect he wd. not make mistakes in arithmetic. ∴ When we detect a mistake we also produce evidence of some moral defect. But a mistake in arithmetic is not the *same* as a sin (e.g. the sin may be only just above zero, where the mistake, as a mistake, is v. serious). In the same way: if a poet were morally perfect, he wd. make the best possible use of his talent. ∴ a defective use implies a moral imperfection. But the poetical fault is not the *same* as the moral.

It all comes down to this: do you think it possible to *try* in poetry & not succeed?

TO MARY NEYLAN (T):

Magdalen College,
Oxford.
Jan 29th 1941

Dear Mrs Neylan

Thanks very much for your kind letter. My own progress is so very slow (indeed sometimes I seem to be going backwards) that the encouragement of having in any degree helped someone else is just what I wanted.

Of course the idea of not relying on emotion carries no implication of not rejoicing in it when it comes. You may remember Donne's *Litanie* 'That our affections kill us not – nor die'. One of the minor rewards of conversion is to be able to see at last the real point of all the old literature which we are brought up to read with the point left out!

22 Logan Pearsall Smith, *Milton and His Modern Critics* (1941).

23 *The Cambridge Review* (21 February 1941), p. 280.

I'm glad your husband likes the job. I won't leave the paper in the Lodge as things go astray there: come across any morning for it. I'm usually free up till 11 o'clock.

Yours (with many thanks)

C. S. Lewis

TO BROTHER GEORGE EVERY SSM (BOD):

Magdalen

Feb. 4th 1941

My dear Every

You touch the root of the whole matter. I'm sure you were right in tracing the *extreme* Richardian (and the Leavisian, so far as it derives from him) view to subjectivism. Since the real wholeness is not, for them, in the objective universe, it has to be located inside the poet's head. Hence the quite disproportionate emphasis laid by them, as by the Romantics before them, on the poet – to the exclusion of the object dealt with, the work of art as a *thing*, and the reader.

I do agree, of course, that a great deal of 'failure' is due to a bad social condition reflected in the whole language. Wd. it help to a final agreement if we distinguished 'literary badness' into

(a.) Less goodness than we hoped or expected (This is a common meaning of 'bad'. A man who says he has had a bad dinner doesn't mean he has been poisoned, nor even that nourishment & palatal pleasure have equalled zero, but only that it's been less good than he thought himself entitled to expect.)

(b.) Mere inefficiency, clumsiness, privation, e.g. 'bad' sentences in our pupil's essays turn on lack of ingenuity in overcoming such difficulties as the confusion of English pronouns – or, on lack of *invention*.

(c.) Positive badness – vulgarity, falsity etc.

I submit that only (c.) really involves moral evil even in the society & *not* in the individual writer who may be its innocent & ignorant victim. (a.) may lead to being in the proper sense 'second-rate' but in that sense the 'second rate' may be 'good' i.e. better than nothing. (b.) is an imperfection but no more evil than the staggering gait and lisping talk of a child.

What really happens is that the (b.) type of badness in the individual leads him in despair, or haste, to help himself to expression from a common stock infected by the (c.) type. E.g. a man of no literary talents, really and discriminatingly moved by a sunset and wanting to do it justice, might possibly help himself to 'the orb of day'. You reply that if he's no literary talents he oughtn't to be writing. That, I think, is true. And critics ought to discourage him. But they mustn't do so by calling him a bad man.

I've read *The Zeal of Thy House*.[24] It is pretty bad.

Yours

C. S. Lewis

P.S. The first sentence of this letter is a good example of (b.) badness thro' haste.

The Problem of Pain *had been finding some grateful and influential admirers, one of whom was the Director of Religious Broadcasting for the BBC, Dr James W. Welch.*[25] *The widespread ignorance of the Christian faith in Great Britain worried him greatly and, looking for people who could help him during this difficult time, he wrote to Lewis on 7 February 1941:*

> *Dear Mr Lewis, I address you by name because, although we have never met, you cannot be a stranger after allowing me – and many others – to know some of your thoughts and convictions which have been expressed in your book* The Problem of Pain. *I should like to take this opportunity of saying how grateful I am to you personally for the help this book has given me.*
>
> *I write to ask whether you would be willing to help us in our work of religious broadcasting. The microphone is a limiting, and rather irritating, instrument, but the quality of thinking and depth of conviction which I find in your book ought surely to be*

---

24 Dorothy L. Sayers, *The Zeal of Thy House* (1937), a play written for the Canterbury Festival.

25 The Rev. James William Welch (1900–67) was educated at Sidney Sussex College, Cambridge, and was ordained in the Church of England in 1927. He was Curate of St Mary's, Gateshead, 1926–9, after which he served with the Church Missionary Society at Oleh, Nigeria, 1929–35. He was Principal of St John's Training College, York, 1935–40, and the BBC's Director of Religious Broadcasting, 1939–42. He was Prebendary of Neasden in St Paul's Cathedral, London, 1942–4, after which he became chaplain to King George VI. Welch was Professor of Religious Studies and Vice-Principal of Ibadan University College, Nigeria, 1950–4.

shared with a great many other people; and for any talk we can be sure of a fairly intelligent audience of more than a million. Two ideas strike me:

(1) You might be willing to speak about the Christian, or lack of Christian, assumptions underlying modern literature . . .

(2) A series of talks on something like 'The Christian Faith As I See It – by A Layman': I am sure there is need of a positive restatement of Christian doctrine in lay language. But there may be other subjects on which you would rather speak.[26]

TO DR JAMES W. WELCH (BBC):

Magdalen College,
Oxford.
Feb 10th 1941

Dear Mr Welch,

Thanks for your kind remarks about my book. I would like to give a series of talks as you suggest, but it would have to be in the vacation. Modern literature would not suit me.

I think what I mainly want to talk about is the Law of Nature, or objective right and wrong. It seems to me that the N.T., by preaching repentance and forgiveness, always *assumes* an audience who already believe in the Law of Nature and know they have disobeyed it. In modern England we cannot at present assume this, and therefore most apologetic begins a stage too far on. The first step is to create, or recover, the sense of guilt. Hence if I give a series of talks I should mention Christianity only at the end, and would prefer not to unmask my battery till then. Some title like 'The Art of being Shocked' or 'These Humans' would suit me. Let me know what you think of this and how many talks and at what dates (roughly) you would like.

Yours sincerely
C. S. Lewis

Lewis next heard from Eric Fenn, Assistant Head of Religious Broadcasting at the BBC.[27] *He wrote to Lewis on 14 February: 'I wonder whether you*

---

26 Justin Phillips, *C. S. Lewis at the BBC: Messages of Hope in the Darkness of War* (London: HarperCollins, 2002), p. 80.

27 Eric Fenn (1899–1995) was a pacifist, and as a result of refusing military service in 1917 he was sent to Wormwood Scrubbs prison. Following the war he took a

would care to consider a series of four Wednesday evening talks (7.40–8.00 p.m.) in August, or alternatively September?'[28]

TO ERIC FENN (BBC):

Magdalen College,
Oxford.
Feb 17th 1941

Dear Mr Fenn

Thanks for your letter. August wd. suit me very well. I shall be happy to see you whenever you find it convenient to come to Oxford. Pray come and lunch – a Thursday or a Saturday would, in most weeks, be the best days for me.

Yours sincerely
C. S. Lewis

TO MARY NEYLAN (T):

Magdalen College,
Oxford.
Feb 20th [1941]

Dear Mrs Neylan

I am sorry I was engaged when you called. I shall of course be delighted to see you on Friday nights whenever you find it convenient if you can face a v. crowded roomful of youngsters and the bus journey home. From 9 till 11 still remains my only free time, when I shall be glad to see you – not that I understand that subject any more than you.

Yours sincerely
C. S. Lewis

At about this stage of the war the Dean of St Paul's, the Very Rev. Walter Robert Matthews (1881–1973) wrote to the Chaplain-in-Chief of the Royal

---

degree at Imperial College, London, after which he trained for the Presbyterian ministry at Westminster College, Cambridge. In 1926 he began working with the Student Christian Movement. He joined the BBC in 1939 as Assistant Director of Religious Broadcasting, leaving the post in 1945 to work on a programme entitled *Think on These Things*. Fenn left the BBC in 1957 and until his retirement in 1968 he was Professor of Christian Doctrine at Selly Oak College, Birmingham.

28 BBC Archives Centre.

Air Force, the Rev. Maurice Edwards,[29] *mentioning a lectureship in his patronage. In these unusual circumstances, he thought it could be a travelling lectureship, and he suggested that, as Lewis might be at a loose end, the Chaplain-in-Chief make use of him. Edwards wrote to Lewis about this, and soon afterwards he and his assistant, the Reverend Charles Gilmore,*[30] *called on Lewis at Magdalen. Gilmore remembered that 'Lewis was diffident of himself but keen to try. I remember that he mentioned that the whole project might well be aborted because the call-up age would reach him the following year. We fixed up details of expenses to be paid by the public purse, and the lectureship could provide his fees.'*[31]

After this meeting the Chaplain-in-Chief informed the chaplains of the RAF that Lewis would be available at weekends to speak on the Christian faith. The first of such talks was given at the RAF base at Abingdon in April.

TO EMRYS EVANS (UC OF NORTH WALES):[32]

Magdalen College
Oxford

March 14th. 1941

Dear Dr. Evans

Please tell the Senate that I am greatly honoured by their invi-

---

29 The Rev. Maurice Henry Edwards (1886–1961) was educated at Queen's College, Cambridge, and Leeds Clergy School. He became a chaplain in the Royal Air Force in 1918, serving in Iraq and Egypt. He was Chaplain-in-Chief of the RAF, 1940–4, after which he was Rector of Acton Burnell cum Pitchford from 1948 until his retirement in 1953.

30 The Rev. Charles James Frederick Gilmore (1908–90) took a BA from St John's College, Oxford, in 1931. After a year at Wycliffe Hall theological college, Oxford, he was ordained in 1932. Gilmore was Curate at Stoke-next-Guildford, 1932–4, and Vicar of St Luke, Battersea, 1934–6. In 1936 he became a chaplain with the Royal Air Force, and in 1949 Assistant Chaplain-in-Chief. He served as Warden of the College of Aeronautics, 1950–2, and adviser to the College, 1968–75. In 1943 he founded and was the first Commandant of the Royal Air Force Chaplains' Society and Society of Moral Leadership.

31 Letter to Walter Hooper quoted in Roger Lancelyn Green and Walter Hooper, *C. S. Lewis: A Biography*, rev. edn (2002), p. 243.

32 (Sir) David Emrys Evans (1891–1966) was educated at University College of North Wales, Bangor, and Jesus College, Oxford. After two years as assistant lecturer in Classics at University College of North Wales, 1919–21, he was the first Professor of Classics at University College, Swansea, 1921–7. Returning to Bangor in 1927, he was Principal of University College of North Wales, 1927–58. His books include

tation.[33] I should much like to give these lectures on *Paradise Lost.*

The only question is whether I shall find myself free when the time comes. I am at present in the state of having promised to undertake some lecturing to the forces which may, or may not, develop into a full time job. If it does, I do not know what my commitments will be. I am therefore in some doubt how to answer your invitation. It may be that almost everyone's plans are at present equally uncertain: if so, a conditional acceptance is a nuisance you may have to face from anyone, and if you choose to face it from me, I accept. If, on the other hand, you can find anyone who is in a position to be more definite, I fully realise that you might very properly prefer him. I await your decision. With thanks.

Yours sincerely
C. S. Lewis

TO FRANK SANDERS (BOD):[34]

Magdalen College,
Oxford.
March 22nd 1941

Dear Mr. Sanders

Thank you very much indeed for the copy of *Elfadore and*

Crefydd a Chymdeithas (1933), *Llais Rhyddid: Detholiad* (1941) and *The University of Wales* (1953).

33 Dr Evans had written to Lewis on 11 March 1941 on behalf of University College of North Wales: 'I am writing on behalf of the Senate of the College to extend to you an invitation to deliver the Ballard Mathews Lectures here next season. Professor Mathews was our first Professor of Mathematics, and he was also a humanist widely read in general literature. It was his desire that his small property should after his sister's death come to the College for the promotion of general culture as distinct from specialist study, but his sister's generosity has enabled us to bring the scheme into action during her lifetime . . . We should be highly honoured if you could find it possible to give a short course of three lectures in the session 1941–42. The lectures would be given in successive nights in the course of a single visit.'

34 Francis Hawkins 'Frank' Sanders (1887–1969), antiquarian bookseller of international reputation, was born and brought up in Barnstaple, Devon. He began his career with W. H. Smith in London and then Minehead. In about 1919 he became business manager to Leslie Chaundy, a well-known figure in antiquarian books at 104 High Street, Oxford. Sanders took over the business in 1924, naming it Sanders & Co. and combining the selling of books with old prints and watercolours. He christened the shop 'Salutation House' after the old building, which had once been the Salutation Inn. Over the years it became a gathering

Mabyna[35] which you so kindly sent me through Mr. Fox.[36] I don't know that I have ever seen this particular game played more prettily. The 'panorama of the gnome'[37] and that whole passage on p. 42 is really exquisite: also the gravely authoritative pedigree of the mice on pp 15 and 16; and the ultra-whimsical simile of the word Egypt on p. 46.[38] I have been trying to find out why *stones of thread* on the first page is so much more effective than *threads of stone* wd. have been.[39] Of course I am devoured with curiosity as to the author, but no doubt you can keep counsel and I must die in suspense!

With very many thanks,

Yours sincerely

C. S. Lewis

TO DOUGLAS BUSH (W):

Magdalen College,
Oxford.
March 28th 1941

Dear Mr. Bush

Thank you very much indeed for *The Renaissance and English Humanism*[40] which I have read with almost continuous excitement to the accompaniment of two opposite feelings: (a) 'Thank Heaven here's a man who has seen through the smoke-screen at last!' (b) 'Drat this man, he's stealing my thunder' – for a great deal of what you say overlaps closely with what I have just lately begun to put into my lectures. Possibly my approach is more radical and in the long run less

---

place for book-lovers and collectors of all ages and personalities. Some of the poets and scholars who became great friends of Sanders were Edmund Blunden, John Betjeman, Roger Lancelyn Green and Martyn Skinner. Sanders retired in 1958, but the business he built up retains his name, Sanders of Oxford, and remains at the original site.

35 Sanders had sent Lewis a copy of the anonymously published *Sir Elfadore and Mabyna: A Poem in Four Cantos* (Oxford: Printed for the author and sold by Messrs. Sanders & Co, 104 High Street, 1935). It was, as he later discovered, by Martyn Skinner. See the letter to Skinner of 23 April 1942.

36 i.e. the Rev. Adam Fox.

37 *Sir Elfadore and Mabyna*, Canto 4, stanza 17, 3.

38 ibid., stanza 32, 6–7: 'As deft and light/As when a quilt doth Egypt write.'

39 ibid., Canto 1, stanza 3, 3.

40 Douglas Bush, *The Renaissance and English Humanism* (Toronto: University of Toronto Press, 1939).

justified, than yours: my line is to *define* the Renaissance as 'an imaginary entity responsible for anything a modern writer happens to approve in the Fifteenth or Sixteenth Century.'[41]

I take a less favourable view of the Humanists than you. I've never quite forgiven them for killing live Latin and erecting the mausoleum of Ciceronianism over its corpse – specially when they themselves have to fall back on that live Latin and do so without gratitude ('quod barbari nostri *circumstantias* vocant' says J. C. Scaliger).[42]

On p. 33 ('such sciences flourished with fresh vigour') you put a neglected truth,[43] but, again, I'd put it more strongly. The Renaissance is the golden age of magic and occultism. Modern writers who talk of 'medieval superstitions' 'surviving' amidst the growth of the 'scientific spirit' are wide of the mark. Magic and 'science' are twins *et pour cause*, for the magician and the scientist both stand together, and in contrast to the Christian, the Stoic, or the Humanist, in so far as both make Power their aim, believe Power to be attainable by a technique, and in the practice of that technique are ready to defy ordinary morality. Of course, one succeeded and the other failed: but that shd. not blind us to the strong family likeness. And that, I think, is the dark side of Renaissance Platonism. Is it not mainly through it that the occultism comes? One more disagreement and I have done.

On p. 90 are you not in danger of countenancing a very prevalent exaggeration of the effect of the new astronomy?[44] I note your quotation

---

41 *English Literature in the Sixteenth Century*, Introduction, p. 55: 'Unfortunately it has, for many years, been widening its meaning, till now "the Renaissance" can hardly be defined except as "an imaginary entity responsible for everything the speaker likes in the fifteenth and sixteenth centuries."'

42 Julius Caesar Scaliger, *Poetices* (1561), III, ii: 'what those barbarous fellows have called circumstances'. See Lewis's treatment of this in *English Literature in the Sixteenth Century*, ch. 1, p. 30.

43 Bush, *The Renaissance and English Humanism*, p. 33: 'The so-called enlightenment did not banish astrology and witchcraft; indeed such sciences flourished with fresh vigour. And countless other irrational and uncritical beliefs and habits of mind persisted not merely among the multitude but among the educated, including such heralds of modernity as Bodin and Bacon and Descartes.'

44 ibid., p. 90: 'Astronomy crystallized the great question, "What do I know?" in a vast and terrifying form. What had been a relatively small world, created by a fatherly God for the benefit of man, who was lord of the rest of creation, became an infinite universe of universes made by natural law, a mechanical system in which human dignity shrank to nothing and God the Father became a logical postulate of motion.'

from Drummond, but have you many more to put beside it? Surely what strikes anyone who comes to the literature of that age primed with the ordinary modern accounts is the scant interest that most people seem to have taken in Copernicus? The idea that he made an upheaval comparable to Darwin or Freud seems to me part of the bluff that you (and, in a smaller way, I) are trying to call.

But all these are nothing beside my agreements. On p. 31 'predetermined by the philosophic outlook of its authors' – yes, I shd. just think so. Pp. 37 and 38 yes, badly needed. P. 43 'gave Pagan writings a place wh. the modern liberal etc.'[45] Oh *grande Sophos . . . ge*![46] A beautiful salvo right where they live. Pp. 45 et seq. on art for art's sake.[47] I shake hands with you on that. Very good on Petrarch too.[48] P. 70 'their view is much nearer the truth,'[49] well said. Very pretty about 'alumni reunions' on p. 78.[50]

P. 85: yes, why *will* no one read Hooker?[51] Why is all that real thought neglected in favour of Bacon's *cul-de-sac* dreams of his unworkable method? P. 91 'antagonism of science & humanism,' quite. But how few of our colleagues seem to know it, though it is there

45 ibid., p. 43: 'Ecclesiastical authority gave pagan writings a place in education which the modern liberal would never dream of giving to religious works; and it was mainly churchmen who copied and preserved the ancient authors for often ungrateful men of the Renaissance to "discover".'

46 'great Wisdom . . . indeed!'.

47 Bush, *The Renaissance and English Humanism*, p. 45: 'The notion of art as self-expression and of criticism as aesthetic disinterestedness is quite modern, and it reached the logical end of its relatively short life in the gospel and practice of art for art's sake.'

48 ibid., p. 50: 'Whatever conflict there may be between Petrarch's religion and the world, there is little between his religion and love of the classics. With all the aesthetic sensitivity of a poet, he does not fail to stress the ethical and religious quality of the ancient authors.'

49 ibid., pp. 69–70: 'When we read in Bacon and Milton that the Reformation, with its appeal to ancient authority, brought about the classical Renaissance, we may say that these men, lacking our long perspective, put the cart before the horse, yet their view is much nearer the truth than that of modern historians who consider the Renaissance essentially irreligious.'

50 ibid., pp. 77–9: 'When we think of the Renaissance humanist's limitless faith in the possibilities of education, we may remember among other things that that faith was not annually sapped by the spectacle of alumni reunions.'

51 ibid., p. 85: 'Medieval ways of thought lasted, powerfully, a very long time; the explorations of reason are circumscribed – or, some might say with equal truth, are inspired – by the same premises for Hooker as for Aquinas.'

staring them in the face as late as the *Dunciad,*[52] *Laputa,*[53] the *Rambler.*

P. 94 'the fundamental questions etc'[54] – I can't tell you how deeply I agree. From p. 97 to the end of that chapter you are really great – as also are pp. 132, 133. I congratulate you heartily on a really great little book – and all, if I may say so, so witty, *merum sal*[55] but without the least taint of that ghastly flippant brightness one gets in Garrod[56] and (latterly) in Livingstone Lowes[57] – a sad substitute for gaiety invented by people who think that not to be grave is necessarily to be merry.

With Milton we come to disagreements again. You can't (come now: sad brow, true maid)[58] you *can't* mean what you say about *Comus* at the bottom of p. 108.[59] Are you sure it's not exactly what it pretends to be – a hymn to the most voluptuous of the virtues, chastity? And (excuse me) have you ever sat down to read it in a quite naïf way in the hope of *doceri cum delectatione*?[60] Because, of course, until one does, one knows no more of its real quality than one can know of a saw by trying to use it as a hatchet.

I make bold to talk this way because I'm a recent convert to a simple

---

52 Alexander Pope, *The Dunciad* (1728, 1742, 1743).

53 The flying island in Jonathan Swift's *Gulliver's Travels* (1726).

54 Bush, *The Renaissance and English Humanism*, p. 94: 'The fundamental questions asked by Plato and Cicero, Erasmus and Montaigne, have been neglected by believers in machinery, and in our time they have been largely handed over to psychologists, sociologists, and exponents of progressive education.'

55 Lucretius, *De Rerum Natura*, Book IV, 1162: 'pure salt' in the sense of 'wit' or 'charm'. Lucretius notes the use of this phrase as a term of loving praise.

56 Heathcote William Garrod (1878–1960) took a degree in Classics from Balliol College in 1901, and as Tutor and Fellow of Merton College, 1901–25, he was considered a presiding genius there. Garrod was Professor of Poetry, 1923–8. His publications include *The Oxford Book of Latin Verse* (1912), *Wordsworth: Lectures and Essays* (1927), (ed.) *The Poetical Works of John Keats* (1939) and *Epigrams* (1946).

57 John Livingston Lowes (1867–1945), American scholar of English literature, was a professor of English at several American universities, and at Harvard University, 1918–45. He is best known for *Convention and Revolt in Poetry* (1919), his brilliant study of Coleridge, *The Road to Xanadu: A Study in the Ways of the Imagination* (1927) and *The Art of Geoffrey Chaucer* (1931).

58 See note 356 to the letter to Eliza Marian Butler of 12 September 1940.

59 Bush, *The Renaissance and English Humanism*, p. 108: 'With all the sensuous passions of a young man and a poet, Milton still holds the precious moly and has not stooped to sensual gratification. Yet the strain of repression is apparent in *Comus*, in Milton's effort to rid himself, as it were, of the sense of inexperience and inferiority to others which his moral strictness has entailed.'

60 'being taught with pleasure'.

view of *Comus* ever since I heard Charles Williams lecture on it last summer. He treated it simply as an exposition of Chastity and the student audience just opened their eyes wider and wider (his lecture being as piquant an unorthodoxy to them as a lecture on *unchastity* wd. have been to their grandparents) and, by Gum, he bowled them, and me, over. You will smile at the idea of a man actually reading *Comus* as a charm (*moly*) against lechery. So indeed wd. I. But isn't that smile just the survival in us of the art-for-arts-sake poison? And is there any way of finding out the real quality of the old books until we make the experiment of reading them as they were meant to be read? It's at least worth trying.

Paradise Lost, too. Try reading it quite seriously as a poem about *obedience* – a descant on Ulysses's speech 'Take but degree away.'[61] It made me sit up when I first did. But we're almost *ad idem* there, as I see from the bottom of p. 115.[62]

Once again, thanks & congratulations. If we both live, and civilisation remains, we may blow a lot of nonsense out of the way.

Yours very sincerely
C. S. Lewis

TO SISTER PENELOPE CSMV (BOD):

As from Magdalen College,
Oxford.
April 10th 1941

Dear Sister Penelope, –

Yes, I will come and address your Junior Sisters next Easter unless 'wife and oxen' have by that time taken the form of incarceration in a German concentration camp, an English Labour Company, or (to pitch on a brighter idea) some sort of Borstal Institution in the lower foot-hills of the mountains of Purgatory. But (if one may say so *salva reverentia*)[63] what very odd tasks God sets us: if anyone had told me ten years ago that I should be lecturing in a convent –! Thanks for the offer of

61 William Shakespeare, *Troilus and Cressida* (1609), I, iii, 109ff.

62 Bush, *The Renaissance and English Humanism*, pp. 115–16: 'We need not query a cheerful epigram, but we may notice that romantic idea which is still to be met, outside universities – namely, that Milton was of the devil's party without knowing it, that Satan was his real hero.' *Ad idem* means 'at one'.

63 'with reverence'.

hospitality in the Gate House, which I accept gratefully, though the Protestant in me has just a little suspicion of an oubliette or a chained skeleton . . . the doors do open outwards as well, I trust.

Thank you very much for the book.[64] It has given me real help. What I particularly enjoy in all your work, specially this, is the avoidance of that curious *drabness* which characterises so many 'little books on religion'. Partly it is due to your Hebraic background which I envy you: partly, no doubt, to deeper causes. Things that particularly pleased me were the true meanings of *Beloved* (p. 8)[65] and *Son* (p. 9),[66] the whole account of the Transfiguration (pp. 16 *et seq*), the passage on Sacrifice (p. 32), the passage 'This was a shock' (on p. 35), on our inability to understand sin (41 and 47), the very important bit about Hebrew & Roman ideas of ransom (52, 53): the really splendid account of *how* God can't help deceiving the devil (56)[67] and the allegorical close. There are, in fact, a good many Gifford Lectures[68] and other such weighty

64 Sister Penelope sent him a copy of her new book, *Windows on Jerusalem: A Study in the Mystery of Redemption* (London: The Pax House, 1941).

65 A Member of CSMV [Sister Penelope], *Windows on Jerusalem*, pp. 7–8: '"Thou art My Son, the Beloved: in Thee I am well pleased." These words stated two facts. First, they declared Jesus to be in very truth Messiah of God, His vice-regent upon earth . . . These words are a reminiscence of what God says in Isa. XLii.1: "My Servant, in whom My soul delights". Jesus, then, is not Messiah only; He is also the Suffering Servant of the Lord.'

66 ibid., p. 9: 'It is quite certain . . . that Messiah and Suffering Servant were very far from being so connected in popular thought, and that Jesus' union of the two rôles in His own person was from the point of view of His contemporaries completely new and startling. That union He Himself expressed later by calling Himself the Son of Man . . . It sounds queer to our ears and queerer still in Greek, for there it is literally "the son of the man", which really means nothing. But in Semitic parlance the phrase was as clear as day: "son of" conveys the idea of unity of nature rather than of derived existence, and the one-like-to-a-son-of-man in Daniel's vision meant simply The Man, the being pre-eminently human, who, as contrasted with the inferior beasts, stands for faithful Israel oppressed by heathen nations.'

67 ibid., pp. 55–6: 'We ourselves are debarred from fully understanding God in the first place by our creaturehood . . . But the devil is debarred from understanding Him, not by his creaturehood only, however superior that may originally have been to ours, but much more by his self-constituted devilhood. Because he has completely repudiated the Divine Likeness in himself, he cannot recognize it in another.'

68 The Gifford Lectures, held at the Universities of Edinburgh, Glasgow, Aberdeen and St Andrews, were established by Adam, Lord Gifford (d. 1887) to 'promote and diffuse the study of Natural Theology in the widest sense of the term – in other words, the knowledge of God'.

tomes out of which I've got less meat (and indeed less efficient cookery!).

You never told me how you got on with the WAFS.[69] I have just started doing something of the same kind with R.A.F. officers and shd. be interested to compare notes. With many thanks and best wishes for Easter.

Yours sincerely
C. S. Lewis

TO MARY NEYLAN (T):

Magdalen
April 26th 1941

Dear Mrs Neylan,

(1) I think I understand what you say about Sarah. Since the total experience (wh. we have inadequately labelled 'maternal jealousy') led you to Him, I agree that some element in it came from Him. It wouldn't follow that the Jealousy considered in the abstract, was good. Cf. a *resentment* at a rebuke wh. is the beginning of a process that leads to real contrition. The resentment in itself is bad, but only the bad concomitant (at that stage perhaps inevitable) of a good thing, self-knowledge. In your experience, I take it, the good thing was the painful realisation of how far you had abdicated your maternal position – a complex privation, of joys missed and duties neglected. The bad element was the 'dog in the manger'[70] indignation at seeing that someone else had picked up what you had dropped. Conjugal jealousy wd. similarly contain good and bad elements, I suppose.

(2) On being 'patted on the head' (in Meldilorn[71] or elsewhere) I have just made some new discoveries. Something like a 'pat on the head' is promised ('Well done, thou good and faithful servant')[72] Link that up with 'entering the Kingdom as a child'[73] – then reflect that being praised by those we ought to please, so far from being the vainest, is the humblest and most creaturely of *all* pleasures. It is our Pride (as

---

69 Either members of the Women's Air Force, or of the Women's Auxiliary Fire Service.

70 A 'dog in the manger' is someone who prevents others from enjoying what is useless to him. The phrase comes from Aesop's fable in which a dog lying in a manger, by his growling and snapping, prevents the oxen from eating the hay placed there for them.

71 The seat of the Oyarsa in *Out of the Silent Planet.*

72 Matthew 25:21.

73 Mark 10:15.

usual) that has excluded from our idea of Heaven the old picture of the divine accolade.

(3) Hyoi's[74] second kind of longing was mainly nostalgia for the past etc. But I'm not sure I'm right: and on the question arising out of it wh. you ask I doubt if I'm a good guide. The important thing for each of us about any book is not whether it is wicked in itself but whether it can be safely read by *me* at this particular moment.

(4) You may say you want to confess your sins to God only. The trouble is that in fact you have confessed a good many of them to me! On the medical level, the amateur practitioner gets *prosecuted* for treating a patient if he is unsuccessful and found out. On the spiritual level, I don't know. I feel pretty sure, however, that if I now give you any wrong advice and the matter comes before any objective spiritual tribunal hereafter, both parties wd. be asked 'Were there no priest in your country?' And quite frankly I am not sure that it is *fitting* for a man who is not protected and supported by the special status of a priest or a doctor to be told too many of his neighbour's secrets – unless, of course, there is some desperate need. It's not a question of being bored at all – more a desire to walk in well established ways wh. have the approval of Christendom as a whole. I leave the decision to you. But one of the things on wh. a confessor cd. give you advice wd. be precisely the proper use to be made of a lay adviser, and the limitations of that use – specially when the lay adviser has no *natural* locus standi[75] as a father, brother or even an old family friend might have.

I hope the sleepwalking is better?

Yours sincerely

C. S. Lewis

Remember me kindly to your husband.

TO MARY NEYLAN (T):

[Magdalen College]
April 30th [1941]

Dear Mrs Neylan

I see from your letter that you have really acted with great circum-

---

74 In *Out of the Silent Planet*, chapter 12, Ransom cannot understand the distinction the *hross* Hyoi makes between two words that both seem to mean 'to long'.

75 'recognized position'.

spection and made every effort to seek advice in more professional quarters! I hope that my last letter, written in ignorance of this, did not sound dictatorial. You may put out of your head any idea of 'not having a claim' on any help I can give. Every human being, still more every Christian, has an absolute claim on me for any service I can render them without neglecting other duties.

When I spoke of some one with more *locus standi* I didn't mean someone 'on whom you had a claim' in the least. I only meant that certain things were most properly discussed *either* where a professional status makes them impersonal *or* where some natural, objective relation between the speakers renders the personal confidence what our forefathers called 'convenient'. Conversations about *principles* (as opposed to particular facts) are another matter. But I think we both agree on the point.

Now, as to a confessor. The two alternatives that occur to me are (a) Milford, (b) A Cowley Father, preferably my own confessor, Father Adams.

The points *for* Milford are that he is a modern intellectual brought up like yourself, a married man conversant with domestic problems, besides being accustomed to hear confessions. The point *against* him is that he seems (from what we saw of him last term) to hold the traditional faith with rather too many concessions to the modern scientific outlook.

The point *against* Fr Adams is that he is much too close to Rome. I had to tell him that I couldn't follow him in certain directions, and since then he has not pressed me. He wd. also, in my opinion, be inferior to Milford as an intellectual guide. On the other hand (a) He certainly understands the human soul for practical purposes v. well indeed. (b) If I have ever met a *holy* man, he is one.

I write this without knowing whether he can take on more penitents than he has at present, for he is very old (an advantage in my opinion) and has had an illness. He knows some psychoanalysis.

I shd. be free at 12 on Tuesday if you cared to call in and give me your views.

If it is not impertinent to say so, I think your husband must have behaved like an angel. I have had the experience myself of remaining an unbeliever when some of my most intimate friends began to believe, and I've experienced the same situation the other way round when I began to change myself. It is an extraordinarily disagreeable one to the unbelieving party and if he is not good may provoke resentment. I'm afraid for a few years I just took the line of being as nasty as I could and saying everything that cd. hurt. God forgive me.

Yours sincerely
C. S. Lewis

The first of the Screwtape Letters *was published in* The Guardian *on 2 May 1941. Thirty more letters followed, one each week. Lewis was paid £2 per letter – but he would not accept the money. Instead, he sent the editor of* The Guardian *a list of widows and orphans to whom the £62 was to be paid. He did the same with the fees the BBC paid for the 'Mere Christianity' broadcasts, and those* The Guardian *paid for the weekly instalments of* The Great Divorce *in 1944–5.*

It never occurred to Lewis that he would have to pay tax on these royalties, and he soon found himself with a huge tax bill. Before things got out of hand Owen Barfield found a solution to the problem. After paying off Lewis's taxes, he set up a charitable trust into which Lewis thereafter directed all his royalties. They named the trust 'Agapony', or 'Agapargyry' = love + money, and from then until his marriage in 1957 Lewis made anonymous gifts of two-thirds of his income. By the time Lewis wrote to Owen Barfield on 20 August 1942 the Agapony was established and Lewis was directing where monies were to be sent. Although he disguised Lewis's name, Barfield devoted a chapter to the Agapony in his book This Ever Diverse Pair *(1950).*[76]

TO MARY NEYLAN (T):

Magdalen College,
Oxford.
May 9th [1941]

Dear Mrs Neylan

I have a reply from Fr Adams. He wd. like you to write to him as soon as you please and suggest a time for going to see him. The first interview will not be the Confession itself but to settle preliminaries. The address is The Rev. Fr. Adams, S.S.J.E., The Mission House, Marston St., Oxford.

76 See note 60 to the letter to Barfield of ?May 1949.

I'm sure you're doing right and that God is leading you and bringing you in pretty fast too. I shall never forget your reply 'It looks like it' when I suggested jealousy as one of the troubles – I never hope to see the human ship take a big wave in better style!

Continue to pray for *me*. I need it all: and may say in general that if I were to tell you as much about myself as you have told me (wh. I shan't!) the record wd. be much blacker than your own.

With all good wishes.

Yours sincerely

C. S. Lewis

Marston St. is about the *second* turn to the right off Cowley Rd. as you are going *away* from Magdalen Bridge.

Lewis had now completed an outline of the four talks he was to give over the BBC in August, which he sent to Eric Fenn for approval.

TO ERIC FENN (BBC):

Magdalen College,
Oxford
May 12th 1941

Dear Fenn

Will this do? I find the more colloquial you are in the actual talks the harder it is to make a close précis. I'm still open to new suggestions about the title.

Yours

C. S. Lewis

TO SISTER PENELOPE CSMV (BOD):

Magdalen College,
Oxford.
May 15th 1941

Dear Sister Penelope

Thanks v. much. I will certainly try to come over for a day as soon as Term and exams are over. We ought to meet about B.B.C. talks if nothing else as I'm giving four in August. Mine are *praeparatio evangelica* rather than *evangelium*, and attempt to convince people that there is a moral law, that we disobey it, and that the existence of a Lawgiver is at least very probable and also (*unless* you add the Christian doctrine of the Atonement) imparts despair rather than comfort.

You will come after to heal any wounds I may succeed in making. So each of us ought to know what the other is saying.

I've given some talks to the R.A.F. at Abingdon already and as far as I can judge they were a complete failure. I await instructions from the Chaplain in Chief about the Vacation. Yes . . . jobs one dare neither refuse nor perform. One must take comfort in remembering that God used an *ass* to convert the prophet:[77] perhaps if we do our poor best we shall be allowed a stall near it in the celestial stable – rather like this!

Yours sincerely
C. S. Lewis

TO ARTHUR GREEVES (W):

[The Kilns]
May 25th 1941

My dear Arthur,

I've been meaning, in a vague sort of way to write to you ever since we heard that Belfast had been blitzed,[78] but I had no notion until we got a letter from Ruth[79] to day that anything had been dropped out our end of town. She says that all my friends are alright so I suppose she wd. have mentioned you if you weren't. It's like the end of the world to think of bombs near Schomberg.[80] Can you let me have a line in the near future?

You said in your last letter that this war was in one way so different from the last (e.g. you and I actually follow the news now! Nay, you have seen and heard the news happening) but in other ways brought the old time back. I feel both points very strongly.

---

77 The story of Balaam's ass is found in Numbers 22:24–31. Beneath this letter Lewis drew a picture of Balaam's Ass, flanked by a nun and a figure wearing a mortar-board. They are seated outside a stable in the radiance of the heavenly city.

78 *The Times* (17 April 1941), p. 2: 'Belfast bore the brunt of the indiscriminate enemy air attacks carried out against Northern Ireland on Tuesday night [15 April]. Shortly after the alert had been sounded high explosives and incendiary bombs were dropped at random over the city. A considerable number fell in residential and shopping areas, causing numerous casualties, many of which it is feared are fatal. Other bombs caused damage to industrial and commercial premises.'

79 Ruth Hamilton (1900–), later Mrs Desmond Parker, was the daughter of Lewis's uncle, Augustus 'Gussie' Hamilton.

80 The Strandtown home of Lily and Gordon Ewart.

Yesterday evening I got a telephone call from a lady who introduced herself as 'a friend of Arthur Greeves' and turned out to be Mrs Pomeroy.[81] I went round to her hotel after dinner and had about an hour and a half of most interesting conversation. She wasn't in the least like what I remembered either in appearance or in mind. I had thought of her as rather vague and perhaps theosophical but she turns out to be very definitely Christian. The talk was all on that subject and I liked her.

About 3 weeks ago I had to make a gramophone record (not a song!) and heard it played through afterwards.[82] Tho' warned to expect a surprise, I was unprepared for the total unfamiliarity of the voice; not a trace, not a hint, of anything one could identify with oneself – one couldn't possibly guess who it was. I realise (an awful moment) that certain imitations of my voice wh. I've heard in Bernagh are much nearer the reality than I supposed. But don't any of you crow; wait till you hear yourselves and then talk if you dare!

Minto is pretty poorly and has a game heart. We are sometimes rather a sad household and then at other times rather better – wh., I suppose, is what the plain truth about any house wd. come down to now-a-days, or indeed in any days.

Warnie has not been recalled to the Army I'm glad to say and is living in his motor boat a few miles away as part of the Upper Thames Patrol. He's painted the boat battleship-grey and bought a blue peaked cap so as to emphasise the fact that he's now part of the navy! Dear Warnie – he's one of the simplest souls I know in a way: certainly one of the best at getting simple pleasures.

I'd love news of everyone at home. How are the McNeills? and Kelsie? and Gundred? and Reid? And your nice friends out at Comber? and I'd like news of *things*. I hope they didn't drop a bomb on the Shepherds Hut or Africa or our own wood. Was it prophetic when we used to walk about those parts talking about the 'giant knocking on the door of the world'? He's knocked now. And mixed up with all this come

---

81 Mrs Pomeroy, from Belfast, was an old friend of Arthur Greeves. She founded and edited a small periodical called the *Odds & Ends Magazine* to which Lewis contributed. No copies have been found. See the letter to Arthur Greeves of 18 September 1919 (*CL* I, p. 466).

82 In May the BBC had Lewis make a 'voice test' in preparation for his first series of broadcasts.

the irresistible, inexcusable, comedy pictures of if-it-had-happened-then, as (a) The Witch of Endor[83] entering the study and saying *very* fast 'If-you-please-Sir-there's-an-incendiary-bomb-in-the-water-closet.' P.B.[84] What's that Mary? W of E (much faster and an octave higher) P.B. Speak up, Mary, speak up etc. (b) Bob *sniffing* to detect gas (c) *Very* allusive and cryptic lecture on the *moral* dangers of public shelters from – well, I cd. select more than one candidate to deliver this.

I'm tremendously busy at present and get hardly any reading done. I have at last read a book by an author we often joked about Phyllis Bottome, called *Private Worlds*,[85] and am about half way through Moberley's *Atonement and Personality*[86] – v. good argument very badly written. I've also read some Peacock, and occasionally refresh myself with a dip into the *Prelude*. I read the *Imitation* pretty nearly every day, but it's rather like creatures without wings reading about the stratosphere. Oh, and I re-read *Woodstock*[87] and found I'd quite forgotten how good it was. Full of ridiculous improbabilities, but how little that matters when a book has got atmosphere and gusto.

So far our mutual positions are exactly the reverse of those we occupied in the last war: you are seeing it, and I am in a back area. While it lasts, Oxford is really nicer than ever at present. I am feasted on friendship and good talk (ranging from religion to bawdy) and kindness and cheeriness all day long.

I don't know what you think but I think a great deal of nonsense is talked about rationing. I've never been hungry yet – in fact the only way it affects me is to plunge me back into the pleasures of early boyhood: I mean food is a subject infinitely interesting and every meal a high light.

I've just been interrupted to go and hear the 6 o'clock news (wh. seems a shade better). I do wish people wouldn't turn it on. Once they've done so you can't help listening, but why submit to this nerve-racking more than *once* a day?

How is Mrs Greeves? Give her my love. I wish we could meet. I

---

83 i.e. Mary Cullen, the cook-housekeeper at Little Lea. See note 38 to the letter of 21 January 1940.

84 'P'daytabird', i.e. Albert Lewis.

85 Phyllis Bottome, *Private Worlds* (1934).

86 Robert Campbell Moberley, *Atonement and Personality* (1901).

87 Sir Walter Scott, *Woodstock* (1826).

never pass a day without remembering you and the Glenmachonians and the McNeills.

Isn't sleep lovely these times? It always was of course, but more so now. And by the way, I wonder how much of the excessive love of sleep in boyhood is due to the outward circumstances being so unkindly?

Yours

Jack

TO MARGARET CARLYLE (W):[88]

Magdalen College
Oxford
June 3rd 1941

Dear Miss Carlyle

I only heard your news from Adam Fox yesterday when he was just going to start for the funeral and I couldn't go with him. After what you said to me the other day I suppose you were in a sense prepared for it, but I know that doesn't really make much difference when the absence actually makes itself felt.

I am very, very sorry and sympathise with all of you deeply. Poor, dear Mrs Carlyle – I can hardly remember a time since I came to Oxford in 1916 when her kindness and humour weren't a part of my life. How good she always was with all us awkward freshmen – how much more important than some tutors and heads of houses whose 'influence on the younger generation' will be solemnly recorded in obituaries and memoirs. Now that the end has come my memory goes back, as I am sure yours increasingly will, to the days before her illness. I think one cd. almost apply to her, as she then was, what Chaucer says of the Duchess, 'She had such list to live, Dulness was of her y-drad.'[89]

One very great consolation you have which some of us haven't had

---

88 Margaret Monteith Carlyle (1896–1972) was the elder of two daughters of the Rev. Dr Alexander James Carlyle, former Fellow and Chaplain of University College, and Rebecca Monteith Carlyle (1862–1941) who died 30 May 1941, the daughter of the Scottish poet and preacher, William Chalmers Smith (1824–1908). The family lived at 35 Holywell Street in Oxford where their home became a social centre for students and their many friends. They had two daughters, Margaret and Mary (1900–72). Lewis came to know them when he was an undergraduate. Rebecca Carlyle collaborated with her husband in writing *Hugh Latimer* (1902).

89 Geoffrey Chaucer, *The Book of the Duchess* (1369), 878–9: 'Therwith hir liste so wel to live,/That dullness was of hir a-drad.'

at such moments – that of having nothing to regret, nothing even omitted. No mother was ever better looked after by her children. Indeed, if you will forgive me for saying something so crude, it is now years ago since I fixed on 35 Holywell as the perfect specimen of family life. One so seldom sees it: and when one does, as at 35, it *looks* so easy and one wonders why more people can't achieve it.

Give my love and sympathy to Dr. Carlyle. I will try to get round and see you all in the near future.

Felix opportunitate mortis of course.[90] But that is cold comfort.

Yours sincerely
C. S. Lewis

On Sunday evening, 8 June, Lewis preached his sermon, 'The Weight of Glory',[91] at evensong in the University Church of St Mary the Virgin, Oxford.

TO R. W. KOSTERLITZ (W):[92]

Magdalen College
Oxford
July 5th 1941

Dear Mr. Kosterlitz

I should very much like to join the study group you mention, but I fear that I cannot become an active member during this long vacation as I am now very busy with exams and as soon as that is over shall be moving almost continuously about the country. If the discussions are being continued next term I shall look forward with pleasure to attending them. With thanks.

Yours sincerely
C. S. Lewis

---

90 'Fortunate in the opportune moment of his death.' Tacitus, *Agricola*, 45: 'Tu vero felix, Agricola, non vitae tantum claritate, sed etiam opportunitate mortis': 'Thou wast indeed fortunate, Agricola, not only in the splendour of thy life, but in the opportune moment of thy death.'

91 2 Corinthians 4:17 'For our light affliction, which is but for a moment, worketh for us a far more exceeding and eternal weight of glory'. This sermon was first published in *Theology*, XLIII (November 1941), pp. 263 and is reprinted in *Screwtape Proposes a Toast and Other Pieces* (London: 1965; Fount, 1998).

92 Rolf Werner Kosterlitz (1906–89) was born in Berlin and took his MD examination at Berlin University. He matriculated at New College, Oxford, in 1941 but never took a degree. He worked in Oxford for most of his life as a psychotherapist.

TO ALEC VIDLER (BOD):

Magdalen
17 August [1941]

Dear Vidler –

(1.) I preached two sermons in S. Mary's and can't remember which was on which date. If the one you've got is on Rev. ii 26–28 beginning 'If you asked twenty good men', I shd. be v. glad for it to be printed in Theology. *The Weight of Glory* was the title. If on t'other hand it is a sermon on Faith beginning 'We are all quite familiar', then I fear it is already bespoke.

(2.) I'm so dreadfully busy travelling the country as a lecturer to the R.A.F. that I can't undertake even a review this long Vac. And also, I don't very much care for reviewing people who have shown me kindnesses as Sampson[93] has, unless it can't be avoided.

Yours
C. S. Lewis

Lewis went up to London every Wednesday evening during August and gave his BBC talks, which he had decided to call 'Right and Wrong: A Clue to the Meaning of the Universe'. He spoke over the air from 7.45 to 8 p.m. on 6, 13, 20 and 27 August. Before the talks were over Lewis was bombarded with questions from his listeners, and he gave another talk on 3 September answering 'Listeners' Objections'.

On 4 September Eric Fenn wrote to Lewis asking if he would give a second series of talks, entitled 'What Christians Believe' and to be broadcast from 4.45 to 5 p.m. on 11 and 18 January and 1, 8 and 15 February 1942. In order for Lewis to arrange the disposal of the fees made from his talks, Fenn gave him the name of Ronald Boswell who was Programme Contracts Director.

93 Ashley Sampson (1900–47) founded the Centenary Press in the 1920s, and after he sold it to Geoffrey Bles Ltd in 1930 he was retained to run it. He was the 'discoverer' of C. S. Lewis. He persuaded Lewis to write *The Problem of Pain* (1946) and other works published by Bles, and his interview with Lewis for the 'Anglican Portrait Gallery' in the *Church of England Newspaper* (4 October 1946) remains a valuable work.

TO ERIC FENN (BBC):

Magdalen
Sept 7th 1941

My dear Fenn –

Right: as far as I can see Sundays Jan 11, 18, Feb 1, 8, 15 are possible and I'll take the job. Thanks for putting me on to Boswell (is he worthy of his name?) to whom I have written.[94]

Yours
C. S. Lewis

TO FRANK SANDERS (BOD):

Magdalen College,
Oxford.
Sept 8th 1941.

Dear Mr. Saunders

Thanks v. much indeed for a delightful present. It arrived just as I was starting on a railway journey and I read it twice through. I'll try to write to Skinner when I get a moment – I'm up to my eyes at present. It is very good stuff. The critics will think it unimportant because it is so Popian and use the word *pastiche* – but really that style is a *lingua franca* and still one of the best ways of getting things said. The 'martyr smiling from her mattress stake' and the storm are really excellent. Give him my heartiest congratulations. With many thanks,

Yours sincerely
C. S. Lewis

TO JOHN GORDON WILLIAMS (BBC):[95]

Magdalen College,
Oxford.
Sept. 30th 1941

Dear Mr. Williams,

I'm afraid in view of my other commitments I shd. be 'over-talked'

---

94 That is, was he worthy to share the name of the great James Boswell who wrote *The Life of Samuel Johnson*? For the biography of Ronald Boswell, see note 5 to the letter of 16 February 1942.

95 The Rev. John Gordon Williams (1906–) was Assistant Director of Religious Broadcasting at the BBC, 1940–50. He wrote to Lewis on 17 September 1941 asking if he 'would consider helping us by giving a series of talks in our Sunday Programme for the Forces'. Williams took a BA in English from the University of

if I accepted the job you kindly suggest for me. I'm talking already to the R.A.F., to the general public, to nuns, to undergraduates, to societies. The gramophone will wear out if I don't take care! With thanks and much regret.

Yours sincerely
C. S. Lewis

TO MARY NEYLAN (T):

Magdalen College,
Oxford.
Oct 2nd [1941]

Dear Mrs Neylan

It's a pity your visits are so 'sudden like'! Owing to my itinerant lectureship to the R.A.F. (a map of my 'missionary journies' wd. be as complicated as those maps of St Paul's wh. haunted our childhood), I am hardly ever at home for more than 3 consecutive nights and unable to arrange anything. I'm off to Aberystwyth to-morrow. I'm glad to learn all goes well including the operation.

The reason why John's return journey[96] is so simple in the book is that I hadn't then begun travelling it and knew v. little about it – in fact 'ignorance, Madam, sheer ignorance'.[97] We both know better now! Cold Virtue has to assimilate the hot dragon, and flabby John the cold, hard one.

For Dante I should get (1) The Temple Classic with English on opposite page.[98] (2) Any Italian text. (3) Hoare's Dictionary which has a little grammar at the beginning.[99]

London in 1927, and then read Theology at Ridley Hall, Cambridge. Following his ordination in 1933, he was Curate of St Luke, Bermondsey, 1932–4. He also served at Holy Trinity, Rotherhithe, 1934–40, and Anfield St Columba in the Diocese of Liverpool, 1953–7, and was Chaplain and Education Officer of SPCK, 1957–72. His books include *Life of Our Lord* (1939) and *Hungry World: The Call for Christian Literature* (1961).

96 John is the pilgrim in *The Pilgrim's Regress*.

97 Boswell, *Life of Samuel Johnson*, vol. I, 1755, p. 293. Boswell wrote of Dr Johnson's *Dictionary*: 'A lady once asked him how he came to define *Pastern* the *knee* of a horse: instead of making an elaborate defence, as she expected, he at once answered, "Ignorance, Madam, pure ignorance."'

98 Dante, *The Divina Commedia*, with prose translation by Herman Oelsner, 3 vols. (London: Dent, Temple Classics, 1900).

99 Alfred Hoare, *An Italian Dictionary* (Cambridge, 1915).

I think the Talks will be published along with some more I am to give in January – but they contain nothing you don't know already.

I've met some wonderful things on my travels – a Baptist air-man who talked and looked like an angel and a Methodist Padre[100] who I hope will be a life long friend.

I'm sorry we keep on missing one another: but term will be more stable than Vac. With all best wishes,

Yours sincerely
C. S. Lewis

TO SISTER PENELOPE CSMV (BOD):

Magdalen College,
Oxford.
Oct 9th 1941

Dear Sister Penelope

I am ashamed of having grumbled. And your act was not that of a brute – in operation it was more like that of an angel, for (as I said) you started me on a quite new realisation of what is meant by being 'in Christ', and immediately after that 'the power which erring men call chance'[101] put into my hands Mascall's two books in the *Signpost* series which continued the process.[102]

So I lived for a week end (at Aberystwyth) in one of those delightful *vernal* periods when doctrines that have hitherto been only buried seeds begin actually to come up – like snowdrops or crocuses. I won't deny they've met a touch of frost since (if only things would *last*, or rather if only *we* would!) but I'm still very much, and gladly, in your debt. The only real evil of having read your scripts when I was tired is that it was hardly fair to them and not v. useful to you.

I have had to refuse a request from Sister Janet. Will you tell her that the 'wives and oxen' are quite real ones?

I enclose the MS. of Screwtape. If it is not a trouble I shd. like you to keep it safe until the book is printed (in case the one the publisher has got blitzed) – after that it can be made into spills or used to stuff dolls or anything.

---

100 The Rev. Joseph Dowell. See note 116 to the letter of 30 November 1941.

101 Milton, *Comus*, 587–8: 'That power/Which erring men call chance.'

102 Eric Lionel Mascall, *Man: His Origin and Destiny* (London: Dacre Press, Signpost, 1941); *God-Man* (London: Dacre Press, Signpost, 1941).

Thank you very much for the photo of the Shroud.[103] It raises a whole question on which I shall have to straighten out my thought one of these days.

Yours sincerely
Clive Lewis

I'm sorry the MS is so disreputable-looking: it's the only one I've got!

TO EMRYS EVANS (UC, NORTH WALES):

Magdalen College,
Oxford.
Oct 30th 1941

Dear Principal

What I have to say about *Paradise Lost* turns out to be pretty bulky. I shall have no difficulty about selecting high lights for 3 lectures, but I'm thinking of subsequent publication. May I take it that it would not be objectionable to your college if I publish (with any publisher I can get and with the sub-title 'expanded from the B.M.[104] lectures 1941') a book much too long to have been actually delivered – say, 60 to 70 thousand words? My own experience is that, when a lecture is the preliminary canter to a book, both gain by it.

Yours sincerely
C. S. Lewis[105]

TO SISTER PENELOPE CSMV (BOD):

Magdalen College,
Oxford.
Nov. 9th. 1941

Dear Sister Penelope –

Did your ears burn last Wednesday night? They should have for I was hearing many things (and all good) of you and of Mother Maribell

---

103 Sister Penelope sent him a picture of the head of the Shroud of Turin from Monsignor Arthur Stapylton Barnes's *The Holy Shroud of Turin* (1934). Lewis had it framed, and it hung on his bedroom wall for the rest of his life.

104 i.e. Ballard Mathews.

105 Lewis gave the three Ballard Mathews lectures on *Paradise Lost* on the three successive evenings of 1–3 December 1941.

from my guest for the night – Bp. Talbot.[106] But I say, Sister, in various senses *quantus Pontifex*![107]

He went down rather like a sack of coals into one of my armchairs and then, not much liking my fire, opened the coalbox and with his bare hand (disdaining the tongs) proceded to fling lumps of coal on it till I thought he was never going to stop. He then reached out his hand for my tobacco, wh. happened to be in sight, filled his pipe and talked till 1.30 the following morning. An overwhelming man . . . but *very* nice. One of my atheist colleagues who sat next to him in Common Room particularly told me he was a nice man: so he must be.

Thank you so much for the head of Our Lord from the shroud. It has grown upon me wonderfully. I don't commit myself to the genuineness. One can never be quite certain. But the great value is to make one realise that He was a man, and once even a dead man. There is so much difference between a doctrine and a realisation.

I am writing, really, for company, for I'm a sad Ass at the moment. I've been going through one of those periods when one can no longer disguise the fact that movement has been backward not forward. All the sins one thought one had escaped have been back again as strong as ever,

> *And all our former pain*
> *And all our Surgeon's care*
> *Are lost: and all the unbearable, in vain*
> *Borne once, is still to bear.*[108]

I re-read your essay on the dog Noonie[109] the other night when v.

---

106 The Rt Rev. Neville Stuart Talbot (1879–1943) was educated at Christ Church and Cuddesdon College, Oxford. Following his ordination in 1909 he was Curate of St Bartholomew, Armley, 1908–9; Examining Chaplain to the Archbishop of York, 1909–10; and Fellow and Chaplain of Balliol College, Oxford, 1909–14. He served as a chaplain in France during the First World War. He became Bishop of Pretoria in 1920, where he remained until he returned to England to serve as Vicar of St Mary, Nottingham and Rural Dean of Nottingham, 1933–43. He was Assistant Bishop of Southwell from 1934 until his death. His books include *The Mind of the Disciples* (1914) and *Thoughts on Religion at the Front* (1917).

107 'what a great priest!'

108 This is a slightly revised version of stanza 5 of Lewis's poem 'Relapse', first published in *Poems*.

109 The essay 'Consider the Dog: A Study in Right Relationship' from Sister Penelope's *Leaves from the Trees*.

tired with great enjoyment. Dogs don't relapse. Cats do, and go wild. I'm a cat.

I've got Ransom to Venus and through his first conversation with the 'Eve' of that world: a difficult chapter. I hadn't realised till I came to write it all the *Ave-Eva* business. I may have embarked on the impossible. This woman has got to combine characteristics which the Fall has put poles apart – she's got to be in some ways like a Pagan goddess and in other ways like the Blessed Virgin. But if one can get even a fraction of it into words it is worth doing.

Have you room for an extra prayer? Pray for *Jane* if you have. She is the old lady I call my mother and live with (she is really the mother of a friend) – an unbeliever, ill, old, frightened, full of charity in the sense of alms, but full of uncharity in several other senses. And I can do so little for her.

Yours
Clive Lewis

TO ERIC FENN (BBC):[110]

Magdalen
Nov. 14th 1941

My dear Fenn –

I'm plugging away at the 5 talks and have nearly finished. I'm thinking of sending copies to 3 theologians (C. of E., R.C., and Dissenting) to see if there's any disagreement. Let us at least be ecumenical. You shall have the scripts in a few weeks.

Sorry, I couldn't do anything on Worship. It's in the church of Michael Robarts that Dr Thorne marries Miss D – either *Framley Parsonage* or *The Small House.*[111]

Yours
C.S.L.

---

110 On 11 November Eric Fenn wrote to Lewis find out how the scripts for 'What Christians Believe' were coming along, and to ask if he would give a broadcast talk on worship.

111 Anthony Trollope, *The Small House at Allington* (1864). In Trollope's *Framley Parsonage* Mark Robarts marries Dr Thomas Thorne to the heiress Martha Dunstable.

TO SISTER PENELOPE CSMV (BOD):

Magdalen College,
Oxford.
Nov. 19th. 1941

Dear Sister Penelope –

Thanks for your kind letters. It was silly to grumble: except that Johnson says 'He that complains acts like a man, like a *social* being,'[112] and it is a curious fact that the advice we can give to others we cannot give to ourselves and truth is more effective through any life rather than our own. Chas. Williams in *Taliessin* is good on this 'No one can live in his own house. My house for my neighbour, his for me.'[113]

I think what really worries me is the feeling (often on waking in the morning) that there's really nothing I so much *dislike* as religion – that it's all against the grain and I wonder if I can really stand it! Have you ever had this? Does one outgrow it? Of course there's no intellectual difficulty. If our faith is true then that is just what it ought to feel like, until the new man is full-grown. But it's a considerable bore.

What you say about 'disappointed with oneself' is very true – and a tendency to mistake mere disappointment (in wh. there is much wounded pride and much of a mere sportsman's irritation at breaking a record) for true repentance. I ought to have devoted a Screwtape letter to this.

Please tell Mother Annie Louisa that I have booked April 20th–22nd. I shouldn't reach Wantage until (I suppose) mid-day or tea-time Monday, but after that will do as I'm told.

Yes – I think the quotation is from Patmore:[114] a very *perfect* poet within his own range.

Yours sincerely
Clive S. Lewis

---

112 Johnson, *The Rambler*, ed. W. J. Bate and Albrecht B. Strauss, vol. I, no. 59 (9 October 1750), 'An Account of Suspirius the Human Screech-owl', p. 318.

113 Williams, *Taliessin Through Logres*. Lewis was paraphrasing lines from 'Bors to Elayne: on the King's Coins': 'the everlasting house the soul discovers/is always another's; we must lose our own ends;/my friend's shelter for me, mine for him.'

114 If Sister Penelope was asking the identity of the author of the poem quoted in Lewis's letter of 9 November 1941 – 'And all our former pain . . .' – it was, as explained in note 108, Lewis's own. He seems to have confused it with a poem by Coventry Patmore.

In his letter to Eric Fenn of 14 November Lewis had said he was thinking of asking three theologians to read the five talks he planned to give on 'What Christians Believe'. The Church of England clergyman who read the scripts was probably the Rev. Dr Austin Farrer, then Chaplain of Trinity College, Oxford.[115] *The Dissenting clergyman was a Methodist, Rev. Joseph Dowell, who at that time was a chaplain with the RAF. The Catholic reader was Dom Bede Griffiths. At the same time, without waiting to hear from these men, Lewis sent a copy of the scripts to Eric Fenn.*

TO JOSEPH DOWELL (BOD):[116]

As from Magdalen College,
Oxford.
Nov. 30th 1941

My dear Dowell –

Here's a job of work for you! These are the proposed scripts of 5 talks I'm doing for the BBC in Jan, and I'm v. anxious to include nothing that all Christians don't agree on. Cd. you possibly find time to read them through and see if orthodox Methodism can give me, on these talks, a *nihil obstat*? I know this is cheek to a busy man, but presume on your goodness.

When are we to meet? You said you might spend a night at Oxford. Do, next term. I still remember our walks & talks as one of the brightest spots of my summer.

Yours
C. S. Lewis

---

115 The Rev. Austin Marsden Farrer (1904–68), philosopher and theologian, read Classics and Theology at Balliol College, Oxford, and took three first class degrees. Following his ordination in 1929 he served his title at All Saints', Dewsbury. He was Chaplain and Tutor of St Edmund Hall, 1931–5, Chaplain and Fellow of Trinity College, Oxford, 1935–60, and Warden of Keble College, Oxford, 1960–8. He was an active member of the Socratic Club, and his books include *Finite and Infinite* (1943), *The Glass of Vision* (1948), *Freedom of the Will* (1958) and *The Revelation of St John the Divine* (1964).

116 The Rev. Joseph Dowell (1907–99) was born in Coventry, and after training as a machine tool draughtsman, he responded to the call of the Primitive Methodist Church. He entered Hartley College, Coventry, in 1928 and on completion of his training in 1931 he served in the Redditch and Newark Circuits. He was a RAF chaplain when Lewis met him. Following demobilisation, he ministered at Champness Hall, Rochdale, then in Northampton, Cradley Heath and Wolverhampton.

On 5 December Eric Fenn sent Lewis his first response to the talks on 'What Christians Believe': 'I have at last had time today to read your scripts. I think they are quite first class – indeed I don't know when I have read anything in the same class at all. There is a clarity and inexorableness about them, which made me positively gasp![117]

TO PATRICIA THOMSON (BOD):[118]

Magdalen College,
Oxford.
Dec. 8th 1941

Dear Miss Thomson

When I said it was 'no good' trying to regard Jesus as a human teacher I only meant that it was logically untenable – as you might say 'It's no good trying to maintain that the earth is flat.'[119]

I was saying nothing in that sermon about the destiny of the 'virtuous unbeliever'. The parable of the sheep & the goats suggests that they have a very pleasant surprise coming to them. But in the main, we are not told God's plans about them in any detail. If the Church is Christ's body, – the thing he works through – then the more worried one is about the people outside, the more reason to get *inside* oneself where one can help – you are giving Him, as it were, a new finger. (I assumed last night that I was talking to those who already believed). If I'd been

117 Phillips, *C. S. Lewis at the BBC*, p. 141.

118 Patricia Tyler Thomson (1921–98), the distinguished editor of Sir Thomas Wyatt, was educated at Sydenham High School and St Hugh's College, Oxford. In 1943 she received a First in English, winning along the way St Hugh's Hurry Prize. She took her BA in 1944 and served in 1945–6 with the Auxiliary Territorial Service. On her demobilization in October 1946 she became an assistant lecturer in English at Sheffield University. In 1954 she accepted a lectureship in English at Queen Mary College, London University, and in 1983 the College made her a Reader. Her books include *The Victorian Heroine* (1956), *Sir Thomas Wyatt and his Background* (1964), *Elizabethan Lyrical Poets* (1967), (ed. with Kenneth Muir) *Collected Poems of Sir Thomas Wyatt* (1969), *Wyatt: The Critical Heritage* (1974) and *George Sand and the Victorians* (1977).

119 Thomson had heard Lewis give a talk in which he said very much what he was later to say in his talk on the BBC on 1 February 1942, and published later as 'The Shocking Alternative' in Book II, ch. 3 of *Mere Christianity*: 'I am trying here to prevent anyone saying the really foolish thing that people say about [Jesus]: "I'm ready to accept Jesus as a great moral teacher, but I don't accept His claim to be God." That is the thing we must not say . . .'

speaking to those who didn't, of course everything I'd said wd. be different.

Fear isn't repentance – but it's alright as a *beginning* – much better at that stage than *not* being afraid.

How interested are you? If you care to come and talk about it I expect we cd. arrange a date. Let me know.

Yours sincerely
C. S. Lewis

TO PATRICIA THOMSON (BOD):

Magdalen College,
Oxford.
Dec. 11th 1941

Dear Miss Thomson –

If you go down to-morrow I am afraid it will be impossible to meet this term. Ring me up or write to me when you come up again and we'll fix a time.

In the meantime, don't let yourself be worried in two incompatible ways. You are wondering whether Christianity is true or false. Remember, if you think it false you needn't bother about all the things in it that seem terrible. If you decide it is true, you needn't worry about not having faith, for apparently you have!

I quite agree any idea of counting up ones good deeds, as if one was in for an exam, is fatal. It was Christianity which first pointed this out. We are not saved 'by merit'. But of all this, when we meet. I suggest George Macdonald's *Phantastes* (Everyman) and *Lilith* & Coventry Patmore's *Poems*[120] & *Rod, Root and Flower* as books that might interest you.

Yours sincerely
C. S. Lewis

TO DOM BEDE GRIFFITHS OSB (W):

[The Kilns]
Dec. 21st 1941

My dear Bede –

(1) I'm extremely glad you've got onto my friend Chas. Williams tho' onto one of his worst books. He is living in Oxford during the

120 Coventry Patmore, *Poems* (1844).

war and we made him lecture on Milton to the faculty, so that (would you believe it, remembering the English lectures of your own period) we actually heard a lecture on *Comus* wh. put the importance where Milton had put it. In fact the lecture was a panegyric of chastity! Just fancy the incredulity with which (at first) an audience of undergraduates listened to something so unheard of. But he beat them in the end.

He is an ugly man with rather a cockney voice. But no one ever thinks of this for five minutes after he has begun speaking. His face becomes almost angelic. Both in public and private he is of nearly all the men I have met the one whose address most overflows with *love*. It is simply irresistible. Those young men and women were lapping up what he said about Chastity before the end of the hour. It's a big thing to have done.

I have seen his impress on the work in the Milton papers when I examined. Fancy an Oxford student, and a girl, writing about Mammon's speech in Book II 'Mammon proposes an ordered state of sin with such majesty of pride that but for the words *live to ourselves*[121] which startle our conscience, we should hardly recognise it as sin, so natural is it to man' (Compare that with the sort of bilge you and I were proud to write in Schools!).

Williams, Dyson of Reading, & my brother (Anglicans) and Tolkien and my doctor, Havard (your Church) are the 'Inklings' to whom my *Problem of Pain* was dedicated. We meet on Friday evenings in my rooms: theoretically to talk about literature, but in fact nearly always to talk about something better. What I owe to them all is incalculable. Dyson and Tolkien were the immediate human causes of my own conversion. Is any pleasure on earth as great as a circle of Christian friends by a good fire?

His stories (I mean Williams') are his best work – *Descent into Hell* and *The Place of the Lion* are the best. I quite agree about what you call his 'affectations' —not that they are affectations, but honest defects of taste. He is largely a self-educated man, labouring under an almost oriental richness of imagination ('clotted glory from Charles' as Dyson called it) which could be saved from turning silly and even vulgar in print only by a severe early discipline which he has never had. But he is a lovely creature. I'm proud of being among his friends.

121 Milton, *Paradise Lost*, II, 254.

(2) Now about the scripts. (a) The claim to forgive sins *is* in S. Mark and all the Synoptics.[122] (b) Yes – I think I gave the impression of going further than I intended, in saying that all theories of the Atonement were 'to be rejected if we don't find them helpful'. What I meant was 'need not be used' – a v. different thing. Is there, on your view, a real difference here: that the Divinity of Our Lord *has to be* believed whether you find it a help or a 'scandal' (otherwise you're not a Xtian at all) but the Anselmic theory of Atonement is not in that position.[123] Wd you admit that a man was a Xtian (and could be a member of your Church) who said 'I believe that Christ's death redeemed man from sin, but I can make nothing of any of the theories as to *how*'?

You see, what I wanted to do in these talks was to give simply what is still common to us all, and I've been trying to get a *nihil obstat* from friends in various communions. (The other dissentient besides you is a Methodist who says I've said nothing about justification by faith.) It therefore doesn't much matter what you think of my *own* theory because that is advanced only as my own. But I'd like to be able to meet you on the other point – how far any theory is *de fide*. The Council of Trent 'made satisfaction' seems to be the real hitch. What was the context? What error was it directed against? Still – don't bother, for I fear I shall have to give up my original hope. I think I could get something you and your friends wd. pass, but not without making the talk either longer or shorter: but I'm on the Procrustes' bed[124] of neither more nor less than fifteen minutes – you can imagine the difficulty.

What did you think of *In Memoriam* on re-reading it? I re-read it (with Barfield) some months ago and thought (1) That the last quarter

---

122 Mark 2:10–11: '"But that you may know that the Son of Man has authority on earth to forgive sins" – he said to the paralytic – "I say to you, rise, take up your pallet and go home".' Cf. Matthew 9:6, Luke 5:24.

123 In Christian theology the Atonement – the 'at-one-ment' – means man's reconciliation with God through the sacrificial death of Christ. There are a number of important references to this 'redemption' of man by Christ in the New Testament, for instance Mark 10:45, John 1:29. St Anselm (c. 1033–1109) explains in his *Cur Deus Homo* that 'Sin, being an infinite offence against God, required a satisfaction equally infinite. As no finite being could offer such satisfaction, it was necessary that an infinite being, i.e. God Himself, should take the place of man and by His death make complete satisfaction to Divine Justice.'

124 In Greek mythology Procrustes had an iron bed on which he attempted to reduce man to one standard. If someone was too long for it, Procrustes cut off the redundant part. If he was too short, he stretched him till he fitted.

is a falling off – and can hardly help being since the poem represents a sorrow neither being transmuted, nor ending in tragedy, but just petering out (2) That the mere difficulty of *construing* some stanzas is v. great. (3) That a great deal of the poetry is simply overwhelmingly good.

About the Son being subject to the Father (as God – of course, obviously subject as Man in the Incarnation) – yes, that's what I think: but was recently contradicted by a theologian. Can you back me up? What is the correct interpretation of 'equal to His Father as touching His Godhead' in the Athanasian Creed?

The Talks will be at 4.40 p.m. on Jan. 11th, 4.45 Jan. 18th, Feb. 1st., 4.40 Feb. 8th, 4.45 Feb. 15th. You look positively fat in the photo – you abbey-lubber!

Yours
C. S. Lewis

TO ARTHUR GREEVES (W):

The Kilns,
Headington Quarry,
Oxford.
Dec 23d 1941

My dear Arthur,

I've had a letter from Tchanie in which she says you say I owe you a letter. I thought your last was in answer to one of mine telling you about Mrs Pomeroy so that the next move lay with you! In fact I still think so. But I had in fact been meaning to write to you for some time in answer to your cheerful and encouraging letter about the Belfast Blitz. (By the way Tchanie praises you to the skies for your 'courage and *decisiveness*' as a Warden. Don't tell her I repeated this to you, because, as Miss Bates[125] says 'It would be so very.' But I thought it right to pass it on. Johnson says in Boswell, if you remember, that one always should pass such things on because 'Sir, it increases benevolence.'[126] Anyway, congratulation. The courage I always knew about – from many hair-raising occasions in your car.)

125 A character in Jane Austen's *Emma*.

126 Boswell, *The Life of Samuel Johnson*, vol. III, 4 April 1778, p. 241. It is actually Boswell who says this to Dr Johnson, who agrees.

I have had a very busy time all this year. I was made Vice President in College and the real President then got ill so that I had all his work to do as well – office work, which as you know is not in my line. I have become quite a dab hand at dictating letters to a secretary. But there were still a great many to be written by my own hand, and committees, telephone calls, and interviews innumerable.

In the second place, all through the Vacation I was going round lecturing to the R.A.F. – always for 2 or 3 days at a time and then home for 2 or 3 days. I had never realised how tiring perpetual travelling is (specially in crowded trains). One felt all the time as if one had just played a game of football – aching all over. None the less I had some interesting times and saw some beautiful country. Perthshire, and all the country between Aberystwyth and Shrewsbury, and Cumberland, are what chiefly stuck in my mind. It also gave me the chance in many places to see and smell the sea and hear the sound of gulls again, which otherwise I wd. have been pining for.

In the third place as the aftermath of those Broadcast Talks I gave early last summer I had an enormous pile of letters from strangers to answer. One gets funny letters after broadcasting – some from lunatics who sign themselves 'Jehovah' or begin 'Dear Mr Lewis, I was married at the age of 20 to a man I didn't love' – but many from serious inquirers whom it was a duty to answer fully. So letter writing has loomed pretty large!

Warnie is still at home. As I think I told you he spent the summer as part of the floating H.G.[127] in his motor boat, but is now in winter quarters at the Kilns. Maureen you know is married – to a most uninteresting little man but she seems to like it! Minto suffers a good deal with arthritis and overwork. Mrs Pomeroy has been in Oxford again but most unfortunately on a day when I couldn't see her.

I've managed in spite of other work to do a little writing. I'm engaged on a sequel to *The Silent Planet* in wh. the same man goes to Venus. The idea is that Venus is at the Adam-and-Eve stage: i.e. the first two rational creatures have just appeared and are still innocent. My hero arrives in time to prevent their 'falling' as *our* first pair did. You will also soon see another book by me called *The Screwtape Letters*, but that was written last year and has been appearing weekly in *The Guardian*.

---

127 i.e. the Home Guard.

It consists in letters from an old devil to a young devil on the art of temptation – you see the sort of thing.

There seems to be little time for reading: and anyway we know now that any book I recommend to you will be one you find unreadable! By the bye, I cherish a hope that the novels of John Galt which I mentioned fairly recently will have proved an exception. At present I'm re-reading Traherne's *Centuries of Meditations*[128] which I think almost the most beautiful book (in prose, I mean, excluding poets) in English. I also read on journies in the summer Graves' *I Claudius*,[129] wh. is quite interesting, but so close to Tacitus and Suetonius that perhaps he doesn't deserve very much credit for it. Dorothy Sayers *The Mind of the Maker*[130] I thought good on the whole: good enough to induce me to try one of her novels – *Gaudy Night*[131] – wh. I didn't like at all. But then, as you know, detective stories aren't my taste, so that proves nothing. I re-read the *Fair Maid of Perth*[132] when I went to Perthshire, and enjoyed it tho' it's by no means one of the best.

I'd give a lot to be able to see you again. I'd like to see how you look in a tin (or Bakerlite) hat. How is Mrs Greeves? Give her my love. To think of Mrs McNeil under fire is almost as strange and unearthly (tho' less pleasant) as an old idea of meeting her in heaven. Do you ever see the other Mrs McNeil now? But I imagine everything is so different under present conditions (including petrol rationing) that all that has gone by the board.

How little you and I guessed when we first knew one another what life had in store for us! And how little we guessed that in this war you were going to see (up to date) so much more of it than I. But I'm beginning to twaddle – why is it that things one feels and thinks extremely deeply sound so platitudinous when they are written down. All good wishes.

Yours
Jack

P.S. I'm giving 5 more BBC talks in Jan. & Feb. at 4.40 on Sunday afternoons, beginning on Jan. 11th.

---

128 Thomas Traherne (c. 1636–74), *Centuries of Meditations* (1908).
129 Robert Graves, *I, Claudius* (1934).
130 Dorothy L. Sayers, *The Mind of the Maker* (1941).
131 Dorothy L. Sayers, *Gaudy Night* (1935).
132 Sir Walter Scott, *The Fair Maid of Perth* (1828).

1942

TO ERIC FENN (BBC):

The Kilns,
Headington Quarry,
Oxford.
Jan 4th 1941 [1942]

My dear Fenn

I hope these reach you in time.[1] I could not get to the job at once and it has proved a tough one. The insertions entail some minor alterations in other places. I shd. be glad to have a fair copy of the whole revised text as soon as possible, to practise on.

Yours
C. S. Lewis

Lewis broadcast his second series of five talks, What Christians Believe, *on 11 and 18 January and 1, 8 and 15 February 1942.*

TO MARY NEYLAN (T):

Magdalen College,
Oxford.
Jan 20th 1942

Dear Mrs Neylan –

Sorry you're in a trough. I'm just emerging (at least I hope I am) from a long one myself. As for the difficulty of believing it is a trough, one wants to be careful about the word 'believing'. We too often mean by it 'having confidence or assurance as a psychological state' – as we have about the existence of furniture. But that comes and goes and by no means always accompanies intellectual assent, e.g. in learning to

1 Lewis was sending Fenn the scripts of his second series of broadcasts.

swim you believe, and even know intellectually that water will support you long before you feel any real confidence in the fact. I suppose the perfection of faith wd. make this confidence invariably proportionate to the assent.

In the meantime, as one has learnt to swim only by acting on the assent in the teeth of all instinctive conviction, so we shall proceed to faith only by acting as if we had it. Adapting a passage in the *Imitation* one can say 'What would I do now if I had a full assurance that there was only a temporary trough',[2] and having got the answer, go and do it. I a man, therefore lazy: you a woman, therefore probably a fidget. So it may be good advice to you (though it wd. be bad to me) not even to try to do in the trough all you can do on the peak.

I have recently been advised by Fr Adams to abbreviate a prayer for other people wh. was becoming so long (as my circle widens) as to be irksome. I have done so, but kept the longer one on two days a week. Result, that having ceased to be the rule and become a kind of extra, it ceases to be irksome and is often a delight. There is danger in making Christianity too much into a 'Law'. Let yourself off something. Relax.

I know all about the despair of overcoming chronic temptations. It is not serious provided self-offended petulance, annoyance at breaking records, impatience etc doesn't get the upper hand. *No amount* of falls will really undo us if we keep on picking ourselves up each time. We shall of course be v. muddy and tattered children by the time we reach home. But the bathrooms are all ready, the towels put out, & the clean clothes are in the airing cupboard. The only fatal thing is to lose one's temper and give it up. It is when we notice the dirt that God is most present to us: it is the v. sign of His presence.

The question about Sarah is why she *wants* not to have to ask the good one to make her good. Wd. it be right (I know so little about children) to point out to her that He *likes* being asked: and that if she *could* be good on her own, taking no notice of Him, that itself wouldn't be good. But ten to one the 2 sticks were primarily a game.

2 Thomas à Kempis, *The Imitation of Christ*, trans. Leo Sherley-Price (1952), book I, ch. 9, p. 79: 'When comfort is withdrawn, do not immediately despair, but humbly and patiently await the will of Heaven; for God is able to restore to you a consolation even richer than before.'

I'm afraid Saturday *is* no good for me, specially now. All goes fairly well with me. My duty to the gudeman and Sarah.

Yours sincerely

C. S. Lewis

Ransom is having a grand time on Venus at present.

The Screwtape Letters *was published by Geoffrey Bles of London on 9 February 1942.*

TO ERIC FENN (BBC):

Magdalen

Feb 9th/42

My dear Fenn –

I want as before to ask the BBC to pay my fees for these five talks direct to the following people in the following proportions,

1. To Miss Webb, 25 Alexandra Rd., Gloucester — 20 guineas
2. To Clergy Widows Fund — 10 guineas
3. To Miss Burton, The Weir, Twyford, Buckingham — 10 guineas
4. To Society of S. John Evangelist, the Mission House, Marston St., Oxford — 10 guineas

I return the cheques already sent. If you want to deduct postage & cost of cheques do it from item 4. Thanks for kind letter.

Yours

C. S. Lewis

TO SIR HUMPHREY MILFORD (OUP):[3]

Magdalen College,

Oxford.

[11 February 1942]

Dear Sir Humphrey

I am amazed at the celerity of your House! A royalty of 10% will do me very well.[4] I enclose a 'blurb' but I am not v. good at this highly

---

3 Sir Humphrey Milford (1877–1952), publisher, was educated at Winchester and New College, Oxford. He joined Oxford University Press in 1900, and served as manager of the London business and publisher to the University of Oxford, 1913–45. Under his management, Oxford University Press became one of the largest publishers in the country.

4 Sir Humphrey had offered Lewis a 10 per cent royalty on *A Preface to Paradise Lost.*

specialised art-form and give you *carte blanche* to hack it about as you please.

Yours sincerely

C. S. Lewis

TO RONALD BOSWELL (BBC):[5]

Magdalen College,
Oxford.
Feb 16th 1942

Dear Mr. Boswell

The Clergy Widows' Fund is conducted thro' the Church of England Pensions Board, The Moorings, Hindhead, Surrey, to whom the cheque shd. be sent, but made payable to the Clergy Widows' Fund.

Yours faithfully

C. S. Lewis

(*not* Rev.!)[6]

TO ERIC FENN (BBC):

Magdalen College,
Oxford.
Feb 25th 1942

My dear Fenn –

Thanks for your kind letter. I'm still wading thro' the correspondence caused by the talks: if you *could* have seen your way to putting them in *The Listener*[7] it wd. have made all the difference to me. I wrote 35 letters yesterday: all out of working hours of course. It 'gets one down' – not to mention postage. I know that this is not your fault – but perhaps you could pass it on.

---

5 Ronald Boswell (1895–1980) was born in Petersfield and educated at Harrow and Balliol, although his Oxford career was interrupted by the First World War. He spent the years 1916–19 with the Royal Army Medical Corps, after which he returned to Oxford. After taking a BA in Classics in 1919, he worked for the publisher, Werner Laurie. He transferred to John Lane in 1921 where he was a director of the Bodley Head. Boswell joined the staff of the BBC in 1935 as Talks Booking Manager, a position he retained until his retirement in 1960. He was also a foundation member of the Programme Contracts Department.

6 When Boswell asked Lewis in a letter of 12 February for the address of the Clergy Widows' Fund, he addressed him as 'The Rev. C. S. Lewis'.

7 The BBC's weekly periodical.

Yes, I'll try to do a series in the Autumn if you like and look forward to seeing you here to discuss it when convenient.[8] My duty to Beales[9] who looked after me a fair treat.

Yours
C. S. Lewis

TO THOMAS WILKINSON RIDDLE (BOD):[10]

Magdalen
March 3rd 42

Dear Dr. Riddle

The cow is milked dry – the tea pot is watered till it's no good calling it tea any longer – my purse is empty. In fact I just can't do an article in the near future. But thanks for asking me.

Yours ever
C. S. Lewis

TO DAPHNE HARWOOD (BOD):

The Kilns,
Headington Quarry,
Oxford
March 6th 42

Dear Daphne

My view of Being-in-love is that (like everything except God and the Devil) it is better than some things and worse than others. Thus it comes in my scale of values higher than lust, selfishness, or frigidity, but lower than charity or constancy – in fact about on a level with

---

8 i.e. a third series of broadcasts.

9 Arthur Charles Frederick Beales (1905–74) was educated at King's College, University of London. He taught at Haberdashers' Askes' Hampstead School, 1928–31, becoming a lecturer in Education, 1933–5. He was a lecturer in Education at King's College, 1935–53, Reader, 1953–64 and Professor, 1964–72. Beales served as Talks Producer of the Religious Broadcasting Department of the BBC, 1941–5. His books include *The Catholic Church and International Order* (1941) and *Education Under Penalty: English Catholic Education from the Reformation to the Fall of James II, 1547–1689* (1963).

10 Thomas Wilkinson Riddle (1886–1983) a Baptist minister, he edited the *Christian Herald* from 1939 to 1980. His books include *The Pathway of Victory* (1911), (with J. K. Maclean) *The Second Picture of the War (The Story of the YWCA War Service)* (1916) and *Matters of Moment: Meditations on Christian Life and Conduct* (1964).

friendship. Like everything (except God and the Devil) it therefore is sometimes opposed to things lower than itself and – in that situation – good: sometimes to things higher than itself and in that situation – bad. Thus Being-in-love is a better motive for marriage than, say, worldly advancement: but the intention to obey God's will by entering into an indissoluble partnership in all virtue and mutual charity for the preservation of chastity and the admission of new souls to the chance of eternal life is better even than Being-in-love.[11]

So far it is fairly plain sailing. The trouble arises when poets and others set up this thing (good in certain conditions with its own proper degree of goodness) as an absolute. Which many do. An innocent and well-intentioned emphasis on the importance of Being-in-love with one's spouse (i.e. its superiority over lust or ambition as a basis for marriage) is in fact widely twisted into the doctrine that only Being-in-love sanctifies marriage and that therefore as soon as you are tired of your spouse you get a divorce. Thus the over-praising of a finite good, the pretence that it is absolute, defeats itself and corrupts the very good it set out to exalt: and what begins by wanting to go beyond the prayer-book idea of marriage ends by reducing marriage to mere concubinage. Treat 'Love' as a god and you in fact make it a fiend.

As to 'Fate', which I call providence – I believe that the coming together of a man and woman, like everything else (e.g. the fall of [a] sparrow)[12] is in the hand of God. In our society the hand is usually

---

11 *The Screwtape Letters*, Letter 18, p. 71: 'The Enemy [God] described a married couple as "one flesh". He did not say "a happily married couple" or "a couple who married because they were in love", but you can make the humans ignore that. You can also make them forget that the man they call Paul did not confine it to *married* couples. Mere copulation, for him, makes "one flesh". You can thus get the humans to accept as rhetorical eulogies of "being in love" what were in fact plain descriptions of the real significance of sexual intercourse. The truth is that wherever a man lies with a woman, there, whether they like it or not, a transcendental relation is set up between them . . . humans can be made to infer the false belief that the blend of affection, fear, and desire which they call "being in love" is the only thing that makes marriage either happy or holy. The error is easy to produce because "being in love" does very often, in Western Europe, precede marriages which are made in obedience to the Enemy's designs, that is, with the intention of fidelity, fertility and good will . . . In other words, the humans are to be encouraged to regard as the basis for marriage a highly-coloured and distorted version of something the Enemy really promises as its result.'

12 Matthew 10:29.

displayed in the form of mutual 'falling in love'. In a society in wh. Our Lord spoke about 'one flesh'[13] this was not so: marriages were usually arranged by parents – and so in the vast majority of times and places. I therefore cannot make 'Falling-in-love' the universal necessary pre-condition. We must always no doubt support it as against any *inferior* one, but not against *any other* one in general. As for Godson Laurence – if and when he asks me my views on the matter (a not *very* likely scene!) of course I must tell him what I think true.

As for 'increasing Authoritarianism' – well! If that doesn't take the bun!! When you have heard half as many sentences beginning 'Christianity teaches' from me as I have heard ones beginning 'Steiner says' from you and Cecil & Owen & Woff – why then we'll start talking about authoritarianism! I humbly trot out a few platitudes about marriage wh. cd. be paralleled in several moralists: you reply with an exact account of which species of angels are concerned in human love affairs! You may be right, and I wrong. But which is the authoritarian?

As for austerity I see exactly what you feel and yet I don't think you've got me. I shd. hate you to believe that I am saying a word against Love – or Poetry or Music or Friendship or even Wine. I think that of all these we must say both 'This also is Thou' and 'Neither is this Thou'.[14] But people like you and me who have been cradled in poetry and suckled on humanism are in so little danger of forgetting the first and such daily danger of forgetting the second. It is so hard to express – I almost feel that Love is all the poets claim *until* people begin saying so. 'How like a god'[15] is a man until he makes the fatal false step of claiming divinity and goes plumb down to devilhood.

And can one forget what sheer misery comes out of the divine (i.e. demonic) pretensions of romantic love – from *Tristan*[16] & *Anna*

---

13 ibid., 19:5–6.

14 Phrases that Charles Williams often used to mean 'This is of God, but not entirely so', as in the chorus of the play *Seed of Adam* (1948).

15 Shakespeare, *Hamlet*, II, ii, 326.

16 There are numerous versions of the Arthurian legend in which Tristan (or Tristram) is a character, the best known of which are Wagner's opera, *Tristan und Isolde*, and Malory's *Le Morte D'Arthur*. For an outline of the legend, see note 66 to Barfield's letter to Lewis of 11 June 1947.

Karenina[17] down to the last poor little suicide pact in the ev.[18] paper? And is it Being-in-love that really makes the happy marriage work? Isn't it something different – higher? Eros won't do without Agape.[19]

Yrs

Jack L.

TO R. W. KOSTERLITZ (W):

Magdalen
March 14th 42

Dear Dr. Kosterlitz

I have been wishing to meet you for some time. I am busy next week. How about Sat. March 28th? Could you call on me here at about 11 a.m.? But you must be prepared to find me only a very amateurish philosopher. With thanks.

Yours sincerely

C. S. Lewis

TO DAPHNE HARWOOD (BOD):

Magdalen,
Oxford
March 25th [1942]

Dear Daphne –

I doubt if we differ as fundamentally as appears. I don't 'pooh-pooh any evolution in morals' but neither do I know the future, and so I cannot say that the recent N.W. European development has come to stay, nor do I know whether it is an improvement.

I am also v. doubtful whether there is any intrinsic affinity between individuals as to make it certain that neither cd. have been perfectly married to anyone else. (It was neither savage nor cynic but that happiest husband and most inconsolable widower Johnson who replied – Cecil will turn it up for you – 'Yes, Sir. With hundreds of thousands of other women.')[20]

---

17 The eponymous heroine of Leo Tolstoy's *Anna Karenina* (1873–7) is a married woman who conceives a passion for a young officer, Vronsky, and is ultimately driven to take her own life.

18 i.e. evening.

19 See note 3 to the letter to Janet Spens of 8 January 1935.

20 Lewis was misquoting a passage from Boswell, *The Life of Samuel Johnson*. See note 218 to the letter to Mary Neylan of 18 April 1940.

But my main feeling is, as I said in my last letter, that what *we* specially need to emphasise is the 'Neither is this Thou' aspect. If one is taught to treat even religious emotion as a mere servant wh. must never be allowed to rule, how much more must one think this of erotic emotion!

All these things, on my view, are capable of *receiving* spiritual value but can't *give* it: and the moment they forget their *creaturely* status they become demons. I think the real difference between us is on a more general topic wh. I can't well go into now – I don't think the conception of *creatureliness* is part of your philosophy at all, and that your system is anthropocentric. That's the 'great divide'. (By the way I *have* had a letter from a civilised and married woman approving this point in *Screwtape*).[21] Love to all.

Yours
Jack Lewis

Dorothy L. Sayers, author of the Lord Peter Wimsey detective novels and a theological polemicist, was editing a series of books known as 'Bridgeheads' that were intended to prepare readers for post-war reconstruction. The first in the series had been her own book The Mind of the Maker. *Sayers had been enormously impressed by* The Screwtape Letters *and had singled out Letter 18 as containing much good sense about love and marriage. About the beginning of April 1942 she asked Lewis if he would write a book on the subject for her 'Bridgehead' series, and the following letter was his reply:*

---

21 Lewis had explained what he meant by 'creatureliness' in *The Problem of Pain*, ch. 5, p. 47 where he defined a 'creature' as 'an essentially dependent being whose principle of existence lies not in itself but in another'. In this letter to Mrs Harwood he was probably referring to *The Screwtape Letters*, Letter 21, pp. 83–4: 'Much of the modern resistance to chastity comes from men's belief that they "own" their bodies – those vast and perilous estates, pulsating with the energy that made the worlds, in which they find themselves without their consent and from which they are ejected at the pleasure of Another! . . . And all the time the joke is that the word "Mine" in its fully possessive sense cannot be uttered by a human being about anything. In the long run either Our Father or the Enemy will say "Mine" of each thing that exists, and specially of each man. They will find out in the end, never fear, to whom their time, their souls, and their bodies really belong – certainly not to *them*, whatever happens.'

TO DOROTHY L. SAYERS (W):[22]

[Magdalen College
April 1942]

Dear Miss Sayers –

But why not write the book yourself? Either a novel, in which the familiar contrast of love-and-marriage *versus* career is replaced by the new (or so old as to be called new) contrast of love-and-misery versus happiness and marriage without 'Love'. Or a treatise. But de Rougemont's (otherwise $\gamma \equiv ?$)[23] *L'Amour et l'Occident* states the case superbly in its last chapter. Still, I expect there's room for more: but I hope you'll do the novel. It wd. soften the blow. Because the job is difficult. One will be accused (and *in a sense* not untruly) of defending simple appetite against *grand passion.*

It raises another question – isn't earlier marriage, so early as to be almost child marriage, quite defensible? But I waver myself now that I start putting it on paper. If we are wrong, clearly we are dreadfully wrong. But that's another argument for doing it in a novel, where [one] can *suggest* more than one wd. feel justified in *stating*.

I know all about the small domestic devils – those that cause ink-springs to arise on empty tables and those that remove passages from books when you want to quote them. I'd like to meet, but don't know when this Vac. I'm doing 'missionary journies' to the R.A.F. all over the country. Are you bidden to a conference on religious Broadcasting that Welch is getting up on May 17th? If so, we may meet there. Excuse paper.

Yours
C. S. Lewis

The French prose is not by me but by one of our evacuees – delightful creatures. I'd never lived with children before – oh that world of pencil-boxes! O bell età dell-oro![24]

---

22 See **Dorothy L. Sayers** in the Biographical Appendix.

23 The Greek letter Γ or γ (gamma) is used in Oxford University examinations to indicate third class. The query mark is there to suggest that perhaps the book was worth a higher, or lower, mark.

24 'O happy golden age!'

TO DOROTHY L. SAYERS (W):

Magdalen
[6 April 1942]

Come and lunch on June 2nd or 3rd – I've booked both. Yes – I understood quite well that you wanted a book for your series: but every word you wrote showed that you had the book in your own head and just straining at the leash. The last letter (with its v. important parallel in autonomy of finance) confirms this impression. All you're doing is to try to get someone else to do the 'ghosting' (or 'son-ing?') But it's no good: you're obviously going to write this yourself. (A good title wd be CARELESS LIVES COST TALK)

C.S.L.

TO SISTER PENELOPE CSMV (BOD):

Magdalen
April 9th. [1942]

Dear Sister Penelope –

The reason your MS took 14 days to travel 15 miles is that it spent 13 days waiting to be posted – sorry! Provided you care to risk that kind of thing and have spare MSS (I never accept *unique* ones) I shd. like to see them all. St. A. has arrived and I will start getting my teeth into it as soon as I can.[25]

Item: on a missionary journey to Plymouth I have been re-reading the *Odyssey*.[26]

Do try the same prescription the next time your rule of life allows you any fiction. I really think it is the best novel in the world.

The Ass is having lumbago: so references to breaking his back, or even references to *backs* at all, are coldly received.

---

25 In one of the notes Sister Penelope attached to Lewis's letters to her she said: 'He refers to my translation of St Athanasius *De Incarnatione*. This had been accepted by S.P.C.K. on Dr Cross' recommendation, and then turned down by their publications committee on the ground that it was not sufficiently literal to be used as a crib! I must have lost at least one letter at this point, for I know that C.S.L. wrote that I must on no account give in to this demand, as my English was quite close enough to the Greek for anyone with any sense at all; and he advised me to try another publisher – "try my Mr Bles." "My Mr Bles" accepted it at once, and C.S.L. wrote the Introduction.' The book was eventually published in 1944. See note 6 to the letter of 19 February 1944.

26 Homer, *Odyssey* (8th century BC).

Perelandra hangs fire for the qualifying reason that they decided half way through to enlarge the edtn.

Yours sincerely
C. S. Lewis

TO JOY PARSONS (BOD):[27]

Magdalen College
Oxford
April 12th [1942]

Dear Mrs. Parsons

Being on the point of setting out for an R.A.F. camp in our grim eastern counties – some place of Nissan huts and loud speakers – my mind naturally looks with what they now call *Nostalgia* to the Palace. This is surely the right moment for thanking the Bishop and yourself. Cathedral chimes, rooks, hot-water bottles, bathrooms that open off bedrooms, elephant-books (it will be *King's Regulations*[28] and Edgar Wallace in my room to-night) never looked more attractive than at this moment. Thank you both very much.

Yours sincerely
C. S. Lewis

TO MARY NEYLAN (T):

Magdalen College,
Oxford
[April 1942]

Dear Mrs. Neylan,

Yes, I will certainly be godfather to Sarah if you wish it.[29] Whether I can be of any use to her (prayers apart) until she is grown up is v. doubtful – I'm not much good with children.

---

27 Joy Parsons (née Streeter) was the wife of the Rt Rev. Richard Godfrey Parsons (1882–1948), Bishop of Hereford, 1941–8. During the course of Lewis's talks to the RAF, he had been invited by the couple to spend the night in the Bishop's Palace in Hereford. Bishop Parsons was educated at Magdalen College, and was Chaplain of University College, Oxford, 1907–11, and Principal of Wells Theological College, 1911–16. He and Joy were married in 1912, and they had one son.

28 *The King's Regulations and Air Council Instructions for the Royal Air Force* (1924–36).

29 Mrs Neylan's four-year old daughter, who was being baptized on 18 April.

The Talks will come out as a booklet in due course. Can't write more as I have um-teen letters to get through before I settle down to scholarship papers.

Yours very sincerely
C. S. Lewis

TO MARY NEYLAN (T):

Postmark: 17 April 1942

Hope to be there on Saturday.[30] All best wishes. C.S.L.

TO MARTYN SKINNER (BOD):[31]

[Magdalen College]
April 23d. 1942

Dear Skinner –

Thanks v. much. I hope you got through Sanders some time ago my great enjoyment of your letters to *Mabaya*.[32] A really good poem. Not in the least a pastiche as the silly people will say but a real proof that the Popian manner is a real *lingua franca* wh. anyone who has anything to say can use for original work. In fact, it is already *less* 'archaic' than the manner of 'Georgian poetry'. (The pother about 'originality' all comes from the people who have nothing to say: if they had they'd be original without noticing it.)

I've been meaning to tackle Hassell[33] (recommended to me by good judges like Fox) for some time. Which book shd. I start on?

It's funny your saying that quantity and distribution of pain is the soul of the problem. Others (e.g. Wilde) have thought that the real knock-out is why anyone or anything should suffer at all, and that one twinge at the tip of one mouse's tail unjustifies all creation. But if you have 'got as far as the Vale of Soul Making idea'[34] that is about as far as my book asks you to go. All I did was to add details about souls

30 Lewis had been invited to attend Sarah's baptism in Iffley.

31 See **Martyn Skinner** in the Biographical Appendix. As can be seen from the letter of 5 November 1947, Lewis later suggested he write a poem on King Arthur.

32 i.e. *Sir Elfadore and Mabyna*. See letter to Frank Sanders of 22 March 1941.

33 Skinner had recommended the poetry of Christopher Hassall (1912–63) who wrote, among other things, *Devil's Dyke, with Compliment and Satire* (1936).

34 *The Problem of Pain*, ch. 6, p. 109. On the 'vale of soul making' see note 54 to the letter to Leo Baker of 24 June 1936.

and the Maker. How can Van Oss believe all that about education after living in schools and universities all his life?[35] Yes, do come and see me,

Yours
C. S. Lewis

TO SISTER PENELOPE CSMV (BOD):

Magdalen College,
Oxford.
May 11th 42

Dear Sister Penelope

Commend me to all whom I met at Wantage. I still look back on the visit with a quite new sort of pleasure – it was not very like anything else that has happened to me so far.

This is a begging letter. There's a v. queer person called Miss Burton (The Weir, Twyford, Buckingham)[36] whom I know by correspondence arising out of the P. of Pain. She read English at Oxford (about your time) is a Christian, has bad arthritis, uses v. violent language, writes illegibly, and lives alone there in digs on a v. small income. I have sent her books and sometimes a little money. She has now been given notice to quit and writes asking if I know of anywhere. I don't. Do you? I had an idea there might be rooms at Wantage known to the convent and partly under its auspices. I imagine she is *difficile* and needs (I don't say 'would welcome' – that might come later!) a little visiting and counsel. Can you possibly help? I don't believe I could place her at Oxford: and, to tell you the bare truth, I am very anxious to keep my acquaintance with her to letters. I get the impression of a tragic, tormented person of the Brontë type, living in torment, ironic, un-

35 Mark Dunbar Van Oss (1897–1979) was educated at Clifton College, after which he served in France with the Royal Flying Corps, 191718. After the war he went to Magdalen College, where he took a First in Classics in 1921. He became a barrister in 1923, but returned to Magdalen in 1940 where he was Fellow of Law and Estates Bursar until 1944. He was the author, with Niall McDermot, of *The Lands Tribunal* (1950).

36 Helen Violet Tryce Burton (1886–1952) was educated at Cheltenham Ladies' College and Somerville College, Oxford, where she took a First in English in 1910. She was private secretary to Lady Gladstone of Hawarden, 1910–14, after which she held a number of posts including that of sister-in-charge of the Convalescent Hospital in Littlestone.

balanced – emphatically not a person to meet if one is of the opposite sex. Can you suggest anything?

The Venus book is just finished, except that I now find the two first chapters need re-writing. I will send you a typed MS as soon as it is typed and you can report on it to Reverend Mother for her consent to the dedication.[37]

The British Academy made a v. stupid audience compared with your young ladies![38] They were all the sort of people whom one often sees getting out of taxis and going into some big doorway and wonders who on earth they are – all those beards and double chins and fur collars and lorgnettes. Now I know.

I haven't had a moment for Athanasius yet, but live in hopes,

Yours sincerely

C. S. Lewis

TO SISTER PENELOPE CSMV (BOD):

Magdalen.

May 15th [1942]

Dear Sister Penelope –

It's writing all these books that has spoiled my fair Italian hand.

Thanks so much for all the information. I have forwarded it to 'step-sister BURTON' as I call the hedge-hogged lady and you may hear from her any time. The tiger-ish qualities are conjectural: it may be only her epistolary style.

I am extremely sorry to hear you have been ill again – it is odd that a few mornings ago I dreamed that you were.

I am establishing quite a friendship with one of the rabbits wh. we now keep along with the deer in Magdalen grove. It was done by the discovery that he relishes chestnut leaves which grow too high for his reach. He doesn't yet allow me any familiarities but he comes and eats

---

37 In her notes to Lewis's letters, Sister Penelope wrote: 'With reference to the dedication of *Perelandra*: I told him that we were usually known as The Community of St Mary the Virgin, or more briefly as C.S.M.V., Wantage; but he would have none of this and put instead "To some ladies at Wantage." More recently this has proved one too many for the Portuguese translator of the book. The dedication as he gives it means "To some wanton ladies"!'

38 Lewis delivered the 1942 Annual Shakespeare Lecture to the British Academy on 22 April 1942. The lecture, 'Hamlet: The Prince or the Poem?' was published in 1943, and it is reprinted in *SLE*.

from my hand. If my jaws were as strong in proportion to my size as his I'd be able to pluck down the pinnacles of the tower with my teeth. But oh!, the great lollipop eyes and the twitching velvet nose! How does He come to create both this and the scorpion?

Jane has got a nasty ulcer on the ankle from knocking it – on a leg that has often had varicose veins: and the maid has not yet come back. So we are in the soup – but her state of mind and heart *very* much better. I don't know who Gillett is. I do hope you'll soon be well again.

Yours sincerely

Br. ASS

TO MRS PERCIVAL WISEMAN (M):[39]

Magdalen.

May 21st 42

Dear Mrs Percival Wiseman –

I enclose a MS[40] – I hope legible. Will you please within four or five days send it on to Miss Jarman, Caludon, Lynch Rd., Farnham, Surrey?[41] The whole series will be published in a month or so by Geoffrey Bles, The Centenary Press.

Yours very truly

C. S. Lewis

TO MRS PERCIVAL WISEMAN (M):

Magdalen.

May 26th [1942]

Dear Mrs. Percival Wiseman –

On the *general* problem of Our Lord's temptations the most helpful remark I know is Westcott's 'Only he who completely resists temptation knows its true strength'[42] – i.e. if you give in at point X you never know

39 Nothing is known of Mrs Wiseman. Her letters from Lewis were given to Magdalen College by someone who knew her.

40 This was probably a manuscript of the second series of BBC talks, *What Christians Believe.*

41 Miss Jarman was one of the beneficiaries of the Agapony fund.

42 Brook Foss Westcott, *The Epistle to the Hebrews: The Greek Text with Notes and Essays* (1892), p. 59: 'Sympathy with the sinner in his trial does not depend on the experience of sin but on the experience of the strength of the temptation to sin which only the sinless can know in its full intensity.'

how fierce it wd. have become an hour later. You only discover the strength of the German army by fighting it.[43]

We are quite ignorant of the real power of our habits until we try to give them up. The *particular* temptation you mention (of loving men more than God) does certainly present difficulties. I don't expect that *was* the cardinal temptation for Him. In the Gospel accounts of the temptation in the wilderness (which, by the way, must come from His own life for they are temptations no mere human has and none cd. have invented) it is the temptation to work miracles – i.e. to set up His own deity in independence of His Father. You and I don't know this temptation, of course, and may be thankful we don't . . . or, after all, *don't we*?

The one you mention is ticklish, because is it not always *really* a way of loving humans too little? I know it sounds odd, but think it over. I mean, as soon as one tries to seek the other person's real good & freedom as opposed to the gratification of ones own affection (wh. often includes some will to power) isn't one driven to loving them in and for God?

Yours sincerely
C. S. Lewis

Lewis was now writing a third series of broadcasts on the subject of Christian behaviour. He did not as yet have a title for this series.

TO ERIC FENN (BBC):

Magdalen College,
Oxford
June 29th 42

My dear Fenn

I *think* (but as you say it must be provisional) that the talks wd. run something like this.

---

43 Lewis used this idea in the seventh of the third series of broadcast talks, given on 1 November 1942 and entitled 'Faith'. It was repeated in *Christian Behaviour*, ch. 7, and *Mere Christianity*, Book III, ch. 11: 'Only those who try to resist temptation know how strong it is. After all, you find out the strength of the German army by fighting against it, not by giving in. . . . Christ, because He was the only man who never yielded to temptation, is also the only man who knows to the full what temptation means – the only complete realist.'

1. Ordinary Ethics – Fair Play.
2. How Christianity makes a difference.
3. Christianity and Pleasure.
4. Chastity.
5. Humility.
6. Charity.
7. Hope and Faith as Virtues
8. The Problem of Faith and Works.

This for the B.B.C.'s eyes. I shd. not recommend 4–8 as *titles*. Am I allowed to say that Aristotle and Xtianity agree in condemning *usury*?

Yours
C. S. Lewis

TO ERIC FENN (BBC):[44]

Magdalen.
[4 July 1942]

I may still be in the thick of exam papers on 15th & 16th. Suggest Saturday July 18th at 11.15 a.m., and shall expect you then unless I hear to the contrary.

C.S.L.

TO LEWIS JOHN COLLINS (LAMBETH PALACE):[45]

Magdalen College,
Oxford
July 5th 42

Dear Padre Collins –

Yes, with pleasure. Since it *is* possible to go and return in one day

---

44 Fenn wrote on 3 July 1942: 'I shall be in Oxford on July 15th and 16th and again over the weekend 17th–19th. Could we meet then for a short session about the talks?'

45 The Rev. Canon Lewis John Collins (1905–82) read Mathematics at Sidney Sussex College, Cambridge, taking a BA in 1927. After reading Theology at Westcott House, Cambridge, he was ordained in 1929. He was Chaplain of Sidney Sussex College, 1929–31, Minor Canon of St Paul's Cathedral, 1931–4, Vice-Principal of Westcott House, 1934–7, and a chaplain in the Royal Air Force Volunteer Reserve, serving at the RAF base at Yatesbury, Wiltshire, 1940–5. He was a Fellow and Chaplain of Oriel College, Oxford, 1938–48, Chancellor of St Paul's Cathedral, 1948–53, Precentor, 1953–70, and Treasurer, 1970–81. His publications include *The New Testament Problem* (1937), *A Theology of Christian Action* (1949) and *Faith Under Fire* (1966).

I think I'd better do so – much tho' I shd. have liked to have accepted your hospitable offer. I suggest August 30th. Have you any suggestions as to what you'd like me to talk *on*?

Yours sincerely

C. S. Lewis

TO LEWIS JOHN COLLINS (LAMBETH PALACE):

Magdalen College,
Oxford
July 12th 42

Dear Padre Collins –

I'll stay the night, if I may. Thanks v. much.

I'm a little surprised (tho' of course, pleased) at the size of the audience you expect. You mean a *voluntary* one, I trust? I shouldn't like to address an audience that had been (even indirectly and by velvet glove methods!) coerced. This means, of course, that I am prepared to risk getting *no* audience: which, indeed, has often happened to me.

Before deciding which of the suggested subjects I'd talk on, I'd like to know whether the audience is likely to consist of believers or enquirers. I ought to have saved you a letter by asking this last time, but I'm in the middle of reading exam papers and my brain is numb. I'll try not to bother you after this!

Yours

C. S. Lewis

Broadcast Talks, Reprinted with some alterations from two series of Broadcast Talks ('Right and Wrong: A Clue to the Meaning of the Universe' and 'What Christians Believe' given in 1941 and 1942) *was published by Geoffrey Bles: The Centenary Press on 13 July 1942.*

TO LEWIS JOHN COLLINS (LAMBETH PALACE):

Magdalen College,
Oxford
July 17th 42

Dear Padre –

The conditions are what I regard as ideal. By all means put me on to talk to the mixed mass first and then let the serious ones come for a follow up in a smaller room afterwards if they like. I have known that work well at other stations.

I shall talk (roughly) on the relation between Christianity and the social order: if you don't think it too flippant it might be called *Christianity isn't a patent medicine.*

Yours
C. S. Lewis

TO ERIC FENN (BBC):

Magdalen.
July 29th [1942]

Sorry about your last visit to Oxford. I was out of College and by the time I got your letter it was too late to write to you at BBC putting you off and you hadn't given me any address in Oxford to find you.

I have now finished script of the 8 talks.[46] Getting them typed is so v. slow and expensive now that I'd rather not do it if it can be avoided. If there is any chance of your being here in the near future I wd. like to give them into your own hand. Not next weekend (I shall be away) but almost any day next week from Tuesday on.

C. S. Lewis

TO SISTER PENELOPE CSMV (BOD):

Magdalen
July 29th 42

Dear Sister Penelope –

(1) The Rabbit and I have quarrelled. I don't know why, unless I gave him something that disagreed with him. At any rate, he has cut me dead several times lately – so fair and so fickle! Life is full of disappointments. 'The stony *hearts* of the conies' is prob. the true reading in that Psalm.[47]

(2) I'm glad to hear you are a little better, but wish you were better still.

(3) After having to abandon S. Athanasius for examining, I have now returned to the *De Incarnatione* and have just finished the long

46 For the third series of broadcasts, on Christian behaviour.
47 Psalm 104:18.

section on Jewish prophecies.[48] If that is the bit you are omitting, I expect you are right. Though it crosses my mind that modern apologetics may have given up too completely the old 'proof from prophecy'. Each individual passage can be explained away as really meaning something else, or accidental: but could it still be argued that to apply this to the whole lot involves stretching the arm of coincidence rather far?

(4) Have you read Martin Buber's *I and Thou*. Tell me what I am to think of it? From Heaven, or (very subtly) from Hell? I'm by no means sure. And why does he limit all true 'meeting' to a Thou-situation? Is there no You-situation? What happens when three friends are together or when a man meets his wife and child?

(5) On Witches. I didn't really mean to deny them, tho' I see I have given that impression. I was interested in them at the moment only as an illustration.[49] I think my considered view wd. be much the same as yours. But if a truth, it is not a truth I am at all anxious to spread.

(6) About 'became Man' *versus* 'a man'. There is you will admit, a v. obvious sense in which He became 'a man' – a man of a particular height and weight, the Son of a particular Mother, who was in one place and time and *not* (in that mode) elsewhere. The Fathers, writing in a language with no indefinite article didn't have to plump for one or the other. Are you correct in saying 'the Person, the Ego, of the incarnated Lord is God'? I had thought there was a human *soul* involved (when we speak of His humanity we don't mean simply His body) and that the human and divine natures together made one Person. Your way of putting it suggests that there was simply a human body with

---

48 Lewis was referring to Sister Penelope's translation of St Athanasius's *De Incarnatione Verbi Dei*, which had been accepted by the London publishers, SPCK, but which was later turned down as not being sufficiently literal to be used by students. The text Lewis was using, and from which Sister Penelope was translating, was *De Incarnatione: An edition of the Greek text by Frank Leslie Cross*, Texts for Students, No. 50 (London: SPCK, 1939).

49 Sister Penelope was referring to the following passage in *Broadcast Talks*, Part I, Talk 2, p. 18: 'One listener wrote and said, "Three hundred years ago people in England were putting witches to death. Was that what you call the Rule of Human Nature or Right Conduct?" But surely the reason we don't execute witches is that we don't believe there are such things.' The same words are found in *Mere Christianity: A revised and amplified edition, with a new introduction, of the three books 'Broadcast Talks', 'Christian Behaviour', and 'Beyond Personality'* (London: Bles 1952; Fount, 1977), Book I, ch. 2, p. 12.

God *substituted* for the human soul one wd. ordinarily have expected. Is this right? I thought not, but I don't know.

(7) I gave up Naomi Mitchison some time ago because of her dwelling on scenes of cruelty. But I recognise real imagination and a sort of beauty in the writing.[50]

(8) I have just sent off to you under a separate cover a MS of *Perelandra*. It's uncorrected, so you can exercise your textual criticism on it. When you, or anyone else whom it concerns, has read it, I shd. like it back with the Rev. Mother's permission (if she gives it) of the dedication.

As for my 'special needs', wh. you kindly ask for, this *Apologist's Evening Hymn* I've just completed, will tell you.

From all my lame defeats and oh! much more
From all the victories I have seemed to score;
From cleverness shot forth in Thy behalf,
At which, while angels weep, the audience laugh;
From all my proofs of Thy divinity,
Thou, who would'st give no sign, deliver me.
Thoughts are but coins. Let me not trust, instead
Of Thee, the thumb-worn image of Thy head;
From every thought, even from my thoughts of Thee,
Oh thou fair Silence! fall and set me free.
Lord of the straight way and the needle's eye,
Take from me all my trumpery lest I die.[51]

Yours sincerely
C. S. Lewis

TO OWEN BARFIELD (W):

[The Kilns
?1 August 1942]

My dear Barfield –

Yes, I think I've understood the poem and it's been worth it.[52] A sinister piece of work. High lights are 'You burn strength tugging at

---

50 He was referring to Naomi Mitchison's *Black Sparta: Greek Stories*. The cruelties in this book are mentioned in the letter to Arthur Greeves of February 1932 (p. 52).

51 The poem is published with slight variations in *CP*, p. 143.

52 It is not known which of Barfield's unpublished poems Lewis was referring to.

that wrist' and 'Lifted light as air The load I only prayed to share.' And the whole idea of what won't come when called but will come (as a different thing) later – is good. The bit on p. 2 from *And launches to sun-filled air* is hard to construe. Does it mean 'launches mantled in air your planet which, till thus launched, was rocky and airless like the Moon'? If so it's a bit Thucydidean in construction: or have I missed the point. As luck wd. have it I too have just littered a pome. See over.

Read Athanasius *De Incarnatione* (SPCK Texts for Students No 50.) and also tell me what to think about Martin Buber* *I and Thou* (publishers T & T Clark). I think it is rather rot but am not sure

Yours
C. S. Lewis

* BUBER (quale nomen!)

TO ERIC FENN (BBC):

The Kilns,
Headington Quarry,
Oxford.
Aug 15th 42

My dear Fenn

The title, for you and me, wd be *Xtian Ethics*. What this is in the vernacular is doubtful. *Xtian Morals*? – *Xtian Morality*? – *Xtian Moral Standards* – *Xtian Behaviour*?

I think the last would be the best, myself. All the other words have been more or less spoiled: I think if Aristotle were writing now he'd call the Ethics 'Behaviour'. Or, wd. they like *The Xtian Technique of Living*?

Yours
C. S. Lewis

TO MR H. MORLAND (T):[53]

Magdalen College,
Oxford.
Aug 19th 1942

The great classical statement of the Anglican position is Hooker's

53 Mr H. Morland, who had probably asked Lewis for a reading list, was writing from 18 Claremont Avenue, Stony Stratford, near Bletchley, Bucks.

Laws of Ecclesiastical Polity (2 vols. Everyman).[54] A good modern book is Essays Catholic & Critical ed. Selwyn (published by S.P.C.K.).[55] Moberley *Atonement & Personality*[56] tho' needlessly long & difficult is good: shd. be corrected by Aulén *Christus Victor*[57] giving a different kind of theory. If you read Gk., St Athanasius, *De Incarnatione* is splendid: if not, look out for a trans. of this shortly to appear.[58] My own greatest debt is to George Macdonald, specially the 3 vols of *Unspoken Sermons* (out of print but often obtainable 2nd hand). Other books you might find helpful are Edwyn Bevan's *Xtianity* & Gore's *Jesus Christ* (both in Home University Library)[59] Bevan's *Symbolism & Belief.*[60] Gore's *Philosophy of the Good Life* (Everyman edtn) Otto's *Idea of the Holy* (Clarendon Press) von Hügel's *Eternal Life* & *Essays & Addresses:*[61] and, going further back, *Theologia Germanica* (Macmillan), Traherne *Centuries of Meditations*, Lady Julian of Norwich *Revelations of Divine Love*, Boethius *De Consolatione Philosophiae* (with trans. in Loeb. Lib.),[62] Augustine *Confessions* (ditto, or in Everyman) & *De Civitate Dei* (not sure where trans. is to be found)[63]

Yours,
C. S. Lewis

---

54 Richard Hooker, *Of the Laws of Ecclesiastical Polity*, 2 vols. (London: Dent, Everyman's Library, 1907). Hooker (c. 1554–1600) developed his doctrines in this long treatise, designed to justify the constitutional structure of the Elizabethan Church. Of the five books which appeared in his lifetime, nos 1–4 were published in 1593, and no. 5 in 1597. Nos 6 and 8 appeared in 1648, and no. 7 in 1662.

55 *Essays Catholic and Critical by Members of the Anglican Communion*, ed. Edward Gordon Selwyn (London: 1926; SPCK, 1929).

56 Robert Campbell Moberley, *Atonement and Personality* (1901).

57 Gustaf Aulén, *Christus Victor* (1931).

58 i.e. Sister Penelope's translation of St Athanasius, *De Incarnatione Verbi Dei*.

59 Edwyn Bevan, *Christianity* (London: Butterworth: Home University Library, 1932). By *Jesus Christ* Lewis probably meant Gore's *Jesus of Nazareth*.

60 Edwyn Bevan, *Symbolism and Belief* (London: Allen & Unwin, 1938).

61 Baron Friedrich von Hügel, *Eternal Life: A Study of its Implications and Applications* (1912); *Essays and Addresses on the Philosophy of Religion* (1921).

62 Boethius: *The Consolation of Philosophy, with the English translations of 'I.T.'* (1609), rev. H. F. Stewart (London: Heinemann, Loeb Classical Library, 1918).

63 St Augustine, *The Confessions of St. Augustine*, trans. E. B. Pusey (London: Dent: Everyman's Library, 1907). Had he known he might have suggested *The City of God*, trans. Marcus Dods (Edinburgh: T. & T. Clark, 1871–2).

TO OWEN BARFIELD (W):

[The Kilns]
Aug 20th [1942]

My dear Barfield –

(1.) Have you read *Esmond*[64] lately? What a detestable woman is Lady Castlewood: and yet I believe Thackeray means us to like her on the ground that all her actions spring from 'love'. This love is, in his language 'pure' i.e. it is not promiscuous or sensual. It is none the less a wholly uncorrected natural passion, idolatrous and insatiable. Was that the great 19th century heresy – that 'pure' or 'noble' passions didn't need to be crucified & re-born but wd. of themselves lead to happiness? Yet one sees it makes Lady C. disastrous both as a wife & a mother and is a source of misery to herself and all whom she meets. This is all irrelevant but I've been reading *Esmond* all day and it rose to the surface.

(2.) Yes: do come, you and Harwood, on Sept 1st. If we think College has had enough of the trio we can dine at the Eastgate: less well, but perhaps more at our ease.

(3.) Thanks for dealing with Mrs Boshell and Mrs Askins.[65]

(4.) Congratulations on recovering £237 for the Agapony. This is stupendous. Tis truly Orphic and I fear to re-read the figure lest it vanish – *feror ingenti circumdata nocte.*[66]

(5.) While Government is reeling under this blow, is it worth while trying to get them to pay for my operation on the ground that it was due to a wound?

(6.) When you ask me to remember you in my prayers, it is like the *Punch*[67] joke where the Doctor says to the patient (a colonel) 'And I think I should recommend a glass of good nourishing wine once a

---

64 William Makepeace Thackeray, *The History of Henry Esmond, Esquire* (1852).

65 Mrs Boshell and Mrs Askins were two of the widows Lewis was helping through the Agapony fund. Mrs Boshell had been befriended by Mrs Moore and at this time was living in a small cottage in the grounds of The Kilns.

66 Virgil, *Georgics*, IV, 497. Orpheus has just looked back at Eurydice, who must therefore return to the underworld. She says as she departs: 'Iamque vale: feror ingenti circumdata nocte . . .': 'And so, farewell: I am borne away, enveloped in a vast night . . .'

67 *Punch, or the London Charivari*, founded in 1841, was an illustrated weekly humorous periodical of literature, history and culture. It finally ceased publication in 1992.

day.' *Patient* 'Oh well – I've taken a bottle of port every night for 20 years, but I don't mind trying to manage an extra glass if you like.'

I am v. sorry you are blue as a whortle-berry within. I feel what people feel when they say 'I'd do anything to amend it': which on closer inspection means, alas, 'I dare to hope that, if the situation really arose, even my cowardice and selfishness wd. not prevent me doing something.' Blessings on you

Yours
C. S. Lewis

TO ERIC FENN (BBC):

[The Kilns]
Fri. Sept 11th [1942]

My dear Fenn

Gloria! Actum est de hac muliere.[68] Look! – from to-morrow (Saturday) ev. till Fri. morning I shall be c/o The Rev. Padre Scutt, No 7, I.T.W. Newquay, Cornwall – in case you had anything urgent to say. What is the *hour* of my talk on Sunday week?

Yours
C. S. Lewis

Lewis's third series of eight talks, entitled Christian Behaviour, *was given on Sunday afternoons from 20 September until 8 November 1942.*

A Preface to 'Paradise Lost' *was published by Oxford University Press on 8 October 1942.*

TO DOM BEDE GRIFFITHS OSB (W):

Magdalen
Oct 13th 42

My dear Dom Bede –

I shouldn't have written quite as I did if I had thought that there was a consensus of theologians in favour of the Anselmic theory.[69] I believed that it was not to be found either in the N.T. or most of the Fathers. If I'm wrong on this, it is a matter of plain historical ignorance.

War & Peace is in my opinion *the* best novel – the only one wh.

---

68 'Glory be! It is all settled with regard to this woman!'

69 See note 123 to the letter to Griffiths of 21 December 1941.

makes a novel really comparable to epic. I have read it about 3 times. What we lose (I'm told) in our translations is the *humour* wh. is an important merit in the real book.

You wouldn't be surprised at the space I give to Dualism if you knew how attractive it is to some simple minds. As for retiring into 'private life', while feeling *very* strongly the evil of publicity, I don't see how one can. God is my witness, I don't *look* for engagements. I don't know the Rances.

Yours
C. S. Lewis

TO THE EDITOR OF *THE GUARDIAN* (*EC*):

[Magdalen College
16 October 1942]

Sir, –

In answer to Mr May's question, I reply that whether the birth of St John the Baptist were a miracle or no, it was not the same miracle as the birth of our Lord.[70] What was abnormal about St Elizabeth's pregnancy was that she was an elderly (married) woman, hitherto sterile. That Zacharias was the father of St John is implied in the text ('shall bear *thee* a son', Luke 1.13).

Of the natural conversion of water into wine, what I said was 'God creates the vine and teaches it to draw up water by its roots and, *with the aid of the sun*, to turn that water into a juice *which will ferment* and take on certain qualities.'[71] For completeness I should, no doubt, have added 'with the aid of the soil', and perhaps other things; but this would not, from my point of view, have materially altered what I was saying. My answer to Mr May's question – where the other raw materials came from – would be the same, whether the list of raw materials be reduced to the mere vegetable and sunlight I mentioned, or extended to bring in all that the skilled botanist might add. I think they came from the same source at Cana whence they come in Nature. I agree with Mr May, of course, that on the hypothesis of the story being

70 Lewis's essay on 'Miracles' appeared in *The Guardian* (2 October 1942), and Peter May criticized it in the issue of 9 October 1942, p. 323. This letter is Lewis's reply to May. 'Miracles' is reprinted in *God in the Dock: Essays on Theology* (London: Bles, 1971; Fount, 1998).

71 *God in the Dock*, p. 7.

fiction, we can attach to it, as our ancestors did to the miracles in Ovid, any number of edifying *moralitates*.[72] What I was doing was to combat that particular argument for its falsity which rests on the idea that, if it occurred, such an event would be arbitrary and meaningless.

Yours sincerely
C. S. Lewis

TO DOROTHY L. SAYERS (W):

As from Magdalen.
Oct 23rd 42

Dear Miss Sayers –

The only question is can I purr loud and long enough for such a 'good Puss'? Thanks very much. And you're that artful, for of course all the part about your humanist friend is positively stroking the cat under the ears. Did he really say all these things? No *Dichtung* mixed with your *Wahrheit*?

Your formula 'good conversation on an interesting subject' reminds me of a man who once told me that to write decent prose needs no more than to have something interesting to say and then say it so as to make the reader feel as you were feeling when you wrote it. In both cases I feel like commenting 'Quite. In this simple medium mastery can be attained by those who have attained mastery'! But it's the subject not the dialogue wd. be my real difficulty in a BBC Screwtape. It wd. be so v. difficult to make the situation *clear*.

Oh Eliot! How can a man who is neither a knave nor a fool write so like both? Well, he can't complain that I haven't done my best to put him right – hardly ever write a book without showing him one of his errors. And still he doesn't mend. I call it ungrateful.

About Shakespeare read and Shakespeare acted. Obviously and *â priori* you're right. Yet as a matter of history, his rise to the position of 'next, if not superior to, Homer' has come largely through reading. Aren't even our productions by now steeped in the *literary* critics? Of course I agree that *any* (tolerable) production will reveal at once several cryingly obvious things one misses in the study: but I wouldn't like to exclude all that he never intended but has come through reading – any

72 'moral lessons'.

more than I want to exclude all we see in the ancients which wasn't there for them.

What is the *seat* of poetry. Take a line of Virgil describing scenery. I've never been to Italy so first I get all the images wrong, substituting English trees and fields for the sort he intended. Then, presumably, I get the pronunciation pretty far from his. Now images & pronunciation *both* being different, what common factor is left between the line he wrote and the line we enjoy? What tiny isthmus connects these two v. different continents?

If your humanist wants comfort he can get it easily. All he needs is to pity instead of hating. Let him say 'Poor young man. He needs to be analysed. Such a pity – they tell me he was quite a promising scholar . . . a tragedy – religious melancholia'. This hardly ever fails to work.

I do hope you'll like Milton. If conditions allow, shd. be read neither more nor less than one Book at a time, at a table, in full evening dress, non-smoking, and semi-aloud. 'Hear the voice of the Bard!'[73]

Yrs. v. sincerely & still purring
C. S. Lewis

TO ERIC FENN (BBC)

[Magdalen College]
Nov. 8th 1942

I should be obliged if you wd. make the cheque for my Xtian Behaviour talks payable to Mrs Boshell c/o Mrs Moore, The Kilns, Headington Quarry, Oxford.

C. S. Lewis

Sometime during the autumn Lewis discovered E. R. Eddison's novel, The Worm Ouroboros *(1922) and it made an instant conquest of him. Lewis later said of Eddison, 'It is very rarely that a middle-aged man finds an author who gives him, what he knew so often in his teens and twenties, the sense of having opened a new door. One had thought those days were past. Eddison's heroic romances disproved it. Here was a new literary species, a new rhetoric, a new climate of the imagination.'[74] He was so*

73 Blake, *Songs of Experience*, 'Hear the Voice of the Bard!'

74 'A Tribute to E. R. Eddison', *Of This and Other Worlds*, p. 55.

delighted with the discovery that he wrote to Eddison, living in Marlborough, Wiltshire, in mock Tudor English:

TO E. R. EDDISON (BOD):[75]

Magdalen College
Oxford
Nov 16th 1942

Honour'd Sir, there is a sawe commonly vsed among our uplandish folk that yf a man pick up were it but a pibble stone or a straw and bestow it in his poke, lyghtlie it shall not fayle but before the yearsend it shall stande him in greter stede than the best treasure ever he ow'd.

Of the which I have right good exaumple by a foolish book (on the *novello*) that came late to my hands, made by som poore seely wench that seeketh a B.Litt or a D.Phil, when God knows shad a better bestowed her tyme makynge sport for some goodman in his bed and bearing children for the stablishment of this reaulme or els to be at her beads in a religyous house.

But all such matters I heere reiecte for the avoydynge of prolixitee. Now this wench, Sir, made mentioun of yr honours historie and heroicall romans entituled *Oroboros*, wherein fondlie comparing of youre eloquent stile to Swinburne she made plain discoverie of her own follie and her ignorance of such good and allow'd auctours in whom I perceive you to be verie well versed, as William of Kelms Cott,[76] Snorri,[77] Homer and Thomas Browne Knight,[78] yet as the sun shall sometimes appeere thorough clowdes I discernd so much of youre deseruings as sente me a great wallop after the said Historie.

In the which booke hauing now read soe fare as to the downfalle and ruinacion of *Garsee*,[79] I were much to blame yf I dyde not do you to wit that in my censure this is the most noble and ioyous book I haue read these ten yeres. Insomuch that if (wh. heuen forbidde) I were its ounlie reder, yet the ioye you hadde in the inventioun and indyting of the said book and I in the reading in it sholde of themselves alone

75 See **Eric Rücker Eddison** in the Biographical Appendix.

76 i.e. William Morris (1834–96), who founded the Kelmscott Press in addition to writing historical romances.

77 Snorri Sturluson (1178–1241), the Icelandic historian.

78 i.e. Sir Thomas Browne, author of *Religio Medici*.

79 Lewis's spelling for 'Carcë'. He means to the end of ch. 32.

vtterlie outweigh and ouergoe all the clam jamfrey and whymperinges of the rakehellie auctours in these latter daies, as the Eliots, Poundes, Lawrences, Audens, and the like.

In good truth, Brother, there is a shrewde lack in your book whereof I made bold a little to snibbe you, in that it conteineth no mappemonnde or card, which were a thing verie necessarie to him that wolde perfectlie vnderstonde all the diverse voyages and travelles, and the whereabouts of all havens, seas, nesses, mountains, straits, rivers, frithes and cities. Item, a table genealogicall sholde have been no small light, and either of these more nedefull than the naked deliverie of times by yeres wherewith you haue garnysshed it.

But there is nothing mortal that hath not his faults. Sir, by these lettres you shall vnderstonde my verie good will and gratitude, and also that there are oon or two faste frends of myne who still, in this duncicall age, delight in noble bookes, that is in straunge adventures, heroicall feates, good maneres, and the report of ferne londes. When yf it sorts with your occasions euere to visit in my poor house and colledge of Sta Marie Maudlin, doubt not to haue the beste chere and feste we can or mai deuyse. From

Your obliged obedient
Servant
C. S. Lewis

Eddison replied on 30 November:

> *Honour'd Sir, I am beholden to you for yr letter, whyche is to mee delectabler than any these long whiles hath come into my hand . . . It aunswereth my hopes unto their hyest strain that one of your renowne for suiting of yr lerninge with yr inventiouns . . . sholde bee moued to appraise this* Worme *in such loftie tearmes of compliment & yet with soe much syncerenes as I must constantlie belieue them . . . Hard it is in this time of Warre to gadde lightlie as a man might aforetime betwixen Oxenford & these downes & habited partes of Wiltshire. Yet doubt not that som daye I shall with gret joye take you at yr worde. Mean whyle, for a kepesake, this boke of* Mistresse of Mistresses, *whyche you being a liker of my* Worme *may find as worthe yr reding. I haue a yet newer booke made publique last yere in Amerique & entitled*

A FISH DINNER IN MEMISON, *but noe publishere haue I yet founde bolde enough to doo it here in Engelonde.*[80]

TO DELMAR BANNER (T):[81]

Magdalen College,
Oxford.
30th November 1942.

Dear Mr. Banner,

Thanks very much indeed for the picture of Webb.[82] As far as I can judge from a photo, it is one of the best modern portraits I have seen for a long time. Yes, I know him well and also knew Brightman. The latter and J. A. Smith both used to live on my staircase; it is a poor place since they left it. Gynes[83] I didn't know, or not to speak of – that was a privilege reserved for undergraduates.

I only wish I could come and see you, specially if it included the chance of meeting Miss Potter.[84] It was the Professor of Anglo-Saxon[85] who first pointed out to me that her art of putting about ten words

---

80 Bodleian Library, MS. Eng. lett. c. 220/2, fols. 34–5.

81 Delmar Harmood Banner (1896–1983), painter, was born of an illustrious family in Freiburg im Breisgau, Germany where his grandfather was an Anglican chaplain. He spoke German until he was seven when the family moved back to England. Educated at Cheltenham College and Magdalen College, he received a BA in History in 1917 before studying art at Regent Street Polytechnic, 1919–27. There he met Josefina de Vasconcellos, who was to achieve fame as a sculptor. She became a Christian partly as a result of his influence, and they were married in 1930. In 1940 they moved to Ambleside in the Lake District, adopting two boys and settling in a farmhouse at The Bield in Little Langdale. Josefina worked in an outhouse at the farm, while Delmar painted landscapes from the summits of the fells. In 1967, through associations with Pelham House approved school in West Cumbria the couple helped found Outpost Emmaus, an activity centre for disadvantaged boys at Beckstones in the Duddon valley.

82 Clement Charles Julian Webb (1865–1954), philosopher and theologian, was educated at Westminster and Christ Church, Oxford, where he took a First in *Literae Humaniores* in 1888. He was a Fellow of Magdalen College, 1889–22, first Oriel Professor of Philosophy of the Christian Religion, 1920–30, and a Fellow of Oriel College, Oxford, 1922–30. Delmar Banner painted his portrait in 1929, and after Professor Webb's death it was presented to Oriel College where it hangs in the Provost's Lodging.

83 J. W. Gynes was Steward of Magdalen College's Junior Common Room, 1914–31.

84 Banner had just painted a portrait of Beatrix Potter (1866–1943), the author of *The Tale of Peter Rabbit* (1901), *Squirrel Nutkin* (1903) and other books for children. The portrait hangs in the National Portrait Gallery.

85 i.e. Professor J. R. R. Tolkien.

on one page so as to have a perfect rhythm and to answer just the questions a child would ask, is almost as severe as that of lyric poetry. She has a secure place among the masters of English prose. He and I have often played with the idea of a pilgrimage to see her, and pictured what fun it would be to shoulder aside the mobs of people who want to show you all the Wordsworth places with the brief rejoinder 'We are looking for Miss Potter' . . . 'I would be at Jerusalem'. With very many thanks.

yours sincerely,
C. S. Lewis

I hope you noted *Rabbit*, *Peter* in index to the Milton book!

TO ERIC FENN (BBC): TS[86]

Magdalen College,
Oxford.
30th November 1942.

My dear Fenn,

Thanks for letting me know about the 'Daily Mirror' – damn their impudence.[87]

When I was last at B.B.C. house, I asked Beales to tell them to send my fee to Mrs. Boshell, c/o Mrs. Moore, The Kilns, Headington Quarry, Oxford. I hope the fact that nothing has yet turned up does not mean that this raised any difficulty.

Best wishes for Christmas.

yours,
C. S. Lewis

TO ARTHUR GREEVES (W):

[Magdalen College]
Dec. 10th 42

My dear Arthur,

It was nice to hear from you again. If you see Tchanie thank her

---

86 'ts' = typescript. Warnie Lewis was now helping his brother with his correspondence, and this is the first letter we have typed by Warnie on his Royal typewriter.

87 The *Daily Mirror* had somehow managed to obtain a copy of Lewis's talk on 'Sexual Morality' and published it on 13 October under the headline 'This Was a Very Frank Talk – Which We Think Everyone Should Read'.

for her letter (received to-day) and tell her I hope to answer it soon. She praises you to the skies, by the way. I sent a copy of my Milton book[88] to her but not to you because you once told me not to send you my books, not for the obvious reason ('I don't know what to do with all these books; the house is R-R-R-otten with books') but because you kindly wanted to buy them!

I begin to see both from her letter and yours what a difference lack of petrol must make; in fact it has, I suppose, pretty well broken up your life by putting nearly all walks and all friends out of bounds. *You* don't complain, but *I* sympathise. (Odd that you and I must often be thinking about our favourite haunts with an *equal* sense of exile – the fact that you're 6 miles from them and I a couple of hundred making no practical difference.) And when we can both re-visit them together again, as I dearly hope we shall, will they be the same? or shall we be the same?

By the way it's all balls about my coming to lecture at Belfast; I'd come hopping if I were asked but I haven't been. It would be lovely.

I was going to say 'I can just picture your room upstairs with me on the sofa in the window and you in your "made to measure" chair' – but suddenly realise I can't quite picture the room. Only one picture comes to mind – the one of the corn field; and, absurdly, the *bed* keeps on creeping in from the days when it was a bedroom. (It wd. be amusing if a bed kept *literally* 'creeping into' a room! Which reminds me, do you object to my using in a story your idea of the dead man coming back into the clothes?)

All pretty well, here. Minto has one of her recurrent varicose ulcers but is surprisingly well in spirits. W. is at home. I have had neuralgia to-day but am otherwise alright – except for rheumatism which has prevented me from sleeping on my right side for nearly a year now. (What a series of rediscoveries life is. All the things which one used to regard as simply the nonsense grown-ups talk have one by one come true – draughts, rheumatism, Christianity. The best one of all remains to be verified –)

I have introduced such a lot of people to Macdonald this year: in nearly every case with success. On my innumerable journeys I've re-read

88 i.e. *A Preface to Paradise Lost.*

Lavengro.[89] Yes, I did read Ld. Elton's book:[90] quite good, I expect, but I'm no judge of that kind of thing.

Did I tell you in my last letter that I'd struck up quite an acquaintance (almost a friendship) with a rabbit in Magdalen Grove who used to come and eat leaves from my hand? Alas, I must have given something that disagreed with him, for he disappeared for about 10 days, and since his reappearance has refused to look at me.

It's a grand day, to day, of low racing clouds and strong wind: you and I cd. enjoy a good walk among whirling dead leaves. Well, 'I must be getting along now' as so many visitors say and then don't get along for half an hour or more. Blessings, and here's to our next meeting

Yours ever
Jack

TO THE EDITOR OF *THE SPECTATOR*:[91]

Magdalen College,
Oxford.
[11 December 1942]

Sir, –

It is not universally true that Christianity means ethics to laymen and doctrine to clergymen. Many laymen who believe the Christian doctrines desire to hear them supported and expounded from the pulpit, and are disappointed when they hear only moral exhortation. I do not think this desire is confined to educated laymen, for I have been present when an airman who had heard a lecture on the historicity of the Gospels exclaimed 'This is the first time I've heard any one advance a reason for believing the Bible might be true.' In my experience we laymen are often more easily shocked than our clergy by clerical disbelief or neglect of doctrine.

Yours faithfully,
C. S. Lewis

---

89 George Borrow, *Lavengro, the Scholar, the Gipsy, the Priest* (1851).

90 Godfrey, Baron Elton, *St George or the Dragon: Towards a Christian Democracy* (1942).

91 This letter appeared under the title 'Religion in the Schools' in *The Spectator*, CLXIX (11 December 1942), p. 553.

TO E. R. EDDISON (BOD):

[Magdalen College]
Dec. xix d. [1942]

I haue delaied, most woorshipfull, to offer you my duetie and therewith thanks for the booke[92] yo˜ hono˜ sente me of late that I might read so far therein as to make known to you withal my censure of the same, which office I will nowe performe, premising, since trouth is the sauce of commendacioun and all haue by complexion and the *Signature* of their souls manie likings and mislikings that stand not upon anie constant points of the art criticall, that I haue lesse stomacke to battles, sieges, trieties and affaires of state (euen in books) than to such straunge questes, remote traveiles, and singular enchanted countries as did in a manere rauysshe me ἐκτος ἐμαυτου[93] in the *Boke of þ˜ Worme*.

Mary, as for yo˜ hono˜s metaphysick mistresses, beatificall *bona robas*,[94] hyper-uranian whoores, and transcendentall trulls, not oonlie my complexioun little delighteth in them but my ripe and more constant ivdgement reiecteth, esteeming them in truth no more but what Geo: Macdonald bringeth us in as *Lilith* in his nobly inuented but ill-languaged romans of the same name, or David Lyndesay of late, under the name *Sullenbode*, in his notable *Voiage and Travell to Arctur˜*.

Wishing the while that yo˜ doctor Van Der Mast[95] had sought higher than Spinoza (who though he saith som things well yet liued after the world sickened) to finde in more allowd philosophers (as Abrabanel,[96] Jamblichus,[97] Plotinus,[98] and Plato) that the Firste Fayre must nedes be of us conceyued as masculine.[99]

---

92 *Mistress of Mistresses.*

93 'out of my wits'.

94 i.e. Italian courtesans (so named after their skirts). Shakespeare, *Henry IV Part II*, III, ii, 25: 'We knew where the *bona-robas* were.'

95 Dr Vandermast who first appears in *Mistress of Mistresses*, ch. 6.

96 Judah Abrabanel (also known as Hebreo León; b. c. 1460). Lewis mentions his *Dialoghi d'Amore* in *A Preface to Paradise Lost*, ch. 9, p. 73.

97 Iamblichus of Chalcis (c. AD 250–c. 330).

98 Plotinus (AD 204/5–270), neo-Platonist whose philosophical essays were collected by Porphyry and arranged into six *Enneads*. 'On its highest level,' said Lewis in ch. 4 of *The Discarded Image*, 'the Pagan resistance can almost be identified with the neo-Platonic school. In it the great names are Plotinus (205–70), Porphyry (233–304?), Iamblichus (ob. 330), and Proclus (ob. 485).'

99 First, Lewis disliked the philosophy talked by Dr Vandermast in *Mistress of Mistresses*, ch. 7. Although Baruch Spinoza (1632–77) is not named, Lewis recognized Vandermast as the mouthpiece of Spinoza; on p. 137 Vandermast

But this I write as a man, and not fullie certein that I haue conceyued you: for to speake criticallie, I well confesse that this secounde book climbeth to a higher stile and disposeth his fable more artificiallie than *þ˜ Woorme* and hath in it manie noble and ioyous inventions, as the garden contriued by V. der Mast,[100] the nymph that becometh a vole,[101] and the bringing in of the Vicar wasshyng his dogges.[102]

Now to trete of yo˜ hono˜'s question concerning the house woman that wrote of your stile, the name, with the book, is goon from me; but she saide it not, as you conceyued me, of evil intent, being rather of those who then most disable an auctour when they most go about to commend him *amici hostibus infestiores.*[103]

For my coming to London as you of grete affability bid me, I beare it euer in minde, but my goings thither are of necessitie so sudden and unaduiced that it shall go harde to do you to wit of it betimes. I woll bidde my booksellers to sende you a foolish trifling romans of my owne,[104] and so commende you to God remaining euer yo˜ hono˜s poore bedesman

C. S. Lewis

Euer expectynge when yo˜ hono˜ shalbe able at yo˜ good leisure to see me in my poore colledge.

---

quotes Spinoza's *Ethics* (1677) II, 6: '*per realitatem et perfectionem idem intelligo*': 'Reality and Perfection are one.' Spinoza is described as a pantheist because he regarded all things as part of God.

Lewis's second objection was that Eddison appeared to conceive of the 'First Fayre' – another name for God – as feminine. The book opens with Aphrodite, the Mistress of Mistresses, promising to fulfil the secret dream of the dying Englishman, Lessingham – a private heaven called 'Zimiamvia' where he shall enjoy her eternally. In his draft reply to this letter of 10 January 1943, Eddison wrote: 'Most auspicious Sir, That I am no philosopher I easily admit, onely an umble lover of Wisdome. I holde that wel sayd of Lessinghame, being about to dye, to that Lady whom, in this master-hour of his life upon erthe, he had begun to see and understand in her very true nature as Queen Aphrodite herself, not Maker indeed but as Conceiver & Bestower, of all Worldes' (Bodleian Library, MS. Eng. lett. c. 220/2, fol. 40).

100 Eddison, *Mistress of Mistresses*, ch. 6, pp. 103–5.

101 ibid., ch. 7, p. 129. Lewis was referring to the scene in which the nymph Campaspe turns into a water-rat.

102 ibid., ch. 5, pp. 80–1.

103 'friends more deadly than enemies'.

104 *Out of the Silent Planet.*

TO E. R. EDDISON (BOD):

[Magdalen College
29 December 1942]

And yo˜ hono˜ had not in a maner given me medicines to make me loue you both for the excellent pieces you have written and yo˜ over indulgent lecture of mine owne, I were now in a fair waye to esteeme you a verie stinkynge hereticke in philosophie, as if forsoothe by cause the First Fayre produceth an infinyte bewtie and hath self-sufficiencie it must nedes be feminyne, when it is a thing openlie manifeste to all but disards and verie goosecaps that feminitie is to itself an imperfection, being placed by the Pythagoreans in the sinister column with matter and mortalitie. Of which we see dailie ensample in that men (unless smitten for the nonce of Cupid's dart) do gladlie withdraw into their own societie and when they would be either merrie or grave stint not to shutte the dore upon Love herself, where we see no woman, tho neuer such a Diana, but will not of good will escape from her sisters and seeke to the conversation of men, as seyking by instincte of Nature so to receive the perfection she lacketh. Accordant thereto is that maxim of the scholes *Materia appetit forman ut virum femina.*[105]

But not to draw this mater owte to infynite argumentes, come soone after our terme is bigunne on Ian. xviiith new stile and solve all in a few cuppes of Rhenish.

You shal shortlie receyue my littil poore boke of a voiauge to Mars[106] wherein, after yours to me, you fare in the exchange as it fell out in the Iliads between Glaucus and Sarpedon when Zeus privily tooke awaie the vnderstanding of the one in so farre that he received a brazen armour for a golden.[107]

Sir, yf you knowe aught of the nuptiall practises and amorous carriages of beares, fayle not to let me knowe, for I haue brought in a

---

105 Aristotle, *Physics*, ch. 1, section 9a: 'Matter seeks out its form, as a woman seeks out a man.' Possibly, however, Lewis was referring to Richard Burton, *Anatomy of Melancholy* (1621), part, 3, sec. 2, mem. I, subs. 2, where the same sentiment occurs.

106 i.e. *Out of the Silent Planet.*

107 In Homer, *Iliad*, 6, 234–6, the exchange of armour is between Glaucus and Diomedes. Glaucus gets the worse of the bargain because his is gold and that of Diomedes bronze.

beare in the book I now write and it shal to bedde at the end with the other.[108]

Beseching yo˜ hono˜ of your good grace and to pardon all my iapes, I remayne your poore bedesman

C. S. Lewis

108 i.e. the bear, Mr Bultitude, in *That Hideous Strength*.

1943

The Abolition of Man, or, Reflections on Education with Special Reference to the Teaching of English in the Upper Forms of Schools *was published by the Oxford University Press on 6 January 1943.*

TO E. R. EDDISON (BOD):

[Magdalen College
19 January 1943]

I send you back, most Worshipfull, the paper you honoured me withal[1] hauving diligentlie reade the same in my coach *in via* and esteeming it a notable ensaumple of your genius though in that veyne among yo˜ Hono˜'s riches which is, as I signified before, less to my peculiar stomack.

Wherin I do chiefly commend that at the end of the 2° and beginning of the 3° shete of *Ỹ old drift of the world*[2] and that other in the sixt *vnder my skin what am I.*[3] Not always, nor perhaps euer, concurring with the scholiast[4] when he *obelizeth*[5] certayne places as troppo staccato, which places did not offend myne eare.

Yf I were to find fault in such small matters, *sed nil*, you know, *in studiis parvum est* seith Quintilian,[6] 'twould be *the Kinge of Beests* on the 2°, which though a verie proper and significant expression hath passed through so manie seely mouths that it reacheth your page somewhat beclobberd.

---

1 Eddison had sent Lewis the Praeludium or first section of *The Mezentian Gate*, the book he was then writing.

2 E. R. Eddison, *The Mezentian Gate* (1958), Praeludium, p. xviii.

3 ibid., p. xxi.

4 A 'scholiast' was one of the ancient commentators who annotated the classical authors.

5 'marked'.

6 Quintilian, *Institutio Oratoria*, Book 10, ch. 3, section 31: '*Sed nihil in studiis parvum est*': 'But there is nothing small in studies'.

Of that preference in me which you haue herde hitherto with so much candour, I know not whether it skills to speake, there being no criticaster so idle as he that blameth a book for not being what it never went about to be, and (if hee should per chance prevail) no friend so mischievous as he who draweth a writer out of his proper and kindlie line. So that all standeth on this question, whether yo˜ hono˜ containing in yourself as it were two souls in *Ouroboros*, the one leaning towards Homer, Morris, Snorri and the like, and toother more enclyning to Swinburne, Beckford, Apuleius and who knows but (at the latter ende) to Flaubert, Baudelaire and Poe – there being (to speake as our cooks do of pottages) a *clere* and a *thick* Eddison, one holding of Pallas and the other of Persephone, whether I say, both humours being intermeddled in your complexion, this increase of the one and diminution of the other is the verie kindly and natural bent of your later growth and your assured path, or no. Which, if it be, my own readier liking for the former should not weigh a feather with either of us. But whether it be so or not I wolde haue yo˜ hono˜ most constantly weigh, ponder, and perpend.

Now for your calling me a *misogynist* by cause[7] I allowe not all your fyne aerie fantasies of femininitee, it is all one as though you should call a man *hater of horses* because he hath it not commonlie in vse to let four grooms bundle his horse into the coache while he himself goeth presentlie into the shaftes to giue Master Bayard[8] his morning dryve. And to think that I wolde smyte any sillie poor drab on the mouth (not to speke of anie noble, wittie, virtuous ladie) and hold such language to her as your beastlie Moorville[9] doth, is as though you supposed me a crewel oppressour of my dogge because I do not, come dinner tyme, set honest Tray[10] in myne elbow chayre with a jack of ale at his right paw and some niceness of napery tyde aboute his nekke and betake myself under table on all iv's to waite for what scrapes he should throwe me.

By the which comedy, to pass ouer the vncomliness of the thing,

7 'because'.

8 'Bayard' was the name of Charlemagne's horse.

9 Lord Morville is a character in *A Fish Dinner in Memison.*

10 'Tray' is the traditional name for a dog, as in Shakespeare, *King Lear*, III, vi, 65–6: 'The little dogs and all,/Tray, Blanch, and Sweet-heart, see, they bark at me.' Cf. Stephen Foster's song 'Old Dog Tray' (1853).

Tray, I warrant, wolde conne me little thanks for ale and napkin but at so soon as he had bent the leg of mutton in his jawes would out of chayre with a great wallop and be doune cruncking on the floore, as who shold saye Maister, tho' you forget the kynde of a man I will not forget the kynde of a hound.[11]

I wayte eurie daie for my newe booke to come from the printers,[12] delaying to sende you the older one[13] till I can send both, so hoping that at least one man in England shall rede them orderlie as they were intended. Wherein I doubt not you shal find as mooch fayre to your complexion as I to myne in yours, and all verie slight.

Is Sir Philip's incomparable *Arcadia*[14] among your books? If it bee not, I conjure you to rede it (not heeding all the fine criticks) for I beleue it was written for you. And Nashe? But here's matter for the chimney corner and the slippered foot.

When does yo˜ Hono˜ come? Greeting you hertely, from my poore chamber *in coll Stae Mar Magd* this xixth daie of Januarie New Style

C. S. Lewis

TO DOUGLAS BUSH (W):

Magdalen College,
Oxford.
Jan 20th 1943

Dear Bush (if we may now drop the honorifics?)

Thank you for your most kind letter. About *Hermione*[15] I wrote in 'ignorance, Madam, sheer ignorance'[16] of some relevant readings in 17th c. texts of the ancients, wh. has since been corrected.

---

11 Eddison replied to this in his letter of 7 February 1943: 'I holde Man & Woman equal in worth & dignity, but in well nighe al particularities els, utterly unequal & diverse, the one sect more excellent in this, the tother in that, & so at evens, all over all, if 'twere possible to measure & match these incommensurables: which . . . is indeed as it ought to be' (Bodleian Library, MS. Eng. lett. c. 220/2, fol. 46).

12 i.e. *Perelandra.*

13 i.e. *Out of the Silent Planet.*

14 Sir Philip Sidney, *The Countess of Pembrokes Arcadia* (1590).

15 15 Lewis's poem 'Hermione in the House of Paulina' had appeared in *Augury: An Oxford Miscellany of Verse and Prose*, ed. Alex M. Hardie and Keith C. Douglas (Oxford: Blackwell, 1940), p. 28. It is reprinted in *CP*.

16 Boswell, *The Life of Samuel Johnson*, vol. I, 1755, p. 293. See note 97 to the letter of 2 October 1941.

Wilson Knight's book[17] was an oddity, wasn't it? A kind of English version of the Nazi creed with Milton as our Rosenberg[18] . . . and, my goodness, what nonsense about Coleridge's *Zapolya*![19] I don't think Milton wd. have seen the contrast – if you mean to suggest one – between virtue as obedience and virtue as reason. I'm not sure that I do myself, either!

The frontier of the OHEL volume settles itself v. comfortably by the mere fact that you have finished your work before me:[20] that gives me a *defined hole* to fill up and I can shape my piece of putty accordingly. I look forward to your book with great pleasure.

yours
C. S. Lewis

TO ARTHUR GREEVES (W):

The Kilns,
Headington Quarry,
Oxford
[January 1943]

My dear Arthur,

For the first time in my life I find myself writing you a business letter. I have to assist someone in writing an academic thesis on A.E. (– Russell, you know) and he says Forrest Reid knew him and knows a lot about him. Incidentally, my pupil, though his name is Budd,[21]

---

17 G. Wilson Knight, *Chariot of Wrath: The Message of John Milton to Democracy at War* (1942).

18 Alfred Rosenberg (1893–1946) was a German political leader who expounded Nazi doctrine in his *The Myth of the 20th Century* (1930).

19 Knight, *Chariot of Wrath*, p. 15: 'What has the British Crown meant during recent years to our own intelligentsia? What place has Coleridge's *Zapolya*, perhaps our most perfect literary realization of goodness and strength in identity, won for itself in our seats of learning? To urge that Shakespeare and Milton, men whose massive poetic statements turn about the poles of the Homeric opposition, stand at the heart of our nation in war and peace, offering an oracular wisdom, appear, to many, absurd. Yet so it is, and it is necessary that we should know it.'

20 Professor Bush had completed his *English Literature in the Earlier Seventeenth Century 1600–1660*, and it was published as Volume VII of the Oxford History of English Literature in 1945.

21 The Rev. Kenneth George Budd (1904–72) a member of Exeter College, wrote a B.Litt. thesis on 'A.E.' (George William Russell) but unfortunately failed his examination in 1945, so the thesis has never been accepted by Oxford University. He published a number of books, one of which was *The Story of Donald Hankey, A*

admires Reid 'consumedly'. Can you (a) Let me have Reid's address, and (b) By judicious conversation put him in the frame of mind in which he will think letters (requiring answers) from an unknown man (called Budd) will be flattering and not boring. This is untrue, of course: that's why it will need such judicious conversation to convince him of it.

Well, how are you? Minto is laid up with one of her terrible varicose ulcers, but W. and I are alright. But it's a weary world, isn't it? My wish for a walk and talk with you is at some times acute ('And what is it at the other times?' said Alice. 'Oh when it's not acute, it is grave,' said the White Knight). As you will have noticed I've been having great luck with my books lately, and it wd. be affectation to pretend I hadn't got much pleasure out of it: but the catch is it increases the amount of letters one has to write almost beyond endurance. I'm pretty well: sometimes sad, other times not. How are the McNeils? – my love and duty to them, and the Glenmachonians.

Except in bed and in trains I get v. little reading done now. Re-read *Middlemarch* in trains last Vac. with great enjoyment, only the marrying Dorothea to Ladislaw at the end is an anticlimax. Also recently read J. Austen's *Sanditon* for the first time: not very good, except for the fat pale man with his basin of cocoa – a little like Bob, one pictures.[22] Am at present browsing in Lambs letters.[23] The 2 vols of *Elia*[24] wh. I so often use and wh. bear the inscription 'From J. A. Greeves. Xmas 1916' are so faded you can hardly recognise the colour now, but fresh as ever inside. Those illustrations still please me as much as ever. (How you must regret having parted with it! Still, you've got *Lore of Proserpine*[25] back, rot you!).

Warnie has grown thin. It's quite interesting seeing the shape of the face coming out: like unpacking a parcel. I'm as bulgy as ever. Let me have a line. It would be a really cheering thing for me – honest! I never

---

Student in Arms (1931). See note 183 to the letter of 27 October 1916 (*CL* I, p. 243).

22 Jane Austen, *Fragment of a Novel Written by Jane Austen: Now First Printed from the Manuscript*, ed. R. W. Chapman (1925), known to members of Jane Austen's family as *Sanditon*. The character Arthur Parker says in ch. 9, 'A large dish of rather weak cocoa every evening agrees with me better than anything.'

23 Charles Lamb, *The Letters of Charles Lamb* (London: Dent, 1935).

24 Charles Lamb, *The Essays of Elia*, 2 vols. (London: Heinemann, 1905).

25 Maurice Henry Hewlett, *The Lore of Proserpine* (1913).

met Mrs Pomeroy again. My love to your mother. Well, I must be getting on. Writing, writing, writing – letters, notes, exam papers, books, lectures. I've enough rheumatism in my right hand now to prevent me from sleeping on that side.

Yours

~~C. S. Lew~~

(Nearly did it wrong!)

Jack

TO MARY NEYLAN (T):

Magdalen,
Oxford.
Jan 31st 1943

Dear Mrs. Neylan –

What frightfully bad luck. And I'm the worst person in the world to write to someone who is feeling weak and listless, not because I have never been in that condition but because I don't myself *dislike* it nearly as much as most people. To lie in bed – to find ones eyes filling with facile tears at the least hint of pathos in ones book – to let the book drop from ones hand as one sinks deeper and deeper into reverie – to forget what you were thinking about a moment ago and *not to mind* – and then to be roused by the unexpected discovery that it is already tea-time – all this I do *not* find disagreeable!

Yes, its funny what horrid young men one meets in Dickens and Thackeray. Of course the *descent* of D. Copperfield[26] is partly due to the fact that no later chapters *could* come up to the early ones. Have you noticed that nearly *all* writers describe childhood (when it is in the first person) well? Jane Eyre[27] is also best at the beginning: and almost every autobiography. But is it also due to the convention whereby Victorian novelists are not allowed to attribute to their heroes peccadilloes (or worse) in respect of chastity? Hence the 'scrapes' of youth all have to be represented by other, less probable, and (to us) more repellent sins? You notice that Tom Jones[28] does not similarly lose our regard as he grows up.

26 The central charcter in Charles Dickens, *David Copperfield* (1849–50).

27 Charlotte Brontë, *Jane Eyre* (1847).

28 The central character in Henry Fielding, *Tom Jones* (1749).

I also had a delightful 'anticlimax' with our reverend friend[29] over quite a different matter. They are among the recurrent pleasures of life. What a mercy to have *another's* voice to liberate one from all the endless labyrinths of the *solitary* conscience!

No. Bears seem to be very modest. No one seems to know anything about their love passages. Perhaps they neither marry nor are given in marriage but gather their young from the flowers as Virgil thought bees did.[30] It would explain why the bear's whelp has to be 'licked into shape' as all authorities agree.

I've re-read *The Ring & the Book*[31] in trains lately with great enjoyment: but don't recommend it to you in your present state! (The *Rose and the Ring* wd. be better).[32]

I shd. think Borrow[33] goes down v. well. But Jane Austen, Scott, and Trollope are my own favourites when ill. I hope you can read this: I become daily less capable of forming the letters I intend.

> *'I write by scratches now; when age comes on*
> *May hardly write at all'*[34]

Now, go to sleep. Blessings.

Yours sincerely
C. S. Lewis

In 1935 Lewis had agreed to write the volume on the sixteenth century for the Oxford History of English Literature. But up to this time, the book continued to lie 'like a nightmare'[35] *on his chest and he was making little progress. There was scant incentive for him to write on the period because his Oxford lectures were almost all on medieval and Renaissance literature. Then came an invitation that pleased Lewis as much as any he ever received, and provided the catalyst for him to begin writing the 'O Hell'*

29 His confessor, Fr Walter Adams SSJE.
30 Virgil, *Georgics*, IV, 149–227.
31 Robert Browning, *The Ring and the Book* (1868–9).
32 William Makepeace Thackeray, *The Rose and the Ring* (1855).
33 George Henry Borrow (1803–81), author of *Lavengro*.
34 Lewis is making a comic allusion to Wordsworth, *The Prelude*, III, 338–9: 'I see by glimpses now; when age comes on,/May scarcely see at all.'
35 See the letter to F. P. Wilson of 25 January 1938.

book. In a letter of 2 February 1943 George Macaulay Trevelyan, the Master of Trinity College, Cambridge, wrote:[36]

> *Dear Mr. Lewis, It is with very particular pleasure that I am writing on behalf of the Council of this College to invite you to give the Clark Lectures for the academic year 1943–4 . . . The lectures are open to the University and the public, but are provided by Trinity College. We should hope to put you up in this College, and I hope usually in this Lodge. Allow me to say how very much I should like to make your better acquaintance, for I am a great admirer of your books from 'The Allegory of Love' onwards.*[37]

Although the Clark Lectures, given on 26 April and 3, 10 and 17 May 1944, formed only a small part of what became English Literature in the Sixteenth Century, *the book was given the subtitle* 'The Completion of The Clark Lectures, Trinity College, Cambridge, 1944'.

TO E. R. EDDISON (BOD):

[Magdalen College
7 February 1943]

As for yo˜ Worships lying at the East Gate or that giant inn of Randulph,[38] I utterlie conspue and reiecte the same, hoping rather that you sholde haue laine in a gvest chamber of this poore colledge if you will soe fare condescende. Faith I can promise yo˜ hono˜ no water rates, voles, lynxes and the like to savour yo˜ bedde withal, and no moore but clene linen and the softe bolstre.

But for the tyme, Tuesdai xvi were in a maner unpossible inas moche as on that night the Dante Societie whereof I am an vnworthie member holdeth its high feast, from the while, being part hooste I cannot nor may not be excused. It were therefore fitting that you sholde come on the xvii (Wednesday) and I wolde looke to see you between the sixt and seventh houre and to lie here and ete a morsel in the morning

36 George Macaulay Trevelyan (1876–1962), historian, was Master of Trinity College, Cambridge, 1940–51.

37 Bodleian Library, MS. Eng. c. 6825, fol. 102.

38 Eddison, having been invited to dine at Magdalen, thought of spending the night at either the Eastgate Inn, across the High Street from Magdalen, or in the huge Randolph Hotel in Beaumont Street.

(tho we holdeth not the notable custom of your owne land to break our fast with a dishe of lobsters & som white wine) and then perforce to parte for I shall be in my besinesse.

Yf this maie not stand, I praie you come on Thursdae xviii, but of all loves to let me haue letters *instanter*[39] doing me to knowe the certeintee of the matter. For the which singular favour, I mean of your intended visit, I shall ever abide yo˜ hono˜s poor bedesman

C. S. Lewis

TO E. R. EDDISON (BOD):[40]

Magdalen College
Oxford
10 February 1943

Neither the maner of the Antients to croune their heads with girlonds nor our later day custom to brave it in plumb colourd taffeta is anie longer in vse among us, nor we doe not euen weare black cloaths, but as verie slouens or hobbinols[41] een fall to our meate in our soiled weeds. A Sorie vsage that came in after the late wars under colour of thrift and hath continued. Soe dailie doth old civilitie decline. (*Ar vas alda*)[42] Lokyng with great ioye and a good stomake to see yo˜ hono˜

C. S. Lewis

Lewis and Eddison met for the first time on the evening of 17 February 1943. After dining in the Hall of Magdalen College, Lewis took his friend to his rooms in New Buildings for a meeting of the Inklings. Present were Warren Lewis, J. R. R. Tolkien and Charles Williams. Eddison wrote to Lewis on 21 February:

> *It is easier to savour such like delectabilities then to write worthily of them . . . Certeyn it is, you have given me a memorie to chew upon . . . beginning with your self & your brother; your good canarie afore dinner; dinner itself in your great shadowy hall with*

---

39 'instantly'.

40 Eddison had replied that he would appear on the evening of Wednesday, 17 February, and asked what he should wear to dine in Magdalen College.

41 'rustics'.

42 *Ar vas alda*: 'It was a year long ago' begins verse 3 of 'The Song of the Sybil', an ancient Scandinavian creation myth in the Elder Edda.

good & honourable company, good ale & good meats sett forth upon shining board fair with glass & ornaments of gold & silver . . .

And so to that quincunciall symposium, at ease about your sea-cole fire, in your privat chaumbre, where (as it seemed to mee) good discourse made night's horses gallop too faste; & so to our goodnight walke & adieux in the gate under your great Towre . . . For my self, I tasted wisdome as wel as good ale at your fireside, all be it, I am much afeared, pouring you out on my parte some provokements in exchange, & talking sometimes indeed as a man will write at a first drafting, or with purpose but to flush a quarry & see whose falcon . . . will mount swiftliest highe enow to strike it downe. If our talk were battledore & shuttlecock, what matter? 'Twas merry talk, & truth will sometimes appere, better than in statu, in the swift flying to & again of the shuttlecock.[43]

TO SISTER PENELOPE CSMV (BOD):

[Magdalen College]
Feb 20th [1943]

Dear Sister Penelope –

I have been putting off my answer to your first letter from day to day in the hope that I shd. be able to send *Perelandra* with it: but tho' the publisher said it wd. be out in Jan. there is no sign of it yet. No doubt there is some hitch with the binders for it has been printed months ago.

My efforts to be patient are now reinforced by the much more sickening disappointment you have had about St. Athanasius. I believe if I were you I shd. *not* re-write it as a crib until I had tried whether publishers wd. not take it in its present form. Try my Mr. Bles,[44] and then Dent. Why shd. it be assumed that no one is capable of reading the *De Incarnatione* except ordinands doing it for an exam (that is what

43 Bodleian Library, MS. Eng. lett. c. 220/2, fols. 51–2.

44 Geoffrey Bles (1886–1957) read Greats at Merton College, Oxford, after which he served in the Indian Civil Service. In 1923 he created his own publishing firm in London, having a great success with Vicki Baum's *Grand Hotel* (1930) and going on to publish some of the most important theologians of the period. Working with him was Ashley Sampson (1900–47), owner of the Centenary Press, who first spotted Lewis and brought him to Bles's attention. Bles bought Sampson's company and amalgamated it with his own, thus becoming the major publisher of Lewis's religious books and some of the Narnian stories.

is behind the demand for a crib) – and ordinands so stupid that they can't see how the Gk. runs from your translation wh., though not barbarously literal, is quite close enough to be used as a crib by anyone who has horse-sense. Don't give in to this absurd demand unless compelled.

The Greek is really extremely easy and your translation, as it stands, supplies what alone ought to be needed – a glossary of unusual *words*. Even from the point of view of weak students a really literal crib is not necessarily so helpful as the SPCK make out: such things tho' Englishing every word are apt to leave the whole unintelligible. Do fight.

I can imagine how you are feeling – feeling something the same myself. It helps one to conceive (analogically) the 'longanimity' of Our Lord in waiting all these centuries to see of the travail of His soul and be satisfied.[45] When will the divine books we were meant to be actually lie on His table all corrected without printer's error or corruption in the text or 'any such thing'?

It is only on *that* side (i.e. the author's desire) that I can admit any real parallel. 'Creation' as applied to human authorship (I'm on your *first* letter now, you see) seems to me an entirely misleading term. We make ἐς ὑποκειμενων[46] i.e. we re-arrange elements He has provided. There is not a *vestige* of real creativity *de novo* in us. Try to imagine a new primary colour, a third sex, a fourth dimension, or even a monster wh. does not consist of bits of existing animals stuck together! Nothing happens. And that surely is why our works (as you said) never mean to others quite what we intended: because we are re-combining elements made by Him and already containing *His* meanings. Because of those divine meanings in our materials it is impossible we shd. ever know the whole meaning of our own works, and the meaning we never intended may be the best and truest one.

Writing a book is much less like creation than it is like planting a garden or begetting a child: in all three cases we are only entering as *one* cause into a causal stream which works, so to speak, in its own way. I wd. not wish it to be otherwise. If one cd. *really* create in the strict sense wd. one not find one had created a sort of Hell?

I enclose the *Hamlet* thing – you have a special right to it since when

45 Isaiah 53:11: 'He shall see of the travail of his soul, and shall be satisfied.'
46 'with regard to what lies at hand'.

I last left your home I was on my way to deliver it.[47] But how dull all ones books are except the one you are waiting for at the moment! – wh. again has an analogical bearing on the parable of the lost sheep. I should have more joy of *Perelandra* at the moment than of 99 books that have had no hitch about them.

My ribs are sore from falling (in the literal sense!) twice!

Yrs. sincerely
Brother Ass.

TO T. S. ELIOT (P):[48]

Magdalen College,
Oxford.
Feb 23rd 1943

Dear Mr. Eliot –

Thank you for your kind letter. I do not think we were really at cross purposes and I did not attribute to you the doctrine that only poets cd. criticise Milton's theology or his character. I attributed to you the doctrine that only poets can criticise his poetry *quâ* poetry, which is what I dissent from.

The matter is ticklish, I admit. If not poets, who can? But it seems to me that the moment one says 'only poets can' the word 'poet' itself is emptied of all content. To discuss your *Note* in detail was not part of my aim. My chapters on the style of secondary epic may imply a criticism on the usefulness of comparing Milton with Henry James or

---

47 i.e. 'Hamlet: The Prince or the Poem?'

48 See **Thomas Stearns Eliot** in the Biographical Appendix. Eliot had written to Lewis about *A Preface to Paradise Lost*, in which Lewis took exception to comments Eliot had made in 'A Note on the Verse of John Milton' in *Essays and Studies*, XXI (1936). In *A Preface to Paradise Lost*, ch. 2, Lewis stated: 'Mr Eliot says bluntly and frankly that the best contemporary practising poets are the only "jury of judgement" whose verdict on his own views of *Paradise Lost* he will accept. And Mr Eliot is here simply rendering explicit a notion that has become increasingly prevalent for about a hundred years – the notion that poets are the only judges of poetry . . . Let us consider what would follow if we took Mr Eliot's view seriously. The first result is that I, not being one of the best contemporary poets, cannot judge Mr Eliot's criticism at all. What then shall I do? Shall I go to the best contemporary poets, who can, and ask them whether Mr Eliot is right? But in order to go to them I must first know who they are. And this, by hypothesis, I cannot find out; the same lack of poethood which renders my critical opinions on Milton worthless renders my opinions on Mr Pound or Mr Auden equally worthless.'

Mr Joyce, but your main contention about bad influences didn't come in my way at all.

Charles Williams is always promising (or threatening!) to confront us with each other [to] hammer all these matters out. I hope the fact that I find myself often contradicting you in print gives no offence: it is a kind of tribute to you – whenever I fall foul of some wide-spread contemporary view about literature I always seem to find that you have expressed it most clearly. One aims at the officers first in meeting an attack!

I'm so glad you agreed about Virgil: if we didn't find ourselves in the very disquieting company of Scaliger I shd. be quite happy!

Yours sincerely

C. S. Lewis

TO E. R. EDDISON (BOD):

[Magdalen College
27 February 1943]

Besides the vsual pleasure I haue in your Ld's letters I was in these last the more eased to vnderstonde parfetlie by the lecture of þe same yt you reste still my good Lorde and are nothing distempered or greued by those saucie and malapert carriages which (I confesse) we vsed to your Lp.[49] on your coming among vs, wherein being as who sholde saie one martyr-lion fallne vnawares ammiddes an whole covine of Xtianes yo˜ hono˜ was somewhat bayted.

In the which vnreverend procesce let the tenour of our former lettres plede for me as one who first going about to dishable and explood yo˜ serenities phylosophie vnderstoode not your ripenesse and reverencie excedynge myne owne in yeres (for hadde I knowne the colour of your mustachios I had not so gracelesslie tweacked em) and then meetynge with yo˜ hono˜ face to face coulde not so soddenlie falle from a wanton sink a pace into a staide pauanne.[50] But your wisdome doubtlesse perceyueth herin a subtle praise inasmoche as tis the lustinesse and inward

49 'lordship'.

50 The galliard was a high-spirited dance from the sixteenth century with five steps to a measure, and was hence known in English as the 'sinkapace' (French *cinque pas*). Thus, Lewis's 'wanton sink a pace'. The pavane, on the other hand, is a slow, stately dance step. Lewis meant that if he had known that Eddison was much older than himself his approach to him would be less like a sinkapace and more like a pavane.

youth of your Ldsp's mind that taketh awaie the propre awfulness of age.

Sir, I am late returnde from New Castle wher I redde a lecture to that Colledge[51] and am now sette down to rede in your excellent *Ichthyophagyes*[52] with singular delyght. Of which romans I can speke no higher praise (though it come somewhat o yo˜ lifte honde) thanne to saie that the sharpnesse of the stile and the strength, rovndnesse, race and verie salt smacke of the persones hadde almost deboshed mee (but my better aungel was to honde) to beleeve in earnest that the verie gretnesse and bewtie lyeth in such high stomacked, self plesing, lecherous, cruel, trecherovs, tyraunts as thise *heroës* of Rerek and Zayana; I mean yo˜ hono˜'s *timocraticall* men whom shallow Mstr Steevens, not knowing Plato his *distinguo*, wolde fobbe off on us for *aristocraticall.*[53]

Sir you are a fulle subtle tempter and stronge enow to catch anie vnripe iudgement in yo˜ nette. Me thinketh whyle I rede in your pages I vnderstonde from withinne by verie felynge what it were to bee one of thise High Dutch captains yt haue twice in our daies mischeued all middle erthe, and doe so enlarge my charitee and confirme my iudgement, ounlie assured that they shal neuer vnderstonde and conteyne my loues as I in a maner doe theres.

The *capitulum* entitvled vii against þe Kynge[54] moulteth in the seconde lecture no fethere of the strengthe it hadde when we herde it.

Alle heer wer so welle content with youre goode companie that nothynge will serue but to renewe that same draught speedily and often. I am ashamed yo˜ hono˜ sholde a dispended tyme on my litel libell of *Payne.* Trewlie it was not for youre reding and yf I wer to wrastle with you˜ Ldsp thise wer not the reasons I wolde a vsed.

---

51 The Riddell Memorial Lectures, later published as *The Abolition of Man.*

52 i.e. *A Fish Dinner in Memison.*

53 In his introduction to *A Fish Dinner in Memison* James Stephens wrote: 'The aristocrat can be as brutal as ever gangster was, but, and in whatever brutality, he preserves a bearing, a grace, a charm, which our fiction, in general, does not care, or dare, to attempt . . . So in these pages, there are villainies, and violences, and slaughterings that are, to one reader, simply devilish. But they are devilish with an accent – as Milton's devil is.' Lewis's point is that if Mr Stephens had read the distinction Plato makes in Book VIII of *The Republic* between Timocratical and Aristocratical men he would know how different they are.

54 Ch. 7 of *A Fish Dinner in Memison*, entitled 'Seven Against the King'.

Gretynge you hertily and resting ever yo˜ hono˜'s poore bedesman in Coll. Stae. Mar. Magd.

C. S. Lewis

Feb xxvjj newe stile 1943.

In Lewis's first letter to E. R. Eddison of 16 November 1942 he complained that The Worm Ouroboros *contained no 'mappemonnde' which was necessary if the reader was to understand 'all the diverse voyages and travelles'. Eddison passed this on to his friend, Gerald Hayes, a cartographer with the Royal Navy. On 21 February 1943 Hayes wrote to Lewis:*

> *This intrusion of a stranger would be inexcusable were it not that I may plead excuse in your letter written some months ago to my friend E. R. Eddison, from wh. he sent me some extracts and in especial that you 'a little snubbed him' on the want of a map for the book 'The Worm Ouroboros'. So indeed I felt when some eighteen years ago, I came on this book . . . With much labour of geometry and calculation I constructed a map for myself from the internal evidence . . . Thus armed I ventured to approach the author for those details which cd. exist in his mind only: and the end was that I drew a large map that secured his approval as a true presentation of all the lands, seas, & countries of his history.*
>
> *Now I have the temerity to ask your acceptance of some rough copies of portions of this (for the whole is too large and dotted with ships, beasts and whatnot to be copied in these busy days) – praying that you will forgive a manifest crudity which is a product of sleep-fighting in the night hours of A.R.P.*[55] *and of a fountain pen, and will regard it as no more than a guiding diagram to help you in your following of the story.*[56]

55 Presumably Hayes was an Air Raid Precautions (ARP) warden. In addition to their regular jobs, these men spent several nights a week patrolling their areas of responsibility making sure that no chink of light showed from any window or door to attract a German air attack.

56 Bodleian Library, MS. Eng. lett. c. 220/2, fol. 53.

TO GERALD HAYES (BOD):[57]

[Magdalen College]
March 3rd 1943

Dear Mr Hayes –

I hardly know whether I can find colours & figures of rhetoric sufficient to express my sense of the delectable & wholly unexpected present you have made me. I have a passion for imaginary maps & look forward to hours of amusement with yours – apart from its decorative value when glazed & hung.

I have now met Eddison & heard him read *Seven against the King* from a *Fish Dinner* which was almost the greatest treat I have ever had in the way of reading aloud – & I claim to be critical since I live in a society who read aloud to one another continually. The richness of the voice, the twirling of the 'mustachio', the bloodthirsty chuckle, were all unforgettable.

I believe (here differing from you) that the *Worm* will never be displaced in my regard by its successors. I don't know about their being more 'truly adult' (unless you use it as the adjective of adultery!). It seems to me that the journey in the *Worm* appeals to things more eternal than the Aphrodite worship of the later books. We outgrow youth far sooner than childhood. But these are personal preferences: the development in art is not disputable. He is certainly a wonderful man – an 'humour' carried to its furthest richness of expansion in the manner, which is still possible in England: a living denial of all the standardisation against which his books so vigorously protest. (The picture of democracy in *Fish Dinner* p. 230 *ad fin* is delicious!)

You must come & look [out] our little confraternity if you ever are in Oxford & receive in person my repeated thanks for what is one of

---

57 Hayes received two letters from Lewis dated 3 and 12 March 1943, which he passed on to Eddison for his delectation. Eddison made copies for his own use and it is these copies (Bodleian Library, MS. Eng. lett. c. 230/1, fol. 44) that are given in the present volume. The map Hayes made for Lewis has survived.

Gerald Ravenscroft Hayes, OBE (1889–1955) was educated at Cranleigh, after which he entered the Admiralty service by open competition. He joined the Hydrographic Department in 1911 and became Chief Cartographer in 1934. In 1946 he transferred to the Secretary's Department where he remained until his retirement in 1953. Hayes was also interested in music, heraldry, painting and sailing. His books include *Introduction to Charts and Their Use* (1944) and *Charting the Seas in Peace and War* (1947).

my notablest treasures. It has given me again what I have not had for years & years, the old pleasure in a 'present'.

I wish I cd. write either modern or court hand as you do!

TO MARTYN SKINNER (BOD):

Magdalen
March 4th [1943]

Dear Skinner

Your letter came most timely for I was just then enjoying your new *Letters*[58] which are so meaty and brisk and bracing that tho' they do not make me pick out particular couplets the whole thing gives me that sense of well-being which (on a successful railway journey or during a party) makes one say 'I'm enjoying this!'.

The relation between the Tao and Xtianity is best seen from Confucius' remark 'There may be someone who has perfectly followed the way: but I never heard of one.' Gaius and Titius[59] were, as you will not be surprised to learn, Australians. Singapore knows what comes of Green Books now.

All the best.

Yours
C. S. Lewis

TO T. S. ELIOT (P):

Magdalen College
Oxford
(appropriately enough) Ash Wed. [10 March 1943]

Dear Mr Eliot –

I'm not sure that we are still not a little at cross purposes, but must not draw you into what might be an interminable argument. I do,

58 Skinner, *Letters to Malaya*. Skinner won the Hawthornden Prize for these poems in 1943. There were to be another four volumes of *Letters to Malaya*.

59 Skinner had mentioned *The Abolition of Man*, in which Lewis had condemned '*The Green Book*' by 'Gaius' and 'Titius'. The real authors were Alec King and Martin Ketley and their book *The Control of Language: A Critical Approach to Reading and Writing*, foreword by W. L. F. Murdoch (New York: Longmans, Green, 1939; 3rd edn London: 1940). Their argument was that all values are subjective and merely statements about feelings.

however, agree that there is a grotesque element in nearly all Renaissance poetry which P.L. has not escaped and wh. one feels more acutely in it than in Tasso's poem[60] just because the thing is superficially more serious. The most gorgeous example (if the subject matter did not make it rather profane to enjoy the joke) is Vida's *Christiad*.[61] The *Lusiads*[62] I know only in translation – and in it they seemed ridiculous.

I agree, as you know, about C.W. – but only, if only he cd. be induced to write more fiction and less criticism! The last novel,[63] in which he had begun to chasten the exuberance of style ought to have been the beginning of a great new development. I'm not likely to be in London for several days on end, I'm afraid, but thank you for your kind suggestion.

Yours sincerely
C. S. Lewis

TO GERALD HAYES (BOD):

[Magdalen College]
March 12th 43

Dear Mr Hayes

My own favourite reading, though it does not overlap yours except at *Amadis*,[64] is somewhat akin – the *Morte Darthur*, the *Orlando Furioso*,[65] the *Faerie Queene*, the *Arcadia*, the *High History of the Holy Grail*[66] & all Wm Morris, but especially his prose romances.

But ought we not both to defend our tastes more stoutly? To all this about being 'grown up' may we not answer that the desire to be grown

60 i.e. *Gerusalemme Liberata.*

61 Marco Girolamo Vida, *Christiad* (1535).

62 Luis de Camoëns, *Os Lusiadas* (1572).

63 i.e. Williams's *Descent into Hell.*

64 *Amadis of Gaul* is a Spanish or Portuguese romance written in the form in which we have it by Garcia de Montalvo in the fifteenth century. It derives from much older stories.

65 Ludovico Ariosto, *Orlando Furioso* (1532).

66 Sebastian Evans, *The High History of the Holy Grail* (1898). This is a translation of the Old French poem, *Perlesvaux*, one of many versions of the Grail legend. Although the *High History* does not entirely unite the theme of King Arthur and the Grail, it is the fullest Perceval romance in existence. On the development of the *High History of the Holy Grail* see Charles Williams and C. S. Lewis, *Arthurian Torso* (1947), ch. 5.

up is itself intrinsically puerile but the love of 'fine fabling'[67] is not. These books were written neither by children nor for children. Because they are now out of fashion they have gravitated to the nursery as the old furniture has – the same is true of fairy-tales themselves. Let us rather congratulate ourselves in retaining (whether we do it in the company of children or not) the taste of more generous & civilised ages than our own.

An early & lasting love of Oriana,[68] Bradamante,[69] Philoclea[70] & the rest at least preserves us from Fiorinda,[71] about whom I think as you do (I told our friend that I had no use for his 'metaphysicall mistresses, hyper-uranian whores, beatifical *bona-robas*, and transcendental trulls'). No, no. From Sophonisba[72] to Fiorinda is a step *back*, however the style (& especially the nomenclature) has been enriched. Good Lord, Sir, would not one simple surgical operation cure a man of all this silly stuff about 'exquisite, ironical beauties' – baggages that they are. But you see you have trod on my loud pedal by mistake.

Seriously, though, if one of the real great heroines of romance walked into Memison wd. not Fiorinda & her crew look suddenly just vulgar – furtive – naïve. Cooks, my dear Hayes, cooks. One wd. notice that they hardly washed behind their ears. One wd. see the snarling inferiority in their smiles.

Yours,
C. S. Lewis

---

67 This famous phrase comes from Richard Hurd (1720–1808). See *Hurd's Letters on Chivalry and Romance*, ed. Edith J. Morley (1911), Letter XII, p. 154: 'Under this form the tales of fairy kept their ground, and even made their fortune at court ... But reason, in the end ... drove them off the scene, and would endure their *lying wonders*, neither in their own proper shape, nor as masked in figures ... What we have gotten by this revolution, you will say, is a great deal of good sense. What we have lost, is a world of fine fabling.'

68 The heroine of *Amadis of Gaul*.

69 The maiden warrior in *Orlando Furioso*.

70 The younger sister of Pamela in the *Arcadia*.

71 Fiorinda, a lady of honour at the ducal court of Zayana, is one of the chief characters in *Mistress of Mistresses*.

72 Sophonisba is a human but immortal queen in Eddison's *The Worm Ouroboros*.

TO DOROTHY L. SAYERS (W):

Magdalen College,
Oxford.
March 18th 1943

Dear Miss Sayers

Allow me to congratulate you on the *Six Other Deadly Sins*[73] of wh. Rieu[74] has just sent me a copy. It is one of the few things which I find, within its limits, perfect – i.e. there is nothing one would wish added or removed or altered.

The bit about avarice and advertisements is specially good. You know the medieval word SALIGIA made of the initial letters of the Seven Deadlies in Latin? Oughtn't we to have a modern one for the names in English? It wd. have to be *Anger* not Wrath and several nice combinations are possible – SEPALAG, PELAGAS, GALASEP etc. But none (that I have yet thought of) has quite the cold, reptilian, insinuating quality of the original *Saligia*.

You must have enjoyed writing it.

Yours sincerely
C. S. Lewis

---

73 Dorothy L. Sayers, *The Other Six Deadly Sins: An Address Given to the Public Morality Council at Caxton Hall, Westminster, on October 23rd, 1941* (London: Methuen, 1943). Sayers begins her book thus: 'Perhaps the bitterest commentary on the way in which Christian doctrine has been taught in the last few centuries is the fact that to the majority of people the word "immorality" has come to mean one thing and one thing only . . . About the sin called *Luxuria* or *Lust*, I shall therefore say only three things. First, that it is a sin, and that it ought to be called plainly by its own name, and neither huddled away under a generic term like immorality, nor confounded with love.' From there she goes on to deal with the 'other six deadly sins': *Ira* or Wrath, *Gula* or Gluttony, *Avaritia* Avarice or Covetousness, *Invidia* or Envy, *Accidia* or Sloth, and *Superbia* or Pride.

74 Emile Victor Rieu (1887–1972), editor and translator, was born in London and educated at St Paul's School and Balliol College, Oxford, where he took a First in Classical Honour Moderations in 1908. In 1910 he joined Oxford University Press, becoming manager of their branch-office in India. In 1923 he returned to England as educational manager of the publishers Methuen. He was managing director, 1933–6. After a break he returned to Methuen in 1940 where he remained until his retirement in 1964. Rieu's promise as a classical scholar and translator came to fruition with the publication of his translation of the *Odyssey* (1946), the first of a new series of Penguin Classics. He went on to translate Virgil's *The Pastoral Poems* (1949), *The Iliad* (1950), *The Four Gospels* (1952) and *The Voyage of the Argo* (1959).

TO SISTER PENELOPE CSMV (BOD):

[Magdalen College]
March 25th 43

Dear Sister Penelope –

I have read *The Holy Seed*[75] with great interest and on the main issue I agree with you as against Welsh.[76] I don't wish any of Isaac's *via dolorosa* away. It is quite true that many of the children will not understand the symbolism. But (a.) All the symbolical passages are quite capable of standing on their own feet as probable and affecting detail for the Isaac story considered in itself. (b.) What they do not understand at the time will go into their semi-conscious mind and help them to understand the Cross years later – will perhaps all the more if they don't remember it. Symbolism exists precisely for the purpose of conveying to the imagination what the intellect is not ready for. Any criticisms I have to offer turn on quite different points.

1. In the first scene. The idea that it will be all the better for ones children if their rich uncle has no child is extremely obvious – to an adult.[77] Is it to a child? I feel sure that it wouldn't have been to me, and therefore wonder whether it does not need plainer statement (e.g. on p. 2 after 'they both laughed', one of the children might say 'But what did Nanny[78] mean about Master's chances?' and the mother might explain. At least if the point is worth bringing in at such length. If you can't afford time to explain it I think it might be omitted).[79]

---

75 In her notes to this letter Sister Penelope said: 'The reference (here and elsewhere) to *The Holy Seed*, as I was then calling it, is to a sequence of Biblical plays which I had been asked to write for the B.B.C. When the work was about two-thirds done, it became evident that those responsible for the production intended so to alter the emphasis throughout the work as to make it the story of man's achievement, rather than that of the saving Work of God. I therefore withdrew it.' The work was subsequently rewritten, and published as 'A Religious of CSMV', *They Shall Be My People: The Bible Traversed in A Course of Reading Plays*, 2 vols. (London: Oxford University Press, 1951).

76 i.e. Dr James Welch, the BBC's Director of Religious Broadcasting, who had commissioned Sister Penelope to write the plays.

77 See 'A Religious of CSMV', *They Shall Be My People*, vol. I, Act II.

78 i.e. Nannar, the Moon-god at Ur on the Euphrates.

79 'A Religious of CSMV', *They Shall Be My People*, vol. I, Act II, 16–19. After Lot's wife, Nuhúia, tells her daughter, Kadmíyah, that God promised the childless Abraham that his people would be 'fruitful and multiply', the conversation between them is as follows:

2. On p. 15 Melchizedech's longish speech[80] is not quite good enough. He's got to have the sense of mystery about him. That means, for purposes of these plays, he must sound like a king out of a fairy tale. Actually in this speech he sounds more like a Bampton Lecturer![81] *Represents, condemnation, include, mediator* all strike the wrong note. I am referring only to the style: the matter is perfectly right. It is easier, of course, to pick holes than to mend them!

If I were trying to do it myself I should make it a speech about the Kings of Salem, not about 'kingship' in general – like a special magic in that family. (The Kings of Salem are not ordinary kings. God has said that we are to etc). On the imaginative level I think the deepest truths enter the mind much better as arbitrary marvels than as universal theorems. Cinderella had to be back at midnight – Psyche must not see Cupid's face – Adam and Eve must not eat the fruit: how much better these statements are than any philosophical generalities about obedience.

The last scene is most moving. 'Am I the lamb'[82] is exactly right – and the *Agnus Dei* will mean more all his life to anyone who has heard this passage as a child. *Coo, what fun!* is perhaps wrong. It suggests a rather younger Isaac than we have had up till then: also, Melchisedech ought to be too wonderful and unearthly for that reaction. One other small point: somewhere (I can't find the place) a character says 'I know *whom* you mean.' *Whom* may be good grammar but it's not how people talk.

Kadmíyah: 'Be fruitful and multiply!' That means, Have lots of children. Mummy, why hasn't Uncle Abraham got any?

Nuhúia: (*evasively*). Oh well, he's got your father dear. He's like a son to him.

Kadmíyah: (*with conviction*). 'Tisn't the same.

80 ibid., Act III, i–iii.

81 In accordance with the will of the Rev. John Bampton (1689–1751), the Bampton Lectures, first given at Oxford in 1780, are given in alternate years in Hilary and Trinity Terms on one of the following subjects: 'to confirm and establish the Christian Faith, and to confute all heretics and schismatics – upon the authority of the writings of the primitive Fathers as to the Faith and Practice of the primitive Church – upon the Divinity of our Lord and Saviour Jesus Christ – upon the Divinity of the Holy Ghost – upon the Articles of the Christian Faith, as comprehended in the Apostles and Nicene Creeds.' The Bampton Lecturer must be a graduate of a university and an Anglican clergyman.

82 ibid., Act II, ii, 13.

I think you may be well pleased with the plays in general. Just a touch of the brush here and there – those last strokes which mean so much – and they'll be complete. Excuse my dreadful hand: I can no longer make letters the shape I intend.

Yours
Brother Ass

TO JAMES GORDON GILLMAN (W):

As from Magdalen
April 5th 1943

Dear Mr Gillman –

I am sorry you have been waiting so long, but you probably have no idea how few and precious are the hours I can give to private reading.

Many of the ideas in your poem interest me.[83] As a poem – well, when a man challenges Dante in subject and then underlines the fact by basing his style on Cary's *Dante*,[84] he's asking for trouble. I think you come out of the scrape pretty well: but it was great literary imprudence to get into it!

Yours sincerely
C. S. Lewis

TO KARL YOUNG (P):[85]

Magdalen College,
Oxford.
April 7th 1943

Dear Young –

Oh tempter! I suspect you of being the *fons et origo* of the whole

83 Gillman had, presumably, sent Lewis a copy of his poem, *The Divine Journey*. See the letter to Sister Penelope of 8 November 1939 about this same book.

84 Dante, *The Vision or Hell, Purgatory and Paradise of Dante Alighieri*, trans. Henry Francis Cary (1814).

85 Karl Young (1879–1943) took his BA from the University of Michigan, and his MA and PhD from Harvard. He was Professor of English at the United States Naval Academy, 1903–5, Professor of English at the University of Wisconsin, 1907–8, and Professor of English at Yale University, 1923–43. He was the author of *The Origin and Development of the Story of Troilus and Criseyde* (1904) and *The Drama of the Medieval Church* (1933).

thing.[86] But it's quite out of the question. I spend all my vacations in trains and all my terms sitting on committees (you see the staff here has become so very small) and I've hundreds of things on hand – I'm like a tea pot that is always pouring out cups and never getting any more tea put in. You'd only get 'dish-wash' if I did come.

Not that I wouldn't enjoy it to the Nth. I'd love to see you again in particular, and I want to meet Bush, and I want to see America, and oh! I want to see blue water and have the feel of being *away*. But it can't be. There are domestic difficulties, too, as I think I told you before: a very aged and daily more infirm mother.

I hope you got my reply to your last letter. We're all pretty full of 'bobaunce'[87] here, though this is balanced in my case by the fact that I am just undergoing my initiation into the mysteries of lumbago. Coghill (did you meet him) is doing a little book on Chaucer[88] and asks me what a *valet* really was. Do you know? Did Chaucer actually make beds – or were all duties already performed by deputy?

Excuse the paper (fit only for much baser purpose) it is all I can get at the moment. With all best wishes.

Yours ever
C. S. Lewis

TO ERIC FENN (BBC):[89]

[Magdalen College]
April 12th [1943]

Not my pigeon, I think. My own history was so mixed up with technical philosophy as to be useless to the general [public] and apart from that I cd. say nothing that would not repeat previous talks. Not that personal 'testifying' isn't most important, but it isn't my gift.

C.S.L.

---

86 The English Department at Yale had invited Lewis there to give some lectures.

87 'boasting', as in Chaucer's short poem, 'La Priere de Nostre Dame', 84: 'Lat not oure alder foo make his bobaunce': 'Let not the foe of all of us make his boast.'

88 Nevill Coghill, *The Poet Chaucer* (London: Oxford University Press, 1949).

89 Eric Fenn wrote to Lewis on 8 April 1943 asking if he would give one of the talks in a series on 'Why I believe in God': 'What we are after is a simple and personal statement from each person concerned of the main grounds on which they have come to believe in God – in other words, an attempt to get an abstract argument in more personal terms' (Phillips, *C. S. Lewis at the BBC*, p. 225).

Christian Behaviour: A Further Series of Broadcast Talks *was published by Geoffrey Bles: The Centenary Press on 19 April 1943.* Perelandra: A Novel *was published by John Lane, the Bodley Head of London on 20 April 1943.*

Lewis had instructed his publishers to send E. R. Eddison copies of Out of the Silent Planet *and* Perelandra, *but they sent a copy of* Perelandra *only. Having read it, Eddison wrote in the draft of a letter to Lewis of Easter Day [25 April] 1943:*

> *Having now read your good gift of this novella of* Perelandra . . . *I am lost in admiration for the solidity of specification of this young world you have discovered behind the thick cloud-envelope of Venus: the detail & sumptuosity of your invention: the way you manage & develop your themes. There is a freshness of morning imbuing your whole world of Perelandra: the morning of life. In particular, your animals please me, & their commerce with human kind: I was ready for this, remembering your handling of that matter in your essay on Pain where your views much took my fancy. And there is morning – what is more, there is divinity in your Queen: in your King too, though his portrait . . . is slighter than hers . . .*
>
> *Now, as for your Eldila. Here, may be, we stray onto slippery ground of personal preferences. 'Angels' in art . . . always strike me as unconvincing. Why, I wonder? True, you come near to pulling them out of their unreality when you make them appear . . . as Ares & Aphrodite. But the pull is momentary only, & the very comparisons it suggests chill me towards their 'appearances' . . . It is, I think, your acceptance of the 'sexless' convention . . . that makes these impressive figures, so far as I am concerned, not unhuman only but undivine. We are told (p. 238) that they are 'transcorporeal intelligences', which I take to mean pure intellects. Well & good. But, surely, they are then* eo nomine[90] *abstractions: whereas your King & Queen (being made, presumably, in the Divine image, in all particulars concrete & perfect) are, compared with these* dieux manqués, *as a falcon is to an aeroplane.*[91]

90 'by that word'.

91 Bodleian Library, MS. Eng. lett. c. 220/2, fols. 62–3.

TO E. R. EDDISON (BOD):

As from Magdalen College,
Oxford.
April 29th 1943

My dear Eddison –

I am just convalescent of a pretty high fever, followed by very low spirits, so your letter came as a welcome pick me up. It takes an author to flatter an author. Who else wd. praise the manage of my rat-trap?[92] It is in these places we spend work, but the common reader is quite unaware of it.

I hardly expected you to like my *daemones eldili*, and demur only to 'sexless convention'. For *convention* read 'tradition', backed up by a sound principle in philosophy, *natura nil agit frustra*,[93] and if these be creatures that do not die to what end shd. they breed? But I confess I prefer them so not on any ascetic ground but to make a rich universe full of *different* creatures: things as different from us as the minerals. To insist on our own sexual life in that translunary world seems to be a *provincialism*. No one asks us to be *eldila*: why shd. we ask them to be men and women? Whether what is transcorporeal is '*eo nomine* an abstraction' is a question for the metaphysics. I think not: your own Spinoza will agree with me. Of course we *prefer* the King and Queen: we are at home there. But neither they nor the eldila are perfect *simpliciter*: i.e. they are not perfect beings but only the one perfect *homo* the one perfect *daemon*. You have not to learn from me that there is only one '*substantia perfecta*'. But we shall never agree on this. I will only conclude with the shortest story I have yet written. '"I tell you I'm a straight line," said the line AB as the circle touched it at the point O. "And I won't be called names. *Tangent*, indeed!" And it lived unhappily ever after.'

---

92 He was referring to the Unman's argument in *Perelandra*, ch. 13, that life is meaningless. '"I get the idea," said Ransom, "that the account a man gives of the universe, or of any other building, depends very much on where he is standing." "But specially," said Weston, "on whether he's inside or out. All the things you like to dwell upon are outsides. A planet like our own, or like Perelandra, for instance. Or a beautiful human body. All the colours and pleasant shapes are merely where it ends, where it ceases to be. Inside, what do you get? Darkness, worms, heat, pressure, salt, suffocation, stink."'

93 'Nature does nothing in vain.' Browne, *Religio Medici*, First Part, section 2, no. xv: 'Natura nihil agit frustra, is the only indisputed Axiome in Philosophy.'

No – the fools were told to send you both books together, but have failed to do it. I have ordered the other to go to you now: but it means your reading back from the greater to the less – the first book ending on a merely satiric note. But Lanes *are* fools. Note that they blab out my whole theme in the blurb, wh. was meant to come over the reader by stealth. Idiots!

The arcturogamie or bears-bridal was for the third book of the trilogy, but I have just read through what is already written (about 300 sheets) and come to the uncomfortable conclusion that it is all rubbish. Has this ever happened to you? A nauseous moment – when the thought of trying to mend it, and of abandoning it, seem equally unbearable.

The bite in the heel is scriptural and wd. have led to something in the third book.[94] I agree UNCO-ORDINATED[95] is frightful. As to why he went up to the mountain – plague on you for an asker of awkward questions! How else should a [man] have reached the top?[96]

I hope you keep well. With many thanks.

Yours
C. S. Lewis

TO ERIC FENN (BBC):[97] TS

Magdalen College,
Oxford.
7th May 1943.

My dear Fenn,

Sorry again. But a talk to the general public on 'Paradise Lost'

---

94 In ch. 14 Ransom discovers that, during their fight, the Unman has bitten his heel. We learn in *That Hideous Strength* that the wound can only be cured when he returns to Perelandra. Lewis was referring to Genesis 3:14–15: 'And the Lord God said unto the serpent . . . I will put enmity between thee and the woman, and between thy seed and her seed; it shall bruise thy head, and thou shalt bruise his heel.'

95 In ch. 16 of the original edition of *Perelandra*, 'uncoordinated' was spelled 'unco-ordinated'.

96 In his letter of 25 April 1943, Eddison wrote: 'I don't think the reader . . . has had any hint of *why* R. has to climb the rose-red Himalayan mountain?' (Bodleian Library, MS. Eng. lett. c. 220/2, fol. 64)

97 Eric Fenn wrote to Lewis on 6 May explaining that the BBC was planning a series of talks on 'certain great Christian books' and asking if he would give one on Milton's *Paradise Lost*.

would be an absolute waste of time. What's the good of telling them they'll enjoy it, when we both know they won't?

yours sincerely,
C. S. Lewis

TO WALTER OGILVIE FIELD (W):[98]

[Magdalen]
May 10th 43

My dear Woff,

Thanks for your letter. You can dismiss all that stuff about being 'out of the picture'. The whole point about the Walk is that all the members are unlike and indispensable. Owen's dark, labyrinthine pertinacious arguments, my bow-wow dogmatism, Cecil's unmoved tranquility, your needle-like or grey-hound-like keenness, are four instruments in a quartette.

Anyway, you are under a simple illusion. You notice when Owen and I are talking metaphysics which you (and Cecil) don't follow: you don't notice the times when Owen and you are talking economics which I can't follow. Owen is the only one who is *never* out of his depth. The thing is an image of what the world ought to be: wedded *unlikes*. Roll on the day when it can function again.

Yours
C. S. Lewis

TO DOROTHY L. SAYERS (W):

Magdalen
May 17th [1943]

Dear Miss Sayers

Thanks awfully![99] I loved the one I heard on the air (I *never* listen

---

98 Walter Ogilvie 'Woff' Field (1893–1957) went up to Trinity College, Oxford, from Marlborough College in 1912. However, he left in 1914 to join the Warwickshire Rifle Regiment, and was promoted to captain in 1916. After seeing action in France and Italy, he was wounded and forced to retire. In 1926 he became a teacher at the Rudolf Steiner School in Forest Row, East Sussex. He was a particular friend of Owen Barfield and Cecil Harwood, and over the years he became a regular participant in the walking tours. See 'Walter Ogilvie Field' in *The Voice of Cecil Harwood*, pp. 283–9.

99 Sayers had sent Lewis an advance copy of her book, *The Man Born to be King: A Play-Cycle on the Life of our Lord and Saviour Jesus Christ* (1943). The plays were

in to anything in the ordinary course) and look forward to reading the whole series. I've had plenty of correspondents like the one you describe – and what I say every man may scratch his own fleas.

The Sluckdrib letter[100] is obviously intended for human consumption. Notice how artfully it labours to remove any uneasiness about Sloth and how it omits the real danger of all controversy with infidels, namely peril to ones own faith. Not of course from the infidel's arguments but from one's own. Never do I find a doctrine less credible than when I have just invented and delivered a telling argument in its defence! So beware.

Yes, the correspondence will last indefinitely – I know – and on days when you were really anxious for some other letter the beast's handwriting will turn up at breakfast – ugh![101] You weren't asked whether you liked souls, I take it. Well it's a 'bleeding shime'.

I'm starting a book on Miracles.[102] Meanwhile is the enclosed any help?[103] And there's some relevant matter in *The Mind of the Maker*.[104] Best wish: you're going to 'see life'.

Yours
C. S. Lewis

---

broadcast over the BBC at monthly intervals between December 1941 and October 1942.

100 The 'Sluckdrib letter', a portion of Sayers's letter to Lewis of 13 May 1943, is written in a style of self-mockery and apes the style of *The Screwtape Letters*. It is found in Dorothy L. Sayers, *Letters*, vol. II, *1937–1942, From Novelist to Playwright*, ed. Barbara Reynolds (1997), pp. 410–12.

101 Sayers had mentioned her correspondence with Mr L. T. Duff, who began writing angry letters to her in March 1943 and who was to continue writing for another year, in her letter to Lewis of 13 May (Sayers, *Letters*, vol. II, p. 413): 'The man keeps on bothering about Miracles; he thinks Hall Caine's *Life of Christ* is the last word in Biblical criticism, and objects violently to the doctrine of Sin, the idea of a Perfect Man without any sex-life, and the ecclesiastical tyranny of the B.B.C. He is in the Home Guard, can't spell, and has a mind like a junk-shop.'

102 Sayers, thinking of Duff's complaints, concluded her letter of 13 May 1943: 'There aren't any up-to-date books about Miracles. People have stopped arguing about them. Why? Has Physics sold the pass? Or is it merely that everybody is thinking in terms of Sociology and international Ethics?' (ibid.)

103 Lewis sent her a copy of his sermon on 'Miracles' published in *Saint Jude's Gazette*, no. 73 (October 1942). An expansion of the same sermon published in *The Guardian* (2 October 1942), it amounts to a miniature version of *Miracles: A Preliminary Study* (1947). It is likely that Sayers's observation about the lack of books on miracles was exactly the encouragement Lewis needed to write his own book on the subject.

104 Ch. 2 of Sayers's *The Mind of the Maker* is entitled 'Free Will and Miracle'.

TO OWEN BARFIELD (W):

[The Kilns
17? May 1943]

My dear Barfield –

As all reviews of *Perelandra* so far have been unfavourable or non-committal you will imagine with what pleasure I read your letter at breakfast.[105] Say what you like, there's nothing like a true friend.

I am thinking of sending you a judicious letter of general remarks on your qualities as a critic – – – The devil of it is, you're largely right. Why can I never say anything *once*? ('Two and two make four. These pairs, in union, generate a quarternity, and the duplication of duplicates leaves us one short of five.') Well, all's one. Plague of these pickled herrings.[106] I had decided before receiving your letter that the novel at present in progress[107] is bosh.

The same post brought a copy of the *Cambridge Review* wh. contained a letter pointing out a real howler in the Milton book.[108] True friends everywhere: genuine amity is ubiquitous and affectionate veracity less

---

105 *Perelandra* was reviewed by Ralph Gardner in *The Cambridge Review*, LXV (20 November 1943), p. 96.

106 Shakespeare, *Twelfth Night*, I, v, 127: 'a plague o' these pickle herring . . . Well, it's all one.'

107 i.e. *That Hideous Strength*.

108 Charles Earle Raven, Master of Christ's College, Cambridge, wrote to *The Cambridge Review*, LXIV (15 May 1943), p. 315: 'When he treats the doctrine of God Mr Lewis looks to St Augustine and follows Professor Saurat to the *Zohar* ['a thirteenth-century Jewish compilation' as Lewis explains in ch. 12 of *A Preface to Paradise Lost*; he goes on to elucidate its connection with Milton and the poem], instead of looking to Calvin and to the Greek Fathers whom the Cambridge Platonists were then reviving, to Joseph Mead and others at College with the poet. Had he done so he would, I think, have recognized that there is much more to be said than he suggests as to the difference between Milton and Augustine on the matter of "Unfallen Sexuality" (Ch. XVII) and, indeed, of sex in general, and that the point about "God retiring himself" (p. 86) need not (indeed in my opinion, certainly could not) be drawn from the *Zohar*. The problems of God's essential, dynamic and moral indwelling and of His mode of creation were freely discussed both by the Fathers and among Milton's contemporaries. Mr Lewis sneers at Milton's Philistine attitude towards Scholasticism (p. 87); but, in spite of Prof. Masson's monumental work, to which he nowhere refers, he seems to have taken little pains to discover the actual content of Christian theology as taught in Milton's time – and this on his own showing is vital to his theme.'

uncommon than we suppose. And take that grin off your ugly face: remove that – hey! Shut up. I'm getting I can't stop it.

Yrs
C.S.L.

TO DOROTHY L. SAYERS (W): TS

Magdalen College,
Oxford.
20th May 1943

Dear Miss Sayers,

Keep the magazine[109] if it simplifies the matter, for I have the MS. Yes – there was going to be a note on the word *because*. I strongly agree about providential cats: see George Macdonald's 'Lilith'.

Have started your book (in bed) but am still in the Preface – very vigorous!

yours sincerely,
C. S. Lewis

TO MR YOUNG (BOD): TS

Magdalen College,
Oxford.
20th May 1943

Dear Mr. Young,

I fully agree about the enormous value of the sort of works you want, but I cannot do it. The details of my own conversion were so technically philosophical on one side, and so intimate on the other that they just can't be used in the way you suggest.[110] Nor, I think, do any talents that I have run in that direction.

yours sincerely,
C. S. Lewis

---

109 *Saint Jude's Gazette* (October 1942).

110 We do not know what kind of book Mr Young asked Lewis to write. See the letter to Vera Mathews of 15 September 1948 in which Lewis mentions that he is writing his autobiography.

TO DOM BEDE GRIFFITHS OSB (W):

[Magdalen College]
May 26th 1943

My dear Dom Bede –

It was delightful to see your hand again. I thoroughly agreed with your article which is badly needed at the moment.[111] Quite a number of pious people are at present attempting what they call 'Christian criticism' and really committing the same *sort* of absurdities as 'Marxist criticism' did. And the error is hard to correct for the reason you mention.[112] If God is 'the Father of lights'[113] from whom comes 'every good and perfect gift,'[114] then *of course* in all good work of any kind one is bound to discover things agreeable to Christianity. It would be worth enlarging your article for publication in some place that reaches more readers.

About Shakespeare I wd. remind you of what you wrote to me several years ago. 'Now that I have become a Christian and read the plays simply as entertainment, I find perfect delight where I found only bewilderment as long as I was looking for a philosophy.' I think you've relapsed into taking art too seriously, and therefore failing to be entertained – or else are in that happy state in which relaxation is not needed, therefore not relished.

Perhaps you also took *Perelandra* too seriously. Although the theme has serious implications, it is primarily a 'yarn' and most of the scenery was meant only to be enjoyable – or to have a spiritual meaning only in the v. general sense of suggesting perfect sensuous happiness. Of course whether the sensuous detail is a *bore* is another matter. I hadn't thought of myself as a rival to Dante!!

---

111 He was referring to Griffiths' review of Edward Hutton's *Catholicism and English Literature* (1942), 'Catholicism and English Literature', *Pax: The Monthly Review of the Benedictines of Prinknash, Glos.*, XXXI, no. 226 (Spring 1943), pp. 40–6.

112 In his review Griffiths argued that the author erred in 'making Catholicism the criterion of value in literature': 'This is the mistake which a Catholic ought above all things to avoid. He must always try to estimate the value of literature as a natural form of human activity, having its own principles and its own perfection . . . It is true that grace perfects nature, but in nothing so much as poetry is it obvious that nature has its own laws of perfection and no amount of grace will make up in the quality of a poem for deficiencies in natural genius.'

113 James 1:17.

114 ibid.

By the way is Milton's idea of angels *heretical*?[115] – I mean is the Thomist account, for you, *de fide*.[116] Blessings on you. Pray for me.

Yours

C. S. Lewis

I liked the article on Friendship. Never heard of S. Ailred[117] before and am glad. The decay of *friendship* – owing to the endless presence of women everywhere – is a thing I'm rather afraid of.

TO DOROTHY L. SAYERS (W):

[The Kilns
30? May 1943]

Dear Miss Sayers –

I've finished *The Man Born to be King* and think it a complete success. (Christie the H.M. of Westminster told me that the actual performances over the air left his 2 small daughters with 'open and silent mouths' for several minutes).

I shed real tears (hot ones) in places: since Mauriac's *Vie de Jesus* nothing has moved me so much. I'm not absolutely sure whether Judas for me 'comes off' – i.e. whether I shd. have got him without your off-stage analysis. But this may be due to merely reading what was meant to be heard. He's quite a possible conception, no doubt: I'm only uncertain of the execution. But that is the only point I'm doubtful on. I expect to read it times without number again.

---

115 Griffiths, 'Catholicism and English Literature', p. 43: 'Mr Lewis in his recent *Preface to Paradise Lost* . . . has shown that *Paradise Lost* is profoundly orthodox in its theology with the exception of only one important matter in regard to the angels.'

116 *A Preface to Paradise Lost*, ch. 15: 'Thomas Aquinas had believed that angels were purely immaterial . . . Hence, for Aquinas, an angel could not eat; when he appeared to do so it was "not actual eating, but a symbol of spiritual eating" (ibid. Ia, Q. LII, Art. 3). And this is the view which Milton goes out of his way to controvert. When his Archangel dined with Adam he did not simply appear to eat, nor was his refection a mere symbol . . . The whole passage becomes intelligible, and much less poetically grotesque, when we realize that Milton put it there chiefly because he thought it *true*.'

117 St Aelred (1109–67) was born in the north of England and became master of the household of King David of Scotland. In 1133 he joined the Cistercian community of Rievaulx in Yorkshire, and later became abbot. His writings include a treatise *On Spiritual Friendship*.

I asked Ransom about the lady's hair.[118] He said 'Oh it was lovely'. 'Yes, but what colour?' – 'Colour? Oh, I dunno. Ordinary sort of colour, you know' – 'But not on top of the green, surely?' – 'I see. How the hell shd. one remember? I never do remember the colour of a girl's hair. Why do you want to know?' – 'Someone asked me' – 'Huh! A woman, I bet' – 'Well as a matter of fact it *was*.' There the matter ended. But he could remember the eyes: they were violet.

Yours sincerely
C. S. Lewis

TO MARGARET CARLYLE (BOD):

The Kilns,
Headington Quarry,
Oxford
May 30th 1943

Dear Miss Carlyle

Mr. McFarlane told me the news about dear Dr. Carlyle a few hours before I saw it in the paper. In spite of his great age – what difference, after all, does age make when it comes to the point? – I was somehow quite unprepared for it. It makes the worst gap yet. I never knew an Oxford without him.

In all those years I have no single memory of him that is not good and happy all through. The memories begin with his paper to the 'Martlets' which was the first 'paper' I'd ever heard in my life and really taught one what Oxford was. And he talked to me then just as if I were his own age (you know, some people have got nicer to one as one went on: he didn't: he *began* nice. One never can quite forget the difference even if one tries). I think that on my own death bed I shall still remember the exact look and tone with which he said 'donkeys'.

I wish I had been able to see more of him these last years: but you know something of my difficulties at home. I write this late at night after a difficult day – Mrs Moore is in great and continuous pain with one of her horrible varicose ulcers.

I'm afraid I've talked of my own feelings instead of sympathising with yours. So much of your father seemed to come uppermost in my

118 Sayers had, presumably, been disappointed that Lewis did not tell his readers the colour of the Lady's hair in *Perelandra*.

mind as soon as I began to write – and all so live and (so to speak) 'bright'-coloured. But I am very sorry for you and your sister – though I don't know that it does much good to say so. I hope there was not much pain. Just *watching* pain is dreadful. And I hope you are not both too pulled down – and that you're not leaving Oxford.

Yours sincerely
C. S. Lewis

TO ARTHUR GREEVES (W):

[Magdalen College]
June 1st 43

My dear Arthur,

The time stretches out longer and longer and I become more hungry for a chat and a walk with you. You may be unrecognisable now! Whenever one meets a friend after long absence these days the first thing one notices is how *thin* he's got.

Things with me are pretty much as usual. Minto still has her nasty varicose ulcer and suffers a great deal with it. Warnie is still with us and is a great help to me as a secretary – he types all my non-personal letters now. Maureen as you know is married.

We are keeping rabbits at the Kilns now, in addition to the hens! But they are very much nicer. As I passed the enclosure in which all the young ones are the other evening, I saw they had all got into a box wh. happened to be lying there. They were all standing (or sitting) up on their hind legs and all facing in the same direction: so that they looked exactly as if they were conducting some kind of evening service – the box looked just like a pew.

It is nice in college at present: as I think I said before, much nicer than in peacetime, for the stormy spirits are away. (Talking of 'stormy', do you know the novels of a woman called Storm Jameson?[119] I had to write to her about a quite different matter the other day and would *like* to have said something nice about her books, but have never read any. Wd. I like them?)

I seem to get v. little reading done these days. One thing I *have* read

---

119 Storm Jameson (1891–1986) wrote numerous novels, including *The Pot Boils* (1919), her first, and a trilogy about a family of Yorkshire shipbuilders, *The Lovely Ship* (1927).

recently is D. Sayers' *The Man Born to be King* wh. I thought excellent, indeed most moving. The objections to it seem to me as silly as the similar ones to *Green Pastures*,[120] wh. I think you and I agreed about.

(By the bye I *did* write and answer your query about L. P. Jacks[121] didn't I – in the long run? Anyway, I'm not going to do so here. Let it be relegated to the world of 'Have you read your Swinburne?' and the controversy about souterains.)[122]

Bryson tells me you have become quite a man of business. Wouldn't it be awful if when I met [you] again you'd become a really practical man in a blue suit and a bowler hat talking rather as my Uncle Gussie did in his prime! There are of course equally awful changes that may occur in me. Perhaps you'll find that I've become a golfer, or a bridge player, or a politician. I sometimes like to think in optimistic moments that you may find me better tempered – heaven knows you well might!

Hatton (do you remember Hatton, my nice quiet college servant?) has been put in a factory and I now have a most awful man who never stops talking.[123] He's told to call me at 7.15 and nearly always wakes me by saying triumphantly 'It's only just five past seven' and giving me a report on the weather which lasts about 10 minutes. Warnie came in dripping wet the other day and said 'It's a bit of luck I met Martin on the stairs' – 'Why?' – 'Because if he hadn't told me I might not have known it was raining.' A good character to put in a book.

---

120 Marc Connelly, *The Green Pastures: a fable suggested by Roark Bradford's southern sketches 'Ol' Man Adam an' his chillun'* (1930). While *The Man Born to be King* was perfectly orthodox, there was, as J. W. Welch says in his foreword to the book, a frantic outburst against the plays by the Lord's Day Observance Society and others who vilified them as 'irreverent', 'blasphemous' and 'vulgar' because an actor was allowed to impersonate Our Lord. One suspects that the chief objection to the plays lay in Sayers's talent for making real things real. Similarly, many objected to *Green Pastures* because it was written in Negro dialect.

121 Lawrence Pearsall Jacks (1860–1955) became Professor of Philosophy at Manchester College (the only Unitarian college in Oxford) in 1903 and served as Principal of the College, 1915–31. At this time Arthur was moving towards Unitarianism, and he seems to have been interested in Jacks because he not only wrote *The Life and Letters of Stopford Brooke* (1917) but was Brooke's son-in-law.

122 On 'souteraines' see the letter to Arthur Greeves of 4 November 1914 (*CL* I, p. 89).

123 William Kembrey Hatton (1900–43), who joined the staff of Magdalen College in 1923, had been Lewis's college servant or 'scout' until September 1941 when he was forced by the war to work in a local factory. He died 25 November 1943. P. W. Martin was employed as Hatton's replacement in October 1941 and remained with the college until May 1944.

Give my love to your Mother and very specially to the McNeills. My handwriting has gone to pot – partly rheumatism.

Yours

Jack

Eric Fenn wrote to Lewis on 11 June 1943:

> *Have you thought any further about the series of more theological talks you were inclined to when I last saw you? We have been considering lately a suggestion made at an informal conference on religious broadcasting . . . namely, the need for a series of talks which would take some of the more abstruse theological doctrines and show what sort of difference they make, both to thought and to conduct.*[124]

TO ERIC FENN (BBC):

Magdalen College,
Oxford
June 16th 43

My dear Fenn –

Sorry: I seem to have lost yr. letter with the Bedford address. Yes, I shd. like to give the sort of series you suggest. Something of this sort,

1. The doctrine of the Trinity
2. The doctrine of the Trinity[125]
3. Creation
4. The Incarnation
5. The Two Natures
6. The Resurrection
7. The Ascension.

Not by these titles. (Perh. 1 & 2 Has God a structure? 3. Creation. 4 & 5 The Human element in God. 6. The defeat of death. 7. The promotion of Man.) Wd. these at all suit?

Yrs

C. S. Lewis

124 Phillips, *C. S. Lewis at the BBC*, p. 228.

125 Lewis expected to devote two talks to the doctrine of the Trinity, but in the end dealt with the subject only in his second talk.

On 23 April Dr James Welch, Director of Religious Broadcasting at the BBC, invited Lewis to take part in a kind of Brains Trust called The Anvil. *As he explained:*

> *The procedure is that we send the questions to you beforehand so that you can prepare the answers in your mind and look up any facts if you want to: though you can put one or two things down on paper, we like the discussion at the microphone to be as spontaneous and unscripted as possible. It would involve three hours from 6.30–9.30 p.m. on Monday . . . Do, please, come over and help us.*[126]

Lewis was laid up with flu at the time, but Warnie wrote on his behalf to say his brother would be pleased to help. It was decided to record The Anvil *on 19 July.*

Meanwhile, Eric Fenn wrote to Lewis on 18 June asking if he might meet Lewis in Oxford to discuss the next series of broadcasts. While there was a shortage of paper everywhere the BBC was astonished at the effect of this on Lewis. Most of his letters were written on thin strips of paper. 'If I may say so,' wrote Fenn in his letter of 18 June, 'your passion for paper economy exceeds anything my imagination can grasp!'[127]

Lewis replied on 1 July – not on a thin sliver of paper, but an entire sheet, leaving four inches by six of blank paper.

TO ERIC FENN (BBC):

The Kilns,
Headington Quarry,
Oxford
July 1st 1943

My dear Fenn –

Alright. I'll come to the Anvil on Mon. July 19th,[128] reporting at

---

126 ibid., p. 226.

127 ibid., p. 229.

128 *The Anvil* was broadcast on 22 July 1943. It was conducted by Dr Welch, who discussed various religious questions with Canon F. A. Cockin of St Paul's Cathedral, Fr Andrew Beck, a Catholic priest, Dorothy Wilson, Minister-in-Charge of the Muswell Hill Congregational Church, and Lewis. An abbreviated transcript of the programme, containing Lewis's full answers, is found in *Mere Christianity: An Anniversary Edition*, ed. Walter Hooper (New York,

BBC House at 6 p.m. Are all questions to be attempted by all candidates? I'm in the thick of examining at the moment, but if you'll name a day to come and lunch with me in College it cd. be managed. Or shd. I turn up early on the 19th and we cd. talk about our other affair then? We shd. perhaps be more at our ease down here, but whichever you like. And what about paper economy now? I trust I can do a handsome thing when put on my metal.

Yours ever.
C. S. Lewis

P.S. You may use the margin of this letter for any purpose you like.

TO MARGARET CARLYLE (BOD):

Magdalen
July 7th 1943

Dear Miss Carlyle

What a lovely surprise packet! I shall treasure it greatly both for its intrinsic charms (it is a *very* attractive little book) and for your father's sake and all your sakes. I am really sorry to have imposed on you the task of answering one more letter of condolence, for I remember in like case what a terrible burden it can be – part of that general un-ending 'kerfuffle' which renders all events, happy and unhappy alike, such a nuisance.

I am very glad to hear you are coming back to Oxford and hope that in quieter times we shall all go on meeting till we are grown into elderly Oxford oddities (the Deneckes and Beneckes and Walkers and Miss Rogers of the 1970's) and tell one another in cracked voices thro' ear trumpets that there are no *characters* in Oxford now.

I have both Aquinas's *Summa's* so it would be πλεονεξία[129] to accept either. With very best wishes to you both.

Yours very sincerely
C. S. Lewis

Macmillan, 1981) and reproduced in the paperback edition of Phillips, *C. S. Lewis at the BBC* (London: HarperCollins, 2003).

129 'too much of a good thing'.

TO I. O. EVANS (W):[130]

Magdalen College,
Oxford.
July 7th 43

Dear Mr. Evans

How extraordinarily kind of you! May I tell you my real feeling? – that since you are a brother 'scientifictionist' or 'scientifictor' (or whatever the word may be) I'd much rather have a copy of one of your own stories if you have one to spare. If not, don't bother. The Sinclair[131] sounds too like the sort of books I often have to read as an examiner of Doctorate theses and wd. therefore be rather a busman's holiday! But in any case, many thanks.

Yours sincerely,
C. S. Lewis

TO JOYCE PEARCE (P):[132]

As from Magdalen
July 20th 1943

Dear Miss Pearce

Go to the top of the class! You seem to have evolved the answer of the best theologians on your own: and I agree with it. You will find what I have to say about it in my little book *The Problem of Pain*. It is to me inconceivable that Nature as we see it is *either* what God intended *or* merely evil: it looks like a good thing spoiled.

---

130 Idrisyn Oliver Evans (1894–1977), author of science fiction, ancient history and popular science, was writing from his home at 53 Waterer Gardens, Burgh Heath, Tadworth, Surrey. His numerous works include *The World of To-morrow: A Junior Book of Forecasts* (1933); *Gadget City* (1944); *The Observer's Book of British Geology* (1949); *Strange Devices: A Story of the Siege of Syracuse* (1950); *Olympic Runner: A Story of the Great Days of Ancient Greece* (1956); *Discovering the Heavens: A Junior History of Astronomy* (1958); *Inventors of the World* (1962); *Peace and the Space Race, and Other Verses* (1976).

131 This work remains to be identified.

132 Joyce Pearce MBE (1915–85) was born in Woking, Surrey and educated at Woking Grammar School for Girls and Lady Margaret Hall, Oxford. On receiving her BA she took a Diploma in Education and from 1939–48 taught at Chichester High School, Horwell Grammar School, Launceston, and Mitcham Grammar School. She returned to Woking and in 1955 founded the Ockenden Venture, now Ockenden International. See Pamela Watkin, *Joyce's Ockenden: The Story of a Vision that Became a Venture for Refugees* (1993).

The doctrine of the Fall (both of man and of some 'gods' 'eldils' or 'angels') is the only satisfactory explanation. Evil begins, in a universe where all was good, from free will, which was permitted because it makes possible the greatest good of all. The corruption of the first sinner consists not in choosing some evil thing (there are no evil things for him to choose) but in preferring a lesser good (himself) before a greater (God). The Fall is, in fact, Pride. The possibility of this wrong preference is inherent in the v. fact of having, or being, a self at all. But though freedom is real it is not infinite. Every choice reduces a little ones freedom to choose the next time. There therefore comes a time when the creature is fully *built*, irrevocably attached either to God or to itself. This irrevocableness is what we call Heaven or Hell. Every conscious agent is finally committed in the long run: i.e. it rises above freedom into willed, but henceforth unalterable, union with God, or else sinks below freedom into the black fire of self-imprisonment. That is why the universe (as even the physicists now admit) has a real history, a fifth act with a finale in which the good characters 'live happily ever after' and the bad ones are cast out. At least that is how I see it.

Yours sincerely
C. S. Lewis

TO J. B. PHILLIPS (BOD):[133]

Magdalen College,
Oxford.
Aug 3rd 1943.

Dear Mr. Phillips –

Thank you a hundred times.[134] I thought I knew *Colossians* pretty

---

133 The Rev. Canon John Bertram Phillips (1906–82), writer, translator and broadcaster, read Classics and Theology at Emmanuel College and Ridley Hall, Cambridge, taking his BA in 1927. Following his ordination in 1930, he was Curate of St John's, Penge, London, 1930–3, freelance journalist and editorial secretary of Pathfinder Press, 1934–6, Curate of St Margaret's, Lee, London, 1936–40, Vicar of Good Shepherd, Lee, London, 1940–4, Vicar of St John's, Redhill, Surrey, 1945–55, Wiccamical Prebendary of Chichester Cathedral, 1957–60, and Canon of Salisbury Cathedral, 1964–9. His many translations and other writings include *Letters to Young Churches: A Translation of the New Testament Epistles, with an introduction by C. S. Lewis* (1947). He wrote an autobiography, *The Price of Success* (1984).

134 In *The Price of Success*, Phillips wrote: 'I sent a copy of my new translation of Colossians to C. S. Lewis, whose work I had been admiring for the last few years. His reply was short and encouraging' (p. 100).

well but your paraphrase made it far more significant – it was like seeing a familiar picture after it's been cleaned.

The third paragraph on p. 4 and the first on p. 5 helped me particularly. The only thing I thought unfortunate is 'Life from nothing began with Him' at the bottom of p. 3. This might mean that Christ was created *ex nihilo*, instead of begotten.[135]

I hope very much you will carry out your plan of doing all the epistles. Of course you'll be opposed tooth and nail by all the 'cultured' asses who say you're only spoiling 'the beauty' of the A.V. – all the people who objected to *Green Pastures* and *The Man Born to be King* and who are always waffling about reverence. But we must kill that!

I hope you'll add a little plain preface – all popular theology, no gas about St Paul's 'personality' or the wild flowers of Palestine – and a really full analytical index. The index by itself will blow to bits all the modern exaggerations of the difference between Pauline & Johannine theology. Heartiest good wishes.

Yours sincerely
C. S. Lewis

P.S. Thanks for all your kind references to my own work.

TO SISTER PENELOPE CSMV (BOD):

Magdalen College,
Oxford.
Aug 10th. 1943

Dear Sister Penelope

I have altered the sentence about 'first intended for students' in the way you suggest. 'Better scholar' will have to stand. The person who translates a book is certainly in some respect a better scholar than the one who hadn't even heard of it till he saw that translation!

I *should* like a few days at Wantage, but things are so bad at home that I'm cancelling several of my R.A.F. engagements. Pray for me, Sister, and for poor Jane (*very* bad with her varicose ulcer) and for

135 In his *Letters to Young Churches*, p. 121, Phillips altered Colossians 1:15 to read: 'He existed before creation began, for it was through Him that everything was made, whether spiritual or material, seen or unseen.'

'Muriel' (a kind of lady gardener & 'help'[136] who is putting off an operation she ought to have, out of funk, and getting hysterical and going into rages, and losing her faith) and for poor dear Margaret (certified 'mental deficient' maid, at times the humblest, most affectionate, quaintest little person you can imagine, but subject to fits of inexplicable anger and misery). There is never any time when *all* these three women are in a good temper. When A is in B is out: and when C has just got over her resentment at B's last rage and is ready to forgive, B is just ripe for the next, and so on!

But out of evil comes good. From praying anxiously for a little of God's peace to communicate to *them*, I have been given more of it myself than I think I ever had before. Which is interesting. You don't get it when you ask for yourself: want it for the sake of the others, you do.

In all His works so sensible,
So deft in all His ways![137]

With my duty to all of you,
Yours sincerely
C. S. Lewis

TO SISTER PENELOPE CSMV (BOD):

Magdalen College,
Oxford.
Aug 16th 1943

Dear Sister Penelope

Thanks for your most kind letter. I am sure you will do me good, tho' in what shape only Maleldil[138] knows. (Would it be irreverent to write some *modern* psalms 'The Lord is always competent: his discretion is the joy of the whole world'?)

Yes, I think I can manage the plays.[139] You will remember my old

136 Muriel Morris was taken on as gardener because their regular gardener, Fred Paxford, had been seconded by the motor car factory in Cowley to assist with war work.

137 Lewis's play on some lines in Cardinal John Henry Newman's hymn 'Praise to the Holiest in the height': 'In all his words most wonderful,/Most sure in all his ways.'

138 The name of The Lord in Lewis's interplanetary novels.

139 i.e. the plays that were later rewritten and published as *They Shall Be My People*.

rule – I receive no *unique* MSS, it *must* be only a copy. And you'd better put the Archdeacon's name and address on it somewhere. There's no knowing just *how* asinine the Ass may be.

Yours sincerely
C. S. Lewis

TO E. R. EDDISON (BOD):

[In Coll. Stae. Mar. Magd.
Oxon
Sept. iv. 1943]

Your lettres, right Worshipfull, being delivered into my hands when I was about to set forth on a vyage and travail are the cause of my ill manners in not making knowne to you my gratefull acceptance of the same.

Which now that I doe, sins I haue fallen into mentioun of my journey I coulde not be excused if I forbore to tell you that I haue been lodged in Quicksands Priorie in the covntrie of Bedforshire where, as is well known to your hono˜ the Osbornes had their principall seate and Dorothy O. wrote her incomparable letters to Sir W. Temple.[140]

In the which hovse when I had awhile considered the noble vaultings, brave staircases, pleasant parlours curiously garnished, and all that statelie landscape of wood and water, I was in a maner transported in a rapture so that I soddenlie brake forth in such words as I conceyue wd. verie well content you, saying, 'What a thing was Aristocracie!'

Now Sir as touching my Marcian storie I well allow yo˜ hono˜'s exception to my *Seroni* and *Pfifltriggi* whose form would be no less irksome, teedyous, loathsome, and vnsavoury to me than to yourself, and no whit to be suffered in a feigned history but that the whole matter of the same standeth vpon the debate or rencountre between kindlie simpathies and antipathies (of th'oone parte) and iudgment of reason (on toother).[141]

---

140 *Letters from Dorothy Osborne to Sir William Temple: 1652–4*, ed. E. A. Parry (1888). The Osbournes lived at Chicksands Priory.

141 In the draft of his letter of 10 August 1943 Eddison gave his impressions of *Out of the Silent Planet*. After the beauty of Tor and Tinidril in *Perelandra*, he was greatly disappointed with the creatures who inhabit Malacandra: 'The Sorns & Pfifltriggi I shd. not myself be eager to consort with, or long look upon: to reap the full advantage of intellectual discourse with them, I shd. wish to conduct it in the dark or blindfold. In this you will recognize again my unfortunate

Marry what little charge you make of the latter where these two jump not presentlie together I am not now to learn. Yet it is worthie of notice how impotent fantasy is (yes in great poets) to invent a form that shall delight save it be patch up of shreds and parcels drawn out of nature.

Sir, to profit in my knowledge of the High Dutch I stvdie dailie now in Mr Grimm, his tales, wherein is much of wit and worth, and also in Dante his Purgatorie which I esteeme everie waie incomparable. With which account of my present estate I must een take leauve, greeting you heartily and resting euer your poor bedesman

C. S. Lewis

TO JILL FLEWETT (T):[142]

The Kilns
Sept 13th 1943

Dear June

Thanks very much for the copy of your father's book.[143] I should be glad to have it if only for the first extract of which I have so often seen the last line quoted but never met it in its place before. I was also interested in the parts of the introduction that deal with metre, because I have to make so many similar explanations in teaching my pupils how to scan Anglo-Saxon verse.

Your father may be interested to know that it involves *both* quantity *and* stress, so that I have to try to get them to understand 'length'. I was pleased with his example *hat-trick* at the bottom of p. xviii. (My favourite is *palely*, which they all know from Keat's 'alone and palely loitering',[144] and which can be compared with the proper name *Paley*. The nicest example of all would be *fish-shop* as against *Bishop* – but then the dunces would say *fish-shop* involved four consonants!)

We all try to hope you'll pass your audition, but we don't always

---

anthropomorphic ideas: a minotaur, a centaur, a titan, a siren, even sphinx, gorgon, or harpy, can be admirable to the eye, for in them humanity's shape is not distort or confounded but merely linked with unhuman attributes' (Bodleian Library, MS. Eng. lett. c. 220/2, fol. 69).

142 See **Jill, Lady Freud** in the Biographical Appendix. Although Lady Freud was given the name 'June' at her baptism, she changed it to 'Jill' when she became an actress.

143 H. W. Flewett and W. E. P. Pantin, *A First Book of Latin Poetry* (1943).

144 John Keats, 'La Belle Dame sans Merci' (1820), 2.

succeed. Bruce behaved with great lack of fortitude during the thunderstorm last night and two of the rabbits made it an excuse for absenting themselves without leave. Pushkin behaved better, but not well. In fact there is a general lack of keenness and discipline among the four-footed members of the household which I deplore. I hope you are all well.

Yours
Jack Lewis

TO SISTER PENELOPE CSMV (BOD):

Magdalen.
Sept. 24th. 1943

Dear Sister Penelope –

I have just finished your cycle.[145] And I would like to say first of all that simply as a thing for me to read it is an eye-opener. I feel I am reaping the fruits of an immense mass of O.T. scholarship without any trouble – getting both the story and *how* the story was written (that part is most interesting) – cutting the ground from under the feet of sceptical higher critics.

All sorts of things come out in a clearer light: and the Annunciation, thus prepared, is more moving than ever.[146] I say 'as a thing for me to read': on the technical question – how it will go over the air and whether the multiplicity of characters and change of scene can be made easy to follow – you will get criticism from those who know better than I.

As literary critic I have one or two adverse criticisms to make. In some of the scenes the *dramatic* form becomes a mere veneer because the matter is essentially descriptive not dramatic. I feel this specially in No. IX. But considering the problem you had to solve this doesn't happen very often.

In *style* I think you often fail of simplicity and concreteness. Sometimes this abstractness is dramatically justified. Ezra as you have painted him (and you make him pretty nasty!) *would* really talk about the 'agricultural aspect' of the ritual.[147] But will children understand it? In other places, however, I think this kind of language creeps in where

145 i.e. *They Shall Be My People.*
146 ibid., vol. I, Play 18, 'The Darkest Hour', II, ii, 2, lines 6–20.
147 ibid., Play 17, 'A People that Dwells Apart', II, iii, lines 19–21.

there is no such dramatic justification. 'The parallel is as close as possible' That's dreadfully lecture-like! Or 'ground under their heel' (for the Assyrian conquest) – it's like a leading article![148]

Surely we ourselves didn't talk like that in 1940. One had got beyond vague metaphors: we were thinking of firing parties and bayonets and concentration camps. In quite a different way 'it hurts God more than it hurts me' won't do because it inevitably reminds one of the traditional schoolmaster and raises a smile.

Finally, unless you are going to write in archaic English throughout, I don't think any character shd. say 'Alas'. It is not living language at all.

You needn't be bothered by this formidable list even if you agree with it. They are surface stains which you cd. quite easily alter by going through it with a fresh mind: like an artist who knows the composition and colouring is alright but the picture needs a little soap and water. It must have been a thundering job and I quite understand your feeling a little flat. Have a good rest. It was very well worth doing.

I've been guilty of Accidia lately! When work is very often interrupted one begins to use it as an excuse for not working even when one could. Things are a bit better and happier in the house now. The lady gardener *is* going to have the operation – in December: and things have been easier between her and Jane. I thank you all for your prayers.

I've written about 6 chapters of the book on Miracles. Did I tell you that this attempt to write on the Supernatural has turned many chapters into sort of hymns on Nature! One never knows what one's in for when one starts thinking. I hope to send your plays on to the Archdeacon to-morrow,

Yours sincerely
Brother Ass

148 ibid., Play 12, 'A Remnant Shall Return', IV, ii.

TO SISTER PENELOPE CSMV (BOD):

Magdalen
Oct. 5th 1943

Dear Sister Penelope

I think the play in which I felt the material to be least dramatic was the Nehemiah one:[149] but your own mind when reading through the script afresh, after you have particularly forgotten it, will find where the criticism applies.

About a publisher, I admit, one who has (like me) had many MSS both rejected and accepted *ought* to be able to advise, but somehow I don't know. My own plan always was to send *first* to the house I fancied best, and then, if they returned it, to try the house I fancied next best – and so on. Rather a simple-minded procedure.

We have just got through a domestic crisis. Poor dear 'Muriel' after putting off her operation indefinitely went completely off the deep end – doctor brought in a psychoanalyst – they wanted us to sign a document putting her into a mental hospital – Jane turned up absolute trumps and refused point blank – a little quiet talk and *truth* (wh. the patient seems never to get from doctors) did what all the experts could not do – and Muriel has departed in her right mind not (thank God) to a mental but to an ordinary hospital.

It was a bad time but I almost venture to say I felt Christ in the house as I have never done before – but alas, such a house for Him to visit!

MS on miracles is still a long way from completion. Thanks for *si vous m'upsettez!*[150]

Yours sincerely
C. S. Lewis

---

149 ibid., Play 17, 'A People that Dwells Apart', I, iv–v.

150 Sister Penelope said in a note about this, 'The story he thanks me for at the end of this letter was this: Winston Churchill was reported to have said to some French notable – not, I think, de Gaulle, "Si vous m'upsettez any more, je vous obliterai!"'

TO MR J. P. PETHAVEL (W):[151]

Magdalen College
Oxford
Oct 13th [1943]

Greetings! I didn't mean that the connection of the Numinous and the Good was *in the long run* doubtful.[152] I meant that it was not obvious in the sense that as they first meet you the experience 'This is an uncanny place' and the experience 'I oughtn't to tell lies', have no *felt* connection.

C. S. Lewis

In a letter dated 'Dec. 1943' the prolific science fiction writer, Arthur C. Clarke, wrote to Lewis as follows:

> *I wish to disagree, somewhat violently, with you over a passage on p. 92 of 'Perelandra' beginning 'He was a man obsessed with the idea . . .' and ending '. . . is to these minds a welcome corollary.' The whole passage seems to be an outburst of unreasoning and emotional panic rather surprising after the acute penetration of 'The Screwtape Letters' which, incidentally, appealed considerably to me notwithstanding the fact that I have never felt much sympathy towards the Christian tradition.*[153]

TO ARTHUR C. CLARKE (BOD):[154]

[The Kilns]
Dec. 7 [1943]

Dear Mr. Clarke –

I quite agree that most scientifiction is on the level of cowboy boys' stories. But I think the fundamental moral assumptions in popular fiction are a v. important symptom. If you found that the most popular stories were those in wh. the cowboy always betrayed his pals to the

---

151 Mr J. P. Pethavel was writing from 38 Corkram Road, Surbiton, Surrey.

152 Mr Pethavel had probably been puzzled by the paragraph in chapter 1 of *The Problem of Pain* which begins, 'The moral experience and the numinous experience are so far from being the same that they may exist for quite long periods without establishing a mutual contact.'

153 Bodleian Library, MS. Eng. lett. c. 220/4, fol. 8.

154 See **Sir Arthur Charles Clarke** in the Biographical Appendix.

crooks and deserted his girl for the vamp, I don't think it *wd.* be unimportant.

I don't of course think that at the moment many scientists are budding Westons: but I do think (hang it all, I *live* among scientists!) that a point of view not unlike Weston's is on the way. Look at Stapledon (*Star Gazer* ends in sheer devil worship),[155] Haldane's *Possible Worlds* and Waddington's *Science and Ethics.*[156] I agree Technology is *per se* neutral: but a race devoted to the increase of its own power by technology with complete indifference to ethics *does* seem to me a cancer in the universe. Certainly if he goes on his present course much further man can *not* be trusted with knowledge

yrs
C. S. Lewis

TO ARTHUR GREEVES (W):

[The Kilns]
Dec 20th 43

My dear Arthur –

I've found it at last! It was in the Union Library, a large green book called *Giant-Land* which on being opened revealed the sub-title *Or the Adventures of Tim Pippin*: by Roland Quiz.[157] This goes back to an earlier stage than the stories I (and probably you) knew as a boy. Our Tim Pippin was in fact the son of the one whose life is here narrated, and this explains certain mysterious allusions to the Granite City and the Subterranean City which used to fascinate me in the ones we knew.[158] It is also rather better. What is very much better is the pictures. These, in our little green books, were the grossest crudities as you no doubt remember, bad pen and ink. In *Giant-Land* you have engravings, some really in the best tradition of that Nineteenth Century school of fairy-tale illustration. Forrest Reid might not disdain some of them. They are better than the text which is pretty poor stuff written

155 i.e. Olaf Stapledon, *Star Maker* (1937).

156 Conrad Hal Waddington, *Science and Ethics* (1942).

157 Roland Quiz (= Richard M. H. Quittenton, 1833–1914), *Giant-Land: Or the Adventures of Tim Pippin*, new edition (1936).

158 Lewis was remembering Roland Quiz's earlier book, *Juvenile Rhymes and Little Stories* (London: 1865).

in a kind of gim-crack glossy style – though there are one or two (not many) traces of true imagination in the episodes.

The one really good idea is that nearly all the giants are *asleep* in an enchanted wood at the beginning. Tim, tho' warned 'Do not wake the giants', foolishly does so. That has the right thrill, hasn't it? But Quiz doesn't seem to know how good it is and wastes it. Some of the semi-comic giants have good names – 'Uncle Two-Heads' and 'Giant Safe-sides'. But on the whole it's poor stuff – though I naturally enjoyed reading it. I find a giant still has a queer fascination for me. Each of those fairy tale dangers has a different flavour, hasn't it? I mean a dragon is quite a different feeling from a giant, and a witch from either. I read *Giant-Land* while invigilating at an exam, and was interested to find that my fellow invigilator had a small son who was interested in almost *nothing* but giants.

My only other adventure of the same sort lately has been reading a lot of Grimm's tales in German. There seem to be about five times as many in the original as there were in any of the translations: many of them v. sinister or harrowingly pathetic. What a lot of *real* peasant suffering and crime must lie behind the repeated stories of cruel step-mothers and of parents who, being unable to feed their children any longer, try to get rid of them and *leave* them in a lonely part of the forest. In the end, after about fifty stories, I find the *predominant* effect is one of depression.

Things are pretty bad here. Minto's varicose ulcer gets worse and worse, domestic help harder and harder to come by. Sometimes I am very unhappy, but less so than I have often been in what were (by external standards) better times.

The great thing, if one can, is to stop regarding all the unpleasant things as interruptions of one's 'own', or 'real' life. The truth is of course that what one calls the interruptions are precisely one's real life – the life God is sending one day by day: what one calls one's 'real life' is a phantom of one's own imagination. This at least is what I see at moments of insight: but it's hard to remember it all the time – I know your problems must be much the same as mine (with the important difference that mine are of my own making, a very appropriate punishment and, like all God's punishments, a chance for expiation.)

Isn't it hard to *go on* being patient, to go on supplying sympathy?

One's stock of love turns out, when the testing time comes, to be so very inadequate: I suppose it is well that one should be forced to discover the fact!

I find too (do you?) that hard days drive one back on Nature. I don't mean walks (there is nowhere to walk to here, the whole neighbourhood is ruined)[159] but little sights and sounds seen at windows in odd moments.

I had a most vivid, tranquil dream about you the other night, just chatting in the old way. Let's hope it will happen sometime. For the rest, I've no news.

I've finished another story which I think of dedicating to Tchanie.[160] Do you think it matters that the heroine's name is also Jane? (In one way it'd be rather fun because she would say *Chain* every time she mentioned the book.)

I also (for a special reason) had to re-read *Guy Mannering* the other day, which I enjoyed enormously. It is one of the few Scotts (*Rob Roy* & *Midlothian* are the other two) in which there's a heroine with some life in her.

I've had a lot of examining work and been pretty busy. I have a cold of course but none of us has flu' so far, thank God. Warnie is flourishing. My old 'scout' Hatton whom you may remember has died.

We've had hard frosts – very beautiful on moonlit nights in Oxford now that there are no lighted windows or street lamps to spoil it. The black out is certainly one of the *pleasanter* results of the war as far as I'm concerned.

Give my love to your mother. Write when you can. All best wishes.

Yours
Jack

---

159 Because of the 'horrible rash of small houses' caused by the building of Morris Motors in Cowley, a few miles from The Kilns. See the letter to Arthur Greeves of 28 March 1937.

160 i.e. *That Hideous Strength*.

TO I. O. EVANS (W):

Magdalen College,
Oxford
Dec 27th 43

Dear Mr. Evans

Thanks for *Cheer the Chief* which I return and which I read with amusement tempered with horror for indeed that sort of thing is too near us to be *quite* funny! I am tempted by your offer of some *Weird Tales*[161] but firmly resist it. Those happy times when one cd. always find time to read and space to house '*one* book more' are gone for me. But thanks for the offer all the same. With all best wishes for the New Year and the new book.

Yours sincerely
C. S. Lewis

The scripts for Lewis's fourth series of BBC talks were completed by 10 December and sent to the BBC. Eric Fenn wrote to him on 22 December:

> *I like them immensely, and think that, as usual, you have achieved a quite astonishing degree of clarity in a very difficult subject. One or two of your analogies seem to me to need a little more scrutiny or possibly qualification.*
>
> *The thing that chiefly worries me is that, so far as I can make out you have worked to a 10 minute script, and not a 15 minute. The average length appears to be about 1,500 words, which is what we usually allow for a 10 minute talk . . . we can either keep them as 10 minute talks, and give away the other five to some other programme, or you could expand by another 600 words.*[162]

161 Evans contributed a number of stories to the magazine, *Weird Tales – The Unique Magazine* which ran from 1923 until 1954.

162 Phillips, *C. S. Lewis at the BBC*, p. 233.

TO ERIC FENN (BBC):

Magdalen College,
Oxford.
Dec 27th 1943

My dear Fenn

I could kick myself for not having used my 15 min. to the full. I *could* add to them but it wd. probably break the unity of each. I suppose I needn't decide till you have sent me back a typed copy – I have no foul copy to work on at the moment. Of course your threatened 'scrutiny' of some of my analogies (the very word has a sinister sound suggesting Scrooge, Screws, Screwtape, scraping and Inland Revenue) may lead to at least 600 additional words in some cases. But, as you know, I'm very biddable when it comes to the point. At any rate let me have a copy as soon as possible.

And you'd better come and dine and spend the night for your Screwtiny, hadn't you? My honour labours still under the lunch you didn't have. Any Thursday or Friday wd. probably do. All best wishes to you and yours.

Yours ever
C. S. Lewis

TO ERIC FENN (BBC):

As from Magdalen
New Year's Eve [1943]

My dear Fenn

Thanks for scripts etc and letter of the 29th. Well, I'll try to expand them to the requisite length and indeed have done so already as regards No 1. It's not going to be so easy with the others. Don't be disappointed if I don't adopt all your suggestions. All that about organisms, for instance[163] – I cd. do it for a Bampton Lecture but this d—d colloquial style is so intrinsically honest that I can't conceal *in it* my ignorance of what really does happen in an organism!

And the Church – it's difficult to go on long about that without

163 We do not have Lewis's original script, but in his letter of 29 December Fenn was referring to ch. 1 of *Beyond Personality*, 'Making and Begetting'.

raising the denominational question.[164] But I'll peg away. I look forward much to having you here for the night. All best wishes.

Yours
C. S. Lewis

164 In his letter of 29 December Fenn expressed worries about the seventh talk, 'Let's Pretend': 'I wonder if this might not be the place to say a bit more about the Christian community? With the exception of one or two references, you don't seem to mention this at all, and the scripts give, therefore, an impression of a purely individualistic approach. In this one, for instance, you are thinking all about one man in relation to God, and not at all about the connection this always establishes with other men' (Phillips, *C. S. Lewis at the BBC*, pp. 237–8).

1944

TO ERIC FENN (BBC):

Magdalen College,
Oxford
Jan 5th 1944

03/R/JEF

My dear Fenn

Here are the interpolations.[1] That for No. 7 is not v. artistically dovetailed but I know the difficulty does arise for some people and for those people it will be hovering in the air all through the last 4 talks. I have not sent the Typescripts for I presume you have a duplicate. Would *Beyond Personality* be a good title for the whole series? I'm glad there's a prospect of seeing you at College. With all best wishes.

Yours
C. S. Lewis

TO DELMAR BANNER (T):

Magdalen
Jan 7th 1944

Dear Banner

How v. kind of you to send me Mr Groom's[2] remarks on *Perelandra.* I am always like other cats glad to be stroked (I take it one shows even more pride by *not* liking praise than by liking it) but this was specially welcome because that is miles and away my own favourite among my books and has had a very bad reception from reviewers.

---

1 See the letters to Eric Fenn of 27 December and New Year's Eve 1943. Lewis had needed to expand the seven talks in his fourth series of broadcasts from ten to fifteen minutes' length.

2 Professor Bernard Groom (1892–1975) read English at Magdalen College, taking his BA in 1918. His books include *A Literary History of England* (1929), *A Short History of English Words* (1934) and *The Diction of Poetry from Spenser to Bridges* (1955).

Despite the preface they all will take it as an 'allegory' and then blame me for not making it clear. Groom has obviously understood it through and through: you and he even go so far as to spell the name correctly which is *very rare*. Commend me to him in all grateful duty.

I don't expect any one he remembers is still at Magdalen except Benecke who is becoming rather vitriolic in his old age. Thanks also for cutting. I missed your letter to *The Times* and shd. much like to see it if you have one to spare.

Less chance now than ever of my getting to your much desired valleys. My domestic difficulties grow worse daily and half my correspondence consists of refusing engagements which I should both like to, and ought to, accept. Be sure and look me up if you are ever in these parts: meanwhile all best wishes.

Yours
C. S. Lewis

TO ERIC FENN (BBC):

Magdalen
Jan 9th 1944
03/R/JEF.

My dear Fenn

I don't think the propriety of the sub-titles (which, I confess, I shd. be unwilling to change) is dependent on our decision about the main title. For it I wd. approve of the following

What Christians think God is like.
What is God like? The Christian answer.
Beyond Personality: or the Christian God.

But I'll *take* any of your suggestions.[3]

I've booked Jan 22nd for you. Lunch will be in my rooms and unless I become unusually greedy it will be there still however late you come!

Yours
C. S. Lewis

Fenn wrote to Lewis on 8 February about the recording of his fourth series of broadcasts:

---

3 The title they finally settled on was *Beyond Personality: The Christian View of God.*

There is rather a serious hitch about the time of your talk . . . The net result is that our Tuesday talk has to be put at about 10.20 p.m. from February 22nd onwards. I explained to the powers that be that this was extremely awkward for you, and attempted to get permission to broadcast from Oxford, but on security grounds, outside broadcasts of that kind have been cut down drastically – so I am afraid we are in a bit of a hole!

We don't like recording talks, and it always drops the temperature in the audience when they hear that it is a recording, but this may be the only thing left to be done. If you possibly could do even some of them 'live' from London at that time (it would mean spending the night in town) we should be enormously grateful, but if this is impossible, we would record the whole seven talks.[4]

TO ERIC FENN (BBC):

Magdalen
Feb 10th 44

Dear Fenn

Pox on your 'powers'! Who the devil is going to listen to anything at 10:20? If it is possible (but I suppose you'd have anticipated my suggestion if it were), cancel the whole thing for this spring and put it on later in the year. If not – I can't spend any Tuesday nights in town, so a talk at 10.20 means catching the midnight train and getting to bed about 3 o'clock. Well, I'll give *three* under those conditions. The rest you'll have to record. I don't mind which.[5]

If you know the address of any reliable firm of assassins, nose-slitters, garrotters and poisoners I should be grateful to have it.

I shall write a book about the BBC – you see if I don't! Gr-r-r-r!!

TO SISTER PENELOPE CSMV (BOD):

Magdalen College,
Oxford.
Feb. 19th. 1944

Dear Sister Penelope –

St. Athanasius arrived the day before yesterday, looking very well

---

4 Phillips, *C. S. Lewis at the BBC*, p. 243.

5 As it turned out, Lewis recorded talks 2, 6 and 7, of which only the last has survived.

dressed.[6] I have not yet had time to read more than your introduction. It gives me real pleasure to have it dedicated to me, though I wd. have deprecated 'witness' if you had given me the opportunity.[7] Apart from the suggestion of martyrdom (!) it carries implications which are rather overwhelming. But I am pleased and grateful all the same.

This is all very bad news about your plays. What I can't quite understand is why your access to the children and Fr. Williamson's must necessarily stand or fall together. No doubt one wishes to get both through: but in sending patrols out into enemy country there is something to be said for making them quite independent so that there will be less chance of *all* being scuppered.

My Talks on the doctrine of the Trinity begin next Tuesday at 10.30. p.m. I am to have a small operation sometime next vac – nothing to worry anyone who had not (as I have) a babyish horror of anaesthetics.[8] I must think over Fr. Williamson's idea about the Prodigal Son, which rather evades me for the moment. We are happy here at the moment because a perfectly saintly girl[9] is staying and helping Jane till May. How is your own health keeping? My duty to Reverend Mother,

Yours sincerely
Brother Ass

Lewis's fourth series of seven talks, entitled Beyond Personality, *was given over the BBC on Tuesday evenings from 22 February to 4 April 1944. These talks were published in* The Listener *in weekly instalments between 24 February and 6 April 1944.*

The popularity of Lewis's BBC Mere Christianity *talks had generated such a large post that he was having difficulty answering it. Warnie was a competent two-finger typist, and he had already begun acting as his brother's secretary. The next letter, to J. S. A. Ensor, is the first example we have of a numbering method Warnie developed. The letter was given*

---

6 *The Incarnation of the Word of God: Being the Treatise of St. Athanasius 'De Incarnatione Verbi Dei'*, trans. 'A Religious of C.S.M.V. S.Th.', introduction by C. S. Lewis (London: Geoffrey Bles: The Centenary Press, 1944).

7 The book is dedicated 'To/C.S.L./Witness and Teacher'.

8 Over the years a piece of shrapnel that lodged in Lewis's chest during the First World War had been working its way towards his lung. The doctors decided it should be removed, and the operation took place in July 1944, probably at the Acland Nursing Home in Oxford.

9 i.e. Jill Flewett.

the reference number 'REF.55/44'. The number on the left probably meant this was the fifty-fifth letter Warnie had typed for his brother in 1944. Having assigned Ensor the number '55' all subsequent letters to him carry that number.

But correspondents did not keep the same number year after year, nor was the method always consistent. The letter to Dorothy L. Sayers of 30 June 1945 was given the reference number '231', probably because that was the 231st letter Warnie typed in 1945. But a month later she is given the number '232'. After this, her reference number, like those of most regular correspondents, changed every year.

TO J. S. A. ENSOR (W):[10] TS

REF.55/44.

Magdalen College,
Oxford.
26th February 1944.

Dear Mr. Ensor,

Thanks for your kind and most encouraging letter. Factories are all-important, and I will try to come and give your group a talk. Could you suggest a date, and what sort of subject? If it could be so timed that I could get home the same night it would make things much easier.

yours sincerely,
C. S. Lewis

TO J. S. A. ENSOR (W): TS

REF.55/44

Magdalen College,
Oxford.
2nd March 1944.

Dear Mr. Ensor,

Thank you for your interesting letter of the 29th: – As regards the nature of the meeting, I leave this to you, but think myself that the smaller meeting would be *much* more useful.

Time and date: – I propose to catch the train arriving at Hayes at 5.46 p.m. on April 18th. As the factory presumably covers a large area, I take it you will send someone to meet me at the station and bring me to the meeting place?

---

10 Ensor was an employee in the head office of Electric and Musical Industries Ltd (EMI), the manufacturers of gramophone records and radios at Hayes, Middlesex.

I propose to talk on 'How can religion be related to modern industry?'
yours sincerely,
C. S. Lewis

TO J. S. A. ENSOR (W): TS

REF.55/44

Magdalen College,
Oxford.
4th. March 1944.

Dear Mr. Ensor,

I'll try that subject if you like: but as I came to believe in God on purely philosophical grounds, it is very hard not to make a talk on this too highbrow. What do you think?

yours sincerely,
C. S. Lewis

TO THE EDITOR OF *THE LISTENER* (*EC*):[11]

Oxford
[9 March 1944]

I agree with Mr W. R. Childe that it is no use to say 'Lord, Lord', if we do not do what Christ tells us: that, indeed, is one of the reasons why I think an aesthetic religion of 'flowers and music' insufficient. My reason for thinking that a mere statement of even the highest ethical principles is not enough is precisely that to know these things is not necessarily to do them, and if Christianity brought no healing to the impotent will, Christ's teaching would not help us.

I cannot blame Mr Childe for misunderstanding me, because I am naturally no judge of my own lucidity; but I take it very hard when a total stranger whom I have never knowingly injured or offended, on the first discovery of a difference in theological opinion between us,

11 The first of Lewis's *Beyond Personality* talks, 'Making and Begetting', was published in *The Listener*, XXXI (24 February 1944), p. 224 as 'The Map and the Ocean'. He had said of the necessity of learning and thinking about Christian doctrines that 'you will not get eternal life by just feeling the presence of God in flowers and music'. He was attacked on this point by Mr W. R. Childe in *The Listener*, XXXI (2 March 1944), p. 245. This letter, Lewis's reply, was published in *The Listener*, XXXI (9 March 1944), p. 273 as 'Mr C. S. Lewis on Christianity'. Childe's reply to Lewis's letter was published in *The Listener*, XXXI (16 March 1944), p. 301.

should publicly accuse me of being a potential torturer, murderer or tyrant – for that is what Mr Childe's reference to faggots means if it means anything.

How little I approve of compulsion in religion may be gauged from a recent letter of mine to the *Spectator* protesting against the intolerable tyranny of compulsory church parades for the Home Guard. If Mr Childe can find any passage in my works which favours religious or anti-religious compulsion I will give five pounds to any (not militantly anti-Christian) charity he cares to name. If he cannot, I ask him, for justice and charity's sake, to withdraw his charge.

C. S. Lewis

TO J. S. A. ENSOR (W):

As from Magdalen College,
Oxford.
March 13th. 1944.

Dear Mr. Ensor,

Now that you mention Questions at the meeting it suddenly occurs to me that the best meetings I've ever had have been *all* questions i.e. I've announced myself as a one-man Brains Trust on moral and religious questions. Wd. your people play up if I did that – I mean, would they have plenty of questions? And if so, is it too late to change? Questions shd. be sent to you in writing (they needn't be signed) and you can open them and read them out. Say 'questions on Xtianity, morals, and connected matters'. What do you think.

Re 'Oxford accent'. To anyone who is interested in this vexed question I wish you'd circulate the *real* answer, wh. is as follows.

(1.) The first time I heard my own voice on a record I didn't recognise it and was shocked. *Moral: A.* No man knows what his own accent is like. *B.* No man's accent is there because he has chosen it. *C.* It may not be the accent he likes. If all my critics cd. hear their own voices they'd be very surprised.

(2.) The whole matter is misunderstood as long as people insist on looking at accents as subjects of approval or disapproval. They are simply accidental phenomena, to be studied as one studies different varieties of beetles. Taken in *that* way they are v. interesting and often reveal much history.

(3.) My own accent is so far from voluntary that I have actually *tried* to retain my original North of Ireland – and apparently failed (Tho' I'm sure I've kept *H*WAT, *H*WITE etc.)

(4.) What do they want me to do? I could try mimicing some other accent but there'd be great danger, at my age, of producing only a horrible mixture.

(5.) The most noticeable feature of the so-called Oxford Accent is what phoneticians call dipthongization e.g. *ka-ut* for *coat*. The slower you speak the more this is exaggerated (indeed v. clear speech will produce it in *any* accent). On the air I'm told to speak slowly – with the result your people deplore. But it isn't *my* fault.

Let me know what you think about the One Man Brains Trust,

Yours

C. S. Lewis

TO THOMAS WILKINSON RIDDLE (BOD): TS

REF.106/44

Magdalen College,
Oxford.
16th. March 1944.

Dear Doctor Riddle,

Thanks for your kind letter of the 15th., and the enclosed present which I look forward to reading. I heard from your son the other day and he seems to be in good form. Be sure and let me know when you are in Oxford again.

yours,

C. S. Lewis

TO MRS PERCIVAL WISEMAN (M):

Magdalen College,
Oxford.
March 20th/44

Dear Mrs Percival Wiseman

I'm afraid the MSS of the talks are going straight to the publisher as soon as the series is over.

Instead I send you a little tract on my views of the future life.[12] You are quite right to keep clear of the Spiritualists. All that is an effort to *cancel* death, to go on getting a pale phantom of the same sort of

12 This was probably his sermon 'The Weight of Glory'.

intercourse with our dear ones which we had when they and we were members of the same world. But we must *submit* to death, embrace the cross.

I think the purpose of the separation is to help us to turn what is merely natural and instinctive affection into real spiritual love of them in Christ. Not that natural affection isn't good & innocent, but it is merely natural – and therefore must first be crucified before it can rise again. Those who try to escape the crucifixion fall in either with charlatans or with delusions from hell: spiritualism often drives people mad. Of course we should pray for our dead as I'm sure they do for us.

Yours sincerely
C. S. Lewis

On 23 March Eric Fenn sent Lewis a copy of a report from the BBC's 'Listener Research people' on the effect produced by the second talk in his fourth series of broadcasts – 'The Three-Personal God'. Fenn commented:

> *One has to bear in mind that this is an attempt to summarize the opinions of a random sample of people who had actually listened. How far it is a clear guide to the reactions of people beyond the sample, it is difficulty to say. But the single most important fact is the sharp division you produce in your audience. They obviously either regard you as 'the cat's whiskers' or as beneath contempt, which is interesting, and ought, I feel, to teach us something, but I can't think what!*[13]

TO ERIC FENN (BBC):

[Magdalen College]
March 25th [1944]

My dear Fenn

Thanks for the suitable lenten reading which I return. What wd. you think of the enclosed as an article for the *Listener* to appear at the end of the Talks?[14]

The two views you report (Cat's whiskers and Beneath Contempt)

---

13 BBC Written Archives Centre.

14 Lewis sent Fenn an 'apologia' replying to listeners' criticism. In the end he decided not to publish it. See his letter to Fenn of 4 April.

aren't very illuminating about *me* perhaps: about my subject matter, it is an old story, isn't it. They love, or hate.

Yours
C. S. Lewis

No paper to be found anywhere to-day![15]

TO FRIEDRICH SAXL (W):[16]

Magdalen College,
Oxford.
March 30th 1944

Dear Dr. Saxl,

I am afraid I can throw no light on this picture of Fortuna.[17] I drew a blank in Ovid, Isidore, Boccaccio. *Lilies* seem, oddly enough, to occur only once in *Roman de la Rose*. What we want is a list of works falsely attributed to Ovid, but I do not know where that is to be found. Have you looked at the IXth century *De Rosae Lilique Certamine* of Sedulius Scotus?[18] That seems the most hopeful single work. Finally, Raby[19] is more likely to know than any man now alive in England. I'm sorry to be so unhelpful.

Yours sincerely
C. S. Lewis

---

15 Lewis's letter was written on the back of Fenn's of 23 March.

16 Dr Friedrich 'Fritz' Saxl (1890–1948), historian of art, was born in Vienna and studied at Vienna and Berlin Universities. He was the founder, with Aby M. Warburg, of the Warburg Institute of the University of London which exists principally to further the study of the classical tradition. His many books include the *Catalogue of Astrological and Mythological Illuminated Manuscripts of the Latin Middle Ages*, 3 vols. (1915–53).

17 There are many drawings and paintings of the Goddess of Fortune, and it is not known which Dr Saxl showed Lewis. It was presumably one of those listed in his *Catalogue of Astrological and Mythological Manuscripts.*

18 Sedulius Scotus (9th century AD), Irish teacher, grammarian and scriptural commentator. His allegorical poem, *De Rosae Lilique Certamine* (*Contention of the Lily and the Rose*) is found in *Poetae Latini aevi Carolini*, ed. E. Duemmler (Berol: 1880–1923), vol. III, p. 231. For a discussion of the poem see *The Allegory of Love*, ch. 2, pp. 85–6.

19 Frederic James Edward Raby, the medievalist, who wrote *A History of Secular Latin Poetry in the Middle Ages* (1934).

TO J. S. A. ENSOR (BOD): TS

REF.55/44

Magdalen College,
Oxford.
31st. March 1944.

Dear Ensor,

(May we at this stage drop the 'Mr.' on both sides?). Right. I am tall, fat, clean shaven, don't wear glasses, and shall be in corduroy trousers, probably with a walking stick. I will look for you at the entrance to Paddington Hotel, just beside the entrance to the Underground.

yours,
C. S. Lewis

TO ERIC FENN (BBC):

Magdalen
April 4th 44

My dear Fenn

I think we'll scrap my 'apologia'[20] altogether on second thought. Replies, except in a real rigorous high-brow controversy, are always a mistake.

Like you, I am not depressed at the reaction. The letters I get myself bear out your Research Report: they are nearly all either violent abuse or extravagant praise. All good wishes for Easter.

Yours
C. S. Lewis

Lewis held a 'One Man Brains Trust' in the Electrical and Musical Industries factory at Hayes, Middlesex, on 18 April 1944. Questions were put to him by Mr H. W. Bowen. Shorthand notes were made, and a typescript sent to Lewis. He revised it a little, and it was printed as a pamphlet entitled 'Answers to Questions on Christianity' in 1944. It is reprinted in Undeceptions *and* EC.

20 This 'apologia' or reply to his critics has not survived.

TO FRANCES YOUNG (P):[21]

Magdalen College,
Oxford.
April 6th 1944

Dear Mrs. Young

I am very, very sorry to hear of your tragic news. In the presence of your own far greater and more intimate loss I am almost ashamed to speak of the loss to scholarship and to myself. I had valued my contacts with your husband very much: I had assumed that we should meet again: I had hoped to do things he would like. I was very much of a beginner, and he of a mature scholar, when he first sought me out, and nothing could exceed his kindness.

It was indeed a model of what such kindness should be, and so rarely is, for while there was no hint of patronage neither was there any silly pretence of our being at the same stage. That was exactly what I liked – and there was such a rich flavour about his mind. His death will be very widely and deeply felt. It was kind of you to write to me at such a time.

You probably know that my views on death are old fashioned and theological. If I elaborated them I should be repeating what you learned from your catechism. I only mention this because it seems a foolish modern hypocrisy on such an occasion not to mention immortality if one firmly believes in it.

Accept my deepest sympathy,
yours very sincerely
C. S. Lewis

TO E. R. EDDISON (BOD):

[Magdalen College]
Long Friday[22] [7 April] 1944

My verie good Lorde youre Ld's letters were deliuered to me euen at such a time when I had it in mynde to write something to youre Hono˜.

Whereof the occasion was that latelie makyng my vyage to London

---

21 Frances Young was the widow of Professor Karl Young, Professor of English at Yale University, 1923–43, who had died on 17 November 1943. Born Frances Campbell Berkeley, she had married Young in 1911, and they had two sons.

22 The Anglo-Saxon term for Good Friday.

and being set dovne in þ˜ same coche with a little Benedictine monke whom I know, we fell into discourse of bookes and the said monke (with whom neither I nor anie of oure friends had fallen vpon such matter before) presentlie asked mee yf I hadde reade through the historical romans of *Ouroboros*, lauding the same to the heavens, and saying he had latelie brought in loue with it the wife of one Farrer a fellowe of the College of the Holie Trinitee.[23]

The whiche seemde to me at first a marveil that wee Christianes who so abhorre youre Ld's *gnosis*[24] yet are your most delighted readers vntill I recalled how naturall phylosophres do reporte that beestes the most infeste to one another by kind, yet yf their commone and greater enemie come among them, falle presentlie into a fashion of amytie: as Plinie crediblie relateth[25] of lyons couching with Unicorns against dragons, Solinus[26] of cats and mice leaguing against Boojums, Orosius[27] of beares and whelpes compassing the death of cockadrills, and almoste innumerable the like instances as your Hono's knowledge I doubt not can multiplie. Wee and your Hono in the like fashion doe together soe hate the androgynous and petrol-nourished monstres of this Age that while it lives we almost lacke leisure for our kindlie and instinctive hatred of one another's tenents,[28] nor can we come armed at you nor you at us till that said monster be putte downe and both our swordes therebie (I suppose) verie much blunted.

For the litel booke of the *Pilgrim*,[29] it is not for your Ldp's reading.

We looke to welcom your Hono˜ in oure poore sodalitie agayne

23 This was Katharine Farrer (1911–72), wife of Austin Farrer. She read Classics at St Anne's College and took a BA in 1933. She taught for a while at Gerrard's Cross, and in 1937 married Austin Farrer who was Chaplain and Fellow of Trinity College, Oxford. She was greatly appreciated as a critic, and Lewis and Tolkien asked her to read a number of their works. Besides translating Gabriel Marcel's *Etre et Avoir* – as *Being and Having* (1949), she published three detective novels, *The Missing Link* (1952), *Cretan Counterfeit* (1954) and *Gownsman's Gallows* (1957).

24 'spiritual beliefs'.

25 Pliny the Elder (AD 23/4–79) in his *Natural History*.

26 Julius Solinus (3rd century AD), author of *Collectanea Rerum Memorabilium*, which is mainly an epitome of Pliny's *Natural History*.

27 Orosius (5th century AD) was a friend of St Augustine, and the author, at the latter's request, of a history of the world up to AD 417.

28 'principles' or 'beliefs'.

29 i.e. *The Pilgrim's Regress*.

when somer maketh longer dayes and som Thursday in the Trinitie Term were for us most convenient. Awaiting advyse of your Hono˜'s pleasure on this matter I verie humblie take my leave,

C. S. Lewis

TO E. R. EDDISON (BOD): TS

REF.203/44.

Magdalen College,
Oxford.
21st. April 1944.

Dear Eddison,

Many thanks for your pleasant letter of the 17th: – Can you come on June 8th. For dinner, bed, and breakfast.

yours sincerely,
C. S. Lewis

In his unpublished 'biography' of his brother, which later became the 'Memoir' to Letters of C. S. Lewis, *Warnie wrote:*

> *In May 1944 Jack received an amusing letter from the Society for the Prevention of Progress, of Walnut Creek, California, inviting him to become a member and requesting him to forward his credentials. The signature on his reply was instigated by one of the Society's rules to which his attention had been called: – Membership and the privileges of the Society are denied to such individuals as Henry A. Wallace[30] and this fellow Beveridge.[31]*

TO THE SOCIETY FOR THE PREVENTION OF PROGRESS (*L*):

[Magdalen College
May 1944]

Dear Sir,

While feeling that I was *born* a member of your Society, I am

30 Henry Agard Wallace (1888–1965) was Vice President of the United States, 1941–5, under Franklin D. Roosevelt. He ran for President in 1948 on the Progressive Party ticket.

31 William Henry Beveridge, first Lord Beveridge (1879–1963), a social reformer and economist, whose 'Beveridge plan' became the blueprint for the present welfare state.

nevertheless honoured to receive the outward seal of membership. I shall hope by continued orthodoxy and the unremitting practice of Reaction, Obstruction, and Stagnation to give you no reason for repenting your favour.

I humbly submit that in my Riddell Lectures entitled The Abolition of Man you will find another work not all unworthy of consideration for admission to the canon.

Yours regressively,
C. S. Lewis

Beverages not Beveridges
(my motto)

TO THOMAS WILKINSON RIDDLE (BOD): TS

REF.279/44

Magdalen College,
Oxford.
17th. May 1944.

Dear Dr Riddle,

Chestnuts! Whiskers! This bloomer has been pointed out several times already.[32] The higher critics will use it to prove that the book was really written 200 years later by five different 'Hands' as they appropriately call them!

All good wishes.
yours sincerely,
C. S. Lewis

32 In *The Screwtape Letters*, Letter 1, Screwtape said that, after his 'patient' had emerged from the British Museum, 'Once he was in the street the Battle was won. I showed him a newsboy shouting the midday paper, and a No. 73 bus going past.' Dr Riddle was one of many who pointed out that it was impossible to see the number 73 bus from there. Lewis corrected this when he was editing *The Screwtape Letters and Screwtape Proposes a Toast* (1961), by altering 'street' to 'streets'.

TO MARTIN MOYNIHAN (BOD):[33]

Magdalen
May 21st 44

My dear Moynihan

You are a perfect correspondent. You bring all sorts of orient treasures of news and ask nothing in return. How I look forward to hearing you tell your tale with feet on the fender here.

I have not heard from your sister since the day she called on me. I hope she won't feel it needs 'courage' to penetrate the lion's den again. I will roar as it were any sucking dove: will play Lion to her Una,[34] as she well deserves for she is a delightful person.

I *did* like *Fives & Logic*[35] very much, and some others too tho' I can't remember them now. The arrangement was that your sister wd. send me a copy of *it*, to try to place, but it hasn't arrived yet.

Talking of Hindus, have you ever heard in India of Martin Lings, a Magdalen pupil of mine about five years before your time, who disappeared with the intention of becoming one? Incidentally apart from your peculiar protection ('there's a divinity that shapes our ends!')[36] can one *become* a Hindu?

There's no news here. We have a new President, Tizzard, a scientist:[37] Ryle of the House has been elected to the chair Collingwood held.[38]

---

33 Martin John Moynihan (1916–), translator and editor of *Letters: C. S. Lewis–Don Giovanni Calabria* (1988) was educated at Birkenhead School and Magdalen College, Oxford, where he read Modern Greats under T. D. Weldon and English under Lewis. On leaving Oxford he joined the India Office and was with the Indian Army (Corps of Guides) during the Second World War, serving with the Punjab Frontier Force on the North West Frontier and in Burma. In 1946 he married Monica Hopwood and joined the Commonwealth and later the Diplomatic Service, becoming HM Consul General, Philadelphia, Ambassador in Liberia and High Commissioner in Lesotho. His books include *The Strangers, and Other Poems* (1946) and *South of Fort Hertz: A Tale in Rhyme* (1956).

34 Spenser, *The Faerie Queene*, I. Una typifies the singleness of the true religion. After she is separated from the Redcrosse Knight she is protected by a lion.

35 This work by Martin Moynihan is unpublished.

36 Shakespeare, *Hamlet*, V, ii, 10.

37 Sir Henry Thomas Tizard (1885–1959), scientist and administrator, took a BA in Chemistry from Magdalen College in 1908. He became a Tutorial Fellow of Magdalen in 1911, but left to serve with the Royal Flying Corps, 1915–17. He was Rector of Imperial College, London, 1929–42, and President of Magdalen College, 1942–6.

38 Robin George Collingwood (1889–1943), philosopher and historian, was a Fellow of Magdalen College, 1935–41, and Waynflete Professor of Metaphysical

I've been giving the Clarke Lectures at Cambridge wh. involved staying with Trevelyan in the Master's Lodge at Trinity. We have nothing like it at Oxford. It is really an Elizabethan palace, room opening out of room like at Hampton Court.

I wonder where this will find you? Φευ γαίας ὅσσον ἀφ ἡμέτερας.[39]

Yours

C. S. Lewis

TO EDITH GATES (W):

Magdalen College,
Oxford.
May 23rd 1944

Dear Miss Gates

Certainly I cannot love my neighbour properly till I love God. As George Macdonald says in his *Unspoken Sermons* (long out of print but if you can get a 2nd hand copy by any means short of stealing, do! It is beyond price)

'And beginning to try to love his neighbour he finds that this is no more to be reached in itself than the Law was to be reached in itself. As he cannot keep the Law without first rising into the love of his neighbour, so he cannot love his neighbour without first rising higher still. The whole system of the universe works upon this principle – the driving of things upward toward the centre.'[40]

On the other hand we have no power to make ourselves love God. The only way is absolute obedience to Him, total surrender. He will give us the 'feeling' if He pleases. But both when He does and when He does not, we shall gradually learn that *feeling* is not the important

---

Philosophy, 1945–68. He is the author (with J. N. L. Myres) of *Roman Britain and the English Settlements* (1936) in the Oxford History of England series. Collingwood was replaced at Magdalen by Gilbert Ryle (1900–76) who had been teaching at Christ Church – the 'House' – since 1924.

39 *Palatine Anthology*, book VII, Leonidas of Tarentum (fl. 274 BC), Poem 740: 'Alas! How far from our own land!'

40 MacDonald, *Unspoken Sermons*, First Series, pp. 194–5. Lewis was paraphrasing the following passage: 'And, beginning straightway to try to love his neighbour, he finds that the empyrean of which he spoke is no more to be reached in itself than the law was to be reached in itself. As he cannot keep the law without first rising into the love of his neighbour, so he cannot love his neighbour without first rising higher still. The whole system of the universe works upon this law – the driving of things upward towards the centre.'

thing. There is something in us deeper than feeling, deeper even than conscious will. It is rather *being*. When we are *quite* empty of self we shall be filled with Him, for nature abhors a vacuum. Of course it is good, as you say, to 'realise' that the source of all our good feelings is God. (That is the right way to deal with pride: not to depreciate the good thing we are tempted to be proud of but to remember where it comes from). But 'realisation' depends on faculties that fail us when we are tired or when we try to use them too often, so we can't depend on it. It is the self you really are and not its reflection in consciousness that matters most.

May I take what is really the closest parallel? No child is begotten without pleasure. But the pleasure is not the cause of life – it is a symptom, something that happens when life is in fact being transmitted. In the same way 'feeling love' is only the echo in consciousness of the real thing wh. lies deeper.

Yours sincerely
C. S. Lewis

TO DOM BEDE GRIFFITHS OSB (W):

Magdalen College,
Oxford.
May 25th [1944]

Dear Dom Bede

Thanks for your letter. I too was delighted with our meeting. About the past, and nothing being lost, the point is that 'He who loses his life shall save it'[41] is *totally* true, true on every level. *Everything* we crucify will rise again: *nothing* we try to hold onto will be left us.

I wrote the other day 'Good and evil when they attain their full stature are retrospective. That is why, at the end of all things, the damned will say we were *always* in Hell, and the blessed we have *never* lived anywhere but in heaven.'[42] Do you agree?

---

41 Matthew 10:39.

42 Lewis was writing *The Great Divorce: A Dream* (1945) at the time this letter was written. The passage he quotes comes from ch. 9 where his guide, 'George MacDonald', says: 'Both good and evil, when they are full grown, become retrospective . . . And that is why, at the end of all things . . . the Blessed will say "We have never lived anywhere except in Heaven," and the Lost, "We were always in Hell." And both will speak truly.'

You're right about C.W.[43] He has an undisciplined mind and sometimes admits into his theology ideas whose proper place is in his romances. What keeps him right is his *love* of which (and I have now known him long) he radiates more than any man I know. Thanks for the name of de Grandmaison.[44] Continue to pray for me as I do for you,

yours
C. S. Lewis

TO C. N. FRANCIS (W):[45] TS

REF.374/44.

Magdalen College,
Oxford.
13th July 1944.

Dear Mr. Francis,

Thank you for your kind and encouraging letter of the 9th: –

No. The only thing I have written on Freud is an essay called 'Psychoanalysis and Literary Criticism' in 'Essays and Studies by Members of the English Association'.[46] (I can't say which volume).

Many thanks for the kind references to my books.

yours sincerely,
C. S. Lewis[47]

TO SARAH NEYLAN (T):

[The Kilns]
July 16th 1944

My dear Sarah –

Thank you very much for sending me the pictures of the Fairy King and Queen at tea (or is it breakfast?) in their palace and all the cats (what a lot of cats they have! And a separate table for them. How sensible!). I liked them very much. It must be nice for them (I mean the King and Queen) having so many currants in their cake. We don't get many now, do we?

I am getting to be quite friends with an old Rabbit who lives in the

---

43 i.e. Charles Williams.

44 This was possibly Léonce de Grandmaison (1868–1927), author of *Personal Religion* (1929).

45 Mr Francis's address was given as 58 Hillmorton Rd., Rugby.

46 See note 74 to the letter of 3 February 1940.

47 The signature was written by Warnie.

Wood at Magdalen. I pick leaves off the trees for him because he can't reach up to the branches and he eats them out of my hand. One day he stood up on his hind legs and put his front paws against me, he was so greedy. I wrote this about it:

A funny old man had a habit
Of giving a leaf to a rabbit.
At first it was shy
But then, by and by,
It got rude and would stand up to grab it.

But it's a very nice Rabbit all the same: I call him 'Baron Biscuit'. Please tell Mummie I thank her for her nice letter.

I didn't have a bad time in the Home but they didn't give me enough to eat and they washed me all over as if I wasn't old enough to wash myself. Have you ever met a hospital-nurse? They are very strong-minded women.

No more now because I am still not quite better. Lots of love to you and everyone else

your affectionate Godfather
C. S. Lewis

TO BARBARA WALL (BOD):[48]

Magdalen College,
Oxford.
July 31st 1944

Dear Mrs Wall

Thank you very much for the last chapter. I enclose cheque for £1–5s: perhaps you will discuss the matter with Colin and let me know the 'war increase' which you already haven't charged me and which all other scribes do and which I am waiting to pay. The amounts so far are much too small. (Colin is a Scotchman and will give sound advice!). Your labours go off to the publisher to-day.

Yours sincerely
C. S. Lewis

---

48 See **Barbara Wall** in the Biographical Appendix. Introduced to Lewis by Colin Hardie, she was currently typing *The Great Divorce.*

TO VIOLET MARY TOY (BOD):[49]

Magdalen College,
Oxford.
Aug 1st 1944

Dear Mrs Toy –

I liked the article.[50] It needs a footnote or addition to the first paragraph making an exception in favour of Charles Williams who has praised Imogen quite as whole-heartedly as you.[51]

On p. 6 you need not *speculate* about Jove standing for God: changes from 'God' in Quarto to 'Jove', 'gods' or 'Heaven' in Folio run through most of the plays wh. exist in both texts and were certainly made in obedience to the 'Act to Restrain Abuses of Players' (1606) wh. forbade the mention of any Divine Name on the stage.[52] I mean you need not speculate on the equivalence *in general*: but of course a play (like *Othello*[53] or *Hen IV*) which is set in Xtian times is different from one where the characters are all theoretically Pagan.

I think myself you are right and that all the presuppositions of *Cymbeline* are really Xtian: but you want to get clear the distinction and perhaps defend your view. I doubt if the words 'sense of comedy' will quite carry the weight you put into them from p. 7 onwards. I see what you mean, but you need to say more – something like 'balance a level mindedness wh. she shares with Sh's great comic heroines'. The ticklish part is p. 5. The quotation *does* suggest something like false modesty (= pride) or frigidity. This is your opponent's strong point

---

49 See **Violet Mary Toy** in the Biographical Appendix.

50 Mrs Toy had sent him a copy of her article 'Defence of Imogen'. It was not published but a copy may be seen in the Bodleian Library (MS. Eng. c. 6043, fols. 84–8).

51 See Charles Williams's treatment of Imogen, heroine of William Shakespeare's *Cymbeline* (1623), in Williams's *The English Poetic Mind* (1932), 'The Cycle of Shakespeare', pp. 104–6.

52 The Act to Restrain Abuses of Players, which was passed by an Act of Parliament in 1606, stated that if 'any person or persons do or shall in any stage play, interlude, show, maygame, or pageant jestingly or profanely speak or use the holy name of God or of Christ Jesus, or of the Holy Ghost or of the Trinity, which are not to be spoken but with fear and reverence, shall forfeit for every offence by him or them committed, ten pounds.' As a result, there are a number of changes between quartos of Shakespeare's plays, printed before 1606, and the folio text, printed in 1623.

53 William Shakespeare, *Othello* (1622).

and I'm not sure you've fully knocked it out of action. But it's a good paper even as it stands.

English (Editor G. Cookson, Truxford Wood, Elstead, Surrey) wd. probably take it. Rejection by T.L.S.[54] had nothing to do with its merits: I expect they don't read MSS except for their own gang – and it's a rotten paper now anyway.

I am glad you are fighting against all that bilge about 'conventional chastity': and I particularly liked your treatment of the scene between Imogen & Iachimo. You know our allies do you? R. W. Chambers two Shakespearian essays in *Man's Unconquerable Mind* and the lecture on *Lear* published since his death:[55] all Charles Williams: and Bethell's new book on Sh. of which the title escapes me.[56] The Raleigh tradition[57] has become madness and people like Tillyard (God bless him, he's the nicest donkey you can imagine)* is blind to the clearest facts. All good wishes.

Yours sincerely
C. S. Lewis

* Not to be quoted!

TO OWEN BARFIELD (W):

[The Kilns]
Aug 22nd 44

My dear Barfield

I have a letter (the second) from a person called P. G. R. BAKER or BALLER or BATIER (illegible. He's half or wholly French). I enclose it. He is certainly a fool and perhaps a lunatic: but he seems v. miserable. I *think* he means he is v. poor.

I have replied telling him that if he sends you a clear objective account of his financial position something may be done for him (I mean, out of the Agapony.) So now you'll know why if six pages of confessions arrive at Palmer's Green.

Almost anyone but you wd. say I was as mad as he for taking any

54 *The Times Literary Supplement.*

55 R. W. Chambers, *King Lear*, 1st W. P. Ker memorial lecture delivered in the University of Glasgow 27th November 1939 (1940).

56 S. L. Bethell, *Shakespeare and the Popular Dramatic Tradition* (1944).

57 Sir Walter Raleigh, *Shakespeare* (1907).

notice of such a rhapsody. I twice determined not to: but there was something so miserable and naggingly miserable about it that I found I couldn't. (Incidentally, I have explained to him that *mollities*[58] does not leave virginity intact!)

I hope your cloud is lifting. It has been in my mind a great many times to-day. 'I would not have you miscarry for the half of my dowry.' I still have no pillar, staff or adminicle that is in the same class as you. In fact, 'Save yourself, Pickwick, for my sake' as Mr. Winkle said, skating madly in the opposite direction.[59]

Yours ever
C. S. Lewis

Ten to one you'll never hear from Bakier. He'll shy off from a solicitor. At least I hope so.

The time had come for Jill Flewett to leave The Kilns to take her place at the Royal Academy of Dramatic Art (RADA) in London. Jill later wrote of the letter that follows:

> *It was very difficult to leave the Kilns – I had been some sort of 'mother's help' – looking after the hens and feeding them was one of my duties – for two years. Paxford was working at Cowley and could only keep a few things going in his spare time. There was no other help apart from Vera Henry who came up and cooked a couple of times a week. Minto had open and painful varicose ulcers and was supposed to lie on a sofa with her leg up as much as possible. I suppose I felt they couldn't manage without me. Also I knew that the burden would fall on Jack as he was already under strain with the demands of his work at Magdalen, the broadcasts and his own writing, while looking after Minto as much as he could.*[60]

58 'effeminacy'.

59 Dickens, *The Pickwick Papers*, ch. 30. Mr Pickwick, while skating, falls through the ice and disappears into the water: '"Keep yourself up for an instant – for only one instant," bawled Mr Snodgrass. "Yes do; let me implore you, for my sake," roared Mr Winkle.'

60 Letter to Walter Hooper of 27 January 2003.

Jill took her entrance examination to the Royal Academy, and although she was offered a place, she returned to The Kilns to help there for another year.

TO WINIFRED FLEWETT (T):[61]

The Kilns,
Headington Quarry,
Oxford.
Sept 5th 1944.

Dear Mrs Flewett

I was very glad to get your letter, for this whole question has been much on my mind. My own opinion is that June ought, in her own best interests, to go to the Academy this coming term. Every argument which my mind brings against this conclusion I regard as a temptation – a keen temptation, because when June goes the only bright spot in our prospect goes with her.

But, putting ourselves out of it, I think she ought to go. From the point of view of her career she is wasting time by staying: she is not getting chances of making friends: and I think she is working too hard. I have told her that this is my view; and since, in talking to June it is no use to appeal to selfish motives (she is, without exception, the most selfless person I have ever known) I told her she had a duty to you and her father in the matter. June's own view is simply and definitely that she will not leave here of her own free will; only if she is made to! The decision obviously rests with you and Mr Flewett.

If you decide to recall her I think you will just have to do it on parental authority. I won't enlarge on what we shall feel in losing her: partly because I don't like thinking of it, and partly because it would sound like begging off the very decision which (my conscience tells me) I ought to advise you to make. But I will say that no gratitude or affection or life-long interest which Mrs Moore and I can feel will ever be adequate to the extraordinary goodness she has shown. We feel we want to thank you both for just being her father and mother!

Yours very sincerely
Jack Lewis

---

61 Winifred Flewett was the mother of Jill (or June) Flewett. See **Lady Jill Freud** in the Biographical Appendix.

P.S. Mrs. Moore sends her best love and knows you will excuse her for not writing at present. She says she doesn't know how she could have come through this time at all without June.

TO SISTER PENELOPE CSMV (BOD):

As from Magdalen College,
Oxford.
Sept 6th. 1944.

Dear Sister Penelope

It is on my conscience that I owe you a letter this long time. All sorts of things have happened to me during it. I've finished another book wh. concludes the Ransom trilogy:[62] the scene is on Earth this time.

I've had an operation for the removal of a piece of shell I got into me in the last war, which, after lying snug and silent like an unrepented sin for 20 years or so, began giving me trouble. How nice modern anaesthetics are compared with the sort I remember from boyhood.

Last of all, and only a few days ago, Jane (you remember my Jane?) has had a slight stroke and lost the power of her left arm. She is in bed and I think will make a full recovery – *this* time. And as usual we are looking, and looking in vain, for domestic help. So have us all in your prayers.

What set me on writing to you to-day was that I re-read a little of your *Windows on Jerusalem* in bed last night and liked it as well as ever. I must thank you again for putting into my mind the very important point about the sub-human, embryonic, incarnation of Our Lord.[63] It always brings to life the words of the hymn 'love so amazing'[64] – wh. are usually deadened by the depreciation the word 'amazing' has undergone since it was written.

---

62 i.e. *That Hideous Strength.*

63 Sister Penelope, *Windows on Jerusalem*, ch. 2, p. 5: 'The Eternal Son began at the beginning with the single cell and, as we all do, recapitulated the entire evolutionary process on the way to birth, touching and renewing life on every level.' Lewis drew on this for his chapter 'The Obstinate Toy Soldiers' in *Beyond Personality* and *Mere Christianity*, Book IV, ch. 5, p. 149: 'The Eternal Being, who knows everything and who created the whole universe became not only a man but (before that) a baby, and before that a foetus inside a woman's body.'

64 Isaac Watts (1674–1748), 'When I Survey the Wondrous Cross'. The hymn concludes with the words 'Love so amazing, so divine,/Demands my soul, my life, my all.'

How are you, Sister? And *quo res summa loco*;[65] I mean, what of the plays?

The world has changed since you and I last met: one finds it difficult to keep pace with the almost miraculous mercies we are receiving as a nation. I never in my most sanguine moments dreamed that the invasion of Europe wd. go quite so well.[66] Query – when Christ tells us to be perfect is it because only He knows how very small an addition to our present efforts wd. break the enemy's line completely? – that perfection wd. cost v. little more than our actual dithering does? But we're all like the boy who takes nearly, but never quite, enough trouble over his prep. and always just spoils it. Remember me to Mother Maribell & Annie Louise.

Yours sincerely
C. S. Lewis

TO G. D. GILLIES (BOD):[67]

[The Kilns]
Sept 15th. 1944

Dear Mr. Gillies

Thank you for your letter. I haven't got the books with me here, but I expect Beeching follows (as always) the first edition.[68] His punctuation, as you rightly say, removes most of the Zohar imbroglio:[69] but if the second edition, which had the poet's sanction and definitely supersedes the 1st, is different, I don't think I shd. feel justified in silencing it. And yet I don't know – your interpretation makes such excellent sense,

Yours sincerely
C. S. Lewis

---

65 Virgil, *Aeneid*, II, 322: 'Where is the crisis?' Aeneas is frantically running around Troy as it burns; he meets Panthus, a priest of Apollo on the citadel, and asks this question.

66 The D-Day landings in France by the Allied forces had taken place, after various delays, on 6 June. Despite fierce German resistance, British, Canadian and American forces succeeded in securing the beachhead by the following day, and the great invasion of Europe was by now well under way.

67 Mr G. D. Gillies was writing from 38a Alexandra Grove, Finchley, London N12.

68 Lewis was probably referring to John Milton, *Poetical Works*, ed. Rev. H. C. Beeching (Oxford: Clarendon Press, 1900).

69 See note 108 to the letter of 17? May 1943.

On 3 October Dr R. S. Lee, Overseas Religious Broadcasting Organizer for the BBC, informed Lewis that the Director of Religious Broadcasting in Australia was interested in having Lewis do a series of talks for them. The BBC had not recorded all his talks, and as the published talks were not available in Australia, Dr Lee asked, 'I wonder whether you will be willing to contemplate doing such another series, and starting it say in about six weeks time. . . . You need not break fresh ground but cover some of the ground you have already been over.'[70]

TO ROY LEE (BBC):[71] TS

REF.214/44.

Magdalen College,
Oxford.
6th October 1944

Dear Mr Lee,

Thank you for your 03/RB/RSL of the 3rd October: –

It would be rather difficult to give a series covering old ground, as all my previous talks have been published in book form: I could not make them *sound* like fresh talks. On the other hand, six weeks notice is not nearly long enough notice for preparing anything new. If you could give me six months, I'd try something. But I daresay this hardly meets your requirements.

Yours sincerely,
C. S. Lewis

Beyond Personality: The Christian Idea of God *was published by Geoffrey Bles: The Centenary Press on 9 October 1944.*

* * *

---

70 Phillips, *C. S. Lewis at the BBC*, p. 262.

71 The Rev. Roy Stuart Lee (1899–1981) was born in Stuart Town, New South Wales, Australia, the son of Kum Sing Lee. He took a BA from the University of Sydney in 1920, and read Theology at the Australian College of Theology. Lee moved to England where, in 1923, he was ordained a priest for the diocese of Bath. After serving as Curate of Forbes, 1922–4, he took a B.Litt. from University College, Oxford, in 1927 and a D.Phil. in 1947. Lee was Vice-Warden of St John's College, Morpeth, Northumberland, 1928–38. While Curate of St Martin in the Fields, London, 1938–47, he spent 1944–7 as Overseas Religious Broadcasting Organizer for the BBC. On leaving the BBC, Lee was Vicar of St Mary the Virgin, Oxford, 1947–61. During this time he did a great deal of pastoral counselling. He was Fellow and Chaplain of St Catherine's College, Oxford, 1961–9. His books include *Freud and Christianity* (1948) and *Principles of Pastoral Counselling* (1968).

Dr Lee had replied to Lewis on 7 October suggesting that he repeat the same talks he had already given for listeners in Australia, and he continued:

> *I would be very pleased indeed to have a new series from you in six months' time, and may I close with that offer now. It would fit in most conveniently if you could begin a series of talks on the Sunday after Easter, that would be April 8th, 1945, which is the six months you asked for.*[72]

However, before Lewis could reply, Dr Lee wrote again on 11 October:

> *Since I wrote to you the other day I have had a cable from the Australian Broadcasting Commission saying that they would appreciate a repetition of your series on Christian Behaviour, which they would record for rebroadcast on the National Stations. I wonder if you would be willing to record the talks for us as you gave them originally, so that we can satisfy their request. I very much hope that you will do them, and be ready to give the first one on November 19th. You can record them all at your leisure in London before that date. When you gave them originally they filled a ten minutes space, but if you desired to make any short additions we can let you have up to thirteen minutes for the talks.*[73]

TO ROY LEE (BBC): TS

REF.214/44.

Magdalen College,
Oxford.
13th October 1944.

Dear Mr. Lee,

I am sorry, but I hardly feel I could give again as Talks what already exists as a printed book – even if my publisher would agree I certainly could'nt do it with any conviction. It is true that most listeners would not have read the book: but some would have, and I think they'd feel a trick had been played on them. It might damage my future utility.

I'm still chewing over the other (1945) proposal.

yours sincerely,
C. S. Lewis

---

72 Phillips, *C. S. Lewis at the BBC*, p. 263.
73 BBC Written Archives Centre.

TO SISTER PENELOPE CSMV (BOD):

Magdalen College,
Oxford.
Oct 21st 1944

Dear Sister Penelope

I meant to send you this before and hope you haven't got it already.[74]

Poor 'Muriel', she got odder and odder and the doctors wd. have put her into an asylum if Jane and I hadn't refused to sign a form. She has now left, and had an operation, and got a job elsewhere. I hope the crisis is tided over. I am almost *sorrier* for her than anyone I have known, because, even if insanity is avoided, the temperament seems one that almost precludes any happiness in this world. And the more one tried to be nice the more complications one seemed to introduce. So we must pray for her always

Yours sincerely
C. S. Lewis

Roy Lee, undeterred by Lewis's previous replies, wrote to him again on 16 October saying he understood his reasons for not wanting to do the old broadcasts again. But he added that the Australian people would be 'disappointed, but it will mitigate their disappointment if I can promise them in the near future a new series of talks from you'.[75]

TO ROY LEE (BBC): TS

REF.214/44.

Magdalen College,
Oxford.
23rd October 1944

(Your 03/RB/RSL,
d.16/10/44).

Dear Mr. Lee,

I hope you won't think that I've simply been wasting time. The idea of a new series for next spring has been before my mind almost daily. After many changes of purpose I have decided not to do it. On previous occasions I have always found, when the proposal came, that

---

74 Lewis enclosed a copy of *Beyond Personality*.

75 Phillips, *C. S. Lewis at the BBC*, p. 264.

I had something suitable for saying in that form, which I wanted to say. This time I don't. And I think you will agree that all success depends on not pumping something up – it must come of its own accord.

If and when I feel I've got a new head of that particular kind of steam, I'll write to Fenn.

I'm sorry you should have been kept waiting.

yours sincerely,
C. S. Lewis

TO CHARLES A. BRADY (W):[76]

Magdalen College,
Oxford.
Oct 29th 1944.

Dear Mr Brady –

Obviously one ought never to thank a critic for praise: but perhaps one can congratulate a fellow scholar on the thoroughness of his work even if the subject of his work happen to be oneself. You are the first of my critics so far who has really read and understood *all* my books and 'made up' the subject in a way that makes you an authority. The results interest me of course because they flatter my vanity as an author.

But there's also an interest of another kind. Here is a man trying to do what all of our profession do, and by the same methods, in the one case where I happen to know already the answers to most of the questions: surely an ideal opportunity for learning something about the efficiency of the methods themselves! The result is encouraging. I have always been haunted by the fear that all our studies of the dead authors (who can't up and protest when we go wrong) may, in spite of careful documentation etc, be quite wide of the mark: on the whole you set that at rest. The *Quellenforschung*[77] is good.

Morris and Macdonald were more or less given you (Morris is more important than you suggest, I think) I admit, but you are the first to stress them properly. On the Tir-na'n-og element, you hit the bull and

76 Charles Andrew Brady (1912–), Professor of English at Canisius College, Buffalo, New York, had sent Lewis two articles entitled 'Introduction to Lewis' and 'C. S. Lewis II' published in the Jesuit periodical, *America*, 71 (27 May and 10 June 1944).

77 'investigation of sources'.

might even have deduced much reading of the early Yeats (worth twenty of the reconditioned 1920 model) and of James Stephens.[78]

Space-and-time fiction: but oddly enough not Rice-Burroughs. But this is probably a mere chance and the guess was a sound one. The real father of my planet books is David Lindsay's *Voyage to Arcturus*, which you also will revel in if you don't know it. I had grown up on Well's stories of that kind: it was Lindsay who first gave me the idea that the 'scientifiction' appeal could be combined with the 'supernatural' appeal – suggested the 'Cross' (in biological sense). His own spiritual outlook is detestable, almost diabolist I think, and his style crude: but he showed me what a bang you cd. get from mixing these two elements. R. H. Benson is wrong: at least I think the *Dawn of All*[79] (the only one I can remember having read) never meant much to me. Chesterton, of course: but more, I think, on thought than on imagination. Rackham, yes: but having mentioned him you just missed tapping my whole Norse complex – Old Icelandic, Wagner's *Ring* and (again) Morris. The Wagner is important: you will see, if you look, how *operatic* the whole building up of the climax is in *Perelandra*. Milton I think you possibly over-rate: it is difficult to distinguish him from Dante & St Augustine. (Tinidril at her second appearance owes something to Matilda at the end of *Purgatorio*).[80]

When you talk about meetings of human races in connexion with Ransom and the Hrossa you say something that was not in my mind at all. So much the better: a book's not worth writing unless it suggests more than the author intended.

The only place where, as it seems to me, your work contains a *warning* for us all is the bit based on the portrait. The whole thing depends upon the portrait's being a good one. In fact it was drawn from a photo by a man who never saw me and, I'm told, is only just recognisable. Memo: let us both remember this the next time we're writing about the 17th century or [an] Elizabethan author and feel inclined to base anything on his portrait! It may not have been at all like him. (Why do we continue to assume that all portrait painters in the past were

78 The literal translation of 'Tir-nan-Og' (from Irish Gaelic) is 'Land of the Young', i.e. the afterlife. Many of Lewis's ideas on this came from W. B. Yeats's *The Wanderings of Oisin and Other Poems* (1889) and James Stephens' *The Crock of Gold* (1912).

79 Robert Hugh Benson, *The Dawn of All* (1911).

80 Dante, *Purgatorio*, XXVIII.

faithful tho' experience in the present tell us that it is the rarest thing for even a good painter to produce a real likeness?)

Tolkien (and Charles Williams, whom I wish you'd do, specially his novels) is most important. *The Hobbit* is merely the *adaptation to children* of part of a huge private mythology of a most serious kind: the whole cosmic struggle as he sees it but mediated through an imaginary world. The Hobbit's successor, which will soon be finished, will reveal this more clearly. Private worlds have hitherto been mainly the work of decadents or, at least, mere aesthetes. This is the private world of a Christian. He is a very great man. His published works (both imaginative & scholarly) ought to fill a shelf by now: but he's one of those people who is never satisfied with a MS. The mere suggestion of publication provokes the reply 'Yes, I'll just look through it and give it a few finishing touches' – wh. means that he really begins the whole thing over again.

I have now had an orgy of talking about myself. But let me congratulate you again on your very thorough and perceptive piece of work. I need not, perhaps, add that if you ever come here our little circle will make a red letter day of it. (By the way, port is usually drunk in *common room*, whereas *oaks* are *sported* in one's own private rooms! But we'll arrange port behind a sported oak for you if you like – though indeed beer and/or tea is our more usual fare). Tell me about yourself if you reply: I'm quite ignorant of modern American letters.

Yours sincerely
C. S. Lewis

TO MR LYELL (T):

Magdalen College,
Oxford.
Dec 6th 1944

Dear Mr. Lyell,

(1) By handing over the natural self to Christ I mean placing it under His orders and trying to will with His will. If a man does that He will usually find that one of the things Christ wills is for him to eat, drink, sleep etc. Not always, but usually. You can't tell in advance what He will tell any man to do about the natural appetites. He may tell one man to be very austere, another to be kinder to the flesh than he has been hitherto.

(2) You are quite right. There wd. be no 'progress' if everyone were living in the Spirit: at least in some senses of the word 'progress'. There might continue to be progress in arts & sciences – why not? But social and economic progress wd. cease, I expect, because all those problems wd. solve themselves in the first year or so. Progress means getting nearer to a desired goal and therefore means not being there already. You don't want the London train to go on progressing after it reached London!

(3) The natural self since the Fall consists of body, soul, & spirit all perverted & self centred and at odds with one another. Animalness (the body & what arises from it) is not in itself bad: what is bad is the rebellious *relation* in wh. it now stands to the other parts. But its rebellion against spirit is less terrible than spirit's rebellion against God.

(4) By central self or spirit I mean chiefly the Will – the ultimate choosing part. It changes itself by its own actions. By *soul* I mean chiefly the imagination & emotions. N.T. does not use a consistent technical vocabulary. For instance in 'Soul take thine ease etc'[81] the passage simply means 'Says I to myself'. I hope this is a bit clearer: but a systematic exposition wd. have to go far beyond the limits of a letter.

Yours sincerely
C. S. Lewis

TO BERNARD ACWORTH (W):[82]

REF.34/44.

Magdalen College,
Oxford.
9th December 1944.

Dear Captain Acworth,

Thanks for your interesting letter of the 8th: – I can't have made

81 Luke 12:19.

82 Captain Bernard Acworth (1885–1963) was the founder and president emeritus of the Evolution Protest Movement. After leaving the Royal Naval College at Greenwich, he served for eighteen years in submarines and commanded the anti-submarine flotilla. Following this, he spent four years in the Torpedo Division of the Naval Staff and was closely associated with the original development of ASDIC, the sonar system for submarine detection. He was naval correspondent for a number of newspapers. His publications include *Navies To-day and To-morrow* (1931), *The Restoration of England's Sea Power* (1936) and *How the War Will be Won* (1940).

my position clear. I am not either attacking or defending Evolution. I believe that Christianity can still be believed, even if Evolution is true. That is where you and I differ. Thinking as I do, I can't help regarding your advice (that I henceforth include arguments against Evolution in all my Christian apologetics) as a temptation to fight the battle on what is really a false issue: and also on *terrain* very unsuitable for the only weapon I have. Atheism is as old as Epicurus, and very few polytheists regard their gods as *creative*. When do you think of coming to see us again? All good wishes.

yours sincerely,
C. S. Lewis

In a letter of 11 December, Dr Lee said, 'I am trying to draw up a schedule of six talks for broadcast on the Sundays during Lent in our Pacific, African, North American and General Overseas Services. At the risk of appearing to pester you, I am writing now to ask whether you would possibly feel inclined to undertake to do all these talks.'[83]

TO ROY LEE (BBC): TS

REF.214/44.

Magdalen College,
Oxford.
15th December 1944.

Dear Mr. Lee,

Thanks for your letter 03/RB/RSL of the 11th: –

No, I think you had better wait until I produce a scheme of my own. The one you present is good in itself, but it is *yours*, and I could'nt do my best work within it. It also overlaps too much with talks I have given already.

yours sincerely,
C. S. Lewis

83 Phillips, *C. S. Lewis at the BBC*, p. 266.

TO LAURENCE HARWOOD (BOD):[84]

[The Kilns
22? December 1944]

My dear Lawrence,

Thank you very much for writing me such a nice Xmas letter. It is very cold here too but I have not got so many colds as usual this year. I think it is because I have got a pair of very thick corduroy trousers, so thick they make me look like a Dutchman or a sailor.

I live in a College here: a college is something rather like a castle and also like a church. It stands just beside a bridge over a river. At the back of the part I live in there is a nice grove of Trees. There are a lot of Rabbits there. One very old rabbit is so tame that it will run after me and take things out of my hand. I call her Baroness Bisket because she is a kind of biscuit colour. There are also stags and deer. The stags – I can't draw them because their horns, which are called

ANTLERS, are so hard to draw – often fight at night and if I lie awake I hear the noise (*click-click* it goes) of their horns tapping together.

So here I sit all day long writing books and setting examination papers and answering letters. Sometimes we kill a deer to eat, the meat is called VENISON. Tell Daddy it is unrationed and I got a great big helping smoking hot the other night – I did enjoy myself but I wished he'd been there.

I'm writing a story with a Bear in it[85] and at present the Bear is going to get married in the last chapter. There are also Angels in it. But sometimes I don't think it is going to be very good.

I'm sorry you don't like cold weather. I do, I love to see the frost all like sugar on the grass and when it makes the fire burn bright. I'm sending you something in this to get a Xmas box with. Well a very happy Xmas and lots of love to Mark, Sylvia, Lois, John, Mummy, Daddy and yourself

from your loving Godfather

Jack Lewis ★ ★ ★ ★ ★ ★ ★ ★

84 See **Laurence Hardy Harwood** in the Biographical Appendix.

85 i.e. *That Hideous Strength.*

1945

TO SISTER PENELOPE CSMV (BOD):

Magdalen
Jan 3d. 1945

Dear Sister Penelope

I am most disappointed to hear that your series of plays will not be given on the air. Indeed it would be difficult to express my full feeling on the subject without seeming actively to *tempt* you to those very emotions which, no doubt, you are in process of successfully knocking on the head! (This is, by the bye, a very ticklish business in social life, isn't it? At least I often catch myself in a moment of sympathy, or vicarious indignation, encouraging in others the passions which, were their case mine, I shd. know it was my business to mortify). O.U.P. *is* separate from Clarendon Press and you should write to Charles Williams, O.U.P., Southfield House, Southfield Rd., Oxford.

I am glad to hear you are going to do another translation. That 17th. century Greek is frightful, isn't it? I have more than once worked out all the contractions and made a list of them but each time I have lost it.

Yes, I *have* written a story called *That Hideous Strength* wh. concludes the Ransom trilogy and which ought to appear about June: but it has no connection whatever with *Who Goes Home*.[1]

I am glad and grateful to hear about Miss Westmacott. Jane is no worse in body: in mind and spirits sometimes very bad, sometimes better. Pray for us always, we are not a very happy house. More and more I am driven to realise what it says in *The Imitation* 'Si vis alios

1 Lewis was referring to his new work, 'Who Goes Home? Or The Grand Divorce', published in *The Guardian* in weekly parts from 10 November 1944 to 13 April 1945. It was published in book form as *The Great Divorce* (1945 [1946]).

pacificare, habe pacem in te ipso'[2] and how I fail to carry it out. All best wishes to yourself and my other friends at Wantage for 1945.

Yours sincerely
C. S. Lewis

After being at The Kilns for about two years, performing innumerable tasks as well as looking after Mrs Moore, Jill Flewett had won the love of everyone there. Now she was leaving to take up her place at the Royal Academy of Dramatic Art. On 2 January Warnie wrote in his diary: 'Our dear, delightful June Flewett leaves us tomorrow, after nearly two years . . . She is not yet eighteen, but I have met no one of my age further advanced in the Christian way of life . . . From a personal selfish point of view I shall feel the loss of June very keenly . . .'[3]

And June wrote of the letter that follows: 'I had to retake the entrance audition to RADA because I had put off my place for so long in order to stay at The Kilns. Unfortunately, on the day, I was still recovering from a tooth abscess in a front tooth, an extraction and a temporary plate – not ideal for an aspiring but inexperienced actress. This particular letter was a well treasured possession.'[4]

TO WINIFRED FLEWETT (T):

The Kilns.
Jan 4th 1945

Dear Mrs. Flewett

Oh what a sad waking up this morning when we realised that June was gone! – but I try to comfort myself by realising that there was a correspondingly happy waking in your house and thinking how long you and she had waited for it and how you deserve it. This is really just a covering letter (as one might say, 'Daughter enclosed') and to try, once again, to express some part of our great gratitude. I have never really met anything like her unselfishness and patience and kindness and shall feel deeply in her debt as long as I live.

It is sickening that the dental trouble should have come just at this

2 Thomas à Kempis, *The Imitation of Christ*, Book II, ch. 3: 'If you wish to pacify others, have peace in yourself!'

3 *BF*, pp. 180–1.

4 Letter to Walter Hooper of 27 January 2003.

time. I gave her a letter for the examiners on this point not because I thought I cd. write a better one than Mr Flewett (!) but because I cd. speak at first hand. She herself doesn't like the idea of using anything that seems like an excuse. I think she is wrong but have an open mind. Mr Flewett knows all about examiners and can give a better opinion than any of us.

Tell June that the Hens were asking for her first thing this morning: that Warnie is even more depressed than usual: and that the cats, under this shared calamity, sank their common differences and slept, mutually embracing, in the same box.

We shall all be on tenter hooks till we hear the result of the exam and will be thinking of her hard to morrow afternoon. Mrs Moore sends her love to June and you with best wishes for the year and hopes that you will soon have good news of your daughter in Egypt.

We are the ghost and ruin of a house . . . Ichabod, Ichabod![5] God bless her (indeed that is just what I keep on telling Him)

Yours sincerely
C. S. Lewis

Maureen Blake gave birth to a son, Richard Francis, on 8 January 1945. Lewis became his godfather.

TO JILL FLEWETT (T):

Magdalen College,
Oxford.
Jan 13th 45

My dear June –

I return the 'literature'.[6] You must know that it is the sort of thing I seldom understand. Miss Anderson, the college secretary, always explains such documents to me here: the idea of anyone sending them to *me* for illuminating comment wd. rouse laughter in Magdalen!

I was interested in your journey to the exam accompanied (in the true style of Livy) by portents: but sorry it was only a clairvoyant. A

5 Cf. 1 Samuel 4:21–2: 'And she named the child Ichabod, saying, The glory is departed from Israel: because the ark of God was taken: and because of her father in law and her husband. And she said, The glory is departed from Israel: for the ark of God is taken.'

6 Jill Flewett had sent Lewis some information about the courses she would be taking.

talking ox or an eagle pursuing five swans on your right as you arrived at RADA wd. have been more fitting.

On my return journey from Rochester two minor portents occurred, one of them v. bad. (1) The pipe you gave me – wh. was just in the bloom of its early maturity, and becoming a pipe fit for Bacchus (or 'Baccus') himself – snapped in two as I was knocking it out. I am desolated.

(2) Humphrey,[7] whom I had met at Paddington, began near Slough to explain to me as much as he understood of Einstein. At Reading everyone else got out and we had the compartment to ourselves for the rest of the way to Oxford. (Of course it *may* have been a coincidence).

I rather liked your syllabus so far as I understood it: but was puzzled by history of drama in the Anglo Saxon period. I shd. have thought that was as briefly and easily learned as the Snakes in Iceland. (You know that story?)[8]

News? Oh, you can guess it all. Bruce is wet, the potatoes are over/under done, Warnie has found some v. sinister bits in the papers and Leonard B.[9] keeps up his appetite wonderfully. The *far* hens have come down to one egg a day, but the *near* ones have gone up to four.

Have you got into the flat yet? And how is your sister? Remember us in your prayers. Love from all.

Yours
Jack

7 Dr Robert 'Humphrey' Havard had since 1943 been serving in the Royal Navy as a medical officer.

8 Boswell, *The Life of Samuel Johnson*, vol. III, 13 April 1778, p. 279: 'Langton said to me afterwards, that he could repeat Johnson's conversation before dinner, as Johnson had said that he could repeat a complete chapter of "The Natural History of Iceland," from the Danish of *Harrebow*, the whole of which was exactly thus: Chap. LXXII. *Concerning snakes*. "There are no snakes to be met with throughout the whole island." '

9 i.e. Leonard Blake.

TO MARGARET FULLER (W):[10] TS

REF.38/1/45.

Magdalen College,
Oxford.
20th January 1945.

Dear Miss Fuller,

Thank you very much for your kind and encouraging letter of 10th December: –

The bit about 'Music and Silence' is from the 'Unspoken Sermons' of George Macdonald[11] – his children's books ('The Princess and the Goblins' 'Curdie and the Princess'[12] etc.) are in your list I hope. He is absolutely first class.

yours sincerely,
C. S. Lewis

TO ARTHUR GREEVES (W):

Magdalen College,
Oxford.
Feb 5 1945

My dear Arthur

Your position, as re-stated in your last letter, is one I entirely agree with. What puzzles me is that you originally brought it forward as a disagreement with my *Beyond Personality*. As about half of that book is taken up with the very doctrine you are now arguing (viz: that all men can become sons of God) I am completely bewildered! I must be a less lucid writer than I thought.

---

10 Margaret Fuller was writing from 235 East 50th Street, Apartment 66, New York City.

11 Fuller had probably asked about the derision of Music and Silence in *The Screwtape Letters*, Letter 22: 'Music and silence – how I detest them both! How thankful we should be that ever since our Father entered Hell . . . no square inch of infernal space and no moment of infernal time has been surrendered to either of those abominable forces.' The inspiration came from George MacDonald, *Unspoken Sermons*, First Series, 'The Hands of the Father', pp. 187–8: 'Nor shall we ever know that repose in the Father's hands, that rest of the Holy Sepulchre, which the Lord knew when the agony of death was over, when the storm of the world died away behind his retiring spirit, and he entered the regions where there is only life, and therefore all that is not music is silence, (for all noise comes of the conflict of Life and Death).'

12 George MacDonald, *The Princess and the Goblin* (1871); *The Princess and Curdie* (1882).

About too much 'emphasis on material things', if you mean on 'What shall we eat and drink and wherewithal shall we be clothed,'[13] I agree. But if you mean sacramentalism, I don't think I do. Isn't Xtianity separated from the other religions just by the fact that it does *not* allow one to exclude or reject *matter*? But the whole question is too big to go into by letter.

I've re-read *Shirley*[14] for the first time almost. In one way C. Bronte seems to me a worse novelist than one wd. have thought possible: such preposterous dialogue, such tawdry rhetoric, such ridiculous devices (like L. Moore's notebook!) and such false scents – all the scenes in the Yorke family lead nowhere. Yet through it all the character of Shirley herself triumphs.

Things are a bit better with us, after an orgy of frozen pipes etc. Some of the beauties not so much of the snow as of the heavy frost wh. preceded it were exquisite. But as you say we are all almost perilously fortunate by modern European standards.

I am hoping for proofs of the new novel, the one dedicated to Janie,[15] any day now and shall be interested to see what you think of it. I have also finished the book on Miracles wh. I've been working at for 'several years'.

It is bitter cold this morning but lovely to see the green earth after all the snow and to hear the birds singing. I have just seen the first celandines in Addison's Walk.

I long to meet again. I imagine each will find the other so *old*-looking as to be almost unrecognisable. God bless you.

Yours
Jack

TO I. O. EVANS (W):

Feb 7th 1945
Magdalen College,
Oxford.

Dear Mr. Evans

Thank you very much for *Gadget City*.[16] I have read it with great

---

13 Matthew 6:31.

14 Charlotte Brontë, *Shirley* (1849).

15 *That Hideous Strength* is dedicated to Jane McNeill.

16 I. O. Evans, *Gadget City: A Story of Ancient Alexandria* (1944).

interest and think it highly original. The gadgets themselves are not very much in my line (I can just about understand the common push-byke and no more) but boys will love them and get a good moral and a lot of knowledge into the bargain. It ought to have a great success.

I am sorry I failed to acknowledge *Woodcraft*[17] wh. reached me alright. I now do so with thanks and apologies. Wishing you all good things.

Yours sincerely
C. S. Lewis

TO MR MCCLAIN (W): TS

REF.119/1/45.

Magdalen College,
Oxford.
7th March 1945.

Dear Mr. McClain,

I always answer fan-mail: not that courtesy and charity do not often sleep, but gratified vanity speaks in their place when they do.

(1). I know no more about publishers than you do about American Radio. I enclose 'Beyond Personality', but have no copy of 'Broadcast Talks'.

(2). I'm afraid a tour in America is out of the question at present, as I have a very old invalid mother to look after and can't be away from home for more than a few days at a time. I'd be glad if you would circulate this to all who are interested, for my continued refusal of offers from U.S.A. is beginning to be given sinister interpretations.

Thanks very much for writing at all. I've an idea that the Dictionary of Illustrations would be fun to do, but would turn out unreadable when one had done it – like all the curry powder extracted from a curry and eaten separately! All good wishes.

yours sincerely,
C. S. Lewis

17 I. O. Evans, *Woodcraft and World Service: Studies in Unorthodox Education. An Account of the Evolution of the Woodcraft Movements* (1930).

TO MARGARET LANDON (W):[18] TS

REF.168/45.

Magdalen College,
Oxford.
April 20th 1945

Dear Mrs. Landon,

Very many thanks indeed for the gift of your 'Anna and the King of Siam'. It kept me reading last night long after I ought to have been asleep. It is fascinating – both in the popular sense that one can't stop reading it, and also in the old sense that it exercises a real snake-like *fascination*. Ugh! that palace is like an opium dream of twenty late Gothic cathedrals all tied together in a tangle and then consecrated to devil-worship.

Do you know G. K. Chesterton's poem 'The Crusader's Return'?[19] He might have been reading your book before he wrote it. I never fully realized what a harem meant before: all those moons, and one dreadful sun, like a horrible parody of a nunnery. And yet the real revelation is the beauties of character which apparently existed among these 'forbidden women'. That sets one thinking. But I must hasten to end before King Mongkut's epistolatory style begins to affect mine – which I feel might happen at any moment.

With many thanks for a real treat, and all good wishes,

yours sincerely,

C. S. Lewis

TO MICHAEL THWAITES (P):[20]

Magdalen College,
Oxford.
April 22nd 1945

Dear Mr Thwaites –

I have just re-discovered your letter among some others which, because they arrived as I was just going to catch a train, were put aside

18 Margaret Landon (1903–93), author of *Anna and the King of Siam* (1945). A friend of hers had asked her to sign a copy for Lewis, and this is his response.

19 G. K. Chesterton, *Collected Poems* (1927), 'The Crusader Returns from Captivity'.

20 Michael Rayner Thwaites (1915–), Rhodes Scholar from Victoria, Australia, was educated at Geelong Grammar School and the University of Melbourne. He matriculated at New College, Oxford, in 1937. While there he won the Newdigate Prize in 1938 and the King's Medal for Poetry in 1940. After taking his BA in 1939

'in a safe place' to be answered when I got back, and were (of course) overlooked. I apologise heartily.

A man who has already your linguistic training might well, I think, begin the Anglo Saxon on his own. You will need E. Wardale *Old English Grammar*.[21] After mastering the alphabet begin with the Accidence (chap 7–10) and go back to the earlier chapters on sound-laws as the references in the Accidence send you back to them for explanation of apparent irregularities.

For texts, the ordinary beginning is first Sweet's *Anglo Saxon Primer*[22] and then his *Old English Reader*.[23] But you, being a classic might well, after a dip in the Primer go on to King Alfred's trans. of Boethius *De Consolatione Philosophiae* (ed. Sedgefield, Clarendon Press).[24] Aided by the original Latin (wh. is done in the Loeb library) you will be able to hammer this out: and it will have the added advantage of making you familiar with one of *the* great European books. (*Verbum* sap.[25] Boethius, with the Vulgate, Virgil, and Ovid *Metamorphoses* are books you cannot read & re-read too often. All medieval vernacular literature is soaked in them).

Whether you can begin O.E.[26] poetry on your own I don't know. But try getting Klaeber's[27] or Chamber's ed. of *Beowulf*:[28] and with it

---

he served in the Royal Naval Volunteer Reserve, 1939–45. He returned to New College in 1946 and took a B.Litt. degree. Thwaites afterwards lectured in the University of Melbourne, 1947–9. He was a branch director of the Australian Security Intelligence Organization (ASIO), 1950–71, and the Assistant Parliamentary Librarian, Canberra, 1971–83. He became an honorary lay canon of St Saviour Cathedral (Goldburn) in 2000. His numerous works include his Newdigate Prize poem, *Milton Blind* (1938), *The Jervis Bay and Other Poems* (1942), *Poems of War and Peace* (1968), *Truth Will Out – ASIO and the Petovs* (1980) and *The Honey Man* (1994).

21 Edith Elizabeth Wardale, *An Old English Grammar* (1922).

22 Henry Sweet, *An Anglo-Saxon Primer* (1882).

23 Henry Sweet, *An Anglo-Saxon Reader* (1876).

24 *King Alfred's Old English version of Boethius De Consolatione Philosophiae*, ed. from the MSS., with introduction., notes, and glossary, by W. J. Sedgefield (Oxford: Clarendon Press, 1899).

25 *Verbum sat sapienti est*: 'A word to the wise is sufficient.'

26 i.e. Old English.

27 *Beowulf and The fight at Finnsburg*, ed. with introduction, bibliography, notes, glossary and appendices, by Friedrich Klaeber (1922).

28 *Beowulf: With the Finnsburg Fragment*, ed. A. J. Wyatt, new edn, rev. with introduction and notes by R. W. Chambers (1943).

Clark Hall's trans. ed. by Wrenn with preface by Tolkien (Allen & Unwin, 1940).[29] This edition is essential for it is Tolkien's part of *metre* wh. is essential. (O.E. verse uses both quality and accent, and your ear is prob. ruined, as mine was, by the false way they teach Latin metre at schools – drastic re-education is required. You were prob. never taught to pronounce the double l in *ille* like the double l in *palely*. It matters enormously).

As to modern literature. You must *not* start out to study it 'as it reveals man's hesitant advance to the idea of a God-created world'. Don't you see you are laying down in advance what a phenomenon is to reveal *before* you have examined the phenomenon? It may reveal that: it may not. You have to *find out*.

I don't think I can lay down any v. definite course of reading. All I can point out is that while you are in the navy and out of reach of libraries and new publications, this is the proper time for solid reading through the big (i.e. long) authors, critical works and histories of lit. can come later. Now is the time for Chaucer, Malory, Spenser, Sidney, Shakespeare, Dryden, Pope, Swift, Johnson, Fielding, Richardson, Cowper, Scott, Wordsworth, Byron, Dickens etc etc.

If you usually keep two books of widely different period and type going together (e.g. *Faerie Queene* & *Tom Jones*) you won't get bored. I myself always index a good book when I read it for the first time noting (a) Linguistic phenomena. (b) Good & bad passages. (c) Customs: meal times, social classes, what they read etc. (d) Moral ideas.

All this reading, tho' dedicated *ad Dei gloriam*[30] in the long run must not be infected by any immediate theological, ethical, or philosophic reference. Your *first* job is simply the *reception* of all this work with your imagination & emotions. Each book is to be read for the purpose the author meant it to be read for: the story *as* a story, the joke *as* a joke. (If you want any explicitly religious reading this can also be made part of your English reading. Read *The Scale of Perfection* (Walter Hilton. Burnes Oates & Washbourne in the *Orchard Books*) Lady Julian *Revelations of Divine Love* (Methuen), Hooker, Thos. Browne, Herbert,

---

29 John R. Clark Hall, *Beowulf and the Finnesburg Fragment: A Translation into Modern English Prose*, new edn, rev. with notes and introduction by C. L. Wrenn; with prefatory remarks by J. R. R. Tolkien (London: Allen & Unwin, 1940).

30 'to the glory of God'.

Traherne (*Centuries of Meditations*) Bunyan, Wm. Law (*Serious Call*), Butler's *Sermons*.[31]

Forgive the handwriting – I have a touch of rheumatism in my right wrist. All good wishes. Be sure and let me know if I can be of any use.

Yours sincerely
C. S. Lewis

TO DR WARFIELD M. FIROR (BOD):[32]

REF.170/1/45.

Magdalen College,
Oxford.
23rd. April 1945.

Dear Mr. Firor,

Thank you for your very kind and encouraging letter: – Family reasons make it impossible for me to plan anything on so large a scale as a visit to America at present – much as I should like to visit a country where 'Perelandra' (my own favourite) seems to be so much more popular than in England. With all good wishes,

yours sincerely,
C. S. Lewis

TO H. LYMAN STEBBINS (BOD):[33]

May 8th 1945
Magdalen College,
Oxford.

Dear Mr. Stebbing –

My position about the Churches can best be made plain by an imaginary example. Suppose I want to find out the correct interpretation

---

31 Joseph Butler (1692–1752), *Fifteen Sermons* (1726).

32 See **Dr Warfield Monroe Firor** in the Biographical Appendix. Firor had invited Lewis to his Wyoming ranch for a holiday.

33 Hart Lyman Stebbins (1911–89) was born in New York City and brought up in the Episcopal Church. After graduating from Yale University in 1933, where he read English, he became an investment specialist. He had been considering the claims of Catholicism, and on 20 April 1945 he wrote to Lewis: 'I would not dare ask you to write to me what you consider to be the arguments which throw the decision to the Anglican and against the Roman Catholic Church. But I do dare ask you if you would do me the great favour of recommending the books which, in your opinion, present these arguments most persuasively' (H. Lyman Stebbins, 'The Boldness of a Stranger', *Laywitness*, 19 (November 1998), p. 7). Lewis responded with the present letter. In the end Stebbins was received into the Catholic Church on 28 May 1946. In 1968 he

of Plato's teaching. What I am most confident in accepting is that interpretation wh. is common to all the Platonists down all the centuries: what Aristotle and the Renaissance scholars and Paul Elmer More agree on I take to be true Platonism. Any purely modern views wh. claim to have discovered for the first time what P. meant, and say that everyone from Aristotle down has misunderstood him, I reject out of hand.

But there is something else I wd. also reject. If there were an ancient Platonic Society still existing at Athens and claiming to be the exclusive trustees of P's meaning, I shd. approach them with great respect. But if I found that their teaching in many ways was curiously unlike his actual text and unlike what ancient interpreters said, and in some cases cd. not be traced back to within 1000 years of his time, I shd. reject these exclusive claims: while still ready, of course, to take any particular thing they taught on its merits.

I do the same with Xtianity. What is most certain is the vast mass of doctrine wh. I find agreed on by Scripture, the Fathers, the Middle Ages, modern R.C.'s, modern Protestants. That is true 'catholic' doctrine. Mere 'modernism' I reject at once.

The Roman Church where it differs from this universal tradition and specially from apostolic Xtianity I reject. Thus their theology about the B.V.M.[34] I reject because it seems utterly foreign to the New Testament: where indeed the words 'Blessed is the womb that bore thee'[35] receive a rejoinder pointing in exactly the opposite direction. Their papalism seems equally foreign to the attitude of St Paul towards St Peter in the Epistles. The doctrine of Transubstantiation insists in defining in a way wh. the N.T. seems to me not to countenance.[36] In a word, the whole

---

founded 'Catholics United for the Faith'. His wife, Madeleine Stebbins, has told the story of her husband's conversion in '50th Anniversary of the Conversion of Our Founder', *Laywitness*, 17 (May 1996), pp. 13–15.

34 i.e the Blessed Virgin Mary.

35 Luke 11:27–8 (Revised Standard Version): 'As he said this, a woman in the crowd raised her voice and said to him, "Blessed is the womb that bore thee, and the breasts that you sucked! But he said, "Yea rather, blessed are they that hear the word of God, and keep it."' Cf. Luke 1:28, 42. Lewis was criticizing the second part of the prayer known as the 'Hail Mary' which in its modern form is: 'Blessed art thou among women, and blessed is the fruit of thy womb, Jesus./Holy Mary, Mother of God, pray for us sinners now and in the hour of our death.'

36 Transubstantiation involves the conversion in the Eucharist of the whole substance of the bread into the Body of Christ and of the wine into the Blood of Christ – only the appearances of the bread and wine remaining. In *Letters to Malcolm*, ch.

set-up of modern Romanism seems to me to be as much a provincial or local *variation* from the central, ancient tradition as any particular Protestant sect is. I must therefore reject their *claim*: tho' this does not mean rejecting particular things they say.

I'm afraid I haven't read any modern books of Roman–Anglican controversy. Hooker (*Laws of Ecclesiastical Polity*) is to me the great formulation of Anglicanism. But the great point is that in one sense there's no such thing as Anglicanism. What we are committed to believing is whatever can be proved from Scripture. On that subject there is room for endless progress. However you decide, good wishes. Mention me in your prayers.

Yours sincerely
C. S. Lewis

By April 1945 the German army was shattered. American and Soviet forces met at the Elbe River on 25 April, and on 30 April Hitler committed suicide. His successor sent General Alfred Jodl to the Supreme Headquarters of the Allied Expeditionary Forces to seek an end to the war. At 2.41 a.m. on 7 May, General Jodl signed for the unconditional surrender of German forces on all fronts. This surrender took effect on 8 May at 11.01 p.m. and the war in Europe was at an end.

TO DOM BEDE GRIFFITHS OSB (W):

Magdalen College,
Oxford.
May 10th 45

My dear Dom Bede

And how did *you* feel on V-Day?[37] I found it impossible to feel either so much sympathy with the people or so much gratitude to God as the occasion demanded. I am sometimes a little awed by the burden of our favours. Every one of us has escaped by a series of Providences,

---

19, pp. 99–101, Lewis later described this theory as 'an object I cannot think ... The command, after all, was Take, eat: not Take, understand. Particularly, I hope I need not be tormented by the question "What is this?" – this wafer, this sip of wine. That has a dreadful effect on me. It invites me to take "this" out of its holy context and regard it as an object among objects, indeed as part of nature. It is like taking a red coal out of the fire to examine it: it becomes a dead coal.'

37 V-Day or VE Day (Victory in Europe Day) was celebrated in Britain and the United States on 8 May 1945.

some not far short of miracles: and it seems to me that the sort of life which wd. be saintly for men less favoured becomes mere minimum decency for us. And how to come up to that standard!

You will remind me that this is precisely the situation we have always been in since our Redemption anyway. True: perhaps one of the great ἔϱγα[38] of a worldly deliverance is to bring that other more fully home to one.

I'm interested in what you say about the serial.[39] Do you think the failure to satisfy is due to lack of real *unity* or development? I mean that the dialogues succeed one another arbitrarily and might have come in any other order and might have gone on a longer or shorter time? Spiritual unity I hope it has: but a book needs musical or architectural unity as well.

By the way, I also have been reading Soloviev but a different book – the one on love.[40] Good, I thought, but just a trifle exaggerated.

And what is odder still I too have been v. much occupied by the idea of the New Creation. I'm absolutely with you. New heavens and earth – the resurrection of the body – how we have neglected these doctrines and indeed left the romantics and even the Marxists to step into the gap.

I'm working at a book on Miracles at present in wh. this theme will play a large part. And here's a funny thing. To write a book on miracles, which are in a sense invasions of Nature, has made me realise Nature herself as I've never done before. You don't *see* Nature till you believe in the Supernatural: don't get the full, hot, salty tang of her except by contrast with the pure water from beyond the world. Those who mistake Nature for the All are just those who can never realise her as a *particular creature* with her own flawed, terrible, beautiful individuality. No time to develop this now – but I thought you'd like to know the thoughts I am drunk with.

I hope you will go on with your own idea of a book on the New Creation.

Oremus pro invicem.[41]

C. S. Lewis

---

38 'works'.

39 i.e. 'Who Goes Home? Or The Grand Divorce'.

40 Vladimir Sergeyevich Soloviev, *The Meaning of Love*, trans. Jane Marshall (1945).

41 'Let us pray for one another'.

In the light of the New Creation all miracles are like *snowdrops* – anticipations of the full spring and high summer wh. is slowly coming over the whole wintry field of space & time.

The same day Lewis wrote to Griffiths, Thursday 10 May, Charles Williams suddenly fell ill and was taken to the Radcliffe Infirmary where he was operated on. The following Tuesday, 15 May, Lewis went to the Infirmary to call on him before joining the other Inklings at the 'Bird and Baby' pub. He learned that Williams had just died. Lewis wrote later:

> *I heard of his death at the Infirmary itself, having walked up there with a book I wanted to lend him, expecting this news that day as little (almost) as I expected to die that day myself. It was a Tuesday morning, one of our times of meeting. I thought he would have given me messages to take to the others. When I joined them with my actual message – it was only a few minutes' walk from the Infirmary but, I remember, the very streets looked different – I had some difficulty in making them believe or even understand what had happened.*[42]

For some while Lewis and Professor Tolkien had been discussing a Festschrift *to honour Williams before peace recalled him to London. Naturally they wanted to include as a contributor Dorothy L. Sayers, who had been so overwhelmed by Williams's* Figure of Beatrice: A Study in Dante *(1943) that it led her to read Dante's* Divine Comedy, *and, a few years later, to undertake a translation.*

TO DOROTHY L. SAYERS (W):

Magdalen College,
Oxford.).
May 17th 1945

Dear Miss Sayers

Like me you will be mourning the death of Charles Williams. Professor Tolkien and I had already been proposing a *Festschrift* for him in the form of a volume of essays by his friends. Tolkien and Mr. Barfield and I had in fact written our contributions. We now want it

42 Preface to *Essays Presented to Charles Williams*, ed. C. S. Lewis (1947).

to go forward as a memorial volume, to be sold for the benefit of his widow. Would you contribute? – any subject you like.[43]

Did I ever tell you my delighted enjoyment of your *Six Other Deadly Sins*? Most scalpel-like.

Yours sincerely
C. S. Lewis

TO T. S. ELIOT (P):

Magdalen College,
Oxford.
May 17th 45

Dear Mr. Eliot

I feel sure that you will, like the rest of us, have felt deeply the death of Charles Williams. Some time ago, when there was no fear of this in our minds, Professor Tolkien and I and one or two others had proposed that when he returned to London we should present him with a *Festschrift* in the form of a volume of essays by his friends. We think that if the plan went forward, now in the form of a memorial volume whereof the profits might be given to his widow, it would be a good thing. The contributions already written are,

On Fairy Tales J. R. R. Tolkien. (His Andrew Lang Lecture)[44]
Immortality A. O. Barfield
Popular Romance C.S.L.[45]

I have wondered whether you would care to contribute an essay? A critique of Charles's own poetry or an account of the man from your hand would be of very great value: but hardly any subject would come amiss.

Secondly (and this question is quite independent of the first) would you consider publishing the book? The O.U.P. would, of course, be in

---

43 Sayers replied on 24 May 1945: 'Thank you; yes – I imagined it would be that type of thing you had in mind, and I will do my best . . . The thing I *want* to write . . . would be something arising out of the Dante job I am doing' (Dorothy L. Sayers, *Letters*, vol. III, *1944–1950: A Noble Daring*, ed. Barbara Reynolds (1998), p. 148).

44 Tolkien's essay, 'On Fairy-Stories' was one of the Andrew Lang lectures delivered at St Andrews University in 1940, and was first published in *Essays Presented to Charles Williams*. It is reprinted in Tolkien's *Tree and Leaf, including the poem Mythopoeia*, 2nd edn, with an introduction by Christopher Tolkien (1988).

45 Lewis's contribution to *Essays Presented to Charles Williams* was eventually retitled 'On Stories', and has since been reprinted in *Of This and Other Worlds*.

some ways the obvious publisher and I have little doubt that Milford would do it: but *sub sigillo*[46] I doubt whether he sells books as well as your firm does.[47]

However you re-act to either question I need not say that your advice would be most welcome.

Yours sincerely
C. S. Lewis

TO OWEN BARFIELD (W):

Magdalen College,
Oxford.
May 18th 1945

My dear Barfield

Thanks for writing. It has been a very *odd* experience. This, the first really severe loss I have suffered, has (a) Given corroboration to my belief in immortality such as I never dreamed of. It is almost tangible now. (b) Swept away all my old feelings of mere horror and disgust at funerals, coffins, graves etc. If need had been I think I cd. have handled *that* corpse with hardly any unpleasant sensations. (c) Greatly reduced my feeling about ghosts. I think (but who knows?) that I shd. be, tho afraid, more pleased than afraid, if his turned up. In fact, all v. curious. Great pain but no mere depression.

Dyson said to me yesterday that he thought what was true of Christ was, in its lower degree, true of all Christians – i.e. they go away to return in a closer form and it is expedient for us that they shd. go away in order that they may do so. How foolish it is to imagine one can imaginatively foresee what any event will be like! 'Local unique sting'[48] alright of course for I love him (I cannot say more) as much as you:* and yet . . . a sort of brightness and tingling.

If you really can't bless (which I question) I suspect that is because you are not, or not yet, quite distinctly a Theist? I meant what I said about the fatal ambiguity of the word 'Nature' in your book. But of this when we meet.

As you see, far from moping I am spoiling for a fight. This may be

---

46 'under seal' or in strict confidence.
47 i.e. Eliot's publisher, Faber & Faber.
48 *CP*, 'Scazons', stanza 2, 2.

a cold wind but it's certainly bracing! Don't forget you're trying to come down again soon. You were wrong about Warnie – I think he feels it as much as any of us.

Yours

C. S. Lewis

*This means *te* not *tu*!

Your play recurs often to my mind. How dreadful it wd. now be if one were reduced to 'He *used to* do this' or 'He *would have* liked that': instead of the βαϱος δοξηϛ.[49]

To put it in a nutshell – what the idea of death has done to him is nothing to what he has done to the idea of death. Hit it for six: yet it used to rank as a fast bowler!

TO MARY NEYLAN (T):

May 20th [1945]

Dear Mrs Neylan –

Forgive me for being silent so long. Yes: de la Mare did write a book about monkeys *The Three Mullah Mulgahs.*[50] I have not read nor even (I think) seen it.

By the way did you see the account of Mouse-Town in the re-opened (London) zoo. I should think Sarah would love it: it would have ravished me at her age. (Perhaps it was already there when you took her to the zoo at Christmas: but you cd. hardly have forborne to mention it if so).

I think what you say about 'grief being better than estrangement' is very true. I am sorry you should have had this grief but, as you describe it, one can't be sorry for the call.

I also have become much acquainted with grief now through the death of my great friend Charles Williams, my friend of friends, the comforter of all our little set, the most angelic. The odd thing is that his death has made my faith ten times stronger than it was a week ago. And I find all that talk about 'feeling he is closer to us than before' isn't just talk. It's just what it does feel like – I can't put it into words.

---

49 'weight of glory'. Cf. Lewis's sermon of that title; see 1941, note 91.

50 Walter de la Mare, *The Three Mulla-Mulgars* (1910).

One seems at moments to be living in a new world. Lots, lots of pain but not a particle of depression or resentment.

By the bye I've finished a selection from Geo. Macdonald (365 extracts) which will come out about Xmas: wd. you (or not) care to have it dedicated to you? I feel it is rather yours by right as you got more out of him than anyone else to whom I introduced his books. Just let me know.

And why should you assume I'm too occupied to see you? Friday mornings in term are bad, but alright in Vac: and Friday afternoons in both. I shd. like a visit (with a week's notice) whenever you find one convenient.

Excuse this paper. It may be less blotched than yours but yours did at least begin life as a real piece of note paper! I'm so glad Dan has got his job made permanent. Blessings!

Yours sincerely
C. S. Lewis

TO FLORENCE (MICHAL) WILLIAMS (W):[51]

Magdalen College,
Oxford.
May 22d 1945

Dear Mrs. Williams

Thank you for your most kind letter. We all knew that your marriage was one in a thousand. I think you will not be offended if I tell you this; that whenever Charles disagreed with anything we had said about women in general, it was a common turn of raillery to reply 'Oh Charles! – of course he's in love, so his opinions on that subject are worthless!'

I feel, in my degree, as you do. My friendship is not ended. His death has had the very unexpected effect of making death itself look quite different. I believe in the next life ten times more strongly than I did. At moments it seems almost tangible. Mr. Dyson, on the day of the funeral, summed up what many of us felt, 'It is not blasphemous', he said 'To believe that what was true of Our Lord is, in its less degree, true of all who are in Him. They go away in order to be *with* us in a

---

51 Florence Sarah 'Michal' Williams was the wife of Charles Williams. See **Charles Williams** in the Biographical Appendix.

new way, even closer than before.' A month ago I wd. have called this silly sentiment. Now I know better. He seems, in some indefinable way, to be all around us now. I do not doubt he is doing and will do for us all sorts of things he could not have done while in the body. Of course this expects no answer. God bless you.

Yours sincerely
C. S. Lewis

TO DOROTHY L. SAYERS (W):

Magdalen
May 23rd 1945

Dear Miss Sayers

Yes: who *does* read this kind of book? That is the cold question wh. comes over me. Still, we can but try. The existing papers are by Tolkien (on Fairy Tales – his Andrew Lang lecture) and by me on Popular Romances. This gives one some unity of subject: i.e. we are both dealing with aspects of the art of story-telling.

If you cared to write *either* on Charles's novels or on your own branch of the art, that wd. fit in admirably. But of course the main thing is to choose a subject you *want* to write about. As for length, I was thinking of the sort of length of essay one meets in *Essays & Studies*: which I suppose to be about 10,000 words. I've never learned to guess what 1000 words look like on the page.

Yes – you'll be having grand fun with the Dante![52] 'Oh my lights and liver!'[53]

Yours sincerely
C. S. Lewis

TO DOROTHY L. SAYERS (W):

Magdalen
May 25th 45

Dear Miss Sayers

I am sure you've struck the right subject. And the learned need it more than anyone else for, as you must know yourself, the last thing

52 Sayers was translating Dante's *Divine Comedy* for the Penguin Classics series.

53 Dickens, *David Copperfield*, ch. 13: 'Oh my lungs and liver, what do you want?'

they ever dream of noticing in a great narrative poem is the *narrative*. (Between Aristotle and Maud Bodkin[54] is there a single critic who ever discusses the nature of *story* at all?) That wd. bring your paper well into line with the subjects up to date. If you cared to do it in a narrative form ('I then noticed' etc) and to drape it round liberal extracts from the Williams–Sayers correspondence (Spenser & Gabriel Harvey[55] and all, you know!) it would be perfect.

I liked your specimen of devilry. Guttlehog and Grobberscritch are α+. For a river in a fairy tale country how do you like Tolkien's *Withywindle*?

Yours sincerely
C. S. Lewis

TO T. S. ELIOT (P):

Magdalen College,
Oxford.
26th May 1945

Dear Mr Eliot

I quite understand the difficulties about paper etc from the publisher's point of view. The connection between the essays so far (at least Tolkien's and mine and one which Dorothy Sayers has promised on the *narrative* power of Dante) is that they are all concerned with *story*, or if you will *mythopoea*: in fact with that element in literature wh. nearly all criticism between Aristotle and Maud Bodkin has left entirely alone. Their connection with Charles is that this was rather his own long suit. But we didn't really aim at more unity than is usually found in a *Festschrift*.

Of course you may, from experience, judge that a book of this type is unsellable: if so, the whole thing may have to be reconsidered. If you do decide that it is worth going on with I think either his novels or his plays wd. be an excellent subject. (I can lend you nearly all the novels)

I'm thinking of lecturing on his poetry next term and perhaps follow-

54 Bodkin, *Archetypal Patterns in Poetry*. See the letter to Eliza Butler of 18 August 1940, note 348.

55 Edmund Spenser and Gabriel Harvey, *Three Letters Between Two Universitie Men* (1580).

ing that up with a book on the subject. I agree about the obscurity and used to tell him he ought to be birched for it.

Yours sincerely
C. S. Lewis

TO SISTER PENELOPE CSMV (BOD):

[The Kilns]
Trinity Sunday
May 28th/45

Dear Sister Penelope

I was intensely interested in the story of your healing of the little dog.[56] I don't see why one shouldn't. Perhaps indeed those to whom God allows a gift in this way should confirm their own faith in it by practising on beasts for in one way they may be easier to heal than men. Although they cannot have faith in Him (I suppose) they certainly have faith in us, wh. is faith in Him at one remove: and there is no sin in them to impede or resist. I am glad it happened.

You will have heard of the death of my dearest friend, Charles Williams and, no doubt, prayed for him. For me too, it has been, and is, a great loss. But not at all a dejecting one. It has greatly increased my faith. Death has done nothing to my idea of him, but he has done – oh, I can't say what – to my idea of death. It has made the next world much more real and palpable. We all feel the same. How one lives and learns. I have often heard of widows and bereaved mothers who 'felt that "he" was now nearer to them than while in the body' and always thought it a sentimental hyperbole. I know better now. As someone said to me just after the funeral 'It is not blasphemous to believe that what is true of Our Lord is true *in their degree* of all who are His. They go away in order to return in a new mode. It is expedient for us that they do. It is thus and thus only that in each case the Comforter comes.' May one accept this?

I am glad things progress favourably about your plays – but wish they wd. buck up and get them out. It is (at least I find it) such a

56 In her note on this letter Sister Penelope said: 'The little dog was a Pekinese I had known from puppyhood. She had had something very much like polio and was badly crippled. Seeing her as part of the redeemed creation, I laid my hands on her in our Lord's name. That was two days before I left the house where she belonged. A fortnight later I heard she was completely well.'

distraction to be engaged in 'placing' a book. That was a subtle design of Screwtape's to have them altered 'not to disturb the childrens' minds' and, in that etiolated form, produced. Of course you were quite right to refuse that. What staggers me is not the wickedness of these people (in fact they may not be wicked at all) but the muddle headedness. If you don't want the *acta Dei* celebrated, why have a series of scriptural plays at all?

The truth is we shall never get on till we have stamped out 'religion'. 'Religion' as it is called – the vague slush of humanitarian idealism, Emersonian Pantheism, democratic politics and material progressiveness with a few Christian names and formulae added to taste like pepper and salt – is almost the great enemy. If one can't talk to a Christian then give me a real believing member of some other religion or an honest clear-headed sceptic like J. S. Mill. One can at least get sense out of them. But I'm losing my temper – and with less right than anyone in the world!

The title *Who Goes Home?* has had to be dropped because someone has used it already. The little book will be called *The Great Divorce* and will appear about August. *That Hideous Strength* is due in July. The Miracle book is finished but will not come out till next year.

Jane is up and down: very liable, I'm afraid, to fits of really bad jealousy – she can't bear to see other people doing the work. Pray for her, dear Sister. With all good wishes.

Yours sincerely
C. S. Lewis

TO DOROTHY L. SAYERS (W):

Magdalen College,
Oxford.
May 29th. 1945

Dear Miss Sayers

The reason why they don't like either the narrative element or low comedy is that these have obvious immediate entertainment value. These prigs, starting from the true proposition that great art is more than entertainment reach the glaring *non sequitur* 'entertainment has no place in great art' – like people who think music can't be 'classical' if there is a catchy tune in it. It is as if, having learned that religious emotion is not the whole spiritual life and erotic pleasure not the whole of marriage, they then concluded that dryness and impotence were essentials. Pack of muddle headed manichaeans who got marks at their prep. school for reading 'good' books wh. they didn't enjoy. Pah!,

Yours
C. S. Lewis

TO T. S. ELIOT (P):

Magdalen College,
Oxford.
June 1st 1945

Dear Mr. Eliot

No, I must have expressed myself clumsily. I was wondering whether you, being the only experienced publisher among us, judged that such a book was unsaleable and wd. therefore not advise us to go on with the scheme *whoever* published it.

I think an essay on the Plays by you wd. be an excellent idea, and I quite understand that you may think the plan feasible *simpliciter* tho' not by Faber & Faber. It was the *simpliciter* I was worried about.

Yours sincerely
C. S. Lewis

TO ANNE RIDLER (BOD):[57]

June 3rd 45
Magdalen College,
Oxford.

Dear Mrs. Ridler –

I feel very inclined to reply, I envy you parts of your obituary. You get in v. essential points wh. I had missed – his scepticism and his way of converting the other person's mere stammer into great truth.[58]

---

57 Anne Ridler (1912–2001) was the daughter of H. C. Bradley, housemaster at Rugby School, and Violet Milford. She was educated at Downe House School, King's College, London, and in Florence and Rome. In 1938 she married Vivian Ridler, printer to the University of Oxford, and they had two sons and two daughters. Her numerous works of poetry, plays, translations and criticism include *Poems* (1939), *Collected Poems* (1994), *Henry Bly and Other Plays* (1950), *A Measure of English Poetry* (1991) and (ed.) *Selected Writings, Charles Williams* (1961).

58 Anne Ridler, 'Charles Williams: A Note in Memory', *The New English Weekly*, XXVII (31 May 1945), p. 63: 'once to have seen the world of ideas (which he inhabited) with his eyes, was to have learnt an entirely new attitude of mind, and

(A higher critic wd. deduce from this either that C. W. had never existed or that one or other of us was quite unhistorical).

It is an interesting fact that everyone almost who has spoken or written to me about his death says something different of him and all true. One feels curiously *un*-depressed, do you find? It has increased enormously one's faith in the next life and I can't help feeling him all over the place. I can't put it into words: I never knew the death of a good man cd. itself do so much good. I don't mean there isn't pain, pain in plenty: but not dull, sullen, sickening, drab, resentful pain.

I'm going to put on a course of lectures on his poetry next term: I'm much interested in what you say about the young poets.

Let us meet when you find it convenient to be in Oxford. I like your things, what I understand of them. Meanwhile, thanks.

Yours sincerely
C. S. Lewis

TO MISS GLADDING (BOD):[59]

Magdalen College,
Oxford.
June 7th 1945

Dear Miss Gladding

I am afraid I don't know any books more elementary than my own wh. wd. help. The truth is that when a person (not herself v. bookish or philosophical) has lost faith under so v. great and bewildering a trial, no *intellectual* approach is likely to avail. But where people can resist and ignore arguments they may be unable to resist *lives.* I am afraid, my dear lady, the only hope lies in you and in any other Xtian friends she has. It is in so far as you succeed in representing Christ to her by all your actions and words that she may, even unconsciously, come to know Him. This is a terrible thing to say to you, but He will make you able to be what you need to be.

---

a perpetual wariness of cant. His own mind contained scepticism and passionate affirmation in an extraordinary balance: it was this that gave him his power of inclusiveness without vagueness, which made one feel that there would be no experience, no perversion or misery, which would be outside his reconciling power, while he yet remained consistent with his dogmatic beliefs.'

59 Nothing is known of Miss Gladding except that her address was Carr Cragg Lodge, Skelwith Bridge, near Ambleside, Westmorland.

For yourself – the trial is your sister in law's trial, not the child's. We know nothing about the life of imbeciles, less than we do about animals. I take it that where the brain does not function the spirit is hardly in this world at all. 'Not at Home' is the real message written across the imbecile's face. It is I think most unlikely that there is anything we cd. recognise as suffering. The *real* child, the soul, is 'miles away'. It is connected with this invalid body and decaying brain only in order that it may go through the process of death which is the turnstile to the resurrection life. What the state of this almost absentee soul is at present no one can know. But you may find out one day that it was particularly blessed. It doesn't look like that of course. But think what wrong conclusions you wd. draw from seeing an anaesthetised person, a drunk person, or even a sleeping person, if we knew nothing about chloroform, alcohol, or sleep.

You will be in my prayers. All good to you – and strength,

Yours sincerely

C. S. Lewis

Be sure your Communions are frequent & regular.

TO MISS GLADDING (BOD):

Magdalen College,
Oxford.
June 18th 1945

Dear Miss Gladding

If we accept Xtianity at all and then also take into account the enormous infant mortality of the human race as a whole (in a 17th century family 12 children of whom 4 grew up seems to be about normal) we *must*, I think, believe that the fact of becoming an animal organism and undergoing bodily death is an essential element in being a risen immortal soul in Christ. Not an essential part of being a blessed immortal spirit of some or other kind (e.g. an angel) but of being a blessed *human* i.e. a creature with a risen body and with that nature to wh. Our Lord was united at the Incarnation. If He wanted only things like angels there wd. have been no point in creating a *human* race at all.

I don't see that this adds to the problems of education which, goodness knows, are thorny enough already. You haven't got to educate people who die in infancy nor (I take it) total imbeciles. You are dealing with souls wh. have what we call a 'normal' human life on earth (tho' in fact only a minority of the human race have reached it). And once they have that it obviously makes a difference how they live it and we can make it easier or harder by good or bad education

Yours sincerely
C. S. Lewis

TO T. S. ELIOT (P):

Magdalen College,
Oxford.
June 21st 1945

Dear Mr Eliot

I took your advice and have now had an answer from Sir Humphrey. He says 'I shall be delighted to publish essays presented to C.W. and so soon as you have the material and will send it to me we will take out estimates and make you a suggestion of terms and prices.' This sounds to my amateur ear as if he thought we meant publication at *our* expense! In which case, no thing doing. But you understand the language better than I do. How do you read it?

Yours sincerely
C. S. Lewis

TO HAROLD ARTHUR BLAIR (W):[60] TS

REF.78/1/45.

Magdalen College,
Oxford.
28th June 1945.

Dear Mr. Blair,

Yes, I will attempt all these; the one I am doubtful about is the R.A.F. officers. If they're absolutely voluntary (no nonsense about

60 The Rev. Canon Harold Arthur Blair (1902–85), was at this time Vicar of Winterbourne Earls with Dauntsey and Winterbourne Gunner, near Salisbury. Besides being Chaplain to the nearby RAF camp, he was looking after Lord Bath's family at Longleat. Blair had asked Lewis to combine a visit to the RAF camp with talks to the Longleat family and a talk to the girls of the Royal School at Bath now evacuated to Longleat. Canon Blair, born in India, was educated at Lancing and St Edmund's Hall, Oxford, where he read Theology. After taking his BA in 1925, he served as a political officer in Ghana where he became an authority on the people of Dagbon. Invalided in 1939, he returned to England and went to Sarum

coming out of politeness) I'll tackle them: but if anything is to be dropped, let it be that.

yours sincerely,
C. S. Lewis

TO DOROTHY L. SAYERS (W): TS

REF.231/1/45

Magdalen College,
Oxford.
30th. June 1945

Dear Miss Sayers,

I have written to Sir Humphrey Milford about the Charles Williams volume, and he replies expressing his willingness to publish: but apparently he imagines we propose to let him do so at our expence. I have replied explaining that we had no such idea – we are seeking no remuneration, and will make over royalties to Mrs. Williams. (You agree, I presume). I wait to see if this will shame him into making an offer.

Yours sincerely,
C. S. Lewis

Lewis had misunderstood Sir Humphrey Milford's letter. Dorothy L. Sayers was incensed that Oxford University Press should expect them to defray the cost of the Festschrift *and she replied to Lewis on 3 July 1945: 'Good God Almighty! And Charles served that firm faithfully for nearly all his life! . . . Does that comic little man expect ME to pay for the privilege of being published by him?* Pay? *PAY? – Or, if it comes to that, YOU?'*[61]

Meanwhile, Sir Humphrey wrote to Lewis on 4 July: 'Good gracious no! You misunderstood my letter. "Terms and prices" only meant a question of royalty and publication price. Of course I realize that you intended a book published at our expense, and that was what I meant too.'[62]

Theological College. After his ordination in 1940 he served in a number of Wiltshire parishes. He was Curate of Sherborne with Castleton and Lillington, 1939–41, Vicar of Winterbourne Earls, 1945–54, Perpetual Curate of Southbroom, 1954–60, and Canon and Chancellor of Truro Cathedral, 1960–75. His books include *A Creed before the Creeds* (1955), *The Ladder of Temptations* (1960), *A Stranger in the House* (1963) and *A Kaleidoscope of Truth: Types and Archetypes in Clement of Alexandria* (1986).

61 Sayers, *Letters*, vol. III, p. 154.

62 Wade Center, Wheaton College.

TO DOROTHY L. SAYERS (W):

REF.232/1/45.

Magdalen College,
Oxford.
6th. July 1945.

Dear Miss Sayers,

You will be as pleased as I am to see the enclosed – a copy of a letter I had from Sir Humphrey yesterday. I will let you know how the matter progresses.

Yours sincerely,
C. S. Lewis

Best quality Sackcloth & Ashes
in sealed packets
delivered in plain vans at
moderate charges
Messrs M. Cato and R. E. Morse[63]

TO T. S. ELIOT (P): TS

REF.232/1/45.

Magdalen College,
Oxford.
6th. July 1945.

Dear Mr. Eliot,

Thanks for your letter of the 27th. June: – You will I'm sure be glad to see the enclosed copy of a letter I have since had from Sir Humphrey. I will let you know how the matter goes on.

yours sincerely,
C. S. Lewis

---

63 ibid., p. 155. In Dante's *Purgatorio*, I, (Marcus) Cato admits penitent souls into purgatory. In her reply of 7 July 1945, Miss Sayers said: 'My menu for tonight shall be:

HUMBLE PIE
IPSISSIMA VERBA
with sharp sauce
FRUITS
meet for Repentance.'

TO OWEN BARFIELD (W):

July 12th 1945

My dear B –

I like this very much indeed.[64] There are two difficulties. The fourth line of the 2nd stanza is to me opaque. Partly because I can't read it. Is it

(Man, therefore) changed the lock

or

Man, therefore I changed the lock?

But neither gives any sense to me. I also agree with Harwood that in the last stanza 'My love! Lucy!' is difficult. I do see what you mean by putting it in the mouth of the returned youth: but dialogue poems are rather difficult any way and this adds another fence. I don't mind the name Lucy as names go. The real thing is that if (or since) you can't get an archetypal name like Egeria, it is doubtful whether you want a proper name at all. I should like 'We're in, Sister!' or something of the sort. The poem makes a piquant pendant to your lines to the Old Adam

I don't know (and wouldn't dream of asking) how far it is *feigned*. If it is autobiographical, I needn't tell you that the experience is a dangerous one for men about our age. No fool like an old (and yet not quite old) one!

Have you read Milton's *De Idea Platonica quemadmodum Aristoteles intellexit*[65] – printed in the Latin poems? Do. Probably intended for a mere joke but develops an astonishing goblin-dancing quality – *Otiosa aeternitas – incedit ingens hominis archetypus gigas.*[66] I've just done a version of it but no time to copy it out this morning.[67]

---

64 Lewis had been asked to criticize one of Owen Barfield's poems, which has never been published.

65 John Milton, *Poems* (1645), '*De Idea Platonica quemadmodum Aristoteles intellexit*' ('On the Platonic form as Aristotle understood it').

66 'Tell, oh Eternity'; 'Lifting to heav'n a head the gods would tremble at.' These are from Lewis's translation of Milton's poem.

67 'From the Latin of Milton's *De Idea Platonica Quemadmodum Aristoteles Intellexit*', a translation by Lewis of Milton's poem, was published in *English*, V, no. 30

You are going it young Copperfield! I wish you all goods.
Yours
C. S. Lewis

Is *Come in, my dear* the perfect ending? I'm not, at all readings, quite satisfied with it.

P.S. Nobody disliked the technique of your *Merman*[68] and I liked it v. much. But what they talked about was the myth. I thought your use of the new line in it gave an effect much like mine on C.W. – wh. has appeared in *Britain To-day*.[69] Wd. you like me to make some public statement that it is *your* metre?[70] In fact this might give you an opening.

Of all the other matter when you will. Yes: one of the main points about any experience is that it shows experiences of that sort to be possible. e.g. the real trouble of meeting a ghost wd. be that you'd then know you might meet another.

TO HAROLD ARTHUR BLAIR (W):

Magdalen College,
Oxford.
July 24th 45

My dear Blair

Thanks for the cheque; I suppose I must mutter to myself, like the said Pooh Bah, 'Well, it will be a useful mortification.'[71]

I have ordered a copy of my *Allegory of Love* to be sent to you and

(1945), p. 195. Lewis introduced it: 'Milton's *De Idea Platonica* was probably intended as a mere academic squib; but genius sometimes laughs at authors' intentions. I hardly dare to hope that this version has preserved the goblin quality of the original: it will be enough if I send some readers to explore for themselves such a neglected and exquisite grotesque.'

68 'The Merman' was published in *The Golden Blade* (1950), and is reprinted in *A Barfield Sampler: Poetry and Fiction by Owen Barfield*, ed. Jeanne Clayton Hunter and Thomas Kranidas, with an afterword by Owen Barfield (Albany: State University of New York, 1993).

69 Lewis's poem 'On the Death of Charles Williams' appeared in *Britain To-day*, no. 112 (August 1945), p. 14. A slightly revised version entitled 'To Charles Williams' was published in *Poems* and *CP*.

70 Barfield scribbled a note at the foot of Lewis's letter saying: 'No (but gesture appreciated). Go on and prosper. When someone accuses *me* of having purloined from *you*, you can unseal your lips, if you will.'

71 W. S. Gilbert and Arthur Sullivan, *The Mikado* (1885), Act II: 'Well, it will be a useful discipline.'

one of C. Williams' *All Hallows Eve* to my kind hostess. The latter may not arrive for some time because Blackwell's were out of stock when I rang them up. The former is to clear up a certain shakiness on the historical side of the (otherwise sound) erotology current at the vicarage! A thousand thanks for all your kindness.[72]

Yours
C. S. Lewis

TO VICTOR M. HAMM (W):[73]

Magdalen College,
Oxford.
Aug 11th 1945

Dear Mr Hamm –

Thank you very much for sending me the offprint of your article on my *Perelandra*.[74]

I should like to be able to repay you with a critique of your critique but, as you may imagine, it is not v. easy for *me* of all people to form an objective judgement! I can only hope you are right.

You are certainly the best Old Solar scholar among my readers so far. MAL- is really equivalent to the definite article in some of the definite article's uses. ELDIL means a lord or ruler, Maleldil '*The* Lord': i.e. it is, strictly speaking, the Old Solar not for DEUS but for

---

72 Canon Blair's letter of 22 April 1969 at Wheaton College explains various details in Lewis's letters to him; this, he wrote, was a 'Letter of thanks for hospitality and cheque for his train-fare – he never asked for fees – and sending my wife "All Hallows Eve", C. Williams, and me "The Allegory of Love". We had a delightful four days of him with the Longleat folk and various other semi-agnostics, and with the R.A.F. officers and men, but had a bad time with the girls' school: the school-marms got at him in a school-marmish sort of way with questions about bringing up children, which he would not answer as he had none of his own. Then a girl asked him what hell would be like, and he said, "Very much like what I'm going through now."'

73 Victor Michael Hamm (1904–?), born in Milwaukee, Wisconsin, on 21 February 1904, received his BA and MA from Marquette University in 1926 and 1928, and a second MA and a PhD from Harvard University in 1929 and 1932. An instructor in English at St Louis University, 1933–4, he was Assistant Professor of English at the College of Mount St Joseph, Cincinnati, Ohio, 1934–7. Dr Hamm returned to Marquette in 1937 as Associated Professor of English, and in 1945 became professor. He is the translator of Pico della Mirandola's *Of Being and Unity* (1943) and the author of *Language, Truth, and Poetry* (1960).

74 Victor M. Hamm, 'Mr Lewis in Perelandra', *Thought*, 20 (June 1945), pp. 271–90.

DOMINUS. (The plural of OYARSA is OYÉRESU, but you couldn't know that!)

The only point I think you are slightly wrong on is that you use the Martian society too boldly as a guide to what Perelandra wd. become later on. But there is no real parallel. The *Incarnation* has come in between. Malacandra belongs to the old order in wh. planetary creatures were subjected to the angels: but the angels kneel before Tor. There is no limit to the future glories of the world wh., needing no redemption itself, yet profits by the Incarnation. You get the idea? And, by the bye, I don't mean the idea of a cosmic language as anything more than fiction.

Well, a thousand thanks. Be sure and look me up if you are ever in these parts.

Yours very sincerely
C. S. Lewis

That Hideous Strength: a Modern Fairy-tale for Grown-ups *was published by John Lane, the Bodley Head on 16 August 1945.*

TO ROY LEE (BBC):[75] TS

REF.214.44.

Magdalen College,
Oxford.
31st August 1945.

Dear Mr. Lee,

Oddly enough I've been thinking lately of trying to do something popular about the Bible: but it would be quite impossible to get it ready by this October, or even October '46. So I must decline.

The Cambridge Chair is a newspaper rumour and untrue.

yours sincerely,
C. S. Lewis

75 Dr Lee wrote to Lewis on 29 August: 'I am writing to you at Magdalen College because I am not sure whether you have yet taken up your Professorship at Cambridge. I am writing to invite you to do one of the talks in a series which I am starting in the middle of October in our overseas networks dealing with the Bible.'

TO THE EDITOR OF *THE GUARDIAN* (*EC*):[76]

[Magdalen College
31 August 1945]

Sir, –

I think your readers should, and will, be interested in the following extract from a letter I have just received; the writer is an invalid lady in a village:

'This used to be a God-fearing village with a God-fearing parson who visited and ran the Scouts ("Lovely troop we 'ad. *And* you should have 'eard our choir of a Sunday," says my bricklayer host). The young were polished up and sent to Sunday school, their parents filled the church to the brim. *Now* they have an octogenarian. No harm in that! My late uncle — at that age was going as strong as most two-year-olds. But this one – I noted for myself, seeing him pass – has been dead for years . . . He does not visit the sick, even if asked. He does nothing. And – listen – he stuck up a notice in the church: *No children admitted without their parents or an adult.* The village . . . went instantly Pagan. I must get away from it. Never before but in the vile pagan West Indies have I been without so much as an *extorted* Holy Sacrament. (*Can* you forbid the church to a Crissom child? – legally, I mean? Pass me a Bishop.)'

TO OWEN BARFIELD (W):

[The Kilns
? September 1945]

My dear Barfield –

Thanks for your generous praise of T.H.S.[77]

I wonder that, being a poet, you shd. fear dolphins. Had you not your harp with you? Then, even had the boat capsized, one of them wd. have brought you singing to land – 'and oh, ye dolphins waft the hapless youth'.[78]

I know nothing about the Maternity Hospital. It must be one of

76 This letter was originally published as 'A Village Experience' in *The Guardian* (31 August 1945), p. 335.

77 i.e. *That Hideous Strength*.

78 John Milton, *Lycidas* (1638), 164.

those cases in wh. your right hand carried out the gospel precept[79] *secundum literam*.[80] By the same token please let me have an agapargyrometrical reading first thing after you come back.

Yours
C. S. Lewis

This literary lion
Emulated Arion:
When other holiday makers went golfin'
He rode his dolphin.[81]

TO CECIL AND DAPHNE HARWOOD (BOD):

The Kilns
Sept 11th 1945

Dear Daphne and Cecil –

Thank you for both your letters. I'm replying to the Minehead address for palaeographical reasons.[82]

About Merlin, I don't think it wd. have made any difference if I did hold your views of the after-world. I mean, of course he wouldn't be *naïf* if he returned from *my* after world any more than if he returned from yours. Whatever the normal *status animarum post mortem*[83] may be, it is feigned that this one man was exempted from it and returned just as he was. (I know they don't really: I was writing a story).

Rê Jane, she wasn't meant to illustrate the problem of the married

---

79 Matthew 6:3: 'But when thou doest alms, let not thy left hand know what thy right hand doeth.'

80 'literally'.

81 The poem is accompanied by a drawing of a man on a dolphin playing his harp and singing 'Ancient fortifications/Sleet behind!'

82 Michael Hall, the Rudolf Steiner school in which Harwood taught, had recently moved from Minehead to Kidbrooke Park, Forest Row, Sussex, and he and his family had moved with it.

83 'state of the soul after death'. Lewis was probably referring to Dante's letter to Can Grande della Scala (1291–1329), a great patron of the arts, to whom he sent a fair copy of the *Paradiso*. The words '*status animarum post mortem*' are found in section 8: 'The subject of the whole work, taken only from a literal standpoint, is simply the state of the soul after death.' See the treatment of this letter to Can Grande in the Introduction to *The Comedy of Dante Alighieri The Florentine: Cantica III Paradise*, trans. Dorothy L. Sayers and Barbara Reynolds (1960), pp. 36ff.

woman and her own career in general: rather the problem of everyone who follows an *imagined* vocation at the expense of a real one. Perhaps I shd. have emphasised more the fact that her thesis on Donne was all derivative bilge.[84] If I'd been tackling the problem wh. Cecil thinks I had in mind, of course I'd have taken a woman capable of making a real contribution to literature.

I'm uncomfortably afraid Cecil is right (with MacPhee) about St Anne's being rather like the House of Lords in *Iolanthe*.[85] All reviewers so far (except *Punch*) have damned the book: comfortingly for different reasons – I mean it can hardly be bad in so many different ways as all that.

I burn to hear more of the poeters. Next term is going to be a whopper, millions of pupils, and I'm no longer allowed to give anyone a meal in College. Love to all.

Yours
Jack

For Daphne – R.C's[86] keep on writing to tell me (like you) that it is a pity that 'knowing so much I shd. be held back from knowing so much more'!

TO ROGER LANCELYN GREEN (BOD):

[The Kilns]
Sept 16th 1945

My dear Green –

I have now read *The Wood That Time Forgot* and this is what I think.[87]

The general *narrative power* is excellent: i.e. on the question whether you have in general the story-telling talent, you may (in my opinion) set your mind at rest. I read it on a railway journey and it carried me

---

84 *That Hideous Strength*, ch. 1, part I, p. 2: 'Jane was not perhaps a very original thinker and her plan had been to lay great stress on Donne's "triumphant vindication of the body". She still believed that if she got out all her notebooks and editions and really sat down to the job, she could force herself back into her lost enthusiasm for the subject.'

85 W. S. Gilbert and Arthur Sullivan, *Iolanthe* (1882), Act II, 'The House of Peers, throughout the war,/Did nothing in particular,/And did it very well.'

86 Roman Catholics.

87 Green later substantially revised 'The Wood That Time Forgot'. Lewis's notes on the final version can be found in his letter to Green of 28 June 1949.

as far as Bletchley (wh. was at chapter VII) without a single flagging of interest. I particularly admired the transition from the natural to the supernatural part. This went just gradually enough to elicit one's faith and by the right stages. I thank you for giving me the authentic thrill: as you did several times.

About the particular myth wh. we find we are dealing with at and after cap. VI I am not so sure. This may be personal: I don't greatly like the Redemption of Ayesha theme myself. I feel more certain, however, that it ought to be managed with less about love: more from the point of view of the children and less from Randal's. Randal seems to me partly good and partly bad. His whole state of mind will be damned as 'morbid' by most modern readers. I don't agree with them: nor do I wish either you or me to be brow beaten by them. But remember Pope – 'make use of every friend *and every foe.*'[88] We must acknowledge that his state of mind *could* easily be morbid and profit by their excessive alarms to be cautious.

I think you should be careful of letting him talk as he does on the bottom of p. 31 and the earlier parts of p. 32. One wants some sort of crispness and driness not obliterating but balancing the wistfulness. His pedantry partly does this, but not enough. He mustn't sigh (p. 36) and say that other people call *Aucassin & Nicolette*[89] silly. It makes him sound weak & unconvincing. You're *inviting* the enemy to attack. A touch of arrogance (á la Yeats) wd. be better.

Some of the verses used for chapter mottoes are not good enough: those on 5, 9, 10, 12 – specially 12 which I think wretched stuff. Of your own poems (child readers will skip them, by the way) I dislike those on pp. 47 and 104. 'What are the wild birds saying' is out of the question: Paul Dombey spoiled it in advance by his 'What are the wild waves saying.'[90]

Now for a matter wh. I wd. not mention if it were not that you and I (obviously) can converse with the freedom of patients in the same hospital. None of these faults is purely *literary*. The talent is certain: but you have a sickness in the soul. You are much too much *in* that enchanted wood yourself – and perhaps with no very powerful talisman

88 Alexander Pope, *An Essay on Criticism* (1711), II, 214.
89 A thirteenth-century courtly story set in northern France.
90 See Charles Dickens, *Dombey and Son* (1847–8), ch. 16.

round your neck. You are in love with your own heroine – wh. is author's incest & always spoils a book. I know all about it because I've been in the wood too. It took me years to get out of it: and only after I'd done so did re-enchantment begin. If you try to stay there the wood will die on you – and so will you!

Have you read C. William's *Descent into Hell.* If not, do so at once (I can lend you a copy). May I show the MS to Tolkien? My brother has read it & likes it v. much.

Yours
C. S. Lewis

TO I. O. EVANS (W): TS

REF.372/44.

Magdalen College,
Oxford.
26th. September 1945.

Dear Mr. Evans,

Many thanks for your kind and encouraging letter of the 24th.

I'm glad you recognised the N.I.C.E.[91] as not being quite the fantastic absurdity some readers think. I had'nt myself thought that any of the people in contemporary rackets were *really* dabbling in Magic: I had supposed that to be a romantic addition of my own.[92] But there you are. The trouble about writing satire is that the real world always anticipates you, and what were meant for exaggerations turn out to be nothing of the sort.

About Merlin: I don't know much more than you do. Apart from

---

91 The National Institute for Coordinated Experiments, the scientific foundation in *That Hideous Strength.*

92 This evil magic is analysed in *That Hideous Strength*, ch. 13, section 4, p. 315 where Dr Dimble says: 'Merlin is . . . the last vestige of an old order in which matter and spirit were, from our modern point of view, confused. For him every operation on Nature is a kind of personal contact, like coaxing a child or stroking one's horse. After him came the modern man to whom Nature is something dead – a machine to be worked, and taken to bits if it won't work the way he pleases. Finally, come the Belbury people, who take over that view from the modern man unaltered and simply want to increase their power by tacking onto it the aid of spirits – extra-natural, anti-natural spirits.' Lewis had pointed out in *The Abolition of Man* (London: Oxford University Press, 1943; Fount, 1999, ch. 3, p. 47: 'For the wise men of old the cardinal problem had been how to conform the soul to reality, and the solution had been knowledge, self-discipline, and virtue. For magic and applied science alike the problem is how to subdue reality to the wishes of men.'

Malory (the Everyman edition[93] and the Temple Classics[94] are both complete) you will get something more in Geoffrey of Monmouth (Temple Classics),[95] and LAYAMON (to be found in the Everyman volume entitled 'Arthurian Chronicles from Wace and Layamon'.[96] For Arthur in general see 'Arthur of Britain' by E. K. Chambers,[97] Collingwood in Vol. I of 'Oxford History of England',[98] and Vinaver's 'Malory'.[99] But the blessing about Merlin (for you and me) is that 'very little is known' – so we have a free hand!

All good wishes.

yours sincerely,
C. S. Lewis

TO JOHN BEDDOW (BOD):[100]

Magdalen College,
Oxford
Oct 7th 1945

Dear Mr Beddow –

Thank you for your most important letter. I am very glad to learn of the existence of the C.W.U.[101] which is exactly what is needed. And

---

93 Sir Thomas Malory, *Le Morte d'Arthur*, with introduction by Professor Rhys, 2 vols. (London: Dent, Everyman's Library [1906]).

94 Sir Thomas Malory, *Le Morte Darthur* (London: Dent, Temple Classics, 1897).

95 Geoffrey of Monmouth, *Histories of the Kings of Britain*, trans. Sebastian Evans (London: Dent, Temple Classics, 1904).

96 *Arthurian Chronicles, Represented by Wace and Layamon*, trans. Eugene Mason, with introduction by Lucy Allen Paton (London: Dent, Everyman's Library [1912]).

97 E. K. Chambers, *Arthur of Britain* (London: Sidgwick & Jackson, 1927).

98 R. G. Collingwood and J. N. L. Myres, *Roman Britain and the English Settlements*, Oxford History of England, vol. I (Oxford: Clarendon Press, 1937).

99 Eugène Vinaver, *Malory* (Oxford: Clarendon Press, 1929).

100 The Rev. Canon John Beddow (1893–1963) was born at Shortheath, Willenhall, Staffordshire, on 14 February 1893. He trained for the priesthood at the House of the Sacred Mission, Kelham, and thereafter spent two years at the University of London. Ordained Deacon in 1916, he was Assistant Tutor at St Paul's Missionary College, Burgh, that year. Upon his ordination as a priest in 1917 for the diocese of Lincoln he was Curate at St Andrew's, Grimsby, 1917–21, and afterwards at St Mark's, Leicester, 1921–6. He was Rector of St Michael's Church, Coppenhall, Cheshire, 1926–48 and Vicar of St Oswald's, Cheshire from 1948 until his death on 9 April 1963. He was made a Canon of Chester in 1946.

101 The Christian Workers' Union, a youth organization which had a branch in Canon Beddow's parish at Coppenhall St Michael.

I agree that it is essential for all 'literature' it issues to its members to be a *translation* into the actual current speech of the people (It has always seemed to me odd that those who are sent to evangelise the Bantus begin by learning Bantu while the Church turns out annually curates to teach the English who simply don't know the vernacular language of England).

But of course I can't write a book for workers. I know nothing at all of the realities of factory life. If one of you will *write* the book, I will *translate* it: i.e. instead of a book by me edited by you, you need a book by you edited by me. That is, if you really need me at all. But are you sure you do? People praise me as a 'translator', but what I want is to be the founder of a school of 'translation'.

I am nearly forty-seven. Where are my successors? Anyone can learn to do it if they wish. It only involves first writing down in ordinary theological college English exactly what you want to say and then treating that just as you treated a piece of English set for Greek prose at school (The parallel is v. close. Popular English differs from 'scholarly' English in v. much the same way as Attic does: i.e. more verbs and particles and fewer abstract nouns). It is also a v. good discipline because nine times out of ten the bit you can't turn into Vernacular turns out to be the bit which hadn't any clear meaning to begin with.

On p. 5 of Fr. Roseveare's pamphlet I read 'There is no need for me to enlarge upon the wide-spread ignorance of Xtian truth wh. is characteristic of our age and generation.'[102] The moment you started to consider 'doing this into Greek prose' you'd see you'd have to get rid of the noun 'ignorance' and that 'characteristic' wd. have to be 'turned'. So in turning it into the vernacular. It wd. finally come out something like 'I need not waste time in telling you that very few people in modern England know what Christianity actually teaches. We need not at the moment ask why this is so or who ought to be blamed for it, etc.'

It is inconceivable that there is no one among you who can do this quite as well as I could: and it is far better that it should be done by those who know at first hand what needs to be said. So my advice is

102 Richard Polgreen Roseveare, *Bridging the Gulf: An Address Given at the First Conference of the Christian Workers' Union, Sheffield, February 1943* (Sheffield: Christian Workers' Union [1943]).

that you get on with it at once (it does one endless good of all sorts as a mere bye-product) and use me as a mere reviser if you want me at all. (Remember that in the Vernacular *creature* means 'beast', a *being* means a 'person'. *Personal* often means 'corporeal', *Primitive* means 'crude' or 'barbarous', and avoid words like *Challenge*, *Tribute* and all newspaper clichés).

I feel I'm talking rather like a tutor – forgive me. But it is just a technique and I'm desperately anxious to see it widely learned. With all good wishes.

Yours sincerely,
C. S. Lewis

TO HARRY BLAMIRES (BOD):[103]

[Magdalen]
Oct. 12/45

My dear Blamires –

I have read your MS.[104] I think your main thesis – that it is time to do for Scott what Bethell has done for Shakespeare[105] – is new, v. important, and true. At any rate, as far as I am concerned, it has illuminated the Waverley novels more than anything I have yet read about them. On your main theme the only thing you *may* be wrong about (I don't know whether you *are*) is your belittlement of the historical element in them. I'm not sure that, besides being what you say, they do not also make a quite new realisation of the past. Trevelyan (the Master of Trinity one, the historian) said to me last summer 'In Gibbon all the characters, Goths, Romans, and Orientals alike are envisaged as 18th. century people. In Macaulay's *History of England*[106] we are made to feel on every page that our ancestors were different from us. I attribute this change almost entirely to the fact that the Waverley Novels have come in between.' He's not a man whose opinion is to be lightly set aside. I suspect Scott is so big that your point and

103 See **Harry Blamires** in the Biographical Appendix.

104 This was the manuscript of a book on 'Scott and his Predecessors' which has never been published.

105 Samuel Leslie Bethell, *Shakespeare and the Popular Dramatic Tradition* (1944).

106 Thomas Babington Macaulay, *History of England* (vols. 1–2, 1849; vols. 3–4, 1855).

Trevelyan's are both true. That is my only cavil with your thesis. I think you have struck gold and made a real critical advance. On minor issues, however, I have some criticisms to make.

In Part I I implore you to retract your disparagement of J. Austen. As it stands it wd. be fatal to you in your first book. You have no idea how ready critics (even scholarly ones) are to seize on some one thing wh. they dislike and then allow it to blind them to everything else in the book. You'll find that 3 out of every 5 reviewers of your book will talk almost exclusively about your views on J. A. If it were a question of conscience I wd. not advise you to conceal your belief on that account. But, far from having a moral duty, you haven't even a logical duty, to attack her. All that is relevant is [to] point out the difference in *kind* between her and the 'dramatic' novelists. You needn't go into degrees of merit at all. If, in spite of this advice, you still want to dispraise her, at least let your censures be grave and civil. As they stand, they are sneering & sometimes cheap.

Ought Lady Morgan not to be mentioned?

With Part II I must confess that, after a v. attractive opening in Pt I, I felt a growing disappointment. I think this comes from the plan of hacking your way through novel by novel. This, as you must have felt yourself, entails intolerable repetition. Cd. you bear to re-cast it? *Either* devoting separate chapters only to the greatest novels or to novels each of wh. heads a certain list, say, of good or bad or other classified specimens: *or else* divide not by novels but by subjects. (Recurrent Elements of Plot – Philosophical Conflicts – Dialogue – Scenic Backgrounds – etc.)

The *concepts* you use do not always seem to me satisfactory. Thus your repeated contrast of intellectual >< emotional or rational >< romantic for me messes up the whole issue. The old Xtian thought of wh. you make Scott the heir wd. have been horrified at your suggestion that avarice & ambition are more 'rational' than love & loyalty. Most of the conduct you call 'emotional' or 'romantic' wd. have seemed to it in conformity with the Divine Reason. If Scott didn't see this (and perhaps he did *not*) that is just what separates him from Dante & Shakespeare. But *you* must see it. I also dislike your use of the word 'Materialism'. That word shd. always be used in its strict philosophical sense. You use it to mean 'utilitarianism' or 'worldliness' or 'egoism': all those wd. be better words.

I also think you make Scott out much more of an egalitarian than he really was. Of course he does see that *sub specie aeternitatis*[107] Edie & Sir Arthur[108] are of one clay. But he also does believe in 'blood' & honour & chivalry quite terrifically. The descent from the Crusade theme to the Honour theme in the *Talisman*[109] was not in his eyes a descent to the ridiculous! You have every right to differ from him: but in places I feel that you have not fully brought into consciousness & faced the enormous difference between his ideology and yours and therefore treat as mere lapses or concessions to plot things that he really deeply felt.

To gain credit for our praise we must admit just blame. You shd. somewhere acknowledge the abominations of Scott's style at his worst, (See *G. Mannering* cap 3 'Above *rolled* the planets, each by its own liquid *orbit* of light distinguished etc.)

I have ventured to scrawl a few marginalia mostly on bad syntax or expressions which seem (to my perhaps old fashioned taste) mere vulgarisms. You are v. fond of the unattached participial clause & of expressions like 'The getting up too late in the morning theme plot technique'.

These are my grumbles. But you've got a first rate book in hand if only you can write it (as I think you can. Many paragraphs are excellent). I wish *I'd* thought of it! All good wishes,

Yours
C. S. Lewis

P. S. I thought *a priori* that the length of Pt I was disproportionate but didn't find any *longeurs* in actually reading it – except possibly the passage on Smollett. But you communicated so much of your own enjoyment in dealing with him that I shd. let the passage stand.

107 'under the aspect of eternity'.
108 Edie Ochiltree and Sir Arthur Wardour are characters in Scott's *The Antiquary*.
109 Sir Walter Scott, *The Talisman* (1825).

TO HERBERT PALMER (TEX):[110]

Magdalen College,
Oxford.
Nov 8?th 45

Dear Mr. Palmer –

What a delightful surprise packet.[111] I've been saying to myself for a long time that you were a poet I must look into – but I confess the day had never come. The truth is I'm v. unfair to contemporaries. When it comes to the point I always ask myself why I shd. go to a bookseller and get something wh. I *may* like when my shelves are full of what I certainly *do* like already.

I don't defend this practice (tho' it has its rewards. Some unanalysable impulse last week sent me back to Rostand's *Cyrano*[112] after over thirty years and I've been drunk as a boy on it ever since). And now vice is rewarded.

I have had great pleasure in your volume. I like best your coarsest and most mallet-like rhythms wh. exactly suit the matter: especially in the *Vampire*, and *Passion*. But also, in a different way, the more elusive ones like *Black Magic* and *Depression*. And it's nice to meet honest rhyming pathos once more in *Girl & Soldier*.[113] (We don't cry enough now a days, that's one of the things that is wrong with us. Achilles cried, Roland cried, Lancelot cried. It's in Shakespeare that characters first start apologising for tears).[114] Thanks v. much.

---

110 Herbert Edward Palmer (1880–1961), poet and literary critic, was born in a Methodist manse in Lincolnshire. After a period as an elementary schoolteacher at Mexborough he attended Birmingham University. From 1899 he taught in various English schools, three French schools, and as a private tutor in Germany. In 1919 he began giving lectures to the Workers's Educational Association, but abandoned teaching in 1921 to devote himself to a literary career. His numerous works include *Two Foemen* (1920); *Two Minstrels* (1921); *The Armed Muse: Poems* (1930); *Season and Festival* (1943); *The Ride from Hell* (1958); and *The Mistletoe Child: An Autobiography of Childhood* (1935).

111 Palmer had sent him a copy of *The Vampire: And Other Poems of a Pilgrim's Progress* (1936).

112 Edmond Rostand, *Cyrano de Bergerac* (1897).

113 Lewis was referring to Palmer's poem, 'The Girl and the Soldier: 1914–18', p. 12, stanza 6: 'Oh, why are your eyes so wild, and your cheeks with fever glowing?/ *Because I'll never see you more, and the last bugles are blowing.*'

114 See, for example, the Duke of Exeter's words in *Henry V*, IV, vi, 28–31: 'The pretty and sweet manner of it forc'd/Those waters from me which I would have stopp'd;/But I had not so much of man in me,/And all my mother came into

About my own verse. Alas, I am not 'that poet who should come'. All the P.R. poems were in the first (1932) edition and most were written a fair time before the book.[115] They are not the dawn of a talent coming but the twilight of a talent going and there has been little since then. I sweated all the blood I had trying to be a poet from about the age of 15 to 30, and did publish (under a pseudonym) a narrative poem[116] wh. reviewers praised. But no one ever bought it and I gave up in the end.

I'm afraid there's a lot of mere personal resentment, even envy (who knows?) in all that part about the Clevers[117] and I've no doubt the history is all muddled. But doubtless you read me to the bottom – i.e. that my experience was much like yours only you've kept on and I gave up. The old wound aches just a little at the touch. Though in graver moods I wonder what on earth or out of it wd. have happened to me if I really had become a successful poet in my twenties. You know what the passion for poetical fame is like at that age – a white hot lust, a blind idolatry, disenchanting all else. Victoriana,[118] by the way, was Edith Sitwell[119] because she was (or I thought she was) doing a sort of half mocking revival of the Victorian scene. I've repented about her since. I think she has real beauty – in verse: the silliness and conceit of some of the critical work puts me out of all patience.

---

mine eyes/And gave me up to tears.' Cf. *English Literature in the Sixteenth Century* (1954), Introduction, p. 52: 'In ancient and medieval literature, as in ancient and medieval life, there is no inhibition about tears. Achilles wept, Aeneas wept, the Roman legionaries wept, Hrothgar wept, Roland wept . . . and Lancelot, to his lasting glory, wept like a beaten child at the healing of Sir Urre . . . In Shakespeare a male character seldom weeps without apologizing for it.'

115 i.e. *The Pilgrim's Regress.*

116 i.e. *Dymer*, published under the pseudonym Clive Hamilton.

117 *The Pilgrim's Regress*, book III, ch. 1.

118 A member of the Clevers in *The Pilgrim's Regress*, book III, ch. 1.

119 Dame Edith Sitwell (1887–1964), poet and critic, was from a literary family. Her brothers Osbert and Sacheverell were also poets. Edith's first volume of verse, *The Mother*, appeared in 1915; her next (with Osbert Sitwell) was *Twentieth-Century Harlequinade* (1916). *Façade* (with William Walton) in 1923 was regarded as extremely witty and probably caused Lewis to cast her as Victoriana in *The Pilgrim's Regress.* It was followed by *The Sleeping Beauty* (1924), a volume of elegiac, romantic poems, one of which Lewis praised in his letter to Warnie of 25 February 1940. Some of her other poems were *Bucolic Comedies* (1923), *Troy Park* (1925), *Street Songs* (1942), *Green Song* (1944), and *Shadow of Cain* (1947). Her prose works include *English Eccentrics* (1933).

I'll try to get P-V-P,[120] but with little hope of success. All books seem unobtainable at the moment. But I hope you won't write much more about those people. Are they worth it?

As soon as they allow us to have guests in College again (they've stopped us since the new rationing) you must come down & dine & spend a night. I can get some people to meet you who share many of your views. I'd like to write more but I've been writing all evening. I'm *very* pleased to have made your acquaintance & look forward to prosecuting it.

Yours
C. S. Lewis

'Two from three leaves ninety one'[121] is really extraordinarily effective *in contextu*:[122] one doesn't quite know why.

'Talking about 'making a world', have you read Eddison's *The Worm Ouroboros*? Good to the taste as home cured ham.

TO T. S. ELIOT (P): TS

REF.231/1/45

Magdalen College,
Oxford.
17th November 1945.

Dear Mr. Eliot,

I could (or at any rate *would*) find the time if I knew the subject. But I'm more an ex-medievalist than a medievalist now, and even in my palmy days I knew very little about the Albigensians.[123] I could'nt without months work, give you an opinion of any value.

Sorry.

yours sincerely,
C. S. Lewis

---

120 Herbert Palmer, *Post-Victorian Poetry* (1938).

121 *The Vampire: And Other Poems*, 'The Vampire', stanza 19, 4.

122 'in context'.

123 The Albigensians, from Southern France, were a branch of the Cathars, a large group of medieval dissenters who proved to be a serious challenge to the Church in the twelfth and thirteenth centuries.

TO JAMES W. WELCH (BBC):[124] TS

REF.214.44.

Magdalen College,
Oxford.
24th November 1945.

Dear Welch,

I am hoping to try the microphone again in the next few years if I may, and am glad to hear that the gate is still open. But this year and next, work will be so fast and furious at Oxford (the full tide of the demobbed pupils is now upon us) that nothing can be done.

With many thanks.

yours
C. S. Lewis

TO DOROTHY L. SAYERS (W):

Magdalen College,
Oxford.
Dec 6th. 1945

Dear Miss Sayers

Yes, by all means send the un-curtailed and *un*-expurgated text to me as soon as it is typed.[125] I mean to make a push at getting every contributor the space he wants: your essay and Tolkien's will both be v. long but I expect Eliot's will be short and so will mine be. You notice of course that Sir Humphrey has retired and been succeeded at the press by some very new-broomish person with a name like Blunderbore or Cumberback.[126] We may split on that rock but I don't think so.

---

124 Dr Welch, former Director of Religious Broadcasting, was now Chaplain to His Majesty King George VI and working part time for the BBC. Writing to Lewis on 22 November he said: 'It is some time since we had a series of broadcast talks from you, and a great many listeners are anxious to hear you again. Have you anything you would like to say during May, June or July of 1946?'

125 In a letter of 3 December, Sayers said she had completed her essay for the *Festschrift* 'which my poor secretary is now slowly reducing to typescript' (Sayers, *Letters*, vol. III, p. 176).

126 Geoffrey Fenwick Jocelyn Cumberlege (1891–1979), after taking his BA from Worcester College, Oxford, served with distinction in the First World War. On his demobilization in 1919 he joined Oxford University Press under Sir Humphrey Milford, succeeding E. V. Rieu as manager of the Indian branch of the Press in Bombay. In 1924 he was appointed president of Oxford University Press in New York, where he remained until 1934 when he returned to England as Milford's principal assistant in the London branch of the Press. In 1945 he was appointed publisher to the University of Oxford. From then until his retirement

Thanks for the kind things you say about *That Hideous Strength*,[127] all the more welcome because it has got a more unanimous chorus of unfavourable reviews than any book I can remember. Apparently reviewers *will not* tolerate a mixture of the realistic and the supernatural. Which is a pity, because (a) It's just the mixture I like, and (b) We have to put up with it in real life. I am so glad you liked the descent of the gods. Mr. Bultitude is described by Tolkien as a portrait of the author, but I feel that is too high a compliment.

I suppose when Stafford Cripps[128] starts controlling publishing we Christian authors will be silenced. What does A do next?

I'm looking forward to your article immensely. With all good wishes,

Yours sincerely
C. S. Lewis

The Inklings had planned a 'Victory Inklings' to celebrate the end of the war, but in the end only three of them – Jack, Warnie and Tolkien – were able to get away. They spent three days, 12–14 December, at the Bull Hotel in Fairford, Gloucestershire – walking, talking, staying up late.[129]

TO DOROTHY L. SAYERS (W):

REF. 232/1/45.

Magdalen College,
Oxford.
14th December 1945.

Dear Miss Sayers,

Although you have so little time to write letters you are one of the great English letter writers. (Awful vision for you – 'It is often forgotten that Miss Sayers was known in her own day as an Author.

---

in 1956 his most significant achievement was the publication, with Cambridge University Press, of the *New English Bible*.

127 Sayers, *Letters*, vol. III, p. 177: 'The book is tremendously full of good things . . . the arrival of the gods is grand and (in a different manner) the atmosphere of the N.I.C.E. is superb. Wither is a masterpiece; even with some experience of official documents and political speeches, one would not have believed it possible to convey so little meaning in so many words . . . Mr Bultitude of course is adorable.'

128 Sir Stafford Cripps (1889–1952), statesman and lawyer, was President of the Board of Trade, 1945–7, and Chancellor of the Exchequer, 1947–50.

129 See Warnie's account in *BF*, pp. 184–5.

We, who have been familiar from childhood with the Letters can hardly realize . . .') But I'm not.

No, Hopkins[130] is not contributing to the volume. A dear creature though.

Yes, I'm all for little books on other subjects with their Christianity latent. I propounded this in S.C.R. at Campion Hall[131] and was told it was 'Jesuitical'.

The Hall Porter at the 'Bull', Fairford likes 'The Man born to be King' (and of such is the kingdom). I've got to have a long talk with you about Socratic Clubs some time soon. In great haste,

yours sincerely,
C. S. Lewis

TO HERBERT PALMER (TEX):

Magdalen
Dec. 15th 1945

Dear Mr. Palmer

You will be wondering by now what has happened to me or perhaps what has happened to my manners. The silence was not, however, due to any lack of appreciation for your most kind present of the two more volumes. The fact is that the last week or so of term & the first week after term is such a jungle of scholarship exams and viva's and committees that I have been unable to keep my head above water at all. Routine work had to go on whatever else was happening: and also – what is the most harassing part of my routine – the never-ending correspondence with people I shall never hear of again.

You have been worse treated because I put you in the class of *real* correspondents. These I tend to keep waiting, while the mere *sine nomine vulgus*[132] (I don't mean to say anything against them: they're very nice, some of them) have to be dealt with punctually or I'd be 'eternally floored'.

---

130 Gerard Walter Sturgis Hopkins, employee of Oxford University Press. See note 126 of the letter to Hopkins of 5 November 1946.

131 The Jesuit college at Oxford.

132 'the many who are unknown to me'. *Selections from Erasmus*, ed. Percy Stafford Allen (1908), ch. VII, 'An Oxford Dinner Party', letter from Erasmus to Johannes Sixtinus, November 1449, about a dinner party in Magdalen College, p. 27.

I thought the *Song of S. & G.*[133] contained some of your v. best work but I must admit the appearance of the *feminine* figure came with a jolt. Another thing that gave me a kick (*kicks* are good, *jolts* bad) was the last 2 lines of *Satiric Sob.* Also *Black Magic* and *David & Goliath.* But I have not really had time, let alone peace within or without, to digest either book.

It is one of the disagreeable signs of increasing age that the act of *receiving* new poetry becomes to me every year more arduous and the moments at which it is even possible become rarer. I am with the Muse now as an old lecher in whom desire outruns performance. I have to watch for favourable moments.

And I am (all these last 6 months) immersed in a v. different poet whom I think great – Charles Williams: the two volumes of his Arthurian poems *Taliessin* and *The Region of the Summer Stars.*[134] Inexcusably difficult, as I always told him, but here there really is something behind the difficulty – that something wh. we all need most in literature at present & wh. I wd. call opaque splendour – thick, rich, solid, heavy – porphyry, gold, diamond.

I *did* get the impression that your danger lies in the direction of writing too much poetry *about* poetry and about the isolated situation in which people like you and me now find ourselves. I say *danger*, not disaster: i.e. the thing hasn't happened but I feel it might, I mean one might so easily develop a *Starrenlied*[135] as monotonous as Mime's.[136] In fact that is how Roy Campbell[137] has frittered away a real talent. There were years of my own life during wh. the literary situation, the ascendancy of the Eliotics,[138] the dominance of the *Criterion* & *Scrutiny* was the daily subject of my thoughts and nagged me like a nagging tooth: but thank God I got out of it. It's no subject for a man to spend his life on. 'Noble rage'[139] is an *ignis fatuus*[140] and always turns in the end to shrill peevishness.

133 Herbert Palmer, *Songs of Salvation, Sin and Satire* (1925).
134 Charles Williams, *The Region of the Summer Stars* (1944).
135 'monotonous song'.
136 Mime is one of the dwarfs in Richard Wagner's *Ring of the Nibelung.*
137 See note 107 to the letter to Roy Campbell of 16 August 1946.
138 The poetry of T. S. Eliot, Ezra Pound and other moderns.
139 Tennyson, *In Memoriam*, XXVII, 1–2: 'I envy not in any moods/The captive void of noble rage.'
140 'deceiving flame'.

I am astonished at what Miss Pitter[141] says and am most deeply rejoiced to find that my work is not (as her rash kindness betrayed her into saying) the 'joy of her life' but the occasion wh. sometimes awakes that joy into activity. The little I have seen of her work I admired very greatly.[142]

This is a v. illegible letter, I'm afraid. That is because I have the rheumatism. We must meet next term. With many thanks

Yours
C. S. Lewis

TO DOROTHY L. SAYERS (W):

As from Magdalen
Dec. 18th (?) 1945

Dear Miss Sayers –

I've romped through your essay for a first reading with v. great delight.[143] There's not a dull moment and some things are superlatively good; the distinction on p. 19 – 'they are great and dead' on p. 24[144] – the very important footnote on p. 43 which might well be made into a whole essay some other day – the part about the mirroring of the theme by the poetic quality, p. 45 – and then, best of all, even great, the whole of pp. 50 and 51.

I am puzzled as to what shd. be done about the quotations. To give English as well as Italian wd, I agree, terribly increase bulk. But aren't you at present translating Dante? If so, why not English *only*, with references so that the reader can look up the original if he wants? (I

---

141 i.e. Ruth Pitter, the poet. See her biography in the Biographical Appendix.

142 See Don W. King, 'The Anatomy of a Friendship: The Correspondence of Ruth Pitter and C. S. Lewis', *Mythlore*, vol. 24, no. 1 (Summer 2003), p. 4: 'In a letter of Nov. 15, 1945, in which [Pitter] comments briefly on several of Lewis's books . . . she writes Palmer: "Are you really going to see Lewis? One of the few people it's worth getting excited over, I think. I know he is a good poet. I daresay he never heard of me, but I wish you would tell him that his work is the joy of my life. One's homesickness for Heaven finds at least an inn there; and it's an inn on the right road. You're absolutely right about his importance – *portentous*."'

143 Sayers's contribution to *Essays Presented to Charles Williams* is entitled '. . . And Telling You a Story: A Note on *The Divine Comedy*'.

144 ibid., p. 15: 'In a twinkling . . . we are pulled back to the tremendous scene and the cosmic realities: this is Mount Purgatory, these are Statius and Virgil, and they are great and dead.'

mean, in most cases. You cd. always keep the Italian for one or two passages where the exact turn of phrase in the Italian was your main point). As it stands I am afraid many bits of the criticism will be unintelligible to those who can't translate the quotations. Will you consider this?[145]

On a separate sheet I add detailed comments and suggestions. Needless to say, you needn't bother about them unless you like: in fact I know you won't.* It's a grand essay. As for *Aeneas at the Court of Dido*, the sentiments are just and the numbers pleasing which is one of Johnson's definitions of poetry – unless I've just invented it.[146]

Yours very sincerely
C. S. Lewis
*i.e. unless you like

TO CHAD WALSH (W):[147]

REF.515/1/45.

Magdalen College,
Oxford.
18th. December 1945.

Dear Mr. Walsh,

Thank you for your kind and encouraging letter of the 30th. November. I'm afraid I've exhausted the (even theoretically) inhabitable planets! But the final one of this trilogy[148] – the scene is Earth – will be published in America any day now.

yours sincerely,
C. S. Lewis

---

145 In the end the quotations from *The Divine Comedy* were given in Italian with English translation.

146 Johnson, *Lives of the English Poets*, vol. I, Life of Abraham Cowley, p. 47: 'It is urged by Dr. Sprat, that the *irregularity of numbers is the very thing* which makes *that kind of poesy fit for all manner of subjects*. But he should have remembered, that what is fit for every thing can fit nothing well. The great pleasure of verse arises from the known measure of the lines, and uniform structure of the stanzas, by which the voice is regulated, and the memory relieved.'

147 See **Chad Walsh** (1914–91) in the Biographical Appendix. On 30 November 1945 Walsh wrote to Lewis praising *Perelandra*, and received this response.

148 *That Hideous Strength*.

TO OWEN BARFIELD (W):

[The Kilns]
Dec. 19. 1945

My dear Barfield –

It was a blow. The others (Tolkien & W.) had preceded me and when I arrived at Fairford station[149] and came forth unaccompanied by you from the train 'dim sadness did not spare that time celestial visages'.[150]

We endeavoured however to obey your advice. We walked. We argued. We were courteous but by no means obsequious. That stretch of country round Fairford shows nothing on a map but is in its own shy way most beautiful when you come to walk it: just a fine English winter beauty of plough & haystack & stubble and bare trees and rooks and dry stone walls and white skies. We found a pub really called the Pig & Whistle which is a thing I never saw before. And in another, can you believe it, a landlady also of her own free hospitality gave us home made ginger-snaps to sweeten our beer with. While at Fairford I read the life of Lewis Carroll:[151] containing the Latin version of the Jaberwock

Coesper erat: tunc lubriciles ultravia circum
Urgebant gyros gimbiculosque tophi.[152]

(*Coesper* as from *coena* & *vesper* cf. *Brillig*). The best line is 'his vorpal blade went snicker-snack' – Persnicuit gladio persnacuique puer.

About W. de la Mare. (1) There was prior evidence, wh. you communicated to me, that he did *not* wish to meet me. (2) The new evidence, on the most optimistic interpretation, does not prove that he *does.* (3) There is no evidence that Tolkien particularly wants to see *him.* (4) And why the Hell should the poor man be made to meet

---

149 Barfield had planned to take part in the 'Victory Inklings' at Fairford, but he was ill and unable to attend.

150 Milton, *Paradise Lost,* X, 23–4.

151 Stuart Dodgson Collingwood, *The Life and Letters of Lewis Carroll (Rev. C. L. Dodgson)* (1898).

152 Collingwood, *The Life and Letters of Lewis Carroll,* p. 144: ''Twas brillig, and the slithy toves/Did gyre and gimble in the wabe', Latin translation by A. A.Vansittart. The English version of the poem 'Jabberwocky' is found in Lewis Carroll, *Through the Looking-Glass and What Alice Found There* (1872), ch. 1.

anyone. On the whole all the elements of the problem can be satisfied by the original and rather subtle solution of doing nothing about it.

But (this is a second problem & you want to keep them quite distinct) I am quite ready for some more poems about Betty, Hetty, or Tetty.[153]

Here's a metrical experiment of mine about the Atomic Bomb overleaf. And – they've relaxed their fierceness about guests in College so I hope you will come & spend a night in college next term. Isn't Harwood's play good?[154]

Yours
C. S. Lewis

The Atomic Bomb.[155]

So: you have found an engine
Of injury that angels
Might dread. The world plunges,
Shies, snorts and curvets like a horse in danger.

Well: comfort her with fondling,
With kindly words and handlings,
But never believe blindly
This way or that. Both fears and hopes are swindlers.

What's here to dread? For mortals
Both hurt and death were certain
Already: our light-hearted
Hopes sentenced from the first to final thwarting.

This makes no huge advance in
The dance of Death. His pincers
Were grim before with chances
Of cold, fire, suffocation, Ogpu,[156] cancer.

---

153 Barfield was writing a series of love poems addressed to a fictional 'Betty'.

154 This is Harwood's play, *A Rope Their Pulley: A Melodrama in Three Acts*, published in *The Voice of Cecil Harwood: A Miscellany*, ed. Owen Barfield (London: Rudolf Steiner Press, 1979).

155 The poem was published, with further alterations, under the title 'On the Atomic Bomb: Metrical Experiment' in *The Spectator*, CLXXV (28 December 1945), and is reprinted in *CP*.

156 An organization that operated in the USSR, 1923–34, to combat counter-revolutionary activities.

Nor hope that this last blunder
Will end our woes by rending
Tellus herself asunder
In one wide flash that fades and leaves no cinder.

Alas!, no mortal gadget
Will dodge the terrible logic
Of history. The long, tragic
Tale ends not till the Master comes to judge it.*

* *Varia lectio.*[157]

The long, tragic
Road will go on, new generations trudge it.

TO CECIL HARWOOD (BOD):

[The Kilns]
Boxing Day [26 December] 1945

My dear Harwood –

The play[158] has one radical fault, but not a fatal one: which is lucky since it can't be removed. The fault is this. When you see things from an unfamiliar angle, as you do by writing from the devil's plane, they ought to be familiar things. I mean it might be fun to paint a man as he would appear if you saw him from below thro' a sheet of glass: it wd. be silly to paint a centaur from that angle. I feel that in art there shd. be strangeness in one direction and ordinariness in another, never strangeness in both.

In *Gulliver* you get strange adventures in a studiously ordinary way. In Virginia Woolf you get v. ordinary life presented in a strange way. But *two* strangenesses is too much.

Your play would have been perfect if what we approached by way of Cinders & Firefly were the kind of moral crisis wh. happens to ordinary people daily: indeed the whole point shd. have been the ordinariness thus revealed in its eternal aspect. But Arnos & Lewti are in fact facing the sort of temptation wh. most human beings can't even imagine and very very few ever experience and that is to me a serious

157 'variant reading'.
158 i.e. Harwood's *A Rope Their Pulley*.

fault. Ordinary lust or jealousy or greed was what we wanted to see – in a play of this kind. It's hard when the devils are so much more human and so much more easy to understand than the mortals.[159]

There. That's all that need be said, and (I repeat) it is not fatal. I think the play in other ways v. good and I was carried through the first two acts without a hitch: and with many a real thrill. The business-like 'examination' of Centi (again *why* such an abnormal name?) is very horrid: and so is 'You are becoming what they call Conscious again.' That really gives one pause: as it was meant to. The finale of Act 3 is also excellent. What I am not so certain about is pp. 1–5. I think there is just a danger of the audience beginning not to listen there and finding it hard to follow.

By the way on p. 3 (Peter's last speech on that page) 'nothing to fight with' can mean in English either 'without weapons' or 'without enemy'.[160] Better substitute some less ambiguous form. I shd. very much like to *see* this play – and v. likely [a] performance wd. prove all my remarks wrong. Is it going to be done?

Oh – I'd nearly forgotten to say that Michael's poem[161] (pp. 6, 7) is good. I don't understand *bow* in l. 15. Is it a misprint? (I've just seen that you probably mean a fiddle-bow.[)] But it's too hard. And creaks – creaks cruelly.

The position in College about guests is now a little easier. I still couldn't have 2 guests to dinner. But what is to prevent you and Owen coming, all three of us dining at a hotel, and then to my rooms for wine, tea, & song? Bedrooms and breakfasts I can manage. Will you and he compare notes and give me some possible dates?

---

159 In his introduction to *The Voice of Cecil Harwood*, Barfield said of the play: 'I . . . suspected that, as a good play should be, it was written to be performed rather than read . . . even without that advantage, most of the difficulties were cleared up by a second and third reading, though I also wondered whether this would have been the case if I had not been acquainted in advance with the figures of Lucifer and Ahriman as they are presented in the Spiritual Science of Rudolf Steiner. Firefly and Cinders – and this is what the reader or spectator must somehow manage, never to let himself forget – are *deceivers*; and they remain so even while they are endowing the two human characters with genuine self-knowledge. It is difficult – but for the very same reason that life itself is difficult.'

160 Harwood, *A Rope Their Pulley*, p. 111: 'When you discover yourself, that is the end of the fight. Then you know there is nothing to fight for, and nothing to fight with.'

161 ibid., pp. 113–14.

You know the old rules ('I lay in my old guard, Hal')[162] – *not* Saturdays or Sundays and term better than Vac. if it cd. be managed. I shd. love it of all things. We three have lived too long merely *in posse*[163] and I am, in your own word, 'hungry'.

Is Kidbrooke nearer London than Minehead was? I hope to see it before I'm too old: but I mustn't be away from home more than the minimum until the conditions of my life change considerably.

I am writing to Laurence in a day or two: but don't tell him I am. Love to you all.

And I append two poems for you to have your revenge on. Oh – yes I *was* astonished at the Betty cycle: and delighted with some of the poetry. The *event* rather startled me. I suppose he's all right: but I'm glad that sort of thing doesn't happen to me!

Yours
C. S. Lewis

The Atomic Bomb[164]

So: you have found an engine
Of injury that angels
Might dread. The world plunges,
Shies, snorts and curvets like a horse in danger.

Well, comfort her with fondlings,
With kindly speech and handling,
But never believe blindly
This way or that. Both fears and hopes are swindlers.

What's here to dread? For mortals
Both hurt and death were certain
Already: our light-hearted
Hopes, from the first, sentenced to final thwarting.

---

162 This is said in imitation of Falstaff speaking to Prince Henry in Shakespeare's *Henry IV Part 1*.

163 'in regard to what might be'.

164 Lewis was constantly revising his poetry, and readers will notice how many alterations he had made in this poem since he sent a copy to Owen Barfield on 19 December.

This marks no huge advance in
The dance of death. His pincers
Were grim before with chances
Of stroke, fire, suffocation, Ogpu, cancer.

Nor hope that this new blunder
Will end our woes by rending
Tellus herself asunder
In one bright moment of preposterous splendour.

As if your paltry gadget
Could dodge the terrible logic
Of history! No: the tragic
Road will go on, new generations trudge it.

Narrow and long it stretches,
Wretched for him who marches
Eyes front. He never catches
A glimpse of the fields each side, the happy orchards.

P.S. I had hoped to return your MS along with this, but can find no envelope big enough. Why will you, like so many other people, make MSS unmanageable by enclosing them in huge sheets of unnecessary cardboard?

TO ARTHUR GREEVES (W):

[The Kilns]
Boxing Day [26 December] 1945

My dear Arthur –

I am sorry to see that it was October last when you wrote to me. But real correspondence (i.e. with my personal friends) is almost impossible in term time now.

You ask me a question about something on p. 323 of *That Hideous Strength*,[165] saying 'Surely God has always been the same loving and

165 Greeves was referring to *That Hideous Strength*, ch. 12, part V where Ransom says: 'Angels in general are not good company for men in general – even when they are good angels and good men. It's all in St Paul. But as for Maleldil [God] himself, all that has changed: it was changed by what happened at Bethlehem.'

heavenly Father and it was the *interpretation* of God that Christ revealed.' I see what you mean but the question is to me v. difficult to answer. On the one hand something really *new* did happen at Bethlehem: not an interpretation but an *event*. God became Man. On the other hand there must be a sense in which God, being outside time, is changeless and nothing ever 'happens' to Him. I think I should reply that the event at Bethlehem was a novelty, a change to the maximum extent to which any event is a novelty or change: but that *all* time and *all* events in it, if we cd. see them all at once and fully understand them, are a definition or diagram of what God eternally is.

But that is quite different from saying that the incarnation was simply an interpretation, or a change in *our* knowledge. When Pythagoras discovered that the square on the hypotenuse was equal to the sum of the squares on the other two sides he was discovering what had been just as true the day before though no one knew it. But in 50 B.C. the proposition 'God is Man' wd. *not* have been true in the same sense in wh. it was true in 10 A.D. because tho' the union of God and Man in Christ is a timeless fact, in 50 B.C. we hadn't yet got to that bit of time which defines it. I don't know if I make myself clear.

Warnie has just been playing me Holst's *Planets*[166] on the gramophone. Have you got them? I distrust my own musical judgements more and more the more I hear really musical people talking and suspect that most of my enjoyment is emotion produced out of my own imagination at rather slight hints (it may even be *accidental* hints) from the music. I therefore don't think it is any very real commendation of the *Planets* to say that I was greatly moved by it. I should be glad to hear your views, if you have got the work. I thought the three last (Saturn, Uranus, Neptune) the best and Jupiter the weakest. Mars, of course, bowls one over but I suppose there is an element of trick in it.

I had great hopes a while ago of getting over to Belfast to give a lecture at Queen's (without some official pretext it seems almost impossible to get allowed onto the Liverpool boat) but dates wouldn't fit and it all fell through, much to my disappointment. I long to see you and the place again. Though I also dread seeing the place. How much has it been spoiled? – I don't mean by the war but by the peace. Is there a

166 Gustav Holst's suite, *The Planets*, was first performed on 15 November 1920.

building estate all round the Shepherd's Hut by now? or a factory half way up Cabra?

We got news of Uncle Gussie's death yesterday.[167] A difficult man to think of from that point of view. He was, as far as one can see, a very selfish man who yet succeeded in avoiding all the usual consequences of selfishness: that is, he was not at all a bore, had no self-pity, was not jealous, and seemed to be as happy as the day was long. I think he illustrates the enormous difference between selfishness and self-centredness. He had plenty of the first: he pursued his own interests with v. little regard to other people. But he had none of the second. I mean, he loved outside himself. His mind was not occupied with himself but with science, music, yachting etc. That was the good element and it was (as I think all good elements are) richly rewarded in this life. Let's hope and pray that it will carry him through where he is now. It may be the little spark of innocence and disinterestedness from which the whole man can be reconstructed.

There's all the difference in the world between a fire that has gone out and one that is *nearly* out. The latter, with skilful treatment, can always be coaxed back to life. It is rather a terrible thing that some people who try really hard to be unselfish yet have in them that terrible self-centredness which he was free from.

I've got a v. rheumaticy shoulder wh. partly explains the bad hand-writing and am threatened with a second small operation on my throat: but nothing to be alarmed about.

Minto is only so-so in health, and often v. unhappy in mind. She is supposed not to get up till lunch time now and hates the inactivity. Luckily she has taken to reading, however, and to my great surprise got through & enjoyed the whole of *War & Peace*. She sends her love and asks if you have any hair left! (I have practically none). I hope your mother keeps fairly well. Give her my warmest love . . . dear, dear, I wonder what you and I will be like when we're old? Shall we do any better?

I suppose I advised you before to get E. R. Eddison's *The Worm Ouroboros* if you ever come across it? But the book famine is very bad: it is one of my difficulties as a tutor that my pupils simply can't get

167 Uncle Gussie – Augustus Warren Hamilton – died at his home in Holywood, Co. Down, on 24 December 1945. He was 79 years old.

any of the books I want them to read. You and I were immensely fortunate in growing up during a period when the supply of good books in cheap editions was practically inexhaustible. Indeed we were fortunate in many ways: in finding one another, in delightful country, in having enough money but not too much

Well, all good wishes

Yours

Jack

1946

TO LAURENCE HARWOOD (BOD):

The Kilns,
Headington Quarry,
Oxford.
Jan 3rd 1946

My dear Lawrence

Thank you very much for your nice letter and card. How I should like to see Kidbrooke, it sounds a lovely place, though in some ways I don't think it could be nicer than Minehead. As it is in Sussex, perhaps you will find the birds called yaffles.[1]

We are having very sharp frosts here. The pond is frozen over but not thick enough for skating yet. Our dog Bruce, who is very old and white-haired now, feels the cold very badly and has to be wrapped up in a blanket at night – he looks very funny in it.

Yesterday the man who lives next door to us came into our garden when we weren't looking and cut down one of our trees.[2] He said it had elm-disease and was spoiling *his* garden, but as he took the wood away with him I call it stealing and we are very angry. He is an old man with a white beard who eats nothing but raw vegetables. He used to be a schoolmaster. He keeps goats who also have white beards and eat nothing but raw vegetables. If I knew magic I should like to turn him into a goat himself: it wouldn't be so very wicked because he is

---

1 i.e. woodpeckers.

2 This was Oswald Byron Powell (1867–1967), who lived at Hawstead (now 58 Kiln Lane), a house older than The Kilns. Powell took a BA from Trinity College, Cambridge, in 1889 after which he taught at Manchester Grammar School. In 1893, the year of its foundation, he joined the staff of Bedales School. Powell was Second Master, 1893–1933, head of the Modern Languages department and conductor of the choir. He moved to Kiln Lane with his wife Margaret (Donington) Powell in 1934, and died there in 1967 at the age of ninety-nine. He is the author of *A Book of German Songs* (1940).

so like a goat already! Don't you think it would serve him right? But I suppose he would then come over and eat the bark of the trees instead of cutting them down, so we should be no better off.

The other thing I might do would be to challenge him to a duel but I suppose he is too old to fight and anyway I am not much good at fencing. Have you ever learned fencing? I think it would be nice.

A few weeks ago I went into an inn near Oxford where the landlady gave me home-made ginger biscuits free along with my cider. Do you wish you had been there? – or don't you like them?

The stars have been wonderfully bright here lately. This house is so funnily built that I have to go up to my bedroom by an outside stairway in the open air. As I get up Sirius (*very* bright and green) looks as if he was sitting just on the top rail, and then when I reach the top I see the whole of Orion. Orion, Cassiopea and the Plough are the only constellations I can be sure of picking out. Do you know any more? (I like Orion the best).

I hope you got a book token I sent you, but don't bother replying if you have too many other letters to write. I have to write about seven a day all the year round: isn't that dreadful? So I must stop this one now and begin the next. All love and good wishes to you and all the others for 1946.

Your affectionate godfather
C. S. Lewis

TO DOROTHY L. SAYERS (W): TS

REF. 46/19

Magdalen College,
Oxford.
7th. January 1946.

Dear Miss Sayers,

I forward the MS as a registered packet by this post.[3] *O noctes cenaeque deum*,[4] I should like to hear from you and Rieu,[5] but it is

3 On 4 January 1946 Sayers returned the revision of her *Festschrift* article, with the following comment: 'I have made the omissions which you suggest, and have written a bit to take the place of the passage that was too near Macaulay, and I have added prose translations of all the quotations.'

4 Horace, *Satires,* II, vi, 65: 'O nights and feasts divine.'

5 In the same letter Sayers said she and her editor, E. V. Rieu, were 'preparing a combined reading . . . of portions of our respective translations, his of the *Odyssey* and mine of the *Inferno*. I should greatly have liked to ask you to make one of the audience.'

quite impossible. I've just finished reading his Odyssey straight through: in fact I could'nt stop it. I suppose that must answer all my particular disagreements ('The refined Calypso'[6] is a bit hard to get over!). With many thanks.

yours sincerely,
C. S. Lewis

TO WARFIELD M. FIROR (B): TS

REF.170/1/45.

Magdalen College,
Oxford.
12th. January 1946.

Dear Mr. Firar,

Many thanks for your kind and encouraging letter of the 1st. You could hardly have sent a more acceptable present than the paper; the shortage here is acute, and your gift had set me wondering daily who the kind anonymous benefactor could be. I thank you for it. Much as I should like to visit your country, I fear that the thing is quite impossible at present: not so much owing to pressure of work – though that is very heavy – but because I have an aged and ailing mother whom, in the existing shortage, or rather absence, of domestic help, it is impossible for me to leave. But I hope the time will come when I shall be able to visit such an interesting country where I seem to have so many kind friends.

With all best wishes for 1946,

yours sincerely,
C. S. Lewis

P.S. May I add my best wishes to your secretary, my fellow-townsman.

The Great Divorce: A Dream *was published by Geoffrey Bles: The Centenary Press on 14 January 1946. (The book was mistakenly dated 'November 1945'.)*

---

6 In Rieu's translation of the *Odyssey* (1945).

TO MRS FRANK L. JONES (W):[7] TS

REF.46/47.

Magdalen College,
Oxford.

Dear Mrs. Jones,

16th January 1946.

The general law is Beneficence.[8] Then come the laws that give certain people a prior claim on your beneficence: people to whom your beneficence is pledged by a promise (Justice), or who have already benefited you (Gratitude), or who are specially weak and pitiable (Mercy) or fellow-citizens (Patriotism) or relatives (Family Affection).

They are all perfectly sound, but the last two must not be allowed to over-ride the others. What I meant in that passage was that Racialism, setting up to be the supreme duty, is the rebellion of one particular moral law against moral law in general.

Thank you for your kind and encouraging letter.

yours sincerely,
C. S. Lewis

TO DOROTHY L. SAYERS (W): TS

REF. 46/19

Magdalen College,
Oxford.

Dear Miss Sayers,

22 January 1946.

Thanks for MS. I am in a *bolge* of pupils and have had not a moment to look at it. Yes, of course I had (and answered) your kind letter: we'll have it out some day about lucidity.[9]

---

7 Mrs Frank Jones was writing from 320 Brookside Road, Darien, Connecticut. She was to become a close pen-friend of the Lewis brothers. After Jack died, Warnie continued corresponding with her for the rest of his life.

8 Mrs Jones wanted to know what Lewis meant in *Out of the Silent Planet*, ch. 20 by 'the laws that all *hnau* know'. In answer to Weston's explanation that he cares only about spreading the seed of man throughout the solar system, the Oyarsa of Malacandra points out that he has isolated a fragment of Natural Law and is ignoring the rest: 'I see now, how the lord of the silent world has bent you. There are laws that all *hnau* know, of pity and straight dealing and shame and the like, and one of these is the love of kindred. He has taught you to break all of them except this one, which is not one of the greatest laws; this one he has bent till it becomes folly and has set it up, thus bent, to be a little blind Oyarsa in your brain.'

9 In her article in *Essays Presented to Charles Williams*, p. 2, Sayers described Dante's diction as 'homely, lucid, and fluent'. In the comments accompanying his letter of 18 December 1945, Lewis responded: '*lucid*. Great Gods!!! Yes, I know it is in *places*: but *lucid* just like that! Whose style wd. you call obscure, I'd like to know!' See

Thanks for the kind things you say about 'Grand Divorce'.[10] It owes more to the Purgatorio than to the Inferno. It all grew out of the Tragedian and the Lady:[11] specimen of a meeting like that of Beatrice and Dante in the Earthly Paradise and what happens when one side won't play.[12]

Have you any idea how far Eliot has got with *his* contribution to the C.W. volume?

yours sincerely,
C. S. Lewis

TO HERBERT PALMER (TEX):

Magdalen
Jan 26th 1946

Dear Mr. Palmer –

I have just read your preface[13] with as much interest and enjoyment as is possible to a man who has had a railway journey, no lunch, and a little pile of examination papers to correct! Thank you very much for letting me see it. I am much too ignorant of the subject to offer you any criticism of the slightest value: beyond pointing out that there is a misprint (*protaginist* for *protagonist*).

No, don't send me an *edition de luxe*: I am in such straights for book-room that the smallest edition of any book is the one I want! Thank you also for your overwhelming compliment to me in the preface. But I shd. feel much happier if you would tone it down a bit. As it stands I think it may do me harm, and if it does me harm it will do you harm too. I am just at that stage when people begin to be a little tired of my name – and the slightest touch of over-praise would raise the groundswell of hostility into a hurricane. (I expect the metaphor is all wrong). So 'draw it mild'.[14]

Sayers's reply of 24 December 1945 in Sayers, *Letters*, vol. III, p. 183. *Bolge* is Dante's word for the lower pits of hell.

10 i.e., *The Great Divorce*.

11 *The Great Divorce*, ch. 12.

12 Dante, *Purgatorio*, XXXI.

13 This was probably a draft preface to Palmer's *Sword in the Desert: A Book of Poems and Verses for the Present Time* (1946).

14 E. Cobham Brewer, *Dictionary of Phrase and Fable* (1898): 'We talk of remarks being highly flavoured, of strong language, of piquant remarks, of spicy words; so that to "draw it mild" refers to *liquor*; let it be mild, not too highly-flavoured, not too spicy and strong.'

About Charles Williams – I can't help saying that you must have been mistaken in thinking he was ever jealous of you: or of anybody or anything.

There are a lot of things in your letter that deserve answering at length but I am a dead man for everything except routine work for the next two months. Meanwhile, thanks again and all good wishes.

Yours
C. S. Lewis

TO SISTER PENELOPE CSMV (BOD):

Magdalen College,
Oxford
Jan 31st 1946

Dear Sister Penelope

I had meant to write to you before now, but life is very crowded. The rush of pupils returning from the forces makes Terms quite different from what they were in war time.

By the way, the returning men are *nice*: far nicer than my generation were when we came out of the army – and a much higher percentage of Christians.

I am delighted to hear that you have finished the sequence and look forward to seeing it in print. Meantime, how does the *De Incarnatione* sell. Did I tell you that the Queen of Belgium[15] (through a lady in waiting) asked me for a copy when it was out of print? ('we stand before Kings'!)[16] No, I didn't know about the Somerset Giants[17] and will try to look up *Country Life* if I can find where the Common Room servants keep the back numbers.

That Hideous Strength has been unanimously damned by all reviewers. About Holst's *Planets*, I heard Mars and Jupiter long ago and greatly admired them but have heard the complete work only within the last 6 weeks. But his characters are rather different from mine, I think.

---

15 This was probably Queen Elisabeth, the Queen Mother of Belgium (1876–1965), the wife of King Albert I (1875–1934). Presumably her lady-in-waiting had written to Lewis.

16 Proverbs 22:29.

17 Harwood Steele, 'The Somerset Giants', *Country Life*, XCIX (11 January 1946), pp. 66–8. The author examines from the air the Somerset Giants, which consist of the signs of the Zodiac, in outline and partly in relief, supposedly laid out in a circle ten miles in diameter near Glastonbury.

Wasn't his Mars brutal and ferocious? – in mine I tried to get the *good* element in the martial spirit, the discipline and freedom from anxiety. On Jupiter I am closer to him: but I think his is more 'jovial' in the *modern* sense of the word. The folk tune on which he bases it is not regal enough for my conception. But of course there is a general similarity because we're both following the medieval astrologers. His is, anyway, a rich and marvellous work.

Jane is up and down: some days miserable and jealous, at other times gentle and even jolly. We have two nice maids at present. My writing gets worse and worse, partly from rheumatism and partly from haste. How do you keep yourself? With all good wishes.

Yours sincerely
C. S. Lewis

TO N. FRIDAMA (P):[18]

Magdalen College,
Oxford
Feb 15th 1946

Dear Mr Fridama,

I was baptised in the Church of Ireland (same as Anglican). My parents were not notably pious but went regularly to church and took me. My mother died when I was a child.

My Xtian faith was first undermined by the attitude taken towards *Pagan* religion in the notes of modern editors of Latin & Greek poets at school. They always assumed that the ancient religion was pure error: hence, in my mind, the obvious question 'Why shouldn't ours be equally false?' A theosophical Matron at one school helped to break up my early beliefs,[19] and after that a 'Rationalist' tutor[20] to whom I went finished the job. I abandoned all belief in Xtianity at about the age of 14, tho' I pretended to believe for fear of my elders. I thus went thro' the ceremony of Confirmation in total hypocrisy. My beliefs continued to be agnostic, with fluctuation towards pantheism and various other sub-Xtian beliefs, till I was about 29.

I was brought back (a.) By Philosophy. I still think Berkeley is

18 Mr Fridama was writing from 4 Hadley Avenue, Clifton, New Jersey.

19 These facts form the basis of *SBJ*, ch. 4.

20 i.e. W. T. Kirkpatrick. See *SBJ*, ch. 9.

unanswerable.[21] (b.) By increasing knowledge of medieval literature. It became harder & harder to think that all those great poets & philosophers were wrong. (c.) By the strong influence of 2 writers, the Presbyterian George Macdonald & the R.C., G. K. Chesterton. (d.) By argument with an Anthroposophist. He failed to convert me to his own views (a kind of Gnosticism) but his attack on my own presuppositions smashed the ordinary pseudo-'scientific' world-picture forever.

On Calvinism. Both the statement that our final destination is already settled and the view that it still may be either Heaven or Hell, seem to me to imply the ultimate reality of Time, wh. I don't believe in. The controversy is one I can't join on either side for I think that in the real (Timeless) world it is meaningless. In great haste.

Yours sincerely
C. S. Lewis

TO DOROTHY L. SAYERS (W):

REF.46/19.

Magdalen College,
Oxford.
28th February 1946.

Dear Miss Sayers,

I thought as much. He's[22] not a *writer* in your sense at all. He's one of these poets (in the worst sense of the word). Shakespeare, Dryden, and Pindar could all deliver the goods to date. I'll write to him as you suggest. There's no sort of good trying to stare *me* out of countenance: I also have my mouse – tho' compared with yours 'tis of the Horatian species (*Mus ridiculus*)!

yours very sincerely,
C. S. Lewis

---

21 i.e. the ideas of the philosopher George Berkeley (1685–1753) regarding the existence of God. In his *Principles of Human Knowledge* (1710) Bishop Berkeley maintained that when we affirm material things to be real, we mean no more than that they are perceived by us. He went on to demonstrate in his *Principles* and *Three Dialogues between Hylas and Philonous* (1713) that material objects continue to exist when not perceived by us because they are the objects of the thought of God. In his letter to Arthur Greeves of 24 July 1917 (*CL* I, pp. 330–1), Lewis urged Greeves to read *Three Dialogues*, 'written to prove the existence of God', the reasoning of which he found 'very subtle but not difficult'. Berkeley played an important part in Lewis's conversion and in *SBJ*, p. 173, Lewis paid tribute to his 'simple, workable, theistic idealism'.

22 i.e. T. S. Eliot.

TO T. S. ELIOT (P): TS

REF.231/1/45.

Magdalen College,
Oxford.
28th February 1946.

Dear Mr. Eliot,

I have nearly all the MSS for the Charles Williams volume. When may I expect yours? I should like to be able to send copy to the O.U.P. by the first week in April. Has Miss Sayers shown you hers on Dante? I think it first class.

yours sincerely,
C. S. Lewis

TO T. S. ELIOT (P): TS

REF.231/1/45.

Magdalen College,
Oxford.
11th March 1946.

Dear Mr. Eliot,

I can't conceal from you, (a), That we are very anxious to go to press about then. We don't want to come after all but the very few have forgotten Charles Williams' death, and we should like to get some royalties into Mrs Williams' pocket as soon as possible. (b). That your absence would in our view cripple the book. One idea has occurred to me, is it possible that you have or will have a *poem* ready, which you would let us use instead of an article? It need'nt have any special connection with Charles Williams. What do you think about the idea?

yours sincerely,
C. S. Lewis

TO T. S. ELIOT (P): TS

REF.231/1/45

Magdalen College.
Oxford.
28th March 1946.

Dear Mr. Eliot,

Thanks for your letter of the 26th: – I look forward to receiving your contribution.

yours sincerely,
C. S. Lewis

TO DANIEL NEYLAN (T):

Magdalen
April 1st [1946]

Dear Neylan

Heartiest congratulations to all concerned.[23] I meant to send a copy of this[24] sooner but have been away. Don't let the gudewife bother to write to me until (distant day for a mother of two!) she has nothing more useful to do. I am delighted that all is well over.

Yours
C. S. Lewis

TO HERBERT PALMER (TEX):

Magdalen College,
Oxford.
April 9th 1946

Dear Mr Palmer

Thank you for your letter of the 8th. If you care to come and dine and sleep the night on Fri. May 17th I should be delighted.

Thanks also for the poem which I liked, and liked progressively more as it went on.[25] The last page builds up excellently. 'Rage & despair. And then the countersign'[26] is a beauty. You are quite right about reviewers. The trouble is not simply that they are bad critics but that they are utterly unreliable for even the most commonplace factual account of a book. But I expect it is a deadly trade and we shd. all become like that if we practised it week in, week out.

Thanks for all the nice things you say about the *Great Divorce*. Let me know if the 17th suits.

Yours sincerely,
C. S. Lewis

---

23 On the birth of the Neylans' second child, Elizabeth.

24 *George MacDonald: An Anthology* (1946), which is dedicated to Mary Neylan.

25 Palmer had sent Lewis a copy of his poem, 'Apocalypse' which appeared a few months later in Palmer's *Sword in the Desert*.

26 ibid., 'Apocalypse', stanza 8, 1.

TO JILL FLEWETT (T):

Magdalen
Easter Monday [17 April] 1946

My dear June

Thanks for your letter and for the Report which I return with congratulations. Minto had recently read, and Maureen and I recently re-read, *Jane Eyre*, so we were thrilled at your success in the part.[27] What an excellent Jane you would make – if the dresser could make you plain enough. I shd. particularly like to have heard you in the scene where Mr Rochester says 'Am I hideous, Jane?' and she replies 'Very, Sir. You always were, you know.'[28] I hope this will be the beginning of many successes.

Minto is pretty poorly and Vera has been away a lot, but we still have Queenie and Flora and might be much worse off.[29] Warnie has just had 'one of his turns' but is better now.[30] I'm being given an honorary D.D. at St Andrew's; a case of Scotch whiskey might have been a kinder compliment but I am very pleased all the same. I enclose my two latest just to complete your set. Please give my duty to your Mother and Father. All here send their loves.

Yours
Jack

Throwing salt over the shoulder is an

Abominable, Arian, Barbarous, Beastlie, Craven, Childish, Damnable, Docetist, Enervating, Ebionite, False, Frenzied, Gentile, Goose-ish, Heathenish, Heretical, Illogical, Impertinent, Judaical, Julianic, Mouldy, Monophysite, Nestorian, Neo-Pagan, Odious, Occultist, Perverse, Puellular, Questionable, Quietistical, Reprobate, Relapsed, Satanic, Sabellian, Troublesome, Theomachic, Unorthodox, Ugly, Vicious,

---

27 June Flewett's first major role at RADA was in a stage production of *Jane Eyre*.

28 Brontë, *Jane Eyre*, ch. 37.

29 Queenie and Flora were maids at The Kilns.

30 June Flewett would have known that Warnie's 'turn' was a euphemism for an alcoholic binge. Warnie had been having trouble with alcohol for a long time. Usually Jack was able to control him when he went on a binge, but it was becoming more difficult. As will be seen from the narrative following the letter to Roger Lancelyn Green of 20 June 1947, Warnie found a way of escaping his brother's protection by going off to Ireland.

Visigothic, Weak-minded, Wilful, Xantippe-ish, Xenodochic, Yahoo-like, Youthful, Zany-ish, Zeal-destroying Practice.[31]

Quoth C.S.L.

TO MR TALBOTT (W):

Magdalen College,
Oxford
April 18th. 1946

Dear Mr. Talbott

Thank you for your letter of March 16th which I accept with gratitude since I am sure that your motive in writing it was charitable. It is clear that we differ on some fundamental points and it follows, of course, that (at least) one of us is in error.

To explore the differences further wd. clearly involve us in a long epistolary controversy and I am not sure that it is either your duty or mine to undertake this. One point of fact you must allow me to correct: it is certainly not 'liberal-minded' religious people who like my books in England. On the contrary it is precisely among them that I find (next to Marxists) my most hostile critics. With all good wishes.

Yours sincerely
C. S. Lewis

TO GEORGE ROSTREVOR HAMILTON (BOD):[32]

Magdalen
April 29th 1946

Dear Mr. Hamilton

I have long wanted to meet you and our common friend Barfield has been trying to arrange it. Your tract on Satan (however erroneous!)

---

31 June remembered that 'at lunch one day, I threw some spilt salt over my left shoulder (as taught by my mother) to ward off evil spirits or bad luck, I'm not sure which. This was my come-uppance' (letter to Walter Hooper of 27 January 2003).

32 (Sir) George Rostrevor Hamilton (1888–1967), poet, writer and civil servant, who was knighted in 1951, was a close friend of Owen Barfield. The son of a clergyman, he was educated at Exeter College, Oxford, where he took a First in Classics in 1911. He joined the Inland Revenue in 1912 and was Private Secretary to the Chairman and Board of Inland Revenue, 1913, Secretary to the Committee of National Debt and Taxation, 1926–9, assistant secretary to the Board of Inland Revenue, 1929–34, head of a special commission on income tax, 1934–50, and Presiding Special Commissioner, 1950–3. For years he was Vice-President of the

does provide an excellent introduction.[33] I love rational opposition and always recommend that little book to my pupils as the best statement of the 'Satanist' case.

I'm with you all the way about Eddison, tho' whether I shall be of any use is doubtful. I've never succeeded in publishing anyone's books but my own, tho' I have v. often tried.[34] I fancy publishers have it as a fundamental rule 'never let your authors persuade you to publish other authors'

I can hardly ever get up to town. Will you come down here and dine (and sleep) some night later in the term – say June 11th? We dine at 7.15 sharp and don't dress. Do.

Eddison is among the most startling literary experiences I have ever had. All modern prose looks *thin* after it. (There are of course thin beauties, and by *thin* I don't mean bad. But it is the opaque blaze in Eddison wh. is so wonderful, the enamel). I don't think Eliot cd. ever like it. It's as if you offered smoking venison and a great port to a man who wanted bread & butter. But I know one *youngster* who admires him: so there's hope.

Are we related by any chance? My mother was an (Irish) Hamilton.

I shall have no time to read your paper till to-morrow evening. I look forward to it.

Yours sincerely
C. S. Lewis

TO T. S. ELIOT (P): TS

REF.231/1/45.

Magdalen College,
Oxford.
3rd May 1946.

Dear Mr. Eliot,

I must apologize for the delay in answering your letter. This was due, not to neglect, but to the necessity of consulting several people who could not all be got together at once.

Royal Society of Literature and President of the Society of Civil Service Authors. His many books include *Bergson and Future Philosophy: An Essay on the Scope of Intelligence* (1921), *Unknown Lovers and Other Poems* (1935), *Collected Poems and Epigrams* (1958) and *Landscape of the Mind: Late Poems* (1963).

33 George Rostrevor Hamilton, *Hero or Fool? A Study of Milton's Satan* (1944).

34 E. R. Eddison died in 1945, and his friend Hamilton was trying to find a publisher for Eddison's unfinished work, *The Mezentian Gate*.

We have now reluctantly come to the conclusion that much as the book will be weakened by the loss of a contribution from you, it might be even more disastrous to postpone publication too long. Perhaps you will find your own way of honouring our friend later and no less effectively.

yours sincerely,
C. S. Lewis

TO ARTHUR GREEVES (W):

[Magdalen College]
May 13th 46

My dear Arthur –

It was more than usually nice to get your letter because I have been for the last few weeks especially haunted by a desire for your society. The picture of some place on a hill beside a wood and you and me talking there floats before me, and I constantly pray that we may meet again in the not-too-far future. But I cannot leave home for more than a night, or two at the outside, now. And this seems likely to be so as long as poor Minto lives.

Oddly enough I had been thinking of Forrest Reid: and indeed in an article (one of two wh. I have just written for *Time & Tide*) I have referred to him as a neglected artist.[35]

The Macdonald anthology,[36] as you see, is not of his verse, wh. I still consider greatly inferior to his prose. In the novels the three things I like are (a) The parts that have something of a fairy tale quality, like the terror of the trees and wind at the beginning of *W. Cumbermede* or the lovely journey 'up Gaunside' in *Sir Gibbie*.[37] (b) (Like you) the melodrama. The older critics are v. unjust to melodrama (c) The *direct* preaching. What I can't stand is the *in*direct preaching – I mean Connie on her sofa in *The Seaboard Parish*.[38] What between him and Scott and an Ulster upbringing I now find no difficulty with the Scotch dialect parts, indeed I like them. They enable him to make characters say

---

35 'Notes on the Way', *Time and Tide*, XXVII (1 June 1946), pp. 510–11. The article is reprinted as 'Different Tastes in Literature' in *Of This and Other Worlds*.

36 *George MacDonald: An Anthology*, ed. C. S. Lewis was published by Geoffrey Bles on 18 March 1946.

37 MacDonald, *Sir Gibbie*, ch. 8. 'Gaunside' is a mistake for 'Daurside'.

38 George MacDonald, *The Seaboard Parish* (1868).

strongly and racily things he wd. spoil in English. I *have* read *The Disciple*,[39] but long ago and don't remember it.

Surely you must be mistaken about hearing *The Planets* on the old gramophone. I cd. take my oath we never had it and I doubt if it was even recorded. Was it even *written*?

About Hell. All I have ever said is that the N.T. plainly implies the possibility of some being finally left in 'the outer darkness.'[40] Whether this means (horror of horror) being left to a purely mental existence, left with nothing at all but one's own envy, prurience, resentment, loneliness & self conceit, or whether there is still some sort of environment, something you cd. call a world or a reality, I wd. never pretend to know. But I wouldn't put the question in the form 'do I believe in an *actual* Hell'. One's own mind is actual enough. If it doesn't seem fully actual *now* that is because you can always escape from it a bit into the physical world – look out of the window, smoke a cigarette, go to sleep. But when there is nothing for you *but* your own mind (no body to go to sleep, no books or landscape, no sounds, no drugs) it will be as actual as – as – well, as a coffin is actual to a man buried alive.

I suppose, like me, you often catch yourself grumbling about 'this rotten government' and realise we are talking just as our fathers talked. My love to your mother, Janie, and the Glenmachonians.

God bless you.

Yours
Jack

TO T. S. ELIOT (P): TS

REF.231/1/45.

Magdalen College,
Oxford.
17th May 1946.

Dear Mr. Eliot,

You cannot regret your absence more than we all do. I agree, by the way, that the plays, as plays, are much the least valuable part of his work.

yours sincerely,
C. S. Lewis

---

39 George MacDonald, *The Disciple and Other Poems* (1867).

40 Matthew 8:12; 22:13; 25:30.

TO OWEN BARFIELD (W):

May 25/46

My dear B

Please send £20 to F. G. Cannan, St Deiniol's Library,[41] Hawarden, near Chester.

Yes, yes. 'Betty in all but three dimensions' frequents the poems. I *like* them alright. I've told you so. Nor did I intend any moral or aesthetic criticism. I only meant that I personally liked other things more. But luckily while the boy writes his poems thro' you, you write yours thro' me: the Birth of Language[42] being pure Barfield.

Yours

C.S.L.

TO OWEN BARFIELD (W):

May 28/46

My dear B –

The moment before I realised that the proposal of adding the fourteeners to your poem was ironical was a dreadful one. I am digesting the 5 Willow-wood Sonnets (4 of D.G.R's and one of yours) and will report as soon as may be.

Meanwhile will you please send £75 (LXXV) to

Miss I. Webb
Bentcot,
Sevenhampton,
near Andoversford
Glos

a poor gentlewoman forced to move house and transport invalid mother by hired ambulance.

Yours

C. S. Lewis

41 St Deiniol's Library, Britain's only residential library, was founded in 1889 by William Ewart Gladstone. The money was sent from the Agapony.

42 Lewis's poem, 'The Birth of Language', which had already appeared in *Punch* (9 January 1946), is quoted below in his letter to Ruth Pitter of 24 July 1946.

TO JILL FLEWETT (T):

Magdalen
May 31st 1946

My dear June

Yes, of course. Whether it is a good choice is another matter – but I suppose you know. I should like to come and hear. I've never heard of Topaze by – is it PAGUOL or PAGUEL?[43] What language? But I'll make enquiries.

The wireless is on making its ghastly noise just before the 9 o'clock signal. Love from all and, as ever, our very best wishes. Remember me to your mother.

Yours
C. S. Lewis

TO OWEN BARFIELD (W):

[? June 1946]

My dear Barfield –

'Frown not! . . .' we frown when we see a child too near a puddle.[44]

Do we *frown* when we see it on the edge of a precipice (skeletons white on the rocks a thousand feet below)? From the literary point of view this is a wonderful crop. Tho' *Punch* is the only paper that wd. now print most of them: and why not?

As to the thing itself – I suppose it is all right, is it? I wish C.W. was alive: this was just his pigeon. His solution was, in a peculiar way, to teach 'em the *ars honeste amandi*[45] and then bestow them on other (younger) men. *Sic vos non vobis.*[46] He was not only a lover himself but the cause that love was in other men. But it's a tickling game. Perhaps I'm taking it all too seriously – but the world is growing chilly and I just couldn't stand any serious miscarriage in your life. ('Save

43 Marcel Pagnol, *Topaze: pièce en quatre actes* (1930).

44 The words 'Frown not' are probably from one of Barfield's poems which cannot be identified.

45 'The art of courtly love' – the name of a work by Andreas Capellanus (fl. 1180s) which Lewis discusses in detail in *The Allegory of Love.*

46 'Thus do ye, but not for yourselves'. The words are the commencement of each of four verses which Virgil wrote but left incomplete, on the occasion when Bathyllus claimed some lines really written by the poet.

yourself for my sake, Pickwick!' said Mr Tupman).[47] I burn to explain to this young woman that a good many people have a concern in your happiness and Gad!, she'd better mind what she's about.

But I hope we meet on Friday.

Yours

C. S. Lewis

TO BARBARA WALL (BOD):

Magdalen.
June 8th 1946

Dear Mrs. Wall –

Thank you very much for *Anna Collett*[48] which I finished last night; with the feeling that I had had a very intense and terrible experience. The only faults I can find are (a.) That Julian Hunter and his mistress, tho' a painfully real character – that talking *at* people in the train on p. 9 is a splendid touch! – does not to the end make clear to me why he is in the story.

(b.) Inferior dialogue on pp. 40, 41 where the sententiousness and even bookishness of much that Anna says (especially 'Alas! We are in this world' etc) sounds like a patch of something you had written years earlier.

But these are trifles. When the thing really gets going it is tremendous: the misery of those elaborately contrived meetings viâ Oxford, the gradual emptying of Anna's whole world, the state in which brown uniform can at once be picked out in any landscape, the strange difference between the real man and the man as written-to (pp. 177, 180: has this been observed before?), the dreadful futile pseudo-prayers, the belief that each new step will somehow be the last – all this really harrowed me. Not that there aren't other good things too. Jack Collett is as sound and real a character as I've met for a long time and an ideal one for his rôle – I mean one has complete sympathy with him and yet one feels his profound unattractiveness. There's also a fine impression of very English ordinary life in all the Angel and hitch-hiking parts. I cd. have done with more of these myself: will there be more someday in a larger, looser novel with a less tragic theme?

47 Dickens, *The Pickwick Papers*. It was in fact Mr Winkle who said this. See note 59 to the letter to Owen Barfield of 22 August 1944.

48 Barbara Lucas [Barbara Wall], *Anna Collett* (1946).

Oh – I'd nearly forgotten: there's a wonderful touch on p. 217 about the bull 'What a chance for hope I let slip!'

You'll be slanged by both sides: old fashioned reviewers will think you too plain spoken and up-to-date ones* will not forgive you for showing adultery in such a horrid light. But it is a very good story. Heartiest congratulations and, once more, thanks

Yours sincerely

C. S. Lewis

* I mean those to whom 'Passion' (preferably pronounced so as to rhyme with *Martian*) is almost a god.

On 6 November 1944 Lewis read a paper entitled 'Is Theology Poetry?' to the Oxford University Socratic Club. In that paper, which anticipated some of the ideas in Miracles: A Preliminary Study (1947), *he said:*

> *Long before I believed Theology to be true I had already decided that the popular scientific picture at any rate was false. One absolutely central inconsistency ruins it . . . The whole picture professes to depend on inferences from observed facts. Unless inference is valid, the whole picture disappears. Unless we can be sure that reality in the remotest nebula or the remotest part obeys the thought-laws of the human scientist here and now in his laboratory – in other words, unless Reason is an absolute – all is in ruins. Yet those who ask me to believe this world picture also ask me to believe that Reason is simply the unforeseen and unintended bye-product of mindless matter at one stage of its endless and aimless becoming. Here is flat contradiction. They ask me at the same moment to accept a conclusion and to discredit the only testimony on which that conclusion can be based.'*[49]

Shortly after 'Is Theology Poetry' was published an anonymous writer complained in The Oxford Magazine *that*

49 'Is Theology Poetry?'was published in the *Socratic Digest*, 3 (1945), and reprinted in *Screwtape Proposes a Toast and Other Pieces* (London: Collins, 1965; Fount, 1998); this passage is on pp. 46–7.

> *Mr Lewis totally rejects the scientific account of the world, because it is constructed by reason, and reason is . . . 'a by-product of mindless matter' and therefore discredited. (Mr Lewis is quite clever enough to know that the scientists may be wrong as to their account of reason, yet right in the results they have achieved by it. If his own account of it makes it trustworthy, why should he reject its scientific discoveries?)*[50]

Lewis replied in the following letter:

TO THE EDITOR OF *THE OXFORD MAGAZINE*:[51]

Magdalen College
[13 June 1946]

Sir, –

If to say that thoroughgoing Naturalism leads to self-contradiction in epistemology is to 'reject science,' then I do 'reject science.' But it is almost embarrassing, after handing out this venerable philosophical chestnut to an audience of undergraduates, to find myself accorded either the odium of a heresiarch or the honours of a pioneer. Your correspondent should consult his philosophical colleagues, who will direct him to more classical forms of the argument than mine: or, if (being a busy man) he wants something short and simple, he can get it from Professor J. B. S. Haldane: 'If my mental processes are determined wholly by the motions of atoms in my brain, I have no reason to suppose that my beliefs are true . . . and hence I have no reason for supposing my brain to be composed of atoms' (*Possible Worlds*, p. 209).[52] Neither Professor Haldane nor I is, of course, arguing, as your correspondent supposes, that a wrong account of the origins of reason would invalidate argument. We are arguing that if a certain account were *true*, argument would be invalidated; and therefore that that account is not true.

50 *The Oxford Magazine*, LXIV (23 May 1946), p. 302.

51 This letter appeared under the title 'Socratic Wisdom' in *The Oxford Magazine*, LXIV (13 June 1946), p. 359.

52 Lewis quoted this in *Miracles: A Preliminary Study* (London: Bles, 1947; Fount, 1998), ch. 3, p. 14.

Yours correspondent's statement ('Mr Lewis adds that the scientists cannot see his difficulty') is false. I said 'many scientists.'

Yours, etc.,

C. S. Lewis

TO GEORGE ROSTREVOR HAMILTON (BOD):

Magdalen
June 17th/46

My dear Palmer,[53] *Animus est vir animae*[54] and in my opinion the types of relation between conscious and subconscious are as various as those between man and wife, ranging from the divorce of schizophrenia through the legal separation of repression and the ordinary cat-and-dog life of most minds to the complete integration in which the distinction is almost overcome. But the question is too hard for any letter I cd. write this morning and concerns not poetry alone but all we do. In a *certain sense* I think all will and all reasoning subconscious i.e. already *over* when you can make them objects. But more at your next visit which I hope will be soon.

My duty to your wife and many thanks, but I have little chance of spending a night in town at present.

By all means tell Blackwell that I love Eddison's works and would write a preface to *The Worm* with pleasure. It won't have the slightest effect on him but one must try!

I haven't got down to Hurnard[55] yet but promise myself a rich feast when this damnable last week of term is over.

Yours

C. S. Lewis

Warnie accompanied his brother to the University of St Andrews in Scotland where, on 28 June 1946, Lewis was made a Doctor of Divinity.

---

53 Lewis had inadvertently written 'Palmer'. This was struck out by Sir George and replaced by 'Hamilton!'

54 Tertullian, *De Anima*, section 679c, 'Treatise on the Soul': 'The intellect is the power of the soul.'

55 *James Hurnard, a Victorian Character: Being Passages from 'The Setting Sun'*, sel. and arranged by G. Rostrevor Hamilton (1946).

One of those who had heard, and been converted by, Lewis's Mere Christianity *broadcasts was the poet, Ruth Pitter.*[56] *In a note on her first letter from Lewis of 13 July 1946, she said:*

> *My first letter to Lewis began 'God bless you.' I had scraped acquaintance through poor Herbert Palmer, who at that time was determined to 'bring out' Lewis as a poet, and who was, I am afraid, very trying in his visits, etc. Palmer knew how much I loved Lewis's work, and wrote asking if I would like to know him. I replied that I would do any honest thing to this end, and duly encouraged by Palmer, I wrote and asked if I might come to see the great man. The trepidation was the usual feeling . . . of sensitive nobodies encountering greatly gifted persons. (It must be awful at the receiving end).*[57]

TO HERBERT PALMER (TEX):

Magdalen College,
Oxford.
July 5 [1946]

My dear Palmer –

You must be wondering why I haven't answered your last, but I've been travelling all over the island since we met. I like the Dragon[58] so far but have only begun it to day: much too short to take on a long journey.

About your not swallowing the Head,[59] it's much nearer fact than you know. It is commonly done with cats' heads in Oxford laboratories and was really tried (unsuccessfully) on a human head in Germany. One can hardly satirise these people – the reality is always more incredible than what one invents.

The mysterious name on the white stone is one's own real name (expressing what God meant you to be when He created you) wh. is to eternity perfectly known to Him & you alone.[60]

---

56 See **Ruth Pitter** in the Biographical Appendix.

57 Bodleian Library, MS. Eng. Lett. c. 220/3, fol. 18.

58 Herbert Palmer, *The Dragon of Tingalam: A Fairy Comedy* (1945).

59 In *That Hideous Strength*, ch. 9, 'The Saracen's Head', the N.I.C.E. keep the head of the scientist Alcasan alive by medicines and infusions of blood.

60 Revelation 2:17: 'He that hath an ear, let him hear what the Spirit saith unto the churches; to him that overcometh will I give to eat of the hidden manna, and will give him a white stone, and in the stone a new name written, which no man knoweth saving he that receiveth it.'

My duty to Miss Pitter. She can know me the moment she pleases.

I shall get onto your poem in a day or two. It's somewhere buried on my brother's table and as he is typing letters for me at the moment I daren't forrage (or forage?) for it. Thanks for the A.E.: but I think he'll sing softer when he meets a real angel.[61] One doesn't take liberties with 'em.

Yours
C. S. Lewis

TO RUTH PITTER (BOD):

Magdalen College,
Oxford.
July 13th 1946

Dear Miss Pitter

Amen! And you too! But what you should be 'trepidant' about in calling on a middle aged don I can't imagine. A Wednesday morning wd. suit me better than a Tuesday or Thursday. Wd. Wed. July 17th. suit? I shall be here all morning.

Yours sincerely
C. S. Lewis

TO THOMAS WILKINSON RIDDLE (BOD):

Magdalen
July 16th 1946

My dear Dr. Riddle

I am very sorry to disappoint you, but I must.[62] This meeting is, as you say, 'different': but it differs in a direction which takes it further away from my capacities. I am primarily an arguer not an exhorter and my target is the frankly irreligious audience: nor do I ever speak my best in a v. large hall with an atmosphere of enthusiasm in it. In fact, of those who can speak at all, I am perhaps the most unsuitable person you could select. Again and again I have gone to meetings about which

---

61 Palmer had probably sent Lewis a copy of 'The Man to the Angel' by 'A.E.' (George William Russell, 1867–1935) which contains the stanza 'All your beauty cannot win/Truth we learn in pain and sighs:/You can never enter in/To the circle of the wise.' See *The Collected Poems of A.E.* (1913).

62 The board of *World Dominion* had invited Lewis to speak at a meeting they were convening at the Royal Albert Hall.

I felt that it was 'not my pigeon' – in obedience to pressure and also in the fear that I might be mistaking for the unsuitable what was merely the (to me) unattractive. But the event has always confirmed my original decision and I have come away feeling that I have wasted people's time. I am sure this meeting is important and excellent: but I must act by my own conviction that I shd. do no real good by speaking at it. When you have to begin by asking 'What on earth cd. I say?' it is a pretty sure sign you should say nothing.

All this is how I shd. feel even if I were a free man. But in fact my professional life is full of arrears of work and my domestic difficulties (an invalid to care for and, soon, no servants) are closing in on me like the contracting cell in Poe. Owing to callers and incessant correspondence I have not yet had a single full morning's work this vacation. So don't be angry if I stick to my refusal. Kind regards to yourself and to your son,

Yours
C. S. Lewis

TO ERIC ROUTLEY (*EC*):[63]

[Magdalen College]
16/7/46

Dear Mr Routley,

The truth is that I'm not in sufficient sympathy with the project to help you. I know that many of the congregation like singing hymns: but am not yet convinced that their enjoyment is of a spiritual kind. It may be: I don't know. To the minority, of whom I am one, the

63 On 13 July 1946 Eric Routley, a minister in the Congregational Church who had been an undergraduate at Magdalen, wrote to Lewis: 'The Hymn Society of Great Britain and Ireland is opening a file of new hymns to which modern hymn-writers are to be asked to contribute. I have been asked to write to you and ask if you will be a member of the panel to whom new hymns may be submitted in order that their merit may be assessed . . .' Eric Routley (1917–82) studied for the Congregational ministry at Mansfield College after taking a BA from Magdalen College in 1939. Ordained in 1943, in 1948 he returned to Mansfield College as a lecturer in church history, librarian, chaplain and director of music. In 1959 he left Oxford to take a church in Edinburgh. See his essay on Lewis, 'A Prophet' in *C. S. Lewis at the Breakfast Table and Other Reminiscences*, ed. James T. Como (1979; new edn, 1992). His two letters from Lewis were quoted in an article entitled 'Correspondence with an Anglican Who Dislikes Hymns', *The Presbyter*, VI, No. 2 (1948), reprinted in *EC*.

hymns are mostly the dead wood of the service. Recently in a party of six people I found that all without exception would like *fewer* hymns. Naturally, one holding this view can't help you.

Yours sincerely,
C. S. Lewis

TO RUTH PITTER (BOD):

Magdalen College,
July 19th 1946

Dear Miss Pitter –

This is about *Trophy of Arms*,[64] not about books that arrived to-day, except to thank you very much (for they came well timed and just as my appetite was growing).

T. of A. is enough for one letter for it has most deeply delighted me. I was prepared for the more definitely mystical poems, but not for this cool, classical quality. You do it time after time – create a silence and vacancy and awe all round the poem. If the Lady in *Comus* had written poetry one imagines it wd. have been rather like this. And your Disdain – 'oh what a deal of scorn looks beautiful': not that it mightn't become a trick if you did it too often, but so far you don't. My special favourites at present are *Eternal Image*, *Heroic Couplets*, *Gentle Joy* (especially the 2nd stanza) *Turn not aside, Shepherd*[65] (of course. It runs in my head as few poems have done since I grew middle aged. Were you right not to preserve that inverted rhythm beyond the first 3 stanzas? Am I being greedy in wishing it went on?) – lovely things in *Thanksgiving for Fair Summer*, *Apology*, *Fair is the Water*, *On a Certain Philosophy* (except for *raiment*[66] wh. is too 'poetical'. No, no: I see you can't help it. There are equal objections to any of the other words. The wound in the language can't be cured by an individual.) *Caged Lion* (perhaps best of all) and *Solemn Meditation*. But there are exquisite things everywhere.

The only one I definitely did *not* like is *The Flower Piece*, wh. seems to me, if you know what I mean, just *too* well written – one can hear

64 Ruth Pitter, *A Trophy of Arms: Poems 1926–1935*, preface by James Stephens (London: Cresset Press, [1936]).

65 ibid., 'Help, Good Shepherd'.

66 ibid., 'On a Certain Philosophy', 20: 'It is but a matter of raiment, as ever with women.'

you doing it. *Cadaverous*[67] in *Storm* is marvellous and 'then alleluia all my gashes cry' just takes one up into regions poetry hasn't visited for nearly a hundred years. Nearly all the Sapphics are good, tho' I usually don't like that meter in English: especially good is 'the silent stars affirm nothing.'[68] I couldn't quite understand the *III Poplars*.

I meant to send you something of mine but I shan't. It all sounds like a brass band after yours. The oil on this American paper begins to reduce me to silence as you see. Why wasn't I told you were as good as this? I expect I may have made a considerable ass of myself on Wednesday. Did I – did I – I hardly dare to put it into words – but I wasn't 'kind' was I? The dreadful suspicion will make me turn all hot on wakeful nights ten years hence.

By the way, I thought there was a deal of waffle in that preface by James Stephens. He hardly *says* anything at all.

By 'kind' I mean patronising. Ugh! Were you fooling me to the top of my bent? I won't forget to return the *Garland*.[69]

Yours sincerely
C. S. Lewis

TO DOROTHY L. SAYERS (W):

Magdalen College,
Oxford.
July 23d 1946.

Dear Miss Sayers,

How does your honour for this many a day? The C.W. essays are all now in the hands of him whom you so properly described as 'that man with a name like Blunderbuss or Bandersnatch'[70] But that's not what I'm writing about. One of Cumberlege's myrmidons has lugged me into helping with a series of 2/6 books, about 15,000 words each, which are to be a sort of library of Christian knowledge for young people in top forms at school. C.W. had already talked to me about it and he and I were to collaborate on a short Xtian Dictionary (about 40 Headings) for it.

By this time you have guessed what is coming. Wd you like to do

---

67 ibid., 'Storm', 1: 'I have seen daylight turn cadaverous.'

68 ibid., 'Of Silence and the Air', stanza 4, 1–2: 'the silent/stars affirm nothing'.

69 Ruth Pitter, *A Mad Lady's Garland* (1935).

70 i.e. Geoffrey Fenwick Jocelyn Cumberlege.

one? They've asked me to approach you – and of course I'm flattered at being thought a suitable 'approacher'. Subjects on wh. books are wanted are 1. What do we mean by God? 2. Who Jesus is. 3. What Jesus taught. 4. Baptism 5. The Holy Ghost. 6. Holy Communion. 7. Prayer. 8. Grace. 9. Week day Xtianity. 10. Xtianity and other religions. 11. The job of the Clergy. 12. Why Xtians disagree. 13. Heaven. 14. The Church of England.

They're giving you first choice, of course. You can do my Dictionary if you like! (there, I can't speak you fairer). Is there any one of these you feel inclined to do? Or one they haven't thought of? Come in and blow us all sky-high. We think of calling it *The Thorn Books*: being elementary as Horn-Books, dealing with thorny questions, from an Anglican point of view (hence Joseph of Arimathea and the Glastonbury Thorn come in) – and the Crown of Thorns. Don't blast me. Good books *have* sometimes been begotten by letters like this!

Yours sincerely
C. S. Lewis

TO RUTH PITTER (BOD):

Magdalen etc
July 24th 1946

Dear Miss Pitter –

I was relieved and pleased to get your letter. It would seem (the case is a little uncommon) that we have a degree of respect for each other's talents wh. almost tends to deadlock and head-on collision! It is as pretty an absurdity as one could wish.

Nothing is more offensive, as I know by repeated experience, than the man who prefers the last book but one to the last book. But I'm going to do so. The *Garland* is the one that pleases me least of all four. This may not have much to do with its merits. One reason, anyway, is that I don't like Spenser's minor poems (I love the F.Q.) nor Drayton's *Nymphidia*[71] nor the whole genre which you are lovingly and very dexterously parodying.

The other two books are full of good, and studded with great work: though there are things I don't yet understand. In *The Spirit Watches*[72]

71 Michael Drayton, *Nimphidia* (1627).

72 Ruth Pitter, *The Spirit Watches* (London: Cresset Press, [1940]).

I don't know what 'the blind stone, the white stone'[73] is. *Old Fashioned Song* is delicious. *Downward Pointing Muse*, tho' only after repeated readings, comes out superb – especially stanza 5 and the last. (I'm not quite sure whether *primal* in 'primal fear'[74] is pulling its weight) *Love & the Child* is the best result in poetry wh. the works of Freud (woolly old wiseacre) have yet produced. *Feliciter audes*, *The Difference*, very good. *Tigress*? – I can't help thinking it needs rhyme: not rhythmically distinguished enough to do without it. *End of Fear* – oh, almost the best of all. The bear's neck, the loved stone, the unmoved breast, by Gum! That's the stuff. On p. 46 I'm hampered by not knowing what a bush-baby is: so can only expect it is good. Thank you for putting Boys (surely the most odious section of the race and standing witness to the Fall) in their proper place on p. 52. So many writers want to idealise the little blackguards.

I'm not sure I've understood *The Bridge*[75] as a whole: but I love 'shapes of sorrow and empty vessels' etc.[76] Nice things in *Seaborn*. The *Cygnet* comes off as well as things like air-raids can come off in poetry. I don't mean because they're modern. But as a rule, the bigger a thing is, physically the less it works in literature. One ghost is always more disquieting than ten: no good fight in a story can have more than a dozen or so combatants: the death of a million men is less tragic than that of one. *Sparrow's skull*: for once the blurb selects rightly. This really breaks the heart and 'harpes the secret tear out of the ee.' One of the great lyrics. *What is There* is excellent. It gives me new light on the Grail story: you remember that all was lost because Percevale failed to ask 'for what does it serve?'[77] *The Bat*, good. *Aged Cupid*: unexpected and savoury.

On An Old Poem alas! it's not true. Poetry is as mortal as man. One's favourite lyric can wear out. A change of language can make the best line first ridiculous, then (ugh!) 'so quaint', then meaningless. A change in education can blot out a whole dead language and

73 ibid., 'The Spirit Watches'.

74 ibid., 'Downward Pointing Muse'.

75 Ruth Pitter, *The Bridge: Poems 1939–1944* (London: Cresset Press, 1945).

76 ibid., 'The Bridge', 3.

77 The story is found in Chrétien de Troyes (fl. 1170–90), *Le Conte du Graal*. It is retold in Charles Williams's *The Figure of Arthur*, which is included in *Arthurian Torso*.

Virgil ceases to be. 'Put not your trust in poets nor in any child of man'

Retrospect, very well. 'An owlish and elvish air'[78] is unimprovable. Excellent bits in *Man accuses Man. Lilies & Wine* – I think I've got it, but am not sure. *But for Lust*: excellent. Your only serious rival here is your own *End of Fear*.[79] *Hill of Kindred*. I like it without understanding it.

Funeral Wreaths. No, no, no. The Moderns have got at you. Don't *you*, of all people be taken in by the silly idea that by simply mentioning dull or sordid facts in sub-poetical rhythms you can make a poem. The effect is certain, but it's not worth getting. You know far better than that.

I send a few of my own. Now remember

(1) I'm not Palmer. You won't wound a sick man by unfavourable comment.

(2). Get clear on what the question is. I know (or think) that some of these contain important thought and v. great metrical ingenuity. That isn't what I'm worrying about. But are they real poems or do the content and the form remain separable – fitted together only by force?

The thing you quoted about 'not the cry of a child but bearded warrior's weeping' I found by chance yesterday. It is not Norse but Finnish: in the Kálevalá (which scans – uu –).[80]

I don't know Finnish but read it in Kirby's translation – 2 vols Everyman.[81] His style is ludicrous but the myths are so good that they come through even that

Yours sincerely
C. S. Lewis

---

78 Pitter, *The Bridge*, 'Retrospect', 3.

79 In *The Spirit Watches*.

80 i.e. the name *Kalevala* is scanned long-short-short-long. (Actually it is four shorts with the stress on the first.)

81 *Kalevala: The Land of the Heroes*, trans. W. F. Kirby, introduced by J. B. C. Grundy (London: Dent, Everyman's Library, 2 vols, [1907]). Lewis made his own translation from Kirby's translation of the *Kalevala*, XXXII, 307–43. It is entitled 'After Kirby's *Kalevala*' and was published in *The Oxford Magazine*, LV (13 May 1937), p. 505. The lines 'not the cry of a child but bearded warrior's weeping' – *Kalevala* VII, 175–7 – are translated by Kirby as 'This is not like childhood's weeping,/Nor like women's lamentation,/But a bearded hero weeping.'

The Birth of Language[82]

How near his sire's careering fires
Does Mercury the planet run;
What wave of heat must lave and beat
That shining suburb of the Sun,

Whose burning flings supernal things
Like spindrift from his stormy crown;
He throws and shakes in rosy flakes
Intelligible virtues down.

And landing there, that candent air
No sooner holds them than they turn
To breathing gods with wreathèd rods
And sandals wing'd and lips that burn.

Due West (the Sun's behest so runs)
They seek the wood where flames are trees;
In crimson shade their limbs are laid
Beside the pure quicksilver seas,

Where thick with notes from liquid throats
The forest melody leaps and runs
Till night lets robe the lightless globe
With darkness and with distant suns.

Awake they spring and shake the wing
And on the trees whose trunks are flames
They find like fruit, with rind and root
And leaves of fire, their proper names;

At taste whereof, in haste and love,
They soar straight up the night's abyss;

---

82 'The Birth of Language' had appeared under the initials 'N.W.' in *Punch*, CCX (9 January 1946), p. 32. Lewis revised it slightly before sending it to Pitter, and it underwent further revision before being published in *Poems*.

Far, far below the arbours glow
Where once they knew Mercurial bliss.

They ache and freeze through vacant seas
Of night. Their nimbleness and youth
Grows lean and frore; their meaning more,
Their being less; life shrinks to truth.

They reach this Earth. There each has birth
Miraculous, a word made breath,
Lucid and small, for use in all
Man's daily needs; but dry like death.

So dim below these symbols show,
Boney and abstract every one;
Yet if true verse but lift the curse
They feel in dreams their native Sun.

To C.W.[83]

If knowledge, like the noonday heat
Uncooled with cloud, unstirred with breath
Of undulant air, begins to beat
On minds one moment after death.

From your rich soil what life will spring,
What flower-entangled Paradise,
Amid green walks what birds will sing,
What med'cinable gums, what spice,

Apples of what smooth gold! But fear
Assails me for myself: the noon
That nourishes Earth can only sear
And scald the unresponding Moon.

83 'To C.W.' (i.e. Charles Williams) is a slightly revised version of 'To G.M.' which appeared in *The Spectator*, CLXIX (9 October 1942). It was further revised before it appeared in *Poems*.

Her empty valleys have no soil,
Her needle-pointed hills are bare;
Water, poured on those rocks, would boil,
And noon lasts long, and long despair.

On Being Human[84]

Angelic minds, they say, by simple intelligence
Perceive the Forms of nature. They discern
Unerringly the Archtypes; all the verities
Which mortals lack or indirectly learn.
Transparent with primordial truth, unvarying,
Pure Earthness and right Stonehood from that clear
High eminence are seen. Unveiled the seminal,
   Huge Principles appear.

The Tree-ness of the trees they know, the meaning of
Arboreal life, how from earth's salty lap
The solar beam uplifts it; all the holiness
Enacted by leaves' fall and rising sap.
But never an angel knows the knife-edged severance
Of sun from shadow where the woods begin,
The blessed cool at every pore caressing us,
   For angels have no skin.

They see the Form of air. But mortals, breathing it,
Drink the whole summer down into the breast; –
The lavish pinks, the new-mown field, the ravishing
Sea-smells, the wood-fire smoke that whispers *Rest*;
The tremor on the rippled pool of memory
Which from each scent in widening circle goes,
The pleasure and the pang – can angels measure it?
   An angel has no nose.

---

84 'On Being Human' was published under the initials 'N.W.' in *Punch*, CCX (8 May 1946), p. 402. Lewis made a few minor changes in the version here, and he made further changes before it appeared in *Poems*.

The nourishing of life, and how it flourishes
On earth, and why, they utterly know. But not
The hill-born, earthy spring, the dark, cold bilberries,
The ripe peach from the southern wall yet hot;
Full-bellied tankards foaming-topped, the delicate
Half-lyric lamb, the new loaf's billowy curves,
Nor porridge, nor the piercing taste of oranges,
  For angels have no nerves.

Far richer they. I know the senses' witchery
Shields us, like air, from heavens too bright to see;
Imminent death to Man the barb'd sublimity
And dazzling edge of beauty unsheathed would be.
Yet here, and in this tiny charm'd interior,
This parlour of the brain, their Maker shares
With living men some secrets in a privacy
  Forever ours, not theirs.

TO DOROTHY L. SAYERS (W):

Magdalen etc
July 29th 1946

Dear Miss Sayers –

Yes. I see your point only too well.[85] I also am haunted at times by the feeling that I oughtn't to be doing this kind of thing. But as the voice, when interrogated, can never give a good reason, I doubt if it comes from above. How is one to decide? If by what other people say – well, your *Six Other Deadly Sins* is about as good as it could be. And if you wrote a book on Sin for this series it wd. certainly be a good one. Against it stands your artistic conscience. I wish I knew what place artistic consciences will hold a moment after death. It might be – and then it might be exactly the reverse. You write such excellent letters that if I were a bad man I should lure you into an epistolary controversy and you wd. find you had written a book for us without knowing it: I shd. simply publish the letters.

---

85 Sayers had told Lewis that her conscience prevented her from writing for the purpose of edifying readers.

Anthropsophists – I have contended with them for weeks on end. They can be awful. But

(a) One of my best friends – a contributor to the C.W. book – is one.[86] His Anthroposophical critique of modern thought was one of the things that opened the way to my conversion.

(b) One of the most disagreeable women I ever knew has definitely improved after 20 years of Anthroposophy. Perhaps the fact that she has also born countless children in that time has something to do with it

(c) Maddening of course when they set up to be Xtians. But compared with the sort of things most of our neighbours believe in, Steiner rises almost to the dignity of good Paganism.

Overhaul the poetical works of Ruth Pitter and when found make a note of (I'm re-reading *Dombey and Son.*[87] This para. has no connection with anything else in this letter)

I'm exceedingly glad you liked *O.S. Planet*. Thanks for the *errata*. I shall never make a proof reader.

Oh ponder well, be not severe! And yet why shd. I pester you? All good wishes. I wish we met sometimes.

Yours very sincerely (if I'm anything 'sincerely' wh. I doubt)
C. S. Lewis

Sayers was provoked by what Lewis called her 'artistic conscience' and she replied on 31 July 1946:

> *Don't let the Devil get away with insinuating that 'only' my* artistic *conscience prevents me from writing this, that and the other to edification. How he does love, to be sure, putting asunder what God has joined! Conscience is conscience; but if you dig out a bit of it and slip the word 'artistic' in front of it he can make it sound something different and quite innocuous. All the same a lie is a lie, and he knows it. Once you start,* for any reason whatsoever, *writing something in which the will does not assent to the undertaking you are beginning to tell lies. And for a time*

86 i.e. Owen Barfield.

87 Charles Dickens, *Dombey and Son* (1847–8) ch. 15, in which 'When found, make a note of' is a favourite phrase of Captain Cuttle.

you can make quite a good-looking job of it (your technique will see to that). But in the end the lie rots inwards and corrupts the art itself.[88]

TO DOROTHY L. SAYERS (W) TS:

REF.46/19.

Magdalen College,
Oxford.
2nd August 1946.

Dear Miss Sayers,

I don't think the difference between us comes where you think. Of course one must'nt do *dishonest* work. But you seem to take as the criterion of honest work the sensible *desire* to write, the 'itch'. That seems to me precious like making 'being in love' the only reason for going on with a marriage. In my experience the *desire* has no constant ratio to the value of the work done. My own frequent uneasiness comes from another source – the fact that apologetic work is so dangerous to one's own faith. A doctrine never seems dimmer to me than when I have just successfully defended it. Anyway thanks for an intensely interesting letter.

yours very sincerely,
C. S. Lewis

On 5 August Sayers replied to the above letter with several pages of protest and explanation which began:

> *To clear up the misapprehension in your last letter would take a small treatise. However, the chief point is that I do not possess anything which I should care to dignify by the name of 'my faith'. All spiritual experience is a closed book to me; in that respect I have been tone-deaf from birth. All the apparatus I have by which to apprehend anything at all is intellect and imagination (or rather, since apart they can do nothing, the imaginative intellect). If or when, from time to time, God is pleased to make any truth clear to me by that means, I can announce it, to the best of my ability, in which I have to call, for lack of a better name, a work of the creative imagination. But if, for any reason, I write anything*

88 Sayers, *Letters*, vol. III, p. 252.

that is not fully apprehended by those means, I produce work that not only is spurious in itself but also falsifies the only instruments I have by which to perceive anything.[89]

TO DOROTHY L. SAYERS (W): TS

REF.46/19.

Magdalen College,
Oxford.
7th August 1946.

Dear Miss Sayers,

Hey! Whoa! You write as if I'd been urging you to do a book. Surely I was very careful not to? The only difference is that I see nothing but doubts where all looks self-evident to you. That may well be because you're a real writer and I'm only a half-timer. Also, because I thought of a work which would be very definitely *applied* art.* But don't bother your head about my views (or doubts) any more.

yours very sincerely,
C. S. Lewis

* i.e. not like asking the wood carver to do you an image but asking him to put up a bookshelf.

TO RUTH PITTER (BOD):

Magdalen etc
Aug 10 [1946]

Dear Miss Pitter –

Certainly a great many good lines have an epithet in them and depend principally on that epithet. But by no means all. Sometimes the work is done by a special use of a Noun:

multosque per annos
sustentata ruet moles et machina mundi.[90]

or

how sweetly flows
That *liquefaction* of her clothes.[91]

---

89 ibid., p. 255.

90 Lucretius, *De Rerum Natura*, V, 94–5: 'The mighty and complex system of the world, upheld through many years, shall crash into ruins.'

91 Robert Herrick, 'Upon Julia's Clothes' (1648).

sometimes by a verb:

> *J'ai mendiee* la mort chez les peuples sauvages[92]

– where to get the effect one wd. almost have to translate 'I have begged death as bread'. Or

> *Forever climbing* up the *climbing* wave[93]

Though here something else, the 'Figure' of repetition, comes in. Sometimes it turns on a Noun metaphorical:

> *Oh my America, my Newfoundland!*[94]

Again and again it turns on Metaphor:

> *The expense* of spirit in a *waste* of shame.[95]

> That from the *nunnery*
> Of thy chaste breast.[96]

> But I beneath *a rougher sea*
> And whelmed *in deeper gulfs* than he.[97]

But in all these there is something you may regard as *equivalent* to an epithet. There is another kind of poetry which seems to do it by simple statement:

> *Thou'll break my heart, thou bonnie bird,*
> *That sings on yonder bough.*[98]

---

92 'I begged for death among the savages.'

93 Alfred, Lord Tennyson, 'The Lotus-Eaters' (1833), Choric Song, iv, 95: 'In ever climbing up the climbing wave.'

94 John Donne, *Elegies*, 'To His Mistress Going to Bed' (c. 1595).

95 William Shakespeare, Sonnet 129 (1609).

96 Richard Lovelace, 'To Lucasta, Going to the Wars' (1649).

97 William Cowper, *Poems*, ed. James D. Baird and Charles Ryskamp (Oxford: Clarendon Press, 1995), vol. III, p. 216, 'The Cast-Away', 65–6.

98 Robert Burns, 'The Banks o' Doon' (1791), 5–6: 'Thou'll break my heart, thou bonnie bird,/That sings upon the bough.'

or

Twenty days and twenty nights
They went in red blood to the knee,
And he saw neither sun nor moon
But heard the roaring of the sea.[99]

No one will say that *bonnie* in the first or *red* in the second has much to do with the result. One might at a pinch say that the apostrophe to a bird in the first and the whole myth in the second are the same kind of thing as an epithet. But then there are still passages where the statement is of the most factual kind and yet (in its context) it is very poetry:

Ronsard me célébrait du temps que j'étais belle[100]

or

Fulsere quondam candidi tibi soles
Cum uentitabas quo puella ducebat
Amata tantum quantum amabitur nulla.[101]

Oh, and what about the *chansons de gestes*?

Roland is dead. God has his soul to Heaven[102]
(Roland est mort. Dieux en ad l'anme aux cieulx)

or

---

99 This is a modernized version, made presumably by Lewis, of Thomas of Erceldoune (fl. ?1220–97), *Thomas Rymer and Queen of Elfland.* See *The English and Scottish Popular Ballads*, ed. F. J. Child (Boston: 1882–98), vol. I, stanza 7, p. 324: 'For forty days and forty nights/He wade thro red blude to the knee,/And he saw neither sun nor moon,/But heard the roaring of the sea.'

100 Pierre de Ronsard, *Sonnets pour Hélène*, 'Quand vous serez bien vieille', II, xliii: 'Ronsard would sing my praise at the time when I was beautiful.'

101 Catullus, *Carmen*, No. 8: 'Once the sun shone bright for you,/when you would go whither your sweetheart led,/she who was loved by me as none will ever be loved.'

102 *The Song of Roland* (12th century), stanza 177, 2397.

Paien unt tort et Chestien unt dreit
(Paynims are wrong and Xians are right)[103]

The truth is that there are a great many different kinds of poetry and extreme roughness (or smoothness) evocative epithet (or plain statement), the metaphorical (or literal) the colloquial (or rhetorical) may all, in their place, rise to perfection. Any attempt to fix *one* of them as *the* secret is really like answering the sort of questions they ask Film-Stars 'What is your favourite colour – or flower – or girl's name?' Once more, read Barfield on Poetic Diction.

That is why Spender's objection to the 'willed quality' in Milton seems to me so bats'-eyed. It is the glory of *one* kind of poetry to sound un-willed, as if it had dropped out of the sky like Blake or else arisen spontaneously in conversation like Donne. But then it is equally the glory of another kind to sound willed: to sound as if one were watching, or even sharing, the building of a huge tower. The willed quality in P.L.[104] is a necessary part of the public and *ceremonial* effect. To demand that Milton shd. have the spontaneity of Catullus or Blake is like demanding that a King at his coronation or a celebrant approaching the altar shd. have the same charm as a child dancing in the waves. Don't we want *both*: both frolics and rituals? At any rate I do. Spender like all the contemporary poet-critics says about Poetry in general what is true only of the kind of poetry liked at the moment –

Thus Wit, like Faith, by each man is applied
To one small sect, and all are damned beside.[105]

Of course you are very right about *Patina* – again see Barfield. No old French poetry got that peculiar Old-Frenchness wh. is to us part of the charm. Half the beauties of the Old Testament did not exist for the writers. I wouldn't be too sure, though, that it is wholly a question of *our* 'projecting' qualities into the old lines. Isn't the fact that hills look blue at a certain distance just as much a fact about them, just as much a mixture of the laws of light and the laws of our eyes, as the

103 ibid., stanza 79, 1015.
104 i.e. *Paradise Lost.*
105 Alexander Pope, *An Essay on Criticism* (1880), 396–7.

fact that those same hills might look green when you were on them? Isn't the fact that past cultures seen from outside have a quality no one cd. have felt from inside just as good a fact as any other? The statements 'We project' and 'They were too close to see' seem to be about equally true. But at any rate the important thing is that we put the individual poet firmly in his place. He is not the creator, only the mother, of something whose father is the Universe or Time: and the child will grow up in its own way & make its own friends long after he's dead.

(Later). This was begun several days ago and was meant only to be an acknowledgement of your v. kind and valuable critique of my things. It developed as you see into a general discourse on Poetry! Now back to our muttons. I am greatly relieved that you think them as good as you do. The *Some believe* one *does* read like a translation: because I fell in love with a metre which is (at any rate still) too difficult for me. The *Epitaph* is only really a squib – someone said it was impossible to write a serious Limerick and this was my answer. I think it is good enough to prove the point but not good enough for much else. The bathos about angels having no nose etc was intended: I wanted a serio-comic effect. This doesn't of course mean that it must be good! The 'tension' you speak of is real. It means that in most of these poems I am enamoured of metrical subtleties – not as a game: the truth is I often lust after a metre as a man might lust after a woman. The effect I want, even if attained, wd. not be of the elusive kind – more like heraldry or enamel – a blaze.

By the way do you know that *buggen* in P. Plowman[106] is pronounced with a DG? GG in Middle English nearly always represents the DG in modern 'Bridge'. The U was somewhere between mod. i and French u as in *Lune*: so that *buggen* wd. rhyme somewhere fairly near *Pigeon*. Has this spoiled the patina?

Yours sincerely
C. S. Lewis

Roy Campbell, the poet, was preparing a programme on Milton for the BBC and asked Lewis's advice on which selections from Milton would be suitable for broadcasting.

106 William Langland (c. 1330–c. 1386), *Piers Plowman*, B, VII, 85.

TO ROY CAMPBELL (BBC):[107] TS

REF.46/289.

Magdalen College,
Oxford.
16th August 1946

Dear Campbell

Oddly enough we were all talking about you last night. Next term you must break away and spend a Thursday night with us in College. (I can do dinner, bed, and breakfast). Meanwhile you are quite as able as I to choose bits from Milton. I suppose a good chunk of L'Allegro and Il Penseroso;[108] Sonnet on Deceased Wife;[109] introduction to P.L. III; evening in Paradise from IV; the end from XII. From Samson the first chorus ('This, this is he')[110] – 'But when their hearts are jocund and sublime'[111] (if you can persuade someone to thump it out like Vachell Lindsay,[112] and not moan or murmur! And give P.R.[113] the go by.

My duty to your wife. My brother asks to be remembered to you, and hopes to see you next term.

yours,
C. S. Lewis

TO DOROTHY L. SAYERS (W):

Magdalen etc.
Aug 19th 1946

Dear Miss Sayers

With one thing and another, including neuralgia, I have only just read and digested your paper on the Faust Legend and the Idea of the

---

107 Roy Campbell (1901–57), South African poet, spent a good many years in England, during which time he worked for the BBC. In 1935 he became a Roman Catholic and fought for Franco in Spain. His works include *The Flaming Terrapin* (1924), *Sons of Mistral* (1941) and *Collected Poems* 1950). For information about his friendship with Tolkien and Lewis see Joseph Pearce, *Bloomsbury and Beyond: The Friends and Enemies of Roy Campbell* (2001).

108 John Milton, *L'Allegro* and *Il Penseroso* (1645).

109 John Milton, *Poems* (2nd edition, 1673), Sonnet XIX.

110 John Milton, *Samson Agonistes* (1671), 115.

111 ibid., 1669.

112 Vachel Lindsay (1879–1931), American author of incantatory ballads, *General William Booth* (1913) and *The Daniel Jazz* (1920) who was known for writing 'jazz poetry'.

113 John Milton, *Paradise Regained* (1671).

Devil.[114] Thanks very much for sending it and for giving me a great deal of pleasure – and knowledge. The part on Göthe, tho' not necessarily the best *per se* was the best *mihi*. I'm afraid I had fallen into the common error of forgetting that Mephistopheles is not G's picture of *the* devil but of *a* devil.

Is *Faust*[115] a profound work or not? I don't know enough German to find out. I know it is a *glorious* work in places: full [of] life and gold in a peculiarly rich German way – *unbegreiflich hohe Werke*,[116] *Lebens goldner Baum*[117] and all. Does something come of it? But tell me about this when we next meet. With very many thanks,

Yours sincerely
C. S. Lewis

TO LAURENCE HARWOOD (BOD):

Magdalen College,
Oxford
Aug 26th 1946

My dear Laurence –

Thank you very much for your interesting letter and for congratulating me about being a Doctor. The most interesting thing about that was the place I went to to be made a Doctor – Saint Andrews. It is a most lovely little town with the sea breaking just under the windows of some of the colleges. There is a ruined castle and a ruined cathedral and miles and miles of sand.

One queer thing is that on this sand I saw no sea-gulls but lots of crows! When I first saw them hopping about on the beach and picking at the sea-weed I said to myself 'Hullo! Why are the gulls all black in Scotland.'

---

114 On 22 February 1945, Sayers gave a lecture at University College London on 'The Faust Legend and the Idea of the Devil'. It was first published in her *Unpopular Opinions* (1946) and is reprinted in *The Whimsical Christian* (1987).

115 Johann Wolfgang von Goethe, *Faust* (1808, 1832).

116 Goethe, *Faust*, Part I, 5, Prologue in Heaven: 'incomprehensibly high works'. In Anna Swanwick's translation of *Faust* (1909–14) the line 'Die unbegreiflich hohen Werke Sind herrlich wie am ersten Tag' is rendered 'Transcending thought, the works eternal Are fair as on the primal day.'

117 Goethe, *Faust*, Part I, 1715: 'Life's golden tree'. In Swanwick's translation the line 'Grau, teurer Freund, ist alle Theorie, Und grün des Lebens goldner Baum' is translated 'Grey is, young friend, all theory: And green of life the golden tree.'

I would have answered your letter sooner but I have been very busy the last few days answering letters from France. We are trying to get two French servants, so we put an advertisement in a French paper and these were the replies. They were all in French, of course, and some of them were very funny. Many of the girls made quite as many mistakes in French grammar as you or I would. (The French call a servant a Bun and spell it Bonne.)

I would like to see you in your canoe: do you use a single or a double paddle? I have not had much swimming this summer because it has been so cold here. But I still think swimming the nicest kind of exercise there is (I think *standing*, just standing still, the nastiest).

This year we have some of the queerest toadstools I have ever seen in our wood, they are the colour of a tomato and have big grey pimples on them. Perhaps you could tell me what they are.

I think your father must be having a lovely time at Falmouth and I wish I knew how to get as many holidays as he does! If I did I should soon come to Kidbrooke and ask you to give me a sail in your canoe. Till then love to all.

Your affectionate godfather
C. S. Lewis

TO RUTH PITTER (BOD):

Magdalen etc.
Aug 28th 46

Dear Miss Pitter –

This is more than driving a bird to a gun.[118] It is more like introducing a phoenix to a fire. Congratulations (and condolences). Of course in any Shoot the Beater's role is a v. humble one. I look forward to your next visit to Oxford. Now I must to work (tho, it's a heavenly late summer morning here: cobwebs and cool wind thro mild sunlight – almost my favourite weather).

Yours very sincerely
C. S. Lewis

118 Pitter said in a note to this letter: 'This alludes to a joke. I cannot quite recall – something like "So-and-so has joined the R.C.'s as a result of reading Lewis" – and a comment about "driving the birds up to other men's guns."'

TO JILL FLEWETT (T): TS

Magdalen College,
Oxford.
10th September 1946.

My dear June,

Hearty congratulations on the double distinction:[119] it looks as if your difficulty about 'volume' was overcome. (I mean volume of sound: one can hardly, under present figure restrictions wish a lady 'volume' in any other sense, nor, without present rations, expect it).

Paxford and Queenie were both out today so I've been henning as well as woodcutting and am rather tired. All send their love. Doesn't Warnie type nicely? – with great feeling and restraint?

Microbe[120] was here today to tea. I sometimes (I think) see your Powell friend at the Socratic. When shall we see you perform again? Minto thanks you for your letter, but can't write at present.

yours (nearly asleep)[121]

P.S. Here's a letter from Minto after all.

P.P.S. Warnie says you will have guessed that he had not heard the good news when he wrote yesterday: he now sends his heartiest congratulations.

Someone at the BBC misunderstood Lewis's letter to Roy Campbell of 16 August 1946, and on 13 September a member of the Copyright Department wrote to Lewis as follows: 'I hear from our Talks Department that you have undertaken to select passages from Milton's poetry for the twenty minute programme . . . For your work in connection with this programme we would suggest payment of a fee of ten guineas.'[122]

---

119 June had achieved a double distinction in the London University Diploma in Drama. This was a degree course at a time when there was no Chair of Drama in England.

120 'Microbe' was Marie-José Bosc, an ex-evacuee from the Sacred Heart School, London.

121 Lewis failed to sign the letter.

122 BBC Written Archives Centre.

TO THE COPYRIGHT DEPARTMENT OF THE BBC (BBC): TS

REF.46/289

Magdalen College,
Oxford.
14th September 1946.

Dear Sir,

I am afraid there has been some misunderstanding. I never undertook this job: I merely scribbled a few suggestions to Mr. Campbell in the course of saying he might properly do it himself. But thank you for your generous offer. I cd. tell you the names of several young men who wd. do it quite as well as I and who need 10 guineas.

yours faithfully,
C. S. Lewis

TO ERIC ROUTLEY (*EC*):

[Magdalen College]
21 September 46

Dear Mr Routley

I can't quite remember my own last letter; but I was wrong if I said or implied that (a) variables, (b) active participation by the people, or (c) hymns, were bad in principle.

I would agree that anything the congregation *can do* may properly and profitably be offered to God in public worship. If one had a congregation (say, in Africa) who had a high tradition in sacred dancing and could do it really well I would be perfectly in favour of making a dance part of the service. But I wouldn't transfer the practice to a Willesden congregation whose best dance was a ballroom shuffle. In modern England, however, we can't sing – as the Welsh and Germans can. Also (a great pity, but a fact) the art of poetry has developed for two centuries in a private and subjective direction. That is why I find hymns 'dead wood'. But I spoke only for myself and a few others. If an improved hymnody – or even the present hymnody – does edify other people, of course it is an elementary duty of charity and humility for me to submit. I have never spoken in public *against* the use of hymns: on the contrary I have often told 'highbrow' converts that a humble acquiescence in anything that may edify their uneducated brethren (however frightful it seems to the educated 'natural man') is the first lesson they must learn. The door is *low* and one must stoop to enter.

Yours sincerely
C. S. Lewis

TO ARTHUR C. CLARKE (BOD): TS[123]

Ref. 46/511

Magdalen College,
Oxford.
24th September 1946.

Dear Mr. Clarke,

Thanks for letting me know. I am afraid I can't get up to London very easily these days: but I wish your lecture every success *except* a practical realization of space travel!

yours sincerely,
C. S. Lewis

TO RUTH PITTER (BOD): TS

Magdalen College,
Oxford.
24th September 1946.

Dear Miss Pitter,

No, I never see American reviews except when a friend sends them, and am glad to have read these. The picture in one is a little puzzling. But I like American reviewers: they do read the book.

yours sincerely,
C. S. Lewis

---

123 On 23 September 1946 Clarke wrote to Lewis: 'You may remember that some years ago I wrote to you disagreeing with your views on the interplanetary question as set forth in "Perelandra". You might be interested to know that I am giving a lecture on that subject in the near future, and if you happen to be in London at the time I should be pleased to see you . . . If I can get a pre-print of the lecture before it is delivered I shall send you a copy in advance to enable you to answer any criticism you may wish to deal with.'

TO RUTH PITTER (BOD):

Magdalen College,
Oxford.
Sept 27th 1946

Dear Miss Pitter

You said there was some chance of your paying another visit to Oxford: I am having a few people to lunch at 1.15 on Wed. October 9th. (the Cecils among them). It wd. give me great pleasure if you wd. join us: and I know my friend Dyson who speaks of your poetry with something like awe very much wants to meet you.[124] You want to ask at the Lodge to be directed to what we call 'the New Room.'

Yours sincerely
C. S. Lewis

TO RUTH PITTER (BOD): TS

Magdalen College,
Oxford.
2nd. October 1946.

Dear Miss Pitter,

Hurrah! But it's not Sir George, only a Fellow of Merton who is a Christian and likes poetry. You are my only lion. Your little narrative is superb.

yours sincerely,
C. S. Lewis

TO ARTHUR C. CLARKE (BOD): TS

Ref. 46/511

Magdalen College,
Oxford.
2nd. October 1946.

Dear Mr. Clarke

Many thanks for the copy of your lecture, which looks most interesting.

yours sincerely,
C. S. Lewis

---

124 Pitter said of this occasion: 'I remember at this lunch Mr. Dyson's saying "Can't we devise something that will get her here to Oxford"? and feeling my chronic Jude-the-Obscure syndrome somewhat alleviated' (Bodleian Library, MS. Eng. Lett. c. 220/3, fol. 30).

TO GEORGE ROSTREVOR HAMILTON (B): TS

REF.46/296.

Magdalen College,
Oxford.
21st October 1946.

My dear Hamilton,

Many thanks for the photo of Hurnard, which I am glad to have: a formidable old buster, as you say. I shall make a note of the 'Book Hand Book', and look forward to your article. I agree with you about poetic diction: which I hear has attained the distinction of being 'put on the Index' by the Faculty of one of the minor Universities. I forgot which.

yours,
C. S. Lewis

TO SISTER PENELOPE CSMV (BOD): TS

REF. 46/521.

Magdalen College,
Oxford.
21st October 1946.

Dear Sister Penelope,

Yes, it is only too true. I begin to be afraid that the villains will really contaminate the moon.[125]

yours sincerely,
C. S. Lewis

---

125 Sister Penelope, long a fan of *Out of the Silent Planet*, had probably drawn Lewis's attention to the news of a spaceship design mentioned in *The Times* (5 September 1946), p. 6, in an article entitled 'Designs for the Future': 'The Council of British Industry announced yesterday, that over 5,000 designs . . . have been accepted for the "Britain Can Make It" Exhibition . . . In the "Designs of the Future" section there will be included . . . A model of a "space ship" that is intended to suggest a probable trend of design for possible inter-planetary flight attempts in the next 20 years. This "ship" model was displayed yesterday, and the designer, Mr. Warnett Kennedy, explained that it is based on existing scientific knowledge and envisages the use of atomic power. It is spherical in shape, and the structure is a geodetic shell, enclosing living and equipment compartments, and a hall containing a navigational screen on which are projected views from a telescopic camera. There is an outer shell of transparent plastics.'

TO WARFIELD M. FIROR (BOD): TS

REF.46/549.

Magdalen College,
Oxford.
21st October 1946.

Dear Dr. Firor,

No indeed, your most kind and much valued presents of stationery did not miscarry; but they reached me without any indication of the sender's name, and consequently I was unable to express my great gratitude for them. We are all looking forward to the arrival of the box of dried fruit: for fruit, like everything else, is very scarce in this country at present. Many thanks.

I note with pleasure that there is a prospect of seeing you in England one of these days. Glad you liked 'Great Divorce'.

yours sincerely,
C. S. Lewis

TO GERARD HOPKINS (OUP):[126]

Magdalen College,
Oxford
Nov. 5th 1946

Dear Hopkins

I am sending to you (registered) by this post the MS. of a work called *Arthurian Torso* which is made up of a prose fragment by Charles Williams and a critique of his Arthurian poems by me. Though I am sending it, it is to be regarded as coming before the O.U.P. *viâ* Messrs. Pearn, Pollinger and Higham of 39–40 Bedford St., Strand, W.C.2, literary agents. It may be known to you that they attempted to send you another MS of the same book some months ago, but it got lost.

Should the Press decide to publish this book, there are two points I had better make.

(1) My permission to use the C.W. fragment was given me by Mrs

126 Gerard Walter Sturgis Hopkins (1892–1961), translator and critic, served the Oxford University Press from 1920 to 1957, first as publicity manager and later as editorial adviser. He was sent to Oxford with other members of the Press at the outbreak of war, and he and Charles Williams were close friends.

Hadfield.[127] What her title to it is, I do not know. I presume that either you or Pearn, Pollinger & Higham will have means of discovering this: I can take no responsibility.

(2) My intention is that all royalties should be paid to Mrs Williams. I take it (literary agents are a quite new phenomenon in my experience) that the actual bargaining will be between the O.U.P. and P.P. and H. May I hope that the O.U.P. will take into account the fact that one chief purpose of this work is to do (financial) good to the widow of your old colleague and their old servant?

As the MS. has gone astray once already I shd. be glad of a note from you telling me of its safe arrival.

You are still 'freshly remembered' among all the Inklings.

Yours
C. S. Lewis

TO HERBERT PALMER (TEX):

Magdalen College,
Oxford.
Nov. 11th 1946

My dear Palmer –

Thank you very much for sending me the book.[128] I have had time for only a first glance at it but am already picking out my favourites: *Spain 1936–39* (I'd never thought of the ghosts of those bulls and horses before – a splendid idea);[129] *Back to the Land* (of course: I remember your reciting it); *Apocalypse*; the subtitle of *Bonfire and Cinders* (almost a poem in itself): *Incantation* ('wheel-sick and brick-sick' is good: only that brick begins to feel quite friendly compared with ferro-concrete):

---

127 Alice Mary Hadfield (1897–1989), born Alice Mary Miller, was educated at Oxford and Mount Holyoke College, Massachusetts. She worked for Oxford University Press in London from 1933 and besides editing a number of books, was librarian at Amen House. While there she became friends with Charles Williams. She married Ellis Charles Raymond Hadfield (1909–96), one of the managers at the Press, in 1945. Mrs Hadfield is the author of *An Introduction to Charles Williams* (1959) and *Charles Williams: An Exploration of His Life and Work* (1983). Because of her interest in Williams's Arthurian writings, she had asked to collaborate with Lewis on *Arthurian Torso*.

128 *A Sword in the Desert: A Book of Poems and Verses for the Present Time* (1946).

129 ibid., 'Spain: 1936–39', stanza 3: 'A wind roved over Europe/Till it found the land of Spain,/Where it stirred a stricken multitude/To spring to life again – /The ghosts of bulls and horses/For a sadist pleasure slain.'

Sirens – and (very much) *Looking Back from the Next Century*, tho' I don't fully understand it.

But I regret *The Present State.*[130] I agree with most of it but it will do neither you nor poetry any good. It will all be discounted as the spleen of a disappointed poet: it will confirm them in their errors by making them feel that nothing but jealousy cd. dream of criticising them – as you and I wd. discount the things said about a girl who'd got married by a girl who hadn't. They might be true but cannot be said by *her* with any chance of being believed. Do stop all this and get on with your own work. 'Fret not thyself because of evil doers.'[131]

I'll look for *Hitler and St. John*. I am so glad you like *Perelandra*: but talking of 'pure creation', *have* you read E. R. Eddison's *The Worm Ouroboros*?

All the best.

Yours

C. S. Lewis

TO RUTH PITTER (BOD): TS

REF.46/509.

Magdalen College,
Oxford.
22nd November 1946.

Dear Miss Pitter,

Thanks. I'm deader than ever with scholarship papers at the moment. One candidate says Jane Austen's humour 'is broad, but exquisitely so'. My brother, who is flattered by your remembrance of him, sends his duty.

yours sincerely,

C. S. Lewis

TO DOM BEDE GRIFFITHS OSB (W):

[The Kilns]
Dec. 20th 46

My dear Dom Bede

No. I don't think I feel like you 'disillusioned'. I think that though I am emotionally a fairly cheerful person my actual judgement of the

---

130 Palmer included in *A Sword in the Desert*, pp. 9–17, an essay on 'The Present State of English Poetry'.

131 Psalm 37:1.

world has always been what yours now is and so I have not been disappointed. The early loss of my mother, great unhappiness at school, and the shadow of the last war and presently the experience of it, had given me a very pessimistic view of existence. My atheism was based on it: and it still seems to me that *far* the strongest card in our enemies' hand is the actual course of the world: and that, quite apart from particular evils like wars and revolutions. The inherent 'vanity' of the 'creature',[132] the fact that life preys on life, that all beauty and happiness is produced only to be destroyed – this was what stuck in my gullet. I agreed most heartily with Lucretius

> *nequaquam nobis divinitus esse paratam*
> *naturam rerum: tanta stat praedita culpa.*[133]

I still think the argument from design the weakest possible ground for Theism, and what may be called the argument from un-design the strongest for Atheism.

Of course my error was in asking how I knew the universe to be so bad: whence came the light wh. discovered this darkness, the straight by which I judged this crookedness?

Hence the v. important part which the Fall (both human and angelic) has played in my thought since I became a Christian. When you say that nothing here (*in hac valle*)[134] has a value in itself, that everything has a value in relation to God, I couldn't agree with you more. And I often, like you, think that all the valuable future may lie with the Christened Chinaman. But one mustn't assume burdens that God does not lay upon us.

It is one of the evils of rapid diffusion of news that the sorrows of *all* the world come to us every morning. I think each village was meant to feel pity for *its own* sick and poor whom it can help and I doubt if it is the duty of any private person to fix his mind on ills wh. he cannot

---

132 Romans 8:20: 'For the creature was made subject to vanity, not willingly, but by reason of him who hath subjected the same in hope.'

133 Lucretius, *De Rerum Natura*, Book 5, 198–9: 'By no means is the natural order of things fashioned for us by a divine agency: so greatly do the imperfections with which it has been endowed stand out.'

134 The phrase comes from the Catholic hymn, 'Salva, Regina' ('Hail, Holy Queen') and the words '*In hac lacrimarum valle*' – 'In this vale of tears'.

help. (This may even become an *escape* from the works of charity we really *can* do to those we know).

A great many people (not you) do now seem to think that the mere state of being *worried* is in itself meritorious. I don't think it is. We must, if it so happens, give our lives for others: but even while we're doing it, I think we're meant to enjoy Our Lord and, in Him, our friends, our food, our sleep, our jokes, and the birds song and the frosty sunrise.

As about the distant, so about the future. It is v. dark: but there's usually light enough for the next step or so. Pray for me always.

Yours
C. S. Lewis

Dorothy L. Sayers had corrected the galley proofs of her essay '". . . And Telling you a Story": a Note on The Divine Comedy' for Essays Presented to Charles Williams *and sent them to Lewis for his approval.*

TO DOROTHY L. SAYERS (W):

Magdalen etc.
Dec. 29/46.

Dear Miss Sayers –

I get to you at last, escaped from Christmas week: a period which (tho' I hope my spiritual man rejoices) my carnal man regards as the most disagreeable of the whole fifty-two. It puts on *fortissimo* the theme of domestic drudgery which is now, I suppose, the main tune in most of our lives.

The *Heart of Stone* is really a brilliant success.[135] It has the first great indispensable merit of not sounding like a translation. 'To the short day and the great circle of shadow'[136] has all the accent of new poetry. And the lines are properly *boney* all through: what critics of my sex (with an assumption which may sometimes imitate yours) call a 'masculine' style. (Though what Eliot meant by calling Dryden the most mascu-

135 *The Heart of Stone* is Sayers's translation of four odes by Dante. It was first printed privately for Christmas 1946, and it is reprinted in Barbara Reynolds, *The Passionate Intellect: Dorothy L. Sayers' Encounter with Dante* (1989), Appendix, pp. 223–35.

136 Reynolds, *The Passionate Intellect*, p. 228, Ode 2, stanza 1, 18.

line of our poets I don't know. He's only masculine in the sense of being unfeminine). Thanks and congratulations.

The idea of *my* being stern with printers on your behalf is at once comic and alarming, seeing as how everyone knows that butter won't melt in my mouth and you inspire a wholesome terror, I'm told, in all publishers, printers, producers, journalists, etc. Now for details.

Title. Right. Let it be *The Divine*

Galley 1. I prefer A. Very definitely. It wd. be a great loss to omit that para. I remove B. Is that right?

Galley 3. This is really insoluble, having lost (what fools we were) the double sense of 'spirit' in English. I think 'breath and water' makes the best of a bad job. 'Sighs and tears' wd. be weak and ordinary in comparison.[137]

Galley 4. The main thing clearly is to quote the text you are translating! Which are you? If 'so dark and intricate is thy utterance'[138] is a water-tight translation of the *parti*[139] reading as well as of the *parli*[140] one, then it doesn't matter. Just let me have a line: I won't risk a ruling on my own.

Galley 10. Agreed.

Galley 12. 'In Poetry' is correct.[141]

Galley 17 The note certainly was not mine. I think it silly. Boswell is not an autobiographer: nor, in my opinion, Pepys: and if they both were, a rule wh. has only two exceptions can certainly be said to be broken 'seldom'. I have crossed all the scholia out and written *stet.*[142]

springava.[143] I have restored the R. Why shd. you quote Mr. Bandersnatch's text if you don't want to?

Galley 23. folgor. I restore your reading[144]

---

137 *Essays Presented to Charles Williams*, p. 4. The question was how to translate Dante's '*spirito ed acqua fessi*'; Sayers translates the couplet: 'The ice that cramped me about the heart melted into breath and water.'

138 ibid.

139 'you depart'.

140 'you speak'; evidently these are alternative readings in the Italian.

141 ibid., p. 15: 'I know no poet who can compare with Dante in the "art of sinking" – and rising again – "in poetry". Not even Shakespeare can do it so swiftly and surely.'

142 ibid., p. 20. Whatever lines were fostered upon the essay, the passage in question now reads: 'Seldom has an autobiographer presented the world with a less heroic picture of himself, or presented his own absurdities so lovably.'

143 ibid., p. 21.

144 ibid., p. 28, note.

Galley 26. Z every time![145]

Galley 28. 'childish-foolish'. I have added a note to say that the hyphen is all important and the dash fatal.[146]

It is a stunning essay and will, by itself, make the book memorable. I've just re-read the *Aeneid* again. The effect is one of the immense *costliness* of a vocation combined with a complete conviction that it is worth it. The whole story is littered with the cost – Creusa, Dido, Anchises, Palinurus, Pallas, Lausus, Camilla. Did he do it so well because the making of the poem had for him the same costliness wh. the founding of Rome had for the characters? All the Alexandrian in him that wanted to write more *Bucolics*,[147] all the countryman that wanted to write more *Georgics*, was sacrificed and long hung (like the Trojan women) *miserum inter amorem Praesentis terrae et fatis vocantia regna.*[148] i.e. the supreme instance of the poet who becomes far better than he was precisely by writing the poem wh. wasn't exactly what he thought he'd like to write. Do I make this clear?

Years aren't what they were, but I wish you a good one.

Yours very sincerely
C. S. Lewis

---

145 ibid., p. 31: 'The excitement, once maintained by encounters with monsters, by perils and escapes, by peripeteia and "strange surprising adventures", is now transmuted into a steadily increasing exhilaration.' In her letter of 19 December Sayers told Lewis: '"strange surprizing adventures" is from the original title-page to *Robinson Crusoe.* The word always looks to me much more "surprizing" spelt that way . . . May I have my "z"?' The editor, apparently, overruled Lewis.

146 ibid., p. 33: '[Beatrice] has used hard words to him, she has called him childish-foolish; but that is only love's way.'

147 *Bucolics* is another name for Virgil's *Eclogues*, a collection of pastoral poems composed between 42 and 37 BC.

148 Virgil, *Aeneid*, Book V, 655–6. At the end of the games, the Trojan Women are tempted to burn the ships and simply stay, rather than proceed to the kingdom Aeneas has promised, 'miserum inter amorem praesentis terrae fatisque vocantia regna': '[suspended] between an unhappy love for lands now to hand and a longing for the kingdom to which the fates were calling'.

TO LAURENCE HARWOOD (BOD):

Magdalen
Dec. 31st 1946

My dear Lawrence

Thank you so much for your nice card and letter. I was glad to see a picture of the new Michael Hall, having heard so much about it. It looks a beautiful place and I hope that I shall be able to see it myself before too long.

Did you like the snow and frost? I did, except for getting up in the morning. We had our pond frozen but not strong enough for skating. I found this out in a funny way. There is a tree with a branch hanging down into the water which spoils one bit for bathing. I have always wanted to cut off the lower end of that branch but could never use a saw from the punt properly: so I thought 'Now's my chance' and went out on the ice – and went through! Luckily I was near the bank so nothing worse happened than having to change my socks. But it is a horrid feeling when ice breaks under you!

It was rather nice here in the floods (did you have any?). The meadow outside my windows looked like a lake and the reflection of the trees in it was beautiful. Most of the deer had been moved into another field before the flood came but two had got left behind on a little island where there was just room for them to stand. They were very miserable till someone went and rescued them.

Talking of animals, a hedgehog came into our kitchen the other night. It didn't seem to be in the least afraid and drank a saucer of milk: when it had finished it got *into* the saucer and settled down to sleep just as if it intended to pass the night there! The chief other live stock in our garden is moles, toads, and owls. I had a very fine view of an owl the other night.

Do you ever notice Venus these mornings at about quarter past seven? She has been terrifically bright lately, almost better than Jupiter.

Any news of John?[149] I enclose a book token with all good wishes for the new year and lots of love to yourself and all the others from

Your affectionate godfather
C. S. Lewis

---

149 John Harwood was at this time in the Royal Navy.

1947

TO ARTHUR C. CLARKE (BOD): TS

Ref. 46/511. Magdalen College,
Oxford.
2nd January 1947.

Dear Mr. Clarke,

Many thanks for the gift of your interesting lecture and the discussion.[1] With all good wishes for the New Year,

yours sincerely,
C. S. Lewis

TO RUTH PITTER (BOD):

Magdalen etc
Jan 4/47

Dear Miss Pitter –

It was nice to hear from you. I am ashamed to have to ask 'Who and what *is* Sir R.S.?':[2] ashamed because I gather from the way you mention him that you must have told me before. I am afraid you must now be let into the secret that no *fact* penetrates my mind until about

---

1 Clarke's lecture on 'The Challenge of the Space Ship', mentioned in Lewis's letter to him of 2 October 1946, was published with a discussion about the lecture in the *Journal of the British Interplanetary Society*, vol. 6, no. 3 (December 1946), pp. 66–81.

2 Pitter supplied this note to the letter: 'Sir R.S. was Ronald Storrs, whom I wished to bring to see Lewis, not only because he was a good classic & much-travelled, but that he had been *Governor of Jerusalem*, which seemed to have a mystical connotation vis-à-vis a great & imaginative Xtian author' (Bodleian Library, MS. Eng. lett. c. 220/3, fol. 34). Sir Ronald Storrs (1881–1955), a Near Eastern expert and governor, was educated at Charterhouse and Pembroke College, Cambridge, where he took a First in Classics. He entered the Egyptian civil service in 1904, and he was military governor of Jerusalem, 1917–20, civil governor of Jerusalem and Judaea, 1920–6, governor of Cyprus, 1926–32, and governor of Northern Rhodesia, 1932–4.

the third repetition: a joke, a thought, a verse, I can remember with the best. But a fact (a fact is roughly anything that cd. be put into the Accusative-with-the-infinitive).

No. I have yet another humiliation to undergo. Can you bear the truth? – *Voyage to Arcturus* is not the parody of *Perelandra* but its father. It was published, a dead failure, about 25 years ago. Now that the author is dead it is suddenly leaping into fame:[3] but I'm one of the old guard who had a treasured second hand copy before anyone had heard of it. From Lyndsay I first learned what other planets in fiction are really good for: for *spiritual* adventures. Only they can satisfy the craving which sends our imaginations off the earth. Or putting it another way, in him I first saw the terrific results produced by the union of two kinds of fiction hitherto kept apart: the Novalis, G. Macdonald, James Stephens sort and the H. G. Wells, Jules Verne sort. My debt to him is very great: tho' I'm a little alarmed to find it so obvious that the affinity came through to you even from a talk about Lyndsay!

For the rest, *Voyage to A* is on the borderline of the diabolical: i.e. the philosophy expressed is so Manichaean as to be almost Satanic. Secondly, the style is often laughably crude. Thirdly, the proper names (Polecrab, Blodsombre, Wombflash, Tydomin, Sullenbode) are superb and perhaps Screwtape owes something to them. Fourthly, you must read it. You will have a disquieting but not-to-be-missed experience.

I think 'nostalgia for the non-existent' (how well I know what you mean) is not the final diagnosis.[4] You wouldn't really exchange a hross, a sorn, and a bubble tree for humans, a cat, and a cherry tree. (A cat of the steely-black kind is no bad substitute for a hross. Seals are better but I wouldn't recommend one till fish is cheaper, and unless you have a *very* large bathroom). But the point is that if you really *were* in Perelandra you wd. still feel the same nostalgia: just as if Wordsworth

3 Besides the fact that *A Voyage to Arcturus* had been serialized on the radio, David Lindsay (1876–1945) had died the previous year, and a new edition of the book, with a note by E. H. Visiak, had just been published in the Connoisseur's Library of Strange Fiction by the London publisher, Victor Gollancz.

4 Pitter said in her note to this letter: 'I had so fallen in love with "Perelandra" that I could not bear to think it would be different on Venus if one could get there. And I so loved the *Hrossa* and the *Sorns* in "Out of the Silent Planet" that there was a pain in my chest for them, as when one is in love at 20. It was this world, our world, that seemed unreal to me then, not theirs' (Bodleian Library, MS. Eng. lett. c. 220/3, fol. 34).

or Proust cd. have gone back to their own past they wd. still have felt it. What you are really wanting will never be in any finite *here* or *now* (God bless us, you know that as well as I do) and the rabbit in Magdalen grove may mediate it as well as a hross. And oh how much sweeter is this *longing* than any other *having*.

Hodgson is right.[5] The pre-human earth already contained suffering. This is why (like our fathers) we must believe in the fall of the angels long prior to the fall of man. Our fall consisted in joining the wrong side in a battle wh. had already begun. I'm inclined to think that the mutual preying of irrational creatures (at least creatures on more or less the same level) *is* evil. Cd. it be without pain?

I'm distressed about your muse. You take it beautifully – the poetic fact, I mean. And of course, in the long run, it doesn't matter, as you say. But it's sad when He locks up our toys: no doubt for a good purpose. I've just had a poem (but then I never was a poet like you) refused by the *Spectator* for the first time – I mean, the first time since I was a youngster. Very tonic: I'd forgotten the *taste* of that little printed slip. What one suffers between the ages of 17 and 22!

I never heard of A. Y. Campbell I'm afraid:[6] nor I don't want Alexander[7] neither, tho' many thanks. By 'Deity' he means 'whatever Nature is going to do next.' Deity *was* [an] organism in the pre-organic period, and *was* mammals in the saurian period, and *was* man among the apes, and now is the super man. It's all nonsense: except for Chapter I (or Introduction, I forget which) where you could, I know, master the distinction between 'enjoyment' and 'contemplation' and so acquire a valuable tool of thought.[8] I shouldn't have said 'all nonsense.' Alexander was a very great man: I only meant to disagree with him!

Finished re-reading the *Aeneid* on Boxing Day. I want to talk about it at length when we meet. Blessings on you.

Yours sincerely
C. S. Lewis

---

5 Leonard Hodgson, *The Doctrine of the Trinity* (1945).

6 Pitter was unable to remember what she said about an A. Y. Campbell, but she thought she may have recommended Archibald Young Campbell's *Poems* (1926).

7 Samuel Alexander, *Space, Time, and Deity* (1920).

8 Lewis was later to devote part of *SBJ*, ch. 14 to this important distinction between 'enjoyment' and 'contemplation' which he found in the introduction to *Space, Time and Deity*.

TO ARTHUR GREEVES (W):

Magdalen
Jan 5/47

My dear Arthur –

I had heard of dear old Mrs McNeill's's[9] death and written to Tchanie before I got your letter: and I have just heard to-night of Forrest Reid's. This must be bad for you. He has been daily in my prayers for a long time and will be. He wasn't a real part of my life, of course, as he was of yours but I liked the man very much – liked him, indeed, better than I cd. find it easy to explain – something about his voice and face and manner.

As for Mrs McNeill – well, what could you and I say about it even if we were together? It's just a flood of queer, absurd, adorable memories, isn't it? – something that you and I cd. both respond to, and in exactly the same way as long as we remained ourselves. I did very much hope to have seen her again. By the way, I told Tchanie in my letter how you and I once, talking about the next world, said how lovely it wd. be if, after all sorts of strange and perhaps terrible adventures, one suddenly (perhaps in a clearing in a huge wood) suddenly heard a voice saying 'Well, Arthur!' and turned round and there the old lady was. Do you remember?

And all this greatly increases my longing to see you again. You know why I can't! I envy you having that 'nurse companion'. The same thing is really needed here but the mere suggestion would almost kill her. And I'm glad to hear of your house too. If only you and I (or you *or* I) doesn't go and die before we have a chance to meet! And yet, if we did no doubt there wd. be some good and loving reason for it. I am (except in bad moods) more convinced of that all the time. We shall meet and be happy together if it is good for us: otherwise not (e.g. I might after all be disappointed in a hope I sometimes cherish that you wd. find me a little less aggressive and dictatorial and arrogant than I have often been in the old days. But who knows? The first argument might shatter all these good resolutions!)

Funny to think we're both elderly, isn't it? And what a sham this business of age is. Do you (except physically) *feel* any older than when

9 Margaret Cunningham McNeill, the mother of Jane McNeill. See note 59 to the letter to Arthur Greeves of 5 November 1933.

we saw the hedge pig and played gramophone records to one another? I don't a bit. My own pupils still seem to me in many ways older than I. Indeed (nice men as many of them are) I am a little worried by the fact that so few of them seem ever to have had youth as we had it. They have all read all the correct, 'important' books: they seem to have no private & erratic imaginative adventures of their own. (I suppose the explanation is that I am the last person who is likely to hear of such things even where they exist. I mean, with me they're all talking 'grown-up' as hard as they can. Yet I don't know: the modern world is so desperately serious. They have a taste for 'books of information' wh. wd. have done credit to your father!)

There's thick snow on the ground and moonlight to-night. God bless you.

Yours
Jack

Do you read *Punch*. The poems signed N.W. wh. sometimes appear there are by me. This is a secret.

On 8 January 1947 Lewis received the following letter from the author and glass-engraver, Laurence Whistler:

> *Dear Mr. Lewis . . . I had lunch today with Andrew Young the poet and his friend Channing Pearce. During last year Young and I found that we had an idea in common, though we had arrived at it independently. It is briefly this: that there is room for a new periodical, mainly (but not exclusively) of a literary and artistic sort, which would have a Christian or at any rate a 'spiritual' point of view. I don't like the second word, but it is difficult to find another. Perhaps I should say, a periodical which would attempt to be within the Tao, in the sense in which you use the word in* The Abolition of Man. *We felt that it is a pity that Horizon's leadership should go unchallenged, and that there are many who would be glad if such a periodical existed. At present, it seems as if the cultural leadership of the young were too much in the hands of those who are, unconsciously perhaps, creating 'Men without Chests' . . .*
>
> *At luncheon today we concluded that a beginning could be*

made if those who are interested would agree to meet. Young offered to hold a house-party at his Vicarage at Stonegates near Tunbridge Wells, and the second weekend in May was suggested (Friday, May 8th). Would you consent to come? Ruth Pitter is wholeheartedly in favour of the plan, and we are very much hoping to induce T. S. Eliot to be there, and Richard Church and a number of others.

When the meeting takes place we can decide on a policy. For the present we have thought that the periodical must avoid appearing exclusively Anglican, and that we should do all we can to bring in Roman Catholics and others of no church who are in sympathy. We thought, too, that it ought to avoid any political bias, and be mainly concerned with literature, art, philosophy and sociology . . .[10]

TO LAURENCE WHISTLER (BOD):[11]

Magdalen College,
Oxford
Jan 9/47

Dear Mr. Whistler

I am pleased, to the point of being excited, by your suggestion. I have said again and again that what we very badly need is a new, frankly high-brow, periodical *not* in the hands of the Left. I have usually added 'If only we cd. find a right-minded capitalist.' Money, I take it, is the first essential.

I entirely agree that it shd. not be specifically Christian, much less Anglican: the Tao (in that sense) is to be the ring fence. In almost all existing periodicals one knows in advance how a certain book will be reviewed: the personal and political bias is no longer even disguised. That is what must be avoided.

I shall be delighted to see you whenever you call. I will also attend the meeting *if I can*: but I am so domestically tied (to the bedside of an elderly invalid) that I can never be sure of being able to leave Oxford. Apart from money – the great question is whether there are enough

10 Bodleian Library, MS. Eng. lett. c. 862, fols. 3–4.
11 See **Sir Laurence Whistler** in the Biographical Appendix.

writers. We must not shipwreck on letting in men of good will who are not first rate.

Yours sincerely
C. S. Lewis

TO MR SMOOT (WHL):

[Magdalen College]
January 1947

Dear Mr Smoot,

. . . I am delighted with your index[12] but I think it would be unwise to put it in the book. You see part of the success of that book depends on luring the ordinary reader into serious self-knowledge *under pretence* of being a kind of joke. A subject index at once gives the bluff away and stamps it as deadly serious. Of course this wd. not deter readers like you. But it is the worldly reader I specially want to catch. With many thanks.

TO RUTH PITTER (BOD):

Magdalen.
Feb 2/47

Dear Miss Pitter –

I want advice. I have written two different versions of a poem and all my friends disagree, some violently championing A and some B, and some neither. Will you give a vote? Firstly, is either any good? Secondly, if so, which is the good one? Don't be in the least afraid of answering No to the first question: kindness wd. only be encouragement to waste more time. The title of both is *Two Kinds of Memory*.

'A' Version

Oh still vacation, silver calm,
Oh Memory the compassionate,
Forever in cool reverie
The cruel past refashioning!

12 Mr Smoot had indexed *The Screwtape Letters* and suggested the index be included in subsequent editions of the book.

But iron Memory, tyrant grip,
Still back into the merciless,
Unalterable halter of
The finished fact coërcing us!

Well did our fabling elders feign
A mild queen in the underworld,
Persephone the ineffable,
The long-lost, the most wonderful;

But made her husband Hades whom
No time nor prayer can mitigate;
On Orpheus, when he forfeited
His bride, he gazed unpitying.

His mercies even are cursed things;
Unworthy for his Elyzium
To barter for his Tartarus,
If there forever, dizzily,

Mechanically, vanished joys
Recur unchanged – Orion on
His quarry and the warrior
Upon his foe still triumphing.

His mirror blinds the spirit. Hers
Is live, though dim, and magical;
Splendour in it and tenderness
Make green the grasses of tragedies,

And joys remembered poise awhile
In air, and soon with arrowy,
Swift flight are off to light upon
The sunshot woods of Paradise.

Who calls such magic falsehood, next
Will tell us that the merriment
And marvel of the harvesting
Belies the corn-seed's burial.

'B' Version

Oh still vacation, silver
Pause and relaxing of severer laws,
Oh Memory the compassionate,
Forever in the thick-leaved woods of reverie
How you refresh the past, how you refashion it!

Yet iron Memory, tyrant
Importunate by night! Whose lucid torture
Still back into the merciless
Unalterable fact and choking halter of
The finished pact, without appeal, coërces us.

Well did our fabling elders
Appoint two differing powers to rule with joint
Authority the underworld;
Persephone, the lost and found, the ineffable
Lady of death and spring, august and wonderful,

And Hades unevaded,
Stern and exact, whom neither prayers can turn
Nor lapse of years can mitigate;
On Orpheus when – the second time – he forfeited
Eurydice, he gazed, precise, unpitying.

His mercies even are cursèd
Mockeries of life, cold, cold as lunar rock,
And all his famed Elyzium
Worthless, if former joys in all their earthliness
Must there recur, mechanically, dizzily,

And round forever, bound for
No goal, caught in a circular rut, the soul
Re-lives her past – Orion on
His quarry, and upon his foe the warrior
Ever pursuing and forever triumphing.

Thus hoarding and recording
He keeps the frozen past. In her it sleeps,
Dreams, stirs – then soft!, the magical
Blendings and tiny changes, till the tenderness
Of budded spring make green the graves of tragedies,

And joys remembered, poising
One moment on the past which was their home,
Spread wings and then with arrowy
Swift flight and airy song are off to light upon
The branches of the sun-shot woods of Paradise.

To call such magic falsehood
Is true – one sort of truth. What can you do
With men who say the merriment
And marvel of the bright, filled ears at harvesting
Is only a lie about the corn-seed's burial?

I could almost make myself hope for your sake – and lest you spend more time and attention on them than is reasonable for me to exact – that both are bad! Otherwise, I have set you a troublesome exercise: the botheration being that you have to read one *first* and can therefore never bring a quite open mind to the second (By the way, B was conceived first but A completed first).[13] All good wishes and don't let this be a nuisance

Yours sincerely
C. S. Lewis

13 Pitter said in her note to this letter: 'Both versions are very fine, of course: the skill in form alone is enough to drive a small poet to despair: and then the melody, so strong and so unforced, and the solemn images and the contrasting moods. Strange how memory is here *polarized*, as though he could not have encompassed the paradisal without retaining a hellish pain in recollection, an ever-fresh wound. (NB. These poems should be read aloud, but only by a strong male voice)' (Bodleian Library, MS. Eng. lett. c. 220/3, fol. 38).

TO RUTH PITTER (BOD): TS

REF.97/47.

Magdalen College,
Oxford.
8th February 1947.

Dear Miss Pitter,

Good. I also was pretty sure of B: the slower rhythm suits the meditative theme, A is too like a jig.[14] *Tiny* is bad, you're quite right.

I think just as you do about the Anglo-Cats.[15] Their prevailing quality is the very non-Catholic one of disobedience. They will obey neither our own book nor Rome.

Thanks for giving me Fredegond Shove's name; but what a name![16]

yours sincerely,
C. S. Lewis

P. S. Is *your* Persephone on view?[17]

TO RUTH PITTER (BOD):

Magdalen etc.
Feb. 12th 47

Dear Miss Pitter –

I'm glad you let me see *P. in H.* I think it a remarkable work. It nearly overcomes the initial difficulty in any poem of that sort: i.e. that the story (as it exists in our minds before we begin reading) is already perfect poetry, so that it is difficult if not impossible to *make* poetry out of it. That, I suppose, is why the greatest myths live in allusions and similes in poems [on][18] other, and less poetical, subjects: and why

---

14 The B version was published, with slight alterations, in *Time and Tide*, XXVIII (7 August 1947), p. 859. It is reprinted in *Poems* and *CP*.

15 i.e. Anglo-Catholics.

16 Fredegond Shove was the author of several volumes of verse including *The Water Mill, From Four Poems by Fredegond Shove, set to music by R. Vaughan Williams* (Oxford: Oxford University Press, 1925).

17 Ruth Pitter, *Persephone in Hades*, 100 copies numbered from 1 to 100 . . . for private circulation only (Auch, France, [1931]). In her note to this letter Miss Pitter said: 'My "Persephone" was a long poem published abroad by Belloc at his own expense. Denis Saurat, always an interesting critic, said of this poem & of poems on myths in general, "The myth must be implicit, not explicit", which substantially agrees with Lewis's kind, painstaking, time-expending critique' (Bodleian Library, MS. Eng. lett. c. 220/3, fol. 41).

18 The manuscript is damaged.

Balder Dead is so inferior to *Sohrab*.[19] The *Life and Death of Jason* does succeed: perhaps by deliberately declining all the more intense poetical appeals.

In your poem the difficulty is much eased for a Xtian reader by the fact that we think all the time of the true version, so that your work becomes a continual simile to *it*. It is full of good things. *Death's filthy garment* (p 8.): reminding me of Thomas Browne's 'I am not so much afraid of death as ashamed of it':[20] the courage of Persephone on 13, 14, and, also on 14, the small stones and the one crocus – tho' *ill-fated* doesn't really help – the 'thunderbolt of insult' (15) – the whole winter scene on 16 – the bit about 'whose heaven is happiness' on 18 – the sense of imminent danger on 19, at 'Frost, strike no deeper.' And what a lot you get into the word 'instruments' on 21! The cream of the whole piece to me is on p. 24 'The flesh like a poor drudge . . . as homespun will.' That is really superb. And I like the speech beginning 'Neighbours' on 40: also the shepherds on 43.

On p. 10 – unless you are playing some delicate metrical trick which I haven't spotted – *Pactolus* is a false quantity.[21] It is Pāctōlŭs surely, like *Cambyses* or *Keir-Hardie*. I was really moved by this poem.[22]

I had poor old H. Palmer to dinner last night and in our flowing cups (they were not numerous for he had to go on to read to a society) your name was freshly remembered. I wish he was not interested in poets so much and more interested in poetry and more still in the things poetry is about. But there's a kind of barbaric greatness about him.

---

19 Matthew Arnold, *Balder Dead* (1832); *Sohrab and Rustum* (1853).

20 Sir Thomas Browne, *Works*, ed. Geoffrey Keynes (London: Faber & Faber, 1964), vol. I, *Religio Medici*, part I, sec. 40, p. 51.

21 Pitter, *Persephone in Hades*, part II, p. 10: 'Who smiled upon that Pactolus of hair.'

22 In a note added to this letter Pitter said: 'On re-reading this letter after more than 20 years, I am impressed anew by Lewis's generosity & the thoroughgoing way he tackles the thankless job of reading & genuinely evaluating another person's poetry (an anguish to most of us). Both his encomiums and his strictures find a home in the heart. But then he was a critic if ever there *was* one. (His "Eng. Lit in the 17th [16th] Cent." in the Oxford U.P. series I can read & re-read for simple refreshment, for the real exhilaration of feeling the scales sway so level). No one is infallible, but I have a strong feeling that Lewis was not fallible in any way that self-discipline could remedy' (Bodleian Library, MS. Eng. lett. c. 220/3, fol. 41).

I'm re-reading the *Prelude*. Always just a little better than one remembers from the last reading, I think,

Yours sincerely
C. S. Lewis

TO MRS FRANK L. JONES (W):

Magdalen College,
Oxford.
Feb 23rd 1947

Dear Mrs Jones –

(1.) The doctrine that Our Lord was God and man does *not* mean that He was a human body which had God instead of the normal human soul. It means that a real man (human body *and* human soul) was in Him so united with the 2nd Person of the Trinity as to make one Person: just as in you and me a complete anthropoid animal (animal body *and* animal 'soul' i.e. instincts, sensations etc) is so united with an immortal rational soul as to be one person. In other words, if the Divine Son had been removed from Jesus what wd. have been left wd. have been not a corpse but a living man.

(2.) This human soul in Him was unswervingly united to the God in Him in that which makes a personality one, namely Will. But it had the feelings of any normal man: hence could be tempted, cd. fear etc. Because of these feelings it could pray 'if it be possible, let this cup pass from me':[23] because of its perfect union with His Divine Nature it unswervingly answered 'Nevertheless, not as I will but as thou wilt.'[24] The Matthew passage and the John passage both make clear this unity of will.[25] The Matthew one gives in addition the human feelings.

(3.) God cd., had He pleased, have been incarnate in a man of iron nerves, the Stoic sort who lets no sigh escape Him. Of His great humility He chose to be incarnate in a man of delicate sensibilities who wept at the grave of Lazarus[26] and sweated blood in Gethsemane.[27] Otherwise we should have missed the great lesson that it is by his *will* alone that a man is good or bad, and that *feelings* are not, in themselves,

23 Matthew 26:39.
24 ibid.
25 Lewis had forgotten that both passages come from Matthew.
26 John 11:35.
27 Luke 22:44.

of any importance. We should also have missed the all important help of knowing that He has faced all that the weakest of us face, has shared not only the strength of our nature but every weakness of it except sin. If He had been incarnate in a man of immense natural courage, that wd. have been for many of us almost the same as His not being incarnate at all.

(4.) The prayer recorded in Matthew is much too short to be long enough for the disciples to go to sleep! They record the bit they heard before they fell asleep.

(5.) It is probable that all the gospels are based on acts and sayings wh. the disciples deliberately learned by heart: a much surer method even now than transmission by writing: still more so among people whose memories were uninfected by too many books and whose books were only MSS. But this is guess work. With all good wishes.

Yours sincerely
C. S. Lewis

Keep clear of psychiatrists unless you know that they are also Christians. Otherwise they start with the assumption that your religion is an illusion and try to 'cure' it: and this assumption they make not as professional psychologists but as amateur philosophers. Often they have never given the question any serious thought

On 8 March 1947 the Marquess of Salisbury (James Edward Hubert Gascoyne-Cecil, 1861–1947), the Conservative MP and speaker on ecclesiastical matters, invited Lewis to join a group, which would include the Archbishops of Canterbury and York, to discuss the future of the Church of England. 'The urgency of the Spiritual situation and the moral deterioration of the world is obvious,' he said.

> *Material progress there has been, especially in our own Country . . . but the moral and spiritual controls appear to be giving way . . . Perhaps the most formidable feature in the moral landscape at this time is profound disillusion and disappointment, and men shrink from contemplating the total failure of the brave new world whose vision used to reassure us twenty years ago. There is a feeling of moral despair. But also on the other hand we may faithfully realize that there is some reaction of hope, and the*

question is put What can we do to be saved? And obviously comes the answering question What can the Christian Church do to help us? . . . Would you join a very small number of laymen (probably less than ten) who feel the urgency of the issue and (of course without in any way committing themselves) meet the Archbishops at Lambeth on the morning of Wednesday, March 26th?[28]

TO LORD SALISBURY (BOD):[29]

[Magdalen College
9 March 1947]

Dear Lord Salisbury

Thank you for your most interesting & important letter. It is unfortunately impossible for me to make a firm promise to come to this meeting (or to do anything else) because my time is almost fully and, what is new, quite unpredictably, occupied by my domestic duties. My mother is old & infirm, we have little and uncertain help, and I never know when I can, even for a day, get away from my duties as a nurse and a domestic servant. (There are psychological as well as material difficulties in my house). But I will come if I possibly can. If I can't, I shall not perhaps be much loss: I am an apologist and a 'rhetor' not a man of affairs nor ever (I suspect) of much practical prudence.

If someone who 'may' come, but is uncertain, had better be written off at once, I shall of course fully understand.

Yours v. truly
C. S. Lewis

28 Bodleian Library, MS. Eng. c. 6825, fols. 91–3.

29 The following is a draft letter in Lewis's hand, written on the verso of Lord Salisbury's letter (Bodleian Library, MS. Eng. c. 6825, fol. 93).

TO GEORGE ROSTREVOR HAMILTON (BOD): TS

REF.46/296. Magdalen College,
Oxford.
11th March 1947.

Dear Hamilton,

Thanks very much for the Book Handbook – how civilized.[30] I'm sorry Hedonicus prefers the Fiorinda books to the Worm. I'm greatly excited by Whistler's project, but you must not be surprised if I'm not at the meeting of conspirators: I'm a tethered man. I will look out for 'The Lamp'.[31]

yours,
C. S. Lewis

TO ROGER LANCELYN GREEN (BOD): TS

REF.177/47. Magdalen College,
Oxford.
12th March 1947.

Dear Green,

I am most sorry to hear of your accident. I'm afraid I can be absolutely no use to you this week. I am in a sad pickle at home with illness in the house, and either tutoring or interviewing every moment in College. Next week, I gather, is no good. Would 'World's End' be better than 'From the World's End'? Congratulations on getting it published.[32]

Yours,
C. S. Lewis

TO FLORENCE (MICHAL) WILLIAMS (W): TS

REF.46/98. Magdalen College,
Oxford.
13th March 1947.

Dear Mrs. Williams,

I have now completed my book on Charles's Arthurian poems, incorporating the MS fragment of his prose 'Figure of Arthur'. The MS of that was sent to me by Mrs. Hadfield, but I presume you are the

30 *The Book Handbook*, a quarterly publication about book collecting, ran from 1947 to 1952.

31 Richard Church, *The Lamp* (1946).

32 Roger Lancelyn Green, *From the World's End: A Fantasy* [1948].

owner. If so, have I your formal permission to use it? Secondly, I hope you will allow me the pleasure of arranging that all royalties made by this book will go to you. Thirdly, may I dedicate it to you? I hope you keep fairly well. If you ever think of revisiting Oxford I hope that you will let me know as all Charles's friends would like to meet you again.

yours sincerely,
C. S. Lewis

TO MRS H. E. GRANT (W):[33] TS

REF.187/47.

Magdalen College,
Oxford.
14th March 1947.

Dear Mrs. Grant,

Many thanks for your most kind and encouraging letter of the 13th. There are, as I am gradually finding out, more Macdonaldites scattered about than one would suppose. The fashions of the vocal 'literary world' give one very little information as to what is really being read. Thank you for your kind invitation, but I have little prospect of being in Hampshire.

yours sincerely,
C. S. Lewis

TO FLORENCE (MICHAL) WILLIAMS (W): TS

REF.46/98.

Magdalen College,
Oxford.
18th March 1947.

Dear Mrs. Williams,

Thank you for your kind letter. Don't entertain false hopes about those royalties: perhaps no one will buy the book and publishing goes at a snails pace these days. Be sure and let me know when you are coming to the Farrers and there shall be a lunch of all the Carolines. I am very glad the novels are coming out again: but why could'nt they do it in his lifetime? I miss him no less than I did the first week.

My brother asks to be remembered to you.

yours sincerely,
C. S. Lewis

---

33 Mrs Grant was writing from Hill Head, Farnham, Hampshire.

TO RUTH PITTER (BOD): TS

REF.97/47.

Magdalen College,
Oxford.
21st March 1947.

Dear Miss Pitter,

Good. Will you and Sir R. Stows[34] lunch with me on May 31st. at 1.15? I've booked the date. 'Miracles' is put off till April. I hope you are well over the measles – it used to be a trifling ailment when I was a boy, but they've improved it since then.

yours very sincerely,
C. S. Lewis

TO LAURENCE WHISTLER (BOD): TS

REF.46/476.

Magdalen College,
Oxford.
21st March 1947.

Dear Whistler,

I have a reply from Ronnie Knox.[35] He can't come to the meeting, but is quite enthusiastically in favour of the project and promises to contribute to the first number.

yours,
C. S. Lewis

---

34 i.e. Sir Ronald Storrs.

35 Monsignor Ronald Knox (1888–1957) took a First in Classics from Balliol College, Oxford in 1910. Ordained in the Church of England in 1912, he was Chaplain of Trinity College, Oxford, 1912–17. A convert to Catholicism in 1917, he was ordained a priest in 1919, and taught at St Edmund's College, Ware, 1918–26. Knox was Catholic Chaplain to Oxford University, 1926–39, Lewis and Tolkien coming to know him at this time. Upon leaving Oxford he worked on translations of the Bible, his New Testament being published in 1945 and his Old Testament in 1949. His numerous books include *A Spiritual Aeneid* (1918), *Let Dons Delight* (1939) and *Enthusiasm* (1950). He was appointed Monsignor in 1936. See Evelyn Waugh, *The Life of the Right Reverend Ronald Knox* (1959).

TO DOM BEDE GRIFFITHS OSB (W):

[Magdalen College]
April 15 [1947]

My dear Dom Bede –

I offer you my congratulations on your new office:[36] my prayers you know you already have. There will certainly, as you anticipate, be a cross somewhere in it, but one mustn't assume crosses any more than consolations. Your remember in the *Imitation* 'The devil does not mind in the least whether he snares us by true or false pictures of the future.'[37] In my experience the cross seldom comes where it is anticipated.

About Hinduism – you will remember that long ago you and I agreed, being still unbelievers, that Hinduism and Christianity were the only two things worth serious consideration.[38] I still think it was a sound decision. And I agree that there is in Hinduism no true idea of the gulf between the Creator and even the unfallen creature. How cd. there be when there is no clear idea of creation – only becoming or emanation – as if the world *were* 'God suffering acutely from divided personality'.

I now believe that refined, philosophical eastern Pantheism is *far further* from the true Faith than the semi barbarous pagan religions (even including all their cruelties and obscenities). The man who rushed with the Maenads[39] on the mountains to tear and eat the beast which also was the god – the immortality wh. in some Semitic paganism the people cd. share, not naturally, but only by union with the divine king – that is far nearer the truth than Hinduism.

---

36 Griffiths had been appointed the new prior of St Michael's Abbey, Farnborough, where he was installed on 29 April 1947.

37 Thomas à Kempis, *The Imitation of Christ*, III, xxx, 7.

38 Describing his conversion to Christianity, Lewis said in *SBJ*, ch. 15, pp. 182–3: 'My chief companion on this stage of the road was Griffiths, with whom I kept up a copious correspondence. Both now believed in God, and were ready to hear more of Him from any source, Pagan or Christian . . . There were really only two answers possible: either in Hinduism or in Christianity. Everything else was either a preparation for, or else . . . a *vulgarisation* of, these. Whatever you could find elsewhere you could find better in one of these. But Hinduism seemed to have two disqualifications. For one thing, it appeared to be not so much a moralized and philosophical maturity of Paganism as a mere oil-and-water coexistence of philosophy side by side with Paganism unpurged; the Brahmin meditating in the forest, and, in the village a few miles away, temple prostitution, *sati*, cruelty, monstrosity. And second, there was no such historical claim as in Christianity.'

39 The followers of Dionysus, the god of wine.

I am inclined to think that Paganism is the primitive revealed truth corrupted by devils and that Hinduism is neither of divine nor diabolical origin but profoundly and *hopelessly* natural: i.e. it displays the natural trend of the speculative intellect *sibi relictus*[40] – the line it will always follow when it escapes savagery and does not receive Grace. Hence such parallel systems as Stoicism, Hegelianism. The importance of the Jews, the absolute rightness of the claim made for them in the O.T., becomes clearer every day. But also, there is a penumbra: the almost miraculous avoidance of the Pantheistic swamp by Plato and (still more) by Aristotle. I no longer want to read Eastern books: except good non-religious philosophers like Confucius.

Yours

C. S. Lewis

TO RUTH PITTER (B):

REF.97/47.

Magdalen College,
Oxford.
27th April 1947.

Dear Miss Pitter,

Sir Ronald Storrs is really very tiresome, for Sundays are *always* impossible. I'll make shift with any other day in the week. Cajole, bully, deceive, if need be. Talk to him 'with sweet, austere composure'.[41] I'm rather shocked at your wasting *your* verse on *my* prose. But I hope it'll only be the irritant to start your real activity. Fruit trees, yes.

yours very sincerely,

C. S. Lewis

Further meetings were planned to discuss Whistler's 'Portico' project, the next at Andrew Young's vicarage on 9 May. Whistler was hoping Lewis would be able to attend, but he was seemingly prevented by his domestic responsibilities. He had, however, diligently prepared a paper setting out his views which he gave Whistler at some time before the meeting. In Whistler's words: 'As C.S.L. could not come, he gave me the following Memorandum, designed to clarify purposes and suggest standards. Alas, it only 'riled' Brother George [Every], to use his own word . . .'[42]

---

40 'left to itself'.

41 Milton, *Paradise Lost*, IX, 272.

42 Bodleian Library, MS. Eng. lett. c. 862, fol. 6.

The second meeting of 'Portico' was held on 9 May 1947 and a third, and last, on 2 July. Afterwards Whistler wrote:

> *Nothing came of the idea, probably because there was no general agreement; certainly because there was no money; and I suspect because it was thought, despite our disclaimers, that Young and I really did want to run it. I wanted* no such thing; *nor, I am sure, did Andrew. Neither of us were fitted to be editors, and I was obscure. We hoped someone qualified would take it out of our hands. C.S.L. believed us, I think, or he would not have been enthusiastic, but I doubt if some of the others did. I learnt then this truth: that though many people will cheerfully* pinch *an idea, few want to take one over as a gift. Good ideas (I think this* was *one) have to occur to the right minds!*[43]

TO LAURENCE WHISTLER (BOD):

[April 1947]

Memorandum

I understand that the impulse behind the project is both religious and cultural: that the two elements are like to be mixed in different proportions in the minds of different individuals present: and that, when we get to details, very different conceptions of the projected periodical will reveal themselves. In case I am unable to be present, I wd. like to lay before the meeting in writing the view which I wd. strongly press.

I think the Periodical ought to come before the public with *no* explicitly religious pretensions at all: its offer should be simply an offer of good poems, good stories, good articles, and good reviews. On the other hand, those who run it should in fact all be Christians. The standard they actually apply in admitting or rejecting contributors should *not* be that of agreement or disagreement with the Christian Faith, but that of agreement or disagreement with what may be called the 'good Pagan' range of rationality and virtue. Thus, while many, perhaps most, contributors would be explicitly Christian we wd. freely admit good work which was not, and might even admit work opposed to the Faith provided the opposition was based on an appeal to reason

43 ibid.

and ethics. What would be definitely and always excluded (a.) Total Scepticism: i.e. attacks on reason and natural morality (b.) Pornography, however high-brow (c.) Cynicism and Sadism however well disguised as 'Realism'. Thus, if they were all now alive, we should admit Aristotle (but not Heraclitus), Lucretius (but not Petronius), Voltaire (but not Anatole France), Hardy (but not Oscar Wilde).

My reason for thinking this is not that I consider the good Pagan standard more important than the Christian, but that I consider the tactics I have suggested more likely in the long run to do what a periodical can towards the conversion of educated people in England: for the following reasons:

1. There are a good many religious periodicals already on the market

2. An explicitly religious periodical must be either denominational or not. There are serious objections to either choice.

3. It would attract only those who are already converted or near conversion.

4. No unbiassed criticism of it wd. occur in the press: it wd. be derided, and welcomed, on purely partisan lines.

5. Every other periodical is becoming more and more of a 'tied house'. That is one of the diseases we want to cure.

6. (which is the really important reason in my mind). In every other age the preaching of Christianity has been able to presuppose the light of nature in its hearers. It was preached to Jews, to those half Jews called *Metuentes*, to Stoics, Epicureans, and polytheistic barbarians. All these had already some kind of ethics, a belief in reason, and often high standards of family, tribal, or civic duty. Where there is total scepticism the call to repentance and the promise of forgiveness *must* fall completely flat. Earlier Xtian preachers were fighting for the Supernatural against Nature. What we are up against is the anti-Natural. The rehabilitation of the Natural (tho' only of course as a preliminary to its conquest by the Supernatural) seems to me the greatest service that a periodical cd. do to-day. (What is the use of quoting 'He that hateth not father and mother and his own life'[44] in a world where many people think all three hateful already?)

I therefore suggest that the title of the periodical shd. be quite unre-

44 Luke 14:26.

vealing and that its real standard shd. discover itself only gradually, by the contents

C. S. Lewis

TO LAURENCE WHISTLER (BOD):

Magdalen
May 2nd 1947

Dear Whistler

I didn't get to the book till to-day.[45] You have succeeded in a thing that usually fails. One dreads the sort of work which as Tacitus said of the *Agricola* (I'm quoting from memory) *pietatis homine aut laudabitur aut excusabitur*.[46] One reads them usually with reverence and sympathy rather than interest.

But greatly to my delight all this was brushed away almost at once, and I mainly thought 'This was an interesting woman': and only later 'Very few character sketches of real people come off, and very very few when the affections of the writer are invoked' (Pity, by the way that successful characters done in hate or derision are apparently so much easier!). The quotations from the letters in many places concern me very much. A great deal of my own difficulty would be solved if I cd. feel the right way about potato-peeling: and the antithesis between coarseness and tawdriness is important. The best bit of all (to my mind) does however come in a poem, the bit about the 'blade of the name' in No I. I thought that really startlingly good – tho' I suppose VI is the best poem as a whole. The shutting up like a fan in X is also good. Some I don't understand: indeed it is rather a worry to me that while my powers of appreciating poetry (when I can make it out) don't seem to be decaying I seem to understand fewer poems every day. Thanks.

You'll let me know what happens at the meeting? Have just read T. H. White's *Mrs. Masham's Repose*[47] wh. I think excellent. The vulgarity wh

45 Whistler sent Lewis a privately printed copy of a book about his first wife, *Jill Furse: Her Name and Her Poems, 1915–1944* (London: Chiswick Press, 1945). One hundred and fifty copies of this book were printed for Whistler in July 1945 by the Chiswick Press and a further 100 copies were made in December 1945.

46 'This will be praised or excused by dint of the pieties of man.' Tacitus, *Agricola*, ch. 3, sec. 3: '*Hic interim liber . . . professione pietatis aut laudatus erit aut excusatus*': 'In the meanwhile, this book will either have been praised or excused for its profession of filial duty.'

47 T. H. White, *Mistress Masham's Repose* (1946).

spoiled *The Sword & Stone* (like a pencil moustache scribbled on the lip of a great statue) seems to have disappeared

yours
C. S. Lewis

TO RUTH PITTER (BOD): TS

REF.97/47.

Magdalen College,
Oxford.
5th. May 1947.

Dear Miss Pitter,

You never told me whether the various means I suggested have succeeded in persuading the 'frugal and temperate knight'[48] to stick to the original date for our lunch – May 31st.

I shall not, alas, be at Whistler's party, but you shall hear my views there.

yours sincerely,
C. S. Lewis

TO MRS DONALDSON (W):

Magdalen College,
Oxford.
May 6th 1947

Dear Mrs. Donaldson

I think I am being rather dense for I don't feel at all certain, after reading your letter several times, what (exactly) I am being asked. One thing I can answer plainly by saying that, so far as I know, there are *no* 'unescapable texts' in Scripture supporting my view of Time.[49] Books where you wd. find something about it are von Hügel's *Eternal Life*, Kirk's *Vision of God*[50] and (among the ancients) Boethius *De Consolatione Philosophiae* wh. you can get with an English translation on the opposite page in the 'Loeb Library'.

There is also an attempt to express it imaginatively at the end of my *The Great Divorce*: tho' whether that wd. make things clearer or darker

48 i.e. Sir Ronald Storrs.

49 Mrs Donaldson had probably asked about *Beyond Personality*, ch. 3, 'Time and Beyond Time'.

50 Kenneth Kirk, *The Vision of God: The Christian Doctrine of the Summum Bonum* (1932).

is not for me to say! When I said in *Beyond P.* that the chance would not last forever I did not mean that future generations wd. not have it.[51] I mean that each individual only has it for a short time i.e. is only alive on this Earth for a short time.

But I still have a feeling that I am missing your point. If you think it worth trying to ask it again I will again try to answer it! With all good wishes,

yours sincerely
C. S. Lewis

TO RUTH PITTER (BOD): TS

REF.97/47.

Magdalen College,
Oxford.
8th May 1947.

Dear Miss Pitter,

Thank you for the *De Porum Moribus*[52] (How does the whole declension go? Puss, Puss, Purrem, Purris, Purri, Purre, Purres, Purres, Porum, Pibus, Pibus?). A very cheerful and companionable work. I think the first piece is the best:[53] so finely observed that I wd. treat it as serious – but that's a foolish distinction.

When am I to see the Spenserians? They'll 'do me good' in a way you probably hadn't thought of. In my job one is always ferreting out the 'Sources' of the great poets. Now (serve me right) I shall be a source myself. I shall know what Lodge wd. feel like while reading *As You Like It*[54] or Brooke while reading *Romeo and Juliet*[55] – or a bulb looking at a hyacinth – or an appetite studying a sublimation – or chaos studying matter.

You are still to fix a date – preferably in Vacation – for our suspended

---

51 Lewis was thinking of the last paragraph of *Broadcast Talks* (*Mere Christianity*, Book II, ch. 5): 'Now, today, this moment, is our chance to choose the right side. God is holding back to give us that chance. It will not last for ever. We must take it or leave it.'

52 Pitter had sent him a copy of her *Pitter on Cats* (1947)

53 'Quorum Porum', i.e. a meeting of cats.

54 The story behind Thomas Lodge's romance, *Rosalyn* (1590) was dramatized by Shakespeare in *As You Like It*.

55 Lewis points out in *English Literature in the Sixteenth Century*, p. 259, that 'Arthur Broke [or Brooke] (ob. 1563) owes his shadowy immortality to the fact that Shakespeare used for a play his *Tragical History of Romeus and Juliet* (1562)'.

lunch. If Sir Thingummy[56] doesn't agree to the first suggestion you make, come without him. We have not yet explored each other's minds so fully that we need a third to keep us going!

Yours sincerely

C. S. Lewis

Miracles: A Preliminary Study *was published by Geoffrey Bles on 12 May 1947.*

TO I. O. EVANS (W): TS

REF.251/47.

Magdalen College,
Oxford.
12th. May 1947.

Dear Mr. Evans,

The Flinties were delightful, and the artist does them a good deal better than he does humans.[57] I want the story to go on. What happened when they had eaten all the rock in Great Britain? Can they swim? If so, don't all land masses simply disappear? I think it is an end-of-the-world theme.

I return it with many thanks.

yours sincerely,

C. S. Lewis

TO BARBARA WALL (BOD): TS

REF.326/47.

Magdalen College,
Oxford.
27th May 1947.

Dear Mrs. Wall,

I am so glad you like it.[58] I don't think I should do much in practice about splitting God up into Genius, Bacchus etc. That is possibly how primitive Monotheism was lost.

yours sincerely,

C. S. Lewis

---

56 i.e. Sir Ronald Storrs.

57 'The Flinties' was a short story by Evans, reprinted in *Science Fiction Through the Ages 2*, ed. I. O. Evans (1966).

58 i.e. *Miracles: A Preliminary Study*.

Now that it is typed this looks rather a portentous letter! And certainly unnecessary. (I didn't really think you were dancing in a dappled fawn skin and waving a thyrsus on Hampstead Heath!)

TO RUTH PITTER (BOD):

Magdalen College,
Oxford.
3rd June 1947.

Dear Miss Pitter,

I shall be happy to see you here for lunch (with or without the errant knight) on – you *said* Wed. June 16th. which does not occur. Do you mean Wed. July 16th or Mon. June 16th. But any will do

yours sincerely,
C. S. Lewis

TO DOROTHY L. SAYERS (W): TS

REF.352/47.

Magdalen College,
Oxford.
5th June 1947.

Dear Miss Sayers,

How kind of you to write.[59] I too thought the Dean of St Paul's very muddled: not only about Time but about my 'treating all the documents as if they were on the same historical level', when I specially said I was'nt dealing with historicity at all.[60] We badly need to revive formal logic.

---

59 Sayers, *Letters*, vol. III, letter of 2 June 1947, pp. 304–5.

60 The Dean of St Paul's, the Very Rev. Walter Robert Matthews, had reviewed Lewis's *Miracles* in *The Sunday Times* (25 May 1947), p. 3: 'Two criticisms may be made . . . He likens miraculous events to material being fed into a machine; the miracle is "fed into" the system of nature, which promptly assimilates it. But some question might arise about the implications of this way of putting the situation. In what sense can an event be said to exist before it happens, and can it be "fed into" nature? The second criticism is more weighty because it affects the next book which we must hope Mr Lewis will write, when he will proceed to deal explicitly with the New Testament miracles. In the somewhat general remarks which he offers in the concluding chapters he seems to take all the documents as of equal historical value. He knows, of course, very well the peculiar nature of the "signs" in the Gospel of John and the contention of many scholars, who have no *a priori* prejudice against the supernatural, that in the same instances, notably the Resurrection appearances, the growth of miraculous or legendary elements can be plausibly conjectured. We shall look forward to the sequel in which, one supposes,

Look: if you hear anything of a new periodical in which Lawrence Whistler is a moving spirit, look on it kindly and contribute to the first number: Monsignor Knox and I are both going to.

The difference between dear old Every and me about stock responses goes all the way down.[61] His intellectual home (if you took away Grace) is with Leavis and *Scrutiny*.

I loved hearing about Elinor and Marianne.[62] You are a real letter writer. I am not. With many thanks.

yours very sincerely,
C. S. Lewis

---

having shown that miracles can happen and that there is no inherent absurdity in believing that the New Testament miracles could have happened, he will give reasons for holding that they actually did happen.'

61 In a previously unpublished portion of her letter of 2 June 1947, Sayers wrote: 'I ran into George Every the other day . . . I gather he thinks your *Abolition of Man* "very dangerous" – he doesn't seem to approve of "stock responses".' Lewis borrowed the term 'stock responses' from I. A. Richards, and made it his own. In the introductory chapter to his *Practical Criticism*, Richards described stock responses as one of the 'chief difficulties of criticism . . . critical traps [that] have their opportunity whenever a poem seems to, or does, involve, views and emotions already prepared in the reader's mind, so that what happens appears to be more of the reader's doing than the poet's. The button is pressed, and then the author's work is done.' In *A Preface to Paradise Lost*, ch. 8, Lewis deplored the exchange of 'direct free play of experience' for willed stock responses such as finding love sweet, death bitter, and virtue lovely: 'In my opinion, such deliberate organization is one of the first necessities of human life, and one of the main functions of art is to assist it. All that we describe as constancy in love or friendship, as loyalty in political life, or, in general, as perseverance – all solid virtue and stable pleasure – depends on organizing chosen attitudes and maintaining them against the eternal flux.'

62 Sayers had purchased two hens which she named Elinor and Marianne after the sisters in Jane Austen's *Sense and Sensibility*. In her letter of 2 June she wrote: 'Elinor is a round, comfortable, motherly-looking little body, who lays one steady, regular, undistinguished egg per day, and allows nothing to disturb her equanimity . . . Marianne is leggier, timid, and liable to hysterics. Sometimes she lays a shell-less egg, sometimes a double yolk, sometimes no egg at all. On the days when she lays no egg she nevertheless goes and sits in the nest for the usual time, and seems to imagine that nothing more is required. As my gardener says: "She just *thinks* she's laid an egg". Too much imagination – in fact, Sensibility' (Sayers, *Letters*, vol. III, p. 305).

TO RUTH PITTER (BOD): TS

REF.97/47.

Magdalen College,
Oxford.
6th. June 1947.

Dear Miss Pitter,
Good. I have booked July 16th., one o'clock.
yours sincerely,
C. S. Lewis

EPIGRAM
Call *him* a Fascist? Thus the rabbit,
Oblivious of their varying merits,
Takes all who share the simple habit
Of eating rabbit-pie, for ferrets.

In 1934 there occurred one of the most startling literary discoveries of the century – a manuscript of Sir Thomas Malory's Morte Darthur *was found in the library of Winchester College. It was contemporary with William Caxton's edition of 1485, but independent of it. Malory scholars had waited in a state of suspense for thirteen years to discover whether the Winchester manuscript would refute or confirm what was known from Caxton's edition. Finally, on 24 April 1947 the three-volume* Works of Sir Thomas Malory, *edited by the great Arthurian scholar, Professor Eugène Vinaver,*[63] *was published. Lewis reviewed it for* The Times Literary Supplement*:*

The predominant ethical tone of Malory's work is certainly not the bourgeois, still less the proletarian, morality of our own day. And, on its own showing, it is not the Christian rule of life; all the chief characters end as penitents. It is aristocratic. It does not forbid homicide provided it is done in clean battle. It does not demand chastity, though it highly honours lifelong fidelity to the chosen mistress. Though it admires mercy it allows private war and the vendetta. And it has no respect at all for property or for laws as such. It is distinguished from heroic morality by its insistence on humility. It can be very accurately called nobility if the noble is defined as the opposite of the vulgar . . .

63 See Lewis's letter to Vinaver of 19 September 1935.

But how different such nobility may be from the virtues of the law-abiding citizen will appear if we imagine the life of Sir Tristram as it would be presented to us by King Mark's solicitors.[64]

That last sentence launched the following lark between Owen Barfield and Lewis. Barfield, using the notepaper of his firm, Barfield and Barfield, and acting as if for King Mark of Cornwall, led off with the first letter to Messrs Inkling and Inkling. Lewis replied as the solicitors Blaise and Merlin, representing Sir Tristram:[65]

To Messrs Inkling & Inkling *BARFIELD & BARFIELD*

Solicitors

11 June 503.

Dears Sirs,

We act for H.M. King Mark I of Cornwall, who has recently consulted us in the matter of the behaviour of your client, Sir Tristram.[66] *It appears that while your client was, at our client's expense and his confidential agent, escorting our client's then fiancée across the English Channel, he took advantage of those very circumstances to seduce this unfortunate lady and has, both*

64 The review appeared in *The Times Literary Supplement* (7 June 1947), pp. 273–4, and was reprinted as 'The "Morte Darthur"' in *Studies in Medieval and Renaissance Literature*, pp. 104–5.

65 *Mark vs. Tristram: Correspondence between C. S. Lewis and Owen Barfield*, ed. Walter Hooper, published in an edition of 126 copies (Cambridge, Mass.: The Lowell House Printers, 1967). The original letters are in the Wade Center.

66 For those unfamiliar with the story, Sir Tristram was brought up at the court of King Mark of Cornwall. As a young knight he defeats and kills Sir Marhalt, the brother of Isoud, Queen of Ireland. King Mark sends him to Ireland to be cured of his wounds by Queen Isoud, who does not know Tristram killed her brother. While in Ireland the knight falls in love with the Queen's daughter, also named Isoud. The Queen discovers that Tristram is her brother's slayer, and he is forced to return to Cornwall. Later King Mark sends Tristram back to Ireland as his ambassador to seek for him the hand of the Princess Isoud. Tristram brings the Princess to Cornwall; her maid, Brangwayn, is carrying a love-potion concocted by the Queen to be given on their wedding night to King Mark and Isoud, which will bind them in love for ever. By mistake the love-potion is drunk by Tristram and Isoud; they are thereafter bound in a tragic and endless passion, but Isoud has nevertheless to marry King Mark. Tristram eventually leaves King Mark's court and, while fighting in Brittany, falls in love and marries a third Isoud (Isoud of the White Hands).

before and since her marriage to our client, been carrying on a criminal conversation with her as and when opportunity offered, at Tintagel and elsewhere. We regret to say that the evidence in our possession removes all doubt of the authenticity of these disgusting allegations.

Our client has of course instructed us to file a petition for divorce on the ground of adultery and we shall be glad to hear from you when it will be convenient for your client to attend at our office to be served therewith. We understand your client is at present in Brittany, living with an unmarried lady who, by a curious coincidence, bears the same name as our client's said wife. You may however take it from us that any misguided attempt to plead mistaken identity is bound to fail.

Meanwhile our client is seriously considering further proceedings in the King's Bench Division against your client for enticement and it will depend on the latter whether the extremely unpleasant publicity which is inseparable from any such proceedings can be avoided or not. We must ask you to let us hear from you within twenty-one days, should your client have any proposal to make for compensating our client – so far as this is now possible – for the grievous injury he has suffered from your client's behaviour, for which we should have thought 'dishonourable' was scarcely an adequate word. No doubt you will, when taking his instructions, point out to him that in assessing the damages, a jury would be required to take into consideration such facts as (a) the previous long and close personal association between our respective clients (b) the fact that your client was at the time employed in a fiduciary capacity in a matter of the utmost delicacy (c) that your client owed to ours at the time not merely the loyalty of an old friend but the allegiance of a tried and trusted subject and (d) the unwritten law of chivalry and the obligation imposed thereby on your client, as the only person of equestrian status on board a small vessel carrying a female passenger of noble rank, even apart from his fiduciary capacity already referred to above.

From the other point of view it will, we gather, hardly be open to your client to minimize *the damage suffered by the Plaintiff in the loss of this lady's consortium!*

We understand from our client that your client has indicated an intention of putting up some kind of defence on the ground of 'irresistible impulse' and even possibly witchcraft. If that is so, you will no doubt advise him as you think fit, but before doing so, you will presumably consider whether, in the eyes of a jury of reasonable and honourable men, the combined obligations referred to under (c) and (d) above could ever in any conceivable circumstances be discharged by anything less than force majeure *in the accepted sense of the term.*

We are, dear Sirs,
As at this time,
Yours faithfully,
Barfield & Barfield

TO BARFIELD & BARFIELD (W):

[Magdalen College
14 June 1947]
þe castle of jv stoons
14-6-503

Dear Sirs,

We have instructed our client Sir T. de Lyonesse K.T.R. to ignore the frivolous letter which has been forwarded to us by Mr. C. S. Lewis. The following considerations have led us to advise him that there can be no serious intention of an action on the part of your client.

1. We are prepared to prove on the evidence of Dr. Gouvernail and Mlle Brangwen that no misconduct occurred during the voyage in the Irish Channel to which you refer.

2. Since H.M. King Arthur of Logres is the overlord of your client and our client is a K.T.R. it is open to him to choose (see Arthur cap. 13. Tit. 24) to answer any allegations of misconduct by wager of battle, as he has already done in the case of the 25 Knights (deceased) whose names will be found in the attached schedule.

Yours faithfully,
Blaise & Merlin

Barfield in turn sent the following replies:

To Messrs Blaise And Merlin — *Barfield & Barfield*
Solicitors
Dear Sirs, — *19th June xxxx 503*

Mark v. Tristram

We are in receipt of your letter of the 14th June.

Acting on the instructions of our client, we have since applied ex parte[67] *to the court of King Arthur sitting at Caerleon for a Rule nisi that the plea which your client seeks to aver according to the second numbered paragraph of your letter, is no longer a good custom. It will not however be necessary for you to appear on behalf of your client and show cause, as we have since received an official communication from Sir Kaye informing us of a Decree delivered orally by his Majesty* ad mensam[68] *on the 17th instant and entitled 'For the Quelling of Garboils and the More Seemly Ordering of the Realm of Logres', by which it is ordered that this dispute be forthwith referred to arbitration and an arbitrator was by the same Decree appointed. In accordance with the usual equitable principles the arbitrator so appointed is the immediate Lord to whom the Defendant owes allegiance. You will be informed in due course of the date and venue for the hearing.*

Yours faithfully,
Barfield & Barfield

To Messrs Blaise And Merlin — *Barfield & Barfield*
Solicitors
19th June xxxx 503

Dear Sirs,

Mark v. Tristram

WITHOUT PREJUDICE

Referring to our open letter of even date, our client writes us that he feels there is 'considerable force' in what you say at the

---

67 A legal term meaning 'on one side only'. 'We have applied *ex parte*' = 'We have applied stating on behalf of our client . . .'

68 'at table'.

conclusion of your letter under reply. We are accordingly to inform you that our client will not in fact take any steps to bring this matter to arbitration provided that your client signs a full and complete Retractatio *of all the works of the flesh, draft of which will first be submitted to and approved by ourselves (we suggest the form which was approved by the Court in* Arthur v. Lancelot *as appropriate).*

We do not know whether your client has any immediate intention of returning to this country, but we feel we can rely on your good selves to explain to him (by express messenger, if necessary) that our own part in this unfortunate affair is purely that of agents acting on instructions. In our experience, this is a point which laymen do not always find it easy to appreciate. May we add, without offence, that we should like to be assured that your junior partner is also thoroughly seised of this point?

Yours faithfully,
Barfield & Barfield

TO BARFIELD & BARFIELD (W):

[Magdalen College
20 June 1947]
þe castle of jv stoons
Die xx jun ano saluaciōis
CCCCCV

To ii lerned clerkes maister barfield and maister barfield gretynge in nōiē dôiî amen and wytte ye well syr tristram of lyones is newlie come ageyne to þis reaulme of logres to Douere and soo wondrouslie enchafed that never feend in helle was moore felle & tedyous inasmuche as some that saw hym when he cam of schippe fell doū for drede and a jentlewoman that was with chylde mis-carried.

And soo by grete adventure he rencountred wyth syr Kaye in a tavern and we knowe not the certeinte of theyr commūnications but wyt ye wel syr tristram hath sent vs a wrytinge as welle under the honde of the said syr Kaye wherein he pleynlie denyeth his wrytinge to your selves and maketh depe othes that yf he wrote þe same he was either dronken or subtilly enchaunted and wiste not what he wrote and calleth all unwrytten and putteth hym all hoolly in the grace of the said tristram outher to lyve or to dye and moore as touching our beloved brother

Merlyon wyt ye wel it stondeth not in our power to let hym to doon his wil for hee is of ful maisterful mood and passing orgulous.

Item he hath this daie departed hence to journey to the citee of London so fell and talentive as no wisard nor magitian was ever more and befoore hys hastie departynge was enraged ayeinst me oonlie for having youre lettres in my hondes that he sodenlie by his crafts transformed me into the likeness and feature of an Asse and soo by great entreatie of many good knights and jentlemen and by cause that I was his olde scholemaister he did consent to restoure me to my kindlie fourme yet imparfaitlie for I know not by what negligēce he hath left me with the unnatural eares and hoofs of that beast whether the lyke peril hangeth over onie other I leve to your best consideraciō.

In the nãe of God,
Maistre Bleyse

TO ROGER LANCELYN GREEN (BOD):

[Magdalen College,
Oxford]
20/6/47

My dear Green

I feel at least as guilty as you; we must both try to do better. Ring me up at 6963 when you get back. Thanks for the kind things you say about *Miracles* and also for the catalogue cutting: but I am no collector. I am glad your story is so far forward.

Yours
C.S.L.

For some time Maureen and her husband had given Jack and Warnie a break from looking after Mrs Moore, spending part of the Easter holidays at The Kilns while Jack and Warnie occupied their house in Malvern. The brothers were in Malvern this year from 4 to 17 April. Warnie became so depressed, however, upon his return to The Kilns – and Mrs Moore – that he wrote in his diary on 17 April: 'I have lost The Kilns: for though I can still force myself to see that it is beautiful objectively, I loathe every stick and stone and sound of it.'[69]

A note of joy, however, was sounded in Warnie's diary on 11 June 1947:

69 *BF*, p. 200.

'The incredible has happened. I am off on my Irish adventure . . . I went in by taxi at 9:15, feeling very guilty at leaving J alone with that horrid old woman in that abominable house, though if I had stopped there I would not have been allowed to do anything to ease his burden.'[70]

He arrived in Ireland on 12 June, expecting to meet his friend, Colonel Herbert Denis Parkin. The Colonel was unable to join him, and Warnie found himself alone in a small cottage at Dunany, County Louth. He began drinking heavily, and when he realized how ill he was he called the local doctor. The doctor had him taken to Our Lady of Lourdes Hospital in Drogheda, some thirty miles north of Dublin. The hospital, and the Medical Missionaries of Mary who ran it, were founded in 1940 by Mother Mary Martin. On discovering how ill her patient was, Mother Mary sent a wire to his brother.

Jack rushed over to Drogheda, arriving there on 23 June. He took a room in the White Horse Hotel and made twice-daily visits to see his brother. Warnie was released from the hospital on 30 June, but instead of accompanying Jack back to Oxford, he continued his holiday there until 27 July. He had found a home away from home in Drogheda, and he was to visit it often for the rest of his life. Jack managed to spend a few days with Arthur Greeves in late June before he returned to Oxford.

TO R. W. KOSTERLITZ (W):

Magdalen
June 29th 47

Dear Kosterlitz

I will with pleasure act as a referee if you think me a suitable person.

Yours

C. S. Lewis

70 ibid., p. 201.

TO PHYLLIS ELINOR SANDEMAN (W):[71]

Magdalen College,
Oxford.
June 31/47[72]

Dear Miss Sandeman

I think that about Houses the answer is this. Nothing rises again which has not died. The natural and possessive love for a house *if* it has been crucified, if it has become disinterested, if it has submitted to sacrifice, will rise again: i.e. the love for a house *you were willing to give up* will rise again. The wilful, grasping love will not – or only rise as a horror.

About the house itself, if the love rises, then all that is necessary to bless it will, I believe, be there. It may not be v. like what you wd. now call 'a house': but you'll see *then* that it was what you really meant by the house.

But the whole point is that you can *keep* forever only what you *give up*: beginning with the thing it is hardest to give up – one's self. What you grab you lose: what you offer freely and patiently to God or your neighbour, you will have. (Your heavenly library will contain only the books you have given or lent! And the dirty thumb marks on the latter will have turned into beautiful marginal decorations – I'm joking of course, but to illustrate a serious principle).[73]

Loving dogs more than children is a misfortune not a sin. *Acting* on that superior love for dogs – i.e. sacrificing the interests of the humans in your household to the animals – is a sin. I think myself that animals wh. have acquired a personality from living with us will probably be restored: but I can only repeat what I said on this point in *The Problem of Pain* (chapter on *Animal Pain*).

---

71 The Hon. Phyllis Elinor Sandeman (1895–1986) had probably told Lewis of her love for Lyme Park, Cheshire, the magnificent house which had been in her family for six hundred years and where she was born and brought up. Her brother, the 3rd Baron Newton, donated Lyme Park to the National Trust in 1946, and she may have asked if one can love a house inordinately. She was the author of *Treasure on Earth: A Country House Christmas* (1952), an account of her childhood at Lyme Park. Born Phyllis Elinor Legh on 9 December 1895, the daughter of the 2nd Baron Newton, in 1918 she married Henry Gerard Walter Sandeman (1885–1953), Chairman of Geo. G. Sandeman Sons & Co. Ltd. They lived in Woodbridge, Suffolk where their two daughters were born. Mrs Sandeman died on 5 April 1986.

72 A mistake presumably for 30 June.

73 Lewis had devoted a paragraph to the 'Heavenly Library' in 'Scraps', first published in 1945 and reprinted in *EC*, p. 346.

Remember, all this is only my guess. I'm not inspired, v. far from it. All good wishes.

Yrs sincerely
C. S. Lewis

TO ARTHUR GREEVES (W):

Magdalen
July 4/47

My dear Arthur

There was no need to apologise about the money. As you anticipated, I got it without difficulty from the hospital – indeed only my nervousness and fussiness cd. ever have made me suppose there'd be any difficulty in doing so. Our meeting was a lovely refreshment but too short.

No more now: the daily letter writing without W. to help me is appalling – an hour and a half or two hours every morning before I can get to my own work.

God bless you.

Yrs
Jack

TO RUTH PITTER (BOD):

Magdalen
July 6th. 1947

Dear Miss Pitter

I like them[74] – and you manage to be closer to the original in verse than some of my continental translators seem to get in prose. I think that XXI probably wd. be taken in a pantheistic sense by a reader who did not start with the doctrine of the Trinity in mind, but so wd. the original. I think XXIII *has* high eloquence – but of course it is hard for me to judge. IX is specially good.

---

74 Pitter said in her note to this letter: 'I had been transcribing the paean of praise towards the end of "Perelandra" into irregular Spenserian stanzas simply as a mnemonic: I wished so much to have these enormous transcendental ideas in a form I could memorize or use wherever I happened to be. They (my verse renderings) have never been in print' (Bodleian Library, MS. Eng. lett. c. 220/3, fol. 52).

I'm looking forward to seeing you (with or without the frugal and temperate knight = FATK) on the 16th.[75]

My Brother, thank God, was out of danger when I reached him on Monday morning last but was at the unearthly city of Drogheda where almost every building is a church or a tavern and what men do but pray and drink or how life is supported in their bodies I can't conceive.

There is some odd quality about great natural beauties (dawn at sea coming jump with the Wicklow mountains) when combined with intense anxiety and great weariness. One wd. expect them to strike less: but it is the acid bites the plate and I shall, I suppose, remember them forever. There are *no* pigs in Ireland now – the people are intensely ugly – and you hear more wit and humour in one day of London than in a week of Drogheda. My Brother was in the care of the most charming nuns.

Yours sincerely
C. S. Lewis

Dear Lady, you've asked for trouble so here it is. Free criticisms invited & all rods will be kissed.[76] I was rather frightened myself by the Great Divorce. – condemned out of my own mouth. I hope you are well. Salutations, in haste

C.S.L.

Donkey's Delight[77]

Ten mortal months I courted
   A girl with bright hair,
Unswerving in my service
   As the old lovers were.

---

75 Sir Ronald Storrs finally agreed to a date, and he and Ruth Pitter dined with Lewis in Magdalen College on 16 July.

76 We do not have Pitter's reply to Lewis, but in her note to these poems she said: 'Magnificent poems to my mind, the technique staggering, vocabulary so wide, learned, & choice, discrimination (moral & spiritual) so lofty. As well might a lion request a mouse to criticize his roaring: and yet I can imagine a lion doing so . . .' (Bodleian Library, MS. Eng. lett. c. 220/3, fol. 52).

77 This poem was published with slight variations under the pseudonym 'N.W.' in *Punch*, CCXIII (5 November 1947), p. 442. A revised version is published in *Poems* and *CP*.

Almost she had learned to call me
   Her dear love, and then
One moment changed the omens,
   She was cold again;
For carelessly, unfairly,
   With one glance of his eyes,
A gay, light-hearted sailor
   Bore away the prize
Unbought, which I had sought with
   Many sonnets and sighs.

In stern desire I turned to
   The high Muses then,
To seek how the unspeakable
   Could be fixed by a pen,
Not to shrink though the ink that
   I must use, they said,
Was my dearest blood, the nearest
   To my heart, the ripe-red.
I obeyed them, I made them
   Many a costly lay,
Till carelessly, unfairly
   A boy passed that way
Who set ringing with his singing
   All the woods and the lanes;
They gave him their favour,
   Lost were all my pains.

I passed then to a Master
   Of a higher repute
Trusting to find justice
   At the world's root.
With rigid fast and vigil,
   Silence and shirt of hair,
The narrow way to Paradise
   I trod with care:
But carelessly, unfairly,
   At the eleventh hour there came,

Reckless and feckless,
  Without a single claim,
A ne'er-do-well, a dare-devil,
  Who smelled of shag and gin;
Before me (and far warmer
  His welcome!) he went in.

I stood still then in the chill
  Of the great morning,
Aghast, until at last –
  Oh, I was late learning! –
I repented, I entered
  Into the excellent joke,
The absurdity, and my burden
  Fell off, as I broke
Into laughter. Soon after,
  I had found my level:
With Balaam's ass daily
  Out at grass I revel,
Now playing, now braying
  Over the fields of light,
Our soaring, creaking *Gloria*,
  Our donkey's delight.

Young King Cole[78]

By enemies surrounded, all venomously minded
  Against him, to hound him to death, there lived a king,
Who was great and merry-hearted. He ate and drank and sported,
  When his wounds smarted, he would dance and sing.

78 'Young King Cole' was published with the title 'Dangerous Oversight' under the pseudonym 'N.W.' in *Punch*, CCXII (21 May 1947), p. 434. It was revised and retitled in *Poems* and *CP*.

With gossiping and stories, with possets and canary,
With goliards and glory, he made the time pass:
His merriment heightened as his territories straitened,
And his grip tightened on the stem of his glass.

When his foes assaulted he arose and exulted
Like a lover as he vaulted onto his gaunt horse,
Sublime and elated. But each time he was defeated,
For the lower gods hated him without remorse.

So his realm diminished; overwhelmed, it vanished,
He held at the finish but a small river isle,
With his Queen, amid the saplings and the green rippling,
With his Fool and his Chaplain; held it for a while.

Till, breathing anger, the Heathen in their hunger,
Came with clangour to the river banks,
With their commissars and harlots, with the bombers and the skirling
Of their pipes, with the snarling and rattle of their tanks.

And fast came the orders for the last King's murder:
From the reedy border the gray batteries spoke
The long endeavour of those strong lovers
Relaxed forever amid stench and smoke.

From their fresh, unpolluted flesh there sprouted
A tree, fair-fruited, its smell and taste
Were big with Eden: every thing was laden
With gold unheeded in the flowery waste.

Past the gossamer and midges, past the blossomy region
Of bees, past the pigeon's green world, towards the blue,
Past the eagles' landings, many a league ascending,
Above the Alps and Andes, infallibly it grew;

And it cast warm joys over vast horizons,
  But its shadow was poison to the evil-eyed.
Yes. They ought to have felled it. They were caught unshielded.
  Paralysed they beheld it. They despaired and died.

Vitrea Circe[79]

The name of Circe
Is wrongly branded
(Though Homer's verses
  Portrayed her right)
By heavy handed
And moral persons
Misunderstanding
  Her danger bright.

She used not beauty
For man's beguiling,
She craved no suitor;
  Sea-chances brought
To her forest-silent
And crimson fruited
And snake-green island
  Her guests unsought.

She watched those drunken
And tarry sailors
Eat nectar-junket
  And Phoenix nests;
Each moment paler
With pride, she shrunk at
Their leering, railing
  Salt-water jests.

They thought to pluck there
Her rosial splendour?

79 This poem was published under the pseudonym 'N.W.' in *Punch*, CCXIV (23 June 1948), p. 543. A revised version is reprinted in *Poems* and *CP*.

They thought their luck there
  Was half divine?
When the feast ended
She rose and struck them
With rod extended
  And made them swine.

No man with kisses
Or eyes she tempted;
Of beddings and blisses
  Knew naught until
There came undream't of
The tough Ulysses,
From fate exempted
  By Pallas' will.

Then flashed above her
(Poor kneeling Circe,
Her snares discovered!)
  The hero's blade.
She lay at mercy,
His slave, his lover,
Forgot her curses,
  Blushed like a maid.

She had none to warn her.
He hacked and twisted
The hedge so thorny,
  It let him pass:
Her awful distance,
Her vestal scorning,
Were bright as crystal,
They broke like glass.

TO DR WARFIELD M. FIROR (BOD):

Magdalen College,
Oxford
July 11th 1947

Dear Dr. Firor

Very many thanks for your most kind parcel of good things wh. I opened yesterday with all the zeal of a child; when I take the various treasures home to my family there will be joy in the house. All was in good condition. I am much moved by your kind thought and by the trouble you have taken.

With much gratitude.

Yours sincerely
C. S. Lewis

TO RUTH PITTER (BOD):

[Magdalen College,
Oxford]
July 21/47

Dear Miss Pitter

(This notepaper with its portentous heading is, need I say, a munificent present from an American).[80] Thanks for the books. I look forward to finding out how rude a potato can be. All the ones I meet are civil enough. I liked the Temperate & Frugal. With my duty,

C.S.L.

TO RUTH PITTER (BOD):

Magdalen.
Aug 9th 1947

Dear Miss Pitter

You know what awful things Americans ask one to do? I have a letter from a lady in dear old Kentucky asking me to look in the London Directory for the address of FERNANDO MARRAINE who lives at

---

80 The headed notepaper, a gift from one of Lewis's American benefactors and which he used for numerous subsequent letters, has printed at the top

C. S. Lewis
Magdalen College
Oxford, England

Harrow on the Hill and is described as a 'professor' of mathematics. This is accompanied by butter (praise) and jam (parcel) so I feel I cannot neglect it: nor can I get to London. Do Directories grow on trees in Chelsea? And could you? If it involves more than a 3 minute's waste of time, don't bother. Commend me to the Frugal & Temperate. He's a charmer.

Yours sincerely
C. S. Lewis

TO MRS E. L. BAXTER (T):

Magdalen College,
Oxford
Aug 19th 47

Dear Mrs Baxter –

First, about Mr. Marraine. I cannot go to London but I have written to a friend who lives there and hope to be able to send you his address in a few days. And yes: thanks very much, tea is always short and always welcome. And thanks again for your most interesting and kind letter. I am sorry I am beaten on the first round by Ramon Novarro[81] by having no photo to send in reply!

I am particularly pleased to have been of any help as a bridge between the parish and the convent. I'm not especially 'high' Church myself but Nuns seem to me the strong argument on that side. They are in my experience almost invariably so very nice – and so happy: much more so *either* than the same number of married women picked at random *or* the same number of monks. I don't know why this should be so.

About precocity, this isn't a change in my style. I have always had two ways of writing, one for the people (to be used in works of popularised theology) and one that never aimed at simplicity (in scholarly or imaginative works). I don't think I could, or ought, to write romances & fantasies in the style of my broadcast talks. And I'm impenitent about *dindle*. You saw at once what it meant and so I've added a lovely word to your vocabulary. Why do you object?

81 Mrs Baxter had, presumably, asked Ramon Novarro (1899–1968), the romantic Mexican film actor, for a photograph.

I've only once written on vivisection and my point was that while it could (just) be defended on Xtian grounds (Man there being really different and superior in kind to the beasts) it cd. not be defended on naturalistic grounds where Man is taken to be really the same kind of thing.

I've never propounded a general position about contraception. As a bachelor I think I shd. be imprudent in attacking it: on the other hand I shd. not like the job of defending it against almost unbroken Xtian disapproval. But it isn't my business.

With many thanks and all good wishes.

Yours sincerely

C. S. Lewis

TO DR WARFIELD M. FIROR (BOD): TS

REF.168/47.

Magdalen College,
Oxford.
5th September 1947.

Dear Dr. Firor,

Is it to your kindness that I owe a handsome supply of stationary which has just arrived from Lucas Bros. Inc., 22/E Baltimore St., Baltimore? There is no other indication of the sender, but if you are the man, please accept my most grateful thanks for your continued kindness to me. I am just a little doubtful though if it is you, for I see you make no mention of such a parcel in your last letter.

With all best wishes,

yours sincerely,

C. S. Lewis

On 6 September 1947 there began a remarkable correspondence in Latin between Don Giovanni Calabria and C. S. Lewis. Don Calabria, a priest of Verona, founded the Congregazione Poveri Servi della Divina Provvidenza (Congregation of the Poor Servants of Divine Providence). Besides this work, Don Calabria was passionately interested in Christian unity, and after reading an Italian translation of The Screwtape Letters *he decided to write to the author. As he could neither read nor write English, he chose the only language he believed they shared – Latin. The Latin correspondence between Don Calabria and Lewis was edited and trans-*

lated by Lewis's pupil, Martin Moynihan, and published as Letters: C. S. Lewis–Don Giovanni Calabria, A Study in Friendship *(1989).*[82] *Published below is Lewis's side of the correspondence, in both the original Latin and Moynihan's translation. Don Calabria wrote on 1 September 1947,*

> *The inspiration of writing to you came to me while I was reading your excellent book called in Italian* Le Lettere di Berlicche. *My purpose is to open my mind to you regarding a problem of the greatest importance, to solve which . . . the times seem to me riper than before. For today, because of this almost universal conflagration of war-madness many boundaries are overthrown, the world is like a field ploughed up with so many troubles and sufferings, many general opinions are changed and rivalries diminished and, in particular, on every side, there appears a great aspiration of all peoples towards reform.*
>
> *All these things seem to constitute anticipations of the solution of that other problem which I have already referred to: namely that of the dissenting brethren whose return to the unity of the Body of Christ, which is the Church, is most greatly desired.*
>
> *This is the sign of the Most Sacred Heart of Jesus manifested in that prayer of His to the Father before He suffered: 'that they all may be one'*[83] *. . .*
>
> *You also seem to me to be able to contribute much in the Lord, with your great influence not only in your own most noble country but even in other lands. How and by what means I leave to your prudence. Poor as I am, I promise to pray strenuously that God and our Lord Jesus Christ will see fit to illuminate and strengthen you that you may be able to perform something of great moment in the Lord's vineyard, so that at last it may be seen that 'there*

82 An Italian edition of the book, published by Don Calabria's own Congregation of the Poor Servants of Divine Providence, includes, besides the Latin originals with Italian translation, a few letters which are not in the English edition. The book is entitled *Una Gioia Insolita: Lettere tra un prete cattolico e un laico anglicano*, Introduzione e note di Luciano Squizzato, Traduzione di Patrizia Morelli (Milano: Jaca Book, 1995).

83 John 17:22.

is one fold and one Shepherd'[84] *. . . I humbly sign myself, yours in the Heart of Jesus . . .*

Don Calabria[85]

TO DON GIOVANNI CALABRIA (V):[86]

Magdalen College
Oxford
Sept. 6th 1947

Reverende Pater,

Epistolam tuam plenam caritate et benevolentia grato animo accepi. Scito et mihi causam doloris et materiam orationum esse hoc schisma in corpore Domini, gravissimum intrantibus scandalum, quod etiam omnes fideles reddit debiliores ad communem hostem repellendum. Ego tamen laicus, immo laicissimus, minimeque peritus in profundioribus sacrae theologiae quaestionibus. Conatus sum id facere quod solum facere posse mihi videor: id est, quaestiones subtiliores de quibus Romana Ecclesia et Protestantes inter se dissentiunt omnino relinquere (episcopis et eruditis viris tractandas) propriis vero libris ea exponere quae adhuc, Dei gratia, post tanta peccata tantosque errores communia sunt. Neque inutile opus: vulgus enim video ignorare de quam multis etiam nunc consentimus – adeo ut hominem inveni qui credebat vos negare Trinitatem Dei! Praeter illud opus, semper putavi mihi quam maxime cum omnibus qui se Christianos appellant fraternaliter conversandum: id quod si omnes strenue fecerint, nonne licet sperare eam dilectionis et operationum unitatem multis annis praecedere, necnon fovere, seriorem doctrinarum redintegrationem? Tertio loco restant (quod validissimum est) orationes.

Consuetudo latine scribendi mihi per multos annos non usitata! Si quem soloecismum fecerim veniam peto.

Oremus pro invicem. Cordialiter paternae tuae caritati me commendo in Domino nostro.

C. S. Lewis

*

---

84 ibid., 10:16.

85 *Letters: C. S. Lewis–Don Giovanni Calabria: A Study in Friendship*, trans. and ed. Martin Moynihan (London: Collins, 1989), pp. 27, 29.

86 See **St Giovanni Calabria** in the Biographical Appendix.

Magdalen College
Oxford
Sept. 6th 1947

Reverend Father,

Thank you for your letter, full of love and goodwill. Be assured that for me too the schism in the Body of Christ is both a source of grief and a matter of prayers, being a most serious stumbling block to those coming in and one which makes even the faithful weaker in repelling the common foe. However, I am a layman, indeed the most lay of laymen, and least skilled in the deeper questions of sacred theology. I have tried to do the only thing that I think myself able to do: that is, to leave completely aside the subtler questions about which the Roman Church and Protestants disagree among themselves – things which are to be treated by bishops and learned men – and in my own books to expound, rather, those things which still, by God's grace, after so many sins and errors, are shared by us. Nor is this a pointless task; for I find that people are unaware how many matters we even now agree on – so much so that I have come across someone who believed that you deny the Three in One God! Over and above that work, it has always seemed to me that I should maintain as much fraternal intercourse as possible with all those who call themselves Christians. If all were actively to do this, might we not hope that this unity of love and action over many years would precede – not to say foster – an eventual reunification of doctrines. Thirdly, there remain – what is most efficacious – prayers.

The practice of writing in Latin is one which for many years I have not kept up! If I have committed any solecism, I ask pardon.

Let us pray for each other. With all my heart I commend myself to your fatherly love in Our Lord.

C. S. Lewis

TO FRANCIS USHERWOOD (P):

Magdalen College,
Oxford.
Sept 9th 1947

Dear Mr. Usherwood,

No, I am sure God has not forced B to give A the job. God's action wd. consist, I believe, in arranging all the circumstances so that

A came at the right moment etc – i.e. in presenting B with the *situation*, on wh. then his free will worked. Ordinary people regard life as a mixture of 'luck' and free will. It is the part usually called 'luck' by which, on my view, God answers prayers.

Yours sincerely
C. S. Lewis

TO MR AND MRS E. L. BAXTER (W):

Magdalen College,
Oxford.
Sept 10th 1947

Dear Mr and Mrs Baxter

Thank you both v. much in anticipation for the parcels. There is good in every situation: I have recovered, at 49, the interest of a child in parcels and in meals! But it is hard on the *really* young.

About stories for children. (a) Don't the ordinary fairy tales really already contain much of the Spirit, in solution? Does not Cinderella give us *exaltavit humiles*,[87] and is not Redemption figured in *The Sleeping Beauty*? (b) For something a *little* more explicit, what about Geo. MacDonald's *The Princess & the Goblins*, *Curdie & the Princess*, *The Wise Woman*,[88] and *The Golden Key*?[89] (c) I have tried one myself but it was, by the unanimous verdict of my friends, so bad that I destroyed it.

With all good wishes.

Yours sincerely
C. S. Lewis

---

87 'He has exalted the humble'. The words are taken from the *Magnificat* (Luke 1:46–55), sung by Mary when her cousin Elizabeth had greeted her as the mother of the Lord.

88 George MacDonald, *The Lost Princess: or, The Wise Woman* (1895).

89 George MacDonald, *Short Stories* ('The Light Princess', 'The Giant's Heart', 'The Golden Key') (1928).

TO DR WARFIELD M. FIROR (BOD): TS

REF.168/47.

Magdalen College,
Oxford.
13th September 1947.

My dear Dr. Firor,

This time at least there is no doubt: for the excellent parcels which reached me today are clearly marked with your name and address. And I feel that the chorus of praise with which it was greeted must have set your ears tingling in Baltimore!

Seriously, I send you my most hearty thanks; if you could live over here for a few months – in a private house I mean, not in an expensive hotel – you would appreciate the enormous difference which it makes if one has just that 'something nice' over and above the monotonous and scanty ration.

With all best wishes,

yours most gratefully,
C. S. Lewis

TO DON GIOVANNI CALABRIA (V):

Magdalen College
Oxford
Sept. 20th 1947

Reverende Pater –

Alteram tuam epistolam, 15mo die Sept. scriptam, grato animo accepi.

Hora, ut dicis, vere Satanae est: sed spei nonnullas scintillas in tenebris video. Communia pericula, communes aerumnae, commune fere omnium hominum in gregem Christi odium et contemptus possunt, Dei gratia, multum conferre ad sanandas divisiones nostras; qui enim eadem, ab eisdem, pro eodem, patiuntur, vix possunt non amare inter se.

Equidem crederem Domini in animo esse (postquam leniora medicamina recusavimus) nos ipsa persecutione et angustiis in unitatem cogere. Satanas ille procul dubio nihil aliud est quam malleus in manu benevoli et severi Dei.

Omnes enim aut volentes aut nolentes voluntatem Dei faciunt: Judas et Satanas ut organa aut instrumenta, Johannes et Petrus ut filii.

Etiam nunc videmus aut majorem caritatem aut certe minus odium inter divisos Christianos esse quam fuit ante C annos: cujus rei mihi videtur (sub Deo) principalis causa esse gliscens superbia et immanitas infidelium. Hitlerus, insciens et nolens, maxime ecclesiae profuit!

Libros quos te missurum esse pollicitus es cum gratiarum actione expecto. Ceterorum mearum operum nullum in Italica lingua exstat: alioquin missurus eram.

Utinam pestifera illa 'Renascentia' quam Humanistae effecerent non destruxerit (dum erigere eam se jactabant) Latinam: adhuc possemus toti Europae scribere.

Orationes tuas, dilecte pater, adhuc oro. Vale.

C. S. Lewis

*

Magdalen College
Oxford
Sept. 20th 1947

Reverend Father,

I was glad to receive your further letter written on the 15th Sept.

The hour, as you say, is indeed Satan's hour. But I see some sparks of hope in the darkness.

Common perils, common burdens, an almost universal hatred and contempt for the Flock of Christ can, by God's Grace, contribute much to the healing of our divisions. For those who suffer the same things from the same people for the same Person can scarcely not love each other.

Indeed I could well believe that it is God's intention, since we have refused milder remedies, to compel us into unity, by persecution even and hardship. Satan is without doubt nothing else than a hammer in the hand of a benevolent and severe God. For all, either willingly or unwillingly, do the will of God: Judas and Satan as tools or instruments, John and Peter as sons.

Even now we see more charity, or certainly less hatred, between separated Christians than there was a century ago. The chief cause of this (under God) seems to me to be the swelling pride and barbarity of the unbelievers. Hitler, unknowingly and unwillingly, greatly benefited the Church!

The books which you have promised to send me I await with gratitude. None of my other writings has been translated into Italian. Otherwise I would have sent them.

If only that plaguey 'Renaissance' which the Humanists brought about had not *destroyed* Latin (and destroyed it just when they were pluming themselves that they were reviving it), we should then still be able to correspond with the whole of Europe.

I still ask, dear Father, for your prayers.

Farewell,

C. S. Lewis

TO JUNE FLEWETT (T):

[The Kilns]
Sept 23/47

Dear June –

As you feared a night in London is at the moment nearly impossible for either of us – especially as you won't be there in the flesh but only in two dimensions. Of course we're looking out with excitement for the film[90] when it comes to Oxford. And congratulations about *The Linden Tree*:[91] will it also come here?

Rê Charles Williams, I was at a lecture on him the other day thronged with his admirers and in the discussion wh. followed someone said 'He does work on the stage alright. I was at a *matinée* of the *House of the Octopus*[92] in London and it generally so gripped the audience that by the last act even those three guffawing schoolboys in the third row had become quiet.' So that's how Warnie and Dyson and I appeared to the world.

Kosterlitz is a nice little man tho' like all central Europeans he doesn't quite understand our English idea of small talk.

The stuff about Substitution comes in all C.W.'s books but most

---

90 June, using her new stage name, Jill Raymond, played Jean Simmons' sister in the film *The Woman in the Hall* (1947), based on the novel by Gladys Bronwen Stern (1890–1973).

91 June played Dinah in the first, nine-month tour of J. B. Priestley's *The Linden Tree: A Play in Four Acts and Two Scenes* (1947), while the play was still on in London. It played in Oxford as part of the tour.

92 Following the publication of Charles Williams's *The House of the Octopus: A Play in Three Acts* (London: Edinburgh House Press, 1945), the United Council for Missionary Education presented a stage version. It was produced by Phyllis M. Potter and performed at the Rudolf Steiner Hall, Park Road, NW1, on 29 September and 8–13 October 1945 at 6.30 p.m., with matinees on Saturdays at 2.30 p.m. June Flewett played the part of Alayu in the play and had lunch with Jack and Warnie before one of the matinees.

clearly I think, in *He Came Down from Heaven* and *Descent into Hell.* It was all meant to be practical & he wd. not have admitted your contrast of 'practical' and 'poetical'.

We're all delighted at your successes and hope that there are 1000's of them ahead and that we shall live to see you rich and famous and still as nice as ever! Minto is v. feeble now but is sleeping better. Love from all.

Yours
Jack

TO DR WARFIELD M. FIROR (BOD): TS

REF.168/47.

Magdalen College,
Oxford.
1st. October 1947.

My dear Dr. Firor,

I am completely at a loss when it comes to thanking you for your last parcel: because I rather doubt if you know what you have done. A ham such as you sent lifts me up into our millionaire class. Such a thing could'nt be got on this side unless one was very deep in the Black Market, and then it would probably set one back about £12–0-0.

And as for the cheese, I found I'd almost forgotten what real cheese tastes like.

I and all my friends are very deeply grateful; you have given an amount of pleasure which you, in your happier country, cannot realize.

yours most gratefully,
C. S. Lewis

P. S. We're boiling it to-morrow. Meantime I go and have a look at it every now and then for the mere beauty of it – the *finest* view in England!

TO DON GIOVANNI CALABRIA (V):

Magdalen College
Oxford
Oct. 3rd 1947

Reverende Pater –

Duos libros (*Amare* et *Apostolica Vivendi Forma*) grato animo accepi. Nomen auctoris non invenio sed puto vestros esse. Lectionem incipere adjuc non potui: nunc enim hora est negotiorum plenissima, qua iuvenes ex feriis in collegium redeunt et nos magistri sentimus primi parentis maledictionem *in sudore vultus* etc.!

Futura otia et voluptatem legendi vestros libros expectamus.

Vale et habe me semper in orationibus tuis,

C. S. Lewis

*

Magdalen College
Oxford
Oct. 3rd 1947

Reverend Father,

I have received with pleasure two books *Amare* and *Apostolica Vivendi Forma*. I do not find the name of the author but I think they are your Congregation's.[93]

I cannot yet begin reading them: because now the time is completely occupied by the return of undergraduates to the College after the vacation and we tutors experience the curse of our First Parent, *in the sweat of thy face etc.*![94]

We look forward to some leisure time to come – and to the pleasure of reading your books.

Farewell, and have me ever in your prayers.

C. S. Lewis

MR E. L. BAXTER (W): TS

REF.414/47.

Magdalen College,
Oxford.
14th October 1947.

My dear Mr. Baxter

We had hardly forgotten the parcel which you were kind enough to send us in August, when another arrives; and such a well selected one too! Believe me, I am most grateful, and so is my household. It will bring into our dietary that little bit extra which just makes all the difference. Thank you very much.

yours gratefully,

C. S. Lewis

93 Don Giovanni Calabria, *Apostolica Vivendi Forma* (1945); *Amare* (1946). Both were published by his congregation, Vescovile Casa Buoni Fanciulli in Verona.

94 Genesis 3:19.

TO MARTYN SKINNER (BOD):

[Magdalen College]
Oct 15/47

Dear Skinner –

I have just finished your admirable *Letters V*[95] wh. you kindly sent me more months ago than I care to remember. I think it is the best yet and full of plums; the personification of peace on p. 13, the descent into Oxford p. 22, Autumn on p. 44 (where the noun *boister* is an excellent neologism), the new hermits' temptations, 56, 57, and the village shop. These for set pieces.

The smaller stabs of pleasure are too numerous to mention and on some pages almost continuous. I pick out for special loveliness the 'open boat, the drifting grave',[96] and 'each temple like a curl'.[97] A beautiful book and terrible too for one, who shares (as I do) your apprehensions. It wd. be less terrifying if one cd. really attribute the murder of beauty to any particular set of evil men: the trouble is that from man's first and wholly legitimate attempt to win safety and ease from Nature it seems, step by step, to lead on quite logically to universal suburbia.

I had a talk with dear old Saunders the other day. He remembers you all with undiminished affection.

We have a change of President – for the better,[98]

Yours
C. S. Lewis

TO DAPHNE HARWOOD (BOD):

Magdalen
Oct 20th 1947

Dear Daphne

How nice to hear from you. About Being and Reason: – it is clear that something must be self-existent (wh. I take it is what you mean

95 Martyn Skinner, *Letters to Malaya, V* (1947).

96 ibid., part I, 134.

97 ibid., part III, 296.

98 Sir Henry Thomas Tizard (1885–1959), President of Magdalen College, 1942–6, was succeeded by Thomas Sherrer Ross Boase (1898–1974), who was President 1947–68.

by 'Being'). I claim to show that Reason must be self existent.[99] There cannot be two independent self-existents. So I conclude that Reason is, or is a characteristic of, Being.

John has returned beautiful as the day[100] but not, I gather, having done much work in the vacation. Wonderful thing, this Heredity![101]

When is Cecil coming to spend an evening and night again? Tuesdays and Fridays preferred. With good wishes to all.

Yours
Jack L.

TO NATHAN COMFORT STARR (W):[102] TS

REF.588/47.

Magdalen College,
Oxford.
3rd November 1947.

Dear Professor Starr,

Many thanks for your most kind and encouraging letter of the 18th October.

Tributes from other men in our own trade are rare and precious to me. A trip to the U.S.A. is out of the question, I'm afraid. I am tied to the bedside of an invalid and bound (like Pope) 'to rock the cradle of declining age'.[103] You will understand. I liked the sonnet, especially the sestet. Not quite sure about 'stark' in the octave. (a.) A bit hackneyed. (b.) Don't like the assonance with 'art'.

Come and see me if you're ever in this luckless country.

yours sincerely,
C. S. Lewis

---

99 Mrs Harwood had probably asked a question about *Miracles*, ch. 4, in which Lewis stated: 'It is . . . obvious that sooner or later you must admit a Reason which exists absolutely on its own. The problem is whether you or I can be such a self-existent Reason.'

100 'Beautiful as the Day' is the title of ch. 1 of E. Nesbit's *Five Children and It* (1902).

101 John Harwood was at this time Lewis's pupil at Magdalen College.

102 Nathan Comfort Starr (1896–1981) received a Ph.D. from Harvard in 1928. He specialised in the Romantic Poets and the Arthurian Legend. He held teaching posts at a number of colleges and universities. He retired from the University of Florida at Gainesville, where he taught for many years, in 1965. His books include *The Dynamics of Literature* (1945) and *King Arthur Today: the Arthurian Legend in English and American Literature, 1901–1953* (1954).

103 Alexander Pope, *An Epistle from Mr Pope to Dr Arbuthnot* (1734–5), 409: 'To rock the cradle of reposing age.'

TO MARTYN SKINNER (BOD): TS

REF.601/47

Magdalen College,
Oxford.
5th. November 1947.

Dear Skinner,

I'd love to be a 'source' for a poet, and hope you'll follow up your narrative ambitions. Why not the long foretold return of Arthur to modern England? Plenty of room for your satiric bent and for as much fantasy as you want.

I know Burnet in part: very important for the old horror of mountains.[104]

yours,
C. S. Lewis

If you'll write the verse I'll provide the Argument!

TO DOROTHY L. SAYERS (W):

[Magdalen College,
Oxford]
Nov 7th 1947

Dear Miss Sayers

I've no idea when Bandersnatch will send us copies of the C.W. book. I've never had a reliable prediction from any of my publishers on that point. It's to be called *Essays presented to C.W.*

I wouldn't say that Richards was woolly or confused, and indeed have always felt rather grateful to him for having worked out a certain view of literature (the only view possible on his basic assumptions) as far as it will go. He is not, I agree, a good critic: but I suppose a man may be worth powder and shot on the nature of criticism without being much of a practitioner. And he asked some of the right questions: no one before him had seriously tried to find out what badness in poetry is. I don't think he got the answer.

As for his being the precursor of my *Green Book* villains,[105] yes. But as in him it is all above-board, a theory advanced for adult consideration

---

104 Thomas Burnet (?1635–1715) was the author of *The Theory of the Earth*, 2 vols (1684–9), a romantic cosmogony, suggested to him by a trip across the Alps.

105 In *The Abolition of Man*. See note 59 to the letter to Martyn Skinner of 4 March 1943.

and argued for, there is no crime in it, only error. The Green Book smuggled it in without argument in a book on a slightly different subject, for children, without probably being even aware that it was controversial. Richards walks up to our mental front door and rings the bell: you needn't buy his stuff if you don't want – 'good morning, no offence'. The others sneak in, or blunder in, through the scullery.

Yours very sincerely
C. S. Lewis

I'm re-reading *The Man Born to be King*. It wears excellently.

TO VERA MATHEWS (W):[106] TS

Ref. 606/47.

Magdalen College,
Oxford.
11th November 1947.

Dear Mrs. Matthews,

Many thanks for your letter of the 5th. November: – Yes indeed, I certainly received your admirable parcel, posted in New York on 23rd. September, and sent you my thanks for it – thanks which it is a pleasure to have the opportunity of repeating – on 6th. November. But this letter I of course did not send to California, but to the address on the parcel, viz. 21952 St. New York, which I assumed to be yours. It was in fact, I take it, the address of the store which despatched it?

I am distressed that you should have been left in doubt about the matter, or worse still, have thought me to be an ungrateful recipient instead of,

yours gratefully,
C. S. Lewis

TO SISTER PENELOPE CSMV (BOD):

Magdalen College,
Oxford.
Nov. 21/47

Dear Sister Penelope

I am very sorry to gather from your letter, tho' characteristically

106 Miss Vera Mathews was writing from 510 North Alpine Drive, Beverley Hills, California.

you say little about it, that Brother Ass is not serving you too well. I am afraid there is no sign of those reviews: *mea culpa.*[107]

I am afraid (there is a certain monotony about this letter) that I am not much more like to get to Wantage than to the Moon. In some ways my domestic situation is better at present for we now have a 'maid' who seems honest & kind, (she has a little girl who makes a noise like the whistle of a railway engine nearly all day: you can't tell whether she is laughing or crying by the sound, equally piercing in either case!) but of course my Mother does not get better – old age is incurable – and I am tighter tied every month.

I am well but very tired: writing nothing except the Lit. History[108] (in vacations) and a few poems (in term) wh. appear in *Punch* – signed N.W. if you ever see it. In fact I am much better off than you! For you find it hard to sleep whereas I find it hard to wake. Paradise, as you say, is the idea. I hope you will be happy and successful in the new work. *Oremus pro invicem.*

Yours sincerely
C. S. Lewis

TO VERA MATHEWS (W): TS

Ref. 606/47.

Magdalen College,
Oxford.
24th November 1947.

Dear Miss Matthews,

It is difficult to find any words in which to acknowledge your continued kindness. I am very glad that my last letter reached you safely, for it was unpleasant to feel that you perhaps thought me indifferent to your goodness. In sending to those behind Mr. Attlee's Iron Curtain,[109] you can never go wrong with MEAT, TEA, and SOAP – soap for washing *clothes* that is; why it should be so I can't imagine, but toilet soap is never as scarce as the other kind.

With renewed thanks and all good wishes,

yours gratefully,
C. S. Lewis

---

107 Sister Penelope had posted to him a parcel of American reviews of her translation of St Athanasius's *De Incarnatione Verbi Dei*, but they never reached him.

108 i.e. *English Literature in the Sixteenth Century*.

109 Clement Attlee (1883–1967), the Labour Prime Minister of Great Britain, 1945–51.

TO DON GIOVANNI CALABRIA (V):

Magdalen College
Oxford
Nov. 25th 1947

Dilecte Pater –

Quamquam vernacula Italica facilior et magis nota mihi est apud Boiardum et Ariostum quam apud hodiernos tractata, *Ut omnes unum sint* grato animo perlegi: in quo multa placent. Nonnulla autem nequeo concedere de quibus pauca rescribam, filiali licentia qua (credo) me uti volebas.

1. De omnipotentia verbi Domini qui ipse Verbum est, quatenus est verbum imperans, consentio. De omnipotentia ejusdem verbi, quatenus oratio est, haesito. Potest enim responderi quod ipse in horto Gethesemane oravit nec impetravit. Deinde, nonne est terribilis veritas, liberum arbitrium mali hominis posse Dei voluntati resistere? Omnipotentiam enim suam modo quodam restrinxit ipso facto creandi liberam creaturam et legimus nescio qua regione Dominum *non potuisse* miracula facere quia defuit fides in hominibus.

2. Totam causam schismatis in peccato esse non pro certo habeo. Concedo nullum schisma esse sine peccato, sed altera propositio alteram haud necessarie consequitur. Ex vestris Tetzel, ex nostris Henricus VIII, perditi homines errant: adde, si vis, ex vestris Papam Leonem, ex nostris Lutherum (quamquam egomet de ambobus mitiorem sententiam darem) sed quid sentiam de vestro Thoma Moro, de nostro Gulielmo Tyndale? Tota opera et hujus et illius nuper perlegi. Ambo mihi videntur esse viri sanctissimi et toto corde amare Dominum: neque hujus nec illius caligas solvere dignus sum. Attamen dissentiunt et (id quod me torquet et attonitum habet) illa dissensio mihi videtur non ex vitiis nec ex ignorantia eorum, immo ex virtutibus et fidei eorum penetralibus oriri – ita ut quo optimi sunt eo maxime dissentiunt. Credo Dei judicium de hac dissensione altius absconditum esse quam tibi videtur: etenim judicia ejus abyssus.

3. Quo scribes Papam esse *il punto d'incontro* fere committis (liceat mihi venia vestra dicere) id quod logici vocant *petitionem principii.* Nam de nihilo magis quam de auctoritate Papae dissentimus: ex qua dissensione ceterae fere omnes dependent.

Quo scribis nos omnes debere quam celerrime contra communem hostem (vel hostes 'nomen Legio est') opponere unitatem caritatis et morum Christianorum, toto corde consentio. Disputationes magis aggravant schismata quam sanant: communis operatio, oratio, fortitudo, communes (si Deus voluerit) mortes pro Christo adunabunt. Dixit Dominus 'si quis fecerit voluntatem Patris, doctrinam sciet' (meis verbis exprimo sensum quia Novum Testamentum latine redditum hodie sub manibus non est). Faciendo veritatem quam iam scimus, in veritatem quam adhuc ignoramus progrediamur. Tunc procul dubio unum erimus: veritas enim una.

Oremus pro invicem: et pro Gallia quae sub periculis jacet. Vale, in Domino

C. S. Lewis

*

Magdalen College
Oxford
Nov. 25th 1947

Dear Father,

Although Italian (the Italian vernacular) is easier for me – and better known – in the pages of Boiardo[110] or Ariosto than the Italian of modern authors, I have read with pleasure '*Ut omnes unum sint*':[111] and much I agree with. Some things, however, I cannot agree with and I shall write back briefly about these, with that filial liberty which I believe you wished me to exercise.

1. About the omnipotence of the Word of God who Himself is the Word: as far as it is a word of command, I agree. As far as it is a word of prayer, I hesitate. For it can be replied that He Himself in the Garden of Gethsemane entreated but did not obtain. Next, is it not a frightening truth that the free will of a bad man can resist the will of God? For He has, after a fashion, restricted His own Omnipotence by the very fact of creating free creatures; and we read that the Lord was *not able* to do miracles in some places because people's faith was wanting.[112]

110 Matteomaria Boiardo (?1441–94), Italian poet who drew on the legends of King Arthur and Charlemagne for his chivalric poems. His principal work was the unfinished *Orlando Innamorato* (1487). See the letter to Arthur Greeves of 25 January 1926 (*CL* I, p. 660).

111 John 17:21: 'that they all may be one'. Lewis was referring to a publication by Don Calabria.

112 Matthew 13:58; Mark 6:5.

2. That the whole cause of schism lies in sin I do not hold to be certain. I grant that no schism is without sin but the one proposition does not necessarily follow the other. From your side Tetzel,[113] from ours Henry VIII,[114] were lost men: and, if you like, Pope Leo[115] from your side and from ours Luther (although for my own part I would pass on both a lighter sentence).[116] But what would I think of your Thomas More[117] or of our William Tyndale?[118] All the writings of the one and all the writings of the other I have lately read right through. Both of them seem to me most saintly men and to have loved God with their whole heart: I am not worthy to undo the shoes of either of them. Nevertheless they disagree and (what racks and astounds me) their disagreement seems to me to spring not from their vices nor from their ignorance but rather from their virtues and the depths of their faith, so that the more they were at their best the more they were at variance. I believe the judgement of God on their dissension is more profoundly hidden than it appears to you to be: for His judgements are indeed an abyss.[119]

3. Where you write that the Pope is 'the point of meeting' you almost commit (if your people will forgive my saying so) what logicians call a *petitio principii* (begging the question). For we disagree about nothing

113 Johann Tetzel (c. 1464–1519), German Dominican, maintained the controversial thesis that indulgences could be obtained for the souls of those in Purgatory, even by people not themselves in a state of grace. His preaching led Martin Luther to issue his ninety-five theses on 31 October 1517.

114 King Henry VIII (1491–1547).

115 Pope Leo X (1475–1521), who was Pope from 1513. His extravagance led him to sell indulgences and offices in the Church to raise money for the construction of St Peter's.

116 Lewis wrote about the Reformation in *English Literature in the Sixteenth Century*: 'In Germany the new theology led into a quarrel about indulgences and thence into a quarrel about the nature of the Church. Whether it need have done so if Leo X had not wanted money, or if Tetzel . . . had not applied to the indulgences grotesquely profane and vulgar methods of salesmanship, may be doubted. In England, Henry VIII, wanting Anne Boleyn and therefore wanting his previous marriage annulled, quarrels with the Pope; caring nothing for Protestant doctrine but accidentally creating a situation in which Protestantism, sometimes exploited and sometimes repressed by government, can become important in England' (pp. 37–8).

117 St Thomas More (1478–1535), Lord Chancellor of England, and zealous defender of Catholicism.

118 William Tyndale (?1494–1536), Protestant Reformer, and translator of the Bible.

119 Psalm 36:6.

more than the authority of the Pope: on which disagreement almost all the others depend.

Where you write that we should all as speedily as possible oppose the common foe (or foes, their name is Legion)[120] with the unity of Charity and Christian living, I agree with my whole heart. Disputations do more to aggravate schism than to heal it: united action, prayer, fortitude and (should God so will) united deaths for Christ – *these* will make us one. The Lord has said 'if anyone will do the will of my Father, he shall know the doctrine'[121] (I put the sense into my own words because today my Vulgate is not to hand). By doing the truth which we already know, let us make progress towards the truth which as yet we are ignorant of. Then, without doubt, we shall be one: for truth is one.

Let us pray for each other: and for France, lying in danger as she does.[122]

Farewell in the Lord,

C. S. Lewis

TO MARTYN SKINNER (BOD): TS

REF.601/47. [Magdalen College]

1st. December 1947.

Dear Skinner,

My own idea (for *you*) would be a series of satiric scenes with one cryptic figure, perhaps rather suspected of being an ass, in the midst of them, until the great moment at which (like Odysseus slipping off his rags and bending the bow) he suddenly leaps out crying 'Logres and the Lord' and smashes all the enemies. But don't let me meddle too much: I've dropped my seed.

yours,

C. S. Lewis

Essays Presented to Charles Williams, edited by C. S. Lewis, *was published by Oxford University Press on 4 December. It contained six essays:*

---

120 Mark 5:9: 'And he asked him, What is thy name? And he answered, saying, My name is Legion: for we are many.'

121 John 7:17.

122 From 1945 to 1947 the Communists were the strongest political group in France and were making desperate attempts to take control of the country. In November 1947 they caused strikes nearly every day, the price of coal went up 60 per cent, 130,00 miners were put out of work and the public services in Paris came almost to a standstill.

'"... And Telling you a Story": A Note on The Divine Comedy*' by Dorothy L. Sayers; 'On Fairy-Stories' by J. R. R. Tolkien; 'On Stories' by C. S. Lewis; 'Poetic Diction and Legal Fiction' by A. O. Barfield; 'Marriage and* Amour Courtois *in Late-Fourteenth-Century England' by Gervase Mathew; and 'The Galleys of France' by W. H. Lewis. It is by any standards an excellent collection of pieces and several, such as those by Tolkien, Lewis and Sayers, have been reprinted numerous times. But, for whatever reason, the book went almost unnoticed. Of the only two reviews it is known to have received, the one in* Time and Tide *was lukewarm, and the other in* Theology *(published in 1948) was hostile.*

TO OWEN BARFIELD (W):

[Magdalen College,
Oxford]
Dec 16/47

My dear B –

Yes, I did read your letter. You must bear with me. Things were never worse at the Kilns. W. is away, so correspondence was never heavier in College. 'Sleep hath forsook and giv'n me o'er'.[123]

I hadn't thought retirement at our age was quite like betrothal: nor how concrete the proposal was. It needs thinking of. In my case the professional job is in some degree a compulsory defence against, and alleviation of, the domestic. Take care. Where there is no office there may be no leisure at all. But of course if it can mean real freedom – God bless it to you.

I am delighted about Orpheus: why do you mock by the word 'Coming'? Not only pleasure but all pleasant duties and I have long been strangers. 'I have shaken hands with delight.'

Your essay[124] is magnificent and I don't know why you are disappointed with it. Tolkien thinks the same & has read it twice. His is v. good too. Mine *thin.* D Sayers perhaps a trifle vulgar in places.

The *Last Don* is delightfully musical. But I don't understand Gaffer (I know it only as = grandfather), nor how I'm to pronounce solecisms nor what knight service has to do with it.

I'm dull: but something stirring comes through. The lines given to

123 Milton, *Samson Agonistes*, 629.

124 In *Essays Presented to Charles Williams.*

Pindar are all out of the real Pindar but shuffled by me – in fact a *cento*. In haste – have wasted most of the morning (soon there will be no mornings) packing up a huge MS sent me unsolicited by a brutal stranger with a name like Van Tripe. Well, all's one.

Yours

C.S.L.

P.S. Of course the real trouble is within. All things wd. be bearable if I were delivered from this internal storm (*buffera infernal*) of self-pity, rage, envy, terror, horror and general bilge!

TO OWEN BARFIELD (W):

[Magdalen College,
Oxford]
Dec 22/47

My dear B –

(This absurd notepaper is a present from an American). I already regret my last letter except in so far as it has produced such a valuable one from you. It was 2/3 temper and melodrama. Thus 'Sleep has forsook and given me o'er' meant 'I have had one or two bad nights lately' plus 'Isn't *Samson Agonistes* fine?'

There is no problem about vocation. Quite obviously one can't leave an old semi-paralysed lady in a house alone for days or even hours: and the duty of looking after one's people rests on us all and is common form. The rage comes from *impatientia*[125] in the strict theological sense: because one treats as an interruption of one's (self-chosen) vocation the vocation actually imposed on one – regards the exam paper actually set as a distraction from the one you wd. like to be doing. Anyway, Maureen is coming for Christmas and W. and I are going to Malvern. I shall do very well.

Verb. Sap – never communicate any troubles of mine again to M. Milne.[126] Through no will of my own I occupy already a larger place in her thoughts than I could wish and the degree of her sympathy is such as to make her miserable and to embarrass me. (All this

---

125 *Impatientia* as understood here means despair, the sense that life is too much to bear. It was *impatientia* which drove Judas to commit suicide.

126 See **Marjorie Milne** in the Biographical Appendix.

under deadly secrecy to all human beings. I wd. not be a *vauntour*).[127]

You're too fond of words like gaffer in poetry I think. Don't imagine I didn't pitch into C.W. for his obscurity for all I was worth.

Yours

C.S.L.

TO LAURENCE HARWOOD (BOD):

[Magdalen College,
Oxford]
Dec. 23/47

Dear Lawrence

You'll wonder at the silly heading of this notepaper: but it is there because it is a present from an American who got it printed like that (I expect there are several Oxfords in America and he wanted it to be clear).

I wonder how you are all getting on? Nothing much has happened to me except that I saw a rabbit *yawn*. I suppose people who keep tame ones have seen it often but this was a wild rabbit and I thought it a v. curious sight. It was a very bored triangular yawn in the middle of a long hot afternoon.

I've also been re-reading Kipling's *Just So Stories*, and have translated all the Runes round that picture of the tusk.[128]

In case you don't know the Runic Alphabet (which is a useful secret writing and supposed to have magical results) it is this:

ᚨ (a), ᛒ (b), ᚳ (c), ⊠ (d), ᛖ (e), ᚠ (f), ᚷ (g),
ᚼ or ᚻ (h), ᛁ (i), ᛄ (j), ᚴ (k), ᛚ (l), ᛗ (m), ᚾ (n)
ᚩ (o) ᛈ (p), ᛉ (q), ᚱ (r), ᛋ (s), ᛏ (t), ᚢ (u), ᚠ (v),

127 'braggart'. Cf. Geoffrey Chaucer, *Troilus and Criseyde*, III, xlv, 6–7: 'a vauntour and a lyere, al is one'.

128 Rudyard Kipling, *Just So Stories For Little Children* (1902). There is a drawing on p. 141 of an ancient ivory tusk, with runes on both sides of the picture. Inside the copy of *Just So Stories* which Lewis was using, and which belonged to his brother, is a page of the proofs of *That Hideous Strength*, and written on the other side is the translation Lewis mentioned to Laurence. It is entitled 'Transliteration of the Runes that face p. 140' and is as follows: 'This is the/stori of/Taffimai/all ritten/out on/an old tusk/if u begin/at the top/left hand/corner/and go on/to the right u can/see for/urself/ the things/as tha h/appened/the reas/on that I/spell so k/ueerli is b/ecause th/ere are/not eno/ugh let/ters in t/he runic/ alphab/et for all the /ourds t/that I ou/ant to us/e to ou/belofed.'

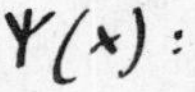 besides the useful letter called Thorn þ = th, and Wen Ƿ = w.

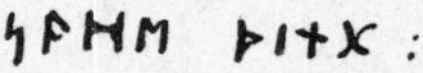[129] e.g. Gk. Λ, Runic , Gk. Σ, Runic . But Kipling mixes up different kinds of Runes and makes rather a muddle.

The other best cipher I know is a disguised form of the old v. simple one wh. you probably know wh. goes like this. Set out the Alphabet thus

A	B	C	D	E	F	G	H	I
J	K	L	M	N	O	P	Q	R
S	T	U	V	W	X	Y	Z	

Now, clearly, 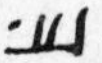 will mean A, 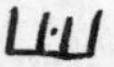 will be E,  will be O and so on. But if you fiddle with it you can get quite nice shapes – 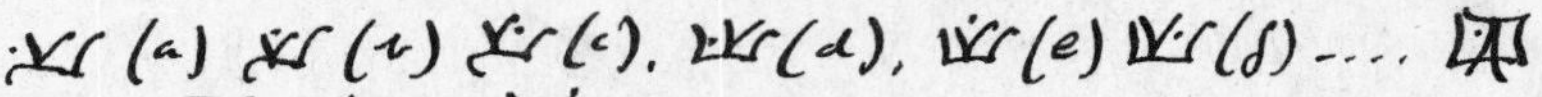 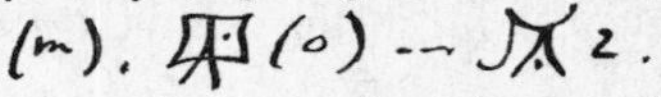. The result looks like a nice Oriental language. So one writes about gods and giants in Runic, and about Caliphs and Ephreets[130] 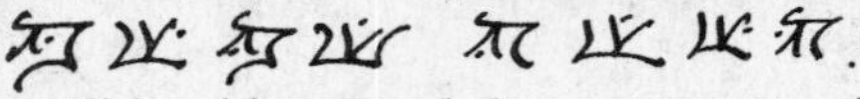[131]

I am sure you will be able to read the secret parts of this letter, but whether you can read the ordinary bits is another matter.

Here's a Christmas box, that is, either 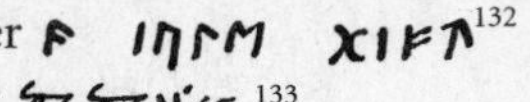[132] or 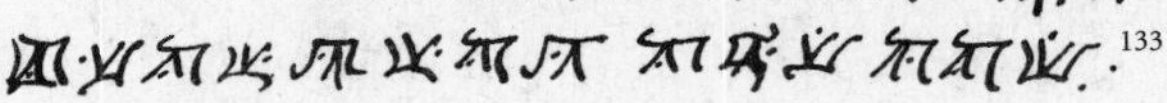[133]

With love to all,
your affectionate
Godfather Lewis

---

129 'If iou know the Greek alfabet iou can see that it and the English and the runic all come origim[n]alli from the same thing.'

130 An Efreet (or Afreet) is a demon of Muslim mythology. In *The Lion, the Witch and the Wardrobe*, ch. 14 an efreet is one of the hideous creatures that join the White Witch in killing Aslan.

131 'Like this'. The horizontal and the thick vertical lines divide the alphabet into groups of three. To interpret each symbol you find the group whose surrounding lines have the same shape as the symbol (ignoring decorative variations), and the dot indicates the letter within the group.

132 'A iule gift'.

133 'Nativity tr[i]bute'.

TO DOROTHY L. SAYERS (W): TS

REF.352/47.

Magdalen College,
Oxford.
29th. December 1947.

Dear Miss Sayers,

Thank you for your good wishes, and for the feline felicities, which are delightful. I think the book *is* nice.[134] Have you seen any reviews? None of us have.[135]

With all the best for 1948,
yours very sincerely,
C. S. Lewis

TO ROMOLO LODETTI (V):[136]

Magdalen College,
Oxford.
Dec. 31. 1947

Frater dilectissime

Quia sermone italico hodierno non calleo liceat mihi latine gratias tibi agere pro benevolis litteris tuis. Oremus pro invicem et speremus

---

134 i.e. *Essays Presented to Charles Williams.*

135 Sayers mentioned in her reply of 1 January 1948 the single review she had seen. *Essays Presented to Charles Williams* was reviewed by Renée Haynes as 'Memorial Searchlights' in *Time and Tide*, 28 (20 December 1947), p. 1370. Barfield's essay was singled out for special praise: 'The most exciting, profound and stimulating of this brilliant group of essays . . . is Mr Owen Barfield's "Poetic Diction and Legal Fiction" which, drawing a parallel between "the paradoxical relation of language to consciousness", explores the very springs of thought.'

136 Dr C. M. Bajetta, who translated this letter into English from the holograph in the possession of Dr Lodetti, provided a note: 'Born at Avio (near Trento, Italy) on 22 June 1921, Dr. Romolo Lodetti had, at that time, just earned his degree in Medicine from the University of Padua and was under the spiritual direction of Don Calabria. After his reading of the Italian translation of *The Screwtape Letters*, he resolved to write to Lewis, being impressed, as he wrote in 1984, by Lewis's "penetrating social and spiritual analysis" of contemporary society: "I wrote complimenting him for his book, but at the same time I felt naturally bound to express my profoundest desire that he would make steps towards the Catholic Church." Lodetti did not consult Calabria (whom he had met as early as 1943) either before or after writing to Lewis. He never wrote to Lewis again: "I considered myself happy with and comforted by the beautiful letter I had received, and I left the rest to Divine Providence – after all, I was at the time quite engaged in social activities and at the beginning of my medical profession." Dr. Lodetti, who has long been a member of the administrative council of the Province of Verona, still lives in that city, where he continues his medical and

nos omnes per unitatem caritatis, virtutis, necnon (fortasse) communionem pro Domino passionum, tandem in diu optatam unitatem doctrinae perventuros esse. Maxime gaudeo Christianum medicum (quae fides in illa arte rara est) salutare. Vale, conservus tuus in Jesu.

C. S. Lewis

In Vigil. Sanctae Circumcisionis Domini.

*

Magdalen College,
Oxford.
Dec. 31. 1947

Dearest Brother,

Since I have little knowledge of modern Italian, allow me to thank you in Latin for your kind letter. Let us pray for each other, and hope that we may all – through the unity of Charity, of Virtue and also (perhaps) through the communion of our sufferings for the Lord – come at last to the long-hoped-for unity of doctrine.[137]

I am very pleased to send my best wishes to a Christian physician (given that faith is rare in that profession).

I am your fellow-servant in Jesus[138]

Written on the eve of the Holy Circumcision of the Lord

C. S. Lewis

---

philosophical research (see his multi-volume *Il corpo umano: per un raccordo mente-corpo-società*, Rome: Edizioni Dehoniane, 1990– in progress. An updated edition of his biography of Calabria has been published as *I fioretti di Don Calabria: episodi, fatti, incontri, dialoghi* (Rome: Edizioni Dehoniane, 1994).'

137 Cf. Ephesians 4:13; where Paul speaks of 'unitatem fidei' (the King James Version is 'till we all come in the unity of the faith'), Lewis has 'unitatem doctrinae'.

138 For this final salutation see Colossians 4:7; Revelation 19:10, 22:9.

TO RHONA BODLE (B):[139]

[Magdalen College,
Oxford]
Dec 31, 1947

Dear Miss Bodle –

I think it possible that what is keeping you from belief in Christ's Divinity is your apparently strong desire to believe. If you don't think it true why do you *want* to believe it? If you *do* think it true, then you believe it already. So I wd. recommend less anxiety about the whole question. You believe in God and trust Him. Well, you can trust Him about this. If you go on steadily praying and attempting to obey the best light He had given you, can you not rely on Him to guide you into any further truth He wishes you to know? Or even if He leaves you all your life in doubt, can't you believe that He sees that to be the best state for you?

I *don't* mean by this that you should cease to study and make enquiries: but that you shd. make them not with frantic desire but with cheerful curiosity and a humble readiness to accept whatever conclusions God may lead you to. (But always, all depends on the steady attempt to obey God all the time. 'He who *does* the will of the Father shall know of the doctrine').[140]

As for books, the v. best popular defence of the full Christian position I know is G. K. Chesterton *The Everlasting Man*. Mascall *The God-Man* might also help.

It is only fair to tell you that my impression is that you are in fact v. much nearer to belief in Christ than you suppose: and that if you really face the opposite view tranquilly (and why be afraid of it unless

---

139 Rhona Bodle was born and brought up in New Zealand. She came to England in 1947 to study the education of deaf children, and taught at Oakdene, a boarding school for girls in Burgess Hill, Sussex. She became interested in Christianity, but could not believe that Christ was God. This led her to read *Broadcast Talks*, *Christian Behaviour* and *Beyond Personality*, and soon afterwards to write to Lewis. In 1950–1 she trained in the Department of Education for the Deaf at Manchester University, after which she taught at Manchester School for the Deaf. Returning to New Zealand in 1952, she taught at the School for the Deaf at Titarangi, Auckland. When she gave her letters from Lewis to the Bodleian Library in 1972 she prepared explanatory notes to accompany them (Bodleian Library, MS. Eng. lett. c. 200/4).

140 John 7:17.

you already know in your bones that the Christian view is true) you will find you don't really believe it – i.e. don't really believe that all you have got out of the books you mention is based on an illusion – wh., if an illusion *at all*, must be a most blasphemous and horrible one. Conversions happen in all sorts of different ways: some sharp & catastrophic (like St Paul, St Augustine, or Bunyan) some v. gradual and intellectual (like my own). No good predicting how God will deal with one: He has His own way with each of us. So don't worry. Continue all your efforts. You are being *steered* by Another: you've only got to row – and therefore the future journey is behind your back.

I'm pretty sure where you'll land, myself, and you will then wonder how you ever doubted it. But you needn't keep looking over your shoulder too often. Keep your eye on the Helmsman, keep your conscience bright and your brain clear and believe that you are in good hands. (No one can *make* himself believe anything and the effort does harm. Nor make himself *feel* anything, and that effort also does harm. What *is* under our own control is action and intellectual inquiry. Stick to that). All good wishes.

Yours sincerely
C. S. Lewis

TO WALDEN HOWARD (W): TS

REF.739/47.

Magdalen College,
Oxford.
31st December 1947.

Dear Mr. Howard,

But Chesterton (whom I love) has done it: I could only water his wine. And the young people won't read Chesterton. I don't think they like paradox. They're all as grave as a government paper now – rot them!

yours very sincerely,
C. S. Lewis

TO MISS H. D. CALKINS (W):[141]

Ref. 740/47.

Magdalen College,
Oxford.
31st December 1947.

Dear Miss Calkins,

Thanks for your most interesting (and amusing) letter. With all good wishes,

yours sincerely,
C. S. Lewis

sorry![142]

141 Miss Calkins was writing from Hutching's Girls High School, 7 Phayse Road, Poona Cantonment, India.

142 He pointed with an arrow to an inkblot.

1948

TO RHONA BODLE (BOD):

[Magdalen College,
Oxford]
3/1/48

Dear Miss Bodle –

I v. much doubt if I'm good enough at prayer myself to advise others. First thing in the morning and last thing at night are good times but I don't find that they are the best times for one's main prayer. I prefer sometime in the early evening, before one has got sleepy – but of course it depends on how your day is mapped out.

'Grudging' tho' a nuisance need not depress us too much. It is the act of *will* (perhaps strongest where there is some disinclination to contend against) that God values, rather than the state of our emotions – the act being what we give Him, the emotions what He gives us (usually, I think, indirectly thro' the state of our body, health etc., tho' there are direct kindlings from Him too. There are *presents*, to be given thanks for but never counted on).

Of course it is very difficult to keep God only before one for more than a few seconds. Our minds are in ruins before we bring them to Him & the rebuilding is gradual. It may help to *practice* concentration on other objects twice a week quite apart from ones prayer: i.e. sit down looking at some physical object (say, a flower) and try for a few minutes to attend exclusively to it, *quietly* (never impatiently) rejecting the train of thought & imagination wh. keep starting up. All good wishes.

Yours sincerely
C. S. Lewis

TO EDWARD A. ALLEN (W):[1] TS

REF.48/18.

Magdalen College,
Oxford.
3rd. January 1948

My dear Mr. Allen,

The excellent parcel which you so kindly sent me on 23rd. November has just come to hand in good condition, and its contents are all that one could desire. How am I to thank you for your continued kindness to me? I can only repeat what I said before, that I am most deeply sensible of it. Times seem to get worse instead of better, and such gifts are a godsend, not only to the consumer, but to the unfortunate domestic caterer.

With all best wishes for 1948,
yours gratefully,
C.S.Lewis

TO JILL FLEWETT (T):

[Magdalen College,
Oxford]
Jan 7/48

My dear June –

(1) Alas, alas! I had some days ago a most disquieting letter from Barfield. It appears probable (tho' not yet certain) that the Govt. is going to disallow the Deed[2] and come on me for income tax for all the money that's gone into it. This does not mean bankruptcy but does mean that at the very best there will only be a very few hundreds left: enough for fivers and tenners to charities and hard cases but nothing at all like what I was able to do before. As I say, this is not certain. If the better alternative shd. still be realised of course I'll let you know.

1 Edward A. Allen and his mother, Mrs Belle Allen, lived at 173 Highland Avenue, Westfield, Massachusetts, and over the years they became pen-friends of the Lewis brothers. Warnie not only typed most of these letters, but largely composed them as well.

2 Lewis was referring to the Agapony fund Owen Barfield had set up in 1941. In a letter to Walter Hooper of 27 January 2003, Lady Freud explained: 'I had written to Jack asking if he could help with college fees for a friend of mine from his Deed of Covenant whereby all royalties from his religious books were given to help with education & did not thereby accrue tax. It was by this means that he paid all my Rada fees for the 2 years of my course.'

It's the devil and all having raised false hopes in poor S.S.[3] As there's nothing confidential about the facts (indeed the more people know about our rulers' anti-charity campaign, the better) you'd best just tell him the whole thing or show him this letter. Hard luck on you too!

(2) Yes I have both the de Rougemont books, the first in the original French edition wh. he sent me.[4] The moral part in the last chapter is excellent but don't you believe a word of what he says about medieval literary history: he has no idea of what evidence is at all.

Well – sorry and ashamed. All the best: we're all going to your film[5] on Friday i.e. Dyson, W. and me.

Yours
Jack Lewis

TO EDWARD A. ALLEN (W): TS

REF.48/18.

Magdalen College,
Oxford.
7th January 1948.

My dear Mr. Allen,

I shall of course give myself the pleasure of writing to your sister, but I should feel churlish if I did not also write to you in reply to your exceedingly kind letter of the 9th December; the knowledge that there is yet another parcel of good things in the 'pipe line' has cheered us up very considerably. Indeed such kindness has its embarrassing side; one can but repeat 'thank you' in various terms, and how cold it looks as an expression of the very deep gratitude which we all feel.

May I say how much I appreciate your 'act of faith'? This goes to the root of the matter I feel: but I must not enlarge on the subject and thus give away to you my gross ignorance of the ABC of international trade!

With very many thanks and all good wishes.

yours gratefully,
C. S. Lewis

---

3 James Seth-Smith (b. 1923) came to know Jill through an interest in the theatre. He is now a journalist using the name James Brabazon. He has published biographies of *Albert Schweitzer* (1975) and *Dorothy L. Sayers* (1981).

4 Denis de Rougemont, *L'Amour et l'Occident* (1939); *Talk of the Devil* (*La Part du Diable*), trans. Kathleen Raine (1945).

5 i.e. *The Woman in the Hall.*

TO DON GIOVANNI CALABRIA (V):

Magdalen College
Oxford
Jan 13th 1948

Dilectissime Pater,

Grato animo accepi salutationes tuas et vota tua. 'Prosint omina' scripsisti et re vera omina fuisse invenio. Nuper enim (quamquam externa meae vitae conditio in melius non mutata est) placuit Domino tranquilitatem magnam, immo hilaritatem, in meum animum infundere. Gratias ago cum timore, quippe qui in mente infixam teneam illam salubrem sententiam in libro *De Imitatione Christi* 'memento in gratia quid sine gratia sis'. Utinam in aeternam constantiam sine vicissitudinis umbrâ pervenissemus!

Octavam instare precum non ignorabam et valde probo. Pro Gallia nuper servata ex tantis tam corporalibus quam spiritualibus periculis gratias agamus. In quotidianis meis orationibus locum semper habes, et medicus quidam Lodetti Veronensis qui nuper fraterna epistola me confortavit. Fortasse vir tibi notus.

Vale, care pater, et semper memoriam facias tui conservi in Christo
C. S. Lewis

*

Magdalen College
Oxford
Jan 13th 1948

Dearest Father,

Thank you for your salutations and your good wishes. 'May the omens be favourable' you have written; and I find that in truth there have been good omens. For recently (although the outward condition of my life has not changed for the better) it has pleased God to pour into my soul great tranquillity – I may even say gaiety. I give thanks not without apprehension as one who keeps firmly in mind that salutary observation in *The Imitation of Christ* 'remember in Grace what you would be without Grace'.[6] Would that we had attained to everlasting constancy with no shadow of turning![7]

6 Thomas à Kempis, *The Imitation of Christ*, III, vii, 3.

7 James 1:17: 'Every good gift and every perfect gift is from above, and cometh down from the Father of lights, with whom is no variableness, neither shadow of turning.'

I was not unaware of the approaching Octave, of Prayers for Unity,[8] and I strongly approve of it.

For France, recently saved from such dangers, alike physical and spiritual, let us give thanks.

In my daily prayers you have ever a place and with you a certain physician Dr Lodetti of Verona who recently encouraged me in a brotherly letter. Perhaps he is known to you. Farewell, dear Father, and may you ever make remembrance of

Your fellow servant in Christ

C. S. Lewis

TO ROY W. HARRINGTON (W):[9]

[Magdalen College,
Oxford]
Jan 19th 1948

Dear Mr Harrington –

Thanks for your most kind letter and for sending me the sermon. About 'back-ground material': the only thing of any importance (if that is) about me is what I have to say. Ought you, as a Pastor, to encourage the public demand for quite irrelevant facts about authors?

At any rate I'm no good at all at that kind of thing. My conversion was much too gradual and intellectual to be described briefly or even interestingly. I haven't got any hobbies. If I have any suppressed desires *ex vi termini*[10] I couldn't know about them. The 'incentive' for my books has always been the usual one – an idea and then an itch or lust to write (as your own Marion Crawford said 'Ink is the most habit-forming of all stimulants'). The one I enjoyed writing least was *Screwtape*: what I enjoyed most was *Perelandra* – but, you see, it all comes to nothing. And don't, on your life, draw on the article in *Time*:[11] which went near to curing me of ever replying to such questions at all.

I hope all this doesn't sound ungracious, it is not meant to be. In

8 The annual Week of Prayer for Christian Unity, now observed worldwide, began in 1908 at the Episcopal Church at Graymoor, New York under the priesthood of Paul James Wattson.

9 The Rev. Roy W. Harrington's address was given as Third and N. Locust Streets, Reedsbury, Wisconsin.

10 'from the force of the term'.

11 Lewis was pictured on the cover of *Time* magazine (8 September 1947), which contained an article entitled 'Oxford's C. S. Lewis. His heresy: Christianity'.

fact I am only revealing what you asked for, one of my favourite 'peeves'. I can't abide the idea that a man's books shd. be 'set in their biographical context' and if I had some rare information about the private life of Shakespeare or Dante I'd throw it in the fire, tell no one, and re-read their works. All this biographical interest is only a device for indulging in gossip as an excuse for not reading what the chaps *say*, wh. is their only real claim on our attention. (I here resist a wild impulse to *invent* some really exciting background – that I am an illegitimate son of Edward VII, married to a chimpanzee, was rescued from the practice of magic by a Russian monk and always eat eggs with the shells on).

If you care to risk loss and damage in the post of course I'll sign any book you like: but if you'd ever seen the inefficiency with wh. I put up parcels you certainly wouldn't.

All good wishes. Sorry for handwriting – I have rheumatism.

Yours sincerely
C. S. Lewis

TO WALDEN HOWARD (W): TS

REF.48/83.

Magdalen College,
Oxford.
20th. January 1948.

Dear Mr. Howard,

This is really very handsome of you, and you could hardly have sent a more welcome gift. I have only to call your attention to the so-called 'Superfine' paper on which I am replying to give you some idea of the luxury of writing on a decent paper at last.

But I'm afraid there is something which even American generosity cannot supply me with: an article called TIME, which was the cause of my previous letter! (its brevity I mean)

yours gratefully,
C. S. Lewis

TO DR WARFIELD M. FIROR (BOD): TS

REF.48/97.

Magdalen College,
Oxford.
22nd January 1948.

My dear Dr. Firor,

Your continued goodness to me becomes positively embarrassing, and I don't know how to thank you; another huge food parcel containing all sorts of good things has just arrived in excellent condition, and how very welcome it is, you can imagine yourself. The parcel is undated, but for purposes of identification I may mention that it contains Plum Pudding, chocolates, jelly, chicken, sardines, lard, syrup, and butter. (It makes ones mouth water even to type it)!

With very many thanks and all good wishes for 1948,

yours gratefully,
C. S. Lewis

TO DR WARFIELD M. FIROR (BOD): TS

REF.48/97.

Magdalen College,
Oxford.
24th January 1948.

My dear Dr. Firor,

What on earth am I to say to you? On Thursday I wrote to you in acknowledgement of an excellent parcel, and today I find myself faced with the task of thanking you for another one, and that a ham no less! No one ever sees a ham these days over here, and even in a good restaurant it is very rarely that you would get a small slice of ham. I shall probably be known in Oxford for months as 'the man who got the ham from America'! Believe me, I am very heartily thankful to you for your great kindness.

yours gratefully,
C. S. Lewis

TO EDWARD A. ALLEN (W): TS

REF.48/18.

Magdalen College,
Oxford.
27th January 1948.

My dear Mr. Allen,

I am quite at a loss for words in which to acknowledge your

continued (I might almost say 'continuous') kindness to me. Your excellent parcel of 22nd November 1947 has just come in, with all its contents in good condition: and very valuable to us they all will be, in view of the rainy day which is rapidly approaching. Cheerful optimists tell me that if the Marshall Plan[12] doesn't go through, our meat ration will be three pence per week.

Once, more, with heartiest thanks, believe me,

yours gratefully,

C. S. Lewis

TO EDWARD A. ALLEN (W): TS

REF.48/18.

Magdalen College,
Oxford.
29th January 1948.

My dear Mr. Allen,

I just don't know what to say in answer to your letter of 23rd January. One, two, perhaps even three parcels can be inadequately but not entirely unsuitably acknowledged, but what is one to say when bombarded with a non-stop stream of kindnesses? Nothing has in my time made such a profound impression in this country as the amazing outburst of individual American generosity which has followed on the disclosure of our economic situation. (I say nothing of *government* action, because naturally this strikes the 'man in the street' much less obviously). The length of time which a parcel takes to cross the Atlantic is a significant indication of the volume of food which must be pouring into England.

As regards the 'Tuxedo' – 'dinner jacket' here, 'le smoking' in Paris – if it does'nt fit me, it will certainly fit one of my friends, and will save some grateful man a year's clothing coupons: and at least £25 cash.

As regards things to send – *don't* send any of that 66 million tons of snow, thanks very much! We still shudder when we think of last

12 The Marshall Plan was named after George Catlett Marshall (1880–1959), US Secretary of State, 1947–9. The Second World War had left the people of Europe hungry and miserable and the economies of most European countries in ruin. By 1947 a worldwide crisis threatened and Marshall proposed a programme of reconstruction, to be set up by the European nations with the assistance of the United States. The Marshall Plan came into effect in April 1948 and over a four-year period the American government appropriated $13.3 billion for European recovery. In 1953 Marshall was awarded the Nobel Peace Prize.

winter.[13] A packet or two of envelopes are almost always welcome; a small thing, but the constant shortage of them becomes very irritating to a busy man after a time. With heartiest thanks for all your great kindness, and best good wishes,

Yours sincerely,

C. S. Lewis

TO VERA MATHEWS (W): TS

Ref. 48/45.

Magdalen College,
Oxford.
7th February 1948

Dear Mrs. Matthews,

Many thanks for your most kind letter of the 3rd: – Letters are unsatisfactory things, and like you, I hope, though for a different reason, we may meet – my reason being that I want to tell you how much I appreciate your great kindness.

yours gratefully,

C. S. Lewis

TO OWEN BARFIELD (W):

[The Kilns]
18/2/48

My dear Barfield –

It was a grand evening: if only we cd. all get back into a state of life where such evenings were more frequent. I look forward to seeing your poem in type as soon as possible – it is not the kind (Cecil's is) that can be fully appreciated when read aloud: but *very* interesting and leads one to hope great things.

There's no chance of my doing anything about the 'virgin senate'[14] in the new future: but even if I cd., I feel that my power to do harm

13 The British winter of 1947 was one of the coldest since records began in 1740. Between 22 January and 17 March snow fell every day somewhere in Britain, and the temperature rarely rose more than a degree or two above freezing.

14 Lewis is quoting the twelfth-century *jeu d'esprit*, *Concilium in Monte Romarici*, a portion of which he translated in his discussion of 'Courtly Love' in *The Allegory of Love*, p. 18: 'When the virgin senate all/Had filled the benches of the hall,/Doctor Ovid's Rule instead/Of the evangelists was read.'

in that quarter is much greater than my power to do good. I enclose D.D.[15]

Yours
C.S.L.

TO EDWARD A. ALLEN (W): TS

REF.48/18.

Magdalen College,
Oxford.
26th February 1948.

My dear Mr. Allen,

You have only got to have a good look at the superfine paper I am using to see how very welcome your kind gift will be. Thank you very much indeed. I'm so glad you did'nt even contemplate using air mail: what a price!

I don't share your fears about the 6 ft. stevedore, for I find that this business of parcels for Europe is being handled with wonderful efficiency; admittedly they take a long time in transit, but that merely shows the astonishing volume of stuff American generosity is pouring into England: and I have yet to hear of a case of a parcel being tampered with. The Customs regulations are a deep and dark mystery; sometimes there is something to pay, sometimes nothing: and no apparent logic about the affair.

With all best wishes and very hearty thanks,

yours sincerely,
C. S. Lewis

TO EDWARD A. ALLEN (W): TS

Magdalen College,
Oxford.
28th February 1948.

My dear Mr. Allen,

P.S. Here's an odd coincidence. Before the time came for my letters to go to the post today, there arrived a magnificent parcel from you, posted on 24th January: no doubt that referred to in your letter of 23rd January, though I have not had the pleasure of opening it yet. A

15 i.e. a copy of the poem 'Donkey's Delight'. See the letter to Ruth Pitter of 6 July 1947.

pleasure which will considerably brighten a grim week end, for the European news is worse than ever. Russia, having made a meal of the Czechs this week, is apparently about to dine off Finland next.[16] But the situation does'nt bear thinking about.

How am I to thank you for your constant kindness? The answer appears to be that it is not possible, and that you must just take my word for it that I am still

most gratefully yours,
C. S. Lewis

TO DR WARFIELD M. FIROR (BOD): TS

REF.48/97. Magdalen College,
Oxford.
2nd March 1948.

My dear Dr. Firor,

The arrival of that magnificent ham leaves me just not knowing what to say. If it were known that it was in my house, it would draw every housebreaker in the neighbourhood more surely than would a collection of gold plate! Even in your favoured country its intrinsic value must have been considerable, and over here it is beyond valuing. I can only repeat, as I have so often and gladly done before, that I am very deeply grateful to you for your great kindness.

With all best wishes,

yours sincerely,
C. S. Lewis

TO EDWARD A. ALLEN (W): TS

REF.48/18. Magdalen College,
Oxford.
10th March 1948.

My dear Mr. Allen,

You will be surprised at getting two letters from me in the same envelope, but the explanation is that your letter of 21st February came

16 Following the Second World War non-aligned Czechoslovakia made the mistake of allying itself with Russia. In February 1948 the Communists carried out a coup, arresting the Czech leaders and installing the leader of the Czech Communist Party. Finland managed to avoid a similar coup by signing a Treaty of Friendship, Cooperation and Mutual Assistance with Russia in April 1948.

in before the post went out. As regards the parcels, I make it *four*, not three. Can I have acknowledged the same one twice? Or – as is more likely – is your generosity so prodigal that you have *forgotten* how many you sent? I cannot now produce the labels, but certainly my letter book shows that I thanked you for parcels on 3rd January, 7th January, 27th January, and 29th January.

On 7th January I had the pleasure of writing to Mrs. Gaynor to thank her for her kindness, but from the way you write now, it rather looks as if the letter never reached her: which is awkward, for if she *has* had my letter, and I now write again, it might seem like a hint that I thought it about time she was sending me another! I wonder could you find out whether she ever heard from me?

I am almost ashamed to hear that there is yet another parcel on the way, for how can I thank you for it? I can only assure you of our continued and very hearty gratitude, and offer you all my best wishes.

yours gratefully,
C. S. Lewis

P.S. The contents seem to me to be all that one could want. Not one person in a thousand would have thought of the tin of lemon juice!

TO VERA MATHEWS (W): TS

REF.48/145.

Magdalen College,
Oxford.
10th March 1948.

My dear Mrs. Mathews,

Your beautiful parcel, posted (I suppose) on 3rd. February has just reached me safely. And I need hardly tell you what joy it has given to all concerned. Coming as it did when the future looks blacker than ever, it was a heartening reminder of the good friends we have in your country: and this feeling that we have sympathazers is one which we cherish in these times when life is pretty grim.

The condition of the parcel was excellent, and it will improve the appearance of my larder by about fifty per cent.

With my heartiest thanks for your kindness, and all good wishes,

yours gratefully,
C. S. Lewis

TO WARFIELD M. FIROR (BOD): TS

REF.48/97.

Magdalen College,
Oxford.
12th March 1948.

My dear Dr. Firor,

Though I have already written to thank you for your grand present of the ham, that letter was written before tasting it: and now having done so, I feel that common decency demands further and heartier thanks.

The fate of the ham was this: we have a small informal literary club which meets in my rooms every Thursday for beer and talk, and – in happier times – for an occasional dinner. And last night, having your ham to dine off, we had a meal which eight members attended. By diligent 'scraping the bottom of the barrel' in various colleges we got two bottles of burgundy and two of port: the college kitchen supplied soup, fish and a savoury: and we had a delightful evening. This by English standards is a banquet rarely met with, and all agreed that they had'nt eaten such a dinner for five years or more.

I enclose a little souvenir of the occasion which may amuse you.[17]

With our very best thanks for all the happiness you gave us,

yours Ham-icably,

C. S. Lewis

As some have not v. legible signatures, I had better say the list runs; C. S. Lewis, H. V. Dyson, Lord David Cecil, W. H. Lewis, C. Hardie, C. R. Tolkien, R. E. Havard, J. R. R. Tolkien. The *order* is just as we happened to be sitting. Tolkien *père* is the senior and T. *fils* the baby.

---

17 On the 'Ham Testimonial' (p. 839) Lewis wrote 'The undersigned, having just partaken of your ham, have drunk your health.' There follow the signatures of the Inklings present at the occasion, accompanied by their titles, explanations of what they did in the Army and their positions at the University. (Bodleian Library, MS. Eng. Lett. C.220/1, fol. 86.)

11/3/48

The undersigned, having just partaken of your ham, have drunk your health:

C. S. Lewis. Fellow of Magdalen, sometime scholar of University College, late 13th Light Infantry

H. V. D. Dyson Fellow of Merton College, Lecturer of University College, University Lecturer in English Literature. ~~Formerly~~ sometime Commoner of Exeter College. Queen's Own Royal West Kent Regt 1915-19.

David Cecil Fellow of New College – ex-Fellow of Wadham College – University Lecturer in English Literature. Commoner of Christ Church.

W. H. Lewis. Royal Military College, Sandhurst, Regular Army 1914–1932, World War II 1939–45. Major, Retired pay.

Colin Hardie Fellow and Tutor in Classics of Magdalen College University Lecturer in Greek and Latin Literature, formerly Director of the British School at Rome, and Fellow, Scholar & Exhibitioner of Balliol College Secretary of the Oxford Dante Society (founded 1876) Sector Warden A.R.P. service. Oxford.

Christopher Reuel Tolkien ∴ B.A. ∴ Undergraduate, of Trinity College ∴ [late R.A.F. & R.N.V.R.] ∴

R Emlyn Havard M.A. D.M. Oxon. B.A. Cantab. late Scholar in Research Fellow University of Oxford, late Lecturer in Physiology Guys Hospital; Demonstrator in Biochemistry University of Oxford, late Surgeon R.N.V.R.

John Ronald Reuel Tolkien M.A. Merton Professor of English Language & Literature, late Professor of Anglo-Saxon (Pembroke College), and exhibitioner of Exeter College, and of the Lancashire Fusiliers (1914–8) and father of the above-named C.R.T.

TO EDWARD A. ALLEN (W): TS

REF.48/18.

Magdalen College,
Oxford.
18th March 1948.

My dear Mr. Allen,

Your kindness to me is so continuous that my secretary now does'nt have to look up your address in the letter book: and I am really ashamed to examine it to see how many parcels I have had from you!

The latest, a stock of stationary posted on 14th February, has just reached me in good condition, and is very very welcome, for the shortage of writing material is, if not one of the most serious, at least one of the most annoying to a busy man. One sees easily why there is a shortage when one noticed a paragraph in the papers that last years stationary bill for one of the govt. departments was £11,000,000!

Believe me, I am very grateful to you for all your goodness to me. With all best wishes,

yours sincerely,
C. S. Lewis

TO WALDEN HOWARD (W): TS

REF.48/248.

Magdalen College,
Oxford.
18th March 1948.

Dear Mr. Howard,

Your very kind gift of stationary, posted on 16th. January, has just reached me in good condition, and I am most grateful for it. It was not only kind, but thoughtful to select such a present, for, whilst of course lack of paper is not our most serious shortage, it is one of the most irritating. And one which the public suspects to be largely unecessary: if our various government departments would *do* more and send out fewer forms, appeals, posters, pamphlets etc., we should get along better I think.

With sincere thanks for your kindness and all good wishes,

yours sincerely,
C. S. Lewis

TO VERA MATHEWS (W): TS

Ref. 48/145.

Magdalen College,
Oxford.
19th March 1948.

My dear Miss Mathews,

Your letter of the 9th. had not prepared me for the magnificent parcel which arrived yesterday; gosh, *what* a present![18] I really don't know how to thank you for it. I wonder do you realize that – so far as I can judge – it represents eight weeks butter rations alone! And as for the bacon, I don't suppose you'd find a piece that size anywhere in the kingdom, outside a grocer's shop. Everything so far as I can see is in as perfect condition as if it had just been bought next door. So far I have sampled the eggs only, and the one I had today was delicious. Your kindness is going to give very deep pleasure to several people, and I assure you I am most grateful to you for it; such treats as these make a very big difference in a somewhat drab existance.

Again very many thanks.

yours sincerely,
C. S. Lewis

TO DOM BEDE GRIFFITHS OSB (W):

[Magdalen College,
Oxford]
25/3/48

My dear Dom Bede –

It was, as always, a delight to hear from you. I think the *essential* difference between Magic and Miracle (leaving out the accidental difference that Magic is usually by means of evil spirits) is that Magic is held to work more or less automatically whereas Miracle is an answer to prayer. Now prayer is a species of request: and the essence of request, whether to God or to a human superior, is that it may or may not be granted, and the essence of faithful and humble Christian prayer is that

---

18 Mathews wrote to Lewis on 18 March 1948: 'Two food parcels have been sent you from here – one on January 7, and another February 3, but to recompense in a measure for the long delay in reaching you, I've placed an order with Marshal Ellis, Ltd. The contents will be sent air-mail, and were chosen from one of their standard assortments: fresh eggs, butter and bacon' (Bodleian Library, MS. Facs. c. 47, fol. 141).

the petitioner is willing that it shd. not be granted ('Nevertheless not as I will but as Thou wilt').[19]

In Magic, on the other hand, I take it that the Magician expects the ceremonial to produce the result by a sort of necessity. Thus, even if there were a real 'white' magic it wd. still be on a lower level than prayer, and not involving a personal relation and the affections but only a skill or technique. Of course the powers of Our Lord, and the possible powers of unfallen Adam, are in rather a different category from either. Magic wd. be the artificial and local recovery of what Adam enjoyed normally: wh. makes a difference. If Our Lord did His miracles *quâ* God and not *quâ* Man then the difference wd. be even greater. (Shakespeare's control over events in the *Tempest* is different in kind from Prospero's)

About the East, and the need for the East in Christendom (to make a full man, the middle wall of the partition being cast down) I agree. Only I wd. make a trichotomy not a dichotomy for I take the Chinese ethos to be at least as different from the Indian as either is from the Western

I'd love to get over & lunch but my present domestic job ('to rock the cradle of declining age')[20] keeps me a prisoner for the middle part of every day. I don't know how to address you in your new *praelatia*: let me know. *Oremus semper pro invicem.*

Yours
C. S. Lewis

TO DON GIOVANNI CALABRIA (V):

Magdalen College
Oxford
27/3/48

Dilectissime Pater

Epistolam tuam plenam (ut soles) caritate grato animo accepi. Dura et inquieta sunt omnia – bella et rumores belli – fortasse non *hora novissima* sed certi *tempora pessima*. Attamen Apostolus iterum atque iterum jubet 'gaudete'. Ipsa naturalis mundi facies jam vere novo renovata proprio modo suo idem jubet. Credo homines hujus aetatis

---

19 Matthew 26:39.
20 See note 103 to the letter of 3 November 1947.

(et inter eos te, pater, et me) nimium cogitare de gentium statu, de rerum saecularium summa. Nonne monet nos auctor *Imitationis* ne nimis implicemur talibus rebus? Non reges, non senatores sumus. Caveamus ne dum frustra de Europae fato cruciamur negligamus aut Veronam aut Oxoniam. In paupere qui ad meam portam pulsat, in matre aegrotante, in juvene qui consilium meum petit, ipse Dominus adest: ergo ejus pedes lavemus. Semper credidi recte sentire illum infidelem Voltaire dum monet *Hortum tuum exerce*: necnon Gulielmum Dunbar (Scoticum poetam qui XVmo saeculo floruit) dum dicit 'vir, place Creatori tuo, et hilari esto animo; totum vero hunc mundum unius aestimemus assis'. Cras celebrabimus gloriosam Christi resurrectionem: tui in sacra communione memor ero. Abeste lacrimae, timores, taedia! Natura nostra cum ipsa Deitate aeterno conjugio adunata in caelum caelorum ascendit. Adhuc nos 'miseros' vocare impietatis esset. Immo, HOMO est creatura cui inviderent angeli si invidere possint. Sursum corda: *forsan et haec olim meminisse juvabit.*

Pro *litania* ista a Cardinale Merry composita, multas gratias ago. Non sciebas omnes temptationes contra quas preces fundit mihi nimium et diu cognitas esse? Desiderio di essere stimato . . . timore di essere rifiutato . . . uhé, compungis me!

Semper oremus pro invicem. Vale.

C. S. Lewis

*

Magdalen College
Oxford
27/3/48

Dearest Father,

I was glad to receive your letter – so full (as is your wont) of Charity.

Everywhere things are troubling and uneasy – wars and rumours of war: perhaps not the final hour but certainly times most evil.

Nevertheless, the Apostle again and again bids us 'Rejoice'.[21]

Nature herself bids us do so, the very face of the earth being now renewed, after its own manner, at the start of Spring.

I believe that the men of this age (and among them you Father, and myself) think too much about the state of nations and the situation of

21 Philippians 4:4: 'Rejoice in the Lord alway: and again I say, Rejoice.'

the world. Does not the author of *The Imitation* warn us against involving ourselves too much with such things?[22]

We are not kings, we are not senators. Let us beware lest, while we torture ourselves in vain about the state of Europe, we neglect either Verona or Oxford.

In the poor man who knocks at my door, in my ailing mother, in the young man who seeks my advice, the Lord Himself is present: therefore let us wash His feet.

I have always believed that Voltaire, infidel though he was, thought aright in that admonition of his to cultivate your own garden: likewise William Dunbar (the Scottish poet who flourished in the 15th century) when he said

> *Man, please thy Maker and be merry;*
> *This whole world rate we at a penny!*[23]

Tomorrow we shall celebrate the glorious Resurrection of Christ. I shall be remembering you in the Holy Communion. Away with tears and fears and troubles! United in wedlock with the eternal Godhead Itself, our nature ascends into the Heaven of Heavens. So it would be impious to call ourselves 'miserable'. On the contrary, Man is a creature whom the Angels – were they capable of envy – would envy. Let us lift up our hearts![24] 'At some future time perhaps even these things it will be a joy to recall.'[25]

For the Litany composed by Cardinal Merry many thanks.[26] You did

---

22 Thomas à Kempis, *The Imitation of Christ*, I, xxi, 11: 'Do not busy yourself with the affairs of others, nor concern yourself with the policies of your superiors.'

23 William Dunbar, *Poems*, ed. James Kinsley (Oxford: Clarendon Press, 1979), no. 68, 'Cuvetyce', p. 191: 'Man, pleis thy makar and be mirry,/And sett not by this warld a chirry.' Lewis adapted the detail of the last line so as to use a Latin phrase from Catullus, poem 5, line 3.

24 'Lift up your hearts' is said in the Preface to the Mass, and is found in the *Book of Common Prayer*.

25 Virgil, *Aeneid*, I, 203.

26 Cardinal Rafael Merry del Val (1865–1930) was educated in England, where he resided for some time at different periods in his career. He acted for some years as private chamberlain to Pope Leo XIII, and was appointed president of the Academia Pontificia in 1899, and Italian Archbishop of Nicosia in 1900. On the death of Leo XIII, he was nominated consistorial secretary, and in 1903 he became Secretary of State to Pope Pius X. Don Calabria had sent Lewis a copy of Cardinal Merry del Val's 'Litanie dell'Umiltà' ('Litany of Humility'), which is reprinted in *Una Gioia Insolita*, pp. 259–60.

not know, did you, that all the temptations against which he pours forth these prayers I have long been exceeding conscious of? *Desiderio di essere stimato . . . timore di essere rifiutato*[27] . . . *Touché*, you pink me!

Let us pray for each other always. Farewell.

C. S. Lewis

TO WARFIELD M. FIROR (BOD): TS

REF.48/97.

Magdalen College,
Oxford.
29th March 1948.

My dear Dr. Firor,

I give it up! I'm beat! My command of the English tongue is insufficient to go on thanking you for your apparently interminable kindness to me. Another enormous parcel has just arrived from you, marked by 'Air Mail'. I have not yet given myself the pleasure of opening it, but if I may judge by the weight, you must have chartered a special plane to carry it over the ocean. But seriously, how is a man to thank you? I can only repeat what I have said so often before, that I am very moved by your goodness, and heartily grateful to you for it.

With all thanks and best wishes,

yours gratefully,
C. S. Lewis

P.S. Some time ago you were kind enough to ask for suggestions for gift parcels. I'll give you one. Put yourself and a ham in the state room of an East bound liner, and come and eat it with us in Magdalen. If you do, you will get the warmest welcome that an impoverished community can give you.

TO VERA MATHEWS (W): TS

Ref. 48/145.

Magdalen College,
Oxford.
29th March 1948.

Dear Miss Mathews,

For the latest token of your continued kindness to me, I owe you not only hearty thanks, but an even heartier apology. I refer to your

27 Del Val, 'Litany of Humility': 'Longing to be thought well of . . . fear of being rejected'.

splendid parcel posted on 9th. January. When it was delivered I don't know, but by some accident was not placed in the usual spot where my mail is left, and in consequence I did'nt discover it until Saturday. You will I'm sure be pleased to hear that the contents are none the worse for the long time which has elapsed sisnce you sent the parcel.

I won't weary you with reiterated thanks: but I must just say once more how very great is the difference which these gifts make in our lives, which would be very drab without them. It is none the less welcome for arriving at the moment when we have just had the official announcement that our cheese ration is to be reduced from 2 to 1½ ozs. a week.

With all best wishes,

yours gratefully,

C. S. Lewis

TO EDWARD A. ALLEN (W): TS

REF.48/18.

Magdalen College,
Oxford.
29th March 1948.

My dear Mr. Allen,

Once more I find myself writing to thank you very heartily for not one, but two parcels: one containing stationary, and the other, which is so heavy I can hardly lift it, containing food. The latter I have not yet opened, but we are licking our lips in anticipation of investigating it later in the day. The stationary parcel came in more apropos than any gift I have received for a long time – today is a public holiday and I was right out of envelopes, just thinking of starting a begging tour of the College, when, lo! In comes your handsome pack of stationary.

The larger parcel by the way was posted on 20th February, and is marked '20' in a circle, apparently by you, not the postal authorities.

The constant kindness which you show to me has long ago exhausted my vocabulary of thanks: I can only assure you once again of my very deep gratitude, and send you all my best wishes,

yours sincerely,

C. S. Lewis

P.S. You won't forget that I am anxious to know whether my letter to your sister thanking her for her great kindness, ever reached her?

TO GILBERT C. PERLEBERG (W):[28]

[Magdalen College,
Oxford]
30/3/48

Dear Mr. Perleberg

This is v. odd. All the arguments you advance as objections to my theory of eternity seem to me to show that you are in exact agreement with me. A doctrine that God 'was' more creative 'at the beginning' than 'now' is absolutely excluded by my view – 'was' and 'at the beginning' being meaningless when applied to the Timeless Being. As I say in *Screwtape* the total creation meets us at every moment.[29] The distinction between miracle and natural event is *not* between what God *once* did and what He *now* does: it is always NOW with Him. The distinction is between divine acts connected with each other in a particular way and divine acts not so connected. Thanks for your kind letter.

Yours sincerely
C. S. Lewis

TO WARFIELD M. FIROR (BOD): TS

REF.48/97.

Magdalen College,
Oxford.
31st March 1948.

My dear Dr. Firor,

Many thanks for your note, which has just arrived. Yes, alas, my address will be the same throughout the summer. For my domestic life is such that I can only get away at rare intervals and then for very short periods.

The continuous stream of your generosity is such that I have rather lost track of the dates of the gifts: but I think that by the time this reaches you, you will have had a *fourth* acknowledgement. So far from complaining of the postal service, this congestion is very heartening to us: for it shows that the Atlantic service is actually overloaded with

28 Mr Perleberg was writing from 357 Tom Hunter Road, Fort Lee, New Jersey.

29 *The Screwtape Letters*, Letter 15: 'The Present is the point at which time touches eternity. Of the present moment, and of it only, humans have an experience analogous to the experience which our Enemy has of reality as a whole; in it alone freedom and actuality are offered them.'

tokens of good will and sympathy from the U.S.A. It would be interesting to know the weight in shipping tons of foodstuffs sent by individual Americans to Europe since the end of the war. I hope you got the joint acknowledgement from all of us who had the good fortune to eat your excellent ham.

With all best wishes and thanks,

yours sincerely,

C. S. Lewis

TO SISTER PENELOPE CSMV (BOD):

Magdalen etc.
8/4/48

Dear Sister Penelope

It is always very nice to hear from you and often (as on this occasion) exciting as well. My mouth wd. water if it were not that my ignorance of geology (and palaeontology) writes NO ADMITTANCE across your story for me at once.[30] It is most attractive: i.e. a most attractive first half of a story. The difficulty, as you see, is what to do when once Head has recognised his gift – and seen Adam wh. might be magnificent. The ending up as a Franciscan is (from the literary point of view) more an *exit* than a climax. Can't there be something in his ordinary life wh. seems to have no connection with the visions yet somehow 'clicks' with them at the end. (Some lifelong worry about one of his parents – drunken father? – fear of heredity – final realisation that all heredities go back to an Adam who was once unfallen? – or: quite conventional picture of Christ derived from bad local church or conventicle – seeming a dead thing beside the shattering reality of the visions – at the end, sudden realisation of the Second Adam through meeting the first?) What fun it is writing other people's books!

Of course I can't at all tell whether you can write a story. You've had good practice in dialogue. I should try it, if I were you.

Alas! my *Miracles* is 'preliminary' only to historical studies wh. the reader must do for himself. I can't start to make myself a N.T. critic at 50!

---

30 Sister Penelope wrote of this: 'Here and elsewhere, the reference is to a story I was trying to write, did write, and rewrite, but it was no good!'

Shall I hear any more of a book on the Psalms you were going to do?[31]

You sound well, for which I praise God: you were far from it when you last wrote. I am overwhelmed with jobs but, as the dear people in the shops and queues say, 'mustn't grumble'

Yours sincerely
C. S. Lewis

TO MARGARET FULLER (W):

Magdalen College,
Oxford.
April 8/48

Dear Miss Fuller

Thanks for the cutting. I am so slow in the uptake that I am not sure I have understood it – are the two nuns a separate story or padding for her version of Screwtape.

Yes, the *Time* article was ghastly: but I suppose no one of sense believes such things. I wouldn't hang a dog on a journalist's evidence myself. Who said I disliked women? I never liked or disliked any *generalisation*.

Frank Baker,[32] who I hadn't heard of, sounds v. sensible.

Yours sincerely
C. S. Lewis

TO WARFIELD M. FIROR (BOD): TS

REF.48/97.

Magdalen College,
Oxford.
16th. April 1948.

My dear Dr. Firor,

In what terms am I to acknowledge – or attempt to acknowledge – your latest generosity? I refer to the two magnificent parcels which

31 This was probably *St. Athanasius on the Psalms: A Letter Rendered for the First Time into English by A Religious of C.S.M.V.* (1949). It was reprinted as an appendix to the second edition of her earlier book and retitled *St. Athanasius on the Incarnation: The Treatise De Incarnatione Verbi Dei*, trans. and ed. A Religious of C.S.M.V., introduction by C. S. Lewis, new edn, revised, with a Letter of St. Athanasius 'On the Interpretation of the Psalms' added as an Appendix (1944; 2nd edition, 1953).

32 It has not been possible to identify Frank Baker.

came in yesterday: one containing another ham, and the other a variety of good things, including a delicious cake. Last night was 'club night' and the latter circulated amid enthusiastic comments, whilst we discussed how to make the fullest use of the noble gift of the ham. (It will give you an illuminating sidelight on English life today when I tell you that the first resolution passed for the impending banquet was 'Every man to bring his own piece of *bread*'!). There is by the way talk of taking bread 'off the ration' after the next harvest, but no one now takes very much notice of such items of official encouragement as our rulers see fit to give us; we have heard this sort of thing too often.

As I have said before, it is impossible to convey in words the great pleasure which your continued kindness gives to me and many others; had you been in my rooms last night – I wish you had been – you would have understood in a way no letter can make you understand, what happiness you have given to a dozen old friends, to say nothing of myself.

With very many thanks and all good wishes,

yours sincerely,

C. S. Lewis

TO EDWARD A. ALLEN (W): TS

REF.48/18.

Magdalen College,
Oxford.
20th April 1948.

My dear Mr. Allen,

Many thanks for your letter of 16th April: –

And for the admirable story of St. Peter and the New Arrival, which you have certainly not spoilt in the telling. It is a pleasure to me to hear that you did not know of what you are so kind as to call my 'prominence in the literary world', for it shows that American generosity is not to be confined to those who are attracting some little notice in their own country. How and in what happy hour for me I wonder, did you select me as the recipient of your continued and much appreciated goodness? You will not misunderstand me if I say that I too am sorry that I have been handed over to the Women's Club: for it gives less opportunity for what is to me a very pleasant correspondence.

As regards the CARE parcels,[33] speaking quite frankly, I think they, and the whole CARE organization, are admirable. Individual tastes differ to such an extent that there may be others who could suggest improvements, but to me and my household they are entirely satisfactory. Not only the selection but the quality of the goods is beyond reproach, and the packing is first rate. I note that there is yet another parcel, serial 29, on the way to me: which will give me the satisfaction of once more writing to you and signing myself,

yours gratefully,
C. S. Lewis

TO VERA MATHEWS (W): TS

Ref. 48/145.

Magdalen College,
Oxford.
23rd. April 1948.

Dear Mrs. Mathews,

Many thanks for your kind letter of the 16th., and for all the nice things you say about my books; to know that they have been of some use to you is both gratifying and encouraging.

I note that with your unwearied kindness, you propose to send me further gifts: absurdly described by you as 'little packages'. I prefer the phrase 'handsome parcels', and when they arrive they will always be very gratefully recieved by my struggling household. I'm told the most annoying of all the shortages are lard – what you folk call 'shortening' – and tea.

With all best wishes, and heartiest thanks for your goodness, past and prospective,

yours sincerely,
C. S. Lewis

---

33 The Cooperative for American Relief Everywhere (CARE) was founded in 1945 when a group of American organizations came together to rush packages to survivors of the Second World War. The first of 20,000 packages reached Le Havre, France, in May 1946. Many millions of CARE packages have since reached various parts of the world. The parcels contained 1lb beef in broth, 1lb steak and kidney, 8oz liver loaf, 8oz corned beef, 12oz luncheon meat, 8oz bacon, 2lb margarine, 1lb lard, 1lb fruit preserves, 1lb honey, 1lb raisins, 1lb chocolate, 2lb sugar, 8oz egg powder, 2lb whole-milk powder and 2lb coffee.

TO EDWARD A. ALLEN (W): TS

REF.48/18.

Magdalen College,
Oxford.
3rd May 1948.

My dear Mr. Allen,

As I contemplate the label of your splendid parcel of 10th April – 'Crisco, beef, ham, and so forth', six lines of it, I fall, at least in mind, into the sin of Gluttony! Incidentally has'nt this gift made a record passage: posted 10th April, received 1st May? I don't remember one coming quicker. There is nothing I can say to you which has not been said before, and not once, but many times; I can but ring the changes on the word 'thank you', and if my expressions seem cold, I can only assure you that the feelings they attempt to express are stronger than ever. I believe that if it was not for you people, this country would starve through sheer incompetence. You will have seen our latest Government 'slapstick' turn – the clothing warehouses so full that the warehouse people are kicking: the goods not being exported: and the country shorter of clothing than ever. Well, well, well!

With all best wishes and heartiest thanks.

yours sincerely,
C. S. Lewis

TO WALDEN HOWARD (W): TS

REF.48/83.

Magdalen College,
Oxford.
3rd. May 1948.

Dear Mr. Howard,

What you will think of my writing on 3rd. May to acknowledge your handsome gift of writing paper posted on 16th. January I'm sure I don't know; but its not my fault. Although the condition of the parcel is excellent, I think it must have *drifted* across!

You could not, in your kindness, have made me a more opportune gift. We have some 7,000 students in residence now, all of course clamouring for paper for theses etc., and the stationer's allocation remains what it used to be when we had about 4,000. You can imagine the result!

With thanks and all best wishes,

yours gratefully,
C. S. Lewis

TO WARFIELD M. FIROR (BOD): TS

REF.48/97.

Magdalen College,
Oxford.
21st. May 1948.

My dear Dr. Firor,

The combinations and permutations by which it is possible to convey thanks for great kindness are limited, and you, with your innumerable gifts, have exhausted my stock; I can only ask you to believe how deeply grateful I am. I refer at the moment to the excellent parcel which arrived yesterday, marked (if this interests you) '48442 Hercules'. What with a fat parcel and the weather, I feel that life is almost liveable. For we are having the best May this country has had this century, and our rulers – very fortunately for us – have not yet been able to discover any satisfactory method of rationing the sunlight.

It is to be hoped that it will hold, for we are to have great doings in academic circles next week when the Princess visits the University – lunches, teas, dinners, visits to various dignitaries, and an open air play.[34] At the female colleges the girls have knocked off ordinary work and are all busy learning how to drop a curtesy: or so rumour has it. I myself will escape with a play and a garden party I think.

Is there no hope of your ever visiting this country?

Once more with all best wishes and thanks,

yours sincerely,

C. S. Lewis

---

34 On 25 May the University of Oxford conferred on Princess Elizabeth – the future Queen Elizabeth II – a Doctor of Civil Law degree. Afterwards the students in Lewis's old college, University College, performed a play for her. The ceremonies concluded with a garden party. See 'D.C.L. Degree Conferred on Princess Elizabeth', *The Oxford Times* (28 May 1948), p. 5.

TO JOHN O. RIEDL (W):[35] TS

REF. 48/393. Magdalen College,
Oxford.
22nd May 1948

Dear Mr. Riedl,

Thank you for your kind invitation of the 4th: –

It is with great regret that I am compelled to decline such a very interesting engagement, but it will be quite impossible for me to leave Oxford this summer, for a variety of reasons.

With all best wishes for the success of your valuable work,

yours sincerely,
C. S. Lewis

TO EDWARD A. ALLEN (W): TS

REF.48/18. Magdalen College,
Oxford.
29th May 1948.

My dear Mr. Allen,

So once more I have to send you my inadequate, but very sincere thanks, not only for the 'tuxedo',[36] but for the impending food parcel – and this is what you call resigning in favour of the Ladies of Westfield! I can only say, as I have so often said before, that I am more than grateful. The extent to which your folk have come to our rescue is amazing, and moving; I knew in a general way of course that very large quantities of gift food, clothing etc. were coming into Britain, but I was none the less surprised to read in a recent debate in the House of Lords that every household in the kingdom benefits by American aid

---

35 John Orth Riedl (1905–92), philosopher, was born in Milwaukee and took his BA and PhD from Marquette University in 1927 and 1930. Riedl taught Philosophy at Marquette, 1930–46, as associate professor, 1944–8, and Professor, 1954–70. During 1946–8 he served as chief of the Catholic Affairs Office of the military government of Germany, and during 1949–52 as chief of the education branch office of the US High Commission for Germany. He had invited Lewis to Nürnberg for the purpose of aiding the High Commission in its 'reorientation work'.

36 In the end, the tuxedo was given to Professor Tolkien's son, Christopher Reuel Tolkien (b. 1924), the youngest member of the Inklings, who was later to edit many of his father's works. See his biography in *CG*.

to the tune of £1–0-0 a week, and has done so for the past *two years.* You may well be proud of yourselves.

Will you please give Mr. Everett Collins my warmest thanks for his kind gift? It has travelled further afield that [than] previous Westfield parcels: none of my own circle could wear it, but it is now adorning the back of a grateful retired Colonel in Surrey, my brother's old commanding officer.[37]

'Just what a Don does?' Like a woman, his work is never done. Taking 'tutorials' occupies the best part of his day, i.e. pupils come in pairs, read essays to him, then follows criticism, discussion etc; then he gives public lectures in his own subject; takes his share in the business of managing the College; prepares his lectures and writes books; and in his spare time stands in queues.

I trust our meeting will not be postponed until the hereafter; why not take a trip over here and distribute some dollars among our hard working and deserving innkeepers?

I will of course write again when the parcel arrives, and in the mean time with all gratitude and best wishes,

yours sincerely,
C. S. Lewis

TO EDWARD A. ALLEN (W): TS

REF.48/18.

Magdalen College,
Oxford.
2nd June 1948.

My dear Mr. Allen,

I'm thinking very seriously of giving up writing to you: and instead, hiring a space in one of the leading American newspapers which will read something like this: – 'Grateful thanks to Mr. E.A. Allen for his weekly kindness'. Seriously though, how is a man to go on expressing the gratitude which he feels for such continuous and great generosity as you show to me? Another beautiful gift, numbered 32, has just arrived in excellent condition, and as I see from the label, is crammed with luxuries quite unobtainable on this side of the water.

If my thanks sound feeble, you will I hope put it down to my lack of literary skill, and not to lack of gratitude. As I have often had the

---

37 i.e. Warnie's friend, Colonel Herbert Denis Parkin.

pleasure of telling you before these parcels just make all the difference between austerity and hardship.

With very profound thanks,
yours sincerely,
C. S. Lewis

TO VERA MATHEWS (W): TS

Ref. 48/145.

Magdalen College,
Oxford.
3rd. June 1948.

My dear Miss Mathews,

There comes a time when continued kindness such as yours leaves the fortunate recipient with nothing to say: for all has been said before! Here is another beautiful parcel just arrived, posted on 12th. April, for which I can only say, as often before, that I am most deeply grateful to you. How welcome it will be when it reaches the house, you may easily guess. Indeed if it was not for the extraordinary goodness of our American friends, I don't know where we'd be; or rather I do know, and the answer is 'in Queer St.'

With all best wishes and heartiest thanks,
yours sincerely,
C. S. Lewis

TO EDWARD A. ALLEN (W):

Magdalen College,
Oxford.
19/6/48

Dear Mr. Allen

What? Another dinner jacket? I do not know how to thank you. I am gradually, at your charge, reclothing all my younger & slighter friends. Your country thus provides us not only with dinners to eat but clothes to eat them in: if only cruel law allowed you to add the potables we shd. live like kings.

As you see, my brother (who drives the typewriter) is away,[38] and I have a rheumatic hand wh. prevents my writing being v. easy either to me or to those who try to read it. You will therefore feel no offence

38 Warnie was on holiday in Ireland.

(perhaps relief!) if I cut it short. A thousand thanks: as Lincoln said on the famous occasion, 'Well, I'm moved.'

Yours very sincerely
C. S. Lewis

TO RHONA BODLE (BOD):

Magdalen etc.
22/6/48

Dear Miss Bodle

Splendid! As long as you keep in your present way – holding fast to God, whether the Incarnation can be accepted or not – you can't go wrong. Because, you see, it is not really you who are holding fast to Him but He to you: and He will bring you to wherever He wants.

I shd. try St. John's Gospel and the non-Pauline epistles if the first three gospels are deadened with familiarity. But why worry? (I don't mean 'Why read & think?': that's obviously right). You are wondering if the Incarnation is true. Well, if it's not true God doesn't want you to believe it. If you are worried by not (or not yet) believing it, then you must in your heart of hearts believe it to be true, for who cd. be so worried at not believing an error!

Your own argument, that you at any rate have come to know God only thro' Christ is a v. strong one: and I don't mind betting you will come to the Xtian belief in the end. But don't read with a determination to do so. Take the books naturally as you wd. any other serious books. And get out of your head expressions like 'theological problem', 'dogma' etc. You are an adult student reading some v. interesting ancient records, with God to guide you. Let them and Him work. And don't get fussed and don't demand quick returns. All is obviously going pretty well. With all good wishes.

Yrs sincerely
C. S. Lewis

TO WARFIELD M. FIROR (BOD):

Magdalen etc.
25/6/48

Dear Dr. Firor

Oh golly! A Ham a month? Did you say a Ham a month? If you added a Phoenix-nest and a Unicorn's horn it wd. hardly be more dazzling. I can only hope (and I almost believe) that you enjoy the sending as much as we do the eating. A thousand thanks – my typist is away and my hand not what it was.

Yours
C. S. Lewis

TO EDWARD A. ALLEN (W):

Magdalen etc
29/6/48

Dear Mr. Allen,

My brother (who drives the typewriter) is away and I have a rheumatic hand, so this will be a short letter tho' so illegible it will probably *seem* long.

Look here! For heaven's sake don't go on sending me parcels on a reduced income! I don't want to be a vampire. You've done enough already to put me in yr. debt for life. See? Leave it to the millionaires – I know that the things you send me are a frightful price in U.S.A. So ease off! Don't drop the *correspondence*: but no parcels.

The big envelopes came alright, but I use them for long (in the spatial sense) letters – agenda for committees, official forms, MSS etc. I haven't the cheek to put my tiny little bits of paper in them! Blessings on you

Yours most sincerely
C. S. Lewis

TO VERA MATHEWS (W):

Magdalen etc.
2/7/48

Dear Miss Mathews

How lovely! Bacon, tea, shortening, what not – and again. A thousand thanks. Typing expert away, as you see, and me hardly able to write legibly. But (if you *can* make it out) believe me our hearts are very warm and we enjoy the kindness and friendship as well as its tangible (and chew-able) results. I really hardly know how to say what I feel: thank you again and again.

Yours sincerely
C. S. Lewis

TO WARFIELD M. FIROR (BOD):

Magdalen etc.
6/7/48

Dear Mr. Firor

A ham so massive that my arm still aches from carrying it to the kitchen arrived this morning. It is not in such perfect condition as it wd. have been in if our dockers had not been on strike but I think the college cook is surgeon enough to remove any infirm member. I must just give up trying to give you adequate thanks.

I do love eating! That's the consolation of living in modern England: one recovers at 50 some of the pleasures of a boy of 13.

Yours ever
C. S. Lewis

TO WARFIELD M. FIROR (BOD):

Magdalen etc.
10/7/48

Dear Dr. Firor

Hurrah! Second Ham arrived to-day. One is at home for domestic consumption: of this I shall make another feast for my friends and 'in our (not 'flowing' but) 'trickling cups'[39] you shall be freshly remembered. When will you join us in person? You are becoming a mythological figure. Future anthropologists, studying our age, will say you were not a man but a Fertility Symbol. I can only express my feelings mathematically

$$\frac{\text{W. M. F.}}{\text{C. S. L.}} = \text{Thanks}^{1000}$$

Yours (replete)
C. S. Lewis

On 25 January 1944, at a service conducted by the Anglican Bishop of Hong Kong, R. O. Hall, Florence Tim-Oi Li had become the first woman to be ordained to the Anglican priesthood. By 1948 the Church of England was under pressure to follow suit. Lewis was made aware of this by a letter from Marjorie Nunburnholme in Time and Tide:[40]

---

39 William Shakespeare, *Henry V* (1600), IV, iii, 55: 'In their flowing cups freshly remember'd.'

40 *Time and Tide*, XXIX (10 July 1948), p. 720.

> *There is so much interest shown today among the public in the Lambeth Conference that your readers may like to know that yesterday, as Chairman of an* ad hoc *Committee on the Ordination of Women to the Priesthood, I delivered a Petition at Lambeth Palace extensively signed by clergy and laity of the Church of England . . . A real need in a great Asiatic Church resulted in one woman, Lei Tim Oi, being ordained in 1943 by the Bishop of Hong Kong to administer the sacraments to a large body who would otherwise have been debarred from receiving them. The Diocesan Synod in Kong Yet in which she ministered circulated a document stating their belief: 'That God is using China's age-long respect for women and her traditional confidence in women's gifts for administration and counsel to open a new chapter in the history of the Church' . . . Many cherished precedents and prejudices are daily being swept away. We feel that women with a vocation for the full ministry have a great opportunity for service to offer to the Church.*

Lewis believed a woman should address the issue, and he wrote to Dorothy L. Sayers.

TO DOROTHY L. SAYERS (W):

Magdalen College,
Oxford
13/7/48

Dear Miss Sayers

I never wake up to anything till it's well under weigh, so news has only just reached me of a movement (starting, I believe, from Chinese Anglicans) to demand that women shd. be allowed Priests' Orders. I am guessing that, like me, you disapprove something which wd. cut us off so sharply from all the rest of Christendom, and which wd. be the very triumph of what they call 'practical' and 'enlightened' principles over the far deeper need that the Priest at the Altar must represent the Bridegroom to whom we are all, in a sense, feminine.

Well, if you do – really I think you'll have to give tongue. The defence against the innovation must if possible be done by a woman. I know you hate being interrupted: but where the job demands 'ANGLICAN (woman): effective dialectical powers: established literary reputation essential,' who else can I turn to? Write an article (or at the v. least a letter) to something – and swear at me as much as you please while doing it.

We haven't had much luck with our C.W. essays, have we? What price M.B.?[41]

It is long since we met: when will you visit Magdalen again?

Yours sincerely

C. S. Lewis

In her reply of 19 July Sayers agreed that the ordination of women would 'erect a new and totally unnecessary barrier between us and the rest of Catholic Christendom,' but she could find no 'theological reason' against it:

> *If I were cornered, and asked point-blank whether Christ Himself is the representative of male humanity or all humanity, I should be obliged to answer 'of all humanity' . . . Incidentally, one has to be very careful with that 'Bridegroom' imagery. It is so very apt to land one in Male and Female Principles, Eleusis, and the womb of the Great Mother. And that sort of thing doesn't make much appeal to well-balanced women, who look on it as just another example of men's hopeless romanticism about sex, and who are apt either to burst out laughing or sniff a faint smell of drains . . .*
>
> *It would be a pity to fly in the face of all the Apostolic Church, especially just now when we are at last seeing some prospect of understanding with the Eastern Church – and so on . . . The most I find I can do is to keep silence in any place where the daughters of the Philistines might overhear me.*[42]

41 'M.B.' was the pseudonym of the reviewer in *Theology* of *Essays Presented to Charles Williams*. See p. 865.

42 Sayers, *Letters*, vol. III, p. 387.

TO SISTER PENELOPE CSMV (BOD):

Magdalen etc
19/7/48

Dear Sister Penelope

Ever since your earlier letter I have been all agog for the next news of the geological romance, so by all means send me the instalments but do not pay too much attention to any criticisms I may make. I see what you mean about the difficulty of changing to the novelist's technique – but you have the great advantage of having written plenty of dialogue before.

I shall, I think be at Oxford all the Vacation *except* the last fortnight of August and shd. very much enjoy a meeting with you at Springfield St. Mary's.[43]

Pesterings of Messrs. John Lane to reprint the *Silent Planet* will obviously be more effective from anyone else than from the author! I hope the 'no news' you give me of your health is good news?

Yours sincerely
C. S. Lewis

TO EDWARD A. ALLEN (W):

Magdalen College,
Oxford.
20/7/48

Dear Mr. Allen

Yet another deliciously heavy and bulky parcel from you has just arrived. You manage like the sunrise to be regular yet always new: if I were as good a letter writer as you are a benefactor my acknowledgements wd. have the same freshness! I can only say yet again, Thanks! I cd. find it in my heart not to regret the state of affairs which has taught me how much kindness there is in America. In all gratitude.

Yours sincerely
C. S. Lewis

---

43 Springfield St Mary's was a youth hostel in Banbury Road, Oxford, run by the Community of St Mary the Virgin.

TO DOROTHY L. SAYERS (W):

Magdalen etc.
20/7/48

Dear Miss Sayers

What a relief – it looked like a letter from America but is really from you. I see your point: but have been goaded into a Notes on the Way for *Time & Tide* which I hope is not too Eleusinian or too drainy.

I'm worse than you – I never get even as far as London.

Yours very sincerely
C. S. Lewis

Lewis's 'Notes on the Way', dealing with the ordination of women, appeared in Time and Tide *in August. Worried not only about the divisions that would result, but a possible change in religion, he said:*

> *Suppose the reformer stops saying that a good woman may be like God and begins by saying that God is like a good woman. Suppose he says that we might just as well pray to 'Our Mother which art in Heaven' as to 'Our Father'. Suppose he suggests that the Incarnation might just as well have taken a female as a male form, and the Second Person of the Trinity be as well called the Daughter as the Son. Suppose, finally, that the mystical marriage were reversed, that the Church were the Bridegroom and Christ the Bride. All this, as it seems to me, is involved in the claim that a woman can represent God as a priest does. Now it is surely the case that if all these supposals were ever carried into effect we should be embarked on a different religion.*[44]

TO SISTER PENELOPE CSMV (BOD):

[The Kilns]
22/7/48.

Dear Sister Penelope

I am so excited by the story that I must write at once tho I cannot send the MS back till I get a big envelope. It is radically sound (i.e. the

---

44 'Notes on the Way', *Time and Tide*, XXIX (August 1948), pp. 830–1. The article was reprinted as 'Priestesses in the Church?' in *Undeceptions* (1971) and *God in the Dock*.

fire is alight) tho' you may have to come back and re-write the first 2 chapters. Chapter 3 is incomparably better and will, I think, do as it stands. Now I will proceed to be a nuisance.

1. I think you let the cat out of the bag (i.e. the fact that their odd experience is a vision of the past) far too soon. This is almost the first explanation that occurs to Ruscombe. I don't think it would occur nearly so quickly in real life: anyway it destroys our curiosity almost before it is aroused. Surely it ought to be kept, at the v. least, to cap 2 (Rayner wd. be the first to suggest it to R) – better, if possible, till much later. Keep us guessing.

2. Is Mr. Ruscombe going to play any real part in the story? If not, why not leave him a bachelor: especially as you have two female characters already, one good (the Vicar's wife) and one excellent, Head's Aunt. I don't feel the Doctor's wife has done any good so far and the domesticities have a slightly perfunctory effect.

3. Too much guide-book in cap 1? I'm not sure about this and some readers may not feel it too much. Try it on one or two others.

4. Rayner is alright in 3 but doesn't quite come off in 2. This is partly because having already let the cat out of the bag and having made him and the Dr. in complete agreement, there is little for the vicar to do but lecture (and he does). If he were propounding, or, better, hinting, the truth to an incredulous Ruscombe the whole dialogue wd. come to life better.

5. On style. You have already erased several eulogistic adjectives from cap 1: go through it now and erase the rest or replace them with real descriptive adjectives. Near the bottom of p. 2 is an example – the sentence 'except for . . . superb.' It's no good *telling us* that things were 'lovely', 'exquisite', and 'superb.' We won't believe you. You must describe them so that *we* say 'lovely' etc. Instead of 'lovely' for shadows I want an adjective telling me about their colour, or texture, or size, or shape, or motion . . . etc. You see? But this is only a surface fault and will 'come out in the wash' with v. little trouble. The dialogue (except when Rayner is allowed to speak too long) is pretty good. I doubt if anyone says 'My boy' or 'my friend' now.

But the great thing is that it has narrative zest, one wants to read on. If you feel in the vein go ahead and don't bother about the first chapters till you've finished. God speed! My *Punch* name is N.W.,

Yours sincerely
C. S. Lewis

As Lewis mentioned in his letter to Dorothy L. Sayers of 13 July, an unfavourable review of Essays Presented to Charles Williams *by 'M.B.' had appeared in* Theology. *In one particularly harsh passage the reviewer had written:*

> *Miss Dorothy Sayers is no more to be suspected of having wished to patronize Dante than Mr Lewis of having wanted to check the growing reputation of the late Charles Williams. Yet for him to imply that Williams was interested in the topics dealt with by the contributors to this volume is surely as misleading as for her to pretend that* The Divine Comedy *is a jolly story of adventure . . . What Williams would have thought privately of this particular hotch-potch we shall never know. But we can guess. Fortunately the memoir with which Mr Lewis introduces it must make difficult the belief that the shimmering dance of Williams's mind would have fallen into step with such ponderous symbols. Yet, before writing one or two sentences of that memoir, Mr Lewis might have asked himself if they would not wound family susceptibilies. In any event, not on what the man was, for he has gone, but on what is left, his own writings, can the reputation of Williams be expected to subsist.*[45]

Sayers sprang into action, sending her response to Theology:

> *Your reviewer, M.B., sees fit to imply that in* Essays Presented to Charles Williams *I (among others) have been so impertinent, or so maladroit, as to offer to the memory of a man I respected a gift that he would have disliked had he been alive to receive it. I may therefore perhaps, without impropriety, mention in your columns how the essay that I contributed to that volume originated. During the last year or so of Charles Williams's life I wrote to him a number of letters on the subject of the* Divina Commedia, *which I was then reading. On September 13, 1944, he wrote to me: 'I very much hope that you will consider turning your letters into some sort of small pamphlet . . .' I agreed to this proposal, on the understanding that he should edit the pamphlet; and he*

45 *Theology*, LI (June 1948), p. 239.

> *was preparing to do this when his death put an end to the project. When I was invited by Dr C. S. Lewis to contribute to the memorial volume,* pietas *seemed to dictate that I should write for it the kind of thing that Charles Williams himself had wished and requested me to write.*[46]

Following the letter from Sayers was a reply from 'M.B.':

> *I am happy to learn that Miss Sayers wrote her piece at the actual instigation of C.W. Certain, when in the body of my note I referred to the quality of the contributions in general that by Miss Sayers was not one of those I had in mind. That my words should give the impression it was must be regretted, but I did not wish to particularize.*[47]

Lewis also felt the need to respond to the reviewer's ad hominem *critique of the book:*

TO THE EDITOR OF *THEOLOGY* (P):[48]

Magdalen College,
Oxford.
27/7/48

Sir –

I accept, though with astonishment, the statement that M.B.'s unfavourable judgement of our *Essays to Charles Williams* was not meant to include Miss Sayers' contribution. What puzzles me is his explanation: he 'did not wish to particularize'. Why not? If a reviewer thinks a book contains some good work and some bad it is his duty to particularize. What is M.B. afraid of? Obviously not of giving pain. And if he thinks we are the sort of people who horsewhip or prosecute or otherwise retaliate on unfavourable reviewers, I assure him he is quite mistaken. I want to hear his real criticism – not particularly of my own essay which is a trifle nor of my preface which has pleased those whom, at such a moment, I chiefly wanted to please.

---

46 ibid. (August 1948), pp. 319–20.
47 ibid.
48 Alec Vidler was still the editor of *Theology*.

The two most serious contributions (apart from Miss Sayers' for which, it now appears, he has a liking hitherto kept secret) are those of Professor Tolkien and Mr Barfield. Why cannot M.B. come out into the open and write a critique on them based on a real examination either of their premises or their logic or both, not on guesses about the feelings of the dead or the bereaved family which are demonstrably wrong? Not a hair of his head will be hurt and it is what your readers have a right to expect from a review.

Up till now *Theology* has an honourable record for genuinely critical reviewing. It is a pity if it is to descend to the vague innuendo so familiar in our ordinary weeklies.

Yours etc
C. S. Lewis

TO I. O. EVANS (W):

Magdalen College
Oxford
28/7/48

Dear Mr. Evans –

I am delighted that you should have liked the Kipling article.[49] I hadn't suspected his dislike for science – I shd. have thought it was mere indifference: but the destinations you mention are certainly interesting. Thanks for writing. But all said & done, what an artist he was!

yours
C.S.L.

TO DON GIOVANNI CALABRIA (V):

Collegium Stae Mariae Magdalenae
apud Oxonienses
Aug. Xmo a.s. 1948

Grato animo, Pater dilectissime, litteras tuas accepi.

Cur dubitas te locum tuum in orationibus meis et adhuc habere et habiturum esse? Nostram rempublicam in lubrico versari recte judicas. Apud nos conflictus est haud acrior quam in Italia sed quodam modo difficilior.

49 'Kipling's World', *Literature and Life: Addresses to the English Association* (1948), reprinted in *SLE*.

Vestri *Sinistrales* (ut ita dicam!) Atheismum suum confitentur, immo jactant, lupi sunt et lupi esse videntur. Nos patimur multitudinem luporum ovilibus vestimentis vestitorum. Eorum qui injustitiam faciunt in re politica multi dicunt se Regnum Domini aedificare; nec dicunt solum sed fortasse credunt. Non enim nostris est corda discernere et caritas nihil malitiae imputat quod potest ex simplici stultitia et ignorantia evenire – 'fert omnia, credit omnia'. Mihi quidem videtur nihil in hoc statu rerum molestius esse quam quod quotidiana pugna contra odium (non dico inimicorum sed nostrum) nos exercet. Nunc etiam novae minae rumoresque belli oriuntur. Attamen saepe recurro ad apostolicum illud verbum 'nulla temptatio nobis accidit nisi quae communis est hominibus – nondum ad sanguinem etc.' Gratias debemus agere pro omni fortuna; si 'bona' est quia bona est, si 'mala' quia operatur in nobis patientiam, humilitatem, et contemptum saeculi et spem aeternae Patriae.

Vale: semper oremus pro invicem.

C. S. Lewis

*

from the College of St Mary Magdalen
Oxford
Aug 10th in the year of salvation 1948

Thank you, dearest Father, for your letter.

Why doubt that you still hold, and shall hold, a place in my prayers?

You rightly judge that our country is in a hazardous state. With us the struggle is not more intense than in Italy but in one way it is more difficult.

Your Leftists – your Sinisters, to put it like that – declare their atheism. Even boast of it. Wolves they are and wolves they are seen to be.[50]

We endure a pack of wolves, dressed in sheep's clothing. Of those who work injustice in politics many say they are building the Kingdom of God. Nor do they merely say it, they perhaps believe it. For we do not have the ability to read hearts, and Charity does not ascribe to malice that which can result from simple foolishness and ignorance – it 'beareth all things, believeth all things'.[51]

50 Cf. Matthew 7:15: 'Beware of false prophets, which come to you in sheep's clothing, but inwardly they are ravening wolves.'

51 1 Corinthians 13:7.

To me nothing in this state of affairs seems more grievous than the struggle against hatred in which we are daily engaged – I will not say the hatred of enemies but of our own people.

Now indeed new threats and rumours of war are arising. Nevertheless I often recur to that word of the Apostle: no temptation has befallen you except what is common to men[52] – 'not yet unto blood, etc.'[53]

We ought to give thanks for all fortune: if it is 'good', because it is good, if 'bad' because it works in us patience, humility and contempt of this world and the hope of our eternal country.

Farewell: and let us pray for one another always.

C. S. Lewis

TO EDWARD A. ALLEN (W): TS

REF.48/18.

Magdalen College,
Oxford.
10th August 1948.

My dear Mr. Allen,

Many thanks for your very kind letter of the 4th, received this morning. And first of all, may I please ask you not to continue your generosity to me whilst you yourself have had a 50% cut in income? (And I am very sorry indeed to hear of it, and hope it will be for a short time only). It would make me very uncomfortable to think that you were denying yourself in order to feed me with luxuries; especially in view of your long continued and quite exceptional kindness in the past. This is not to say that my mouth does'nt water at the thought of the roast beef in the pipe line: it does!

I quite agree with you that Mr. Hoffman has a man size job in front of him;[54] he has so far as I can judge, made a good impression so far, which is a big start. And I feel that the task is being tackled in the right way, i.e. insistance on Europe helping *itself*, not merely standing by to collect American money. What a mess though, Sir Stafford Cripps has made of the offer of American advice in turning up our industries! I cannot imagine why he did'nt keep the scheme quiet until he had talked over the trades unions.

---

52 ibid., 10:13.

53 Hebrews 12:4.

54 Paul Gray Hoffman (1891–1974) was the administrator of the Marshall Plan.

I note what you say about the drought; its very different here. We have unlimited rainwater, and if only we could export our surplus to you, we would be on our feet in a few months!

With many thanks, and all good wishes for a speedy improvement in your business,

yours sincerely,
C. S. Lewis

Owen Barfield was greatly disappointed that, following his conversion, Lewis refused to argue about those things they had discussed in the days of their 'Great War' – one of which was Anthroposophy. In a talk given in 1985 Barfield said, 'What I wanted to do was to see what relation there was between his "stance" after his conversion and the kind of opinions he held before it, and also to see how far we were still in accord.'[55] *The following letter is one of the few instances where Lewis was willing to continue their argument.*

TO OWEN BARFIELD (W):

[The Kilns]
Aug 19. [1948?]

My dear Barfield –

You have won to this extent that I find myself, against my resolve, once more embarking on epistolary controversy with you – how it all comes back.

First, as to 'all religions but Xtianity'. My real distinction is 1. Polytheism simple. 2. Pantheism. 3. Platonism (the last phase, *Timaeus*),[56] Judaism, Islam & Xtianity.

Next, I think we prob. differ about the meaning of *creation*. I take it to mean 'to cause to be, without pre-existing material (= to cause both the form & matter of) *something pre-conceived in the Causer's thought wh., after creation, is other than the Cause.*' The *élan vital* as conceived by Bergson (Shaw never clears the question up) does not

55 *Owen Barfield on C. S. Lewis*, ed. G. B. Tennyson (1989), 'Lewis and/or Barfield', p. 106.

56 Plato's *Timaeus* describes how the Creator made the world a single spherical living thing, having both soul and body.

create in this sense.[57] It works into *a pre-existing matter*, blindly & tentatively, and does not make but become living organisms. Stoicism in practice is always, I admit, tending towards genuine Theism: but where do I find a clear statement of creation? And is one not constantly urged in Stoic writings to 'live according to' φύσις[58] not because it is righteous and you not, nor because it is creator and you creature, *but* because it is Whole and you Part – a relation not only distinct from creation but hardly consistent with it.

Further, the point is not simply 'righteous', 'creative' etc but 'righteous not a-moral', 'creative not inert'. For there are many who wd. agree on the attributes without denying their opposites, believing in a *coincidentia oppositorum*.[59] That is what I wanted to oppose. As for 'mapping' I have seen what were v. literally maps in Theosophical books, belts of colour with names like Nirvana, para-Nirvanah, mapa-para-nirvana etc. But I did think that the higher you got the more *coincidentia oppositorum* you'd get. The whole question is v. close to your other one about Reason. I can't help using the same word for our reason and the Divine Reason, because I think that in creating rational creatures God created things wh., quâ rational, are like Himself. *When I say that one is not the other* I am not *referring* primarily to the difference

57 In his *Creative Evolution* (1911), Henri Bergson conceived the notion of the *élan vital* or vital impulse as directing evolutionary growth. George Bernard Shaw was not familiar with Bergson's work when he wrote *Man and Superman: A Comedy and a Philosophy* (1903) in which his characters discuss the 'Life Force' which bears some similarity to Bergson's *élan vital.* Cf. Lewis's comments on Creative Evolution in *Mere Christianity*, Book I, ch. 4, p. 22: 'The wittiest expositions of it come in the works of Bernard Shaw, but the most profound ones in those of Bergson. People who hold this view say that the small variations by which life on this planet "evolved" from the lowest forms to Man were not due to chance but to the "striving" or "purposiveness" of a Life-Force. When people say this we must ask them whether by Life-Force they mean something with a mind or not. If they do, then "a mind bringing life into existence and leading it to perfection" is really a God, and their view is thus identical with the Religious. If they do not, then what is the sense of saying that something without a mind "strives" or has "purposes"?'

58 'nature'.

59 'coincidence of opposites'. Lewis probably had in mind Nicholas of Cusa who defined *coincidentia oppositorum* thus: 'As a certain kind of unity perceived as coincidence, a unity of contrarieties overcoming opposition by convergence without destroying or merely blending the constituent elements' (Nicholas of Cusa, *Selected Spiritual Writings*, trans. and introduced by H. Lawrence Bond (1997), p. 366).

of quality or degree (tho' this is no doubt immense) but *to distinction of substance*: rejecting the whole-and part relation in favour of the creator-creature one, i.e. unsaying what I said in the *Summa*. I mean, say, that my acts of attention are not a part or element in God's act of attention, that He has in fact given me a subjectivity other than His. What is the secret doctrine wh. you suspect me of 'popularising' I don't know.

The poem wh. so sweetly carried my mind back to *Spirits in Bondage* never occurred there. Has Marjorie Milne told you she wants to make a ballet out of *Dymer*? Good news about the *Unicorn*.[60] When a few more Inklings are back I'll arrange a suitable evening when you can be sure of a good audience.

Yours
C. S. Lewis

Lewis's next communication to Barfield is not dated, but it was probably written about this time. Barfield had finished his verse drama, Orpheus, *which he had begun in the 1930s and it was to be produced by the Sheffield Educational Settlement at The Little Theatre, Shipton Street, Sheffield, on 25 September 1948. Barfield asked Lewis to write a blurb for the occasion, and the blurb, exactly as given below, was reproduced on the programme. It is also printed on the back cover of* Orpheus: A Poetic Drama.

TO OWEN BARFIELD (W):

[The Kilns
? August 1948]

I await with great interest the public reaction to a work which has influenced me so deeply as Barfield's *Orpheus*. On the technical side it presents us with a variety almost as rich as that of the *Shepherd's Calendar*.[61] I hope this will not be mistaken for virtuosity. The alliterative lines, the trochaics, the couplets, the blank verse and the lyrics are in reality so responsive to the different states of being they embody, that they serve the same purpose as dramatic orchestration. They mediate a drama which the Orpheus in each of us will understand best if he at first leaves the Eurydice in him free to follow the images and the melodic development. It

60 Although Barfield was apparently led to believe that he had found a publisher for his long narrative poem, 'The Unicorn', it has never in fact been published.
61 Edmund Spenser, *The Shepheardes Calender* (1579).

is a mystery (not a 'problem') drama. It executes in us a reunion of which we always stand in need; never more than at present.

C. S. Lewis

1. Why do I feel a cad to be writing blurbs for you?
2. It is better than I remembered. How can they *not* see!

CSL

TO SISTER PENELOPE CSMV (BOD):

Magdalen etc
31/8/48

Dear Sister Penelope

The new chap II is a great improvement and keeps up the proper excitement. It will do v. well and the few criticisms I make concern the surface – i.e. skin troubles (like pimples) not disease at the heart.

P 3. 'voice – tense with interest.' Perfectly good *in itself* but the word *tense* has been so overworked by cheap writers that we can't use it now – thus the innocent suffer for the guilty. I doubt if we really need anything about her voice at this moment. If we do perhaps you can find the *mot juste*.

P 4. 'had nothing outward seen' is not clear: nor do I think that many people wd. say it in conversation – it sounds like German. (Perhaps 'You mean you've seen Pan, as you call it, – had the blind unreasoning terror – when you didn't *see* anything?')

At bottom of same page 'but in your case . . . before it came.' Bad. Manages to be as clumsy as real conversation and at the same time as stiff as a bad lecture. Also no mortal wd. *say* (tho' some wd. *write*) 'in that you felt'. ('You and M. felt that you were meeting Pan. But you were seeing things too, weren't you? I mean, things you hadn't been seeing a moment before?'?)

P. 6. At bottom. 'A good few folk.' In the fear of making him like a parson in an old fashioned novel you are making him 'matey' or 'straight-talkey' like some parsons in real life. Wouldn't he really say 'a good many people'

Chap V I devoured with great enjoyment. Again, it is radically sound. P. 5 at top: does a grin go through a telephone? *Ne vedi stesso né che posse!*[62]

---

62 'You do not see either yourself or what you can do.'

Chap IV (sorry I'm putting things in the wrong order). The same.

On P. 2 comes my only doubt about content as opposed to style. What you say about priesthood is v. good, but I am not quite sure whether at that point the occasion is quite adequate to the importance of your generalisation: or, to be more accurate, whether it *seems* adequate, for the seeming is more important almost than the being. Won't you want to say this later on at some more critical moment?

P. 3 'it was just topping . . . I just loved.' Aren't you making Head talk too much like a child? I admit that in real life he might *say* these words but the impression wd. be modified by his manly face & voice. On the printed page you don't have them and therefore must be careful. ('It bowled me over. I'd not been on the sea before. I liked the motion. I liked the gulls. The old seals, too: they kept on bobbing up . . .')

P. 10 'if so be that the difference in size.' That Bampton Lecture manner again! ('if it's really true that the difference'?)

You may go ahead with confidence: the bones and muscles of the story are good, and the faults are all surface ones that can, whenever you please, come out in the wash.

In correcting dialogue it is useful to imagine it being acted on the stage or at least read aloud. Is there anything which, before a large audience, you wd. feel embarrassed at – anything which an actor wd. find it difficult to say? It must always *sound* like real conversation but must be in reality clearer and more economical than that. Literature is an art of *illusion*. You must be enjoying yourself: and I am hungry for more,

Yours sincerely
C. S. Lewis

TO RUTH PITTER (BOD):

Magdalen etc.
Aug 31/48

Dear Miss Pitter

On a railway platform this morning (I am just back from Malvern) I made a resolution. I said 'I will no longer be deterred by the fear of seeming to press for an opinion about my poems from writing to find out whether R. P. is dead, ill, in prison, emigrated, or simply never got my letter.' So it was with great pleasure that I found yours awaiting me. I have an inkling (but no more) of what you mean by False-Absolute

Football. Do you mean (a.) A pretence of kicking, or attempt to kick, false beliefs about more easily than I should or can? (b.) Being too 'boisterously at ease in Sion,'[63] treating the real Absolute in too rollicking a style? Or more briefly is it false football with the real Absolute or real football with false absolutes?[64]

About Eddington [Eddison]. Yes. A shocking and startling greatness. This, as regards style, increases in the later books, but there is spoiled for me by a horrid Aphrodite mysticism which even renders some of his women nearly vulgar. But I am v. glad to hear of the Omnibus.

I agree about August. In that fell month summer can only plead

'Know that I too, even I, was once a spring.'[65]

Everything horrid that ever happened to me was in an August.[66] But courage! Divine September, the grey mornings, the beady cobwebs, the delicious hint of frost in the evening, is at hand. There are hibernating animals: why no aestivating animals? I wd. be one, if I might.

Yours sincerely
C. S. Lewis

TO VERA MATHEWS (W): TS

Ref. 48/145.

Magdalen College,
Oxford.
1st. September 1948.

My dear Miss Mathews,

Many thanks for your kind note of the 27th. August: – No, I'm afraid I did'nt get the parcel you refer to; the last you were good enough to send me was posted at Beverly Hills on April 12th. But this does not necessarily mean that you are entitled to jump down your shop-

---

63 Amos 6:1: 'Woe to them that are at ease in Zion.'

64 Pitter said in a note on this letter: 'Oh dear, I was quite taken up with the idea of "False-Absolute Football": it sounds diverting, but I cannot for my life recall what it was supposed to mean. Drat the man for destroying letters (and yet the suffocating tyranny of paper justifies him)' (Bodleian Library, MS. Eng. lett. c. 220/3, fol. 58).

65 This is a version of the last line of Lewis's poem 'Late Summer', published in *Poems* and *CP*: 'Mortals remember, looking at the thing/I am, that I, even I, was once a spring.'

66 His mother had died on 23 August 1908.

man's throat! The parcel may have been stolen on the English side, or on board ship.

Though I regret the loss of the gift, I am none the less grateful to you for your goodness in thinking of me and sending me yet another.

With all best wishes and thanks,

yours sincerely,

C. S. Lewis

TO EDWARD A. ALLEN (W): TS

REF.48/18.

Magdalen College,
Oxford.
4th September 1948.

My dear Mr. Allen,

Once more I have to write to thank you for your exceeding kindness in sending me yet another excellent parcel: posted on the 24th August, and marked (48).

My scientific friends tell me that the entire structure of the human body is renewed once in every seven years. If the apparently unceasing flow of your generosity continues, I shall, in common gratitude, have to put a placard on my back stating that 'this body has been reconstituted entirely by the generosity of Edward A. Allen Esq., of Westfield, Mass. U.S.A.'! Seriously though, I do wish as I have already told you, that you would put a brake on your kindness while you yourself are feeling the effects of short time; I feel very uncomfortable at the thought that you may be denying yourself in order to send luxuries to me.

I take it that your short time indicates not a saturation of the home market, but a shortage of purchasing power due to inflation? That is the situation with which we are faced at the moment; I see that the clothing concessions for instance have not resulted in an increased sale of home market goods. The stuff is in the shops, but people can't buy. Though with us the problem is complicated by the inferior quality of so much of the stuff on the home market.

Please accept once again all which I can offer you, namely my very heartiest thanks for your great kindness: and with all best wishes to you and yours,

yours gratefully,

C. S. Lewis

TO VERA MATHEWS (W): TS

Ref. 48/145.

Magdalen College,
Oxford.
15th. September 1948.

My dear Miss Mathews,

You will by this time be thinking what a remarkably rude man I am in not thanking you earlier than this for your excellent parcel of the 14th July, and the letter of the same date in which you say so many kind things about me. The fact is that the parcel duly arrived and was duly enjoyed by all, but appeared to be anonymous – the letter having, by some domestic blunder, been mislaid, and only having come to light yesterday. I apologize humbly, and with some annoyance, for I should not like you to think that I accept your repeated kindnesses as a matter of course. Please forgive me.

As regards new books, I am at present busy with my autobiography,[67] but cannot say when it will be published: and am also still pegging away at what is known here as 'Oh! Hell': 'Oxford History of English Literature', for which I am doing one of the volumes.

Again with many thanks and all good wishes, and hoping that we may someday meet,

yours sincerely,
C. S. Lewis

TO WARFIELD M. FIROR (BOD): TS

REF.48/97.

Magdalen College,
Oxford.
21st. September 1948.

My dear Dr. Firor,

Most of the great musicians have tried their hand at 'variations on a theme': and I wish I could borrow some of their expertise in order to add a little freshness to my thanks for your great and continued kindness to me. Your latest gift (which I have not yet opened) has just arrived, and by air too! It was accompanied by a pompous official document from British Airways, demanding a receipt, which I have just sent off. The number of the parcel is 72955. If you could see the average shopping basket which the housewife brings home in this country, you

---

67 i.e. *SBJ*.

would know how great is my gratitude to you; things seem to get worse instead of better, and 'points' goods, i.e. tinned extras, have now almost disappeared from the shops. Your generous parcel – judged by shaking it – is full of just that sort of supply, and you can imagine what excitement there will be when I open it tonight.

Believe me, I am deeply touched by your very great kindness.

With all best wishes,

yours gratefully,

C. S. Lewis

TO WARFIELD M. FIROR (BOD): TS

REF.48/97.

Magdalen College,
Oxford.
24th. September 1948.

My dear Dr. Firor,

Many thanks for your kind letter of the 8th. September, and the glad news that there are parcels on the way. I do wish I had some other way of expressing my own (and my friend's) great gratitude to you for the many kindnesses you have done us. I will of course acknowledge the parcels as and when they arrive.

What a tragedy about the ham! Nothing arouses so much excitement amongst my friends as the welcome news that 'a Firor ham' has arrived; and we have eaten many a noble supper at your expense, not forgetting to drink your health in whatever liquour was available. However, so far as I know, it is the only one that has ever gone astray, so whilst we may regret, we must'nt grumble.

With renewed thanks, and all best wishes,

yours sincerely,

C. S. Lewis

P. S. Change of address noted.

TO WARFIELD M. FIROR (BOD): TS

REF.48/97.

Magdalen College,
Oxford.
25th. September 1948.

My dear Dr. Firor,

I don't think my letter of yesterday had been in the post box an hour, when my servant came staggering in with *three* enormous parcels from you. One marked 'provisions', the other two marked 'Ham 13½ lbs' and 'Ham 13½ lbs. REPLACEMENT'. I need hardly enlarge on the delightful surprise, for I had thought that ham gone for good and all, and then to get two – Well, you'd just have to come over and try life on this side for a bit to understand how we feel about such a windfall, and how extremely grateful we are to you for your kindness. Indeed I wish you could join one of our 'ham feasts': you would meet a very grateful group of friends of mine (and of yours at second hand), who would be delighted to express their thanks in person.

With hearty good wishes,

yours gratefully,

C. S. Lewis

TO RUTH PITTER (BOD):[68]

[The Kilns]
Sept 26/48

'Shall I tell her the truth? . . . dare I? . . . but she is a poet and can envisage calm All circumstance . . . and pitee renneth soon in gentil herte[69] . . . and she is my even-Christen and I mustn't lie to her . . . tell the truth, and shame the Divell.'[70] Thus Conscience and I.

My very approved good Ladie and deerest dread, mislike me not forever for these news: wherein I must plainlie confesse that by cause of my unluckie absence from home and of these late autumnall heates

---

68 Pitter said in a note to this letter: 'At the little house in Essex which had been my mother's, we had a large vinery: I have never seen nor heard of any other place where a cottage had a 40-foot vinery to it. We had got quite good at managing it, too. I had noticed that Lewis had a special feeling about grapes. So have I. Of all fruits they are the most wholesome, graceful, beautiful, various: the plant is "de toute beauté", the modest flower ravishing in scent: then there is wine (which of course one would not make from table grapes, but we did make splendid vinegar from the thinnings & prunings). And most of all, the sacred associations & imagery. I had sent Lewis a sample of a specially highly flavoured grape, the Tokay Frontignan: but the luck was out. Because his absence from home was one reason the grapes had gone off, he imagined it was all his fault, and he chose to apologize in "Middle English"' (Bodleian Library, MS. Eng. lett. c. 220/3, fol. 60).

69 Geoffrey Chaucer, *The Canterbury Tales*, The Knight's Tale, 1761: 'For pitee renneth soone in gentil herte.'

70 Shakespeare, *Henry IV Part 1*, III, i, 58–9: 'And I can teach thee, coz, to shame the devil/By telling truth: tell truth and shame the devil.'

and also inasmuch as yr gratious packet laie together with sundrie giftes from the American (which, as I well vnderstoode, were full of salt flesh and the like which needed not to be presently disposed) ther fell vpon me no little neglicence. Whereby it came about yat I vnhoused not yr. Ladieships gift vntill – howe shall I saie it – vntill that cautell in yr. letter 'Note þe smelle' had become infinitely superflvous. To saie all in brief (for the avoidynge of prolixitie) that corrupcion which we must pacientlie look for in our owne persons had already trivmphde on the raisins which should have pampered the same.

O tempus edax rerum.[71] O goode apothecarie, an ovnce of civet to sweeten my imagination. Wherein I sorrowe not soo moche for the losse of the carnall solace which I might have enioyde in the eatynge and manducation of the noble berries as for the frustration of your singular (intended) favour and courtesie. Conceive that my thankes are never the lesse but my shame the greater: and for all loves so meddle pitee with daunger that I maie now as ever subscribe myselfe yr. La'ps humble seruant and poore bedesman

C. S. Lewis

TO DOM BEDE GRIFFITHS OSB (W):

[The Kilns]
27/9/48

My dear Dom Bede –

This is all extremely interesting. Pedagogically I shd. have thought you were in some danger of overloading the syllabus.

I fully agree with your remarks about India. I even feel that the kind of union (with God) wh. they are seeking is precisely the opposite to that which He really intends for us. We all once existed potentially in Him and in that sense were not other than He. And even now inorganic matter has a sort of unity with Him that we lack. To what end was creation except to separate us in order that we may be reunited to Him in that unity of love wh. is utterly different from mere numerical unity and indeed presupposes that lover & beloved be distinct?

Thus the whole Indian aim seems to me to be *backward* towards a sort of unity wh. God deliberately rejected and not onward to the true one. If mere unity (as opposed to union) is the aim all Creation seems otiose.

71 Ovid, *Metamorphoses*, XV, 234: 'O time that devours all things'.

As for the Chinese, all I know is the *Analects* translated by Waley.[72] From that the transition to truth seems much easier: for Confucius ends up by saying 'This is the Law, but I do not know of anyone who has kept it.' Doesn't that canal us straight into St. Paul? Such are the thoughts that occur to me on the spur of the moment. I hope you will have every blessing in your new post.

Yours
C. S. Lewis

TO RUTH PITTER (BOD):

[The Kilns]
29/9/48

Dear Miss Pitter

I was silent about yr. criticism because I was still chewing it and have been early taught Not to Speak with my Mouth Full. And I'm still chewing and can't really quite eat it. (a.) Because of a deep suspicion that the charge of False Absolute Football is really only a rationalisation of a deep & inarticulate (and prob. correct) feeling that mine isn't really poetry at all – a feeling repressed by your kindness and liking for my prose work and coming out in this form. (b.) By an understanding of the charge (supposing it not to be a rationalisation) wh. is still v. imperfect. But I'll try some more on you anon, and we may hammer it out.

I'm greatly flattered to be read in flu' since for my own flu' I always go back to *The Wind in the Willows* while the temperature is really high, and progress to Scott or Wm. Morris (laced with Trollope) as I get sane. The *one* Gk. Chorus you know is one of the *many* I don't.

I hope the flu' is well over: guard against a backhander.

Why don't you write a story – if there's really no poetry coming? It's such fun after sweating over verse: like free-wheeling.

Yours sincerely
C. S. Lewis

Because Ruth Pitter's side of the correspondence has not survived it is not known what she said in reply to Lewis's persistent question as to whether his poems were 'really poetry at all'. Looking back on the matter twenty

72 Confucius, *The Analects*, trans. Arthur Waley (1938).

years later, she supplied this note about Lewis's letter of 29 September 1948:

> *Now I wonder.* Is *his poetry after all not? About how many poets or poems would readers agree 100% or even 50%? 'The peaks of poetry are shiftingly veiled, and different readers catch different glimpses of the transcendental.'*
>
> *I should like to know more about the actual process of conception in his case. Did his great learning, & really staggering skill in verse inhibit the poetry? Did he ever (like most of us) catch some floating bit of emotional thistledown & go on from that, or did he plan on a subject like an architect? (Producing perhaps short epics?)*
>
> *He had a great stock of the makings of a poet: strong visual memory, strong recollections of childhood: desperately strong yearnings for lost Paradise & hoped Heaven ('sweet desire'): not least a strong primitive intuition of the diabolical (not merely the horrific).*
>
> *In fact his whole life was oriented & motivated by an almost uniquely-persisting* child's *sense of glory and of nightmare. The adult events were received into a medium still as pliable as wax, wide open to the glory, and equally vulnerable, with a man's strength to feel it all, and a great scholar's & writer's skills to express and to interpret. It is almost as though the adult disciplines, notably the technique of his verse, had largely inhibited his poetry, which is perhaps, after all, most evident in his prose. I think he wanted to be a poet more than anything. Time will show. But if it was* magic *he was after, he achieved this sufficiently elsewhere.*[73]

73 Bodleian Library, MS. Eng. lett. c. 220/3, fols. 63–4.

TO CHAD WALSH (W):

Magdalen etc
Oct 8/48

Dear Walsh

I've looked through the 2 chapters and made a few corrections.[74] You have been a little misled about my normal term-time day: you saw me in the last week of summer term when most of my pupils were doing exams and I was very free. The normal term time routine is

9–10 Correspondence

10–1 Pupils (except Tue. wh. I try to keep free from 11–1)

5–7 Pupils

and I am sleeping in College not coming in of a morning. Vacation, I sleep at home and am usually at Bodley from 9.30 till 1. I hope this won't entail much re-writing. I can't judge the chapters otherwise any more than one's own photo.

All congratulations on the new daughter and 1000 thanks for the parcel. In great haste as this is the black morning before term begins. My brother and I join in kindest regards

Yours

C.S.L.

TO EDWARD A. ALLEN (W): TS

REF.48/18.

Magdalen College,
Oxford.
8th October 1948.

My dear Mr. Allen,

I hope I shall not be suspected of 'cupboard love' (is the expression used in your country?) if I say how delighted I am to hear that you are back on full time once more: and I hope you will long continue to be so. To know that there is another parcel on the way is very heartening, and fills me with grateful anticipations.

Certainly we are all much in need of cheering up just at present – winter coming on, war just round the corner etc. etc. Even in the U.S.A., if we can judge from what we read in our press, war in the not

74 Lewis had two visits from Chad Walsh during the summer of 1948 regarding Walsh's book, *C. S. Lewis: Apostle to the Skeptics* (New York: Macmillan, 1949). See **Chad Walsh** in the Biographical Appendix.

distant future seems to be regarded as inevitable. So make the most of your holidays while you can. I enjoyed your too short description of your trip. Yes, I have always heard of the beauty of your 'fall', and the other day I was much impressed by its loveliness on the screen: having paid one of my rare visits to the cinema to see 'Bambi'.

Yes, Psalm 24 would be excellent for the purpose you suggest; but I fear U.N.O. is as dead as the League of Nations was still-born in fact.:[75]

With hearty thanks and all best wishes for the coming winter,

yours sincerely,
C. S. Lewis

TO EDWARD A. ALLEN (W): TS

REF.48/18.

Magdalen College,
Oxford.
15th October 1948.

My dear Mr. Allen,

I write to you in sackcloth and ashes. Here is an address which by this time I have very good reason for knowing as well as my own, and I must needs leave out the name of your home town! It was certainly trying your Postal Authorities a little high to expect them to track down 173, Highland Ave, Mass! With all best wishes,

yours sincerely,
C. S. Lewis

TO VERA MATHEWS (W): TS

Ref. 48/145.

Magdalen College,
Oxford.
18th. October 1948.

Dear Miss Mathews,

Many thanks for your letter of 12th. October, which I was glad to get. It is kind of you to speak as you do about the parcels, but let me assure you that to me, next to their goodness, their frequency is their most remarkable feature.

I am flattered that you should want one of my photos; I *think* I have

75 The League of Nations was founded in 1920 to promote international co-operation and peace. It was proposed in 1918 by President Woodrow Wilson although the United States never joined it. It turned out to be powerless, and it was dissolved in 1945. The United Nations Organization was established the same year to replace it.

some somewhere, and am now going to embark on a search for them.

With all best wishes,

yours sincerely,

C. S. Lewis

Arthurian Torso, Containing the posthumous fragment of The Figure of Arthur by Charles Williams, and A Commentary on The Arthurian Poems of Charles Williams by C. S. Lewis *was published by Oxford University Press on 21 October 1948.*

Dorothy L. Sayers had already read Arthurian Torso, *and wrote to Lewis on 22 October 1948:*

> *There is to-day far too little straightforward interpretative criticism. Everybody insists on doing 'creative' criticism – which means that the critic simply uses his author as a spring-board from which to leap off into an exposition of his own views about the universe . . . we need the pure interpreter, who will sit down before a poem, or whatever it is, with humility to it and charity to the reader, and begin by finding out and explaining what the author actually did say, before he starts to explain what the author ought to have said and would have said if he had been as enlightened a person as his critic. A friend of mine, after toiling through several unintelligible books about modern poetry, said plaintively: 'I want a critic who will say: "This is a poem about a bus; this is what the poem says about the bus; this is the conclusion the writer draws from his observation about the bus; I think he has said it well (beautifully, badly, etc.) for the following reason." After that he can say what he likes, and I shall know where I am.'*
>
> *I intend a compliment when I say that your critical portion of* Arthurian Torso *seems to me to explain in just the desired manner that 'this is a poem about a bus'; and I shall buy another copy and present it to my friend.*[76]

76 Sayers, *Letters*, vol. III, p. 401.

TO DOROTHY L. SAYERS (W):

Magdalen etc.
Oct 26. 48

Dear Miss Sayers

I am just getting over a bout of gastric flu' and cd. not have a better tonic than your kind and (as always) most interesting letter. I am absolutely with you about criticism: or, should I say, absolutely with you in feeling that we have far too much criticism and far too little *commentary*. Even scholars have abandoned the latter. They're always producing 'texts', accurate to every comma, but never explaining a hard line: if one wants help one still has to go back to the Wartons, Todds, Malone's etc.[77] (McKerrow's Nashe is an honourable exception).[78]

I can't, in my present condition, play back your two Dante gobbets at all. I had never thought of an equivoque in *pietà* or *passion porta*. But you're almost certainly right. And I think you are very likely right about the ladies of Burma too.[79] That's what I want to happen – i.e. that I shall be only the starting point of *Williamswissenschaftslehre*.[80]

It wd. be interesting if you're right in saying that a cuckold can't be a hero.[81] Menelaus in the *Odyssey* is an old dear (and so is Helen) but

---

77 These are the distinguished eighteenth-century literary critics Joseph Warton (1722–1800) who published an *Essay on the Writings and Genius of Pope* (1756, 1782); his brother Thomas (1728–90), the author of *The History of English Poetry*, 3 vols. (1774–81); Henry John Todd (1763–1845), editor of Milton's *Poetical Works*, 6 vols. (1801); and Edmond Malone (1741–1812), Shakespearian scholar who wrote *An Attempt to Ascertain the Order in Which The Plays Attributed to Shakespeare Were Written* (1778). Lewis acknowledged his debt to these scholars in *An Experiment in Criticism* (1961) ch. 11, p. 121: 'I have owed, and must continue to owe, far more to editors, textual critics, commentators, and lexicographers than to anyone else. Find out what the author actually wrote and what the hard words meant and what the allusions were to, and you have done far more for me than a hundred new interpretations or assessments could ever do.'

78 Thomas Nashe, *Works*, ed. R. B. McKerrow, 5 vols (1904–10).

79 In an unpublished portion of her letter of 22 October 1948, Sayers mentions a connection between lines of Dante's *Inferno* and some lines in Charles Williams's *Region of the Summer Stars*, 'The Prayers of the Pope', section 14, 58–60: 'The roses of the world bloomed from Burma to Logres;/pure and secure from the lost tentacles of P'o-l'u,/the women of Burma walked with the women of Caerleon.'

80 Lewis joins 'Williams' and 'Wissenschaftslehre' ('theory of science') to become 'the theory of science of Williams'.

81 In the unpublished portion of Sayers's letter of 22 October 1948, she remarks that 'Whoever handles the Arthurian matter, Arthur never succeeds in being the hero

I suppose not a hero, Soames is, maugre the author, the most interesting person in the *Forsyte Saga*[82] (a book one does not *go back* to, I find). Arthur is a hero alright in Layamon, but only a war hero. It looks as if you were right. But A. has other disqualifications besides his horns. Once his court was made the nucleus of 'adventures' he was bound to fade: sinks into the Headmaster. By the way, how I *hate* all the great mistresses except Helen – Isoud, Guinevere, Anna Karenina: and how much nicer to be the cuckold than the lover if one had to be either! Poor old Vronski!

I wish I were a better proof reader, but I'll never learn. I also wish you sometimes came to Oxford. With many thanks & my duty,

yrs. very sincerely
C. S. Lewis

TO ROGER LANCELYN GREEN (BOD):

Magdalen
Nov 4/48

My dear Green

I am afraid Sat (and Sunday) are always *dies non* for me. It is during the week end that my domestic duties fall most heavily on me and Monday morning gives me the same 'Stand easy' feeling that others have on Saturday at lunch time!

All afternoon, from 1 to 5, also are periods of home-duty so that if you had called you wd. not have found me. Please give my thanks & compliments to your wife and my regret at having to refuse yr. and her kind invitation.

I will lend you *M. of M's*[83] with pleasure if you will call in for it any morning.

Yrs
C. S. Lewis

---

futurus . . . The unfortunate fact seems to be that you cannot make a heroic figure out of a cuckold.'

82 i.e. Galsworthy, *The Forsyte Saga*.

83 i.e. E. R. Eddison, *Mistress of Mistresses*.

TO JOHN WAIN (*L*):[84]

[Magdalen College]
6 November 1948

My dear Wain

I am wondering whether you have thought of applying for the tutorial fellowship in English at New College? I understand (this is of course strictly confidential) that they have a strong candidate who is an old New College man but they are not *settled* to elect him, i.e. if a definitely stronger candidate puts in they will elect that candidate. I know you are well thought of by D.C.,[85] it is therefore possible that you might be the stronger candidate if you applied. If you were out of a job of course it wd. be obvious that you shd. try for this. As things are, I don't know if you will wish to or not. I shall never be satisfied myself until you are at Oxford: and this job wd. no doubt be better paid than your present one. On the other hand it wd. probably mean more work and of course, house-hunting. I don't know that I cd. add anything by writing at greater length. Think it over for twenty-four hours and let me know.

TO WARFIELD M. FIROR (BOD): TS

REF.48/97.

Magdalen College,
Oxford.
6th. November 1948.

My dear Dr. Firor,

Your generosity has reached such proportions that if I were less scrupulous (and greedy), I should have no difficulty in setting up in the Black Market provision trade on the side! Two more magnificent parcels – 71399 HAM, and 68378 HERCULES – have just arrived in excellent condition. To tell you once more how very deeply grateful I, or rather we, are, is to say nothing. I can only hope that I will at least

---

84 John Wain CBE (1925–94), novelist and critic, was a member of the Inklings. He read English at St John's College, Oxford, but was sent to Lewis for tuition. After taking his BA in 1947 he became a lecturer in English Literature at the University of Reading where he remained until 1955. Soon afterwards he moved to Oxford as a freelance author, becoming Professor of Poetry in 1973. His novels include *The Contenders* (1958) and *A Winter in the Hills* (1970). His *Sprightly Running: Part of an Autobiography* (1962) includes an account of tutorials and meetings at both the Inklings and the Socratic Club.

85 i.e. Lord David Cecil.

sometime have the pleasure of thanking you face to face. There are signs – very faint ones I admit – of things improving a little over here: some extra sugar is promised, and we are to have 2 ozs. of shortening per week instead of one, but only for the winter. However, let us be thankful for even the smallest mercies!

We are still a bit bewildered by your Presidential election: having for months been assured that the only feature of interest in a very dull contest was what Dewey's majority would be. I gather that to the Americans themselves, the result was as unexpected as to the outside world.[86]

Once more, very many thanks to all your great goodness to me and mine: and with all best wishes for a happy Christmas,

yours gratefully,
C. S. Lewis

TO OWEN BARFIELD (W):

Magdalen College
Oxford
Nov 10/48

I wonder whether what you say about depressions does not mark an advance in self criticism and objectivity – i.e. that the very same experiences wh. wd. once have led you to say 'How nasty everyone (or the weather, or the political situation) is at present' now leads you to say 'I am depressed' – a Copernican revolution revealing as motion in the self what in ones more naïf period was mistaken for motion in the Cosmos. (True, your last letter shows some decline in your critical powers: but we have all been warned that an inability to appreciate new poetry comes with years!) But I'm serious about the other suggestion. I also will soon be fifty.[87] Just the twenty years more now![88] A happy birthday to you. If the knowledge that for some 25 years you have been

86 The 1948 Presidential election was between Thomas E. Dewey and Harry S. Truman. *The New York Times* had declared Dewey's election as President 'a foregone conclusion', and nearly all pollsters and opinion-makers predicted a Dewey win. Yet Truman's victory was overwhelming: he carried twenty-eight states with 303 electoral votes to Dewey's sixteen states with 189 electoral votes.

87 Barfield was fifty on 9 November 1948.

88 Psalm 90:10: 'The days of our age are threescore years and ten; and though men be so strong that they come to fourscore years: yet is their strength then but labour and sorrow; so soon passeth it away, and we are gone.'

always food (and often physic as well) to my mind and heart contribute to it, well it is so.

C.S.L.

TO VERA MATHEWS (W): TS

Ref. 48/145.

Magdalen College,
Oxford.
13th. November 1948.

Dear Miss Mathews,

Many thanks for your note of the 5th., and I'm so pleased you liked the photo.

I really don't know what to say when you tell me that another of your so-called 'small parcels' is on the way; I seem to have exhausted all the possible ways of saying 'thank you'. But please believe me, my gratitude remains as deep and as sincere as ever. Yes, tobacco is still I'm sorry to say both short and dear, and a little of it is always welcome; I'm not particular about the brand.

Again many thanks, and with all good wishes to you for a happy Christmas,

yours sincerely,
C. S. Lewis

TO CHAD WALSH (W): TS

REF.48/281.

Magdalen College,
Oxford.
13th November 1948

My dear Mr. Walsh,

This is really extremely kind of you, and I am most heartily grateful. I refer of course to your splendid parcel of 13th October, which has just come in, and in good condition. You will have seen enough of our way of living while you were here, to realize just how welcome the fat is. We shall now look forward with more equanimity to our eighth austerity Christmas. How are you? And how goes the book? Let us hear something of you. My brother asks to be kindly remembered to you.

Again many thanks indeed, and all good wishes for a happy Christmas,

Yours sincerely,[89]

---

89 The letter is unsigned.

Ronald Lewin of the BBC's Talks Department wrote to Lewis on 16 November 1948 asking if he would 'undertake a talk giving an appreciation of the novels of Charles Williams'. This was partly because, as he said, the novels were being reprinted,[90] *but also because 'we should like to take the opportunity of recording this talk by you for our permanent collection of archive recordings; we have only one very brief recording of your voice in our permanent collection'.*[91]

TO RONALD LEWIN (BBC): TS

REF.48/16.

Magdalen College,
Oxford.
17th November 1948.

Dear Mr. Lewin,

T. S. Eliot would do it better and carry more weight with that audience. There's also Miss Sayers. But if it comes down to me or nobody, I will do it. I am v. busy and not v. well and wd. like to be passed over provided this wd. not miss a chance of helping C.W.'s sales.

yours sincerely,
C. S. Lewis

TO EDWARD A. ALLEN (W): TS

REF.48/18.

Magdalen College,
Oxford.
20th November 1948.

My dear Mr. Allen,

Many thanks for your most kind and interesting letter of the 6th, which gave me great pleasure. In this matter of food gifts, your continued goodness has long since passed the point at which even one of the professional eulogists of the seventeenth century could have found any fresh terms in which to express his gratitude: and I can now only hope that you will believe that, if the acknowledgements get colder, the

---

90 BBC Written Archives Centre. Between 1946 and 1948 Faber and Faber reprinted Charles Williams's novels.

91 While the BBC had recorded three of the *Beyond Personality* talks, the only one to survive is the last of the series, recorded on 21 March 1944. Mr Lewin, however, was probably referring to the recording the BBC made on 27 February 1948 of Lewis reading the preface to *The Great Divorce*. A list of Lewis's surviving recordings is given in *CG*, pp. 779–80.

gratitude which I am incapable of expressing gets warmer. Thank you once more.

I have an uncomfortable feeling that Sir J. B. Orr[92] is right, and that the danger we are facing is not World War III but World Famine I; I recently was horrified by an article which put the trouble, not in the dim future, but about 200 years ahead. Can we really be destroying our own future at such a reckless rate?

Over here, it is very difficult to make anything of the Presidential election. The Socialist press hails it as a triumph for socialism, and proclaims that the U.S.A. has come over to 'modern democracy', i.e. state ownership, beaurocracy, and all the joys of present day English life. The Conservatives say that America has once more recorded an emphatic vote for true freedom etc, etc. So what have you?

Once more many thanks, and all best wishes to you and yours for a happy Christmas,

yours gratefully,
C. S. Lewis

On receiving Lewis's letter of 17 November, Ronald Lewin answered on 25 November that he was sorry Lewis was unable to undertake a talk on Charles Williams and that 'We feel that unless you wish to give the talk we would prefer to postpone it'.[93]

TO RONALD LEWIN (BBC): TS

REF.48/16.

Magdalen College,
Oxford.
26th November 1948.

Dear Mr. Lewin,

Thanks for your letter 04/HT/RL of the 25th. But I have not made myself plain. I can and will do a talk on Charles Williams if you can't, or don't want to, get anyone else to do so. Indeed I have draughted it

---

92 Sir John Boyd Orr, later Lord Boyd Orr (1880–1971). In 1946, when director-general of the Food and Agriculture Organization of the United Nations, Orr set up an International Emergency Food Council, with thirty-four member nations, to meet the post-war food crisis. His proposal was, however, turned down in 1947 when neither Britain nor the United States would vote for it. He wrote *Food: The Foundation of World Unity* (1948).

93 BBC Written Archives Centre.

already, on the chance that the people whom I suggested might refuse.

yours sincerely,
C. S. Lewis

TO RUTH PITTER (BOD):

Magdalen etc
Dec 6th. 1948

Dear Miss Pitter

Thank you very much. I feel a little guilty at bombarding you with these things but my men friends (none of whom is as good a poet as you) give such contradictory opinions that I must have a Court of Appeal. No, I didn't want the other MSS back and of course glow all over at the use you have put *B. of Language* to.[94]

Three of us re-read *Sohrab & Rustum* the other night. It worked as well as ever. But *how* does he move so by just writing simple factual sentences connected by *and's*? 'And I got up and then I had a bath' – that's the *sort* of thing he keeps on saying, and one's heart is half broken as one reads.* Yet he can, in prose and sometimes in verse, be elsewhere almost silly. I sometimes wonder whether we know anything about poetry.[95]

If the horrible commercial racket and general nuisance of 'Xmas' allows it, I hope you will have a happy 'Christmas'.

Yr. most obliged
C. S. Lewis

* It has nothing to do, tho' he may have thought it has, with Wordsworth's nonsense about the real language of men![96]

---

94 Lewis had sent Pitter a copy of his poem 'The Birth of Language' which was published in *Punch*, vol. CCX (9 January 1946), p. 32, and is included in *CP*.

95 Of this question, Pitter said in her notes: 'I am never sure myself that a reader, however subtle & discriminating, has taken my most secret meaning: there are layers, from the most obvious to the most intangible, and I watch like a cat to observe who has taken the latter, if indeed any such there be: for we must be prepared to admit that these very innermost things may be *chimaerae.* And of course there are meanings in our own work that we have never seen, and when others point them out we are quite astounded' (Bodleian Library, MS. Eng. lett. c. 220/3, fol. 67).

96 In the Preface to William Wordsworth and Samuel Taylor Coleridge, *Lyrical Ballads, With a Few Other Poems* (1798), Wordsworth wrote: 'The first volume of these Poems ... was published, as an experiment, which, I hoped, might be of some use to ascertain, how far, by fitting to metrical arrangement a selection of the

TO EDWARD A. ALLEN (W): TS

REF.48/18.

Magdalen College,
Oxford.
6th December 1948.

My dear Mr. Allen,

Did you ever read two amusing American books, 'Letters of a Self-Made Merchant to his Son', and the sequel, 'Old Gorgon Graham'?[97] I am put in mind of them by the tale of the man who offered to pay a fellow down on his luck $100.00 a month until he found a job; the thanks for the first cheque took six pages of manuscript; the eighth month the man wired 'My cheque not to hand. Expedite and explain'. The moral being that if you continue to bombard me with luxuries at this rate, I can see the time coming when I say to my secretary, 'tell Mr. Allen I've recieved the parcel, and the quality of the so-and-so was poor: and don't let it occur again'!

But all jokes apart, what am I to say about your goodness to me? Judging from the label (all that I've yet seen), there are enough good things here to provide a Christmas dinner and then a New Year party on top of that. Thank you very much indeed, and m[a]y your own Christmas be the brighter for the knowledge that you have so greatly improved mine.

With all best wishes,

yours sincerely,

C. S. Lewis

TO RUTH PITTER (BOD):

Magdalen.
Dec 11th 48

Dear Miss Pitter

But why do the *other* kinds of poetry continue to be produced in maturity or even old age? One can't write *Winter's Tale* or *Samson Agonistes* or the *Philoctetes*[98] by looking after No. 1.

---

real language of men in a state of vivid sensation, that sort of pleasure and that quantity of pleasure may be imparted, which a Poet may rationally endeavour to impart.'

97 George Horace Lorimer, *Letters of a Self-Made Merchant to his Son* (1903); *Old Gorgon Graham: More Letters from a Self-Made Merchant to his Son* (1904).

98 Sophocles, *Philoctetes*, a tragedy produced in 409 BC.

Is it rather that the characteristic experiences of youth demand the lyric and those of age, being (when any good at all) more concatenated and woven into wholes, demand the big poem? A flash of love-liking, a bird's song, a momentary depression, can hardly appear to age with that apparent isolation & self-sufficiency wh. they have in youth. One knows where they come from and where they go to and it is *that* one wants to talk about – the summer not the swallows? But I wouldn't know.

Yours
C. S. Lewis

Goethe, I'm told, kept on pouring out first class lyric to the end. But that is because he kept on having love affairs – a recipe I wd. deprecate.[99]

TO JOHN BETJEMAN (VIC):

Magdalen College,
Oxford.
Dec 17/48

Dear Betjeman

A student of yr. works placed in my hands last night a piece of XIXth century didactic hardware so edifying in tendency & hideous in design that we all felt you were the one man in England who cd. fully appreciate it. It awaits you in my rooms whenever you care to call for it. If I am not in you will easily recognise it on the table, and we wish you joy of it as an 'Exmas Box'.[100]

Yours
C. S. Lewis

---

99 Of this letter Ruth Pitter wrote: 'Beautiful letter, but he doesn't reflect that nowadays everybody has to do chores and is constantly interrupted – it is almost lyrics or nothing, especially for women. Taking to invalidism is an idea, but not so easy now: or to get oneself accepted as a Guarded Flame & be surrounded by stooges (horrible).

'Being in love, to be sure, does get one airborne, but only in hops of varying length, and is not to be relied on for much more than half a century: and even for this, the chores make everybody so careworn and unresponsive after youth is past. Never mind, poetry has perhaps always been done against odds' (Bodleian Library, MS. Eng. lett. c. 220/3, fol. 70).

100 Betjeman was a connoisseur of almost everything Victorian; this may have been a volume of Victorian verse.

TO WARFIELD M. FIROR (BOD): TS

REF.48/97.

Magdalen College,
Oxford.
20th. December 1948.

My dear Dr. Firor,

It is characteristic of your great kindness that you should not only send me another of those excellent hams, but should have timed it to arrive at the beginning of Christmas week; our Christmas dinner begins to assume a very different aspect with ham on the menu! I am quite at a loss for words to tell you what these kindnesses of yours have meant to my household, my friends, and myself. To begin to do so I should have to try to give you the whole background of our daily lives over here, and then would probably fail.

Food production and economics are right off my line, but I was uncomfortably impressed by an article I read some little time ago in an American periodical, in which the author claimed that the danger ahead of us was not World War III, but World Famine I; then others tell me that the whole problem is one of mal-distribution: and yet others, that it is obsolete farming.

With deepest thanks, and all best wishes for a happy and successful New Year,

yours sincerely,
C. S. Lewis

TO ROGER LANCELYN GREEN (BOD):

[The Kilns]
Christmas Eve 1948

My dear Green

(Why do you 'Mr.' me?) As you supposed Sunday night is quite impossible.

But you have already given me a very happy Christmas: merely looking thro' the book for that delicious gustatory 10 minutes has already loosed my knees and ravished me. 'Stay me with flagons, comfort me with apples.'[101] I trust I have some degree of fortitude in adversity but in the stronger grip of Sweet Desire I am as helpless as a schoolgirl. The Freudians say all this is a substitute for sex: I'm more

101 Song of Solomon 2:5.

inclined to suspect that sex and wealth & fame and wine and travel and all things except God are only a substitute for this! Blessings on you.

Yours
C. S. Lewis

TO WARFIELD M. FIROR (BOD) TS

REF.48/97.

Magdalen College,
Oxford.
29th. December 1948.

My dear Dr. Firor,

How deceptive voting figures can be. We also have a government elected by a majority which is really a minority. I am writing to Dr. Johnson[102] to explain that the tea in my mental teapot will not yield another cup at present: but I'm very delighted to hear of your Christian medical students. No more useful people could be imagined.

With all our best wishes for the New Year. You have made our past year a great deal brighter than it would have otherwise have been.

yours sincerely,
C. S. Lewis

TO LAURENCE HARWOOD (BOD):

Magdalen
Dec 29th 1948

My dear Laurence

Thanks for your interesting letter. Instead of having a fat goose we had a thin turkey, so I expect you had the best of the bargain. We have had a little ice on the pond but nothing near thick enough for skating.

I shall be interested to hear what Lois[103] thinks of Dartington Hall. I once had as my pupil a girl who was a mistress there,[104] and it seemed to me that the more sensible that girl became the less she approved of

---

102 It was well known that Dr Samuel Johnson had an inextinguishable thirst for tea. Lewis had probably been asked by a friend of Dr Firor, also named Johnson, to write an essay for publication.

103 i.e. Lois Harwood (b. 26 January 1926), Laurence's sister.

104 i.e. Mary Neylan.

Dartington. (Perhaps you had better not hand that bit of information on to Lois).

What an excellent thing to have read nearly all the Waverley novels.[105] At your age I had only read the medieval ones (*Ivanhoe*, *Q. Durward*, *The Talisman* etc) and didn't discover the more modern ones (*Waverley*, *G. Mannering*, *Antiquary* etc) till I was at Oxford. I now like those in the second list better than those in the first, but I think both lots very good and never get tired of them. What I like is that Scott doesn't skimp things, but tells you how everyone was dressed and what they ate and drank and what sort of houses they lived in, and the weather – which is what I always want to know though some people find it boring.

I hated Dickens as a boy. I think the illustrations put me off. Long before I could read I used to turn them over and over as picture books, not liking them, indeed rather frightened by them, but fascinated. The very smell of that edition (you have noticed that every book has its peculiar smell: in fact the smell of some books, next to that of new shoes, is one of the best smells there is, I think) – the very smell of that edition had a sort of horror about it. Luckily I've got over it now and was re-reading *Pickwick* just before Christmas. But I've never gone back to *O. Twist*.[106] Wd. you advise me to? *Gt. Expectations* is one of the best.

I have just read about a curious medieval method of proving your answer to a multiplication sum, and I am wondering if anyone at Michael Hall can explain why it works. I multiply, say, 12 by 63 and get the answer 756. I now want to find if I've done it right. I add the two digits of 12 (1 & 2) and get 3. I then add the two digits of 63 (6 & 3) and get 9. I multiply 3 x 9 and get 27. Then add 2 + 7 and get 9. Now I tackle the answer, 756. I add all its digits (7 + 5 + 6) and get 18. Add those digits 8 + 1 and get 9. The fact that I get 9 for both operations shows that my answer was right. Or here's another example:

---

105 Sir Walter Scott's first novel, *Waverley*, was an immediate success, and he followed it up with what are known as the 'Waverley novels'; these include *Guy Mannering, The Antiquary, The Black Dwarf* (1816), *Old Mortality* (1816), *Rob Roy, The Heart of Midlothian, The Bride of Lammermoor* (1819), and *The Legend of Montrose* (1819). Scott also wrote a number of historical novels, including *Ivanhoe* (1820), *Quentin Durward* (1823), and *The Talisman.*

106 Charles Dickens, *Oliver Twist* (1837–8).

22		2 + 2 = 4		
13		1 + 3 = *4*		
66			16	1 + 6 = 7
22				
286	2 + 8 + 6 = 16			1 + 6 = 7

Probably the explanation is quite simple and anyone less rotten at Maths than I am will see it at once.

I rather envy your Father having 'business' that takes him to Switzerland. Mine never takes me anywhere half so nice: does yours? You don't think this mysterious business, if we could follow him (invisible) and watch, would turn out really to be tobogganing and ski-ing and smoking cigars and having eight course dinners?

The cat keeps jumping on the chair and I must stop. I never knew any animal so bad at taking a hint. Love to all and best wishes for the New Year.

Your affectionate Godfather,
C. S. Lewis

TO EDWARD A. ALLEN (W): TS

REF.48/18.

Magdalen College,
Oxford.
31st December 1948.

My dear Mr. Allen,

Many thanks for your welcome letter of the 18th: welcome I hasten to add not merely for the news that you are still not tired of supporting me and mine, but for the pleasure of hearing from you again.

I stand amazed and ashamed at the statistics of your giving during 1948, and more especially when I reflect that you were on 'short time' for a portion of the year. Even in your generous country, there must be few men who have done so much to help us through our hard times. I am glad to say that the sense of what we owe America is almost universally appreciated over here, both by press and public. The Press in particular has been doing good work in hammering it home that this endless stream of gifts comes, in the main, not from millionaires, but from ordinary folk like ourselves; at first there may have been a slight tendency to think that the rich man's table was so abundantly supplied that the crumbs could easily be spared. Our people are hardly to be blamed for this: their knowledge of the U.S.A. is drawn exclusively from the pictures emanating from Hollywood, from which the man in the street gathers that *all* American incomes scale upwards from a minimum of £6,000 a year or thereabouts.

Yes, your dentist can hardly be said to err on the side of effusiveness, can he? I too have seen a lot of talk about dentist's earning under our state scheme, but have no first hand information on the subject: and I'm inclined to think it must be exaggerated. If not, their position is very different to that of the doctors; a doctor gets some 17/- per year out of the £13 contributed by each patient. The balance goes in pensions, funeral expenses, administrative expenses, and so on. One would like to know the percentage of the last item, but this they take care not to tell us.

You ask what we most need? Sugar and tea are the two things which are most difficult to get in anything like sufficient quantities at the moment, but almost anything is welcome. I have'nt myself had any experience of the 'unpalatable staples' you refer to; all my parcels have been excellent. *No* bacon can be too fat in a country which is permanently short of fats.

Once more with deepest thanks to you and your Mother for your great kindness, and all our best wishes for a happy and prosperous New Year,

yours sincerely,
C. S. Lewis

TO WARFIELD M. FIROR (BOD) TS

REF.48/97

Magdalen College,
Oxford.
31st. December 1948.

My dear Dr. Firor,

Overseas Associates Inc. has just delivered – in perfect condition as usual – another of those delicious hams: leaving me, also as usual, with nothing whatever to say. For who can go on putting any conviction into a 'thank you' which has been so often reiterated as mine? All I can tell you is that my gratitude is as warm as it always was, and that I do say 'thank you' with a warmth which I fear is lacking from this note.

I was very sorry indeed not to be able to do that article for your friend; but, as I explained to him, most of the bad articles that get written are turned out by men who feel that they must 'pump up' something for the occasion.

Tomorrow it will be 1949. One of my chief recollections of 1948 will be that, by your kindness, it has been a much happier year than it otherwise would have been.

With all best wishes,

yours sincerely,

C. S. Lewis

1949

TO DOROTHY L. SAYERS (W): TS

REF.5/49.

Magdalen College,
Oxford.
1st. January 1949

Dear Miss Sayers,

Hurrah! Pussius Catius never wrote a better Analect. The 'region of the summer stars' is a quotation from Taliessin's song in the Mabogi-nion[1] and (between ourselves) I doubt if C.W. attached more than an 'emotive' significance to it. I dare'nt begin to think of the zones, roofs, and proofs.[2]

Your letter shines amid the day's mail like a good deed in a naughty world. The Christmas holydays are the time when all the nuisances in the world choose to write to me – I expect to you too. I do hope we can meet in the summer. All good wishes and many thanks.

yours sincerely,
C. S. Lewis

I'm reading North's Plutarch. Once one gets off the ones read as 'sources' to Shakespeare (wh. naturally aren't the ones good in themselves) they're wonderful stuff. Recommend Timoleon & Marcellus.[3]

---

1 Sayers wanted to know where the title of Charles Williams's poem, *The Region of the Summer Stars*, came from. *The Mabinogion* is a collection of Welsh tales composed between the second half of the eleventh century and the end of the thirteenth, but based on older oral tradition. Most contain Arthurian legends. The first English translation was made by Lady Charlotte Guest in 1838–9 which included 'The Story of Taliesin' which is a later Welsh legend including several songs attributed to Taliesin.

2 In her letter of 31 December 1948 Sayers mentioned being puzzled by Williams's *Taliessin Through Logres*, 'The Coming of Galahad', last stanza: 'But he: "Proofs were; roofs were: I/what more? Creeds were; songs were. Four/zones divide the empire from the Throne's firmament.'

3 See note 10 to the letter to Warnie of 11 January 1939.

TO VERA MATHEWS (W): TS

REF. 12/49.

Magdalen College,
Oxford.
3rd. January 1949.

Dear Miss Mathews,

Gratitude being the only return that I can make you for your continued kindness, it is coals of fire upon my head to find you signing your later [letter] of the 28th. December 'yours gratefully'! I need hardly say how much I am looking forward to the arrival of your latest gift, and how much it will be appreciated in my home. It will take no hurt for being six weeks on the road, but I think you exaggerate a little. Did'nt your last one arrive within the month?

With all best wishes to you for a happy and prosperous 1949,

yours *most* gratefully,
C. S. Lewis

TO DOROTHY L. SAYERS (W): TS

REF.4/49.

Magdalen College,
Oxford.
5th. January 1949.

Dear Miss Sayers,

C. C. J. Webb once read a paper on Siger[4] to the Dante Society, and he would probably love to be asked. Write to him c/o Magdalen.

C.W. did'nt have to *have* a rhyme at that moment.[5] *Hoofs* (equals the Tartar invasions) would have been nice!

yours sincerely,
C. S. Lewis

4 In a letter of 3 January 1949 Sayers asked why Dante was so keen on Siger of Brabant (d. 1281), who is mentioned in *Paradiso* X, 136. Siger was a master of arts in Paris, and leader of Latin Averroism during the sixth and seventh decades of the thirteenth century.

5 In the last stanza of Charles Williams's 'The Coming of Galahad'. See note 2 to the letter to Sayers of 1 January 1949.

TO WARFIELD M. FIROR (BOD): TS

REF.23/49

Magdalen College,
Oxford.
5th January 1949.

My dear Dr. Firor,

The year is only five days old, and already I find myself trying to perform the pleasant task of thanking you for your continued kindness to me and mine. Your beautiful parcel of groceries has just arrived, and I cannot tell you how very welcome it is: for this year we are being encouraged to further effort by the promise that now *real* austerity is about to begin! One is reminded forcibly of the old tale of the horse which was trained to live on one bit of straw a day. However, thanks mainly to you, we are in the position of being able, not only to face quite a bit of austerity ourselves, but to help less fortunately placed neighbours.

I leave town this evening for an eight days rest in the country: at Malvern, about sixty miles to the west of us; we shall be a batchelor party in a borrowed house – my doctor, my brother, and myself. And the chief item of our baggage is your last *ham* which has been carefully kept on the ice for this occasion. A kind farmer friend in the neighbourhood has sent us a duck: and promises some eggs. So you can see we are going to have a holiday which a Black Market King might envy! I need hardly say that we shall have many grateful thoughts of you as we eat that ham.

With many thanks indeed, and all best wishes for a prosperous and happy 1949,

yours sincerely,
C. S. Lewis

TO DON GIOVANNI CALABRIA (V):

Magdalen College,
Oxford
Jan XIV. 1949.

Laeto animo, Pater dilectissime, epistolam tuam in die Natali Domini scriptam accepi eo gratiorem quia tam solemni horâ me in memoria habere voluisti. Noli dubitare quin locum usitatum in orationibus meis teneas. Nunc vero montes et maria nos dividunt nec scio quâ sis formâ corporis; placeat Deo ut olim in resurrectione corporum et inenarrabili illâ novitate congrediamur.

Quod ad meos labores pertinet, nollem te spe inani fallere. Iam quinquagesimum annum ago. Fervorem scribendi et priscum quidquid erat ingenii decrescere sentio: neque (credo) lectoribus, ut solebam, placeo. Multis aerumnis laboro. Domus mea inquieta, muliebribus rixis vastata, *inter tabernacula Kedar habitandum est*. Grandaeva mater, longa valetudine confecta, diurnae curae mihi est.

Ora pro me, Pater, ut semper in mente habeam praeclaram istam sententiam 'si vis pacificare alios, tene *te* in pace'. Haec scribo non quasi querelas sed ne forte credas me opera componere. Si Deo placuerit ut plura scribam, benedictus sit; si non placuerit, iterum benedictus sit. Fortasse animae meae saluberrimum erit et famam et ingenium perdere ne in vanam gloriam (malam pestem) lapsurus essem.

De istis parvis 'magnis viris' quorum mentionem fecisti, tacebo. Magna minantur et magna pollicentur; utraque (fortasse) vana. Sollicitudo de rebus futuris frustra angit mentes mortales. Attamen, confiteor, saepe cogimur dicere 'Quousque, Dominine?'

Vale.

C. S. Lewis

*

Magdalen College,
Oxford
Jan XIV. 1949.

With a joyful heart, dearest Father, I received your letter written on the day of the Lord's Nativity – all the more welcome for this, that you were willing to remember me in so solemn an hour.

Do not doubt that you hold your accustomed place in my prayers. Now, indeed, mountains and seas divide us; nor do I know what your appearance is in the body. On some day hereafter, in the resurrection of the body, and in that renewal beyond our telling, God grant that we may meet.

As for my own work, I would not wish to deceive you with vain hope. I am now in my fiftieth year. I feel my zeal for writing, and whatever talent I originally possessed, to be decreasing; nor (I believe) do I please my readers as I used to. I labour under many difficulties. My house is unquiet and devastated by women's quarrels. I have *to dwell in the tents of Kedar*.[6] My aged mother, worn out by long infirmity,

6 Psalm 120:5: 'Woe is me, that I sojourn in Mesech, that I dwell in the tents of Kedar!'

is my daily care. Pray for me, Father, that I ever bear in mind that profoundly true maxim: 'if you wish to bring others to peace, keep thyself in peace.'[7]

These things I write not as complaints but lest you should believe I am writing books. If it shall please God that I write more books, blessed be He. If it shall not please Him, again, blessed be He. Perhaps it will be the most wholesome thing for my soul that I lose both fame and skill lest I were to fall into that evil disease, vainglory.

About these little 'big men' of whom you make mention, I shall keep silent. They threaten much, they promise much, and equally, perhaps, in vain. Concern for the future distresses mortal minds in vain. However, we are often, I confess, compelled to say 'How long, O Lord?'[8]

Farewell.

C. S. Lewis

TO VERA MATHEWS (W): TS

REF. 12/49.

Magdalen College,
Oxford.
15th. January 1949.

My dear Miss Mathews,

It would be almost impertinent to say that the parcel posted on 14th. November fulfilled my expectations: for when have you not sent a gift which exceeded them? I am just back from a week in the country, and have'nt yet had time to open it, but the 'bill of fare' on the label is a feast in itself; it is with a particular delight that I read '1 tea' – a thing of which my household uses large quantities, and which, in the jargon if [of] the day, is with us always 'in short supply'. Thank you very much indeed for this and all past kindnesses.

With all best wishes to you during 1949,

yours sincerely,

C. S. Lewis

---

7 Thomas à Kempis, *The Imitation of Christ,* II, iii, 1.
8 John 10:24.

TO EDWARD A. ALLEN (W): TS

REF.48/18.

Magdalen College,
Oxford.
17th January 1949.

My dear Mr. Allen,

With characteristic kindness you have chosen to wish me a happy New Year not by letter, but by an enormous parcel of good things: your No. 54, sent on 24th October last, which arrived over the week end in perfect condition. That any should go to such trouble and expense for your friends – if I may so describe myself – is amazing and touching. I refer not so much to the content of this handsome consignment but to your admirable packing and addressing. It is no wonder that the task absorbed 220 hours of your time during 1948. I can think myself capable if positions were reversed, of *ordering* a parcel for you at some shop, but I fear my self-sacrifice would not extend so far as to undergo all the patient labour which you put into your gifts.

There remains nothing that I can say, except, as so often before, that I am deeply grateful for all your goodness to me.

With my best wishes,
yours sincerely,
C. S. Lewis

TO ARTHUR GREEVES (W):

[Magdalen College]
Jan 20/49

My dear Arthur,

I hope you have not thought badly of me for not writing sooner. The news[9] reached me (from Kelsie, as well as Janie) just as term was starting and I have hardly had a moment to myself till now. But I've been thinking of you in plenty and trying to imagine how you might be feeling. I know you have long dreaded this final break up. And I suppose you now find that you miss your Mother more than you expected. But it's really such a mix up of sensations at such times: 'comfortless excitement' is how I wd. describe it. My *reason* tells me

9 Arthur's mother, Mary Margretta Greeves, died on 1 January 1949, aged eighty-seven.

that you will now be freer and there is perhaps more chance of seeing you in England: but I *feel* something quite different – as if a new gap had opened between us, as if this somehow cut us off from the happy past. (Not that it was very happy, really: you know what I mean.) For you, of course, the wrench will be v. big, all the bigger because the same home life in wh. you grew up has gone on so very long without a real break. I am glad you – and she – were not harrowed with a long or painful illness.

What happens now? Where will John go?[10] Poor John. And poor Mrs Greeves: she was always kind to me. I expect you are writing innumerable letters at present, so of course I look for no answer.

God bless you, my oldest friend: you, and she, will be in my prayers.

Yours

Jack

Warnie of course sends his sympathies: what rot it all sounds between you and me!

TO WARFIELD M. FIROR (BOD): TS

REF.23/49

Magdalen College,
Oxford.
22nd. January 1949.

My dear Dr. Firor,

Your bounty (see *Antony and Cleopatra*) 'an autumn is that grows the more by reaping'.[11] Only yesterday I said to myself, How I should like to see America if only one could see the quiet parts of it, and not the cities – things which in every country interest me only if I want to hear an opera or buy a book! And you anticipated me.

But it's all impossible. An old invalid ties me to home. A visit to another continent is as impossible to me as one to the Moon. Oh what a pity! To think that I might as your guest have seen bears, beavers, Indians, and mountains! How did you know what I wanted? Meanwhile, the only chance of a meeting is that you should visit this island prison.

---

10 Arthur's brother, John Greeves (1892–1969), was unmarried and had been living with his mother.

11 Shakespeare, *Antony and Cleopatra*, V, ii, 87–8: 'an autumn 'twas/That grew the more by reaping'.

To all my set you are by now an almost mythical person – Firor-of-the-Hams, a sort of Fertility god.

God bless you.

yours regretfully,
C. S. Lewis

TO EDWARD A. ALLEN (W): TS

REF.48/18.

Magdalen College,
Oxford.
24th January 1949.

My dear Mr. Allen,

All very well to say cut down on the adjectives, but the adjective is the only method of expression of gratitude which is available to the Englishman in this 'brave new world'. Would you like a letter which told you what wonderful weather we were having for February, and finishing off 'P.S. By the way thanks for that parcel'. But I will certainly quote the numbers in future. I don't in fact think any of your gifts to me have ever gone astray. No, envelopes are as hard to get as ever, and will be very welcome.

As I've so often told you, I'm no economist, and this new world beats me. Why is a nation not in the same position as the individual? Supposing you strike a bad patch, what is your domestic policy of spending? Surely, Rent, insurance, food, clothes, general necessities, and luxuries, in that order. Here it is hard to get envelopes but perfectly easy to get champagne and gin. I agree with Mr. H. C. Urey:[12] but his idea is such obvious commonsense that he will doubtless be labelled as an impracticable crank.

yours ever,
C. S. Lewis

---

12 Harold Clayton Urey (1893–1981), who won the Nobel Prize for Chemistry in 1934, was Director of War Research of the Atomic Bomb Project at Columbia University, 1940–5. He moved to the Institute for Nuclear Studies at the University of Chicago in 1945 as Distinguished Service Professor of Chemistry and became Martin A. Ryerson Professor in 1952.

TO I. O. EVANS (W): TS

REF.83/49.

Magdalen College,
Oxford.
24th. January 1949.

Dear Mr. Evans,

(1). I thought parts of 'King Kong' (especially where the natives make a stand after he's broken the gate) magnificent, but the New York parts contemptible.

(2). I've just read 'Flying Saucer'[13] and thought it a good satiric romance. Some minor touches – the American woman objecting to the 'Martian's' nudity – were admirable. The difficulty was, obviously, to get an Ending, and I'm not quite sure that this was solved, i.e. is there a lack of climax? But well worth reading, and many thanks for sending it.

yours sincerely,
C. S. Lewis

TO EDWARD A. ALLEN (W): TS

REF.48/18.

Magdalen College,
Oxford.
28th January 1949.

My dear Mr. Allen,

When I contemplate this beautiful parcel, I wonder how many of those 220 hours in 1948 were spent in packing for me; personally, being unable to do up a parcel which would hold together from here to the other side of Oxford, I regard your handiwork with envy.

You will think that this is a very odd beginning to a letter of thanks: rather as if one were to send a man a dozen eggs and he replied with praise of the egg shells. My excuse is that the outside of your egg is all that I have yet seen, though I am vastly intrigued by the label; here are 22 lbs. of good things which will give us all much joy and comfort for a long time to come. And what can I say? Nothing more than what I have so often had the great pleasure to say before, namely 'thank you very much for your continued kindness to us'.

I see disquieting accounts in our papers of conditions in the U.S.A.

---

13 Bernard Newman, *The Flying Saucer* (1948).

– short time, heavy drop in sales etc., and foreboding of a slump. I hope however that this is mere 'dope' to keep us contented with conditions inside the 'Iron Curtain'.

With all my best thanks and best wishes,

yours sincerely,

C. S. Lewis

TO SISTER PENELOPE CSMV (BOD):

Magdalen etc
Jan 31/49

Dear Sister Penelope

Alas! As to the next move, I never, in my own frequent early disappointments, hit upon any subtler plan than flinging the MS. at one publisher after another, and was always too ignorant to select the publishers except by fancy and rumour. In other words, a large supply of sealing wax, brown paper, and fortitude is called for. You might of course try a magazine. As I never read one I can't tell you what ones now publish serials at all – but you must have some friends who are less ignorant than I.

As regards Bles's points – (1) When we last met, if you remember, I expressed an anxiety lest what promised to be a Space-and-Time story with a moral was turning into a 'straight' religious novel with recurrent Space-and-Time interludes. If that is what they mean by their antithesis of 'human interest' and 'religious propaganda' I shd. see what they mean. But I'm not sure that they do. At any rate I take it that a drastic re-writing wd. be psychologically impossible to you at the moment. If all else fails perhaps in a few years?

(2) I did also think (and say) that if more than one character in a story had time-vision some reason ought to be invented for the coincidence. Your two cousins don't settle the matter for *real* life doesn't need to be probable (seldom is!) but stories do.

(3) For a *nom de guerre* – I don't know. G. H. Pevensey, S. Claydon, are names that come into my head. Or, in a different vein Ithacensis (Penelope being an Ithacan).

We're hobbling along at home: 'mustn't grumble' as they say. I'm very disappointed about the book, and will try to console myself with Athanasius.

If it comes to re-writing I still feel that there are *two* different books striving together in your MS. You may have to write both.

Yours sincerely

C. S. Lewis

TO VERA MATHEWS (W): TS

REF. 12/49.

Magdalen College,
Oxford.
1st. February 1949.

My dear Miss Mathews,

Your generosity is so copious that I sometimes get the impression that half my time (the pleasantest half) is spent in writing you woefully inadequate notes of acknowledgement! Your very fine gift, date undecipherable, has just reached me, in good condition, and I hasten to send you my heartiest thanks, not only on my own behalf, but on that of all who will ultimately be sharers in your kindness; for your parcels, if I may so express it, have a wide circulation. Dr. Johnson you remember once said that 'there was no Irishman so wretched that he had not another Irishman as his client'. The situation as regards food is something like that with us now; few of us don't get something occasionally from the U.S.A. and few of us fail to share it with those less lucky: so you can imagine how much sharing there is to be done by those like myself who, thanks to your kindness, are so well stocked with good things.

Again many thanks, and with all best wishes,

yours sincerely,

C. S. Lewis

TO DAPHNE HARWOOD (BOD): TS

REF.106/49.

Magdalen College,
Oxford.
2nd February 1949.

Dear Daphne,

Thanks for your kind letter. Is'nt Wolfram himself derived from Chrestien?*[14] But no time now.

---

14 Chrestien is the Old French spelling of Chrétien (de Troyes).

Love to all.
yours sincerely,
Jack Lewis

* Not of course that he wd. be any less important on that account.[15]

TO WARFIELD M. FIROR (BOD): TS

REF.23/49

Magdalen College,
Oxford.
4th. February 1949.

My dear Dr. Firor,

I much fear that a zealous 'new broom' of a servant has been 'tidying' the portion of my rooms set aside as a warehouse for storage of your unconsumed benefactions. At least, to my horror, I have just come across a parcel from you which I have not marked 'ack.'[16] How long it has been here I don't know; it is from Overseas Associates Inc., number 73575 Hercules, and has a 'Merry Christmas' label, with a shield of the Stars and Stripes. Your address I see is given as 107 Longwood (?) Rd. I am ashamed to think that it may have been unacknowledged to you for a considerable time. Fortunately it is one of those excellent consignments of tinned goods, so no harm is done: but I turn pale to think it might just as easily have been a ham!

If I have thanked you for this parcel already, please forgive me for troubling you again: and if I *have'nt*, please accept my humble apologies for a blunder which was not of my making. In any case I have the opportunity of once more thanking you for all your kindness to me.

With all best wishes,
yours sincerely,
C. S. Lewis

P.S. I hope I do right in addressing to Calvert St. as usual?

---

15 Mrs Harwood had probably asked which version of the story of Perceval and the Holy Grail came first – that of Chrétien de Troyes who wrote *Perceval* or *Le Conte du Graal* or that of Wolfram von Eschenbach (fl. 1200–20) whose principal work, *Parzival*, was composed early in the thirteenth century. The later author's work contains many elements which did not appear in the *Perceval* of Chrétien, and is a great work in itself.

16 i.e. 'acknowledged'.

TO EDWARD T. DELL (P):[17]

[Magdalen College,
Oxford]
4/2/49

Dear Mr. Dell –

(1.) As you doubtless know, it was the opinion of some 'Fathers' that our unfallen human race would have been, as you say, 'translated'. Naturally, I have no *doctrine* on such a purely speculative point. You must not confuse my romances with my theses. In the latter I state and argue a creed. In the former much is merely supposed for the sake of the story.

(2.) I cannot claim to have a clearly worked out position about the Bible or the nature of Inspiration. That is a subject on which I wd. gladly learn: I have nothing to teach.

(3.) Everyone who accepts the teaching of St. Paul must have a belief in 'sanctification'.[18] But I should, myself, be v. chary of describing such operations of the Holy Ghost as 'experiences' if by experiences we mean things necessarily discoverable by introspection. And I should be still more chary of mapping out a series of such experiences as an indispensable norm (or syllabus!) for all Christians. I think the ways in which God saves us are probably infinitely various and admit varying degrees of consciousness in the patient. Anything wh. sets him saying 'Now . . . Stage II ought to be coming along . . . is this it?' I think bad and likely to lead some to presumption and others to despair. We must leave God to dress the wound and not keep on taking peeps under the bandage for ourselves.

(4.) I don't know Dr. Brightman's views,[19] and don't know what Personalism is. But I certainly do not believe in a limited God – except

---

17 See **Edward Thomas Dell Jr** in the Biographical Appendix. Facsimiles of his letters from Lewis are in the Bodleian Library and Wheaton College.

18 Dell wrote in his letter of 1 February 1949: 'Our church teaches a Wesleyan doctrine called Sanctification. Its ethic is the idea of Holiness which is the imitation of Christ. Wesley taught that the experience was a second crisis and that it corrected the "bent to sinning", mentioned in Charles Wesley's hymn, as well as being the occasion for the coming of the Holy Spirit into the heart' (Bodleian Library, MS. Eng. lett. c. 220/4, fol. 67).

19 *Personalism in Theology, a Symposium in Honor of Albert Cornelius Knudson, by associates and former students*, ed. Edgar Sheffield Brightman (Boston: Boston University Press, 1943).

in so far as He chooses to limit Himself (e.g. by giving some of His creatures free will)

(5.) I firmly believe that God's life is non temporal.[20] Time is a defect of reality since by its v. nature any temporal being loses each moment of its life to get the next – the moments run through us as if we were sieves! God forbid that we shd. think God to be like that. On the eternal Now read Boethius, von Hügel's *Eternal Life* etc. Also St. Peter (?) who adds to the old maxim '1000 years in His sight are but as a day' the v. important opposite 'and a day as 1000 years'[21]

With all good wishes,

Yours sincerely

C. S. Lewis

TO RHONA BODLE (BOD):

[Magdalen College,
Oxford]
Feb 10/49

Dear Miss Bodle –

I doubt whether I, or anyone else, needs to interfere. The route you are following at present seems to be the right one. Adding to Pascal's 'if you had not found me you wd. not seek me'[22] (a sentence I have long loved), the very obvious further step 'And if I had not drawn you, you wd. not have found me,' and seeing both in the light of Our Lord's words 'No man cometh to me unless the Father have drawn him'[23] – well, it is pretty clear that you are being conducted. 'Follow-my-leader' is a good enough guide now. Thinking as you now do of Christ you will not be able for long to set aside the sayings wh.

---

20 Dell commented in his letter of 1 February 1949: '[Gordon Parker] Bowne in his *Metaphysics* [1898] says that time and space are only necessities of the finite mind and not necessary to God. Some of us say that since God is a personality that time is real to Him – and necessary. Others of us maintain that in-time is no more necessary than in-space to Him. Your reference to the eldil not "waiting" in "Perelandra" for instance' (Bodleian Library, MS. Eng. lett. c. 220/4, fols 67–8).

21 2 Peter 3:8: 'One day is with the Lord as a thousand years, and a thousand years as one day.'

22 Blaise Pascal, *Pensées*, trans. W. F. Trotter (1996–7), Section VII, Morality and Doctrine, no. 553: 'Console thyself, thou wouldst not seek Me, if thou hadst not found Me.'

23 John 14:6.

proclaim Him to be more than man ('Before Abraham was I AM'[24] – 'I AM and hereafter ye shall see the Son of Man etc'[25] – 'Thy sins are forgiven thee'[26] – 'I am the Vine').[27]

I didn't listen in (I never do) to the discussion you mention: but I quite agree that people are far too concerned about the 'modern' man and this-that-and-the-other man. Why not, as you say, just *man*? You are always in my prayers.

Yours sincerely
C. S. Lewis

TO WARFIELD M. FIROR (BOD): TS

REF.23/49

Magdalen College,
Oxford.
11th. February 1949.

My dear Dr. Firor,

'Yours to hand, contents noted'.

Gratitude evaporates through a typewriter, and I often feel acutely that my letters thanking you for your continued and great goodness do in fact boil down to the first line of this; but I feel now, if I may say so, that you know me well enough to understand that if the expression is weak, the sentiment which prompts it is warm. Without your help, life for me and mine would be a very differing business.

I don't know how far one is to trust American news in our papers; they all talk of a big slump impending in the States, heavy and increasing unemployment etc. I am no economist, but I fail to understand how there can be a slump in a country which has such huge potential foreign markets as has the U.S.A. I am still full of regrets at the thought of the summer I might have had with you, if things had been otherwise. Is there no chance of your coming to England in the near future? Though why you should visit this bleak island I don't know: but I should like the chance of thanking you personally for all that you have done for me.

yours sincerely,
C. S. Lewis

---

24 ibid., 8:58.
25 Matthew 26:64.
26 ibid., 9:2.
27 John 15:1.

TO EDWARD A. ALLEN (W): TS

REF.48/18.

Magdalen College,
Oxford.
16th February 1949.

My dear Mr. Allen,

Many thanks for your interesting and amusing letter of the 31st of last month, and particularly for the story about the two tins of spam; it would be of little help to me if a similar accident happened in our street. At my time of life I should merely be trampled to death in the rush! You 'ate eggs and eggs' did you? And don't you realize how lucky you were! We eat 'fish and fish'. The normal family in this country – the family in fact which has no Edward Allen to come to its rescue – eats fish as its main meal at least five times a week. And will soon be eating it seven times a week as far as I can see, for we now have quarrelled with the Argentine; what the rights and wrongs of the case are, I don't know. We claim that the Argentines are trying to stick us up, and they say that they have no divinely appointed mission to supply England with meat at England's price.[28]

So there is yet another evidence of your extreme kindness to me on its way. What can I say about it? Only as I have so often said before, 'thank you very very much'. Easily said, and unsatisfactory; but you I hope realize how deeply I do feel your goodness. I am struck and rather mystified by the restriction on tea; if it had been say *fat*, of which there is a world shortage, I could have understood it. But surely a 'hard' currency country like yours can have no difficulty in getting tea in any quantity it likes to pay for?

I will let you know of course how the parcel fares. With renewed thanks and all best wishes,

yours sincerely,
C. S. Lewis

---

28 Under the terms of the 'Andes Agreement', Argentina was to supply England with 400,000 tons of meat during the succeeding twelve months. However, when the agreement ended 108,000 tons remained unshipped. Argentina's government said they would supply the rest of the meat, but at a price almost double what Britain had been paying. Several agreements were broken by Argentina who wanted more money than Britain was able or willing to pay. Supplies of meat from Argentina were not resumed until April 1951.

TO WARFIELD M. FIROR (BOD): TS

REF.23/49

Magdalen College,
Oxford.
17th February 1949.

My dear Dr. Firor,

I see it is just a week ago since I last had the pleasure of thanking you for a parcel, and today you surpass yourself by sending me not *a* parcel, but *three* parcels! And one of them a ham no less! My first feelings are those of a hungry schoolboy, my second, regret that you cannot be here to make one at the impending feast. If you believe in the old wives tale of 'sympathetic attraction', your ears will burn in a few days time at the heartiness with which a select party will drink your health whilst consuming your bounty. I am indeed a very lucky man to have such a friend as you, and only wish that an epistolatory could be converted into a personal contact; but I live in hopes that you may still consider such an 'exchange post' as you thought of for this year.

Once again, very many thanks for your great and continued kindness, and with all best wishes,

yours sincerely,
C. S. Lewis

TO I. O. EVANS (W):

28/2/49

Dear Mr. Evans

Thanks for your kind letter and for enclosing the C.S.A.[29]

I'm with you on the main issue – that art can teach (and much great art deliberately set out to do so) without at all ceasing to be art. On the particular case of Wells I wd. agree with Burke,[30] because in Wells it seems to me that one has *first* class pure fantasy (*Time Machine, First Men in the Moon*) and *third* class didacticism: i.e. I object to his novels with a purpose not because they have a purpose but because I think them bad. Just as I object to the preaching passages in Thackeray not because I dislike sermons but because I dislike bad sermons. To me, therefore, Wells & Thackeray are instances that obscure the issue. It must be fought on books when the doctrine is as good on its own

29 I. O. Evans, *The Coming of a King: A Story of the Stone Age* (1950).
30 Burke remains to be identified.

merits as the art – e.g. Bunyan, Chesterton, (as you agree) Tolstoi, Charles Williams, Virgil. All good wishes.

Yours

C. S. Lewis

TO VALERIE PITT (BOD):[31]

1/3/49

Dear Miss Pitt

Not proven, I think. The first passage might for all I can see refer only to microbes or small insects. The second is panpsychism: where from, I don't know. But I don't see anything to tie either down to *De Nymphis* – tho', mind you, it is now some time since I read that pleasant book.[32] I feel that if Shelley had been using it he wd. have been delighted to tell us in his Notes. Godwin by the way (P.J. V I.) mentions Salamanders living in the Sun.[33] Keats' *Song of 4 Faeries*[34] gives the 4 orders: but I expect from the *Rape of the Lock*.[35]

Yours sincerely

C. S. Lewis

---

31 See **Valerie Joan Pitt** in the Biographical Appendix. Lewis's letter of 1 March 1949 concerns the B.Litt. thesis Pitt began writing on Percy Bysshe Shelley in 1947.

32 Pitt had perhaps asked Lewis about the source of two passages from Shelley dealing with natural spirits which she believed had come from Paracelsus, *Liber de Nymphis, Sylphis, Pygmaeis et Salamandris et Caeteribus Spiritibus* (1515). She may have found an early source that suggested to her that someone had preceded Shakespeare in *A Midsummer Night's Dream* as the inventor of *small* fairies, and Lewis apparently doubted the reference. This subject is dealt with in some detail in *The Discarded Image*, ch. 6, 'The *Longaevi*', where Lewis discusses the various kinds, and sizes, of faeries.

33 Godwin, *Enquiry Concerning Political Justice*, Book V, Section 1: 'He that knows the mind of man . . . must himself have been an actor in the scene, have had his own passions brought into play, have known the anxiety of expectation and the transport of success, or he will feel and understand about as much of what he sees as mankind in general would of the transactions of the vitrified inhabitants of the planet Mercury, or the salamanders that live in the sun.'

34 John Keats, *Lamia* (1820), I, 1–6: 'Upon a time, before the faery broods/Drove Nymph and Satyr from the prosperous woods,/Before King Oberon's bright diadem,/Sceptre, and mantle, clasp'd with dewy gem,/Frighted away the Dryads and the Fauns/From rushes green, and brakes, and cowslip'd lawns.'

35 Alexander Pope, *The Rape of the Lock* (1714), Canto I, 57–66: 'The Sprites of fiery Termagants in Flame/Mount up, and take a *Salamander's* name./Soft yielding Minds to Water glide away,/And sip, with *Nymphs*, their elemental Tea./The graver Prude sinks downward to a *Gnome*,/In search of Mischief still on Earth to roam./The light coquettes in *Sylphs* aloft repair,/And sport and flutter in the Fields of Air.'

TO WARFIELD M. FIROR (BOD): TS

REF.23/49

Magdalen College,
Oxford.
3rd. March 1949.

My dear Dr. Firor,

My secretary has been ill for a few days, and I have been more than usually busy; which things coinciding have caused a regrettable delay in thanking you for your goodness in sending me one of the now familiar, but ever welcome 'Hercules' parcels: and as usual, packing, condition, and quality leave nothing to be desired. I have long since exhausted all my thanks, and can now only leave you to infer them: for I feel sure that you know that I *am* thankful.

Why conditions should continue to be so bad over here I'm unable to guess. That Belgium, as a 'hard' currency country should be better off than the rest of us is understandable; but why Denmark, or France, where I see in this morning's paper[36] – a reputable one – that *all* rationing is to end in July. But these are deep problems (though dealt with I fear by shallow minds), so with very hearty thanks to you for all your goodness, I will turn to my task once more.

yours sincerely,
C. S. Lewis

TO EDWARD A. ALLEN (W): TS

REF.48/18.

Magdalen College,
Oxford.
3rd March 1949.

My dear Mr. Allen,

Pkge. 81, posted Springfield Mass, Brightwood Sta. 31/1/49, arrived good condition stop contents checked with label and found correct stop.

Come now, you can't complain that is'nt a nice short business like answer!! But joking apart, I refuse to be done out of my 'six or eight adjectives'; it would be inhumane to expect it, when adjectives are all that I have to offer. It would take a good deal more nerve than I possess to complain about what was in a gift parcel, even if there were anything

36 Lewis did not read the newspapers, and this is one of those incidences where Warnie was not only typing a letter but expressing some of his own thoughts.

to complain of; but honestly, I can't think of a single item that won't be of the utmost value – and thank you very very much.

yours sincerely,
C. S. Lewis

P.S. It's just occurred to me that I heard at home the other day that what we are short of is not toilet soap, but washing soap. Do you talk about 'washing' soap? What we mean by it is soap to wash clothes.

TO FRANK D. LOMBAR (W): TS

REF.145/49.

Magdalen College,
Oxford.
3rd. March 1949.

Dear Mr. Lombar,

Your beautiful parcel would have been acknowledged earlier had it not been for the illness of my secretary. Would you please convey to the National Association of Evangelicals[37] my very deep thanks for their kindness. It may be true that all of us over here have, in a strict dietetic sense, 'enough to eat'; but only those who have endured this sort of 'sufficiency' for a number of years, can appreciate its deadly dullness. Nor indeed is there any agreement between our various experts as to whether we have even that sufficiency. So you can understand what a difference it makes to us when our diet is supplemented by such luxurious gifts as yours.

With very many thanks and all good wishes,

yours sincerely,
C. S. Lewis

TO WARFIELD M. FIROR (BOD):

Magdalen etc
4/3/49

Dear Dr. Firor

This is very good news (Belfast is my native town and my Mother was a B.A. of Queen's). You must manage at least a dinner, night, and

37 Frank D. Lombar was in charge of relief material for the National Association of Evangelicals which describes itself as 'a coordinating agency facilitating Christian unity, public witness, and cooperative ministry among evangelical denominations, congregations, educational institutions, and service agencies in the United States.'

breakfast here.[38] I've probably told you how I live – tied to an invalid with one night out (i.e. one night in College) a week. That night is normally a Thursday and can never be a Sat. or Sunday. So ear-mark a week day as early as possible (preferably a Thursday) and let me know. All who have feasted on your hams will be anxious to meet you.

To allow that my main (or exclusive!) interest in an American slump turns on philoprogenitiveness of hogs wd. imply that my interest in them was itself hoggish. Still, I'm glad that they at least will not cease to do their duty.

With heartiest welcome.

Yours

C. S. Lewis

Besides being 'tied to an invalid' – Mrs Moore – Lewis was also having difficulty with Warnie who wrote in his diary on 4 March: 'I emerged from the Acland yesterday morning, where I had been as a finale to the wearisome cycle of insomnia – drugs – depression – spirits – illness. The saddest feature of the thing is that I can see that J. assumes it to be spirits – insomnia – drugs – depression – spirits – illness. But his kindness remains unabated.'[39]

TO VERA MATHEWS (W): TS

REF. 12/49

Magdalen College,
Oxford.
7th. March 1949.

My dear Miss Mathews,

I should have been writing to you in any case this morning, for oddly enough your very kind gift of the 4th. February and your letter of the 2nd. arrived within a post of each other. It is like your kindness to insist on the pleasure which you give to yourself in continuing to send me these excellent parcels, and flattering to my amour propre to see the reference to 'favourite author': but you must allow me once more to say how deeply grateful I am to you for all your goodness.

We too hope that we may soon want for nothing, but it would be

38 In July 1949 Dr Firor visited Belfast and Oxford, where he spent the night in Magdalen College as Lewis's guest. After dining in Hall he attended a meeting of the Inklings in Lewis's rooms.

39 *BF*, p. 225.

the most blatant wishful thinking to suppose that day is near; in fact in many ways we seem to get worse off, viz. in the case of our meat squabble with the Argentine.

I take this opportunity to tell you how ashamed most of us are at the persistent refusal of our government to make any public acknowledgement of the debt we owe to America; as some one pointed out in a letter to the papers yesterday, every *third* meal we eat is 'on America': but this must be officially soft-pedalled in support of the theory that we owe our national 'recovery' (!) to the Socialist government entirely,

With many thanks and all good wishes,

yours sincerely,

C. S. Lewis

When Roger Lancelyn Green dined with Lewis in Magdalen College on the evening of 10 March he recorded in his diary that there followed a 'wonderful talk until midnight: he read me two chapters of a story for children he is writing – very good indeed, though a trifle self-conscious.'[40] *The story was* The Lion, the Witch and the Wardrobe, *and it seems possible that Lewis had already completed it, or at least a first draft, for he told Roger Lancelyn Green that 'he had read the story to Tolkien'.*[41]

Was this the beginning of Narnia, or a new start to another story? When Chad Walsh visited Lewis in the summer of 1948 he said Lewis talked 'vaguely of completing a children's book which he has begun "in the tradition of E. Nesbit."'[42]

If it was The Lion, the Witch and the Wardrobe *he was referring to, Lewis was having a difficult time with it. It seems likely that Lewis got stuck, and that the story remained where it was until the early months of 1949. Later, when asked about the inspiration of* The Lion, the Witch and the Wardrobe, *he said:*

> *The* Lion *all began with a picture of a faun carrying an umbrella and parcels in a snowy wood . . . suddenly Aslan came bounding into it. I think I had been having a good many dreams of lions about that time. Apart from that, I don't know where the Lion*

40 Green and Hooper, *C. S. Lewis: A Biography*, ch. 11, p. 309.
41 ibid.
42 Chad Walsh, *C. S. Lewis: Apostle to the Skeptics* (1949), p. 10.

> *came from or why He came. But once he was there He pulled the whole story together, and soon He pulled the six other Narnian stories in after him.*[43]

Although Lewis may have continued to discuss The Lion, the Witch and the Wardrobe *with Tolkien and others, it is first mentioned in the letter to Owen Barfield of 30 May 1949.*

The BBC's Drama Script Editor, Lance Sieveking, had written to Lewis on 8 March 1949 about a 'suggested play' based on The Screwtape Letters. *It was being written by the Rev. Leonard John Bowyer, Vicar of Norbury, Derbyshire, and was, according to Sieveking, 'the story of a man ruined by self-pity through the activities of Screwtape's nephew, Wormwood. The framework of the play would be the interviews between Screwtape and Wormwood.' 'We should like him to finish the play,' said Sieveking, 'but of course, before going any further, we must consult you.'*[44]

TO LANCE SIEVEKING (BBC):[45]

REF 03/D/LS Magdalen College,
Oxford
11/3/49

Dear Mr. Sieveking

I have no objection to Mr. Bowyer's taking what in my opinion he needs for his purpose from my book; but in this MS I think he

---

43 'It All Began with a Picture . . .', *Of This and Other Worlds* (London: Collins, 1982; Fount, 2000), p. 64.

44 BBC Written Archives Centre.

45 Lancelot 'Lance' de Giberne Sieveking (1896–1972), author, playwright and producer, was educated at St Catharine's College, Cambridge, after which he served with the Royal Navy and the Royal Navy Air Service during the First World War. He joined the BBC as assistant to the Director of Education, 1924–6, after which he produced plays for the BBC, 1927–31. After serving with the Canadian Broadcasting Corporation, 1938–9, he returned to England as Regional Programme Director, 1942–4, and Drama Script Editor, 1946–50. He retired in 1956. His many books include *Bats in the Belfry: The Collected Nonsense Poems of Lancelot de Giberne Sieveking*, illustrated by John Nash, with introductions by G. K. Chesterton & Max Beerbohm (1926), *The Stuff of Radio* (1934) and *A Private Volcano: A Modern Novel of Science and Imagination* (1950). Sieveking wrote and produced the first dramatization of *The Lion, the Witch and the Wardrobe*, which was broadcast on radio in six forty-minute parts in September–October 1959.

takes more than he needs and some things he would be better without. All he really wants is the general diabolical framework, the Lowerarchy. He had much better not use the same two devils (by name) as I did, though he might well make *his* two refer to *my* two. *Above* all he shd. not in his conclusion reproduce my last *Letter*. His own dialogue is good and he wd. make a far better ending by relying on his own powers than by borrowing.

In a word, I shd. be honoured at being an 'influence' on his work, at supplying some 'ideas', but not at having actual characters, names, and words taken over. And in taking this line I think I consult his interest as much as my own. The detailed borrowings are only vestigial, a hang-over from his original idea of dramatising my whole book which ought to have disappeared when he wisely rejected that plan in favour of an original work employing the same 'machine'.

That is my view: of course you would also have to find out from G. Bles whether he wd. agree that modified form of Mr. Bowyer's plan which I describe.

Yours sincerely
C. S. Lewis

What a delightful man Bazley is, isn't he?[46]

TO EDWARD A. ALLEN (W): TS

REF.48/18.

Magdalen College,
Oxford.
12th March 1949.

My dear Mr. Allen,

What, *again*! Really, I don't know what to say. This time it is parcel No. 86, posted on February 18th.

Just as I was about to deal with it I noticed from the label that the alternative recipient was my very old friend Professor Tolkien: my conscience smote me: we are in Lent: could there be any better mortification of the flesh than to send *him* the parcel? He has no Mr. Allen to look after him, and his wife has been in poor health most of the

46 Sir Thomas Stafford Bazley (1907–97), third baronet, was Lewis's pupil at Magdalen College, 1927–30. On leaving Oxford he founded Marigold Health Foods. During the Second World War he served as an intelligence officer with the Ministry of Information.

winter. So, I admit with unregenerate regret, I have send the gift over to Merton College with your compliments. I hope you will not think that my act shows any disparagement of your great kindness – far from it; a last lingering look at the label shows me only too well the treat which I have forfeited!

Once more with very many thanks, and all best wishes to you,

yours sincerely,

C. S. Lewis

TO RHONA BODLE (BOD):

[Magdalen College]
15/3/49

Dear Miss Bodle

(1) I wonder if the first one in this volume[47] wd. help at all. (2) Have you ever thought what a rum thing *your own* incarnation is? All good wishes.

Yours sincerely

C. S. Lewis

TO WARFIELD M. FIROR (BOD): TS

REF.23/49

Magdalen College,
Oxford.
22nd. March 1949.

My dear Dr. Firor,

You *swamp* me with your kindness. Here this morning is another excellent parcel, and what can I say to you in thanks for it except what I have so often said before? It is a poor consolation that you are visiting Oxford this year, and that we all look forward eagerly to your visit. The welcome that we look forward to giving you will probably be a slice of Spam and a glass of port! But what is that in comparison to what you have done for me and my friends? But at any rate of this you can be assured, that your welcome will be a very hearty and grateful one.

With many thanks and all good wishes,

yours faithfully,

C. S. Lewis

P. S. Have you by any chance taken to making me anonymous gifts?

47 The sermon, 'Transposition', in *Transposition and Other Addresses* (1949).

There arrived the other day, without any distinguishing mark, a *turkey* (not in a tin, the real bird). Do I owe this to you?

TO EDWARD A. ALLEN (W): TS

REF.48/18.

Magdalen College,
Oxford.
24th March 1949.

My dear Mr. Allen,

Until his tragic death a few weeks ago, we have had for a long time an enormously popular radio act over here called ITMA – 'It's that man again'.[48] My secretary put me in mind of it when I handed over to him the label – but not the contents – of your parcel of the 21st. (?) Febry. (And you will be so good as to note that there is no adjective in front of the word 'parcel')! Not that you are going to escape the adjectives, for as I said the other day, adjectives are all I have to offer you: what else can I send you? The good book tells us that it is 'more blessed to give than to recieve';[49] but what the good book does not mention is that it is much harder to receive than to give! But all foolery apart, I feel sure that you know by now how really grateful I am to you for your continued, in fact I may say continuous, kindness to me.

We have just had a pleasant surprise over here. The Government has published one of its innumerable 'White Books' on recovery etc. And, tucked away in small print in it, is an acknowledgement that we owe a 'large measure of our present prosperity (!)' to the generosity of the U.S.A. So far as I know this is the first time that our labour government has acknowledged that there *is* any American generosity.

With all best wishes,
yours sincerely,
C. S. Lewis

---

48 The name of the radio comedy *It's That Man Again* derived from a catchphrase: whenever Hitler made a new territorial claim in the months before the Second World War, the newspaper headlines would proclaim 'It's That Man Again!' The programme, set on a commercial radio ship, began in July 1939 and was broadcast weekly from September 1939. The scripts were written by Tommy Handley and Ted Kavanagh, and the show ended after the episode of 6 January 1949 on the sudden death of Handley, who had been its star performer.

49 Acts 20:35.

TO WARFIELD M. FIROR (BOD): TS

REF.23/49

Magdalen College,
Oxford.
25th. March 1949.

My dear Dr. Firor,

The Baltimore–Oxford 'pipe line' continues to flow with evidence of your kindness. I have just received the excellent parcel which arrived at Southampton on the 19th., to whose contents we all look forward eagerly: even more eagerly than usual, for we have just had another cut in our meat ration. But I suppose as the poet says:–

But things like that you know must be
After a famous victory

I hope that your plans are taking shape comfortably for your visit to Northern Ireland and England. What a pity that your time is so short. I count on your giving me at least as much of it as will enable you to dine, wine, sleep and breakfast here in Magdalen. I look forward to meeting you and telling you in the flesh that I am

yours gratefully,
C. S. Lewis

TO EDWARD T. DELL (BOD):

Magdalen etc.
28/3/49

Dear Mr. Dell

By *experience*[50] I mean 'That part or result of any event which is presented to consciousness'. Thus in a Toothache the total event is a complex physiological, bio-chemical, and (in the long run) atomic

50 In a letter of 24 March 1949 Dell wrote: 'I have wondered, in reading your letter [of 4 February 1949] whether we mean the same thing by "experience". I believe that the work of the Spirit is both crisis and progressive in character. I do not believe, as you say, that one should "peek under the bandage" while God, in His own way (suited to the patient's particular personality) does His own mysterious work. Yet in a larger sense there must be recognition of sin and the methods or means whereby we come to God to have Him dress the wound. These methods may vary in form but essentially they must include repentance, forgiveness, consecration and the infusion of Christ's indwelling Spirit' (Bodleian Library, MS. Eng. lett. c. 220/4, fols. 71–2).

event: what is presented to consciousness, i.e. the *Pain*, I call an *experience*.

Thus to your question (1.) I reply *Sin* is the turning away of the will from God. But the *experience* of sin will differ in different people: e.g. to an uninstructed person it may appear in consciousness merely as disobeying human authority, or taking a legitimate indulgence. That sin-as-it-really-is is *ever* fully present to human (as opposed to diabolical) consciousness at the moment of commission, I doubt. The rebellion of the will is nearly always accompanied with *some* fogging of the intelligence.

2. On Original Sin I have said what I think in my *Problem of Pain* chap. 5.

3. No – no other book soon.

4. I hope some day to write an autobiography wh. will tell *what I know* (= the experience) of my own conversion. But the real event, as known to God, will differ from this as much as the total event 'decaying tooth' differs from the pain.

5. Yes: an American, or anyone else, wishing to enter Magdalen shd. write to The Secretary for Admission, Magdalen College, Oxford.

We've all learned to be careful of paper here! The *A. of L.*[51] is out of print: and I don't know anything about old copies of Wesley. I shd. think you were just as likely to get them thro' an American bookseller as through an English. In haste,

Yrs. sincerely
C. S. Lewis

TO OWEN BARFIELD (W):

[The Kilns]
4/4/49

Your rebuke for not reading letters has caused me more shame and pain than it is at all likely you intended. I had hoped I read all yours – and indeed the passage you mention does now come back to me. It's a long time ago, you know, and so many things happen (Dog's stools and human vomits have made my day to day: one of those days when you feel at 11 a.m. that it really must be 3 p.m.) Unfortunately April 21st won't do, nor May 5. Anything else.

---

51 i.e. *The Allegory of Love.*

The Elizabethans called strong beer 'Merry-go-Down'

I hope I'm not Andromeda too

Did I ever mention that Weston, Devine, Frost, Wither, Curry and Miss Hardcastle[52] were all portraits of you? (If I didn't, that may have been because it isn't true. By gum, tho', wait till I write another story.)

Plus aux bois?[53] We will, Oscar, we will.[54]

Henry 7th had some mastiffs hanged for fighting a Lion: said they were rebelling against their natural sovereigne. That's the stuff. Also, had his own hawk decapitated for fighting an eagle.

Talking of beasts and birds, have you ever noticed this contrast: that when you read a scientific account of any animal's life you get an impression of laborious, incessant, almost rational economic activity (as if all animals were Germans) but when you study any animal you know – what at once strikes you is their cheerful fatuity, the pointlessness of nearly all they do. Say what you like, Barfield, the world is sillier and better fun than they make out.

What you'll miss if you take your revenge by not reading this letter,

Yours

C. S. Lewis

TO EDWARD A. ALLEN (W): TS

REF.48/18.

Magdalen College,
Oxford.
5th April 1949.

My dear Mr. Allen,

If it is'nt one Westfield benefactor, it's another; on Saturday I had notice from Mrs. Smith that she was going to be kind enough to send me a parcel, and now it is you again! But I've said all that I can say on this topic before. Apropos, have you noticed that our government is beginning to make a few soft pedalled, half hinted expressions of

52 These are all the villains in *That Hideous Strength*.

53 From the French song, '*Nous n'irons plus aux bois*', 'We shall no longer go to the forest' (1920), words by Théodore de Banville (1823–1891), music by St John Lucas (1879–1934).

54 An allusion to the anecdote according to which Oscar Wilde is said to have expressed admiration for one of the remarks of James McNeill Whistler. Said Wilde to Whistler: 'I wish I had said that.' Whistler's reply: 'You will, Oscar, you will' (Joseph Pearce, *The Unmasking of Oscar Wilde* (2000), p. 85).

gratitude to U.S.A.? I suppose they must be frightened in case your government turns off the tap, or at any rate reduces the volume of help.

Mea culpa, mea maxima culpa! As you say (and as my secretary says) I *would* elect to show my vicarious generosity by giving away the one parcel which was specially intended for me. No, Tolkien has *not* returned my stationary, but I'll be after him as soon as he gets back from Edinburgh University where he is giving a course of lectures at the moment.

Many thanks for the snaps, which I have studied with much interest. Really one gets to know a man from his letters – if you can't meet him – and not from his photo, but it is interesting to see at last what you look like. Incidentally, the one of your mother is better than the one of yourself, and the *sea* is better than either of you; I can hear it breaking on that beach. It is now many years since I have had a seaside holiday, and I long for one again. I have not at the moment a snap available to send you in return, but when I do, you will see that I am a *global* rather than a world figure!

I shall of course write again when your parcel arrives. And in the meantime, with kindest regards to your mother,

yours sincerely,
C. S. Lewis

TO WARFIELD M. FIROR (BOD): TS

REF.23/49

Magdalen College,
Oxford.
6th. April 1949.

My dear Dr. Firor,

I begin to wish I was more statistically minded, for I should like to know how many hundredweight of pig my friends and I have eaten at your expense. And here is yet another noble ham arrived today, which gladdens my eyes, and to the demolition of which we all look forward eagerly.

How eagerly you may well imagine, if the news of our squabble with the Argentine has got into your papers. The 'Daily Mail' has been conducting a sort of poll on whether we should accept the Argentine terms or fight it out, and got a thirty to one vote in favour of fighting it out: which I find consoling from the point of view of our national morale. But an ounce of meat per day is'nt going to be very exhilarating; though its lucky the matter came to a head with summer approaching instead of winter.

Of your great kindness to me I have spoken inadequately, but so often that the well of inspiration runs dry; I can only assure you of my continued great gratitude (and that of my friends). Thank you very much. I look forward to your arrival on these shores.

With all best wishes,

yours sincerely,

C. S. Lewis

TO VERA MATHEWS (W): TS

Ref. 12/49.

Magdalen College,
Oxford.
6th. April 1949.

Dear Miss Mathews,

Many thanks for your letter of the 2nd. and for the Easter Card. I am pleased, but ashamed to think that you should keep the very inadequate notes in which I try to acknowledge your continued kindness to me. I could wish them to be better and longer for your sake, but I am so hard driven that I cannot lift my nose from the grindstone for more than a few minutes at a time.

I too am Irish, and entirely sympathize with you about dictation from what in the cant of the day is called 'the highest level': but what do you happy people know about it after all? Try living in 'free' England for a bit, and you would realize what government interference can mean! And not only interference, but interference in a 'school marm' form which is maddening. For instance, one of our rulers the other day defended rationing, not on the only possible grounds, i.e. the economic, but on the ground that in the old days housewives bought the food which they knew their husbands and families *liked*: whereas now, thanks to the rationing, they are forced to provide their households with 'a properly balanced diet'. There are times when one feels that a minister or two dangling from a lamp post in Whitehall would be an attraction that would draw a hard worked man up to London!

You overwhelm me with your news that there are *three* parcels for me in the pipe line: and all I have to offer you in return is warm thanks and my best wishes to you and your father for a happy Easter.

I shall of course write again when the parcels arrive.

yours sincerely,

C. S. Lewis

TO VERA MATHEWS (W): TS

REF. 12/49.

Magdalen College,
Oxford.
9th. April 1949.

Dear Miss Mathews,

Thank you, once more, very much. Alas, yes, Magdalen College is the address which will find me in July and August – except for a very few days, if I am lucky.

The difficulty about filming THAT HIDEOUS STRENGTH is the rarity of tame angels and bears in this country![55]

yours,

C. S. Lewis

TO VERA MATHEWS (W): TS

REF. 12/49.

Magdalen College,
Oxford.
14th. April 1949.

My dear Miss Mathews,

This becomes absurd! I feel that what I want is some form of thanksgiving letter which I can get printed and send you to put on your mantel piece, for how is a man to go on acknowledging your kindness every day – or very nearly everyday! Your beautiful parcel of 15th. March, which has just come in, has raised these thoughts. But I think you must know by now that if my thanks are necessarily feeble, the gratitude is strong. Believe me, I am truly grateful.

With all best wishes,

yours sincerely,

C. S. Lewis

---

55 Mathews wrote to Lewis on 5 April 1949: 'I was re-reading THAT HIDEOUS STRENGTH the other day and thought what a magnificent motion picture it would make. Of course, to be done right, it would have to be made in England and would probably cost a fabulous amount, but what a fine job someone could do with it' (Bodleian Library, MS. Facs. c. 47, fol. 155).

TO KATHLEEN ANDREWS (BOD):[56]

REF.211.49. Magdalen College,
Oxford.
18th April 1949.

Dear Miss Andrews,

A pamphlet sponsored by a Ham and Tongue defies all criticism – though this one looks interesting on its own account. Very, very many thanks.

The educational prospect is very black everywhere. The consolation is that as our classical system never succeeded in making most of the boys classical, so probably all the new schemes will fail too.

With all good wishes and much gratitude,

Yours sincerely,

C. S. Lewis

TO WARFIELD M. FIROR (BOD): TS

REF.23/49 Magdalen College,
Oxford.
22nd. April 1949.

My dear Dr. Firor,

I have managed to steal a Monday to Friday in the country; at eleven this morning I was on top of the Malvern hills – larks singing in a blue sky, lambs bleating, the wind rustling in the grass.

At 7.30 (it is now 10 p.m.) I stepped out of the train, very disgruntled, at Oxford, and made my way up here to start a new term tomorrow. Judge what a cheering sight it was to find, amongst a heap of dull mail, your parcel with a *ham* in it – providing immediate spiritual refreshment, and promising speedy bodily solace. It could'nt have arrived at a better moment, and the thought of it is sending me to bed in a comparatively philosophic state of mind.

Thank you my dear Dr. Firor very much indeed: and think of me next week when I shall be eating it and, with my friends, subscribing myself,

yours very gratefully,

C. S. Lewis

---

56 Miss Andrews was writing from Box 79, Bloemfontein, OFS, South Africa.

TO WARFIELD M. FIROR (BOD): TS

REF.23/49

Magdalen College,
Oxford.
26th. April 1949.

My dear Dr. Firor,

You put me in something of a quandary; I can see that the time is coming when I shall either have to give up acknowledging your kindness, or else get my secretary to produce a 'common form' letter to send to you. Not that my gratitude grows less – on the contrary it increases – but simply that I have exhausted all possible forms of saying 'thank you'. But this 'lease lend' traffic has gone on for so long – substantial benefits eastward and thanks westward that I flatter myself that by now, however feeble my thanks may sound on paper, you know that they are none the less heartfelt. And so, for your latest very kind gift, may I say once more 'thank you very much indeed'.

yours sincerely,
C. S. Lewis

TO VERA MATHEWS (W):

REF. 12/49.

Magdalen College,
Oxford.
26th. April 1949.

My dear Miss Mathews,

There is a considerable difficulty in acknowledging your kindness – for after all, there is a limit to the number of ways in which one can say 'thank you'. We have Biblical authority for believing that it is 'more blessed to give than recieve': but what the Bible does not point out is that it is more *difficult* to recieve than to give! So if my expression of thanks is feeble, I hope you will understand that it is none the less very sincere. I am referring to your parcel of the 21st. March, which I have not yet opened, but I know that with your gifts I am perfectly safe in acknowledging without doing so. Only one thing on the label intrigues me – I am wondering what 'Wheathearts' are: but no doubt I shall find out before I am much older.[57]

---

57 Mathews replied on 10 May 1949: 'I'm always so happy to hear the packages have arrived safely, and as regards the food situation here, in contrast to that in Britain at the moment, my father says to tell you to be consoled by the fact that America has the highest percentage of ulcers in the entire world!' (Bodleian Library, MS. Facs. c. 47, fol. 160).

With very many thanks, and all good wishes,
yours sincerely,
C. S. Lewis

TO J. S. GOODRIDGE (P):[58]

Magdalen College,
April 26th 1949

Dear Mr Goodridge

Thank you for your most kind letter. I have always found your son a most interesting and sympathetic pupil. I can't promise you a First Class for him in the exam, though he is, in my opinion, certainly a First Class man. The difficulty is that his natural way of developing a subject is one that demands more space (and time) than exam. conditions allow. A long, patient, 'sequacious' essay, advancing on a wide front, is his line: and when he has to condense for an exam. answer the best qualities of his work do not always survive the process.

Oddly enough, he is a quite admirable condenser (indeed, the best I know) of other peoples' thoughts – as we all saw from his Minutes when he was Secretary to the Socratic Club. But when he comes to his own thoughts – growing as he writes – well, it is like asking Hooker to write like Tacitus! He is of course quite well aware of the problem himself and *may* solve it. If he does not, you need feel no doubt (his tutors will feel more) that he has a very fine mind.

About his future, he seems almost perilously unworldly. He is looking for a vocation, not a mere job, and when he finds it neither you nor anyone else will be able to hold him back.

I am glad you agree with me about the value of MacDonald. I had

58 J. S. Goodridge was the father of Lewis's pupil, Jonathan Francis Goodridge (1924–84) who served with the Intelligence Corps, 1943–6. He matriculated at Magdalen in 1946 and read English under Lewis. He was an active secretary of the Socratic Club, 1947–8, becoming a friend of G. E. M. Anscombe, Fellow of Philosophy at Somerville College, and editing the double issue of *The Socratic Digest* (1948) which contains her 'Reply to Mr C. S. Lewis's Argument That "Naturalism" is Self-Refuting'. In the end Goodridge took a Third in English in 1949, and a Diploma in Education in 1950. He was Senior Lecturer in English at St Mary's College, Strawberry Hill, and Senior Lecturer in English at the University of Leicester, 1965–84. He founded and edited *The Catholic Teachers' Journal*, 1959–63. His books include (trans. into modern English) *Piers the Ploughman* (1959) and *The Raw Side* (1978)

hoped my Anthology might lead to a reprinting of some of his books, but it has not yet done so. Yet I keep on getting letters from people who have found him as helpful as you and I do: the last, oddly enough, was a Jesuit!

Yours sincerely
C. S. Lewis

TO KATHLEEN ANDREWS (BOD):

REF.211.49.

Magdalen College,
Oxford.
30th April 1949.

Dear Miss Andrews,

Your precious gift arrived this morning, and has been opened with much excitement. I don't know how many 'points' would be needed for 8 lbs of meat: but, drawing a bow at a venture, I should say one's whole stock for 18 months or two years!

Of your kindness I find it difficult, or rather impossible to speak as I would like to; I can only say 'thank you very much'.

With all best wishes,
yours gratefully,
C. S. Lewis

TO OWEN BARFIELD (W):

[The Kilns
? May 1949]

This is really great news about B & B. tho' I know that for you the stirring up of all those old hopes & fears is a doubtful pleasure.[59]

---

59 Out of the tension between his life as a solicitor and his longing for a life of literature and philosophy, Barfield wrote a story about a London solicitor whose psyche is so divided between the pedestrian world of his profession and the imaginative world of his desiring that his two identities have different names. 'Burden' is the humourless, practical-minded solicitor and 'Burgeon' his idealistic alter ego or 'sleeping partner' who is screaming silently inside to get out. The story, originally titled 'Burden and Burgeon', is told in the first person by Burgeon, who always speaks of Burden as of another person. Chapter 6 is about a client named Ramsden who is based on Lewis, and deals in a humorous way with the charitable trust Barfield set up for his friend. The story was published under the pseudonym, G. A. L. Burgeon, and the title changed to *This Ever Diverse Pair* (1950).

Ambivalent they call it now-a-days: a useful adjective for it applies to pretty well everything –

> There's *the divel in't,*
> *All is ambivalent*

As the Chorus of Textual Critics say at the end of my forthcoming *Gurton in Cheedle* just after K. Stephen has descended *ex machina* to explain that Hodge's breeches are really the pair he thought too dear. Can you wangle for me to review B & B anywhere?[60]

TO EDWARD A. ALLEN (W): TS

REF.48/18.

Magdalen College,
Oxford.
9th May 1949.

My dear Mr. Allen,

Faithful to your instructions to ration the adjectives, and go large on the facts, I hasted to acknowledge parcel No. 93, containing tinned bacon and soap – not in the same tins one hopes – ditto sausage: soap powder: tea and lump sugar. 'What a feast to set before a king' as we used to sing in the old nursery days! And it has'nt produced any music from the 'four and twenty blackbirds', it has produced a loud and inharmonious chorus from those of my household. I should really I suppose own up to you that we are enjoying your kindness under false pretences: for I saw in the press recently that one of our rulers had been making a speech in which she said that the British housewife now enjoyed a healthier and better balanced diet than in 1939. The speaker left the hall not only alive, but uninjured, which I regard as the finest testimony to British chivalry I've ever heard of.

I suppose that by this time you will be thinking of that delightful bathing beach of yours again; even over here we are thinking of putting away our fur lined boots and our hot water bottles.

---

60 Lewis reviewed *This Ever Diverse Pair* under the title 'Life Partners' in *Time and Tide,* vol. XXXI (25 March 1950), p. 286: 'It is not a sad book relieved by jokes, nor (worse still) a comic book with a nagging undertone of melancholy. It is a high and sharp philosophic comedy, more fully a work of art and more original than anything I have read for a long time. I wished it longer – which shows, perhaps, that it is the right length.'

With once more many thanks for your great kindness, and – if I may be allowed – with kindest regards to your mother,

yours sincerely,

C. S. Lewis

TO VERA MATHEWS (W):

REF. 12/49.

Magdalen College,
Oxford.
16th. May 1949.

My dear Miss Mathews,

Your very kind gift of the 5th. should have been gratefully acknowledged before this: but I have been much handicapped by the absence of my secretary, who has been (and still is) in hospital. But I feel that by now you know me well enough not to have suspected that the delay was due to mere carelessness. As usual, your parcel is excellently chosen, and all the items will be a domestic success. And, also as usual, I have nothing to offer in return except my very best thanks.

With all good wishes,

yours sincerely,

C. S. Lewis

P.S. I am overwhelmed with pleasure and shame; at the very moment of 'going to press' I find that it is *two* parcels which are unacknowledged. There is also that of the 12th. April. Where would my household be without your goodness?

TO ROGER LANCELYN GREEN (BOD):

Magdalen College
Oxford
18/5/49

Dear Green

Cd. you come & dine on Tue. June 14th? (Meeting in Smoking Room at 7 o'clock)

Yours

C. S. Lewis

TO EDWARD T. DELL (P):

[Magdalen College,
Oxford]
26/5/49

Dear Mr. Dell –

The trouble about writing so many letters as I have to is that one can't remember them: I'm afraid I don't know what I wrote to you before.

There surely is a mean between Rigid Syllabus and Total Lack of direction.[61] As to 'describing' God, there are, after all, quite a number of propositions about Him wh. you know on the authority of Scripture. As to the *way*, you know there is only one – Christ. And you know that the first step is repentance, and after that, attempted obedience.

I take it that what St Paul means by Sanctification[62] is the process of 'Christ being formed in us', the process of becoming like Christ – so that the title of the medieval book (wh. I hope you read) *The Imitation of Christ* is a formula for the Christian life. And no doubt sanctification wd. be the correction both of our congenital or original *sinfulness* and of our actual particular sins. I haven't seen that the distinction is v. important, since the latter are the expression of the former.

As you know, theologians have disagreed about the extent of our depravity. Need we know that as long as we know that it needs to be set right and are ready to submit to the cure? (The Doctor will know whether my broken leg is a simple or a compound fracture: all I've got to do is to turn up at the surgery and set my teeth).

I'm not a good enough theologian to give any note that wd. be safe

---

61 In his letter of 13 May 1949 Dell wrote: 'I am left with the problem of preaching either "seek God (who I really cannot describe) in your own way (but not in mine)" or "this is the absolute and one path to God – there is no other." I think both are extremes. But where is the balance? I think that a rigid syllabus or the total lack of any direction can both lead to their respective presumptions and despairs' (Bodleian Library, MS. Eng. lett. c. 220/4, fol. 77).

62 ibid.: 'I'd also appreciate your thoughts on these questions: 1. What do you think St. Paul means by sanctification? 2. Is sanctification primarily related to sins men commit or the depravity of man? 3. How extensive is depravity in man? You indicate a stained spirit – yet there is the remaining tension or "frontier" between nature and spirit in man. 4. What is the "witness of the spirit" of Rom. 8:16?'

on Rom VIII. 16.[63] You are trying to use a rough knife as a razor: I'm not qualified to give the guidance you need. These things I need to learn, not teach. With all good wishes,

Yours sincerely
C. S. Lewis

TO RHONA BODLE (BOD):[64]

[Magdalen College,
Oxford]
28/5/49.

Dear Miss Bodle

Knox is better literature than Moffatt but he has to translate the Vulgate not the Gk.[65] This really makes v. little difference but the Rabbi will make play with it so she'd better have Moffatt.

I also suggest G. K. Chesterton's *Everlasting Man.* And can't she counter-attack if the Rabbi doesn't believe in miracles? If he doesn't believe in the signs & wonders in Egypt, or the passage of the Red Sea, or the miracles of Elijah, then quite clearly he is not holding the real Jewish faith. She is quite entitled to say 'If you want me to remain a Jewess send me a real Jew not a Jewish Modernist.' And as I don't think they'll be able to find her one, she can then ask how it is that there are still real Christians and no real Jews.

I quite agree with you about not using one's job for propaganda: but once the pupil raises the question I think one has a free hand.

Yours sincerely
C. S. Lewis

If they do find her a *real* Jew then the battle moves onto a different front: but, I think, half their weapons wd. be gone.

The Lion, the Witch and the Wardrobe *had been completed by now,*

---

63 Romans 8:16: 'The Spirit itself beareth witness with our spirit, that we are the children of God.'

64 Bodle had a pupil in her school who wanted to learn about Christ, and she asked Lewis for help.

65 Ronald Knox, *The New Testament of Our Lord and Saviour Jesus Christ: Newly Translated from the Vulgate Latin* (1944); Moffatt, *The New Testament: A New Translation.*

and as Lewis had decided to dedicate it to his god-daughter, Lucy Barfield, he asked her parents, Owen and Maud Barfield, to read it.

TO OWEN BARFIELD (W):

[Magdalen College,
Oxford]
30/5/49

No, no, I don't mean it for Harwood: will you post it back at your leisure? The fur coats can easily be altered easily. The chances of getting shut in cupboards is much more serious and less easily altered. I don't know why Maud shd. feel let down: fur *is* nice, otherwise there wd. be no temptation to trapping and one *does* find it in wardrobes. But that will be altered.[66]

The Beavers aren't there to prevent you taking it too seriously, but to supply the snug & homely and to give information. I'd have liked that chapter as a child.

Yours
C.S.L.

TO MAUD BARFIELD (BOD):[67]

[Magdalen College,
Oxford]
4/6/49

Dear Maud

(If I may venture so far after so many years!) I had a very nice letter from Lucy and will be thinking of her to-day. I also replied.

Owen has told me about the two main snags, from your angle, in the story. The fur can easily be removed. I am afraid I was not thinking of the fur trade at all, but only of the fact that you wd. almost certainly find fur coats in an old wardrobe. Much more serious is the undesir-

---

66 Barfield's wife was concerned about the inhumane trapping of animals, and when she read the manuscript of *The Lion, the Witch and the Wardrobe*, she mentioned this to Lewis, as well as her fear of children locking themselves in wardrobes. Because of this Lewis included a warning in ch. 1 of the story: '[Lucy] had, of course, left the door open, for she knew that it is a very silly thing to shut oneself into a wardrobe.' In fact, there are *five* such warnings in the first five chapters of the book.

67 Maud Barfield was the wife of Owen Barfield. See **Matilda ('Maud') Douie Barfield** in the Biographical Appendix.

ability of shutting oneself into a cupboard. I might add a caution – or wd. this only make things worse? With kindest regards.

Yours
Jack L.

TO VERA MATHEWS (W): TS

REF. 12/49.

Magdalen College,
Oxford.
4th. June 1949.

My dear Miss Mathews,

The portable grocery store which you packed and sent to me on 11th. May has just arrived in good condition: and though I have at the moment got no further than reading the invoice, I forsee that your kindness is going to provide the whole household with an excellent Whitsun holiday. We are all most grateful for your kindness.

Here things go from bad to worse so far as I can see; in addition to chronic shortage of dollars, we are now beginning to panic about the repercussions of the financial crisis which is said to be coming in your country. Cripps tells us that we must work as we have never done before, to which the working man has so far responded with a series of unofficial strikes. At the moment we have a docker's strike (so good for our export trade), an impending railway strike (designed to ruin their fellow worker's holiday at Whitsun), and a milk trade distributor's strike. However, thus far and no further: enough of our troubles.

With many thanks again, and all best wishes,

yours gratefully,
C. S. Lewis

On 10 June Warnie went to Malvern for the weekend, and when he returned on 13 June he found an ambulance at the door. Jack was so ill he was taken to the Acland Nursing Home. The next day Warnie wrote in his diary:

> *J was light headed during the night, and obviously a very sick man when I went into see him; he is having injections of penicillin every three hours. I could get little out of Humphrey except that it is 'a very serious illness for a man of fifty' – Humphrey explained*

to me that J's real complaint is exhaustion . . . he added that when he got him on his legs again, he would insist that he accepted no responsibility for J's health unless he took a good holiday away from The Kilns. I got home sick with fright and savage with anger, and let her ladyship have a blunt statement of the facts: stressing the exhaustion motif and its causes. I ultimately frightened her into agreeing to grant J a month's leave.[68]

Warnie also sent the following letter to Edward A. Allen:[69]

REF.48/18. *Magdalen College,*
Oxford.
18th June 1949.

Dear Mr. Allen,

For a long time past I have been writing – or rather typing – to you at my brother's dictation, and, as we 'muck in' together in the suburbs, I have also for a long time past been benefiting by the 'crumbs which fall from the rich man's table'![70]

May I take this happy chance of thanking you personally for all the vicarious good you have done me. (e.g. on Monday night your dinner jacket: Tuxedo I believe is the American name – will be adorning me at a cocktail party. How you got it through as second hand I don't know, for I can't find a flaw in it anywhere).

My brother I'm sorry to say is in hospital with what has become a very common complaint over here: a thing called Streptococcus (?) Throat. He was taken in on Monday last with a very high temperature, was delirious on Tuesdy., and the doctor was very anxious on Wednesday – could'nt get anything out of him except that it was 'a serious complaint for a man of fifty'. You can imagine my anxiety, for he has been my most intimate male friend since the days when we used to play robbers together under the dining room table.

However, thank God, he has made a marvellous recovery, under a treatment of having penicillin administered to him every three

---

68 *BF*, p. 226.
69 The original of this letter is in the Wade Center, Wheaton College.
70 Luke 16:21.

hours all round the clock; and when I went in to see him this morning I found him sitting up in bed smoking a cigarette.

Would it be an impertinence to take this opportunity of offering my kindest wishes to your mother?

yours sincerely,

W. H. Lewis

TO ARTHUR GREEVES (BOD):

As from Magdalen
June 21st 1949

My dear A –

I have not your address and fear that a letter W. sent some days ago to Bernagh may not have reached you.[71] I have been ill and am ordered a real change. I'm coming home (Belfast) for a month. I aim at crossing about July 4th – it depends on when I can get a sailing ticket. And of course I want to be with you as much as possible. Can you find me a nice little hotel (or decent rooms) near your cottage? If you wd. care for us to go somewhere else for part of the time together (e.g. Ballycastle or Hilltown or what not) I'm your man. I shall be free for once. The sooner you reply the happier I shall be. It seems too good to be true.

Yours
Jack

I am assuming that you wd. like to be with me as much as I wd. like to be with you! – I hope this is not vanity

TO OWEN BARFIELD (W):

[The Kilns]
June 23 [1949]

My dear B –

I am humbled (I think that is the right word) by your great news.[72] I wish I cd. be with you. Welcome and welcome and welcome.

No, of course it won't mean the end of the Great War. Donkey's

---

71 Since his mother's death in January, Arthur had moved into a cottage at Silver Hill, Crawfordsburn, County Down.

72 Barfield was baptized on 25 June 1949 in St Saviour's Church, Uckfield, Sussex.

Delight and Brave Little Belgian doesn't bother me at all.[73] Resentment (wh. *will* raise its forbidden head) is such a painful experience that I honestly believe the discovery that the other man is not what we thought him and that it is *we* who were asses wd. involve a relief that wd. easily outweigh the humiliation. You really feel just the same. And we shd. still be able to enjoy the exquisite rotundity of his head – ours, if we are asses, being so much the reverse.

Who on earth is Henry Balmforth?[74] Poor old Melisande.[75] In the Temple question it depends a good deal on what he means by *debauchee*: but I think on *any* meaning he is wrong.

Have written a stunning poem but can't copy it out now. I find a few days high temperature impair the hand nerves & muscles v. much. So long. God bless you.

Yours
C. S. Lewis

TO ARTHUR GREEVES (BOD):

Magdalen etc
June 23/49

My dear Arthur,

Hurrah! I was beginning (with all the morbid anxiety of a convalescent) to wonder if you were away or ill. Now for plans. The *Inn* wd. suit me down to the ground. Thanks for asking me to the cottage but I think the relation of guest & host prevents friends from getting the most out of one another. The one feels responsible & the other feels grateful and the old *camaraderie* is lost. So make it the Inn please.

I cross by Heysham on the night of Mon. July 4th and leave Ireland on the night of Thurs. Aug. 4th. And now, do you think of booking me a room for that whole time or should you and I go away together

---

73 Barfield had probably asked Lewis to forgive him for not asking him to be his godfather at the baptism. The poem 'Donkey's Delight', a copy of which is attached to the letter to Ruth Pitter of 6 July 1947, is Lewis's explanation of *why* he felt no resentment.

74 The Rev. Henry Balmforth (1890–1977) was Canon of Ely and Principal of Ely Theological College, 1941–56, and Chancellor of Exeter Cathedral, 1956–73. He is the author of *The Christian Religion: A Brief Account* (1945) and other works of apologetics.

75 Presumably this is a reference to the character Melisande in Maurice Maeterlinck's play, *Pelléas et Mélisande* (1892). The play was made into an opera by Claude Debussy, first performed in 1902.

to some Ulster sea-side place or mountain place for a week or so during my stay? I shall be equally content either way, so just do what you prefer. It all seems too good to be true.

I suppose there's a Ry. Station at Crawfordsburn? I always prefer train to bus with luggage.

God bless you.

Yours (all of a dither)

Jack

P.S. Have you ever had injections every 3 hours.

P.P.S. I much prefer *inns* to *hotels*. Cheaper too, I expect.

TO RHONA BODLE (BOD):

[Magdalen College,
Oxford]
24/6/49

Dear Miss Bodle

Welcome home! And thank you for writing to tell me:[76] this has been a wonderful week, for I have just heard that my oldest friend is to be baptised on Saturday.

No, one can't put these experiences into words: though all writing is a continual attempt to do so. Indeed, in a sense, one can hardly put anything into words: only the simplest colours have names, and hardly any of the smells. The simple physical pains and (still more) the pleasures can't be expressed in language. I labour the point lest the devil shd. hereafter try to make you believe that what was wordless was therefore vague and nebulous. But in reality it is just the clearest, the most concrete, and the most indubitable realities which escape language: not because *they* are vague but because language is. What goes easily into words is precisely the abstract – thought about 'matter' (not apples or snuff) about 'population' (not actual babies), and so on. Poetry I take to be the continual effort to bring language back to the actual.

God bless you: mention me sometimes in your prayers.

Yours sincerely

C. S. Lewis

---

76 In her note to this letter Bodle said: 'I wrote telling how my doubts had all dissolved in a wordless illumination of the mind.'

TO DOM BEDE GRIFFITHS OSB (W):

[Magdalen College,
Oxford]
27/6/49

My dear Dom Bede

I have just emerged from the Acland (*streptococcus*) and my future plans are uncertain – I mean, for the Vac. I might possibly be able to look you up but doubt if it is possible.

I think the fact that you and I both at the time of our conversions had the feeling that we might be taking part in a Christian Renaissance is a disadvantage to us. It may even imply a drop of mere, what class shall I call it?, Vogue, Movementism, Historicism, Worldliness, in our then state of mind which has to be brought to a painful crisis before it can be cured. In so far as our Faith to any degree at all (even .0001%) leaned on hopes of some speedy triumph for Christendom (for which we have no Promise) it was not real Faith. It is not for us to know the times and the seasons.[77] My own *feelings* move up and down.

I think a glance at my correspondence wd. cheer you up: letter after letter from recent converts, by ones and by twos, often (which is most helpful) married couples with children. Of [course] it amounts to nothing by the standards of world statistics. But are they the right standards? I sometimes have a feeling that the big mass-conversions of the Dark Ages, often carried out by force, were all a false dawn, and the whole work has to be done over again. As for the virtuous heathen, we are told that Our Lord is the saviour 'of all men' though 'specially of those that believe'.[78] As there is certainly vicarious suffering is there not also vicarious faith?

Oh, by the way, Barfield was baptised last Saturday: have him in your prayers.

I have two lists of names in my prayers, those for whose conversion I pray, and those for whose conversion I give thanks. The little trickle of *transferences* from List A to List B is a great comfort. At any rate 'Fear not, little flock.'[79]

Yours
C. S. Lewis

---

77 Acts 1:7: 'And he said unto them, It is not for you to know the times or the seasons, which the Father hath put in his own power.'

78 1 Timothy 4:10.

79 Luke 12:32.

Roger Lancelyn Green, in an attempt to turn his story The Wood That Time Forgot *into 'a fairy tale for grown-ups', had revised it, scrapped the last two chapters and written four new ones to give it a completely new ending – of which Lewis approved. The book, however, remains unpublished as it would appear to owe too much to* The Lion, the Witch and the Wardrobe. *Given below are Lewis's notes on the final version of* The Wood That Time Forgot*:*

TO ROGER LANCELYN GREEN (BOD):

[Magdalen College]
28 June 1949

[page]
1 The magic city of towers etc.
2 A sort of Peter Pan
3 'ticuarly (Ought the word to be so clearly localised?)
6 A [strange] feeling of awe.
7 Cut out *infinitely*?
18. Are we hearing too much about what the wood felt like?
30 'It suggests mystery and romance'
33 Isidore? Alanus?
42 [strangely] silent.
47 tractor [pulling – instrument]
45 The poem won't do: anyway young readers will skip it.
46 I hate the word bosom myself.
48 *Save only I me*?
48–49. Something better than 'a strange, hissing voice' and 'We shall meet again'
51 'thrilling and romantic' *No*!
52 D. feeling comforted at her superior danger is excellent
59 Omit 'isn't it all rather wonderful'?
60 Of course you want to get them separate, but *would* R adopt such an extremely foolish plan?
64 'A [strange] dark house.' Or even 'a house'?
76 A thundering good chapter. The varied reactions of the three children are excellent.
82 Omit *horrible*
What wd. Elena know about rehearsals and plays? (This is but the journey: the battle with sharps is still to come?)

93 *came through the door. Went* through?
97 quickly, almost faster. I wd. prefer *quickly, almost more quickly* (where there is exact repetition of thought there shd. always be exact repetition of words).
99–100 *I begin to feel – to come.* Cut it all out? (It may not be only Joanna who is a bit bored!)
104 You raise an interest in R's one friend which you do nothing to satisfy. I'm not happy about this whole speech. It suggests the intrusion of autobiographical elements which are of no *legitimate* interest to the reader. And the more you pile up R's loneliness and wishes, the more you make us fear that Elena *is* only a succubus.
114 [Tense] silence. No, no! This is not the *Sunday Express*!
117–118. This speech of Agares is excellent. And so is the fact of the children's joining the enemy. Bravo!!
131. This is a fine chapter
134 [Dark] grove of [mysterious] fir trees Surely, better wet their shoes than stop to take 'em off at a moment like this.
142 I never thought you cd. make the sound of plane so welcome!

TO DOROTHY L. SAYERS (W):

[Magdalen College,
Oxford]
30/6/49

Dear Miss Sayers –

Yes. I remember my astonishment in world war I at hearing a French labourer spout out to his mate that he was taking a *promenade obligatoire*.[80] What one-horse affairs all languages except English are after all! But of course the fact that Dante couldn't have understood certain difficulties in any English version of his work does not remove or even mitigate them. And the trouble is *not* that either *speech* or *little* is a 'low' word.[81] Nothing low about Crashaw's 'oh little All, in thy embrace'[82] or about 'a speech of Burke's'. My objection is that I can't

80 'obligatory walk'.
81 *The Comedy of Dante Alighieri The Florentine: Cantica I Hell <L'Inferno>*, trans. Dorothy L. Sayers (London: Penguin, 1949), XXVI, 121: 'My little speech made every one so keen . . .'
82 Lewis was probably remembering Richard Crashaw's 'Hymn of the Nativity', 83–4: 'Great little one! whose all-embracing birth/Lifts earth to heaven, stoopes heav'n to earth.'

hear the *combination* 'my little speech' being said except in a half comic self-deprecatory manner.

You see, if it was anything like so short as Ulysses' *orazion*[83] we shd. hardly call it a speech at all except facetiously. I think to satisfy me you'd have to jettison *picciola*. And I daresay the problem is insoluble. They often are. What wd. one do if one was translating *Beowulf* about *suhtergefaederan*, 'uncle and nephew'?[84]

About the Jansenism (if that is what it is). Did you notice that a poet in *The Listener* the other day wrote

Anyone happy in this time or place
Is daft or corrupt.[85]

Set that beside the Stoic maxim 'The *sapiens* will be happy on the rack' and one gets the measure of the change. Is it beginning with Keat's praise of 'those to whom the miseries of the world Are miseries and will not let them rest'?[86] I think they'd tell us that it will be time to laugh when no one is being starved or tortured. Not quite easy to answer. But I think it does come from the optimistic-revolutionary illusion that the woes of the world can be rapidly and decisively cured. We who think them chronic are more cheerful: wh. is not really a paradox. If one is hurrying a hurt man into an ambulance with the knowledge that he can be saved if you get him to hospital in time, of course one doesn't joke. But if one is alleviating (year in, year out) the sufferings of an invalid who will never be quite well till the Resurrection, then for his sake as well as one's own cheerfulness, even gaiety, must be encouraged. . . . the importance of *not* being earnest.

By the way, why does the best fantastic lit. come from happy periods & the grimmest realism from ours? Makes hay of the ordinary views about 'Escapism' & 'Compensation'

Yrs sincerely
C. S. Lewis

---

83 In Dante, *Inferno*, XXVI.

84 *Beowulf*, 1164.

85 Roy Fuller, 'Translation', stanza 7, 1–2: 'Anyone happy in this age and place/Is daft or corrupt' (*The Listener*, XLI (20 December 1949), p. 1027).

86 John Keats, *The Fall of Hyperion* (1856), I, 148–9.

Sometime in June Roger Lancelyn Green visited Lewis at Magdalen and found him at work on a sequel to The Lion, the Witch and the Wardrobe. *It was a story about Digory who can understand what the trees and animals say. However, when he cuts a branch off a friendly old oak tree to help Polly next door, the gift is lost, and he can no longer understand trees and animals. Soon afterwards Digory receives a visit from his god-mother, Mrs Lefay, who is endowed with magic arts – but there the story stuck.*[87] *It was to be several years before Lewis discovered how that story should develop, and it was eventually published in 1955 as* The Magician's Nephew.

In his conversation with Green about the story of Digory and Polly, Lewis mentioned his interest in people being summoned or pulled by magic across time and space. This idea seems to have lain dormant until the morning of 17 September when, as he wrote to Vera Mathews, 'a good idea for a (children's') story . . . arrived this morning'. He almost certainly meant Prince Caspian: The Return to Narnia *(1951). The manuscript of that story was completed and sent to Roger Lancelyn Green for comment before Lewis met Pauline Baynes, the illustrator of* The Lion, the Witch and the Wardrobe, *on 31 December 1949.*

TO ARTHUR GREEVES (BOD):

Magdalen College
Oxford
July 2nd 1949

My dear Arthur –

Thanks for your most kind and comforting letter – like a touch of a friend's hand in a dark place. For it is much darker than I feared. W's trouble is to be called 'nervous insomnia' in speaking to Janie and others: but in reality (this for yr. private ear) it is Drink. This bout started about ten days ago. Last Sunday the Doctor and I begged him to go into a Nursing Home (that has always effectively ended previous bouts) and he refused. Yesterday we succeeded in getting him in: but alas, too late. The Nursing Home has announced this morning that he is out of control and they refuse to keep him.

87 By an irony of fate, this 'Lefay Fragment' is one of the few Narnian manuscripts to survive (Bodleian Library, Dep. D. 811). It is published in Walter Hooper, *Past Watchful Dragons: The Narnian Chronicles of C. S. Lewis* (1980).

To day a mental specialist is to see him and he will be transferred, I hope for a *short* stay, to what is called a hospital but is really an asylum.[88] Naturally there is no question of a later Irish jaunt for me this year. A few odd days here & there in England is the best I can hope for.

Don't imagine I doubt for a moment that what God sends us must be sent in love and will all be for the best if we have grace to use it so. My *mind* doesn't waver on this point: my *feelings* sometimes do. That's why it does me good to hear what I believe repeated in your voice – it being the rule of the universe that others can do for us what we cannot do for ourselves and one can paddle every canoe *except* one's own. That is why Christ's suffering *for us* is not a mere theological dodge but the supreme case of the law that governs the whole world: and when they mocked him by saying 'He saved others, himself he cannot save'[89] they were really uttering, little as they knew it, the ultimate law of the spiritual world.

God bless you.

Yours

Jack

TO DOM BEDE GRIFFITHS OSB (W):

[Magdalen College,
Oxford]
5/7/49.

My dear Dom Bede

I think I see what you mean by men's *imaginations* having once been Christian. But I wd. put it a different way. I wd. say that a particular world-picture which included, along with the (so to speak) *coarser factual* elements of Christianity, a lot of other things (Feudalism, Ptolemaic Astronomy, Neo-Platonic Demonology etc) was the assumed background, just as Evolution etc is now. I don't think an acceptance of this was necessarily of religious significance any more than the modern background implies any real scientific spirit in most of those who hold it. Simply to accept the Redemption & Heaven & Hell as fact, when the climate of opinion makes real acceptance inevitable, need not be

88 The Warneford Hospital in Warneford Road, Oxford.
89 Matthew 27:42; Mark 15:31.

faith: the devils so accept it.[90] Was it not a *kind* of 'knowing Christ according to the flesh'.[91]

I heard Marcel lecture in Oxford, talked to him, and was much more impressed with his goodness than with his intelligence.[92] It is definitely *not* my philosophy.

Yours
C. S. Lewis

TO J. A. CHAPMAN (BOD):[93]

[Magdalen College,
Oxford]
6/7/49

Dear Chapman

Kitty Lea[94] has sent on to me the MS. of your *Wordsworth*.[95] It has not found me at a moment when my judgement is up to much, for I have just emerged from the Acland where I have been punctured and filled up with penicillin every three hours, till I seemed to be an organism midway between a beer barrel and a pin-cushion.

Perhaps that is why your MS. does not strike me as easy reading: but I doubt if it was intended as such. No one could mistake it for the work of a fool or a shallow man. Some might complain that it is more continually *passionate* than either the medium (prose) or the activity

---

90 James 2:19: 'The devils also believe, and tremble.'

91 Romans 1:3.

92 Gabriel Marcel (1889–1973), French Catholic philosopher, playwright and critic. Lewis met Marcel when he addressed the Oxford University Socratic Club on 18 February 1948. A summary of his paper on 'Theism and Personal Relationships' is found in the *Socratic Digest*, no. 4 [1948], pp. 78–9.

93 John Alexander Chapman (1875–1957) joined the India Office in 1905, and was sent to work at the principal government institute in Calcutta in January 1911; he became Librarian of the Imperial Library at Calcutta in August 1911. He retired from the India Office in 1930. Chapman combined his interest in India and Indian literature with an interest in the literature of his own country, and his many books include *Religious Lyrics of Bengal* (1926), *India, its Character, a Reply to Mother India* (1928), *Papers on Shelley, Wordsworth & Others* (1929) and *Wordsworth and Literary Criticism* (1932).

94 Kathleen Lea (1903–99) was educated at Lady Margaret Hall, Oxford, where she took a First in English in 1924. She was Librarian and Lecturer at Westfield College, London, 1926–37, and Tutor and Fellow in English at Lady Margaret Hall, 1937–71.

95 There is no record of this book on Wordsworth being published.

(criticism) quite allows. There are two, to be frank, sentences which are extremely difficult to read – I mean, to read to oneself: that you, reading aloud, wd. make them sound fine I don't doubt. And there are transitions of thought that it took me some time to follow. How do we get from Wordsworth on Snowdon to female 'campaigners?' But perhaps in all these objections *penicillinium locutum est.*[96]

Bits I whole-heartedly liked were – A. The *excursus* on knowledge, epic poetry, and Sayyid Abre M. B. In *Coleridge & the L. of Passion.* p. 7 *et seqs* the doctrine of different degrees in our possession of different words C. In *W's Authority* pp 1, 2. the distinction between W. and Keats, Arnold was here exquisitely wrong. D. *Ibid* p. 2 on self-deception.

I am not convinced by the thesis of cap 1 that W's boyish experiences were *toto caelo* different from those of the overwhelming majority of boys. To convince me you must not only show me the positive (that W's experiences had a certain quality) but also the negative (that other boys' experiences have not). And how can this negative be proved? Since the other boys are by definition not poets they can never express their experiences and therefore we can never know how different they are from the poet's. I certainly think I had Wordsworthian experiences as a boy; and if (in desperation) you discount this by saying that I am a very minor poet, I counter by saying that I shared them with another boy who has never developed any powers of expression at all.[97] Wordsworth, as you admit, is on my side. So is Keats (For every man whose soul is not a clod has visions and wd. speak if he had loved, And been well nurtured in his mother tongue. *Vision of Hyperion* I)[98]

In *Dante* p. 2 I am uneasy about the dictum that our appreciation cannot equal the joy of creation: not because I think it does equal it but because I think there is a difference in kind between two joys which makes comparison of degree inappropriate. I don't say there is nothing in common: but they seem to me as distinct as the pleasure of dancing is from that of watching a dance, or the pleasure of singing from that of listening to song: or the pleasure of teaching from that of learning. But I know how few agree with me on this.

---

96 'it's the penicillin talking'.

97 No doubt he had in mind Arthur Greeves.

98 Keats, *The Fall of Hyperion*, I, 13–15: 'Since every man whose soul is not a clod/ Hath visions, and would speak, if he had loved/And been well nurtured in his mother tongue.'

I expect this is a silly letter but the best I can do at present. Your MS is a most damnable shape & won't fit into the biggest envelope I fear. I will try to send it off to-day: but my talents as a putter up of parcels are nil.

Yours
C. S. Lewis

TO ARTHUR GREEVES (BOD):

[Magdalen College,
Oxford]
6/7/49

My dear Arthur –

I think the view you express in your letter is the same I hold, and indeed I fancy I have stated it in print.[99] I do not hold that God 'sends' sickness or war in the sense in which He sends us all good things. Hence in Luke xiii.16 Our Lord clearly attributes a disease not to the action of His Father but to that of Satan. I think you are quite right. All suffering arises from sin.

The sense in which it is also God's will seems to me twofold (a) The one you mention: that God willed the free will of men and angels in spite of His knowledge that it cd. lead in some cases to sin and then to suffering: i.e. He thought Freedom worth creating even at that price. It is like when a mother allows a small child to walk on its own instead of holding it by her hand. She knows it may fall but learning to walk on one's own is worth a few falls. When it does fall this is in one sense contrary to the mother's will: but the general situation in wh. falls are possible *is* the mother's will. (In fact, as you and I have so often said before 'in one way it is, in another way it isn't!)

(b) The world is so made that the sins of one inflict suffering on another. Now I don't think God allows this to happen at random. I think that if He knew that the suffering entailed on innocent A by the sins of B wd. be (in the deep sense & the long run) *bad* for A, He wd. shield A from it. And in that sense I think it is sometimes God's will that A should go through this suffering. The supreme case is the suffering that our sins entailed on Christ. When Christ saw that suffering drawing near He prayed (Luke xxii.42) 'If thou be willing, remove this

99 See the chapters on 'Human Pain' in *The Problem of Pain*.

cup from me: nevertheless not my will but thine.' This seems to me to make it quite clear that the crucifixion was (in the very qualified sense wh. I've tried to define) God's will. I do not regard myself as disagreeing with you, but as holding the same view with a few necessary complications which you have omitted.

Warnie is now definitely better as far as this bout is concerned: but we dare not assume that it is the last. As long as there was no one but him to leave in charge at the Kilns and as long as he is a dipsomaniac it *seems* impossible for me to get away for more than a v. few days: but I don't doubt at all that if it is good for us both (I mean, you & me) to meet and have some happiness together it will all be arranged in ways we can't now foresee.

I've just finished re-reading *War & Peace*. The great beauty of *long* books is that however often you read them there are still large tracts you have forgotten.

Yours
Jack

TO VERA MATHEWS (W):

[Magdalen College,
Oxford]
11/7/49

Dear Miss Matthews

My secretary and I are both convalescents (nothing serious) but I am a stage ahead of him, so here goes.

The *cruces* about the Lord's Prayer are good specimens of a large class. My brother as a child took the words to be '*Hallow* would be thy name'[100] and always wondered why, if the Almighty wanted to be called Hallow, He didn't call Himself Hallow. One's elders always explained everything except the bits one didn't understand; and I often read in the face of a pupil after I've been expounding a *crux* in *Beowulf* that I have made exactly the same omission.

How odd to think of *Dymer* turning up again.

I hope your intuition is right, and I daresay it is. It isn't easy to see a future for a country which sprouted into a population far too large for it on the strength of an immense overseas trade and an empire and

100 Matthew 6:9; Luke 11:2: 'Hallowed be thy name.'

has largely lost both – just as it's hard to see a future for Vienna with no Austrian Empire. But the only certain thing about the future is that, whether for better or worse, it is always quite different from what we expect.

The pipeline makes a lovely gurgling all the time. You must try not to grow weary of thanks. Are you right about May? I have no trace of a parcel on the 2nd, but one of all delectable things in tins posted by you on May 11th. and acknowledged on June 4th. Your goodness is a nice thing to think about in these times; 'so shines a good deed in a naughty world.'[101]

Yours very sincerely,
C. S. Lewis

TO VERA MATHEWS (W): TS

REF. 12/49.

Magdalen College,
Oxford.
12th. July 1949.

Dear Miss Mathews,

Had I waited to answer you another 24 hours, I should have been able to let you know that the pipe line was not only gurgling, but also *delivering*. Your noble parcel of 6th. June has just arrived, and in a house even more than usually disorganized, will be a Godsend. I have'nt opened it yet, but the bill of fare reads excellently.

We are in the middle of a heat wave, a dock strike, a financial crisis, and an impending railway strike: so this unfortunate country is even more unpleasant than usual. My brother, who has lived in the tropics, tells me that England in hot weather is one of the nastiest countries he knows. You I suppose live far enough south to *prepare* for hot weather: a thing we never did, even in the wealthy pre-war era.

With very many thanks and all good wishes,
yours sincerely,
C. S. Lewis

---

101 William Shakespeare, *The Merchant of Venice* (1600), V, i, 90.

TO RHONA BODLE (BOD): TS

REF. 121/49.

Magdalen College,
Oxford.
22nd. July 1949.

Dear Miss Bodle,

I don't think you are looking for impossibilities, but you are asking for information I do not possess.[102] You would be shocked if you knew how few modern books of that general sort I have read.

Very sorry, and all good wishes. I am catching a train presently, so this letter probably won't be signed by me.

yours sincerely,
C. S. Lewis

It is, after all!

TO ARTHUR GREEVES (BOD):

[The Kilns]
27/7/49

My dear Arthur

My telephone number in College (i.e. from 9 a.m. to 1 o'clock) is 3151: at home (i.e. from 1.45 to night, except on Thursday when I'm usually out) is 6963. I will take the train to Helen's Bay.

A horrid cloud has appeared on the horizon. Warnie shows some signs of getting ill with a nervous complaint he has had before. If he *does*, of course the whole scheme will fall through. I am in an agony of hopes & fears as you may imagine: meanwhile proceed on the assumption that all will be well.

It wd. be better if the door of my prison had never been opened than if it now bangs in my face! How hard to submit to God's will.

Don't tell Jane you haven't got me a room for the whole time. Of course I want to see her but not to stay with her.

Hope for the best.

Yours
Jack

---

102 In her note to this letter Bodle said: 'I don't remember just what I asked for. I think a list of books on a similar line to Toynbee's "Civilization on Trial" [Arnold Toynbee, *Civilization on Trial* (1948)] which made an impression on me at that time.'

TO ARTHUR GREEVES (BOD):

[Magdalen College,
Oxford]
27/7/49

My dear Arthur –

Good, I'm glad we are really agreed. The one thing I forgot to say in my other letter (and I think you will agree with it too) is that we make a great mistake by quoting 'thy will be done' without the rest of the sentence 'on earth *as it is in Heaven*'.[103] That is the real point, isn't it? Not merely submission but a prayer that we may be enabled to do God's will *as* (in the same way as) angels and blessed human spirits do it, with alacrity & delight like players in an orchestra responding spontaneously to the conductor.

I don't think I can make a second attempt to get to Co. Down. W. himself is going away (without me) soon and of course I must be on duty then. I'm taking a few short trips (long week ends) instead: there's a difference between that & any Irish holiday long enough to be worth taking. But I have (faint) hopes of another year. He has been completely tee-total now since he came out of hospital. If only he cd. keep it up! Perhaps he will. I had thought, like you, that 'others depending on us' might be an incentive, but you see this broke down as soon as it was tried. I think it wd. work with an ordinary temptation, but not with what is really a recurrent obsession – i.e. almost as much a medical as a moral problem. If we cd. get a 12 months' clean bill of health from him I shd. feel much freer.

The whole affair has done at least this good that it has made us write to one another again! If you call this scrawl writing – my hand has gone all to pot. God bless you.

Jack

TO MARY NEYLAN (T):

[Magdalen College,
Oxford]
30/7/49

Dear Mrs Neylan

I found the coat about two minutes after you had gone and pursued you with it hot-foot but in vain. It is now in the lodge.

---

103 Matthew 6:10.

I thought there must be something more than health in the change I detected. To put it quite bluntly you looked much prettier.[104]

I've no right to an opinion about Venice or Spain. I don't suppose either is in the least like what I imagine. Venice used to have the name of being unhealthy at any rate in the summer. Has it ceased to be malarial? And are the canals still sewers?

My fairy tale went to the publisher yesterday – it's for younger readers than Sarah by now. I couldn't manage *Little Women*[105] myself but good judges like it. Love to all.

Yours sincerely
C. S. Lewis

TO SISTER PENELOPE CSMV (BOD):

Magdalen College
Oxford
1/8/49.

Dear Sister Penelope

Brother Ass got what used to be called tonsilitis but is now dignified by the name of Streptococcus. By dint of pricking him with needles-full of Penicillin every three hours they got the old moke out to grass again with wonderful speed and he now brays as well as ever.

I don't really know how to advise you about *The Morning Gift.* I didn't even know it was possible to get guarantees of the kind you suggest. Fabers I shd. think more hopeful than G.B.[106] I wd. quite like to read it some time (when you have a spare MS) but I don't want to write any more prefaces for a good bit: I think my name has come before the public in that way too often and ceases to do much good either to those for whom I write the prefaces or to me.

Yes I read Farrer's Lectures, but not the book on Revelation.[107] I think he is α +. And I'm very glad you're doing St. Bernard.[108]

104 Mary Neylan probably told Lewis something which confirmed his belief that she was making spiritual progress.

105 Louisa May Alcott, *Little Women* (1868–9).

106 i.e. Geoffrey Bles Ltd.

107 Austin Farrer, *The Glass of Vision*, The Bampton Lectures for 1948 (1948); *A Rebirth of Images: The Making of St John's Apocalypse* (1949).

108 A Religious of CSMV [Sister Penelope], *St Bernard: On the Love of God* (London: Mowbray, 1950).

You don't say how *you* are, except that you're 'tired.' Don't overtax Brother Ass.

Yours sincerely
C. S. Lewis

TO MISS BRECKENRIDGE (*L*):

[Magdalen College]
1 August 1949

Don't bother about the idea that God 'has known for millions of years exactly what you are about to pray'. That isn't what it's like. God is hearing you *now*, just as simply as a mother hears a child. The difference His timelessness makes is that this *now* (which slips away from you even as you say the word *now*) is for Him infinite. If you must think of His timelessness at all, don't think of Him *having* looked forward to this moment for millions of years: think that to Him you are always praying this prayer. But there's really no need to bring it in. You have gone into the Temple ('one day in Thy courts is better than a thousand')[109] and found Him, as always, there. That is all you need to bother about.

There is *no* relation of any importance between the Fall and Evolution. The doctrine of Evolution is that organisms have changed, sometimes for what we call (biologically) the better . . . quite often for what we call (biologically) the worse . . . The doctrine of the Fall is that at one particular point one species, Man, tumbled down a moral cliff. There is neither opposition nor support between the two doctrines . . . Evolution is not only not a doctrine of *moral* improvements, but of biological changes, some improvements, some deteriorations.

TO VERA MATHEWS (W): TS

REF. 12/49.

Magdalen College,
Oxford.
5th. August 1949.

Dear Miss Mathews,

Many thanks for your kind letter of the 30th. July. I'm glad to say that a series of short holidays this vacation has put me into pretty good trim for next term. Yes, I think that your epigram about Bevin and

109 Psalm 84:10.

Bovril touches the spot; when we are blamed for the slowness of our recovery, it is not always remembered that ten years of indifferent nutrition is a heavy handicap, especially to the middle aged.

I see from this morning's paper that we are getting a shocking bad press in your country at the moment, and I don't wonder at it. The only laugh in a deplorable business is an interview between one of our Cabinet Minsters and your Mr. Snyder;[110] the former is reported to have said impressively that without a further big dollop of Marshall Aid, the British government would fall – to which Mr. Snyder replied airily that the fall of the present British government would produce no unfavourable repercussions on any section of Congress, and would be hailed with relief by many. Curtain and exeutn [exeunt] omnes!

We are so full of our own troubles that we have'nt much time for following yours, and in any case I'm no great newpaper [sic] reader; but I gather that my namesake, the miner's leader,[111] is a thorn in your flesh. The fact is that only a return to Christianity can save the world, and I'm sure you won't think us ungrateful for American aid if I say that golden ointment for Europe is merely a palliative for the symptoms and not a cure for a deep seated disease.

But none the less I am looking forward greatly to the golden ointment you are sending, and which I know from long experience, will do a lot to soothe my complaint.

With many thanks and all best wishes,

yours sincerely,

C. S. Lewis

TO VERA MATHEWS (W): TS

REF. 12/49.

Magdalen College,
Oxford.
6th. August 1949.

Dear Miss Mathews,

You will be surprised at my writing you twice in forty eight

---

110 John Wesley Snyder (1895–1985) was Secretary of the Treasury in the Truman administration, 1946–53.

111 John Llewellyn Lewis (1880–1969) was President of the United Mine Workers of America, 1920–60.

hours: but I feel I must let you know at once that your lovely parcel posted on 6th. July was waiting for me on my desk this morning when I got in.

It has so often been my pleasant duty to tell you what I think of your gifts that, as the older writers put it, I am 'gravelled for matter'; I can only say, as I have done before, thank you very much indeed for your great kindness.

I see there is a novelty on the menu this time – fruit cocktail. In this sultry weather it sounds delicious, and we look forward to experimenting with it this evening: 'we' being myself and my brother – [who] in the course of twenty years wandering in the army, has I observe learnt enough of foreign languages to be able to say 'here's how' in Russian, Chinese, Japanese, Tamil, and Hindustani!

With many thanks and all best wishes,

yours sincerely,

C. S. Lewis[112]

TO DAPHNE HARWOOD (BOD):

As from Magdalen College
Aug 8th 1949

Dear Daphne

It was all lovely and seems already very far away in the past. Thank you both very much for giving me such a good time – I don't think any other jaunt has done me so much good in every way. (Now that I've written it that sentence seems to make it sound as if it had been like medicine! – but that wasn't what I meant).

I am venturing to send you an American parcel, of which I get far more than my fair share. It's rather a dip in the lucky bran-tub for some contain really nice things like bacon and tongues and others contain such nonsense as paper-table-napkins or tinned pine-apple. I hope your dip will be lucky.

You've no idea what it's like coming back to a house in the middle of a building-estate after the sylvan glories of Kidbrooke.

Whoever finds my pencil may keep it! I got a new one in London with great difficulty. It is far below East Grinstead and the shopping centre: and the beer is not so good as at Withyam.

---

112 The signature is in Warnie's hand.

My duty to Lady Olivier: my compliments to Louis (? Spelling?): my blessing and good wishes to Laurence: and my love to Sylvia, of which she may pass on any she doesn't need to the Rabbit family: and all these to Cecil and yourself with never so many thanks and wishes that you will both have a really restful time at the Laytons (Leighons? Latents?). NOTHING to the Duchess.

Your most obliged
Jack L.

TO MARY VAN DEUSEN (W):[113] TS

REF.66/49.

Magdalen College,
Oxford.
9th August 1949.

Dear Mrs. Van Deusen,

Thanks for your very interesting letter of the 3rd.

I don't feel I could write a book on Prayer: I think it would be rather 'cheek' of my part.

All good wishes.

yours sincerely,
C. S. Lewis

TO VERA MATHEWS (W): TS

REF. 12/49.

Magdalen College,
Oxford.
10th. August 1949.

Dear Miss Mathews,

When you told me recently that there was something for me in the pipe line, I envisaged *a* parcel, not a bombardment of parcels! Here is another beauty arrived this morning whose label arouses most greedy anticipations.

It is really extraordinarily kind of you, and I am most grateful: for, as I said in my last letter, things don't improve over here. I was in a grocer's shop the other day – in a queue as usual – and got into talk with my neighbour, a visitor from Paris, who told me that food prices in England run about double what they do in a French city.

---

113 Mrs Van Deusen, writing from New York State, was one of the Americans Lewis was to correspond with for years.

So you can imagine what a windfall your handsome gift makes. With many thanks and all best wishes,

yours sincerely,
C. S. Lewis

On 13 August 1949 Lewis signed a contract with Geoffrey Bles Ltd for the first Chronicle of Narnia. The book was to be called The Lion, the Witch and the Wardrobe.

TO RUTH PITTER (BOD):

Magdalen, etc
Aug 13th 1949

Dear Miss Pitter

It is maddening that you should have been in Oxford without our meeting. Why did you put such confidence in Report?

I should love to come and lunch with you, thanks, and let us by all means read our works. But it can hardly be till the second half of September: I think Barfield was confused when he said August. Will September do for you? – when the world begins to stir again and one puts back the eiderdown and there are cobwebs of a morning?

I long for it.

Yours very sincerely
C. S. Lewis

TO GEORGE ROSTREVOR HAMILTON (BOD):

Magdalen etc
Aug 14th 49

My dear Hamilton

Thank you very much for the book,[114] which I have just finished, not only with interest but with excitement. The point about *The* (and, drat it, you have made me self-conscious about using it! – it occurs only once in your letter) is brilliantly novel and I think you have diagnosed rightly. Nothing you say is too strong for the condemnation of that publicised privacy – like 'bloods' talking esoterically in very loud voices in order to be overheard by admiring new boys!

---

114 George Rostrevor Hamilton, *The Tell-Tale Article: A Critical Approach to Modern Poetry* (1949).

My real difference from you in this book (and it may be one of experience, not theory) comes on pp. 104 *et seq*. I am not sure that I can find in myself this incompleteness of landscape or this completeness of art. I grant that the real landscape has no edge, much less a frame: but that seems to me to mean that while it forfeits the completeness of a good picture, it also avoids the incompleteness of a bad one. I grant too, that the real landscape carries me beyond itself, but then so does the work of art.

By the way wd. you admit this – that to lose the sense of man's greatness is *not* fatal when men think something else great instead? Man can show pretty small in the Psalms, Pindar, Aeschylus, and Lucretius: but the poetry remains glorious because God, or the gods, or *Natura* are great. The modern predicament is that having voted Man into the chair and *then* lost belief in Man, there is *no* glory left.

I'd like v. much to meet again and in defiance of good manners ask you to come down for a week day night almost any time this or next month. Do if you can. This is neither conceit nor a hypertrophy of hospitality but simply that I am a man in chains, especially at this time of year. Will you suggest a date?

Yours
C. S. Lewis

TO SISTER PENELOPE CSMV (BOD):

[Magdalen College,
Oxford]
Aug 16th. 49

Dear Sister Penelope

The Morning Gift read in its entirety proves *very much better* than I thought. It held me completely and I sat up after my usual bedtime to finish it, not out of friendship but out of the sheer incontinence of curiosity.

Your preface removes many of my objections. But need you mention Adam in it? By so doing you rouse expectations wh. it is almost impossible to fulfil, whereas if he comes as a surprise (an 'uncovenanted' delight) your treatment will do very well.

The film magnate with the plastic face is a great success and infuses new interest just when the story needs it. It also suggests powers of bold characterisation wh. you have not displayed earlier in the book.

Rayner is a difficulty. He doesn't (for me) really come to life as a character until he loses his wife. Up to then he is in danger of being a mere mouthpiece of doctrine: especially in the Museum chapter. I don't mean that what he says is dull, far from it. But one is interested in *it*, not in *him*: a book cd. do for Head all he does.

The public, even the Christian public, will dislike the 'white' marriage of Lisa & Head. I think it is artistically right and beautifully led up to by his playing St. Joseph in the Nativity Play. But what about the Moral Theology of it? Wd. a good *directeur* not have told Lisa she was suffering from a *scruple*?

The writing is generally satisfactory but I'd go through it for *clichés*. (e.g. '*all* too little' on cap I. p.1 – '*sands . . . running out*' p183 and 'three score and ten' *ibid*. All so stale by now that they repell).

What revision you will find possible at this stage I don't know. Anything that *increases* the vision parts and decreases the others wd. be good. Perhaps Head's first experiences as a churchgoer (*after* the Baptism wh is excellent & must not be changed) might be made less agreeable: we adult converts don't always take to the services quite so easily as he. Anything (even oddities) that wd. bring Rayner to life wd. be an enormous gain, and I have a feeling there may be a real character (perhaps with hints from an actual person) waiting for you round the corner. Don't be timid: let your imagination & humour have their heads. You must stick to the White marriage, but perhaps a better reason cd. be found for it. If Lisa were physically doomed not to sterility but to death-if-she-bore-a-child I shd. feel happier. That provides a motive for Head's sacrifice wh. we can all enter into.

But with or without revision I like it. I will leave it in the lodge to-morrow.

Yours sincerely
C. S. Lewis

The simile of Our Lord leading an old man down to age like an old horse brought tears to my eyes. I wish I had thought of it myself – sheer beauty

TO MRS BELLE ALLEN (*L*):

Magdalen etc.
Aug. 16/49.

Dear Mrs Allen,

I should think I *do* like salt water in all its forms; from a walk on the beach in winter when there is not a soul in sight, or seen washing past (rather like beaten copper) from the deck of a ship, or knocking one head over heels in great green, ginger-beer-coloured waves. I grew up close to it, but there's no chance of getting there now. On the other hand I have discovered the joys of shallow river bathing . . . It is like bathing in *light* rather than in water; and having walked for miles, you can *drink* it at the same time . . . We also are in a drought and heat wave.

P.S. C is for CLIVE – no connection with the iniquitous Anglo-Indian of that name.[115]

TO RUTH PITTER (BOD):

Magdalen
Aug 17/49

Dear Miss Pitter

That week wd. do v. well. Thursday 22nd wd. not be the best day (tho' possible) and Wed 21 wd. be baddish. That leaves Mon, Tue, and Fri. Wd. any of these do?

I have never been in the Barfieldian part of Sussex till a few weeks ago. If I had I wd. indeed feel exasperated at having missed you: though why the mind is more offended at missing something so narrowly than at just missing it is a difficult question.

Isn't Withyham[116] a delight?

Yours most sincerely
C. S. Lewis

---

115 Mrs Allen had asked what the initials 'C.S.' meant. 'Clive' was given him at baptism because it was a good name, with no connection to the British soldier and statesman, Robert Clive (1725–74), known as Clive of India. His other Christian name, 'Staples', was given in memory of his great-uncle, The Rt Hon. John Staples (1736–1820), MP for Co. Antrim.

116 A small village in East Sussex.

TO WARFIELD M. FIROR (BOD):

Magdalen
Aug 17/49

Dear Dr. Firor –

(I wd. prefer to begin 'Dear Firor', but as you mister me and I am the younger man I suppose I mustn't) Thank you for your letter of July 16th. It shd. have had a quicker reply but I also have been travelling – though my journies wd. hardly be visible at all on any map of yours drawn on a reasonable scale.

You gave me a brief rule for writing to you when you were here; *Thoughts not thanks*. Well, here goes.

First, about Lanier, who arrived safely. He is really a very remarkable poet. No doubt, since his work is so intimately connected with the landscape, a foreign reader loses a good deal. But enough comes through. Mind you, I think that in the longer lyrics the over-all effect is not quite so good as that of the individual phrases: but what a phrase maker he is – the 'burly-bark'd man-bodied Tree'[117] – 'green leagues of hilly separation'[118] – 'stood as if Death had the form of a deer'.[119] Above all, fixing a life-time in a line, 'the soul's sad growth o'er stationary friends.'[120] I am ashamed to have been ignorant of him so long. I meet no one here who has read him, though one old professor cd. tell me his dates. That is rather characteristic of academic life – to know everything about a man except what matters. I have also gathered from an encyclopedia that the *Song of the Chatterhoochee*[121] is his most celebrated poem: but the one that comes next in this edition (*From the Flats*)[122] seems to me far better: so does *Clover.*[123]

When you were here you started the subject of Praise as Worship, which has led me to some bewilderment. Take the traditional language: *glorifying*, i.e. literally 'making glorious' what is already not only glorious but Glory itself and the source of all other glory – *magnifying* what is

117 Sidney Lanier, *Poems, Edited by his Wife, With a Memorial by William Hayes Ward* (New York: Charles Scribner, 1884), Hymns of the Marshes, no. 1, 'Sunrise', 19.
118 ibid., 'The Waving of the Corn', 22.
119 ibid., 'The Revenge of Hamish', 9.
120 ibid., 'To Bayard Taylor', 62.
121 ibid., p. 24.
122 ibid., p. 26.
123 ibid., p. 19.

already infinite – *exalting* what is already highest. At first it is hard to see what all this means. It sounds like the most fatuous flunkeyism, like telling a rich man that he is rich: and I am sure that this impression has a powerful and repellent effect on modern people, especially in democracies. I take it the truth is that in so far as a creature sees God it cannot help in some way (not of course necessarily by words) telling Him what it sees (silence might be one way). Its 'praise' is a necessary reaction: the divine light sent back to its Source from the creature which has become its mirror. The sun is not brighter because a mirror reflects it: but the mirror is brighter because it reflects the sun.

On a lower level this necessity of telling the object what it is has been experienced by every man in love. True, he *may* tell the girl she is pretty in order to please her: but he'd have to tell her anyway. Thus 'exalting the Lord' is in reality indistinguishable from *seeing* Him. There's no question of flattery or even courtesy about it: the moment the Creator–Creature relation is normal (in the proper sense of the word *normal*) praise or worship is there automatically. The picture of Heaven as perpetual worship, a place, in the hideous words of the hymn

Where congregations ne'er break up
And Sabbaths have no end,[124]

which has tormented many a luckless child (finding one Sabbath per week a ration only too liberal!) comes alright when one sees the real meaning: the perpetual worship *is* the perpetual vision, the perfect exercise of all one's faculties on the perfect Object. Of that, one cd. never have too much: of its simulacrum, 'worship' as we know it down here, one easily can.

I am glad the Prague affair was successfully concluded without your personal intervention. All who met you thought much about that journey: and all hope to see you here again.

Yours
C. S. Lewis

124 Anne Knox, 'The Model Church' (1872), stanza 5.

TO RUTH PITTER (BOD):

[Magdalen College,
Oxford]
Aug 19/49

Dear Miss Pitter

I've booked Tue 20th and assume 1 o'clock as the time.[125] Aided by Owen's knowledge of undergrounds for the ocean voyage and by your mappemonde for the estuary-work after we've got into soundings I have great hopes of our safe arrival. It's a grand map: perhaps a heraldic bus or two (in lieu of dolphins) . . . ? but one can't have everything.

I append my latest Short,

your most obliged
C. S. Lewis

Epitaph.[126]
My grave my pillory, by this blabbing stone
  Forbidden to rest unknown,
I feel like fire my neighbours' eyes, because
  All here know what I was.
Think, stranger, of that moment when I too
  First, and forever, knew.

TO RUTH PITTER (BOD):

Magdalen etc.
Aug 24/49

Dear Miss Pitter

Oh no, no, no, you must review *The Tell Tale Article*. I have already corresponded with Hamilton about it and he is coming to stay the night on Friday and a favourable review from me wd. now be collusion and an adverse one wd. be treachery and anyway I haven't read the modern poets. You needn't talk any more than you want about Humanity. There's any amount to say about poetic style: and as you must read it anyway you'd better get a free copy.

---

125 Ruth Pitter had invited Lewis and Owen Barfield to have lunch with her at 55A Old Church Street, Chelsea, London, on 20 September.

126 This poem first appeared under the title 'Epitaph in a Village Churchyard' in *Time and Tide*, XXX (19 March 1949), p. 272, and it appears as 'Epigrams and Epitaphs', no. 16, in *Poems* and *CP*.

I re-read most of *The Bridge*[127] last night. A lot of it is stunning good, you know. I'd tell you which if the book wasn't out at home and me in here.

Yours ever
C. S. Lewis

TO EDWARD A. ALLEN (W):

Magdalen College,
Oxford
Aug 25/49

Dear Dr. Allen

Yet once again hearty thanks for a fine parcel which has arrived in excellent condition to-day. I don't know how we should get on without you. My brother who drives the typewriter is away and my hand is nearly dropping off from letter writing, so you'll forgive brevity – and the horrible scrawl! I'm none the less grateful inside!

Yours sincerely
C. S. Lewis

TO VERA MATHEWS (W):

Magdalen College,
Oxford
Aug 26/49

Dear Miss Mathews

'The cry is still *They come*'[128] The beneficent storm of parcels still fills the air over Beverly Hills, unparalleled (there's a nasty word to spell) since Danae's golden shower.[129] A lovely one arrived yesterday. I have to do all my own letters at present so that any hand writing I ever had has gone to the blazes and 'over the paper I fall asleep And scrawl them on in a dream'. I'd like to do better for *you*, but can't.

---

127 Ruth Pitter, *The Bridge: Poems, 1939–1944* (1945).

128 William Shakespeare, *Macbeth* (1623), V, v, 2: 'The cry is still, "They come."'

129 In Greek mythology Danae was the daughter of Acrisius, King of Argos. An oracle foretold that Acrisius would be killed by Danae's son, and to prevent this he confined Danae in a tower. But Zeus loved Danae, and he visited her in a shower of gold. From this union was born Perseus who, in the course of many adventures, accidentally kills his grandfather.

Will you accept this v. inadequate scribble from a tired wrist but a grateful heart?,

Yours sincerely,
C. S. Lewis

TO OWEN BARFIELD (W):

Magdalen
Aug 29 [1949]

My dear B –

Owing to an accident in Mrs Moore's ash-tray your letter reached me in the state you see. To a ripe textual critic, however, this presents no serious difficulty. The first hiatus I fill up thus:

for your most obliging
hat's what makes me feel I enjoy
your, as also Dr. Johnson's
t being as exhilarating as 100
parody showing how not *to write the*
airy blend of much Oph
I am
The joke.

Hiatus 2
y poems
they found all my work most
, if I had any more, to
short a time I found
stened but esemplastically
[iouns desperatus]

To be serious – *why* did you do anything so asinine as sending them the whole bunch at one go?[130] A more perfect recipe for rejection I can hardly imagine. Tho' I joke I am a little sick at these numbers. There's something v. wrong when the best of the lighter Bettiana[131] can't get into our only paper of light verse. Like all rejections of one's own, or

130 Barfield had sent a volume of his poems to a publisher.
131 i.e. Barfield's poems addressed to or about 'Betty'.

friend's work, it launches a kind of threat at one's *world*: with, for me, the rider 'If they think him bad what value shd. I attach to their liking me?' Possibly you'd thought of that!

When are you coming to spend a night with me? We both have fewer pleasures every day: let us snatch almost the only one left (fortunately the best) while we can. If even youth's stuff will not endure, how much less middle age?

Yours
C.S.L.

TO 'MRS LOCKLEY' (*L*):[132]

[Magdalen College]
2 September 1949

Apparently I was mistaken in thinking that to condone the infidelity and submit to the arrangement your husband suggests would be *wrong*. My adviser of course says that it is impossible to him to 'give a fair ruling without knowing more of the parties'. But with that reservation he suggests (1) Mrs A shd. refuse to have intercourse with her husband, otherwise carry on, completely ignoring the mistress. (2) Mr A must never mention the mistress in his house nor when he has seen her, nor shd. he let Mrs A. or anyone else have any suspicion when or where he meets the mistress. I can't myself quite see the point of No. 2, and I take it that anyway it is impracticable . . .

On the actual practical arrangements I don't feel that I – an elderly bachelor and the most amateurish of theologians – can be useful. Where I *might* help, on the internal and spiritual problems for yourself, you obviously do not need my help. All the things I would have said to most women in your position (about charity, submission to God's will, and the poisonous nature of indulged jealousy, however just the case) you clearly know already. I don't think it can do you any harm to know that you have these graces, provided you know that they are *Graces*, gifts from the Holy Spirit, and not your own merits. God, who foresaw your tribulation, has specially armed you to go through it, not without pain but without strain; not a case of 'tempering the wind to the shorn

132 'Mrs Lockley' is a pseudonym Warnie gave this correspondent in *L*. In later years he was unable to remember her actual name. Her letter is concerned with the fact that her husband had taken a mistress.

lamb'[133] but of giving the lamb a coat proportional to the wind. On all *that* side you have only to go on as you are doing. And you certainly needn't worry at all about there being any material for psychotherapy in you . . .

One point in your story looms large in my mind – the fatal consequences of your husband's lack of faith in you when he did not get those letters. For this is just how *we* also might desert God. If nothing, or nothing we recognise comes through, we imagine He has let us down and reject Him, perhaps at the very moment when help was on its way. No doubt your husband may have been readier to desert you because a quite different temptation had already begun. But then that applies to the God-Man situation also . . .

TO R. W. CHAPMAN (T):

[The Kilns]
Sept 6/49

My dear Chapman

My copy of your J.A.,[134] long since ordered, has at last arrived and I have just finished it, with great delight.

(But why the deuce didn't you print a Tree to serve as a map through the forest of cap 1? I've had to do one of my own on the end-leaf and even now I believe I've got it wrong. I've only got in one Martha. Are there *two* – as sentences on pp 54 and 55 darkly suggest).

It is all good. Cap 7 is of course the best fun and you hit a great many boundaries. I'm all on your side. The critics who complain of her irreligion have, I suspect, the same sort of idea about religion that a schoolboy has about being a sailor or an amorous young bachelor about marriage: no idea of routine & permanent taken-for-granted background. All the novels are didactic. Who else (except Shakespeare) ever seriously punished & rebuked a comic character like Mr Bennett?[135] How *underlined* is the repentance of Marianne 'If I had died in that illness it wd. have been self destruction.'[136] And for J.A. the

133 Henri Estienne (c. 1531–98), *Les Prémices* [1594]. 'Dieu mesure le froid à la brebis tondue': 'God tempers the wind to the shorn lamb.'

134 R. W. Chapman, *Jane Austen: Facts and Problems: The Clark Lectures, Trinity College, Cambridge, 1948* (Oxford: Clarendon Press, 1949).

135 In Jane Austen's *Pride and Prejudice*.

136 Austen, *Sense and Sensibility*, ch. 46.

Crawfords[137] are damned from the outset: they talk lightly of serious matters! No good, with her, pleading charm!

How revealing on p. 132 (of your book) is 'even in this world': showing the basic assumptions. She thought she wd. have suited Crabbe: I think she'd have suited Johnson even better. Again & again I feel that the J.A. novel is fundamentally like a *Rambler* – at any rate in the bark & steel.

Her books have only 2 faults and both are damnable. They are too few & too short. Yours shares one of these.

All those Nicholsons[138] etc on the letters are like a lot of louts who have blundered into a private house and are annoyed to find the authoress talking like a lady about her own concerns, instead of giving an 'interview' to a journalist

Yours

C. S. Lewis

TO 'MRS LOCKLEY' (*L*):

[Magdalen College]

6 September 1949

Telling these things to someone you approach as a consultant is no more disloyalty than revealing one's body to a doctor is indecent exposure. With a trained confessor this, as it were, *disinfectant* situation would be even more so.

I don't think the arrangement the old man suggested is 'dishonest'. I think his advice turns on the fine but important distinction between *enduring* a situation which is some one else's fault and *sanctioning* it in a way wh. makes one an accessory. After all, your husband has no right to have it both ways and you have no duty (or right) to make him feel as if he had. It wd. do him no harm to realise that this affair is *just as much* adultery as if it were 'furtive visits to a prostitute' . . .

137 Henry and Mary Crawford are characters in Jane Austen's *Mansfield Park* (1814).

138 Harold Nicolson's review of Jane Austen's *Letters*, ed. R. W. Chapman (1932) in *The New Statesman and Nation* (26 November 1932) is quoted in Chapman, *Jane Austen: Facts and Problems.*

TO DON GIOVANNI CALABRIA (V):

E Collegio Stae Mariae Magdalenensis
apud Oxonios
Sept. X A.D. mdccccxlix

Dilecte Pater,

nuper in scriniis meis inveni epistolam tuam quam benevolo animo scripsisti Paschâ praesentis anni. Credo me nullum responsum misisse: quo silentio meo nihil minus civile, minus humanum, fieri potuit. Culpam agnosco, veniam peto. Nolo autem te credere aut memoriam tui ex animo aut nomen tuum ex orationibus meis quotidianis excidisse. Nihil enim aliud in causa erat nisi perpetuus scribendi labor necnon (ne nimis me exculpare videar) accidia quaedam – mala pestis et (credo) VII istorum mortalium vitiorum in me validissimum, quamquam hoc de me pauci credunt.

Ex brevi valetudine, Deo gratia, sanatus sum. Passus sum morbum quem medici olim *tonsilitim* anglice appellabant nunc vero splendidiore titulo *streptococcum*. Febris haud modica incumbebat et horas quasdam deliravi . . . o quam bene poeta vester scripsit de animis perditis qui *han perduto il ben dell intelletto*: quid enim supplicium atrocius? Nam dum mens alienatur nobismet videmur multo cogitationis negotio laborare syllogismos contexere, quaestiones subtilissimas tractare, nescientes tamen quid sit de quo cogitamus. Operatio mentis adest, opus abest.

In hac insula gravis carentia imbris nos vexat. De aliis nationibus taceo. Quid enim ad me nisi ut magis magisque teneam infixa cordi Dominica verba 'Audituri estis praelia et opiniones praeliorum. Videte ne turbemini'?

Vale, mi pater, nec cesses ex paterna caritate apud communem Dominum (verum Deum et solum verum Hominem, ceteri enim nos omnes, post Adami lapsum, semihomines) mentionem mei facere

vester,
C. S. Lewis

*

from the College of St Mary Magdalen
Oxford
10th September in the year of Our Lord 1949

Dear Father,

I have just found in my desk the letter which you so kindly wrote at Easter this year. I think I have sent no reply: nothing could be less civil than this silence of mine, nothing less human. I acknowledge my fault, I ask pardon. But I do not wish you to believe either that your memory has fallen from my mind or that your name has fallen from my daily prayers. For nothing else was responsible for it except the perpetual labour of writing and (lest I should seem to exonerate myself too much) a certain Accidia, an evil disease and, I believe, of the Seven Deadly Sins that one which in me is the strongest – though few believe this of me.

From a brief illness, God be thanked, I am recovered. I had what the doctors once used to call in English 'tonsilitis': but now by a more splendid name, 'streptococcus'. Fever laid on me a heavy hand and for some hours I was delirious . . . o how well has your poet written of the lost souls who 'have lost the good of the intellect': for what torture is more dreadful than that? For while the mind is alienated from us, to ourselves we seem to toil away with much effort of thought, to knit together syllogisms, to treat of the most subtle questions – not knowing, however, what it is we are thinking about. The *working* of the mind is there, but not its *work*.

In this island we are troubled by a severe drought. About other nations I say nothing. For what is required of me unless more and more to hold fixed in my heart our Lord's words: 'Ye shall hear of wars and rumours of wars. See that ye be not troubled'?[139]

Farewell, my Father; and of your fatherly charity cease not to make mention of me before our common Lord (true God and the only true Man – for all we others, since the Fall of Adam, are but half men).

Yours,
C. S. Lewis

TO 'MRS LOCKLEY' (*L*):

Magdalen College
12? September 1949

I don't think your objection to 'setting yourself up as a judge' is cowardly. It may spring from the fact that you are the injured party and have a v. proper conviction that the plaintiff cannot also be on the Bench. I also quite realise that he didn't feel the sin as a Christian wd.: but he must, as a man, feel the dishonour of breaking a promise. After

139 Matthew 24:6.

all constancy in love thunders at him from every love-song in the world, quite apart from our mystical conception of marriage . . .

As you say, the thing is to rely *only* on God. The time will come when you will regard all this misery as a small price to pay for having been brought to the dependence. Meanwhile (don't I know) the trouble is that relying on God has to begin all over again every day as if nothing had yet been done . . .

The reason why I am saddled with many people's troubles is, I think, that I have no natural curiosity about private lives and am therefore a good subject. To anyone who (in *that* sense) enjoyed it, it wd. be a dangerous poison.

TO VERA MATHEWS (W):

Magdalen College,
Oxford.
Sept. 17th 1949

Dear Miss Mathews

Parcel 'Insured number 4662' and containing all manner of delights has just arrived. That, with an exquisite autumn morning (much the best season of the year for me: anyone else may have all my summers if they'll give me their autumns, or Falls as you say, instead) and a good idea for a (children's') story which also arrived this morning, I suppose from the subconscious, bode well for a good day.[140]

Talk of 'hands across the sea' – *spoons* or *plates* across the sea is more like it. You almost attain the dignity of a myth in my mind. Ceres or Ge or Cybele.[141] With all this talk (the autumn feeling, the stirring and waking, must have got into my head) I see I haven't even said 'Thank you' yet. But I've been meaning to say nothing else. Blessings on you.

Yours sincerely,
C. S. Lewis

---

140 After completing *The Lion, the Witch and the Wardrobe* and making a false start on *The Magician's Nephew*, Lewis probably meant that he received the idea for *Prince Caspian* on the morning of 17 September.

141 Ceres, the ancient Italian corn-goddess, was commonly identified in antiquity with Demeter. The Greek goddess Ge, whose Roman name was Gaia, is usually known as Mother Earth. Cybele is the mother-goddess of Anatolia.

TO VERA MATHEWS (W):

Magdalen College
Oxford
Sept. 21/49

Dear Miss Mathews

I think it was the day before yesterday that I acknowledged a parcel reg. no. 4662, but it isn't the '8 lb. roast' one. (By the way *this* letter is in answer to yours of the 17th – how un-businesslike I am). Coffee for some reason is *not* scarce with us: no doubt owing to an oversight on the part of our masters. And we use no black pepper as far as I know. Your typing looks perfectly professional to me but I'm sure I cd. never learn to do the like with or without a stenographic school. I am the clumsiest person with my fingers that ever existed. If Man is defined as a tool-using animal, I am not human. With continuous thanks.

Yours sincerely
C. S. Lewis

TO RUTH PITTER (BOD):

Magdalen College
Oxford
Sept 22. 1949

Dear Miss Pitter

The Tray arrived (and I could no more pack like you than paint like you) to create general delight and put up my domestic stock. No one had been the least impressed when I said I was going 'to lunch with a poet in Chelsea', which sounded good enough to me: but now that you have risen to be 'someone who paints lovely trays' it is a different matter.[142] (If we were Victorians I shd. almost certainly say they had discovered new *traits* in yr. character – but all these simple,

142 In her note to this letter Pitter said: 'Lewis came with Owen Barfield to lunch in Chelsea with Kathleen O'Hara & myself. He is alluding to the end of the party, when I spread on the floor a number of painted trays & invited them to choose one each. (Except during the wars, I have earned a living by painting things. From 1930, in partnership with Miss K. O'Hara, I ran a business employing 12 or 14 people, and we made quite a bit of money. We were proud of having done this on our capital of about £600, starting in the great recession, and enduring some hardship at first. We still think our painted things were the best in the trade.)' (Bodleian Library, MS. Eng. lett. c. 220/3, fol. 81).

demure, chuckling pleasures are now forbidden us). The only snag is that I detect already a tendency to call it The Good Tray and prevent its ever being used.

Still, they can't stop me reading the poem.[143] I think even better of it after two readings than I did at the recital: it may well be the best you have done. I'm not absolutely certain whether in the last stanza 'The beam Intolerable' (good, but good in a high Miltonic manner) is not waiting to be replaced by something a shade more piquant. (When I say I'm not certain, I mean I'm not certain). As a mere matter of interest – nothing to do with the poem – I think in my experience Despair belongs typically to childhood. I doubt if my enfeebled adult frame could bear the blacknesses which were quite common when one's age was still in single figures.

You gave us a lovely day. A fine hazy air of cornucopia ('beyond all Rule or Arte, enormous bliss')[144] hangs over it. See Milton's sonnet To Mr. Lawrence, which all fits except that the repast in our care was hardly 'light'.[145]

My only regret is that my acquaintance with the *Blitzekatze*[146] doesn't prosper as I shd. have wished. My duty to your colleague; it was a great pleasure to meet her,

yours vastly obliged
C. S. Lewis

TO 'MRS LOCKLEY' (*L*):

Magdalen College
22 September 1949

The intellectual problem (why children lose one or both parents in this way and other ways) is no harder than the problem why some women lose their husbands. In each case, no doubt, what we regard as a mere hideous interruption and curtailment of life is really the *data*, the concrete situation on which life is to be built . . . When the *data*

143 Pitter's 'The World is Hollow'.
144 Milton, *Paradise Lost*, V, 297: 'Wild above rule or art; enormous bliss.'
145 John Milton, Sonnet XVII (1673), 9: 'What neat repast shall feast us, light and choice'. Pitter said of the cornucopia: 'It was autumn, and I had taken some trouble to bring from the fruity Essex bower the richest specimens of grapes, pears, plums, & peaches: we arranged them on a large silver tray with sprays of vine-leaves etc' (Bodleian Library, MS Eng. lett. c. 220/3, fol. 81).
146 'Blitzekatze' was Pitter's cat, found in the ruins after an air raid.

are of the kind we naturally like (wealth, health, good fathers or husbands) of course we tend not to notice that they are data or limitations at all. But we're told that they are: and what seem to us the easiest conditions may really be the hardest ('How hardly shall they that have riches' etc.)[147] . . .

TO 'MRS LOCKLEY' (*L*):

[Magdalen College]
27 September 1949

Yes, yes, I know. The moment one asks oneself 'Do I believe?' all belief seems to go. I think this is because one is trying to turn round and look *at* something which is there to be used and work *from* – trying to take out one's eyes instead of keeping them in the right place and seeing *with* them. I find that it happens about other matters as well as faith. In my experience only v. robust pleasures will stand the question, 'Am I really enjoying this?' Or attention – the moment I begin thinking about my attention (to a book or a lecture) I have *ipso facto* ceased attending. St Paul speaks of 'Faith actualised in Love'.[148] And 'the heart is deceitful':[149] you know better than I how very unreliable introspection is. I shd. be much more alarmed about your progress if you wrote claiming to be overflowing with Faith, Hope and Charity.

TO VERA MATHEWS (W): TS

REF. 12/49.

Magdalen College,
Oxford.
29th. September 1949.

Dear Miss Mathews,

I shall have to ask you to be very indulgent to me over your letter of the 24th. August: which should have been answered long ago, but I held it over until my secretary came back from his holidays. And now that he *is* back, I don't think it can be answered at all! For during the cleaning out of these rooms, the record of all my correspondence since the 24th. May has been lost. You can imagine what a plaguey catastrophe it is.

---

147 Mark 10:23: 'How hardly shall they that have riches enter into the kingdom of God!'

148 Galatians 5:6.

149 Jeremiah 17:9.

All I can say with certainty is that no parcel of yours has ever been unacknowledged.

Very many thanks for all your goodness.

yours sincerely,
C. S. Lewis

TO EDWARD A. ALLEN (W): TS

REF.48/18.

Magdalen College,
Oxford.
29th September 1949.

My dear Mr. Allen,

I have to acknowledge your latest kindness 'blind': for the gift from the American Stationary Co. is so beautifully done up that I shall have to get the assistance of the local burgular to find out what's in it. But as it has come from you, I know it's going to be something good.

It seems a long time since I have heard from you. I hope all goes well? *Your* suit is just back from walking 400 miles in Ireland – on my brother – where it was much admired. My brother, who sends his kind regards, is of course full of the joys of life in that favoured isle, where they are all getting ready to make money our [out] of you people next year when you come over on devaluated money.

With my best regards to your mother, and my best thanks for the gift,

yours sincerely,
C. S. Lewis

TO VERA MATHEWS (W): TS

Ref. 12/49.

Magdalen College,
Oxford.
1st. October 1949.

Dear Miss Mathews,

Your latest parcel, the fresh meat one, has just arrived, and I need hardly say how grateful I am for your kindness. Thank you very much. Will you be very angry with me when I tell you how I have disposed of it? I have taken the liberty of re-addressing it and – I admit not without a sigh – have sent it to a lady in London who does not find it easy to make both ends meet, and to whom it will be a real Godsend.

Don't think that this is a circumlocutory way of saying that I don't like beef: far from it. But I like to share the good things with which your generosity so constantly supplies me.

But my thanks to you remain as warm as if I were about to eat it myself.

yours sincerely,
C. S. Lewis

TO ARTHUR GREEVES (BOD):

[The Kilns]
12. 10. 49

My dear Arthur

I couldn't agree with you more. One of the worst bye-products of a bad habit is the nervous expectations and infuriating vigilance it creates in the sufferer's family, and also in him, if he's trying to fight it. Your recipe is the right one: but, of course, much easier to understand than to carry out. (Wh. reminds me of a book I read wh. recommended as a cure for Forgetfulness – can you believe it – *Memory*!)

I thoroughly enjoyed Jane's visit and I wished you had been with us. If there were any changes in her I thought they were all for the better.

Autumn weather here is beautiful enough to break your heart. I've just re-read *The Woman in White.*[150]

Yours
Jack

TO WARFIELD M. FIROR (BOD):

Magdalen etc.
Oct 15. 1949

My dear Firor –

To-day the less pleasant side of Autumn has showed itself for the first time. Up till now it has been paradisal, the sort of weather which for some reason excites me much more than spring: cool, cobwebby mornings developing into the mildest sunlight, and exquisite colours in the woods. It always gives me *Wanderlust* & 'divine discontent' and all that. To-day we have had a low, dirty, smoke-coloured sky racing overhead and a steady down-pour. That, however, has no causal

150 Wilkie Collins, *The Woman in White* (1860).

connection (chronology proves it) with the subject that is uppermost in my mind and has been for some days: Old Age.

You are a bit further on the road than I am and will probably smile at a man whose fifty-first birthday is still several weeks ahead starting his meditation *de senectute.*[151] Yet why? The realisation must *begin* sometime. In one way, of course (no, in two) it began much earlier. (1.) With the growing realisation that there were a great many things one wd. never have time to do. Those golden days when one could still think it possible that one might some time take up a quite new study: say Persian, or Geology, were now definitely over. (2.) Harder to express, I mean, the end of that period when every good, besides being itself, was an earnest or promise of much more to come. Like a pretty girl at her first dance: valued not chiefly for itself but as the prelude to a whole new world. Do you remember a time when every pleasure (say, the smell of a hayfield on a country walk, or a swim) was big with futurity and bore on its face the notice 'Lots more where I come from'? Well there's a change from that to a period when they all begin to say 'Make the most of me: my predecessors outnumber my successors.'

Both these two feelings – the twitch of the tether and the loss of promise I have had for a long time. What has come lately is much harsher – the arctic wind of the future catching me, so to speak, at a corner. The particular corner was the sharp realisation that I shall be compulsorily 'retired' in 1959, and the infernal *nuisance* (to put it no higher) of patching up some new sort of life somewhere.

You will not suppose I am putting these things as lamentations: that, to a man older than oneself, wd. be very odd. They are merely the *data.* (Add, of course, among them, the probable loss of friends, especially if, like me, one has the impudent habit of making more friends among one's seniors than among one's juniors). And as usual the result of all this (wd. you agree?) is almost entirely good.

Have you ever thought what it wd. be like if (all other things remaining as they are) old age and death had been made optional? *All other things remaining*: i.e. it wd. still be true that our real destiny was elsewhere, that we have no abiding city here and no true happiness, *but* the un-hitching from this life was left to be accomplished by our own

151 'on old age'; an allusion to Cicero's work of that name.

will as an act of obedience & faith. I suppose the percentage of *di-ers* wd. be about the same as the percentage of Trappists is now.

I am therefore (with some help from the weather and rheumatism!) trying to profit by this new realisation of my mortality. To begin to die, to loosen a few of the tentacles which the octopus-world has fastened on one. But of course it is continuings, not beginnings, that are the point. A good night's sleep, a sunny morning, a success with my next book – any of these will, I know, alter the whole thing. Which alteration, by the bye, being in reality a relapse from partial waking into the old stupor, wd. nevertheless be regarded by most people as a return to health from a 'morbid' mood!

Well, it's certainly not that. But it is a *very* partial waking. One ought not to need the gloomy moments of life for beginning detachment, nor be re-intangled by the bright ones. One ought to be able to enjoy the bright ones to the full and at that very same moment have the perfect readiness to leave them, confident that what calls one away is better.

We still hope for another visit from you. I shd. have many things to thank you for if you had not forbidden me.

Yours
C. S. Lewis

TO VERA MATHEWS (W): TS

REF.12/49.

Magdalen College,
Oxford.
15th. October 1949.

My dear Miss Mathews,

Soup, sugar, tea, ham cheese etc., etc, etc! Who says there is any hardship in living in England these days? But then unfortunately we have not all got a Miss Mathews to keep us out of trouble! Very many thanks indeed. I'm so glad you approved of the manner in which I disposed of the beef.

We are lucky in one respect this year; after a glorious and prolonged summer, we are now having a lovely autumn. Indeed today there is nothing, except the colour of the leaves, to show that it is not high summer still.

With all best wishes,
yours gratefully,
C. S. Lewis

P.S. I forgot to say that your parcel is the one which was posted on 12th. of last month.

TO RHONA BODLE (BOD):[152]

[Magdalen College]
24/10/49

Pish! There's nothing to be proud about. The whole situation is that of being lent a dignity that doesn't belong to me – the child being allowed to give the penny to the bus conductor, the dog being given the newspaper to carry home.

Or, looked at another way, the really efficacious intercession is Christ's, and yours is *in* His, as you are *in* Him, since you became part of His 'body', the Church. Read Charles Williams on Co-inherence in almost any of his later books or plays (*Descent of the Dove,*[153] *Descent into Hell, The House of the Octopus*)

C.S.L.

TO EDWARD T. DELL (P):[154]

Magdalen College,
Oxford.
Oct 25/49

Dear Miss [sic] Dell

(1.) You'll get all the 'sidelights' you can want on me in Chad Walsh's *C. S. Lewis, Apostle to the Skeptics*, (American) Macmillans, 1949.

(2.) My 'attitude' to other men or movements of the day is usually

---

152 Miss Bodle had told Lewis she feared 'spiritual pride when people asked you to pray for them'.

153 Charles Williams, *Descent of the Dove: A Short History of the Holy Spirit in the Church* (1939).

154 In his letter to Lewis of 21 October 1949 Dell said: 'I'm now teaching in this institution . . . and have been invited to join a group of professors and instructors who are members of the somewhat right-wing fundamental Church of the Nazarene who sponsor this college. We are seeking a positive gospel for the modern, thinking, questioning man . . . I have been asked to review your thought, the scope of your work, and a bit of your background . . . I would appreciate (1) any information or sidelights you might care to give on yourself, (2) your attitude to other men or movements, and (3) how you evaluate or regard your own place in the world as a Christian thinker' (Bodleian Library, MS. Eng. lett. c. 220/4, fol. 79).

profound Ignorance – if ignorance *is* an attitude. I think D. Sayers *Man Born to be King* has edified us in this country more than anything for a long time. Chas Williams is my other great light in our own time. (3.) How on earth cd. a man 'evaluate' his own position?. (4.) St. Paul's epistles are full of prayers 'involving the will of others' and Our Lord's prayer for St. Peter is also of that kind. So there is no doubt such prayers are right. (5.) I am tied to the care of an invalid here & couldn't possibly get to America for a lecturing tour (6.) Thanks v. much: a little stationery wd. be a v. welcome gift.

Caveat – there's no question of 'seeking a positive gospel' for modern man: only of seeking how to make him understand the existing & immutable gospel. All good wishes.

Yrs sincerely
C. S. Lewis

TO RHONA BODLE (BOD):

Magdalen
Oct 26/49

Dear Miss Bodle

I have never seen any more difficulty about praying for the dead than for the living, and it is quite clear that God wishes us to do that. How He uses, or why He shd. use, our prayers, I do not pretend to say, but I am attracted by Pascal's saying that 'God has instituted prayer to lend to his creatures the dignity of Causality.'

I wonder whether this sonnet wh. I wrote years ago, tho' not a v. good poem, makes clear what I think. It is the fact that II Kings xix.32 and Herodotus[155] give these different accounts of the mysterious fading away of a great army! –

The Bible says Sennacherib's campaign was foiled
By an angel: but Herodotus declares, by mice –
Innumerably nibbling all one night they toiled
To eat away his bow-strings as warm wind eats ice.

But muscular archangels, I suggest, employed
Six little jaws to labour at each slender string

155 Herodotus, *Histories*, Bk. II, 141.

And by their aid (weak masters though they be) destroyed
The smiling-lipped Assyrian, cruel-bearded king.

No stranger that Omnipotence should choose to need
Small helps than great! Not strange, then, if His action lingers
Till men have prayed, and suffers our weak prayers indeed
To move as very muscles His delaying fingers,

Who, in His longanimity and love for our
Small dignities, holds back awhile His eager power.[156]

Yours sincerely
C. S. Lewis

TO J. R. R. TOLKIEN (P):[157]

[Magdalen College,
Oxford]
Oct 27. 1949

My dear Tollers –

Uton herian holbytlas[158] indeed. I have drained the rich cup and satisfied a long thirst. Once it really gets under weigh the steady upward slope of grandeur and terror (not unrelieved by green dells, without which it wd. indeed be intolerable) is almost unequalled in the whole range of narrative art known to me. In two virtues I think it excels: sheer sub-creation – Bombadil, Barrow Wights, Elves, Ents – as if from inexhaustible resources, and construction – the construction Tasso aimed at (but did not equally achieve) wh. was to combine the variety of Ariosto with the unity of Virgil. Also, in *gravitas*. No romance can repell the charge of 'escapism' with such confidence. If it errs, it errs in precisely the opposite direction: the sickness of hope deferred and the merciless piling up of odds against the heroes are near to being too painful. And the long coda after the eucatastrophe, whether you intended it or no, has the effect of reminding us that victory is as

156 A slightly different version of this poem was published under the title 'Sonnet' in *The Oxford Magazine*, LIV (14 May 1936), and it was revised again before it appeared in *Poems*.

157 This letter was written after Lewis had finished reading the typescript of *The Lord of the Rings*, which Tolkien had just completed.

158 'Let us praise hobbits.'

transitory as conflict, that (as Byron says) 'There's no sterner moralist than pleasure'[159] and so leaving a final impression of profound melancholy.

No doubt this is increased for me by the circumstances in which I heard most of it for the first time: when there was great danger around us but, in me at any rate, a happier heart than now. But that only accounts for a small part of my total impression. I am sure it is in itself a great and hard and bitter book which, tho I love it, I shall never open without a certain shrinking. It will rank, along with the *Aeneid* as one of what I call my 'immediately sub-religious' books.

Indeed (unexpectedly) the general aroma seems to me more like the *Aeneid* than anything else, in spite of all your Northernness. This is partly because both (a.) Are so often sylvan (b.) Have *strategy*, as distinct from mere combat, (c.) Suggest an enormous past behind the action.

All the alliterative verse I liked.

Of course this is not the whole story. There are many passages I cd. wish you had written otherwise or omitted altogether. If I include more of my adverse criticism in this letter that is because you have heard and rejected most of them already (*rejected* is perhaps too mild a word for your reaction on at least one occasion!) and even if I now convinced you on any point, the conviction wd., I take it, be too late to bear fruit. And even if all my objections were just (which is of course unlikely) the faults I think I find cd. only delay & impair appreciation: the substantial splendour of the tale can carry them all. *Ubi plura nitent in carmine non ego paucis offendo maculis.*[160]

I congratulate you. All the long years you have spent on it are justified. Morris and Eddison, in so far as they are comparable, are now mere 'precursors'.

The *mappemound* is, as you warn me, now inaccurate. But on a rather different point – do you mean the Shire to be so *large*?

I miss you very much

Yours
Jack Lewis

---

159 George Gordon, Lord Byron, *Don Juan* (1819–20), III, lxv, 8.

160 Horace, *Ars Poetica*, 351–2: 'verum ubi plura nitent in carmine, non ego paucis offendar maculis': 'Indeed, when much glistens in a poem, I shall not be offended by a few blemishes.'

TO VERA MATHEWS (W): TS

REF.12/49.

Magdalen College,
Oxford.
29th. October 1949.

My dear Miss Mathews,

And thick and fast
They came at last,
And more and more and more![161]

As Lewis Carroll sings: not oysters in your case, but the very much more appreciated articles in your parcel of the 3rd. October. All of which will be given their usual welcome, and the pudding will no doubt be 'laid down' in the larder for Christmas.

Things here remain as bewildering as usual; I see in this morning's paper that Sir Stafford is much shocked to discover that English folk are in the habit of sending to Ireland for parcels of groceries – and has arranged with the Customs people to put a stop to that nonsense. Well, well, well!

With many thanks and all good wishes,
yours sincerely,
C. S. Lewis

TO VERA MATHEWS (W):

Magdalen etc.
Oct. 31st 1949

Dear Miss Mathews –

I couldn't agree with you more about the commercial rush of 'Xmas' as distinct both from the Christian festival of Christmas and the old Germanic feast of Yule. This idiotic exchange of cards which have nothing to do with the Nativity by people who care nothing about Our Lord – this maddening interchange of presents which no one wants to receive – the monstrous annual campaign of advertisements with their venal geniality – the aching feet of the shopper and the shop-girl – the waste of the world's wealth in producing all this rubbish of gadgets

161 Lewis Carroll, *Through the Looking-Glass and What Alice Found There* (1871), ch. 4, 'The Walrus and the Carpenter', stanza 9.

and 'novelties' – *faugh!* Giving toys to children and food to the hungry (as you do!) is very well: but two grown-ups exchanging a patent cigarette lighter (a dozen boxes of matches wd. be far more use) against a patent calendar (that doesn't work) seems to me abysmal.

About deer.[162] They're not exactly tame. They scatter away, a dappled gleam across the 'Grove' (rather like my Bragdon Wood, only not so large) whenever I walk through it, and then all group at a safe distance, stags in front & women & children behind. They have however learned that tourists, divided from them by a fence, will give them eatables and to this they will come trooping: and once or twice I have got v. near a young faun that had not yet learned sense. At this time of year the young stags fight a good deal (just below my windows): their pig-like grunts & the klick-klick of interlocking antlers have been familiar night noises to me for twenty-three years. But they're not pets: we kill every now & then and eat venison. I believe the herd was here before the college was founded, so they are our oldest members. Of course your father mustn't picture them like elks or mooses. They're little chaps: the senior stag is about the height of a v. small pony, but of course incomparably slenderer & more fragile – exquisite, perhaps decadent, late flower of an ancient beast-aristocracy.

Once more, thanks: and we don't in the least mind whether all the good eating falls at 'Xmas' or not!,

yours sincerely,
C. S. Lewis

TO RHONA BODLE (BOD): TS

REF.121/49.

Magdalen College,
Oxford.
3rd. November 1949.

Dear Miss Bodle,

I'm very ill qualified to give you a list. What about Kirk's *Vision of God*, E. L. Mascall's *The God-Man*, and Charles Williams' *The Descent of the Dove*? But I really just don't know the literature. Old books

162 In her letter of 25 October 1949 Mathews wrote: 'My father wants me to tell you he is keenly interested in the tame deer he has read about in Magdalen Park, and wonders whether they've been there long, what they're fed, etc. Being unable to answer even one of his questions, I turn most beseechingly to you' (Bodleian Library, MS. Facs. c. 47, fol. 177).

I expect I've mentioned before: *The Imitation*, Hilton's *Scale of Perfection* (Burnes and Oates),[163] Anon, *Theologica Germanica* (Macmillan),[164] Traherne, *Centuries of Meditations*, Lady Julian, *Revelations of Divine Love*.

All good wishes.

yours sincerely,
C. S. Lewis

TO RHONA BODLE (BOD):[165]

[Magdalen College,
Oxford]
9/[11]/49

Dear Miss Bodle

Congratulations. You are daily in my prayers.

Caveat – don't count on any remarkable sensations, either at this or your first (or fifty first) Communion. God gives these or not as He pleases. Their presence does not prove that things are especially well, nor their absence that things are wrong. The intention, the obedience, is what matters.

Yours sincerely
C. S. Lewis

TO DOROTHY L. SAYERS (W): TS

REF.5/49.

Magdalen College,
Oxford.
9th November 1949.

Dear Miss Sayers,

Hurrah! I look forward to your Inferno very much, all the more because I was re-reading your C.W. essay on Dante last night with great enjoyment. I expect I *shall* find you loud pedalling the comic element more than I approve, but it is much better to have *your* Dante as *your*

---

163 i.e. Walter Hilton, *The Scale of Perfection*, with an introduction from the French of Dom M. Noetinger (London: Burns and Oates, [1927]).

164 *Theologia Germanica*, trans. Susanna Winkworth, with preface by the Rev. Charles Kingsley and a letter to the translator by the Chevalier Bunsen (London: Macmillan, 1907).

165 Bodle had informed Lewis she was being confirmed in December.

Dante than to have a compromise between it and some one else's. That's the only way a translation can be really alive.

No – I know (and care) little about the Existentialist nonsense. I would'nt dream of writing a preface.[166] I think it is mainly philosophical *melodrama*. (Do what you like, provided you make a fuss about it).

All thanks and blessings,

yours sincerely,

C. S. Lewis

TO VERA MATHEWS (W): TS

REF.12/49.

Magdalen College,
Oxford.
9th. November 1949

My dear Miss Mathews,

Your parcels are so large, and arrive at such very frequent intervals, that I am beginning to be ashamed to meet my servant's eye when he brings in the post.

Your latest has no date stamp, which is odd; but is the one containing fruits, jellies, tea, chocolate, plum pudding, and other attractions too numerous to mention. It has seen fit to arrive on a pouring wet morning, as I am recovering from a cold, and could not have chosen a more favourable moment to give its cheerful message.

Many thanks indeed.

yours sincerely,

C. S. Lewis

TO DOROTHY L. SAYERS (W):

Magdalen
Nov 11/49

Dear Miss Sayers –

The book[167] arrived just after I'd written to you the other day and

---

166 Sayers, *Letters*, vol. III, p. 464. In her letter of 4 November 1949 Sayers wrote: 'By the way, Methuen's asked you to write a preface to Helmut Kuhn's *Encounter with Nothingness* [Helmut Kuhn, *Encounter with Nothingness, An Essay on Existentialism* (1949)] in our "Bridgeheads" series? . . . I suggested your name for this.'

167 *The Comedy of Dante Alighieri The Florentine: Cantica I Hell <L'Inferno>*, trans. Dorothy L. Sayers (London: Penguin, 1949).

I have just reached the third Bowge. This speed on my part, resulting as it does from inclination and rather frowned on by my literary conscience, tells us one thing about your version: you have got (what you most desired) the quality of an exciting story. On that side you may record almost complete success.

Next: I think the metrical audacities are nearly all effective in their places, i.e. as things in your poem. How far they are like anything in Dante – I mean, 'operate as Dante does' – is another matter. They have on me the effect (notably in the journey by Wyvern, XVII) of making D. rather like Browning. That is certainly better than making him like Milton. I shd. say that on the whole they are everywhere doing more good than harm.

The colloquialisms will be the largest of all hostile criticism. That you are no doubt prepared for. I approve a great many of them: just now & then, however, I feel they suggest not intimacy & directness but flippancy – like Byron's *Don Juan*. 'Dear me' (XVI. 118) has an old ladyish air. But I don't think you need bother too much about the point. As you said, there's no 'definitive' translation any more than a definitive performance of the Ninth Symphony. Every live rendering must sacrifice some things to achieve others. You have chosen to get in Dante the lively 'scientifictionist' at all (reasonable) costs, and as all your predecessors chose to get in the *altissimo poeta*[168] at *all* costs, this was the right thing to do. It is a strong, exciting, view of Dante from one particular angle, and that is worth any number of timid, safe versions. Your version of any passage will always be *one* of the things I shall take into account in trying to understand any difficult place: and that, which those who haven't thought on the matter, wd. take for faint praise, is, as you know, saying a lot.

The sheer work of the thing, the untiring quality and inexhaustible cleverness (there are hardly any *creaks*) fill me with astonished admiration. How do you keep it up? Oh – best of all – it *frightens* me more than any translation I've seen. I am being 'compurgated' & edified. Notes & maps excellent. I'm ready for the *Purgatorio* as soon as you like. And many thanks.

Yrs. sincerely
C. S. Lewis

---

168 'the most exalted of poets'. Lewis was encouraging Sayers not to attempt to imitate Dante's sublime poetry but his vivid story-telling.

TO HARRY BLAMIRES (BOD): TS

REF.433/49.

Magdalen College,
Oxford.
14th November 1949.

My dear Blamires,

Your modest and good manners are greater than you know: most requests of this kind come from total strangers, *with* the MS enclosed, and no stamps or envelope.

For a preface, No. That work begins to be dangerous to me and perhaps to the writer concerned. But I'll gladly read the MS.[169]

Perhaps when I've finished it, you could come up for a night and talk it over?

Yours,
C. S. Lewis

TO DOROTHY L. SAYERS (W):

[Magdalen College,
Oxford]
15/11/49

Dear Miss Sayers

I've finished it now. There's no doubt, taking it for all in all, it is a stunning work. The real test is this, that however I set out with the idea of attending to your translation, before I've read a page I've forgotten all about you and am thinking only of Dante, and two pages later I've forgotten about Dante and am thinking only about Hell. *Brava, bravissima.*

Your obliged
C. S. Lewis

TO RUTH PITTER (BOD): TS

REF.447/49.

Magdalen College,
Oxford.
17th. November 1949.

Dear Miss Pitter,

I should be delighted if you used your Spenserians for that purpose, and don't really see why you should need my permission. The Hen (in

---

169 Harry Blamires, *Repair the Ruins: Reflections on Educational Matters from the Christian Point of View* (1950).

your poem) is lovely: unfortunately the hens I meet are'nt very like her. But it's a noble poem.

yours sincerely,
C. S. Lewis

TO DON GIOVANNI CALABRIA (V):

[Magdalen College,
Oxford]
19/11/49

Delectissime Pater

Remitto ad te epistolam hodie acceptam in qua et oculos meos (jam admodum debiles) et parvam meam vestri vernaculi sermonis peritiam superavit chirographiae difficultas. Ne nomen quidem viri possum legere; sententiarum *disjecta membra* modo intellexi! Hanc chartam (Sibyllinum librum!) tibi remitto ne auctor, vir procul dubio plenus caritate, credat me inhumaniter neglexisse. Si Anglice vel Latine manu scripserit aut si Italice dactylographica machina usus fuerit communicatio intra nos fieri poterit. Interea et scriptori et tibi mitto fraternas aut filiales salutationes illas praesertim quae ad hoc beatum tempus pertinent quo nos iterum Bethlehem petimus et Sanctum Infantem; quem oremus ut nos, aetate et longa consuetudinae peccandi confectos novos homines reddat et ducat in regnum suum ubi nisi sub specie infantis nullus introitus est. Gaudeo quia Dominus qui ceteras miserias nostras omnes suscepit non voluit senilitatem suscipere; in Uno Vero Homine aeterna juventus. Valete et tu et ignotus ille scriptor.

C. S. Lewis

*

[Magdalen College,
Oxford]
19/11/49

Dearest Father

I send back to you a letter which I received today in which the difficulty of the handwriting was too much both for my eyesight – my eyes are now rather weak – and for my limited experience of your language. I cannot even read the name of the writer:[170] I can scarcely

170 This letter, from Don Paolo Arnaboldi, is reproduced in Appendix 6 of Don Calabria, *Una Gioia Insolita*, pp. 261–2.

understand the 'scattered limbs' of his sentences. I send you back this letter (a Sibylline book!) lest the writer, a man without doubt full of charity, should think that I have discourteously neglected him.

If he had written in English or in Latin, or if in Italian he had used a typewriter, communication between us would have been possible.

Meanwhile both to the writer and to you I send greetings fraternal and filial respectively, especially those greetings which belong to this blessed time wherein we again seek Bethlehem and the Holy Child. Let us pray to Him that, weakened as we are by age and the long habit of sinning, He may make new persons of us and lead us into His Kingdom – that Kingdom into which there is no entry except in the likeness of a child.[171] I rejoice that the Lord, who took upon Him all our other miseries, willed not to take old age: in the One True Man, lives youth everlasting.

Farewell, both to you and to the unknown writer,

C. S. Lewis

TO DOROTHY L. SAYERS (W):[172]

Magdalen etc.
Nov. 21/49

Dear Miss Sayers

(1.) I *did* really like Mr. Kuhn's book,[173] but does that qualify one for pronouncing on it in public? How can one praise a man's exposition of a subject when one's own knowledge of that subject is derived almost wholly from him? A pupil cannot be an independent judge of his master's knowledge. No doubt this is often ignored by critics (I have read reviews of my own academic works wh. wd. sound v. learned and judicious to the general reader but in which I cd. see that the reviewer's knowledge of the subject was derived wholly from me. Now that is an imposition on the public.

(2.) You win hands down with your reminder that Byron and

171 Matthew 18:3.

172 Sayers, *Letters*, vol. III, letter of 18 November 1949, p. 465: 'I've had a lot of nice letters about the *Inferno*, but I think yours is the very nicest, because you understood so well what the thing's all about, and what a translation aims at, and why it is bound to be one thing or the other and can't very well be two incompatible things at once.'

173 i.e. Helmut Kuhn's *Encounter with Nothingness*.

Browning are our most Italianate poets.[174] Unless I ask 'But *is* Dante?' He's v. unlike the others I read, Boiardo, Ariosto, & Tasso.

(3.) About metre. Yes. All the metrical phenomena you mention are there. The question is whether they have the same effect as in English. Your anapaestic (and other such) lines affect my ear as irregularities, with the pleasure or displeasure proper to irregularities, because they are heard against the imagined norm of *And singing masons building roofs of gold.*[175] Now you maintain that all lines in D. are heard against the (supposedly identical) norm of *Nel mézzo dèl cammín di nóstra vita.*[176] But when I hear Italians reading it they don't seem to have that norm. They seem to have in their ears something mid way between the mere equality of syllable wh. is French metre and the iambic pattern of English *plus* (what we have *not* got in English) a strict and strong caesura. More like

Nel mézzo del cammín –
  Di nóstra víta

That's why I think your English 'irregularities', even when they are the same, are in a sense *not* the same. For an Italian I doubt if a half line like *l'ultime fasce*[177] is really different (in metre) from *di nostra vita*: nothing like so different anyway as Milton's

What words have passed thy lips ÁDAM SEVÉRE[178]

is from

With hideous ruin and COMBUSTION DOWN[179]

---

174 Sayers, *Letters*, vol. III, p. 467: 'I fancy all my verse is to some extent influenced by Browning, whom I read at an impressionable age. I still think he is a very much greater poet and metrist that he is nowadays given credit for being; and what's more, I recognize echoes of him sometimes even among the moderns, who probably don't know what they are echoing. He may not be a bad model for translating Dante, because he was steeped in him and Italy. So was Byron – it is interesting that my faults should remind you of two of our most Italianate poets.'

175 William Shakespeare, *Henry V* (1600), I, ii, 198: 'The singing masons building roofs of gold.'

176 Dante, *Inferno*, I, 1.

177 ibid., XXIV, 111.

178 Milton, *Paradise Lost*, IX, 1144.

179 ibid., I, 46.

But it is v. hard to prove because Italians who really understand English verse don't grow on every bush, and the others will say anything.

(4.) There were several passages when you 'rose', thus answering one's anxious question 'This is all very fine, but what'll she do with the *Paradiso*?' Ulysses on the whole was one of them: 'the uninhabited world behind the sun',[180] good. But, dear lady, *my little speech*[181] – it does conjure up vicars and bazaars! It cannot be said in Eng. without a mock modest smirk. In 114 you neutralise the effect of our *little* by adding *last.*[182] Of course, if you ask me how one *is* to render *orazion picciola*, I don't know. (*Few words* wd. have been much worse, even closer to the parish hall. Tubbs on the poop with a glass of water on it and a chairman!) *C'est facile aux speculatifs d'ètre sevères.*[183]

Yours sincerely
C. S. Lewis

TO DOROTHY L. SAYERS (W): TS

REF.5/49.

Magdalen College,
Oxford.
23rd. November 1949.

Dear Miss Sayers,

No, no. The last syllable of Tottenham, followed by the C of Court, is long is'nt it? I suggest 'Down at Abingdon' as a quantitative and not accentual dactyl – and – spondee.

About Ulysses: hypocricy, yes; but is *orazion picciola* a normal, modern, conventional term like 'a little speech'?

yours sincerely,
C. S. Lewis

TO JILL FLEWETT (T): TS

Magdalen.
24th November 1949.

My dear Juin,

I was very glad to get your letter, and we both look forward very

180 *The Comedy of Dante Alighieri The Florentine: Cantica I Hell <L'Inferno>*, XXVI, 117.

181 ibid., 121.

182 ibid., 115: To this last little vigil left to run.'

183 'It is easy for theoreticians to be severe!'

much to seeing you again and having a talk – to say nothing of lunch.

Saturday is always a very bad day with Jack, so if you can possibly manage it, make it Monday 12th December. We would be waiting for you at the Royal Oxford Hotel from 12.45 onwards. Do you know the R.O.? It's the big yellow hotel which is more or less opposite the L.M.S. Railway Stn. (I refuse to talk about these places as 'British Railways').

This stern affair of the coffee? How are we going to manage it if there are two entirely separate lunch parties. Is G.B.S. a teetotaller?[184] Supposing we were to make it 12.30 at the R.O., and she was to come in for a cocktail with us before going on to lunch with Rowse?[185] would not that be simpler? If we once begin drinking coffee somewhere at about 2.30, there is no knowing how long the entertainment may continue, and after all it's *you* we want to see!

Let me know further details in due course.

As I'm writing anyway, let me take this opportunity of sending you my little Christmas present. Would that it were more, but remember I belong to the second most despised and downtrodden class in the community. (The *first* is the one man business; he is even more hated by the London School of Economics than the pensioner-rentier. Don't ask me why)!

With all best love, and kind regards to your mother from us both,

yours,
Warnie
Jack

TO DOROTHY L. SAYERS (W):

[Magdalen College,
Oxford]
Nov 28/49

Dear Miss Sayers

Of course we go by sound, not spelling. Thus NG in *singer* is only one consonant, but in *finger* it is two. And if *Tottenham* were really three syllables at all the first wd. be short, tho' accented. But I agree (after yr. letter) that it isn't. To a true Londoner it is perhaps a long

184 i.e. novelist Gladys Bronwyn Stern, who wrote *The Woman in the Hall.*

185 Alfred Leslie Rowse (1903–97), the poet and historian, was a Fellow of All Souls' College, Oxford.

monosyllable – it certainly wd. have been to the footman in *Sylvie & Bruno* who made a single syllable out of Your Royal Highness.[186] I can only get it to a spondee – *Totnm*. Good examples of the lengthening power of a real double consonant occur in

Bĭshŏp <> Fĭsh shop
Sãtrap <> Rat trap

And of course (you beat me down all the time) one mustn't give in too much to vulgar associations or every phrase will be contaminated. The Girtonienne is illuminating.[187] Cf. a pupil of mine to whom I said 'At last you've admitted that Lamb gives pleasure' and who replied 'That's just the trouble. No one has any *right* to give *pleasure*.' I'm for Christ against Epicurus, but no words can express my championship of Epicurus against *Scrutiny*, Existentialists, and 'all that'.

Yours (in orderly retreat)
C. S. Lewis

TO VERA MATHEWS (W):

Magdalen College,
Oxford.
28th. November 1949.

My dear Miss Mathews,

I don't know if Wodehouse's Bertie Wooster stories ever came your way; Bertie was the typical brainless 'dude' of his period, and in acknowledging your parcels would have said something like – 'I say, my dear old thing, you know, what about it I mean to say, eh? what?'

---

186 Lewis Carroll, *Sylvie and Bruno* (1889, 1893), ch. 1: ' "She's with the Warden, I believe, y'reince!" the Chancellor replied with a low bow. There was, no doubt, a certain amount of absurdity in applying this title (which, as of course you see without my telling you, was nothing but "your Royal Highness" condensed into one syllable).'

187 i.e. a student of Girton College, Cambridge. Sayers may have told Lewis about the 'Cambridge pupil' mentioned to her by Barbara Reynolds who said of her translation of *Inferno*: 'It makes me laugh and I just go on and on reading.' Sayers replied on 26 November 1949: 'That is most delightful, and even more encouraging than all the approval of the wise and learned. . . . Perhaps I have made them laugh at Dante, when they "ought" to be trembling at the thought of Hell! – but if they don't read and don't enjoy what they read, they will never even begin to learn to shudder' (*Letters*, vol. III, p. 472).

Or in other words 'I am overwhelmed by your continuing generosity.' If the parcels keep on arriving at this rate, I shall soon be reduced to Bertie's stuttering incoherences.

But seriously, I am most grateful. I think you would be pleased if you knew how wide a circle of people benefit from your kindness: for we always try to share some of your things with less fortunately situated neighbours.

Many thanks and good wishes.

Yours sincerely,
C. S. Lewis

TO VERA MATHEWS (W): TS

REF. 12/49.

Magdalen College,
Oxford.
30th. November 1949.

Dear Miss Mathews,

Many thanks for your kind and interesting letter of the 23rd. One of my reasons for hoping I may some day visit your country is to see your variety of animal life in those great enclosures which we have no room for in this little country. A year ago a friend in Baltimore offered to take me to his holiday home in the mountains and introduce me to bears galore:[188] would that I had been able to accept!

No, I don't think that I have a favourite cake: but the whiskey one sounds most exciting, and if your efforts to bake the perfect whiskey cake should be crowned with success –!

This is most uncommonly kind of you about the bacon, butter, and eggs, and all will sing your praises when the consignment arrives; yes, I understand your feelings about waste at a time like this. But it would ill become *us* to be self-righteous about it: partly because any degree of luxury life here now affords is entirely due to American generosity: and mainly because in our prosperous days, we wasted food without the slightest regard to the needs of those less plentifully provided than ourselves.

With all best wishes once more,

yours sincerely,
C. S. Lewis

---

188 See the letter to Warfield M. Firor of 22 January 1949.

TO CHAD WALSH (W): TS

REF.150/49.

Magdalen College,
Oxford.
30th November 1949.

Dear Walsh,

All our prayers and good wishes go with you in your Ordination.[189] Thanks for the curio.

And I stand by to receive the book.[190]

Yours,
C. S. Lewis

TO EDWARD T. DELL (P): TS

REF.409/49

Magdalen College,
Oxford.
2nd. December 1949.

Dear Mr. Dell,

Your very kind gift of stationary has just arrived, and I am most grateful for it. I suppose we can hardly consider paper and envelopes to be prime necessities of life, but the convenience of having such things at hand when you want them, is great: instead of having to divert my secretary to hunt them through the town, with consequent waste of time and temper to us both!

With many thanks and all best wishes for Christmas,

yours sincerely,
C. S. Lewis

TO WARFIELD M. FIROR (BOD):

Magdalen etc.
Dec 5/49

My dear Firor –

I knew I should provoke (and deserve) a smile by my references to old age. But what counts is not the age so much as the prospect; not the mileage travelled or ahead, but the view from this bend in the road. I grudged the passing years in childhood because they were

---

189 Chad Walsh was ordained into the Episcopal Church on 21 December 1949 and became an associate rector at St Paul's Church in Beloit, while continuing his teaching duties as Professor of English at Beloit College.

190 This was probably Walsh's book, *C. S. Lewis: Apostle to the Skeptics.*

bringing me nearer to School and I thought that to be a schoolboy wd. be much less pleasant than to be a child. And as it turned out, I was quite right. I did not grudge them as a young man because I thought having a job and acquiring a reputation wd. be nicer than wishing and hoping for them. I was right again. But don't let me pursue a useless and querulous line of thought.

Yes, I *have* thought (tho' with no background of biology like yours) about rhythm and recuperation: perhaps, in my thought, more strictly *renewal* – the way things come back, changed, yet the same. We are all only too familiar with this in the case of sins or diseases which we hoped we had left behind. How terribly like a malignant tumour a vice is – the big, drastic operation which one screws oneself to face, the apparent cure, and then, remorselessly, gradually, the return –

And all our former pain
And all our surgeon's care
Are lost, and all the unbearable (in vain
Borne once) is still to bear.[191]

(This is at least as true of mental vices as of those we loosely call bodily). But it does work with the good things as well. At any moment something may sink an artesian well right down into one's pent self and old joy, even old power, may come rushing up. That is why I think that *Resurrection* (what ever it exactly means) is so much profounder an idea than mere immortality. I am sure we don't just 'go on'. We really die and are really built up again.

Now this – though I didn't foresee the fact till this minute – links up with what you were saying about the Peace of God. (By the way, I don't think 'incomprehensible' in the Creed[192] or 'passing comprehension'[193] mean what is usually thought. It doesn't mean, I am told, simply *unintelligible*, like a book in an unknown tongue. It means not

---

191 This is a slightly revised version of 'Relapse', stanza 5, published in *Poems* and *CP*. It was quoted in Lewis's letter to Sister Penelope of 9 November 1941.

192 He was referring to the passage in the Athanasian Creed which speaks of 'The Father incomprehensible, the Son incomprehensible: and the Holy Ghost incomprehensible'.

193 Philippians 4:7: 'And the peace of God, which passeth all understanding, shall keep your hearts and minds through Christ Jesus.'

thinkable-out, not capable of being fully summed up or intellectually mastered). I am sure you are right, that is power. Our idea of peace expresses only the negative results of it: the exclusion of care, haste, fear etc. but not the positive thing that excludes them. So someone who had never bathed might think of a swim only as absence of clothes, absence of solidity in touch with one, etc: but not what really counts, the cool, yielding embrace of the water. But (here comes the connection with what I was saying, and also the rub) does it not come exactly in proportion as we have, in some sense, *died*.

I am concerned about that at present, chiefly as a result of reading William Law. It's all there in the New Testament, though. 'Dying to the world' – 'the world is crucified to me and I to the world'.[194] And I find I haven't begun: at least not if it means (and can it mean less) than a steady and progressive disentangling of all one's motives from the merely natural or this-worldly objects: like training a creeper to grow up one wall instead of another. I don't mean disentangling from things wrong in themselves, but, say, from the v. pleasant evening which we hope to have over one of your hams to-morrow night, or from gratification at my literary success. It is not the things, nor even the pleasure in them, but the fact that in such pleasures my heart, or so much of my heart, lies. Or to put it in a fantastic form – if a voice said to me (and one I couldn't disbelieve) 'you shall never see the face of God, never help to save a neighbour's soul, never be free from sin, but you shall live in perfect health till the age of 100, v. rich, and die the most famous man in the world, and pass into a twilight consciousness of a vaguely pleasant sort forever' – how much wd. it worry me? How much compared with another war? Or even with an announcement that I shd. have to have all my teeth out? You see? And what right have I to expect the Peace of God while I thus put my whole heart, at least all my strongest wishes, in the world which he has warned me against?

Well, thank God (for there is still part of me, a tiny little infantine voice somewhere amidst all the strong, confident *natural* voices, which can just thank Him, or perhaps only thank Him for being able to wish to thank Him) we shall not be left to the world. All His terrible resources (but it is we who force him to use them) will be brought against us to detach us from it – insecurity, war, poverty, pain,

194 Galatians 6:14.

unpopularity, loneliness. We must be taught that this tent is not home. And, by Jove, how terrible it would be if all suffering, including death itself, were *optional*, so that only a v. few voluntary ascetics ever even attempted to achieve the end for which we are created. *A propos* – dare we gloss the text 'Strait is the way and few there be that find it'[195] by adding 'And that's why most of you have to be bustled and badgered into it like sheep – and the sheep-dogs have to have pretty sharp teeth too'! I hope so.

No, I don't know Conybeare & Howson.[196] I usually do my epistles with the aid of separate commentaries.

R. B. MacCallum lives at Pembroke College, Oxford: Dr. R. E. Havard at 28, Sandfield Rd., Oxford.

You over-awe me with your Hebrew!

We shall drink your health to-morrow night.

Thanks (as always) and good wishes,

Yours

C. S. Lewis

TO RUTH PITTER (BOD):

[Magdalen College,
Oxford]
Dec 10/49

Dear Miss Pitter

Will you lunch with me at 1.15 on Sat. Dec 31st. after the Conference?[197] The only other members of it that I'm asking are Miss Milne and Mr. Barfield – i.e. it is to be not a continuation but an antidote or antimasque. Now, do.

Yours sincerely

C. S. Lewis

195 Matthew 7:14.

196 William John Conybeare and John Saul Howson, *The Life and Epistles of St Paul* (1852).

197 Pitter said in her notes: 'This was a small conference on the subject of "Women in the Priesthood"' (Bodleian Library, MS. Eng. lett. c. 220/3, fol. 87).

TO HARRY BLAMIRES (BOD): TS

REF.433/49.

Magdalen College,
Oxford.
12th December 1949.

My dear Blamires,

I've now read the MS, mostly with great interest and approval. When can you come over and talk about it? I suggest you come and dine (come to my rooms, *not* dressed, at 6:55) and sleep on the night of Thursday 22nd December. You can be off after an 8.15 breakfast on the Friday morning.

yours,
C. S. Lewis

TO PAULINE BAYNES (W):[198]

[Magdalen College,
Oxford]
Dec. 17/49

Dear Miss Baynes

I was with Mr. Bles last week and wd. like to congratulate [you] on your drawings for my story,[199] which I thought really excellent. I love (and I think children will love too) the wealth of vigorous detail – if only there were going to be more room for it when they are reduced in size. I wish we were doing a folio!

I hope we may have several meetings as the work goes on. Meanwhile – as a preliminary – wd. there be any chance of your coming to a little lunch party I'm giving on Sat. Dec. 31st at 1.15? It wd. give me great pleasure. I think Bles said you live not too far away from Oxford.

The *Farmer Giles*[200] drawings were exquisite and in quite a different genre.

Yours sincerely
C. S. Lewis

198 See **Pauline Diana Baynes**, the illustrator of the Narnian stories, in the Biographical Appendix.
199 i.e. *The Lion, the Witch and the Wardrobe.*
200 J. R. R. Tolkien, *Farmer Giles of Ham*, embellished by Pauline Diana Baynes (1949).

TO MR YOXALL (W): TS

REF.488/49.

Magdalen College,
Oxford.
17th. December 1949.

Dear Mr. Yoxall,

I'll try: but I'm very ignorant of what has been written on our own times, and shall do it very badly.

yours sincerely,
C. S. Lewis

TO EDWARD T. DELL (P):

[Magdalen College,
Oxford]
19/12/49

Dear Mr. Dell

I don't think the idea that evil is an illusion helps.[201] Because surely it is a (real) evil that the illusion of evil shd. exist. When I am pursued in a nightmare by a crocodile the pursuit and the crocodile are illusions: but it is a real nightmare, and that seems a real evil. (Whenever one says 'This isn't a real so-and-so', is it not a real something else? e.g. if this is not a real pink rat it is real delirium, if this pupil is not a real sufferer from headache he is a real liar – and so on).

I don't feel I can advise on the American educational scene. One must not of course distort or suppress the sciences. It is rather, I suppose, a question of reducing them to their proper place – hypotheses (all provisional) about the *measurable* aspects of *physical* reality. Sometimes the adjustment between these hypotheses and the quite different pictures we get from Theology, Philosophy, and Art, has to be left in

---

201 In a letter of 12 December 1949, Dell wrote: 'I'm wondering whether or not Hegel's idea of evil as an illusion hasn't merit. The evil seems to have its ground of being as the "discreative force" (as Edwin Lewis calls it) or a parasite on creativeness which is the positive reality, good. Happenings are usually judged evil on the basis of a set of values which sinful men adopt. (i.e. when premature death comes we automatically say it is evil on the thesis that "living forever in this existence is the highest value".) Thus, if man could get his criterion adjusted he would see that all so-called evil is in actuality not evil at all. Of course sin is another problem and its presence has produced situations which victims of man's sin will call evil. These are the products of sinful society' (Bodleian Library, MS. Eng. lett. c. 220/4, fols. 82–3).

suspense – as discrepancies within the sciences themselves are left in suspense. The popular works of Jeans & Eddington are helpful here, but not to be too loud pedalled for other scientists don't always agree. There are good books by Sherwood Taylor.[202]

Thanks v. much for the admirable stationery.

With all good wishes.

Yours sincerely

C. S. Lewis

TO VERA MATHEWS (W): TS

REF.12/49.

Magdalen College,
Oxford.
19th. December 1949.

Dear Miss Mathews,

How perfectly splendid, with Christmas only five days off; eggs for breakfast forsooth! I am really quite overwhelmed by people's kindness. With your appetizing gift, what should arrive but a ham from some friend in Canada. So I foresee a happy marriage between the two parcels, at which feast we shall raise our cups of (rationed) tea and drink your health.

On looking more closely at the parcel, I see I should give you the countersign '30576 Maple Leaf, £11.50'. It sounds like some sort of secret society, does'nt it? But I am implored on the label to quote it in all communications. So there you have it.

Christmas looks like being pretty bleak for most people over here, and our Food Minister Mr. Strachey has – very wisely I think – chosen Christmas shopping week to go and give a pep talk to his ground nut experts in Central Africa.[203] Let us be thankful for the smallest mercies: from there he can't at any rate give us a Father Christmas talk on the air!

With many thanks and all my best wishes,

yours sincerely,

C. S. Lewis

---

202 Frank Sherwood Taylor (1897–1956) graduated in Chemistry from Lincoln College, Oxford, in 1921. After teaching at Queen Mary College, London, 1933–8, he was curator of the Science Museum, Oxford, 1940–50, and director of the Science Museum, London, 1950–6. His numerous books on scientific subjects include *The World of Science* (1936) and *An Illustrated History of Science* (1955). During his years in Oxford he spoke at the Socratic Club.

203 John St Loe Strachey (1901–63), Minister of Food in 1946, was in 1949 involved in the abortive Tanganyika ground-nut scheme.

TO RUTH PITTER (BOD):

[Magdalen College,
Oxford]
Dec 22/49

Dear Miss Pitter,

Has a letter either way gone astray? I'm still in suspense as to whether you will lunch with me here after the conference at 1.15 on Dec 31st. I do hope you can. Cd. you let me have word? – I want to know my numbers.[204]

Yours sincerely
C. S. Lewis

TO EDWARD T. DELL (P): TS

REF.409/49

Magdalen College,
Oxford.
26th.December 1949.

Dear Mr. Dell,

Many thanks for the little Biblical anthology; so much better than the routine Christmas Card of commerce.

With all best wishes to you for 1950,

yours sincerely,
C. S. Lewis

TO CHAD WALSH (W): TS

REF.150/49.

Magdalen College,
Oxford.
28th December 1949.

My dear Walsh,

Only this very morning I was saying to my brother that I wish some kind friend would send us some tea, or sugar, or both. And lo and behold, you appear on that cue like the fairy in a pantomime: to say nothing of all the other good things. (We in fact opened the parcel as soon as it arrived to get at the type ribbons).

I hope the ordination took place as you intended on the 21st? We have both thought of you during the last few weeks.

---

204 Miss Pitter noted: 'Telegraphed immediately, 11.15 a.m. 24.12.49' (Bodleian Library, MS. Eng. lett. c. 220/3, fol. 91).

With all best wishes from both of us for 1950, and hoping to see you in that year.

yours sincerely,
C. S. Lewis

TO MR YOXALL (W):

[Magdalen College,
Oxford]
28/12/49

Dear Mr. Yoxall

We must be more definite. The Jews may have had their own use of hyperbole but the last direction in wh. they wd. have used it was to deify a man. The absolute chasm wh. they put between Jahveh and His creatures was just the thing that cut them off from Pagans. No other race cd. have told the stories they told about Moses & Elijah and yet left these persons absolutely, sheerly human.

What was Jesus condemned for by the Sanhedrin? Surely His declaration 'I am etc.' must have been recorded right?[205]

Of course you're right – all the other points depend on the divinity, and even if they could be believed [without] it wd. not be specially interesting.

yours sincerely
C. S. Lewis

---

205 Luke 22:66–71: 'When day came, the assembly of the elders of the people gathered together, both chief priests and scribes; and they led him away to their council, and they said, "If you are the Christ, tell us." But he said to them, "If I tell you, you will not believe; and if I ask you, you will not answer. But from now on the Son of man shall be seated at the right hand of the power of God." And they all said, "Are you the Son of God, then?" And he said to them, "You say that I am." And they said, "What further testimony do we need? We have heard it ourselves from his own lips."'

TO DOROTHY L. SAYERS (W):

Magdalen College
Oxford
Dec 28/49

Dear Miss Sayers,

You have done *Vergine madre*[206] beautifully. Hearty congrats. and thanks. 'No more now' – you know what this season means to people in our job! Oh the mails: every bore in two continents seems to think I *like* getting letters. One's real friends are precisely the people one never gets time to write to.

Yours sincerely
C. S. Lewis

206 Dante, *Paradiso*, XXXIII, 1: 'Virgin mother'. Lewis may have been referring to Sayers's translation of 'Donna è gentil nel ciel' in *Inferno*, II, 94 as 'Heaven hath a noble Lady'.

BIOGRAPHICAL APPENDIX

ADAMS, Father Walter Frederick, SSJE (1871–1952), Lewis's confessor and spiritual director, was born at 32 Richmond Terrace, Clifton, on 30 January 1871 the son of the Reverend Frederick Morice Adams and his wife Mary Trevenen Grylls. He read Theology at Keble College, Oxford, and took his BA in 1894. After a year at Wells Theological College, he was ordained deacon in 1896 and priest in 1897. He was Curate of St James the Apostle and Martyr in Bream, Gloucester, 1896–9, and he then served at St Mark, Gloucester, 1900–3, and St Saviour, Roath, 1903–13.

He joined the Society of St John the Evangelist, Oxford, in 1913 and was professed in 1916. This society of mission priests and laymen, the oldest Anglican community for men religious and popularly known as the 'Cowley Fathers', was founded in 1865 by Robert Meux Benson (1824–1915), then Vicar of St James's, Cowley, Oxford.

As a missionary priest Fr Adams served the Society at their mission house in Cape Town, South Africa, 1921–3, at Cuthbert's Mission House, Tsolo, Cape Province, 1923–7, and at St John's Mission House, Mazagon, Bombay, 1930–1. He returned to the community house in Oxford in 1931 where he spent the rest of his life. He was well known as a conductor of retreats and much liked as a preacher. C. S. Lewis began going to him for confession in 1940, and recommended him to others. Much of the thought that Lewis became familiar with is found in Fr Adams's *Thoughts from the Notebooks of a Priest Religious* (London: Faith Press, 1949). He is the author (with G. Shaw) of *Triumphant in Suffering* (London: A. R. Mowbray, 1951).

Fr Adams died in Oxford on 3 March 1952. Lewis gave the following account of his spiritual mentor's death in a letter to Don Giovanni Calabria of 14 April 1952:

> *Pray for me, especially at present when I feel very much an orphan because my aged confessor and most loving father in Christ has just died. While he was celebrating at the altar, suddenly, after a most*

> *sharp but (thanks be to God) very brief attack of pain, he expired; and his last words were, 'I come, Lord Jesus.' He was a man of ripe spiritual wisdom – noble minded but of an almost childlike simplicity and innocence.*[1]

Lewis, however, was misinformed about Fr Adams's death; he died, not at the altar, nor even in church, but peacefully at the house of friends in Headington. For more information about Fr Adams, and a photograph, see 'Cowley Fathers – a Monastic Experience' in Bleakley, *C. S. Lewis: At Home in Ireland.*

BARFIELD, Matilda Douie 'Maud' (1885–1980), the wife of Owen Barfield, was born in Carlisle, Cumberland, on 3 March 1885, the daughter of Dr William Jones Douie, M.D., and Helen (McFarlan) Douie. After the family moved to Sevenoaks, Kent, Maud, as she was known, became a professional dancer and worked with the theatrical producer and designer Gordon Craig (1872–1966). She and Owen Barfield, both members of the English Folk Dancing Society, met in St Anthony in Roseland, Cornwall when the Society was touring Devon and Cornwall in the summer of 1920. They were married in the Church of St Jude-on-the-Hill, Golders Green, London on 11 April 1923, and they made Long Crendon, Buckinghamshire, their first home.

In his diary Lewis described his first meeting with Maud Barfield in the autumn of 1923: 'She is very quiet, a little shy, I think: "homely" both in the good and the bad sense of the word. I like her, and I think I should like her more, the more I saw of her.'[2] Thereafter the Barfields frequently visited Lewis in Oxford, and Maud became a close friend of Mrs Janie King Moore. Despite the difference in their ages and the fact that Maud disliked Anthroposophy, Lewis and Mrs Moore agreed that the Barfields were happily married, and got on 'better than the majority of married people'.[3]

In 1925 the Barfields moved to London to help with Owen Barfield's literary career. Unfortunately, his plans had to be abandoned when Barfield's father lost the services of a brother in the family law firm, Barfield and Barfield. In 1929 Owen joined the firm, and he spent the next twenty-eight years as a solicitor. Unable to have any of their own,

1 *Letters: C. S. Lewis–Don Giovanni Calabria*, p. 69.
2 *AMR*, note, 1923, p. 277.
3 ibid., 26 January 1927, p. 439.

the Barfields adopted three children: Alexander (b. 30 January 1928), Lucy (2 November 1935–3 May 2003),[4] Lewis's god-daughter, to whom he dedicated *The Lion, the Witch and the Wardrobe*, and Jeffrey (b. 9 June 1940),[5] to whom Lewis dedicated *The Voyage of the 'Dawn Treader'* (1952). Although Maud had always liked Lewis, she credited him in particular with saving Jeffrey. The boy's own mother had been unable to provide for him, and the Barfields agreed to foster him for a while. However, when it came time to give him up, Mrs Barfield could hardly bear it and she turned to Lewis for help. Lewis took on Jeffrey's school fees and other expenses, making it possible for the Barfields to keep him. This turned out to be very fortunate: Jeffrey lived at home during the whole of his adopted mother's life, and was a great help to her.

Because Lewis wanted to dedicate *The Lion, the Witch and the Wardrobe* to their daughter, Maud and Owen Barfield were among the first to read it in manuscript. Lucy qualified as a professional teacher of music, and it was a matter of great distress to her parents when, in the 1960s, she developed multiple sclerosis; she was to spend almost half her life in a wheelchair. However, being known as the dedicatee of *The Lion, the Witch and the Wardrobe* turned out to be a more precious legacy than anyone had foreseen in 1949.

Shortly after Owen Barfield retired in 1959 he became a visiting scholar in many American colleges and universities. Maud accompanied him on a number of these trips, and sometimes gave lectures on folk dancing. When the family moved to Orchard View, Dartford, Kent, in 1969 their house became a favourite resort of numerous American friends. Maud was a woman of great gentleness and kindness. She enjoyed company, and many will recall two of her favourite recollections. She and her mother were in Hyde Park on 20 June 1887 and saw Queen Victoria on her way to Westminster Abbey to celebrate her Golden Jubilee. Another favourite memory was seeing the American contemporary dancer, Isadora Duncan (1878–1927) perform in London on 22 February 1900.

Even in old age, Maud remained a kind and entertaining hostess. She loved the company of cats and dogs, and when her eyesight began to fail one of her greatest pleasures was hearing the novels of Sir Walter Scott read aloud. When over ninety she became reconciled to Anthroposophy. She died at Orchard View on 13 February 1980.

4 See the short biography of Lucy Barfield in *CG*, p. 758.

5 See the short biography of Jeffrey Barfield in *CG*, pp. 759–60.

BAYNES, Pauline Diana (1922–), illustrator of the Chronicles of Narnia, was born in Brighton on 9 September 1922, the daughter of Frederick William Wilberforce Baynes and Jessie Harriet Maude (Cunningham) Baynes. Pauline spent her first five years in India where her father was a commissioner in the Indian Civil Service. On returning to England she was educated at Beaufort School, Camberley, and in 1937 she followed her older sister, Angela, to Farnham School of Art. In 1939 she went to the Slade School of Fine Art in London, which was evacuated the same year to the Ruskin School in Oxford and remained there until 1948.

She was very busy during the Second World War. Farnham Castle had become the Camouflage Development Training Centre of the Royal Engineers, and Pauline and Angela worked there during 1940–2 as assistant model-makers. It was while she was there that Pauline did her first illustrations, which accompanied some of the tales in the *Perry Colour Books* (1942–63). She next went to Bath to draw charts for the Admiralty Hydrographic Department, remaining there from 1942 until 1945. At the end of the war she taught art at Beaufort School in Camberley, 1946–7.

Her professional work began after she happened to draw a picture in the margin of a letter to a friend. It was shown to Frank Whittaker of *Country Life* magazine, and this led to a commission to illustrate three books by Victoria Stevenson: *Clover Magic* (1944), *The Magic Footstool* (1946) and *The Magic Broom* (1950). Before she had completed these commissions she illustrated a book of her own, *Victoria and the Golden Bird* (1948).

Baynes's long association with J. R. R. Tolkien and C. S. Lewis began with Tolkien's intense dislike of some illustrations his publishers had chosen for his book, *Farmer Giles of Ham* (1949). George Allen & Unwin Ltd had commissioned Milein Cosman to illustrate the story, and Tolkien wrote to them on 5 August 1948 complaining of the 'fashionableness' of the drawings which he thought 'wholly out of keeping with the style or manner of the text'.[6] The publishers then contracted Pauline Baynes to provide illustrations for *Farmer Giles*. Tolkien was delighted. 'They are more than illustrations,' he wrote to Allen & Unwin on 16 March 1949, 'they are a collateral theme. I showed them to my

6 *The Letters of J. R. R. Tolkien*, ed. Humphrey Carpenter (1981), pp. 130–1.

friends whose polite comment was that they reduced my text to a commentary on the drawings.'[7]

A few months after this Lewis asked Baynes to illustrate *The Lion, the Witch and the Wardrobe*. As Tolkien had read the manuscript of *The Lion* it is almost certain he showed Lewis the illustrations to *Farmer Giles of Ham*. But this may not be the only reason Lewis wanted her to illustrate his book. In an interview on 19 July 1978 Baynes said:

> *C. S. Lewis told me that he had actually gone into a bookshop and asked the assistant there if she could recommend someone who could draw children and animals. I don't know whether he was just being kind to me and making me feel that I was more important than I was or whether he'd simply heard about me from his friend Tolkien.*[8]

Lewis signed a contract with Geoffrey Bles Ltd for *The Lion, the Witch and the Wardrobe* on 13 August 1949, after which Mr Bles formally commissioned Baynes to do the illustrations. They were completed and ready for Lewis to see when he met Bles during the second week of December 1949. Lewis hoped his readers would not be conscious while reading the Narnian stories of the parallels between them and the Gospels, and Baynes's experience was exactly what he hoped for. 'I didn't see it at all,' she said, 'until after I had finished drawing *The Lion, the Witch and the Wardrobe*, but I must admit that when I was drawing Aslan going through all the awfulnesses, when he was being tortured, I was crying all the time.'[9]

Baynes met Lewis for the first time at a luncheon party in Magdalen College on 31 December 1949. He was so impressed by her traditional style of drawing that he asked her to illustrate all the Narnian stories. By the time *The Lion* was published on 16 October 1950, Lewis had completed *Prince Caspian* (1951) and *The Voyage of the 'Dawn Treader'*, and on 5 January 1951 he sent Pauline a map of Narnia to illustrate not only the first two stories, but those he was yet to write. Accompanying the map, which is in the Bodleian Library[10] and reproduced as a postcard, was a note: 'My idea was that the map should be more like a medieval map than an Ordnance Survey – mountains and castles drawn – perhaps

7 ibid., p. 133.
8 Hooper, *Through Joy and Beyond*, p. 120.
9 ibid.
10 Bodleian Library, MS. Eng. lett. c. 220/1, fol. 160.

winds blowing at the corners – and a few heraldic-looking ships, whales and dolphins in a sea.'[11] When we compare these simple instructions with the map in the end pages of *Prince Caspian*, and Baynes's poster-sized map of Narnia published in 1968, we realize how much our picture of Lewis's imaginary world owes to the skill and imagination of Pauline Baynes. It was the perfect marriage of author and illustrator. Remembering him some years later, Baynes described Lewis as

> *the most kindly and tolerant of authors – who seemed happy to leave everything in my completely inexperienced hands! Once or twice I queried the sort of character he had in mind – as with Puddleglum & then he replied, but otherwise he made no remarks or criticism, despite the fact that the drawings were very far from perfect or even, possibly, from what he had in mind. I had rather the feeling that, having got the story written down & out of his mind, that the rest was someone else's job, & that he wouldn't interfere. As I remember, he only once asked for an alteration – & then with many apologies – when I (with my little knowledge) had drawn one of the characters rowing a boat facing the wrong direction!*
>
> *When he* did *criticize, it was put over so charmingly, that it wasn't a criticism, i.e. I did the drawings as best I could . . . and didn't realize how hideous I had made the children – they were as nice as* I *could get them – and Dr Lewis said, when we were starting on the second book, 'I know you made the children rather plain –* in the interests of realism *– but do you think you could possibly pretty them up a little now?'*[12]

By the time the Narnian stories came to an end Pauline Baynes was helping Professor Tolkien again. He wanted illustrations, he told her on 6 December 1961, that were 'bright and clear visions of things that one might really see'.[13] The result was Baynes's charming mock-medieval drawings for Tolkien's *The Adventures of Tom Bombadil* (1962). A few years later she illustrated his *Smith of Wootton Major* (1967). The same year that Pauline won the Kate Greenaway Medal for her illustrations

11 C. S. Lewis to Pauline Baynes, 5 January 1951. Bodleian Library, MS. Eng. lett. c. 220/1, fol. 154.

12 Letter to Walter Hooper of 15 August 1967, Bodleian Library, MS. Eng. lett. c. 220/1, fols. 162–3.

13 *The Letters of J. R. R. Tolkien*, p. 312.

to Grant Uden's *Dictionary of Chivalry* (1968) the Tolkiens moved to Bournemouth, and it was while living there that Professor and Mrs Tolkien came to know Pauline's husband.

In the early months of 1961 Pauline met Fritz Otto Gasch. He was born 21 September 1919 in Auerswalde, Saxony, Germany, and after being taken prisoner while serving in the Afrika Korps was brought to England, via the USA, as a prisoner of war. They married on 25 March 1961. 'We only knew each other a few months before we decided to get married,' she said. 'Meeting Fritz was the best thing that ever happened to me; he was a splendid man and a wonderful husband who was completely tolerant of his wife's obsession to draw!'[14] Following their marriage they settled in the village of Dockenfield, near Farnham, where Fritz was a garden contractor. He accompanied Pauline on visits to the Tolkiens, and he went with her to the United States in 1970 for the unveiling of the world's largest crewel embroidery, designed by Baynes for the Plymouth Congregational Church in Minneapolis. This good man died on 28 October 1988.

Pauline Baynes has illustrated over a hundred books, some of the best known of which are Amabel Williams-Ellis's *The Arabian Nights* (1957) and *Fairy Tales from the British Isles* (1960), Hans Christian Andersen's *Andersen's Fairy Tales* (1963), Richard Barber's *Companion to World Mythology* (1979) and Beatrix Potter's *Country Tales* (1987). She has also written and illustrated a number of books, among which are *The Song of the Three Holy Children* (1986), *How Dog Began* (1986), *Good King Wenceslaus* (1987), *Noah and the Ark* (1988) and *In the Beginning* (1991). She is, in addition, the editor and illustrator of *Thanks Be to God: Prayers from Around the World* (1990).

As the Chronicles of Narnia have become more and more famous, Baynes has been kept busy providing more illustrations. A special edition of *The Lion, the Witch and the Wardrobe*, published by HarperCollins in 1991, contains her original illustrations as well as seventeen additional full-page illustrations in colour. For the centenary of Lewis's birth in 1998 Baynes was commissioned to colour the original black and white illustrations in all seven books (London: HarperCollins, colour edition, 1998). A special 'anniversary edition' celebrating the fiftieth birthday of *The Lion, the Witch and the Wardrobe* contains the original illustrations in colour, the seventeen full-page illustrations, and Baynes's map of

14 *CG*, p. 626.

Narnia (London: HarperCollins, 2000). Those who prefer black and white illustrations should not worry. There are numerous editions of the Chronicles which contain all the original black and white illustrations, the most recent of which is the boxed set brought out by HarperCollins in 2001. We already know what C. S. Lewis thought of her beautiful work. When *The Last Battle* won the Carnegie Medal for the best children's book of 1956 she wrote to congratulate him. Lewis replied on 4 May 1957: 'Is it not rather "our" Medal?'[15]

BETJEMAN, Sir John (1906–84), Poet Laureate, was born in London on 28 August 1906, the son of Ernest Betjemann and Mabel Bessie (Dawson) Betjemann (John changed the spelling of his name to 'Betjeman' when a young man). He was educated at Highgate Junior School, 1915–17, the Dragon School, Oxford, 1917–20, and Marlborough College, 1920–5. He matriculated at Magdalen College in 1925, and was one of C. S. Lewis's first pupils. The entries on him in *AMR* provide evidence of the fact that he would not work, with the result that he failed the University's Divinity examination. After being 'rusticated' for a term, he chose not to take his final examination and he left Oxford without a degree. His chief complaint about Lewis was that he would not support him, and his case against his erstwhile tutor is made in a letter to Lewis of 13 December 1939 which Betjeman probably never posted:

> *In order to get a post in the inevitable prep-schoolmastering to which all unsuccessful undergraduates of my type are reduced, I needed written testimonials from the President of my college, the headmaster of my school and my tutor. I applied to you for a testimonial and you told me you could not say anything in my favour academically (at tutorials you frequently told me I had 'no literary style', and would only get a third and I certainly did little or no work for you as a consequence). So on this testimonial the only thing you said was that I was kindhearted and cheerful. It lost me three decentish jobs before I realized that I would be wiser not to show this testimonial in future.*[16]

From the time he left Oxford Betjeman began making Lewis a figure of fun. In *Ghastly Good Taste* (1933) he wrote: 'Finally, the author is

15 Bodleian Library, MS. Eng. lett. c. 220/1, fol. 158.

16 John Betjeman, *Letters, Volume One: 1926–1951*, ed. Candida Lycett Green (1994), p. 250.

indebted to Mr C. S. Lewis . . . whose jolly personality and encouragement to the author in his youth have remained an unfading memory for the author's declining years.' However, in later years Betjeman admitted that he was partly to blame for failing at Oxford and in a letter to Martyn Skinner of 23 February 1960 he admitted: 'Lewis was my undoing at Magdalen as well as my own temperament.'[17]

Betjeman's first two volumes of poems, *Mount Zion* (1931) and *Continual Dew* (1937), show a poet already well formed. His poetical career flourished when he published *Old Lights for New Churches* (1940) and *A Few Late Chrysanthemums* (1954). A delightful man, Betjeman was passionately devoted to the Church of England. He served on the Oxford Diocesan Advisory Committee, 1946–78, and for a number of years he was on the London Diocesan Advisory Committee. Lewis and Betjeman were eventually reconciled and they corresponded from time to time. But despite Lewis's efforts, they never became close friends. In 1960 Betjeman won the Queen's Gold Medal for Poetry. He was elected a Companion of Literature by the Royal Society of Literature in 1968 and he was knighted in 1969. He was chosen as Poet Laureate in 1972. In the 1970s Betjeman began suffering from Parkinson's disease, and he died on 19 May 1984. See Bevis Hillier, *Young Betjeman* (1988) and *John Betjeman: New Fame, New Love* (2002).

BLAKE, Leonard James (1907–89) was born in Hendon, Middlesex, on 7 October 1907, the son of Arthur Blake and Ethel (Mitchell) Blake. He began his musical career at the age of nine as a choirboy at Hendon Parish Church. In 1925 he was awarded the Royal Amateur Orchestral Society's scholarship to the Royal College of Music, where he met Maureen Moore. On leaving the College in 1929 he became music master at Twyford Preparatory School in Winchester. He was Director of Music at Worksop College, 1935–45, and at Malvern College, 1945–68. He was very active on behalf of the Royal School of Church Music, and was editor of *English Church Music*, 1938–58, persuading Lewis to contribute an essay 'On Church Music'. Blake married Maureen Moore on 27 August 1940 and the couple had two children, Richard Francis, Lewis's godson, who was born on 8 January 1945, and Eleanor Margaret born on 16 November 1949. On his retirement in 1968 the family moved to Winchcombe where Blake became organist and choirmaster

17 John Betjeman, *Letters, Volume Two: 1951–1984*, ed. Candida Lycett Green (1995), p. 183.

at Winchcombe Parish Church. He died on 2 August 1989. For more information, see **Dame Maureen Dunbar of Hempriggs** in the Biographical Appendix to *CL* I.

BLAMIRES, Harry (1916–) was born in Bradford, Yorkshire, on 6 November 1916, the son of Tom Blamires and Clara (Size) Blamires. He went up to University College, Oxford, in 1935 and was Lewis's pupil in English Literature until his graduation in 1938. After holding various teaching posts, in 1948 he became head of the English department at King Alfred's College, Winchester and later Dean of Arts and Sciences. He retired early to turn full-time writer in 1976, settling in Keswick, Cumbria. He subsequently lectured widely in the USA and was Visiting Professor of English at Wheaton College in 1987. He was awarded a D.Litt. by Southampton University in 1993. His theological works (numbering over a dozen books) include the classic *The Christian Mind* (1963), which has never been out of print. His output in literary criticism and history has been even larger and includes *The Bloomsday Book* (later *The New Bloomsday Book*), the celebrated guide to James Joyce's *Ulysses*, used continuously by students since it appeared in 1966. His most recent work has been in the field of English usage (*The Penguin Guide to Plain English*, 2000).

CLARKE, Sir Arthur Charles (1917–) was born in Minehead on 16 December 1917, the son of Charles Wright Clarke and his wife Mary Nora (Willis) Clarke. He was educated at Huish's Grammar School, Taunton, after which he moved to London and worked in the Exchequer and Audit Department, 1936–41. His apartment became the headquarters of the British Interplanetary Society, and in 1949 he became its chairman. He served in the Royal Air Force, 1941–6, specializing in radar, and during his time in service he sold his first science fiction stories. In 1945 he published a paper, 'Extra-terrestrial Relays',[18] proposing a technology that proved to be the forerunner of communication satellites. After the war Clarke went to King's College, London, where he took a B.Sc. with honours in Physics and Mathematics in 1948. His novel, *Prelude to Space* (1951), was written in three weeks during the summer of 1947. He was an assistant editor of *Physics Abstracts*, 1949–51, and since 1952 he has been a full-time writer. In the 1950s Clarke

18 Arthur C. Clarke, 'Extra-terrestrial Relays', *Wireless World* (October 1945), pp. 305–8.

became interested in undersea exploration and moved to Sri Lanka. He was knighted in 1998. Clarke's numerous books include *The Sands of Mars* (1951), *Childhood's End* (1953), *Earthlight* (1955) and *2001: A Space Odyssey* (1968). See Neil McAleer, *Arthur C. Clarke: The Authorized Biography* (1992) and *From Narnia to A Space Odyssey: The War of Ideas Between Arthur C. Clarke and C. S. Lewis* (New York: 2003).

DELL, Edward Thomas, Jr (1926–) was born in Atlanta, Georgia on 12 February 1923. A member of the Church of the Nazarene, he was educated at Eastern Nazarene College, Wollaston, Massachusetts. He took a BA in 1948, and it was while working on a degree of Bachelor in Theology at Eastern Nazarene that he began corresponding with Lewis. After Dell converted to the Episcopal Church he studied for a BD in Theology, and he was ordained an Episcopal priest in 1956. In 1954 he married Carol Jane Carr, and they had three children. Dell was a curate at St John's Church, Roxbury, Massachusetts, 1955–6, and on the parish staff at St Paul's Church, Millis, Massachusetts, 1956–61. Dell's most important work has been in periodicals. He was book review editor, associate editor and managing editor of *The Episcopalian*, 1968–73. He founded the serials *Audio Amateur* in 1970 and *Speaker Builder* in 1980. His published works include *Of Mockingbirds and Other Irrelevancies* (Francestown, New Hampshire: Marshall Jones Co., 1993). On his retirement he moved to West Peterborough, New Hampshire. Facsimiles of his letters from Lewis are in the Bodleian Library and Wheaton College.

EDDISON, Eric Rücker, CB CMG (1882–1945) was born at St Helen's, Adel, Yorkshire, on 24 November 1882, the son of Octavius Eddison and Helen Louisa (Rücker) Eddison. Adel is only a few miles from Leeds, and 'Ric', as Eddison was known, became friends with another boy from the city, Arthur Ransome (1884–1967), who is best remembered for *Swallows and Amazons* (1930) and other novels for children. As Ransome recalled in his autobiography, the pair received much of their early education together:

> *[Ric's] father was Octavius Eddison, a Leeds solicitor, whose saddle-horse I have seen, in those leisurely days, tied up outside his office in the middle of Leeds. His uncle, Dr John Eddison, was a friend of Andrew Lang's. Both lived at Adel, a few miles further out of Leeds*

> *than Headingley. Ric was about my own age. He and I shared first a governess, a kindly, comfortable Miss Glendinning . . . The Eddisons' dog-cart used to take her to Adel, picking me up on the way . . . Miss Glendinning was presently succeeded by a long series of unlucky tutors.*[19]

Eddison's juvenilia, in the Bodleian Library, provide evidence of how early in his life he and Ransome loved stories of high romance. At the same time Eddison was devoted to Homer and the lyrical poetry of Greece. He went on to develop a love for Icelandic, and taught himself the language when he went away to Eton. Eddison matriculated at Trinity College, Oxford, in 1901, where he read Classics. He took his BA in 1905 and in 1906 began work with the Board of Trade.

Eddison served as private secretary to successive Presidents of the Board, 1915–19, and was then Controller of the Profiteering Act Department, 1920–1. In 1923 he became Secretary to the Imperial Economic Conference. He was Comptroller of the Companies Department, Board of Trade, 1924–8, Head of Empire Trades and Economic Division in the Department of Overseas Trade, 1928–30, and in 1930 became Deputy Comptroller-General in the Department of Overseas Trade. He was made a Companion of the Order of St Michael and St George in 1924 and a Companion of the Order of the Bath in 1929, both honours being awarded for his services to the Board of Trade.

In 1909 Eddison married Winifred Grace Henderson, and they had one daughter, Jean Gudrun Rücker Latham (1910–2002). Eddison was a civil servant of distinction, and during his years with the Board of Trade he and his family lived in London. In 1939 Eddison retired from the Civil Service in order to devote more time to his writing, and the family moved to Dark Lane House, Marlborough, Wiltshire.

Eddison's fame rests on his four major works – *The Worm Ouroboros: A Romance*, illustrated by Keith Henderson (London: Jonathan Cape, 1922; New York: Albert & Charles Boni, 1926); *Mistress of Mistresses: A Vision of Zimiamvia*, with decorations by Keith Henderson (London: Faber & Faber, 1935; New York: Dutton, 1935); *A Fish Dinner in Memison* (New York: Dutton, 1941); and *The Mezentian Gate*, frontispiece and decorations by Keith Henderson (London: Elek Books, 1958).

19 Arthur Ransome, *Autobiography*, ed. Rupert Hart-Davis (1976), p. 37. See Ransome, *Autobiography*, Plate 1, for a photo of the young Ric Eddison and Arthur Ransome, along with their tutor, Mr Pegg.

The last three of these form a trilogy set partly on earth and partly in a world of imagination, Zimiamvia. According to Ransome:

> The Worm Ouroboros *was a book of strange power, a story of fantastic heroes in a fantastic world, written in a consistent, fastidious prose that seemed devised for that purpose. The language, the place-names and the names of the heroes were for me an echo of those ancient days when Ric and I produced plays in a toy theatre with cardboard actors carrying just such names and eloquent with just such rhetoric. Gorice, Lord Goldry Bluszco, Corinius, Brandoch Daha seemed old friends when I met them nearly forty years later. Ric throughout his life had a foot in each of two worlds, and the staid official of the Board of Trade was for ever turning from his statistics to look out over the towers of Koshtra Belorn.*[20]

The Worm Ouroboros was Lewis's favourite of Eddison's books, and in his copy he listed the dates of six times he read it, although it is known that he read it more often than that. In 'A Tribute to E. R. Eddison' which first appeared on the cover of the posthumous *Mezentian Gate*, Lewis described Eddison's novels as 'a new literary species, a new rhetoric, a new climate of the imagination'.[21]

But much as Lewis liked Eddison's books, and the author himself, he shared some reservations about them with Eddison's close friend, Sir George Rostrevor Hamilton. In an important work of appreciation, 'The Prose of E. R. Eddison', Hamilton touched on what he and Lewis regarded as a both a strength and a weakness in the Zimiamvian trilogy:

> *The truth is that Eddison fell deeply in love with his imagined world, from Fiorinda to the least blade of glass and, like a lover, he could see nothing amiss. He is completely serious and takes his stand on philosophy, reducing Truth, Beauty and Goodness to one ultimate value, Beauty: a thing you may only do, if in Beauty you include not only sensuous beauty of form and beauty of action but also – and not dependent on these – beauty of character, according to the highest conception of Good. It is his failure to recognize this which I regard as the chief defect in Eddison's Utopia. And yet to bring it into the open is to risk a loss of perspective: for this fault has the*

20 Ransome, *Autobiography*, p. 38.
21 'A Tribute to E. R. Eddison', *Of This and Other Worlds*, p. 42.

> *same root as his virtue, so that one may almost say – felix culpa.*[22] *It was just because he saw with the eyes of a lover that he was able to present this world with so amazing a vitality.*[23]

Eddison's other works include (arr.) *Poems, Letters and Memories of Philip Sidney Nairn* (London: 1916), *Styrbiorn the Strong* (based on *Styrbjarnar þaettr Svíakappa*), illustrated by Keith Henderson (London: Jonathan Cape, 1926; New York: Albert & Charles Boni, 1926) and (trans.) *Egil's Saga Skallagrimssonar, done into English out of the Icelandic with an introduction, notes, and an essay on some principles of translation* (Cambridge: Cambridge University Press, 1930; New York: Greenwood Press, 1968).

Eddison died on 18 August 1945. He had maintained his friendship with Ransome, who recalled: 'Of us two Ric was always the leader, and throughout our lives the tone of our relationship was exactly what it had been when he was Ric (short not for Eric but for Fredericius) and I was Bony (short for Bonifacius), enacting terrifying scenes in the Adel nursery.'[24] Eddison was a splendid letter-writer and in 1968 his daughter, Jean Latham, presented the Bodleian Library with many of her father's papers, including letters to Lewis, Gerald Hayes, and others.[25] The manuscripts of Eddison's published works are held in Leeds Public Library.

ELIOT, Thomas Stearns (1888–1965), poet, playwright, critic and publisher, was born in St Louis, Missouri, on 26 September 1888. After taking a BA and a MA from Harvard in 1909 and 1919, Eliot decided to become a professor of philosophy and began a doctoral dissertation. Harvard granted him a travelling fellowship, which involved spending 1914–15 at Merton College, Oxford.

While there he met the American poet Ezra Pound (1885–1972), and it was largely through Pound's influence that he gave up philosophy for poetry. Pound helped him to publish some of his early poems; one of

---

22 'happy fault'. The phrase, '*O felix culpa quae talem et tantum meruit habere redemptorem*': 'O happy fault . . . which gained for us so great a Redeemer', is found in the Easter Liturgy of the Catholic Church.

23 George Rostrevor Hamilton, 'The Prose of E. R. Eddison', *English Studies* (1949), p. 48.

24 Ransome, *Autobiography*, p. 38.

25 Bodleian Library, GB 0161, MS. Eng. misc. b. 105, c. 456–7, c. 469, d. 654–6, e. 598–9; MS. Eng. lett. c. 230–2.

these was 'The Love Song of J. Alfred Prufrock' which was included in Eliot's first volume of poems, *Prufrock and Other Observations* (1917). In 1915 Eliot married Vivien Haigh-Wood, and during their first year of marriage Eliot taught at Highgate Junior School – where John Betjeman was one of his pupils. Eliot worked for Lloyds Bank, 1917–25, and in 1922 he founded the influential literary periodical, *The Criterion* (1922–39), where his poem *The Waste Land* was published. In 1925 Eliot left Lloyds to become a director of the publishing firm of Faber & Gwyer, which became Faber & Faber in 1929.

In 1927 Eliot became a British subject and he was baptized in the Church of England on 9 June 1927. He became an active churchman, and his High Anglicanism was charted in *Four Quartets* (1935–42). He did much to revive poetic drama, and in 1935 he published his drama about the martyrdom of St Thomas à Becket, *Murder in the Cathedral* (1935). Eliot wrote numerous volumes of verse and criticism; one of his best-known critical works is *Notes Towards the Definition of Culture* (1948). His wife Vivien, after years of mental illness, died in 1947. In 1957 he married Valerie Fletcher, with whom he lived very happily for the rest of his life. In 1948 Eliot received the Nobel Prize for Literature, and the Order of Merit. Eliot died on 4 January 1965.

From the time Lewis came across *Prufrock* he disliked Eliot's poems intensely, and he had Eliot in mind when he told his father on 6 June 1920 that he did not think the possibilities of 'metrical poetry on sane subjects'[26] exhausted. If there is one poem of Eliot's that typifies what Lewis hated it is 'The Love Song of J. Alfred Prufrock', which opens: 'Let us go then, you and I,/When the evening is spread out against the sky/Like a patient etherized upon a table.'[27] The comparison of evening to 'a patient etherized upon a table' violated what Lewis called proper stock responses, and nowhere is his case more persuasively argued than in *A Preface to Paradise Lost*:

> *By a Stock Response Dr I. A. Richards means a deliberately organized attitude which is substituted for 'the direct free play of experience'. In my opinion such deliberate organization is one of the first necessities of human life, and one of the main functions of art is to assist it. All that we describe as constancy in love or friendship, as loyalty*

26 *CL* I, p. 492.

27 T. S. Eliot, *The Complete Poems and Plays* (1969), p. 13, 'The Love Song of J. Alfred Prufrock', 1–3. Compare Eliot's poem with Lewis's 'Confession' in *CP*.

> *in political life, or in general, as perseverance – all solid virtue and stable pleasure – depends on organizing chosen attitudes and maintaining them against the eternal flux . . . I have heard Mr Eliot's comparison of evening to a patient on an operating table praised, nay gloated over, not as a striking picture of sensibility in decay, but because it was so 'pleasantly unpleasant.' . . . That elementary rectitude of human response, at which we are so ready to fling the unkind epithets of 'stock', 'crude', 'bourgeois', and 'conventional', so far from being 'given' is a delicate balance of trained habits, laboriously acquired and easily lost, on the maintenance of which depend both our virtues and our pleasures and even, perhaps, the survival of our species.*[28]

In the end, Lewis realized he had lost his battle on behalf of poetry, and he turned his attention to matters he could do something about. In 1959 Lewis and Eliot were appointed members of the Commission to Revise the Psalter, and when they met things were totally different. Lewis told Walter Hooper about it in the summer of 1963: 'You know I never liked Eliot's poetry, or even his prose. But when we met this time I loved him.'[29]

EVERY, Brother George, SSM (1909–2003) and his twin brother, Edward, were born on 3 February 1909 at Ottery St Mary, Devon, where their father, the Rev. George Every, was vicar. He was educated at King's School, Ottery St Mary, 1917–21, the Choir School, Winchester College, 1921–2, and the King's School, Worcester Cathedral, 1922–6. In 1926 he went to University College of the South-West (now the University of Exeter), where he took his BA in 1929. While there his special subject was supervised by the distinguished Catholic historian, Christopher Dawson (1889–1970), and he left with first class honours.

Instead of becoming an academic, as might be expected, Every became in 1929 a student-tutor at the Society of the Sacred Mission (SSM), an Anglican theological college at Kelham near Newark in Nottinghamshire. The SSM was a community of priests and laymen founded in 1893 by Fr Herbert Kelly. Its tasks were to train men to give their lives to the divine service through missionary work or the study of theology. In 1903 the Society settled at Kelham, its mother house for seventy years.

---

28 *A Preface to Paradise Lost*, ch. 8, pp. 53–5.

29 Green and Hooper, *C. S. Lewis: A Biography*, ch. 13, pp. 389–90.

Every remained a student-tutor at Kelham until 1933. Following his profession as a lay brother in that year, he then served as Assistant Librarian until 1973. Applications to Kelham dropped from four hundred a year before the war to less than forty in 1971, and the college closed in 1973. What remained of the Society moved to new priory buildings at Willen, near Milton Keynes.

Over the years Every had given much thought to the schism between the Catholic Church and the Eastern Churches as discussed in his book, *The Byzantine Patriarchate, 451–1204* (1947), and by the time the Second Vatican Council was meeting (1962–5) it was evident to him that the teaching of the Council had not only cleared up aspects of that schism but settled his problems with Catholicism. 'My sense of involvement with these,' he said in the preface to *A Christmas Collection* (2001), 'when the College at Kelham was closing in 1973 led me to make my submission to Rome.' Every was received into the Catholic Church in the Benedictine Priory of Christ the King, Cockfosters, by Dom Edmund Jones OSB on 17 March 1973. He was Assistant Librarian at the Catholic seminary, St Mary's College, Oscott, 1973–84. He taught a number of courses there until his retirement in 1995. Despite the fact that in his old age George Every's hearing was impaired, his mind remained as agile as ever and he continued to be a loved member of St Mary's College. He died on 2 September 2003.

George Every's books include (with J. D. C. Pellow and S. L. Bethell) *Selected Poems* (1945); *The Byzantine Patriarchate, 451–1204* (1947; rev. edn 1962); *Poetry and Personal Responsibility: An Interim Report on Contemporary Literature* (1949); *The High Church Party, 1688–1718* (1956); *Lamb to the Slaughter* (1957); *Light Under a Door: Poems about Christmas* (1958); *The Baptismal Sacrifice* (1959); (ed.) Herbert Kelly, *No Pious Person: Autobiographical Recollections* (1960); *Basic Liturgy: A Study of the Structure of the Eucharistic Prayer* (1961); *Misunderstandings Between East and West* (1965); *Christian Mythology* (1970; rev. edn, 1987); *Understanding Eastern Christianity* (1980); (sel. and ed. with Richard Harries and Kallistos Ware) *Seasons of the Spirit: Readings Through the Christian Year* (1984); and *A Christmas Collection: Poems of Incarnation and History* (Leominster: Gracewing, 2001).

FIROR, Dr Warfield Monroe (1896–1988) was born in Baltimore, Maryland on 7 November 1896. He received his AB in 1917 from Johns Hopkins University and his MD in 1921 from the Johns Hopkins

University School of Medicine. He remained at Johns Hopkins for residencies in both neurosurgery and surgery and became a faculty member and surgeon there.

Dr Firor played a major role in the national effort to raise the level of training in surgery and lectured on medicine throughout the United States. He conducted research on the effects of tetanus toxin on the spinal cord and investigated the treatment of diseased adrenal glands with hormone implants. Among Firor's surgical contribution was the introduction of intestinal antisepsis in preparation for colon surgery. In 1939 he was awarded the gold medal from the American Medical Association. His work was far reaching, and in 1959 he supervised the building of a hospital in Seoul, Korea.

Dr Firor had a cabin in the Rocky Mountains, and it disappointed him that Lewis was never able to accept his invitation to have a holiday there. Even so, he enjoyed their single meeting in Oxford in 1949. His generosity was endless. Besides supplying Lewis with numerous hams and other foods over a period of years, he donated his collection of letters from Lewis to the Bodleian Library, and his financial donations made it possible for Walter Hooper to edit several volumes of Lewis's papers. 'You are a fairy-tale character,' Lewis said in a letter of 14 April 1950, 'your bounty (as Cleopatra says) is an autumn that grows the more by reaping.'[30]

Johns Hopkins awarded Dr Firor an honorary doctorate in 1981. Following his death on 12 August 1988 the Johns Hopkins School of Medicine founded the Warfield M. Firor Chair of Surgery. There is a collection of Firor's papers and interviews in the Alan Mason Chesney Medical Archives at Johns Hopkins. Dr Firor was a Presbyterian Elder in the Franklin Street Church, Baltimore. See his essay on 'Divine Intercession' in *Theology Today*, XV, no. 4 (January 1959).

FLEWETT, June: see **Lady (Jill) Freud**

FOX, Rev. Adam (1883–1977), an Inkling, was born in London on 15 July 1883. He was educated at Winchester College and University College, Oxford, taking his BA in 1906. He taught at Lancing College, 1906–18. Fox was ordained in 1911 and was Warden of Radley College, 1918–24. After teaching at the Diocesan College, Rondenbosch, 1924–29, he was

30 Shakespeare, *Antony and Cleopatra*, V, ii, 87–8. Bodleian Library, MS. Eng. lett. c. 220/1, fol. 127.

elected Dean of Divinity at Magdalen College, thus beginning a friendship with Lewis. In 1937 Fox published a narrative poem, *Old King Cole*, which led to his becoming Professor of Poetry, 1938–43. In 1942 Fox became a Canon of Westminster Abbey, where he remained until 1963. He died 17 January 1977 and his ashes are buried in Poet's Corner, Westminster Abbey. See his biography in *CG*.

FREUD, Lady (Jill) (1927–) was born June Beatrice Flewett in London on 22 April 1927, the daughter of Henry Walter Flewett (1892–1970) and Winifred 'Freda' (Johnson) Flewett (1896–1967). Her father was Senior Classics Master of St Paul's School, London, and the Senior Examiner for London University of School and Higher Certificates in Latin and Greek.

Jill, as she is known, was born and brought up a Roman Catholic and educated at Sacred Heart Convent in London. However, as war loomed closer and closer, Sacred Heart, like many other schools, began rehearsing for an evacuation. At the outbreak of the Second World War in the autumn of 1939 Jill and her two sisters, aged five and fifteen, were sent to the comparative safety of Oxford. Jill lived for a while with the unmarried 'Misses Butler' – who had been three of the children in Lewis Carroll's circle of friends. By the summer of 1942 Jill knew she would not be going back to the Butlers' and the following September she was interviewed for a place at The Kilns by Janie King Moore. It was agreed that Jill would take up residence there the following September. However, the school returned to London where she completed her School Certificate and left school in July 1943. Mrs Moore invited her to The Kilns for two weeks' holiday, but in the end she stayed there for two years.

England was in the middle of the war, and because the gardener, Fred Paxford, had been called to work in a munitions factory close by, extra hands were needed to look after the family's twenty-five chickens, three rabbits, and huge vegetable garden. Mrs Moore, now seventy-three and suffering from varicose ulcers, could not have managed without Jill. They kept hens, and the burden of feeding and looking after them fell on her. Jill had been accepted for a place at the Royal Academy of Dramatic Art; however, because she was so greatly needed at The Kilns, she put off her attendance several times. When she finally did go it was necessary to retake the entrance examination.

At the time of writing there is no one still alive who was on such close terms with Mrs Moore and the Lewis brothers as was Jill. In reminiscences published in 1983 she provided an intimate picture of life at The Kilns during the war, incidentally answering the question of what happened to Mrs Moore's letters from Lewis. She wrote:

> *To Mrs Moore, Lewis showed the greatest loving care. He waited on her, filled her hot water bottle, made her a hot drink, saw that she was tucked in each night. The only time I ever heard Jack Lewis's voice rise in annoyance with her was once when she had said something derogatory about his brother. She was strong-willed, and had a great sense of humour. Mrs Moore and Jack Lewis had happy times together. She adored him absolutely. Her whole life was centred around him and around him alone . . . When she became ill she took all Jack's letters, piles of letters she had received from him over a period of about twenty-five years, and I think also the letters from her son, Paddy – Lewis's great friend who was killed in the First World War – and threw them all into the old-fashioned boiler in the kitchen. She burned them all.*[31]

Although C. S. Lewis was already famous in Oxford, and despite the fact that Jill had read some of his books, it was some time before she became aware that he and the 'Jack' Lewis of The Kilns were the same man. As she wrote about him years later:

> *Here was this man whom I'd been chatting away to quite freely and I suddenly realized that he was somebody who could see into my inner soul and what an awful person I was. At 16 that was very devastating. Of course I fell madly in love with him. It was a tremendous crush, and I would have lain down and he could have walked all over me for the next two years . . . Every smile, every kind word was like daylight, like the summer. I just took the crumbs that I was offered. He took a lot of trouble with me. He'd lend me a book and then talk to me about it as if my idiot childish opinions were of any interest. Minto once told me he thought I was very intelligent. I think he regarded me in a very benevolent way as a very young student. He would coach me in that sense. He was also . . . totally over the*

31 Jill Freud, 'With Girls at Home', *In Search of C. S. Lewis*, ed. Stephen Schofield (South Plainfield, New Jersey: Bridge Publishing Inc., 1983), p. 58.

top about what a wonderful thing I'd done for them and how they couldn't manage without me.[32]

She greatly underestimated herself and the impression she made on everyone. On 2 January 1945, the evening before she left for the Royal Academy, Warnie wrote in his diary:

Our dear, delightful June Flewett leaves us tomorrow, after nearly two years, for London and the Dramatic School where she is to be taught to be an actress. She is not yet eighteen, but I have met no one of any age further advanced in the Christian way of life. From seven in the morning till nine at night, shut off from people of her own age, almost grudged the time for her religious duties, she has slaved at The Kilns, for a fraction 2d. an hour; I have never seen her other than gay, eager to anticipate exigent demands, never complaining, always self accusing in the frequent crises of that dreary house. Her reaction to the meanest ingratitude was to seek its cause in her own faults. She is one of those rare people to whom one can venture to apply the word 'saintly' . . . From a personal selfish point of view I shall feel the loss of June very keenly: for in addition to her other virtues, she is a clever girl, and with her gone, it means that when J is away, there is no one to talk to in the house.[33]

As the letters in this volume bear witness, the Lewis brothers never ceased to regard Jill with the highest affection; and she, in turn, felt the same about them.

Jill was very successful in her career, and having taken her Diploma in Drama from London University in 1947, with an Acting Diploma from the Royal Academy of Dramatic Art, she appeared in her first film role under her screen name, 'Jill Raymond'. It was *The Woman in the Hall* (1947) in which she played the sister of Jean Simmons. Of course Jack and Warnie went to see the film, and they were present when Jill appeared at the Oxford Playhouse in J. B. Priestley's play, *The Linden Tree* (1947). There were to be many more roles in films, television, radio and, most of all, the live theatre, in which her greatest interest lay.

Jill was in the lounge of the Arts Theatre Club, London, on 2 April 1950 when she was introduced to the writer, Clement Freud, son of

32 Phillips, *C. S. Lewis at the BBC*, pp. 176–7.
33 *BF*, pp. 180–1.

Ernst and Lucie Freud, brother of the painter Lucian Freud and grandson of Sigmund Freud. Clement was born in Berlin in 1924 but his family came to England in 1933, refugees from the Nazis. Clement and Jill were married at St James's Church, Spanish Place, on 4 September 1950. Jack Lewis was unable to attend, but Warnie was there and wrote about the reception afterwards: 'Was welcomed at the door by Mrs Flewett, who said all manner of nice things to me and then passed on to where Clement and June were receiving their guests: kissed the latter by special command, which was the only enjoyable part of the function.'[34]

The Freuds were to have four children, Nicola (b. 1951), Dominic (b. 1958), Emma (b. 1962) and Matthew (b. 1963). In 1973 Clement Freud was elected MP for the Isle of Ely and for the next fourteen years Jill was kept busy as an MP's wife. Even so, she continued her acting whenever she could. Clement Freud was knighted in 1987 and in 2003 became Rector of St Andrews University.[35] In 1980 Jill founded Jill Freud and Company, an actors' non-profit-making company, which produces theatre seasons in Southwold and Aldeburgh in Suffolk. Of Lady Freud's achievements, perhaps the one that would have pleased Lewis most was the Honorary Degree of Civil Law she received from the University of East Anglia in 2001 'for services to the theatre'.

GIOVANNI Calabria, St (1873–1954), founder of the Congregation of the Poor Servants of Divine Providence, was born on 8 October 1873 in Verona, Italy, the son of Luigi Calabria and his wife Angela Foschio. They were a very poor family, and after his father's death Giovanni had to interrupt his fourth year of elementary school to find work. Fr Pietro Scapini prepared him privately for admission to the seminary but before this could take place he had to undertake two years of military service.

Having finished his military service, Giovanni resumed his studies. One cold night in 1897, upon returning home from a visit to the sick, he found a boy crouching on his doorstep. He picked him up and cared for him in his own home. This was the beginning of his work for orphans and abandoned boys. Not long afterwards he founded the Pious Union for Assistance to the Sick.

He was ordained a priest on 11 August 1901, after which he served as a curate at St Stephen's, Verona. Besides visiting the hospitals, the

34 ibid., p. 234.

35 See Sir Clement Freud's autobiography, *Freud Ego* (2001), which contains photographs of Jill and her family.

prisons and the poor, Don Giovanni set out to rescue orphans from the streets. He became parish priest of St Benedict's al Monte in 1907, and on 26 November 1907 conceived the idea for his great 'work'. This was the San Zeno Orphanage, or Casa Buoni Fanciulli (Home of Good Children) in Verona. The following year he settled with many of his orphans in a quarter of the city known as San Zeno in Monte. To help with the work, Don Giovanni established a congregation of priests and laity to be called the Poor Servants of Divine Providence. By the time this congregation was approved by the bishop on 11 February 1932 it numbered some 150 priests and laymen, attached to about twenty houses in the provinces of Verona, Vicenza, Ferrara, Milan, Rome and other parts of Italy. Nowadays those students who enter the congregation are housed, fed and given an elementary education. After this they are free to enter any seminary or religious missionary institute they like. These poor children – who now number over 2,500 – are looked after and prepared for life. In 1910 Don Giovanni founded a female branch of this order, the Poor Sister Servants of Divine Providence. It received diocesan approval on 25 March 1952 and pontifical approval on 25 December 1981.

In 1947, the year Don Giovanni's Congregation of The Poor Servants of Divine Providence was approved by Pope Pius XII, he began corresponding with C. S. Lewis. Don Giovanni had for a long time been passionately interested in Christian unity, and after reading an Italian translation of *The Screwtape Letters* – *Le Lettere di Berlicche* (1947) – he wrote to the author. He did not know English, and the only language he believed them to share was Latin. In his first letter to Lewis of 1 September 1947, he mentioned the octave of prayer for unity: 'You . . . seem to me to be able to contribute much in the Lord . . . I promise to pray strenuously that God and our Lord Jesus Christ will see fit to illuminate and strengthen you that you may be able to perform something of great moment in the Lord's vineyard.'[36] Thus began a correspondence which was precious to both men, and from which Lewis received great encouragement.

Don Giovanni had an unerring sense of how and when to comfort and stimulate his friend. After receiving Don Giovanni's letter of Christmas Day 1948 encouraging him to write more, Lewis replied:

36 *Letters: C. S. Lewis–Don Giovanni Calabria*, p. 29.

> *My house is unquiet and devastated by women's quarrels . . . My aged mother, worn out by long infirmity, is my daily care . . . These things I write not as complaints but lest you should believe I am writing books. If it shall please God that I write more books, blessed be He. If it shall not please Him, again, blessed be He. Perhaps it will be the most wholesome thing for my soul that I lose both fame and skill lest I were to fall into that evil disease, vainglory.*

Almost immediately afterwards Aslan bounded into Lewis's life, and he wrote *The Lion, the Witch and the Wardrobe.*

The two men corresponded until Don Giovanni's death on 4 December 1954, after which Lewis maintained a correspondence with another priest of the Congregation, Don Luigi Pedrollo. It was reported that on the eve of his death Don Giovanni 'made his last act of charity, offering his life to God for the dying Pope Pius XII. The Lord accepted this offer, for while he was dying, the Pope mysteriously and unexpectedly recovered and lived for another four years.'[37]

Don Giovanni was beatified by Pope John Paul II in Verona on 17 April 1988 and canonized by Pope John Paul in Rome on 18 April 1999. On the latter occasion the biography of him that appeared in the Vatican newspaper mentioned that a Jewish woman doctor, who had been in hiding from Nazi-Fascist persecution in one of Don Giovanni's religious institutes, had written to the Pope that 'Every instant of his life was a personification of St Paul's marvellous hymn on charity.'[38] 'Giovanni Calabria's entire life,' Pope John Paul said at his canonization, 'was a living Gospel, overflowing with love: love for God and for his brothers and sisters, especially the very poor.'[39]

The correspondence between Lewis, St Giovanni, and Don Luigi Pedrollo was published with the original Latin and an English translation by Martin Moynihan as *Letters: C. S. Lewis–Don Giovanni Calabria, A Study in Friendship* (1988). There is also a scholarly Italian edition of the correspondence, with some additional letters between Lewis, St Giovanni and Don Luigi Pedrollo, entitled *Una Gioia Insolita: Lettere tra un prete cattolico e un laico anglicano,* edited by Luciano Squizzato and translated by Patrizia Morelli (Milan: Editoriale Jaca Book SpA, 1995). *Una Gioia Insolita* contains biographies of Lewis, St Giovanni

37 *L'Osservatore Romano* (21 April 1999), p. 2.
38 ibid.
39 ibid., p. 1.

and Don Luigi Pedrollo, as well as an exhaustive list of works by and about St Giovanni Calabria.

GREEN, Roger Lancelyn (1918–87), in his lifetime the world's leading authority on Victorian children's books, was born on 2 November 1918 in Norwich. He was the eldest of two boys and two girls born to Gilbert Arthur Lancelyn Green and Helena Mary Phyllis (Sealy) Green. Major Gilbert Lancelyn Green, retired from the Army, was in Norwich taking a course in agriculture when Roger was born. Roger was two years old when the family moved back to Poulton Hall, Poulton-Lancelyn, Wirral, Cheshire, an estate his ancestors had held for almost nine hundred years. This ancient estate is entailed, which means there is a predetermined order of succession through the male line, and which also ensures it cannot be bequeathed at pleasure or sold.

Roger was educated at Dane Court, Pyrford, Surrey, and Liverpool College. However, because of ill health during his childhood he was educated privately for a number of years. In the summer of 1937 he visited Greece for the first time, and thus began a lifelong passion for Greek myth and legend. That autumn he matriculated at Merton College, Oxford, where he took an honours degree in English Language and Literature in 1940. This was a good time to read English at Oxford because C. S. Lewis was giving his enormously popular 'Prolegomena' lectures on Medieval and Renaissance literature. Lewis hardly ever remembered to bring a watch to these lectures and usually borrowed one from the nearest undergraduate. Since Green regularly sat almost at Lewis's feet during the Michaelmas Term of 1938–9, Lewis began borrowing his watch. Soon afterwards Lewis invited Green to port and coffee, and their long friendship began. After taking his BA in 1940, Green stayed on in Oxford to write a B.Litt. thesis on Andrew Lang (1844–1912) who had been a student and a Fellow of Merton. The thesis, 'Andrew Lang as a Writer of Fairy Stories and Romances' (1944),[40] was supervised by Professor J. R. R. Tolkien, who became another lifelong friend.

In time Roger Lancelyn Green was to make the most significant contribution to the retelling of fairy tales and legends since that made by Andrew Lang. But this was still in the future. On leaving Oxford he pursued a number of brief careers: he was a teacher, an antiquarian

40 Bodleian Library, MS. B.Litt. d. 336.

bookseller and an actor. Humphrey Carpenter's *OUDS: A Centenary History of the Oxford University Dramatic Society* (1985) contains a photograph of him taking the part of Biondello in the Society's Diamond Jubilee production of *The Taming of the Shrew* given in Wadham College in June 1945.

Green was exempted from military service, and he returned to Oxford in 1945 where for the next five years he served as Deputy Librarian of Merton College. Merton has preserved its Old Library which dates from the fourteenth century. Among its treasures are medieval books still chained to lectern desks, and Chaucer's own astrolabe. He served as the Noble Research Fellow at Liverpool University, 1950–2.

Over the years his interest in Victorian writers had been growing, and while playing one of the pirates in a production of J. M. Barrie's *Peter Pan* (1911) in 1942–3 he became fascinated by the story of the boy who did not want to grow up. This led to the writing of his highly acclaimed history of its production, *Fifty Years of Peter Pan* (1954). It was, however, his pioneering study, *Tellers of Tales: Children's Books and their Authors from 1800 to 1968* (1946; rev. edn, 1969), that set him apart as an authority on Victorian children's literature. He went on to write *Andrew Lang: A Critical Biography* (1946). It was followed by *The Story of Lewis Carroll* (1949). Carroll very quickly became one of Green's greatest interests, and after the biography he edited *The Diaries of Lewis Carroll* (1954) and *The Works of Lewis Carroll* (1965). Writing was as natural to him as breathing, and from his pen there flowed biographies of many of the great Victorian and Edwardian storytellers, among them *A. E. W. Mason* (1952), *J. M. Barrie* (1960) and *Mrs Molesworth* (1961).

On 31 March 1948 (chosen because it was Andrew Lang's birthday) Green married June Burdett, who was to become the perfect wife and companion. They began married life at 119 Woodstock Road, Oxford, where their first son, Scirard, was born on 27 October 1949. They were not to remain in Oxford much longer. When Roger's father, Major Gilbert Lancelyn Green, died on 17 June 1947, his eldest son, by order of succession, became the thirty-first lord of Poulton. By this time Green had decided to devote himself to writing, and in 1950 he returned to live at Poulton Hall. This great house is as much a 'major character' in Green's life as C. S. Lewis's childhood home, Little Lea, was in his.[41] He

41 *SBJ*, ch. 1, p. 6: 'The important thing about the move [to Little Lea] was that the background of my life became larger. The New House is almost a major character in my story.'

described in the following terms the beautiful arcaded Queen Anne Library:

> *It is an odd shock to come out of the light, comparatively modern-looking passage which one would have called Victorian at the very earliest, and step over a single threshold right back to the reign of Queen Anne. For the Library is of that date, and has not been altered in any respect . . . since 1750 or earlier: even the glass in the windows is unaltered (for the windows can rarely have been opened since the eighteenth century!) . . . Some years ago I showed the Library to my old friend, the poet Dr Gordon Bottomley, and his comment after a few moments of surprised silence was: 'This might be the library of one of the smaller colleges at Oxford or Cambridge!' . . . There are one hundred and thirty-one shelves containing in all four thousand four hundred and ninety six volumes, which were roughly catalogued by my father when he was still convalescing from a serious leg-wound received in the first World War.*[42]

The Public Orator of Liverpool University referred to this room when Green received an honorary doctorate in 1981: 'Of such a family and in such a house he was born to saga and romance!'[43]

It was at the end of this elegant room that Roger Lancelyn Green wrote most of his books and letters. Because he was such a good reteller of *other* writers' tales his own stories for children have been overshadowed. They include *The Wonderful Stranger* (1950), *The Luck of the Lynns* (1952), *The Secret of Rusticoker* (1953), *The Theft of the Golden Cat* (1955), *Mystery at Mycenae* (1957), *The Land of the Lord High Tiger* (1958) and *The Luck of Troy* (1961).

The first of these was written in 1949 while Green was still in Oxford, and when C. S. Lewis was finding his way into Narnia. Tolkien was one of the first to read the manuscript of Lewis's *The Lion, the Witch and the Wardrobe*, and he didn't like it. 'I hear you've been reading Jack's children's story,' he said to Green. 'It really won't do, you know! I mean to say: "*Nymphs and their Ways, The Love-Life of a Faun*". Doesn't he know what he's talking about?'[44] Green, on the other hand, was delighted

42 Roger Lancelyn Green, *Poulton-Lancelyn: The Story of an Ancestral Home* (1948), p. 26.

43 Obituary of Roger Lancelyn Green, *The Daily Telegraph* (12 October 1987), p. 20.

44 Green and Hooper, *C. S. Lewis: A Biography*, p. 307.

with it and over the years he proved an invaluable critic and supporter of what he dubbed 'The Chronicles of Narnia'.

Lewis, in turn, gave Green advice about some of his classic 'retellings' of traditional myths and legends. Lewis's own favourite was *King Arthur and the Knights of the Round Table* (1953) which is based on Malory and other Arthurian sources. 'It's even *better* than Malory,' Lewis said to Green. 'Well, no, not that good, but you know what I mean.'[45] Many of his retellings have become classics, including *The Adventures of Robin Hood* (1956), *The Saga of Asgard*, later renamed *Myths of the Norsemen* (1960), and *Heroes of Greece and Troy* (1960). Other favourites of Lewis's were *Tellers of Tales* and a book dedicated to Lewis – *Into Other Worlds: Space-Flight in Fiction, from Lucian to Lewis* (1957). These, like all his books, were lucid and eloquent.

Roger Lancelyn Green was a gentle and faithful friend. He made many friends during his life, and retained all of them. He was genuinely interested in others and gave one his full attention. His capacity for happiness seemed infinite, but this did not mean he was undiscriminating. He could be very frank, but always with courtesy. Lewis greatly valued his help with the Chronicles of Narnia. As a friend of Lewis and Tolkien, he was a welcome guest at meetings of the Inklings, and over the years he attended many of their Tuesday morning gatherings.

Lewis visited Roger and June at Poulton-Lancelyn several times, and came to know Scirard and Roger's other two children, Priscilla (b. 17 November 1951) and Richard (b. 10 July 1953). Roger was for many years editor of *The Kipling Journal* and was an early member of the Sherlock Holmes Society of London. After his son Richard acquired a taste for the Sherlock Holmes stories, it was natural that he should help him set up a replica of Holmes's study at 221B Baker Street in one of the attics of Poulton Hall. Green's guests will remember the excitement that awaited them after dinner when they were conducted up to Holmes's study to talk with the great detective about a problem. 'I could tell from the sound of your footsteps,' young Sherlock Holmes might begin, 'that you had a fall recently. The scratch on your shoe was caused by a dog-leash which pulled you over. Would you like to tell me about it?'

Richard Lancelyn Green went on to become the leading authority on Sir Arthur Conan Doyle and Sherlock Holmes. He edited (with John Michael Gibson) *A Bibliography of A. Conan Doyle*, foreword by Graham

45 Roger Lancelyn Green in conversation with Walter Hooper.

Greene (Oxford: Oxford University Press, 1983), the Oxford (World's Classics) edition of *The Adventures of Sherlock Holmes* (Oxford: Oxford University Press, 1993), and many other works.

Roger Lancelyn Green had visited Greece almost every summer since 1937 and when he and June discovered that Lewis and his wife Joy wanted to go during the summer of 1959, they suggested a trip together. Joy was dying of cancer, and the Greens turned what might have been a nightmare for the Lewises into some of the happiest days of their lives. The story of what Lewis called their 'pub-crawl through the glittering isles of Greece' was recorded in Green's diary and is found in the work he wrote with Walter Hooper, *C. S. Lewis: A Biography* (1974; fully revised and expanded edn, 2002).

Of the many honours heaped upon him, those he valued most were the dedication to him of Lewis's last book *The Discarded Image* (1964) – a collection of the 'Prolegomena' lectures he heard thirty years before – and an Honorary D.Litt. from the University of Liverpool in 1981. He was beside himself with grief at Lewis's death, but faced his own with serenity. He wanted to be around for the centenary of Lewis's birth in 1998, but it was not to be. He had accomplished much, and Poulton would pass into the capable hands of his son, Scirard, who had already given him a grandson. When Parkinson's disease made it impossible for him to write, he rang his friends instead. 'This is my letter,' he would explain. He died at Poulton Hall on 8 October 1987 and is buried with many of his ancestors beneath the shadow of St Andrew's Church, Bebington.

GRIFFITHS, Dom Bede, OSB (1906–93) was born Alan Richard Griffiths in Walton-on-Thames, Surrey, on 17 December 1906, the youngest of the three children of Walter Griffiths and his wife Harriet Lilian (Frampton-Day). Alan's father, a devout Anglican, was a manufacturing chemist from Liverpool who entered into a partnership with an uncle which caused him to lose all his money. Alan was four at the time, and soon afterwards the family moved to New Milton, Hampshire. When he was fourteen the family moved to the Isle of Wight and a few years later to Burghclere, near Newbury in Berkshire.

Alan was educated at Christ's Hospital in Horsham, Sussex, and after winning a scholarship to Magdalen College he matriculated in October 1925. His arrival there coincided exactly with Lewis's first term as Fellow of English. He read Classical Moderations, but instead of going on to

Greats, he elected to read English. Lewis was his tutor, but, as Griffiths pointed out in his autobiography, *The Golden String*:

> *Lewis was at this time no more of a Christian than I was, but he had been through the same phrase of romanticism as I was then passing through, and had reached a more rational philosophy of life . . . When I explained to him my reasons for reading English Literature. He protested vigorously against my view of life, but he was naturally unable to convince me, as I was not open to reason on the subject . . . I had ceased to practise any form of Christianity, and I regarded Christianity as a religion of the past, which had ceased to have any significance for the present day.*'[46]

During his years at Magdalen Griffiths made lasting friends of two other students, Hugh Waterman[47] and Martyn Skinner (see **Martyn Skinner** below). After taking his degree in 1929 Griffiths was undecided about what he wanted to do; Lewis persuaded him to remain in Oxford and read some philosophy to make up for not having read Greats. The books that affected him the most were Dante's *Divine Comedy* and St Augustine's *Confessions*, which Lewis persuaded him to read in the original Latin.

Griffiths, Waterman and Skinner were keen to shun civilization for a while and do without the products of the industrial revolution, to live as 'man has been compelled to live for the greater part of his history'.[48] In April 1930 they bought a small cottage at Ford Farm in the Cotswold village of Eastington where they lived as simply as they could for part of a year. They grew their own vegetables and drew water from the village tap. It was at Ford Farm that Griffiths first began reading the Bible. Following what he called an 'Experiment in Common Life',[49] he returned to Burghclere where he read the New Testament and the *Summa Theologica* of St Thomas Aquinas. Not long afterwards Griffiths became a believer and he was soon thinking of taking orders in the Church of England. However, before he got far with his plans he returned to Ford Farm in the summer of 1932 to reconsider.

46 Dom Bede Griffiths, *The Golden String* (1954), ch. 2, p. 30.

47 For the biography of Hugh Waterman see note 5 to the letter of 8 January 1936.

48 Griffiths, *The Golden String*, ch. 4, p. 61.

49 ibid., p. 60.

While there he read John Henry Newman's *Essay on the Development of Christian Doctrine* (1845) and everything changed. He later wrote:

> *What Newman showed of the Papal authority he showed also of all the other doctrines . . . All alike could be seen to be organic developments of the original doctrine of the Gospel, evolving by the same law as an oak tree develops from an acorn, or an embryo into a complete animal. Newman enumerated seven principles by which the genuineness of the development could be tested and distinguished from a corruption. They were the preservation of its type, the continuity of its principles, its power of assimilation, its logical sequence, its power to anticipate the future and to conserve the past, and finally its chronic vigour. Each of these tests was then scientifically applied to the doctrine of the Roman Church and it was shown how it answered to the test . . . I saw that the living Church, which could show a continuous evolution from the day of Pentecost and whose doctrine had been built up through successive centuries through the guidance of the indwelling Spirit, was none other than the Church of Rome.*[50]

Almost immediately Alan Griffiths found himself drawn to Catholicism, and he visited the Catholic Church of St Nicholas in Winchcombe. He got to know the parish priest, Father Wilfrid George Palmer (1871–1939), and on 5 December 1932 Fr Palmer took him to Prinknash, the Benedictine priory near Winchcombe. After less than a month there Griffiths decided to become a Catholic, and he was received into the Catholic Church at Prinknash on Christmas Eve 1932 by the Prior, Dom Benedict Steuart. That same day he made his first Communion at Midnight Mass at St Nicholas, Winchcombe. Shortly afterwards he decided to try his vocation as a monk at Prinknash, which at that time contained about thirty monks who lived in an old Cotswold manor house overlooking the Malvern Hills. Griffiths remained there, and on 20 December 1933 he was clothed as a novice. He had been greatly moved by the *Ecclesiastical History of the English People* by St Bede 'The Venerable' (c. 673–735), and he took the name 'Bede', becoming known thereafter as Dom Bede Griffiths. He made his solemn vows on 21 December 1937.

50 ibid., ch. 7, p. 112.

Griffiths loved writing and wrote so well it was natural that he be asked to contribute articles and book reviews to *Pax: The Monthly Review of the Benedictines of Prinknash*. From the time he became convinced of the truth of Catholicism, Griffiths tried to argue the merits of their respective churches with Lewis. In this he was disappointed. 'I had better say once and for all,' Lewis said in a letter of 4 April 1934, 'that I do not intend to discuss with you in future, if I can help it, any of the questions at issue between our respective churches.' They remained friends, but, said Griffiths, 'It meant that I could never really touch on much that meant more to me than anything else, and there was always a certain reserve therefore afterward in our relationship.'[51] Even so, Lewis showed great respect for his old pupil. Griffiths was ordained a priest on 9 March 1940, and when Lewis was writing his BBC scripts on *What Christians Believe* he asked Griffiths to check them for orthodoxy.

On 29 April 1947 Griffiths was installed as Prior at St Michael's Abbey, Farnborough. He had not been there long before he began to express thoughts not entirely compatible with those of the Church. He thought Catholicism had much to learn from Protestant denominations and the religions of India. Whereas in his early letters to Lewis he was chiefly concerned with differences, he was now concerned with similarities. He began inviting Anglican groups to Farnborough for discussions, and from ecumenism he went on to consider those things Christians had in common with Jews, Muslims, Buddhists and Hindus. Soon he was attracting a great many visitors, and he became something of a cult figure. As romantic as this might have seemed to those outside the priory, Griffiths's primary responsibility was to the monks in his charge, and his old superior at Prinknash, Abbot Wilfrid Upson, was worried. On 18 December 1951 Abbot Wilfrid arrived at Farnborough, and two days later Griffiths was sent to the new Scottish priory at Pluscarden as novice master.

It was at Pluscarden that Griffiths wrote his autobiography, *The Golden String* (1954); the book appeared the same year that Lewis published *Surprised by Joy*, which is dedicated to Dom Bede. *The Golden String* is beautifully written and proof that, in that work at least, Griffiths shared Lewis's gift of making his writings about other people's books into literature in its own right. But whereas at Farnborough Griffiths had been quite discreet about his interest in Eastern religions, in *The Golden String* he is much more open:

---

51 Dom Bede Griffiths, 'The Adventure of Faith', *C. S. Lewis at the Breakfast Table*, p. 19.

> *For centuries now, Christianity has developed in a westerly direction, taking on an ever more western character of thought and expression. If it is ever to penetrate deeply into the East it will have to find a correspondingly eastern form, in which the genius of the peoples of the East will be able to find expression. For Christianity will never realize its full statue as a genuine Catholicism, that is, as the universal religion of mankind, until it has incorporated into itself all that is valid and true in all the different religious traditions.*[52]

It would be unfair to equate Griffiths's position in this book with so many of those writing today who, without knowing what other religions actually believe, advocate a synthesis of them all. Griffiths went on to make the perfectly orthodox point that 'If we believe that in Christ is to be found the revelation of Truth itself, then we must recognize that all truth wherever it is to be found is contained implicitly in Christianity.'[53] Lewis would have agreed with that, but he and others were worried that Griffiths did not understand other religions as well as he thought.

Father Benedict Alapatt, an Indian Benedictine born in Europe, was visiting Pluscarden in 1954, and he asked Griffiths to join him in setting up a foundation in India under the auspices of Prinknash. His abbot found it a very difficult decision, but after making it clear that the ultimate decision lay with the Vatican, he gave Griffiths permission to go. Griffiths arrived in India in 1955 and on 14 August of that year he and Father Benedict moved to their new home, a place ten miles from Bangalore which they called Nirmalashram, 'The Monastery of the Immaculate'. After they had waited a long while, the Vatican rejected their request.

Griffiths was, of course, very disappointed. But soon afterwards he became friends with a Cistercian monk, Father Francis Mahieu, who was also trying to found a monastery in India. They asked their respective authorities if they could found a monastery that was, strictly speaking, neither Cistercian nor Benedictine. Permission was given and on 21 November 1956 the two priests left for Kerala on the south-west coast of India. After a great deal of hard work they founded Kurisumala Ashram, a Benedictine community. As most Catholics in Kerala belonged to the Syrian Church they used the Syrian liturgy in Mass. Very soon they adopted the saffron habit of the Hindu *sannyasi*, and

---

52 Griffiths, *The Golden String*, ch. 10, pp. 154–5.
53 ibid., p. 155.

following the style of Indian peasants, they worked a plot of land. Their new community grew quickly and attracted many vocations. It was clearly a success. A few years later Griffiths outlined in *Christian Ashram* (1966) or *Christ in India* (1967), as the book is called in the United States, his ideas about how Indian Catholicism and the future universal Church might develop. He had reason to feel hopeful because one of the documents of the Second Vatican Council (1962–5), the 'Declaration on the Relation of the Church to Non-Christian Religions', stated:

> *The Catholic Church rejects nothing of what is true and holy in these religions. She has a high regard for the manner of life and conduct, the precepts and doctrines which, although differing in many ways from her own teaching, nevertheless often reflect a ray of that truth which enlightens all men. Yet she proclaims and is in duty bound to proclaim without fail, Christ who is the way, the truth and the life (Jn. 1:6). In him, in whom God reconciled all things to himself (2 Cor. 5:18–19), men find the fullness of their religious life.*[54]

Griffiths was certain Christianity could be enhanced by Hindu spirituality, and he believed the 'Declaration' gave him the right to try to establish an ashram where Christians and Hindus could enjoy contemplative life together. On 15 August 1968 he moved eastwards to Shantivanam, in Tamil Nadu, where he joined two French monks, Fathers Jules Monchanin and Henri le Saux who founded Saccidananda in 1950. Together they adapted it to become a more fully Indian community, which they called the Saccidananda Ashram. They lived in thatched huts and, though they preserved the Benedictine model of manual work, study and prayer, their prayers included texts not only from the Bible and Catholic tradition but from the *Vedas* (the Hindu sacred texts), the *Koran*, and the *Granth Sahib* of the Sikhs. Under Dom Bede's guidance Shantivanam Ashram became a centre of contemplative life, inculturation and interreligious dialogue. While there he published *Vedanta and Christian Faith* (1973), *Return to the Centre* (1976), *The Marriage of East and West* (1982), *The Cosmic Revelation* (1983) and *A New Vision of Reality* (1989).

Every two or three years Griffiths returned to Europe and travelled

54 Vatican Council II, 'Declaration on the Relation of the Church to Non-Christian Religions', *The Conciliar and Post Conciliar Documents*, 2 vols, ed. Austin Flannery, OP (1975; rev. edn 1988), vol. I, paragraph 2, p. 739.

to the United States on lecture tours. In 1979 the Benedictine East-West Dialogue Board invited him to become a 'roving lecturer' and this led him to visit many American monasteries. As a result of his books and personal appearances Griffiths won numerous admirers, particularly among the young. But many of his fellow Catholics, not least in India itself, felt he was selling the Christian faith short by what they regarded as an attempt at syncretism. Lewis was one of those who criticized his understanding of Hinduism. 'The whole Indian aim,' Lewis said in a letter of 27 September 1949, 'seems to me to be *backward* towards a sort of unity which God deliberately rejected and not onward to the true one.' Besides the charge of syncretism, Griffiths sometimes went out of his way to attack the official teaching of the Church.

On 25 January 1990 Griffiths had a stroke and for some days his life was in the balance. But he improved and in May of that year he made another trip to the United States where he gave the John Main Lectures at New Harmony, Indiana, which were published as *The New Creation in Christ* (1992). Soon afterwards he completed what was to be his final book, an anthology of world scriptures showing how all religions begin and finally end in nonduality. *Universal Wisdom: A Journey through the Sacred Scriptures* was not published until 1994.

Meanwhile, during 1992 Griffiths gave more 'roving lectures' in the United States before going on to visit Germany, Austria and England, where he met Cardinal Basil Hume, the Benedictine Archbishop of Westminster. While in London he spoke at the Anglican church of St James, Piccadilly, which was so packed that people were forced to stand in the aisles and the crowds overflowed into the street. From London he went to Australia where he met the Dalai Lama. On his return to Shantivanam in October 1992 he found an Australian film team waiting to make a film about his life. They managed to complete *A Human Search* a few days before he had another stroke on 20 December 1992.

He was taken to the City Hospital at Trichy, and this time the damage was found to be very great. But Griffiths's resolve was greater and he was back at Shantivanam by Christmas. On 24 January 1993 he suffered another stroke which completely disabled him. Dom Bede Griffiths died in his beloved Shantivanam Ashram on 13 May 1993, leaving devoted followers throughout the world feeling like orphans. For more on his life see Shirley Du Boulay, *Beyond the Darkness: A Biography of Bede Griffiths* (1998).

GRIGGS, Alice (1871–1966), Lewis's neighbour, was born Alice Snelgrove in Bishopstoke, Hampshire, on 24 April 1871. This delightful woman married the Reverend David Barnes Griggs (1870–1934) on 29 December 1899. David Griggs took a BA from Exeter College in 1907, and thereafter held a number of ecclesiastical appointments, including a curacy at St Aldate's Church, Oxford, 1901–5. He became Rector of Portland, Dorset, in 1909, returning there after service as a chaplain during the First World War. He died while serving as Vicar of Hoddesdon.

Shortly afterwards, Alice Griggs and her sister-in-law, Miss Rhoda Rose Griggs, who was born in Portsea, Hampshire, on 16 May 1874, moved to Tewsfield where they became close friends of Mrs Moore and Lewis. Although there were not many years between the two ladies, Rhoda Griggs was still referred to as 'young Miss Griggs' even after she reached ninety. Of all their neighbours, these were the ones Lewis and Warnie knew best and longest. Alice Griggs died at Tewsfield on 8 May 1966, and Rhoda died there on 19 June 1969.

Warnie's admiration for Rhoda Griggs knew no bounds when she stood up to Mrs Moore. In June 1949 Jack was hospitalized for exhaustion and ordered to take complete rest. While Mrs Moore showed enormous concern for their dog Bruce, she was not so solicitous about Lewis. On 15 June, while Jack was still in hospital, Warnie wrote in his diary:

> *A most remarkable interview with Miss Griggs . . . It appears that Minto [Mrs Moore] has at last worn out even that good woman's charity; Miss G really* angry, *stamped her feet and waved her clenched fists during a tirade on M's selfishness: told me with such pride that on entering M's room she had forestalled any possible Mintonic opening with the words, 'No, I don't want to hear anything about Bruce's health, I want to hear about Dr. Lewis's health'!*[55]

HARWOOD, the Honourable Daphne (1889–1950) was born in London on 18 October 1889, the daughter of Sydney Haldane Olivier, Lord Olivier (1859–1943), Colonial Secretary of Jamaica, 1900–4, and Governor of Jamaica, 1907–13. Her mother was Margaret (Cox) Olivier. She read the Medieval and Modern Languages Tripos at Newnham College, Cambridge, taking her BA in 1913. She then began teaching. At a conference in Manchester College, Oxford, in August 1922 she first

55 *BF*, p. 226.

heard Rudolf Steiner lecture. The same summer she met Cecil Harwood in Cornwall, and it was she who introduced him to Anthroposophy.

The following summer Daphne Olivier attended an educational conference at Ilkley in Wharfedale, Yorkshire, 4–18 August 1923, where Steiner lectured on 'Education and the Spiritual Life of Today'. During the conference she and several other teachers expressed a desire to found a co-educational day school in England on the basis of Steiner's educational principles and along the lines of the Waldorf School in Germany. Steiner approved, and a Founders' Committee purchased a house in London big enough to accommodate 200 children. Daphne Olivier was one of the four young women chosen by Steiner to teach there. While the school was still under discussion Cecil Harwood accompanied her to the Second International Conference of the Anthroposophical Society held at Torquay, 9–23 August 1924. Rudolf Steiner gave a course of lectures on 'True and False Paths of Spiritual Investigation', and during the conference he suggested that the four women teachers would do well to have some male assistance. Pointing to Harwood, he said, 'What about him?' Cecil Harwood was dedicated both to the school and to Anthroposophy from that time. The New School, as it was called, was founded in January 1925, with Olivier and Harwood as two of its original five teachers.

Harwood and Daphne were married on 14 August 1925. Over the years the Harwoods worked in a number of Rudolf Steiner schools in London, Minehead, and (from 1945) Kidbrooke Park, Forest Row. They had five children: John Olivier (b. 31 May 1926); Lois Gillian (b. 26 January 1929); Laurence Hardy (b. 12 June 1933), who was C. S. Lewis's godson (see **Laurence Hardy Harwood** below); Mark Peredur (b. 4 October 1934); and Sylvia Marion (b. 16 May 1937). Daphne Harwood died at Kidbrooke Park on 14 July 1950. For further details of her life see **Cecil Harwood** in the Biographical Appendix to *CL* I.

HARWOOD, Laurence Hardy, OBE, FRICS (1933–), the second son of Alfred and Daphne Harwood, was born on 12 June 1933 when his father was teaching at the Michael Hall Steiner Waldorf School in London. When war broke out in 1939 the school was evacuated to Minehead, Somerset, and it was here that Laurence began his education. In 1945 the school moved to its permanent location at Kidbrooke Park, Forest Row, Sussex. Like his father before him, Laurence went to Christ Church, Oxford, but after two years illness forced him to leave. Laurence worked on farms in Westmorland before, with Lewis's help and encouragement, attending the Royal Agricultural College, Cirencester, 1954–7. After qualifying as a Chartered Land Agent and surveyor, he took up the post of Assistant Factor with the British Aluminium Company at Fort William in Scotland where he remained until 1960. He then joined the National Trust as Assistant Area Agent for East Anglia, remaining an employee of the Trust until his retirement in 1996. In 1968 he became the Trust's Regional Director for the Northumbria Region. After eleven years he was promoted to Regional Director for the North West, a post he held until 1991. In 1992 the Trust appointed him National Adviser on Countryside and Coastal Strategy Planning. He was awarded the OBE for services to conservation with the National Trust. In 1968 Laurence married Janet Wiles, and they had two children, Matthew Henry (b. 20 September 1968) and Alice Daphne (b. 10 December 1969). His marriage was dissolved in 1987, and in August 1992 he married Melissa Donne Stone in California.

Over the years Laurence became very close to Owen Barfield, who often visited Laurence in Northumberland. By the time Cecil Harwood died in 1975, Barfield was an old man himself and found it difficult to travel. Laurence saw that the close links between them remained intact by visiting him frequently.

LINGS, Martin (1908–) was born in Clifton on 24 January 1909, the son of George Herbert Lings and Gladys Mary (Greenhalgh) Lings. He matriculated at Magdalen College in 1929 and read English under C. S. Lewis. During his years at Magdalen he became a close friend of another of Lewis's pupils, Adrian Hugh Paterson (1909–40). After taking his BA in 1932, Lings lectured in the University of Kaunas, Lithuania, on Anglo-Saxon and Middle English, 1935–9. From 1940 until 1951 he held a lectureship in English Literature at Cairo University where he lectured mainly on Shakespeare.

While he was teaching in Lithuania Lings read the books of the Sufi scholar, René Guénon (1886–1950), who founded the Traditionalist School, and it was as if he had 'been struck by lightning'.[56] Guénon was living in Cairo, and Lings began corresponding with him about his books. He wrote as well to his friend Paterson, knowing he would have the same reaction. Paterson was in need of work, and soon afterwards

56 Martin Lings, 'René Guénon', *Sophia: The Journal of Traditional Studies*, vol. I, no. 1 (Summer 1995), p. 5.

accepted a lectureship at Cairo University. When Lings went to Cairo to visit Paterson in 1939 he found him already a member of Guénon's household. Both men, through the influence of Guénon, converted to Hinduism and Traditionalism. According to the Traditionalist School, 'The term *Tradition* refers to the concept that all authentic religions derive from a single Primordial Tradition and are therefore equally valid paths to Salvation. *Traditionalism* is therefore the school of religious studies that strives to illuminate the unifying Principles underlying the various manifest Traditions of the world.'[57] A year later, 1940, Lings and Paterson went out riding in the desert when Paterson's horse ran away with him and the young man was killed. Eventually, Lings took Paterson's place in the Guénon household.

Lewis was disappointed when Lings converted to Traditionalism (see his letter to Dom Bede Griffiths of 14 September 1936). But Lings was determined on this new life. Lings's first work, *The Book of Certainty: The Sufi Doctrine of Faith, Vision and Gnosis* (1932; revised, expanded edn, 1992), was published under his Arabic name, Abu Bakr Siraj ud-Din. Martin Lings returned to England in 1952 and took a degree in Arabic from the University of London. He was Assistant Keeper of the Department of Oriental Printed Books and Manuscripts at the British Museum and the British Library, 1955–70, and Keeper, 1970–4. Besides his many scholarly books, he published *The Elements and Other Poems* (1967), the preface to which contains some interesting observations about his friendship with Lewis, *The Heralds and Other Poems* (1970) and *Collected Poems* (1987). His other works include *What is Sufism?* (1975), *Muhammad: His Life Based on the Earliest Sources* (1991) and *Symbol and Archetype: A Study of the Meaning of Existence* (1991).

MILNE, Marjorie (1907–77) was born in Gonda, India, on 2 December 1907 of Scottish Presbyterian parents, both of whom were doctors with the Indian Medical Service. Marjorie became an Anglican while at Cambridge University where she worked for the Student Christian Movement. She then became a nun with the Sisters of the Epiphany in India. She was a devout Anglo-Catholic and, after returning to Britain in the mid-1930s, she did several jobs. In 1945 she and a friend founded an ecumenical retreat centre near Northampton. In 1951 she sold all her worldly possessions and began living a life of faith.

57 *Tradition: English-Language Traditionalist Material on the Internet*, www.kiva.net/julianus/tradition.html

It was while living in Oxford during the 1940s that she came to know Lewis and Owen Barfield. Marjorie was given to 'enthusiasms', and her adulation for Lewis led her to want to make him a national Christian leader. Her admiration for his poem *Dymer* led Lewis to dedicate the second impression (1950) to her. See Marjorie Milne, 'Dymer: Myth or Poem?', *The Month*, VIII (September 1952).

Having idolized Lewis for a while, he went the way of other objects of her veneration, when she dropped him. Unfortunately, she destroyed his letters to her. In 1962 she moved to Glastonbury and lived there for the rest of her life. She died there on 28 August 1977. Her biographer, Brian Frost, said of her:

> *Marjorie was a woman of many strong convictions, which often brought her into opposition with others but her conflicts seemed to find a resolution near the end of her life . . . At the root of her vision was the search for a new England. It was why she lived at Glastonbury, where she felt some of the earliest Christian traditions in the British and Irish islands lay. That new England had to be post-industrial and ecologically sensitive, she maintained. It could then take its place in the world of nations, purged of the false in its past, and especially in the Commonwealth, of which she was a passionate advocate.*[58]

Her story, with photographs, is told in Brian Frost, *Glastonbury Journey: Marjorie Milne's Search for Reconciliation*, introduction by Lesslie Newbigin (Oxford: Becket Publications, 1986).

NEYLAN, Mary (1908–97) was born Mary Shelley in Watlington, Oxfordshire, on 3 August 1908, the daughter of Hugh Alexander Shelley, a wood carver, and Maud (Baldwin) Shelley. At the age of nine she became a boarder at St Katherine's School in Wantage, run by the Community of St Mary the Virgin. She left it two years later because of illness, and returned to Watlington. From there she went to Reading University, where she was taught by Hugo Dyson, one of the Inklings. In 1929 she became a pupil at St Hugh's College, Oxford, but she was sent to Magdalen to be tutored by Lewis. After receiving her BA in 1932 and a Diploma in Education the following year, in 1933 Mary began teaching

58 *An Unknown Glastonbury Mystic: The reflections of Marjorie Milne, through prose, poetry & prayer*, compiled by Brian Frost, illustrations by Dennis Richard and preface by Dr Robert Runcie (1989), p. 7.

at Dartington Hall, Devon. She was living in Bradenham, Buckinghamshire, when on 30 August 1934 she married Daniel Neylan (1905–69), a schoolmaster and the son of the civil servant, Sir Daniel Neylan. They were to have two children, Sarah Shelley (b. 1938), and Mary Elizabeth (b. 1946). Mary Neylan's article, 'My Friendship with C. S. Lewis', was published in *The Chesterton Review*, vol. XVII (August/November 1991), pp. 405–6. She died on 9 February 1997.

C. S. Lewis was godfather to the Neylans' first child, Sarah, who was born in Dartington on 15 January 1938. After school Sarah went on to become an artist and muralist. One of her most popular works is found in the waiting room of the X-ray Department in the Radcliffe Infirmary in Oxford which she painted to look like a conservatory. She has pointed out that although sick people may be too ill to enjoy the art, their relatives find it helps them get through hours of anxiety. On 31 December 1960 she married Christopher Patrick Tisdall, at that time a lieutenant in the Royal Navy. They had four children.

PENELOPE, Sister, CSMV (1890–1977) was born Ruth Penelope Lawson in Clent, Worcestershire, on 20 March 1890. She was the daughter of the Reverend Frederick Robert Lawson, Vicar of Clent, 1878–1908, and his wife Laura Penelope (Anstice) Lawson.

Penelope loved Clent, but in September 1908, when she was nine, she went to Worcester High School, which in 1914 was renamed the Alice Ottley School after its first headmistress. The school was founded by the great Tractarian clergyman, the Reverend William John Butler (1818–94), who also founded, in 1848, the Community of St Mary the Virgin, Wantage, the first Anglican religious order to come into existence since the Reformation. The Tractarians were adherents of the nineteenth-century High Church movement which embraced an earlier sacramental Catholicism. Sister Penelope considered it one of her greatest blessings that she had been taught by Miss Alice Ottley, another notable Tractarian. It was under Miss Ottley that she developed a devotion to the Blessed Virgin Mary and a love of Greek and Latin. In her 'spiritual autobiography', *Meditation of a Caterpillar*, she described two 'fundamental things' in Miss Ottley's teaching which affected her decision to enter a religious order:

> *The first was that it was my duty as a Christian to examine my conscience before Communion, and to confess to God specifically*

what I found amiss . . . The other thing she taught me personally and unknown to herself, on the evening of 15 March 1904 . . . I knew with overwhelming certainty that she was living in a world of most intense reality, to which I was as yet a total stranger. I was outside it utterly, but it existed.[59]

In 1912 she entered the Convent of the Community of St Mary the Virgin at Wantage, becoming Sister Penelope CSMV. Some years later she wrote a 'Tribute to Two Tractarians' – Alice Ottley and Beresford James Kidd (1863–1948) – in which she expressed disappointment that one left the Alice Ottley School with 'a great love and reverence for the English Church' but with 'very little doctrine'.[60] The Mother Superior at Wantage showed great perspicuity in sending Sister Penelope to Oxford to study theology for she yearned for the hard, clear facts of doctrine. Dr Kidd, Warden of Keble College, lectured on Church history, and he took Sister Penelope under his wing, allowing her to attend his lectures and giving her private coaching. As she recalled:

His lectures were enthralling; even with his rather dry delivery and total lack of any striving for effect they made those early centuries live before one's eyes. In them, as in his books, he used perfect English, simple and dignified as is St Leo's Latin, and never an unnecessary word nor one misused . . . But those lectures conveyed far more than just the sheer delight in well-told human history, great thought that was. They taught us living doctrine.[61]

Dr Kidd later published those same lectures as *A History of the Church to A.D. 461* (1922). It is possible that he was aware of the effect he and his books would have on his pupil because Sister Penelope's chief contribution to Christianity has been mainly that of translating the Fathers of the Church – St Athanasius, St Hugh of Victor and others – and never using an 'unnecessary word' nor misusing one.

It was not customary at that time for nuns to write under their own names, and during her lifetime Sister Penelope's books were published

59 A Religious of CSMV [Sister Penelope], *Meditation of a Caterpillar* (London: Faith Press, 1962), pp. 27–8.
60 A Religious of CSMV [Sister Penelope], 'Tribute to Two Tractarians', *Theology*, LI (December 1948), p. 457.
61 ibid., p. 458.

under the names 'A Member of CSMV' and later 'A Religious of CSMV'. One of her first books, *The Wood for the Trees: An Outline of Christianity* (1935) contains not only a wealth of Christian knowledge written in beautifully clear English, but also her defence of the Church of England. Some readers wrote to her about what seemed to them an anomaly: her acceptance of a church that had severed its connection with the Roman Catholic Church. The closest she came to defending her position is found in this 'Outline' where, writing about the English Reformation, she said:

> *The breach with Rome was not effected here by any movement of popular desire: it was chiefly the work of the potentate upon whom, a few years before, the Pope had bestowed the title Defender of the Faith for writing a book against Luther. Now Pope met Pope, and it was the royal Pope who won. Failing to obtain the consent of the Holy See to his divorce from Katharine of Aragon, Henry VIII declared* himself *the Supreme Head of the Church in England; and when excommunicated by the Pope took no notice. You cannot justify his demand for divorce, nor his subsequent action, nor the Pope's reply: both acted wrongly, but there it is . . . The Church of England became a real* via media, *retaining all the essentials of Catholicity and with singular freedom for development.*[62]

Sister Penelope had just completed a new book, *God Persists: A Short Survey of World History in the Light of Christian Faith* (1939) when she came across Lewis's *Out of the Silent Planet* and was overwhelmed. She wrote to him on 5 August 1939:

> *It provokes thought in just the directions where I have always wanted to think; and wherever it is most delightfully suggestive one senses the most profound scriptural basis . . . There are bits – Augray's views about the different sorts of bodies, the relations of the unfallen creatures with Oyarsa, their social order, their peaceful awareness of the spiritual world – which are more lovely and more satisfying than anything I have met before.*[63]

62 A Member of CSMV [Sister Penelope], *The Wood for the Trees* (3rd rev. edn, 1959), ch. 22, pp. 178, 181.
63 Bodleian Library, MS. Eng. c. 6825, fol. 60.

Thus began a friendship and a fruitful correspondence which lasted for the rest of Lewis's life. He spoke of Sister Penelope as his 'elder sister' in the Faith because she, more than anyone, helped him appreciate the Catholic side of Anglicanism. She was not the immediate cause of his going to confession, but he knew it was something they shared. In 1941 she gave him a photo of the Turin Shroud. Coming from anyone else, he might not have accepted it, but he wrote to her on 9 November 1941 that 'It has grown upon me wonderfully . . . There is so much difference between a doctrine and a realization.' He kept the photograph on the wall of his bedroom for the rest of his life.

Lewis and Sister Penelope met for the first time when he went to Wantage in 1942 to address the junior sisters of the community. Afterwards Lewis decided to dedicate *Perelandra* to the sisters of the Community of St Mary the Virgin, and the book is hence dedicated to 'Some Ladies at Wantage'. It amused Sister Penelope that this appeared in the Portuguese translation as 'To some wanton ladies'. She had a delightful sense of humour and enjoyed telling the story of how, when she was a girl, she heard a missionary preach on the evils of alcohol. 'Bring up your son to hate the bottle,' he said, 'and when he is a grown man he will never depart from it!' Lewis, in his turn, had a great influence on Sister Penelope; and while she helped him appreciate St Athanasius, she learned a great deal from him about translating into the 'vernacular'.

Between 1935 and the time of her death Sister Penelope published dozens of books – histories, instruction, devotion, plays – some of the best of which are *The Wood for the Trees*, *God Persists* and *They Shall be My People* (1952). However, it is likely that her translation of the Greek and Latin Fathers will be her most enduring monument. The best is probably the translation she made with Lewis's encouragement, *St Athanasius: On the Incarnation of the Word of God* (1953). Perhaps her own favourite was the one she made near the end of her life, *Hugh of St Victor: Selected Spiritual Writings* (1962). She wrote hundreds of book reviews, all of which do what she did best – give instruction. Unfortunately they have never been collected and published.

In person Sister Penelope was charming. She possessed one of the most beautiful voices one is likely to hear. One of her friends, Walter Hooper, remembers that every time he visited the convent he was greeted by an elderly nun who said, 'Sister Penelope has never grown up! She's still a girl!' Sister Penelope certainly shared with Lewis the combination of a childlike enthusiasm and a mature intellect. Nothing was beneath her notice, and the most trivial things underwent transformation. Not long before her death in the convent on 15 May 1977 Sister Penelope was given charge of the garden, the pond and some half-dozen ducks. It was inevitable that they should be named after saints. Once when Sister Penelope spotted one duck go after another she was heard to say, 'Naughty Anselm! I *saw* you peck Polycarp!'

PITT, Valerie Joan (1925–99) was born in Peckham on 14 February 1925, the daughter of William Bygrave Pitt, an aircraft fitter, and Elizabeth Marjorie (Dixon) Pitt. Her family was deeply rooted in the socialist and trade-union traditions of south London. Valerie was educated at Mary Datchelor Girls' School, London, and at St Hugh's College, Oxford, where she took a First in English in 1946. While an undergraduate she came under the influence of the theologian Austin Farrer, Chaplain of Trinity College, and was received into the Anglican Church. She was elected Secretary of the Socratic Club, of which Lewis was President, during the Michaelmas Term of 1944, and it is because of her excellent keeping of the minutes that much of the Society's history was written and preserved. During her years at Oxford Valerie Pitt came to admire Lewis as both theologian and English scholar, and this led her to correspond with him over the years. She was one of the first to welcome Lewis to Cambridge when he was elected Professor of Medieval and Renaissance Literature.

Pitt began writing her B.Litt. thesis on Percy Bysshe Shelley in 1947. Eventually, as her ideas matured, she became more interested in Shelley's moral ideas, and the completed thesis bore the title 'The Development of Shelley's Thought with Special Reference to His Theory of Good and Evil'. She was awarded the B.Litt. in 1955. Pitt was by now a lecturer in English at the University College of South Wales and later became a lecturer in English at Newham College, Cambridge. In 1958 she returned to London as Principal Lecturer in charge of a Division of Humanities at Woolwich Polytechnic, an establishment which over the next thirty years she saw transformed into Thames Polytechnic and then into the University of Greenwich. In 1971 she was elected head of the School of Humanities, becoming one of the first 'polytechnic professors'. She retired in 1986.

Valerie Pitt was a devoted member of the Church of England, her mentors being Farrer and Archbishop Michael Ramsey. Many of her theological reflections went into the journal *Prism*, the organ of a new breed of Anglo-Catholics. In 1965 she was elected to the Church Assembly where on 29 June 1967 she introduced a resolution calling for the admission of women to holy orders. During the thirty years she served as a member of the General Synod she fought hard to expose ecclesiastical nonsense and to encourage serious theological reflection. She died on 4 January 1999. Her published works include *Tennyson Laureate* (1962) and *The Writer and the Modern World: A Study in Literature and Dogma* (1966). See the obituary of Valerie Pitt in the *Church Times* (22 January 1999), p. 6.

PITTER, Ruth (1898–1992) was born in Ilford, Essex, on 7 November 1897, the eldest of the three children of George Pitter and his wife Louisa (Murrell) Pitter. Both parents were primary schoolteachers and Ruth's education began at home when they hit upon the scheme of bribing her to learn English poetry by heart. This was done at rates between a penny and sixpence, depending on length, for each poem in Francis Palgrave's *Golden Treasury* (1861). She was able to recite for the rest of her life reams of Wordsworth, Tennyson, Shakespeare and others. Soon after she was born the family moved to the new London suburb of Goodmayes. At the age of five Ruth went to Downshall Elementary School, and in her twelfth year she moved to the Coburn School at Bow.

When Ruth and her sister and brother, Olive and Geoffrey,[64] were children they were taken for walks in Hainault Forest, part of the ancient hunting forest of Epping. Later the family rented a cottage on Crabtree Hill in the forest. Although primitive beside their suburban home, Ruth began to look upon this as her real home, and it was to appear often in her poems. She was five when she wrote her first poem. She recalled:

> *I was sitting on the back doorstep when suddenly there came into my mind, overwhelmingly, an image of something we had seen on one of our walks – a desolate and abandoned place. It was the first thing that ever gave me a poetic sensation. My eyes filled with tears of a strange new kind. Seizing my stump of blue pencil and a bit of torn paper I began in painful capitals: 'The old mill stands with broken shaft . . .'*[65]

64 Olive went on to become a successful novelist under the pseudonym Shirley Murrell, and Geoffrey became an architect and surveyor as well as a spare-time painter of distinction.

65 Arthur Russell, 'Faithful to Delight: A Portrait Sketch', *Ruth Pitter: Homage to a Poet*, ed. Arthur Russell, introduction by Lord David Cecil (1969), p. 22.

When she was only twelve her father took her to meet A. R. Orage, the editor of *New Age*, who first published one of her poems. For the next twenty years or so Ruth's poems were constantly appearing in *New Age* and the *New English Weekly*. Some of these went into her first volume of poems, *First Poems* (1920). She next published *First and Second Poems* (1927).

Ruth Pitter was only seventeen when the First World War broke out, and as the family could not afford to send her to university, she became a junior temporary clerk in the War Office. Working there from 1916 to 1918 left her in poor health. She then became a painter – a very good one – for the Walberswick Peasant Pottery Company in Suffolk. They made simple furniture and other wares and decorated them in peasant styles. At the end of the war the company moved to London, and Ruth with them. By 1930 a slump had made her employment precarious, and she and a fellow worker, Kathleen O'Hara (b. 14 March 1885), twelve years her senior, began a similar business of their own called Deane and Forester. They set up house together in Chelsea, and remained together until O'Hara's death many years later. By this time the demand for painted furniture had died away, and trays and other 'gift goods' painted with flowers now sold best. Besides her painting Ruth Pitter found time to write poetry, and during the 1930s she published *Persephone in Hades* (1931), *A Mad Lady's Garland* (1934), *A Trophy of Arms: Poems 1926–35* (1936) – which won the Hawthornden Prize in 1937 – and *The Spirit Watches* (1939).

By the beginning of the Second World War in 1939 she and O'Hara had a thriving business employing about twelve people. The war, however, ended this and at the fall of France on 18 June 1940, they took work in a factory that made crucibles, among other items. During this time Ruth first heard of C. S. Lewis. Her friend Lord David Cecil wrote to her on 1 February 1941, 'I shared [your poetry] with C. S. Lewis the teacher of literature at Magdalen here & a very remarkable man – he wrote a book on medieval romance called The Allegory of Love, which is a superb piece of vital, vivid criticism – & he was deeply struck & went off to buy your poems.'[66] On 13 July 1942 she wrote to Cecil about a book that had made an instant conquest of her. 'I have found,' she said, 'the book which has excited me more than anything has done for long time – "The Screwtape Letters".'[67]

66 Don W. King, 'The Anatomy of a Friendship: The Correspondence of Ruth Pitter and C. S. Lewis, 1946–1962', *Mythlore*, vol, 24, no. 1 (Summer 2003), p. 3.
67 ibid.

In addition to their factory work Pitter and O'Hara both had office jobs – by the end of the war they were utterly exhausted – and Ruth was reduced almost to despair by the machine shop. Stopping in the middle of Battersea Bridge one dreadful night she knew she could not go on.

The answer came soon afterwards when she heard Lewis giving his *Mere Christianity* talks over the BBC. From there she went on to read every word of his she could find, and she was converted to Christianity, 'driven to it,' she wrote to a friend on 1 January 1948, 'by the pull of C. S. Lewis and the push of misery'.[68] Ruth considered becoming a Catholic, but in the end she clung to her baptism in the Church of England and decided, 'I will belong to the traditional church of my country. Never mind about Henry VIII; it is the church into which I was born and into which I was baptized . . . This is the church for me.'[69] Finally, having wanted to meet him for years, Pitter wrote to Lewis in July 1946 asking if she could visit him. They met for the first time on 17 July 1946.

Finally the war ended; Ruth and Kathleen O'Hara had made enough from their business to be able eventually to buy a house, and they decided to continue their work at home, 55A Old Church Street, Chelsea. By this time their work was painting trays, and her friend Arthur Russell described it in 1969 thus:

> *Her work bears comparison with the best flower-painting on porcelain. Though stylized, it has a poet-botanist's realism . . . On one small tray she may show the wild strawberry fruit at three distinct stages of ripeness, as well as bud and flower. Yet she achieves her effects by shorthand of crisp strokes and blobs, each meaningful and none niggling. The result is always graceful and delicate . . . No design that she paints in her seventies has the air of tired repetition; each petal, leaf and stem looks as if the painter had made a fresh close scrutiny of the original.*[70]

During all this time Pitter had managed to spend a few hours a day writing poetry, and in 1941 she published *The Rude Potato*, which was

---

68 ibid., p. 16.
69 Russell, 'Faithful to Delight', p. 29.
70 ibid., p. 31.

followed by *Poem* (1943), *The Bridge: Poems 1939–44* (1945), *Pitter on Cats* (1946) and *Urania* (1950).

By now Ruth had a country base, a cottage in Felstead, Essex, which her mother had bought in 1930. After Mrs Pitter died in 1941, Ruth's sister lived there for some years. There Ruth taught herself how to grow, train and prune the vine, and she regretted leaving all this behind when the cottage was given up in 1952. That same year Ruth and O'Hara bought a house in the little village of Long Crendon, Buckinghamshire, within easy reach of Oxford and London. It was set within two and a half acres of old nursery-garden and orchard, and here Ruth's life expanded.

Her first volume of poems to be published after she moved into her new home was *The Ermine: Poems 1942–1952* (1953) which won the William Heinemann Award. In 1955 a committee consisting of Sir John Masefield, Nevill Coghill, Walter de la Mare, Charles Morgan, Gilbert Murray, Vita Sackville-West and Sir Osbert Sitwell unanimously awarded her the Queen's Gold Medal for Poetry. It was the proudest day of Pitter's life when she received the Gold Medal from the hands of Her Majesty Queen Elizabeth II at Buckingham Palace.

This honour was followed by a number of appearances on BBC Television's *Brains Trust* programmes (1955–61) in which she proved a delightful participant. During these years Ruth Pitter and Lewis visited one another regularly. On three occasions between 1953 and 1955 Lewis's former pupil, George Sayer, drove Lewis to Long Crendon, dropped him off at Ruth's house and collected him later. As Sayer wrote,

> *It was obvious that he liked her very much. He felt at ease in her presence – and he did not feel relaxed with many people. In fact, he seemed to be on intimate terms with her. The conversation was a mixture of the literary and the domestic. They discussed Eddison's romances and the poems of R. S. Thomas and Andrew Young. Each suggested amusing and improbable books for the other to write . . . After one visit in 1955, he remarked that, if he were not a confirmed bachelor, Ruth Pitter would be the woman he would like to marry.*[71]

The only time Pitter met Lewis's future wife, Joy Gresham, was at a luncheon Lewis gave at the Eastgate Hotel on 1 February 1954. Despite

71 Sayer, *Jack: C. S. Lewis and His Times*, ch. 19, p. 211.

Lewis's hope that they would become friends, neither took to the other. On 1 January 1957, when Joy was in hospital shortly before he married her, Lewis wrote to Ruth saying: 'I am sure she would love a letter from you.' Pitter wrote later,

> *I had been taught in youth that a woman's friendship with a married man must be by grace and favour of his wife, and as Joy recovered and lived on so amazingly, I did from time to time write to her: but there was never any reply, so I decided to be thankful for this correspondence and friendship with so rare a creature as Lewis, and to leave it at that.*[72]

After Lewis's marriage in March 1957 he and Pitter exchanged few letters, and she last saw him on a visit to Oxford on 15 August 1962. A number of Lewis's friends hoped he would marry Pitter, and after Lewis's death one of them mentioned this to her. 'Would you have accepted?' he asked. She smiled, but gave no answer.

During the next thirty years Pitter published a good many poems both new and old: *Still by Choice* (1966), *Poems 1926–1966* (1968), *End of the Drought* (1975), *A Heaven to Find* (1987) and *Collected Poems* (1990). She was made a Companion of Literature in 1974 and a Commander of the British Empire in 1979. But there was sadness as well. Her friend of many years, Kathleen O'Hara, died on 18 March 1973. During the years she and O'Hara had operated their business in London Ruth suffered an injury to her eye from hot enamel, and late in her life she became totally blind. She endured this with the same fortitude with which she had lived her life. Unspoiled by her many honours, Ruth Pitter died on 29 February 1992. Let some of her verses serve as an epitaph:

> *Even so, dread God, even so my Lord!*
> *The fire is at my feet, and at my breast the sword;*
> *And I must gather up my soul, and clap my wings, and flee*
> *Into the heart of terror, to find myself in thee.*[73]

POCOCK, Guy Noel (1880–1955), author, editor, scholar and teacher, was born in London on 15 May 1880, the son of Noel Lewis Pocock, a solicitor, and Alice Jane (Popham) Pocock. He was educated at St John's

---

72 Bodleian Library, MS. Eng. lett. c. 220/3, fol. 142.

73 Ruth Pitter, *Collected Poems* (1990), 'The Sparrow's Skull', stanza 6.

College, Cambridge, after which he taught for ten years at Cheltenham College. He then joined the staff of the Royal Naval College, Dartmouth. In 1923 he gave up teaching in order to devote himself to writing and editing. Apart from writing many novels and school books such as *Brush Up Your Reading* (1942), he edited numerous anthologies of modern prose and poetry. With Sir Arthur Quiller Couch he edited the 'King's Treasuries of Literature' series, which included *Herodotus: Stories and Travels*, ed. Guy Pocock (1932). During the 1930s he edited a number of books for J. M. Dent, which included Lewis's *Pilgrim's Regress*. In 1934, while continuing his literary work, Pocock joined the staff of the Talks Department at the BBC, becoming head of the department. In 1940 he left the BBC to return to Cheltenham where he taught for the remainder of the war. His novels include *Knight's Gambit* (1929), *Stubbs at Fifty* (1937), *Then They Pulled Down the Blinds* (1940) and *Design for a Staircase* (1954). Guy Pocock died on 19 March 1955.

SAYERS, Dorothy Leigh (1893–1957), novelist, translator, theologian, was born in 1 Brewer Street, Oxford, on 13 June 1893, the only child of the Reverend Henry Sayers and Helen Mary (Leigh) Sayers. Henry Sayers, who had been a student at Magdalen College, was Headmaster of the Christ Church Cathedral School, and his daughter was born in the house provided for him. Dorothy was baptized on 15 July in Christ Church Cathedral by her father. In 1894 the family moved with the choir school into 3 Brewer Street, and this was Dorothy's home until she was four and a half years old.

In 1897 the family moved to Huntingdonshire, in the fenland of East Anglia, where Mr Sayers had been offered the living of St Mary's, Bluntisham-cum-Earith, and it was here Dorothy grew up. There were numerous relatives nearby, and Dorothy developed a close friendship with her mother's niece, Ivy Shrimpton, who was eight years older.

On 17 January 1909 Dorothy became a boarder at the newly opened Godolphin School in Salisbury. From the beginning, she seems to have been very happy there. She did exceptionally well in French and music, playing both the piano and the violin. While there she won a scholarship to Somerville College, Oxford.

Dorothy arrived in Oxford on 11 October 1912, and after passing preliminary examinations settled down to read an Honours course in Modern Languages. She was thrilled to be back in the city of her birth, and with many cousins in Oxford at the same time she had a busy social life. One of her greatest pleasures was singing in the Bach Choir, which was conducted by Sir Hugh Percy Allen (1869–1946), later Professor of Music at Oxford. Of Dorothy's many 'crushes' at Oxford the most significant occurred upon simply seeing the young man who won the Newdigate Prize in 1913. 'I fell head over ears in love with him on the spot,' she wrote to Catherine Godfrey. 'His name is Maurice Roy Ridley . . . He has just gone down from Balliol, so I shall see him no more.'[74] Years later, when she and her friend from Somerville, Muriel St Clare Byrne,[75] were casting about for an actor to play her hero, Lord Peter Wimsey, in a theatre production of *Busman's Honeymoon*, Dorothy happened to be in Oxford. She wrote to Muriel on 6 March 1935: 'My heart is BROKEN! I have seen the *perfect* Peter Wimsey. Height, voice, charm, smile, manner, outline of features, *everything* – and he is – THE CHAPLAIN OF BALLIOL!! *What* is the use of anything?'[76] The Chaplain of Balliol was none other than Maurice Roy Ridley (1890–1969).[77]

After taking a First in her finals in 1915, Dorothy took a job with Blackwell's Bookshop, Oxford. During the two years she spent there she published two volumes of verse, *Op. I* (1916) and *Catholic Tales and Christian Songs* (1918). In the end she found office work tedious, and finding herself adrift in 1919 she accepted a job teaching English at L'Ecole des Roches, a boarding school near Verneuil in Eure, in the south of Normandy.

After a year in France, Dorothy returned to England. Until this time Oxford University had not regularized the position concerning degrees for women and Dorothy was among the first group of women who, on 14 October 1920, were formally invested with BA degrees. Armed with a first class degree in French, she set about looking for employment. She found some work translating French documents, and in the autumn of 1920 she landed a temporary post at Clapham High School. She spent her Saturdays reading books on criminology in the Reading Room of

---

74 Dorothy L. Sayers, *Letters*, vol. I, *1899–1936: The Making of a Detective Novelist*, ed. Barbara Reynolds (1995), letter to Catherine Godfrey, 29 July 1913, p. 79.

75 Muriel St Clare Byrne (1895–1983) OBE, met Dorothy at Somerville College where she read English, 1914–17. After taking her BA in 1917, she was a lecturer at the Royal Academy of Dramatic Art, 1923–55. Besides publishing many books, she edited the letters of Arthur Plantagenet, Viscount Lisle, between 1533–1540. They are published as *The Lisle Letters*, 6 vols. (1981).

76 Sayers, *Letters*, vol. I, p. 345.

77 There is a photograph of Roy Ridley in Barbara Reynolds, *Dorothy L. Sayers: Her Life and Soul* (1993), p. 57. See Ridley's biography on p. 306.

the British Museum, and in a letter to her mother of 22 January 1921 she mentioned the idea for what was to be her first detective novel: 'I have chosen this moment to be visited with ideas for a detective story . . . [It] begins brightly, with a fat lady found dead in her bath with nothing on but her pince-nez.'[78]

This was the genesis of the novel *Whose Body?* (1923) in which the corpse wearing pince-nez is not a fat lady but a Jewish man. It was in this story that Dorothy's aristocratic detective, Lord Peter Wimsey, made his first appearance. In the summer of 1921 Dorothy went home to Bluntisham where she completed *Whose Body?* and began a second novel, *Clouds of Witness*. She was already toying with the idea of subsequent Lord Peter stories. While trying to find a publisher for her first novel, Dorothy accepted a job as a copy-writer with the London advertising firm of S. H. Benson where she remained until 1931.

During the time Dorothy was writing *Whose Body?* she fell deeply in love with John Cournos, a Russian Jew born in Kiev in 1881, now working in London for the Foreign Office and the Ministry of Information. His first novel, *The Mask*, was published in 1919 and he was working on another. Dorothy wanted marriage and children, but Cournos wanted intercourse with no commitment. Although Dorothy regarded sex outside marriage as 'a bitter sin',[79] she also had a strong objection to the use of contraceptives. After she broke up with Cournos, she reproached him for soiling their love by suggesting the use 'of every dirty trick invented by civilization to avoid the natural result'.[80] In October 1922 Cournos moved to America.

Her emotional life in ruins, Dorothy turned to a man very different from Cournos, a virile motorcyclist and car salesman, Bill White.[81] She knew he would seem an odd sight at her parents' home, but she took him there for Christmas 1922. Back in London Dorothy's novel, *Whose Body?* was published, and she and Bill White became lovers. When Dorothy became pregnant Bill wanted neither marriage nor the child. To avoid breaking the hearts of her elderly parents, Dorothy kept the matter secret from everyone.

Dorothy spent a fortnight with her cat in a cottage in Hertfordshire

78 Reynolds, *Dorothy L. Sayers: Her Life and Soul*, p. 101.
79 ibid., p. 141.
80 ibid., p. 112.
81 There is a photograph of Bill White in Reynolds, *Dorothy L. Sayers: Her Life and Soul*, p. 120.

thinking out her problem. She then went to a maternity home, Tuckton Lodge in Southbourne, where she gave birth to her son, John Anthony, on 3 January 1924. Her friend and biographer, Barbara Reynolds, said of this difficult time: 'There were no telegrams, no letters of congratulation, no flowers and presents from delighted grandparents. Above all, no visit from a proud and beaming father. The loneliness of her situation had just begun.'[82]

Dorothy had to work in order to survive, and a few days before her son was born she turned to her cousin Ivy Shrimpton for help. At this time Ivy was living with her mother Amy at 45 Oxford Road, Cowley, Oxford and making a living caring for orphaned children. When Dorothy mentioned John Anthony to Ivy in a letter of 1 January she pretended he was someone else's baby, but after Ivy agreed to look after the child, Dorothy wrote again on 27 January with 'Strictly Confidential' particulars about him: 'My dear, everything I told you about the boy is absolutely true – only I didn't tell you he was my own!'[83] Except for Ivy, John Anthony himself, and the man she later married, she never told anyone else the secret of her son's birth. She delivered John Anthony to Oxford a few days later and was back at work at the beginning of February 1924. (In 1928 Ivy moved with John Anthony into a cottage called The Sidelings at Westcott Barton, fourteen miles from Oxford, and there he grew up.)[84]

On returning to S. H. Benson, Dorothy tried to interest Bill White in his son, but he did not want to be involved and a few months afterwards he took up with someone else. A year later, however, Dorothy met the man she would marry. He was Oswald Arthur 'Mac' Fleming (1881–1950), who had risen to the rank of captain during the First World War and was now writing for *News of the World* under the name 'Atherton Fleming'. He had married someone else in 1911 and had two daughters. The marriage had collapsed some years before, and when Dorothy met him he was a reporter on crime and motor racing, and had published a book about the First World War, *How to See the Battlefields* (1919). He and Dorothy were married in a register office on 13 April 1926. In the end it was not a happy marriage. But, for the time

82 ibid., p. 125.

83 ibid., p. 127.

84 There are photographs of John Anthony and Ivy's cottage at Westcott Barton in James Brabazon, *Dorothy L. Sayers: The Life of a Courageous Woman*, preface by Anthony Fleming (1981), opposite p. 220.

being, Dorothy was more settled than she had been for years. They maintained a flat at 24 Great James Street, London, and in 1928 they bought a house at 14 Newland Street, Witham, Essex.

Dorothy's writing prospered. The second Lord Peter Wimsey novel, *Clouds of Witness*, was published in 1926, to be followed by ten more detective novels, *Unnatural Death* (1927), *The Unpleasantness at the Bellona Club* (1928), (with Robert Eustace) *The Documents in the Case* (1930), *Strong Poison* (1930), *The Five Red Herrings* (1931), *Have His Carcase* (1932), *Murder Must Advertise* (1933), *The Nine Tailors* (1934), *Gaudy Night* (1935) and *Busman's Honeymoon* (1937). If it is true that Lord Peter Wimsey must take second place in popularity to Agatha Christie's Hercule Poirot, Dorothy L. Sayers nevertheless reigns supreme as the Queen of Crime when it comes to the quality of her writing. Her detective novels are works of real literary skill.

It is recorded that a boy wrote in a school essay: 'Then there was Miss Dorothy L. Sayers who turned from a life of crime to join the Church of England.'[85] Actually, Dorothy was still enjoying her life of crime when she made her mark as a theologian. In 1928 George Bell (1881–1958), Dean of Canterbury Cathedral and later Bishop of Chichester, brought drama back into the church with his launching of the Canterbury Festival. In 1928 he arranged for the production of John Masefield's *The Coming of Christ*, the first dramatic performance in an English cathedral in modern times. Other performances at Canterbury had been T. S. Eliot's *Murder in the Cathedral* in 1935, followed by Charles Williams's *Thomas Cranmer of Canterbury* the following year. In 1936 Sayers was invited to write a play for the Festival.

She was unsure what to do until it was explained to her that a play did not have to be historical, that it might be a celebration of artists and craftsmen. Within a few months she was committed to the project, and the result was *The Zeal of Thy House*, which was about the rebuilding of the cathedral choir by William of Sens after a fire in the twelfth century destroyed the original Norman structure. It was first performed on 12–18 June 1937, after which it went on tour. From this point on Dorothy L. Sayers became a public person, one whose opinions on religious matters were regarded as of much consequence.

To Dorothy the play about William of Sens had given birth to one

---

85 Janet Hitchman, *Such a Strange Lady: An Introduction to Dorothy L. Sayers (1893–1957)* (1975), p. 133.

of her most important ideas, that of craftsmanship and the relationship between a workman and his work. On 1 December 1939 she wrote to the Guild of Catholic Writers that she was getting together 'a group of people, mostly writers, to do books, articles, lectures, etc. about national reconstruction . . . We shall try to quicken the creative spirit which enables man to build . . . systems in the light of his spiritual, intellectual and social needs. We aim at the Resurrection of Faith, the Revival of Learning and the Re-integration of Society.'[86]

Before the tour of *The Zeal of Thy House* had ended, the BBC invited Sayers to write a nativity play for their Children's Hour. This turned out to be important for Dorothy because it gave her an opportunity of making the Incarnation of Christ real and immediate. She shared C. S. Lewis's conviction that people needed to hear the Gospel in the 'vernacular', the language people actually speak. The result was *He That Should Come*, performed in 1939. This, in turn, led to one of her most ambitious projects. On 5 February 1940 the Director of Religious Broadcasting, the Reverend Dr James Welch,[87] invited her to write a series of thirty-minute plays on the life of Our Lord. She replied on 18 February that if she did do it,

> *I should make it a condition that I was allowed to introduce the character of Our Lord Himself, and to present the play with the same kind of realism that I used in the Nativity play* He That Should Come. *I feel very strongly that the prohibition against representing Our Lord directly on the stage or in films . . . tends to produce a sense of unreality which is very damaging to the ordinary man's conception of Christianity. The device of indicating Christ's presence by a 'voice off', or by a shaft of light, or a shadow, or what not, tends to suggest to people that He never was a real person at all, and this impression of unreality extends to all the other people in the drama, with the result that 'Bible characters' are felt to be quite different from ordinary human beings.*[88]

There were to be enormous difficulties for both Dorothy L. Sayers and the BBC, but in the end her series of twelve plays, *The Man Born*

86 Reynolds, *Dorothy L. Sayers: Her Life and Soul*, pp. 307–8.
87 See the biography of the Rev. James William Welch, note 25 before the letter of 10 February 1941.
88 Sayers, *Letters*, vol. II, pp. 146–7.

to be King, was broadcast at monthly intervals from December 1941 to October 1942, and published in 1943.[89] It was one of the author's greatest triumphs. While all this was going on Dorothy and Muriel St Clare Byrne began putting Dorothy's notions about 'Creativeness' into action by editing a series of books to be called 'Bridgeheads'. The first volume in the series was Sayers's *The Mind of the Maker* (1941). It was an invitation to C. S. Lewis in 1942 to write a book for the series that initiated their correspondence.

For several years Dorothy L. Sayers had signed her letters to her son 'Cousin Dorothy'. However, in 1935 Dorothy and her husband 'adopted' John Anthony, and when he went off to Malvern College it was as 'John Anthony Fleming', the 'oldest son of Oswald Atherton Fleming'. At the same time he was told to call Dorothy 'Mother'. Meanwhile, she had reason to be proud of her son for he had won a scholarship to Balliol College in 1942. After serving with the Technical Branch of the Royal Air Force for several years Anthony read Modern Greats at Balliol College, and took a first class degree in 1948. His tutor was Roy Ridley.

Sayers had come to know Charles Williams after he wrote a glowing review of *The Nine Tailors*, and they corresponded about their various projects. However, it was the publication of Williams's *The Figure of Beatrice* (1943) that led her to read *The Divine Comedy* of Dante Alighieri (1265–1321). The effect was dynamic and led to her last great undertaking, a translation of *The Divine Comedy*. Barbara Reynolds recounts the story of this 'new enchantment'[90] in *The Passionate Intellect: Dorothy L. Sayers' Encounter with Dante* (1989). The first result of her interest in Dante was a great rush of letters to Charles Williams, and after his death to C. S. Lewis. Her translation of the first part of the *Comedy* was published in 1949 as *The Comedy of Dante Alighieri the Florentine, Cantica I: Hell*. She was working on the next volume when Mac became ill, and she broke off to nurse him. He died suddenly on 9 June 1950. Her cousin Ivy Shrimpton died nine months later, and Dorothy handed the administration of Ivy's estate over to her son, who was now using the name Anthony Fleming. Dorothy continued with her work, and the next volume of the translation was published in 1955 as *The Comedy of Dante Alighieri the Florentine, Cantica II: Purgatory*.

By this time Dorothy L. Sayers was such a popular and loved figure

89 See Phillips, *C. S. Lewis at the BBC*, ch. 14, '*The Man Born to be King*'.
90 Reynolds, *Dorothy L. Sayers: Her Life and Soul*, p. 353.

that it would have been impossible for her to retreat into her study. She was working on the last part of *The Divine Comedy* when on 13 December 1957 she went to Cambridge to attend the baptism of Barbara Reynolds, thereby becoming Barbara's godmother. After a couple of days at Cambridge she returned to Witham. She went up to London on 17 December to see a portrait of herself by Sir William Hutchison, after which she returned home by train. She had just gone downstairs to feed her three hungry cats when she fell forward at the foot of the stairs and died. Her body was found the next morning.

She had appointed Muriel St Clare Byrne as her executor, and the day after her death Anthony Fleming went to see Muriel and revealed who he was. The ashes of Dorothy L. Sayers were buried in the tower of St Anne's Church, Dean Street, London, and Lewis composed a panegyric[91] for the memorial service held for her at St Margaret's Church, London, on 15 January 1958. A few months before his own death on 26 November 1984, Anthony Fleming said of his mother: 'She did the very best she could.'[92]

Sayers's translation of Dante was completed by Barbara Reynolds and published as *The Comedy of Dante Alighieri the Florentine, Cantica III: Paradise*, translated by Dorothy L. Sayers and Barbara Reynolds (1962). Her letters, edited by Barbara Reynolds, are published in four volumes: *1899–1936: The Making of a Detective Novelist* (1995); *1937–1943: From Novelist to Playwright* (1997); *1944–1950: A Noble Daring* (1998); *1951–1957: In the Midst of Life* (2000). The two major biographies are James Brabazon, *Dorothy L. Sayers: The Life of a Courageous Woman*, preface by Anthony Fleming (1981) and Barbara Reynolds, *Dorothy L. Sayers: Her Life and Soul* (1993).

SKINNER, Martyn (1906–93) was born in Acton on 24 August 1906 the son of Sir Sydney Martyn Skinner and Emelie Madeline (Belling) Skinner, and educated at Berkhamsted, Clifton, and Magdalen College, Oxford, where he read History, 1925–8. He was just discovering nature, art, music and the romantic poets, and he left Oxford without a degree. Because of a crippling paralysis which struck him early in life, Skinner was left permanently lame. Fortunately, he had a private income, and this made it possible for him to devote his time to writing poetry. In

91 'A Panegyric for Dorothy L. Sayers' is found in *Of This and Other Worlds*, pp. 104–8.

92 Reynolds, *Dorothy L. Sayers: Her Life and Soul*, p. 346.

1935 he published at his own expense, and with the help of his friend Frank Sanders, a poem in four cantos, *Sir Elfadore and Mabyna*. In 1938 he married Pauline Giles, and they had six children, Jonathan (b. 1940), Anthony (b. 1942), Charlotte (b. 1944), Catherine (b. 1948), Benjamin (b. 1950) and Daniel (b. 1956). By the time the first of his children was born Skinner had settled down as a farmer at Ipsden in Oxfordshire.

During the 1940s he published in five parts his first major poem, in heroic couplets, *Letters to Malaya: Written from England to Alexander Nowell MCS of Ipoh* (Parts I and II, 1941; Parts III and IV, 1943; Part V, 1947). This poem won him the Hawthornden Prize in 1943, and it amused Skinner to reflect that he was the only working farmer to have won the Hawthornden, as well as being the only poet to win a prize for his malting barley. As can be seen from the letter of 5 November 1947, Lewis later suggested he write a poem on King Arthur. The result was Skinner's great epic poem, *The Return of Arthur: A Poem of the Future* (1955–9). His other works include *Two Colloquies* (1949), *Alms for Oblivion: Passages Selected from his Five Long Poems* (1983) and a play, *Old Rectory, or The Interview* (1970–7). See *Two Men of Letters: Correspondence Between R. C. Hutchinson, novelist, and Martyn Skinner, poet, 1957–1974*, ed. Rupert Hart-Davis (1979). Martyn Skinner died on 24 October 1993.

TILLYARD, Eustace Mandeville Wetenhall (1889–1962) was born in Cambridge on 19 May 1889, the son of Alfred Isaac Tillyard and his wife Catherine (Wetenhall) Tillyard. Alfred Tillyard was at one time the mayor of a Cambridge borough. After studying at the Collège Cantonal at Lausanne and Perse School in Cambridge, Tillyard read the Classical Tripos at Jesus College, Cambridge. He took Firsts in both parts, going thereafter in 1911 to study at the British School of Archaeology in Athens. He returned to become a Fellow of Jesus College, 1913–15, but left to serve in the First World War as a captain with the British Expeditionary Force in France and Greece, 1915–19. For his distinguished work in Greece he was awarded an OBE. His Greek experience was to bear more fruit after the war, his first book being *The Hope Vases: A Catalogue and a Discussion of the Hope Collection of Greek Vases* (1923). He was a University lecturer in English at Cambridge and returned to Jesus College in 1934 as a Fellow.

Lewis's controversy with Dr Tillyard began when he found Tillyard complaining that in Milton's *Paradise Lost* such matters as style 'have concerned the critics far more than what the poem is really about, the true state of Milton's mind when he wrote it.'.[93] Lewis dubbed such criticism 'The Personal Heresy', and he replied in a paper entitled 'The Personal Heresy in Criticism' in which he maintained that one approached the poet by 'sharing his consciousness, not by studying it'.

> *I look with his eyes, not at him. He, for the moment, will be precisely what I do not see; for you can see any eyes rather than the pair you see with, and if you want to examine your own glasses you must take them off your own nose. The poet is not a man who asks me to look at* him; *he is a man who says 'look at that' and points; the more I follow the pointing of his finger the less I can possibly see of* him.[94]

Following the publication of this essay in *Essays and Studies*, Tillyard defended his position in 'The Personal Heresy in Criticism: A Rejoinder'.[95] Lewis's Johnsonian relish for argument was aroused and he replied to Tillyard's 'Rejoinder' with another article entitled an 'Open Letter to Dr Tillyard'.[96] Tillyard had more to say and his second response, along with another 'Rejoinder' from Lewis and a third response from Tillyard, were published with the original three essays as a book entitled *The Personal Heresy: A Controversy* (1939).

In 1945 Tillyard became Master of Jesus College, a position he held until his retirement in 1954. His many works include *Milton* (1930), *The English Epic Tradition* (1936) and *The Elizabethan World Picture* (1943). Dr Tillyard died in Cambridge on 24 May 1962. See Basil Willey's obituary notice in *The Proceedings of the British Academy*, vol. XLIV (1963), pp. 387–405.

TOLKIEN, Father John Francis Reuel (1917–2003), who came to know Jack and Warnie well over the years, was born in Cheltenham on 16 November 1917. He spent his early years in Oxford and then in Leeds where his father, J. R. R. Tolkien, was Reader, and then Professor of English Literature, at the University of Leeds. In 1925 the family

93 E. M. W. Tillyard, *Milton* (1930), p. 237.

94 'The Personal Heresy in Criticism', *Essays and Studies*, vol. XIX (1934), p. 15.

95 E. M. W. Tillyard, 'The Personal Heresy in Criticism: A Rejoinder', *Essays and Studies*, vol. XX (1935), pp. 7–20.

96 'Open Letter to Dr Tillyard', *Essays and Studies*, vol. XXI (1936), pp. 153–68.

returned to Oxford when Tolkien was appointed Rawlinson and Bosworth Professor of Anglo-Saxon. John was educated at the Dragon School, Oxford, and at the Oratory School in Caversham near Reading. In 1936 he matriculated at Exeter College, Oxford, where he read English Literature. On taking his BA in 1939 he spent several months at St Mary's College, Oscott, and in November 1939 he went to the English College in Rome. Professor Tolkien was soon to become very anxious about him. In May 1940, weeks before Mussolini declared war on France and Britain, John and his fellow-students had some narrow escapes getting home. Having arrived back, they continued their studies in Lancashire. John Tolkien was ordained a priest on 10 February 1946 and said his first Mass at St Aloysius, Oxford.

Fr Tolkien spent the next forty-eight years serving in a succession of parishes in the Diocese of Birmingham. He was at St Mary and St Benedict, Coventry, 1946–1950, English Martyrs, Sparkhill, Birmingham, 1950–7, Our Lady of Sorrows, Knutton, Staffordshire, where he was part-time chaplain at the University of Keele, 1957–66, and Our Lady of the Angels and St Peter in Chains, Stoke-on-Trent, 1966–87. By this time Fr Tolkien was seventy, and he was delighted to be able to spend the next five years only a few miles from Oxford at St Peter's, in the quiet Oxford village of Eynsham. While there he collaborated with his sister, Priscilla, on *The Tolkien Family Album* (1992). This lovable priest retired to Oxford in 1994 and up to the end of the century was chaplain to the De La Salle Brothers in Banbury Road. He died in the Green Gates Nursing Home, Oxford, on 22 January 2003.

TOY, Violet Mary (1889–1952) was born Violet Mary Doudney on 5 March 1889 in Barkby, Leicestershire, and moved with her family to Thurnby when she was a baby. She was educated at Miss Odell's school in Thurnby, and at Ashby-de-la-Zouch Grammar School. Violet entered St Hilda's College, Oxford, in 1908 and read English. However, because of the regulations at Oxford regarding women she was not able to take her BA and MA until 1921.

By 1912 suffragettes in prison had begun going on hunger strikes and the government, determined to avoid these women becoming martyrs, had introduced a regulation, known as the 'Cat and Mouse Act', allowing them to be released as soon as they became ill. Once recovered, the suffragettes had to return and complete their sentences. In June 1912 Violet was sentenced to two months hard labour in Holloway Prison for breaking a window in the Home Secretary's house as a suffragette protest against the Cat and Mouse Act. She was forcibly fed in prison but was released in July 1912 on an undertaking given by her father that she would not in future engage in militant suffragette activity.

Violet gained the London Teaching Diploma in 1912 and taught in a number of girls' schools. During this time she published poems in *The Poetry Review* (September/October 1916) and *St. Hilda's Hall Verse: Selected Poems*, ed. H. C. Hughes (1922). She taught in Canada, 1922–4, and at Queen Anne's School, Caversham, 1924–6. In 1926 she went to Constantinople to teach at the English High School for Girls. She returned to England two years later and in June 1929 married Sidney Toy (1875–1967), a writer on fortifications. They had three sons and lived at the Cloisters, The Temple, London. In 1939 they moved to Epsom, Surrey, where Violet took up teaching at a local preparatory school and at Epsom College. She died on 14 January 1952.

VIDLER, The Reverend Dr Alexander Roper (1899–1991), editor of *Theology*, was born in Rye, East Sussex, on 27 December 1899. Educated at Selwyn College, Cambridge, he took his BA in 1921. Following his ordination in 1923, his first curacy was St Philip's in Newcastle upon Tyne. It was at this time that he became a supporter of the Labour Party and began making a name for himself as a spokesman for the 'liberal Catholic' parishes. Vidler was Warden of St Deiniol's Library, Hawarden, 1939–48, Canon of St George's Chapel, Windsor, 1948–56, Fellow of King's College, Cambridge, and Dean of King's College, 1956–67.

About the same time that Vidler was appointed editor of the monthly journal *Theology* in 1939 – a position he retained until 1964 – he became drawn towards the neo-orthodoxy then fashionable. However, it was not long before he discovered aspects of the Protestant and Reformed tradition he had hitherto neglected and he wrote at length about them. During his latter years, when he was Dean of King's College, his modernism disappointed orthodox believers.

Lewis's powerful indictment of the demythologizers resulted from reading Vidler's *Windsor Sermons* (1958). Shortly after the book's publication, Lewis happened to dine at the Anglican Theological College, Westcott House, Cambridge, with the Principal, Kenneth Carey (later Bishop of Edinburgh). When Carey was called out of the room, Lewis apparently picked up a copy of Vidler's book and read 'The Sign at

Cana'. According to Lewis's account, 'A book of Alec Vidler's happened to be lying on the table and I expressed my reaction to the sort of theology it contained . . . One thing led to another and before we were done I was saying a good deal more than I had meant about the type of thought which, so far as I could gather, is now dominant in many theological colleges.'[97] Carey recalled that when he asked Lewis what he thought about it, he 'expressed himself very freely about the sermon and said that he thought it quite incredible that we should have had to wait nearly 2,000 years to be told by a theologian called Vidler that what the Church has always regarded as a miracle was, in fact, a parable!'[98]

Kenneth Carey invited Lewis to address the students of Westcott House on the subject. On 11 May 1959 Lewis read them a paper entitled 'Fern-seed and Elephants', in which he predicted that

> *A theology which denies the historicity of nearly everything in the Gospels to which Christian life and affections and thought have been fastened for nearly two millennia – which either denies the miraculous altogether or, more strangely, after swallowing the camel of the Resurrection strains at such gnats as the feeding of the multitudes – if offered to the uneducated man can produce only one or other of two effects. It will make him a Roman Catholic or an atheist.*[99]

Alec Vidler's many books include *The Modernist Movement in the Roman Church* (1934); (with Wilfred L. Knox) *The Development of Modern Catholicism* (1938); *God's Judgement on Europe* (1940); *Natural Law: A Christian Re-consideration* (1946); *Windsor Sermons* (1958); (ed.) *Soundings: Essays Concerning Christian Understanding* (1962); *Objections to Christian Belief* (1963); *F. D. Maurice and Company* (1966); and *A Variety of Catholic Modernists* (1970). In 1977 he published *Scenes from a Clerical Life: An Autobiography*. Following his retirement Alec Vidler returned to Rye, where he died on 25 July 1991.

WALL, Barbara (1911–) was born Barbara Lucas in London on 9 October 1911, the daughter of Perceval and Madeline (Meynell) Lucas. She is

---

97 *Fern-seed and Elephants and Other Essays on Christianity*, ed. Walter Hooper (London: Collins, 1977; Fount, 1998), p. 86.

98 Letter to Walter Hooper from Kenneth Carey quoted in *Fern-seed and Elephants*, p. 86, n. 2.

99 *Fern-seed and Elephants*, p. 87.

the sister of Christian Hardie, who was the wife of Colin Hardie, Lewis's colleague at Magdalen College and a fellow Inkling. During the Second World War Lewis was looking for someone who would type his books, and Colin Hardie introduced him to Barbara, who was living in Oxford. She typed *That Hideous Strength*, *The Great Divorce* and *Miracles*. *The Great Divorce* is dedicated to her.

Barbara was educated at St Paul's Girls School in London. She met her husband, the writer Bernard Wall (1908–74) when both were involved in London's Catholic Workers Movement in the 1930s. Together they founded the *Catholic Worker* newspaper. In 1935 they married and they had two daughters. She has written a number of theological books under the name Barbara Wall, including *And Was Crucified* (1939) and *Great Saints and Saintly Figures* (1963), and she and Bernard wrote several books together, including *Thaw at the Vatican* (1964). Her novels, all written under her maiden name, include *Stars were Born* (1936), *The Trembling of the Sea* (1936), *Anna Collett* (1946), *More Ado About Nothing* (1969) and *Widows and Widowers* (1979).

WALSH, Chad (1914–91), poet and teacher, was born in South Boston, Virginia, on 10 May 1914. He took a BA in French from the University of Virginia at Charlottesville in 1938, and a D.Phil. in English Literature from the University of Michigan in 1943. Walsh served as a research analyst with the United States War Department, 1943–5. In 1945 he joined the English Department of Beloit College, Beloit, Wisconsin, eventually becoming Professor of English, Writer in Residence and Poet in Residence. He was Chairman of the Department of English, 1962–70. He was ordained in the Episcopal Church on 21 December 1949, and from then until his retirement in 1977 he served as an assistant at St Paul's Episcopal Church, Beloit.

In 1938 Walsh married Eva Tuttle and they were to have four daughters, Damaris, Madeline, Sarah-Lindsay and Alison. In 1945 he came across a copy of Lewis's *Perelandra*, and his life was greatly changed:

> *I was struck first of all by the sheer beauty of the book. It transported me into a kind of Elysian Fields – or better yet unspoiled Eden, inhabited by the innocent and unfallen. . . . Here at last was science fiction as science fiction at its fullest development should be . . . In* Perelandra *I got the taste and the smell of Christian truth. My senses as well as my soul were baptized. It was as though an intellectual*

> *abstraction or speculation had become flesh and dwelt in its solid glory among us.*[100]

Walsh first wrote to Lewis on 30 November 1945, and the following year he published an essay, 'C. S. Lewis: Apostle to the Skeptics' in *The Atlantic Monthly* (September 1946). Little was known about Lewis in America at this time, and at his wife's urgings, he began expanding his *Atlantic* essay into a book. He had several meetings with Lewis in the summer of 1948, and the following year Macmillan of New York published the enlarged *C. S. Lewis: Apostle to the Skeptics*. It was the first book about Lewis, and it remains one of the best. His description of Lewis's conversation is one of the plums of the book, and has never been surpassed. 'The comparison with Dr. Johnson,' wrote Walsh, 'has a grain of truth in it, as I discovered to my cost':

> *Lewis – at least on the occasions when I was with him – never crushed an opponent with the brusqueness of Boswell's hero, but he has a sharp, quick-moving mind, impatient of vagueness and half-formed ideas. He is swift to press home his advantage when somebody begins talking without fully thinking out what he is talking about. Such was my experience when I tried to defend surrealist art. Next day I thought of many excellent arguments, but at the moment I could offer nothing except thoughts in the process of gestation, and Lewis expertly pushed me to the wall and left me pinned there. However, the manoeuvre is performed so smoothly, and in such a friendly, manly way, that it seems a compliment and act of respect. And Lewis, when occasionally pushed to the wall, can admire the skill of the pusher.*[101]

One of those who read Walsh's book was Joy Davidman, and as a result of writing to thank him for the book they became friends. This emboldened Joy to begin writing to Lewis. Although her correspondence with Lewis has not survived, Joy wrote to Walsh on 27 January 1950 about the first letter she received from Lewis: 'Just got a letter from Lewis in the mail. I think I told you I'd raised an argument or two on some points? Lord, he knocked my props out from under me unerringly;

100 Chad Walsh, 'Impact on America', *Light on C. S. Lewis*, ed. Jocelyn Gibb (London: Bles, 1965), p. 107.

101 Chad Walsh, *C. S. Lewis: Apostle to the Skeptics* (1949), ch. 2, pp. 12–13.

one shot to a pigeon. I haven't a scrap of my case left.'[102] In the summers of 1951 and 1952 Joy and her husband, William Gresham, visited the Walshes at their summer home at Lake Iroquois in Vermont. Chad and Eva liked both of them, but they felt a special attachment to Joy.

Soon after the second visit to Vermont, Joy visited Lewis in Oxford, and in 1953 she moved there with her two sons. When Chad, Eva and their children visited Lewis in the summer of 1955 they found Joy spending a great deal of time at The Kilns. 'My wife,' wrote Walsh, 'firmly declared, "I smell marriage in the air."'[103] During the difficult years that followed, when Joy was found to have cancer, and she and Lewis were married, they found it natural to confide in Chad Walsh. It was no doubt because of his friendship with both that Lewis dedicated *The Four Loves* (1960) to Walsh. Walsh paid a final visit to Lewis in 1961.

Chad Walsh published numerous volumes of poetry and Christian apologetics, which include *Stop Looking and Listen: An Invitation to the Christian Life* (1948); *Early Christians of the 21st Century* (1950); *Campus Gods on Trial* (1953); *Behold the Glory* (1956); *Nellie and Her Flying Crocodile* (1956); *Knock and Enter* (1959); *From Utopia to Nightmare* (1962); *The Unknown Dance* (1964); *Doors into Poetry* (1970); *End of Nature: Poems* (1969); *God at Large* (1971); *Hang Me Up My Begging Bowl* (1981).

His critical writings about Lewis include 'Impact on America' in *Light on C. S. Lewis*, ed. Jocelyn Gibb (1965); 'The Man and the Mystery' in *Shadows of Imagination*, ed. Mark R. Hillegas (1969); 'The Re-education of the Fearful Pilgrim' in *The Longing for a Form*, ed. Peter J. Schakel (1977); the Afterword to the Bantam edition (1976) of *A Grief Observed*; and *The Literary Legacy of C. S. Lewis* (1979). There is also a collection of Walsh's reviews of the books of C. S. Lewis, *Chad Walsh Reviews C. S. Lewis* (San Francisco, Mythopoeic Press, 1998).

Following his retirement from Beloit College, Walsh and his wife retired to their home at Lake Iroquois, and there they entertained many of those who wanted to know more about Lewis. Chad Walsh died on 17 January 1991. His letters to Lewis are held in the Wade Center at Wheaton College, with copies in the Bodleian Library. There are collec-

102 Lyle W. Dorsett, *And God Came In* (1983), ch. 3, p. 70.
103 Chad Walsh, Afterword to *A Grief Observed* (New York: Seabury Press, Bantam Books, 1976), p. 140.

tions of his own writings in the Newberry Library in Chicago and in the Roanoke College Library, Salem, Virginia.

WHISTLER, Sir Laurence (1912–2000), glass engraver, writer, poet, and architectural historian, was born on 21 January 1912, the son of Henry Whistler and Helen (Ward) Whistler. He was the younger brother of the painter and stage designer, Rex Whistler (1905–44). Laurence was educated at Stowe and Balliol College, Oxford, where he took his BA in 1934. He won the Chancellor's Essay Prize in 1934, and the King's Gold Medal for Poetry in 1935. His interest in glass engraving began in 1934 and arose from his awareness that Elizabethan gentlemen inscribed verses on window glass with diamond points. On coming across the master glass engravers of the eighteenth century, he began training under the tutelage of his brother Rex. After discovering his vocation he met and married the actress Jill Furse in 1939. It was to be a cruelly short marriage as she died in October 1944, his brother Rex having been killed in Normandy a few months earlier.

On leaving Oxford he was commissioned to write his first biography, *Sir John Vanbrugh, Architect and Dramatist* (1938). Whistler joined the army in 1940, and was commissioned an officer in the Rifle Brigade in 1941, becoming captain in 1942. On his return to civilian life he wrote two biographies of his brother, *Rex Whistler: His Life and His Drawings* (1948) and *The Laughter and the Urn: The Life of Rex Whistler* (1985). There were a number of volumes of poetry as well, including *The World's Room* (1949) and *The View From This Window* (1956).

Whistler's technical skill as a glass engraver steadily increased, and he is now chiefly known for having revived and transformed the art of glass engraving. His work includes engraving on goblets, church windows and panels. Thousands of visitors a year are drawn to St Nicholas's Church in Moreton, Dorset, to see the only church in the world filled with engraved glass. His many clients included members of the Royal Family. One of his most notable pieces was commissioned by Queen Elizabeth, the Queen Mother, to celebrate the birthday of King George VI in 1949. Laurence Whistler, a man of great gentleness and modesty, was knighted in June 2000 and he died on 19 December 2000. See his autobiography, *Initials in the Heart* (1964).

WILLIAMS, Charles Walter Stansby (1886–1945), novelist, poet, dramatist, biographer, critic, theologian, was born at 3 Spencer Road (now

Caedmon Road), London, on 20 September 1886. He was the surviving member of twins born to Richard Walter Stansby Williams, a chronometer maker, and his wife Mary (Wall) Williams. Charles was baptized at St Anne's Church, Finsbury Park, on 7 November 1886, and from earliest memory he was a passionate member of the Church of England. In 1894 the family moved to 15 (now 360) Victoria Street, St Albans, twenty miles from London, where Walter Williams opened a little shop that sold artist's materials.

In 1894 Charles went to St Albans Abbey School and in 1898 he won a County Council scholarship to St Albans Grammar School (now St Albans School). It was there he made his first great friend, George Robinson. In 1901 both boys gained Intermediate Scholarships to University College, London. Charles, however, had to leave before the session of 1903–4 because the family could not afford to keep him there. In 1904 he began work at the Methodist Bookroom, and there he became friends with Frederick Page who found a job for him with the Oxford University Press. On 9 June 1908 Williams began working for the Press, which was then at Amen Corner, in Ave Maria Lane off Ludgate Hill, close to St Paul's Cathedral, and he never left it. Charles worked under Page in the Paper, Printing, and Proof-reading Department.

In 1910, while reading the proofs of a reissue of Henry Francis Cary's translations of Dante's *Divine Comedy*[104] Williams was struck by Dante's account of how his love for Beatrice eventually took him through Hell and Purgatory to Paradise and the Beatific Vision of the Trinity. 'But this is *true*,' he said to himself.[105] He was thus led to the idea of the 'Beatrician experience', the recovery of the vision which would have been common to each of us if Man had not fallen.

In his first book, *The Silver Stair* (1912), he explained how earthly love can be a staircase to God. Despite the obscurity of his verse, the fullest expression of the 'Beatrician experience' is found in Williams's Arthurian poems, *Taliessin Through Logres* (1938) and *The Region of the Summer Stars* (1944). Williams was to go on developing this theory of 'Romantic Love' for the rest of his life, principally in 'The Theology of Romantic Love' in *He Came Down from Heaven* (1938) and *The Figure of Beatrice* (1943). The clearest expression of it is found, however, in

104 *The Vision or Hell, Purgatory and Paradise of Dante Alighieri*, trans. Henry Francis Cary.

105 Dorothy L. Sayers, *The Poetry of Search and the Poetry of Statement* (1963), p. 73.

C. S. Lewis's 'Commentary' on Williams's Arthurian poems in *Arthurian Torso* (1948).

The 'Beatrician experience' was already being tested first hand. A few months after he began work with Oxford University Press, Williams met Florence Sarah Conway (b. 23 May 1886 in London), a teacher whose father, James Conway, was manager of Hallam's ironmongery shop in St Albans. They first met at a parochial children's Christmas party, and Florence recalled this meeting years later:

> *For the first five minutes of our meeting I thought him the most silent withdrawn young man I had ever met. For the next five minutes I thought him the nicest young man I had ever met. For the rest of the evening I thought him the most talkative young man I had ever met, and still the nicest.*[106]

After they became engaged Florence began protesting about Williams's habit of chanting verse aloud in public places. This led him to nickname her 'Michal' after Saul's daughter who mocked David when he danced before the Lord.[107] Williams was unfit for the army and so continued at the Press during the First World War. He and Florence were married on 12 April 1917 and went to live in a flat in Hampstead. Michal continued to teach until their son, Michael Stansby Williams, was born on 18 June 1922. Although Williams never wavered in his belief that Romantic Love is an actual state, one of his friends, Anne Ridler, revealed that 'Their marriage was a tempestuous and a true one. No one who heard Charles Williams speak of the institution of marriage could doubt that he knew it to have been the ground of his own growth, though he never spoke of it as a grace that is easily won.'[108]

In 1924 the Press moved into larger premises in Amen House, Warwick Square. Williams was delighted with the move. Meanwhile, he was supplementing the family income by giving evening lectures for London County Council. Michal published a work called *Christian Symbolism* in 1920, and after half a dozen volumes of verse Charles Williams published his first novel, *War in Heaven* (1930). This was the first of

106 Florence Williams, 'As I Remember', *Episcopal Churchnews* (12 April 1953), quoted in the introduction to Charles Williams, *The Image of the City and Other Essays*, sel. Anne Ridler (1958), p. xvii.

107 2 Samuel 6:16.

108 Williams, *The Image of the City*, p. xviii.

what have been called his 'spiritual shockers'[109] and with a burst of inspiration – very like that behind Lewis's Chronicles of Narnia – Williams followed it up with *Many Dimensions* (1931), *The Place of the Lion* (1931), *The Greater Trumps* (1932), *Shadows of Ecstasy* (1933), *Descent into Hell* (1937) and *All Hallows' Eve* (1945).

These have always been Williams's most popular books. Their appeal lies in what Lewis called a mixture of 'the Probable and the Marvellous'. Said Lewis,

> *We meet in them, on the one hand, very ordinary modern people who talk the slang of our own day, and live in the suburbs: on the other hand, we also meet the supernatural – ghosts, magicians, and archetypal beasts. The first thing to grasp is that this is not a mixture of two literary kinds . . . Williams is really writing a third kind of book which belongs to neither class and has a different value from either. He is writing that sort of book in which we begin by saying, 'Let us suppose that this everyday world were, at some point, invaded by the marvellous. Let us, in fact, suppose a violation of frontier.'*[110]

Lewis was bowled over by *The Place of the Lion*, and he wrote to Williams on 11 March 1936,[111] praising the book and inviting him to a meeting of the Inklings. As it turned out, Williams was proofreading Lewis's *Allegory of Love* and was on the point of writing to him. 'After this,' said Lewis, 'we soon met and our friendship rapidly grew inward to the bone.'[112]

At the outbreak of the Second World War Charles Williams was one of the staff that Oxford University Press transferred to Oxford. He arrived in Oxford on 7 September 1939 and moved into 9 South Parks Road, while Michal and their son remained in London. Lewis was of course delighted to see him, and Williams was soon attending the twice-weekly meetings of the Inklings on Thursday evenings in Lewis's rooms in Magdalen College and Tuesday mornings at the Eagle and Child pub.

Williams missed London, which he loved passionately, but no one

---

109 Preface to *Essays Presented to Charles Williams*, ed. C. S. Lewis (1947), p. viii: 'I first heard of Charles Williams a great many years ago when a man who was sitting next to me at dinner (Dr R. W. Chapman) asked me if I had read any of his novels. He described them as "spiritual shockers".'

110 'The Novels of Charles Williams', *Of This and Other Worlds*, pp. 34–5.

111 All Lewis's letters to Charles Williams are found in this volume.

112 *Essays Presented to Charles Williams*, Preface, p. viii.

could have received a warmer welcome to Oxford. Lewis went out of his way to introduce him to friends and put his extraordinary gifts to use. In the *Festschrift* which Lewis and others had hoped to offer Williams, Lewis gave this description of the man.

> *In appearance he was tall, slim, and straight as a boy, though grey-haired. His face we thought ugly: I am not sure that the word 'monkey' has not been murmured in this context. But the moment he spoke it became, as was also said, like the face of an angel – not a feminine angel, a spirit burning with intelligence and charity.*[113]

The Inklings were all warm towards Williams, but the fact that he was a newcomer did not exempt him from criticism. After one meeting Lewis told his brother that following a discussion of 'the most distressing text in the Bible' ('narrow is the way and few they be that find it')[114] one of the Inklings 'almost seriously expressed a strong wish to burn Williams'.[115] At other times they were highly complimentary. All Lewis's friends would have agreed with what he said in a letter to Dom Bede Griffiths of 21 December 1941. Williams was 'largely a self-educated man, labouring under an almost oriental richness of imagination'. Lewis did not want that 'oriental richness of imagination' to be squandered and when he detected slovenliness and obscurity in the things Williams was writing he said what he thought. 'Don't imagine I didn't pitch into C.W. for his obscurity for all I was worth', Lewis told Owen Barfield in a letter dated 22 December 1947.

Oxford's English Faculty was depleted by the war, and it was not long before Williams was drafted in to give lectures. Some were outstandingly good. The most popular of these were a course on Milton delivered during Hilary Term 1940. Lewis's delight in Williams's lecture on *Comus* on 5 February 1940 is an indication of their quality. Writing to his brother about the lecture on 12 February, Lewis said: 'I have at last, if only for once, seen a university doing what it was founded to do: teaching Wisdom.' The essence of these lectures survives in Williams's Preface to *The English Poems of John Milton*, ed. H. C. Beeching (London: Oxford University Press, new edn 1940). On 18 February 1943 Oxford University awarded Williams an honorary MA. Meanwhile Williams

113 ibid., p. ix.

114 Matthew 7:14.

115 See the letter to Warnie of 5 November 1939.

spent most weekends with his wife, and he was able to see a good deal of his son who worked part of this time at Blackwell's Bookshop and lived with his father in South Parks Road.

Besides University lectures and his work for the Press, Williams managed to write six books while he was in Oxford, the most notable of which were *The Figure of Beatrice* in 1943 and the last of the 'spiritual shockers', *All Hallows' Eve* in 1945. *The Figure of Beatrice* was to bring him a new friend. Dorothy L. Sayers was so excited by the book that, after a long and profitable correspondence with Williams, she was led to make a new English translation of Dante's *Divine Comedy*.

The war in Europe ended on 8 May 1945, but on 10 May Charles Williams was seized with pain. He was taken to the Radcliffe Infirmary where he was operated on, while Michal rushed to Oxford from London to be with him. On 15 May Charles Williams died of an acute intestinal obstruction. He was buried on 18 May in the cemetery of St Cross Church, Holywell, Oxford. Beside him lie the bodies of his wife, Michal, who died on 2 February 1970, and their son Michael who died, unmarried, on 27 June 2000. The grave is lovingly tended by people from Oxford and elsewhere.

INDEX

Abbotsford: 60n, 91
Abelard. Peter: 245
Aberdeen University: 432n
Aberystwyth (Cardiganshire): 378, 492, 493, 504
Abingdon (Berkshire): 39, 485
Abrabanel, Judah: *Dialoghi d'Amore*, 541
Abraham: 390n, 565n, 916
Academia Pontificia: 844n
Achilles: 678, 679n
Acland, Sir Robert: 321
Acland Nursing Home (Oxford): 302, 943–4, 948, 954
Act to Retrain Abuses of Players: 620
Acworth, Bernard: letter to: 632–3; *How the War Will be Won*; *Navies To-day and To-morrow*; *Restoration of England's Sea Power*, 632n
Adam: 180, 207, 244, 289n, 314, 338, 450, 462, 464n, 566, 577n, 664, 842, 848, 967, 978, 979, 1028n
Adams, Rev. Frederick Morice: 1015
Adams, Mary Trevenen: 1015
Adams SSJE, Father Walter: biography, 1015–6; *Thoughts from the Notebooks of a Priest Religious*, 1015; (with G. Shaw) *Triumphant in Suffering*, 1015; men. 453n, 482, 483, 507, 551
Adderbury: 2n
Addison, Joseph: 15n, 309
Addison's Walk (Magdalen College): 15, 244, 296, 298, 300, 330, 357, 377, 640
Adelaide: 2n, 323n
Adelaide University: 323n
Adey, Lionel: *C.S. Lewis's Great War with Owen Barfield*, 55n
Adirondack Mountains: 212n
Admetus: 269
Adonis: 1, 35
Admiralty Hydrographic Department: 1018
Adullam, Cave of: 26n
Adultery: 560, 782, 975, 977
'A.E.': see George William Russell
Aelred, St: *On Spiritual Friendship*, 577n; men. 577
Aeschylus: 192, 967
Aesop: 480n
Aesthetics: 35, 41, 108n, 205, 401n
Affection: 408, 423, 511n, 522
Africa: 1011
Afrika Korps: 1021
Agape (Charity): 6, 73, 147, 153, 154n, 158, 165n, 202, 234, 257, 408–10, 496, 510, 511, 513, 523, 641, 748, 803, 804, 822, 868, 983, 1085
Agapony Fund: 483, 530, 621–2, 669, 711, 827–8
Aghalee (Co. Down): 133n
Agnosticism: 424, 444, 702
Alanus ab Insulis: *De Planctu Naturae*, 149, 949
Alapatt, Fr Benedict: 1047
Albania: 359
Albert I of Belgium, King: 701
Albigensians: 680
Alcott, Louisa May: *Little Women*, 961
Aldeburgh (Suffolk): 1036
Alexander, Samuel: *Space, Time, and Deity*, 754
Alfred, King: *Old English version of Boethius De Consolatione Philosophiae*, 643; *Orosius*, 264; men. 42, 326n
Alice Ottley School (Worcester): 1055
Allegory: 141, 142, 154, 438–9, 441, 479, 601
Allen, Mrs Belle: letter to: 969; men. 827n, 931
Allen, Edward A.: letters to: 827, 828, 832–4, 835–6, 836–7, 840, 846, 850–1, 852, 854–6, 856–7, 858, 862, 869–70, 876, 883–4, 891–2, 894, 899–900, 907, 909, 910–11, 917, 920–1, 925–6, 927, 930–1, 938–9, 944–5, 973, 984
Allen, Sir Hugh Percy: 1066
Allen, Percy Stafford: 683n
Alliteration: 197, 872
All Saints, Highfield (Oxford): 21n
All Souls College (Oxford): 71n, 301n, 414n, 416n, 1002n
Alps, The: 810n
Altmark: 355, 385
Amadis of Gaul: 562, 563
Ambient, Mark (and Lionel Monkton and Howard Talbot): *The Arcadians*, 51
America/Americans/U.S.A.: 641, 645, 731, 809, 832, 835, 848, 856, 862, 863, 869, 876, 880, 883–4, 889, 892, 899–900, 908, 910–11, 912, 916, 923, 927, 929, 931, 944, 963, 989, 1004, 1017, 1049, 1067
America: 629n

American Medical Association: 1032
American Review: 163
Amersham: 2n
Amos: 352, 875
Andersen, Hans Christian: *Andersen's Fairy Tales*: 1021
Andes Agreement: 917n, 931–2
Andreas Capellanus: *The Art of Courtly Love*, 712n
Andrew Lang Lectures: 650, 654
Andrews, Kathleen: letters to: 934, 937
Andromeda: 930
Angels: 278n, 337, 450, 493, 512, 569, 577, 585, 634, 660, 667, 692n, 718, 727, 747, 843, 844, 956, 960, 989, 1085
Anglicanism: 134–6, 176–7, 178–9, 225n, 226, 234n, 256, 757, 859–61, 1043, 1046, 1053, 1057, 1058
Anglo-Catholicism: 94, 134, 164n, 272n, 285, 303n, 417n, 443, 762, 1029, 1053, 1055, 1059, 1060
Anglo-Saxon (Old English): 44, 113n, 168, 182n, 264, 297n, 341, 349n, 537, 589, 611n, 638, 643–4, 1052, 1075
Anglo-Saxon Chronicle, The: 280
Annagassan (Co. Louth): 90n
Anne, Queen: 1041
Annunciation, The: 31, 590
Anscombe, G.E.M.: 'Reply to Mr C.S. Lewis's Argument That "Naturalism" is Self-Refuting', 936n
Anselm, St: *Cur Deus Homo*, 464, 502, 531
Anstey, F.: *Vice Versa*, 342
Anthropomorphism: 189, 589n
Anthropology: 403n, 859
Anthroposophical Society: 1051
Anthroposophy: 55, 56, 107–8, 130, 162, 195, 300, 383, 420–21, 703, 729, 870, 1016, 1017, 1050–1
Anthroposophy: 106n
Antigone: see Sophocles
Anti-Nature/anti-Natural: 368, 672n, 773
Anvil, The: 582–3
Aphrodite: 542n, 560, 569, 875
Apocatastasis: 451n
Apocryphal New Testament: 142
Apollo: 269, 625n
Apologetics, 526, 527, 573, 633, 730
Apostles, The: 35, 201, 227n, 283n, 765
Apostles' Creed, The: 255n, 566n
Apuleius: *Cupid and Psyche*, 41–2; men. 546
Aramaic: 266
Archer, Rev. Charles Frederick: 370n
Archer-Hind, Richard Dacre: 157–8
Architrenius: 451
Ardglass (Co. Down): 85
Ares/Mars: 569, 693, 910
Argentina: 917, 923, 931–2
Argument: 136, 178–9, 427
Arians: 5
Ariosto, Ludovico: *Orlando Furioso*, 562, 563, 813, 814, 990, 1000
Aristotle: *De Anima*, 15n; *Metaphysics*, 153; *Physics*, 543; *Politics*, 395; men. 176, 188, 193, 242, 245, 326, 418, 422, 523, 528, 646, 655, 664, 771, 773
Armageddon, Battle of: 345
Army Educational Corps: 275
Arnaboldi, Don Paolo: 998n
Arnold, Matthew: *Balder Dead*; *Sohrab and Rustum*, 763, 893; men. 252, 378n, 391, 401n, 455, 464, 955
Arrochar (Dunbartonshire): 115
Art: 390–1, 1010
Art for Art's Sake: 476, 478
Arthur, King: 518n, 562n, 673, 723n, 783, 784, 785, 809n, 810, 814n, 816, 887, 1042, 1073
Arthurian Chronicles, Represented by Wace and Layamon, 673
Arthurian Legends: 809n, 902n, 1042
Arthurian Society, The: 166
Artistic Conscience: 728, 729–31
Arts Theatre Club (London): 1035
Arundel (Sussex): 74
Arundel Castle: 74
Ascension, The: 581
Asclepius: 269n
Asgard: 449, 1042
'Ashton', 'Mrs': 135n
Askins, Jane King: (Mrs Moore's mother): 309
Askins, Michael: 169, 171
Askins, Molly: 169, 171, 530
Askins, Dr Robert: 169n
Askins, Rev. William James (Mrs Moore's father): 309n
As they pass the gay cafes: 50
Asia: 69–70
Astrology: 475n, 702
Astronomy: 237, 407n, 475, 953
Athanasian Creed: 255, 268, 417, 503, 1006
Athanasius, St: *Incarnation of the Word of God*, 516n, 520, 525–6, 528, 529, 554–5, 602–3, 701, 812n, 849n, 911; *Letter on the Psalms*, 849n; men. 1056, 1058
Atheism: 633, 747, 868, 1077
Athelney (Somerset): 338
Athens: 227, 646
Atlantic Monthly: 1079
Atomic Bomb: 688, 691–2, 909n
Atonement, The: 22–3, 35, 451n, 484, 502
Attlee, Clement: 812
Aucassin and Nicolette: 671
Auden, Wystan Hugh: 197, 424, 429, 536, 556n
Audio Amateur: 1025
Auerswalde (Germany): 1021
Augustine of Hippo, St: *City of God*, 214, 233, 529; *Commentary on the First Letter of John*, 194; *Confessions*, 190, 225, 529, 1044; *Sermons*, 194; men. 227, 574n, 612, 630, 824

INDEX

Aulén, Gustaf: *Christus Victor*, 529
Austen, Jane: *Emma*, 211, 503; *Letters*, 977n; *Mansfield Park*, 977; *Northanger Abbey*, 10, 210; *Pride and Prejudice*, 404, 976; *Sanditon*, 549; *Sense and Sensibility*, 342, 779n, 976; *The Watsons*, 320; men. 68, 182n, 203n, 317, 551, 676, 746, 976–7
Austin, John Langshaw: 354–5, 403, 408
Australia: 2n, 404, 561, 625, 1049
Australian Broadcasting Commission: 627
Australian Security Intelligence Organization: 643n
Austria: 1049
Authorized Version of the Bible: 586, 822n
Auxiliary Territorial Service: 452, 499n
Avery Hill Training College: 360n

Babbitt, Irving: 145n, 146
Bacchus: 1, 638, 777
Bach, Johann Sebastian: 11, 391
Bach Choir: 1066
Bacon, Roger: 475n, 476
Bagehot, Walter: 21
Bailey, Cyril: *Greek Atomists and Epicurus*; *Legacy of Rome*; *Phases in the Religion of Ancient Rome*; *Religion in Virgil*, 344n; men. 344–5
Baird, James D.: (with Charles Ryskamp) *Poems of William Cowper*, 732
Bajetta, Carlo M.: 821n
Baker, Frank: 849
Baker, Henry: 76n
Baker, Henry Williams: (ed) *Hymns Ancient and Modern*, 417
Baker, Henry William: 'The King of Love My Shepherd Is', 387
Baker, Leo: letters to: 161–2, 195–8; men. 518n
Balaam: 485n
Balaam's Ass: 485, 792
Balder: 1, 35
Balfour, Arthur James: *Foundations of Belief*, 240
Ballads: 26–8, 733
Ballard Mathews Lectures: 473n, 494
Balliol College (Oxford): 15n, 17n, 27, 102n, 283n, 292n, 306, 316n, 336n, 403n, 495n, 498n, 509n, 564n, 769, 839, 1066, 1071, 1081
Ballycastle (Co. Antrim): 22, 52, 945
Balmforth, Rev. Henry: *The Christian Religion*, 946n; men. 946
Baltimore (Maryland): 798, 803, 928, 1004, 1031
Balzac, Honoré de: *Le Curé de Tours*; *Le Père Goriot*, 298
Bambi (the film): 884
Bampton, Rev. John: 566n
Bampton Lectures: 566, 598, 874
Banbury: 2n
Bangalore: 1047
Banner, Delmar: letters to: 537–8, 600–1
Banville, Théodore de: 930n
Baptism: 135n, 722
Baptism by Desire: 135
Baptist Church: 493
Barber, Richard: *Companion to World Mythology*, 1021
Barbour, John: *Bruce*, 42
Barfield, Alexander: 1017
Barfield, Arthur Edward: 232–3, 1016
Barfield, Christian Matilda 'Maud': biography: 1016–17: letter to: 942–3; men. 18
Barfield, Elizabeth: 418
Barfield, Jeffrey: 1017
Barfield, Lucy: 942, 1017
Barfield, Owen: letters to: 55, 56–7, 76–8, 78–9, 87–8, 104–7, 155–6, 172–3, 198–9, 217–18, 222–3, 228–33, 247–9, 259–61, 266–9, 418–21, 527–8, 530–1, 574–5, 621–2, 651–2, 664–5, 668–9, 687–9, 711, 712–13, 817–19, 834–5, 870–3, 889–90, 929–30, 937–8, 942, 945–6, 974–5;
Writings: (with C.S. Lewis) *A Cretaceous Perambulator*, 155n; *Barfield Sampler*, 665n; 'Lewis and/or Barfield', 870; *Mark vs. Tristram: Correspondence between C.S. Lewis and Owen Barfield*, 781n; 'The Merman', 665; *Orpheus: A Poetic Drama*, 158, 162, 222, 228, 248, 817, 872–3; *Owen Barfield on C.S. Lewis*, 870n; *Poetic Diction*, 439, 734; 'Poetic Diction and Legal Fiction', 649, 817, 821n, 867; 'Philosophy of Samuel Taylor Coleridge', 106; *Romanticism Comes of Age*, 106n; *The Silver Trumpet*, 198; (as by G.A.L. Burgeon) *This Ever Diverse Pair*, 483, 937–8
Unpublished writings: 'English People', 172n; 'Note on Pain', 56, 63; 'The Tower', 55, 162; '*Tertium Quid*', 156; 'The Unicorn', 872; men. 10–11, 17–8, 38, 39, 71–4, 103, 107n, 137, 139, 161, 162, 169, 182, 195, 203, 239, 241, 244, 247, 313, 343, 350, 377n, 381–8, 434–5, 483, 502, 512, 572, 690n, 703, 707, 729, 827, 924, 947, 948, 966, 969, 971, 981n, 1008, 1016–17, 1052, 1054, 1085
Barfield and Barfield, Solicitors: 11n, 1016
Barkby (Leicestershire): 1075
Barley Mow (Blewbury): 17–8, 69
Barnes, Mgr. Arthur Stapylton: *Holy Shroud of Turin*, 494n
Barrie, J.M.: *Mary Rose*, 124; *Peter Pan*, 949, 1040; men. 1040
Barth, Karl: *Commentary on Romans*, 351n; men. 165, 351, 404
Basle (Switzerland): 351n

Bate, W.J.: 229n, 497n
Bateson, Frederick Wilse: *English Comic Drama*; *English Poetry and the English Language*, 415n; men. 415
Bath (Somerset): 316, 317, 1018
Bath, Marquess of: 661n
Bathsheba: 196n
Battles, Ford Lewis: *Calvin Catechism*, 289n; men. 289, 293
Baudelaire, Charles: 546
Baum, Vicki: *Grand Hotel*, 554
Bawdy: 16, 26–8
Baxter, Mr and Mrs E.L.: letter to: 797–8, 802, 807
Baynes, Angela: 1018
Baynes, Frederick William Wilberforce: 1018
Baynes, Jessie Harriet Maude: 1018
Baynes, Pauline: biography: 1018–22; letter to: 1009; *Good King Wencelaus*, 1021; *How Dog Began*, 1021; *In the Beginning*, 1021; *Noah and the Ark*, 1021; *The Song of the Three Holy Children*, 1021; *Thanks Be to God*, 1021; *Victoria and the Golden Bird*, 1018; men. 952
Bazley, Sir Thomas: 925
BBC (British Broadcasting Corporation): 330n, 469–71, 483, 484–5, 486, 490–2, 496, 498–9, 503, 505, 506, 508, 509–10, 515, 518, 521, 522–3, 525, 528, 531, 533, 534, 538, 565n, 568, 571–3, 581–3, 597–9, 601–2, 603, 608, 610, 626–9, 667, 681, 735–6, 739–40, 891, 892–3, 924–5, 1046, 1062, 1063, 1065, 1070–1
BBC Copyright Department: letter to: 740
Beales, Arthur Charles Frederick: *Catholic Church and International Order*; *Education Under Penalty*, 510n; men. 510, 538
Beatific Vision, The: 191, 1082
Beatrician Experience, The: 1082
Beauford School (Camberley): 1018
Beaulieu Abbey: 125
Beck, Fr Andrew: 582n
Beck, Leslie John: 292n
Beckett, Sir Eric: 63, 71–4, 155, 162
Beckford, William: 546
Bedales School: 696n
Beddow, Canon John: letter to: 673–5
Bede, St: *Ecclesiastical History of the English People*, 1045; men. 326, 353
Bedford, Grosvenor C.: 421n
Bedford College (University of London): 306n
Beecham, Sir Thomas: 151
Beeching Henry Charles: (ed) *The Poetical Works of John Milton*, 625; (ed) *The English Poems of John Milton*, 1085
Beerbohm, Max: 924n
Beethoven, Ludwig van: Symphony no. 3 'Eroica', 128; Symphony no. 5, 128, 151; Symphony no. 7, 128; Symphony no. 9, 170–1, 996; men. 101, 175
Belfast: 12n, 112, 115–16, 131, 212n, 294n, 301, 485, 503, 539, 693, 921, 922n, 945
Being: 808–9
Being-in-Love: See Eros
Belgion, Montgomery: 379n
Belgium: 920
Bell, George Kennedy Allen: *Christianity and World Order*, 278n; men. 278, 1069
Belloc, Hilaire: 762n
Beloit College (Beloit, Wisconsin): 1078, 1080
Belton, Rev. John Thomas: 133
Benecke, Paul Victor Mendelssohn: 15, 282, 283, 347, 363, 429, 432, 601
Benedict IX, Pope: 283n
Benedictines: 5n, 612, 1045–9
Bennett, Joan: letters to: 209–11, 215, 255–6; *Five Metaphysical Poets*, 209n, 215n; (ed) *Seventeenth Century Studies Presented to Sir Herbert Grierson*, 209, 210, 211–12; *Sir Thomas Browne*, 209n; men. 211
Bennett, Stanley: *English Books and Readers*; *Life on the English Manor*; *Medieval Men and Women*, 435n; men. 209n, 435
Benson, Robert Hugh: *The Dawn of All*, 630
Benson, Fr Robert Meux: 1015
Benson, S.H.: 1067, 1068
Bentley, Geoffrey Bryant: 351n
Beowulf: 9n, 16, 182, 297n, 643, 951, 957
Berdyaev, Nicolas: *Freedom and the Spirit*, 465n, 466
Bergson, Henri: *Creative Evolution*, 870–1; men. 708n
Berkeley, George: *Principles of Human Knowledge*; *Three Dialogues*, 703n; men. 225, 702–3
Berkshamsted School: 1072
Berkshire Down: 49, 71, 111
Berlin: 416n, 425n, 489n, 1036
Berlin University: 403n, 489n, 609n
Bernagh (Arthur Greeves's home): 13, 86n, 88n, 131, 486, 908, 945
Bernard of Clairvaux, St: 451, 961
Berners, Lord (John Bouchier): 52n
Bethell, Samuel Leslie: 'Christianity and Culture', 401n, 412, 446, 447; (with G. Every and J.D.C. Pellow) *Selected Poems*, 1031; *Shakespeare and the Popular Dramatic Tradition*, 621, 675
Betjeman, Sir John: biography: 1022–3; letters

to: 226–7, 895; *A Few Late Chrysanthemums*, 1023; *Continual Dew*, 1023; *Ghastly Good Taste*, 1022–3; *Letters*, I, 1022; *Letters*, II, 1023; *Mount Zion*, 1023; *Old Lights for New Churches*, 1023; men. 474n, 1029
Betjemann, Ernest: 1022
Betjemann, Mabel Bessie: 1022
Bethlehem: 693, 998, 999
Bevan, Edwyn: *Christianity*, 529; *Symbolism and Belief*, 375, 529
Beveridge, William Henry, Lord: 613, 614
Beverly Hills (California): 875, 973
Bhagavad-Gita: 218
Bible/Scriptures: 23, 112n, 142, 179n, 218, 227, 351, 380, 422, 451n, 540, 646, 647, 667, 769, 775, 815n, 914, 989, 1012, 1044, 1085
Biblical Criticism: 573n
Bibury (Gloucestershire): 317
Biography, 281
Birmingham: 152
Bird, Rev. Henry Edward: 7
'Bird and Baby' pub: see Eagle and Child
Birkbeck College, University of London: 69n
Birkenhead School: 615n
Birth Control: 18, 424
Bishopstoke (Hampshire): 1050
Blackwell's Bookshop/ Publisher (Oxford): 666, 716, 1066, 1086
Blair, Rev. Harold Arthur: letters to: 661–2, 665–6; *A Creed Before the Creeds*; *A Kaleidoscope of Truth*; *The Ladder of Temptation*, 662n
Blair, Mrs Harold Arthur: 666
Blaise: 783, 784, 785–6
Blake, Arthur: 1023
Blake, Eleanor: see Eleanor Dunbar
Blake, Ethel: 1023
Blake, Leonard James: biography: 1023–4; men. 325, 405–6, 430, 431, 405, 638, 786
Blake, Richard Francis: see Sir Richard Dunbar of Hempriggs
Blake, William: *Marriage of Heaven and Hell*, 249; *Songs of Experience*, 534; *Songs of Innocence*, 160; men. 734
Blamires, Charles Wright: 1024
Blamires, Harry: biography: 1024; letters to: 675–7, 997, 1009; *The Bloomsday Book* (*New Bloomsday Book*); *The Christian Mind*; *The Penguin Guide to Plain English*, 1024; *Repair the Ruins*, 997
Blamires, Mary Norah: 1024
Blanchett, Rev. Arthur William: 277, 279, 287, 290, 342, 417, 426
Bleakley, David: *C.S. Lewis – At Home in Ireland*, 19n, 305n, 1016
Bleiben, Rev. Thomas Eric 'Peter': 272, 278, 299, 306, 312, 335, 353, 354, 363, 417, 432
Blenheim Palace: 293, 310, 359–60
Bles, Geoffrey: 516n, 554, 911, 925, 961, 1009, 1019
Bletchley (Buckinghamshire): 246, 528n, 671
Bloemfontein (South Africa): 934n
Blumenau, Ralph: *History of Malvern College*, 293
Blunden, Edmund: *Undertones of War*, 106; men. 474n
Bluntisham-cum-Earith (Huntingdonshire): 1065, 1067
Board of Trade, The: 1026, 1027
Boase, Thomas Sherrer Ross: 808n
Boccaccio, Giovanni: 609
Bodin, Jean: 475n
Bodkin, Maud: *Archetypal Patters in Poetry*, 439–40, 655
Bodle, Rhona: letters to: 823–4, 857, 915–16, 926, 941, 947, 959, 988, 989–90, 993–4
Bodleian Library (Bodley): 14n, 220, 368, 450n, 452n, 883, 1019, 1025, 1026, 1032, 1080
Boehme, Jacob: 40
Boethius: *Consolation of Philosophy*, 374, 465, 529, 643, 775, 915; men. 42, 140n, 158
Boiardo, Matteomaria: *Orlando Innamorato*, 813, 814, 1000
Boleyn, Anne: 815n
Bonaventure, St: 146n
Bond, H. Lawrence: 871n
Bone, Gavin David: *Anglo-Saxon Poetry*; *Beowulf in Modern Verse*, 297n; men. 297–8
Bone, John H.: *Aerial*, 191
Bone, Sir Muirhead: *The Western Front*, 298n; men. 298
Bonn University: 437n
Book Handbook, The: 743, 767
Book of Common Prayer, The: 255n, 380n, 380, 392–6, 422, 511, 844n
Bookham: see Great Bookham
Booth, William: 736n
Borrow, George: *Lavengro*, 540, 551
Bosanquet, Bernard: *A History of Aesthetic*; *Knowledge and Reality*, 157n
Bosc, Marie-José 'Microbe': 739
Boshell, Mrs: 530, 534, 538
'Bosphorus' (Warnie's boat): 244n, 270–1, 312, 377, 437, 486, 504
Boswell, James: *Journal of a Tour of the Hebrides*, 426; *Life of Samuel Johnson*, 4, 40, 48–9, 50, 62, 71, 89, 222, 329, 334, 337, 373, 393, 432, 491n, 492, 503, 513, 547, 638; men. 491, 749
Boswell, Ronald: letter to: 509; men. 490
Bottome, Phyllis: *Private Worlds*, 487

Bottomley, Gordon: 1041
Bournemouth (Dorset): 222
Bourdillon, Francis Bernard: 316, 397
Bourdillon, Mary Dorothea: 316, 397
Bowen, Marjorie: 413
Bowne, Gordon Parker: *Metaphysics*, 915n
Bowyer, Rev. Leonard John: 924–5
Brabazon, James (James Seth-Smith): *Albert Schweitzer*, 828n *Dorothy L. Sayers*, 828n, 1068n, 1072; men. 828
Bradenham (Buckinghamshire): 1055
Bradford (Yorkshire): 1024
Bradley, H.C.: 658n
Bradley, Violet: 658n
Brady, Charles A.: letter to: 629–31; men. 151n
Brains Trust: 1063
Bramber (Sussex): 72–3
Brangwayn, Mlle: 781n, 783
Brasenose College (Oxford): 17n
Breckenridge, Miss: letter to: 962
Brendon (Somerset): 319, 339
Brett-Smith, Herbert Francis: 26n, 365
Brewer, E. Cobham: *Dictionary of Phrase and Fable*, 700
Bridgeheads: 1071
Bridges, Robert: *The Spirit of Man*, 306; men. 63
Bridgetown (Somerset): 387
Brightman, Edgar Sheffield: (ed) *Personalism in Theology*, 914
Brightman, Rev. Frank Edward: *English Rite*, 76n; men. 76, 428, 429, 537
Brighton (Sussex): 1018
Bristol (Gloucestershire) : 10, 317
Britain To-day: 665
British Academy, The: 520
British Aluminium Company: 1052
British Interplanetary Society, 752n, 1024
British Museum: 369n, 614n, 1066–7
British School (Rome): 839
British School of Archaeology (Athens): 1073
British Union of Fascists: 291n
Broadcasting House (BBC): 538, 583
Brontë, Charlotte: *Jane Eyre*, 291, 550, 706; men. 389
Brontë, Charlotte: *Shirley*, 640
Brontë, Emily: *Wuthering Heights*, 31–2, 34; men. 389
Brooke, Arthur: *Tragical History of Romeus and Juliet*, 776
Brooke, B.J.: *Wild Orchids of Britain*, 297n
Brooke, Stopford: 580n
Browne, Sir Thomas: *Religio Medici*, 6n, 376, 535n, 570, 763; men. 6, 20, 44, 83, 209n, 535, 644
Browning, D.C.: 370n
Browning, Robert: *The Ring and the Book*, 551; men. 68, 996, 1000
Bruce (Mrs Moore's dog): 309, 316, 322, 362, 371, 377, 404, 430, 432, 590, 638, 696, 1050
Bruce, Robert: 313
Bryn Mawr: 145
Bryson, John Norman: 102, 214, 580
Buber, Martin: *I and Thou*, 526, 528
Buchan, John: *Memory Hold-the-Door*, 366; *The Three Hostages*, 103; men. 125
Buck, Pearl: *The Good Earth*, 69
Buckingham Palace: 1063
Budd, Rev. Kenneth George: *The Story of Donald Hankey*, 548n; men. 548–9
Buddha/Buddhism: 70, 307, 328, 329, 464, 1046
Bull Hotel (Fairford): 682, 683, 687
'Bultitude' (Whipsnade Zoo): 84
Bunyan, John: *Pilgrim's Progress*, 160, 387, 439; men. 89, 441, 824, 919
Bunsen, Chevalier: 994n
Burghclere (Berkshire): 1043, 1044
Burke, Edmund: *Reflections on the Revolution in France*, 34; men. 950
Burma: 29, 615n
Burnet, Thomas: *The Theory of the Earth*, 810
Burns, Robert: 'The Banks o' Doon', 732
Burroughs, Edgar Rice: 237, 630
Burton, Helen Violet Tryce: 508, 519–20
Burton, Richard: *Anatomy of Melancholy*, 653n
Bush, Douglas: letters to: 452, 474–8, 547–8; *Classical Influences in Renaissance Literature*, 221n; *English Literature in the Earlier Seventeenth Century*, 221, 548; *John Milton*, 221n; *Pagan Myth and Christian Tradition*, 221n; *The Renaissance and English Humanism*, 474–8; men. 221–2, 568
Butler, Catherine Elizabeth Barradouth: 437
Butler, Eliza Marian: letters to: 437–46, 448–9; men. 477n, 655n
Butler, Joseph: *Fifteen Sermons*, 645
Butler, Samuel: *Way of All Flesh*, 62
Butler, Theobald Fitzwalter: 437n
Butler, Rev. William John: 1055
Butlers, Miss: 1033
Byrne, Muriel St Clare: *The Lisle Letters*, 1066n; men. 1066, 1071, 1072
Byron, George Gordon, Lord: *Don Juan*, 991, 996; *Vision of Judgement*, 210, 211; men. 163, 361, 644, 999–1000

Caedmon: 182n
Caerleon: 238, 784
Caine, Hall: *Life of Christ*, 573n

Caird, Edward: 15n
Cairo: 1052
Cairo University: 24n, 1052, 1053
Caius College (Cambridge): 351n
Calabria, Angela Foschio: 1036
Calabria, Don Giovanni: see Giovanni Calabria, St
Calabria, Luigi: 1036
Calcutta: 293, 321n, 954n
Calcutta University: 360n
Calkins, Miss H.D.: letter to: 825
California: 811
Calvin, John: *Institutes*, 289n; men. 351, 574n
Calvinism: 73, 447, 703
Camberley (Surrey): 323
Cambridge: 1072
Cambridge Bibliography of English Literature: 415n
Cambridge Platonists: 574n
Cambridge Review, The: 466, 574n
Cambridge University: 152, 209n, 215n, 229, 246, 284, 351, 407n, 435, 437n, 616, 1059
Camoëns, Luis de: *Os Lusiadas*, 562
Campbell, Archibald Young: *Poems*, 754
Campbell, Mary (wife of Roy Campbell): 736
Campbell, Roy: letter to: 736; *Collected Poems*; *The Flaming Terrapin*; *Sons of Mistral*, 736n; men. 684, 735, 739, 740
Campbell College (Belfast): 97n, 116
Campion Hall (Oxford): 683
Cana: 532, 1077
Canaan: 144, 263n
Canada: 1011, 1076
Canadian Broadcasting Corporation: 924n
Can Grande della Scala: 669n
Canisius College (Buffalo, N.Y.): 629n
Cannan, F.G.: 711
Canterbury Cathedral: 184–5, 186, 278n, 469n, 1069
Capability Brown: 362
Cape Town (South Africa): 1015
Capital Punishment: 250
Capron, Rev. Robert 'Oldie': 292
Cardiff: 412, 421, 424
CARE (The Cooperative for American Relief Everywhere): 851
Carlisle: 244, 460n, 1016
Carlyle, Rev. Edgar Frederick: (with R.W. Carlyle) *History of Medieval Political Theory*, 399n; (with Rebecca Carlyle) *Hugh Latimer*, 488n; men. 399, 489, 578–9
Carlyle, Margaret Monteith: letters to: 488–9, 578–9, 583
Carlyle, Mary (daughter of Edgar Frederick Carlyle): 579, 583
Carlyle, Rebecca Monteith: (with E.F. Carlyle), *Hugh Latimer*, 488n; men. 488–9
Carlyle, Sir Robert Warrand: 399n
Carlyle, Thomas: *Past and Present*, 20, 23; *Sartor Resartus*, 23; men. 2n, 210, 402, 428
Carnegie Medal, The: 1022
Carpenter, Humphrey: (ed) *Letters of J.R.R. Tolkien*, 182n, 1018; *OUDS: A Centenary History of the Oxford University Dramatic Society*, 1040
Carritt, Edward Frederick: letter to: 220; 'Christianity and Culture', 401n, 412, 446; men. 401, 410
Carroll, Lewis: *Sylvie and Bruno*, 1003; *Through the Looking-Glass*, 687, 992; men. 687, 1033, 1040
Carter, Reginald: *He and His*, 363–4
Cary, Henry Francis: (trans) *The Vision or Hell, Purgatory and Paradise of Dante Alighieri*, 567, 1082
Carey, Rev. Kenneth: 1076–7
Cassiopeia: 697
Castlereagh Hills (Co. Down): 151
Castlerock: 18
Castor: 381, 388
Casualty Clearing Station: 296
Cat and Mouse Act: 1075–6
Catcombe (Wiltshire): 387–8
Catherine of Aragon, Queen: 1057
Catholic/Catholicism: 5, 134–6, 143–4, 152, 164n, 170, 176–8, 178–9, 183, 213, 224–5, 226, 256n, 257, 349, 358, 379, 405, 416n, 435, 451, 510n, 576n, 645–7, 670, 703, 736, 738n, 747n, 757, 762, 769, 813–16, 860–1, 863, 1033, 1045–9, 1062, 1077
Catholic Church, The: 482, 645–7, 799, 800, 801, 821n, 1028n, 1031, 1045–9, 1057
Catholic Teachers' Journal, The: 936n
Catholic Worker: 1078
Catholic Workers Movement: 1078
Catholic Writers, Guild of: 1070
Catholicon Anglicum: 166
Catterick (Yorkshire): 270, 274
Catullus: *Carmen*, 733; men. 734
Cavalcade: see Noël Coward
'Cave', 'The' (club for English dons): 26–7, 306, 365
Caxton, William: 166n, 780
Cecil, Lord David: *Stricken Deer*, 182; men. 182, 742, 838, 839, 888, 1060n, 1061
Cecil, James Edward Hubert Gascoyne-, fourth Marquess of Salisbury: letter to: 766; men. 765–6
Cecil, Rachel, Lady: 742
Cecilia, St: 267n
Centenary Press: 289n, 554n
Ceres: 980
Cervantes, Miguel de: *Don Quixote*, 250
Chamberlain, Neville: 231

Chambers, Sir Edmund Kerchever: *Arthur of Britain*, 673; *Sir Thomas Wyatt*, 166n, 211; *Timelessness of Poetry*, 355; men. 355–6
Chambers, Raymond Wilson: *Beowulf*, 168, 643; *Man's Unconquerable Mind*, 326–7, 621; *On the Continuity of English Prose*, 326; *Thomas More*, 168n; men. 168
Chancellor's Essay Prize (Oxford): 1081
Chapel-en-le-Frith (Derbyshire): 158–9, 160n
Chapman, John Alexander: letter to: 954–6; *India, its Character*; *Papers on Shelley, Wordsworth & Others*; *Religious Lyrics of Bengal*, 954n
Chapman, Robert William: letters to: 203, 976–7; *Jane Austen*, 203n; *Jane Austen: Facts and Problems*, 976; *Jane Austen's Letters*, 977; *Letters of Samuel Johnson*, 203n; *Portrait of a Scholar*, 17; men. 1084n
Charity: see Agape
Charlemagne: 546n, 814n
Charterhouse School: 319, 415n, 752n
Chastity: 345–6, 478, 501, 511, 514, 523, 550, 621, 780
Chaucer, Geoffrey: *Book of the Duchess*, 488; *Canterbury Tales*, 56, 879; *Fortune*, 141; *La Priere de Nostre Dame*, 568n; *Troilus and Criseyde*, 359, 819; men. 42, 91, 141, 397, 477n, 644, 1040
Chaundy, Leslie: 473n
Chavasse, Rev. Claude Lionel: *Bride of Christ*, 379n, 381; men. 19, 404
Checkers (Oxford): 435
Cheltenham: 1074
Cheltenham College: 437n, 519, 537n, 1065
Cheltenham School: 150n
Cherbourg School (Malvern): 57, 95
Cherwell, The: 300, 330n
Cherwell Edge: 349
Chesney, Alan Mason: 1032
Chester (Cheshire): 131
Chesterton, Gilbert Keith: *All Things Considered*, 352; *Collected Poems*, 642n; 'The Crusader Returns', 642; *Everlasting Man*, 375, 823, 941; *Orthodoxy*, 375; men. 28, 183, 198, 630, 703, 824, 919, 924n
Chesterton Review, The: 1055
Chicago: 411
Chichester: 1069
Chichester Cathedral: 585n
Chicksands Priory: 588
Child, F.J.: (ed) *The English and Scottish Popular Ballads*, 733n
Childe, W.R.: 605–6
China: 1, 44–5, 57, 64, 67, 85, 350, 431n
Chinese, the: 36, 90, 842, 881
Chivalry: 251, 434n, 782, 938
Chrétien de Troyes: *Perceval/Le Conte du Graal*, 723n, 912, 913n
Christian X, King: 389n
Christian Herald: 510
Christian Literature: 181, 193–4
Christian Renaissance: 145–6
Christian Re-union: 226, 234
Christian Scholar's Review: 141n
Christian Social Union: 399n
Christian Unity: 798, 799, 803, 804, 814, 816, 829, 830
Christian Workers' Union: 673–5
Christie, Agatha: 1069
Christie, John Traill: 6, 10, 15, 20, 60, 577
Christ Church 'The House' (Oxford): 196n, 278n, 286n, 370, 378n, 379, 403n, 428n, 495n, 537n, 615, 839, 1051
Christ Church Cathedral (Oxford): 1065
Christ Church Cathedral School (Oxford): 1065
Christ's College (Cambridge): 167n, 351n, 574n
Christ's Hospital School: 1043
Church, Alfred John: *Stories from Homer*, 439
Church, Richard: The Lamp, 767; men. 757
Church, Richard William: 367n
Churchill, Winston: *Marlborough*, 399; men. 425n, 592n
Church Missionary Society: 469n
Church of England: 250–2, 278, 285, 428n, 469n, 722, 765–6, 813–16, 859–61, 863, 1023, 1029, 1043, 1044, 1056–7, 1059, 1062, 1069, 1076–7, 1082
Church of Ireland: 19n, 132–3, 702
Church of the Nazarene: 988n, 1025
Church Stretton (Shropshire): 240
Church Times: 1060
Cicero: *De Legibus*, 334; *De Republica*, 31; *De Senectute*, 986; *Somnium Scipionis*, 31; men. 477n
Cinderella: 566, 802
Circe: 794–5
Cistercians: 1047
City of London School for Boys: 307
Clacton (Essex): 339
Clapham High School (London): 1066
Clarendon Press, The: 169–70, 203n, 635
Clarendon Press Institute: 302
Clark Lectures, The: 552, 616
Clarke, Rev. Alured George: 21
Clarke, Sir Arthur C.: biography, 1024–5; letters to: 593–4, 741, 742, 752; 'The Challenge of the Space Ship', 752; *Childhood's End*, 1025; *Earthlight*, 1025; 'Extra-terrestrial Relays', 1024; *Prelude to Space*, 1024;

The Sands of Mars, 1025; *2001: A Space Odyssey*, 1025;
Clarke, Charles Wright: 1024
Clarke, Mary Norah: 1024
Classical Moderations: 431n, 432n, 564n, 1043
Clemenceau, Georges: 399
Clement VII, Pope: 1057
Clement of Alexandria: 662n
Clent (Worcestershire): 1055
Clergy Widows' Fund: 508, 509
Clifton (Gloucestershire): 1015
Clifton College: 519n, 1072
Clive, Robert (Clive of India): 969
Clough, Arthur Hugh: 220n
Cockin, Canon F.A.: 582n
Coghill, Carol: 398–9
Coghill, Elspeth: 398–9
Coghill, Nevill: *The Poet Chaucer*, 568; men. 26n, 99, 182, 183, 288, 302, 365, 381, 398–9, 403, 1063
Coincidentia Oppositorum: 871
Co-inherence: 988
Coleridge, Samuel Taylor: *Aids to Reflection*, 204; *Biographia Literaria*, 205n; (with William Wordsworth) *Lyrical Ballads*, 893n; *Zapolya*, 548; men. 72n, 106–7, 477n, 955
Collège Cantonal (Lausanne): 1073
Collier, John: *Tom's A-Cold*, 111, 128
Collingwood, Robin George: (with J.N.L. Myres) *Roman Britain*, 616n, 673
Collingwood, Stuart Dodgson: *Life and Letters of Lewis Carroll*, 687
Collins, Everett: 855
Collins, Rev. Lewis John: letters to: 523–5; *A Theology of Christian Action*; *Faith Under Fire*; *The New Testament Problem*, 523n
Collins, Wilkie: *Moonstone*, 210; *Woman in White*, 985
Colombo: 21
Combe Martin (Somerset): 339
Comber (Co. Down): 131
Commission to Revise the Psalter: 1030
Communism: 218, 236n, 327, 328, 344, 345, 358, 368, 456n, 816n, 836
Community of St Mary the Virgin: 261n, 520, 862, 1054, 1056–9
Como, James T.: (ed) *C.S. Lewis at the Breakfast Table and Other Reminiscences*, 719n, 1046
Compensation: 951
Conciliar and Post Conciliar Documents: 1048n
Concilium in Monte Romarici: 834n
Condlin, J.W.A.: 18–9, 75, 355, 368, 384, 385
Confession, auricular: 452, 453, 481, 482, 483, 977, 1015, 1055–6, 1058
Confirmation: 702, 994n
Confucius: *Analects*, 881; men. 561, 771
Congregation of Sisters of the Holy Cross: 140n
Congregation of the Poor Servants of Divine Providence: 798, 799n, 1037–8
Congregation of the Poor Sisters of Divine Providence: 1037
Congregational Church: 383, 719
Connelly, Marc: *Green Pastures*, 580, 586
Conrady, Mrs: 341
Conscience: 351, 501, 551, 623, 676
Conscientious Objection: 233–4, 251, 344–5, 398
Constantinople: 1076
Contemplation: see Enjoyment and Contemplation
Contraception: 798, 1067
Conversion: 914, 929, 948
Conway, James: 1083
Conybeare, John: (with John Saul Howson) *The Life and Epistles of St Paul*, 1008
Cookson, G.: 621
Cooper, John Phillip: (with Joan Thirsk) *Seventeenth-Century Economic Documents*; (ed) *Wentworth Papers*, 415n; men. 414–15
Copernicus: 476, 889
Cornwall: 239n, 781, 1016, 1051
Corpus Christi College (Oxford): 354n, 415n, 460n
Cosman, Milein: 1018
Country Life: 701, 1018
Countryman, The: 69
County Down: 960
Cournos, John: *The Mask*, 1067; men. 1067
Courtly Love: 141, 142, 148n, 186, 190, 379, 712, 834
Covent Garden: 84, 112n, 114, 137, 138
Coverdale, Miles: 422n
Coward, Noël: *Cavalcade*, 114–15
Cowley, Abraham: 686n
Cowper, William: 'On the Loss of the *Royal George*', 259; 'The Cast-Away', 732; *Poetry & Prose*, 21; men. 68, 89, 182n, 644
Crabbe, George: 68, 455, 977
Craftsmanship: 1070
Craig, Gordon: 1916
Cranbrook School (Sydney): 323
Cranmer, Apb. Thomas: *Remains of Thomas Cranmer*, 278n; 185, 278
Crashaw, Richard: 'Hymn of the Nativity', 950; men. 209n, 215n
Crawford, Francis Marion: 830
Crawfordsburn (Co. Down):
Creation: 581, 770, 870–1, 880
Creative Evolution: 870–1
Creatureliness: 514
Criminology: 1066
Cripps, Sir Stafford: 682, 869, 943, 992
Criterion, The: 157, 684, 1029
Croce, Benedetto: *Aesthetics*, 108; men. 157, 252, 391

Crosby, Kate (with A.D.B. Wood) *Terrace and Courtyard Gardens*, 65n
Cross, Frank Leslie: *De Incarnatione: An Edition of the Greek Text*, 516n, 525–6, 528, 554–5
Cross-Channel Boats: 86–7
Crossman, Richard Howard Stafford: *Backbench Diaries of Richard Crossman*, 130n; *Diaries of a Cabinet Minister*, 129n; men. 129–30
Crown of Thorns: 722
Croydon (Somerset): 386
Crucifixion, The: 957
Cuddesdon (Oxford): 18
Cuddesdon College: 2n, 495n
Cullen, Mary: 329, 487
Culture: 252, 332–3, 351n, 401n, 446, 447, 1029
Cumberland: 504
Cumberlege, Geoffrey Fenwick Jocelyn: 681, 721, 749, 810
Cupid: 6n, 41, 566
Cupid and Psyche: 41
Cuthbert's Mission (Cape Province): 1015
Cybele: 980
Cynicism: 773
Czechoslovakia: 231, 836

Dacca University: 360n
Dadaists: 437
Daily Mail: 10, 337n, 931
Daily Mirror: 538
Daily Telegraph, The: 1041n
Dalai Lama, The: 1049
Danae: 973
Danby, Frank: see Arthur Frankau
Dane, Clemence: *White Ben*, 308
Dane Court (Pryford, Surrey): 1039
Daniel: 479n
Dante Alighieri: *Divine Comedy*, 82, 135n, 142, 442, 492, 630, 649, 654, 681, 685–6, 699n, 704, 817, 864–7, 1044, 1071, 1086; *Inferno*, 82n, 163, 700, 886n, 950–1, 994–5, 995–6, 997, 999–1000; *Paradiso*, 82n, 135n, 669n, 903, 1001, 1014, 1072; *Purgatorio*, 82n, 135n, 589, 630, 700, 996; *The Vision or Hell, Purgatory and Paradise of Dante Alighieri* (trans. Henry Francis Cary), 567; men. 16, 164, 184, 219, 288, 292, 348, 391, 576, 649, 655, 669n, 676, 831, 955
Dante Society: 348, 552, 839, 903
Dark Ages: 948
Darling, Charles John, Baron: 319
Darlington (Durham): 275
Dartington Hall School: 254n, 314, 378, 897–8, 1055
Darwin, Charles: 476
David, King: 26n, 196n, 684, 1083
David of Scotland, King: 577n
Davidman, Joy: see Joy Gresham
Davis, Bernard Eustace Cuthbert: *Edmund Spenser*, 313n; (ed. with Elizabeth Davis) *Poets of the Early Seventeenth Century*, 313n; men. 313–14, 340–2
Davis, Elizabeth: 313n
Dawkins, Richard MacGillivray: 227, 348, 403
Dawson, Christopher: *Beyond Politics*, 398; men. 1030
Day, Michael: 301n
D-Day Landings: 625
Deane and Forester: 1061
Death: 119–20, 258, 262, 267, 281, 423, 581, 608, 639n, 652, 653, 656, 659, 660, 669, 688, 692, 783, 970, 986–7, 989, 1008
Debussy, Claude: 946n
Dee, Dr John: 335–6
De fide: 179, 502, 577
Defoe, Daniel: *Robinson Crusoe*, 750n; men. 308
De Gaulle, Charles: 592n
De la Mare, Walter: *The Fleeting*, 127; *Three Mulla-Mulgars*, 652; men. 260, 687, 1063
De La Salle Brothers: 1075
Dell, Carol Jane: 1025
Dell, Rev. Edward T.: biography: 1025; letters to: 914–15, 928–9, 940–1, 988–9, 1005, 1010–11, 1012; *Of Mockingbirds*, 1025
Demeter: 223, 980n
Democracy: 372, 391, 394–5, 398, 455, 548n, 560, 657, 892
Demonology: 449
Demythologizers: 1076–7
Denmark: 389n, 920
Dent, J.M.: 95, 170, 1065
Dent, J.M. (Publishers): Letters to: 100–1, 109, 126
Denton (Oxford): 18
De Peyer, Charles Hubert: 150
Derbyshire: 158–9, 160
Descartes, René: *Discourse on Method*, 42; *Mediations on First Philosophy*, 7n; men. 475n
Despair: 139
Detective stories: 33, 34, 97, 112, 505, 1066–9
Deuteronomy: 149
Devil, The: see Satan
Devils: 205n, 426–7, 505, 512, 512, 515, 594, 642, 924–5, 954
Devotion: 136
Dewey, Thomas E.: 889
Diana: 543
Dickens, Charles: *David Copperfield*, 550; *Dombey and Son*, 671, 729; *Great Expectations*, 898; *Old Curiosity Shop*, 181; *Oliver Twist*, 898; *Our Mutual Friend*, 210; *Pickwick Papers*, 92, 325, 391, 445, 622, 712–13, 898; men. 344, 644, 898
Dijon: 437
Diomedes: 543n
Dionysius the Pseudo-Areopagite: 245
Dionysus: 35, 770n
Discussion Group (Magdalen College): 287–8, 292, 295, 296, 330

Disney, Walt: *Snow White*, 242
Divinity School (Bodleian Library): 293, 339, 346
Dixon, Arthur Lee: 416
Dobrée, Bonamy: *Early Eighteenth Century*, 167n; men. 167, 221
Dobson, Quentin Burrington: 356–7
Dockenfield (Surrey): 1021
Doctrine, Christian: 22, 35, 135, 146, 268–9, 495, 540, 646, 648, 730, 800, 801, 823, 914, 918–19, 962, 1045, 1056
Dods, Marcus: 529n
Dominicans: 815n
Donaldson, Mrs: letter to: 775–6
Donne, John: *Elegies*, 732; *Litanie*, 464, 467; men. 209n, 210, 215n, 353, 670, 734
Dorset: 241
Dorsett, Lyle W.: *And God Came In*, 1080
Dostoevsky, Fyodor Mikhailovich: *Brothers Karamazov*, 32; *Crime and Punishment*, 334
Douglas, Clifford: *Social Credit*, 382n
Douglas, Gavin: 221, 235
Douglas Scheme, The: 382
Douie, Helen McFarlan: 1016, 1017
Douie, Dr William Jones: 1016
Dowell, Rev. Joseph: letter to: 498; men. 493n, 502
Downes, A.H.: 451
Downpatrick (Co. Down): 132
Doyle, Sir Arthur Conan: *Sherlock Holmes*, 34; *Sir Nigel*, 410
Dragon School (Oxford): 428n, 1022, 1075
Dragons: 595
Drayton, Michael: *Nimphidia*, 722
Drew, Victor: 276
Drogheda (Co. Louth): 90n, 790
Dromore (Co. Down): 309n
Drummond of Hawthornden, William: 475
Dryads: 919n
Dryden, John: *A Song for St Cecilia's Day*, 267; men. 210, 644, 703, 748–9
Dualism: 532
Du Bartas, Guillaume de Salluste: *Divine Weeks and Works*, 364–5
Du Boulay, Shirley: *Beyond the Darkness: A Biography of Bede Griffiths*, 1049
Dublin: 165, 170, 787
Duemmler, E.: (ed) *Poetae Latini aevi Carolini*, 609n
Duff, L.T.: 573n
Dulverton (Somerset): 338
Dumas, Alexandre: *Three Musketeers*, 102–3
Dunany (Co. Louth): 787
Dunbar, Eleanor: 1023
Dunbar, William: *Poems*, 843, 844; men. 221–22
Dunbar of Hempriggs, Dame Maureen: 1, 3, 4, 8, 10n, 11, 15, 20n, 44, 58, 75n, 86–7, 90, 128, 131–3, 254n, 276, 277, 279, 281, 290, 308, 312, 315, 316, 317, 325, 331, 359, 361, 363, 389, 405–6, 416n, 430, 431, 432, 434, 504, 579, 637, 706, 786, 818, 1023–4
Dunbar of Hempriggs, Sir Richard: 637, 1023
Duncan, Isadora: 1017
Dundrum (Co. Down): 132
Dunkery Beacon (Somerset): 318, 383
Dunleer (Co. Louth): 309n
Dunlop Rubber Co.: 300n
Duns Scotus: 134n
Dunster (Somerset): 338, 385, 388
Düsseldorf: 416
Dwarfs: 242
Dyson, Henry Victor Dyson ('Hugo'): (with John Butt) *Augustans and Romantics*, 360–1; men. 1, 16–7, 26n, 254, 273, 278, 279, 286, 288–9, 291, 322, 351, 359–60, 365, 382, 385, 424–5, 432, 501, 651, 653, 656, 742, 805, 828, 838, 839, 1054
Dyson, Margaret: 16, 382

Eagle and Child pub ('Bird and 'Baby'): 182, 649, 1084
Early English Text Society: 166n
Earth, The: 431–2, 686
East Anglia University: 411n
Eastbourne: 63, 71
Eastern Nazarene College (Massachusetts): 1025
Eastgate Hotel (Oxford): 288, 368, 530, 552, 1063
East Grinstead (East Sussex): 964
Eadale (Derbyshire): 159
Eddington, Sir Arthur Stanley: 407, 1011
Eddison, Eric Rücker: biography, 1025–8; letters to: 535–6, 541–7, 552–3, 557–9, 570–1, 588–9, 611–13; (trans) *Elgil's Saga Skallagrimssonar*, 1028; *A Fish Dinner in Memison*, 537, 546, 558, 560, 1026, 1027; *The Mezentian Gate*, 545, 708, 1026, 1027; *Mistress of Mistresses*, 536, 541–2, 563, 887, 1026, 1027; *Poems, Letters and Memories of Philip Sidney Nairn*, 1028; *Stybiorn the Strong*, 1028; *The Worm Ouroboros*, 534–6, 541, 542, 546, 559, 560, 563, 612, 680, 694, 716, 746, 1026, 1027; men. 534, 536–7, 553–49, 559–61, 569, 708, 716, 875, 991, 1063
Eddison, Helen Louisa: 1025
Eddison, Dr John: 1025
Eddison, Octavius: 1025
Eddison, Winifred Grace: 1026
Eden: 338
Eden, Anthony: 425n
Edinburgh University: 15n, 336n
Edward VI, King: 278n
Edward VII, King: 831
Edwards, Rev. Maurice: 472, 485

Egypt: 204n, 472n, 637
Einstein, Albert: 75, 638
Élan Vital (Life Force): 870–1
Electric and Musical Industries (EMI): 604–5
Eleusis: 861, 863
Elfland: 103
Elgar, Edward: *Enigma Variations*, 151–2
Elijah: 941, 1013
Elias, Kathy: 353n
Eliot, George: *Middlemarch*, 257, 327, 549; *Romola*, 257
Eliot, T.S.: biography: 1028–30; letters to: 556–7, 561–2, 650–1, 655–6, 658, 661, 663, 680, 704, 708–9, 710; 'A Note on the Verse of John Milton', 556; *Complete Poems and Plays*, 1029; *Four Quartets*, 1029; 'The Love Song of J. Alfred Prufrock', 1029; *Murder in the Cathedral*, 1029, 1069; *Notes Towards the Definition of Culture*, 1029; *Prufrock and Other Observations*, 1029; *The Waste Land*, 163, 1029; men. 94, 134, 157, 163–4, 247, 252, 424, 429, 443, 533, 536, 681, 684, 700, 703, 708, 748–9, 757, 891
Eliot, Valerie: 1029
Eliot, Vivien: 1029
Elisabeth of Belgium, Queen: 701
Elizabeth, St: 532, 802
Elizabeth, Princess (later Elizabeth II): 283, 853, 1063
Elizabeth, Queen (the Queen Mother): 283, 1081
Elizabeth I, Queen: 42, 335
Elton, Oliver: *Essays and Addresses*, 303n
Ely Cathedral: 351, 946: 946n
Ely Theological College
Emmanuel College (Cambridge): 209n, 351n, 435, 585n
Emotions/feelings, 391, 396, 467, 514, 616–7, 632, 635, 644, 657–8, 764–5, 826, 908, 953, 994
English: 621, 664
English Association, The: 867n
English Church Music: 1023
English Club (Magdalen College): 415
English College, The (Rome): 378n, 405, 1075
English Folk Dancing Society: 1016
English High School for Girls (Constantinople): 1075
English Hymnal, The: 417
English Martyrs, Church of (Sparkhill): 1075
English School (Oxford University): 9, 16, 26–7, 66, 81–2, 113, 397, 430n, 431n, 500–1, 1039, 1075
English School (Cambridge University): 209
English Studies: 1028n
Enjoyment and Contemplation: 754
Ensor, J.S.A.: letters to: 604–5, 606–7, 610
Entwhistle, William James: *European Balladry*, 398
Ephesians, Letter to: 9
Epicurus/ Epicureans: 41, 344n, 633, 773, 1003
Episcopal Church (USA): 1005n, 1025, 1078
Episcopal Churchnews: 1083
Episcopalian, The: 1025
Epistles, The: 22–3, 35, 136, 227n, 586, 646
Epson College (Epson): 1076
Erasmus, Desiderius: *Selections*, 683; men. 477n
Eros (Being in Love): 147, 153, 154n, 158, 165, 379, 391, 392–7, 408m 510–11, 512–13, 515, 543, 653, 730, 779n
Escapism: 951
Essays and Studies: 157n, 210n, 342n, 618, 654, 1074
Essays in Criticism: 415n
Essays Presented to Charles Williams (ed. C.S. Lewis): 649–51, 654–5, 658, 661, 662–3, 681, 697, 699, 700, 704, 708–9, 710, 721, 729, 810, 816–17, 821, 861, 864–7, 1084, 1085
Estienne, Henri: *Les Prémices*, 975–6
Eternity: 847
Ethics: 594, 773
Eton College: 1026
Eucharist, The: 301, 646n
Eurydice: 162, 438, 760, 872
Eustace, Robert: (with D.L.Sayers) *The Documents in the Case*, 1069
Evans, Sir David Emrys: letters to: 472–3, 494; *Crefydd a Chymdeithas*; *Llais Rhyddid*; *University of Wales*, 473n; men.
Evans, Idrisyn Oliver: letters to: 584, 640–1, 672–3, 777, 867, 910, 918–19; *Cheer the Chief*, 597; *Coming of a King*, 918; *Discovering the Heavens*, 584n; *Gadget City*, 584n, 640–1; 'The Flinties', 777; *Inventors of the World*, 584n; *Junior Book of Forecasts*, 584n; *Olympic Runner*, 584n; *Peace and the Space Race*, 584n; (ed) *Science Fiction Through the Ages*, 777n; *Woodcraft and World Service*, 641; *World of To-morrow*, 584n
Evans, Sebastian: 562n, 673n
Eve: 338, 496, 566
Every, Rev. Edward: 1030
Every SSM, Br George: biography: 1030–1; letters to: 446–8, 454–7, 466–7, 468–9; *A Christmas Collection*, 1031; *The Baptismal Sacrifice*, 1031; *Basic Liturgy*, 1031; *The Byzantine Patriarchate*, 1031; *Christian Discrimination*, 454–6; *Christian Mythology*, 1031; 'In Defence of Criticism', 446; *The High Church Party*, 1031; *Lamb to the Slaughter*, 1031; *Light Under a Door*, 1031; *Misunderstandings Between East and West*, 1031; 'The Necessity of

Scrutiny', 252, 253, 332, 446; *Poetry and Personal Responsibility*, 1031; (with R. Harris and K. Ware) *Seasons of the Spirit*, 1031; (with J.D.C. Pellow and S.L. Bethell) *Selected Poems*, 1031; *Understanding Eastern Christianity*, 1031; men. 252–4, 771, 779
Every, Rev. George: 1030
Everyman Library: 42
Evil: 121–5, 468, 1010
Evolution: 633, 870–1, 953, 962
Evolution Protest Society: 632n
Ewart, Charles Gordon: 19n, 116, 485
Ewart, Gundreda 'Gunny': see Gundreda Forrest
Ewart, Hope: 116n
Ewart, Sir Ivan: 279
Ewart, Kelso 'Kelsie': 116n, 279n, 486, 907
Ewart, Mary, Lady: 116n
Ewart, Mary Elizabeth 'Lily': 19–20, 116, 485n
Ewart, Sir Robert Heard 'Bob': 116n, 127, 279n, 357n, 487, 549
Ewart, Sir William Quartus: 116n
Exeter Cathedral: 946
Exeter College (Oxford): 19n, 57n, 99n, 289, 292n, 381, 403, 548n, 707n, 839, 1050, 1075
Exford (Someset): 318
Existentialism: 995, 1003
Exmoor: 333, 337, 377n

Faber & Faber: 301n, 650–1, 658, 891n, 961, 1029
Fairies: 385, 400, 919
Fairy Tales: 171, 198, 456, 566, 589, 595, 650, 654, 655, 802, 1039
Faith: 274, 427, 506–7, 523, 573, 652, 656, 659, 770, 948, 983, 987
Fall of Man, The: 262, 450, 455, 460, 463, 585, 632, 723, 747, 754, 962
Falling in Love: 13, 65, 512
Falmouth (Cornwall): 738
Fancy: 204, 205n
Fantasy: 456, 589, 797, 918
Farnham (Surrey): 1021
Farnham Castle (Surrey): 1018
Farnham School of Art (Surrey): 1018
Farrer, Rev. Austin: *A Rebirth of Images: The Making of St John's Apocalypse*, 961; *Finite and Infinite*, 498n; *Freedom of the Will*, 498n; *Glass of Vision*, 498n, 961; *Revelation of St John the Divine*, 498n; men. 498, 612n, 768, 1059
Farrer, Katharine: (trans) *Being and Having*; *Cretan Counterfeit*; *Gownsman's Gallows*, *Missing Link*, 612n; men. 768
Fascism: 327, 328, 780
Fate: see Providence
Fathers of the Church: 206n, 526, 531, 566n, 574n, 646, 914, 1056, 1058
Fauns: 919n, 1041
Faust, 736–7
Fear No More: A Book of Poems for the Present Time: 356n
Feelings: 427
Felix Culpa: 1028
Felstead (Essex): 1063
Feminine: 108, 543, 749
Feminism: 424n, 543, 546, 1075
Fenn, Eric: letters to: 471, 484, 491, 496, 506, 508, 509–10, 522–3, 528, 531, 534, 538, 568, 571–2, 581, 582–3, 582–3, 598–9, 600, 601, 602, 608–9; men. 470–1, 490, 496, 597
Ferrara (Italy): 1037
Feudalism: 953
Field, Walter Ogilvie 'Wof': letter to: 572; men. 162, 321–2, 382, 388, 512
Fielding, Henry: *Tom Jones*, 550, 644; men. 644
Fifth-Columnist: 428
Filmer, Robert: *Patriarcha*, 314
Findon (Sussex): 73
Finland: 311, 337, 350n, 836
Firor, Dr Warfield M.: biography: 1031–2; letters to: 645, 698, 744, 796, 798, 803, 806, 832, 836, 838, 845, 847–8, 849–50, 853, 857–8, 859, 877–9, 888–9, 896, 897, 900–1, 904, 908–9, 913, 916, 918, 920, 921–2, 926–7, 928, 931–2, 934–5, 970–1, 985–7, 1005–8; 'Divine Intercession', 1032; men. 1004n
Fitzgerald, Maurice H.: 421n
Flannery OP, Fr Austin: (ed) *Conciliar and Post Conciliar Documents*, 1048n
Flecker, James Elroy: *A Ship, an Isle, a Sickle Moon*, 312
Fleming, Atherton 'Mac' (Oswald Arthur): *How to See the Battlefields*, 1068; men. 1068–9, 1071
Fleming, John Anthony: 1068, 1071, 1072
Flewett, Henry Walter: (with W.E.P. Pantin) *A First Book of Latin Poetry*, 589; men. 623, 637, 706, 1033
Flewett, Jill: see Jill Freud
Flewett, Winifred: letters to: 623, 636–7; men. 706, 712, 1033, 1036
Florence: 220n, 411n, 658n
Foligno, Cesare Carolo: 349
Folkstone (Kent): 339
Food and Agriculture Organization: 295n
Foord-Kelcey, Rev. Edward: biography, 2; men. 2–3, 31, 38, 39, 61, 62, 83–4, 92, 169, 325, 340
Foord-Kelcey, Mrs Edward: 2
Ford Farm (Eastington): 1044
Foreign Office, The: 71n, 282n, 292n, 316n, 416n
Forman, Maurice Buxton: 196n
Forrest, Gundreda 'Gunny': 116n, 151, 279n, 357n, 486, 549
Forster, E.M.: 252
Foster, Stephen: 546n

Fox, Rev. Adam: biography: 1032–33: *Old King Cole*, 1033; men. 15, 282, 287, 293, 342, 355–6, 359–60, 425, 474, 488, 518
Fox-hunting: 2, 434
France: 14, 231, 285–6, 344, 357, 358, 363, 368, 402, 412, 437, 451, 495n, 519n, 572n, 625n, 738, 814, 816, 829, 839, 851n, 920, 1061, 1073, 1075
France, Anatole: 773
Francis, C.N.: letter to: 618
Franciscans: 848
Franco, Francisco: 368, 736n
François de Sales, St: *Introduction to the Devout Life*, 301
Frankau, Arthur: 209
Franklin Street Church (Baltimore): 1032
Frederick the Great: 273, 402
Frederika Louisa, Queen (wife of Frederick the Great): 402
Freedom: 398
Free love: 424n
Free Will: 409–10, 453, 585, 764, 802, 813, 814, 915, 956
Freiburg-im-Breisgau (Germany): 537n
French Revolution, The: 429n
Freud, Sir Clement: *Freud Ego*, 1036n; men. 1035–6
Freud, Dominic: 1036
Freud, Emma: 1036
Freud, Ernst: 1036
Freud, Jill, Lady: biography: 1033–6; letters to: 589–90, 637–8, 706–7, 712, 739, 805–6, 805–6, 827–8, 1001–2; men. 603, 622–3
Freud, Lucian: 1036
Freud, Lucie: 1036
Freud, Matthew: 1036
Freud, Nicola: 1036
Freud, Sigmund: 476, 618, 723, 1036
Freudians: 896–7
Fridama, N.: letter to: 702–3
Friendship: 101, 150, 174, 228, 408, 510, 512, 577, 653, 685n, 779n, 858
Froissart, Jean: *Chroniques*, 52–3
Frost, Brian: *An Unknown Glastonbury Mystic: The Reflections of Marjorie Milne*, 1054
Fuller, Margaret: letters to: 639, 849
Fuller, Roy: 'Translation', 951
Furse, Jill: 774, 1081

Gabriel, Archangel: 74
Gaia: 980n
Gainsborough, Thomas: 341
Galahad, Sir: 249, 903n
Galsworthy, John: *Forsyte Saga*, 64, 127, 887
Galt, John: *The Entail*, 327; men. 505
Galway, Miss: 341
Gardner, Ralph: 574n
Garnett, Maxwell: 416n
Garrod, Heathcote William: *Epigrams*; *Oxford Book of Latin Verse*; *Poetical Works of John Keats*; *Wordsworth*, 477n; men. 477
Gasch, Fritz Otto: 1021
Gates, Edith: letter to: 616–17
Gems of Literature, Elegant, Rare, and Suggestive: 309–10
General Theological Seminary (New York): 370n
Genesis: 354, 390n, 423, 571, 807
Geneva: 32, 379n
Genius: 149, 154, 777
Geoffrey Bles Ltd (London): 1019
Geoffrey of Monmouth: *Histories of the Kings of Britain*, 673
George, St: 337n, 1026
George V, King: 114n
George VI, King: 469n, 681n, 1081
George Allen & Unwin Ltd: 1018
Germany/Germans: 128, 129n, 231, 269, 270, 276, 277, 290, 291, 311, 352–3, 355, 368, 389n, 402, 404–5, 414, 416n, 425, 426, 435, 478, 522, 625n, 647, 717, 737, 740, 854n, 873, 930, 1049, 1051
Gethsemane: 258, 266–7, 764, 813, 814
Ghana: 661n
Ghosts: 651, 665
Giants: 144, 171, 594–5
Gibb, Jocelyn: (ed) *Light on C.S. Lewis*, 1079n, 1080
Gibbon, Edward: *The History of the Decline and Fall of the Roman Empire*, 675
Gibbon Club, The: 344
Gibraltar: 1, 14n
Gibson, John Michael: (with Richard Lancelyn Green) *A Bibliography of A. Conan Doyle*, 1042–3
Gifford Lectures, The: 479
Giggleswick School: 360n
Gilbert, Sir Martin: *Second World War*, 269–70
Gilbert, W.S. and Arthur Sullivan: *Iolanthe*, 670; *The Mikado*, 665
Gillies, G.D.: letter to: 625
Gillman, James George: letter to: 567; *Divine Journey*, 285, 567
Gilmore, Rev. Charles James Frederick: 472
Gilson, Etienne: *Moral Values*; *Philosophie au Moyen Age*; *System of St Thomas Aquinas*, 142; *La Théologie Mystique de Saint Bernard*, 451
Giovanni Calabria, St: biography: 1036–9: letters to: 800–1, 803–5, 806–7, 813–16, 829–30, 842–5, 867–9, 978–9, 998–9; *Amare*, 806, 807; *Apostolica Vivendi Forma*, 806, 807; *Letters: C.S. Lewis – Don Giovanni Calabria*, 615n, 799, 800, 1015–16; *Una Gioia Insolita: Lettere tra un prete cattolico e un laico anglicano*, 799n, 844n, 998n, 1038; men. 798–800, 821n, 1015–16
Girton College (Cambridge): 209n, 1003

Gladding, Miss: letters to: 659–61
Gladstone, William Ewart: 711n
Gladstone of Hawarden, Lady: 519n
Glasgow: 111, 115
Glasgow University: 147n, 366
Glastonbury: 701n, 1054
Glastonbury Thorn: 722
Glaucus: 543
Glendinning, Miss: 1026
Glenmachan/ Glenmachonians: 116n, 131, 279n, 357, 367, 488, 549, 710
Gloucester: 5n, 363, 508
Gnosticism: 451n
God the Father: 7, 8, 13, 21, 37, 43, 71, 74, 90, 92, 105n, 108, 118–20, 121–5, 128, 134, 135, 136, 137, 146, 149, 153, 158, 161, 162, 163, 169n, 174, 177, 189, 201, 206, 207, 223–4, 225–6, 232, 233, 236n, 244, 258, 262–3, 264, 265n, 266–9, 277, 278n, 283, 327, 351, 357, 372, 379, 390, 391, 394, 396, 401n, 408–10, 411, 421, 423, 427, 431–2, 449, 455n, 458–66, 475n, 478–9, 480, 483–4, 499–500, 502, 503, 507, 510, 511, 514n, 519, 522, 526–7, 532, 535, 541, 543, 555, 565–6, 568n, 571n, 576, 581, 585, 587, 591, 592, 595, 601, 605, 616–7, 620n, 621, 632, 637, 646, 647, 656, 668, 684, 692–3, 703n, 717, 722, 730, 733, 740, 747, 764–5, 770, 776n, 777, 788, 799, 800, 801–2, 803, 804, 813–16, 817, 823–4, 826, 829–30, 841–2, 847, 848, 857, 860, 863, 864, 868, 870–2, 880, 897, 904, 905, 908, 914–15, 928n, 929, 940, 944, 953, 956–7, 959, 960, 962, 967, 971, 975–6, 978, 979, 980, 989–90, 994, 1006n, 1007, 1013, 1015, 1038, 1064
Godfrey, Catherine: 1066
Godfrey, Baron Elton: *St George or the Dragon*, 540
Godolphin School (Salisbury): 1065
Godwin, William: *Political Justice*, 224, 919
Goethe, Johann Wolfgang von: *Das Märchen*, 441; *Dichtung und Wahrheit*, 260n; *Faust*, 737; men. 895
Golden Blade, The: 665n
Golden Cross Restaurant (Oxford): 102, 365, 400, 424–5
Goldsmith, Oliver: *Deserted Village*, 352
Goliath: 683
Gollancz, Victor: 753n
Gomorrah: 218
Gonda (India): 1053
Good, The: 1027
Goodridge, Jonathan Francis: 936; (trans) *Piers the Ploughman*; *The Raw Side*, 936n
Goodridge, J.S.: letter to: 936
Good Shepherd, The: 9
Goodness: 283, 373
Googe, Barnabe: 236
Gordon, George Stuart: 271, 275, 288
Gordon, Mrs George Stuart: 288
Gordon, Janet: 288
Gore, Charles: *Jesus of Nazareth*, 125, 529; *Philosophy of the Good Life*, 321, 324, 375, 529
Gospels, The: 1, 5, 9, 22–3, 31, 35, 70, 266, 374–5, 522, 540, 765, 989, 1019, 1045, 1077
Gouvernail, Sir: 783
Gower, John: *Confessio Amantis*, 149
Graham, David: (ed) *We Remember C.S. Lewis*, 11n
Grahame, Kenneth: *The Wind in the Willows*, 347, 881
Grace: 194, 362, 368, 447–8, 722, 771, 779, 800, 801, 829, 975
Graf Spee: 305n
Grail, Holy: 35, 562, 723n, 913n
Grandmaison, Léonce de: *Personal Religion*, 618n; men. 618
Grand Siecle: 6
Grant, Mrs H.E.: letter to: 768
Granth Sahib: 1048
Graves, Robert: *I, Claudius*, 505
Gray, Thomas: *Elegy Written in a Country Church-Yard*, 361
Great Bookham: 66, 101, 117, 402, 413
Great Marlow: 2n
'Great War': 55n, 107–8, 199, 870, 945
Greece: 52, 1026, 1039, 1042, 1043, 1073
Green, Candida Lycett: (ed) John Betjeman, *Letters*, Vol. I, 1022; *Letters*, Vol. II, 1023
Green, Frederick C.: 76n
Green, Gilbert Lancelyn: 1039, 1040
Green, Helena Mary Phyllis Lancelyn: 1039
Green, June Lancelyn: 1040, 1042, 1043
Green, Priscilla Lancelyn: see Priscilla Lancelyn West
Green, Roger Lancelyn: biography, 1039–43; letters to: 236–7, 670–2, 767, 896, 887, 896–7, 939; *The Adventures of Robin Hood*, 1042; *A.E.W.Mason*, 1040; *Andrew Lang*, 1040; (with Walter Hooper) *C.S. Lewis: A Biography*, 472n, 923, 1030, 1043; *Diaries of Lewis Carroll*, 1040; *Fifty Years of Peter Pan*, 1040; *From the World's End*, 767; *Heroes of Greece and Troy*, 1042; *Into Other Worlds*, 1042; *J.M.Barrie*, 1040; *King Arthur*, 1042; *The Land of the Lord High Tiger*, 1041; *Luck of the Lynns*, 1041; *The Luck of Troy*, 1041; *Mrs Molesworth*, 1040;

Green, Roger Lancelyn – *cont.* *Mystery at Mycenae*, 1041; *Myths of the Norsemen*, 1042; *Poulton-Lancelyn*, 1041; *The Saga of Asgard*, 1042; *The Secret of Rusticoker*, 1041; *The Story of Lewis Carroll*, 1040; *Tellers of Tales*, 1040, 1042; *The Theft of the Golden Cat*, 1041; *The Wonderful Stranger*, 1041; (unpublished) 'The Wood That Time Forgot', 670–2, 949–50; *Works of Lewis Carroll*, 1040; men. 474n, 706n, 923, 952
Green, Richard Lancelyn: (with J.B. Gibson) *A Bibliography of A. Conan Doyle*; 1042–3; (ed) *The Adventures of Sherlock Holmes*, 1043; men. 1042–3
Green, Scirard Lancelyn: 1040, 1042, 1043
Green, T.H.: 15n
Green Gates Nursing Home (Oxford): 1075
Greeves, Arthur: letters to: 1, 11–4, 22–5, 33–5, 51–4, 64–7, 85–7, 92–3, 95–7, 101–4, 110–12, 113–26, 126–9, 150–2, 159–61, 165, 169–72, 174–5, 179–81, 190–1, 212–14, 215, 274, 412–13, 485–8, 503–5, 538–40, 548–50, 579–81, 594–6, 639–40, 692–5, 709–10, 755–6, 789, 907–8, 945, 946–7, 952–3, 956–7, 959–60, 985; men. 21, 83–4, 131, 202n, 279n, 304n, 310n, 440n, 527n, 703n, 787, 814n, 955n
Greeves, John (brother of Arthur Greeves): 908
Greeves, Joseph (father of Arthur Greeves): 756
Greeves, Mary Margretta Gribbon (mother of Arthur Greeves): 22n, 25, 33, 54, 97, 104, 129, 131, 161, 165, 172, 175, 214, 274, 413, 487, 505, 581, 596, 694, 710, 907–8
Greeves, Thomas Jackson: 66, 413
Gregory VI, Pope: 283n
Grensted, L.W.: *Psychology and God*, 376
Gresham, David: 1080
Gresham, Douglas: 1080
Gresham, Joy: 1043, 1063–4, 1079–80
Gresham, William: 1080
Grief: 652
Grierson, Sir Herbert: *Cross Currents in English Literature*, 211; *Essays*, 428n; *Milton and Wordsworth*, 211; men. 209n, 361
Griffiths OSB, Dom Bede: biography 1043–9; letters to: 133–7, 150, 176–9, 187–90, 191–5, 200–3, 216–17, 224–6, 233–4, 256–8, 325–7, 390–2, 422–3, 500–3, 531–2, 576–7, 617–8, 647–9, 746–8, 770–1, 841–2, 880–1, 948, 953–4; *A Human Search* (documentary film): 'The Adventure of Faith', 1046; *Christian Ashram* (*Christ in India*), 1048; *Cosmic Revelation*, 1048; *Golden String*, 178n, 1044, 1045, 1046, 1047; *Marriage of East and West*, 1048; *New Creation in Christ*, 1049; *New Vision of Reality*, 1048; *Return to the Centre*, 1048; *Universal Wisdom*, 1049; *Vedanta and Christian Faith*; 1048; men. 55, 56, 63–4, 71–4, 152, 230–1, 379n, 498, 1053, 1085
Griffiths, Elaine: 349
Griffiths, Harriet: 1043
Griffiths, Walter: 1043
Griggs, Mrs Alice: biography: 1050; men. 108n, 279, 342, 417
Griggs, Rev. David Barnes: 1050
Griggs, Miss Rhoda Rose: biography: 1050; men. 279, 281, 342, 417
Grimm, Jacob Ludwig Carl: 589, 595
Grimm, Wilhelm Carl: 589, 595
Groom, Bernard: *Diction of Poetry from Spenser to Bridges*; *Literary History of England*; *Short History of English Words*, 600n; men. 600–1
Guardian, The: letters to: 532–3, 668; men. 367, 389, 404, 422, 426n, 483, 504, 573n, 635
Grundy, J.B.C.: 724n
Guénon, René: 204, 1052
Guest, Lady Charlotte: (trans) *The Mabinogion*, 902
Guillaume de Lorris (and Jean de Meun): *Romance of the Rose*, 142, 149, 438, 440, 609
Guinevere, Queen: 887
Guy's Hospital (London): 839
Gynes, J.W.: 537

Haberdashers' Askes' Hampstead School (Hampshire): 510n
Habich, Eduard: 79n, 114
Hades: 759, 760
Hadfield, Alice Mary: 745; *An Introduction to Charles Williams*; *Charles Williams: An Exploration of His Life and Work*, 745n; men. 744–5, 767
Hadfield, Ellis Charles Raymond: 745n
Haggard, Henry Rider: *People of the Mist*, 33, 40; men. 120, 144
Hainault Forest (Essex): 1060
Haiti: 295n
Haldane, John Burton Sanderson: 'Auld Hornie', 236n; *Possible Worlds*, 236–7, 255, 407, 594, 715
Halifax, Lord (Edward Frederick Lindley Wood): 366–7
Hall, John R. Clark: (ed) *Beowulf*, 644
Hall, Joseph: *Virgidemiarum*, 334
Hall, Bishop Ronald Owen: 859–60

Ham Testimonial, The: 839
Hambledon (Buckinghamshire): letter from: 109
Hamilton, Augustus Warren 'Gussie': 212, 279, 313, 485n, 580, 694
Hamilton, Sir George Rostrevor: letters to: 707–8, 716, 743, 767, 966–7; *Bergson and Future Philosophy*, 708n; *Collected Poems and Epigrams*, 708n; *Hero or Fool? A Study of Milton's Satan*, 707–8; *Landscape of the Mind*, 708n; 'The Prose of E.R. Eddison', 1027–8; *The Tell-Tale Article*, 966–7, 972; *Unknown Lovers*, 708n; men. 972
Hamilton, Rev. Thomas Robert: 68n, 80, 132n, 390
Hamm, Victor: letter to: 666–7; (trans) *Of Being and Unity*; *Language, Truth, and Poetry*, 666n; 'Mr Lewis in Perelandra', 666–7
Hampton Court: 616
Hanbury-Sparrow, Arthur Alan: *Land-Locked Lake*, 103, 104–6, 156n; *Gilt-Edged Insecurity*, 162; men. 156, 162
Handley, Tommy: 927n
Hankey, Donald: 548n
Hansel and Grettel: 299
Hardenburg, Friedrich Leopold von ('Novalis'): *Heinrich von Ofterdingen*, 440; men. 441, 753
Hardie, Alex M.: (with K.C. Douglas) *Augury*, 547n
Hardie, Christian: 288n, 435, 1078
Hardie, Colin: 288, 292, 435, 619, 838, 839, 1078
Hardy, Thomas: *Dynasts*, 223–4; men. 218, 773
Harrington, Rev. Roy W.: letter to: 830–1
Harris, Richard: (with G. Every and K. Ware): *Seasons of the Spirit*, 1031
Harrow School: 292n, 460n, 509n
Hart-Davis, Rupert: (ed) Arthur Ransome, *Autobiography*, 1026n; (ed) *Two Men of Letters: Correspondence Between R.C. Hutchinson, novelist, and Martyn Skinner, poet, 1957–1974*, 1073
Hartford Seminary: 289n
Harvard University: 145n, 221n, 287n, 415n, 477n, 567n, 666n, 1028
Harvey, Gabriel: (with Edmund Spenser) *Three Letters Between Two Universitie Men*, 655
Harvey, John W.: 204n
Harwood, Alfred Cecil: letters to: 138–40, 155, 199–200, 216, 669–70; *A Rope Their Pulley*, 688, 689–90, 692; *Voice of Cecil Harwood*, 199–200, 688n, 690n; *Way of a Child*, 420; men. 7, 39, 55n, 64, 71, 108, 129, 130, 137, 156, 162, 199, 230, 238, 239, 261, 299–300, 315, 318–22, 338, 339, 377n, 381–8, 512, 513, 530, 572, 634, 664, 809, 834, 899, 942, 965, 1051
Harwood, Alice Daphne: 1052
Harwood, Hon. Daphne: biography, 1050–1; letters to: 107–8, 129–30, 238–9, 510–13, 513–4, 669–70, 808–9, 912–13, 964–5; men. 216, 318, 382, 420, 634
Harwood, Janet: 1052
Harwood, John Olivier: 238, 299, 318, 420, 634, 751, 809, 1051
Harwood, Laurence Hardy: biography: 1051–2; letters to: 634, 696–7, 737–8, 751, 819–20, 897–9; men. 130, 216, 238, 318, 512, 691, 965
Harwood, Lois: 634, 897–8, 965, 1051
Harwood, Mark: 634, 1051
Harwood, Matthew Henry: 1052
Harwood, Melissa: 1052
Harwood, Sylvia: 634, 965, 1051
Harwood, Rev. William Hardy: 383n
Hassall, Christopher: *Devil's Dyke*, 518
Hatton, William Kembrey: 276, 323, 580, 596
Havard, Grace: 365
Havard, Dr Robert Emlyn 'Humphrey': 182, 313, 324, 342, 344, 358, 365, 405, 416–17, 425, 432, 436, 501, 638, 838, 839, 904, 943–4, 1008
Hawthornden Prize: 561n, 1061, 1073
Hayes, Rev. Ernest William Carlisle: 19, 132
Hayes, Gerald: letters to: 560–1, 562–3; *Charting the Seas in Peace and War*; *Introduction to Charts and Their Use*, 560n; men. 559–60, 1028
Hayes, Renée: 821n
Hayes (Middlesex): 604
Hayley, William: 259n
Hazlitt, William: 21n
Headington Quarry: 2–3, 7n
Headington School: 86n
Healing: 656
Healy, John: 233n
Healy, Michael: 19n
Heath-Stubbs, John: (ed) *Collected Plays by Charles Williams*, 410n
Heaven: 177, 235, 241n, 256, 265n, 324, 403, 451, 453, 459, 465, 474, 481, 507n, 526, 585, 617, 685n, 703, 733, 843, 844, 863, 868, 869, 882, 952, 960, 971, 1014n
Hebert, A.G.: 147n
Heber, Reginald: 321
Henty, George Alfred: 273
Herbert, George: 209n, 215n, 376, 644
Hebrew: 263n, 264, 266, 479, 1008
Hebrides: 48
Hector: 267n
Hegel, Georg Wilhelm Friedrich: 771, 1010n

Hegelianism: 771
Heidelberg: 416n
Helen of Troy: 197, 306, 886, 887
Helensburgh (Dunbartonshire): 111n, 115
Helen's Bay (Co. Down): 959
Hell: 135n, 218–19, 256n, 438, 450–1, 453, 465, 466, 526, 585, 608, 617, 639n, 666n, 687, 703, 710, 953, 997, 1082
Helsinki: 311n
Hemans, Felicia: *Forest Sanctuary*, 259; men. 309
Henderson, Keith: 1026, 1028
Hendon (Middlesex): 1023
Henn, Thomas Rice: *The Bible as Literature*, 112n; *Longinus and English Criticism*, 112; letter to: 111
Henry, Vera: 90, 133, 315, 336, 365, 366, 622, 706
Henry VII, King: 930
Henry VIII, King: 813, 815, 1057, 1062
Heraclitus: 773
Hereford (Herefordshire): 517
Herodotus: *Histories*, 320, 989
Herrick, Robert: 'Upon Julia's Clothes', 731
Herrtage, Sidney J.H.: 166n
Hertford College (Oxford): 370n
Hewitt, Richard Thornton: 277, 400
Hewlett, Maurice Henry: *Lore of Proserpine*, 549
Heysham (Lancashire): 946
Highgate Junior School (London): 1022, 1029
High History of the Holy Grail: 65, 562
Hill, George Birkbeck: 246n
Hillegas, Mark R.: (ed) *Shadows of Imagination*, 1080
Hillier, Bevis: *John Betjeman*; *Young Betjeman*, 1023
'Hillsboro': 75, 297n
Hilltown (Co. Down): 945
Hilton, Walter: *The Scale of Perfection*, 326, 644, 994
Hindenburg University: 416n
Hindhead (Surrey): 509
Hindus: 173, 615, 1046–9
Hinduism: 204, 225, 318, 329, 770–1, 1053
Hippolytus: 269n
Historicism: 948
Hitchman, Janet: *Such a Strange Lady*, 1069
Hitler, Adolf: 128, 129n, 231, 289, 291, 351n, 367, 368, 389, 391, 404n, 408, 425, 647, 804, 927n
HMS Achilles: 305n
HMS Ajax: 305n
HMS Cossack: 355n
HMS Exeter: 305n
Hoare, Alfred: *Italian Dictionary*, 492
Hodge (the cat): 71
Hodgson, Ethel Margaret: 370
Hodgson, Rev. Leonard: *Doctrine of the Trinity*, 754; men. 370
Hoffman, Paul Gray: 869
Holland: 289, 414, 416
Hollywood (California): 900
Holst, Gustav: *The Planets*, 693, 701–2, 710
Holy Communion: 30, 42–3, 67, 132–3, 301, 371, 377, 394, 411, 426, 660, 722, 843, 844, 994
Holy Grail: 65
Holy Sepulchre, The: 639n
Holy Spirit, The/ Holy Ghost: 23n, 358, 448, 566n, 620n, 632, 656, 717, 722, 975, 1006n
Holy Trinity, The: 417, 581, 603, 764, 789, 800, 801, 863, 914, 928n, 940n, 941n, 1082
Holy Trinity Church (Headington Quarry): 2, 7n, 8–9, 21, 30, 42, 118, 174, 272, 273, 277–8, 279, 284, 290, 299, 306, 324, 335, 342, 352–3, 354, 359, 362, 365, 377, 417, 426, 432
Holy Trinity, Headington Quarry, Oxford, 1849–1999: 272
Home Guard: see Local Defense Volunteers
Home Rule (for Ireland): 10
Homely, the: 21, 103, 181
Homer: *Iliad*, 267, 543, 564n; *Odyssey*, 456, 516, 564n; men. 164, 360, 533, 535, 546, 548n, 794, 1026
Homosexuality: 229
Hone, Sir Brian William: *Critic Practice and Tactics*, 323n; men. 323–4, 325, 404
Hong Kong: 859, 860
Hood, Basil: *Count of Luxenbourg*, 50n
Hooker, Richard: *Of the Laws of Ecclesiastical Polity*, 528–9, 644, 647; men. 476, 936
Hooper, Walter: (with R.L. Green) *C.S. Lewis: A Biography*, 472n, 923, 1030, 1043; *C.S. Lewis: A Companion & Guide*, 15n, 88n, 127n, 181n, 182n, 213n, 282n, 288n, 292n, 854n, 891n, 1016n, 1017, 1033; 'The Lectures of C.S. Lewis in the University of Oxford and Cambridge', 141n; *Past Watchful Dragons: The Narnian Chronicles of C.S. Lewis*, 952n; *Through Joy and Beyond*, 160n, 1019; men. 1020, 1032, 1041n, 1058
Hope: 523, 983
Hope, Edward: biography, 58
Hopkins, Gerard Manley: 294, 339, 683
Hopkins, Gerard Walter Sturgis: letter to: 744–5; men. 293–4
Horace: *Ars Poetica*, 991; *Odes*, 300–1; *Satires*, 697; men. 703
Horizon: 756
Horner (Somerset): 319, 339, 384
Horspath (Oxfordshire): 371
Horwood, Chesney: 16
Houghton, Rev. Ralph Edward Cunliffe: *Influence of the Classics on the Poetry of Matthew Arnold*, 378n; men. 378

Housman, A.E.: *A Shropshire Lad*, 248; men. 252, 326n
Howard, Walden: letters to: 824, 831, 840, 852
Howson, John Saul: See John Conybeare
Hrothgar: 679
Hughes, H.C.: (ed) *St Hilda's Hall Verse*, 1076
Hughes, Thomas: *Tom Brown's Schooldays*, 69n
Hugh of Victor, St: 1056, 1058
Hugh-Jones, Edward Maurice: biography, 28–9; (with E.A.Radice) *American Experiment*, 28n; *Woodrow Wilson and American Liberalism*, 28
Hugh-Jones, Mrs Edward Maurice: 28–9
Huish's Grammar School (Taunton): 1024
Hull, R.F.C.: 440n
Humanism/Humanists: 134n, 145n, 474–8, 512, 534, 804, 805
Humanitarianism: 657
Hume, Cardinal Basil: 1049
Humility: 261, 346, 356, 372, 447, 523, 764, 780, 844–5, 868, 869
Hunt, Leigh: 421
Hunter, G.K.: 167n
Hunter, Jeanne Clayton: 665n
Hurd, Richard: *Letters on Chivalry and Romance*, 563
Hurnard, James: *Setting Sun*, 716; men. 743
Hutchinson, R.C.: (ed. Rupert Hart-Davis) *Two Men of Letters: Correspondence Between R.C. Hutchinson, novelist, and Martyn Skinner, poet, 1957–1974*, 1073
Hutchison, Sir William: 1072
Hutton, Edward: *Catholicism and English Literature*, 576n
Huxley, Aldous: 24
Hyde Park (London): 1017
Hymn Society of Great Britain and Ireland: 719n
Hymns: 719–20, 740–1
Hymns Ancient and Modern: 417, 456

Iamblichus of Chalcis: 541
Ibadan University College (Nigeria): 469n
Ibsen, Henrik: 441
Iceland: 638
Icelandic: 197, 1026
Idealism: 15n, 108, 133–4, 145, 225, 703n
Ideologies: 416
Ilford (Essex): 1060
Ilfracombe (Somerset): 339
Ilkley (Yorkshire): 1051
Imagination: 12, 171, 191, 201, 204, 205n, 234n, 375, 389, 424n, 432, 439, 445, 477n, 501, 527, 534, 565, 595, 630, 632, 644, 693, 730, 756, 797, 924n, 953
Imitation of Christ: see Thomas à Kempis
Immaculate Conception, The: 179
Immortality: 216, 233, 611, 651, 1006
Imperial College (London): 471n, 615n
Imperial Library (Calcutta): 954n
Imperial News Bulletin, The: 303
Incarnation, The: 192, 451n, 462, 526–7, 581, 624, 667, 693, 764–5, 857, 863, 904, 905, 1070
India: 5n, 328–9, 376n, 564n, 615, 661n, 842, 880, 1018, 1047–8, 1049
Indian Civil Service: 70, 1018
Indian Medical Service: 1053
India Office: 615n, 954n
Indulgences: 813, 815
Inklings, The: 16n, 99n, 181–2, 219, 283, 288–9, 293–4, 336, 342, 359–60, 365 404–5, 410, 416–17, 433, 436, 501, 553–4, 560, 649, 682, 736, 745, 838–9, 850, 872, 879, 888n, 1032, 1042, 1078, 1084, 1085
Innocent III, Pope: *On the Misery of the Human Condition*, 269n
Institut Catholique (Paris): 134n
Interplanetary Society: 344
Institute for Medieval Studies (Toronto): 134n
Ipsden (Oxfordshire): 1073
Iraq: 472n
Ireland: 10, 131–3, 144, 787, 856, 928, 984
Irenaeus, St: *Adversus Omnes Haereses*, 451; men. 451, 453
Irish, the: 38
Iron Curtain, The: 911
Isaac: 565, 566
Isaiah: 228n, 351, 555
Isidore of Seville: 609, 949
Islam: 329, 870
Isle of Wight: 125, 1043
Isoud, Queen: 781n
Isoud/ Isolde, Princess: 512n, 781–6, 887
Isoud of the White Hands: 781n
Israel: 263, 637n
Italy/Italian: 231, 349, 359, 368, 405, 572n, 867, 868, 1000–1, 1036–8
It's That Man Again: 927

Jacks, Lawrence Pearsall: *Life and Letters of Stopford Brooke*, 580n; men. 580
Jackson, Robert Wyse: *Jonathan Swift*, 405
Jacob: 192
Jamaica: 1050
James, St: Epistle, 84–5, 169, 576, 829, 857, 954
James II, King: 510n
James, David Gwilym: *Scepticism and Poetry*, 424
James, Henry: 556
Jameson, Storm: *The Pot Boils*; *Lovely Ship*, 579n; men. 579
Janet, Paul-Alexandre: *Histoire de la Science Politique*, 120
Jansenism: 951
Japan: 44–5, 46, 67, 269
Jean de Meun: see Guillaume de Lorris
Jeans, Sir James: *Mysterious Universe*, 431; men. 407, 1011

Jehovah's Witnesses: 344, 345
Jenkin, Alfred Kenneth Hamilton: letters to: 239–43, 244–7; men. 222
Jenkyns, Henry: 278n
Jeremiah: 983
Jersey: 403n
Jerusalem: 538, 624, 752n
Jesuits: 73, 683
Jesus Christ: 1, 35, 43, 93, 125, 135n, 146, 154n, 177, 186, 191–4, 208, 227, 233–4, 258, 265, 266–9, 283, 307, 351n, 369, 374–5, 381n, 390n, 391, 395, 408, 410, 417, 448, 449, 462, 479, 492n, 493, 494, 495, 499, 502, 503, 512, 521–2, 526–7, 532–3, 555, 566n, 572–3, 586, 592, 605, 608, 620n, 624, 625, 631, 639n, 646, 651, 653–4, 656, 659, 660, 693, 722, 747, 748, 764–5, 799–800, 803, 804, 813–16, 822, 823–4, 829–30, 842, 843, 844, 848, 857, 861, 863, 904, 905, 915–16, 928, 940, 941n, 948, 953, 956–7, 968, 978, 979, 988, 989, 998, 999, 1003, 1006n, 1013, 1037, 1047, 1048, 1049, 1070–1
Jesus College (Cambridge): 1073, 1074
Jesus College (Oxford): 6n, 70, 424n, 472n
Jews: 128, 276, 396, 416n, 771, 773, 941, 1013, 1046
Joachim, Harold Henry: 292
Job, Book of: 327n
Jodl, General Alfred: 647
Johannes Sixtinus: 683n
John, St: Epistles, 194n, 857; Gospel of, 70, 122, 208, 764, 778n, 799–800, 813, 814, 816, 823, 857, 905, 906, 915, 916; Revelation, 463, 490, 717, 822n, 961; men. 9n, 586
John the Baptist, St: 192, 532
John Lane The Bodley Head: 862
John Main Lectures: 1049
John Paul II, Pope: 1038
Johns Hopkins University (Baltimore): 1031–2
Johnson, Dr Samuel: *History of Rasselas*, 402; *Lives of the Poets*, 246, 406, 686; *Memoirs of Charles Frederick, King of Prussia*, 402; *Rambler*, 228–9, 408, 477, 497, 977; *Vanity of Human Wishes*, 373; men. 2n, 4, 40, 48–9, 50, 53, 68, 71, 203, 210, 222, 242, 304, 309, 319, 329–30, 337, 362, 393, 406, 426, 432, 492, 503, 513, 547, 638, 644, 897n, 912, 974, 977, 1079
Jones, Mrs Frank L.: letters to: 699, 764–5
Jonson, Ben: *Works*, 81; men. 164, 373, 491n
Joseph, St: 31, 968
Joseph of Arimathea: 70, 232, 722
Joseph (son of Jacob): 354
Journal of the British Interplanetary Society, 752n
Jove: 187, 620, 1008
Joy (as inconsolable longing and 'sweet desire'): 12, 88n, 882, 896–7, 985
Joyce, James: *Ulysses*, 1024; men. 163, 252, 557
Judaism: 35, 70, 870
Judas Iscariot: 577, 803, 804, 818n
Julian of Norwich, Lady: *Revelations of Divine Love*, 369–70, 377, 392, 418, 529, 644, 994
Julius Solinus: *Collectanea Rerum Memorabilium*, 612
Jung, Carl: *Archetypes and the Collective Unconscious*, 440
Jupiter (the planet): 230, 298, 312, 348, 693, 701–2, 751
Justification by Faith, 502
Just War: 250–2
Juvenal: 163

Kaemke, Ernst: 353n
Kafka, Franz: *The Castle*, 199, 439, 440; *Trial*, 439; men. 440
Kalevala: 724
Kant, Immanuel: 418, 421, 466
Kate Greenaway Medal: 1020
Kavanagh, Ted: 927n
Kaye, Sir: 784, 785
Keats, George: 196n
Keats, Georgiana: 196n
Keats, John: *Endymion*, 11–12, 13; *The Fall of Hyperion*, 951, 955; *Hyperion*, 11; 'La Belle Dame sans Merci', 589; *Lamia*, 919; *Letters*, 196, 518; Ode to a Nightingale', 268; *Poetical Works*, 477n; men. 247n, 309, 421, 454, 955
Keble, Rev. John: *The Christian Year*, 321n; men. 303n, 321
Keble College (Oxford): 28, 182n, 277n, 302, 365n, 403n, 498n, 1015, 1056
Kedar: 905
Keele University: 28n
Keir, Sir David Lindsay: 17, 245
Kelly, Fr Herbert: *No Pious Person*, 1031; men. 1030
Kenchew, Mr: 58–60
Kennedy, Warnett: 743n
Kentucky: 796
Ker, William Paton: 326n
Kerala: 1047
Kernan, Julie: 375
Keswick (Cumbria): 1024
Ketley, Martin: (with Alec King) *The Control of Language*, 561, 810–11
Kidbrooke Park (Forest Row): 669, 691, 696, 738, 964, 1051
Kidd, Rev. Beresford James: *A History of the Church to AD 461*, 1056; men. 1056
Kidlington (Oxford): 19n
Kierkegaard, Søren Aabye: 440
Kilkeel (Co. Down): Letters from: 86–7, 131–3; men. 132, 133n
Kilns, The: letters from: 14–21, 22–5, 25–32, 33–5, 45–8, 48–51, 51–4, 55, 56–7, 57–63, 67–76, 76–9, 85–6, 88–90, 90–1, 92–3, 95–7, 101–4,

104–7, 108–9, 113–21, 126, 126–9, 150–4, 156–8, 159–61, 169–72, 174–8, 176–8, 198–9, 203, 212–14, 217–18, 222–4, 238–43, 244–7, 247–9, 260–1, 264–9, 272–84, 286–325, 333–67, 371–90, 397–412, 414–19, 421–2, 424–37, 441–8, 485–8, 500–6, 510–13, 527–8, 530–1, 548–50, 574–5, 577–9, 582–3, 589–90, 594–6, 618–9, 625, 634, 636–7, 656–7, 668–72, 692–7, 746–8, 805–6, 834–5, 863–4, 870–3, 879–81, 929–30, 937–8, 945–6, 959, 976–7, 985; men. 1, 2, 8, 13, 6–15, 17, 18, 21, 25–6, 31, 38, 44, 47, 53, 64–7, 90, 108n, 117, 130, 160, 190, 213, 261, 270, 273, 281, 286–7, 295–6, 304–5, 309–10, 311–15, 333, 336, 340, 342, 359, 365–6, 370–1, 377, 383, 389, 399, 400–1, 407, 415, 430, 434, 486, 530n, 538, 579, 586–7, 622–3, 636, 696n, 738, 751, 767, 786–7, 817, 905, 944, 957, 959, 1033–5, 1080

King, Alec: (with Martin Ketley) *The Control of Language*, 561

King, Don W.: 'The Anatomy of a Friendship: The Correspondence of Ruth Pitter and C.S. Lewis', 685, 1061

King, Venerable Francis: 309n

King, Jane: 309n

Kingdom, Rev. Henry Paul: 292

King Alfred's College (Winchester): 292n, 1024

King Kong (film): 120, 910

King's College (Cambridge): 1076

King's College (University of London): 510n, 658n, 1024

King's Gold Medal for Poetry: 1081

King's Regulations and Air Council Instructions for the Royal Air Force, The, 517

King's School (Ottery St Mary): 1030

Kingsley, Charles: *Hereward the Wake*, 33–4, 41; *Water-Babies*, 288; men. 232n, 994n

Kinsley, James: 844n

Kipling, Rudyard: *Barrack-Room Ballads*, 306; *Departmental Ditties*, 389n; 'Heriot's Ford', 306; 'If- ', 306; *Just So Stories*, 819; *Kipps*, 64; *Light that Failed*, 306; *Limits and Renewals*, 388n; 'McAndrew's Hymn', 7, 306; *Plain Tales from the Hills*, 328; *Seven Seas*, 7n; men. 223, 385, 867

Kipling Journal, The: 1042

Kirby, W.F.: (trans) *Kalevala*, 724

Kircher, Athanasius: *Iter Exstaticum Coelestre*, 237

Kirk, Kenneth: *The Vision of God*, 775, 993

Kirkpatrick, William Thompson ('Great Knock'): 75, 444, 702

Klaeber, Friedrich, (ed) *Beowulf*, 643

Knight, G. Wilson: *Chariot of Wrath*, 548

Knox, Anne: 'The Model Church', 971

Knox, John: *First Blast of the Trumpet*, 19n

Knox, Monsignor Ronald: *A Spiritual Aeneid*; *Enthusiasm*; *Let Dons Delight*, 769n; (trans) *The New Testament*, 769n, 941; *The Old Testament*, 769n; men. 769, 779

Knudson, Albert Cornelius: 914n

Koeppler, Heinrich: (with M. Garnett) *A Lasting Peace*, 416n; men. 416

Koran, The: 1048

Kosterlitz, Rolf Werner: letters to: 489, 513, 787; men. 805

Kranidas, Thomas: 665n

Kreyer, Lt-Col. and Mrs J.A.C.: 38, 279n

Kuhn, Helmut: *Encounter with Nothingness*, 995n, 999

Kurisumala Ashram: 1047

Kuwait: 411n

Labour Party: 10, 150n

Lady Margaret Hall (Oxford): 147n, 584n, 954n

La Fontaine: *Les Amours de Psyché et de Cupidon*, 6

Lake Iroquois (Vermont): 1080

Lamb, Charles: *Essays of Elia*, 95, 255, 428, 549; *Last Essays of Elia*, 349; (with Mary Lamb) *Letters*, 72–3, 549; *Letters* (Everyman), 84; men. 6, 89, 222, 1003

Lambeth Conference: 860

Lambeth Palace: 766, 860

Lamp-Post, The: 270n

Lancashire: 1075

Lancashire Fusiliers: 839

Lancing College: 15n, 1032

Landon, Margaret: letter to: 642; *Anna and the King of Siam*, 642

Lang, Andrew: 650, 654, 1025, 1039, 1040

Langland, William: *Piers Plowman*, 141, 735, 936n

Langlois, Ernest: 438n

Language: 36–7

Lanier, Sidney: *Poems*, 970

Larne (Co. Antrim): 18

Larne Harbour (Co. Antrim): 333

Laski, Harold Joseph: *Danger of Being a Gentleman*, 336

Latham, Henry: *Pastor Pastorum*, 283

Latham, Jean: 1026, 1028

Latimer, Hugh: 353n, 488n

Launcelot, Sir: 678, 679n, 785

Laurel Bank School (Glasgow): 147n

Laurie, Werner: 509n

Law, William: *An Appeal to All That Doubt*, 5, 13, 40; *Serious Call to a Devout and Holy Life*, 5, 13, 40, 645; men. 1007

Law Journal Report: 69
Lawlor, John: *C.S. Lewis: Memories and Reflections*, 248n, 369n
Law of Inattention: 983
Lawrence, D.H.: 252, 455n, 536
Lawson, Frederick Henry: biography, 17
Lawson, Rev. Frederick Robert: 1055
Lawson, Laura Penelope: 1055
Layamon: *Brut*, 673, 887
Laywitness: 645n
Lazarus: 764
Lea, Kathleen: 954
League of Nations, The: 44–5, 884
Lean, Edward Tangye: 181
Leavis, F.R.: 252, 467, 468, 779
L'Ecole des Roches: 1066
Leda: 381n
Lee, Kum Sing: 625n
Lee, Rev. Roy Stuart: letters to: 626–7, 628–9, 633, 667; *Freud and Christianity*; *Principles of Pastoral Counselling*, 626n; men. 627
Lee, Sidney: 355
Lee, Stephen Grosvenor: 286–7, 347, 378
Leeds (Yorkshire): 1025
Leeds Clergy School: 472n
Leeds Public Library: 1028
Legends: 1039, 1042
Lehar, F.: 50n
Le Havre: 90, 279, 851n
Leibniz, Gottfried Wilhelm: 188n
Leider, Frida: 79n
Lenin, Vladimir Ilich: 119
Leningrad: 350n
Leo I, St: 1056
Leo X, Pope: 813, 815
Leo XIII, Pope: *Aeterni Patris*, 134n, 179n; men. 844n
Leonidas of Tarentum: Poem 740, 616
Leprechauns: 240, 344
Le Saux, Fr Henri: 1048
Lesotho: 615n
Le Tréport: 333
Lewes (Sussex): 71–2
Lewin, Ronald: letters to: 891, 892–3
Lewis, Agnes: 353n
Lewis, Albert James 'P'daytabird' (father of CSL): 14, 14n, 15n, 18n, 19n, 34, 44, 54, 57, 61, 104, 111, 116n, 127n, 133n, 161, 220n, 273, 279n, 294n, 311, 313, 328, 329n, 340, 355, 361, 364, 421–2, 426n, 487, 1029
Lewis, Charlton T. Lewis (and Charles Short): *Latin Dictionary*, 149
Lewis, Clive Staples: 'afforestation; of Kilns, 2, 4, 15, 25–6, 29–30, 37, 46, 62–3, 66–7, 80–1, 90, 95, 96, 217, 380, 397, 414, 417; Agapony fund, 483, 508, 530, 711, 827–8; age, on, 755–6; animals, observations of, 6, 44, 118, 128, 179–80, 214, 288, 316, 362, 495–6, 520–1, 525, 540, 543–4, 551, 571, 618–9, 634, 656, 737, 751, 754, 788, 819, 899, 993; Anglican-Catholic controversy, 135–6, 150, 170, 176–7, 178–9, 226, 234, 256–7, 502, 645–7, 813–16, 863; arguer, is an, 718; autobiographical writings, 77–8, 79, 87; bathing, 81, 117; BBC talks, 490, 508, 522–3, 524, 531, 601–2, 603, 608–9, 626–9, 633, 797, 891, 892–3, 1046; Bible, on, 9; book-annotating, 53; Christian reunion, on, 234, 256–7; Christmas card, hatred of, 307–8; Chronicles of Narnia, 923–4, 941–3, 952, 980, 1018–22, 1018–22, 1042; church-going, 8–9; churchmanship, 285; cold, love of, 8; confession, 452, 453, 1015; conversion to Christianity, 1, 467, 501, 575, 702–3, 729, 747, 824, 830–1, 870, 929, 948; dating of letters, 14; detective stories, 64; dogmatic Christianity vs. quasi-Christian slush, 351; duty towards the elderly, 818; effect on others, 605–6, 608–9, 610; estimate of self, 755; evacuated children, and, 270, 273, 274, 276, 277, 279, 282, 289, 290, 451, 515; evaluating other people's writings, 763n; examining for Schools and Scholarships, 81–2, 85, 91, 111, 127, 358, 363, 523, 524, 583, 584, 595, 683, 700, 746; exhaustion, 943–5; fairy-tale, failure with, 802; friendships, 35, 174; genius, on, 82; happiness, on, 334–5, 373, 379, 409; holidays in Ireland, 86–7; honorary D.D., receives, 706, 716; Hooker, the great formulation of Anglicanism, 647; humanized animals, 264–5; hymns, dislike of, 719–20, 740–1; Inklings meetings, 16, 181–2, 283; interruptions, on, 595, 818; invigilating, 80, 111; Ireland, love of, 132; language, on, 36–7; laziness (Accidie), his besetting sin, 422, 591, 978, 979; letter-writing, on, 601, 641, 683, 707, 948, 980; *Lion, the Witch and the Wardrobe*, writes, 923–4, 941–3; loves, the four, 6, 73, 101, 147, 150, 153, 154n, 158, 165, 174, 202, 228, 234, 257, 379, 391, 392–7, 408–10, 423, 510–13, 514, 522, 530, 577, 653, 779n; *Magician's Nephew* started, 952; men and women, 172, 507, 541–2, 546–7, 716, 860, 861, 863; 'Mere Christianity' ('common ground'): 135–6, 179, 502; miseries of the world, how to feel about, 350, 419, 747–8, 842–5, 951; modern fiction, 64–5, 66; musical

evenings at home, 128, 152; Narnia, beginning of, 923; 'Nat Whilk', use of: 218n; 'nostalgia for the non-existent' (longing), 753–4; ordinary day, 14–5; Pauline Baynes chosen to illustrate Narnia, 1019–20; pets, 6, 11; P'daitaism, 20n; 'peeve' favourite: 831; planets and stars, interest in, : 36, 230, 298, 312, 397, 413, 431–2, 528, 686, 693, 697, 701–2, 725, 726, 743, 751, 910, 919; pleasure in using English forcibly, 187–8; poet, effort to become, 679, 684; poetry, Ruth Pitter on his, 882; praying for the dead, 989; Prolegomena lectures, 140–1, 212, 236, 246–7, 1039, 1043; pseudonym, 'Nat Whilk' or 'N.W.', 424n; *Perelandra*, favourite among books, 600; *Prince Caspian*, idea for, 952, 980; pupils, 24; rational opposition, love of, 708; Religion vs. Christianity, 657; Royal Air Force, talks to, 485, 490, 492, 493, 504, 515, 517, 523–5, 586, 661–2, 665–6; sacraments, 43; *Screwtape Letters*, conception of, 426–7; sermons, 489; Stagnation Party, interest in, 369; talent for writing, 905–6; theological reading, 5, 40; 'translator' of Christian doctrine, 673–5; T.S.Eliot, case against, 163–4; tutorials, 15–6, 20, 767; twitch of the tether and loss of promise, 986; United States, invitations to, 567–8; Vine President of Magdalen, 504; Wagner's operas, 77, 78, 79, 84; walks, solitary, 299, 300, 304, 309, 357, 370–1, 379–80, 401, 540, 596; ways of writing, 797; weather, interest in, 22, 74, 96, 117–8, 128, 171, 174–5, 239, 241, 284, 304, 323, 330, 340, 357, 359, 397, 540, 875, 966, 985; Williams, Charles, death of, 649–54, 656, 659; worries about brother, 44–7, 54, 67, 939, 943–4, 952–3, 959, 960

Writings (published): (with Owen Barfield) *A Cretaceous Perambulator*, 155; *A Grief Observed*, 1080; 'A Panegyric For Dorothy L. Sayers', 1072; *A Preface to Paradise Lost*, 246n, 450n, 494, 508–9, 531, 538, 539, 541n, 556, 574, 577, 779n, 1029–30; 'A Sacred Poem', 247n, 249, 252; 'A Tribute to E.R. Eddison', 534, 1028; 'A Village Experience', 668; *The Abolition of Man*, 545, 558, 561, 614, 672n, 756, 779n, 810–11; 'After Kirby's *Kalevala*', 724n; *All My Road Before Me*, 46n, 58n, 286n, 291n, 297n, 336n, 416n, 1016, 1022; *Allegory of Love*, 1, 98, 127, 141n, 142, 148n, 149n, 154n, 168, 169–70, 173, 174, 181, 184, 186, 190, 191, 195, 197, 199, 203, 552, 609, 665–6, 712n, 834n, 929, 1061, 1084; 'Answers to Questions on Christianity', 610; 'Apologist's Evening Prayer', 527; (with Charles Williams) *Arthurian Torso*, 562n, 655–6, 723n, 744–5, 767–8, 885–6, 1083; 'Autobiographical Poem', 77–8, 87; *Beyond Personality*, 597–9, 600, 601–2, 603, 605–6, 626, 628, 639–40, 775, 776, 823n, 891n; 'The Birth of Language', 711, 725–6, 893; 'Bluspels and Flalansferes', 107n; *Boxen*, 270n, 349, 410, 437–8; 'Break, Sun, my crusted earth', 356n; *Broadcast Talks*, 470–1, 484–5, 486, 490–2, 496, 498, 502, 503, 504, 505, 506, 509–10, 518, 521–2, 524, 526, 776n, 823n, 1046; *Christian Behaviour*, 408n, 522–3, 525, 528, 531, 534, 538, 569, 627, 823n; 'The Christian in Danger' (see 'Learning in War-Time'); *Christian Reflections*, 252n, 333n, 362, 401n; 'Christian Reunion', 234n; *Christian Reunion and Other Essays*, 234n; 'Christianity and Culture', 252, 332–3, 446–7 (an essay); 'Christianity and Culture', 412 (a letter); *Chronicles of Narnia*, 554n, 924, 1041–2; *Collected Letters of C.S. Lewis I*, 3n, 7n, 8n, 10n, 16n, 20n, 69,, 75n, 76n, 83n, 99n, 111n, 116n, 127n, 132n, 133n, 151n, 157n, 202n, 239n, 279n, 304n, 334n, 353n, 388n, 390n, 426n, 486n, 549n, 814n, 1029n; *Collected Poems*, 137n, 527n, 547n, 651n, 665n, 687, 762n, 790, 792–5, 875n, 893n, 972n, 1006n; 'Conditions for a Just War', 250–2; 'Dangers of National Repentance', 367; 'Dante's Similies', 348n; 'Different Tastes in Literature', 709; *Discarded Image*, 141n, 153, 541n, 919n, 1043; 'Donkey's Delight', 790–2, 835, 945–6; 'Donne and Love Poetry in the Seventeenth Century', 209, 210; *Dymer*, 98, 112, 172, 679, 872, 957, 1054; 'The Efficacy of Prayer', 276n, 362; *English Literature in the Sixteenth Century*, 168, 221–2, 235–6, 246n, 475n, 551–2, 679n, 812, 815n, 877; 'Epigrams and Epitaphs', 972n; 'Epitaph in a Village Churchyard', 972; *Essay Collection*,

Lewis, Clive Staples
Writings – *cont.*
234n, 250–2, 276n, 308n, 362, 367n, 434n, 610, 788n; (ed) *Essays Presented to Charles Williams*, 649–51, 654–5, 658, 661, 662–3, 681, 697, 699, 700, 704, 708–9, 710, 721, 729, 810, 816–8, 821, 861, 864–7, 1084, 1085; 'Essence', 356n; 'Fern-seed and Elephants', 1077; *Fern-seed and Elephants and Other Essays*, 1077; *The Four Loves*, 154n, 408n, 1080; 'From the Latin of Milton's *De Idea Platonica Quemadmodum Aristoteles Intellexit*', 664; (ed) *George MacDonald: An Anthology*, 653, 705, 709, 768, 937; *God in the Dock*, 532, 863n; *The Great Divorce*, 483, 617, 619, 635, 648, 657, 698, 700, 705, 744, 775–6, 790, 891n, 1078; 'Hamlet: The Prince or the Poem?', 520n, 555–6; 'Hermione in the House of Paulina', 547; 'Is Theology Poetry?' 714–15; 'It All Began with a Picture . . .', 923–4; 'Kipling's World', 867; *The Last Battle*, 135n, 1022; 'Late Summer', 875; 'Learning in War-Time' (= 'The Christian in Danger'), 353n, 451; 'Lefay Fragment', 952; *Letters: C.S. Lewis – Don Giovanni Calabria*, 615n, 799–801, 904–6, 1038; *Letters of C.S. Lewis*, 975n; *Letters to Malcolm*, 137n, 646n; *The Lion, the Witch and the Wardrobe*, 820n, 923–4, 941–3, 949, 952, 961, 966, 980n, 1009, 1017, 1019, 1038, 1041–2; *The Magician's Nephew*, 952, 980n; *Mark vs. Tristram: Correspondence between C.S. Lewis and Owen Barfield*, 781n; *Mere Christianity*, 408n, 483, 499n, 501–2, 503, 522n, 526n, 717, 871n, 1062; *Mere Christianity: An Anniversary Edition*, 582n; 'Miracles', 532–3, 573n; *Miracles: A Preliminary Study*, 573, 591, 592, 640, 648, 657, 715n, 769, 777, 778, 786, 809n, 848, 1078; 'The Morte Darthur', 781; 'Mr C.S. Lewis on Christianity', 605–6; 'The Necessity of Chivalry', 434; 'The Novels of Charles Williams', 1084; *Of This and Other Worlds*, 236n, 242n, 534, 650n, 709n, 924n, 1027n, 1072n, 1084n; 'On Being Human', 727–8; 'On Church Music', 1023; 'On Science Fiction', 242n; 'On Stories', 649, 817, 866; 'On the Atomic Bomb', 688–9, 691–2; 'On the Death of Charles Williams', 665; 'Open Letter to Dr Tillyard', 210n, 1074; 'Our English Syllabus', 422n; *Out of the Silent Planet*, 218, 219–20, 233, 234–5, 236–7, 242, 254–5, 261–2, 264, 376, 413, 450, 458, 459, 480–1, 504, 542, 543, 547, 569, 571, 588–9, 630, 667, 699n, 729, 743n, 753n, 862, 1057; 'Pattern', 230; 'Peace Proposals for Brother Every and Mr Bethell', 401n, 446; *Perelandra*, 182n, 496, 504, 508, 517, 520, 527, 547, 554, 556, 569, 570–1, 574, 576, 578, 588n, 593–4, 600–1, 630, 645, 666–7, 686, 741n, 746, 789n, 830, 915n, 1058, 1078–9; (with E.M.W. Tillyard) *The Personal Heresy: A Controversy*, 157n, 248n, 249, 256, 260, 443, 1074; 'The Personal Heresy in Criticism', 156n, 210n, 1074; *Pilgrim's Regress*, 87–8, 92–3, 94–5, 97–101, 103–4, 109–10, 126, 127, 128, 156, 164n, 170, 176–7, 193–4, 256n, 265, 285, 314, 376, 450, 492, 612, 679, 1065; 'Poem for Psychologists and/or Theologians', 356n; *Poems*, 218n, 495n, 665n, 725n, 726n, 727n, 762n, 790n, 792n, 794n, 875n, 972n, 990n, 1006n; 'Prayer', 137n; *Present Concerns*, 434n; 'Priestesses in the Church?', 863; *Prince Caspian*, 952, 980, 1019, 1020; *The Problem of Pain*, 289, 302, 308, 342, 353n, 392, 409n, 449–50, 458–66, 469, 470, 514, 518, 519, 558, 569, 584, 593n, 788, 929, 956n; 'Psycho-analysis and Literary Criticism', 342, 618; *Reflections on the Psalms*, 322n; *Rehabilitations*, 249, 255, 422n; 'Relapse', 495, 1006; 'Religion in the Schools', 540; Review of G.A.L. Burgeon (Owen Barfield), *This Ever Diverse Pair*, 938n; Review of Claude Chavasse, *The Bride of Christ*, 379n; Review of Denis de Rougemont, *Passion and Society*, 379n; Review of E.K.Chambers, *Sir Thomas Wyatt*, 166n; Review of Logan Pearsall Smith, *Milton and His Modern Critics*, 467; 'Scazons', 651n; 'Scraps', 788; *The Screwtape Letters*, 426–7, 483, 493, 497, 504–5, 508, 511n, 514, 533, 573n, 593, 614n, 639, 753, 758, 798, 799, 821, 830, 847, 849, 924–5, 1037, 1061; *The Screwtape Letters and Screwtape Proposes a Toast*, 614n; *Screwtape Proposes a Toast and*

Other Pieces, 489n, 714n; *Selected Literary Essays*, 107n, 217n, 520n, 867n; *The Silver Chair*, 213; 'Socratic Wisdom', 715n; 'Sonnet', 218, 990; *Spirits in Bondage*, 872; *Studies in Medieval and Renaissance Literature*, 348n, 781n; *Studies in Words*, 209n; *Surprised by Joy*, 47n, 55n, 75n, 77n, 83n, 116n, 134n, 292n, 342n, 410n, 702n, 703n, 754n, 770n, 877, 929, 1040n; *That Hideous Strength*, 342n, 348n, 544, 571, 574, 596, 624, 634, 635, 640, 657, 667, 668, 672–3, 682, 686, 692, 701–2, 717, 819n, 930, 933, 993, 1078; *Timeless at Heart*, 234n; 'To C.W.', 726–7; 'Transposition', 926; *Transposition and Other Addresses*, 353n, 926; 'Two Kinds of Memory', 758–62; *Undeceptions*, 610, 863n; 'Vitrea Circe', 794; *The Voyage of the 'Dawn Treader'*, 1017, 1019; 'The Weight of Glory', 489, 490, 607, 652; 'What the Bird Said Early in the Year', 15n; 'Why I Am Not a Pacifist', 234n; 'William Morris', 217; 'Xmas and Christmas', 307n; 'Young King Cole', 792–4

writings (unpublished), 'Metaphysices contra Anthroposophos' (or 'Summa'), 55, 107, 199, 872; 'P'daita Pie', 50; 'Prose "It"' (early unpublished autobiography), 87

Lewis, Edwin: 1010n
Lewis, Eileen: 353
Lewis, Florence Augusta 'Flora' (mother of CSL): 19n, 68n, 116n, 288, 305, 708, 747, 875n, 921
Lewis, John Llewellyn: 963
Lewis, Richard (father of Albert Lewis): 305n
Lewis, Richard (brother of Albert Lewis): 111n, 115, 310, 314, 329, 332, 353
Lewis, Warren Hamilton 'Warnie' (brother of CSL): letters to: 1–11, 14–21, 25–32, 36–44, 45–8, 48–51, 57–63, 67–76, 79–85, 90–1, 131–3, 270–3, 272–3, 275–84, 286–325, 333–71, 376–90, 397–412, 414–18, 421–2, 423–8, 430–7; *Brothers and Friends*, 5n, 14, 30n, 270n, 319n, 337n, 636, 682, 786, 787, 922, 943–4, 1035, 1036, 1050; 'The Galleys of France', 817; 'Memoir', 613; men. 14, 30n, 34n, 44–5, 54, 64, 85, 89, 92, 95, 97, 101, 111, 115–17, 125, 127, 128, 137, 143, 152, 156, 161, 169, 182, 213, 240, 244, 270, 274, 285–6, 413, 451, 486, 501, 504, 538n, 539, 549, 553, 579, 580, 582, 596, 603–4, 618n, 637, 638, 652, 672, 682, 687, 699, 706, 736, 739, 746, 786–7, 789, 790, 805, 818, 827n, 828, 838, 839, 840, 855, 856, 858, 883, 890, 902n, 904, 908, 920n, 922, 927, 931, 935, 939, 943–5, 952–3, 957, 958, 959, 960, 864, 964, 973, 983, 984, 1005, 1012, 1034–6, 1050
Lewis, W. & R., Rope Manufacturers: 111n
Lewis, William 'Limpopo' (brother of Albert Lewis): 111n, 115, 310, 314, 389, 418, 421
Lewis Centenary Stone: 15n
Lewis Papers: 14, 49–50, 85
Leyland, Margaret: 270n
Leyser, Karl Joseph: *Medieval Germany*; *Rule and Conflict in an Early Medieval Society*, 416n; men. 415–6
Liberia: 615n
Life Force: see *Élan Vital*
Lilith: 255, 541
Limbo: 255n, 256
Lincoln, Abraham: 857
Lincoln Cathedral: 144, 376n
Lincoln College (Oxford): 166n, 167n, 416n, 1011n
Lindsay, David: *Voyage to Arcturus*, 151, 170, 236, 440, 541, 630, 753
Lindsay, Vachel: *The Daniel Jazz*; *General William Booth*, 736
Lings, George Herbert: 1052
Lings, Gladys Mary: 1052
Lings, Martin: biography, 1052–3; *Book of Certainty*, 1053; *Collected Poems*, 1053; The *Elements and Other Poems*, 1053; *The Heralds and Other Poems*, 1053; 'René Guénon', 1052; *Muhammad: His Life Based on the Earliest Sources*, 1053; *Symbol and Archetype*, 1053; *What is Sufism?*, 1053; men. 24, 39, 90, 204, 615
Lisle, Arthur Plantagenet, Viscount: 1066n
Listener, The: letter to: 605–6; men. 509, 603, 951
Literae Humaniores (Classics): 403n, 432n, 707n, 752, 769n, 1026, 1044
Literary Criticism: 156–7, 163–4, 209–12, 253–4, 533–4
Literature and Life: 867
Li Tim-Oi, Florence: 859–60
Little Lea ('Leeboro' and 'Leeborough'): 17, 20, 36, 95, 114, 116n, 133, 297, 305, 329n, 330, 332, 487, 1040
Little People (faerie folk): 395, 400
Little Theatre, The (Sheffield): 872
Liturgy: 76n
Liverpool: 165, 693, 1043
Liverpool College: 1039
Liverpool University: see University of Liverpool
Livy: 637
Llewellyn, Evan Clifford: *Influence of Low Dutch on the English Vocabulary*, 425n; men. 424–5, 430–1

Lloyd, Frank: 114n
Lloyd George, David: 399–400
Lloyd's Bank: 1029
Local Defense Volunteers/ Home Guard: 425–6, 432, 433, 434, 436, 447, 573n, 606
Loch Lomond: 115
Loch Long: 115
Locke, Hubert G.: 353n
Locke, John: *Two Treaties of Government*, 314
Lockhart, John Gibson: *Memoirs of the Life of Scott*, 60, 89, 91, 96, 102
'Lockley', 'Mrs': letters to: 975–6, 977, 979–80, 982–3
Lodetti, Dr Romolo: letter to: 821–2; *I Fioretti de Don Calabria*; *Il corpo umano: per un raccordo mente-corpo-società*, 822n; men. 829, 830
Lodge, Thomas: *Rosalyn*, 776
Logic: 134n, 150, 292n, 373, 689, 691, 778, 867
Logres: 245, 247n, 249n, 253, 497, 684, 783, 784, 785, 816, 886n
Lombar, Frank D.: letter to: 921
London: 54, 222, 239, 244, 270n, 293n, 421, 790, 797, 805, 932, 964, 984, 1016, 1026, 1050, 1051, 1061, 1062, 1064, 1067, 1069, 1072, 1082, 1083, 1084, 1086
London County Council: 1083
London Philharmonic Orchestra: 170n
London School of Economics: 341n, 1002
Long Crendon (Buckinghamshire): 1016, 1063
Longfellow, Henry Wadsworth: *Hiawatha*, 222
Longinus: 112n
Longleat House: 661n, 666n
Lord's Day Observance Society, The: 580n
Lord's Prayers, The: 957, 960
Lorimer, George Horace: *Letters of a Self-Made Merchant to his Son*; *Old Gorgon Graham*, 894
L'Osservatore Romano: 1038
Louis XVI, King: 427
Lovelace, Richard: 'To Lucasta, Going to the Wars', 732
Lowes, John Livingston: *Art of Geoffrey Chaucer*; *Convention and Revolt in Poetry*; *Road to Xanadu*, 477n; men. 477
Lubbock, Percy: *Earlham*, 362
Lucas, Frank Laurence: *Decline and Fall of the Romantic Ideal*, 209–10, 211
Lucas, Madeline: 1077
Lucas, Perceval: 1077
Lucas, St John: (ed) *Oxford Book of French Verse*, 6; men. 930n
Luccombe (Somerset): 318, 338–9
Lucian: 1042
Luck: 802
Lucretius: *De Rerum Natura*, 477n, 731, 747; men. 344n, 773, 967
Ludlow (Shropshire): 240
Luke, St: Acts of the Apostles, 227n, 927, 935, 948; Gospel of, 31, 93, 136, 192, 453, 502n, 532, 646, 764, 733, 802, 857, 944, 948, 956–7, 957, 1013; men. 9, 13
Luther, Martin: 165n, 232n, 813, 815, 1057
Lutheran Church: 352n, 353
Luxborough (Somerset): 386
Lyddiatt, Frederick David: 15, 80
Lyell, Mr: letter to: 631–2
Lyme Park (Cheshire): 788
Lyndsay, David: 235
Lynmouth (Somerset): 339

Mabinogion, The: 902
McAleer, Neil: *Arthur C. Clarke*, 1025
MacCallum, R.B.: 1008
McCarthy, Desmond: 336, 428
Macaulay, Rose: *Mystery at Geneva*, 32; men. 273, 276, 277
Macaulay, G.M.: 52n
Macaulay, Thomas Babington: *History of England*, 675; men. 697n
McClain, Mr: letter to: 641
McClurg, William Moncrief: 212n
McDermot, Niall: 519n
MacDonald, George: *Diary of an Old Soul*, 172; *The Disciple*, 710; (ed. C.S. Lewis) *George MacDonald: An Anthology*, 653, 705, 709, 768, 937; 'The Giant's Heart', 802; 'The Golden Key', 802; 'The Light Princess', 802; *Lilith*, 118–20, 124, 125, 263, 500, 541, 575; *Phantastes*, 22, 263, 453, 500; *The Princess and Curdie*', 639, 802; *The Princess and the Goblin*, 639, 802; *The Seaboard Parish*, 709; *Short Stories*, 802; *Sir Gibbie*, 263, 709; *Unspoken Sermons*, 376, 529, 616, 639; *Wilfred Cumbermede*, 419, 709; *The Wise Woman*, 802; men. 43, 66, 92, 96–7, 103, 183, 396, 438–9, 404n, 451, 539, 617n, 629, 703, 753, 936–7
MacDonald, Greville: 118
MacDonald, Ramsay: 10
Macdonald, William: 84
McEldowney, Mary McQueen: 'The Fairy Tales and Fantasies of George MacDonald', 96–7
McFarlane, Kenneth Bruce: 57, 59, 127, 578
MacKail, John William: 443
McKenna, Stephen: *Confessions of a Well-Meaning Woman*, 349
Mackenzie, William James Millar: *British Government Since 1919*; *Free Elections*; *Power, Violence, Decision*, 336n; men. 336n, 370, 408

McKerrow, Ronald B: (ed) *The Works of Thomas Nashe*, 397n, 886
MacKinnon, D.M.: *Vexilla Regis*, 259; men. 332
Maclean, J.K.: 510n
McNeill, James Adams: 97n, 127n
McNeill, Jane 'Tchainie': 97, 127, 151, 169, 342n, 357, 400, 413, 486, 487, 503, 538–9, 549, 581, 596, 710, 755, 907, 952, 959, 985
McNeill, John T.: 289n
McNeill, Mary Cunnigham: 97, 127n, 413, 486, 487–8, 505, 549, 581, 755
Machiavelli: 236
Madeleva CSC, Sister: *Chaucer's Nun*; *Four Last Things*; *Knights Errant*; *Lost Language*; *My First Seventy Years*; *Pearl*; *Penelope*; *Selected Poems*, 140n; letters to: 140–3
Maenads: 770
Maeterlinck, Maurice: *Pelléas et Mélisande*, 946
Magdalen College (Oxford): letters from: 1–11, 36–44, 78–9, 79–85, 87–8, 97–8, 107–8, 109–13, 126, 129–30, 138–43, 155–6, 163–7, 172–3, 179–81, 187–98, 195–8, 199–203, 209–12, 214–17, 218–22, 224–9, 233–5, 243, 247, 249–54, 255–60, 261–4, 270–1, 285–6, 325–7, 332, 367–71, 390–7, 412–13, 420–1, 422–4, 437–40, 448–9, 452–7, 459–85, 488–500, 506–10, 513–27, 528–9, 531–48, 550–73, 575–7, 579–82, 583–9, 590–3, 597–618, 619–25, 626–33, 635–6, 639–55, 657–68, 672–86, 697–710, 712–46, 748–805, 806–34, 835–63, 866–70, 873–9, 883–929, 930–7, 938–45, 946–59, 960–76, 977–85, 985–1014; men. 1, 4, 5, 15–6, 24–5, 30, 36, 38–9, 46–7, 57–8, 64, 74, 76, 140, 150n, 164n, 178n, 181–2n, 190n, 229, 248, 271, 272, 275–6, 277n, 286–8, 290, 292, 295, 296, 298, 299, 300, 311, 314, 329, 333, 335–6, 346–7, 348, 356, 357, 376n, 377–8, 398–9, 403, 404–5, 411, 413, 414–7, 432, 436, 468, 504, 517n, 519n, 520, 525, 530, 536, 537, 540, 547, 552–4, 579, 583, 601, 615, 618–9, 622, 634, 637, 667, 683n, 690–1, 701, 719n, 742, 751, 754, 763, 790n, 808, 839, 845, 846, 861, 883, 903, 921–2, 923, 925n, 928, 929, 933, 936, 959, 993, 1009, 1019, 1022, 1033, 1043–4, 1052, 1061, 1065, 1072, 1078
Magdalen College School (Oxford): 291n
Magdalene College (Cambridge): 209n
Magic: 475, 672, 841–2
Magnificat: 802n
Mahieu, Fr Francis: 1047
Malapropisms: 69, 415
Malone, Edmond: *An Attempt to Ascertain the Order in Which They Plays Attributed to Shakespeare Were Written*, 886
Malory, Sir Thomas: *Morte D'Arthur*, 65, 89, 117, 166–7, 217, 512, 562, 644, 673, 1041; (ed. E. Vinaver) *The Works of Sir Thomas Malory*, 780–6
Malvern: 72, 240n, 242, 786, 818, 874, 904, 934, 943
Malvern College: 95, 190n, 293, 333n, 334, 426n, 1023, 1071
Malvernian: 310
Mammon: 177n
Manchester: 152
Manchester College (Oxford): 580n, 1050
Manchester Grammar School: 696n
Manchester University: 336n, 823n
Manchuria: 44–5
Mandell, Gail Porter: *Madeleva*, 140n
Manicheeism: 392, 753
Mannerheim Line: 350
Mannin, Ethel: 424
Mansfield College (Oxford): 719n
Marcel, Gabriel: *Etre et Avoir*, 612n; men. 954
Marcellus: 902
Marcus Aurelius: 41, 463
Marett, Robert Ranulph: *Hope and Charity in Primitive Religion*; *Sacraments of Simple Folk*, 403n; men. 403
Marhalt, Sir: 781n
Marigold Health Foods: 925n
Maritain, Jacques: 134
Mark, St: Gospel of, 9n, 93, 429n, 480, 502, 813, 816, 857, 983
Mark of Cornwall, King: 781–6
Marlborough (Wiltshire): 534, 1026
Marlborough, John Churchill, Duke of: 399
Marlborough College: 178n, 307, 323, 324, 572n, 1022
Marlowe, Christopher: 164, 235
Marquette University: 666n, 854n
Marraine, Fernando: 796, 797
Marriage: 379, 392–7, 511–13, 513–4, 515, 658, 669–70, 730, 817, 975–6, 977, 979–80, 982
Mars: 220, 234n, 235n, 237, 242, 413, 543, 569, 701–2
Marshall, Jane: 648n
Marshall, George Catlett: 833n
Marshall Plan: 833, 869, 963
Marsh Baldon: 17
Martha (sister of Mary): 396
Martin, Mother Mary: 787
Martin, P.W.: 580n
Martlets Society: 399n, 579
Marvell, Andrew: 209n
Marx, Karl/Marxists: 157, 351, 648, 707
Mary, Blessed Virgin: 31, 74, 263n, 265n, 381, 396, 496, 526, 646, 747, 802, 1014, 1047, 1055

Mary Datchelor Girls' School (London): 1059
Mary (sister of Martha): 396
Mary, Queen: 114n
Mary Magdalen, St: 536
Mascall, Rev. Eric Lionel: *The God-Man*, 493n, 823, 993; *Man: His Origin and Destiny*, 493n; men. 250–2, 259
Masculine: 108, 541, 749, 860
Masefield, Sir John: *The Coming of Christ*, 1069; men. 1063
Masochism: 106
Mason, A.E.W.: 1040
Masson, David: *The Life of John Milton*, 574n
Materialism: 94, 105n, 145, 146, 157, 189, 449, 657, 676
Mathew OP, Father Gervase: 'Marriage and *Amour Courtois* in Late-Fourteenth-Century England', 817
Mathews, Vera: letters to: 811, 812, 834, 837, 841, 845–6, 851 856, 858, 875–6, 877, 884–5, 890, 903, 906, 912, 922–3, 932–3, 935–6, 939, 943, 957–8, 962–4, 965–6, 973–4, 980–1, 983–4, 984–5, 987, 992–3, 995, 1003–4, 1011; men. 575n, 952
Matthew, St: Gospel of, 9n, 23, 93, 189, 192, 234, 266, 283, 328, 359, 361–2, 381n, 394, 408, 410, 450–1, 480, 502n, 511, 617, 640, 669, 710, 764–5, 813, 814, 842, 857, 868, 916, 953, 957, 960, 978, 979, 998, 999, 1008, 1085
Matthews, Very Rev. Walter Robert: 471–2, 778n
Mauriac, François: *Vie de Jésus*, 213, 375, 577
Maurice, F.D.: 1077
May, Peter: 532–3
Mead, Joseph: 574n
Medical Missionaries of Mary: 787, 790
Melbourne, Lord (William Lamb): 182n
Melbourne Church of England Grammar School: 323n
Melchior, Lauritz: 79n
Melchizedech: 390, 566
Memory: 758–61
Mendelssohn, Felix: 15n
Medium Aevum: 142, 166n
Menelaus: 305, 886–7
Mercury (the planet): 725, 726, 919n
Meredith, George: *The Egoist*, 210–11, 341
Merlin: 348n, 669, 672–3, 781, 783, 784–6
Merry del Val, Cardinal Rafael: *Litany of Humility*, 843, 844–5
Merton College (Oxford): 16n, 17n, 99n, 102n, 167, 195, 271n, 292n, 431n, 477n, 554, 839, 926, 1028, 1039, 1040
'Mesopotamia': 330, 377
Metaphors: 205n, 591, 732, 734
Methodist Bookroom (London): 1082
Methodist Church: 493, 498, 502, 678n
Methodist College (Belfast): 97n
Methuen Publishers: 564n
Metre: 643, 665, 721, 1000
Metuentes: 773
Meyer, Margaret: 312
Michael, St: 1026
Michael Hall School (Forest Row): 572n, 669n, 751, 898
Michael Hall School (London): 7n, 1051
Michael Hall School (Minehead): 300, 669n
Middle Ages: 143
Middle English: 9n, 42, 65, 168n, 1052
Midhurst (Sussex): 74
Milan: 1037
Milford, Sir Humphrey: letter to: 508–9; men. 21n, 187, 651, 661, 662–3, 681
Milford, Rev. Theodore Richard: *Foolishness to the Greeks*, 376n; men. 376, 482
Milford-on-Sea: letter from: 121–6
Mill, John Stuart: 70, 464, 657
Miller, J.: 76n
Milne, Marjorie: biography: 1053–4; 'Dymer: Myth or Poem?', 1054; men. 818–19, 872, 1008
Milton, John: *Comus*, 345–6, 477–8, 493, 500–1, 720, 1085; *De Idea Platonica Quemadmodum Aristoteles Intellexit*', 664; *Il Penseroso*, 197, 736; *L'Allegro*, 736; *Lycidas*, 668; *Paradise Lost*, 20, 82, 221, 246n, 338, 415, 425, 450, 473, 478, 494, 501, 534, 562, 571–2, 574n, 577, 687, 707–8, 734, 736, 771, 982, 1000, 1073; *Paradise Regained*, 736; *Poems*, 664n, 736; *Poetical Works*, 625; *Samson Agonistes*, 736, 817, 818, 894; 'Sonnet on Deceased Wife', 736; Sonnet XVII, 982; men. 11, 164, 211n, 221n, 309, 335, 339, 360, 406, 422n, 467, 476n, 548, 556, 558n, 630, 739, 740, 982, 996
Milwaukee (Wisconsin): 666n, 854n
Minehead (Somerset): 300, 315, 318, 320, 321–2, 323, 381–3, 384, 385, 386, 388, 473n, 669, 691, 696, 1051
Miracle Plays: 31, 74
Miracles: 522, 532–3, 591, 640, 648, 649, 778, 841–2, 941, 1077
Misogyny: 546
Mitchison, Naomi: *Black Sparta*, 52, 64, 527
Mitford, Unity Valkyrie: 291
Moberley, Robert Campbell: *Atonement and Personality*, 487, 529
Molière, *Comedies*, 76; *Tartuffe*, 29; men. 76
Modern Quarterly: 236n
Moffatt, James: *New Testament*, 375, 941; *New Translation of the Bible*, 375, 422; *Old Testament*, 375
Molesworth, Mrs: 1040

Monchanin, Fr Jules: 1048
Monkton, Lionel (with Mark Ambient and Howard Talbot): *Arcadians*, 51
Monmouth School for Girls: 3n, 128
Mons, Angels of: 337
Montague, C.F.: 298n
Montaigne, Michel Eyquem de: 477n
Montalvo, Garcia de: 562n
Monteith, Charles Montgomery: *Omnipresence of the Deity*; *Oxford*, 309n; men. 309, 414
Montevideo, Battle of: 305
Montgomery, Robert: 309
Month, The: 1054
Moon, The: 36, 528, 726–7, 743, 812, 908
Moore, Alice Hamilton: 281–2, 287, 294, 297, 377, 413
Moore, Edward Frances Courtenay 'Paddy' (son of Mrs Moore): 496, 1034
Moore, George: 34
Moore, Hubert Stuart: 234n
Moore, Mrs Hubert Stuart: see Evelyn Underhill
Moore, Mrs Janie King Askins ('Minto'): 1, 3–4, 6n, 11, 13, 25, 31, 37, 38, 44, 46, 58, 75n, 80, 86–7, 90, 91, 125, 128, 130, 131–3, 165, 169, 171, 180, 181, 213, 247, 259, 261, 270, 274, 276, 279, 281, 287, 290, 294, 297, 303, 305, 311, 313, 314–5, 325, 331, 333, 336, 362, 363, 388, 389, 397, 400, 405, 413, 418, 430, 434, 436, 486, 496, 521, 534, 538, 539, 549, 578, 579, 596–7, 591, 592, 595, 603, 622, 623, 624, 628, 636, 637, 641, 657, 694, 270, 706, 709, 719, 739, 755, 757, 766, 786–7, 806, 812, 818, 843, 844, 905–6, 922, 944, 974, 989, 1016, 1033–4, 1038, 1050
Moore, Maureen: see Dunbar of Hempriggs, Dame Maureen
Moore, Dr Robert: 297n
Morals/morality: 192, 257
More, Paul Elmer: letters to: 145–6, 156–8, 163–5; *The Greek Tradition*, 145n; *New Shelburne Essays*, 145n; *Platonism*, 157; *Sceptical Approach to Religion*, 145–6; *Shelburne Essays*, 145n; men. 646
More, Sir Thomas: *Utopia*, 170; *Workes of Sir Thomas More*, 170; men. 326, 813, 815
Morelli, Patrizia: 1038
Morgan, Charles: 252, 1063
Morgan, Lady (Sydney Owenson): 676
Morland, H.: letter to: 528–9
Morley, Edith J.: 563n
Morpheus: 158
Morgan, Charles: *The Fountain*, 66
Morris, John Humphrey Carlile: 286, 354–5
Morris, Muriel: 587, 591, 592, 628
Morris, William: *Child Christopher and Goldilind the Fair*, 40; *Dream of John Ball*, 24; *Earthly Paradise*, 8n, 218; *House of the Wolfings*, 218; 'Land East of the Sun and West of the Moon', 7–8; *Life and Death of Jason*, 41, 763; *Love is Enough*, 24; *The Roots of the Mountains*, 111, 218; *The Well at the World's End*, 218; *The Wood Beyond the World*, 24, 33, 40; men. 89, 103, 217–18, 223, 535, 546, 562, 629, 630, 881, 991
Morris Motors (Oxford): 160n, 213, 596n
Morrison, Sheila: 404
Moses: 144, 1013
Mosley, Diana, Lady: 291n
Mosley, Sir Oswald: 291n
Mount Holyoke College (Massachusetts): 745n
Mountains of Mourne: 97, 132
Moy (Co. Tyrone): 370
Moynihan, Martin: letter to: 615–6; (trans) *Letters: C.S. Lewis – Don Giovanni Calabria*, 615n, 799, 800n, 1038; *South of Fort Hertz*; *The Strangers*, 615n
Moynihan, Monica: 615n
Mozart, Wolfgang Amadeus: *Magic Flute*, 441
Muir, Edwin: 439n
Muir, Willa: 439n
Mulcaster, Richard: *Elementarie*, 235
Munich Crisis, The: 231, 418
Murdoch, W.L.F.: 561n
Murray, James: 414
Murray, Gilbert: 366, 1063
Murrell, Shirley: 1060n
Murry, J. Middleton: *Studies in Keats*, 247n
Music: 639
Musical Comedy: 50–1
Muslims: 173, 328, 820
Mussolini, Benito: 368, 408, 1075
Muswell Hill Congregational Church: 582n
Myres, J.N.L. (with R.G. Collingwood) *Roman Britain*, 616n
Mystere de la Poesie, Le: 436–7
Mysticism: 189, 201, 206, 207–8, 234n, 235
Mythlore: 685n, 1061n
Mythology (Classical): 1, 381n, 44, 973, 1039, 1042
Mythology/Mythical (General): 1, 8, 12, 35, 172, 1753, 186, 221n, 237, 262, 438, 439, 445–6, 453, 665, 671, 733, 762–3, 820
Mythopoeia: 389, 655

Nairn, Philip Sidney: 1028
Napoleon Bonaparte: 128, 338, 421, 429n
Nash, John: 924n
Nashe, Thomas: *The Unfortunate Traveller*, 397; *Works*, 886; men. 236, 547
National Association of Evangelicals: 921
National Portrait Gallery (London): 537n
National Socialism: 353n

National Trust, The: 1052
Natural Law/Moral Law: 470, 475n, 484–5, 526n, 699, 773, 881
Naturalism: 715, 733
Nature: 175, 186, 188, 207, 208, 225n, 321, 349, 368, 447–8, 456n, 459, 584–5, 591, 596, 648, 651, 672n, 754, 842, 843, 967
Nazis: 229, 290n, 346, 352n, 409–10, 428, 532, 548
Nehemiah: 592
New College (Oxford): 17n, 28n, 129, 182n, 272n, 323n, 489n, 508n, 642n, 839, 888
New English Dictionary: 329n
Neo-Platonism: 326–7, 541, 953
Neo-Scholasticism: 134n, 176
Neptune: 696
Nesbit, E.: *Five Children and It*, 809n; men. 923
New Age: 1061
Newberry Library (Chicago): 1081
Newbigin, Lesslie: 1054
Newbury (Berkshire): 1043
Newbury (Somerset): 384
Newcastle (Northumberland): 275, 460n, 558
Newcastle (Co. Wicklow): 132
Newdigate, Sir Roger: 159n
Newdigate Prize: 159, 642n, 1066
New English Bible: 682n
New English Dictionary: 166n
New English Weekly, The: 658n, 1061
Newman, Bernard: *Flying Saucer*, 910
Newman, Cardinal John Henry: *Essay on the Development of Christian Doctrine*, 1045; 'Praise to the Holiest in the Height', 587
New Milton (Hampshire): 1043
Newnham College (Cambridge): 437n, 1050, 1059
Newquay (Cornwall): 531
News of the World: 1068
New Statesman and Nation: 129n, 329–30, 447, 977n
New Testament: 22–3, 136, 169, 201, 375, 380, 531, 585–6, 632, 646, 710, 778n, 848, 1007, 1044
New York: 120n, 645n, 681n, 811, 910, 965n
New York Times, The: 889n
Newry (Co. Down): 309n, 436
Newton, 2nd Baron: 788n
Newton, 3rd Baron: 788n
New Zealand: 823n
Neylan, Sir Daniel: 1055
Neylan, Daniel: letters to: 214, 705; men. 211n, 376, 378–9, 396, 468, 481, 482, 508, 653, 1055
Neylan, Elizabeth: 705, 1055
Neylan, Mary: biography: 1054–5; letters to: 113, 211–12, 214, 254–5, 371–6, 392–7, 467–8, 471, 480–4, 492–3, 506–8, 517–8, 550–1, 652–3, 960–1; 'My Friendship with C.S. Lewis', 1055; men. 314, 392, 513n, 619, 705, 897–8
Neylan, Sarah: see Sarah Tisdall
Nicene Creed, The: 255n, 566n
Nicholas of Cusa: *Selected Spiritual Writings*, 871
Nicodemus: 70
Nicolson, Harold: 977
Niebuhr, Reinhold: *Interpretation of Christian Ethics*, 324
Niemöller, Else: 352–3
Niemöller, Martin: *Exile in the Fatherland*, 353; *From U-Boat to Concentration Camp*, 353n; men. 352–3
Nimmo, William P.: 309
Nirmalashram: 1047
Nirvana: 871
Nobel Prize: 833, 909n, 1029
Noetinger, Dom M.: 326n
Norbury (Derbyshire): 924
North, Sir Thomas: (trans.) Plutarch: *Lives of the Noble Grecians and Romans*, 447, 902; men. 243, men. 242
North China News: 63
Northernness: 171, 175, 991
Norway: 355n, 400, 402, 403, 406, 449
Norwich: 369, 411, 1039
Nous n'irons plus aux bois: 930
Novalis: see Hardenburg, Friedrich Leopold von
Novarro, Ramon: 797
Nuffield, Viscount, William Richard Morris: 160n, 213, 428
Numbers: 144, 485
Numinous: 593
Nürnberg (Germany): 854
Nurbunholme, Marjorie, Lady: 859–60
Nursery Rhymes: 171
Nygren, Anders: *Agape and Eros*, 147, 153–4, 158, 165
Nymphs: 919, 1041

Oakdene School (Sussex): 823n
O'Brien, Sir Frederick Lucius: 22, 35n
O'Hara, Kathleen: 981n, 982, 1061–4
O'Neill, Joseph: *Land Under England*, 160
Obedience: 202, 371–2, 464n, 478, 548, 940, 987, 994
Objectivism: 468, 889
Odysseus: 816
Ockenden International: 584n
Odds & Ends Magazine: 486n
Oelsner, Herman: 492n
Officers' Training Corps: 303, 365n, 426n
Ogden, Charles Kay: *Basic English*; *Basic Words*; (with I.A.Richards) *The Meaning of Meaning*, 107
Ogden, Samuel: *Sermons on the Efficacy of Prayer*
Ogpu: 688
Old Age: 986–7, 998, 999, 1005–6
Old Cleeve (Somerset): 388
Old English: see Anglo-Saxon
Old Inn (Crawfordsburn): 946

Old Icelandic: 630
Old Testament, The: 144, 351, 375, 380, 401n, 421, 451, 590, 734, 771
Olderfleet Castle: 333
Olivier, Margaret, Lady: 965, 1050
Olivier, Sydney Haldane, Lord: 108, 1050
Omar Khayyam: 203
Omnipotence, Divine: 461n, 813, 814, 990
Onions, Charles Talbot: *Advanced English Syntax*, 414n; men. 414, 432
Opie, Redvers: 286–7, 346, 378, 408, 413
Orage, A.R.: 1061
Orange Order: 368
Oratory School (Caversham): 1075
Orchard View (Dartford, Kent): 1017
Order of Merit: 1029
Order of St Michael and St George: 1026
Order of the Bath: 1026
Ordination of Women: 859–61, 863, 1008, 1012, 1060
Oriel College (Oxford): 102n, 203n, 282, 523n, 537n
Origen: 381, 451
Original Sin: 450, 929
Originality: 518
Orion: 697, 759, 760
Orosius: 612
Orpheus: 158, 162, 222–3, 228, 248, 759, 760, 817, 872–3
Orr, Sir John Boyd: *Food*, 892n; men. 892
Orthodox (Eastern) Church: 861, 1031
Osborne, Dorothy: *Letters from Dorothy Osborne to Sir William Temple*, 588
Ottery St Mary (Devon): 1030
Ottley, Alice: 1055
Otto, Rudolf: *Idea of the Holy*, 204, 285, 529
Our Lady of Lourdes Hospital (Drogheda): 787, 790
Our Lady of Sorrows ((Knutton): 1075
Our Lady of the Angels and St Peter in Chains (Stoke-on-Trent): 1075
Outpost Emmaus: 537n
Ovid: *Metamorphoses*, 880; men. 533, 609, 834n
Owl and the Nightingale, The: 75
Oxfam: 376n
Oxford Aristotelian Society: 15n
Oxford City Corporation: 3n
Oxford City Home Guard Battalion: 437, 504
Oxford Dante Society: 288n
Oxford English Dictionary: 414n
Oxford High School: 416n
Oxford History of English Literature: 167–8, 221–2, 235–6, 452, 548, 877
Oxford Magazine, The: letter to: 715–16; men. 60, 170n, 218n, 311n, 349n, 429n, 714–16, 724n, 990n
Oxford Movement, The: 303n, 321n, 417n
Oxford Playhouse: 349–50, 1035
Oxford Times: 3n, 853n
Oxford University C.S. Lewis Society: 155n
Oxford University Dramatic Society: 365n
Oxford University Examinations: 81–2, 85, 91, 111, 113, 297
Oxford University Press: 183n, 184, 272, 564n, 635, 650–1, 662–3, 681, 683n, 704, 744–5, 1082–6
Oxford University Socratic Club, The: 498n, 683, 714, 888n, 936, 954n, 1011n, 1059

Pacifism: 233–4, 251–2, 258, 277, 400, 401, 470n
Pagans/Paganism: 1, 8, 12, 24, 35, 133–4, 135n, 193, 194, 218, 221n, 233, 256, 476, 496, 541n, 620, 702, 770–1, 772, 773, 1013
Page, Curtis Hidden: 29n
Page, Frederick: 1082
Pagnol, Marcel: *Topaze*, 712
Pain: 56, 63, 118, 196, 258, 302, 308, 343, 458–66, 518, 579, 651, 653, 659, 754, 866, 929, 975, 1007
Palatine Anthology: 616n
Palestine: 70, 411n, 586
Palgrave, Francis: *Golden Treasury*, 1060
Palmer, Herbert Edward: letters to: 678–80, 683–5, 700–1, 705, 745–6; *Armed Muse*, 678n; *The Dragon of Tingalam*, 717, 718; *Mistletoe Child*, 678n; *Post-Victorian Poetry*, 680; *Ride from Hell*, 678n; *Songs of Salvation*, 684; *Sword in the Desert*, 700, 705, 745–6; *Two Foemen*, 678n; *Two Minstrels*, 678n; *Vampire, And Other Poems*, 678, 680; men. 724, 763
Palmer, Fr Wilfrid George: 1045
Pan: 873
Pantheism: 133, 134, 145, 177–8, 207, 208, 657, 702, 770, 771, 789, 870
Pantin, W.E.P. (with H.W. Flewett) *A First Book of Latin Poetry*, 589
Papacy, The: 257, 281, 368, 646, 813, 815–16, 886n, 1045, 1057
Papworth, Mr (Lewis's dog): 6, 44, 118, 128, 180m 214, 430
Parables (of Jesus): 192, 1077
Paracelsus: *Liber de Nymphis*, 919
Paradise: 78, 460, 464n, 726, 761, 812, 882, 1082
Paris: 903n
Paris, Prince of Troy: 197
Paris: 103, 166n, 219n, 379n, 816nski
Parker, Desmond: 485n
Parker, Henry Michael Denne 'Wounded Buffalo': 296, 298, 336, 346–7, 362, 366–7, 426
Parker, Ruth Hamilton: 485
Parkin, Major Herbert Denis: 5–6, 275, 787, 855
Parry, E.A.: 588n
Parson, Joy: letter to: 517

Parson, Bishop Richard Godfrey: 517
Parson's Pleasure: 331
Pascal, Blaise: *Pensées*, 915; men. 227, 989
Pater, Walter: *Marius the Epicurean*, 34–5, 41
Paterson, Adrian Hugh: 24, 1052–3
Patmore, Coventry: *Poems*, 500; *Rod, The Root and The Flower*, 257, 500; *Unknown Eros*, 257; *Victories of Love*, 257; men. 184, 185, 497
Paton, David M.: *Blind Guides?*, 284
Paton, Lucy Allen: 673n
Patrick James: *Magdalen Metaphysicals*, 15n
Paul, St: Colossians; 585–6, 822n; I Corinthians, 62, 69, 285, 394, 868, 869; II Corinthians, 201, 489; Ephesians, 193, 822; Galatians, 23, 193, 194, 201, 983, 1007; Hebrews, 390, 521n, 868, 869; Philippians, 327, 842, 843, 1006; Romans, 193, 266, 351n, 747, 940, 941, 954; I Timothy, 410, 94; men. 40,8 136, 326, 396, 455, 492, 586, 646, 692, 824, 881, 914, 989
Pax: 176–7, 178, 224–5, 576n, 1046
Paxford, Frederick William: 'He Should Have Been a Parson', 11n; men. 213, 310, 331, 382, 587n, 622, 739, 1033
P'daitas/ism: 20, 21, 29, 75, 300, 313, 321, 324, 340, 377, 401
Peace: 233n, 278n, 418, 1007
Peace of God: 1006, 1007
Peacock, Thomas Love: *Crotchet Castle*; *Headlong Hall*; *Nightmare Abbey*, 436n; men. 487
Pearce, Channing: 756
Pearce, Joseph: *Bloomsbury and Beyond: The Friends and Enemies of Roy Campbell*, 736m; *The Unmasking of Oscar Wilde*, 930n
Pearce, Joyce: letter to: 584–5
Peckham (London): 1059
Pedrollo, Don Luigi: 1038, 1039
Peele, George: *Arraignement of Paris*, 197; *David and Bathsabe*, 196–7; *Life and Works*, 196n
Pegg, Mr: 1026n
Peg's Paper: 389
Pellow, J.D.C.: (with G. Every and S.L. Bethell) *Selected Poems*, 1031
Pembroke College (Cambridge): 2n, 752n
Pembroke College (Oxford): 2n, 31, 380, 839, 1008
Penelope CSMV, Sister: biography, 1055–59; letters to: 261–6, 285–6, 450–2, 453–4, 478–80, 484–5, 493–4, 494–6, 497, 516–7, 519–21, 525–7, 554–6, 565–7, 586–8, 590–2, 602–3, 624–5, 628, 635–6, 656–7, 701–2, 743, 811–12, 848–9, 862, 863–4, 873–4, 911–12, 961–2, 967–8; *God Persists*, 261n, 262–3, 1057; *Hugh of St Victor: Selected Spiritual Writings*, 1058; (trans.) St Athanasius, *The Incarnation of the Word of God*, 516, 520, 525–6, 529, 602–3, 701, 812, 911, 1058; *Leaves from the Trees*, 264–5, 495–6; *Meditation of a Caterpillar*, 1055–6; (trans) *St Athanasius on the Psalms*, 849; *St Bernard: On the Love of God*, 961; *Scenes from the Psalms*, 265, 285, 383, 422, 423; *They Shall Be My People*, 565–7, 588, 590–1, 592, 603, 635, 656–7; 'Tribute to Two Tractarians', 1056; *Windows on Jerusalem*, 479–80, 624; *The Wood for the Trees*, 1057; men. 449–50, 567n, 1006n
Pentecost: 1045
Pepys, Samuel: 749
Perceval, Sir: 562n, 913n
Perleberg, Gilbert C.: letter to: 847
Perlesvaux: 562n
Perry Colour Books: 1018
Perse School (Cambridge): 1073
Persephone: 223, 546, 759, 760
Perseus: 973
Personalism: 914
Perthshire: 504, 505
Peter, St: I Peter, 23, 857; II Peter, 915; men. 646, 850, 989
Petersfield (Hampshire): 509n
Pethavel, J.P.: letter to: 593
Petrarch: 236, 475
Petronius: 773
Pharisees: 70, 125, 192, 374, 453
Phelps, Lancelot Ridley: 282
Philadelphia: 615n
Philistines: 861
Phillips, Eric George: *Advanced Mathematics Course*, 403n; men. 403
Phillips, Rev. John Bertram: letter to: 585–6; *Letters to Young Churches*, 585n, 586n; *The Price of Success*, 585
Phillips, Justin: *C.S. Lewis at the BBC*, 470n, 568n, 581n, 582n, 597, 599n, 602, 627, 628, 633, 1035, 1071
Philology: 9n, 414n
Philosophy/Philosophers: 15n, 142, 143, 164, 176, 188–9, 191–3, 196, 198, 202, 204, 220n, 225n, 292n, 311, 330, 340, 341n, 344, 354n, 372–3, 403n, 420, 514, 537n, 543, 557, 568, 570, 575, 576, 580n, 612, 616n, 702, 765, 854n, 954, 1010, 1027, 1028, 1044
Philosophy, Politics, Economics: 28n, 150n
Phipps, Mrs Harry Joseph 'Phippy': 297, 324, 333, 342
Phoenix, the: 5, 857
Physics Abstracts: 1024

Pico della Mirandola: *Of Being and Unity*, 666n
Piety: 352
Pig and Whistler (Fairford): 687
Pigiebotism: 8n
Pike, Magnus: 315
Pindar: 703, 818, 967
Pious Union for Assistance to the Sick: 1036
Pirie-Gordon of Buthlaw, Christopher Martin: 411
Pitt, Elizabeth Marjorie: 1059
Pitt, Valerie: biography: 1059–60: letter to: 919; *Tennyson Laureate*; *The Writer and the Modern World*, 1060
Pitt, William Bygrave: 1059
Pitter, Geoffrey: 1060
Pitter, George: 1060–1
Pitter, Louisa Murrell: 1060, 1063
Pitter, Ruth: biography: 1060–64: letters to: 718, 720–1, 722–8, 731–5, 738, 741–2, 746, 752–4, 758–64, 769, 771, 775, 776–7, 778, 780, 789–95, 796–7, 874–5, 879–80, 881, 893, 894–5, 969, 972–3, 981–2, 997–8, 1008, 1012; *A Heaven to Find*, 1064; *A Mad Lady's Garland*, 721, 722, 1061; *A Trophy of Arms*, 720–1, 1061; *The Bridge*, 723, 724, 973, 1062; *Collected Poems*, 1064; *End of the Drought*, 1064; *The Ermine*, 1063; *First and Second Poems*, 1061; *First Poems*, 1061; *Persephone in Hades*, 762, 1061; *Pitter on Cats*, 776, 1063; *Poem*, 1063; *Poems 1926–1966*, 1064; *The Rude Potato*, 1062; *The Spirit Watches*, 722–3, 724, 1061; *Still by Choice*, 1064; *Urania*, 1063; 'The World is Hollow', 982; men. 151n, 685, 711n, 717, 729, 757, 835n, 881–2, 946n
Pittsburg Theological Seminary: 289n
Pius X, Pope: 844n
Pius XII, Pope: 368, 1037
Planets/Stars: 75, 348, 413, 431–2, 528, 693, 697, 701–2, 725, 726, 743, 751, 812, 908, 910, 919
Plato: *Apology*, 201; *Gorgias*, 120; *Phaedo*, 147n, 248; *Phaedrus*, 12: 20; *The Republic*, 558; *Timaeus*, 157n, 870; men. 31, 145n, 157, 180, 227, 245, 326, 391, 477n, 646, 771
Platonic Forms: 180, 245, 664
Platonism: 235, 326, 450, 475, 646, 870
Pleasure: 13, 19, 23, 25, 33, 44, 47, 54, 65–6, 75, 92, 101, 111, 125, 132, 156, 183, 187–8, 190, 462–3, 477, 480–1, 519, 523, 617, 657, 986, 1003
Pliny the Elder: *Natural History*, 612
Plotinus: *Enneads*, 541
Plough, The: 697
Pluscarden Abbey: 1046, 1047
Plutarch: *Lives of the Noble Grecians and Romans*, 243
Pluto: 197
Plymouth (Devon): 516
Plymouth Congregational Church (Minneapolis): 1021
Pocock, Alice Jane: 1064
Pocock, Guy: biography, 1064–5; letters to: 94–5, 97–9, 108–10, 126; *Design for a Staircase*, 1065; (ed) *Herodotus*, 1065; *Knight's Gambit*; *Stubbs at Fifty*; *Then They Pulled Down the Blinds*, 1065
Pocock, Noel Lewis: 1064
Poe, Edgar Allan: 546, 719
Poet Laureate: 1023
Poetic Diction: 743
Poetry Review, The: 1076
Poggio (Mrs Moore's dog): 418, 430
Poland: 269, 270, 271, 311, 350, 389n
Political Philosophy
Political Science: 120
Politics: 352, 399–400
Pollux: 381, 388
Polytheism: 189, 449, 633, 733, 870
Pomeroy, Mrs: 486, 503, 504, 550
Poole, Reginald Lane: *Benedict IX and Gregory VI*; *Illustrations of the History of Medieval Thought*, 283n; men. 283
Pope, Alexander: *An Epistle from Mr Pope to Dr Arbuthnot*, 809, 842; *An Essay on Criticism*, 671, 734; *Dunciad*, 477; *Rape of the Lock*, 919; men. 212, 361, 429, 518, 644
Pope-Hennessy, Dame Una: *Laird of Abbotsford*, 60
Poppelbaum, Hermann: *Man and Animal*, 129
Porlock (Somerset): 318, 319, 320, 339, 384
Pornography: 456, 773
Porphyry: 541
Portadown (Co. Armagh): 102
'Portico' Project: 756–8, 767, 769, 771–4, 779
Portland (Dorset): 1049
Port Meadow: 59
Portsea (Hampshire): 1050
Portugal: 9, 1058
Potiphar: 354
Potiphar's wife: 354
Potter, Beatrice: *Country Tales*, 1021; *Peter Rabbit*, 171, 537n, 538; *Squirrel Nutkin*, 171, 537; men. 537–8
Potter, Phyllis M.: 805n
Poulton Hall (Cheshire): 1039–43
Pound, Ezra: 164, 536, 556n, 684, 1028–9
Powell, Margaret: 696n
Powell, Oswald Byron: *A Book of German Songs*, 696n; men. 696–7
Powicke, Sir Maurice: 240
Powys, Llewelyn: *Damnable Opinions*, 159–60
Praise of God: 322, 970–1
Prayer: 48–9, 135, 172–3, 202, 206, 225, 264, 276n, 361–2, 367, 391, 392, 410, 411, 427, 436, 453, 461, 496, 507, 517, 587,

Prayer – *cont.* 618, 628n, 722, 813, 814, 826, 841–2, 905, 906, 956–7, 960, 962, 965, 978, 979, 989–90, 994, 1005
Presbyter, The: 7
Presbyterians: 43, 164n, 471n, 703
Pride: 125, 188, 189, 267, 480–1, 585
Priesthood: 859–61, 863
Priestley, J.B.: *The Linden Tree*, 805, 1035
Princeton University: 134n, 145n, 163
Princeton University Library: 145n, 164n
Prinknash Abbey: 5n, 126, 152, 176n, 576n, 1045, 1046, 1047
Prism: 1059
Proceedings of the British Academy, The: 1074
Proclus: 541n
Procrustes' Bed: 502
Prodigal Son, The: 192
Progress: 632
Prometheus: 418–19
Protestant: 165, 178, 213, 368, 379, 479, 646, 647, 800, 801, 815n, 1046
Proust, Marcel: 754
Prouty, C.T.: 196n
Proverbs: 701
Providence: 48–9, 511–12, 647–8
Prudentius (Aurelius Prudentius Clemens): 98
Pryce-Jones, David: *Unity Mitford*, 291n
Psalms, The: 265, 285, 322n, 525, 587, 746, 813, 815, 849, 884, 889, 905, 962, 967
Psyche: 6n, 41, 566
Psychiatrists: 765
Psychoanalysis: 94, 329, 372–4, 376, 482
Psychology/Psychologists: 477n, 489n, 765
Psychotherapy: 976
Punch: 424, 429, 530–1, 711n, 712, 725n, 727n, 756, 790n, 792n, 812, 863, 893n
Purgatory: 302, 478, 815n, 1082
Puritanism: 23
Pusey, E.B.: 529n
Pythagoreans: 543, 693

Quakers: 22n, 72–3, 432
Queen Anne's School (Caversham): 1076
Queen Mary College (University of London): 313n, 499n, 1011n
Queen's College/University (Belfast): 17n, 102n, 240n, 245, 693, 921
Queen's College (Cambridge): 28, 472n
Queen's College (Oxford): 182n
Queen's Gold Medal for Poetry: 1023, 1063
Queen's Own Royal West Kent Regiment: 839
Quick, Rev. Oliver Chase: letter to: 460–66; *Christian Sacraments*; *Doctrines of the Creed*; *Ground of Faith*, 460n; men. 376, 458
Quiller-Couch, Sir Arthur: 1065
Quintilian: *Institutio Oratoria*, 545
Quittenton, Richard M.H. ('Roland Quiz'): *Giant-Land*, 213–14, 594–5; *Juvenile Rhymes*, 594n
Quiz, Roland: see R.M.H. Quittenton

Raby, Frederic James Edward: *A History of Secular Latin Poetry*, 609
Racine, Jean: 164
Rackham, Arthur: 273, 630
Radcliffe Camera: 368
Radcliffe Infirmary: 182n, 649, 1054, 1086
Radford, Dr Mary Cowper: 281
Radley College: 15n, 1032
Radice, Edward Albert (with E.M. Hugh-Jones) *American Experiment*, 28n
Raleigh, Sir Walter (1552?-1618): 236
Raleigh, Sir Walter (1861–1922): *Shakespeare*, 621; men. 224
Ramsey, Archbishop Michael: 1059
Randolph Hotel (Oxford): 552
Ransome, Arthur: *Autobiography*, 1025–7, 1028; *Swallows and Amazons*, 1025; men. 1025–28
Rastell, William: 170n
Rationalism: 176, 204, 443, 772, 881
Rationalist Press Association: 75
Raven, Rev. Charles Earle: *Gospel and the Church*, 351n; men. 351, 574n
Reading (Berkshire): 16, 381, 388
Realism (in literature): 389, 454, 456, 682, 773
Reason: 88n, 110, 146, 188, 189, 192, 194, 204, 233, 274, 427, 466, 548, 588, 676, 714–15, 772–3, 808–9, 871, 907
Redemption: 953
Redesdale, Lord: 291n
Reformation, English: 271n, 346, 381, 476n, 510n, 1055
Reid, Forrest: *Apostate*, 12n; *Private Road*, 12n; *Uncle Stephen*, 12n, 13; men. 12, 22, 112, 214, 274, 486, 548–9, 595, 709, 755
Religion: 189, 200, 225n, 250, 263, 285, 335, 352, 365, 373, 439, 440, 444, 445, 479, 487, 497, 540n, 605, 606, 640, 657
Renaissance, The: 196, 221n, 236, 246–7, 271n, 450, 474–8, 551, 562, 646, 804, 805
Renwick, William Lindsay: *Complaints*, 148
Repentance: 940
Repton School: 6n
Resurrection, The: 35, 217, 377, 581, 778n, 843, 844, 904, 905, 951, 1077
Reynolds, Barbara: (with Dorothy L. Sayers) *The Comedy of Dante Alighieri The Florentine: Cantica III Paradise*, 669, 681, 1072;

Dorothy L. Sayers: Her Life and Soul, 1066, 1067, 1068, 1070, 1071, 1072; (ed) Dorothy L. Sayers, *Letters*, Vol. I, 1066; (ed) Dorothy L. Sayers, *Letters*, Vol. II, 573n; (ed) Dorothy L. Sayers, *Letters*, Vol. III, 650n, 662n, 778n, 779n; *The Passionate Intellect: Dorothy L. Sayers's Encounter with Dante*, 748n, 1071; men. 1072
Rhetoric: 444
Rhodes House: 323
Rhodes Scholars: 323–4, 642n
Rhys, Ernest: 84
Rice-Oxley, Leonard: 26n, 365, 398, 403
Richard, Dennis: 1054n
Richards, I.A.: (with Charles Kay Ogden) *The Meaning of Meaning*, 107n; *Practical Criticism*, 209n, 779n; *Principles of Literary Criticism*, 209n; men. 209–10, 252, 443, 468, 810, 811, 1029
Richardson, Samuel: *Pamela*, 246; men. 644
Riddell Memorial Lectures: 558, 614
Riddle, Thomas Wilkinson: letters to: 510, 607, 614, 718–19; *Pathway of Victory*; *Matters of Moment*; (with J.K. Maclean) *The Second Picture of the War*, 510
Ridler, Anne: letter to: 658–9; *A Measure of English Poetry*; 'Charles Williams: A Note in Memory', *Collected Poems*; *Henry Bly*; (ed) Charles Williams, *The Image of the City and Other Essays*, 1083; (ed) Charles Williams, *Seed of Adam and Other Plays*, 289n, 512n; (ed) *Selected Writings, Charles Williams*, 658n
Ridler, Vivian: 658n
Ridley, Rev. Maurice Roy: 26n, 306, 1066, 1071
Ridley Hall (Cambridge): 277n, 492n, 585n
Riedl, John Orth: letter to: 854
Rieu, Emile Victor: (trans) *Iliad*, 564n, 697n; *Four Gospels*, 564n; Odyssey, 564n, 697n, 698; *Pastoral Poems*, 564n; *Voyage of the Argo*, 564n; men. 564, 681n, 697
Rievaulx (Yorkshire): 577n
Ritualism: 23
Rivers, Lord: 5
Rivière, Michael Valentine Briton: *Late in the Day*; *Poetical Works*; *Selected Poems*, 411n; men. 410
Roanoke College (Salem, Virginia): 1081
Roberts, Michael: 247n, 253
Robespierre, Maximilien: 429n
Roebuck Restaurant (Oxford): 418n
Robin Hood: 1042
Robinson, George: 1082
Robson-Scott, William Douglas: 69, 415
Rocky Mountains: 1032
Roger de Coverley, Sir (from *Spectator*): 352
Roland: 678, 679n
Rolfe, Frederick ('Baron Corvo'): *Hadrian the Seventh*, 143–4
Romances (literary): 5, 12, 24, 33–4, 103, 116–17, 262, 797
Romania: 142
Romantic Poets: 177–8, 223, 468, 648
Romantic Love: 1082, 1083
Romantic Theology: 184, 185
Romanticism: 88n, 110, 186, 224–5
Romantics (in English School): 9n,
Rome: 9, 134n, 344n, 378, 405, 658n, 750, 1036, 1038
Rondenbosch (South Africa): 1032
Ronsard, Pierre de: *Sonnets pour Hélène*, 733
Roosevelt, Franklin D.: 613n
Rootsie Tootsie: 50
Ros, Amanda McKittrick: *Delina Delaney*, 348–9; *Irene Iddlesleigh*, 294, 297; *Poems of Puncture*, 294n;
Rosenberg, Alfred: *Myth of the 20th Century*, 548
Roseveare, Rev. Richard Polgreen: *Bridging the Gulf*, 674
Rossetti, Christina: 260
Rostand, Edmond: *Cyrano de Bergerac*, 678
Rostrevor (Co. Down): letter from: 133–7; men. 132
Rougemont, Denis de: *L'Amour et l'Occident* (*Passion and Society* or *Love in the Western World*): 379, 391, 511, 515, 828n; *La Part du Diable* (*Talk of the Devil*), 828n; men. 379, 380
Rousseau, Jean-Jacques: 398
Routh, Martin Hugh: 295
Routh, Martin Joseph: 295
Routley, Rev. Eric: letters to: 719–20, 740–1; 'A Prophet', 719n; 'Correspondence with an Anglican Who Dislikes Hymns', 719
Rowse, Alfred Leslie: 1002
Royal Academy of Dramatic Art (RADA): 622, 623, 636, 637–8, 706, 827n, 1033, 1035, 1066n
Royal Agricultural College (Cirencester): 1051
Royal Air Force: 313n, 471–2, 473, 480, 485, 490, 492, 493, 504, 515, 517, 523–5, 586, 661–2, 665–6, 1024, 1071
Royal Air Force Chaplains' Society: 472n
Royal Air Force Volunteer Reserve: 523n
Royal Albert Hall: 718n
Royal Army Medical Corps: 297n, 509n
Royal Army Service Corps: 1, 5n, 14, 45, 85
Royal Belfast Academical Institution 'Inst': 301, 414
Royal College of Music: 1023
Royal Engineers: 1018
Royal Field Artillery: 336n

Royal Flying Corps: 519n, 615n
Royal Inniskillen Fusilliers: 301n
Royal Institute of International Affairs: 316n
Royal Military College (Sandhurst): 839
Royal Naval College (Dartmouth): 1065
Royal Naval College (Greenwich): 632n
Royal Navy: 295n, 299n, 305n, 560, 638n, 751, 924n, 1055
Royal Navy Air Service: 924n
Royal Navy Volunteer Reserve: 313n, 643n, 839
Royal Oxford Hotel: 1002
Royal Society of Literature: 708n, 1023
Royal Society of Medicine: 277
Rudolf Steiner Hall (London): 805n
Rudyard (Derbyshire): 158
Rudyard Lane (Derbyshire): 158–9, 160n
Rugby School: 658n
Runcie, Dr Robert: 1054n
Runcorn (Cheshire): 131
Runes: 819–20
Ruskin, John: *Modern Painters*, 210; men. 20, 119
Ruskin School of Fine Art (Oxford): 1018
Russell, Arthur: (ed) *Ruth Pitter: Homage to a Poet*, 1060, 1062
Russell, George William 'A.E.': *Collected Poems*, 718; men. 548n
Russia: 276, 311, 350, 368, 437n, 647, 836
Rye (East Sussex): 1076, 1077
Ryle, Gilbert: 615, 616n
Ryskamp, Charles: (with James D. Baird) *Poems of William Cowper*, 732

Sabatini, Rafael: 103
Saccidananda Ashram: 1048, 1049
Sacramentalism: 640
Sacraments: 43, 403n
Sacred Heart of Jesus: 799
Sacred Heart School (London): 739n, 1033
Sackville-West, Victoria 'Vita': 360, 1063
Sacrifice: 1, 35
St Alban's Abbey School (St Albans): 1081
St Alban's School (St Albans): 1082
St Aldate's Church (Oxford): 1050
St Aloysius Church (Oxford): 1075
St Andrew's Church (Bebington): 1043
St Andrew's Church (Headington): 7n
St Anne's Church (Finsbury Park): 1082
St Anne's Church (Dean Street, London): 1072
St Anne's College (Oxford): 291n, 349n, 612n
St Benedict's al Monte (Verona): 1037
St Catharine's College (Cambridge): 112n, 924n
St Catherine's College (Oxford): 16n, 435, 626n
St Cross Church (Oxford): 1086
St Deiniol's Library: 410, 711, 1076
St Edmund Hall (Oxford) 370n, 498n
St Edmund's College (Ware): 769n
St George's Chapel (Windsor): 1076
St Helen's (Adel, Yorkshire): 1025
St Hilda's College (Oxford): 1075
St Hilda's Hall Verse: 1076
St Hugh's College (Oxford): 113, 293, 499n, 1054, 1059
St James Church (Cowley): 1015
St James's Church (Piccadilly, London): 1049
St James's Church (Spanish Place, London): 1036
St James the Apostle (Bream, Gloucestershire): 1015
St John's Church (Roxbury, Massachusetts): 1025
St John's College (Cambridge): 1064–5
St John's College (Oxford): 297–8, 341n, 472n, 888n
St John's Mission House (Mazagon, Bombay): 1015
St John's Training College (York): 469n
St Jude-on-the-Hill (London): 1016
St Jude's Gazette: 573n, 575
St Louis (Missouri): 145n, 1028
St Louis University (Missouri): 666n
St Margaret's Church (London): 1072
St Mark's, Dundela (Belfast): 19n, 116, 132, 381
St Mark's Church (Gloucestershire): 1015
St Martin in the Fields (London): 626n
St Mary and St Benedict (Coventry): 1075
St Mary's College (Notre Dame): 140n
St Mary's College, Oscott (Birmingham): 280, 1075
St Mary's College (Strawberry Hill): 936n
St Mary the Virgin (Oxford): 353, 376n, 489, 490, 626n
St Michael's Abbey (Farnborough): 770n, 1046
St Michael's Church (Coppenhall): 673n
St Michael's Church (Oxford): 272n
St Nicholas's Church (Moreton): 1081
St Nicholas's Church (Winchcombe): 1045
St Patrick's Cathedral (Dublin): 405, 469n
St Paul's Cathedral (London): 469n, 471–2, 523n, 778, 1082
St Paul's Church (Beloit, Wisconsin): 1005n, 1078
St Paul's Church (Millis, Massachusetts): 1025

St Paul's Missionary College (Burgh): 673n
St Paul's Girls' School: 341n, 1078
St Paul's School (London): 460n, 564n, 1033
St Peter's Basilica (Rome): 815n
St Peter's Church (Eynsham): 1075
St Peter's Church (Winchcombe): 1024
St Peter's College (Oxford): 340–2, 378
St Petersburg: 166n
St Philip's Church (Newcastle): 1076
St Saviour Cathedral (Goulburn): 643n
St Saviour Church (Roath): 1015
St Saviour's Church (Uckfield, Sussex): 945n
St Stephen's Church (Verona): 1036
St Stephen's House (Oxford): 19n
St Thomas Hospital (London): 2n
Sadducees: 125
Sadism: 106, 222, 773
Salisbury: 661n
Salisbury, Marquess of: see Cecil, James Edward Hubert Gascoyne-
Salisbury Cathedral: 585n
Salisbury Plain: 71n
Salter, John: 244n
Salter, Stephen: 244n
Salters' Boatyard: 244, 270n
Salva, Regina: 747
Sampson, Ashley: (ed) *Famous English Sermons*, 353; men. 289n, 353n, 490, 554n
I Samuel: 637
San Zeno in Monte (Verona): 1037
Sanctification: 914, 940
Sandeman, Gerard Walter: 788n
Sandeman, Honourable Phyllis Elinor: letter to: 788–9; *Treasure on Earth*, 788n
Sanders, Francis Hawkins 'Frank': letters to: 473, 491; men. 518, 808, 1073
Sanders of Oxford: 473n
Sargent, Malcolm: 170
Sanhedrin: 1013
Sarpedon: 543
Sarum Theological College: 661n
Satan: 246n, 262, 266–7, 327, 329, 448, 478n, 479, 510, 511, 514n, 639n, 689, 707–8, 729, 737, 747, 770, 803, 804, 879, 956
Satanic: 753
Saturn: 348n, 693
Saul: 1083
Saunders, Frank: 5
Saurat, Denis: *Milton: Man and Thinker*, 574n; men. 762n
Savernake Forest (Wiltshire): 111;
Saxl, Friedrich: letter to: 609; *Catalogue of Astrological and Mythological Illuminated Manuscripts*, 609n
Sayer, George: *Jack: C.S. Lewis and his Times*, 190n, 1063; men. 190, 379n
Sayers, Dorothy L. Sayers: biography, 1065–72; letters to: 515–6, 533–4, 564, 572–3, 575, 577–8, 649–50, 654–5, 657–8, 662–3, 681–3, 682–3, 697–8, 699–700, 703, 721–2, 728–9, 730, 731, 736–7, 778–9, 810–11, 860–61, 863, 886–7, 902, 903, 950–1, 994–5, 995–6, 997, 999–1001, 1002–3, 1014; *Aeneas at the Court of Dido*, 686; '. . . And Telling you a Story: A Note on *The Divine Comedy*', 681, 685–6, 697, 699, 704, 721, 748, 749–50, 817, 864–7, 994; *Busman's Honeymoon*, 1069; *Catholic Tales and Christian Songs*, 1066; *Clouds of Witness*, 1067, 1069; *The Comedy of Dante Alighieri The Florentine: Cantica I Hell Inferno*, 950–1, 994–5, 995–6, 997, 999–1000, 1003, 1014, 1071; *The Comedy of Dante Alighieri The Florentine: Cantica III Paradise*, 669n, 1072; *The Comedy of Dante Alighieri The Florentine: Cantica II Purgatory*, 1071; (with R. Eustace) *The Documents in the Case*, 1069; 'The Faust Legend and the Idea of the Devil', 736–7; *The Five Red Herrings*, 1069; *Gaudy Night*, 505, 1069; *Have His Carcase*, 1069; *The Heart of Stone*, 748; *He That Should Come*, 1070; *Letters*, Vol. I, *The Making of a Detective Novelist*, 1066, 1072; *Letters*, Vol. II, *From Novelist to Playwright*, 573, 1070, 1072; *Letters*, Vol. III, *A Noble Daring*, 650, 662, 681n, 699n, 729–31, 778n, 861, 885, 999n, 1003n, 1072; *Letters*, Vol. IV, *In the Midst of Life*, 1072; *The Man Born to be King*, 572–3, 575, 577, 580, 586, 683, 811, 989, 1070–1; *The Mind of the Maker*, 505, 514, 573; *Murder Must Advertise*, 1069; *The Nine Tailors*, 1069; *Op. I*, 1066; *The Other Six Deadly Sins*, 564, 650, 728; *The Poetry of Search and the Poetry of Statement*, 1082; *Strong Poison*, 1069; *Unnatural Death*, 1069; *The Unpleasantness at the Bellona Club*, 1069; *Unpopular Opinions*, 737n; *The Whimsical Christian*, 737; *Whose Body?*, 1067; *The Zeal of Thy House*, 469, 1070; men. 252, 514, 604, 864–7, 885, 891
Sayers, Helen Mary: 1065, 1067
Sayers, Rev. Henry: 1065, 1067
Scaliger, Julius Caesar: *Poetics*, 475, 557

Scandinavia: 389
Scapini, Fr Pietro: 1036
Scepticism: 773
Schakel, Peter J.: (ed) *The Longing for a Form*, 1080
Schofield, Stephen: (ed) *In Search of C.S. Lewis*, 1034
Scholasticism: 134–5, 142, 176, 188–9, 205, 285, 574n
School Certificates: 155n, 303, 307, 343, 425
Schools, Examination: 80, 524
Schorr, Friedrich: 79n
Science/Scientists: 129, 143, 189, 235, 262, 372–4, 406–7, 475, 476, 482, 594, 714–16, 924n, 953, 1011
Science Fiction: 151, 584, 593–4, 630, 753–4, 910, 911, 918, 1024–5
Science Museum (Oxford): 1011n
Scott, Sir Walter: *The Abbot*, 47, 53; *The Antiquary*, 47, 53–4, 677, 898; *The Black Dwarf*, 898; *The Bride of Lammermoor*, 898; *Fair Maid of Perth*, 505; *Guy Mannering*, 89, 596, 677, 898; *The Heart of Midlothian*, 53, 61, 596, 898; *Ivanhoe*, 898; *The Legend of Montrose*, 898; *The Monastery*, 47, 53; *Old Mortality*, 909; *The Pirate*, 91; *Quentin Durward*, 898; *Rob Roy*, 47, 596, 898; *The Talisman*, 677, 898; *Waverley*, 60n, 64, 203, 898; *Woodstock*, 487; men. 2n, 41, 42, 60, 61, 89, 91, 102, 551, 644, 674–7, 709, 881, 1017
Scutt, Rev. John Melville: 531
Scrutiny: 252, 332–3, 446, 684, 779, 1003
Second Coming, The: 345
Sedgefield, W.J.: (ed) *King Alfred's Old English version of Boethius De Consolatione Philosophiae*, 643
Sedulius Scotus: *De Rosae Lilique Certamine*, 609
Segar, Robert: 46–7
Self-examination: 202
Selly Oak College (Birmingham): 471n
Selworthy (Somerset): 321
Selwyn, E.G.: (ed) *Essays Catholic and Critical*, 375, 529
Selwyn College (Cambridge): 1076
Seneca, Lucius Annaeus: *Epistles*, 257
Sennacherib: 218, 989
Seth-Smith, James: see James Brabazon
Seven Deadly Sins: 978, 979
Seventh Day Adventists: 344, 345
Sewell, Anna: *Black Beauty*, 353
Sex: 119, 379, 392–3, 434, 444, 511n, 538n, 569, 570, 574n, 861, 896–7, 975
Shafer, Robert: *Paul Elmer More*, 165
Shakespeare, William: *Antony and Cleopatra*, 130, 267, 908, 1032; *As You Like It*, 443, 776; *Cymbeline*, 620–1; *Hamlet*, 64, 374, 512, 520n, 555–6, 615; *Henry IV, Pt. I*, 258, 412, 620, 691, 879; *Henry IV, Pt. II*, 541; *Henry V*, 678–9, 859, 1000; *King Lear*, 244, 546, 621; *Macbeth*, 973; *Measure for Measure*, 326–7; *The Merchant of Venice*, 958; *Midsummer Night's Dream*, 172, 349–50, 919n; *Much Ado About Nothing*, 271, 433; *Othello*, 620; *Richard III*, 271; *Romeo and Juliet*, 168, 776; *Sonnets*, 732; *Taming of the Shrew*, 261, 1040; *The Tempest*, 172, 268, 842; *Troilus and Cressida*, 149, 478; *Twelfth Night*, 112, 574; *Winter's Tale*, 170, 894; men. 2n, 236, 259–60, 356, 370, 378n, 442, 533, 548n, 576, 644, 675, 676, 703, 749n, 831, 886n, 902, 976, 1052
Shanghai: 1, 14, 25, 44–5, 46, 49, 54
Shankill (Co. Down): 133n
Shantivanam Ashram: 1048, 1049
Sharrock, Roger: 160n
Shaw, George Bernard: *Back to Methuselah*, 255; *Man and Superman*, 871; men. 28, 441, 870
Sheed, Frank: 170, 177
Sheed and Ward Publishers: 170, 177
Sheffield Educational Settlement: 872
Sheffield University: 499n
Sheldonian Theatre: 151, 170n
Shelley, Hugh Alexander: 1054
Shelley, Mary: see Mary Neylan
Shelley, Mary Godwin: 224n, 421
Shelley, Maud: 1054
Shelley, Percy Bysshe: *Adonais*, 224; *Prometheus Unbound*, 418; *Witch of Atlas*, 224; men. 119, 421, 919, 1059
Shenstone, William: 246n
Sherburn, George: *Early Career of Alexander Pope*, 212;
Sherley-Price, Leo: 507n
Sherlock Holmes Society: 1042
Shillingford (Oxford): 18
Short, Charles: see Charlton T. Lewis
Shove, Fredegond: *The Water Mill*, 762
Shrewsbury: 504
Shrimpton, Amy: 1068
Shrimpton, Ivy: 1065, 1068
Shroud of Turin: 494, 495, 1058
Siam: 642
Sibelius, Jean: *Tapiola*, 151; men. 171, 175, 181
Sidelings, The: (Westcott Barton): 1068
Sidney, Sir Philip: *Arcadia*, 547, 562, 463, 644
Sidney Sussex College (Cambridge): 19n, 469n, 523n
Sieveking, Lance: letter to:

924–5; *A Private Volcano*; *Bats in the Belfry*; *The Stuff of Radio*, 924n
Sigar of Brabant: 903
Silence: 639
Simmons, Jean: 805, 1035
Simon Bolivar: 290n
Simon of Cyrene: 232
Simpson, Evelyn M.: 81n
Simpson, Joseph: 222n
Simpson, Percy: 81–2
Sin: 391, 422, 423, 450, 466n, 467, 479, 502n, 573n, 765, 788, 929, 940, 956, 1007, 1010n
Sinai: 149n
Sinodun Hill (Berkshire): 18
Sino-Japanese War: 44–5, 46, 67
Sirius: 697
Sisam, Kenneth: 167
Sisters of the Epiphany: 1053
Sitwell, Dame Edith: *Bucolic Comedies*, 679n; *English Eccentrics*, 679n; *Green Song*, 679n; *The Mother*, 679n; *Shadow of Cain*, 679n; *The Sleeping Beauty*, 357, 679n; *Troy Park*, 679n; *Twentieth-Century Harlequinade*, 679n; men. 94, 679–80
Sitwell, Sir Osbert: 679n, 1063
Sitwell, Sacherverell: 679n
Skeat, Walter William: *Chaucer Canon*, 141
Skinner, Anthony: 1073
Skinner, Benjamin: 1073
Skinner, Catherine: 1073
Skinner, Charlotte: 1073
Skinner, Daniel: 1073
Skinner, Emelie Madeline: 1072
Skinner, Jonathan: 1073
Skinner, Martyn: biography, 1072–3; letters to: 518–19, 561, 808, 810, 816; *Alms for Oblivion*, 1073; *Letters to Malaya*, 561, 808, 1073; *Old Rectory*, 1073; *The Return of Arthur*, 1073; *Sir Elfadore and Mabyna*, 473–4, 491, 518, 1073; *Two Colloquies*, 1073; (ed. Rupert Hart-Davis) *Two Men of Letters: Correspondence Between R.C. Hutchinson, novelist, and Martyn Skinner, poet, 1957–1974*, 1073; men. 178, 491, 1023, 1044
Skinner, Pauline: 1073
Skinner, Sir Sydney: 1072
Slade School of Fine Art (London): 1018
Sleeping Beauty: 802
Smeaton, Oliphant: 370n
Smith, David Nichol: *Shakespeare in the Eighteenth Century*; *Some Observations*, 195; men, 195n, 405
Smith, Horace: *Rejected Addresses*; *Tin Trumpet*, 309n; men. 309
Smith, John Alexander: *De Anima*, 15n; men. 15, 76, 282, 311, 537
Smith, Logan Pearsall: *Milton and His Modern Critics*, 467
Smith, Sydney: *Elementary Sketches of Moral Philosophy*, 310
Smollett, Tobias: 361, 677
Smoot, Mr: letter to: 758
Snorri Sturluson: 535, 546
Snow, George Robert Sabine: 4
Snowden, Philip, Viscount: 10
Snow White and the Seven Dwarfs, 242
Snyder, John Wesley: 963
Snyder, Susan: 364n
Soaking Machine/Soak: 304, 339, 347, 349, 384, 386, 433
Socialism: 923
Society for the Prevention of Progress: letter to: 613–14
Society for the Promotion of Christian Knowledge (SPCK): 492n, 516n, 526n, 529, 555
Society of the Sacred Mission, The (Kelham): 252, 446, 673n, 1030–1
Society of St John the Evangelist, 453n, 483, 508, 1015–16
Socrates: 192
Socratic Club: See Oxford University Socratic Club
Socratic Digest: 714n, 936n, 954n
Soloviev, Vladimir Sergeyevich: *The Meaning of Love*, 648
Somerset Giants: 701
Somerset Light Infantry: 839
Somerville College (Oxford): 431n, 519n, 1065–66
Song of Roland, The: 733–4
Song of Solomon: 896
Sophia: 204n, 1052n
Sophocles: *Antigone*, 456; *Philoctetes*, 894; men. 164
Sorbonne, The: 292n
Soul, the: 11, 78, 118–20, 149, 172, 191, 194, 196, 207, 208, 518–19, 632, 660, 669n, 764, 1064
Southampton: 928
Southampton University: 1024
South Boston (Virginia): 1078
Southern California C.S. Lewis Society: 270n
Southey, Robert: *Letters*, 421
Southwold (Suffolk): 1036
Space Travel: 216, 235, 236–7, 741, 743n
Spain: 42, 368, 736n, 745, 961
Speaker Builder: 1025
Spectator, The: letter to: 540; men. 69, 352n, 606, 687n, 726n, 754
Speculum: 142
Spender, Stephen: 734
Spens, Janet: letters to: 147–9, 153–4, 223–4; *An Essay on Shakespeare's Relation to Tradition*, 147n; *Elizabethan Drama*, 147n; *Spenser's Faerie Queene*, 147–9, 154; *Two Periods of Disillusion*, 147; men. 513n
Spenser, Edmund: *Faerie Queene*, 11, 53, 67–8, 147–9, 154, 170, 177, 203, 224, 264, 562, 615, 644; 'Mutabilitie Cantos', 147; *The Shepheardes Calender*, 872; (with Gabriel Harvey) *Three Letters Between Two Universitie Men*, 655; men. 55, 98, 313n, 722

Spinoza, Benedict de: *Ethics*, 542n; men. 225n, 570
Spiritualism: 335–6, 352, 607–8
Springfield St Mary's (Oxford): 862
Squizzato, Don Luciano: (ed) *Una Gioia Insolita*, 799n, 844n, 998n 1038
S.S.Pladda: 414
Stadhampton (Oxford): 18
Staël, Anne-Louise-Germaine, Madame de: *Corinne*, 202
Stalin, Joseph: 391, 408
Staples, Rt. Hon. John: 969n
Stapleton, Olaf: *Last and First Men*, 236; *Star Maker*, 594
Starr, Nathan Comfort: letter to: 809; *The Dynamics of Literature*; *King Arthur Today*, 809n
Stebbins, H. Lyman: letter to: 645–7
Stebbins, Madeleine: 646n
Steele, Harwood: 'The Somerset Giants', 701
Steele, Sir Richard: 352n
Stein, Gertrude: *Tender Buttons*, 219n; men. 164, 219
Steiner, Rudolf: 55n, 420–1, 512, 572n, 669n, 690n, 729, 1051
Stephens, James: *Crock of Gold*, 120, 630; men. 558, 720n, 721, 753
Stern, Gladys Bronwen: *The Woman in the Hall*, 805, 828, 1002, 1035; men. 1002
Sterne, Laurence: *Tristram Shandy*, 38
Steuch, Augustine: 188n
Stevens, Courtney Edward 'Tom Brown': 282, 347
Stevenson, Robert Louis: *Lay Morals*, 312; *Strange Case of Dr Jekyll and Mr Hyde*, 156; men. 365
Stevenson, Victoria: *Clover Magic*; *The Magic Broom*; *The Magic Footstool*, 1018
Stewart, H.F.: 529n
Stock Responses: 779n, 1029–30
Stocks, John Leofric: 341n
Stocks, Mary Danvers Brinton, Baroness: *Fifty Years in Every Street*, 341n; *Hail Nero*, 341; *History of the Workers' Educational Association*, 341n; *My Commonplace Book*, 341n; men. 341
Stoics/Stoicism: 70, 374, 448, 464, 475, 764, 771, 773, 871
Stoker, Willard: 349n
Stokes, Sally: 341
Stone, Eric: *Oxfordshire Hundred Rolls of 1279*, 365n; men. 365
Storrs, Sir Ronald: 752, 769, 771, 775, 777, 778, 790, 796, 797
Story/Stories: 33, 34, 655
Stowe School (Buckinghamshire): 1081
Strachey, John St Loe: 1011
Strachey, Lytton: 31
Strandtown (Belfast): 97n, 341, 342n, 485
Stratford-on-Avon: 259, 260, 261, 271
Strauss, Albrecht B.: 229n, 497n
Student Christian Movement: 336, 346n, 353n, 376n, 471n, 1053
Style, literary: 20, 448, 590–1
Sub-Creation: 555, 589
Subjectivism: 468, 561
Substitution: 201, 805–6
Suetonius: 505
Suffern, Lilian 'Lily': 68
Suffern, William: 68n
Sullivan, Arthur: see W.S.Gilbert
Sun, The: 725, 919
Sunday Express: 950
Sunday Pictorial: 294
Sunday Times: 336n, 337n, 366, 428n, 778n
Superman, The: 754, 871n
Supernaturalism: 285, 591, 682, 733
Surrealism: 437
Swans (on Kilns pond): 11n, 306
Swanwick, Anna: 737n
Swanwick (Hampshire): 284
Sweden: 398
Sweet, Henry: *An Anglo-Saxon Primer*, *An Anglo-Saxon Reader*, 643; men. 264n
Swift, Jonathan: *Gulliver's Travels*, 308, 477, 689; men. 308, 405, 644
Swindon (Wiltshire): 306
Swinburne, Algernon Charles: 24, 223, 306, 535, 546, 580
Switzerland: 351n, 379n, 899
Sydenham (Belfast): 305n
Sydenham High School (London): 499n
Sylvester, Josiah: 364n
Symbolism: 157, 438, 439, 565, 1083
Syrian Church: 1047

Tacitus: *Agricola*, 418, 489, 774; men. 505, 936
Talbot, Howard (with Mark Ambient and Lionel Monkton): *The Arcadians*, 51
Talbot, Bishop Neville Stuart: *Mind of the Disciples*; *Thoughts on Religion at the Front*, 495n; men. 495
Talbot, Mr: letter to: 707
Tao, The: 561, 756, 757
Tassell, Douglas Spencer Montagu: 426
Tarzan: 237n
Tasso, Torquato: *Gerusalemme Liberata*, 68, 203, 562, 990, 1000
Taunton (Somerset): 317, 383
Taylor, Jeremy: *Whole Works*, 4–5, 13, 321n; men. 20, 43, 353
Taylor, Sherwood: *Illustrated History of Science*; *World of Science*, 1011n; men. 1011
Taylor, Vincent: *The Atonement*, 451
Taylor, William: 29, 75, 282, 340, 380
Temple, The (London): 1076
Temple, Sir William: 588
Temptation: 266–9, 426–7, 507, 521–2, 960
Tennyson, Alfred, Lord: *In Memoriam A.H.H.*, 241,

502–3, 684; 'The Lotus-Eaters', 732; *The Princess*, 103; men. 68
Tennyson, G.B.: (ed) *Owen Barfield on C.S. Lewis*, 870n
Tertullian: *De Anima*, 716; *De Exhortatione Castitatis*, 327
Tetzel, Johann: 813, 815
Tewsfield: 38n, 108, 279n, 1050
Textual Criticism: 451
Thackeray, William Makepeace: *History of Henry Esmond*, 530; *Pendennis*, 82, 83; *The Rose and the Ring*, 551; men. 82–3, 550, 918
Thame (Oxfordshire): 281
Thames Polytechnic (London): 1059
Theism: 145, 431, 651, 747, 871
Theologia Germanica: 232, 529, 994
Theology: letters to: 250–2, 866–7; men. 243, 247n, 252–4, 259, 262n, 332–3, 351, 379n, 381, 401, 412, 446, 451n, 490, 817, 861n, 865–6, 1076
Theology Today: 1032
Theosophy: 486, 702, 871
Theresa of Avila, St: 107
Thirsk, Joan: 415n
Thomas, R.S.: 1063
Thomas, Rev. Wilfrid Savage: 2–3, 8–9, 21n, 42, 272n
Thomas, Mrs Wilfrid Savage: 2
Thomas à Becket, St: 1029
Thomas à Kempis, *Imitation of Christ*, 23, 487, 507, 635–6, 770, 829, 843, 844, 905, 906, 940, 994
Thomas Aquinas, St, (and Thomism): *Summa Theologica*, 55n, 134n, 135n, 176, 179n, 194n, 205–6, 207, 251, 402, 466, 577, 583, 1044; men. 134n, 142n, 144, 146n, 228n, 418, 461n, 476n
Thomas of Erceldoune, *Thomas Rymer and Queen of Elfland*, 733
Thompson, James Matthew: letter to: 428–9; *Annotated Psalter*, 429n; *Collected Verse*, 429n; *Jesus According to Mark*, 429n; *My Apologia*, 424, 427–8, 433n; *Napoleon Bonaparte*, 429n; *Robespierre*, 429n; *Through Facts to Faith*, 429n
Thomson, Patricia Tyler: letters to: 499–500; (with K. Muir) *Collected Poems of Sir Thomas Wyatt*; *Elizabethan Lyrical Poets*; *George Sand and the Victorians*; *Sir Thomas Wyatt and his Background*; *Victorian Heroine*; *Wyatt: The Critical Heritage*, 499
Thought: 666
Thrale, Hester Lynch, Mrs: *Thraliana*, 406n; men. 31, 203n
Thrills: 441
Thucydides: 528
Thwaites, Michael: letter to: 642–5; *Honey Man*; *Jervis Bay*; *Milton Blind*; *Poems of War and Peace*; *Truth Will Out*, 643n
Tillyard, Alfred Isaac: 1073
Tillyard, Catherine: 1073
Tillyard, Eustace Mandeville Wetenhall: biography, 1073–4; *The Elizabethan World Picture*, 1074; *The English Epic Tradition*, 1074; *The Hope Vases*, 1073; *Milton*, 156n, 248n, 1073–4; (with C.S. Lewis) *The Personal Heresy: A Controversy*, 157n, 248n, 249, 256, 260, 1073–4; 'The Personal Heresy in Criticism: A Rejoinder', 1074; men. 210n, 2311, 222, 248, 621
Timberscombe (Somerset): 388
Time: 18, 703, 735, 775–6, 778, 831, 847, 915, 962
Time (magazine): 830, 849
Time and Tide: 434, 709, 762n, 817, 821n, 859–60, 863, 938n, 972n
Timelessness of God: 703, 775–6, 847, 915, 962
Times, The: 46, 79n, 112n, 271, 290n, 349n, 355n, 425n, 601, 743n
Times Literary Supplement, The: 621, 780–1
Tim Oi Li, Florence: 859–60
Timoleon: 902
Tintagel: 782
Tir-nan-Og (Land of the Young): 629–30
Tisdall, Christopher Patrick: 1055
Tisdall, Sarah: biography, 1055; letters to: 618–9; men. 254, 314, 480, 507, 508, 517, 518, 652, 705, 961
Titarangi (New Zealand): 823n
Tizard, Sir Henry: 615, 808n
Todd, Henry John: 886
Tolkien, Christopher: (ed) *Tree and Leaf*, 650n; men. 838, 839; men. 854n
Tolkien, Edith (wife of JRRT): 297, 301, 925–6, 1021
Tolkien, Fr John Francis Reuel: biography, 1074–5; (with Priscilla Tolkien) *The Tolkien Family Album*, 1075; men. 280, 378, 405
Tolkien, John Ronald Reuel: letter to: 990–1; part in Lewis's conversion, 1; proposals for English School, 9n; beginning of Inklings, 16; member of 'Cave', 26n; translation of *Owl and the Nightingale*, 75; grew up on William Morris and George MacDonald, 103; as Catholic friend, 136; to attend *Ring of the Nibelung*, 137; and medieval word, 166; too busy to write volume on Old English Literature for Oxford History of English Literature, 168; founding of Inklings, 181–2; introduced to *Place of the Lion*, 183; on Barfield's

Tolkien, John Ronald Reuel – *cont.* *Silver Trumpet*, 198; *The Hobbit* published, 212; and Walking Tour, 222; his Icelandic Society, 227n; 'a real philologist', 264; descended from Saxon nobility, 273; his son John, 280; and Charles Williams, 283; reads part of *Lord of the Rings* to Inklings, 288–9; his trials, 297; Inklings meet in his home, 302; Monday meetings with Lewis, 335; reads chapter of *Lord of the Rings* to Inklings, 336; at Williams's Milton lecture, 339; sees *Midsummer Night's Dream*, 349; on cremation, 358; and Hugo Dyson, 360; at 'Cave', 365; a Spanish friend, 368; a walk with Lewis, 377–8; son in Rome, 378; at Pembroke College, 380; news from Rome, 405; at Inklings meeting, 416–17; importance of Earth, 431–2; Inklings meeting, 436; one to whom *Problem of Pain* dedicated, 501; on Beatrix Potter, 537–8; meets E.R.Eddison, 553; and Katharine Farrer, 612n; 'a very great man', 631; remarks on *Beowulf*, 644; *Festschrift* for Charles Williams, 649, 650; and Withywindle, 655; and Roger Lancelyn Green, 672; describes Bultitude as portrait of Lewis, 682; at 'Victory Inklings', 682, 687; and Walter de la Mare, 687; and Roy Campbell, 736n; and Ronald Knox, 769n; likes Barfield's 'Poetic Diction and Legal Fiction', 817; signs 'Ham Testimonial', 838, 839; hears Lewis read *Lion, the Witch and the Wardrobe*, 923–4; given food parcel, 925–6; at Edinburgh University, 931; Lewis on *Lord of the Rings*, 990–1; Pauline Baynes illustrates *Farmer Giles of Ham*, 1018–19; Baynes illustrates *Adventures of Tom Bombadil* and *Smith of Wootton Major*, 1020; move to Bournemouth, 1021; supervised R.L. Green's thesis, 1039; on *The Lion, the Witch and the Wardrobe*, 1041; and R.L. Green, 1042;
  Writings: *Adventures of Tom Bombadil*, 1020; *Farmer Giles of Ham*, 1009, 1018–19; *The Hobbit*, 96, 264, 631; *Letters of J.R.R. Tolkien*, 181–2, 1018n, 1020; *Lord of the Rings*, 288–9, 302, 631, 655, 990–1; 'On Fairy-Stories', 650, 654, 681, 817, 867; *Tree and Leaf*, 650n; men. 1074–5
Tolkien, Priscilla: (with John Tolkien) *The Tolkien Family Album*, 1075
Tolstoy, Leo: *Anna Karenina*, 512–13, 887; *Resurrection*, 433–4, 436; *War and Peace*, 433, 531–2, 694, 957; men. 919
Torquay (Devon): 1051
Totalitarians: 368
Tottel, Richard: 235
Tower of Glass, The: 19n, 84
Toy, Sidney: 1076
Toy, Violet Mary: biography: 1075–6; letter to: 620–1
Toynbee, Arnold: *Civilization on Trial*, 959n
Tractarians: 1055, 1056
Traditionalism: 204n, 1052, 1053
Traditionalist School: 204, 1052
Traherne, Thomas: *Centuries of Meditations*, 505, 529, 645, 994
Trajan, Emperor: 135n
Transfiguration, The: 479
Translation/s: 533–4
Transposition: 207
Transubstantiation: 646
Trappists: 987
Trent, Council of: 502
Trevelyan, George Macaulay: 552, 616, 675, 676
Trevor-Roper, Hugh Redwald: *Archbishop Laud*, 336–7
Trichy (India): 1049
Trinity, The Holy: 74, 146
Trinity College (Cambridge): 157n, 335n, 552, 616, 675, 696n, 976n
Trinity College (Oxford): 414n, 415n, 498, 572n, 612, 839, 1059
Trinity College (Dublin): 133n, 309n
Tristram/Tristan, Sir: 512, 781–6
Trojans, The: 267n
Trollope, Anthony: *Autobiography*, 456–7; *Barchester Towers*, 280, 314n, 352; *Framley Parsonage*, 334, 496; *The Small House at Allington*, 496; *The Warden*, 314n; men. 82, 144, 298, 354, 363, 364, 551, 881
Trotter, W.F.: 915n
Troy: 77, 625n, 1041
Truman, Harry S.: 889n, 963n
Truro Cathedral: 662n
Tuckton Lodge (Southbourne): 1068
Tunisia: 295n
Tupper, Martin: *Proverbial Philosophy*, 63
Turner, Bradwell Talbot: 355n
Turner, Sir Eric Gardner: 432
Turner, John Symonds: 360
Twyford (Buckinghamshire): 508, 519
Twyford Preparatory School (Winchester): 1023
Tyers, Tom: 337
Ty-Isa (or Tigh-Essa): 305
Tykes (dog): 11
Tylor, Edward Burnett: *Anthropology*, 75, 76
Tyndale, William: 813, 815

Uden, Grant: *Dictionary of Chivalry*, 1021

Ulreich, John C., Jr: 222n
Ulysses: 795, 951, 1001
Underhill, Evelyn: letters to: 234–5, 459–60; *Letters*, 459n; *Life of the Spirit*; *Mysticism*; *Worship*, 234n; men. 458
Unicorns: 857
Unitarianism: 580n
United Council for Missionary Education: 805n
United Mine Workers of America: 963n
United Nations Organization: 884, 892n
United States Naval Academy: 567n
University College (Cardiff): 424n
University College (Oxford): 15n, 69n, 157n, 220n, 356, 399n, 406n, 410, 488, 517, 626n, 839, 853n, 1024
University College (London): 168n, 182n, 236n, 433n, 737n, 1082
University College (Swansea): 472n
University College of North Wales (Bangor): 472n
University College of South Wales (Cardiff): 425n, 1059
University of Birmingham: 414n, 678n
University of Chicago: 909
University of Durham: 286n
University of East Anglia: 1036
University of Edinburgh: 195n, 931
University of Exeter: 1030
University of Florida (Gainesville): 809n
University of Freiburg-im-Breisgau: 16n
University of Greenwich (London): 1059
University of Hong Kong: 24n
University of Kaunas (Lithuania): 1052
University of Keele: 1075
University of Leeds: 167n, 182n, 271n, 1074
University of Leicester: 936
University of Liverpool: 1040, 1041, 1043
University of London: 69n, 432n, 492n, 739n, 1033, 1035
University of Manchester: 166n, 240n, 341n, 365n, 437n
University of Melbourne: 642n
University of Michigan: 567n, 1078
University of Naples: 349n
University of North Carolina: 14n
University of Padua: 821n
University of Reading: 16n, 316n, 501, 888n, 1054
University of St Andrews (Scotland): 650n, 706, 716, 737, 1036
University of Sydney: 626n
University of Victoria (British Columbia): 55n
University of Vienna: 416n, 609n
University of Virginia: 1078
University of Wisconsin: 567n
Upper Thames Patrol: 486
Upson, Abbot Wilfrid: 1046
Uranus: 694
Urey, Harold Clayton: 909
Urre, Sir: 679n
Usherwood, Francis: letter to: 801–2

Vanbrugh, Sir John: 1081
Van Deusen, Mary: letter to: 965
Van Oss, Mark Dunbar: (with N. McDermot) *Lands Tribunal*, 519n; men. 519
Vansittart, A.A.: 687
Vasconcellos, Josefina de: 537n
Vatican, The: 1038, 1047, 1078
Vatican Council II: 'Declaration on the Relation of the Church to Non-Christian Religions', 1048; men. 1048
Vaughan, Dorothea 'Dotty': 86, 315
Vaughan, Herbert: 209n, 215
Vaughan, Thomas: 43
V-Day: 647
Vedas: 1048
Venice: 961
Venus: 197
Venus (the planet): 348, 397, 496, 504, 508, 520, 569, 751
Verne, Jules: 753
Verona (Italy): 798, 829, 830, 843, 1036–8
Vicenza (Italy): 1037
Victoria, Queen: 1917
Vida, Marco Girolamo: *Christiad*, 562
Vidler, Rev. Alec: biography: 1076–7; letters to: 243, 247, 253–4, 255, 259, 332, 412, 490; *A Variety of Catholic Modernists*; *The Development of Modern Catholicism*; *F.D. Maurice and Company*; *God's Judgement on Europe*; *The Modernist Movement in the Roman Church*; *Natural Law*; *Objections to Christian Belief*; *Scenes from a Clerical Life*; (ed) *Soundings*, 1077; *Windsor Sermons*, 1076–7; men. 401, 866n
Vienna: 958
Vinaver, Eugène: letter to: 166–7; *Malory*, 166n, 673; 'Malory's *Morte d'Arthur* in the Light of a Recent Discovery', 166, 167n; *Rise of Romance*, 166n; *Tale of the Death of King Arthur*, 166n; (ed) *The Works of Sir Thomas Malory*, 166n, 167, 780
Vincent of Beauvais: *Speculum Naturale*, 141
Vincent of Lerins, St: *Commonitorium*, 452
Virgil: *Aeneid*, 61, 62, 156, 257, 625, 750, 754, 843, 844, 991; *Georgics*, 51, 61, 223n, 530, 551, 750; *Pastoral Poems*, 564n; men. 164, 288n, 344n, 534, 557, 712, 724, 919, 990
Virtue: 772
Vivisection: 798

Virtuous Unbeliever, The: 256, 499
Visiak, E.H.: 753
Voltaire: *Candide*, 125; *Micromégas*, 237; men. 773, 843 844
Von Hügel, Friedrich: *Essays and Addresses*, 529; *Eternal Life*, 529, 775, 915; men. 234n
Voyage of the Argo: 564n
Vulgate, The (Latin version of the Bible): 814, 816, 941

Wace: *Roman de Brut*, 673
Waddington, Conrad Hal: *Science and Ethics*, 594
Wade Center (Wheaton College): 14n, 666n, 1080
Wadham College (Oxford): 46n, 71n, 182n, 283n, 313n, 1040
Wagner, Richard: *Rhinegold*, 77, 107, 112, 114; *Ring of the Nibelung*, 77n, 137, 138, 223, 630, 684; *Siegfried*, 77, 78, 79, 84, 114; *Siegfried Idyll*, 171; *Tristan und Isolde*, 512n; *Valkyrie*, 114; men. 11, 51, 175, 441
Wain, John: letter to: 888; *A Winter in the Hills*; *The Contenders*; *Sprightly Running*, 888n
Walberswick Peasant Pottery Company (Suffolk): 1061
Waldorf School (Germany): 1051
Wales: 71
Waley, Arthur: 881n
Walking Tours: 17–8, 39, 49, 55, 56, 63–4, 71–4, 103, 155, 158–9, 239–40, 241, 244, 310, 316–22, 333, 337–9, 376–7, 381–8, 572
Wall, Barbara: biography, 1077–8; letters to: 619, 713–13, 777–8; (as Barbara Wall) *And Was Crucified*, 1078; (as Barbara Lucas) *Anna Collett*, 713–14, 1078; *Great Saints and Saintly Figures*, 1078; (as Barbara Lucas) *More Ado About Nothing*; *Stars were Born*, 1078; (as Barbara Wall with Bernard Wall) *Thaw at the Vatican*, 1078; (as Barbara Lucas) *The Trembling of the Sea*; *Widows and Widowers*, 1078
Wall, Bernard: 1078
Wallace, Edgar: 75, 517
Wallace, Henry Agard: 613
Walsh, Alison: 1078
Walsh, Chad: biography: 1078–81; letters to: 686, 883, 890, 1005, 1012–13; *Behold the Glory*; *Campus Gods on Trial*; *Chad Walsh Reviews C.S. Lewis*, 1080; 'C.S. Lewis: Apostle to the Skeptics' (essay), 1078; *C.S. Lewis: Apostle to the Skeptics*, 883, 890, 923, 988, 1005, 1079; *Doors into Poetry*; *Early Christians of the 21st Century*; *End of Nature*; *From Utopia to Nightmare*; *God at Large*; *Hang Mr Up My Begging Bowl*, 1080; 'Impact on America', 1078, 1080; *Knock and Enter*; *The Literary Legacy of C.S. Lewis*; 'The Man and the Mystery'; *Nellie and Her Flying Crocodile*; 'The Re-education of the Fearful Pilgrim'; *Stop Looking and Listen*; *The Unknown Dance*, 1080
Walsh, Damaris: 1078
Walsh, Eva: 1078, 1080
Walsh, Madeline: 1078
Walsh, Sarah-Lindsay: 1078
Walton, William: 679n
Walton-on-Thames (Surrey): 1043
Wanderer, The: 220n
Wantage (Berkshire): 261n, 519, 586, 636, 812, 1055, 1056, 1058
Wapping (London): 317
War: 233–4, 250–2, 260, 278n
Warborough (Oxford): 18
Warburg, Aby M.: 609n
Warburg Institute (University of London): 609n
Ward, William Hayes: 970n
Wardale, Edith Elizabeth: *An Old English Grammar*, 643
Ware, Bishop Kallistos: (with G. Every and R. Harris) *Seasons of the Spirit*, 1031
Warfield M. Firor Chair of Surgery: 1032
Warneford Hospital: 953n
War Office: 1061
Warrack, Grace: 369n
Warrington (Lancashire): 131
Warsaw: 271, 310
Warton, Joseph: *Essay on the Writings and Genius of Pope*, 886
Warton, Thomas: *History of English Poetry*, 886
Watchet (Somerset): 382
Waterman, Hugh: 178, 1044
Watford (Hertfordshire): 292n
Watkins, Pamela: *Joyce's Ockenden*, 584
Watlington (Oxfordshire): 1054
Watson, Thomas: 236
Watts, Isaac: 624
Wattson, Rev. Paul James: 839n
Waugh, Evelyn: *The Life of the Right Reverend Ronald Knox*, 769n
Webb, Clement Charles Julian: 537, 903
Webb, I.: 711
Webb, Miss: 508
Webbe, William: 236
Webster, John: 164
Week of Prayer for Christian Unity: 829, 830
Weird Tales: 597
Welch, Rev. James William: letters to: 470, 681; men. 469–70, 515n, 565n, 580n, 582, 1070
Weldon, Thomas Dewar: 336n, 370, 434, 615n
Wellesley College: 286n
Wellesz, Egon Joseph: 416
Wells, H.G.: *First Men in the Moon*, 237, 442, 456, 918; *The Time Machine*, 131,

918; men. 353, 454, 630, 753
Wells Theological College: 2n, 272n, 292n, 517n, 1015
Wenlock Edge (Shropshire): 240
Wenvoe (Cardiff): 412, 425
Wenvoe Camp (Cardiff): 412
Wesley, Charles: 914n, 929
West, Priscilla Lancelyn: 1042
Westcott, Bishop Brook Foss: *Epistle to the Hebrews*, 521–2
Westcott House (Cambridge): 376n, 523n, 1076–7
Westfield (Massachusetts): 827n, 854, 855, 876, 930
Westfield College (University of London): 313n, 340–2, 854n
Westminster Abbey: 15n, 1017, 1033
Westminster Cathedral (London): 435n
Westminster College (Cambridge): 471n
Westminster School: 6n, 378n, 537, 577
West Peterborough (New Hampshire): 1025
Wheatley (Oxford): 18
Wheaton College (Illinois): 1024, 1025
Whimsical: 6
Whipsnade Zoo: 2, 83–4
Whistler, Helen: 1081
Whistler, Henry: 1081
Whistler, James McNeill: 930n
Whistler, Jill: 774n
Whistler, Sir Laurence: biography: 1081; letters to: 757–8, 769, 772–5; *Initials in the Heart*, 1081; *Jill Furse*, 774; *The Laughter and the Urn: The Life of Rex Whistler*; *Rex Whistler: His Life and His Drawings*; *Sir John Vanbrugh*; *The View From This Window*; *The World's Room*, 1081; men. 756–7, 767, 771–2, 779
Whistler, Rex: 1081
White, Agnes Romilly: *Gape Row*, 151, 175
White, Bill: 1067, 1068
White, Terence Hanbury: *Mistress Masham's Repose*, 774–5; *Sword in the Stone*, 456, 775
White, William Luther: 182n
Whitehead, Alfred North: 421
White Horse Hotel (Drogheda): 787
Whittaker, Frank: 1018
Whitty, Kathleen: 10, 126
W.H.Smith: 473n
Wiblin, Vida Mary 'Smudge': 291
Wicklow Mountains: 790
Wilde, Oscar: 34, 518, 773, 930
Wilferd, Jacklyn: 353n
Wilhelmina of the Netherlands, Queen: 414n
Wilkinson, Cyril Hackett: 304, 323–4
Will, Act of: 632, 764, 826
Willen (Milton Keynes): 1031
Willey, Basil: *Seventeenth Century Background*, 212; men. 1074
William Heinemann Award: 1063
William of Ockham: 134n
William of Sens: 1069
Williams, Charles: biography, 1081–6; letters to: 183–7, 218–20, 227–8; *All Hallows' Eve*, 666, 1084, 1086; (with C.S. Lewis) *Arthurian Torso*, 562n, 655–6, 723n, 744–5, 767–8, 885–6, 1083; *Collected Plays*, 410n; *Cranmer of Canterbury*, 185; *Descent into Hell*, 218–19, 245, 501, 562, 672, 806, 988, 1084; *Descent of the Dove*, 988, 993; *The English Poetic Mind*, 620; *Figure of Beatrice*, 649, 1071, 1082, 1086; *The Greater Trumps*, 1084; *He Came Down from Heaven*, 227–8, 806, 1082; *The House by the Stable*, 289; *The House of the Octopus*, 805, 988; (ed Anne Ridler) *The Image of the City*, 1083n; *Judgement at Chelmsford*, 248; *Many Dimensions*, 187, 197–8, 249, 1084; *Poems of Conformity*, 184, 186–7; *Place of the Lion*, 180–1, 183, 197–9, 200, 245, 249, 501, 1084; Preface to *The English Poems of John Milton* (ed. H.C.Beeching, 1940), 1085; *The Region of the Summer Stars*, 684, 886n, 902, 1082; *Seed of Adam and Other Plays*, 289n, 512n; *Shadows of Ecstasy*, 1084; *The Silver Stair*, 1082; *Taliessin Through Logres*, 245, 247n, 249, 252, 497, 684, 903, 1082; *Terror of Light*, 410; 'The Theology of Romantic Love,' 1082; *Thomas Cranmer of Canterbury*, 1069; *War in Heaven*, 218, 1083; men. 184–5; 243n, 263, 272, 278, 283, 293–4, 335, 336–7, 339, 345–6, 357, 360, 389, 415, 459n, 478, 500–1, 553, 557, 562, 618, 621, 631, 635, 649–54, 656, 658–9, 661, 662–3, 665, 697, 699, 700–1, 704, 708–9, 710, 712, 726–7, 729, 744–5, 768, 810, 816–17, 819, 821, 861, 864–7, 891, 892–3, 919, 989
Williams, Florence 'Michal' (wife of Charles Williams): letters to: 653–4, 767–8; *Christian Symbolism*, 1083; 'As I Remember', 1083; men. 650, 662, 704, 745, 1083, 1084, 1086
Williams, Rev. John Gordon: letter to: 491–2; *Hungry World*; *Life of Our Lord*, 492
Williams, Mary: 1082
Williams, Michael Stansby: 1083, 1084, 1086
Williams, Rev. Norman Powell 'Nippy': *Ideas of the Fall*, 450

Williams, Ralph Vaughan: 762n
Williams, Richard Walter Stansby: 1082
Williams, T.: *Every Man His Own Lawyer*, 319
Williams-Ellis, Amabel: *Arabian Nights*; *Fairy Tales from the British Isles*, 1021
Wilson, Dorothy: 582n
Wilson, Frank Percy: letters to 168, 221–2; *English Drama 1485–1585*, 167n; men. 167–8, 235–6, 397n, 551n
Wilson, Harold: 129n
Wilson, Woodrow: 28n, 884
Winchcombe (Gloucestershire): 1023
Winchester Cathedral: 370n
Winchester College: 166n, 278n, 508n, 780, 1030
Windsor Castle: 114n
Winkworth, Susanna: 232n, 994n
Wireless World: 1024
Wisdom: 1085
Wiseman, Mrs Percival: letters to: 521–2, 607–8
Wish-Fulfilment: 454, 457
Witchcraft: 475n
Witches: 526, 595
Witham (Essex): 1069
Withyham (East Sussex): 964, 969
Wodehouse, P.G.: *Right Ho Jeeves*, 271; men. 219, 1003–4
Woking (Surrey): 584n
Woking Grammar School for Girls: 584n
Wolfenden, John: 164n
Wolfram von Eschenbach: *Parzival*, 913n
Women's Air Force: 480
Wood, Arthur Denis Blackford: men. 65–6; (with Kate Crosby) *Terrace and Courtyard Gardens*; *Grow and Cook It*; *Practical Garden Design*, 65n
Woody Bay (Devon): 339
Woolwich Polytechnic (London): 1059
Wootton Courtney (Somerset): 338, 383–4
Worcester Cathedral: 1030
Worcester College (Oxford): 11n, 303n, 323, 681
Worcester High School: 1055
Wordsworth, William: (with S.T.Coleridge) *Lyrical Ballads*, 893; *The Prelude*, 39, 55, 154, 247, 273, 424, 487, 551, 764; *White Doe of Rylstone*, 40; men. 56, 211n, 397, 425, 477n, 538, 644, 753–4, 954–6
Workers' Educational Association: 678n
Worksop College (Nottinghamshire): 1023
World Dominion: 718n
World War I: 2n, 5n, 167n, 240, 274, 278, 286n, 296, 307, 345, 352n, 357, 365n, 376n, 385, 426n, 435, 487, 495n, 509n, 603n, 681n, 747, 924n, 950, 1034, 1041, 1050, 1061, 1068, 1073
World War II: 190n, 230–1, 240, 260, 269–70, 271, 272, 273, 274, 275, 277–8, 288n, 290–1, 293, 305, 307, 309, 310, 323, 325, 335, 344–5, 346, 350, 352–3, 355, 357, 358–9, 367, 368, 379, 385, 396, 399, 400, 402, 404–5, 406, 413, 416, 423, 425–6, 432, 435, 436, 451, 485, 487, 504, 505, 514, 522, 591, 596, 615n, 625, 647, 701, 833, 836n, 851n, 925n, 927n, 1018, 1033, 1061, 1075, 1084
Wormwood Scrubbs Prison: 470n
'Wounded Buffalo': see Henry Michael Denne Parker
Wrenn, Charles: *Beowulf*, 182n, 644; *Poetry of Caedmon*; *Study of Old English Literature*, 182n; men. 182, 283, 294, 416–17
Wyatt, A.J.: 643n
Wyatt, Sir Thomas: 166n, 211, 499n
Wycherley, William: 163
Wycliffe Hall (Oxford): 472n
Wyndham, George: 243n
Wynkyn de Worde: 326n
Wynyard School ('Belsen'): 47, 292, 390
Wytham (Oxfordshire): 220

Xmas and Christmas: 992–3

Yale University: 567n, 568n, 611n, 645n
Yang, Gladys Tayler: 431n
Yang, Hsien-yi: 430–1
Yatesbury (Wiltshire): 523na
Yeats, W.B.: *Last Poems and Two Plays*; *Purgatory*, 303n; *The Wanderings of Oisian*, 630
YMCA: 360n
Yonge, Charlotte M.: *Heir of Redclyffe*, 303n; men. 303, 310, 315
Young, Andrew: 756, 771, 772, 1063
Young, Francis: letter to: 611
Young, Karl: letter to: 567–8; *Drama of the Medieval Church*; *Origin and Development of the Story of Troilus and Criseyde*, 567n; men. 611
Young, Mr: letter to: 575
Yoxall, Mr: letters to: 1010, 1013
YWCA: 510n

Zacharias: 532
Zeus: 269n, 381n, 543, 973n
Zion: 875
Zodiac: 701n
Zohar: 574n, 625
Zola, Emile: 157
Zulus: 352

THE COLLECTED LETTERS OF
C. S. LEWIS

VOLUME I

BOOKS BY C. S. LEWIS

AVAILABLE FROM HARPERSANFRANCISCO

Mere Christianity

Mere Christianity Journal

The Screwtape Letters (with "Screwtape Proposes a Toast")

Miracles

The Abolition of Man

The Great Divorce

The Problem of Pain

The Weight of Glory

A Grief Observed

George MacDonald: An Anthology

A Year With C. S. Lewis

The Collected Letters of C. S. Lewis Volume II

ALSO AVAILABLE FROM HARPERCOLLINS

The Chronicles of Narnia:

The Magician's Nephew

The Lion, the Witch and the Wardrobe

The Horse and His Boy

Prince Caspian

The Voyage of the Dawn Treader

The Silver Chair

The Last Battle

THE COLLECTED LETTERS OF
C. S. LEWIS

VOLUME I

Family Letters 1905–1931

EDITED BY WALTER HOOPER

HarperSanFrancisco
A Division of HarperCollins*Publishers*

On the cover: Background C. S. Lewis handwriting image supplied by the Marion E. Wade Center, Wheaton College, Wheaton, IL.

HarperCollins books may be purchased for educational, business, or sales promotional use. For information please write: Special Markets Department, HarperCollins Publishers, 10 East 53rd Street, New York, NY 10022.

HarperCollins Web site: http://www.harpercollins.com

HarperCollins®, ®, and HarperSanFrancisco™ are trademarks of Harper-Collins Publishers.

PREVIOUSLY PUBLISHED AS A HARDCOVER EDITION IN 2004

Library of Congress Cataloging-in-Publication Data is available.

ISBN-13: 978–0–06–088449–9
ISBN-10: 0–06–088449–5

05 06 07 08 09 RRD(H) 10 9 8 7 6 5 4 3 2 1

CONTENTS

Preface vii
Abbreviations xiii

Letters:
1905–1910 1
1911–1912 15
1913 21
1914 46
1915 101
1916 159
1917 265
1918 351
1919 424
1920 471
1921 515
1922 589
1923 604
1924 617
1925 637
1926 657
1927 676
1928 745
1929 782
1930 856
1931 946

Biographical Appendix 978
Index 1025

PREFACE

'A heavy responsibility rests on those who forage through a dead man's correspondence and publish it indiscriminately.' Thus C. S. Lewis wrote to his father, Albert Lewis, on 5 June 1926 about *The Letters of Sir Walter Raleigh* which both were reading. Sir Walter Raleigh (1861–1922), whom Lewis had known, was the first Professor of English at Oxford (1904).

'The funny thing,' Lewis went on to say, is that Raleigh's 'views on the things of the spirit ... are not really in opposition to the atmosphere of Christianity. Whatever he thought about the historical side of it, he must have known...that the religious view, whether literally true or not, was at any rate much more *like* the reality than the views of the scientists and rationalists.'

It is surprising to find C. S. Lewis – the *clearest* of writers – attempting to create vagueness by his use of the phrases 'not really', 'the religious view' and 'the historical side'. He was 28 and had been a Fellow of Magdalen College for nine months. But since he ceased to believe in Christianity at the age of 14, he had been hiding his atheism from his father. In trying to make Raleigh's beliefs appear more orthodox than they were, 'Jack', as he was known to his friends, may have expressed the anxiety he felt about his father discovering *his* unbelief.

Only three years later, 1929, Albert Lewis died. Shortly before his father's death Jack converted to theism, a change that did much to unite his private beliefs with his public face. Then two years after this came the step which did away with the need for subterfuge altogether. On 28 September 1931 Jack was taken to Whipsnade Zoo in his brother's sidecar. 'When we set out,' he later said in *Surprised by Joy*, 'I did not believe that Jesus Christ is the Son of God, and when we reached the zoo I did. Yet I had not exactly spent the journey in thought. Nor in great emotion. "Emotional" is perhaps the last word we can apply to some of the most important events. It was more like when a man, after long sleep, still lying motionless in bed, becomes aware that he is now awake.'

Family Letters is the first of what is to be a three-volume collection of C. S. Lewis's letters. It covers the period November 1905 to 18 October

1931, from the first letter we have of Lewis's, written when he was seven, up to his acceptance of Christianity as true. To prevent the book from being too long it was necessary to leave out a few letters, but the volume contains about 95 per cent of the letters from that period. Many of the letters I have omitted were weekly 'regulation' letters from Jack to his father from his various schools. I have also left out certain letters to Owen Barfield and Cecil Harwood. In these Lewis was primarily arguing philosophical points or criticizing his correspondents' poetry. It was thought these letters would be of comparatively marginal interest to most people or of relatively small significance in the larger story.

When Albert Lewis died, Jack and his brother Warren, or 'Warnie', found their father had preserved masses of family papers going back to 1850. The papers were moved to Oxford, and Warnie spent much of 1933 to 1935 copying them. He undertook this enormous task using the hunt-and-peck system on his little Royal typewriter. Both brothers added valuable editorial notes along the way, and the papers were bound into 11 volumes entitled 'Memoirs of the Lewis Family: 1850–1930', now widely referred to as the 'Lewis Papers'. The original of the Lewis Papers is in the Marion E. Wade Center at Wheaton College in Illinois, with microfilms in the Bodleian Library, Oxford, and the Southern Historical Collection at the University of North Carolina at Chapel Hill. Any dubious spelling or dating in the Lewis Papers is impossible to check against the original manuscripts. When Roger Lancelyn Green and I borrowed the Lewis Papers for help in writing *C. S. Lewis: A Biography*, Warnie urged us (letter of 1 April 1967) to 'take the greatest care of them – for there is only this one copy in existence, and the originals from which all material was drawn were burnt by Jack in 1936'. It is unlikely that Lewis would have thought publishing letters from this collection an 'indiscriminate' use because he helped to assemble them.

The Lewis Papers came into use when Warnie wished to commemorate his brother after Jack's death in 1963. 'I intend to see what sort of a hand I make at a "Life and Letters" of dear Jack,' he wrote to me on 8 February 1964. 'Not exactly a L. & L. in the usual sense, for of course I shall not use anything he has himself told us in *Surprised by Joy*. It will be more what the French 17th Cent. writers used to call *Mémoires pour servir* etc.' That book eventually became *Letters of C. S. Lewis*, edited, with a Memoir by W. H. Lewis (1964). However, because Warnie originally set out to write a biography, not edit a volume of letters, he restricted his brother's letters to what are, in effect, quotations. None of the family letters quoted in *Letters of C. S. Lewis* is complete. I hope those who enjoyed reading fragments of Lewis's letters to his father and brother in the 1966 *Letters* and the Enlarged Edition of 1988 will be pleased to find them here in their entirety.

While the volume includes letters to Owen Barfield and other friends he met at Oxford, most were written to Albert Lewis, Warnie and his boyhood friend Arthur Greeves. Some of the best of those he wrote to Warnie arose out of Warnie's long stay in South Africa with the Army Service Corps. He knew Warnie would be lonely so far away and that he found letters companionable. 'As we talk a good deal of odd fragments out of books when we are together,' Jack wrote to him in March 1921, 'there's no reason why we should not reproduce the same sort of tittle-tattle. Perhaps one of the reasons why letters are so hard to write and so much harder to read is that people confine themselves to news – in other words think nothing worth writing except that which would not be worth saying.'

The letters to his father are by no means all *news*, but they differ from the ones to Warnie and Arthur in being more or less obligatory reports from his various schools. There are times when news is very interesting too, and on occasions we find Jack begging his father for precisely that, *news*. One of the turning points in this volume comes soon after 1925 when his ideas *are* the news. Jack, now a don at Magdalen College, writes to his father as an independent young man and we see that seminal work of literary history, *The Allegory of Love*, taking shape before our eyes.

Jack Lewis was later to regret that he was so cavalier about dating his early correspondence, and my guess is that it was Albert Lewis who preserved the postmarks of many of his son's letters. This helped Warnie when arranging them in the Lewis Papers. Sometimes he did not even have a postmark to guide him, and in some instances where he failed I had the advantage of comparing the family letters to those written to Arthur Greeves, and vice versa. In one of the many undated letters to his father (2? April 1919), Jack said, 'Did you see the "very insolent" review of me on the back page of the Times Literary Supplement last week?' I found the review in *The Times Literary Supplement* of 27 March 1919, and we are able to see almost exactly where the letter fits.

The letters to Arthur Greeves were published in 1979 as *They Stand Together: The Letters of C. S. Lewis to Arthur Greeves (1914–1963)*, a book which has been out of print many years. The originals of all the Greeves letters in *Family Letters* are in Wheaton College, with copies in the Bodleian. Jack described Arthur as his 'First Friend'. 'I had been so far from thinking such a friend possible,' he said of him in *Surprised by Joy*, 'that I had never even longed for one; no more than I longed to be King of England.' The letters to Arthur are exactly the balance needed for those Jack wrote to his father, not merely because they were young men of the same age with similar interests, but because Arthur was his confidant. The only clear statement we have about Lewis's religious beliefs as a teenager was made to Arthur in October 1916. 'All religions, that is, all mythologies to give them their proper name,' he wrote on 12 October 1916, 'are merely man's own invention.' And when, following the death of his father, he began to look at Christianity, and himself, in a new light, he confided in Arthur. 'You are my only real Father Confessor', he said.

And it was to Arthur that Jack confided his teenage sexual fantasies beginning with the letter of 28 January 1917. Years later, when he re-read the letters in which this subject is mentioned, he told Arthur (1 October 1931): 'I am now inclined to agree with you in *not* regretting that we confided in each other even on this subject, because it has done no harm in the long run – and how could young adolescents really be friends without it?' Before his death, Arthur, as an old man, sought to make his friend's letters more respectable by scribbling over those passages in which this particular excess of youth had appeared. In deciding what to do about this, I came to the conclusion that if I omitted these passages, but retained the letter of 30 January 1930 in which Lewis accuses himself of the deadly sin of Pride, I would be treating the teenage lusts of the flesh with a seriousness they don't deserve. My solution in this volume is the same one I used when the letters were first published in 1979. The passages which Arthur, for whatever reason, scribbled through are found in brackets shaped like this – < >.

I should include an Editorial Note at this point. We have none of the letters Arthur wrote to Jack during the years covered in this book, but it is clear Arthur was always pleading with Jack to put dates on his letters. Jack rarely complied, and as a result the letters to Arthur were harder to date than the ones to his father. As I explained in the Editor's Note I wrote for *They Stand Together*, I used various methods of dating, including comparing the various nibs Jack used in composing the letters. Lewis almost always wrote with an old-fashioned nib pen that is dipped into an inkwell as one writes. Each nib writes slightly differently and it is possible to see which letters were written with which nib. It is not a method to condemn. When Lewis dictated letters to me, he always had me read them aloud afterwards. He told me that in writing letters, as well as books, he always 'whispered the words aloud'. Pausing to dip the pen in an inkwell provided exactly the rhythm needed. 'It's as important to please the *ear*,' he said, 'as it is the eye.'

What Lewis was not concerned with was how the page looked. He preferred to save paper, and most of his letters were not divided into paragraphs. I have taken the liberty of introducing paragraphs, with the result, I hope, that Lewis's clearly ordered ideas stand out and are more enjoyable to read. I have tried throughout to preserve Lewis's spelling. This was easy when transcribing from the original letters to Arthur, but I suspect that Warnie silently corrected some of his brother's frequent misspellings.

Following the name of every person to whom a letter is addressed I have indicated where the reader might consult the original letter, if there is one, or where in the Lewis Papers he will find the copy used in this book. Thus 'To his Father (LP III: 82)' means 'Lewis Papers, Volume III, page 82'. In the case of the letters to Arthur Greeves the reader will notice that sometimes I refer to letters being in both Wheaton and the Lewis Papers (e.g. W/LP). This means that the original, from which the Lewis Papers version was copied, is now in Wheaton. Jack borrowed many of his letters from Arthur so Warnie could include them in the Lewis Papers. I am not sure what happened, but those dated 1 and 8 February 1916 and those which run from 7 March 1916 to 27 September 1916 seem to have got lost because these only exist as copies in the Lewis Papers. The initial 'B' means the original is in the Bodleian, and 'P' means it is in a private collection. It should not be difficult to consult the letters on either side of the Atlantic because the Bodleian and the Wade Center have a reciprocal arrangement which means each has copies of what the other has. Thus, those letters cited as in 'W' (Wade Center), such as the Barfield letters, may also be consulted in 'B' (Bodleian).

Nearly all the letters in this volume were written to people so important in Lewis's life that I did not feel it would be enough to identify them with a mere footnote. The solution was to include short biographies in a Biographical Appendix.

I hope my friends will be as satisfied as I am by the appearance of this volume for I have been tireless in seeking their knowledge and advice. I wish to thank in particular Dr A. T. Reyes, Professor James Como, Father Seán Finnegan, Professor Emrys Jones, Dr Barbara Everett, Madame Eliane Tixier, Professor G. B. Tennyson, Dr Stephen Logan, Miss Priscilla Tolkien, The Rt Hon. David Bleakley MP, Michael Ward, Andrew Cuneo, Edward Nelson, Jonathan Brewer, Paul Tankard, Edward De Rivera, Fr Jerome Bertram, Brother Alexander Master and the Fathers and Brothers of the Oxford Oratory.

No editor could have been served so well by his publishers as I have been. I am very grateful to Kathy Dyke, managing editor of

HarperCollins*Religious*, for guiding the book through to press, and to many others. My thanks to all concerned.

Walter Hooper
27 March 1999
Oxford

ABBREVIATIONS

AMR = *All My Road Before Me: The Diary of C. S. Lewis 1922–1927*, edited by Walter Hooper (1991).

BF = *Brothers and Friends: The Diaries of Major Warren Hamilton Lewis*, edited by Clyde S. Kilby and Marjorie Lamp Mead (1982).

CG = Walter Hooper, *C. S. Lewis: A Companion and Guide* (1996).

LP = unpublished 'Lewis Papers' or 'Memoirs of the Lewis Family: 1850–1930' in 11 volumes.

'Memoir' = Memoir by W. H. Lewis contained in *Letters of C. S. Lewis*, edited with a Memoir by W. H. Lewis (1966), and reprinted in *Letters of C. S. Lewis*, edited with a Memoir by W. H. Lewis, revised and enlarged edition, edited by Walter Hooper (1988).

SBJ = C. S. Lewis, *Surprised by Joy: The Shape of My Early Life* (1955).

1905–1910

The Lewises were a happy family. Albert Lewis[1] *had prospered as a police court solicitor, and on 18 April 1905 the family moved from the semi-detached Dundela Villas, where Warnie and Jack were born, into a house Albert had specially built for his wife, Flora.*[2] *This was 'Little Lea', one of the new 'big houses' of Strandtown, a lovely area of Belfast. Outside, the family looked over wide fields to Belfast Lough, and across the Lough to the mountains of the Antrim shore.*

Albert and Flora, like most Anglo-Irish parents, wanted their children to be educated in English public schools, and on 10 May 1905 Flora took Warnie,[3] *who was eight, across the water to Wynyard School in Watford, Hertfordshire. In complete innocence she was delivering her son into the hands of a madman. The headmaster, Robert Capron or 'Oldie' as the boys called him,*[4] *'lived in a solitude of power,' Jack was later to write, 'like a sea-captain in the days of sail'* (SBJ *II). In two years' time he would have a High Court action taken against him for cruelty. For the time being Warnie joined the dwindling band of some dozen boys who lived in the pair of semi-detached houses which made up Wynyard School.*

Meanwhile, Jack was tutored at home, his mother teaching him French and Latin and his governess, Annie Harper,[5] *teaching him everything else. He was almost eight when he wrote this first letter to Warnie:*

1 See **Albert James Lewis** in the Biographical Appendix.
2 See **Florence Augusta 'Flora' Lewis** in the Biographical Appendix.
3 See **Warren Hamilton 'Warnie' Lewis** in the Biographical Appendix.
4 See **Robert Capron** in the Biographical Appendix.
5 Miss Annie Harper was governess to the Lewis boys from 1898 to 1908.

TO HIS BROTHER (LP III: 63):

Little Lea.
Strandtown.
[c. November 1905]

My dear Warnie

Peter[6] has had two un-fortunate aventures since I last wrote, however they came out all right in the end. No. 1, Maude[7] was in her room (*up there* remember) heard *Peter howling*. When she came down, what do you think? sitting on the floor ready to spring on Peter was a big *black cat*. Maude chased it for a long way. I was not able to help matters because I was out on my bych.

The next adventure was not so starling, never the-less it is worth while relating that a mouse got into his cage.

Tim[8] got the *head staggers* the other day while running on the lawn, he suddenly lay down and began to kick and foam at the mouth and shudder.

On Halow-een we had great [fun?] and had fireworks; rockets, and catterine wheels, squbes, and a kind of thing that you lit and twirled and then they made *stars*. We hung up an apple and bit at it we got Grandfather[9] down to watch and he tried to bite. Maud got the ring out of the barn-brach and we had apple dumpling with in it a button a ring and a 3 penny bit. Martha got the button, Maude got nothing, and I got the ring and the 3 pence all in one bite. We got some leaves off the road the other day, that is to say the roadmen gave us some that they had got off the road, in fact they wanted them because they make good manure. I am doing french as well as latin now, and I think I like the latin better. Tomorrow I decline that old 'Bonus,' 'Bona,' 'Bonum' thing, but I think it is very hard (not now of course but it was).

Diabolos are all the go here, evrrey body has one except us, I don't

---

6 Jack's canary.

7 Maude and Martha were housemaids at Little Lea.

8 Tim was the family dog of whom Lewis said in *SBJ* X: 'He may hold a record for longevity among Irish terriers since he was already with us when I was at Oldie's [1908–10] and did not die till 1922...Poor Tim, though I loved him, was the most undisciplined, unaccomplished, and dissipated-looking creature that ever went on four legs. He never exactly obeyed you; he sometimes agreed with you.'

9 Grandfather was Richard Lewis (1832–1908), the father of Albert. See **The Lewis Family** in the Biographical Appendix.

think the Lewis temper would hold out do you? Jackie Calwell has one and can do it beautifully (wish I could)

your loving
brother Jacks

TO HIS BROTHER (LP III: 75–6):

Little Lea.
Strandtown.
[c. 1906]

My dear Warnie

I am sorrey that I did not write to you before. At present Boxen is *slightly* convulsed.[10] The news has just reached her that King Bunny is a prisoner. The colonists (who are of course the war party) are in a bad way: they dare scarcely leave their houses because of the mobs. In Tararo the Prussians and Boxonians are at fearful odds against each other and the natives.

Such were the states of affairs recently: but the able general Quicksteppe is taking steps for the rescue of King Bunny. (the news somewhat pacified the rioters.)

your loving
brother Jacks.

TO HIS BROTHER (LP III: 79):

Little Lea.
Strandtown.
18 May 1907

My dear Warnie,

Tommy is very well thank you. We have got the telephone in to our house. Is Bennett beter again, as he has been ill you see that you are not the onley boy who stayes at home.

We have nearly seteld that we are going to france this summer, all though I do not like that country I think I shall like the trip, wont you. I liked the card you sent me, I have put it in the album. I was talking to the

10 Boxen was a world invented by Jack and Warnie a year or so before this time, and about which Jack was to write many stories and histories involving the characters mentioned here – King Bunny, General Quicksteppe and others. Much of this juvenilia has been published as *Boxen: The Imaginary World of the Young C.S. Lewis*, ed. Walter Hooper (1985).

Greaves through the telephone I wanted Arthur but he was out and I onley got Thom.[11]

I am sorry I can't give you any news about Nearo, but I have not got anny to give. The grass in the front is coming up nicely. It is fearfully hot here. I have got an adia, you know the play I was writing. I think we will try and act it with new stage don't say annything about it not being dark we will have it up stairs and draw the thick curtains and the wight ones, the scenery is rather hard, but still I think we shall do it.

your loving
brother Jacks

TO HIS BROTHER (LP III: 80):

Little Lea.
Strandtown.
[August 1907?]

My dear Warnie

Thank you very much for the post-cards I liked them, the herald was the nicest I think, dont you. Now that I have finished the play I am thinking of writeing a History of Mouse-land and I have even gon so far as to make up some of it, this is what I have made up.

Mouse-land had a very long stone-age during which time no great things tooke place it lasted from 55 BC to 1212 and then king Bublich I began to reign, he was not a good king but he fought gainest yellow land. Bub II his son fought indai about the lantern act, died 1377 king Bunny came next.[12]

Your loving
brother Jacks

---

11 See the Biographical Appendix for **Joseph Arthur Greeves**, a boy who lived across the road from the Lewises.

12 This 'History of Mouse-Land' is found in *Boxen*, op. cit., pp. 39–41.

TO HIS FATHER (LP III: 82):

[Pension Petit-Vallon,
Berneval,
Près Dieppe]
4th Sept. '07.[13]

My dear Papy,

excuse this post-card being so dirty, but in our rooms everything is so dusty. It is still lovely weather still. I was sick and had to go to bed but am quite beter now. I hope you are all right. Are Tommy and Peter all right?

your loving son,
Jacks.

TO HIS BROTHER (LP III: 105):

Tigh-na-mara,
Larne Harbour,
Co. Antrim.
[May 1908][14]

My dear Warnie

how are you geting on. Mamy is doing very well indeed. I am sending you a picture of the 'Lord Big',[15] I forgot until it was too late that she was screw not paddle, but of course there might be 2 boats in the same line that have one name. Did I tell you about going to chains memorial?[16] It is a funny old place, one thing that struck me was the thickness of the walls. The light (as I suppose you know) is worked by gas, while I was there the man broct two mantles. Did you get my letters? one of them had a home drawn post card on it, I got yours and now I had beter stop, as there is nothing to say.

your loving brother,
Jacks

---

13 This was to be the last holiday Jack and Warnie took with their mother. They travelled to London, and from there they went on to Berneval in France, where they were on holiday from 20 August until 18 September.

14 Jack was here on holiday with his mother.

15 Lord Big, a frog, is the most memorable of the Boxen characters.

16 Warnie Lewis wrote: '"chains memorial" is a lighthouse at the entrance to Larne Harbour, erected to the memory of James Chaine, a prominent local landowner; he is buried in an upright position, in unconsecrated ground, overlooking the harbour' (LP III: 105).

Flora Lewis had been ill for months and an operation on 15 February revealed she had cancer. The following month she seemed better, but during this period of uncertainty Albert Lewis's father died on 24 March. The last letter from Flora Lewis in the Lewis Papers was written to Warnie on 15 June 1908. 'I am sorry not to have been able to write to you regularly this term,' she said, 'but I find I am really not well enough to do so. I have been feeling very poorly lately and writing tires me very much. But I must write today to wish you a happy birthday' (LP III: 106). Flora was very ill, and the impending tragedy at Little Lea resulted in Warnie being brought home at the end of June. Following another operation, she died at home on Albert's forty-fifth birthday, 23 August 1908. The following month Jack accompanied his brother to Wynyard School in Watford, and the next letter is the first Jack wrote to his father after his arrival there.

TO HIS FATHER (LP III: 140):

[Wynyard School,
Watford,
Hertfordshire
19? September 1908]

My dear Papy,

I suppose you got our telgy-graph to say that we were all right.

It was rather rough crossing, poor Warnie was very sea sick, I was sick once. Unfortunately Warnie was sick again in the train, also the breakfast car was so full that we could not get anything to eat till a long way after Crewe, we were both very hungry but when at last it came Warnie could not eat any worth talking about. When we arrived at Euston we saw both our trunks and plaboxs, the side of mine was dinged in. When we got to Watford the play-boxs were missing, evedently (though Warnie gave him 3d.) the porter had omitted to put them in at Euston. The railways officials think they can find them.

I cannot of course tell you yet but I think I shall like this place. Misis Capron and the Miss Caprons are very nice and I think I will be able to get on with Mr. Capron though to tell the truth he is rather eccentric.[17]

17 Robert Capron was assisted in his teaching by all the members of the family, his wife Ellen Barnes Capron (1849–1909), his son Wynyard Capron (1883–1959), and his three daughters, Norah, Dorothy and Eva. See **Robert Capron** in the Biographical Appendix.

Anything we want Warnie is telling you about in his letter.
your loving son,
Jacksie

TO HIS FATHER (LP III: 147):

[Wynyard School]
Postmark: 29 September 1908

My dear Papy

Mr. Capron said some-thing I am not likely to forget 'curse the boy' (behind Warnie's back) because Warnie did not bring his jam in to tea, no one ever heard such a rule before.

Please may we not leave on Saturday? We simply *cannot* wait in this hole till the end of term.

your loving
son Jack

TO HIS FATHER (LP III: 149):

[Wynyard School]
Postmark: 3 October 1908

My dear Papy

We are getting on much better since Aunt Any's visit.[18] We went up to the Franco-British exhibition and enjoyed it very much, but I suppose Aunt Any has told you all about it.

Warnie was just a little sick last night and had to go to bed early and take 2 pills, he is quite well today but did not go to church. I do not like church here at all because it is so frightfully high church that it might as well be Roman Catholic.

You must excuse me writing a long letter as I have a lot of people to write.

your loving
son Jacks

---

18 Annie Sargent Harley Hamilton (1866–1930) was the wife of Flora's brother, Augustus 'Gussie' Hamilton, who undertook much of the care of Jack and Warnie following their mother's death. A Canadian by birth, she married Augustus Hamilton in 1897, and was thereafter Flora's best friend. Lewis said of her in *SBJ* III: 'In her I found what I liked best – an unfailing, kindly welcome without a hint of sentimentality, unruffled good sense, the unobtrusive talent for making all things at all times as cheerful and comfortable as circumstances allowed. What one could not have one did without and made the best of it. The tendency of the Lewises to reopen wounds and to rouse sleeping dogs was unknown to her as to her husband.'

The contrast between what was said of the church the boys of Wynyard attended – St John's Church, Watford – and what it meant in retrospect *is very great. In a little diary kept at Wynyard and dated November 1909, Jack said:*

> *We...marched to church in a dismal column. We were obliged to go to St John's, a church which wanted to be Roman Catholic, but was afraid to say so. A kind of church abhorred by respectful Irish Protestants. Here Wyn Capron, the son of our Head Master, preached a sermon better than his usual ones. In this abominable place of Romish hypocrites and English liars, the people cross themselves, bow to the Lord's Table (which they have the vanity to call an altar), and pray to the Virgin.* (LP III: 194)

Recalling it some years later in SBJ *II, he said:*

> *I have not yet mentioned the most important thing that befell me at [Wynyard]. There first I became an effective believer. As far as I know, the instrument was the church to which we were taken twice every Sunday. This was high 'Anglo-Catholic.' On the conscious level I reacted strongly against its peculiarities – was I not an Ulster Protestant, and were not these unfamiliar rituals an essential part of the hated English atmosphere? Unconsciously, I suspect, the candles and incense, the vestments and the hymns sung on our knees, may have had a considerable, and opposite, effect on me...What really mattered was that here I heard the doctrines of Christianity (as distinct from general 'uplift') taught by men who obviously believed them.*

TO HIS FATHER (LP III: 151):

[Wynyard School]
Postmark: 25 October 1908

My dear Papy,

Did you get my letter? Is Maud still with you, I hope so. How is your back?

I am very sorry you are so much annoyed at Mr. Capron's letter, but it is quite untrue, Warnie is not lazy.[19] How is Ant Any? And now you must excuse me writing such a short letter, but as every day is the same as the last I have little or nothing to say.

your loving
son
Jacks

TO HIS FATHER (LP III: 154):

[Wynyard School]
Postmark: 22 November 1908

My dear Papy,

There are only 3 more Sundays this term, next one is my birthday. The term brakes up on 17th Thursday. How is your back? We have thought of a splendid new idea; a book club, it is going to be started next term, Warnie is going to get the Pearson's, and I the Strand. Field is getting the Captain.[20]

I find school very nice but it is frightfully monotenis.

with love
from
Jacks

TO HIS FATHER (LP III: 155):

[Wynyard School
27? November 1908]

My dear Papy,

How are you feeling? As to what you say about leaving I cannot know quite what to say, Warnie does not particularly want to, he says it look like being beaten in the fight.

---

19 On 22 October, Mr Capron wrote to Albert Lewis saying: 'Not only is Clive an exceptionally bright, intelligent, and most lovable little boy, but he is also very keen and eager to learn. Would that I could write to you in the same strain of Warren! Ever averse to effort, physical and mental, he grows worse, and I am almost driven to regard his indolence in the light of a disease' (LP III: 150).

20 These were three magazines for boys. *Pearsons Magazine* ran from 1903 to 1936; *The Strand Magazine* was an illustrated monthly which aimed at 'cheap, healthful literature' in the form of stories and articles – Arthur Conan Doyle's *Adventures of Sherlock Holmes* was among its first serials – and ran from 1891 to 1950; *The Captain*, another magazine for boys, ran from 1899 to 1924.

In spight of all that has happened I like Mr. Capron very much indeed. Have you still got Maud? How are they all down at Sandycroft? Give Joey my love and tell him I will write to him as soon as I have time.[21]

Your loving
son Jacks

TO HIS FATHER (LP III: 173):

[Wynyard School]
Postmark: 21 February 1909

My dear Papy,

According to certain authorities this is half term Sunday, others are inclined to think it will fall sometime during the week. But almost everyone is unanimous on the fact that next Sunday will be well over half term.

This week many things of interest are happening here, according to rumour, Peckover, Reis, and a few others are going soon. Peckover we know is for certain, we being in close privy confidence with him. Between us and the other boys great changes are taking place; a secret society got up by 'Squivy' included everyone but us. However Peckover (who has up till now been Squivy's chum) does not seem to think that Squivy is the best of friends, so he more or less sided with us in preference. He contrived to make Jeyes and Bowser assume an aspect of friendship towards us, and enmity towards Squivy. So Squivy and his toady Mears remain together, under the blissful delusion that they are still popular, and in the case of a row would be staunchly supported by every boarder but us. I am delighted to observe Squivy's popularity and power gradually disappearing. Peckover is leaving because Mr. Capron gives him such a bad time of it here (assisted by Wyn), and in reality, Peckover has been shamefully handled. John Burnett is leaving for a similar reason. Reis (being a day boy, and a nasty one at that), I have not bothered to look into his case.

---

21 'Sandycroft' was the Belfast home of Albert's brother, Joseph Lewis (1856–1908) who died on 3 September 1908. He was a marine consulting engineer. In 1880 he married Mary Tegart, and they had five children, of which Joseph or 'Joey' (1898–1969) was at this time Jack's best friend. See **The Lewis Family** in the Biographical Appendix.

I may mention that the day boys have taken no part in what I am telling about Squivy.

Thanks for the '1st men in the moon',[22] I have already finished it and enjoyed it very much. Is Aunt Annie any better, please tell me all about her, and *your* back in the next letter you write.

your loving
son Jacks

P.S. Peckover begs me to tell you not to tell anything about what I've told you.

J.

TO HIS FATHER (LP III: 175):

[Wynyard School
28 February 1909]

My dear Papy,

Thank you very much for the note paper. Did you get the letter I wrote on Friday (at least I think it was Friday) night? A rather amusing incident occurred yesterday afternoon. We went for a walk in the afternoon and those day boys who wished, came with us too. And it so happened that Poppy, the brother of John, and Boivie (the sociable Swede) came with us. Now Boivie is a Swede, and therefore a good old northerner, and like us, hates anything that savours of the south of England: so I mentioned in the course of our conversation how intensely I hated the churches down here: 'There're so high' said I. 'Oh, yes', replied Boivie 'the ones in Denmark are much nicer, look there (pointing to a church across the road) look how high the steeple is'. And he didn't mean it as a joke either.

Now as there is not much news I must stop.

your loving
son Jacks

On 28 July 1909 Warnie won his release from Wynyard School, and on 16 September he arrived in Malvern, Worcestershire, to begin his first term at Malvern College.

---

22 H.G. Wells, *The First Men in the Moon* (1901).

TO HIS FATHER (LP III: 185–6):

[Wynyard School]
Postmark: 19 September 1909

My dear Papy,

I arrived safely (as you heard in the telegraph), after a pleasant journey. Oldy met me at Euston as you said, but as his train was late, he was not at my platform. However, I got my luggage attended to all right, and met him on the Watford platform. Euston is not nearly so muddling as I thought, and coming back to here next term I don't think Oldy need meet me here.

I am sorry to say that there are no new boys this term, but there is a rumour that Oldy is going to have a private pupil (whatever that may mean) later on. He is over sixteen and stands 6 ft. 2., according to Oldy, but then I don't believe that.

There are thirteen weeks this term, which sounds a lot, but it will soon go past, at least I hope so.

Have you heard any more from Warnie, and if so how is the old chap getting on? I hope to send an epistle to him today. I have not seen the day boys yet, as school does not begin in earnest until tomorrow morning. 'And now as the time alloted for correspondance is drawing to a close' etc. But now I must stop, with love and good wishes,

yours loving son,
Jack

P.S. Don't forget to write very plainly in your letter which I am expecting tomorrow.

TO HIS FATHER (LP III: 195–6):

[Wynyard School
16? December 1909]

My dear Papy,

This time next week I will be at home with you. Isn't it just splendid? One of the causes of writing this letter to you is to remind you to send the journey-money (not that I think you would ever forget); but last time it came *just in the nick of time*, which made Warnie rather anxious.

I don't think I will have the microscope for Christmas. In order to study entomological specimens, it would of course be needful to kill them: and to go about exterminating harmless insects, with no other motive in view than the gratification of one's own whimsical tastes does not seem to me very nice, when I look at it in that light. Of course it must be said that death to the insect is painless and quick; and that certain kinds of beetles (and other insects as well), when turned on their backs, cannot move. One could study these species through the microscope without killing them. However, the arguments against *practical* entomology are, I think, much stronger than those for it. Consequently I have decided not to have the microscope for Christmas, and it would be nicer not to know what I am going to get.[23]

Yesterday (Wednesday) we went for a paper chase. Mears and I were the hares, which was rather absurd, seeing that we are the two worst runners in the school, and know less about the country than the others. Both you and I know that I have got hardly any 'puff', and so you will be surprised to read as I was to find, that I kept up all right. We ran for a good long way, and however got caught in the end. I can tell you I slept well afterwards. Today we are all very, very stiff.

As the end of term draws nearer and nearer, we must soon decide all about the journey home. I think I had better go by Liverpool; for if I could arrange to meet Warnie at Lime St. Station, it would no longer be necessary for you to come over.

Now I must stop: with much love,
your son,
Jacks

TO HIS FATHER (LP III: 209–10):

[Wynyard School]
Postmark: 21 May 1910

My dear Papy,

I am writing to you today (Saturday) because we are going to St. Alban's to see Wyn ordained tomorrow.

We have quite settled down to the term here, and the time is beginning to fly: I hope it will go quickly with you too.

I have been thinking about the school question, but the more I think the more difficult it seems to arrive at any *definite* conclusion. Of course half formed, nebulous, impossible ideas will bubble up spontaneously.

---

23 Jack apparently got over his scruples about the microscope, for he received one for Christmas.

Yesterday (Friday) we went to church in the morning and afternoon; in the afternoon a great many boy scouts were present. Somehow I don't think 'Wee Georgie' (minus the Wood) will be *very* popular at first: but what is this to Shakespearian students like you and I who know what happens –

'After a well graced actor leaves the stage.'[24]

The other day we had a general knowledge examination: it was very exciting. I got 62 marks out of 100, and was second, Bowser was first. Thank goodness Squiffy came out miles below Bowser and I. If I cannot triumph over Squiffy in games and out of school, I will do my level best to triumph over him in work (which I *can* do), and which is perhaps a far better way of getting my own.

If you are 'thinking long' because this is a long term, remember that the holidays are long in proportion.

your loving
son Jacks

P.S. Have you seen the comet? We have not.

24 William Shakespeare, *Richard II* (1595), V, ii, 24.

1911–1912

That was Jack's last term at Wynyard. The school had been foundering for a long time, and now with too few pupils to provide him with a livelihood, it sank beneath the headmaster's feet. Mr Capron wrote to Albert on 27 April 1910 to say he was 'giving up school work'. After the boys left in July, Mr Capron was inducted into the little church at Radwell on 13 June 1910. It did not last. He began beating the choirboys, and had to be put under restraint. He died in the Camberwell House Asylum on 18 November 1911.

Jack spent one term, between September and December 1910, at Campbell College, Belfast. Then in January 1911 he and Warnie travelled together to Malvern, Warnie to Malvern College and Jack to the little preparatory school, Cherbourg School, which lay only yards from the College. It was made up of about twenty boys between the ages of 8 and 12, and had been founded in 1907 under the headmastership of Arthur Clement Allen (1868–1957). After the stultifying effects of Capron's teaching, with its 'sea of arithmetic' and a 'jungle of dates, battles, exports, imports and the like, forgotten as soon as learned' (SBJ *II), Jack experienced something like a renaissance at Cherbourg, which in* Surprised by Joy *he calls 'Chartres' after the most glorious cathedral in France. 'Here indeed my education really began. The Headmaster, whom we called Tubbs, was a clever and patient teacher; under him I rapidly found my feet in Latin and English'* (SBJ *IV).*

TO HIS FATHER (LP III: 226–7):

[Cherbourg School,
Malvern
January 1911]

My dear Papy,

Warnie and I arrived safely at Malvern after a splendid journey. Cherbourge is quite a nice place. There are 17 chaps here. There are three masters, Mr. Allen,[1] Mr. Palmer, and Mr. Jones, who is *very* fat.

It is only going to be a ten week term I think, so there are 79 more days.

Luckily we escaped all Pinguis's Malvern friends and were able to travel alone.

Malvern is one of the nicest English towns I have seen yet. The hills are beautiful, but of course not so nice as ours.

Two or three chaps here remember Mears.

Are you sure you have packed my Prayer Book? I cannot find it anywhere. If you find it at home, please send it on as soon as possible, and some stamps.

The weather here is miserably cold, and the air is thin and rarified: one can see ones breath all the time. One good thing is that we have hot water in the mornings, which we didnt have either at Campbell or Wynyard.

I haven't discovered the 'small museum' yet, and I am inclined to think it is a minus quantity.

Now I must stop.

yours affectionate
son,
Jacks

---

1 Arthur Clement Allen (1868–1957), the headmaster, was educated at Repton and New College, Oxford, where he read Classics. After taking a BA in 1891 he was a teacher at Silloth School from 1902 until 1907 when he founded Cherbourg School. In 1925 he moved the school to Woodnorton, Evesham, and the school closed officially when he retired in 1931.

TO HIS FATHER (LP III: 228):

[Cherbourg School]
Postmark: 5 February 1911

My dear Papy,

Sunday come round again – hurray! We had great fun this week, we went to the 'Messiah'.[2] It was only an amateur performance, but still it was simply lovely. I heard our old friends 'Comfort ye', and 'I know that my Redeemer liveth'. The former was specially well sung by a stout and hideous gentleman with an excellent voice.

On Wednesday we went for a walk across the flat side of Malvern and a funny thing happened. We were going through some fields when some one said 'look out', and we cleared off the path to make way for a college run which was coming. First came some big chaps with blue shields on their shirts, some distinction, I don't know what. Then came a motley crowd, and then!: A familiar voice said 'Hullo Jack', and looking round, I saw Pinguis himself. There he was. Its rather a comfort to know that he likes running.

That reminds me, the College breaks up on the 4th of April, and we do not [leave] till some days later. I suppose however you will arrange that I always go home on the same day as Pinguis. Be sure and tell me in your next letter what you think about this: I am positive you will agree. So when it gets near April 4th, just write to Mr. Allen and tell him about my coming home early. If you don't do this I don't know how we shall manage, for I couldn't face this complicated Malvern journey alone.

Last week we had some very bitter weather, but we did not feel it much as we wore our sweaters under our greatcoats. The other day we went off for a ripping walk over the hills, right across into Wales, a good step on the other side, and home through a sort of cutting.

Only nine more weeks if I come home on the 4th.

Yours loving

son,

J.

---

2 *Messiah*, an oratorio by George Frideric Handel, was first performed in 1752.

TO HIS FATHER (LP III: 239):

[Cherbourg School]
May 14th [1911]

My dear P.,

Thanks very much indeed for the money. I certainly did have a great fright, I could not think what had become of it. However I realised that it must have got left behind. I am glad to hear that Warnie has got his shove, where is he in his new form? I was pained and surprised to hear that you were not producing 'an old soldier and his wife', they would have been a novelty if nothing else.

We have found this time that it is much more comfortable to have lunch at Shrewsbury and go on by a later train.

Thank goodness that old pig Jonah has left, so I shall be able to enjoy myself this term. In his place we have got a chap named Turner, he is quite decent. In fact he is a very queer fellow indeed, I do not understand him and I think there is a good deal more to find out about him than anyone guesses. He is very quiet. Next week we are going to see Benson[3] in 'The Merchant of Venice'.[4] Of course Malvern has a rotten theatre, but it always gets very good things, I can't think why.

I enclose a photo of the characters in our play (that we had last term), in their stage costumes. The people from left to right are back row, Clutterbuck,[5] Nadin, front row, Me, Maxwell, Bowen.

your loving son
Jack

---

3 Sir Frank Robert Benson (1858–1939), English actor-manager, founded his own Shakespearean company. Beginning in 1883 he took his company on tours, producing all Shakespeare's plays with the exception of *Titus Andronicus* and *Troilus and Cressida*.

4 William Shakespeare, *The Merchant of Venice* (1600).

5 Jack Ernest Clutterbuck (1898–1975) went from Cherbourg School to Malvern College where he was a pupil from 1912 to 1915. After training at the Royal Military Academy, Woolwich, he received a commission in the Royal Engineers and served in the First World War. He went to Trinity Hall, Cambridge, and took a BA in 1922. After more than twenty years in the army, during which he reached the rank of brigadier, he was Chief Engineer of the G.I.P. Railway in Bombay, 1946–47. He retired in 1950. The photograph is reproduced in Walter Hooper, *Through Joy and Beyond: A Pictorial Biography of C.S. Lewis* (1982), p. 31.

TO HIS FATHER (LP III: 284–5):

Cherbourg.
Malvern.
Postmark: 5 May 1912

My dear P.,

We arrived safely here on the Friday, as you know by our telegram, and found that Cherbourg, contrary to all expectations, had come back on Wednesday, and I was late. I did not weep.

On the boat after you had gone, a solid phalanx of 'young persons' lined up on the quay and sang 'let's have a game of ring of roses'. You *would* have enjoyed it. The Malvern weather is exactly like the home – rotten. We have two new masters this term: the 1st a monstrosity of 6 ft., 6 ins height whom I don't like at all, so far as I have any opinion yet. He is called Eden. The other is of reasonable height, and, so far as we can see, fairly decent. But that remains to be seen. There is a new matron, Miss Gosling, who seems to be passably inoffensive – but of course is not nearly as decent as Miss Cowie.[6] The small master's name is Harris.[7] I hate starting a new term with an absolutely new staff, and *such* a new staff too.

---

6 The school matron, Miss G.E. Cowie, had been forced to leave, and she was now replaced by Miss Gosling. Writing about Miss Cowie in *SBJ* IV, Lewis said: 'No school ever had a better Matron, more skilled and comforting to boys in sickness, or more cheery and companionable to boys in health...We all loved her; I, the orphan, especially. Now it so happened that Miss C., who seemed old to me, was still in her spiritual immaturity, still hunting...She was...floundering in the mazes of Theosophy, Rosicrucianism, Spiritualism; the whole Anglo-American Occultist tradition...Little by little, unconsciously, unintentionally, she loosened the whole framework, blunted all the sharp edges of my belief. The vagueness, the merely speculative character, of all this Occultism began to spread – yes, and to spread *deliciously* – to the stern truths of the creed. The whole thing became a matter of speculation.'

7 We meet Percy Gerald Kelsal Harris again in the letter of 16 February 1918, but it should be noted that Harris is the master referred to in *SBJ* IV as 'Pogo' and about whom Lewis said: 'Pogo was a wit, Pogo was a dressy man, Pogo was a man about town. Pogo was even a lad. After a week or so of hesitation (for his temper was uncertain) we fell at his feet and adored. Here was sophistication, glossy all over, and (dared one believe it?) ready to impart sophistication to us...After a term of Pogo's society one had the feeling of being not twelve weeks but twelve years older.' P.G.K. Harris was born in Kinver, Staffordshire, on 31 August 1888. From King's School in Taunton he went up to Exeter College, Oxford, in 1907. That he left without a degree may be explained by those very qualities which delighted his pupils at Cherbourg. But he was to show an entirely different sort of mettle in the approaching war. For a photograph of Harris see Walter Hooper, *Through Joy and Beyond: A Pictorial Biography of C.S. Lewis* (1982), p. 30. Harris is the man standing on the left in the back row.

We left Liverpool this time by the 2.40 instead of the 12, and I think we will do so next time; it is a better train.

your loving
son Jack

The Lewis Papers *contain no letters from Jack written between that of 5 May 1912 and the one below. The lacuna is possibly explained by the fact that whatever letters he wrote have not survived. However, a more likely explanation is that his energies were being poured into writing of a different sort. His personal 'Renaissance' began when he came across the Christmas issue of* The Bookman *for December 1911 and saw the words* Siegfried and the Twilight of the Gods, *with a picture by Rackham illustrating the first part of Richard Wagner's* Ring of the Nibelung *saga. 'Pure "Northernness" engulfed me,' he said, 'a vision of huge, clear spaces hanging above the Atlantic in the endless twilight of Northern summer'* (SBJ *V). This love of myth led him between the summers of 1912 and 1913 to write 819 lines of an epic called* 'Loki Bound' *which was Norse in subject and Greek in form. He was as well a frequent contributor to* The Cherbourg School Magazine, *in which his articles are remarkable achievements for one so young. But for the moment, however, he had his mind set on winning a Scholarship to Malvern College.*

It was also at this point that Jack became an unbeliever. A major cause was the 'Occultist fancies' he had picked up from the matron of Cherbourg, Miss G.E. Cowie. He got into his head that 'No clause of my prayer was to be allowed to pass muster unless it was accompanied by what I called a "realisation", by which I meant a certain vividness of the imagination and the affections. My nightly task was to produce by sheer will-power a phenomenon which will-power could never produce' (SBJ *IV). There were also unconscious causes of doubt.*

> *One came from reading the classics. Here, especially in Virgil, one was presented with a mass of religious ideas; and all teachers and editors took it for granted from the outset that these religious ideas were sheer illusion. No one ever attempted to show in what sense Christianity fulfilled Paganism or Paganism prefigured Christianity...Little by little, with fluctuations which I cannot now trace, I became an apostate, dropping my faith with no sense of loss but with the greatest relief.* (SBJ *IV*)

1913

TO HIS FATHER (LP IV: 1):

Cherbourg.
Sunday.
Postmark: 6 January 1913

My dear Papy,

This scholarship question is going to be settled then once for all, in the coming week; the best or the worst will soon be known. It always seems to me a comforting fact before any important event concerning whose result one is anxious, that one's own varying expectations about it can make no difference to the event. At any rate, I have tried, and the rest must remain to be seen. Tubbs was talking to our friend S.R. James[1] the other day about the affair, and we learn thence that Greek, which has been somewhat of a bugbear, is not a very important subject – that the most necessary things are French and English; my French of course is rather poor, but I think I can do alright in English. But perhaps we had better not think too much about the event until it is over. What shall happen shall happen, and in the mean time we hope.

I expect I shall see W. down at the Coll. when I am there, which will be a good thing, as I have not heard from him for a long time.

On Wednesday we went to see Benson's company in 'Julius Caesar'[2] which was very enjoyable. Benson himself as Mark Anthony acted as badly as anyone possibly could, overdoing his part exceedingly, and in places singing rather than speaking the words. Thus in the famous speech to the people we hear 'all' pronounced with four syllables in the passage – 'So are they all, all honourable men'. The rest of the company were however good, especially a man called Carrington as Brutus, and

---

1 The Rev. Canon Sydney Rhodes James (1855–1934) was the headmaster of Malvern College 1897–1914. His story is told in *Seventy Years: Random Reminiscences and Reflections* (1926).

2 William Shakespeare, *Julius Caesar* (1623).

Johnston as Caesar. Although I do not join with Warnie in condemning Shakespeare, I must say that in a good many plays he has missed alike the realism of modern plays and the statliness of Greek tragedies. Julius Caesar is one of his best in some ways.

The cricket trousers arrived thank you, and fit excellently. Will you please send me some envelopes.

your loving
son Jack.

TO HIS FATHER (LP IV: 26–7):

[Cherbourg School]
June 7, 1913
Saturday.

My dear Papy,

As you say, it was most unfortunate, more than unfortunate, that I should fall ill just now.[3] I had, as I thought, discussed the coming exam with myself in every possible light, but just the one thing I had not taken into account happened. For a while I thought I should not be able to do the papers at all, so that even the chance of doing them in bed was a relief. I did not start till late on Tuesday evening when I did Latin and Greek grammar and Latin Prose: I am afraid I did horribly badly in the Greek, though tolerably well in that days Latin and in the Latin translation and verses which came on Wednesday.

That afternoon came the essay paper which was one after my own heart, the three alternative subjects being 'The qualities of a successful soldier' 'The possibility of an universal language', and 'West is west and East is east, and never the twain shall meet'. I chose the last and applied it chiefly to the Indian question. It was much admired by Tubbs and by some masters at the College.

On Thursday I had a 'General paper' including History and Geography, Scripture and English, in which I got on alright but had not time to finish, a rather difficult French paper, and as a finale, Arithmetic and Algebra, which I think I did rather better than I anticipated.

Thus you have a brief schedule of my three days in bed. Not what one would choose for pleasure, but still what might have been worse. And I

3 Jack fell ill on about 1 June and had to retire to bed. He nevertheless managed to take the exams in the infirmary between 3 and 5 June.

hear you have written something to our common respected friend on the subject of a scholarship elsewhere, to the effect that I have some objection to going to any other school than Malvern but that you keep an open mind.[4] Very true. As a natural result I am honoured by the very well meant but rather importunate advice of the said respected friend that I should try for a scholarship elsewhere if I fail here. He is a great man for sticking to his guns; a man of purpose. I foresee that I shall find it very difficult to help taking his advice, which I by no means want to take. The good pedagogue has Uppingham at present in his eye for me. Now of this school I know absolutely nothing, good or bad. For this reason I do not like the idea of it – it is a leap in the dark. Of course for that matter Cherbourg, which has proved a success, was also a leap in the dark to a certain extent. But don't write anything of this to the good pedagogue. I have so far looked with ostensible favour on Uppingham when talking with him of the matter, as, having been ill and working hard on scant food for some days, I do not really feel disposed yet to enter into a controversy which I know will prove sharp. I suppose by going in for an Uppingham scholarship I do not bind myself to go to that school.

I cannot help wanting to go to the Coll. For one thing for two years now – and two years recollect are quite a long time at the age of fourteen – I have been expecting to go to Malvern, not indeed with any great fervour, for I am happy here, but with as much pleasure as I look on any public school, and it has become rather a rooted idea. Then again, I know a good deal more of Malvern than I do of any where else, and it is in a sense familiar already. As well, I shall still be at the town of Malvern, and since I must needs spend the greater part of the year in England I had sooner do it here than anywhere else.

I am very glad indeed that Warnie has at last decided definitely on some career, as I know this will lift a great weight from your mind. I confess that I don't know why you speak – as you have always spoken – so disparagingly of the Army Service Corps. It cannot be, can it, that you really liked the idea of putting W.[5] into the L.N.W.R.? I admit that there are great and lucrative posts to be gained in this company; greater than in the Army Service Corps. But the depths of drudgery for the less

---

4 He was referring to Mr Allen who on 2 June wrote to Albert saying, 'I believe you want him to go to the college here; if not, he might have a try for some other school which holds its Exams later' (LP IV: 25).

5 Warnie was very often referred to in correspondence with family and friends as 'W.'

successful are also greater. In the A.S.C., W., it is true, may not follow a great career, but, what is far more important, he will be always doing congenial work and mixing with other gentlemen; not with every railway clerk who may wear loud spats and button the last button of his waistcoat.[6]

I have got up today for a short time (Saturday), and am feeling almost all right. Hoping that your boils are better, and you are otherwise in good health, I am

your loving son,
Jack

TO HIS BROTHER (LP IV: 49–50):

Cherbourg.
Gt. Malvern.
[1? July 1913]

Dear old W.,

I have just heard from home the following statement, 'I suppose you know that I am in further and worse trouble about Warnie'.[7] What has happened? You haven't been sacked have you? Whatever it is, I should be the last person to tell you that the plate is hot after you had burned your fingers, so we will look on the bright side as much as possible. After all we have always been justly famed for extracting the maximum of pleasure from the most depressing circumstances: let us live up to it.

I am afraid P. will be in a very cheerless mood for the hols. If we cannot have mental enjoyment from the atmosphere of Leeborough[8] we can always fall back on our own resources and make the most of the physical comfort which, at their worst, the holidays always afford. Rows after tea

---

6 Warnie had just begun thinking of entering the Army Service Corps, the one career he was always sure he wanted, while his father favoured a job with the London and North Western Railway.

The Army Service Corps, which supplied food, weapons and other necessities to the troops, began in 1794 as the Corps of Waggoners. Over time it evolved until in 1888 it was recreated the Army Service Corps. In 1918, in recognition of its good work, it became the Royal Army Service Corps. It was renamed the Royal Corps of Transport in 1965. See John Fortescue, *The Royal Army Service Corps: A History of Transport and Supplies in the British Army*, vol. I (1930). Volume II by R. H. Beadon was published in 1931.

7 Albert's letter to Jack of 30 June 1913 (LP IV: 41). Warnie had been caught smoking.

8 'Leeborough' was Jack's and Warnie's private name for Little Lea. It had the advantage of yielding the adjectives 'Leeburian' and 'Leborough', as in a volume of their Boxen drawings called 'Leborough Studies Ranging from 1905–1916'.

and penitentiary strolls in the garden are not pleasant: but a soft bed, a nice Abdullah, a lazy walk with Tim, an occasional Hippodrome or Opera House, have their consolation and a sound gramophone can always refresh the jaded ear. But even now, in a rather dark hour, I do not dispair of P's cheering up a bit for the hols; for, as good luck would have it, my scholarship has brightened things.

Please write soon (how often have I made that request and received no answer to it), and tell me exactly what has happened, and also tell me your arrangements for the journey home. We break up on Tuesday 29th July, and you as I understand, the following Wednesday. So I suppose we shall go on the Tuesday. *Do* write immediately and tell me about this matter. Don't spend all your journey money. Cheer up.

your affect.
brother Jack.

P.S. Send a cab up for me first, and then down to S.H., and let it be in *plenty* of time. J.

In a letter to his father of 12 December 1912, Warnie told his father that, while he knew smoking was against the rules at Malvern College, he would like his permission to smoke 'in moderation' elsewhere (LP III: 317). Mr Lewis replied on 14 December, 'School smoking I condemn unreservedly...But outside that – at dinners etc., where it would make you odd or uncomfortable not to smoke a cigarette – smoke it and smoke it with a clear conscience, *knowing that you would not be ashamed to tell your father what you had done. But in school it is different' (LP III: 318). No trouble seems to have come of this and Warnie was made a prefect on 9 March 1913. About this time he decided on a career in the army and, careless of College rules, he was involved in several escapades. In June 1913 he was degraded from the prefectship after being caught smoking at school. Warnie had hoped to remain at Malvern until Christmas 1913 so that he could be there for Jack's first term, but while the headmaster, Canon S.R. James, was willing to reinstate him in his position as a prefect in July 1913 he would not allow him to remain another term. It was Warnie's wish at this time to enter the Royal Military College at Sandhurst and pass from there into the Army Service Corps (ASC). For this Warnie would need to pass the entrance examination to Sandhurst and his father began considering how he might prepare for this.*

TO HIS FATHER (LP IV: 44–5):

Cherbourg.
6/6/13 [6 July 1913]

My dear Papy,

I have been extremely worried since I got your last letter. No: I do not know what has happened to W. I have had no news either of him or from him since the day when I heard that he had been degraded. What has happened? Surely he has not been expelled? I often had fears as to what he might do at Malvern, but I never thought it would come to this. It is of no use my writing to him for information, as he seems to consider the answering of letters a superfluous occupation. Of course I know that all this is worse for you than for me, but it is very unpleasant for both of us: what has he himself got to say upon the matter? However, please let me know as soon as you can what the exact position of affairs is: in the meantime I can only hope that my fears have no foundation; for after all, the great majority of the troubles which I have at one time or another anticipated, have never come to pass. But after all, the process of self consolation, if it were not such a terrible business, would be almost funny. We are ready to turn and twist the facts until they bear no resemblance to the original thing. Perhaps one could not go on at all without doing so. Perhaps however if W's school career has been a failure, he may do better in the future.

Thank you very, very much for your kind suggestion about the present. You are really making too much of this scholarship.[9] Nevertheless, there is nothing that I should prize more than a nice edition of Kipling, whose poems I am just beginning to read and to wonder why I never read them before – a usual state of mind, in the literary way, for me at Leeborough.

Today we leave our letters open and the authorities insert a printed notice of the date of breaking up. Its rather singular to notice the familiar landmarks – in a metaphorical sense – that cluster round as we reach the last weeks of the term – and there are only three more now. Nevertheless I hardly watch the flight of time with my usual eagerness. In spite of several rows both fierce and long drawn out, both with masters and boys, I have really been very happy at Cherbourg; and Malvern is unknown ground. More important than this is the fact that we shall see each other again in a short time.

---

9 On 9 June Jack won a classical entrance scholarship to Malvern College.

Looking forward to which, I am,
your loving
son Jack.

TO HIS FATHER (LP IV: 45–6):

Cherbourg.
Gt. Malvern.
8/7/13.

My dear Papy,

I was more pleased than I can say to get your letter. Bad as the news is, it is not the worst, and it is always a relief to have certainty after a prolonged spell of suspense. I am afraid I cannot carry out your suggestion of letting W. speak first: shortly after I wrote my letter to you, I decided to write to him, partly because I hoped for an answer from the College which would naturally reach me before one from Belfast, and I could bear it no longer, partly to cheer W. up since no recriminations can improve the accomplished facts, and partly to settle arrangements about the journey home. In this letter I asked him of course, what exactly had happened, but I have received your answer. You are right in your supposition that I should resent being left in the dark, and I am very thankful that you wrote and told me everything.

Do not say in a letter that 'you must stop, or else begin to pour out all your troubles, which would be unfair'. It would not be unfair; it would be wise. For, in the first place you would derive some comfort from the mere action of putting them into words, and, in the second place, I trust that they would be lighter after we had talked them over together in our letters. This small thing, this act of discussing and sympathizing over matters, is all the help I can give you at present, but, such as it is, I give it, as you know, very gladly.

Perhaps you will be somewhat cheered up by the visit of our Scotch relatives: but to be honest, I have spoken too fiercely and too often against society to endeavour now to preach in its favour.

I was very interested by what you told me about Jordan.[10] Who knows

---

10 In a little piece called 'My Life During the Exmas Holadys of 1907', Jack paid tribute to the postman: 'Our postman is called Gordon [Jordan] and is a very nice and sensible man, and often sets me an essay to wright, the subject of which he provides' (LP III: 90). In his letter to Jack of 30 June 1913, Mr Lewis congratulated Jack on his scholarship, saying: 'I met Jordan the postman the other night, and as he used to set you essays, I thought I would tell him. He was as pleased as Punch. He said "Sir, the next time you're writing will you say – Jordan is delighted." ' (LP IV: 41).

but that I owe more to those early little essays in the old days than you or I imagine? For it is to this uneducated postman that I owe the fact that I was acquainted with the theory of essay writing, in however crude a form, at an age when most boys hardly know the meaning of the word. To him, of course, next to you and to the fact of my being born in a race rich in literary feeling and mastery of their own tongue, and in that atmosphere of culture which has always shrouded the study both at Dundela and Leeborough. Nowhere else have I met that peculiar feeling – that literary ether. Perhaps Archburn would have it were it not for the cats. No school ever had it, and libraries are too public. Thank goodness I shall soon be in it and with you.

Yet I do not enjoy saying goodbye to Cherbourg: a good many things happy and unhappy have happened there, and I like the place.

What a curious business about that post card. Thanks for sending it. Its rather alarming to think that our letters can go astray like that.

your loving
son Jack.

At the beginning of September Albert Lewis thought of asking his old headmaster at Lurgan College in County Armagh, William T. Kirkpatrick[11] *(1848–1921) if he would prepare Warnie for the Sandhurst examination. Following his retirement from Lurgan in 1899 Mr Kirkpatrick had moved with his wife to 'Gastons', Great Bookham in Surrey, where he usually had one residential pupil each year whom he prepared for university or college examinations. He agreed to tutor Warnie and the latter arrived at Great Bookham on 10 September 1913.*

Jack arrived in Malvern on 18 September to begin his first term as a scholar of Malvern College – or 'Wyvern' as he called it in his autobiography. Like Warnie before him, Jack was a member of School House.

11 See **William Thompson Kirkpatrick** in the Biographical Appendix. Mr Kirkpatrick had a number of nicknames, including 'The Great Knock', 'Knock' and 'Kirk'.

TO HIS FATHER (LP IV: 71–2):

[Malvern College,
Malvern.
21? September 1913]

My dear P.,

I arrived safely as you know by the telegram – reaching Malvern at about half past five. Most of the other new boys had arrived, but one or two didn't come until the following day. So far everything has been very pleasant indeed.

Luckily I am going to get a study out of which the old occupants are moving today. There will be three other people in it – Hardman,[12] Anderson,[13] and Lodge.[14] The last of these is an intolerable nuisance, but the Old Boy manages these things and it can't be helped.

I have seen quite a lot of W's friend Hichens,[15] who seems frightfully pleased at being head of the house; going about with a huge note book and a blue pencil, taking down quite unneccesary things.

Yesterday we made our first acquaintance of Smugie[16] – a queer, but very nice old man who goes on as if taking a form were a social function – 'a quaint old world courtesy' as you read in some book. There is one

---

12 (Sir) Donald Innes Hardman (1899–1982) was Jack's study-mate in School House. On leaving Malvern he went to Hertford College, Oxford. While serving in the First World War during 1916–19 he joined the Royal Air Force and became a professional serviceman. He was promoted to wing commander in 1939, air commander in 1941, air commander of South East Asia 1946–47, and was chief of air staff and organization 1954–57, retiring in 1958.

13 Edward Anderson (1898–1928) was a member of School House 1913–17. After leaving Malvern he served in the war as a 2nd lieutenant. He later moved to Northern Rhodesia, dying there in November 1928.

14 Kenneth Ernest Lodge (1899–?) was a member of School House 1913–17. During the war he served overseas as a 2nd lieutenant with the Duke of Lancaster's Own Yeomanry. He was promoted to captain and remained in the army.

15 Fitzgerald Charles Cecil Baron Hichens (1895–1977) was at Malvern 1909–14 and was the head of School House when Jack arrived in 1913. From Malvern he went to Exeter College, Oxford, but soon left there for Sandhurst from where he passed into the Duke of Cornwall's Light Infantry in 1915, becoming a captain in 1918. Following the war he resigned from the army and obtained a regular commission in the Royal Air Force, in which he became a wing commander. He retired in 1943.

16 'Smugie' or 'Smewgy' was Harry Wakelyn Smith (1861–1918) who taught Classics and English to the Upper Fifth and for whom Jack was to have great affection. He had been educated at St John's College, Oxford, and he joined the staff of Malvern in 1885. In *SBJ* VII, Lewis said: 'Except at Oldie's I had been fortunate in my teachers ever since I was born; but Smewgy was "beyond expectation, beyond hope". He was a grey-head with large spectacles and a wide mouth which combined to give him a froglike

other new boy from the School House in the Upper V – Cooper, who is quite all right.[17] We begin ordinary work on Monday.

Could you please send me some plain socks, black, which are 'de rigeur' here. My size is rather uncertain, but get them almost as big as your own, for I have a large foot. I have not heard from W. yet. Hoping you are not 'thinking long', I am,

your loving
son Jack

TO HIS FATHER (LP IV: 77):

Malvern.
28/9/13.

My dear Papy,

I hope you don't object to the use of red ink, which is unavoidable, as our study has no black. Thanks very much for the money, note paper and socks. As you advise, I am being careful not to be rooked, and have already refused countless offers of utterly worthless merchandise. I have made the acquaintance of W's friend Captain Tassell, who is quite an interesting study.[18]

---

expression, but nothing could be less froglike than his voice. He was honey-tongued. Every verse he read turned into music on his lips...He first taught me the right sensuality of poetry, how it should be savoured and mouthed in solitude...Had he taught us nothing else, to be in Smewgy's form was to be in a measure ennobled. Amidst all the banal ambition and flashy splendours of school life he stood as a permanent reminder of things more gracious, more humane, larger and cooler. But his teaching, in the narrower sense, was equally good. He could enchant but he could also analyse. An idiom or a textual crux, once expounded by Smewgy, became clear as day.' This deeply loved man died in his little house in the school grounds, where he lived alone, on 13 November 1918, a victim of the influenza sweeping Europe that year.

17 Harry Richard Lucas Cooper (1899–1936), of Oxford, entered Malvern as a minor scholar in 1913. When he left in 1918 he ranked as the second boy in the school, head of School House, a cadet officer in the OTC and a football star. From Malvern he went to Christ Church, Oxford, where he took his BA in 1922. He worked for the Imperial Bank of India, and in 1924 was employed in the Calcutta office.

18 Douglas Spencer Montague Tassell (1872–1956) took a BA in 'Greats' at Christ Church, Oxford, in 1894 and began teaching classics at Malvern in 1905. On the retirement of the geography master in 1928 he took over the teaching of geography. Perhaps his greatest work, and that which gave him most satisfaction, was with the Officers' Training Corps. In 1909 he was put in charge of the Malvern contingent of the OTC, which he commanded until 1919 when he was awarded the Territorial Decoration. Warnie wrote of him: 'In appearance he was a jaunty, dark haired, short mustached, dark eyed little man, very much the soldier with a permanent expression of busy irritation' (LP IV: 73). It was he who first reported Warnie for smoking.

Talking about W., I have heard from him since I came back. He seems to be settling down to the routine a la maison Gastons.

The work here is very heavy going, and it is rather hard to find time for it in the breathless life we lead here. So far that 'breathlessness' is the worst feature of the place. You never get a 'wink of peace'. It is a perpetual rush, at high pressure, with short intervals spent in waiting for another bell. Roll is called several times each day, which of course helps to crowd up the time. However, I suppose this sense of being eternally hustled will wear off as things settle down. On the whole, it is very pleasant so far, and, which is a help, I like Smugie.

There is another thing that is worrying me rather. That is the fact that I miss Lea Shakespeare hours for drawing. Both of these subjects I should like to continue, but one must be dropped. What do you advise me to do? If we decide to give up the drawing, I suppose you can arrange that with the authorities.

I get on very well with the people in my own study, which is a great comfort. How is every thing at Leeborough?

your loving
son Jack

TO HIS BROTHER (LP IV: 78–9):

[Malvern
15? October 1913]

My dear W.,

I was very glad to hear from you and acknowledge my remisness in writing, but honestly I am being worked to death by Smugy – with whom however I get on very well – not a moment of peace.

True, no 24 is rather near the pres. room, but both Hardman and I have extraordinary luck about fagging. One thing is that we are in the same study as that fat beast Lodge, whom everyone hates, so that if a pre. comes in he is sure to fag Lodge before us. I have only had to clean boots twice so far.

I have, among other things, written an article to appear in the 'Malvernian' under the name Hichens – whom I like best of the pres.[19]

---

19 For whatever reason his article did not appear in *The Malvernian*.

I don't see all the horrors which you heaped on Browning.[20] He's always very decent to me. Bourne gets very much mobbed as a pre.[21] I am in Walter Lowe's math set.[22] Were you ever there?

Two very exciting things have happened. A drawing of mine, which we had to do for Smugy as one of the questions in W.E., was pinned up on the Upper V door for a week, and the James came down and said it was spirited. Also an English poem of mine in imitation of Horace was 'sent up for good' to Jimmy.[23] Consequently I have to go down to South Lodge and copy the poem into his great book tomorrow.

Isn't the Fish a glorious man?[24] Smugy keeps on asking about you. As he is so interested in O.M's., you ought to write to him if you have time. He *is* a decent old Kod,[25] isn't he? Recruit drill is at present the chief joy of my life. I got a Coll. pres. for skipping clubs the other day. Jervis I

---

20 Stanley Forrester Browning (1896–1917) became a member of School House in 1910 and by the time he left at the end of summer term of 1914, he had been a house prefect and in the second eleven at football. In 1914 he joined the Royal Flying Corps, and was a captain in that branch of the service when he was killed in action 3 May 1917.

21 John Arthur Watson Bourne (1896–1943) was at School House 1910–14, during which time he was a house prefect. During World War I he was a captain in the RAF. He then worked as an engineer in the technical and research department of a petroleum company. During World War II he served as a captain in the Royal Signal Corps. He died in March 1943.

22 William Walter Lowe (1873–1945) entered Malvern in the winter of 1888. When he left in 1893 he was junior chapel prefect, captain of the football eleven, and had been four years in the cricket eleven. From Malvern he went to Pembroke College, Cambridge, where he received a BA in 1896. He returned to Malvern as an assistant master in 1896, and was house master 1913–32. He retired in 1932 and died in May 1945.

23 i.e. Canon James, the headmaster.

24 'The Fish' was Henry Geoffrey Curwen Salmon (1870–1933) who went up to Jesus College, Oxford, in 1888 on a Classics scholarship. He joined the staff of Malvern College in 1901 and taught French and German to the sixth form. In 1914 he helped prepare the third edition of the *Malvern Register*, and he was entirely responsible for the fourth edition of 1924. When he retired from teaching in 1929 he was appointed secretary of the Malvernian Society, which work he undertook with enthusiasm for the rest of his life.

25 In his *Glossary of Words in Use in the Counties of Antrim and Down* (1880), William Hugh Patterson (1835–1918) defined 'cod' as '(1) *sb.* a silly, troublesome fellow. (2) *v.* to humbug or quiz a person; to hoax; to idle about. "Quit your *coddin'*."' (p. 22). Warnie said, 'It has however a third meaning, namely an expression of humourous and insincere self depreciation; an Ulsterman will say of himself, "Amn't I the square oul' cod to be doin' so and so?"' (LP IV: 306). Jack Lewis used the expression often, and he seems to have invented the diminutive 'codotta' or 'Kodotta' which appears occasionally in his letters. A notebook of his poems written about this time was entitled 'Metrical Meditations of a Cod'.

rather like,[26] but Bull II hasn't come back yet.[27] It is a good business that I have got into a study with a decent lad. I like Hardman II very much.[28]

By the way, you *don't* enclose the Col. Rena May [list] whatever you may think you do. How goes the History? You must manage to come down to the House Supper. Everyone would be awfully bucked to see you. I shall write and tell P. that I am nervous about going home alone if you like. This is being written in the breathless interval between Supper and Prayers, so I must chuck it now.

your loving
brother Jack

TO HIS FATHER (LP IV: 87–8):

[Malvern]
Postmark: 19 October 1913

My dear P.,

I hope you did not think that I was incurring reckless expense when I wrote to you for the money. The way you are rooked at Malvern by subscriptions, loans, and the fines which are shabbily arranged, is perfectly appalling. Thanks very much indeed for the five shillings.

The poem after Horace was, I am glad to tell you, somewhat in the nature of a success. It was top of the form and was sent up to the James. 'Being sent up for good' is a privilege enjoyed only by our form and the Upper Sixth and is rather a ceremony. I had to go down to Smugy's house and copy the poem into a vast old volume of his, containing the works and signatures of all those who have been 'sent up for good' since 1895. I was of course greatly interested to read the other poems and things in the book: some of them are really very good. I enclose the

---

26 Edwin Cyril Jervis (1896–?) was at School House 1911–15. On leaving Malvern he went to Sandhurst. He joined the Duke of Wellington's Regiment in 1916, was made a lieutenant in 1917 and during the war was seriously wounded. He received the Military Cross.

27 Charles Edward Bristow Bull (1900–77) was at School House 1912–15. During the war he served in the OTC. After the war he was private secretary to Aylesbury Brewery Co. Ltd, and also an actor.

28 This was the younger brother of Jack's study companion. Wallace George Hardman (1897–1917) was at School House 1911–14. After leaving Malvern he was a 2nd lieutenant in the Manchester Regiment, and was killed in action near Kut on 9 January 1917.

poem which it may interest you to see. Smugy's house is a queer little nook of the world, exactly typical of its owner.

I am inclined to agree with you that it will be a pity to lose Mr. Peacocke. He was neither a great preacher nor reader, but he was an educated gentleman, which is something to say in these times.[29]

I hope this business of Aunt Minnie[30] will turn out all right. Coming on top of the trouble about Norman it is very hard lines, and I should imagine that the Moorgate household is one of the worst fitted to receive trouble, as there is always, even when things are at their brightest, a certain gloom there.

It certainly is a grievous pity that Shakespeare filled Romeo and Juliet[31] with those appalling rhymes. But the worst thing in the play is old Capulet's preposterous speech to the guests. Still, it is a very fine tragedy. So is the Greek play that we are doing. It is quite unlike all that stiff bombast which we are accustomed to associate with Greek tragedy. There is life and character in it.

your loving
son Jacks

'"Carpe Diem" after Horace'
'In the metre of "Locksley Hall"' (Tennyson)

When, in haughty exultation, thou durst laugh in
Fortune's face,
Or when thou hast sunk down weary, trampled in
The ceaseless race,
Dellius, think on this I pray thee – but the
Twinkling of an eye,

---

29 The Rev. Gerald Peacocke, who succeeded Thomas Hamilton as rector of St Mark's, was leaving. He was the son of the Most Rev. Joseph Ferguson Peacocke, Archbishop of Dublin, and was educated at Trinity College, Dublin where he took the Hebrew Prize in 1892. He was ordained priest in 1894, and was curate of Carnmoney, Co. Antrim, 1893–6. After four years in Holywood, Co. Down, he was rector of St Mark's, Dundela, 1900–14. He was prebendery of Geashill, Co. Offaly, 1914–23, and Archdeacon of Kildare 1923–44.

30 Aunt Minnie was the wife of Albert's brother, William Lewis (1859–1946). See **The Lewis Family** in the Biographical Appendix.

31 William Shakespeare, *Romeo and Juliet* (1597).

May endure thy pain or pleasure; for thou knowest
Thou shalt die,
Whether on some breeze-kissed upland, with a
Flask of mellow wine,
Thou hast all the world forgotten, stretched be-
Neath the friendly pine,
Or, in foolish toil consuming all the springtime
Of thy life,
Thou hast worked for useless silver and endured
The bitter strife:
Still unchanged thy doom remaineth. Thou art
Set towards thy goal,
Out into the empty breezes soon shall flicker
Forth thy soul,
Here then by the plashing streamlet fill the
Tinkling glass I pray
Bring the short lived rosy garlands, and be
Happy – FOR TODAY.

TO HIS FATHER (LP IV: 90–1):

[Malvern]
Postmark: 26 October 1913

My dear P.,

I hope it did not seem that my act of sending you the poem was meant for a 'draw', which it was not. All the same, thanks very much for the P.O. which has restored 'the firm' to its pristine health and prosperity.

Anderson, one of the people in our study, has just received a huge crate of pictures from home which will enable us to sell some of our older pictures and raise capital. I had not been able to see about the extra copies of the Cherbourg magazine, as I have not yet been up to see Tubbs. I think however that I am going up today, when I shall be able to transact all my business.

On Thursday we had our field day and it was really a great affair. We started for the place, which is quite near Malvern about an hours march, at ten o'clock. W's friend Captain Tassell was in great form, mounted on a steed of which he was obviously terrified. Of course no one knew in the least what was meant to be happening, but we all dashed about, lying down and firing at intervals: on the whole it was very enjoyable.

You ask me what type of person one meets at Malvern: I will tell you. The average Malvernian may be, in fact usually is, a very good fellow in reality, but he always does his best to make himself out as bad as possible. Never believe his own account of his thoughts, deeds, or ideals. It is always far worse than the truth. Beyond this very childish and thoroughly British foible, there are very few faults in him. When you break through the shell of foolish affectation, you find him an honest kind hearted manly enough sort of fellow. At least that is how six weeks acquaintance of him strikes me. To use for once the phrase you have condemned, 'I may be wrong'. But I think not.

Yesterday there was a lecture in the Gym by that man Kearton who came to the Hippodrome last holidays. I must confess that I thought him very poor indeed. So we did not miss much by leaving that 'popular house of entertainment' alone.

The mother of Stone,[32] one of our House Pres., has died this week and he has consequently gone home. It is a very nasty business.

your loving
son Jack.

TO HIS BROTHER (LP IV: 96):

[Malvern
2? November 1913]

My dear W.,

Although always quite ready to fall in with your wishes whenever they are within the bounds of possibility, I always like to point out some of the more glaring absurdities in the same. It has not occurred to you that this simultaneous attack on the paternal purse will savour somewhat too much of preparation. But to proceed. The following is what I intend to write home, coming at the end of a long and cheerful letter, when he will be bucked.

'I have heard from W. again in the course of this week, and he seems to be comfortable with Kirk, although still working at high pressure. He mentions in this last letter, as he has done frequently before, that he entertains an idea of coming down here at the end of the term and

32 Noel Herbert Stone (1895–1918) was at Malvern 1910–14. After training at Sandhurst he joined the Worcestershire Regiment and was promoted to captain in 1917. He fought in France and was killed in action near Amiens on 27 April 1918.

travelling home with me as we did in the old times. This of course would be exceedingly pleasant for me, especially as most of the other new boys here have got friends coming down at the end of term; and it is undoubtedly pleasanter as well as more economical to travel in pairs than singly. The Old Boy, who by the way is one of the real good points about Malvern, has asked once or twice after W., and expressed a hope that W. will come down some time soon. Of course I am aware all this has nothing to do with me, but still he seems to have set his heart on it, and as I gather from the tone of his letter he has not mentioned it to you...'

As I said, it looks rather artificial, and can't be made much better. How are you getting on, old man? I hope this thing will work, as I am looking forward to another journey in the good old style. As you will notice in my epistle, I have made it the Oldish and not the James who wants you to come down.[33] I think that his name will carry more weight.

So far I am having a very good time here. You ask me what I think about Jacks.[34] I'll tell you. He's always most awfully nice to me, spends half hall talking to me about you and Smugy and things, and never fags me or drops me; but all the same I can't blind myself to the fact that he is an absolute _____ to most other people. But of course that doesn't worry me.

We had field day on Thursday at Malvern. I have managed to get into my house section, 'mirable dictu',[35] although I mob all the recruit drill. I can't go on now.

your affect.
brother Jack

---

33 'The Old Boy' or 'The Oldish' was George Gordon Fraser (1870–1958), the headmaster's assistant in the management of School House. He entered the College as a day boy in 1879 and remained until 1885. On leaving there he went to London University where he obtained a degree in 1889. In 1895 he became an assistant master at Lord William's School, Thame, and in 1895 he went in the same capacity to Forest School. In 1901 he was appointed an assistant master at Malvern, and in 1917 he became house master of No. 9 House, which position he held until 1927.

34 Stopford Brooke Ludlow Jacks, JP, FRSA (1894–1988), son of Professor L.P. Jacks, entered School House in 1910 and left in 1915. During the war he served with the artillery, became a major, and won the Military Cross. He took a Diploma in Economics in 1920 from Balliol College, Oxford, and became a director of Messrs. Greg and Co., cotton spinners, Manchester. He served as a governor of the Royal College of Arts, chairman of HM Prisons for Women, president of the Prestbury Petty Sessions, and a governor of Malvern College.

35 *Mirabile dictu*, 'Wonderful to relate'.

TO HIS BROTHER (LP IV: 101–2):

[Malvern
9? November 1913]

My dear W.,

You don't seem to be having a bad time at Gt. Bookham with your visits to 'The Laughing Husband' and the Hippodrome etc. I wouldn't boom these diversions over loudly in the paternal ear, as, innocent though they may be in themselves, yet they would not convey an impression of 'good hard work'. You may bet your boots I've heard enough about 'warm singlets and drawers etc.' to last me for a life time. P. tells me that 'when I come home he's going to take me in hand and see that that chest of mine gets as sound as a bell'. I wonder what that means?

I don't really know that a house tie would be worn with a black suit, but we'll see. Anyhow you must provide the tie as I am too 'stoney' for anything. I am amused to see that you have fallen into the excellent Marathon trap of spending 20/- where 5/- would do. As well, I wonder if 'Miss Thompson' would have heard about it. No one in T. Eden's shop ever seems to have heard of anything, do they?

It'll be a great weight off your chest when this filthy exam is over, so I am glad that it is comparatively soon.[36] I should think you ought to pass fairly easily if you've been oiling with Kirk. I am longing to find out from you in the hols what Kirk is really like. A *kod* of the first water I should imagine by all reports.

At the end of this term we really must get Jarnfeldt's Preludium.[37] I heard it again at the Classical Orchestral Concert, and was more than ever charmed with it. Perhaps too you are right about this Marathon scheme. We can talk that over anon.

P. of course refuses to accept your scheme of taking the trip to Malvern as a birthday and Xmas gift. At least he writes to me, 'W of course with his usual ingenuity says that this trip is going to be his Christmas and birthday present. But that is not quite the way I do things'. By the way, are we travelling home a day early or do you want to stay for the House Supper? I don't mind staying a bit if you like, only it is so close to Xmas with that fearful problem of P's present.

yours Jack.

---

36 Warnie was preparing to take the entrance examinations (25 November–2 December) for Woolwich and the Royal Military College at Sandhurst.

37 Armas Järnefelt, *Praeludium* (1904).

TO HIS FATHER (LP IV: 104–5):

[The Sanatorium,
Malvern]
Postmark: 24 November 1913

My dear Papy,

I am sorry to hear that you are 'thinking long', but, as you know, there is a good reason for the absence of letters as this is the first day I have been able to write. As you say, I have a lot of things to talk about and the first is Smugy's half term report.

I must confess that I was very disappointed in it. But I should have expected it all. For, the fact of the matter is about this Greek Grammar, that I know very little indeed: and the consequence of this is that what the rest of the form are running over in a sort of casual way for the third or fourth time, I am often learning for the first time in my life. This of course makes it rather difficult to keep up with the running. Then again, there are a lot of points of Greek grammar which I learnt up in furious haste at Cherbourg in the last few moments before the exam – and of course forgot again. These have to be faced with a half knowledge which is worse than ignorance, because it only muddles one's brain. But all these things should come right in time; as I flatter myself I am not cursed with 'an inability to grasp the elements' of any reasonable subject. As for the place in form, I was prepared for it to be poor, as the general standard of the form is rather beyond me – seeing that with the exception of the other scholars it consists of people who have filtered through to Smugy's care just at the end of their Malvern career. However, I get on well with Smugy and really that is half the battle.

You need not have been so worried about my temporary indisposition. It is only one of those trifling, although irritating chills to which I am subject in the winter months. Anyway, the worst of it is over now, as I am up in my room at the San. today. The San. is about the most curious place I have ever been in. I arrived here a week ago on Friday and was placed in a bed in a large and many windowed apartment, in one corner of which a fire was cheerfully engaged in belching forth dense clouds of smoke, which rendered it well nigh impossible to see or breathe. Conquering a natural terror of at once becoming unconscious in such an atmosphere, I resigned my self to sleep that night – but not for long. I soon discovered to my cost that the room in which I had been deposited was directly over the kitchen. I was apprised of this fact by the musical efforts of the domestic staff, whose vigorous and unwholesome concert was prolonged far into the night. But the funniest thing about this place is the noises that one hears in the morning. I really cannot imagine what the staff do. Judging from the loud peals of laughter and the metallic clangs which strike my ears before breakfast daily, they engage in hand to hand combat with the fire irons.

After a short period of the smoky room I was removed to a smaller but much more comfortable chamber where I still remain. Here my only trouble is the determined 'quacking' of a body of geese imprisoned somewhere in the neighbourhood.

As for your kind enquiries about the approaching natal gift, I have made up my mind that I should like 'The Rhinegold and the Valkyries' to match the 'Siegfried and Twilight of the Gods' which I have got.[38] I think however that the purchase of the book had better be deferred until Xmas when I can talk to my friend Carson in person.

I am glad to hear that W. is coming down at the end of the term as it is nicer travelling 'in comp.' than alone. I must stop now. How are you yourself keeping these days?

your loving
son,
Jack.

TO HIS FATHER (LP IV: 108–9):

The Sanatorium,
Thursday or Friday.
(I am not quite sure what
day it is today)
Postmark: 28 November 1913

My dear Papy,

I have advanced yet another stage and am now enjoying the priveledge of being downstairs in the San. That is, instead of sitting up in my bedroom, I have been moved to a sitting room where I can look out upon the hideously ugly garden of the San. And yet there is a homely

38 Jack already had the last two parts of Wagner's *Ring* cycle, *Siegfried and the Twilight of the Gods*, translated by Margaret Armour, with illustrations by Arthur Rackham (1911). For Christmas his father gave him the volume containing the first two parts, *The Rhinegold & The Valkyrie* (1910).

touch about this garden. It is full of laurels that will never grow because of the wind: we've seen these before haven't we?

I have been condemned by the school doctor, as soon as I go back, to join the ranks of people who do 'special exercises for delicate chests' in the gym. This is a piece of 'sconce' after your own heart, and I have no doubt that you will be more pleased to hear about it than I was. Your remarks about the sealskin etc. strike me as being both in questionable taste and the products of a fevered imagination rather than of a sane mind. But still, the human mind is so constituted that the bizarre must ever appeal more potently than the normal. Which is a consolation.

Congratulations on your victory at the Pattersonian musical festival. You'll be becoming quite a noted Strandtown diner out if you are not careful.

Talking about social functions reminds me of some wild fantastic talk of another dance this year.[39] Don't let us spoil the Xmas holidays by a chore as colossal as it is disagreeable, and as disagreeable as it is unnecessary. No one else gives a dance on two consecutive years. Nip this matter in the bud 'which has a bitter taste' and of which 'sweet will *not* be the flower'. (Do you remember the quotation?) But seriously, I hope no such folly is really toward. It is quite bad enough having to attend the functions of others without adding to the nuisance ourselves. Please convey to Aunt Annie and the other conspirators that you are determined not to hear of it, as I am sure you are. For one thing it is a considerable and uncalled for expense, and an expense of the most annoying kind – namely where you get absolutely no return for your money: unless *you* derive any great pleasure from hovering about among the noisy and objectionable throng who have invaded the pristine seclusion of Leeborough. But I don't fancy that you do. I am certain that I don't.

---

39 'Christmas will be here almost immediately,' Albert wrote to Warnie on 9 November 1913, 'and amongst other questions that must be decided is the all important one – are we to have a dance or not? No doubt our friends expect it. To me of course the thing is an expensive nuisance. But I don't want you and Jacks to drop out of things here' (LP IV: 99). 'No dance!!' replied Warnie on 10 October (LP IV: 101). Jack hated dancing, and years later he wrote in *SBJ* III: 'It was the custom of the neighbourhood to give parties which were really dances for adults but to which, none the less, mere schoolboys and schoolgirls were asked...To me these dances were a torment...How a small boy who can neither flirt nor drink should be expected to enjoy prancing about on a polished floor till the small hours of the morning, is beyond my conception.'

One good thing is that there are only three more weeks or so this term. I suppose W. will have both tickets when it comes to travelling. Is it next Tuesday or the Tuesday after that his exam comes off?

As to your remarks about the school san., in spite of smoky chimneys and a villainous domestic staff, there are a good many worse places to spend a few weeks of a long winter term. There are plenty of books and fires, and I always derive a certain savage pleasure in sitting with my feet on the fender, watching through the window a body of my unfortunate fellow beings setting off for a run across that cold, dismal golf links that always reminds me of the moorland in 'Locksley Hall'.

Talking about 'Locksley Hall', I have discovered a tattered copy of Tennyson's works here, buried among the sixpenny novels and illustrated weeklies, with which I have spent a few enjoyable afternoons reading 'In memoriam'[40] and some other things that one ought to know.

your loving
son Jack.

TO HIS FATHER (LP IV: 111):

The Sanatorium,
St. Andrew's Rd.,
Sunday.
Postmark: 30 November 1913

My dear P.,

I am now I think really quite better and shall be leaving the San. in a few days. It is funny, isn't it, how soon you get accustomed to a new kind of life? I've been down here for a fortnight or so, and I have grown so used to it that I could almost believe that Malvern never existed. But I shall be amply reminded of its life shortly. I am beginning to go out now on those intensely dull convalescent walks – progressing at two miles an hour, muffled up like an arctic explorer, and getting in the bits of sunshine. Thanks very much for the postal order which arrived yesterday. One good thing about being down at the san. is that it prevents your spending money, which is always an advantage.

For three days during this week I have had a companion – one Waley[41]

---

40 Alfred, Lord Tennyson, *Locksley Hall* (1842), *In Memoriam A.H.H.* (1850).

41 Reginald Philip Simon Waley (1897–1951) was a member of School House 1911–15. On leaving Malvern he served as a 2nd lieutenant in the Royal West Kent Regiment. In 1923 he went to work on the Stock Exchange.

of the School House, who had a boil on his arm and talked an amazing amount of agreeable nonsense. I pretended to be interested in and to understand his explanation of how an aeroplane engine works, and said 'yes' and 'I see' and 'really' at suitable intervals. I think I did all that was required very well.

However I am very pleased that he's gone, as I find my own society infinitely more agreeable than his, and prefer Tennyson to lectures, however learned, on aeronautics. That's just the perversity of fate. Anyone else who'd been down here alone for a fortnight would have been longing for a companion and of course wouldn't get one, while I, who have been thoroughly enjoying the solitude, (so rare a blessing at school), must have not only a companion, but a talkative one, dumped down. However it was only for three days.

You were saying the other day that when you sat doing nothing of an evening you passed the time in day dreams. I used to day dream a tremendous lot, but these last few days I find when I sit down in a nice chair in front of the fire that I get up an hour later and realise that I've been thinking about absolutely nothing. Is this a sort of mental stagnation I wonder.

Have you seen to the quashing of that dance conspiracy yet? Don't dare to answer in the negative. At any rate there *must* be no dance *for me*; nor for any other rational being I hope. So let that matter receive your immediate attention. You have your orders. Now we may go on.

I suppose the winter has set in at home by now, as it has here. But a very different kind of winter is the good old Belfast 'rainy season' from the English equivalent. Have you been winning any more musical laurels? That is a deed of daring do which should be set up in 'letters all of gold' (vide 'brave Horatius')[42] under a statue in the hall representing you with a symbolical lyre and 'plectrum'. (Look 'plectrum' out in a dictionary of classical terms).

your loving
son Jack.

---

42 Thomas Babington Macaulay, *Lays of Ancient Rome*, 'Horatius', LXVI, 6.

TO HIS FATHER (LP IV: 115):

School House,
Malvern College.
Postmark: 8 December 1913

My dear Papy,

I am now once more safely ensconced in the house, and so my illness is officially dead and buried. Unfortunately I have missed the Lea Shakespeare exam., in which I think I might have done something. However, these things will happen. There are only two more weeks 'and odd days' as they say in Romeo and Juliet,[43] now. I suppose we shall revise this week and have exams. next, so that the routine is practically over. Write and tell me about W's exam as soon as possible.

We have settled down into real winter weather here, which is always rather pleasing.

I notice in your recent correspondance an absence of any answer to my remarks re the quashing of the dance conspiracy. What is the meaning of this? Am I to understand that it has not been duly slain and buried? If not, why not? As I said before – 'you have your orders'. They were put before you in a plain and forcible manner so that you have no excuse for misunderstanding them. I hope to hear by return of post that the matter is now a thing of the past.

I can quite believe that the Peacockean platitudes were a come down after grandfather's production.[44] Yes: that is a very appropriate text.

During the course of my walks abroad while I was at the San., I met Mr. Taylor, the old Cherbourg drawing master whom you met. He was very distressed because he had heard that I had given up my drawing at the Coll., but was consoled by my assurance that it was only a temporary fixture so long as it clashed with English. We had a very pleasant little chat indeed.

Today was the Repton match, and I suppose Cherbourg was there, but I didn't notice them. It ended in a draw of one all after a very exciting game.

---

43 Shakespeare, *Romeo and Juliet,* I, iii, 15.

44 Mr Peacocke, the rector, gave his last sermon at St Mark's on 30 November. Remembering Thomas Hamilton's farewell sermon from the same pulpit, Albert wrote to Warnie on 30 November saying that Mr Peacocke's sermon was 'an extraordinarily poor performance even for him. I remember an old man some thirteen years ago preaching a farewell sermon from the same place, and I have never been more deeply touched by spoken words in my life' (LP IV: 110).

Allow me to observe that your noisy salutations to this insolent physician are not at all apropos and also were in somewhat questionable taste. I cannot write any more now.

your loving
son Jack.

1914

The year began with anxiety about the entrance examination to Sandhurst that Warnie had taken in November. But more than that was at stake. Albert was worried about what his son could do with his life, and this had been a question he put to Mr Kirkpatrick more than once. After tutoring him for four months, in preparation for Sandhurst, Mr Kirkpatrick wrote to Albert on 18 December 1913, saying:

> *You ask me as to his abilities. They seem to be good enough. But observe, a question of that nature cannot be answered in the abstract, for the will power, the moral element is involved. You never know what you can do until you try, and very few try unless they have to. Warren had a nice easy time, but no more so than the other fellows he associated with, many of whom were so well off that it did not matter from the economic point of view if they ever did anything or not. Years of association with such boys must have an effect in modifying the outlook. I do not see anything wrong with Warren apart from this slack, easy going quality. He has been blessed by Nature with two of her best gifts – good health and good nature. But it is too late now to make him interested in knowledge. The day for that has gone by. What he needs now is to be at work of some kind, and as soon as possible. I trust there can be little doubt of his passing, and if so, he should go to Sandhurst at once. The life may not be too strenuous, but it will be strenuous enough for him. The mere fact that he has set his mind on it is most important, and I think the army is now no bed of ease. Is he adapted for the life and will he succeed? These are questions very hard to answer. He does not want to go into any business, and dislikes exertion, drudgery, push and all the rest of it. He will probably discover that he cannot escape these things, even in the army. I should like to see a little more ambition in his composition – that*

> *is the main defect; but something of the kind may come in time. I have warned him that his present ideas may not be his ideas when he is a little older – a hard saying for a boy of course.* (LP IV: 118–19)

On 9 January the Civil Service Commissioners published the results of the November examinations, and the Lewises were elated to learn that Warnie passed 21st out of 201 successful candidates for Sandhurst. The first 25 candidates were awarded 'Prize Cadetships' which secured them admission to the College at half fees, and a grant of £50 on obtaining a commission. On 3 February Warnie and Jack crossed, Warnie to the Royal Military College, Camberley, Surrey, for the first time, and Jack back to Malvern.

TO HIS FATHER (LP IV: 130–1):

Gt. Malvern,
Sunday.
7th Feb. [1914]

My dear P.,

Thanks for the cutting which has been read with great interest. In addition to the natural unpleasantness of crossing on a bad night, I am annoyed at having broken my record, as I was sea sick on Tuesday for the first time in my life. It is not a pleasant experience. W. was very ill too, which is strange, as we both thought to have got over that danger.

The rest of the journey to Malvern was pleasant enough, and on my arrival I was pleased to find that Hardman and Quennel[1] had moved into the new study, which is a great success. Like somebody's cocoa, it is 'grateful and comforting'. So far, to my surprise, the weather has been quite mild and springlike, so I hope to get rid of the cold I had when I left home.

Smugy, I am sorry to say, waxed humorous over my illness, observing in that hoarse whisper of his that I must be 'a very delicate flower'. He must be excused of course, as the opportunity was too good for him to

---

1 William Eyre Hamilton Quennel (1898–?) entered School House the same term as Jack, and left Malvern in 1916. From there he went to Sandhurst, and in 1917 was gazetted into the 7th Dragoon Guards. He was promoted to lieutenant the same year. After the war he trained to be a doctor at St Bartholomew's Hospital, London. During World War II he served as medical officer in the Essex Yeomanry.

miss. I suppose it is a priviledge of old age. Otherwise he has been very pleasant, almost effusive, which is an unusual state of affairs with him.

I find there are even less than eight weeks more this term, which of course is good news for both of us. Quennel has already disappeared from the arena with a cold and an ear ache. We hear to our inexpressible joy that the good matron is leaving this term. More than we dared to hope. And, in considering about future possibles, it is a comfort to know that whatever happens, we can't get anything worse.[2]

There must be a lot of talk at home about the Greeves affair. What was the dinner like? When you write be sure and tell me all the latest developments. 'The case', as Sherlock Holmes would say, 'is not devoid of interest.'

What is W's address? I know it is Camberley, but there are a lot of codotta about companies and so forth, are there not?

I am afraid I must again 'bite your ear' for ten shillings. An unexpected outrage has occurred. A tax of five shillings a head is being levied for the Old Boy's leaving present, and another five for that of the James. I consider this rather stiff, but I am afraid it must be done. Please send it as soon as possible. I suppose the hat will be going round for various leaving presents all through this term. Another of the fees one has to pay for the benefit of a Public School education. But I think these places are doomed. Books like 'The Horrovians' form the thin end of the wedge.[3] It will end in a terrible debacle. I must stop now.

your loving
son Jack.

TO HIS FATHER (LP IV: 137–8):

[Malvern College]
Postmark: 16 February 1914

My dear Papy,

Thanks very much indeed for the unexpected donation and also for the exacted fund. 'An excellent thing – money' as an old friend of ours is wont to observe.

---

2 'The good matron' was Miss Backhurst, of whom Warnie wrote: 'She was better known and abominated by many generations of School House boys under her usual appellation of "The Old Bitch". She was a weak, spiteful, fussy, prying old woman, absurdly sensitive on the point of dignity, and like so many stupid women, always seeing ridicule where none was intended' (LP IV: 131).

3 Sir Arnold Lunn, *The Harrovians* (1913).

Although others at Malvern have proved wanting in perspicacity with regard to Warnie's brilliant successes, I was glad to see that Smugy was free from the general reproach. He lost no time in congratulating me warmly, and asking me to convey all the appropriate remarks to W. in my next letter. Such things are perhaps not great acts of kindness. But they serve to mark the difference between those who care for their old pupils and those who do not. Indeed the more I see of that remarkable old man, the more I like and admire him. I wish you knew him. If ever you come to visit Malvern again, you must not leave without making his acquaintance.

This week he has set us a job at which I hope to be able to do something. The alternatives were,

- a poem in imitation of Horace asking a friend to stay with you at the most beautiful spot you know.
- b A picture of a specified scene from Sophocles.
- c An original ghost story.

As you have probably guessed, I chose the first. I invited an imaginary friend to stay at Castlerock. As that would be impossible in verse I changed it to Moville, which is a little village near the former, as you remember. I treated the cliffs, seas, etc. at some length, and have taken pains over it. It is to be shown up tomorrow, and I hope it will be a success. I have written again in the metre of Locksley Hall; it is to be hoped that Smugy will not think that this shows a lack of invention or variety. If he does, I shall point out that some people like Pope and Addison wrote all their poems in the same metre. But of course Horace was a greater man than either of those. However, after a lot of thinking I came to the conclusion that no other metre would do as well. Horace is really impossible to translate: but I think we can imitate him in tolerable style. Everything so far is very pleasant in the Upper V.

How can people advocate a 'modern' education? What could be better or more enjoyable than reading the greatest masterpieces of all time, under a man who has made them part of himself? And against this some are foolish enough to oppose algebra and French verbs! The Greek Grammar has not yet put in an appearance. We are turning our attention to Latin where, of course I get on better.

I have seen Dr. Mackay who orders me to continue those annoying breathing exercises and not to play footer. The latter is a great comfort. The other a useful annoyance.

By the way I find I need another coat here. The present one is getting, not shabby, but tired looking, and the other is too small. Could you get Cummings to make me a new black coat to *exactly* the same measurements as the last. Only three buttons. Or, if it be more convenient, is there an old one of W's that would do?

Hichens has been down at the Sanatorium and has just come back. On a walk today I met Tubbs who asked me to go up to Cherbourg tomorrow. I think I shall.

your loving
son Jack.

TO HIS FATHER (LP IV: 152):

[Malvern College]
Postmark: 18 March 1914

My dear Papy,

Please excuse my delay in answering your letter. But I have had no time for any of my private affairs for all this week. I think that your criticism on the report are perfectly just; but I would like to remind you that not only does this persecution get harder to bear as time goes on, but that it is actually getting more severe. As for the work indeed, things are now much brighter, and I have been getting on all right since half term.

But, out of school, life gets more and more dreary; all the prefects detest me and lose no opportunity of venting their spite. Today, for not being able to find a cap which one gentleman wanted, I have been sentenced to clean his boots every day after breakfast for a week. It is after breakfast that the form goes through their translation together. From this I am cut off. When I asked if I might clean them in the evening (an arrangement which you observe would have made no difference to him), I received a refusal, strengthened by being kicked downstairs.

So we go on. These brutes of illiterate, ill-managed English prefects are always watching for an opportunity to drop upon you. There is no escape from them, night or day. There is some consolation in knowing that every one else is in the same box: all my friends too, are utterly miserable and tired of life. Perhaps you ask why we don't complain to the Old Boy. Sometimes a poor creature, driven wild by injustice and oppression, does try it. The Old Boy of course does his best: but what is the result? The prefects return to the persecution of the boy with renewed vigour. The place is systematically made uninhabitable for him, and he usually leaves. So that way is barred.

Please take me out of this as soon as possible but don't, whatever you do, write to the James or the Old Boy, as that would only make matters worse. Thank goodness there are only 2 weeks more; that must be our wee bit of 'silver lining'. You can't think how I'm longing to get back to you and Leeborough again. See and keep quite well yourself.

your loving
son Jack.

TO HIS FATHER (LP IV: 155):

[Malvern College]
Postmark: 22 March 1914

My dear Papy,

What a good thing the police did *not* turn up to arrest Craig.[4] If they had, I suppose you would be in the thick of it now.

No: I think I had better wait till the Tuesday and attend the House Supper. Not that I want to of course, but Maxwell and all the other Irish boys are waiting as it is Jimmy's last term, and you can't very well go early this time. So please book the berth for that night.

In common justice I feel that I ought to correct the notion which, very naturally, I have given you of Hichens. It is only fair to say that he is always ready to do anything he can for me or for anyone else. But the truth of the matter is that, though nominally head of the house, he has to mind his P's and Q's very carefully. The *real* head of the house is a splendid physical animal called Browning, who is one of the worst cads I have ever met. But he certainly *has* got 'guts' and bends the other prefects to his will with a rod of iron. They are all afraid of him. But Hichens, although neither clever or strong minded, is a kindly and gentlemanly sort of person. I have no complaints against him. But we are now so near

4 James Craig, first Viscount Craigavon (1871–1940), statesman. He was born in Belfast and was the MP for East Down 1906–18; MP for Mid-Down 1918–21; parliamentary secretary to the Ministry of Pensions 1919–20 and to the Admiralty 1920–1. He was chief secretary to Sir Edward Carson in opposing home rule, and was active in organizing means of resistance in Ulster. He was the first prime minister of Northern Ireland 1921–40. Captain Craig, as he was in 1914, was a very popular figure in the North of Ireland, and his house was about a hundred yards from Little Lea.

the end of the term that I am beginning to take a philosophical view of things: all will soon be over.

Although the papers are full of it, the people here don't seem to grasp the Ulster situation very much: one person asked me this morning if it was *for* Home Rule or against it that the volunteers were being formed.

Last night we had a lecture about Russia which was quite interesting.

your loving
son Jack.

Jack arrived at Little Lea on 25 March. His father, knowing how desperately unhappy he was at Malvern, was already in correspondence with Warnie about the matter. 'Your news about Jack is unpleasant,' Warnie said on 23 March,

> *but to me at least, not unexpected: from the moment he first came home and told me his opinion of the Coll., I was afraid it could only be a matter of time until he made the place too hot to hold him. I remember asking if it was not a splendid feeling at the end of a house match when you realised that your own house had won: "I saw a lot of boys throwing their caps in the air and making unpleasant noises: yes, I suppose it is an interesting study"...I had an idea that Malvern would weave its influence round Jacks as it did around me, and give him four very happy years and memories and friendships which he would carry with him to the grave...I am all in favour of sending him to Kirk. There would be no one there except Mr and Mrs K for him to talk to, and he could amuse himself by detonating his little stock of cheap intellectual fireworks under old K's nose.* (LP IV: 156–7)

Albert replied on 29 March:

> *I honestly confess that knowing Jack's mind and character, I am not greatly surprised to find him and a Public School unsuited to one another. In saying that I blame neither the one nor the other. He is simply out of his proper environment, and would possibly wither and decay rather than grow if kept in such surroundings...What is to be done? For a boy like Jacks to spend the next*

> *three or four years alone with an old man like Kirk is almost certain to strengthen the very faults that are strongest in his disposition. He will make no acquaintances. He will see few people and he will grow more into a hermit than ever. The position is a difficult one and gives me many anxious hours.* (LP IV: 160)

Albert asked Mr Kirkpatrick what he advised, and in his letter of 17 April he suggested that he send Jack back to Campbell College in Belfast. 'The Campbell College is at your door,' he said. 'If he went there, he would be in contact with you, which ought surely to count for much at this period of growth...It is very kind of you to think of sending him to me, but do you not think it a little premature?' (LP IV: 165). Mr Lewis persisted, almost begging Mr Kirkpatrick to accept him. 'If he can hold on through this summer,' Mr Kirkpatrick replied on 30 April, 'I hope I shall be ready (if I am spared) to receive him in the autumn, if you are still in the same mind then. And here let me say that I feel almost overwhelmed by the compliment to myself personally which your letter expresses. To have been the teacher of the father and his two sons is surely a unique experience' (LP IV: 167). Although Jack didn't want to go back to Malvern for even one more term, Mr Lewis got him to agree to it as an 'experiment'. If it became too bad, he would leave.

Sometime in mid-April, while this debate was going on, Jack came to know his 'First Friend'. 'His name was Arthur [Greeves]' he wrote in SBJ *VIII,*

> *and he was my brother's exact contemporary; he and I had been at Campbell together though we never met...I received a message saying that Arthur was in bed, convalescent, and would welcome a visit. I can't remember what led me to accept this invitation, but for some reason I did.*
>
> *I found Arthur sitting up in bed. On the table beside him lay a copy of* Myths of the Norsemen.[5]
>
> *'Do you like that?' said I.*
>
> *'Do you like that?' said he.*
>
> *Next moment the book was in our hands, our heads were bent close together, we were pointing, quoting, talking – soon almost*

5 H.M.A. Guerber, *Myths of the Norsemen from the Eddas and Sagas* (1908).

shouting – discovering in a torrent of questions that we liked not only the same thing, but the same parts of it and in the same way...Many thousands of people have had the experience of finding the first friend, and it is none the less a wonder; as great a wonder...as first love, or even a greater. I had been so far from thinking such a friend possible that I had never even longed for one; no more than I longed to be King of England.

TO HIS FATHER (LP IV: 169–70):

[Malvern College]
Postmark: 3 May 1914

My dear Papy,

I suppose, when I come to think of the matter, it was rather foolish of me to write and ask for 'a coat', without specifying what kind. One is apt to imagine at times that the person to whom you speak can keep up with your thoughts, whether they are expressed or not. What I want is a common or garden jacket coat, same measurements as the last, and with not more than three buttons on the front.

There are now only some five weeks more. Thank goodness!! For to tell the truth, Malvern is hardly the place for a long stay. I think it would be as well to stick to our original plan of leaving at the end of the term. It is rather heavy going; the ceaseless round of fagging, hunting for clothes and books that have been 'borrowed', and other jobs that have to be done in what is euphemistically known as your 'spare time', gets very trying. It is literally true that from the time you get up in the morning till the time you go to bed at night, you have not a moment to spare.

And the worst of it all seems to be that I am not getting on too well in form. It's discouraging. Whether it is that I haven't time to do it, or that I'm losing my mental faculties, or the fact that it is getting harder, I don't know: but the fact remains that things aren't as they should be. Goodness knows, I work as hard as I can. But it's all uphill. For instance, if you are hoping to do some of your surplus work in the interval between breakfast and morning school, it is very hard to have to give up that time to cleaning boots for some great big brute of a prefect at the bottom of the school. Then of course, as all your arrangements have been thrown out of joint, you don't know the lesson. And you can't give Smugy the real explanation. My chief dread is that he may get a bad impression, and I prize his opinion as much as that of any one. Then again, the whole atmosphere of the place is so brutal and unsavoury. In one word, it *won't do.*

Of course this is no new discovery. We both agreed last holidays that it was only an experiment, and I am now giving the result of that experiment. There is no need for you to worry or to do anything other than we have already thought of. But I consider it better to let you know straight away that this place is a failure, than to leave the botch over until it is irreparable. I suppose Kirk's is the best place for me. At any rate one of these 'English Public Schools', so famed in song and story, is not. To get on well at one of these, one needs to have a constitution of iron, a hide so thick that no insult will penetrate it, a brain that will never tire, and an intelligence able and ready to cope with the sharp gentlemen who surround you.

But these places are doomed. Books like the 'Harrovians' are the thin end of the wedge: and I don't mind saying that if you came back in a couple of hundred years, there would be no Public Schools left. That is a sort of consolation: for, among other things, one learns here a power of hating with an almost incredible intensity. However, I suppose this sort of education is found to be suitable for some people. But on others it comes rather hard.

To turn to a brighter topic, I am very pleased to hear that W. is getting on well at Sandhurst. His letters to me are very cheerful, and at the same time more serious than some of his communications have been. All these facts point in the right direction.

In the mean time, how are things in the ancient and honourable city of Belfast? Perhaps all this unpleasantness in a foreign land has its use, in that it teaches one to love home and things connected with home all the more, by contrast. I suppose the aggravation of the social nuisance, which always accompanies Xmas has now died down. And what are the attractions at the popular houses of entertainment? Among other things that I want to know, has the great fire mystery been solved yet? It destroys my mental picture of Leeborough if I am not sure whether there still be a wall between the hall and the study or not. However, I am glad to say that I shall be able to see the whole thing for myself at no very distant date.

It is now half term, and there are only four or five weeks more. They will not be long in the going. I wonder is there any truth in the idea that a wise man can be equally happy in any circumstances. It suddenly struck me the other day that if you could imagine you were at home during the term, it would be just as good as the reality.

your loving
son Jack

TO HIS FATHER (LP IV: 173–4):

[Malvern College]
Postmark: 17 May 1914

My dear P.,

I must really apologise elaborately and profusely for having left you letterless this week: but the fact is that this has been my first opportunity.

First of all, you will be interested to learn that our friend Browning has not, as he anticipated, been raised from the position of House Pre. to that of School Pre. Instead, a humble and inoffensive person named Parker[6] has been placed above him; at which you may well imagine his chagrin and my delight.

The new headmaster[7] has created a good impression here already by making the servants clean our boots – thereby abolishing the most obnoxious source of fagging. So far he has spoken very little indeed, but when he speaks it is in a pleasant voice and in good English. He wastes no time. All this shapes very well, although (thank goodness) I shall not see much of his career.

Smugy's wit on my late return did not exercise itself in my presence. But on the first day, as I am told, he expressed a fear lest I had been 'killed in the war'. Ah, well! These people will soon learn that war is not a subject for joking; so for that shall we too.

The worst part of the summer term is the fact that we have to keep out of doors nearly all our time; but here one notices the great advantage of being in the Upper School, and therefore allowed to go into the

6 Gerard Parker (1896–?) was in School House 1910–14, and was school prefect. After leaving Malvern he went to Sandhurst, passing from there in 1915 into the Devon Regiment. He was promoted to lieutenant in 1917 and during the war he was mentioned in despatches. He made captain in 1926, and retired in 1931.

7 Canon James had been succeeded as headmaster by Frank Sansome Preston (1875–1970) who had been educated at Marlborough College and Pembroke College, Cambridge. He was an assistant master at Marlborough 1899–1914, and headmaster of Malvern 1914–37.

Grundy Library at all hours of the day – it proves a great refuge when the 'house' is out of bounds.[8]

I have received a letter from Arthur Greeves. Intimate to him the fact that a suitable reply is being composed at our leisure. Note the royal plural. Well, it's a good thing that two weeks at any rate have gone. How are the 'rheumatics' keeping? I suppose by this time you are in the depths of the house cleaning ceremony: have the study and hall been knocked into one, or any other funny thing happened?

This term in the Grundy I have discovered a new poet whom I must get, Yeats. I never read any of his works before, and both what he says and the way he says it, please me immensely. Do you know him or care for him at all?

Just one bit of 'Kodotto' before we stop. In the study or in *your* dressing room (not mine), you will find a little black book of Warnie's, a Greek Testament. I should be very glad if you would send it here as soon as possible.

your loving
son Jack

TO HIS FATHER (LP IV: 179–80):

[Malvern College]
Postmark: 31 May 1914

My dear Papy,

Many apologies again for these same 'epistolary shortcomings'. But the days this term are so very full, and are spent so much out of doors that it is very hard to polish off the weekly letter with anything like regularity.

What a nuisance that old arm is to be sure. However, I expect that when the fine weather sets in it will improve. I am sorry that in asking you to procure my Attic pentateuch I was compelling you to embark upon a voyage at once perilous and disagreeable and arduous (Johnsonese again). I hope that by the time this letter reaches you, the study wall will have been replaced and the stately hall of Leeborough will smile upon guest and inhabitant with its pristine splendour and hospitality. Of

8 In *SBJ* VII Lewis said that while 'Smewgy' was the major blessing of Malvern, the other 'undisguised blessing of the Coll was "the Gurney", the school library; not because it was a library, but because it was a sanctuary. As the negro used to become free on touching English soil, so the meanest boy was "unfaggable" once he was inside the Gurney.'

course in restoring the 'main library' you are careful to alter the appearance of the room as little as possible. It would be a pity if I came home to a strange house. In the meantime I hope that the small library has been allowed to remain untouched?

This week I am glad to say that the Greek grammar has been going a good deal better; I hope this will continue, as it would be a pleasure to secure a good report of these people before I left. Happily Browning has been ill at the Sanatorium since last Monday, which has kept him out of mischief for *one* week at least. Last week I got out of the library the works of our present poet laureate, Bridges, who did not impress me a bit;[9] but I have now struck better ground in Charlotte Bronte's 'Wuthering Heights',[10] which although melodramatic like all her books, shapes very well indeed.

Before I close I must request you to forward a little of the 'ready' as owing to exorbitant subscriptions, fines, and the expenses of the summer term, our whole study has run out of cash. As long as one of us was flush the other two could live upon him, but when all three are in this condition it is impossible.

I hope that your arm will not remain 'hors de combat' very long.

Your loving
son Jack

TO ARTHUR GREEVES (W/LP IV: 180–1):

[Malvern College
5 June 1914]

Dear Arthur,

I really must apologize for having kept such a long and unjustifiable – silence. But the readiest means of mending that fault are those of writing fully and at once – which I now propose to do. To begin at the beginning, you had hardly been outside Little Lea for twenty minutes when a chance of not going back seemed to be held out to me, only, as you may guess, to be snatched away again. When we came to pack up my last few belongings, what should happen but that no key was to be found for my trunk! High and low we searched, but not a sign of it. My father

9 Robert Bridges (1844–1930), Poet Laureate from 1913. His poetry appeared in a single volume in 1912, and this was probably what Lewis was reading.

10 Emily Brontë, *Wuthering Heights* (1847).

was in despair: how was I to go back? How long would it take to have a new lock fitted? For a few moments I had a wild hope of staying at home. What was my disgust, when, almost at the last moment, Annie[11] turned up with the required artical, and off I had to go!

Since then, I have lived or existed as one does at School. How dreary it all is! I could make some shift to put up with the work, the discomfort, and the school feeding: such inconveniences are only to be expected. But what irritates me more than anything else is the absolute lack of appreciation of anything like music or books which prevails among the people whom I am forced to call my companions. Can you imagine what it is like to live for twelve weeks among boys whose thoughts never rise above the dull daily round of cricket and work and eating? But I must not complain like this, I suppose. Malvern has its good points. It teaches one to appreciate home, and to despise that sort of lifelessness. If I had never seen the horrible spectacle which these coarse, brainless English schoolboys present, there might be a danger of my sometimes becoming like that myself. But, as it is, I have had warning enough for a lifetime. Another good point about Malvern is the Library, which is one of the best-stocked I have ever been in – not that anyone but myself and two or three others care twopence about it, of course! I have here discovered an author exactly after my own heart, whom I am sure you would delight in, W.B. Yeats. He writes plays and poems of rare spirit and beauty about our old Irish mythology. I must really get my father to buy his books when I come home. His works have all got that strange, eerie feeling about them, of which we are both proffessed admirers. I must get hold of them, certainly.

You can hardly tell how glad I was to hear that you were learning theory. It is a positive shame that you should go about with all those lofty strains running in your head, and yet never set pen to paper to perpetuate them. Of course, take the 'Loki Bound' MS.[12] over to Bernagh,[13] anytime you feel inclined to compose a little operatic music. Thank you very much indeed for undertaking the job of the gramaphone. I suppose by this time it is restored to its former condition. It makes me furious to think of your being able to walk about your house and ours and all the

11 Annie Strahan was the cook-housekeeper at Little Lea, 1911–17.

12 The tragedy, Norse in subject and Greek in form, which Lewis was writing.

13 The Greeves's home in Circular Road was directly across from Little Lea.

beautiful places we know in the country, while I am cooped up in this hot, ugly country of England. Where is your favourite walk? I hope that by this time you are quite recovered and are able to go about freely without fear of injury. County Down must be looking glorious just now: I can just picture the view of the Lough and Cave Hill from beside the Shepard's Hut. Sometime next holydays, you and I must make a journey up their before breakfast. Have you ever done that? The sunrise over the Holywood Hills, and the fresh stillness of the early morning are well worth the trouble of early rising, I can assure you.

Since I have touched on the subject of health, I must ask a few questions of a disagreeable nature, on a matter which I have very near my heart. I have now had no direct letter from my father for over three weeks, and I hear that he is very ill. I would be very thankful indeed if you would go over and see him sometimes, and try and cheer him up: then you could tell me exactly how he is, and whether what I have heard has been exagerated or not – although I really don't deserve a reply to this after the shameful way I have treated you with regard to letters. But I feel sure you won't mind writing just a few lines, to tell me about yourself and family, and the state of various other things, besides my father's health. As I am sure you are tired by this time of a long and melancholy letter, I will stop.

Yours affectionately
Jack Lewis

TO HIS FATHER (LP IV: 190–1):

[Malvern College]
Postmark: 22 June 1914

My dear Papy,

Since I last wrote to you, I received, with your knowledge as I gather, a letter from Annie, short and comfortless enough to be sure, but still something to keep me from alarm. The most promising thing about her communication was that she promises me a letter from you at no very distant date. Do not force yourself to write until you feel thoroughly fit – but when you can, let me have a rare budget of news and reflections to compensate for the weeks 'that the locust hath eaten'.[14] Above all, don't forget to tell me all about yourself. I will spare you the trite expressions

14 Joel 1:4.

of sorrow and hope for your recovery; between those who know each other so well, such remarks are out of place, and I am sure you have had enough of that sort of thing. I should like to encourage you to cheer up if I thought I should have any success in that line; I must at any rate mention one consoling circumstance – namely that it is now half way through this dreary term, and is only five weeks till we shall be together again. This week you will get the report: and I hope and pray, not without confidence, that it will do nothing to add to your discomfort. I think I have now crossed the Rubicon in Greek Grammar, and am now happily arrived at the safe side of it. Mr. Smith [Smugy] has been very kind to me indeed, and I think we shall part friends.

This week I have been reading a most remarkable book which has created a great impression. It is 'The Upton Letters',[15] a series of letters from a school master at 'Upton College' to a friend whose health confines him in Madeira. They purport to have been actually written on such an occasion and not for publication; and indeed the utter absence of plot, or in some cases even of connection, make this seem to be true, although their wonderful beauty argues against it. But to come to my point: the great revelation of the book is the statement made somewhere that we 'ought not to write about our actions but about our thoughts'. How wonderfully true. We busy ourselves, you and I, telling each other about the weather and the little trivial happenings of each day, while the thoughts of our hearts, the really great experiences of our selves, are seldom spoken of. Of course this is rather rhetorical and letters written entirely on those lines would tend to become monotonous. But the saying struck me so forcibly at the time that I thought I would mention it to you.

This week the natural course of our life has been torn up as it were, by a cyclone in the form of speech day. I suppose you will be able to read Preston's speech in the Times, and give your own verdict upon it.[16] For my part, I did not see much merit in it – a few trite maxims, a few of the usual jokes, and that was all. In fact if the truth must be told, Preston is not a big man. He is, as far as I can see, a learned and courtly gentleman of captivating manners, but not the person who can save the ruin of a tottering school. Malvern would seem to be fated by the gods never to

15 Arthur Christopher Benson, *The Upton Letters* (1905).
16 *The Times* (2 June 1914), p. 9.

secure the right man as her headmaster. It is gratifying for me to think that I may live to see the end of this place. Perhaps that is an ungenerous thought: and I should hesitate to bestow my loathing so heartily on anything, even an inanimate object, if I did not think that it would be a real benefit for the country if this place were suppressed.

At this time of the year especially, one sees how awfully the place misses its mark. The whole of our spare time is given up to the great business of our life – cricket. Cricket is played with intense seriousness, and the players are usually in a very bad temper with themselves and everyone else, owing to the strain put on their minds by such a stupendous affair. Now for me, work is the business of the term: I am tired when I come out of school, and should like some recreation. Unfortunately, I am frankly and desperately bored by the recreations that are forced upon me. And yet it is obvious that one must have compulsory games at school: but if you do, as it seems, they are given this ludicrous preponderance and become for some the absorbing interest of their life, and for others a bogie and an incubus.

I enclose a few verses in imitation of Ovid, which were top of the form last week and well spoken of by Smugy. Do you care for that metre? There are a great many rhymes in it, which makes it difficult; but the thing that I want to learn is 'to move easily in shackles' (I wonder who said that? Do you know?)

Before I close I must again make shift to bite the paternal ear; as the 10/- which you were kind enough to send has been absorbed in paying off old debts and buying back for the study things which had been sold in the days of extreme embarrasment. I hope you won't think this extravagant.

See you take care of yourself, and write as soon as you are able.
your loving
son Jack

The following poem was enclosed with the letter above. The words underlined by 'Smewgy' are in capital type, and his remarks are in brackets.

'Ovid's "Pars estis pauci"'

(Metre copied from a chorus in Swinburne's 'Atalanta in Calydon')

I.
Of the host whom I NAMED
As friend, ye alone
Dear few!, were ashamed
In troubles unknown
To leave me deserted; but boldly ye cherished my cause as your own.
(Yes.)

II.
My thanks shall endure
– The poor tribute I paid
To a faith that was pure –
Till my ashes be laid
In the urn; and the Stygian boatmen I seek, an impalpable shade.
(Yes, but not Ovid.)

III.
But nay! For the days
Of a mortal are few;
Shall they limit your praise
Nay rather to you
Each new generation shall offer – if aught be remembered – your due.

IV.
For the lofty frame (hardly scans.)
That my VERSES ENFOLD,
Men still shall acclaim
Thro' ages untold;
And still shall they speak of your virtue; your honour they still shall uphold.
(Yes.)

TO HIS FATHER (LP IV: 192–3):

[Malvern College]
Postmark: 29 June 1914

My dear Papy,

On Friday I got a letter from you for the first time since this trouble, and glad I was to get it. It has been a bad business, but I am glad to see that you are over the worst of it now. Be careful of yourself, and take care that you don't go back to your ordinary routine until you are thoroughly fit.

My mental picture of home is disturbed to a certain extent by your mention of a fire. Here, we are in the middle of a magnificent summer: day succeeds day with the same cloudless sky and parched earth, and the nights are hot and comfortless. But on the whole, fine weather is agreeable, and has, I think, a certain effect on the spirits. Thank you very much for the money, which will enable 'the firm' to live 'en prince' until the time of our exile be over, and I return to a lovelier country to lead a happier life.

On the Tuesday of this week an unusual thing happened. Smugy asked myself and another boy in the same form and house, by name Cooper, to motor over with him to a little place called Birchwood in the country, where we had tea at an inn, and took a long delightful walk through fields and woods to a place where we were again picked up by the car, and thus home again. It was indeed very kind of the old man, as I am sure he sees quite enough of us in school hours. We went through a very beautiful piece of country, far, far away to the N. West of the hills where we could never go in an ordinary walk. To me, tired as I was of the flat, plain, and ugly hills of Malvern, this region, with its long masses of rolling hills and valleys, variegated by close mysterious woods and cornfields, together with one or two streams, was an enchanted ground. The Malvern hills loomed as a dark mass not far off the horizon: seen at this distance, they had lost their sharpness of outline, and looked weird and unreal, but very beautiful.

Here, in the middle of all this, we came upon the little cottage which used to be the summer resort of Elgar,[17] the composer, formerly an intimate friend of Smugy's. The latter told us that Elgar used to say he was

17 Sir Edward Elgar (1857–1934), composer, who rose to international fame about 1900 through his choral and orchestral music. He was living in Worcester at this time.

able to read a musical score in his hand, and hear in his mind not only the main theme of the music, but also the different instruments and all the side currents of sound. What a wonderful state of mind!

This week I have taken a course of A.C. Benson's essays, which have impressed me very favourably indeed. Do you know them? He has a clear, simple, but melodious style, second as I think only to Ruskin, and the matter is always suggestive, weighty, and original. He always makes you think, which a book ought to.

your loving
son Jack

TO HIS FATHER (LP IV: 196–7):

[Malvern College]
6/7/14

My dear Papy,

I was glad to get your letter on Saturday, as I was beginning to grow somewhat anxious about you. I am glad indeed to hear that you are on the mend, and hope that the term 'mending' will soon be out of place. So the report has come at last. Though I could have wished for something more effusive, still it is pleasing to note that it is an improvement on the last one, and I hope that the next in its turn will be a proportionate advance. Yes. I think the old man has some regard for me, but, it must be remembered that even if I were to return next winter, I should no longer be under him, as all our form are getting a shove to make way for the influx of new scholarship people.

This week I have enjoyed the doubtful privilege of having two teeth extracted, both of which had been bothering me a good deal off and on this term. The dentist, who is a thoroughly competent official, pronounced his verdict that as they had been tinkered with over and over again, and were now hopelessly rotten, they had better come out. So out they came, with gas, and I think it was a good job.

I am at present engaged in reading Newman's poems:[18] do you know them at all? They are very, very delicate and pretty, and are like nothing more than one of those valuable painted Chinese vases which a touch would destroy. I must except from this criticism the 'Dream of

18 John Henry Newman, *Verses on Various Occasions* (1868).

Gerontius',[19] which is very strongly written. But the rest are almost too delicate for my taste: it is a kind of beauty that I can't very much appreciate.

We have had two thunderstorms this week, and their combined efforts have left the ground pretty much under water, which is a great relief, as it puts an end to that eternal cricket. I wonder which is the more fatiguing, being made to play oneself, or watching others play it? We have plenty of both here, and both are compulsory.

But to turn to a better theme, do you realise that there is barely a month more this term; and I am already beginning to look forward to the end of it. That, I think, is one of the really priceless pleasures of youth – this joy of home coming, the gradual approach to the familiar surroundings etc. – as an old friend of ours once said on another subject, 'it can't be beat'.

Which reminds me, has Arthur got the gramophone mended yet?

your loving
son Jack

TO HIS FATHER (LP IV: 197–8):

[Malvern College]
Postmark: 13 July 1914

My dear Papy,

Although there has been no letter this week, I do hope that you have not had a relapse or anything, and that you are getting on all right.

This week we have had a Repton match here, and other things which must now be told. A nice impression truly these people will take back of Malvern and the Malvernians! One evening, during the game called 'crockets' (which is a kind of impromptu cricket played with soft balls on the stretch of gravel outside S.H.), two real knuts from Repton strolled up, and began watching at a distance: this is what they saw. Browning, whose ball had been hit over into Mr. Preston's garden, turned round to

19 Newman's *Dream of Gerontius* depicts the journey of the soul to God at the hour of death. In 1900 it was set to music by Elgar, who regarded the work as his masterpiece. Lewis came to like the *Dream* very much in later life and in a discussion of Purgatory in chapter 20 of *Letters to Malcolm* (1964) he said 'the right view returns magnificently in Newman's *Dream*'.

an inoffensive person called Hamley,[20] who has just been made a prefect, and demanded the latter's ball. This request was very naturally refused: whereupon our friend Browning proceeds to take it by force, and with many blows and oaths, succeeded in ejecting the other down the bank. Then, noticing the not unnatural mirth of the Reptonians at the sight of two public school prefects fighting and rolling in the mud like street boys, he turned round and told them in terms which I cannot reproduce, 'not to grin at *him*', with a great emphasis on the last word.

So this is our public school dignity, politeness and hospitality which we are always hearing about! These are the institutions that all other civilised countries envy us for, and would imitate if they could. Bah! I for one, will be glad to be rid of them all, and would like to see the day when they are abolished. But as for this Browning, perhaps we judged him too harshly. It is very true that we never know the data for any case but our own. I hear he is not happy at home: so that, although it may be that he is such a beast that he cannot be well treated, yet on the other hand it may be that he has been made into a beast. One never knows.

Last week we had an essay on the difference between Genius and Talent, and mine has been 'sent up for good', the ceremony which I told you of.[21] Only three weeks more now.

your loving
son Jacks

On Saturday, 19 September 1914 Jack arrived at Great Bookham to be met at the station by the man he'd heard about all his life, W.T. Kirkpatrick. 'I came prepared,' he later wrote in SBJ *IX,*

> *to endure a perpetual luke-warm shower bath of sentimentality. That was the price I was ready to pay for the infinite blessedness of escaping school...One story of my father's, in particular, gave me the most embarrassing forebodings. He had loved to tell how once*

20 Cedric Edwin Hamley (1899–1997) was an exact contemporary of Jack Lewis in School House, having arrived in the third term of 1913. He left in 1915 and served in the war with the London Rifle Brigade. He was afterwards a 2nd lieutenant in the RAF, and a captain in the 3rd London Fusiliers from 1922–28. He worked in the family business, C. Hamley Ltd. in London.

21 It is reproduced in LP IV: 198–200.

at Lurgan when he was in some kind of trouble or difficulty, the Old Knock, or the dear Old Knock, had drawn him aside and there 'quietly and naturally' slid his arm round him and rubbed his dear old whiskers against my father's youthful cheek and whispered a few words of comfort...And here was Bookham at last, and there was the arch-sentimentalist himself waiting to meet me...He was over six feet tall, very shabbily dressed...lean as a rake, and immensely muscular. His wrinkling face seemed to consist entirely of muscles, so far as it was visible; for he wore moustache and side whiskers with a clean-shaven chin like Emperor Franz Joseph. The whiskers, you will understand, concerned me very much at that moment. My cheek tingled in anticipation...

Apparently, however, the old man was holding his fire. We shook hands, and though his grip was like iron pincers it was not lingering. A few minutes later we were walking away from the station. 'You are now,' said Kirk, 'proceeding along the principal artery between Great and Little Bookham.' I stole a glance at him. Was this geographical exordium a heavy joke? Or was he trying to conceal his emotions? His face, however, showed only an inflexible gravity. I began to 'make conversation' in the deplorable manner which I had acquired at those evening parties and indeed found increasingly necessary to use with my father. I said I was surprised at the 'scenery' of Surrey; it was much 'wilder' than I had expected.

'Stop!' shouted Kirk with a suddenness that made me jump. 'What do you mean by wildness and what grounds had you for not expecting it?' I replied I don't know what, still 'making conversation'. As answer after answer was torn to shreds it at last dawned upon me that he really wanted to know. He was not making conversation, nor joking, nor snubbing me; he wanted to know. I was stung into attempting a real answer. A few passes sufficed to show that I had no clear and distinct idea corresponding to the word 'wildness', and that, in so far as I had any idea at all, 'wildness' was a singularly inept word. 'Do you not see, then,' concluded the Great Knock, 'that your remark was meaningless?'...By this time our acquaintance had lasted about three and a half minutes; but the tone set by this first conversation was preserved without a single break during all the years I spent at Bookham...If ever a man

came near to being a purely logical entity, that man was Kirk...Some boys would not have liked it; to me it was red beef and strong beer.

TO HIS FATHER (LP IV: 212):

[Gastons,
Great Bookham,
Surrey]
Sept. 21st [1914]

My dear Papy,

I arrived, as you heard by the telegram, at Great Bookham in perfect safety and with all my effects. Today is Monday and you must excuse my not writing yesterday as some friends of Mine Host's called in the afternoon when I had intended to do this.

Need I say how thoroughly satisfied I am with Bookham, Gastons, and their inhabitants. You already know all about Kirk – more than I do probably – and W. has spoken of Mrs. K., whom I like exceedingly.

The country is absolutely glorious. I took my first tour of exploration this afternoon, and went through the outskirts of a large forest. One was strongly reminded of 'As you like it'.[22] The village is one such as I have often read of, but never before seen. The little row of red roofed cottages, the old inn, and the church dating from the Conquest might all have stepped out of the Vicar of Wakefield.[23] How Arthur would enjoy this place!

Another point of gratification is that I have at last, triumphantly, found a dirtier railway than the Co. Down. (I wonder have you any shares in the London & S. Western?) Kirk's son,[24] who is in a volunteer camp near here called for an hour or so last night. We get the 'Whig' here, which gives a touch of home. I hope you are keeping in good health

---

22 William Shakespeare, *As You Like It* (1623).

23 Oliver Goldsmith, *The Vicar of Wakefield* (1766).

24 George Louis Kirkpatrick (1882–1943) was the only child of Mr and Mrs Kirkpatrick. He was born 23 May 1882 when his father was still headmaster of Lurgan College, and educated in England at Charterhouse 1896–99. From there he went to work for the electrical engineers, Browett, Lindley & Co., English Makers of Patricroft, Manchester. When Mr Kirkpatrick retired from Lurgan he and Mrs Kirkpatrick moved to Manchester to be near him. Now Louis was in a camp near Great Bookham. He was general manager of Bruce Peebles & Co. (Engineers) in Edinburgh from 1932 until his death in 1943.

and spirits and letting Tim sleep indoors. Of course there are sewing meetings and all the usual war codotta at Bookham. To finish up – it is a brilliant success.

your loving
son Jack

P.S. Any signs of the photos? J.

TO ARTHUR GREEVES (W/LP IV: 212–13):

'Gastons'
Grt. Bookham.
Surrey.
Saturday
Sept / 14
[26 September 1914]

My dear Arthur,

If it were not that you could answer me with my own argument, I should upbraid you with not having written to me. See to it that you do as soon as you have read this.

And now – what do I think of it? After a week's trial I have come to the conclusion that I am going to have the time of my life: nevertheless, much as I am enjoying the new arrangement, I feel sure that you would appreciate it even more than I. As for the country, I can hardly describe it. The wide expanse of rolling hill and dale, all thickly wooded with hazel and pine (so different from our bare and balder hills in Down) that is called Surrey, is to me, a great delight. Seen at present, in all the glory of a fine Autumn, it may be better imagined than described. How I wish that I could paint! Then I could carry home a few experiences on paper for my own remembrance and your information. But the village wd. please you even better. I have never seen anything like it outside a book. There is a quaint old inn that might have stepped out of the 'Vicar of Wakefield', and a church that dates from before the conquest. But it is no good enumerating things: I cannot convey the impression of perfect restfulness that this place imparts. We have all often read of places that 'Time has forgotten' – well, Great Bookham is one of these!

I have only just discovered that you put my name in that book.[25]

25 Arthur had given him H.G. Wells' *The Country of the Blind, and Other Stories* [1911].

If I had seen it earlier I shd. have sent it back. You have no right to be so foolishly generous! However – many, many thanks. When one has set aside the rubbish that H. G. Wells always puts in, there remains a great deal of original, thoughtful and suggestive work in it. The 'Door in the Wall', for instance, moved me in a way I can hardly describe! How true it all is: the *SEEING ONE* walks out into joy and happiness unthinkable, where the dull, senseless eyes of the world see only destruction & death. 'The Plattner Story' & 'Under the Knife' are the next best: they have given me a great deal of pleasure. I am now engaged in reading 'Sense & Sensibility'. It is, undoubtedly, one of her best. Do you remember the Palmer family?[26]

In Greek, I have started to read Homer's Iliad,[27] of which, of course, you must often have heard. Although you don't know Greek & don't care for poetry, I cannot resist the temptation of telling you how stirring it is. Those fine, simple, euphonious lines, as they roll on with a roar like that of the ocean, strike a chord in one's mind that no modern literature approaches. Better or worse it may be: but different it is for certain.

I hope everything went off successfully on the eventful Teusday, and also that you are now recovered from your cold. You know my address: you have no excuse for silence, Sir!! No Philip's concerts this year at Belfast, I am told.

Yrs. (Expecting a letter)
C. S. Lewis

---

26 In Jane Austen's *Sense and Sensibility* (1811).

27 Homer, the Greek poet generally believed to have lived in about the eighth century BC, is famous for his two epics, the *Iliad* and the *Odyssey*. Mr Kirkpatrick wasted no time preparing Lewis to undertake these Greek masterpieces. 'We opened our books at *Iliad*, Book I,' Lewis wrote in *SBJ* IX. 'Without a word of introduction Knock read aloud the first twenty lines or so in the "new" pronunciation, which I had never heard before...He then translated, with a few, a very few explanations, about a hundred lines. I had never seen a classical author taken in such large gulps before. When he had finished he handed me over Crusius' *Lexicon* and, having told me to go through again as much as I could of what he had done, left the room. It seems an odd method of teaching, but it worked. At first I could travel only a very short way along the trail he had blazed, but every day I could travel further...I was beginning to think in Greek. That is the great Rubicon to cross in learning any language.' Lewis was using Gottlieb Christian Crusius, *A Complete Greek and English Lexicon for the Poems of Homer and the Homeridae: Illustrating the Domestic, Religious, Political, and Military Condition of the Heroic Age, and Explaining the Most Difficult Passages*. Translated with corrections and additions by Henry Smith. New Edition revised and edited by Thomas Kerchever Arnold (1862).

TO HIS FATHER (LP IV: 214):

[Gastons]
Monday.
Postmark: 30 September 1914

My dear Papy,

Thanks very much for the two letters which I received all in due course. Yes: I think that will be the best plan about the photos. Only, please send me two copies, as I want to give one to some one else at Malvern.

I am now at the end of my first week at Bookham, and can again tell you that it is everything that can possibly be desired. Both in work and leisure it is of course incomparably beyond any of the arrangements we have tried yet.

This week end an old pupil and friend of Kirk's was staying with us – one Oswald Smythe, who hies from Bembridge and is about twenty five years of age. Do you know who that would be? We are going on with friend Homer at what – to my ex-Malvernian mind – is a prodigious rate: that is to say we have polished off a book in the first week. At Malvern we always took a term to read a book of that sort of stuff.

Today I did a thing that would have gladdened your heart: walked to Leatherhead (for Bookham does not boast a barber) to get my hair cut. And am now looking like a convict – Yes thanks I have plenty of underclothing, and the cold is a good deal better!

There is a good deal of war fever raging here, as is natural. I am glad to hear that those 'five righteous' have been found. But five thousand would be more to the point. What is all the local news? Tell Arthur the next time you see him that I am eagerly expecting a reply to my letter. I suppose the winter has closed in at home by this time: but we are still having quite summer weather here – which I rather resent. Mrs. Kirk plays the piano beautifully, which is one of the great assets of Bookham. There is also a movement on foot to make me learn to play bridge: but I am wriggling as hard as is compatible with manners.

your loving
son Jack

P.S. Who is the 'Mr. Dods'[28] that Kirk mentions?

War had been building up for some time, and it was now imminent. The heir to the Hapsburg empire, Archduke Franz Ferdinand, was assassinated in Sarajevo on 28 June 1914. Linking the assassination to the government of Belgrade, on 23 July Austria despatched to Serbia an ultimatum which could only be answered in two ways: Serbia must become for all practical purposes a conquered province of the Austrian Empire, or it must accept a declaration of war. On 28 July Austria declared war on Serbia, and on 29 July Russia mobilized her south-western army. That same day in London, Winston Churchill proposed to the British Cabinet that the European sovereigns should 'be brought together for the sake of peace'.[29] *Germany refused, and on 31 July Russia mobilized against Germany. That same day Britain asked France and Germany to respect Belgian neutrality, to the maintenance of which Britain was committed by a treaty signed in 1839. France agreed to do so, but Germany gave no answer. Then, on 3 August Germany declared war on France. Hitherto Britain had stood aside, but the question of Belgian neutrality raised a problem and on 3 August Britain sent an ultimatum to Berlin demanding there be no attack on Belgium. On 4 August Germany entered Belgium, and that night Britain declared war on Germany. By midnight on 4 August five empires were at war: the Austro-Hungarian Empire against Serbia; the German Empire against France, Britain and Russia; the Russian Empire against Germany and Austria-Hungary; and the British and French Empires against Germany.*

Because of war-time needs, Warnie's training had been accelerated from two years to only nine months. On 1 October he was commissioned a 2nd lieutenant in the Army Service Corps and sent to the base at Aldershot in preparation for being sent to France on 4 November.

---

28 Eric Robertson Dodds (1893–1979), classical scholar, was from Banbridge, County Down. He was educated at Campbell College, and University College, Oxford. At this time he was reading *Literae Humaniores* at University College. He took his BA in 1917. Dodds was Lecturer in Classics at University College, Reading 1919–24, Professor of Greek at the University of Birmingham 1924–36 and Regius Professor of Greek in the University of Oxford, 1936–60. See his autobiography, *Missing Persons* (1977).

29 Martin Gilbert, *First World War* (1994), p. 25.

TO HIS FATHER (LP IV: 225–6):

[Gastons]
Monday [5?] Oct./14

My dear Papy,

Thanks very much for the photographs, which I have duly received and studied. They are artistically got up and touched in: in fact everything that could be desired – only, do I really tie my tie like that? Do I really brush my hair like that? Am I really as fat as that? Do I really look so sleepy? However, I suppose that thing in the photo is the one thing I am saddled with for ever and ever, so I had better learn to like it. Isn't it curious that we know any one else better than we do ourselves? Possibly a merciful delusion.

You ask about our church at Bookham.[30] I thought I had mentioned it in my first description of the village. However, at the risk of repetition, you shall be informed. It is of pre-Norman structure, and is, like all these old churches, no particular shape. There are various plates of bronze dedicated by 'So and so, gentleman, to his beloved ladye who etc., etc.' The organ is out of tune: the singing execrable. The Vicar is a hard working, sincere and cheerful fellow, but, as Miss Austen would say, of 'no parts'. It is, in its own way, very, very beautiful. Yes, I go every Sunday.

I wonder did you notice the article on Nietzche in last Sunday's Times Literary Supplement,[31] which demonstrates that although we have been told to regard Nietzche as the indirect author of this war, nothing could be farther removed from the spirit and letter of his teaching? It just shows how we can be duped by an ignorant and loud mouthed cheap press. Kirk, who knows something about N., had anticipated that article with us, and is in high glee at seeing the blunder 'proclaimed on the housetops.'

I am very glad to hear that Warnie has at last safely arrived in that state of bliss, our British Army. What happens to him now, do you know?

The weather here is perfectly ideal: sharp frosts at night, and clear, mild sunshine in the day: this is really the nicest country I have ever seen, outside – of course – Co. Down. The places about here in the

---

30 St Nicolas Church, the earliest parts of which were built in the 11th century, is mentioned in the Domesday Book. The Reverend George Shepheard Bird was rector 1905–26. Jane Austen went to St Nicolas often when her godfather was vicar.

31 'The Nietzschean Way', *The Times Literary Supplement* (1 October 1914), p. 442.

woods are alive with pheasants, as the usual shots are at the front: they are so tame that you can come within a few paces of them.

On Saturday the household went over to the famous Boxhill, which however I thought not nearly so pretty as some of the places nearer Gastons.

I can still say that a larger knowledge of our new stunt gives nothing but deeper satisfaction. We have at last struck the real thing in education, in comfort, in pleasure, and in companions. I could almost believe that Malvern had never existed, or was merely a nightmare which I am glad to forget. Paper and time at an end.

yr. loving son,
Jack

TO ARTHUR GREEVES (W/LP IV: 214–7):

Gt. Bookham
[6 October 1914]

Dear Arthur,

I will begin by answering your questions & then we can get on to more interesting topics. The plot of my would-be tragedy is as follows: (The action is divided into the technical parts of a Grk. tragedy: so:)

I. Prologos.
Loki, *alone before Asgard, explains the reason of his quarrel of the gods: 'he had seen what an injustice the creation of man would be and tried to prevent it! Odin, by his magic had got the better of him, and now holds him as a slave.* Odin *himself now enters, with bad news.* Loki *(as is shewn in the dialogue) had persuaded the gods to make the following bargain with the Giant, Fasold: that if F., in one single winter, built a wall round Asgard, the goddess Freya should be given him as his concubine. The work is all but finished: the gods, repenting of the plan, are claiming Loki's blood.*

II. Parodos.
Thor, Freya *&* *the* Chorus *enter. After a short ode by the latter, Thor complains that* Loki, *who is always the gods' enemy has persuaded them to this plan, well knowing that it would come to no good.* Loki *defends his actions in a very scornful speech, and the two are only kept from blows at the request of* Odin *&* Freya.

Odin, *though feeling qualms on account of their ancient friendship, agrees to* Loki's *being punished if the latter cannot devise some way out of the difficulty by the next day, (when 'the appointed Winter' is up). The others then withdraw leaving Loki alone with the* Chorus. *He has been cringing to Odin up till now, but on his exit bursts out into angry curses.*

III. Episode I.

The Chorus *pray to the 'spirits of invocation' to help* Loki *to find a plan. His only desire is to be able to save his own head and plunge the gods into even deeper morasses. A long dialogue ensues between him & the* Chorus, *the result of which is this plan: that* Loki *will send a spirit of madness into* Fasold's *horse which always accomplishes the greater part of the work. (Vide 'Myths of the Norsemen'). The* Chorus *agree & Loki sets off to Jarnvid (Ironwood) to instruct the spirit.*

IV. Episode II.

It is now quite dark. The Chorus *are singing a song of hope & fate, when* Fasold *enters with his horse, dragging the last great stone. He stops & converses with the* Chorus. *In the dialogue which follows, the genial, honest, blundering mind of* Fasold *is laid open: and his frank confession of his fears & hopes for* Freya, *and his labours, forms a contrast to the subtle intrigues of the gods. At last he decides to move on. He urges the horse: but at that moment the frenzy siezes it: it breaks from its traces & gallops off, kicking its master and leaving him senseless in the snow. Presently he recovers, and after a very sad & indignant accusation of the gods, goes off to mourn 'his vanished hope'. He cannot now hope to gain the 'dear prize' for which 'he laboured all those months'! The morning is all ready at hand*

V. Episode III.

Loki, Thor *&* Freya *return. All are in high spirits, and exult over the success of the plan. To them enters* Odin. *By the appearance of the god, we guess that something is wrong. On being questioned his explanation (greatly condensed) is this. 'The gods' empire rests on treaties. Therefore on honour. When that honour is broken their* *doom is at hand. Loki has conquered the Giant, how? By Fraud. We have broken faith and must prepare for the twilight of the gods.' As soon as the general shock has passed off,* Thor *turns upon* Loki *and says that he is the cause of all this.* Loki, *seeing that he has accomplished his design, throws off the mask of humility that he has been wearing, and, confessing that it was all his plan, bursts forth into fearful [cursings?] upon* Thor *and* Odin. *Since* Loki *cannot be killed by any known weapon, Thor purposes to pinion him on an adjacent boulder (etc. Vide 'Myths of the N's') as a punishment.* Odin, *though without enthusiasm consents, and he is bound. (Thor, Freya, Odin go off).*

VI. Exodos.

Loki, *bound to the rock, is indulging in a satyric dialogue with the* Chorus, *when Odin returns. As soon as* Loki *sees him he bursts into violent abuse.* Odin *has come to offer him pardon & release: 'He (*Odin*) is a lonely god: men, gods, & giants are all only his own creatures, not his equals & he has no friend – merely a crowd of slaves.* Loki, *who had been brought forth* with *& (*not by*) him by Fate, had supplied one. Will he be reconciled?'* Loki, *however, casts his offer back in his teeth, with many taunts. Seeing that they can effect nothing* Odin *&* Chorus *withdraw & the tragedy ends.*

Such then, in brief, is the skeleton of my poor effort poor indeed in its intrinsic worth, and yet not so poor if you could set it to soul-stirring music. As an opera the parts would be like this.

LOKI	Tenor (?)
ODIN	Baritone
THOR	Basso (of course)
FREYA	Soprano
FASOLD	Basso
LEADER of the CHORUS	Contralto (she has quite a lot to do, here & there)

Of course you would readily see what musical points could be made. Nevertheless I cannot refrain from giving you a few of my ideas. To begin with, Loki's opening speech would be sombre and eerie, – expressive of the fire-god's intrigueing soul, and endless hatred. Then (*Parados*) the first song of the chorus would be bright and tuneful, as a relief to the dramatic duet that precedes it. The next great opportunity for 'atmospheric' music comes (Episode I) where the theme of the 'spirit of madness' is introduced. *You* can well imagine what it ought to be like. Then (Episode II) we would have a bluff, swinging ballad for the huge, hearty giant; and of course the 'madness motive' again, where the horse breaks lose. Then some 'Dawn' music as a prelude to (Episode III) and Odin's speech about their position! What an opening for majestic & mournful themes. But the real gem would be some inexpressibly sad, yearning little theme, where (Exodos) Odin expresses his eternal loneliness. But enough!, enough! I have let my pen run away with me on so congenial a subject & must try & get back to daily life.

As for my average 'Bookham' day, there is not much to tell. Breakfast at 8.0, where I am glad to see good Irish soda-bread on the table begins the day. I then proceed to take the air (we are having some delightful, crisp autumn mornings) till 9.15, when I come in & have the honour of reading that glorious Iliad, which I will not insult with my poor praise. 11–11.15 is a little break, & then we go on with Latin till luncheon, at 1.0. From 1.–5.0, the time is at my own disposal, to read, write or moon about in the golden tinted woods and vallies of this county. 5–7.0, we work again. 7.30, dinner. After that I have the pleasant task of reading a course of English Literature mapped out by Himself.[32] Of course, that doesn't include novels, which I read at other times. I am at present occupied with (as Eng. Lit.) Buckle's 'Civilization of England',[33] and (of my own accord) Ibsen's plays. Hoping to hear from you soon, with all your views & suggestions for Loki, I am.

Yrs. sincerely

C. S. Lewis

P.S. If you begin composing in earnest you'll find the libretto in my study upstairs. J.

32 i.e. Mr Kirkpatrick.

33 H.T. Buckle, *History of Civilization in England* (1857; 1861).

TO HIS FATHER (LP IV: 229–39):

[Gastons]
Postmark: 13 October 1914

My dear Papy,

I am astonished to hear that the Glenmachonians[34] are still so foolish as to stick to the Russian delusion: as Kirk has pointed out several times, this extraordinary rumour, and the credit paid to it, is a striking illustration of the way in which a mythology grew up in barbarous or semi-barbarous ages. If we, with all our modern knowledge fall into an error so ludicrous and so unfounded, it is hardly to be wondered at if primitive man believed a good deal of nonsense.

Our household has an addition this week in the person of Mrs. K's theatrical friend Miss MacMullen, who is staying here for a week or ten days. 'Soul! She's a boy!' Altho' perfectly well she sees fit to travel down to Gastons with a bath chair, a maid, and a bull dog. However, they are the only faults, and they are amusing Kodotta.

This is the most extraordinary place I have ever seen for weather: we have had bright sunshine, frost, and not a spot of rain ever since I arrived. The touch of frost, unaccompanied by any wind to blow the leaves off their branches, has converted the country into a veritable paradise of gold and copper. I have never seen anything like it. Everyone at Bookham is engaged in a conspiracy for 'getting up' a cottage for Belgian refugees:[35] a noble scheme I admit: carried out however in a typical fussy 'Parishional' way. Some of Kirk's comments are very funny.

Any news from the Colonel?[36] When is he off to the front? Did you ever at Lurgan read the 4th Georgic?[37] It is the funniest example of the colossal ignorance of a great poet that I know. It's about bees, and Virgil's natural history is very quaint: bees, he thinks, are all males: they find the young in the pollen of flowers. They must be soothed by flute playing when anything goes wrong etc., etc.

---

34 The Ewart family who lived in nearby Glenmachan House. See **The Ewart Family** in the Biographical Appendix.

35 For some weeks the Germans had been intent on reaching the Belgian and French coastline. In an attempt to prolong the defence of their port city, Antwerp, the Belgian government appealed to Britain for troops. Thousands of British troops rushed to the aid of Antwerp, but by 10 October it was impossible to hold it against the Germans. By this time tens of thousands of Belgian refugees had arrived in England.

36 A nickname given Warnie by his father and brother.

37 Virgil (70–19 BC), the greatest Roman poet, wrote four 'Georgics', which are didactic poems in hexameters on Italy and traditional ways of rural life.

I hope that your dental troubles are now gone and that you are quite well in other ways (Yes – it is a bad cold Joffer!) I am scanning the horizon for a brown suit. I suppose you have settled down to winter weather and customs by now at home.

your loving
son Jack

TO ARTHUR GREEVES: (W/LP IV: 220–2)

Wednesday
[14 October 1914]
Bookham

My dear Arthur,

Although delighted, as always, to find your letters on my plate, I was very sorry to hear that you were once again laid up: I hope, however, that it is nothing more than a cold, and will soon pass away.

I was very glad to hear your favourable criticism of 'Loki' (and I hope it is genuine) and to see that you are taking an interest in it. Of course your supposed difficulty about scoring is a 'phantasm'. For, in the first place, if we do compose this opera, it will in all probability never have the chance of being played by an orchestra: and, in the second place, if by any chance it were ever to be produced, the job of scoring it would be given – as is customary – to a hireling. Now, as to your budget of tasteful and fascinating suggestions. Your idea of introducing a dance after the exit of Odin etc, is a very good one, altho' it will occasion some trifling alterations in the text: and, speaking of dances in general, I think that you are quite right in saying that they add a certain finish to both dramatic & operatic works. Indeed, when I was writing them, there were certain lines in the play which I felt would be greatly 'helped out' by appropriate movements. Thus the lines

'The moon already with her silvery glance, –
The hornèd moon that bids the high gods dance'

would suggest some good moonlight music both in motion and orchestra.

Turning to your remarks about illustrations, I must confess that I have often entertained that idea myself; but, thinking that, since you never spoke of it, there was some radical objection on your part, I never liked to suggest it. Now that I am undeceived in *that* direction, however, need I say that I am delighted with the idea? Your skill with the brush, tho' by no means superior to your musical abilities, has yet a greater mastery of the technical difficulties. I have only to cast my eyes over the libretto to conjure up a dozen good ideas for illustrations. (1) First of all, the vast, dreary waste of tumbled volcanic rock with Asgard gleaming high above in the background thrown out into sharp relief by the lurid sunset: then in the foreground there is the lithe, crouching figure of Loki, glaring with satanic malignity at the city he purposes to destroy. That is my conception of the Prologos. (2) Then Odin, thundering through the twilit sky on his eight footed steed! (what a picture.) (3) Again, Freya, beautiful, pathetic and terrified making her anguished entreaty for protection. (4) A sombre study of the moonlight choral dance that you so wisely suggested. (5) The love-sick Fasold raging in impotent fury when he discovers that he has been cheated. And (6) last of all, Loki, bound to his rock, glaring up to the frosty stars in calm, imperturbable and deadly hatred! And so on & so on. But you, with your artist's brain will doubtless think of lots of other openings. I do sincerely hope that this idea will materialise, and that I shall find on my return a whole drawer full of your best.

I am afraid this is rather a 'Loki' letter, and I know that I must not expect others to doat on the subject as foolishly as do I. I am going to ask for 'Myths and legends of the Celtic Race'[38] as part of my Xmas box from my father: so that, as soon as I put the finishing touches to 'Loki Bound', I can turn my attention to the composition of an Irish drama – or perhaps, this time, a narrative poem.[39] The character of Maeve, the mythical warrior Queen of Ireland, will probably furnish me with a dignified & suggestive theme. But, we shall see all in good time.

Mrs Kirkpatrick, the lady of this house, had not played to me at the time of writing my last epistle. But since then she has given me a most delightful hour or so: introducing some of Chopin's preludes, 'Chanson Triste',[40] Beethoven's moonlight Sonata,[41] Chopin's March

38 T.W. Rolleston, *Myths and Legends of the Celtic Race* (1912).

39 Whether Arthur Greeves ever attempted any part of his share in the musical drama is not known, but Lewis's lyric text of 'Loki Bound' filled 32 pages of a notebook. The only part of this which has survived consists of 819 lines reproduced in LP IV: 218–20.

40 Pyotr Il'yich Tchaikovsky's *Chanson Triste* was first performed in 1878.

41 The nickname of Ludwig van Beethoven's piano sonata No. 14 in C sharp, Opus 27, No. 2 (1802).

Funebre,[42] The Peer Gynt Suite[43] & several other of our old favourites. Of course I do not know enough about music to be an authoritative critic, but she seemed to me to play with accuracy, taste & true feeling. So that there is added another source of attraction to Great Bookham. For the value of Mrs K's music is to me two fold: first it gives me the pleasure that beautiful harmonies well executed must always give: and secondly, the familiar airs carry me back in mind to countless happy afternoons spent together at Bernagh or Little Lea!

Strange indeed is my position, suddenly whirled from a state of abject terrorism, misery and hopelessness at Malvern, to a comfort and prosperity far above the average. If you envy my present situation, you must always remember that after so many years of unhappiness there should be something by way of compensation. All I hope is that there will not come a corresponding depression after this: I never quite trust the 'Norns'.[44]

I have come to the end now of my time & paper and, I daresay, of your patience. While I remember; it would be as well for you to keep that sketch of the plot of Loki, so that we can refer to it in our correspondence, when necessary.

Yrs. very sincerely
Jack Lewis

P.S. Have the Honeymooners come home from Scotland yet? (J.)[45]

TO HIS FATHER (LP IV: 232):

[Gastons]
Postmark: 18 October 1914

My dear Papy,

Although fully alive to the gravity of the situation and grateful for the kindness of your suggestion, it was not without a smile that I read your last letter. I hardly think that the siege of Bookham will begin before Xmas, so that I need not come home just yet. And seriously, why not study the lilies of the field?[46] All your worry and anxiety will not help

---

42 Frédéric Chopin's *Marche Funêbre* was first performed in 1827.

43 Edvard Grieg's piano solo, the *Peer Gynt Suite* No. 2 (1893).

44 The female Fates of Norse mythology.

45 The 'Honeymooners' were probably Arthur's brother, Thomas Greeves, and Winifred Lynas, who were married on 22 September 1914.

the war at all: and the truest service that we who are not fighting can do is to conduct our lives in an ordinary way and not yield to panic.

The good ladies of Bookham are now in the highest state of felicity, having secured a formidable family of seven Belgian refugees, which they have duly installed in a cottage selected for the purpose. Luckily the mother of the family speaks French, so that the educated ladies of Bookham can talk to her: but the rest of the family speak nothing but Flemish. Yesterday I went with Mrs. K. to see them: tried my French on the mother and bombarded the others out of a phrase book with subtile converse like 'Good morning: are you well: we are well: is the child well: it is fine: it is wet: is it wet etc.' Of course they are not gentlemen; but very respectable and intelligent bourgeois.

Young Kirk was employed at his camp the other day in unloading a train of seriously wounded soldiers from the front: from whom he learned that the newspaper stories of German atrocities (mutilation of nurses, killing wounded etc.) were not in the least exaggerated.

I hope the dental troubles are a thing of the past. I suppose the Scotch Greevous honeymooners have returned by now, and that Arthur is back to work. He tells me that there is some talk of his going to Portrush with Mrs. Greeves,[47] which I should think was a chilly operation at this time of year.

The Gastonian arrangement continues to give every possible satisfaction that anybody could ask for: and the country is lovelier than ever. The theatrical lady is still here, so that when young Kirk comes down from his camp to spend the week end, we are quite a pleasant sized party. I am off to bed now, so good night.

your loving
son Jack

TO ARTHUR GREEVES (W/LP IV: 222–3):

[Gastons
20 October 1914]

My dear Arthur,

Many thanks for the letter, which I hope is becoming a regular 'institution', and apologies for my comparative slackness in replying.

---

46 Matthew 6:28: 'Consider the lilies of the field, how they grow; they toil not, neither do they spin.'

47 This was Arthur's mother, Mrs Mary Margretta (Gribbon) Greeves. See **Arthur Greeves** in the Biographical Appendix.

When I read your description of the boring evening I thought for a while of writing you a letter full of 'war' – to hear your views afterwards. But, to be serious, what would you? Is the trivial round of family conversation ever worth listening to, whether we are at war or no? I can promise you that it is not at Little Lea and if Bernagh is different it must be an exceptional household. The vast majority of people, too, whom one meets outside the household, have nothing to say that we can be interested in. Their circle of interests is sternly practical, and it is only the few who can talk about the really important things – literature, science, music & art. In fact, this deadly *practicalness* is so impressed on my mind, that, when I have finished Loki, I am resolved to write a play against it.

The following idea has occurred to me: in Irish mythology the ruling deities are the light & beautiful Shee: but, we are told, before these came, the world was ruled by the Formons, hideous and monstrous oppressors. What are the exact details of the struggle between the two parties I do not know. But it ought to make a good allegorical story, in which the Formons could be taken as typical of the stern, ugly, money grubbing spirit, finally conquered by that of art & beauty, as exemplified by the lovely folk of the Shee. However, of course, this is only a castle in the air.

I sympathize with your difficulty in drawing a horse, as I have often made the attempt in the days when I fancied myself in that line. But of course that counts for nothing: as the easiest of your sketches would be impossible for me. But there are heaps of pictures in which you need not introduce the animal. I hope the music has started in real earnest by now. The longer I stay at this place, the better I like it. Mrs. K., like all good players – including yourself – is lazy and needs a lot of inducement before she performs.

yours sincerely
C. S. Lewis

TO HIS FATHER (LP IV: 234):

[Gastons
25? October 1914]

My dear Papy,

You have surpassed yourself. The popular press, of whose reliability the Russian rumour is an example, remarks on the possibility of an invasion: the idea, after being turned over in your mind, appears in your next letter, clothed as 'it is *absolutely certain* that he is going to invade England'[48] Surely, Joffer, this is rather hyperbole? The one thing that Britain can depend upon is her fleet: and in any case Germany has her hands full enough. You will perhaps say that I am living in a fool's paradise. 'Maybe thon'. But, providing it only be a paradise is that not preferable to a wise and calculating inferno? Let us have wisdom by all means, so long as it makes us happy: but as soon as it runs against our peace of mind, let us throw it away and 'carpe diem'.[49] I often wonder how you came to have such a profound and genuine philosopher for your son, don't you?

I received and duly posted your letter to the Colonel: though why it should reach him any more easily from Bookham than from Belfast I don't know. It seems to me outrageous that you can't get a letter through. I suppose he *is* still at Aldershot and that they are allowed to receive letters? I think the 'my bankers'[50] wheeze is immense. The brother of that Smythe fellow, who was staying here some days ago, has lost his arm and is coming home. It begins to come home to you as a personal element, doesn't it? At present the only solution which Kirk will allow probable, is the absolute exhaustion of one, or more likely both parties: and that is a revolting prospect, is it not?

Last week I went up to town with Mrs. K. and the theatrical lady to the Coliseum to see the Russian ballet, which was very good: but the rest of the show seemed to me to be neither better nor worse than an average bill at our own old Hippodrome.

---

48 The rumour that Germany would invade England persisted for a long time and worried Albert greatly. It may have started with an article in *The Times* (15 October 1914) entitled 'Will Invasion be Tried?' in which the war correspondent said: 'Now that the war is reaching the climax of its violence we must anticipate that all the living forces of Germany will be thrown into the conflict, and that the German navy will no longer remain inert. We must expect to be attacked at home, and must not rest under any comforting illusions that we shall not be assailed. As an attack upon us can have no serious object, unless the intention is to land an expedition in England for the purposes of compelling us to sign a disastrous peace, it is well that we should look the situation calmly in the face, and reckon up not only Germany's power to do us harm, but also our power of resistance and means for improving it' (p. 4).

49 'Seize the day'. Horace, *Odes*, Book I, Ode 11, l.8, in which the poet urges Leuconoe to take thought for the present and not to worry inordinately about the future.

50 In a letter of 12 October, in which Warnie asked his father for a loan, he explained that he was owed money by Sandhurst and that 'I have communicated with my bankers' (LP IV: 229).

I hear from my Malvern correspondent, in the thankfulness of his soul, that it is half term. How different is his lot as he counts up the tardy lapse of hard, dreary, cheerless week after week, to mine: where the weeks slip away unasked and unobserved as at home. I am glad to see that the Captain was mentioned in despatches, and cannot see that there would be anything wrong in congratulating Hope.[51] I am giving up the usual end of the letter tag about Gastons 'giving all satisfaction', as you may safely assume that things continue better than I could describe.

your loving
son Jack

TO ARTHUR GREEVES (W/LP IV: 233–4):

Gt. Bookham
Wednesday
[28 October 1914]

Dear Arthur,

You ask me what a shee is: I reply that there is no such thing as '*A*' Shee. The word (which, tho' pronounced as I have spelled it, is properly in Irish spelled 'Shidhe') is a collective noun, signifying 'the fairies', or the gods, – since, in Irish these powers are identical. The common phraze 'Banshee', is derived from 'Beän Shidhe' which means 'a woman of the Shee': and the gods, as a whole, are often called 'Aes Shidhe', or 'people of the S.' The resemblance between this word '*Aes*' and the Norse '*Aesir*' has often been noted as indicating a common origin for Celtic & Teutonic races. So much for the etymology. But the word has a secondary meaning, developed from the first. It is used to indicate the 'faery forts' or dwelling places of the Shee: these are usually subterranean workings, often paved and roofed with stone & showing an advanced stage of civilization. These can be seen in a good many parts of Ireland. Who *really* built them is uncertain: but scholars, judging by the rude patterns on the door posts, put them down to the Danes. Another set say that they were made by the original inhabitants of Ireland, previous *even* to the Celts, – who of course, like all other Aryan people primarily came from Asia.

---

51 Their cousin, Hope Ewart (1882–1934), married Captain George Harding (1877–1957) in 1911 and they went to live in Dublin. Harding joined the army in 1900 and had been a member of the Army Service Corps since 1901. He was promoted to major in October 1914. He gained the DSO during the war and retired in 1928 with the rank of colonel.

I am sorrey that my epistle is rather late in arrival this week: but what with people bothering from Malvern, and letters to be written home, I have not had many free evenings. I feel confidant of your always understanding that, when my letters fail to arrive, there is a good, or at least a reasonable explanation. Now that I have threshed out the question of Shee, and apologized, I don't know that there is much to write beyond hoping that 'Loki' is proceding expeditiously in music & illustration.

Last week I was up with these people to the Coliseum: and, though of course (which by the way I see no prospect of) I had sooner have gone to some musical thing, yet I enjoyed myself. The Russian Ballet – and especially the music to it – was magnificent, and G. P. Huntley in a new sketch provoked some laughter. The rest of the show trivial & boring as music halls usually are.[52] At 'Gastons' however, I have no lack of entertainment, having been recently introduced to Chopin's Mazurkas, & Beethoven's 'Sonate Pathétique'.[53]

No: there is no talk yet of going home. And, to tell you the truth, I am not sorry: firstly, I am very happy at Bookham, and secondly, a week at home, if it is to be spent in pulling long faces in Church & getting confirmed, is no great pleasure – a statement, I need hardly say, for yourself alone.

Yrs.
Jack Lewis

TO HIS FATHER (LP IV: 239–49):

[Gastons]
Postmark: 3 November 1914

My dear Papy,

If suddenly there descends upon innocent Leeborough a monstrosity of brown paper containing school books from Malvern, don't lose your head: or in other words, Porch[54] having asked me what to do with some books I had forgotten, was asked by me to send them home, which he may do at any time. I do *not* want you to send them on.

---

52 The programme at the London Coliseum between 19 and 24 October included the Imperial Russian Ballet's performance of *Fleurs d'Orange* and G.P. Huntley acting in Eric Blore's *A Burlington Arcadian*.

53 Ludwig van Beethoven, Sonata No. 8, 'Pathétique' (1799).

54 Robert Bagehot Porch (1875–1962) was a pupil at Malvern College 1888–94. From there he went to Trinity College, Oxford, receiving his BA in 1898. He joined the staff of Malvern College in 1904 and taught there most of his life.

This fellow Smythe who lost his arm at the front, has been telling all sorts of interesting things to Mrs. K., who was up to town to see him last week. I think they ought to be collected and published under the title of 'The right way to get shot'. One is relieved to hear that it is not painful at the time.

What do you think of this latest outrage perpetuated by the slander, ignorance, and prejudice of the British nation on those who alone can support it? I mean of course the shameful way in which Prince Louis of Battenberg has been forced to resign.[55] He is, I hear, the only man in the Admiralty who knows his job: he has lived all his life in England: his patriotism, loyalty, and efficiency are admitted by all who have a right to judge. And yet, because a number of ignorant and illiterate clods (who have no better employment than that of abusing their betters) so choose, he must resign. This is what comes of letting a nation be governed by 'the people'. 'Vox populi, vox Diaboli',[56] we might say, reversing an old but foolish proverb.

I suppose things in Belfast are much in the same condition as usual. I hope a few people are clearing off to the front. Some of those people one meets on the Low Holywood Road would be improved by shooting. Any news from *our* representative in the Army? I suppose he will hardly be out of England yet? I am so pleased at not forgetting to post the letter you sent to him that I shall be furious if you don't get an answer. Has it ever struck you that one of the most serious consequences of this war is what Kirk calls 'the survival of the *un*fittest'? All those who have the courage to do so and are physically sound, are going off to be shot: those who survive are moral and physical weeds – a fact which does not promise favourably for the next generation.

We are beginning to make a feeble attempt at winter here, but the weather is still beautifully mild. I hope you are keeping fit and in good spirits – (Yes thank you Papy, my cold is a good deal better!)

your loving son,
Jack

---

55 Prince Louis of Battenburg (1854–1921) was born in Austria. He moved to England when he was a boy and had risen through the ranks of the Royal Navy to become First Sea Lord. Despite all that Winston Churchill could do, as first lord of the Admiralty, Prince Louis was forced to resign. He relinquished his German titles and the family name was changed to Mountbatten.

56 'The voice of the people is the voice of the Devil'.

TO ARTHUR GREEVES (W/LP IV: 236–7):

[Gastons
4 November 1914]

Dear Arthur,

I suppose that I should, as is usual in my case begin my epistle with an apology for its tardiness: but that form of adress is becoming so habitual as to be monotonous, so that it may be taken for granted.

I was, if I may say so, not a little amused to hear you say in an off-hand manner 'The Celts used to retire to them in time of war', when antiquarians have been disputing for ages: but of course you have grounds for your statement I admit. Your souteraines are, I imagine, but another variety of the same phenomena as my Shidhes: when I said 'doorposts' I did not imply the existence of doors, meaning only the stone pillars, commonly (I believe) found at the entrances to these excavations.

Great Bookham and the present arrangement continue to give every satisfaction which is possible. But there is one comfort which must inevitably be wanting anywhere except at home – namely, the ability to write whenever one wishes. For, though of course there is no formal obstacle, you will readily see that it is impossible to take out one's manuscript and start to work in another's house. And, when ideas come flowing upon me, so great is the desire of framing them into words, words into sentences, and sentences into metre, that the inability to do so, is no light affliction. You, when you are cut off for a few weeks from a piano, must experience much the same sensations. But it would be ridiculous for me to pretend that, in spite of this unavoidable trouble, I was not comfortable. Work and liesure, each perfect and complete of its kind, form an agreeable supplent to the other, strikingly different to the dreary labour and compulsory pasttimes of Malvern life. The glorious pageant of the waning year, lavishing her autumn glories on a lovely countryside, fills me, whenever I take a solitary walk among the neighbouring hills, with a great sense of comfort & peace.

So great is the selfishness of human nature, that I can look out from my snug nest with the same equanimity on the horrid desolation of the war, and the well known sorrows of my old school. I feel that this ought not to be so: but I can no more alter my disposition than I can change the height of my stature or the colour of my hair. It would be mere affectation to pretend that sympathy with those whose lot is not so happy as mine, seriously disturbs the tenour of my complacence. Whether this is the egotism of youth, some blemish in my personal character, or the common inheritance of humanity, I do not know. What is your opinion?

I am reading at present, for the second time, the Celtic plays of Yeats.[57] I must try & get them next time I am at home. Write soon, and tell me all that you are doing, reading & thinking.

Yours,
C. S. Lewis

TO HIS FATHER (LP IV: 240–1):

[Gastons
8? November 1914]

My dear Papy,

If bounty on the part of his weary audience could stop the sermon of the philosopher, I should be compelled to close our controversy of the paradise and inferno: but even the four, crisp, dainty postal orders (for which many thanks) cannot deter me from exposing the logical weakness of your position. The arguments, as you will recollect, upon which I based my theory, were briefly as follows: that when evils cannot be averted by him who suffers them, i.e. you and I, who *cannot* go into the army – he would do well to shut his eyes and pretend that they do not exist. For the evil, being in itself a fixed quantity, can neither be multiplied or diminished when it actually descends: but the agony of anticipation may be attenuated to nothing. Bearing these facts in mind, your imaginary dialogue, lively and picturesque tho' it may be, is irrelevant: since your two friends are presumably in a position to volunteer, and their case therefore offers no parallel to our own. In short, you have shifted the ground of argument by substituting the description of a satanist for the demonstrations of a philosopher.

I carried out to the letter your directions about Warnie: or in other words, as he arranged nowhere I met him nowhere. A pity. But who are we to cavil at the arrangements of this great man. Seriously however, I know what your feelings must be when, to the annoyance arising from his shipshod methods at such a moment, is added the anxiety of his

57 W.B. Yeats had published many Celtic plays. Lewis may have been thinking of his *Plays for an Irish Theatre* (1911).

present position at the front.[58] Let me offer however such consolations as the case permits of. If, by the Grace of God, he returns unscathed from this hideous masque of death, it will be a sadder and wiser Warnie than he who went away: the indiscretions of a raw Malvern school boy. If, as we both hope and pray, this turns out to be the case, we may indeed feel, that in one home at least, this outburst of the primitive savagery of man will not have been without a compensation.

In the meantime, your worry about Palmes[59] need not be of much importance. I had the honour of meeting this gentleman on one of W's visits to Malvern: he is a harmless, amiable idiot who will make no fuss, and the sum that he lent is, I believe, trifling. Surely too, it is rather hard to call a man a cad, just because he demands his own money back: even if he does so (I am convinced through sheer empty headedness) on a P.C.

Hoping that this will find you in good health and tolerable spirits, I remain,

your loving son,
Jack

TO ARTHUR GREEVES (W/LP IV: 239):

[Gastons
10 November 1914]

Dear Arthur,

It is the immemorial privilege of letter-writers to commit to paper things they would not say: to write in a more grandiose manner than that in which they speak: and to enlarge upon feelings which would be passed by unnoticed in conversation. For this reason I do not attach much importance to your yearnings for an early grave: not, indeed, because I think, as you suggest, that the wish for death is wrong or even foolish, but because I know that a cold in the head is quite an insufficient cause to provoke such feelings. I am glad Monday found you in a more reasonable frame of mind.

---

58 Warnie crossed to France with the Army Service Corps on 4 November. They were part of the British Expeditionary Force stationed at Le Havre.

59 Guy Nicholas Palmes (1894–1915) entered Malvern in 1908, and left in 1911 for the Royal Military College at Sandhurst. He joined the Yorkshire Light Infantry at the beginning of the war and was promoted to lieutenant in 1915. He was killed in action near Ypres on 9 May 1915.

By the way, I hear nothing about music or illustrations now! Eh? I hope that this can be accounted for by the fact that both are finished. I suppose the former has been performed in the Ulster Hall, by this time, and the latter exhibited – where? Here the sentence comes to a stop: for I have suddenly realized that there is no picture gallery in Belfast. It never occurred to me before what a disgrace that was. I notice, too, that you answer my questions about 'doing' and 'reading' but keep a modest silence about 'thinking'. It is often difficult to tell, is not it? And seldom advisable: which makes me think about the hard question of truth. Is it always advisable to tell the truth? Certainly not, say I: sometimes actually criminal. And yet, useful as it is for everyday life, that doctrine will land one in sad sophistries if carried to its conclusion. What is your view?

The other day I was in Guildford (it is a glorious old English town with those houses that [get] bigger towards the top; a Norman castle; a street built up a preposterous hill; and beautiful environments) where I picked up a volume of Wm. Morris's lyric poems in that same edition in which you have 'The Wood at the Worlds end'.[60] So delighted was I with my purchase, that I have written up to the publisher for the same author's 'Sigurd the Volsung':[61] which, as I need hardly tell you, is a narrative poem, dealing with Siegfried (=Sigurd) & Brünhilde, as described in the legends of Iceland, earlier than those of Germany. What is your opinion of Ainsworth? I see you are reading his 'Old St. Pauls'.[62] I must confess I find him dreary – a faint echo of Scott, with all the latter's faults of lengthiness and verbosity and not of his merits of lively narrative & carefully-welded plots.

When you talk about the difficulty of getting the necessary materials for one's pursuits, I am thankful that, in my case, when the opportunity is at hand, the means – paper & pen – is easily found. Whereas you, unfortunately, need a piano or a box of paints and a block of drawing paper.

I hope there will be some relics of us left when we have settled that question of souteraines.

Yrs sincerely
Jack Lewis

---

60 He meant William Morris's *The Well at the World's End* (1896).
61 William Morris, *Sigurd the Volsung* (1876).
62 William Harrison Ainsworth, *Old St Paul's* (1841).

TO HIS FATHER (LP IV: 244–5):

[Gastons
13? November 1914]

My dear Papy,

I was glad to receive your letter this evening (Friday) as I was beginning to get anxious: and thought that I would write my reply at once while your words were still in my head. I must admit that my defence of Palmes was founded on a misconception of his plans – which is excusable, in as much as, if you saw the gentleman in the flesh, you would never imagine that he had the intelligence for such an idea.

After this magnanimous confession of my defeat, I cannot refrain from observing that there is no reply to my last step in the 'Paradise-Inferno' controversy. But as no further disputation is possible after my crushing and exhaustive demonstration, that is not much to be wondered at.

Although perhaps the occasion demands a graver view, I cannot restrain a smile when I think of the colonel staying at a first class hotel in 'Haver' and strutting about in his uniform like a musical comedy hero.

It seems a great pity this confirmation should occur when it does, thus cutting out at least a week of valuable time. Although fully sensible that it is of course of more importance than the work, yet if it could possibly be managed at some more convenient date in the near future, I should think it an advantage. I believe there is one held at Easter, which I might attend with less derangement of our plans. I would ask you to consider this point before mentioning the matter to Kirk. I am not quite clear from your letter as to what you propose to do. As I read it, three interpretations are admissable.

a That you bring me home for the necessary time and send me back for the odd weeks.
b That you add from Dec. 6th – Xmas on to the ordinary holidays.
c That you have ordinary length holidays, only beginning on the 6th and ending earlier.

Of these alternatives, (a) is practicable enough, but necessitates a tiresome and expensive amount of extra travelling: (b) is agreeable, but wasteful of time and quite unthinkable. (c) is not only extremely alien from all our usual plans, but would also put Kirk to a great deal of trouble and annoyance. So that none of the three is really satisfactory. However, you will discuss the point in your next letter. If this Kodotta about cross channel boats goes on much longer, the matter will not rest in our hands.

Hoping for a continuance of health on your part, as well as an improvement in spirits, I am

your loving son,

Jack

TO ARTHUR GREEVES (W/LP IV: 282):

[Gastons

17 November 1914]

My dear Arthur,

Do you ever wake up in the morning and suddenly wonder why you have not bought such-and-such a book long ago, and then decided that life without it will be quite unbearable? I do frequently: the last attack was this morning à propos of Malory's 'Morte D'Arthur', and I have just this moment written to Dent's for it. I am drawing a bow at a venture and getting the Everyman two-shilling 'Library' edition.[63] What is it like, do you know? As for the book itself, I really can't think why I have not got it before. It is really the English national epic, for Paradise Lost[64] is a purely literary poem, while it is the essence of an epic to be genuine folk-lore. Also, Malory was the Master from whom William Morriss copied the style of his prose Tales.

Which reminds me of your criticism of the 'Well'. I quite see your point, and, of course, agree that the interests of the tale reach their climax in the great scene at the World's End: my reply is that the interest of the journey home is of quite a different nature. It is pleasant to pick up all the familiar places and characters and see the same circumstances applied to the heroe's new role of 'Friend of the Well'. The Battle-piece at the end is very fine, and the ending, tho', as was inevitable, conventional, leaves one in a pleasant, satisfied state of mind. The only part that I found really tedious was Roger's historical survey of the Burg & the

63 *Le Morte D'Arthur* is the title generally given to the cycle of Arthurian legends by Sir Thomas Malory, finished in 1470 and printed by Caxton in 1485. The version Lewis began with was *Le Morte d'Arthur by Sir Thomas Malory*, with an introduction by Professor Rhys, 2 vols., Everyman's Edition [1906].

64 John Milton, *Paradise Lost* (1667).

Scaur. In fact, Roger was only a lay-figure brought in to conduct the Ladye's machinations with Ralph, and why he was not allowed to drop into oblivion when they were over, I cannot imagine.

How I run on! And yet, however many pages one may fill in a letter, it is only a tithe of what ten minutes conversation would cover: it is curious, too, how the thoughts that bubble up so freely when one meets a friend, seem to congeal on paper, when writing to him.

I wonder what you, who complain of loneliness when surrounded by a numerous family and wide circle of friends, would do if you could change places with me. Except my grinder and his wife, I think I have not spoken to a soul this week: not of course that I mind, much less complain; on the contrary, I find that the people whose society I prefer to my own are very few and far between. The only one of that class in Bookham, is still in the house, though they tell me she is up and about.[65] Of course, as they say at home, this solitude is a kind of egotism: and yet I don't know that they are right. The usual idea is that if you don't want to talk to people, you do so because you think they're intellectually your inferiors. But its not a question of inferiority: if a man talks to me for an hour about golf, war & politics, I know that his mind is built on different lines from mine: but whether better or worse is not to the point.

My only regret at present is that I cannot see Co. Down in the snow: I am sure some of our favourite haunts look very fine. We have been deeply covered with it all week, and the pine wood near hear, with the white masses on ground and trees, forms a beautiful sight. One almost expects a 'march of dwarfs' to come dashing past! How I long to break away into a world where such things were true: this real, hard, dirty, Monday morning modern world stifles one. Progress in health and spirits and music! Write soon and give all your thoughts, actions, readings and any local gossip, for the benefit of

yours sincerely
Jack Lewis

65 This was probably Mrs Kirkpatrick's 'theatrical' friend, Miss MacMullen, whom Lewis mentioned to his father on 13 October.

TO HIS FATHER (LP IV: 246):

[Gastons]
Postmark: 20 November 1914

My dear Papy,

I received your answer this evening and decided to be guided by your views, or in other words my objections to the 'Monstre' holiday are not insuperable. Break the news gently to Kirk, as I am not sure he will relish the interruption.

I hope you will enjoy prosecuting dear Mr. Russell:[66] he will probably give you 'something to be going on with' in the way of back chat. Tell me any news of Warnie as soon as you hear it. I will stop now, as this is only a 'letter extraordinary'.

your loving
son Jack

Lewis returned to Belfast on 28 November and was confirmed in St Mark's on 6 December. Writing of this in SBJ *X, he said: 'My relations to my father help to explain (I am not suggesting they excuse) one of the worst acts of my life. I allowed myself to be prepared for confirmation, and confirmed, and to make my first Communion, in total disbelief, acting a part, eating and drinking my own condemnation.'*

TO HIS BROTHER (LP IV: 276–7):

[Little Lea,
Strandtown.
[22 December 1914]

W ȧdeljė jíltate

A'itéw suggnẃmhn ^moi m̀h ĝrajai[67] – but perhaps I'd better write in English. This has become such a habit you know, but I beg your pardon.

It is a pity that you happen to be at the front just now, as – at last – an Opera Company came to Belfast while you were away. It was the 'Moody Manners', but that you have heard P. talking about. They were quite

66 Mr Russell was a harmless, but terrifying, lunatic who was for many years a well-known figure in and around St Mark's.

67 'O dearest brother, I am sorry not to have written.'

good, though somewhat early Victorian in the way of scenery and gestures. We went to 'Faust'[68] and 'Trovatore'.[69] The former was perfectly glorious, well sung and everything. It is a very good opera and of course knowing a good deal of the music and having read Goethe, I enjoyed it very well. Of course I have discovered that it is no use expecting to hear the overture or preludes to the acts at Belfast, as everyone talks all the time as if nothing were going on. Il Trovatore, as we have always agreed, is a very mediocre thing anyway, and, with the exception of the soprano and baritone, was villainously sung. I don't want to hear it again.

On the following Friday we got badly let down: the Glenmachonians Greeves's and I had made up a party to go to 'Samson and Delilah',[70] which we were all looking forward to immensely. Imagine our feelings when the cod at the door told us it has been changed to 'Fra Diavolo' – a very inferior comic opera of Auber's![71] I seem to be fated never to get fair treatment from that theatre management. Fra Diavolo impresses on one how very badly the comic opera needed reform when Gilbert and Sullivan came to the rescue:[72] it is the old style – bandits, a foolish English earl, innkeepers 'and sich'. It was without exception the greatest drivel I ever listened to. There has been nothing worth noticing at the Hippodrome lately. Those two people – I've forgotten their names – who do the sketch about the broken mirror, were at the Opera House last week. The Opera House is now in the grip of that annual monstrosity the Grand Xmas Panto. I suppose I ought to be reconciled to it as fate by now. One good thing is that Tom Foy is coming, but of course the whole thing will be awfully patriotic.

I like your asking why I didn't go to meet you in town. You omitted the trifling precaution of telling me your address – or did you intend that I should go up to a policeman in Piccadilly and ask, 'Have you seen

---

68 An opera by Charles Gounod, based on the *Faust* of Johann Wolfgang von Goethe, and first produced in 1859.

69 *Il Trovatore*, an opera by Giuseppe Verdi, was first performed in 1853.

70 *Samson et Dalila*, an opera by Camille Saint-Saëns, was first performed in 1877.

71 Daniel Auber's opera *Fra Diavolo* was first performed in 1830.

72 W.S. Gilbert (1836–1911), playwright and librettist, and Arthur Sullivan (1842–1900), composer, together wrote many very popular operettas. They include *The Pirates of Penzance* performed in 1879, *The Mikado* performed in 1885, and *The Yeoman of the Guard* performed in 1888.

my brother anywhere?'

The new records are a most interesting and varied selection, comprising 'The calf of gold' from Faust, with a vocal 'Star of Eve'[73] on the other side: the Drinking and Duel scenes from Faust: Saint Saen's 'Danse Macabre':[74] Grieg's 'March of the Dwarfs':[75] and 'Salve Minerva' from Faust. There are also several new books, but most of them are not in your line: the only two you might care for are the works of Shelley and Keats.

We were up at Glenmachan yesterday (Monday) evening to a supper party of Kelsie's where you went representing a novel.[76] All the usual push were there of course, and I quite enjoyed it. A number of people besides, whom I had never seen before, also turned up. There was one rather pretty thing whom Lily[77] is arranging as 'suitable' for Willie Greeves[78] – in opposition I suppose to the Taylor affair. Of course it is all

---

73 'Bright Star of Eve' is from Charles Gounod's *New Part Songs* (1872 or 1873).

74 Camille Saint-Saëns's orchestral work *Danse Macabre* was first performed in 1872.

75 'March of the Dwarfs' is a piano piece in Edvard Grieg's *Lyriske Stykker* (1891).

76 Their mother's sister, Mrs Lilian 'Lily' Suffern (1860–1934), wrote to Warnie on 3 February 1915 about the book party. 'On 21st Dec.,' she said, 'Kelsie gave a book party which was very amusing....Some of the books were very good – too good for me, for I couldn't guess them. Your father's was *Edged Tools*, a fan and a knife. Clive's was *The Three Musketeers* – a bit of paper with "Soldier's Three" on it, it made us all mad because it was so plain, and we did not (many) guess it. Miss Murray's was a cutting from that day's Newsletter of the birthdays – *The Newcomes*. Another cutting from the Newsletter won the prize – Advt. of rise in the price of coals – *The Sorrows of Satan*. No one hardly guessed Hugh McCreddy's – yet it was very good – a picture of a man with his mouth wide open in a laugh – *L'Homme Qui Rit*. I had a picture of the Kaiser, nicely framed in ribbon – *The Egoist* (Meredith). Everyone guessed it *The Lunatic at Large*. Three old ladys sitting talking (picture of), tied with green ribbon was *Gossips Green*. Willie Jaffe's was bad – a black African with a white line down it – *Across the Dark Continent*' (LP IV: 289–90).

(Henry Seton Merriman wrote *With Edged Tools* (1894); Alexandre Dumas wrote *The Three Musketeers* (1844–5); William Makepeace Thackeray wrote *The Newcomes* (1853–4); Marie Corelli wrote *The Sorrows of Satan* (1895); Victor Hugo wrote *L'Homme Qui Rit* (1869); George Meredith wrote *The Egoist* (1879); Joseph Storer Clouston wrote *The Lunatic at Large* (1899); Alice Dudeney wrote *Gossips Green* (1906); and Sir Henry Morton Stanley wrote *Through the Dark Continent* (1878).)

Kelso Ewart (1886–1966) was the fourth child of Lady Ewart, the cousin of Flora Lewis, and her husband Sir William. See **The Ewart Family** in the Biographical Appendix.

77 Mary Elizabeth 'Lily' Greeves (1888–1976) was Arthur Greeves's sister. She married Lewis's cousin Charles Gordon Ewart (1885–1936) on 15 December 1915. See **The Ewart Family** in the Biographical Appendix.

78 This was Arthur's brother, William Edward Greeves (1890–1960).

very nice, but don't you thank the gods you haven't got a sister?

One other piece of local gossip is so funny that you really must hear it. Do you know a vulgar, hideous old harridan on the wrong side of 40, a Miss Henderson, who lives at Norwood Towers? She's just the sort of creature who would live there. Well the latest wheeze is that you meet her every time you go to Glenmachan, running after Bob.[79] And the beauty of the thing is that she makes Bob bustle about and talk to her and flirt with her. I know you can't imagine Bob 'courtin'. I promise you it is a thing of beauty. While admiring the creature's energy in getting a move on anyone like him, I don't want her to get into the connection even as remotely as the sister in law of my second cousins.

You're becoming quite a hero in your absence, and I can always command a large and attentive audience by spinning yarns about 'The other day my brother, who is at the front etc.' Hope is here now, and the Captain was home for a few days – I suppose you saw that he is now a Major? Why couldn't you manage to get a few days off? You would at any rate have a change of clothes and diet if you did. Last week we went to the Messiah with Carrie Tubb[80] as soprano – she can sing, but she's as ugly as the day is long. The contralto, altho she hadn't much of a voice, was an improvement in that way – really quite a magnificent creature. Rather like the woman whom we met in France going about with the Katinarsky's. I wondered if it was the same, but I suppose not, as the other would be younger. Of course Handel is not your ideal or mine as a composer: but it is always fair to remember that he wrote in the days of spinets and harpsichords, before anyone had discovered that there could be any point in music beyond a sort of abstract prettiness. Of course the inappropriateness of his tunes is appalling – as for instance where he makes the chorus repeat some twenty times that they have all gone astray like sheep in the same tone of cheerful placidity that they'd use for saying it was a fine evening.

Yes: the Kirk arrangement is absolutely *it*. The war is mainly interesting to him as illustrating some remark he made to 'Mr. Dods' fifty years ago. The only trouble about Bookham is our dear Mrs. Crutwell. I don't

---

79 Robert Heard Ewart (1879–1939). See **The Ewart Family** in the Biographical Appendix.

80 Carrie Tubb (1876–1976) was an English soprano much in demand as an oratorio singer. She was a favourite singer of operatic excepts, notably the final scene of Richard Wagner's *Götterdämmerung*.

know if it was the same in your time, but she has lately developed a mania for 'seeing young people enjoying themselves' – and you know what that means. Write some time.

Yours, Jack

P.S. Did you ever get the letter I wrote from Larne?

1915

TO HIS FATHER (LP IV: 285–6):

[Gastons
24? January 1915][1]

My dear Papy,

I have arrived and settled down here in due course, and everything progresses favourably, including the German. We had it snowing hard all day on Thursday, beautiful snow and bright frosty sun until Saturday, and are now enduring the thaw. (Yes; I did change my socks. No; there are no holes in my shoes. Yes, thanks, I have plenty of warm underclothing.) I hope you have by this time got rid of your cough, and, did I not know the utter futility of so doing, I should advise you to be careful. However, as you will doubtless reply, my playing the anxious adviser of a patient who will not obey orders, is rather like Satan rebuking sin.[2] But all joking apart, do take any care of yourself that you reasonably can, and don't refuse harmless precautions for no reason.

That Smythe boy, the brother of the one who lost his arm, was home for a few days and lunched at Gastons on Wednesday: he tells us that his brother is going out again as soon as he is better – so hard are we pressed that even cripples whose worth is known will be taken in some departments! What this argues as to the paucity of our troops in general, and the old officer's contempt for the new volunteers who are to come, you will readily imagine. Smythe also directly contradicts the reports of the newspapers about the Indian troops whom he declares to be worthless, and absolutely unfitted for trench fighting: they have too, an unpleasant habit of not burying their dead, which contributes a good deal to the

1 Albert Lewis, like so many others, had for some months previously feared that England would be invaded by the Germans, and this explains why his son was not allowed to return to Great Bookham until 16 January 1915.

2 Mark 3:26: 'If Satan rise up against himself, and be divided, he cannot stand, but hath an end.'

discomfort of European men anywhere near. But of course this is only one man's story, and the longer this war goes on the less credulous we become. Kirk has many amusing reflections, as usual, on the present crisis, especially when the curate came in yesterday at afternoon tea and told a number of patriotic lies about Germany and the Germans. Kirk then proceeded with great deliberation to prove step by step that his statements were fallacious, impossible, and ridiculous. The rest of the party including Mrs. K., Louis, and myself enjoyed it hugeously.

Thanks for my Classical Library which I have received. In the course of the week I shall return Munro's Iliad I–XII[3] which was *not* asked for: after which fact has been explained gently to Carson you will tell his remains to give you in exchange Merry's Odyssey I–XII,[4] which *was* asked for. Kirk also tells me to ask for 'Tacitus's Agricola',[5] any edition *except* Macmillan's.

your loving son,
Jack

TO ARTHUR GREEVES (W/LP IV: 286–7):

[Gastons
26 January 1915]

My dear Arthur,

I wonder would hunting be good sport? The matter ocurred to me, not because I am really interested in it, but because I have just returned from a compulsory chase – trying to find out where the bit at the top of page 2 of your letter was meant to come in. Now, faint & perspiring, I am enjoying the fruits of my labours.

By this time you will probably have finished 'Villette'.[6] What do you think of the ending? I can just hear you saying, 'Cracked – absolutely!'. It certainly is most unsatisfactory, but yet a touch of genius. I fancy it is the only novel in existence that leaves you in a like uncertainty. Merriman is a far cry from the Brontes. Both of course are good, but while they should be sipped with luxurious slowness in the winter evening, he may

---

3 Homer, *Iliad, Books I–XII*, with an introduction, a brief Homeric grammar, and notes by D.B. Monro (1884).

4 Homer, *Odyssey, Books I–XII*, with an introduction, notes, etc. by W.W. Merry (1870).

5 Cornelius Tacitus (c. AD 55–117), the greatest historian of ancient Rome, in AD 98 published *Agricola*, a biography of his father-in-law, Julius Agricola.

6 Charlotte Brontë, *Villette* (1853).

be read in a cheap copy on top of a tram. And yet I don't know: of course his novels are melodrama, but then they are the best melodrama ever written, while passages like the 'Storm' or the 'Wreck' in the Grey Lady, or the Reconciliation between the hero and his father in 'Edged Tools', are as good things as English prose contains.[7]

The remark about the Maiden Islands was really quite smart for you. You might have it framed? Also such gems of orthography as 'simpathise' and 'phisically' which appeared in your last correspondance, tho' of course I, being almost as bad, have no right to complain.

The weather here is perfectly damnable, there having been scarcely a couple of hours' sunshine since I left home. Now that my friends have gone, there is nothing to do but sit & read or write when it rains, and consequently I have nearly finished The Morte D'arthur. I am more pleased at having bought it every day, as it has opened up a new world to me. I had no idea that the Arthurian legends were so fine (The name is against them, isn't it??) Malory is really not a great author, but he has two excellent gifts, (1) that of lively narrative and (2) the power of getting you to know characters by gradual association. What I mean is, that, although he never sits down – as the moderns do – to describe a man's character, yet, by the end of the first volume Launcelot & Tristan, Balin & Pellinore, Morgan Le Fay & Isoud are all just as much real, live people as Paul Emanuel or Mme Beck.[8] The very names of the chapters, as they spring to meet the eye, bear with them a fresh, sweet breath from the old-time, faery world, wherein the author moves. Who can read 'How Launcelot in the Chapel Perilous gat a cloth from a Dead corpse' or 'How Pellinore found a damosel by a Fountain, and of the Jousts in the Castle of Four Stones', and not hasten to find out what it's all about?

To obey my own theory that a letter should tell of doings, readings, thinkings, I will conclude by saying that I am trying to find some suitable theme for my Celtic narrative Poem: there are heaps of stories but mostly too long. Fare-thee-well.

Yours sincerely
C. S. Lewis

N.B. This was written on the same day as I got your letter, but I forgot to post it. Mille pardons. J.

---

7 Henry Seton Merriman, *The Grey Lady* (1895); *With Edged Tools* (1894).
8 Paul Emanuel and Mme Beck are characters in *Villette*.

TO ARTHUR GREEVES (W):

[Gastons
2 February 1915]

Dear Arthur,

The first essential point for a letter writer to master is that of making himself intelligable to his reader. Or, to come down from my high horse, what was the (it?) in brackets meant for? A thousand pardons for my dulness, only I utterly failed to follow your wheeze: please explain in your next epistle.

I am deep in Morte D'Arthur by this time, and it is really the greatest thing I've ever read. It is strangely different from William Morris, although by subject & language they challenge comparison. One is genuine, and the other, tho' delightful, must, of course, be only an artificial reproduction. You really ought to read your copy of it, or at any rate parts of it, as the connecting chain between book and book is not very tightly drawn. I don't think it can be the Library Edition, that those people have sent me, as it does not agree with your description at all, being bound in plum-coloured leather, with pale-blue marker attached. However, partly through my keenness to read the book & partly because it was a very handsome binding, I did not send it back.

By the way, is there anything the matter with my father, as I have not heard from him for some time now? Or perhaps it is only this submarine nonsense that makes the conveyance of letters uncertain: which reminds me, that, though I do not usually take much interest in the war, yet it would be unpleasantly brought home to me if I had to spend my holydays in England.[9]

Your remarks á propos of loneliness are quite true, and I admit that what I said before was rather not, as uncongenial companions produce in reality a worse desolation than actual solitude.

I am glad to hear you have read Esmond:[10] it is one of my favourite novels, and I hardly know which to praise most, the wonderful, musical, Queen Anne English, or the delicate beauty of the story. True, I did rather resent the history, and still maintain, that when a man sets out to

---

9 There were, in fact, a good many German submarines operating in the Irish Sea at this time. Lewis's father was particularly upset over the raid near Fleetwood on 30 January 1915 when the Germans sank the *Kilcoan*, a collier designed by his brother Joseph.

10 William Makepeace Thackeray, *Henry Esmond* (1852).

write a novel he has no right to ram an European War down your throat – it is like going back to Henty![11] Did you ever try that arch-fiend?

I am surprised that there is no snow in Ulster as we had a week of good, thick, firm, 'picture' snow – and very much I enjoyed it. And other things too! She is better now, up & about, and we have progressed very rapidly. In fact the great event is actually fixed – fixed! – do you realize that? I don't think I've ever been so bucked about anything in my life, she's an awfully decent sort.[12] But I suppose this is boring you, so I must cut short my raptures – & my letter.

Yours

Jack

TO HIS FATHER (LP IV: 292–3):

[Gastons]

Postmark: 3 February 1915

My dear Papy,

As you will be by this time accustomed to my using 'this week' as synonymous with 'next week', I will make no further mention of that matter than to say that the Iliad which you are to exchange is being sent by the same post as this. I must confess to extraordinary dullness in failing to catch any point – if point there be – in your remark, 'now for a nasty one': 'I found a Homer'. Why a nasty one? The fact that you have begun to suffer from a mania for sending poor, unnecessary unoffending books about the channel is nothing which should disturb the peace of mind of the philosophers of Gastons.

Talking about the channel reminds me of this morning's news. Of course the really important feature of this submarine work is not so much the actual danger to goods and individuals as the inevitable 'scare' which it will cause, and the injury to business arising from that. I suppose this was their intention. As for the Zepplin talk, it seems to me to be

11 George Henty (1832–1902), while serving with the army in the Crimea, became a war correspondent. Following this career in many countries, he became successful as the author of stories for boys mainly based on military history. *Out in the Pampas* (1868) was followed by some 35 other titles.

12 A family of Belgian refugees were evacuated to Great Bookham in the autumn of 1914. Lewis began visiting them with Mrs Kirkpatrick, and became infatuated with one of the young girls in the family. He doubtless discussed his feelings for her with Arthur Greeves during the Christmas holidays. As to how much truth there was in what he wrote and said about the Belgian girl, see Lewis's letter of 1 October 1931.

rather childish folly on the part of the Germans: a few babies and an odd chimney stack cannot afford a recompense proportionate to the labour, expense and danger of managing an aerial raid. The only point is the moral influence, which again depends entirely on the amount of 'guts' of the victims.

I am glad to hear that the new Kiplings are poems, as we have had none of them yet. The question as to whether he was a greater poet or proseur is one of those everlasting things. Perhaps however, we may admit that someone else might possibly have written his best poems, but there is only one man alive who could have written 'Kim' or the 'Jungle books' or 'Puck'.[13] I am not sure whether I have read the Seven Seas or not. Is it there that the ballads about the prehistoric Song-Man and Picture Man (the story of Ung) occurs?[14] I remember they make a very interesting criticism on artists and their public, ancient and modern, and impressed me greatly.

We have had one day of spring and are now paying for it by a wind and a rain that would take you off your feet. My German is progressing with such alarming success that I am rather afraid they will put me under suspicious as a spy! Keep well.

your loving son,
Jack

TO HIS FATHER (LP IV: 296–7):

[Gastons]
Postmark: 13 February 1915

My dear Papy,

As Spenser naively remarks at the beginning of about the thousandth canto of his poem,

'Oh, what an endlesse work I have in hand',[15]

so might a parent doomed to supply an ignorant philosopher with the forgotten necessities of life echo the sentiment. Or in other words there

13 Rudyard Kipling, *Kim* (1901), *The Jungle Book* (1894); *The Second Jungle Book* (1895); *Puck of Pook's Hill* (1906).

14 Albert Lewis had just acquired Kipling's *The Seven Seas* (1896), which contains 'The Story of Ung'.

15 Edmund Spenser, *The Faerie Queene* (1590, 1596), Book IV, Canto xii, 1.

is 'still one river to cross', and I really do think this will be the end. What I want is a copy of the *Helena* of Euripides,[16] which you will find kicking its heels somewhere in the little end room. The shoes have just arrived, for which many thanks: and by the way, when I want to pay for anything, we'll let you know boss, don't worry.

I am very annoyed that an opera company should come while I am away from home, although indeed it is a common enough state of affairs. Perhaps we are accustomed to regard John Harrison as an oratorio singer and it would be rather a shock to hear him in opera, although I have often seen records of him in operatic songs. I think you would be wise if you raised the energy to go. Perhaps Uncle Hamilton and Aunt Annie would care to take you – do you think so?

They must be having a rotten time at Glenmachan: 'les jeunes maries' particularly are making a bright start, aren't they? What one always feels about these troubles is that they are so hard on poor Bob.[17] Is it not cruel when a poor fellow is doing his best, working away at his music all night and slaving like a nigger to make things bright and cheerful for everyone else, never letting his conversation flag, saving many a dull hour from ennui and always unselfishly making his wishes subservient to the comfort of the household – is it not hard that he should meet trouble like this? And yet – you will hardly believe it – I have heard people so brutal as to suggest that this 'angel in the house' ought to be at the front!

Everything here is pretty much as usual. The weather is delightful and Kirk's thoughts turn even lightlier than of old to agriculture. His chief 'stunt' at present is to point out the fact that he is the same age as Balfour,[18] and ask whether he (K) would stand any chance of getting a job as Headmaster now: and if not, is he to understand that the care of a few schoolboys calls for more qualities of youthful energy and intellect than that of the British Empire? Well, perhaps he's right; we have often heard him say so at any rate.

I have been reading this week a book by Swinburne from the Library, a 'Study on Shakespeare'.[19] This is my first experience of his prose, and I think I shall make it the last. 'Apt alliteration's artful aid' may be all right in verse, but it is undoubtedly vicious in prose, as also are words like

---

16 *Helena*, a play by the Greek poet Euripides, was produced in 412 BC.

17 Lewis is mocking his cousin Robert Heard Ewart.

18 Mr Kirkpatrick and Lord Balfour (1848–1930), were born in 1848, making them 67.

19 Algernon Charles Swinburne, *A Study of Shakespeare* (1880).

'plenilune', 'Mellisonant', 'tautologous', 'intromission'. And yet at the same time there is great force in the book, and his appreciation of the subject is very infectious.

your loving son,
Jack

P.S. You might give me the Colonel's address in your next letter. J.

TO ARTHUR GREEVES (W):

[Gastons
16 February 1915]

Dear Arthur,

When I received your epistle, which certainly did not weary one by its length, I was in one of my black moods: like Saul, my evil spirit was upon me.[20] Having just had a sufficient glimpse of home and of my brother to tantalize but not to satisfy:[21] having lost, if not for good, at least for this term, an unparalleled opportunity: and finding a very objectionable visitor in possession of my grinder's house, you may well imagine that I was in no mood for an extra irritation. I had just, too, been out for a walk, mon dieu, a nightmare! Splashing thro great puddles beneath a leaden sky that rained and rained! However, enough of this.

You ask me what was the matter with me when I was at home. Thank you: I believe I enjoyed excellent health. Of course it is true, that we saw a good deal more of our relations than we wanted, and had none too much time to ourselves: but of course, you, or any member of your household, are always welcome.

As to the other grievance, it really is phenominal ill luck. Of course, like all the rest of her sex she is incapable of seeing anything fair, and when she had been persuaded after a good deal of difficulty to do this, and then I failed to turn up, it is only to be expected that I am 'left'. In any case, it would be impossible now; as she has gone with her mother for a week to visit some other Belgians in Birmingham.[22] But perhaps you are tired of my 'affaires'.

---

20 1 Samuel 16:23: 'The evil spirit from God was upon Saul.'

21 Warren had only just returned from France, and having a week's leave, he and Jack spent part of it together at home. Jack returned to Great Bookham on 9 February.

22 Presumably the Belgian girl he had written about in his previous letter.

To go back to the question of holydays (I started to try and write an 'essay-letter', but can't keep it up; excuse me if I meaunder a bit), the last straw came on Sunday afternoon when we were snatching a few moments rest before going off to visit our various relations: who should walk in – but – but – but – Henry Stokes!!!! Dear boy! How thoughtful of him! How kind! What a pleasure for us all! After that, my brother suggested that if ever he got another week's leave, we should spend it on the Maidens.

You must imagine me writing this in my bedroom at about 11 o'clock, as that damned guest makes it impossible to be comfortable downstairs. Although it was quite spring weather before I went home, a thin snow mixed with rain is falling outside. In spite of all my troubles, I am quite bucked with life to night, and if only the water were hot enough for a bath I should be in heaven. I wonder what you are doing just now?

Which reminds me, you are drifting into a habit of morbid self-pity lately: all your letters are laments. Beware of the awful fate of growing up like that. I never, for my part, saw what was meant by such terms as 'the releif of confiding ones troubles' and the 'consolations of sympathy': my view is, that to mention trouble at all, *in a complaining way*, is to introduce into the conversation an element equally painful for everyone, including the speaker. Of course, it all depends on the way it is done: I mean, simply to mention them, is not wrong, but, by words or expression to call for sympathy which your hearer will feel bound to pump up, is a nuiscance.

What a good friend I am, to sit up writing all this stuff to a creature who, just because he 'doesn't feel like it' gives me no more than a couple of lines. Write soon, like a good friend, and tell me all about yourself, and all the local gossip. I am damnably tired, and there's something the matter with the gas, and I've come to the end of my paper. So I must dry up.

Yours
Jack

TO HIS FATHER (LP IV: 302–3):

[Gastons]
Postmark: 3 March 1915

My dear Papy,

I hope this pause in your correspondence does not mean a pause in your health; it is now, in the words of the poet, 'a long time, in fact a ver-ray considerable time' since your hand writing appeared on the hall table. One might write a paper on characters according to different days of the week: how a Monday table is associated with a letter from Arthur and a Tuesday table with one from you: although, as it would appear sir, in this case it has lately joined

'The inheritors of unfullfilled renown'[23]

and become as blank and barren as its surly brothers of Saturday and Sunday. Of course we would not forget Wednesday with its 'Punch' or Thursday with its Literary Supplement, which is getting by the way poorer and poorer every week (like chalk, you know.)

I don't know that anything of world shaking importance has happened here: we have had snow and thaw, snow and thaw alternately, with plenty of rain, wind and frost thrown in to make things pleasant. Since Saturday however, there has been some sunshine, and we are hoping for better things.

The good ladies of Bookham still come regularly to tea, and I have the priviledge of hearing what Mrs. Grant-Murray would do if she were in Kitchener's place,[24] and all about Miss Milne's new maid. The discovery of German spies too, is an art in which they excell: how I wish I knew enough German to let drop a few words occasionally, just as if I had slipped into it by accident! It is a great pity that Kirk won't come in to afternoon tea, as his commentaries on the whole kodotta would be great.

I essayed a new author the other day whom we have often heard praised and of whom I hoped great things – Landor: but the book I got, a series of imaginary letters called 'Pericles and Aspasia'[25] proved rather disappointing. Indeed I am afraid my appreciation of English prose is

---

23 Percy Bysshe Shelley, *Adonais* (1821), XLV, 397.

24 Lord Kitchener (1850–1916) was Secretary of State for War.

25 Walter Savage Landor, *Pericles and Aspasia* (1836–7).

very limited, and I certainly cannot fatten on mere prose when the matter is not interesting. However, as the Colonel said in his essay on 'Kenilworth',[26] the 'book is not wholly without merit'. I forget whether you said you had ever read him or not?

I suppose we must soon begin to make arrangements about the Easter Holydays – I will not give up that spelling: however there is no hurry as the actual feast comes very late, and it is better to take off the summer term and add on to this. One might observe in passing – purely as a matter of general interest of course – that we must by now have got past half term.

Write soon if you are alright, and tell me all the gossip.

your loving
son Jack

P.S. Has that English word 'got' ever struck you? In reading this letter I couldn't help thinking of it. It is made to mean almost anything – J.

TO HIS FATHER (LP IV: 303):

[Gastons
7? March 1915]

My dear Papy,

In the bad old days when I was still in the gall of bitterness at Malvern, we used sometimes to hear of schools that had a mid term holiday, and congratulate ourselves on being superior to such kodotta. But it proves to be no bad institution after all. Of course it is short: but then how pleasant to feel at the end that one has only half a term to get through. And one appreciates a week at half term more than the same time in the middle of the holiday. I have not heard from the Colonel since we parted at Euston, but I suppose he arrived at Saille all right – (if that is how you spell it.)

That Gerald Smythe of whom I told you, who lost an arm in the war, was staying with us last week. He is really wonderful: he has only been out of bed about a month and is going back to the front again next week. It does one good to see a person thoroughly cheerful under circumstances like his, and actually eager to be there again. Even in so short a time he has learnt to be quite independant, and can cut his food, light

26 Sir Walter Scott, *Kenilworth* (1821).

his pipe, and dress – tho' how a man can tie a tie with one arm, I don't know.

Did you read Lloyd George's speech the other day introducing the remark about the German potato bread – 'I fear that potato bread more than all Von Kluck's strategy'.[27] Although, as you have seen, I don't often read the newspapers, I was glad when Kirk pointed that out to me. Most of the people one hears rather laugh at that bread 'wheeze', but I rather think Lloyd George's is the wiser view. In the way of reading, I have been taking a course of 'Poems and Ballads', which, with the exception of the 'Coign of a cliff'[28] I had almost forgotten. It is rather pleasant to discover a book which is already at home for future use.

The weather here is very miserable, and I don't think there has been an hour's sunshine since I came back. Kirk asked me to write for Aeneid VII and VIII, published at 1/6 each by Cambridge University Press, editor Sedgwick.[29] I am afraid these requests for books are rather numerous, but of course it is Kirk's to command, mine not to question why, etc.

I have heard nothing from you now since the holydays, except the scant note of which you so rightly said 'This is not a letter'. I sincerely hope you are not hors de combat. Do drop me a line soon and let me know.

your loving son,
Jack

---

27 David Lloyd George (1863–1945), Minister of Munitions, gave a speech on 28 February in which he appealed for an end to labour disputes. 'We laugh at things in Germany,' he said, 'that ought to terrify us. We say, "Look at the way they are making their bread – out of potatoes, ha, ha." Aye, that potato bread spirit is something which is more to dread than to mock at. I fear that more than I do even von Hindenburg's strategy, efficient as it may be. That is the spirit in which a country should meet a great emergency, and instead of mocking at it we ought to emulate it.' *The Times* (1 March 1915), p. 10.

28 Algernon Charles Swinburne, *Poems and Ballads*, Second Series (1878). The poem entitled 'A Forsaken Garden' begins 'In a coign of the cliff between lowland and highland'.

29 *Publius Vergili Maronis Aeneidos: Liber VII*, edited by Arthur Sidgwick (1879); *The Aeneid of Vergil: Book VIII*, edited with notes and vocabulary by Arthur Sidgwick (1879).

TO HIS FATHER (LP IV: 304):

[Gastons
21? March 1915]

My dear Papy,

In connection with the 'question before the house', I have, as you may have anticipated, only one answer. Apart from the natural inclination to go home if possible, it occurs to me that there is no knowing where such a period of non-homecoming might end. If we could be sure that this policy of frightfulness would be over by midsummer, I should not hesitate to spend Easter in England. But it would be illogical to stay here *now* on account of the submarines and cross *then* in spite of them. So that there is the frightful prospect of living on opposite sides of the channel for two, five, or six years.

That of course is unthinkable; and it is on that ground chiefly that I should recommend going home.

A minor point to be considered is that it would be as well to make use of my return ticket while it is still available. The same idea would make me inclined to travel by Fleetwood – for which my ticket is available – in preference to Larne and Stranraer. The difference in the length of the crossing is, I should say, by no means commensurate with the extra expense, and in comfort Fleetwood is probably superior. If these ideas fall in at all with your own, I should suggest that I leave Bookham on Thursday week (the 1st April), which would mean arriving home on the morning of Good Friday. That just leaves a comfortable space of time in which you can write to K. about it.

Last week end was busily employed in reading through De Quincey's 'Confessions'[30] as a whole, for the first time, from which I derived great satisfaction. How much of it is true? The whole thing reads so like a novel that I am rather incredulous. Anyway it is certainly a splendid piece of English prose, especially in the rhetorical passages where he shows such a happy knack of getting pleasantly off the point. Thanks for the Aeneids: though, with the holydays near, if I had thought, I might have let it stand over.

As you say, our inability to cope with the submarine menace is a very serious thing; but not half so far reaching, so degrading, so essentially rotten as the behaviour of our working classes, who, tho' so highly paid

30 Thomas De Quincey, *Confessions of an English Opium Eater* (1822).

that they can afford to have three days off per week when nominally at work, yet because of some petty jealousies of their own are refusing to turn out the goods necessary to the military operations which the country is engaged upon. As K. points out, we are the only country which when the war broke out was 'free' from militarism, and yet about to engage in civil war: and we are now the only one that cannot secure peace among its working classes. But enough of all this. The weather, as usual of late, is disgusting except for one 'pet' day on Sunday. Hope to see you next week.

your loving son,
Jack

TO ARTHUR GREEVES (W):

[Gastons
30 March 1915]

Dear Arthur,

How I pity you people who never have known the pleasures and the pains – which are an integral part of the pleasures – of a regular interchange of home-coming and school going. Even the terrors of Malvern were almost justified by the raptures with which one hailed the periodic deliverance. Here, where the minor disadvantages of my sojourns at Bookham are just enough to act as a foil to the pleasures of home, but not so great as to make the earlier part of the term unhappy, the arrangement is ideal. The satisfaction with which a day boy looks forward to a period of rest from his work, can be but the faintest shadow of a boarder's feeling towards his return from temporary exile.

These last few days! Every little nuiscance, every stale or tiresome bit of work, every feeling of that estrangement which I never quite get over in another country, serves as a delightful reminder of how different it will all be soon. Already one's mind dwells upon the sights and sounds and smells of home, the distant murmuring of the 'yards', the broad sweep of the lough, the noble front of the cave hill, and the fragrant little glens and breazy meadows of our *own* hills! And the sea! I cannot bear to live too far away from it. At Belfast, whether hidden or in sight, still it dominates the general impression of nature's face, lending its own crisp flavour to the winds and its own subtle magic to horizons, even when they conceal it. A sort of feeling of space, and clean fresh vigour hangs over all in a country by the sea: how different from the stuffiness of

Bookham: here the wind – that is to say, the true, brisk, boisterous irresistable wind – never comes.

And yet, I would not for a moment disparage the beauty of Surrey: these slumbering little vallies, and quaint farmsteads have a mellow charm of their own, that Ulster has not. But just now my End-of-Term feelings will not allow me to think of that. 'But why', you will ask 'am I treated to these lyrical raptures?' Indeed, Sir, I hardly know. My father wrote a few days ago, and asked if we should risk the submarines and come home, or not. I of course said that we should, – advancing many sage arguments thereto, and suggested leaving here next Friday. I have not been answered yet, but hope to goodness it is coming off. Anyway, a wave of End-of-Terminess came over me to night, and, as I had to communicate with someone, so you, poor fellow, got let in for this!

I had a letter from 'Her'[31] the other day, which is all satisfactory, Must shut up now.

Yours
Jack

Jack arrived in Belfast for his Easter holidays on 1 April and was there till 30 April. During this time he wrote the first poems he considered worthy of preservation. One of those written during this holiday was 'The Hills of Down', and it is found in his Collected Poems *(1994). From this time until he went up to Oxford in 1917 Lewis wrote 52 poems which he copied into a notebook bearing the name 'Metrical Meditations of a Cod'. Fourteen of the 'metrical meditations' are found in* Spirits in Bondage.

TO ARTHUR GREEVES (W):

[Gastons
4 May 1915]

Dear Galahad,[32]

I am surprised! Have you actually come down to enjoying such stuff as 'The Breed of the Treshams'?[33] I never (for which the gods be

---

31 i.e. the Belgian girl.

32 Lewis has borrowed the name from Malory. In *Le Morte d'Arthur* Galahad is the son of Launcelot and Elaine, and destined because of his immaculate purity to achieve the Holy Grail.

33 John Rutherford, *The Bread of the Treshams* (1903).

thanked) saw or read it, but the name is enough. I admit, I should like to have seen The Shrew,[34] and novelties in the way of staging are always rather interesting. I much prefer on the stage – and everywhere for that matter – quiet, tasteful, plain decorations, to tawdry, splendid things.

I feel my fame as a 'Man-about-the-Gramaphone' greatly put out by your remarks à propos of Lohengrin Prelude Act III,[35] as, I must confess, I never heard of it on Columbia. I do hope it is a good *record*, as I should like to have it very much: what is the Venusbury music like?[36] Is it that wild part that comes at the end of the Tannhaüser overture? Of course you know the Columbia edition of Schubert's Rosamunde[37] has long been at Little Lea, but when last I played it to you, I seem to remember a *non* favourable verdict from you. I am so glad that you have gotten (That's correct, you know. 'Got' isn't) the Fire Music,[38] as I have been hesitating over it for ages, and your success or failure will decide me. Oh! I had better stop writing about this, as it makes me 'think long': not, if you please, in a sentimental way, but with a sensible desire for my books and you and our Gramaphones etc.[39]

However, I have gott*en* (notice – again) one great addition to my comfort here, in the discovery of a 'Soaking-machine', which conveniences are very scarce in England, owing to the strict customs which prevent the mildest trespassing. My new palace, is at the foot of a great oak, a few yards off a lane, and hidden therefrom by a little row of shrubs and small trees. Completely private, safe from sun, wind or rain, and on the ridge of the only rising ground (you wouldn't call it a hill) about here. There, with a note book and pencil, I can be as free to write, etc, as at home. So if your next letter comes in pencil, on a sheet torn from a pocket book, you needn't be surprised. I must find some more of these places as summer goes on, for it is already too hot to walk far.

---

34 William Shakespeare, *The Taming of the Shrew* (1623).

35 Richard Wagner's opera *Lohengrin* was first performed in 1850.

36 The title Richard Warner had chosen for his opera was *The Venusberg*, but he changed it to *Tannhäuser* when he learned that certain wits were making a joke of it. The opera was first performed in 1845.

37 Franz Schubert's *Rosamund* was first performed in 1823.

38 The 'Fire Music' is the Interlude to Act III, scene 3 of Richard Wagner's opera *Die Walküre*, or *The Valkyrie*, first performed in 1870 and part of his *Ring of the Nibelung* cycle.

39 For information on music recorded on gramophone records see Francis F. Clough and G.J. Cuming, *The World's Encyclopaedia of Recorded Music* (1952).

I bought yesterday a little shilling book about Wm. Morris, his life and his work,[40] which is rather interesting. To me, at least, for I am afraid *you* have given up that old friend of ours.

To say that you have something 'sentimental' to say, and not to say it, is to be like Janie McN.[41] with the latest scandal, that everyone is told *about* and no one is told. I don't quite follow your letter in places. What is the connection between all the rubbish about 'that nuiscance Arthur' (you know how all your friends ridicule and dislike that sort of talk) and the wish that I should become sentimental perforce? By the way, I am perhaps more sentimental than you, but I don't blow a trumpet about it. Indeed, I am rather ashamed of it. Feelings ought to be kept for literature and art, where they are delightful and not intruded into life where they are merely a nuiscance.

I have just finished 'Shirley'; which I think better than either 'Jane Eyre'[42] or 'Villette'. You must read it. What a letter; every sentence seems to begin 'I'. However, a good healthy dose of egotism is what you need, while you might pass on a little of your superfluous modesty to Bookham. Sorry you've returned the old Meistersingers,[43] but think the Beka better value.

Yours

Jack

P.S. What is the name of the 'Galloping Horse' piece by Chopin,[44] I want to make Mrs K. play it.

---

40 Arthur Clutton-Brock, *William Morris: His Work and Influence* (1914).

41 Jane ('Janie') Agnes McNeill (1889–1959) was the daughter of James Adams McNeill (1853–1907), headmaster of Campbell College 1890–1907, and Margaret Cunningham McNeill. Mr McNeill had at one time been Flora Lewis's teacher, and he and his wife and daughter lived near the Lewises in 'Lisnadene', 191 Belmont Road, Strandtown. When he was young Jack Lewis both liked and disliked Janie. As time went on he realized that Jane, who would have liked to have gone to university, had remained home to look after her mother. He came to admire her much, and in time they became devoted friends. He was also close to Mrs McNeill, whose company he greatly enjoyed. *That Hideous Strength* is dedicated to Janie. See her biography in *CG*.

42 Charlotte Brontë, *Shirley* (1849); *Jane Eyre* (1847).

43 *Die Meistersinger von Nürnberg*, an opera by Richard Wagner, was first performed in 1868.

44 Arthur did not seem entirely sure what this 'Galloping Horse' piece was. In Lewis's next letter of 11 May, he said to Arthur, 'Why didn't you give me the number of the Polonaise: and what cheek to say "I think it is in A Flat" – when a journey downstairs would make sure.' If he had looked carefully Arthur might have discovered that it was not one of Chopin's Polonaises, but one of his Mazurkas.

TO ARTHUR GREEVES (W/LP IV: 316–17):

[Gastons
11 May 1915]

Dear Galahad,

Tut! Tut! Must I change your soubriquet? From being the spotless knight of the Grail, are you going to turn philosopher and meet me on my own ground to dispute my shadowy quibbles about the proper sphere of sentiment? Galahad becomes Merlin: who knows but that you may 'grow besotted of a damosel', like him, and like him, I may find you when I come home bound fast under a great stone, making a piteous wail to all who pass. And what a relief for the neighbourhood! I think I shall nominate a suitable damosel – say Miss Bradley or Sal Stokes – to besott and bind you. By the way, à propos of Miss Bradley, has she yet recovered (or better still died) from that peculiarly interminable complaint of hers, which prevents the gramaphone being played up at Glenmachen?

But to go back to the sentiment controversy, your objection is nonsense. You argue that sentiment is delightful in art, because it is a part of human nature. Quite right. From that, you deduce that it ought not to be confined to that sphere of human nature where it *is* delightful – viz. art. That is almost as sensible as to say that trousers are delightful only because they are a part of human clothes: therefore they ought to be worn, not only on the legs, but every where else. Do you maintain that it is a highly commendable and philosophical act to wear trousers, say, on your head? My point is that art is a recepticacle of human thought: sentiment, emotion etc make up that section of human thought which are best suited to fill that definite receptical – and no other. For why, when we have found the best place to keep a thing, should we keep it in other places as well, or instead? By the analogy of the trousers I have shown how ridiculous that would be. As for your idea that to be young, one must be sentimental, let us go into it. Young children are practically devoid of sentiment: they are moved only by bodily pain: young men are a little more sentimental, middle aged ones considerably more so, and old ones the most mawkishly so of all. Sentiment, you see, is a distinct mark of age.

Ah! Having gott*en* (N.B.) that off our chest, we can proceed to other matters. That little book about Wm. Morris has interested me so much – or re-awakened the old interest – in him, that I have just written up for

'The Roots of the Mountains' in Longman's pocket edition:[45] it is about the Goths, and is praised in that book as one of the best of the prose Romances. What is the good of getting Anderson in Everyman?[46] It is true, the tales have considerable merit in ipso (that's Latin and means 'in themselves', Ignorant!): but yet, if any book ever needed or was greatly improved by fancy binding, that is it.

The word Soaking-Machine can hardly be styled 'slang', being, as it is, coined by myself for private circulation: I thought you knew what it meant. The word 'soak' means to sit idly or sleepily doing nothing, and a S'ing machine is [a] place for this operation, i.e. a comfortable seat. Surely I must often have said to you in the course of our walks 'Let's find a soaking-machine' or 'Here's a good soaking-machine'?

I despair of making head or tail of any of your gramaphonic talk, where your extraordinary loose and obscure use of words like 'latter' etc makes havoc of the sense. Do you mean that you had another record of the Venusburg music, before you heard it with Lohengrin, à l'autre côté? Or do you know what you mean? Or, lastly, do you mean anything at all. I write such enormous letters (which you probably never read to the end) that, from the way Mrs K. keeps looking at me, I believe she fancies it a billet doux. Why didn't you give me the number of the Polonaise: and what cheek to say 'I think it is in A Flat', when a journey downstairs would make sure.

It has been raining for almost 36 hours here, which is not very cheerful. The idea of spelling melodrama 'mello-drama' is really quite 'chic': I should take out a patent on it, if I were you. I hope you are in good spirits these days, and that the lady of the office window is kind & in good health. Write soon: you've know idea how welcome your letters are. By the by, you might tell the girl in Osborne's to send on the monthly catalogues to my address here, which you can tell her – Columbia, H.M.V., Zono, Beka, are the chief. Valde.

Yours
Jack

---

45 William Morris, *The Roots of the Mountains* (1890). The Longman's Pocket Library edition was published in two volumes in 1913.

46 Hans Christian Andersen, *The Mermaid and Other Fairy Tales*, translated by Mrs Edgar Lucas, with coloured illustrations by Maxwell Armfield, Everyman's Library [1914].

TO HIS FATHER (LP IV: 312–13):

[Gastons]
Postmark: 13 May 1915

My dear Papy,

I suppose I must apologise for being a little behindhand with my bulletin; but I confess I don't understand the remark about 'punishing accidents'. I am really sorry if you have been nervous, but I thought the telegram would suffice to set you at ease. However, let me assure you here and now that I and my luggage arrived quite safely at Bookham: there has been no question of accidents at all.

Hard times these must be at Leeboro: I have managed to escape the spring gales both at home and here. Thanks for your exertions about my room, which I hope will prove successful in keeping it from shifting. Perhaps 'key-lashing' as an extreme measure would be advisable.

I think the idea of permanent Sunday luncheon at the Rectory is excellent:[47] perhaps a series of weekly lectures under the title of 'Anticipation and Realization; their genesis, distinctions and development: together with an excursus on their relations to the Greenshaketything', would contribute greatly to the gaiety of the occasion. With that disinterested devotion to science, that noble generosity which has always characterised my actions, I not only place the material at your disposal but actually relinquish all claim to authorship. It would be but folly to deny that I experience some natural pangs – but no! Far be it from me to

47 Albert and his sons were delighted with the new rector of St Mark's. This was the Reverend Arthur William Barton (1881–1962) who was born in Dublin and had gone, like Warnie and Jack, to Wynyard School. He took his BA from Trinity College, Dublin in 1903, and his BD in 1906. He was ordained in 1905 and was curate at St George's, Dublin, from 1904 until 1905, and curate of Howth from 1905 to 1913. From 1912 to 1914 he was head of the university settlement at Trinity College Mission in Belfast. He was instituted as rector of St Mark's, Dundela, on 6 April 1914, and remained there until 1925 when he became rector of Bangor. In 1927 he was made Archdeacon of Down, and in 1930 he became Bishop of Kilmore, Elphin and Ardagh. In 1939 Barton became Archbishop of Dublin and Primate of Ireland, which post he held until his retirement in 1956. In his description of Barton Warnie said, 'There must have been few who met him and did not like him, and he was soon to become a constant and welcome visitor at Little Lea. He was a man of sunny temperament, with a great sense of fun, and a caressing voice; he brought into the rather narrow air of a Belfast suburb the breath of a wider culture and a more humane outlook; his society was refreshing. What was of more importance, he was an excellent and conscientious Priest, who found the religion of his parish sunk into mere formalism under the regime of his slothful predecessor, and who set on foot a renaissance' (LP IV: 178).

divert the publication of philosophical enlightenment into a channel for the aggrandisment of personal glory. No! Not even when, from the stately halls of Purdysburn[48] conferred upon you by a grateful and adoring country, you watch the fame of my achievements heaping its most succulent favours upon your own head – not even then, I say, will a sigh of regret escape from the gullet of self sacrifice.

We had some real summer weather for a few days after I came back, but it has seen fit to pour in torrents today. There is nothing of much interest here except that I have heard a nightingale for the first time. I think I mentioned before that they are as common as sparrows about here – in fact they are rather too numerous. In my conceit (Elizabethan), the song of these birds is one of those few things that does really come up to its reputation: at any rate I never heard anything else at all like it.

'But enough of these tropes' (as Bacon says at the end of an essay about Masques and stage plays.):[49] let me soon have another letter as long as a Lurgan spade. The coat has arrived.

your loving son,
Jack

P.S. That cat about *accidence*, I guess has cold feet about jumping, eh?

TO ARTHUR GREEVES (W/LP IV: 323–4):

[Gastons
25 May 1915]

Dear Galahad,

B-r-r-r! Behold me coming with locusts & wild honey about my loins (or is it sackcloth & ashes) to kneel and tremble and apologise for my letterless week. However, qui s'excuse, s'accuse, as the French say, and if you want to seek the real author of the mischief you must go up to heaven, and find the four and twenty elders sitting in a row, as St John says, falling on their faces on the sea of glass[50] (which must hurt rather but apparently is the 'thing' up yonder), and William Morris in white raiment with a halo.

48 Purdysburn was a lunatic asylum.

49 'But enough of these toys', Francis Bacon said in 'Of Masques and Triumphs', *Essays or Counsels, Civil and Moral* (1625).

50 Revelation 4:4–10.

Or, in other words, 'The Roots of the Mountains' is the chief cause of my silence. It is not, however, in spite of all this, nearly so good as the first volume of 'The Well at the World's End', although the interest is better sustained throughout. To begin with, I was desparately dissapointed to find that there is nothing, supernatural, faery or unearthly in it at all: in fact, it is more like an ordinary novel. And yet there are many compensations: for, tho' more ordinary than the 'Well', it is still utterly different from any novel you ever read. Apart from the quaint and beautiful old English, which means so much to me, the supernatural element, tho' it does not enter into the plot, yet hovers on the margin all the time: we have 'the wildwood wherein dwell wights that love not men, to whom the groan of the children of men is as the scrape of a fiddle-bow: there too abide the kelpies, and the ghosts of them that rest not',[51] and such delightful names as The Dusky Men, The Shadowy Vale, The Shivering Flood, The Weltering Water etc. Another thing I like about it is that the characters are not mediaeval knights but Norse mountain tribes with axe & long-sword instead of horses & lances and so forth. However, though it is worth having and well worth reading, I don't know if its really worth buying. The next time I get a Morris Romance it will be one of the later ones, as the 'Roots' is one of the first, when, apparently, he hadn't yet found his feet in prose work.

On Saturday last we were over at a little village near here, where Watts the painter lived:[52] there is a little gallery, a lovely building, designed by himself, containing some of his quite famous pictures like 'Orpheus & Euridyce', 'Endymion', 'Sir Galahad' etc, which I always thought were in the Louvre or the Tate or some such place. Of course I don't really quite understand good painting, but I did my best, and succeeded in really enjoying some myself, & persuading the other people that I knew a tremendous lot about them all.

What a grand dialectician, our Little Arthur is!![53] You reply to my elegant tirade against sentiment by stating your old thesis that it ought

---

51 *Roots of the Mountains*, op. cit., vol. I, ch. 3, pp. 24–5: 'Therein are Kobbolds, and Wights that love not men, things unto whom the grief of men is as the sound of the fiddle-bow unto us. And there abide the ghosts of those that may not rest; and there wander the dwarfs and the mountain-dwellers, the dealers in marvels, the givers of gifts that destroy Houses.'

52 The painter and sculptor George Frederic Watts (1817–1904) who lived for some years at 'Limneslease' near Compton in Surrey.

53 Presumably a reference to the notorious Victorian children's lesson book *Little Arthur's England* (1835) by Lady Calcott.

not to be suppressed, without a single reason. You don't admit my arguments, and yet make no endeavour to answer them. And because I choose trousers for an example you say that it is 'very funny'. Moi, I didn't know trousers were funny. If you do, I picture your progress from the tram to the office something thus: 'Hullo! Good lord, there's a fellow with trousers over there! And there's another. Ha-Ha – Oh this is too screaming. Look – one-two-three more – ' and you collapse in a fit of uncontrollable merriment. Doesn't this sort of truck fill up the paper? But in point of fact, I've lost your last letter, and so don't quite know what to talk about.

Thanks for carrying out my message to Miss Whatdoyoucallher? about the monthly catalogues, which are now arriving in due order. That's rather a pretty girl, the H.M.V. infant prodigy 18 year old soprano, but she doesn't seem to sing anything worth hearing. Hear your brethren are going to join a friend's ambulance corps, whatever that may be. Give them my congratulations and all the usual nonsense one ought to say on such an occasion. I hope they will get on famously and come back with Victoria crosses and eye-glasses, which seem to be the two goals of military ambition.

It is hot as our future home down below, here, but the country is looking delightful, & I have found one or two more SOAKING MACHINES (I will use that word if I want to) and so am quite comfortable. I hear you have taken to getting heart fits in the middle of the sermon at Saint Marks and coming out – I only wish you'd teach me the trick.

And now, the kind reader, if there still is one, is going to be left in peace. Do write soon, and forgive your suppliant

Jack

TO HIS FATHER (LP IV: 313–14):

[Gastons]

Postmark: 25 May 1915

Dear Papy,

I don't seem to have heard from you for some time now, but I suppose I am a little behindhand myself. There has been great excitement here this week end: when I came home from Church on Sunday morning I found a note waiting for me to say that Kirk and Mrs. Kirk had gone to Bristol where they had heard by a telegraph that Louis was in hospital. It appears he got a mild species of sun stroke while working with big guns down there at a place called Lydd. It was not very serious – in fact I gather somewhat of a mares nest – and K. is back this evening while Mrs. K. is staying at Bristol for a few days.

We have started our real summer here, and it is pretty warm. How does the weather suit the home farm, where I hope the tragic gardeners are in good form? What between pigeons and gardeners and white Homburg hats, Leeborough must present quite a seasonable spring idyll (with a double 'l'.)

Mrs. K. and I were over at a place called Compton beyond Guildford on Saturday, where the attraction is a little pottery for fancy tiles and sich, founded by my friend William [Morris], who, as you know, besides being a poet was a wall paper designer, a potter, a hand loom weaver and everything else you can think of. Nearby is a gallery of Watts's pictures. He, it appears, was one of that same set, and there are a lot of quite swell things there, such as his 'Paolo and Francesco', 'Orpheus and Euridyce', and 'Found Drowned' etc., which I always imagined to be in some big place like the Louvre or Tate. It was quite interesting.

Any news from the Colonel lately? I have not heard from any one except Arthur for a long time now, so do try and raise a letter soon. Or is this silence a result of a literal obedience to my last advice a propos of lectures to the members of the Select Vestry? I hope the doctors don't think it serious.

There are plenty of nightingales about now, and in fact they are rather a nuisance. I am afraid this is rather a scrappy letter, but I am writing rather late at night, just before going to bed, and am a bit sleepy. I should like to know what is going on at Leeborough just now. I suppose these are the days of no fires, and sunset on the seat behind the laurels, with the crows coming home overhead, and Tim on the look out for wasps.

I hope you are keeping well and cheerful. Write again soon.

your loving,

son,

Jack

TO HIS FATHER (LP IV: 322–3):

[Gastons
28? May 1915]

My dear Papy,

I am sorry to hear that the mental digestion of my parent is so weak, and blame myself for giving it such strong meat. Perhaps a course of 'Decalettes, pure and simple things', or nursery rhymes would meet the case. (Now we can proceed to the letter.)

Of course it is a very good thing that Bernagh is contributing to the forces, but one cannot help thinking that a better choice than the 'Friend's Ambulance Corps' – which really does sound rather sleepy – might have been made.[54] However, I suppose 'those also serve'[55] though the trenches impress the outside spectator more than an ambulance corps. A propos of conscription, I sincerely hope that one of two things may happen. Either that the war may be over before I am eighteen, or that conscription may not come into force before I have volunteered. I shouldn't fancy going out to meet the others – as a conscript. I see the *Daily Mail* is being burnt everywhere for advocating the plan.[56] How excellent a proof of the necessity of a petty little plan like sending an envelope full of ashes – or most likely it was a woman. There is absolutely no news here, and the weather is very hot. Mrs. K. has now returned again from Bristol where she left Louis getting on all right.

I like your garden picture. I can imagine the whole scene, and especially the conversation with the Greeve's on the road, we have heard so many like it before. The country at home must be looking delightful now, and I wish I could see it, but most of all the sea. If Bookham were not so far inland it would be delightful too – and indeed to do it justice it is very pretty. The remark about the fates is excellent from a literary point of view, only I don't like to think of you thinking those sort of things in such a place – and with a white Homburg hat too. And yet I

---

54 Several generations of the Greeves family had been members of the Society of Friends (Quakers). However, Arthur Greeves's grandparents had been converts to the Plymouth Brethren and it was in this denomination that Arthur had been brought up. The family retained its connection to the Friends.

55 John Milton, Sonnet 16, 'When I consider how my light is spent' (1673): 'They also serve who only stand and wait.'

56 The letters columns of the papers had been filled with talk of the pros and cons of conscription. However, the Military Service Act, which brought in conscription, did not come into being until 10 February 1916.

remember that Swinburne has some remark about the impossibility of changing 'wings for feet, or feet for wings'. I suppose if we Lewis's are made in that mould of reflective gravity which troubles deepen into melancholy, it is the price which we pay for a thoughtful and feeling mind. About the question of retrospect and anticipation (dangerous word for you, sir), there is a sentence in one of W. Morris's prose tales that I am reading at present, which tho' perhaps not strictly in point, is yet well worth remembering in its archaic charm and quaint nobility: – 'Thus then lived this folk in much plenty and ease of life, though not delicately nor desiring things out of measure. They wrought with their hands and wearied themselves: they rested from their toil and feasted and were merry: tomorrow was not a burden unto them, nor yesterday a thing that they would fain forget: life shamed them not, nor did death make them afraid.'[57] There is another way of looking at life: impossible it may be in a sophisticated age, and yet I think he would be a happy man who could do so.

What time do my letters reach you in the day? In letter writing one ought to know when and where the other person reads, as it makes more of a semblance to real conversation. I must dry up now.

your loving son,
Jack

TO ARTHUR GREEVES (W):

[Gastons
1 June 1915]

Dear Galahad,

Your interesting epistle which I have read with wonder and delight, contains the following gems of Arthurian style

A. 'I don't suppose you will object to *my* coming with *me*.'

B. 'Read this with *discust*.'

C. 'I am talking now of *sensulity*.'

Dear old Galahad! That's an unusually good budget even for you: I am afraid this 'sensulity' of yours – I never saw the word before but I suppose you know what it means – must be beginning to tell on you.

As to your first question, the only holyday I propose to take is a week or so with my relations at Larne, and my father's offer, which I take to be

57 *Roots of the Mountains*, op cit., vol. I, ch. 1, p. 13.

purely formal, I would not much care to accept. I hope you will be sensible enough to spend your holydays at home with me, seeing each other and talking & going for long walks over the hills, instead of going off to some godless place by the sea. My point is that I should be going to my Aunt's in any case, and 1 week or so from home is quite enough for me: as well, I don't think it very decent to leave my father any longer. But don't let this prevent your going somewhere. All I want to point out is, that my refusal of a joint holyday, is not from a design to avoid you, but because I don't want to be away from home too long. Of course, if you would condescend to honour Larne with your presence while I am at my Aunt's, I should be very bucked to see you: but you might be bored. However, we can talk all this over when we meet at the end of July.

Odeon records are the most fascinating and delusive bait on the Gramaphone market. Cheap, classical, performed by good artistes, they present a jolly attractive list: but they wear out in a month. Of course there are exceptions, and I can play you some selections from Lohengrin which I have on that make, and which have worn well. On the whole however, I wouldn't advise anyone to get Odeon records, as a short-lived record is one of the most dissapointing of things. I foresee, by the way, that your way of getting records is like Jane McNeil's way of getting books – that is you use a shop like a free library: whenever a record is worn out, back it goes to the shop, and you have a new one in its place. Which reminds me, my monthly catalogues for this month haven't turned up yet, so you must shout at Miss Thompson.

With reference to your remarks about sensuality – je vous demande pardon – 'sensulity', I don't know I am sure, why you have been suffering especially in this way just now. Of course when I was particularly so last term, there was a reason, about whom you heard perhaps more than you wanted. You ought to be past the age of violent attacks of 'EPW TÍKA (Greek); as well you are Galahad the spotless whose 'strength is as the strength of ten, because your heart is pure'. Perhaps you would understand now, what you didn't understand when I started the subject last hols, <what I mean by the 'sensuality of cruelty': again perhaps you would not.>

Last week I got a copy of that little book of yours on Icelandic Sagas, which I found very interesting, and as a result I have now bought a translation of the 'Laxdaela Saga'[58] in the Temple Classics edition. I never saw a Temple Classic before; did you? In binding, paper, & 'forma' (by which I include the aspect of a typical page, its shape, spacing, lettering etc) they are tip top, and justify the boast of 'elegance' made in their advertisements. They are, I think, far better value than Everyman's at the same price.

As to the Saga itself I am very pleased with it indeed: if the brief, simple, nervous style of the translation is a good copy of the original it must be very fine. The story, tho', like most sagas, it loses unity, by being spread over two or three generations, is thoroughly interesting. Just as it was interesting after the 'Well at the World's End' to read the 'Morte', so after the 'Roots', a real saga is interesting. I must admit that here again the primitive type is far better than Morris's reproduction. But that of course is inevitable, just as Homer is better than Vergil.

Sorry to hear my father is so low, but I write to him regularly, and the last was really rather a long and good effort. Hope you're all well at Bernagh.

Yours
Jack

TO ARTHUR GREEVES (W):

[Gastons
8 June 1915]

Dear Galahad,

I seem to have trod on somebody's corns over this question of a holyday: I expressly said that I did not wish to keep you at home on my account if you wished to go elsewhither. To be brief, my whole answer was that I refused your kind proposal because I was already booked, adding that I should not care to take another holyday in addition to that at Larne. Now what is your grievance – for grievance you must have or you would not write such good grammar. Is it because I won't throw up my previous invitation in favour of yours? That would be rude. Is it because I will not accompany you on another holyday? That is selfish of you, to expect me to give [up] my fleeting sojourn at Leeborough for

58 *Laxdaela Saga*, translated by M.A.C. Press, Temple Classics (1899). This 13th century Icelandic saga is the tragic story of several generations of an Iceland family, and in particular of Gudrun who causes the death of a man she loves but fails to marry.

your amusement. Is it because I mildly suggested that you need not go for a holyday? There was never any obligation on you to accept such a scheme. And as for your hot weather – je me moque de cette là, it is bitterly cold to-night! How funny that I always prove everything I want in argument with you but never convince you!

Now, having despatched our inevitable weekly dialectical passage-at-arms (by the way, you have never replied to my theory of trousers), we may proceed to the letter. I admit that the 'I hope you are all well' is a blot on my character that can hardly be wiped out: I didn't think I had sunk*en* so low as that, and will try to reform.

I thought you would agree with me about Mansfield park:[59] I should almost say it was her best. I don't remember the names very well, but I think I rather liked Edmund. Do get a Temple Classic. You will bless me ever after, as they are really the best shillings worth on the market. I hope I may prove a false prophet about the Odeon records, and that you will have better luck in them than I. Now that it is drawing a little nearer my return, I begin to hanker again for my gramaphone: but I am not consoled even with the catalogues, so you must stir up the damosel again. I am still at the 'Laxdaela Saga' which is as good as ever, and I insist upon your reading it too.

On Saturday I met the prettiest girl I have ever seen in my life (don't be afraid, you're not going to have to listen to another love-affair). But it is not her prettiness I wanted to tell you about, but the fact that she is just like that grave movement in the Hungarian Rhapsody (or is it the 'dance'?) that I love so much.[60] Of course to you I needn't explain how a person can be like a piece of music, – you will know: and if you play that record over, trying to turn the music into a person, you will know just how she looked and talked. Just 18, and off to do some ridiculous war-work, nursing or something like that at Dover of all places – what a shame!

By the way, that would be a rather interesting amusement, trying to find musical interpretations for all our friends. Thus Gordon[61] is like the Pilgrims chorus from Tannhaüser, Kelsie a bit like the Valkyries[62] only

---

59 Jane Austen, *Mansfield Park* (1814).

60 He had in mind Franz Liszt's Hungarian Rhapsody No. 1, first performed in 1851.

61 Charles Gordon Ewart (1885–1936) was the second son of Sir William Quartus Ewart. See **The Ewart Family** in the Biographical Appendix.

62 He means her character was like Wagner's *Die Walküre.*

not so loud, Gundred[63] like the dance-movement in Danse Macabre, and Bob like a Salvation army hymn. We might add yourself as a mazurka by Chopin, wild, rather plaintful, and disjointed, and Lily like, well – a thing of Grieg's called 'The Watchman's Song'[64] that you haven't heard. I think I must write a book on it.

By the way (all my sentences seem to begin like that) I am very sorry this is a bit late, but I was writing to my father and brother last night. Now, good night, Galahad, and be good and talk sense the next time you do me the honour of arguing with me.

Yours
Jack

P.S. What about the question of 'sensulity'?

TO HIS FATHER (LP IV: 319–20):

[Gastons]
Friday [18 June 1915]

My dear Papy,

I am writing this immediately after reading your letter, but I mean it to belong to next week. Perhaps I shall not post it till Monday to equalize the dates, but at any rate it is much easier to write to you just after reading yours. I somehow seem to be unable to write to you properly now-a-days: perhaps because we make jokes nearly all the time when we are together, and household humour, though the funniest of all things to those who understand (a propos of which, read the first Roman story in 'Puck of Pook's Hill'),[65] can't really be written down. Whereas if I try to be serious, I merely succeed in being 'stuffy'. The last word describes exactly what I mean. However, as Plato says, the written word is only a poor faint shadow of real conversation, in which, among people who know each other well, the merest suggestion explains a train of thought which the most elaborate written explanation leaves obscure, lifeless and formal.[66] Still, as it would be expensive to telephone to you every week

63 Gundreda Ewart (1888–1975) was one of the daughters of Sir William Quartus Ewart. See **The Ewart Family** in the Biographical Appendix.

64 From Edvard Grieg's *Lyriske Smaastykker* (1867).

65 i.e. 'A British Roman Song'.

66 He is referring to Plato's *Phaedrus*, 278a.

with trunk calls – do you remember the lady in 'The Whip'?[67] – we must do the best we can.

I think we may reasonably hope that the war will be over before it begins to concern me personally. At the same time, the knowledge that I had gone as soon as possible to the front would not, I fancy, be a very substantial comfort to me if I arrived there as a conscript. All the people on whom that name has fallen would be lumped together without distinction in the minds of our Tommies – who indeed might be excused for feeling some warmth in the circumstances. Then there is the other possibility that Europe will be at peace before I am eighteen. In that case I believe my career at Oxford would be, if anything, a little easier than usual, owing to lack of competition. It would be ghastly however to reckon up that condition as an advantage – when we remember what it means. I am sorry for your sake that 'Mr. Carr'[68] has gone, but after all, from his point of view, it was inevitable. There is not much objection made to the teeth now, it seems!

I will certainly write to the Colonel as soon as you send me his address, which I am not quite sure of. I don't think I will make it a birthday letter, which – from me at any rate – would not appeal to him: I may find some 'crack' however to interest him. Isn't it interesting to note the different things we expect from different people? If I imitated your style exactly, and could write a letter to the Colonel almost the same as a typical one of yours, the result would be merely irritating: if you tried the same experiment with my style, or absence of style, the result would be the same. Yet both, I believe, would be acceptable from the right authors.

This is a digression: to go back to Warnie, it certainly must be very depressing to see so many of the Malvern lot – for whom he had a regard as genuine as it was inexplicable – dropping off like this. 'It is an ill wind' – the proverb is rather old. But one result of the war to us seems to be that you and W., if I may say so, understand each other better than you have done for some time.

I am learning lots of things here besides the Classics – one of them being to take cold baths: and such an artist I am becoming that you will hardly know me when I get home for the brevity of my sojourn in the

67 *The Whip*, a play by Cecil Raleigh and Henry Hamilton, had been performed for the first time in 1909 and was having a revival.

68 Willie Carr, Albert's managing clerk, apparently after being rejected for the army on account of his teeth in the earlier days of the war, had now been accepted.

bath room and the prodigious amount of noise I make over it. The weather is still hot and a trifle oppressive here, but agreeable in the morning and evening.

I have been devoting this week to the reading of Othello,[69] which I like as well as any Shakesperian play I have read. The part of Iago, to my mind, is something of a blemish, and the fact that his pitiless malignity has absolutely no motive leaves him rather a monster (in the Classical, not the newspaper sense of the word), than a human character. But then of course Shakespeare at his best always works on titanic lines, and the vices and virtues of Lear, Macbeth, Hamlet, Othello, Desdemona, etc., are magnified to a pitch more splendid and terrible than anything in real life.[70]

If I leave here on the 30th July, so as to arrive home on the last Saturday of that month, the exact half of the term ought to have fallen about four hours ago. That will make the usual twelve weeks. Only six more now! That sounds perhaps too like the old days at Malvern, but don't suppose that because I will be glad to see you again, I am not happy and more than happy at the K's.

your loving,
son,
Jack

TO ARTHUR GREEVES (W):

[Gastons
29 June 1915]

Dear Galahad,

Did the Norns or Dana holy mother of them that die not, weave for us in that hour wherein our mothers bare us, that never should we write to each other without the first page being occupied by argument? Because, whether by the decree of fate or no, this has always been the case. First it was Shee v. Souteraines, then Tears v. Trousers, and now Larne v. Leeborough – which by the way means Little Lea. How you can have known me so long without picking up the words & tags which I use every day passes my understanding – unless I am to conclude that you are asleep half the time I am talking to you, which is very probably so.

69 William Shakespeare, *Othello, The Moor of Venice* (1622).

70 These are the central characters in William Shakespeare's plays *King Lear* (1608), *Macbeth* (1623), *Hamlet* (1603) and *Othello*.

Well about this infernal holyday: as your infantile brain – for which I have catered on this envelope – is incapable of swallowing my previous very elementary argument, I will explain my position once more in very simple terms, as follows: –

I have eight weeks vacations.

I have been invited to stay 10 days with Mrs Hamilton.[71]

I have accepted her invitation.

I intend to keep that promise

I don't want to be any longer away than 10 days.

I don't want to keep you at home on that account.

I therefore decline your kind proposal.

I am very sorry

I hope you understand. How's that?

It may be true that it is easier to assign music to people we know, than to conjure up people to fit the music, but I deny that anyone's character is really unlike their appearance. The physical appearance, to my mind, is the expression and result of the other thing – soul, ego, ynch, intellect – call it what you will. And this outward expression cannot really differ from the soul. If the correspondence between a soul & body is not obvious at first, then your conception either of that soul or that body must be wrong. Thus, I am 'chubby' – to use your impertinent epithet, because I have a material side to me: because I like sleeping late, good food & clothes etc as well as sonnets & thunderstorms. The idealistic side of me must find an outlet somewhere, perhaps in my eye, my voice or anything else – you can judge better than I. And the other side of me exists in my countenance because it exists also in my character.

'But', I hear you saying, 'this is all very well. Only what about the practised flirt with the innocent schoolgirl face & the murderer with a smile like an old woman?' These are only seeming exceptions. The girl has or imagines she has that sort of disposition somewhere in her, or it wouldn't be on her face: as a matter of fact, it is always 'innocent' (which means ignorant) people who do the most outrageous things. The murderer too, may be really a peaceful, kindly 'crittur', and if circumstances drive him to violence, the initial mould of the character and therefore of the face remain just the same.

71 This was Jack's maternal grandmother, Mrs Mary Hamilton, then living at Archburn, Knock. See **The Hamilton Family** in the Biographical Appendix.

I remember reading in a book called 'The open Road'[72] an extract from Hewlet's 'Pan and the Young Shepherd'[73] which I thought splendid. Thanks to our Galahad's detestable handwriting I can't tell whether your book is the 'Lore' or the 'Love' of P. In any case I have never heard of it before, but, from your description, am very eager to read it. I also saw a copy of this author's 'Forest Lovers'[74] in Carson's last hols, but it did not attract me much. Is this new one in a decent edition?

I am glad to hear that you are keeping up the 'illustrative' side of your art, and shall want you to do some for my lyric poems. You can begin a picture of my 'dream garden' where the 'West winds blow'. As directions I inform you it is 'girt about with mists', and is in 'the shadowy country neither life nor sleep', and is the home of 'faint dreams'. With this Bädekers guide to it, you can start a picture. You remember, I scribble at pen and ink sketches a bit, and have begun to practise female faces which have always been my difficulty. I am improving a very little I think, and the margins of my old Greek lexicon as well as my pocket book now swarm with 'studies'.

Only four weeks now till I shall be home again! Isn't that a buck, at least for me – and no one else in the world really counts of course. What nonsense you talk about that 'poor man', my father. I am afraid it is true that he must bore Lily, but there is no fear of her boring him. I sympathize however, with the havoc which he must have wrought with a serious musical evening.

How is your gramaphone progressing, by the way, and how many records have you listed up to date? I am so sorry if this Liliputian writing has blinded you for life, but we have run out of the other sort of note paper.

Well kaire moì (Farewel)

Jack

P.S. Have begun the 'Proffessor'[75] and as read far as the heroe's arrival at Brussels. It is shaping very well. I believe you have read it have you not – J.

---

72 *The Open Road*, compiled by E.V. Lucas (1905).

73 Maurice Hewlett, *Pan and the Young Shepherd* (1898).

74 Maurice Hewlett, *Lore of Proserpine* (1913); *Forest Lovers* (1898).

75 Charlotte Brontë, *The Professor* (1857).

Warnie arrived in Bookham from France on 4 July 1915 and Jack, after some resistance from Mr Kirkpatrick, was permitted to accompany him home. He returned to Bookham on 9 July.

TO HIS FATHER (LP V: 1–2):

[Gastons
10? July 1915]

My dear Papy,

In reply to your note which has just this minute been handed to me, I suggest to your notice the following considerations. In the first place you ask 'why were you told £1-10s?' I am not aware that I ever told you anything at all about the subject: the sum of money – whatever it was – was handed by Kirk to Warnie at the request of the latter, who took charge of it throughout, together with both tickets and every other arrangement. It never passed through my hands, and I am not prepared to say with any certainty what it amounted to. I do not remember mentioning the matter while at home. You have therefore applied to the wrong quarter.

Secondly, supposing for purposes of argument that I did tell you that it was £1-10s, what then? As I have already pointed out, I had nothing to do with the money, and Warnie not I, was responsible for its being borrowed. It follows that I could have had no conceivable motive for misrepresenting the amount. If there was to be any blame attached, it was not I who incurred it: I need never even have mentioned it. Accordingly, if I said anything untrue, it must have been through a mere error – and even at that an error by which I could gain nothing.

Thirdly, do not be annoyed if I descend to a rather crude, a fortiori line of argument. The tone of your letter, no less than the haste with which it was dispatched, suggests an ugly suspicion. This can of course be very easily answered. Setting aside all question of honour, I ask you to credit Warnie and myself with commonsense. Granted then, that for some inscrutable reason we wanted to conceal the amount he borrowed from Kirk, would we have been such fools as to have told a lie which must inevitably be detected as soon as the latter wrote to you? And of course, we would have known that K. must write to you to get his money back.

And so, it follows that either Kirk is wrong, or else if Warnie gave you the wrong figures it must have been by accident. That I knew nothing of it, and was not concerned in the transaction, has already been shown.

Last of all, if anything in this letter should seem to indicate that I am hurt or offended, I assure you it is not the case. I am perfectly convinced that your note was not meant to be insulting, though, from its nature, it could hardly help it. In any case it is as well to make things clear, even at the risk of some little superfluous violence. I am,

your loving son,
Jack

TO HIS FATHER (LP IV: 321–2):

[Gastons
19? July 1915]

My dear Papy,

I sincerely hope this silence of yours doesn't mean anything wrong with your health. Arthur says you didn't seem very well the last time he was over at Leeborough, so I am not quite easy in my mind. If however anything is wrong, you might tell Aunt Annie to write to me with particulars, and also to forward W's address, which since I wrote for it in my last letter has become even more necessary as he has now written to me. I should not like him to think that he is forgotten or that his letter has not reached me, but I cannot reply to him until I hear from you.

Not even in Bookham can one be safe from the hoi polloi; a stubborn refusal to learn tennis is no longer a protection among people who will inflict croquet instead. I was out on Wednesday for tea and croquet and again today (Saturday) for the same entertainment, plus a great deal of conversation. However, this I suppose is part of the curse inherited from our first parents: my private opinion is that after the words 'In the sweat of thy brow shalt thou earn thy bread'[76] another clause has dropped out from the original text, running 'In the exasperation of thy souls shalt thou attend social functions'. On the whole, though I do not of course know anyone as well as at home, I like a good many of those I meet: the world indeed (as you have reminded me on innumerable occasions), is full of nice people. And if it must be full at all, I suppose it is as well that they should be nice.

Talk, of course, runs mostly on the war. I have always thought it ridiculous for people to talk so much on a subject of which, in the

76 Genesis 3:19.

majority of cases, they are really very ignorant. Books, art, etc., passing trivialities and even gossip are topics on which everyone can speak with more or less authority. We prefer however to pass our time in criticism of politics, or at present the war – subjects on which only specialists should speak. This endless criticism by ignorant men and women of public men, whose positions they do not understand, I always hear with annoyance.

The Colonel writes to me cheerfully though briefly, and wants an answer. I suppose he tells me nothing that you don't know already. Bathing and a sack of books seem to be his chief consolations in 'this detestable country.'

I have been reading nothing since Othello but a translation from the Icelandic, and stray articles etc. In Greek we have begun Demosthenes. Of course oratory is not a sort of literature that I appreciate or understand in any language, so that I am hardly qualified to express an opinion on our friend with the mouthful of pebbles. However, compared with Cicero, he strikes me as a man with something to say, intent only upon saying it clearly and shortly. One misses the beautiful roll of the Ciceronian period, but on the other hand, he is not such a — blether.[77]

Do try and write soon, or, if the worst comes to the worst, get Aunt Annie to do so.

your loving,
son,
Jack

TO ARTHUR GREEVES (W/LP IV: 299–300):

[Gastons
24 July 1915]

Dear Galahad,

I have debated more than once as to whether you would prefer a tired and perfunctory letter written in good time during the week, or a fresh and willing [one] a few days late on Saturday evening. Thinking that you would choose the latter, and knowing I would – here we are.

---

77 Demosthenes (383–322 BC) was a great Athenian orator and statesman, and Cicero (106–43 BC) a great Roman orator and statesman. Neither, however, attracted Lewis, who writing years later in *SBJ* IX said: 'Kirk did not, of course, make me read nothing but Homer. The Two Great Bores (Demosthenes and Cicero) could not be avoided.'

What on earth are you doing reading the Sowers?[78] A Russian mystery-story full of wise diplomatists and impossible women – it ought to be clad in a bright red cover, with a crude picture of Steinmitz saying 'The Moscow Doctor – and your prince!!!' from the head of the stairs, and set on a railway bookstall. But, perhaps I am wrong. Of course it has points, but you are worthy of better things. Never read any George Eliot[79] myself, being no great hand at novels but admire your energy in that line.

Talking about books, I am determined to teach you to like poetry, and will begin next hols. on Coleridges 'Christabel'. Don't be put off by the name. It is exactly the sort of romantic strangeness and dreaminess you & I like, a sort of partner to the Ancient Mariner,[80] as Danse Macabre is to the March of the Dwarfs.

Also – I hope all these schemes aren't boring you – you are going to help me to improve my drawing next hols. Figures I can do tolerably, but from you I must learn the technique of the game – shading, curves, how to do a background without swamping the figures etc. Of course this will all be in pen and ink which is the best medium for my kind of work – I can imagine your smile at my calling such scribbles 'work', but no matter. I am longing to get home again now, and expect I shall arrive next Saturday.

Yes Mrs K. has played the Polonaise; we found the right one without difficulty, and tho' she made some remarks about the hardness of it I at length persuaded her. Now, you know, I never flatter: so you may take it as solemn truth when I tell you that, if I admired your playing before, I understood its true value far better when I compared [it] with Mrs K. – by no means a contemptible craftsman. To hear the lovely galloping passages rendered correctly, even well, but without your own frank enjoyment of the work, your sympathy with the composer and your inimitable fire and abandonment (this sounds like an essay but I mean every word of it), was a revelation. You threw yourself into it, and forgot yourself in the composer: Mrs K sat there, amiable, complacent and correct, as if she were pouring out tea. Now, while they're not all as bad as she, still you alone of the people I have heard play set to the matter

78 Henry Seton Merriman, *The Sowers* (1896).

79 George Eliot (1819–80), the English novelist whose real name was Mary Ann Evans.

80 Samuel Taylor Coleridge, *Christabel and Other Poems* (1816); *The Rime of the Ancient Mariner* (1798).

properly. And for that reason, a piece, by you, if it were full of mistakes (tho' of course it wouldn't be) would be better than the same piece faultlessly played by – say, Hope Harding.[81] This is a rare gift of yours: you should yet do great things with it: you are a fool if you don't cultivate it. Perhaps, because you paint and read as well as play, you realize the imagination of a composer's mind perfectly, and can always bring out to a sensible (in the old sense of the word) listener anything at all that there is in the notes. Of course, all this is the praise of an amateur: but the praise of an honest amateur who has a genuine, tho' non-techniqual taste for music, is worth something at least.

I agree with you that the music of Lohengrin, so far as I know it is delightful: nor do I see what is wrong with the story, tho' of course the splendid wildness of the 'Ring'[82] must be lacking. On the whole, however, I am not sure that any music from it I know, is not perhaps cast in a lower mould than 'Parsifal'[83] & the 'Ring'. Although, indeed the prelude – which you wouldn't listen to when I played it – is quite as fine I think as that from 'Parsifal'.

What is your opinion of W. Jaffe – little Vee-Lee?[84] He did one thing for which he can never be forgiven – dropping in and staying till eleven on the first night of my brother's leave. The Hamiltons came over on another, so we had only one evening alone together in peace and comfort. On the whole, tho', he is a decent crittur, I suppose. Have you ever heard their gramaphone? I wonder what its like.

Which reminds me, did you hear the new Glenmachen record – a solo by the Russian base – Chaliapin[85] from 'Robert Le Diable'.[86] The orchestration is absolutely magnificent and the singing as good. I only wish I could afford 'the like of them', don't you?

---

81 i.e. Lewis's cousin, Mrs George Harding (*née* Charlotte Hope Ewart, 1882–1934).

82 Lewis loved all Richard Wagner's music, especially the *Ring of the Nibelung* cycle comprising *Das Rheingold* (*The Rhinegold*) first performed in 1869; *Die Walküre* (*The Valkyrie*), first performed in 1870; *Siegfried* and *Götterdämmerung* (*The Dusk of the Gods*), both performed for the first time in 1876.

83 *Parsifal*, an opera by Wagner, first performed in 1882.

84 William Jaffé, a friend of Albert Lewis, was the son of Sir Otto Jaffé who was twice Lord Mayor of Belfast.

85 Chaliapin was Fyodor Ivanovich Shalyalpin (1873–1938) who was generally considered the greatest singer of his day.

86 *Robert le Diable*, an opera by Giacomo Meyerbeer, was first performed in 1831.

I shan't write again this term now – jolly glad it's so near the end.
Yours
Jack

TO HIS FATHER (LP V: 9):

[Gastons]
Moon Day.
(A good codotta that.)
[28 July 1915]

My dear Papy,

I was very glad to get both your letters, and sorry if I worried you at a busy moment. Willie's absence must be a great discomfort, and of course I shall understand if letters are short or overdue just at present. No. A registered letter is no equivalent to 'speaking sharply' to one, and I am therefore in no need to the German gentleman's remorse – or 'again-bite' to be Teutonic. But at sixteen we will do much for excitement, a new experience. 'What' said I to myself 'tho' the shades of Plato and Sophocles wait upon my pleasure, the treasures of Rome, the brilliance of France, the knowledge of Germany attend my nod? I am out of the world here. While the great war of all histories, nations and languages is waged hard by, shall I remain like a dormouse, inactive, apathetic. A thousand times no', (as a friend of yours in Punch said on a memorable occasion), 'I will have excitement I will taste of new experiences, soul-stirring adventures' – and gripping my hat with a cry of 'D'audace et toujours d'audace'[87] I rushed out into the night and – sent a registered letter!

I don't know that there is any news here: that Macmullen girl, the theatrical lady, is staying here just at present. The summer here is one of the worst Kirk remembers, being very wet and making a special point of raining whenever the poor people are trying to mow or make hay. Fortunately the amount of corn we grow at home is insignificant as regards the country's needs. All the same, at a time like the present every little counts, and if this sort of thing is going on all over England it is rather a pity.

(Later on.) I have spent a ghastly evening being used as a lay figure by Miss Macmullen for bandages – as she is going to volunteer to something or other. I have been treated successively for a broken arm, a

87 '"Boldness and ever more boldness" from G. J. Danton in *Le Moniteur* (4 September 1792).'

sprained ankle, and a wound in the head. This, with the adjoining complement of pins, small talk etc., is a good night's work. I can now sympathise with your attitude towards the excellent game of 'hair cut or shaved'. Ah well, I suppose half an hour's codotta with some bits of lint is not a great sacrifice to the war. Still, I am really too exhausted to write any longer, and everyone is going to bed.

your loving
son Jack

Jack arrived in Belfast on 31 July and was there for the next eight weeks. Mr Kirkpatrick expected him to continue with some work, and he wrote to him on 17 August saying:

> *I suggest you should order...the following: Plato:* The Phaedo, *if you have not got it. Demosthenes:* De Corona. *Tacitus:* The Annals. *Aeschylus:* The Agamemnon...*I expect you are browsing at present on the pastures of general literature, and this of course is as it should be. If however you find English too easy and sigh for more worlds to conquer, I recommend the perusal of any German book you may happen to come across.* (LP V: 12)

During this time Lewis added six more poems to his 'Metrical Meditations of a Cod', at least two of which are included in his Collected Poems.

TO HIS FATHER (LP V: 128–9):

[Gastons
17? September 1915]

My dear Papy,

After a week of mutual waiting for a letter, I suppose it is my duty to take up the pen. Things have been so developing here in various ways that I have not really had time to settle down. A wonderful thing has happened – yesterday I got a fellow pupil![88] It is a nephew of Mrs. Howard Ferguson's who is to come and read with Kirk for the paymaster's

88 The fellow pupil was Terence Forde (1899–?), the ward of Mrs Howard Ferguson. He had been brought up in Manchester, and after moving to Ireland he attended Campbell College, from which school he was sent to Mr Kirkpatrick.

department of the navy, and is about my own age. Of course it is just a bit of crumpled rose leaf to have this inroad, but as he will spend nearly all his time at Leatherhead taking special classes for chemistry and solid mathematics – whatever that name of terror may mean – one cannot complain. He seems a decent poor creature, though of course not wildly interesting. Mrs. Ferguson came down with him on Saturday and went away the same evening. I suppose you have met her? I thought she was exceedingly nice, and was interested to hear all the Lurgan and Banbridge gossip which Mrs. K's questions called forth, until Kirk could stand it no longer and broke in with a fifteen minute lecture on the Budget.

The boy himself was at Campbell before he came here, and I can still remember enough to pick up acquaintance in common and to criticise 'the old place'. I hear to my surprise that Joey[89] is a 'knut' cricketer in his House Eleven: one never hears these tit-bits at home.

It is a good deal warmer here than in Ireland and my cold is consequently getting better – you will be relieved to hear. Kirk is still going strong and Bookham is looking its prettiest. Any sign of the new overcoat yet? But of course it will not really be needed till much later in the year. Tell me too if you hear anything from W. I must now stop and go to bed, which I feel justified in doing because I am one up on you in the way of letters.

your loving
son Jack

P.S. Don't forget to tell me when you write, how that cold of yours is. Jack.

TO ARTHUR GREEVES (W/LP V: 21–2):

[Gastons
5 October 1915]

My dear Galahad,

I can't really see why you have any more right to grouse at my not writing than I at you, but we will let it pass. And in the meantime, what

89 This is Jack's cousin, Joseph 'Joey' Tegart Lewis. See note 21 to letter of 27 November 1908. Joey entered Campbell College, Belfast, in 1906, and was still a pupil there. See **The Lewis Family** in the Biographical Appendix.

do you think? It is a bit thick when one has fled from Malvern to shun one's compeers in the seclusion of Surrey wilds, to be met by a damned fellow pupil of my own age – and sex![90] Isn't it the limit? Moreover he is a hopeless fellow with whom I despair of striking up any friendship that can be at all amusing – you know, the usual sort with absolutely no interest in any of the things that matter. Luckily, however he spends the greater part of his time taking special classes at Leatherhead, so that I still have my afternoon walk alone. Indeed, I suppose it is easier to put up with one philistine at Bookham than with five-hundred at Malvern, but still, the thing is a nuisance on which I had not counted.

I wish indeed that I had been with you at Portrush, of which your description sounds most attractive. I once visited Dunluce Castle years ago when I was staying at 'Castle Rock', but being a kid did not of course appreciate it as much as I would now.

It is very annoying that after waiting all the holydays for those Columbia records, I should just manage to miss them: mind you tell the girl to send me on the monthly lists of Zono, Columbia & H.M.V. I noticed by the way that the Zono list contains an attractive record with the 'Seranade' and 'Church Scene' from Faust.[91] Do you remember the latter – that magnificent duet outside the Church, with organ accompaniment where Gretchen is hunted about the stage with Mephisto behind her? You must hear it and tell me your impressions.

I thought you would enjoy 'Shirley'. Don't you see now what I meant when I said that love, apart from physical feelings, was quite different to friendship? If not you must have a brain like a cheese. There is not really much resemblance either between Louis & Gordon or Shirley & Lily. Can you imagine G. behaving to Lily the way Louis does at times to Shirley? I am afraid that, much as I like him, G. hasn't got it in him. Lily of course is not unlike S., but not so much of a 'grande dame', if you know what I mean.[92] When I said that K.[elsie Ewart] was like a valkyrie I meant of course in her appearance – or rather in her open-air appearance. When however you see her in artificial light, both in clothing & natural colouring she is like some thoughtful, exquisite piano piece of Chopin's – you'd know which better than I.

---

90 i.e. Terence Forde.

91 i.e. the opera by Charles Gounod.

92 The comparison is between Louis and Shirley, characters in Charlotte Brontë's *Shirley*, and Gordon Ewart and Lily Greeves who were to be married on 14 December 1915.

By the way, tell your sister that I have already written to thank her for the boot-bags, and that when the love she says she's sending arrives I will write and thank her for it too.

I have been reading the 'Faerie Queen' in Everymans both here and at home ever since I left you and am now half way thro' Book II.[93] Of course it has dull and even childish passages, but on the whole I am charmed, and when I have made you read certain parts I think you will appreciate it too.

Talking about poetry, if you have not done so already, go over to Little Lea and borrow Swinburne's 'Poems and Ballads' 2nd Series at once. Read 'The Forsaken Garden', 'At Parting' (I think that is the name, it begins 'For a day and a night love stayed with us, played with us')[94] 'Triads' 'The Wasted Vigil' and 'At a month's End'. The latter especially you must read from end to end as a commentary on the love parts of 'Shirley', only that in this case the man who tried to tame some such fierce & wonderful character failed instead of succeeding. Then you will relish all the lovely verses at the end, especially that beginning 'Who strives to snare in fear and danger / Some supple beast of fiery kin'.[95] Then tell me your impressions. Hope this hasn't bored you.

I am jolly glad to hear that you are at last starting with Dr Walker[96] and shall expect to find great 'doings' in your musical line when I come back. Write soon and don't forget the catalogues

Yours

Jack

TO ARTHUR GREEVES (W):

[Gastons

12 October 1915]

My dear Galahad,

I am frightfully annoyed. I have just been to Guildford to hear Ysaye[97] and enjoyed it no more than I do the barking of a dog. The

---

93 Edmund Spenser, *The Faerie Queene*, 2 vols., Everyman's Library [1910].

94 Swinburne, *Poems and Ballads*, op. cit. 'At Parting' begins: 'For a day and a night Love sang to us, played with us.'

95 The lines from 'At a Month's End' are: 'Who snares and tames with fear and danger/ A bright beast of a fiery kin.'

96 Dr Lawrence Walker of Belfast was a teacher of music.

97 Eugène Ysaÿe (1858–1931), the Belgian violinist and conductor whose style of playing was considered unconventional and highly original.

apalling thought comes over me that I am losing by degrees my musical faculty: already, as you know, I cannot enjoy things that used to drive me wild with delight, and I suppose in the course of time I shall become absolutely insensible – just like Henry Stokes or my brother or anyone else. There was also a woman called Stralia, a soprano, who sang one lovely thing from 'Madame Butterfly'[98] and lots of stuff I didn't understand. I havenot the faintest idea what Ysaye played, and I never want to hear it again. I listened as hard as I could, shutting my eyes and trying in vain to concentrate my attention, but it was all just meaningless sound. Of course violin solos were never much in my line but even so, it should not be so bad as this. Now I suppose I have lost your sympathy forever and am set down – who knows but it may be rightly – as a Goth and philistine. But it really is torture to feel things going out of you like that. Perhaps after all, the taste in music developed by a gramaphone is a bad, artificial, exotic one that dissapears after a certain point ... The Lord knows!

You ask me how I spend my time, and though I am more interested in thoughts and feelings, we'll come down to facts. I am awakened up in the morning by Kirk splashing in his bath, about 20 minutes after which I get up myself and come down. After breakfast & a short walk we start work on Thucydides – a desperately dull and tedious Greek historian[99] (I daresay tho', you'd find him interesting) and on Homer whom I worship. After quarter of an hour's rest we go on with Tacitus till lunch at 1. I am then free till tea at 4.30: of course I am always anxious at this meal to see if Mrs K. is out, for Kirk never takes it. If she is I lounge in an arm chair with my book by the fire, reading over a leisurely and bountiful meal. If she's in, or worse still has 'some people' to tea, it means sitting on a right angled chair and sipping a meagrue allowance of tea and making intelligent remarks about the war, the parish and the shortcomings of everyones servants. At 5, we do Plato and Horace, who are both charming, till supper at 7.30, after which comes German and French till about 9. Then I am free to go to bed whenever I like which is usually about 10.20.

As soon as my bed room door is shut I get into my dressing gown, draw up a chair to my table and produce – like Louis Moore, note book

98 *Madame Butterfly*, an opera by Giacomo Puccini, was first performed in 1904.

99 Thucydides (c. 460–c. 400 BC) wrote a history of the Peloponnesian War which is one of the greatest historical works of all time. One of its most noteworthy passages is Pericles's Funeral Oration over the Athenians who had died in the war.

and pencil. Here I write up my diary for the day, and then turning to the other end of the book devote myself to poetry, either new stuff or polishing the old. If I am not in the mood for that I draw faces and hands and feet etc for practice. This is the best part of the day of course, and I am usually in a very happy frame of mind by the time I slip into bed. And talking about bed, I wish you and your family would have the goodness to keep out of my dreams. You remember my telling you that I dreamed that you and Lily & I were walking along North Street when I saw a ghost but you & she didn't? That was at Port Salon. Well, last night found the same 3 walking somewhere in town, only this time the place had been captured by the Germans. Everyone had escaped and we were hurrying along in terror through the deserted streets with the German soldiers always just round the corner, going to catch us up and do something terrible. Dreams are queer things.

You ask me whether I have ever been in love: fool as I am, I am not quite such a fool as all that. But if one is only to talk from firsthand experience on any subject, conversation would be a very poor business. But though I have no personal experience of the thing they call love, I have what is better – the experience of Sapho,[100] of Euripides of Catullus[101] of Shakespeare of Spenser of Austen of Bronte of, of – anyone else I have read. We see through their eyes. And as the greater includes the less, the passion of a great mind includes all the qualities of the passion of a small one. Accordingly, we have every right to talk about it. And if you read any of the great love-literature of any time or country, you will find they all agree with me, and have nothing to say about your theory that 'love=friendship+sensual feelings'. Take the case I mentioned before. Were Louis & Shirley ever friends, or could they ever be? Bah! Don't talk twaddle. On the contrary, the mental love may exist without the sensual or vice versa, but I doubt if either could exist together with friendship. What nonsense we both talk, don't we? If any third person saw our letters they would have great 'diversion' wouldn't they?

In the meantime, why have no catalogues reached me yet? By the time this reaches you, you will I hope have read your course of Swinburne I mapped out, and can send me your views. So glad you too like the

100 Sappho (b. c. mid-7th cent. BC), a poetess born in Lesbos. Only 12 of her poems have survived.

101 Gaius Valerius Catullus (c. 84–c. 54 BC), one of the most versatile of Roman poets, who wrote love poems, elegies and satirical epigrams with equal success.

'Faerie Queen', isn't it great? I have been reading a horrible book of Jack London's called 'The Jacket'.[102] If you come across [it] anywhere, don't read it. It is about the ill-treatment in an American prison, and has me quite miserabl. Write soon.

Yours

Jack

TO HIS FATHER (LP V: 24–5):

[Gastons]

Postmark: 22 October 1915

My dear Papy,

The state of our library at Leeborough must be perfectly apalling: how such a collection of ignorances and carelessnesses could have got together on the shelves of our room passes my comprehension. As well, where is the beautiful quarto edition? What is a quarto? I don't believe you have the vaguest idea, and should not be surprised if the edition in question is merely an 8vo., (– no, that doesn't mean 'in eight volumes', though I too thought so once.) In fact there are a whole lot of things in your letter that I don't understand. What are 'vagrom' men might I ask? I have consulted all the dictionaries at Gastons and failed to find the word. 'But enough of these toys' as Verulam remarks.[103]

Kirk has just called my attention to an amusing article in the papers which I daresay you have read.[104] It appears that a Radley boy who had been allowed home for a day to see his brother who was going to the front, overstayed his leave by permission of his father, and on his return was flogged by the Head. If you remember, there was good reason because it turned out that the journey was out of joint or something, so that the fellow couldn't get home and back in time. Moreover, the father sent a telegram. Well the boy and the father have brought an action, and now we come to the point. One of the witnesses called by the schoolmaster to defend his conduct was a certain Canon Sydney Rhodes James, sometime headmaster of Malvern. As Kirk points out, it is amusing to see that he alone was picked out of all England to defend a pedagogue from the boy he had flogged: so far he 'outshone millions tho' bright'.

102 Jack London, *The Jacket* (1915).

103 This is from the essay by Francis Bacon referred to in the letter of 13 May 1915. Bacon was the Baron of Verulam.

104 See *The Times* (21 October 1915), p. 4 and (22 October 1915), p. 5.

Unfortunately the judge, who I fancy must have known his man, decided that Jimmy's theories of school management would be off the point, and did not call him. The evidence I suppose would have consisted in an illuminated discourse on 'the young squirm's' conduct.

The chief amusement here is the Zeppelins. We saw the bombardment of Waterloo station going on that last time they were here: at least that is what we were told it was. All you could see were some electrical flashes in the sky caused by the bombs, and of course it was too far away to hear anything. Now that people know that they are about, we are always hearing them going over at nights, but it usually turns out to be a motor byke in the distance. Once we heard the noise of the thump of a hammer at Guildford, and people said that was the dropping of bombs, but I have my doubts.

Isn't Jimmy good this week in Punch? I am glad to hear that Lily and Gordon are not going out of the neighbourhood, as they would make a bad gap. The sponge etc. must be having a long journey, but I hope they are like the mills of the Gods.[105]

your loving
son Jack

TO HIS FATHER (LP V: 31):

[Gastons]
Postmark: 11 November 1915

My dear Papy,

As sole companion on a desert island, as a friend to talk to on the night before one was hanged, or, as in the present case, for a helper when one lies stunned in a muddy road, whom would we choose rather than Bill Patterson?[106] Ah! Bill. He is a joy for ever, is he not? – to himself. When you talk about the collision as you do, I take it to be mostly codotta: if I thought otherwise, I would be seriously alarmed. In any case, you must not allow this tendency to dissipation to run away with

105 'Though the mills of God grind slowly, yet they grind exceedingly small.' Friedrich von Logau, *Sinnegedichte* (1654), 'Desz Dritten Tausend, Andres Hundert' no. 24 (translated by Henry Wadsworth Longfellow).

106 William H.F. 'Bill' Patterson, the son of William Hugh Patterson (1835–1918) who wrote *A Glossary of Words in Use in the Counties of Antrim and Down* (1880), was addicted to puns and was a recognized Strandtown wit. He published a volume of verse under the initials W.H.F., *Songs of a Port* (Belfast, 1920).

you at a time like the present when one sees the angel of death flapping his wings from the shores of Totting to hordes that dwell in the skirts of the rising sun, and things of that sort – instead of which, you go about indulging in debauches at the dentist's. Is this not worthy of the severest censure?

I see no reason to congratulate the Times on its recruiting supplement in any way, nor the country on the necessity (which it allows to remain) for such publications being made. I am afraid that we must admit that Kipling's career as a poet is over. The line to which you refer is the merest prose, as well as very bad metre. And why is the word 'stone' introduced, except to rhyme with o'erthrown?[107] On the other hand, if his career be over, we may say that it is creditably over, and if I, for one, had such a record of poetry behind me I should be well satisfied. I conceive that Kipling is one of those writers who has the misfortune in common with Longfellow, of always being known and liked for his worst works. I mean his poetry to the agaraioi means merely the Barrack Room Ballads,[108] which, however original and clever, are not poetry at all. 'The brightest jewels in his crown' as the hymnal would say, are, I suppose, 'The Brushwood boy',[109] 'Puck of Pook's Hill', 'The jungle book' and various of the scattered poems, among which I should place first the dedication piece about 'my brother's spirit' and 'gentlemen unafraid'. 'The last rhyme of true Thomas', 'The first and last Chantry' and several others which I forget.[110] He is less of a scholar than

---

107 Included in *The Times* of 3 November 1915 was *The Times Recruiting Supplement*, on page 16 of which was a poem Rudyard Kipling composed for the occasion. The first verse of the poem, 'For All We Have and Are', is as follows:

For all we have and are,
For all our children's fate,
Stand up and meet the war,
The Hun is at the gate!
Our world has passed away
In wantonness o'erthrown.
There is nothing left to-day
But steel and fire and stone.

108 Rudyard Kipling, *Barrack-Room Ballads and Other Verses* (1892).

109 'The Brushwood Boy' is one of the stories in Kipling's *The Day's Work* (1908).

110 The 'dedication piece' which refers to 'my brother's spirit' and 'gentlemen unafraid' is the dedication poem to Wolcott Balestier in *Barrack-Room Ballads*; 'The Last Rhyme of True Thomas', 'The First Chantey' and 'The Last Chantey' are found in *The Seven Seas*.

Newbolt,[111] but he is also freer from conventional and obvious sentiment: his metres are often too clever. With it all however, I think he will survive, if any of the present crew do. Except Yeats, I don't know of any other who is in the least likely to.

I myself have been reading this week a book by a man named Love Peacock, of whom I had not heard, but who seems to be famous. He was a contemporary of Lamb, Hazlitt, Byron etc., and an intimate friend of Shelly. The book is a farcical novel called 'Headlong Hall',[112] and very amusing.

As to the overcoat, I agree with you that it will be better to leave the business till the holydays, as the effort to make Bamford understand anything at all under any circumstances whatever is by no means child's play. I hope you have not any urgent desire for the other one. According to my computations the half term was about three days ago. As I must now go and add to the glories of Greek literature by a very choice fragment of Attic prose, good night.

your loving son,
Jack

TO HIS FATHER (LP V: 22):

[Gastons
15? November 1915]

My dear Papy,

The youth's name is Terence Ford, and I know nothing more about him except that he lived in the suburbs of Manchester during his father's lifetime. As I never see anything of him except on Sundays – for he spends all day at Leatherhead – I am quite reconciled to his presence and even enjoy hearing his talk about Campbell, which makes me by contrast more sensible of my present good luck. By the way, who is your friend Lord Bacon? I don't remember any such name in English literature: in fact the name Bacon itself never occurs, to my knowledge, except as the family name of Lord Verulam. (Ahh! A body blow, eh?).

I am sorry to hear about your gums. Are you sure your dental artist is a competent man? A change of advisers often works wonders in medical

111 Sir Henry John Newbolt (1862–1938) was educated at Clifton College and Corpus Christi College, Oxford. He is remembered particularly for his nautical ballads published in *Admirals All and Other Verses* (1897).

112 Thomas Love Peacock, *Headlong Hall* (1816).

matters. I always envy the Chinese for their excellent arrangement of paying the doctor while in health and, on falling ill, ceasing it until a cure has been effected. Perhaps you might suggest such an arrangement to the dentist.

I am still busy with my 'heavy winged Pegasus' as you call Spenser, and still find him delightful. He is a very lotus land, a garden of Proserpine to people who like pure romance and the 'stretched metre of an antique song'.[113] You should give him another trial some time, though not in our abridged edition which leaves out a lot of valuable stuff. I have also been reading in library copies, Schopenhauer's 'Will and idea',[114] and Swinburne's 'Erectheus' which is another tragedy on Greek lines like 'Atalanta',[115] though not so good in my opinion. Schopenhauer is abstruse and depressing, but has some very interesting remarks on the theory of music and poetry.

Kirk, I need hardly say, is strong on him, and will talk on the subject for hours – by the way, the real subject to get him on just now is the Mons angels.[116] You should drop him a cue in your next letter: you know – 'a man was telling me the other day that he had seen with his own eyes' or something of the kind. And while we are on the subject of the war, I am sure you have noticed the excellent blank verse poem in this week's 'Punch' entitled 'Killed in action'.[117] I read it with great pleasure, and thought at the time that it would appeal to you.

The weather here is a perfect joke, warmer than July, bright sunshine and gentle breezes. Personally I have had quite enough summer, and should not be sorry to bid it goodbye, though Kirk persistently denounces this as a most unnatural state of mind. I am rather curious to know what the new case of books at home contains. Tell Arthur if you see him, that there is a letter owing to me.

---

113 William Shakespeare, Sonnet 17 (1609).

114 Arthur Schopenhauer, *The World as Will and Idea* (1883–6).

115 Algernon Charles Swinburne, *Erechtheus* (1876); *Atalanta in Calydon* (1865).

116 The Battle of Mons, on the Western Front, began on 23 August 1914. For the whole of that day the British held the line against the Germans with greatly inferior numbers. A legend began within two weeks of the battle that an angel had appeared 'on the traditional white horse and clad all in white with flaming sword'. Facing the advancing Germans the angel 'forbade their further progress'. Martin Gilbert, *First World War* (1994), p. 58.

117 'Killed in Action' by R.C.L. is found in *Punch*, Vol. CXLIX (13 November 1915), p. 310.

your loving
son Jack

P.S. Was there any talk about Lord Bacon?

TO ARTHUR GREEVES (W/LP V: 23–4):

[Gastons
16 November 1915]

My Furious Galahad,

Horace has pointed out that if you buy an article after knowing all its defects, you have no right to quarrel with the seller if you are dissatisfied.[118] In the present case, since I told you how slack I was, and openly admitted that I could not promise to keep up a regular correspondance, you have no ground for grumbling if you find that I was speaking the truth. Should you, however, show any disposition to a brief exercise in that fascinating art, I have another excellent excuse: your letters are always shorter than mine: so much so that if I remain silent for a week or so, my amount of letter-writing for the term will still be a good bit bigger than yours.

As a matter of fact I have really had nothing to say, and thought it better to write nothing than to try and pump up 'conversation' – in the philistine sense of the word. I have read nothing new and done nothing new for ages. I am still at the Faerie Queene, and in fact have finished the first volume, which contains the first three books. As I now think it far too good a book to get in ordinary Everyman's I am very much wondering what edition would be the best. Of course I might get my father to give me that big edition we saw in Mullans' for a birthday or Xmas present: but then I don't really care for it much. The pictures are tolerable but the print, if I remember, rather coarse (you know what I mean) and the cover detestable. Your little edition is very nice, but rather too small, and not enough of a library-looking book. How much is it, and what publisher is it by? I believe I have heard you say that it can be got in the same edition as your 'Odyssey', but then that is rather risky, because the illustrations might be hopeless. Write, anyway, and tell me your advice.

By the way those catalogues have never come yet; you might wake the girlinosborne's up. I hope you are right about my music not being a

---

118 Horace, *Epistles*, 2. 2. 17–19.

whim: could you imagine anything more awful than to have all your tastes gradually fade away? Not a bad subject for a certain sort of novel! And talking about music, how did you enjoy Ysaye:[119] you don't say in your letter. Yes: his brother did play when they were at Guildford: one of his things was a Liebestraum by Liszt, which I did appreciate to a certain extent. Mrs K. has got a new book of Grieg's with a lot of things in it that I am just longing to hear you play: the best is 'Auf den Bergen',[120] do you know it? A lovely scene on mountains by the sea (I imagine) and belled cattle in the distance, and the snow and pines and blue sky, and blue, still, sad water. There's a sort of little refrain in it that you would love. You must try and get hold of it.

Since finishing the first volume of Spenser I have been reading again 'The Well at the World's End', and it has completely ravished me. There is something awfully nice about reading a book again, with all the half-unconscious memories it brings back. 'The Well' always brings to mind our lovely hill-walk in the frost and fog – you remember – because I was reading it then. The very names of chapters and places make me happy: 'Another adventure in the Wood Perilous', 'Ralph rides the Downs to Higham-on-the-Way', 'The Dry Tree', 'Ralp reads in a book concerning the Well at the World's End'.

Why is it that one can never think of the past without wanting to go back? We were neither of us better off last year than we are now, and yet I would love it to be last Xmas, wouldn't you? Still I am longing for next holydays too: do you know they are only five weeks off.

By the way, I hope you have read 'your Swinburne' by now: anyway, when you go up to night to the room I know so well you must go and have a look at the 'Well at the W's End'. Good-night.

Yours
Jacks

119 This is Théo Ysaÿe (1865–1918), a pianist and composer, brother of Eugène.
120 'Auf' den Bergen' is a piano solo from Edvard Grieg's *Folkelivsbilleder* (1872).

TO HIS FATHER (LP V: 33):

[Gastons]
Postmark: 19 November 1915

My dear Papy,

By all accounts I have missed a treat by being lost in a Surrey village during these recent 'elemental disturbances' as the man in Bret Harte says – or was it Mark Twain? I love this sort of melodrama in weather, and a night when the cross-channel boats can't put out is just in my line. Of course we never have any real wind here. The winter however has now set in for good, and ever since Monday there has been a hard frost with a little snow. They have been glorious days all the same, mostly without a cloud in the sky, and a blazing sun that is bright and dazzling but quite cold – grand weather for walking. I love the afternoons now, don't you? There is something weird and desolate about the perfectly round orange coloured sun dropping down clear against a slatey grey sky seen through bare trees that pleases me better than all those cloud-cities and mountains that we used to see in summer over the Lough in the old days when the crows were going home. There never seem to be such sunsets latterly, do there?

Your friend Byron is not (I devoutly hope) immortal, though his poem about the Assyrians unfortunately is.[121] It shares that rather deluding longevity with about half a dozen other nightmares such as 'The village clock has just struck four', 'It was the schooner Hesperus', 'Under the spreading chestnut tree'[122] etc.: to which list one might add the poems of Ovid, the novels of Dickens, and the complete works of Wordsworth.

Many thanks for the welcome postal order. Talking about money, when you next write to Warnie you might remind him of a business matter which seems to be rather hanging fire, and tell him that I am not only like Barkis, willing but also waiting.[123] I have acted upon your excellent advice and at last written to Arthur. There is, as yet, no answer, but

---

121 George Gordon, Lord Byron, *The Destruction of Sennacherib* (1815), l. 1: 'The Assyrian came down like the wolf on the fold'.

122 'It was the schooner Hesperus' is l. 1 of Henry Wadsworth Longfellow's *The Wreck of the Hesperus* (1839); 'Under the spreading chestnut tree' is l. 1 of Longfellow's *The Village Blacksmith* (1839).

123 Barkis is the character in Charles Dickens' *David Copperfield* (1849–50) who sent a message by David to Clara Peggotty that 'Barkis is willin'.'

in the meantime I am investing in a very good suit of sackcloth reach-me-downs and a dozen bottles of best quality ashes.

I am glad that you have been installed as a member of the permanent staff of St. Mark's, and hope that 'the management will continue to secure the services of this enterprising artist during the forthcoming season' as the critics say in another department of life.[124] Yes: I am sure you will read the lesson as it has not been read in St. Mark's for some time, although perhaps as you say, you appreciate it too well to do it justice.

I am rather sorry to hear that I have missed an opera company at all, even if a bad one. I suppose it is useless to ask if you have patronized it – unless perhaps you have been compelled to by Uncle Hamilton on the look out for a free stall.

Hoping the results of the accident are disappearing, I am
your loving,
son,
Jack

TO HIS FATHER (LP V: 33–4):

[Gastons]
Postmark: 24 November 1915

My dear Papy,

I am sorry if my intentional silence on this subject in my last letter has proved, as it well might, rather provoking. You will readily understand however my motives for not wishing to take any unnecessary responsibility in so delicate a point. My position, like that of Gilbert's policeman, 'is not a happy one'.[125] While really anxious not to add in the least to your worries, at the same time I have no wish to do anything that Warnie would afterwards consider mean or unpleasant. Since however you ask my opinion, I reply that the new point of this being the last leave he is likely to get certainly makes a considerable difference from our point of view as well as from that of K. It is no business of mine to sit in judgement on Warnie's actions, and from that it seems to me to be hard luck that he should not get a few days at home with us both before settling down to – an indefinite period. Of course, as you say, he may be exaggerating, but I can only go upon the information that we get.

---

124 Albert had been appointed a church warden at St Mark's for the third time.

125 W.S. Gilbert and Arthur Sullivan, *The Pirates of Penzance* (1879), Act II.

You will understand I am sure that it is almost entirely for his sake that I should suggest such an arrangement. A few rather breathless days at home are not such a prize that I should make much exertion to secure them on my own account. In the absence of any authority from you I have judged it better not to make any mention of the matter to K. I hope this was right as I was not at all sure what I ought to do.

Believe me Papy I am very sorry indeed that we are all worrying you in this way. I have told you what I feel about it, but it remains really a question between you and him. I wish only to act, if possible, in a manner agreeable to you both, or failing that, to help *you* as far as I can and fall in with your wishes. I am not at all sure that I have said exactly what I wanted in this letter, or made my position perfectly clear. The post with your letter came in very late, just as I was going to bed, and I am writing this rather hastily. It cannot be posted till tomorrow morning (Wednesday). I hope your side is getting better, as also the teeth.

your loving
son Jack.

P.S. I need not of course point out to you that I should hardly like to have any of this letter quoted to Warnie – but of course you understand that. J.[126]

TO HIS FATHER (LP V: 36–7):

[Gastons]
Postmark: 4 December 1915

My dear Papy,
This has been a week of surprises. As Chaucer says,

'One might a book make of it in a story'[127]

126 Albert replied on 26 November 1915: 'I was glad to get your kind and sympathetic letter. I have done as you would wish. I have just written to Warnie to say that inasmuch as he says he will not get leave again until the end of the war, I have altered my decision and have written to you to hold yourself in readiness to leave when he calls. I shall write to K. and send your travelling money later. You may tell K. what is impending if you like' (LP V: 34).

127 Chaucer, *Troilus and Criseyde*, bk. V, l. 585: 'Men mighte a book make of it, lik a storie!'

On Thursday, having a faint suspicion that things wouldn't pan out as we expected, like Dido 'Omnia tuta timens'[128] I made no preparation beyond walking down to the station to meet what I judged a likely train (excuse the 'ation' jingle in that sentence). Today however, being convinced that Warnie would really turn up, I clothed myself in glad rags, packed my handbag and was just putting on my shoes preparatory to a second walk to the station when your telegram arrived. So we must expect him on Sunday week!

Kirk advised me to make an arrangement about meeting him in town, since it will be a Sunday and the trains therefore different, he might not find time to come down here between his arrival in London and the departure of the boat train. Entre nous I don't think such a plan desirable – I hate meeting people in strange places, and especially W., as we always manage to bungle things in between us. Nor indeed should it be necessary: on the last occasion, as you will remember, he crossed on a Sunday and found no difficulty. Moreover, even if you wrote to arrange it with him as soon as you get this, your letter would scarcely reach him in time, and he would certainly have no time in which to reply. If you think otherwise, of course you will arrange accordingly and let me know.

It has rained steadily for several days now, and in spite of the unsettled conditions I have been reading a lot. I have now finished the first volume of the Faerie Queene and am going through an English Literature of Kirk's by Andrew Lang.[129] Lang is always charming whatever he does – or 'did' as we must unfortunately say, and this book is very good. More a rambling record of personal tastes than a set handbook, but all the better for that reason. There has also been from the London Library a book called 'Springs of Helicon' by Mackail[130] – you know, Professor of Poetry at Oxford and *the* man on Wm. Morris. This is a study on Chaucer, Spenser and Milton and I enjoyed it immensely. He has quite infected me with his enthusiasm for the former, whom I must begin to read. He talks of other works, 'the legend of good women', 'Troilus and Cresseide' as being better than the tales.[131] It is from Troilus and

128 Virgil, *Aeneid*, IV, 298: 'Incline to fear where all was safe...'

129 Andrew Lang, *History of English Literature* (1912).

130 John William Mackail, *Springs of Helicon: A Study in the Progress of English Poetry from Chaucer to Milton* (1909); *The Life of William Morris*, 2 vols. (1899).

131 i.e. Chaucer's *Legend of Good Women* and *Troilus and Criseyde* are better than his most popular work, *The Canterbury Tales* (composed 1387–1400).

Cresseide that he quotes that priceless line to which I treated you on the first page: I think it is rather great, don't you?

There is also a 'Greek Literature' by Gilbert Murray,[132] the bad verse-translator, which I have read with dire anger, as he degrades Homer from a poet into a 'question' and prefers that snivelling metaphysician Euripides to Aeschylus.

I suppose the great wedding is over by now? Or shall W. and I be let in for it? I hope you have not let the news of the coming visit trickle through to the ears of the sociable ágoraîoi?[133] Thanks for the 'crowns for convoy', which I am sure will be quite sufficient.

your loving son,
Jack

Jack was home from 21 December 1915 until he returned to Great Bookham on 21 January 1916. Warnie was on leave from France, and Mr Lewis had both his sons home together.

132 Gilbert Murray, *A History of Ancient Greek Literature* (1897). Murray (1866–1957) was Regius Professor of Greek at Oxford 1908–36, and a distinguished translator of Greek plays.

133 People who frequent the agora (market place), i.e. the common people.

1916

Jack was at Little Lea when, on 8 January, The Times *published the Military Service Act, which was expected to come into effect soon. In a section concerning the 'Obligation of unmarried men to serve' it stated that included among those who would have to serve were: 'Every male British subject who, on the fifteenth day of August nineteen hundred and fifteen – (a) was ordinarily resident in Great Britain; and (b) had attained the age of eighteen years and had not attained the age of forty-one years; and (c) was unmarried or was a widower without children dependent on him' (p. 8).*

In a 'Service Act Proclamation' published in The Times *on 4 February 1916 King George V ordered that the Military Service Act come into operation on 10 February 1916. Even then, Jack had reason at this time to think he might not be required to serve.* The Times *of 8 January had published, along with the Military Service Act, notification of 'A Bill to make provisions with respect to Military Service in connection with the present war' (p. 8). 'Exemptions,' it declared, would include 'Men who are resident in Great Britain for the purpose only of their education or for some other purpose.'*

While the Military Service Act went into effect on 10 February, the question of exemptions for Irishmen was debated by the Government for many months, during which time Jack did not know whether he would qualify for exemption or not. By the time it was clear that exemption would *apply to him, and that he was not required to serve, he had decided that he should serve nevertheless.*

TO HIS FATHER (LP V: 48–9):

[Gastons]
Postmark: 31 January 1916

My dear Papy,

One of the small consolations that a long experience of the continual change from term to holidays and vice versa brings, is the ability to settle down at once. I feel now as if I had been here for several months and have quite got into the old routine again. Everything at Bookham is of course in statu quo – I believe it would still be a hundred years hence. It is beautiful spring weather, as it was at home when I left you, and if only one could have that matutinal cup of tea, life would have nothing more to offer.

I spent the afternoon last Saturday in town, at the Shaftesbury, where there was a matinée of Carmen:[1] the singing was very poor, especially our friend the bass, whose rendition – I fancy that is the correct term – of the Toreador song was a thing to make the angels weep. Carmen herself however was quite good, and the tenor tolerable, so that on the whole I might have fared worse. With the opera itself, apart from the performance, I was very pleased. Just about the right percentage of the tunes was (it ought to be 'was' not 'were' oughtn't it?) familiar to me, and the ones which I had not heard before 'discoveries'.

This afternoon I have been a long walk to a perfectly delightful village[2] that I had never found out before, and I wish you could see it. It is rather like some of the places described in the 'Upton Letters' only more so. One old house – a thing as thick as a cottage and a good deal longer than Leeborough, all built on different levels, bears the legend '1666'. The best things however are the dragons and other monsters on the roof. Another most excellent codotta is the White Horse where you can drink tea, and a parlour that was used in the coaching days, and has not, by the look of it, been furnished since. If only they would dust the butter it would be quite ideal.

The 'Faerie Queen' which I told Mullens to send here as soon as it came has now arrived, and I am very pleased with it. If a bill comes from Osbornes for those records, please send it on at once as I have a cheque of W's. made out (or whatever the phrase is) to T.E.Osborne to pay it withal. However, no bill ought to arrive as I am asking Arthur to tell the 'young person' to send it here. And by the by, talking about cheques, I am not sure whether I asked you to take the cheque out of my cash box in the little end room and turn it into money some time before next holidays. Would you please do this? Hoping you are carrying on all right.

your loving
son Jack

---

1 *Carmen*, an opera by Georges Bizet, first performed in 1875.
2 The village in question was Dorking.

TO ARTHUR GREEVES (LP V: 50–1):

[Gastons
1 February 1916]

Dear little Archie,

Oh Gods of friendship, has such devotion ever been witnessed as mine! I am just at the beginning of a heavenly new book, I am just at the end of a long day's work, and yet I spend my spare time in writing letters. I hope you duly appreciate the sacrifice of a fresh young heart offered up on the savage altar of[3] – well to get on.

On the Saturday[4] in London I wasted 7/6 on going to a matinee of Carmen. There was no one in the cast of whom I had heard before and no one whom I want to hear again. Carmen herself was tolerable, but the rest, especially the Toreador, were fiendish. With the opera too I was awfully disappointed, although there is certainly a lot of beautiful music in it – particularly in the preludes to the acts (oh, one thing was good – the orchestra: they played that intermezzo that I have exquisitely) and in the scene among the mountains. But one does get so sick of all the tedious melodrama, all the blustering orchestration, and sticky tunes of good old fashioned operas. Then too there are a pair of villains in it who have a ghastly resemblance in their clownings to that other pair in Fra Diavolo – do you remember those awful creatures? So on the whole I was very fed up with this world by the time I reached dear Bookham. I find – of course – my beloved fellow pupil.

Since then I have been cheered up by the arrival of my new 'Faerie Queen' in the red leather Everyman. I can't see why you so dislike this edition: and if you have noticed the effect that their backs have when two or three are together in a shelf I am sure you do really appreciate them. I have read a good chunk of this and have also re-read Jane Eyre from beginning to end – it is a magnificent novel. Some of those long, long dialogues between her and Rochester are really like duets from a splendid opera, aren't they? And do you remember the description of the night she slept on the moor and of the dawn? You really lose a lot by never reading books again.

The other book – which I am denying myself to write to YOU, yes YOU of all people – is from the library by Blackwood called 'Uncle Paul'.[5]

---

3 Algernon Charles Swinburne, *A Forsaken Garden* (1878): 'As a god self-slain on his own strange altar'.

4 29 January 1916.

5 Algernon Blackwood, *The Education of Uncle Paul* (1909).

Oh, I have never read anything like it, except perhaps the 'Lore of Proserpine'. When you have got it out of your library and read how Nixie and Uncle Paul get into a dream together and went to a primaeval forest at dawn to 'see the winds awake' and how they went to the 'Crack between yesterday and tomorrow'[6] you will agree with me.

It was most annoying not getting my new records before I came back, wasn't it? Tell the girlinosbornes – the next time you go to see Olive – to send the bill for them to my address here at once. I do hope my Caruso[7] 'E lucevan e stella'[8] is going to be a success. Talking about that thing, does it convey anything to you? To me it seems to be just abstract melody. The actual scene I believe is a man on the battlement of a castle writing a letter – but you have probably read Tosca in that beastly potted opera book.

I was interested in what you said about the 'Brut'.[9] You ought to get it in Everyman.

Yours
Jack

TO HIS FATHER (LP V: 51–2):

[Gastons
6? February 1916]

My dear Papy,

Thanks very much for the cheque, which I enclose, signed as you told me. I am afraid however that I must trouble you again: one of my pairs of shoes has finally given out 'beyond the hope of uttermost recall' and I want you please to get me a new pair, or else tell Annie to do so. The mysterious piece of paper which I am sending is a map of my foot so that the knave in the shop will know what size to give you. I am very sorry if this is a nuisance, and will take care next term to set out well equipped with hats, coats, shoes and other garments, like the men in the furnace.

---

6 ibid., ch. X, p. 130; ch. XIV, p. 182.

7 Enrico Caruso (1873–1921), Italian tenor who made his first public appearance in Naples in 1894, and whose powerful, wonderfully pure voice made him one of the greatest singers of the century.

8 'E lucevan le stelle'—'and the stars shone'— is a song from Giacomo Puccini's opera *La Tosca*, which was first performed in 1900.

9 Layamon (*fl.*1200), *Brut*. Lewis was referring to *Arthurian Chronicles, Represented by Wace and Layamon*, translated by Eugene Mason, with an introduction by Lucy Allen Paton, Everyman's Library [1912].

That business about Warnie's commission, though of course important in itself, is as you say a nice example of war office methods. If big things are managed in the same way as these small ones, it promises well for the success of the war doesn't it? Another thing also struck me: we have often wondered and laughed at some of the people who have commissions. It becomes even funnier when one reads the formula, 'reposing special trust and confidence in your loyalty, courage, and good conduct': we remember that the Jarvey[10] who drove the Colonel up to the office last time was one of those who hoped soon to enjoy this 'special trust and confidence.'

By the way, you should get that 'Spirit of Man', Bridge's anthology,[11] that everyone is talking about. Mrs. K. has it from the library at present: it is one of the prettiest little books I have seen for a long time, and there is a lot of good stuff in it. One 'nice point' is that the names of the authors are printed at the end of the volume and not under each piece: it is very amusing – and somewhat humiliating – to see how many you know.

This business about matriculation and enlisting is 'very tiresome', as the Mikado said.[12] Are you [sure] that it applies to those who are under age, and who are also Irish? If so, as you say, we must think it over together. Of course in dealing with such a point we must always remember that a period of something more than a year elapses between the time of joining up and one's getting any where near the front.[13] However, it can wait until we are together at Easter.

And now my dear parent, as the time alloted to correspondence is drawing to its close, I fear I must relinquish – or in other words it is time for Church. You will observe that this is one of those houses where we rise so early on Sundays that there is a long interval between breakfast and our Calvinistic exercises.

your loving son,
Jack

---

10 i.e. a hackney-coachman.

11 Robert Bridges, *The Spirit of Man: An Anthology in English and French From the Philosophers & Poets made by the Poet Laureate in 1915 & Dedicated by gracious permission to His Majesty the King* (1916).

12 W.S. Gilbert and Arthur Sullivan, *The Mikado* (1885), Act II.

13 The preliminary selections of persons to be conscripted were apparently going on at this time.

TO ARTHUR GREEVES (LP V: 53–4):

[Gastons
8 February 1916]

My dear Arthur,

You lucky devil! It makes me very envious to hear of all these good things going on at home while I am languishing in the wilds of Surrey.

I am surprised to hear that you never heard of Barkworth,[14] as I have seen his name in the musical part of the Times and other papers: I believe he is one of the promising musicians of the day – that is if there are ever going to be English musicians and an English school of opera. Personally I should have been very much interested to hear his 'Romeo and Juliet'. If the only fault is that it is blustering, you might say the same of the 'Flying Dutchman'[15] or the 'Valkyrie', mightn't you? What did poor Willie Jaffe think of it? (I suppose you mean him by W.J. –) Hardly in his line I should fancy. I am sure 'Pagliaci' and 'Cavalleria' were lovely, and I would especially like to have seen 'Rigoletto', because I know the plot.[16]

I quite agree with you that a gramophone spoils one for hearing opera: the real difficulty is to find for what a gramophone does not spoil one. True, it improves your musical taste and gives you opportunities of hearing things that you might otherwise never know: but what is the use of that when immediately afterwards it teaches you to expect a standard of performance which you can't get, or else satiates you with all the best things so that they are stale before you have heard them once on the stage? Or in other words, like everything else it is a disappointment, like every other pleasure it just slips out of your hand when you think you've got it. The most striking example of this is the holiday which one looks forward to all the term and which is over and gone while one is still thinking how best to enjoy it.

By all this you will gather that I am in a bad temper: well, so I am – that bloody little beast my fellow pupil has sneaked upstairs for a bath

---

14 John Edmund Barkworth (1858–1929) was an English composer educated at Rugby, Oxford and the Royal College of Music. His chief work, an opera based on Shakespeare's *Romeo and Juliet*, was first performed on 7 January 1916.

15 *Der Fliegende Hollander* ('The Flying Dutchman'), an opera by Richard Wagner (1843).

16 *I Pagliacci* (1892) is a short opera by Ruggiero Leoncavallo; *Cavalleria Rusticana* (1890) a short opera by Pietro Mascagni; and *Rigoletto* (1851) is an opera by Giuseppe Verdi.

and I can now hear him enjoying it and I know there will be no hot water left for me. They only raise hot water here about once a month.

However. Let us proceed: do you read Ruskin at all? I am sure you don't. Well I am reading a book of his at present called 'A joy for ever',[17] which is charming, though I am not sure you would care for it. I also still employ the week ends with the Faerie Queene. I am now in the last three books, which, though not much read as a rule, are full of good things. When I have finished it, I am going to get another of Morris' romances, or his translation of one of the sagas – perhaps that of Grettir the Strong.[18] This can be got either for 5/- in the Library edition (my 'Sigurd the Volsung'[19] one) or for 3/6 in the 'Silver Library' (like my 'Pearl Maiden').[20] Which would you advise?

By the way, why is your letter dated Wednesday? It has arrived here this evening – Tuesday – am I to understand that you posted it tomorrow, or that you have been carrying it about in your pocket for a week?

Isn't it awful about Harding? I hear from my father that Hope is going out.[21] I suppose that by this time the jeunes mariés have got into Schomberg.[22] Why are your letters always so much shorter than mine? Therefore I stop.

Yours,
Jack

17 John Ruskin, *The Political Economy of Art* (1857), the title of which was later changed to *A Joy for Ever.*

18 William Morris, *Grettir Saga: The Story of Grettir the Strong*, translated from the Icelandic by Eiríkr Magnússon and William Morris (1869).

19 William Morris, *Völsunga Saga: The Story of the Volsungs and Niblungs, with Certain Songs from the Elder Edda*, translated from the Icelandic by Eiríkr Magnússon and William Morris (1888).

20 Henry Rider Haggard, *Pearl Maiden* (1903).

21 Major George Harding, who was married to the former Charlotte Hope Ewart, had contracted double pneumonia in Sicily, where he had been sent to make the preliminary administrative arrangements for the transfer of a British Expeditionary Force to the Italian front. His wife was allowed to join him in Sicily, and she travelled overland alone via France and Italy.

22 The home of the newlyweds, Gordon and Lily Ewart.

TO HIS FATHER (LP V: 56–7):

[Gastons]
Postmark: 26 February 1916

My dear Papy,

'Well I calls it 'ard' as your friend used to say of the 'alf hour: I am accustomed, nay I am hardened to missing opera companies: but that I should be exiled in the wilds of England while Robin W. Gribbon and Lucius O'Brien[23] are visiting Belfast – this is too utterly all but. But why might I ask are these nonconformist canals reciting in the school house of Saint Mark?[24] What have they to do with us? Let them get behind us. Joking apart, one might get a 'running river of innocent merriment' out of their efforts, 'extremely stretched and conned with cruel pains'. Perhaps however you have your own reasons for reverencing the school house. Is it not the theatre of an immortal rendition of that 'powerful' role of Gesler,[25] and also of an immortal brick-dropping re an immortal preacher? There too the honey tongued tenor of Garranard – but we will draw a veil over the painful scene.

There is a certain symmetry of design in your list of books, a curiosa felicitas, a chaste eloquence and sombre pathos in the comments, 'See no. 40' and 'see no. 2' which I cannot but admire. I don't know how they have bungled it, but so long as I actually have two copies of the 'Helena' it will be all right, as Mullen's will make no difficulty about exchanging the unused one. If however the second copy exist (not exist*s*) only on paper – why there we have the sombre pathos.

I am rather surprised at your criticism on 'The Spirit of man', and consider the reference to 'rescuing' both otiose and in doubtful taste. Of course it must be read, not merely as an anthology, but in the light of its title and avowed purpose, and we must not be disappointed when we

---

23 Robin W. Gribbon of 'Ardvarna', Strandtown, was Arthur Greeves's cousin on his father's side. His son, Charles Edward Gribbon (1898–1938), achieved distinction as an artist. (Sir) Frederick Lucius O'Brien (1869–1974) was Arthur's cousin on his mother's side. He had been educated at the Friends' School, Lisburn, and Bootham School in York. He was the first chairman of the Northern Ireland Housing Trust, 1945–60, and during his life he held many civil and governmental positions in Belfast. He and Arthur often travelled together.

24 They were both Quakers.

25 He is referring to Gioacchino Rossini's opera, *Guillaume Tell*, first performed in 1829. The opera is based on Friedrich von Schiller's play, *William Tell* (1804). William Tell is arrested for failing to salute the Austrian hat which is set upon a pole, and compelled by Gesler to shoot at the apple which is placed upon his son's head.

find certain favourites left out because they could not rightly claim a place in such a scheme. In this sense indeed the book is rather an original work than a collection of poems: for just as the musician may weave together a symphony by using the melodies of others arranged to express himself, so I take it Bridges is here working out an idea of his own: and the medium he chooses – as one might choose marble and another chalk (which you know is deteriorating terribly) – is the collective poetry of his predecessors. Or indeed, if I am reading too much into him, this would be a plan for a better anthology than has yet been written. One thing in the book I admit is indefensible – the detestable translation from Homer, which, though you may hardly recognise it, is meant to be in the metre of 'Oh! let us try'. For this Bridges ought to get 'something with boiling oil'.[26]

After a January so warm and mild that one could almost have sat in the garden, we have suddenly been whisked back to winter. It has snowed all day today, and is freezing hard tonight on top of it. I am very sorry to hear what you tell me about Hope: as you say, it must be terribly lonely and trying for her out there, and I am afraid the patient brings a very second rate constitution to the struggle.

your loving son,
Jack

P.S. I forgot to say the list of books, with one exception, is correct. J.

TO ARTHUR GREEVES (W):

[Gastons
28 February 1916]
Monday

My dear Galahad,

I suppose that by this time there is wrath and fury against me: however, there is no excuse, and you must just thole, as they say.

I don't know what it is like with you, but for this last week we have had the most lovely snow here. There is no wind, so where the snow 'falleth, there shall it lie':[27] which means that when you walk through the

26 He means Robert Bridges is to blame because he translated the two pieces from Homer in *The Spirit of Man*.

27 Ecclesiastes 11:3: 'In the place where the tree falleth, there shall it be.'

woods every branch is laden like a Christmas tree, and the mass of white arranged in every fantastic shape and grouping on the trees is really wonderful. Don't you love to walk while it is actually snowing? I love to feel the soft, little touches on your face and see the country through a sort of haze: it is so exquisitly desolate. It reminds one of that scene in 'The Lore of Proserpine'.

Poor thing! I do like the way, because a fellow asks you to join a corps, that you complain about 'your troubles'. May you never do worse! It reminds me of the story of Wellesly and his rich friend: W. had been going on one of his preaching tours round the country, riding alone in all weather, being put in the stocks, insulted, & stoned by the mob, in the course of all which he stayed for a night at the luxurious mansion of the friend. During the evening, a puff of smoke blew out of the grate, whereupon the host exclaimed 'You see, Sir, these are some of the crosses which I have to bear!'[28] Indeed, however, I 'can't talk' as you would say, for of course I am an inveterate grumbler myself – as you, of all people have best reason to know.

By the way, do you know a series of rather commonplace little volumes at 1/6 each called the Walter Scott Library? I have just run across them: they are not particularly nice – though tolerable – but the point is that they sell some things I have often wanted to get: among others Morris' translation of the 'Volsunga Saga' (not the poem, you know, that I have, but a translation of the old Icelandic prose saga) which cannot be got in any other edition except the twelve guinea 'Works', of which you can't get the volumes separately.[29] If only the edition were a little decenter I'd certainly get it.

---

28 *The Works of John Wesley*, ed. Albert C. Outler, vol. 3 (1986), Sermon 108 'On Riches', para. 8: 'Nearly related to anger, if not a species of it, are *fretfulness* and *peevishness*. But are the rich more assaulted by these than the poor? All experience shows that they are. One remarkable instance I was a witness of many years ago. A gentleman of large fortune, while we were seriously conversing, ordered a servant to throw some coals on the fire. A puff of smoke came out. He threw himself back in his chair and cried out, "O Mr Wesley, these are the crosses which I meet with every day!" I could not help asking, "Pray, Sir John, are these the heaviest crosses you meet with?" Surely these crosses would not have fretted him so much if he had had fifty instead of five thousand pounds a year!' (pp. 526–7). The 'gentleman of large fortune' was Sir John Phillipps (c. 1701–64).

29 *The Collected Works of William Morris*, with introduction by his daughter May Morris, 23 vols. (1910–15). The *Works* were limited to 1,050 copies.

Perhaps you laugh at my everlasting talk about buying books which I never really get: the real reason is that I have so little time here – indeed only the week-ends as I spend all the spare time on week-days in reading French books, which I want to get more fluent in. However, I am now nearing the end of the 'Faerie Queene', and when that is done the Saturdays & Sundays will be free for something else. Really, whatever you say, you have much more time than I.

I wonder why Osborne's have sent no bill to me yet? I am not sure whether I asked you to give them my adress and tell them to send in the account or not: anyway, be a sport, and do so – AT ONCE. I have had a grisly dissapointment this week: Mrs K. said she was going away for a fortnight & I was gloating in the prospect of privacy & peace. But it has turned out a mare's nest. Ochone!

be good,
Jack

TO ARTHUR GREEVES (LP V: 58–9):

[Gastons
7 March 1916]
Tuesday

My dear Galahad,

I was very glad to get your interesting letter – which was fortunately longer than some of them – as I was beginning to wonder what had become of you; I think your 'lapse' this term puts you on a level with mine last, so that we can cry quits and admit that we are both sinners.

I have had a great literary experience this week. I have discovered yet another author to add to our circle – our very own set: never since I first read 'The well at the world's end' have I enjoyed a book so much – and indeed I think my new 'find' is quite as good as Malory or Morris himself. The book, to get to the point, is George Macdonald's 'Faerie Romance', *Phantastes*,[30] which I picked up by hazard in a rather tired Everyman copy – by the way isn't it funny, they cost 1/1d. now – on our station bookstall last Saturday. Have you read it? I suppose not, as if you had, you could not have helped telling me about it. At any rate, whatever

30 George MacDonald, *Phantastes: a Faerie Romance* (1858). Lewis was reading the Everyman's Library edition of 1915.

the book you are reading now, you simply MUST get this at once: and it is quite worth getting in a superior Everyman binding too.

Of course it is hopeless for me to try and describe it, but when you have followed the hero Anodos along that little stream to the faery wood, have heard about the terrible ash tree and how the shadow of his gnarled, knotted hand falls upon the book the hero is reading, when you have read about the faery palace – just like that picture in the Dulac book – and heard the episode of Cosmo, I know that you will quite agree with me. You must not be disappointed at the first chapter which is rather conventional faery tale style, and after it you won't be able to stop until you have finished. There are one or two poems in the tale – as in the Morris tales you know – which, with one or two exceptions are shockingly bad, so don't TRY to appreciate them: it is just a sign, isn't it, of how some geniuses can't work in metrical forms – another example being the Brontes.

I quite agree with what you say about buying books, and love all the planning and scheming beforehand, and if they come by post, finding the neat little parcel waiting for you on the hall table and rushing upstairs to open it in the privacy of your own room. Some people – my father for instance – laugh at us for being so serious over our pleasures, but I think a thing can't be properly enjoyed unless you take it in earnest, don't you? What I can't understand about you though is how you can get a nice new book and still go on stolidly with the one you are at: I always like to be able to start the new one on the day I get it, and for that reason wait to buy it until the old one is done But then of course you have so much more money to throw about than I.

Talking about finishing books, I have at last come to the end of the Faerie Queene: and though I say 'at last', I almost wish he had lived to write six books more as he hoped to do – so much have I enjoyed it. The two cantos of 'Mutabilitie' with which it ends are perhaps the finest thing in it, and if you have not done so already, you should read them whenever you have the time to spare.

I am now – by the same post – writing for a book called 'British Ballads' (Everyman)[31] in the chocolate binding of which I used to disapprove: so you see I am gradually becoming converted to all your views.

---

31 *British Ballads: English Literature for Schools*, ed. Arthur Burrell, Everyman's Library [1914].

Perhaps one of these days you may even make a Christian of me. Yes: I have at last heard from the girlinosbornes: but like the minstrel in Scott,

> *'Perhaps he wished the boon denied'*[32]

as the bill is rather a staggerer and my finances are not very blooming at present – I am thinking of sending it out to my brother to pay.

I well remember the glorious walk of which you speak, how we lay drenched with sunshine on the 'moss' and were for a short time perfectly happy – which is a rare enough condition, God knows. As Keats says 'Rarely, rarely comest thou, spirit of Delight'.[33] I do hope we shall have many more pleasant hours such as that the days are running in so fast now, and it makes me so sad to think that I shall have only two more sets of holidays of the good old type, for in November comes my 18th birthday, military age, and the 'vasty fields'[34] of France, which I have no ambition to face. If there is good weather and you get some days off next hols., we should go for some walks before breakfast – the feel of the air is so exquisite. I don't know when I can expect to come home.

Jack

TO HIS FATHER (LP V: 60–1):

[Gastons]
Postmark: 10 March 1916

My dear Papy,

'I wonder' said Demetrius, and so do I. You know it is a terrible thing for a young boy to get into the hands of a rascally old firm of solicitors to be cajoled into signing all sorts of mysterious documents. How do I know to what I have committed myself? Perhaps my three moors are being made over, or you are putting an entail on my little place in Rome. (What is an entail) Ha! Ha! The missing heir. Indeed the whole proceeding savours of the novelette: you must cut your moustache shorter and call yourself Richard or Rupert. However, I herewith enclose the enigmatic slip of paper, with the forged signature inked over 'avec d'empressement' (French language). By the way, I see that I have acknowledged £16-13-10. Well what became of this...this...business...this tea business?

---

32 Sir Walter Scott, *The Lay of the Last Minstrel* (1805), Introduction.

33 The lines are in fact from Shelley's 'Song' (1824).

34 William Shakespeare, *Henry V* (1600), Prologue, 12.

I hope you have read your Times Literary Supplement this week: do you see that the commonwealth of letters is the richer by a great new poet? Now let the stars retire for the sun has risen: let Hemans and M'K-itrick Ros[35] be silent, for Mr. Little has come! It is really too good to be missed. I love the fine impassioned address to the sea, as much greater than Tennyson's 'Break, break, break'[36] as that is than the one in the Prometheus, the one you will have noticed beginning

> *'Oh, wave! Thy clemency is open*
> *To shrewd suspicion'.*[37]

What melody! What masterly phrazing and gorgeous imagery! We may pass over such minor beauties as the lioness which becomes the 'formidable sultaness' and go on to the last piece which contains the gems about the 'golden brawn' of the sunrise, the 'various viands of the rainbow' and nature 'gorgeous, great, gratuitous'. Why this is a more exquisite song than the other about 'Presumption, pride, pomposity', though there is a certain likeness. This I suppose is the modern school that has got beyond Tennyson. Well perhaps they have: but I for one had sooner walk on the earth than soar on any Pegasus which bears such a disquieting resemblance to a rocking horse.

St. John's, the school at Leatherhead whither my fellow pupil is wont daily to repair for gentlemanly and vertuous discipline and schooling in the humane letters, has got an epidemic of influenza and is breaking up for the term. So I suppose we shall have our well beloved Ford more in evidence now. Tell Arthur to write. I am sorry to hear what you say about Grandmother: I feel that we ought to have seen more of her, but it was not easy.[38] Your loving,

son,
Jack

---

35 Two terrible poets. Mrs Felicia Dorothea Hemans (1793–1835) published her first volume of *Poems* when she was 15. Amanda McKittrick Ros (1860–1939), known as 'the World's Worst Writer', was the author of *Irene Iddesleigh* (1897) and *Poems of Puncture* (1915). It became a customary feature of Lewis's Inklings meetings at Magdalen College to bet that no one could read a passage from *Irene Iddlesleigh* without a smile.

36 Alfred, Lord Tennyson, *Break, Break, Break* (1842), ll. 1–2: 'Break, break, break, / On thy cold grey stones, O Sea'.

37 Philip Francis Little, *Thermopylae and Other Poems* (1916), reviewed as 'An Uncertain Voice' in *The Times Literary Supplement* (9 March 1916), p. 116.

38 Lewis's mother's mother, Mary Warren Hamilton (b. 16 December 1826) died on 22 March 1916. See **The Hamilton Family** in the Biographical Appendix.

TO ARTHUR GREEVES (LP V: 63–4):

[Gastons
14 March 1916]
(You ought to know the date.)

My dear Galahad,

It must have been a very old Everyman list on which you found 'Phantastes' as one of the new ones, since, to my knowledge, the copy I got had been on the bookstall for weeks. Everymans with us have gone up 1d. in the shilling: I suppose it is just the same at home? By the time you get this you will probably have finished Phantastes, so you must give me your verdict on it as a whole: when one has read a book, I think there is nothing so nice as discussing it with some one else – even though it sometimes produces rather fierce arguments.

I too am rather disappointed. The 'British Ballads' has come, and though I am awfully bucked with the edition – I can't think why I didn't appreciate it before. This must be a triumph for you – the reading matter is not nearly so good as I expected. For one thing, instead of being all made up of real old ballads as I hoped, it is half full of silly modern imitations and even funny ones. Don't you loathe 'funny' poetry? However, as it is not your style of book, I suppose I am boring you.

All the same, when you begin to write a letter you just go on babbling – at least I do – without thinking whether the person at the other end is interested or not, till you come to the last page and find that you haven't really said what you wanted to. But perhaps that sort of rambling is the right kind of letter. I don't know whether you personally write that way or not, but the result is charming, and you can't think how eager I am to see the atrocious but familiar scroll waiting for me on the hall table. And yet, every letter is a disappointment: for a minute or two I was carried back to your room at Bernagh – don't you remember rooms by their smells? Each one has its own – and seem to be talking to you, and then suddenly I come to the end and it's all only a little bit of paper in my hand and Gastons again. But come. We are being mawkish. I think you and I ought to publish our letters (they'd be a jolly interesting book by the way) under the title of lamentations, as we are always jawing about our sorrows. I gather it was that beastly girl in Mayne's who 'flared up' as you say. Aren't they rude in that place? I think we ought to start a movement in the neighbourhood to boycott them. Only we'd have to join in it ourselves, which would be a pity.

No: I have never yet seen Kelsie's book. I daresay she doesn't know that I take an interest in such things, and you are lucky in having a reputation as a connoisseur which makes you free of every library in Belmont – tho' there aren't very many to be sure. I am afraid our Galahad will be growing a very stodgy mind if he reads nothing but Trollope and Goldsmith and Austen. Of course they are all very good, but I don't think myself I could stand such a dose of stolidity. I suppose you will reply that I am too much the other way, and will grow a very unbalanced mind if I read nothing but lyrics and fairy tales. I believe you are right, but I find it so hard to start a fresh novel: I have a lazy desire to dally with the old favourites again. I think you'll have to take me in hand and set me a 'course' when I come home.

By the way what about the piano and the gramophone these days? We don't seem to talk of music so much now as we did: of course your knowledge on that subject is so much greater than mine that I can really only express a philistine's taste. Are you still going to Walker? For my part, I have found my musical soul again – you will be relieved to hear – this time in the preludes of Chopin. I suppose you must have played them to me, but I never noticed them before. Aren't they wonderful? Although Mrs K. doesn't play them well, they are so passionate, so hopeless, I could almost cry over them: they are unbearable. I will find out the numbers of the ones I mean and we will have a feast next holidays.

By the way, you speak in your last letter of the difference between music and books: I think (to get back to an old argument) it is just the same difference as between friendship and love. The one is a calm and easy going satisfaction, the other a sort of madness: we take possession of one, the other takes possession of us: the one is always pleasant the other in its greatest moments of joy is painful. But perhaps I am rating books and friendship too low, because poetry and great novels do sometimes rouse you almost as much as music: the great love scenes in Shirley for instance, or the best parts of Swinburne etc.

I am sorry I always make the mistake about your address. Hullo – I've done it again.

Yours,

Jack

TO ARTHUR GREEVES (LP V: 64–5):

[Gastons
21 March 1916]

My dear Galahad,

So here we are at the weekly letter, and very glad I am too; but Heavens! – how the weeks run on don't they? While I was at Malvern I used to count the days and long for the end of term, so of course time crawled; now-a-days when I am quite comfortable the whole thing goes on far too quickly. And it's all so many days, months etc., not of the term or the year, but of one's life – which is tiresome. 'Help!' I hear you muttering, 'Is he going to moralize for four pages?' (Cheer up, I'll try to hold it in.)

I'm awfully bucked to hear that you think the same about Phantastes as I, though if you only began to enjoy it in the eleventh chapter, you must have missed what I thought were the best parts – that is to say the forest scene and the faery palace – or does that come after chapter XI? You will gather that the book is upstairs and that I am too lazy to go and get it. I hope that by this time you have bought 'Sir Gibbie'[39] and will be able to advise me on it. Some of the titles of his other books are, to me at least, even more alluring than the one you quote: for instance 'At the back of the north wind'.[40]

Isn't it funny the way some combinations of words can give you – almost apart from their meaning – a thrill like music? It is because I know that you can feel this magic of words AS words that I do not despair of teaching you to appreciate poetry: or rather to appreciate all good poetry, as you now appreciate some. This is however off the point: what I meant to say was that lots of his titles give me that feeling. I wish there were more in Everymans, don't you?

Talking about Everymans, do you know what their 1/6 binding is like? I can't remember whether you have anything in it or not, but I have been thinking of trying it, so tell me what you know on the subject. What? you ask, still new books? Well really the length of the Faerie Queene was a godsend, because so long as I turned to it every week-end with the regularity of clockwork I could keep my money in my pockets: now however the temptation to get a nice new book for the longed for Sunday rest is overwhelming.

---

39 George MacDonald, *Sir Gibbie* (1879).

40 George MacDonald, *At the Back of the North Wind* (1871).

I am glad to hear that you have moved into Lily's room as I think you – or 'we' shall I say in selfishness – will be more comfortable there: at the same time I have a sort of affection for the old one where we have had such good times: we should call it 'joyous garde'.[41] Still, I am longing to find myself in your new quarters with all the old talk, the old music, and the old fingering of rich, friendly books.

You know, Galahad, that though I try to hide it with silly jokes that annoy you, I am very conscious of how unfair our friendship is, and how you ask me over continually and give me an awfully good time, while I hardly ever bring you to us: indeed though he is a good father to me, I must confess that he – my father – is an obstacle. I do hope you understand? You know how I would love if I could have you any time I liked up in my little room with the gramophone and a fire of our own, to be merry and foolish to our hearts content: or even if I could always readily accept your invitations without feeling a rotter for leaving him alone. I don't know why I've gone off into this discussion, but perhaps it is just as well. Indeed the only thing to be done is to get my father married as quickly as may be – say to Mary Bradley. Or lets poison old Stokes and give him the widow. In which case of course our imagined snuggery in the little end room would be brightened up by a charming circle of brothers and sisters in law.

I know quite well that feeling of something strange and wonderful that ought to happen, and wish I could think like you that this hope will some day be fulfilled. And yet I don't know: suppose that when you had opened the door the Ash had REALLY confronted you and turning to fly, you had found the house melting into a haunted wood – mightn't you have wished for the old 'dull' world again? Perhaps indeed the chance of a change into some world of Terreauty (a word I've coined to mean terror and beauty) is in reality in some allegorical way daily offered to us if we had the courage to take it. I mean one has occasionally felt that this cowardice, this human loathing of spirits just because they are such may be keeping doors shut? Who knows? Of course this is all nonsense and the explanation is that through reading Maeterlink,[42] to improve my French, too late at night, I have developed a penchant for mystical

41 Sir Launcelot's castle in the Arthurian legend.

42 Maurice Maeterlinck (1862–1949), Belgian poetic dramatist and essayist, achieved great popularity with *L'Oiseau bleu* (1908) and its translation *The Blue Bird* (1909).

philosophy – greatly doubtless to the discomfort of my long suffering reader.

By the way, is the girlinosbornes beginning to ask about my bill yet – which is not paid? Write soon AND LONG mon vieux, to,

yours,
Jack

TO HIS FATHER (LP V: 70):

[Gastons]
Postmark: 1 April 1916

My dear Papy,

The little plans of mice and men, it would seem, must a' gang aft aglee.[43] You ask me when I am thinking of going home. Well I *was* thinking of the 15th, as instructed by the Colonel, so that his next leave would fall nicely at the end of my holydays. Mrs. K. suddenly turns up with the pleasing news that Terry is going on Tuesday the 4th., and Osbert Smythe with mother is coming down on the same date to convalesce from a wound, and – ah – when was I thinking of going home? Or in other words, after a little pow-pow, I have been 'kicked out' (Perhaps they were right to dissemble their love, but why –).[44] So I fear me Tuesday it must be. I hardly think a letter from you can reach me before that, so I shall borrow from K. By the way, Terry tells me that all the Belfast boats are off; if this is so, will you please wire and tell me, as in that case I shall have to go by Larne: I suppose the same ticket and payment of difference will do – or is the fare by Larne just the same? Of course if Liverpool and Fleetwood are still running, I will go by either – whichever is running on Tuesday night. In any case please wire and tell me. I am sorry to be such a nuisance, but it is quite as annoying for me, and more so for W. Sunt lacrimae rerum.[45]

your loving son,
Jack

---

43 Robert Burns, 'To a Mouse' (1786): 'The best laid schemes o' mice an' men / Gang aft a-gley.'

44 Isaac Bickerstaffe, *An Expostulation* (1789): 'Perhaps it was right to dissemble your love, / But – why did you kick me downstairs?'

45 Virgil, *Aeneid*, I, 462: 'Sunt lachrimae rerum et mentem mortalia tangunt' ('There are tears for those things and they touch the minds of men.')

P.S. On second thoughts, Monday would be better if you get this in time; if I go on Tuesday I shall have to travel with Terry and a lot of his friends, which would be terrible – for one thing I know they don't want me. So Monday be it: please wire. J.

Lewis was at home from 5 April to 11 May 1916. Writing to Albert about him on 7 April 1916, Mr Kirkpatrick said:

> *The very idea of urging or stimulating him to increased exertion makes me remind him that it is inadvisable for him to read after 11 p.m. If he were not blessed with such a store of physical health and strength, he wd. surely grow weary now and then. But he never does. He hardly realizes – how could he at his age – with what a liberal hand nature has bestowed her bounties on him...I notice that you feel adverse at present to let him enter the university at the close of next Autumn...But as far as preparation is concerned, it is difficult to conceive of any candidate who ought to be in better position to face the ordeal. He has read more classics than any boy I ever had – or indeed I might add than any I ever heard of, unless it be an Addison or Landor or Macaulay. These are people we read of, but I have never met any.* (LP V: 74)

Mr Kirkpatrick wrote again on 5 May 1916:

> *The case of Clive is very perplexing, but let us make a few points clear. I think he ought to be able to gain a classical scholarship or exhibition at entrance in any of the Oxford Colleges next Novr. or Dec., when the exams are held. But suppose I gave my opinion that he could with advantage do another years work with me. Do you not see what you are in for? Clive will be 18 in Dec., and if he remains in this country after that date, strictly speaking one month after that date, he will be liable for military service. There is no escape from that now...Ireland is exempt from the Act. Will it be brought in, as Carson[46] before, and now Captain Craig have asked?*

46 Edward Henry Carson, Baron Carson (1854–1935), Ulster leader, was attorney general of Ireland.

> *I find it hard to believe it. But we shall see. At any rate we may give up the idea that the war may be over before Jany. 1917...What is to become of the Eng. Universities under this new Conscription Act? I cannot say, but I do not see how they are to go on. Suppose Clive gained an entrance exhibn. next Decr. He would not be able to attend lectures. At the end of one month he would be liable to conscription.* (LP V: 78–9)

Albert replied on 8 May 1916: 'Clive has decided to serve, but he also wishes to try his fortune at Oxford' (LP V: 79).

TO ARTHUR GREEVES (LP V: 80–1):

[Gastons
16 May 1916]

My dear Galahad,

I wonder what you are doing tonight? It is nearly ten o'clock and I suppose you are thinking of bed: perhaps you are at this moment staring into the good old bookcase and gloating over your treasures. How well I can see it all, exactly as we arranged it a few days ago: it is rather consoling for me to be able to follow you in imagination like this and feel as if I were back in the well-known places.

Now let us get on with what you really want to hear; no, I did not go to the 'Starlight Express'[47] nor could I see it in the 'Times' list of entertainments. Perhaps after all it is not an opera but a cantata or something. What I did go to see was a play called 'Disraeli'[48] which I liked immensely, though I am not sure the Meccecaplex would have cared for it. It's about the real Disraeli[49] you know, the part being taken by Dennis Eadie – whom you saw in 'Milestones'[50] didn't you; he looks exactly like the pictures of the said politician in the old Punches. However, it is a thoroughly interesting play and I shall never repent of having seen it:

47 *The Starlight Express*, a play based on Algernon Blackwood's *A Prisoner in Fairyland* (1913), with incidental music by Edward Elgar, was first performed on 29 December 1915.

48 Louis Napoleon Parker's *Disraeli* was first performed on 23 January 1911.

49 Benjamin Disraeli (1804–81), first Earl of Beaconsfield, was Prime Minister 1868 and 1874–80. He published a number of novels, including *Vivian Grey* (1826), *Coningsby* (1844), *Sybil* (1845) and *Tancred* (1847).

50 Arnold Bennett and Edward Knoblauch's play *Milestones* (1912).

I think you agree with me that a good sensible play is far better than a second rate opera, don't you?

By the way, you have really no right to this letter, old man: that one of yours which you have been talking about all the holidays is not here, and Mrs K. says that nothing came for me while I was away. So now I shall be no longer content with your continual 'as I said in my letter', but will expect it all over again – especially the remarks about 'The Back of the Northwind' (by the way doesn't it sound much better if you pronounce that last word 'Northwind' as one word, with the accent slightly on the first syllable?).

Talking of books – you might ask, when do I talk of anything else – I have read and finished 'The Green Knight',[51] which is absolutely top-hole: in fact the only fault I have to find with it is that it is too short – in itself a compliment. It never wearies you from first to last, and considering the time when it was written, some things about it, the writer's power of getting up atmosphere for instance, quite in the Bronte manner, are little short of marvellous: the descriptions of the winter landscapes around the old castle, and the contrast between them and the blazing hearth inside, are splendid. The last scene too, in the valley where the terrible knight comes to claim his wager, is very impressive.

Since finishing it I have started – don't be surprised – 'Rob Roy',[52] which I suppose you have read long ago. I really don't know how I came to open it: I was just looking for a book in the horribly scanty library of Gastons, and this caught my eye. I must admit that it was a very lucky choice, as I am now revelling in it. Isn't Die Vernon a good heroine – almost as good as Shirley? And the hero's approach through the wild country round his Uncle's hall in Northumberland is awfully good too.

In fact, taking all things round, the world is smiling for me quite pleasantly just at present. The country round here is looking absolutely lovely: not with the stern beauty we like of course: but still, the sunny fields full of buttercups and nice clean cows, the great century old shady trees, and the quaint steeples and tiled roofs of the villages peeping up in their little valleys – all these are nice too, in their humble way. I imagine

---

51 The 14th century poem *Sir Gawain and the Green Knight*. Lewis was reading the prose translation by E.J.B. Kirtlan (1912).

52 Sir Walter Scott, *Rob Roy* (1818).

(am I right?) that 'Our Village'[53] gives one that kind of feeling. Tell me all about your own 'estate' as Spenser would say, when you write.

Have you finished 'Persuasion'[54] and has the De Quincy come yet, and what do you think of both? Have there been any particular beauties of sun and sky since I left? I know all that sounds as though I were trying to talk like a book, but you will understand that I can't put it any other way and that I really do want to hear about those kind of things.

This letter brings you the first instalment of my romance: I expect you'll find it deadly dull: of course the first chapter or so must be in any case, and it'll probably never get beyond them. By the way it is headed as you see 'The Quest of Bleheris'. That's a rotten title of course, and I don't mean it to be permanent: when it's got on a bit, I must try to think of another, really poetic and suggestive: perhaps you can help me in this when you know a bit more what the story is about.

Now I really must shut up. (That's the paper equivalent of 'Arthur, I'm afraid I shall have to go in a minute'.) Oh, I was forgetting all about Frankenstein.[55] What's it like? 'Really Horrid'?, as they say in 'Northanger Abbey'.[56] Write soon before I have time to feel lonely.

Yours,
Jack

TO ARTHUR GREEVES (LP V: 82–4):

[Gastons
22 May 1916]
Monday. 10 o'clock.

My dear Arthur,

Many, many thanks for the nice long letter, which I hope you will keep up for the rest of the term, in length. I see that it has taken four days to reach me, as it came only this morning, so I don't know when you will be reading this.

I am rather surprised at your remark about 'Persuasion', as it seemed to me very good – though not quite in her usual manner. I mean it is more romantic and less humorous than the others, while the inevitable

53 Mary Russell Mitford, *Our Village: Sketches of Rural Life, Character, and Scenery*, 5 vols. (1824–32).

54 Jane Austen, *Persuasion* (1818).

55 Mary Wollstonecraft Shelley, *Frankenstein* (1818; 1831).

56 Jane Austen, *Northanger Abbey* (1818).

love interest, instead of being perfunctory as in 'Emma'[57] and 'Mansfield Park' is the real point of the story. Of course I admit that's not quite the style we have learned to expect from Jane Austen, but still don't you think it is rather interesting to see an author trying his – or her – hand at something outside their own 'line of business'? Just as it is interesting to see Verdi in 'Aida'[58] rising above himself – though I suppose I have no right to talk musical criticism to you – or indeed to anybody.

I am glad that you are bucked with your De Quincy, and am eager to see the paper. By the way I suppose you notice that the same series can be got in leather for 5/-. I wonder what that would be like. I am thinking of getting the two volumes of Milton in it, as soon as I am flush or have a present of any sort due to me: one wants to get a person like Milton in a really worthy edition you know. Tell me what you think about this.

On Wednesday I had a great joy: I went up to town with the old woman[59] (by the way I have just seen the point of your joke about 'byre' and liar. Ha! Ha!) to see the Academy.[60] I have never been to one before, and therefore cannot say whether this year's was good as they go: but anyway I enjoyed it immensely and only one thing – your company – was lacking to make it perfect. How I wish we could have been there to enjoy some things together – for there were ones that would have sent you into raptures. Particularly there was a picture called 'Nature groaning' that exactly reminded me of that wet walk of ours, although the scene was different: it represented a dull, gloomy pool in a wood in autumn, with a fierce scudding rain blown slantways across it, dashing withered leaves from the branches and beating the sedge at the sides. I don't suppose that makes you realize it at all, but there was a beautiful dreariness about it that would have appealed to you. But of course it is really no good trying to describe them: I wish you would get that Academy book which one always finds in a dentist's waiting room so that we could compare notes. If you do, you must particularly notice 'The Egyptian Dancers' ['A Dancer of Ancient Egypt'], 'The Valley of the Weugh or Sleugh' or something like that ['The Valley of the Feugh'] (a glorious snow Scene), 'The deep places of the earth', 'The watcher' and a lovely faery scene from Christina Rosetti's 'Goblin Market'. It costs only a

57 Jane Austen, *Emma* (1816).

58 *Aida*, an opera by Giuseppe Verdi, first performed in 1871.

59 Mrs Kirkpatrick.

60 The Royal Academy of Art, London.

shilling I think and tho' of course the black and white reproductions lose a lot, still they are quite enjoyable.[61]

Talking about pictures etc., I was very pleased with your description of the mist and the night sky: you are by no means such a contemptable artist in words as you would like people to believe – in fact to be honest, if you weren't lazy you could do big things – and you have brought a very clear picture to my mind: one does get topping effects over the Lough sometimes, doesn't one? Really, after all, for sheer beauty of nearly every kind, there is no place I know like our own good county Down.

I am still at 'Rob Roy' which I like immensely, and am writing by this post for the first volume of Chaucer's 'Canterbury Tales' in the Everyman 2/2 edition:[62] am I wise? I have dipped into them very often latterly in the Kirk's horrible old copy, and think I shall like them, while, as I told you before, the paper of that Everyman is especially nice. I have also got a French prose romance of 'Tristan and Iseut'[63] which promises very well as far as I can see: in the meantime however since like all French firms' books it is paper back, I have sent it away to be bound in a very tasty binding of my own choice. Tell me more about 'Frankenstein' in your next letter so that I may decide whether to buy it or no. Any new records? I imagine that the success of your late venture may buck up your taste for your gramophone may it not?

This brings you the next chapter of my infliction. By the way I don't know how I actually wrote it, but I certainly meant to say 'The quest of Bleheris' and [not] 'of THE Bleheris', since Bleheris is a man's name. However, as I wrote to you before, that title is only waiting until I can get another better one. Your advice as to fighting and brasting exactly falls in with my own ideas since like Milton I am,

> '*Not sedulous by nature to indite*
> *Wars............*'[64]

---

61 A complete list of the art works at the Royal Academy Exhibition can be found in *The Exhibition of the Royal Academy of Arts*, no. 148 (1916). But Lewis is referring to *The Royal Academy Illustrated* (1916) which contains photographs of most of the paintings mentioned here.

62 *Chaucer's Canterbury Tales for the Modern Reader*, prepared and edited by A. Burrell, Everyman's Library (1908).

63 *Le Roman de Tristan et Iseut*, Traduit et Restauré par Joseph Bédier, Préface de Gaston Paris (Paris [1900]).

64 Milton, *Paradise Lost*, IX, 27–8.

I am afraid indeed that like 'Westward Ho'[65] my tale will have to dawdle about a bit in the 'City of Nesses' before I can get poor Bleheris off on his adventures: still you must do your best.

Oh vanity! vanity! to think that I can waste all this time jawing about my own work. Oh, one thing: I can't agree with you that Kelsie is at all like Diana Vernon: for if – to talk like Rashleigh,[66] 'My fair cousin' has a fault, it is a certain deadly propriety and matter-of-factness that will creep in even when she's at her best, don't you think so.

And now I've scrawled for a whole hour (it's just striking) so good night.

Jack

TO HIS FATHER (LP V: 81–2):

Gastons,
Great Bookham.
28/5/16.

My dear Papy,

I hear from the colonel that you are expecting a letter:[67] so, as they say of a sheep in a picture book, 'here it is', although, to be exact, I don't see why I should owe you one – the score so far this term being exactly equal on both sides.

Well, how have things been since I left home? I hope the laurels are coming on nicely. Everything here is of course very much the same, and the weather is glorious. On my way back I went to a play that would have appealed to you – 'Disraeli', which you will remember to have seen reviewed in Punch's 'At the play'.[68] If the real man was at all like the character in the piece he certainly must have been a prince of cards. I suppose that most of the bon mots that I heard at the Royalty are actual historic ones, preserved in his letters and so forth. I wonder too whether it be true to life when, having said good thing, he is represented as making his secretary take a note of it 'For Manchester next week: that'll just about suit Manchester'. Which reminds me how are you getting on with the fourteenth – or is the twentieth volume of his life?[69]

---

65 Charles Kingsley, *Westward Ho!* (1855).

66 Diana Vernon and Rashleigh are characters in *Rob Roy*.

67 Warnie was on leave, and at Little Lea, 19–25 May.

68 *Punch*, vol. CL (12 April 1916), p. 252.

69 Mr Lewis had probably been reading William Flavelle Monypenny's *The Life of Benjamin Disraeli*, 6 vols. (1910–20).

The only other excitement I can think of was a jaunt up to town with Mrs. K. to see the Academy, last Saturday. I had never been to one before, and therefore cannot say whether this was good, as they go, or not. At any rate it seemed to me that there were a lot of very nice things there, while even watching the other watchers was a great amusement.

My reading at present is very sober and old fashioned – 'Rob Roy' and the 'Canterbury Tales', both of which are most satisfactory. The former I suppose you have read years ago: at least I have tracked to its lair one of your favourite quotations, 'Do not mister or Campbell me: my foot is on my native heath and my name is MacGregor'.[70] But what a pity it is to see such good 'yarning' as Scott's spoilt and tripped up at every turn by his intolerably stilted and pedantic English. I suppose we must thank Dr. Johnson and 'Glorious John'[71] for first making such prose possible.

I met Warnie on Friday, according to instructions, and saw him go off by his 4.0 troop train. I am sorry to hear from him that you are bothered with some sort of rheumatism, and hope that it is now on the mend.

your loving
son Jack

P.S. I am one up in letter now: so don't forget to write soon. J.

TO ARTHUR GREEVES (LP XI: 259–60):

[Gastons
30 May 1916]

My dear Galahad,

I don't know whether you quite realized how mysterious your last letter was: on page III I read 'have just begun a tale called "Alice for short"'. Very good, say I, remembering William de Morgan's novel of that name:[72] but you are 'doubtful whether you'll finish it': remembering the size of the volume on our landing book case I am not surprised: then I read on a bit and see that you 'daren't let it out of your hands, even to me'. Ah! Ce devient interèssant (is there an accent on that word?), I think something tremendously improper. But imagine my even greater confusion on learning that de Morgan's long and heavy looking novel is a

70 *Rob Roy*, ch. XXXIV.

71 John Dryden (1631–1700), so called both for his writings and for the fact that he was the first Poet Laureate to be officially so designated.

72 William De Morgan, *Alice-for-Short* (1907).

continuation of Alice in Wonderland![73] Of course as soon as I turned the page I saw that you meant 'began to write' and not 'began to read' as I had naturally thought, being as you know cracked absolutely.

Well as to the information itself: I cannot urge you too strongly to go on and write something, anything, but at any rate WRITE. Of course everyone knows his own strength best, but if I may give any advice, I would say as I did before, that humour is a dangerous thing to try: as well, there are so many funny books in the world that it seems a shame to make any more, while the army of weird and beautiful or homely and passionate works could well do with recruits. But perhaps your 'Alice' is not so much humorous as lyric and fantastic? Anyway, you might as well send me along what you have done and let me have a look at it: at the worst it can't be more boring than 'Bleheris' and of course it's much easier to criticise each other's things on paper than viva voce: at least I think so.

And by the way, while I'm on this subject, there's one thing I want to say: I do hope that in things like this you'll always tell me the absolute truth about my work, just as if it were by someone else whom we did not know: I will promise to do the same for you. Because otherwise there is no point in sending them, and I have sometimes thought that you are inclined not to. (Not to be candid I mean). So I shall expect your MS – 'Alice' or anything else you have done – next week.

'Rob Roy' is done now, and (to pay you out for your remarks about 'Persuasion') I must admit that I only skimmed the last three or four chapters: the worst of a book with a plot is that when the plot is over, the obvious 'fixing up' is desperately tedious. On the whole however it was jolly good, and some of the scenery passages, as you say, are gorgeous: particularly where Frank is riding 'near the line' with the Bailey and the latter points out the Highland Hills – do you remember? That bit is almost as good as the scene where Clement Chapman shows Ralph the Wall of the World. But I suppose you would think it sacriledge to compare Morris to Scott. So would I for that matter, only the other way round.

You ask about the binding of my 'Tristram': well of course, apart from the binding itself, all French books are far poorer than ours: this one for instance cost 2/- (2fr.50) although it was only a paper back, of about the

73 Lewis Carroll, *Alice's Adventures in Wonderland* (1865).

same size as my Gawain: the binding will come to another 2/- or perhaps 2/6. That sounds a lot: but after all if you saw a nice leather bound book in a shop of that size and were told it cost 4/-, I don't think it would seem very dear. Of course it is true I may very likely be disappointed in it, but then, not being a prudent youth like you, I have to take risks occasionally.

With the Chaucer I am most awfully bucked: it is in the very best Everyman style – lovely paper, strong boards, and – aren't you envious – not one but two bits of tissue paper. When I've collected enough in that way, I shall be able to put tissue in all my better class Everymans. As to the contents, although I looked forward to them immensely, they have proved even better than I hoped: I have only had time so far to read the 'Prologue' and 'The Knight's Tale' (that's Palamon and Arcite you know), but I adore them. The tale is a perfect poem of chivalry, isn't it? And the pathos of Arcite's death is really wonderful, with the last broken appeal,

> *'Forget nat Palamon that gentil man'* [74]

and the cry of 'Mercy Emelye'.[75]

But God! there I go on talking like a book again, and you a poor invalid who ought to be consoled. Seriously though, I hope you'll be quite alright by the time you read this: I don't like to hear of your being in bed so often, especially as it affects your spirits so. However, cheer up, and whenever you are fed up with life, start writing: ink is the great cure for all human ills, as I have found out long ago.

I quite appreciate what you say about my father, to whom I wrote on Sunday: but after all he hasn't written to me, and as he had Warnie with him I thought he could 'thole'. Still you are quite right in what you say and I must be more regular in future.

I thought you would like De Quincy, and hope you will go on reading him: it is always nice to feel that one has got a new friend among the book world, isn't it? What an old miser you are though. I suppose I shall have to buy the Academy book myself now: and rest assured that you will never see one page of it. It is strange that 'Frankenstein' should be badly written: one would expect the wife of Shelley to be a woman of taste, wouldn't one?

---

74 *The Canterbury Tales*, 2797.
75 ibid., 2808.

As to my brother's talk about another 'E Lucevan le Stelle' I'm afraid the front must have turned the poor boy's brain: considering how I pined after your copy for over a year it wasn't very likely that I should have forgotten one if I had it. What put the idea into his head I can't think.

Have been to Leatherhead baths for a swim today and am terribly stiff, as I always am after the first bathe of the year. Sorry this is not much of a letter this week, old man, but it's after 11, and everyone is going to bed. This brings you the next instalment of Bleheris – criticise freely.

Yours,
Jack

TO ARTHUR GREEVES (LP V: 84–6):

[Gastons
6 June 1916]

My dear Arthur,

I was rather surprised to see the note paper of your last letter, and certainly wish that I could have been with you: I have some vague memories of the cliffs round there and of Dunluce Castle, and some memories which are not vague at all of the same coast a little further on at Castlerock, where we used to go in the old days. Don't you love a windy day at a place like that? Waves make one kind of music on rocks and another on sand, and I don't know which of the two I would rather have.

As to your remarks about my 'promise' to join you on some future holiday, I must call your attention to the fact that all I promised was not to contract any engagement with my Aunt that could stand in the way of it, always warning you that I might not go anywhere. However I hope to do so, and will certainly try my best.

By the way, in future, if possible, don't write your letter on so many different 'levels', so to speak: I keep them all on a pin now, and so far, all being written the same way up, I have been able to turn to any one I wanted, like a book: the latest one is a hard nut to crack. Always grumbling you see.

You may well ask 'when' my 'Tristan' is coming: I have asked the same question myself more than once, and it's beginning to be like those famous Columbia records the holydays before last. As to the binding, if it is what the girl in the shop told me, it will be boards with leather back, and those little triangular pieces of leather on the corners. I don't know if you understand this description, so I have drawn it for you: though perhaps indeed you find the picture quite as hard. In other words it is a glorified edition of the 2/- Everyman. The reason I'm not quite certain is that the girl showed me a much larger book done in the same style, only red. As I didn't care for the colour, she said she thought it could be done like that in brown; so I'm still waiting the result.

With my last parcel – the Canterbury Tales – I got Macmillan's and Dent's catalogues, where I find much of interest: I suppose you know it all already however. For instance I never knew before that Macmillans would send you – through a bookseller – books on approval. Of course when things are so out of joint as you're only allowed to keep them for a week, perhaps you could hardly manage it over in Ireland. Being so near town myself, I think I shall try it, wouldn't you? I also notice that Dents have a series of 'Classiques Francaises' corresponding to the English Everymans Library. Does that mean that they'd be bound the same way? Among them I'm very pleased to find a rendering of the 'Chanson de Roland' into modern French:[76] this, as you probably know, is the old French epic, equivalent to our Beowulf,[77] and for years I have been wondering how to get it. Now, as things sometimes do, it just turns up. Of course talking about Beowulf reminds me again what hundreds of things there still are to buy: if you remember it has been 'the next book I'll get' ever since you have known me.

I know very well what you mean by books getting tiresome half way through, but don't think it always happens: for instance 'Phantastes', 'Jane Eyre', 'Shirley' (which in fact only begins to get interesting about then) might be cited – good word that – as examples. Tell me more about 'John Silence'[78] when you write, and also let me know the publisher and price, as I have forgotten again and may want it one of these days.

I don't like the way you say 'don't tell anyone' that you thought 'Frankenstein' badly written, and at once draw in your critical horns with the 'of course I'm no judge' theory. Rot! You are a very good judge

76 *La Chanson de Roland*, Traduction Nouvelle D'Après les Textes Originaux [1911].

77 *Beowulf*, a poem in Old English generally dated to the eighth century and surviving in a 10th century manuscript. It tells the story of the Geatish hero, Beowulf, and is the most important poem in Old English.

78 Algernon Blackwood, *John Silence: Physician Extraordinary* (1908).

for me because our tastes run in the same direction. And you ought to rely more on yourself than on anyone else in matters of books – that is if you're out for enjoyment and not for improvement or any nonsense of that sort. Which reminds me, I came on a phrase in Maeterlinck the other day which just suits my views about youth and silly scientific learning. 'L'ignorance lumineuse de la jeunesse',[79] the luminous ignorance of youth is exactly our strong point, isn't it?

Great God, how I must be boring you! But you ought to know by now that your friend Chubs with a pen in his hand is a very dangerous object: that extemporising goes a bit far at times: though seriously, to harp back to the eternal subject of self – I think Bleheris has killed my muse – always rather a sickly child. At any rate my verse, both in quality and in quantity for the last three weeks is deplorable!! Before you get any further in the aforesaid romance, let me hasten to warn you that when I said [of] the first chapter, that Bleheris was like you, I hadn't really thought of what I should make him. However I take that back, so that in future when my poor hero does anything mean you won't think I am covertly preaching at you.

In odd moments last week I read an excellent novel by – you'd never guess – Bernard Shaw. It is called 'Love among the Artists', and is published in Constable's shilling series.[80] I want you to get it: there are one or two extraordinary characters in it, and I think the whole gist of the thing, all about music, art etc. would appeal to you very strongly. Tell me if you do. I wonder what the good author who takes his own works so seriously would think if he knew that he was read for pleasure to fill up the odd moments of a schoolboy. If you do get the book, don't forget to read the preface which is very amusing.

I can't understand why you are willing to let me see your tale in the holydays, but are unwilling to send it by post. I refuse point blank to read it in your presence: that means that you spend your time thinking of what the other person is thinking and have no attention left to give to the work itself. So you may as well send it along.

Since I last wrote to you I have found the thought of a book done and yet not done intolerable, and therefore gone back and finished 'Rob Roy'.

---

79 The phrase is from Maurice Maeterlinck's 'L'Intelligence des Fleurs', which Lewis found in his *Morceaux Choisis*, with an Introduction by Georgette Leblanc (Paris, 1911), p. 181.

80 George Bernard Shaw, *Love Among the Artists*, Constable's 1/- Series (1914).

I am very glad I did so, as otherwise I should have missed the very vigorous scene in the library, and the equally satisfactory death of Rashleigh.

I have written from 10 to quarter past 11 and the others are going up; so good night my Galahad,

from yours,

Jack

TO ARTHUR GREEVES (LP V: 89–90):

[Gastons
14 June 1916]

My dear Arthur,

I must begin by apologizing for being a day late this week: I suppose by this time you have worked up quite a flourishing grievance. However, you will be glad to know that there is a genuine excuse this time – not just laziness. The reason is that there were visitors here last night, and tho I don't usually turn up on these occasions, I was so warmly urged 'just to come into the drawing room for a minute or two when I had finished my work' that I really couldn't refuse. So the hour between 10 and 11 which on Tuesday nights is usually taken up with your letter was lost.

The reason why Mrs K. pressed me was that the visitors were some neighbours of ours and with them a girl who is staying with them – that's an elegantly arranged sentence for a literary man – who has a voice and is being trained for opera. Well I am certainly glad I didn't miss it, as she has a very fine contralto and sang two good songs – your record from 'Orfeo'[81] and a very queer thing of Debussy's which I would like to hear again. Of course with that exception she sang rubbish, as the fools asked for it: horrible old ballads like 'Annie Laurie' etc. Still it was worth sitting talking about the war and wasting my time even for two good things. Why are singers always so plain I wonder?

I can't help smiling at the thought of your sitting in the garden on Sunday morning, as we have had nothing but thunderstorms for the last week and it has just now turned so cold that we've gone back to fires. There, I'm talking about the weather! By the way I don't know if you ever noticed how topping it is to see a fire again suddenly in the middle of June: it is so homely and cozy and is like having a bit of the good old Winter back again.

---

81 *L'Orfeo*, an opera by Luigi Rossi, was first performed in 1647.

The remark about the cows with which you credit me really comes from your newly made friend De Quincy. I think it is just before the description of the flood – the 'Bore' as he calls it. Look it up and see if I'm right.[82] Anyway I quite agree with it: but perhaps even nicer is a humorous looking old horse, living contentedly in a field by himself, it's those little things that keep one from being lonely on a walk – there is one horse here that I have got to know quite well by giving him sugar. Perhaps he may save me from a witch some day or lead me home in a fog?

You will be amused to hear that my 'Tristen' has not YET come: that is nearly three weeks now, and I am beginning to get angry. You ask at what shop it's being done: well you see it's being worked indirectly through the village stationer here who will send books to be bound for you in London, I don't know where. The reason for its taking so long, I imagine is that the wretch really waits until he has several to do and then makes one parcel of them so as to save himself the postage. In any case I shall not give him another opportunity, as there are people in the neighbouring town of Leatherhead who bind books themselves.

I am glad you like 'John Silence' and must get it too. I have now read all the tales of Chaucer which I ever expected to read, and feel that I may consider the book as finished: some of them are quite impossible. On the whole, with one or two splendid exceptions such as the Knight's and the Franklin's tales, he is disappointing when you get to know him. He has most of the faults of the Middle Ages – garrulity and coarseness – without their romantic charm which we find in the 'Green Knight' or in Malory. Still, I only really expected to enjoy some of the Tales, and feel that the book was worth getting for their sake. I am not sure whether you would like him or not, but you should certainly not start poetry with him.

Which reminds me, have you ever carried out your plans of reading 'Jason'?[83] I am wondering what I ought to get next, or whether I ought to save money and read some of the Gastons books – perhaps finish the Brontes or take up another Scott. I have found that Sidney's romance the 'Arcadia'[84] is published at 4/6 by the Cambridge University Press (what

---

82 The passage occurs in the 'Introductory Narration' of Thomas De Quincey's *Confessions of an English Opium Eater* (enlarged edition, 1856).

83 William Morris, *The Life and Death of Jason* (1867).

84 Sir Philip Sidney, *The Countesse of Pembrokes Arcadia* (1590).

are they like?) and am strongly tempted to get it. One thing that interests me is that Sidney wrote it for his sister, the Countess of Pembroke, sending it to her chapter by chapter as he wrote it as I send you 'Bleheris'. Perhaps we were those two in a former state of existence – and that is why your handwriting is so like a girl's. Though even my self conceit will hardly go as far as to compare myself with Sidney.

What a queer compound you are. You talk about your shyness and won't send me the MS of 'Alice', yet say that you are willing to read it to me – as if reading your own work aloud wasn't far more of an ordeal. By the way I hope that you are either going on with 'Alice' or starting something else: you have plenty of imagination, and what you want is practice, practice, practice. It doesn't matter what we write (at least this is my view) at our age, so long as we write continually as well as we can. I feel that every time I write a page either of prose or of verse, with real effort, even if it's thrown into the fire next minute, I am so much further on. And you too who have been so disappointed at the technical difficulties of composing, won't you find it a relief to turn to writing where you can splash about, so to speak, as you like, and gradually get better and better by experience? Or in other words, I shall expect an MS of some sort with your next week's letter: if I don't get it, I may have recourse to serious measures.

I like the way you say 'why don't' I 'take' a day in town! As if I could just stroll down one morning and say that I wasn't going to do any work today: no Galahad, that sort of thing may do in Franklin Street, but where people WORK – note that word, you may not have met it before – it can't be did.

I am being fearfully lacerated at present: thinking that Pindar is a difficult author whom we haven't time to read properly, Kirk has made me get it in the Loeb library – nice little books that have the translation as well as the text.[85] I have now the pleasure of seeing a pretty, 5/- volume ruined by a reader who bends the boards back and won't wash his filthy hands: while, without being rude, I can't do anything to save it. Of course it is a very little thing I suppose, but I must say it makes me quite sick whenever I think of it.

In case you despair of ever getting rid of the 'City of the Nesses', I promise you that in the next chapter after this one Bleheris actually does

85 *The Odes of Pindar, including the Principal Fragments*, with an introduction and an English translation by Sir John Edwin Sandys, Loeb Classical Library (1915).

get away. Don't forget the MS when you write, and tell me everything about yourself. Isn't this writing damnable?

Yours,
Jack

The time had come for Lewis to apply to an Oxford college, and it was to this end that Mr Kirkpatrick had been preparing him. Seventeen colleges then made up the University of Oxford, and the question before Lewis was which to apply for. The practice at the time was to list at least three on the entry form, stating one's order of preference. The 'big group' of colleges mentioned in the following letter to his father included New College, Corpus Christi, Christ Church, Oriel, Trinity and Wadham, and of these New College became Lewis's first choice. Before being accepted by a college, Jack had to sit a scholarship examination in the subject he wished to read, Literae Humaniores, *or Classics, to be given in December 1917. If accepted by an Oxford college, this would not make him a member of Oxford University. For that he would need to pass Responsions, the entrance examination administered by the University. Meanwhile, in preparation for the scholarship examination, Mr Kirkpatrick obtained some of the examination questions used in previous years so that he and Jack would have a better idea of how to prepare.*

TO ARTHUR GREEVES (LP V: 93–5):

[Gastons
20 June 1916]

My dear Arthur,

I do wish you would be serious about 'Alice': whatever else is a matter for joking, work – in this particular sense of the word – certainly is not. I do really want to see something of yours, and you must know that it is impossible to write one's best if nobody else ever has a look at the result.

However, I told you I would proceed to serious measures, so here is my manifesto. I, Clive Staples Lewis, student, do hereby give notice that unless some literary composition of Arthur Greeves be in my possession on or before midnight on the last night of June in the year nineteen hundred and sixteen, I shall discontinue from that date forward, all communication to the said Arthur Greeves of every kind, manner, and description whatsoever, until such composition or compositions be forwarded. 'So there' as the children say. Now let us go on.

'Oh rage, Oh desespoir'! Alas I am undone. All men are liars. Never, never get a book bound. You will gather from this that 'Tristan' has arrived and is a complete and absolute failure. When I told them to bind it in brown leather, with corner pieces etc., I imagined that it would look something like Kelsie's Dickens or like a 2/- Everyman. Wouldn't you have thought so? Well as a matter of fact, though in a sense they have done what I told them, yet the total effect, instead of being booky and library like, is somehow exactly like a bank book or a ledger. For one thing the leather – though I must say excellent in quality – is very dark and commercial looking, and the cloth between the back and triangular bits is the absolute abomination of desolation. As if this wasn't enough – the edges of the paper were before nice, and artistically rough. Well what do you think the brutes have done? They have smoothed them down and coloured them a horrible speckled red colour, such as you see in account books. You can imagine my absolute fury.

True, it is some consolation to find the book itself good beyond what I had expected: it gets the romantic note (which the French don't usually understand) very well indeed. One or two little descriptions are full of atmosphere. In particular, what could be better for Lyonesse – glorious name – as we imagine it, than this simple sentence: 'Climbing to the top of the cliff he saw a land full of vallies where forest stretched itself without end.' I don't know whether you will agree with me, but that gives me a perfect impression of loneliness and mystery. Besides its other good points, it is very, very simple French, so that if you think of starting to read that language this would make a very good beginning.

I am sorry to hear about the 'Beowulf', and if it is at all like what I imagine, surprised as well. Of course you were always less patient of the old fashioned things than I, and perhaps it is not a good translation. However (seriously) I may buy it from you at a reasonable price, if I like the look of it, just to match my 'Gawaine' – that is unless I get Morris's 'Beowulf'[86] instead, which is rather too dear at 5/-.

Your remarks about music would seem to lead back to my old idea about a face being always a true index of character: for in that case, if you imagined from the music of the soul either of Gordon or of this

86 *Beowulf*, translated by William Morris and A.J. Wyatt (1892).

mysterious 'fille aux cheveux de lin'[87] one would be bound to imagine the face too – not of course exactly, but its general tone. What type of person is this girl of whom Debussy has been talking to you? As to your other suggestions about old composers like Schubert or Beethoven, I imagine that, while modern music expresses both feeling, thought and imagination, they expressed pure feeling. And you know all day sitting at work, eating, walking etc., you have hundreds of feelings that can't (as you say) be put into words or even into thought, but which would naturally come out in music. And that is why I think that in a sense music is the highest of the arts, because it really begins where the others leave off. Painting can only express visible beauty, poetry can only express feeling that can be analysed – conscious feeling in fact: but music – however if I let myself go on such a fruitful subject I should take up the rest of this letter, whereas I have other things to tell you.

What is nicer than to get a book – doubtful both about reading matter and edition, and then to find both are topping? By way of balancing my disappointment in 'Tristan' I have just had this pleasure in Sidney's 'Arcadia'. Oh Arthur, you simply must get it – though indeed I have so often disappointed you that I oughtn't to advise. Still, when you see the book yourself, you will be green with envy. To begin with, it is exactly the sort of edition you describe in your last letter – strong, plain, scholarly looking and delightfully – what shall I say – solid: that word doesn't really do, but I mean it is the exact opposite of the 'little book' type we're beginning to get tired of. The paper is beautiful, and the type also.

The book itself is a glorious feast: I don't know how to explain its particular charm, because it is not at all like anything I ever read before: and yet in places like all of them. Sometimes it is like Malory, often like Spenser, and yet different from either. For one thing, there is a fine description of scenery in it (only one so far, but I hope for more) which neither of them could have done. Then again the figure of the shepherd boy, 'piping as though he would never be old'[88] rather reminds me of the 'Crock of Gold'.[89] But all this comes to is that Sidney is not like anyone else, but is just himself. The story is much more connected than Malory: there is a great deal of love making, and just enough 'brasting and

87 'Flaxen-haired girl'. Lewis was thinking of the prelude by Claude Debussy, 'La Fille aux cheveux de lin'.

88 Sidney, *Arcadia*, Bk. I, ch. 2.

89 James Stephens, *The Crock of Gold* (1912).

fighting' to give a sort of impression of all the old doings of chivalry in the background without becoming tedious: there is a definite set of characters all the time instead of a huge drifting mass, and some of them really alive. Comic relief is supplied by the fussy old king of Arcadia – rather like Mr Woodhouse in Emma – and his boor, Dametas. The only real fault is that all the people talk too much and with a tendency to rhetoric, and the author insists on making bad puns from time to time, such as 'Alas, that that word last should so long last'.[90] But these are only small things: true, there is a good deal of poetry scattered through it which is all detestable, but then that has nothing to do with the story and can be skipped. I'm afraid this description won't help much, but I am just longing for Saturday when I can plunge into it again. (I mean the book, not the description.)

So much have I chattered that I have hardly any more room left. No, I have never yet read any of Christina Rosetti's poems, though, as you have heard me say, I love her brother Gabriel Rosetti. I believe she is very good, and a faery picture illustrating the 'Goblin market'[91] which I saw in the Academy attracted me very much. That is certainly a lovely edition of Lily's, though of course not worth [getting], unless somebody presented it to you. A nice sentiment truly! But you understand.

I see that I have scribbled a note about illustrations on this week's instalment (of course each is written a fortnight before you get it). Well do have a try: or rather that is a patronizing thing to say: I mean, do exert yourself. I am afraid my poor description won't inspire you much. I wonder do you really know what Cloudy Pass[92] looks like?

Well, they're going to bed now. It is eleven o'clock so I suppose you yourself are already in that happy place. Don't forget my manifesto.

Yours,

Jack

---

90 Sidney, *Arcadia*, Bk. I, ch. 1.

91 The picture was by Hilda Hechle.

92 In his story *The Quest of Bleheris.*

TO HIS FATHER (LP V: 86–7):

[Gastons
23 June 1916]

My dear Papy,

There is certainly something mysterious about the 'machinations of the Knock', as one might put it in the title of a novel; because, though I had not thought of it before, his success with Warnie is an unanswerable point against him. As to the Smythe business, however, I understand that mathematics were taught by him at some school in Manchester to which he went every day. But still, we are not flying so high as Woolwich. Tell me what Kirk says in answer to your letter. I do not think that there is anyone at Malvern whose advice I should prefer to Kirk's on the question of Oxford: unless indeed I were to amuse myself by writing to Smugy and asking in an off-hand way whether it was Oxford or Cambridge he was at!

No; to be serious, I think we must rely chiefly on K. and on our own judgement. There is of course a considerable temptation to risk it and try for a Balliol: it was Balliol we always thought of, before we knew as much as we do now, and I must admit there is still a glamour about the name. On the other hand, Dodds says in his letter that the prestige of Balliol is on the decline, and quotes as Colleges in the big group, New, Corpus, Christ Church, Oriel, Trinity, and Wadham. Of course these are all merely names to us both, but the first three and Trinity are generally admitted to be in the first rank, while Dodds speaks with particular admiration of New, and Kirk assures me that now-a-days Christ Church is little if at all inferior to Balliol in scholarship. Bearing all this in mind I am afraid we should hardly be well advised in following,

> *'The desire of the moth for the star'*[93]

when the star in this case is so perilous, and perhaps after all does not differ from another in glory so much as we have been led to expect. A further point to remember is that New College – of which Kirk has got a prospectus – substitutes for verse a paper of French and German translation instead of prose; which of course is far better from our point of view.

---

93 Percy Bysshe Shelley, 'To—: One word is too often profaned' (1824).

If then we decide to enter the big group, as I think we must, it remains to consider in what order we shall put down our Colleges. I should suggest Christ Church first, as undoubtedly the biggest name of the six, and after it perhaps New: and then the others in any order, keeping Wadham to the last.

It is a great relief to hear your news about the exact terms of the Military Service Act, as in this case I ought to be able to get a commission of some sort at home, or even a nomination from Oxford. At any rate, since there is no hurry – detestable expression, but let it pass – we can leave the matter to be discussed at ease in the seclusion of Leeborough.

If you have had even two hot days at home, you need not complain of the weather. We have had,

'Clouds instead an ever during dark'[94]

continual rain, and such bitter cold that on one or two evenings we have been obliged to light the fire: I believe it is just as bad all over England.

I am at present enjoying a new literary find in the shape of Sir Philip Sidney's 'Arcadia', which I got at a venture and found better than I expected: though like De Quincy's and Southey's epics, 'I expect that I enjoy the priveledge of being the sole reader of this work'. Talking about books, I hope you noticed the leader in this week's Literary Supplement – on Edgar Allen Poe?[95] I never heard such affectation and preciosity; the man who thinks the 'Raven' tawdry just because it is easily appreciated, and says that in 'The choice of words Poe has touched greater heights than De Quincy' ought – well, what can we say of him?

I am sorry to hear what you say about Cousin Quartus:[96] he seemed to be as brave and cheerful as usual last holydays.

By the way I have had to expend 6/6 on a Pindar and a Lucan which K. wanted me to get from London, thinking that Mullan's would be too slow. If a kind parent would like to refund – !

your loving son,
Jack

---

94 Milton, *Paradise Lost*, III, 45: 'But cloud instead and ever-during dark'.
95 *The Times Literary Supplement* (22 June 1916), pp. 1–2.
96 This was Sir William Quartus Ewart (1844–1919) of Glenmachan House. See **The Ewart Family** in the Biographical Appendix.

TO ARTHUR GREEVES (LP V: 97–8):

[Gastons
28 June 1916]

My dear Arthur,

For some reason your letter didn't reach me until this morning (Wednesday) so I am afraid that this will be a day late. I have been longing to get to my answer all day: and now that the time is come I hardly know how to collect my thoughts – they have been buzzing so in my head ever since breakfast.

First, ten thousand thanks for the enclosure. You know that I never flatter my friends – in fact my faults are in the other direction: so you may accept as a truth how this first sample of your work has knocked me all of a heap. Really, Galahad, I had no idea you could do anything like this: it is splendid. The only fault I have to find is that there is not enough of it. The idea of all the things round the river being in love with your hero – and I suppose the river too – showing their affection – is beautifully suggestive: I am longing to see it worked out – for by the way, on no account must you think of giving up after so happy a beginning. What I like particularly is the way which – according to the advice of friend Horace – you get straight into the middle of your theme right away, without any such dull descriptions as open Bleheris. The whole description of the river, etc., is done (in my poor opinion) with great skill: it sort of carries you away from the world into a dim, summery dream in some landscape more lovely than reality. Isn't the very word 'punt' very descriptive of summer and cool green reaches?

And now I am going to be so bold as to make a few suggestions: not that I think I am better 'up' in such things than you, but because it is good for both parties to be criticised, and I wish you would do the same to me. Well then, I don't know if it be true with other people, but in my own case, I have always found that if you are in at all good form when you write, corrections made afterwards are usually for the worse. Certainly most of yours are not improvements: for instance in several cases you have changed the word 'that' to which, as

that) happened long ago.
which)

Of course it is a small point, but don't you think 'that' is more simple, natural, and dignified than 'which'? The latter is indeed rather business like. Nor do I see why 'extremely old' should be written over the plain 'very old'. The second point is this: does your own judgement approve the sentence, 'shook her silvery sheen'? The alliteration, I think, would be a bit daring even in verse, and I am sure cannot be allowed in prose.

Now, I suppose you think me meddlesome and impudent. Well, though perhaps I am given to finding spots in the sun, I still appreciate its brightness: I repeat, though my opinion of you as a friend could not be higher than it was, my opinion of you as an author has risen by leaps and bounds since this morning. You MUST go on with this exquisite tale: you have it in you, and only laziness – yes, Sir, laziness – can keep you from doing something good, really good. By the way, before we go any further, I must say in fairness, that when you find those roses playing a more prominent part in the life of my Bleheris, it is not cribbed from your willow tree! I had thought out my plot – what there is of it – before I left home.

I am very glad to hear that you have bought C. Rossetti's poems: partly because I want to be able to look at it myself in the comfort of your sofa – mind the springs – and also I am glad you are beginning to read poetry. Which reminds me, a propos of your tale, you should read the bit in Morris's 'Jason' about Hylas and the water nymphs. I think it is in Book II – at any rate you can see from the headings – and it would not take you more than half an hour. As to the illustrated edition of his early poems, I believe we once saw it together in Mullen's, but so far as I remember, weren't greatly impressed; or am I thinking of something else? You don't tell me what you are actually reading at present, for you can't be living entirely on lyrics: have you finished 'John Silence' yet, and what is your final verdict on it?

In the mean time the 'Arcadia' continues beautiful: in fact it gets better and better. There has been one part that Charlotte Bronte could not have bettered: where Philoclea the heroine, or rather one of the heroines, is beginning to fall in love unconsciously with a man disguised as a girl: and she does not know the secret: the delicacy and pathos of her wrestlings with a feeling which of course she can't understand, as told by Sidney are – well I can't explain what they are like: there is one scene where she goes out by moonlight to an old grove, an haunted place, where there is an altar to 'the wood gods of old',[97] and lies looking up at the stars and puzzling about things, that is equal to if not better than the scene where Jane Eyre wakes up on the moor – do you remember? On the other hand, of course there are parts YOU might not have patience with: in the old style, where people relate their own adventures with no direct bearing on the main story: yet even this, to me, is interesting – so quaint and so suggestive of the old romantic world.

Besides this, I have read nothing lately, except a foolish modern novel which I read at one sitting – or rather one lying on the sofa, this afternoon in the middle of a terrible thunderstorm. I think, that if modern novels are to be read at all, they should be taken like this, at one gulp, and then thrown away – preferably into the fire (that is if they are not in one's own edition). Not that I despise them because they are modern, but really most of them are pretty sickly with their everlasting problems.

I am glad to hear that you have started illustrating my tale: your criticism about not making long conversations is a very sound one, though I fear I can't keep up to it. For instance, after this chapter the next two are, I am afraid, taken up with a conversation between Bleheris and the people he meets at an inn. Still, as it is necessary to what follows, you must try and get through it. This chapter is a failure: I particularly wanted to show what sort of a person he is and how he develops, but have only made him ridiculous.

I am interested in what you tell me of the Bronte country. Fancy a real living original of Heathcliffe?[98] What must he have been like.

Now it is time for bed, so good night mon vieux, and don't forget another instalment in your next letter.

Yours,
Jack

TO HIS FATHER (LP V: 91–2):

[Gastons
30? June 1916]

My dear Papy,

I can't understand why Kirk has not answered your letter. He never mentioned it to me, and until I heard from you I did not know that you

97 Sidney, *Arcadia*, Bk. II, ch. 4.

98 Heathcliff is the central figure in Emily Brontë's *Wuthering Heights*.

had written: perhaps it has gone astray – like your subscription to the chocolate fund!

At any rate, after reading what you said, I asked him whether a modern language could be substituted as you suggest: he replied that he thought this was so, but pointed out that of course this did not include mathematics, and that the latter would consist of a good deal of graphical work and other things which he – though goodness only knows why – does not feel fit to teach. If the worst comes to the worst, I suppose I could grind mathematics in the holidays: but all things considered I think we should look on the Sandhurst scheme as a "pis aller"[99] if it be found impossible to get a commission by influence or any other way.

You see the difficulties of entrance, though not insurmountable, are still serious, and it is well to remember that, as Harding told us, if I get a permanent commission, it may not be easy to leave the army immediately after the war. Do you think we could manage to work the business through our political friends? Kirk assures me that even now this is not difficult, and if it could be done, it would certainly be far the best plan. Failing this, I should suggest some volunteer institution from Ulster if any of these are still in existence.

Since we last wrote, I have been in communication with Oxford: missives have been elicited from Balliol, and I was glad to hear that if you go in for a scholarship, you are not expected to matriculate as well. It is rather a question however whether Balliol should be our mark: in order to prevent it getting the pick of the candidates, there is an arrangement by which Balliol and one or two insignificant colleges stand in a group by themselves outside the 'big group' which, like 'Pooh-Bah'[100] comprises 'everything else' worth talking about. Now in each of these two groups you put down the Colleges in the order you wish, and are put into one of them according to your place in the exam. You are of course 'stuck' in the group for which you enter. Under these circumstances, unless you are absolutely sure of success, it might be better to leave Balliol alone, seeing that if I miss it I have only a very few fall-backs, and those not of the first water. Tell me what you think? At any rate it is one comfort that Kirk's talk about matriculation was all moonshine: the scholarship exams take place in December. What between Oxford and the Army I am beginning to think that we would be better advised to sell all we have, take a cottage

99 'The thing to do if the worst happens.'

100 A character ('Lord High Everything Else') in Gilbert and Sullivan's *The Mikado*.

in Donegal, and cultivate potatoes for the good of the nation. Still, I suppose we really have very little to grumble at.

If it is not strange to say so, I am glad to hear that Dick is safely wounded:[101] it is by far the best thing that can happen to a man in the trenches, and the really unlucky ones are those who 'bear the labour and heat of the day'[102] unhurt for over a year – always it would seem in the long run to be killed after returning from a leave.

Things look pretty black at present, don't they? The North Sea battle, though perhaps not so bad as we thought at first, is certainly a very serious business, and our attitude towards the 'rats' was rather that of friend Tim than of the sportsman 'digging them out'. What exactly will the loss of Kitchener mean?[103] 'De mortuis...'[104] now of course, and for my own part I never approved of arm chair criticism.

How noble of poor Bob to give up his sister to the war!

Your loving
son Jack

As we have seen, for some time now letters had been passing between father and son, and father and Mr Kirkpatrick, regarding Jack's future. All were agreed that he should try for a place at Oxford, and Jack was due to sit for a scholarship examination there on 5 December. However, with one son already in the army, and the war growing worse every day, Albert Lewis was very anxious to keep Jack out of the service. According to the Military Service Act 'every male British subject who had attained the age of eighteen and ordinarily resident in Great Britain' was liable for enlistment in the army. On the other hand, the exemption mentioned at the beginning of this chapter – that of a man resident in Great Britain 'for the purposes of his

101 'Dick' who had been 'safely wounded' in France is Richard Lewis (1890–), eldest son of Joseph Lewis (1856–1908), and thus Albert's nephew. He joined the Sports Battalion in 1914 and finished the war as a company sergeant major, with a Distinguished Conduct Medal.

102 Matthew 20:12: 'These last have wrought but one hour, and thou has made them equal unto us, which have borne the burden and heat of the day.'

103 Lord Kitchener, Secretary of State for War, was in the British cruiser, the *Hampshire*, on the way to Russia when on 5 June it was sunk by a German submarine. Kitchener was killed.

104 The phrase 'De mortuis nil nisi bonum' ('Speak not evil of the dead') is originally a Greek expression ascribed to Chilon, a Spartan ephor of the sixth century BC. It is not known who first translated the original Greek into the proverbial Latin that we have.

education only' was now in effect. Jack was Irish, and the exemption applied to him. But contrary to his father's wishes, Jack insisted that he would not apply for the exemption, and he was determined not to be talked out of it by either father or tutor.

TO ARTHUR GREEVES (LP V: 103–5):

[Gastons
4 July 1916]

My dear Arthur,

So you feel hurt that I should think you worth talking to only about books, music, etc.: in other words that I keep my friendship with you only for the highest plane of life: that I leave to others all the sordid and uninteresting worries about so-called practical life, and share with you those joys and experiences which make that life desirable: that – but now I am getting rhetorical. It must be the influence of dear Sidney and his euphuism I suppose. But seriously, what can you have been thinking about when you said 'only' books, music, etc., just as if these weren't the real things!

However, if I had thought for a moment that it would interest you, of course you are perfectly welcome to a full knowledge of my plans – such as they are. Indeed I imagined that you had a pretty clear idea about them: well, 'let us go forward', to quote from a certain romance: being Irish, I hear from my father that the fact of my being educated in England will not bring me under the new act. I am therefore going to remain as I am until December when my Oxford exam comes off. After that, I shall of course join the army: but in what exact way, I don't at present know any more than you do. So there you have the whole yarn.

I may just remark in passing that you should by this time know better than to waste pity on your friend Chubs for 'worrying' about it: did you ever see him worrying about anything? I have learnt by now that whatever plans you make in this world, everything always turns out quite differently, so what is the use of bothering? To be honest, the question has hardly crossed my mind once this term. Now I don't mind in the least telling you all this, and if you wanted to know I don't see why you never asked before. But then I am a coarse-grained creature who never could follow the feelings of refined – might I say super-refined? – natures like my Galahad's.

The annoying part is that you have taken up your letter (and here am I taking up mine!!) with this, to the exclusion of all sorts of interesting things that I wanted to hear: for instance, you must tell me more about Hardy. We have all heard of him till we are sick of it, and so I should like to hear the opinion of someone I know. What sort of a novel is it? Would I like it?

But of course the first thing I looked for in this evening's letter was to see if there was an instalment there. I have now read it over again with last week's to get the continuous narrative, and with the same pleasure. Did you quite realise what a splendid touch it was for Dennis to hope 'nobody would steal his clothes'? Somehow the practical, commonsense realism of that, increases the fairy-like effect of what follows enormously. I don't know if I can explain it, but it sort of brings the thing just enough in touch with reality to make it convincing, without spoiling its dreaminess. Also the idea of his seeing her face not directly, but in the water, is somehow very romantic. By the way, I hope you don't really think that I hinted for a moment that your willow was borrowed from my roses: how could you know what my roses were going to do about five chapters ahead? Above all, don't change anything in the plan of your tale on that account. Perhaps, as you say, we both took it unconsciously from 'Phantastes', who in his turn borrowed it from the dryads, etc. of classical mythology, who are a development of the primitive savage idea that everything has a spirit (just as your precious Jehovah is an old Hebrew thunder spirit): so we needn't be ashamed of borrowing our trees, since they are really common property.

Your reply to my criticism is typically Galahadian: but though in your case I am sure it is more sincere than it looks, still this excessive modesty is rather absurd. You may be dissatisfied with it (though I don't see why), you may be uncertain of yourself, but still in your heart of hearts you don't think of 'The Water Sprite' as 'that rubbish of mine', now do you?

Do you know what your tale has done? It has made me sorry that I began Bleheris in the old style: I see now that though it is harder to work some effects in modern English, yet on the whole my way of writing is a sort of jargon: however, we must do the best we can. I was very glad to hear that you liked the Sunken Wood, especially as the next two chapters are stodgy conversation. I am afraid Bleheris never gets into the wood: but you ought to know that the 'little, hobbling shadow' doesn't live more in that wood than anywhere else. It follows nervous children upstairs to bed, when they daren't look over their shoulders, and comes and sits on your grandfather's summer seat beside two friends when they have talked too much nonsense in the dark. I hope you have an illustration ready for this chapter?

I am still at the 'Arcadia', which you will gather from this is a long book, though not a bit too long. I won't make you sick of it before you see it by starting to sing its praises again: I only promise you that I am still as keen on it as when I began. By the way, now that we are both writing, and know how much work there is in a short instalment that can be read in a few minutes, you begin to realize the labour of writing a thing say like the 'Morte D'Arthur'.

I gather from your silence that you are doing nothing in the gramophone way? Ask the Girlinosbornes whether my new record of 'Is not His word like a fire'[105] (ordered last holidays) has come yet or not. I hope it will be waiting for me when I get home: which event – do you realize – will happen in about a month. This term has gone terribly quickly and been very pleasant, but all the same I shall not be sorry to take up my other life again.

What new books are there of yours to see? I am longing to have a look at your De Quincey and 'Rossetti'. By the way, I suppose you never looked up the passage about the 'bore' nor the one in William Morris about Hylas and the nymphs? I have now finished my Tristan, which is really delightful: it is the saddest story on earth I think, don't you? I have written for the French Everyman translation of 'Roland' which ought to have come by now, but hasn't. I am interested to see what the binding is like, aren't you?

You will see by the scrawl that I am trying to write about a million miles an hour as everyone has gone to bed. So goodnight old man: send another instalment next week, I am so interested in your adorable fairy.

Yrs.,
Jack

P.S. By the way, one criticism just to keep you from getting your head turned. Don't talk about Dennis as 'our young friend' or 'our hero' – the last is like a newspaper: at least you may take it as a suggestion just for what it is worth. – J.

105 From Felix Mendelssohn's oratorio *Elijah*, first performed in 1846.

TO HIS FATHER (LP V: 102–3):

[Gastons
7 July 1916]

My dear Papy,

Your 'essay' and letter arrived, and Kirk read me a great part of the former. I think what you say about Christ Church is probably right, although Kirk tells me that there is most certainly a reading set, which one could live in. However, Dod[d]s specially recommends New, and as you say yourself, both it and Oriel are in the first rank. On the other hand, I am afraid that there will be no more 'Guards Regiments' anywhere by the time I reach Oxford: the old 'bloods' have mostly been shot, and the atmosphere of an after-war England will not be conductive to the birth of a new generation. Fortunately, there is no hurry about the question, and we can talk it over together in comfort next holidays.

Yes! It would be true irony if we ran upon something of the James or Capron type again; our little portrait gallery for that never-written novel is already getting crowded. By the way, what do you think of the new arrangement about Ulster? Kirk has talked about it for nearly a week: not that he has any views on either side, but he seems to find a pleasure in balancing off all the arguments for and against the proposal: so well has he succeeded that I am beginning to think 'That way lies madness.'[106] No sooner have we made up our minds on one side, than we are immediately floored by a new point that he brings up on the other. What do you think about it?

I must deprecate those very questionable references to my unfortunate last term's exodus from Gastons: if I saw that the goodwife of the house was, like Martha 'careful over many things,'[107] and then tactfully suggested that I might go home, what do you find extraordinary in such an action? At any rate, though we have our faults, we don't make ourselves ridiculous in an open carriage, nor lose our way in a country we have known from childhood. To be sensible, I suppose the term will end, as you say, at the end of July.

Many thanks for both your enclosures. The letter was from my old Malvern study companion Hardman: he is going to be conscripted at Christmas, and wants to know what I am going to do. I am writing to say

106 Shakespeare, *King Lear*, III, iii, 21: 'O! That way madness lies; let me shun that.'
107 Luke 10:41.

that I don't know yet, but will tell him as soon as our plans are settled. Of course if it turned out to be convenient, I should like to have a friend with me in the army, but it is hardly worth while making any special provisions for so small a matter. We shall see how it all works out.

Your reference to the two books is tantalizing. I quite agree with you that they should be put in a safe place: and the safest place in Leeborough is a certain 'little end room' where all the footsteps point one way. I for my part am still at my 'Arcadia' which I find excellent.

The weather here is ridiculous: wintry colds alternating with hot, close fogs, and an occasional thunder shower. I don't know what the farmers will do.

your loving
son Jack

TO ARTHUR GREEVES (LP V: 106–8):

[Gastons
11 July 1916]

My dear Arthur,

I am very glad to hear that you are getting to like Jason: I agree with you that the whole description of Medea – glorious character – going out by night, and of her sorceries in the wood is absolutely wonderful, and there are other bits later on, such as the description of the 'Winter by the Northern River' and the garden of the Hesperides, which I think quite as good. Curiously enough I have just started the 'Argonautica'[108] the Greek poem on the same subject, and though I haven't got very far – only in fact to the launching of Argo – it is shaping very well. It will be interesting to compare this version with Morris's, although indeed the story of the Golden Fleece is so perfect in itself that it really can't be spoiled in the telling. Don't you find the very names 'Argo' and 'Argonauts' somehow stirring?

I thought a person like you would sooner or later come to like poetry: by the way, of course you are quite right when you talk about thinking more of the matter than of the form. All I meant when I talked about the importance of form was to carry a little further what you already feel in prose – that is how some phrases such as the Wall of the World, or at the Back of the North Wind affect you, partly by sound partly by association,

108 Apollonius Rhodius (c. 295–215 BC), *Argonautica.*

more than the same meaning would if otherwise expressed. The only difference is that poetry makes use of that sort of feeling much more than prose and produces those effects by metre as well as by phrase. In fact, the metre and the magic of the words should be like the orchestration of a Wagnerian opera – should sort of fill the matter by expressing things that can't be directly told – that is, it expresses feeling while the matter expresses thought. But I daresay I have given you my views on the subject before. I am very flattered that you remember that old line about the 'garden where the west wind' all these months, and will certainly copy out anything that is worth it if you can find me a shop in dear Belfast where I can buy a decent MS book: I have failed in that endeavour so far.

So we are to be treated to more and more modesty? Indeed Arthur if I could get a little of your diffidence, and you a little of my conceit we should both be very fine fellows. This week's instalment is quite worthy of the other two, and I was quite disappointed when it broke off. The reeds 'frightened out of their senses' and shouting in 'their loudest whisper' are delightful. 'Our Lady of the Leaf' might be kept in mind as a possible title if you don't care for the present one.

You are rather naive in telling me that you 'have to sit for a minute thinking' and 'find the same word coming in again' as if these weren't the common experiences of everyone who has ever written. I haven't noticed any smallness in the vocabulary you employ for your tale, and anyway that's just a matter of practice. By the way, even if you didn't mean it, I hope you see now what I am driving at about the remark of Dennis as to his clothes. As to the 'sitting for ten minutes', I don't believe that good work is ever done in a hurry: even if one does write quickly in a burst of good form, it always has to be tamed down afterwards. I usually make up my instalment in my head on a walk because I find that my imagination only works when I am exercising.

Can you guess what I have been reading this week? Of all things in the world 'Pendennis'![109] Isn't this the one you find too much for you? I am nearly through the first volume and like it well so far: of course one gets rather sick of Pen's everlasting misbehaviour and the inevitable repentance going round and round like a mill wheel and there doesn't seem much connection between one episode and another. All the same, it has a sort of way with it.

109 William Makepeace Thackeray, *The History of Pendennis* (1849–50).

That feast the 'Arcadia' is nearly ended: in some ways the last book is the best (though a little spoiled I admit by brasting) and here the story is so like the part of Ivanhoe where they are all in Front-de-Boeuf's castle, that I think Scott must have borrowed it.[110] Your remarks about C. Rosetti's poems are very tantalizing and I am longing to see them. How I do love expensive books if only I could afford them. Apropos of which, do you know anything of the artist Beardesley?[111] I fancy he was the man who started the modern school of 'queer' illustrations and the like: well I see you can get for £1.5s. a 1 vol. edition of Malory with his illustrations, published by Dent. What do you think it would be like? I only wish it was Macmillan and so we could have it on approval.

You are quite wrong old man in saying I can draw 'when I like'. On the contrary, if I ever can draw, it is exactly when I don't like. If I sit down solemnly with the purpose of drawing, it is a sight to make me 'ridiculous to the pedestrian population of the etc.'. The only decent things I do are scribbled in the margins of my dictionary – like Shirley – or the backs of old envelopes, when I ought to be attending to something else.

I am quite as sorry as you that I can't see my way to working Bleheris back into the Sunken Wood, for I think the idea might be worked a bit more: but don't see how it is to be done without changing the whole plan of the story.

The immediate prospects of my getting married 'agreeably or otherwise' as you kindly suggest, are not very numerous: but if you are getting uneasy about an invitation, rest assured, when the event comes off, if you behave you shall have one.

It was strange that Mrs K. should get Hardy's 'Under the Greenwood Tree'[112] out of the library last week, though I never got a chance of looking into it: somehow I don't fancy Hardy is in my line, but then I always have a prejudice against people whom you're always hearing about.

You say nothing about music now-a-days, and I am afraid I scarcely think of it: it annoys me hugely to think of the whole world of pleasures that I used to have and can't enjoy now. Did you see a long article in the Times Literary Supplement[113] about the 'Magic Flute'[114] which is on at the

110 Sir Walter Scott, *Ivanhoe* (1819), ch. XXI.
111 Aubrey Vincent Beardsley (1872–98).
112 Thomas Hardy, *Under the Greenwood Tree* (1872).
113 'The Magic Flute' (unsigned), *The Times Literary Supplement* (29 June 1916), pp. 1–2.
114 Wolfgang Amadeus Mozart's opera *The Magic Flute* was first performed in 1791.

Shaftesbury? How I wish I could go up and hear it and also 'Tristan and Isolde'[115] – though if I did it would be a disappointment in all probability.

I am furious because in answer to my order for the 'Chanson de Roland' I am told it is out of print, which is very tiresome. Here I enclose another chapter, really all conversation this time, but can promise you a move next week. Don't forget your own instalment which I look forward to very eagerly. Good night.

Yours,
Jack

TO HIS FATHER (LP V: 105–6):

[Gastons
14? July 1916]

My dear Papy,

This must be nipped in the bud: there can be no question of that. Get your lady friend's visit over before the end of this month, at all costs, or else bid them avaunt till the winter.[116] What should I do, left alone all day to face a situation of that sort? As well, the whole thing is tyranny, extortion, infliction, profligacy and arrogance of the worst sort, and therefore not to be borne. Have they not already taken more than their fair share of reprisals for our own visit so long ago? This 'breakfast is a charming meal' business can be overdone: however, a man can but die once, so I suppose destiny must take its course.

This is big news from the front, though whether it will have any permanent effect or not, of course we can't say. The Ulster Division – what there are of them now – must have silenced the yapping politicians for ever.[117] I suppose the losses are felt very heavily in Belfast: here, nobody seems to have noticed anything.

Yes, that wheeze about 'pulled through' ought to 'supply a long felt want': it can be used on every occasion and ought to live for a very long time. I am sorry if any obscurity on my part gave rise to the 'savage emphasis,' but then his ordinary style of conversation is so – I think the

---

115 *Tristan and Isolde*, an opera by Richard Wagner, was first performed in 1865.

116 Albert's brother William, with his wife and daughter, were proposing a visit. See **The Lewis Family** in the Biographical Appendix.

117 Since the beginning of the war, the Ulster Volunteer Force had been gathering momentum, and they had now forced the War Department to accept them as an integral part of the British army.

word is 'nervous' in its 18th Century sense, that best describes it – that we must not pay too much attention to such things. I think, as you say, that things point to New, but of course we will keep an open mind in the meantime.

The literary event of the week is our respected laureate's ode in the Times Literary Supplement:[118] truly a most remarkable production, though I am afraid like the honest Major in 'Patience,' I must confess that 'it seems to me nonsense'.[119] To do the man justice, the lines about Homer, the ones about the birds, the beginning of the vision, and a few other passages, are rather fine. But the habit of throwing in an odd rhyme here and there is rather uncomfortable: still, if you can lay your hand upon it (the Pattersonian pun is quite a mistake, owing to haste, as it is getting late and the others are going up) you might keep this number.

I am at present in the middle of a book called 'Pendennis' which I should advise you to read unless I knew your prejudice against the author: however, one of these days you will come round and 'see my point.'

your loving,
son,
Jack

TO ARTHUR GREEVES (LP V: 111–13):

[Gastons]
Tuesday evening, the I
don't know whath,
[18] July /16.

My dear Arthur,

I can't understand why you should want to know the dates on which these gems of wit were written: if you should ever happen to look at them in the future, a date is a meaningless thing and it won't really help you to see a few numbers written on the top. For my part, when I read your old letters, I don't think about such nonsense. I classify them not by time but by the stage in our thoughts at which they were written:

118 He was referring to Robert Bridges' 'Ode on the Tercentenary Commemoration of Shakespeare', *The Times Literary Supplement* (6 July 1916), p. 319.

119 Gilbert and Sullivan, *Patience*, Act I. It is Patience who says: 'Well, it seems to me to be nonsense.'

I say 'Ah, that was when we were talking about Loki, this was when we talked much about music and little about books, we didn't know each other so well when this was written' and so on. Which is far more sensible than saying, 'This was September 1914, that was August 1915.' As well, the fact that everyone else puts a date on their letters is to me an excellent reason for not doing so. Still, if you are really concerned about it, I suppose I must 'bow myself in the house of Rimmon'.[120] Since I have gone so far as to put a date however, you can't be so unreasonable as to suggest that it should be the right one.

I am awfully bucked about 'Twelfth Night':[121] I thought at the time you remember, that Heath Robinson's illustrations were absolutely perfect – quite as good as Rackham's, though of course in a different style. If I remember aright there is a splendid one on the line 'How full of shapes is fancy'[122] and also some fine evening cloud effects – not to mention the jester in the rain and the delightfully 'old English' garden scenes.

I am longing, as you say, to be at home and to go over all our treasures both old and new: – so of course we shall be disappointed in some way. As you say, you are extravagant, but I too at present buy one book as soon as I have finished another.

The 'Arcadia' is finished: or rather I have read all there is of it, for unfortunately it breaks off at a most exciting passage in the middle of a sentence. I will not praise it again, beyond saying that this last 3rd. book, though it has no such fine love passages as the 2nd., yet (despite the brasting), for really tip-top narrative working the interest up and up as it goes along, is quite worthy of Scott.

This week's new purchase consisted of Milton's 'Paradise Lost' – in the same edition as my Mandeville[123] – and 'John Silence' in the 7d. edition. Just as one sometimes has a spell of being disappointed in new books, so at other times you keep on getting one treat after another. For the first few pages of John Silence I was hardly in the right mood: but after that it fairly swept me off my feet, so that on Saturday night I hardly dared to go upstairs. I left off – until next week end – in the middle of the 'Nemesis of Fire' – Oh, Arthur, aren't they priceless? Particularly the 'Ancient Sorceries' one, which I think I shall remember all my life. Oh, that evil

---

120 2 Kings 5:18.

121 *Shakespeare's Comedy of Twelfth Night*, with illustrations by W.H. Robinson [1908].

122 William Shakespeare, *Twelfth Night* (1601), I, i, 14.

123 *The Travels of Sir John Mandeville*, modernized and edited by A.W. Pollard (1900).

dance, and the 'muttering the old, old incantation'! The feeling of it all chimed with a lovely bit of 'Paradise Lost' which I read the same evening where it talked of the hounds that,

> '. . . *Follow the night hag, when, called*
> *In secret riding through the air she comes*
> *Lured with the smell of infant blood, to dance*
> *With Leopard witches, while the labouring moon*
> *Eclipses at their charms.*'[124]

Don't you like the Leopard witches? How you will love Milton some day! By the way we may remark in passing that John Silence is one of the nicest 7d's in paper and so forth that I have ever seen. I wonder how people would laugh if they could hear us smacking our lips over our 7d's and Everymans just as others gloat over rare folios and an Editio Princeps? But after all, we are surely right to get all the pleasure we can, and even in the cheapest books there is a difference between coarse and nice get up. I wonder what a book called 'Letters from Hell' published at 1/- by Macmillan would be like?'[125]

This week's instalment I enjoyed especially: the idea of the hair so beautiful to the eye so coarse to the touch is very suggestive, and you keep us in fine doubt as to whether your faery is going to turn out good and benevolent or terrible. You complain that your tale is commonplace, but I don't know anything that you think is like it, and I hope that you will really never think of giving it up unfinished – all the same, if you do – for which I can see no earthly reason – don't be discouraged, because we very rarely succeed in finishing a first work. If you saw the number of 'beginnings' I have made! By the by, there is one little point I must grouse at this week. You say that the faery resumed her 'normal' size. What was her normal size? We saw her first as a little figure on a leaf, and she hasn't changed since. Do you mean that she took on human size? Of

---

124 Milton, *Paradise Lost*, II, 662.

125 [Valdemar Adolph Thisted], *Letters from Hell*, Given in English by Julie Sutter, with a Preface by George MacDonald (Richard Bentley & Son 1885; reprinted by Macmillan, 1911). This curious book was first published in Denmark in 1866, and later translated into German. Julie Sutter's English translation of 1885 was made from the German version. Who knows? the book may have played some part, years later, in the genesis of Lewis's *Screwtape Letters* (1942).

course a few trifling changes when you revise will make this quite clear. The point of names is rather difficult: 'Dennis' I like, but the old Irish attractions of 'Desmond' are very strong. I really don't know what I should advise.

I am sorry you disapprove of my remarks in the romance. But you must remember that it is not Christianity itself I am sneering at, but Christianity as taught by a formal old priest like Ulfin, and accepted by a rather priggish young man like Bleheris.[126] Still, I fear you will like the main gist of the story even less when you grasp it – if you ever do, for as is proper in romance, the inner meaning is carefully hidden.

I am really very sorry to hear about your new record, but so many of your Odeons have been successful that I cannot reasonably have the pleasure of saying 'I told you so'. Talking about music, I have at last found out the exact number of the Chopin piece I like so well – it is the 21st Prelude. Look it out, and tell me if it is not the best music in the world?

I am afraid it is mere foolishness to praise that rhyme of mine as you do. Remember, you know exactly the occasion that gave rise to it, and can read between the lines, while to others it would perhaps be scarcely intelligible: still it is nice to be able to please even one reader – as you do too, for all your talk. In a way that sort of double-meaning in the title 'Lady of the Leaf' would be rather fascinating I think.

I am glad to hear your remarks about the different pleasures of painting, writing etc. I quite agree with you, 'work' of this kind, though it worries and tortures us, tho' we get sick of it and dissatisfied with it and angry, after all it is the greatest pleasure in life – there is nothing like it. Good night old man.

Jack

P.S. Is Dennis in bathing things all this time, or 'au naturel'? The point is not without interest.

---

126 The passage Arthur probably objected to occurs in Chapter V, where we are told that before Bleheris set out on his quest: 'He made his confession devoutly to father Ulfin, and was shriven of his sins, and took holy water in a little flask to bear with him for a defence, if he met any evil thing by the way. Poor boy!, that deemed in his folly that a priest's bauble, a dream-thing woven out of the hopes of man's self and then called "holy", might avail him aught against the great and terrible powers of the earth!'

P.P.S. Up in my room I have just read over the whole 'Watersprite' again. I have not done it justice in this letter, the whole story is topping and the air of mystery that hangs about Her makes one very keen to go on. I am not putting this in because I want to pleasure you, but because it just strikes me at the moment and must come out. Go on and prosper – there goes half past. So gute nacht du lieber kamarad, bon soir mon vieux.

J.

TO HIS FATHER (LP V: 114–15):

[Gastons]
21st July 1916.

My dear Papy,

I was just beginning to get up what I considered a very legitimate 'grouse', but must admit that you offer the best of reasons for the offence. I am glad that you enjoyed their visit,[127] and wish that I could have been one of the party: – at least so I may now say with safety when 'the tyrranny is over past'.[128] Many thanks for your indulgent permission to take a Scotch trip – never fear, we'll keep your place in order.

Kirk tells me he has sent you a list of the Scholarships and Exhibitions at colleges in the big group, which we will be able to go over together in the holidays. It is cheering to see that we have some fifteen to come and go over, most of them in the first rank.

My fellow sojourner at Gastons is going home this day (Friday) week, so I think it would be best for me to choose the following Monday. I forget what state the cross-channel routes are in at present, but if Fleetwood is going I had sooner travel by it: failing that by Liverpool with Larne as a pis aller. So if you could book a stateroom for the 31st, and forward a few 'crowns for convoy' I shall do myself the honour of waiting on you at Leeborough on Tuesday morning the first. (You may notice the phrasing of the last sentence, the insidious influence of that excellent man, Major Pendennis.)[129]

I had not heard before about Dick[130] and was very glad and proud of

127 Albert's brother William, his wife Minnie, and their daughter Clare, were at Little Lea from 7 to 13 July.

128 Psalm 57:1.

129 A character in Thackeray's *Pendennis*.

130 i.e. Richard Lewis, the son of Joseph Lewis. See note 101 to letter of 30? June 1916.

the news. As you say, he has plenty of 'guts' if only he has the luck to stick out. Things look a little brighter at the front now, though I am afraid it will need many such successes to bring the business to an end. Kirk went up to London on Wednesday to see the elder Smythe boy, who is at home wounded, for the third time.

'Summer is a-cummen in'[131] here at last, and we have actually had no rain since Saturday.

your loving
son Jack

TO ARTHUR GREEVES (LP V: 115–17):

[Gastons]
July 25 1916 and be d-d to you.

My dear Arthur,

That thrice accursed fellow pupil of mine is at present sitting up in the work room so I cannot go and steal a page from his exercise book to write on, as I have been doing all the term – you must be content therefore with these odd scraps: indeed I don't see why I should write at all, as by writing both the first and the last letter of this term I have treated you to two more than you deserve; however, I will make a note that it is your turn to begin after the holidays.

You are quite mistaken if you suppose that in asking about Dennis' bathing things I suggested that he OUGHT to have them on – I only wanted to get a perfectly clear picture: still I don't see any parallel between him and Bleheris in knickerbockers (a very funny word – that or Bickerknocker would be a good name for a dwarf if either of us should want one), because I take it your story is modern. But of course I quite agree that your hero is far better without them. It seems rather unnatural though to pass over any question of embarrassment in absolute silence: the fey of course, as a non-human being, may be excused, but poor Dennis might at least be allowed to blush when he comes round. Handled delicately and without any foolish humour – I am quite serious – the point might be worked a little more: what think you? Morris – who I always think manages to be as good as gold and at the same time beautifully sensuous, would have revelled in it. This week's instalment is excellent, and your references to the Sea and the sea

131 Anonymous, *Cuckoo Song* (c. 1250), l. 1: 'Sumer is icumen in'.

gods give me great anticipation of what may happen next: that next number which I am longing to get – from your own hand.

You must be easily satisfied if you think that I flatter you – when I scarcely let a sentence go past without pricking holes in it: you must also have funny ideas about my rate of composition if you think I have already finished Bleheris. As a matter of fact I write one chapter every Sunday afternoon, and having started before I came back, am always two instalments ahead of the one you get: the general course of the story was mapped out from the start, but of course is changed pretty freely whenever I like. When I said that you wouldn't like the 'gist' of the thing, I meant nothing to do with what you call 'shocked' or 'immodest' (though I admit that when the heroine turns up she is in fairly sharp contrast to Alice the Saint), but that the meaning of it all is somewhat anti-Christian: however, the story and not the allegory is the important part.

I have now finished that adorable (to quote our friend Ch-anie)[132] 'John Silence': I still think 'Ancient Sorceries' the best, though indeed all, particularly the 'Fire' one, are glorious. In the last one the opening part, all about those lovely Northern Islands and the camp life – wouldn't you love to go there? – is so very beautiful that you feel almost sorry to have the supernatural dragged in. Though the idea of the were-wolf is splendid. At what point of the story did you begin to guess the truth?

My last budget of books includes a French Everyman copy of a poet called Chenier[133] (a poet you might perhaps like some day, when you come to read French verse) and a 13d. Macmillan copy of Walter Pater's 'Renaissance',[134] in the same edition as the 'Letters from Hell' I suppose. That book (Hell) by the way is not by Dostoevsky I think, because I fancy I read somewhere that it is translated not from the Russian but from the Swedish: I have noticed too (did I tell you before) that this edition has a preface by our friend Macdonald, the author of Phantastes. We must certainly get it, as the Macmillan 1/- series are, to my mind, very nicely got up. The French Everyman is quite different from the English

---

132 The pronunciation of the name of their friend Jane or 'Janie' (thus 'Ch-anie' and even 'Tchanie') McNeill by 'Ch-anie's' mother – which pronunciation Lewis delighted in imitating.

133 André Chénier (1762–94), *Poésies*, Classiques Françaises [1916].

134 Walter Pater, *The Renaissance: Studies in Art and Poetry*, Second Edition, Revised (1912).

one – I am not sure yet whether I like it more, or less – you must judge for yourself.

It is a terrible responsibility to have to guide my Galahad in poetry: a false step might turn you away altogether! I don't think I should advise Milton: while there are lots of things in him you would love – the descriptions of Hell and Chaos and Paradise and Adam and Eve and Satan's flight down through the stars, on the other hand his classical allusions, his rather crooked style of English, and his long speeches, might be tedious. Besides it is written in blank verse (without rhymes) and people who are beginning to read poetry don't usually care for that. But of course you are different, and for all I know you might. You must have a good look at it in my copy and see what you think.

Endymion[135] is top-hole in places, in fact nearly all the time, though somewhat 'sticky': it would be a very good thing to try, I think, if you would not scruple to skip whenever you found it dull: the third book especially, where he wanders at the bottom of the sea, would appeal to you strongly. The only other poems I can suggest are Arnold's 'Tristan and Isolde' or 'Balder Dead'[136] (though this is in blank verse) or some of the stories in Morris' 'Earthly Paradise'[137] or perhaps some of the other Rossetti's pieces; these of course you could finish in a few hours, and some of them are not really very good. If you get an edition of Keats perhaps you would like 'St Agnes Eve'[138] – it is shorter than Endymion, written in Spenser's metre, and very romantic – though perhaps rather 'sticky' also. In sympathy with your new investment, having finished 'Pendennis' of which I am heartily sick by now, I have begun to read 'Twelfth Night' which is a charming little romance, don't you think? The opening speech about the music is the best.

Can't understand it being 'too hot to practise' as it is absolute winter here. Bah, there you see I am talking about the weather, like any fool! If I can get away – I haven't promised, mind – I should be pleased with all my heart to go to Portsalon: indeed whenever (correctly used in this sentence) I have thought of a holiday with you, that place has come into my mind: however, we can discuss all this when we meet – next week. Can you realize? I am so looking forward to seeing you again old man, and I

135 John Keats, *Endymion* (1818).

136 Matthew Arnold, *Tristram and Iseult* (1852); *Balder Dead* (1853).

137 William Morris, *The Earthly Paradise* (1868–70).

138 John Keats, *The Eve of St Agnes* (1820).

do hope and pray that nothing will turn up to disappoint us. I expect to arrive home on Tuesday: there is some faint danger of my father's staying at home, but if not, perhaps you could get a day off? Oh, how we will look over all these new books together: I have something ravishing to show you in the way of paper, but that can wait.

I am writing at present a rather lengthy (for me that is) poem about Hylas, which you shall see if it is a success: but perhaps it will never be finished. By the way, I have come to the Hylas part in the Greek Argonautica. He doesn't go into it nearly as fully as Morris, but in some ways it is better. In this version the various nymphs – mountains, Oreads, wood nymphs etc., are dancing by moonlight when they hear a mortal blundering through the wood. So they all scatter to their various trees, streams etc., and this particular one, as Hylas bent down to fill his pitcher, caught him round the neck and pulled him down; and so to bed, bon soir tu excessivement pudibonde.

Jack

TO ARTHUR GREEVES (LP V: 121–2):

[Little Lea,
Strandtown,
Belfast]
18/9/16.[139]

My Dear Galahad,

It seems a mockery to think that we were talking so lately about how much better we were in our letters than in conversation – I don't feel like that when I actually sit down to write for the first time. Somehow my being at home instead of at Bookham makes it seem strange to be away from you: it is only so few days ago that we were ragging about together in your bedroom. And now you must brush your teeth alone!

But first of all I will answer your questions. The journey home was absolutely damnable: I had to wait an hour at Letterkenny, and an hour and a quarter at Strabane. You may judge of my boredom when I tell you that I was reduced to buying a 'Novel' magazine[140] – because everything

139 Some time after Lewis arrived home on 1 August, he and Arthur went on holiday to Portsalon in Co. Donegal. While Arthur stayed on at Portsalon – this letter being addressed to him there – Lewis returned to Belfast. He crossed over to England on 22 September.

140 *The Novel Magazine* was published between 1905 and 1936.

else on the bookstall was even more impossible. My father seemed in very poor form when I got home, and fussed a lot about my cold: so everything is beastly, and I have decided – of course – to commit suicide again.

This morning I visited Mullans on your little job, but their copy of the Kaleva[141] was much too old and shop-soiled to satisfy you, while I couldn't find one in Maynes at all: this being so I didn't know quite whether you meant me to order one or not – at any rate I did NOT. I am sending you – as a peace offering – a little present, which may arrive by the end of this week: change it if you don't care for it – or when you have read it.

I was very much interested in your description of those lakes, tho' I must say that considering my eager desire to see them, both this year and last, it was particularly kind of you to go just after I had left – but not a word of that to the others. I can quite imagine how fine it must have been – rather like the 'Star Bath'[142] as I picture them. The mist's gradual creeping up would have been great. After all, mountain scenery is in some ways the best, isn't it – excepting our own hills with their exquisite little corners of such homely and 'intime' beauty, which are in a different class. How I do wish I could still be with you during the next fortnight! You must let me know whatever you do, and tell me all the funny or exciting 'adventures' that turn up, and I won't feel quite out of it.

To go back to books: I found my Milton Vol. II waiting at Mullans and am very pleased with it, except that the yellow wrapper is in bad condition and can't be worn when it is on its shelf. I have also bought a 7d. Macmillan book by Algernon Blackwood called 'Jimbo, a fantasy'.[143] Although you have never mentioned it, I dare say you know that there is such a book – I never heard of it myself. I am keeping it to read in the train when I go back (Friday night), but I have to restrain myself every moment – it looks so awfully appetizing. If it turns out to be good, of course I will let you know. What are you reading? Try Phrynette[144] if you

---

141 *Kalevala* ('Land of Heroes') is the national epic poem of Finland.

142 During his Easter holiday Lewis added seven more poems to his 'Metrical Meditations of a Cod'. One of these was 'Star Bath' which was possibly suggested by an account of some lakes near Portsalon and was later included in *Spirits in Bondage: A Cycle of Lyrics* (1919).

143 Algernon Blackwood, *Jimbo: A Fantasy* (1909).

144 Marthe Troly-Curtin, *Phrynette and London* (1911); *Phrynette Married* (1912).

can't get anything else. I am still at The Newcomes and the Faerie Queene, reserving the Milton for next term, while in the mornings in bed I am going over 'Sense and Sensibility' again – which I had nearly forgotten. Do you remember Mrs Jennings and Marianne Dashwood and the rest?

On Sunday night my father and I had supper at Glenmachan, whither came the Hamiltons from Knock. K.[elsie] has a scheme for going down with them and me to Larne for a day, which I hope will come off, as I am very dull, and lonely and fed up – indeed I shall not be sorry to leave home.

I needn't apologize for giving you no instalment this week, as you are in the same state, but I will try and do better next time. This letter is perhaps a bit short, but so is yours – we have neither of us yet got our sea legs. Let me hear from you by Tuesday at the very latest, a good long one, as I need a lot of cheering up. Good bye old man,

yours,
Jack

TO HIS FATHER (LP V: 125):

[Gastons]
27/9/16.

My dear Papy,

I hope you got the telegram all right this time: at least it was sent on Saturday afternoon. I had a very tolerable journey, and I think my cold is gone. How is yours? Kirk is very pleased with the Trinity papers and we find them very useful: most of them of course are rather harder than those I shall have, as a Trinity Scholarship is not an entrance scholarship at all, but is taken when you have been 'up' for a year – at least so I am assured. But of course the greater includes the less, and if we master these the other will be all the safer. I am sending back some of the German books which he thinks unsuitable, but we have enough for the present.

Thanks for the letter from Arthur which you forwarded. When he wrote, 'the gaiety of nations'[145] had been increased by Gordon's developing a bad knee which prevented him from walking! On the whole it must

145 Samuel Johnson, *Lives of the English Poets* (1779–81). In the life of 'Edmund Smith' Dr Johnson said the death of David Garrick 'eclipsed the gaiety of nations'.

have been a cheery little party after my leaving them – tho' *that* in itself was perhaps enough to depress any holiday-makers. But of course you will never hint for a moment to anyone that I had anything but panegyrics to say about Portsalon. These people are all so throughother [*sic*] that you never know who will hear what, as Mrs. K. would say.

Everyone here says that they heard the last London raid, though I ingloriously slept all night. With that exception, everything in the war way seems to be going well, doesn't it? It is hot summer weather here without the least suggestion of autumn, which I dislike very much. Kirk is in very good form, although he does not remember M. Henry. About the Westminster confession I have not yet asked.

The collars which Annie was to send me have arrived. I don't know exactly how postage rates are running, but I hope you didn't sell the gramophone or your new picture to raise it. Some day when you have a lot of money and time to spare, I might ask you to send me three catalogues – Macmillan's, Dent's and a French one, which you will find on the table farthest from the window, on the microscope box, in the little end room. Of course at present, ruined as you are by these freights of cellar linen, I shouldn't dare!

your loving
son Jack

TO ARTHUR GREEVES (LP V: 123–4):

[Gastons]
27th./9/16.

My dear Galahad,

I think you must be going dotty with all your talk about when I'm going back, seeing that I said in my first letter that Friday (last) was already fixed. At any rate you must have found out by now, and will understand why I am late in answering your letter, which only reached me today. As you say, it seems years and years since I left: I have quite dropped back into the not unpleasant, though monotonous routine of Bookham, and could almost believe that I had never left it. Portsalon is like a dream. I heartily agree with you that it must have been nice to have the Lounge all to yourselves.

Now to books: I told you didn't I that I had bought Blackwood's Jimbo did I not? I finished it on Sunday and am awfully bucked with it – a very good 7d. worth. It is quite in Blackwood's best manner, and you will specially love the last thirty pages or so – they are terrific. Get it at once. I hope you are not praising 'Letters from Hell' out of politeness, for I really want to know what it is like. I saw it once in a second hand bookshop at Guildford nearly a year ago: looking over the first few pages I thought it excellent, but of course it may not be so good later on. How many books seem to promise such a lot at the start and then turn out disappointing. Whereas good, stodgy books like Scott have all their interesting parts in the middle and begin with reams of dry-as-dust. Talking about stodge, I finished 'The Newcomes' before leaving home, and certainly enjoyed the end better than any parts except the scenes at Baden. Of course it is a great novel, but I am very thankful to have got it off my chest. I should advise you to get the 2/6 volume containing Milton's minor poems,[146] which I am now reading: I am sure they are better to begin on than P.L. I am now at 'Comus', which is an absolute dream of delight. I am sure you would love it: it is like a play written on an episode from the Faerie Queene, all magic and distressed ladies and haunted woods. It is lovely in books the way you can just turn from one sort of beauty to another and never get tired.

I was sorry to find no instalment in your last letter, tho' of course if you have completely lost interest in poor Papillon it is no good forcing yourself. I will consent to your trying a novel only on the condition that it be sent to me, chapter by chapter. I too am wondering whether I should not chuck Bleheris and start something else: partly I have so many ideas and also I think the old fashioned English is a fatal mistake. Any good things that are in it or would be later on, can be worked in elsewhere. In a way it is disheartening to remember how keenly we were both starting out on our tales this time last term and see the result. But still we have both much experience and practice gained, and we got a lot of pleasure out of them while they lasted: the danger is that we get to turn too easily from one thing to another and never get anything done.

I didn't go to see anything in London, I really don't know why – I was a bit tired, nothing seemed to attract me much, and also, having started 'Jimbo' in the train, was eager to get to it again. One part of my journey I enjoyed very much was the first few miles out of Liverpool: because it was one of the most wonderful mornings I have ever seen – one of those lovely white misty ones when you can't see 10 yards. You could just see

146 John Milton, *Paradise Regained and Minor Poems*, ed. F.E. Bumby [1910].

the nearest trees and houses, a little ghostly in appearance, and beyond that everything was a clean white blank. It felt as if the train was alone in space, if you know what I mean.

I think you are very wise not to take that puppy from K[elso Ewart]. Unless you are a person with plenty of spare time and real knowledge, it is a mistake to keep dogs – and cruel to them. Have you got the Kaleva yet, tell me when you do and what you think of it. I wonder where you are at this moment? Have you reached home yet? Tell me all the news when you write, what you're reading etc. and whether you are going back to your taskmaster Tom at once.[147] I am not nearly so fed up now as I was, and hope you are the same. The country at home was beginning to look nice and autumn-y, with dead leaves in the lanes and a nice nutty smell (you know what I mean) so I suppose it is getting better still. Here it is horrible bright summer which I hate. Love to all our friends such as the hedgepig etc.

Yours,
Jack.

TO ARTHUR GREEVES (W):

[Gastons]
Oct. Ugh! 10/4/16!! [4 October 1916]

My dear Arthur,

I believe it is Lamb who says somewhere that he does not know whether it is more delightful to set out for a holiday or return from one: perhaps you hardly agree with him! Though I am sure he hated his office (read 'The Superannuated Man')[148] quite as much as you do. But of course he means, I suppose, the getting back to home, to ones books etc and not to work. However I suppose you are gradually getting 'broken in'.

The beastly summer is at last over here, and good old Autumn colours & smells and temperatures have come back. Thanks to this we had a most glorious walk on Saturday: it was a fine cool, windy day & we set out after lunch to go to a place called 'Friday Street' which is a very long walk from here through beautiful woods and vallies that I don't know well.[149] After several hours wandering over fields & woods etc. with

147 Arthur was assisting Tom Greeves in his brother's business.
148 Collected in Charles Lamb's *Essays of Elia* (1823).
149 Friday Street, Surrey, about 10 miles south of Great Bookham.

the aid of a map we began to get lost and suddenly at about 4 o'clock – we had expected to reach the place by that time – we found ourselves in a place where we had been an hour before! *You* will understand that while the others were only annoyed at this, I felt je ne sais quoi de dreamlike and terrifying sensation at the idea of wandering round in circles through these big, solemn woods; also there was a certain tinge of 'Alice-in-W-ism' about it. We had a lot of difficulty in at last reaching the place, but it was glorious when we got there. You are walking in the middle of a wood when all of a sudden you go downwards and come to a little open hollow just big enough for a little lake and some old, old red-tiled houses: all round it the trees tower up on rising ground and every road from it is at once swallowed up in them. You might walk within a few feet of it & suspect nothing unless you saw the smoke rising up from some cottage chimney. Can you imagine what it was like? Best of all, we came down to the little inn of the village and had tea there with – glory of glories – an old tame jackdaw hopping about our feet and asking for crumbs. He is called Jack and will answer to his name.

The inn has three tiny but spotlessly clean bedrooms, so some day, – if the gods will, you & I are going to stay there. The inn is called the 'Stephen Langton' and dates from the time of that gentleman's wars against the king or the barons or somebody (you'll know I expect),[150] tho' of course it has been rebuilt since. I don't like playing the guide-book, but it was so ravishing that I had to tell you. We were so late getting there that it was dark soon after we left, and often going astray we didn't get home till ten o'clock – dead beat but happy.

Partly because the country we saw that day was so like it I have been reading again the second volume of Malory, especially the part of the 'Sangreal' which I had forgotten. With all its faults, in small doses this book is tip-top: those mystic parts are very good to read late at night when you are drowsy and tired and get into a sort of 'exalted' mood. Do you know what I mean? You so often share feelings of mine which I can't explain that I hope you do: mention this subject when you next write. Besides this I have finished 'Comus' with great enjoyment: I have also re-read for the thousandth time 'Rapunzel' and some other favourite bits of Morris, while through the week I have read an excellent novel of

150 Stephen Langton (d. 1228), Archbishop of Canterbury, in his later life supported the regency in its struggles against baronial insubordination.

Vachell's 'The Paladin'[151] which you have probably read too and also dipped often into Boswell's 'Life of Johnson'.[152] Being entirely made up of conversation I don't think it is a book to be read continuously, tho' it is very good fun in bits: you are thinking of getting it I believe. I agree with you that I must read some more books in the particular 'genre' of 'Our Village' etc, but there are so many things to read that I don't know where to begin. I forget what edition you are getting of the 'Scenes of Clerical life'[153]

As to the fate of sad Papillon, I will look at the exact place of leaving-off when I go upstairs & write it down somewhere in pencil: unless you decide to go on with it don't waste time & energy copying the rest but send me instead the first drafts of your new work. I should be glad, though, to see you going on with it and have the complete tale, for there is good stuff in it: however, I can't preach in this respect now! Loki & Dennis & Bleheris, all our operas, plays etc go one way; perhaps they are caught like Wan Jadis in the Grey Marish on the way to the country of the past![154] For my part I am at present engaged in making huge plans both for prose and verse none of which I shall try. I begin to see that short, slight stories & poems are all I am fit for at present & that it would be better to write & finish one of such than to begin & leave twenty ambitious epic-poems or romances. I wait eagerly either for another instalment of the Watersprite or else some new venture from you: you shall have the first thing I do, if I ever do anything.

How I wish I had been with you at Mr Thompson's.[155] Everything seems to have happened well after my departure – I suppose you say no wonder! what a female-minded person I am getting! I would cross out that remark as peevish & 'cattish', but it would make a mess and you would only wonder what was underneath. Take it as unsaid.

Have you got or begun the 'Kalevala' yet? Give me your first impressions when you do. Papillon has got to where they are both under the

---

151 Horace Annesley Vachell, *The Paladin, As Beheld by a Woman of Temperament* (1909).

152 James Boswell, *The Life of Samuel Johnson* (1791).

153 George Eliot, *Scenes of Clerical Life* (1858).

154 Wan Jadis is a young man in Lewis's 'Bleheris'. In chapter XI this 'sweet and comely youth' is caught in a swamp named the 'Grey Marish'. Lewis was later to use the name 'Jadis' in the Chronicles of Narnia for the Queen of Charn who becomes the White Witch.

155 James A. Thompson was a resident of Strandtown and of some consequence in the congregation of St Mark's, Dundela.

water and ends with the words 'it shot him much farther than he had intended so that he nearly lost sight of the fairy'. Looking at it revives my enthusiasm. Do go on with it if you can: certainly send me the rest provided this doesn't interfere with any new work. Now good night Galahad the 'haut prince' as Malory [would] say,

yours
Jack

P.S. Poor puppy!! What a life it'll have! I shall poison it in kindness when I come home!

P.P.S. Why do your letters never come till Wednesday now?

TO HIS FATHER (LP V: 129–30):

[Gastons]
10/6/16 [6 October 1916]

My dear Papy,

Many thanks for the catalogues, which were necessary to my peace of mind. I shouldn't try the 'conceit' if I were you, as two can play at that game, and you might get a number of strange parcels.

Since I last wrote, that awe-inspiring person the Tutor for Entrances of Balliol has deigned to forward us last year's scholarship papers for that college – although we are I think quite determined now on the big group. He distinguished himself by doing the very thing that we have so often discussed – addressing his envelope to the 'Rev. T.W. Kirkpatrick', thinking I suppose that no one except a clergyman could possibly be entrusted with the youth of a nation. The papers themselves were pretty much what we expected, and not discouraging. The subject for an English essay – with no alternative – was 'Diplomacy' which is rather a mouthful. It would involve a good deal of history. Kirk has been growing very enthusiastic on the superior composition of these papers to the Trinity ones, which indeed were rather unintelligently drawn up. Some of the pieces in the scholarship exams are desperately hard, while others in the Fellowship ones are ridiculously easy: of course it is the competition and the standard required which really makes the difference. I agree with you that a 'course' would be much worse than this scheme: for while it is true that a man can always learn a course, another can always learn it better.

I am reading at present a book whose scene is laid in Oxford and which tells one a good deal about the University (not Tom Brown),[156] 'Lady Connie' by Mrs. Humphrey Ward.[157] She is a favourite of yours, is she not? I have never read her until now, and she seems to have many points. She is rather a pedant tho', insists too much on her 'culture', and tells us a great deal about tanagra Statues, Titainesque effects, discoveries in Crete, Euripides, Goethe, etc., etc. You know what I mean.

We have yet another pupil here now – a boy who comes every morning to do Spanish. He is reading for the Foreign Office. It seems a lovely language, and so easy that I can imagine 'even Warnie' taking to it. I wish I could prevent Arthur's invasions, but don't know quite how to do it.

your loving
son Jack.

TO ARTHUR GREEVES (W):

[Gastons]
(The 12th. Oct., I think) [1916]

My dear Arthur,

It was unfortunate that I should choose a word like 'exaltation' which is so often used in connection with religion and so give you a wrong impression of my meaning. I will try to explain again: have you ever sat over the fire late, late at night when you are very drowzy & muddle headed, and it is no use trying to go on with your book? Everything seems like a dream, you are absolutely contented, and 'out of the world'. Anything seems possible, and all sorts of queer ideas float through your mind & sort of vaguely thrill you but only mildly & calmly. It is in this sort of mood that the quaint, old mystical parts of Malory are exactly suitable: you can read a chapter or two in a sort of dream & find the forests of 'Logres & of Lyonesse' very agreeable at such a time – at least I do.

As to the other question about religion, I was sad to read your letter. You ask me my religious views: you know, I think, that I beleive in no religion. There is absolutely no proof for any of them, and from a philosophical standpoint Christianity is not even the best. All religions, that is, all mythologies to give them their proper name are merely man's own

156 Thomas Hughes, *Tom Brown's Schooldays* (1857); *Tom Brown at Oxford* (1861).
157 Mrs Humphrey Ward (Mary Augusta Ward), *Lady Connie* (1916).

invention – Christ as much as Loki. Primitive man found himself surrounded by all sorts of terrible things he didn't understand – thunder, pestilence, snakes etc: what more natural than to suppose that these were animated by evil spirits trying to torture him. These he kept off by cringing to them, singing songs and making sacrifices etc. Gradually from being mere nature-spirits these supposed being[s] were elevated into more elaborate ideas, such as the old gods: and when man became more refined he pretended that these spirits were good as well as powerful.

Thus religion, that is to say mythology grew up. Often, too, great men were regarded as gods after their death – such as Heracles or Odin: thus after the death of a Hebrew philosopher Yeshua (whose name we have corrupted into Jesus) he became regarded as a god, a cult sprang up, which was afterwards connected with the ancient Hebrew Jahweh-worship, and so Christianity came into being – one mythology among many, but the one that we happen to have been brought up in.

Now all this you must have heard before: it is the recognised scientific account of the growth of religions. Superstition of course in every age has held the common people, but in every age the educated and thinking ones have stood outside it, though usually outwardly conceding to it for convenience. I had thought that you were gradually being emancipated from the old beliefs, but if this is not so, I hope we are too sensible to quarrel about abstract ideas. I must only add that ones views on religious subjects don't make any difference in morals, of course. A good member of society must of course try to be honest, chaste, truthful, kindly etc: these are things we owe to our own manhood & dignity and not to any imagined god or gods.

Of course, mind you, I am not laying down as a certainty that there is nothing outside the material world: considering the discoveries that are always being made, this would be foolish. Anything MAY exist: but until we know that it does, we can't make any assumptions. The universe is an absolute mystery: man has made many guesses at it, but the answer is yet to seek. Whenever any new light can be got as to such matters, I will be glad to welcome it. In the meantime I am not going to go back to the bondage of believing in any old (& already decaying) superstition.

See! I have wasted 3/4 of my letter on all these dry bones. However, old man, you started the subject and I had to have my turn. Yes, I wish you had really been with me on the walk to Friday-Street: how you and I, alone, would have gloried in those woods and vallies! But some day we will go and spend a week there at the inn, get up at 5 every morning & go to bed at 8, spending the interval sitting by the lake and talking to the Jackdaw. He can only say 'Caw' so that will be a nice change after my torrents of conversation!

I have written up for 'Letters from Hell' and it ought to be here by the end of the week. I am looking forward to it immensely and will enjoy being able to talk it over with you. You ask me what 'special' book I am reading at present: you must remember that I read seriously only on week-ends. When I last wrote my week-end books were 'Comus' and the Morte Darthur; last week-end, 'Comus' being finished, its place was taken by Shelley's 'Prometheus Unbound'[158] which I got half through. It is an amazing work. I don't know how to describe it to you; it is more wild & out of the world than any poem I ever read, and contains some wonderful descriptions. Shelley had a great genius, but his carelessness about rhymes, metre, choice of words etc, just prevents him being as good as he might be. To me, when you're in the middle of a fine passage and come to a 'cockney' rhyme like 'ru*in*' & 'pursu*ing*', it spoils the whole thing – makes it vulgar and grotesque. However some parts are so splendid that I could forgive him anything. I am now, through the week, reading Scott's 'Antiquary'.[159] I suppose you have read it long ago: I am very pleased with it, especially the character of the Antiquary himself, the description of his room, and the old beggar. Tell me your views when you write – it is nice gradually to get more & more into each other's style of reading, is it not – you with poetry and I with classical novels?

As to Bleheris, he is dead and I shan't trouble his grave.[160] I will try and write something new soon – a short tale, I expect – but am rather taken up with verse at present, in my spare-time; which gets less and less as the exam. draws nearer. However I look eagerly for the first chapter of your novel, or failing that, the next leaf of Dennis.

It is an amazing thing to call the 'Kalevala' tame: whatever else it is, it is not tame. If a poem all about floods & primeval spirits and magic and talking beasts & monsters is not wild enough, I really don't know what to say! However, chacun à son gout! As to the Milton I daren't advise you –

---

158 Percy Bysshe Shelley, *Prometheus Unbound* (1820).

159 Sir Walter Scott, *The Antiquary* (1816).

160 'The Quest of Bleheris' lies in a very distinguished 'grave'. The manuscript is now in the Bodleian Library (MS. Eng. lett. c. 220/5, fols. 5–43).

both volumes are so good, if you care for him. You don't give any criticism on 'Evelina';[161] do so, when you write.

It is a lovely moonlight night (a brau' brich' minlich' nicht, do you remember). I wish you were here. Goodnight

J.

TO HIS FATHER (LP V: 132):

[Gastons]
12th October 1916

My dear Papy,

We have all been plunged in misery here for the last week because no one can remember the context or the author of a quotation that we all know as well as our own names. It started by Mrs. K. seeing it in the 'In Memoriam' part of the paper and asking casually what it was from: since then we have ransacked our memories and books of reference in vain. You will laugh us to scorn when I tell you that it is the familiar,

'E'en as he trod that day to God
So walked he from his birth,
In simpleness and gentleness
And honour and clean mirth.'[162]

but I am dashed if I can remember where it comes from. Some time I am sure it is Kipling, and again in other moods it seems impossible. Try and enlighten us.

You are rather too severe on the 'Diplomacy' essay: it is not – in my poor conceit – that the subject is not bounded enough, but that it is too bounded. It hems the candidate down to a field of historical and even technical knowledge that they have no right to expect of him. Now an essay on 'air' in a scientific exam would be very proper, and even an essay on virtue would have no vice about it. You may produce that 'mot' as one of your own when you next meet Bill Patterson 'that sprightly caliph' on the top of his tramcar. Before leaving the subject of exams, I must remark that the Oxford papers do not include one on 'accidents' which is

---

161 Frances Burney, *Evelina* (1778).
162 See note 167 to letter of 19 October 1916 for the actual source of this quotation.

a relief: tho' of course if I am going to break down in that way, I shall have plenty of opportunities in the composition.

I am sorry to hear of your being laid up, and even Arthur's assurance that he is 'going to call on my father some time soon' does not quite make up for it. If the weather at home is the same medley that we have here, I am not surprised. It is alternately hot, damp and warm, or cold and windy. I wish we could settle down to good winter weather and habits.

I have finished 'Lady Connie' and though it does not end as well as it begins, it was good enough to make me determine to read some more of hers next holidays. Since then I have been dipping into Boswell, whom I grow to like better and better.

Thanks for the enclosure which was a letter from my old Malvern study companion, who is in some mysterious affair called the 'Artist's Rifle.' Did you ever hear of it? I confess I don't know what claim Hardman has to be an artist.

Hoping you are quite set up again by now,
I am,
your loving
son Jack.

TO ARTHUR GREEVES (W):

[Gastons]
(Forgotten the date) [18 October 1916]

My dear Arthur,

Frequently in arguing with you by letter I have had to ask you to read what I say carefully before you rush on to answer it. I distinctly said that there was once a Hebrew called Yeshua, I think on p. 2 (II!!) of my letter: when I say 'Christ' of course I mean the mythological being into whom he was afterwards converted by popular imagination, and I am thinking of the legends about his magic performances and resurrection etc. That the man Yeshua or Jesus did actually exist, is as certain as that the Buddha did actually exist: Tacitus mentions his execution in the Annals.[163] But all the other tomfoolery about virgin birth, magic healings, apparitions and so forth is on exactly the same footing as any other mythology. After all even your namesake king Arthur really lived once (if

163 Cornelius Tacitus, *Annals* (c. 116), Bk. XV, sect. 44.

we are to believe the latest theories) but it doesn't follow that Malory's old book is history. In the same way there was such a person as Alexander the Great, but the adventures which the Middle Ages related of him are nonsense. It is generally thought, too, that there was such a man as Odin, who was deified after his death: so you see most legends have a kernel of fact in them somewhere. Indeed, these distinctions are so very obvious, that if you were not my best friend I should almost suspect you of wilfully misunderstanding me through temper.

Later on you ask me why I am sad, and suggest that it is because I have no hope of a 'happy life hereafter'. No; strange as it may appear I am quite content to live without beleiving in a bogey who is prepared to torture me forever and ever if I should fail in coming up to an almost impossible ideal (which is a part of the Christian mythology, however much you try to explain it away). In fact I should think it horrible to feel that if life got too bad, I daren't escape for fear of a spirit more cruel and barbarous than any man. Then you are good enough to ask me why I don't kill myself. Because – as I have said to you before – in spite of occasional fits of depression I am very well pleased with life and have a very happy time on the whole. The only reason I was sad was because I was dissapointed in my hope that you were gradually escaping from beleifs which, in my case, always considerably lessened my happiness: if, however, it has the opposite effect on you, tant mieux pour vous! As to the immortality of the soul, though it is a fascinating theme for day-dreaming, I neither beleive nor disbeleive: I simply don't know anything at all, there is no evidence either way. Now let us take off our armour, hang up our swords and talk about things where there is no danger of coming to blows!

Yes, I quite agree that the metre of the Kalevala is tedious & the word 'tame' exactly describes it. It doesn't sort of rise to the subject at all, but is always the same whatever is happening. If you give this up – and there is no point in going on unless it takes your fancy – don't let it quench your rising taste for poetry. I must really fulfill my long standing purpose and settle down to some more books of the 'Cranford'[164] type: your description has made me quite enthusiastic, so without fail tell me the edition you have got it & all your Austens etc in? I finished 'The Antiquary' this afternoon, and it thoroughly denies our old wheeze about

164 Elizabeth Cleghorn Gaskell, *Cranford* (1853).

most books getting tiresome halfway through. It gets better and better as it goes on, and I have not enjoyed anything so much for a long time. I believe I shall soon become almost as devoted to Scott as you are: I begin to feel that sort of 'repose', which you like, in turning to him. Which of his should I try next? I shall be glad to hear your views on 'Lavengro'[165] when you have read it, also by whom this mysterious 1/- edition is published.

And now I must turn to 'Letters of Hell'. I suppose I must have looked forward to it too much: at any rate – I will tell the truth – I have failed to read it, have not enjoyed it a bit and have put it away in my drawer unfinished. There! Am I fallen in your eyes forever? I don't really know why I disliked it so much, because I could see all the time that there was good in it if only I could appreciate it – which makes it all the more annoying. For one thing I expected beauties of the phantastic type, and in reality it turns out only a novel. For the parts about Hell are after all only a setting for the story of his previous life – a story which seemed to me so far as I read it supremely commonplace. The characters are all absolutely crude – wicked rich men of the melodramatic type and miraculously innocent angels of heroines. The only part I liked was the vision of paradise, which struck me as good. Still, when both you and Macdonald praise the book, I am ready to beleive that the fault must be in me and not in it.

Thanks for the instalment: as the post only came in at 9 o'clock I can't read it yet or I won't get my letter to you done till bedtime – but you shall have my verdict ('impudence' say you) next week. Do either go on with this tale or start something new: I am trying to make out the plan of a short tale but nothing 'comes'. That is an awful waste, that book W[arnie] gave my father: wouldn't you love an edition with that binding and paper, only the size of my Kipling, say of the Brontës or James Stephens or Macdonald? Talking about Kipling it is time you began him: try 'Rewards & Fairies'[166] and if the first story in it 'Cold Iron' doesn't knock you head over heels, I don't know what will. Good night, they're all gone up, and I have tired you by now 'I *do* talk *so*.'

Jack

---

165 George Borrow, *Lavengro* (1851).

166 Rudyard Kipling, *Rewards and Fairies* (1910).

P.S. (In the bedroom) It is much more wintry to night, and when I came up the curtains were not drawn and the room was full of moonlight, bright bright as anything. It is too cold to sit looking at the glorious night but it *is* beautiful! I shake your hand. Goodnight. I wish you could come & 'grind' at Gastons. Ugh. Horrible cold sheets now

J.

TO HIS FATHER (LP V: 133–4):

[Gastons]
19/Oct./16.

My dear Papy,

Yes! That was a bad lapse of memory, and now that the mystery is solved, I wonder how I could possibly have forgotten it. Perhaps the fact of its being printed as 3 lines (the 'God' and 'trod' rhymes having lines to themselves) had something to do with it. Still, it was a nasty blunder, and I thought I knew my Kipling better than that. Like all quotations from good authors, it is much finer in its setting than when we read it alone: that whole poem ought to settle for good and all K's question as to whether Kipling be a poet.[167] He could be 'spoken to' as poor Uncle Bill was on a similar occasion.

Many thanks for the 'Spectator' which I shall certainly keep for the sake of the poem. It is, I quite agree with you, a really notable piece of work, quite above the average. The verse beginning 'Life? – 'Twas a little thing to give' is glorious, and also the last two lines

'Who bartered for Youth's diadem
The dross of after years.'[168]

I wonder is there any country outside these islands where about every 10th man is a poet, as seems to be the case with us? I wish somebody of real taste would collect all the verse that is appearing in the papers at present and make a selection – it would be the best anthology ever published. As to F.S. Boas I know him well from a book of his on

---

167 The Kipling quotation comes from the prefatory/dedicatory poem to the *Barrack-Room Ballads* (1892). It has no title in the original but simply follows a separate dedicatory page to Wolcott Balestier.

168 'Ulster on the Somme' by F.S. Boas, *The Spectator* (14 October 1916), p. 443.

Shakespeare[169] that Kirk has, but it never struck me that there was any relationship. Perhaps it was he who 'lectured on Herrick'? The nephew I don't remember, though he must have been at Campbell in my time.

The other article has a lot of sense in it: the writer must be like K's friend, of whom I told you, who could give anyone points in classical literature without knowing Latin or Greek. That Butcher and Lang translation of Homer[170] is very good, and so is Bacon's bit of Lucretius, tho' not as beautiful as his own suggestion that 'it be with pity'. Of course I suppose only the very greatest poetry will stand translation: fancy a French prose version of Swinburne.

I am at present reading a book which you would enjoy, 'The letters of Dorothy Osborne to Sir William Temple'.[171] In case you have forgotten who they were, you can turn to Macaulay's essay on the latter.[172] They lived in Cromwell's time, and the letters are very quaint. In the notes the editor also quotes an account of the 'remove these baubles' scene by an eye-witness, who was apparently a member of the old aristocracy and tells us indignantly how the Lord Protector came into the House in 'grey worsted stockings'.[173] They had their own way of writing love letters in those days: Mistress Osborne begins hers 'Sir' like a letter to a newspaper, and ends up 'your humble servant' or 'your faithful friend'. Almost a la Gordon.

your loving
son Jack.

TO ARTHUR GREEVES (W):

[Gastons]
25th Oct 1916

My dear Galahad,

As usually happens in these sort of things the violent controversy that we have been having for the last three weeks (& which I quite agree with you in giving up) has obscured the original subject of the discussion 'exaltation'. I want to know if you understand that sort of 'fey'

---

169 Frederick Samuel Boas, *Shakespeare and his Predecessors* (1896).
170 *The Odyssey of Homer*, done into English by Samuel Henry Butcher and Andrew Lang (1879).
171 *Letters from Dorothy Osborne to Sir William Temple: 1652–4*, ed. E.A. Parry (1888).
172 'Sir William Temple', *The Works of Lord Macaulay*, 12 vols. (1898), vol. IX, pp. 1–110.
173 *Letters from Dorothy Osborne*, introduction to letter 17 (24 April 1653), pp. 75–6.

state of mind which I described, or tried to describe, as coming on when one is very drowzy. Say what you think of this in your next letter. The question arose out of the 'Morte' which I have now read from the beginning of the Quest of the Grael to the end, thus finishing the whole thing. I certainly enjoyed it much better than before, and wished that I had the first volume here as well. The quietness of the end, and the description of Arthur's death are particularly good – you must give it another try sometime.

It was silly of me to ask you about 'Cranford' etc, as I have a MacMillan's list here and could have looked them up myself if I had had the sense: but I suppose you regard that as a big 'if'! I can understand that it is not pleasing to have these in the same edition as the Jane Austens, tho' for me of course it would make a nice change. I don't know when I shall buy some new books, as I am at present suffering from a flash of poverty – poverty comes in flashes like dulness or pleasure. When I do it will be either 'Our Village', 'Cranford' or Chaucer's 'Troilus & Cressida', if I can get a decent edition of it. By all accounts it is much more in my line than the 'Canterbury Tales', and anyway I can take no more interest in them since I have discovered that my Everyman edition is abridged & otherwise mutilated. I wish they wouldn't do that ('Lockhart',[174] you say, is another case) without telling you. I can't bear to have anything but what a man really wrote.

I have been reading the quaintest book this week, 'The Letters of Dorothy Osborne to Sir William Temple' in Everyman. I suppose, as a historian you will know all about those two, but in case you don't they lived in Cromwell's time. It is very interesting to read the ordinary everyday life of a girl in those days, and, tho' of course they are often dull there is a lot in them you would like: especially a description of how she spends the day and another of a summer evening in the garden. It is funny too, to notice that, just like us, she says that she never wished very hard for anything in her life without being dissapointed. But then I suppose everyone in the world has said that sometime or other. It is perhaps not a book to read straight through but well worth having.

My other reading – in French – has been Maeterlinck's 'Oiseau Bleu': of course I have read it before in English and seen it on the stage, as you know, but I am absolutely delighted to read it again. Now that I have the

174 John Gibson Lockhart, *Memoirs of the Life of Sir Walter Scott*, 7 vols. (1937–8).

original I wish you would adopt my English version, which is yours forever for the taking whenever you care to walk up to my room at home and find it on the little open bookcase. You could do it to day when you are home for lunch: I don't know why you have never read this glorious book before, but please do as I suggest & (though it is always dangerous, as we know, to recommend) I think you will have some real joy out of it. The scenes in the Temple of Night and in the Kingdom of the Future are exactly in our line.

Unfortunately we have not got a complete set of Scott here – only odd Everyman copies of which 'The Fair Maid of Perth' is not one. The earlier period is of course all the better for me, in fact to be honest I am childish enough to like 'Ivanhoe' better than any of his, and next to it 'Quentin Durward'. What is 'Guy Mannering' like? The alternative title of 'The Astrologer' sounds attractive but of course it may not have much to do with it.[175]

How's the poor, miserable, ill-fated, star-crossed, hapless, lonely, neglected, misunderstood puppy getting along? What are you going to call him, or rather, to speak properly, how hight he? Don't give him any commonplace name, and above all let it suit his character & appearance. Something like Sigurd, Pelleas or Mars if he is brisk and warlike, or Mime, Bickernocker or Knutt if he is ugly and quaint. Or perhaps he is dead by now, poor little devil!

The book you refer to is 'How to Form a Literary Taste' by Arnold Benett:[176] the edition is pretty but the book is not of any value. The very title – as if you set out to 'learn' literature the way you learn golf – shews that the author is not a real book-lover but only a priggish hack. I never read any of his novels & don't want to. Have you? By the way, he is a rather violent atheist, so I suppose I shall meet him by

'The fiery, flaming flood of Phlegethon',[177]

as good old Spencer has it. I am sure Lockhart's Life of Scott would be good, but 5 vols. at 3/6 each is too much: at any rate I had sooner get

175 Sir Walter Scott, *The Fair Maid of Perth* (1828); *Ivanhoe* (1820); *Quentin Durward* (1823); *Guy Mannering* (1815).

176 Arnold Bennett, *Literary Taste: How to Form It, with Detailed Instructions for Collecting a Complete Library of English Literature* (1909).

177 Spenser, *Faerie Queene*, I, v, 33, 3: 'And come to fiery flood of *Phlegeton*'.

Boswell if I were going to make a start on biography. I have read to day – there's absolutely no head or tale in this letter but you ought to be used to that by now – some 10 pages of 'Tristam Shandy'[178] and am wondering whether I like it. It is certainly the maddest book ever written or 'ever wrote' as dear Dorothy Osborne would say. It gives you the impression of an escaped lunatic's conversation while chasing his hat on a windy May morning. Yet there are beautiful serious parts in it though of a sentimental kind, as I know from my father. Have you ever come across it?

Tang-Tang there goes eleven o'clock 'Tis almost faery time'.[179] Don't you simply love going to bed. To curl up warmly in a nice warm bed, in the lovely darkness, that is so restful & then gradually drift away into sleep...Perhaps to enjoy this properly you must stay up till 11 working fairly hard at something – even a letter like this – so as to be really hungry for sleep. At home, like you, I often get started off on a train of thought which keeps me awake: here I am always too tired tho' goodness knows, eleven is early enough compared with some peoples times. It is strange, somehow, to read about concerts & Bill Patterson's visits etc; when I am at Bookham everything at home seems a little unreal. Each of you (i.e. my friends) is quite real by him or herself but 'en bloc' you seem like something out of a book. I wish I had been with you at D. Garrick.[180] I have always heard it was good. I shall not soon forget that morning at the far end of the strand, with the pleasant 'Frightfulness' of the Waves. I can still remember exactly what it felt like in the water and also running up to the cave. Take it all in all, we've had many pleasant times in our lives, & of these many (in my case) the most part together. You'd think I was bidding you an eternal farewell the way I'm going on. There's quarter past, so I'll say 'Good morning' not 'Night' for you read this at breakfast, don't you? I'm turning out the gas. Bon soir!

Jack

By the way, what sort of voice has a 'cracked turnip'. See your last letter.

---

178 Laurence Sterne, *The Life and Opinions of Tristram Shandy*, 9 vols (1760–7).

179 William Shakespeare, *A Midsummer Night's Dream* (1600), V, i, 372.

180 Thomas William Robertson, *David Garrick* (1864), a comedy in three acts.

TO HIS FATHER (LP V: 134–5):

[Gastons]
27/Oct./16.

My dear Papy,

Far be it from me to plead in extenuation of the disgusting freak of Algy that it was only fun. The debauches of a ruffian are not the less disgraceful because they are the product of levity, and Nero is said to have fiddled – about which I have my own views – on a famous occasion. As a matter of fact, to be serious, if Elia's theory that 'the best puns are the worst'[181] is true also of Limericks, Swinburne's Majorca one is a masterpiece, and so is the next one about Birmingham – though on the whole I would agree with you in preferring the 'deserted garden'.

I was very sorry to hear of the death of 'A Student in arms', whose book I read last holidays as you may remember.[182] I never met anything exactly like it before, it is wonderfully original and beautiful. Nothing in it however, if I remember aright, quite reaches the level of this last article, a wise and charming piece of work – and doubly so from the exquisite appropriateness with which it comes from the pen of a man who died a few days after writing it. As you say, there is almost something divine about the way in which he sums up his beliefs and his views on death, just as though he knew the end was coming and meant to finish off his work. The substance of this paper resembles Bernard Shaw's cry, 'Why not give Christianity a trial?' – so far at least as the writing of a scholar and a gentleman can resemble that of a Philistine. Indeed nowadays there seems to be a tendency in that direction: there is some possibility of getting back it appears, to what Christ actually did teach, and clearing away all the additions His followers have been tacking on for the last twenty centuries.

Before leaving the subject of 'Student in Arms', I must draw your attention to what seems a mis-print in the sentence marked. Surely the full stop should come after 'discouraged', and not after 'offend'. The author first states a general principle 'Anxious responsibility is discouraged', and then

---

181 Charles Lamb, 'That the Worst Puns are the Best', *The Last Essays of Elia* (1833).

182 *A Student in Arms*, with an Introduction by John St Loe Stracher (1916) was published anonymously. Lewis and his father had seen a piece in *The Spectator*, vol. 117 (21 October 1916), pp. 466–7, entitled 'In Memory of "A Student in Arms" (Second Lieutenant Donald Hankey, Killed in Action on the Somme, October 12th, 1916).'

about characters & 'problems' to a time when hunting, fighting, eating, drinking & loving were all a man had to think of it. And lastly, always remember it's a translation which spoils most things.

As to 'Malory' I liked it so awfully this time – far better than before – that I don't know what to say. How can I explain? For one thing, to me it is a world of its own, like Jane Austen. Though impossible, it is very fully realized, and all the characters are old friends, we know them so well: you get right away in those forests and somehow to me all the adventures & meetings & dragons seem very real. (I don't beleive that last sentence conveys my meaning a bit) Then too I find in it a rest as you do in Scott: he (M. I mean) is so quiet after our modern writers & thinks of his 'art' so little: he is not self-conscious. Of course he doesn't describe as Morris does, but then he doesn't need to: in the 'Well' you feel it is only a tale suddenly invented and therefore everything has to be described. But the Round Table is different: it *was* a hundred years ago & shall be a hundred years hence. It wasn't just made up like an ordinary tale, it grew. Malory seems to me almost a historian: his world is real to me, his characters are old friends whom you get to know better & better as you go on – he is a companiabl author & good when you're lonely.

I suppose this sounds all rot? But after all when you say it 'doesn't suit you' you strike at the root of the matter. Perhaps you can't enjoy it just as I couldn't enjoy Green's Short History:[187] it is not my fault that I don't like oysters but no reasoning will make me like them. This controversy has proved even more expansive than the other: if you had given me any excuse for going on with the 'exaltation' one I'm afraid I should never get to bed to-night. By the way I suppose at 10 o'clock when I am beginning your letter you are just getting into bed? Remember at 10 next Wednesday night to imagine me just spreading out your one in front of me and starting to jaw. But seriously, do I bore you. I have taken up such reams about 'Boewulf' etc. It is easy to explain a thought, but to explain a feeling is very hard.

Last week-end I spent in reading 'The Professor'. It forms a nice sort of suppliment to Villette – something [like] the same story told from the man's side. I liked the description of Hunsden extremely & also the detestable brother. I do wish she had left out the awful poetry in the proposal scene: they are the worst verses in the language I should think. Its

187 John Richard Green, *Short History of the English People* (1874).

difficult to understand how a woman of Ch. Brontës genius could help seeing how bad they were. But on the whole it is a very enjoyable book, tho' not of course to be compared with her other three. What did you think of it?

Yes, I shall be home for Xmas, rather earlier in fact. This exam.[188] will take place in the first week of December and when it is over I shall come straight home. I am beginning to funk it rather: I wish you were in for it with me (so as to be sure of one, at least, worse than myself). I wish I could see 'The Winter's Tale': it, 'The Midsummer's Nights Dream' & the Tempest are the only things of Shakespeare I really appreciate, except the Sonnets.[189] It is a very sweet, sort of old fairy-tale style of thing. You must certainly see it. As to Bennet's book, if a person was really a book-lover, however ignorant, he wouldn't go and look up a text book to see what to buy, as if literature was a subject to be learned like algebra: one thing would lead him to another & he would go through the usual mistakes & gain experience. I hate this idea of 'forming a taste'. If anyone like the feuilletons in the 'Sketch' better than Spenser, for Heaven's sake let him read them: anything is better than to read things he doesn't really like because they are thought classical. I say, old man, it's beastly kind of you to keep the 'Country of the Blind' till I come. Of course if you hadn't told me I should have thought you would throw it off the top of the tram. Ha-Ha-Ha-Ha, likewise He-He-He! (You do love that sort of writing!) By the way why do you call it your dog if it lives at Glenmachen? I suppose in the same way as you like Shakespeare but I don't like reading him? Can't write more to night, your last letter was very short –

J.

TO HIS FATHER (LP V: 142):

[Gastons]
3/11/16.

My dear Papy,

This is a surprise. I can hardly account for it, if it be true – a jump from the rank of second Lieutenant to that of Captain is very unusual, is it not?[190] Even among the temporary people. However, I suppose you will

188 The scholarship examination for Oxford.

189 William Shakespeare, *The Winter's Tale* (1623); *The Tempest* (1623); *Sonnets* (1609).

190 Warnie, who was with the 3rd Company 7th Division in France, had been promoted to temporary captain on 1 October.

know all about it in your next letter from Big Brother, who will doubtless communicate the facts with much codotto. I only hope we shall not be disappointed in any way.

I thought that I had told you about the colleges, but apparently not. We have finally burned our boats and sent in my name for the big group. This has not been without a good deal of hesitation, but I think on the whole it was the wisest plan. There are very strong arguments on both sides, and we can only hope for the best. The man at New tells us that the candidates for scholarships will be either lodged in the colleges or directed to 'digs' selected by the University – apparently Alma Mater takes more care than we supposed, for even her sons elect (Bow! Bow!). He is going to write again of course, and indeed I am surprised that we have not heard from him yet. As to the 'Accidents' I really can't see on what principle my Latin and Greek proses may be quite good for five days and come out with some awful blunder on the sixth – which is what happens. I am sure I take as much trouble on one day as on another. It is at times a bit disheartening, but we pray that the exam may not come on an 'off' day. In the German Kirk thinks I am doing better.

I am reading at present, what do you think? Our own friend 'Pilgrim's Progress'.[191] It is one of those books that are usually read too early to appreciate, and perhaps don't come back to. I am very glad however to have discovered it. The allegory of course is obvious and even childish, but just as a romance it is unsurpassed, and also as a specimen of real English. Try a bit of your Ruskin or Macaulay after it, and see the difference between diamonds and tinsel.

It is one of those afternoons here when the sky is the colour of putty and the rain comes down in sheets for hour after hour: perhaps we are beginning the winter at last. Tell me all the further news about the 'captaincy' as soon as you know anything.

your loving
son Jack.

---

191 John Bunyan, *The Pilgrim's Progress* (1678; 1684).

TO ARTHUR GREEVES (W):

[Gastons
8 November 1916]

My dear Arthur,

You certainly have all the luck! I should give anything to be at home for these operas. (Cant get a decent pen so you'll have to do with pencil this week) As I can't see them myself I can only hope & pray devoutly that they will be badly sung & staged, your seat be uncomfortable, yr. neighbours talkative & your escapade detected by your terrible parent – Amen.

To be serious: if I were going to three of them I should choose Aida & the Zauberflut[192] straight off without hesitation: the latter is of course old fashioned but, to me – tho' of course my views on music are those of an ignoramus – the formal old beauty of old music has something very attractive about it. At all events a thing with an overture like that must be good. As to the libretto, my ideas are rather hazy, but an article on it which I read last year in the 'Times' gave me the impression of something rather nice & fantastic. These two then I'd certainly go to: in the third it is more difficult to decide. 'Tales of Hoffman'[193] I thought was a comic opera – at any rate I am sure it's not in the first rank. 'Carmen' & 'the Lily'[194] are out of the question – the latter being an awful hurdy-gurdy, tawdry business by all accounts. Perhaps on the whole you would get more pleasure out of 'Faust' than any: here too you'd have the dramatic interest as well. 'Pagliacci' & 'Cavaleria' you have seen haven't you? – Though of course that's no reason why you shouldn't see them again.

'En passant' I don't exactly 'despise' your opera-book. I think it very useful like a Greek grammar or a time-table, but no more a 'book' in the proper sense than they are. For instance I should never think of getting 'Bradshaw's Railway Guide' printed on hand made paper with illustrations by Rackham, wd you? And talking about Rackham I saw in my French list the other day an edition of Perrault's 'Contes'[195] 'avec gravures en couleurs de Rackham' for 1 fr. 95 (at the present rate of exchange

192 i.e. Mozart's opera *Die Zauberflöte* (*The Magic Flute*).

193 *Tales of Hoffman*, an opera by Jacques Offenbach, first performed in 1881.

194 *The Lily of Killarney*, an opera by Julius Benedick (with libretto by John Oxenford and Dion Boucicault, based on the latter's play, *The Colleen Bawn*), was first performed in 1862.

195 Charles Perrault, *Histoires et Contes du Temps Passé* (1697).

about 1/6, I suppose). If its the same Rackham that wd. be wonderful value, wouldn't it? Though I daresay Perrault himself (the French 'Hans Anderson') would not be up to much, – coming as he did of the most prosaic nation on earth.

It is hardly fair to be sarcastick about my 'controversies' as you deliberately asked for both of them. I am afraid I have not made my views on old literature very clear but it can't be helped. The word 'feuilleton' is French, I suppose, originally but quite naturalized. (By the way can the whole of Bernagh not raise a French dictionary? I might give you one in calf for an Xmas box!) It means the horrible serial stories that run in the daily papers: if you've never happened to glance at one it's worth your while. They are unique! Yes, Sir!, it IS correct to say 'if he like' & not 'if he likes' – tho' a little pedantic.

I thought you would enjoy 'The Antiquary'. The scene on the beach is fine & tho' it hadn't struck me before the whole scenery of 'Fairport' is rather like Portsalon. What I liked best was the description of the antiquary's room at Monkbarns – I wish I could fill up my room with old things like that – also the scene where the doting old woman sings them the ballad at her cottage, but perhaps you haven't come to that yet. Of course the hero – as usual in Scott – is a mere puppet, but there are so many other good characters that it doesn't much matter.

What fiddlesticks about Malory being only a translation: I wish you were here that I could have the pleasure of stripping every shred of skin from your bones and giving your intestines to the birds of the air. What do you mean by saying 'It' is 'an old French legend': the 'Morte' includes a hundred different Arthurian legends & as you know the Arthur myth is Welsh. Of course he didn't invent the legends any more than Morris invented the Jason legends: but his book is an original work all the same. Just as the famous 'Loki Bound' of Lewis is based upon a story in the Edda, but still the poem is original – the materials being re-created by the genius of that incomparable poet. As a matter of fact I am at present reading a real 'old french' romance 'The High History of the Holy Graal' translated in the lovely 'Temple Classics'.[196] If I dared to advise you any longer – . It is absolute heaven: it is more mystic & eerie than the 'Morte'

196 *The High History of the Holy Graal* was translated (from the first volume of *Perceval le Gallois*, ed. C. Potvin) by Sebastian Evans, with illustrations by Edward Burne-Jones (1898).

& has [a] more connected plot. I think there are parts of it even you'd like.

I am also reading Chaucer's minor poems ('World's Classics',[197] a scrubby edition but the only one I can find) and am half way thr[ough] 'The House of Fame', a dream poem half funny & half fantastic that I like very much. But the print, tho' clear, is very small. As to 'The Letters of D.O. to W.T.' I suggest you had better have a look at them in my copy before you do anything. There is a lot in them I think you would like but also a good deal that is dull.

I got this morning a letter from His Majesty the King of the Fiji isles expressing his pleasure at your gift. How much he appreciates it may be seen in his own terse and elegant words 'Oor mi dalara bo chorabu plat-lark pho'.

We have had glorious storms here & a big old elm at the bottom of the garden is down by the roots. There is something majestic about a giant tree lying dead like this.

By the way take care of that weak heart of yours: it seems pretty sure that CONSCRIPTION is coming to Ireland now. I for one shall be jolly glad to see some relations of mine (and some of yours) made to behave like men at last. Goodnight, old man –

Jack

TO HIS FATHER (LP V: 143):

[Gastons]
9th Nov. 1916.

My dear Papy,

As it happened I had heard from Warnie himself shortly after my letter to you and thus got the truth about the promotion.[198] I think we really have a right to plume ourselves on this – the double step is so very rare. You say 'if inside the next year it is made permanent': is there any prospect of that's happening? If so we had better go and live with him or else get him to make us a separation allowance each. In the mean time avoid your bricklaying friend who may have something to say to you on

197 Chaucer, *The Minor Poems*, ed. Walter W. Skeat (1888).

198 Warnie wrote to his father on 30 October saying: 'I have at last got my step. I have got the temp. rank of Captain, dated back to 1/10/16 – exactly two years from the date I got my Commission' (LP V: 139).

the subject of 'temporary' commands. (Ah, these conversations between a brick layer and a brick dropper!)

Your encouragements – even the salts – are very pleasant to read, and it is always a great comfort to be assured that if I lose, I lose nothing more than a scholarship. As to the real prospects of that, they are on the knees of the gods, and possibly the 'putty sky' when I last wrote to you had something to do with my impressions. The consolation of having deserved a thing is perhaps one we should all rather apply to our rivals than to ourselves.

I don't think I shall need any new clothes as I have three good suits (1) besides my everyday one, and two should be enough to take with me. Should I take the dress suit now that we know I shall not go to an hotel? And by the way, when the man says lodgings are to be 'found', does he mean that we get them free?

The hero of 'Lady Connie' was certainly a detestable fellow, though I must admit that in places I found something rather attractive about him. At the auction of the pictures he is particularly great. But on the whole, as you say, the book is unsatisfactory, and she ought to have married the Pole What's his name. We are all reading Clodd's memoirs[199] here, which you will have seen reviewed everywhere. It is rather disappointing though, and the best story in it is the one about the Shah of Persia quoted in the Spectator 'Library Supplement'. There is a certain vulgarity about Clodd: he seems rather too pleased with his famous friends. I like last week's 'Romance' by the Student in Arms very much – in some ways as much as the other, tho' perhaps you will not agree with me.[200]

We have got over the rain at last after one or two fearful storms in which a fine old elm at the bottom of the garden, the pride of Kirk's

---

199 Edward Clodd (1840–1930), banker and author, had just published his *Memoirs* (1916).

200 An essay entitled 'Romance' by 'A Student at Arms' (Donald Hankey) was published posthumously in *The Spectator*, vol. 117 (4 November 1916), pp. 544–5. The sentiments expressed by the young soldier are so like those Lewis was later to hold that they are worth illustrating by these last sentences of the essay: 'For those boys who hate the war, and suffer and endure with the smile that is sometimes so difficult, and long with a great longing for home and peace – some day some of them will look back on these days and will tell themselves that after all it was "Romance," the adventure which made their lives worth while. And they will long to feel once again the stirring of the old comradeship and love and loyalty, to dip their clasp-knives into the same pot of jam, and lie in the same dug-out, and work on the same bit of wire with the same machine gun striking terror into their hearts, and look into each other's

heart, and of fabulous age, has come down. Today it is sunny and cold. That was a bad business in the Irish Sea, wasn't it?

your loving
son Jack.

(1). That's a funny mistake. I suppose I'm trying to make adjectives agree in English. – J.

TO ARTHUR GREEVES (W):

[Gastons
15 November 1916]

Dear Arthur,

I must begin my letter this week by heartily apologizing for some foolish remarks which I thoughtlessly directed against a book for whose merits your approval should have been to me and to all who enjoy the honour of your friendship a sufficient guarantee. As you very properly remind me, I am profoundly ignorant of the scientific side of music in which you specially excel, while my aesthetic judgements on the subject are modelled upon the sane and temperate example of your own criticism. What amends I can make by studying with diligence the admirable work which you commend, shall immediately be made: for, believe me, I am not insensible of the kindness and indulgence which a man of your education has displayed in such musical discussions to a boy so ill informed as I.

Your verdict upon Macdonald's tale was worthy of so shrewd and serious a gentleman as yourself: I can well understand that the puerilities which attract a schoolboy may indeed seem [a] waste of time to an experienced business man. I am not a little ashamed of my own lightheadedness, and am resolved to turn my attention to that excellent study of history with which you beguile your leisure. Here may I take the liberty of expressing my ardent and continued admiration of those

---

eyes for the same courageous smile. For Romance, after all, is woven of the emotions, especially the elemental ones of love and loyalty and fear and pain. We men are never content! In the dull routine of normal life we sigh for Romance, and sometimes seek to create it artificially, stimulating spurious passions, plunging into muddy depths in search of it. Now we have got it we sigh for a quiet life. But some day those who have not died will say: "Thank God I have lived! I have loved, and endured, and trembled, and trembling, dared. I have had my romance"' (p. 545).

qualities which make you the ornament of the society to which you belong: first and foremost the practical nature of your character which enables you to relinquish in a moment those trivial fairy tales and such like useless inventions: then your habits of economy and regularity, your sound knowledge of the Lord's Word, your unaffected piety, your knowledge of modern thought, the perfect control of your temper, the justness of your sentiments and – above all – the elegance of your language.

Well! we'll drop it now, as I want some room left for a chat: but honestly thats the sort of answer your last letter seemed to expect. Goodness!, you gave me an awful dressing down! And all because I dared to make a joke on a book of yours that has been a recognised subject for fooling this year or so. Perhaps, however, you just happened to be in bad form when you wrote, so I needn't take it too seriously. Or, what is more likely, J. M.[201] has been annoying you and I come in for the aftermath. Anyway, language such as I have just read is not pleasant, and I was on the point of writing a very rude letter. But I remembered, what I do hope you will remember old man, that real friendships are very, very rare and one doesn't want to endanger them by quarelling over trifles. We seem to be always sparing now a days: I dare say its largely my fault (tho' in this case I really don't know why you're so angry) but anyway do let us stop it. Perhaps my nerves are a bit on edge as I get nearer to this abominable exam., and that makes me irritable. But I'll try to do my best if you will.

So I may imagine you this evening just about now coming from dinner at Lily's with Mr. Thompson, with the memory of 'Aida' from last night and the prospect of the 'Magic Flute' to-morrow! I would give much to be in your place, and more to be in the same place with both of us there. I am very interested to hear what you think of the 'Flute', so mind you give me a special account of it – and accounts of the others also. Aida, of course, if well sung and staged must be enjoyable. I do hope you found them all three so, for that matter.

It must be lovely to really appreciate music (I am not fooling now). My taste for it was always that of a philistine and I am afraid even that is leaving me now. Perhaps it is as well I was not with you, or I might just have sat eating my heart out because I couldn't enjoy what I would have enjoyed in those delightful days when we first 'discovered' one another. But even if music fails I still have books!

---

201 Janie McNeill.

And talking about books I am surprised that you don't say more of the 'Golden Key':[202] to me it was absolute heaven from the moment when Tangle ran into the wood to the glorious end in those mysterious caves. What a lovely idea 'The country from which the shadows fall'! It is funny that we should both have the same idea about the Temple Classics. I was almost sure they were out of print and only wrote on the off chance for the Pilgrims' Progress (did I mention it? I have read it again and am awfully bucked) and then for the 'Grael'. I wonder would Mullan's tell you a thing was out of print just because they didn't think it worth while to get you the few we'd want At any rate, for paper etc they are far the prettiest cheap books I know, and if you still think of getting 'The Compleat Angler'[203] I should advise you to try this edition. The 'set' of the print and the notes in the nice broad margin are what I particularly like – Also the frontispieces – in some. My 'Grael' has a lovely one (in the extreme mediaeval style of course) in each volume by Burne-Jones & a title page design that reminds me of the Goodfridaymusic. I envy you, having your Letters of D.O. to W.T. in the Wayfarers – a very nice series except for the end leaf if I remember right – mine is only the 1/- Everyman and rather shop-soiled at that!

Was Mr. Thompson as nice as ever last night? He is a man I should love to meet again – but here too you have all the luck. Are you still reading 'The Antiquary' and does it still please you as much as ever? Here I am at the end of my letter and I had meant to give you a long jaw about some beautiful frost & mist effects I saw on Saturday evening (like Oldbuck's article on Castrametation) but you will have to pine without it. I must say I heartily agree with your remarks about autumn. There are some lovely colours here, & though I fancy there are finer 'cold' looking afternoons at home, the woods here are perhaps even richer.

Time to dry up now. My head is splitting, & my feet are like ice so I suppose if you were here you'd explain to me how & why I was in for a cold. Well I'd be glad to have you even on those terms. Good-night & do be indulgent to my many failings. There's a frost –

J.

---

202 George MacDonald, *Short Stories* ('The Light Princess', 'The Giant's Heart', 'The Golden Key') (1928).

203 Izaak Walton, *The Compleat Angler* (1653).

TO HIS FATHER (LP V: 145–6):

[Gastons]
19th Nov. 1916.

My dear Papy,

It is Sunday – though not very early in the morning – and so I am afraid this letter will be late: but yours did not arrive until yesterday and this is really the first time I have had. I have heard of the failing of my spelling in many places, at many seasons, and from many sources (even the 'for a boy of your age it is scandalous' or sometimes 'ludicrous' has a familiar ring) and I am only too well aware of the truth. However, we must hope for the best. As to the other little episode, we must record 'marker, one up!' But you have forgotten to say what the word was: I should like to know.

In spite of the tutor's obliging promise to find, or to use the safer form 'discover' lodgings, a letter arrived from him two or three days ago with a form for entrance in which, among other things, he wants 'your adress during examination' – but no word of advice. I accordingly wrote at once to my Malvern friend, who replied saying that he could not tell of any place, but that candidates as a rule write and ask the college. I did this and got an answer saying he would let me know of some place 'presently' and in the meantime I am to fill up the rest of the form and send it. This I am doing today, putting down the colleges in the order we arranged. He also asks for my birth certificate, which is rather a nuisance. Perhaps you had better see about that exemption business.

I was very sorry when I read the letter from my friend Cooper. His people have gone bankrupt and he has come through a very rough time, although he does not say anything about leaving the Coll. It must be very hard lines on him and he was a thoroughly good fellow. I had asked to be remembered to Smugy and the old man has wished me every success and advised me to read my 'Little Thompson' via Cooper.

It is snowing fast as I write, and has been since yesterday evening. Kirk is actually in bed this morning 'with a cold'. This is so very rare with him that I confess it makes me a little uneasy. Thanks very much but I think your suit case or Warnie's will do very well for the present trip, and we can talk about the other later on.

your loving
son Jack.

TO ARTHUR GREEVES (W):

[Gastons
22 November 1916]

My dear Arthur,

I quite agree with you and hope we shall have no more controversies at any rate for the present: for, as you say, it is too much to hope that we should live in peace and good will for more than a few weeks continuously. In passing I must explain that when I said your 'language was not pleasant' I only meant the general tone of what you said – 'diction' or 'sentiments' as Jane Austin would have delighted to put it. I wasn't using 'language' in the slang sense of the word meaning swearing – for of course I don't mind 'language' of that sort in itself. However, this is only a lesson in English & has nothing to do with the argument, which we will consign to the swarthy mere of Acheron!

Which reminds me I am no longer in a position to take your advice about 'Letters from Hell' as we had a jumble sale for the red cross or something in 'our village' last week and I contributed this. A mean enough offering indeed but they tell me it sold for 1/6! I am at present enjoying the malicious pleasure of expecting that the buyer will be as dissapointed as I was.

What a pity about the 'Magic Flute': I particularly wanted to hear your impressions of it. I am surprised to learn that it is 'comic' (a horrid word to describe a horrid thing) tho' of course it may only be nice humour of the fantastic kind. Your description of Aida is most tantalizing, and I would love to have been there. Even if I had found that I could no longer enjoy the music – tho' I think I am still up to Verdi – I could always have amused myself by talking to you or coughing loudly in the middle of the best passages! Seriously, did they play that lovely prelude well and did the Belfast boors give you a chance to hear it in peace? I daresay I am wrong about the 'Wayfarer's Library': but whatever the end-leaves be like I remember that the whole effect is good. Have you looked at 'Dorothy Osborne' yet and do you think you will like her? I am desperately in love with her and have accordingly made arrangements to commit suicide from 10 till 4 to-morrow precisely. I wonder does the 'Wayfarer' series publish my latest discovery – the most glorious novel (almost) that I have ever read. I daresay you have read it already or at any rate you must have hearded it praised too often to need my advice. It is Nathaniel Hawthorne's 'House with the Seven

Gables'.[204] I love the idea of a house with a curse! And although there is nothing supernatural in the story itself there is a brooding sense of mystery and fate over the whole thing: Have you read it? See if it is in the 'Wayfarers' as I want to get an edition of my own as soon as possible.

I am afraid I have really no memories! I had clean forgotten your ever speaking to me about the 'Golden Key': tho' I well remember setting off in the cab that grey, early morning and waiting for L. & G.[205] at the station! How funny Gordon was with his stiff back! That sounds a strange thing to say but you know what I mean. But after all has not Hewlett (or is it some one else) told us that the fairies have the shortest memories of all! So short that they cannot even remember their lovers from one new moon till the next.

I must say I admire your pluck in taking back 'The Antiquary' after so many years! But as you say the books we buy or return doesnt make much matter to Macmullans. I was sure you'd like the Antiquary very much. I tried to start 'Guy Mannering' on Saturday but some how it didn't grip me. As to the 'mist scene' I am afraid tho' it was very beautiful at the time it will hardly come to life again,

> *'inimitable on earth*
> *By modle or by shading pencil drawn.'*

I will leave you to imagine it.

Your imagination by the way has had a long enough rest by now. I have so far purposely refrained from saying anything about further instalments of 'Papillon', for fear, since you seemed to have no inclination to go on with it, that it might only hinder you from starting something new. But apparently this is not coming off. Do let us have something – tale, novel, what you will. I am revolving plans for a sort of fantasy much shorter than Bleheris and – which I hope will be an improvement – in modern English. I don't know exactly when I shall inflict the first instalment upon you, but like the people in Northanger Abbey you may be prepared for something 'really horrible'.

Talking about 'Northanger' I have been condemned during this last week to watch Mrs K. reading it in her own edition – your one. I wish

---

204 Nathaniel Hawthorne, *The House of the Seven Gables* (1851).
205 Lily and Gordon Ewart.

you could have seen it. It is not that she actually dirtied it, but what is almost worse she held it so rudely and so close over the fire that the boards have developed a permanent curve and the whole book has a horrible twist! It went to my heart all the more because it was your copy: at least I couldn't get that idea out of my head[.] Must stop now sorry I was late starting to night.

Jack

TO HIS FATHER (LP V: 146–7):

[Gastons]
Tues. 28th Nov. 1916.

My dear Papy,

This is not a proper letter – I will write you that later on when I have got yours. Meanwhile I am writing only to ask you to send me either your suit case or Warnie's as soon as you get this, for the fateful day is next Tuesday. Although the tutor said he would write and tell me of lodgings and also the place of the exam he has as yet done neither of these things: but I suppose its alright. Write soon to your

loving son,
Jack.

TO ARTHUR GREEVES (W):

[Gastons
29 November 1916]

Although by experience I am somewhat shy of recommending books to other people I think I am quite safe in earnestly advising you to make 'the Gables' your next purchase. By the way I shouldn't have said 'mystery', there is really no mystery in the proper sense of the word, but a sort of feeling of fate & inevitable horror as in 'Wuthering Heights'. I really think I have never enjoyed a novel more. There is one lovely scene where the villain – Judge Phycheon – has suddenly died in his chair, all alone in the old house, and it describes the corpse sitting there as the day wears on and the room grows darker – darker – and the ticking of his watch. But that sort of bald description is no use! I must leave you to read that wonderful chapter to yourself. There is also a very good 'story in a story' – curiously resembling the Cosmo one[206] tho' of course not so

206 Cosmo von Wehrstahl in MacDonald's *Phantastes.*

openly impossible. I intend to read all Hawthorne after this. What a pity such a genius should be a beastly American!

I am sorry to hear of your infatuation (very much inFATuation)* for a certain lady, but you need not despair, nor do I propose to call you out; we will divide mother & daughter between us, and you can have first choice! I really don't know which would be the worse do you?

That is certainly a glorious prelude to Aida. Do you remember that first afternoon last hols! How dissappointed we were at first and yet how we enjoyed ourselves afterwards sitting under those trees in the evening (or rather late afternoon) sunlight & throwing pencils & poems from one to the other? Well, we shall soon be there again if all goes well. I am going up for this damnable exam next Monday, shall be back here not later than Saturday & home on the following Monday if not sooner. So that is all well, but I wish to hell next week was over. Don't you sympathise with me? Pray for me to all your gods and goddesses like a good man!

No the Meagre One was not born with a squint: but long, long, long ago, so long ago that Stonehenge had a roof and walls & was a new built temple, he killed a spider. The good people of his day, outraged at this barbarity, stuck a dagger thro his nerve centre which paralyzed him without making him unconscious, seated him on the altar at St. Henge's temple & locked him up with the spiders son. The latter began to spin a solid mass of cobwebs from the Opposite corner. Very very slowly through countless years the web grew while the poor Meagre One – who couldn't die – developed a squint from watching it getting nearer. At last after countless ages Stonehenge dissapeared under an enormous mass of web & remained thus till one day Merlin hapenned to set a match to it and so discover what was inside: hence the myth of Merlin's having 'built' St. Henge's. To this day if you go there at sunrise & run round it 7 times, looking over your shoulder you can see again the wretched prisoner trying to struggle as the horrid sticky strands close round him. Cheap excursion trains are run for those who wish to try it.

The Tales of a Grandfather[207] in a rather scrubby but old edition has lived in the study these ten years, so you may try a taste of it before risking your money. I imagine it is in rather a childish style, tho' of course you know more about Scott than I do.

207 Sir Walter Scott, *Tales of a Grandfather* (1745–6).

I am sorry to hear that you have not yet begun your novel, and as I am sending you four pages of punishment I trust you will let me have something in your next letter. Which reminds [me] I don't know what my address will be at Oxford so you must just write to Bookham as usual. Do go on with the good work. What about taking that magic story Mr Thompson told us, for instance, toning down the supernatural parts a bit & making a Donegal novel of the Bronte type? Or else working that local idea of the Easelys[208] and all. Remember the second attempt will be easier & pleasanter than the first, and the third than the second.

Talking about the Easeleys, whether I read 'Guy Mannering' or no I shall not take to skimming as Kelsie does – for much as we esteem our beautiful and accomplished cousin – as Mr Collins[209] would have said – I don't think I shall follow her in literary matters. I am quite sure that every thing bad is true of your cousin Florence: she and her sister are young women who need transportation – as also my cousins at Bloomfield.[210] But indeed if only those who deserved to have books had them! – who besides you & me would there be to support the booksellers?

We have had some glorious frosty mornings here, with the fields all white & the sun coming up late like a red hot ball behind the bare woods. How I do love winter. We have had a book of Yeats' prose out of the library, and this has revived my taste for things Gaelic & mystic. Ask Mullan's if he knows a book called 'The Rosacrutian Cosmo Conception' or any on that subject. Gute Nacht. I wish I were dead –

Jack

*Ha! Ha! Poor little Bill, he only tries to be agreeee-able.

---

208 Lewis was to remember this idea of a novel cast in modern-day Ulster. In about 1928 he wrote two chapters of a novel about a family called Easley, which fragment is which is found in LP IX: 291–300.

209 The pompous and silly clergyman in *Pride and Prejudice* who was so obsequious to persons of high social station.

210 The wife and children of Joseph Lewis (1856–1908). See **The Lewis Family** in the Biographical Appendix.

TO HIS FATHER (LP V: 152–3):

[Gastons]
Friday Dec. 1st 1916

My dear Papy,

I am sorry I did not tell you earlier that the exam was so soon, but the idea was so familiar in my own mind that I only just realized, the day when I wrote to you, that I had never given you the date. I suppose by the time this reaches you, you will have sent off the suit case etc., but even if you have not had time, I dare say Mrs. K. would have something that would serve. So far, that pestilent knave at New College has failed to keep his promise of letting me know about lodgings: however, if the worst comes to the worst I can always go to an hotel, though of course this will be more expensive for you and less convenient for me.

We have also seen about this exemption business. K. and I both thought the matter beyond us, so we decided to consult my solicitors (Don't forget the 'my' – or is 'my man of business' the better expression) at Leatherhead. Having only a limited knowledge of solicitor's offices – purely provincial in fact – I was duly impressed. He was a state solicitor – a little, bald, figetty man, in a dingy black suit, and he advised me to put my case before the Chief Recruiting officer at Guildford. I wrote to the latter and today, after a long interval, have a reply saying that I am exempt from the Military Service Act, but that I must get registered at once: which I shall do either this afternoon or tomorrow.

The cold here is quite as bad as with you, and it freezes every night. This week I have been reading 'The House of the Seven Gables' which I have often heard praised but never met before. Have you? It is well worth the reading. As to coming home, the Oxford authorities, whose principle apparently is to worry the candidate by every concievable sort of mystery, have given me no idea how long the exam lasts. But I shall write to you about that from Oxford next week. I suppose I want only a day or two to get back from here and bring my trunk from Bookham. Many thanks for the enclosure – I wish it were for my sixteenth birthday, with two years more of Gastons life ahead.

your loving
son Jack.

Lewis went up to Oxford for the first time on Monday, 4 December 1916, to sit for a scholarship examination. He described this visit in SBJ *XII where he says he found lodgings in the first house 'on the right as you turn into Mansfield Road out of Holywell'. The examination, given in Oriel College, took place between 5 and 9 December, after which he returned to Great Bookham.*

TO HIS FATHER (LP V: 156):

[1 Mansfield Road,
Oxford
7 December 1916]

My dear P.,

This is Thursday and our last papers are on Saturday morning so I will cross on Monday night if you will kindly make the arrangements. We have so far had General Paper, Latin Prose, Greek and Latin unseen, and English essay. The subject for the latter was Johnson's 'People confound liberty of thinking with liberty of talking'[211] – rather suggestive, tho' to judge by faces, some did not find it so.

I don't know exactly how I am doing, because my most dangerous things – the two proses – are things you can't judge for yourself. The General paper was ideal and each of the unseens contained a piece I had done before. I am surprised at the number of candidates, tho' I can find only one going to New, a Harrow boy who sits opposite me.

The place has surpassed my wildest dreams: I never saw anything so beautiful, especially on these frosty moonlight nights: tho' in the Hall of Oriel where we do our papers it is fearfully cold at about four o'clock on these afternoons. We have most of us tried with varying success to write in our gloves. I will see you then on Tuesday morning.

your loving son,
Jack.

211 *Boswell's Life of Johnson*, ed. George Birkbeck Hill, 6 vols. (Oxford: Clarendon Press, 1934), 7 May 1773, vol. II, p. 249.

He crossed over to Belfast on 11 December and his rather fearful worries about the examination were laid to rest when he received a letter of 13 December from the Master of University College, Reginald W. Macan,[212] *who said: 'This College elects you to a Scholarship (New College having passed you over). Owing to your having furnished us with no Oxford address, I am obliged to send this to your home. I should have been glad to see you and ascertain your plans. Will you be so good now as to write to me and let me know what you propose to be doing between this time and next October' (LP V: 159–60). An announcement of this award appeared in* The Times *of 14 December, along with the news that University College had awarded Jack not only a Scholarship but an Exhibition – an additional financial endowment.*

The question for Jack, his father, and Mr Kirkpatrick was what Jack should do *until the following October. Jack was keen to begin his studies, and in replying to the Master of University College, he said he had 'formed no plans for the intervening time' and that he would be glad of the Master's 'guidance in the matter' (LP V: 160).*

While they waited to hear from the Master, Albert Lewis wrote at once to thank Mr Kirkpatrick for all he had done to secure Jack the Scholarship. Those who have read C. S. Lewis's tribute to Mr Kirkpatrick in Surprised by Joy *will be interested in what the 'Great Knock' thought of his pupil. In his letter to Albert Lewis of 20 December, Mr Kirkpatrick said:*

> *The generosity of your heart has led you to express yourself in terms altogether too complimentary to me. I ask you, what could I have done with Clive if he had not been gifted with literary taste and the moral virtue of perseverance? Now to whom is Clive indebted for his brains? Beyond all question to his father and mother. And I hold that he is equally indebted to them for those moral qualities which though less obvious and striking than the intellectual, are equally necessary for the accomplishment of any great object in life – I mean fixity of purpose, determination of*

212 Reginald Walter Macan (1848–1941), Master of University College 1906–23, was born in Dublin. He was educated at Christ Church, Oxford, where he took Firsts in the subjects Lewis would be reading, Classical Honour Moderations (Greek and Latin classical writers) and *Literae Humaniores* or 'Greats' (philosophy and ancient history). His publications include *Goethe in Rome* (1914) and *Herodotus and Thucydides* (1927).

> *character, persevering energy. These are the qualities that carried him through. I did not create them, and if they had not been there, I could not have accomplished anything. All this is so perfectly obvious that it is hardly worth emphasizing...As a dialectician, an intellectual disputant, I shall miss him, and he will have no successor. Clive can hold his own in any discussion, and the higher the range of the conversation, the more he feels himself at home.* (LP V: 165)

Over Christmas Jack received a letter from the Master of University College. It has not survived, but Albert Lewis provided the gist of it in a letter to Warnie of 31 December. Dr Macan, he said, wrote to Jack

> *asking him what his intentions were in regard to Military Service, and informing him at the same time that all their Scholars are with the Colours, save one who is hopelessly unfit physically. Pretty plain speaking that! So now I have to start to look for a commission for Jacks. Failing that, I am afraid that he must either chuck Oxford or go into the ranks. Apparently it is a moral impossibility for a healthy man over 18 years of age to go into residence at Oxford.* (LP V: 172–3)

Mr Kirkpatrick, again, solved the deadlock. He thought Jack should take Responsions, the University entrance examinations, and have this out of the way. In his letter to Albert of 2 January 1917 he pointed out that Mathematics 'form an important element in this exam.' and that Jack 'could very usefully employ a good part of the day in working up a subject for which he has not only no taste, but on the contrary a distinct aversion' (LP V: 174). It was further decided, as Jack mentioned in the letter to his father of 8 February, that if all his ideas about Oxford 'fell through', he would try for the Foreign Office. For this reason Mr Kirkpatrick planned for him to learn Italian, German and Spanish.

1917

TO HIS BROTHER (LP V: 176–7):

[Little Lea]
Postmark: 8 January 1917

My dear APB,[1]

Many thanks indeed for the letter and the most acceptable enclosure, which arrived, thank goodness, while P.[apy] was out, and so was saved from going the same road as my poor legacy. For you know I got £21 (is that the amount?) the same as you, but of course I have never seen a penny of it: my humble suggestion that I might have a pound or two was greeted with the traditional 'Ah, such nonsense.'

Congers on being made a real Lieut., which of course I suppose is far more important than the temporary Captaincy. Is there any chance of your being made a real Captain when this war is over – which I hope to God will be before my valuable person gets anywhere near it.

I quite agree with what you say about 'C. S. Lewis (Malvern.)'. Though of course I pulled a long face about it, I took very good care that Malvern should appear in the form I filled up: moreover, when people asked me what Coll. I was at I replied in the best manner 'Mawan': I saw no necessary to add 'two years ago'. It has been very comfortable at K's but there's no need to publish the fact: indeed I have now got to that stage when I am beginning to sentimentalize about the Coll. I had a very decent letter from old Smugy in which he also congratulated you.

1 Jack sometimes addressed Warnie as 'APB' and, in turn, Warnie addressed his brother as 'SPB'. When Warnie and Jack were very young their nurse, Lizzie Endicott, when drying them after a bath, threatened to smack their 'pigieboties' or 'piggiebottoms'. In time the brothers decided that Warnie was the 'Archpiggiebotham' and Jack the 'Smallpiggiebotham' or 'APB' and 'SPB'. Thereafter they used these terms of one another, particularly in their correspondence. For a discussion of 'pigiebotism' see the letter to Warnie of 2 August 1928.

Oxford is absolutely topping, I am awfully bucked with it and longing to go up, tho' apparently I am not to do this until next October. I hope you'll be somewhere near in England when I am at O. after the war, and will be able to come over and look me up in 'my new home' as the private school prospectuses say.

A large parcel of records to you arrived the day before yesterday and we took the liberty of opening them. As you know, they contain the 'Persian Garden' set and the 'Bing Boy' ones. The former are very satisfactory; have you heard them yourself, or did you get them on chance? The others of course aren't my line, but are very good in their own genre, tho' the patter in some of the Geo. Robey[2] ones is not very easy to hear until you 'get used to them like'.

I am going back to the Knock to read for my next exam. Responsions[3] (whatever that may be) on the 18th or 20th of January. After I've passed them, unless I hear against from my Coll. I shall probably join up here at home and not go up till after the war. Is there any possibility of leave?

yours,
SPB

P.S. Quite agree with your remarks about Wilson[4] and his friends. But what else do you expect from a set of squatters and damned money grubbing puritans like the Yanks? You remember Wilde's wheeze, 'When good Americans die they go to Paris' – 'But where do bad Americans go when they die?' – 'Oh, they go to America'. – J.

Lewis left Belfast on 25 January 1917, arrived in Oxford on the 26th, and called on the Master of University College on the 27th. The Master promised that if he passed the Responsions to be given between 20 and 26 March he could come up to Oxford at the beginning of Trinity Term in April. From Oxford, Lewis returned to Great Bookham on 27 January to prepare for the forthcoming examinations.

2 (Sir) George Robey (1869–1954), a music-hall comedian who appeared in a number of silent comedy films.

3 Oxford's entrance examination.

4 Woodrow Wilson (1856–1924), President of the United States from 1913 to 1921.

TO HIS FATHER (LP V: 179):

Great Bookham
[28 January 1917]

My dear Papy,

You will know from my two telegraphs that I got through my journey all right, tho' with some annoyance from very crowded trains and long stops at unheard of stations.

At about half past 11 on the Saturday morning I went to Univ. and was led across two quads, one behind the other, to a house in a beautiful old walled garden. This was the ogre's castle. He was a clean shaven, white haired, jolly old man, and was very nice indeed.[5] He treated me to about half an hour's 'Oxford Manner', and then came gradually round to my own business. Since writing last, he had made enquiries, and it seems that if I pass Responsions in March I could 'come up' in the following term and join the O.T.C.[6] This plan he thinks the best, because I should have far more chance of a commission from the Oxford O.T.C. than from anything else of the sort. The only disadvantage is that, as my scholarship doesn't begin until next October, I should not get any 'emolument'. However as he says, in the meantime I am to go on reading for Responsions, and the rest can be settled as we go along. After that he made me stay to lunch with his wife and niece and 'so to the station'. I am very pleased with my ogre after all.

It is colder in England, both here and at Oxford, than I have ever felt it anywhere in my life – perfectly awful. I hope you stayed in the house last week and will be able to do so for some part of the next until you have shaken off your cough. As usual, that 'shockin' cold of mine is disappearing on this side, to be replaced by the usual term time chilblains. The Knock is in very good form, although I have heard no talk about the 'carte blanche' so far.

Let me hear from you soon, and have good news of the cough.

your loving
son Jack.

---

5 The Master of University College.

6 Officers' Training Corps.

TO ARTHUR GREEVES (W):

[Gastons
28 January 1917]

My dear Galahad,

(If you are still to be Galahad after all) here I am at last, on Sunday evening, once more starting the first letter of a term. Well, I left you on the telephone at four of the clock, and I will go over my adventures, to get you thoroughly bored before we start talking.

The crossing was rough and cold, and we were late getting into Fleetwood; after which the train thought it wd. be best to wait for an hour before starting. We dawdled on to Crewe and there waited for another hour, tho' I didn't mind this as it gave me an opportunity of breaking my fast. So by very slow stages I got to Oxford at 6 o'clock. I took the same rooms as before, had a comfortable night, rose at 9.30, bathed, shaved, breakfasted in great ease and so sallied forth.

After wandering about the place and buying a second-hand copy of the 'Gesta Romanorum'[7] (of which more anon) I took my courage in both hands and knocked up the Master of University. He turned out to be a very, very nice old boy and after settling our business he made me stay to lunch. His wife and niece were there, both very decent, <indeed the latter wouldn't be a bad subject for the lash.> But what pleased me most was the masses upon masses of books in his house: among which I saw, tho' of course I couldn't look at it properly, a volume of that glorious new Malory – the one like my 'Psyche'[8] you know. So you may imagine I left Univ. very much relieved and delighted.

(Here my borrowed fountain pen loses its temper) The 'Gesta Romanorum' (you read about it in Mackail's 'Life of W.M.')[9] is a collection of mediaeval tales with morals attached to them: they are very like the Arabian Nights, tho' of course the characters and setting are chivalric instead of Eastern. It is not a first class book but it only cost me 1/- and

---

7 The *Gesta Romanorum* is a collection of fictitious stories in Latin, compiled in the 14th century and first published about 1472.

8 The story of 'Cupid and Psyche', which Lewis read over Christmas, is one episode in *The Golden Ass* of Apuleius (b. c. AD 114). He read it in *The Story of Cupid and Psyche*, translated by William Aldington, Temple Classics (1903). The long gestation of Lewis's *Till We Have Faces* (1956) probably began with this reading of the 'Cupid and Psyche' story.

9 J.W. Mackail's *The Life of William Morris*.

helps to while away an hour or so between serious things. I also bought at Oxford a copy of the poet Collins in the same edition as my Gray[10] (you know?) I don't know if you would care for him, but I like him quite well: you can look him up in your History of Literature and see what it says. I also bought a French Book on the Poetry of the middle ages[11] – so you see dear Oxford is a dangerous place for a book lover. Every second shop has something you want. Meanwhile I am going on with the 'Life' and besides Collins have read over the 1st Book of Paradise Lost again. I think I shall go through the whole poem this term, and if you begin it some day soon it would be interestin to keep side by side. About books, don't forget to tell Walter to send hither the Lambs & the Macaulay so soon as they come. The cold here is beyond words.

I can see my way clear to the end of 'Dymer'[12] now and will let you have an instalment next Sunday: three more will finish him, and after that I shall expect something from you. For my own part, I should like to write some short narrative poem if I could – about the length of a Book of 'Jason'.[13] I am tryin to think of some subject, at once romantic, voluptuous and homely. You must excuse (tho' Im sure I don't care a damn if you don't, mon vieux!) this writing, as it is being done across my knee.

<'Across my knee' of course makes one think of positions for Whipping: or rather not for whipping (you couldn't get any swing) but for that torture with brushes. This position, with its childish, nursery associations wd. have something beautifully intimate and also very humiliating for the victim.>

Quite enough for a first letter. Good bye, my old Archibald (you are fut a-a-ille) –

Jack

---

10 *The Poetical Works of Gray and Collins*, ed. Austin Lane Poole, Oxford Editions (1917). The poets are William Collins (1721–59) and Thomas Gray (1716–71).

11 Gaston Paris, *Littérature Française du Moyen Age* (1912).

12 Over the Christmas holiday, Lewis began a prose tale called 'Dymer'. Though the prose 'Dymer' is no longer extant, he was to begin a narrative poem about the same hero in 1918, which poem was to go through many revisions until it was eventually published in 1926 under his pseudonym 'Clive Hamilton'.

13 Morris, *The Life and Death of Jason*.

TO ARTHUR GREEVES (W):

[Gastons
31 January 1917]

My dear Arthur,

I was specially glad to get this letter of yours, both because it is longer than your usual ones (I hope you will keep this up) and because there are several good items in it.

First, I am glad you are starting French: I knew you would find no difficulty if once you began. Dont slack off after the first week or so, but don't read French on ordinary work day evenings when you are tired. Keep it for week ends. I should think 'Les Miserables'[14] pretty tough reading in any language, but then you like that sort of thing. As well, you always have your translation to save you dictionary turning. By the way, whether in French or English, you simply must read this book of Maeterlink's on death.[15] It is full of most interesting stuff, and even where you don't believe his theories they always have a sort of romantic interest. One case he tells of reminds me of 'John Silence'!, it is so wierd: but I mustn't spoil it by an outline.

I was also glad of your adventure in the billiard room. See how the Gods lead you on of their own accord! <I am given to understand that the idea of suffering yourself appeals to you more than that of inflicting. It used to be so with me, and perhaps the experienced victim does get a more vivid voluptuous sensation than the operator – at first. But of course once you are really in pain you can't think of anything else while the operator grows keener all the time.>

(In passing, can you imagine a horribler book, in paper, illustrations & binding than the 'History'?) Just before supper I finished the 2nd volume of Mackail's 'Life of W.M.' There is nothing nicer than to lay aside a book with a certain satisfaction at getting it settled with and yet having enjoyed it thoroughly, is there? I certainly know Morris better than I did before, tho' in a way his character is a dissapointment. You can't really think there's any resemblance between him and me? Of course I would give mine eyes to be like him in some ways, but I don't honestly think my temper is quite so bad.

As to the other point I often think he must have been <a special devotee of the rod.> Do you remember in the 'Well at the World's End' where

14 Victor Hugo, *Les Misérables* (1862).

15 Maurice Maeterlinck, *La Mort* (1913).

a man at the Birg of the Four Friths says that the advantage of slave girls as opposed to wives is that we need care nothing for their ill humours <'so long as the twigs smart and the whips sting'? That sentence is dragged in quite unnecessarily and is exquisitely worded.>

Item (as Morris says in his letters) the 2nd Vol. of Macaulay[16] is come, in excellent condition. The leaves are all stuck together and lump in ridges and make the right crackly noise. Thanks for sending it, old man: I wish indeed you were coming the same journey. How perfectly happy we could be here, walking and talking together and both doing work we liked.

Your suggestion that I did not want your company in the cab, is purely rhetorical, I hope. You must know that I wanted it very much, although I cant talk about those sort of things the way you do. It seems to me indecent somehow, if you know what I mean.

I am sorry to hear that you're fed up, and, although nobody who gets enough food and clothing in a world where most are hungry and cold has any business to talk about 'misery' I do sympathise with you exceedingly. I wish to goodness (or to Jeshua shall we say?) that you could get out of the office. If only you had work that you liked you'd feel a different being in spite of loneliness and so on. I know I can always turn to pleasant work for comfort as a last resource. But what's the good of telling you this! I think your father and mother should be shot for keepin' you in that hole, <while the only other member of your family whom I am interested in could be punished in an other way – to the general enjoyment of the operator, and to the great good of her soul.>

Dear! Dear! How the theme comes back. To change it, I had a lovely walk this afternoon in the snow. As I walked up the village street the ground and house tops were thick, and it was coming fluttering down à la Debussy. But best of all, the blacksmith's place was open, and you could see the red forge glowing inside. Can't you imagine it?

I long to see the picture you have made of that lane in THE wood. Any more designs for the 'Poems'? That first little one is such a success that you must do lots of tail-peaces and such.

No: I didn't see 'La Bohème',[17] and it took from 2–6 to get from Oxford to here. Good night, old sinner, <and imagine yourself the slave

16 Thomas Babington Macaulay, *History of England*, 5 vols. (1849–61).

17 *La Bohème*, an opera by Giacomo Puccini, was first performed in 1897.

of some Eastern queen who whips you – I mean when you next go North.>

I am just going to have the first bath since seeing you, as there has been no hot water. –

<Philomastix>

TO ARTHUR GREEVES (W):

[Gastons
1 February 1917]

Just a scrape to thank you a thousand times for the books[18] which have just come. Can you really spare them? It is most awfully good of you and I am very pleased with them, especially when I think of the other edition which is certainly not so nice, tho' I hope you will come to think otherwise.

I wrote to you on Wednesday as usual, which letter will now have reached [you] & will write again next Wednesday after getting your next. You say 'Arethusa'[19] is lovely: have you bought it or got a copy from the library? In any case I am very glad you have started it. Isn't Omobono a lovely character, and also the slave dealer's wife? I think it a very good romance all round. Having finished Morris I am reading a silly book of Anstey's 'The Talking Horse',[20] before settling down to Macaulay. I never heard you speak of Anstey, but you should read him certainly: this book is fantastic & almost as ridiculous as 'Alice' tho' of course in a more ordinary way.

The snow is nearly gone now, but the country still keeps a wintry look which is lovely & the mornings a wintry nip which is not. You'll be glad to hear that I've started a 'friendly' tobacco-pipe instead of the cigarettes you so object to. Glad your interest in R. is increasing, but more of this elsewhere – Addio,

Jack

---

18 Charles Lamb's *Essays of Elia*.

19 Francis Marion Crawford, *Arethusa* (1907).

20 F. Anstey, *The Talking Horse and Other Tales* (1892).

TO ARTHUR GREEVES (W):

[Gastons
7 February 1917]

My dear Arthur

I must begin by explaining why there is no instalment with this letter. On Sunday, when I should have written one I spent the whole day most delightfully skating on a lake at a place called Wisley near here, which you reach by a road through the woods. As it is now thick snow again you can imagine what a topping walk it is. The winding road covered with snow, the bare trees with their snow covered branches & the sunlight falling thro' them in bars on the ground also covered with snow. Absolutely lovely, especially as the air is very dry and the sky clear.

To day I have been to the same place to skate again & the ice is now rather cut up. I was in pleasant company (NO – not that sort) and enjoyed it greatly, especially the walk back. The moon was out, & starting under a clear starry sky we gradually walked into a cold white fog. The white of the ground and the white of the fog became indistinguishable and you seemed to be floating in a sort of silver cloud, broken by the red light of a railway signal at the station. This is a vague description, but I think you'll understand.

How I do love *real* winter like this! The thermometer in the hall stands at 7° to night, the water in my jug is solid to the bottom and all the pipes are frozen up. If you look out for a moment through the willow-pattern of frost on the windows you see this lovely haze of snow & mist & moonlight. What with the general beauty of the world and my lovely hours of skating I have not been so bucked for a long time.

My French is under rather different conditions from yours, as I read from 10–11 every night except on Wednesdays when I write to you. I have really never counted exactly how much I cover and it wd. not be accurate to count by pages, as they vary so in size and in type. I shouldn't read for more than an hour at a time in your case, certainly not for a whole afternoon. I never read Perrault myself but I am sure he is good (A. Lang praises him) and you may remember that there is an edition of him with illustraggers by Arthur Rackham – I forget the details however. What would you say to the 'Contes Fantastiques' of Charles Nodier, in that nice blue Collection Gallia at 1/-?[21] Some of these tales you would

21 Jean Charles Nodier, *Contes Fantastiques* (1914).

like tho' some seemed to me dull. Then again why not get something in that 1/6 Dents edition with the lovely paper, say Voltaire's 'Contes' (very amusing) or the shorter tales of Georges Sand, – you can see the list. I have now made a good start on my second volume of Macaulay, which is admirable. What a nice man James must have been! But before starting this I read in a library copy two of F. W. Bains Indian Tales 'The Descent of the Sun' & 'The Heifer of the Dawn'.[22] They are translations from the Sanskrit and are 'really rather adorable'. A little too weird, perhaps, for your solid tastes; but you should certainly have a look at them in Lily's copies.

It is most exasperating of you to say you have come to a conclusion which will dissapoint me, but you don't want to put it in paper. What tawdry nonsense! If any person did read our letters, he would be an ill-bred cad & therefore we shouldn't mind what he saw. But anyway I will be really annoyed if you don't clear up the mystery in your next letter. My own <Philomastix> is only a harmless piece of Greek affectation: 'philo' is the same word you see in 'philosopher' 'philologist' etc, and means 'fond of' while <'mastix' is the ordinary word for a whip.>

I think I can understand your getting tired of Iceland before Morris left it: but didn't you like the Faroe Islands? That part reminded me of our mountain walks at Portsalon, didnot it you? I rather expected some fuller criticism on Arethusa, and would like to know your final verdict when you write. Tho' of course it's not in the rank of 'real books', I have a sentimental affection for it from reading it over ever since I was about ten. I am now through the first two Books of Paradise L. and really love Milton better every time I come back to him, &, what is more to the point, I think his merits are of a [kind] you'd appreciate. However, if Harrap won't let you have a copy till 1919, our plan [of] reading in harness goes 'off'. I can quite understand the interest of the Welsh marches at the time of the Wars of the Roses – especially as it was in that place & that time that our good friend Thomas Malory lived (see introduction to the Morte). I am now reading in French this book on French literature of the Middle Ages which to me at least is very interestin. By the way Maeterlink's book on Death is in the usual horrid, expensive continental paper back – still this gives you the exciting task of getting it bound.

Good night for the present – <Philomastix ΦΙΛΟΜΑΣΤΙΞ,> you can learn that amount of Gk. letters to mystify the unlettered!)

---

22 Francis William Bain, *The Descent of the Sun* (1903); *A Heifer of the Dawn* (1904).

Next morning – colder still! Remember to clear up the mystery when you write & if you like I'll destroy the letter –

J.

TO HIS FATHER (LP V: 185):

[Gastons]

Postmark: 8 February 1917

My dear Papy,

The 'momentous decision' about German was simply – that we had dropped it and taken up Italian instead! I thought K. would have explained this in his letter, but it makes no difference as, by a little management we have found it possible to fit in both. This means that if all my dreams of Oxford fall through and I were reduced to something really desperate like trying for the Foreign Office, I should have three modern languages in my pocket. Italian quite comes up to K's promises about its easiness and on Sunday I read the first 200 lines of Dante with much success. By the end of term I should be able to read it as easily as French.

And talking about the end of the term, would you please send me £2/2 some time soon, which is the fee to the University for entrance at Responsions?

You are certainly most unfortunate in getting this kind of weather for your convalescence. Is it as bad at home as it is here? We are having real winter, and so far I have had three days excellent skating. Besides the ice, there is fine dry snow everywhere, usually with bright sunshine, which is very pleasant. The water in my 'giraffe' is solid, right through to the bottom, every night, and yesterday evening the thermometer in the hall was at 7 degrees. However, on the whole, I like this sort of weather, tho' the pipes are now all frozen up, which makes rather a nuisance. I suppose however you have already seen all this in the papers.

What do you think about America? Kirk says it will be a great disadvantage if she comes in, tho' I don't quite understand how: he also assures us that we shall be starving before next summer, which indeed (unless you are right in hoping to see it over by then) seems like to be.

your loving

son Jack.

P.S. If you are sending me some of that thermogenic wool, wouldn't it be kind to let the Knock have a little too?

TO ARTHUR GREEVES (W):

[Gastons
15 February 1917]

You begin on this page

Cher Ami,

One of the vertues of snow is that it chiefly teacheth and instructeth us for to loven and cherish the greene grasse – certainly I never appreciated grass until about Teusday when the snow began to melt and after so many days whiteness it was nice to see the old homely fields again, all pale and washed looking, with drifts still lying in the hollows.

Your letter, although dated a long while ago (9th) only arrived this morning, Thursday: so that I am afraid this will not come to your hands at its wonted time. Which is your fault, not mine.

<If the whole mystery was that you didn't love the Rod as I do – well there's no mystery about that. Very, very few are affected in this strange way and I am only surprised that you can enter into my feelings even so much as you do. As a matter of fact, just as the other – the normal desire has a poignant sensual side and a vague sentimental side, so that has too. I can understand your being able to like the *idea*, and yet not having your physical feelings raised by the thought of the 'mastix' – . . . .[23] Is this at all your state of mind? Yes, that business about stepping on Zoe appeals> strongly to the sentimental or theoretical side of this feeling. But we are getting too sticky. Passez outre!

Item, I am reading such a splendid book in German, by a man called Chamisso 'Peter Schlemichl's Wundersame Geschichte' (The Amazing Adventures of Peter Schlemichl).[24] It is about a man (modern) who sells his shadow to a wizard: his subsequent adventures are treated chiefly in the absurd 'Alice' style but there is a sort of core of horror lurking in it all the time, that is to me very attractive. I see from the introduction to my copy that there are several translations: I should certainly advise you to get it out of the library – except in a specially nice edition it is perhaps hardly worth buying. I am writing to night to see about an edition of 'Undine' in the original. I also have seen in a book on German literature

---

23 The dots represent the approximately 15 letters that Arthur had written over, and which are indecipherable.

24 Adelbert von Chamisso, *Peter Schlemihls Wunderbare Geschichte* (1853).

the name of some of Fouqués other books – Thiodolf the Icelander, The Magic Ring etc.[25] Sweet lord! how one does want to read everything. I am nearly through Macaulay Vol. II, which I have enjoyed immensely, especially the part about Oxford: I am sorry Obadiah Walker should have been at Univ![26] However, Shelley & I goin there should make up for it.[27]

Cher ami, j'ai a confession to make. I have thee told a lie. A certain operation is NOT called going North at Malvern. I invented this phraze so that you & I might have some convenient & safe way of referring to that thing. It wd. be unpleasant to have to use the ugly expressions which slang has evolved & this one has the advantage of being quite meaningless to an outsider. But I couldn't have stopped and explained all this to you in the middle of that breathless night walk.

I do so hope you will enjoy the opera: and if I could only be at home worrying you & making little plans for going to them (I couldn't leave my father of course) I'd risk being dissapointed. One sort of music still holds me as much, or indeed more than ever – piano music. I suppose the gods are doing this to console me. By the way, here's a bright idea, perhaps the gods have a touch of my disease & that is why the world is tortured so every day. I wonder could that be work[ed] into a mystical story. Which reminds me, when is your novel comin? The Bible (which you don't read) has very hard things to say of people who put their hand to the plough and turn back.[28] There was great promise in poor 'Papillon' – imagination, charm – the technical part you will learn by practice. Buck up!

At any rate I am sending you Dymer's next excursion, and have begun the poem. The subject is 'The childhood of Medea', & it will leave off where the most poems about her begin – shortly after her meeting with Jason. It will describe her lonely, frightened childhood away in a castle with the terrible old king her father & how she is gradually made to

---

25 Friedrich Fouqué, Baron de la Motte, *Undine* (1811); *Thiodolf the Icelander* (1815); *The Magic Ring* (1812).

26 Possibly because Obadiah Walker (1612–99), the Master of University College 1676–88, was a Roman Catholic who was imprisoned in the Tower because of his religious beliefs. See the two-part essay 'Obadiah Walker' by A.E. Firth in *University College Record*, Vol. IV (September 1962), pp. 95–106 and Vol. IV (October 1964), pp. 261–73.

27 Shelley was expelled from University College in 1811 for circulating a pamphlet, *The Necessity of Atheism* (1811), which he had written with Thomas Jefferson Hogg.

28 Luke 9:62: 'And Jesus said unto him, No man, having put his hand to the plough, and looking back, is fit for the kingdom of God.'

learn magic against her will.[29] Of course I'll make a mess of it 'cracked absolutely', but there's a fine subject in all that for someone who knew how to manage it. I wish Morris or Apollonius had made a poem about that. Descriptions of childhoods & gradual growing up are very fascinating I think.

Glad you are coming to like your Lamb, tho I don't think you can love it so well as I do mine. His novel is called 'Rosamund Gray' isn't it?[30] It was published anonymously and some one (someone like poor little Bill,[31] I suppose) said that

Friends coming up to examine it
Observe a good deal of Charles Lamb in it.

What is it like. Yes!, isn't the collection Gallia awfully dainty. As soon as I've finished my book on French Literature of the Middle Ages I think I'm going to tackle 'Notre Dame';[32] It is rather in your line & mine too, isn't it? Do you know I believe I shall come to like history kwite as much as u do? What nonsense about the Heiffer of the Dawn; you never told me a syllable. The Silver library is very nice but is the Library Edition (like My Sigurd[33] you know) not worth the difference? I heartily recomend the E[arthly] Paradise (never having read it) and intend to buy a copy myself as soon as I have finished the Paradise Lost. Have been reading Malory, the 'Beaumains' part again & cant understand how anyone can help loving him. But you always were a cross sent to try me, cher ami, so cher ami good night. Is this letter long enough, because it's all your going to get anyway.

<ΦΙΛΟΜΑΣΤΙΞ>

29 Lewis's primary sources for the story of Medea were Apollonius Rhodius's *Argonautica* and William Morris's *Life and Death of Jason*, both of which are mentioned in his letter of 11 July 1916.

30 Charles Lamb, *A Tale of Rosamund Gray and Old Blind Margaret* (1798). It was not published anonymously as Lewis thought.

31 William Hazlitt (1778–1830), who was a friend of Charles Lamb.

32 Victor Hugo, *Notre Dame de Paris* (1831).

33 Morris, *Sigurd the Volsung*. See note 61 to letter of 10 November 1914.

TO HIS FATHER (LP V: 187):

[Gastons]
Friday.
Postmark: 16 February 1917

My dear Papy,

First of all, many thanks for the enclosure which I have sent off to the pundits, and thus got the whole of that business off my chest. After mature deliberation I decided that it would be just as well not to send £1-19-6 with a note, '6d. deducted for telegraphic peculation' – the plan which first occurred to me.

I am sorry that my last letter did not arrive in time to prevent you from discharging your volley of pebbles. K. told me that he heard from you and that he was writing to 'put you in possession of the facts', which I suppose means that you are being put in your place.[34] At any rate I hope you will approve of the present arrangement. Certainly Italian gets better and better, and will be an excellent counterblast to Big Brother's 'fine wandering knowledge of the Spanish language'. I think that after some twenty years work, I may be able to make something out of German too.

Talking about Big Brother, I heard from him yesterday. He seems to have had a touch of fever again, and wants to know why there are no letters from Little Lea. This weather out there must be rather offensive. The snow is gone here, but the frost has kindly come back again, just to keep us from thinking long. I am very glad to hear the news of your recovery, and hope it will be permanent.

---

34 In his letter to Albert of 14 February Mr Kirkpatrick said: '[Clive] has actually dropped nothing, only that the amount of Classical reading has been somewhat curtailed. He goes on with German, which, tho' not directly required at Oxford, will we hope be of service to him in the future. But he has taken on a new language – Italian. This may seem a bold venture to be accomplished in seven weeks. And, no doubt, there are many teachers who would pronounce the proposal little better than folly. But you may be quite sure I wd. not have undertaken such a task if I had not seen my way to make it a success. Italian is just the kind of language that Clive can get into easily, and already inside a fortnight he is reading *I Promessi Sposi* (a Senior Grade book) with more success and a great deal more interest than anything he has done in German. Of course his knowledge of Latin is a great service to him in the new venture, and with an ordinary pupil I should not have thought of making such an experiment. If he gets a good grammatical knowledge here before he goes, it is half the victory. All he wants afterwards is Spanish, and then he will have the full complement of modern languages required for the Foreign Office' (LP V: 186–7). *I Promessi Sposi* (1827) – 'The Betrothed' – by Alessandro Manzoni is held by many to be the greatest Italian literary work after Dante's *Divine Comedy*.

Yes! This is not the first time that I have had buttons sewn on me by an opera company. However, I am sure I shall have a full account of their performances by an 'eye-witness'.

your loving
son,
Jack.

TO ARTHUR GREEVES (W):

[Gastons
20 February 1917]

Cher Ami,

Il y a je ne sais quoi de charme in your style of writing a letter on a number of loose sheets in devil knows what order. It is so nice when you think that the pleasure of reading it is over to suddenly come on half a page more hiding somewhere. I wish I wasn't such friends with you – it takes away from ones independance: I hang on Teusday evenings and Wednesday mornings for your letter just like a schoolgirl and am quite put out if it doesn't turn up.

Item, it is very annoying for a habitual liar like me, when he does tell the truth for once to be accused of invention: however, tho' my little confession was quite true, many of my statements are so 'Of imagination all compact'[35] that I can't blame you for disbelieving this one. It is a pity tho' that you always fix on the true ones to suspect and swallow down the lies with avidity!

I am sorry that you don't like Mackail's second volume. I suppose I am a bundle of contradictions, but I must say socialism does interest me. When you think of the way labourers in the factory live at home, – men & women slaving from half past five in the morning to six at night at hard, monotonous work in hideous rooms full of shrieking machinery year after year, with never a moments pleasure except when they are drunk (and you can't blame them) it really does make you feel that the whole thing is wrong. Aren't you ashamed to think of us, blessèd prigs, with our books and music and little grumbles about nothing, dawdling along (your office is absolute Paradise & idleness compared with their lives) while half or more than half the people are slaves. As much slaves as ever there were in Rome, their only liberty being liberty to starve

35 Shakespeare, *A Midsummer Night's Dream*, V, i, 8.

when the torture becomes unbearable! However I am not going to afflict my cher ami with a political letter, but I just wanted to explain why I can't help thinking about those things.

By the way, what do you mean by <the whip in music? At any rate the mere sound of a whip doesn't affect me in the least. There's no special virtue in a whip – hundreds of other methods of mild torture are just as good.>

I am glad I wasn't there to have the last remnants of my Wagnerian taste murdered by a garbled Tannhaüser. Aye me! how our tastes and feelings have changed since the days when Wagner was the great common ground of talk, when Morris was only a name (perhaps you wish he were still) and I had never read Charlotte Brontë. A propos of which, having finished Macaulay (an admirable book, tho' of course the writer is too much of a whig and puritan for my taste: the old cavaliers were at any rate gentlemen) I am beginning 'Mansfield Park' again, after a futile effort to read 'Vanity Fair'.[36] I waded knee deep into the marish of endless characters, sentimentalism & platitude and then really could not go on. Why is it I can't appreciate Thackeray?

It is difficult to choose between two such perfect flowers as the 'Crock of Gold' & 'Phantastes'. The former has a beautiful sense of nature and open air, and a certain voluptuousness that the other ha'nt, but then there is nothing in it quite so fine as the faery palace[37] or the place where Anodos comes out on the sad sea shore and throws himself into the waves[38] – or

---

36 William Makepeace Thackeray, *Vanity Fair* (1848).

37 *Phantastes*, ch. X: 'The stream bore my little boat with a gentle sweep round a bend of the river; and lo! on a broad lawn, which rose from the water's edge with a long green slope to a clear elevation from which the trees receded on all sides, stood a stately palace glimmering ghostly in the moonshine: it seemed to be built throughout of the whitest marble. There was no reflection of moonlight from windows – there seemed to be none; so there was no cold glitter; only, as I said, a ghostly shimmer. Numberless shadows tempered the shine, from column and balcony and tower. For everywhere galleries ran along the face of the buildings; wings were extended in many directions; and numberless openings, through which the moonbeams vanished into the interior, and which served both for doors and windows, had their separate balconies in front, communicating with a common gallery that rose on its own pillars...Though I was there for many days, I did not succeed in mastering the inner topography of the building, so extensive and complicated it was.'

38 ibid., ch. XVIII: 'I stood one moment and gazed into the heaving abyss beneath me; then plunged headlong into the mounting wave below. A blessing, like the kiss of a mother, seemed to alight on my soul; a calm, deeper than that which accompanies a hope deferred, bathed my spirit. I sank far into the waves, and sought not to return...

the story of Cosmo.[39] You see!, what memories crowd up. Still the homely, Irish beauty of the other is topping: so is the humour both of the philosopher and the policemen. The philosophical parts (I mean the serious philosophical parts at the beginning of some chapters) I don't understand, but they stir me in some strange way that they probably wouldn't if I really could follow them.

<By the way, cher ami, you must have a very depraved taste if you like THAT passage best in Dymer tho'> I admit twas pleasant to write. Perhaps it is true what the Greek poet in the Anthology says: 'Sweet is water to the thirsty man, and to the weary mariners sight of land is sweet. But sweeter than all it is when one bed holds twain that love, and the queen of Cypris is praised of both.'[40] Queen of Cypris, you know, is Aphrodite. I have no intention of giving up Dymer, tho' I fear he will dissapoint you.

The childhood of Medea has progressed to some two hundred and twenty lines, in the metre of 'Jason' – tho' I am trying not to imitate Morris too much. The subject of course is far too good for a schoolboy of eighteen to blunder at, but I think I shall try & go on. I write it whenever the fit takes me, in a pocket book, so you will not see it till tis done.

My Responsions exam begins on Teusday 20th of March and I cast me to be home before the following Monday. You say you hope to have some more 'breathless' walks. I can undertake to manage the 'breathless' part either by strapping a sponge bag onto your head, or by compelling you to advance up the steepest hills at the double. I have finished my book on French Literature (admirable, excellent, exquisite) and started a very interesting work 'Les Confessions' de Rousseau[41] – <qui avait, lui aussi, un penchant pour la verge qui consacre a ce sujet adorable quatre pages.>[42] Altogether a 'really rather lovely' book. <His taste is altogether for suffering rather than inflicting: which I can feel too, but it is a feeling more proper to the other sex.>

I opened my eyes; and, looking first up, saw above me the deep violent sky of a warm southern night; and then, lifting my head, saw that I was sailing fast upon a summer sea, in the last border of a southern twilight.'

39 Cosmo von Wehrstahl whose story is told in chapter XIII.

40 The *Greek Anthology* contains over six thousand epigrams found in various Greek authors and ranging over 17 centuries. The words Lewis quoted are from a poem by Asclepiades, found in the *Greek Anthology*, bk. 5, poem 169.

41 Jean-Jacques Rousseau, *Les Confessions* (1781–8).

42 'who had, he too, a penchant for the rod, [and] who dedicates to this delightful subject four pages'.

The pleasures of spring have been jawed about so often that I am rather shy of saying anything about the lovely weather that has succeeded to the snow here. Do you know what it feels like when you go out for the first time without an overcoat and feel all the nerves funny up the back of your legs and see the clouds blowing about a really blue sky? All the same I know spring too well to really like her. She invariably makes you feel lonely & dissatisfied & long for

'The land where I shall never be
The love that I shall never see.'[43]

You know what I mean?

Yrs.,

J.

<Philom.>

<VERGERS POUR LES VIERGES>

TO ARTHUR GREEVES (W):

[Gastons
28 February 1917]

Cher Ami,

Thou art fool: you take tremendous care about putting in anything too <*philomastigian*> for fear it should be seen and then go and stick in a reference to a certain lady of my passion, making it quite clear whom you mean so that it *really would* matter if somebody got hold of it. However, they shan't.

But as to that lady, I remember that you did not agree when I suggested <her as a suitable subject for the lash>, on that eventful night. But surely now that you have seen her again you must agree with me. Is she not absolutely perfect from head to heel – and moreover <the necessary part of the body – one of the most beautiful parts anyway – shaped with an almost intolerable grace? The gods> – whom I'm always abusing – certainly produced a masterpiece in her: even to see her walk across the room is a liberal education. Ah me, <if she had suffered indeed half the stripes that have fallen upon her in imagination she would be well

43 For the source of these lines see note 44 to the letter of 28 February 1917.

disciplined.> Of course I don't say that it is quite my own ideal type of beauty. But then who ever is? After all 'The love that I shall never see' is better both in body and soul than all the real women on earth.

Which reminds me, that couplet (a beauty isn't it) is NOT by me – I wish it were. Andrew Lang quotes it somewhere, but I have never been able to discover the author. Whoever it be, he deserves immortality for those two lines alone.[44]

Item, I have read nearly all Tacitus, his short works the Agricola & Germania, the Histories & am now at the Annals.[45] At first I absolutely hated him, partly because I had not then learned to appreciate history, partly because his twisted and obscure style (he is called 'the Latin Carlyle' & 'the Latin Meredith', so you can imagine) at first repelled me. Now, however, I am grown to be very fond of him indeed. I have just finished the 14th and am beginning the 15th book of the Annals – all about Nero. Some of N's depravities are so fearful as to be almost funny, aren't they? I expect that like me, it will especially interest you as being the source of 'Quo Vadis'.[46] The only other author of ancient history I can recommend is the Greek historian Herodotus.[47] He combines the pleasure of real history & the charm of romance: he tells all about Egypt & Persia and the wonder of Babylon & the Hyperboreans who live beyond the North Wind, & the gryphons who guard their gold in the Scythian deserts etc. I am sure a good translation of him would provide you with agreeable reading.

Since writing last I have read for the first time 'The Tenant of Wildfell Hall'.[48] In spite of some excellent passages it is a bad book. People who have been brought up as gentleman don't even when drunk, fight and beat their wives in their hostesse's drawing room. It is all very melodramatic & gives you the impression of being written by a lady's maid. However the beginning and the end, the part outside Helen's own

44 The lines 'The land where I shall never be / The love that I shall never see' are by Andrew Lang and are found in his *History of English Literature* (1912), p. 579, which book Lewis was reading in 1915. Lewis was, however, quoting from memory. Lang's actual lines are 'The love whom I shall never meet, / The Land where I shall never be'.

45 Cornelius Tacitus, *The Life of Agricola* (c. 98); *Germania* (98); *Histories* (c. 116).

46 Henryk Sienkiewicz, *Quo Vadis?* (1896).

47 Herodotus (c. 480–c. 425 BC) is known as the 'father of history'. His *Histories*, the first great prose work in European literature, deal with the struggle between Asia and Europe and culminate with the Persian invasions of Greece.

48 Anne Brontë, *The Tenant of Wildfell Hall* (1848).

narrative, are topping & I had rather have read it than not. I am now beginning Mrs. Gaskell's 'Life'[49] in the household edition & love it already. The description of Haworth with the moors going up behind it is heavenly – wouldn't you like that sort of country – tho' of course not better than our own. You will be glad to hear that in the introduction to this copy, that ill-bred journalist Clement Shorter gets well slated & is shown to have most maliciously [mis]represented lots of things.

Your description of 'John Inglesant'[50] is not very appetising: as to the subject about Catholics and Protestants, I fear me that my views would only annoy you (comment 'Has that ever prevented you from stating them if you wanted to?' Ah well! ...) Doesn't it seem ages ago, cher ami, since we sat that day in the library looking down on the street and trying to talk? I *am* looking forward to a return homeward. Responsions is the entrance exam to the University: for you see, tho' I have got a scholarship at one college, I don't belong to the whole show.

'The Confessions' of Rousseau (to jump from one subject to another) quite apart from THAT splendid passage, continue very interesting indeed. The description of his wanderings and adventures is rather like that of De Quincey – perhaps even better. It would be rather long for you at present but you should keep it in your mental list of French books to be got.

I do hope you are really speaking the truth about Dymer in all your flattery. As he draws near his end I am getting quite anxious lest I should not finish him. You will understand with what pleasure I look forward to being able to say 'Well, there is a book written: long or short, good or bad, there it is by itself and done.' How I wish I could make you start writing again so that we could have all these little wheezes in common as we do everything else.

Item, the

'springs voluptuous pantings'[51]

still go on, damn them! It has now got to the stage when real comfort in bed must be given up till next winter. If you keep on the clothes you had

49 Elizabeth Cleghorn Gaskell, *The Life of Charlotte Brontë* (1857).

50 Joseph Henry Shorthouse, *John Inglesant* (1881).

51 Percy Bysshe Shelley, *Alastor* (1815), l. 11.

last week you will be asphyxiated, if you lay them off you will have, not cold, but a lonely, comfortless sense of thinness. All the same I must admit it is lovely to hear the birds of a morning and feel the sun on your back as you're getting into your bath. Voilà de l'éloquence à propos d'a worn out theme: but honest all the same, and therefore pardonable. Do you know, cher ami, that it is at great cost I write hard like this up to the very moment of going to bed? I never sleep well on the nights of writing – all the ideas buzzing in my head keep me awake.

Which reminds me, you will be releived to hear that 'Medea's Childhood' after struggling on for 300 turgid lines has been quietly made into spills for my 'tobacco pipe' – all those fine landscapes and vigorous speeches, devoted to real use at last![52] En effet, it is a failure. I can quite share your annoyance about the Essays. There are a hundred things I meant to say in this letter and haven't. My feet are cold & there is a moon. Look at the lady we mentioned & think. Good night old fool: have finished P. Schlemihl.

TO HIS FATHER (LP V: 189–90):

[Gastons]
Thursday.
1st March 1917.

My dear Papy,

I have waited thus long in the hope of dragging some communication out of you: for to treat the parcel of Greek grammar – for which however many thanks – as a substitute for your weekly letter would be a very bad precedent. However, although you are not entitled to one now, I suppose I must make allowances. 'Colonial manners' don't you know. By the way, I hope the letterlessness, to coin a pretty word, of last week doesn't mean that you are laid up again? Arthur says that he met you 'the other day', but of course I don't know when that was. So try and let me have a letter some time soon, just to see how things are going.

This Responsions exam. begins Tuesday the 20th of this month, and I hope to be with you on the following Monday at the latest, but much

52 While Lewis may have destroyed the version of 'Medea's Childhood' he first mentioned in his letter of 15 February 1917, he returned to the theme a year and half later. In his letter to Arthur of 14 July 1919 he said of the second version, 'The "Medea" is very nearly finished, and will be about twelve hundred lines.' For the only surviving lines of the poem see the letter of 18 September 1919.

more likely on the Friday. If the exam does not end until the Saturday I may have to stay in Oxford over the Sunday, which will be rather a nuisance – tho' of course there would be points about it too. The spring is coming on by leaps and bounds here, but I'm afraid I can't share the usual raptures. Mrs. K. is already beginning to say 'Really it's almost too hot with the fire today' which is a very disconcerting sign. I must admit there is something nice about those birds in the mornings – the creatures that you and I would call swallows, but which Kirk (after a short preamble on the amazing ignorance of elementary natural history shown by some people), puts down as 'house martins'. I think Blodo's 'Oh no sir', delivered in the Blodo voice would be a suitable reply.

My condiscipulus Terry, whom I am beginning rather to like, was 'called up' last week, but managed to get exempted after some bother. How glad I am that my fate is once for all settled for good or bad.

I have got out of the library an old name of ours, 'The Chronicles of Froissart'[53] in two enormous folios from the Kelmscott Press – Morris's thing you know. But it is rather dull after all. I foresee great difficulty in getting German and Italian books later on, but I suppose the covers of Oxford may yield to beating.

Let me hear from you soon.

your loving
son Jack.

TO ARTHUR GREEVES (W):

[Gastons
6 March 1917]

Cher Ami,

I think sometimes that we have spoiled everything by starting this subject. For one thing, we always are like the ladies in Jane Austin, who each want to talk about her own concerns and neither to hear the other's. <I mean, you are interested in a brand of *That* which doesn't appeal to me, and I in one that doesn't appeal to you.>

But it is not only that: I happened this morning on an old letter of yours from the days of Papillon, full of enthusiasm about books and music and scenery, which somehow made me feel that we were on a

53 *Froissart's Chronicles*, Kelmscott Press, 2 vols. limited to 160 copies on vellum (1897). The *Chronicles* of Jean Froissart (c. 1337–c. 1410) were first translated into English by John Bourchier in 1523–5.

much higher level then, much more removed from the common mob. And yet I do not see that it is sensible to pretend that these things don't exist, when we are both really very sensual at heart. Rather, when we first started the subject, I didn't think it would be quite the same: I fancied there was a way of treating such themes with gravity, delicacy and real, honest appreciation of the good things of the world, that could sort of fall into line with our other interest in literature and so on: that we could raise the subject to our level instead of falling to its. Nor can I see exactly how we have failed in that ideal: yet – without blaming you in the very, very, least – when I had read your letter this evening I felt that something was wrong.

Perhaps I was just in a particular kind of mood, but more likely it was the unhappy reference to Catullus that finished me. For Catullus (you saw him in my big Medici volume) though I have only read ⅓ or so of him, is to me one of the really sacred poets, some of his tiny little things leave me really breathless – in particular one bit about that wander-lust feeling in the Spring, which he describes beautifully; in fact he is one of my gods, I put him on a level with Morris or Keats. You can understand what a sudden shock it gave me <to think of anyone approaching him from your point of view. It was blasphemy>: mind, I don't blame you in the very least, still less do I suggest that I wouldn't have felt just the same in your position <(I may remark in passing that in the parts of Catullus I have read there is no allusion to your particular taste).> All the same it set me thinking – and I have just tried to jot down the substance of it. In a way we have spoiled our paradise.

All the same, having gone thus far, there is no good trying to go back – it would be horrible to keep an artificial silence and feel that there was something there all the time. Let us talk of these things when we want, but always keep them on the side that tends to beauty, and avoid everything that tends to sordid-ness <and beastly police court sort of scandal out of grim real life (like the O. Wilde story).> Cher ami, please, please don't think this is preaching. I don't pretend that I have done so any better than you, but I am only suggesting plans for the future: for I am sure you have felt at times as I do now.

You will have gathered that I am in bad form to-night:

'Oh Galahad, my Galahad,
The world is very lone and sad,

The world is old and gray with pain
And all the ways thereof are bad.'

For one thing it is most annoying to think that I shall only have 3 weeks holiday this Easter: for another, as it draws to its close, I begin to regret the very happy time I have spent at Bookham. As well Mrs Gaskell's Life, though a book quite beyond all praise, especially in the description of scenery, has regularly given me the blues, so sad is the story it tells. When God can get hold of a really first rate character like Charlotte Brontë to torture, he's just in his element: cruelty after cruelty without any escape. How little right we have to grumble at any little discomforts of ours.

Cher ami, of course that lady is not my ideal, and I agree with you that she is much too big. I wonder would you think my ideal even pretty if I could produce her in bodily form! I have her very clearly in my mind however & could recognize her at once if such a person came into existance. The girl in the last instalment of Dymer is the one from the witch's house of course: it was dark when they met there, and in the morning Dymer left her still sleeping – so of course he knew her but she had never seen him. But I admit, that was so long ago that you may be pardoned for having forgotten. I am afraid this instalment is a failure. I have made three attempts at it and am not at all satisfied. Both in prose & verse & my everyday work the thing I take most pains with are always the poorest. Regardez comme je suis égoiste! Half the time I talk about the state of my soul & the other half of my own book.

Item, 'Peter Schlemihl' is the name of that German 'admirable' book about the man who sold his shadow. I am very pleased to have read it. I am now (in German) at 'Sintram'[54] a tale by Fouqué. It has some good eerie touches in it, but none of the homely beauty of 'Undine' – indeed 'tis rather tawdry as a whole. The edition is so horrible that it ought to emanate from 'Satan & Co.' & sometimes I have a ghastly suspicion that it is 'scripted': for these school editors are absolutely without conscience & wouldn't hesitate to mutilate a book and then publish it without a word of explanation.

By the way, did you know that the 1/- Nelson French series had several other bindings? I have got a 4/- 'half-polished morocco' one at

54 Friedrich Fouqué, Baron de la Motte, *Sintram* (1862).

which you will 'fly with delight'. It is Victor Hugo's 'Hans d'Islande'[55] (Islande=Iceland, not island, you know) of which a book on F. literature says 'it is founded on a modern Icelandic tradition of a man-beast who lives among the mountains.' So I hope it will be good. The whole set of Hugo built up in that binding would be splendid.

I have finished 'Paradise Lost' again, enjoying it even more than before. Really you must read it sometime soon. In Milton is everything you get everywhere else, only better. He is as voluptuous as Keats, as romantic as Morris, as grand as Wagner, as wierd as Poe, and a better lover of nature than even the Brontes. A propos of which, there are certainly some true Bronte touches in 'The Tenant of Wildfell (lovely name) Hall', especially in the homely gathering of the first chapter and some fine descriptions of the moors. Those moors must be lovely. Mrs. Gaskell's excellent description has quite fired me – not that any scenery could quite fill the place of our own dear glens and fields. I do hope we shall have some really good rambles among them soon: we must be careful never to talk of 'That' in the precincts of the Sacred Wood – as well, our vegetable loves, the hazels & brambles, might be jealous. Have your 'Essays' come yet? I wrote to Mullans a long time ago for the 3rd volume of the History which of course has not come. If this goes on I shall get all my books from London both in term and holydays. Yet that would be against all my principles.

'Our azure sister of the Spring'[56] is so annoyed at my praises of winter that she has retired and left the field to snow and slush. And the bare trees are all waving to and fro and sighing, and the drenching rain is blowing sideways out of a gray sky today altogether a very fine spectacle. I got onto one of the big Roman roads (theres something fine about feeling that a road runs away to Carlisle behind you) and trudged for miles watching the dead leaves floating along the swollen gutters. A most fascinating amusement, have you ever tried it?

I have written for the 'Faithful Sheppeardess'[57] in the Temple Dramatists. What are they like? I have also got a Chatto & Windus list with some interesting news in it. My usual smoking nowadays is one of those

55 Victor Hugo, *Han d'Islande* (1823).

56 Percy Bysshe Shelley, 'Ode to the West Wind' (1819), l. 9: 'Thine azure sister of the spring'.

57 John Fletcher, *The Faithful Shepherdess* (1610).

very long old fashioned clay pipes. The sort that Milton may have smoked. You should try one. It is the cheapest and one of the best ways of smoking & you can understand the 'old world charm' of it. I wish there wasn't a week to wait for your next letter, make it as long as long as long. Good night, mon vieux.

TO HIS FATHER (LP V: 192):

[Gastons]
8/3/17.

My dear Papy,

I am very sorry that you should feel hurt about the boots. I must admit that I was hitherto under the impression that Warnie proposed to write and pay for them himself, in which case there would have been no reason to bring to your notice what I was sure you would regard as an extravagance. I argued that at any rate it was his affair and not mine, that it was not my business. Whenever I am in doubt what to do, it is always my rule to do nothing. I suppose I was wrong to follow it in this case, and am very sorry you should have been troubled.

The Oxford arrangement is rather more than an assurance that 'nothing will be decided until I go into residence'. I take it that we have settled that my military career will begin through the Oxford O.T.C. next term, and after that everything will be in the hands of the authorities – so that we have nothing more to worry about. At any rate that is what I meant in my last letter. The exam, as you know, begins next Tuesday week. With many abject apologies for my old, old offence, may I ask you to send me before that time, the waistcoat of my new brown suit? There are several brown waistcoats in my room, but you will know this one by the bright blue lining.

The food allowances are beginning to be short enough here. Like you, we find the meat plenty, but the bread rather short. Potatoes have almost disappeared among the poorer people and are no longer an every day dish anywhere. Of course it would be absurd to complain at present but it looks very black for the future, if this submarine business goes on. Kirk complains of the surplus potatoes held up in Ireland. By the way how is our ill fated front lawn coming on?

Some time before I arrive home I am posting a parcel addressed to you, with as many books as possible, to gain weight, and room in the suit case. At present I am reading Mrs. Gaskell's 'Life of Charlotte Bronte' which is admirable. After a glimpse of spring, we are back to a blowing frost.

your loving
son Jack.

TO HIS FATHER (LP V: 193–4):

[Gastons]
14th March /17.

My dear Papy,

It is rather difficult to give you any idea of what monies numbered I shall need for this trip. Last time, the journey to Oxford and back and the stay there came to a little over £5, did it not. This time of course there will be the journey from Oxford to Liverpool (or Fleetwood) as well.

Which reminds me, I will write and tell you as soon as I know which will be the better way and on what night I am crossing. If my examination takes me till midday on its last day, I might have difficulty in catching that evening's boat and so have to waste another day. I don't know when Malvern breaks up, but I have hopes of seeing my friend Cooper this time.

I suppose the wierd looking parcels of my books have arrived by now, and shall be glad to hear of their safety. I spent a long morning on Saturday rummaging the second hand dealers of Charing Cross Road (vide Lamb) for them: these foreign books (except French of course) are a great difficulty now.

Of course there is no formal promise about military service, but even if we wanted to (which we don't) we couldn't very well help joining the O.T.C. next term, when I am being allowed to go up for that very purpose. You don't mention your health, so I hope the cough has disappeared. We have had some more snow and several days and half days of the densest clamniest fog you ever heard of outside London.

Another of Mrs. K's nieces is staying here at present: they seem to be inexhaustable. I am looking forward to a glorious vista of potatoes in plentiful Ireland.

your loving
son Jack.

TO ARTHUR GREEVES (W):

[Gastons
14 March 1917]

Cher Ami,

I have just been debating whether the pleasure of getting a letter will outweigh the dissapointment of finding a very short one: for without anything from you to provoke argument I don't know how long I can go on gassing. See how concieted I am grown, as if in my letters shortness would not be the best recommendation.

Well to proceed (and recite the following verses of the poet) I was delighted to hear of your illness, which I did yesterday from M. mon père and to day from Mme. vôtre mère & your own scrawl. I hope you will be just nicely convalescing when I turn up – well enough to go out, but of course not nearly well enough for Niffleheim (or Frankleheim). Seriously, unless it is [a] very painful or opressive illness I always get some pleasure out of 'keeping my bed'. Especially if you are sick enough to have a fire! There is something beautifully cosy about meals brought up on a tray, and after a frugal but thoroughly enjoyable breakfast I love to pile up my pillows, call for a choice pile of bright volumes and settle down to an endless read: if there be snow falling so much the better.

I say 'bright volumes' advisedly, because all books are not suitable for bed reading. Books of the 'Phantastes' & 'Crock of Gold' type are best; some new ones if possible, several old favourites, a trashy novel from the library (trashy, but not bad, if you know what I mean) AND some picture books of the Rackham & Robinson type. I should find 'Jason' very good company too. By the way don't imagine I'm trotting all this out as sort of 'advice to invalids': its only that the subject naturally came up & I couldn't lose an opportunity of airing my own tastes. Expect you wont agree with any of them. I suppose the Titian print is great company: or can you see nothing but reflexions in it's glass from where you sit?

Cher ami, 'Han d'Islande' in its lovely binding is the best book I've read for many a day. It is about Norway in the 16th century, a good historical romance, gets along quicker than Scott tho' without any of the hiccupping style that annoys us in Dumas. Although there is no supernatural element there is a great deal of the terrifying and the 'macabre'. Hans himself, a sort of ugly & ferocious Rob Roy, with a dash of Alberich in his character and appearance is a real treat. There are also excellent descriptions of scenery among the mountains and ruins. Altogether a book I should very heartily recommend you. Amn't I good to write to you instead of readin it at this moment? The III vol. of my Macaulay has come at last in a shocking shop soiled copy, but I suppose I shall have to keep it.

You will see from the tag in this week's Dymer that I have begun Italian, which is the easiest language of the world.[58] I shall be able to shew you one charming edition in that language next hols. My adress after Teusday is,

C/o Mrs Etheridge,
1 Mansfield Road,
Oxford.

'No more now' as the housemaids say. Goodnight.

P.S. I wonder what you really thought of my last letter

Lewis returned to Oxford on 20 March and lodged in the same digs as before. Responsions began on the 21st and he returned home on 27 March, soon afterwards learning that he had been ploughed in algebra. He was, however, allowed to come into residence in Trinity Term so as to be able to pass into the army by way of the University Officers' Training Corps. He arrived in Oxford on 26 April and matriculated on the 28th. From an academic point of view he was supposed to be reading for Responsions, and shortly after his arrival he began algebra lessons with John Edward Campbell (1862–1924) of Hertford College.

On 30 April Lewis joined the Officers' Training Corps and had a physical examination. He weighed 13 stone, or 182 pounds, and measured 5 feet 10¾ inches. In the official records, the officer commanding wrote under 'Special Remarks': 'Likely to make a useful officer but will not have had sufficient training for admission to an O.C.U.[59] *before end of* June.'

58 Writing to Jack's father on 18 April 1917, Mr Kirkpatrick said: 'I conceived, with the enthusiastic assent of the pupil, of course, the bold conception of mastering the Italian language in half a term. And we did it. None but a quite exceptional student could have attempted it, much less succeeded in it.' (LP V: 203).

59 Officer Cadet Unit.

TO HIS FATHER (LP V: 194):

[University College,
Oxford]
Postmark: 20 March 1917

My dear P.,

Many thanks for the money: I am sorry to have given you the trouble of wiring it. I find I can cross by Fleetwood on Friday night. Have arrived here this morning and exams begin to morrow. Your letter came just before I left Bookham. As usual it is colder here than any where else. This is our shop: second tower belongs to some other coll.

yours J.

TO HIS FATHER (LP V: 206–7):

[University College]
Postmark: 28 April 1917

My dear Papy,

I hope that you have got both my wires. The second I could not send off till the morning, as the post offices were all shut by the time I knew anything to tell you last night.

The effect of the war here is much more startling than I could have expected, and everything is very homely and out of order. The College at present numbers 6 men, of whom 4 are freshmen! Others are coming all the time, but I do not think we shall be more than eleven all told. Last night we had dinner not in Hall but in a small lecture room, and none of the dons appeared. Hall is in possession of the blue-coated wounded, who occupy the whole of one quad: incidentally, the second tower (in the p. card) does belong to us after all.

The first thing that strikes you is the enormous size of the rooms. I imagined a 'sitter' something smaller than the little end room. The first one they showed me was rather larger than our drawing room and full of most beautiful oak. I wasn't left there however, and am now in a much humbler, and very nice set, on the other side of the quad.[60] It is a pity in a way that all the furniture and pictures really belong to a man who may be coming back after the war – it saves me expenses, but it prevents me from having what I want.

---

60 Lewis was in set no. 5 on Staircase XII of the Radcliffe Quad. Most of the rooms in this quad were occupied by the wounded.

I have been to see the Dean,[61] who turns out to be a beardless boy of about 25, and also my tutor, who is also the bursar.[62] They don't appear to suggest any real reading while I am in the Corps, but the Bursar has promised to find me a coach for elementary mathematics, if possible. Corps does not begin till Monday evening for which short respite I am very thankful. I think it will be quite cheap living in this 'vast solitude': the only serious expenses so far have been £2-10 for uniform (which seems very reasonable), and £1-9 for cap and gown (which does not). It seems that the adress of 'University Coll.' will find me quite safely. Hoping that you are keeping well and cheerful and that you will soon write,

I am,
your loving son,
Jack.

TO ARTHUR GREEVES (W):

[University College
28 April 1917]

Cher Ami,

I wonder how much description will be tolerable for you to hear and me to write. I am so full of new things that I don't know where to begin, and yet nothing has really happened so far. I will try to tell you at least my first adventures in some detail.

Heavily laden with suitcase, parcels and coats I arrived at the great gate of Univ. at about 5 o'clock. From the porter's lodge a sandy-haired man emerged and shouted 'Jo'. Somewhat timidly I came further in and asked 'Can you tell me where my rooms are, – my name is Lewis.' Yes, Sir,' said the man. 'Can't say where you'll be, Sir, the Dean hasn't come up yet – Jo!' Jo now appeared.[63] 'Show Mr Lewis into Mr

61 John Clifford Valentine Behan (1881–1957) was Dean 1914–17. He was the first Rhodes Scholar to come from the state of Victoria, Australia, and he was made a Fellow of Law at University College in 1909.

62 Arthur Blackburne Poynton (1876–1944), Lewis's tutor. He came up to Balliol College in 1885 and was one of the most distinguished undergraduates of his generation. After taking a First in Classical Honour Moderations in 1889 and a First in *Literae Humaniores* in 1890 he was elected a Fellow of Hertford College. In 1894 he moved to University College as Fellow and Praelector in Greek. He was the Master of University College from 1935 to 1937.

63 Cyril 'Joe' Haggis (1890–1967), a college scout, came to the College in 1908, and retired, at the age of 65, after 43 years of service. See *University College Record*, Vol. V (September 1967), pp. 111–12.

Crawford's[64] old rooms' said the sandy haired man. Jo took my various baggage and led the way along one side of the quad (I was very relieved to see no one about). Then he led me up three very bare noisy flights of stairs, between stone walls, dark with tiny windows, halted before a room, and throwing open the 'oak' and the inner door said 'Here you are, Sir. Your servant'll be here in arf an hour, and if these aren't the right rooms, he'll tell you Sir.'

You can imagine, ami, with what intense excitement I stepped into the first varsity rooms I'd ever seen. The first thing that struck me with amazement was the size. I had expected something rather less than the little end room at home. What I saw was a very low-roofed, rather uneven-floored room somewhat larger than the study at home. The furniture was of dark oak very richly carved, and valuable I should think. On the floor was a red carpet with great profusion of rugs. Besides the old furniture was a big modern sofa & several very easy chairs. There was also a little bed-room and a cupboard. I was awfully bucked with it and went on sitting down in one chair after another, and opening and shutting the 'oak' after Jo had left me.

I looked down on the quad. and saw a tall youth in spectacles talking to the porter. I began to wonder what I should do. Did one wear a gown for hall? How did one sit in hall? The question of wearing a gown was solved soon, because I heard someone in the opposite room saying to someone else 'Oh no, no gowns.' Presently I went down into the quad to prospect – but be of good cheer, cher ami, I am not going to keep up this detailed description much longer. I must try and give you a general account of the college in shorter terms.

The rooms I am in now are very nice tho' not so magnificent as the first ones (which turned out to be wrong). They really belong to a tremendous blood who is at the front – at least the furniture is all his. Of course this takes away from me the pleasure of choosing the things for myself; but then it is much better done than I could have afforded. There is a grand piano – couldn't we have great times, ami? It is getting to be

64 Edward Hugh Martin Crawford (1894–1973) was a graduate of Dalhousie University, Nova Scotia. He matriculated in 1914 as a Rhodes Scholar. He took a Second in Jurisprudence in 1916, and a BCL in 1920. He was called to the Canadian Bar in 1920, having spent the latter years of the war in a munitions factory. During World War II he served with the Royal Canadian Air Force.

quite homely to me this room, especially when I come back to it by fire-light and find the kettle boiling. How I love kettles!

Dinner is not in Hall now, as there are only 12 men in college, but in a small lecture room, and the dons don't turn up. For all other meals the scout brings you a cover in your rooms; tea etc you make for yourself. So far, I have done absolutely nothing. The Dean refuses to map out any plans for me, on the ground that the Corps will take me all my time. Corps doesn't begin till Monday afternoon.

Now as to the human part of the place. None of the older men (from last or previous terms, I mean) take any notice of us freshmen, except to ask us for the salt and that sort of thing. There are 3 freshmen counting myself. One of them is quite impossible, and I and the other one, a certain Edgell,[65] have lived mostly together so far. He is writing letters in my rooms at the moment. Well what like is he? I can hardly say. First of all, in tastes he is no friend of ours. He doesn't read, and is interested in mechanics – ugh! However, he can talk not without interest on a good many subjects, among which we reached religion, when I was foolish enough to tell him my own views. 'Natheless he so endured.'[66] He is very useful to me, because his father was at Univ. and has told him all the tricks of the trade. He also makes excellent cofee, and so I am sticking to him at present. Later on, as I get to know more people, perhaps I shall find some real friends here also.

The only other thing I can think of that may interest you – in that way – is the Shelley memorial which you would love. I pass it every morning on the way to my bath. On a slab of black marble, carved underneath with weeping muses, lies in white stone the nude figure of Shelley, as he was cast up by the sea – all tossed into curious attitudes with lovely ripples of muscle and strained limbs. He is lovely.[67] <(No – not since I came back. Somehow I haven't even thought of it.)>

---

65 Lawrence Fayrer Arnold Edgell (1898–1950) after receiving his BA in 1923, read Theology at Wycliffe Hall, Oxford, and was ordained in the Church of England in 1927. After some years with the Church Missionary Society in Persia, he returned home and was the vicar of several churches, his last being in Shalford, Essex, from 1946 until his death.

66 Milton, *Paradise Lost*, I, 299.

67 The drowned figure of Shelley lying on a slab of Connemara marble was carved by Edward Onslow Ford. It lies under a dome designed by Basil Champneys. The monument was originally intended for the Protestant cemetery in Rome, where Shelley is buried, but it was presented to the college by Lady Shelley.

Well, there you have all my news. Now let us talk about yourself. So write at once and tell me everything, and be of good cheer. We get potatoes every day here. – Addio,

Jack

TO HIS FATHER (LP V: 208–9):

[University College]
Wednesday.
Postmark: 3 May 1917

My dear Papy,

I was delighted to see your letter at the bottom of my staircase this morning, and was only sorry to hear that you are 'hipped'. Of course I know that that can hardly be otherwise,

'and on my knees
I too have prayed that it should be amended'

though I do not know how. It is terrible to think of the lonely life you now have to lead, and I do most earnestly hope and pray that you may find some way out of it. So far as the knowledge of my comfortable and healthy circumstances here can add to your happiness – well 'Make it so'; I have nothing but good to report so far. The Corps proves very much more agreeable than the Malvern one – every one is so friendly and reasonable, you feel that you are there to learn, and not merely to be bullied by sergeants. I have found a mathematical coach, a very pleasant Scotsman, a Mr. Campbell of Hertford, who has almost promised to get me through 'Smalls' [Responsions] next term.

As to the other matters, whatever vices one is likely to develop here must be those native to the University: the huge mass of military people who are settled in Oxford count for nothing. You see the actual varsity O.T.C. is only a small body: outside it is a mob of cadets freshly come from other O.T.C.'s, and here training for commissions. They are rather a bad lot, and certainly an ill bred lot, especially the Flying Corps, who, like most people in dangerous things, are busily engaged in eating and drinking on their splendid pay, for tomorrow they die. Against all these the old feud of TOWN and GOWN is rather in force. Thank goodness none are quartered in Univ. But even then we shouldn't know them. Beyond the 'commons' mug of ale supplied with our lunch, bread and cheese, I see no drinking here.

I have met several Malvernians, including my sometime study companion Hardman, whom I was sorry to find in the ill-famed Flying Corps, quartered opposite us in Queen's. However, I was glad to have a crack with him over old times: some people, like some books, do not read so well when we open them after a long interval. Yet the charm of 'Do you remember' will carry on a conversation with anyone.

I paid cash for the gown but not for the uniform. The bills will come in at the end of term, and I think will include nothing but tailor, grocer (for necessaries not supplied by College, tea, sugar, butter etc.) and Battels. These are sent me weekly to check, but aren't paid till the vac. Of course I shall try to keep everything down, tho' my fresher's ignorance of shops sometimes makes me pay more for something than I need have done. Am learning to row.

your loving son,
Jack.

P.S. Please let me have Warnie's adress, of which I am not quite sure. J.

TO ARTHUR GREEVES (W):

[University College
6 May 1917]

My dear Galahad,

I am afraid this letter is not punctual and I am further afraid that many of my letters this term will not be punctual. We do not do really much here, but somehow the whole day is frittered away in little things. As for going on to my diabolical romance – tis out of the question. Your last letter is lost, so what shall I jaw about?

Well first, let me most earnestly advise you to get Gautier's 'Un Trio de Romans'[68] when you next want a French book. It is really excellent; one story rather reminds me of the Cosmo episode in 'Phantastes'. I am afraid I shall get too many in that edition, it is so very convenient. The 2nd vol. of the Earthly Paradise stands in my bookcase here, but I have progressed only a few pages since coming up. However I am going to make out a regular time-table for each day & try if I cannot get more

68 Théophile Gautier, *Un Trio de Romans* (1852).

time like that. When you are not made to work and when there is such a lot to do, it is very hard to get on with things.

It is most glorious weather here now and we spend most of our spare afternoons on the river. Edgell knows something about rowing, so I am gradually learning through many blunders. We ran someone down today (Sunday) greatly to the amusement of the assembled river: but as the other wasn't a varsity man of course it didn't matter!

My chief 'cross' at present is my friend, or rather my companion, Edgell, whose limitless piety I don't think I can endure any longer. He has all your particular faults, cher ami, with none of your merits. He is economical, methodical to the verge of insanity. He is fully convinced of his own moral superiority, and lectures me on my 'weakness of character'. Still, I suppose I must stick to him until I get to know some of the senior men a bit better!

Don't imagine however that I'm grumbling. The place is on the whole absolutely ripping. If only you saw the quad. on these moonlit nights with the long shadows lying half across the level, perfect grass and the tangle of spires & towers rising beyond in the dark! Oh ami, ami, what times we could have here together: you really must come. What talks we could have in the privacy of these rooms by firelight while the kettle was boiling. Item, you must get a ground room if you come, as even I begin to find the dashing up & down stairs rather tiring. I am finding a whole lot of Malvernians here – a new one every day. How lovely the country must be at home now – I hope you are still on half time and are having some nice afternoons <(– in that way?)> in the garden. Which reminds me, I have 'Digestive' biscuits every day for tea, & always wish I was sharing them with you instead of with that six feet of spectacled priggery!

The book shops here are rather adorable, and also our college library. Still better is the Library of the Union Society (a club everyone belongs to) where I spent this morning turning over one book after another and enjoying myself hugely. My books have not finished binding yet, but of course I shall give you a full account so soon as they arrive. The Maeterlink's are to be plain dark blue cloth, and the 'Literature Française au Moyen Age' in green linnen. I'm afraid this [is] all the length of letter I can raise. Do reply soon and at full length.

TO HIS FATHER (LP V: 210–11):

[University College]
Postmark: 12 May 1917

My dear Papy,

I hope you will forgive a little delay in my answering your last letter, as I wanted to wait until I had seen my coach Mr. Campbell again, and could give an answer to your question. A rather awkward and at the same time rather pleasing thing has happened. (Incidentally Mr. Campbell turns out to be the uncle of my Malvern friend Hardman, who, as I told you, is here in the Flying Corps). Well, when I asked him about fees, he said he didn't want any. I replied, with very many thanks, that the matter of course concerned my father and not me, and that I was sure you wouldn't allow him to do any such thing. He said that he regarded the thing as a service done to Univ., to which society he was under many obligations: that if my father wanted to get rid of some money, he could give it to some deserving charity: and that if you sent it to him, that is what he would do with it. I repeated that of course it had nothing to do with me – that I would write to you about it. I then bear my retreat, with renewed thanks. Whatever you decide to do, I suppose you will write to him. The address is:

J.A.Campbell Esq.
Hertford College,
Oxford.

When you imagine how boring it must be for a real mathematician and an F.R.S. to teach such elementary stuff, you will understand the extent of his goodness. I have liked him exceedingly from the first. As you say, it is a thousand pities that this is not the real Oxford. The more I stay here the more I hope that I shall see it again as it ought to be.

Of course I am keeping my classics up as much as I can, tho' it is not always easy to find time for everything, especially as 'sporting your oak' is not allowed when there are so few men in College. Yes, there are plenty of shellfish of the crab kind to be found in the waters both of the 'Isis' and the Cherwell: also knocks on the chin, and eloquence from people you collide with. Some other freshers and I had 'brekker' with the Master this morning – a thoroughly enjoyable function. How very nice everyone I've met so far seems to be! The only possible exception is the Dean, who is – in manner – like Uncle Pumblechook,[69] only more so: his favourite conversational fallback is that chilling word 'Oh.' Your friend David Garrick was here last week, but I didn't go.

your loving
son Jack.

TO ARTHUR GREEVES (W):

[University College
13 May 1917]

Cher Ami,

As you seem able to bear my boring accounts of life here, I may give you a little more. To-day, for instance, (Sunday) has so far been a very prosperous and a not untypical day. I woke at about 7 o'clock with the pleasing reflection that there was no early parade and read Wm. Morris and Gautier till 8.30. I then went down to the bathroom and had first a hot & then a cold bath – which is 'done' here.

We are gradually getting to know people and a very senior man, Butler,[70] has asked us to 'brekker' (breakfast) this morning. I arrived in his rooms a little too early, and thus had an opportunity of studying his books, which I always consider the best introduction to a new acquaintance. I was pleased to find Keats, Shelley, Oscar Wilde, Dante & Villon, as well as Plutarch & one of the lately executed Sinn Fein poets:[71] for Butler is an Irishman & a nationalist. I was just trying to find out the publisher of the nice Plutarch when Butler arrived with the other guests, Edgell & a certain Edwards[72] & we sat down to brekker. I like Butler exceedingly. Of

69 'Uncle Pumblechook' was the Lewises' nickname for G. Herbert Ewart (1857–1924), the brother of Sir William Quartus Ewart, and the managing director of the family business of William Ewart and Son, Belfast.

70 Theobald Richard Fitzwalter Butler (1894–1976) who was to achieve great distinction as a lawyer, was called to the Bar, Inner Temple, in 1921, became Master of the Bench in 1960, and Chancellor of the Diocese of Peterborough in 1962.

71 He is referring to Joseph Mary Plunkett (1887–1916), known as one of 'The 1916 Poets'.

72 John Robert Edwards (1897–1992) grew up in Manchester and attended Manchester Grammar School. He graduated from Univ. in 1920 with a Second in Greats. He began work in business, but he could not be parted from the Greek and Latin classics, and he had a remarkable career as a teacher. He taught classics at Chigwell School and Merchant Taylor's School, Crosby, until 1931. He was then appointed headmaster of Grove Park Grammar School, Wrexham, where he remained until 1935. He went from there to the Liverpool Institute High School as headmaster where he remained until his

course he talked a good deal to me about Ireland: it seems that he knows Yeats quite well, & also Gilbert Murray. Otherwise the talk turned on books. Can I confess that I had certain spiteful pleasure in seeing Edgell, who has been lecturing me on morals & motor bykes for the last fortnight, very much out of his element in such a conversation?

After brekker we all decided that a bathe would be a very sound plan. Some kind friend lent me a bycyle and thus we set out. It was a perfectly lovely morning with a deep blue sky, all the towers & pinnacles gleaming in the sun & bells ringing everywhere. We past down through quieter streets among colleges and gardens to the river, & after about quarter of an hour's ride along the bank came to the bathing places. Here, without the tiresome convention of bathing things we enjoyed a swim. The bathing place is a lovely backwater surrounded by those *level* (you know the sort) daisied & buttercuped fields & overhung by those short fluffy trees – named – I don't know.[73]

So about 11.30 we arrived back at college and I am come straight thence to the Union. 'The Union' is a club to which nearly everyone in the varsity belongs. It has a writing room of strictest silence, where I am scribbling this, and an admirable library where I have already passed many happy hours and hope to pass many more. Oh, Galahad, you simply must come up after the war. This at present is only a shadow of the real Oxford, yet even so I never was happier in my life. Do make an effort!

By the way my books have finished binding and are absolutely ripping. In a fit of extravagance I am getting two more done. One is an Apuleius: he as you know wrote the book in which the 'Cupid & Psyche' story occurs. I have found his complete works in the college library and their brooding magic no less than their occasional voluptuousness &

---

retirement in 1961. Writing to me on 6 January 1978, he recalls that Lewis in 1917 'could join in any discussion on any subject and talk fluently and knowledgeably; he was particularly interested in those early days in religion and was particularly challenging in his scepticism'. See *University College Record*, Vol. X, No. 4 (1992), pp. 93–4.

73 'Parson's Pleasure' lay north of Magdalen College, where two branches of the Cherwell come together to form the area known as 'Mesopotamia', after the ancient country between the Tigris and the Euphrates. It was known as 'Parson's Pleasure' in the 17th century and it seems always to have been used by men for bathing and sunbathing in the nude. It was customary for ladies to disembark from their punts before reaching 'Parson's Pleasure' and walk around to a series of metal rollers where they could pick them up again. In recent years it has been turned into a park.

ridiculous passages have made me feel that I must get a copy of my own. What lots I shall have to show you when I come down!

But voila que je suis égoiste![74] I have done nothing but jaw about myself. However reply by jawing about yourself & tell me all you are reading & thinking & how things go forward at home.

Jack

TO HIS FATHER (LP V: 212–13):

[University College]
Postmark: 17 May 1917

My dear Papy,

I think your note to Campbell will fit the occasion very well. His job at Hertford is that of Bursar – but I fancy he is undertaking this only for the time of the war. He is a fellow (all people like Bursars and Deans are Fellows as well it would appear), and a mathematical tutor. I am often alone in his room at Hertford, but I have not seen anything but technical books so far, except one vol. of our own edition of De Quincy. However, I must take further reconnaissances. He is really an awfully nice chap, though very Scotch.

Our 'military duties' are as light as they well could be. We have a morning parade from 7 till 7.45, and another from 2 till 4, with occasional evening lectures on map reading and such like subjects. I am afraid I must tell you that the chances of getting into the gunners are pretty pale, as 'Only those cadets who can be shown to have some special knowledge of mathematics' will be recommended for them.

The early morning parade of course makes it impossible for us to go to chapel, except to the Celebration on Sundays. I am afraid that I usually find the place in possession only of us freshers and the dons. As to St Mary's,[75] I have not been yet. The last two Sundays were so fine that having been to the early service, I felt justified in going off to bathe after 'brekker'. I have however found out enough about it to realize that it is rather different from what we imagine. There are only a few prayers, and a very long sermon, usually more of a philosophical and political than of

74 'But there it is: what an egoist I am!'

75 The Church of St Mary the Virgin. This medieval church, which was largely rebuilt in the 15th and early 16th centuries, dominates the High Street and is directly across the street from Univ. It has for centuries been closely associated with the University, and is referred to as the 'University Church'.

a religious nature: in fact it is more a Sunday lecture room than a church in the true sense. The best place to go for a fine service is the Cathedral at 'The House' as Christ Church is called: it is typical of the House that it should have the Cathedral of the diocese for its chapel!

Getting the right to use the Bodleian is a long job; I have been recommended for a 'reader' by my tutor, but must wait a week or so until I am elected. In the mean time the College Library and the 'Union' library supply me with more books than I am ever likely to read. The Union is particularly interesting to me because it bears on its walls the remains of the frescoes which Morris, Burne-Jones, Watts and Rosetti painted – only to fade immediately through some impurity in the plaster.

How I hope that you'll be able to come up and see me here some day when this troublesome war is over! I see Wells has written a new book – apparently working out some of the theories hinted at in 'Mr. Britling'.[76] We have had a round of dissipation this week, going to 'brekker' with nearly all the senior men. It appears that they ask you, but that freshers aren't supposed to ask anyone to anything their first term. There is an Irishman here called Butler who was in Serbia with Dod[d]s and worked his passage home with him: he is a violent Home Ruler.

your loving
son Jack.

TO ARTHUR GREEVES (W):

[University College
20 May 1917]

Cher Ami,

I wonder if we could not arrange our letters so that they don't always cross. I mean, as things at present are, you will not have got this until you have written your own replying to my last. This spoils the 'conversational' effect of letter writing. However, I am afraid Sunday is now my only possible time, and if it is yours too I am afraid there is no help for us.

I am glad to hear that you like Milton: I was sure he would appeal to you. The language is, I admit, not always easily understood: tho' using English words, he often builds his sentences on a Latin framework which

76 H.G. Wells, *The Soul of a Bishop: A Novel – with just a little love in it – and Conscience and Religion and the real Troubles of Life* (1917); *Mr Britling Sees it Through* (1916).

makes it almost meaningless to a purely English reader. Some words, too, he uses in very strange ways. For instance, when, at the opening of the 3rd Book you come to the line

> *'Or hear'st thou rather pure ethereal stream'*[77]

remember that 'hear' means in this place 'hight', i.e. 'to be called'. What he wants to say is 'Shall I call thee rather "Pure, ethereal stream." ' Don't you love all the descriptions of Hell? (Item. When reading about the Shetlands in 'The Pirate'[78] I was disconsolate because I thought I should never see them. In reading about the scenery of Hell, I need have no such uneasiness!) You will also love the parts about Eden when you come to them.

The chief event in things of art this week has been my discovery of Albert Dürer. I don't know if you have heard of him before: he was a German engraver of the 16th century, and I have often heard him referred to as the 'most Romantic of engravers', the 'Founder of the Fantastic school in Art' etc. Yesterday I came across some postcard reproductions of his pictures, and bought some. I daresay they will dissapoint you, but I like them greatly: especially one 'Study of an old Man's Head'. Although not a modern, you can easily see that he is the father of Rackham and all this modern school of fantastic illustrators. But all this must wait for full discussion when I come down, & we can go over them side by side.

Life goes on very pleasantly here. Besides Butler (whom I mentioned in my last letter) the other most interesting person here is a man named Edwards. He is not a very attractive person, and has a rather unpleasant accent (tho' not so bad as some of my friends have!): what interests me about him is that he was an atheist till lately, and is now engaged in becoming a Catholic, or is very near it. He came into my rooms last night, and sat till about 12. We had a long talk about religion, Buddhism, poetry and everything else. How I like talking!

As to the other man, Butler, I like him better the more I know him (Item. He often comes to Portsalon so we may see him sometime). He is, however, not an immaculate character. I had often heard that he was

77 Milton, *Paradise Lost*, III, 7.
78 Sir Walter Scott, *The Pirate* (1821).

very amusing when drunk, but I had no experience until last night. At about 10, he burst into my room exclaiming 'God bless you, God bless you.' He sank down on my sofa but soon rolled onto the floor, repeating in tragic accents 'I would that I were dead, and lying in the woods with the corpses of the great ones of Erin about me. (This is all out of some nationalist poet) None is unhappier than I, save only the great yellow bittern.' He continued lying on the floor reciting, expressing an ardent desire to go and kiss the Dean, and calling on the 'Holy Mother of God', until Edwards and a rather pointless man called MacNicholl[79] came in to see the fun. We began to try to get him to bed, but he begged in pathetic tones to be left there on the floor for just ten minutes and swore 'by the Holy Ghost and by Venus Aphrodite' that he would go then. By about 11 we did actually succeed in getting him out. His mood had changed now and instead of wanting to lie 'dead in the wood' he wanted 'To be in the pine forest in the white arms of Aphrodite'. You see how a man of taste & reading preserves his natural character even when dead drunk. He used the most beautiful language. I went for a bathe with him this morning and he seemed almost quite recovered. He is going to lend me a copy of the nationalist poet from whom he was quoting from.

I have finished the 2nd vol. of Wm. Morris, all except the last story of 'Ogier the Dane'.[80] I don't think I shall order the next until I come down, as I have so little time for reading here. By the way – don't ever imagine, as I used to, that access to good libraries is an inducement to reading. Among thousands of interesting books it is impossible to settle down to one. Yes, I did and do think of Papillon on the river – especially when we pass pretty people.

Yours
Jack

79 John Milne MacNicholl (1898–), son of Douglas McNicholl of Abergele, Denbighshire, matriculated in 1917, but in 1918 enlisted as a 2nd lieutenant in the Royal Horse Artillery and served in Palestine. He did not return to Oxford to finish his degree.

80 'Ogier the Dane' is one of the stories in *The Earthly Paradise*.

TO ARTHUR GREEVES (W):

[University College
27 May 1917]

Cher Ami,

First, lest we forget, I must answer your question. I do not know yet when I shall get down nor for how long: it is certain that we shall not be down for the whole vac., but even so, I think we shall be at home longer than a school holiday. I hope to be able to tell you exactly in my next letter.

You say that your books have come at last from Denny, and then add that you may give up buying books altogether. Am I to gather that this last parcel (consisting of what?) is very dissapointing? Personally I am being rather extravagant. This week's purchases include the poems of Thomson and Renan's 'Vie de Jésus'.[81] The Thomson here mentioned is not the modern but an 18th century man, whose best thing is a poem in Spencerian stanzas called 'The Castle of Indolence'.[82] Tis as good as the title suggests. The other (Nelson's 1/- edition), Renan's 'Vie de Jesus' you will probably have heard of: it is a life of 'Jeshua' written from a free thinker's point of view, and is very beautiful in style. I think you would not care for it, but I like it immensely. I have also ordered a copy of the first volume of Tennyson in a new edition by Macmillan. It is excellent in paper and title page & so on, but the binding is a kind of semi-limp leather that I don't much care for. However, as it is the only tolerable edition of Tennyson that I can hear tell of, I thought it fit to be bought. Dunsany's book was reviewed in the Times Literary Supplement some time ago, where they spoke of him as an experimenter in prose style.[83] I should like to see his 'Tales of Wonder', but I do not think it would be worth 5/-. Another good book I am reading at present (from the Union Library) is Andrew Lang's and R. Haggard's 'The World's Desire'[84] of which you have heard Chainie[85] speak very, very, very often. Item, tell Chainie that I am coaching with a friend of hers, Mr Campbell of Hertford.

---

81 Joseph Ernest Renan, *La Vie de Jésus* (1863).

82 James Thomson, *The Castle of Indolence* (1748).

83 The review of Edward Dunsany's *Tales of Wonder* (1917) is found in *The Times Literary Supplement* (12 April 1917), p. 172.

84 H. Rider Haggard and Andrew Lang, *The World's Desire* (1891).

85 i.e. Janie McNeill.

The other morning I was surprised by Gundrede,[86] (up for the day) Mrs and Cherry Robbins.[87] G. of course has gone but of the other two I have seen a good deal. Cherry is not pretty unfortunately but she is what I call a really ripping kind of person – an awfully good sort, and (greatest recommendation to us) a lover of books.

No – all days are not so pleasant as the Sundays. On week days I am called by my scout at 7.0. I tramp down to the parks for early parade, from which I return to bath and brekker at about 8.45. I then work till 1, have lunch, and set off for another parade from 2 till 4. At 4 I come back, have tea (either in college or at the Union) and go down to the river for a bathe. I get back to college at about 5.30, and then read English until dinner at 7. In the evenings I work mildly or talk or sometimes play cards or even go for a byke ride, getting to bed at about 11. It is on the whole a very pleasant life.

To-day (Sunday) Butler had brekker with me and afterwards we bathed. We had a long talk on the rival merits of Swinburne & Keats, the improbability of God, and Home Rule. Like all Irish people who meet in England we ended by criticisms on the invincible flippancy and dulness of the Anglo-Saxon race. After all, there is no doubt, ami, that the Irish are the only people: with all their faults I would not gladly live or die among another folk.

Edgell – the other fresher of whom I have spoken – gets more and more wearisome every day: he is the most priggish, illiterate and narrow-minded ass I ever met. His chief subject of conversation is his relatives, especially his brother and cousin who have been killed at the front. Well of course I respect them for it, and I sympathise with him for loosing them. At the same time, I don't think they need be dragged into every single conversation, on every opportunity!

The country about here with its two rivers and its tall poplars, though not exciting is now beautifully fresh and green and sleepy. How I look forward to the hills of Down, the little copses and the view over the

86 Lewis's cousin, Gundreda Ewart, who was with the Voluntary Aid Detachment, was home on leave from France where she had been nursing at various camps.

87 Mrs Kittie Robbins (wife of Colonel Herbert E. Robbins) was the sister of Mary, Lady Ewart – and so first cousin to Lewis's mother. Her daughter 'Cherry' was with the Voluntary Aid Detachment at a military hospital in Oxford during the war.

lough! I am sorry my letters from here cannot be so long as they were from Bookham, but I really have not time. Addio,

yours,

Jack

TO HIS FATHER (LP V: 215–6):

[University College]
Postmark: 28 May 1917

My dear Papy,

Coals, did you say? At present all my windows are open, my blinds are pulled down on the sunny side; the quad., with its roasting stonework is simply baking under a 'heaven as brass above me'.[88] These sort of days are topping on the river, but not so nice for bayonet practice, and route marches and such like entertainments. I will find out from the Adjutant exactly when we O.T.C. people come down and for how long: rumours vary a good deal, but I think our vac. will be shorter by several weeks than the ordinary one, but as long or longer than a school summer holidays. However, I expect that I shall be able to give you more definite information in my next letter.

This week I have had adventures. On Tuesday in the middle of the morning I had happened to come down and walk across the quad. to see if there were any letters in the porch, when I was hailed as 'Jack' by a group of ladies on the far side. At first I couldn't see who they were, but they turned out to be Gundreda (up for the day), Aunt Kittie and Cherry Robbins. They had come in to look at College quite by accident, not knowing that I was there. Since then I have seen a good deal of them. What a dear old lady Aunt Kittie is! And how typical of her set: we happened to talk about Cromwell the other day, and when Cherry and I ventured on some criticisms, the true greatness of old Noll was explained to us by a reminder that 'Cromwell's mother was some connection of ours'! Here we have the spirit of history; wouldn't it appeal to the Knock?

Dod's friend Butler is a poetical and sentimental complete separationist, interested in the pronunciation of Gaelic: by the way, Dods is

88 Lewis possibly had in mind John Webster's *The Duchess of Malfi* (1623), IV, ii, 25: 'Th'heaven ore my head, seems made of molton brasse.' This, in turn, may be related to the curse in Deuteronomy 28:23: 'And thy heaven that is over thy head shall be brass, and the earth that is under thee shall be iron.'

coming up to take his degree at the end of this term, so I shall have an opportunity of meeting him.

I should be glad if you would send the little book on philosophy so soon as you can, as I want to make a start on this subject and the College Library has nothing quite elementary enough for a beginner. At present I am reading Renan's 'Vie de Jésus', which I think an admirable book, and a great lesson in good manners to other free thinkers.

I have had to pay cash (£2.10) to the Quartermaster for my uniform, and 15/6 for a pair of service boots. I don't want to bother you unneccessarily, but this has been rather a drain on resources, and I should be glad if you could refund it.

your loving
son Jack.

TO ARTHUR GREEVES (W):

[University College
3 June 1917]

Cher Ami,

I am delighted to hear that you have at last arriven at 'The Victorians'.[89] The criticism that most of these novels begin with a very interesting part about the childhood and then get more conventional as they go on is only too true – at least for us who are attracted by 'childish things'.[90] In this case I think it is certainly true that the school scenes are the best (very good in every way). But there is no very violent slump in the interest and I for one followed the rest of it very eagerly. She is a most excellent character.

Last Sunday I began reading Blackwood's 'Prisoner in Fairyland'[91] in the Union Library, & liked it immensely. But I think I shall wait until they publish it in the 7d edition & then get it for myself. My other book 'The Castle of Indolence' goes on excellently: it is quite a good imitation of Spencer, and has a certain shy humour mixed with it, which Spencer himself has not. I am also, in Italian, reading Ariosto's 'Orlando Furioso',[92] from which there are many stories in your Andrew Lang romance book. It is in the same edition as my Tasso which you have

89 Netta Syrett, *The Victorians* (1915).
90 1 Corinthians 13:11.
91 Algernon Henry Blackwood, *Prisoner in Fairyland* (1913).
92 Ludovico Ariosto, *Orlando Furioso* (1532).

probably forgotten: I am just reading a canto here & a canto there, and it is very good, really suggesting 'Phantastes' more than the Faery Queen.

How beautiful Donegal must be now! I often think how lovely twould be if you could take up this city of Oxford bodily and put it down somewhere

'By a northern sea'[93]

between the mountains of Donegal. I am afraid the river would have to go, though!

I hope you are right as to the possibilities of my finding my particular kind of love. <Butler tells me that the person to read on my subject is a Frenchman of the 17th century called the Visconte de sade>:[94] his books, however, are very hard to come by.

I cannot understand Denny's behaviour to you, as they never gave me any trouble at all. How you would love the shops here! At home you have to hammer what you want into their thick heads: here they know all about publishing and literature (Sanskrit or Russian if you want!) & your only effort is to conceal your ignorance.

I do wish you were here: what long and private talks we could have. Somehow the place seems to lend itself to endless conversation. Butler came in and sate till twenty to two last night. The piano too would be a perpetual joy, for Cherry was playing it when she was in here to tea the other day, and says it is quite good. I suppose Cherry has only met you for a few moments, as I have never heard you speak of her. She is a real sportsman, the sort of person I really like. Quel domage que sa figure n'égale pas son ésprit![95] Yet after all she is plain in rather a pleasing kind of way when you get to know her. Mrs Robbins I also like immensely.

In prose at present I am reading one of those 'Home University Library' books on 'Psychic Research'.[96] It is a subject in which my old interest is awakening: so far the phenomena are certainly extraordinary,

---

93 Lewis probably had in mind Andrew Lang's lines: 'St Andrews by the Northern Sea, / A haunted town it is to me', *Almae Matres* (1884).

94 Comte Donatien Alphonse François de Sade (1740–1814), known as the Marquis de Sade, was a French novelist. His obsession with a particular sexual perversion caused his name to be given to the word 'sadism', meaning a love of cruelty.

95 'It's too bad that her figure isn't in the same class as her wit.'

96 William Fletcher Barrett, *Psychical Research* [1911].

tho' I fear they do not actually prove the agency of real spirits – yet. They tell me that Dodds, who is coming up next week is very interested in the subject also, so I shall be able to have a talk about it.

I quite agree with you that cards are the most utter and senseless and losing waste of time ever invented, and I never play them from inclination but only because you can't go on refusing the same people if you have nothing to do. We have had a college group [photo] of our 9 surviving undergrads. so I will be able to point out to you all these characters.

Item, somebody pointed me out Bridges[97] in the street the other day. How I should like to meet him! Really cannot spare a second longer, now old man. Write soon & LONG, returning good for evil –

Yours
Jack

TO HIS FATHER (LP XI: 261):

[University College
3? June 1917]

My dear Papy,

Thank you for the enclosures and also for the enquiries (a nice, rythmical sentence by the way). I am glad to find that my money 'pans out' quite sufficiently, and is indeed just about the average. I mean the amount of pocket money is about the same as that of other people, though of course many have an allowance out of which they pay all their own bills – in which case the actual pocket money will vary with the ups and downs of their Battels. To give you some idea of the latter, I enclose mine as supplied so far. (These do not include groceries as explained before). I am pleased to see that they decrease from the beginning of term onwards. The first week was necessarily expensive, chiefly through ignorance, 'in which accomplishment' as De Quincey says, 'I excel'.

My scout is a very fatherly old man who has been here for forty-six years, and is really exceedingly good about keeping my expenses down: he once even told me to change my socks when they were wet!!! His only failing is an impentrible (or -able) deafness which causes many conversations of the 'It's a fine day' – 'No, not much to pay' type.

I am afraid you must not build anything on the idea of my rowing, as I have almost given it up in favour of canoeing. You see a row boat can

97 i.e. Robert Bridges, the Poet Laureate.

be used only on the big river, where you run into all the real rowing men, as the Cherwell (much prettier and more interesting) soon gets too narrow for rowers to pass each other. Besides, there is to me something very attractive about one of these little canoes – so very light and so all-to-yourself. Perhaps when we all come back again from the war, and there is no O.T.C., I will take up rowing again.

The O.T.C. gets more interesting as we go on. We spend a good deal of our time in 'the trenches' – a complete model system with dug outs, shell holes and – graves. This last touch of realistic scenery seems rather superfluous. But then our C.O., a certain Colonel Stanning, is quite cracked.

I have nearly finished Renan, whom I find delightful. He seems to have written a good many other books on different subjects. I am going to borrow Wells' new book from a man in College called Edwards, who is thinking of becoming a Catholic. He is an ardent Newmanite, and we have some talk on literary subjects. Someone pointed me out our present poet-laureate, Bridges (1), on the river last Wednesday.

your loving son,
Jacks

(1) Its just occurred to me that you might have known the name anyway. Apologies! – J.

On Thursday 7 June, Lewis joined a cadet battalion and was sent across Oxford to be billeted in Keble College for a four-month course in soldiery. It has already been pointed out that as an Irishman Lewis was exempt from the Conscription Act. Normally a member of the OTC is not part of the regular army, and membership in it may be resigned at will. However, during the war members of the OTC were 'embodied', that is, became part of the army. As a result they were liable to be treated as the needs of the army required. Keble College had been used since January 1915 for the training of officers, and Lewis was one of many from Oxford and other places who arrived there on 7 June. He found himself sharing a room with Edward Francis Courtenay ('Paddy') Moore,[98] who came into the Oxford OTC from Bristol where he had been a pupil at Clifton College.

98 See **Edward Francis Courtenay 'Paddy' Moore** in the Biographical Appendix.

Paddy, who was the same age as Lewis, was born near Dublin of Anglo-Irish parents, Courtenay Edward Moore and Janie King Moore.[99] *When they separated in 1907, Mrs Moore took Paddy and his sister Maureen*[100] *to live in Bristol where she had a brother. When it was known that he would go into the army through the Oxford OTC, Mrs Moore and Maureen came with him and took rooms in Wellington Square.*

TO HIS FATHER (LP V: 218):

[Keble College,
Oxford]
Postmark: 8 June 1917

My dear Papy,

Just a line in a hurry, to let you know how things go. I have not been able to write to you before. Well of course this is not an agreeable change, but it was the natural next step in any pilgrimage towards a commission. The cadet batallion, which I joined yesterday (of course it has nothing to do with the varsity) is quartered in Keble. There are several gentlemen among it, and I am fortunate in sharing a room with one. It is a great comfort to be in Oxford, as I shall still be able to see something of my Univ. friends and Cherry.

As to Responsions, I may or may not be able to persuade them to give me three days' leave to do it in: if they do, I should not think that under the circumstances my chances of passing would be very bright. At any rate, six months service with the colours will exempt me from it.

As to the artillery, I am afraid that only those who have 'some special knowledge of mathematics' will be recommended. About leave we don't know anything yet. I am sorry I can't write any more to cheer you up, but we must both of us thole for a while. My tips etc. on leaving College have cleared me out, so could you let me have something to go on with? Write to the old address at Univ. as I can call for letters there at any time.

your loving
son Jack

---

99 See **Janie King Moore** in the Biographical Appendix.
100 See **Dame Maureen Dunbar of Hempriggs** in the Biographical Appendix.

TO HIS FATHER (LP V: 218–9):

[Keble College
10? June 1917]

My dear Papy,

I am sorry that your last letter had to wait some time for an answer: I am afraid that, whenever I hear from you, I can only reply on a Saturday or a Sunday.

And now for some account of the new life. Well at first when I left my own snug quarters and my own friends at Univ. for a carpetless little cell with two beds (minus sheets or pillows) at Keble, and got into a Tommy's uniform, I will not deny that I thought myself very ill used. However, as What's-his-name said, 'I have had many misfortunes in life, but most of them never happened to me'.

I have quite recovered, and am now leading a very happy life, tho' not of course the life I would have chosen. In many ways it is a better life: I have never worked until now, and it is high time that I began. As to my companions, they are really divided into three lots. The first and largest lot consists of rankers who have been out for some time and have come here to get commissions. These are mostly jolly good chaps: clean, honest, infinitely good natured. As they have come here to be made into 'officers and gentlemen' their own naive conceptions of how gentlemen behave among themselves lead them into an impossible politeness that is really very pathetic. Most of our set get on very well with them. The next lot (about one third of the whole) consists of cads and fools pure and simple. They don't need much description: some of them are vicious, some merely doltish, all vulgar and uninteresting. They drop their h's, spit on the stairs, and talk about what they're going to do when they get to the front – where of course none of them has been. Then comes the third lot, our own set, the public school men and varsity men with all their faults and merits 'already ascertained'.

My chief friend is Somerville, scholar of Eton and scholar of King's, Cambridge, a very quiet sort of person, but very booky and interesting. Moore of Clifton, my room companion, and Sutton of Repton (the company humourist) are also good fellows. The former is a little too childish for real companionship, but I will forgive him much for his appreciation of Newbolt. I must not pass over the knut, De Pass, also of Repton, our regnant authority on all matter of dress, who is reported to wear stays: nor Davy, the Carthusian, who remembers my Sinn Fein friend as a prefect at Charterhouse.[101]

The daily round is of course pretty strenuous, and leaves little time for dreaming or reading. However, I eat and sleep as I have never done before, and am getting rid of some adipose tissue. I will give you full information about leave as soon as I have any. Captain Moberly himself an old Oxonian, is a delightful man, and I am sure he will do anything he can for me about an extension of time for travelling. It would be 'a bit too previous' to ask him at present.

I think I mentioned that Dodds had come up for his schools. Both he and Butler got Firsts, Dodds in Literae Humaniores, Butler in Law. Although of course they should both be serving, still a college with only nine undergraduates cannot help being proud of two Firsts. The conquering heroes gave a dinner on Saturday last, to which I attended and helped to celebrate the event. Both are now gone down, but Butler has promised to write to me.

There is no need to do anything at present about my clothes etc. They are carefully put away in my rooms at Univ., and can stay there till my course is ended, when I can bring the whole lot home together. By the way, my new adress is No. 738 Cadet C. S. Lewis, 'E' Company, Keble College, Oxford. Be of good cheer, your loving son,

Jack

TO ARTHUR GREEVES (W):

[Keble College
10 June 1917]

My dear Arthur,

I must admit that you have a very reasonable ground of complaint against me. But you must remember that my whole way of life has now completely changed, and that I have practically no time for reading or writing except at week-ends. However I will try to do better in future, tho' I hope that you, who have more time to yourself, will give me longer

101 Martin Ashworth Somerville (1898–1918) became a member of King's College, Cambridge, in April 1917. During the war he served as a member of the Rifle Brigade in Egypt and Palestine, and died 21 September 1918 of wounds received in action. The others, all born in 1898, were: 'Paddy' Moore of Clifton College, Alexander Gordon Sutton and Denis Howard de Pass of Repton School, and Thomas Kerrison Davey of Charterhouse School. The 'Sinn Fein' friend was Theobald Butler.

letters than you get: just as, when I get to the trenches, tho' I may not be able to write to you at all, I shall hope to hear from you at regular intervals. This may seem a one-sided bargain: yet surely it is fair, that when one of us has escaped and the other has got into this military nonsense, the freeman should make some allowances for the slave.

I will only tell you very shortly of the new life as there is not much of interest. It is a great change to leave my own snug room at Univ. for a carpetless room, with beds without sheets or pillows, kept miserably tidy & shared with another cadet, at Keble. However, tho' the work is very hard & not very interesting, I am by now quite reconciled to my lot. It is doing me a lot of good (days of trench digging and route marching under a blazing sun are a fine cure for tendencies in THAT direction) and I have made a number of excellent friends – especially Somerville, a scholar of Eton & King's (Cambridge) who is very well up in books. My room-mate Moore (of Clifton) is quite a good fellow too, tho' a little too childish and virtuous for 'common nature's daily food'. The advantages of being in Oxford are very great, as I can get week end leave (from 1 o'clock Saturday till 11 o'clock p.m. Sunday) and go to Univ. where I enjoy the rare luxury of sheets & a long sleep.

Last week end was a great success. Butler and Dodds (Dodds a Campbellian and Univ. man whom you must have heard of) both got 'Firsts' in their Schools and gave a dinner to celebrate the event, at which, for the first time in my life, I was royally drunk. <I am afraid I must have given myself away rather as I went round imploring everyone to let me whip them for the sum of 1*s*. a lash!> All this happened at Exeter in the rooms of an Indian called Gokeldas: but as I was not the only person in that condition, the Dean of Exeter got fed up with the row and sent round a notice that Mr Gokeldas' guests must leave the College at once. I have absolutely no recollection of the walk home, and in fact, tho' I remember leaving Exeter, knew nothing more till I woke up on the floor of my own room at about 9 next morning.[102]

The story that you have a headache after being drunk is apparently quite a lie <(like the other one about going mad from THAT).> But the

102 He seems not to have exaggerated the degree of his intoxication: the Indian he calls 'Gokeldas' was Madhavji Dharamsi Moraji Gokuldas (1896–1931), a member of Brasenose College, and it was probably in Brasenose, rather than in Exeter, that the party occurred. The Dean of Brasenose was W.T.S. Stallybrass (1883–1948), who became Principal of the college in 1936.

interesting part is that Butler, having muddled recollections of my last night's <desire to whip,> challenged me on the subject, and we had a long conversation. <He's not himself that way inclined. He has come across the thing in the course of his varied reading. The right name for it is sadism, so called from its great originator of the 16th century, M. Le Vicomte de Sade whose history we looked up in a French 'Dictionaire de la Bibliographie Nationale'.>

Butler (and nearly every one else) has now gone down, so that this week end I have lived very quietly, but no less happily in an empty College, sleeping late, and reading my new volume of Maeterlinck's plays.[103] Two of them I have read before in English ('Pelleas & Melisande', 'L'Interieur') but all could be read with pleasure a score of times. They all have a peculiar mystic dreamlike atmosphere about them, and tho' much more possible are somehow much more wierd than 'L'Oiseau Bleu', especially the 'most musical, most melancholy' 'Alladine et Palomides', where Palomides may be the Malory Palomides or may not.

I have also been spending more time than usual in the College Library, dipping here and there. Did I tell you that there was a queer little volume in Latin by Cornelius Agrippa the great magician (mentioned in Cosmo's episode)? Unfortunately the print is so execrable and the worms have done their work so well that I cannot make much of it: but I love to have it in my hands, and think of all the wizards who have centred their hopes on it – perhaps on this very copy, for it is some 300 years old.[104]

I have also read a good deal of Spencer in a big folio and of my favourite Johnson. On taking up my Homer this morning it was shocking to find how strangely the Greek came to me after three weeks soldiering. I do hope I shall not forget all I know, and come back from the war a great empty-headed military prig!

Yesterday afternoon I spent on the river with Cherry Robbins, in whom I am pleased to find an ardent admirer both of Arthur Rackham & of Wagner. She has heard 'Die Walküre' at Covent Garden & has read the Ring in my edition. She says that the stage is a terrible come down to those who have seen Rackham's pictures first and that she listened with

103 Maurice Maeterlinck, *Alladine et Palomides, Intérieur, et La Mort de Tintagiles, Drames Pour Marionnettes* (1894).

104 He is writing about either Vol. I or Vol. II of the *Opera* (Lugduni: Per Beringos Fratres [1531]) of Henricus Cornelius Agrippa (1486–1535) of Nettesheim. The book which he handled is now in the Museum of the History of Science.

her eyes shut most of the time. The 'Wotan' however was splendid, and really terrifying. She is also very keen on Norse mythology, and for this reason praised the Ring above 'Parsifal' or 'Lohengrin'. Although the subject did not arise, I rather think from some phrazes she let fall about Norse & Christian mythology, that I shall find another agnostic here. How sad that so interesting a girl is not beautiful (tho' she is certainly not nearly so plain as I at first imagined) Even sadder that she should like Browning and have a morbid appetite for photography!!

I am in a strangely productive mood at present and spend my few moments of spare time in scribbling verse. When my 4 months course in the cadet battalion is at an end, I shall, supposing I get a commission allright, have a 4 weeks leave before joining my regiment. During it I propose to get together all the stuff I have perpetrated and see if any kind publisher would like to take it. After that, if the fates decide to kill me at the front, I shall enjoy a 9 days immortality while friends who know nothing about poetry imagine that I must have been a genius – what usually happens in such cases. In the meantime my address is

No 738 Cadet C. S. Lewis
'E' Company,
Keble College
Oxford.

Write me a nice long letter and help to keep up other interests amid all this damned military show.

Yours as ever
Jack

TO HIS FATHER (LP V: 224–5):

[Keble College]
Postmark: 18 June 1917

My dear Papy,

First of all, many thanks for the liberal enclosure, which has made life much more 'sunny' again: though indeed I have no right to grumble about my present position. The change was bound to come, and could not be expected to be an agreeable one. But this being so, it could not have been better than it is. Being in Oxford is a great comfort, and there is an unusually high percentage of Public School men in this Battalion.

Moore, my room mate, comes from Clifton and is a very decent sort of man; his mother, an Irish lady, is staying up here and I have met her once or twice. As to my friends in Univ., they are accounted for in various ways. The only other two who were in the O.T.C. with me are both under eighteen and a half. Edwards, the embryo Roman Catholic, is physically unfit. Butler, the Home Ruler, is not serving for political reasons.

The weather here is terribly hot, and we are all getting into wonderful training under it: however, I can well afford that sort of thing, as you know. It seems that we get a four days leave after the first month of our course. Unless they will allow me extra time for travelling, I don't exactly know what to do with my four days. If you could come up for a week we could both stay at Univ. (one is allowed to have a guest staying in College), and have a very nice little time. Think about it and see if you couldn't manage – seriously.

I don't know of any special Cadet Batallion (or is it Battalion?) for the artillery. Don't you think it would be better to give up that idea? A person who gets ploughed in Smalls in not likely to master Trigonometry etc: as well, every one else puts up with the Infantry, and I think we ought to do so too.[105]

I hope this kind of weather suits a man who lives in 'a rotten house'. And that the same man is carrying on well and cheerfully. Please explain to Warnie that I have hardly time to write, and ask him to let me have a line or two when he can.

your loving
son Jack

---

105 Albert Lewis was becoming frantic with worry about Jack, and was seeking a way to have his son transferred from the infantry into the artillery, particularly to the gunners, where he believed he would be safer. The infantry was composed of foot-soldiers, who were closest to the enemy and the first to lose their lives. Artillery was the great killer of the First World War; it is thought that artillery fire caused up to 70 per cent of battlefield deaths. But whereas the infantry were in close contact with the enemy, the artillery were firing from some distance behind them, and their position was perhaps somewhat safer.

TO ARTHUR GREEVES (W):

[University College
8 July 1917]

Cher Ami,

The best, in fact the only really important tale in Gautier's little book was the last one 'Avatar',[106] which I would have had you read first & read the other two or not, as might seem worthwhile afterwards. It was this third one that I compared, not to Phantastes as a whole, but to the Cosmo story – which, you know, has rather a different flavour from the main book. I must admit that the resemblance is rather a vague one: still, I am sure that you will like 'Avatar' if you give it a trial. In French I am going on with this new volume of Maeterlinck's plays. The last one 'La Morte de Tintagiles' is even better than Palomides, and quite one of the eeriest and most overwhelming things I have struck yet – though I am not quite sure if I understand what the author is driving at. You must certainly get this volume, or borrow mine someday.

'From a College Window'[107] is one of the 5 or 6 Benson books that I have read: but as the titles are so vague, I never can remember which is which. I enjoyed them all very much, they are nice companionable reading for lonely men. Perhaps the 'Upton Letters' was the one that pleased me best.

I was sure that you wd. like 'Balder Dead': I used to prefer it to 'Sohrab'[108] tho' I don't now. All the same it is a topping piece of work, especially the journey, as you say, and the description of the ghosts, and the ending with its impressive pause before the glorious line

'At last he sighed & set forth back to Heaven.'[109]

Doesn't it all make you think of the dear old days when we were writing our great opera on Loki & Odin & the rest? Indeed I am recalled to our earlier stage by other things as well: for all morning I have been reading the German text of 'Siegfried'. The splendid first Act has quite stirred up my old Wagnerian enthusiasms, & for the first time this twelve months or so I have really felt the want for a gramophone. Of course a great deal

---

106 Théophile Gautier, *Avatar, or, The Double Transformation* (1888).

107 Arthur Christopher Benson, *From a College Window* (1906).

108 Matthew Arnold, *Sohrab and Rustum* (1853).

109 Arnold, *Balder Dead*, III, 566.

of my pleasure in it is owing to Rackham's pictures: still it is lovely wild poetry &, like everything else, much better in its own language. The edition is the same as my one of the Dutchman & I can get the other three parts of the Ring in the same: when I have them all I think I shall bind the 4 thin volumes into one nice book & have a really good edition to my library.

This week end, as you gather, I am again spending in Univ. But the Dean says I can't come any more, as the Scouts are going for the holidays!! Damn him! Do you know, Ami, I am more homesick for this College than ever I was for Little Lea. I love every stone in it: I do wish we could be here together after the war!

Last night, at about nine o'clock I wandered out into the deserted quad. & after 'strolling' for some time went up a staircase where nobody ever goes in these days into the oldest part of the College. The windows here are all tiny & ivy covered & stained so that it was very dark already. I walked up & down long passages with locked rooms on each side, revelling in 'desolation'. The 'oaks' of these rooms were mostly (as I say) locked, but by good luck I found one open & went in. On the inner door the faded name 'Mr Carter' greeted me: inside was a tiny room, smaller than my own at home, very dark & thick with dust. It seemed almost sacrilege to turn on the lights in such a forsaken place, but I simply had to inspect it. The furniture was all just as the owner must have left it & his photos were there on the wall. I also inspected his books (mostly ordinary Everymen) including 'Lavengro', 'Tristram Shandy', [Edmund] Burke's Speeches & 'Tom Jones'.[110] I suppose this sounds trivial to you; but perhaps you can picture the strange poetry of the thing in such a time & place. I wonder who Carter is, and if he has been killed yet, & why he left his pile of music so untidily on the dressing table?[111]

I had another thrill too, when I got up (quite dark by now) into a sort

---

110 Henry Fielding, *Tom Jones* (1749).

111 Arthur Norwood Carter (1891–1983), whose rooms Lewis was in, matriculated as a Rhodes Scholar from New Brunswick, Canada, in 1913. On 4 August 1914 he was commissioned a lieutenant in the 8th York and Lancaster Regiment, and he served in France during 1915. He was awarded the Military Cross on 6 March 1918. On returning to Oxford he took a shortened war course in jurisprudence in 1919, and he received his BCL in 1920. He sent two sons – also Rhodes Scholars – to University College.

of attic place full of old trunks etc. & heard a strange thumping noise just beside me. I was mystified for a while, till I realized that I was just behind the big college clock & this was the ticking of it. You know how sad & grand a big clock sounds in a lonely place! These are all rather conventional remarks, but I really did get into a great mood among all the cobwebs. When I came back into the quad & saw all the empty windows staring at me all round, I turned a bit creepy & was glad to get back to my rooms & settle down on the 'Faerie Queene', & another book, which I must tell you about.

This is a book on William Morris in the 'English Men of Letters Series' by Alfred Noyes[112] which I took out of the Library. It is chiefly interesting for its venomous hostility towards Mackail's great 'Life of W.M.' which it loses no opportunity of attacking. This of course is rather petty: but I must admit that the book has some very good points about it, & certainly appreciates 'Jason' far better than Mackail does.

Yes, I must say that the society of some interesting person of the other sex is a great anodyne in a life like this – especially if it is one of the very few people who share our own pet tastes – Wagner, Rackham and the rest. Cherry has been away on leave this last week, and I find this causes quite a gap in my routine. A propos, when is there any prospect of your long expected visit being paid to Oxford. If you were here for a week-end I could come & stay with you somewhere in the town, & I think that the time would pass pleasantly.

It is pouring with rain outside as I write. If I do ever send my stuff to a publisher, I think I shall try Maunsel, those Dublin people, and so tack myself definitely onto the Irish school. What castles in the air – but still better have a cloud castle than no castle at all –

Yours,
Jack

TO HIS FATHER (LP V: 227–8):

[Keble College]
Postmark: 18 July 1917

My dear Papy,

Many thanks for your nice long letters: as before, it has to wait till Sunday for an answer, but I hope you were not expecting one sooner.

112 Alfred Noyes, *William Morris* (1908).

Life here goes on pretty much in the usual way, except that the work gets rather more interesting and involves less actual 'sweat of the brow' than at first. We do a good deal of night work, which I rather like, and which leads to getting up later in the morning. The weather too has grown cooler, and today it is raining.

Dodds' particular foible is also nationalism. I don't know that it is pure cant either in his case or in Butler's: certainly the argument from 'being at an English university' hardly seems very cogent unless you are going to come down on the Englishmen who were at German universities before the war. Does the fact of going to be educated in a country give that country any claim on your services? After all, you *pay* them for the education. Which reminds me that the Bursar has written to say that I am to have my scholarship money for this term and knock off some other term for it after the war. He says that this arrangement has been made with people in my position. I don't know whether we are being 'done' in any subtle way or not, but I suppose there is no objection to the plan so far as you are concerned.

You are allowed week end leave here every week, provided that you do not go out of Oxford. The last four weeks I have spent it over at Univ., enjoying all my old luxuries over again. Now however the Dean – Who as I remarked is a superior person – has vetoed the plan; on the ground that College is kept open in vacation for men who want to read 'and not for use as an hotel'. I suppose he is quite right in a way, but it is rather a pity.

You can't imagine how I have grown to love Univ., especially since I left. Last Saturday evening when I was sleeping there alone, I spent a long time wandering over it, into all sorts of parts where I had never been before, where the mullioned windows are dark with ivy that no one has bothered to cut since the war emptied the rooms they belong to. Some of these rooms were all dust sheeted, others were much as the owners had left them – the pictures still on the wall and the books dust covered in their shelves. It was melancholy in a way, and yet very interesting. I have found one room that I have mapped out to be my own when I come back.

At present I am reading a countryman of ours, Bishop Berkely, 'that silly old man' as Andrew Lang calls him: in fact, one of our few philosophers and a very interesting fellow, whom I always admired for the courage with which you find him standing up to the ogre in Boswell.[113]

Are the other poems in 'The Old Way'[114] man's book as good as the one we know? Talking of modern poetry, some of the rebels who were shot in Easter week seem to have had the root of the matter in them.

Could you let me have some money to get boots for my officer-pattern uniform. I find the cadet school so far much more expensive than the Varsity. When does W. get his leave?

your loving
son Jack

TO HIS FATHER (LP V: 230–1):

University College,
Oxford.
Postmark: 22 July 1917

My dear Papy,

I have to thank you for two letters and for moneys numbered. Pay there was none at first, except for the old soldiers: but the War Office has at last discovered our existence, and on Friday I drew 7/-, the first money I have earned. It ought to be hung on a watch chain.

---

113 Mr Kirkpatrick had encouraged Lewis to read various works of philosophy in preparation for the day when he would begin his studies in *Literae Humaniores*. In the last few months he had become very interested in 'Subjective Idealism' or 'Idealism', the predominant philosophy at Oxford. At this time Lewis was immersing himself in the subjective idealism of Bishop George Berkeley (1685–1753) as propounded in his *Principles of Human Knowledge* (1710). The Bishop held that when we affirm material things to be real, we mean no more than that they are perceived. What annoyed Lewis about 'the ogre in Boswell' – that is, Dr Johnson – was the famous remark recorded in Boswell's *Life of Samuel Johnson*, vol. I, p. 471. On 6 August 1763 Boswell wrote: 'After we came out of the church, we stood talking for some time together of Bishop Berkeley's ingenious sophistry to prove the non-existence of matter, and that every thing in the universe is merely ideal. I observed, that though we are satisfied his doctrine is not true, it is impossible to refute it. I shall never forget the alacrity with which Johnson answered, striking his foot with mighty force against a large stone, till he rebounded from it, "I refute it *thus*."' As Bishop Berkeley never met Dr Johnson, he had no chance of 'standing up' to him. Lewis had confused the Bishop with his son, who was also named George. This George Berkeley (1733–95) met Dr Johnson shortly after he came up to Oxford in 1752, and when Dr Johnson made fun of the Bishop's abortive scheme for a missionary college in Bermuda the young George walked out of the room. He subsequently refused Dr Johnson's repeated requests for permission to write a Life of Bishop Berkeley.

114 Ronald Arthur Hopwood, *The Old Way and Other Poems* (1917).

You say that you should talk to me 'not of the Muse'. Indeed the reverse is quite the truth, for I make every effort to cling to the old life of books, hoping that I may save my soul alive and not become a great, empty headed, conceited military prig. I am finding out that the military ideal in our army differs from the German one only in degree and not in kind. The Sergeant Major told us the other day that 'soldiering is more than 'arf swank. You've got to learn to walk out as if the bloody street belonged to you. See?' We are also encouraged in every way to be pharisees and pat ourselves on the back for being in khaki, and stare rudely at apparently eligible young men whom we meet in mufti. Well I hope that neither I nor any of my friends – and I have done well here in the way of friends – will ever attain to that degree of soldierhood. The promised four days' leave will come in about a fortnight's time: I am sorry that I cannot let you know more definitely. I shall of course come home the quickest way, there being no question of 'lucre' when a paternal government provides you with a pass.

As to your suggestions about the Artillery, I fear I cannot follow you in this matter. Let us have it out. I have put down my name for the artillery first, and after that for the infantry. To which on the advice of my friends, I have added 'King's Own Scottish Borderers' in brackets. Of course this second alternative which I have put in would not make any difference to the first if they were disposed to have me in the gunners. But, as I have mentioned before, they specially insist on a knowledge of advanced mathematics. It is true that you might get me in by influence. But would it not be very wrong for mere reasons of safety, to push me into a responsible position for which I know I am absolutely unfit? If you are fortunate (and how few fathers are today) in having one son in a perfectly safe job, do you think we should try to alter the natural cause of events for the sake of the other? As minor considerations, I may add that I am come to like the idea of the K.O.S.B.'s very much, because two friends of mine will be going at the same time. When you have thought it over, I am sure you will not even want me to change my mind.

On Saturday I drank tea with a dear old gentleman named Goddard, formerly an undergrad. of Balliol and now a don at Trinity.[115] What

115 He must have misunderstood the name. There was no don named 'Goddard' at Trinity College in 1917.

interested me most was his opinion of Jowett[116] (here usually pronounced to rhyme with 'poet') who, he said, had spoiled the scholarly tone of Balliol by a vulgar running after lions. Surely Jowett must have trodden on Mr. Goddard's corns some how, or is there any truth in this verdict?

Of Swinburne's prose, I have read the book on Charlotte Bronte, and the smaller one on William Blake.[117] It is undoubtedly very bad prose (I did not find the coarseness) but it is so vigorous that you can forgive it. Don't forget to keep Wells' 'God the invisible King'[118] in the house, as I am longing to read it.

your loving
son Jack

TO HIS FATHER (LP V: 231):

[Keble College]
Postmark: 24 July 1917

My dear Papy,

I am very sorry to have left you so long without a letter: we have been hopelessly rushed for the last week, the idea being I suppose to get the last ounce out of us before we go on our mouthful of leave. Which reminds me, I think that I forgot to tell you the exact date when I should get home – which was just as well, for the date has now been changed. According to the new arrangement, our leave is from 12 noon on Wednesday the 8th of August till 12 midnight on the following Sunday. As they have refused to allow me any extension for travelling, this will mean arriving home on Thursday morning and leaving on Saturday night. However, 'smallest contributions thankfully recieved' must be our spirit I suppose.

As soon as possible I want you to find out whether Fleetwood or Liverpool is running on Wednesday night, book me a berth, and let me know which it is – by wire. (Be careful to put 'E' Company on it, as there

116 Benjamin Jowett (1817–93) was the Master of Balliol College from 1870 to 1893. He was ordained in 1845 but his theological liberalism, particularly evident in his essay 'The Interpretation of Scripture', was hotly debated. Jowett's classical learning was, however, almost unrivalled during his years in Oxford. He was an Oxford figure and the subject of innumerable stories.

117 Algernon Charles Swinburne, *Note on Charlotte Brontë* (1877); *William Blake* (1868).

118 H.G. Wells, *God the Invisible King* (1917).

is another C. S. Lewis in another company, also at Keble. I keep on getting letters of his, and vice versa.)

Please forgive me for a short letter, as I want to go to bed. We shall have the more to talk about when I come back.

your loving
son Jack

TO ARTHUR GREEVES (W):

University College,
Oxford.
24/7/17

Cher Ami,

How horribly conventional to be writing on ordinary note paper just like other people – why I'll be putting the date at the top soon if I'm not careful. A propos de Maunsel, you say that the patriotic motive could have no influence on me. Well perhaps that may be deserved: tis true that I have no patriotic feeling for anything in England, except Oxford for which I would live and die. But as to Ireland you know that none loves the hills of Down (or of Donegal) better than I: and indeed, partly from interest in Yeats and Celtic mythology, partly from a natural repulsion to noisy drum-beating, bullying Orange-men and partly from association with Butler, I begin to have a very warm feeling for Ireland in general. I mean the real Ireland of Patsy Macan[119] etc, not so much our protestant north. Indeed, if I ever get interested in politics, I shall probably be a nationalist (another subject for us to quarrel on, you see). Of course one sound reason for choosing Maunsel is that they are only a second-rate house and therefore more likely to give me some attention.

I suppose that by now you are nearly at the end of 'Avatar', and see what I meant by comparing it to the Cosmo story. It is an excellent little novel, I think, as voluptuous and magical as only you and I can appreciate. The titles of Benson's essays which you quote bring back memories of pleasant mornings over my tea in bed at home.

Good God, if only I could get back to it all! And yet I am not nearly so unhappy as I ought to be. This week I have been reading the works of Bishop Berkely, an eighteenth century country man of ours, &

119 Patsy Macann is a character in Stephen's *The Demi-Gods* (1914).

philosopher. Published under the title of 'Principles of Human Knowledge etc'[120] in the Everyman. The part I have been reading is 3 dialogues written to prove the existence of God – which he does by disproving the existence of matter. The reasoning is very subtle but not difficult. Look here, oh my Galahad, philosophy is a subject I am just arriving at, so why shouldn't we start abreast & read it side by side. After Berkely I shall try Hume or Descartes also in Everyman. What do you say? Expend 1/- on Berkely and have a go on those 3 Dialogues!

Your idea of the old wizard, up in the clock-tower, the in dwelling spirit of this dear college since Alfred's time,[121] is excellent; and when I am in the mood again I must write on it either in prose or in verse (outher in verse, as Malory would say).

You must remember a copy of Pater's 'Renaissance' badly stained with hair oil in my cupboard. I tried to read it some time syne when I knew even less of liter[ature] and art than I do know now, & I found it rather stiff. Pater is called a great prose stylist – but except Malory, Bunyan, Ruskin and the Authorised Version of the Bible, I am afraid I have not much ear for prose style.

I find that we get 4 days leave in about 3 weeks. Unless they allow me some time for travelling it will mean very little time at home for me, and of that little even less can be devoted to you: though you know my wishes. However I trust we shall have some few hours of happiness together. How I long to see your new books & to shew you mine – especially the ones I got bound, which I hope you will approve. Then too I will choose that present which you have so kindly offered to give me. (And so there will be no sinful waste on postal orders to worry the just.)

I must dry up now. Sorry this letter is late, but I lost it when half finished & have found it again in a pocket only to-day (Teusday).

Yours
Jack

120 George Berkeley, *A New Theory of Vision and Other Writings (A Treatise Concerning the Principles of Human Knowledge. Three Dialogues between Hylas and Philonous)* (1710), with an introduction by A.D. Lindsay, Everyman's Library [1910].

121 University College, according to some histories, was founded by Alfred the Great.

TO ARTHUR GREEVES (W):

University College,
Oxford.
[4 August 1917]

Cher Ami,

Before I go on to anything interesting I must just have one little growl at you about something in your last epistle. You express a fear that my father 'may take into his head' to stay at home during my day or two of leave. Well I resent this 'take into his head' tone. A man is living absolutely alone: both his sons are in the army and one of them – who will soon be 'out' and in the infantry, not the A.S.C. or the Friends' Ambulance Corps – gets the first day's leave he has had since joining. And then you talk about the man 'taking it into his head' to see something of him! I am afraid that my father will most certainly 'take it into his head' to stay at home. But I hope to be able to see something of my Galahad, though I fear not much.

I was interested to hear that you liked Tristram Shandy – I think I told you about seeing a copy of it in one of the deserted rooms of Univ. Personally I have tried in vain to see the good points of it. The absolute disconnection or scrappiness, the abundant coarseness of an utterly vulgar, non-voluptuous sort and the general smoking-room atmosphere of the book were too much for me. In all these points it is the direct opposite of our quiet, balanced & delicately humourous Jane Austen. Tell me more about it in your next letter and try to shew me its merits: one often learns to appreciate a book through one's friends in this way. What edition are you reading it in?

I am delighted to hear that you enjoyed Comus – it is agreed to be one of the most perfect things in English poetry, and if you prefer it to Paradise Lost you have Saintsbury[122] (but not little me) to back you up. Don't you love the opening speech

'Above the smoke & stir of this dim spot . . .'[123]

– which always reminds me of our walks over the clean hills when we look down into the Nibbelheim below. Also the descriptions of the forest

122 George Edward Bateman Saintsbury, *Short History of English Literature* (1898).
123 John Milton, *Comus* (1637), 5.

and the weird sounds that lonely shepheards have heard on its outskirts are very weird. I think the best thing of all is the last song with its allusions to

> *'Hesperus and his daughters three*
> *That sing about the golden tree',*[124]

– so beautifully lonely and romantic. I hope you won't give up your idea of reading Berkely; he is, I should think, a very good philosopher to begin on: perhaps that little book in the Home University series 'Problems of Philosophy'[125] would help too.

By the way I have forgotten to tell you any news about leave. It was going to be from next Friday till next Teusday, but that has been changed. It is now going to start on Wednesday[126] 9th & go on till that Sunday midnight. A lot depends on whether I can get any extension for travelling, which is still

> *'in even poise.'*[127]

If I can't it will be pretty poor.

You have started the question of prose style in your letter and ask whether it is anything more than the 'literal meaning of the words'. On the contrary it means less – it means the words themselves. For every thought can be expressed in a number of different ways: and style is the art of expressing a given thought in the most beautiful words and rythms of words. For instance a man might say 'When the constellations which appear at early morning joined in musical exercises and the angelic spirits loudly testified to their satisfaction'. Expressing exactly the same thought, the Authorised Version says 'When the morning stars sang together and all the sons of God shouted for joy.'[128] Thus by the power of style what was nonsense becomes ineffably beautiful. See?

Talking about 'Comus', I forgot to mention my new edition of it. The binding is not interesting. The paper is a kind of parchment (like your

---

124 ibid., 982–3.
125 James Hervey Hyslop, *Problems of Philosophy, or, Principles of Epistemology* (1905).
126 A mistake for Thursday.
127 Milton, *Comus*, 410: 'an equal poise'.
128 Job 38:7.

Omar Khayyam) and it is illustrated by the person who did 'Tchainie's' copy of the 'High History of the Holy Grael'. A thoroughly desirable book of which I hope you will approve.

Have lots to talk about but no time, and too dead tired as we were up till 2 o'clock last night doing 'attack' and then got up at the usual hour of 6.30 again this morning.

Yours
Jack

Albert Lewis recorded in his diary that Jack arrived home in his uniform on Thursday 9 August, and was there until he left Belfast on Saturday 11 August. Warnie was able to get over to see his father from 14 to 21 August, after which he paid Jack a visit in Oxford on 22 August before returning to France.

TO HIS FATHER (LP V: 231–2)

[Keble College]
Postmark: 27 August 1917

My dear Papy,

You must have been wondering what had come over me, but the crowded time I have been having since I left home will serve as some excuse. First of all came the week at Warwick, which was a nightmare. I was billeted with five others in the house of an undertaker and memorial sculptor. We had three beds between six of us, there was of course no bath, and the feeding was execrable. The little back yard full of tomb stones, which we christened 'the quadrangle', was infinitely preferable to the tiny dining room with its horse hair sofa and family photos. When all six of us sat down to meals there together, there was scarcely room to eat, let alone swing the traditional cat round. Altogether it was a memorable experience.

We came back on Saturday, and the following week I spent with Moore at the digs of his mother who, as I mentioned, is staying at Oxford. I like her immensely and thoroughly enjoyed myself.

On Wednesday as you know, Warnie was up here and we had a most enjoyable afternoon and evening together, chiefly at my rooms in Univ. How I wish you could have been there too. But please God I shall be able to see you at Oxford and show you my 'sacred city' in happier times.

Since coming back I have finished 'The angel of pain'[129] (which I give full marks) and started an interesting book of Wells', 'A modern Utopia'.[130] Being interested in an author is a very different thing from liking him, isn't it? I will send you the college group some day next week if I can get cardboard. I have asked the grocers for their bill. Hoping to hear from you soon,

your loving son,
Jack

TO HIS FATHER (LP V: 232–3) :

[Keble College]
Postmark: 10 September 1917

My dear Papy,

I was very glad to get your letter, for, though my own sins in that line are as scarlet, I must admit that I was beginning to get a little bit anxious. It was such a pity that Warnie and I could not be home together – and yet too, in a way, it spread out the 'invasion' of your young hopefuls longer for you. Warnie seems to have thoroughly enjoyed his leave, and I am sure the 'drag' exists only in your imagination.

I can quite understand your refusal of Aunt Hamilton's warm and timely invitation. In three days time I bid fair to understand it still better: for – have I told you – the next amusement on our programme is a three days bivouac up in the Wytham hills. As it has rained all the time for two or three days, our model trenches up there will provide a very unnesseccarily good imitation of Flanders mud. You know how I always disapproved of realism in art!

I will send you 'The angel of Pain' in a few days: just at present my friend Mrs. Moore has borrowed it.

As time gets on towards the end of our course, we are more and more crowded and live only in hope for the fabulous amounts of leave we are going to get before we're gazetted. Tell Arthur I simply *can't* write.

your loving
son Jack

---

129 Edward Frederic Benson, *The Angel of Pain* (1906).
130 H.G. Wells, *A Modern Utopia* (1905).

TO HIS FATHER (LP V: 233):

[Keble College]
Postmark: 24 September 1917

My dear Papy,

I hope I was not grousing in my last letter, for though this may not be the life I had chosen, yet a little hard work never did any one any harm, and I might be much worse off. The sleeping out on Cumnor hills (there were only two nights of it) illustrated some old theories of anticipation etc. – but I needn't go through it. In point of fact, sleeping out of doors proved delightful. You have a waterproof groundsheet, two blankets, and your haversack for a pillow. There was plenty of bracken to make a soft bed, and I slept excellently. You wake up in a flash without any drowsiness, feeling wonderfully fresh. Both nights were fine, but of course it would be horrible in the wet.

Our final exam comes off next Tuesday: and remembering my wonderful faculty for failing in easy exams (vide Smalls) I don't feel too confident. There seems some doubt as to when we get away after it, but probably before the end of this week. In any case I shall stay on here with the Moores over the Sunday, and wire exact date of my crossing to you later. We get a free warrant home, but I should be glad if you would send me the Samaritan's 'two pence' for oil and wine en route. Is the Wilkes you mention the same man who showed his ear in cotton wool to the Commons?

ever your loving
son Jack

P.S. Please send your next letter to University with 'To be called for' on it, as I may be in Keble or at the Moores or anywhere. Yours J.

Jack took his Responsions ('Smalls') examination on Tuesday 25 September. The next day he received a temporary commission in the regular army, and was given a month's leave. His father, waiting in tense anticipation for a visit, was to be deeply hurt by what happened. On Saturday 29 September Jack went with Paddy and his family to their home at 56 Ravenswood Road, Bristol, and remained there until he crossed over to Ireland on Saturday 12 October, giving his father a pittance of a visit. It was while he was there that Paddy learned that he had been placed in the Rifle Brigade, and he crossed to France in October.

This stay with the Moores was to have far-reaching consequences. It was the last time Jack and Paddy were to be together. The slaughter of junior officers at this period in the war was very great, the youngest paying the highest price. Twenty-three per cent of the men in University College lost their lives in the war. Jack and Paddy knew how slim their chances were, and Paddy's sister, Maureen, recalls hearing Paddy and Jack promise one another that if only one survived the war the survivor would look after Paddy's mother and Jack's father. Mrs Moore knew of the promise too, and was later to mention it to Mr Lewis.

TO HIS FATHER (LP V: 234):

56 Ravenswood Road,
Redland,
Bristol
Oct. 3rd [1917]

My dear Papy,

I suppose you must have been wondering what had become of your prodigal son all this time. Rather a chapter of adventures has occurred, and I will hasten to recount them – in the best journalese style.

We got away from Keble on the Saturday, and instead of staying in Oxford with the Moores I came down here to their home at Bristol – within a mile or so of Clifton school. On the Sunday we went and saw the latter, including the Chapel where I failed to find 'Qui procul hinc ante diem etc,' which in fact does not exist. The place is fine, but inferior to Malvern.

On Monday a cold (complete with sore throat) which I had developed at Oxford, went on so merrily that Mrs Moore took my temperature and put me to bed, where I am writing this letter (Wednesday). I am quite better now however, and shall cross on Monday night.

Looking forward to seeing you soon again, I am
your loving
son, Jack

P.S. The exam was alright, as you promised me. They don't publish either places or marks, but only tell you whether you failed or not.

Jack arrived in Belfast on Friday 12 October, and on the 16th he was gazetted into the Somerset Light Infantry. He left home on Thursday 18 October to join his regiment at Crownhill, South Devon.

TO HIS FATHER (LP V: 237–8):

3rd Somerset Light Infantry,
Crownhill,
South Devon
Monday. 5.5 p.m. [22 October 1917]

My dear Papy,

I have waited till now so that I could tell you what an ordinary working day here is like. Incidentally the phrase 'working day' is merely façon de parler: but more of that anon, as you will first be anxious to hear what sort of thieves I have fallen among. I should say the gentlemen are about 65 per cent of the whole crowd of officers, which is quite as large a majority as one has a right to expect now-a-days. One or two of them I think I shall like, though of course it is hard to say at present. It must be admitted that most of them are hardly after my style: the subjects of conversation are shop (Oh! for the ancient taboo that ruled in officers messes in the piping times of peace) sport and theatrical news recurring with a rather dull regularity – that is in the few moments of conversation which interrupt the serious business of bridge and snooker. However, they are for the most part well bred and quite nice to me. So that if this new life rouses no violent enthusiasm in me, it is on the other hand quite bearable or even pleasant.

The 'work' is a very simple matter. All the men nearly are recruits, and the training is carried on by N.C.O.s. All you do is to lead your party onto parade, hand them over to their instructor, and then walk about doing nothing at all. This you do for several hours a day. It is a little tiring to the legs and I think will finally result in atrophy of the brain. However, it is very much better than hard work, and I am quite satisfied.

I was a bit too previous in wiring from Plymouth station that Crownhill was a barracks. It turns out to be a village of wooden huts, set up in the hills amid really very beautiful scenery. Besides the officer's mess – which is a sort of glorified golf club-house – we each have our own room, with a stove in it. When this is lit, it is really very snug, tho' of course huts are always a little more draughty than even 'r-r-r-rotten' houses!

So my verdict you see is quite favourable. The life, so long as I am in England, will be rather dull, but easy and not unpleasant. There is no need to transfer into any other infantry regiment. So at least I think now: of course I may change. I had a rather tiresome journey and got to Bristol at 12.

Hoping that the new domestic is a success[131] and that you are tolerably comfortable.

your loving
son Jack

TO ARTHUR GREEVES (W):

3d Somerset Light Infantry,
Crown Hill,
Plymouth
Sunday [28? October 1917]

Cher Ami,

'At last' you will say, and I admit I should have written long ago. I am the more sorry to have to begin my letter by saying something rather ungracious. Since coming back & meeting a certain person[132] I have begun to realize that it was not at all the right thing for me to tell you so much as I did. I must therefore try to undo my actions as far as possible by asking you to try & forget my various statements & not to refer to the subject. Of course I have perfect trust in you, mon vieux, but still I have no business to go discussing those sort of things with you. So in future that topic must be taboo between us.

And now to tell you all the news. I am quite fairly comfortable here, we are in huts: but I have a room to myself with a fire in it & so am quite snug. The country is glorious – very wild & hilly & we are up a good height ourselves. From the camp I can enjoy a fine landscape – nice cosy little bits of green country with cottages & water & trees, then woodier

131 Annie Strahan (1884–1972), the cook-housekeeper at Little Lea since 1910, had decided to retire and set up a cake shop in Belfast. She was to remain a valued friend of the Lewises, and Albert lent his house and resources to her for a wedding party in November 1917 when she married John McCrea. Albert gave his services as a solicitor to the McCreas, and he always took a great interest in their five children. Mrs McCrea was succeeded at Little Lea by Mary Cullen who was to remain with the family until the break-up of Little Lea in 1930.

132 Mrs Moore.

hills rising at last into big, open moors that make up the horizon. It is especially lovely in the mists of early morning or of night.

There is very little work to do here, so you will see that I might be worse off. I even manage to get a little reading done. At present I am engaged on Hawthorne's 'Transformation' in the Bohn's 1/- edition. In spite of repeated advice from me I don't think you have ever read this man. This one is very good indeed & has a lot about painting in it & some fine descriptions of Italian scenery. It is better than 'The Scarlet Letter',[133] but, of course, not so good as 'The House with the Seven Gables'. I have also got the 1st 2 volumes of Malory in the Temple Classics. The frontispieces are from designs by Beardsley.[134] They are v. good in the extremest style of mediaevalism – perhaps rather affected. One is of the finding of Excalibur & the other of someone giving Tristam a shield. In the Excalibur one, Merlin is shewn as a not very old clean-shaven but beautifully wizened man. Not what I'd have imagined him but good all the same. I have also bought in the ordinary Everyman 'Adam Bede' (by George Eliot)[135] because it was the only thing I could find – the bookshops in Plymouth are rotten. I rather like the look of it and it is one of the best kind of Everyman as regards paper & type.

There is a rumour that we are all going to Ireland to quell the Sinn Feiner in a day or two – but the above address is safe to find me. Better not send the MS. book[136] till we're sure where I'll be.

Adieu mon ami, write soon
Jack

TO ARTHUR GREEVES (W):

[Crown Hill,
Plymouth
4? November 1917]

My dear Arthur,

To your last three letters, which, with all respect, indicate a sad falling under influences which I thought we had killed, I might make a

133 Nathaniel Hawthorne, *Transformation* or *The Marble Faun* (1860); *The Scarlet Letter* (1850).

134 Malory, *Le Morte d'Arthur*, Temple Classics (1897).

135 George Eliot, *Adam Bede*, Everyman's Library (1859).

136 The manuscript volume of his poems, 'Metrical Meditations of a Cod', some of which he hoped to publish.

very long reply indeed: but as free criticism is notoriously dangerous, even among friends of our standing, I will content myself with saying 'Don't be a damned fool' and je passerai outre.

I am so sorry that you have never heard before that 'Green'[137] arrived safely, for which many thanks. I rather thought I had told Mrs Moore, but perhaps she forgot to pass the information on, or, which is more likely, I forgot to give it in the first place. I approve most thoroughly of this shelter of yours in the garden, it will make a resort where we can always have privacy, even when everyone else is at home.

I shall certainly be in Ireland, by the way, though when & for how long I don't know. By the way (to descend into practical matters) after your leave, you go to a battalion at home until you are posted 'overseas' again. In my case the 3d Somersets to which I shall go is at Holywood Barracks, so that if I have a short respite before going out again, during *that* time also I shall be able to come up and see you of an afternoon. You will be glad to hear that I have revised my former 'patriotic' views about having a hospital in Craigavon: and I now regard a Tommy whether wounded or not as an abominable sight, especially among the scenes of home.

I am much obliged to you for the suggestion that I am now become 'a cheer-oh young man' (by the way, in my experience, only lodging house landladies etc. refer to people as 'young men') and if I had the energy would take my revenge by playing the part of one: but it would be too fatiguing.

I think the only real change that you will find in me is an increasing tendency towards philosophy; which has grown in the course of many interesting talks with my good friend Johnson,[138] whom I hope to meet after the war as a scholar of Queens at Oxford. I think you would like him for his literary tastes and for a morality as strict as your own, but based on reasonable, not religious grounds: in music you would have many a quarrel with him and perhaps consider him a prig when he

137 i.e. Green's *Short History of the English People*. See letter of 1 November 1916.

138 Laurence Bertrand Johnson (1898–1918) was elected a scholar of Queen's College, Oxford, in the spring of 1917 but, being commissioned a 2nd lieutenant in the Somerset Light Infantry on 15 April 1917, he was never able to matriculate at the University. Lewis was to see a good deal of him over the next months, and not only did he like him better upon closer acquaintance, but he was to write a deeply affectionate reminiscence of him many years later in *SBJ* XII.

pronounces Chopin to be 'sugary' – his severe tastes apparently do not fall below Bach & Wagner. Debussy, strange to relate, he does not know.

Both he and all the other literary people whom I have met since I left home for Oxford, have made me feel how deep is my ignorance of modern, that is to say, *contemporary*, literature, especially poetry. I have often sat in amazed silence amid glib talk of Rupert Brooke,[139] Masefield,[140] Chesterton,[141] Bottomley[142] etc. But after all I suppose our steady nibbling at older works is a safe-guard against 'crazes' – deadly things that arise so easily about a new writer. At the same time I am often surprised to find how utterly ignored Yeats is among the men I have met: perhaps his appeal is purely Irish – if so, then thank the gods that I am Irish.

But philosophy or metaphysics is my great find at present: all other questions really seem irrelevant till its ones are solved. I think you should take it up – its probings would at least save you from the intellectual stagnation that usually awaits a man who has found complete satisfaction in some traditional religious system.

By the way, you never told me what Carpenter's <'The Intermediate Sex'[143]> was like (– or did you? Yes, I think you did). I don't much fancy a book – 'something like the psalms' – it sounds as if it were that detestable thing known as 'prose-poetry' which is usually the cave of Adullam for those who can write NEITHER prose NOR poetry. But perhaps I have not quite understood you.

Since I have been here I have had one parcel from Denny's containing 'The Ultimate Belief' by Clutton-Brock[144] and 'Eighteenth Century Studies' (in the Wayfarers' Library) by Austin Dobson.[145] Clutton Brock wrote a monograph on Wm. Morris in the 'Home University Series'[146] – that is

---

139 Rupert Brooke (1887–1915), a young poet of beauty and charm whose reputation was enhanced by the posthumous publication of his *1914 and Other Poems* (1915) and *Collected Poems* (1918).

140 John Masefield (1878–1967), perhaps Lewis's favourite modern poet, published over 50 volumes of verse, and became Poet Laureate in 1930.

141 G.K. Chesterton (1874–1936), Catholic poet, novelist, journalist, and Christian apologist. His works were to have a deep and lasting impression on Lewis. His *Orthodoxy* (1909) and *The Everlasting Man* (1925) contributed towards Lewis's conversion.

142 Gordon Bottomley (1874–1948), a poet whose works Lewis wrote to Greeves about on 12 September 1918.

143 Edward Carpenter, *The Intermediate Sex* (1908).

144 Arthur Clutton-Brock, *The Ultimate Belief* (1916).

145 Henry Austin Dobson, *Eighteenth-Century Essays* (1914).

146 i.e. *William Morris: His Work and Influence*, op. cit.

all I knew about him until this new book of his was on everyone's lips. I expected it to be a fat tome at 12/6 but it turned out to be a mere pamphlet in size (though not in format) published by Constable at 2/6. I should like you to read it: it is partly about education, but is of great general interest and has given me new points of view, especially on the subject of morals. Hitherto I had always thought there were only two possible views of morals: either, if you believed in a religion, that they were a god-imposed law: or, if you did not, that they were merely rules for convenience – 'The rules of our prison-house' as Blake called them. This man gives a third possibility which is very interesting – regarding them as a kind of art, an object to be pursued for its own beauty. He says several other good things – also on aesthetics. The other book is just what I expected – pleasant & chatty & good to read in bed tho' not wildly exciting or original.

In your last letter – the 'neglected' one, written apparently on the model of Mrs Gumadge in one of Dicken's books[147] – as far as I remember you don't tell me much about your reading. I was glad to hear in a former letter that you liked Benvenuto Cellini – of course your knowledge of history would make it even more interesting to you than to me. The references to <'That'> were slightly involved and may easily have escaped you: I could scarcely find them again. I think you *would* like Andrew Lang's translation of the Odyssey: the Iliad is much less pleasing,[148] mind you don't try it.

I wonder have those walks in sun & rain vanished forever? I wonder shall I ever live as I lived then? However we must get on as best we can: I shouldn't drop that romance of yours except to begin something else. Burton's advice to the melancholy you know was 'be not idle, be not solitary'[149] – which has been corrected to 'be not idle when you are solitary'.

Good bye, now, cher ami, write to me soon and tell me all your thoughts and doings.

Yours
Jack

147 Mrs Gummidge in Charles Dickens' *David Copperfield* (1850) – a 'lone lorn creetur'.

148 Andrew Lang (with S.H. Butcher), *The Odyssey* (1879); (with W. Leaf and E. Myers), *The Iliad* (1883).

149 Robert Burton, *The Anatomy of Melancholy* (1621), part I, sec. ii, mem. 2, subs. 6.

TO HIS FATHER (LP V: 240–1):

[3rd Somerset Light Infantry,
Crownhill,
South Devon]
Postmark: Belfast, 5 November 1917

My dear Papy,

We are all in great excitement here. News has come round that we are under short notice to proceed to Ireland on active service. That means that everything has to be got ready and we may or may not go at the end of it. They sometimes do these things you know just to see how quickly a Battalion can get 'short hove' as grandfather used to say. Of course we are all hoping it is true, as 'active service' in Ireland, whatever exactly it may mean, will be a great deal pleasanter than in France. Have you any idea what it could be about? The wildest rumours are afloat here about new Sinn Fein risings and one man actually says that the Germans have landed on the Shannon!

Apart from all nonsense of that sort, there certainly does seem some hope of a job that might keep us at home, if we are all going to Ireland together. Everything is being taken as if for real work there – ammunition, field dressings, even anti-gas appliances. After all, very probably it will turn out to be only a war office stunt to smarten us up, and nothing may happen.

Thanks muchly for the proofs. I will return them in a day or two after deliberation. The ones of us both together are excellent as photographs, but I think a little theatrical and 'posed'. The ones of me alone are so monstrous in size, aren't they? Warnie's one was much more natural and more what one expects a photograph to be than those enormous heads. The slight blurring of the shoulder in two or three doesn't matter much I think: of the likeness or unlikeness of course I can hardly judge. In the 'joint' photographs, I think the one of you looking at me is excellent: the full face not so good. I will give you my final verdict when I send them.

I have really been very lucky in getting here, as I like most of my companions, and the percentage of gentlemen is distinctly high. Paddy Moore, in the Rifle Brigade, seems to have got in with a most terrible lot of outsiders, so after all our separation was a blessing in disguise. He also seems to be much harder worked than I. Curiously enough there are two

Malvernians here, Perret[150] and Routh,[151] neither of whom I knew at the Coll: the former is quite a good sort. There are also two Oxonians, the Padre, formerly of Christ Church, and a man named John who was up at Exeter.

Thanks. I am well supplied with books just at present. After this Irish business has been settled one way or the other, if I still have time for reading, I may ask you to send me some of my own books from home – in which case of course, I can give you exact geographical descriptions of their disposition.

Hoping that you are well and that the domestic arrangement goes on 'as well as may be expected', I am,

your loving
son Jack

TO HIS FATHER (LP V: 241):

Telegraphed from Bristol
5.55 p.m. 15 November 1917

Have arrived Bristol on 48 hours leave. Report Southampton Saturday. Can you come Bristol. If so meet at station. Reply Mrs. Moore's address 56 Ravenswood Road Redlands Bristol. Jack.[152]

TO HIS FATHER (LP V: 242):

[56 Ravenswood Road,
Redland,
Bristol]
Postmark: 15 November 1917

My dear Papy,

I have just got your wire. I am sending off another to explain things more clearly: I'm awfully sorry, but I can't think how I failed to make it plain in the first. It is perfectly wretched giving me such short leave – 48 hours is no earthly use to a person who lives in Ireland and

---

150 Frank Winter Perrett (1898–), of London entered Malvern in the third term of 1912. After leaving in 1915 he served as a lieutenant in the 3rd Somerset Light Infantry. After the war he worked for some years as a planter.

151 Douglas James Lionel Routh (1895–) entered Malvern in 1913, and served in World War I from 1914–19 as a captain with the Somerset Light Infantry.

152 Mr Lewis wired back: 'Don't understand telegram. Please write. P.'

would have to spend about two days and nights travelling. Please don't worry, I shall probably be a long time at the base as I have had so little training in England. Can't write more now: must go and do some shopping. I return the proofs. I should like one of each I think. I'll let you know my address in France as soon as I can.

your loving
son Jack

TO HIS FATHER (LP V: 242):

Telegraphed from Bristol
11.20 a.m. 16 November 1917

Orders France. Reporting Southampton 4 p.m. on Saty. [17 November][153] If coming, wire immediately. No need alarm. Shall be at base. Jack.

TO HIS FATHER (LP V: 243):

[France]
1st Somerset Light Infty.
3 I.B.D.
21/11/17.

My dear Papy,

This is really a very sudden and unpleasant surprise. I had no notion of it until I was sent off on my 48 hours final leave, in fact I thought they were ragging me when they told me. I am now at a certain very safe base town[154] where we live comfortably in huts as we did at Crownhill. I am being innoculated this afternoon and have 48 hours off duty afterwards. By the way, has Gundrede come out again? You might let me know, as she was at this town before and meant to come back here.

I suppose we have no reason to grumble: this was bound to come sooner or later. There is no need to worry for a good time yet, and I'll try and let you hear every day when there is. Have got to go on parade in a

---

153 Immediately upon their arrival at Southampton on 17 November, Lewis went with his battalion to France.

154 Lewis was at Monchy-Le-Preux. One of the poems in his *Spirits in Bondage* (1919) is named 'French Nocturne (Monchy-Le-Preux)' and if it was not written there, it is about the effect the place had on him.

few minutes, so must stop. Shall be able to write you a proper letter off duty tomorrow.

your loving
son Jack

Albert Lewis was desperately worried about his son, and upon receipt of this letter he wrote to Colonel James Craig – later Viscount Craigavon (1871–1940) – who was MP for the East Division of County Down, asking for his help in getting his son transferred from the infantry to the artillery. He believed he would be safer with the gunners. Colonel Craig replied on 3 December 1917 that 'Before any steps are taken in this matter, it will be necessary for me to have a letter from [CSL.] personally, expressing his wishes to be transferred, and explaining that his present Commanding Officer will recommend him' (LP V: 247). Mr Lewis sent a copy of this correspondence to Jack.

TO HIS FATHER (LP V: 249):

[France]
13 December 1917

My dear Papy,

Your letter arrived today, and I must answer it at once – with apologies. Of course you will understand that work and a certain inevitable share in the life of the regiment do not leave me much time to myself.

The letter of which you forwarded me a copy is rather a surprise, and I hope you will not be disappointed at my answer to it. Some arguments in favour of staying in the infantry have arisen since we were last together. In the first place, I must confess that I have become very much attached to this regiment. I have several friends whom I should be sorry to leave and I am just beginning to know my men and understand the work.

In the second place, if the main reason for going into the gunners is their supposed safety, I hardly think it is enough. On this part of the front the guns are exposed to almost as heavy shelling (and it is shells that count far more than rifle fire) as the infantry: if their casualties are fewer that must be because their total strength is so much smaller. Then, again, nobody holds out any hopes of my getting recommended by the

C.O. He would be sure to reply (and not without reason) that it would be expensive and wasteful to take a half-trained infantry officer home again and turn him into a gunner. Our C.O. – a Lt. Colonel Majendie – is a splendid fellow for whom I have a great admiration, and I should be sorry to cut so poor a figure in his eyes as I must do in trying to back out as I get nearer the real part of my job.[155] Of course I fully understand that it is rather late for me to talk thus; and beyond the right which you have to guide me in any case, you have ample grounds for claiming that I should stick to our arrangement. Yet I think you will sympathize with what I have said above.

I am at present in billets in a certain rather battered town somewhere behind the line. It is quite comfy, but of course the work is hard and (which is worse) irregular. I have just finished 'Adam Bede' which I liked immensely – but don't send me any more of hers as I know a shop (or rather canteen here) that has them – in the Tauchnitz edition.

By the way I owe you some money for the things you bought and which should have been paid for out of my first allowances. I enclose a blank cheque to 'square' it.

Good night. Try not to worry and write soon.

your loving
son Jack

TO ARTHUR GREEVES (W):

[France]
14/12/17

My dear Galahad,

Just the proverbial few lines to answer your letter & to thank you for writing to Mrs Moore – she appreciated it very much and you may perhaps understand how nice & homely it is for me to know that the two people who matter most to me in the world are in touch.

I do get a certain amount of time for reading here, but of course it takes a long time to eat up a whole book in such small mouthfuls. I have just finished 'Adam Bede'. As you know, it is the first of hers I have read,

155 Vivian Henry Bruce Majendie (1886–1960) had been educated at Winchester College and Sandhurst. As commander of the 1st Battalion of the Somerset Light Infantry he was eminently suited for writing *A History of the 1st Battalion The Somerset Light Infantry (Prince Albert's) July 1st 1916 to the end of the War* (1921). He ended his long and useful career in the army as a major-general, and he retired in 1946.

and I earnestly advise you to read it. Of course as in so many of the older novelists there is a feeble happy ending stuck on to a tragedy: but the greater part of it is excellent. I am now reading a book of Balzac's called 'Le Père Goriot'.[156] It is rather a grim, realist production but quite good. I am writing home for Boswell, Milton, and another George Eliott in the Everyman.

I don't know when I can give you a decent letter but I may manage a note like this fairly often. Write as often & long as you can, mon ami, it's a great comfort –

ever yours
Jack

(Never tell mon père when I write to you – J)

On 29 November Warnie Lewis, who was still in France with the 4th Company, 7th Divisional Train, was promoted to captain. On 23 December he arrived in St Omer to begin a course at the Mechanical Transport School of Instruction.

TO ARTHUR GREEVES (W):

[France]
New Year's Eve [1917]

Cher Ami,

So glad to hear from you again yesterday evening. My last correspondent from Strandtown was 'Chanie' who wrote me a very typical would-be facetious letter – <she certainly is an apalling woman and I shall> never forget her on various occasions profaning our sacred haunts & soaking machines with her chatter. Do you remember the day we heard or thought we heard her in the wood and fled through many devious paths. Oh I'd just love to have another of those walks, particularly now in the snow – I suppose there's snow at home too, it is just thawing here. Don't think I've lost the taste for all that life.

I hope I have gained the new without losing the old and if we were all three – you know my meaning – together somewhere I'm sure we could be very happy, without any clash of interests. Apologies for not telling

156 Honoré de Balzac, *Le Père Goriot* (1834).

you much 'about myself' in my last letter. You know we always avoided practical details & anyway I assume that you hear all that from another source.

I am delighted to find that you appreciate 'Yeats' – I think the eeriness of that opening conversation in 'The Countess Kathleen' is splendid – rather like 'Christabel' in a way

> *'What can have made the grey hen flutter so?'*[157]

By the way will you send on my MS. book – the Metrical Meditations one – to Ravenswood Rd – I have yielded to oft repeated suggestions that it should go there.

Write as much as you can & as often

Yours

Jack

157 William Butler Yeats, *The Countess Cathleen* (1892), i, 1.

1918

TO HIS FATHER (LP V: 256–7):

[France]
4 January 1918

My dear Papy,

Your letter, with the enclosure for which I thank you very much, arrived the day before yesterday. Before going any further, I should say in answer to your question that I find my pay quite sufficient for all my needs and comforts. I am glad that I shall not have to bother you in that way.

I have thought a good deal about the question that is uppermost in both our minds, and talked it over with some of my friends. The arguments in favour of staying where I am seem overwhelming, and I have finally made up my mind to do so. I am very sorry that you should have taken trouble unnecessarily, and I hope that my decision will not be a disappointment to you. From what you say in your last letter, I think you agree with me that the gunners are not really preferable for safety or society. I have been up in the trenches for a few days (which I will speak about later on) attached to a company for instruction, and the number of shells that went singing over our heads to fall on the batteries far away behind, did not – as you may imagine – weaken my affection for the infantry!

I am now back again on a course of bombing, where I live with the bombing officer, a very nice fellow, of literary tastes, in a quite comfortable billet. The work, involving a good deal of chemical and mechanical questions, is not of the sort my brain takes to readily, but as long as one is safe and has an unbroken nights sleep, there is nothing to grouse about I suppose.

You will be anxious to hear my first impressions of trench life. This is a very quiet part of the line and the dug outs are very much more comfortable than one imagines at home. They are very deep, you go down to them by a shaft of about 20 steps: they have wire bunks where a man can sleep quite snugly, and brasiers for warmth and cooking. Indeed, the chief discomfort is that they tend to get *too* hot, while of course the bad air makes one rather headachy. I had quite a pleasant time, and was only once in a situation of unusual danger, owing to a shell falling near the latrines while I was using them.

I think I told you that I had read 'Adam Bede' and am now at 'The Mill on the Floss',[1] which I like even better. Do you know of any life of George Elliot published in a cheap edition? If you can find one, I should like to read it.

Thank you muchly for the smokeables. The pipes have been soaked in whiskey, according to the dictum of experts, and are going very well. I also thank you from my heart for your last letter that defies definition. I am very proud of my father.

With such wishes for the New Year as still seem possible,

I am,
your loving son,
Jack

TO ARTHUR GREEVES (W):

No 10 British Red Cross Hospital[2]
Le Tréport
France.
2/2/18

My dear Galahad,

Here I am safely ensconced in a bed in hospital, miles away from the line, thank the gods, and therefore at last in a position to write you a more or less respectable letter. The news of my illness will have been given you by Mrs Moore, so there is no need to waste words on that.

I was sorry to hear that you were in trouble over the death of your cousin:[3] I did not think that you had been so attached to him. Your letters are always very sad now. I hope you are not letting yourself 'fall into

1 George Eliot, *The Mill on the Floss* (1860).

2 After some months on the front line Lewis fell ill with pyrexia, or 'trench fever' as the troops called it. On 1 February he was admitted to this hospital where he was to remain until 28 February.

3 Thomas Malcolmson 'Malcolm' Greeves (1895–1917) was the son of Alfred Greeves of 'Fernbank', Belfast. He attended Campbell College 1907–13. During the war he served as a flight sub-lieutenant with the Royal Navy, and was killed in action on 23 December 1917.

a melancholy' as Johnson would have said in some severe letter to his Boswell. Now is the time to rally all your interests about you & to paint & write for dear life.

I must admit fate has played strange tricks with me since last winter: I feel that I have definitely got into a new epoch of life and one feels extraordinarily helpless over it. How I should love one of our old afternoons again when we sat in your drawing room and discussed our tea and digestive biscuits: we were usually discontented over something but we had many a good laugh. As for the older days of real walks far away in the hills & journies out of town on the top of the tram – ma foi, that was the golden age infinitely remote 'mais ou sont les neiges d'antan'.[4] Perhaps you don't believe that I want all that again, because other things more important have come in: but after all there is room for other things besides love in a man's life. As well, you should trust in me after I have given you so much confidence.

How rude of me! – to come thus far without thanking you for your parcel. Let me hasten to do so. I am still reading the 'Lavengro' (although I'm sorry to say both books were rather crushed when they arrived) & like it very well though of course I am most violently out of sympathy with the author at times – when he is loudly patriotic (as in the idiotic passage about painters in chapter XXI) or when he indulges in vulgar invective against the parent church. Of course *that* is probably agreeable enough to you – eh?, old puritan. I am also reading Boswell vol. II and enjoy very much renewing my acquaintance with all these great old gentlemen. It is the ideal book to read out here and to keep me in touch with all the quiet literary pleasant things in the world – one feels so cut off at times among all these godless philistines. However I'm having an excellent time here doing nothing – if only it could last.

You are lucky you know; it must be grand to look forward to an endless prospect of regular nights' sleep & comfortable chairs & good meals & books & everything decent & civilized.

Well, good bye for the present mon vieux, keep true to the old interests – and don't let your relations influence you too much. You see I begin to fear for you now I can't watch over you & guard you against evil!

Yours
Jack

4 François Villon, *Le Grand Testament* (1461), 'Ballade des dames du temps Jadis': 'But where are the snows of yesteryear?'

TO HIS FATHER (LP V: 282):

British Red Cross and Order of St. John[5]
[France]
9 February 1918

My dear P.,

Just a line. I am much better now and hope to be up in a few days. In spite of its alarming name, Pyrexia is not much more serious than influenza. I shouldn't build on the idea of leave in which to recuperate, I'm afraid that's only for people who have been very ill indeed. This little turn is however not a bad thing, as it has kept me out of the line and in a good bed for a season. I will write again and at greater length when I get up.

your loving,
son,
Jack

TO ARTHUR GREEVES (W):

[No. 10 British Red Cross Hospital,
Le Tréport,
France]
12/2/18

My dear Galahad,

Your letter dated the 24th January 19*17* (sic) arrived a few days ago. It has certainly been a famous time, – a year and a month – in coming.

Your account of the various meetings with your friend Mr Thompson reads rather like our Boswell. 'I met him at luncheon at so-and-so: I dined with him at etc.' From which you will gather that I am still reading my '*Bozz*-well' (you remember the proper way of pronouncing it?) and enjoying it very much: it is such a rest to come back to after everything else. I also have a confession – to wit that I have given up Lavengro at any rate for the present. I gave up everything, of course, during a bad spell with high temperature which I have had since I last wrote to you: and now I feel no inclination to return to him. I don't object to the scheme of the book; in fact I think that in other hands, say A. C. Benson's, it might

5 On 2 February 1918 the War Office informed Albert Lewis that Jack 'was admitted to 10th Red Cross Hospital, Le Tréport on February 1st, suffering from slight Pyrexia'.

be charming. But my lack of sympathy with, nay by now my violent hostility to the author, prevents me from enjoying it. I expect you will think me rather foolish over this.

How do you like the tour to the Hebrides?[6] That book follows naturally after one has read the Life. I remember taking up the Everyman copy of it in a shop in Oxford (oh! for those bookshops in 'The Broad' – how we could ramble there!) & liking the paper and type.

I am sorry 'Tommy' has gone as he must have brightened up your 'circle' a good deal. <Are you still bound to him by the chains of desire as well as by 'pure' friendship?> I consider your reasons for not going to stay with him seem to me, with all due respect to be rot. A person with a weak heart may need quiet & may have to take care not to tire himself etc but Lord-a-mercy, short of actual hardships, why should he be more uncomfortable than other people? Of course you know best, but I must say if I ever thought you were refusing to come and stay with me for like cause I should think pretty poorly of your excuses – and your friendship. Not that I think you would, old man: I flatter myself that you could endure a few discomforts if we were together again.

'Shall we ever be the same again'[?] Oh, how far we have travelled, you and I. To think of the things we've done: do you remember that day we walked up the glen in the rain, & everything was soaking? Or the evening up in Tiglath's field at dusk – the only real evening walk we ever had? Or the days of scheming over Loki when I first shewed you any work of mine, and you used to play over bits from the unborn opera? And the night when we first broached the 'nameless secrets of Aphrodite' and walked up and down that bit of road in the dark? And now – well, umph. However, we may have good times yet, although I have been at a war and although I love someone.

You talk about the days of our book-discussing as being far off, but indeed I think they're the only thing that has survived, I still want to hear all you are reading & I am still buying books. Apropos I have written home (London, I mean) for 'The Autobiography of Benvenuto Cellini' (Everyman)[7] which I'll talk about some other time. Fancy you beginning to care for old books! I was beginning to love some of the old books in

6 James Boswell, *The Journal of a Tour to the Hebrides* (1785).

7 *The Memoirs of Benvenuto Cellini written by Himself*, translated by Anne Macdonell, Everyman's Library (1913).

the college library at Univ. Of course London is the place, I suppose, for rumaging second hand shops.

You don't tell me what you are reading: always remember that it keeps us in touch. I'm afraid you'll be on very stodgy stuff – but then I'm getting stodgy too. After Benvenuto I'm thinking of reading Lockhart's 'Life of Scott' or else a life of 'G. Eliot'. Hers ought to be interesting. She had an affair with De Musset.[8] Is there any other edition of Green's Short History than the one that both our fathers have? Please answer this. Good bye now, old man, try to keep in touch and feel to me as you used to –

Yours
Jack

TO HIS FATHER (LP V: 285–6):

No. 10 British Red Cross Hospital,
Le Tréport
16 February 1918

My dear Papy,

Your letter has remained unanswered for some time, and if I had literally fulfilled my promise of 'writing when I got up', I fear the time would have been longer still. 'Trench fever' sounds a formidable name enough – like 'prison fever' in the days of the Bloody Assize I always think, but it is not usually a troublesome business. In this country it is called P.U.O. which, I am told, stands for 'Pyrexia unknown origin': which in plain English means merely a high temperature arising from the general irregularity of life at the front. In my case however, after they had got me down to normal, I had a relapse, and was pretty ill for a day or two. I am now however on the highroad to recovery, though still in bed. I consider this little turn as an unmixed blessing: even if I get no leave by it – and I'm afraid that is not very likely – I shall have had a comfortable rest from the line. The place where I have been dropped down is a little fishing village so far as I can make out. There are cliffs and a grey sea beyond – which one is very glad to see again – and from my own window pleasant wooded country. They tell me Dieppe is about eighteen miles away: and that makes one remember . . . eheu fugaces![9]

---

8 He is probably thinking of Alfred de Musset's affair with the French novelist, George Sand.

9 During part of August and September 1907 the Lewis brothers spent their last holiday with their mother near Dieppe. See letter of 4 September 1907.

This is indeed distressing news about Gunny: I hope the successful backwoodsman does not propose to return to his native heath with his booty, when the war is over.[10] However, we must rejoice that our qualms about a certain Hebrew neighbour were baseless. How is Cousin Quartus – he was in a poor way when I left home.

By the way (I can't remember whether I told you before or not) the Captain of the Company I am in is the Harris who used to be a master at Cherbourg: I think you met him once. He impressed me in those days, but I find him very disappointing. I wonder is it my own fault that so many of my old acquaintances I have run up against since leaving my shell at Bookham 'Please me not'? I suppose these things are to be expected.[11]

---

10 Gundreda Ewart was being courted by Captain Geoffrey Burbage, an army officer from Canada. Their engagement was announced in January 1919 but was broken off a few months later.

11 This is the same Percy Gerald Kelsal Harris, 'Pogo', mentioned in note 7 of the letter of 5 May 1912. Harris was commissioned a lieutenant in the Somerset Light Infantry on 1 February 1915 and on 6 October 1917 he was promoted to captain. He had made a poor showing at Cherbourg House, but he cuts an heroic and dashing figure in Everard Wyrall's official *History of the Somerset Light Infantry (Prince Albert's) 1914–1919* (1927). Wyrall describes the bravery at Verchain which caused Harris to receive the Military Cross with this citation: 'For conspicuous gallantry near Verchain on 24 October 1918. At the river bank, in the darkness, considerable confusion and difficulty were experienced in throwing the bridges, owing to the heavy machine-gun fire. It was entirely due to his example and efforts that the bridges were thrown and that the men were able to cross. He subsequently led his company to a further objective, and carried out a personal reconnaissance across the open under heavy machine-gun fire, obtaining very valuable information' (p. 354). A bar was added to that Cross as a result of Harris's gallantry at Preseau on 1 November 1918. Wyrall wrote of it: '"Preseau" – it was here that the 1st Somerset Light Infantry ended its glorious record of fighting in the Great War...Assisted by Company Sergeant-Major R. Johnson, Captain P.G.K. Harris rallied his men and ordered them to charge. The whole line sprang forward with a cheer and, with the bayonet, flung the Germans back' (p. 356).

It is, however, in Lt Col. Majendie's *History of the 1st Battalion The Somerset Light Infantry* that the Cherbourg 'Pogo' of uncertain temper is seen as a man, not less glossy perhaps, but far more admirable than the one Jack remembered. 'During the clearing of Preseau,' wrote Colonel Majendie, 'Captain P.G.K. Harris, M.C., was the chief performer in an incident which gave rise to some merriment. He was standing at the top of some cellar steps collecting prisoners, when a German came up from below "kamerading" with such enthusiasm that he collided with Captain Harris and knocked him down. Captain Harris sat down violently on top of a dead German, and in his efforts to rise put his hand on the dead man's face. This was too much for Light Company's Commander; he leapt at the offender and, mindful of his Oxford days, caught him such a left under the jaw that the unhappy German did not recover consciousness for some time' (p. 120).

You kindly ask if there is anything you could send. The next time you are in Mulllan's, I should be 'beholden' if you would ask them to look out some cheap edition of Burton's 'Anatomy of Melancholy' and send it to me, or the 1st. volume of it. You remember it used to be a fancy of mine, and somebody has recommended it to me lately. If the only edition is in a fairly large book, let them send it all the same – I can find room for it. What are you reading? You see I make some desperate attempt to keep in touch with a life beyond the one which we lead here. I hope you keep well in body: so long as I am in hospital you may keep easy in mind. How I wish your hopes about leave could be realized. Of course it is possible, but I don't think there is much chance. By the way, offer Warnie all my congratulations upon his recent glories when next you write. That at least is a blessing: he won't be doing badly in the soldiering line if he is to be a Captain after the war at his age. Well good bye for the present: write soon again.

your loving
son Jack

TO ARTHUR GREEVES (W):

[No. 10 British Red Cross Hospital]
21/2/18

My dear Galahad,

Your last letter would have been answered earlier but for two reasons. 1, that as my last apparently crossed yours I thought you had something to go on with; 2 when I had actually started writing to you the other day, duty suddenly called to me and made me write to M. mon père instead. So you see your good precepts have stood in your own way!

I will dispose of the immensely uninteresting subject of my own health shortly – I am up again now and was out for the first time yesterday. Indeed I am beginning to tremble as to how long I shall be left here – but of course I may have the good luck of another relapse: but I doubt it, the gods hate me – and naturally enough considering my usual attitude towards them.

The country round, so far as I could see in yesterday's walk, quite comes up to expectation. I in vain tried to get onto a road leading to the cliffs and the sea, but, like the house in 'Alice in Wonderland' they evaded me. I struck a very pretty little village however: the houses are mostly clay walled, which gives them a lovely colour, and are very ramshakle.

The roofs are all of old old tiles and there are lots of old stone crucifixes, with their little offerings of grass & beads & things on them. Catholic Christianity is certainly more picturesque than puritanism. But what pleased me most was an old granary with little kinds of arrow slits under the eaves through which you could see oats or corn or whatever it was projecting: it gave you the impression of the place being filled to bursting and was somehow very homely, snug and comfortable. There are also pigeons all over the place, lodged in dovecots of the real old type that you see in pictures. Another nice thing was the orchards, where you could look along the bright grass among the tree stems – very like our wood at home just above and beyond the vicious dog. Wandering about the sleepy country reminded me of Bookham days – what a paradise of peace and quiet interests that was with our weekly letters so full of life & always following up some new idea.

I hardly realized till your last letter that of course from your present liesure you must look back with a kind of horror to the days when you had to go into town. Yet we had a few minutes of 'good talk' sometimes in that sordid old office – which, by the way, if I had a bunk in one corner, I should now regard as an almost incredibly luxurious billet – actually windows and a fireplace.

I am longing to see those old English romances of yours: I think that *is* the kind of book I had rather hunt out second hand than buy brand new and obvious in a shop. If, as I imagine from your account they suffer from being too thin, could you not have them bound together in some good solemn half leather & strong boards. The girl in Ovenell's, Broad St., Oxford assured me they could make a good job of binding books together like that. I am sure your cautious soul would never risk it, but I think you'd be quite safe in sending them to Ovenell's with instructions. She would understand & a good shop like that would certainly do it with taste. If it suits the style of the book you could have a guilt top as well.

I wait anxiously for your answer as to there being any other edition of Green's Short History – but I'm afraid there is NOT. I feel inclined to read history somehow. By the way I must recommend the 'Autobiography' of Benvenuto Cellini which I am now three quarters way through. I expect you know who he was – a Florentine designer born in 1500. The book professes to be a sober 'life' but seems to me most impossible. He lives like a character in a Dumas novel: he is often attacked in the street by five or six men, all of whom he kills wounds, or puts to flight: he is shut up in a castle (with a 'castellan' who is mad & imagines himself to be a bat), and makes a most wonderful escape – letting himself down by a rope of sheets *of course* – He goes with a magician to practice sorcery in the ruins of the Colisseum and after the magician had 'conjured for more than two hours many thousands of spirits began to appear' so that the whole amphitheatre was full of them threatening to come inside the magic circle. And perhaps what would appeal to you most is the background of great historical figures by whom he is patronized – two popes, cardinals both of France and Italy, Lorenzo & Cosimo de' Medici, the King of France and his powerful & spiteful mistress Madame d'Etampes, the Emperor. It is like a grand historical romance, with the added pleasure that it is, at least for the most part, true: how I look forward to reading it in the Italian when (and if) I get back to real life. It is also a good Everyman speciman: the paper is thin & crisp, the print just a comfortable size & the margins larger than usual – making a very pretty page. But I could talk forever about it. I should very, very strongly recommend you to get it as in the historical way it may appeal to you even more than to me. <It touches in one place tho' very briefly on your penchant, and is from time to time interesting in 'that way'.> I expect you are now heartily sick of the subject!

The 1st volume of Johnson has arrived and I am now started on it: I also discovered among the piles of trash of the hospital Blackwood's 'Incredible Adventures'[12] and a ragged copy containing some of Tennyson. Of the former I have read 2 stories, excellent of his style but I feel it a waste of time in these precious days. Tennyson, too, never raises any great enthusiasm in me. I am starting G. Eliot's 'Middlemarch'[13] to night. So, you see I am in clover. Do write soon again or I shall begin to feel neglected –

Yours
Jack

12 Algernon Henry Blackwood, *Incredible Adventures* (1914).
13 George Eliot, *Middlemarch* (1871–2).

TO HIS FATHER (LP V: 291–2):

[No. 10 British Red Cross Hospital,]
Le Tréport
22 February 1918

My dear Papy,

Your letter of the 17th has just arrived, with the enclosure, for which many thanks: a widening experience of other people's parents has taught me to value these things more than I once did, both for themselves and what they mean. That suggests literary possibilities: there is already a book called 'Other people's children',[14] but why not a companion volume 'Other people's parents' – in our schooldays we have most of us suffered from time to time at the hands of these irrelevant beings.

It is one of the punishments – to be sure, richly deserved – of a bad correspondant, that when at last he does write, his letter usually crosses the next one from his victim. I hope that you have before this got the longer letter which apparently had not come when you wrote yours.

I don't think there is need to worry if at any future time you hear of my being in hospital merely with illness. Even supposing it to be fairly serious, it is a more natural and easy kind of danger than that of the front: as well, there is always the rest, the unaccustomed comforts, and at the end the possibility of leave. In this case I am afraid I have not been bad enough.

I am sending you in this two photographs of my room at Univ. They were taken by my friend Moore shortly before I left Oxford, but remained undeveloped for a long time and have lately been sent to me by his mother. The room is not of much personal interest, as everything in it belonged to another man – I think I mentioned that at the time. But I daresay you may care to see them. Do you remember it used to be one of my dreams that I might some day entertain you and the Knock there together. As you said, 'That would be a symposium of the gods'. What crack there would have been! With what an added zest we would have drunk in the man's 'statements of fact' in the hope of chuckling over them between ourselves later on. Who knows? At any rate we can hope that you and I will some time see Oxford together.

The picture of our Warnie attending an A-murican proffessor's lecture from the chair of Poker is good. But I'm afraid the psychology of the

14 John Habberton, *Other People's Children* (1877).

card player will always baffle me as it has baffled you. I had as soon spend the evening building card houses – much sooner watch the picture in the red of the fire.

I have discovered that optimism about the war increases in an inverse ratio to the optimist's proximity to the line. Was our Colonel so hopeful a month ago? But indeed I'm afraid I must live up to our family reputation, for certainly I can't see any bright prospects at present. The conditions at home are almost as bad as anything we once fabled of starvation in Germany: spirits will be more pacific every day on short commons: there seems to be 'spiritual wickedness in high places'[15] (I think it was Smugy who told us that this text should be rendered 'wickedness of spirits in the upper regions of the air' – Satan being 'Prince of the air' and the evil hosts finding there the parade ground par excellence).

Poor old Mr. Patterson! As you say, we cannot miss a single detail out of the picture of home without a sense of regret. The longer we are absent from it and the more different the scenes in which we are compelled to live, the more eagerly we prize even its most irrelevant features. The sight of Campbell across the fields – the hideous palm like thing beside the front avenue – the broken glass in the etching in the upstairs passage. Mr. Patterson was en[titled] to some fame too for his famous mot 'Not convenient'. We avoided him often in our walks and are sorry that there will be no necessity to avoid him again.[16] He was, in short, one of the 'old familiar faces'.[17]

Now there is a thing we quote very often, but I never read till the other day the little poem of Lambs from which it comes: I don't know if you were in the same plight: if so, it would give you a few minutes pleasure – if it is in any of our imperfect editions of Lamb.

I am ordering a couple of books of Vergil from my bookseller in London, and if I find that I get on with these I shall order something equally pleasant and simple in Greek. German and Italian I fear must go to the wall: of course I read a French book from time to time and seek opportunities of speaking it – but one sees very little of the natives. I am also still at Boswell, and have also begun 'Middlemarch'. You see I am quite 'caught' by George Eliot's books.

15 Ephesians 6:12.

16 William Hugh Patterson (see note 25 to letter of 19 October 1913) died on 6 February 1918.

17 Charles Lamb, 'The Old Familiar Faces', l. 3: 'All, all are gone, the old familiar faces'.

I have now almost written my pen out of ink, and – perhaps my reader out of patience: but 'out of the abundance of the heart'[18] and as well there will be days when I cannot write much. I have been out once or twice, and can't say how much longer I shall be here. Write as often and as long (grammar!) as you can.

your loving,
son Jack

TO HIS FATHER (LP V: 301):

[France
5 March 1918]

My dear Papy,

I have been living at such a rush since I left hospital that it needed this battle and your probable anxiety to make me write. I am out of the fighting area, but of course we are not enjoying the old peaceful trench warfare I knew before Le Treport. We have just come back from a four days tour in the front line during which I had about as many hours sleep: then when we got back to this soi-disant rest, we spent the whole night digging. Under these conditions I know you will excuse me from much letter writing: but I will try and let you know that I am safe from time to time.

your loving son
Jack

TO HIS FATHER (LP V: 304):

[France]
8 April 1918

My dear Papy,

Just another hurried line to tell you that I am still safe and well. We have had a fairly rough time, though we were not really in the thick of it. I have lost one or two of my best friends and in particular a fellow called Perrett who used to be at Malvern, and who got a bit in the eye. It is a long time since I heard from you.

your loving son
Jack

---

18 Matthew 12:34.

The Germans launched their great spring offensive on 21 March with the additional troops drawn from the Eastern Front following the collapse of Russia. This was the worst crisis of the war and it galvanized the War Cabinet into action. The Prime Minister, David Lloyd George, took over the direction of the War Office on 23 March and the nation was soon transporting 30,000 men a day to France. Even so, the Allies were disintegrating, and on 3 April Marshal Foch took over supreme command. He was just able to halt the advance of the Germans when they were within 40 miles of Paris. 'With our backs to the wall and believing in the justice of our case, each must fight to the end,' declared Field Marshal Douglas Haig, chief of the British forces on the Western Front. The Germans' second putsch came on 9 to 25 April. On 3 April Lewis was among those who took part in the Battle of Arras. The particular part of the battle he took part in was centred on Riez du Vinage. In his official History of the 1st Battalion The Somerset Light Infantry (Prince Albert's) July 1st 1916 to the end of the War, *Everard Wyrall gives an account of the battle that took place between 14 and 16 April:*

> *As the leading Somerset men approached the eastern exits of Riez, the enemy launched a counter-attack from east of the village and the northern end of the Bois de Pacaut. This counter-attack was at once engaged with Lewis-gun and rifle fire and about 50 per cent of the Germans were shot down. Of the remainder about half ran away and the other half ran towards the Somerset men with their hands in the air crying out 'Kamerad!' and were made prisoners...*
>
> *When dawn broke on the 15th a considerable number of Germans in full marching order were seen: they were advancing in twos and threes into shell holes from houses north and north-east of Riez and from the northern end of Bois de Pacaut. Heavy rifle fire and Lewis-gun fire was opened on them, serious casualties being inflicted, and if a serious counter-attack was intended it was definitely broken up, for no further action was taken by the evening: his stretcher-bearers were busy for the rest of the day...*
>
> *About noon on the 16th the enemy opened a trench-mortar and artillery fire on the line held by the Somerset men...A little later he was observed massing immediately north-east of Riez with the obvious intention of wresting the village from the Somersets...About 2 p.m. the Germans were seen retiring in twos and*

threes: they had given up the struggle, having found the stout opposition put up by the Somersets impossible to break down. The results of this minor enterprise were splendid: (i) The village of Riez du Vinage had been captured; (ii) a battery of British field guns and a battery of 4.5 howitzers, taken by the enemy, had been recaptured; (iii) sixteen light machine guns and four heavy machine guns were taken: a Vickers gun was also recaptured – making a total of 21; (iv) a heavy mortar on wheels was taken, but it was not possible to get it away before the Somersets were relieved; (v) at least one German battalion, or the equivalent, was put out of action; 135 prisoners were taken: 60 dead Germans were seen in the village and probably 200 other casualties were inflicted on the enemy. A statement in the Battalion Diary, however, to the effect that 'never before have such targets been presented, or such execution done by the bullet', is hardly correct, for during the War there were many instances of the enemy's troops advancing in massed formation and being shot down in hundreds, if not in thousands. That the Somerset men had taken full advantage of the opportunities presented them, is shown by the fact that one Lewis gunner fired 2,000 rounds from his gun during the period, whilst a rifleman fired in one day from his own rifle 400 rounds.

The casualties of the 1st Battalion between 14th and 16th April were: 2/Lieut. L. B. Johnson died of wounds (15/4/18) and 2/Lieuts. C. S. Lewis, A. G. Rawlence, J. R. Hill and C. S. Dowding wounded: in other ranks the estimated losses were 210 killed, wounded and missing. (pp. 293–5)

TO HIS FATHER (LP V: 307):

[Liverpool Merchants Mobile Hospital,
Étaples]
16 April 1918

My dear Papy,

I am slightly wounded and am now in Hospital and will let you know my definite address as soon as possible.

yours,
Jack[19]

19 This note was written in an unknown hand, presumably that of a hospital nurse.

TO HIS FATHER (LP V: 307):

[Liverpool Merchants Mobile Hospital,
Étaples]
17 April 1918

My dear P.,

I have come down the line and my address is 'Liverpool Merchants Mobile Hospital, Etaples'. Getting on all right but cant write properly yet as my left arm is still tied up and its hard to manage with one. Please write soon.

your loving son,
Jack

Shortly after Jack was taken to the hospital at Étaples, on the Strait of Dover, his father received a telegram from the War Office saying: '2nd. Lt. C. S. Lewis Somerset Light Infantry wounded April fifteenth' (LP V: 308). Albert interpreted this to mean 'severely wounded', and was of course very worried. Warnie, having completed the course at the Mechanical Transport School of Instruction, had been stationed at a camp near the village of Behucourt near Doullens since 8 March. On learning from his father on 24 April that Jack had been 'severely wounded', he borrowed a motor bike and rode the 50 miles from Doullens through Frévent, Hesdin and Montreuil to the hospital at Étaples. 'You can't let your mind dwell on imaginary fears,' he told his father on 13 May, 'when you are trying to get your best out of machinery – roaring along the straight bits of road and nursing your engine over the rough' (LP V: 315). He made the return trip as soon as he had seen his brother, and writing to his father on the evening of 24 April, he said:

> *I don't know who was responsible for the phrase 'severely wounded', but it gave me a desperately bad fright. As a matter of fact you will be glad to hear that [Jack] is not much the worse, and is in better spirits than I have seen him for a long time. He was in great fettle and we had a long crack...A shell burst close to where he was standing, killing a Sergeant, and luckily for 'It' [Jack] he only stopped three bits: one in the cheek and two in the hands: he then crawled back and was picked up by a stretcher bearer.* (LP V: 309)

TO HIS FATHER (LP V: 312–13):

[Liverpool Merchants Mobile Hospital,
Étaples]
4 May [1918]

My dear Papy,

Many thanks for the smokes and also for the letter which I was particularly glad to get, as I had not heard from you for so long. I am very sorry – and angry – that you [have] been through a lot of unnecessary worry and anxiety owing to the carelessness of some fool at the War Office, who – as Arthur informs me – told you some rubbish about my being hit in both arms and in the face.

As a matter of fact I was really hit in the back of the left hand, on the left leg from behind and just above the knee, and in the left side just under the arm pit. All three were only flesh wounds. The myth about being hit in the face arose, I imagine, from the fact that I got a lot of dirt in the left eye which was closed up for a few days, but is now alright. I still can't lie on my side (neither the bad one nor the other one) but otherwise I lead the life of an ordinary mortal and my temperature is alright. So there is no need for any anxiety at all.

I was surprised the day before yesterday by a visit from two ladies – a Miss McConnell and a friend. Apparently you know her brother. Ought I to? For the life of me I can't remember any one of that name. Whoever she is she was very agreeable and it didn't make any difference.

The correspondants of mine – Mrs. Moore and a man called Johns in the Somersets – seem to think that a number of letters to me were sent to my home address when I first went to Le Treport. If you have any letters of mine, will you please send them on? I suppose they haven't been silly enough to send my valise home have they?

Warnie has been down to see me and seems in good health and spirits. If only leave would start again he might manage to be at home with me as he is due for it now.

I hope you are keeping well and not worrying about me, for as you see, I am getting on excellently.

your loving son
Jack

TO HIS FATHER (LP V: 316–17):

Same adress.
[Étaples]
14/6/18 [14 May 1918]

My dear Papy,

Thank you for the letter, the enclosure, and the other 'far wandered' letters. I must confess that when Warnie turned up here I didn't realise through what possible difficulties or by what exertions he had come: I understand now 'video proboque'.[20]

I expect to be sent across in a few days time, of course as a stretcher case: indeed whatever my condition they would have to send me in that way, because I have no clothes. This is a standing joke out here – the mania which people at the dressing stations have for cutting off a wounded man's clothes whether there is any need for it or not. In my case the tunic was probably beyond hope, but I admit that I mourn the undeserved fate of my breeches. Unfortunately I was unconscious when the sacrilege took place and could not very well argue the point.

I am doing exceedingly well and can lie on my right side (not of course on my left), which is a great treat after you have been on your back for a few weeks. In one respect I was wrong in my last account of my wounds: the one under my arm is worse than a flesh wound, as the bit of metal which went in there is now in my chest, high up under my 'pigeon chest' as shown: this however is nothing to worry about as it is doing no harm. They will leave it there and I am told that I can carry it about for the rest of my life without any evil results.

Aunt Lily[21] keeps up a sharp fire of literature – Browning, Emerson, Mill (on 'the subjection of women")[22] and 'The Scotsman'. How on earth can I be supposed to be interested in 'The Scotsman'? However there are

---

20 Ovid, *Metamorphoses*, Book 7, ll. 19–21: 'sed trahit invitam nova vis, aliudque cupido, / mens aliud suadet: video meliora proboque, / deteriora sequor'. 'But a strange force drags me against my will, and desire persuades me one way, reason another: I see the better and even approve it – still, I follow the worse.'

21 Mrs Lilian 'Lily' Hamilton Suffern, who is mentioned in note 73 to the letter of 22 December 1914, was the sister of Florence Hamilton Lewis, and Jack's aunt. She was an ardent suffragette who had quarrelled with everyone in her family. She had been married to a Scotsman, William Suffern, who died in 1913. Although she was constantly on the move, she was living in Edinburgh at the time. Mrs Suffern was particularly fond of Jack and bombarded him with books and a pseudo-metaphysical correspondence. See **The Hamilton Family** in the Biographical Appendix.

22 John Stuart Mill, *The Subjection of Women* (1869).

one or two Scotch patients here to whom I hand it over: so I can truthfully tell her that they 'are read and enjoyed'.

My friend Mrs Moore is in great trouble – Paddy has been missing for over a month and is almost certainly dead. Of all my own particular set at Keble he has been the first to go, and it is pathetic to remember that he at least was always certain that he would come through.

In spite of Aunt Lily's library I have been battening on other fare. 'Old Mortality'[23] which I found disappointing, and now 'Barchester Towers'[24] with which I am delighted. This brings me to Martha's wedding.[25] (The connection being 'What a pity that she too has not married a Bishop, since she could run a diocese at least as well as Mrs. Proudie').[26] Give her any message from me which you think suitable. Hoping that you keep well and cheerful, I am,

your loving son
Jack

Although his mother did not receive confirmation until September, Paddy Moore died in March 1918 during the battle at Pargny. The story of his part in the war was summarized, from information supplied by Mrs Moore, in his school magazine The Cliftonian, *No. CCXCV (May 1918), p. 225:*

> *2nd-Lieutenant E.F.C. Moore. He joined the Rifle Brigade after the usual training, and was in action in France in the great German attack which began on March 21. He was reported missing on March 24, and it is now feared that he cannot have escaped with his life. The Adjutant of his battalion writes: 'I have to tell you that your very gallant son was reported missing on the 24th of last month. He was last seen on the morning of that day with a few men defending a position on a river bank against infinitely superior numbers of the enemy. All the other officers and most of the*

23 Sir Walter Scott, *Old Mortality* (1816).

24 Anthony Trollope, *Barchester Towers* (1857).

25 Martha, the cook at Little Lea, was getting ready to marry a clergyman and move to Glenavy, County Antrim.

26 'Mrs. Proudie', a character in *Barchester Towers* and all Trollope's subsequent Barsetshire novels, is the tyrannical wife of the Bishop of Barchester.

men of his company have become casualties, and I fear it is impossible to obtain more definite information. He did really fine work on the previous night in beating off a party of Germans who had succeeded in rushing a bridgehead in our lines. We all feel his loss very deeply, and I cannot express too strongly our sympathy with you.'

TO ARTHUR GREEVES (W):

[Liverpool Merchants Mobile Hospital,
Étaples
23 May 1918]

My dear Arthur,

I was so glad to get your answer to day as it is the first 'answer' I've had for a long time – thro' my own neglect I admit.

I think your criticisms on my 'Literary Supplement' letter[27] were quite just, but I must give two reasons why I was led to write in such a style. In the first place I was rather stung by your gratuitous supposition that I had become a 'cheer-oh young man', and this naturally urged me into the opposite extreme of being what somebody calls 'a university prize prig'. Of course I don't mean to say that I didn't write throughout of things that really interested me and which I expected to interest you: but the general tone was probably influenced by that feeling. The second reason is this. The personal element naturally found a large field in my letters from Bookham and Univ. where all my life and surroundings were of interest to us both: but here, where everything I do & suffer is dull and repulsive, I don't turn to description and details which would bore me to write and – probably – you to read. If you think that I look to you only for abstract interests and no longer yearn for the old intimacy, the teas, the laughter the walks and the comparing of books – you are very much mistaken, mon ami.

(Talking about comparing of books, if you are still minded to sell your Trollope you will now find a purchaser in me. A chance copy of 'Barchester Towers' has quite converted me and I am now all a-gog to read his others, so that I will certainly take your whole set if I may. By the way, this is an advantage – the only one – of being in the army: I have always plenty of money for anything I want. To any one in my irresponsible

27 So called because of his lengthy comments on Cellini's *Memoirs*.

position the despised pay of a second lieutenant is a never-empty purse, unless he chooses to waste it on prostitutes, restaurants and tailors, as the gentiles do.)

When I see you face to face I will tell you any war impressions quite freely *at your request* – and not otherwise: for it is very proper that you should make use of me if you ever happen to want to know how certain things feel – but on the other hand there is no reason why I should bore you with a subject that we have always disliked, if you do *not* want.

Congratulations old man. I am delighted that you have had the moral courage to form your own opinions <independently,> in defiance of the old taboos. I am not sure that I agree with you: but, as you hint in your letter, <this penchant is a sort of mystery only to be fully understood by those who are made that way – and my views on it can be at best but emotion.>

You will be surprised and I expect, not a little amused to hear that my views at present are getting almost monastic about all the lusts of the flesh. They seem to me to extend the dominion of matter over us: and, out here, where I see spirit continually dodging matter (shells, bullets, animal fears, animal pains) I have formulated my equation Matter= Nature=Satan. And on the other side Beauty, the only spiritual & not-natural thing that I have yet found. Does all this bore you?

I think my stilted style must be due to the fact that I read 'Old Mortality' a short time ago and am at present in the midst of 'Guy Mannering'. The former I thought very disappointing but am quite pleased with the latter, tho', truth to tell, I enjoyed 'Barchester Towers' much more. I have got here but not yet begun Blackwood's new book 'The Promise of the Air':[28] perhaps you read the verdict of the Times L.S. that this is his first really serious book.[29] I hope it may be true.

Strange! how wrongly one can read the simplest sentence: just reading over part of your letter I have realised for the first time that when you say you were 'driven' to town you mean driven in the car: I thought you meant 'driven' by circumstances of some sort. Now theres one of those little things which are useless on paper but would have made us roar with laughter if we were together.

---

28 Algernon Henry Blackwood, *The Promise of Air* (1918).

29 *The Times Literary Supplement* (9 May 1918), p. 219.

By the way, are you allowed to go up & downstairs freely these days? If so, it occurs to me that it would be a very good idea for you to act as a sort of librarian to the little-end-room when I return to my penance. I mean, the key would be left in the bookcase and I should like you to go there frequently & see that they were alright, and borrow or examine anything you wanted & put in suitable places any new volumes I sent you. This would keep me in touch with my books to some extent and save the room from looking disused when I come back. What do you say?

I have only come across a few references to the Dorian customs: I hope Carpenter does not fall into the error common to enthusiasts, of reading into ancient institutions more than is really there. However, of course I have never studied the subject and can't give an opinion.

I was to have been sent across to England last night, but we were heavily bombed, so of course all traffic stopped. It is interesting to note that an air-raid here frightened me much more than anything I encountered at the front: you feel so helpless in bed, knowing you can't walk or anything even if you get out of it. Unless the same things happen again I shall probably go, or at least the night after. I suppose it would be out of the question for you to come and see me in hospital in England for a few days? It would be a great something to look forward to & it would give you an opportunity to meet Mrs Moore.

I am tired now, old man, after a very disturbed night & a stifling day so I will dry up & just enclose a little song I wrote the other day, which I hope you will approve –

Yours ever
Jack

Song

Faeries must be in the woods
Or the satyr's merry broods,
Tritons in the summer sea,
Else how could the dead things be
Half so lovely as they are?
How could wreathèd star on star
Dusted o'er the wintry night,
Fill thy spirit with delight

And lead thee from this care of thine
Through a land of dreams divine
To the dearest heart's-desire,
Unless each pale & drifting fire
Were indeed a happy isle
Where eternal gardens smile
And golden globes of fruit are seen
Twinkling thro' the orchards green
Where the Other People go
On the soft sward to and fro?
Atoms dead could never thus
Wake the human heart of us,
Unless the beauty that we see
Part of endless beauty be,
Thronged with spirits that have trod
Where the bright foot-prints of God
Lie fresh upon the heavenly sod.[30]

TELEGRAM TO HIS FATHER (LP V: 319):

25 May 1918

Am in Endsleigh Palace Hospital, Endsleigh Gardens, London, Jack.

TO ARTHUR GREEVES (W):

[Endsleigh Palace Hospital,
Endsleigh Gardens,
London
29 May 1918]

Cher Ami,

I am sitting up in bed in the middle of a red sunset to answer this evening's letter straightaway. Your letters set me thinking of so many old interests that I cannot go on with my book.

First a word or two as to my present estate: I am in a vastly comfortable hospital, where we are in separate rooms & have tea in the morning & big broad beds & everything the heart of man could desire and best

30 This poem was later to appear under the same name, but with considerable alterations, in Lewis's *Spirits in Bondage* (1919), pp. 73–4. It is reprinted in his *Collected Poems* (1994).

of all, in close communication with all the bookshops of London. Of course you can easily understand what other and greater reasons there are for me to be happy. There are still two pieces of shrapnel in my chest, but they give me no discomfort: <Mrs Moore and> I are always hoping that it *will* start to give some trouble and thus secure me a longer illness (This is quite like the Malvern days again, isn't it?).

The thing in your last letter with which I most want to disagree is the remark about Beauty and nature; apparently I did not make myself very clear. You say that nature is beautiful, and that is the view we all start with. But let us see what we mean. If you take a tree, for instance, you call it beautiful because of its shape, colour and motions, and perhaps a little because of association. Now these colours etc are sensations in my eye, produced by vibrations on the aether between me and the tree: the real tree is something quite different – a combination of colourless, shapeless, invisible atoms. It follows then that neither the tree, nor any other material object can be beautiful in itself: I can never see them as they are, and if I could it would give me no delight. The beauty therefore is not in matter at all, but is something purely spiritual, arising mysteriously out of the relation between me & the tree: or perhaps as I suggest in my Song, out of some indwelling spirit behind the matter of the tree – the Dryad in fact.

You see the conviction is gaining ground on me that after all Spirit does exist; and that we come in contact with the spiritual element by means of these 'thrills'. I fancy that there is Something right outside time & place, which did not create matter, as the Christians say, but is matter's great enemy: and that Beauty is the call of the spirit in that something to the spirit in us. You see how frankly I admit that my views have changed: I hope I don't bore you.

<I admit the associations of the word paederasty are unfortunate but you should rise above that. As well what does 'Uranian' mean – it ought to mean 'Heavenly' as far as my knowledge goes, and I will stick to the word that I understand in preference.>

I don't agree with you about Trollope's being mamby pamby: in fact the sentimental part seems to me very slightly sketched and only to serve as a turning point for all the delightful 'Austinesque' work about the Mrs Proudie's etc. I have now read the 'Warden' and am more than half way through 'Dr Thorne'.[31] I cannot understand why you got tired of him, I

31 Anthony Trollope, *The Warden* (1855); *Doctor Thorne* (1858).

should have thought he was so very much in your line: but indeed one can never really say what will please another person.

I told you I was reading Blackwood's new one 'The Promise of Air': it is very disappointing, being merely a long & tedious expansion of a theory that could have been explained in a single essay. Although it is in story form nothing ever happens: I'm afraid if he goes on being 'serious' after this fashion we shall have lost a good romancer for a bad mystic.

Can you imagine how I enjoyed my journey to London? First of all the sight and smell of the sea, that I have missed for so many long and weary months, and then the beautiful green country seen from the train: I suppose its because I've been shut up in a hut so long, but I think I never enjoyed anything so much as that scenery – all the white in the hedges, and the fields so full of buttercups that in the distance they seemed to be of solid gold: and everything such a bright, bright green. I am sure our hills look lovely now and the wood must be full of life and sweet smells.

Yes, after all our old conversations I *can* feel otherwise about the lusts of the flesh: is not desire merely a kind of sugar-plum that nature gives us to make us breed, as she does the beetles and toads so that both we and they may beget more creatures to struggle in the same net: Nature, or the common order of things, has really produced in man a sort of Frankenstein who is learning to shake her off. For man alone of all things can master his instincts.

From my window I see a big flat plain of houses and beyond that actually a green hill with trees on it, which I am told is the aristocratic district of High Hampstead. In the foreground is the Euston station hotel – bringing old, old memories. 'Mais ou sont les neiges.'

Your quotation from Pater expresses my attitude to philosophy exactly: I don't really think it will teach me the truth, but I do think it will supply me with thoughts & feelings that I may be able to turn into poetry. As you turn all kinds of nourishment into blood. I was glad to see Willie (I suppose 'Bill' since his marriage)[32] he seems in good form.

Good bye, old man, write by return.

Yours ever

Jack

---

32 Arthur's brother, William Edward Greeves, who married Marion Janet Cadbury on 14 February 1918.

TO HIS FATHER (LP V: 320–1):

Endsleigh Gardens.
[London]
30 May 1918

My dear Papy,

I hope that you got my telegram and that I will soon hear from you, and not only hear but receive a visit in the aristocratic neighbourhood of Euston. You will be able to come over, will you not, if only for a few days? We must get Kirk up to meet you and have a famous crack. In the meantime, will you please send me my new brown suit, and also, if possible, a pair of black brogue shoes: I ought to have several. It is allowed to wear ordinary clothes here until I can get a uniform made. This is merely a note, as you are already heavily in my debt in the matter of letters. Hoping to hear soon, I am

your loving son
Jack

TO ARTHUR GREEVES (W):

[Endsleigh Palace Hospital,
London
3 June 1918]

My dear Arthur,

Your letter of the 1st arrived this morning. I am very sorry that you are getting bored with our 'tree' argument (the Dry Tree as it might well be called from the nature of the discussions to which it gives rise) for I am afraid I cannot let the subject drop without refuting the heresies which you started in to-day's letter.

First, as to the colour of the atom, I would remind you that atoms are regarded as all identically the same – as the original world-stuff, and if therefore they had colour all things would be coloured the same. And to analyse colour ninety-two million miles away the action of certain vibrations in the sun sets up a wave on the ether which travels to the atom under your consideration: this sets up certain other vibrations in the atom which again sends off another wave along the ether towards your eye. When this reaches the tissue of your eye it sets up more action which travels along a nerve and produces in your brain a sensation which we call greenness. Here for the first time we reach the colour – in your brain, not in all these vibrations of atoms. Magnify your atom to infinity, and still your consciousness has no *direct* communion with it. All you can ever say is that certain sensations arise in your brain: you suppose (which in itself was doubted by Berkeley and other idealists) that there is some exterior cause for these: but what that exterior cause is like in itself you do not know and never can know. Suppose this vibration from the atom never happened to strike an eye, but went on for ever into space – where then is your greenness? No – the whole exterior world can only make itself known to us by certain sensations which it produces on our brain in a complicated manner, and it is simply a habit of mind which makes us call these impressions (colour, shape, sound etc) the thing-in-itself. Hence as I said before, beauty cannot be in the material thing.

Of course there is another simpler argument, without going into abstruse regions. If beauty were really in the tree, then two people who both had normal eyes would be bound to see the same beauty. But nothing is easier than to find two people one of whom would see beauty and the other see no beauty in the same tree. Therefore the beauty cannot be in the tree but in some obscure and non-material point of view or relation between the mind of the perciever and the sensations which the tree – very indirectly – causes in that mind. I have done: are you bored beyond endurance?

Perhaps you feel that we are wandering away from the grounds that supplied our earlier interests in common and first brought us together. I hope not: I like to think of our interests as a circle which may increase in size but whose centre is always the same. For myself I think I am true to the old cannons – romantic beauty, eeriness, terror, homeliness, solidity – & absurdity. These were the gods we worshipped in the golden age, were they not mon vieux?

By the same token, I have been reading since this morning an incomparably homely book, of which I am having a copy sent to you – 'The Private Papers of Henry Ryecroft' by G. Gissing (Constable 1/-).[33] Gissing's name I have often heard, but I have no idea what else he wrote. This is a collection of very loose, spontaneous essays, about books and other quiet interests – including food. He has some splendid things to say about the glory of 'tea', so homely & cheery after a long walk. There is hardly a bad piece in the whole book, and it is a very companionable

33 George Robert Gissing, *The Private Papers of Henry Ryecroft* (1903).

volume to fill up the spaces of serious reading with, or to read over a lonely meal.

Are you lonely these days, or are you over-much oppressed with visitors? I should like to hear from you a fuller account of your cousin Gribbon: I remember him – with a shudder – at Campbell. I hear he is enormously clever and knows all things: I expect he will pulverize me – rusted as I am with a year's barbarity – if I should ever meet him.[34] But I mustn't talk thus or you will perhaps think, like somebody in a French play 'que je vous fasse l'honneur d'etre jaloux'.[35]

Spenser, I am sure, would be greatly surprised to hear that Britomart was a type of [illegible] – considering she is represented as loving Artegall the knight of Justice; I don't remember her being described as having a 'man's heart' in the real Faerie Queene, and the book which you mention probably uses that phraze in the conventional sense as 'having a man's courage'. But how I love to hear you say 'I came across so-and-so in a book this morning': it conjures up such visions of those old happy hours when I sat surrounded by my little library and browsed from book to book. You, who have never lost that life, cannot understand the longing with which I look back to it.

By the way, haven't you got a reddy-brown MS. book of mine containing 'Lullaby' and several other of my later poems? I wish you would send it here, as I have decided to copy out all my work of which I approve and get it typed as a step towards possible publishing. Even if nobody will have them a complete typed copy would be a great convenience.

Wouldn't it be glorious if I were writing you the last letter of a term at Bookham, perhaps with an 'instalment', with all the rich harvest of the pleasant term behind me and the glorious liesure of the long summer holidays (with after dinner walks to the shrine of Tigliath-Pileser) before me. I knew then that those were good days, but I think now that I didn't prize them enough. Ahem!, the sunset appears to be making me sentimental: & yet its not sentiment at all but very certain truth. Doesn't the word 'ahem' breathe of old-fashioned novels?

---

34 Arthur's cousin Charles Edward Gribbon (1898–1938), mentioned in note 23 to the letter of 26 February 1916, had been a pupil at Campbell College 1904–14, and became a professional artist. Some of his pictures were bought by the Friends of the National Collection of Ireland.

35 'that I should do you the honour of being jealous'.

You accuse me of talking, 'as your own father might talk': and perhaps that is one thing you may find in me now – a vein of asceticism, almost of puritan practice without the puritan dogma. I believe in no God, least of all in one that would punish me for the 'lusts of the flesh':[36] but I do believe that I have in me a spirit, a chip, shall we say, of universal spirit; and that, since all good & joyful things are spiritual & non-material, I must be careful not to let matter (= nature = Satan, remember) get too great a hold on me, & dull the one spark I have.

Yours ever
Jack

TO HIS FATHER (LP V: 326–7):

Endsleigh Palace Hospital
[London]
12 June 1918

My dear Papy,

Thank you for both the letters, as the 'essay with enclosures' has followed me here, and indeed arrived shortly after the one I wrote, venturing to suggest that my score of letters was still one up. Peccavi: I most humbly apologise. 'And you wid a bronchitis in you.' (By the way it is not a whole shell in me, only a bit of one.) Seriously, I hope that before this you have got over any suggestion of the old trouble: you cannot be too careful in warding it off.

The brown suit arrived safely, together with some collars and ties which I had forgotten to ask for, but which either you or Mary had thoughtfully put in. I am now up and dressed and have been out a few times: you can well imagine how delightful it is for me to wear decent clothes again – to have pockets without buttons, and to be able to change one's tie from day to day. I have written to the transport officer of the battalion about my valise, but so far there is no answer: poor man, I expect he has other things to think about than my kit. And – who knows – perhaps even now a Teutonic unter offizier is sleeping in my blankets and improving his English on my bits of books.[37] Which reminds me,

36 *Book of Common Prayer*, the Catechism: 'I should renounce the devil and all his works, the pomps and vanity of this wicked world, and all the sinful lusts of the flesh.'

37 Warnie wrote to his father on 7 June saying: 'It is splendid to know that our "It" [Jack] is safely home at last. I confess it made me very uneasy when I heard that those damned hounds had been bombing base hospitals. And talking about that, did you see

though the reproach is usually the other way, on the only occasion when we took any prisoners, I was able to talk a little German to their officer, though he could speak no English to me.

My first day out here was enlivened by a taxi accident – some girl with a lorry ran into the cab in which I was, causing considerable damage to both machines but doing no harm otherwise. Since then I have had a solicitor's clerk round here asking me interminable questions: I have often been reminded of your friend's answer, 'I thought some damned fool would be sure to ask me, so I measured'. I consider that when the fates arrange little varieties of this sort for a man in search of peace, it is a very doubtful 'jeu d'esprit'.

I have since added to my new knowledge of Trollope 'The Warden' and 'Dr. Thorne'. Although it may seem strange that Warnie and I both neglect books that are at home and then afterwards read them elsewhere, there is a reason. A book must find you in the right mood, and its mere presence on a shelf will not create that mood, tho' it lie there for years: as well, when you meet 'in a strange land'[38] a book that is associated with home, it has for that very reason an attraction which it would not have at ordinary times. I am now at work, and very much at work on Hume's 'Treatise of Human Nature',[39] a new Maeterlinck and a new volume of Swinburne. I keep up a very brisk fire of correspondence on Literary and pseudo-scientific subjects with my Aunt Suffern: at this distance she is entertaining, but in a tête à tête 'no, a thousand times no'.

By the way, I have never seen anything but the proofs of those photos of us both, and I should be glad if you would send me the best. Which reminds me, what was the final verdict on your portrait? Is it still a sojourner in the drawing room? But we must settle all these things when I come home.

It is a great pity that you are laid up: there would be points about London for us two – I should like to go with you to the Abbey and the Temple and a few other places. (Just as I am making Arthur green with envy by my accounts of Charing Cross Road, 'a mile of bookshops'.) On Sunday I am going down to Bookham to see the sage: if only you could

---

that the fellow who was caught red handed was admitted into the hospital he had bombed, and had his wound treated. I'd have given him treatment forsooth.'

38 Exodus 2:22: 'I have been a stranger in a strange land.'

39 David Hume, *A Treatise of Human Nature* (1739).

make the same pilgrimage! I must go and be massaged now, take care of yourself.

your loving son,
Jack

TO ARTHUR GREEVES (W):

[Endsleigh Palace Hospital,
London]
Monday [17 June 1918]

My dear Galahad,

Now will I make you envious. On Friday night I went to Drury Lane to hear 'The Valkyrie'.[40] The dream of years has been realised, and without disillusionment: I have had thrills and delights of the real old sort, I have felt as I felt five years ago.

We had difficulty in getting seats, and from those which we had we could only see one side of the stage. I was also much worried by the people that sat near us. Not that they were philistines and talked, but their very enthusiasm made them a nuisance. One little man in front of me was so moved that at several interesting points he stood up, until at last I became so exasperated that I caught him by his coat tails and pulled him into his seat. Another, who was following the score, kept on giving vent to quite audible criticisms such as 'Louder, Louder!' or 'No, no, no' whenever the conductor's design differed from his own.

But the performance was beyond all words. The first act as you remember is in Hunding's hut with the tree growing in it: and towards the end you remember how Siegmund draws the sword and how they throw open the great doors at the back. This showed us a most beautiful scene of distant snow covered peaks and a wild valley. The lighting gave a really unusual impression of spring moon light, and that combined with the glorious love-music of the orchestra (you remember the spring song?) simply swept you away – and then all the time creeping in under this the faint horn blown motive of the sword and the far-off tinkling hammers to remind you of the Niblungs – oh, ami, it was simply heaven! But the next act which opens in 'A wild rocky place' – represented not conventionally but with real sympathy – and Brünhilde singing 'Moi-a-

---

40 The performance on 14 June of Wagner's *The Valkyrie* was conducted by Sir Thomas Beecham and there is a notice about it in *The Times* (15 June 1918), p. 3.

a-hei' (you know) was even better. She, it is true, was a trifle full-breasted and operatic, but as the interest of the scene went on, one forgot that. Wotan was magnificent whenever he came on, and all his music is splendid – there are whole hours of music just as wonderful as the little bits we know: the singing was in English, and so clear and un-strained that with my knowledge of the story, I could follow nearly all the dialogue, and so all the poetic and romantic pleasure came to help the musical. As a spectacle the third act was the best, where Brünhilde is hiding from Wotan. The stage is almost dark, lit only from time to time by flashes of lightening, as the angry god draws nearer and nearer and at last enters in a glare of red light, glinting on the huge raven-wings of his helmet and the rings of his mail – one gleaming figure in that sinister gloom – and the music, I cannot describe it. Most unfortunately it was so late that I had to come away before the end, and miss the fire music: but I was so full of delights that I could hardly find it in my heart to grumble.

Looking back, what pleases me most was the training of all the singers together and the entire absence of strain: none of your Italian screaming and contortions. There was no famous name in the caste, and no-one except Brünhilde had a voice of any unusual power: but the beauty was that they never tried to sing louder than they could, and were content to sacrifice power to real beauty – playing into each other's hands and making it all musical dialogue NOT mere duets. You felt that they all loved the Ring and took it seriously not merely as an opportunity for noise. Sieglindë particularly, with a sweet voice and clear enunciation, *acted* very well, quietly & naturally not in the usual operatic style. And oh! the blessèd absence of a chorus! So you have my verdict that if the Ring is all like this it quite comes up to our old dreams, and that all Italian opera is merely a passtime compared with the great music-drama of Wagner. In spite of all our efforts we could not get a programme and so I cannot send you one.

To descend from the windswept eerie's of the swan-maidens to a further argument about the Dry Tree may seem bathos: but as you have agreed to go on with it, let us do so. The subject is of great interest too.

Of course we all start with the idea that our senses put us in direct contact with reality – you think that your eyes are windows by which your brain 'sees' the world. But science teaches you that your eye, or rather the nerve of your eye, is merely a telegraph wire. It's vibration produces a feeling in your brain which we call colour etc.: but what the

Something at the other end which starts the vibration may be, of this no human being can have any conception. No increase of our sensory keenness, no microscope or teloscope can put us in any direct relation with the Thing: we still remain dependant on this long chain of communications, travelling by vibration from atom to atom: and we can never have any proof that the sensation which it produces in our brain conveys any true idea of the external Thing. Nay the thing *must* be quite different from our conception of it: for we necessarily concieve it in terms of the senses – we think of any object as having a certain size, shape, colour and feel. But all these are only the names of our own sensations: take size, which may seem at first to be outside ourselves. On the table lies my pipe: if I wish to have an idea of the size of this I naturally handle it: in other words I send out a *will* from my brain (which I call 'moving my hand') and presently a set of impressions come back to me – smoothness, hardness, width and the rest. It is true that at the same time as these come along my touch-nerves another set of brown-ness, shininess, rotundity etc come along my visual-nerves. And if I repeat the action ten times I find that the same set of sight-impressions always accompanies the same set of touch-ones: in other words what looks a pipe, always feels a pipe too. But this brings me no nearer to the real pipe: I can only think of it as long, brown, smooth, hard and rounded: therefore think of it wrongly, since length, smoothness, brown-ness, hardness and rotundity are feelings in my brain, and cannot belong to the real pipe at all. (Shape, which was bothering you, is of course on the same footing as colour or hardness: it can only be apprehended thro' the same chain of communication, by the senses of touch or sight, and therefore is in me not in the external Thing). Hence you see we are driven to the conclusion that we have no knowledge of the external world: that it is concievable that there IS no external world at all, and that if it does exist it must be quite different from our usual ideas of it. A good many modern scientists think that 'matter' consists of atoms which are not (as we used to think) small solid bodies but merely points of force and that all the phenomena of matter can be attributed to the inter-action of these forces. If you are still interested in these subjects I will talk in another letter about the various conclusions which philosophers have drawn from this ignorance which we are forced to acknowledge, and the ways by which they have tried to escape from it.

I have sent you two books from Hatchards' of Picadilly: whether you have them already or would care to have them, I can't say, but you will have no difficulty in changing them. I finished my last letter in rather a hurry, and can't remember whether I referred to your drawing in them: I am glad you are going on with it. The absence of models, as far as hands, limbs, folds of clothes, etc go could be helped by the looking-glass, which I imagine is an excellent teacher. How fine it will be when you can get me up in your room again and show me all your new work and all your new treasures. I too shall have plenty for you to see: I have sent home a fine edition of Yeats which I have been wanting for ages, and have bought here Dent's Malory with designs by Beardesly. It is a beautiful book, with a handsome binding, good paper and a fair page: there are lovely chapter headings and decorations, and somehow a great big book suits Malory, doesn't it? In that same shop, Bain's, where I got this they showed me some of Morris's Kelmscott Press books, including the Chaucer, very rare and now at £82. I suppose it is bad taste on my part, but I don't care for Morris's type, it is much too ornate and difficult to read. Ordinary old black-letter I should much prefer.

By the way, <if you have alone established 'Uranianism' in your own mind as something virtuous and natural, I must remind you that for men in ordinary sexual arrangements, a promiscuous desire for every beautiful person you meet is usually disapproved of. Your talk about continually meeting people and having to conceal your feelings suggests that you have no intention of confining yourself to one love: but perhaps I have misunderstood you.>

On Sunday we were down at Bookham and I called at Gastons. You can imagine how strange it was to go back now among those old scenes and people.

I think I have talked enough now. Addio, write by return.

Yours

Jack

TO HIS FATHER (LP V: 329–31):

[Endsleigh Palace Hospital,
London
20? June 1918]

My dear Papy,

On Sunday I made my pilgrimage. Even to go to Waterloo was an adventure full of memories, and every station that I passed on the way down seemed to clear away another layer of the time that passed and bring me back to the old life.

Bookham was as its best: a mass of green, very pleasing to one 'that has been long in city pent'.[41] As I walked up to Gastons the familiar road was crowded with good people coming back from church, and I passed many a stuffy old couple whom I remembered well, though none of them recognised me. It was like being a ghost: I opened the gate of Kirk's garden almost with stealth and went on past the house, to the vegetable garden and the little wild orchard with the pond, where I had sat so often on hot Sunday afternoons, and practised skating with Terry when the long frost began two years ago.

And there among the cabbages, in his shirt and 'Sunday' trousers, there sure enough was the old man, still digging and smoking his villainous pipe. His back was towards me and I had come within a few paces of him before he turned and saw me. And so I was led into the house with much triumph and displayed to Mrs K., whom we found fussing with the maid just as of old. I have seldom spent a more delightful afternoon: what 'crack' we had, what reminiscences, how often my opinions were shown to be based ('bazed' as the sage pronounces it) on an insufficient knowledge of the subject! When I told him that it was by an English shell I was hit, it called forth a magnificent Tirade on the 'simple mathematical problem' of calculating how a gun's range would shorten as it got heated by firing – on the 'every school boy knows' lines.

I have bought an edition of Yeats[42] which I ordered the bookseller to send home and which should have arrived by this time. Of course I need not add that you are welcome to open the parcel, if you would care to. Arthur at any rate would like to see it, and if you replace the books in their boxes they will be safe from dust and damp until I come home. I hope you do not think it extravagant in me to have bought such a thing, for I knew it was a limited edition which would be very much dearer in a few years' time. In the same shop where I made this purchase, I'm afraid I gave myself away badly. What first tempted me to go in was a battered copy of Burton's Anatomy: as you know, I had been looking for this and thought here was an opportunity of picking up a cheap second hand

41 John Keats, 'To one who has been long in city pent' (1817), l. 1.

42 This was probably *The Collected Works of William Butler Yeats in Verse and Prose* in eight volumes, published in 1908 by the Shakespeare Head Press.

copy. I went in and requested a courtly old gentleman to let me see it. 'H'm', said I, glancing over the dirty little volume, 'it seems rather worn: haven't you a newer copy?' The gentleman looked at me in rather a pained way and said that he had not. 'Well, how much is it?' I asked, expecting a considerable reduction. 'Twenty-five guineas' said my friend with a bland smile. Ye Gods! Just think of it: there was I for the first time in my life fingering a really valuable old edition and asking for a 'NEWER' copy. I turned hot all over: and even you as you read, will blush for the credit of the clan. However, the old gentleman was very forgiving: he turned his treasury inside out for me. He showed me priceless old copies of Vergil and Rabelais, books from the Kelmscott Press, including the Chaucer at £82 and strange forgotten waifs of French literature with stiff engravings 'from the age of snuff boxes and fans'. And so what could I do but bring away the Yeats? Apropos of Beardsley, he told me that the 'fleshly' artist had often been in that shop and had finally gone the way of all mortal things without paying his account. Well, 'et ego in Arcadia Vixi,'[43] it is something to have been in the shop of James Bain even for an hour.

It seems that now-a-days one is sent from hospital to be kept for some time in a 'convalescent home' before going on leave. Of course I have asked to be sent to an Irish one, but there are only a few of these and they are already crowded: we must not therefore expect too much. But wherever I am I know that you will come and see me. You know I have some difficulty in talking of the greatest things: it is the fault of our generation and of the English schools. But at least you will believe that I was never before so eager to cling to every bit of our old home life and to see you. I know I have often been far from what I should in my relations to you, and have undervalued an affection and a generosity which (as I said somewhere else) an experience of 'other people's parents' has shown me in a new light. But, please God, I shall do better in the future. Come and see me. I am homesick, that is the long and the short of it.

I have been once or twice to the English Opera at Drury Lane and seen among other things my long desired 'Valkyrie' and Faust again – full of reminiscences of course. This week Mrs. Moore has been up on a visit to her sister who works at the War Office, and we have seen a good

---

43 'I too have lived in Arcadia.' Lewis was here altering the anonymous tomb inscription, 'Et in Arcadia ego', which is often depicted on classical paintings.

deal of each other. I think it some comfort to her to be with someone who was a friend of Paddy's and is a link with the Oxford days: she has certainly been a very, very good friend to me.

I was much cheered this afternoon by a visit from Kelsie [Ewart]: who is in excellent spirits but looked to me very poorly – perhaps it is my imagination. I will wire to you as soon as there is any talk of my being moved. Do not count on Ireland: but at all events, come. The wound on my leg is still bothering me a bit, although it was the smallest I had. The bandage – just above the knee – is always slipping, and descended to my ankle the other day in the middle of Piccadilly, necessitating urgent calls for a taxi.

Good night: nurse the old chest and write soon and long,
your loving son
Jack

TO HIS FATHER (LP VI: 17–18):

[Ashton Court,
Long Ashton,
Clifton, Bristol
29 June 1918][44]
Saturday.

My dear Papy,

Surely this is the most unfortunate thing that ever happened to us! I was prepared to be disappointed in my efforts to be sent to an Irish convalescent home, but this is the very acme of ill luck. When they finally told me in London that I could not go to Ireland, they asked me to choose some part of England: at first I said London, thinking that this would be more convenient for you than any provincial town, but this could not be done. I then elected Bristol, where I could have the society of Mrs Moore, and also of Perrett of the Somersets, whose being wounded some days before myself I mentioned to you. Little could I foresee what was going to happen: we are still close prisoners, and have had several tests of blood and excreta taken – the one painful, the other disgusting.

All the 'gilded youth' among the patients, who have no interests in themselves, of course grow more troublesome being confined. The place

44 Lewis, as he mentions in this letter, hoped to be transferred to an Irish hospital, but he was sent to Ashton Court instead, arriving there on 25 June.

echoes to the crack of their billiard balls and their loud, tuneless whistling: I was very miserable for the first few days until I discovered a little, almost disused writing room at one end of the house. Here I can sit in comparative safety and read Burton's anatomy[45] which I have had sent from town.

If I should happen to get the disease I suppose all my bits of things will be burned. I could sit down and cry over the whole business: and yet of course we have both much to be thankful for. When a man can sleep between sheets as long as he will, sit in arm chairs, and have no fears, it is peevish to complain. If I had not been wounded when I was, I should have gone through a terrible time. Nearly all my friends in the Battalion are gone. Did I ever mention Johnson who was a scholar of Queens? I had hoped to meet him at Oxford some day, and renew the endless talks that we had out there. 'Dis aliter visum',[46] he is dead. I had had him so often in my thoughts, had so often hit on some new point in one of our arguments, and made a note of things in my reading to tell him when we met again, that I can hardly believe he is dead. Don't you find it particularly hard to realise the death of people whose strong personality makes them particularly alive: with the ordinary sons of Belial who eat and drink and are merry, it is not so hard.

But I must not enlarge on a melancholy subject: I have no doubt that we are all three of us pretty low. However, 'better luck next time': this cannot last for ever and I hope yet to have a visit from you. As for my own health it is pretty good, although the wound in the leg – the smallest of the three – is still giving some trouble. The house here is the survival, tho' altered by continual rebuilding, of a thirteenth-century castle: the greater part is now stucco work of the worst Victorian period (à la Norwood Towers) but we have one or two fine old paintings and a ghost. I haven't met it yet and have not much hope to – indeed if poor Johnson's ghost would come walking into the lonely writing room this minute, I should be glad enough. Greatly to my chagrin the library is locked up. The park is several miles in extent, very pleasant and stocked with deer: once or twice while wandering in the bracken I have suddenly come

45 Lewis's copy of Burton's *The Anatomy of Melancholy* was one brought out by Chatto & Windus in 1907. Lewis kept this edition all his life and some of its many annotations were no doubt made at Ashton Court.

46 'It seemed otherwise to the gods'. Laurence Bertrand Johnson (see note 138 to letter of 4 November 1917) was killed by the shell which wounded Lewis.

upon the solemn face and branching antlers of a stag, within a few feet of me. He examines me for a moment, then snorts, kicks up his heels, and is gone: a second later, head after head comes up – his panic has reached the rest of the herd, and they too scamper off after him like the wind.

A most generous and welcome consignment of smokeables came this morning. Communication with the town is scanty now of course, and this is a most welcome addition to our diminishing stocks: what is more, such little attentions are infinitely cheering when one is dull, lonely and disappointed. With many thanks and best love, I am

your loving
son Jack

P.S. Please let Arthur know my change of address and tell him that I will write soon. yours, J.

TO ARTHUR GREEVES (W):

[Ashton Court,
Long Ashton,
Clifton, Bristol
17? July 1918]

My dear Arthur,

I am truly sorry to have left you so long without a letter. My best excuse is that already 'my hand aches and my eyes grow weary' with writing, for I am at present busily engaged in copying out the final version of my poems: in a few days the new MS. will be ready for the typist and when it returns thence it will begin the round of the publishers. I shall start with the famous houses and go on until I have exhausted all that I can hear of: even if it is unsuccessful all round, I may pick up some useful criticisms, and at any rate it will be well to have a typed copy.

Of course the book now is very different from the one you have, by the insertion of several new pieces and the alteration or omission of some of the old. The arrangement I find particularly difficult and besides I am beginning to grow nervy and distrust my own judgement. It is so hard to know whether you are improving or spoiling a thing.

This will partly explain my silence, tho' of course I know I should have written. But, ami, you must never suppose when I don't write that this means any change in my feelings or any loss of touch with the old life – put it down to laziness or forgetfulness or other occupations rather than to that. When I have got the MS. off (it used to be my love but is now becoming more my tyrant!) I will write you a longer and better letter. In the meantime I will just run over my news up to date and then say good-bye.

My last adventures before leaving town were a visit to 'Faust' and to 'Tosca'.[47] With the former I was disgusted: the crowded stage, the conventionality, the noisy comic-opera scenes of drinking, the choruses etc were really too much after the 'Valkyrie'. The church scene was very well done I admit: but on the whole I got very little pleasure out of it. Of course if I were a real musician like you I should appreciate this kind of music too 'in its own way' and get a sort of critical & historical interest out of it to make up for the sheer ecstasy of modern music: but then literature is my province, and in music I can only afford to enjoy the music that really suits me. By the way they had the whole ballet, which is very rarely done now I suppose, as a separate scene. The dancing was very uninspired and I didn't care for the music, but you would have agreed with me in praising the setting – which was a wild open place done in the style of Heath Robinson: in the back ground was a typical absurdly beautiful mountain of his, and steep little vallies, and big masses of pink cloud. The whole was lighted to represent early summer morning and gave a fine impression of loneliness.

'Tosca' I revelled in: from beginning to end I enjoyed it, and it seemed to my untutored ears to be very well sung – tho' not of course with the solemnity of the 'Valkyrie' (you see I cannot help harking back to that, it was immeasurably beyond anything I had seen or hoped to see so gloriously un-operatic – in the silly sense). Puccini certainly has a wonderful richness of orchestration and a sort of continuity – hasn't he? None of those nasty gaps that you have in 'Faust' where one 'number' (loathsome word) has ended and the other begins, like pieces in a concert: 'E lucevan le stelle' was quite up to expectations.

The books which you returned did not arrive until I had left London – but don't bother about that: I have decided to keep 'Peacock Pie'[48] and can easily dispose of the others. As it seems impossible to get what would

---

47 The production of Giacomo Puccini's opera, *Tosca* (1900), which Lewis saw on 21 June is reviewed in *The Times* (22 June 1918), p. 3.

48 Walter de la Mare, *Peacock Pie: A Book of Rhymes* (1913).

suit you 'by the light of nature' I am sending you the wherewithal to choose for yourself at Mullan's. This is an unconventional way of giving a present, but you are too sensible to mind that. I will tell you all my details in my next letter. Bear with me.

Yours ever
Jack

TO HIS FATHER (LP VI: 11):

Ashton Court.
Monday.
[29? July 1918]

My dear Papy,

You can imagine how mystified I was by an envelope from the U.V.F. – the contents too were unexpected.[49] In some ways this scheme has given me to think: you see the Board which sate upon me in London gave me two months convalescence which will be finished on the 4th of August. It appears however in this hospital, if you are quiet and inoffensive and keep yourself well out of the notice of the authorities, you may be often left for several weeks after your time. The great danger about this change would be that of getting the reply 'If you are so anxious to move, we will have you boarded at once and discharged from hospital.' Such a procedure would of course hasten my return to France. The amount of leave I get after hospital (whatever it may be) will not be influenced by the time which I have spent in the former, and it is therefore to our interest to prolong the hospital period to the utmost. The smaller Irish hospitals are notoriously strict and up to time with their Boards.

I must admit too, I should be sorry to give up the idea of your coming to visit me here: it would give me great pleasure for you to meet Mrs. Moore, and I feel that this visit to me is the only excuse on which you will ever get away for a while from Belfast and the office. If you were at the office all day and I had to be back at the hospital at 6 or 7 every night, it would be hardly worth while coming to a hospital at home. Here we could have a delightful little holiday together.

I am the more ready to put off any change because of the fact which I had forgotten to tell you – namely that the 3rd Somersets are in

49 Albert Lewis was trying to get Jack into the Ulster Volunteer Force, hoping this way to get him transferred to Ireland.

Holywood Barracks, and during the period of home service which will follow my leave I shall be able to dine with you every evening, and perhaps even to sleep at home: I shall also be able to get a week end off from time to time. For all these reasons I have thought it better to make no move in the matter. Write and tell me what you think: I hope you will come over here and talk the matter over in person. This is of course only a 'business' letter: I will write again to take away any reproach in the matter of correspondence.

your loving
son Jack

TO ARTHUR GREEVES (W):

[Ashton Court,
Bristol]
Wednesday [7 August 1918]

My dear Arthur,

The fact of trying to publish a book at once makes you regard publishers in quite a new light. When you sit down to consider where you will send it first, you immediately realize the enormous prestige of Macmillan – when you come to think of it, everyone who is published by them gains a certain importance from that very fact. I looked upon acceptance by them as a goal almost beyond hope, and sent my MS. to them first. Needless to say it has come back, accompanied by the following note: – 'Dear Sir, We duly received your manuscript entitled "Spirits in Prison: A cycle of lyrical poems", by Clive Staples, and regret to say that we do not see our way to undertake its publication. Some of the shorter nature poems seem to us to have no little charm, but we do not feel that the collection as a whole would be likely to appeal to any considerable public. We beg therefore to return the MS. with thanks. We are, yours faithfully, Macmillan and Co. Ltd.'

This is at any rate courteous and I suppose not very discouraging: perhaps, however, they always sweeten their refusals with some little complement. However that may be, I am determined not to lose heart until I have tried all the houses I can hear of. I am sending it to Heinneman next – they seem to publish a fair amount of new poetry. From the title which I have given my collection, you will gather that it differs in many ways from the one which you possess.

I find I am getting very slack and idle. My serious reading at present is

Burton's Anatomy of Melancholy, as published in one big volume by Chatto & Windus at 7/-.[50] The paper and type are of a good, plain quality, but the binding is not attractive. I get on with it very slowly, and have intermixed with it a new book called 'A Schoolmaster's Diary',[51] which interests me being mainly on education and literature. I also read a good deal of Wordsworth in my Everyman. You remember perhaps how violent my criticisms on him once were, but I am becoming a reformed character. I feel very weak and tired these days and inclined to lose interest in anything that needs continued attention. If only I could get my book accepted it would give me a tremendous fillip and take my mind off the future. In my present mood few things have pleased me more than Macdonald's 'The Goblin and the Princess',[52] which I borrowed from Maureen Moore. This child has a well stocked library of fairy tales which form her continual reading – an excellent taste at her age, I think, which will lead her in later life to romance and poetry and not to the twaddling novels that make up the diet of most educated women apparently. I am getting the Life of Thomas More in the Temple Classics.[53]

Forgive me if I don't write any more, I don't feel like it to day. It is terribly hot, which you know I hate.

Yours

Jack

TO ARTHUR GREEVES (W):

[Ashton Court,
Bristol
31 August 1918]

My dear Arthur,

In spite of the loneliness and melancholy of which you complain I must begin by congratulating you on the excellent time which you had in Dublin and the interesting people whom you met. Indeed I think you are

---

50 Richard Burton, *The Anatomy of Melancholy; What it is with all the Kinds Causes Symptoms Prognostics & Several Cures of It, In Three Partitions with the Several Sections Members & Subsections Philosophically Medicinally Historically Opened & Cut Up by 'Democritus Junior' ['Robert Burton'] with a Satirical Preface Conducing to the Following Discourse* (Chatto & Windus, 1907). See note 45 to letter of 29 June 1918.

51 Stuart Petre Brodie Mais, *A Schoolmaster's Diary* (1918).

52 George MacDonald, *The Princess and the Goblin* (1871).

53 Ann Manning, *The Household of Sir Thomas More*, with *The Life of Sir Thomas More* by William Roper, Introduction by Ernest Rhys, Temple Classics (1906).

as much to be envied as anyone I know: you live in comfort, surrounded by interests, in pleasant society, and are not a slave of the state and do not have the menace of France hanging over your head. When you were toiling in the office how you would have looked forward to this time if you had known it was coming! How many men to-day, living in holes and mud heaps, driven, hunted, terrified, verminous, starved for sleep, hopeless, would give their very souls to change places with you even for twenty four hours. And yet of course we can all be discontented in any circumstances, and I dare say I should be just the same in your place.

So you are inclining to the New Ireland school are you? I remember you used rather to laugh at my Irish enthusiasm in the old days when you were still an orthodox Ulsterman. I am glad you begin to think otherwise: a poetry bookshop for Ireland, in Dublin, would be a most praiseworthy undertaking: it might also bring out some monthly journal on Irish literature, containing reviews of contemporary books, articles on classical Gaelic literature and language, and a few poems and sketches. The idea is fascinating: if you could get some big man to take it up. I should like very much indeed to meet your friend Parker: it is a grand idea to build a house after a dream. What talks you all must have had. Were they purely literary or did they talk anything about religion and philosophy? I suppose that set are mostly mystics, rosacrutians and the like. Here I must indulge my love of preaching by warning you not to get too much bound up in a cult. Between your other penchant .... and the Irish school you might get into a sort of little by-way of the intellectual world, off the main track and loose yourself there. Remember that the great minds, Milton, Scott, Mozart and so on, are always sane before all and keep in the broad highway of thought and feel what can be felt by all men, not only by a few. Attractive as they are these side-tracks are always a little decadent if one lives wholly in them. But I suppose your good solid old faith in history and 'stodge' will keep you from that danger.

It is partly through this feeling that I have not begun by sending my MS. to Maunsels: it would associate me too definitely with a cult and partly because their paper and binding are rather poor. I suppose none of your friends have any influence at Maunsels that might be of use to me?

I have just finished reading a very pleasant book called 'The Four Men', by Hillaire Belloc.[54] I always imagined that his books were of a very

54 Hilaire Belloc, *The Four Men: A Farrago* [1912].

different kind but this is rather in the style of Lavengro, only, it seems to me, more homely and humorous: in one or two places where the four wanderers sit in a little forest hut smoking and telling tales it rather reminds me of the 'Crock of Gold'. I began to read the 'Egoist'[55] and after five pages came to the conclusion that it was one of the worst books I had ever seen or heard of. I don't know how you can stand Meredith's affectation. By the bye, 'The Four Men' is in the 1/- Nelson blue edition with quite nice pen and ink sketches. I should not advise you to try Burton. I have got stuck with him and I think he would be less in your line than in mine. Oh don't you sometimes feel that everything is dead? I feel, and apparently you feel, a sort of impossibility in getting on solidly with any serious book in the way we used to do.

Yours
Jack

TO HIS FATHER (LP VI: 26–7):

Ashton Court,
Long Ashton,
Clifton.
3 September 1918

My dear Papy,

Ever since my last letter to you I have been almost daily expecting to hear from you, and I am rather surprised that neither my answer to your proposal nor my suggestion that you should come over here has met with any reply. Have you not yet decided on a date for coming over? It is four months now since I returned from France, and my friends laughingly suggest that 'my father in Ireland' of whom they hear is a mythical creation like Mrs Harris.[56]

As to my decision, I think you will agree that it has already justified itself. I am now nearly a month over my time, and even if I were boarded tomorrow this would be so much to the good. Of course in the present need for men, being passed fit by a board would mean a pretty quick return to France. I am afraid there is not much possibility of the 'job at home' which you once thought might be the result of my wounds: although not quite well I am almost 'fit' now in the military sense of the

55 George Meredith, *The Egoist* (1879).
56 The mythical friend of Mrs Gamp in Charles Dickens' *Martin Chuzzlewit* (1843–4).

word, and depend only on the forgetfulness of the authorities for my continued stay in hospital. Of course this has nothing to do with my leave.

I hope there is nothing wrong and that I shall soon hear from you again and see you here. I know there are difficulties in the way, but I suppose they are no more serious now than when Warnie was at home. With best love, I am,

your loving son,
Jack

TO HIS FATHER (LP VI: 30–1):

Ashton Court,
Long Ashton.
Clifton.
9 September 1918

My dear Papy,

I write in haste to give you a piece of news which I hope will please you not much less than it did me. You are aware that for some years now I have amused myself by writing verses, and a pocket book collection of these followed me through France. Since my return I have occupied myself in revising these, getting them typed with a few additions, and trying to publish them. After a refusal from Macmillans they have, somewhat to my surprise, been accepted by Heinemann. Wm. Heinemann thinks it would 'be well to reconsider the inclusion of one or two pieces which are not perhaps on a level with my best work'. I have sent him some new ones as substitutes for these and things are going on well, although his absence from town on a fortnight's holiday will cause a delay in coming to a definite arrangement about money.

I don't know when I may hope actually to see the book, but of course I will send you a copy at once. It is called 'Spirits in Prison: a cycle of lyrical poems by Clive Staples'. The paper and printing will probably be detestable, as they always are now-a-days. This little success gives me a pleasure which is perhaps childish and yet akin to greater things.

Hoping that I shall soon have some answer from you, I am,

your loving son,
Jack

TO ARTHUR GREEVES (W):

56 Ravenswood Rd.,
Redland,
Bristol.
[12 September 1918]

My dear Arthur,

The best of news! After keeping my MS. for ages Heinemann has actually accepted it. 'Wm. Heinemann' – apparently there is a real Mr Heinnemann – writes to say that he 'will be pleased to become its publisher'. He adds that it may be well to re-consider the inclusion of some of the pieces 'which are not perhaps on a level with my best work'. I wrote back thanking him and telling him there were a few new pieces that he might care to use as substitutions for ones he omits. An answer came back this time from a man called Evans, the managing director asking me to send the new pieces and saying that Heinemann himself was out of town for a week or so.[57] I sent him 5 new poems by return – and so things are going on very well although I'm afraid Heinemann's holiday will cause some delay. You can imagine how pleased I am, and how eagerly I now look at all Heinemann's books and wonder what mine will be like. I'm afraid the paper will be poor as it always is now in new books.

It is going to be called 'Spirits in Prison'[58] by Clive Staples & is mainly strung round the idea that I mentioned to you before – that nature is wholly diabolical & malevolent and that God, if he exists, is outside of and in opposition to the cosmic arrangements. I'm afraid you will find a good many of your favourite ones left out: I thought very carefully over them but I think we all have to follow our own judgement in the end.

On no account tell my father that you know anything about it, as he might be hurt at not having been taken into my confidence: I will let him know myself when I next write (I have written to him since at your instance) and you must hear it from him as news or else pretend that you have just heard. *Of course* don't say anything to the Strandtown fraternity.

I am glad to see that you are more cheerful in your last letter. I don't think I shall follow your advice to try George Meredith again. There is so

---

57 These letters from William Heinemann (1863–1920) and Charles Sheldon Evans (1883–1944) of 3 and 5 September respectively are found in LP VI: 31–2.

58 1 Peter 3:19: Christ 'went and preached unto the spirits in prison'.

much good stuff to read that it is wasteful to spend time on affectations. You are quite right about Emerson.[59] I often pick him up here for an odd quarter of an hour, and go away full of new ideas. Every sentence is weighty: he puts into paragraphs what others, seeking charm, expand into whole essays or chapters. At the same time his tense concentration makes him painful reading, he gives you no rest. I don't know why you object to his style – it seems to me admirable. Quel dommage that such a man should be an American.

I have read (in a borrowed copy) 'King Lear's Wife' and also 'The End of the World' which is in the same volume.[60] Bottomley's play seems very closely copied from Yeats, but very good. I prefer the other on the whole – tho' I think better of humanity and believe that quite ordinary folk would face 'The fire that was before the world was made' with less hysteria than Huff and his circle.[61]

Must stop now – good bye –

Yours

Jack

P.S. Board[62] is overdue & may it continue so.

TO HIS FATHER (LP VI: 34):

Ashton Court,
Long Ashton,
Clifton.
14 September 1918

My dear Papy,

I am sorry that you should have been so troubled as you were when you last wrote to me, and sorrier still that I should have been to any extent the cause of it. At the same time it is only fair to add that I do not entirely acquiesce in the blame which you lay upon me. Above all, the joking reference to 'Mrs Harris' which you take 'au pied de la lettre'

---

59 Ralph Waldo Emerson (1803–82).

60 *Georgian Poetry 1913–1915*, ed. E[dward] M[arsh] (1915). 'King Lear's Wife' is by Gordon Bottomley (pp. 3–47) and 'The End of the World' by Lascelles Abercrombie (pp. 195–239).

61 A line from Act I of 'The End of the World' (p. 205). Huff is a character in that play.

62 The army medical board who would decide whether or not Lewis should return to active duty.

was quite harmlessly meant. I do not choose my friends among people who jeer, nor has a tendency to promiscuous confidence ever been one of my characteristic faults. However perhaps it was tactless, and there is no need to go into it further.

Many thanks for the 'monies numbered' and the parcel. Those Virginian cigarettes which you have sent me several times are a good brand. Are matches obtainable at home? We are very badly off for them here: hardly any tobacconist will give you a box, and grocers only give a small weekly allowance to their regular customers.

I was very much cheered by your telegram. Such things are the most valuable part of the successes which they accompany. I hope I have not led you to expect too much: the publisher is only the first fence in our steeplechase – the book may still be badly reviewed or not reviewed at all, may fail to sell, or your own taste and judgement may be disappointed in it. The news I need hardly say should be communicated with discretion to the 'hoi polloi'. Heinemann is still out of town, so nothing further can be done just at present.

I expect this letter will again cross yours, but it seems our fate.

your loving son,

Jack

TO HIS FATHER (LP VI: 36–7):

Ashton Court,
Long Ashton,
Clifton.
18 September 1918

My dear Papy,

Many thanks for your cheering and encouraging letter and for the enclosure. I knew that I could count on your sharing my interests on this subject and already the suggestions you make are most valuable.

It had quite escaped my notice that Hichens had written a novel called 'Spirits in prison', but now that you mention it, I think that you are right – or perhaps it is 'A spirit in Prison' – the resemblance at any rate is close enough to hit that title on the head.[63] I don't know whether I shall be able to find another that expresses so aptly the general scheme of the book, but we must do our best. The sub-title 'A cycle of lyrical poems' was not

63 Robert Hitchens, *A Spirit in Prison* (1908).

given without a reason: the reason is that the book is not a collection of really independant pieces, but the working out, loosely of course and with digressions, of a general idea. If you can imagine 'In Memoriam'[64] with its various parts in different metres it will give you some idea of the form I have tried to adopt. Such merit as it has depends less on the individual than on the combined effect of the pieces. To call it a cycle is to prepare the reader for this plan and to induce him to follow the order of the poems as I have put them. Probably he will not, but we must do our best.

At the same time I admit that the word 'cycle' is a very objectionable one. The only others which I know to express the same thing are 'series' and 'sequence' and of those the former is hardly definite enough and the latter in my opinion more affected and precieux than 'cycle' itself. Of course one could dispense with a sub-title altogether, but I rather approve of the old practice by which a book gives some account of itself – as 'Paradise Lost – a heroic poem in twelve books' – 'The Pilgrim's Progress – being an account of his journey from this world to the next'. Perhaps you can suggest some simpler and more dignified way of saying that the book is a whole and not a collection.

My only reason for choosing a pseudonym at all was a natural feeling that I should not care to have this bit of my life known in the regiment. One doesn't want either officers or men to talk about 'our b—y lyrical poet again' whenever I make a mistake. But perhaps it is silly to attach importance to that. Simply 'Clive Lewis' would be better in many ways than any faked name. The objections to the name 'Staples' had not occurred to me, but I am afraid they are only too true. At one time I thought of anagraming Lewis into 'Wiles' or 'Welis' but I give it up as a trifle fantastic. On the whole it is more straightforward to put ones own name on the cover to take its fortune, and since I agree with you about Staples, we may as well drop the disguise altogether.

Mrs. Moore had received news at last of her son's death: I suppose it is best to know, and fortunately she never cherished any hopes. Never a day passes but I thankfully realize my great good fortune in getting wounded when I did and thus being spared the very deadly months that followed.

With best love,
your loving son,
Jack

64 Tennyson, *In Memoriam A.H.H.*

TO HIS FATHER (LP VI: 45–6):

Ashton Court,
Long Ashton,
Clifton.
Postmark: 3 October 1918

My dear Papy,

Thank you for your letter and for the parcel of cigarettes. I am well enough off for underclothing etc., and have been able to get a local tailor to make a quite satisfactory khaki suit to replace the one which was cut up at the dressing station.

Now as to the question of this word 'cycle'. In its primitive sense it does undoubtedly mean, as you say, simply a wheel or circle. I think however that there is lots of precedent for using it to mean a series. For one thing, to use your own example, Wagner's 'Ring' is called a cycle: for another, the German lyric poets have always used the name 'a song cycle' to describe a series of songs, and following them, Tennyson wrote 'The Swallows – A Cycle', which was set to music by Sullivan.[65] Again, in critical books hasn't one often heard it used in that way? 'The cycle of legends clustering round the Grail Story', or say that 'The Iliad probably represents the combination of a whole cycle of "independant lays"'. Why the word should be used in that sense I don't know, but I think there is sufficiently good authority. I think 'Spirits in Bondage' would be a good substitute for the old title and would sound well: 'Spirits in Bonds' would not do so well, and suggests tiresome jokes about whiskey. I think it is only natural to describe it as a Cycle of poems, just to say 'a cycle' is rather unintelligible. After all I'm not claiming that they are good poems – you know the schoolboy's definitions, 'Prose is when the lines go on to the end of the page: poetry is when they don't.'

The more I think of it the less I like anonymity. If it wasn't for the army I'd let my own name take its chance. Don't you think Clive is too famous a surname to take as a nom de plume (just as we thought Staples too notorious)? Of course we must always remember that the people who are most likely to talk of 'our b****y poet' are also the least likely to hear anything about it; they don't haunt bookshops, nor do they read literary papers.

---

65 Those works of Alfred, Lord Tennyson set to music by Arthur Sullivan are *The Foresters* (1892) and *The Window* (1871).

I read and posted the letter which you enclosed for Mrs Moore. It seemed to me up to the high standard of your usual letters on such occasions.[66] I have heard lately that Somerville, whom I have mentioned to you, is gone too. With him the old set completely vanishes.[67]

I hope that the domestic troubles have by now reached some solution. I'm afraid that question will be very acute, even after the war: over here it is a mark of great good luck and of a large income for people in our position to have maids at all.

Your loving
son Jack.

On the following day Germany appealed to President Wilson for an Armistice; the request was either refused or ignored.

---

66 A draft of Albert Lewis's letter to Mrs Moore reads as follows: '[21 September 1918] Dear Mrs. Moore, Two days ago I heard from Jacks that all hope of Paddy's safety must now be abandoned. I hope I may write of him as "Paddy" for I felt as tho' I had known him intimately for a long time. I shall not offer you the commonplaces of consolation – about duty and patriotism. When all that is said – and truthfully said – the terrible fact remains – the irremediable loss – the bitter grief. I do however offer you with intense sincerity my true and earnest and deep sympathy and sorrow in your great loss. For all your kindness to my son which I here again ask permission to acknowledge, I am deeply grateful. Believe me, with much sympathy, yours most sincerely, Albert Lewis' (LP VI: 42).

67 Those who made up 'the old set' are mentioned by name in Lewis's letter from Oxford of 10 June 1917. Paddy Moore died at Pargny in March 1918. Martin Ashworth Somerville, also of the Rifle Brigade, served in Egypt and Palestine and was killed in Palestine on 21 September 1918. Alexander Gordon Sutton, who was with Paddy in the 2nd Battalion of the Rifle Brigade, was killed in action on 2 January 1918. Thomas Kerrison Davy, of the 1st Battalion of the Rifle Brigade, died of wounds received near Arras on 29 March 1918. Lewis assumed that Denis Howard de Pass – 'our regnant authority on all matters of dress, who is reported to wear stays' – had died as well. He was reported 'wounded and missing' on 1 April 1918. As it turned out, de Pass of the 12th Battalion of the Rifle Brigade had been taken prisoner by the Germans. Following the repatriation in December 1918 he not only continued to serve in the First World War but fought in the Second as well. From 1950 until his death in 1973 this once fashionable dresser was a dairy farmer at Polegate in Sussex.

TO ARTHUR GREEVES (W):

No 3 Officers' Mess,
Perham Downs Camp,
Ludgershall, Hants.[68]
[6? October 1918]

My dear Arthur,

No, you were wrong, I have not gone on my leave; I was only out for a night at Mrs Moore's. I have now however had my board, over a month late I'm glad to say, and been sent for further convalescence to a camp here. This is Salisbury Plain, a place much cursed by most army people who are sent there because it is in the heart of the country and cannot therefore afford them the only pleasures of which they are capable. Personally I quite like it: it consists of long low hills, grassy and rather grey looking except in bright sun and very few trees. Of course it is rather spoilt by the city of wooden huts that is called a camp, but even these look quite well towards dusk when there are rows of light in the windows.

By this time you have probably got a parcel containing Beardesly's Malory and the Works of Corneille, which I have sent to you for safe keeping. Be sure and let me know what you think of both. Even if you don't care for the designs (and they are a little decadent and 'genre') I think you will like the general get up of the Malory. The Corneille is in a sort of good, solid old fashioned style, which I have grown to like: the plates of course *as* illustrations are idiotic but there is something solid and grand about them. Corneille is not half such a dull author as some people might imagine – don't take him at Tchaine's valuation. Down here I am reading Dante's 'Purgatorio' in the Temple Classics edition with a crib on the opposite page.[69] So 'ave the mighty fallen.

I told you that Wm. Heinemann was away for a fortnight, but he should be back now and I am expecting to hear from him any day now. I had a shock a short while ago when I saw a book of poems 'Counter-Attack' by Siegfried Sassoon[70] (a horrid man) published by him at 2/6 in a red paper cover and horrid type. I do hope they will give me something better than that.

---

68 Lewis was moved here on 4 October.

69 *The Purgatorio of Dante Alighieri*, the text with a translation by Thomas Okey, edited by H. Oelsner (1900).

70 Siegfried Sassoon, *Counterattack* (1918).

I have also been reading here the 1916–1917 books of Georgian Verse,[71] in which I liked particularly the bits from Robert Nichol's 'Faun's Holiday'. How a man who wrote them could also write such howling gibberish as 'The Assault' must remain a mystery. I believe you have his 'Ardours and Endurances'[72] haven't you? If so you might give me the details as to publisher, price and edition.

Mrs Moore has managed to get rooms in a tiny cottage here, where they keep rabbits and pigs. It is all very rural but not very sanitary. Write soon.

Yours
Jack

P.S. Don't say anything about my being moved, as I don't want my father to start trying to get me moved again.

On 4 October a German and Austrian 'Peace Note' was sent to President Woodrow Wilson, asking him to agree to an armistice. They made it clear that this was not a surrender, but an attempt to end the war without conditions that would be harmful to Germany and Austria. On 8 October Wilson rejected the Peace Note, insisting that a first condition of an armistice was the evacuation of all occupied territories.

TO HIS FATHER (LP VI: 50):

[No. 3 Officers Mess,
Perham Downs Camp,
Ludgershall,
Hants.]
10th [October 1918]

My dear Papy,

Thanks for the parcel, also the little note with enclosure. The 'Kassandra' cigarettes – one wonders vaguely why the 'K' and what language – are a pre-war luxury and much appreciated by us all.

By this time I expect you have my last letter and I may soon hope for your answer. Isn't the news excellent, or do you still distrust it? Peace and

71 *Georgian Poetry 1916–1917*, ed. E[dward] M[arsh] (1917).
72 Robert Nichols, *Assault and other War Poems* (1918); *Ardours and Endurances* (1917).

success have been so often held up to us that I admit one scarcely dares to have definite hopes again. I was very pleased however by the wise and temperate tone of Wilson's reply, which contrasted favourably with the blood and thunder vulgarity of the American press. But hush! We must not speak that way now when Britain has come to be mentioned as 'one of the Allies of the States': I never thought I'd live to see that – Wilson the head of the confederacy and England his humble retainer.

With best love,
your loving son,
Jack

TO ARTHUR GREEVES (W):

No 3 Officers Mess,
Perham Downs Camp,
Ludgershall,
Hants.
Sunday [13 October 1918]

My dear Arthur,

'Savernake Woods', doesn't that breathe of romance? It is the sort of name one would expect to find in Maurice Hewlett or Geoffrey Farnol, but as a matter of fact it is not invention at all – I have been in Savernake Woods this morning.

You get clear of the village, cross a couple of fields and then a sunken chalky road leads you right into the wood. It is full of beech and oak but also of those little bushy things that grow out of the earth in four or five different trunks – vide Rackham's woodland scenes in the 'Siegfried' illustrations. In places, too, there has been a good deal of cutting down: some people think this spoils a wood but I find it delightful to come out of the thickets suddenly to a half bare patch full of stumps and stacks of piled wood with the sun glinting thro' the survivors. Green walks of grass with thick wood on either side led off the road and we followed one of these down and found our way back by long détours, tho' not before a comfortable 'soaking machine' had been discovered and enjoyed.

By the way, talking about Siegfried, is it not an abomination the way the Germans have named their trench systems after the heroes of the Ring? The other day they were defending the 'Alberich line' and now they have been driven back to 'Brünnhilde'. Anything more vulgar than the application of that grand old cycle to the wearisome ugliness of modern war I can't imagine.

It was strange the way not only our letters but our thoughts crossed about 'the good old style' of the Corneille: the binding was of my own choice. How had both books stood their journey? As long as our views agree to this extent you need not be afraid of that 'getting farther and farther away' of which you always complain. We shall of course have a great many new subjects to talk of when we meet again, and a good many old ones to talk of quite differently, but that is an advantage.

I only wish I *was* busy 'correcting my proof-sheets': I have heard nothing more from Heinnemann although he must be back from his holiday by now. I have horrid fears sometimes that he may have changed his mind and be getting ready to return them – but then it would have been so easy for him to have done that in the first place.[73] Of course there is none of the fighting element in my book, but I suppose it has some indirect bearing on the war.

Funnily enough I had been reading a little handbook on Schopenhauer last week:[74] though I have never read him seriously I have often dipped into him at Kirk's and the old man's talk was saturated with Shopenhauer-esque quotations and ideas. There is certainly much worth reading in him: his views on love, for instance, though they are far from being the whole truth, give nevertheless an excellent account of the actual origin of love – what he forgets is that it is man's peculiar glory to make out of something which nature created for her own biological purposes something else which is spiritual and which nature would have no interest in. That is our triumph. Of course he is not really a philosopher at all in the technical sense.

Am still going on slowly with the Purgatorio. Write soon a good long screed

Yours

Jack

73 Mr Heinemann's enthusiastic letter of 8 October (LP VI: 49) was sent to Ashton Court and had not yet caught up with him.

74 Arthur Schopenhauer (1788–1860). Lewis was probably reading *The Wisdom of Schopenhauer*, ed. W. Jekyll (1911).

TO ARTHUR GREEVES (W):

Teusday [15 October 1918]
Same place.

My dear Arthur,

Many thanks for the book,[75] it was most unexpected and delightful. It is nicely got up, but has suffered a little from tight strings on the journey. I haven't begun to read it seriously yet but all that I have seen pleases me. I at once looked up the poem 'The Gift of Song' which you mentioned, and I thoroughly agree with you. It has a beautiful dreamy movement and the sound follows the sense exactly; also, what is more it has that depth and mystery which a lyric should have if you are to read it again and again. I liked too the 'Canticle' in Danaë and indeed all the Danaë pieces, and there are fine passages in the verses on somebody's death – the ones where the last lines all rhyme to 'Despair'. Didn't you like that description of the snow outside the firelit window at Oxford. The war poetry is, at least, no worse than the rest of its kind. Nichols is very different from that great mass of modern poets, who copy the faults but not the merits of Rupert Brooke, and who are so intolerably clumsy and ugly in form. He stands quite apart and seems to me the best of the younger lot whom I have come across – much better than Brooke himself for instance. I'm afraid I shall never be an orthodox modern – I like lines that will scan and do not care for descriptions of sea-sickness.

Now for a little growl: if you realised what I'd got to go back to you wouldn't be so damned keen on my having another board. And you should understand that the longer it is before you see me the longer that evil day is put off.

Talking about Schopenhauer have you read anything about his views on music? He regards the arts in general as the only escape from the Will, and music in particular as the supreme escape and perhaps in itself the fundamental Reality. It is rather finely worked out and should appeal to you.

I am so glad you have got into that school at last: I hope they will do you good and lead you on to a proper development of your natural bent. After all interesting and arduous work is about the one thing to save us from melancholy – your besetting disease (I had almost written 'sin').

The Purgatorio, or even the whole Divine Comedy with the Inferno and Paradiso, is much shorter than the Faerie Queene. Without Latin I

75 i.e. *Ardours and Endurances* by Robert Nichols.

am not sure that even your knowledge of French & the crib would carry you through: but if you would care for a translation remember that Cary's version in blank verse is supposed to be the best piece of verse-translation ever written.[76] Don't get Longfellow's or any of the modern ones, they are all (I'm told) bad. Gilbert Murray is a very sound man, and his translations should be good – I have never more than glanced at them, not being fond of Euripides myself.[77]

I got Mrs Moore's sister in town to call on Heinemanns, which she did on Wednesday last and they said they'd written the day before, but it must have been lost. That of course accounts for the delay and I hope to hear some day soon.

The hills and all our favourite walks should be lovely just now – Hadn't heard about K.'s arm.

Yours
Jack

TO HIS FATHER (LP VI: 53–4):

Officers Mess,
No. 3 Camp,
Perham Down.
Andover,
Hants.
Oct. 18th 1918

My dear Papy,

I have had a board at last, and been moved to this 'Command Depot' for an unspecified period. This is the usual step after leaving hospital, unless one is well enough to be passed for general service. Of course I am still far from this, but one doesn't usually remain here very long. It is a sort of a glorified hospital here, although we live in a mess and wear uniform: the best feature is that we have rooms to ourselves, which is a pleasant change after hospital wards.

I have just had a letter from Heinemann's which has taken some time to come round through Ashton Court. He accepts some new pieces I had sent him and mentions a few he wants rejected. He also objects to a 'too

76 *The Vision or Hell, Purgatory and Paradise of Dante Alighieri*, trans. Henry Francis Cary (1814).

77 *Hippolytus and The Bacchae of Euripides, and the Frogs of Aristophanes*, trans. Gilbert Murray (1902).

frequent use of certain words' and points to one or two places that seem weak and which I might alter. 'After that' he suggests we might come to terms, a point on which I am quite ready to agree with him. I am hoping to get a day off some time next week and run up to town and see him: that will be much better than a long series of letters. With most of his omissions and objections I agree, and shall have no difficulty in making changes, tho' there are one or two cases in which I am determined to stick to my guns. One must trust ones own judgements sometimes.

I was quite amused at your story of the origin of 'Spirits in Bondage' tho' that would not be a sufficient argument against it. Of course I remembered the text about 'the spirits which are in prison' and it is that which seemed to give the old title its significance which 'Spirits in bondage' could never have. I think perhaps we should stick to 'Prison'. I shall ask Heinemann whether that novel by Hichens really exists; he ought to know.

By the way, what about Clive Hamilton for a pseudonym? It will be a complete disguise to outsiders, transparent to 'our ain folk', and will be a name which we have the best of reasons to love and honour.[78]

Many thanks for the enclosure. I am very sorry to hear about the drawing room floor which used to be 'the brightest jewel in our crown'.

your loving
son Jack

78 'Clive Hamilton' is the pseudonym Lewis eventually chose to appear under. Unluckily for Lewis, in a 'List of Poetry' from Heinemann found in the back pages of *Spirits in Bondage*, the book is advertised as the work of 'George Lewis': 'Crown 8vo. Cloth 3s.6d. net. Lieut. G.S. Lewis, who is 20 years of age, was at Malvern College when the war broke out. In 1916 he took a classical scholarship at University College, Oxford, and a year later received his commission in the Somerset Light Infantry. He was wounded in front of Lillers in April, 1918.' C.S. Evans wrote to Lewis on 7 April 1919 saying, 'I do not know how the "C" became changed into "G" and hence by a natural deduction into "George", except that we have another poet whose name is George Hamilton' (LP VI: 106).

TO HIS FATHER (LP VI: 58–9):

No. 3 Officer's Mess,
Perham Downs Camp.
Ludgershall,
Hants.
27th[26th?] Oct. 1918

My dear Papy,

I succeeded in getting my day off to see Heinemann yesterday, after being stopped last week through a very ridiculous incident of a kind that is common in the army. In order to get leave for a day you have to write down your name, the time of leaving, and your destination in the book which is then signed by the medical officer. Last week the book was lost: no objection was made to my going on either military or medical grounds, but – how could I go without the book? A suggestion that I might write the particulars on a slip of paper which could then afterwards be put in the book was treated as a sort of sacrilege. After a week however it occurred to the Adjutant (who must be a man of bold originality and signal generosity) that we might spend half a crown on a new book, and so I was able to go after all.

Heinemann was out when I reached the office and I was shown in to the Manager, a man called Evans, quite a young fellow and very agreeable. Afterwards Heinemann himself came in and I was with him for about three-quarters of an hour. He produced a typed agreement of which, with many 'hereinafter's and 'aforesaid's, the gist is that they are to publish the book 'at their own expense, in such style and to be sold at such price as they deem best' and that I am 'to receive the following royalty: 10% of the profits on the published price of 12 out of every thirteen copies sold'. It concludes with a stipulation that they should have the refusal of my next work, if any. Whether I am being well or ill treated I am of course too ignorant to say: but I suppose, poetry being such an unprofitable branch of publishing, I have no reason to be dissatisfied. He also told me that John Galsworthy (who publishes with them) had seen my MS and wanted to publish a certain poem in a new monthly called 'Revielle' which he is bringing out in aid of disabled soldiers and sailors. I naturally consented, both because it is pleasant 'laudari a laudato viro' and because it is an excellent advertisement. Before I left he said he would go on with the printing at once and might be able to have the proofs ready for me in three weeks. He is a fat little man with a bald head, apparently well read, and a trifle fussy – inclined to get his papers mixed up and repeat himself.

Thank you very much for the cigarettes and tobacco – I was just out of the latter. I am sending you the last batch of photos of the child, taken in Bristol some time ago and only now developed. Let me know what you think of them.

Lunch in London on omlettes, fish, hors d'oeuvres and other non-coupon dishes was alright – but what about one scone and cup of tea at 1/6?

your loving son,
Jack

P.S. By the way I've never had any finished copies of those last photos taken at home – could you please send me some. J.

TO ARTHUR GREEVES (W):

[Perham Downs Camp,
Ludgershall]
Saturday [2 November 1918]

My dear Arthur,

Many thanks for your letter (what a conventional opening!) which shows you much more cheerful and contented than you were in the last. I am delighted about these classes at the technical, and I am sure, tho' it may be tiring at times, that you will feel much the better for them both in your painting and spirits. What sort of people do you meet there? I suppose they are of all ages, sexes and classes, but you ought with luck to find plenty of interesting folk in a place of that sort.

I suppose I *was* the last person to whom the bramble spoke. Your reference to her does carry one back to the old days that were so happy although one hardly realized how happy at the time (another frightfully conventional remark, but you can't help feeling that it's true). It is terrible to think how quickly an old order changes and how impossible it is to build it up again exactly the same.

I wonder will there be many changes when we meet again? Maureen told me the other day that I was greatly changed since she first knew me, but, with the impenetrable reticence of a child, declined to say in what way. Personally I don't feel very different. I suppose I am a bit broader – more tolerant of people different from ourselves and readier to see the good points in a well-meaning philistine – but I think my interests and ambitions are pretty much the same. You, I imagine from your letters, are a good deal broader, and have developed considerably, especially in your taste for poetry: your dip into the slightly decadent but charming 'celtic' circle at Dublin has certainly made you less of a Northerner. You were once a trifle bigoted about catholicism: that has passed. I suppose we are each of us different from being away from the other: we had perhaps learned to think & even read too much with an eye on the other's criticism. However we shall have enough to talk about for years, when once we get going.

By the way these rather stuffy reflections are holding up all my real news. Last Friday, or rather last Friday week, I made a journey to London to see Heinemanns.[79] You will understand well how pleasant it was to walk in under a doorway, adorned with the 'windmill' we have so often seen, feeling that I had some right to be there. I offered a card to a young woman who said that she thought Mr H. was out, would I see the manager? I was led through innumerable corridors, thro' all sorts of offices, past armies of typists and shown into a rather dingy room. C. S. Evans, the manager, was a young man, pale and fair &, I think, a gentleman. He was very nice to me and quite enthusiastic about the book and especially about one piece. John Galsworthy, he said, had read the MS. and wanted to put this piece in a new Quarterly which he is bringing out for disabled soldiers & sailors called Reveille: of course I consented.[80] While we were talking he was interrupted to speak on the telephone. I listened to quite a long technical conversation (if you can call *one* end of a telephone conversation) apparently with a female interlocutor on 'some designs for endleaves' – all of which, as you would heartily agree with me, was very interesting.

Later on H. himself came in. He was a little, fat bald man, very agreeable and fussy, but, as far as one could see, a really literary not a mere business man. We fixed up all the formalities about terms and he hopes to let me have the proofs in about three weeks.

---

79 On 25 October.

80 When it was discovered that Robert Hitchens had published a book under the title *Spirits in Prison* in 1908, Lewis (who altered his pseudonym to 'Clive Hamilton') changed the title of his to *Spirits in Bondage*, a phrase borrowed from Milton's *Paradise Lost*, I, 658.

I returned home treading on air and bought a copy of Reveille – the August number & the first. It included only one poem, by Kipling so I suppose I should be satisfied with the company. So at last dreams come to pass and I have sat in the sanctum of a publisher discussing my own book (Notice the hideous vulgarity of success already growing in me). Yet – though it is very pleasant – you will understand me when I say that it has not the utter romance which the promise of it had a year ago. Once a dream has become a fact I suppose it loses something. This isn't affectation: we long & long for a thing and when it comes it turns out to be just a pleasant incident, very much like others.

The country is gorgeous, it is so still that hardly a leaf has fallen & I have never seen such autumn colours anywhere. There are lovely beech woods down beyond Savernake with winding roads thro' them and some fine old houses hidden away. They are all like a big yellow flame now – and a lovely autumn smell. Am sending you a new photo to-morrow

Yours
Jack

TO HIS FATHER (LP VI: 62–3):

No. 3 Officer's Mess,
Perham Downs Camp,
Ludgershall.
Hants.
3 Sept. [November] 1918

My dear Papy,

The first parcel of smokeables *did* arrive safely despite its perilous transit through Ashton Court and was acknowledged in my last letter: I am therefore the richer by your qualms on that subject and acknowledge my 'dutiful thanks' for both.

You may make your mind easy on the question of the War Office's 'tricks', as my removal to a command depot is quite in order. At the same time I am afraid I shall have to disappoint you on the two months leave as I am not likely to get nearly so long. The idea doubtless arose in your mind from the fact that officers discharged from hospital and still convalescent, were formerly sent home and told to report for a board again in two, three or even six months' time. This however was

'In the olden
Time long ago'

It was found that the average uniformed bounder had only two interests – alcohol and women – and that two months' undisturbed indulgence in his natural tastes left him very much less fit than when he began. As well, men were continually being forgotten, and there were even cases of officer's desertion: consequently tho' Majors 'et hoc genus omne'[81] still get their sick leave, we unfortunates convalesce in hospitals and depots and get some leave as a sop after we are cured. As usual, the innocent suffer for the guilty, but this is too common an event to surprise either you or me. Any attempt to 'work' things is dangerous: we had a hopelessly unfit man at Ashton, who, on trying to be sent to a different hospital, was boarded and sent to France. It's a way they have in the army.

Since you have asked about the state of the exchequer – I find my pay quite sufficient for ordinary purposes and even for such mild luxuries as I want. It would be quite unfair for a person in my position to expect pocket money from his father. Distinct from these ordinary expenses however, I would mention the quite *extra*-ordinary one of getting a new uniform (for which I am sending you the receipt) and boots, very cheap at 36/-. If you don't agree with me in calling this an extra-ordinary expense, say so of course quite frankly, I shall not be at all hurt. There was also a revolver which I have not replaced. Perhaps indeed the whole bill should be sent in to 'A firer of gun, name and location uncertain'!

I was wrong in calling 'Reviellé' a monthly, it is a quarterly. I have bought a copy of the first number (which is dated August) to spy out the land. It contains only one poem – by Kipling, not at his best, and is rather more technical and propagandist than I had hoped. However, it will be a useful enough means of drawing attention to ones existance.

Yes – a year and six days is a long stretch enough: indeed my life is rapidly becoming divided into two periods, one including all the time before we got into the battle of Arras, the other ever since. Already last year seems a long, long way off. However, there appears to be some prospect of the whole beastly business coming to an end fairly soon.

your loving son,
Jack

---

81 'and all that sort'.

TO HIS FATHER (LP VI: 65–6):

No. 3 Officer's Mess,
Perham Down Camp,
Ludgershall,
Hants.
10th Nov. 1918

My dear Papy,

I have three things to acknowledge with thanks – cigarettes, photos, and a cheque. As to the photos, the only case in which I am really able to judge of the likeness is the 'crack' one. This I think is very good indeed and greatly superior to any of the single photos of you which have yet appeared. It is unfortunate that they all have such serious technical imperfections of blurring. I will direct the Bristol photographer to send you some copies of the new one which you like – of course without the account: this is my show.

Although one does not wish to live in a fool's paradise or be foolishly confident, yet I do think the present course of events is such as to render the question of trying to get a home job rather less important than it was a month ago. In twenty four hours time it may have ceased to have any meaning at all. Of course even if we do get peace, I suppose I shall take some time in escaping from the army. But in no position should I stand a better chance of a speedy discharge than in my present one of convalescent officer at a Command Depot. Our attitude therefore must simply be to 'stand by'. I do not know what your views on the present situation are, but suppose you have reached the situation prophesied by George Harding in which you and Hope will no longer be able to 'have a real good talk'.

Of course the question whether Heinemann is treating me well or no has often been in my mind, and I have come to the conclusion that such an agreement is all that we have a right to expect. We must remember that even when poetry has a 'succès fou' it is still less profitable to the publisher than even fairly good fiction. As Evans said to me, 'We don't expect to make a commercial success out of poetry: we only publish it – well simply because its good'. This of course may be an exaggeration, but surely there is a good deal of truth in it? I was particularly careful to find out exactly what the 'first refusal' clause committed me to. I began by asking if this would prevent me writing a magazine article if ever I wanted to. Evans said 'Of course not' and added, 'All the clause means is this, Mr. Lewis. You send us your next MS. If we don't like it we shan't take it: if you don't like our terms you won't let us have it'. That seems a straight enough proposition. There was no suggestion at all that I should *have* to sell them at the same terms as the first.

Since you ask, such compliments as I was payed by Heinemann were of a somewhat peculiar nature – their object being to impress upon me the great honour that was being done me, and the majesty of the firm. 'Of course Mr. Lewis we never accept poetry unless it is really good' and more in that strain – with mental reservations on my part as I remembered some specimens. He merely said that Galsworthy 'admired' the one he wanted for Reveillé.

We have been innoculated against the influenza here. If it is at all bad at home I should get it done. It is not worth one's while risking ones life over a thing like that and the innoculation is very mild. It proved an effective check in Paris and why it has not been more widely used here, goodness only knows.

With many thanks for everything and best love,
I am your loving son,
Jack

On 11 November, Albert Lewis wrote in his diary: 'Armistice signed. War ended. Thanks be to God.'

TO HIS FATHER (LP VI: 68–9):

Officers' Command Depot,
Eastbourne.
Suffolk [Sussex]
[17? November 1918]

My dear Papy,

As you see, I have been moved again. That is to say I have in the literal sense covered several hundreds of miles of country, but in the military sense I have not moved at all. In other words, 'Command Depot' itself has moved: as a step towards demobilisation the officers who were scattered at various depots over the country have been collected into a special depot for officers here. As to the great news which is uppermost in our minds, I can only echo what you have already said. The man who can give way to mafficking at such a time is more than indecent – he is mad. I remember five of us at Keble, and I am the only survivor: I think of Mr Sutton, a widower with five sons, all of whom have gone. One cannot help wondering why. Let us be silent and thankful.

The question of how to get most quickly out of the army has of course occupied me too. I wrote to Macan explaining my position and asking whether Colleges propose to make any representations to the powers on behalf of the Sam-Browned freshmen who wanted to get back – for I had heard that something of that kind was being done. He replied in a kind and even cordial letter that I was not likely, so far as he knew, to be discharged for several months, and that the head of the U.T.C.[82] was writing to me. The latter wrote to me saying that if I could get passed by a board as 'unfit for at least three months' I could go back to Oxford in khaki and on army pay, for what they call 'an intensive course of University training' on the chance of not being disturbed again. This seems to me however rather a cat and mouse business, and for another thing, I don't think any board is likely to pass me as unfit for three months. As regards wire pulling, we must remember that there are thousands of other young men in the same position, each thinking that his own claims for an early release are particularly pressing: I doubt if personal influence is likely to alter the plan of demobilisation much. Of course too there is the danger of being passed fit for that army of occupation.

We're a nice pair! In the same letter you say – quite truly – that I have never told you to what extent I am likely to be disabled by the wound, and also that you are in Squeaky's hands for trouble – unspecified.[83] Well let's make a bargain. Here is my health report, and in return I shall look for a full account of your own bother. The effects of the wound in general movement are practically nil. I can do everything except hold my left arm straight above my head, which I don't want to do anyway. The effects on general health are very small: I have had one or two stoppages of breath which I am told are not unusual after a chest wound and which will soon disappear, and of course I still get tired easily and have a few headaches in the evenings. On the nerves there are two effects which will probably go with quiet and rest...[84] The other is nightmares – or rather the same nightmare over and over again. Nearly everyone has it, and

82 University Training Courses.

83 'Squeaky Dick', as Richard Whytock Leslie, MD (1862–1931) was known to many, was the Lewis family doctor.

84 The Lewis brothers removed a passage from this letter when it was typed for the Lewis Papers.

though very unpleasant, it is passing and will do no harm. So you see I am almost 'in statu quo'. I certainly don't think the removal of the piece would be advisable.

The proofs of the book are expected any day and it will probably be out in the Christmas list. I hope you will not be disappointed in it. Have you any news of when Warnie is likely to be home?

With best love and heartiest congratulations on the good fortune we have both shared, I am,

your loving son,
Jack

TO ARTHUR GREEVES (W):

Officers' Command Depôt,
Eastbourne.[85]
Monday 2nd [December 1918]

My dear Arthur,

Many thanks for your letter. I am sorry to have left you so long without anything; the chief reason was the bustle of being moved here. At first I thought it abominable – it is [a] much worse camp than the Ludgershall one – but now that the others[86] have come down of course I spend most of my time out.

You are wrong in supposing that I am doing no reading, indeed I don't know why I have not kept you up to date. I have just finished the life of Browning (Everyman) by Dowden[87] which was a most interesting book – just what the life of a writer should be in my opinion, i.e mainly about his work, not all futile personal details & dates. Moved by this I read his (B's) 'Paracelsus'[88] which I liked much better than I expected. Of course a good deal of it is not what we used to call poetry in the good old days, but there are some bits of the real stuff and it is all full of interest.

But the great event is that I have learned to enjoy Shakespeare. I bought an Everyman copy of the Comedies[89] and am just finishing 'Measure for Measure'. Isn't it funny the way you come round to things you

---

85 Lewis was moved here about the middle of November.

86 Mrs Moore and Maureen.

87 Edward Dowden, *Robert Browning* (1915).

88 Robert Browning, *Paracelsus* (1835).

89 *Shakespeare's Comedies*, with biographical introduction by Oliphant Smeaton and prefatory notes by D.C. Browning (1906).

used to hate? I think the characterisation is excellent & there are fine passages of poetry. Don't you like Claudio's piece about,

> '*worse than worst*
> *Of those that wayward & uncertain thought*
> *Imagines howling*'?[90]

I am also reading Virgil & Euripides 'Alcestis'.[91]

At the same time I am doing a lot of writing again. I have just finished a short narrative, which is a verse version of our old friend 'Dymer', greatly reduced & altered to my new ideas. The main idea is that of development by self-destruction, both of individuals & species (as nature produces man only to conquer her [*sic*], & man produces a future & higher generation to conquer the ideals of the last, or again as an individual produces a nobler mood to undo all that to-day's has done). The background proceeds on the old assumption of good *outside & opposed to* the cosmic order. It is written in the metre of Venus & Adonis:[92] 'Dymer' is changed to 'Ask' (you remember Ask & Embla in the Norse myths) & it is in the 3rd person under the title of 'The Redemption of Ask'. I am wondering what you will think of it. I am also at work on a short blank verse scene (you can hardly call it a play) between Tristram & King Mark & a poem on Ion, which is a failure so far.

By the way have you thought of getting the Xmas Bookman? I suppose not & I am in despair because it has all been bought up in advance. It is a thing I always want to get & it will be especially desirable this year as it may have a review of my book in it. Item, the proofs have NOT come yet but we live in hopes.

It is almost incredible that the war is over, isn't it – not to have that 'going-back' hanging over my head all the time. This time last year I was in the trenches, & now – but, come!, the tendency to moralize is getting the better of me. The child[93] is writing another fairy tale – rather the plan of 'Puck of Pook's Hill' I fancy.

Yours
Jack

---

90 William Shakespeare, *Measure for Measure* (1623), III, i, 124 (slightly misquoted).

91 Euripides (480–406 BC), *Alcestis*.

92 William Shakespeare, *Venus and Adonis* (1593).

93 The 'child' is probably Maureen Moore.

TO HIS FATHER (LP VI: 74–5):

Officer's Command depot,
Eastbourne.
8th Dec. 1918

My dear Papy,

I have put off answering your birthday letter and thanking you for the enclosure in the hope that your answer to my last, which is now due, would arrive. I am anxiously awaiting your views on the University Training Corps business: until I hear these I am rather uneasy about taking even such negative action as is implied in doing nothing.

The first disappointment of 'this publishing business' reached me last week and has probably by now reached you. Of course Galsworthy had every right to change his mind on the merits of my piece, but I will admit that I was rather annoyed to find that neither he nor Heinemann saw fit to tell me the fact. I first knew of it by seeing a copy of 'Reveillé' on the local book stall.[94] However these things are common enough in the lives of even real writers, and there is no need to grouse. Let us go and solace our hearts with Mr. Nichol's more successful chef d'oeuvre.

As you have probably seen in the papers, we are all going to get 12 days 'Christmas leave'. I use the inverted commas advisedly as mine seems likely to be in January. I suppose it would be unreasonable to expect them to let us all go at the same time, and you and I won't quarrel with dates. It has been a long time coming and a time unpleasantly and wastefully spent, but thank God it is over at last. By the way, although, as I understand, I am entitled to a vote, I have not yet received any of the 'Election Communications' which have fallen to the lot of most men I know. Perhaps you can advise the constituency that it is in danger of losing the support of an influential voter! I suppose we are all voting for the Coalition, though I must confess I distrust them most heartily and look for no liberty as long as they are in power. Most of us here would be ready to vote for Lucifer himself if he rose up in red velvet and sulpher whispering the word 'Discharged'. But I see we are not to be 'discharged' but demobilized and kept on a leash for the rest of our lives. Sometimes when I think of this I feel inclined to go and steal a red flag from the neighbouring golf course.

Could you please send me a Greek Lexicon which you will find – I hope – in the little end room, and also Sophocles 'Oedipus Rex' or

94 The publishers had decided not to include Lewis's poem in issue No. 2 of *Reveille*.

'O.Tyrrannus'[95] which you will find among three blue volumes of Sophocles in the middle of the second shelf from the top of the bookcase furthest from the window. If you also had room for Tasso's 'Gerusalemme Liberata'[96] from the top shelf, I should be 'eternally beholden to you'.

At my suggestion Mrs Moore has come down here and is staying in rooms near the camp, where I hope she will remain until I go on leave. It is a great relief to get away from the army atmosphere, although for that matter I have been lucky in finding several decent fellows, including even another aspirant for poetical laurels – a most amusing card. It is fine country down here and I am glad that chance has given me its hills and cliffs to walk on. Certainly, if nothing else, the army has shown me some bits of England that I would not otherwise have seen.

I hope for your letter soon and that it will bring no bad news of that 'trouble' of yours.

With love and thanks,
your loving,
son,
Jack

TO HIS FATHER (LP VI: 76):

Officers Command Depot,
Eastbourne,
Sussex.
Dec. [16?]th, 1918.

My dear Papy,

Thank you very much for the letter and enclosure and also for the two books which arrived today in excellent condition. I have already wired to you the dates of my leave:[97] a list of the periods alloted to each of us has been posted up here, and, as was to be expected, the coveted dates which would include Christmas fall to the Majors and Captains 'et hoc genus omne'. If however you can let Warnie know in time, I should think he would have no difficulty in getting his leave postponed. Everyone of course will be trying to get home for Christmas day, and it ought to be easy to change with someone who had got a later date against his will.

95 Sophocles (496–406 BC), one of the great Greek tragedians, wrote *Oedipus Tyrannus*.
96 Torquato Tasso, *Gerusalemme Liberata* (1581).
97 The telegram to his father of 16 December reads: 'Leave tenth to twenty second January.'

I quite agree with you that it would be most disappointing if even now our little gathering were broken up.

Of course I shall be only too pleased if any influence of yours could succeed in getting me a discharge, though at the same time I am afraid it will be a very difficult business. As you have probably seen in the papers, we are to be drafted on our demobilization in 'Class Z Reserve' where I suppose we shall remain ready for the next scrape that some Labour government in the future may get the country into. I don't want to be pessimistic, but there does not seem much hope of ever being quite free of the army again. To get a discharge might be possible on the score of unfitness, but I do not think that my degree of military unfitness will be sufficient to serve our turn.

What you have to say on the Reviellé question makes me feel rather a fool: no doubt it must be as you say. The only thing that bothers me is this. Surely Heinemann will get my book out before the next quarterly season begins? – and if so, is it usual for a periodical to publish an extract from a book *after* that book itself has appeared? However, it is quite an unimportant sideshow.

About the 'University Training Course', I still think as I thought before that it would be almost useless for me to try and get that 3 months verdict from a board. I only wanted to see if you thought the thing so desirable that you would wish me to try on the off chance. Since we both look eye to eye on the matter and are not inclined to jump at any disguised backwater of the army (you can still see the brass buttons under the gown!), we may let it drop.

So far my readings both in Latin and Greek have been a pleasant surprise: I have forgotten less than I feared, and once I get the sound and savour of the language into my head by a spell of reading, composition should not come too hard either. In English I have started friend Trollope again – 'The Small House at Allington'.

I hope that trouble of yours is really better – as you say, it is an unpleasant complaint and leads to a good many inconveniences.

With best love, your loving son,

Jack

TO HIS FATHER (LP VI: 77):

Officers Command Depot,
Eastbourne,
Sussex.
Dec. 22nd. 1918

My dear Papy,

The selection of possible books here was so small that I was really driven to this as a last resource: if you have it already, or if you do not like it, I expect that Mullen's will be gracious and change it.

The slippers were got for the benefit of corns and sore feet. I should like them to have been better, but as you know, the war has pretty well drained the English shops of leather goods.

With my very best love and heartiest wishes for a happy Christmas, a speedy reunion, and a prosperous and peaceful New Year for us all, I am,

your loving son,
Jack

Jack had told his father that his leave was not until 10 to 22 January. Warnie, who was in France, was unable to alter the dates of his leave and he arrived in Belfast on the morning of 23 December. Jack was discharged from the hospital on 24 December, and he found himself demobilized from the army. There was not enough time to alert his father before he set off for home. In his diary of 27 December Warnie wrote: 'A red letter day today. We were sitting in the study about 11 o'clock this morning when we saw a cab coming up the avenue. It was Jacks! He has been demobilized thank God. Needless to say there were great doings. He is looking pretty fit. We had lunch and then all three went for a walk. It was as if the evil dream of four years had passed away and we were still in the year 1915. In the evening there was bubbly for dinner in honour of the event. The first time I have ever had champagne at home. Had the usual long conversation with Jacks after going to bed' (LP VI: 79). Following this reunion, Jack returned to Oxford on 13 January 1919 to begin the Classical Honour Moderations course in Greek and Latin literature. He was living in University College, still in Room 5 on Staircase XII. Mrs Moore and Maureen found rooms nearby in the home of Miss Featherstone at 28 Warneford Road, Oxford. Meanwhile, Jack's father had been urging him to write to the War Office about a possible pension, and the next letter was written in Oxford but 'as from' his home in Belfast.

1919

TO THE SECRETARY, WAR OFFICE (PUBLIC RECORD OFFICE):

Little Lea,
Strandtown,
Belfast
Jan 18th 1919

Sir,

On the 26th of September 1917 I was appointed from the Oxford University O.T.C. to a temporary commission in the Regular Army. I joined the Somerset Light Infantry on the 16th October and crossed to France on the 17th of November. I was severely wounded near Lillers on the 15th April 1918 and remained in Hospitals and Command Depôts until the 24th December 1918 when I was demobilised. I have up till now recieved neither gratuity nor pension. I shall be obliged by your informing me when I may expect a communication on the subject.

I am, Sir,
Your obedient servant,
C. S. Lewis

TO ARTHUR GREEVES (W):

[University College,
Oxford
26 January 1919]

My dear Arthur,

I was agreeably surprised to hear from you so soon: perhaps you will be equally surprised to hear that I have already performed your commissions if not to your satisfaction at any rate vastly to my own. I found two complete editions of the Larger Temple Sh.,[1] one new and the other second

1 *The Works of Shakespeare*, ed. Israel Gollancz, 12 vols., 'The Larger Temple Shakespeare' (1899).

hand at 36/-. In neither case would they sell separate volumes and I therefore got the 36/- one myself with malicious glee! It is a little bit battered in some volumes but absolutely clean inside and has the real pre-war guilding, and good edges. Slowly as I can afford [it] I must get them re-bound.

As to the Gibbon they showed me specimen volumes of two editions both by Methuen: the larger one at 10/6 a volume was about the size of your 'British Empire' book & very similar in paper and type: the binding was a somewhat unpleasant ribbed blue cloth with elaborate gilding on the back – not unlike my Benedetto Croce. The smaller was the one which my father has, beautifully fresh & clean: I have therefore asked them to order this,[2] explaining that it would be no use unless they could get you the complete set – which they seem fairly confident of doing. I suppose this is what you would like done? I certainly envy you such a nice book if they *do* get a complete set: where will you put it? I am very pleased indeed with my Shakespeare.

Now for some account of myself and my doings. My day is as follows: called at 7.30, bath, chapel and breakfast – in Hall.* Owing to the lack of coal and servants we are having all our meals in Hall this term. Next term we hope to go back to the traditional and much more pleasant arrangement of having breakfast and lunch in our own rooms. After breakfast I work (in the library or a lecture-room which are both warm) or attend lectures until 1 o'clock when I bycycle out to Mrs Moore's.

They are installed in our 'own hired house'[3] (like St Paul only not daily preaching & teaching). The owner of the house has not yet cleared out & we pay a little less than the whole for her still having a room. She is an elderly maiden lady and – I am not joking – a saint. She gets up early every morning and goes to church – very high Anglican – through the bitter frost. In spite of protests she brings Mrs Moore a cup of tea in the morning: she can hardly be persuaded to use her own kitchen, which by the arrangement should be common to us both. Altogether a most remarkable character – and very given to good works. At another house we tried we met a Miss Tennyson, niece of the poet.

After lunch I work until tea, then work again till dinner. After that a little more work, talk and laziness & sometimes bridge then bycycle back

2 Edward Gibbon, *The History of the Decline and Fall of the Roman Empire* (1776–88), ed. J.B. Bury, 7 vols., 'Methuen's Standard Library' (1905–6).

3 Acts 28:30: 'And Paul dwelt two whole years in his own hired house, and received all that came in unto him.'

to College at 11. I then light my fire and work or read till 12 o'clock when I retire to sleep the sleep of the just. At this little end of the day I have read three Acts of King John which I like immensely. At that time of life he wrote much more simply: the verse has a more correct flow and the characters are easily understood. Don't you like Constance, especially her speech about death & the scene between Pandulph & the Dauphin just afterwards?[4] Also, whether working or not I always end the day by looking into Bridges. He is so quiet and has something for every mood.

(From this [point] on you may read the letter to my father if you want.) The place is more beautiful than ever in this weather: every morning when I am called I see a lovely picture out of my window: a battlemented tower and three bare trees against the cold, cold red of the morning: then looking out you see the grass of the quad. powdered in white and all the old stone of the roofs white too and pinched with cold. However one can get quite warm in the library or the Junior Common Room: of course it is in the former I work – if only you could smoke there, it would be ideal: the temptation to spend all your time rambling over the interesting modern books & the great old worm-eaten folios has to be sternly resisted!

Now for a piece of good luck – I go to lectures by Gilbert Murray twice a week, on Euripides 'Bacchae'. Luckily I have read the play before and can therefore give him a freeër attention: it is a very wierd play (you have read his translation, have you not?) and he is a real inspiration, – quite as good as his best books, if only he didn't dress so horribly, worse even than most dons. I go to Christchurch to hear him and to Balliol to hear a man called Bailey on Lucretius, who is very amusing.[5] He began by saying 'I hope none of you gentlemen have got my edition of this book[6] as it was written in my unregenerate days.'

One of the things that worries me is that every lecturer you go to tells you of about 5 books 'you should all have access to', which comes expensive. Some, of course, can be got second hand: my regular book-monger keeps his second-hand stock downstairs in a 12th century crypt, at one period haunted by Guy Faulkes.[7] Some of the best bits of Oxford seem to

4 William Shakespeare, *King John* (1623), III, i, 29ff.

5 Cyril Bailey (1871–1957) was Classical Tutor at Balliol College.

6 *Lucreti De Rerum Natura Libri Sex. Recognovit brevique adnotatione critica instruxit C. Bailey* [1899].

7 This was Mr H.G. Gadney's bookshop at 2 and 3 Turl Street. It later became the Turl Cash Bookshop – taking its name from the fact that Mr Gadney never gave credit. The 12th century crypt, haunted by Guy Fawkes, is now 'The Crypt' of the Mitre restaurant.

be underground – hidden away beneath prosaic grocers, hotels and tobacconists. Another thing that bothers me is the terrible independence with which you have to work here: I only see my tutor once a week and at other times it is very trying to reflect after a long day's work that you may have been simply wasting your time ever since you got up. On the whole, however, I get on fairly well & the amount of reading I've done stands me in good stead. Of course there is very little time for ordinary reading, which has to be confined to the week-end as it was at Kirk's. At present I am still at the Philosopher book which is excellent.

I have found one old friend, Edwards, who was here when I was last up and, as an 'unfit' has been here all the time. It is good to be back and doing something one is interested in. I bless my good fortune every night when I hear the hours strike, lying in my bed. One chime takes it from another with varying notes, getting fainter & fainter, as though the whole great city were turning over and settling itself to sleep in the cold, cold night. That Debussy thing keeps on running in my head. I hope the biliousness is gone, & that you are getting on with your varying works: anything in the writing line?

Yours
Jack

* I mean breakfast only in hall – not bath & chapel as well.

TO HIS FATHER (LP VI: 82–3):

University College,
Oxford.
Jan. 27th 1919

My dear Papy,

Before giving any account of myself and my doings, I should let you know what we have missed. The letter from Aunt Lily[8] which you forwarded to me announced that she would soon be arriving in Belfast 'for two days'. She proposed to come and see the Hamiltonians 'we could walk down together and have a good talk on the way; perhaps that nice boy Arthur Greeves would join us'. May one be permitted to hope that the good lady has been even better consoled by a good talk with you. I can just see the picture.

8 Jack's aunt, Mrs Lilian Hamilton Suffern. See note 21 to the letter of 14 May 1918.

After a quite comfortable journey (which showed me that 1st. Class travelling is very little different from 3rd) I arrived here somewhat late in the evening. The moon was just rising: the porter knew me at once and ushered me into the same old rooms (which by the way I am going to change).[9] It was a great return and something to be very thankful for. I was also pleased to find an old friend, Edwards, who was up with me in 1916, and being unfit, has been there all the time. There is of course already a great difference between this Oxford and the ghost I knew before: true, we are only twenty eight in College, but we *do* dine in Hall again, the Junior Common Room is no longer swathed in dust sheets, and the old round of lectures, debates, games, and whatnot is getting under weigh. The reawakening is a little pathetic: at our first[10] we read the minutes of the last – 1914. I don't know any little thing that has made me realise the absolute suspension and waste of these years more thoroughly.

The Mugger[11] preached a quite memorable sermon on the first Sunday evening. It was very plain, even homely in style, not what one expected, but it grew on one, and I admire the restraint where 'gush' would have been so fatally easy. By the way, I have not been asked to see the Mugger yet, but I gather he has a waiting list and is working slowly through it. We have quite a number of old members who were up before the war and are a kind of dictionary of traditions.

Now as to work: I am 'deemed to have passed' Responsions and Divinity and it was open to me either to take Honour Mods or go straight on to 'Greats'[12] – as you know, the final fence. In consideration of my wish to get a fellowship, Poynton,[13] who is my tutor, strongly advised me not to avail myself of this opportunity of slurring over Mods. I presume I was acting as I should when I followed his advice. Except for the disadvantage of starting eighteen books of Homer to the bad I find

9 Room 5 on Staircase XII.

10 i.e. the first meeting of the Junior Common Room.

11 The Master of University College, R.W. Macan.

12 'Greats' or *Literae Humaniores* is the study of philosophy and ancient history. Midway in the student's second year he takes the first public examination in what is called Classical Honour Moderations, an examination in Greek and Latin. It is possible, however, to go directly to 'Greats' which is the second part of *Literae Humaniores*. Given the choice, Lewis decided not to bypass Classical Honour Moderations.

13 Arthur Blackburne Poynton is mentioned in note 62 to the letter of 28 April 1917.

myself fairly alright: of course the great difference after Kirk's is that you are left to work very much on your own. It is a little bit strange at first, but I suppose hard work in any lines will not be wasted. The best thing I go to is the series of lectures by Gilbert Murray, which are very good indeed: I always feel much the better for them.

The coal difficulty is not very serious. We have all our meals in Hall, which, if it abolishes the cosy breakfast in one's rooms and the interchange of 'decencies and proprieties' is a little cheaper: we shall go back to the old arrangement as soon as we can. The library, one lecture room, and the Junior Common Room are always warm, and the two former are quite quiet: then for the evening we can afford a modest blaze at one's 'ain fireside'. Our little body gets on very well together and most of us work. The place is looking more beautiful than ever in the wintry frost: one gets splendid cold colouring at the expense of tingling fingers and red noses.

I hope the water works in front of the dining room windows is being restored, and that you are keeping well. How is the finger?

your loving son,
Jack

TO HIS FATHER (LP VI: 85–6):

University College,
Oxford.
4th Feb. 1919

My dear Papy,

Although, as you say, your letter was not a 'real' one, the absence of a successor to it leads me to believe that the word is again with me. Before this I hope that you have got mine. Thank you for the enclosure which so far I have failed to change as they ask me for my 'certificate'. If you have it I had better get it or else send you the other thing to change. The private letter which you enclose was rather funny: it thanks me for a subscription to the 'Strandtown Sewing Guild' – which I have never heard of. I suppose it was really given by you – or is W. a keen amateur of sewing guilds?

With regard to things in general here I don't know that I have much to add to my last letter. I find the work pretty stiff, but I think I am keeping my head above water. Poynton is, so far as I can judge, quite an exceptionally good tutor, and my visits to him are enjoyable as well as useful – although he objects to my style of Greek prose – 'I don't care very much for treacle *or* barley sugar myself'. So you have bequeathed to me some remnant of the old Macaulese taint after all. I drank tea with him last Sunday. Another man from Univ. went with me and the party consisted of Mrs and Miss Poynton, two girl undergraduates, and ourselves. As a matter of fact our host did nearly all the talking and kept us very well amused: he is an excellent if somewhat unjust raconteur. He came up to Balliol under Jowett and had a lot to say of the great man. It's funny you know, they all laugh at him, they all imitate his little mannerisms, but nobody who ever met him forgets to tell you so.

Much to my surprise I have had 'greatness thrust upon me'.[14] There is a literary club in College called the Martlets, limited to twelve undergraduate members: it is over three hundred years old, and alone of all College Clubs has its minutes preserved in the Bodleian.[15] I have been elected Secretary – the reason being of course that my proposer, Edwards, was afraid of getting the job himself. And so if I am forgotten of all else, at least a specimen of my handwriting will be preserved to posterity. Someone will read a paper on Yeats at our next meeting: we are also going to have one on Masefield and we hope to get Masefield himself (who lives just outside)[16] to come up and listen to it and give a reply.

I have a very bad piece of news for you: Smugy is dead.[17] Sometime in the middle of last term he fell a victim to flu. I suppose I am very inexperienced but I had come to depend on his always being there – to quote a specimen of his Little Thompson, to welcome me back some day to criticise the book. Poor old man! I heard this from my friend Cooper who is up at Christchurch. As he is in a most expensive College and arrayed in glory, I suppose – and hope – that there has been a change in the family fortunes.

14 Shakespeare, *Twelfth Night*, II, v, 161.

15 The Martlets somehow acquired the reputation of dating 'from dim antiquity' but their first meeting was in 1892. The minute books are in the Bodleian Library under the shelfmark MS. Top Oxon. d. 95/1–5. There is an article on 'The Martlets' by P.C. Bayley in the *University College Record* (1949–1950). Walter Hooper's 'To the Martlets' in *C.S. Lewis: Speaker and Teacher*, ed. Carolyn Keefe (1971) contains the minutes of the papers Lewis read to the society between 1919 and 1940.

16 i.e. outside Oxford.

17 Harry Wakelyn Smith, who taught Classics and English at Malvern College. See note 16 to the letter of 21 September 1913.

I am afraid all this must sound rather selfish to you in the Bolshevik darkness of Belfast: but you have my sympathy – if only nothing worse comes of it. The Clyde business seems to have been settled without a concession, and that is the best sign we have.[18]

With best love,
your loving son,
Jack

TO ARTHUR GREEVES (W):

[University College
9 February 1919]

My dear Arthur,

I am really sorry that I did not write you your letter as I should last week. At present I am working at such high pressure that if anything unexpected turns up it must swallow something else. So long as nothing interrupts my routine I get on just comfortably, with a little time to spare at week ends for reading: when something does, I am stranded. However I hope to be more regular in future. Last Sunday I had to go out to tea with a don here called Poynton who is my tutor.

The place has been looking just lovely in the snow. As you come out of our college gate you see All Souls and just beyond it the grey spire of St Mary's Church: you know what real Gothic is like: all little pinaccles with every kind of ornament on them and in the snow they look like a wintry forest hung up against the dark sky, and always associated in ones mind with the sound of bells. Just beyond St Marys you come into a solemn silent square with the great dome of the Bodleian in the middle: you can imagine how fine it looks with the white carpet underfoot. But I must send you some penny postcards.

I expected my father read you about the 'Martlets', a literary club I have joined: I only hope it won't absorb valuable time. The great treat is the prospect of whistling John Masefield up from his villa in the suburbs of Oxford to read us a paper. I must really get some of his books when

18 Over the years the high price of shipbuilding caused the well-known shipbuilders, Messrs. Yarrow and Co., to move their works from the Thames at Poplar up to Scotstoun on the Clyde (near Glasgow). Nevertheless, because labour problems continued to hound shipbuilding even in Scotland, it was announced in *The Times* of 4 February 1919 (p. 9) that Yarrow and Co. would gradually transfer part of their production to the Pacific coast of North America at Vancouver.

I have any time. I see from this week's Supplement[19] that he has just published another volume of narrative poems. Judging by the quotations it is execrably bad.

Tea at the Poynton's was quite amusing by the way: he is a very humorous old man who says the funniest things in a monotonous, melancholy voice. He showed us some books of Russian fairy tales – he is learning the language. They were badly printed on poor paper but exquisitely illustrated and illuminated: the designs were all 'flat' of course but very effective, and in one or two cases very simple colouring produced the best impressions of evening or cold or so forth.

The only man of much interest whom I have met in College is Blunt.[20] His father is a don at Christ Church,[21] and he was at Winchester where he acted a minor part in a production of Yeat's 'On Baile's Strand'[22] with the young Asquith[23] as 'The Fool' – some wd. say an appropriate part! He has also met Kipling and Bergson,[24] neither of whom impressed him in talk tho' he professes to admire the latter. Of course he is a trifle affected and omniscient like all these people who stayed out the whole numbing time at 'one of our great public schools' but he is really appreciative of some kinds of literature, especially Morris, Yeats and Maeterlinck which of course pleases me. I also find that another man in college called Paisley[25] has written some poems which that man Mais (who wrote 'Diary of

19 John Masefield's *A Poem and Two Plays* (1919) was reviewed in *The Times Literary Supplement* (30 January 1919), p. 54.

20 Henry Pyot Blunt (1898–1955) took his BA in 1922. He was with the Bombay Burma Trading Corporation, Rangoon, 1922–26; an assistant master in the Upper Canada College, Toronto, 1927; with the John Lewis Partnership in 1936; Minister of Food in 1939; with the Commercial Corporation in 1942; and Minister of Food 1947–52.

21 Herbert William Blunt (1864–1940) who was Tutor in Philosophy and Librarian of Christ Church 1888–1928.

22 W.B. Yeats, *On Baile's Strand* (1904).

23 The Hon. Anthony Asquith (1902–68), fifth son of the 1st Earl of Oxford and Asquith.

24 Henri Bergson (1859–1941), a French philosopher who developed a philosophical position in opposition to scientific materialism. During his undergraduate years Lewis read Bergson's *Essai* (1889) and *L'Évolution Créatrice* (1907).

25 (Sir) Rodney Marshall Pasley (1899–1982) was educated at Sherborne School, after which he served as a 2nd lieutenant in the Royal Field Artillery during 1914–18. He took his BA from University College in 1921, after which he became an assistant master at Alleyn's School, Dulwich, 1921–5; vice-principal of Rajkumar College at Rajkot, India, 1926–8; assistant master at Alleyn's School, 1931–6; headmaster of Barnstaple Grammar School, 1936–43; and headmaster of Central Grammar School, Birmingham, from 1943 until his retirement in 1959.

a Schoolmaster and an introduction to 'The Loom of Youth'[26]) is 'trying to get published'. The thing rather sniffs of modernism, of general Alec-Waugh-ishness. I don't know Paisley very well but I shall be interested to see the book when and if it comes out. I wish I could hear anything of my own: I am sure I shall be white haired before it sees daylight!

In reading I am still at the philosopher book, have finished King John and am reading Troilus & Cressida – a very good play. I progress so slowly that I shall have little to chronicle in this way for a long time. The Gibbon for you has not turned up yet but I shall order them to send it immediately.

'The family' has been greatly taken with your photo: they didn't expect you to be so good-looking! & Mrs Moore asks me to ask you for one for herself and sends her love.

I wonder are you right about George Elliot not living? Perhaps so, for even already one hears less of her than of the Brontes: but there is a sort of balance and sanity, a good-breeding even about them & especially 'Middlemarch' that you don't get in the Brontes. You said you *had* read Gilbert Murray's translation of the Bacchae didn't you? I think I shall write one myself some day: his doesn't satisfy me at all!

I am glad to hear you are still working. Do get on with the writing: as you said yourself it at least needs no physical energy and I am sure you only need to stick at it. The cold here is simply awful – thats not a conventional remark, because it is. Oh, by the way, somebody else *did* ask me who wrote the librettos of Wagner's operas – I nearly expired. Two such ignorami in one world is *too* much.[27]

Yours
Jack

P.S. Nearly all this is fit for 'publication' except one sentence.[28]

TO ARTHUR GREEVES (W):

[University College
16 February 1919]

My dear Arthur,

Many thanks for your letter. Your account of strike life at home

---

26 Alec Waugh, *The Loom of Youth* (1917).

27 Lewis was thinking of Richard Wagner's *Ring of the Nibelung* cycle, for which Wagner wrote both libretto and music.

28 He did not want his father to see the reference to Mrs Moore.

was very amusing – rather trying to have your model eaten! Only why were you painting those sort of things? 'Faute de mieux' I suppose!

About the Gibbon, Blackwell's have at last heard: you can get only three volumes and there is no talk of a reprint. Would you like me to try and get a complete set of that larger edition by the same publisher? I think I described it to you before, but I can't say I should advise it myself: the type is a little bit larger but it has no other advantage & is certainly not worth the difference in price.

I have bought two copies of drawings by Albrecht Dürer. You will find a good article about him in the Encyclopedia Brittanica. I have always looked upon [him] as the founder of the fantastic & illustrative school now represented by Rackham and Heath Robinson. This view is probably quite wrong historically but I am sure you would recognize the similarity in the very lines and shadows. These two are 'S. Jerome' and the 'Prodigal Son'. The first is very dark, and shows a heavy Gothic chamber: in the light of the single window sits an old wizardy figure pouring over a monstrous book. The room contains the typical insignia of mediaeval sorcery – a crocodile hung on the wall. At the saint's feet sleep together a lion and a dog. I do wish Dürer had illustrated 'The Faerie Queene'. The best thing about the 'Prodigal Son' is the drawing of the swine, which are really like great, wild boars, shaggy and tusked, and recalling somehow in their fantastic strength the dwarfs in Rackham. The background containing the thatched buildings of the sty and the 'tangled spires' of a house is – le Romance même. I haven't had time to study the prodigal himself and so don't describe him. I hope they will be framed by Teusday. There are several others in a shop here – from 2/6 each and a few shillings more for framing. I wonder would you like them? There are a lot I would like to get but some of his best backgrounds are spoilt by nude female figures of the most brutal and deliberate ugliness I've ever seen. I can't think what he is trying to do in these cases – whether they are done in malice or whether that seemed beautiful in his day.

I am still reading the philosopher book: there is something to be said for reading so little, you take it in better. Of course in work I am reading as fast [as] I can & am more than half way through the Iliad. I have to read all Homer, all Virgil, all Demosthenes & all Cicero, besides four Greek plays and a special subject instead of verse. I think in my case it will be Logic, but am not quite sure.

By the way when are you going to get Lang's translation of Homer? I suggest you should get 'The World's Desire' the romance about Helen that he wrote in collaboration with Rider Haggard (a good blend!) and then his Oddyssey after that. 'World's Desire' is so Homeric that you would pass from one to the other insensibly. By the way people from Christ Church tell me they have a don there who tells you to translate Homer in the style of Pope and sternly quells anything like Morris or Chaucer. Can you believe that such barbarism survives in the 20th century, such an absolute lack of historical sense?

Did I describe to you our meeting of the 'Martlets' on Yeats,[29] I think I did. I have got to read a paper on Morris at the next but one. I fought hard against undertaking this extra time devouring job, but had to in the end. Luckily I shall have no difficulty in finding things to say, and I really have read nearly all his important works – which is a very rare qualification in people that read papers at college societies.

Winter has broken up here and it is quite warm. Once or twice in the mornings I have been able to sit in my own rooms without a fire and the window open. One of the annual joys is the first day you go out without an overcoat.

I have been talking to Pasely, the man whose poems Mais is trying to get published. He says he is of an old-fashioned type, not at all a modernist and has promised to show me his things. He was at the same school with Alec Waugh and confirms the story of his getting the order of the boot.

You don't say anything about your own writing: mine of course is compulsorily 'off'. I think it would do you [a] lot of good to start something and perhaps send me instalments in the old way.

Many thanks for the photo.

Yours

Jack

Lewis thought he was probably holding a temporary commission in the regular army, with perhaps a small pension, and on 18 February he sent the War Office exactly the same letter he had written to them on 18 January, complaining that he had 'received neither gratuity nor pension', and asking for clarification on the matter. He was to be disappointed and embarrassed by the reply. In their letter of 20 February the War Office said:

---

29 The minutes of this meeting, held on 12 February, are found in the Bodleian: MS. Top. Oxon. d. 95/3, fos. 64–6.

You have been released from actual military duty from 24th December inclusive. Subsequent to this date you will not be entitled to army pay and allowances, neither shall any period during which you are so released count towards any gratuity, nor for non-effective benefits, nor will you be eligible for promotion during that period...You will be liable to recall for Military duty only in the event of urgent military necessity before the termination of the present war, but such liability of service is not a bar to you taking up civil employment, emigration, or repatriation overseas. (Public Record Office and LP VI: 91)

TO HIS FATHER (LP VI: 91–2):

University College,
Oxford.
23rd Feby. 1919

My dear Papy,

Many thanks for your letters and the enclosures. Certainly our friends 'the master starred with gold and splashed with red' have surpassed themselves over my commission. I remember Peard well at Crownhill: I do not remember his having been to France since, so we may suppose that for the last two years he has been able to devote all his energies to the cultivation of his epistolary style. The result is highly praiseworthy. You write complaining that A is B and he replies that on the contrary you can find by reference that B is A. As you say however, we cannot let the matter rest there. The immediate danger you spoke of has been warded off, at any rate for a time, and I think you can safely continue your correspondence with this very worthy young man.

I return the two oracular letters about the gratuity. I can hardly believe that they are trying to cheat me altogether, as it has been repeated time after time in every newspaper that we are all to have them – wounded or unwounded. I met a man from Keble the other day who had never been out, but who was demobilized with a pension of 10/- a week on the strength of 'ill-health contracted while in the service'. Perhaps we might mention to the masters that I went in Class A and came out B: that I can't take any violent exercise: and that I still have other trouble we wot of. Certainly if we do get Bolshevism in England, the treacherous and dishonest beaurocracy has earned it. Have you read the story of the eight officers sent back on leave from Cologne in the middle of the recent cold in a cattle truck without even straw, and no stops – seven of whom died? Save us from our friends.[30]

By the way I notice that the war bond thing you sent me expires on the first of next month. Will you please send me the certificate with your next letter, as they won't change it otherwise. Thank you for the pyjamas which are quite warm enough. Spring has come in with a rush, and once or twice in the morning I have been able to sit in my room with no fire and the windows open.

I am glad to hear that Malvern intends to do the right thing about Smugy. Let me know what the Colonel intends to do and I will do like wise. I should rather like to know the subject they will choose for the H.W. Smith Prize. I suggest the study of Horace as suitable to the old man's tastes. Cooper has a photo of him taken shortly before his death: he seemed to have got much thinner, and that, with the size of his eyes, had given him a somewhat frog like appearance, but it was the same genial face. On the questions of his possible criticisms of the book we are left to endless conjecture: whether he would have thought them too outspoken or not, he would probably have found them too polemical, too turbid, lacking the classical quiet and detachment for which he looked in his favourite books – Horace, Milton, the Arabian Nights, R.L. Stevenson. 'I hate being written *at*' he once said.

I am glad to hear that Belfast has recovered, and hope you are none the worse for the wearisome weeks you have been through.

With best love,
your loving son,
Jack

TO HIS FATHER (LP VI: 86–7):

University College,
Oxford
[28?] Feb. 1919

My dear Papy,

This week we have surpassed ourselves – besides crossing in fact, our letters have crossed in substance as well. It is rather strange that

30 Albert Lewis would not allow the matter to rest. After writing to the War Office on behalf of his son, on 28 March they paid Jack a 'wound gratuity' of £145 16s 8d. After further correspondence, and a medical examination, he was paid a 'further wound gratuity' of £104 3s 4d.

Warnie and I should both be foregathering with Old Malvernians so far apart. I am glad to see that affairs at home have not gone beyond inconvenience, although that is bad enough: our own strikers however seem to have shown a certain decency and sense of order which others did not.

We continue here in much the same way and I am beginning to fall into the routine. On Wednesday I drank tea with the Carlyles – Dr. Carlyle, as I think I said, is one of the Don members of the Martlets.[31] He is also the College Chaplain, and in describing our daily services to a lady, Poynton rather maliciously said, 'Carlyle reads as much of the service as he can remember', which is only half justified. He is a foxy looking old gentleman of Scotch extraction with an ultra-clerical voice: wife and daughters not very remarkable. The most interesting thing about him is his house in 'Holywell', one of the oldest streets. It is inconspicuous from outside, as its fine old gables have been cut down into a 'classic' balustrade during the barbarism of the 18th century, but it is almost perfect inside: grand old stone fireplaces, little leaded panes and beamed ceilings. I suspect however that it is a trifle damp and not unknown to the mice.

We have woken up to a white quad (if not quite a white world) for two or three mornings, and I believe there has been some skating. It is certainly very pretty, but I for one shall be glad when it is gone.

By the way, from what you say about 'Mods' and 'Greats' I am inclined to think that I may have given you a wrong impression. It is not really a question of 'cultivating fallow ground' by Mods., for as a matter of fact, 'Greats', being more philosophical and less strictly Classical, would be really rather easier to me as I am at present. The only thing is that when a question of Fellowships rose later on, people might feel that they could never be quite sure of you unless they knew what you had done in Mods. However, from that point of view it is equally the right course to take.

I have had a letter from Aunt Suffern and I gather than the two 'Arundel Prints' are coming. She hopes that 'the prevailing tint of my rooms is

---

31 The Rev. Alexander James Carlyle (1861–1943) was a political philosopher, ecclesiastical historian and social reformer. He was ordained in the Church of England in 1888, and became a Fellow and Chaplain of University College in 1893. He had to give up the fellowship when he married in 1895, but he continued to serve the College as a lecturer in politics and economics and as chaplain. He was the mainstay of the Christian Social Union. His works include the *History of Mediaeval Political Theory in the West*, 6 vols. (1903–36), which he wrote in collaboration with his brother, Sir R.W. Carlyle.

brown' as otherwise they will not enjoy their full splendour. In the present condition of the post I think it is very doubtful if they will ever arrive at all.

Would you please ask the 'skeery old woman' to fish me out a suit of pyjamas and send them?[32] I find I have left myself rather short. I hope that the floods around Leeborough are by now subsiding – or perhaps you have had a little skating in front of the dining room windows. Heinemanns remain as silent as the grave.

your loving son,
Jack

P.S. I have sent off the various army forms. Any news about getting out of that Special Reserve commision?

TO ARTHUR GREEVES (W):

[University College]
Sunday [2 March 1919]

My dear Arthur,

I was rather under the impression that I *had* kept to the weekly arrangement this last time. At any rate you will observe that I am answering your last at once for it only came yesterday.

You seem to be lucky in your theatrical fates at home. I should very much like to have seen 'The Importance of Being Ernest',[33] tho perhaps some of it would be lost on the stage. So far as I can remember I don't agree with you about the feeble ending. The beauty of it is that it entirely rejects probability or sentiment – would that all our society farces did the same – and gives itself up to a sort of glittering and classic nonsense that reminds me strongly of 'Alice in Wonderland'.

I have Layamon's Brut and Wace's translated in the one Everyman volume[34] – or rather the parts of them about the Arthurian period. Wace you remember was 'a french clerke, well could he write' who copied

---

32 The 'skeery old woman' was Mary Cullen, the successor to Annie Strahan in 1917 as cook-housekeeper at Little Lea. She was called this because of a certain breathless manner. She was devoted to Albert Lewis whom she served for the rest of his life. On the break-up of Little Lea in 1930 she became a cook in a public kitchen, and lived in a house which had belonged to Albert, rent free. (LP VI: 87).

33 Oscar Wilde, *The Importance of Being Earnest* (1895).

34 This is the *Arthurian Chronicles, Represented by Wace and Layamon* [1912] mentioned in note 9 to letter of 1 February 1916.

Layamon's poem in French rhyming couplets, with more style but less vigour. Wace is famous for his 'rationalising' remark about a magic fountain he went to see in Broceliande, and, being the wrong sort of man, of course did not find the marvels 'A fool I went, a fool I returned.'[35] Layamon I quite liked tho' I didn't finish it. Of course his battles are fatiguing, but the whole thing is very 'heroic' – much more like Boewulf than Malory. Arthur cleaves the Dane Skallagrim to the teeth and exults over him just like the warriors in the Iliad. On the other hand the passing of Arthur is really more romantic than in Malory, who, you remember, makes Avalon a really existing valley where the great king is buried. Brut, however, knows better 'They say he abideth in Avalon with Argante the fairest of all elves: but ever the Britons think that he will come again to help them at their need'[36] – a great deal of which I copied in a poem rejected by Heinemann – on whom ten thousand maledictions. Every week nearly in the Times Supplement I see a new book of poems published by him, but never mine. I can't think why he took it at all at this rate. I shall probably write to Evans to day – with the usual result.

As your letter arrived yesterday afternoon (Saturday) I couldn't follow your commands about going for the Gibbon-hunt at once. I am still at the philosopher book, tho' nearly finished. The later & more modern chapters are pretty difficult – Spencer and William James etc, who do not so easily fit into formulae as simple minded gentlemen of the Locke or Paley type. I thought you would like 'The Private Papers of Henry Ryecroft'. I don't know that the 'soothing qualities' were what struck me most, but no! – I'm thinking of 'The Corner of Harley Street'.[37] Now I remember: don't you like his remarks about cooking? Also on spiritualism he expresses a feeling I have sometimes experienced – mechanical reaction I suppose. We do get quite good things at the theatre but when should I have time to go? The only one I regret was Maeterlinck's 'Burgomaster of Stilmonde':[38] but it was only two nights, and the waste of an evening and the rush there would have been to get seats put me off.

To go back 'to the last remark but one' for a minute, as Alice says, that book of mine on Epic and Heroic Poetry gives a very good account of Layamon: reading it I have often wished you could get a complete crib

35 ibid., p. x.
36 ibid., p. 264.
37 Peter Harding, *The Corner of Harley Street* (1911).
38 Maurice Maeterlinck, *Le Bourgmestre de Stilmonde* (1919).

instead of only the Arthurian bit. Geoffrey of Monmouth is in the Everyman is he not? I am waiting to try and get a copy of him in the Latin[39] – perhaps there is one in the College Library. If only one had time to read a little more: we either get shallow & broad or narrow and deep.

At our last meeting of the Martlets a man called Wyllie read a paper on Newbolt.[40] I hadn't thought the subject *very* promising but he quoted a great many good things I hadn't known – especially a very queer little song about grasshoppers that you must read if you can get hold of it: so different from the usual patriotic business, tho' that is good too, until you've read sixty odd pieces on exactly the same lines. I have had a most interesting talk with Pasely and seen his poems. I mentioned him before, didn't I? Mais is trying to get him published. He has written one long piece that I envy him very much, and a number of pretty enough things – no stuff in them, the sort of things that are as common and not quite as good as wildflowers. But the one piece was really extraordinarily good. I wonder will he do the same again? At the meeting, by the way, some bright person was found to make a defence of vers libre.[41]

I got a letter the other day from an unknown member of the female sex – an undergraduate apparently – asking me to play my part in National Reconstruction by joining the Oxford University Socialist Society. As it was a printed circular I didnt 'feel called upon' to answer it.

I think the ugly figures in Dürer go beyond your suggestion – there is spite in every line: they were probably fancy portraits of ladies who didn't ask him to dinner. But it would be unfair to judge him by these explosions of ill temper. By 'verse' in exams I mean the composition of Latin & Greek verses, which is the usual subject to take: if you don't do them, you do something else. Of course it is nothing to do with the verse or prose that you read.

We are having some lovely days here now, and it must be just glorious in the country: thank goodness there is plenty of greenery in Oxford.

---

39 Geoffrey of Monmouth (d. 1154), *Historia Regum Britanniae* (Paris, 1508); *Histories of the Kings of Britain*, trans. Sebastian Evans, Everyman's Library [1912].

40 Basil Platel Wyllie's paper, read at the meeting on 26 February, was entitled 'The Poetry of Henry Newbolt'. Bodleian: MS. Top. Oxon. d. 95/3, fos. 67–9.

41 'An interesting discussion on "Vers Libre", arising out of one poem quoted by Mr Wyllie, then followed. Mr Pasley maintained that this school was not entirely free from a certain charlatanism, but the Society was interested to find in Mr [Geoffrey Odell] Vinter an enthusiastic defender of this kind of composition.' MS. Top. Oxon. d. 95/3, fo. 69.

There is no decent edition of Chaucer except the fabulously expensive Medici press one and even that only gives the Canterbury Tales – except of course the Everyman Canterbury Tales which is garbled and modernised: by a ridiculous arrangement whenever they come to an obscene passage they slip back into the real language.[42] Chaucer was very like Dickens – a virtuous, bourgeois story teller fond of highly moral vulgarity & indecency for its own sake, incapable (at the Tales period not in his early life) of appreciating romance.

Yours
Jack

TO HIS FATHER (LP VI: 96–7):

University College,
Oxford
5th March 1919

My dear Papy,

I was glad to get your letter, after a somewhat longer interval than usual and a hint that you were rather under the weather. Arthur also tells me that you have not been well. If this flu' is at all bad in Belfast I most strongly advise you to get inoculated. It will cost you only a few hours discomfort and, whatever people may tell you about its efficacy or otherwise, it undoubtedly did stop the pest in our camp at Ludgershall.

Thank you for your offer about the Smugy memorial: but you remember what David said on a similar occasion about 'that which cost naught'.[43] I am sending them a cheque for £2 and if you still wish to, you had better make yours a separate present in your own person. By the way, talking about subscriptions, I was asked the other day for one to a testimonial for the commandant of Ashton Court – a most peevish and ill tempered old maid whom we all hated, patients and nurses alike. I wish the adoring public could know what a few of these 'kind workers for our wounded' are really like.

I return with many thanks the certificate and the other two official documents. The one which promises that I shall not be called up for further service except in the case of another emergency in the present war was very pleasing to me – not that I set any value on their promise, but it

42 Charles Cowden Clarke, *Tales from Chaucer*, Everyman's Library [1911].
43 2 Samuel 24:24.

would be nice to be able to show their dishonesty in print if they tried to trick me again. With regard to the other, I am thinking of changing my bank to one in Oxford, as I have to get my cheques cashed at odd shops and depend on their convenience. Have you any advice to give me on this point?

I don't think that anyone who takes the trouble to read my book through will seriously call it blasphemous, whatever criticism he may make on artistic grounds.[44] If he does not, we need not bother about his views. Of course I know there will be a number of people who will open it by chance at some of the gloomiest parts of Part I and decide 'Swinburnian Ballads' and never look at it again. But what would you do? If one writes at all – perhaps like Talleyrand many 'don't see the necessity' – one must be honest. You know who the God I blaspheme is and that it is not the God you or I worship, or any other Christian. But we have talked over this before. Arthur tells me that you have a copy of Reveillé with my thing in it.[45] They have omitted to send me one – 'who am I?' as Knowles said.

I look like having a busy time next week: I am reading in Chapel, saying grace in Hall, writing a paper on Morris for the Martlets, finishing

44 Although *Spirits in Bondage* was not published until 20 March 1919, Albert and Warnie Lewis had read it and Jack's atheism was evident to both. Exchanging views about the poems, Albert said to Warnie on 27 January, 'I don't know what your candid opinion may be as we had not an opportunity of comparing notes. Mine is very distinct. Some of the poems I think excellent – one or two better than excellent. The spirit which pervades the book, at times at all events, I should have liked different. But when every word of criticism or disparagement has been spoken, it remains something more than a creditable performance for a boy of 19' (LP VI: 82). 'While I am in complete agreement with you,' Warnie replied on 28 January, 'as to the excellence of parts of "IT'S" book, I am of opinion that it would have been better if it had never been published. Even at 23 one realises that the opinions and convictions of 20 are transient things. Jack's Atheism is I am sure purely academic, but even so, no useful purpose is served by endeavouring to advertise oneself as an Atheist. Setting aside the higher problems involved, it is obvious that a profession of a Christian belief is as necessary a part of a man's mental make up as a belief in the King, the Regular Army, and the Public Schools.' Mr Lewis knew that his younger son's dislike of Malvern was a cause of irritation and embarrassment to the older brother, but when he learned that Warnie had taken Jack to task over the book, he wrote to him on 9 March saying: 'He is young and he will learn in time that a man has not absolutely solved the riddle of the heavens above and the earth beneath and the waters under the earth at twenty. I am not going to slop over but I do think that if Oxford does not spoil him...he may write something that men would not willingly let die' (LP VI: 98).

45 'Death in Battle' from *Spirits in Bondage* appeared in *Reveille*, No. 3 (February 1919).

the Iliad, and dining with the Mugger. I hope to be able to eat and sleep a little as well! As the time goes on I appreciate my hours with Poynton more and more. After Smugy and Kirk I must be rather spoiled in the way of tutors, but this man comes up to either of them, both as a teacher and as a humorous 'card'. Gilbert Murray is, I'm afraid, not very much good for exams., tho' his literary merits are unsurpassed.

I will write to the Bristol photographer and speak 'severely'. What do you think of the Canadian Bolshevists? I wonder is there anyone found now a days to disparage – as we once did – the great Victorian age? 'They were the glory, we are the decline'.

I hope you are better by now. Take care of yourself and don't run risks.

your loving son,
Jack

TO HIS FATHER (LP VI: 100):

University College,
Oxford
Saturday 15th [March 1919]

My dear Papy,

This is 'out of its due time'[46] as you are still in my debt. I am writing to tell you that the 'Varsity term ends today and the College term on Monday. I shall be staying up for a week more, following Poynton's instructions.

After that I shall go down to help Mrs Moore with her move at Bristol: she has had to come back to clear out the house. There seems to be considerable difficulty about getting anywhere else. London and Bristol are both hopeless: I have suggested here, but that seems equally impossible. I can't understand where the influx of people is coming from.

Of course the expenses of the journey I shall pay myself, and not include in the 'Term' – which, by the way, will also not include this term's Battels, as, by an absurd arrangement, we don't get our bills until we come up next term.

My effort in Reveillé – I was sorry to see the old reading – is in curious company, isn't it? No word from Heinemann's still.

46 1 Corinthians 15:8.

I was surprised to hear from Aunt Lily that G. had broken off her engagement.[47] I wonder what your view on the subject is?

your loving son,

Jack

TO HIS BROTHER (LP VI: 104):

University College,
Oxford
[2? April 1919]

My dear W.,

Many thanks for both letters. I got the first one alright, and wrote for the French book at once, waiting to answer you until I could send it. The reason of my silence in general is that I have got to work like Hell here – I seem to have forgotten everything I know.

If you are on the look out for a cheap modern edition of Chesterfield's letters,[48] I will see what I can do, but I feel inclined to reply in Tommy's irreverent style, 'Wot 'opes'. About St Simon you will find it much easier to write to Paris for a French edition: when you had finished with it you could send it on to me to be bound and pressed – after which you would find it as good as new. I don't know of a crib to it.[49] To take up P's style, have you ever noticed a book at home 'very much on the same lines', the Memoirs of Count Gramont, written in French by a Hamilton who was a hanger on of the grand monarque, and translated?[50]

In the name of all the gods why do you want to go into the 'Russian Expeditionary Force'? You will drag on a post-less, drink-less, book-less, tobacco-less existence for some months until the Bolshevists finally crush us and then probably end your days at a stake or on a cross.

The typewriting of private letters is the vile invention of business men, but I will forgive you on the ground that you were practising.

---

47 His cousin Gundreda Ewart had just broken off her engagement to Captain Geoffrey Burbage.

48 Philip Dormer Stanhope, Earl of Chesterfield, *Letters to his Son*, 2 vols. (1774); *Letters to his Friends*, 3 vols. (1777–8).

49 Warnie was to remember all his life the discovery in St Omer on 3 March 1919 of an abridgement of the *Mémoirs* of the Duc de Saint-Simon. He was writing to Jack from France for information about the whole of Saint-Simon's *Mémoirs* which he was keen to acquire. Out of this grew his lifelong interest in the court of Louis XIV and the *Grand Siècle*, and the writing of his seven books on that period.

50 *Memoirs of Count Gramont*, ed. Gordon Goodwin (1903).

There doesn't seem to be any week end leave at Oxford except for the U.P.A., which aren't so easily accepted as in the army.

Did you see the 'very insolent' review of me on the back page of the Times Literary Supplement last week?[51] There will be woe and consternation on the home front. I have been meeting a lot of O.M's.[52] this term, mostly people who sat under Smugy with me. I'm sorry to give you such a scrappy letter, but – quite bona fide – I really am burning the midnight oil these days.

yours
Jack

P.S. The only echo of Bolshevism in Oxford was the following jeu d'esprit: five or six bright spirits from Balliol sent up a long wire to the Daily Mail telling of an attempt by the 'Red' people to burn down Oxford, which only succeeded in burning down a cabstand: the lie never appeared and seems to have fallen rather flat.

TO ARTHUR GREEVES (W):

[University College]
Monday [5 May 1919][53]

My dear Arthur,

Many thanks for your letter. I had meant to write to you yesterday whether I heard or not, but when the time came I was not feeling well and so it got put off till to-day.

My first news I'm afraid will plunge you into despair. The copy of Morris's Odyssey which I had seen last term is gone and they could produce only a rather dirty one in its place! I felt I had better not order a copy, as you [are] rather afraid of doing that – tho' I think it is a case of 'nothing venture, nothing win', you'll *have* to order a book sometime again.

51 *Spirits in Bondage* received the following review in *The Times Literary Supplement* (27 March 1919): 'These lyrics are always graceful and polished, and their varied themes are chosen from those which naturally attract poets – the Autumn Morning, Oxford, Lullaby, The Witch, Milton Read Again, and so on. The thought, when closed with, is found rather often not to rise above the commonplace. The piece which most arrested us was "The Satyr."'

52 Old Malvernians.

53 Lewis would have seen Arthur when he was in Belfast from 2 to 24 April.

I was in some anxiety to see my new rooms, having left them in a ghastly state from my luckless attempt at distempering, and having heard nothing from the man whom I had told to paper them. Of course he hadn't done it, but by way of compensation the distemper had dried out excellently – all my splotches and thick & thin variations had disappeared. It is a nice quiet greyish blue: of course it is rather untidy and splashed about the woodwork a bit, but you don't notice that very much. It suits the two Dürers very well and also the Venus. There is also *one* good piece of furniture, a small bookcase of dark oak. You would agree with me in liking the beam in the ceiling and the deep windows and the old tree that taps against them, recalling Phantastes and Wuthering Heights. When it gets into leaf I shall look out into a mass of greenery with glimpses of the old walls across and of the grass below – such a scene as the redoubtable Heath Robinson did in your 12th night.[54]

But all this you shall see for yourself. I shall go to the dean as my tutor to-morrow and ask him then about the 'guest-room'. By the way I was annoyed to find that I had left behind all the pictures you gave me. Will you please send them as soon as possible: you can understand my desire to get fixed in and see all my household gods around me. How is the Rackham-esque drawing of the hills going on? I hope it will be a great success: it was certainly a splendid idea to do that particular bit in that style.

I have nearly finished the Venus poem and am full of ideas for another, which Gilbert Murray gave me the hint of in a lecture – a very curious legend about Helen, whom Simon Magus, a gnostic magician mentioned in the Acts,[55] found living as a very earthly person in Antioch and gradually recalled to her who she was and took her up to Zeus again, reborn: on their way they had to fight 'the Dynasties' or planets – the evil powers that hold the heaven, between us and something really friendly beyond – I have written some of it, but of course I get hardly any time either for reading or writing.

I have not quite finished the third volume of Gibbon, and it still pleases me as much as ever it did, in fact all the more as I go on. The only attitude you can adopt towards my father's underhand and contemptible efforts to get information out of you (he apparently judges

---

54 Shakespeare's *Twelfth Night*. See note 120 to letter of [18] July 1916.

55 Acts 8:9–24.

your character by his own) is the one you rightly do already – as you say, ignore it; and if he becomes unbearable, go away. You throw out merely a hint about the Glenmachonians' remarks on my book: tell me all they say when you write, you can easily understand how interested I am. I am glad you liked the Patriotism book, many parts of it sounded attractive: the Masefield one I hope to get one of these days.

We have had one meeting of the Martlets at which a very dull looking youth read a surprisingly good paper on Synge:[56] it has really quite encouraged me to try him again, tho' I feel some grains of prejudice against what I remember of him – perhaps because he has become a cult, which few writers escape now a days. I am afraid I have not got to know any of the Balliol poets yet, and am not sure that I shall be able to manage it – I don't see very many people and I don't think Pasely himself meets them very often.

I hope by this time you're sailing the seas of Gibbon (the new counterpart to the old 'Have you read your Swinburne?') and not feeling too depressed with the world in general – that 'The thing's not becoming intolerable!' in fact.

We are having lovely weather here and I shall soon begin to bathe. Don't forget the pictures.

Yours
Jack

TO HIS FATHER (LP VI: 122):

[University College,
Oxford]
11th May 1919

My dear Papy,

Many thanks for your letter and also for the enclosed cheque for £19.12.8. That amount includes all the charges both for tuition and

56 Edward Fairchild Watling (1899–1990) matriculated at University College in 1918. He took a Second in Classical Moderations in 1920, and a Third in Greats in 1922. On leaving Oxford he went to King Edward VII School, Sheffield, where he taught classics for 36 years. He will be remembered for his idiomatic and highly readable translations of the classics. These include Sophocles's *Theban Plays* (1947) and Seneca's *Four Tragedies and Octavia* (1966). See *University College Record*, Vol. X, No. 3 (1991), pp. 115–17. He read his paper on 'The Plays of J.M. Synge' at the 192nd meeting of the Martlets on 30 April. Bodleian: MS. Top. Oxon. d. 96/3, fos. 71–2.

college expenses and may serve as a base for future calculation, tho' of course there may be slight differences from term to term.

I was very glad to hear the good news about May:[57] if she was really as bad as they suppose when I left home, they have certainly every reason to be thankful for a very extraordinary recovery.

I have not yet heard from the war office, but, having regard to their usual leisurely methods, I suppose it is not yet time to take any fresh step. I am right, am I not, in supposing that it is from London and not from Dublin that I must expect further communication? We are having real summer weather here, and in our stone walls, without any wind, it is already rather oppressive. The river of course is refreshing, and as my room does not get the morning sun, I can be fairly cool there with all the windows open.

I am sorry that you have no encouraging news from Campbell. Perhaps, after you have given him a fair trial, it might be advisable to see some English surgeon and get a new point of view.

We have all been much amused here by the historic insolence of the German delegates at Versailles. I am afraid however that the matter has a very serious side, and some are already beginning to hint that we may be back in uniform again before it is all over.

Thank you for the letter from Warnie which you sent on: he suggests, as perhaps he has already done to you, that we should go out and see him in France for a few days this summer.

your loving son,
Jack

TO HIS FATHER (LP VI: 126–7):

[University College,
Oxford]
25th May 1919

My dear Papy,

Close upon the heels of your letter came one from the War Office in which I was instructed to place myself in communication with the G.O.C. Southern Command at Salisbury with a view to this Medical Board. I have acknowledged, and shall get myself examined by a local doctor tomorrow.

---

57 May Lewis (b. 1887) was the daughter of Albert's brother, Joseph Lewis.

As for the investments, I think on the whole that the Commercial Debentures would be the most promising: the security, you say, is perfectly good, and in any case I suppose with small sums one should always prefer a good rate to mere safety.

Many thanks for the cake which ate excellently: I enclose a small note of 'appreciation' to the Witch of Endor[58] – it was really rather good of the old creature to suggest the enterprise.

I have not written to Evans, as I found a circular from a Press Association cutting to which I have replied, enclosing 10/-. The results so far have been a very interesting review on 'The Principles of Symbolic Logic' by C. S. Lewis of the University of California. I am writing back to tell them that they have got rather muddled. Symbolic Logic forsooth! I started reading it without noticing the title and was surprised to find myself – as I thought – being commended for a 'scholarly elucidation of a difficult subject'.

As nearly everyone here is a poet himself, they have naturally no time left for lionizing others. Indeed the current literary set is one I could not afford to live in anyway, and tho' many of them have kindly bought copies of the book, their tastes run rather to modernism, 'vers libre' and that sort of thing. I have a holy terror of coteries: I have already been asked to join a Theosophist, a Socialist, and a Celtic society.

By the way, the distinction which one finds in such books as Tom Brown[59] by which the poor, the industrious, and the intellectual, are all in one class, and the rich, brainless and vicious, all in another, does not obtain. Some 'poor scholars' are bad lots, and some of the 'gilded youth' are fond of literature.

I am exceedingly sorry about May. I had hoped that after she turned the corner, the recovery would be easy. The suffering is perhaps the worst feature of the case – danger is so much easier to bear.

I think the work is progressing 'according to plan' and Poynton is still most satisfactory.

We are having a heat wave at present, but manage to survive with the help of bathes. I find I can't swim half the distance I used to, and am

58 Mary Cullen, the cook-housekeeper at Little Lea, was often referred to as the 'Witch of Endor'. See note 31 to the letter of 2 March 1919.

59 Hughes, *Tom Brown's Schooldays*.

rather stiff after that. Hoping that your own trouble is on the mend, I am,

your loving son,
Jack

For some time Mr Lewis had been worried about the prominence of Mrs Moore in Jack's life, and he and Warnie were beginning to discuss it. 'The Mrs Moore business is certainly a mystery,' Warnie wrote to his father on 10 May, 'but I think perhaps you are making too much of it. Have you any idea of the footing on which he is with her? Is she an intellectual? It seems to me preposterous that there can be anything in it. But the whole thing irritates me by its freakishness...Probably the whole dread mystery is a product of our own imaginations' (LP VI: 118). 'I confess I do not know what to do or say about Jack's affair,' replied Mr Lewis on 20 May:

> *It worries and depresses me greatly. All I know about the lady is that she is old enough to be his mother – that she is separated from her husband and that she is in poor circumstances. I also know that Jacks has frequently drawn cheques in her favour running up to £10 – for what I don't know. If Jacks were not an impetuous, kind hearted creature who could be cajoled by any woman who has been through the mill, I should not be uneasy. Then there is the husband whom I have always been told is a scoundrel – but who some of these days might try a little amiable blackmailing. But outside all these considerations that may be the outcome of a suspicious, police court mind, there is the distraction from work and the folly of the daily letters.* (LP VI: 123)

On 3 June Warren wrote to his father saying,

> *I am greatly relieved...to hear that Mrs Moore* HAS *a husband: I understood she was a widow; but as there is a Mr Moore, the whole complexion of the business is altered. We now get the following very unsatisfactory findings. (1) Mrs Moore can't marry Jacks. (2) Mr Moore can't blackmail him because 'IT' hasn't enough to make it a paying risk. (3)* You *can't be blackmailed because you*

> *wouldn't listen to the proposition for one moment. But the daily letter business* does *annoy me: especially as I have heard from Jacks* once *since January of this year.* (LP VI: 129)

Although Mrs Moore received a small amount of money from her husband, the main expense of their joint home seems to have fallen on Jack. As Warren mentioned in his 'Memoir': 'since an allowance calculated to suit a bachelor living in college was by no means enough for a householder, Jack found himself miserably poor'. In 1919 the average cost of living in an Oxford college was about £60 a term. (At this time £1 was worth about US$5.) Jack's scholarship from University College was worth about £80 a year, but after paying his college expenses he was left with only about £11 per term. Albert Lewis was giving his son £67 per term, as well as paying incidental expenses.

TO ARTHUR GREEVES (W):

[University College,
Oxford]
Monday [2 June 1919]

My dear Arthur,

I really was ashamed of myself when I got your letter: I had put off my weekly one to you from day to day, hoping to work it in 'some day soon' and hardly realized how long I'd let it go. My letter-writing time last week was rather upset by a long standing debt to Aunt Lily, which simply *had* to be done and an unexpected letter from W.

Now as to all the important questions (1) Come whenever is convenient and let me know beforehand when I may expect you (2) I am afraid you can only get a guests [room] for one or two nights in College, therefore (3) You had better stay in 'The Mitre' in High Street which is the best and also the nearest to College (4) Would you like me to book you a room there.

Thanks very much for the pictures: the two best, the garden one and the tree in the new Soaking Machine are better than I remembered. I am having them both framed. The little Rackhamesque one I am not sure yet how I will treat. It gives me pleasure and has indeed a *special* appeal that the ordinary kind of drawing has not, but I can't find any place I think it would suit. We shall see.

It is perfectly lovely now both in town and country – there are such masses of fruit trees, all white. One big cherry tree stands in the Master's garden just below my windows and a brisk wind this morning had shaken down masses of leaves that lay like snow flakes on the bright smooth grass. Then beyond the lawn you see the gable end of the chapel.

I usually go and bathe before breakfast now at a very nice little place up the Cherwell called 'Parson's Pleasure'.[60] I always swim (on chest) down to a bend, straight towards the sun, see some hills in the distance across the water, then turn and come again to land going on my back and looking up at the willow trees above me. It is a most romantic bathe and rather like William Morris – as one of his characters would 'wash the night off'. I have been reading at breakfast lately 'The Water of the Wondrous Isles',[61] which is more romantic tho' not so well-constructed as 'The Well at the World's End': all the same I have enjoyed it immensely with quite the old thrill, his witches and wanderers I can usually rely on. He is so inexhaustible!

How very funny about Bob, and how typical of Kelsie! Is it that she hides her opinions – I mean on other subjects as well as this – or that she has none.

I have NOT 'woken up and found myself famous' yet but I have slunk into a modicum of notoriety it would seem. At the last meeting of the Martlets I was asked by a man called Hartman[62] whether I was 'the famous Lewis' jokingly of course. It appears that some of the extreme literary set at Balliol and Exeter, the writers of 'vers libre' etc, who run the yearly Books of Oxford Poetry had got the book and asked Hartman if he knew a Lewis at Univ. and if that was the man. The result is that several people are going to buy it who might not have otherwise done so. On Wednesday I am to meet at Hartman's rooms a man called Childe

60 See note 73 to letter of 13 May 1917.

61 William Morris, *The Water of the Wondrous Isles* (1897).

62 Cyril Hughes Hartmann (1896–1967), elder son of George Hartmann of Thames Ditton, Surrey, was educated at Charterhouse and matriculated at Oxford in 1914. He took a Third in Modern History in 1920 and a B.Litt. in 1922. On leaving Oxford he became a successful author, writing mainly on literary and historical subjects. His many books include *La Belle Stuart: Memoirs of Court and Society in the Times of Francis Teresa Stuart, Duchess of Richmond and Lennox* (1924), *The Cavalier Spirit and its Influence on the Life and Work of Richard Lovelace (1618–1658)* (1925), *Charles II and Madame* [1934], and *Cudleigh, Lord High Treasurer of England (1630–1673)* [1937].

who edits these books of Oxford Poetry[63] & tho' I am sure I shall disapprove of him and his views it will possibly be useful. Hartman himself is rather an interesting character: his mother was a member of the set that included Oscar Wilde and Whistler[64] and would have included Swinburne if it could. He said he had once met Wilde but did not remember much about it. Lucky man, he was in Spain all thro' the war!

I am afraid I shall never get on with the Gibbon as I go now; although I still like it as much as ever it is awfully hard to keep the connection in my head with so many other irons in the fire. If I once give it up I shall be lost!

Hardly writing anything at all except a few lines yesterday for the Helen poem, and bits for a short one I thought of doing on 'Nimue'. What are the possibilities of the subject? Awfully sorry to hear you've been laid up again: you mustn't do too much when you're here.[65]

Yours

Jack

P.S. Haven't heard from my esteemed parent for some time; has he committed suicide yet?

TO HIS BROTHER (LP VI: 133–4):

University College,
Oxford
9th [June 1919]

My dear W.,

'Sir,' said Dr Johnson, 'you are an unsocial person.' In answer to the charge I can only plead the general atmosphere of the summer term which is the same here as it was at school: whatever energy I have has to be thrown into work and, for the rest, the seductive influence of the river and hot weather must bear the blame. Term ends some time in July, but I shall be staying up for part of the vac. Would the early part of September

63 Wilfred Rowland Childe (1890–1952) was the editor (with T.W. Earp and A.L. Huxley) of *Oxford Poetry 1916* (1917) and (with T.W. Earp and Dorothy L. Sayers) of *Oxford Poetry 1917* (1918).

64 The artist James Abbott McNeill Whistler (1834–1903).

65 Arthur visited Lewis in Oxford from about 20 to 28 June, during which time he met the Moores. From Oxford he went to London to consult a heart specialist.

do for your leave: one doesn't get any chance of fine weather or of endurably warm sea water any earlier in Donegal.

I quite agree with you that we could have quite an excellent time together at Portsalon – if we were 'both' there; if, as you suggest, we were 'all' there, I suppose we could endure as we always have endured.

You ask me what is wrong with P......[66] which he describes as exceedingly painful and horribly depressing. I don't meet the doctors myself and therefore, in the case of a man who would hold precisely the same language about a boil or a wasp's sting, it is impossible to say how bad he is: I am afraid however it is rather a serious bother.

There is also a second thing wrong with him – namely that he is fast becoming unbearable. What the difficulties of life with him always were, you know: but I never found it as bad as when I was last at home. I needn't describe the continual fussing, the sulks, the demand to know all one's affairs – you might think I was exaggerating as you have been out of it for so long. I wish to the Lord we had a small income of our own to fall back on in case of emergencies.

The third piece of information was drawn out of Arthur with some difficulty, and will appeal to your sense of humour. It began by a conversation which he overheard between the Gudeman and his lady mother, after they had just met P. The phrases 'It's a pity', 'It's sad to see him going that way', 'I've been afraid for some time' were repeated with true puritan gravity. The real fun began when Arthur managed to drift into the study unannounced one day. There he found our revered parent sprawling in an arm chair, very red in the face and drowsy. For some time he merely stared and refused to give any answer to any remark. Poor Arthur wondered what to do, till his host finally solved the question by saying in a husky voice, 'I'm in great trouble, you'd better go away'. No evidence as to what this 'great trouble' was has ever been forthcoming, so I think we may with probability, if not quite certainty, breathe the magic word of *al-cohol*, 'the subtle alchemist who in a trice' etc.! Of course no one objects to a man getting blind occasionally – although it is interesting to remember his merciless tirades on drink – but there is something unpleasant about this solitary tippling. He might have gathered some of his friends to share the fun.

Thanks very much for getting three copies of the book: one to Jacks, if Jacks père approves of it, might help me to get something into 'The

66 Part of this sentence was removed when the letter was copied into the Lewis Papers.

Hibbert', which as you know he edits.[67] I am pleased that you liked 'The Star Bath'[68] as you have been, so far, its only admirer. I have tried with perhaps not very much energy to find those books for you, but Arthur is coming up next week and I shall send him hunting while I want to work. At the same time I should think from my own experience that ordinary English translations are usually too free to be much use as cribs.

The scenery of Donegal would suit us both better than the continent – good old mountains and heather, rather grey and grim. One usually finds quite pleasing people in the hotel which would serve to break up the eternal trio. Write and let me know your plans, I shall try to answer sooner this time.

yours,
Jack

TO HIS FATHER (LP VI: 151–2):

Oxford
Sat. June 29th [1919]

My dear Papy,

I have put off answering your letter until I got Arthur away, who departed with much reluctance yesterday. I have a short note from him this morning telling his first London adventures, which include a discovery of the fact that the specialist whom he went to see has retired some years ago. One would have thought that his people or his home doctor might have found this out before he was sent.

As regards the matter which you particularly mention, there was less need of 'expedition' because I had already communicated with the colonel and had an answer from him: his letter I presume contains substantially the same information which he gave to you.

My own position is this: the academical term has just ended, but owing to 'Comem,' and various schools, hardly anyone has gone down yet. In practice, the summer term really continues for a fortnight or three weeks after its official decease. Beyond this, Poynton has advised me to stay up for some time and work. I am inclined to agree with him: home, while it has every material, has few moral incitements to steady

67 Lawrence Pearsall Jacks (1860–1955), the editor of the *Hibbert Journal*, was a lecturer in philosophy at Manchester College, Oxford, from 1903, and Principal of the College 1915–31.

68 One of the poems in *Spirits in Bondage*.

reading. My own books, my MSS, the supply of new literature, our kind friends, and the telephone are all temptations: here, when the oi polloi go down, there is a melancholy desertion which leaves you simply nothing to do but work.

Under these circumstances I should suggest first that Warnie should change his leave, *if possible*. If this is absolutely out of the question I suppose he will divide his time between Leeborough and Oxford. It naturally occurs to me here that you were hoping to get away for a bit this summer. Where could you pass your holiday better than Oxford? The three of us could certainly spend our afternoons in a punt under the willows at least as comfortably as we did at Dunbar, and the Mitre, honoured with so many famous ghosts, would be an improvement on the Railway Hotel! Let me know in your next letter what you propose to do.

I have not been able to get hold of a complete copy of the June 'Bookman', but the cutting which the agency sent me is pasted into a little book in which I am collecting such shreds of criticism as I can get hold of.[69] My friends tell me that I am at a disadvantage for literary success because I lack the 'gift of self advertisement'. My only reply – not expressed aloud – 'thank heaven'!

Murray certainly seems to hold rather moderate views of the Mugger's accomplishments: I have lately been noticing in his history of Greek Literature the references to Mr Macan's conclusions on this and that

---

69 The review of *Spirits in Bondage* in *The Bookman*, vol. LVI (June 1919), p. 108, is the best Lewis received. 'There is nothing indefinite here,' wrote Francis Bickley. 'Mr Hamilton is as positive as Pope. From his forty short poems one can reconstruct his cosmogony. There is, it seems, somewhere "far too far off for thought or any prayer", a god who created the world but subsequently lost interest in it; nearer and more active is a lesser god, who is also Satan, and is responsible, among other unpleasantness, for the war; then there is the world of men, who suffer from and are degraded by this second god's irresponsible iniquities; lastly, there is the world of fairies whither, if one is as fortunate as Mr Hamilton, one may escape for beauty and peace; like Mr Maurice Hewlett, Mr Hamilton is friend of Desponia, and he has seen Angus. And with all these orders of being he deals competently. One might search his book for an accent out of place or a false rhyme; I do not think one will be rewarded. He writes so well that he does not fear to challenge comparison with his greatest predecessors. (He had even the hardihood to collocate the adjectives "old" and "unhappy".) Confidently he claims a place in the great tradition, and I think he makes his claim good. For there is beauty and dignity, a fine bitter vein and a fine courage, in his work, and good craftsmanship is one of the major virtues of poetry.'

subject. They are very polite, and this perhaps is what makes them so desperate.[70]

The town is expecting the news of the peace and preparing for it with all kinds of modern fireworks which 'make a noise exactly like a heavy shell'. I don't know that I am very fond of that kind of noise. Meanwhile they are starving and torturing in Russia and the Polish women are out digging trenches against Hindenburg's invasion. Should one laugh – or cry?

I hope that you are keeping up to the mark and that the old trouble shows some signs of improvement.

your loving son,
Jack

TO ARTHUR GREEVES (W):

[University College
14 July 1919]

My dear Arthur,

I suppose you have already decided about my remissness as a correspondent that 'The thing is intolerable': and perhaps I have been more ready even than usual because I have to convey to you a piece of information which as Miss Austin[71] says may produce 'the cruelest sense of mortification'. It is about the song: on the more technical side of the question Miss Plowman will write to you but I can give you some outline.[72] It appears, to speak frankly, that you will have to learn a great deal more about composition, and even about more elementary points of technique before you can hope to do yourself justice. It is not merely a question of embellishing or pruning what you have done to suit arbitrary rules. As far as I can gather, the real trouble is that your weakness on these points leads you, so to speak, to run your ideas into moulds already prepared by compositions which you unconsciously remember, and therefore appear to be less original than you are. Do I make it clear?

---

70 Gilbert Murray, *A History of Ancient Greek Literature* (1897).

71 i.e. Jane Austen.

72 Mary Plowman was the elocution mistress as well as a teacher of music at Headington School, where Maureen was a pupil. In time she became friends with Maureen's mother and Lewis and was a frequent visitor at their house. During her lifetime she published four books: *Monologues and Duologues* (1909); *The Letters of Paul Durrant* (1918); *The Vicar* (1919); *Get Out of Your Cage* [1934]. Her opinion was sought about a piece of music Arthur had just written.

It seems to me the inevitable result of a lack of formal knowledge: it is like an essay by a schoolboy who gives you a sentence of his own here and there and then ends up the sentence with a remeniscense of Macaulay. I don't think myself that in any art this argues a real lack of originality: it merely shows that he is 'groping about in worlds not realised' and his thought clutches at any ready-made clothing which seems fairly suitable. But Miss Plowman's letter will make all clear.

Now I do hope you won't let yourself be discouraged by what her friends have said. If without any knowledge you had succeeded in giving yourself a chance it would have been very wonderful: that you have not, was only to be expected, and I certainly think you have no reason to give it up. When I was at Bookham I twice went in for the lyric competition in the Bookman, once with 'Night! black Night' and again with the piece which appears as 'Ad Astra' in the MS. & 'Victory' in the printed book.[73] Both were complete failures – failed of the first prize, failed of the second, failed even of a mention. This was much worse than what has now happened to you! Besides you could not be in a better position than you are for going on: you have absolutely unbounded liesure – you don't have to work at odd moments stolen from your 'work' in the other sense like the rest of us: according to this specialist your heart is not so bad as you have supposed: good feeding and a little more exercise which good feeding will enable you to take will set you up. A course of solid but agreeable work with hopes and dreams ever in view would be the best thing for your nerves & spirits. That is, of course, unless you decide to take up painting or writing *really* seriously instead. Now that you have made a sort of landmark in your routine by coming to England, do try not to slip back into the old ways: do not give in to depression – and give everything up as soon as difficulties arise. Remember all we dreamed and did in the golden age of Bookham. I think I have nearly talked myself out now, & it is a wonder if you have put up with it.

Since you left I have read the 'Talisman',[74] merely because Maureen happens to be 'doing it' at school and it was lying about. Of course it is one of his poorest: the rapid episodes and impossible disguises remind us of what monstrosities the Romantic movement could and did commit in its infancy. I imagine Walpole's 'Castle of Otranto'[75] and the 'really

73 *Spirits in Bondage*, p. 16.

74 Sir Walter Scott, *The Talisman* (1825).

75 Horace Walpole, *The Castle of Otranto* (1765).

horrid' Gothic romances of Mrs Whats-her-Name[76] were something in this style. The subject however is fascinating, and Saladin is a great figure. I wonder where one could read something else about the Crusaders & the Saracens – do you know of anything? I suppose for the next six years or so I shall have no time to get thro' Tasso[77] in the original! I am now reading an Everyman crib to 'Marco Polo'.[78] The descriptions of innumerable Eastern towns would probably bore you, not having my appetite for collecting useless information: but I think you would like it once he reaches China and describes the wonderful court of the great Khan Khublai (Coleridge's Khubla Khan): the royal park with its palaces & pavilions and lakes 'full of all kinds of birds and bridges' reminds one of a willow pattern plate. There is also an excellent introduction by John Masefield and as a book this copy is a very favourable specimen of Everyman. This and the Talisman have begun to revive my interest in the East which was swept aside by Morris and Malory about the time I first knew you.

I hope you are avoiding my father as much as possible. Keep me posted however in all that may occur. I wired to him the other day to ask if W. had come home, and as he calls the latter 'Warren' in his reply I conclude he is in a temper about something or other.

The 'Medea' is very nearly finished, and will be about twelve hundred lines.[79] The main interest hangs on the family relations of the horrible old king and his daughter, whom I imagine as a sort of Emily Brontë, only more of a wolf – some of her father's bad blood coming out. The defect of the poem as a whole will be – heaven help us! – dulness.

I picture to myself your pleasure in arranging all your new books and getting settled down again: I do hope you will keep well and do something – perhaps I might get an instalment some day. Give me a full account of what you saw in town, especially about Cyrano.[80] The Minto[81] sends her love & says she is very pleased with the doctor's report on you:

---

76 Mrs Ann Radcliffe who wrote *The Mysteries of Udolpho* (1794).

77 i.e. Tasso's *Gerusalemme Liberata*.

78 *The Travels of Marco Polo the Venetian*, with an Introduction by John Masefield, Everyman's Library [1908].

79 Lewis mentioned an earlier version of the poem 'Medea' in his letters of 15, 20 and 28 February 1917. For more on this second version see his letter of 18 September 1919.

80 Presumably the play *Cyrano de Bergerac* (1898) by Edmond Rostand which Greeves could have seen in London.

81 The nickname used by Lewis and Greeves for Mrs Moore.

she also tells me to add that she has been expecting a letter from you by every post, and her 'face falls' three times a day. The hot weather comes back. Cheer up & write soon & don't shoot yourself yet.

Yours
Jack

TO HIS BROTHER (LP VI: 141–2):

University College,
Oxford
Teusday 22nd [July 1919]

My dear A.P.B.,[82]

I have just got your letter to which I am replying immediately. Of course I see your point, and am greatly relieved to hear from you as I had – of course – lost your adress and wanted to get into touch with you. Now will you please wire me at Univ. and let me know the day and approximate time of your arrival at Oxford: I will then report at the station at a suitable hour. If by any chance I am absent from parade you must drive to Univ. and wait for me, even if I do not turn up at once. The porter will have means of getting on to me if I am out. The programme you sketch is very attractive and it would be grand to have ignorance exposed by the Knock again. You understand why I behave so queerly – the effort to avoid being left alone at Leeborough. With you to back me up however, I have no doubt that we shall depart up to scheduled time. I doubt if this letter will reach you before you leave – in which case I hope it will *not* be forwarded.

yours ever,
Jack

Warnie arrived in Oxford on 23 July to begin his holiday with Jack. They were in London for the next two days, and on the 25th they visited Mr Kirkpatrick in Great Bookham. On 26 July they crossed to Ireland to stay with their father until 22 August.

The already uneasy relations between Jack and his father were considerably worsened by an event described by Mr Lewis in his diary of 6 August:

82 'Archpiggiebotham'. See note 1 to letter of 8 January 1917.

> *Sitting in the study after dinner I began to talk to Jacks about money matters and the cost of maintaining himself at the University. I asked him if he had any money to his credit, and he said about £15. I happened to go up to the little end room and lying on his table was a piece of paper. I took it up and it proved to be a letter from Cox and Co stating that his a/c was overdrawn £12 odd. I came down and told him what I had seen. He then admitted that he had told me a lie. As a reason, he said that he had tried to give me his confidence, but I had never given him mine etc., etc. He referred to incidents of his childhood where I had treated them badly. In further conversation he said he had no respect for me – nor confidence in me.* (LP VI: 161)

On 22 August Warnie and Jack set off for Dublin where they visited a friend of Warnie's, Dr Horace Stratford Collins, house surgeon at Doctor Steeven's Hospital, Dublin. Jack returned to Oxford from Dublin on 24 August to find that Mrs Moore had left 28 Warneford Road and taken a flat in the home of Mr and Mrs Albert Morris at 76 Windmill Road, Headington.

This rupture between Jack and his father was to last a long time. On 5 September Mr Lewis wrote in his diary:

> *I have during the past four weeks passed through one of the most miserable periods of my life – in many respects the most miserable. It began with the estrangement from Jacks. On 6 August he deceived me and said terrible, insulting, and despising things to me. God help me! That all my love and devotion and self-sacrifice should have come to this – that 'he doesn't respect me. That he doesn't trust me, and cares for me in a way.' He has one cause of complaint against me I admit – that I did not visit him while he was in hospital. I should have sacrificed everything to do so and had he not been comfortable and making good progress I should have done so...The other troubles and anxieties which have come upon me can be faced by courage, endurance, and self-denial. The loss of Jacks' affection, if it be permanent, is irreparable and leaves me very miserable and heart sore.* (LP VI: 167)

TO ARTHUR GREEVES (W):

Sunday [24 August 1919]
'Hill View'
Windmill Rd.
Highfield
[Oxford]

My dear Arthur,

Just a line to let you know of my arrival and of this change of address – the Minto having left Uplands and come here. Our landlady is a funny old woman, the wife of an Indian engine driver: I sleep on the sofa which quite satisfies my moderate demands on the world's comfort though it would hardly do for you.

We had quite a pleasant day in Dublin. I liked W's friend, who is house-surgeon in Steeven's hospital where he has a very pleasing little set of rooms. Have you ever been in Steeven's? There is a fine little library – despite some shocking portraits – containing some letters of Swift's. This letter begins to read like a guide book, so I will pass on.

Pass on to what? We are all well here and the Minto sends her love and tells me to thank you for all your labours on our behalf in the matter of letters etc[83] and also for the butter which we are still eating. She expects to go to France in a week or so now, which is rather horrible. What a pity you couldn't come over and bear me company in the solitudes of Highfield. By the way there is a thing I want you to do. No sooner had we got outside the gate on Friday than I remembered I had left the Reviews of my book[84] behind, which I particularly wanted to bring. Would you please go across some morning when his Excellenz is out and get them: they are in the bottom shelf of the miniature roller-top desk thing that stands on the table of the little end room nearest the window. They are in a white envelope – please see about it, will you, and send them on.

Have not been doing much in the way of reading so far but the Hell-story is nearly finished. Write soon and tell me all developments.

Yours
Jack

---

83 Lewis and Mrs Moore exchanged daily letters whenever he was in Ireland, and to avoid Albert Lewis knowing about this (though he did in fact know) Mrs Moore addressed hers to Arthur's home.

84 i.e. the reviews of *Spirits in Bondage*.

TO HIS FATHER (LP VI: 168–9):

University College,
Oxford
13th Sept. 1919

My dear Papy,

I was rather under the impression that you were a letter in my debt and have consequently waited from day to day in the expectation of hearing from you. However that may be, you have outdone me in taciturnity and the move falls to me.

We are having very hot weather here until today when it has, to my great relief, broken in mists and rain. However I can usually manage to get cool in my room and am getting through a good deal of work. Having regard to the coal situation, indeed, it is to be hoped that we shall not have a long winter.

From the newspapers you appear to be having a lively time in Ireland. I know of course that there was an extensive 'Papish' party in Belfast, but I am surprised to see that Larne has also been the scene of a raid. I should have thought that it was almost the type of a 'decent wee Presbyterian town' with not a spark of disaffection in it.

While at home I forgot to ask you for the certificate of my War Bond, without which I cannot turn the Dividend Warrant of June 1st into money. Will you therefore please forward it to me? I should also be glad if you would let me have Warnie's latest address.

We are living here in the anticipation of two interesting arrivals – Yeats for good[85] and Bergson for a second visit. The former I hope to meet, but I suppose I shall not see the latter unless he gives a lecture. Such are the important events that exercise our little community.

your loving son,
Jack

TO ARTHUR GREEVES (W):

[University College]
Thursday [18 September 1919]

My dear Arthur,

Your first letter, to quote Dr Johnson, 'was in such a strain of peevish discontent and unmanly resolution as could afford little comfort to a

85 The poet W.B. Yeats had moved to 4 Broad Street, Oxford.

friend or satisfaction to a philosopher.' Hem! Well, perhaps it wasn't so bad as all that: but I hope that the bad spirits which seem to have resulted from mountains, sea and pleasant society have been banished by the charms of Bernagh.

You seem to have had some adventures in rescuing my reviews from the jaws of Excellenz! How fortunate that you had really borrowed some books to carry off the scene with. 'De Profundis'[86] is hardly more than a memory to me. I seem to remember that it had considerable beauties, but of course in his serious work one always wonders how much is real and how much is artistic convention. He must have suffered terribly in prison, more perhaps than many a better man. I believe 'The Ballad of Reading Gaol'[87] was written just after he came out, and before he had had time to smelt down his experiences into artificiality, and that *it* rather than 'De Profundis' represents the real effect on his mind. In other words the grim bitterness is true: the resignation not quite so true. Of course one gets very real bitterness in D.P. too – as in the passage where he waited at the railway junction. Hartman's mother was a member of the Wilde set, and Hartman knows the person (refferred to in the book by initials) who waited to take off his hat – but I've forgotten who it was. 'The Ideal Husband'[88] is not, I think, one of the best.

I have written to and had an answer from Excellenz. He observes that he was pleased to get my letter and would have been more pleased to see in it 'some expression of regret for the terrible things I had said to him'. You see, he still insists on occupying the position of joint judge, jury and accuser, while relegating me to that of prisoner at the bar. So long as he refuses to acknowledge any faults on his side or to attribute the whole business to anything but my original sin, I do not see how he can expect a real or permanent reconciliation.

The Minto has returned from France: on which subject you will probably hear from her own pen. Since then we have moved into the flat which is very comfortable. Of course there has been a tremendous amount of work settling in but we begin to see daylight now.

On getting back to England I had the pleasure of looking over my 'Medea' of which I told you and finding that it was all hopeless and only fit for the fire! Nothing daunted however I bade it a long farewell – poor

86 Oscar Wilde, *De Profundis* (1905).

87 Oscar Wilde, *The Ballad of Reading Gaol* (1898).

88 Oscar Wilde, *An Ideal Husband* (1899).

still-born – and consoled myself by turning the 'Nimue' from a monologue into a narrative, in which form it may do. It appears in 'stanzas' of my own invention and is rather indebted to 'St Agnes' Eve' with touches of Christabel and some references to contemporary politics – by way of showing how much better I could manage the country if they made me Prime Minister. Sounds promising, DON'T it? It relates the events of a single evening – Merlin coming back & catching Nimue at last. This is the first stanza, do you think it any good?

'There was none stirring in the hall that night,
The dogs slept in the ashes, and the guard
Drowsily nodded in the warm fire-light,
Lulled by the rain and wearied of his ward,
Till, hearing one that knocked without full hard,
Half-dazed he started up in aged fear
And rubbed his eyes and took his tarnished spear
And hobbled to the doorway and unbarred.'[89]

You will perhaps be surprised to hear that I am reading 'The Prelude'[90] by way of graduating in Wordsworth-ism. What's even funnier, I rather like it! I'm coming to the conclusion that there are two orders of poetry – real poetry and the sort you read while smoking a pipe. 'The Prelude' nearly always on the second level but very comfortable and interesting all the same – better than Rousseau's Confessions in something the same style. You read it, didn't you? I expect like me you recognised lots of the early parts from recollections of your own childhood. I fancy the first Book is the best.[91]

I sent 'Hippolytus' to the Odds & Ends Magazine[92] but I haven't seen it yet. I shall be interested in trying to pick out Mrs Pomeroy's contribution. Does she write prose or verse?

---

89 These are the only surviving lines of Lewis's poem about Medea which he had mentioned frequently in his letters to Arthur. There are two further references to it in his letters of 11 April 1920 and 4 November 1925.

90 William Wordsworth, *The Prelude: or, Growth of a Poet's Mind* (1850).

91 In response to the question put by *The Christian Century* (6 June 1962): 'What books did most to shape your vocational attitude and your philosophy of life?' Lewis listed 10 books, of which one is Wordsworth's *Prelude*. See *CG*, p. 752.

92 Mrs Pomeroy, a Belfast lady and friend of Arthur Greeves, founded and edited the *Odds & Ends Magazine* to which Lewis contributed. I have been unable to discover any

The country is just beginning to think about Autumn. We have had some lovely walks. There are delightful 'rights of way' about here through fields and wood, all over styles made of single old stones – rather Druidical looking.

Write soon again. The family sends their love.

Yours

Jack

TO ARTHUR GREEVES (W):

University College.
[18 October 1919]

My dear Arthur,

I am sorry to have left your last letter so long without an answer: of course the beginning of the term is accompanied with a lot of business which fills up my time. And I am afraid there is another cause which operates against you – namely that the idea of writing to you is inevitably associated with that of writing to Excellenz, a task for which I have so little relish that, in my cowardly way, I keep it as much out of my mind as possible.

I should have spared my 'sarcasm' if I had known that it would 'cut you to the heart': that susceptible and sorely-tried organ of yours should not offer itself so readily to the knife: and, as you see, Johnson was much *more* severe. Not of course that I consider myself entitled to the great man's privilege of colossal rudeness. But we follow as we may.

I am not very fond of Euripides' Medea: but as regards the underworking of the possibilities which you mention, you must remember that the translation has to be rather stiff – tied by the double chains of fidelity to the original and the demands of its own metres, it cannot have the freedom and therefore cannot have the passion of the real thing. As well, even in reading the Greek we must miss a lot. We call it 'statuesque' and 'restrained' because at the distance of 2500 years we cannot catch the subtler points – the associations of a word, the homeliness of some

---

copies of the *Odds & Ends Magazine*. However, among the literary fragments preserved in the Lewis Papers (VIII: 165–7) is a portion of the 'Hippolytus' poem no doubt referred to here. The poem was to go through various transformations, from 'Hippolytus' to 'Wild Hunt' to 'The King of Drum' until it finally became 'The Queen of Drum' which is found in Lewis's *Narrative Poems* (1969).

phrazes and the unexpected strangeness of others. All this we, as foreigners, don't see – and are therefore inclined to assume that it wasn't there.

I quite see the humour of your idea about Excellenz's double life and clandestine marriage. I don't think it *has* evaporated on paper. But, oh ye gods, what fun there would have been if he had been at home when Mrs Pomeroy arrived! What mysteries and suspicions he would have spun.

Yeats has taken up his residence in Oxford, and some of us are going to beard the lion in his den one of these days. Perhaps we shall get him to read a paper to the Martlets: perhaps we shall be kicked out. But I think his vanity is sufficient to secure us a good reception if we come with the obvious purpose of worshipping devoutly.

I finished the Prelude and liked it. It is about as bad as a poem could be in some ways but one considers the great passages not too dearly bought at the price of the rest. Since then I have read Geoffrey of Monmouth's 'History of the Kings of Britain'. I don't think you would care much for it, there are a good many dull battles and his Arthur is merely contemptible. Where he really is good is in the early part. Who would not hear about the first coming of Brut, and Bladud (our first aeronaut, the British counterpart of Daedalus), and the birth of Merlin and the building of Stonehenge (its delightful alternative name being The Dance of Giants) and Vortigern and Lear and Locrine? One learns a little too. 'Kaer' apparently is British for 'city'.[93] Hence Leil builds Kaer-Leil (Carlyle) and Kaer-leon is the city of legion. 'Kaerleon of the legions' (as I call it in Nimue) what a name! Also I have been looking into Macdonald's poems in bookshops lately: now-a-days I am too poor to buy anything without long consideration. They look much better than I thought before. I have been so long with Wordsworth and philosophers that I want something mystical – pure unadulterated imagination.

One gets lovely autumn bits even in town now. The other day I was sitting under the tower of Magdalen on a bus. The big bells were just chiming five and the tower was turning paler and paler every minute. The trees were getting ghostly and everything had just one word 'frost'. I do love to feel the winter coming on.

---

93 Hence 'Cair Paravel', castle of the kings and queens of Narnia in Lewis's Chronicles of Narnia.

The Minto is frightfully busy and hasn't written to a creature except her sister since she came back, but when she has time you will be among the first claimants. We are both delighted to hear that you are coming to London[94] at last and shall expect to see you here for a week end whenever you can come. I do hope the London idea will set you up & start a new 'era' (hideous word) in your life. I am writing to Excellenz tomorrow (Sunday). Owing to the darned strike I have had no copy of Odds and Ends yet but am living in hopes.

Yours
Jack

TO HIS FATHER (LP VI: 170–1):

University College,
Oxford.
Postmark: 20 October 1919

My dear Papy,

I have had rather a miserable time with a heavy cold and sore throat which has sent me to bed early in the evenings and generally kept me from doing the things which I ought. Otherwise I should have answered your letter before. I seem to have got rid of it now.

Many thanks for your packet of War Office papers. I filled them all up, supplying the facts as you suggested, and got more forms in return which I filled up again. Like most of these papers, it involves signing for the money which you haven't yet got, and this signature – rather funnily it seems to me – constitutes a sort of cheque which you pay into your bankers. It is also loaded with deadly threats against 'people making false declarations'.

I had already seen about the death of Cousin Quartus[95] in the Times before I got your telegram. For this I suppose one should have been prepared, and indeed for himself, poor man, it was no tragedy. Yet I had come to think of his always being there: it will be a sad thing to go to Glenmachan now. As far back as I can remember he has always had a big place in our life – always the same kindly, courteous old gentleman. I am of course writing to Cousin Mary, although I think such letters are of little use. There is a great deal that we could all say, and say honestly, but it usually sounds conventional on paper.

94 Arthur was thinking of going there to study art.
95 Sir William Quartus Ewart died on 17 October. See **The Ewart Family** in the Biographical Appendix.

It is very cold here, but fortunately I have a fair amount of coal left over from last term and can therefore afford a reasonable period of fire every day.

As regards the other matter of which you spoke in your letters, I must ask you to believe that it would have been much easier for me to have left those things unsaid. They were as painful to me as they were for you. Yet, though I have many things to blame myself for, I should blame myself still more if I had tried to establish the relations you refer to by any other means than that of saying frankly what I thought. I did not speak in anger; still less for the purpose of giving pain. But I am sure you will agree with me that the confidence and affection which we both desire are more likely to be restored by honest effort on both sides and toleration – such as is always necessary between imperfect human creatures – than by any answer of mine which was not perfectly sincere.

your loving son,

Jack

1920

TO LEO BAKER[1] (B):

Little Lea,
Strandtown,
Belfast.
12th Jan. 1920.

My dear Baker,

The fact of being at home, which to me is a synonym for busy triviality, continual interruption and a complete lack of privacy, must be my best excuse for not having written to you before. I should have thanked you, too, long ago for the card which you sent me with my MSS. The poem, seen for the first time in print, was excellent: the first line carries you away into a strange country, a grave childlike kind of Christmas-land, homely yet strangely interesting and even awe-inspiring. I find, however, on reading the poem over, plenty of melody but not enough harmony: it does not leave a continuous music in the ear.

This is intolerable, you know, about your health: I had never reckoned on such a sublunary consideration breaking up our salon. Doubtless you have already decided what to do, so any advice on my part comes – happily – too late. 'Safety first' as the posters say, must of course be your motto and no one would advise you to risk your permanent health for even the delights of Pasley's society and mine: but, unless my wishes deceive me, I should think that interest and occupation at Oxford would be better for you than remaining in town with or without a job. I am afraid everything will be broken up if you are staying next term. You are rather a key-stone, you know.[2] Pasley will tend gradually toward modernism, I to mediaevalism; Hartman will go on being brilliant, but

1 See **Leo Baker** in the Biographical Appendix.

2 Baker matriculated at Wadham College in October 1919. Because of ill-health he was unsure of coming back to Oxford for the Hilary Term.

there will be no cohesion. I was hoping to have many more conversations with you on the subjects which we have in common, and perhaps become your amateur disciple in mysticism. However – do try and come up.

About Munro's refusal and the new step, if any, to be taken, we can hardly talk without meeting.[3] I feel, as a matter of conscience that we should try to get the thing published, though I do not feel any great joy at the prospect.[4] Everything hinges on our view of Munro's opinion. If he is right we must make him wrong,

yours very truly
Clive Lewis

TO ARTHUR GREEVES (W):

[University College]
Teusday [3? February 1920]

My dear Arthur,

I shall expect to hear from you soon that your plans are settled: I suppose it is useless to hope that you have still any intention of going to Harrogate, though you may tell your advisers, for their comfort, that it is absolutely warm and springlike in England.

You will be surprised when you hear how I employed the return journey – by reading an H. G. Wells novel called 'Marriage',[5] and perhaps more surprised when I say that I thoroughly enjoyed it; one thing you can say for the man is that he really is interested in all the big, outside questions – and the characters are intensely real, especially a Mr Pope who reminds me of Excellenz. It opens new landscapes to me – how one felt that on finding that a new kind of book was waiting for one, in the old days – and I have decided to read some more of his serious books. It is funny that I – and perhaps you – read the old books for pleasure and always turn to contemporaries with the notion of 'improving my mind'. With most, I fancy, the direct opposite is so.

---

3 H.E. Monro (1879–1932) founded a poetry bookshop in 1913 to encourage its sale and for publishing the series *Georgian Poetry*, edited by Sir Edward Marsh. He had refused to publish the poems Lewis sent him.

4 Lewis and Baker were getting together an anthology of poems entitled 'The Way's the Way' which they hoped would be published by Basil Blackwell.

5 H.G. Wells, *Marriage* (1912).

But I must work like ten devils this term and bid good-bye to general reading except for an odd hour on Sundays. I read the Bacchae[6] over yesterday – for the last time before the exam: to rush through great poetry at top speed is not, of course, the right way to appreciate it, but one gets a peculiar value out of such a flying survey now and then. I realized, for one thing, how very quickly the terrible story happens: in the morning the old men with the magic youth in them are going out to the mountains, and before evening you have the stupid anger of Pentheus, the capture of the God and his quiet, ominous words to his captor, his escape, the swift madness of Pentheus, the catastrophe, and then it is all over and the long years of misery follow the one fatal mistake when mortal wisdom met immortal passion. You did like it didn't you?

I was in Baker's rooms with Pasley last night: Pasley departed early and the conversation between us two fell on shadowy subjects – ghosts and spirits and Gods. You may or may not disbelieve what followed. Baker began to tell me about himself: how he had seen things ever since he was a child, and had played about with hypnotism and automatic writing: how he had finally given it all up, till now 'things' were coming back of their own accord. 'At one time' he said 'I was afraid to look round the room for fear of what I might see.' He also stated confidently that anyone could compel a ghost to appear, that there were definite ways of doing it: though of course the thing you 'fished up' might not be what you wanted – indeed *quite* the contrary. The greater part of his views I will reserve for our next meeting: what I wanted to tell you was the effect on me. I got, as it were, dazed and drunk in all he said: then I noticed his eyes: presently I could hardly see anything else: and everything he said was real – incredibly real. When I came away, I moved my eyes off his, with a jerk, so to speak, and suddenly found that I had a splitting headache and was tired and nervous and pulled to pieces. I fancy I was a bit hypnotised. At any rate I had such a fit of superstitious terror as I have never known since childhood and have consequently conceived, for the present, a violent distaste for mysteries and all that kind of business. Perhaps he is a bit mad.

The Minto was so pleased with your bag and so was Maureen with her box which I think is quite charming. I have decided to come out and

6 *Bacchae* is a tragedy by Euripides produced c. 405 BC.

'dig' at Headington altogether next term.[7] Hope you're alright.

Yours

Jack

TO HIS FATHER (LP VI: 179):

University College

Sunday.

Postmark: 4 February 1920

My dear Papy,

Many thanks for your letter and also for the instructions to Aunt Suffern. I don't in the least want to consume large quantities of oranges or anything else, but if it must be, I suppose she will rest content with such an arrangement. I only hope she will not waste too much of our substance in riotous living.

The parcel you were asked to register contained my old trench coat which I thought might be better than a big coat for wet but warm days. I had left it with her of Endor and given instructions that it should be sent on and that 'the captain would register and address it'. However it has now arrived safely, and as there have been no 'wet, warm days' the delay has done no harm.

I am preparing to wait upon my great aunt Warren[8] this afternoon, with transports as moderate as those of the Colonel. I think this particular form of introducing strangers by letter, on the theory that blood is thicker than water ('and a good deal nastier' as someone added) is one of the most irritating of social amenities. It always reminds me of two hostile children being shoved into a room and told to 'have a nice game' together.

I hope you will like Mexico:[9] most interesting characters those old 'conquistadors' with their strange mixture of avarice, religion, and

---

7 Undergraduates were normally required to spend three terms in College, after which they were allowed to move into University-approved 'digs' or lodgings. Lewis meant that at the end of Hilary Term he planned to live with the Moores. About the time this letter was written the Moores moved from 76 Windmill Road, Headington, into the house of Mrs John Jeffrey, a butcher by occupation, in 58 Windmill Road.

8 Warnie included a note about this lady in LP VI: 179: 'I am unable to trace "great aunt Warren"; she cannot however have been a Warren by blood, for all the five sisters of Mary Hamilton [his maternal grandmother] were married. The three brothers of Mary Hamilton were also married, and I presume that it is the wife of one of them who is referred to.'

9 Albert Lewis was probably reading Charles Reginald Enock's *Mexico* (1909).

brutality. I am inclined to agree with you – and Mrs Ward – about the lack of charm in Wells: but there are other qualities as important, if less delightful. I am now reading 'Lavengro' at breakfast every morning and should like it very much if one could cut out the anti-Catholic propaganda.

We are still having wonderful weather here and I hope to get in a good walk today. The new suits have arrived and are most satisfactory.

your loving son,

Jack

TO ARTHUR GREEVES (W):

[University College]
Saturday [14? February 1920]

My dear Arthur,

I was very glad to see from your letter that you have at last escaped from Ireland. New scenery, pleasant society, books to read and an empty hotel to read them in – what could be nicer? I hope you have got over your usual 'unsettlement' at leaving home: certainly it is good that you have left: it is not the disadvantages of home but its comforts that kill – lazy comfort gets hold on one like spiders-web, doesn't it? I hope you told Mrs P.[10] that it was 'lack of time' decided me to give up 'Odds & Ends', not that I thought it pretty bad? You are so tactful you know!

You will be glad to hear that I have started Lavengro again (at breakfast) and though I still dislike the anti-Catholic propaganda and the rhetorical passages where the inspiration failed him and he filled up with the usual style of the period, I feel the charm as I did not feel it before and find the book hard to put down. I think with authors as with people we meet, when one finds an objectional feature the best thing is to trace it back to some central point of character from which it originates. When a thing is explained it loses half its nastiness, 'tout comprende c'est tout pardonner'.[11] I have therefore found an explanation which might account for

10 Mrs Pomeroy.

11 Madame de Staël (1766–1817) said in *Corinne* (1807), bk. 18, ch. 5, 'Tout comprendre rend très indulgen' ('To understand everything makes one very indulgent'). There are two similar phrases, 'Comprendre c'est pardonner' ('To understand is to forgive') and 'Tout comprendre c'est tout pardonner' ('To understand everything is to forgive everything') which are attributed to Madame de Staël but are not found in her works. The phrases are probably misquotations of – or indeed improvements on – the sentence in *Corinne*.

Borrow's rampant protestantism – it lies in the extreme Northernness or Saxon-ism of his nature. He thrilled, as we once did, to everything Norse, even the skull of Dane. I am glad to see that he knew the Kalevala. Hence, of course, a thoroughly Southern, Latin & Mediterranean thing like the Church was antipathetic and he worked up reasonable explanations to support the feeling which was really independent of them. I think the descriptions of the walk thro' the snow and the fairy-smith are admirable.

Did you see the Times Review of a new poem 'Mansoul' by Charles Doughty?[12] Doughty is an old poet and traveller whom I have heard mentioned now & then by the 'people who really know', always with a profound if distant respect. The review persuaded me to buy Mansoul, which is the strangest thing to be written in 1920 – an epic poem in 6 books, of which I have read two and a half so far. Now, mark, for this is important if I'm right – I think it was one of the *really* great things that will stand out like Dante or Milton, and, if so, isn't it wonderful to be alive when it has come out. It is very, very difficult, being written in a curious grammar which leaves out nearly all the pronouns: this is wicked, but even through it you can see the signs of a great work. It is a sort of journey into the underworld, where various ancient sages are interviewed on the meaning of life: we have a glimpse of hell, too, and some fine well-at-the-worlds-end kind of scenery in the first book: later on, I see, there are very learned & very English fairy passages. On the whole its more like Spenser than Milton.

Damn Tchaine's impudence for thinking I am to be a critic: the only thing in the world I could criticize really well is her wonderful self.

It is frosty here again, and there has been beautiful twilight to-day with the cold red light behind the black trees. All of us and chiefly the Minto find this place[13] more and more intolerable as time goes on: but all our hopes of a change seem to become will o' the wisps (do you remember that song – at Portsalon – ye gods!!) when we are hottest on the trail.

I have decided to send you some spelling-notes every time I write until you improve. To day I suggest 'digging' and 'asthma' as preferable to 'diging' and 'asma'.

Yours
Jack

12 Charles Montagu Doughty, *Mansoul, or the Riddle of the World* (1920). Reviewed in *The Times Literary Supplement* (22 January 1920), p. 49.

13 Mrs Jeffrey's house at 58 Windmill Road.

TO ARTHUR GREEVES (W):

22 Old Cleeve
Washford,
Somerset.
[2 April 1920]

My dear Arthur,

I don't know what you must think of me by now. Sometimes I try to console myself by saying that you would have written again yourself unless you had been sufficiently occupied in the interval. All the same I know the fault is mine – but hear my tale.

First of all came some weeks of hard work before the exam. Then the exam[14], itself for eight days, on the first day of which this swollen gland in my throat appeared again, much larger this time and more painful. I had a night with practically no sleep and could hardly eat anything – I think sanatogen saved me in the end. After the exam, I had a few cheery days packing up all my books etc (heart-breaking task!) preparatory to living at Headington next term. Then when I got out there, relations with our landlady had become so intolerable – the Minto will describe it to you some day – that we had to leave at once – and as the place we are going next term was not ready we had no other alternative but to decamp and leave our effects with various friends. More days of packing, pulling & hawling cases, arranging and re-arranging in boiling weather. We had seen an advertisement of a cottage here for a month and taken it on chance, so desperate were we. Thus finally, after the most loathsome and degrading scenes with our landlady and landlord, who nearly became violent, we departed – all of us pretty nearly done. The Minto and I still dream of the Jeffreys. I shall never get the taste of that woman out of my mind – 'not uglier follow the night-hag'.[15] But now that we are here, to quote Milton again, 'This turn hath made amends.'[16]

You do not, of course, know where old Cleeve is: nor did I till a week ago. It is not far from the end of the world: from a delightful thatched cottage with big low rooms *and* modern arrangements we look out on a

---

14 These were the examinations for Classical Honour Moderations which began on 4 March. The results were already known and, curiously, Lewis failed to tell his friend that he took a First, an announcement of which appeared in *The Times* (1 April 1920), p. 18.

15 Milton, *Paradise Lost*, II, 662: 'Nor uglier...'

16 ibid., VIII, 491.

sea of fruit trees. The village is so small as hardly to deserve the name: and all round there is not a single straight line in the landscape. From the sea which is about a mile to our right to the black mountains on our left the hills are piled together like eggs in a basket, with the most charming villages nestling between them and orchards and streams everywhere and primroses as thick as the lights from the town at home on every bank. Across the water is the hazy outline of Wales – the Arthurian country round Kaerleon and the Usk, I believe. Those same 'Black Hills' on the extreme left of our landscape I have been trying to reach for some time and succeeded this morning (Good Friday). They are rather of the same type as Divis[17] – very black and grim. On one side I looked down into our own homely and rolling valley, on the other to more and more hills with deep gorges between where fir woods sometimes straggled up the sides. Then I went half way down a deep fold in the hill where a stream ran under queer gray trees and there were rocks to sit on, for the bracken and heather were wet. There I rested in an enormous silence and gradually the old feeling came into my mind. You know what I mean – a feeling associated with Wagner and the Well at the Worlds End, which I haven't had for over a year now. I wish I had my copy of The Lore of Proserpine here – it is just the place to read it in.

You can't imagine what a relief it is to be down here, away from work and exams and rows and packing and luggage! I am writing a good deal and also reading. Before we left Oxford I read Romola.[18] Certainly there is great comfort in these old-fashioned historical novels with a slow but not languid movement and plenty of work in them. I have forgotten whether you have read it or not. Since then followed Washington Irving's Life of Mahomet,[19] a silly and scanty book on an interesting subject and Lowes Dickinson's 'The Meaning of Good'.[20] You should read the latter if you get hold of it – it introduces you to a good many points of view in philosophy without being at all technical or pedantic. I am now at 'Waverley'[21] which I like very much so far and 'Prometheus Unbound'.

---

17 Mount Divis in Co. Antrim.

18 George Eliot, *Romola* (1863).

19 Washington Irving, *Lives of Mahomet and his Successors* (1850). The *Life of Mahomet* was published separately in Everyman's Library (1911).

20 Lowes Dickinson, *The Meaning of Good* (1901).

21 Sir Walter Scott, *Waverley* (1814).

I am writing to my father on Monday to tell him that I shall not be home this Vac. – I really can't face him on top of everything else – but you had better pose as having heard nothing about me or my movements if you should be compelled to meet him.

The Minto has a nasty cold but I think the place is doing her good – she sends her love and hopes that your stay in England has done you good. And now, don't be fed up with me for my long silence: write and tell me how your world goes on – I only hope you are having as good a time as I at present have without the purgatory through which I passed to reach it.

Yours
Jack

TO HIS FATHER (LP VI: 183):

22 Old Cleeve,
Washford,
Somerset
4 April 1920

My dear Papy,

I am glad to be able to begin with a bit of good news. I did get a first after all. Unfortunately that is almost all I can tell you, as the names in each class are given only in alphabetical order and I can see no possibility of finding out places or marks. Now as to our movements: as this is the shortest vac., and also as I felt in need of some 'refresher' I thought it a good opportunity of paying off an engagement with a man who has been asking me for some time to go and 'walk' with him.[22] We are at present at this tiny little village in a perfectly ideal cottage (which is, so to speak, his people's Teigh-na-mara) from which base we shall set out when the weather clears.

We are quite alone and live an idyllic life on eggs, bully beef and – divine treasure – an excellent ham which Aunt Lily very opportunely sent. The country is delightful, consisting of high moors with charming valleys full of orchards between them, and everything is a mass of white blossom. It is on the borders of Somerset and Devon. Our address will of course be moveable but letters sent here will reach me after some delay. I am sorry to desert you for the present, but it had to be polished off sooner or later.

---

22 This of course is a fabrication as Lewis was here with Mrs Moore and Maureen.

I am just getting over a rather tiresome cough and cold and am beginning to feel much better than I have done for a long time. I have brought Waverley to clean out my mind – there is great comfort in these solid old books.

I have celebrated the occasion by sending a poem to the Hibbert Journal, but I very much doubt if they will accept anything by so unknown a person as myself. At any rate they will probably take about a month to deliberate.

Thank you very much for both the cheques. I hope the teeth are now giving no trouble and also that the official shooting season has not set in yet at Belfast. Does the last murder mean that the Orange people are replying?

your loving
son Jack

TO ARTHUR GREEVES (W):

22 Old Cleeve,
Washford,
Somerset.
Sunday [11 April 1920]

My dear Arthur,

Your letter gave me great pleasure both because it was the first after a long pause (for which I was responsible) and also because it had a cheerfulness and resolution which have long been strangers to you. If the mind really reflects the body you must be enormously better. Is it possible that the good days are at last dawning again? I can't say how pleased I should be to see you strong and able to do things and doing them: above all don't get a relapse either mental or physical, and incidentally excuse what may sound a patronising tone and put it down to the best motives. As we cannot have that 'long talk' you mention, we must try to discuss things as well as possible on paper.

One thing I should take as data – whatever you do, let it be something that will take you from Belfast. Absence cured you: nothing, I fancy, is more likely to un-cure you than a long period at Bernagh. I can't put into words the effect which surroundings familiar even to staleness and the sort of heavy impetus of all that has passed are likely to have. And Ireland itself – much as I love and 'desire it all my days' as Homer says, if other things were equal – I think there is some truth in my own 'Irish

Nocturne'.[23] Look it up, not as a poem but as a theory and tell me if you agree.

It would please me beyond everything if you could realize your plan of coming to Oxford. Though of course I could not see you so often nor so regularly as at home we should be constantly meeting, and once you get 'settled' – which you would in time – I think the life would be splendid for you. You would find an enormous choice of congenial friends, and you can have no idea how the constant friction with other and different minds improves one. You would have none of the reasons (either of circumstance or temperament) which make my circle small and would, I hope, soon 'know everybody'. The difficulty is to find an ostensible pretext for Oxford. What the exact conditions of entering are since Greek has been withdrawn I do not know: but perhaps merely to be here, *not* as an undergraduate would leave you freer to develop on your own lines – though of course a degree is useful in itself and gives you, as you say, some object in life. You might come up to study some particular period of history – not as an undergraduate – and to use the old documents etc in the Bodleian: always provided you can trust yourself to be busy and happy without a definite task and exams. Your father could easily afford it: would he approve. Of course you can frankly use my presence as a reason for wanting to be here!

Except for my own pleasure the Slade[24] is undoubtedly the best plan, and I suppose it is that you really have in view. I don't see on what principle the doctor could veto it and yet allow any of the other plans.

I suppose you are not really serious about the poultry farming? The Minto has plenty of experience in that line and says that IF you could get the ground and house at Headington you could run a partnership with her and she would undertake to make it pay! You know best whether you could really be happy in what is called an outdoor life.

In fact if the doctor forbids the Slade, I suppose it comes down to pursuing something definite in private – but I hope NOT at home. I do most strongly fear the effects of another dull, empty winter at Bernagh. I know you don't like to apply to your father again very soon but if nothing else turns up you should make an effort at all costs to be away, here

23 'Irish Nocturne', *Spirits in Bondage*, pp. 18–19: '...I know that the colourless skies / And the blurred horizons breed / Lonely desire and many words and brooding and never a deed.'

24 The Slade School of Fine Art, University College, London.

or anywhere, for as long as possible. You wouldn't care to turn your attention to philosophy – seriously, I mean, not just as ordinary reading? I am just starting it soon for my next exam. and we could keep each other up by letter.

I didn't at all agree with you about the difficulty of 'getting into' Waverley. I personally would not have a sentence of those early chapters curtailed: they showed me Scott in quite a new light, describing the childhood and development of the hero in his world of imagination. I can't help feeling that when he wrote this Scott had a higher sense of responsibility to his own characters – took them more seriously and worked out their natural growth more thoroughly – than in his later novels. Isn't the scene at the end where Waverley finds the old Baron of Bradwardine by the guidance of the idiot David Gellatley simply typical Scott – and delightful.

I saw a scene the other day that was typical Scott too – the Castle of Dunster. It stands on a little wooded hill just at the mouth of a long valley with very steep sides half-covered by fir-woods and just from its gates downwards straggles the single broad street of a drowsy village[25] with an old fountain: and the upper storeys of the cottages project in Elizabethan style. But it can only be described in language of Scott's period.

I am glad you saw 'Dear Brutus'.[26] 'Don't go into the wood!' – how well that first act works up to the supernatural of the second. I hope the 'Dream-child'[27] was good – everything depends on her. And that reminds me, the best news of all in your letter was that you are writing again. I won't repeat all my old wishes on the subject: but I still think it most unlikely that all the romance and imagination which are in you should evaporate in nothing more than appreciation of other people's work. Of course the thing's always difficult for a man who begins after his own critical faculties are fully grown. A child, if easily discouraged, is also easily satisfied and his powers grow with his ideals. But I hope you will make up your mind to go through with a good deal of trouble.

Look at me – I am still working at my poem on Merlin and Nimue. It has been in succession – rhymed monologue – rhymed dialogue – blank verse dialogue – long narrative in stanzas – short narrative in couplets –

---

25 Dunster, Somerset.

26 Sir James Matthew Barrie, *Dear Brutus* (1917).

27 *The Dream-Child* is the young daughter who exists only in the dream-world of Act II of *Dear Brutus*.

and I am at present at work on a blank verse narrative version. I hope I am not wasting my time: but there must be some good in a subject which drags me back to itself so often. You see, as Chaucer says,

We toilen ever and poren in the fire
And for all that we fail in our desire.[28]

Since finishing Waverley I have started Heroes and Hero-Worship[29] and finished the first lecture, which I read long, long ago when I first knew you, in the days when everything to do with the Norse lore was honey to me. Even now, when I have found so much better, I can't help regretting the extraordinary keenness and singleness of *wish* that one had then.

Write soon and I will really try to keep up a regular interchange in the 'good, old' style. I hope that you will go on as you now are: remember how others have kept themselves full of hope and life in worse predicaments – and excuse my ever preaching.

Yours
Jack

P.S. I never got the last letter you mention. If you can please say *when* it was sent, for we are afraid those damned Jeffreys are keeping our letters. Love from all.

TO HIS FATHER (LP VI: 184–5):

22 Old Cleeve,
Washford,
Somerset.
April 11th 1920

My dear Papy,

I was very sorry to hear that I had allowed you first to learn the news about Mods. from a stranger. I had put off writing until I was clear of Oxford and half thought that you might see it in the Times[30] as soon

---

28 Chaucer, *Canterbury Tales,* 'The Canon's Yeoman's Tale', 670–1: 'We blondren evere and pouren in the fir, / And for al that we faille of oure desire.'

29 Thomas Carlyle, *On Heroes, Hero-Worship, and the Heroic in History* (1841).

30 The results of the Classical Moderations examinations were mentioned in *The Times* of 1 April 1920 (p. 18).

as you could have heard it from me. As a matter of fact the Oxford news is so hid in a corner of the paper that it quite naturally escaped you.

I had quite forgotten about Aunt Warren. She must be pretty old, and dresses (with cap and white collar) in a style which makes her look rather more so. At the same time there is nothing senile in her conversation or manner. We talked chiefly about Glenmachan and Irish politics. The only one of 'the girls' present was Daisy, who is, I suppose, over forty. She struck me as being ecclesiastical in a high degree: for instance from her point of view the chief argument in favour of expelling the Turks from Europe was 'that it would re-establish the Patriarch at Constantinople and thus create a balance to the Papacy'. After the Armenian massacres, not to mention the war, *that* would hardly have appeared to me – nor to you I presume – the most important reason. There was a very attractive child whose parents are in India: but I like the old lady the best of the three.

As you see, we have not yet moved: indeed the weather has not encouraged us to set out, though it has not prevented us from a great deal of walking. It is more beautiful here almost than any place I have ever seen – whether in the valleys full of orchards or up on the big heathery hills from which one looks down on the sea and the Welsh coast away on the horizon.

You need not have any fears about our cuisine here. Remember we are almost in Devon and the clotted cream of the country is a host in itself: also – shades of Oldie – the real 'Deevonshire' cider in every thatched and sanded pub.[31]

A few miles away is a little fishing town called Watchet, which saw at least one interesting scene in its obscure history: it was here that Coleridge and the Wordsworths slept (or 'lay' as they would have said) on the first night of their walking tour. During that afternoon the germ of the Ancient Mariner occurred in conversation and in the inn at Watchet the first lines were jotted down.

I should think Brighton is not yet so intolerable as it will become in summer. I fancy the Colonel – and perhaps all of us – stands a good chance of being back in France soon unless the situation clears. God bless the French! and a murrain on Lloyd George and his impudent note!

31 Robert Capron ('Oldie'), his former headmaster at Wynyard School, was from Devonshire.

I am sorry to hear that you have been poorly again. Have you ever tried Sanatogen as a tonic? Someone recommended it to me when I had my gland and was feeling rather poorly. It certainly gave me sleep, though not an opiate, and I think bucked me up all round.

your loving son,
Jack

TO HIS FATHER (LP VI: 187–8):

University College,
Oxford.
May 1st 1920

My dear Papy,

I found your letter waiting for me when I came up, and in the business of seeing new tutors, starting new lines of work, lunching with the said new tutors etc., etc., this is almost the first opportunity I have had of answering you.

As to 'finance' I agree with what you say. I understand that the arrangement was for you to lodge £30 at the beginning of each term: and the reason why no dates were mentioned was that doubtless a person with a mind like mine (or 'mentality' as a really modern writer would say – I know you love the word!) never knows the dates of the terms unless he has a calendar by him. I think however that this is sufficiently definite: and if you would kindly send me that amount before the beginning of each term, and also do so now, we shall be alright. You will not mind my applying to you for some 'extra' expenses which may from time to time occur.

I have two tutors now that I am doing 'Greats', one for history[32] and one for philosophy.[33] Of course I am sorry to have parted brass rags with

---

32 George Hope Stevenson (1880–1952), Lewis's history tutor, was born in Glasgow and educated at Glasgow University. He took a First in Greats from Balliol College and in 1906 he was elected Praelector in Ancient History at University College where he remained until his retirement in 1949. His contributions to Roman history include *Roman History* (1930) and *Roman Provincial Administration* (1939). He was a keen Anglo-Catholic and for many years was church warden at St Margaret's Church in Oxford.

33 Edgar Frederick Carritt (1876–1964), Lewis's tutor in philosophy, was Fellow of Philosophy at University College, 1898–1941. He was an excellent lecturer, combining a very logical procedure with commonsense illustrations. In 1902 he was the first member of the faculty to lecture on aesthetics. Some of his lectures were amplified and published

old Poynton: the other two are much younger men, but seem quite nice. We go to the philosophy one in pairs: then one of us reads an essay and all three discuss it. I wish you could hear the 'crack', it is very amusing. Luckily I find that my previous dabbling in the subject stands me in good stead and for some time I shall have only to go over more carefully ground through which I have already meandered on my own.

I expect that what you feel about travel would be endorsed by a great many other people of your own age, who, as you say, have never really wanted a shilling in their lives. As far as I can see it is only the few who can do it without the least sacrifice who bother to see the world at all: the majority will not give up anything for it and would sooner afford a car to go round Stangford on, than see Greece or Cathay – if there really is a Cathay. One is amazed at the resolution of a real traveller like Herodotus, whom I am reading at present: knowing apparently no language but his own and relying on merchant caravans and dragomans with a smattering of Greek, he had yet penetrated to Babylon and seen the hanging gardens and the temple of Bel-Baal I suppose – and up the Nile as far as Elephantine where there were rumours of the land of dwarfs beyond – the Pygmies of course. Or Marco Polo – whom you should read: books of travel are a great resource.

I can't understand the Irish news at all. One of the most curious things is the rapprochement which seems probable between English Trades Unionism and Sinn Fein. I was always confident that the religious differences, the 'odium theologicum' would prevent a junction between the two. If they really do work together I think it is all up for England and Ireland.

How are the teeth getting on?

your loving son,

Jack

---

as *Theory of Beauty* (1914), *Philosophies of Beauty* (1931) and *Ethical and Political Thinking* (1947). Mr Carritt, a Socialist and supporter of the left wing, was not a Christian. An argument he had with Lewis years later is mentioned in Lewis's 'Christianity and Culture' found in *Christian Reflections* (1967). See 'Edgar Carritt' in the *University College Record*, Vol. IV (October 1964), pp. 235–43.

TO ARTHUR GREEVES (W):

[University College]
Monday [3? May 1920]

My dear Arthur,

Your last letter reached me the day after my return here and this is positively the first opportunity I have had of answering it. I must deal first of all with your definite questions. Ist As far as I can make out (for, indeed, the whole subject is still very uncertain) Greek will still be compulsory for Responsions in June but *not* for those in October and after. IInd I do not consider the choice of a college very important, much less so than that of a house at school. There are one or two you should avoid, as Christchurch and Magdalen for their expense, or Keble and Jesus for their vulgarity. Wadham is a very nice, quiet place and not too big. My great friend Baker is there and finds a great many pleasant people. There is no reason why Univ. should be 'out of the question', tho there is equally no reason why you should prefer it, especially now that I am living out. IIId I do not think that most colleges have entrance exams. in addition to Responsions. But on that and on the question of coming up before you take Responsions you had better write to the Bursar of the college you decide on and get definite information. It is much better to open such a correspondence than to rely on unofficial snippets like mine. I should say that you hoped to come up to So-and-So and ask I. for a syllabus of the Responsions subjects, II. whether you must take them before you come up – and any other questions that may occur to you. I do not think that anyone can fail in 'Smalls' after the removal of Greek, unless, like myself, he is incapable of elementary mathematics![34]

I do not quite gather if your going to Oxford is still only a pis-aller for the Slade or whether you now mean to come in any case. I most sincerely hope you will, for I can imagine nothing that would do you more good. I feel rather nervous, lest, if it disappoint you, the responsibility may rest with me. It is a pity Caesar is such a dull book, but I suppose you'll have to stick it. With care and going slowly at first you should easily pick up your Latin again. Perhaps indeed the historian in you may find interest where most of us cannot: of course it is mainly military history but if you once see it in perspective as an important step in the evolution of Europe you may not be too hopelessly bored.

---

34 Lewis was now exempt from having to pass Responsions in mathematics by virtue of being a serviceman.

How splendid to hear of you on the hills again: I can imagine what you felt in reaching at last that Mecca of ours after being exiled so long. There is much better scenery elsewhere no doubt, but as long as I live those little bits of wood and field will be an enchanted country to me. I think you touch on the great problem of writing when you put off describing your walk because the feeling of it is already past. If only the moment of inspiration cd. be identical with that of composition! As Chénier says 'Le Coeur seul est poète'[35] – only the heart, not the poor intellect trying to recapture it with his words and craft. Have you tried anything more in the writing line since? but I daresay your mind and your time are fully occupied in other ways.

We find our new quarters much more to our liking (so far) than we expected, though very expensive.[36] It is a great relief to be living here and not trailing back in every night. Our landlady is a strange character – with a mystery about her: but that needs a whole letter if not an Algernon Blackwood story to describe.

Our Anthology[37] (you know what I mean) goes to the publishers finally to-morrow and will be out for the Autumn sales. I am not just too satisfied with it, but Blackwell[38] seems to think it will pay its way and even leave a little profit with its five authors.

I am very sorry to find that my friend Baker is leaving at the end of this term: he is in every way the best person I have met in Oxford. I wonder what you will think of his poems. I say nothing of reading as I have been busy working and seeing people ever since I came up. The Minto sends her love and is like me delighted to hear of the revolution in your plans.

Just one more thing – if you really believe that painting is your job rather than a life of letters, don't let this obscure that object. There is plenty of time for both, I suppose, but the real thing must always be the background of ones mind, mustn't it? Hoping that nothing will occur to set you back in anyway – how conventional the words are, but I do most intensely mean them.

---

35 André Chénier (1762–94), *Les Elégies*, viii, 2: 'L'art ne fait que des vers, / le coeur seul est poète' ('Art only makes rhymes, / The heart alone is a poet').

36 Lewis and the Moores now had rooms in the home of Mrs Marshall, at 'Courtfield Cottage', 131 Osler Road, Headington.

37 i.e. 'The Way's the Way'.

38 Mr (later Sir) Basil Blackwell (1889–1984), the distinguished Oxford bookseller and publisher. He joined the family firm of B.H. Blackwell in 1913, and that same year established a publications department separate from the bookshop.

Yours
Jack

P.S. Your other letter has turned up.

TO HIS FATHER (LP VI: 188):

[University College,
Oxford]
Wednesday
Postmark: 25 May 1920

My dear Papy,

Please forgive my not having acknowledged your note sooner – I half expected a letter to follow. Many thanks for putting in the cheque. I have been in bed for some days with a mild form of this flu' but am better now. The heat here is something terrible – we are almost a city of dreadful night.

your loving son,
Jack

TO ARTHUR GREEVES (W):

[University College]
Sunday [6? June 1920]

My dear Arthur,

You certainly seem to be working with a vengeance now, and I daresay you find a great deal of effort necessary. I shouldn't go too hard at the beginning: certainly I should not advise work on walks. I am a great believer in having your periods of rest, complete rest, however short they may be: ten minutes absolute 'slack' is far more useful than an hour of the half in between business.

The Latin Constructions did at one time seem rather a 'slough', I remember. The great thing is to pin them onto the nearest English equivalent constructions. Thus, for instance, if you have 'He said I was a fool', instead of thinking mechanically for the Accus. & Inf. rule, remember simply to say in English 'He declared me to be a fool'

dixit
– then you get it at once *declaravit* } *me stultum esse*'.

Always make the verb of saying 'declare' in English. Similarly the Ablative Absolute has a parallel in the Irish idiom: as you might have '*He kept on talking while I waited*' which in the language of Meehawl Mac-Murrahu would [be] 'He kept on talking, so he did, and me waiting' – there you have it (leaving out the 'and' of course) 'mê expectante'. I am afraid I don't know the difference between a final and consecutive clause in English *or* Latin! – I always do what sounds right in either, but of course you can't begin that way. 'That I may get a copy' would certainly be Pres. Subj. 'ut librum procurem'. I shouldn't kill myself trying to get ready for 'Smalls' by any particular time, though, of course, the sooner the better.

You will be interested to hear that I met your friend Robert Nicholls the other day. He is much less beautiful than the frontispiece to 'Ardours & Endurances' would lead you to suppose: as the particular grin which makes that big mouth tolerable in the photo cannot be kept up in conversation! He also sees fit to wear enormous goggle spectacles rimmed with thick, dark horn which covers most of his cheeks. He is a pleasant fellow, though rather overpowering and Tchanie-like (could a suitable match be arranged? I have no doubt the 'ardours' could be found on her side, but would the 'endurances' on his be forthcoming?) He went over the 'Wild Hunt' with me, suggesting several emendations, most of which I (and Baker) thought definitely bad – or rather he goes on a peculiar theory which may be good for him, but is not good for me.

Certainly the little trivial things such as shaving, cooking, eating and the like run away with a lot of time. I have had some days in bed with flu and been generally very lazy, reading 'Kim'[39] and Trollope's 'Small House at Alington'.[40] I am also, in the evening, reading Virgil through again: I do hope you will someday be able to read Latin with enjoyment – tho' perhaps that seems to you at present a contradiction in terms.

I saw 'Romance'[41] in Oxford in 1917 before I went into the army (antequam militiam suscepi!)[42] and liked it pretty well, though there is really only one character in it – the woman. If she is good, parts of it are really very fine – and oh!, I forgot the other character, Tomaso, the

---

39 Rudyard Kipling, *Kim* (1901).

40 Anthony Trollope, *The Small House at Allington* (1864).

41 The play *Romance* by Edward Brewster Sheldon was performed first in New York on 10 February 1913, and for the first time in England on 30 September 1915.

42 'before I went into the army'.

monkey. I expect you will see in it the same people whom I saw (censeo te in illâ fabulâ visurum esse eosdem histriones quos ego!!)

I hope this last bout of hot weather has not set you back. You really shouldn't grudge any time spent on walks: now that you feel better able to get about it must be delightful to visit the old haunts. By the bye, I hope you keep the week-ends quite free from work: what can be better than to get out a book on Saturday afternoon and thrust all mundane considerations away till next week. You never get the same pleasure out of books as when you come back to them from these periodical exiles. I doubt if the amount of history you'd require for Smalls would really be much use to you afterwards: and I am quite sure that it would for the moment be more troublesome than the literature.

Wonderful to relate W. has been home and back again without giving us the honour of a visit.[43] Miss Plowman was here the other night. The Minto sends her love and hopes to see you soon 'flusht with victory'.

Yrs
Jack

P.S. 'Realize' not 'reallize'. How is Gundred's portrait getting on. How well you'll look in a commoner's gown!

TO HIS FATHER (LP VI: 189–90):

University College,
Oxford
6th June 1920

My dear Papy,

A better case could have been made out for your not writing: technically I might be the defendant, since your letter, of whatever length, was the last given or received. At any rate it's a very nice point. I'm sorry to hear that you also have been ill: I hope it is not a return of the old trouble. Mine of course was nothing more than troublesome and now I am all right.

What exactly is Big Brother doing now? I presume that he hasn't really started to keep a stud of two cars – I suppose one is being sold to get another: perhaps he too is getting sold over the deal. How we all get let down over the things on which we plume ourselves! Nothing will

43 Warnie, who was now stationed at Aldershot in Hampshire, was in Belfast on leave from 23 to 29 May.

convince Warnie that he is not a great financier, while I continue in the face of all experience to imagine myself a 'very parfait'[44] traveller. Thus Johnson considered that he was 'a very polite man'.[45]

I thought I had said something about the Anthology. It is being got up as a kind of counterblast to the ruling literary fashion here, which consists in the tendencies called 'Vorticist'. Vorticist poems are usually in 'vers libre' (which means they are printed like verse, but neither rhyme nor scan, a line ending wherever you like). Some of them are clever, the majority merely affected, and a good few – especially among the French ones – indecent: not a sensuous indecency, but one meant to nauseate, the whole genus arising from the 'sick of everything' mood. So some of us others who are not yet sick of everything have decided to bring out a yearly collection of our own things in the hope of persuading the gilded youth that the possibilities of metrical poetry on sane subjects are not yet quite exhausted because the Vorticists are suffering from satiety. Of course we may end by proving just the opposite, but we must risk that: there will be a polemical preface and the first number is to appear in the autumn. We call it 'The way's the way'[46] which is a quotation from Bunyan (a writer of books you know)!

I have had to do some restocking of foot gear as the Somersetshire hills finished some old veterans. The bill for three 'solings' with rubbers (which add to the weight of the foot but keep you dry and make the leather last much longer) and one new pair is £3.18.0. It seems to me rather excessive, but my friends all tell me that it is low for the times. If you think this may fairly be counted an extra, would you please let me have the amount some time?

I don't think even Arthur can fail to pass Responsions now that they have abolished Greek – unless indeed he stumbles, as I did, over elementary mathematics. He tell me you have been 'very kind' in 'giving him advice', which I gather means telling him how to write a letter. I remember once when he was here he had to write a card about getting a room

44 Chaucer, *Canterbury Tales*, 'General Prologue', 72: 'He was a verray, parfit gentil knyght.'

45 *Boswell's Life of Johnson*, op. cit., vol. III, p. 54, n. 1.

46 John Bunyan, *The Pilgrim's Progress*, ed. James Blanton Wharey, 2nd ed. revised by Roger Sharrock, Oxford English Texts (Oxford: 1960), pt. II, p. 237: 'Some have wished that the next way to their Fathers House were here, that they might be troubled no more with either Hills or Mountains to go over; but the way is the way, and there's an end.'

in London: we were in committee about that for the best part of twenty four hours. However, judging by his recent letters, there is a great mental and physical improvement.

We have had a bus strike here. The President of the Liberal Club and the President of the Labour Club, with followers, very foolishly addressed the world at large from chairs the other evening: and a warm scene between mixed workers and undergraduates on each side was only interrupted by the appearance of the Proctors: whereupon the undergraduates fled from the Proctors and the Proctors, with less success, fled from the mob. This, you see, is true democracy.

your loving son,
Jack

P.S. I have had my board and am certified for a 20% disability: we shall hear in time what that means.

TO ARTHUR GREEVES (W):

[University College]
Saturday [19 June 1920]

My dear Arthur,

The new syllabus for 'Smalls' certainly looks attractive. Quite putting aside the question of interest, I should advise you to take the literature. There is a lot of work in making up even a short period of history: but, for a person who has acquired the habit of reading, it should be really very easy to pass on the plays and the Milton and even on the Bacon. Of course you will have to read the books several times and make yourself master of all the biographical details etc: since you do not naturally remember things 'to quote' you must simply (as many another) learn by heart the 'pivot' passages which illustrate important qualities. Thus in Milton I you would quote 'That to the height of this great argument / I may assert eternal Providence / And justify the ways of God to Man'[47] to illustrate the moral purpose, as a commentator would say, and the passage about 'Faery-elves'[48] (near the end) for his Romanticism: and find out from the notes where he is imitating the classics or the Italians etc. Never having done this kind of thing I can't say what are the best

47 Milton, *Paradise Lost*, I, 24–6 (slightly misquoted).
48 ibid., I, 781.

annotated editions of these books: but doubtless any 'English master' at Campbell could tell you. I scarcely think that you ought to need any tuition for the English: nor would I recommend Helen – <the unspeakable Helen>. Can you get hold of any old papers on the subjects to give you an idea of the sort of questions they ask? That is a very great help. The one and only method in reading Latin is to go slowly and scientifically at first, looking for the verb etc in the old childish way: to rush like a bull in a china shop is fatal. As for the composition, it must be taught. Whether you enjoy it or not, the mere working for this exam. will do you an enormous amount of good: you have no idea how routine work and exactness improve the brain. I, for instance, have gained enormously in clearness and honesty of thought from my last year's work. I am reading Bergson now and find all sorts of things plain sailing which were baffling a year ago.

Without a scholarship I do not think you can manage on less than £300 a year: £250 might be just possible, but most uncomfortable and your attention would be everlastingly settled on money matters. (Some colleges, by the way, have musical scholarships: would you have any chance for one of those?).

I hope you won't mind my calling your attention to one other necessity – that of a drastic revision in your methods of spelling, which are at present a trifle too eccentric for general acceptance. I am afraid if the first page of your English paper contained such peculiarities as 'unprepaired', 'Hellen', 'reallized', 'overate' (over-rate?) it might prejudice an examiner! (It has just struck [me] that of course 'overate' would be the past tense of 'over-eat' but that can't be what you mean – I never over-eat your abilities.) This, of course, is a matter which can easily be put right: and I know that you are not bothering about it in a letter to me, as indeed there is no reason why you should.

Our anthology 'The Way's the Way' is to come out in autumn. The contributors are Carola Oman[49] (the daughter of the historian), Margaret Gidding (a friend of Pasley's), Pasley, Baker and myself. My own pieces are 6 in number, one of which is the longish 'Wild Hunt' which I think you saw: it was sent, in a slightly different form to 'Odds & Ends'.

49 Carola Mary Anima Oman (Lady Denanton), (1897–). Her father, Sir Charles William Chadwick Oman (1860–1946), had been a Fellow of All Souls College, Oxford, since 1883.

Most of the others I think you have seen, but you would not remember them by their names. Blackwell has the audacity to talk of 'five or six shillings' as a price for the book and seems to hope for a profit: I suppose he ought to know, but I feel dubious.

You ask about Baker, and I hardly know how to describe him. He was at a mixed school of a very modern type, where everyone seems to have written, painted and composed. He is so clairvoyant that in childhood 'he was afraid to look round the room for fear of what he might see'. He got a decoration in France for doing some work in an aeroplane over the lines under very deadly fire: but he maintains that he did nothing, for he was 'out of his body' and could see his own machine with 'someone' in it, 'roaring with laughter'. He has a bad heart. He was a conscientious objector, but went to the war 'because this degradation and sin might be just the very sacrifice which was demanded of him'. He maintains that everything in Algernon Blackwood is quite possible: and though the particular cases may be fictitious, 'things of that sort' are quite common. He is engaged to be married. In appearance, he is about my height, with very fair hair, glasses, remarkable eyes and according to the Minto, rather like you. I like and admire him very much, though at times I have doubts on his sanity. He is almost exactly my own age. He is quite different from Pasley, who represents rather the best type of the average English 'nice boy' and combines literature and athletics.

It is really quite delightful here. I walk into Oxford every morning down a green lane[50] and across the bridges and islands of the Cherwell: they are all white with may and quite deserted at that time. I have had one bathe. The Minto and I 'drank a dish of tea' with Miss Plowman the other day, and came away a trifle 'bethumped with words'.[51] I should like to see her and Tchanie together.

I am trying to imagine what your life is like these days, and always hoping that nothing will turn up to change your mind. What hours do you work? and do you find time to go for walks? You must begin to write something now, whether good or bad, in order to acquire a faculty of expression: for of course, whatever you take up here, you will do a lot of essay writing. It is simply splendid to think of all the difference between now and a few months back: perhaps you are hardly enjoying

50 Cuckoo Lane which runs parallel to Headington Hill.

51 Shakespeare, *King John*, II, i, 466: ''Zounds! I was never so bethump'd with words.'

the change yet, but I have no doubt there is a good time coming. If you can pass a year or two here with success, learning what you want to know and making friends, you will still be able to go back to the painting. The loss of time is serious: but more, far more than compensated by the extra power and brain you would take to your work. Write soon or I shall augur a relapse.

Yours
Jack

TO HIS FATHER (LP VI: 192):

[University College]
Sunday.
Postmark: 23 June 1920

My dear Papy,

I am very sorry to hear of Mr Henessy's death.[52] Although you did not often mention him I think I have heard you say that he visited you in the office nearly every Saturday: it is just that sort of regularity in a friendship which, on each separate occasion, may be taken for granted and may count for little, but which in its cumulative effect is very strong. I too in a short space of time have lost some of the best friends I had: but of course the long years of intercourse knit a closer bond than even the warmest of friendships which the war cut short after a few months. You are wrong in supposing I never met him: though I do not know when, I distinctly remember him coming out to lunch, long ago, in Mammy's time, and even have some hazy idea of what he looked like. He was a biggish man was he not, and wore a short beard?

Now for a dramatic bit of news. Picture me yesterday strolling along 'the High' neither fearing nor purposing any evil in the world. Suddenly, as happens when one is wool gathering, I found my eyes fixed on a face that came towards me. Curious...I should know it...ah, yes, some woman who happens to be rather like Mrs McNeill. But no: there is a growing uneasiness: it *is* Mrs McNeill[53] and – horror of horrors – 'Tchainie' is with her. Next minute the streets of this learned city echoed to her stentorian greeting. Tomorrow we are 'going to have tea somewhere' for the wonder and admiration of my fellow citizens.

---

52 E.G. Henesy, who died on 9 June 1920, was one of Albert's closest friends. He was the manager of the East Downshire Steamship Co. Ltd. at Dundrum, Co. Down.

53 See note 41 to letter of 4 May 1915.

I know from experience how slow Arthur is to accept alterations in a letter. But is it not true that we are all least ready to be corrected in the things which we do worst? My friend Baker for instance will let you criticize his poetry (which is good) ad infinitum: but any logical argument about his views on religion, philosophy, or politics (which are what Johnson calls 'undigested') is treated with the polite tolerance of unassailed superiority.

Thank you very much for the cheque. An appreciative College has awarded me £5 worth of books as a prize for getting a 1st. The other man in Univ. who did likewise of course had chosen his several weeks ago: I, after nearly giving up the problem as insoluble, have just sent in my list.

I enclose a sketch of the real Poynton. He not only has two sons, but a daughter. Didn't I ever tell you about Carlyle and the daughter's christening?

your loving son,
Jack

TO ARTHUR GREEVES (W):

[University College]
Sunday [27? June 1920]

My dear Arthur,

Do you think Davis[54] is a good teacher? I should be sorry to weaken your confidence in him, but I don't like his just passing over the Oratio-Obliqua and saying you won't get anything as hard in Smalls. I think with care and patience – but so few schoolmasters have any patience – anyone could be led to master a reported speech in Caesar: and it is just possible you might get an equally difficult Unseen. My Unseen was the passage from Statius (Davis will show it you) beginning 'Crimine quo merui juvenis, placidissime divum':[55] it is a lovely little poem; have a look at it and see if you can make it out.

---

54 Robert Furley Davis (1866–1937), who took his BA from St John's College, Cambridge, in 1888 and his MA in 1896, was the senior Classical master at Campbell College from 1902 until his retirement in 1931.

55 Statius, *Silvae*, V, iv, I. The full Latin text is: 'Criminie quo merui, iuvenis placidissime divum, quove errore miser, donis ut solus egerem, Somne, tuis?' which is translated: 'O youthful Sleep, gentlest of the gods, by what crime or by what mistake of mine have I deserved that I alone should lack your gifts?'

I have had a delightful windfall: £5 worth of books as a prize from College for getting a First. Oh ye gods, if this had come four or five years ago, what raptures and debatings, what making and re-making of lists had been! As it was I had great difficulty in making them out at all, being perpetually haunted by the fear that I should afterwards find out that I had got all the things I really did NOT want. It is a dismal sign of breaking up and old age that I look forward to their arrival with very luke warm pleasure. The nicest among them all will be Hall's 'Ancient History of the Nearer East'[56] – which bears to some extent on my work in Herodotus, but goes beyond it.

This subject of ancient history is now one of my absorbing interests: Herodotus is pure delight, and so are the modern writers who comment on [him]. Isn't the magic of mere names wonderful? Babylon, Nineveh, Darius, the Pharaohs – I revel in every trace of them – and to see things piecing together: a story in Herodotus and a story in the Book of Kings, backed up by an inscription newly unearthed in Mesopotamia or a scrap of Persian legend! However, this may not interest you.

'Abraham Lincoln'[57] came here last term and all the world except me went to see it: I have heard it praised by everyone. It is very cheering to see these 'literary' plays with verse in them like the Dynasts[58] and Drinkwater's one, on the stage at all. Fifty years ago I don't suppose they'd have got a hearing.

My imagination boggles at the idea of you – or myself – on a motor byke. When you come up here I suppose you will become one of the young men who toot-toot-toot up and down the High clad in overalls: and instead of the Muses it will be spanners and magnetos and intermezzos and cut-outs and petrol that will fill our conversation. Ah well!, I must move with the times. I can't quite rise to a motorbyke but perhaps I could get a scooter (Picture – Excellenz and myself going to Church on scooters 'Ah – these scooters are r-r-r-otten tools: the thing's intolerable')

This letter was begun I don't know how long ago. 'Sunday' is all I can find at the top: but whether it was a week or a fortnight ago I can't say. I'm sorry: a mood of laziness has been upon me. It has been one of those

---

56 H.R.H. Hall, *The Ancient History of the Near East* (1913).

57 John Drinkwater, *Abraham Lincoln*, first performed 12 October 1918, was published in 1919.

58 Thomas Hardy's *The Dynasts* (1904–8) was first performed as a play on 15 November 1914.

periods when we do nothing because we always feel tired and feel tired because [we] do nothing. Also – Tchanie is here: I have chust returned from lunching with her and her amiable mother, with the usual exhausting effect. Mrs McNeil has made several exquisitely ridiculous remarks in her solemn style, but they would be spoiled on paper. Tchanie has been strongly urging the advantages which would result from your having Helen as a tutor: and, though you may fancy that I have been talked over, I would advise you to think of it. When I said before that you didn't need a tutor for English, I am afraid I was thinking rather of the mere 'getting up' of the books: for essays etc you really do need someone to put you up to those little tricks of vocabulary and rounding off sentences which may seem trivial but which examiners demand. Whether Helen is the best person you can get, is, of course, quite a different story: if you had any authority outside Tchanie's for believing her to be good, I should not let any personal dislike stand in the way. Who are the alternatives? The divine mother & daughter have mentioned some other McNeil at Wadham who appears to be a friend of yours:[59] did you ever speak to me of him? – you know I can never remember names. The publication of our Anthology has been put off to an indefinite date because of a printing strike: I shall improve the interval by correcting my contributions out of recognition.

The only book I have read with satisfaction lately is Mackail's 'Lectures on Poetry':[60] I think he is one of my favourite moderns – he always has just the right point of view and deals with the right subject: he has sent me back to 'Endymion' which I read for some time in a church porch yesterday afternoon. Otherwise books have been absorbed in the general inertia of this time. I hope you are having exactly opposite experiences.

Yours
Jack

59 William Martin McNeill, who matriculated in 1919.
60 John William Mackail, *Lectures on Poetry* (1911).

TO HIS FATHER (LP VI: 195–6):

University College,
Oxford
25th July 1920

My dear Papy,

I should have answered you before but I have been engaged in entertaining the Colonel. He, despite the efforts of a tyrannical and slave driving general staff, is still managing to keep body and soul together and to sustain his labours with that equanimity for which he is justly famed. Contrary to your fears, he, as yet, [has] only one car: which he proposes to sell and buy another. As soon as his leave begins he is going to motor me to Liverpool, via Malvern, and so home. I am still debating whether I can sufficiently brace my nerves to such an ordeal.

But indeed one should not at the present moment talk in joke about ordeals: for by all accounts you are approaching a real one at home. Do the 'Times' accounts of the Belfast rioting exaggerate or the reverse?[61] I am glad to note that so far it has been mainly confined to its traditional grounds at the other end of town, and also that it usually takes place 'after hours'. A wise man these days will do well to survey the situation chiefly from the study. When I come home I shall (like Lundy in the play) buy a favour with green on one side and orange on the other, turning the appropriate colour outwards according to circumstances. What between this business at home and the Bolshevists nearly in Germany, one feels inclined to despair. Are all efforts made for the world as utterly barren in results as the terrible effort of this war has undoubtedly proved?

Your mention of the charms of biography reminds me of a book I saw the other day which would be much in your line – a translation of the diary kept by the late Shah of Persia during his tour of Europe. This is indeed to 'see ourselves as others see us'. Thus for instance 'the people of London are taught to pay great respect to their police, who are comely young men in a peculiar uniform: whatsoever offends them is judged worthy of death'. Or again (on the way from Dover) 'the train proceeded at such a speed that fire came out of the wheels and set one of the coaches ablaze: the mechanics extinguished the fire: then we continued

---

61 *The Times* (24 July 1920), p. 12: 'Night fighting in Belfast, 23 July. Little more than a mile away from the City Hall are lying over 100 casualties and at least 13 dead. For the greater part of the night a triangular contest of soldiers, Protestants and Catholics has gone on intermittently in several widely-separated areas.'

our journey'. Still better, (referring to Edward VII as Prince of Wales in kilts): 'Now the peculiarity of Scottish costume is this – that the legs are left bare to the thighs'. This is a greater treasure than the Young Visiters:[62] but I have room for only one more quotation. 'The waves rose and a violent storm began: the great Wazeer, the (here follow several unpronounceable officials) etc. were much disturbed. Thanks to Allah, We retained Our composure'.[63] (Room for an illustration by George Morrow[64] I think!)

I had nearly forgotten to tell you that Uncle and Aunt Hamilton[65] were here for a night on their tour. If any man has ever been successful in screwing the honey out of life it is he. One cannot help admiring the skill with which he knows exactly how far selfishness can go without rebounding on himself: he has learned to a nicety how much every plank will bear. At the same time this worldly wisdom which has an appetite for everything and yet can be content with little, which knows what can be got out of life and does not expect more, would be almost a virtue, so pleasant is it and so sensible, if it were not centred completely on self. He made one good 'mot' here – that 'England would be an excellent country to tour in were it not for the Cathedrals'. I hear that you were very nearly asked to take John in their absence but were finally rejected in favour of Glenmachan. No doubt you feel the affront bitterly. Hoping that you are otherwise well.

your loving son,
Jack

---

62 *The Young Visiters* (1919) is a comic masterpiece. It was written by Daisy Ashford (1881–1972) when she was a child. It was found in 1919 and sent to Chatto & Windus who published it with an introduction by J.M. Barrie, who insisted on meeting the author in order to discover if it was genuine.

63 Nasir Al-Din, *The Diary of H.M. The Shah of Persia during His Tour Through Europe in A.D. 1873*, translated by J.W. Redhouse (1874), ch. IV.

64 George Morrow (1870–1955) was a book illustrator from Belfast who was a regular contributor to *Punch*.

65 Augustus 'Gussie' Warren Hamilton (1866–1945) was the brother of Flora Lewis. He was known as possessing a remarkable degree of 'matter of factness'. After leaving Strandtown School he was apprenticed to the firm of MacIlwaine, Lewis and Co., and on completing his time, he went to sea as an engineer with the Ulster Steamship Company. On one of his voyages he met and fell in love with a young lady from Canada, Anne Sargent Harley (1866–1930), who later became his wife. After leaving the sea, Augustus settled in Belfast and founded the firm of Hamilton & McMaster, marine boilermakers and engineers. 'He was,' Warnie Lewis wrote of him, 'one of that rather uncommon type of man, thoroughly selfish and mean in money matters, who yet possesses qualities which make his society welcomed in any company' (LP II: 155). See **The Hamilton Family** in the Biographical Appendix.

TO HIS FATHER (LP VI: 198–9):

University College,
Oxford
Aug. 11th 1920

My dear Papy,

Thanks for your letter and the enclosure. Of this latter I scarcely know what to make. Your interpretation of it as meaning that I am still in the army seems inevitable. The fact being that hundreds of us who asked for temporary commissions in the regulars were, on the quiet, given permanent commissions in the special reserve. But unless my memory plays me very false, all the newspapers published a statement some time ago to the effect that those in my position would be 'deemed to have resigned' their commissions unless they wrote expressing a wish to the contrary before a certain date. Is it of any use for me to write and mention this? In the meantime I am making all enquiries I can about the subject. If anything should happen so suddenly as to prevent my 'concerting a plan' with you, I could, as a last resource, go to the solicitor here. At all events its no good blinding ourselves to the fact that if another emergency occurs, everyone will be pushed into it again by public opinion or conscription, commission or no: to be out of the army would mean only a few months lease of freedom. I cannot say that I now face such a prospect with anything more than resignation – once was enough. However, I am convinced that this country cannot now go to war: if we try, it will be a case of fighting our English revolutionaries at home, and then we shall all have our backs to the wall and nothing will matter much.

In all seriousness, I think we have now arrived at the point where a wise man can do no more than wait for the end with what grace he can: and it is hard to summon much grace if you meet as many traitors and cranks in our own class as I do here, hankering for the blessing of Soviet rule at once. Only boys of course, as you will say: but it is usually a few fools who start the shooting which the wise heads cannot stop.

I quite forgot to tell you the result of my board: perhaps it was so sweet a morsel that I feared to part with it – I was awarded £20 down in lieu of further pension! I wrote and protested on the ground that even the last board had given me a 20% disability which I understood entitled me to something more. They said the matter could not be reconsidered. The ultimate result of this will be I suppose that I am counted 'fit' again for anything that may turn up: the immediate result is that I shall have to ask you to make up the extra £50 per annum. I am sorry to have to do so, but the necessity of keeping my allowance, as it was with the pension, depends on the same conditions of life everywhere, which makes me reluctant to ask.

Under the unwritten laws of social humbug the Henry's[66] certainty that you would not come if asked did not justify them in passing you by. You were quite right not to send a present. The weather here is almost frosty, and it usually rains. I think it likely that the Colonel and I may advance by rail after all.

your loving son,
Jack

TO LEO BAKER (B):

27 Old Cleeve,
Washford,
Somerset.
[14? August 1920]

My dear Baker,

You tell me you have nothing specific to write about: but I have a thousand such. I could a tale unfold!..but I will not reduce your several hairs to the condition of quills upon the fretful porpentine. Let it suffice to say that I have lived this many a day in the realms of nightmare,

– I have sat down by Babylonian streams
And hanged my harp upon funereal trees –[67]

in a world of incredible problems that offer one the alternative 'Heads I win, tails you lose' of plans feverishly made and remade, of things once deemed impossible yet undertaken, from dire necessity at the last moment. A faint pallor of daylight, however, now streaks the East: we

66 The 'Henrys' were contemporaries of Warnie. Robin Henry was something of a character in Strandtown. He and his wife, the former Molly Robertson, had both been pupils of Miss Annie Harper, and they formed a good-looking pair. During the war Robin Henry served in the artillery.

67 Lewis's lines are based on Psalm 137:1–2 (Coverdale version): 'By the waters of Babylon we sat down and wept: when we remembered thee, O Sion. / As for our harps, we hanged them up: upon the trees that are therein.'

have a house in view! But I am not yet 'full of beans' again, either in mind or body.

I was glad to hear that you are reading my two canonical poets: though how you can take Milton and Spenser together, I do not at all understand. All historians of literature have told me, like you, of their points in common: but, tho' interesting, how artificial do these verbal likenesses appear compared with the real difference of the faery atmosphere and the divine. Spenser says 'The waies thro which my wearie steps I guide in this delightful launde of faerie, are so exceedingly spatious, and wide, and sprinkled with such swete varietie...etc',[68] but the other 'Sad task! – yet argument not less but more heroic than the tale of'[69] – I forget the words but you can find them. Or again, to take a passage where the Miltonic thunder seems somehow wearisome and forced beside the 'falling close' of Spenser, compare 'Hurled headlong flaming from the etherial sky to bottomless perdition – there to dwell, with adamantine chains and penal fire'[70] with 'And Nature's selfe was vanished whither no man wist'[71] – surely the most wonderful alexandrine ever written. To see Milton's real greatness one need but notice the fresh joy and reality of his Eden after the over-ripe stanzas which describe the garden of Acasia, tho' that is partly in the subject. I do, however, like to pick up in the Faerie Queene the germs of Milton's phrazes.

This is one of the privileges of art, that all things are in common: imitation, if it is forgotten, matters not, and, if it lives, is justified and does not diminish the originality of the borrower. The notion of literary property was brought by philistines from the valley of the gorribeen-men into Helicon where it has no weight nor meaning. All poetry is one, and I love to see the great notes repeated. Homer and Virgil wrote lines not for their own works alone but for the use of all their followers. A plague on these moderns scrambling for what they call originality – like men trying to lift themselves off the earth by pulling at their own braces: as if by shutting their eyes to the work of the masters they were likely to create new things themselves.

---

68 Spenser, *Faerie Queene*, VI, Preface, 1, 1–2.

69 Milton, *Paradise Lost*, IX, 13–16: 'Sad task! Yet argument / Not less but more heroic than the wrath / Of stern Achilles on his foe pursued / Thrice fugitive about Troy wall.'

70 ibid., I, 45.

71 Spenser, *Faerie Queene*, VII, vii, 59, 9.

'Damme' says Wellington in the Dynasts 'Where does he suppose I am to get reinforcements from'.[72] Where do you suppose a hermit like myself is to find new recruits for our Guild? About this same Guild, by the way, I went to see Barfield[73] before I left Oxford but found him about an hour gone. We must not make the mistake of trying too hard to beat up followers: indeed perhaps we must not make the mistake of trying too hard about anything: of this sacred Anthology of ours I am heartily sick. It appears now as clear as daylight that Blackwell does not want it, though he may bring it out, for all that, in his own good time. The chief motive for sticking to such a water-logged craft is the disappointment which I think Pasley would feel if he were marooned. I have had his revised version of the old man sent to me, with many corrections, but not of great importance. The more often I read his work in comparison with the rest of the anthology the more do I feel that we have consistently under-estimated him, tho' more by inference and assumption than by direct statement. When all these things reach the public, the modernist vigour of Vision and Tumult and the other one about 'Against the sky rode he' will make a noise that may surprise us, – agreeable, I hope, for the greatness of our hearts. I have done revised versions of Nimue and The Wild Hunt: the latter, I hope, is improved beyond recognition. At least I have reached a state from which I usually augur well – that wherein one looks back on the first version (once pleasing enough) as impossible, and thanks the gods for having escaped it.

Since I began this letter some two or three days ago I have been recuperating in most divine scenery. There are moors here, not so big nor high as those beyond Minehead, but sufficient for perfect beauty and solitude: indeed I have seldom found anywhere quite so alone. For a whole morning I saw nothing but ants (enormous ones) and a hawk: and from them you look down to the most wonderful hills and gorges and more moors on the one side, and on the other to the channel with Wales beyond it. Up there the emptiness, if it says anything, seems to say 'Admire if you will, but you have nor lot nor part in me'. I am constitutionally incapable of the harmony you feel. The more beautiful and desolate it is, the more I feel myself a trespasser: there is always someone waiting over the crest to warn me off. We also rode through glorious hill

72 Hardy, *The Dynasts*, VII, vii (slightly misquoted).

73 See **Owen Barfield** in the Biographical Appendix. He came up to Wadham College, Oxford, on a Classical Scholarship in 1919 and was introduced to Lewis by Leo Baker.

country to Porlock and saw Exmoor, far off, as Alan Quartermain saw the mountains of Suliman Berg.[74] This town has a church of St. Dubricius who, you may remember, crowned and annointed Arthur. (I forget whether this is in Malory, but it certainly is in the guide book.)[75]

I am sorry your job has not materilized. It seems as if the best thing you could do would be to return to Oxford. When I come within reach of typists again, I will try to send you the new Wild Hunt.

yours
C. S. Lewis

Is this good, bad or indifferent? –

Oh that a black ship now were bearing me
Between the stars of the sky
And the answering stars of the sea!, –
And the wind to throb, and I
On the decks to be sitting, awake
Watching the foamdrops break
In fire from her prow:
Passing a moon-drencht island, pale, a Hesperian clime
Where the apple hangs on the bough
And the blood-red life, with no repining
Is full of shouting, a giant, terrible, shining,
Till the guttering of the candle and the gathering home of time.

P.S. I am very sorry that I shall (I hope) be assisting a move into the house at the time you ask me to come to you. But I will tell you latter for certain.[76]

74 In Rider Haggard's novel *King Solomon's Mines* (1886).

75 The church in Porlock Lewis wrote about is dedicated to St Dubricius, whose name is sometimes spelled 'Dubric' or 'Dyfrig'. St Dubricius (d. c. 550), as he is usually called, is one of the most important saints of South Wales. He was a monk and a bishop, who worked mainly in the Hereford-Gwent area. Very little is known about him. He does not appear in Malory, but in Geoffrey of Monmouth's 12th-century *Historia Regum Britanniae* (VIII, 12), is given credit for crowning King Arthur.

76 Leo Baker's reply to this letter, dated 16 August 1920, is found in LP VI: 199–200.

On 20 August Jack joined Warnie at Aldershot Camp in Farnham, Hampshire. They travelled in Warnie's motorcycle and sidecar to Liverpool, and from there they crossed the Channel to Belfast, arriving at Little Lea on 26 August. They stayed with their father until 23 September.

TO LEO BAKER (B):

[University College
25 September 1920]

My dear Baker,

I was delighted to get your letter. You seem to have dropped – or dropt, as Pasley would like us to write – into a job which is pleasant though somewhat arduous. What a lucky thing for Harpenden!

Now, to get this damned anthology of[f] my chest: it has been sent back to Basil, who has now kept it in silence for a fortnight. He talked about being able 'to meet us in some way': I pointed out on behalf of the Big Three that we could meet him to precisely the extent of £0.0s.0d. In spite of this he still wanted to see the MS again, but I am quite sure he will never publish it. Pasley and I both think that if he does not, we ought to give up the plan: let me know whether you agree.

I have been absolutely incapable of writing a line for heaven knows how long: as I have to do two essays – one philosophical & one historical – every week and have also been writing a paper for the Martlets, this is perhaps not to be wondered at.

I am more worried by what goes on inside me: my imagination seems to have died: where there used to be pictures that were bright, at least to me, there is now nothing but a repetition of the trivialities and worries of the outer life – I go round and round on the same subjects which are always those I least want to think about. Perhaps, after all, these experiences are not brilliantly original nor wonderfully tragic – so don't think I am taking myself too seriously. After all, what is the object of writing to friends except that of talking oneself into a state of self importance and the belief that ones own perversities are matter of universal sympathy.

Pasley is in great form mentally, tho busily engaged in killing himself in trying to run. He announced his engagement (in deadly secrecy) the other day: so do not assume knowledge of the same unless you had heard before. He is also writing poems in what he calls 'rhythm'. I am using all my powers of persuasion to guide 'rhythm' away from vers libre and towards the unrhymed lyric. Do you remember a poem in unrhymed quatrains, which he showed us both? He has revised it and I think it is now one of his best –

> *'gold and silver moons*
> *That wonderfully sing their glories up.'*

He is certainly much better than he was last term.

Thanks for the theory of poetry. The most valuable part of it, and the part which shd. be insisted on is that 'a poet who is only a poet is not the greatest poet'. The assumption that a great poem must have nothing in it but poetry has 'worked like madness in the brain'[77] of too many of us. On the other hand Coleridge's definition 'the best words in the best order'[78] has always seemed to me bad: for it would apply to good prose: or it would apply even to any piece of writing that fulfilled its purpose. Thus 'The train will leave at 7.30' gives us the best words (for the purpose) in the best order, i.e. we cannot improve upon them. Wordsworth indeed might have written 'The hissing locomotive with her line / Of labouring coaches from the platform side / Shall take departure ere the moving index / On that high, grim chronometer etc': but this wd. be worse words in a worst order. Coleridge's position does not (to me) therefore involve what you say. It is in your 1 (b) 'Words used for the purpose they alone can serve' that you really get to the heart of the matter. All this talk that every critic gives us about vision etc is darkening counsil: for vision, exaltation, criticism of life etc are not poetry, but the subject of poetry: and not the peculiar subject of poetry but the subject of all art. What we want to find is – that which is proper to poetry alone: what is the method by which poetry *and no other art* performs the duties shared with all art? Doubtless you would answer that in the same way as I wd. & come to a definition something like this 'Poetry is the art of utilizing the informal or irrational values of words to express that which can only be symbolized by their formal or conventional meanings.' These values include chiefly sound & association: also of course their 'group' sound or rhythms which are above and beyond their individual sounds: here is the meaning & justification of metre. Hence the value of the test 'Could this be said as well in prose?': if the answer is in the affirmative the poem is

77 Coleridge, *Christabel*, II, 413.
78 Samuel Taylor Coleridge, *Biographia Literaria* (1817), Ch. XIV.

condemned. As to all those other things – inspiration, purpose, nobility, wisdom etc, there are two answers. (1.) These are not peculiar to the art of poetry but common to all art: it is unfair, therefore, to include them in the definition of poetry. (2) If a man was not an artist (i.e. had not these other possessions) he cd. not have things inexpressible by ordinary speech to tell us, cd. not therefore be a poet. So our definition, narrow as it may seem at first sight, implies all that is necessary. You see that my theory has nearly everything in common with yours, but I think you still show some confusion between poetry itself and the objects of poetry.

Your invitations are delightfully couched. I have not forgotten at Cornwall 'there are no route marches, no dreadful excursions & no political debates: we do only those things that are proper to hermits'. I hope you won't think it the usual social lie, when I again have to refuse them. Please thank your Aunt and convey my apologies.

I shall have to spend Christmas in Ireland: it is very difficult for me ever to get away. You can understand that when you have a nominal home in one place & a real home somewhere else, the disposal of ones person even for a few days makes demands that can't be met. I am very sorry, not to be able to come. I wish I could ask you to visit us at Oxford sometime when term is over: but the gods only know where or in what quarters we may be then. If your journeyings ever bring you to Oxford I needn't tell you how glad I should be: why you insisted on going down is still a mystery to me.

I haven't had time yet to go and look Barfield up but hope to do so soon: you don't mention the Guild, so I hope it has not gone the way of all ideals.

You will be interested to hear that in the course of my philosophy – on the existence of matter – I have had to postulate some sort of God as the least objectionable theory: but of course we know nothing. At any rate we don't know what the real Good is, and consequently I have stopped defying heaven: it can't know less than I, so perhaps things really are alright. This, to you, will be old news but perhaps you will see it in me as a sign of grace. Don't mistake the position: its no cry of 'all's well with the world':[79] its only a sense that I have no business to object to the universe as long as I have nothing to offer myself – and in that respect we are all bankrupt.

---

79 Robert Browning, *Pippa Passes* (1841), I, 228: 'All's right with the world!'

Write again: forgive my atrocious habits as a correspondant –
Yours
C. S. Lewis

TO HIS FATHER (LP VI: 169):

University College,
Oxford
9th Oct. [1920]

My dear Papy,

Once again, in the words of the immortals, we have resumed our round of steady work, relieved and sweetened by hearty play. I would have written earlier but I have been rather incapacitated by a bite from a playful cat – merely a scratch at the end of my forefinger, but enough for a while to prevent one laying it to a pen with any comfort. It is now alright.

I was sorry to see the other day news of our friend Heineman's sudden death. The papers have been so covering him with eulogy since he went that I begin to feel glad I met him, if only for once – Vergilium vidi tantum!'[80] In this case however I think the virtues are not wholly of the tombstone nature: a great publisher is really something more than a mere machine for making money: he has opportunities for doing things for the best of motives, and if one looks round most of our English houses, I think he avails himself of them as well as anyone can expect. I always put up a fight for the tribe of publishers here where so many young men with manuscripts have nothing too bad to say of them.

We are having the most delightful weather here – it ought to mean a saving of coal against the lean days, if the strike comes off: tho' I suppose the amount of coal used for domestic purposes is trifling compared with the consumption in factories – 'and the like' as Knock says. The look of the streets here has been very much altered by these quaint caps and gowns which the women have started wearing since they came into their inheritance – but I daresay you have read of it in the papers.[81]

80 'I have seen the so great Virgil!' Ovid, *Tristia*, IV, x, 51.

81 On 17 February 1920 a statute was passed making women full members of the University.

I hope you are keeping well: it is strange to be once more in circles where Irish politics show only a certain way above the horizons. English people are terribly indifferent.

your loving son,
Jack

TO HIS FATHER (LP VI: 211–12):

University Coll.
Postmark: 8 December 1920

My dear Papy,

I am afraid your opinion of my powers as a correspondant will not have increased. As a matter of fact I have been interrupted by a journey to Cambridge, followed by some days in bed. It is not, I hope, too late to thank you for the cheque and also for Bill's book.[82] A notable work that! I have not yet summoned up enough courage to write to him, nor found words wherewith to congratulate him on this grotesque firstborn. I suppose one can always fall back on comparisons and say which are better than others, even in depths like this.

My journey to Cambridge was on this wise. You may remember that a society of Martlets at Pembroke, Cambridge sent representatives to our society of that name: on this occasion four of us were sent to pay a return match. The trip was rendered both cheaper and pleasanter by the fact that one of the four lives there, and very kindly put us all up. I read them a paper on narrative poetry.[83] Of course I don't know what they thought of it, but at any rate nothing was thrown at me. We dined with them first. It was a wretched night, which having attempted to freeze, had finally decided instead on a sleety rain. The old library of their college, where we had dinner, was very badly heated, and what between that and going about their quadrangle in the chilliness of evening dress and the rain, I got rather a nasty chill – whereof I am just now recovered.

---

82 Their friend of many years, Bill Patterson, had just published under the initials W.H.F. a small volume of verse entitled *Songs of a Port* (Belfast: McCaw, Stevenson & Orr, 1920).

83 This was Lewis's first visit to Cambridge and it took place on his 22nd birthday, 29 November 1920. Lewis was elected President of the Martlets on 15 October 1919 and he was prevailed upon to retain the position until 13 June 1921. The paper he read in Cambridge on 'Narrative Poetry' was the same he had read to the Oxford Martlets on 3 November 1920. The paper has not survived but the minutes of the Oxford meeting are reproduced in Walter Hooper's 'To the Martlets' in *C.S. Lewis: Speaker and Teacher*, op. cit., pp. 44–5.

It was very interesting next day to see Cambridge. In many ways it is a contrast: there is something, I can hardly say whether of colour or of atmosphere, which at once strikes a more northern, a bleaker and a harder note. Perhaps the flatness of the country, suggesting places seen from the railway beyond Crewe, has something to do with it. The streets are narrow and crowded: the non-university parts depressing enough. Some things – such as King's College Chapel, in which I was prepared to be disappointed – are indeed beautiful beyond hope or belief: several little quadrangles I remember, with tiled gables, sun dials and tall chimnies like Tudor houses, were charming. One felt everywhere the touch of Puritanism, of something Whiggish, a little defiant perhaps. It has not so much Church and State in its veins as we. The stained windows in the Halls show figures like Erasmus[84] and Cranmer.[85] Oxford is more magnificent, Cambridge perhaps more intriguing. Our characteristic colour is the pale grey, almost the yellow of old stone: their's the warm brown of old brick. A great many Cambridge buildings remind one of the Tower of London. Most of the undergraduates whom I met I liked very much. Their dons, as judged by those who were at the 'do', are certainly inferior to ours in charm of manners and geniality. One I thought hardly a gentleman.

I am afraid you took my remark about 'a small book' rather too literally – I meant only an essay for my tutor: I am hardly up to writing historical monographs (for publication) just yet. I have however been recommended to try for the Vice Chancellor's Essay Prize next April. The subject is 'Optimism' under which heading one could include almost anything one wanted to write about. My point of view will be mainly metaphysical and rather dry. It would be a splendid advertisement if I could pull it off, but of course competition is very keen.

---

84 Desiderius Erasmus (1466/9–1536), the Dutch humanist, was the most renowned scholar of his age. Besides reviving many Classical texts, he edited the Greek New Testament with his own translation into Classical Latin. Drawn to Cambridge by St John Fisher (1469–1535), Vice-Chancellor of Cambridge University, Erasmus was the first teacher of Greek there.

85 Thomas Cranmer (1489–1556), Archbishop of Canterbury from 1533 to 1553, was educated at Jesus College, Cambridge, and became a Fellow in 1523. He was Henry VIII's chief instrument in overthrowing Papal supremacy in England. His theology was influenced by the Continental Reformers, and he achieved his ambition of providing the Church of England with the *Book of Common Prayer* (1549).

Thanks for the enclosures. I suppose the War Office business is now settled, although apparently the army cannot exist without my services as a full Lieutenant. I really don't think I can go to Mrs Shillington's dance[86] and hang about uselessly cumbering the ground – which is all a non-dancer can do.

The same storm which you mention seems to have done damage all over England. I hope the trouble at Leeborough is not serious.

your loving son,
Jack

P.S. W. was over here some time ago. He says that in the photo Kirk is wearing 'his ordinary expression', which shows how he has changed since the old days.[87]

TO LEO BAKER (B):

[University College
22 December 1920]

My Dear Baker –

The Way's the way to bankruptcy, paying cash down and heavy loss: and for this reason Edmund Gosse those lovely lines will never see. And oh! to think with what a shock we crush the hopes of Clutton Brock;[88] and luckless G. K. Chesterton is fated not to look thereon. The blow has fallen. Basil refuses to publish the dam' thing unless we raise some money – I forget how much, but more than we thought possible. Please find enclosed, our own babes from the ruined crêche. My own feeling of relief is something wonderful and has inspired me to write several immortal poems in the last few days. I am sending you the revised version of the Wild Hunt and await your criticism. I am crossing to Ireland to-morrow, where my address will be Little Lea, Strandtown, Belfast.

---

86 Lewis had been invited to a party at the home of Mrs Shillington in Belfast. He and Warnie were there visiting their father from 24 to 30 December.

87 On 10 October 1920 Warnie took a photograph of Mr and Mrs W.T. Kirkpatrick at their home in Little Bookham, Surrey. It is the only known photograph of the 'Great Knock', and it is reproduced in Walter Hooper, *Through Joy and Beyond: A Pictorial Biography of C.S. Lewis* (1982), p. 35.

88 Lewis is only having fun. He did not expect any of these men to see their poems. Sir Edmund Gosse (1849–1928) was a poet who had been friends with some of the Pre-Raphaelites; Arthur Clutton-Brock (1868–1924) was an essayist, critic and journalist who contributed frequently to *The Times Literary Supplement.*

Heard Lohengrin with great delight, for the first time, since I wrote to you: (this letter is so childish that I almost continued 'It was very nice'). I have not time today to discuss your theory of poetry: we seem to be prettily [*sic*] agreed on fundamentals, tho' there are still points of difference – real ones, not 'misunderstandings'. Am writing again,

yours

C. S. Lewis

1921

TO HIS FATHER (LP VI: 226):

Oxford Union Society
[Oxford]
Jan. 19th [1921]

My dear Papy,

I was sorry to hear that you were not well. I suppose it was the final stage of the nasty cold which you had when I left, and hope that it has now 'dragged its slow length' to completion. Warnie will have told you of our pleasant journey to Liverpool. I travelled the rest of the way in great comfort and had an excellent lunch on the train. After so many lean years during the war it is quite strange to see a dining car again. The country was flooded everywhere as far as Oxford: I have never seen anything like it, and I suppose it will be very serious.

I have been very busy ever since I came up with my essay on Optimism, which I find has to be earlier than I thought. Indeed I have almost lived with my pen to the paper. It has been one of those rare periods that we all have now and then when everything becomes clear and we see the way before us. So I thought I must utilise it at all costs: I felt like the horse in Masefield's new poem, when he was winning the steeple-chase, 'my day, my day, I shall not have another'.[1] For this reason I did not write to you on Sunday.

I don't know that there is anything new here to record: if there is, I have probably missed it, being for the nonce a troglodyte in the truly paternal manner. I have had one of the usual voluminous letters from Aunt Lily. It has turned cold here and very frosty of nights: but it is dry and bracing and pleasanter than the sort of deluge you are perhaps still having at home. Tell big brother that I have e'en now taken his bundles of literature to one he wots of and they will be done in three

1 John Masefield, *Right Royal* (1920), Pt. I, p. 8 (slightly misquoted).

weeks.[2] You might also tell him to occupy his spare time looking round the study for a little green book called 'Skeleton Outlines of Greek History':[3] and if he will send it, I shall be his debtor. I am writing this at the Union in great haste before lunch, and cannot stay longer: next week I shall not be so busy. Hoping that you are now better and possibly none the worse for a few days Nirvana in bed and away from the Court.

your loving son,

Jack

TO HIS FATHER (LP VI: 229–30):

Oxford Union Society
[Oxford]
Friday Jan. 21st [1921][4]

My dear Papy,

I certainly deserve the wrath of all my family, for I had scarcely sent off my last letter to you when I discovered that the missing book had never been taken home at all. Perhaps I should have let you know this: but having heard that you were in bed, I supposed that the quest would be confined to Big Brother and that his usual self restraint would have prevented his researches from being carried to any tedious length. However – !

My history tutor has handed me over to a gentleman at Magdalen whom he recommended by telling me that he was a grandson of Mendelsohn's: a trifle irrelevant I thought. The exchange was presented to me in the form of a compliment and I am quite satisfied with it. The reason I mention it is because the new man deserves to be known to fame. I had not been many minutes in his room until I had an uneasy sense of strange yet familiar neighbours. When he went out for a moment I discovered what it was – pigs! Do not mistake me: not live pigs: but pigs of china, of bronze, of clay, of wood, of stuff and of stone: pigs jovial and pigs quizzical, kindly pigs and severe pigs, Falstaffian pigs and pigs philosophical. I counted 28 in a few seconds and had still not

2 Warnie had returned to Belfast on 14 January, to remain with his father until he embarked on 9 March 1921 for Sierra Leone. He had sent his brother four volumes of *Mémoires de Mlle de Montpensier*, ed. Pierre Adolphe Chéruel (Paris: 1858) to be bound.

3 Evelyn Abbott, *A Skeleton Outline of Greek History* (1900).

4 This letter bears the postmark 2 p.m. 29 January 1921.

got beyond the mantelpiece. This porcine seraglio of a lonely old bachelor is one of the little comedies I would not have missed for a good deal. And yet how wise! Here are companions for every mood, who need practically no upkeep and are never untrue or unkind. I think I must give him a new one: perhaps one of those balloon pigs filled with gas, so that it would hover against the ceiling – and be drawn down by a windlass at night to rest, like a Zeppelin in some little 'hangar'.[5]

I am very sorry to hear that you were laid up so long, and hope that you now have quite shaken it off. I have had a bit of a cold, but it is now gone, and beyond the perennial need of having my hair cut, I think you would pass me as 'all present and correct'. I am still smoothing and varnishing the work on Optimism.

Here is a story that will please the Colonel. The other night at the 'Martlets' old Carlyle read a paper. He is a foxy looking old gentleman with a cleanshaven face as red as a berry and straight hair the colour of snuff – a very comical face and a high croaking voice. He began by saying that he ought to apologise for his paper 'because – H'm – to tell you the truth – I had meant to publish it – but – H'm – H'm – it was so unsatisfactory that – I – I just sent it to an American magazine.' That's the proper spirit!

How very like our great army on which the sun never sets – I mean all the muddle about Warnie's sailing: I don't much envy him his voyage if this weather continues.[6] It is a little unkind to tantalise me with these glimpses of the social joys – Pumblechooks party – a quiet chat with John – symposium chez the apple man: this to me a poor scholar in Grub St! But I am sure it was unintentional, and I grudge no one his innocent pleasures.

your loving son,
Jack

---

5 The history tutor was Paul Victor Mendelssohn Benecke (1868–1944), the great-grandson of the composer Felix Mendelssohn. He became a Fellow of Magdalen College in 1893 and taught Classics until his retirement in 1925. He lived in Magdalen with his vast collection of pigs for the rest of his life. Lewis's reminiscences of Benecke are found in Margaret Deneke's *Paul Victor Mendelssohn Benecke (1868–1944)* (Oxford: [1954]), pp. 31–4.

6 The War Office had informed Warnie that he was under orders to sail to Sierra Leone on 12 January, but the orders were sent to Aldershot and forwarded from there to Sierra Leone. As a result, the ship sailed without him, and he had to wait until 9 March to embark on another one.

TO HIS FATHER (LP VI: 242–3):

Oxford Union Society
[Oxford]
16th Feb. [1921]

My dear Papy,

I am afraid I have been on this occasion remiss. I have been pretty busy and that, coupled with the laziness which follows a 'cold in the nose' and one or two outstanding letters to Aunt Suffern and a few others, have kept me going. Correspondance is unhappily no true parallel to conversation: and it is just when one would be most ready for a talk in the odd hour of the day when one shoves ones work from one and lights the pipe of peace, that one is least ready to sit down and write a letter. I often wonder how the born letter writers whose 'works' fill volumes, overcame this difficulty.

The colonel is certainly in luck, and I do not see how even the logic of the army can hold him responsible for not having been ordered abroad. I have a sort of feeling – a mere presentiment – at the back of my mind, that he will never reach Sierra Leone: a fate which will worry him more than you.

My bookseller has just sent me a bill for the books which I have got since I began to read 'Greats'. I tried originally to neutralise the outlay by selling again most of those which I had for 'Mods.', but this did not carry me far. I hope you will not consider it unreasonable if I ask you for a contribution of £5, since I cannot comfortably meet this out of income. Prices of necessary books are appalling: a Joseph's 'Logic'[7] at 12/6, a 'corpus' of Greek inscriptions at 15/-, an edition of Aristotle's Ethics at 12/6 etc., etc. For some reason – presumably because of the increased number of undergraduates – second-hand books have practically disappeared from the market here. One cannot rely entirely on libraries for some works of reference which are constantly in use, tho' I particularly resent expenditure on books which I shall never open once I am through the examination schools. The £5 of course does not include any thing I got 'because I thought I would like to have it', whether bearing on my subject or not.

The tale of Tchanie and Lily's absurd remark about the Strandtown 'season' is good. I met a friend of the said Tchanies the other night at the

7 Horace William Brindley Joseph, *An Introduction to Logic* (1906).

Carlyles, a girl called Helen Waddell[8] whom you may have heard of. When last I saw her she was lying face downwards on the floor of Mrs McNeill's drawing room, saying rather good things in a quaint Belfast drawl which poor Allan Smiles[9] himself could hardly have beaten. Though she behaved differently here, it was a strange sensation to see a little bit of our queer native world in such a different milieu. Que diable [allait-il] faire dans cette galere?[10]

I hope Arthur is not really going to the South of France because he is tired of the Slade: if that is so, I am afraid I shall find it hard to feel any sympathy with him again. It will be a disease of the soul rather than of the heart, and an incurable one, which we shall then have to bewail in him.

If the Colonel is at home again, will you show him the cutting which I enclose: he will remember having seen this strange creature here in the Union, and who could forget the 'voluminous trousers'.[11] There is a Chaucerian or Dickensian 'mine host' in a little inn near Cumnor where I sometimes call on my walks abroad who has told me that the old man

---

8 Helen Waddell (1889–1965), medieval scholar and translator, was educated at Victoria College and Queen's University, Belfast. She went up to Somerville College, Oxford, in 1920, and after taking her degree she spent the years 1923-5 in France learning the language and attaining familiarly with the Latin poetry of the fourth to the twelfth centuries. On her return she gave a course of lectures at Lady Margaret Hall, Oxford, on 'The Wandering Scholars'. She lived mostly in London after this, and published many books, the most famous of which are *The Wandering Scholars* (1927), *Medieval Latin Lyrics* (1929) and a novel, *Peter Abelard* (1933). She was a close friend of Jane McNeill, but except for this one reference above neither she nor Lewis mentioned each other in their correspondence. Lewis was, however, an admirer of her books, and in *The Allegory of Love* (1936) he says of *The Wandering Scholars*: 'Of the literary merits of Bernardus, the reader can judge best by comparing the account I have just given with the equally favourable, but differently directed, account of Miss Waddell, who touches nothing which she does not adorn' (ch. II). See Felicitas Corrigan, *Helen Waddell: A Biography* (1986).

9 Alan Smiles was a neighbour of the Lewises. He joined the Royal Irish Rifles in 1914 and was killed in battle in 1916.

10 Molière, *Les Fourberies de Scapin*, II, vii. A literal translation is, 'Why on earth did he ever get on board that galley?' but, in Lewis's context, 'What on earth was he doing there?'

11 Jack sent his father an article from *The Times* (5 February 1921), p. 11, entitled 'Death of an Oxford Character'. 'The death was announced yesterday,' it said, 'of Mr Herbert Jackson, a well-known Oxford "coach" and one of the oldest non-collegiate students. He was a remarkable personality, and his utter indifference to his dress, shown in the cravat, short coat, and voluminous trousers which he habitually wore, made him a distinctive figure in the streets of Oxford and at University ceremonies.'

used often to be there years ago – 'and 'e didn't 'arf look after his self sir. I've seen 'im polish off an 'ole duck and 'arf a pound of cheese and a couple of pints o' bitters – reg'lar as anything 'e would' – which sounds an exaggeration.

It has been very cold here – frost and wind. I often pity the heroes whom I see on the river in things like summer underclothes. I suppose they'd pity me too, in a less kindly manner, if they knew that such a mortal existed.

your loving son,
Jack

TO LEO BAKER (B):

Union Society,
Oxford.
Feb 25th 1921

My dear Baker,

When I read your letter I was so glad that, if I were not a respectable middle aged suburbanite, I should have gone and got drunk. I am staying up until this term next year, so, tho I shall pass a little before you, we have some time before us.

Next to the news of your return – which I accept too thankfully to ask for reason or motive – I was pleased, tho not maliciously, to hear that you had entered *questa salva selvaggia ed aspre et forte*,[12] the Dantesque mood, and begun to doubt. I can foresee clearly your ultimate return to the house hold of faith, but anticipate great good from your excursion. 'Blind faith' is indeed unsuitable for us who are alive now: we know too much and see life too widely and it is culpable not to make use of our widened landscape. The comfortable little universe with heaven above and hell beneath, an absolute up and down and a bare six thousand years of recorded history, could furnish you well enough with a world-view that a man could write in his pocket book and have done. But we haven't got that now, and I feel that we ought to use our own data even if they lead only to destruction.

It is hard to criticize the little poem you sent me: I shall try to do so later on. At present it seems to me like the landscape it describes, full of mist opening only here and there into oases of something you can get

12 *The Vision or Hell, Purgatory and Paradise of Dante Alighieri*, op. cit., Canto I, l. 5: 'That forest, how robust and rough its growth'.

hold of. I was a bit thrown off the rails by expecting it to be heroic blank verse, but I think it will come on acquaintance to please my ear. The fine rhythm of 'God the father almighty' tho' borrowed from the prayer book, comes in with such a gracious surprise that it becomes your own. But of this more when I have digested it. I look forward to hearing the music: tho' I hope it is not going to mean a permanent turning away from poetry. I suppose it is the stress of work which has absorbed your energy and prevented you from writing anything lately.

The same thing has happened to Pasley – indeed between schools and being engaged he has lost all interest in the muse. At the same time I think I like him better now than ever I did (have I said this before?). There are other things besides vision – lots of them.

What a splendid picture of you as a Nabob! – tho I hope your leg has released you before this from your enforced royalty.

It has been wonderfully springlike here, and I have been reading Prometheus Unbound and going for long walks – particularly interested lately in cloud scenery. This coming luck of yours is unlike things that really happen: like reversing time and raising the dead. Am busy on my old Venus re-cooked as a narrative with Ossian[13] & Niamh[14] instead of Venus & Tannhauser:[15] a wonderful subject 'if answerable style I can obtain'.[16] I shall try to send you something without a letter in a few days.

yrs
C. S. Lewis

TO LEO BAKER (B):

Oxford Union,
[4? March 1921]

My dear Baker,

As you say, this is indeed terrible. A letter railing upon the gods or fates means no great thing in my mouth but I was disturbed to see that

---

13 i.e. Oisin, a legendary Gaelic warrior and bard, as found in W.B. Yeats' narrative poem, *The Wanderings of Oisin* (1889).

14 In Irish mythology, Niamh is the daughter of Manannán the sea-god. She fell in love with Oisin, carried him off, and kept him with her for 300 years. She allowed him to return to his country on condition that he not set foot on the earth. He disregarded the caution and as a result lost his youth and became a blind, old man.

15 Tannhäuser is a German Minnesinger or lyric poet of the 13th century. He becomes enamoured of a beautiful woman who beckons him into the grotto of Venus.

16 Milton, *Paradise Lost*, IX, 20.

they have brought you also to this pass: partly indeed from a certain jealousy wherewith I am used to reserve pessimism to myself and keep my friends as a body of consolers, but partly because I argue from it something seriously wrong. I hope it will turn out to be merely the psychological result of your body's impertinent interference, and not some 'stroke of fortune': I hope you're not in pain: 'pain the perfect misery, the worst / Of cuts', there's nothing else to say about it. As a matter of fact, I fancy you would bear pain a great deal more wisely than I, who am an arrant coward and ready to run to earth even in annihilation at the first touch of our lady Dolores:[17] the enforced idleness and monotony of illness, on the other hand, you probably resent far more than I. There must be a drop of Oriental blood in me: I am so often content to sit or lie still for hours together thinking nothing and hardly even imagining anything. Beyond Suez they call it the Kaf, I think. I am rather like a cow, you see: you, rather more like a blue bottle. In short you probably need the South for your mind as much as for your body – is there any chance of you going abroad?

Barfield, whom I have looked up after a term's inexcusable neglect on both sides, tells me you were in excellent form when he last met you. He has given me his 'Tower' to read, which you have seen, I believe. In spite of many obvious faults – languor of metre, indirect egotism, too great frequency of similes and a forced novelty of phrazing – in spite of all this I am amazed at its power and feel that we have never yet treated him with sufficient respect. Its solid and real and has its feet on terra firma: it is organically connected with life as a whole, not a mere panel of odd experiences, in a word its central. That's what I envy him and what our best moderns, Brooke and Flecker[18] and de la Mare, seem to lack. Yeats even hasn't got it: Masefield has or had it in some degree. The description of the 'musical endings' and 'little blunt verses' remembered from fairy tales and the dream which follows are, I think, really capital. On the other hand, I cannot tolerate the prologue. Tho' in theory all shd. come within the poet's range, yet in practice there are some things one simply can't say without making the reader, or at least a reader like me, either uncomfortable or disposed to mock. At any rate, Barfield can't do it: it

17 From Dolour, 'Our Lady of Pain', as Dolour or Pain is sometimes called.

18 James Elroy Flecker (1884–1915), poet and playwright whose Eastern work *Hassan* Lewis wrote about to Arthur Greeves on 23 February 1931.

hasn't come off, tis a shameless piece of spiritual indecency. It is mere instinct given direct and not sublimated by vision. What do you think about it? The recurring motive of the tower, I'm afraid, will give the psycho-analysts something to talk about in their usual vein.

I was interested to hear about your music – you attempt formidable subjects: will there be any chance of your sending either of the songs here. Barfield has a friend called Mitchell, a baritone, who sang pleasantly enough when I was with them the other night. He is also digging with the poet Harwood;[19] do you know any of his work? But I am a little alarmed, all the same, so jealous I am, to see you flirting ever so innocently with the other muse. Even if I could do it, I should feel it a kind of adultery in me and fear to be finally discovered and cast off by both. Which is inconsistent, for I am even now busied with my Essay on Optimism for the Vice Chancellor's prize. I have written four or five poems since the end of last term, one quite recently. I suppose I can hardly expect you to go to the trouble of copying out any of your new ones: if you ever feel so disposed, send them to me, even without a letter if you haven't time.

We must really try to harden ourselves to the difficulties of correspondence, which are very real. It is just those odd hours of the day when one shoves ones work from one and lights a pipe that one would most readily talk if a friend was present and yet is least disposed to write a letter. However we ought to be able to conquer this.

Thanks for your criticisms of the Wild Hunt (Barfield, by the way, condemns it as 'derivative'). Rê the last line, 'sincerity' is a vague word: it is *not* my own view I give, but my own view from the position of Hippolytus – from that mood which makes the subject of the whole poem, and which comes to us all at times and shd. be taken into account. I hope you will be better before this reaches you: don't work yourself to death whatever job you do, you have other functions more important for which you will in 'the perfect witness of all-judging Jove'[20] be more accountable. – and do try to give me another letter soon

Yrs

C. S. Lewis

---

19 See **Cecil Harwood** in the Biographical Appendix. Harwood matriculated at Christ Church, Oxford, in 1919. After taking his BA in 1921 he and Owen Barfield had 'digs' together at Bee Cottage in Beckley, a few miles from Oxford.

20 Milton, *Lycidas*, 82.

P.S. Paisley has won a College prize (£5) for the historical essay: he is full of life and happiness & looking for a job against his going down at th' end of next term. Faces what seems to me awful difficulties in 'the grand manner,' has written no poetry lately and I'm rather afraid he's not likely to.

TO HIS FATHER (LP VII: 261–2):

Oxford Union Society
[Oxford]
19th March [1921]

My dear Papy,

I have put off writing from day to day, partly in the expectation of a letter from you, which your last note seemed to promise, and partly at first because I thought that the Colonel would call here on his way to the world's end. I suppose he has arrived by now at the incredible place.[21] Here, amid cold March winds, my imagination has a sort of shock when it tries to paint those poster like blue skies and to think of him sitting in flannels and panting. I have so long forsaken the illiberal study of geography that I would not now give up my ignorance for a good deal. To me, and I expect to you, everywhere beyond the equator is a vague romance: I have an idea that if Warnie went for a walk a little way south he would come to the coast of Coromandel and be able to get an autograph from the Yongi Bongi Bo himself. Please let me have his address as I have promised ('the triumph of optimism over experience')[22] to try and send him a monthly newsletter.

I have been taken recently to see the mighty Yeats.[23] It was the weirdest show you ever saw, and I fear he is a Kod. You sit on hard antique chairs by candlelight in an oriental looking room and listen in silence while the great man talks about magic and ghosts and mystics: I should have loved to have had Kirk there. What fluttering of the dovecote! It is a pity that the real romance of meeting a man who has written great poetry and

---

21 Warnie sailed on the ship *Appam* for Sierra Leone on 9 March 1921. He arrived at Freetown, Sierra Leone on 19 March.

22 *Boswell's Life of Johnson*, op. cit., vol. II, 7 December 1770, p. 128: 'A gentleman who had been very unhappy in marriage, married immediately after his wife died: Johnson said, it was the triumph of hope over experience.'

23 The meeting with W.B. Yeats took place on 14 March and is described fully in Jack's serial letter to Warnie of March–April 1921.

who has known William Morris and Tagore[24] and Symons[25] should be so overlaid with the sham romance of flame coloured curtains and mumbo-jumbo.

It is bitterly cold here and I have been a little bothered with what would be called growing pains if I were a bit younger, but would now be dignified by the name of rheumatism. I have written a piteous and I hope convincing reply to the letter you enclosed. 'Optimism' is going to the typist next week.

Hoping to hear from you and that you keep well.

your loving son,

Jack

TO HIS BROTHER: (A SERIAL LETTER, WRITTEN ON VARIOUS DATES IN MARCH–APRIL 1921; LP VI: 284–9)

University College.
[Oxford]

My dear W.,

I am waiting to hear your address from M. L'Oiseau Pomme de Terre,[26] and in the meantime have begun – tho' with what promise of continuance I don't know – my journal letter. As nothing ever happens to me it will be filled, if at all, with trivialities and things that have interested me from day to day. As we talk a good deal of odd fragments out of books when we are together, there's no reason why we should not reproduce the same sort of tittle-tattle. Perhaps one of the reasons why letters are so hard to write and so much harder to read is that people confine themselves to news – or in other words think nothing worth writing except that which would not be worth saying. All that should be said by way of preamble has already been better said by Lamb in his letter to a friend at the Antipodes. I feel the same difficulty: I cannot imagine in what kind of melodramatic setting you will be reading this. I hear that

24 Rabindranath Tagore (1861–1941), the eminent Bengali poet. His *Gitanjali: Song Offering* (1912) won the Nobel Prize for Literature in 1913.

25 Arthur William Symons (1865–1945) whose early volumes of poetry included *Days and Nights* (1889) and *London Nights* (1895). He is largely remembered as a leading spirit of the Decadence movement and a defender of 'Art for Art's Sake'.

26 The Lewis brothers were enthusiastic nicknamers. Since boyhood they had been amused by their father's 'low' Irish pronunciation of 'potatoes' as 'p'daytas'. As a result, he became 'The P'dayta' or 'The P'daytabird' – and now, with Warnie in Sierra Leone where French is spoken, 'Monsieur L'Oiseau Pomme de Terre'.

your 'preposterous box' on the 'East India-man' was not to your liking. Well, you would be a soldier: you must keep a stiff upper lip about it and button up your coat. Here we have sleet and that sort of wind that freezes you when you go out drest for summer: if you do otherwise, 'the wild winds whist' and the sun comes out a good 80. But I will be on with my journal: the dates are only approximate.

March 1st

Going into College today I met Hamilton-Jenkin[27] in the porch, who carried me to his rooms in Merton Street. Jenkin is a little, pale person with a smooth green face, not unlike a lizard's. He was too young for the war and I always look on him as rather a child, though some people think I am wrong in this. I mention him for the amusing passages he showed me from two books. One was a Tour of the County of Cornwall written in the 17th Century: an admirable codology. Under the heading of Beastes we find (after those of Venerie and Draught) Rats. These are described as 'not only mischievous by day for their devouring of clothes, writings and meats, but cumbersome by night for their rattling and jaunting as they gallop their galliards in the roof'. This sentence I at once learnt by heart. 'The slow six legged crawler' which in Cornwall infest all but the 'cleanly home bred' are also worth recording.[28]

The other book approaches the tall end of your period from a strange angle. It is the newly discovered autobiography of a Cornish smuggler who was one of the first 'methodies': apparently finding this employment compatible with his religion. The joke was that he managed to get himself imprisoned in France with some 'of the best people' waiting to be guillotined. They seem to have been very nice to him and asked him to sing – for in his own Cornwall he was accustomed to go out into a lonely place and sing 'so that I suppose I could be heard for a mile off': which he did 'for fear of giving offence'. He was however worried how to avoid too much society without offending until 'the Lord provided him a little place under the stairs'. This strange character I thought worth mentioning.[29]

---

27 See **Alfred Kenneth Hamilton Jenkin** in the Biographical Appendix. Jenkin was born in Cornwall and matriculated at University College in 1919 where he read English and was a member of the Martlets.

28 Although the passages are slightly misquoted they come from Richard Carew's *The Survey of Cornwall* (1602), p. 22.

29 *The Autobiography of a Cornish Smuggler (Captain Harry Carter, of Prussia Cove) 1748–1809*, with an Introduction and Notes by John B. Cornish (1894).

Jenkin himself is an enthusiastic Cornishman and some are bored with his persistency in talking of his native scenery, habits, language and superstitions. I rather like it. He put on a little linen cap which he wears when 'he goes down mines'. Cornwall of course is all mines: they are full of beings called Nackers whom one hears knocking at the ends of the lonelier galleries. The workmen leave little bits of their food for them, for they are terrible bringers of good and bad luck – rather like Leprechauns as I understand. Jenkins has only one vice: that of writing very sad poetry which he sometimes shows me. It is usually about Cornwall.

March 12th

Everyone was going down today. Such days have all the atmosphere of a school end of term with its joy taken out of it – body without soul. I hate it: and lest empty rooms and stacks of suit cases should not be sufficiently offensive, we have the intolerable institution of Collections.[30] This is the worst relic of barbarism which yet hangs about the University. From 9 until noon the Master with all his 'auxiliar fiends' sits at the high table in Hall and one by one sheepish or truculent undergraduates, as their names are called, walk up the long emptiness, mount the dais, and stand foolishly gaping while he delivers a little homily. In my case he always used to say the same thing. 'Well Mr Lewis, I – ah – I – have nothing but – ah – satisfaction to express as regards – ah – ah. We expect great things of you.' Apparently he has now given up expecting great things of me.

Now you, lolling in your punkah while the lotuses fly over a pagoda coloured sky etc, may think me very weak: but it is extraordinary that any ceremony which is designed to make you feel like an inky schoolboy will succeed in making you feel like an inky schoolboy. I doubt if even the P'daytabird could have invented anything more subtly undermining of one's self-respect than that early morning procession up a big hall to be complimented by an old gentleman at a table. Try to imagine it and then add the idea of nine o'clock in the morning: and that your collar has broken loose from its stud at the back: and that there's a smell of last night's dinner about: a fly on your nose: a shaving cut beginning to bleed – but no, it is too painful.

30 'Collections' means either the informal college examination at the beginning of each term to test a student's progress in his work, or the reports given orally at the end of a term by the tutor.

While waiting my turn I had a smart faux pas with an old monument called

'A Mr Wilkinson, a clergyman'

(as the immortal line runs) who is reading for the Church.[31] He used to be President of the Martlets when I was secretary and I have had fiery passages with him in 1919. He had been to see the Queen given a degree the day before and I dropped some vague remarks about 'this upholstered poker business'. But, would you believe it, I'd stumbled on a true loyalist who thought her a fine woman and gave me a severe telling-off! It was a day of misfortunes. Wilkinson looks very like Gordon[32] grown fatter. He once read us a paper on Drinkwater,[33] holding a little bundle of paper close to his face and speaking a thin whisper out of the corner of his mouth: but it soon developed into a philosophical argument by Wilkinson, which lasted till one o'clock, much to the annoyance of the unphilosophical owner of the rooms, who wanted to go to bed.

March 13th

It being Lord's Day I waited after breakfast on Pasley in his rooms at Unity House: this is a cottage in a lane by Headington Church where the buildings are so ruinous that it looks like a bit of France as the cant goes – well FAIRLY like it. Pasley is my oldest ally: he used to write poetry but is now too engrossed in history and he has also become engaged – that fatal tomb of all lively and interesting men. Unity House is ruled by a strangely ugly woman whose only accomplishment is an illegitimate born to a captain of artillery who once lodged there. So at least she tells Pasley: but I find these villagers are so eager to present the

31 Donald Frederick Wilkinson enlisted in the army in 1914. In 1915 he was commissioned a captain and served with the King's (Liverpool Regiment) in France and Belgium 1915–17. He was awarded the Military Cross in 1917. He matriculated at University College in 1918 and read *Literae Humaniores.* He took his BA in 1921, and his MA in 1925. After reading Theology at St Stephen's House, Oxford and Cuddesdon College, Cuddesdon, he was ordained in the Church of England in 1924 for the diocese of Southwark. After a number of impressive appointments, he was Rector of Beckley, Sussex, from 1931 to 1947.

32 i.e. Gordon Ewart.

33 John Drinkwater (1882–1937), a poet and critic, some of whose poems Lewis had seen in the five volumes of *Georgian Poetry* published between 1912 and 1922.

world with a 'gentleman's' son and so proud to have done it, that it may be mere idle boasting. This is no exaggeration but plain truth – they burst with pride and lose their heads in proportion as they lose their figures. Headington is a sink of all the iniquities and improbabilities: but perhaps I shall devote a whole 'Account' to that – and become known as 'Headington Hamilton' which rolls off the tongue at least as well as Corsica Boswell. By the same token I saw an EDITIO PRINCEPS of Bozzy's Corsica[34] for 5/- the other day.

But where was I? Nothing to say after all but that I had an excellent walk with Pasley: he described to me the humours of the new constitution of Tzecho-Slovakia, which I wish I cd. remember. We sat in a wood full of primroses. Damnit, how generations of P'dayta's have teased the language till the very name of a primrose sounds sentimental: when you come to look at them, they are really rather attractive. I walked Pasley off his legs and we lunched chez moi on rabbit pie – our common fare at present – Pasley and Mrs Moore having a lively conversation on money in view of his intent shortly to try 'this marrying business'.

March 14th

I received this morning a letter from my obliging friend Stead.[35] Stead is rather a punt: I think you saw me stop to speak to him one day in the Corn.[36] He is an undergraduate but also curate of a parish in Oxford. He writes poetry. The annoying thing is that it's exactly like

---

34 James Boswell, *An Account of Corsica* (1768).

35 William Force Stead (1884–1967) was born in Washington, DC, and graduated from the University of Virginia in 1908. That same year he was appointed to the US Consular Service, serving as vice-consul in Liverpool and Nottingham. He was ordained in the Church of England in 1915 and served as a curate at Ross-on-Wye until he matriculated at Queen's College, Oxford, in 1917. He took his BA from Queen's in 1921 and his MA in 1925. Stead was Chaplain of St Mark's Anglican Church, Florence, Italy, from 1922 to 1924. He served as Chaplain of Worcester College, Oxford, from 1925 to 1933 when he converted to the Catholic Church. Stead was a friend of T.S. Eliot, whom he baptized on 9 June 1927. He published many volumes of poems, and besides having this interest in common with Lewis, his wife, the former Frances Goldsborough, was the sister of Mary Goldsborough, who married Dr John Askins. Dr Askins was Mrs Moore's brother, so Frances Stead, being sister to Mrs Askins, was Mrs Moore's sister-in-law's sister. At the beginning of World War II, Stead returned to the Consular Service in order to help his country. He went back to the United States in August 1939. His published poems include *Verd Antique* (1920), *The Sweet Miracle* (1922) and *Festival in Tuscany* (1927).

36 i.e. Cornmarket Street, Oxford.

mine, only like the bad parts of mine: this was my own original opinion and it has been confirmed by others. Perhaps you can imagine the sensation I experienced in reading it. Stead's letter was to say that he had mentioned to Yeats – whom he knows – 'my double claim to distinction as an Irishman and a poet' and would I come along this evening and see him?

I accordingly repaired after dinner to Stead's lodging in Canterbury Street. He is a married man: his wife is an American: she is the sister of a woman who is married to a brother of Mrs Moore's. She was a woman of implacable sullenness who refused even to say good evening to me: beside her at the fire sat an American gentleman who was apparently left to console her for the absence of her husband. This was a very amiable person: he was 'studyin' when I entered, but politely laid his book down. You know the sort of face in which a long promontory of nose (eagle build) projects from between two rounded hills of cheek (cherub build)? Picture this surmounted by a pair of horn spectacles and made of a texture rather like cod's roe: then add that this face beams but can contribute to the crack only by saying 'That's right' at the end of everyone's remark. In these rather nasty surroundings Stead was finishing a very nasty meal of cold fish and cocoa: but he soon put on his coat and after asking his lady why there were no stamps in the house and receiving no answer, swung out with me into the usual Oxford theatrical night. Trusting soul to leave his wife unguarded in such society!

Yeats lives at the end of Broad St, the first house on your right as you leave the town. I can assure you I felt a veritable Bozzy as I reflected that I was now to meet at last WILLIAM BUTLER YEATS![37] But enough of that. We were shown up a long stairway lined with rather wicked pictures by Blake – all devils and monsters – and finally into the presence chamber, lit by tall candles, with orange coloured curtains and full of things which I can't describe because I don't know their names. The poet was very big, about sixty years of age: 'awful' as Bozzy says: grey haired, clean shaven. When he first began to speak I would have thought him French, but the Irish sounds through after a time. Before the fire was a

37 William Butler Yeats (1865–1939) and his wife, the former Georgie Hyde-Lees, had moved to 4 Broad Street, Oxford, in April 1919. Lewis admired Yeats' poetry when the poet was a romantic. However, as Yeats moved further and further into mysticism and theosophy, Lewis began to feel repulsed; he had seen other lives ruined by theosophy. Mrs Yeats was pregnant at this time, and on 22 August 1921 she gave birth to their son, Michael Yeats.

circle of hard antique chairs. Present were the poet's wife, a little man who never spoke all evening, and Father Martindale.[38] Father M. is a Catholic Priest, a little twinkling man like a bird, or like Puck, whom I take to be an atheistical dog. I used to go to his lectures in the old days: he is a mocker. Everyone got up as we came in: after the formalities I was humbly preparing to sink into the outlying chair leaving the more honourable to Stead, but the poet sternly and silently motioned us into other ones. The meaning of this I have not fathomed: 'twas very Pumblechookian.[39]

Then the talk began. It was all of magic and cabbalism and 'the Hermetic knowledge'. The great man talked while the priest and Mrs Yeats fed him with judicious questions. The matter I admit was either mediaeval or modern, but the manner was so XVIII Century that I lost my morale. I understood how it is possible for a man to terrify a room into silence: and I had a ghastly presentment that something would presently impel me to up like that 'unknown curate' and say 'Were not Vale Owen's revelations, Sir, addressed to the passions?'[40] And then as Max Beerbohm says 'Bang' the suddenness of it! However I remembered that Johnson WAS really dead and controlled myself. Indeed some good angel guided me: for presently I really had something to say – a case mentioned by

---

38 Father Cyril Charlie Martindale SJ (1879–1963) was a member of the Jesuit college, Campion Hall, and he lectured in the faculty of *Literae Humaniores*. He began life as a bookish little boy, and he took a First in Classical Honour Moderations in 1903 and a First in Greats in 1905. After his ordination to the priesthood in 1911, he taught at Stonyhurst. He returned to Oxford to lecture in Classics in 1916. During the war he surprised everyone with an unsuspected ability to minister to the spiritual needs of the wounded, and a remarkable ability to communicate with people very unlike himself. In 1927 he joined the staff of the Jesuits' Farm Street Church in London, where his spiritual clientele was drawn from every level of society, from dukes to dustmen. He involved himself with numerous good enterprises, including settlements for working-class boys in the East End of London. Far from being an 'atheistical dog', as Lewis suspected, he preceded Lewis as a broadcaster and writer who could translate theological doctrines into simple, everyday language. He published numerous biographies of such contemporaries as Robert Hugh Benson, and many works of Christian apologetics. See Philip Caraman, *C.C. Martindale* (1967).

39 'Pumblechook' was the nickname of G. Herbert Ewart (1857–1924). See note 68 to the letter of 12 May 1917.

40 George Vale Owen (1869–1931) was a clerical spiritualist admired by Sir Arthur Conan Doyle. His *magnum opus* was *The Life Beyond the Veil*, 4 vols (1920–1). He also wrote *Problems which Perplex (mainly psychic) explained by question and answer* (1890), *The Outlands of Heaven* [1923], *What Happens after Death* [1924], and *How Spirits Communicate* [1926].

Coleridge which was most apposite and indeed crying for quotation on something just said. But thank God I didn't: for a minute later the priest did.

> *YEATS (thumping his chair): 'Yes – yes – the old woman in Coleridge. That story was published by Coleridge without the slightest evidence. Andrew Lang exposed it. I've never had a conversation on the subject that SOMEONE didn't bring in Coleridge's old woman. It is anonymous in the first place and every one has taken it over without question. It just shows that there's no limit to the unscrupulousness that a sceptical man will go to – '*
> *MARTINDALE: 'Oh surely Mr Yeats – '*
> *YEATS: 'Yes! There is a Professor living in Oxford at this moment who is the greatest sceptic in print. The same man has told me that he entered a laboratory where X (some woman whose name I didn't catch) was doing experiments: saw the table floating near the ceiling with X sitting on it: vomited: gave orders that no further experiments were to be done in the laboratories – and refused to let the story be known.'*

But it would be only ridiculous to record it all: I should give you the insanity of the man without his eloquence and presence, which are very great. I could never have believed that he was so exactly like his own poetry.

One more joke must be recorded. Stead presently told us a dream he had had: it was so good that I thought it a lie. YEATS (looking to his wife): 'Have you anything to say about that, Georgie?' Apparently Stead's transcendental self, not important enough for the poet, has been committed to Mrs Yeats as a kind of ersatz or secondary magician. Finally we are given sherry or vermouth in long and curiously shaped glasses, except Martindale who has whiskey out of an even longer and more curiously shaped glass, and the orgy is at an end. Try to mix Pumblechook, the lunatic we met at the Mitre, Dr Johnson, the most eloquent drunk Irishman you know, and Yeat's own poetry, all up into one composite figure, and you will have the best impression I can give you.

March 18th etc.

About this time I recieved a letter from Pdaytaheim in which I was informed that 'as the vacation was only ten days long' he supposed I should not be coming down, tho' it would have been 'very pleasant' if I had. Three cheers for inaccurate information, said I, and flung my hat in the air! For about a week after this we had the most beautiful spring weather. I took to push-biking and slacked off work a good deal. The country round here is not bad: for summer or winter at their best, one wants mountains and sea, but just at present it is quite good enough to be in an ordinary English county. Whatever else you lack you always have fruit trees with white blossom (looking like cauliflowers) and winding road and nice little stone villages, each with its pleasant church and pub: and what, after all, is wrong with a low raftered bar parlour in the Thames valley, with foxes in glass cases and a pint of good draft cider? On such occasions I usually take a little note book and write down whatever occurs to me. On Easter Monday the publican at Garsington was very polite to me and asked me to go into the front parlour 'if I had some writing to do'. I elected to stay where I was: but how true to the countryman's attitude! We 'write', they 'have some writing to do' on rare occasions – just as they might have 'some digging' or 'some darning' TO DO. I usually get back for a late tea and after consuming much soda bread and drinking Johnsonian cups, sit under the one tree in our tiny strip of garden and read a little of the good Plato.

March 19th

Here is a thing worth remembering – a propos of our old discussion of the ancestral conception of God as 'an old gentleman in a blue dressing gown etc'. It is a remark of Chateaubriand's (you will probably think I am inventing it, but it's quite true) quoted by Emerson – 'Si Dieu a fail l'homme a son image, l'homme l'a bien rendu.'[41] Serve him right!

March 21st

Having met Stead yesterday in the Broad with his wife and of course with our friend of the nose, I was told that the great man had expressed himself sorry not to have been able to see more of me owing to his argument with the priest, and would I come again with Stead [the] next night?

41 'Si Dieu nous a faits à son image, nous le lui avons bien rendu' ('If God created us to his image, we returned him the compliment'). The quotation is actually from Voltaire's *Le Sottisier*.

This night we were shown to a study up in the ceiling and entertained by him alone: and, would you believe it, he was almost quite sane, and talked about books and things, still eloquently and quite intelligently? Of course we got on to magic in the end – that was only to be expected. It was really my fault, for I mentioned Bergson. 'Ah yes,' said he, 'Bergson. It was his sister who taught me magic.' The effect of this statement on Aunt Suffern (already in paroxysms of contempt over what I had already told her about Yeats) ought to be amusing.

We spoke of Andrew Lang. YEATS: 'I met him once – at a dinner somewhere. He never said a word. When we began to talk afterwards, he just got up and took his chair into a corner of the room and sat down facing the wall. He stayed there all the evening.' Perhaps Lang didn't like wizards! Of the 'great Victorians' he said: 'The most interesting thing about the Victorian period was their penchant for selecting one typical great man in each department – Tennyson, THE poet, Roberts, THE soldier: and then these types were made into myths. You never heard of anyone else: if you spoke of medicine it meant – (some 'THE Doctor' whose name I've forgotten): if you spoke of politics it was Gladstone.'

This is especially interesting to us as explaining the mental growth of a certain bird we wot of. ('Well all said and done boys, he was a GREAT man.') So home to bed more pleased with our poet than I had been on the last occasion: and rather thankful that L'Oiseau Pomme de Terre hadn't been there to explain that 'you can see he's a disappointed man' after every adverse criticism on any living writer. Oh, before I leave it, Stead told me he had shown Yeats a poem: Yeats said he thought 'IT WOULD DO VERY WELL' to set to music! Stead thinks this is a compliment. H'mh!

TO HIS FATHER (LP VI: 269–70):

University College,
Oxford.
March 28th [1921]

My dear Papy,

I am glad that you sent me the wire. I am a poor reader of papers and should have been very sorry, through ignorance, to let such a thing pass in silence. Poor old Kirk![42] What shall one say of him? It would be a

42 Mr W.T. Kirkpatrick died at his home, Gastons, Great Bookham, Surrey, on 22 March 1921.

poor compliment to that memory to be sentimental: indeed, if it were possible, he would himself return to chide the absurdity. It is however no sentiment, but plainest fact to say that I at least owe to him in the intellectual sphere as much as one human being can owe another. That he enabled me to win a scholarship is the least that he did for me. It was an atmosphere of unrelenting clearness and rigid honesty of thought that one breathed from living with him – and this I shall be the better for as long as I live. And if this is the greatest thing, there are others which none of us will forget: his dry humour, his imperturbable good temper and his amazing energy – these it is good to have seen. He was a unique personality with nothing inconsistent about him – except the one foible about the Sunday suit: the more one sees of weakness, affectation and general vagueness in the majority of men, the more one admires that rigid, lonely old figure – more like some ancient Stoic standing fast in the Roman decadence than a modern scholar living in the home counties. Indeed we may almost call him a great man, tho', as it happened, his greatness was doomed to reach so small a circle. I should have liked to have seen him once again before this happened. I have of course written to Mrs K.

You ask whether I am satisfied with my Optimism, and I am afraid I hardly know. For one thing I almost know it by heart, and consequently can least of all judge it impartially: for another, it is so very ill typed that the usually helpful effect of cold print is neutralised by mere irritation. At a charge of £1.7s. for an essay of about 11,000 words I should not have expected such petty annoyances as MEDONISM for HEDONISM, NOW for WORD, paragraphs run together, question marks in the wrong place etc., etc. But, as Knowles says, 'Who am I'.

At any rate, it has given me, in parts, as much trouble as anything I have ever done and I shall be glad to have it launched into the registrar's box for good and all and to leave the rest on the knees of the gods. Only don't expect any results. You see I am afraid I have rather fallen between two stools: it has to aim at being both literary and philosophical, and, in the effort to accomplish the double object, I have made it too literary for the philosophers and too metaphysical for the dons of English Literature. These are the pitfalls with which the walks of Academe are digged. Such things are written for a tiny public of appointed judges, and you never know what their particular point of view is going to be: they are only human beings and must have tastes and tempers of their own, but one can't find these out. It must be difficult to be quite fair to an essay which expresses some view that you have been denouncing to a submissive Senior Common Room for the last half century, however good it may be.

I should dearly love to get away for a bit, but, as you say, for so short a time, the expense and the interruption of work is hardly worth it. The Colonel must have had an unpleasant journey: I wish he would keep a diary which we could compare with that of Grandfather Hamilton in the same waters.[43] Two generations of sub-tropical Atlantic and Hamilton temperament would be worth studying!

I hope you are keeping tolerably well: my growing pains are better. I don't think I 'ever heard tell of' rheumatics being traced to absence of underclothing: but an old wound always gives you some degree of rheumatism as a souvenir. I was asked to the Yeat's again last Saturday: there was only one other guest and the great man was much saner: he talked less of magic and more of literature, including a good story about Andrew Lang for which I haven't room here – but remind me. The country is full of white apple blossom.

your loving son,
Jack

TO HIS BROTHER: (A CONTINUATION OF THE SERIAL LETTER: LP VI: 289–91)

[University College]
April 20? [1921]

I am afraid I had already let my diary languish for some time, less from being tired of it than from shame to repeat endlessly little descriptions of walks and talks, when yours arrived. The mail day for your land is on the 26th, but as term has now begun again I had better keep its adventures, if any, for my next. Whether during term I shall be able to keep a journal I don't know. In the meantime you have not lost many items of interest.

---

43 Warnie, who was still in Sierra Leone, *was* keeping a diary at this time. Their maternal grandfather, the Rev. Thomas Robert Hamilton (1826–1905), was ordained a clergyman in 1853, and in 1854 he was appointed a chaplain in the Royal Navy. He served with the Baltic squadron of the fleet throughout the Crimean War, and in other parts of the world until he retired from the navy in 1870. The diaries he kept during his naval career form part of the Lewis Papers. See **The Hamilton Family** in the Biographical Appendix.

There was a show at the child's[44] school to which I went, sneaking in alone a whimsical and unobserved male among miles of petticoat. Of course they did the ghost scene from Macbeth: great success if some lout in the audience hadn't giggled at the entrance of the ghost. The ghost, I should add in justice, was really very good: but they all took up the laugh like sheep and 'Macbeth's' chances of tragic effect were ruined. Perhaps also I should not let Miss Ploughman pass unrecorded.[45] She is the music mistress at this school, who called here the day after the coal strike had been declared and said 'Well you know, I don't think that there's going to be any strike after all'; she is not however, as this remark seems to imply, brainless, but suffers from an excess of energy, being jerky in her movements. She looks like a Spaniard and pours forth a stream of continuous conversation in a VERY loud voice with the rich intonation of a teacher of elocution. She has published one book.

About the coal strike itself you have, I suppose, heard AD NAUSEAM from the papers: what it means to me personally is that I have done a good deal of wood sawing. Have you ever sawed wood? If not, you probably have an idea that one sets the saw lightly on the log, gets to work, and continues steadily deepening until the two halves fall apart. Not a bit of it: you set the saw lightly on the log and then try to move it. It darts aside with a sound like a swallow, and you wrap a handkerchief round your hand: when the blood has soaked through this you go into the house and get some court plaster. Next time you go more cautiously and after the saw has chirped a whole song, a bit of bark comes off: by this time you are fairly warm. Then you really get to it: back and forward you go, changing uneasily from your left to your right, feeling the blisters arise on your hand, while the shadows lengthen and the sweat pours down. When you go to bed that night, the 'big push' has got about as far as you see in the cut, and you get visions of getting through that log on your thirtieth birthday. I have now become quite good at it and sometimes even get a degree of enjoyment out of it when the day is fine and it goes well. Pasley has turned up the other day: everyone has drifted in since.

Many thanks for your most interesting letter. What a queer end of the world backwater – just like the places we used to imagine out of God

44 The 'child' is Maureen Moore, a pupil at Headington School.

45 i.e. Mary Plowman. See note 72 to letter of 14 July 1919.

knows what sea stories but, still more 'all made out of the carver's brain'.[46] I certainly never thought to hear anything like H.M.S. 'Dwarf' in real life: and how very homely to have a telescope and a Lloyd's register! You will have plenty more to tell me in your next letter: I haven't quite got my picture yet. What type of mountains are they? I assume they don't rise to snow: I know they can't be heathery: and I have a suspicion they are not smooth green like the hills at Malvern. So you see I am at a loss for them. The cockchafers[47] are the last word. It is the terror of such specimens of nature's vulgar horseplay which will keep me confined to Europe all my days. You don't mention the white people you meet. Have you heard of a civilian called Bathgate or Wimberley – these are people who Mrs Moore mentions as 'having government jobs' in Sierra Leone. By the way, does Sierra Leone mean in practice just the town, or do people live anywhere else?

I am very glad you have become a convert to Milton: what put you on to him and what parts have you been reading? I wonder will you ever get to the end of the Bible:[48] the undesirable 'primitives' around you will enable you to appreciate the Hebrews who were Class A primitives after all.

What a queer thing that black man (v. Lamb on 'our brothers')[49] is: he's been there as long as anyone else and has never advanced one quarter of a step. Perhaps the really strange thing is that the others have. Let me know when you write if you get the Times Literary Supplement: if not I will send you cuttings that are in your line. Also tell me whether you want this to continue: is there anything you'd like to hear LESS of?

---

46 Coleridge, *Christabel*, I, 179–80: 'Carved with figures strange and sweet, / All made out of the carver's brain.'

47 Cockchafers are a coleopterous insect which come from the chrysalis late in May and fly with a whirring sound.

48 In March Warnie decided to use his free time in Sierra Leone by reading the Bible through. His idea was to read five pages per day, and when he wrote to Jack he had just finished Leviticus.

49 In Charles Lamb's 'Imperfect Sympathies', in *Essays of Elia*, he said: 'In the Negro countenance you will often meet with strong traits of benignity. I have felt yearnings of tenderness towards some of these faces – or rather masks – that have looked out kindly upon one in casual encounters in the streets and highways. I love what Fuller beautifully calls – these "images of God cut in ebony".'

TO HIS FATHER (LP VI: 294–5):

[University College]
April 23rd [1921]

My dear Papy,

I am sorry to hear that you have been unwell. If you have been having our weather I am not surprised – days of bright spring, alternating with frosts, biting winds, and snows, or often all these mixed in one day. It has indeed the charm of variety, but, unlike that other variety 'custom can' easily 'stale it'.[50]

On top of this, or rather arranged by some malicious power to coincide with the cold, comes the strike, and as Pepys says 'Lord knows what disorders we shall fall into'. Once or twice it has looked like becoming a very ugly business. On this subject you are the optimist to my pessimist, and I hope you are right. No doubt it was very wise of the government to call up the reserve, thus meeting at one stroke the unemployment and the results of the unemployment, but these queues of volunteers, the lorries in the streets and the uniformed figures are too unpleasantly familiar to most of us – and suggestive. What a good thing we drew our foot out of that net!

I can of course appreciate your feelings about poor Kirk's funeral.[51] Stripped of all wherewith belief and tradition have clothed it, death appears a little grimmer – a shade more chilly and loathsome – in the eyes of the most matter of fact. At the same time, while this is sad, it would have been not only sad but shocking to have pronounced over Kirk words that he did not believe and performed ceremonies that he himself would have denounced as meaningless. Yet, as you say, he is so indelibly stamped on one's mind once known, so often present in thought, that he makes his own acceptance of annihilation the more unthinkable. I have seen death fairly often and never yet been able to find it anything but extraordinary and rather incredible. The real person

50 William Shakespeare, *Antony and Cleopatra* (1623), II, ii, 243: 'Age cannot wither her, nor custom stale'.

51 The Lewises had long known that Mr Kirkpatrick was an atheist. However, writing to Warnie on 21 April, Mr Lewis told him how painful he found the arrangements for Mr Kirkpatrick's body: 'There was not to be a funeral – no service, no ceremony, no flowers, and he was to be cremated. My whole soul rose in revolt at the thought. The dear old man to be spirited away furtively – like an unclean thing – and burned!' (LP VI: 292).

is so very real, so obviously living and different from what is left that one cannot believe something has turned into nothing. It is not faith, it is not reason – just a 'feeling'. 'Feelings' are in the long run a pretty good match for what we call our beliefs.

I have had a letter from Warnie, probably stating much the same as he has written to you. He certainly seems very pleased with his new billet so far: and it must be a breath of home to find his office provided with a Lloyd's Register and a telescope. He is apparently reading Milton and the Old Testament, both I fancy works which enjoy a very limited circulation on the West Coast!

I find that I am run pretty near the end of my tether by now and would be glad if you will put in the new money at once. We are hobbling along on wood fuel at present but that is soon to be limited: gas also is threatened and with it presently, electricity. If this lasts a month longer, England will be in a pretty state.

No news of Optimist yet and no man knoweth when it may be expected – so we can all enjoy our hopes undisturbed by facts for a while longer.

your loving son,
Jack

TO HIS FATHER (LP VI: 308–9):

University College,
Oxford
May 9th [1921]

My dear Papy,

I must apologise for having delayed till now to answer your letter and acknowledge 'the needfull', for which, tho' belated, many thanks. (That's a bad sentence: I mean the THANKS are belated, of course, a confusion that could hardly occur in any language except English. However, letters do not aim at literary precision.)

It seems almost a pity to have cashed the dividend: such relics of civilisation and commerce will soon have a historical interest if this country goes the way it is treading at present. Of course it is not a question of wages: it is one side of the big underground movement which is working other troubles than those of labour at present. The most dangerous feature of the whole thing has developed since you wrote – I mean the 'sack of Aldershot' by the Reservists with a red flag.[52] The levity of English people is incorrigible – and encouraging. Most of the men I have met take the view, having been at Aldershot during some period of their soldiering, that the sooner it is all destroyed the better. As our friend at the Hippodrome says, 'I won't go back to Aldershot'!

I am beginning my period of Roman history and this has sent me back to Tacitus whom I read with Kirk. It is the strangest and in a way the pleasantest sensation. The old phrases come up inevitably in his own voice and manner, not only by the usual force of association, but also because Tacitus is a grim, sardonic author whose hardest sayings Kirk relished and made his own. One seems to remember those days in the little upper room with the photograph of Gladstone and the gas stove all the more often now that they are absolutely finished and shut up.

The weather continues pretty cold here and there are still a good many soldiers passing to and fro. I don't know that the Colonel's letter to me was very discursive: the Lloyd's Register in his office and his dislike of the natives and cockchafers were the chief points. But for the climate it would not be a bad job for troglodytes and readers like ourselves: fortunately he has a streak of that in him. For the average officers with no mind and no resources it must be a terrible business and a nurse of all the solitary vices: it is a curious necessity that always casts these sort of jobs – Lighthouses, wireless stations etc. – on the men least fitted for them by nature.

There is still no news of Optimism, and by now little optimism among those who await the news. I should have thought that they could have decided on the productions before this: an unsettled possibility like that becomes in the end a nuisance at the back of one's mind.

your loving son,
Jack

52 *The Times* (9 May 1921), p. 10: 'A riot which caused material damage, and which, it is believed, was instigated by Bolshevist sympathizers in military uniform, occurred in Aldershot last night…The actual rioters may have numbered between 60 and 80; the party who marched with them under the red flag, it is estimated numbered about 500.'

TO HIS BROTHER (LP VI: 315–19):

[University College]
May 10th [1921]

My dear W.,

The younger Pliny has a good letter in which he says to a friend 'If any one asks you at Rome what you have done today, you reply perhaps, I have been to a betrothal, I have assisted at so and so's coming of age, I've been to vote for somebody etc. That day and each day it seems necessary: it is only when you review the series of days from the seclusion of the country that it seems futile.'[53] I quote this a propos: for tho' I have less time to describe things now that term has begun, I don't know that I can spend even that setting down so many nothings.

From your last letter – in which I was sorry to see that you had not got mine – I gather that you don't get the papers. Still, I suppose I needn't describe the coal strike, the split in labour which now alas appears to be healing: nor the calling up of the reserves: nor the sack of Aldershot by 2000 of those same Reservists, a red flag at their head. All this you will get (with appropriate comments) from another source. You may imagine meantime how glad I am to have got safely out of the Ersatz before all this began.

Here term is still new enough to be interesting. It is still pleasant to see fewer foreign visitors pacing the High with guide books and taking photos of spires – where I know they'll get them crooked – and to see one's friends again instead. Pasley was the first to wait upon us, in a blinding snow shower, a few days before term began.

As you will never meet them (nor indeed will I), it is no breach of confidence to touch on the grim humours of his future 'in-laws'. A mother of the Mrs Greeves type, who has all the money but is nevertheless incapable of resisting her husband, a retired army officer, busily engaged in trying to see if his constitution will 'keep' by being sufficiently soaked in spirits. This indeed has been his life work, and the devil of it is that it seems likely to 'keep' a good bit yet. He wd. not be worth mentioning save for one trait which brings him into our circle. After having been on a binge for several days, after having exhausted all the months money, his favourite remark is 'Well, well, after all, we're a happy family.' Another good P'daytism: to the daughter (Pasley's fiancée)

53 Pliny the Younger (AD 61 or 62–c. 113), *Letters*, No. 9 to Minicius Fundanus.

reduced to great straits and learning typing, altho' they ought to be fairly comfortably off: 'Don't forget to let me know any time a little money would come in handy.' As Pasley, in the true language of a historian wd. say if he could live in Leeborough a while, 'A very good parallel.'

A great friend of mine, Baker of Wadham, has come up again after being down for a couple of terms. I often amuse myself by thinking how you and he would worry each other: not so much by direct antagonism as by being absolutely unable to understand one another. Have you ever met a person who talks habitually in metaphors and doesn't know that they are metaphors? He has certainly the perverseness and troublesomeness of speech which betoken greatness: his poems are like rooms full of exotic and insolent ornaments, but with nowhere to sit down. However, I introduced him only to lead up to an idea which may tickle you. Seated together in Wadham gardens (one of the few WILD gardens in Oxford, full of bluebells and old trees) during one of our rare glimpses of fine weather, I was talking to him about magic (of course: it's the burning subject) and the difficulty of getting enough data even to disbelieve: then it transpired that the secrets books are attainable only to the esoteric Masons. Now of course all the little P'daytas and Squeakies are fed on EXoteric faked rituals ('so they tell you').[54] But what a fine discourse on the black art we can have one of these days at Leeborough. 'Well the idea of any sane man – ' 'Pa!' (in a warning voice) 'Do you seriously mean Warren – ' 'Brother, here is this man himself initiated into the abominable rites of the most powerful magical association in existance etc. etc.' But the picture of M. L'Oiseau P. de T. as a wizard will remain. Some of the 'Horrid names' used in incantations (Shadai, Gogiol) seem made for his particular intonation.

The only strictly social function I have attended so far this term was tea with the Carlyles in their most charming house in Holywell. It is a place I greatly envy: long uneven rooms with beams in the ceiling and wide stone grates where a little kind of brazier sits in a deep cave of Dutch tiles. I need hardly say that in Oxford houses all such things were unearthed only fairly recently: the XVIII Cent. had very decently covered them over with plaster, 'substituting' as they wd. doubtless have said 'elegance and civility for Gothic rudeness'.

The principles on which tea fights are conducted at the Carlyles is this: you are given a seat by someone and when you have had a reasonable

54 He is referring to the fact that Albert Lewis was a member of the Freemasons.

time to get to the interesting part of the conversation, Mrs C., a rather fatuous woman, gets up and says, 'Mr Lewis, go and talk to Professor Smith' or 'Mr Wyllie, I think you know my daughter' or whatever it may be: then every single pair is shuffled. When you've got fairly settled, the same thing happens again: as some one said, it is like nothing so much as a game of cricket with nothing in it but an umpire calling 'over'. I had my longest 'spell' between Pasley and a lady whom the elder Miss C. describes as 'my little sister'. She is reading our School: she is a damned socialist and is contributing moneys to the miners: she laughs all the time: worst of all she is an optimist. Her face suggests an intensely anxious rabbit.

By the rule of the house of course Pasley and I had scarcely started trying to instil a little pessimism when she said, 'Oh, I must get Father to talk to you'. OVER! When that had subsided I recovered consciousness beside Dr Carlyle. He has every reason to be an optimist: a man who can hold a parish AND a College Chaplaincy (you remember Poynton's remark 'Dr Carlyle repeats as much of the service as he can remember') without being a Christian, and who has lived on the bounty of a Royal Foundation for the last century while being a Socialist, ought to be. All the same he's a dear old man with a thin brick red face and very straight white hair and never takes anything seriously. People talk about the Oxford manner and the Oxford life and the Oxford God-knows what else: as if the undergraduates had anything to do with it. Sitting beside this worthy priest I felt that it is really a thing we are quite outside: the real Oxford is a close corporation of jolly, untidy, lazy, good for nothing humorous old men, who have been electing their own successors ever since the world began and who intend to go on with it: they'll squeeze under the Revolution or leap over it somehow when it comes, don't you worry. When I think how little chance I have of ever fighting my way into that unassuming yet impregnable fortress, that modest unremovability, that provokingly intangible stone wall, I think of Keats's poison

> *'Brewed in monkish cell*
> *To thin the scarlet conclave of old men.'*[55]

Which reminds me, did you ever read Daudet's 'L'Immortel'? It is a novel about the Academie Francaise: if you like sheer cool premeditated

---

55 John Keats, *The Fall of Hyperion*, I, 49–50 (slightly misquoted).

insolence you should order this by the next mail – tho' perhaps I should warn you that it is only a couple of hours reading, and you may like books that last, on the world's end. However, it is a book that might have been written by Kirk – I will quote from the preface, which is a good testimony to its character – 'Les insinuations de quelques journaux voulant faire de *L'Immortel* l'expression d'une vulgaire cacune de candidat evincé, m'oligent a mettre en tête [de cette nouvelle édition] la lettre que j'ecrevais il y a cinq ans: "Je ne me presente pas, je ne me suis jamais presenté, je ne me presenterai jamais a L'Academie".'[56] I suppose this is for P'daytas 'Ah, he's a disappointed man you know. I await Moore's Abelard with interest: I have never read anything by him. I gather it is of incredible length.[57]

I mentioned Kirk just now, almost by accident. The resources of conversation are silenced before his death. Is there anything you could say which he wouldn't rise and denounce as 'the grossest absurdity'? Better to treat it in our own way and picture him addressing to Jehovah, when first presented, the famous Voltarian alexandrine

'Je soupçonne entre nous que vous n'existez pas'[58]

or telling Aristotle that his logic (this is a real Kirkian remark which he once made) 'has the distinction of never having been of the slightest use to any human being'. All this is only after all our interpretation of the Miltonic counsel

'[For] so to interpose a little ease
Let our frail thoughts dally with false surmise.'[59]

Today the 11th, little Jenkin[60] appeared after lunch and bade me go for a bike ride. As I had decided to work, I thought this would be an excellent opportunity of breaking my resolution. Jenkin has his own principles of

56 Alphonse Daudet, *l'Immortel, Moeurs parisiennes* (1888): 'The insinuations of some newspapers that wish to make the author of *L'Immortel* sound like a common rejected candidate voicing his feelings, force me to start [this new edition] with a letter I wrote [to *Le Figaro*] five years ago: "I am not a candidate to the Académie, I have never been one and never shall be."'
57 George Augustus Moore, *Heloïse and Abelard* (1921).
58 Voltaire: 'Between us, I suspect that you do not exist.'
59 Milton, *Lycidas*, 152.
60 A.K. Hamilton Jenkin.

push biking, the maxim being that 'where I go my machine can go'. He rides over moors and once carried it down a cliff in Cornwall. After stopping for a drop of the negus at Garsington in the same little pub whither I went (v. last letter) on Easter Monday, we rode along the top of a long hill where you look down into a good, woody English valley with the Chilterns, rather sleek and chalky – like greyhounds – on the horizon. It was a grey day with clouds in muddled perspective all round. Just as the first drops of rain began to fall, we found a young man looking as if he were going to be hanged, crossing a field. He turned out to be one Groves[61] of Univ., who is now gone down and incarcerated at a High Church Theological Seminary in the neighbouring village of Cuddesdon. 'He would have liked to ask us in to tea, but couldn't – indeed oughtn't to be talking to us – because they were having a QUIET DAY.' Ye gods: a lot of young men shut up together, all thinking about their souls! Isn't it awful?

After this it was quite fresh and lively to investigate an old wind mill near Wheatley: it has the sort of atmosphere we felt at Doagh and a little copper plate over the door with a figure of a bird on it. Under it was a word variously read by Jenkin and myself as County and Cointy. I do not know what this all was about. Jenkin keeps on picking up stones and telling you that it is iron here.

We rode over Shotover Hill: through sandy lanes with gorse on each side and passing occasional warm comfortable English barns and haystacks. Most attractive sign posts, 'Bridle path to Horsley' – a bridle path always sounds mysterious. And dozens of rabbits and whole bunches of bluebells: and a view far off between the two slopes of Forest Hill and the little house where the first Mrs Milton used to live. About the time he wrote L'Allegro and Il Penseroso he would often be riding over here from his home to court her – God help her!

While on the subject of Milton I should remark that I haven't had time yet to solve your puzzle out of Comus. Give me a hint as to whether the motto refers to (1) Sierra Leone or (2) yourself or (3) Diary writing. If to (1), perhaps you will prefer after a few months, 4 lines from Paradise Lost – about 'a universe of death, which God by curse/Created evil, for evil only good – where nature runs perverse and breeds all

61 Sidney John Selby Groves (1897–1970) was ordained in 1922. He was vicar of Sonning from 1942 to 1965 and a canon of Christ Church.

monstrous, all prodigious things etc.'[62] I say this because in your last letter you already seem to be finding it unattractive. You have omitted so far all reference to the human element – the 'other fellows': and I await with interest some account of your visit to H.M.S. Dwarf. What loathsome place to go for a walk in – that's one thing about the Daudel[63] (have you made any use of the same). I suppose snakes can't JUMP into it? Why didn't you try this Cambridge reptile with a whiff of grapeshot or a little of the cannister?

We had a visit this afternoon from Dr Macran.[64] He nearly fills up our little suburbanite garden and his loud, spasmodic Irish conversation can be heard by all the neighbours. (Our neighbours by the way include members of Univ.) Cranny, as we call this atheistical priest, was full of wonderful things that happened. He lives in the tiny village of Childrey, where, judging by his own appearance, he must keep a strange household. Here he recently had the adventure of entertaining compulsorily an old schoolfellow of his son's, who brought down some funny little touring company and insisted on Cranny taking a lorry to the nearest railway station to conduct the company of 14 members. He then proceeded to cover that small village with posters, explaining that the specimens of fine English comedy to be given shortly in the village hall, were 'under the patronage of Dr Macran': this, of course, being unauthorised. Cranny arrived the next evening to see the show: he found the same man conducting a furious quarrel with his leading comedian at the door, after which he fainted. And so on.

Here's another: a neighbouring clergyman while proceeding to Oxford, met a notable thievish charwoman of Childrey in the train. The parson (who must have been blind to the world) insisted on inviting this

---

62 Milton, *Paradise Lost*, II, 622–6:'Created evil, for evil only good; / Where all life dies, death lives, and Nature breeds, / Perverse, all monstrous, all prodigious things, / Abominable, unutterable, and worse.'

63 What Jack refers to as the 'Daudel' or 'Dawdle' was Warnie's motorcycle and sidecar.

64 The Rev. Dr Frederick Walker Macran, 'Cranny' (1866–1947) was an old friend of Mrs Moore and her brother, Dr John Askins. He was born in Ireland and took a BA from Trinity College, Dublin in 1886. After serving in a number of parishes in Co. Down, he moved to England and was the rector of Childrey from 1905 to 1923. He is the man Lewis refers to in *SBJ* XIII as 'an old, dirty, gabbling, tragic, Irish parson who had long since lost his faith but retained his living...All he wanted was the assurance that something he could call "himself" would, on almost any terms, last longer than his bodily life.' There is a good deal about him in *AMR*.

lady to tea somewhere in Oxford: after the meal he said, 'I'm feeling a little faint: you must give me your arm' and proceeded to walk her up and down the Corn telling her scandalous stories about Cranny. Strange mortals these knights of the cloth are! But you would have been amused if you had seen me seated by Cranny in the smoking room of the Union this morning, before an audience of amazed old men: he has 24 hours growth on his face, one trouser turned up and the other down: one tail of his coat was coming away from the main body and he had apparently failed in the arithmetic of his fly buttons. He expounded Thomas Aquinas, modernism, Stead's religious position, the views of a Univ. don called Emmet on the divinity of Christ, of which the point is that he was only a man but you can still apparently go on being a parson if you say 'We don't worship Jesus Christ, only the Christ THAT WAS in Jesus' – a beautiful distinction. Anyway to have heard scraps of our crack would have thought he was delivering 'a straight talk with boys' – however they must have heard it ALL, anyway, so I needn't worry what the effect of 'scraps' would have been.

23rd [May 1921]

Am just finishing this off. Thanks for your other letter: it is very sad to hear that you have not yet got mine, but I hope you will have by this. I suppose I needn't add anything by way of public news: even without papers the main things will reach you – that Egypt is rioting – that the relations and children of R.I.C.[65] men are being murdered in London by Sinn Fein – that the coal strike is still on – that the Japanese Prince has visited Oxford – that sharks and octopuses have appeared on the English coast for the first time within memory. This last is really the climax: a jelly fish was quite enough. Hoping to hear again soon.

yours,
Jack

---

65 Royal Irish Constabulary.

TO HIS FATHER (LP VI: 325–7):

[University College,
Oxford]
29 [May 1921]

My dear Papy,

Thank you very much for your wire and the letter: I am very glad to have been able to send you good news.[66] I had almost lost heart about the thing, it dragged on so long. Everyone has been very nice about it, particularly the Mugger who is delighted, and this ought to be of use to me later on. Some of my congratulations indeed have made me feel rather ashamed, coming from people whom I have been used to class generically as 'louts'. By louts I denote great beefy people unknown to me by name, men with too much money and athletic honour, who stand blocking up passages. If looks could kill I'm afraid they would often have been in danger as I shouldered my way through them. Now they have weighed in with polite remarks and gratified my vanity with the grand-paternal 'No. Does HE know ME?' I suppose the explanation is that in their view we have done so badly on the river that any success – even in so unimportant a field as letters – should be encouraged.

I have also had a letter from Blackwell offering to see me about publishing it, and have, as a formality, written to Heinemann's. In any case I am not sure what to do about that: I shall certainly not spend any money (nor allow you to, tho' I know you gladly would) on forcing it into print if publishers won't take the risk. I have always thought that a bad thing to do. Perhaps publication in some periodical might provide a compromise: it would remind people that I exist and yet it would not give too permanent a form to any opinion or argument that I may outgrow later on. At worst, if any one would like it, it would mean a five pound note and enable you and everyone else to read it decently printed instead of in type. If all these plans fall through, or if they are likely to take a long time, I will get another copy done and send it to you.

You must not expect too much: the trains of argument are rather dull and I am afraid this effect is not neutralised by anything more than adequacy in the form. No purple patches – hardly a faint blue. But I must drop the annoying habit of anticipating your judgement.

66 On 24 May the University announced that the Chancellor's Prize for an English Essay was won by C.S. Lewis, and Jack immediately informed his father of this by telegram. No copy of 'Optimism' survives in either the University or the Lewis family papers.

Before I stop egoising I must tell you one other fact. The 'proxime accessit' or next best was, as you have probably seen in the Times, a man called Brundrit[67] of Wadham. He is a frequent speaker in the Union and the editor of an 'advanced' magazine: that is to say he inclines to the Bolshevik left and doubtless managed to make Optimism a political subject. I am very glad to have been able to do even this much towards removing the common reproach that the revolutionaries here have all the brains – indeed it is generally true: the real Tories have nothing but beautiful voices and long banking accounts.

I am very sorry to hear about W's letters going astray. He has apparently not got mine. I can quite understand that letters mean a good deal at the world's end, and I have broken all precedent in giving him long screeds full of English scenery and atmosphere. Do you suppose that he has given us an insufficient address? Let me know if you hear anything that will throw light on the matter. I suppose this is the Government's return for increased rates of postage!

I have been reading the oddest book lately – Newman's 'Loss and Gain.'[68] I never knew that he had written a novel. As fiction or drama it is of course beneath contempt, but it has some real satirical humour. Do you know it? The picture of the then Oxford, with its ecclesiastical controversies etc., is something more remote from my experience whether real or imagined, than ancient Britain or modern Cathay.[69] I haven't heard anything about the prize – I think it is in money – not very much – and there are some books from College.

I too thought about Kirk. We are all old, disillusioned creatures now, and look back on the days of 'buns and coffee' through a long perspective and only seldom come out of our holes: the young men up from school in their immaculate clothes think we have come to clean the windows when they see us. It happens to everyone here. In your first year you drink your sherry and see people: after that your set narrows, you haunt the country lanes more than the High, and cease to play at being the undergraduate of

67 Daniel Fernley Brundrit, of Wadham College, took his BA in 1921.

68 John Henry Newman, *Loss and Gain: The Story of a Convert* (1848).

69 He was thinking of the grip of the Church of England on the University since the Reformation. Until 1854–6 no student could take a degree without subscribing to the Thirty-Nine Articles, the set of doctrinal formulae which define the Anglican Church's dogmatic relation to the controversies of the 16th century. It was not until 1871 that religious tests were no longer required of University officials.

fiction. 1919 seems further off than France at times. So I need not avail myself of your kindly suggestion – there will be no revelry by night.

your loving son,

Jack

TO HIS FATHER (LP VII: 14):

[University College,
Oxford]
Postmark: 17 June 1921

My dear Papy,

This is a bad business about the rabbit hole: and it is cold comfort to reflect that your misfortune is to be traced solely to your insatiable desire for the society of your fellow men. I know of few things, in a small way, more painful than a sprain. I hope it has not been so bad as to keep you awake at nights: one can stand any amount of discomfort during the day time, if only one can get sleep: it is after that the real rub comes.

It is not easy to know what to do about publishing my essay. I must begin by thanking you very heartily for your suggestion: if, after you have heard what I have to say and after you have read the essay – which I will try to send this or next week – you still feel the same, I will do as you wish. At the same time I think we should be wiser to let the matter alone. I can only find three motives for publishing anything – fame, money or reputation, in the narrower sense that may help ones career indirectly. I presume that in the present case the last of these three is the important one: and in this, I do not think that publication will be of any use. My essay itself, however treated, will soon be forgotten except by my own family and friends: THE FACT of my having won the prize will be recorded and may some day turn the balance in my favour. Several of our dons have advised me (with infinite degrees of tact which are funny to watch) not to go into print: many have regretted it in similar circumstances: whatever merits there are in prize compositions are much better kept to make the basis of a real book later on, when wider reading and fresh thought have given the chance to make better use of any really original idea you have blundered on. This seems to be the general view, and there is much to be said for it. I do not of course mean that publication would be an absolutely bad thing: but I already regret one or two things in Spirits in Bondage and (however different its sphere) there may be parts of Optimism, both in style and manner, which I shall have outgrown in a few years. I labour the matter because I want you to accept my point of view, if you do accept it, DE JURE and not DE FACTO. At all events it is only reasonable that you should see it yourself before you make any decision. I am tempted to alter one or two sentences (on which you will easily lay your finger) but shall restrain myself – and except for the translation of some quotations it will be as it went into action.

Cousin Mary and Kelsie[70] have been here for a few days – the former looking very aged since I last saw her. I gather she has been sent to England by medical advice. The worthy Graham[71] was with them: he does not approve of Oxford I think.

A friend of mine who is going down this term is starting schoolmastering on £330 a year: on the strength of 'being expected to get a first' – so that even if I had to mark time at that job for a year or two before getting a fellowship, it would not be so bad as it once was. My tutor knows of one or two places which will be vacant here next year: however, if I do well in schools, I have some hope of getting a berth forthwith. I only hope I shall not collapse just at the end into stupidity as many a better man has done.

I have [had] nothing from W. for a long time: hoping the ankle is well again by now.

your loving son,
Jack

TO HIS FATHER (LP VII: 20–1):

[University College,
Oxford]
Monday 27th [June 1921]

My dear Papy,

I ought perhaps to have written before this about a remarkable thing that has happened: but, as you will see when you have read this letter, I have had my full these last three days. The 'thing' is a cheque made out by you to me for £19-8-9 and dated May 1919, wh., greatly to my surprise, I have unearthed between the pages of an old manuscript

70 Cousin Mary, the reader may recall, is Lady Ewart of Glenmachan House, Belfast. Kelso, or 'Kelsie' is her daughter. See **The Ewart Family** in the Biographical Appendix.

71 Samuel Graham was the Ewart family's coachman and family friend.

book. What the legal and formal position may be in such a case I have no idea; as however the money was intended for me and as its loss at the time, tho' not noted INTELLECTUALLY by such a muddle head as myself, must have occasioned some discomfort and exhausted the remains of my army money, I have felt justified in sending it in. I should not of course have done so, even with a stranger, without letting him know. I hope you will agree with what I have done: if not, you must let me know.

So much for that: the event of last week was one of the unforeseen consequences of my winning Optimism. I had almost forgotten, if I had ever known, that 'prizemen' have to read portions of their compositions at our ceremony of the Encaenia.[72] Being of the troglodytic nature I have never before exerted myself so far as to assist at this show: but having been now compelled, I am glad.

It is a most curious business. We unhappy performers attend (tho' it is at noon) in caps, gowns, and FULL EVENING DRESS. It was held in the Sheldonian Theatre: I think Macaulay has a purple passage about 'the painted roof of the Sheldonian'[73] under which Charles held his last Parliament. During the long wait, while people trickled in, an organ (much too large for the building) gave a recital. The undergraduates and their guests sit round in the galleries: the 'floor' is occupied by the graduates en masse, standing at barriers in all their war paint. At noon the Vice Chancellor enters with his procession of 'Heads of Colleges, Doctors, Proctors, and Noblemen' – a very strange show they make, half splendid and half grotesque, for few don's faces are fit to bear up against the scarlet and blue and silver of their robes.

Then some 'back chat' in Latin from the Vice Chancellor's throne and the Public Orator led in the persons who were to receive honorary degrees: with the exception of Clemenceau and Keyes (the Zeebruge man), they were not well known to the world at large. Keyes was a very

72 The Encaenia is Oxford University's annual commemoration of founders and benefactors, at which honorary degrees are given and prize compositions recited.

73 Macaulay, *History of England*, vol. II, ch. viii, p. 446: 'When her Chancellor, the venerable Duke of Ormond, sate in his embroidered mantle on his throne under the painted ceiling of the Sheldonian theatre, surrounded by hundreds of graduates robed according to their rank, while the noblest youths of England were solemnly presented to him as candidates for academical honours, he made an appearance scarcely less regal than that which his master made in the Banqueting House of Whitehall.'

honest looking fellow and Clemenceau the tough, burly 'people's man' whom one expected: but what was beyond everything was the Canon of Notre Dame, a great theologian apparently, with some name like Raffitol.[74] Such a picture of a great priest with all the pale dignity that one had imagined, I never saw. If the words 'love at first sight' were not tied down to one kind of feeling only, I would almost use them to express the way this man attracted me. He would have appealed to you immensely.

After the honorary degrees, the Professor of Poetry[75] made an 'oration' in Latin, chiefly about colleagues who had died during the last year: this was my first experience of spoken Latin and I was pleased to find that I could follow and enjoy it. The performance of us prizemen was of course very small beer after all this. We had been instructed to read for about two minutes each: I had some difficulty in finding a short passage which would be intelligible by itself. I was, of course, nervous: I am also told that I was the first of our little band whom Clemenceau looked at: but as I do not know WITH WHAT EXPRESSION he looked, nor whether he speaks English, we must remain in doubt whether this was a compliment or not.

I have had a good lesson in modesty from thus seeing my fellow prize men. I was hardly prepared for such a collection of scrubby, beetle-like, bespectacled oddities: only one of them appeared to be a gentleman. Any I spoke to sounded very like fools, perhaps like Goldsmith, they 'writ like an angel and talked like poor Poll'.[76] It brings home to one how very little I know of Oxford: I am apt to regard my own set, which consists mainly of literary gents, with a smattering of political, musical and philosophical – as being central, normal, and representative. But step out of it, into the athletes on one side or the pale pot hunters on the other, and it is a strange planet.

---

74 Georges Clemenceau (1841–1929) was Prime Minister and Minister for War of France from 1917 to 1920. Sir Roger Keyes (1881–1929) was Admiral of the Fleet from 1920 to 1929 and the hero of Zeebrugge. The Canon of Notre-Dame de Paris was the Rt. Rev. Monseigneur Pierre Battifol (1861–1929), a distinguished church historian.

75 William Paton Ker (1855–1923), Fellow of All Souls' College, Oxford, and Quain Professor of English Language and Literature at the University of London, was the author of many books on English, Scottish and Scandinavian literature.

76 David Garrick's imaginary epitaph on Oliver Goldsmith.

I have hardly left room to answer your letter. As to 'a berth', that may all be put on one side for the present. I am sorry you didn't go and get yourself made an O.B.E.[77] or something when George-by-the-grace-of-God came to Belfast.[78] I suppose it is useless to hope for any fruit from his speech: from today's paper Ulster seems to be beating her big drum harder than ever, with a zeal excusable more than praiseworthy. You don't mention how the leg is getting on. I hope my MS will reach you next week.

your loving son,
Jack

P.S. By the bye – if you may answer such questions – is there a real difference between Esoteric and Exoteric Masonry: and have the magicians – I know some – any justification for associating all their stuff with the Masonic inner circle. I should be glad of a little hard facts. – J.

TO HIS BROTHER (LP VII: 24–9):

[28 Warneford Road,
Oxford]
July 1st [1921]

My dear W.,

I was delighted to get your letter this morning; for some reason it had been sent first to a non-existent address in Liverpool. I had deliberately written nothing to you since those two you mention: not that I was tired of the job, but because I did not feel disposed to go on posting into the void until I had some assurance that my effusions would reach you. That seemed a process too like prayer for my taste: as I once said to Baker – my mystical friend with the crowded poetry – the trouble about God is that he is like a person who never acknowledges one's letters and so, in time, one comes to the conclusion either that he does not exist or that you have got the address wrong. I admitted that it was of great moment: but what was the use of going on despatching fervent messages – say to Edinburgh – if they all came back through the dead letter office: nay more, if you couldn't even find Edinburgh on the map. His cryptic reply was that it would be almost worth going to Edinburgh to find out.

77 Officer (of the Order) of the British Empire.
78 King George V was in Belfast on 22 June to open the Parliament of Northern Ireland.

I am glad however that you have ceased to occupy such a divine position, and will do my best to continue: tho' I hope it won't be for fifteen months.

Here another term has blossomed and faded: that time moves has I believe been observed before. I have lived my usual life: a few lectures, until – as happens about half way through the term – I got tired of them all: work, meetings with friends, walks and rides, solitary or otherwise, and meetings of the Martlets. These birds by the by were all invited to dinner by the don Martlets a few weeks ago, and I again had the opportunity of peeping into the real Oxford: this time through the medium of a very excellent meal ('with wine' as Milton says with the air of a footnote) in cool, brown oaky rooms. I have been thinking of a formula for it all and decided on 'Glenmachan turned male and intellectualised' as fairly good.

The great event of MY term was of course 'Optimism'. I must thank you for your congratulations before going on: THEY were provoked by the event, but the consequences of it will move your ribaldry. 'Prizemen', the Statutes say, 'will read at the Encaenia portions of their exercises (I like that word) – their exercises chosen by the Professor of Poetry and the Public Orator.' Sounds dam' fine, doesn't it? But the Statutes omit to mention the very cream of the whole situation – namely that the prizemen will appear in full evening dress. Fancy me entering the Sheldonian at 11.30 a.m. on a fine June morning in a cap, gown, boiled shirt, pumps, white tie and tails. Of course it was a 'broiling' day as the P'daytabird would say, and of course, for mere decency I had to wear an overcoat.

However, I managed to make myself audible, I am told, and beyond nearly falling as I entered the rostrum, I escaped with success (They DO actually call it a rostrum, so that I was delighted: for the whole gallery of the Damerfesk[79] seemed to gaze at me, and the jarring ghosts of Big, Polonius and Arabudda to lend me countenance.)[80] This was really the fault of one not unlike our Arabudda – old Ker the professor of poetry, who, having earlier in the proceeding delivered his Latin oration,

79 The 'Damerfesk' is described in *SBJ* V as the 'common legislative assembly' of Boxen. Unlike that of England, it was not doomed to one fixed meeting place, but could meet anywhere the joint sovereigns chose.

80 Lord Big (a frog), Polonius Green (a parrot) and Sir Charles Arabudda (a fish) are characters from the world of 'Boxen' which Jack and Warnie created as boys. See note 10 to letter of [c. 1906].

decided to remain sitting in the rostrum instead of going back to his own stall. This (in the language of Marie Stopes)[81] 'made entry difficult if not impossible' for us prizemen: in my anxiety to avoid the burly professor, I stumbled over a raised step and nearly fell backwards. This must have appeared curiously enough to those who were on a level with, or higher than the rostrum: but the best effect of all was from the floor, from which, owing to the height of the front barrier and the big velvet cushion on it, I appeared simply to sink through a trap and rise again like a jack-in-the-box. However, I rallied my sang froid and bawled defiant remarks on the universe for two minutes. It is a good thing that the P'daytabird was not present or he would have been sorely put to it – especially if you had been beside him, giddy with laughter (You can imagine his asking me afterwards 'Did you do it to annoy me?').

I will send you a copy of my essay, since you ask for it, though I do not think it will be much in your line. Some of the insolent passages may amuse you: I hope you will like the way I dealt with the difficulty of 'God or no God'. To admit that person's existence would have upset my whole applecart: to deny it seemed inadvisable, on the off chance of there being a Christian among the examiners. I therefore adopted the more Kirkian alternative of proving – at any rate to my own satisfaction – that it 'really made no difference whatsoever' whether there was such a person or no. The second part of my essay you may use as a mild test whether you are ever likely to come to metaphysics or not. I look forward with some trepidation to discussing it at home: for his 'reading of the thing' will doubtless differ vastly from my writing of it.

Clemenceau took an honorary degree at this same ceremony and, tho' an imposing figure, suffered by contrast to the other two Frenchmen presented with him. There's no doubt that a butty, tho' a genius, remains a butty still. With him were Canon de Notre Dame Raffitol, a perfect picture of a great priest, and the Duc de Broglie.[82] From a great deal of snobbish reference, which sounded less vulgar in Latin, I gather he is of a great house. Do you know anything of it?

---

81 Marie Stopes (1880–1958) was an early sex reformer who devoted herself to birth control.

82 Louis-Victor, 7th Duc de Broglie (1892–1987), French physicist of a distinguished noble family, is best known for his research on quantum theory, and for his discovery of the wave nature of electrons. He was awarded the Nobel Prize for Physics in 1929.

I had not meant, in my other letters, to bring any serious charge against the Oxfordshire country. Tried by European standards it takes a lowish rank: but I am not such a fool as to deprecate any decent country now, and rather wrote in deprecation for fear you'd fancy I was 'writing up' a place [in] which you would remember no particular beauties. Of landscapes, as of people, one becomes more tolerant after one's twentieth year (which reminds me to congratulate you on your birthday and ask what age it makes you.[83] The rate at which we both advance towards a responsible age is indecent). We learn to look at them not IN THE FLAT as pictures to be seen, but IN DEPTH as things to be burrowed into. It is not merely a question of lines and colours but of smells, sounds and tastes as well: I often wonder if professional artists don't lose something of the real love of earth by seeing it in eye sensations exclusively?

From the house where we are now living there are few good walks, but several decent rides. Last Saturday we rode to Standlake. In the heat of the day – we are having drought here too – it was an heroic undertaking. Don't come down on me with any traveller's tale about 'what real heat is': I know with my intellect that it is much hotter in Africa, but put any honest man on a treeless road, uphill, in an English summer, and he can't really imagine anything is hotter. We had to begin by climbing the 'warm green muffled Cumnor hills':[84] a long pull, all on foot. You have a fine, but conventional view of Oxford as you look back: but we really enjoyed nothing until beyond Cumnor we sunk into the long grass by the side of the road under one of the deplorably rare trees and tackled our luncheon basket. A local pub supplied beer for me and lemonade for the children, and we had a basket of cherries. After this it became better and when after a long and pleasant decline through corkscrew lanes full of meadowsweet (that's the white, dusty stuff with a nice smell, you know) we reached Bablocke Hythe, it was quite delightful. Beyond this the country is very flat, but tree-y: full of villages rather too 'warm and muffled': they make you feel like a bumble bee that has got into damp cotton wool.

Our objective was a cottage in Standlake about the letting of which during the summer Mrs Moore was going to see. Here (tho' our purpose failed) we were rewarded by meeting a wonderful old woman, the owner,

---

83 Warnie turned 26 on 16 June.
84 Matthew Arnold, *The Scholar-Gipsy*, VII, 9.

Mrs Penfold, who talked of her husband as 'Penfold' without the Mr, just like a character in Jane Austen. This I am afraid you will hardly credit, but it is true all the same. Although flat and almost too blankety for a man to strike a match in, this country is much favoured of the Muse.

A few miles beyond us was Kelmscott, where Wm Morris lived and built that 'red house' whose brick nudity first defied the stucco traditions: from it, all the pretty villas of our day are directly descended. A little to our right at Stanton Harcourt (where Jenkins is always going to take me) is an old Manor with a tower room where Pope wrote his famous parody – which he called a translation – of the Iliad.[85] And of course, as you know, every mile smells of Arnold. We were not far from 'the Fyfield elm': we had 'crossed the stripling Thames'[86] and saw in the distance near Cumnor what I took for the 'plot of forest ground called Thessaly'.[87] Oh by the way I have found the ideally bad edition of Thyrsis and the Scholar Gipsy.[88] It was lying in Blackwells between grey boards with very black type: illustrated with photographs – one to almost every two stanzas. For 'what sedged brooks are Thames's tributaries'[89] you had a bed of rushes taken close, as you would for a plate in a natural history handbook, with a water rat in the middle: but best of all – there's a line somewhere I can't remember, about a 'battered merchant-man coming into port': for this we had two cutter racing yachts!! How are such things possible: and yet people will buy this and like it and be very proud of it. I am writing in our little strip of garden at five past ten and it is getting too dark to see: I will in and drink some of the eveningmilch.

The next time I am in town I will order the books you ask for. Cary's Dante (not the Inferno alone, but the whole Comedy) is published in the Everyman. You may remember I got it last Christmas in the Oxford edition which suffers from intolerably small print, but gains from having Flaxman's interesting designs.[90] It is supposed, as you know, to be one of the very few

85 Alexander Pope, *The Iliad*, 6 vols. (1715–20).

86 Arnold, *Scholar-Gypsy*, VIII, 4: 'Crossing the stripling Thames at Bab-lock-hithe'.

87 ibid., XII, 5: 'Above the forest-ground called Thessaly'.

88 Matthew Arnold, *The Oxford Poems of Matthew Arnold – 'The Scholar Gipsy' and 'Thyrsis' – illustrated...Portrait, Ordnance Map, and 76 photographs. By Henry W. Taunt* (Oxford: Henry W. Taunt & Co. [1909]).

89 Matthew Arnold, *Thyrsis* (1866), XI, 10.

90 *The Vision or Hell, Purgatory and Paradise of Dante Alighieri*, trans. H.F. Cary, with Introduction and Notes by E.G. Gardner (London: Everyman's Library, 1908); the same translation, illustrated by John Flaxman (London: Oxford University Press, 1910).

really good translations in existance. If you get sick of the Inferno, you will, on my advice, skip to the Purgatorio: about the last quarter of it is the heart of the whole book – tho' perhaps, as was unkindly said of the Good Friday music – it owes something to its surroundings: perhaps one has to go through the Inferno to appreciate the relief. Rochefocauld[91] I think can be got in the same series as my little volume of Voltaire's Contes.

I agree with your refusal to support George Moore in his blackmail.[92] The theory is that he publishes privately because he can't put up with modern print and paper: tho' I am sufficient of a kod myself to like beautiful type and to be discontented with the usual commercial sort, I think it a bad plan – because it rejects the real reader – who is always a poor man, and admits the parvenu who would buy 'culture'. Incidentally I have an unreasonable and purely A PRIORI belief that Geo. Moore is a bit of a quack. If I were more of a P'dayta I should invent some reasons – or what he wd. take to be reasons – for this idea, but I am ready to leave it admittedly unreasonable.

Since we last communicated, Cousin Mary and Kelsie have visited Oxford. I was summoned for my first audience after dinner on a breathless evening, threatening thunder. Dripping with sweat, I climbed up the stairs of the Mitre to the private room where they had for the nonce established their holy of holies. They had a fire going! They had just finished dinner: a few minutes later a substantial meal of tea, cakes, bread and butter was brought up. The two ladies did it ample justice. I was the only non-juror. The conversation was all of Ireland. The following thesis was put forward. (1) That there were no atrocities committed by the Crown forces. (2) That it was no wonder the Crown forces did ANYTHING considering what they had to put up with. (3) That in any case it was all the fault of the English government.

---

91 François, Duc de La Rochefoucauld, *Réflexions ou Sentences et Maximes Morales* (1665). Lewis was probably talking about *The Moral Maxims and Reflections of the Duc de La Rochefoucauld*, trans. G. Stanhope, with notes by G.H. Powell (1904).

92 George Augustus Moore (1852–1933), the Anglo-Irish novelist, two of whose best known works were *Esther Waters* (1894) and *Heloïse and Abelard* (1921). Jack and Warnie had been reading an article by Moore entitled 'A Communication to Book Collectors' in *The Times Literary Supplement* (10 March 1921), p. 157, in which Moore announces his plans to revive the art of printing. There was no blackmail in the formal sense. Jack was thinking of the difficulty Moore caused the publisher, William Heinemann, over publishing a special edition of *Esther Waters*.

Kelsie tells me that she met Turner[93] in town on the day of the elections: 'he's had one vote in Larne, and another in Belfast, and he'd have another before he went home'. The corruption appears to have been something that wd. make an Englishman's hair rise. I was told that the Sinn Feiners made a great attempt at intimidation. ME: 'But how could that be? I thought they were in a minority?' C.M.: 'Oh, well they thought they'd try anyway.' A story of a 'decent man' shooting Catholics outside one of the booths was advanced – apparently as a proof of Sinn Fein intimidation, and the whole wound up with the statement that 'English people didn't understand'.

Next day at lunch a woman living in N. Oxford and called Cousin Bessie[94] was present: conversation ran on purely family lines. 'And how are Hugh's boys?' – 'Ah, I'm afraid he's wild' – 'Oh my, what a pity' (from C.M.) – 'Of course SHE thought she was going to live at Warrenscourt – oh no, it wouldn't have done at all – poor Uncle Jack – everyone told him you know – and what about the boy – they say he's wild too.' The number of people who were disposed of in the single word 'wild' was very funny. I wonder what exactly it means? Are we wild do you think? Or tame? However the real final deluge of Glenmachonianism and the concerted movement of the whole symphony – came on Saturday evening when I dined alone with Kelsie. She always had her on days and her off days: and for many years now there have been times when I found têtes a têtes with her longer by mental measurement than the clock would vouch for. But on this occasion, honestly it was so boring that there was an air of insanity about it all: connected perhaps with the terrible heat and with that crowded tiny dining room at the Mitre. She never paused. Stories that I have heard from those same lips so often before followed one another: somebody was engaged and somebody else had broken off an engagement: the inevitable discussion of the Greeves's: had I heard about so and so: did I remember what Willie Jaffé had done on such and such an occasion?

---

93 Warnie provided the following information in LP VII: 27: 'Turner had formerly been the Glenmachan butler, and at this time was the Major Domo of the Olderfleet Hotel at Larne Harbour, which in fact I believe he owned. I was once shopping there when some of the Ewarts arrived at the hotel, driven of course by Graham. The latter greeted his former fellow servant in the following encouraging manner – "Well Turner, are ye not dead yet?"'

94 Warnie says of her in LP VII: 27: 'Presumably Bessie Geraldina Gundred [Warren], daughter of Rear Admiral J.B. Warren and Mary St Ledger, and therefore a first cousin of Lady Ewart's: Lady Ewart's mother, Charlotte Heard being a sister of the Admiral's.'

When we went up to the private room again, I could do no more. Wrapping my gown round her head to stifle her cries, I seized our cousin by the left ankle and precipitated her from the window. She flew out over the High in a great arc: the strolling butties and undergraduates looked up and shouted. But to my horror, just as she descended on one of the pinnacles of St Mary's spires, her dress developed a certain balloon like quality: instead of breaking into a thousand pieces she rose up on the giddy ledge and, just as I lost consciousness, I could hear her proclaim distinctly to the whole town 'I once saw an awfully funny thing happen to a girl at Aldershot – .' I can't quite swear to all this having happened exactly as it is here set down: but something like it must have taken place, since the undoubted fact remains that I did get away.

Good old Glenmachan with its faint, unmistakable smell: can't you hear the soft 'whoosh' of the rubber thing on the cloak room door and the 'tuff tuff' of the gas engine a little further off? And then one thinks of all sorts of things – long afternoons in the very old days when we were more like burglars than guests. Do you remember how one used to feel turning down that avenue homeward at about 5 o'c some summer's afternoon when there was a row on? Or at the last day of the holidays? By Jove it was a refuge for battered p.b[95] during their stormy youth. Certainly it has no more convinced disciple than myself: but it won't bear transplanting: move the Court to the Mitre and it is simply a joke as you would realise if you had seen it.

The steps by which you became a Miltonian are very interesting. Can one quite have done by labelling him a republican and a puritan? Puritanism was after all (in some of its exponents) a very different thing from modern 'dissent'. One cannot imagine Milton going about and asking people if they were saved: that intolerable pride is the direct opposite to sentimentalism. He really had the vices and virtues of the aristocracy – writing for 'fit audience tho' few'.[96] He always seems to look down on the vulgar from an almost archducal height. 'How charming is divine philosophy. Not harsh and crabbed as dull fools suppose.'[97] The DULL FOOLS are the ordinary mass of humanity, and though it has its ridiculous side, that deliberate decision of his, taken at my age 'to leave

95 'Pigieboties' or 'Piggiebottoms'.

96 Milton, *Paradise Lost*, VII, 31: 'and fit audience find, though few'.

97 Milton, *Comus*, 476.

something so written that posterity wd not willingly let it die'[98] takes a little doing. Paradise Regained I only read once: it is a bit too much for me. In it the Hebrew element finally gets the better of the classical and romantic ingredients. How can people be attracted to things Hebrew? However, old Kirk really summed up Milton when he said 'I would venture to assert that no human being ever called him Johnnie'.

By the way, on a ride the other day I passed an inn which the landlord had seen fit to call 'The Olde Air Balloon'. What a splendid name for the P'daytabird – who, by the way, is threatening to come here in a few days, thanks to the persistent endeavours of Uncle and Aunt Hamilton, backed, according to his account, by your advice. I wish you'd mind your own business, Master P. B. I have told him I've been moved out of College, so the business resolves itself into my presenting my abode here as ordinary digs – and keeping him out of them as much as may be. Luckily Pasley will be up for his viva and 'a friend sharing with me and working very hard' ought to be a sufficient deterrent. I think too, that if I walk the Old Air Balloon out here in the present insupportable heat, once will be enough for him. The temperature is over 90 in the shade: even the water at Parson's Pleasure has reached 71. Though still the only comfortable place (where I spend many a happy hour) this takes the real bite and shock out of a bathe.

One great beauty at present is that they are mowing the meadows on the far side, and as you splash along with your nose just above the dark brown water, you swim into the smell of hay. But to expiate over the delights of an English river would be really unkind to you. You will probably await my next with interest, in which you will hear of the success or failure of the paternal visit. What an anachronism he will be here: of course he may not come: I have suggested that 'if he really is going away, some little place to ourselves later on would be much more enjoyable than a Hamilton obbligato – perhaps N. Wales' – which as the hereditary cradle of true Pdaytism, ought to be a draw.

Thanks for the passage about H. Walpole and the Bozzy bird: its simply splendid. Try and let me hear again soon: I will write as soon as I am out of my present pother.

yrs,

Jack

Books and MSS following on in due course.

98 Milton, *The Reason of Church-Government*, Second Book (slightly misquoted).

TO ARTHUR GREEVES (W):

[University College
June 1921]

My dear Arthur,[99]

I am ashamed that this has been so long delayed. Now that you have been caught, though late, in the snares and cares of this wicked world you will be able to understand how the time rushes past, how you have scarcely time to notice a new week beginning before it is Saturday again, and thence at a single stride into the middle of the next. And always like a mountain piles up the list of things that you must put off, books you want to read, people to see, letters to write.

So many things have happened since we last met that it is no use to attempt chronology: I may as well begin with what is, I must admit, uppermost in my mind – this Chancellor's prize, that you ask about. It is set every year for the whole university and decided by seven judges chosen in rotation. The subject this year was 'Optimism'. Suitable to my family, as you probably guess! The actual prize is £20 in money (that is in strict secrecy – I don't want the fact disclosed at home until it has to be) but of course it is much more valuable as a means of self advertisement and may help me towards a job one of these days: it serves a little to mark you out from the crowd. I liked the subject and took a lot of trouble and am consequently very pleased. The essay may possibly be published – I don't know yet: in any case I don't think anyone at home will care much for it – its rather dull and metaphysical.

The other thing which I suppose you would be most interested to hear about will be my two visits to Yeats. I really cannot do this justice in the space of a letter, but will give you something to go on with. His house is in Broad Street: you go up a long staircase lined with pictures by Blake – chiefly the 'Book of Job' and the 'Paradise Lost' ones, which thus, en masse, have a somewhat diabolical appearance. The first time I came I found a priest called Father Martindale, his wife and a little man with a grey beard who never spoke, sitting with him. It was a very funny room: the light was supplied by candles, two of them in those 6-ft. candle-sticks that you see before the altar in some English churches. There were

99 Arthur gave up his idea of going to Oxford when he was permitted to enrol in the Slade School of Fine Art in London. He entered the Slade in January 1921 and took lessons three times a week until he left in December 1923. His address while in London was 66 Torrington Square and, later, 49 Leinster Gardens.

flame-coloured curtains, a great many pictures, and some strange foreign-looking ornaments that I can't describe. The company sat on very hard, straight, antique chairs: except Mrs Yeats who lay on a kind of very broad divan, with bright cushions, in the window. Yeats himself is a very big man – very tall, very fat and very broad: his face also gives one the impression of vast size. There would have been no mistaking which was THE man we had come to see, however many people had been in the room. Grey haired: about sixty years of age: clean shaven: glasses with a thick tape. His voice sounded rather French, I thought, at first, but the Irish shows through after a bit. I have seldom felt less at my ease before anyone than I did before him: I understand the Dr Johnson atmosphere for the first time – it was just like that, you know, we all sitting round, putting in judicious questions while the great man played with some old seals on his watch chain and talked.

The subjects of his talk, of course, were the very reverse of Johnsonian: it was all of magic and apparitions. That room and that voice would make you believe anything. He talks very well and not unlike his own printed prose: one sentence came almost directly out of 'Per Amica Silentia Lunae'.[100] The priest was guardedly sceptical but allowed himself to be argued down. One gets the impression (as I have sometimes got it from others) of a tremendous amount of this sort of thing going on all round us. Yeats – 'learnt magic from Bergson's sister' – 'for a long time I wondered what this dream meant till I came across some Hermetic students in London, who showed me a picture of the same thing I had seen' – 'ah yes – So-and-so: he went in for magic too, but his brain wasn't strong enough and he went mad' – 'at that time I was going through what are known as Lunar meditations etc, etc'. You'll think I'm inventing all this but it's really dead, sober truth. The last two or three years have taught me that all the things we used to like as mere fantasy are held as facts at this moment by lots of people in Europe: perhaps, however, you have run across it in town.

The second time I went to see Yeats, the talk ran more on literature: it also was very interesting, better in some ways than the other, but I haven't time to describe it – beyond recording the fact that he is an enthusiastic admirer of Morris prose romances: which shd. give us confidence.

100 W.B. Yeats, *Per Amica Silentia Lunae* (1918).

That constitutes about all my real news: otherwise it has been all the usual thing. I walk and ride out into the country, sometimes with the family, sometimes alone. I work: I wash up and water the peas and beans in our little garden: I try to write: I meet my friends and go to lectures. In other words I combine the life of an Oxford undergraduate with that of a country householder: a feat which I imagine is seldom performed. Such energies as I have left for general reading go almost entirely on poetry – and little enough of that.

If my letters fail by their rarity, yours tell me very little about yourself. I have had no news yet, save very indirect snippets, as to how you are getting on with the Slade. Have you met any interesting people? What is your day made up of ? I await with interest the results of this 're-arrangement of your face'. Have you become infected with futurism and do you intend to practice it on yourself? Will something of this sort be the result? Seriously, I hope you won't have too bad a time.

Like you, I am too hard up to think of leaving Oxford except for a compulsory tête-a-tête with Excellenz. There is an awful suggestion of his coming over to England on a motor tour with the Hamiltons, calling of course at Oxford. What on earth that might lead to I daren't even begin to imagine: my only consolation is that the difficulty of removing him from Little Lea will probably prove insurmountable.

Kelsie and Cousin Mary have been here for a few days & are going tomorrow: I think they intend to 'look you up' in London. Just between ourselves I have been bored to death with them: I came in a thunderously hot evening to find them sitting in a private room at the Mitre with a big fire blazing – then an ample meal of tea & cakes an hour after their dinner. Well I don't know: they have been very kind to me all my life and are in many ways excellent people: but just seeing them here suddenly, out of their setting, the main impression is of provincialism, narrow Ulster bigotry and a certain sleek unreality – so hardly will a rich woman enter into the Kingdom.

Try to let me have an answer to this & I'll try to answer *that*. Let me know *between what dates* you'll be at Bernagh: I must try to get my compulsory visit coinciding with you. The Minto sends her love and sympathies for the nursing home.

Yours
Jack

TO LEO BAKER (B):

28 Warneford Road,
Oxford.
[July 1921]

My dear Baker,

You must have almost given me up by now. I don't know how it has been. I have had a good deal of bothers of one sort and another, that have induced me, in my lazy way, to let work and with it things more obligatory, go their own way. First of all, thanks for the Gospel of Buddha:[101] in so far as it is a gospel, an exposition of ethics etc, it has not perhaps added much to what I knew of the subject, tho' it has been very pleasant reading. On the metaphysical presuppositions of Buddhism, it has given me new light: I did not realize, before, his denial of the Atman: that is very interesting. I cannot at present believe it – to me the Self, as really existing, seems involved in everything we think. No use to talk of 'a bundle of thoughts' etc for, as you know, I always have to ask 'who thinks?' Indeed Buddhism itself does not seem to make much use of the non-Atman doctrine, once it has been stated: and it is only by torture that the theory of re-birth is made compatible with it. Perhaps he has confused a moral truth with a metaphysical fallacy? One sees, of course, its inferiority to Christianity – at any rate as a creed for ordinary men: and though I sometimes feel that complete abnegation is the only real refuge, in my healthier moments I hope that there is something better. This minute I can pine for Nirvana, but when the sky clears I shall prefer something with more positive joy.

I wonder what is to be done about your question of Beauty? The popular theory among contemporaries is that Beauty is simply expression: as soon as a shape or a sound becomes a means by which I find the expression or 'objectification' of myself, it is beautiful. That is why (they say) that even things 'uncomely & broken' find their aesthetic value in the right place. Not satisfied with this view myself: for it makes it indifferent *what* is expressed. E.g. a face that expressed cruelty, stupidity or greed would be beautiful if only it expressed them thoroughly. They wd. probably say that greed etc are themselves 'inexpressive' of the *idea* of the individual – the thing he is tending to be, his potential completeness. To me it seems that a great many different emotions are united in the

101 Paul Carus, *The Gospel of Buddha According to Old Records* (1895).

perception of beauty: it may turn out to be not a simple thing but a result of unions. For one thing nearly all beautiful sights are to me chiefly important as *reminders* of other beautiful sights: without memory twould be a poor affair. The process presumably has a beginning but once going it grows like a snowball. Could it be that joy remembered ('Which now is sad because it has been sweet')[102] is a necessary element in Beauty? There is too, I think, a purely sensuous element: that such and such notes or tints (*in themselves* – not in their combinations) just happen to satisfy our nerves of hearing & sight – as certain foods satisfy those of tastes. This wd. be rather a condition of beauty, perhaps, than an element in it. One thing is plain, that the statements continually made about Beauty's being pure contemplation, stirring no impulse, being the antithesis of the practical or energizing side of us, are wrong. On the contrary beauty seems to me to be always an invitation of some sort & usually an invitation to we don't know what. A wood seen as 'picturesque' by a fool (who'd like a frame round it) may be purely contemplated: seen as 'beautiful' it seems rather to say 'come into me'. But this is getting away from your point – much more important – whether its objective & has a real right & wrong apart from our opinions. One always feels that it has. But I don't understand: it must be objective & yet how can it? Don't quite know what you mean about the organs of generation appearing beautiful: I never thought that.

Pasley is with us at present for his viva: he is very worn out and somewhat depressed – changing in the most curious way. He has got into spiritualism and is very keen. It was only the end of last term he said to me that he had no interest in immortality – 'with ordinary luck a man ought to have lived all there was in him to live by the time he reaches old age'. That's quite changed now & he finds life 'weary stale unprofitable'[103] if theres no immortality. See how they run!

I have been very busy – as I had been some time ago – writing a new & v. different version of the 'Foster' poem: it is being very troublesome & at present will not get itself finished but now & then I have great hopes of it. I am afraid this [is] rather a spidery letter. By the way I hope you are vastly improved before this in body & mind and have met good

102 Shelley, *Prometheus Unbound*, II, i, 9.

103 Shakespeare, *Hamlet*, I, ii, 133–4: 'How weary, stale, flat, and unprofitable / Seem to me all the uses of this world.'

adventure. I shall try to write again, and shall be greatly delighted to hear from you.

Yrs
C. S. Lewis

TO HIS FATHER (LP VII: 33):

University College,
Oxford
9th July [1921]

My dear Papy,

Many thanks for your letter and for 'this of' the cheque. It was no one's fault but my own that it was not sent in at the proper time: my brain seems to be a very poor engine for carrying the day to day facts of existance in my head.

The colonel seems to write to us both about the same time: and what you tell me of his letters would sometimes suggest that he kills two birds with one stone by means of carbon paper – if his ink did not disprove it. I am very glad, at last, to find that my letters are now reaching him. I think the introduction of monkeys at Leeborough would be a dangerous precedent. Tim, for one, would go off his head.

I am truly delighted to hear that you think it at last possible to weigh anchor from home: and there are certainly great attractions about your coming here. Is it safe – I am so afraid that any change may mean a change to the negative course of status quo – to suggest that if you can get away, we might utilise the opportunity better? Here of course there is the charm of much which I do not underrate because it is now family, and which would naturally have a peculiar interest for you. On the other hand there will be very little privacy. I have been moved out of College and you will probably find me sharing with a man who is up to his eyes in work. That means we can't spend much time on my own hearth: and, for the rest, I think we should prefer each other neat rather than with a permanent Hamilton soda (Hamilton paying the soda of course?). What do you say to a few weeks later on somewhere in Westmorland or N. Wales? We might 'do' a little bit of country by walks, rather than a big bit by motor. But let me know. It is in these directions that my own fancy inclines: the great thing is to GET AWAY – hither if you like, elsewhere if you like – but AWAY.

Have you seen a recent amusing illustration of Wilde's theory that nature copies art? that a real Captain Kettle has appeared in the bay of

Syracuse: complete even to the beard: and told the public prosecutor, the British Consul, and the Italian officers 'The minute any of you gentlemen sets foot on my deck, I'll brown her up'. By James!

I have been looking at Shaw's new books in the library once or twice. It seems 'curiouser and curiouser'[104] as Alice said. The drought and the heat wave here are something beyond description.

your loving son,
Jack

In the end, Mr Lewis decided to visit his son in Oxford, and he set off on one of his rare holidays, the last and the most enterprising he was ever to take. On 20 July he joined his brother-in-law and sister-in-law, Augustus and Anne Hamilton, and they travelled in their car across Wales. At Albert's request, the party spent their first night in Betws-y-Coed, Caernarvonshire, for it was here in 1894 that Albert and Flora spent the first part of their honeymoon. They then proceeded to Oxford where they were joined by Jack on 24 July. Together they toured much of southern England.

TO HIS BROTHER (LP VII: 49–58):

28 Warneford Road
Oxford
7 August [1921]

My dear W.,

You heard in my last letter of the consternation into which our little household was thrown by the threatened and hardly precedented migration of the P'daytabird. I have so much history to record that I must bustle on from that point. By rights I should tell you of all the preparations that were made: how Pasley came up at a whistle, like the faithful comrade in arms he is, to be the man who was digging with me and to 'lend artistic verisimilitude':[105] how the little back room was dressed up in the semblance of an undergraduate's digs, where women never set foot. But the story would be too long. The gods spared me the

104 Carroll, *Alice's Adventures in Wonderland*, ch. 2.

105 Gilbert and Sullivan, *The Mikado*, Act II. Pooh says: 'Merely corroborative detail, intended to give artistic verisimilitude to an otherwise bald and unconvincing narrative.' It is repeated in the letter of 28 May 1923.

need of this Palais Royal farce with its uneasy tendency to degenerate into something more like Grand Guignol.[106]

It so worked out that the Irish party only stopt at Oxford for their midday eating and then took me with them for a week. My compulsory holiday took me through so much good country and supplied me with such a rare crop of P'daytisms that it gives me really too much epic matter to write about. I shall try to give you any information that may interest you as prospective pilot of the Dawdle through the same parts: but of course you must not take it for as accurate as Michelin.

The first and by far the funniest piece of scenery I saw was my first glimpse of the Old Air Balloon himself, outside the Clarendon in Cornmarket. You've no idea how odd he looked, almost a bit shrunk: pacing along with that expression peculiar to him on a holiday – the eyebrows half way up his forehead. I was very warmly greeted by all; and with the exception of Aunt Annie, we took a short stroll before lunch. I was in a great flutter for fear of meeting some fool who might out with any irrelevance, but everything passed off well.

I learned that he found the heat intolerable, that he had not slept a wink since he left home, that he had a feather bed last night at Worcester – which Uncle Hamilton thought a great joke. He seemed dazed by his surroundings and showed no disposition to go and see my rooms, tho' he observed that College had 'treated me very shabbily as they distinctly mentioned free rooms as one of the privileges of scholars' – a statute by the by completely unknown at Oxford, however familiar at Leeborough. We lunched heavily at the Clarendon: I succeeded in getting some cold meats (suitable to a shade temperature of near 90) in spite of the frequently advanced proposition that it would be 'better' (how or why?) for us 'all to have the table d'hote'.

We addressed ourselves to the road as soon as the meal was over.[107]

---

106 The Grand Guignol was a type of English theatre which made its appearance in Britain in 1908 and which has appeared from time to time ever since. It specialized in short, one-act horror plays. There was for a time an English company which called itself 'Grand Grignol'. Both took their name from the Théâtre du Grand Grignol which operated in Montmartre during the 19th century and which specialized in short plays of violence, murder, rape, ghostly apparitions and suicide.

107 In his letter to Warnie of 22 August Mr Lewis wrote: 'Shortly after our arrival, the "Lad" drifted in with a few belongings in a borrowed handbag. He looked a bit washed out, but was in great spirits. After a capital lunch we started out again. I had not much time in Oxford...I did not see the river or Univ. "It" seemed a bit shy of the role of showman and of course I did not press for more than he offered' (LP VII: 73).

Uncle Hamilton's car is a 4-seater Wolsley: I have forgotten the horse power. It is pale grey and wears a light hood. Our direction was South and West, so we ran out over Folly Bridge and towards Berkshire, thro' pleasant but tame wooded country. The weather was oppressively hot, even in an open car which our uncle keeps almost permanently over thirty-five miles an hour: when you dropped to twenty at a turn or a village a stifling heat leaps up round you at once. This first run was almost the only one where Excellency sat behind me, and it was about half an hour south of Oxford that he made his first mot, and one of the best of his life, by asking 'Are we IN CORNWALL YET?' Honest Injun, he did!

I don't know if you have a map with you: we drove by Nailsworth, Cirencester, Tetbury (I think) to Malmesbury ('MAWMSbury, Gussie' from the O.A.B.) where we hoped to lie. The people here have a very barbarous, uncivil custom of closing hotels, even to resident visitors, on a Sunday – this being Sunday. In this quandary various proposals were raised: the P'daytabird was in favour of going on to Bath and going to the largest hotel there – being reduced to a painful uneasiness when we told him that he could get supper, not dinner, of a Sunday evening in these small towns. Here and elsewhere through the tour Uncle H. displayed great skill in his family tactics of amusing all parties with a frivolous appearance of a discussion while he was preparing his own plans.

It ended by our pushing on to a place called Chippenham, which we made about five o'clock, and, liking the house where we had tea, we took rooms for the night. Aunt A. and I were sent to look at them, and the O.A.B., despite of all his pother of the feather bed overnight refused (of course) to look at them. 'If they satisfy you, Annie, they'll satisfy me.' Chippenham is one of (I suppose) a thousand English towns that one has never heard of, but once having seen, remembers kindly. It is perhaps about the size of Wrexham, but as different as the south from the north. Here are quiet streets with nice old ivied houses, at a strange variety of levels, so that you can look into their gardens, with a little river running through them, and very fine trees. These streets widen occasionally into what are called squares, being, after the manner of English country towns, any other shape in Euclid rather than a square.

Our hotel was very comfortable and nearly empty. After dinner of course we 'strolled'. I had some Leeburian talk with the O.A.B. and afterwards some, of another sort, with our uncle – about God: a monstrous unlikely subject under such conditions. He finds the proof of intelligible work, of a mind something like his own in the universe, because the universe does after all work: it is not all higgledy piggledy. The conversation was perhaps not worth saving, but he has great merits as a talker: he has many gaps in his thinking, but it is all absolutely his own – he never takes anything over. If he covers familiar ground he still uses maps of his own making.

I found him a wonderful antidote to the P'daytabird: the latter was made happily miserable by a Salvation Army band which played the Dead March from Saul up and down the streets – why I don't know. When we got back to our hotel we sat for a time in the dark hall on a very comfortable sort of benching, and the O.A.B. offered us drinks.

Uncle H. wd have some beer and so would I. O.A.B. (in his 'desperate' voice): 'I'll have a bottle of soda water. Here! Waitress: two half pints of bitter beer and a bottle of soda water – (pause) – and if you'd just put a little Scotch whiskey in it.' (The waitress goes and returns.) 'Here you are Gussie. Is that my soda water?' Waitress: 'Yes sir – with the whiskey in it.' O.A.B.: 'Hm'h.' (Roars of laughter from Uncle H.) This was truly in our best manner, wasn't it?

The next morning I was early astir, after an excellent night and a bath, to buy some aspirin surreptitiously at the nearest chemist's, having had a headache the night before but I never used it again. What is pleasanter than a hotel breakfast in a strange town – porridge, crisp fried fish, and an ample plinth? I have never outgrown the child's belief that food grows better with every mile further from our usual table (except tea, which I can never get good outside my Oxford residentiary).

On this second day I had a typed itinerary to keep me right: the Oxford journey, being unrehearsed, was not on it. In our seats at about ten. We drove through a hilly country, the weather being a little cooler, by Bath, Farrington Gurney and Chewton Mendip to Wells. The landscape has everything, tho' on a small scale: rocks, hills, woods and water. Chiefly you run along the sides of winding valleys. The villages and their churches are very pleasant.

At Wells I distinguished myself in a way to make you laugh: (should I remind you that it is the Cathedral city of the diocese of Bath and Wells?) We were not quite certain of our whereabouts, and seeing a military looking old gentleman standing on the pavement, I lean out and shout 'What's this place, sir?' M.O.G. (in a tone of thunder) 'The City of

Wells!' A minute later an irreverent little boy jerked a finger at the M.O.G. and informed us 'E's the Mayor'.

The whole street seemed to be in laughter. As Uncle H. said, it must have been the word 'place' which stuck in his gorge: we should have asked 'What great city are we now approaching?' I profited however by this lesson, and after Uncle H. had given me an itinerary and a look at the maps he had I steered our course very satisfactorily. The P'daytabird only advanced so far as to get hold of the Michelin every day and look up hotels: usually he looked up some place HE thought suitable to lie at: very often it was wrong – once or twice it was a place we had stopped at the night before.

We lunched at Wells after seeing the Cathedral. I do not know whether such things come into your horizon: I at any rate am no architect and not much more of an antiquarian. Strangely enough it was Uncle H. with his engineering more than the O.A.B. with his churchmanship that helped me to appreciate them: he taught me to look at the single endless line of the aisle, with every pillar showing at once the strain and the meeting of the strain (like a ships frame work inverted): it certainly is wonderfully SATISFYING to look at. The pleasure one gets is like that from rhyme – a need, and the answer of it following so quickly, that they make a single sensation. So now I understand the old law in architecture 'No weight without a support, and no support without an adequate weight'. For the rest, Wells is particularly rich in a wilderness of cloisters all round the Cathedral where one can cut the cold and quiet with a knife. There is a fine castle with the only real drawbridge I ever saw, just across the Close.[108]

We lunched pretty well in this city (I daren't call it a town) and were on the road by two. Henceforward the P'daytabird nearly always took the front seat since this seemed to please him. We ran through Westbury, Cheddar ('Are we in Cheshire, Gussie?' asked the Balloon), Axbridge, Highbridge, Bridgewater etc., into Somerset. All this was country I knew (towards the end), having stayed twice in the village of Old Cleeve: for this reason I had been able to name Dunster to Uncle H. as a likely stopping place. I had at first been rather troubled lest my apparent knowledge of the place should lead to long and tedious questioning from the

108 He means the Bishop's Palace, separated from the Cathedral by a moat. He refers to it again in his letter of 21 October 1925.

P'daytabird: but I found him advancing from his own resources that I had got to know it while stationed at Plymouth ('They're both in Devonshire aren't they?') – and did not pursue the subject.

Here it begins to be very beautiful. Through the village of Nether Stowey we climbed up through the Quantocks: they are a tremendous barrier of moor, with the most wonderful valleys, called 'combes', running up them. From the high ground we looked down into the last valley in Somerset – a little piece of ground that I love as well as any I have ever walked in. On your right is the Bristol Channel with the faint line of the Welsh coast beyond it. Ahead are the enormous hills of [the] Devonshire border, the beginnings of Exmoor, with Minehead just this side of them where they go down to the water. On the left are the lower moors, known as the Black Hills, and all between the pleasantest green country with no end of red iron streams, orchards, thatched villages and buried lanes that wind up the hills in leafy cuttings.

I pointed the Welsh coast out to the O.A.B. He replied, 'Ah, the thing's got twisted. It ought to be round to our left.' How I should like to draw a P'daytamap of England! It was a curious sensation for me to scoot down the Quantocks into Williton and on through Washford, passing at forty miles an hour through country that I had often walked.

We made Dunster at about 4 o'clock, and had our first engine trouble just as we drew up at the Luttrell Arms: my ignorance reduces me to saying that it 'was the gear jammed somehow'. Later on you may be able to gather what was really the matter. Uncle H. treated the business with admirable sang froid: his faculty of never being ruffled is a great virtue in a companion, and if life was confined to this kind of intercourse I really think it would cover all his other sins. The O.A.B. insisted on standing by with an expression like a pirate flag, making irritating suggestions: I made one or two attempts to remove him, in sympathy with our uncle, but of course they were unsuccessful. Later on he discussed the situation with me in private. I remarked that Uncle Gussie took it very well. O.A.B.: 'Ah Jacks, you don't know the fellow as I do. Making a mess of things like this just hits him on his sore point: he's as vain as a peacock. He's just fuming under the surface. That's why I waited: just to smooth things over'. Why by the way is any misfortune that happens to anyone but himself always described in P'daytesque as the sufferer's 'having made a mess of something'? It was finally arranged to have the car towed into Minehead, about two miles further on, where there is a well appointed garage: Uncle Hamilton was afraid that he would have to get a new part from Birmingham: the P'daytabird was strongly in favour of taking a 'day of rest tomorrow'.

For the present, however, we could do nothing but wait: and it was fortunately in the most delightful place. One of the many mountain valleys that I mentioned before ends in a small wooded hill attached to the main mountain by a sort of isthmus. The little hill is crowned by Dunster Castle: the village of Dunster winds up the isthmus, consisting chiefly of a very broad lazy street with old houses. The Luttrell Arms itself is a sixteenth-century building with embrasures for musketry fire on either side of the porch. Just opposite its door is a curious octagonal erection with a tiled roof, used I suppose for market purposes in wet weather. It was 'pierced by a ball' from the Castle during the Civil Wars. I remarked that this gave one a visible specimen of the trajectory of the old cannon: to which Uncle Hamilton very shrewdly replied that unless one knew whether it was AIMED at the thing or not, it told one nothing.

I am afraid that from my description this may sound a typical guide book village: as a matter of fact there is nothing really curious enough in it to attract the tourist, and it is more completely tucked away than anywhere. Wherever you look, through every V left by two meeting gables, you see the hills, so close that they seem to go straight up and the rare paths in the heather look perpendicular: it gives one a great sense of snugness. Only from the little garden at the back of the hotel do you get an unexpected view across to the cliffs by Watchet and the Bristol Channel. Nobody talks loud, nobody walks fast, rooms are deep and shady, chairs have their backs well broken so that you can't sit down without an 'Ah!', hotels are never crowded at Dunster. It has a personality as definite as, though antithetical to, Doagh. It has changed hands only once; from the De Mohuns to the Luttrells in almost mediaeval times. It's off the main road: nobody goes there: when I saw the car towed off to Minehead I had a notion that nobody ever leaves it either. Oh what a place for a soak – but not for a 'day of rest' with the P'daytabird. After an excellent dinner we strolled: Aunt Annie and I both climbed the nearest ridge – a very stiff scramble – and left the uncles behind, being rewarded with a fine view over Exmoor and the Channel: then, after the evening beer in the little garden, to bed.

Next morning was very warm again: the male section of the party – one of them most unwillingly, to wit myself – walked to Minehead to see if the car was done: the mechanic thought it would be quite alright. We drove it back and decided to take the road after lunch. The P'daytabird was now quite in love with Dunster (which he called 'Dernster', 'Deemster' and other wierd names) and was still talking of a day of rest. I noticed that he was usually in love with somewhere we had left: after anything good he could hardly be brought to admit merits anywhere else, and when he was, the whole process began over again. Thus for the first days, if you ventured to praise anything, you were told it was not to be compared with the Welsh mountains: after that it was Dunster that blotted every other halt than Land's End: when I left him he had settled down to the view that 'none of these places come up to' Salisbury.

But to proceed, we ran very comfortably through Minehead and immediately began to climb, tho' still on tolerable surfaces. We passed one barrier and saw the first real Exmoor ahead – tremendous mountains and awful gradients: but we weren't there yet and dropped into Porlock, a very pleasant town at the bottom of the moors. All through Devon and Cornwall a valley and a town are synonymous: 'they all live in holes' as Uncle Gussie said. At Porlock we had [a] choice of two roads: one the 'old' road and the other a private venture which the local lord of the soil supports by a shilling toll.

We paid our toll and Uncle G. was just changing gear in preparation for the next appalling hill when it stuck again. Telephoned back to Minehead for the same mechanic. More buttoning up of coats and stiffening of upper lips as per previous night. Aunt Annie and I went and looked at the Church – we found it cooler both psychologically and physically – for the sun was terrific (none of your traveller's advice here!). Apparently there is a bar that fits into a hollow cylinder where the gear works: and the Wolseley people 'have a catch of' making everything a perfect fit: which means that everything is just a little too tight when the metal gets hot. The bar was reduced by sand paper when the relief car came, and we had no more trouble with it. We were held up there for some three-quarters of an hour, greatly to the annoyance of the other traffic: and the heat as we stood still made us very glad to be in motion again.

Our objective was now Lynmouth, a very short run which would be occupied entirely in climbing up and down over the next shoulder of Exmoor into the next hole. Let me here solemnly warn you against ever attempting this ride on the Dawdle. The toll road is generally detestable in surface and hardly anywhere – after the first hundred yards – broad enough for two cars to pass: it ascends at a gradient which is habitually worse than Broadway hill and which seems all but impossible, especially at the inner corners of the twenty odd hairpin bends by which it reaches the top. The humourist who owns it has also left it without any kind of barrier at the outside, and everywhere the banking is all wrong.

I must confess that mountain scenery is often seen most impressively when I for one wd be least ready to enjoy it. To look back as you attack an almost perpendicular corner, down an enormous cliff: to see other hills piled up on the far side of the gorge and, in their unusual perspective from such a position, giving the whole scene a gauchmaresque appearance: to look forward at the same moment and see the road getting even worse ahead to the next bend: to remember that the cheery man from the garage told us that a car backed over into the sea further along this road a few days ago: to wonder what exactly you'd do if one of those char-a-banc came down – on my life I had the wind up. We did reach the top somehow, where nature played another practical joke by plunging us into a cold winter's day with a misting rain. It was fine here all the same: an enormous stretch of moor all round you, and a car going all out over a single road, which was now straight if it was rough. It reminded me of the opening chapter of Meriman's 'Sowers'. The descent from this into the next hole was even worse than the ascent. You just wind down the cliff edge on a road about seven ft wide, which touches, at times, the pleasant gradient of 1/4½. That's not my own conjecture, it's from some guide book of Uncle H. The view over the sea below you wd be very fine – on foot.

We were exceedingly glad to drop into Lynmouth, a little town wedged into this next wooded gorge round the edge of a broad, brown, stony river: the heights all round are perhaps too beetling, and to live there permanently would be like living at the bottom of a well. Our hotel had a veranda above the river, where we sat very pleasantly after the four o'clock and watched a water rat manoeuvring from stone to stone.

I had to share a room with Excellency here, and I am not likely to forget the fact that it was the scene of a typical episode. We all walked out after dinner and up the road which we were to follow next day. Uncle Hamilton and I outstripped the others. It was a fine evening, delightfully cool and dewy. The road was good: it wound up the sides of big gorges that kept opening out of one and other into mysterious and chaotic landscape – 'forest on forest piled'. Looking back you saw the sea in the V shaped opening between the hills. Whenever you were still the sound of that stream under the trees many feet below and the EEe-ee of bats worked a kind of counterpoint on the general theme of silence. We walked faster: we talked most entertainingly. Finally we reached the top where these valleys, getting shallower and shallower, at last come out on the surface of the moor. We sat under a haystack enjoying the smell and the air of a good starless, moonless English country night.

We arrived back at the Hotel about eleven, and, incredible to relate, our Uncle gave me a drink. But when I reached my room, 'twas to be greeted by the O.A.B. in shirt and 'drawers' with the apostrophe 'Jacks, why did you do it?' How much real nervousness, how much pique and desire for drama went, and in what proportions, to making up a scene at once ridiculous and unpleasant, I cannot say. But the sound of the stream under our window drowned the puffings and blowings of the O.A.B. In fairness I should record how earlier that day, P'daytism had blossomed into something like grandeur: which it reaches at times, because of rather than in spite of its absurdity. After arriving there had been some discussion as to which hotel we should lie in. Aunt Annie suggested that the one we finally chose was rather too big. O.A.B.: 'IT'S NO BIGGER THAN WE ARE.' If only he had the right, no one could quarrel with his power to assume the grand manner.

I find that I have very few distinct images left of the next day's run, but I know that it was wild and beautiful. From this [point] onwards all the roads are bad. We ate Mittagessen at Clovelly. It carried the West Country tradition of living in holes to its logical conclusion, consisting simply of a stairway some 250 yards long with whitewashed houses on each side, ending in a cove and a jetty. The local tramway consists of a dozen well cared for donkeys on which lazy people travel up and down: goods are carried or trailed in a kind of wooden sledge. The bump bump from step to step is one of the most characteristic sounds of the place. Commercial enterprise has made the place convenient as a halt, for there are several eating places varying from the trimly modest and artificially rural where you can get galantines, salad and wines, to the frankly 'vulgar, easy, and therefore disgusting' where you can get – I suppose – mutton pies and brandy balls.

The O.A.B. strongly disapproved of going down to the cove before lunch, or indeed afterward over that infinite staircase: and it certainly was a very slippery and tedious journey of which you could say in Miltonic phrase

'Each stair mysteriously was meant, *nor stood*
There always'[109] – *where one's foot expected it.*

Arrived at the beach, he sternly refused the unanimous advice of his companions to facilitate his ascent by mounting one of the donkeys. Doubtless because he thought it unbecoming to his dignity: we continued to press him, for precisely the same reason: but he would not. After a hearty lunch, we proceeded.

This day we passed into Cornwall. I have always imagined Cornwall a place of rocky heights and gulfs. At first I was very disappointed: for, to be candid, it is so like County Down or parts of Antrim that it felt uncanny. The same absence of bright colours, the same cottages, the same sloping, somewhat bare hills, grey rather than green. The only thing that disturbs the illusion is the continual engine houses of the tin and copper mines: they are like this,[110] some in use and more half decayed. I can hardly remember a landscape which had not a dozen of these silhouetted on the horizon: they rather increase the general celtic dreariness and 'oddness' (you know what I mean) which bring it so close at times to our own country – a thing by the by far more insidious than the sensuous idleness of richer scenery. Are any 'flower coloured fingers' of the tropics half so numbing as the tepid morsels of putty that such places 'put down into your brain'?

The hills never rise into mountains, but are heaped together like eggs as far as the eye can reach, and the road winds on and on between them. The gates are coming off their hinges: the loose stones that divide the fields are all getting scattered. 'They'll do rightly – ach, never bother your head.' Then every little while you drop on one of the mining settlements: a valley probably, not unlike the back areas in France, splashed with great dirty pools and ringed round with enormous conical piles of shingle: and narrow gauge railways threading in and out like fussing insects among the debris. Why does a metal mine have such a glamour and a coal mine not?

The show parts of Cornwall – the parts one has read about – are all on the coast. We lay this night at Tintagel, storied name. There is a generally diffused belief that this place is connected with King Arthur: so far

109 Milton, *Paradise Lost*, III, 516–17.
110 He included an illustration in the original letter.

as I know from Malory, Layamon and Geoffrey of Monmouth, it is not:[111] it is really the seat of King Mark and the Tristram story. This has not however deterred some wretch, hated by the muse, from erecting an enormous hotel on the very edge of the cliff, built in toy Gothic, and calling it the King Arthur's Hotel. The interior walls are made of cement with lines stamped on them to represent stone. They are profusely illustrated with toy armour from Birmingham: a Highland target, suitable for Macbeth, jostles a reproduction of late Tudor steel plate and is lucky to escape a Cromwellian helmet for its next door neighbour. In the centre of the lounge, with the *Sketch* and *Tatler* lying on it, is – of course – THE Round Table. Ye Gods!! Even the names of the Knights are written on it. Then there are antique chairs – on which very naturally we find the monogram K. A. stamped.

I have not yet exhausted the horrors of the place: I was glad to see a book case in the lounge. All the books were uniformly bound, and I was surprised to see such unlikely titbits as the Ethics of Aristotle and the works of the Persian epic poet Firdausi. I solved the mystery by finding out that they were a uniform series of Lubbock's HUNDRED BEST BOOKS!!![112] How I abominate such culture for the many, such tastes ready made, such standardization of the brain. To substitute for the infinite wandering of the true reader thro' the byways of the country he discovers, a char-a-banc tour. This whole place infuriated me.

But the coast was wonderful: very like the Antrim coast only better: foreland after foreland stretching away on each side, and just in front of us, joined by a narrow ridge of rock and grass the huge Tintagel rock. There is a little sandy bay between it and the mainland. There are some remains of fortification on it, but not very old: nature has however so marked it for a stronghold that I could imagine its having been a fort almost immemorially. In the evening I extracted honey even from the hundred best books by reading an excellent play of Molière's. I cannot remember the title but it is the one from which the famous phrase 'Tu

---

111 Lewis is wrong here. Tintagel is given in Malory, Layamon and Geoffrey of Monmouth as the castle where King Uther Pendragon was wedded to Igraine, and where their son Arthur was born. It was subsequently the home of King Mark of Cornwall.

112 The choice of the hundred best books was made by the critic and biographer, Sir Percy Lubbock (1879–1965).

l'as voulu, Georges Dandin'[113] comes. Do you know him at all? We left Tintagel after breakfast. By the way it is of course pronounced Tingtagj-le: which was a sufficient reason for the P'daytabird's insisting on calling it TIntagEL, with a hard G. I find (like Bozzy) that 'I have preserved no record of the O.A.B.'s conversation during this period'.

We passed through a perfectly abominable town, Redruth. It was about here that a stinging rain, that might equally be described as a fast moving fog, attacked us. At Penzance we put up our side screens and excluded the view, but nothing would deter Uncle Hamilton from going on to Land's End: I indeed thoroughly agreed, but I was his only supporter. Of the last bit of England I saw nothing. Hot clothes began to steam under the screen and hood: outside there was only a genuinely celtic greyness: the road winds abominably and has no surface. My chief recollection is of Aunt Annie shouting 'Gus, don't run into that post!' We began to pass several hotels, nearly every one of which announced that it was the 'last hotel in England'. Some of them looked as if this was perfectly true. Our Uncle scorned them all and drove ahead till we reached the real end of the world where the road stops on a cliff outside the really last hotel.

It was pouring with rain and blowing a terrific gale. It is a place well worth seeing. The cliffs go down sheer, and one is so to speak in a salient. The same driving mist continued all the time we were there, clearing up for ten minute intervals with extraordinary suddenness every now and then. When this happens the blue suddenly leaps out of the grey and you see the clouds packing all along the cliff for miles, while a light house or some rocks about three and a half miles out turns up from nowhere. Indeed the appearance and disappearance of this place is what I most remembered. It has almost the regular phases of a revolving light: first the blank mist – then the outlines rather ghostly in it – then golden – then quite clear with hard outlines and waves breaking on it – then blurred again and so back into the fog. Watching it from behind the thick plate windows of the very snug hotel, I found there was something curiously soporific about it – this most 'debatable land' that comes and goes, as if it winked at you with confiding solemnity. Whenever the rain thinned we went out and climbed as near the cliffs as was safe and watched the enormous breakers.

---

113 *George Dandin, or le Mari Confonda*, is a 'comédie-ballet' by Molière first performed in 1667. Dandin, the hero of the comedy, is a tradesman who marries a nobleman's daughter and suffers many humiliations. His bitter refrain is, 'Vous l'avez voulu, George Dandin' ('You've got what you wanted, George Dandin').

We had – A big lacuna occurs here: some pages of journeying have been lost and you will perhaps be relieved to hear that I do not propose to rewrite them. Dartmoor and New Forest must remain unsung. Three more vignettes I give and then I will leave the tour.

The first is simply to record our monster run in one day from Lyndhurst in the New Forest, thro' Camberley, Maidenhead and Oxford to Warwick, including our only headlight voyage.

The second is a good P'daytism – or shall I report as Minister of Experimental Philology a new word for an old thing – shall a P'daytism be a Balloon play or Ballonenspeil? – which occurred at Warwick. Uncle Hamilton could get no cover for the car which had to spend the night – a threatening night, in an open yard. When I lamented this fact, the O.A.B. replied 'Ah well, the holiday's nearly over now'. This remark contains so many distinct trains of thought and pure P'dayta ethics that you may spend a wet afternoon in disentangling them.

My third – as the Acrostics say – is connected with a certain Cathedral city in the North Midlands where I found the masterpiece of comic or satiric statuary. It represents a little eighteenth-century gentleman with a toy sword. I cannot explain how cunningly a kind of simpering modesty is combined with a certain profound vanity in this figure. Perhaps the eyes looking down the nose and the smug smile have something to do with it – perhaps it is the stomach thrust forward or the conventionally statuesque pose of the feet, as if to support a figure of heroic proportions, and then at once belied by the stiff little doll to which they really belong. Or, on second thoughts, perhaps it owes something to the colossal figure on the other pedestal, older and less ingenious work, obviously meant to be the centre and obviously made into the fool of the piece by its compulsory second. At any rate the effect is too funny for laughter: real genius went to make it. Need I add that the town was Lichfield and that the statue bore the mystic name – BOSWELL.

From Lichfield I returned to Oxford by train:[114] I am going home in a few days, but you had better send your next as usual to Univ. I was

114 In a letter to Warnie of September 1921 Mr Lewis wrote of the conclusion of his holiday: 'At Lichfield I parted company with Jacks very sorrowfully. He returned to Oxford and we pursued our journey. We lunched that day at Shrewsbury, another nice old town, with one of the very best hotels I have been in. From there we headed north. We had tea at Llangollen whose attraction is a very fine river. We were back in Capel Curig [Wales] that night...We spent two nights at Capel Curig – descended from there on Birkenhead "and so home"' (LP VII: 87).

delighted with your letter and have much to say in answer which must at present wait. I liked particularly your description of the rains – I can see that. Just one word about Paradise Regained – surely the real reason for the shrinkage of Satan is the very proper one that since the great days of P. Lost, he has spent sixty centuries in the Miltonic Hell? It comes out in his great speech beginning 'Tis true – I am that spirit unfortunate.'[115] Thanks for the photo. I hope the various delights of the season have left you in peace. I enclose my essay.

yours,
Jack

TO HIS FATHER (LP VII: 74–5):

Oxford Union Society
[Oxford]
Aug. 22nd [1921]

My dear Papy,

I hope that by this time you have begun to recover from your holiday and that the exhaustion of resting has left you. I am glad that you had at last the opportunity to return again to your favourite tit bit of the Welsh mountains. Certainly we had a famous tour: it deserves to be commemorated as Johnson's was to the Hebrides, but I am unfit for the job and find my recollections already in confusion. The elements of enjoyment and hazardous adventure were so well mixed that I do not know whether we should be more thankful to have gone or safely to have returned. I at any rate have felt much the better for it.

I have been pretty busy since I came back; and unless I were to tell you of the Roman Emperors I have murdered or the antinomies of pure reason that I have digested, I do not know that I have any news – except of bills! ominous item for all parents. Several worthy men whose services I unavoidably used seem all to have remembered the fact at once. There was a dentist who stopped a tooth: some one else obliged with a new pair of shoes and repairs: there was also a pair of flannel trousers. I regret two white shirts, as I should have had them but I found I had only one from Leeborough and it was indelibly stained. I also have had to get some new socks: those made by poor Annie's husband went to holes at once. As the conclusion of the whole matter I hope you will not think it extravagant

115 Milton, *Paradise Regained*, I, 358.

if I ask you for £7.18.6. Clothes and such are not usually a heavy item of my expenditure.

I have not forgotten the Magdalen inscription and am making you out a facsimile: but think again of my 'Laus fortius irritare' – the praise of brave men is their irritation – ask Barton about that. I have no news from Warnie since I got back, nor from anyone else. The drought has finally broken up, and we are now enjoying cool and rain.

I wish you could hear all the nonsense that is talked here about politics. In the meantime, thanks once again, very heartily for our capital jaunt.

your loving son,
Jack

TO HIS FATHER (LP VII: 80–1):

Oxford.
Aug. 31st, 1921

My dear Papy,

'For this relief much thanks'[116] says Bernardo when he is bitter cold and not a mouse is stirring. Thanks very much indeed for the generous enclosure.

As you say, the change from society for which 'lively' would at times have been too mild an epithet, and from the constant variety of our moving seats to the routine of ordinary work, is one that we are rather acutely conscious of at first. I still feel that the real value of such a holiday is still to come – in the images and ideas which we have put down to mature in the cellarage of our brains, thence to come up with a continually improving banquet. Already the hills are getting higher, the grass greener, and the sea bluer than they really were: and, thanks to the deceptive working of happy memory, our poorest stopping places will become haunts of impossible pleasure and Epicurean repast.

As for myself, I do not propose, as you may be sure, to spend the whole vac. here. I will do what I can: but I must 'sit to my book' for a little while yet. The fault of our course here is that we get so little guidance and can never be sure that our efforts are directed exactly to the right points and in the right proportions. I suppose that is part of the education – part at any rate of the game.

---

116 Shakespeare, *Hamlet*, I, i, 8.

I expect you have heard from Warnie before this. I had a letter since my return, the first for a considerable time. I am sorry to hear that he has had a bad attack of boils, followed by prickly heat: but he seems better now and is in excellent spirits and reading Dante. The revolutions which Africa has produced in his literary polity are really amazing. I am still working whenever I have half an hour to spare, at my account for him of our journey. It would be amusing and WILL no doubt be amusing for him to compare the two versions. We shall differ in selection and (so confused does one get) even on matter of fact, where a map will often show both authorities equally wrong. Uncle Hamilton on the other hand would be able to give exact information about every stage and distance – but totally incapable of describing anything at all.

I have had a touch of neuralgia, occasioned as I believe, by getting some water into my ear when washing and failing to get it out again. People tell me this is impossible and even suggest that the pains could not be of the types and in the places where I described them. I am rather disposed to take the view 'D–am it Cole, she ought to know. She's sitting on it.' Otherwise, I am in excellent form and acquiring new energy and spirits, as I always do, from the first nip of cold which is already beginning to steal into the air.

I keep on hearing of 'battle, murder and sudden death'[117] in the streets of Belfast. How long is this to continue I wonder? To me peace is so obviously the good and the condition of all other goods that perhaps I do not sufficiently appreciate the motives of those, in any party, who wish to settle everything by shooting. I hope you are keeping well, and that you already wear your shrapnel helmet when traveling on a tram.

your loving son,
Jack

TO HIS FATHER (LP VII: 92–3):

[University College,
Oxford]
Sunday
Postmark: 25 October 1921

My dear Papy,

I must first acknowledge with many thanks the needful, of whose appearance a letter from Cox informs me. Beyond a rather difficult

117 *Book of Common Prayer*, the Litany.

thesis from Aunt Suffern that is all that has reached me from the outside world since my return. The change from summer into severe Oxford winter increases the sharp contrast of the two worlds. I find certain home figures, some of those who habit on the edges of our world, like Bob and John, very phantasmal after I have crossed the Irish Sea.[118] W. owes me a letter, but it does not come. I really have no news.

Days here pass in a kind of hurricane. I am at lectures all morning: none of them yet shows signs of being bad enough to drop. One steals hours from work to talk to ones friends, hurries to meet and hurries to go away. The 'adorable dreamer' as some cove once called this city is less like dreaming than anything I know. Perhaps it is the cold that gives people the extra speed I observe in the streets – or is it only the contrast with the infinite leisure of the Circular Road. I find that considerable interest attaches to the great adventure of having been in such a place as Belfast. It is a curious paradox that Other Irishmen report such complete quiet from Dublin. By the by I mentioned that yarn about a certain public figure and his double role (the one I heard on the boat) to an Irishman yesterday, and he said he had already heard it. So the rumour, however ridiculous, is wide spread.

My journey here, though not unpleasant, deserves to be remembered for the continual misinformation. They seem to work with half a dozen different time tables in England now. Indeed the disorganization of all the ordinary conveniences of life, the general thorough badness of everything from a Gold Flake[119] upwards, is what impressed me most in this year of grace.

I hope you are keeping well and that your Uncle Hamilton has taken you for another of his nice rides.

your loving son,
Jack

TO HIS FATHER (LP VII: 93–4):

Union Society,
Oxford
30th
Postmark: 30 November 1921

118 Jack had just returned from several weeks with his father at Little Lea.
119 Jack's favourite brand of cigarettes.

My dear Papy,

Very many thanks for your kind note of good wishes and for the enclosure. It's a dreadful age, isn't it? By next year however I hope you will be finished at long last with my education and that I shall be unloading for the benefit of an astonished world the cargo that I have been so long in taking aboard.

I have had a touch of flu'. At least I suppose it may be called flu' since anything of the cough and cold variety now goes by that name. Although it has not been severe it has taken some time to shake off – this must be my defence for not having written before. I have also been warned by Aunt Kitty[120] that I am soon to be invited to London to assist at the wedding of some cousin infinitely remote. Her name appears to be 'Fireryee' or something of that sort. (Aunt Kitty's writing is awful). Of course I shall not go – can't you see me. You will be glad to hear however that 'dear old Bob' has been with them to Tonbridge and 'has been SUCH a help in making arrangements and in ENTERTAINING THE YOUNG COUPLE'. Truly an excellent air at Tonbridge that can do such things with our Bob.

I am afraid that my weakness in yielding to the Colonel's request for a copy of Optimism has reduced the poor man to permanent silence. I must try to get some sort of letter off to him before Christmas. A dread portent has arisen above our horizon here – an immoralist, nihilist, determinist, fatalist. What are you to do with a man who denies absolutely everything? The joke is that he's an army officer on a course. He talks you blind and deaf. The more I see of him the clearer does my mental picture become of his brother officers en masse – imploring him to take advantage of a two years course at Oxford – or Cathay or the Moon.

It is very cold here, but that is alright once you are used to it. I hope you keep well. The alarums and excursions of which I read daily in the paper are coming unpleasantly near places which you cannot choose but frequent.

Always reflect that the man who omits any possible and reasonable caution is simply a fool. But 'Lord knows what disorders we shall fall into'. With many thanks again.

your loving son,
Jack

120 This is Mrs Kitty Robbins mentioned in note 87 to the letter of 27 May 1917.

1922

Warnie arrived at Little Lea on 7 April 1922, having been awarded a leave of six months.

TO HIS FATHER (LP VII: 129–30):

[University College]
May Day [1 May 1922]

My dear Papy,

Many thanks for your letter and also for the allowance which Cox have duly acknowledged. Also convey to the Maga Endoricana (that's scholarship) the thanks of the humblest of her servants: the rain of satisfaction has descended on the desert of appetite and the palate of enjoyment has signed the contract of marriage with the incarnation of perfect plumcakes, and the adamantine strength of sugar has been the Cadi. In the name of Allah (the compassionate, the all powerful) – 'thus far into the bowels of the cake have we dug down without impediment'. It has been praised of many and eaten of not a few, so if your unexpired portion is less than a ton, put it in your trench mortar and igniting the fuse, take cover and poop it in the direction of Oxford. With examinations in my head this at once leads to suggestions – curious the way the mind works – 'Trace the probable path of a plum cake projected from Strandtown to Oxford, noting any archeological or other etc.'

The news of Warnie's return is good and surprising. The news of his irreduced tissues is neither good nor surprising. But here is a good story for a tropical veteran. Coming the other day to a stream bridged by a single plank, I was just going to cross when, Lo, a khaki and black snake as long as my arm and as thick as the handle of a cricket bat. Yah! Where are the tropics now? It's my belief that this Sierra Leone business has been greatly exaggerated. As a matter of fact my snake was dead: it can't have been naturally as fat as that, but it would be accounted for by mortification. The colonel will tell you about dead 'balloon' horses in France.

I hope you will both believe my snake story and thereby show your originality, for no one else has. The popular theory is that it was a toy one, put there by little boys, and that the little boys were watching behind a hedge while I threw stones at it (à la Willie Jaffé) to see if it was dead.

In a country pub the other day I had a wonderful conversation with an old ranker who got a commission during the war and was at Drumshambo, Co. Leitrim: though sentenced to death twice by the I.R.A.,[1] he thinks the Irish 'very nice people' and rather inclines to the view that the English are to blame for most of the trouble. These old soldiers of fortune who have been everywhere are surely a unique and pleasing feature of our time? And does not his view – whether right or wrong – of the Irish question, illustrate the extraordinary fairness of the English masses. I should like to hear a French or a German Tommy after being in a similar situation.

It keeps very cold here, and mocks one with spring sunshine without heat. I am very busy, but very fit. I hope you have been reading about the Royal Commission on Oxford in the papers, and that the pundits are 'satisfied' with it. What the papers don't mention is that the Commission is composed entirely OF OXFORD MEN. However, Geddism is beginning to be felt in other ways. People who are trying for the Home Civil tell me there is not one vacancy this year and probably none next. Yet in the lower ranks it is full of conscientious objectors who got there during the war. The 'Grand Guignol' has been here, but I did not go. I hope you are well and in good form.

your loving son,
Jack

TO HIS FATHER (LP VII: 140–1):

[University College]
May 18th [1922]

My dear Papy,

Many thanks for your letter. Your news of a post at our back gate was, I must admit, rather a shock to the imagination when I first read it. I hope it will not 'draw the enemy's fire'. You will be in a position of the front area people in France, when they used to put up a notice for the benefit of Warnie's friends ET HOC GENUS OMNE, 'Don't raise a dust:

1 Irish Republican Army.

we live here, you don't'! Are you searched every morning on your way into town?

And now I want to talk about my plans. You will remember a talk we had when I was last at home. On that occasion I repeated to you a conversation which had taken place some time before between one of my tutors and myself. I had asked him for a testimonial, preparatory to giving my name to the employment agency. Instead of giving me one he advised me very earnestly not to take any job in a hurry: he said that if there was nothing for me in Oxford immediately after Greats, he was sure that there would be something later: that College would almost certainly continue my scholarship for another year if I chose to stay up and take another school, and that 'if I could possibly afford it' this was the course which he would like me to take. He ended with some complimentary remarks.

I was not particularly keen at the time about doing so: partly on your account, partly because I did not care to survive most of my contemporaries. At that time there seemed to be one or two things in view – a vacant fellowship at Lincoln, another at Magdalen. Soon however it 'transpired' (I know you love the word) that one of these was to lapse and the other be filled from its own college without open election. I thought of the Civil Service: but as my tutor says, 'There is no Civil Service now'. Thanks to the Geddes axe there will be none next.[2]

The advice of my first tutor was repeated by my other one: and with new points. The actual subjects of my own Greats school are a doubtful quantity at the moment: for no one quite knows what place classics and philosophy will hold in the educational world in a year's time. On the other hand the prestige of the Greats school is still enormous: so that what is wanted everywhere is a man who combines the general qualification which Greats is supposed to give, with the special qualifications of any other subjects. And English Literature is a 'rising' subject. Thus if I cd. take a First or even a Second in Greats, AND a first next year in English Literature, I should be in a very strong position indeed: and during the extra year I might reasonably hope to strengthen it further by adding some other University prize to my 'Optimism'.

---

2 Sir Eric Geddes (1875–1937) was from August 1921 to March 1922 chairman of the committee appointed by the Chancellor of the Exchequer to advise on all questions of national expenditure. In his report, published in *The Times* (10 May 1922), p. 18, he mentions the need to economize in education.

'While I yet pondered' came the news of a substantial alteration in the English Schools. That course had formerly included a great deal of philology and linguistic history and theory: these are now being thrown over and formed into a separate school, while what remains is simply literature in the ordinary sense – with the exception of learning to read a very few selected passages in Anglo-Saxon, which anyone can do in a month. In such a course, I should start knowing more on the subject than some do at the end: it ought to be a very easy proposition compared with Greats. All these considerations have tended to confirm what my tutor advised in the first place.

You may probably feel that a subject of this sort ought to be left for discussion by word of mouth: but, while I do not want to hurry you, my decision must be taken in the near future, as, if I stay up, I must apply to College for permission to do so and for the continuation of my scholarship; if not, I must beat up the agency at once. And after all, I do not know what discussion can do beyond repeating the same points over again. The facts – I hope my account is intelligible – naturally suggest all the pros and cons. I ought, in fairness, to say that I am pretty certain I can get a job of some sort as I am: but if it comes to schoolmastering, my inability to play games will count against me. Above all, I hope it is clear that in no case will Greats be wasted.

The point on which I naturally like to lean is that the pundits at Univ. apparently don't want me to leave Oxford. That is rather a loathsome remark for any man to make about himself – but no one overhears us, and it really is relevant. Now if, on all this, you feel that the scheme is rather a tall order and that my education has already taken long enough, you must frankly tell me so, and I shall quite appreciate your position. If you think that the chance thus offered can and ought to be taken, I shall be grateful if you will let me know as soon as may be. It is just possible that I might be able to help towards this extra year by getting a thing called the John Locke scholarship, but I have not yet discussed this with my tutor, and, as it is quite in the air, it can hardly be taken into account in what military men call 'appreciating the situation'.

My only bit of news is the adventure, if so you can call it, of seeing the Asquiths.[3] It happened while I was waiting in a queue to see a ballet to

3 These were Herbert Henry Asquith (later Earl of Oxford and Asquith, 1852–1928), who was Prime Minister 1908–16, and his second wife, Margot, whose magnetic personality proved to be something of a liability to her husband. Volume II of *The Autobiography of Margot Asquith* had just been published.

which I went because several of my friends were performing. She – Mrs Asquith – is much, much worse than even the memoirs or the photographs have made me believe. But the joke of the thing – for which I mentioned it – was the buzz of the crowd 'Mrs Asquith – Mrs Asquith' and the total indifference of everyone to poor old Asquith himself, flopping heavily out of the car behind her. How are the mighty fallen!

I enclose some old papers from the History Schools on which the Colonel may test how much knowledge of his period he has gained from these years of memoir reading.[4] I have got a poem accepted by a periodical called the Beacon – but I don't know when you'll see it. The usual plan is to wait one month for a reply, three more for the proofs, two more for its appearance, and Lord-knows-how-many-more for payment.[5]

your loving son,

Jack[6]

Lewis took his examination for Literae Humaniores *or 'Greats' during 8 to 14 June, and he was now waiting to hear the results.*

TO HIS FATHER (LP VII: 163):

University College,
Oxford
Wednesday [21 June 1922]

My dear Papy,

I have waited for some days to try and get a bird's eye view from a distance before telling you anything – only to find how difficult it is to form or keep any opinion of what I've done. With the history papers where I can look up facts and see how near or far I was, it is easier: and on these I think I have done pretty fairly – in one case, very much better than I expected. But my long suit is the philosophy and here it is like trying to criticize an essay you wrote a week ago and have never seen again, nor ever read over. Sometimes I feel I have done badly, sometimes that I have done brilliantly. Last night however I got a little light from my tutor who repeated the following conversation he had had with one of the

4 Memoirs of those in and around the court of Louis XIV.

5 It took longer than he thought. The poem, 'Joy', was published in *The Beacon*, III, No. 31 (May 1924). It is reprinted in *Collected Poems* (1994).

6 Mr Lewis sent a telegram at once saying, 'Stay on.'

examiners. 'One of your young men seems to think that Plato is always wrong' – 'Oh! Is it Simpson?' 'No.' 'Blunt? Hastings?'[7] 'No, man called Lewis: seems an able fellow anyway.' So that is good as far as it goes.

On the whole I may sum up: I don't at all know whether I have got a first or not, but at least I know that there was nothing in the nature of a debacle. Of course the VIVA[8] is still ahead, and there the family ability to bluff on paper will be no use. The Runic Salda will never do across the viva table. Luckily we had a spell of cool weather for the exam, which for six hours writing a day for six days is a great blessing. I hope you are keeping well.

your loving son,
Jack

TO HIS FATHER (LP XI: 263–4):

Univ. Coll.
July 20th [1922]

My dear Papy,

I am now close to my viva and of course on that subject I have nothing new to tell you. The details of the examination for the Magdalen Fellowship have however been published at last. The subjects are, as was expected, identical with those of Greats: but it is also notified that candidates may send in a dissertation on any relevant subject in addition to competing on the papers. I felt at once that this gave me a great pull. To choose your topic at your ease, to strike out your own line and display a modicum of originality – these, for men of our ilk, are more promising roads to victory than mere answering of questions. Indeed this condition is a rare bit of luck and of course I am all agog to begin. Naturally I shall not sit seriously to the work until my viva is over.

Under these circumstances you will understand that I cannot promise an early return home. I must see how I get on. No doubt this is disappointing for us all: but apart from that – on the score of health – you need have no misgiving. I am in excellent form at the moment and I shall not play the fool: midnight oil and ten hours a day were never my passion, and I am careful about the daily walk. Being confident on that

7 Philip Overend Simpson, Henry Pyot Blunt, and John Maurice Hastings – all of University College.

8 *Viva voce* ('by or with the living voice') or oral examination.

score I feel it would be folly to throw away any chance for the sake of an immediate holiday. Also – odious factor – in my present position it is advisable to be on the spot, to be seen, to let people remember that there's a young genius on the look out for a job. In the meantime I find the financial water a trifle low. I have had examination fees and a few odd wardrobe repairs to pay and I look forward to more expenses, including tipping, when I take my degree. The dates of terms naturally make a long interval between my spring and autumn allowances, but it has not been worth bothering you about before, and last year the Chancellors Prize helped to fill up. I had hoped to combine a little light tutoring with my own work – which would have been useful experience apart from the shekels – but I was too late and the possible jobs in Oxford were filled up.[9] Could you then let me have £25? I am sorry to 'cut and come again' but you will understand the reasons.

I thought I had got hold of a temporary job for next year the other day. It was before I knew full details of the Magdalen fellowship, and consisted of a classical lectureship at University College, Reading. For geographical reasons I had hoped that this would combine – by means of a season ticket – the diplomatic or 'advertisement' advantages of keeping in touch with Oxford with the advantages of a salaried post. This however turned out impossible. As well, pure classics is not my line. I told them quite frankly and they gave the job to some one else. Perhaps also I was too young. My pupils would nearly all have been girls. The funny thing was that the head of their classical department and one of the committee who interviewed me was Eric Dods. I had lunch with him in Reading and some talk. He is a clever fellow, but I didn't greatly take to him somehow.[10]

Arthur has been staying in Oxford.[11] He was painting and I was working, but we saw a good deal of one another. He is enormously improved

---

9 Lewis meant he could not get any tutoring with University College. He was feeling the financial pinch badly, and he had decided to strike out on his own and look for students. He ran the following advertisement in *The Oxford Times* on 23 June, 30 June and 7 July 1922: 'Undergraduate, Classical Scholar, First-class in Honour Moderations, University Prizeman will give TUITION, Philosophy, Classics, to Schoolboy or Undergraduate in Oxford, August, September. Highest references – Write D3, 183, "Times' Office, Oxford."'

10 This is E.R. Dodds, first mentioned in note 28 to the letter of 30 September 1914. Dodds was a lecturer in classics at University College, Reading, 1919–24, and Lewis's interview with him on 24 June is described in his diary (*AMR*), pp. 54–5.

11 Arthur's visit is described in *AMR*. While in Oxford he stayed with Lewis and the Moores at 28 Warneford Road.

and I didn't feel the qualms which I once should have about introducing him to people. He is not a brilliant talker and he seldom sees a joke but his years in London are brightening him up amazingly. His painting is getting on and he did one landscape here which I thought really good.

I hope you all do well. Belfast now figures less in the Daily Mail and silence, I suppose, is now best news.

your loving son,
Jack

TO ARTHUR GREEVES (W):

28 Warneford Rd.,
Oxford
[25 July 1922]

My dear Arthur,

We were all glad to get your letter and not only for the enclosure as you might maliciously say! Although we may seem to you at times ribald spectators we really feel the greatest sympathy for your present restoration to the paternal roof tree.

We all miss you very much and so, no doubt, do our neighbours. Veronica[12] is so heart broken that she has not sent us any word since. We duly delivered your message to Miss Wibelin[13] who has her exam. to morrow and is in an awful state of nerves. Baker is rehearsing for his play but is out nearly every day: it is going to be perfectly absurd and we are trying to arrange for Miss W., Maureen and me to go to it together.[14] The Doc is not very well and is going to Brittany in a few weeks.[15] Baker, by

---

12 Veronica FitzGerald Hinkley was a native of Oxford and a member of Lady Margaret Hall. She had just finished Schools and she took her BA in 1922.

13 Vida Mary Wiblin (1895–1937) was born in Oxford and matriculated at the Society of Oxford Home-Students (later to become St Anne's College) in 1920. She received her Bachelor of Music in 1924. She went on to read for a degree in Latin and Greek and took her BA in 1926. From 1926 to 1937 she was musical director at Magdalen College School, where she was a well-known and loved figure. Vida Mary was a close friend of the 'family', and in return for giving Maureen violin lessons, Lewis tutored her in Latin.

14 Leo Baker was admitted to hospital, suffering from nervous exhaustion, after finishing Schools. Mrs Moore arranged for him to come and convalesce at 28 Warneford Road, where he was to remain for some weeks. The play, *Glorious England* (1922), was by Baker's friend Bernice de Bergerac. It was performed in the priory gardens of Christ Church on 31 July.

15 'The Doc' was Mrs Moore's brother, Dr John Hawkins Askins (1877–1923). He was born in County Louth and educated at Trinity College, Dublin, where he obtained a

the bye, met an American woman in London who has devoted the last twenty years of her life to astrology. Without the least knowledge of his intended career she told him that he was going on the stage and prophesied early success.[16] I fancy this is telepathy and that the 'astrology' is all rot. I don't and won't see what stars have to do with it.

Ever since you left, it has been beastly weather, but to day was beautiful. We have the french window open in the dining room and a glorious night outside – there was a fine sunset awhile ago over the church tower.

Such a tragedy! On Friday we found the poor 'dam' Vee' lying dead in the hall, poisoned apparently. Before we were out of mourning for him a tiny fluffy black kitten from across the way began to visit us – and we really believe it is his son, for Vee led the devil of a life.

Do you remember my mentioning the Chanson de Roland in the old days? It is the Norman epic about Charlemagne etc, written in the eleventh century: I have been reading a copy with the Norman on one page and the French translation opposite.[17] It is exceedingly fine.

You have made a mistake about the cheque which should have been only £4-10s., and Minto remembers she owed you 2/1 so I enclose the balance of 12/2 with many thanks. Minto was most distressed at forgetting the 2/1 when you were going & we both hope you were not short for the journey.

Everyone sends best love (except Tibbie who is in a bad temper because of the intrusions of 'Vee's' son who ate all her supper and you should have seen her face). Minto specially asks me to say how much we enjoyed your being here & to add both our hopes that you will soon repeat your visit.

Bachelor of Medicine in 1904. He was commissioned a lieutenant in the Royal Army Medical Corps in 1915, and was promoted to captain in 1916. He was wounded in January 1917. Following his marriage to Mary Emmet Goldsborough, of Washington, DC, they lived in Clevedon, where their daughter Peony was born. Dr Askins' heath seems to have been broken by the war, and after his discharge he devoted much of his time to psychoanalysis. Shortly before 1922 he and his family moved to Iffley, just outside Oxford, to be near his sister. His wife's sister, Frances, was married to William Force Stead. See note 35 to the letter of 14 March 1921.

16 For some time it had been Leo Baker's intention to go on the stage. In his diary (*AMR*) for 28 August 1922 Lewis describes his visit to London to see Baker in his first professional role.

17 He was reading this 12th century poem in Léon Gautier's edition, *Le Chanson de Roland: Texte critique, accompagné d'une traduction nouvelle, et précédé d'une introduction historique par L. Gautier* (Tours, 1872).

Yrs. ever
Jack

P.S. Miss Wibelin says she's going to write to you. Lucky Choseph! Maureen has finally decided to leave school & devote her time entirely to music.

TO HIS FATHER (LP VII: 184–5):

University College,
Oxford.
July 26th [1922]

My dear Papy,

Very many thanks for the enclosure.[18] 'There's a power of wash-boards in that' as Meehawl Macmurrachu said when he found the crock of gold.[19] It is very kind of you to tell me to possess my soul in patience, when the patience has rather to be practised on your side. But let us hope that my unique merits will soon be appreciated and that I shall be able to rely on the inexhaustible patience of the tax payer and the sainted generosity of dead benefactors. In the meantime thank you and again thank you.

I have wondered, as you suggest in your letter, whether I unduly decried my own wares before the Readingites. I think, on the whole, that I behaved wisely: I am, after all, nothing remarkable as a pure scholar, and there is no good hiding what is so easily in their power to find out. As well one produces only misery for oneself don't you think, by taking on jobs one is not up to. Biting off more than you can chew is about the most poisonous sensation I know. As for the girls, if one considers only their faculties, it might seem an easy task. But then they would be reading for the same exams as the men: and that being so, the 'weakness of the sex' (assuming that they are dunces) would make the proposition all the tougher. It is a strange irony that Dodds who is a born pure scholar, spends his time lecturing on philosophy. As you say, however, the loss is hardly to be regretted: but there is a mean spirit somewhere in most of us that strives under all circumstances to explain away the success of the other fellow. The other jobs I hear of are mostly in America. In the wild

18 Mr Lewis sent his son £30.

19 Stephens, *The Crock of Gold*, ch. III.

west they seem to have a passion for young classical and other lecturers from English Universities, and offer what seem good salaries too: but of course that would be a counsel of desperation.

A curious little case was brought to my notice by a man the other day. A large asylum has sold some ground to Magdalen College. On the ground stand some cottages inhabited by tenants of whom the asylum wishes to be rid, but can't. The only access to these cottages is a path running through the ground bought by Magdalen. The Asylum, in selling, mentioned no right of way. Neither buyer or seller will allow the cottagers to go across, and they are in a desperate state. The interesting point is that a story goes that any road by which a body has once been carried out to burial becomes a legal entry to the house from which it was carried out. This is 'the custom of the country'. Have you ever heard it? It sounds pretty good rot, but such things usually have an origin, and England's full of quaint old survivals.

This is certainly the most miserable attempt at summer that I remember. I don't know if it's the same with you, but here we have perfectly autumnal mornings with mist and that indescribable thin smell that you get in October.

The storm centre seems now thoroughly shifted to Dublin. Long may it continue so! – a wish not so malevolent as it may sound. I hope you are keeping in the pink.

your loving son,
Jack

On 28 July Lewis had his viva for 'Greats'. On 1 August he and the Moores moved into a house they came to know well over the years – 'Hillsboro', at 14 Western Road, Headington, which road has since been renamed Holyoake Road. They remained there until 5 September when they returned to 28 Warneford Road. On 4 August Jack learned that he had taken a First in Greats, and he straight away wired his father this good news.

*Warnie arrived in Oxford for a visit on 3 August and took a room at the Roebuck Hotel in Cornmarket. Jack had begun keeping a diary (*AMR*) on 1 April 1922 and we are able to follow in detail Warnie's main purpose in coming to Oxford – an attempt to persuade his brother to visit Little Lea in September. At the same time, Warnie refused to go out and meet Jack's* *'family'. He later changed his mind, and he met Mrs Moore and Maureen for the first time on 5 August. The next day he moved into 'Hillsboro' where he remained until 26 August.*

In October Lewis began reading for the English School. On 13 October he had his first meeting with his English tutor, F.P. Wilson,[20] *and on the day following he had his first tutorial in Anglo-Saxon with Edith Elizabeth Wardale*[21] *of St Hugh's College.*

TO HIS FATHER (LP VII: 263–5):

[University College,
Oxford]
28th [October 1922]

My dear Papy,

Your letter and wire both deserved an earlier answer, but you know when one is busy how easily tomorrow becomes the day after and that, the next week end. I judged that you would see my fate in the Times.[22] This needs little comment. I am sorry for both our sakes that the 'hasting days fly on with full career and my late spring no bud nor blossom showeth'.[23] But there's no good crying over spilt milk and one must not repine at being fairly beaten by a better man. I do not think I have done myself any harm, for I have had some compliments on my work. One

20 Frank Percy Wilson (1889–1963), Lewis's tutor in English, took a BA in English from Birmingham, and then a B.Litt. from Lincoln College, Oxford. While serving in the Warwickshire Regiment during World War I he was badly wounded on the Somme. He returned to Oxford in 1920 as a University lecturer, and was appointed Reader in 1927. He was Professor of English at the University of Leeds 1929–36, and Merton Professor of English Literature at Oxford 1947–57. He was one of the editors of the *Oxford History of English Literature*, and he it was who invited Lewis to contribute *English Literature in the Sixteenth Century* (1954) to that series.

21 Edith Elizabeth Wardale (1863–1943) entered Lady Margaret Hall, Oxford, in 1887, and moved a year later to the recently opened St Hugh's Hall (now College). After obtaining a First in Modern Languages she became Vice-Principal and Tutor at St Hugh's and Tutor to the Association for the High Education of Women. She was Tutor in English at St Hugh's until 1923. Her publications include *An Old English Grammar* (1922) and *An Introduction to Middle English* (1937).

22 It was announced in *The Times* of 12 October 1922 that the Fellowship in Philosophy at Magdalen College, which Lewis had applied for in July, went to Henry Habberly Price (1899–1984). In 1935 he became Wykeham Professor of Logic and a Fellow of New College. He and Lewis were to debate a number of times at the Socratic Club.

23 John Milton, sonnet, 'On Being Arrived at Twenty-Three Years of Age', ll. 3–4: 'My hasting days fly on with full career, / But my late spring no bud or blossom shew'th.'

examiner, at any rate, said I was 'probably the ablest man in for it', but added that my fault was a certain excess of caution or 'timidity in letting myself go'. I fancy this means that I do not sufficiently use the kind of answer which is typified in the 'RUNIC SALDA', and that should be easy to alter. For the rest, except for the extra drain on you, I should be glad enough of the opportunity or rather the necessity of taking another School. The English may turn out to be my real line, and, in any case, will be a second string to my bow.

I very much appreciate your enquiries about the adequacy of my allowance, and hasten to assure you that it leads to no such privations as you imagine. I will be quite frank with you. It is below the average, but that is balanced by the longer period of time over which it has been spread. It leaves no margin for superfluities, but I am lucky in having found cheap digs and, as my tastes are simple and my friends neither rich nor very numerous, I can manage alright – specially as you have been always very ready to meet any extraordinary charges. I am very grateful for the slow period of incubation which you have made possible – and have no mental reservations on the subject. On the contrary, I very often regret having chosen a career which makes me so slow in paying my way: and, on your account, would be glad of a more lucrative line. But I think I know my own limitations and am quite sure that an academic or literary career is the only one in which I can hope ever to go beyond the meanest mediocrity. The Bar is a gamble which would probably cost more in the long run, and in business, of course, I should be bankrupt or in jail very soon. In short, you may make your mind easy on this subject.

As to looking run down – I suppose I am turning from a very chubby boy into a somewhat thinner man: it is, at all events, not the result of a bun diet. Your letter explains the wire (for which, thanks). I don't know whether my ear is getting very dull, but I must confess I did not notice the high lyrical strain until it was pointed out to me. Consequently I was completely baffled by the word 'copyright' and weighed the rival theories of a clerical error or a mental derangement on your part, with some interest. But now I catch the swing of it – oh that septennial spring!

I am drumming ahead like anything with my Anglo-Saxon, and it is great fun. One begins it in a Reader constructed on the admirable system of having nearly all the text in one dialect and nearly all the glossary in another.[24] You can imagine what happy hours this gives the young student – for example, you will read a word like 'WADO' in the text: in the glossary this may appear as WEDO, WAEDO, WEODO, WAEDU, or WIEDU. Clever bloke, ain't he? The language in general, gives the impression of parodied English badly spelled. Thus the word 'CWIC' may baffle you till you remember the 'quick and the dead' and suddenly realize that it means 'Alive'. Or again TINGUL for a star, until you think of 'Twinkle, twinkle little star'.

By the way I was quite wrong about Miss Waddell: it turns out to be Miss Wardale – an amazing old lady who is very keen on phonetics and pronunciation. I spend most of my hours with her trying to reproduce the various clucking, growling and grunted noises which are apparently an essential to the pure accent of Alfred – or Aelfred as we must now call him: as in that immortal work of Cornelius Jagenal's 'The upheaving of Aelfred' – 'Brother, what would you do if you felt a sudden etc., etc.' There does not seem to be very much excitement here about the election. As a B.A., I shall have a vote for the University, which is rather comic. And, by the same token, when you're next addressing a letter to me – and there is a propriety, a decency, an idoneity – Very cold these days!

I went to the Martlets the other night: now that I am doing English, I shall have to go regularly and take it seriously. We had a paper on Burns, read – of course – by a Scotsman: with libera-r-r-r-al quotations. I doubt if the Englishmen followed much of it. Of Burns I'm afraid I must say with Kirk 'Ach, I'm no good at that sort of thing'.

This is bad business about McGrigor's – I hope the Colonel had not much in it – I fancy not.[25] You remember the yarn about the officer who, being known to have a balance of £100, was tried for 'conduct unbecoming an officer and a gentleman'.[26]

I hope you are flourishing. Any more Artesian wells?

your loving son,

Jack

---

24 He is referring to Henry Sweet's *Anglo-Saxon Reader* (1876).

25 Warnie, who on 4 October became the assistant to the office in charge of the RASC at Colchester, had about £25 in McGrigor's Bank when it failed.

26 *Articles of War* (1872), 'Disgraceful Conduct' Article 79: 'Any officer who shall behave in a scandalous manner, unbecoming the character of an officer and a gentleman shall...be cashiered.'

On 23 December, Jack met Warnie in London and they visited their father in Belfast for Christmas. Jack remained at Little Lea until 12 January 1923, when he returned to Oxford and his work in the English School. His holiday in Ireland is covered in AMR, *pp. 156–78.*

1923

TO A.K. HAMILTON JENKIN (B):

28 Warneford Road,
Oxford
April 21st [1923]

My dear Jenkin,[1]

I'm afraid this is almost unpardonable. I have outraged all decency towards you and every one else lately. My excuses are poor enough. Your card arrived on the day on which I had to go down to Bristol to the funeral of the poor old Doc. After all his troubles, after all our efforts against the nerve trouble, he died quite suddenly of heart failure – bloody business.[2] Since then there have been no end of minor bothers – a move to a new house with all its attendant labours and infuriating difficulties and incidental money worries.[3]

Also I have got myself thoroughly rattled about the future. I also absolutely forgot your card as if it had never been for the first few days. Afterwards it joined that huge mass of postponed correspondance which all this time has lain like a cloud at the back of my mind and driven me crazy. As to the answer (if its any use now) I can only say *don't count me in any arrangement*. If I get a pupil in the long Vac and make some money I may be able to come down for a time *late* in the long Vac. But as far as I see now it is long odds I shan't be able to. Can you accept the apology? I know that the fact one is plagued and depressed and tired is

---

1 Jenkin had taken his BA in 1922, written a thesis on Richard Carew, and had now returned to his native Cornwall.

2 The harrowing story of Dr John Askins' madness while staying with Mrs Moore and Lewis at 28 Warneford Road is told in *AMR*, pp. 201–18. He died on 5 April and his funeral was on 10 April.

3 Lewis and the Moores had been decorating 'Hillsboro' at 14 Holyoake Road, preparatory to returning there on 30 April.

not really an excuse for being uncivil. I can only 'cry your mercy' – I am like the first chapter of the Return[4] –

Yrs ever
C. S. Lewis

P.S. Your Chaucer Primer is in my desk & will be returned at request.

TO ARTHUR GREEVES (W):

28 Warneford Rd.
April 22nd [1923]

My dear Arthur,

Your letter was very welcome. We have been through very deep waters. Mrs Moore's brother – the Doc – came here and had a sudden attack of war neurasthenia. He was here for nearly three weeks,[5] and endured awful mental tortures. Anyone who didn't know would have mistaken it for lunacy – we did at first: he had horrible maniacal fits – had to be held down. We were up two whole nights at the beginning and two, three or four times a night afterwards, all the time. You have no idea what it is like. He had the delusion that he was going to Hell. Can you imagine what he went through and what we went through?

Arthur, whatever you do never allow yourself to get a neurosis. You and I are both qualified for it, because we both were afraid of our fathers as children. The Doctor who came to see the poor Doc (a psychoanalyst and neurological specialist) said that every neurotic case went back to the childish fear of the father. But it can be avoided. Keep clear of introspection, of brooding, of spiritualism, of everything eccentric. Keep to work and sanity and open air – to the cheerful & the matter of fact side of things. We hold our mental health by a thread: & nothing is worth risking it for. Above all beware of excessive day dreaming, of seeing yourself in the centre of a drama, of self pity, and, as far as possible, of fears.

After three weeks of Hell the Doc. was admitted to a pensions hospital at Richmond: and at first we had hopeful accounts of him. But the poor man had worn his body out with these horrors. Quite suddenly heart failure set in and he died – unconscious at the end, thank God. Of course I cannot pretend to have the same share in it as poor Minto, but I

4 Thomas Hardy, *The Return of the Native* (1878).
5 Between 23 February and 12 March.

am very, very sorry – tho to me the horrors he suffered here were much more heartrending than his death could ever be.[6] As you will understand we are all rather run down and dead tired, in mind at any rate. Isn't it a damned world – and we once thought we could be happy with books and music! We are at present engaged in moving to another house.

Your letter is rather cryptic. I gather you objected to your Irish visit more than ever – and so we shall every time till the bitter end. One thing in your letter however is excellent – I mean what you say you feel about your work. Thats the stuff! As you say, work is the only thing (except people of course, the very few people one cares about) that is worth caring about. I find it hard to imagine your way of thinking in painting – the technical side counts for so much more with you than with poets. One thing I take it is sure for all the arts – that the 'noble thoughts' and 'beautiful ideas' and 'vision' and all the other rot that appeals to amateurs is just what does *NOT* count for twopence: its the man who sees how to do something, that matters. I am glad you read Strachey's Victoria[7] – a capital book. In the intervals of packing etc I am working away at routine work for exams – chiefly the dull mechanical parts for wh. alone I am fit just at present. If you can make your visit to Oxford later than May you will be more likely to see something of us, for we're in the devil of a muddle at present. With love and good wishes from all the family.

Yrs ever
Jack

TO HIS FATHER (LP VIII: 119–20):

Univ. Coll.
May 27th [28] [1923]

My dear Papy,

I do not care to think how long it is since I last wrote to you. I have made some attempts to do so before this, but they have all collapsed under the pressure of work, or of the mere trifling and lassitude which is the reaction to work. You wrote to me that a disinclination to write

---

6 It would be difficult to exaggerate the effect of this experience on Lewis. He does not reveal Dr Askins' name in his autobiography, but it is the 'Doc' he has in mind when he cites a friend's madness as one reason for 'a retreat, almost a panic-stricken flight, from all that sort of romanticism which had hitherto been the chief concern of my life' (*SBJ* XIII).

7 Lytton Strachey, *Queen Victoria* (1921).

letters was 'one of the marks of approaching old age' which you felt or thought you felt. If that were true, what a premature senility is mine! It is a very ridiculous and a very wretched confession that I can hardly remember any period since I was a child at which I have not had a crowd of unanswered letters nagging at the back of my mind: things which would have been no trouble if answered by return but which hang on for weeks or months, getting always harder to write in the end, and contributing their share to the minor worries that lay hold of us when we have the blues or lie awake. That anyone should let himself maintain such a standing army of pinpricks would be incredible if it were not fairly common. Perhaps you will plead guilty yourself to a homefelt recognition of the state I am describing: if not, you are one of the proud minority. Our Colonel, on the principle of 'diamond cut diamond' knows how to defeat this laziness in another because he is so familiar with it himself. At Whitsun he wrote to me saying he would arrive for the week end unless he heard to the contrary: that at any rate means that no one can keep him waiting for a reply!

He came from Friday evening to Monday.[8] He is at present deep in Gibbon[9] and is very enthusiastic about it. I envy him his routine work – in itself apparently not uninteresting and finished definitely at four o'clock with the rest of the day free for general reading, with no uncertainties or anxieties. Despite the frittering away of time over drinks and gossip in the mess and the low mental level of the society, I cannot help feeling that for him the military life has solved the problem of existance very well.

The result of the Exeter fellowship has not yet been announced: but I have heard it said that it is one of those elections in which no electing is done: that they have had some pet candidate of their own in view from the beginning and are in fact merely delaying in order to 'give an air of artistic verisimilitude'. The rumour of course is unofficial but it came from a donnish source and is only too likely to be true. When I first heard it, it completely knocked me over: it was one of the biggest disappointments I have had in recent years. While ready enough to take my chance in an open field, I was disposed to question the candour or even the honesty of a College that set everyone's wits and hopes to work and

8 Warnie was there from 29 March to 2 April. See *AMR*, pp. 225–7.

9 Gibbon, *The History of the Decline and Fall of the Roman Empire.*

perhaps induced some to change their plans in order to give the false appearance of an election to what was in fact a kind of co-option.

I have since dismounted from my high horse of indignation and admit that this is the way in which the world is run and that a man may as well get used to it. Your own view of the Exeter project was quite right as far as fact goes: it WOULD be a small thing, about £200 a year and would be very rightly rejected on that account – if I had a supply of more lucrative and equally congenial openings at my feet or if you were a plutocrat who could, without feeling the strain, keep me indefinitely in my present position while I waited for the ideal job.

These however are 'IF'S and ANDS' according to the proverb. In the concrete situation I felt that the Exeter pittance was the shadow of a great rock in a thirsty land.[10] It would have given me exactly what I wanted: a means of subsistence during five years in which I could have gone on with my work, frequented the senior philosophical and literary societies, made myself known to all the important people, and produced a learned thesis after which it would go hard but I found a place here easily enough.

Your other argument about 'changing horses' is one that naturally occurs. Partly, one's conclusion on that depends on weighing chances and risks, not between a bird on the hand and one in the bush, but between two in the bush – which no two people will ever do quite alike. Partly – well I have taken the English school in such a very short time that a little interruption cannot make matters much worse. If I pull through it will be thanks to knowing most of the work before, and to a lucky faculty (which has always helped me till now) of being in spate at the right moment.

Our summer here consists of sleet, frost and east winds: tho' the summer invasion of Americans has come punctually enough. I mention this because they introduce a good American story which you may not have heard. In the old days of primitive sheriff rule in the western states a man was hanged and shortly afterwards his innocence was proved. The local authorities assembled and deliberated on the best method of conveying the news to the inconsolable widow. It was felt that a too sudden statement would be a little 'brutal' and the Sheriff himself, as the man of

10 Isaiah 32:2: 'As rivers of water in a dry place, as the shadow of a great rock in a weary land.'

greatest refinement, was finally deputed to wait upon the lady. After a few suitable remarks on the figs and the maize, he began with the following, 'Say Ma'am, I guess you've got the laugh of us this time!'

After my eloquent analysis of the state of the mind of the man who doesn't answer letters it would perhaps be incongruous to expect an early reply from you: but I shall hope for the best. I am very sorry not to have answered you before and thanked you for the enclosure, which I do now – if that did come after the gap, for indeed I am not sure. I hope you are in good health in spite of the vile weather: I, of course, have a cold.

your loving son,
Jack

TO HIS FATHER (LP VIII: 132–3):

[University College]
July 1st [1923]

My dear Papy,

Your letter came through unusually quickly and I am answering it after having slept on it. Before everything else let me thank you heartily for what it contains. I hope some day to repay these long years of education in the only way in which they can be repaid – by success and distinction in the kind of life which they aim at. But that is partly in the power of fortune and in the meantime I can only record that I am not foolish enough to take these things for granted and that the thought of how much you are doing for me is often, even insistently, before my mind.

The Exeter Fellowship, as you may have read in the Times, has been awarded – but not to the youth whom the rumour pointed out: what is more, not even to an Exeter man. The winner is a Balliol man and I am told is engaged in some archaeological work in Athens: this fact – that he already had some concrete job on hand which involved residence abroad and which needed money – must naturally and on the whole justly, have weighed very strongly in his favour and made him an almost deadly rival for the rest of us. The upshot, then, is that the rumour was false, and this fellowship at any rate, was awarded on its merits. While the realisation of the rumour might have been more flattering to our vanity, the actual result, as you will see, is – as far as it goes – an answer to the misgivings about influence which you mention in the first part of your letter and which, of course, I have felt quite as strongly as you. I will now turn to your next point.

I should not be a son of yours if the prospect of being adrift and unemployed at thirty had not been very often present to my mind: for of course the worrying temperament of the family did not end in your generation, and to quote Jeremy Taylor[11] 'we were born with this sadness upon us'. But, shaking off all that is temperamental and due to momentary fits of optimism and pessimism, I can only put the situation thus. I have, and of course shall have, qualifications that should, by all ordinary probability, make a tolerable schoolmastering job practically certain whenever we decide to give up Oxford as hopeless.

The same qualifications also put me fairly high in the rank of candidates for academic jobs here. The Magdalen people told my tutor quite recently that they thought my work for their fellowship quite on a level with that of the man who won it, except that it was 'more mature'. But of course the number of other hungry suitors with qualifications equal to mine, tho' not very large, is large enough to put up a well filled 'field' for every event: and the number of vacancies depends, as in other spheres, on all sorts of accidents. What it comes to is that there is a pretty healthy chance here which would, on the whole, be increased by a few years more residence in which I should have time to make myself more known and to take some research degree such as B.Litt or Doc. Phil. and which would be, perhaps, indefinitely or permanently lost if I now left. On the other hand, even apart from the financial point of view, I very keenly realise the dangers of hanging on too long for what might not come in the end.

Speaking, for the moment, purely for myself, I should be inclined to put three years as a suitable term for waiting before beating a retreat. We would hope of course that something would come along sooner than that, but I should take three years as a fair trail of the chances. I think too that there may possibly be a vacancy in Univ. by that time. It is unfortunate – or I feel it so – that even while we are on this subject, I have to ask you for some present money for expenses which I have had to meet. Some of them are rather old and have been paid. The items are, book bill £6-15, new shoes and repairs to old £2-7, grey flannel trousers £1-2-6, fees for examinations £5, two terms fees for Miss Wardale £8-15-1. I am afraid they loom rather big, but I do not think there is anything that could have been avoided.

11 Jeremy Taylor (1613–67), the Anglican bishop and writer.

The English School is come and gone, tho' I still have my viva to face. I was of course rather hampered by the shortened time in which I took the school and it is in many ways so different from the other exams that I have done that I should be sorry to prophesy. I have the chance of a little job examining for the 'Oxford Local' some time next month. It will mean very little money and a good deal of rather disagreeable work, but I shall take it because it will remind people of me and may lead to more lucrative work of the same kind some other time.

I am sorry to hear about the Goodman.[12] Although there is a good deal about him which I don't care for, he is such a familiar figure and has been a subject for 'wheezes' so long, that I can't help feeling what Macaulay calls 'a kindness for him' – and he has always been pleasant in his quaint way whenever I met him. I am afraid poor Mrs Greeves must be having a bad and anxious time.

The weather here is now warm and quite different from what you described at home. Once more with many thanks and hopes that all this business will solve itself soon,

your loving son,
Jack

On 16 July the University announced the examination results of the English School, and the following morning Jack wired his father the good news: 'A First in English.' Some time later, when compiling the Lewis Papers, Warnie made the following observation on his brother's achievement:

> *When we reflect on the circumstances of Clive's life during the time he was reading this School – the shortness of the period at his disposal, his ill health, the constant anxiety inseparable from supporting a family out of an undergraduate's allowance, his fears for the future, the unceasing domestic drudgery, the hideous episode of Dr John Askins' final illness, and the move to Hillsboro – we are*

12 Proverbs 6:19: 'The goodman is not at home, he is gone a long journey.' The 'goodman' (i.e. good man) or head of the house referred to here is Arthur's father, Joseph Greeves. He was very ill and had gone into the nursing home where he died on 20 February 1925.

> *astounded at the extent of an achievement which must rank as easily the most brilliant of his academic career.* (LP VIII: 140)

Arthur Greeves, who was still a pupil at the Slade School of Art in London, arrived in Oxford on 11 July and spent a fortnight with Lewis. There seems to have been a temporary 'cooling-off' between them, possibly owing to the fact that each was surrounded by new friends and new ideas. Arthur was comfortable with Lewis, but not with his Oxford friends. In his diary, Lewis said that when Arthur arrived on 11 July 'we renewed our earlier youths and laughed together like two schoolgirls' (AMR, *p. 256). However, a few days later he wrote with disappointment that Arthur*

> *is changed...Someone has put into his head the ideal of 'being himself' and 'following nature'. I tried on one occasion to point out to him the ambiguity of that kind of maxim: but he seems to attach a very clear meaning to it – namely that the whole duty of man is to swim with the tide and obey his desires...He has taken over from psychoanalysis the doctrine that repression in the technical sense is something quite different from self-control.* (AMR, p. 257)

As he mentioned to his father, Lewis needed money badly, and no sooner had Arthur Greeves left Oxford, than he began correcting English essays for the School Certificate. These Certificates have disappeared, but they were a kind of miniature 'Schools' introduced by the Board of Education in 1905. Every boy and girl who had reached the age of 16, and who had not left school at the age of 14, was allowed to sit these examinations. The universities of Oxford and Cambridge had a large say in what went into them. To obtain a Certificate one was required to pass a minimum of five subjects of which English, Maths and Latin were mandatory. Upon completing the Certificate to the satisfaction of the Oxford and Cambridge Schools Examination Board one could, if one hoped to enter Oxford or Cambridge, take either the Board of Education's Higher School Certificate or Responsions – the 'entrance examination' administered by the two universities.

TO A.K. HAMILTON JENKIN (B):

Hillsboro,
Western Rd.,
Headington.
12th August [1923]

My dear Jenkin,

I'm so sorry your letter was not answered before – I've been having the hell of a job correcting the English Essays for the Higher Certificate, blue pencil in hand, twelve hours a day. You've no idea what its like. Fancy reading essay after illiterate essay on 'The Conquest of the Air' every single one telling you about Montgolfier[13] and his little fire balloons and ending up with a forward glance at the possibilities of the Helicopter. Now what might a helicopter be?

As to the important business – I'm afraid it looks like a dud. Our P.G.[14] (an atrocious little blackguard of a French nouveau riche boy with negro blood in him and the manners of a swine) does not go till after the first fortnight of September and then I'm afraid I shall have to go to Ireland for a bit. If the Blackguard shd. go a bit earlier (wh. I think is just possible) I will let you know at once and try to come – that would be early in Sept.

Yours, hot, hustled & fed up
C. S. Lewis

TO HIS FATHER (LP VIII: 161–3):

[University College]
22nd Nov. [1923]

My dear Papy,[15]

You wrote your first (and last) few lines before my letter reached you and I have been continually expecting an answer to mine. This,

13 Joseph Michael Montgolfier (1740–1810), the French aeronautic inventor. He and his brother Jacques (1745–99) built and went up in the first practical air-balloon (1783).

14 Paying guest.

15 Jack spent the period 22 September to 10 October with his father at Little Lea. Mr Lewis wrote in his diary on 11 October: 'While Jacks was at home I repeated my promise to provide for him at Oxford if I possibly could, for a maximum of three years from this summer. I again pointed out to him the difficulty of getting anything to do at 28 if he had ultimately to leave Oxford' (LP VII: 156).

combined with the usual reasons of a dilatory man, has eked out my silence to its present length.

I have a certain amount of news to give you, all of an inconclusive character. To get the least agreeable item over first, I am afraid old Poynton has proved a broken reed in the matter of pupils: I believe, because he put off the job too long. He is an oldish man and habitually overworked so I do not judge him hardly, tho' I was rather disappointed.

I had a really cheery conversation with my old history tutor, Stevenson – honest fellow, whom nature intended for a farmer: by which I mean no depreciation of his scholarship but an appreciation of his character. He told me that my name was much mentioned in connection with the vacant fellowship and suddenly exclaimed 'And I don't mind telling you, in my opinion it will be a scandal if you don't get a fellowship at this College or some College soon.' He also spoke of me to the new Master in the hope that the latter's wide acquaintance with journalism might give me a temporary lift by getting me some reviewing to do. Not to make the story too exciting I will tell you at once that this came to nothing.

It led however to an interview with the new Master – Sir Michael Sadler,[16] the education expert. I was very favourably impressed: he is much younger and more interesting than his predecessor and I fancy there is less of the 'to be sure the Bursar does that' business about him. He congratulated me on my past successes and added 'We will do whatever we can for you'. He gave me a new book on Wordsworth to review in a given number of words, which I found as difficult a job as I have ever done. He was however pleased with my effort which he pronounced 'Very much to the point' and wrote to six editors, including your friend Strachey, on my behalf. None of them could find room for me, but he tells me that there is still some hope for the future: and tho' I place very little confidence in it, it is as well to have established personal relations with the rising sun.

---

16 Sir Michael Ernest Sadler (1861–1943), educational pioneer and patron of the arts, was educated at Rugby and Trinity College, Oxford, where he took a First in *Literae Humaniores* in 1884. He served with the Education Department 1895–1903, after which he was Professor of Education at the University of Manchester 1903–11, and Vice-chancellor of the University of Leeds 1911–23. He was Master of University College, Oxford, 1923–34.

I have got quite recently ONE pupil, tho' not through Poynton. He is a youth of eighteen who is trying to get a Classical scholarship. I am to coach him in essay writing and English for the essay paper and general papers which these exams always include. I fear we shall win no laurels by him. I questioned him about his classical reading: our dialogue was something like this: –

> *SELF: 'Well Sandeman, what Greek authors have you been reading?'*
> *SAND (cheerfully): 'I never can remember. Try a few names and I'll see if I can get on to any.'*
> *SELF (a little damped:) 'Have you read any Euripides?'*
> *SAND: 'No.'*
> *SELF: 'Any Sophocles?'*
> *SAND: 'Oh yes.'*
> *SELF: 'What plays of his have you read?'*
> *SAND (after a pause): 'Well – the Alcestis.'*
> *SELF (apologetically): 'But isn't that by Euripides?'*
> *SAND (with the genial surprise of a man who finds £1 where he thought there was a 10/- note): 'Really. Is it now? By Jove, then I HAVE read some Euripides.'*

My next is even better. I asked him if he were familiar with the distinction that critics draw between a NATURAL and a LITERARY epic. He was not: you may not be either, but it makes no difference. I then explained to him that when a lot of old war songs about some mythological hero were handed down by aural tradition and gradually welded into one whole by successive minstrels (as in the case of 'Homer') the result was called a natural epic: but when an individual poet sat down with pen in hand to write Paradise Lost, that was a literary epic. He listened with great attention and then observed 'I suppose Grey's Elegy is the natural kind.' What idiots can have sent him in for a Scholarship? However, he is one of the cheeriest, healthiest, and most perfectly contented creations I have ever met with.

I am still weighing alternative schemes for my thesis in an unproductive but I hope not unprofitable indecision. I hope to get it straightened out before I come down. Whatever I fix on I see a good deal of work ahead. I hope you have got over the bad turn I left you in and are as well as anyone can be in this suffocating cold. Getting up and going to bed are two evil moments these days.

your loving son,
Jack

1924

TO HIS FATHER (LP VIII: 180–2):[1]

[University College]
Monday [4 February 1924]

My dear Papy,

You will explain your long silence as an answer to mine – at least I hope there is no more serious reason for it than that and the desultoriness in correspondence which you claim as one of the penalties, if it is not rather one of the privileges, of the years beyond fifty. I, like the judge, have other reasons.

As soon as I had met people here I heard of a new will-of-the-wisp, a poor Fellowship at St John's now vacant and calling out for candidates. The warning that preference would be given to 'founder's kin and persons born in the County of Stafford' did not seem sufficient to deter me from trying my luck. At first I thought of sending them my old dissertation which I had written for Magdalen: but no man cares greatly for his own things when once the bloom is off them, and I decided in the end to write a new one. I was in pretty good form, but I was pressed for time: and of course there is a waste of time when one flings oneself back into work which one has abandoned for a few months – the old harness will not at once sit easily. It was only after I had sent this in that I discovered how small my chances must necessarily be. I had supposed – and who would not – that the preference for natives of Staffordshire etc. meant only a preference, others things being equal.

I find however that if any candidate appears who claims such preference and who has in addition either a SECOND in Greats or a FIRST in any other final school, he must be elected. I do not of course know in fact whether there is such a candidate in the field, but Stafford is a large

1 Warnie was still stationed at Colchester, and he and Jack travelled together to Little Lea where they were with their father from 9 to 28 December 1923.

county, and we may be sure that the founder was some philoprogenitive old fellow who, like Charles II in Dryden, 'scattered his Maker's image through the land'.[2] In short we may expect a defeat with almost complete certainty. I suppose that a privileged class of 'persons born in Staffordshire and founder's kin' is in the nature of things no more absurd than any other privileged class, though at first it struck me oddly. But in this long quest for a job I have determined to suppress all questionings about the justice of things and the comparative value of my own and other people's qualifications. Such feelings, once admitted, would be fatal.

I was particularly pleased, in a testimonial which my philosophy tutor gave me on this occasion, to read the following passage: – 'He has not only real enthusiasm for knowledge, as distinct from its emoluments, but an unusual originality in pursuing it on his own lines. He seems to me the sort of man who is most likely to do something that would justify endowment, though there are some who have directed their studies more immediately to its attainment.' I am afraid I inherit from you abilities that make it easier to produce than to advertise the goods.

This then occupied my first weeks. And I had hardly looked about me when a most irritating thing happened. I got chicken pox and am only now out of quarantine. I have of course been quite well enough to write for some time but I don't know whether you have had this complaint and thought it better not to chance infecting you: I am told that the older you are the less likely it will be to 'take', but the worse if it does. I had a pretty high temperature at the beginning and some very uncomfortable nights of intense perspiration, but it soon passed off. The danger of cutting any of the spots on my face of course made shaving impossible till this very day and I had a fine beard. I have left the moustache which would excite 'poor Warren's' envy, but I shall probably get tired of it in a few weeks. It is very stiff, and all the hairs grow in different directions and it is thicker on one side than on the other.

The greatest annoyance was of course that I could not get any light literature except what I happened to have in my hands. Here however comes 'the soul of virtue in things evil'. I have been converted to Thackeray. Somebody lent me a copy of Vanity Fair and as it was that or counting the cracks in the ceiling, I read that – almost at once with toleration

---

2 John Dryden, *Absalom and Achitophel* (1681), l. 10.

and soon with respect and enjoyment.[3] I think of course that it *is* a little jaundiced: the meanness of nearly all the characters is too much, and, what is worse, the author doesn't always know, I'm afraid, quite HOW mean they are. But this is amply made up for by its life, its pathos, and above all, its humour. Minerva House, Jos Sedley both at home in Vaux-all and in Brussels, the Crawley ménage, the old aunt at Brighton, old Osborne saying, 'Jane, turn the cook out of the house tomorrow' and the Pumpernickel scenes at the end – all these simply beat Bannagher![4] The Waterloo scenes are splendid. How wise of him to avoid the temptation of a battle chapter – and how he gives you the feeling of war by those two slight references to the firing, heard far off the first day and a little nearer the second day!

Rawdon is I think one of the best characters in the book – he *Grows* so – begins as a comic figure sketched from the outside, and then gradually grows more and more human. But I must stop: I felt that I owed Thackeray a recantation in full. It's rather funny that I have since read 'Lady rose's daughter' by Mrs H. Ward[5] which opens with a situation taken consciously or unconsciously from Vanity Fair.

And now I am afraid I must fulfill friend Staples'[6] suggestion, 'Sons bleeding you?' You know of course that my Scholarship is at an end. It was nominally a scholarship of £80 a year. What I actually got out of it was about £11 a term. Sometimes it would be a little more or a little less, but it generally averaged out to £33 a year. My 'battells' or accounts for the last term from College show me that this time I am £3.4.3 to the bad instead of £11 to the good. (The items are not very enlightening – 'Domus Fund', 'Establishment Charges' and 'Service' which means I suppose that the porter says 'good morning' to me.) This amount will I think vary from term to term but will hardly go above £3.10. You will see that this leaves me with an annual reduction of income of £43.10s. I had

3 See the reference to *Vanity Fair* in the letter to Arthur Greeves of 20 February 1917.

4 In Ireland there is the phrase 'It beats Banagher!' or, in the local dialect, 'It bates Banagher!' which means that Banagher is the benchmark of excellence. Banagher, in County Londonderry, is a small town south of Dungiven, with a church founded by Muriedach O'Henry in the 12th century. I owe this reference to the Rt. Hon. David Bleakley, CBE.

5 Mrs Humphrey Ward, *Lady Rose's Daughter* (1903).

6 Robert Ponsonby Staples, who was distantly related to Jack and Warnie through the Hamiltons, was described by Warnie as 'one of the most remarkable and scandalous characters of his time in the North of Ireland' (LP III: 128).

hopes of being able to make up that in other ways – pupils and the like – but they have not been realised and I am afraid I must ask for help. I do not like increasing your charges – but as Kirk said, 'All this has been said before'.

I have lost Sandeman. He got good marks in his English in the Scholarship he tried for near Christmas and his mother and his other coach said the nicest things of me, when dash it if the fool doesn't go and break his leg. Then of course his mother, seeing a long interruption ahead and knowing that his chances depended on hard cramming, wrote to ask me what I thought. What chance had he? Was it worth going on? You may imagine that I chewed up many a pen and drew many a face on my blotting paper before I answered that letter, but of course, in common honesty, I had to say that his chances were not big. Perhaps I said it rather more plainly because I hear that they are poor – the father is bad or dead or something. At any rate Mrs Sandeman has decided to give the game up, thanking me for all the trouble I have taken with Austin – I have been SO helpful etc., etc. Poor Woman! – she says of her own son, 'I have tried every means I can think of to rouse some intellectual interest'.

I hope I shall hear from you soon – indeed, according to precedent, this will probably cross a letter of yours. It is miserably cold here and I am rather tired of four walls. I don't know that I have any other news. I have been reading the debates very conscientiously since the new government came in. Did you see Chamberlain's amusing speech?

your loving son,
Jack

TO HIS FATHER (LP VIII: 193–5):

[University College]
March 6th [1924]

My dear Papy,

I am sorry to hear about the flu'. You may remember that I had it about this time a year or two ago: and I well remember the black lethargy and depression which succeeds it. It is a period during which all seems 'weary, stale, unprofitable, flat': when all the thoughts which each one of us (I suppose) keeps at arms length, come in and take possession of the mind, till one is amazed at one's own ingenuity in finding out new sources of regret for the past and anxiety for the future. It is always rather 'shocking' – in the original literal sense of the word – to find how closely our states of mind depend on the states of our bodies. One reads now and then in the paper of people who have committed suicide through 'depression after flu' and one always thinks it rather absurd until one's own turn comes. However, it is unhealthy to chew the cud of these bad things. It is a horrible time, to be forgotten as soon as may be: and I suppose we should consider ourselves fortunate if it does not lead to pneumonia or any of the other complications which sometimes follow it.

After having said this, I trust I shall not be thought unsympathetic if I confess that the episode of the boiler, coming where it did in your letter, really had its funny side. Though it is very far from funny at the time, there is something absurd in the sudden descent to such a very prosaic incident – from the solemn world despair that we get after flu'. I do indeed remember the last time it burst. I remember your coming up in the twilight of a winter's morning to wake Warnie with the tragic announcement 'The boiler's burst': and the exquisitely unconcerned 'Is it?' with which 'as a door on its hinges so he on his bed etc.' I always regard that dance as one of the Hamilton's masterpieces. You and I certainly neither desired nor enjoyed it. The colonel may have had some pleasure of it: but I think the lion's share fell to Our Uncle and Aunt and their friends.

And now to business. The Univ. Fellowship has not been filled up. You may have read in the papers that a new 'Chaplain Fellow' has been elected, but that of course is a different job. If I don't mention it, it is because there is nothing new to say about it. Just at present a new and very good vacancy at Trinity (I mean Trinity, Oxford of course) has appeared, for which an election is to be held in the summer, and I shall certainly go in for it.

As to money: I had rather you had explained in detail what you 'don't follow' in my arithmetic, but I trust there is nothing seriously wrong with the figures I gave you and will proceed accordingly. What is more serious is your reference to £30 extras last year. The only part of this which I can at present identify are the extra tuition and the book bill. The former of course was purely abnormal and will not occur again. The book bill was naturally increased by my turning to a new subject. I try to use the libraries as much as possible: but when one is reading for a particular exam there are over a hundred other people taking the same books out of the libraries – and of course there are some things one must have at command. My expenditure on books will be less in future. I have a book bill due to be paid some time soon which is under five pounds: if you will pay that I think I can undertake to find myself for books in the future – tho' since you tell me to be frank, I will say that this may not always be easy. The rest of the £30 you mention is, I suppose, made up by items of clothing. I presume it does not include my two suits? As to clothing, I'm afraid that even if you increase my allowance as you suggest, I cannot undertake to find myself. I mean that my loss of the scholarship and my outlay on clothes would not be balanced by an addition of £40 or £50.

I cannot see how to cut down my expenses on clothing. You know I think that it does not go to fancy waistcoats or kid gloves. And I have some ties that date from before the war! Flannel trousers are an item that I have to repeat pretty often: they ARE ill wearing things, but if I didn't wear them I should need suits more often than I do. On shoes I admit that I am hard and have to get a good deal of 'soling' done: but I am afraid this reads rather as if I were defending myself against a charge of extravagance, which you will justly reply you never made: but you must not think that. I am only trying to put down the facts of the question as they actually occur to me from day to day in order to make my conclusion more reasonable and intelligible to you. And the conclusion is this. You ask me where £85 a term to 'cover everything' would be sufficient. If by 'covering everything' you mean covering my books, shoes, shirts, socks and other items that I have hitherto sent you, I am afraid it would not. As I said, if you wish it, I will try to undertake my own books in the future, and, at any rate to cut them down. I will also abandon the new dinner jacket suit that was mooted, and you must not imagine that I would feel that sort of curtailment as any hardship. As for a new overcoat, the one you gave me when I left home suits and fits me so well that the question need not be considered. But I do not think that I can manage to keep myself in minor articles of clothing.

I'm afraid this may seem to you but a charter of indefinite expenses for the future. Well then, to say all, if it is too much, you must tell me so. You have done all and more than all I can expect of you, and if you tell me that these extra years are too heavy, I assure you that I shall never, even in my secret thought, criticise such a decision. If on the other hand, you see fit to lodge £85 a year and to pay for such extras in the way of clothing, etc. as may occur, I will try to make them as little as I can.

I must point out however that it is much easier to save on the big items I have mentioned – the dress suit and overcoat – than on those necessary articles which have so often to be replaced. If you will give me a dress suit when I get a job, I ought to be able to tide over these years without any more 'suitings' from you at all. If, till they are over, you can lodge £85 a term and make it retrospective for the present year, while paying for my smaller articles of clothing, I think I can manage. And whether you can do this or not, I have nothing but deepest gratitude for the past.

I am not fretting against enforced idleness, for I am not idle, though I have made a change in my work. I started work experimentally on Dr Henry More[7] – a 17th Century theologian – with the idea of 'doing' him for a D.Phil. And I had a great deal of fun out of him before I stopped. He told me a great many curious 'facts' in natural history. You never knew that the leader of a flock of cranes carried a large stone in his mouth when in flight: the reason being, that when they alight, all the others go to sleep, but the leader, as soon as he does, is awakened by the sound of the stone falling. Or who would have thought that elephants had a religion and performed purificatory rites to the new moon? He was a very holy man, this More: his contemporary biographer tells us that his body 'at the putting off of his cloathes, exhaled sweet herbaceous smells, and his urine had the natural savour of violets'.[8]

---

7 Henry More (1614–87), Cambridge Platonist, was educated at Christ's College, Cambridge, became a Fellow of the College in 1639, and remained there for the rest of his life. Those works of his which Lewis was reading included *An Antidote Against Atheism* (1653), *An Explanation of the Grand Mystery of Godliness* (1660) and *The Immortality of the Soul* (1659). In them More sought to vindicate theism against the materialism represented by Thomas Hobbes. He did this particularly by emphasizing the instinctive reasonableness of divine truth. If it seems odd that Lewis should be interested in More, it is not because he believed in God, but because he believed in the importance of morals and ethics. During 1924 he was to write a number of papers on ethics, including 'The Hegemony of Moral Values' mentioned in note 9 to the letter of 9? March 1924.

8 Richard Ward, *The Life of the Learned and Pious Dr Henry More, Late Fellow of Christ's College in Cambridge* (1710), pp. 123–4: 'He hath told us...That not only his own Urine, had naturally the Flavour of Violets in it, but that his Breast and Body, especially when very Young, would of themselves, in like manner, send forth flowry and Aromatic Odours from them; and such as he daily almost was sensible of, when he came to put off his Clothes, and go to bed. And even afterwards, when he was Older, about the end of Winter, or beginning of Spring, he did frequently perceive certain sweet and herbacious Smells about him; when yet there were no such external Objects near, from whence they could proceed.'

I had not however gone very far in this naïf wonderland without deciding that I was on a fool's errand. The D.Phil. would add very little to my Firsts in the way of qualification: and in the mean time I should be letting my knowledge of philosophy and above all my Greek rust. I have determined instead to go on vigorously improving my philosophy and classics and also to learn some history – history being the gate to an All Souls fellowship, at which I must have my try. If to the consciousness of the long burden I am imposing on you and to the obstinate fears and despondences of the unemployed I added idleness, I should, I think, be mad. Work is our drug and we run to it as others do to drink.

The chicken pox has left no marks. Since your verdict on the moustache, tho' you had not seen it, agreed with that of everyone who had seen it, it has come off and I no longer front a stranger in the mirror. I think you were wrong about Warnie having had chicken pox 'as a little fellow'. I am almost sure he had it at Malvern. Uncle Bill, who was passing, came and looked at him through the window of the San. I was at Wynyard at the time.

Just two words more about Vanity Fair. I think an example of Thackeray's Waterloo art even better than that end of the chapter, is the passage where Dobbin pulls Osbourne out from Becky's and says, 'The enemy have crossed the Sambre and our left is already engaged'. That's the stuff! My second point is 'It was a damned unfriendly act?' Was Rawdon right? Is it a man's duty in the circumstances to shove his oar in?

your loving son,
Jack

TO HIS FATHER (LP VIII: 198):

[University College
9? March 1924]

My dear Papy,

'This won't do'. You really must not take so to heart my budget of expenses and economics, which was written, I can assure you, with no intention of producing such an effect on you. 'Cheese paring shifts and devices' has a bleak sound. But let us not be the dupes of words. It is natural for young men who have not yet made their way in the world to 'live close': you have had your share and I daresay a lion's share of this in your young days. I have everything to be pleased about and to be grateful for so long as I can peruse the goal I wish – how many have been forced into uncongenial drudgery before they had time to look round?

This is only a line to thank you and to answer your letter – but I must just mention a pleasant little success I had the other day when I read a philosophical paper to a rather unpleasant society who had brought the Professor of Moral Philosophy there to reply to me without telling me beforehand.[9] This worthy Professor said a lot of nice things which I discounted as 'manners': but what really mattered was that he said my idea was 'quite NEW' to him and 'very attractive' and advised me to publish it in 'Mind'. And as I heard him repeating the word 'new' to people in another group when we had broken up, I believe he really meant it.

your loving son,
Jack

TO HIS FATHER (LP VIII: 217–18):

[University College]
April 27th [1924]

My dear Papy,

Your letter with 'advertisement' as they say of doings with Cox's, is better than your word. We have now talked of this subject so much that I can say no more than that I thank you very heartily. I must also acknowledge your cheque for a dividend. 'The blessings that surround my path...'!

I have been exercised in the slightly unpleasant duty of getting all things in readiness for my application for the Trinity Fellowship – getting testimonials and talking to one or two people who will write unofficially for me. I also went to a dinner where I met the present philosophy man from Trinity[10] whose successor I should become if I were elected. This was done no doubt to give me an opportunity of impressing him with my unique social and intellectual qualifications. Unhappily the whole conversation was dominated by a bore who wanted to talk (and

9 In his diary of 6 March Lewis gives an account of how he read a paper on 'Hegemony of Moral Values' to the Oxford University Philosophical Society in Manchester College. The Professor of Moral Philosophy who commented on his paper was William Ross David (1877–1971) of Oriel College.

10 The Fellow of Philosophy at Trinity was Harold Arthur Pritchard (1871–1947). He was White's Professor of Moral Philosophy 1928–37 and the author of *Kant's Theory of Knowledge* (1909).

DID talk) about the state of India, and I suppose I hardly exchanged ten words with the Trinity man. However, it may have been just as well. A man who knows he is on show can hardly be at his best: and I was told that this Trinity man is a very shy, retiring, moody old man and difficult to talk to. In the meantime I send in my application and wait – reminding myself that the best cure for disappointment is the moderation of hopes.

I have just come across a book which I think you would find very much in your line. It is the diary of one William Allingham[11] (whom I never heard of before) a minor poet born at Ballyshannon, who lived in London in the very hey-day of the great Victorians. He was on intimate terms with Tennyson, Browning, Ruskin, Carlyle, Thackeray and the pre-Raphaelites, and the book consists chiefly of their conversations with him. Tennyson and Carlyle are the protagonists and there is any amount of good crack. One cannot help noticing however that none of the lot comes out of it half so well as old Johnson with his Boswell. They are not so savage of course: but what they gain on him in manners they lose in snap or 'pep'. But you ought to get hold of this book.

One never reads a printed diary without wishing to be a diarist oneself. What would I not give for a diary of my days in France – or better still a diary of Bookham recorded from day to day. One can imagine it – 'This morning at breakfast Kirk continues our argument on the date of the Old Testament. Asks have I read Puffendorf – Schliemann – Webster.[12] Argument closed. Mrs X, Y, and Z to tea. Bridge was intended. Kirk, driven in by rain, talked to them about physiological anthropology instead. All left early. Mrs K very snappy at supper time'.

I can't remember if I told you about my last visit to Aunt Lily.[13] I went out by bus. The conductor did not at once understand where I wanted to stop, and a white bearded old farmer chipped in, 'You know, Jarge – where that old gal lives along of all them cats'. I explained that this was exactly where I did want to go. My informant remarked, 'You'll 'ave a job to get in when you DO get there.' He was as good as his word, for when I reached the cottage I found the fence supporting a wire structure about

11 William Allingham, *A Diary* (1907).

12 The men Lewis heard Mr Kirkpatrick mention frequently were probably: Samuel Pufendorf (1632–94), the first German professor of natural and international law; Friedrich Daniel Ernst Schleiermacher (1768–1834), a German theologian; and Max Weber (1864–1920), the German pioneer of the analytical method of sociology.

13 A fuller description of this visit is found in Lewis's diary, *AMR*, pp. 302–3.

nine feet high which was continued even over the gate. She does it to prevent her cats escaping into the main road. On this occasion she presented me with a print of an old picture, 'St Francis preaching before Pope Honorious' because, she said, the Pope was a portrait of me. It is not one of her fads, for I do really see the likeness myself. I suppose nature has only a limited number of faces to use after all.[14]

The weather cleared up for Easter here, but it is still rather cold. I hope you have quite got rid of the last traces of flu' by now. With many thanks again,

your loving son,
Jack

TO HIS FATHER (LP VIII: 225-6):

[University College]
Sunday [11 May 1924]

My dear Papy,

I have a bit of good – or fairly good – news. Some nights ago I was summoned to call on the new Master after dinner, there to meet Farquharson[15] and my old philosophy tutor Carritt,[16] and when I arrived the following 'transpired'. Carritt it appears is going for a year to teach philosophy in the University of Ann Arbor, Michigan, and it was suggested that I should undertake his tutorial duties here during his absence and also give lectures. As soon as I heard the proposal I said that I was already a candidate for the vacancy at Trinity. To this they replied that they had no intention of asking me to sacrifice the possibility of a

---

14 The picture of 'St Francis preaching before Honorius III' is Number XVII in the 'Legend of St Francis' which Giotto painted around the walls of the upper basilica of St Francis in Assisi. It is reproduced in Elvio Lunghi, *The Basilica of St Francis at Assisi* (1996), pp. 84–5.

15 Arthur Spenser Loat Farquharson (1871–1942) went to University College, Oxford, in 1890 and took a First in Greats. After a short time as a schoolmaster he returned to University College in 1899 as a Fellow and remained there for the rest of his life. From 1900 until the outbreak of the First World War he held the office of Dean. During the war, when he was chief postal censor, he took missions to France, Belgium and Italy, and he was twice mentioned in despatches. He became a lieutenant-colonel in the Territorial Army in 1918, and was made a CBE in 1919. He taught philosophy to the men reading Greats, and later to those reading the new school of Philosophy, Politics and Economics. He was a keen student of military history, and a great admirer of Marcus Aurelius, the soldier-philosopher.

16 For information about Mr Carritt see note 33 to the letter of 1 May 1920.

permanent job: it would be understood that if I were elected to Trinity I should be released from my engagement to Univ. – unless indeed Trinity were willing to let me do both tasks and I felt able to do so.

This being settled, I of course accepted their offer. I was a little disappointed that they only offered me £200 – specially as I anticipate that when living in and dining at high table I shall hardly be able to economise as much as I do now. I am afraid that I shall still need some assistance from you. Of course Carritt's job must be worth more than that: I imagine he is keeping his *fellowship* and I am getting his *tutorial* emoluments and of these, Farquharson, who is 'taking a few of the senior men' is getting a share. Being under Farquharson's suprintendance will be in some ways troublesome: and indeed I have already had a specimen of his fussy futility. I sent in to the Master as the title of my proposed lectures for next term 'The Moral Good – its place among the values.' Within an hour I had a notice brought out to my digs by special messenger 'Farquharson suggests "position" instead of "place". Please let me know your views at once.' There's glory for you,[17] as Humpty Dumpty said! Well, it is poorly paid and temporary and under the shadow of Farquharson, but it is better to be inside than out, and is always a beginning. The experience will be valuable.

You may imagine that I am now pretty busy. I must try to get through most of the Greats reading before next term and do it more thoroughly than ever I did when I was a candidate myself. I must be ready for all comers and hunt out the bye ways which I considered it safe to neglect in my own case. There can be no throwing dust in the examiner's eyes this time. Preparing my lectures will however be the biggest job of all. I am to lecture twice a week next term, which comes to fourteen hours talking in all. You who have been so much on your legs, can tell better than I what a lot of talking a man can do in one hour. I rather fancy I could really tell the world everything I think about everything in five hours – and, Lord, you hear curates grumbling because they have to preach for twenty minutes a week. However, as Keats remarks somewhere, 'Demme, who's afraid?': we must learn that slow deliberate method dear to the true lecturer. As Farquharson remarked (without the ghost of a smile) 'Of course your first lecture would be INTRODUCTORY'. I felt like replying, 'Of course: that's why I always skipped YOUR first lectures'!

17 Lewis Carroll, *Through the Looking-Glass* (1872), ch. 6.

As a prospective candidate I dined at Trinity the other night. I found out afterwards that this is a better sign than I thought, for Ewing[18] ('the rabbit' you remember) is also a candidate, remarked to me 'Price of Magdalen is a very dangerous man – he has been asked to dinner'.[19] 'But', said I with unfeigned surprise, 'surely they will ask all the candidates?' 'Oh dear me, no' said Ewing, 'only those who are in the running.' I held my tongue of course, while feeling, as I have often done lately, that this whole struggle for jobs is very degrading. It puts you in unpleasant relations with other people, and although one is perfectly innocent, one feels ashamed. This however is not what I meant to say. The interesting thing is that the President of Trinity[20] turns out to have been a bosom friend of Smugy's. He's quite a nice old man, but shy and a poor talker and I couldn't get him to talk about Smugy as I should have liked. I was very favourably impressed with the Trinity people.

In the smoking room after dinner we were just of a number for conversation to be general and I had one of the best evenings imaginable, the 'crack' ranging over all things. A burlesque element was supplied by their Senior Tutor, a disreputable old man in Holy Orders and in liquor, who, finding that I came from Univ., regaled us with some stories of Farquharson. So if Trinity don't give me a Fellowship, at least they gave me a very good time. All the same Ewing is right, 'Price of Magdalen' is 'a dangerous man' and I clip my hopes accordingly.[21]

'Mr Rogers'[22] is a name that I can remember almost as far back as I can remember anything. I am very sorry to hear of his death and even

---

18 Alfred Cecil Ewing (1899–1973), also of University College, took a First in Greats in 1920, and a D.Phil. in Philosophy in 1923. He was a Lecturer in Moral Science in the University of Cambridge from 1931 until 1954 and Reader in Philosophy at Cambridge from 1954 until 1966.

19 H.H. Price who, in 1922, had been awarded the Fellowship at Magdalen that Lewis applied for. See note 22 to the letter of 28 October 1922.

20 The Rev. Herbert Edward Douglas Blakiston (1862–1942) was President of Trinity College from 1907 until 1938.

21 He was right to do so. On 7 June Lewis had a letter from the President of Trinity College informing him they had made their decision. They elected H.H. Price to the Fellowship.

22 Edgar Rogers (1863–1924) of County Down was educated at the Royal Academical Institution, Belfast, and the Queen's College. In 1882 he joined the tobacco manufacturing firm of Murray, Sons and Co., of which he became the managing director. He was a friend of Albert's of long standing, and he was a frequent visitor to Little Lea.

sorrier that he should have fallen on evil days before the end. The roll of casualties in your letter reminds me of one of the little trap doors in the Vision of Mirzah.[23] Young men are supposed to think themselves immortal, but the subject is not very often out of my mind for a long time together. It is however a subject that will keep, God knows.

It has rained for a week here.

your loving son,

Jack

TO HIS FATHER (LP VIII: 256–7):

[University College]
Sunday [10? August 1924]

My dear Papy,

I should have answered your last generous letter earlier but for the last three weeks I have been busy from morning to night examining.[24] To examine is like censoring letters in the army or (I fancy) like hearing confessions if you are a priest. Beforehand it seems interesting – a curious vantage point from which to look into the minds of a whole crowd of people 'as if we were God's spies':[25] but it turns out to be cruelly dull. As the censoring subaltern finds that every man in his platoon says the same things in his letters home, and as the priest, no doubt, finds that all his penitents confess the same sins, so the examiner finds that out of hundreds of girls and boys of all social classes from all parts of England, scarcely a dozen make themselves memorable either for original ideas or amusing mistakes.

The paper which I corrected most of was on David Copperfield and Kinglake's Eothen:[26] and the first question was 'Contrast the characters of Uriah Heep and Mr Micawber'. So one takes up ones first sheet of answers and reads 'Uriah Heep is the finished type of a rogue: Mr Micawber on the other hand is the portrait of a happy go lucky debtor'.

---

23 In Joseph Addison's *Vision of Mirzah* (1711) Mirzah has a vision of human life as a bridge. As the multitudes pass over, some drop through concealed trap-doors into the flood beneath.

24 Lewis was working, except for a short lunch break, from 8 a.m. to 7 p.m. correcting examinations for the Higher School Certificate.

25 Shakespeare, *King Lear*, V, iii, 17.

26 Alexander William Kinglake, *Eóthen: or traces of travel brought home from the East* (1844).

Then one plods on to the same question answered by the next candidate and reads 'Mr Micawber is the finished portrait of a happy go lucky debtor, while Uriah Heep is a typical (or perhaps 'typicle') rogue'. And so it goes on through all the weary hours of the day till ones brain reels with Uriah Heep and Mr Micawber and one would willingly thrash the editor or whoever it is who has supplied them with that maddening jargon about the 'finished portrait of a rogue'.

I must set down on the credit side the fact of having been thus forced to read Eothen. I know of course that it has stood in red cloth, skied near the ceiling in the bookcase nearest the study door, since I can remember – unmoved by twenty spring cleanings, the Russian Revolution, and the fall of the German Monarchy. I don't know whether this is one of the books you have advised me to read or not. It is even possible (such things have been known) that Eothen has lived there all these years in the study bookcase undisturbed not only by the Russian Revolution, but equally by the hand of its owner. (It was Sir Otto[27] was it not, who observed 'But this isn't cut Mr Lewis'?) At any rate I most strongly advise you to give yourself a very pleasant evening by taking down Kinglake. If you don't feel a stomach for the whole thing at least read the interview between the Pasha and the 'possible policeman of Bedfordshire' in the first chapter and the Surprise Sataleih in the last, for humour: and for ornate prose I should recommend the opening of the chapter on Constantinople, the part beginning 'the stormy bridge of the Doge is the bowing slave of the Sultan'. The Colonel was over here shortly before my durance began and I have converted him to my new idol: so you must by all means 'come in' and share the spoil – unless of course you really have read it already.

I have seen enough of the papers to imagine that Ulster must be pretty well humming with politics just at present: and indeed I suppose

27 Sir Otto Jaffé (1846–1929) was first mentioned in note 84 to the letter of 24 July 1915. He was a Jewish general merchant and linen manufacturer who was born in Hamburg and who became a resident of Belfast in 1848. He was twice Lord Mayor of Belfast (1899–1900 and 1904–5) and was knighted in 1900. He was an LL.D. of the Royal University of Ireland, and President of the Belfast Natural History and Philosophical Society 1906–8. In 1879 he married Paula Hertz, and they had two sons, Arthur (b. 1880) and William (b. 1883), who was a friend of Albert's. Warnie said that 'On the outbreak of the Great War the family was subjected to a cruel and stupid social persecution on account of its German origin, as a result of which Sir Otto and Lady Jaffé left Belfast and settled in London' (LP III: 124).

the situation is as serious now as it ever has been since the trouble started. Clap on top of this comes Macdonald's rushing through the treaty with Russia without the King's name on it.[28] What did you think of that? Is there any force in the legal defence put forward in the Times? It seemed to my lay eye to be great nonsense.

You must excuse me for a shortish letter. After my long spell with the blue pencil I am in an indolent mood which would be very pleasant if I could give it its head: but I must start and tackle my lectures tomorrow. I have ordered a dinner jacket suit at the same tailors: for that and for all else that your letter contained, many thanks.

I had almost forgotten to say that on the occasion of W's last visit I went over to Colchester for the night in order to come back with him in the sidecar.[29] The new byke is a noble machine and we stopped to eat our lunch at a railway bridge near Watford which used to be the regular goal of our walks when we were at Wynyard. Here we sat on the slope of the cutting looking down on the L.N.W.R. main line on which we used to gaze in the old days when it was the only object of interest in the landscape. It was strange to find that the said landscape was quite an ordinary, even pleasant English countryside: and it was almost impossible to realise the appalling blankness and hostility which it once wore. In those days we had not grown used to the English colouring (so different from Ulster): our interests and appreciation of nature were limited to the familiar: rivers might wind and trees bloom in vain – one saw it all only as an abominable mass of earth dividing one by hundreds of miles from home and the hills and the sea and ships and everything a reasonable man could care for.

We were puzzled for some time as to why the line was invisible from a fence on which we used to sit to watch it: until W. hit on the simple truth that some trees which had been little trees in 1909 had become big trees in 1924. That's the sort of moment that makes the youngest of us feel old. We also passed a large park in Hertfordshire whose famous name I know very well at the moment but it won't come into my

28 James Ramsay MacDonald, the Labour Prime Minister, was trying to get his Anglo-Soviet treaty passed. A draft of the proposed treaty, dealing with commerce and navigation between Great Britain and Northern Ireland and the Soviet Union, appeared in *The Times* of 8 August.

29 For an account of this outing with Warnie on 3 July see *AMR*, pp. 341–2.

head.[30] W. tells me that it is one of the places where you spoke on the Irish question in your young days. I don't know if he is right.

your loving son,
Jack

TO HIS FATHER (LP VIII: 260–1):

[University College]
Postmark: 28 August 1924

My dear Papy,

As you say, it becomes uncanny. Whenever I 'remember me of my sins' I know that this will happen, and usually, as in the present case, I fear I clinch the matter by forgetting for a day or so to post my letter. Thanks for the dividend.

When I came to the part in your letter where you speak of how God does temper the wind to the shorn lamb I fairly laid it down and laughed. A joke by letter seldom has this effect: it usually arrives but the ghost of a spoken joke – it reaches the intellect without disturbing the face. But the image of Warnie as a shorn lamb, and of the expression with which he would say 'What d'you mean?' if you tried to explain to him WHY he was funny as a shorn lamb, was too much for me. But though you didn't mention it, I know very well WHO tempered the wind in the present case.

I am plodding on with my fourteen lectures – I am at number five, or rather have just finished it. I think I said before that I am not writing them IN EXTENSO, only notes. The extemporary element thus introduced is dangerous for a beginner, but READ lectures send people to sleep and I think I must make the plunge from the very beginning and learn to TALK, not to recite. I practise continually, expanding my notes to imaginary audiences, but of course it is difficult to be quite sure what will fill an hour. Perhaps I will experiment on you when I come home! The laborious part is the continual verifying of references and QUOTING. As Johnson says 'a man can write pretty quickly when he writes from his own mind: but he will turn over one half a library to make one book.'[31]

---

30 Warnie appended a footnote to this letter in LP VIII: 257 suggesting that the place is probably Hatfield, the seat of Lord Salisbury.

31 *Boswell's Life of Johnson*, op. cit., vol. II, 6 April 1775, p. 344 (slightly misquoted).

And of course when one is trying to TEACH one can take nothing for granted. Hitherto I have always talked or read to people to whom I could say 'You remember Bradley's stunt about judgement' or 'The sort of business you get at the beginning of Kant'. But of course that won't do now – and the deuce of it is that when you actually look the passage up you always find that they either say more or less than you want. Consequently I spend my days running from library to library, or hunting things from the index of one book to another. By the way, in ORAL instruction, how many times do you have to say the same thing before people tumble to it? You should be able to answer that.

While it comes into my head – a propos of the photo of Warnie bathing – I take it it is the one of his FLOATING which he showed me: telling me at the same time that one of his colleagues had remarked 'It is one of the sights of the summer to see Lewis ANCHORED off the coast'. This should have come with my first paragraph, but I hadn't found your letter at that stage.

I was very much impressed by what you tell me about affairs at home. I know you must have often thought that W. and I treated the Irish question very lightly: indeed you once told me that my views were 'like those of every other Englishman'. This I think was natural: our trip to France had naturally altered the proportion of things and both views are explicable. The latest developments however have brought me much nearer to your way of looking at it. If there is a bust up now, the consequences will by no means end in Ireland. I cannot see how in the long run it could avoid leading to a repetition of the Curragh incident: and what that would mean with the present government is a nasty problem.[32]

---

32 In 1913 some 500 delegates of the Ulster Unionist Council, which had been formed in 1905 to bring together unionists' associations, nominated a provincial government which would take office if the Home Rule bill was passed. This group, which planned to resist Home Rule, called itself the Ulster Volunteer Force. It numbered over 84,000 men and it imported many thousands of rifles and other arms which were distributed all over Ulster. In March 1914 it was decided that a military force must be ready in the Curragh – the chief military training camp 32 miles south-west of Dublin. However, when the commander-in-chief of the army in Ireland demanded that any officer who was unwilling to invade Ulster must be dismissed from the forces, Sir Hubert Gough (1870–1963), the brigadier-general commanding the 3rd Cavalry Brigade at the Curragh, prepared to resign rather than initiate military operations against Ulster. This became known as the 'Curragh incident' or the 'Curragh mutiny'.

There has hardly been a day's sunshine here for months and most of the harvest is being lost. A propos, I had a little communication today asking me to contribute to the Salvation Army harvest thanksgiving! I can't understand why so many religious people keep up this dishonesty. For surely it is pure humbug to return thanks for what you haven't got?

I don't know that I have any news except that I was caught by Aunt Lily in the street the other day: that I am meeting her to lunch in some restaurant tomorrow: that I have had my hair cut: and am to have my dinner jacket tried on this week. I hope you keep well.

your loving son,
Jack

TO HIS FATHER (LP VIII: 263):

Univ. Coll.
Wednesday.
Postmark: 15 October 1924

My dear Papy,

My maiden lecture yesterday went off alright in a sense – the only difficulty was the audience.[33] They put me down for the same time at which a much more important lecture by an established man was being held elsewhere.[34] They also, by a misprint, put me down as lecturing at Pembroke, not at Univ. In these conditions it is not to be wondered at if no one came at all. As a matter of fact FOUR people turned up! This of course is not very encouraging. But I shall not let it come between me and my rest. Better men than I have begun in the same way and one must be patient. As long as Mr Pritchard's highly essential lectures are held at the same time as mine, I can hardly expect anyone to come to me. Don't be worried about it.

Otherwise everything goes well. All my new colleagues are kindness itself and everyone does his best to make me feel at home – especially dear old Poynton. I find the actual tutoring easy at the time (tho' I am curiously tired at the end of the day) and have already struck some quite good men among my pupils. I have seen only one real dud so far – a man

---

33 Lewis's first lecture in the University of Oxford, on 'The Good, its position among values', was delivered at 10 a.m. on Tuesday 14 October.

34 Harold Arthur Prichard, Fellow of Philosophy at Trinity College, was lecturing at this same time on 'History of the Theory of Knowledge (Descartes, Locke, Berkeley, Hume)'.

who celebrated his first hour with me by telling me as many obvious lies as I have heard in a short space.

I have paid the bill for my dress suit – ten guineas, less 10/6 discount so that it was actually £9.19.6.

I have both the parcel of books and the handkerchiefs, for wh. many thanks. I have the College football captain among my pupils and am busy making up THAT subject also in order to be able to talk to him.

your loving son,
Jack

Warnie arrived in Oxford on his motorbike and sidecar on 20 December, and he and Jack set off for home the next morning. They drove to Liverpool on the motorbike, crossed the Irish Sea by ferry, and arrived at Little Lea on the morning of 23 December. They remained with their father until 10 January.

1925

TO HIS FATHER (LP VIII: 274–5):

[University] College
Thursday
Postmark: 11 February 1925

My dear Papy,

You should have heard from me before, but I have hardly been in a position to write. I spent the first fortnight of the term in bed with flu. I am very much afraid my organism is acquiring the HABIT of getting this troublesome complaint every time it becomes prevalent. As you have had it yourself and as you doubtless remember the curious psychological results it produces in the convalescent stage – the depression and dead alive feeling – I need not describe them. In my own case the spirits are not greatly improved by the necessity of having a tooth drawn as soon as I was fit for it. However it came out yesterday with gas, and the relief of having that off my chest has so cheered me that I think it has chased away the last dregs of the flu depression. So now 'my bosom's lord sits lightly on the throne'.[1] It has actually not rained today – and all is for the best.

W. and I had a magnificent ride back and I was sorry he had not his camera with him. From Shrewsbury to Oxford was all perfect: an orgy of woods, hills, broad rivers, grey castles, Norman abbeys and towns that have always been asleep. I wish I could describe Ledbury to you. It consists of about four broad streets in which every second house is of the Elizabethan type, timbered and white, with gables to the front. It is set in the middle of delightful rolling country and the end of Malvern hills comes down to the town end. Best of all, no one has yet 'discovered' it: it has not become a show place and the inhabitants are quite unaware that there is anything remarkable about it. Ludlow too I would like you to

1 Shakespeare, *Romeo and Juliet*, V, i, 3.

see: with its castle, former seat of the Earl of the Marches, where Comus was first performed. But after all, where can you go in the South and West of England without meeting beauty?

I don't think I have much news. All goes on as usual here – that is to say very pleasantly on the whole though with some sense of strain and little leisure. My lectures have gone off rather better this term though it's still very much a case of 'fit audience though few'.[2] My most persevering auditor is an aged parson[3] (I can't image where he comes from) who takes very copious notes and darts dagger glances at me every now and then. Some one suggests that he is a spy sent out by the board of faculties to detect young lecturers in heresy – and that he keeps on coming with the idea that if he gives me enough rope I shall hang myself in the end. There is also a girl who draws pictures half the time – alas, I have done so myself!

I hope you are keeping pretty well. This is the most trying time of the year I think. Even here far inland we have such gales that I thought the house was coming down. I say 'house' because the part of College which I am in is an old sixteenth century house which somehow got incorporated. Nevertheless the primroses are out in the College gardens. How are the corns? – mine are rather better.

your loving son,
Jack

TO HIS FATHER (LP VIII: 287–9):

[University College
April 1925]

My dear Papy,

Many thanks for your letter. I am sorry to hear of your 'rotten Easter': mine was redeemed by the glorious two days trip with Warnie.[4] Otherwise I was pretty well hustled during the vacation, working against time to prepare for this term, which, to tell the truth, I began in rather a tired state. As you once said to me, 'Talking is the most exhausting of all occupations'.

---

2 Milton, *Paradise Lost*, VII, 31: 'Fit audience find, though few.'

3 This was the Rev. Frank Nightingale who had gone to the University of London after being a clergyman in the Church of England since 1894, and who had now retired to Oxford.

4 This was another trip by motorbike and sidecar, on 6–8 April.

The trip was delightful. I was pleased to revisit Salisbury and see it more thoroughly. I well remember my former visit. 'It was a Sunday' and NOT very early in the morning, as you doubtless recollect, when we stopped for a few minutes in Uncle Hamilton's headlong career and heard morning prayer going on in the Cathedral. At that time I did not agree with you and cared for it less than Wells or Winchester.

This time as we came into sight of Salisbury, where, on those big rolling downs that spire can be seen from fifteen miles away, I began to have my doubts. Later, when we had had tea and strolled into the Close I decided that it was very good in its own way but not in my favourite way. But when we came out again and saw it by moonlight after supper, I was completely conquered. It was a perfect spring night with the moon nearly full, and not a breath of wind stirring nor a sound from the streets. The half light enhanced its size, and the sharp masses of shadow falling in three great patches from the three main faces of one side emphasized the extraordinary simplicity in which it differs so from say, Wells.

That is the real difference I think, and what repelled me at first: the others, mixed of a dozen styles, have grown from century to century like organic things and the slow history of secular change has been built into them. One feels the PEOPLE behind them more: the nameless craftsmen in this or that gargoyle which is different from every other.

Salisbury, on the other hand, is the idea of a master mind, struck out at once for ever. Barring mechanical difficulties it might have been built in a day. Doesn't Kipling talk of the Taj-Mahal as 'a sigh made marble'? On the same metaphor one might say that Wells is an age made into stone and Salisbury a petrified moment. But what a moment! The more one looks the more it satisfies. What impressed me most – the same thought has come into everyone's head in such places – was the force of Mind: the thousands of tons of masonry held in place by an idea, a religion: buttress, window, acres of carving, the very lifeblood of men's work, all piled up there and gloriously USELESS from the side of the base utility for which alone we build now. It really is typical of a change – the medieval town where the shops and houses huddle at the foot of the cathedral, and the modern city where the churches huddle between the sky scraping offices and the appalling 'stores'. We had another good look at it in the morning light after breakfast – when the plump and confident members of the feathered chapter cooing in the very porch added a new charm. W. says that Salisbury is Barset: if so, we must be standing near where the Warden said 'I'm afraid I shall never like Mrs Proudie' and the Archdeacon took off his hat to 'let a cloud of steam escape'.[5]

On our run that day we stopped at Stonehenge – a very fine morning and intensely quiet except for a battery practising over the next ridge. It was the first time I had heard a gun fired since I left France, and I cannot tell you how odd the sensation was. For one thing it seemed much louder and more sinister and generally unpleasant than I had expected: as was perhaps natural from the general tendency of memory to minimize, and also from the solitude and quiet of the place. I thought (as I had thought when we revisited Watford) how merciful it would be if we could sometimes foresee the future: how it would have carried me through many a long working night in the trenches if I could have seen myself 'seven years on' smoking my pipe in the oldest place in the old, safe, comfortable English fields where guns fire only at targets. But on the whole, however, it would not be a comfortable privilege: though I have no doubt at all that it is accorded to some – but like all these mysterious leaks through of Something Else into our experience it seems to come without rhyme or reason, indifferently chosen for the trivial or the tragic occasion. I don't know why I have blundered into this subject, which may not interest you: you must put it down as a momentary eruption of that sense of irremediable ignorance and bewilderment which is becoming every year more certainly my permanent reaction to things. Whatever else the human race was made for, it at least was not made to know.

This is my last term 'in the bond' at Univ. and there is still no word of the Fellowship. I begin to be afraid that it is not coming at all. A Fellowship in English is announced at Magdalen and of course I am applying for it, but without any serious hopes as I believe much senior people including my own old English tutor[6] are in for it. If he gets it I may get some of the 'good will of the business': I mean some of the pupils at Univ., Exeter and elsewhere whom he will have to abandon. These continued hopes deferred are trying, and I'm afraid trying for you too. About money, if you will put in £40 – if you think this is reasonable – I shall be on the pig's back.

5 Trollope, *Barchester Towers*, ch. VI.
6 F.P. Wilson.

My best pupil[7] is in great trouble. He went down in the middle of last term to attend his father's deathbed. He came up late at the beginning of this term, having been detained at home while his mother was operated on for cancer. To make matters worse this poor fellow has been left very badly off by his father's death, and it was even doubted last term whether he would be able to go on with his course. It is really extraordinary how long troubles are in letting go when they have once fastened on an individual or a house. If only he had a decent chance he would almost certainly get a first: he is in addition a very modest decent chap. One feels very helpless in coming continually into contact with such a case. If I were an older man, or again if I were his contemporary, I might be able to convey some sense of sympathy: but the slight difference in age, or some defect in myself, makes an insurmountable barrier and I can only feel how trivial or external and even impertinent my 'philosophy' must seem to him at such a moment.

I am sorry if this is rather a scrappy letter – and likewise rather smudged and meanly written. I have been writing in pauses between pupils, and odd moments. You must not think that I am forgetful in my long silences. I have often things to say to you day by day, but in the absence of VIVA VOCE conversation they die away and the time and mood for a set letter do not come so easily.

I have been into Hall and common room afterwards and heard an interesting thing. Do you remember Mrs Asquith's saying in that detestable autobiography that she once asked Jowett if he had ever been in love? He replied 'Yes' and being asked what the lady was like, replied 'Violent – very violent.' Apparently the lady was really Florence Nightingale. Poynton and Farquharson both knew of it. For her 'violence' see Strachey in 'Eminent Victorians'. The story – a strange tragi-comedy – seems to have been common property. Both the parties were irascible and opinionated and quarreled nearly as often as they met: and yet the affair hung on for a long time.

I hope you are fairly well and going along comfortably.

your loving son,

Jack

---

7 This pupil's name was Harold Henry Cox (1901–74). He matriculated at University College in 1919, and despite the troubles Lewis mentions, he succeeded in taking a First in Greats in 1927. He went on to become Tutor of Philosophy at Lincoln College, Oxford.

In his diary of 20 May Albert Lewis wrote: 'While I was waiting for dinner Mary came into the study and said "The Post Office is on the phone". I went to it. "A telegram for you." "Read it." "Elected Fellow Magdalen. Jack." "Thank you." I went up to his room and burst into tears of joy. I knelt down and thanked God with a full heart. My prayers had been heard and answered.'

Preserved with Mr Lewis's papers was this cutting from The Times *of 22 May 1925:*

> *NEW FELLOW OF MAGDALEN COLLEGE. The President and Fellows of Magdalen College have elected to an official Fellowship in the College as Tutor in English Language and Literature, for five years as from next June 15, Mr Clive Staples Lewis M.A. (University College). Mr Lewis was educated first at Malvern College. He won a scholarship in classics at University College in 1916, and, (after war service) a first class in Classical Moderations in 1920, the Chancellor's prize for an English essay in 1921, a first class in Literae Humaniores in 1922, and a first class in the Honour School of English Language and Literature in 1925.* (LP VIII: 290)

TO HIS FATHER (LP VIII: 291–2):

Univ. Coll.
26th May 1925

My dear Papy,

First, let me thank you from the bottom of my heart for the generous support, extended over six years, which alone has enabled me to hang on till this. In the long course I have seen men at least my equals in ability and qualifications fall out for the lack of it. 'How long can I afford to wait' was everybody's question: and few had those at their back who were both able and willing to keep them in the field so long. You have waited, not only without complaint but full of encouragement, while chance after chance slipped away and when the goal receded furthest from sight. Thank you again and again. It has been a nerve racking business, and I have hardly yet had time to taste my good fortune with a deliberate home felt relish.

First of all, as I told you, I thought that I had my own tutor Wilson as a rival, which would have made the thing hopeless. But that I found to be a false rumour. Then I wrote to Wilson and Gordon (the Professor of

English Literature)[8] for testimonials, relying on them as my strongest supports. Within twenty four hours I had the same answer from both. They were very sorry. If only they had known I was going in for it...they thought I had definitely abandoned English for philosophy. As it was, they had already given their support to my friend Coghill of Exeter.[9] Once more, they were exceedingly sorry, and remained mine sincerely etc.

This was enough to make anyone despair: but mark how the stars sometimes fight for us. Two days later came news that Coghill had been offered a fellowship by his own College and had withdrawn from the field. Wilson's testimonial – a very good one – came by the next post. Gordon said he wouldn't write anything as he was going to be consulted personally by the Magdalen people, but he would BACK me. This of course was much better than the testimonial. Still, I hardly allowed myself to hope. Then came a letter from Gordon – 'CONFIDENTIAL'. 'I was asked my opinion about the candidates yesterday and I put my money on you. I think your chances good, but of course one never knows what the spin of the coin may do in such things.' This, I said to myself, is at least nearer than I've ever got before: but don't hope, don't build on it.

Then came an invitation to dine at Magdalen on Sunday a fortnight ago. This showed only that I was one of the possibles. Then came the LITTLE problems that seem so big at the time. Was Magdalen one of the Colleges where they wore white ties and tails, or did they wear dinner jackets and black ties? I asked the Farq. and he advised white tie and tails: and of course when I got there I found everyone in black ties and dinner jackets. These dinners for inspection are not exactly the pleasantest way of spending one's evening – as you may imagine. You can hardly say 'He'll enjoy it when he gets there'. But I must say they carried off as well

---

8 George Stuart Gordon (1881–1942) became Magdalen College's first Fellow of English in 1907. He was Professor of English at Leeds University 1913–22, after which he returned to Oxford as the Merton Professor of English. Sir Walter Raleigh had inaugurated a discussion class for those reading English Literature, and Gordon continued this practice when he became Merton Professor. Lewis was a member of the discussion class and he wrote about it in *AMR*. He was to see a good deal of Gordon when he was President of Magdalen College from 1928–42.

9 Nevill Henry Kendall Coghill (1899–1980) matriculated at Exeter College, Oxford, in 1919. He and Lewis read English together. See **Nevill Coghill** in the Biographical Appendix.

as could be asked a situation which must be irksome to the hosts as well as to the guest. So far so good.

Then came a spell of thundery weather of the sort that makes a man nervous and irritable even if he has nothing on his mind: and the news that Bryson[10] and I were the two real candidates. Bryson comes from home and knows Arthur: but of course I mention his name in the strictest possible secrecy. One afternoon, in that week, I saw the said Bryson emerging from Magdalen: and ('so full of shapes is fancy')[11] felt an unanswerable inner conviction that he had won and made up my mind on it.

On the Saturday Warren[12] (1) met me in the street and had a vague tho' kindly conversation with me. On Monday I had a very abrupt note from him asking me to see him on Tuesday morning, with the curious addition, 'It is most important'. I didn't like it at all: it suggested some horrible hitch. Was I going to be viva-d on Anglo-Saxon verbs or asked my views on the Thirty Nine Articles?[13] We had thunder that night, but a poor storm and not enough to clear the air: and Tuesday rose up a grey clammy morning when one sweats every time one moves and the big blue bottles settle on your hands. This sounds like writing it up to an exciting conclusion: but it WAS a nasty morning and it WAS quite exciting enough for me at the time.

---

10 John Norman Bryson (1896–1976) was educated at the Queen's University, Belfast and Merton College. He was a lecturer at Balliol, Merton and Oriel Colleges 1923–40, when he became Fellow of English at Balliol College. He retired in 1963.

11 Shakespeare, *Twelfth Night*, I, i, 14.

12 Sir Thomas Herbert Warren (1953–1930) made his mark at Clifton College where he was head of the school and scholar-elect of Balliol College. When he came up to Balliol in 1872 Benjamin Jowett was Master and the college was at the height of its reputation. Warren took Firsts in Classical Moderations (1873) and *Literae Humaniores* (1876). In 1877 he was elected to a prize fellowship at Magdalen. Besides being a brilliant scholar and able to stimulate his pupils, he came to know them as personal friends. In 1885, at the age of 32, he was elected President of Magdalen, an office which he held until 1928, a period of 43 years. He threw himself into developing the college, and it was a marked tribute to the position he held in the University and outside it that in 1912 King George V chose it for the Prince of Wales. His contribution to classical scholarship was an edition of the first five books of Plato's *Republic* (1888). The two great literary enthusiasms of his life were Virgil and Tennyson, and there are reflections of both in his two volumes of verse, *By Severn Seas* (1897) and *The Death of Virgil* (1907).

13 The set of doctrinal formulae proposed by the Church of England in the 16th century as a method of defining its dogmatic position. See note 69 to the letter of 29 May 1921.

I got to Magdalen, and, would you believe it, he kept me waiting for HALF AN HOUR before he saw me. The choir boys were practising in the tower close by. When he did see me it turned out to be all formalities. They were electing tomorrow and thought me the 'strongest and most acceptable candidate'. Now IF I were elected would I agree to this, and would I be prepared to do that, and did I understand that the terms of the fellowship implied so and so. The only thing of the slightest importance was 'would I be prepared, in addition to the English pupils, to help with the philosophy.' (This, I imagine, stood me in good stead: probably no other candidate had done English as well as philosophy.) I need hardly say that I would have agreed to coach a troupe of performing bagbirds in the quadrangle: but I looked very wise and thought over all his points and I hope let no subservience appear. He then gave me a long talk about the special needs of Magdalen undergraduates – as if they were different from any others! – all as if I had been elected, but without saying I had been. During the whole interview he was cold and dry and not nearly so agreeable as he had been on the Saturday. He finally dismissed me with a request that I would hang about Univ. the following afternoon in case I were called for.

And then next day – about 2.30 – they telephoned for me and I went down. Warren saw me, told me I had been elected and shook hands: since he has written me a very nice letter of congratulations saying that he believes they may congratulate themselves. It is a fine job as our standards go: starting at £500 a year with 'provision made for rooms, a PENSION, and dining allowance'. The election for five years only in the first case of course means only that in five years they have the chance of getting rid of you if you turn out 'hardly one of our successes'. One hopes, in the ordinary course of events, to be re-elected.

A cat 'met me in the day of my success'[14] and bit me deeply in the right thumb while I was trying to prevent it from attacking a small dog. In fact, to go on with the Shakesperian allusion, I came 'between the fell incensed points of mighty opposites'.[15] By dint of poultices I have now reduced the inflammation, and this is the first day I have been able to write with ease. It would have been better sooner if I had not been forced daily to answer as best I could the kind congratulations which have

14 Shakespeare, *Macbeth*, I, v, 1 (slightly misquoted).
15 Shakespeare, *Hamlet*, V, ii, 60–1.

reached me. I must cut it short now. It has been an egotistical letter, but you asked for it. Once more, with very hearty thanks and best love,

your loving son,
Jack

(1) I mean the President of Magdalen of course, not Big Brother.

TO HIS FATHER (LP VIII: 297–9):

[University College]
Aug. 14th [1925]

My dear Papy,

Since our last interchange of letters I have been almost continuously employed in my usual summer task of examining. This year I had been promoted from the post of examiner to that of awarder. An awarder is one who besides examining himself revises the marks of the other examiners and so produces a final verdict: the principle being that if Mr A gives six marks where I should have given eight, then 85 should count for a pass in the candidates I have looked over, while his will get through on 75 or 80. In each department there are two awarders, one from Oxford and one from Cambridge, and the work is done alternately year by year in either university. This year it was at Cambridge and about forty Oxford people went over.

We were all put up in Queens College where I must say they did us like fighting cocks. It is all paid for by the 'Board' which I take it means the taxpayer, through the ministry of education. As I knew many of the Oxford people I had quite a good time. Cambridge is beautiful beyond description: more so, in many ways, than Oxford. My rooms looked out over the river. Unfortunately our work took from 9 a.m. till 7 p.m. and so I had little time to see the town. My Cambridge colleague was a man of no breeding – the sort of person who referred to the candidates as 'kiddies' – but quite a pleasant fellow and we got on comfortably together.

We were a good deal delayed by the carelessness of the examiners whose work we had to use: some of them were erratic and a great deal of the marking had to be completely revised. We also had to deal with the difficult problem of papers which seemed to have been tampered with by a schoolmaster after they had left the boys' hands. We came to the conclusion that the evidence was not strong enough to justify us in making such a serious accusation – but I still feel rather uncomfortable about it.

By an arrangement previously made, W. biked over from Colchester to take me there for the week end on the Saturday. We got away by five o'clock and after a journey through pleasant but tame country, we made Colchester at nine. The authorities have again taken advantage of our Colonel's good nature. The mess has broken up and every one has gone on maneuvers: W. has had to sacrifice the hope of long days in the saddle and short nights in the open air, forced marches and alarms and excursions under the suns of Salisbury plain, and content himself as best may with a suburban lodging house, short hours, books, and sea bathing. He bears up very well.

On Sunday he took me to the sea where we had a capital swim: it is the first time for several years that I have been in salt water. We saw a good deal of the country on Monday. As I said before, Essex and Suffolk are tame: but what nature lacks is compensated by the works of men and I have never seen a countryside so thickly studded with fine buildings. Every second village has a parish church that might be an abbey, a Tudor manor house, a ruined Norman keep, a full blown castle, or at least a venerable inn. I left him on Tuesday.

The only other event of importance since I last wrote has been my formal 'admission' at Magdalen. It is a formidable ceremony and not entirely to my taste. Without any warning of what was in store for me, the Vice-President (a young fellow called Wrong[16] whom I have since got to know on the Cambridge jaunt) ushered me into a room where I found the whole household – it is large at Magdalen. Warren was standing and when Wrong laid a red cushion at his feet I realized with some displeasure that this was going to be a kneeling affair. Warren then addressed me for some five minutes in Latin. I was able to follow some three quarters of what he said: but no one had told me what response I ought to make and it was with some hesitation that I hasarded DO FIDEM as a reply – copying the formula for taking your M.A. This

---

16 Edward Murray Wrong (1889–1928), a Canadian, was educated in Toronto and at Balliol College, Oxford, where he took a First in Modern History in 1913. He was elected a Fellow of Magdalen College in 1914. He was vice-principal of Manchester College of Technology 1916–19, after which he returned to Magdalen. His publications include *The British Empire* [1916], *Charles Butler and Responsible Government* (1926) and *History of England, 1688–1815* [1927]. E.M. Wrong was a man of enormous grace and charm, and his early death was the cause of grief to all who knew him. See his obituary in *The Times* (16 February 1928), p. 14.

appeared to fill the bill. I was then told (in English) to kneel. When I had done so Warren took me by the hand and raised me with the words 'I wish you joy'. It sounds well enough on paper but it was hardly impressive in fact: and I tripped over my gown in rising. I now thought my ordeal at an end: but I was never more mistaken in my life. I was sent all round the table and every single member in turn shook my hand and repeated the words 'I wish you joy'. You can hardly imagine how odd it sounded by the twenty fifth repetition. English people have not the talent for graceful ceremonial. They go through it lumpishly and with a certain mixture of defiance and embarrassment as if everyone felt he was being rather silly and was at the same time ready to shoot the first man who said so. In a French or Italian university now, this might have gone off nobly.

I had also forgotten to tell you – or did I tell you before – that previous to the examining I had a few days in London with a married friend of mine called Barfield, and met Arthur by accident in a theatre. But I have a feeling that I have written this to you already. The mind – or at any rate MY mind – plays tricks in these things. In a way I share your regret that when the opening came it did not come at Univ. I shall never find a common room that I did not like better: and every break in the continuity of one's associations is in some degree unpleasant. No one likes, even at my age, to see any slice of life being finally turned over to the past.

As to the other change – from Philosophy to English – I share your feeling less. I think you are mistaken in supposing that the field is less crowded in Philosophy: it seems so to you only because you have more chance of seeing the literary crowd. If you read 'Mind' and one or two other periodicals of the sort as regularly as you read the Literary Supplement, you would probably change your view. I think things are about equal in that way. On other grounds I am rather glad of the change. I have come to think that if I had the mind, I have not the brain and nerves for a life of pure philosophy. A continued search among the abstract roots of things, a perpetual questioning of all that plain men take for granted, a chewing the cud for fifty years over inevitable ignorance and a constant frontier watch on the little tidy lighted conventional world of science and daily life – is this the best life for temperaments such as ours? Is it the way of health or even of sanity? There is a certain type of man, bull necked and self satisfied in his 'pot bellied equanimity' who urgently needs that bleak and questioning atmosphere. But what is a tonic to the Saxon may be a debauch to us Celts. And it certainly is to the Hindoos.

I am not condemning philosophy. Indeed in turning from it to literary history and criticism, I am conscious of a descent: and if the air on the heights did not suit me, still I have brought back something of value. It will be a comfort to me all my life to know that the scientist and the materialist have not the last word: that Darwin and Spencer[17] undermining ancestral beliefs stand themselves on a foundation of sand; of gigantic assumptions and irreconcilable contradictions an inch below the surface. It leaves the whole thing rich in possibilities: and if it dashes the shallow optimisms it does the same for the shallow pessimisms. But having once seen all this 'darkness', a darkness full of promise, it is perhaps best to shut the trap door and come back to ordinary life: unless you are one of the really great who can see into it a little way – and I was not.

At any rate I escape with joy from one definite drawback of philosophy – its solitude. I was beginning to feel that your first year carries you out of the reach of all save other professionals. No one sympathises with your adventures in that subject because no one understands them: and if you struck treasure trove no one would be able to use it. But perhaps this is enough on the subject. I hope you are well and free from corns, sore gums and all other 'crosses'.

your loving son,
Jack

Jack visited his father in September, and this time they got on very well. His having a job, and no longer being dependent upon his father, removed the tension between them, and both seemed at ease. In his diary for 13 September, Mr Lewis said: 'Jacks arrived for holidays. Looking very well and in great spirits' (LP IX: 7). On 1 October he wrote: 'Jacks returned. A fortnight and a few days with me. Very pleasant, not a cloud. Went to the boat with

17 Herbert Spencer (1820–1903), philosophical and scientific thinker whose publications include *First Principles* (1862), *Principles of Biology* (1867) and *Principles of Ethics* (1893). He was the chief exponent of agnosticism in 19th century England. He divided the whole of reality into the knowable (the principles of science) and the unknowable (the principles of religion). He affirmed that progress was the supreme law of the universe.

him. The first time I did not pay his passage money. I offered, but he did not want it' (LP IX: 29).

Following his return to Oxford, Lewis divided his time between Magdalen and 'Hillsboro' which he shared with the Moores. During term he slept in his college rooms – Staircase III, Number 3, of New Buildings – and visited the 'family' at 'Hillsboro' in the afternoons. When term ended the routine was reversed, and he lived at 'Hillsboro' and came into Magdalen whenever there was a need to do so. However, from the time he moved into Magdalen he was to have two homes until his retirement many years later.

TO HIS FATHER (LP IX: 37–8):

Magdalen College
Oct. 21st 1925

My dear Papy,

When we discussed the question of furnishing my rooms before I left, I thought it a very remote contingency. It was rather a crushing blow to find that I had to get everything – and for three spacious rooms: the extent of College's bounty being some linoleum in the smaller sitting room and a washstand in the bedroom. It is hard to say on what principle fellows are provided with washstands but left to provide their own beds: unless it is a symbol of the combined VIGILANCE and purity which is so characteristic of their corporate life. Carpets, tables, curtains, chairs, fenders, fire irons, coal boxes, table covers – everything – had to be bought in haste. It has cost me over £90, although I was able to pick up some things second hand. It sounds an alarming total, but I do not think I have been extravagant; the rooms certainly do not look as if they had been furnished by a plutocrat.

My external surroundings are beautiful beyond expectation and beyond hope. To live in the Bishop's Palace at Wells would be good but could hardly be better than this. My big sitting room looks north and from it I see nothing, not even a gable or spire, to remind me that I am in a town. I look down on a stretch of level grass which passes into a grove of immemorial forest trees, at present coloured with autumn red. Over this stray the deer. They are erratic in their habits. Some mornings when I look out there will be half a dozen chewing the cud just underneath me, and on others there will be none in sight – or one little stag (not much bigger than a calf and looking too slender for the weight of its own antlers) standing still and sending through the fog that queer little bark or hoot which is these beasts' 'moo'. It is a sound that will soon be as familiar to me as the cough of the cows in the field at home, for I hear it day and night. On my right hand as I look from these windows is 'his favourite walk'.[18] My smaller sitting room and bedroom look out southward across a broad lawn to the main buildings of Magdalen with the tower beyond it. It beats Bannaher!

As to the 'College' in the other sense – as a human society – I can say little yet. One's first impressions of a new set are changed many times in the first month. They are all very nice to me. The general tone of the place strikes as a rather slack and flippant – I mean among the Dons – but I may very well be mistaken. Sambo[19] hardly ever appears. The most surprising thing is that they are much less formal than Univ. They don't dress for dinner except when the President dines, on which occasion a warning notice is sent round to our rooms. Again, there are an enormous number of us compared with Univ., and we meet much more often. Thus we breakfast and lunch in Common Room; meals in your own rooms (which I had thought universal at Oxford) being unknown here either for Dons or undergraduates. The latter are a little aloof from the rest of Oxford: not entirely thro' affectation but because as a matter of geography we are 'at the town's end': or, as someone said, we are the beginning of suburbia. I have very few pupils at present, wh. of course is helping me to improve my reading. They are quite nice fellows.

I had a most amusing journey with Arthur. When we got to the steward's office nothing was known of the berth which he professed to have booked and for a time it looked as if we should have to sit up all night. He really took the prospect much better than I had expected, but not so well as to deprive me of considerable enjoyment.

We are having real autumnal weather here: some pleasant bright days of frost but mostly damp and fog. I hope you have not yet succumbed to the seasonable cold in the head.

---

18 The favourite walk of Joseph Addison (1672–1719), the essayist and poet known for his contribution to *The Spectator*. When he was a Fellow of Magdalen he lived in New Buildings and greatly enjoyed the walk which runs northward from the College buildings and which has been known since the 19th century as 'Addison's Walk'. Lewis would have been surprised to know that on 13 May 1998 a C.S. Lewis Centenary Stone was erected in Addison's Walk on which is inscribed his poem about Addison's Walk – 'What the Bird Said Early in the Year' – found in *Poems* (1964) and *Collected Poems* (1994).

19 Nickname of the President of Magdalen.

your loving son,
Jack

TO A.K. HAMILTON JENKIN (B):

Magdalen College,
Oxford.
Nov. 4th [1925]

My dear Jenkin,

Your letter speaks of a possible meeting in the flesh. If I looked up from my study in New Buildings & saw you coming across the lawn I would fling a book in my pupils face and outstrip the winds in getting downstairs.

I cannot at present ask you to Hillsboro where Mrs Moore, alas, lies in bed sick of the varicose veins: but if you care for a night or two in College (preferable a Monday and Tuesday, not a week end), and if you were prepared to amuse yourself in the afternoons when I am out at Headington – why, then, we might look forward to two long evening talks and I can hardly express in temperate language how much the prospect pleases me.

Have you ever lived among deer? The windows of my Northern room look into the grove. There is a flat stretch of grass receding into big forest trees (all day long at present the leaves are eddying up the sky from them and the wind among them at night is magnificent). There is nothing in sight, not even a gable, to remind me that I am in a town: and over this grass the 'little dappled fools'[20] come right up to beneath my window. One morning there will be seven there chewing the cud in close squadron: next day not one in sight, till I go down to the bathroom. The window there is level with the ground and on these autumn mornings one gets a delicious earthy freshness and a horizontal view of dew and cobwebs along the turf: and perhaps one tiny solitary stag nibbling quite close to the sill as if he were the first animal in the world. But best of all is to hear them at night. They don't moo and they don't neigh, but they have two sounds. The one is a thin little hooting, rather like a faint cough, and most unearthly. The other (mark the catholicity of these beasts) the other is absolutely indistinguishable from the grunting of old fat pigs. And this last being most unpoetical and an anticlimax in the

20 Shakespeare, *As You Like It*, II, i, 22: 'the poor dappled fools'.

eyes of the universe, is really the best. If only to hear this you should come.

You shd. come if only to enter Magdalen after dark across the grove by my master key – on a moonlight night. With such a key at such an hour of night under such massy archways, through the length of such blind walks that sudden opened out into the freckled moonshine of tall groves, so secret and so wrapped Medea went by stealth to gather the enchanted herbs that did renew old Aeson.[21]

In plain prose there are two or three moments in that night entry by these successive posterns that I do it for the love of it when I might just as well go in past the porter's lodge. And if there is no moon (dazzlingly white among the trees after a long dark cobbled passage) perhaps instead there will be thick darkness and drumming rain and the hoofs of the deer (invisible) scampering away – and ahead the long lighted line of the cloisters in New Buildings. I wish there was anyone here childish enough (or *permanent* enough, not the slave of his particular and outward age) to share it with me. Now, it is that I am unfortunately in my meetings, or that I am growing a shell 'unprofitably travelling towards the crab', or is it that no man makes real friends after he has passed the undergraduate age? Because I get no forr'arder since the old days.

I go to Barfield for sheer wisdom and a sort of richness of spirit. I go to you for some smaller and yet more intimate connection with the feel of things, for a certain gusto and complete *rightness* of palate: to Harwood for 'humours' and the appreciation of them. I speak now of the points in which you severally excel, tho' of course your functions change and cross: and in a certain juncture of the planets each may play the other's part. Indeed I have expressed all the parts inadequately – specially Harwood's. But the question I am asking is why I meet no such men now. Is it that *I* am blind?

Some of the older men here are delightful: the younger fellows are none of them men of understanding. Oh for the people who speak one's own language: men and women in their different ways. A man can spread his legs out with them and talk: he can get something new from them. It is odd that only old friends bring *new* talk. With the others

21 Lewis is here remembering his poem on 'Medea' as mentioned in his letter to Arthur Greeves of 18 September 1919.

(those of our generation or a year or so older) 'whereso'er I turn my view / All is strange but nothing new.'

But a fig for them. If I wasn't worried to death about Mrs Moore's illness I should be on the pig's back. I have hardly any pupils at present and so am learning a little in my leisure. I am easy financially for the first time in my life: the material beauty of my surroundings is beyond all that I can desire – in its own style of course.

Thanks for your letter. The shooting star & the ninth wave must have been the thrill at second hand. I read Mrs G's Bronte years ago and don't remember it well, but I know what you mean (tho' not in connection with that book). Do try and come up. Regards and salutations from all here.

Yrs,
C. S. Lewis

TO HIS FATHER (LP IX: 42–3):

Magdalen College
Dec. 4th [1925]

My dear Papy,

It is strange if I forgot to acknowledge the cheque in a letter which I wrote primarily for that purpose. It is like going upstairs for a handkerchief and coming down with a book – a kind of adventure which overtakes even the wise. Let me hasten to cry MEA CULPA and also acknowledge with many thanks the two enclosures of your last.

I have had a nasty blow – don't be alarmed, it concerns neither life, limb or reputation. I was already worried about the difficulty of preparing an English lecture in the time at my disposal, but by dint of choosing a short subject which I know well (XVIII century precursors of the Romantic movement) I hoped to be able to acquit myself well enough. What was my displeasure on finding, when the rough draft of next term's lecture list was sent me, that my old tutor Wilson was lecturing on 'English Poetry from Thompson to Cowper'.[22] Now of course my 'precursors', with the exception of some critics and other prose writers, are just the poets from Thompson and Cowper. It is in fact the same subject under a different name. This means that, being neither able nor willing to rival Wilson, I am driven to concentrate on the prose people of whom

22 James Thomson (1700–48) and William Cowper (1731–1800).

at present I know very little. I have as hard a spell cut out for me between now and next term as I have ever had. Of course all the more easy and obvious subjects which will leap to your mind are long since occupied by the bigwigs.

The immediate consequence is that I am afraid I shall scarcely be able to take more than a week at home at Christmas. To compensate for this I shall try to get across at Easter. I am sorry to disappoint you (and myself): but it is only one of the many evils which I see following from this bad hunch about the lecture. At the very best it means working much harder for a much poorer result. Of course no one, least of all Wilson himself, is to blame.

I have very nearly had flu but by dint of keeping my rooms and fireside for two days, have succeeded in turning the corner without going to bed.

I dined at Balliol the other night for the first time. 'We were not amused'. Although it was supposed to be a guest night par excellence and I was one of a crowd of guests, more than half the Balliol Dons did not turn up. They were (heaven help us) at a boxing match and of those who did appear many slipped away to the spectacle as soon as we left the table. The dinner was cold. Worst of all we had our wine afterwards in a common room which is next door to a Laboratory and (there is no other word) stinks. The Master of Balliol is a very bad host: what is euphemistically called a 'shy' man and what one suspects to be either conceited, lazy, or a dull man.[23] But come, come: this is not the way to return hospitality. 'Nor to offer it' one might add.

This is the hardest winter I have known for a long time. For many weeks the earth has been as iron under my feet and the heaven, not as brass, but as grey steel or ground glass above me. But for the pressure of these lectures I would give myself up to some days skating. A little snow fell over a fortnight ago, and every flake has remained unthawed to decorate the trees and to make the telegraph wires like old fashioned woolly bell ropes.

I have only been back to Univ. once – to a Martlet's dinner. It is strange how soon the places we leave assume the charm of the past. I could almost sentimentalize over the Farq. – or well ALMOST!

---

23 Alexander Dunlop Lindsay, Baron Lindsay of Birker (1879–1952), read Greats at University College. After teaching for a few years in Scotland, he returned to Oxford in 1906 as Fellow of Classics at Balliol College. He was Master of Balliol from 1924 to 1949.

I cannot help being glad for the moment about W's change of prospect. Is there no chance that this dilly dallying may go on indefinitely until he retired without sight of India?

I hope you are well and standing the cold.

your loving son,

Jack

P.S. How does one get a copy of one's birth certificate? Can you let me have one or shall I write myself to Somerset House or the Tower of London or the National Gallery or wherever they keep these things? They want it for some sort of Insurance Scheme by which I contribute to my own pension.

1926

TO HIS FATHER (LP XI: 265–6):

[Magdalen College]
Monday Dec. [January] 5th [1926]

My dear Papy,

I hope the cold has now gone. At best, I am afraid it will leave you weakened and shaken. It is the first week or two after one has got about again that is the dangerous part of such things: I hope you are taking all possible precautions.

Warnie and I had a rather interesting journey back.[1] First there was the episode of the friendly and intoxicated stranger in the smoking room of the Liverpool boat: but I feel that the Colonel's pen will do that story more justice than mine. Secondly there was the amazingly erudite fellow traveller in the train. I suppose he had gathered from our conversation – W. was reading Evelyn's diaries – that we were bookish people, but he let several hours pass before he quite suddenly chipped in, in a rather apologetic manner. I surmise that he lives among people who do not share his tastes and it is a relief to him to talk about them. He did not speak with the voice of an educated man, but his reading was curious: Pepys, Evelyn, Burnet, Boswell, Macaulay, Trollope, Thackeray, Ruskin, Morris and 'The Golden Bough'.[2] He seemed to be some kind of architect or decorator.

Now this is the sort of thing I like. To have a literary conversation in the study at Leeborough or the common room at Magdalen is (by comparison) nothing, because one remains in the charmed circle of one's own set and caste: there is nothing to refute the accusation of being out of the world, of playing with things that perhaps derive a fictitious value from the chatter of specially formed groups. But to talk over the same

1 Jack and Warnie were with their father at Little Lea from 20 until 28 December.

2 Sir James George Frazer, *The Golden Bough* (1890).

things with a man whose aitches are uncertain in a third class carriage – this restores one's faith in the value of the written word and makes one feel suddenly at home in one's country. It is the difference between grapes in a greenhouse and a hillside of vines.

The other interesting thing in our journey was the new scenery produced by the floods. Round about Warwick (you remember Warwick) for miles at a time there was nothing but water between one hedgerow and the next – and then the little hills made into islands. A village on a rise with 'the decent church that fronts (or is it *crowns*) the neighbouring hill'[3] has a very fine effect. You probably spotted the enclosed picture in today's Times, but I send it in case you have not. The long building to the right of the tower is 'New Building' which Gibbon,[4] who lived in it, called 'a stately pile'. The arrow points to the line whose windows belong to (1) Brightman[5] (the mechanical toy man) at the top. (2) 'J.A.'[6] ('nothing to

---

3 Oliver Goldsmith, *The Deserted Village* (1770), 12: 'The decent church that topt the neighbouring hill.'

4 Edward Gibbon (1737–94), author of *The History of the Decline and Fall of the Roman Empire*, lived in New Buildings 1752–3.

5 Frank Edward Brightman (1856–1932), liturgist of the Church of England, had been an undergraduate at University College, Oxford. He took a First in Mathematical Moderations (1877), a First in *Literae Humaniores* (1879) and a First in Theology (1880). He was ordained in 1885, having been made in 1884 an original librarian of Pusey House. He held that post until he was elected a fellow of Magdalen in 1902. There he remained until his death in 1932. He was one of the most learned scholars who flourished at the turn of the century. Amongst his publications is his monumental work, *The English Rite*, 2 vols. (1915), in which he set out the sources of the Book of Common Prayer and the changes from 1549 to 1662. See H.N. Bate's 'Frank Edward Brightman' in *Proceedings of the British Academy*, vol. XIX (1933). With reference to Lewis's verse 'We were Talking of dragons, Tolkien and I' in the essay on 'The Alliterative Metre' in *Selected Literary Essays* (1969), I asked Professor Tolkien the source. In his reply of 20 February 1968, he said: 'I remember Jack telling me the story of Brightman, the distinguished ecclesiastical scholar, who used to sit quietly in Common Room saying nothing except on rare occasions. Jack said there was a discussion on dragons one night and at the end Brightman's voice was heard to say, "I have seen a dragon." Silence. "Where was that?" he was asked. "On the Mount of Olives," he said. He relapsed into silence and never before his death explained what he meant.' *The Letters of J.R.R. Tolkien*, ed. Humphrey Carpenter (1981), p. 389.

6 John Alexander Smith (1863–1939), philosopher and classical scholar, was educated at Edinburgh and Balliol College where he took a First in *Literae Humaniores* in 1887. He became a fellow of Balliol in 1891 after which he was the Waynflete Professor of Moral and Metaphysical Philosophy and Fellow of Magdalen 1910–36. He was a distinguished scholar of Aristotle, and his translation of *De Anima* appeared in 1931. For the intellectual influence of J.A. Smith and other Oxford philosophers see James Patrick, *The Magdalen Metaphysicals: Idealism and Orthodoxy at Oxford, 1901–1945* (1985).

be gained by stammering over the word consciousness'). (3) Myself. (4) Ground Floor, and undergraduate rooms. You can imagine from the picture what a magnificent view I now have when the park has been converted into a lake. On a fine day when the sky makes the water blue and the wind fills it with ripples, one might almost take it for an arm of the sea. Of course I am not forgetting the serious side of the floods: but after all, what would you? I can't save the life of Dutch peasants or the pockets of Warwickshire peasants by refusing to enjoy the beauty of the thing as it appears from my window.

I am getting on nicely, or at least enjoying myself, over the lectures. New facts and new connections between old facts turn up every day. Do you remember an essay of Arthur Benson's about travelling by rail through a countryside where one has walked as a child?[7] He describes how he saw all sorts of things which he had known all his life 'linking up' in new ways. The big field with the stile, when one used to look out into the unknown world, turned out to be only *the other side* of the field with the duck pond which one passed on another walk. The *two* big *woods* turned out to be one little plantation dividing two familiar walks. He goes on to describe the peculiar pleasure which these discoveries gave him. That is the kind of pleasure I am enjoying at present. For instance if you have known long ago that the Wartons[8] wrote a certain kind of romantic poem full of phrases from Milton, and that Collins[9] did the same sort of thing: and if you have hitherto regarded these as two isolated facts: how delightful to find out suddenly that the Wartons and Collins were at school together and made a sort of poetry club there as boys and had evolved it together. This is only one example. Something like it turns up every day. Coincidences, accidents, isolated phenomena,

---

7 Benson, *Upton Letters*, letter of 4 August 1904, pp. 177–82.

8 Joseph Warton (1722–1800), one-time headmaster of Winchester College, published poems and odes. But he is best known as a critic of wide knowledge and good judgement. His *Essay on the Writings and Genius of Pope* (1756, 1782), distinguishes between the poets of 'the sublime and pathetic' and the 'men of wit and sense' such as Shakespeare, Spenser and Milton. His brother Thomas Warton (1728–90) was Professor of Poetry at Oxford 1757–67 and became Poet Laureate in 1785. He edited the works of Milton, but is best known for his celebrated *History of English Poetry*, 3 vols. (1774–81).

9 William Collins (1721–59) was educated at Winchester College (where he met Joseph Warton), and then Oxford. Later when he moved to London he became a friend of Dr Johnson, and he is mentioned in Dr Johnson's *Lives of the English Poets*. Collins's *Odes on Several Descriptive and Allegoric Subjects* (1746) has had considerable influence.

are disappearing all the time and being replaced by intelligible connections. 'Linking up' in fact. It is a most satisfying process. Let me have a line soon to say how you are, even if you can't manage a letter.

your loving son,
Jack

TO HIS FATHER (LP IX: 70–2):

Magdalen College.
Sunday
Postmark: 25 January 1926

My dear Papy,

There was no need for any apologies about the affair of the cheque. I was of course puzzled for the request for the return of an unknown cheque and wondered why you had not taken the more obvious step of 'stopping' it. In any case however I am so often guilty of dilatoriness in such matters that I can hardly complain if I am sometimes suspected in error.

As to the German measles – will you think me affected if I number a small illness among the minor pleasures of life? The early stages are unpleasant but at least they bring you to a point at which the mere giving up and going to bed is a relief. Then after twenty four hours the really high temperature and the headache are gone: one is not well enough to get up, but then one is ill enough not to want to get up. Best of all, work is impossible and one can read all day for mere pleasure with a clear conscience.

I re-read some of my favourite Jane Austens and read for the first time that jolly, unexacting tale, Quentin Durward.[10] I even took the chance of going on with my neglected Italian and got through several cantos of Boiardo:[11] an interminable fairy-tale kind of a poem, full of dragons and distressed damsels, without the slightest moral or intellectual significance. It is suited to the atmosphere of a day in bed with the snow falling outside: the drift, the holiday from all sublunary cares. Then one returns to a primitive and natural life as regards sleeping and waking. One dozes when the doze comes unsought and if one lies castle building at night one does not mind because there is no getting up in the

---

10 Scott, *Quentin Durward*. See note 175 to letter of 25 October 1916.

11 Matteomaria Boiardo, *Orlando Innamorato* (1487).

morning.[12] But of course all these delights have to be paid for: the first few days back to work when legs still ache and hours are long, are an unwelcome shock of earth – and that, I think, is the really bad part of it. I hope you are now past that stage.

I read with pleasure your account of how you had dealt with John.[13] It is a miserable business. But while nothing can alter one's contempt for John, my sympathy for the girl is modified by my settled conviction that John was certain to cause unhappiness sooner or later to any decent woman who had the bad luck to care about him. The real misfortune came long ago when they got engaged: something of this sort could then be foreseen, and it is better that it should have come in the form of a jilt than later, through the divorce courts, after years of unhappy marriage. That any process could have made John different, I don't believe. He is as perverted in heart as he is feeble in head. He has no natural goodness of feeling to supply his lack of any kind of principles, and no inherited tradition of decent behaviour to act as a curb on his selfishness. None of that family has any notion of self control. In the case of Lily and Arthur you see this illustrated over small things and merely leading to bad manners: greediness at table, pettish discontent over trifling inconveniences, the perpetual 'I want'. In John's case the circumstances only are different. If one has no notion of restraint I suppose it is largely a matter of accident whether one commits great or small faults. But Lord! how my tendency to preach is running away with me. Better say simply that John is a rotter and leave it at that. And perhaps I ought to put in a word for Arthur who, after all, is an old friend of mine. At least he knows what is wrong with him and, I think, makes some effort to overcome it. As to Lily – what would she NOT do if she really wanted to?

I have given my first lecture.[14] I suppose my various friends in the English Schools have been telling their pupils to come to it: at any rate it was a pleasant change from talking to empty rooms in Greats. I modestly

---

12 Lewis was later to write in the last chapter of *The Allegory of Love* (1936): 'Johnson once described the ideal happiness which he would choose if he were regardless of futurity. My own choice, with the same reservation, would be to read the Italian epic – to be always convalescent from some small illness and always seated in a window that overlooked the sea, there to read these poems eight hours of each happy day.'

13 This is Arthur Greeves's elder brother, John Greeves (1892–1969), of whom there is a description in LP III: 305.

14 At noon on Saturday, 23 January, Lewis gave the first of his eight weekly lectures on 'Some Eighteenth Century Precursors of the Romantic Movement'.

selected the smallest lecture room in College. As I approached, half wondering if anyone would turn up, I noticed a crowd of undergraduates coming into Magdalen, but it was no mock modesty to assume that they were coming to hear someone else. When however I actually reached my own room it was crowded out and I had to sally forth with the audience at my heels to find another. The porter directed me to one which we have in another building across the street. So we all surged over the High in a disorderly mass, suspending the traffic. It was a most exhilarating scene. Of course their coming to the first lecture, the men to see what *it* is like, the girls to see what *I* am like, really means nothing: curiosity is now satisfied – I have been weighed, with results as yet unknown – and next week I may have an audience of five or none. Still it is something to be given a chance.

We have been as heavily snowed up here as I ever remember to have been since that winter long ago at home when you had to walk along the bank by the roadside to reach the tram. It was fine, dry, powdery snow while it lasted and the College looked very beautiful under it. The slush and dirt of the thaw is now over. I hope to have a letter from you soon,

your loving son,
Jack

TO NEVILL COGHILL (B):

Magdalen College,
Oxford.
[3 February 1926]

Dear Coghill

I am in hopes that this, whatever its literary merits, will at least help to make clear what I was trying to express last night: and last night's conversation in its turn may make cantos VII & VIII more intelligible. If you are disposed to any *detailed* criticism (a task I nowise impose on you) please put it in pencil on the margin.[15]

15 Lewis had been working on his narrative poem, *Dymer*, since 1922, and Nevill Coghill was one of the first ones he showed it to, asking for his criticism. Recalling this in his 'Approach to English', Coghill said: 'He showed me [*Dymer*] during the early days of our acquaintance, towards 1924. He told me he had been visited many years before by a dream or myth that had remained completely mysterious to him, and yet compelling. It held his imagination though he could not explain its significance. He had made a poem of it, he said. I asked him to let me see it, and presently it arrived, a thickish folder of typewritten cantos in rhyme-royal. It was the first time that I had been

Can you come & dine to day week (the 10th) at 7.15. I want to get down to it about some of the very difficult things we raised last night: but you needn't have read Dymer by then – you shan't be viva'd! I was delighted with de la Mare: its the real thing all thro' and like cool water after Yeats and — fill in to taste,

yrs
C. S. Lewis

By the bye the MS. is confidential: I don't want it known that I am writing 'pomes'.

TO NEVILL COGHILL (B):

Magdalen College,
Oxford.
Feb. 4th 1926

My dear Coghill

It is as if you had given me a bottle of champagne – a dangerous moment and difficult to reply to. For any one of my temperament there is always a certain difficulty in quite believing praise, especially from a new reader. It is not exactly modesty – more a sort of fear that we must be leaving something out of account. Yours, however, is of the best sort. Waiving any application to myself your remark about 'the delight of giving admiration in exchange' is quite a new light to me and enables me to understand better a great deal of my own experience as a reader.

Your remarks on the Masefieldian lines go to the root of the matter – I should say the *bad* Masefieldian lines, for, in some points, one wd. not be in the least ashamed to have learned from him. The 'pretense of carrying more weight of beautiful meaning' is absolutely true. I shall be very glad to have any passages where that happens pointed out to me: the thing has gone on so long now that it is hard to spot them for myself. As to 'slickness', I am sure I have often deluded myself and tried to delude the reader that way. All the same, it is not quite plain sailing here. The early parts *must* have a certain neat, shallow speed – they must appear rather cheap compared with the later because that phase of the journey *was* cheap, wasn't it. Of course I know we are here up against the devil of

entrusted with an original work of such weight and I read it with all the excitement natural in one who is first privileged to see new work by a new poet.'

a problem: how to present bores without being a bore, or second-rateness without being second rate: complicated by the fact that the reader must be made to share that stage with Dymer and feel the spell himself.

As to the other side – it pleases me more than I can tell that you *recognize* the spiritual experiences. I was afraid that they might be private or not of this age. Also you relieve me of my two greatest anxieties *a.* Whether Canto III was mere vulgar nonsense *b.* Whether the 'redemption by parricide' myth in general wd. seem simply preposterous & shocking.

Dymer hardly felt mediocrity *after* waking (my dear Sir, how uncannily well you have understood it!) because he died i.e. the special problem of adolescence worked itself out to a finish. We feel it because we are in a different problem now: all Dymer's problems are past history to us and we live where he never came. At least I think that is true.

With many thanks, & hoping to see you Wednesday

yrs

C. S. Lewis

P.S. Of course *I'm* not Dymer: I am about to him as he to his son. At any rate he has done his best to kill me these three years!

TO HIS FATHER (LP IX: 102–4):

Saturday 5th June 1926
Magdalen

My dear Papy,

While not disposed to question the strictly mathematical parts of the reasons submitted in your letter, I suggest that you omit the real question. Did you reply to my last letter? Was the move with you or with me? However, let the move be where it will, I was wrong to leave it for such a length of time. As often before, I can only plead that what has no special date and may be done tomorrow as well as today, is hard to do at all.

I hear with delight from Warnie that you propose to visit England this summer. Let us determine that no light reason shall be allowed to upset this plan, and no difficulty be made into an impossibility. My idea is that I should cross to Ireland for part of my usual time and that we shd. then return to Oxford and you spend some days with me in College. There is a set of guest rooms on this very staircase, so we should be very snug and able to hob nob a'nights without going out of doors. We could dine in Common Room (not dressed) or go to an ordinary in the town as we preferred, and you would have an opportunity of sauntering about the city and its fields with more leisure than Uncle Hamilton's peremptory programme allowed us. Then, if possible, W. would come up for a week end and we might proceed to London or elsewhere. Do make every effort to realise the plan. Now that I am in College we have a pied à terre in England which seems to have all the advantages and none of the drawbacks of a hotel, and which certainly ought to make visits more possible than they have ever been before. It is rather important to try and fix a date, and I should be glad to know when you think you could get away.

But I know what I do in raising the point of 'date'. At least I presume it is from you that I inherit a peculiar tendency by which a chill comes over the happiest designs as soon as a definite detail of time or place is raised. At first all is attractive and like a floating island, detached from the actual world: at the mention of a date, obstructions crowd upon the mind: arrangements to be made, difficulties to be overcome, and all the repellent lumber of packings, boats, time tables and interrupted habits rush in and 'quench the smoking flax'.[16] The odds are that the whole scheme, if injudiciously pressed at that moment becomes a sort of bugbear. Is this a true bill? It is of me, I know only too well. The only remedy seems to be to remember that every happiness we have attained in the past depended on the lucky moments when we were not cowed by the 'lumber'. (Lord! Was there ever such a young fellow for preaching at his elders? He cannot take up his pen but a steady flow of doctrine begins. Perhaps it comes from taking pupils.)

A heavy responsibility rests on those who forage through a dead man's correspondence and publish it indiscriminately. In those books of Raleigh's[17] we find, as you say, letters like 'a glass of good champagne' side by side with mere squibs thrown off in high spirits or mere grumbles written when he was liverish. Notice how Liverpool, India and Oxford all come up for castigation in turn. Much of this should never have seen

16 Isaiah 42:3.

17 *The Letters of Sir Walter Raleigh (1879–1922)*, ed. Lady Raleigh, with a Preface by D.N. Smith, 2 vols. (1926). In 1904 Sir Walter Raleigh (1861–1922) became the first holder of the new chair of English Literature at Oxford, and in 1914 he was elected Merton Professor of English Literature.

print. The anti-religious passages are odd. Something must be allowed for the mere turn of his language which was always violent and dogmatic – like Johnson. When he says 'Jesus Christ made a mess of it'[18] I doubt if he really *means* much more than another might mean by saying 'Even the teaching of the Gospel seems to involve fundamental difficulties'. But I am speaking without book and of course it all depends on the context. In so far however as his remarks show a real ignorance of the importance of Christianity as (*at least* and on my view) one of the biggest and most venerable things in the history of the mind – in so far as they refuse to allow to it even that reverent consideration which any educated person must allow, say, to Greek Philosophy, or the Renaissance, or Buddhism – to that extent they are merely silly and unenlightened. On the other hand, so far as they are merely using terms of expression which are offensive to religious feeling in order to express legitimate, tho' may be very erroneous, views about Christianity, I think they are covered by the fact that they occur in private letters. On the whole I must confess that the reading of the letters, much as I enjoyed them, did not raise my opinion of Raleigh. When all allowance has been made for the haphazard nature of casual letter writing, it remains true that there must be some flaw in a man who is always blessing or damning something or other. There are *too many ecstasies* and the opposite. The funny thing is that his own view on the things of the spirit, in a large sense – I mean about what is really valuable and what is not, and about the position of mind in the world – are not really in opposition to the atmosphere of Christianity. Whatever he thought about the historical side of it, he must have known perfectly well (everyone seems to be getting to know now) that the religious view, whether literally true or not, was at any rate much more *like* the reality than the views of the scientists and rationalists.[19] I daresay the whole thing springs from some prejudice contracted in early boyhood. You speak of '*comfort* to tens of millions of men and women' and this

18 ibid., vol. II, p. 287, letter to John Sampson of 2 December 1905: 'Jesus Christ didn't fetch it off.'

19 ibid., vol. I, p. 19, letter to his sister Alice of 4 March 1885: 'I am a good deal depressed at the way people mix up their beliefs with unessentials. The probability of a future life, the existence of God, the case for miracles, the validity of conscience are all hopelessly muddled so that if I say that my conscience is not justly called the voice of Christ I am excommunicated from the sympathy of people with whom I am in the deepest accord on essentials.' Vol. II, p. 324, letter to John Sampson of 26 December 1907: 'Give me Christ and morals – not Christianity and moralists.'

just reminds me to quote a sentence from Raleigh's 'Wordsworth' to show him at his best. 'The vision shown to the pure in heart does not fulfill, it corrects their desires'.[20] I do this to adjust the balance, lest I should seem to have forgotten that 'with all his faults etc., etc.'

I have been bothered into the last job I ever expected to do this term: taking a class of girls once a week at one of the women's Colleges.[21] However, I am not engaged to be married yet, and there are always seven of them there together, and the pretty ones are stupid and the interesting ones are ugly, so it is alright. I say this because as a general rule women marry their tutors. I suppose if a girl is determined to marry and has a man alone once a week to whom she can play the rapt disciple (most fatal of all poses to male vanity) her task is done.

Otherwise things go on as usual. Nearly all my pupils went off during the strike to unload boats or swing batons or drive engines.[22] The best strike story I have heard was about engines. A train (with amateur driver) set out from Paddington to Bristol, first stop Bath. When it reached Bath *half an hour* earlier than normal express time, every single passenger got out of that train and refused to enter it again. Apparently the genius in the engine had just opened the throttle full, said to the stoker 'Carry on', and left the rest to fate.

A boy I knew at Merton drove an engine for twenty seven hours. At the end he never could remember whether the last light he had seen was green or red. Sometimes he painfully shunted back to see: but he found that if he did that once, he wanted to do it again. There were surprisingly few accidents. Warnie had some ugly adventures in London but if he has not told you, perhaps they are not to be committed to the *written* word.

---

20 Walter Raleigh, *Wordsworth* (1928).

21 Lewis's diary, *AMR*, contains details of the class he gave to the young ladies of Lady Margaret Hall.

22 Lewis is writing about the General Strike. It began as a result of the Samuel Committee recommending cuts in the wages of miners. The owners of the mines, however, while accepting a cut in wages, argued for longer hours, and at the end of April they locked the miners out of the pits. The Trades Union Congress called a meeting and agreed a 'national strike'. They hoped that such a threat would force the Government to settle. But Stanley Baldwin, the Prime Minister, called off talks with the Trades Union Congress because printers refused to print an anti-union article in the *Daily Mail*. Beginning on 3 May workers in transport, iron and steel, electricity, gas, building and newspaper printing all stopped work. Every town had its own strike committee which tried to keep essential supplies moving. While the miners refused to give in, the TUC called off the strike.

We of course had to stay on as long as any pupils were left, and it had just got to the point of our having got to go when the thing ended. I don't mind telling you I was in a funk about it. Docking was filled up and I would sooner have gone to the war again than been a constable. The necessity for either moral or physical courage is bad enough, but the two together are 'a bit thick'. I could make some shift to stand and have things thrown at me: I could make such shift to lift up my voice in an angry crowd. But to have the spiritual ordeal first and then the physical! As well, I haven't got the right voice or face for 'moving on' people. The first time I spoke they wouldn't hear me: the second time they'd say 'F—off!: the third time I'm afraid they'd simply laugh. In fact I had come down to thinking of inglorious canteen work when the whole nightmare came to an end.

Well, I must go to bed. I think I am beginning, as you say, to feel my feet under me. Every one is very pleasant. I am examining in a fellowship examination in the autumn – rather a sudden reversal of positions. You diddle me over Falstaff: it certainly is surprising when taken out of context.

your loving son,
Jack

TO A.K. HAMILTON JENKIN (B):

Magdalen
Sept. 8th [1926]

My dear Jenkin,

When your hymeneal epistle[23] reached me I was spending my days in correcting exam papers and my nights chiefly in thinking about toothache – nature having then favoured me with particular opportunity for a first hand study of that phenomenon. With the immense superiority of a miserable man who was startled at the shallowness of character shown by people who married and were given in marriage while my tooth ached: I reflected that so they had done in the days of Noe until the flood came and swept them all away.[24] Since then, as leisure

23 A few months earlier Hamilton Jenkin married Luned Jacob, the daughter of the writer, W.W. Jacob.

24 Reflecting on the marriage of his friend Rodney Pasley in 1922, Lewis said in his diary of 9 July 1922, 'A friend dead is to be mourned: a friend married is to be guarded against, both being equally lost' (*AMR*, p. 66).

and ease have gradually returned, I confess that my judgement of your exploit has progressively softened. From scorning it as impertinent, I tolerated it as pardonable: from toleration (it was even at that moment when the fumes of the gas began to leave my brain and I heard a voice say, Rinse your mouth out with this)[25] I proceeded to approval. The thing was innocent: even laudable: nay profitable, comfortable, and a cause of gratulation. You see that at no earlier moment could I properly have taken in hand to offer you (as I now do) the heartiest congratulations and the very best wishes (even to a Shandëan particularity of curious beatitude) of Mrs Moore and myself.

Indeed there was something in your manner of announcing it – with the parenthetical ease of a man borrowing a box of matches – which hardly invited a formal reply. 'It was not unpremeditated'. Egad, was it not? Well, the lady is fortunate: I am sure you are too. You have as much of the gift of happiness as any man I know, barring donkies, and I am sure you will taste domesticity (the Augustans wd. have said 'vertuous love') with the same fine palate you have applied to mines, birds, woods, wind, rain, fires, crime, letters and ghosts.

Authors ought to marry author's daughters (a notable tongue twister) as they may be supposed to be already inured to living with genius. It must be a wonderful experience. (1) Please recommend me to your wife and, even in my absence, remit the friendship with her new seal, which as Lamb says, you know, is needful.

I have had an infernally busy summer, writing lectures, and have nothing to tell you: except that I grow daily more and more doubtful in all subjects. Once more heartiest congratulations and best wishes to you both,

Yrs

C. S. Lewis

(1) I mean marriage, not 'living with genius'.

25 Addressing the subject of Purgatory, Lewis said in *Letters to Malcolm* (1964), ch. 20: My favourite image on this matter comes from the dentist's chair. I hope that when the tooth of life is drawn and I am "coming round", a voice will say, "Rinse your mouth out with this." *This* will be Purgatory.'

Jack was unable to persuade his father to travel to Oxford for a visit. He did, however, manage a visit to Little Lea from 11 to 20 September. He was with his father when the narrative poem he had been working on since 1922, Dymer, *was published by J.M. Dent on 18 September. As with* Spirits in Bondage, Dymer *was published under the pseudonym 'Clive Hamilton'.*

TO CECIL HARWOOD (B):

Magdalen College,
Oxford.
Postmark: 28 October 1926

My dear Harwood,

Thanks for your letter. I can think of a thousand replies to what you say about Cantos I and II, but you must be right, as Barfield, the reviewer in the New Leader (my best so far), and the only don who is in my confidence, all think the same.[26] Securus judicat.[27] That is one of the many quotations of which my knowledge is purely functional: one knows where it applies, but what the de'il it was about I never discovered.

About powers other than reason – I would be sorry if you mistook my position.[28] No one is more convinced than I that reason is utterly inadequate to the richness and spirituality of real things: indeed this is itself a deliverance of reason. Nor do I doubt the presence, even in us, of faculties embryonic or atrophied, that lie in an indefinite margin around

26 *The New Leader*, Vol. XIII, No. 53 (15 October 1926). In this periodical of the Labour Party, C. Henry Hamilton said of *Dymer*: 'In a lucid and dramatic Tale we follow the adventures of Dymer revolting from the standardized society in which he was born, he fled into the Wood of the World; and there, one by one, and through bitter experience, he sloughed off those unreal selves that life in the Perfect City had endowed him with. It is an allegory, at once so live and satisfying that we could well accept it as a Tale and leave it at that. But when the excitement of the drama slackens in memory the significance of the poem strikes home, and we know that Dymer is Everyman, his heritage the heritage of us all to-day – though not, alas! to all of us comes his unfolding. A fine poem, indeed, marred only by an opening canto that is commonplace in comparison with the rest of the work' (p. 15).

27 Lewis was thinking of the phrase 'Securus judicat orbis terrarum' – 'The world is a safe judge' – which he came across in John Henry Newman's *Apologia Pro Vita Sua* (1864), ch. III. It comes from St Augustine's *Contra Epistolam Parmeniani*, iii, 3.

28 He means as regards Anthroposophy. Cecil Harwood and Owen Barfield had become believers in Rudolf Steiner's Anthroposophy in 1923, and Lewis was totally opposed to it. What follows is an explanation of why he cannot accept Anthroposophy.

the little finite bit of focus which is intelligence – faculties anticipating or remembering the possession of huge tracts of reality that slip through the meshes of the intellect. And, to be sure, I believe that the symbols presented by imagination at its height are the workings of that fringe and present to us as much of the super-intelligible reality as we can get while we retain our present form of consciousness.

My scepticism begins when people offer me explicit accounts of the super-intelligible and in so doing use all the categories of the intellect. If the higher worlds have to be represented in terms of number, subject-and-attribute, time, space, causation etc (and thus they nearly always are represented by occultists and illuminati), the fact that knowledge of them had to come through the fringe remains inexplicable. It is more natural to suppose in such cases that the illuminati have done what all of us are tempted to do: – allowed their intellect to fasten on those hints that come from the fringe, and squeezing them, has made a hint (that was full of truth) into a mere false hard statement. Seeking to know (in the only way we can know) more, we know less. I, at any rate, am at present inclined to believe that we must be content to feel the highest truths 'in our bones': if we try to make them explicit, we really make them untruth.

At all events if more knowledge is to come, it must be the wordless & thoughtless knowledge of the mystic: not the celestial statistics of Swedenborg,[29] the Lemurian history of Steiner,[30] or the demonology of the Platonists. All this seems to me merely an attempt to know the super-intelligible *as if it were a new slice of the intelligible*: as though a man with a bad cold tried to get back smells with a microscope. Unless I greatly misunderstand you, you are (in a way) more rationalist than I, for you would reject as mere ideology my 'truths felt in the bones'. All this, by the bye, is meant for exposition, not argument.

---

29 The Swedish scientist and mystical thinker, Emanuel Swedenborg (1688–1772).

30 Rudolf Steiner (1861–1925), founder of Anthroposophy. He was educated at Vienna University and worked for several years on an edition of Goethe. In 1902 he became the leader of the German section of the Theosophical Society. He later rejected the eastern associations of the society and in 1913 founded the Anthroposophical Society as an independent association. His aim was to develop the faculty of spirit cognition inherent in ordinary people and to put them in touch with the spiritual world from which materialism had caused them to be estranged. His works include *The Bible and Wisdom* (1923), *Anthroposophy and the Social Question* [1933] and *Cosmic Christianity and the Impulse of Michael: Karma in the Life of Individuals and in the Evolution of the World* (1953). Anthroposophy was condemned by the Catholic Church in 1919.

I should dearly like a visit. Term ends on Dec. 11th, but I am not quite certain whether I shall be able to interpose a weekend between that and the beginning of a scholarship examination. But I will do my best. But seriously, are you certain that I shall not be a bother? I know that even an intimate friend cannot come to a house without disturbing to some extent the even tenor of its way – and there's the *parvus puer*.[31] Please make quite sure about this: and above all don't let Daphne persuade herself that it won't be a bother, because she thinks you'd enjoy having me. The fact that you have inflicted the whole of Dymer on her

(Unhappy fate the poet's wife attends
– He reads his own stuff, and he reads his friends')

has given me such large idea of her altruism, that I am afraid.

Barfield spent a night with me in college last week and we had a golden evening. With best wishes to all of you,

yrs
C. S. Lewis

TO MRS LILY SUFFERN (P):

Magdalen College,
Oxford
[November? 1926]

My dear Aunt Lily

A copy of this[32] has been set aside for you ever since publication, but I lost your address many months ago and so it has stood over. You gave me a bad fright in your letter – it was a relief to get to the doctor's revised verdict. Do let me know if there is anything more to know. Both you and I have had dealings with pain and death: I hope we can talk to each other with soldierly freedom. You will tell me everything, won't you?[33]

I am sure your attitude is the right one: half the people who die are killed off by fright at the names of diseases – often falsely diagnosed! But quite apart from this present trouble, is it really wise to live so entirely

31 'little boy'.
32 i.e. *Dymer*.
33 Lewis's Aunt Lily had cancer.

alone? You know you nearly fell into your well out at Thame...of course there are difficulties and a stupid housemate is a cross: but perhaps a fairly wholesome kind of cross.

Harley[34] is priceless. The incurable vulgarity of mind in our Holywood relations is a thing I shudder at: incurable, because it is accompanied by conceit.

What luck having the £250 to publish with – but surely it hasn't got down to publishing at your own expense. Surely even in this country there must be someone sufficiently alive to be interested in what you are saying. I long to see it as I still have only some idea of it in its earlier forms.

I am well, except for a cough, and live in the midst of (probably) too much beauty and too much comfort for soul's good: the only corrective is – well, not real overwork, but a continued succession of jobs, social and academic, which fritter away one's time.

As to Dymer – I always rely on you for plain honest criticism. The first four Cantos you have seen already: the last four are the best, I think, and certainly the most in your line. It has had one or two good reviews and is promised another, but I am still in Harley's position about sales.

I shall be very anxious to hear from you again as soon as possible. As regards all practical advice, you are much better informed than I am: I only beg you not be foolish and undertake more than you can manage. Can't you have even a girl in to help? It is dreadful to think of you in a cottage alone, falling thro' ceilings etc. I wish I could do anything that might be of help to you. Is there anything I possibly can do? Is there anything I can send you – you must be out of reach of most of the resources of civilisation. In the mean time, I can only assure you of my deepest sympathy in all the bothers you have had and my intense admiration of your courage. I saw the following dedication in a book the other day, and it made me think of you 'To —, —, and —, who had nothing in common except that they were not governed by fear and desire and you cd. believe what they said.' That is simple and sound, isn't it? With best love and best wishes in every way,

your affectionate nephew
Clive

---

34 Harley Hamilton was the daughter of Gussie and Annie Hamilton.

TO ARTHUR GREEVES (W):

[Magdalen College
December 1926]

My dear Arthur,

I was on the point of writing to find out where you were, when your letter arrived.[35] Of course I am sorry that we shall not meet at Christmas, but I quite understand that after your long spell of home you are not eager to return.

About the play[36] – of course I ought not really to speak without knowing more details of your new ideas than I do: but I can not help thinking that the introduction of incest is a mistake. I think it is quite legitimate for a man to take incest as his main theme, if he is really interested in a tragedy of it or the various moral and psychological problems which it raises. And in that case I shd. regard any moral objection to his work as invalid. But it is a very different thing for him simply to throw it in as the makeweight in a play whose real purpose and interest lie elsewhere. *That*, I think, might be legitimately objected to. At any rate it would irritate the best kind of spectator by diverting his attention from your real theme into the realm of mere pathology, and attract the wrong kind who will always find sexuality (specially abnormal sexuality) more interesting than anything else. Besides, you bring it in only to make things 'more so'. Wasn't it just that desire for the 'more so' which spoiled so many Elizabethan plays – piling horror on horror and death on death till the thing turns ridiculous? It's quality not quantity that counts. If you can't make tragedy out of the story as it was, you won't be any the more able to do so by the help of the unnatural. I think, myself, the whole feeling about incest is very obscure – almost a savage taboo, and not really moral at all: that makes it, to me, rather external and superficial. Again, won't it force you to load your play with improbabilities & long explanatory dialogues? I don't know if Gribbon is in your confidence about the play. If he is, you should discuss my view with him and try to reach a conclusion. The Banshee may be a good idea enough – it all depends, as you know, on the way it is introduced.

Minto and Maureen are well and send their love. I have had rather a nasty term with a cough wh. has kept me awake at nights and a good

35 From Paris, where Arthur Greeves had gone for a visit.

36 Arthur's play 'Trees', which was never published.

deal of work. I don't know how Dymer is selling, if at all. One thing is most annoying: you remember that the T.L.S. reviewer wrote a very kind letter, promising a good review.[37] It has not yet appeared. No doubt it will in time, but it is too late now to give a lead to other papers – wh. wd. have been its chief value. I am learning Old Norse and thus beginning to read in the original things I have dreamed of since before I really knew you. Dreams come true in unexpected ways.

yrs
Jack

P.S. I don't know the French for C/O. Is it 'chez' or 'au son soin de'?

37 Hugh l'Anson Fausset (1895–1965) wrote to Lewis on 29 September saying: 'I have just read and reviewed your Dymer for the Times Literary Supplement, but as some weeks will probably elapse before the review gets printed, I wish to send you a line to say what a remarkable achievement I consider your poem to be. I have not read any poem recently which has so impressed me by its inevitability of expression and by the profundity of its metaphysic. I use the word "metaphysic", unpleasant as it is, because it is by its metaphysical reach that your poem stands head and shoulders above most modern verse. But it is a metaphysic which is wholly and quite incalculably translated into terms of image and symbolism, and this seems to me the final test of greatness in poetry' (LP IX: 130–1). Fausset's review appeared in *The Times Literary Supplement* (13 January 1927), p. 27. See note 8 to letter of 30 March 1927.

1927

On 19 September Warnie learned that he had been selected to attend a six-month course in economics at London University beginning on 4 October. He was able to travel with Jack to Belfast on 21 December to be with their father for Christmas. On 18 January 1927 Mr Lewis wrote in his diary: 'Warnie and Jacks returned tonight by Fleetwood. As the boat did not sail until 11 o'c. they stayed with me to 9.30. So ended a very pleasant holiday. Roses all the way' (LP IX: 139).

TO HIS FATHER (LP IX: 165–8):

Magdalen
March 30th 1927

My dear Papy,

I was sorry both to hear of the eclipse of the visit scheme and of your disappointing state of health. As to the former, if it stood by itself, I would reply (adapting Falstaff) 'Are there not trains? Are there not motor buses? Are there not men of war in side cars?'[1] Why should your movements depend on the erratic and extremely hazardous aurigations of a boiler maker?[2] On the score of economy, trains have it every time. On the score of safety I can think of no method of travelling which is not superior to a seat in Uncle Gussie's car.

Of course, if you are not well enough to move at present, that is a different matter. Your account of the swelling on the right knee elicited the word 'gout' from the only knowledgeable person I mentioned it to. I know there is a sort of semi-jocular attitude adopted by everyone towards the suggestion that he himself is suffering from gout. The connection between gout and port wine is so strong in our minds that we

1 William Shakespeare, *Henry IV, Part 2* (1600), I, ii, 84–7: 'Is there not wars? Is there not employment? Doth not the king lack subjects? Do not the rebels want soldiers?'

2 i.e. Uncle Gussie Hamilton.

forget how flimsy it is in physiology. Did Grandfather or Grandmother suffer from it? I don't really see what you *can* do in the long run except go to some doctor who will really diagnose the complaint and really prescribe the proper treatment. I am quite sure you *will* do this in the end, and I cannot see what you will gain by postponing it. If you propose to offer up several months of pain as a sacrifice on the altar of old acquaintance, I reply that such an offering will not have the least effect. If Squeaky is going to be offended, he will be just as offended a month or an year hence as he would be tomorrow.

Of course on this question in general – the question of patronizing or dealing with the people you have always dealt with, even if they are not the best – I am entirely of your mind. I have never regretted Gillespie and his hexagonal wheel,[3] and if I lived at home would continue to use Gillespie all my life. But there must come a limit – a point at which the inefficiency of the man and the importance of the service in question absolutely demand a change. Hang it all, even you wouldn't suggest that because I've known Warnie a long time I ought to trust him as an interpreter on a holiday in Spain.

The scene of Squeaky in the office is a masterpiece and made me roar with laughter. One is re-assured to find that the comic spirit remains undefeated in the 'vile body'.[4] 'Fiat mixtura'[5] is the real titbit – to prevent Mopsi from sending you up the *aqua pura* in a separate bottle, as he would so naturally have done if left to himself. It reminds me of the President's latest exploit, when we met to elect a Proctor (it falls to each College in turn to choose one of its own Fellows as Proctor). When the election had been made the President said that a formal notice had to be sent to the Vice-Chancellor at once 'so perhaps Mr Benecke' (Benecke is about sixty years of age) 'you wouldn't mind going round: and then you must ring at the door and hand it to the maid'. As some one said, it only needed the additional injunctions 'and remember to wipe your feet and take a clean handkerchief' to make it really complete.

While I'm on this, I must tell you another. We are putting up a new building. In the committee that met to discuss it, someone suggested an

---

3 Mr Gillespie was a taxi driver.

4 Philippians 3:21.

5 'Let them be mixed.' Presumably Squeaky (i.e. Dr Richard Leslie) imagines Mopsi (the chemist) will not mix the aqua pura with the other unidentified substance unless Squeaky gives clear directions to the contrary.

architect's name, adding by way of explanation, 'that's the man who built Liverpool Cathedral'. To which the President at once retorted with an air of closing the matter, 'Oh, I don't think we want anything quite so large as that'.

He has at last announced his intention of retiring, so I suppose we shall live in the excitement of an election for the next year. He has certainly had a wonderful run for his money, and tho' a very laughable, is also a very lovable old fellow. He has the ludicrous, without the odious side of snobbery. He may have reverenced a Prince or a Duke too much, but never in his life did he despise or snub a poor scholar from a grammar school. When snobbery consists *only* of the admiring look upward and *not* of the contemptuous look downward, one need not be hard on it. A laugh – no unfriendly laugh – is the worst it deserves. After all, this kind of snobbery is half of it mere romance. A man may like Kings and Lords not so much because they have patronage to bestow as because he connects them (unconsciously no doubt) with stories and histories read at school. There is what is supposed to be a portrait of Sambo in 'Rough Justice' by C.E. Montague,[6] which just misses what I have been describing and represents him as a snob of the *un*pardonable type. It might interest you all the same, and the book is worth reading on other grounds. But don't believe him about Sambo.

I have had a pretty busy term, but good on the whole. I had been suffering a good deal before I went home at Christmas from sleeplessness, and from depression and nervousness (including nightmares) at nights. At first the change didn't seem to have done me much good and I was rather worried about myself, but after the first few weeks of this term the devils departed and I am now in excellent fettle. Nightmares are rather delightful things *afterwards*. As remembered (not heaven help us, as endured) they often have a sublimity and strangeness which one couldn't reach with the waking mind. It is dangerous to tell them – they sometimes sound flat to everyone except the dreamer. But here is one so good (it seems to me) that I must hand it on. I dreamed that I was walking among the valleys of the moon – a world of pure white rock, all deep chasms and spidery crags, with a perfectly black sky overhead. Of course there was nothing living there, not even a bit of moss: pure mineral solitude. Then I saw, very far off, coming to meet me down a narrow ravine,

6 Charles Edward Montague, *Rough Justice* [1926].

a straight, tall figure, draped in black, face and all covered. One knew it would be nicer not to meet that person: but one never has any choice in a dream, and for what seemed about an hour I went on till this stranger was right beside me. Then he held out an arm as if to shake hands, and of course I had to give him my hand: when suddenly I saw that instead of a hand he had a sort of metal ring which he closed round my wrist. It was sharp on the inside and hurt abominably. Then, without a word, drawing this thing together till it cut right to the bone, he turned and began to lead me off down the same long valley he had come from. It was the sense of being on the moon you know, the complete desolateness, which gave the extraordinary effect.

This Vac., besides the usual 'College Meetings', 'Tutorial Boards' etc., is involved in an Entrance Examination for which I have been nabbed. It is pleasant not to have pupils appearing at regular hours, but otherwise I am as busy nearly as in term, and if I can get away for two or three nights to do a walk somewhere, shall consider that I have done very well.

I never realised the proper question to ask oneself about reviews until it was put to me the other day by a friend who has published, and therefore been through the mill himself. It is of course 'What kind of a review *would* really satisfy you?' If honestly answered the question will lead one to demand for oneself a sort of *succès fôu*[7] with large headlines – a degree in fact of recognition which could never be won now-a-days by any book of the sort one tries to write. Fausset's review really says as big things as I could, with any reason, wish for.[8] The question 'Is epic now possible?' has

7 'A huge success'.

8 In his review of *Dymer*, found in *The Times Literary Supplement* (13 January 1927), p. 27, Hugh l'Anson Fausset said: 'Mr Hamilton's poem is notable because it is in the epic tradition and yet is modern in idiom and reflects a profoundly personal intuition. The hero of the old epic kills monsters, giants, and dragons and these are rather symbols of the malign forces of nature with which the primitive man lives in constant conflict, than images of those forces as they war against the spiritual possibilities in the nature of man. As the epic ceases to be a primitive expression it ceases also to be symbolical and becomes allegorical. Its giants and dragons remain and its heroes contend against them with more and more knightly circumstance. But his adventures are only a pictorial tapestry woven for its own sake, to which a moral interpretation is somewhat arbitrarily attached. And doubtless the prejudice which exists against the epic as a modern art form is due to a belief that in civilized hands it must prove an impure form, a form in which substance and form are not necessarily related. Mr Hamilton has disproved that belief by showing that, in modern epic, the spiritual may be translated into terms of the physical, as inevitably in the primitive epic the physical was translated into terms of the imaginative. He has shown this more convincingly than Mr Masefield in Dauber, with

been a stock question for years. Taking the word 'epic' to mean his sense, there is no candidate between Milton and our own times. He puts up Masefield as a possible, and prefers me. He says I have brought back under modern conditions something that has seemed impossible since the days of myth – for I think he includes the Miltonic along with the Spenserian in his sentence about 'allegory' and 'knightly circumstance'. I don't mean of course that he thinks I am better than Milton and Spenser, but that I have brought back something lost before (and during) their time. If what he said were true, it wd. mean that I was a very considerable turning point. Of course he is wrong: whatever merits Dymer has are not really of the epic kind. But that is another question. He may be going in a direction which I think wrong but I certainly cannot demand that he should go further.

We live in the most absurd age. I met a girl the other day who had been teaching in an infant school (boys and girls up to the age of six) where the infants are taught the theory of Evolution. Or rather the Headmistress's version of it. Simple people like ourselves had an idea that Darwin said that life developed from simple organisms up to the higher plants and animals, finally to the monkey group, and from the monkey group to man. The infants however seem to be taught that 'in the beginning was the Ape' from whom all other life developed – including such dainties as the Brontosaurus and the Iguanodon. Whether the plants were supposed to be descendants of the ape I didn't gather. And then people talk about the credulity of the middle ages! A propos of this can you tell me who said 'Before you begin these studies, I should warn you that you need much more *faith* in science than in theology'. It was Huxley or Clifford or one of the nineteenth century scientists, I think. Another good remark I read long ago in one of E. Nesbitt's fairy tales – 'Grown ups know that children can believe almost anything: that's why they tell you that the earth is round and smooth like an orange when you can see perfectly well for yourself that it's flat and lumpy.'[9]

---

which his poem may be usefully compared, because Dymer's experience is throughout metaphysical. His ordeal is not on the high seas, but in swamps and places of his own soul's making...'

9 'Grown-up people find it very difficult to believe really wonderful things, unless they have what they call proof. But children will believe almost anything, and grown-ups know this. This is why they tell you that the earth is round like an orange, when you see perfectly well that it is flat and lumpy.' E. Nesbit, *Five Children and It* (1902), ch. I.

Almost the only interesting thing that has happened to me lately was a visit from a young German. He called to see me because he is a friend of a friend of mine in London. The friend had written asking me to be civil to him. He turned out to be more like a comic picture of a German in a war time Punch than you would have thought it possible for a living man to be. I mean, his neck went up quite straight from the back of his collar into his head, and he had hardly any hair. But this was nothing to the joys of his conversation. I asked if he had served in the war. He replied after deep thought (he is a high falutin sort of a fellow, philosophical, theosophical, very spiritual – *geistlic* I think he'd call it) 'Ach...I could not bring to my mind the reality of that life...I could not connect myself systematically with this war, this soldat...so I became very ill'. I wish I'd known that tip in 1919. I refrained from asking him the German for 'to swing the lead'.

His next was almost as delicious. He was already engaged to dine at Christ Church, and I was going out to lunch, so the best that I could do (by way of fulfilling the requests of our mutual friend) was to ask him if he could come in and have a talk and a drink that evening after dinner. He said he would if he could. Next day a postcard arrived saying that tho' our engagement had been of a vague kind, still he thought he would write and apologise for not coming as 'his consciousness not was quite pure'. By the by, while everyone can see the joke, how many can correct him here? I mean make absolutely clear to a foreigner the difference between 'consciousness' and 'conscience', within the limits of a postcard? I gave up the attempt: it really turned out too difficult. Of course it is easy enough if there is a German word for 'conscience' as opposed to 'consciousness' – but I don't know whether there is. I think French uses 'la conscience' for both, while on the other hand the Latin 'conscientia' is hardly ever used for 'consciousness'.

I dined the other night at an Italian Professor's, who is a Fellow of Magdalen,[10] and sat next to a Frenchwoman who has met Mussolini. She says he is a rhetorician, and escapes from questions he doesn't want to answer into a cloud of eloquence. I asked if she thought him a charlatan. She said no: he quite believes all his own gas, like a school boy, and is

10 Cesare Carolo Foligno (1878–1963), Italian scholar, was Taylorian Lecturer in Italian at Oxford University 1909–15, and Serena Professor of Italian and Fellow of Magdalen 1919–40. He was Professor of English at the University of Naples 1940–53.

carried away by it himself. It interested me very much as being true to type – Cicero must have been just that sort of man. She also claimed to have said to him 'Yes, I have heard all the rhetoric, now I want the real answer', which I took leave (silently) to disbelieve. But my host told me that it is almost certainly true, for she appears to be a sort of Aunt Lily on the grand scale, who meets the biggest lions by accident and tells them their own business. A good remark about lions was made the same evening (by a lady). 'When I meet that sort of person I am always divided between two fears: one that he will speak to me: the other that he won't.'

This letter has grown to an intolerable length. I have discovered the real secret of letter writing. (I mean the secret of quantity of course. Quality is another matter.) It is to write a letter when you have another task you ought to be doing. For instance I proposed this morning to finish a few notes on English sound laws (which are not gay), badly needed for next term. Then when you get to the really nasty part of course as usual one's thoughts begin to stray. 'Why not write that letter' comes as a seduction rather than an admonition. Hinc illae.[11] You ought to try it. I hope I shall profit by it to the extent of many pages the next time you decide to spend an evening with your accounts – if the rheumatics allow you.

I quite see that the hotel in Donegal is in some way unattractive. But temperance and plain diet are to be had everywhere. May I suggest that nothing hinders – indeed the Lenten season encourages, – you and the Colonel to make Leeborough during the coming week into a *temperance hotel* with *plain but plentiful food*. Dumb bells and 'Instant Postum' you know.

your loving son,
Jack

P.S. Did I tell you that I was asked to tea by a pupil not long ago and noticed a copy of Dymer in his bookcase? That is fame.

11 'Flitting from this to that'.

TO HIS BROTHER (LP IX: 224–31):[12]

[Hillsboro,
Western Avenue,
Headington,
Oxford]
Easter Monday [18 April 1927]

My dear W.,

I had both your communications and remain about as wise as before. We, or at any rate Minto, will scan the papers daily: but in what *part* of the press will the information be given? In the shipping? Or the Gazette? We will do our best, but I doubt very much whether this will be posted till we have had word from you?

Mr Papworth[13] continued to manifest his disapproval of the proceedings until we were out of Oxford and almost starting the ascent of Cuckoo Lane: in fact he showed every flattering degree of attention compatible with his 'beastly kind' (wh. sounds more beefy and affecting somehow than our modern 'animal nature'). He is still frequently struck by a resemblance to you in some grocer or roadmender of portly habit and springs to investigate. You will be surprised to hear that while I write this, Minto is out to dinner. This results from the chief event since you left – the arrival of 'un ami' of Florence de Forest – not staying here, thank heavens. He is a little Swiss commercial traveller, 'Villie Goût', as smart as a bandbox, and very polite. Beyond making horrible noises in clearing his 'pipes' (a la Sir Roger)[14] and being intensely ugly, he is really quite harmless, tho' of course very vulgar. He and Florence absolutely insisted on Minto's dining with them at the Eastgate tonight, and won the day. They know how to move their monde, as you will see from this fact and also when I tell you that they made me take them up Magdalen Tower this morning – as well as round the College. When I showed them

12 On 11 April 1927 Warnie set sail on the troopship *Derbyshire* for Shanghai where he would remain for almost three years.

13 Mr Papworth, or Baron Papworth, was Lewis's and Mrs Moore's dog. They had many dogs and cats over the years, but Baron Papworth, who died in 1937, was always their favourite.

14 Sir Roger de Coverley, a delightful character in *The Spectator*, the periodical conducted by Sir Richard Steele and Joseph Addison. *The Spectator* ran from 1 March 1711 to 6 December 1712, and part of 1714. In issue No. 269 (by Addison) of 8 January 1712 Sir Roger de Coverley could be heard 'upon the Terrace hemming twice or thrice to himself with great Vigour, for he loves to clear his Pipes in good Air'.

the deer he made one of those extremely simple French jokes with which Maurice and M. Zée have familiarised us.[15] I had explained that these deer were descendants of a herd wh. had been there before the College was founded (that is quite true by the by, or as true as a College tradition need be), and I added 'So you may say they are the oldest members of the College'. 'And ze most intelligent?' returned M. Goût.

I was really glad they made me go up the Tower. I think I only tried to take you up but I didn't then know where the key was to be had. It was superb on top. There was a magnificent sky of blue and white, and the whole cluster of roofs and towers simply blazed in sun light. One also gets the effect of the town in its frame – it is just small enough for there to be a margin of green hill beyond the roofs on every side, except north-ward, where trees play the same role. Then the lawn in the cloister quad-rangle below – it is far enough away to look more perfect than any grass could be. 'Velvet' and 'shaven' were no longer poetical metaphors applied to *it*. It gave me a good idea of the peculiar kinds of beauty one must get from a low flying aeroplane.

We have a visitor at present, a Miss Whitty,[16] a music teacher of Mau-reen's at Bristol, who is one of Minto's lame ducks. 'Sir, he is poor, he is miserable, and that is recommendation enough to Johnson'. But while ill health, poverty and overwork may justify her presence in Hillsboro, they can hardly justify her appearance in this letter. I cite her because she clears up a problem. You must have wondered very often for *what* public illuminated texts of Kipling's 'If',[17] calendars with a thought for every day, mottoes in crackers, Easter cards, etc., etc., etc. were produced. Now I know. To Miss W. these are food and drink. It is most embarrassing. She is really struck by a 'Thought for the week' in the Sunday Pictorial and will *read it out*. You know how those things are, even when you glance at them in turning over the pages of the paper. But you can have no conception what they *sound* like if actually pronounced during a pause at the breakfast table. There are things extant in print which, one took it for granted, had never, would never reach the viva voce level of

15 The Frenchmen, Maurice Delangues and Monsieur Zée, had been paying guests at one time. See *AMR*, 1 August–9 September 1923, for the period Maurice Delangues was with them.

16 Kathleen Whitty, who had been Maureen's music teacher in Bristol, often visited the Moores in Oxford.

17 Rudyard Kipling, 'If–' (1910).

existance. I will inflict one only on you – and am rather chary about it even on paper, well impounded in inverted commas. 'No one is utterly useless in this world who helps to lighten another's burden'. We needn't bother about 'in this world': they all take care to tell you that they refer to 'this world' or 'this life'. It gives a sort of atmosphere. But just look at the rest. To lighten someone's burden can only mean to do him a service, which again can only mean to be useful to him. So that the gem precisely informs us that if you're any use you can't be useless. The length of the oscillation my mind performs – from the extreme of subtlety, reading Coleridge's Biographia Literaria till the lunch bell goes – to the extreme of platitude when I reach the table!

I forget if you know the Biographia. A good deal of it is too philosophical to interest you, but the earlier chapters on Christ's Hospital under Bowyer are an interesting supplement to Lamb's account, and there is lots of good literary criticism. As an attempt at a book (as opposed to mere Coleridgean talk) it is preposterous. Indeed it contains, nay *consists of*, the best unconscious bit of literary joke that was ever played. In about the 2nd or 3rd chapter Coleridge makes his famous distinction between imagination and fancy,[18] and decides that he must explain what imagination really is. In the Coleridgean style (it must be exactly like his conversation) this very naturally involves a preliminary sketch of the history of the theory of the association of ideas from Aristotle down to his own time, which leaves one more or less ready to begin a flanking movement on the main subject, via Kant, Fichte, Schelling, Spinoza, the Neo-Platonists, and the mystics. Somewhere half way through the book, after a suggested theory of knowledge in general and a development of Cartesianism along new lines (with a few mild ten page

18 Coleridge, *Biographia Literaria*, ch. XIII: 'The imagination then I consider either as primary, or secondary. The primary imagination I hold to be the living power and prime agent of all human perception, and as a repetition in the finite mind of the external act of creation in the infinite I AM. The secondary I consider as an echo of the former, co-existing with the conscious will, yet still as identical with the primary in the kind of its operation. It dissolves, diffuses, dissipates, in order to re-create; or where this process is rendered impossible, yet still, at all event, it struggles to idealize and to unify. It is essentially *vital*, even as all objects (as objects) are essentially fixed and dead. Fancy, on the contrary, has no other counters to play with but fixities and definites. The fancy is indeed no other than a mode of memory emancipated from the order of time and space; and blended with, and modified by that empirical phenomenon of the will which we express by the word *choice*. But equally with the ordinary memory it must receive all its materials ready made from the law of association.'

episodes of the anecdotal, critical and religious type) we actually get into touch with the enemy's outpost line. We see 'Imagination' as a chapter heading. We beat to quarters (or whatever it is) and are all ready when suddenly our author quotes a letter from 'a friend' advising him after all *not* to give an account of imagination. While you are still wondering what this is put in for, Coleridge, remarking 'that this judicious letter produced *immediate conviction* in his mind'[19] has quietly closed the chapter – and the fixture is off. 'And what good came of it at last, quoth little Peterkin'.[20] The answer is *nothing* – nothing whatsoever.

It reminds me of my friend Barfield who recently wrote me a letter full of plans for our Easter walking tour and added in the last line 'Wash out, Beckett[21] has just rung up to say he couldn't manage such a day' – but solemnly posted and sent it all the same. We start on this walk tomorrow, assembling at Goring station at 2.30 – a loathsome hour to begin at, but it couldn't be helped. We shall lie our first night at East Ilsey. We propose to walk through Lambourn on the downs and Savernake Forest to Marlborough: thence on to the Plain, and Salisbury itself is not beyond our ambitions. We had originally planned a more adventurous tour over Exmoor, but it proved too long for the short holidays of some and the purses of others.

April 26th

I arrived back from my travels at lunch time yesterday and found your letter, posted at Gib.,[22] awaiting me. It had come in fact the day after I left. It left me with a fine impression of boundless leisure and sea air, that is particularly tantalizing in view of the recollection that term begins on Friday. The arrival of income tax forms this morning drives home my irritation with this hanky-panky which keeps a few hundreds of self-indulgent fellows like you fooling about in the Mediterranean on my money in order to fill the pockets of the 'China Merchants'. However, you may be in less pleasant circumstances by the time this reaches you, so I must suppress the note of envy. Still, provided that you don't meet

19 ibid.

20 Robert Southey, 'The Battle of Blenheim' (1800), ll. 12–13.

21 (Sir) Eric Beckett (1896–1966), who often walked with Barfield, Lewis and the others, took a First in Jurisprudence from Wadham College in 1921. He was a Fellow of All Souls College 1921–8. He was called to the Bar in 1922 and was assistant legal adviser to the Foreign Office 1925–45 and legal adviser 1955–8.

22 i.e. Gibraltar.

with a war in China, every ordinary boredom and discomfort which may await you is a price almost worth paying for a free trip half round the world, well fed, unworked, and in tolerably congenial society. (You must be putting on flesh at a desperate rate.)

I thought we had mentioned Squire Western's choice of table talk before.[23] It goes to the root of the matter, doesnt it? By the way I have never been able to share that popular feeling about Western as a fine type of bluff, honest, genial Englishman: he seems to me one of the four or five most intolerable people in fiction (I mean to meet: of course he is excellent in a book). *Tom Jones* goes far to explain why Johnson and his set didn't like the country. I can quite imagine that a countryside of highwaymen and the rural jokes of the period, inhabited by Westerns and Blifils would have led him to 'abstract his mind and think of Tom Thumb':[24] for one can hardly imagine him knocking them down with folios. At least, if he had made the attempt, he would have liked the country even less after it than before it. He would have dismissed Mr Square as an infidel dog, and I dont feel that he would have got on with Thwackum. Sophia is good. She comes during that lucid interval when good heroines were possible in novels written by men, when the restoration tradition by which a heroine must be a whore was dead, and the Victorian tradition by which she must be a fool had not been born.

Now for my own adventures. I was joined [on 19 April] at Oxford station by two others and we proceeded together to Goring.[25] One of them was new to the game and turned up carrying a Tommies pack filled square like a tommy's pack, for inspection. On the way we extracted from it a large overcoat, a sponge, four shirts, a heavy tin mug holding about a pint, two strong metal cigarette cases of pudaita proportions, and a number of those insane engines which some people associate with holidays. You know – the adaptable clasp knife which secrets a fork at

23 In Henry Fielding's *The History of Tom Jones* (1749).

24 Percival Merritt, *The True Story of the so-called Love Letters of Mrs Piozzi* (1927), p. 70.

25 The friends who met Lewis in Oxford for a walk on the Berkshire Downs were Owen Barfield and Cecil Harwood. They were joined at Goring by Walter Ogilvie 'Wof' Field (1893–1957). Field came up to Trinity College, Oxford, from Marlborough College in 1912. He left to join the Warwickshire Rifle Regiment in 1914, and in 1916, having continued his studies, he took a war degree from Trinity College. He was promoted to captain in 1916, and after seeing action in France and Italy he was wounded and forced to retire in 1919. In 1926 he became a teacher at the Rudolf Steiner School in Forest Row, East Sussex.

one end and a spoon at the other, but in such a way that you could never really use the fork and the spoon together – and all those sort of things. Having recovered from our delighted laughter and explained that we were going to walk in an English county and not in Alaska, we made up the condemned articles into a parcel wh. we compelled him to post home from Goring. It weighed about seven pounds. Our fourth met us at Goring station.

After tea in the garden of the lock keeper at Goring lock – we ate it sitting just beside the weir, dipping our hands into the water and enjoying the rush and the noise – we set out N.N.W. In half an hour the suburbanity of Goring was out of sight. We soaked for a long time in a winding valley with all the bigness of downs opening behind and the richer Chiltern country towards Henley rising in the distance. We were on the broad grass track of the Icknield Way, the grass very short and fine and perfectly dry, as it is nearly all the year round in these chalk hills. It was an afternoon of lovely sunshine with a pleasant light wind, and a lark overhead displayed all its accomplishments. That night we slept at East llsley which (I think) you and I went through on our way to Salisbury.

We spent nearly the whole of Wednesday [20 April] following the Icknield Way along the northern edge of the downs, overlooking the Wantage valley on our right. Around us, and to our left, the country had all the same character: close smooth grass, very pale in colour, deliciously springy to the foot: chalk showing through here and there and making the few ploughed pieces almost cream colour: and, about three to a mile, clumps of fir, whose darkness made them stand out very strikingly from the low tones of the ground. The extent of prospect was (or seemed to be) larger than any I have seen, even from the highest hills I have been on – just wave after wave of down, and then more of them, for ever. The air is very clear here and one sometimes sees a hay stack or a farm on a ridge, so distinct and at the same time so remote that it is like something seen through the wrong end of a telescope. We had tea at Lambourn and slept at Aldbourne.

Thursday [21 April] opened with discussions. A survey of the maps showed a lamentable discrepancy between the route we wanted to follow and the possible places for lunch. Then emerged the dark and hideous prospect of 'taking' lunch. Perfectly simple you know. Buy some bread and cheese before we start and have lunch where we like. Makes you independant you know. Drinks? Oh, get a few oranges if you don't feel inclined to carry a bottle of beer in your pack for the first ten miles. I need hardly say that our novice – the Knight of the Adaptable Jack Knife – was entirely in favour of a scheme which promised to restore his original conception. I of course, who had seen days spoiled this way before, was the head of the opposition. The wrong party won. We stuffed our packs with bread, butter, cheese and oranges. The only thing I look back on with satisfaction was that the butter, at any rate, was not in my pack. Then we set off.

The first mile made us thoroughly aware of the fact that the wind (wh. had been in our faces since Goring) had risen to a gale. The next three miles left no one in any doubt of the fact that when a strong wind blows in your face all day, it parches your throat and chaps your lips without cooling your body. We were now in sight of 'Barberry Castle', a Roman Camp, for the sake of seeing which all this folly had started. The exponents of the 'carry your lunch' school had now reached the stage of indulging in a quite unusual degree of praise of the scenery and the pleasures of walking tours, on the 'this is fine' lines. But long before we had reached the top of that disastrous camp they slunk in silence, and only the malcontents (Barfield and myself) felt inclined to talk. In fact we talked quite a lot.

When we reached the top we found ourselves in one of those places where you can neither speak for the hurricane nor open your eyes for the sun. Beyond the suggestion (mine) of performing on the wind (and the Romans) a certain physiological operation disallowed by English law and by polite conversation, we were silent here. Turning up our collars and pulling our hats down hard on our heads, we couched under a scrannel gorse bush wherever prickles and sheep dung left a space, and produced our scanty and squalid meal. The appearance of the butter faintly cheered us (all of us except the man among whose socks and pyjamas it had travelled), but it was a sight that moved mirth, not appetite. The last straw was the oranges, wh. proved to be of the tough, acrid, unjuicy type, which is useless for thirst and revolting to taste.

The midday siesta (that great essential of a day's walking) was out of the question in that abominable camp, and we set off gloomily S.W. Barfield and I dropped behind and began composing in Pope-ian couplets a satire on the people who arrange walking tours. Nothing cd have been happier. At a stroke every source of irritation was magically changed into a precious fragment of 'copy'. By the time we had walked three miles we were once more in a position to enjoy the glorious country all round us. Five o'clock found us descending a slope full of druidical stones, where we started three hares successively so close that we had nearly trodden on them, into the village of Avebury.

Avebury overwhelmed me and put me into that dreamlike state which is sometimes the reward of being very tired. Imagine a green ancient earthwork with four openings to the four points of the compass, almost perfectly circular, the wall of a British city, large enough to contain broad fields and spinneys inside its circuit, and, in the middle of them, dwarfed by its context, a modern village. Obviously here was the capital of a great king before the Roman times. We had been passing British things all day – stones, mounds, camps etc. But it was extraordinary to find a Berkshire village inside one. Here we had tea gloriously, in the orchard of an inn: and took off our shoes, and ordered a fresh pot and more hot water, and fair copied the satire and lay on our backs and talked Oxford reminiscences and smoked pipes.

Then Wof – he's the jack knife man – did a sensible thing by returning after a moment's absence and saying 'If you're not very keen on *walking* to Marlborough there's a man here with a milk cart who will take us in'. So we sat among milk cans (which are just the right angle to lean against) and bumped and rattled along the Bath road (of Pickwickian and coaching memories) into Marlborough. Field is an old Marlburian but we were too tired to let him show us the sights. He told us however (what will interest you) that the fine old Georgian building which faces you as you enter the school precincts was an inn on the Bath road in the old days. Pleasant days they must have been.

Next day [22 April] we walked about four miles into Savernake Forest. It is not to be compared with the Forest of Dean, but well worth an hour or so. It is the typically English kind of wood – nearly all big oaks with broad mossy spaces between them and deer flitting about in the distance. Leaving the forest we struck westward into the vale of Pewsey, and were threading about little woods and fieldpaths for an hour or so. After our windy days on the Downs this was a pleasant change: the richness of the colours, the soft burring of the wind (now harmless) in the little trees, and the flowers everywhere were specially delightful by contrast. We crossed a fine rise called Hansell Hill: a thing rising so abruptly on both sides that it was like a gigantic tumulus. From the top of this we had one of the finest views in England. Northward, the Berkshire Downs, huge even in their apparent extent, and huger to our minds because we had spent two whole days walking on them. Southward, across the valley, rose the edge of the Salisbury plain.

We came down the side of that hill over a big spur called the Giant's Grave and lunched admirably in the village of Ocue – beer and bread and cheese followed by a pot of tea, and then a game of darts: you know the apparatus for that game which one finds in pubs. Shortly after lunch we had the best 'soak'[26] I've ever had in a walk, by turning out of a little grassy lane into a wood where the grass grew soft and mossy, and there were solid clumps of primroses the size of dinner plates: not to mention a powdering of those little white flowers – wood anemones. We laid ourselves flat on our back with packs under our head for pillows (for it is in the beauty of a pack that it can thus convert into a regular bed a flat ground otherwise useless for soaking): some rash attempts at conversation were ignored and we spent an hour with half shut eyes listening to the burring of the wind in the branches, and an occasional early bumble bee. The remainder of the day brought forth a bad bit of wrong map reading: but this also is among the delights of a journey: for it found us ambling into our tea stopping place along the grassy tow-path of an all but obsolete canal, where we had never meant to go and which was all the better for that. We lay at Devizes: a poor inn.

Next day [23 April] we struck south across the vale of Pewsey. We expected to be bored in this low ground which divides the Berkshire Downs from Salisbury Plain: but it turned out a pleasant morning's tramp through roads with very fine beech trees and a tangle of footpaths. Even if it had been dull, who would not make sacrifices to pass through a place called Cuckold's Green. (We passed Shapley Bottom two days before.) I myself was for tossing a pot of beer at Cuckold's Green, which we might have done by going two hundred yards out of our course, but the other two being both married, ruled that this was no place to rest a moment longer than we need. So did literary associations render possible a joke that the illiterate would hardly venture on. (In passing, if one had lived in the 17th century, what a horrible fate it

26 The reader should remember the definition of a 'soaking machine' in the letter to Arthur Greeves of 11 May 1915: 'The word "soak" means to sit idly or sleepily doing nothing, and a S'ing machine is [a] place for this operation.'

would have been to live at Cuckold's Green. 'Your servant sir. Your wife tells me that you are carrying her to the country in a few days. Pray sir where do you live?' 'Cuckold's Green.' By the age of forty one wd be quite definitely tired of the joke.)

We lunched this side of the climb on to the Plain, and crawled up on to that old favourite afterwards. It pleased me as much as ever: more than all, after being given tea by a postmistress, with boiled eggs and bread and jam at lib., for which she wanted to take only 6d. Oddly enough, up there in the chalk of the plain, that village was almost completely under water. Our evening walk, up and down mile after mile of unfenced chalk road with smooth grey grass all round and sheep and young lambs (so numerous that in places they were deafening), and a mild setting sun in our faces, was heavenly.

But what no one can describe is the delight of coming (as we came) to a sudden drop and looking down into a rich wooded valley where you see the roofs of a place where you're going to have supper and bed: specially if the sunset lies on the ridge beyond the valley. There is so much mixed in it: the mere physical anticipations as of a horse nearing its stable, the sense of accomplishment and the feeling of 'one more town', one further away into the country you don't know, and the old never hackneyed romance of travelling (not of 'travel' wh. is what you are doing and wh. no doubt has its own different pains and pleasures). It always seems to sum up the whole day that is behind you – give it a sort of climax and then stow it away with the faintly melancholy (but not unpleasant) feeling of things going past. This town I am gassing about was Warminster. Here we had the ill luck to come into a fair: so that half an hour after that quiet moment on the edge of the Plain (with the first stars just coming out) we were treading our way through the noisy and sweaty crowds of a narrow street, lit up by naked gas flares and bellowing with the steam organs of roundabouts and the voices of cocoa-nut-shy people. We even had confetti on us. And alas! all the hotels were in that street. Luckily it was a Saturday so they had to stop at midnight. (Let us here bless that much abused Puritan Sunday of ours which gives rest to the labouring classes and peace to ours.) So after ham and eggs, cider, bread, cheese, marmalade and tea, we had a philosophical discussion (or so it seemed at the time) till twelve o'clock, and so to bed, all three of us in a room: where as long as I lay awake I heard the showmen (v. tired poor fellows) taking down their shows. Their conversation was of a purely military kind. 'Wot the f—g 'ell are you doin Jarge?' 'Where's that bl—dy f—g hammer?' 'I 'ant got yet bleedin' 'ammer. Go and f—g well b—r yerself' etc. etc.

Next day [24 April] we walked all morning through the estates of the Marquis of Bath, in a very old and fine forest on a hillside. About a mile and a half below us on the hillside we saw the house – a rather tiresome place on the lines of Blenheim, with three lakes – and we emerged at one o'clock into a village just outside one of the park gates. The atmosphere here is feudal, for the hostess of our mittagessen pub would talk about nothing but His Lordship, who apparently lives here all the year round and knows everyone in the village. We asked how old he was. 'O, we don't think 'im old', she replied, which stumped me. The rest of that day was so intensively complex in route and so varied in scenery (also we were so embroiled in conversation) that I give no account of it. Suffice it that 8 o'clock found me in a hot bath at Shepton Mallett which is just under the eastern end of the Mendips and half a day's march from Wells. So that if you take Goring in the right way (really a suburb of London) and if you take Wells as being just outside Bristol, we might say (the P'daitabird undoubtedly *would* say) that we had walked across England. At any rate, another day and a half and we could have dipped our hands in the Bristol Channel. 'There's glory for you' as Humpty Dumpty said! Next day we all returned home by train.

I have spent so long (to my entertainment more perhaps than yours) on my tour that I must huddle up everything else. I had your letters from Gib. and from Aden and also the long letter forwarded by the P'daita Bird, wh. I read with very great interest and enjoyment. The description of the Red Sea coast (how differently one imagines it when Milton says 'The red sea coast whose waves ov'erthrew / Busiris and his Memphian chivalry')[27] particularly took my fancy and has really enriched me with a new conception.

I sympathise with you in your uncongenial society and above all in your P.T. I suppose there are two points of view for a trooper in the tropics, (1) 'Well you can't possibly take exercise *here*'. (2) 'Well, a man must do something to keep himself sweet in a place like this'. I need hardly say that the one point of view as compared with the other seems to me as light to darkness. It is most chilling to reflect how long you must wait

27 Milton, *Paradise Lost*, I, 306–7.

before you get this: but it has really been impossible to get it finished any sooner.

And now for Lamb's final division of a letter – 'puns'. I think I have only two. (1). The story of a man[28] who was up with me, and who was the only genuine maker of malapropisms I ever met: but this one I never heard till the other day. It appears that while having tea with the 'dear Master of University' he conducted a long conversation with the ladies, chiefly re places to stay for one's holidays, under the impression that the word 'salacious' meant 'salubrious'. You can imagine the result. But what you can't imagine is that when the Mugger himself, whose brow had been steadily darkening for some minutes (during which he had heard his daughters told that they wouldn't like Devonshire very much because it wasn't very salacious) finally decided to cut it short and broke in with 'Well Mr Robson-Scott, how do you like Oxford?' Robson-Scott turned to him with imperturbable good humour and said 'Well to tell you the truth sir, it isn't so salacious as I had hoped.'

This fellow Robson indulged also – as I well remember – in a kind of complicated misfire of meaning: rather like a rarefied or quintessential p'daitaism. Two I can vouch for. When arriving with me late somewhere he observed panting, 'We might have known that it wd. take us longer than it did.' Another time, in a debate, he said, 'I quite agree with Mr So-and-So's point *as far as it goes* – but it goes much too far.' You will see how easily this sort of thing wd. pass for sense in the heat of the moment.

(2). I don't know if this can rank as a pun, but I'll put it down. When S.P.B. Mais (whose Diary of a Schoolmaster we have both read) got a 3rd in English here, the examiners told him they were very sorry, but added by way of consolation that he 'was the very best Third they had ever examined'. On which Raleigh[29] remarked 'It is bad enough for a man to get a Third: but to be pointed out as the most brilliant Third of your year is damnable.'

(3). I've just remembered another – rather more suitable. An old pupil of mine who is now a master at Stowe came to see me the other day. Among other things, he told me that the moral tone there was very

28 William Douglas Robson-Scott (1900–80), who matriculated at University College in 1919, and in 1923 took a First in English Literature. He became Professor of German Language and Literature at Birkbeck College, University of London.

29 i.e. Sir Walter Raleigh, the first Professor of English at Oxford.

high. I told this to a cynical colleague whose reply was, 'From what I saw of Stowe, the grounds are so large and so well wooded that the moral tone couldn't help being high'. By the by, the moral tone at Stowe seems to be really insane. What are boys thinking of? This master (my pupil) said 'Damn' in a game of rugger. Whereupon, if you please, a deputation of prefects waits upon the Headmaster to complain. They have just succeeded in stopping bad language in their houses: and what are they to do if master etc., etc. I must say if I were the Headmaster I should be tempted to the P'daita policy of thrashing the lot. Or better still 'I'd teach them to say damn if I had to lie under their beds all night' (Perhaps no bad expedient for the purpose!).

Well, I must stop. I have taken pupils, and walked Mr Papworth, and played bowls and it is near twelve o'clock. I look forward to your next letter. The family all send their good wishes to which I add my own – the sum total being a speedy return.

yrs.
J.

Warnie arrived in Singapore on 10 May, and from there his ship made its way to Kowloon on mainland China, a few miles from the island of Hong Kong, arriving there about 15 May. Writing to Jack on 7 June, he said:

> *I am second in command of the Base Supply Depot, with [Captain J.E.] Drysdale as my O.C., which naturally is as pleasant an arrangement as could have happened...Broadly speaking I am a cross between a ship's officer and a wharf manager. A steady succession of store ships arrive at our wharf with supplies from home or Australia and it is my duty to receive and check them and stack them in the 'godown' as they call it, which is the local name for a warehouse.* (LP IX: 237)

He went on in the same letter to describe their commanding officer, Colonel G.E. Badcock, 'who is really,' he said,

> *I believe the most excessively unpleasant man I have ever met in the whole of my life. To describe him properly would need a letter in itself, but briefly he is a pompous bully with a thoroughly common*

> *mind. He has some ability, but his real talent is that of a showman. His advertising is really admirable, and he has what amounts to a genius for assimilating the ideas of other men, and text books, and later on reproducing them as his own.* (Ibid.)

Warnie mentioned Colonel Badcock in a letter to his father of 14 June:

> *This fellow is, with one solitary war time exception, the most objectionable man I have ever served under in my life. I personally have not fallen foul of him yet, but I fear it is only a matter of time till I do so...Short of some maddened soldier putting a bullet in him, I see no prospect of escape, for he is one of those great oxes of men whom no climate appears to affect...In the mean time he is determined to get something for himself out of this show if he kills every officer and man under him in doing it.* (LP IX: 241)[30]

Colonel Badcock was to make the first five months in China almost intolerable for Warnie.

---

30 In fact, Colonel Gerald Eliot Badcock (1883–1966) was a distinguished soldier. He was born in Murree, India, on 26 August 1883, the son of General Sir Alexander Robert Badcock (1844–1907), and was educated at Wellington College and Pembroke College, Cambridge. He was commissioned a 2nd lieutenant in the Army Service Corps in 1904, promoted to captain in 1912, adjutant in 1914, major and then brevet lt.-colonel in 1918, and colonel in 1931. From 1915–19 he was Assistant Director of Transport for the Middle East Force and the Egyptian Expeditionary Force. He became Commanding Officer of the Royal Army Service Corps in China in 1927, but returned to England in 1929 to serve as Chief Instructor at the Royal Army Service Corps Training College at Aldershot, 1929–31. From there he went on to become an instructor at the Senior Officers' School at Sheerness, 1931–3. He was Assistant Quartermaster General for the War Office from 1934 until his retirement in 1936. Colonel Badcock served as Bursar of Clifton College, Bristol, 1936–9, after which he was re-employed by the War Office as Director of Salvage, 1940–44. On his retirement he moved to Dorchester where he died 13 January 1966. He is the author of *A History of the Transport Services of the Egyptian Expeditionary Force, 1916–1917–1918* (1925), and an autobiographical work (which contains his photograph), *Two Generations: General Sir A.R. Badcock, Colonel G.E. Badcock* [1933].

TO HIS FATHER (LP IX: 234–6):

Magdalen College,
Oxford.
Saturday.
[28 May 1927]

My dear Papy,

Your wire, which arrived this morning, contributed more to my grandeur than to my peace of mind. It contributed to my grandeur because it happened to be the third communication of an urgent nature which I had received during that hour, and the pupil who was with me, seeing me inundated with these messages and telegrams, must doubtless have supposed that I was the hub of some mighty academical, or even national intrigue. I am sorry you were bothered. I had not thought my silence had been long enough to give you serious anxiety, though it was longer than I wished. If I had written before I could only have given you a line, for the summer term is always the busiest and my days are very full.

Many thanks for the 'Wandering Scholars'.[31] I have so far been able to read it only bit by bit, a quarter of an hour daily, between being called at 7.30 and getting out of my bed at 7.45. It is difficult to judge such a book, for the matter is so extremely interesting to me and my appetite of ignorance so sharp set, that I have paid little attention to the style and disposition. And of course there is always an impossibility in forming a real judgement of a work of scholarship unless you have independent knowledge of the author's raw material. I cannot say how she has *handled* the stuff when I depend on her for knowing the stuff at all. I think, on the whole, that it is a delightful book, tho' rather over-written (all the things she mentions can't really be as good as she claims) and too emotional. But, after all, it tells me much that it is very hard to find elsewhere and will be very useful to me: one cannot ask for much more.

Now for a more important matter. W. and I both agreed that heaven and earth must be moved to get you out of Ireland this summer – preferably to some place where rheumatics are cured. The Colonel's parting instructions were given with characteristic emphasis 'Take him to Droitwich and just get him *boiled in mud* or whatever it is they do to people there.' And I agreed, and promised to do my best. I don't insist on

31 See note 8 to letter of 16 February 1921.

the boiling and the mud: but I do frankly think that it would be absurd for a man who has otherwise a very tolerable constitution to sit down with 'close lipped patience, sister of despair' under rheumatism while all the natural cures (muds, waters etc.) and all the modern electrical cures remain untried. Confess that the man who could be induced to wearing zinc in his boots and drinking (what was it you were advised to drink – an onion soaked in gin, or port or mustard?) but who could not be induced to try what has cured hundreds, is in an indefensible position.

I therefore propose that part or all of my annual holiday should be spent in some such places as I have suggested with perhaps a few days here in Oxford – as our jam after our powder. I know there are difficulties. What have you ever done in which there was not? A man of your age and in your position cannot really be the slave of business engagements. I know too that the thought of an hotel in a 'spa' does not fill you with rapture: but even a troglodyte can't find the presence of strangers as painful as sciatica. And after all, once the plunge is made, would there not be a sort of holiday spirit that would descend on us in such a place and make us no unpleased spectators of the 'stir'. The change of diet alone, and of hours and of way of life is I think a pick-me-up. I know I have always found it so. Monotony is no better for the body than for the mind. Now the first essential of this scheme is to concert our movements. August would be impossible for me. That leaves September and the early part of October. Whether you have time or inclination to write me a long letter or not, please let me have a line soon giving me at least the outline of a scheme possible for you. I have really set my heart on the plan and very earnestly hope that an indulgence of my wishes and a reasonable care for yourself will combine to persuade you to the effort (it cannot really be a very great one) of making arrangements and removing obstacles. If you will fix a time for getting away I will start finding out details at once (I wish W. were here, he'd do it far better and serve you up five alternative operation orders worked out to a half minute at every station, while you waited. But alas – !)

Yes. There is no good balking the fact that this China journey is a bad business, a piece of rotten luck. I confess that when he sailed I was horribly uneasy. By this time (if I can judge at all from the papers) the chance of a war in China is greatly lessened and I am more cheerful. If the trouble clears up I don't see why he might not be home again in eighteen months or so. Of course there is the danger that, once he is out there, he may be put into some peacetime Eastern station for ordinary duty. But I am not really very much afraid of that. It is certainly what would seem reasonable and economic to you and me if we ran the British army. But one hasn't observed that *they* act that way. Even if they designed him for ordinary duty in China soon, they wd. be quite likely to bring him home again first, and we should gain while the tax payer lost.

His letters are of the greatest interest and very good. How the travels of anyone we know suddenly light up the waste places of the Atlas. I suppose the Red Sea coast is described in hundreds of books: but we had to wait till Warnie went East before we ever heard about it.[32] (I always imagined it flat and sandy myself.)

There is no need to bother about my health, and, even when busiest, I usually get my daily walk. I work as a rule from 9 till 1, from 5 till 7.15 (when we dine) and then after dinner till about 11 or 12. This you see gives me time for a good long tramp every afternoon. Nightmares I am afraid are hereditary in more senses than the one you meant. The thing, or what it stands [for] is in the blood of not one family but of the creature called Man.

I had to see Sambo about something this morning and he asked me if I were writing anything. I said I hoped to in a few years (I am hoping to write a book about Sir Thomas More and Erasmus and the people of that time. But my ordinary work gives me v. little time for the necessary reading and it will be a slow, slow business). He then said 'Oh. I was told that you had just published a considerable poem anonymously.' So I had to own up. He wouldn't say who his informant was, but asked if he might see the work: so of course I am presenting him with a copy, and will let you know his comments if he makes any. I foresee that all conversation with him henceforth must run on the lines of 'We authors, Ma'am.'[33]

One never knows what one will run across in the course of one's reading. You will be interested in the following extract from an essay by

---

32 In a letter to his father of 25 April 1927, Warnie described the area around the Red Sea thus: 'Sullen grey white rocks and cliffs, soaring up into fantastic peaks and towers of rock, baking away eternally at a temperature of perhaps 130, in utter desolation – no sign of any living thing, no blade of grass nor tree – just nothing. I imagine that the mountains of the moon, if one could visit them, would give the same horrid impression of the end of all things' (LP IX: 198).

33 Benjamin Disraeli to Queen Victoria following the publication of her *Leaves from a Journal of Our Life in the Highlands 1848–61*(1869).

Sir William Temple written in 1690, just after William and Mary had come to the Throne. 'I shall conclude with a saying of Alphonsus, surnamed the Wise, King of Aragon – that among so many things as are by men possessed or pursued in the course of their lives, all the rest are baubles, besides old wood to burn, old wine to drink, old friends to converse with, and old books to read.'[34] There! I'll bet a hundred pounds to a ha'penny you didn't guess how that quotation was going to end when you began to read it. 'Alphonsus the Wise' seems to have lived in the fourteenth century. I know nothing else about him. But perhaps this is enough and tells one all one wants to know.

Well, I must to bed. 'So to bed' as Pepys says. I am sorry you were worried. Be sure and let me have an answer to my main question and in the meantime, good night.

your loving son,
Jack

TO ARTHUR GREEVES (W):

[Magdalen College
26 June 1927]

My dear Arthur,

Knowing the state of your finances I couldn't find it in my conscience to keep the whole of your extremely kind and unexpected present, and herewith return £1. The other I retain with very many thanks, and shall devote it to a pleasant edition of Thomas Browne in three volumes which I saw lately: or perhaps I shall get Dryden's plays in a folio wh. I think sells for about that amount. De la Mare's poems I have had for a long time and I read them more often than any other book. I put him above Yeats and all the other moderns, and in spite of his fantasy find him nearer than any one else to the essential truth of life.

I was sorry to hear such a poor account of my father from you. Of course three weeks in an English hotel with him would for me have all the disadvantages of my usual spell at home without any of the advantages: but I feel bound not only to make the suggestion but to try and bring it to reality. This by itself would give me unhappy anticipations of this summer, but I am much more bothered by the possibility of Minto's

34 'On Ancient and Modern Learning', in *Essays of Sir William Temple*, vol. II (1822), pp. 93–4.

having to have an operation – not, thank heavens, a very serious one, but her bad veins make even a slight one unpleasant. At present things seem more hopeful than they did a few weeks ago, and it may not be necessary: but you can imagine that we are all pretty uneasy.

I am glad to hear that you are still working on the play, and think that the new idea you have of the Trees is a great advance. I haven't read the essay of Clutton Brock's[35] which you mention, but the theory – that out of the deep reservoirs of nature (the caverns of Erda) we draw power and inspiration which *we* make good or evil – is a familiar and favourite one of my own. If you will re-read what I make the girl say in Canto VIII of Dymer you will get my view on that subject better expressed than I can hope to put it in a letter, and summed up in the line 'With incorruptibles the mortal Will corrupts itself.'[36] But I will read the Clutton Brock as soon as I come across it and see what he says. I like and agree with most of his work.

I am realising a number of very old dreams in the way of books – reading Sir Gawain in the original[37] (you remember my translation of it in a companion volume to my translation of Beowulf) and, above all, learning Old Icelandic. We have a little Icelandic Club in Oxford called the 'Kólbitar':[38] which means (literally) 'coal-biters', i.e. an Icelandic word for old cronies who sit round the fire so close that they look as if they were biting the coals. We have so far read the Younger Edda and the Volsung Saga: next term we shall read the Laxdale Saga. *You* will be able to imagine what a delight this is to me, and how, even in turning over the pages of my Icelandic Dictionary, the mere name of god or giant catching my eye will sometimes throw me back fifteen years into a wild dream of northern skies and Valkyrie music: only they are now even more

---

35 Arthur probably mentioned Arthur Clutton-Brock's 'The Adoration of the Magi' in *Essays on Art* (1919), pp. 1–2.

36 *Dymer*, VIII, xv, 5–6.

37 He had recently acquired *Sir Gawain and the Green Knight*, ed. J.R.R. Tolkien and E.V. Gordon (1925).

38 See **J.R.R. Tolkien** in the Biographical Appendix. J.R.R. Tolkien became Professor of Anglo-Saxon at Oxford in 1925, and in *AMR*, pp. 392–3, Lewis mentions their first meeting on 11 May 1926. Tolkien began at Oxford the study of Old Icelandic texts. At the same time he founded a society called the Kolbítar or 'Coalbiters' for the purpose of reading the Icelandic sagas and myths in the original Old Icelandic or Old Norse. It was through this society, which Lewis joined in 1926 or 1927, that Lewis and Tolkien became friends.

beautiful seen thro' a haze of memory – you know that awfully *poignant* effect there is about impression *recovered* from ones past.

I feel great sympathy with your situation at home and can just imagine it this wet Sunday morning on which I write – with St Mark's bell ringing in the distance and 'the O'Mulligan'[39] trotting off to Church. Talking about home, have you seen Helen Wadell's book. I am sure Tchanie is never tired of talking of it. It is specially interesting to us because when you have read it you see what an enormous influence H.W. has had on Tchanie: the book is full of passages that Tchanie wd. have written herself if she could. I know now where Tchanie's dreadful serious moments (when she recites!) come from. Alas poor Tchanie! 'I was chust saying to Chanie.' So Gundred is married.[40] Tout change! I hope you will keep me informed as to what my father is *really* thinking of doing. As I said before, I shall press the English trip: but I have a secret conviction that it will not come off, and we shall probably meet this summer as usual. With many thanks again, and with love from all here.

Yours
Jack

TO HIS BROTHER (LP IX: 252–8):

Hillsboro
July 9/27

My dear W.,

This particularly unpleasant paper is a direct result of the great war, for I went to the door today and met an ex-service man selling writing pads. This was 1/3. It happens about twice a week and as Minto's excellent principles never allow her to send the poor devil empty away, we have an enormous supply of expensive paper of the worst quality. However it has jogged me into starting a fresh letter to you.

The Term has now been over some weeks, for which I am not sorry. It produced one public event of good omen – the carrying in Congregation

39 Miss Lizzie Mulligan and her sister who lived on Glenfarlough Road, about 200 yards from Little Lea, had been friends of Lewis's mother. Albert and his sons referred to her affectionately as 'the O'Mulligan' as she passed Little Lea and Bernagh on her way to St Mark's.

40 On 15 June 1927 Gundreda Ewart married Colonel John Forrest, formerly of the Royal Army Medical Corps, who had just become the secretary of the Royal Victoria Hospital in Belfast.

of a Statute limiting the number of wimmen at Oxford.[41] The appalling danger of our degenerating into a woman's university (nay worse still, into *the* women's university, in contradistinction to Cambridge, *the* men's university) has thus been staved off. There was fierce Opposition of course, our female antagonists being much more expert than we in the practice of 'whipping' in the parliamentary sense.

Since the victory the papers have been full of comment from such people as Sybil Thorndike, Lady Astor, Daisy Devoteau, Fanny Adams and other such notable educational authorities. They mostly deplore (especially in the Daily Mirror and the Little Ha'penny Sketch) one more instance of the unprogressiveness of those 'aged Professors'. The word 'academic' is also worked hard: tho' how the politics of an academy could, or why they should, cease to be 'academic', 'might admit of a wide conjecture'.

But the question of the age of the anti-feminists is an interesting one: and the voting (we have no secret franchise) revealed very consolatory facts. First came the very old guard, the octogenarians and the centurions, the full fed patriarchs of Corpus, the last survivors of the days when 'women's rights' were still new fangled crankery. They were against the women. Then came the very-nearly-as-old who date from the palmy days of J.S. Mill, when feminism was the new, exciting, enlightened thing: people representing as someone said, 'the progressiveness of the 'eighties'. They voted for the women. Then came the young and the post-war (I need not say I trust that I did my duty) who voted solid *against*. The arrangement is quite natural when you think it out. The first belong to the age of innocence when women had not yet been noticed: the second, to the age when they had been noticed but not yet found out: the third to us. Ignorance, romance, realism. The queer thing was that one solitary woman voted against her sex. She has since married and given up her job. *Una de multis face nuptial digna*: your Horation apprenticeship will carry you as far as that.[42]

But what irritated me beyond bearing during the whole thing was the re-iterated statement made even by people on our side, that, if we ought

41 The principle that 'the university has a right to remain predominantly a men's university' was asserted in a statute passed in the University on 14 June 1927. For more on this issue see the chapter on 'Women' in *The Twentieth Century* (ed. Brian Harrison), volume VIII of *The History of the University of Oxford* (1994).

42 Horace, *Odes*, Book 3, poem 11, ll. 33–4: 'One of the many worthy of the bridal torch'.

on principle to put up a show, it was really no good, because 'it was bound to come'. If I remember rightly your friend Drysdale,[43] on the only occasion I met him, indulged in the same fatalism. It is a very remarkable thing, this kind of view. Because the 18th century was fond of personifying abstractions ('Corruption has seized the provinces' etc.) and because Carlyle carried that further and gave us a tinge of poetry in his French Revolution,[44] whence it passed into every writer who wants to write impressively on poetical and historical subjects, we have now reached a stage at which causes, movements, tendencies etc. are talked of as if they were real things who did things: as if it were Bolshevism, not Bolsheviks, who fomented revolutions, and the revolutionary spirit, instead of the revolutionary spirits, which made men drunk. The natural corollary is that the world is managed by beings such as 'Woman' or 'The Locarne spirit' and real human beings are pawns in their hands. Now a days you can resist a given spirit or tendency only by hitching yourself to its equally spirituous or tendentious opponent – much like an ancient Egyptian who, helpless himself against the name of a god, can put it across it by means of the name of an higher god. I was just going to describe this as the return to polytheism. But the polytheists were more sensible for they accepted their positions as pawns because they believed in their gods. And if the wiseacre really believed in the beings to whom he attributes all public events (as I wd. be quite prepared to do with certain reservations) I cd. forgive him. But he is the first man to denounce you for a mystic if you hint that there might really be an entity such as the 'spirit of the age' over and above the human beings acting in that age. He is thus in the remarkable position of suspending everything on a peg which (he believes) isn't there, and preaching the uselessness of human endeavor because we are helpless in the hands of – Nobody. However, the subject seems to be carrying me further than I foresaw.

Much more important in the term's history was a private event in Magdalen common Room which lasted only a minute – but that minute should have recalled Lamb from the dead. The hero is Brightman,[45] that very old prebendary, whom some call Lob: for 'he looked elvish by his countenance' (he is less than five feet high, clean shaven, bald, and round

43 Captain J.E. Drysdale was Warnie's officer in command in China.

44 Thomas Carlyle, *History of the French Revolution* (1837).

45 Frank Edward Brightman. See note 5 to letter of 5 January 1926.

as a barrel). A former fellow who had returned to dine, rallied him in the words, 'Well, Brightman, I suppose you're as ready to bur'rn me at the stake as ever?' referring I suppose to some old theological dispute. Mark the answer: Lob, ignoring the main question as too obvious, waited a moment and then reflectively added the rider, 'You're a Scotchman amongst other things'.

I haven't yet made up my mind as to whether this is a pudaita story or not. Sometimes I think it is just in his line (being closely parallel to 'but there are other reasons') at others I am desperately afraid of some such complex reply as 'Why, is this fellow Bunkman a Scotchman himself?' Indeed perhaps its resemblance to 'there are other reasons' is an additional danger and may lead to the familiar (yet ever new) infuriating beginning 'Sure this is only the old wheeze of so-and-so' with the net result that having ventured on a story yourself you are forced to laugh at a very old story of some one else's.

The rest of the term was mainly occupied by the nonsense connected with Commem. Magdalen gave a ball which you would not suppose could have concerned me: but it did, for they put up a huge marquee between the cloisters and New Building, which not only spoiled all the beautiful spaciousness but on windy nights groaned and creaked like a ship under sail and kept me awake.

Sailing boats reminds me – I have just read Smollet's *Roderick Random*[46] which, as you probably know, is our chief literary document for the life of the navy in the 18th century. It is there that Captain Whiffle orders the officer out of the cabin because he cannot stand the stink of him. His picture as a whole is much what I expected – infernal. The resigned but bottomless contempt of all ranks for their senior officers, the certainty that everything is being mismanaged, and that the staff are fools and cowards is especially interesting: I suppose it is the normal state in all armies and navies. The book as a whole belongs to a type whose disappearance I do not much regret: the autobiographical novel in the form of memories of one who relates his misfortunes (for he is very unfortunate): that is, a string of frauds, oppressions and accidents piled on the hero in such a way as to give him the opportunity of fluctuating rapidly through all social strata, now 'a fine gentleman', now in a sponging house, pressed, imprisoned, etc. At one time he becomes a foot

46 Tobias George Smollett, *The Adventures of Roderick Random* (1748).

soldier in a French regiment. It is all very lively and will hold your attention wherever you open it: but the author's determination to ring the changes and show every side of the life of his times, by making it certain that whatever the hero is doing at the moment, some accident will completely reverse the position in the next ten pages, prevents the development of any continuous interest. Like Tom Jones, it uses the device of a story in a story and Roderick is constantly meeting people who at once tell him their story. (You will remember one instance of this in Tom Jones). This, together with the rambling episodes, recalls the structure (tho' not of course the atmosphere) of the Faerie Queene. In fact in reading this, Tom Jones, and Evelina[47] (which I have also read recently for the first time) I was struck by the real identity of method between the mediaeval romance and the early novel, and also by the wonderful reform that Scott and Jane Austen effected in reaching the modern complex but unified plot.

By the way, can you suggest why it is that when you read Boswell, Walpole's letters, or Fanny Burney's diary you find the 18th century a very delightful period, differing from ours chiefly by a greater formality and 'elegance' of manners whereas when you turn to the novel (including Evelina), you suddenly step into a world full of full-blooded, bawdy, brutal, strident, pull-away-the-chair barbarity? The sea captain in Evelina who supplies the comic element does so by playing a series of tricks on an elderly French lady, whom he addresses as 'Madam Frog', throws into ditches, and trips up in the mud. What is the common denominator between this and Johnson's circle? And which is true? Perhaps both are and one sees what the Doctor meant when he said that in a jail the society was commonly better than at sea.

But I mustn't spend too long on books for I have the ludicrous adventure of my own to tell. Unfortunately it needs a good deal of introduction to render it intelligible, but I think it is worth it. Mme Studer is the widow of M. Studer[48] who died recently under distressing circumstances. She had been temporarily insane once during his lifetime: and tho' there was no serious fear of a relapse, her state of mind after his death, together with some traces of hysteria and more depression than even the

---

47 Fanny Burney, *Evelina, or a Young Lady's Entrance into the World* (1778).

48 Mrs Studer was the wife of Paul Studer (1879–1927), Taylorian Professor of the Romance Languages in the University of Oxford, who died 23 January 1927. They were both Swiss, and had three children.

death of a husband seemed to justify, led most of her friends to keep an eye on her. Minto went to see her pretty regularly. So did (the heroine of my story) a Mrs Wilbraham. She is what is called 'a brave little woman' (tho' it is not known what dangers she ever had to encounter) and is never idle. She brings up her daughter in the light of lectures on child psychology delivered by professors whose own children never get born at all or are notable puppies. She is a spiritualist: a psychoanalyst, but does not believe in the theories of Freud because they are so horrid: she weighs the babies of poor women: her business in fact is universal benevolence. 'If only one feels that one can be of some use in the world ...' as she often says.

Well, the other night I was just settling down to translate a chapter of the Edda, when suddenly Minto called me out of the dining room and said 'Mrs Wilbraham is here. She says Mrs Studer has twice tried to commit suicide today. She's got a taxi here and wants me to go and see the doctor at the Warneford.[49] We shall have to get a nurse for Mrs Studer.' I said I'd come along, because Minto has been rather poorly and I didn't know what she might be let in for. So Mrs W., Minto and I drove off to the Warneford. I remained in the taxi while the two ladies went in to see the Doctor. It was about half past nine, dusk and raining. At an unlighted window just opposite stood a very pale man with a long beard who fixed his eyes on the taxi with insane steadiness for half an hour without ever blinking or moving as far as I could see: to complete the picture (you'll hardly believe it) a large black cat sat on the window sill beneath him. (I always imagined they kept the patients in back rooms or something or at any rate had bars on the window.) I liked this so little that in desperation I tried to start a conversation with Griffin the taximan (also your garager when you are at Headington). 'This is an unpleasant place, Griffin', said I. He replied promptly 'You know sir you can't put her in without a doctor and a magistrate'. I then realized that he thought we were there for the purpose of 'putting in' either Minto or Mrs W. In my dismay, not quite decided what I meant, I blurted out 'Oh I hope that won't be necessary' – and when he replied 'Well it was the last time I got one put in 'ere' I realized that I had hardly improved matters.

49 The Warneford Hospital opened in 1826 as the Oxford Lunatic Asylum, and in 1843 it took the name Warneford Asylum. The asylum was purpose-built, and it recreated the atmosphere of a country gentleman's house, with a chapel and landscaped grounds.

The others emerged at last with a Nurse Jones and we started off for the Studer's. But now the question was what to do? Madame would certainly refuse to have a strange young woman thrust upon her for the night for no apparent reason: as her husband was dead and her relatives abroad, no one had any authority over her. And even if we wished, no doctor would certify her as insane on the evidence of a child – the only person who ever claimed to have seen the attempt at suicide. Mrs Wilbraham said it was all perfectly simple. She would stay hidden in Mme Studer's garden all night. Nurse would be put up in the bungalow of a stranger opposite Madame's house. She must herself stay in the garden. It was no good arguing. It was her duty. If only her nephew was here! If only she could have a man with her, she confessed, she would feel less nervous about it. I began to wish I'd stayed at home: but in the end of course I had to offer.

No one raised the question as to why the Nurse had been prevented from going to bed at the Warneford in order to be carried half a mile in a taxi and immediately put to bed in another house totally unconnected with the scene of action, where she could not possibly be of the slightest use. The girl herself, who was possibly in some doubt as to who the supposed lunatic might be, remained in a stupefied silence.

I now suggested as a last line of defence that nothing wd be more likely to upset Mme Studer than to find dim figures walking about her garden all night: to which Mrs W. replied brightly that we must keep out of sight and go very quietly. 'We could put our stockings on outside our boots you know.' At that moment (we were all whispering just outside a house further down in the same street as Madame's, and it was now about eleven o'clock) a window opened overhead and someone asked me rather curtly whether we wanted anything, and if not, would we kindly go away. This restored me to some of the sanity I was rapidly losing, and I determined that whatever else happened, four o'clock should not find me 'with my stockings over my boots' explaining to the police that I was (v. naturally) spending the night in some one else's garden for fear the owner might commit suicide.

I therefore ruled that we must keep our watch in the road, where, if we sat down, we wd be hidden from the window by the paling (and, I added mentally, wd be open to arrest for vagabondage, not for burglary). Several neighbours had now turned up (all women, and nearly all vulgar) to revel in excitement, and Mrs W. (while insisting on the absolute necessity of letting no one know – 'it would be dreadful if it got about poor thing') gave each newcomer, including the total strangers, a full account of the situation. I came home with Minto, drank a cup of tea, put on my great coat, took some biscuits, smokes, a couple [of] apples, a rug, a waterproof sheet and two cushions, and returned to the fatal road. It was now twelve o'clock. The crowd of neighbours had now melted away: but one (neither vulgar nor a stranger) had had the rare good sense to leave some sandwiches and three thermos flasks. I found the brave little woman actually eating and drinking when I arrived. Hastily deciding that if I were to lie under the obligations of a *man* I wd assume his authority, I explained that we should be really hungry and cold later on and authoritatively put a stop to that nonsense. My next step was to provide for my calls of nature (no unimportant matter in an all night tête-à-tête with a fool of an elderly woman who has had nothing to do with men since her husband had the good fortune to die several years ago) by observing that the striking of a match in that stillness wd easily be heard in the Studer's house and that I wd tiptoe to the other end of the road to light my pipe.

Having thus established my right to disappear into the darkness as often as I chose – she conceded it with some reluctance – I settled down. There had been some attempt at moonlight earlier, but it had clouded over and a fine rain began to fall. Mrs Wilbraham's feminine and civilian vision of night watches had apparently not included this. She was really surprised at it. She was also surprised at its getting really cold: and most surprised of all to find that she became sleepy, for she (after the first ten minutes) had answered to my warning on that score with a scornful 'I don't think there's much danger of that!' However all these hardships gave her the opportunity of being 'bright' and 'plucky' as far as one can be in sibilant whispers.

If I could have been quit of her society I wd have found my watch just tolerable – despite the misfortune of finding my greatcoat pockets stuffed with camphor balls (Minto is very careful about moths) which I flung out angrily on the road, and then some hours later forgetting this and trying to eat one of the apples that had lain in those pockets. The taste of camphor is exactly like the smell. During the course of the night my companion showed signs of becoming rather windy and I insisted on playing with her the old guessing game called 'Animal, Vegetable, or Mineral'. (Incidentally I thought I would find it more interesting than her conversation.) After assuring me that she was thinking of an animal, a live animal, an animal we had seen that night, she had the impudence to announce in the end that 'it' was the 'voice of an owl we had heard' – which shows the working of her mind. However my story is over now, and when I have added that the crows had been 'tuning up their unseasonable matins' a full half hour before any other bird squeaked (a fact of natural history which I never knew before) I may dismiss Mrs-Ruddy-Wilbraham from my mind.

The whole affair has suggested to me the idea of an admirable short story for wh. we have all the characters ready. Let Mrs W. suspect the P'daytabird of insanity on the Witch of Endor's information: and then have your story told in the first person by him. He finds himself receiving visits from crowds of strangers on the flimsiest pretexts, who relieve one another from eight till twelve (because it's dangerous to leave him alone): he finds, or learns from the Witch of Endor, of the gradual but steady disappearance of all *cutlery*: the denouement might come when on one of his rare nights alone he suddenly finds the study plunged in total darkness and after calling 'Mary' repeatedly at the study door, blunders down into the lower regions where by the light of a match he discovers a brave little woman (with her stockings over her boots) who says soothingly 'Its alright Mr Lewis, I just came in to turn the gas off at the metre' – and a moment later his 'What on earth...' coinciding with her signal whistle to those without, he might find himself overpowered by a miscellaneous collection of people (mostly 'cattle') who had been spending the night in the wash house.

I was agreeably surprised yesterday morning by your letter from Hong Kong – or the mainland opposite, which gives me a lively impression of your present predicament.[50] You will not be able to appreciate the

50 'As regards our friends the Chinese,' Warnie wrote on 7 June 1927, 'the West African is a curious person with many odd habits but you never lose the sense of a common humanity shared with him, and the same is of course true of the Indian. But it is impossible to visualize these disgusting creatures as human beings at all or even as animals. One somehow has a freakish feeling that some extraordinary accident blew them off another planet into China. To take the few illustrations I have so far encountered, what are you to make of a race who nod their heads when they mean "no" and shake them when they mean "yes" – where the corpse is the only person who does not attend his own funeral – where a group of friends are chatting at a street corner and on one being knocked down by a lorry and fatally injured, the others, after bursting into a peal of laughter, stroll on and leave him to die in the road – where the

point of William James'[51] remark that the great presumptive argument against personal immortality was 'What are you going to do with the Chinese?' One can't help feeling that when people are so very different as all that, one has no business to be connected with them at all. The society of things human (or roughly human) in form but in nothing else must be v. injurious. The only things I have ever read or heard about their culture exactly agree with your account: not that one can place much reliance on your friend Ahmed Din, if he is a Moslem, as I presume by the name: you remember Mackail's description of Islam as being 'polygamous methodism' – I mean they have the name of looking on all other cultures much as a Plymouth Brother looks on the ungodly. Surely A. Din's primary grudge against the Chinks is that they are *idolaters* – and the rest follows. However, I expect that in this case he is quite right. Their national vanity is confirmed by everything that one hears of them. Didn't we both read somewhere that the typical Chinese reaction to any new invention is an elaborate historical research ending with the statement 'Sure this is only the old so-and-so business that we invented in the nth Dynasty'. I am alarmed by the great philologist Jesperson[52] who argues (v. cogently) that the English language is rapidly moving towards a structure and syntax of wh. the Chinese is the only other example.

I have no difficulty in imagining a day grey and drizzling as an English November 'seeing as how' we have lived under such days for a week or so, relieved by the mutterings of a chronic thunderstorm. The popular theory is that the weather is all 'caused by the eclipse', the eclipse which has been 'news' in the papers long before and after its occurrence: or as

---

language is such that a Chinaman from two hundred miles away would not understand what a Hong Kong Chinaman is saying?...This detachment from the human family is difficult to explain but I honestly believe that if I saw a dozen Chinamen hit by an H.E. shell I should feel nothing but a mild disgust at the mess. Another of their characteristics is I am told an immense conceit and a self satisfaction with their own civilization which appears to me quite unwarranted. My informant is one Ahmed Din, an Indian tailor, and a very clever man, with whom I had a most interesting chat the other day. He knows Chinese and has read a lot of their literature, from which he contemptuously denies them any claim to a culture' (LP IX: 239).

51 William James (1842–1910), American philosopher. He was Professor successively of Psychology (1887–97) and Philosophy (1897–1907) at Harvard University. In his *Varieties of Religious Experience* (1902), he distinguished between 'once-born' and 'twice-born' religious types, and made a scientific analysis of conversion.

52 Otto Jesperson, *Language, its Nature, Development and Origin* (1922), ch. XVIII, xix–3, 'Structure of Chinese', pp. 369ff.

Rose Macaulay wd. say, it produced 'amazing crowds' and in them were 'many well dressed women'. Unfortunately it was not visible from Headington. What I can't understand is why, if the moon is constantly revolving round the earth, it gets directly in the light of the sun only once in a century or so: I shd. have imagined that it would happen about twice a year. None of the elaborate explanations in the papers touch this point, so I suppose it must just be given up.

I wrote to the OAB shortly after your departure professing my eagerness to take an English holiday with him in some health resort this year, and putting the case for it as strongly as I could: my letter has had the usual result of reducing him to several weeks of complete silence. If you ever want to make sure of *not* hearing from him, the infallible method is to ask him some question which requires a definite decision of his to answer it. I've never known it fail: and I must confess that I react in precisely the same way myself. How easy to answer an important letter: how impossible to answer any of those inexcusable epistles which insolently *demand* an answer.

Joynson Hicks[53] (did you know that he was the leading light of the survivors of English Evangelicalism and as such has been a centre of opposition to the Papistical tendencies of the new Prayer Book?[54] Now, continue to be a Tory if you dare) – well this Joynson Hicks said yesterday that troops were being rapidly recalled from China. I suppose that is too good to be true, and wouldn't have been said if it were true.

Well, examining begins tomorrow and this letter, with all other rational activities, must end. Write when you can. All here send their affectionate compliments.

yours,

J.

---

53 Sir William Joynson Hicks (1865–1932), statesman, was Home Secretary 1924–9, and prominent in the defeat of the Prayer Book revision of 1927–8.

54 Early in 1927 the bishops of the Church of England completed a revision of the Book of Common Prayer. It was different in many ways from all previous Prayer Books, and it was rejected by the House of Commons on 15 December 1927. *The Book of Common Prayer with the Additions and Deviations Proposed in 1928*, as it is known, was published in 1928. While it does not have official approval, it is used by some parishes. For Albert Lewis on the 1928 Prayer Book see note 19 to the letter of 13 April 1929.

TO HIS FATHER (LP IX: 260–2):

[Magdalen College]
July 29th. [1927]

My dear Papy,

I was glad to hear from you. A letter from Arthur some time ago had let me know that you were still suffering from the old complaint and I was therefore more pleased to hear that there was at least some relief than disappointed to hear it was not greater.[55] I am a little surprised at your response to the programme of being 'boiled in mud'. Neither of us of course would choose Harrogate or any similar place for pleasure: that may be taken as a starting point to any discussion on the subject – tho', I repeat, the unpleasantness must not be exaggerated. (Damme Sir, are we to be frightened of some retired colonels and rich old maids?) I suggested it purely and simply on medical grounds and your reply strikes me rather as if I had said to a man with toothache 'Why not go to a dentist?' and he had answered 'You're quite right – I will go out. But I won't go to a dentist. I'll go and get fitted for a new pair of boots.' However, I am so pleased at your agreement on the main issue, that of going away, that I must not press the other too hard. It would be only reasonable to be guided by Joey in this matter. If he has any faith in mud baths etc., surely we can manage to combine the business with pleasure, even on the site of the mud baths. I am delighted to hear that you have changed your Doctor at last.[56]

As for Joey – after all I may as well be frank. As a matter of cool judgement, no doubt, I do disapprove his behaviour during the war: on the other hand, like all us Celts, I am a born rhetorician, one who finds pleasure in the forcible emotions independently of their grounds and even to the extent to which they are felt at any time save the moment of speaking. Like the obscure poet whom I saw mentioned in the local newspaper at Caerleon, I love to 'ride like a cork on the ocean of eloquence': and

55 Mr Lewis had been seized by lumbago during the night of 17 June, and for a fortnight he was completely prostrated by it.

56 He had exchanged Dr Leslie for his nephew Dr Joseph 'Joey' Lewis (1898–1969). 'Joey' was the son of Albert's eldest brother, Joseph. His career at Campbell College, Belfast, and medical schools had been brilliant. In 1928 he was appointed bacteriologist to the Belfast Infirmary, and he became one of the leading blood specialists in Northern Ireland. It annoyed Jack, however, that he had not served during the war. See **The Lewis Family** in the Biographical Appendix.

whenever you hear me inveighgling in 'Ercles vein' you must take this into account. A tirade against war shirkers is an exhilarating after dinner exercise: but while not wholly unreal it implies no such heartfelt animosity as would jibb at Joey's attendance even on myself. Certainly if the choice is between Squeaky and Joey one can't hesitate. I hope you will commit yourself to the 'blood specialist's' hands from this day forth and profit by it.

I am just in the few days lull between my two 'fittes' of summer examining. I have finished reading the boys' answers in Oxford, and next week I go to Cambridge for the pleasanter (and more profitable) business of awarding. I had rather a heavy dose of it this time, and the strain took the form of giving me neuralgia. At least my dentist, after striking probes into me, punching me in the face, and knocking my teeth with small hammers – accompanied with the blatantly impertinent question 'Does that hurt?' (to which the proper reply seems to be a sharp return blow at *his* jaw with the words 'Yes, just like that') – my dentist I say, assured me that there was nothing wrong with my teeth and therefore it must be neuralgia. I managed in spite of it to sleep pretty well by dint of soaking my feet in water as hot as I could stand, immediately before going to bed. This is an excellent plan if you have to work right up to bedtime and your head is in a whirl, as it draws the blood away to the extremities and makes you stop thinking.

My labours were rewarded by some good things from the candidates (who are school boys under sixteen). The definition of a *Genie* as 'an oriental spirit inhabiting bottles and buttons and rings' is a rather rare example of a correct answer which is funny. 'A *Censer* is one who incenses people' is more of the familiar type. In answer to a question from a paper on *Guy Mannering* 'Would you have liked Colonel Mannering as a father? Support your answer by an account of his behaviour to Julia', one youth sagely replied that he would. It is true that Mannering was cold, suspicious, autocratic etc., 'but he was very rich and I think he would have made an excellent father'. That boy should be sent to the City at once: he has the single eye. But the best of all came from a paper (set by me) on Macbeth.

> Question*: Give the context of, 'Throw physic to the dogs, I'll none of it.'*[57]

57 Shakespeare, *Macbeth*, V, iii, 47.

> Answer: *'Macbeth said these words near the end of the play. He was feeling uneasy before the battle and Seyton told him he ought to take some medicine.'*

It is very interesting to speculate what would have happened if Seyton *had* done this. Would the line have run 'Throw Seyton to the dogs, I'll none of him.' Yet, incredible as the mistake may seem, it was repeated (of course with small variations) in some fifteen or twenty papers. In one, Seyton suggested the dose not only for Macbeth but for his soldiers as well.

As I have spent ten days or so glued to my table at this task I have naturally not much news. Sambo, after asking for Dymer and being sent a copy, has made neither comment on it or acknowledgment of the gift. I suppose he is waiting to read it in his holidays, or else has forgotten all about [it]. The other hypothesis – that his feelings about it were 'too deep for words' is rendered improbable because I have dined with the Warrens since: so at least he has decided not to cut the acquaintance over the head of it.

Now let me see if anything else has a curious, but quite independant parallel to your 'but there are other reasons' story. A Scotchman, formerly a Fellow of this College, came to dine, and rallied old Brightman (with whom I suppose he had had theological arguments in the old days) by saying 'Well Brightman, I suppose ye're still as ready to bur-r-rn me as ye always were'. To which Brightman, ignoring the main question as too obvious for an explicit answer, replied meditatively 'You're a Scotchman amongst other things'.

My only other recent adventure was a purely literary one – that of quite accidentally picking up *The Woman in White*[58] and reading it: a book of course now practically unknown to anyone under forty. I thought it extremely good of its kind, and not a bad kind. But what spacious days those were! The characters, or at least all the wicked ones, flame in jewels and the hero is so poor in one place that he actually travels *second class* on the railway. I have decided to model my behaviour for the future (socially I mean, not morally) on that of Count Fosco, but without the canaries and the white mice.

---

58 Wilkie Collins, *The Woman in White* (1860).

Another curious thing is the elaborate descriptions of male beauty, which I hardly remember to have seen since Elizabethan poetry: or do the 'noble brow, the silky beard' and the 'Manly beauty' still flourish in fiction which I don't happen to have read? Of course only third rate people write that kind of novel now, whereas Wilkie Collins was clearly a man of genius: and there is a good deal to be said for his point of view (expressed in the preface) that the first business of a novel is to tell a story, and that characters etc. come second. Aristotle thought the same about tragedy.

Warnie seems to be having a rotten time.[59] The only consolation seems to be that (as far as one can judge from the papers) things look like clearing up in China and he may be sent back sooner than we expected. I shall be pretty busy all August, but will get across as soon as I can in September. I hope we shall have a famous jaunt. I am going bald at a prodigious rate and in a few years time you will have a better head of hair than either of your sons. What sort of a wig would you recommend?

your loving son,
Jack

TO HIS FATHER (LP IX: 264–5):

Magdalen.
Aug. 12th [1927]

My dear P.,

So sorry – I find I forgot to send the enclosed with my last letter. I am back from Cambridge, where I had the usual unwholesome combination of high living (we are fed splendidly, both food and drink being free) and sedentary occupation.

I heard a rather impressive thing while I was there. While we were at work one morning, some one came in and informed my Cambridge colleague of the death of a common friend. When the other had gone, my friend told me the story. Mr — (I forget the name) was a Fellow of a Cambridge College. Shortly before the war his pancreas went badly out of order, and finally ceased to work at all. The ordinary doctors could do little for him: but as he was a rather distinguished bio-chemist, and lived among bio-chemists, he managed to get along somehow on the

59 Things were worse than Jack and his father thought. On 12 July Warnie went into the 3rd British General Hospital with a fever and an outbreak of boils over his entire body.

experiments that he and his circle tried on him: but he was subject to frequent attacks and (what worried him the most) could never do more than about two hours work a day. Three weeks ago one of his bad turns came on. Whereupon he said to his doctor, 'Look here doctor, would it make any difference to you professionally if a patient of yours chose to die of starvation?' The Doctor (who must have been an unusual man) said it would not. The patient immediately put his plan into action and from that moment no food passed his lips. He was constantly visited by his friends and refused to discuss his own situation, while indulging with all his former spirit in science, politics, and banter – banter of the rather schoolboyish quite unintellectual type which is so common in England. My colleague's informant had been to see him a few days ago: and the last words of the patient (now almost a skeleton) had been 'Well bye bye – thank the Lord I shall never have to be your partner at Bridge again!' There is a story in Pliny's letters of a Roman[60] who chose exactly the same plan in similar circumstances: but he seems to have spent his last hours in rhetorical 'last words' and Stoic platitudes about contempt of death. Perhaps I shouldn't say 'platitudes': the Roman was probably quite sincere. But the difference of temperament strikes one.

The other story I heard at Cambridge was very funny tho' very blasphemous. However, as it was told to me in the presence of an Archdeacon by a B.D., two laymen may be excused for enjoying it. It is told of Phelps the Provost of Oriel,[61] but will do equally well for anyone who 'has a good conceit of himself'. Phelps dreamed that he had died and reached the gate of heaven. Here a resplendent being, bowing obsequiously, said 'Very pleased to see you, Mr Provost I'm sure. Right straight on up the stairs.' At the top of the stairs a much more resplendent being, respectful rather than obsequious, met him. 'Ah, Provost, delighted to see you. Just turn to your right.' Following these directions he suddenly found himself in front of a throne in a blaze of light. 'Why my dear Phelps' exclaimed the Occupant. 'This is delightful', then rising 'Why – bless me – I beg your pardon – I'm afraid I've got your chair!'

Have you any views as to *where* you and I shd. go, if we don't get boiled in mud? I had thought of N.Wales, some of the mountainous

---

60 Pliny, *Letters*, Bk. I, letter to Calestrius Tiro.

61 Lancelot Ridley Phelps (1853–1936), Provost of Oriel College, Oxford 1914–29.

places. But possibly that wd. be too relaxing, and too wet in September.

your loving son,
Jack

P.S. The blots on this page are not my tears – it rained on to my table while I was away at lunch.

TO ARTHUR GREEVES (W):

The Folly,
Perranporth,
Cornwall.
Aug 24th [1927]

My dear Arthur,

A thousand apologies. We have come down here for a bit to set us all up, specially Minto, and you can imagine that the almost nomadic grandeur of family packing and family travelling, combined with the pleasant, yet crowding, picnic life we are now leading, has left me little liesure for writing. Still, I certainly ought to have let you have a line if only to acknowledge the cheque, and am very sorry that I did not. Very many thanks: but I still protest that it is an excessive gift from poor you to me. However, if you are going to challenge me to a duel in case I return it again, I will see what I can do towards spending it. Again, many many thanks.

As to showing my father the play. I think his criticism, tho' formal, is valuable on questions of *style* for a speech or essay or the narrative parts of a novel. Whether it wd. be much use for *dialogue*, I am hardly prepared to say. The general philosophy and meaning and all that, would not, I think, interest him, nor would he take very much trouble to understand it. He would assure you that he knew exactly what you meant and then substitute something of his own: probably identifying your view with some very superficially similar view expressed in some book he had read, in the words 'Sure this is the old business of so-and-so.' I fancy, however, he wd. have a pretty good eye for theatrical effect, specially on the humorous side. I am afraid I cannot be much more conclusive, and you must decide for yourself. After all you know his literary conversation nearly as well as I do. One thing you must be warned of. If he thinks the whole thing bosh he will be much too kind to tell you so: and at the same time he is habitually *rather* contemptuous of local literary endeavours. It would be hard for you to excite his admiration, and yet he will be determined not to hurt you.

I expect to be home on the 5th of September – leaving the others here. The doctor thought Minto ought to get away – she is much better and really (but touch wood!) has made a remarkable escape from the trouble that threatened her. We are having a delightful time and the best surf bathing I've had since our old days at Portsalon. As I write I look out on a deep blue sea and a golden sand, divided by twenty yards of pure white foam. *Of course you won't mention at home that I am not in Oxford.*

I am busy all morning at rather dull and mechanical work, and fit in more at odd times when I can. Looking forward to seeing you again, & with many thanks.

Yrs
Jack

In his letter of 7 July 1927 (LP IX: 248–52) Warnie told his brother that since he'd been in China Colonel Badcock had

> *succeeded in 'breaking' two Majors, a Captain, and a Subaltern: when I say 'breaking' I do not mean that they have been cashiered, but that they are being sent home with reports that they are inefficient... This reign of terror under which we live does not make existence in the tropics any pleasanter. I personally am sufficiently convinced of the reality of our danger to intend warning the O.A.B. that I do not think I can last out the year and that I expect to be home and workless by December.*

Jack and Mr Lewis did not know it yet, but Warnie left the hospital in Kowloon on 1 September after being transferred to the convalescent camp at Wei-Hei-Wei in northern China. He and other patients sailed to Shanghai, arriving there on 4 September and from there they travelled on to Wei-Hei-Wei which they reached on 7 September.

A serious consideration for Warnie was that if he remained and did foreign service for three years he would not have to go abroad for another six years. On the other hand, if he returned home now his stay in China would not count as part of the necessary period abroad, and it would all have to be done again some other time. Before he went to Wei-Hei-Wei, Colonel Badcock told him of a vacancy coming up in the Army Service Corps in Hong Kong. Offered the post, Warnie accepted it, to discover later that while he was convalescing in the north, the 15th Infantry Brigade broke up and Colonel Badcock and one of the regiments returned to England.

TO HIS BROTHER (LP IX: 270–6):

[Perranporth,
Cornwall]
3 September [1927]

My dear W.,

Many thanks for your letter describing the beastliness of the Colonel and the missionary's wife, the beauty of bathing, and the demonology of the Chinese.[62] I think it is always very difficult to 'evaluate' these superstitions – I mean to gauge the amount of barbarism and stupidity which they imply in those who believe in them. What exactly does the fact that English dinner parties have been ruined by having thirteen at table prove about English civilization? The idea however of running

62 'It is the incredible, cruel evil beastliness of the fellow [Colonel Badcock],' Warnie wrote to Jack on 7 July 1927, 'which makes me wonder whether there was not after all something to be said for the ancient personal existence theory of the Devil. However I have no right to use you as a safety value for blowing off this festering hate with which we go to bed at night and get up in the morning...Speaking of devils, these appear to play a very big part in the life of the Chinese – another proof I think that they are not the "perfectly polite" people of popular legend, but distinctly on the low level of humanity...When a Chinese house is being built, the tops of the scaffolding poles have large bunches of grass tied to them: the explanation is simple – with no roof on the house it would be an obvious temptation to any out of work devil to drop into the interior, wait till the place was inhabited, and then annoy its tenants...Last year, during the Hong Kong strike, there was an enormous number of deaths by motor car accidents in the streets of Hong Kong, which the authorities not unnaturally attributed to suicide owing to trade depression: but it turned out to be nothing of the sort. The prevalent scarcity of work was attributed by every intelligent Chinese to the malignancy of that personal devil who stalks at most men's heels...We landed at about nine o'clock at the end of a narrow wooden jetty at the bathing beach, and, walking up the smooth perfectly white sand to the bamboo and wattle bathing club, secured two cubicles against our afternoon dip. As we watched the blue water rippling round the spur of sponge cake looking rock which guards the beach and the waves breaking on the sand, I said to [Drysdale] that one of the most comforting things in life is that wherever you may be sent, a wave breaking on a beach looks the same and sounds the same: if you are serving on a coast you can never be entirely cut off from the old familiar life' (LP IX: 248–50).

across in front of a car in order to get your follower squashed, is certainly immense: I cannot decide whether it argues a great sense of humour or a great absence of humour. The colonel nuisance has all my sympathy: that sort of thing, or the more or less constant danger of it, is the snag which wd. make a military life intolerable to me, and it is chiefly for the escape from that that I congratulate myself on having ceased to be a boy.

I confess I can't look at the prospect you suggest (I hope not very seriously) without complete dismay. A recrudescence in middle life of the 'What are you going to be' menace, continued through months of residence at Leeborough – a continual urgence of the desirability of 'going into' anything that would remove you to that undiscovered country 'the colonies' – this would be extremely unpleasant. Still, with your 'little bit of savings' to spend on luxuries, you could always hope to grow a Leeborough skin (as we did in the old days) wh. would render you insensible to diatribes. The old expedient of just sitting there with 'that wooden face' and going on with your books would have to come into play again: and perhaps the new expedient of replying (to the dear old question) 'a pudaita' might now be actually put into practice. One pictures the problem of a career ceasing to be a practical problem at all and becoming merely a periodical outlet for the OAB's spleen – a storm at whose appearance one philosophically buttoned up the collar and raised the umbrella. (Another possible repartee that occurs is 'What are you going to be?' – 'A blue gentleman').

Or perhaps it would be better for you to put the whole thing on a different footing from the start and take up the position of the dominant and adult son to the oppressed 'Pa' and always to anticipate the storm by taking your place on the hearthrug with legs astride and hands in pockets and bellowing 'Pa! You and I had better understand one another'.

It is true that the financial framework of the scene does not at once adapt itself to such treatment: but as Johnson says of Pastoral Poetry, the artist must use his skill in keeping out of sight those parts of his subject which are mean and disgusting.[63] However I had better beware as you say

63 Johnson, *Lives of the English Poets*, op. cit., vol. III, Life of William Shenstone: 'The four parts of his *Pastoral Ballad* demand particular notice. I cannot but regret that it is pastoral; an intelligent reader acquainted with the scenes of real life sickens at the mention of the *crook*, the *pipe*, the *sheep*, and the *kids*, which it is not necessary to bring forward to notice, for the poet's art is selection, and he ought to shew the beauties without the grimness of the country life' (p. 356).

of the 'selection of two presents' and not joke too long about a subject which may (tho' I trust the possibility is very remote) have become more serious by the time this letter reaches you.

Now for my own history. My period of examining passed over with its usual accompaniment of neuralgia and oaths, relieved by the one excellent boy who defined 'a genie' correctly, yet more than correctly, as 'an eastern spirit inhabiting bottles and buttons and rings'. Pretty good for a boy. I was also pleased with a youth who, being asked to write a letter to a friend recommending Guy Mannering, wrote to his brother recommending it and saying 'I think you wd. be interested in the character of Colonel Mannering, he is so like our father': and then later in a paper *on* Guy Mannering in which I had set the question 'Would you have liked Colonel Mannering as a father?' – illustrate your answer etc. – began decisively 'I would not have liked Colonel Mannering as a father in the least'.

Then came my usual week at Cambridge, where, despite long hours I revisited King's College Chapel, sauntered round the Backs, and bathed in the Cam, under a pearl-coloured sky simmering with summer river haze from morning till twilight. Even the hours of work passed not disagreeably in the company of my very vulgar and uneducated but not unpleasant and amusing Cambridge colleague. You shd. have heard us going over the work of a female examiner called Helen Laybourne who was v. bad and gave us a lot of trouble, chanting with one voice full of meaning 'I would I were where Helen lies'.[64]

I returned from Cambridge and almost immediately set out with Minto, Maureen, Florence de Forest and Baron Papworth, for Perranporth (Cornwall) where I am now writing. On Sunday (it is now Friday) I set out for P'daitaheim: whether to spend my days interminably strolling in the cemetery-like walks of a hydro garden or drinking two o'clock buckets of sherry in the study, I don't yet know: for of course it is still quite uncertain whether he can be got to move or not.

In the mean time I sit looking out on a tawny strip of sand (four miles of it in length but I can't see all from here) and the bluest shiningest sea that a home dweller like me has ever seen – the one divided from the other by about twenty yards of Chinese white varied with something like champagne – row after row of full Atlantic rollers. Beyond them the

64 Ballads (anonymous), 'I wish I were where Helen lies.'

sea is unstained with a single fleck of foam, except on the point (about three miles half right from where I sit) and there one sees the white go perpendicularly up the rocks. Except the fishing fleet which comes and goes in the offing every three days there is hardly a boat to be seen from this place: once or twice from the highest cliffs I have seen a steamer, usually at sunset, sitting apparently immovable against the end of the world.

Of course there is a drawback to Cornwall. All along this coast the bathing is a death trap except at full tide, which means that we are reduced to one bathe a day (for who, in real life, can bathe at 6 a.m. and 6.20 p.m.) when, for the excellence of it, one would willing (like Wordsworth) 'make one long bathing of a summer's day'.[65] I have never had such surf bathing in my life: not so much here as at St. Agnes' Cove, a few miles S.W., where we go nearly every day. When you have got in up to your belly you get the waves already broken – a solid wall of foam about a foot and a half high (above the level water this side) and about ten feet broad. Then when you have put down your head with a smack, and spluttered through this, you get to business. They come in at places, where you're in your depth between the waves, far higher than a man. They are kindly creatures if taken the right way, and I daily slide up into hollowing breakers which, at first, I would have thought dangerous. The excitement is to guess when they will break. You see the bright bottle green mass of water before you and you bob over it like a floating gull and it keeps its thunders till it is behind you. Usually it crashes just before you reach the top and then you go hurtling back, kicking and spitting, and stand up finally far inland with spent water swimming round your ankles. But when you actually get it in the break, anything may happen. Usually you go far under and if you try to swim your arms are worked rapidly round and round – the movements in the root of a wave being apparently circular. The other day however, turning my back rapidly to the breaking wave, I had the rather remarkable experience of having my head actually in the hollow cave under the curl (which has been seen so often from the outside): so that I saw a second of shining water before my still *unwetted* face, much like a tourist passing between rock and water under Niagara.

My pen has run away with me thus far before I recall that you also have been bathing, and that you even take the wind out of my sails in

65 Wordsworth, *The Prelude*, I, 290.

advance by observing that a falling wave is the same all the world over. We have therefore studiously described to each other the *one* element in our experiences which is common to us both. However I think the interest of any description is great in proportion to the extent to wh. (Lord – what a sentence) one already knows the thing described: i.e. the less it is needed the more one is prepared to listen to it.

Baron Papworth by the sea has removed for ever the reproach of cowardice. As long as only the girls and I are in he contents himself with galloping to and fro in the inch of water where the waves have retreated, barking at the top of his voice. Then when Minto goes in a moment later, he is to be seen steadily swimming after her, ploughing *through* every wave like a tramp, his hair all back from his nose, showing how thin and rapier muzzled he is and indeed making him look rather like a torpedo or an ocean going ant eater. Nothing will stop him, tho' swamped and scuttled times without number. This heroic practice makes him much sweeter than your nose will remember him: except when its beneficial effects are frustrated by the fact that he finds sea water acts on him as a violent purgative. The only other things I have to say about the sea proper are (1) That I quite agree that to lose the *sound* of a sea bathe wd. be to lose a great deal of the delight, (b) that Florence, in her bathing things, is an almost perfect figure of the plumper type.

As to Cornwall itself: the basic formula is 'The County Down country plus the Antrim Coast'. The resemblance of the interior to Co. Down is quite remarkable: the same white cottages, the crumbling dry stone walls, the patchy fields, small and rather oddly shaped, and the bleak colouring. But when you have got this well into your mind's eye you must proceed to moderate it a bit. First of all, magnify the hills to about the Antrim size, while keeping them in the main strictly to the Co. Down quality. That is, tho' big, they are not long gaunt bluish hogbacks, but all criss cross, rounded, and higgledypiggildy. If Co. Down was described (Kelsie says it was) as 'eggs in a basket', this is turkey's eggs in a basket. Then you must add (what is rare in Down) masses of heather and gorse, not crowning the hills which would give them the mountain look, but most often on the sides of valleys where they are steep: and when you reach the valleys themselves, specially the narrower ones, you may give up the Co. Down idea altogether.

Here an utterly different country meets you, a richness like the Devonshire combes, a hot labyrinth of lanes beside streams that flow glass clear over red and yellow stones, lanes very deep sunken and full of ferns, with occasional sub-tropical things (I have not seen a palm but they grow here) lanes that go through absolute tunnels of vegetation, dank and green, buzzing with bees and darted through by huge dragon flies. The grasshoppers are noisier than I ever heard them, and sing long after sunset. If you can picture these winding valley-strips of a more luxurious and exotic world inconsequently trickling (each with a lovely stream) though the bottom of a Co. Down landscape you will get some idea of this wonderful place.

Yet the most characteristic feature is still untold – and one wh. I am afraid will go far to render the rest unpicturable. I have been speaking of the narrower valleys – those shaped like the human anal cavity. But now suppose you have just come to the brink of a broader, more saucer like depression. Here you are almost sure to find heathery sides sloping down to a floor of flat grey stones and clay (just what one imagines lava ground like) with here and there a very old slag heap: a sort of great raw gash of abandoned industrialism with the engine house of a mine (*always* like this but of course in very various stages of decay) brooding over an odd litter of miscellaneous buildings that have long been quarries to the neighborhood, of things like mill wheels idly suspended, of artificial oblong pools with a last green stagnant trickle on the floor of – Lord knows what! You can't walk a mile without coming to a mine: there are rather more in the valleys than on the hills: but every hill-horizon too, shows three to six variations of the engine house theme, the high tower like building and the slightly higher stumpy chimney. Silhouetted against the sky far off, as I see it every night, it has the exact appearance of a giant's armchair. The deserted mines outnumber those at work almost as the dead outnumber the living. Of course it is only the comparatively modern ones that are marked by engine house, or still unvegetated slag.

One comes across other relics that may be Elizabethan, Saxon, Roman, or even British: sometimes a shaggy low lintelled doorway opening inconsequently into the side of a hill, where only one man cd. enter at a time, and, frankly, nothing would induce me to be that one: often, miles from anywhere, one finds a reddish stream coming out of such a doorway and perhaps very old timbers still making the door posts. Or else, you are plodding along on the heathery slope of a valley and suddenly see a place, about the size of Hillsboro's drawing room, fenced (or stone walled) about. Go nearer and you see a plain round hole: its sides, of green or red and usually dripping rock, are visible for twenty feet or so and then disappear into darkness. If you throw a fair sized stone down you hear it go '*BANG-BANG*-BANG-BANG-bang-bang' with decreasing noise from side to side on its journey down: but you never hear any *final* noise to that journey. The 'bangs' just get less and less and fade insensibly to nothing. Few ideas give me (as the 18th century wd. have said) such 'pleasing horror' as that of the bottom of the shaft in a mine abandoned, say, about the year the Armada was defeated. A working mine would be bad enough.

By the bye there is *one* more modification in the original 'Down-and-Antrim' scheme – namely that, owing to mineral wealth the sea cliffs are nearly all red: solid rock of course and beaten into every spire and arch of ruinous architecture, but red as garden clay. If you take all this that I have tried to describe and put over it a bluer sky, and round it a bluer 'poster' sea than Ireland ever dreamt of, you will have the best I can do for you about Cornwall: but nothing can describe the feeling with which, from brooding over the deserted mine shaft and throwing your stone down it, you suddenly *return* (as if you yourself had been in a deadly place) to the riot of sunshine and gorse and birds and wind about you. I think even the Baron feels those holes in the ground to be rather awful.

The only Cornish city I have been to is Truro. The town is an ordinary little market town, much less pleasing than any in the 'homely' counties between Morlockheim and the West Country: in fact so true is the Co. Down element in my Cornish recipe that Truro has more than a flavour of Newtownards about it. The Cathedral is the poorest, almost, that I have ever seen. This is a rough idea of it: a very tall square central tower supporting a spire, and four narrow towers or pinnacles of the same sort at the four corners, but all so thin in proportion to their height that it gives the impression of one of those buildings that figure on the lid of a child's box of bricks and for the construction of wh., no sensible child has ever used the bricks.

The history of this abortion is a painful mystery to me. The West Front is adorned with statues of Edward VII and of obviously Victorian and Edwardian prelates, and it appears to be of exactly the same date as the rest – the whole thing being of one texture, a rather ugly and very new looking pale stone, cut small, and the joinings between the blocks aggressively black and staring. On the other hand the interior contains a 16th century monument (none earlier so far as I could see). Do you suppose the monument is the sole survivor of a small old cathedral which was replaced wholesale by a contractor in the reign of the late King? Anyway, the whole thing is a deplorable business (except the height of the interior which has a fine effect) and it is made worse by the fact that *one* of the cupolas is bright green copper coloured – the rest all pale stone.

The main object of my visit was to get a book, having finished Martin Chuzzlewit which I brought down. And here let me digress for a moment to advise you v. strongly to make one more effort with Dickens and make it on Martin Chuzzlewit if only for the sake of an account of 19th century America. In loathing for America you will at last find what you and Dickens have in common. For sheer cruelty and uproarious farce with a horrid essential truth (every American without exception whom Martin meets is first introduced to him as 'one of the most remarkable men in our country, sir')[66] it beats everything. Of course to enjoy it, or any other Dickens, you must get rid of all idea of realism – as much as in approaching William Morris or the music hall. In fact I should say he is the good thing of which the grand Xmas panto. is the degeneration and abuse: broadly typical sentiment, only rarely intolerable if taken in a jolly after dinner pantomime mood, and broadly effective 'comics': only all done by a genius, so that they become mythological. Just try Mr Tigg, the blue gentleman in Martin Chuzzlewit. You will never meet a blue gentleman like him: and certainly Turner's *mot* 'Don't you wish you could?' wd. here be answered by a very decided 'No'. But he is what every blue gentlemen is trying to be – a sort of eternal Platonic form of blue gentleman. But this is all by the way.

I had assumed that as Truro was a cathedral city, it must have at least a clerical intelligentsia: and if that, a decent bookshop. It appeared to have only a Smith's and a faded looking place that seemed half a news agents. At the door of this I stopped an elderly parson and asked him whether this and Smith were the only two booksellers. He said they were: then a few moments later came back walking on tip toes as some parsons do, and buzzed softly in my ear (he had a beard) 'There is an S.P.C.K. depot further down this street'. This almost adds a new character to my

66 Dickens, *Martin Chuzzlewit*, ch. XVI: '"Jefferson Brick," he observed after a short silence, in commendation of his correspondent, "is one of the most remarkable men in our country, sir."'

world: henceforth among my terms of abuse none shall rank lower than 'he's the sort of man who'd call an S.P.C.K. depot a bookshop'.

I discovered however that my unpromising bookshop had a second hand quarter upstairs. This at first was depressing as it appeared to consist entirely of two sections: one labeled 'books on Cornwall', the other 'Second hand rewards'. That also is a valuable new idea. I suppose a Truro child, after having spent a sufficient number of year's study of the S.P.C.K. depot, may be examined by a beard-buzzing clergyman on tiptoe and then, if successful, receive a 'second hand reward' (the second hand rewards ranged from Paley's evidences[67] to the 'Queen of the upper Fourth', so he has no need to complain). However in the end I discovered an upper garret where there were at last some *books*. I had v. little money and the selection was poor. I got inter alia the poetical work of 'Armstrong, Dyer, and Green' with lives and prefaces to all three by the Rev. Gilfillan.[68] He lived in the early 19th century and wrote lives and prefaces to everyone in the 'British Poets'[69] – those long thin greyish backed volumes ('Of which I have an hondred in my celle') with fine large type of the period when they still had generosity and elegance and were only just beginning to lose beauty. Gilfillan is incredible. Here is a little passage from his preface to Dyer. 'The painter himself too, becomes one of the finest objects in the landscapes of earth as seen sitting motionless under the rainbow, and perchance in his reverie dropping his pencil into the bubbling stream, or copying with severe sympathy the cataract with a rain of bright berries and green leaves descending on him...thus at the young Dyer etc.'[70]

As for my poets, Dyer you will remember as the author of 'The Fleece',[71] perhaps the best example of that curious 18th century growth, the commercial epic – cf. Also 'Cyder'[72] and 'The Sugar Cane'.[73] Armstrong

67 William Paley, *A View of the Evidences of Christianity* (1794).

68 *The Poetical Works of Armstrong, Dyer and Green*, with memoirs and critical dissertations by the Rev. George Gilfillan (1858).

69 George Gilfillan (1813–78), a Scottish dissenting minister, literary critic and editor, was a champion of 'Spasmodic' poetry – poetry which described interior psychological drama, and which was violent and verbose. His *Gallery of Literary Portraits* ran to three series published in 1845, 1850 and 1854.

70 *The Poetical Works of Armstrong, Dyer and Green*, p. 102.

71 The biography of John Dyer (1700–57) is found on pp. 101–14 of *The Poetical Works of Armstrong, Dyer and Green*. *The Fleece*, included in this volume, was originally published in 1757.

72 John Philips, *Cyder* (1708).

73 James Grainger, *Sugar-Cane* (1764).

wrote a similar poem in Miltonic blank verse on 'The Art of preserving Health'.[74] I have read it with huge enjoyment. It is beyond all parody as the specimen of the noble art of making poetry by *translating* ordinary sentences into 'Miltonic' diction. Thus 'some people can't eat eggs' is rendered,

Some even the generous nutriment detest
Which, in the shell, the sleeping embryo rears.[75]

(Where 'rears' I suspect is a misprint for 'bears.') If one eats too much fat,

The irresoluable oil
So gentle late and blandishing, in floods
Of rancid bile o'erflows: what tumults hence
What horrors rise, were nauseous to relate.[76]

One is surprised to learn that even then some people took cold baths,

To fortify their bodies, some frequent
The gelid cistern: and, where nought forbids
I praise their dauntless heart.[77]

Is 'cistern' merely poetical for a bathtub? – or did they really bathe in cisterns? If so, I agree about their dauntless hearts. I can't imagine anything nastier than a dip in the cistern off the Leeborough attic. Green, I confess, I had never heard of. He wrote a poem on 'The Spleen'.[78]

While I am on this subject I should mention the even stranger bookshop at Newquay. It bore the legend 'New and Second Hand Bookseller'. But when I went in, the following dialogue occurred. 'Where are your

---

74 The biography of John Armstrong (1709–79) is found on pp. v–xxii of *The Poetical Works of Armstrong, Dyer and Green*. *The Art of Preserving Health*, included in this volume, was originally published in 1744.

75 *The Poetical Works of Armstrong, Dyer and Green*, p. 16, *The Art of Preserving Health*, Bk. II, 111–12.

76 ibid., pp. 15–16, Bk. II, 83-6.

77 ibid., p. 15, Bk. III, 292–4.

78 The biography of Matthew Green (1696–1737) is found on pp. 233–8 of *The Poetical Works of Armstrong, Dyer and Green*. His poem, *The Spleen*, included in this volume, was originally published in 1747.

second hand books?' 'They're all in private rooms'. 'Well can I see them?' 'No. They're all locked up.' 'Aren't they for sale?' 'No.' What do you make of that? The other great disadvantage of Cornwall is the beer. It costs 4d a half pint and (though draught) tastes like Bass – the lowest level surely that beer can attain. Draught cider seems to be unknown. I wonder what the miners drink – 'metheglin'[79] or 'majogony' do you suppose?

I hope you will continue your admirable letters on the same scale as long as you are abroad: they also deserve Johnson's praise – but we must not degenerate into admiration of each other's epistolary style or the thing will become self conscious. My next will be sodden and stuffy with the fumes of Leeborough: and can hope, at best, for a fine P'dayta-crop. I enclose some photos and good wishes from all.

Yours,
Jack

TO HIS BROTHER (LP IX: 290–1):[80]

Belfast Steamship Company Limited
S.S. Patriotic.
Oct. 5th 1927

My dear W.,

Tho' I am uncertain when my next proper letter to you will be written, I should be unpardonable if I failed to salute you on an occasion over which your spirit so emphatically presides. (You will perceive that at the moment of writing I am not absolutely sober). The cry of 'Any more for the shore' has gone round. Arthur, who saw me off and drank with me (nay! at *his* expense) has just gone. The 'flip, flip' of the boots of Belfastians on the rubber floor of the saloon deck is heard on all sides. In a moment we shall shove off. I gave the P'daytabird *four* solid weeks and a day: tomorrow I shall be in Oxford.

Of course it proved impossible to get him away. He had just put himself under the injection treatment of our cousin the 'blood specialist': and his first line of defence thus turned on the necessity of 'giving this serum business a fair trial'. He couldn't go away and break it for a few

79 Metheglin is a spiced or medicated form of mead peculiar to Wales.

80 Lewis was with his father at Little Lea from 6 September until 5 October. This portion of a letter, written aboard the SS *Patriotic* as it was about to leave Belfast, was enclosed with the bulky instalment dated 'Dec. 12th' and the whole was posted to Warnie on 16 December.

weeks. ('These serums are a funny business Jacks. You know there're made of – ' 'Yes, yes, I remember you told me the other night.' 'Well, you know it's really very funny. They take a swab of your throat – ' 'Yes, I know, very funny.' 'Aye, but that's not the cream of the joke. The other two ingredients are your own urine and your own excrement.') These details I have heard at least twice a week for the last month.

His second defence was a pure windfall. A letter from Uncle Dick gave it him. Eileen was coming over to stay at Sandycroft.[81] That provided his second defence. 'Well you know, I *couldn't* go away now. Uncle Dick will expect me to [do] my little bit of manners – I'll have to have that girl up to dinner and all that sort of thing' – a suggestion wh. was converted in a few days to 'I tell you what I'll do. I'll ask her to *tea* some day.' So the attempt to get him boiled in mud, which I made sincerely and even importunately, was a complete failure. A usual Leeborough holiday took its place, with an inordinate number of P'dayta Days. It is cruelest of all when he comes home on Monday at 11.30. To be given just enough time to decant the brisk liquour of Monday morning and then to have the cup dashed from your hand.

It was specially annoying this time because I wanted to be very busy putting into action my project of an Encyclopedia Boxoniana. I have worked through the texts down to The Locked Door[82] and at Christmas hope to be able to begin the actual encyclopedia. Big 4 (the one you know best) will be by far the largest article and B the longest letter (Bob, Bar, Bradley, Bradshaw, Bublish, Bumregis, Brus (vin de), Bears, Benjamin I, Benjamin VI, Benjamin VII, Boj, Bojaren, Borata, Boys, the, Big I, Big II, Big III, Big IV – all lengthy). I find the work fascinating: the consistency between the very early texts and the ones we usually read is much greater than I dared to hope for: and an odd sentence in the Locked Door or the Life of Big will fit into a narrative written in Wynyard or pre-Wynyard days in the most startling way. I suppose it is only accident, but it is hard to resist the conviction that one is dealing with a

---

81 'Uncle Dick' was Richard Lewis (b. 1861), one of Albert Lewis's four brothers and two sisters. See **The Lewis Family** in the Biographical Appendix.

At the time this letter was written, Jack and Warnie seem never to have met Richard Lewis nor any of his family. 'Sandycroft' was the home of C.S. Lewis's great-grandfather, Joseph Lewis (1803–90), in Saltney, Flintshire. Richard and his daughter Eileen were going to visit members of the Lewis family still living there.

82 'The Locked Door' is one of the many histories and stories of Boxen that Lewis wrote as a boy. See note 10 to letter of c. 1906 to Warnie Lewis.

sort of reality. At least so it seems to me, alone in the little end room. How it will appear tomorrow in Magdalen Common Room or a month hence to you in How Kow is another matter.

We're off. The screw turns. I had stewed steak for lunch today and boiled mutton for supper dinner. I am going to eat some supper. Can you forget the flavour of one's first non-P'dayta meal. (I was mistaken. The screw has stopped again.)

TO HIS FATHER (LP XI: 266–8):

[Magdalen College,
Oxford
29? November 1927]

My dear Papy,

Many thanks for your letter.[83] My own long silence has the cause (I wish it were also the excuse) which you suggest. I have got my evenings nearly full up this term. On Monday nights I entertain as many of my own pupils and other undergraduates as care to come and join in the reading of an Elizabethan play: I was driven to institute this because I saw no other way of persuading them to get through the enormous number of plays they are supposed to read (I am often tempted to curse the fertility of our Elizabethans). On Wednesdays some of the junior pupils come to read Anglo-Saxon with me.[84] The actual work is usually done by half past ten: but they are comfortably by the fire and like to sit on and talk – and after all, it is part of ones job to get to know them – so that evening is usually full up till midnight. Then there are functions which occur fortnightly: the Kolbitar or Icelandic Society, and a fortnightly philosophical supper with Hardie[85] and some others.

None of these engagements is onerous in itself, indeed they are all agreeable: but when you add to them the inevitable interchange of invitations to dinner, an occasional visit, and an odd night when one is tired and goes to bed early, it leaves few evenings free in term time. My mornings are

83 Mr Lewis's letter of 23 November is found in LP IX: 306–7.

84 These became known as Lewis's 'Beer and Beowulf Evenings'. During these sessions he introduced his pupils to mnemonic devices he invented for learning Old English, they chanted *Beowulf* aloud, and the beer-jug was passed around.

85 William Francis Ross Hardie (1902–90), educated at Balliol College, became a Fellow of Philosophy at Magdalen in 1925. He was Fellow and Tutor in Philosophy at Corpus Christi College, Oxford 1926–50, and President of Corpus Christi 1950–69.

of course occupied with tutoring or preparation for it: and even my afternoons are sometimes invaded by a college meeting. a meeting of the Tutorial Board, or a meeting of the English Faculty. This is not to say that I am overworked: a labourer or a tram driver might justly describe all that I have enumerated as a round of strenuous idleness. But if I am as free as any man can hope to be from 'work' in the original and proper sense of drudgery (the curse of Adam), in revenge, I have as little leisure, in the sense of vacant time, as I can well have.

I do not think the accounts of Hogarth in the newspapers were exaggerated – except in so far as a natural feeling about the newly dead, a wish to do the best you can for a man, affects all obituary notices and funeral orations whatsoever.[86] Most of his work lay rather outside my own sphere: though I read the 'Ancient History of the Near East'[87] when I was doing Greats (a work of immense learning which includes much of the best results of Assyriology, Egyptology, and Babylonian, Greek and Hittite archaeology, while remaining fairly short and almost popular). I also read his 'Wanderer in the Levant'[88] which is purely popular and gives you a sort of essay like account of his experiences in the Near East, not as a scholar, but as a traveller.

He did not dine in very often and I seldom talked to him – only once had a real conversation with him and that was about Doughty's poetry.[89] He was a very fine looking soldier like man: straight as a ramrod: but there was something which I at least found a little uninviting in his face – a tinge of that haughtiness, almost cruelty, which you see so often in the faces of people who have got into the habit of lording it among coloured races east of Suez. (You can trace the thing I am referring to in many of the episodes and reflections, even in the style, of Kinglake's

---

86 David George Hogarth (1862–1927), scholar and traveller, took his degree from Magdalen in 1885. He travelled and excavated in Asia Minor, Cyprus, Egypt and Knossos, many of which places are discussed in his books. In 1908 he became Keeper of the Ashmolean Museum, Oxford. According to a note Lewis wrote on the presidential elections (LP IX: 307–9), most of the Fellows of Magdalen were hoping to elect Hogarth as their next President when he died suddenly on 6 November 1927. An obituary appeared in *The Times* (7 November 1927), p. 14.

87 Hogarth did not write a book with that title. Lewis was probably thinking of Harry Reginald Hall's *The Ancient History of the Near East: from the earliest times to the Battle of Salamis* (1914).

88 David George Hogarth, *A Wandering Scholar in the Levant* (1896).

89 The poetry of Charles Montagu Doughty, which Lewis mentioned in his letter to Arthur Greeves of 14 February 1920.

Eothen).[90] Still it is no doubt easier to wear kid gloves and think of the brotherhood of man when we are in Little Lea or Oxford than it would be in Arabia. That is the excuse which W. would certainly urge for all those Anglo-Indian officers, sea captains, and others in whom I find this disturbing element. And I allow it. But wouldn't you agree (tho' I find it constantly forgotten) that there is all the difference in the world between saying that a thing is excusable and saying that it needs no excuse? As if 'the driver couldn't prevent the train leaving the rails' means the same as 'the train is still on the rails'.

They had great fun at the Union last week. Birkenhead came to speak.[91] The first thing that worried him was the private business in which two gentlemen got up and discussed the library list – additions to the library of the Union being a subject which naturally comes up in private business. On this occasion the merits of *Smith in Journalism*[92] by P. G. Wodehouse, *That Ass Smith*[93] by the same author, and *The Wreck of the Birkenhead*[94] were hotly canvassed. The noble lord was understood to make some observations to those around him in which the word 'schoolboys' figured.

Then the debate began. The first speaker produced the good old ancient Wadham story of how Smith and Simon[95] had decided what parties they were to follow in their political careers by the toss of a coin the night before they took schools. You will hardly believe me when I tell you that Smith jumped up: 'baseless fabrication' – 'silly, stale story' – 'hoped that even the home of lost causes had abandoned that chestnut, etc. etc.' – and allowed himself to be sidetracked and leg pulled to such an extent that he never reached his real subject at all. It seems to me impossible that a man of his experience could fall to such frivolous tactics: unless we accept the accompanying story that he was drunk at the time, or the even subtler explanation that he was *not*.

Many thanks for the birthday wishes and the birthday present. I will select the latter in the next few days and let you know. I am not sure that

---

90 For Kinglake's *Eóthen* see note 26 to letter of 10? August 1924.

91 Lord Birkenhead, or F.E. Smith (1872–1930), read Law at Wadham College, and was Lord Chancellor of England from 1919 until 1922.

92 P.G. Wodehouse, *Psmith, Journalist* (1915).

93 *That Ass Smith* is not a Wodehouse title.

94 William Gilly, *The Wreck of the Birkenhead* (1873).

95 John Allsebrook Simon, first Viscount Simon (1873–1954), statesman, was, like Lord Birkenhead, educated at Wadham College. He was Lord Chancellor between 1940 and 1945.

I shall not get a picture instead of the books. I am sorry to hear that the electrical treatment is not more permanent in its results: but I still stick to my original theory that a change of air and diet must be at least the *first* step towards a cure. The weather of course is very much against you at present: at least if ours is at all like yours. We have had no sight of the sun now for these four days, and fogs more dense and more frequent than I ever remember. Most of these mornings it has been so damp that the door handles are wet to the touch.

your loving son,
Jack

Warnie left the convalescent camp at Wei-Hei-Wei at the end of September and travelled to Shanghai en route to Hong Kong to rejoin his unit. While awaiting passage headquarters decided to leave him in Shanghai for the next 18 months in command of the Shanghai Supply Depot. This was much to his liking because he was told that his foreign service would be completed in 18 months, after which he could return home. However, there was a sudden change of plans and on 18 October he was posted to Hong Kong. Upon his arrival there on 21 October, Colonel Badcock ordered him straight back to Shanghai. Apart from his delight in returning to Shanghai, Warnie soon had the pleasure of learning that he was finally free of Colonel Badcock who on 14 November returned to England to become training instructor at the Royal Army Service Corps Training College at Aldershot.

TO HIS BROTHER (LP IX: 320–5):

[Magdalen College]
Dec. 12th. [1927]

I enclose a fragment written when and how, you will see. I had hoped to continue it in reasonable time: but the monthly letter has proved an impossibility during the term. My evenings for the fortnight in term run thus. *Mon*. Play reading with undergraduates (till Midnight). *Tue*. Mermaid club.[96] *Wedn*. Anglo-Saxon with undergraduates. *Thurs*. – *Frid*. – *Sat*. – *Sunday*. Common room till late. *Mon*. Play reading.

96 The Mermaid Club was founded in 1902 'to promote the reading and study of the Elizabethan and post-Elizabethan drama'. Lewis was President of the Mermaid Club in Michaelmas Term 1927.

Tue. Icelandic Society. *Wedn*. Anglo-Saxon. *Thurs*. Philosophical supper. *Fri*. – *Sat*. – *Sunday*.

As you will see this gives at the very best only three free evenings in the even weeks, and two in the odd. And into these two everything in the way of casual entertaining, correspondence and what we used to call 'A-h-h-h!' has to be crammed. Without increasing the Ah-h-h to any tolerable proportions I can well find myself at the end of eight such weeks with my letter still unwritten. Even if this fails to convince you, you will be satisfied with the ironical vengeance which now falls upon me – when I find myself sending off to you that note from the Liverpool boat within a few days of my revisiting the same boat again, this time with a nasty error in the direction of her bows.[97] How loathsome now are all those details with which I tried to create the atmosphere for you! The smells and sounds will all be there again next week: but the one fatal error of direction dashes them all. Before leaving this now ancient subject, perhaps I should give you some account of my stay in P'daytaheim.

I have already mentioned your father's refusal to move and his frivolous reasons. For the rest, he suffered a good deal from his complaint while I was there. It is always difficult with him to estimate the exact amount: but it was I think fairly bad, tho' a little improved. I cannot understand what his doctors are up to. In England one always hears drastic dieting prescribed for rheumatic complaints – with a special reduction (or complete prohibition) of animal foods. I asked him if they had said nothing on that subject: to which he very characteristically replied 'No. I asked Joey if I ought to give up my little drop of whiskey and he said it didn't matter.' It was quite useless to point out that diet (even his) did not consist exclusively of whiskey. As regards his 'parts' he was often agreeable and cheerful. The chief change I notice in him with advancing years is a very rapidly 'increased rate of increase' in the coarseness of his conversation. With some such prelude as 'It's not a nice subject but – ' or, more ominous still, 'You're a man now and we can talk – ' night after night he launches forth on what for its blueness and its salacity may well be called an *ocean* of stories. There was one about a man who had to empty his bowels in a Co. Down Railway carriage: and when I had been told (with illustrative gestures) how 'these fellows'

97 He is referring to the fact that he was returning to Little Lea for Christmas. Lewis was with his father from 21 December until 11 January 1928.

spread a newspaper on the floor and how 'this chap got down' on his hunkers and 'did the best he could', I discovered that *that* – the mere fact – was the whole point of the story.

There were also occasions on which he appeared in his earlier manner. One morning I had gone down to the hall early to get a morning cigarette (that will conjure up in your mind the whole quality of a day in mid-holidays when you have let yourself run out of non-P'dayta cigarettes). I saw a letter from Barfield for me: but didn't take it, knowing that it would be a long piece of argument not suited for reading in bed. I returned to bed and in due course was summoned to the bath room. Before I had locked the door I heard him shouting up from the hall, 'Here's a letter for you.' I shouted 'Thanks' and banged the door. In an incredibly short time he was rattling at the door (he must have wolfed his breakfast abominably). Admitted to wash his teeth, he repeated in an aggrieved voice 'You've got a letter waiting for you. D'you not want it?' I continued drying myself as soon as he was gone and after dressing came down stairs. As I reached the lowest step a voice from the cloakroom boomed out 'You'll find that letter on the hall table.' As I was perfectly easy in my mind about this particular letter, I could not refrain from leaving it where it lay while I went to ring the dining room bell. In a moment he was after me (now hatted and coated) with the letter in his hand. That episode was pure fun: this that follows was of the kind that is funny in memory but was insufferable at the time.

One afternoon Arthur and I went for a long walk over the hills round Divis. I said 'I don't know when we shall be back.' He said 'That's all right, my son, I'll wait dinner till you come.' I explained 'very loud and clear' that he was not to wait: if I didn't turn up at the right time, would he please go on and I would have some cold supper with tea whenever I got back. To my surprise he actually consented: the arrangement was most distinct and I set off with my mind at ease. At 8.30, after a glorious afternoon I came in: my feet sore, my cheeks cool, my mind full of heather and sky, with not a care in the world. That mood does not live long after you have crossed the threshold of Leeborough. I found him in the hall. 'I waited as long as I could,' he said, 'I'm sorry.' I explained with some heat that I thought we had arranged he was not to wait. To which he returned in a low voice, 'Well get your boots off and take your bit of dinner' – then, opening the glass door, 'Mary! Master Jacks is in now.' I was then brought to the dining room and given a disgusting meal of soup, joint, vegetables and pudding, which had been kept hot for me. The O.A.B. *standing* in the room in various attitudes of resignation until I had finished. I resolved that night that once and for all I would put an end to this tomfoolery and repeated a few days later the experiment of saying I would be late for dinner and should prefer a cold meal when I came in. His preference for a grievance was apparently not proof against a second night's abstinence and this time the scheme worked to admiration. I had cold supper with tea, alone, in almost non-Leeburian comfort.

Emboldened by this I actually took the unprecedented step of dining in town with Arthur and an Oxford man called Bryson[98] one night! No objection was raised: indeed he entered into the project so keenly and discussed how we should 'handle the thing' so often that I was heartily sick of the affair long before it came off. It became such an *affair*. The whole point was an evening's escape into the haphazardness and absence of fussiness which one longs for so at home. But (he always has an unsuspected trump card) he contrived, without raising a finger in objection, to banish all that. Where would we go? Would we dress? How would we arrange about meeting? It would be a bad business *if* – and here a thousand perverse hypotheses which he contrived to make real for the moment. Still – to be seated in a hotel, eating an ordinary dinner and drinking your wine, indulging in ordinary chat, and then to reflect that Belfast is outside the window, is a marvellous sensation. I discovered to my surprise that Bryson (whom I always regarded as an imposing junior Don) was in just the same state at home as Arthur and myself.

During my month in Ireland I had the most glorious jaunts. You can walk nearly all the way from Craigantlet to Helen's tower through thick woods, crossing the road only once. You can drive out to Hannah's Town (at the Western extremity of Divis range) and then spend all afternoon coming over the mountains to Ligoniel. We did it on an afternoon when there were some moving clouds overhead, but all the more distant sky towards the horizon was a pale transparent blue: and the distant objects very clear. At our first halt we could see, (1) *Half left* – a rolling blue green plain stretching out to the Mournes: the Mournes, as you know, jagged like mountains in a romance, and of such a pure blue colour that you felt, if a bird flew behind them, you could have seen it *through* them. (2) *Straight ahead* – the heather sloping down in big folds to the road we

98 i.e. John Bryson. See the letter of 26 May 1925.

had left: beyond that a deep narrow valley filled with woods. Beyond the valley the ground rose, studded with white cottages and crossed with hedges, to a well peaked conical hill – one side wooded with steeply perpendicular pines. (3) *Half right* – the expanse of Lough Neagh, shining like the roof of a greenhouse, and more mountains beyond it. (4) *Full right*: like this, over the shoulder of our own slope a very remote rocky looking slice of Antrim for the first time – where I think you have preceded me. That valley with the rock rampart on one side and the woods below and the open spaces on the high moors at the head of the valley, with their glimpses of the Scotch coast, are among the best things I have seen.

At the moment of writing I have forgotten the order of places and distances: I remember working out at the time that a walking tour in those parts, starting from Larne or perhaps from Belfast would be quite possible. Shall we make a resolution to do it together when we are next both at home? My dinner in town has proved that the pleasant things of life can be carried out during a P'daytaholiday. Do not let us put off all these projects for amelioration of the Irish visit which we have so often discussed. By the way the O.A.B. was with us on our ride to the Glens: and said, 'The last time I was in Cushendun was on a Boxing day – bitterly cold, and I had to set off for here and leave you boys: a miserable business it was.' It is odd that the memory of that occasion has entirely faded from my mind. Yet it must have been epic. The house to ourselves all day in the Wynyard period and Christmas food! Possibly we should date there the memorable artillery engagement with mince pies.

It comes into my head for no reason at this point to tell you that I have read Coningsby: having been informed that his grandfather (drawn by the way from the same original as Thackeray's Lord Steyne[99]) has found a very suitable seat in the house for him, he objects that his principles will not allow him to support the ministry: and receives from the old man the reply 'You'll go with your family, boy, like a gentleman, and not start talking about principles as if you were an adventurer.' But apart from this you, who have always been a Tory, and yet felt some uneasiness at finding yourself in the same boat as all the canting and comfortable exploiters of sweated labour, will find just what you want in Dizzy: Toryism at its extreme of opposition to the 'Manchester School' and anxious

99 In *Vanity Fair*.

to restore (as he calls it) '*the estate* of the peasantry' in the place of the Whig created '*class* of the poor'.[100]

And while we are on 'estates', you will probably be surprised to hear (as I was to read) that King Alfred, translating Boethius and interpolating a passage of his own, says that a king must have as tools for his work 'the three estates' (tha threo gerferscipu), prayer men, money men and work men'. (A moment later he comfortingly mentions *beer* as another essential.) This seems to show that the conception goes back pretty far in mediaeval theory: Alfred came to the throne in 871. But possibly to you – more acquainted than I with European history – this may be stale news.

I also (while at home) bought a capital Montaigne in three very large quartos with magnificent type: printed (oddly enough) in London cum privilegio regis in the early XVIII century – 1712 I think.[101] I found the French more difficult than I expected: also the matter at once more seriously valuable as thought (in some parts) and more deliciously absurd (in others) than I had ventured to hope. Some of his 'facts' go beyond anything in Burton.[102] Do you remember the story of the man who could break wind in time with a tune, and the other who broke wind continuously for forty years and then died? The only thing one gets rather bored with is the endless succession of stories from Plutarch – 'Agesilaus being besieged by the Epirotes –' 'Scruma Nonius, being made aedile etc.' Plutarch is one of those unhappy authors whom we are bored with years before we read him. Shakespeare is almost another: and you may add Blake, Pascal and Montaigne himself. It is curious the boredom which broods over certain things. Why is 'The Empire' such a dull subject?

I have done very little reading outside my work these last months. In Oman's 'Dark Ages'[103] I have come up against a thing I had almost forgotten since my school days – the boundless self assurance of the pure text book. 'The four brothers were all worthy sons of their wicked father – destitute of natural affection, cruel, lustful, and treacherous.' Lewis the Pious was 'a man of blameless and virtuous habits' – tho' every other sentence in the chapter makes it plain that he was a sh-t. 'Charles had

---

100 Disraeli, *Coningsby*, bk. III, ch. 3.

101 *Les Essais de Michel seigneur de Montaigne, avec des notes etc. pas Pierre Coste*, 3 vols. (1724).

102 Robert Burton's *Anatomy of Melancholy*.

103 Sir Charles Oman, *The Dark Ages 476–918* (1893).

one lamentable failing – he was too careless of the teaching of Christianity about the relations of the sexes.' It is so nice too, to be told without a hint of doubt who was in the right and who was in the wrong in every controversy, and exactly why every one did what he did. Yet Oman is quite right: that is the way – I suppose – to write an *introduction* to a subject. Indeed I have confessed this in turning to him because Gibbon, however delightful to read, simply won't do, if, starting from scratch, you want to get a clear skeleton outline which you can afterwards colour in at leisure. There is also this advantage in Oman, that you can see when he is being silly: with Gibbon one is up against a really clever man and I expect that much besides 'infidelity' is 'artfully intermixed'.

I am almost coming to the conclusion that all histories are bad. Whenever one turns from the historian to the writings of the people he deals with there is always such a difference. What is in my mind at present is (on the one hand) Beowulf and Alfred and the Sagas, and (on the other) Gibbon and Oman about 'the barbarians'. What common measure is there between 'Odoacer had alienated the sympathies of his Italian subjects by seizing a third of the land to reward his veterans' and 'Oft Scyld Scefing overthrew the mead benches of many a kindred. The dwellers round had to obey him across the whale's way. That was a good king...So shall a young hero *do good* and give lordly gifts, that his retainers may repay him when war comes.'[104] The implication (always present) in the first version that Odoacer oughtn't to have given the land to his men, or that any choice in the matter could have occurred to him, as against the perfectly untroubled sincerity with which the other describes the hero as 'doing good' in scattering the 'lordly gifts' (acquired no doubt at the cost of 'alienating the sympathy' of someone) makes one despair. Then 'his veterans' – memories of Chelsea Hospital! Of course one can see in some sense that the two passages refer to the same sort of fact. But what is left of the 'fact' if you take away both its two 'appearances'? And if you plump for *one* of them, is that historical truth? I wish there was a good translation of Beowulf. Isn't this good? (The funeral of Scyld Scefing). 'They bore him down to the brim of the sea: there rode in harbour – with rings at her bows – ice-hung, eager, the atheling galley. They laid in her their beloved lord, their giver of rings, in the galley's

104 *Beowulf*, ll. 4–24.

waist... They let the sea carry him away. No one knew who took in that cargo.'[105]

I hear with pleasure of your separation from the unpleasant Colonel, of your sea voyagings, and that you think to spend on 18 months in 'furrin parts'. The Shanghai news looms very formidable in the papers at this distance: but I comfort myself by the reflection that the state of Belfast when we have been there, would often have read much the same.

I was delighted with your account of the American. You remember Carritt's mot concerning them – 'they lisp in numbers for the numbers come'.[106] If you cast back your mind, when we were at Wynyard we were in exactly that phase: it gave us a pleasure at which I still blush to din into peoples ears the fact that Belfast had the largest gantry in the British isles or had launched the largest ship afloat. But we have outgrown it: it would now give me no appreciable thrill to convince the fellows of Magdalen that my father was the largest batata in Europe. If the analogy between peoples and individuals were sound, I suppose we should have to forgive the Americans for being in a state which we once passed through ourselves. But the analogy is nonsense. I never can see why a fat middle aged American whose ancestry (in the purely biological sense of course) must stretch back as far as any one else's, and whose nation started with all the history of European culture as a jumping off point, should be excused any of his vulgarity on the score of youth. Incidentally they didn't start the business about being 'young' and shouting, hallooing, and indulging in horseplay until the earlier stages of their career were well over.

There is none of the breezy and laborious rawness of Whitman[107] in Hawthorne[108] or Lowell – of whom I have received from the O.A.B. the handsome complete set that has languished in 'my' dressing room for so many years.[109] I read most of the essays before crossing back to England.

---

105 ibid., ll. 28–52.

106 Alexander Pope, *An Epistle from Mr Pope to Dr Arbuthnot* (1734–5), 125: 'I lisp'd in Numbers, for the Numbers came.'

107 The American poet, Walt Whitman (1819–92), whose *Leaves of Grass* (1855) Lewis had read.

108 Lewis mentioned Nathaniel Hawthorne's *The House of Seven Gables*, *The Marble Faun* and *The Scarlet Letter* in his letters of 22 November 1916 and 28? October 1917.

109 *The Writings of James Russell Lowell*, Riverside Edition, 10 vols. (1890).

His hatred of his fellow countrymen is far from being the only endearing characteristic about him. In addition to the literary essays – always worth reading – there is one on winter which need not be ashamed to show its face in any collection. Lowell, sir, is a book that a man may be proud to have stand on his shelves. And Hawthorn I admire beyond words: and 'I have a sneaking affection' for Longfellow. But in none of these is there the faintest trace of this abominable 'youth'. Longfellow is never happy unless he is in the dark ages: Hawthorne takes some old building dating from the New England times and weaves out of the very few centuries at his disposal an air of antiquity which is not often attained even in Europe where we have so much *arithmetically* greater a past to conjure with. (By the by, what a wonderful conceit of Thomas Browne's referring to the age of the long lived antediluvians – 'an age when living men might be antiquities'.[110] Query: *Would* a living man a thousand years old give you the same feeling that an old building does? I think there is a good deal to be said for Alice Meynell's theory that one's idea of antiquity and the standard one measures it by, is derived entirely from one's own life.[111] Certainly 'Balbec and Tadmor'[112] (whoever they may be) could hardly give one a more weird sense of 'ages and ages ago' than some early relic discovered in the drawers of the little end room often does.

One has one's own 'dark ages'. But I daresay this is not so for everyone: it may be that you and I have a specially historical sense of our own lives. Are you often struck, when you become sufficiently intimate with other people to know something of their development, how *late* their lives begin so to speak? I mean these men you meet who seem to have

---

110 Sir Thomas Browne, *Religio Medici* (1642), Pt. I, sect. 42.

111 Alice Meynell, *The Colour of Life* (1896), 'The Illusion of Historic Time': 'When a child begins to know there is a past, he has a most noble rod to measure it by – he has his own ten years. He attributes an overwhelming majesty to all recorded time. He confers distance. He, and he alone, bestows mystery. Remoteness is his. He creates more than mortal centuries. He sends armies fighting into the extremities of the past. He assigns the Parthenon to a hill of ages, and the temples of Upper Egypt to sidereal time. If there were no child, there would be nothing old. He, having conceived old time, communicates a remembrance at least of the mystery to the mind of man' (pp. 89–90).

112 Baalbek or Balbec is the ancient city of Coele-Syria, forming part of modern Lebanon. It was a centre of the worship of Baal. The ancient city of Tadmor is better known by its Roman name, Palmyra. It stood in an oasis of the Syrian desert, and its remains include a huge temple of Bel.

read everything, done everything, and yet they were pure barbarians until they left school, and had turned twenty perhaps before they began to be interested in the things that interest them now?

When I was at home I committed the unpardonable folly of telling your father that a man called Hogarth was one of the 'possibles' for our new President. Two results follow. (a) That his election was henceforth treated as absolutely certain. (b) His powers as infinite. (c) His name became Hogg-arth (to rime with 'Sogarth' in 'Sogarth Aroon'). By the end of the month I was pretty tired of 'Well is this new President of yours, this Hogg-arth, an able chap?' and 'Well, I suppose Hogg-arth will put a stop to all that'. But since then Hogarth has died. I have already had a letter observing 'So Hogarth is not going to be the new President at all.' Can't you already see the career of 'poor Hogarth' as one of the stock figures of Leeborough conversation henceforth – forever linked with 'John Burnett' and 'Prendergast'.[113] The crop of P'daytaisms was poor: all his energies have now been thrown into pronunciation and philology. This time, in answer to his 'his – to use a word I hate – mentality' I ventured to tell him that he used the word mentality more often than anyone I knew.

You will be seriously alarmed to hear that so far this winter I have followed my hot bath every morning by a cold shower. I mention it, not because I think the fact can give you any pleasure, but because of the happy turn given to it by my friend Harwood who visited me for a few days this term. 'Ah yes' he said, 'the hardening treatment. I used to do it too. Then I realised that one ought to be hardened to all extremes of temperature: so I harden myself now by living in overheated rooms.'

Well, there is no good in prolonging the agony. I must send off by this post a letter to Coast Lines for a berth. Unless your life at present is much nastier than I suppose it to be, I have a claim on your sympathies.

yrs,
Jack

113 John Burnett, who lived in Watford, was at Wynyard School with Warnie and Jack and was their closest friend there. He paid a visit to Little Lea in the summer of 1909. He is mentioned in the letter of 28 February 1909, and several times in the diary Jack kept in 1909. See LP III: 158–61. Prendergast is probably another school friend.

1928

TO HIS FATHER (LP IX: 329–31):

Magdalen.
Feb. 25th. 1928

My dear Papy,

I am afraid I have been a sad defaulter. The truth is that one finds oneself in the middle of term before there is time to look round, and this particular term has not been a very good one with me. First of all, I walked out through the College garden one fine Sunday morning and slammed the door of it on my finger. I wrapped a handkerchief round it to stop the bleeding and gave utterance to a few 'blasphemies', but until I had set out to a place where I could get it dressed and had very nearly fainted on route, I hardly realised what a nasty knock it was. Luckily it was the left hand, but I had some pain and great inconvenience with it. Then I developed a series of colds and a troublesome cough which kept me for some weeks in that border line condition wherein one manages to stumble through the daily round but slinks to bed very soon after dinner (when this is possible) and wakes muddy and unrefreshed. In the end it would not be denied. In spite of my coyness I found that I would have to keep my annual assignation with our lady influenza. A few days in bed soon settled that (this comes rather unfortunately after the assignation metaphor – a consequence not foreseen by the writer) and I am now on my legs again and indeed much better than I have been for many weeks.

The chief event has been the death of one of our fellows, Wrong,[1] which you may have seen in the papers. He was Vice President when I first joined: and had invited me to become Pro-Proctor with him as a junior Proctor – which could not be done as I was just a term too little from my matriculation to be eligible. He was always extremely friendly

1 See note 16 to letter of 14 August [1925].

to me, and I liked him as well as any one in College. He was that very rare and very delightful thing, a colonial aristocrat – being of an old Canadian family. His grandfather was one of the last people to fight a political duel; to which he was challenged on whatever corresponds to the floor of the 'House' in Canada. The blend is curious. It is odd to find a man who has canoed in Hudson bay and knows all about trapping and skunks and Indians, and yet who has distinction in the lines of his face and tradition in his outlook. No doubt, like other good things, it is disappearing: the influx of commercial democracy and the rule of the Bosses from the States will soon put an end to that element in Canada, just as (I am told) it has always swamped some things in their own vaunted southern states. He had (as Johnson would have said) 'a great deal of literature', though his own subject was history, and I have had much good crack with him about books. He was even responsible himself for a thin volume of poetry – whose merit it would be unkind now to discuss. He was one of the most brilliant of our men, and we shall have trouble in filling his place. Our 'Mods' tutor is also leaving us: so with his place, Wrong's, and the President to fill, we shall live this summer in a riot of elections. The great consolation is that Sambo cannot take part in the choosing of his own successor: if he could, heaven knows what Homeric length of meetings, speeches, committees, memoranda, and what not might await us!

I have had one letter from Warnie since I left, but it largely duplicated his last to you. I cannot help envying him the richness of his subject matter. My own life is hard to turn into matters for letters. You make the same complaint I know of yours: but at least you have the advantage, that you can write trifles to me because I know the people and places concerned. If you tell me you had a very jolly evening's chat with John Greeves or went and had a slap-up dinner with excellent champagne at Uncle Hamilton's, that is of interest because I know who John Greeves and Uncle Hamilton are. If I, on the other hand, were to tell you how I enjoyed Bircham's[2] brilliant and original views on Hamlet last night, or what a pleasant talk I had the other day with Nicholl Smith[3] (statements

2 Arthur Christopher Halsey Bircham (1908–) was one of Lewis's least promising pupils. He took his BA in 1926 and his MA in 1929.

3 David Nichol Smith (1875–1962) was a senior man in the University. He was Fellow of English at Merton College from 1921 until he became Merton Professor of English Literature in 1929.

by the way as probable as those I have put in your mouth), it would convey nothing.

However, I see that the main thing is to go on talking: for this wheeze brings into my head the fact that I did really have a very good evening the night before last when I exercised for the first time my newly acquired right of dining at Univ. – an exercise which must be rare because it is so damned expensive. Poynton, the Fark, Carritt and Stevenson, as luck would have it, were all in that evening and it was delightful to revisit the whimsical stateliness of that particular common room. There's no getting away from the fact that we at Magdalen are terribly 'ordinary' beside it. We are just like anyone else: there, every single one of them is a character part that could be found nowhere outside their own walls.

I wonder is there some influence abroad now-a-days that prevents the growth of rich, strongly marked personal peculiarities. Are any of our contemporaries 'characters' as Queen Victoria or Dizzy or Carlyle were 'characters'? I am not asking the ordinary question whether we produce greater or smaller men. 'To be a character' in this sense is not the same thing as 'to have character'. For instance, I suppose Abraham 'had character', but no one ever thought of calling him 'a character': your friend in the Rocket, on the contrary, was lacking in character, but he distinctly was 'a character'. There seems to be no doubt that the thing is growing rarer. Or is it that you need to be at least elderly to be a character? In that case, each generation, seeing the characters all among its elders, would naturally conclude that the phenomenon was passing away. Or perhaps it goes further yet. Perhaps the secret of being a character in the very highest degree is to be dead, for then the anecdotes cluster and improve unchecked.

But all this is from the purpose. What I began on was the difficulties of letter writing. I fear

> *'The fault, dear Brutus, is not in our stars*
> *But in ourselves.'*[4]

for the born letter writer is quite independent of material.

Have you ever read the letters of the poet Cowper?[5] He had nothing –

---

4 Shakespeare, *Julius Caesar*, I, ii, 139–40.

5 *The Letters and Prose Writings of William Cowper*, ed. James King and Charles Ryskamp, 5 vols. (1979–96).

literally nothing – to tell any one about: private life in a sleepy country town where Evangelical distrust of 'the world' denied him even such miserable society as the place would have afforded. And yet one reads a whole volume of his correspondence with unfailing interest. How his tooth came loose at dinner,[6] how he made a hutch for a tame hare,[7] what he is doing about his cucumbers[8] – all this he makes one follow as if the fate of empires hung on it.

Some authors, on the other hand, are far below themselves in their letters. Notably Charlotte Brontë and Mrs Gaskell whose life I re-read again while I was laid up. I had forgotten one of the best unintentionally funny things in literature until I saw it again. It comes where a letter written by Charlotte immediately after her profligate brother's death has been quoted. The situation is genuine tragedy. After giving the letter, Mrs Gaskell proceeds 'The dear friend to whom these affecting lines were written was unfailing in her sympathy for the poor worn mind and harassed frame and shortly afterwards sent her a present of a shower bath.'[9] (I cannot resist thinking of the idea of giving presents of this sort instead of letters of condolence. 'Poor so and so, I must send his wife a vacuum cleaner tomorrow'. It would be 'brutal' to work it out in detail: but undeniably a good idea.

I find that when I left home I came away without (1) a cardigan jumper, (2) a mackintosh. If you can conveniently lay your hands on these and direct the Witch of Endor to send them to me, I shall be much obliged. Try to let me have a letter in the near future – I hope it will contain a favourable account of your health and doings.

your loving son,
Jack

TO HIS FATHER (LP X: 2–3):

Magdalen.
March 31st.[1928]

My dear Papy,

Many thanks for the parcel which arrived safely. I should have acknowledged it earlier but I was in hope that I would have heard from

6 ibid., letter to Lady Hesketh of 17 December 1787, vol. III, p. 73.

7 ibid., letter to *The Gentleman's Magazine* of 28 May 1784, vol. V, pp. 40–1.

8 ibid., letter to William Unwin of 3 July 1782, vol. II, pp. 63–4.

9 Gaskell, *The Life of Charlotte Brontë*, ch. XVIII: 'The kind friend, to whom she thus wrote, saw how the poor over-taxed system needed bracing, and accordingly sent her a shower-bath.'

you before now. I hope that your continued silence has no worse cause than 'a truant disposition'[10] and the enticements of forty winks of a Sunday afternoon. Try to let me have a line – if no more – in the course of the next week or so to let me know how you are getting on. I have had no word from the Colonel either for a great while.

I have succeeded, at last, in shaking off the ailments of one of the most troublesome terms I have yet had. I forget whether I told you that after the squashed finger and the flu, I developed a swollen gland under my tongue. A doctor soon put my mind at rest about it, but of course before consulting him I had plenty of opportunity of listening – specially at night – to all the grim suggestions which the selfishness and cowardice of one's uncorrected 'natural man' pours into ones ear on such occasions. The nail, by the by, *is* going to come off and at present hangs by a thread, looking very black and ugly and catching in everything. It reminds me of the far off days when one used to get a shilling for pulling out one's own tooth. I await with much philosophical interest to see how a new nail grows.

My studies in the XVIth Century – you will remember my idea of a book about Erasmus – has carried me much further back than I anticipated. Indeed it is the curse and the fascination of literary history that there are no real beginnings. Take what point you will for the start of some new chapter in the mind and imagination of man, and you will invariably find that it has always begun a bit earlier: or rather, it branches so imperceptibly out of something else that you are forced to go back to the something else. The only satisfactory opening for any study is the first chapter of Genesis.

The upshot of all this is that the book will be a very different one from what I imagined, and I hope to try a preliminary canter in a course of lectures sometime next year. In the mean time I spend all my mornings in the Bodleian:[11] and the evenings in trying, for the hundredth time, to get a real working knowledge of the German language, since in my present occupation I find my ignorance of it up against me at every turn. For example, the only history of mediaeval Latin literature is in

10 Shakespeare, *Hamlet*, I, ii, 169.

11 The Bodleian, one of the oldest libraries in the world, is the library of the University of Oxford. Those parts of it, including the 'Duke Humfrey Library', that Lewis used to work in, were built in the 15th and 16th centuries and are some of the most beautiful buildings in Oxford.

German. The authoritative edition of an old French poem I shall have to read is in German. And so on. But I am making progress.

If only you could smoke, and if only there were upholstered chairs, the Bodleian would be one of the most delightful places in the world. I sit in 'Duke Humphrey's Library', the oldest part, a Fifteenth-Century building with a very beautiful painted wooden ceiling above me and a little mullioned window at my left hand through which I look down on the garden of Exeter where, these mornings, I see the sudden squall of wind and rain driving the first blossoms off the fruit trees and snowing the lawn with them – At the bottom of the room the gilt bust of Charles I presented by Laud, faces the gilt bust of Strafford – poor Strafford.[12]

The library itself – I mean the books – is mostly in a labyrinth of cellars under the neighbouring squares. This room however is full of books (duplicate copies I suppose, or overflows) which stand in little cases at right angles to the wall, so that between each pair there is a kind of little 'box' – in the public house sense of the word – and in these boxes one sits and reads. By a merciful provision, however many books you may send for, they will all be left on your chosen table at night for you to resume work next morning: so that one gradually accumulates a pile as comfortably as in ones own room. There is not, as in modern libraries, a forbidding framed notice to shriek 'Silence': on the contrary a more moderate request 'Talk little and tread lightly'. There is indeed always a faint murmur going on of semi-whispered conversations in neighbouring boxes. It disturbs no one. I rather like to hear the hum of the hive, and it is pleasant when someone steps into your box and says 'Hello, are *you* here?'

As you may imagine one sees many oddities among one's fellow readers – people whom I have never met elsewhere and who look as if they were shut up with the other properties every night. Positively the only drawback to the place is that beauty, antiquity and over-heating weave a spell very much more suited to dreaming than to working. But I resist to the best of my abilities and trust in time to become innoculated. (The

---

12 William Laud (1573–1645) became prominent in the Church of England under King Charles I, and in 1633 he was made Archbishop of Canterbury. He defended the Anglican Church as a national institution, and supported the King in his struggle against the Commons. As Archbishop of Canterbury he enforced uniformity in the Church. In 1640 Parliament impeached him of high treason, and he was beheaded in 1645. The Earl of Strafford (1593–1641), chief adviser to Charles I from 1639, was impeached by the Commons in 1640. He was executed, with the King's assent, in 1641.

practice of opening the window in one's box is not, I need hardly say, encouraged.) In such a life as this, what news should there be?

By the time this reaches you, you will probably have heard the result of the boat race – with the same very moderated grief as myself. Perhaps you will also have heard that there is a religious revival going on among our undergraduates. Which is true. It is run by a German-American called Dr Buchman.[13] He gets a number of young men together (some reports say women too, but I believe not) and they confess their sins to one another. Jolly, ain't it? But what can one do? If you try to suppress it (I am assuming that you agree with me that the thing is unhealthy) you only make martyrs.

The rumour that Big Bill Thompson[14] is to be the new President of Magdalen is untrue, and should be contradicted.

your loving son,
Jack

TO HIS BROTHER (LP X: 37–43):

[Hillsboro]
All Fool's Day, 1928
Postmark: 24 April 1928

My dear W.,

Once again I have found it impossible to keep up my letters to you during the term. This will be a chronic complaint and I am afraid you will have to accept it as a law of nature.

My last letter, if I remember rightly, was ironically begun on the return from the summer visit to P'daytaheim and finished only on the eve of the Christmas visit. I have thus a new 'holiday' period to record, which is almost barren in events. The P'dayta crop was singularly poor. The only item worth remembering was his curious contribution to the problem of venereal disease, to the effect that obviously it must have

---

13 Frank Buchman (1878–1961), the American founder and director of the Oxford Group, was a pupil at Mount Airy Seminary, Philadelphia, and entered the Lutheran ministry. On a visit to England in 1908 he was converted by a sermon he heard on the Atonement. He took up evangelistic work among the students of Pennsylvania State College, and from 1915 on he travelled widely preaching to student congregations, including some at Cambridge and Oxford. In 1938 he began his work of Moral Re-Armament, which stressed the role of individuals in transforming society.

14 Big Bill Thompson (1869–1930) was mayor of Chicago.

begun with women and spread thence to men. Being asked why, he replied 'Sure how could a man have given it to a woman if he hadn't got it from a woman herself?' This is unanswerable.

Another illuminating remark was made in answer to some casual remark of mine as to the control of one's imagination – I was talking, I think, about not letting one's mind brood on grievances or fears. He replied 'What on earth do you mean by controlling the imagination? One controls ones appetites.' That is the whole psychology of his generation in a nutshell, isn't it? A man sits thinking of negus and making 'iron rules' not to drink any, with much contortion of the face and muttered 'oh Lords' until the inevitable moment when he finds some excellent reason for breaking the iron rules. The idea of a simpler method – that of applying his mind to something else and using a little concentration – would never occur. The discussion ended (of course) with the infuriating statement that we were not 'ad idem' on the 'connotation' of the word control.

Which reminds me of the splendid definition of an egoist which he read to me out of Punch in happy unconsciousness of its application. 'An egoist is a man who thinks that all the words he doesn't understand are misprints.' He said I ought to write it down. I told him I should certainly remember it. He said, 'Well I bet you if I ask you tomorrow you won't know.' Next evening just as he was about to leave the study, he suddenly whipped round (in the 'I'll tell you another thing' style) and bellowed out in a voice that made me jump out of my skin, 'Jacks!! What's an *optimist*?'

We had indeed a good deal about words, because I had given him Fowler's 'Modern English Usage', a kind of prig's dictionary which contains such entries as 'METICULOUS, see vogue words,' and 'CACHINNATION, see Humour, polysyllabic', and which agrees with him about nearly everything. I really lacked the courage to give him another picture. I added to Fowler the new Nineteenth Century volume of the Dictionary of National Biography. Both these proved to be the most successful jumping jacks we have ever struck on, without exception. Both were intolerable nuisances also, lending themselves fatally well to the 'Now there's a very funny thing' style of conversation. My third and last was Max Beerbohm's 'Zuleika Dobson'[15] which was much less

15 Max Beerbohm, *Zuleika Dobson* (1911). In this novel a beautiful young lady comes to Oxford to visit her uncle, who is Warden of Judas College. It is Eights Week, and all the young men fall madly in love with Zuleika. When she rejects them, they throw themselves in the Isis and drown.

successful because he insisted on trying to find a hidden meaning in it. 'I wonder what this fellow's driving at...' 'AH, he's got some meaning in all this you know.' Apart from these there is little to record.

We had the usual regrets that you were in the army and the usual astonishment that you didn't appear to be nearly as unhappy as a man of your income ought by all reason to be. We had the usual discussions on theology, drifting off into something else as soon as one had cleared one's ground to begin. His health was tolerable, I thought. But there will be no more calculable days or weeks of non-p'dayta time at home. That is a problem that you and I will have to have a very serious talk about one of these days.

The little end room and all it stands for is rapidly becoming uninhabited territory. My Encyclopedia Boxoniana made hardly any progress at all. And I have not yet done going through the texts, let alone making the actual entries.[16] And even when he does go to town, he may return any time between eleven and three. By the way, what is the explanation of the fact that even if he returns at one o'clock when the lunch ought to be already cooking, the domestic staff immediately goes into p'dayta hours and puts the meal back to two or two thirty? He tells us that it is by no order of his, but I strongly suspect that he's hiding something from us. I find the bucket of sherry a very poor consolation for the disturbance of my day. Talking of sherry you will be surprised to hear that I have been at last moved on to the whiskey roster. I have even overshot you to such an extent that lemon, hot water, and sugar bowl now appear nightly together with the whiskey. The new regimen is accompanied of course with many ponderous jocosities of look, word, and wink, and a frequent use of that very offensive word 'boozing'. This can hardly fail to redound to your advantage. You being now the old guard and I the novice, no doubt the jokes and insinuations (and also the suggested alternative of 'your' Burgundy and soda) will hence forward be transferred to my lot. But I hope there will be no nonsense about continuing in the medium of whiskey the good old theme of the large and the small suitcase. (With what resignation will he explain to visitors, nay with what viciousness 'They each have their whiskey now'. Or more pointedly, 'Yes, when I take my little drop they each have a tumbler of whiskey.')

---

16 Lewis did not complete his Encyclopedia Boxoniana. However, what he did write is contained, with most of his Boxen stories, in *Boxen*, op. cit.

One of the misfortunes of my position is that my reading contains less and less that I can share with my non-professional friends. Except Pickwick[17] (a *very* overrated work) I have read hardly anything this term which you would care to hear of. At present I am deep in medieval things.[18] I find I shall have to try to 'get' some Old French. Don't you think this is rather jolly. In one of those gardens in a dream, which mediaeval love poetry is full of, we find the tomb of a knight, dead for love, covered with flowers. Then: –

> *'Oysiaus i ot: por l'ame del signor*
> *Qui la gisoit, cantent de vrai amor.*
> *Quant il unt fain, cascuns baise une flor,*
> *Ja puis n'arunt ne faim ne soif le jor.'*[19]

I am still so ignorant that I don't know what 'i ot' (1) or 'Ja' mean, but I suppose it can be v. roughly Englished,

> *'And birds that for the soul of that signor*
> *Who lay beneath, songs of true love did pour:*
> *Being hungered, each from off the flowers bore*
> *A kiss, and felt that day no hunger more.'*

The odd thing is that one would expect the same rime going all through to be monotonous and ugly: but to my ear it produces a beautiful lulling like the sound of the sea. I fancy one pronounces the N's less nasal than the modern French N, and almost certainly makes a real syllable out of the mute E's. In quite a different vein I like the mere baldness of this address to ladies,

> *'Toutes estes, seres, ou futes,*
> *De fait ou de volonte, putes.'*[20]

---

17 Charles Dickens, *The Pickwick Papers* (1837).

18 As Lewis mentions in his letter to Owen Barfield of 27 May 1928, he was 'starting a book on...the Romance of the Rose and its school'. This is the first reference to what would become Lewis's first, and perhaps greatest, work of literary history, *The Allegory of Love: A Study of Medieval Tradition* (1936).

19 *Li Fablel dou Dieu d'Amours*, ed. Achille Jubinal (Paris: 1834), stanza 112, p. 31. This was the first publication of this 13th century poem.

20 Guillaume de Lorris and Jean de Meun, *Le Roman de la Rose*, ll. 9155–6. Lewis was using *Le Roman de la Rose*, ed. Ernest Langlois (Paris: Société des Anciens Textes Français,

where you can easily guess the meaning of *putes* if you don't know it already – and also understand the insolence of Swift in calling his flying island 'La Puta'.[21] Which leads to another question. The only modern editions of 'The Romans de la Rose' are old fashioned enough to print asterisks for certain words. So you get,

> *'Car volontiers, non pas enirs*
> *Mist Diex en C****** et en v***
> *Force generacion.'*[22]

We all see what c...... and v.. are. Do you know the words? And is c...... the same as its modern English equivalent? I think you and I ought to do a little old French together, where your superior knowledge of the modern language and my wider experience of language in general would put us at the same point. We might begin with Aucassin and Nicolette,[23] to which, if I remember rightly, you first introduced me. Also, sooner or later, you will be bound to look back at the mediaeval roots out of which your France grew.

1914), and either he or Warnie made some errors in transcribing these lines. They are: 'Toutes estes, sereiz e fustes / De fait ou de volenté putes.' ('All women are, will be, or were – either de facto or by intent – whores.') The best modern edition of *Le Roman de la Rose* is that of Félix Lecoy (Paris, Les Classiques Français Du Moyen Age, 1965–70). In his edition the same lines are numbered 9125–6 and are given as: 'Toutes estes, serez et fustes, / de fet ou de volenté, pustes.' The *Romance of the Rose* is a 13th century French allegorical romance in octosyllabic couplets. It is cast as an allegorical dream-vision, and describes a young man's initiation into love and his efforts to possess the rosebud of which he is enamoured. The first 4,058 lines were written c. 1230 by Guillaume de Lorris (d. 1237) and the remaining 17,622 lines of the poem were written c. 1275 by Jean de Meun. About a third of the whole was translated into the Middle English *The Romaunt of the Rose*, the first part of which may be by Chaucer. The poem, discussed in *The Allegory of Love*, ch. III, is central to Lewis's understanding of courtly love. On courtly love see note 72 to the letter of 3 November 1928.

21 In Jonathan Swift's *Gulliver's Travels* (1726).

22 *Le Roman de la Rose*, ed. Langlois, ll. 6965–6: 'Car volentiers, non pas enviz, / Mist Deus en coilles e en viz.' *Le Roman de la Rose*, ed. Lecoy, ll. 6935–6: 'car volentiers, non pas enviz / mist Dex en coillons et en viz *force de generacion*.' (*The Romance of the Rose*, translated by Frances Horgan (1994): 'For it was by his own will rather than against it that God in his wonderful purpose put the generative power into the testicles and penis, in order that the race would live forever, renewed by new births.'

23 *Aucassin and Nicolette* is a 13th century courtly story in French. It is composed in alternating prose and songs, and believed to be a pastiche of the excesses of courtly love. The story tells of how Aucassin, the son of Count Garins of Beaucaire, loves Nicolette, a Saracen captive. The Count opposes their love and imprisons them. They escape, and after many adventures, they are married.

(1) On second thoughts 'ot' must be an old preterit of avoir, and i ot equals il ya avait.'

April 15th

Last week end I was away on my Easter walking tour, and as Sundays are the only days I can spare for these 'loose undigested pieces' this has had to lie fallow for a fortnight. You should take a box of English maps away with you whenever you go abroad: recalling old jaunts and planning new ones would be a great solace to you and you would also be able to follow any itineraries I write. And, by the same token, don't you approve of the suggestion made by a friend of mine that there shd. be a set of new conventional signs to put on one's map: e.g. [24]means here we bathed our feet in a cool stream. [25]Here we drank beer: [26]bad beer: [27]fleas in beds here, and so forth.

My own Oxford sheet at least shows the right tendency in bearing crossed swords, the sign of a battle, at the point of N.W. of Chipping Norton where you and I contended with that puncture in the teeth of a gale. As I presume that you haven't your maps with you, I shall not give you a detailed account of our journey. It was the inexhaustible Cotswolds again, as all of us this year happened to be too straitened for time and money to attempt a longer walk. I say 'inexhaustible' advisedly. This year, within a mile or so of country we had walked before, we found valley after valley and wood after wood as beautiful as ever, and whole days of country different totally in character from what we had already seen. The Bathurst estate beyond Cirencester is a place we must revisit when you come home. You can take the whole breakfast to lunch walk in the glorious woods and then emerge into the open in time to lunch at the most glorious village on the edge of the Stroud valley, which winds away as far as you can see, delightfully wooded and watered. (The first Lord Bathhurst, I am told, was raised to the peerage for inventing a new kind of toilet paper for Queen Anne. I have often heard of honours won by getting up the ....[28] of one's superiors. Perhaps this is the origin of the expression. Now there is an idea quite silly enough to write to *Notes and*

24 Here there is a drawing of a pipe.

25 Here there is a drawing of a beer mug.

26 Here there is a drawing of a beer mug with a slash through it.

27 Here there is a drawing of a flea.

28 Warnie deleted a word here.

Queries or the *Spectator* about – if only public prejudice didn't render it impossible on other grounds.)

Shortly after this one passes the western mouth of the (now disused) canal tunnel that runs under the Chilterns. It is very awe inspiring and suggests the mouth of the Styx. It seems in the nature of things that one real blunder should be produced by each walking tour. This time we committed the folly of selecting a billeting *area* for the night instead of one good town: i.e. we said 'Well here are four villages within a mile of one another and the map marks an inn in each, so we shall be sure to get in somewhere.' Your imagination can suggest what this results in by about eight o'clock of an evening, after twenty miles of walking, when one is just turning away from the first unsuccessful attempt and a thin cold rain is beginning to fall. Yet these hardships had their compensations: thin at the time, but very rich in memory. One never knows the snugness and beauty of an English village twilight so well as in the homelessness of such a moment: when the lights are just beginning to show up in the cottage windows and one sees the natives clumping past to the pub – clouds meanwhile piling up 'to weather'.

Our particular village was in a deep narrow valley with woods all round it and a rushing stream that grew louder as the night came on. Then comes the time when you have to strike a light (with difficulties) in order to read the maps: and when the match fizzles out, you realise for the first time how dark it really is: and as you go away, the village fixes itself in your mind – for enjoyment ten, twenty, or thirty years hence – as a place of impossible peace and dreaminess. Failure to find lodging brings to my mind the excellent story of the Golden Opportunity which I heard for the first time the other day. I hope it is new to you.

'They say and they sing and relate' that a young man on a walking tour found himself benighted once in Scotland with only a tiny farm house in sight. Knocking at the door, he was greeted by a gaunt God-fearing man who told him to get out of that: when suddenly the voice of the farmer's young wife from behind said, no, let the laddie in. So the farmer reluctantly admitted him. At supper an excellent meat pie was produced. The young man was very hungry, but when the hostess offered him a second helping, the God-fearing man said 'Na. Na. The rest of yon pie's for ma breikfast': so it was put away. Upstairs was only a single bed. The guest got in first: then the God-fearing man: then the wife. They had hardly had time to close their eyes when a voice from without bellowed up 'Jock! Jock! Come down man, the grey coo's goin' to calve.' Unwillingly for many reasons did that God-fearing man arise, and bundling his long white nightshirt into his trousers, shuffle away. Then 'Young man' said the hostess softly, 'He maun be oot there twa hours at the least. It's a golden opportunity.' 'By Gad, maam, you're right. It *is* a golden opportunity' replied the guest fervently, as he leapt from the bed: and going downstairs swiftly, finished to the last morsel that very excellent meat pie.

I sincerely hope this is a really modern story, for it would show that the mind of the nation was not yet spoiled. But it has a suspiciously Chaucerian flavour, and I expect we shall meet [it] in the middle ages again some day. What pleases me so much is the idea of the breakfast party next morning, on one side 'Hell hath no fury like a woman scorned':[29] on the other the G.F.M., up most of the night and breakfast-less.

Our own adventures in the inhospitable billeting area ended by the miserable expedient of walking on five miles of main road into that most loathsome city, Cheltenham: in the outskirts of wh. – you will find this hard to believe – we found a brilliantly lighted hotel, echoing with music, in the midst of a garden, and *no gate* into it anywhere so far as we could discover. The wind blew and the rain poured. We walked on until we had clearly passed the hotel grounds: then we walked back. But we found no gate and I am still divided as to whether it was merely a Christina dream[30] or an extension of the view taken up in that hotel where you and I were asked whether we'd be wanting anything more after our tea and where (if you remember) we concluded that the proprietors regarded us as a nuisance. You may imagine how glad we were to get down to it when we did finally reach an hotel in the middle of Cheltenham. Though I have decided not to be topographical (in your lack of

29 William Congreve, *The Mourning Bride* (1697), III, viii: 'Heaven has no rage, like love to hatred turned, / Nor Hell a fury, like a woman scorned.'

30 In the Preface he wrote for the second impression of *Dymer* (1950) Lewis explained that: 'In those days the new psychology was just beginning to make itself felt in the circles I most frequented at Oxford. This joined forces with the fact that we felt ourselves (as young men always do) to be escaping from the illusions of adolescence, and as a result we were much exercised about the problem of fantasy or wishful thinking. The "Christina Dream", as we called it (after Christina Pontifex in Butler's novel), was the hidden enemy whom we were all determined to unmask and defeat.'

maps), I must just put on record the delightful valley in which Temple Guiting stands – a place we ought certainly to visit.

I had almost forgotten to tell you of another snatch of holiday – only a week end – which I had immediately after term when a colleague motored me down to his bungalow at Rhossilli in the Gower peninsula. This, as you probably know, lies on the south coast of Wales, near the mouth of the channel. The bottle neck is closed by the formidable city of Swansea. The tide of people of leisure and taste (who, by the by with their cars, villas and bungalows, really spoil sport for us far more than the bluecoat and the burley) having looked at Swansea, very naturally go further. But once past that detestable town (I once v. nearly tried for a job there) you find yourself in a solitude of bare hills, limestone cliffs and crags, coves well wooded, and more Norman castles than I ever believed possible. As the peninsula is a dead end leading to nowhere but a harbourless sea, nothing comes down its road: even tramps have long since decided not to walk down and have to walk back. There is nothing spectacular: no real mountains and no *great* cliffs – rather the sort of cliffs that is sheep bitten grass half the way up and then breaks into grey spires. (Limestone is the pale grey rock that tends to go pointy. How useful these sciences are after all!). The whole of the western end of Gower is owned by an old lady who, because she will not sell any of her land for building – in other words will not raise her income by rendering her home uninhabitable – is described as eccentric. Blessings on her.

My visit would have been pleasanter if my host had not discovered in himself elements of the Burnetto-Desmond[31] which I had no previous means of discovering. I could have pardoned his firm adherence to the Take-Lunch-With-You school on our daily expeditions – being a malady specially incident to married men – but his fixed idea about picking up any bit of odd timber on the way home for firewood was what really annoyed me. His account of the thing was 'If I see a nice bit of firewood when we're in sight of home, I sometimes bring it along with me.' The *fact* was that any time after lunch on an all day walk, not he, but *we*, began to burden ourselves with every lump and spar of timber we could find. In my simplicity I had joined in planning a walk that would bring us home along four miles of sand (A wonderful bathing beach it would

31 This is private language between the Lewis brothers, and it seems to mean the artificial, the contrived, the opposite of what was to them comfortable and natural.

be in summer, and not a human habitation). Little did I realise that his praises of a beach walk were inspired by something very much more lively than aesthetic appreciation and that the word which flashed across his mind was 'Driftwood'. I had indeed wondered whether it might not be tiring to walk so far on sand. It was. By six o'clock I was feverishly engaged in keeping his attention fixed on the horizon for fear he would notice the foreparts of a wrecked rowing boat which we were passing. By half past six I heard, to my inexpressible horror, that even *metal* objects came in very useful, and saw him stop to look longingly at an old anchor which four men could not have lifted. Whether he smelts them or chemically produces one of those heats in which iron will burn I stayed not to inquire. However, I had a very pleasant week end on the whole: and how few people has one followed into their native haunts without finding some such drawback.

The only disadvantage in the place was the ever present danger of his latrine: whereof he only appraised me as my hand was on the latch after breakfast the first morning, by remarking casually that I'd better not drop a match down it as he de-odorised it with a highly inflammable chemical. To throw a cigarette end or a match down the rears is an action so natural that I was always in terror of the place. It reminds me of what someone told me about his school where a continuous channel underneath united a row of rears, and it passed for an excellent witticism to set fire to a mass of toilet paper and launch it burning on the stream – thus, according to naval traditions, introducing as it were a fire ship under the bottoms of a man's acquaintances.

It is a long time since I've heard from you, and I am not even clear when exactly your oriental spell comes to an end. All here are pretty fit. I re-read The Man of Property[32] in the mornings in bed last week. I didn't change my views at all about the general merits of it, but was surprised not to have noticed before [that these] who are meant (I suppose) to be sympathetic are really v. like the rest. If anyone contended that Irene herself is a typical Forsyte it wd. be quite easy to make out a case for him. Do you observe that no disinterested action is anywhere recorded of her? One also discovers that Soames is much more broadly drawn in the early parts of the Man of Property than anywhere else in the saga – much more a figure of satire. He is described as 'mousing' along the street. I

32 John Galsworthy, *The Man of Property* (1906), the first of his Forsyte novels.

don't think Galsworthy would have used the word later on. Indeed I wish he'd kept more to the original level: I want more of the glorious Forsytism, the soup and port and saddle of mutton and family gatherings and less of the ordinary novelistic 'pash' – less about young Jolyon's feelings and Irene's hips. I don't think I like Galsworthy in his tender vein. A man so sensual ought not to be so serious about it. All those scents and sunsets – we all know it's bosh really. But a great book, whenever he stops writing a novel and just tells us about the Forsytes.

yrs,
Jack

TO OWEN BARFIELD (W):

[Hillsboro]
Whitsunday [27 May 1928]

My dear Barfield,

After an unconscionable delay for which no excuse was offered, Messrs. Brooks have been out to view the 'property' at Crendon.[33] They sent me a letter saying that the matter seemed rather difficult and would I come to call on them. I replied that I would if they wished: but added that I had already said all I had authority to say, and that if it were a question of interpretation, my interpretation would have no more warrant than theirs and they had better write to you direct. I hope you won't attribute this to mere laziness. It is quite clear that I can't really move an inch without again referring to you, and, that being so, it seems absurd for the resulting correspondence to go round from you to me and me to Brooks. What is the train to do at my station beyond having the doors opened and slammed again and the wheels tapped? So I hope you are now in communication with them.

I have just got a copy of Poetic Diction – having just learned of its appearance from a marvelously absurd review in the T.L.S.,[34] where the critic fiddles about for a paragraph with the main argument, obviously

33 Owen Barfield and his wife, Maud, loved the country and it was their wish to return to the small village of Long Crendon where they had lived for a while. Long Crendon is about 14 miles from Oxford. See **Owen Barfield** in the Biographical Appendix.

34 *Poetic Diction: A study in Meaning* began as Owen Barfield's B.Litt. thesis at Oxford, and it had just been published. It was reviewed in *The Times Literary Supplement* (17 May 1928), p. 375.

unable to make anything of it and very much afraid of giving himself away, and then with almost audible relief grasps at some parenthetical remark of yours about Lamb, and having at last got something he can understand, begins eagerly 'But surely Mr Barfield is wrong in calling Lamb a minor poet' – But you must not be angry with him: the poor man was having a very bad time and this was the shadow of a great rock in a thirsty land. I spent ten minutes after breakfast this morning trying to lend the book to J.A.[35] but like the two girls in Sense and Sensibility he 'resolutely and fervently' declined the invitation.[36] People will never borrow the books you want to lend, but always the others. I haven't yet re-read it, but am rather astonished at what I have seen so far. In Appendix IV iii you quote with approval a passage from Steiner where he seems to be saying just what I always say and you always deny.[37] That the subject is a product of thought and not its author is almost my ἀρχή.[38] I think in general that I am going to agree with the whole book more than we thought I did. We are really at one about imagination as the source of meanings i.e. almost of *objects*. We both agree that it is the *prius* of truth. But I can't write about it now.

When are you coming home? I must see someone sane again soon. Just by the bye – and you must not repeat it to anyone, even myself – this college is a cesspool, a stinking puddle, faex Romuli,[39] inhabited by

---

35 i.e. J.A. Smith who is mentioned in note 6 to the letter of 5 January 1926.

36 Austen, *Sense and Sensibility*, ch. 20: 'eagerly and resolutely'.

37 Barfield quotes the following passage from Rudolf Steiner's *Philosophy of Spiritual Activity*, pp. 51–2: 'Thinking must never be regarded as a merely subjective activity. Thinking transcends the distinction of subject and object. It produces these two concepts just as it produces all others. When, therefore, I, as thinking subject, refer a concept to an object, we must not regard this reference as something purely subjective. It is not the subject, but thought, which makes the reference. The subject does not think because it is a subject, rather it conceives itself to be a subject because it can think. The activity of consciousness, in so far as it thinks, is thus not merely subjective. Rather it is neither subjective nor objective; it transcends both these concepts. I ought never to say that I, as individual subject, think, but rather that I, as subject, exist myself by the grace of thought.'

38 'Origin' or 'First Cause'.

39 Lewis believed there to be some truth in the accusations he was making, but he was primarily having fun with a friend who he knew would understand the exaggeration. There is an instance of *Faex Romuli* – dregs of Romulus – in Cicero's *Letters to Atticus*, 21.8: '[Cato] speaks in the Senate as though he were living in Plato's Republic instead of Romulus's cesspool [*Romuli faece*].'

Fals-Semblant,[40] Favel,[41] Mal-Bouche[42] and Losengeres:[43] things in men's shapes climbing over one another and biting one another in the back: ignorant of all things except their own subjects and often even of those: caring for nothing less than for learning: cunning, desperately ambitious, false friends, nodders in corners, tippers of the wink: setters of traps and solicitors of confidence: vain as women: self-important: fie upon them – excepting always the aged who have lived down to us from a purer epoch. Don't you think it dammed unfair to have resisted all youthful temptations to cynicism and then to have ones lines cast in a sewer where all that the cynic asserts in general happens for the nonce to be true?

I forgot. We have *one* honest man. He preaches what he practices: tells you openly that anyone who believes another is a fool, and holds that Hobbs alone saw the truth: tells me I am an incurable romantic and is insolent by rule to old men and servants. He is very pale, this man, good-looking, and drinks a great deal without getting drunk. I think he is best of our younger fellows and I would sign his death warrant to-morrow, or he mine, without turning a hair.[44] Don't conclude that all Oxford colleges are like this: I've seen a good deal of them, and I know.

---

40 Fals-Semblant – false appearing – is found in John Gower's *Confessio Amantis* (1390), II, 1879–8: 'Of Falssemblant if I schal telle, / Above alle othre it is the welle / Out of the which deceipte flowethe.'

41 Favel is the hero of Gervais du Bus's *Roman de Fauvel* (1310–14). In this story Fauvel is an anthropomorphic horse, the ultimate hypocrite, and one who turns everyone else into hypocrites too. The expression 'curry favour' comes from him. Another example of Favel as insincerity is found in William Langland, *Piers Plowman* (written about 1367–70), II, 22–3: 'To-morewe worth the marriage made of Mede and of Fals; / Favel, with fair speche, had forgid them togidere.' 'Tomorrow would be the marriage of Reward and Deceit, / Favel with fair speech, had given them to one another.'

42 Mal-Bouche means evil mouth, as in Sir Richard Ros, *La Belle Dame* (c. 1460), 741: 'Male-bouche in courte hath great commaundement.'

43 Losengeres are the traitors who turn up in almost every courtly romance, spy on lovers and betray them, as in Chaucer, *The Legend of Good Women*, 352: 'For in youre court ys many a losengeour.'

44 Lewis was almost certainly describing Thomas Dewar Weldon (1896–1958). He took a BA from Magdalen in 1921 and was Fellow and Tutor of Philosophy there 1923–58. There is a good deal about Weldon in Lewis's *AMR*. Weldon is also one of the subjects of the nine 'portraits' Lewis wrote about his colleagues in about 1927 and which are found in *AMR*, pp. 482–3. It seems likely that Weldon is the man Lewis was writing about in *SBJ* XIV in which he said: 'Early in 1926 the hardest boiled of all the atheists I ever knew sat in my room on the other side of the fire and remarked that the evidence for the historicity of the Gospels was really surprisingly good. "Rum thing," he went on. "All that stuff of Frazer's about the Dying God. Rum thing. It almost looks as if it had really happened once."' This may have occurred on the night of 27 April 1926,

I have written no poetry since. Last Vac. I spent mostly in Bodley starting a book on – what do you think? – the Romance of the Rose and its school. I'll explain the choice when we meet, till when roll on the time. Love to both of you.

yrs.,
C. S. Lewis

I've no right to ask for a letter after my endless silences: but if you had a wet afternoon or so it would be a very meritorious act.

TO OWEN BARFIELD (W):

[Magdalen College
7? June 1928]

My dear Barfield,

When I asked you I forgot that that evening wd. find me in the middle of examining in B6. Can you both take Wednesday June 13th instead, and will Mrs Barfield lie at Headington & you lie at Magdalen that night? I hope this presents no difficulties. I enclose a scrap of paper to pull the controversy together: I have been trying very hard to see whether I could find my trace of consciousness of *thinking pure* and am concluding definitely *Wal – I don't believe it*. Let me have a line.

Yrs.,
C. S. Lewis

TO OWEN BARFIELD (W):

[Magdalen College
8? June 1928]

Come on Tuesday next and let your lady wife come and lie at Headington while you stay in College, for both will be very welcome. I haven't read Aeschylus this long time but I don't mind having a shot. The Prometheus is a bit easier than the Agamemnon.[45] You cd hardly expect

---

about which Lewis says in *AMR*: 'In the evening...Weldon came in. This meant whiskey and talk till 12.30...We somehow got on the historical truth of the Gospels, and agreed that there was a lot that could not be explained away.' See Martin Moynihan's 'C.S. Lewis and T.D. Weldon', *Seven: An Anglo-American Literary Review*, vol. 5 (1984), pp. 101–5.

45 Aeschylus (525–456 BC) was a Greek tragic poet, two of whose plays are *Prometheus Vinctus* and *Agamemnon*. Lewis and Barfield often met for the purpose of reading Greek plays or other works of literature. Lewis mentions their reading *Prometheus* together on 25 January 1927 (*AMR*, p. 436).

the man in the T.L.S. to know the esoteric doctrine of myths. By the bye, we now need a new word for the 'science of the nature of myths' since 'mythology' has been appropriated to the myths themselves. Would 'mythonomy' do? I am quite serious. If your views are not a complete error this subject will become more important and it's worth while trying to get a good word before they invent a beastly one. 'Mytho-logic' (noun) wouldn't be bad, but people wd read it as an adjective. I have also thought of 'mythopoeics' (cf. 'Metaphysics') but that leads to 'a mythopoeician' wh. is frightful: whereas 'a mythonomer' (better still 'The Mythonomer Royal') is nice. Or shall we just invent a new word – like 'gas'. (Nay Sir, I meant nothing.)

I am writing a great new poem – also a Mnemonic rime on English sound changes in octosyllabic verse

(Thus Æ to Ĕ they soon were fetchin',
Cf. such forms as ÞÆC and ÞECCEAN.)

which will be about as long as the Cursor Mundi, & great fun.

Arrive about 3 o'clock on Tuesday, if that suits you. P.S. Wd 'Mythologics' do?

C.S.L.

TO HIS FATHER (LP X: 73–5):

July 10th [1928]
Magdalen.

My dear Papy,

It is so long now since I have heard either from you or from Warnie that I begin to wonder whether I am one of the men who came out of the earth full grown in a Greek story and had neither kith nor kin. Try to let me have a few lines soon if you can possibly manage it.

Since I last wrote to you I have had a visit from Uncle Dick and Aunt Agnes.[46] I had them to lunch and they had me to dinner and we met once or twice in between: after my first suggestion of taking Uncle Dick to the top of Magdalen Tower had been refused, they showed no desire to solicit, or even to tolerate my services as a showman. It was the oddest

46 This is Albert's brother, Richard Lewis, and his wife Agnes. See **The Lewis Family** in the Biographical Appendix.

sensation to see him again and brought a great many submerged memories to life. After the first embarrassment, which I always feel in meeting that queer mixture of the intimate and the stranger – a rarely seen relation – I liked them both extremely. I found that my picture of him had got rather badly mixed up with Uncle Bill,[47] greatly to its disadvantage. That was all swept away in the first ten minutes. But what surprised me most of all was that, apart from his parrot nose and grey hair, his appearance reminded me strongly of you: and not only his appearance but his turns of expression and even something of his voice that kept on becoming audible even through the top dressing of Scotch. This set me thinking on the strange persistence of a family type and how it breaks through differences of environment. I could not help wondering whether the same voice was really present beneath *my* southern English as it was beneath his Scotch. That the appearance is there, we have all heard *ad nauseam*: and there are certainly traits of a common character both welcome and unwelcome, which I am sometimes startled to observe in myself. As I said to him 'We're a cantankerous lot' to which Aunt Agnes replied 'Indeed you are', but he 'Speak for yourself.' Of course he hardly came up to my childhood's memories of the 'funny' Uncle Dick. But he has certainly a great sense of humour, and to watch him enjoying the joke is almost as good as the joke itself. His stories are not as good as yours and are drawn from a narrower field, but they have gusto. To an irreverent member of the younger generation, of course the best fun of all was the attitude of not unkindly pity – on the 'Poor Warren' lines – which he adopted throughout when speaking of you or Uncle Bill. Aunt Agnes is a dear. In fact if they liked me anything like so well as I liked them, the meeting may be pronounced a brilliant success.

I have actually begun the first chapter of my book.[48] This perhaps sounds rather odd since I was working on it all last vac., but you will understand that in a thing of this sort the collection of the material is three quarters of the battle. Of course, like a child who wants to get to the painting before it has really finished drawing the outline, I have been itching to do some actual *writing* for a long time. Indeed – you can imagine it as well as I – the most delightful sentences would come into

47 Uncle Bill or 'Limpopo' was William Lewis. See **The Lewis Family** in the Biographical Appendix.

48 i.e. *The Allegory of Love*.

one's head: and now half of them can't be used because, knowing a little more about the subject, I find they aren't true. That's the worst of facts – they do cramp a fellow's style. If I can get it – the first chapter – to the stage of being typed, I shall bring a copy home for your amusement.

I should warn you, by the by, that Erasmus and all that has had to be postponed to a later book. The actual book is going to be about mediaeval love poetry and the mediaeval idea of love which is a very paradoxical business indeed when you go into it: for on the one hand it is extremely super-sensual and refined and on the other it is an absolute point of honour that the lady should be some one else's wife, as Dante and Beatrice, Lancelot and Guinevere etc. The best introduction is the passage in Burke about 'the unbought grace of life'.[49]

I am intending by the way to pay you my summer visit in *August* this year instead of at the usual time. This is because the whole of the later part of the Long[50] will be occupied with the preliminary stages of the Presidential election, specially the informal conversations which matter most. I am particularly anxious to be there, with one or two others, at the early parts and see what is going on: for – I am almost ashamed to tell you – I am beginning to be rather disillusioned about my colleagues. There is a good deal more intrigue and mutual back-scratching and even direct lying than I ever supposed possible: and what worries me most of all, I have good reason to believe that it is not the same in other colleges.

---

49 Edmund Burke, *Reflections on the Revolution in France* (1790), ed. Conor Cruise O'Brien (Penguin Classics: 1986), p. 170: 'The age of chivalry is gone. – That of sophisters, oeconomists, and calculators, has succeeded, and the glory of Europe is extinguished for ever. Never, never more, shall we behold that generous loyalty to rank and sex, that proud submission, that dignified obedience, that subordination of the heart, which kept alive, even in servitude itself, the spirit of an exalted freedom. The unbought grace of life, the cheap defence of nations, the nurse of manly sentiment and heroic enterprize is gone! It is gone, that sensibility of principle, that charity of honour, which felt a stain like a wound, which inspired courage, whilst it mitigated ferocity, which ennobled whatever it touched, and under which vice itself lost half its evil, by losing all its grossness.'

50 i.e. Long Vacation. Oxford's academic year is divided into three terms and three vacations. Each Oxford term consists of a period of eight weeks, beginning on a Sunday. In each of these terms there is a period of eight weeks known as Full Term. (1) Michaelmas Term is the first of the academic year and it begins on and includes 1 October and ends on and includes 17 December; (2) Hilary Term begins on and includes 7 January and ends on and includes 25 March or the Saturday before Palm Sunday; (3) Trinity Term begins on and includes 20 April or the Wednesday after Easter, whichever is the later, and ends on and includes 6 July. Long Vacation runs from the end of Trinity Term to the start of Michaelmas Term.

Of course it may simply be that, being rather an innocent in practical matters myself, and having been deceived once or twice, I have rushed too hastily to conclusions: as they say a simple man becomes too knowing by half when he once becomes knowing at all. Let us hope so. But the bad thing is that the decent men seem to me to be all the old ones (who will die) and the rotters seem to be all the young ones (who will last my time).

I have a bad cold, I think from sleeping in a damp bed at the cottage of a friend (whose wife was away) last week. Is it of any use to ask how you are? I mean will one get an answer? I earnestly hope that your long silence means nothing bad.

your loving son,
Jack

TO HIS BROTHER (LP X: 75–81):

Hillsboro.
Begun Aug. 2nd. [1928]

My dear W.,

Your letter of the 23rd June reached me yesterday and just gave me the mental pick-up required after my annual week's penance as an examiner. It has even stimulated me to begin an early reply, for though I had not said in my wrath that I'd see you farther if I wrote until I heard from you again, still I was certainly allowing your silence to act as a sort of makeweight with my own idleness. At the moment I can't clearly recollect when I last wrote to you or how much has happened since.

To start with something I am certain of, I have recently made the acquaintance of Uncle Dick and Aunt Agnes, who came for a few days to Oxford towards the end of last term. I think I remember you once wishing that we had been old enough to appreciate the spectacle of the three P'daytas together when that conjunction (good idea – in the astronomy of our island there would be a P'dayta constellation so that you would have 'The Greater P'dayta in Negus' or something of that sort) – when that conjunction occurred at Helensburgh. Failing that, the next most interesting thing was to see one of the other P'daytas alone, and I profited by it.

The result that emerges clearly is the overwhelming steadiness of the type: there are differences between the Pomum Terrestre Albertense and the Pomum Terrestre Ricardense, but they are a mere nothing compared to the resemblances. (What ghastly speculations this raises about myself, you may easily imagine). To begin with, the faces are very much alike: and so are the voices. But it's the style of conversation which simply hits you in the chest. You know what I mean...the indefinable allusiveness, knowingness, the tipping the wink, the pantomime. The language in which 'They raised a subscription' becomes 'So these Johnnies (jerk of the head towards the imaginary Johnnies) had to take the hat round (wide opened eyes and head suddenly lowered, with expression suggesting the worst come to the worst) and then of course we had to put our hands in our pockets (imitative gesture) and see what could be done' etc. Under the heading of *manner* I should perhaps record how – after I had given them a posh lunch *with wine* in College – having asked me to dinner in the Clarendon, he suddenly beamed into that expression of hospitality to the Nth with a touch of roguery and one-of-the-boys-ness known only to P'daytas and said 'Well Jacksie, as this is a special occasion I think I may order two *pints*, eh?'

So much for manner. As for matter, it consisted entirely of wheezes: not only like the P'dayta wheezes but often the identical wheezes. Of course he is a man of far less erudition than your father, and the wheezes were drawn from a narrower field: nothing of the literary or legal element came in. Rather what we may call the McGlusgie element – stories about men getting their heads broken and then being arrested for making a disturbance – what makes only a part of the P'dayta's repertory made Uncle Dick's whole stock in trade. It is quite a sound sort of humour of course, and we all appreciate it – indeed I submit that an intensive appreciation of it is one of the few genuinely P'dayta traits which has descended to you in fuller measure than to me. However, Uncle Dick doesn't tell his stories nearly so well as the P'daytabird, and indeed recalls him less vividly in the humour of the thing than in the intolerable quantity and in the merciless determination to extract from you the last guffaw – you know: repeating the denouement and saying 'Eh? What?' when your jaws are already aching. I hate a joke used as a thumbscrew. Indeed it just occurs to me at the moment of writing that the proper answer to the P'daytesque 'Well it was very funny' is 'Yes – it *was*! Half an hour ago.'

In one way he is above the P'daytabird – he doesn't whine. He described, in answer to my enquiries, the difficulties of his business etc. (Of course you know he's 'ruined') with the same humour he applied to everything else and without a touch of the Limpopo or P'daytesque self-pity. That is all to the good. On the other hand he descends to conversational depths which the P'daytabird knows not, such as carrying in his pocket case a joke (of the McGlusgie type) which he has cut from a comic paper and producing it suddenly for your delectation. Now that is the sort of thing which I thought was only done by people in trains.

You must not imagine from all this that I didn't like him. We got on admirable, and if when I first saw him from my window stumping towards new buildings with his large block hat and respectable umbrella, I felt a moment's qualm, it was checked by the memory of Sir Willoughby when he saw his naval relative walking up the drive with his carpet bag.[51]

One great subject of conversation which we had in common was the P'daytabird himself. Of all the jokes, Uncle Dick enjoys his brother James the best. Your father's faculty of getting stung financially in every undertaking was referred to again and again with gusto. He also said that both the O.A.B. and Uncle Limpopo were born old. And the moral of that is, Master Pigibuddie, that you and I needn't imagine that we are necessarily outside the orbit of P'datism when we laugh at it – perhaps we are then fullest inside, for they all find each other ridiculous.

Of course the alternative is to say that Uncle Dick is not a P'dayta. Sometimes I almost think not: specially when having written home and said 'he referred to you and Uncle Bill with a vaguely humorous tone on the "poor Warren" lines' – wh. I thought would amuse him – I got a reply 'I know very well the tone you refer to. Anyone who is not up to concert pitch all the time is only shamming and needs to pull himself together and be shaken up. It is, I confess, an attitude that I am sometimes very tired of.' There certainly is a wide rift there. But all it comes to is that Uncle Dick's unpardonable offence in the eyes of his brothers is courage. He will not join the Crying Club. He has all the typical P'dayta troubles – suffers from lumbago and his business is going to the dogs – but he will *not* take them in the right way. He makes jokes of them. Still, they are P'dayta jokes. He has the P'dayta dislike of animals. He has the P'dayta habit of drifting away from a subject the moment it becomes interesting – the movement of his mind is from story to story by association of words, not from topic to topic by association of ideas. I think we must

51 Sir Willoughby Patterne is the egoist in George Meredith's novel *The Egoist*.

call him a P'dayta – say, a 'P'dayta with courage' – a sweet P'dayta – a clam.

As for Aunt Agnes, she is one of those very reliable, solid, affectionate, dull wives and mothers who are so profitable and comfortable to their own menfolk, but not very interesting to anyone else: a walking justification for that mixture of Northern respect and Oriental suppression which is the essentially P'daytesque answer to the female sex – and not a bad answer either. While hunting for a definition to fit Uncle Dick my mind threw up a phrase, I think, of yours 'a *new* P'dayta'. Do you remember who you coined it for?

And talking of memory ('dear me, it's a funny thing the way the human mind works') I can tell you about Pongee.[52] We did get it from print, but not from the book about Tibet. A person called the 'Crown Prince of Pongee' was referred to in a children's story in a magazine long ago, and the word passed into our stock much as 'Lord Bugabu' passed into it from the P'dayta conversation – you remember of course that Bugabu is a name for a lord whenever the O.A.B. is in his democratic mood. Could anyone say whether he hates or loves a lord most? (Did I tell you his good remark when I was last at home, and had told him that Lord Chelmsford[53] was a possible new President of Magdalen, and he observed 'Ah he wouldn't be a suitable man' – admitting a little later that he confessed he didn't know *who* this fellow Chelmsford might be. But that of course was done with an air which made it an additional argument against Chelmsford.)

It was odd your mentioning Dr Thorne, as I had just re-read the book. He, you remember, 'hated a lord and would have died in defence of the House of Lords.'[54] What do you think of Thorne as a character? I felt he would have been nicer if the author hadn't been so determined to make him so nice. He's just a little bit too manly with his basins of tea and his suppressed emotions. I am afraid, brother, he gulped. As in the

52 Pongee is a place in the geography of Animal-Land or Boxen. See 'History of Animal-Land' in *Boxen*, op. cit., p. 43.

53 Viscount Chelmsford, or Frederick John Napier Thesiger (1868–1933) had been educated at Winchester College and Magdalen College. He was trained in jurisprudence and was Viceroy of India 1916–21, and First Lord of the Admiralty in 1924. In 1929 he was re-elected a Fellow of All Souls, Oxford.

54 Trollope, *Doctor Thorne*, ch. III: 'It is hardly too much to say that he naturally hated a lord at first sight; but, nevertheless, he would have expended his means, his blood, and spirit, in fighting for the upper house of Parliament.'

only extant chapter of your father's public school novel 'A swallowing sound was heard'. But this is really rather rot I suppose, and all books need an allowance for the emotional code of their times. Yes – the dinner given by the Duke of Omnium is almost incredible and suggests Roman society more than anything else. I am so ignorant that for all I know things may be very much the same still. If you or I became celebrities of some sort and were asked to a crush at some great house tomorrow, I wonder how exactly we would be treated?

At any rate, after reading Jane Austen, Trollope, and Thackeray a man must give up the pleasure of talking about the coarse snobberies of the nouveaux riches. *All* the evidence shows that as far as that goes, the aristocracy was not a bit better than the plutocracy which has replaced it. They may have differed in other ways: but for downright crudity in throwing their weight about, can one really see a pin to choose between the modern millionaire and say Lady de Bourgh, the de Courcys, Lord Chesterfield?[55] I know that we are told that they did all with the grace of unconsciousness, but it doesn't sound at all as if they did.

I am glad you like the Lives of the Poets.[56] There is no subject on which more nonsense has been talked than the style of Johnson. For me his best sentences in writing have the same feeling as his best conversation – 'pop! it was so sudden'. I don't know anyone who can settle a thing so well in half a dozen words. I have read a good deal of the Rambler[57] last term, which is supposed to be more Johnsonian than the Lives. But he does the dagger business – or no, it's more like a mace, but a mace properly used is not a cumbersome weapon – what is there clumsy about choosing an infinitesimal point of time in which quietly to break a man's head with a perfectly directed tap of a sledge hammer? – he does it again and again.

You know that the Rambler is a mass of moral platitudes – and infuriates the French critics who say that they haven't come to their time of life to be told that life is short and that wasted time can never be recovered. Johnson, anticipating that kind of objection, simply remarks

55 Lady Catherine de Bourgh is a character in *Pride and Prejudice*; the De Courcy family are characters in *Doctor Thorne*; Lord Chesterfield (1694–1773) was a distinguished statesman who is remembered in connection with Dr Johnson's *Dictionary*.

56 Johnson, *Lives of the English Poets*, 3 vols., ed. George Birkbeck Hill (1905).

57 *The Rambler* was a twice-weekly periodical in 208 numbers issued by Dr Johnson between 20 March 1750 and 14 March 1752.

'People more frequently require to be reminded, than to be instructed'.[58] What more is there to say? or again 'The natural process of the mind is not from enjoyment to enjoyment but from hope to hope'.[59] That would be a page of whining and snivelling in Thackery – ah, which of us, dear reader, has his hearts desire etc., etc.

Better still, this on marriage: 'Marriage is not otherwise unhappy than as life is unhappy.'[60] I can't say that would be a whole novel with the moderns because the whole novel would not get as far as that. The author would make a great fuss about how Pamela got on Alan's nerves and how in the end they decided that life was a failure, and would be praised for his fearless criticism of the institution of marriage, without ever getting one glimpse of the fact that he was merely describing the *general* irritatingness of daily life, as it happens in the case of married people. Johnson just knocks a whole silly literature aside. He has been through all that (Ibsen and Wells and such) before it was written. But the Lives are the best – specially Savage, Dryden and Pope. I can imagine that the atmosphere, the Englishness, is specially delightful to you in 'furrin parts'. To me, the queerest thing about Johnson is that he is by no means an enthusiastic critic and yet he always makes me want to read the people he talks of even when I know that I shall dislike them.

I remember your precious account of Wei-Hei-Wei and rather envy you. Except for my twenty one days Field Punishment[61] we shan't be able to manage a holiday this year, and we are having one of our rare really hot summers – when a lane by a brickyard is not to be thought of – the first since that terrific one when you were in Sierra Leone. Its first sweets are long over. The flowers wither on their stalks in the garden, the pea pods are shriveled and yellow, the soil is mere dust, red roses are bleached white, and white are also brown. There is no dew either morning or evening. Wasps are very plentiful and to go for a walk is to make yourself the leader of a column of flies. In fact it is rich man's weather, pleasant only on a sea shore with flannels and long long drinks.

---

58 *The Rambler*, No. 2, 'On Looking into Futurity': 'Men more frequently require to be reminded than informed.'

59 ibid., No. 2: 'The natural flights of the human mind are not from pleasure to pleasure, but from hope to hope.'

60 ibid., No. 45, 'Causes of Marital Disagreement': 'Marriage is not commonly unhappy, otherwise than as life is unhappy.'

61 He means the three weeks he was to spend at Little Lea from mid-August until the second week in September.

I must allow that earlier in the year – just before term began – I had a delightful week end at a farm house in the Forest of Dean. As you know, I have walked in those parts before, but never stayed there. It is, I think, the most glorious *inland* place I know. Imagine two clumps of forest, one about the size of Island Magee, the other about the size of a quadrilateral whose corners are St Marks, Holywood, Helen's Tower and Canadian Villas. Both occupy very hilly, almost mountainous ground, and are divided by a couple of miles of fields. The smaller one is cut by the deep gorge of the Wye, a broad, brown, rattling river with islands in it. Though they are quickly being destroyed as forests – for the Crown fells far more quickly than it replants and indeed is quite a wanton forester – they are still almost untouched by trippers, and excellently solitary: almost uncannily so on an all day walk if one gets into the fir districts where birds don't sing and happens to be for a moment out of the sound of a stream (Mr Papworth by the way decided at once that the whole forest was a dangerous place, and always kept close to heel). Here and there in the wood you come on a little old farm house with a few acres of clearing, surrounded by a hedge and approached by a road so desolate that it is hardly different from the green 'rides' that pierce the wood in every direction. In these 'islands' of farms – in one of which we stayed – there is the most comfortable sense of being tucked away miles deep from the world, of being snugged down in a blanket, of having found a lee shore. We lived in a world of country butter and fresh eggs and boiled fowl, of early hours and hens lazily squawking (*not* crowing, just making that long drawling sound that they make). The nights were noisy with the sounds that keep no right thinking man awake – owls, a very good nightingale, and once the barking of a fox. 'A pleasant land of drowsyhead it was...'[62] But as a matter of fact it isn't the drowsiness that really counts, its the sense of being 'well away' – of having avoided the 'Crewe Train'.[63]

I read that admirable book some months ago and instantly thought of you. There are two passages in it which I shall always remember. (A) When the mother in law explains to the heroine that 'doing out a room' means taking all the furniture out and then putting it back again, and

62 Thomson, *The Castle of Indolence*, I, 6: 'A pleasing land of drowsyhead it was.'

63 Rose Macaulay, *Crewe Train* (1926). The book is dedicated to 'The Philistines, the Barbarians, the Unsociable, and those who do not care to take any trouble'.

she (i.e. the heroine) 'could not help wondering whether the same end might not be attained by leaving it where it was.'[64] (B) When she tells her husband that she thinks she is going to have a child, and keeps on saying 'Of course it may pass off' until he exclaims in exasperation 'I wish you wouldn't talk about it as if it were the measles.'[65] Another admirable passage is the first review of his novel. Have you noticed that in almost every one of Rose Macaulay's novels there is a character something like this – a person who just lives in some private world of her own (it is always a woman in these novels) and lets the whole life of the other characters slip by, anxious only not to be forced into adult, practical, moral, or immoral, social, or economic life? In *Orphan Island* there is the girl who is interested only in islands: in *Potterism* the girl who is always going away to see battleships launched and pretending to be a naval officer: and in the *Lee Shore* the same thing, treated more seriously and perhaps less sincerely, is the whole theme.

The *Crewe Train* goes far to answer that old question in natural philosophy whether there can be in nature such a thing as a female PB.[66] I take it the heroine is one: and so, in a less degree, the corresponding characters in the other books. Of course in Rose Macaulay they all have – and they are the *only* characters in the books who do have – a touch of poetry about them: an earthy poetry like that of Caliban: hence Denham's cave, and the other girl's islands. And perhaps that is foreign to the true nature of PBism. I am not absolutely certain about this, for there may be a kind of poetry about a brewing outfit. But I think not. The great ideal projection of PBism in Boxen is a world which has almost every charm *except* that of poetry. The only character who ever showed the slightest trace of an aesthetic side was Polonius Green,[67] who did enjoy the opera. I wonder how we could define the genuine PB spirit. *Idleness* won't do: any fool can be idle. Perhaps 'idleness raised to the dignity of a principle and pursued by at least two idlers in common, with the zest of a conspiracy'. I am sure there must be an element of conspiracy, of making common cause against a stubbornly un-idle world: and that, in its turn, necessitates at least two. *Quaere* in a perfectly idle world

64 ibid., pt. III, ch. VI, p. 298 (slightly misquoted).

65 ibid., pt. II, ch. VIII, pp. 155–6 (slightly misquoted).

66 i.e. a female piggiebottom. See note 1 to letter of 8 January 1917.

67 'Ah it's cod,' said Macgoullah despairing the opera in 'The Locked Door' (*Boxen*, op. cit., p. 80). '"Cod!?" cried the musical Green aghast, "I'd like to see you write it!"'

could there be such a thing as a Pigiebotie? Must he not be a pilgrim flying from the City of Industry, a brand snatched from the fire of Energy? A door bolted on the inside against a crowd of Bernetto-Desmonds who would fain get in, not to share but to shatter what is inside, seems to be essential. Again, a Pigiebotie must be *conscious* of idling and approve of it. He must not merely like to sit still, but he must also like to think of himself sitting still, or even like to think of himself *liking* to sit still. He must be rewarded by the pleasures of a good conscience which applauds his own immobility. He must say 'A-h-h-h' not only with his lips, but in spirit. He is the only true 'Quietist'. He sitteth down like a giant and rejoiceth *not* to run his course. He eateth all things, neglecteth all things, moveth not himself, is not waked up.[68] Observe – no man is really a Pigiebotie when tired. Aching limbs and unconquerable yawns sink us all into a common mass: Burnetto-Desmonds and Pigibudda snore together. There is no merit in lying down when you can't stand up. The Pigiebotie slumber must come not by merit but by grace. It is, brother, a Mystery of Inactivity.

You know the only real disadvantage of poetry as against negus – since you make the comparison – is that there's less of it. It sounds astonishing but English poetry is one of the things that you can come to the end of. I don't mean of course that I shall ever have read everything worth reading that was ever said in verse in the English language. But I do mean that there is no longer any chance of discovering a new long poem in English which will turn out to be just what I want and which can be added to the Faerie Queene, The Prelude, Paradise Lost, The Ring and the Book, the Earthly Paradise, and a few others – because they aren't any more. I mean, in the case of poems one hasn't read, one knows now pretty well what they're like, and knows too that tho' they may be worth reading, they will not become part of ones permanent stock. In that sense I have come to the end of English poetry – as you may be said to have come to the end of a wood, not where you have actually walked every inch of it, but when you have walked about in it enough to know where all the boundaries are and to feel the end near even when you can't see it: when there is no longer any hope (as there was for the first few days) that the next turn of the path might bring you to an

68 A play on 1 Corinthians 13:7, in which Charity 'beareth all things, believeth all things, hopeth all things, endureth all things'.

unsuspected lake or cave or clearing on the edge of a new valley – when it can no longer conceal anything.

This reminds me by the way – I'm afraid I must be a P'dayta, for I made a P'daytism the other day: I began talking about the world and how it was well explored by now and, said I 'We know there are no undiscovered islands'. It was left for Maureen to point out the absurdity.

Well, as the Tommies say, 'no more now' (and by the way, *all* the writers of the Paston letters[69] – XV Century you know – end up just in the same way). I go to Ireland at the end of the week. I think the Everyman volume of Fletcher[70] is the best form for you to read the Faithful Shepherdess in, and will have it sent. I don't think you can get Chatterton in any cheap edition but I will make enquiries. I shan't go more than 10/- without further instructions. They are mostly bosh to my mind.

yrs,
Jack

TO HIS FATHER (LP X: 94–6):

[Magdalen College
3 November 1928]
Saturday.

My dear Papy,

Thank heavens our electioneering troubles are nearly over. This day fortnight we shall all be locked into chapel like so many Cardinals and proceed to make a President and then goodbye to the endless talk and agreements and disagreements and personalities that I have lived in since term began. A subject of this sort hanging in the air manifests itself chiefly by a plethora of informal meetings which naturally spring up on those few hours and days when the ordinary routine has left one a little freedom. As I have anyway a rather heavy time table this term – chiefly, alas, those philosophy pupils whom I share with Weldon and whom he regards as his if they turn out well and mine if they turn out ill – I am now heartily sick of the whole business.

At the same time I have added to my occupations in other and I hope more hopeful ways. Two or three of us who are agreed as to what a

69 This is a collection of letters preserved by three generations of the Paston family of Norfolk, written between c. 1420 and 1504.

70 Francis Beaumont and John Fletcher, *Select Plays*, with an Introduction by G.P. Baker, Everyman's Library (1911).

College ought to be, have been endeavouring to stimulate the undergraduates into forming some sort of literary society. In any other Colleges the idea that undergraduates should require, or endure, stimulus in that direction from the dons, would be laughable. But this is a very curious place. All College societies whatever were forbidden early in the reign of the late President – an act which was then necessitated by the savagely exclusive clubs of rich dipsomaniacs which really dominated the whole life of the place. This prohibition succeeded in producing decency, but at the cost of all intellectual life. When I came I found that any Magdalen undergraduate who had interests beyond rowing, drinking, motoring and fornication, sought his friends outside the College, and indeed kept out of the place as much as he could. They certainly seldom discovered one another, and never collaborated so as to resist the prevailing tone. This is what we wish to remedy: but it had to be done with endless delicacy, which means, as you know, endless waste of time.

First of all we had to make sure that our colleagues would agree to the relaxation of the rule against societies. Then we had to pick our men amongst the undergraduates very carefully. Luckily I had been endeavouring already for a term or two to get a few intelligent men to meet one another in my rooms under the pretext of play reading or what not, and that gave us a lead. Then we had to try to push those chosen men v. gently so that the scheme should not appear too obviously to be managed by the dons. At present we are at the stage of holding a preparatory meeting 'at which to discuss the foundation of a society' next Monday – so the whole show may yet be a dismal failure.[71] I hope not: for I am quite sure that this College will never be anything more than a country club for all the idlest 'bloods' of Eton and Charterhouse as long as undergraduates retain the schoolboy's idea that it would be bad form to discuss among themselves the sort of subjects on which they write essays for their tutors. Ours at present are all absolute babies and terrific men of the world – the two characters I think nearly always go together. Old hearts and young heads, as Henry James says: the cynicism of forty and the mental crudeness and confusion of fourteen.

I sometimes wonder if this country will kill the public schools before they kill it. My experience goes on confirming the ideas about them

71 This society, named the Michaelmas Club, was founded by Lewis and his Magdalen colleague, Kenneth Bruce McFarlane (1903–66), a distinguished medieval historian who was Tutor in Modern History.

which were first suggested to me by Malvern long ago. The best scholars, the best men, and (properly understood) the best gentlemen, seem now to come from places like Dulwich, or to be wafted up on country scholarships from secondary schools. Except for pure classics (and that only at Winchester, and only a few boys even there) I really don't know what gifts the public schools bestow on their nurslings, beyond the mere surface of good manners: unless contempt of the things of the intellect, extravagance, insolence, self-sufficiency, and sexual perversion are to be called gifts.

Arthur came and went and I think enjoyed his visit. He was a little alarmed at the idea of rising at 7.30, but did not mind it when it came to the point – indeed decided that a long morning was so valuable that he wd. stick to 7.30 rising when he got back to Bernagh. Good resolutions! I piloted him away from unsuitable people and those whom he met he got on with admirably. It was very pleasant to have him – but I could not help reflecting on another guest who has a nearer claim on my best arm chair and reading lamp and whose visit has been already very long delayed. But it needs Uncle Dick to talk to you on a subject like that!

The first chapter of my book is finished and typed and the only two people who have seen it approve. The unfortunate thing is that nobody in Oxford really knows anything about the subject I have chosen. I may have made some elementary blunder which the French people – who have so far mainly studied the matter – would pounce on in a moment.[72] However, my translation of some Old French into contemporary English

72 In the letter to his father of 10 July Jack had mentioned the 'mediaeval idea of love' he was writing about in *The Allegory of Love*. The technical name for this idea is 'courtly love', and the definition which Lewis provides in the first chapter of his book will help the reader understand it. 'Everyone has heard of courtly love, and every one knows that it appears quite suddenly at the end of the eleventh century in Languedoc...The sentiment, of course, is love, but love of a highly specialized sort, whose characteristics may be enumerated as Humility, Courtesy, Adultery, and the Religion of Love. The lover is always abject. Obedience to his lady's slightest wish, however whimsical, and the silent acquiescence in her rebukes, however unjust, are the only virtues he dares to claim. There is a service of love closely modelled on the service which a feudal vassal owes to his lord...The whole attitude has been rightly described as a "feudalization of love".'

(forgery is great fun)[73] has passed Onions[74] who knows more than anyone else about the English of that period.

I am afraid this has been an egotistical letter. But it is dull work asking questions which you can't (at any rate for the moment) give a reply to. You do not need to be told that I hope you are keeping fairly well and that I shall be glad to hear if this is the case. For myself – if you came into the room now you would certainly say that I had a cold and that my hair needed cutting: what is more remarkable: you would (this time) be right in both judgements.

your loving son,
Jack

Mr Lewis had been following the presidential election at Magdalen College with great interest, and when he opened The Times *on 19 November he learned that Magdalen had elected Professor George Gordon. He remembered that Gordon had supported Jack for his election to a Fellowship (see letter to A.J. Lewis of 26 May 1925), and when he wrote to Jack on 25 November he said: 'I hope his election is acceptable to you. I am heartily glad the thing is over' (LP X: 96). Jack replied with this brief but clear account of the whole process.*

TO HIS FATHER (LP X: 97):

Magdalen
[27? November 1928]

My dear Papy,

Many thanks for your letter and kind offer. I think I shall take the liberty of rolling Christmas and birthday into one and get myself another picture.

---

73 What, in the end, Lewis attempted was much harder than translating Old French into modern English. He was translating into what he hoped would pass as Middle English for he felt this would carry the 'flavour' of the period more nearly. His translations are considered one of the great successes of his book.

74 Charles Talbut Onions (1873–1965) was a distinguished lexicographer and grammarian. He joined the staff of the Oxford English Dictionary in 1895. He was appointed a Fellow of Magdalen College in 1923 and was a lecturer in English at Oxford 1920–27 and Reader in English Philology 1927–49.

I am not dissatisfied with the election. The history of the thing was this. *Stage 1. Hogarth* put forward with almost universal approval. Hogarth dies. *Stage 2. Chelmsford* put forward by all the Winchester interest and *Craig*[75] put forward by Weldon and his friends – to be their puppet. *Stage 3. Benecke* put forward by party including myself who dislike both *Chelmsford* and *Craig. Stage 4.* Absolute determination of the *Craig*-ites not to have *Chelmsford* – absolute determination of the *Beneck*-ites not to have *Chelmsford* or *Craig. Stage 5. Benecke* leading by a long way. *Stage 6.* Proposal of *Gordon.* Satisfies *Craig*-ites as being at any rate better than *Chelmsford*: satisfies *Beneck*-ites as better than *Chelmsford* or *Craig. Stage 7. Benecke* v. *Gordon. Stage 8.* No clear majority for Benecke possible. Fear of letting in *Chelmsford* if the *Craig*-ites and *Beneck*-ites quarrel about *Benecke* and *Gordon. Stage 9.* Agreement of the two parties on *Gordon*, which then outvotes the remnant of the *Chelmsford* and *Craig* people. So, as you say, it is more or less of a compromise.

I hope to come down on Friday next (i.e. crossing Friday night) and shall have to leave home on 5th January.

your loving son,
Jack

75 Edwin Stewart Craig (1865–1939) was a demonstrator in the electrical laboratory of the University of Oxford 1905–13 and a Fellow of Magdalen 1918–30. See Lewis's 'portrait' of him in the Magdalen College Appendix, *AMR*, pp. 476–7.

1929

TO HIS FATHER (LP X: 100–1):

Magdalen.
Sunday.[3 February 1929]

My dear Papy,

What an unhappy career this group photograph has had! Before visiting the shop again I should be glad to know more exactly what condition it was in when it arrived and whether I am justified in making a fuss about it.

As I expected, my return to England plunged me into a winter compared with which our little cold snap at home was positively balmy. The fields were covered with snow all the way on my train journey south, there has been some skating, indoor temperatures in rooms without fires have fallen below freezing point, and I have woken more than once to find a tumbler partially full of ice on the table beside my bed. In fact – to make a confession – I have so far bowed to the rigours of the season as to start using a hot water bottle, a luxury which I had hitherto regarded as an indulgence for holiday times at Leeborough. I told Hatton[1] apologetically that I thought it was the beginning of middle age: to which he replied 'Oh don't say that sir' in the same voice of unconvincing gravity with which he might have made the same answer if I had said I thought I was getting delirium tremens. Can you remember the first occasion on which you habitually had about you a servant younger than yourself? It gives one a feeling of antiquity I find, because servants, from the early days when one watched them at work in the kitchen, have always belonged so essentially to the grown up world.

I look in vain for any item of news fit to be extracted from the uneventful routine. Let me see. Brightman – your friend Toys – has had

1 W.K. Hatton, who joined the staff of Magdalen College in 1923, was Lewis's 'scout' or college servant.

influenza but has happily got over it. The new President and his family have not yet moved into the Lodgings, where the work of putting in bathrooms which is now going forwards, throws a new light on the venerable domestic economy of the previous regime.

My current lecture (on Elyot,[2] Ascham,[3] Hooker[4] and Bacon[5]) has attracted as a distinguished member of its audience the Mother Superior of the local hostel for papish undergraduettes – I suppose because I fired off by an attack on Calvin. If you hear indirectly that the Church of Rome is hoping for a distinguished convert among the young Oxford dons you will know how to interpret it.

---

2 Sir Thomas Elyot (c. 1490–1546) is the author of the *Boke of the Governour* (1541), a treatise on education and politics which displays the particular influence of the classics and Plato in particular. It illustrates as well the evolution of English prose. As a result of it Elyot was appointed ambassador to Charles V. His other works include *The Image of Governance* (1540) and *The Castel of Helth* (c. 1536). His translations did much to popularize the classics in England. Lewis's fullest treatment of Elyot is found in bk. II, ch. 3 of *English Literature in the Sixteenth Century* (1954), where he says 'Elyot is a well informed man, not a scholar; a sensible man (for the most part), not a deep thinker. As a stylist he has perhaps higher claims.'

3 Roger Ascham (1515/16–68) distinguished himself at St John's College, Cambridge, and became the college reader in Greek in 1540. His *Toxophilus* (1545) is a delightful treatise on archery. It is set in the form of a dialogue between Toxophilus (lover of shooting) and Philologus (lover of books). In 1554 he became Latin secretary to Queen Mary, but he was allowed to continue being a Protestant. In his last years he wrote *The Scholemaster* (1570), of great value to education, which was published posthumously. Lewis's fullest treatment of him is in *English Literature in the Sixteenth Century*, bk. II, ch. 3, where he says Ascham 'is everyone's friend...His delightful, and delighted, temperament has flowed into his writing.'

4 Richard Hooker (?1554–1600), theologian, was a Fellow of Hebrew at Corpus Christi College, Oxford, 1577–84. He was the greatest of all apologists of the Elizabethan Settlement of 1539, and the finest advocate that Anglicanism has ever had. He developed his doctrines in his massive treatise, *The Laws of Ecclesiastical Polity* (1593, 1597). Lewis delighted in Hooker, and wrote at length about him in *English Literature in the Sixteenth Century*, bk. III, ch. 2, where he speaks of the *Polity* as a 'work of prudence, of art, of moral virtue, and...of Grace'.

5 Francis Bacon (1561–1626), a barrister, was elected to Parliament in 1584. He became Lord Chancellor in 1618. His writings are of various kinds. His best-known works are *The Advancement of Learning* (1605) and *Essays* (1597). Writing about Bacon's *Essays* in *English Literature in the Sixteenth Century*, Epilogue: New Tendencies, Lewis said: 'If Bacon took his title from Montaigne, he took nothing else. His earliest essays resemble essays by Montaigne about as much as a metallic-looking cactus raised on the edge of the desert resembles a whole country-side of forest, filled with light and shade, well stocked with game, and hard to get out of.'

The undergraduates have just brought off a good rag by getting a copy of the university seal and circularizing all the garages in Oxford with a notice purporting to come from the Vice Chancellor and Proctors and rescinding an order made last term by which all these places were compelled to shut for undergraduate use at eleven. Unfortunately this excellent joke was disclosed before it had had any time to run its course.

Oh – I had nearly forgotten my exploits as a printer. I am attending a lecture for postgraduates on Bibliography this term, and we were all taken to the Clarendon Press last Thursday to examine a hand press, to set up our own names, and to print them on a broadsheet. The episode was rendered more amusing by the fact that J.A. happened to meet me on my way to the Press and insisted on attaching himself to the party, greatly to the surprise of the instructor, who, I could see, all the time was trying to puzzle out who or what he was. The venerable philosopher delayed us by asking the printers a number of questions, none of which they could understand and lecturing them in return on a variety of subjects from cookery to bookbinding, and ended up by printing his own name upside down – which however we corrected in proof, so it does not appear in the enclose 'lelult'. I hope you notice the grace and feeling – the creative touch – of my own rendition of our name!

Well, as I say, I have nothing to say, and this is only a word of chat, 'hoping it finds you as it leaves me' – or rather not, as I have a vile cold. I hope you are keeping tolerably well.

your loving son,
Jack.

P.S. I find I have been carrying this in my pocket for a day or so. This however gives me the chance of opening it again to insert two things which I had forgotten.

(1) Two of my reviews from the Oxford Magazine.[6]

6 The first of these items was Lewis's review (unsigned) of Evelyn Waugh's *Rossetti: His Life and Works* which appeared in *The Oxford Magazine*, XLVII (25 October 1928), pp. 66, 69. The second was a review of Hugh Kingsmill's *Matthew Arnold* in *The Oxford Magazine*, XLVII (15 November 1928), p. 177, signed 'C.S.L.'

(2) My best thanks for my birthday picture which is both beautiful in itself and suited to its place, so that it makes a great change in my room. It has been much admired.

J.

TO ARTHUR GREEVES (W):

[Magdalen College
March 1929]

My dear Arthur

I am very sorry your message has been so long delayed. If you remember my way of life, you will know that I am kept in by pupils all morning, that I then have to go out to Headington, that I then return to pupils again after tea – after which the shops are shut. It really is with the greatest difficulty that I ever get free in the streets of Oxford to visit shops. I ought, I confess, to have *made* the occasion, but I want to plead in my defence that it is not, as you, forgetting, probably suppose, a question of just walking out any old day and doing it. Term ends soon (don't say so at Leeboro) and I will really try to get it done.

I admit freely that I was in the wrong and apologise. I wish you could avoid writing things like <'Am I so soon forgotten.'> You had a right to be annoyed: but you certainly did not really think that my failure to do an errand for you betokened any change in a friendship that has now lasted the greater part of our lives: and if you had thought so, this was hardly a manly or a sensible way of opening the subject <(If I had left the letter lying about anyone wd. have supposed it was from a girl whom I had deserted and who was just going to have a baby!)> I am sorry to have inconvenienced you, but hope the matter is not mortal.

Yrs

Jack.

TO HIS BROTHER (LP X: 118–23):[7]

[Hillsboro]
Postmark: 13 April 1929

My dear W.,

I am ashamed of my long idleness, though indeed the gap between my last and your last was almost as long as the gap between your last and this. I must admit too, that I am moved to write at this moment by the selfish consideration that I heard last night a thing which you of all people ought to hear – you know how one classifies jokes according to the people one wants to tell them to – and am therefore uneasy till I have unloaded it.

The other night an undergraduate, presumably drunk, at dinner in the George covered the face of his neighbour with potatoes, his neighbour being a total stranger. Whether this means simply that he flung the contents of the potato dish at him or (as I prefer to think) that he seized him firmly by the short hairs and systematically lathered him with warm mash, my informant could not say. But that is not the point of the story. The point is, that being haled before the Proctors and asked why he had done so, the culprit, very gravely and with many expressions of regret, pleaded in so many words 'I couldn't think of anything else to do!'

I am sure you will share my delight at this transference of the outrage from the class of *positive* to that of *negative* faults: as though it proceeds entirely from a failure of the inventive faculty or a mere poverty of the imagination. One ought to be careful of sitting near one of these *unimaginative* men. The novel idea can be worked equally well from either end: whether one thinks of the mohawk bashing your hat over your eyes with the words 'Sorry old chap, I know its a bit hackneyed, but I can't think of anything better' – or of some elderly P'dayta exclaiming testily 'Ah what all these young men lack now-a-days is initiative' as he springs into the air from the hindward pressure of a pin.

With *the* P'daytabird I had quite a good three weeks at Christmas. The arrangement about the jumping jack at your sole charges (for I accepted your offer and you will have had the account by now) had this

7 Writing to his father on 11 February 1929 Warnie said, 'Unless something very unexpected happens, I should leave Shanghai early in November and will be with you shortly after Christmas. This means that I shall complete a foreign tour with a total of two years and say eight months abroad' (LP X: 103–4).

inconvenience, which we should have foreseen, that no effort on my part seemed to make him understand that the present was from you as well as from me. If you have said nothing implying responsibility in any of your letters, I am afraid you have had no credit: if you *have*, I must by now (with shoulder shrugs and upward jerks of the head) stand suspected of 'a very shabby business'. I hope, by the way, that besides getting the bill for the jumping jacks, you have also got Chatterton[8] and The Faithfull Shepherdess.[9] Of the former, as you know, I have a very poor opinion – the dirge 'Sing unto my roundelay' being to my mind the only item in his tremendous fake which has real merit. But the Faithfull Shepherdess I love. Ones pupils, trained in 'just opinions' tell one it is artificial: not that the criticism would worry you with your penchant for Versailles shepherds and shepherdesses. But what is the really interesting thing about it is the way it manages to keep the homely L'allegro-and-Il Penseroso-[10] English-village-and-country feeling going along with the pastoral conventions. The priest of Pan is exactly like a country parson.

By the by, I thoroughly agree with you about Scott: in fact I think that even his most fanatical admirers have 'given up' his heroines (with the exception of Die Vernon and Jeanie Deans)[11] and his love scenes. But then one gives that up in all XIX Century novels: certainly in Dickens and Thackeray. And when you have ruled that out, what remains is pure delight. Isn't it nice to find a person who knows history almost entirely by tradition? History to Scott means *the stories remembered in the old families*, or sometimes the stories remembered by sects and villages. I should say he was almost the last person in modern Europe who did know it that way: and that, don't you think, is at the back of all his best work. Claverhouse,[12] say, was to Scott not 'a character' out of Macaulay (or Hume or Robertson) but the man about whom old Lady so and so tells one story and about whom some antediluvian local minister's father

8 Thomas Chatterton, *Poems*, ed. Sidney Lee, 2 vols. (1905).

9 See note 56 to letter of 6 March 1917.

10 John Milton, *L'Allegro* and *Il Penseroso* are companion poems published in 1645.

11 Die Vernon is the heroine of *Rob Roy*, and Jeanie Deans the heroine of *The Heart of Midlothian*.

12 John Graham of Claverhouse (?1649–89) was a royalist officer employed by the Scottish Privy Council in executing the severities of the government in Scotland during the reigns of Charles II and James II. He was determined to raise the Highlands for James, and was killed at the battle of Killiecrankie. He figures prominently in Scott's *Old Mortality*.

told another. Printed and documented history probably kills a lot of this traditional local history and what is finally left over is put in guide books (When nothing else can be said about an old church you can always say that Cromwell stabled his horses in it.)

Scott was only just in time to catch it still living. This (so historians tell me) has had one unforeseen result, that Scotch history has ever since been more neglected than that of any other civilized country: the tradition, once stamped by Scott's imagination, has so satisfied curiosity that science has hardly ventured to show its head. It is a pity that no one similarly caught the tradition in England – tho' probably there was less to catch.

I suppose the Scotch were a people unusually tenacious of old memories, as for example Mr Oldbuck. I am not sure that The Antiquary is not the best. Do you remember his efforts to get the hero to write an epic on the battle of ? in order to work in his excursus on castramentation?[13] On the other hand it has perhaps the worst heroine of all. Of heroines, there is something to be said for Julia Mannering ('Yes sir. And is my future friend red headed?' 'I am sure we all thank Mr. Sampson for the extraordinary countenance he has shown us'.) The beginning of Guy Mannering is excellent. What an admirable P'dayta the old Laird is: and what an admirable description of P'daytism the jumble of thoughts in his conversation. But of all the Scott characters I know, I give the palm to three above all the others – the Baron of Bredwardine, Cuddy Headrigg, and Baillie Mickle (sic) Jarvie.[14] I am very fond of Dandie Dinmont[15] too. By the way – it is very unfair – but did you too like me hate the name of Dandie Dinmont long before you knew who he was?

And that brings me to the very curious fact that nothing militates so much against Scott as his popularity in Scotland. The Scotch have a curious way of rendering wearisome to the outside world whatever they admire. I daresay Burns is quite a good poet – really: if only he could ever escape from the stench of that unmerciful haggis and the

13 Sir Walter Scott, *The Antiquary* (1816), vol. I, ch. 14. Lewis was referring to the battle of Mount Graupius between the Roman general, Agricola, and the Caledonians in 82 or 83 AD as recounted by Tacitus. Mr Oldbuck maintained that the battle took place on the site of his house, Kaim of Kinprunes (an imaginary name). Castramentation is the art of laying out a military camp.

14 The Baron of Bredwardine is a character in *Waverley*; Cuddie Headrigg a character in *Old Mortality*; and Bailie Nichol Jarvie a character in *Rob Roy*.

15 Dandie Dinmont is a character in *Guy Mannering*.

lugubrious jollities of *Auld Lang Syne*. What a world it opens upon – the 'kail yard' school – beside the bonny briar bush – Mansie Wauch.

I have just suddenly (as I write) seen what is the trouble about all this Scotchness. When you want to be typically English you pretend to be very hospitable and honest and hearty. When you want to be typically Irish you try to be very witty and dashing and fanciful. That is to say, the typical English or Irish mode consists in the assumption of certain qualities which are in themselves quite pleasant. But the typically Scotch consists not in being loud or quiet, or merry or sad, or in any recognizable quality, but just in being *Scotch*. You make roast beef the English dish because it is nice (or fairly nice), and the rose is a pleasant flower. But the haggis and the thistle never could have any merit beyond their sheer, unredeemed, monumental Scotchness. I notice that the nicest Scotch people claim to be Picts. This theory of Scotchness probably comes to me from some excellent remarks of Hazlitt's on respectability which I read in the summer. A good many people have tried to find out why respectability is contemptible, but I think only Hazlitt has got it right.[16] He points out that if you are describing a person, and there is any quality in him which is at all pleasing, you mention *that*. You say 'He is an amusing man' or 'He is a good shot' or even that 'He is very good looking'. It is only when there is nothing whatsoever to say in his favour that you come down to 'He is a very respectable man': i.e. the 'respectable' is that which we have agreed to respect although there is nothing respectable in it. ('Scotch' things similarly are those which even a Scot can find no reason for liking other than their Scotchness).

---

16 William Hazlitt, *The Plain Speaker: Opinions on Books, Men and Things* (1826), Essay XXXI 'On Respectable People': 'There is not any term that is oftener misapplied, or that is a stronger instance of the abuse of language, than this word *respectable*. By a *respectable* man is generally meant a person whom there is no reason for respecting, or none that we choose to name; for if there is any good reason for the opinion we wish to express, we naturally assign it as the ground of his respectability. If the person whom you are desirous to characterize favourably, is distinguished for his good nature, you say that he is a good-natured man; if by his zeal to serve his friends, you call him a friendly man, if by his wit or sense, you say that he is witty or sensible; if by his honesty or learning, you say so at once; but if he is none of these, and there is no one quality which you can bring forward to justify the high opinion you would be thought to entertain of him, you then take the question for granted, and jump at a conclusion, by observing gravely, that "he is a very respectable man." It is clear, indeed, that where we have any striking and generally admitted reasons for respecting a man, the most obvious way to ensure the respect of others, will be to mention his estimable qualities.'

What a very Conradian adventure with your engineer![17] As to have, you may be quite sure that some scotch people do say 'has' for 'hae' as the consequence of h*a*ve. The proper verb is 'have' as we pronounce it. H*a*ve is a lengthening of this which occurred originally in sentences where the emphasis fell on the word *have*, but afterwards became stereotyped in certain parts of the country and at certain periods. 'Have' and 'H*a*ve' are both good English in certain parts of the country and in [the] XVII Century: so that when Milton writes (Comus – the lady's song.)

> '*if thou have*
> *Hid them in thine airy cave.*'[18]

it is not, as we are apt to suppose, a bad rime: he probably pronounced it like that. H*a*ve lasted longer in Scotland than in England: but a whole nation, depend upon it Sir, does not carry about a word like *have* without often (i.e. in some districts) dropping the end and thus giving *hae* (hay).

As to the doctrine that to profess no philosophy is to *have* a bad philosophy, I am not conscious of having borrowed it from anywhere and could not tell where to look for it in a book, but of course I may have done. On the other hand the idea is one obvious enough to strike a good many people independently. Your engineer sounds a very typical Scotch philosopher, judged by his library. I would warn you that a 'Scotch philosopher' means something much more than a philosopher who happens also to be a Scotchman: almost as much more as a Welsh Rabbit or

---

17 In his letter of 23 October 1928 Warnie wrote of a sea voyage to Hong Kong. 'The most interesting person on board,' he said, 'was the Chief Engineer who was a character straight out of Kipling – such a man as I had always believed never existed outside novels...I first came across him one night after dinner when a few of us collected in the saloon for a mouthful of the port, and McAndrew's Hymn being mentioned, he expressed his warmest approval of it...This and some more chat led to an invitation to adjourn to his room and inspect "ma buiks". It was a severe shock after a discussion on Kipling to arrive at his room and come bolt under a withering collection of philosophy – Spencer, Comte, and similar books. I had to mumble something about having no philosophy, which was met with "When ye say ye haaaave no pheelawsophy, Cap'n, ye only mean ye haaave a bad pheelawsophy." Is this remark a philosophical cliché or is it pure coincidence that you should have made exactly the same remark to me some years ago? By the way it is only apparently in funny stories that Scotchmen say "hae" for "have" – actually they say "haaaave" with a very broad vowel sound as I have tried to describe it above' (LP X: 92).

18 Milton, *Comus*, 237–8: 'Hid them in some flowery cave'.

a Prairie Oyster. The Scotch School represents all that is most negative, analytic, and dry: in fact what you think of all metaphysics is true of the Scotch type. Now I give you my word that when I started to write this I had no intention of talking about the Scotch at all: and yet my two attempts to break away from the subject have proved entire failures. Let us throw off the incubus – .

The P'daytabird was in pretty good form while I was at home. The P'daita crop was poor. The only goodish one was as follows. 'Lord Hugh Cecil is a fine chap. You know he took a very moderate line over the prayer book: he didn't object to this reservation business – '[19] (I'm sorry but now that I come to write it down I find that I have forgotten the ins-and-outs of this one, and after some attempt to puzzle it out, I think I had better give it up. This looks as if it were deliberately done to tantalise you, but it isn't.)

I think you asked in your last letter whether Uncle Dick perpetrated genuine P'daitisms. I must confess that during our rather short time together I did not succeed in collecting a single unambiguous example. The nearest he got to it was his complete indifference to the remoter consequences of his own views, as I described before: but I am afraid that hardly amounts to P'daitism. In a way it would be disappointing if we found that our own P'daita was the only perfect specimen in the family. I have just seen that that leaves open to you a very silly and obvious retort.

I had a glorious day of walking in Antrim with Arthur while I was at home. We reached the top of Glengariff by car at about 11 o'clock, and walked till dark, not in the glens, but on the moors above the northern wall of the valley. There was hoar frost on the heather and ice on most of

19 During 1927–28 Lord Hugh Cecil (1869–1956) was active in the Church Assembly which brought forth the Revised Prayer Book of 1928. It was, greatly to his disappointment, rejected by the House of Commons. One of their reasons for rejecting the 1928 Prayer Book was its recommendation of 'Reservation', the practice of keeping the consecrated Host enshrined in a tabernacle for the purpose of Holy Communion and for communion of the sick. Jack Lewis later recalled what his father said about the matter, for he recorded the incident in 'Pudaita Pie' as follows: 'He remarked "Lord Hugh Cecil is a fine chap. Though he is a high churchman, he is a *sane* high churchman over this prayer book business." "Indeed," replied his interlocutor, "what line does he take?" – "Well, I confess I don't remember, but I expect you'd find it was very much what I take myself. You know, *I've* no objection to reservation." – "I see. But that would hardly prove his moderation as a high Churchman, for surely it was just the high Church party that wanted reservation?" "I can't quote you chapter and verse, but that's my impression of the man."' On the 1928 Book of Common Prayer see note 52 to the letter of 9 July 1927.

the streams, looking startlingly white wherever the peat water emerged at a break. The sun was trying to break through all day, but hardly succeeded further than to make clouds scatter and gleam and smoulder along the big peaks inland, with a series of wonderful apocalyptic end-of-the-world effects, or occasionally to send a watery gleam across the slopes. Up there it is more solitary than Exmoor, and I don't think I ever passed a day in grander desolation. We had a magnificent tea in what looked like a pigsty but was really a Post Office: seated one on each side of a wood fire (the only light in the room) and eating new soda bread under the directions of the post mistress who charged us 6d. each.

I often wonder, specially lately, whether you are right (if you still hold the opinion) in thinking Ireland the right country to live in, with all its drawbacks. Certainly the actual country appeals to me more every time I go home. In fact I am coming round by a long circuit to a position not unlike that of our Wynyard days: a different position, because I find more and more a something in almost every Irish scene which you can't get elsewhere, and which, though not better in itself, is better *for us*. I think 'roughness without severity' is the nearest one can get to it. It is grand and desolate and yet somehow one feels at home. We really must manage that Irish walking tour when we are next at Leeborough together. I amused myself while at home by working out an itinerary which of course I have since lost, and found that a reasonable walk could be arranged through Ballynahinch, Newcastle and Rostrevor. The first day would have to cover about twenty five miles, which is of course more than one wants: but it is better that a big journey shd. fall on the first than on the second day, and after that it panned out pretty well. As for your ridiculous contention that you will be out of condition when you arrive in England, I understand that there are admirable facilities for exercise on a modern liner, and what between dumb bells, the gymnasium, quoits, and deck tennis, you ought to arrive lean and bronzed.

Someone called A. Tilley has just published a book called The Decline of the Age of Louis XIV[20] (Cambridge University Press 25/-) which has been very well recieved, so you had better make a note of it. I have had a week in bed with 'flu since I began this letter, during which I re-read *The Antiquary*, *Sense and Sensibility*, and *Pickwick*. The latter I shall not read

20 Arthur Tilley, *The Decline of the Age of Louis XIV: or, French Literature 1687–1715* (1929).

again. I thought I had won my freedom of it last year, but a second reading brought back my old invincible distaste. The language and conception seem to me exactly those of the crudest comic passages in our own Boxoniana, and without the charm of old associations I can't swallow it.

My week in bed gave me the pleasure of emerging into a world quite different from the one I had left – all the hedges out, the daffodils under the trees, and birds singing. We have started keeping hens at Hillsboro who provide us with from three to four fresh eggs a day (that's rather a silly remark – they cd. hardly lay stale ones) and make the most beautifully rural and leisurely noises while one is lying between sleeping and waking in the morning. On Friday I set off on my annual walking tour: this time we start from Salisbury and hope to end up on the coast of Lyme Regis. I look forward to renewing my acquaintance with that cathedral; you remember our excellent Daudelspiel.[21]

I was much interested to hear of the new phase of your musical history. I, as you know, have long been a great admirer of Beethoven, though I probably know much less of him than you. I put him about on a level with Milton and in very much the same kind – taking Puccini to be the same as Swinburne, Mozart as Shelly, Verdi as Tom Moore. It is curious how one finds oneself all along the line coming to like the *drier* flavours as ones palate grows older – or rather, the really tip top people like Milton and Beethoven have the richness and sweetness *as well as* the staying power of the dry.

I find I am 'bringing in gabble' and had better make an end on't. Is it next Christmas that I may look to see you? You have been an infernal time away.

yrs,
Jack

TO ARTHUR GREEVES (W):

[Magdalen College
22 April 1929]

My dear Arthur,

I have had ten days in bed with flu', four days walking tour from

21 On 6–8 April 1925 Warnie and Jack had taken a trip on Warnie's 'Dawdle' or 'Daudel', a motorcycle with sidecar. They had gone to Salisbury during that 'Daudelspiel' or 'Daudel-play'.

Salisbury to Lyme Regis and a week with Minto and family in a Sussex farmhouse – of which items only the walking tour had better be communicated to the P'daitabird – but before all this I visited Blackwells and looked up their Lamb. After investigating such copies as I could lay my hands on (viz. two) in private and finding that neither of them contained the missing letters I consulted the man who thought they might have some second hand old sets in stock, but thought wrongly. I am sorry if it has been my dilatoriness that led to this negative result, but trust that even when you have learned by heart all the remaining letters (and, dear me, what a convenience that will be to *me*!) the lack of those ten will not drive you to desperation (Of course, perhaps, the most sensible thing would be for both of us to blow our brains out).

I am also, and more seriously sorry that I wrote you rather a snarky[22] letter when we last communicated, and tried to turn an apology into an accusation, which was a very unhandsome thing to do. I hope you will allow for end of term feeling and frayed nerves.

We arrived back from Sussex to day and travelled within a couple of miles of Bookham, all up the Dorking valley which I know so well. It very nearly made me weep, I got such a rich poignant whiff of memory from the old days – Phantastes, Bleheris, Dymer, Papillon, T. Edens Osborne all jumbled up. But as you know, one has the secret of these memories now and knows how to extract the spiritual sweet without falling into mere desire and regret.

While ill, I re-read both *Sense & Sensibility* and *The Antiquary* and most strongly advise you to read the latter again, and specially notice the effect of Elspeth in her earlier scenes.

Yrs
Jack

TO HIS FATHER (LP X: 125–6):

Magdalen.
Sunday.[19 May 1929]

My dear Papy,

I hope your recovery from the winter 'flu has been permanent. My own prolonged cold, having lasted out the term, worked up into a sore

22 Lewis Carroll, *The Hunting of the Snark* (1876), Fit IV, ll. 33–4: 'For the Snark's a peculiar creature, that won't / Be caught in a commonplace way'.

throat and temperature and a few days in bed about Easter time. This finally got rid of the trouble and was not unpleasant. It gave me the excuse to be idle and the chance to re-read some old favourites – including *The Antiquary*. Read the Antiquary. I think it contains the cream of Scott's humour and very nearly the cream of his tragedy.

I also re-read Pickwick, but this, as you know, I can hardly call an old favourite. Indeed I have only read it once before. This time I hoped I had at last got the secret and become a real convert: but my second reading has broken the spell, I am a relapsed heretic. It won't do. I like the Wellers, both father and son, and I like the trial: but Eatanswill and Mrs Leo Hunter and Bill Stumps, his Mark, seem to me laboured and artificial, and I can't forgive him for showing us poor Jingle in prison and repentance. The whole spirit in which we enjoy a comic rogue depends on leaving out the consideration of the consequences which his character would have in real life: bring that in, and every such character (say Falstaff) becomes tragic. To invite us to treat Jingle as a comic character and then spring the tragic side on us, is a mere act of bad faith. No doubt that is how Jingle wd. end in real life. But then in real life it would have been our fault if we had originally treated him as a comic character. In the book you are forced to do so and are therefore unjustly punished when the tragedy comes.

I had four days away from Oxford and spent them walking with my usual party – friends from my undergraduate days – from Salisbury to Lyme Regis. Luckily I need not describe Salisbury to you. It will be enough to say that I have now seen it three times and each time with increasing admiration. But I made the mistake of attending a week day evensong. (We assembled at Salisbury in the afternoon, starting our walk on the following morning.) There was no music, and the psalms were read. Four fat and spongy clergymen, two on each side, in a little week day chapel at the back of the main altar, scampered and simpered through the job in a way that really disgusted me. It is perhaps too much to expect any intense spiritual quality in the reading of men who have to do it every day (and yet why are they in the church if the thing means so little to them as that?). But I think one is entitled to expect the decency of clear and unaffected pronunciation and such a general appreciation of the mere literary qualities of the service as ought to belong to any educated men. I know I should be ashamed to read out a recipe as abominably as they read out the psalms. Then one looked round at the

Cathedral and the contrast between those who built it and those who now officiate in it was pretty steep.

Our walk was delightful but I can't sit down to describe all the pleasant villages and windy hills that we walked, or all the shady rookeries and old towns that we rested in: it is a wonderful country and we had wonderful talk and forgot our various professions and discontents and got through the serious arguments in the ten miles before lunch and came down to mere fooling and school-boy jokes as the shadows lengthened. I came back quite set up in body and mind.

I have done most of the second chapter of the book but can't get it ready for typing before the end of this term. You may have noticed that I have recently been enlightening the literary world through the correspondence columns of the Times Literary Supplement.[23] I missed the copy in which my letter appears, so I don't know whether the world shaking truths have been conveyed to the public with that accuracy – that *meticulous* accuracy – which they deserve. I am now waiting for a reply letter which will begin 'Your correspondant seems to be unaware...'

I have a capital story which is quite new to me. The hero is a certain Professor Alexander, a philosopher, at Leeds, but I have no doubt that the story is older than he. He is said to have entered a railway carriage with a large perforated cardboard box which he placed on his knees. The only other occupant was an inquisitive woman. She stood it as long as she could, and at last, having forced him into conversation and worked the talk round (you can fill in that part of the story yourself) ventured to ask him directly what was in the box. 'A mongoose madam.' The poor woman counted the telegraph posts going past for a while and again could bear her curiosity no further. 'And what are you going to do with the mongoose?' she asked. 'I am taking it to a friend who is unfortunately suffering from delirium tremens.' 'And what use will a mongoose be to him?' 'Why, Madam, as you know, the people who suffer from that disease find themselves surrounded with snakes: and of course a mongoose eats snakes.' 'Good Heavens!' cried the lady, 'but you don't mean

23 His letter on 'The Kingis Quair' appeared in *The Times Literary Supplement* (18 April 1929), p. 315. 'The Kingis Quair', which means 'The King's Book', is a poem of 379 lines of rhyme-royal used by King James I of Scotland while he was a prisoner in England and at about the time of his marriage to Lady Jane Beaufort. In his letter Lewis attempts to explain the connection between the 'apparently rambling' introduction and 'the poem which follows'.

that the snakes are real?' 'Oh dear me, no said the Professor with imperturbable gravity. 'But then *neither is the mongoose*!'

I hope this is not an old chestnut.

your loving son,

Jack

'Why are they in the church,' Lewis asked about the clergymen in Salisbury Cathedral, 'if the thing means so little to them as that?' This concern with sincerity is perhaps the first indication of a huge change in Lewis's spiritual life. For it was about this time – we don't know the exact date – that Lewis came to believe in God, though not yet in Christ. Speaking of his conversion to Theism, he said in Surprised by Joy:

> *You must picture me alone in that room in Magdalen, night after night, feeling, whenever my mind lifted even for a second from my work, the steady, unrelenting approach of Him whom I so earnestly desired not to meet. That which I greatly feared had at last come upon me. In the Trinity Term of 1929 I gave in, and admitted that God was God, and knelt and prayed: perhaps, that night, the most dejected and reluctant convert in all England. I did not then see what is now the most shining and obvious thing; the Divine humility which will accept a convert even on such terms. The Prodigal Son at least walked home on his own feet. But who can duly adore that Love which will open the high gates to a prodigal who is brought in kicking, struggling, resentful, and darting his eyes in every direction for a chance of escape? The words* compelle intrare,[24] *compel them to come in, have been so abused by wicked men that we shudder at them; but, properly understood, they plumb the depth of the Divine mercy. The hardness of God is kinder than the softness of men, and His compulsion is our liberation. (*SBJ *XIV)*

24 Luke 14:23 (Vulgate): 'Et aid dominus servo: Exi in vias, et sepes: et compelle intrare, un impleatur domus vea.' 'And the lord said unto the servant, Go out into the highways and hedges, and compel them to come in, that my house may be filled.'

TO ARTHUR GREEVES (W):

Magdalen College,
Oxford.
May 19th [1929]

My dear Arthur,

I enclose a letter wh. I have been waiting to send you for ages.[25] Of course I am delighted to hear of your coming to Oxford to-morrow, but hope that you will stay in College with me. You will remember that last time you found the hardships of Collegiate life worse in anticipation than in experience. If you insist on going to a Hotel try the Eastgate which is cheap & quiet & just beside Magdalen. Let me have a line or wire at once. I am looking forward tremendously to meeting again

Yrs
Jack

TO HIS FATHER (LP X: 127):

Magdalen College,
Oxford
Monday 18th [17 June 1929]

My dear Papy,

I was hoping to have elicited a letter from you before now. I have heard neither from you nor from the Colonel for a long time – not that I'm much better myself, but I think I am one up on both of you at the moment.

I am thinking of taking my summer holiday earlier than usual this year – from three to four weeks from the 12th or 13th of August. We ought to have the hottest part of the year then, and I hope you will be able to take most of your time off. But I have been burdened with a job – a friend wants me to look after his dog while he is in Switzerland. I am certainly of all his friends the best acquainted with the beast, and I have agreed. Can you tell me whether there is any difficulty – e.g. quarantine etc. – about bringing him into Northern Ireland and out of it again. Perhaps I ought also to ask whether there is any difficulty about bringing him into Leeborough? I can vouch for his cleanliness, courtesy, and other canine virtues. I think you will rather like him.

25 Presumably the letter of 22 April.

I have just finished a week of examining for the Pass Degree here, which of course means examining the extreme dullards. I got one delightful sentence in a paper on *Paradise Lost*, about Adam and Eve praying 'before they *turned in*' at night.

Hoping you are tolerably well and also hoping for an early answer (after you have 'taken legal advice' about the dog question!).

your loving son,

Jack

TO HIS FATHER (LP X: 140–2):

[Magdalen College]
Sunday [7 July 1929]

My dear Papy,

Many thanks for your letter on 'this dog business'. I begin to see, in the uncertainty of my friend's plans, a faint gleam of hope that the whole question is going to solve itself, and I shall arrive home blessedly dogless. As to your cautions about the looking after another man's dog – depend upon it I did not consent until every decent subterfuge had been tried. If, as I hope, the scheme falls through, how cheaply I have earned my credit. And then people say that virtue isn't rewarded.

I am sorry to hear of your poor health. Ought we not to think of spending part of my time away from Leeborough? I will go any where you wish – even to Moorgate.[26] Think of this, but don't pin yourself to a date without consulting me again. I am still undecided (it depends largely on when I finished Chapter II of the book) whether August 12 or something like August 25th or 24th would be best for me. I expect that a change of air, scene, and diet would do you more good than many nostrums. (I wonder what precisely a *nostrum* is and why it is so called?)

I am busy at the book at present, and next week shall start examining. This year, by all accounts, I have an ugly row to hoe. As I have probably told you before, every group of Awarders consists of one Oxford and one Cambridge man, and they shift them about from year to year. This time I have lost my Cambridge colleague with whom I have worked very pleasantly for the last four years, and getting instead a man whom everyone has warned me against. (How I hate, except in the most formal

---

26 The home of William Lewis in Glasgow. Albert's brothers in Scotland were pressing him to visit them.

composition, that 'against whom' instead of the more natural form.) He has quarreled with every previous colleague he has had and it remains to see whether I shall fare better. He is old too, which makes the matter worse: it is easier to stand ones rights to contemporaries without the appearance of insolence. Can you suggest any spiritual exercises – perhaps our old friend 'Calvinistic exercises' would do – suitable as a prophylactic against loss of temper in trying circumstances? There ought to be somewhere a Collect for the Use of Examiners.

I don't think I have much news to tell you. My days – like the man in the poem – 'are passed among the dead', that is in the Bodleian, which I have already described to you; and as to these said dead themselves you may have heard more of them than you wish in August, for I shall certainly bring you a chapter to read. It remains however a very pleasant way of spending one's time, tho' I shall be glad to get out of this windless hollow and see the sea again.

I am in good health and form, except for a kind of summer rash which gives me occasionally the sensation of being covered with fleas. I shall be glad when it is gone. I haven't much time for general reading but I have been amusing myself in the 'Sweet o' the night' – the odd half hour before going to bed – with an anthropological book of Andrew Lang's called 'Myth, Ritual and Religion'.[27] Among other things it gives the Zulu deluge story – a story which in some or other form as you know turns up in every mythology. Apparently at one time all the animals and men were like to die of thirst. The reason was that a huge frog had swallowed all the water: after which of course he was larger than ever. The remaining inhabitants of the world laid their heads together and decided that their only chance was to force the frog to disgorge by inducing him to laugh. They therefore assembled and each of them did the funniest thing he could think of. The frog, for a long time, like Queen Victoria, was not amused: but at last the eel stood on the tip of its tail and this was too much for him and he laughed so that he fairly split himself and all the water ran out and made a huge ocean in which most of the world was drowned. But the story is, to my mind, less funny than what follows. Lang quotes it from the record of some missionary, who, after listening for several days to stories of this kind, began in turn to produce for the enlightenment of the poor heathen his own account of the world,

27 Andrew Lang, *Myth, Ritual and Religion* (1887).

starting off with the story of creation as it is told in Genesis. The result was disappointing. 'The savages' we are told 'laughed consumedly and replied that he could expect no one but old women to believe such a story as that'. A missionary goes I suppose prepared for hardships and danger: but its a bit hard to be ridiculed for pulling the long bow by an audience who believed the story about the frog and twenty others of the same kind. This is the altar-cloth and the door-mat with a vengeance.

We have been suffering for weeks here from the most shocking drought – flowers withering on their stalks, our bowling pitch in the quadrangle yellow as straw, and the earth cracking everywhere. It has now broken up in the most terrific hailstorms – I got wetter in fifteen minutes yesterday than I have often got during a whole wet afternoon on the hills at home. Luckily the hay is all in, but corn will be in a bad way.

Oh – I had nearly forgotten my best bit of news. Weldon[28] is going to be away for two terms. I can hardly tell you with what glee I look forward to seeing the place even temporarily rid of that sinister presence.

your loving son,
Jack

TO ARTHUR GREEVES (W):

Magdalen College,
Oxford.
[16 July 1929]

My dear Arthur

It is only to-day that we have made up our minds about our arrangements for the summer. As far as I can see, I shall be in Ireland from the 12th of August onward, for three to four weeks. I very much hope that this will fit in with your plans, as it will be impossible for me to fit it in either later or earlier. I will make a note of the *Rebel Passion*.[29]

Bryson told me you were going to visit these parts? Is that untrue? And, by the way, could you let me know whether there is any difficulty about bringing dogs into Northern Ireland? Can you let me have an answer.

Yrs
Jack

---

28 For information on Thomas Dewar Weldon see note 44 to letter of 27 May 1928.
29 Katharine Burdekin, *The Rebel Passion* (1929).

TO HIS FATHER (LP X: 142–3):

Magdalen.
July 17th.[1929]

My dear Papy,

Well – the dog business is finally settled and I shall not have to burden myself (or you) with the animal. And I propose to come home on August 24th. All this being made plain you can now go ahead with any plans you came to make about this joint holiday. I, as I have said, am ready to agree with anything, in fact – like another travelling companion of yours –'I'm a mere parcel.'[30] Whether you prefer to seek out some quiet place on our own, or whether domestic comforts and long standing invitation recommend Helensburgh,[31] is all one to me. I must say I should like to do that journey up the Kyles of Bute once again. These however are points of detail. On the main issue (like Kirk's farewell) everything has been said before.

This week a curious thing has happened. I have had a letter from Malvern stating that 'Malvern College Ltd' has been wound up and the school has now been put under a board of governors, and asking me to allow my name to be put up for election as one of them. As they are to number over a hundred the honour is not so overwhelming as at first appears. In my first heat I composed a very fine letter declining on the ground of my 'limited knowledge of public school life and, still more, my imperfect sympathy with the aims and ideals of public schools'. This I enjoyed doing: but then alas 'the native hue of resolution was sickled o'er with the pale cast of thought'.[32] I reflected that this would get about and that the great junta of masters and old boys of various schools

---

30 Jack was quoting his mother's father, Grandfather Thomas Hamilton. In a little biography Warnie provided of him in the Lewis Papers he said: 'Albert's attachment of Florence ("Flora") Hamilton, had begun about the year 1890, when the Revd. Thomas was 64 years old. The Rector, with considerable astuteness realized at an early stage in the proceedings that the attachment could be made to serve his own purposes; he was a man much addicted to short jaunts or holidays...In the unfortunate Albert, he was to find not only a courier, but also on many occasions, a disbursing officer... "I'm a mere parcel" he would say genially, leaving Albert to make all the arrangements. But at any hitch, especially at any overcharge, the geniality gave place to loud, bitter, and worse still, public complaints, which shamed the sensitive Albert to the soul' (LP I: 4–5). See **The Hamilton Family** in the Biographical Appendix.

31 The little town near Glasgow where Albert's brother, Richard Lewis, lived.

32 Shakespeare, *Hamlet*, III, i, 84–5.

would pass from one to the other the word – 'If you have a boy going to Oxford, I shouldn't recommend Magdalen. Lot of queer fish there now. Cranks etc. etc.' So I funked it, tore up my first letter, and wrote an acceptance. I hope I should have been able to hold out against the purely prudential considerations ('funk' is the simpler word) if I had not been supported by the feeling, as soon as I had cooled, that membership of such a huge board would be purely nominal, except for the ring of 'insiders', and that therefore if I refused I should be only making a storm in a teacup. But won't Warnie be tickled? – if I remember, you and I discussed this situation purely as a joke when I was last at home.

Try to let me have a line when you feel like it. Don't be put off writing altogether because you feel unequal to an essay – just a note to say that you have made up your mind where we are going. I should also be glad to hear some news of the Colonel and of when he is coming back. He is badly in my epistolatory debt.

your loving son,
Jack

TO ARTHUR GREEVES (W):

[Magdalen College
18? July 1929]

My dear Arthur,

Good man. I shall book for the 12th and look forward to our journey together as a very bright spot.[33] I had of course thought of the possibility of my father & you and I going away together, but don't want to raise false hopes in you or me in case it doesn't come off. It would be just as good for him & of course infinitely better for me.

If you are wondering where to go for a few days out of London, I shall be at Cambridge from the 8th to the 10th.[34] I shall be working all day till 6 p.m., so it wd. be absurd for you to come to *see me*: but if on other grounds you cared to visit that ancient city we might have a couple of evenings together. I shall have a sitting room to myself in Queens. However, that's as it may be.

---

33 Greeves was residing in London and, as his time was very much his own, Lewis hoped he would accompany him to Belfast on 12 August.

34 August 8–10 when he would be examining in English Literature at Cambridge.

Thanks again & again for coming home – my faithful Arthur! I'm dead tired examining all day.

Yours
Jack

When Albert's brother, Dick, visited him during the first week of July he thought he looked very unwell. After that, Uncles Dick and Bill began urging him to see a doctor. Then come some ominous entries in Albert's diary. Saturday 20 July: 'The old pain began,' he said. 'Never so violent before. I spent a wretched night.' Sunday 21: 'Mary rang up Leslie at 10 o'c. Leslie in England attending a medical conference and wd. not be home till Thursday or Friday. Mary rang up Joey. He was in Newcastle for the weekend but wd. be home at 7 o'c. I decided I must endure until the morning.' Tuesday 23 July: 'Irwin and Joey here before 10 o'c. Irwin...did not think any operation wd. be necessary, but I must go into a nursing home and be washed out and next morning Xrayed.' Friday 26: 'Went from home to Dr Beath. Xrayed. Result rather disquieting. Joey drove me out to Little Lea' (LP X: 143–4). Not long after this Albert wrote to Jack about his illness, and Jack also had a letter from Uncle Dick expressing concern.

TO ARTHUR GREEVES (W):

Hillsboro,
Western Rd.,
Headington
July 25th [1929]

My dear Arthur,

I have had bad news from home. First a letter from my Scotch uncle commenting on my father's poor state of health, saying that he is losing wait and that they suspect 'something internal', and urging me to get him away for a holiday. Second, a letter from my cousin Joey to say that they are putting him into a nursing home for inspection to-day (the 25th) but, thank goodness, saying that they don't suspect any growth, though they do suspect some inflammation.

The way in which this concerns you and me in common is this (a) I shall have to spend a good deal longer with him this summer than usual (b) I shall have to do my best to get him away for part of that time and as long a part as possible, and it will probably have to be to our relations in Scotland. As far as my selfish wishes go this, of course, is the last thing on earth: but you will easily see that I've got to try and bring it about. I shall go home on the 11th or 12th of August. Now it is extremely likely that with all my efforts *either* I shall not be able to get him away at all *or* I shall be able to do so only after hammering away at persuasion for some considerable time. In the first event I need hardly say how glad I should be if you and I cd. both have together in Ireland this longer-than-usual spell. In the second event (which is more probable and which, probable or not, it is my duty to try to bring about) I hope I shall not have the chagrin of being at home *alone* for a fortnight or so and then setting off for the loathsome Scotch relations just as *you* arrive in Ireland and thus missing our time together for the year.

Poor Arthur, I have so B-g—red you about that you will hardly know whether you are on your head or your heels! I only lay this before you because you suggested in your last letter that you wd. have been coming home earlier if *I* had not proposed coming later. You will not feel hardly if you remember from your own experience how horrible one feels when the people whom one ought to love, but doesn't very much, are ill and in need of your help & sympathy;[35] when you have to *behave* as love wd. dictate and yet feel all the time as if you were doing nothing – because you can't give what's really wanted. Among other things I have to face the prospect that it may be my duty to get him permanently over here – with God knows what upsets & difficulties for everyone I care about – you, Minto, Warnie, myself, everyone.

Do let me have a line as soon as you possibly can: at best, to say you will come home (with me) on the 12th: at worst a word of good cheer. Isn't it all beastly. Poor, poor, old Pdaitabird, I cd. cry over the whole thing

Yrs
Jack

TO HIS FATHER (LP X: 152–3):

[Magdalen College]
Postmark: 5 August 1929

My dear, dear Papy,

I am very glad you have written. I had heard the news and was anxious to write, but hardly knew how to do so. I will, of course, come

35 Arthur's father, Joseph Greeves, had died on 19 February 1925.

home at the first moment. Unfortunately I have to go to Cambridge on the 8th for this examining, but will cross to Ireland on the 12th. Don't bother to write yourself if you are not up to it, but see that I am informed.

I gather from what I heard that there is much that is hopeful in the first photo. It would be silly to pretend that this can set worries at rest for either of us; there is surer ground – at least for you – in the wonderful spirit, as shown in your letter, with which you are taking it. I wish I could convey to you one tithe of the respect and affection which I felt in reading it. For the rest, what can I say to you that is not already understood? What can any of us do for one another except give a handshake and a good wish, and hope to do as well when our own time comes to be under fire. It has been a bit of a strain this last week to keep my mind on examination papers for nine hours a day, and I am specially glad that you have written. I was told everything in confidence, I didn't know that you knew I knew, and I could do nothing. I wish I could come straight away but I can hardly get out of Cambridge now. I know what hospitals and nursing homes are like – there at any rate I can sympathize with some experience.

Whatever the next few days brings forth I hope you will make no decision about your treatment without letting me know. I don't of course mean to postpone such decision (necessarily) till next week: but see that I am told. Of course if there is serious trouble, you will have other advice than that of the Belfast crowd.

With all my love and my best wishes – I wish there was anything more useful I could offer – your loving son,

Jack

TO HIS BROTHER (LP X: 182–3):

Leeborough.
Sunday, Aug. 25th. 1929.
In the study, 8.30. p.m.

My dear W.,

This is a line to let you know that P. is rather seriously ill. The first I heard of it was from Uncle Dick about a month ago when I was still in Oxford, and then, in answer to my inquiry, from Joey who is attending him. The trouble is abdominal. The first fear was of course cancer. Xray photos cannot apparently disprove this with certainty, but their evidence, I'm glad to say, is all against it and according to Joey the other features of the case render it very improbable. We must not of course kid ourselves by saying impossible. The present diagnosis is that he is suffering from a narrowing of the passage in one of the bowels. The ordinary cure for this is the operation known as short circuiting: but they had hoped that if he would go on a light diet he would manage to get along, not in perfect health but in tolerable comfort, without being operated upon – or at any rate that the operation would be indefinitely postponed.

I came home immediately after my Cambridge examining and found things at this point. He was up and pretty well. About a week ago however he had an attack in the night of a sort of convulsion and shivering – they call it *rigor* – of which I only learnt next morning. This was not regarded as a very serious symptom by either Joey or Squeaky, but they kept him in bed. Next night when I took his temperature about nine I found it 103 and got the surgeon McConnell (a colleague of Joey's in the case from the start) out to see him about midnight. He was light headed but the temperature fell in the morning. Since then he has been monkeying up and down and of course he has been in bed. This evening they have told him that it is pretty certain that he will have to have the operation. They are to consult again in a few days and we shall then know for sure. He is taking it extraordinarily well. I shall of course stay until the operation is over, unless they postpone it till Christmas. AS FOR YOU, I suppose it would be (a) Impossible, (b) Useless for you to get special leave as the affair is pretty sure to be settled before you could get home.

I have a great many things on other subjects to say – on Liverpool Cathedral and the new Liverpool boat and so forth – but this is only a note for necessity. I have been up the most of a good many nights with the P'daitabird and can't leave the house long enough to get decent walks, so am rather tired and do not feel in form for a letter. This is from the little end room at about 10. p.m. What a pity you're not here. In spite of the worrying situation we should find redeeming features about Leeborough under the present regime. When one is alone it is by no means so pleasant. Thanks for your last letter and excuse me for this scrawl. Remember I have the Leeborough demoralization on me as well as the cures of a patient. And by Gum, both ones *morals* and ones morale are hard put to it.

Of course the present emergency does not cancel immemorial rules. If your letter arrives P. may be – lets hope to goodness he will be – up again, and you must write therefore only what can be shown. When I am creeping about at night at present, or looking at his fire, I often derive a sort of whimsical pleasure from thinking of the long training in stealth for quite different purposes of which he is now the object in a new sense. I'm sorry that you have had an envelope in my handwriting, of which the contents will disappoint you so much as this.

I am just going to creep on tiptoe to the cellar – the key being very sensibly in my charge – to get a mouthful of the whiskey.

yours,
Jack[36]

TO HIS BROTHER (LP X: 183–90):

[Little Lea]
Aug. 29th. 1929[37]

My dear APB.,

To be frank, you owe this second letter to a typically Leeburian situation. I had mentioned to the P'daitabird that I was writing to you, and this has provoked such a hailstorm of advice and warning – I must write on the thinnest paper and I must go to Condlin[38] to get the right sort of envelope – and of questions – how am I getting on with my letter to the Colonel – that there is nothing for it. Sooner or later I must satisfy him with the touch and sight of a letter that by its size will not [be] too obviously a notification of his illness and therefore a cause of alarm to him. And I think it would be really too unkind to send you a wad of toilet paper.

---

36 To this letter Warnie appended a note in the Lewis Papers: 'It is perhaps as well that the reader should be reminded at this point of the "time lag" in the whole of the Belfast–Shanghai correspondence. The above letter for instance, dated Aug. 25th, was posted in Belfast on Aug. 27th. It was not endorsed "via Canada" and would therefore have been despatched by the long sea route via Suez: i.e. it could not have reached Shanghai, at the earliest, until 43 days later, or the 9th October. Warren's letters to Belfast, being written to catch a particular steamer running on the short sea route (i.e. via Canada or the U.S.A.) would be reaching Belfast some 32 or 33 days after they were written' (LP X: 183).

37 This letter, which was endorsed 'via Canada', reached the army post office in Shanghai on 11 October.

38 J.W.A. Condlin had been Albert's managing clerk since 1917.

Things are no better since I last wrote, and I am really very despondent about him. Yet it would be an offence against Pigiebotian ethics to seal ourselves up therefore in perpetual solemnity: and, however you may feel in China, I on the spot can only get through my days and nights by allowing myself an enjoyment of the old humours, which, needless to say, show through even this situation. If only it did not always raise anxiety, the daily visit of the Doctor would be irresistibly funny. The patient's utter refusal to answer to the point, his hazy accounts (on the familiar 'mouthful' principle) of what he has eaten, and his habit of replying to some such question as 'Have you noticed any change in yourself?' with a sudden 'Doctor! I'm perfectly satisfied in my own mind that the root of all this trouble etc. etc.' and his subsequent belief that the doctor has propounded to him the grossly improbable theory which he had in fact propounded to the doctor – all this you will be able to imagine on the slightest of hints from me. It was very alarming the night he was a little delirious. But (I cannot refrain from telling you) do you know the form it took? The watercloset element in his conversation rose from its usual 30% to something nearly like 100%.

And though, thank heavens, he has never been lightheaded since, this percentage has not been much reduced. Indeed I may be said to live at present in a dominantly excretory world: for you must add to his merry tales all the serious conversation on such subjects which his condition entails, and all the reminiscences of family illness to which this leads...The funniest event was the borrowing of a commode from Bernagh. The moment Arthur had left me, promising to return with this humble piece of apparatus, of course Janie[39] turned up to make kind enquiries. You know the difficulty she finds in getting out of a room; and when that is conquered, the further difficulty of getting off a doorstep. Picture me standing with her at the hall door, keeping one eye on her and doing my little bit of conversation while with the other I watched the corner for the appearance of Arthur followed by the Bernagh chauffeur trundling a commode in a wheelbarrow.

However, perhaps all this water closet world is appropriate to me at the moment as I have just finished the formidable task of reading the whole of the works of Rabelais. The original 17th century translation can now be had uncut in a single fat volume at 6/- with very good print

---

39 i.e. Janie McNeill. See note 41 to letter of 4 May 1915.

and paper.[40] I had to read him for the light he throws on the Renaissance in general and his particular influence on our own Elizabethans. Would I advise you to do the same? I hardly know. He is very long, very incoherent, and very, very stercoraceous. But you must base no opinion of him on what you hear from uneducated people who have never read any other comic book written before the reign of Queen Victoria and are therefore so blinded by a few familiar words when they first see them in print that they never go on seeing the drift of a page, much less a chapter, as a whole.

The first surprise is that about a quarter of the book is perfectly serious propaganda in favour of humanist education. The comic parts are mostly satires on the papacy, monasticism, and scholastic learning. The free farce of the Miller's Tale[41]-cum-Decameron[42] type is really only about a third of the whole. There is a great deal of quite sincere piety and humanity of a pleasant Shandeyian,[43] Montaignesque type. Some of the aphorisms must be added to our stock at once. 'The greatest loss of time that I know is to count the hours' – 'Drunkards live longer than physicians'. Some of the preposterous humour is excellent. I like the scene where in visiting a certain island they are taken to witness 'the ceremony of a bursting', and while they are on the way hear 'a loud report like the cleaving of a tree' by which they gathered that the man had burst already. I like the gentleman 'whose life was a perpetual dinner' and the abbot, who, being asked on his deathbed to allow his successor to take over, replied that 'the last f—- he should utter would be the f—- of an abbot'. The word 'utter' is here specially pleasing and in indexing Rabelais – without which, in the case of so shapeless a work, to have read it is the same as not to have read it – I enjoyed making the entry 'ABBOT, last utterance of'.

Some of the satire – tho' satire tends always to bore me – is very 'sly', to use a good old word which we moderns have dropped or degraded

---

40 François Rabelais, *Gargantua & Pantagruel*, prefaced by Life of Rabelais by Henri Clouzot, illustrated by 525 vignettes by Joseph Hémard (London: Joseph Hamilton, 1927).

41 In Chaucer's *Canterbury Tales*.

42 A collection of tales from many sources by the Italian author Giovanni Boccaccio, and assembled in their definitive form between 1349 and 1351.

43 After Laurence Sterne's character in *Tristram Shandy*. See letter to Arthur Greeves of 25 October 1916.

without finding a better to fill its place. The 'clergyhawks' (clergy of course) were shown to Pantaguel in their cage. It was explained to him that they were originally men who came over from a neighbouring country called Want o'Bread ('a cruel country where the days are of a weary length') and were turned into birds. Pantaguel remarks that he quite believed this, for they looked very *like* men: in fact if he hadn't been told, he would never have known that they *had* been turned into birds at all. You must have a look at this author and see if he is for you. At the least one is always pleased to have turned a name into a memory. I shall write no more tonight. By an unpardonable folly I have forgotten to secure the cellar key this evening and am fain to experiment on that curious Victorian drink, sherry and soda. This is from the little end room at 11.15 of a chilly August night. Don't try sherry and soda. I have just had my first sip. It tastes just like sherry only less so.

Next day. [30 August]

Leeboro is a curious place. My sherry and soda, tho' mawkish to the taste, made me quite drunk last night. Today is in our worst manner. I am just going out to buy him a new bottle of ink. I have assured him there is a bottle in the little end room with which I am writing daily: but he does not think this will be sufficient for a dozen cheques which he has to endorse, and there is no arguing with a sick man so I must waste my short time out in a journey to Strandtown: and lucky at that – for his idea was a journey to Condlin who would direct me to a suitable stationers, and it was only with difficulty he was brought to admit that Strandtown might supply some writing fluid that would do at a pinch until tomorrow, when of course I must go into town and get some of 'the proper' ink. As this sort of thing happens every hour of every day you will understand that I need an outlet of frankly heartless laughter if I am to keep my temper. How the servants put up with his glaring injustice to them I don't know. Almost every day he decides on his lunch at about 1 and then is furious because he does not get it before two.

But in spite of this I have a growing respect for him. He faces the major issue very pluckily, and from his reminiscences, in which he is at present indulging very freely, I get a more acute impression of the abominable rock from which he was hewn. One should rather be surprised that he has gone so far than annoyed that he has gone no further. Some glimpses I have had lately of old Ty-isa show it as a positive sink.[44] His own going to Lurgan, happily as it turned out, appears to have been originally a penal measure – in fact 'a serious quarrel ending in his going to a Boardingschool'. He had a scrap with Limpopo in their bedroom and Uncle Dick at once went and shouted downstairs to the Grandpadaita to come up for 'they couldn't stand this fellow James any longer'. (Of course there may be a Richardian version of this story too, but even if untrue it is significant).

The next is worse. You may have forgotten that we had on the P'daita side an Aunt Jenny KIONE (is that the spelling?) who by the by was 'a really *lovely* girl – big black lustrous eyes and fuzzy hair and all the rest of it'. She had a female friend who came and lived with her at Ty-isa for eleven years. And the P'daitas, who so far seem wonderfully patient, didn't like the friend. Then Jenny married Kione and arranged with the consent of her husband that her friend was to come and live with them in their new home.[45] 'We all' – that is the Grand-pudaita and all his pouting, puffing, black-as-a-thundercloud hobble-de-hors – 'We all said if the Kiones had that woman to live with them all connection between the two households was at an end'. And she *did* have her to live with her and her husband: and all connection *was* at an end. I ventured to suggest that

---

44 'Ty-isa' in Lower Sydenham, Belfast, was the home of Albert's parents, Richard Lewis (1832–1908) and Martha Gee Lewis (1831–1903). The Lewis family moved there in 1870, and it was their home until Martha Lewis's death in 1903. After the sale of Ty-isa in 1903, Richard Lewis lived with each of his sons in turn until he moved into Little Lea in 1907. See David Bleakley, *C.S. Lewis – At Home in Ireland* (1998) for a photo of Ty-isa.

45 Although Albert Lewis was ill when he was talking to Jack about his sister, Sarah Jane 'Jeannie' (1856?–1901), it helps explain why the relations between Jeannie and her family were strained. Jeannie's friend, Miss McConnell, was living with the Lewis family at Ty-isa when, in 1882, Jeannie became engaged to Thomas Heron Keown. They were married the following year and Miss McConnell accompanied them to their home in Duncairn Gardens, Belfast. Jeannie and her husband had four children, Sarah, Thomas, Richard and Henry. Mr Keown owned Dundela Villas (where Warnie and Jack were born) and he rented this to Albert Lewis after the latter had married Flora Hamilton. Following the Lewis family's move to Little Lea, Thomas Keown and his family moved into Dundela Villas. Despite the fact they lived so close together, Jeannie rarely saw any of the Lewis family, and when she was dying, Flora wrote to Albert on 27 June 1901 saying, 'I am very sorry to hear of Mrs Keown on your mother's account. Does she know about it? I wonder would Mrs Keown like to see any of you? You know I have always had the feeling that she would have liked to be friends with us, she always, on the few occasions I met her, seemed glad to talk to me and to hear about the children. It seems dreadful to think of her dying like that, away from you all' (LP II: 321).

her husband was perhaps the person to decide whom he would allow to stay in his own house. The reply was delightful – 'Ah he was a weak creature.' It is part of my duty as a nurse to redouble my hypocrisy and to refrain from all vexatious argument, but such an unheard of violation of personal liberty put my self control to the pin of its collar. Can't you see them all? And what on earth would one do if one was married and a crowd of one's relations in law (including that colossus of rancid butter, Bill – plumbago Bill) suddenly turned up and said 'If you have a friend of your wife's to stay with you, we'll cut you and her'. I know what line I'd take.

I crossed this time by the new Liverpool boat. I had not heard of her until my porter on the landing stage volunteered the information that I'd be crossing by the, it sounded like 'Ulstermanic'. I thought it an odd name but nothing like so bad as the name they have actually given her[46] – a pleasure boat name as you rightly say in a letter which reached us three or four days ago. Now as regards comfort below decks, this is the very best boat I have ever been on. The extraordinary width of the berths is the most striking feature. Though I had a cabin without a porthole the ventilator was so efficient that I had to put my head under the clothes: and there is hot and cold in the basin in your stateroom. But as a ship she is disgusting. The deck hamper is piled up almost to the top of the funnels – the squat oval toy funnels of the motor boat. There is no place at all for open air walking except the boat deck. She sails an appalling height out of the water. The internal decorations are the worst example of fake taste I have ever seen. As the ship sails to *Ireland*, some brute has had the idea of doing her up internally in what he would probably call 'the olde Irishe cottage style'. The ceiling of the chapter house is covered with faked beams: the walls are adorned with targets and spears: and (would you believe it) their walls are painted to represent the rough stone work of a cottage. What should be done with the man whose idea of decorating a ship is to try and make you think that she is built throughout of undressed stones and mortar? But let us give honour where honour is due. In this chapter house the chairs are comfortable, the open floors are spacious: and it opens on to a verandah (also in 'olde Irishe cottage' style) looking aft where you can sit and enjoy the air under cover. But tis a bad business on the whole. It only remains to

46 *Ulster Monarch.*

disguise the engines as spinning wheels and dress the officers in plush breeches and cutaway coats with shillelaghs,[47] to make the stewardesses into colleens,[48] and to substitute a huge electrically twanged harp on each funnel for the horn, and then the crowd of annual English visitors for this infernal motor race will feel really comfortable.

I must take my mouthful of the negus and go to bed. I have had a trying day. I would give a pint of blood – nay, what's more a tooth (stipulating for a general anesthetic) if you would throw a pebble at the window and announce your unexpected return. The little end room as I write shows all the traces of occupation by a solitary and disgruntled Pigibudda. You know – the extraordinary litter of a dozen P'daita books which one is still trying to read concurrently and the dozen more which one has abandoned but not returned to their places: the two or three dusty volumes, neither P'daitesque or Pigiboetean which one has fished out from among the flies and gurglings of the attic with the vague idea that they might be interesting: the packets of Gold Flake deplorably empty and the tins of P'daita cigarettes deplorably full. I have reached the stage of looking long and fixedly at the photo of the Oldish. Its simply frightful at present because one never gets a real solid hour to work without interruption, and one can never get a decent jaunt into Down or Antrim: the two great mainstays against sheer undiluted Leeburianism (a dreadful thing when taken alone) are thus removed.

[31 August] This is the next day at 12.30. I have been continuously on the run since I got up – going to the McNeills to fetch the various jellies and confections with which they daily supply us – their decency to the O.A.B. all along has been extraordinary – helped your father to shave, giving him cheques to sign and endorse. If I start to work now I shall be interrupted by the doctor before I have well got my head into it, so I may as well put in ten minutes conversation with you.

After finishing your letter-portion last night and wiping up the deluge occasioned by opening one of those remarkable soda water bottles, I read a few pages of Macaulay's letters. My reading them pleased the patient and as I have to do them some time or other I may as well do it now when it provides a common topic for our conversations. They are not uninteresting. Do you know that Macaulay developed his full

47 An Irish cudgel of blackthorn or oak.

48 An Anglo-Irish name for a girl.

manner as a schoolboy and wrote letters home from school which read exactly like pages out of the Essays? This is very illuminating. He was talking about the nature of government, the principles of human prosperity, the force of the domestic affections and all that (you know the junk) at the age of fourteen. He could not at that age have *known* anything about them: least of all could he have known enough for the flowing generalizations which he makes. One can see quite clearly that having so early acquired the *talk* he found he could go on quite comfortably for the rest of his life without bothering to notice the *things*. He was from the first clever enough to produce a readable and convincing slab of claptrap on any subject whether he understood it or not, and hence he never to his dying day discovered that there was such a thing as understanding. Don't you think the last word on him is Southey's statement – 'Macaulay's a clever lad, and a clever lad he'll remain' – ?[49]

The most interesting thing in the book so far is the picture of the remains of the real old Whig aristocracy (Toryism you know is incurably vulgar in England, whatever it may have been in France or the Highlands: illiterate squires, place hunters in Parliament, and farmer Georges in long succession on the throne) at Holland house. The account of old Lady Holland's conversation is very pleasing. 'Mr Macaulay, ring the bell. Allen there is not enough turtle soup for you, you must be content with gravy soup. Mr Craddock, take that candle into the next room and show Mr Smith the portraits. Lord Russell, put down that screen: you will spoil it.'[50] This is all verbatim. The parts which excite my contempt for the author most are the letters from India. He is not, of course, an oppressor, a mere Collector of Bogley Wallah. He is conscientious and even tolerant. But it's impossible to conceive any man walking through an ancient civilisation more completely cased in the armour of Holland House, Manchester, nineteenth century 'progress', and general cocksureness that spinning jennies and spelling books are the ultimate secret of life, and that anything other than these exists simply to be first ridiculed, then patronized, and finally 'improved'.

49 Sir George Otto Trevelyan, *The Life and Letters of Lord Macaulay* (1876), vol. I, ch. 3, p. 138. The remark was not made by Robert Southey (1774–1843), but by John Wilson ('Christopher North') in response to an attack by Macaulay on Southey.

50 ibid., vol. I, ch. 4, pp. 209, 235. These comments by Lady Holland were made on several occasions, and are recorded in Macaulay's letters to his sister, Hannah More Macaulay, of 30 May and 25 July 1831. Lewis misquoted the command given Mr Craddock, for it is 'Mr Allen, take a candle and show Mr Craddock the picture of Buonaparte.'

It is Grandfather Hamilton over again, with Liberalism instead of Evangelicalism. He laughed consumedly at the first native he saw, not for anything the man said or did, but simply and solely because he was 'black'.[51] (Damn it, master Pigiebotie, I should have had time to do some work after all!) I don't say this is a crime: but doesn't it just reveal in a flash the provincial and the urchin under the veneer of general culture? He was also apparently responsible for one of the greatest absurdities in the Empire – I mean the fact that I as a Lower Certificate examiner get papers by little Mohammedan girls in Purdah on, say, *Ivanhoe*: a story which rests at every turn on what the Germans call *Frauendienst* – the mediaeval knight and lady romantic ideal, *place aux dames*, breaking of lances, and 'all that'. What on earth it can mean to them I have often wondered. Well when Macaulay arrived in India, the Company was just agitating the question of native education, and had fixed up the only scheme by which any real education was possible: an education of Indians in their own classics, Sanskrit and Persian, conducted on European lines – i.e. according to the standards demanded by European scholarship.

Macaulay (who of course could hardly speak a syllable of even the vernacular, let alone any classical Oriental language) wrote a minute which is a real masterpiece of Philistinism and P'daitism.[52] First of all you have the familiar device of the false parallel. To teach native scholarship would be as if Europe at the Renaissance, instead of studying Latin, and Greek, had gone back to Norman French or Anglo-Saxon. Notice the delicious implication that English (an alien contemporary language)

---

51 ibid., vol. I, ch. 6, p. 334: In 1833 Macaulay was appointed to the Supreme Council of India, and on 10 June 1834 he arrived at Madras. 'On the 10th June the vessel lay to off Madras; and Macaulay had his first introduction to the people for whom he was appointed to legislate in the person of a boatman who pulled through the surf on his raft. "He came on board with nothing on him but a painted yellow cap, and walked among us with a self-possession and civility which, coupled with his colour and his nakedness, nearly made me die of laughing." '

52 ibid., vol. I, ch. 6, pp. 370–2: 'On the 2nd February [1834], Macaulay ... produced a minute in which he adopted and defended the view of the English section in the Committee... "We have to educate a people who cannot at present be educated by means of their mother-tongue. We must teach them some foreign language. The claims of our language it is hardly necessary to recapitulate. It stands pre-eminent even among the languages of the West. It abounds with works of imagination not inferior to the noblest which Greece has bequeathed to us... What the Greek and Latin were to the contemporaries of More and Ascham, our tongue is to the people of India." '

is to India as Greek, Latin (ancient native languages) are to Europe. Don't forget that even inside the parallel Macaulay knows exactly nothing of Norman French or Anglo-Saxon, but he is quite sure that there is nothing in them. How should there be – he never learned them.

Then comes the master stroke. He 'suspects' that Sanskrit is little superior to Anglo-Saxon, 'in some departments, such as history, certainly inferior'.[53] That is, while the reader is still being amused by the false parallel, he is bowled over by a 'how much the less, therefore' argument based on a comparison of two literatures *both* absolutely unknown to the writer and the reader! It is worth remarking that the clever lad, as he wrote the minute, was really creating the Babu.[54] For what is a Babu but a man sufficiently servile to take pride in having imperfectly acquired the jargon of a culture which he cannot assimilate and which he would never have attempted to master but for purely financial reasons? 'Muddlejee-All-Buggard-Up, Failed Calcutta Entrance' is the natural epitaph of Macaulay's education policy in India. You remember Raleigh: 'Macaulay – God's ape. He stinks in my nostrils'.[55] And mine. Yours too I trust.

This is Saturday night. The patient is rather better...Another thing almost too good to be true is that someone in town advised him, as a cure for rheumatism, to carry a pudaita in each pocket – which he actually tried. Oh, and another interesting thing. He was talking, as often, about the insolence of Uncle Hamilton and said 'You know, what I don't like about Gussie is that he never says these desperately insolent things when we're alone. It's always to raise a laugh from you boys at my expense.' I wonder does he regard 'that fellow Gussie' as the origin of the whole anti-Pudaita tradition. If so, a certain remark overheard on the stairs that eventful night so many years ago must have gone deep.

The great consolation about Leeborough at present is my control of the meals. As soon as I came home and found P. on light diet I said I would make things easier for him by giving up my own meat for lunch.

---

53 ibid., vol. I, ch. 6, p. 372: 'The literature of England is now more valuable than that of classical antiquity. I doubt whether the Sanscrit literature be as valuable as that of our Saxon and Norman progenitors. In some departments – in history, for example – I am certain that it is much less so." '

54 A native of India who has acquired some superficial education in English.

55 *The Letters of Sir Walter Raleigh*, op. cit., vol. II, p. 278, letter to David Nichol Smith of 3 July 1908: 'Macaulay – God's Ape – he stinks in my nostrils. Cheap, vain, poor, noisy, blind.'

I substituted bread and cheese, cream crackers and butter, and fruit. This may not appeal to you: but the glory is that I can have it when I choose. There has not been a day for the last fortnight on which one o'clock has not seen me sitting down to my cheese, fruit and wine in a dining room with the windows open. A little effort of imagination will enable you to realize what a comfort this is. I maintain the same arrangement during the week end. Fancy a Leeboro *Saturday* with light lunch at *one* instead of a gorge at half past two, and then high tea (cold roast chicken and ham tonight) at seven! Again, during the first bad nights when I had to sit up I got 'the old woman' to give me a cup of tea before she went to bed. This excellent practice has been continued ever since, so that between tea at 10.30 and negus at 11.30 I get through my evenings very well. If only I wasn't constantly bothered about the P'daitabird (for one never knows really what the next temperature may bring forth), if only I could get decent walks, and if only I could get some more work done, it wouldn't be a bad life. A formidable list of exceptions! It's like the poacher in Punch 'If I get three more after the one I'm after now, I shall have caught four'...[I] break off here and drink my drop of spirits.

By the way we had tonight the old stunt about whiskey being an unpalatable drink. Incidentally all the doctors without exception say that he has done and is doing himself harm with it. Joey says that when he mentions this to the patient, the patient simply laughs at him – and has ruled that there's no good trying to stop it as the good which cd. now be done by cessation would be less than the psychological irritation. He gave me a real fright as I was going out of the gate the other day, having left him as comfortably settled up for the afternoon as I could. He suddenly appeared at his window shouted at me in a voice that made me think some terrible crisis had come I...[went] tearing upstairs to find the real tragedy: he had suddenly discovered that I was going out with the cellar key in my pocket – and apparently the 'odd dregs' in the *two* bottles which he keeps in the wardrobe were not enough to last him the afternoon. There is a very serious side to all this, but I agree with Joey: and I'd go a long way before I'd be leagued with the doctors to deprive the poor old chap of what is about his only pleasure. Let us hope Rabelais is right. Well now for the negus. Stand by for the intolerable moment of opening a P'daita soda water bottle. (If I die of alcohol some day, how ironically this last sentence will jostle the parenthesis before it.)

Sept. 3rd.

The surgeon and Squeaky and Joey have all consulted today and decided on an operation. He is taking it like a hero. By the time this reaches you all will be settled for good or ill. It has been the devil of a day as you may imagine, infernally nerve racking and painful and I'm dead sleepy. I shall post this tomorrow. I had meant to write more, but I'm too tired. As to *facts*, theres nothing more to add. Anyway this can't reach you in time to give any information.

yrs,
Jack

By the by, tho 'special leave' is clearly out of the question, I think, if all goes fairly well at the operation, you would have a real claim to preferential treatment as regards the first boat instead of the second, on grounds of U.P.A.[56] Whether there is any chance of its being regarded, you know better than I.

TO OWEN BARFIELD (W):

Little Lea,
Strandtown,
Belfast
Sept. 9th 1929

My dear Barfield,

Many thanks for your letter. I am not sure that the distinction between 'intimacy' and 'familiarity' is really very profound. It seems to be largely a matter of accident that you know so little of my previous history. I know more of yours because we meet in England: if we had met in Ireland the position would be reversed. Again, we do not much narrate our past lives, but this is because we have so much else to talk about. Any day might have started a topic to which such narrative would have been relevant, and out it would have come. Consider how many bores whose history you know well after a short acquaintance, not because familiarity has in their case replaced intimacy but because they had nothing to say and would not be silent.

I am not saying that there is nothing in the distinction. When the parties are of different sexes it may be more important. I suppose a good

56 Uniformed Personnel Allowance.

Greek was familiar with his wife and intimate with his εταιρα.[57] But between men I suspect that intimacy includes familiarity potentially. Now with a woman, of course, no degree of intimacy includes any familiarity at all; for that there must be στοργη[58] or ερϖσ[59] or both.

The test really is this. When you have talked to a man about his soul, you will be able, whenever the necessity arises, say, to assist him in using a catheter or nurse him through an attack of dysentery, or help him (if it should so happen) in a domestic problem. This is not so in the case of a woman.[60]

As for my present situation, it frightens me for what it implies. I argue thus: 1. I am attending at the almost painless sickbed of one for whom I have little affection and whose society has for many years given me much discomfort and no pleasure. 2. Nevertheless I find it almost unendurable. 3. Then what in heavens name must it be like to fill the same place at the sickbed, perhaps agonised, of someone really loved, and someone whose loss will be irreparable? A formidable argument *a fortiori*. No doubt under 1. it is proper to include the fact that if lack of real affection spares some pains, it introduces others. Where every kind word and forbearance is the result of calculated duty, and where all we do leaves us still rather ashamed, there is, I suppose, a particular *kind* of strain which would be absent from the other situation. There is also, in this present case, though no spiritual sympathy, a deep and terrible physiological sympathy. My father and I are physical counterparts: and during these days more than ever I notice his resemblance to me. If I were nursing you I should look forward to your possible death as a loss lifelong and irremediable: but I don't think I should shrink from the knife with the sub-rational sym-pathy (in the etymological sense) that I feel at present.

Having said all this I must proceed to correct the exaggeration which seems to be inherent in the mere act of writing. Who was it said that disease has its own pleasures of which health knows nothing? I have my good moments to which I look forward, and perhaps, though the whole

57 'Friend'.
58 'Affection'.
59 'Love', as that between a man and woman.
60 We find here Lewis defining those loves which later became the subject of his book *The Four Loves* (1960).

tone of the picture is lowered, there is as much chiaroscuro as ever. When my patient is settled up for the night I go out and walk in the garden. I enjoy enormously the cool air after the atmosphere of the sick room. I also enjoy the frogs in the field at the bottom of the garden, and the mountains and the moon. I often get an afternoon walk when things are going well, and my friend Arthur Greeves – the 'friend' of It[61] you know, who mentioned the beech tree in his letter – sees me every day, and often twice a day. Some of my consolations are very childish and may seem brutal. When Arthur and I talk late into the night there is, even now, a magical feeling of successful conspiracy: it is such a breach, not of course of the formal rules, but of the immemorial custom of a house where I have hardly ever known freedom. There is pleasure of the same kind in sitting with open windows in rooms where I have suffocated ever since childhood: and in substituting a few biscuits and fruit for the Gargantuan mid-day meal which was hitherto compulsory, I hope this is not so uncharitable as it sounds. I do not suppose I look after him the worse for it.

At any rate, I have never been able to resist the retrogressive influence of this house which always plunges me back into the pleasures and pains of a boy. That, by the bye, is one of the worst things about my present life. Every room is soaked with the bogeys of childhood, the awful 'rows' with my father, the awful returnings to school: and also with the old pleasures of an unusually ignoble adolescence By the way, that is just the point about intimacy *containing* familiarity. If it ever became really relevant to some truth that we were exploring in common I could and would expand the last sentence into detail: on the other hand I have not the slightest inclination to do so. i.e. what would be an *end* for familiars is only an instrument for intimates. I enclose a few epigrams on which I would like your opinion. With many thanks,

yours
C. S. Lewis

Jack had been nursing his father at home for over a month when, in the second week of September, Mr Lewis was admitted to a nursing home at

61 'It' was Lewis's early name for what he later defined as 'Joy' in his autobiography, *Surprised by Joy*.

7 Upper Crescent, Belfast. An operation discovered carcinoma of the colon, and for a while he seemed to rally. The doctors thought he might live for some time and, following their advice, Jack returned to Oxford on 22 September. On Tuesday 24 September he received word that his father was worse, and he left for Belfast immediately. He was too late to see him: his father died of cardiac arrest on Wednesday 25 September. His funeral was in St Mark's, Dundela, on Friday 27 September, after which he was buried beside his wife Flora in the city cemetery. The day before, the Belfast News-Letter *and the* Belfast Telegraph *published long obituaries. 'The death of Mr Lewis,' said the* Telegraph, *'removed from our midst a strong upright man, a faithful friend, a keen and able advocate, a cultured and educated gentleman, and by his death the city in which his brilliant professional career was spent is appreciably the poorer.'*

Warnie had not yet received the two letters from Jack about his father's illness when on 27 September he wrote in his diary:

> *I got down to the office at quarter to nine [and] Lee handed me a cable: it was from J., handed in at Belfast at 4.20 p.m. yesterday – 'Sorry report father died painless twenty fifth September. Jack.' In a dull nagging way it is hurting me more than I should ever have imagined it would have done...All day I have been seeing pictures of him at his best, jumbled up in no chronological sequence – Saturday evening tram rides and visits to the Hippodrome with late supper afterwards in Malvern days...I am glad that the last time we spent together was also one of the happiest we ever had – the first week of April 1927 – unclouded by the emotionalism with which he would have spoilt it had he known that I would be half way to China before the month was out. I suppose it is cowardly to be glad that I was not at home for the final scene: saying goodbye is a thing which I shirk whenever possible, but the final goodbye is almost unendurable: at times Mammy's is still a horribly vivid memory...Mixed, perhaps rather callously, with my feelings about P., is the wrench of losing Leeborough, the Leeborough of the little end room and the attics, and of our room, and rare warm summer afternoons in the garden with the gramophone. And worst of all, being pulled up by the roots...The thought that there will never be any 'going home' for me, is hard to bear. I'd give a lot at this minute for a talk with J.* (LP X: 192)

TO HIS BROTHER (LP X: 194–5):

Hillsboro
Sept. 29th. 29.

My dear APB,

By this [time] you will have had my cable and the two letters written from Leeboro. As there is a good deal of business I will only give you the bare facts. The operation, in spite of what they prophesied, discovered cancer. They said he might live a few years. I remained at home, visiting him in the Nursing Home, for ten days. There were ups and downs and some bad spasms of pain from flatulence (apparently the usual sequence to abdominal operations) going over the wound: but nothing really dreadful. Quite often he was himself and telling wheezes, tho' of course he was often wandering from the dopes.

By this time I had been at home since Aug. 11th and my work for next term was getting really desperate, and, as Joey said, I might easily wait several weeks more and still be in the same position – i.e. not really making the progress he should, but not likely to take a sudden turn for the worse. I therefore crossed to Oxford on Saturday Sept. 22. On Tuesday 24 I got a wire saying that he was worse, caught the train an hour later, and arrived to find that he had died on Tuesday afternoon.[62] The immediate cause seems to have been some blood moving on to the brain: at least that is how they interpreted it. The facts were that he never woke on Tuesday, and remained all that day in a state of unconsciousness with a rising temperature. Now for business.

1. *The business in the office is being carried on under the name of Mr Hayes, solicitor, of Belfast.* (The reason is as follows. The moment the news got about there would be applications by other solicitors for the work of the big permanent clients, such as the Corporation, and the Railways, and therefore, before we could sell the business, there would be no business to sell.[63] It is therefore necessary to tell these clients 'Business

62 Jack is confused about the dates. He crossed to Oxford on Saturday, 21 September, and received a wire about his father on Wednesday, 25 September. Albert Lewis died on 25 September.

63 The *Belfast News-Letter* of 26 September 1929, citing Mr Lewis's many clients, said that besides being Prosecutor for the Belfast Corporation 'he acted in the Police Courts for the Belfast Harbour Commissioners (since 1924); and for the Belfast Water Commissioners; the Belfast branch of the National Society for the Prevention of Cruelty to Children; the Belfast & Co. Down Railway Co.; the Great Northern Railway; the Post Office, and the Ministry of Labour'.

as usual.' but tho' Condlin *in fact* does all the work, it cannot legally be done except under the auspices of a qualified solicitor. Mr Hayes receives no payment for lending his name, but any *new* business which accrues during his nominal reign goes to him. I gave authority for this step to be taken, on the advice of Condlin, seconded by Limpopo (I wish I had time to tell you my adult impression of *him*!)

2. *Condlin is sending you a copy of the Will and as soon as possible, an estimate of the Estate.* (In the will, we are given equal shares. Before the operation however the P'daitabird said that, having regard to the insecurity of your career and the comparative security of mine, he would like to leave you more than me: in fact to divide the whole in the proportion of 3 to $2^1/2$: it being understood however that if Magdalen failed to re-elect me, or any other such contingency made me as insecure as you, you would restore equality. This statement I have made known to Condlin. It has of course no *legal* status).

3. *There are two methods of disposing of the business.* a. *Sale outright for a lump sum.* b. *The Drage method.* – i.e. the purchaser to make us a fixed annual payment for a given term of years (I mean fixed in amount of course – *not* a fixed percentage of his takings).

Condlin would advise accepting (b) if the purchaser who on other grounds is most desirable insists on having it so: i.e. not to turn down a good offer solely because the payment is to be deferred.

4. *I have postponed the sale of Leeborough until your return, retaining the Witch of Endor as a housekeeper.* This, I am afraid will sound very uneconomic. But,

a In the state of my work I cannot spend the fortnight or three weeks more in Ireland which would be necessary for cleaning the house out and dividing what we wanted to keep from what we wanted to sell.

b My decisions as to what we wanted to keep might not agree with yours.

c Frankly Pigibuddie it would really be too bloody to sit down and do it alone in that house now.

d I can't let anyone like the Hamiltons do it at *their* discretion because – well you know *two* good reasons for that.

e I can't shut it up and leave it empty because damp and rats would render it unsaleable in a few weeks.

f Also, I confess I should be sorry to give up the idea of you and I having one more stay there together before it goes. (I have of course got rid of the gardener and house maid, ordered all papers to cease – except a 'Tally' for the Witch – and impressed upon her that it is no longer a rich house.)

5. Nearly all the silver – i.e. all except a few knives and forks for you and me at Xmas – including much that has been locked up in a trunk in the attics since Mamy's death – has been packed and sent to the bank.

I think that is all. Please if you possibly can let me have a line by return to say whether you agree with these steps: and also if there is any further certainty when you are coming back. I have lots more to say but, as you may imagine, what between the last few days and piles of my own work and replying to letters of condolence, I am pretty well cooked. You have still every right to work the U.P.A. as regards the date of sailing if it is likely to be any good,

yours,
Jack

P.S. Limpopo is *much worse* than I remembered (h'm – wha'?)

P.P.S. He drinks too – *our* whiskey – and ordered a taxi on his own bat on Thursday in which he kept me driving about all day. Old associations are so strong that it was only afterwards that I realised that *we* were paying for it. (h'm – wha'?)

TO HIS BROTHER (LP X: 197–9):

Hillsboro.
Oct. 17th 1929

My dear W.,

I got your letter of Sept. 27th yesterday and am more disappointed than I can say to hear that you will not be home till April. My pleasant fancy of a last stay at Leeborough together must, among other things, be abandoned.

Perhaps after all the reality would have turned out to be a gloomy, or at any rate an uneasy one. In the meantime someone is already approaching Condlin about the purchase. I am waiting to hear from Condlin the price we can reasonably or without flagrant unreason, demand. The trouble is that this man wants possession by Dec. 1st, and the term doesn't end till Dec. 7th., and the week end, which is all the absence I could take in term, would be utterly useless towards clearing it out. I shall of course attempt to get the purchaser to be content with possession a little later: but if he won't he won't: and if I can't get the house cleared in time for him, I can't. So don't blame me if I let him slip – you see I am in a cleft stick.

Now as to this terrible clearing out itself. To be absolutely safe from selling anything you want to keep my right line would be to store the whole contents of the house until your return: but the price of storage and deterioration wd. eat up or even reduce to a minus quantity the product of the sale. I think therefore I must sell all the furniture except the Chippendale bookcase in the drawing room, the bureau in the study, a bookcase or so, the grandfather clock, the two hall chairs from great grandfather's Welsh farmhouse, and some such oddments. All silver, jewelry and crockery I shall bring to Oxford and keep for your consideration.

As to books, the situation is difficult and I think I can only go on the principle of selling nothing but absolute rubbish. E. g. I don't *suppose* you want to keep the Dumas but you just *may*, so it can't be sold. The picture of Grandp'daita I propose to give to Joey. There may be first editions among the novels and so forth. Pictures are even worse. The P'daita portraits of course can't be sold. We owe Joey a very handsome present for his really very assiduous attendance unpaid, at all hours of the day and night: he is the only member of the family who is propagating: it is not a good picture: and he can't refuse it.[64] Medici prints will be kept: the other pictures (except of course photos) I suppose can be knocked down. 'Relics', MSS or both, of all three generations I shall of course strictly preserve.

As regards money, £1200 is the best offer for the business, and the law library may sell for £500. The list of investments you will understand better than I. The funeral expenses were £55.10.0. Doctors, surgeons, and nursing home have not yet come in. £100, by his directions, (with my v. hearty approval) are to be given to the Witch of Endor.

---

64 The 'P'daita portraits' are probably the oil portraits of Albert Lewis, Grandfather Richard Lewis and Grandfather Hamilton painted by A.R. Baker. As explained in note 186 of Lewis's letter to his father of 27 October 1916, all three P'daita portraits went with Lewis to Oxford. Baker's portrait of Albert Lewis is still in Magdalen College.

What you say in your letter is v. much what I am finding myself. I always before condemned as sentimentalists and hypocrites the people whose view of the dead was so different from the view they held of the same people living. Now one finds out that it is a natural process. Of course, on the spot, ones feelings were in some ways different. I think the mere pity for the poor old chap and for the life he had led really surmounted everything else. It was also (in the midst of home surroundings) almost impossible to believe. A dozen times while I was making the funeral arrangements I found myself mentally jotting down some episode or other to tell him: and what simply got me between wind and water was going into Robinson and Cleaver's to get a black tie and suddenly realising 'You can never put anything down to his account again.' By the way, a great deal of his jollities and wheezes remained to the end. One of the best things he ever said was the day before I left – four days before his death. As I came in the day nurse said 'I've been telling Mr Lewis that he's exactly like my father.' P. 'And how am I like your father?' N. 'Why, he's a pessimist.' P. (after a pause) 'I suppose he has several daughters.'

As time goes on the thing that emerges is that, whatever else he was, he was a terrific *personality*. You remember 'Johnson is dead. Let us go to the next. There is none. No man can be said to put you in mind of Johnson.'[65] How he filled a room! How hard it was to realise that physically he was not a very big man. Our whole world, the whole Pigiebotian world, is either direct or indirect testimony to the same effect. Take away from our conversation all that is imitation or parody (sincerest witness in the world) of his, and how little is left. The way we enjoyed going to Leeborough and the way we hated it, and the way we enjoyed hating it: as you say, one can't grasp that *that* is over. And now you could do anything on earth you cared to in the study at midday or on Sunday, and it is beastly.

I sympathise with you in the strange experience of returning to a British Isles which no longer contains a P'daitaheim. I hope that when all your books are set up (presumably in the non-glassed little end room bookcase) in Magdalen, where you can always have an empty sitting

65 'Johnson is dead. – Let us go to the next best: – there is nobody; – no man can be said to put you in mind of Johnson.' The words are those of William Gerard Hamilton and are quoted by James Boswell in his *Life of Johnson*, op cit., vol. IV, p. 42.

room to which you can repair at all hours, I hope that a leave at Hillsboro will be able to pass not unpalatably. Its no good pretending that its the old thing, but there you are.[66]

You may be grateful for your absence at present in one way. Two nights out of three I sit down at 10 o'clock after my own work to do an hour's business correspondance with Condlin. Hardly my long suit! By the by about the *proportion* between your share and mine, I think you ought to know that I have mentioned and shall mention it to no one alive except Condlin: so you need not feel that you are facing a public opinion that cd. misunderstand or criticise.[67] Write when you can.

yours,
J.

TO ARTHUR GREEVES (W):

Magdalen College,
Oxford.
Monday [28 October 1929]

My dear Arthur,

A straggling letter in diary form is in process of composition and will be posted in due course:[68] the present is written for practical purposes and contains a proposal wh. I make with some diffidence. However I must take my courage in both hands: here goes.

Warnie is not coming home till April. Therefore the proposed visit by him and me to Leeborough to clear it out at Christmas will not take place. But unless a purchaser turns up I am disposed to leave the house as it stands until his return. The danger is that if I do not do something this vac. a purchaser may suddenly spring on me next term wanting immediate possession, when I could only run across for a week end at

---

66 A letter from Mrs Moore of 27 October was placed in the envelope with Jack's. In it she wrote: 'I do hope you will always look on Hillsboro as a home and that you will come straight to us on your return in April...We hope some day to get a larger house, when things would be more comfortable for you, so please do think of our home as your home, and be assured always of a very hearty welcome' (LP X: 197).

67 As soon as he received this letter on 2 November, Warnie sent a telegram to Jack saying, 'Equal shares, otherwise agree proposals including retention Leeborough. Home early April. Warnie' (LP X: 199).

68 Portions of the 'letter in diary form' which he writes about here were composed before this and the next two letters, but all are given in the order in which the individual items were received by Greeves.

the most, and it wd. be almost impossible to do the whole job in the time. I have therefore decided at least to make a start at the end of the present term. I want to have Minto with me and she v. much wants to come: partly that she may have a look at household things of whose value W. and I are ignorant, partly because we shd. both like her to have seen my old home before it goes. But I cannot (and she agrees) take her to Leeborough. There are ghosts there who wd. not be happy to see her nor anxious to make her happy. Also, it wd. look like the traditional insolence of an heir, trampling on the old king's laws before the crown is warm on his head. But I could take her to Bernagh as a mutual friend of yours and mine.

So what I want to know is could you possibly put the pair of us up (only us two – no Maureen, no cats & no dogs) for a week from Dec. 7th to Dec. 15th. This is the cheekiest proposal I have ever made to any one in my life: but – well, my want is urgent, you are my oldest friend, and I think I can count your mother such too. If it is inconvenient, don't be afraid to say so. I wait for an answer v. eagerly.

Yrs
Jack

TO ARTHUR GREEVES (W):

Magdalen College,
Oxford.
[4? November 1929]

My dear Arthur,

A thousand thanks! I was 'all in a flutter of spirits' when I got your letter for my proposal seemed to me & still seems extraordinarily cool. I am now trying to prevent my anticipations from running so high as to ensure their own disappointment. Lovely sunrise through tall elms twinkling over the frosty grass this morning.

Yours
Jack

TO ARTHUR GREEVES (W):

Magdalen College,
Oxford.
[11? November 1929]

My dear Arthur,

Yes, it is *Sunday*[69] morning we shall arrive on, all being well. If you arrive by 9.30 I expect we shall have breakfasted on board, being then hungry, wh. will be no harm as we can then be washing and changing etc while you are at breakfast. I *have* primed Minto. I presume you have primed your mother. Provided they don't hurt one another their cross purposes & misunderstandings will be very funny. Selah!

Yours
Jack

TO ARTHUR GREEVES (W):

[Hillsboro]
Thursday Oct 3rd [1929][70]

My dear Arthur,

I have decided to write a snippet to you every odd time when I have a moment and thus gradually to fill up a letter. This is the first snippet. I am feeling better. Oh how delicious the gradual recovery from a time of horror is. There is a good description in *The Ring & the Book* of this: where a man speaks of beginning to feel again 'the comfortable feel of clothes And taste of food'.[71] Remember also Herbert's poem – *The Flower* I think – 'I once more feel the sun and rain And relish versing.'[72]

It is much colder here and from my window I see the lawn covered with yellow leaves: the long drought had shrivelled them so that they drop early this year at the first touch of cold. I am sleeping solid and it is a delight to wake up each morning with the sense of peace and safety and home. Then I sing in my bath & take Mr Papworth for a run before

69 Sunday 8 December – when Lewis and Mrs Moore arrived in Belfast and where they remained until 20 December.

70 This is the first portion of the 'letter in diary form' mentioned in the letter of 28 October 1929.

71 Robert Browning, *The Ring and the Book* (1868–9), X, 1710: 'The healthy taste of food and feel of clothes'.

72 George Herbert, 'The Flower' (1633), 38–9: 'I once more smell the dew and rain / And relish versing...'

breakfast, eating my apple the while. Unfortunately the morning has to be given to uninteresting work done as fast as I can manage to get through it – a process which would rob even voluntary work of its interest. How thankful you should be that you never have tasks which are not chosen by yourself. And yet I don't know. So many things have now become interesting to me because at first I had to do them whether I liked them or not, and thus one is kicked into conquering new countries where one is afterwards at home.

Oct. 4th

Yesterday Barfield came to lunch and afterwards took me out for a drive-and-walk – you see you are not the only friend I sponge on. We walked in the flat fields by the Thames near Iffley. I wonder if you remember Iffley, where the Norman church is. I sat on the bridge at Iffley lock with you and Minto's doctor brother, Johnnie, (the one who died) and we talked about sailing up the Amazon.[73] It was a luminous grey day yesterday with a fresh wind that curled the river into crisp waves. A fleet of ducks that passed us were going up and down about as much (in proportion to their size) as fishing smacks in a real swell. We also saw two swans and their cygnets. As often happens with the best of friends we were not in a very good talking mood – only that pleasant sense of security that comes from being with those who understand you.

Last night I told Minto about your nursery rime book, and we went all through 'The dog began to bite the pig' together, and then the House that Jack built. She said she so wished to be a grandmother so as to tell them to her grand-children. I said that now that she has big spectacles and her eyes look very big through them she could do it most impressively.

To day I worked in the morning and afternoon and walked into town by Cuckoo Lane and Mesopotamia[74] after tea. The real autumn tang in the air had begun. There was one of those almost white skies with a touch of frosty red over the town, and the beginnings of lovely colouring in the college garden. I love the big kitchen garden there. There is something very attractive about rows of pots – and an old man potting – and

73 On 18 July 1922, Lewis wrote in his diary, 'The Doc. gave us a vivid description of his sail 1500 miles up the Amazon. Speaking of exploring central Brazil, Arthur said "That's the sort of thing I'd like to do!!"' *AMR*, p. 73.

74 See note 73 of letter to Arthur Greeves of 13 May 1917.

greenhouses and celery trenches. I suspect that 'trench' was a delicious earthy word (like 'ditch') before it was spoiled by the war associations. I saw both a squirrel and a fat old rat in Addison's walk, and had glimpses of 'it'.

I think almost more every year in autumn I get the sense, just as the mere nature and voluptuous life of the world is dying, of something else coming awake. You know the feeling, of course, as well as I do. I wonder is it significant – in stories nymphs slip out of the tree just as the ordinary life of the wood is settling down for the night. Does the death of the natural always mean the birth of the spiritual? Does one thing never sleep except to let something else wake. Milton found that his genius was never in full tide except in autumn and winter.

We have our first fire to night. Mr Papworth is asleep in his basket and Minto is listening-in[75] and mending on the sofa.

Oct. 6th

I have nothing to tell you about books these days. The mornings and afternoons are occupied with making notes on *Loves Labour's Lost*,[76] the last of those four plays which I have been making up all this summer & which will also be associated with this time in my mind. The evenings so far have been nearly always occupied in answering letters of condolence or business correspondence from Condlin. Last night was an exception and I read a short new book, Foligno's *Latin Thought in the Middle Ages*,[77] which I strongly suspect of being Fascist propaganda. When a man is very anxious to emphasise (what everyone admitted before), the greatness and influence of Rome, and to suggest that even yet we have not fully appreciated it, my suspicions are awakened – perhaps unjustly. I also glanced through A. E. Houseman's *Shropshire Lad*[78] for the hundredth time. What a terrible little book it is – perfect and deadly, the beauty of the gorgon. I think you know it.

I have not yet started meditation again. The difficulty is to find a suitable time. These are not suitable days for sitting out of doors: indoor times are occupied with work or conversation. In bed at night – well

75 i.e. to the radio.

76 William Shakespeare, *Love's Labour's Lost* (1598).

77 Cesare Carolo Foligno, *Latin Thought During the Middle Ages* (1929).

78 A.E. Housman, *A Shropshire Lad* (1896).

work and Headington make me so sleepy that I have never yet mustered the resolution to tackle such a difficult job when the pillow and the sheet and the rain on the window are wooing me to glide away into drowsiness. (By the way I don't ever remember a time when the coming of sleep was such a positive pleasure to me as it has been since I left Ireland: and by the way there is a fine passage on that subject in Barfield's novel.)[79] Then in bed in the morning, at early-tea time, I am still sleepier. When I go back into College perhaps I shall be able to fit in five minutes after breakfast. (Memo: can meditation be combined with emptying of the bowels? What a saving of time, specially for a constipated man like you.)

To-day, Sunday, I worked till lunch. After lunch, dug up the hen-run and worked again till tea. All this time it was raining hard. After tea it cleared and I sallied forth for a v. good walk. There was a very high wind, the trees were waving, and a lot of tattered rain clouds were scudding across the sky, unusually low. I walked down Cuckoo Lane and into the Private Road[80] where I had a magnificent view of Oxford below me all gleaming in a sudden dazzling gold break in the cloud. I came home through the fields to old Headington, where the colouring in the hedgerows was rich. But these winds are bringing the leaves down too quickly.

Oct. 10th

We haven't been having a very nice time for the last day or so as Mr Papworth has been seriously ill, which bothers me not only for the poor beast's sake, but also for Minto's, who takes it so to heart and gives herself so much extra work about it. I am also very busy getting ready for term. You can well imagine how I dislike all these preparations because they are always associated with leaving my homely timeless days at Hillsboro and going back to the solitude of my college bedroom and the routine of a time-table. Of course college and ones own rooms & books have their charm: but you know what I mean – especially late at night when people go away and you find that you have let the fire [go] out.

79 The novel 'English People', which has never been published.
80 Pullens Lane.

I am slowly reading a book that we have known about, but not known, for many a long day – Macdonald's *Diary of an Old Soul*.[81] How I would have scorned it once! I strongly advise you to try it. He seems to know everything and I find my own experience in it constantly: as regards the literary quality, I am coming to like even his clumsiness. There is a delicious home-spun, earthy flavour about it, as in George Herbert. Indeed *for me* he is better than Herbert.

Oct. 15th?

I have been back in College for about a week and find I can't go on with this very well. I may try to start another on a more purely diary model. The return to College and its regular routine has done me good: the lag ends of recent horrors have begun to fade in my mind. I am very busy this term, but the beautiful weather over-rides everything.

Yrs
Jack

TO ARTHUR GREEVES (W):

[Magdalen College]
Thursday Oct. 17th [1929]

Altho I had not gone to bed till one and had then been kept awake by the brilliant moonlight in my room (after walking a half hour in the same moonlight thro' the grove with Griffiths[82]) I woke perfectly refreshed after one of those sleeps deeper than usual which sometimes comes to us in a short night. Went round the walks with Griffiths after breakfast and both enjoyed the bright yellow leaves floating on the water. He packed off and set out to bicycle home to Newbury at 10.

---

81 Though it may not have been the copy he was reading at the time, Lewis owned the 'New Edition' of *The Diary of an Old Soul* (1885) which contains the inscription in MacDonald's hand, 'Charlotte Kölle with kindest regards from George & Louisa MacDonald. April 27, 1885.' It contains, as well, an inscription in Lewis's hand, 'Later: from C.S. Lewis to Joy Davidman, Christmas 1952.'

82 Alan Richard Griffiths (l906–93) matriculated at Magdalen in 1925 and read English under Lewis. In *SBJ* XV, Lewis speaks of him as his 'chief companion' on the road to Christianity. In 1931 Griffiths was received into the Catholic Church, and in 1936 he took his solemn vows as a Benedictine monk, at which time he took the name Dom Bede Griffiths. In 1955 he was sent to India, and he remained there for the rest of his life. The story of his joint pilgrimage to the Faith with Lewis is found in *The Golden String* (1954).

From 10 to 1 pupils. Out home for lunch. Dug the hen run, dug worms for the hens, and took Tykes[83] for the short walk which is all he can manage at present: then at 3.30 walked v. quickly up Shotover getting back about 4.15 for tea. Left home at 5 and got back for pupil at 5.30.

My new book on Marlow[84] had come which I read after dinner. It is chiefly concerned with the appalling career of Poole,[85] who was one of those present when Marlow was murdered: an incredible person who was receiving pay from the Papists for carrying letters to Mary Queen of Scots and also from the govt. for spying on the Papists and Mary: at the same time engaged in litigation with the husband of a woman who visited him while in prison for debt.

Dropped in on Christie[86] for half an hour and was in bed by 11.15 after reading my daily verse from *The Diary of an Old Soul.*

Mon. Nov. 4th – After breakfast returned to College from home where I had been spending the week end in the hope of getting rid of my flu'ey cold. I had foolishly taken last week end out there in bed, had to get up too soon, and consequently felt v. poorly all week. No pupils on Monday morning. Spent the whole time till lunch answering letters and setting examination papers. A dull job, rewarded by those sudden gleams of fugitive association that have the habit of starting up only when the intellect is fully engaged on something else.

Home for lunch. Dug the hen run and dug for worms. Worms are a case in which the extension of a name has altered a physical feeling for me. From reading Beowulf and the Edda the word 'Worm' in the sense of 'dragon' has become so familiar to me that I always think of these humble twisters as poor relations of Fafner and Jormungander; their kinship with the monstrous has taken from them the merely disgusting and I can now lift them in my fingers without a shudder. Even if I could not, earth is such a lovely thing that it reconciles one to all its contents. As Minto always says 'There's comfort in the clay.' Took Mr Papworth for his walk.

---

83 Another name for Mr Papworth, Lewis's dog.

84 Frederick Samuel Boas, *Marlowe and His Circle* (1929).

85 Robert Poley or Robert Poole was a government agent so deeply involved in plots and counterplots that no one knew whose side he was on. Boas devotes ch. 2 of his book to him.

86 John Traill Christie (1899–1980) was Fellow and Classical Tutor at Magdalen from 1928 to 1932; headmaster of Repton School, 1932–7; headmaster of Westminster School, 1937–49; and principal of Jesus College, Oxford, 1950–67.

The leaves on the ground are now very thick in Cuckoo Lane. A white liquid sky with horizontal bands of darker grey and a white sun behind them. Not a breath of wind. I had hoped to go and see old Foord-Kelcie[87] after the walk but I am still rather groggy and was tired & sweating when I came back so I did not.

Into college after tea. I intended to write a page or so for you before dinner, but answering letters to Condlin filled up the whole time. After dinner the Michaelmas Club met in my rooms. (An undergraduate society wh. McFarlane and I were instrumental in founding a year ago.) Acton,[88] a funny little chap with a cockney accent but the best philosopher as well as the most earnest and *real* thinker in College – nothing blasé about him – read an excellent paper on *Pessimism*. It had the touch of reality about it – quite unlike most young men's pessimism. A fairly good discussion afterwards till about 11.45 when the Club broke up. McFarlane stayed with me till 12.30 talking by the fire, to the accompaniment of the stags grunting in the grove outside. V. tired.

Tue. Nov. 5th – One of *our* days. Woke to a great roaring wind that kept the trees in the grove rising and falling with the motion and noise of seas all morning while the leaves fell in showers. Work all morning and home at 1 o'clock, where the Barfields, a pleasant surprise, turned up after lunch. Mrs B.[89] stayed with Minto while he and I took a short walk. Talked chiefly about his novel (this seems to be a practice of my friends!). He said among other things that he thought the idea of the spiritual world as *home* – the discovery of homeliness in that wh. is otherwise so remote – the feeling that you are coming *back* tho' to a place you have never yet reached – was peculiar to the British, and thought that Macdonald, Chesterton, and I, had this more than anyone else. He doesn't know you of course[90] – who, with Minto, have taught me so much in that way <(in *that* way? No, no.).>

---

87 The Rev. Edward Foord-Kelcey (1859–1934), a retired clergyman who entered Pembroke College, Oxford, in 1884 and whose last preferment before moving to Oxford was Great Kimble in Buckinghamshire. There is a short biography of him by Lewis in LP XI: 24–5.

88 Harry Burrows Acton (1908–) matriculated in 1927 and took a First in PPE (Philosophy, Politics and Economics) in 1930. In 1931 he became an assistant lecturer in philosophy at University College, Swansea.

89 Owen Barfield had married Matilda 'Maud' Douie (1885–1980), a professional dancer and producer, in 1923. See **Owen Barfield** in the Biographical Appendix.

90 He means they didn't know one another well. They met for the first time at 28 Warneford Road on 7 July 1922, on which occasion Greeves drew a sketch of Barfield. See *AMR*, p. 65.

Had to be back in Oxford by 5 to attend Simpson's[91] class on Textual Criticism (no, no, Arthur – *T*extual) which I am learning this year in order to teach next. After dinner read with Ker[92] (a pupil) some of the fragments of Anglo-Saxon poetry. Immensely fine. There's one begins with a man going to the window & looking out and saying 'No. This light is not the day breaking, nor a fiery dragon, nor is the house on fire. Take your shields & swords.'[93] Ker shares to the full my enthusiasm for the saga world & we had a pleasant evening – with the wind still roaring outside.

Wed. Nov. 6. – A nasty day. Work all morning. Then lunch in college, which I hate, as there was a college meeting at 2: at which everything went the way I didn't want it to go. I had just time to rush out home, take Mr Papworth for a run and have tea, returning to give my lecture at 5, take a pupil at 6, dine at 7.15 and receive a visit from a pupil with a terrible stutter at 8.30. Fortunately McFarlane came in at about ten wh. encouraged this poor fellow – to his own relief as much as mine – to take himself off. We then made cocoa and chatted till eleven. V. tired and – the old phraze – v. much 'entangled in the world' & v. far in spirit from where I would be.

Thurs. Nov. 7th. – Got an unexpected free evening off owing to a pupil's having another engagement and like a fool wasted it lounging about in the smoking room till after 10 talking to various people whom I don't greatly care for of subjects I'm not greatly interested in. Such fools we are.

---

91 Percy Simpson (1865–1962) was educated at Selwyn College, Cambridge. After taking a degree in 1887 he taught at Denstone School until 1895. In 1888 he embarked on what was to be his life's work: the annotation of Ben Jonson's plays. Over many years, Simpson, his wife Evelyn M. Simpson and C.H. Herford edited the 11 volumes of Jonson's *Works* (1925–52). In 1913 he arrived in Oxford to work for the Clarendon Press, and was almost at once invited to help as a lecturer in the English Faculty. In 1914 he was appointed first librarian of the new English faculty library, a post which he held until 1934. Simpson also lectured on textual criticism for students reading for the B.Litt. degree. Lewis, who had learned textual criticism from Simpson, began teaching his own class for B.Litt. students in the Trinity Term of 1930 when his subject was 'The Text of Milton's *Comus*'.

92 Neil Ripley Ker (1908–82) matriculated in 1928, and was a Fellow of Magdalen and Reader in Paleography from 1946 to 1968. He brought to the study acute powers of observation, and included among his distinguished works are the *Catalogue of Manuscripts containing Anglo-Saxon* (1957) and *Medieval Manuscripts of Great Britain* (1969 onwards).

93 The opening lines of *Finnsburg*, ed. George Hickes (1705).

Dec. 3rd. – I tried hard to keep this up but it wouldn't do. Awful business correspondence with Condlin filled up any spare hours I had of an evening. I have also got rather into a whirl as I always do in the latter part of the term. I have too many irons in the fire – the Michaelmas Club, the Linguistic Society, the Icelandic Society, and this and that. One week I was up till 2.30 on Monday (talking to the Anglo Saxon professor Tolkien[94] who came back with me to College from a society and sat discoursing of the gods & giants & Asgard for three hours, then departing in the wind & rain – who cd. turn him out, for the fire was bright and the talk good?), next night till 1 talking to someone else, & on Wednesday till 12 with the Icelandics. It is very hard to keep ones feet in this sea of engagements and very bad for me spiritually.

I am trying not to look forward too much to next week. How odd it will be to sleep in Bernagh – and to walk into Leeborough with Minto. I wonder does the future hold for us things as strange to our present point of view as *this* is to our old one? Barfield's novel[95] is finished and already refused by one publisher. To day there is a fog, and all the trees quite bare now.

In spite of the failure so far I intend to keep up the effort of continuing a journal letter to you. In the Vac. it shd. be easier than in the term, and perhaps habit will at last teach me to fit a portion however small into my day's routine. But you must do the same. Think how we shall enjoy the product when we are old.

Yrs
Jack

P.S. Give my love to your mother and v. many thanks for having us.

TO HIS BROTHER (LP X: 211–18):

Hillsboro.
Dec. 21st 29

My dear APB,

Thank you for your letter of the 2nd Nov. and specially for your generous decision about the money – though it would be mere

94 J.R.R. Tolkien is mentioned in note 38 to the letter of 26 June 1927. See also **J.R.R. Tolkien** in the Biographical Appendix.

95 i.e. 'English People'.

hypocrisy to pretend it was unexpected. When you say that we have lived long on a communal basis, I am afraid I cannot help reflecting that it has largely been a communism in which I have played the receiving proletarian to your bleeding capitalist: that however is a form justified by the best models. As to the proportions of the money – P's decision was based on the belief that I was safely and amply provided for while you, despite the surprising quantity of 'music' you got out of life, were very poor at the moment and liable to be axed in the near future. I feel justified in taking half because he was of course ignorant that more than one shared my income, and also much too sanguine about the safety of my job. But I want it to be clearly understood that if you get axed (*absit omen*),[96] and I still have a job, we shall then revert to unequal portions.

This all sounds as if I were in hourly expectation of being turned out of my fellowship, but that is not exactly what I mean. I am simply taking into account the fact that re-election – for which I come up next summer – though very usual is not inevitable or merely formal and depends on far reaching wangles. I do not think it at all probable that the Tutorial board would care to set the ominous precedent of refusing to recommend one of its own members for re-election (too many can play at that game once it is started), but there are anti-English Schools and anti-SPB and the thing is conceivable. All this must sound very strange to you, but you must try to realise what a real democracy like a College means. Suppose Sir, that your continued employment depended on the votes of the other officers in your unit, and that some one (who also rather disliked you personally) wanted your place for an officer of a different type e.g. wanted a horse transport bloke *instead*, it being impossible to increase the strength...you see the sort of situation which results. There is no reason to be seriously worried about it, and I have already spent longer on the subject than I intended.

Now as to other business. I think I told you in my last letter that a purchaser was nibbling at Leeborough. After inspection he decided not to buy. The episode however gave me rather a fright. If another purchaser turned up next term, what was I to do? He would probably want immediate possession: and, much as you might want to spend another fortnight there in April, I take it you would not wish to do so at the cost of three thousand odd pounds – that would be a curious commentary on our old slogan 'it's a

96 'May this omen be absent' or in this instance, 'Heaven forbid!'

very *cheap* hotel'. Again, the house is so unsaleable that if you turned down one purchaser you might never get another: and pleasant as it may be now to reflect that 'we still have Leeborough', the same reflection will rather pall if we are making it fifteen years hence. On the other hand I could not get over for more than a couple of nights in term: so that if such a situation arose, I should probably have to let the place be turned out and a sale held with very little supervision. This alternative was clearly quite out of the question. I accordingly decided to go over at the end of last term and sort things into such an order that if I had to give sudden authority for a sale, no great prying or larceny could go on. I decided to take Minto with me, partly to give her a change, and partly to have her advice about china and linen, and as I felt it wd. be a breach of decorum to take her to Leeborough, we both billeted ourselves at Bernagh for about ten days, arriving back in Oxford today. The following is a record of what I have done.

(1) *All keeps* in the way of books I have put in the study: i.e. all your books, all my books which I wish to keep, all P'daita books which I know that I want or suspect that you want. The *Cambridge Modern History*[97] and the big translation of Dumas are the inclusions that I felt most doubtful about: but if we finally condemn them they will sell as well a year hence as now.

(2) All Boxonian and pellesmonic documents (after one last unsuccessful search for that *ignis fatuus* Zoe Pasquali)[98] I have carefully collected into the playbox and placed in the study.

(3) *Other papers.* These are all in the study in the other playbox and the big chest from the cistern attic. 1. Family letters. Of Grandfather and Grandmother Lewis and Granduncle Thomas Lewis (neither of whom could spell), I have kept all. Of Mammy's and P's letters I have kept all except bills, receipts, invitations and the like. Of Uncle Bill and Uncle Dick I have kept a selection (These are such utter rubbish that it was kind to keep any considering the enormous bulk of papers I dealt with). Hamilton letters there were hardly any, but I kept all I could find. All letters of yours (i.e. to and from you) I kept. I took the liberty of removing the envelopes towards the end, as space was by this time becoming a serious question.

97 *The Cambridge Modern History*, planned by the late Lord Acton, edited by Alphonsus William Ward, George Walter Prothero, Sir Stanley Leathes and Ernest Alfred Benians, 13 vols. (1902–12).

98 That 'deceiving flame', Zoe Pasquali, was presumably a character in a Boxen story that has not come to light.

2. *Diaries.* Grandfather's (Hamilton), yours and fragments of diary by P. 3. Documents relating to Mammy's academic career, your Mention etc., all of course kept. In the time at my disposal it was quite impossible to arrange these three classes of papers in any sort of order, so I am afraid that both chest and playbox will have to be turned out to find any given piece. What I can say for sure is that I have destroyed nothing of yours that I could find. I would have assembled them if I had found them even remotely assembled – but you know what it is like in Leeborough. It had to be simply a case of taking drawer after drawer, as you came to them, and going on doggedly, often for hours at a stretch.

(4) *Pictures.* (a) All *photographs* of yours are either in the drawers of P's study desk, or with the papers in the chest and playbox. (This means of course that at first I began putting photos in with the letters but later found them too big an item). Family photos e.g. of Mammy, P., ourselves etc, are all in the drawers in the study desk. Various endless photos of our cousins at various ages, or of utterly unknown people, I destroyed. Malvern and Army groups and other large framed photos are all in the study. (b) the two grandfather portraits, the 3 P'daita portraits, the 2 Medicis, the pictures from the little end room, the drawings from the hall, are in the study.

(5) Forrest Reid (a novelist and friend of Arthur's)[99] and Arthur, with the aid of the leading booksellers catalogues, picked out for me the cream of the novels by which I mean the cream, not from the reading, but from the collector's standpoint. Here I had to make a decision of my own. I decided, I hope not wrongly, that you would as soon read your *Man of Property* in a contemporary edition as in a first, listed by booksellers at £17.10.0. I have therefore brought back with me a packing case full of the most valuable of these: a trunk follows containing the less valuable, but still too good to be knocked down at an auction. I shall have about twenty copies of the list typed and send it to several booksellers and take the best offers I get. I ventured to act without authority because the Galsworthys are now about as high as they are likely to go.

---

99 Forrest Reid (1875–1947), the novelist, was living in Belfast at this time. His story is told in his two autobiographies, *Apostate* (1926) and *Private Road* (1940). There are several references to Arthur Greeves and J.N. Bryson in Russell Burlingham's *Forrest Reid: A Portrait and a Study* (1953). A portrait of Reid, painted by Greeves, is in the possession of the Royal Academical Institution, Belfast.

(6) *The Dud books* I have collected altogether on the floor of the landing and some bedrooms. Arthur and Reid have promised to bring a librarian to see them as lending libraries often offer more for ordinary novels in decent condition than a bookseller buying by weight.

(7) *Clothes*. 1. All clothes of yours except obviously antediluvian dress softs and infantile shirts have been kept, including a great deal which I am pretty sure is useless. 2. All P's clothes that are in reasonable condition have been kept to provide knockabouts for us. 3. Mammy's clothes were a very difficult problem. a. some things are in cardboard boxes in the study. I suppose we had better give them as presents to people like Aunt Annie. These are ones in which the material has intrinsic value. b. some small intimate things I burned. c. some things which had no intrinsic value I gave to the Witch of Endor to dispose of among poor people as she chose. All clothes of P's and yours are in the wardrobe in his dressing room. Condemned clothing (i.e. hopelessly small, torn, or moth eaten) I have partly given to the Witch, partly brought back to give to the very frequent people who ask for clothes at our door. I hope this was a right disposal. You can't sell such things and to destroy it all (incidentally, how would you set about it?) in a country where dozens of people have no coats, seems rather harsh.

(8) *Archpigiebotian miscellanies*. The heavy canvas parcel (damnably heavy) in P's dressing room, the topees, the horrid rubble of spurs, and iron spikes in the same room, the maps, the steel box, the African spear, and everything unintelligible which looked like being yours, I have conveyed to the study.

(9) *Silver and jewelry* all packed and in the bank except a few things too large, like lamps, and a few things of small value overlooked, which I gathered up and put in the study: besides a modicum for our own table use in the spring if (as I still hope) we are there together again.

(10) *China and glass*. Minto thought very little of this was good, and what was good was often cracked and defective. A small selection at her advice I put in a special place in one of the pantries and notified the Witch – who agreed about the small value of this item as a whole. (She has served in several big houses and is also a *very* loyal Leeburian, so I think her opinion good.).

(11) The piano I have sold for £18.0.0 to one French, who came out to value the contents of the house for death duties. Condlin, Arthur, and Minto all advised my acceptance of this figure and indeed were surprised

that we got it. (Such payments are made to the account of C. S. Lewis Exctr. of A. J. Lewis decd., at the Bank of Ireland so that there is no danger of their getting mixed up with my private account at Barclay's Bank in Headington. I should have preferred to have cheques made out to us both, but this is much too simple for the Law who prefer that the present executor (for of course I act qua executor and not as one of the heirs) should act entirely on his own, so that the other executors can have a chance to sue him as and when they turn up).

(12) *Mammy's collection of stamps.* P. frequently mentioned this to me and intended it to be sold. In fact he left in the album a note dated 1929 saying 'Some of these may be worth money' – a note which I have of course preserved as one of the best and least P'daita-ish actions of his life. The best stamps in the album were forgeries, so that I was glad to sell it for four pounds.

(13) I have also sold (a) to Reid: *The Graphics*[100] and the 'famous trials' for £3.2.6. As the *Graphics* can be bought for 6d a volume, we have no reason to be dissatisfied. (b) To Arthur: *the Smaller Temple Shakespeare*[101] and some oddments for £4.6.6.

(14) *Furniture.* I have placed in the study (or left there) the desk, the sofa, the tables, the two screens, grandfather's chair from the little end room, the soft study chair, one of the drawing room arm chairs, the little end room armchair, four upright armchairs from the drawing room. I have labeled *not for sale* the two hall chairs, the glazed drawing room bookcase, Mammy's desk in drawing room (which I can find no key to unlock), the cloak room settle, the two little end room bookcases, and the grandfather clock. (Gramophone, telescope, and microscope also in the study).

Having got thus far, I begin to fear that the impression produced on you will be much as if I had written 'I have moved all the study furniture into our bedroom and carefully placed all our bedroom stuff in the hall: I have had the water closet seats pulled out and refixed in the little end room at a very moderate cost: I have sunk a swimming bath in the croquet lawn and been fortunate to dispose of a bushel of parsley to Bob

---

100 *The Graphic* was a periodical which ran from 1869 to 1932, after which it was continued as *The National Graphic.*

101 He was probably referring to *The Temple Shakespeare for Schools*, 8 vols. (1902), which had been preceded by *The Temple Shakespeare*, ed. Israel Gollancz, 40 vols. (1894–97) and *The Larger Temple Shakespeare*, ed. Israel Gollancz, 12 vols. (1899, 1900).

Ewart for 9½d. The collection of bowler hats I am bringing to England to distribute among the dealers who offer the best figures...'

But what my proceedings really boil down to is this: All real treasures and relics are now in the study. All *valuables* are either in the Bank of Ireland or (like the first editions) in Magdalen. Therefore, if a good purchaser appears suddenly this term wanting immediate possession, I can sell the house and hold a sale of effects at Leeborough, carefully excepting from the sale the whole study and certain things outside the study which I have labeled. I have made the division and can give orders to carry it into effect at a moments notice. In making it I have no doubt committed several errors of judgement and still more of negligence – it is very hard to avoid mistakes in going through thousands of articles. I feel pretty confident that you will not blame me for having made the divide on my own. The only alternatives were to risk the loss of a very considerable sum of money or to leave the division to make itself during a two days visit from me surrounded by auctioneers and relations. The only thing I have left wholly out is the trunk of 'characters' in the attic. If you are home before the house is sold, we can act together: if not, it can go to storage with the things in the study.

Of course it is very likely that no one will buy before April – and you may add 'Or after': and it is one of the disadvantages of what I have done that in that case you will return to a Leeborough hideously changed by my conversion of the study into a store. But I can say quite honestly from my experience of the last ten days that I believe it will be a damned sight pleasanter to get it all at once like that than to watch it gradually assume that aspect. I certainly had the idea that we could still have a few days of the old type, but as soon as you get there you see that it's quite impossible. As there are no silences in the Arctic circle, because there's no noise, so there can be no nonp'daita days when there's no P'daita. If we are there together in April the only thing to do is to give up from the start any idea that it is the real thing again. If we start on that basis we may get along quite well: on any other you'll find that it gives you the blues like the devil.

As to the points in your letter. Re *List of Securities*. Of course in the question of dividing this I shall do nothing till you come home. Like you, I can make very little of it: indeed I cannot sometimes resist a smile at the idea that he keeps the secret of 'his little bit of savings' as tenaciously as ever. But there are certainly a good many steam tramways. As to *what Condlin means* – for the Lord's sake don't ask me. A very short interview with Condlin invariably reduces me to the state of wondering which of us is mad. As for gratuities: to the Witch of Endor £100 by P's own request. To Condlin – I should like to be decent to him, but have no idea what one can do. His social and financial status are so very indeterminate that I am not sure whether he falls in the class to whom one gives money or the class to whom one gives keepsakes. I am rather afraid he falls in that class to whom one gives money, but only in enormous quantities. We must talk this over when we meet.

Window – I am greatly attracted by this idea, but have no idea what the cost would be.[102] I suggest as a preliminary that the sum realised by the sale of Mammy's jewelry* should be set aside as the basis of a fund for this purpose. *Silver*. The whole question of valuables kept by me, for of course I shall keep more than you (furniture etc.) is rather a problem. Everything has been valued for probate, so that I suppose we had better add up the values of all articles kept by either of us: and the man with the heavier list (i.e. SPB) hands over the difference. The other way is to auction everything and let us appear as bidders, but I don't fancy that. I think the best thing would be to hand over our several keeps (excluding communal keeps) for re-evaluation by some competent person – the value for probate being a little lower than real market value. We should then get a sum like this.

Realised by the sale.	*£x.*
W's share of this	*£x/2*
J's share of this	*£x/2*
But W. keeps	*£30*
J. keeps	*£150*
J. pays W. £150 – 30	*£120*
W. now has	*x/2 plus 120 (plus 30's worth)*

i.e. x/2 plus 150
J. now has x/2 plus 150's worth
i.e. x/2 plus 150

102 In 1935 Jack and Warnie gave a stained glass window to St Mark's, Dundela, in memory of their parents.

This is no doubt a cumbersome way of representing a simple operation but you know that these things are not my long suit.

One of the pities of the present state of affairs seems to be that it is impossible for either of us to write the other a real letter. I will try to break the spell by giving you some account of my adventures since you last heard from me before the great divide. The chief adventure is the quite new light thrown on P. by a closer knowledge of his two brothers. One of his failings – his fussily directed manner 'Have you got your keys etc.' – takes on a new air when one discovers that in his generation the brothers all habitually treated one another in exactly the same way.

On the morning of the funeral Uncle Dick arrived before breakfast and came to Uncle Bill who was sleeping in the spare room. I drifted in. After a few greetings, it was with a shock of mild surprise that I heard Limpopo suddenly cut short a remark of Uncle Dick's with the words 'Now Dick, you'd better go and take off your collar, huh, (gesture) and wash yourself and that sort of thing, eh, and have a bit of a shave.' To which his brother, with perfect seriousness replied 'Now how had we better handle the thing, eh Jacks? You'd better go to the bathroom first and I'll go downstairs and get a cup of tea. Bill, you'd better lie down (gesture) and cover yourself up and I'll come and tell you...' *Limpopo* (cutting in) 'Well Dick, get along downstairs, huh, and Jacks will go and tell you, wouldn't that be best, eh?'

Later in the day we had a session of the wardrobe committee quite in the old manner: and in the afternoon I was told 'Jacks, show Mrs Hamilton that coat you found. Isn't it a splendid fit, huh, might have been made for him, wha'?'

Another light came to me during the visit to the undertakers: the whole scene had such an insane air of diabolical farce that I cannot help recording it. After a man with a dusty face had approached me with the assurance that he had buried my grandfather, my mother, and my uncle, a superior person led us into an inner room and inquired if we wanted 'a suite of coffins'. Before I had recovered from this – and it sounded like the offer of some scaly booking clerk at an hotel in hell – the brute suddenly jerked out of the wall a series of enormous vertical doors, each one of which when lowered revealed on its inner side a specimen coffin. We were quite surrounded by them. Slapping one of them like a drum with his resonant hand he remarked 'That's a coffin I'm always very fond of' and it was then that the 'light' came.

Limpopo – and even Limpopo came as a relief in such an atmosphere – put an end to this vulgarity by saying in his deepest bass 'What's been used before, huh? There must be some tradition about the thing. What has the custom been in the family, eh?' And then I suddenly saw, what I'd never seen before: that to them family traditions – the square sheet, the two thirty dinner, the gigantic overcoat – were what school traditions and college traditions are, I don't say to me, but to most of our generation. It is so simple once you know it. How could it be otherwise in those large Victorian families with their intense vitality, when they had not been to public schools and when the family was actually the solidest institution they experienced? It puts a great many things in a more sympathetic light than I ever saw them in before.

But apart from these two lights, what I carried away from those few days was the feeling (perhaps I mentioned it before) that all the other members of that family were only fragments of our own P'daitabird. Uncle Dick has the wheezes, but only the crudest of them and none of the culture. In Joey you see the wheeze side of the character gone to seed – the man whose conversation is nothing but giggles. In Limpopo, of course you see simply all the bad points without any of the good: with the additional property of being an outrageous bore, which is the one thing P. never was at any time.

His idea of conversation is almost unbelievable. On the evening of the day of his arrival, after dinner, having been supplied with whiskey, he drew up the little wooden seated study chair to the fire, and having placed his little tubby body in it and crossed his flaccid hands on his belly, proceeded to enunciate the following propositions. 'I usually leave town about quarter to six, huh, and then I get out to Helensburgh about quarter past and walk up to me house, eh, and then I (Jacks I'll have another drop of that whiskey) put on an old coat, huh, then I come down and have something to drink and a bit of a chat with your Aunt Minnie, huh, and then...' Without any exaggeration, he kept me up till 1.30 with this drivel. The last night, when the Hamiltonians were there, was much better. Limpopo explained that he had given up dealing with Hogg. 'The last suit he sent me...the trousers came up to my chin (gesture)...I was very nearly going to law with him.' *Uncle Gussie*: 'I think you should. You should have gone into court wearing that suit.' *Limpopo* (with profound gravity) 'Oh, I wouldn't like to have done that, huh.'

While in Ireland we had two days off from work. On one the Greeves's motored us up the coast road and up the glens of Antrim: on the other Uncle Gussie and Aunt Annie took us down to Cloghy to their cottage at the end of the Ards. The beauty of both drives you know without need of description. Which reminds me, come what may, you and I must have that walk to the Mournes: after a fortnight or so of breaking up and other horrors at Leeborough, it would be just the thing to get the taste out of our mouths. I don't know that I have any other news. I seem to have read nothing except for work – indeed to have had no normal life or leisure – for ages. One scrap worth quoting comes to my mind from a Wynyard letter of yours which I read before putting it into the box. It began 'Mrs Capron died today and we are all very sorry about it. Mr Capron is in a very bad temper over it.' *Ex ore infantium*[103] – could that be bettered? One book I did read during P's illness was 'All quiet on the Western front':[104] but perhaps I mentioned that to you before.

I suppose I shall hear from you again before April – let me have exact dates of arrival as soon as you can. By the way, do they schedule troopships to arrive at a certain day – or week – or month? I feel more bored at present than I ever remember feeling.

yrs,
Jack

* If any. Jewelry is not v. easy to sell at present I hear.

P.S. If we had both volumes of the 1st Editn. of the Jungle Book[105] we could probably get £40 or £50 for it: but after hunting high and low I can find only one.

---

103 Matthew 21:16 (Vulgate): 'Out of the mouths of babes and sucklings [thou has perfected praise].'

104 The German author Erich Maria Remarque (1898–1970) published his great novel of the First World War under the title *Im Westen Nichts Neues* (1929). Arthur Wesley Wheen's English translation, *All Quiet on the Western Front*, was published the same year.

105 Kipling, *The Jungle Book*. They had a 1897 reprint of *The Jungle Book*, first published in 1894, but a first edition of *The Second Jungle Book* (1895) and they retained both of them.

TO ARTHUR GREEVES (W):

Hillsborough,
Headington,
Oxford.
[27 December 1929]

My dear Arthur,

The perfect guest again! An awful thing has happened: I find that I have not got with me my three most valuable keys. I have wired to the Ulster Monarch[106] & had an answer to say that they cannot be found. My last hope is that they are in the study. Will you please look and then let me know, but do *not* send them till further notice. There are three tied together with string, two ordinary looking keys and one very short & shiny one. They may be in the key hole of my father's desk – i.e. the small one in the key hole & the other two hanging from it – or on the top of the same desk. As one of the keys is my college key which will cost me £100 if I lose it, I am rather in a stew & shall be glad to have a line as soon as possible. Just like me, you will say.

Many thanks & much love from us both. Minto is writing in a few days.

Yrs

Jack

P.S. Of course have a look elsewhere, but if they're not in the study I expect they're a gonner. If you get them please take them home with you (after making sure that the desk is locked) & guard them carefully till further notice. Shall write as soon as I can.[107]

[Hillsboro
1929]
Dec. 21st

Although if I had had my choice I should have preferred some real talk between you and me alone, still I think it worth while to say that I felt something very pleasant in our final chat with John[108] and our drinking on board the Ulster Monarch. On occasions that are rather melancholy a plunge into the cheery and homely world of 'good fellows' and women has something of the same wholesome effect as a romp with

---

106 The cross-channel boat on which Lewis and Mrs Moore returned from Ireland on 20 December.

107 Greeves wired on 28 December to say he had found the keys.

108 Arthur's brother, John Greeves.

dogs or children; it was specially appropriate to this visit too, since the main thing that I bring away with me is a new view of John. Besides, as Barfield said when Christie interrupted us one night that he was staying in College, it is rather important that friends should occasionally share together their experience of a third person.

Dec. 22nd

I think the L.N.W.R. mainline must run through the dullest country in the British Isles – tho' of course no country is without some charm. I read *Grace Abounding* in Everyman, having (you remember) read *Mr Badman* in the same volume on the way over. *Grace Abounding* is incomparably the better of the two. Some of the sentences in it reach right down. 'But the milk and honey is beyond this wilderness'[109] – 'I thought I could have spoken of his love and his mercy even to the very crows that sat upon the ploughed lands before me'[110] – 'I could not find that with all my soul I did *desire* deliverance.'[111] Of course a great part of it paints the horrors of religion and sometimes almost of insanity. What do you make of the curious temptation that assailed him just after he had been converted and felt himself united to Christ; when a voice kept saying 'Sell Him, sell Him': sometimes for hours at a stretch, until in mere weariness Bunyan blurted out 'Let Him go if he will'[112] – which afterwards led him into despair, believing he had committed the unpardonable sin?

I suppose this is the same mental disease of which you and I have felt a trace in the impulse to throw ones new book in the fire – some strange twist that impels you to do a thing because it is precisely the one thing of all others that you *don't* want to do.

I should like to know, too, in general, what you think of all the darker side of religion as we find it in old books. Formerly I regarded it as mere devil worship based on horrible superstitions. Now that I have found, and am still finding more and more, the element of truth in the old beliefs, I feel I cannot dismiss even their dreadful side so cavalierly. There must be something in it: only what?

---

109 John Bunyan, *Grace Abounding and The Life and Death of Mr Badman*, with an Introduction by G.M. Harrison, Everyman's Library [1928], preface, p. 6.

110 ibid., para. 92, p. 31.

111 ibid., para. 194, p. 34.

112 ibid., para. 139, p. 44.

Dec. 23rd

Delighted to get back to my books again and did a good morning's work on Chaucer, mostly textual problems. Too wet for anything but a short walk after lunch. In the evening wrote part of a long letter to Warnie. I find I am (so far) surprisingly little upset about the affair of my keys.

Dec. 24th

Into town in the morning to get my hair cut, and then, before lunch, began indexing my Bunyan. I had a lovely walk in the afternoon – a perfect winter day with mellow sunlight slanting through a half frosty mist on the grey fields, the cosy farms, and the tall leafless elms, absolutely unmoving in the air. On my way back the sun was down and it was cold. I passed two men engaged in penning sheep and walked just by the baa-ing crowd, whose breath looked like smoke.

At seven in to College to dine, which I didn't much enjoy as I got an awful bore called Parker[113] on my left and on my right the Italian professor[114] whose English is so bad that I can't understand *him*, and who is so deaf that he can't understand *me*.

At 9 o'clock we went up into hall for the Christmas Eve revels, which of course I have never seen before. The hall looks very noble with its green branches, and a roaring fire and the centre cleared, and a Christmas tree. Female guests, including, of course Minto and Maureen, were in the musicians gallery. From 9 to 10 the choir gave us the first part of the *Messiah*: a great mistake, I thought, with only a piano at our disposal for accompaniment. Then came an interval during which those who had no guests remained in hall for supper and to watch the choir boys having *their* Christmas supper, which is the best sight of all: I, and others in the same plight, went down to common room to feed our ladies on sandwiches and hot negus and talk small talk. We returned to hall to find lights out and candles lit on the tree and to hear carols: all the really good ones like the Coventry Carol and *In dulci jubilo* and one by Byrd that I never heard before. This last comes just on the stroke of midnight

---

113 Henry Michael Denne Parker (1894–1972), Fellow and Tutor in Ancient History at Magdalen College. Lewis usually referred to him as the 'Wounded Buffalo' or 'Wounded Bison'. See his portrait of him in *AMR*, 'Magdalen College Appendix', pp. 480–1.

114 Professor Cesare Foligno. See note 10 to the letter of 30 March 1927.

after the Vice President has sent a message to the ringers to begin the peals. I had been rather bored with the proceedings earlier in the evening but at this moment the glorious windy noise of the bells overhead, the firelight & candlelight, and the beautiful music of unaccompanied boys voices, really carried me out of myself. We then have sack passed round in a loving cup and pledge one another and so break up: home by taxi at about 12.30.

Taking it all in all, with the walk and the evening, and the blessed sense of charity, so rare in me, – the feeling, natural at such a moment that even my worst enemies in college were really funny and odd rather than detestable, while my friends were 'the many men so beautiful'[115] – this was as good a day as I could wish to have. If only it wasn't for those damned keys!

Dec. 25th

A slack day. All up very late after our debauch of the night before. Went for several short strolls with Mr Papworth, but no real walk. My afternoon one, about five o'clock was the best: an evening of bitter wind with the trees lashing one another across a steel coloured sunset. Afterwards – as a Christmas treat! – I read a modern novel, H. G. Wells' *Meanwhile*[116] which deals chiefly with the General Strike, and contains very good comic elements. You and I ought to read, think and talk of these things more than we do.

Dec. 26th

Another lazy day. Went in to College at about 10.30, by arrangement to go for a walk with McFarlane. We were on the road by about eleven. Neither of us was at first disposed for more than desultory chat. The trudge out of Oxford was tedious (as always) and I did not really begin to enjoy myself till we had climbed Cumnor Hill. Once through the beautiful grey and mossy village of Cumnor, I became extremely pleased with everything. Walking on unfrequented paths, we hardly met a soul: the sky was palest blue, without a cloud or a breeze, and the weak sun laid a lovely unity of pale colour over the ploughed fields, the haystacks and the church towers in each village. 'Unity of colour' is not just a phrase – I mean that everything, except the woods (which of course were brownish-black) and the crows, was almost the same colour of chilly greenish grey.

---

115 Coleridge, *The Rime of the Ancient Mariner*, Part IV, 236.
116 H.G. Wells, *Meanwhile* (1927).

As we dropped down the far side of the hill the floods began to spread themselves out wider and wider below us. Where the Thames should have been there was a sheet of water about a mile broad, intersected with the tops of hedges and polled willows. We began to wonder whether we could reach the ferry at Bablock Hythe. I was in favour of taking off shoes & stockings, not, of course, to wade the river, but to wade the shallow flood to the real river bank where the ferry begins. McFarlane however couldn't as one of his feet was bandaged under the sock as the result of wearing a tight shoe yesterday. However, when we got there, and called, the man at the pub brought a punt not only across the river but across the floods to where we stood. Once over, we feasted in the pub on bread & cheese, beer, and a following cup of tea – my invariable walking lunch. It left us in that delightful state which (I remember) Harwood once described – 'One is neither full nor hungry and goes on like a ship.' As it was boxing day, no one was working in the fields, and all was so still that the wheeling starlings made quite a noticeable noise.

You know how it sometimes is when you are out for a day's jaunt – as it has so often happened to you and me – that there comes a period when things are getting better and better every moment till suddenly one says 'Oh!' or 'By God!' and that is IT – the centre of the whole day, the thing one will remember it by. Such was the moment when the old man came over the gate in the frost-mist up by our wood: or when we saw the fire that night near the house of the sinister old man who sold lemonade: or when we were shown into the postmistress's cottage above the glens of Antrim. To day was of course totally different from all these. It happened by luck that two things came at the same moment.

We came round a turn into the village of Stanton Harcourt and suddenly got a view of the towered manor house and the church, across a farmyard, where a very fine old horse with a white star on his forehead was looking at us across a half gate. That was the first thing. And at the very same moment – this is the second thing – the ringers in the church began practicing their peal. It sounds poor on paper, but the thing about it was the sense of absolute peace and safety: the utter homeliness, the Englishness, the Christendom of it. And then I thought of Antrim only a week or so ago, and what you said (in the rainbow and sleet scene on Divis – itelf another instance of this *apex* in the day's outing) about the 'broad-mindedness' of the infinite – Antrim that's desolate and keen in July, Stanton Harcourt and all the sleepy Cumnor country (isn't the very name Cumnor good) which is snug and dreamy and like cotton wool even in winter.

Perhaps it is less strange that the Absolute should make both than that we should be able to love both. Bacon says 'The whole world cannot fill, much less distend the mind of man.'[117] (By the way, that is the answer to those who argue that the universe cannot be spiritual because it is so vast and inhuman and alarming. On the contrary, nothing less would do for us. At our best, we can stand it, and could not stand anything smaller or snugger. Anything less than the terrifyingly big would, at some moments, be cramping and 'homely' in the bad sense – as one speaks of a 'homely' face. You can't have elbow room for things like men except in endless time and space and staggering multiplicity.)[118]

A few miles beyond Stanton Harcourt – in the tower of that manor house, by the way, Mr Pope translated 'his Iliads'[119] – the peace of the afternoon was broken by brutes in the distance firing guns. The only good result of this was that it started a pair of white owls to blunder across our road, stupid with the daylight, poor chaps, and very grotesque to see. We had tea at Eynsham, and sitting over the fire in the pub there we fell (at last) into serious conversation – about the rival claims of reason and instinct. We continued this on the homeward journey – a long stretch of road (we dared not try the tow-path in the floods) which would have been dull by daylight. Now that the stars were out it was good enough. The remains of the sunset was before us, and all between us and it seemed to be water. McFarlane observed that it was one of the rare occasions on which night seemed a tangible thing: and looking back I saw what he meant, for the darkness and stars did seem to come up at our backs and then stop just over our heads, while in front was twilight.

We got back to Oxford, very happy but very footsore and tired, at about 6.30, and I was home (by bus) at about 7. Finished *Meanwhile*

117 A conflation of several lines of Francis Bacon's *The Advancement of Learning* (1605), First Book, I, 3.

118 Cf. 'Dogma and the Universe', in Lewis's *God in the Dock: Essays on Theology*, ed. Walter Hooper (London: Fount Paperbacks, 1979); *God in the Dock: Essays on Theology and Ethics*, ed. Walter Hooper (Grand Rapids: Eerdmans, 1970). 'What sort of universe do we demand? If it is small enough to be cosy, it would not be big enough to be sublime. If it is large enough for us to stretch our spiritual limbs in, it must be large enough to baffle us...It is to be expected that His creation should be, in the main, unintelligible to us.'

119 Alexander Pope, *The Iliad*, 6 vols. (1715–20).

after supper and took a hot bath to cure my stiffness – this being the first real exercise I have had for ages. It only needed a more perfectly receptive companion – such as you – to have made it one of the really great days: not that McFarlane is half bad, and one ought to learn to like more, and more different, people.

Dec 27th

Worked at Chaucer all morning. After lunch as I was carrying a plate into the scullery I suddenly got one of those vivid mental pictures that memory sometimes throws up for no apparent reason – a picture of the deep stony and brambly vallies on the side of Scrabo, wet and grey as they were one day when you and I came down that way. 'Jesus, the times this knight and I have had!'[120] (That's from Henry IV. Read it all, but specially the scene where Falstaff meets his old acquaintance Shallow in the country – one of the best 'Do you remember' conversations in any book that I know.)

After lunch Maureen took Mr Papworth for a walk, which always gives me a blessed liberation to go where I choose: for much as I like Mr P., his presence is a considerable restraint. You can't go *that* way because there is a dog that fights: and you can't go *that* way because there are sheep and you have to keep him on the lead. In fact it is rather like Dick Swiveller's walks in London.[121] I bussed into College, took out the second chapter of my book[122] & left it at the house of a Professor in Marston who had promised to give me his views on it. Thence home up the hill under grey and windy skies with a little rain. I tried my practice of keeping myself free from thought – a mere sponge to sense impressions – for a certain part of the way. Later I hope to resume the higher stage of meditation proper. Went on with Chaucer before supper: afterwards wrote to Condlin, Aunt Annie, Uncle Bill, Uncle Dick and you.

Dec. 28th

Went to Barfield's to day for my stay. Thanks awfully about the keys – your wire was a great relief. When will *your* big letter arrive? –

Yours

J

---

120 A conflation of lines 228–9 and lines 236–7 in Shakespeare's *Henry IV, Part 2*, III, ii.

121 A character in Charles Dickens' *The Old Curiosity Shop* (1841).

122 i.e. *The Allegory of Love*.

1930

TO ARTHUR GREEVES (W):

[Hillsboro]
3rd Jan 1930

My dear Arthur,

By now I hope you have my long letter and are well advanced with your long reply. You shall have another gripping instalment, D.V., in the course of the next ten days. We both enjoyed your description of your visit to the witches den,[1] most of which I read aloud to Minto. I am now, as you will already have guessed, going to give you the opportunity of paying her another one! This time it is my cheque book (Bank of Ireland) – which is unlikely to be in my Father's desk – tho' it may be, my dear fellow, it may be – and may be in the study or at Bernagh. If found it could be sent by post: and any odd collars or handkerchiefs left at Bernagh would be convenient packing. Don't hate me for ever!

Yours
Jack

TO ARTHUR GREEVES (W):

[Hillsboro
13? January 1930]

My dear Arthur:

Thurs Jan 2

Got home to day from four day's stay with Barfield. For the first two days his wife and adopted baby[2] were away, so we had the house to ourselves – alas that you and I never have such an uninterrupted feast of each other's society.

---

1 i.e. 'The Witch of Endor' (Mary Cullen), the cook-housekeeper at Little Lea.
2 Alexander Barfield (b. 1928).

We had promised ourselves some solid reading together, and in spite of the temptations of conversation and walking, we stuck to it: Aristotle's *Ethics* all morning, walk after lunch, and then Dante's *Paradiso* for the rest of the day.

The latter has really opened a new world to me. I don't know whether it is really very different from the *Inferno* (B. says its as different as chalk from cheese – heaven from hell, would be more appropriate!) or whether I was specially receptive, but it certainly seemed to me that I had never seen at all what Dante was like before. Unfortunately the impression is one so unlike anything else that I can hardly describe it for your benefit – a sort of mixture of intense, even crabbed, complexity in language and thought with (what seems impossible) *at the very same time* a feeling of spacious gliding movement, like a slow dance, or like flying. It is like the stars – endless mathematical subtility of orb, cycle, epicycle and ecliptic, unthinkable & unpicturable, & yet at the same time the freedom and liquidity of empty space and the triumphant certainty of movement. I should describe it as feeling more *important* than any poetry I have ever read. Whether it has the things you specially like is another question. It is seldom homely: perhaps not *holy* in our sense – it is too Catholic for that: and of course its blend of complexity and beauty is very like Catholic theology – wheel within wheel, but wheels of glory, and the One radiated through the Many.

One night we sat up till four, and heard the cock's crowing as we went to bed: a very good moment, and who shall I ever find to share it with me fully? For *you* would be too sleepy, and Barfield doesn't really taste a thing like that as keenly as you and I. They have a most delightful house, an ex-farmhouse with many outbuildings and an orchard: in one of the most beautiful villages I know. We had one very good walk among the floods, and one very good sky.

Frid. Jan 3

In the Bodleian all morning. Back after lunch, arriving there at 3 o'clock to find it shutting! Bought the new book on Malory by Vinaver[3] at 15/-, which is necessary for work, but not worth the price.

---

3 Eugène Vinaver, *Malory* (1929).

Sunday Jan 5th

I spent the morning finishing a long letter on philosophical subjects which I had carried about with me all the time in Ireland, to my friend and former pupil, Griffiths. It was owing to this that you have no Saturday's instalment from me: and if you knew how long Griffiths had waited for an answer you would not grudge it to him.

In the afternoon I had a most delicious walk, in that rarified afternoon sunlight which I have tried to describe so often. It is the peculiar glory of the English winter. Apart from a period of meditation – mind-emptying, I mean – which was fairly successful, I was on the whole as free from thought and fancies as I have been for a long time. Two moments are worth preserving.

One, when I suddenly paused, as we do for no reason known to consciousness, and gazed down into a little ditch beneath a grey hedge, where there was a pleasant mixture of ivies and low plants and mosses, and thought of herbalists and their art, and what a private, retired wisdom it would be to go groping along such hedges and the eaves of woods for some herb of virtuous powers, insignificant to the ordinary observer, but well known to the trained eye – and having at the same time a stronger sense of the mysteries of living stuff than usual, specially the mysteries twining at our feet, where homeliness and magic embrace one another.

The second was a stiffish five minutes up-hill towards a hedge of small trees and bushes, behind wh. the sun was setting. A keen frosty wind in my face: all beyond me flaming yellow, and on that yellow, in perfect black, the rich and varied pattern of the hedge, looking quite flat, so that the whole had a Chinese or Japanese appearance.

In the evening I started to read the Everyman volume of Jacob Boehme[4] which I had ordered sometime ago. The Dialogue at the end, called the Supersensual Life, was fairly easy going, and I should advise you to get and read it at once. Then I turned back and began the longer work, the Signatura Rerum. I could see at once that I was reading the most serious attempt I had ever met to describe (not to explain, for he speaks as one who has seen and his description *is* his explanation) – to describe the very mystery of creation and to show you the differences

4 Jacob Boehme, *The Signature of all Things, with Other Writings* [translated by John Ellistone], Introduction by Clifford Bax, Everyman's Library [1912].

actually coming into being out of the original One and making a world and souls and good and evil. Almost at the same time, I saw, alas, that it was hopelessly beyond me: yet tantalising for I could just grasp enough to be quite sure that he was talking about something tremendously real, and not merely mystifying you.

I had two quite distinct experiences in reading it. (a) Certain sentences moved and excited me although I couldn't understand them – as the mysterious words in the Crock of Gold, which Aengus told the Philosopher. In case they may have the same effect on you I quote two of them: 'That the nothing is become an eternal life and has found itself, which cannot be, in the Stillness.'[5] – 'The wrath extinguishes and the turning orb stands still, and instead of the turning a sound is caused in the essence.'[6] (b) At certain points a feeling of distress, and even of horror. I had always assumed, in my way, that if I could reach the things Boehme is here talking about, I should *like* them! There is something really very dreadful in this second chapter of the Signatura. (You'll think I'm putting this on *just a little bit*. Honestly, I'm not.) I intend to try and get hold of some good commentator on this book, if there is one, and worrey out the meaning.

In the meantime, I wish to record that it has been about the biggest shaking up I've got from a book, since I first read *Phantastes*. It is not such a pleasant experience as Phantastes, and if it continues to give me the same feeling when I understand more I shall give it up. No fooling about for me: and I keep one hand firmly gripped round the homely & simple things. But it is a real book: i.e. it's not like a book at all, but like a thunderclap. Heaven defend us – what things there are knocking about the world!

Monday [Jan. 6]

Morning's work in town as usual and to the station at 1.30 to see the Harwoods whose train was stopping there for ten minutes. I shall always think of you in connection with him, as through your imitations of his manner, he has become one of our stock characters. It was a silly and useless tryst – nothing can be less like conversation than chatter at a carriage door with a man in the presence of his wife and two babies –

---

5 ibid., ch. II, para. 18, p. 16.
6 ibid., ch. II, para. 19, p. 16.

and I only kept it to return a pair of skates wh. he left in my rooms last winter.

I walked as usual after lunch, dropping in on the way to see if old Foord-Kelsie would accompany me. I think I have mentioned him to you – a retired country parson of 80, who drives his own car, carpenters, and mends everyone's wireless. He is an irreplaceable character – a great reader, specially of *Tristram Shandy*, Boswell, & *Pickwick* – and as redolent of English country life as an old apple in a barn. He is deliciously limited: cares for no poetry but Shakespeare, distrusts all mysticism and imagination, and all overstrained moods. Yet you could not wish him to be otherwise: and inside this almost defiantly human and mundane framework there is such tenderness of heart that one never feels it bleak. He was in his workshop when I arrived, with shavings all about his ankles, making a cover for the font of old Headington Church. He would not come out, and I stayed to shout conversation for fifteen minutes above the thudding and singing of his circular saw. We had a bit of everything: an outburst against Shaw, a broad story, and then, as always, onto Tristram Shandy. 'Wonderful book – oh a wonderful book. You feel *snug* when you read that – you get in among them all in that little parlour. And my uncle Toby – ah (a *very* parsonical, long-drawn, almost devotional *a-a-ah*) ah, a beautiful character. And the jokes – I'm sure I don't know how the rascal thought of it all – the rascal!' I wish you could have seen him saying all this, bending down as he shoved a beam of wood against the saw, with one dear old wrinkled eye screwed up and held close to the work. You must hurry up and come and see me before he dies, for he of all people should be added to our stock characters.

Wed. January 8th

I have just got your excellent letter. I find I am getting great pleasure out of this correspondence – both the writing and the reading. It recalls old times. I quite agree with what you say about letters being haphazard and informal – in their choice of subject. Things ought to come up just as they do in conversation. The actual expression is a different matter. There is such a thing as being unnaturally natural – I mean it doesn't really come naturally to most of us to write exactly as we speak. I say this in self defence, lest you should think I am sometimes trying to be literary. (There's a good example. I should never say *lest* in conversation, but it comes naturally to me in writing perhaps because *lest* is four letters and *for fear* is seven.) My only attempt is to get across the picture in my mind: and in order to do that one *has* to choose ones words, because there is no chance of correcting a wrong impression as we shd. in conversation. As for the diary form, that is not much more than a framework, to keep one going from evening to evening.

I agree about the not looking forward to the time when we shall reread them. But one's between the devil and the deep sea. That pleasure in the future is the chief spur to diary-writing: and yet to think of it makes the thing artificial. Still, I suppose one can play hide and seek with ones own mind in that way: e.g. in playing a game. You've got to hoodwink yourself into thinking that winning is important, or else it is no fun: and at the same time you've got to remember that it is not important, or else it ceases to be a game.

I liked your description of your second visit to Leeborough – like Arthur at Orgoglio's castle. And I'm glad you have the Smaller Temple. That smell will always carry you back to the old days. Chevasse[7] really has a *talent* for evil, hasn't he? I've had a very busy day, and lots more to do, so good-night. (Tidying up I came across the old prose Dymer the other day. Emotions and comments can be supplied to taste!)

Thurs 9th

Another day all on Chaucer. What I am actually doing is going thro the parts of the Canterbury Tales which I know least with the aid of several commentators, making copious notes and trying to get really 'sound' on them. You see there has been a new edition since my undergraduate days, so that most of my knowledge – it was never very exact – on Chaucer, is out of date. This sounds dull, but as a matter of fact I take great pleasure in it.

What a glory-hole is the commentary of an old author. One minute you are puzzling out a quotation from a French medieval romance: the next, you are being carried back to Plato: then a scrap of medieval law: then something about geomancy: and manuscripts, and the signs of the

7 The Rev. Claude Lionel Chavasse (1897–1983), of an Anglo-Irish family, was educated at Haileybury College and Exeter College, Oxford. Following his ordination he was curate of St Mark's, Dundela, 1928–31. He served a number of parishes in County Cork, and was vicar of Kiddington, Oxon, 1947–57. For information about his early life see his essay 'An Irish Setting' in *To Nevill Coghill from Friends*, collected by John Lawlor and W.H. Auden (1966).

Zodiac, and a modern proverb 'reported by Mr Snooks to be common in Derbyshire', and the precession of the equinoxes, and an Arabian optician (born at Balk in 1030), five smoking room stories, the origins of the doctrine of immaculate conception, and why St Cecilia is the patroness of organists. So one is swept from East to West, and from century to century, equally immersed in each oddity as it comes up, and equally sudden in ones flight to the next: like the glimpses (oh how I hate the word *vignette*) that you get from an express train, when the cart going under the bridge seems to be a little world in itself, until it is replaced – instantaneously – by the horses running away from the line in the next field.

About Bunyan – I had forgotten the passage you mention in which a share in judging the damned is held out as one of the pleasures of the saint. I quite agree that it is horrid. As to whether it is contrary to the spirit of Christ – it is certainly not contrary to the letter: for he himself in the Gospels (if I remember rightly) does hold out that very reward to the disciples – 'And ye shall sit on twelve thrones judging the twelve tribes of Israel.'[8] In spite of all my recent changes of view, I am still inclined to think that you can only get what *you* call 'Christ' out of the Gospels by picking & choosing, & slurring over a good deal. However that's as may be. Of course in Bunyan's case, one must remember the persecution he had undergone – which makes his vindictiveness more pardonable than the intolerance of those you speak of who have never suffered anything at the hands of the 'ungodly'.

To day has been a day of howling wind and low, fast-driving clouds, but no rain. On my afternoon walk my 'NO THINKING' period was rather more successful than usual. I find as I go on that one becomes more conscious of ones thought by trying to stop. After shoving out the obvious loud thought, one listens to the whispered thought underneath. When one has checked that, I suppose there will be another layer underneath! Perhaps it is thought all the way down. Anyway, it is not a bad thing to get even this far: to step out of the thinking and listen to it going on. Perhaps it will teach you to control it better when you step back into the stream. Of course the trouble of writing about it is that the words inevitably mean more than one intends: as these, for instance, sound as if I'd got far further than I really have – wh. wasn't

8 Luke 22:30: 'That ye may eat and drink at my table in my kingdom, and sit on thrones judging the twelve tribes of Israel'.

the effect I wanted to produce. Oh! my hand is tired. I've been writing on and off nearly all day.

Frid 10th

It will probably be short commons to night for I have been pretty hard at work all day, except for walk, and I feel rather tired. My life tends to go in spurts. When I am interested in a subject, my interest drives me like a daemon, and for a few days the time at meals (or the time spent in digging the hen run and rinsing plates and talking) seems as if it would never be done and let me back to work. And for the first few days I feel as if I could never be tired. Then suddenly, one evening, (tho the interest remains) virtue has gone out of me, and my legs ache and I feel as if I could do nothing. So I shall do slightly different work to morrow. Another lovely day. I think January, when it is fine, is one of the most exquisite months in the year. I love these skies with level alternate bars of pale yellow and of grey, exactly the grey of a grey horse. Also one seems to hear almost as many birds as in spring.

The others were out for tea, and I had another go at Boehme. Much the same effect. I must try him again in different circumstances and at a different time of the year, to see if it is some trick of my health or of the weather that makes this book have such an astonishing effect on me. On the whole, this time there was a little less of the sinking feeling, and a little more understanding. But there is no question that it is full of the most lovely sentences: 'That many a twig withers on the tree is not the tree's fault, for it withdraws its sap from no twig, only the twig gives forth itself too eagerly with the desire: it runs on in self will, it is taken by the inflammation of the sun and the fire, before it can draw sap again in its mother and refresh itself'[9] – 'He breaks self-hood as a vessel wherein he lies captive, and buds forth continually in God's will-spirit, with his desire regained in God, as a fair blossom springs out of the earth'[10] – 'If the soul did but truly know that all beings were its mothers, which brought it forth, and did not hold the mother's substance for its own, but for common.'[11]

9 Boehme, *The Signature of all Things*, ch. XVI, para. 36, p. 219.
10 ibid., ch. XV, para. 31, p. 203.
11 ibid., ch. XV, para. 8, p. 198.

I suppose by now you are at, or finished, Henry IV. Isn't Hotspur a wonderful picture of the kind of hearty public school 'no nonsense' type?

I am afraid this correspondence is sure to languish on my side after the end of next week when term begins: it will be your turn then to put your back into it. A letter a day keeps the apples away. (Why not a new slogan – 'Daily castration Prevents Master Bation' – 'Who goes daily to Wadham, he Need have no fear of sodomy' – 'Decapitation each night Teaches you to spell right' – 'Tchanie each afternoon Cures heresy soon.') By the way, I am saddened about the McNeills.[12]

Sunday [Jan. 12]

I have had a letter from Warnie, in which he says that he particularly wants to keep *Mother Goose's Fairy Tales* 'the first book of my own which I ever had – this is written in the front of it'.[13] I find something very pathetic in this sudden streak of sentiment in so unsentimental a character, and I expect you will feel the same, and therefore will not mind facing the Witch again and transferring this book (it is probably on the landing or the room opposite my father's) to the study. At the same time would you (wu-u-u-d) you please send me the MS. book catalogue that Minto made. It is shoved in on top of the books in one of the shelves of the big bookcase on the north wall of the study – i.e. it is probably now behind one of the grandfathers' portraits. I am sorry to keep on sending you on these errands. You must feel rather like Crusoe rowing out to the wreck every few days to bring off a bag of tools or a tin of biskets (That is, by the way, an old and good way of spelling *biscuits*) I expect a good long letter from you any day now –

Yours
Jack

---

12 It is not clear what this means. While neither Janie McNeill nor her mother were ill, they were deeply saddened over the death of Mr Lewis. Janie visited Albert daily during his last illness, and upon his death Mrs McNeill offered Warnie their spare room when he was in Belfast. See their letters to Warnie of 7 January 1930 in LP X: 224–5.

13 The actual title is *Mother Goose's Nursery Rhymes, Tales and Jingles* (London: Frederick Warne and Co. [1890]). Inscribed in it is a note from Albert to Warnie: 'Badgie, his first book from his Papy. Novr. '96.'

TO HIS BROTHER (LP X: 228–32):

Hillsboro,
Western Rd.
Headington,
Oxford.
Jan. 12th. 1930.

My dear W.,

I was very glad to see your handwriting yesterday, tho' a little disappointed at the thinness of the envelope. However, perhaps it would be artificial to try to keep up an ordinary correspondence at present: and even if one starts with the idea 'I'll polish off the business in the first page or so and then go on to a real letter' as I did in my last – the first few pages seem to exhaust all one's desire for writing.

Do you find that the present state of affairs produces a permanent condition of – so to speak – comfortless excitement? Every thing is unsettled: all the old *structure* of things has collapsed and the complete liberty of making plans exactly as we choose, which one would once have sighed for, turns out to be in practice merely a bewildering impossibility of envisaging the future at all.

For the moment however, you will be most anxious to hear about the present, or, as it will be for you, the past. Well up to date Leeboro has not been sold. I will become very anxious as the time draws nearer your return. If a really good offer, *plus* a demand for immediate possession turns up, say, a fortnight before you are due at Liverpool, I really think I shall go out of my mind. And I am afraid, whatever happens, you are bound to be in the pretty b—y situation of setting your foot on shore in complete uncertainty as to whether we can go to Leeboro or not. I think however there is nothing for it but to leave the place (as it is at present) on the houseagent's books, with fires still burning and the Witch still in possession, and to accept the first good offer we get, while secretly hoping that no such offer will come till after April. It is not at all (as one passage of your letter seems to suggest) a question of the cost of upkeep. It is not 'Can we afford to keep it three – or ten – months longer before selling it?' but 'Can we afford to refuse any good offer for a thing that may turn out to be unsaleable?' Can we afford to gamble on the off chance of there being a second good offer *at all*? (Remember, there hasn't been *one* yet.) That is, we are not in the position of an impoverished Victorian Colonel wondering whether he can afford to go on hunting for one season more, but rather in that of a middle aged Victorian spinster wondering if she can safely refuse *any* proposal.

This infernal 'two presents' system – which began by being a joke and has ended by being an incubus – has naturally reduced most of your logical divisions and subdivisions of alternative possibilities to matchwood. To take the points that survive:

As to book keeps. I had already placed in the study as keeps, *The Bab Ballads*,[14] *Out of the Hurley Burley*,[15] *Through the forbidden land*, and Ludwig's *Kaiser Wilhelm*.[16] I am very sorry that I did not know about *Mother Goose*: but I have just finished a letter to Arthur (which will go by next post) asking him to look out for it and, if he can find it, to put it in the study. I cannot say that I distinctly remember having handled it in my recent labours, but I know the book you mean.

The trunk in the attic.[17] I entirely agree with you. Our only model for dealing with our world is the heavenly P'daita's method of dealing with this: and as he has long since announced his intention of ending the universe with a general conflagration, we will follow suit. If you and I are together for it, I should even propose – 'I am serious sir' – that we reduce all the characters to their original lead and bury the solid pig that will result. Rolling stock can of course only be buried as you can't melt tin except in a furnace. I should not like to make an exception even in favour of Benjamin. After all these characters (like all others) can, in the long run, live only in 'the literature of the period': and I fancy that when we look at the actual *toys* again (a process from which I anticipate no pleasure at all), we shall find the discrepancy between the symbol (remember the outwards and visible form of *Hedges, the Beetle* – or *Bar* – or even *Hawki*) and the character, rather acute. No, Brother. The toys in the trunk are quite plainly corpses. We will resolve them into their elements, as nature will do to us. As to *stage sets*: I can't remember whether I did come across some and put them in the chest of paper keeps in the study, or whether I merely decided that if I did come across any I would do so. The solid bits – houses, banks etc – I think should be

14 W.S. Gilbert, *The Bab Ballads* (1925).

15 Charles Heber Clark, *Out of the Hurly-Burly, or, Life in an Odd Corner, by Max Adeler* [1874].

16 Emil Ludwig, *Kaiser Wilhelm II* [1926].

17 i.e. the trunk containing the Boxen toys.

burned: but a few side and back sheets should be preserved in *Leeboro Studies*.[18]

The New little end room The most jarring comment on this proposal reached me before the proposal itself, in the form of a rather offensive letter from that old harridan Aunt Mary,[19] to the following effect – that she had heard that Little Lea was going to be sold: that she supposed I knew about the two book cases of Uncle Joe's that P. has 'stored' for him: that she very much wanted to have them: could she send and have them taken away at once: she had expected to see me at Christmas etc. etc. The minute I read it I knew in my bones that it was our little end room book-cases. I replied: that I should certainly not hold a sale without giving my relations the chance of mentioning to me any articles which did not belong to you and me: that I had never heard of the articles she mentioned, but if she would describe them I would order them to be set aside, so that she need have no fear of their being confused with other things: (I very nearly wrote 'of our own things' but decided to make no *admission* of her claim until I was forced): that if she really required them for immediate use, of course we must make some other arrangement: but that I should very much prefer not to start dismembering the house before you returned.

By the same post I forwarded to Condlin an abstract of both letters and asked his advice, which I expect in a day or two. Of course if they are really hers (as I suspect) they will have to be given to her: but I don't choose to be jostled into settling these sort of things single handed the moment a greedy and possibly mendacious old woman tackles me. Well that is the first and great comment on your plan of a new little end room.

The second is that to my mind the question largely turns on another: if we can succeed in getting another and larger house than Hillsboro, and you (as I hope – but this comes in a later paragraph) are with us, should such a room be there or in College. Thirdly, apart from these questions, your proposal is one that I partly agree with and partly disagree with. It

18 'Leeborough Studies' or 'Leeboro Studies' is described in the 'Encyclopedia Boxoniana' (*Boxen*, op. cit., p. 201) as: 'A series of drawings of all period collection in two exercise books with limp yellow covers'. The 'Studies' are now in the Wade Center, Wheaton College, Wheaton, Illinois.

19 This was Mrs Mary Tagert Lewis (1868–1941), the widow of Albert's brother, Joseph. See **The Lewis Family** in the Biographical Appendix.

runs in your letter 'A place where we can always meet on the common ground of the past and *ipso facto* a museum of the Leeborough we want to preserve'.

Now my view would run 'A place where we can always meet on the common ground of the past and present and *ipso facto* a continuation and development of the Leeborough etc.' You see, Pigiebuddie, a *museum* is preciously like a *mausoleum*. An attempt at exact reconstruction (supposing it could succeed – wh. it can't in a room of quite different size and shape –) would fix the externals of a certain period for ever. But if you and I had gone home and lived at Leeborough, that is precisely what wouldn't have happened. Sooner or later we should have substituted good prints for the groups. As our library grew, new bookcases would have come. In the mere course of time the long thin table would have finished the process which it had already made a good start on, of falling to pieces. A thing fixed in imitation of the little end room as it is, can only be a perpetual reminder that that whole life is not *going on*. If it were going on, it would gradually change. The mere act of setting up your present French library introduces a new element. The unavoidable presence of my books (I have about twice as many there now as there were in the Little End Room) introduces another.

I want to give full weight to two considerations (1) That distance, and a long fast, makes the little end room even more poignant a picture to you than to me. (2) That the general trend of our lives, you having never had any real kind of *chez toi* except it, has some effect. Whether I ought to set against this the fact that by temperament – as opposed to circumstances – I am probably the more sentimental bloke of the two, is doubtful. I don't think I am really being influenced by considerations of my own convenience – because in any case I should *have* to keep a great many non-Pigiebotian books in that room: and I can quite honestly say that I am, to the best of my knowledge, not influenced at all by any Forsytian desire to 'call my rooms my own' or nonsense of that sort. On the contrary I had already proposed to myself that some room – whether in a house or in College – (College has certain advantages) should become in the fullest sense '*our room*' and in that way be a 'new little end room'. And of course such a room would naturally contain most of the Leeboro relics that we shall keep. And further, you and I would tackle the problem of fitting up this room together just as if we had bought a house and were tackling it there. In all this we are in full agreement.

What I [am] thinking [is] that an attempt to imitate the little end room in detail would be a mistake. A mistake in sentiment, for it could only mean that we were embalming the corpse of something that isn't really dead, and needn't die at all. An aesthetic mistake – because we don't really want to have the taste of our schooldays established as a boundary for our whole lives: and also, you can't really fit up a room with complete neglect of its actual shape and size. A utilitarian mistake because you'll find in practice that the draughts and lights of *this* room and the habits of *this* life demand their own treatment. But perhaps all this argument is unnecessary: firstly because we shall probably not have the bookcases, and secondly because, once you get here, with things round you, and the actual room in front of you, you will probably develop ideas about our arrangements quite as quickly – and quite as independently of mere imitation – as I shall. No doubt we shall have differences: well, we must quarrel about them and settle in the old way.

What I am chiefly talking against in all this is the faint implication that the *past* is the only 'common ground' on which we can meet. I think, perhaps this is an occasion for frankness – a virtue which should be very sparingly used, but not never. I have no doubt that there have been times when you have felt that, shall we call it, Pigiebotianism was in danger of being swallowed up by, shall we say, Hillsborovianism: at such moments you may even have felt that the past was the only common ground – that wearing the national costume had become, as in Wales, an archaic revival. I am very sorry to have been the cause of such a period (this is not an apology but a statement) – but isn't that period itself passed? We have both changed since the real old days, but, on the whole, we have changed in the same direction. We are really much nearer together now than in the days when I was writing ridiculous epic poems at Cherbourg and you were wearing scarcely less ridiculous patent leathers at the Coll.

Now, as to your own plans. If you decide to become a full and permanent member of the household, you will be very welcome to all of us: and I must confess that it doesn't seem good enough that the two Piggiebudda should spend so much of their life divided by the whole breadth of the planet. Having laid this down as a starting point, you won't I hope think that I am trying to dissuade you if I put up certain signposts. e.g. I Suppose you do realize that to exchange an institutional for a domestic life is a pretty big change. (I take it for granted obviously that as a permanent member you neither could nor would wish to have, even remotely, the guest status.) Both kinds of life have their discomforts: and *all* discomforts are in a sense intolerable. The great thing is to choose with one's eyes open. Can you stand as a permanency our cuisine – Maureen's practising – Maureen's sulks – Minto's burnetto-desmondism – Minto's mare's nests – the perpetual interruptions of family life – the partial loss of liberty? This sounds as if I were either sick of it myself or else trying to make you sick of it: but neither is the case. I have definitely chosen and don't regret the choice. What I hope – very much hope – is that you, after consideration, may make the same choice, and not regret it: what I can't risk is your just floating in on the swell of a mood and then feeling trapped and fed up. Of course to weigh it fairly one must compare the best of this sort of life with the best of the other, and the worst of this with the worst of the other. What one is tempted to do is just the opposite – when one is exasperated in a home, to compare it with one of those splendid evenings one had in a mess or common room. Of course what one ought to do is to weigh it against the evening with the mess bore. On the whole my judgement would be that domestic life denies me a great many pleasures and saves me a great many pains.

There is also this further point. I spoke above of Pigiebotianism and Hillsborovianism. I presume that if you join us you are prepared for a certain amount of compromise in this matter. I shall never be prepared to abandon Pigiebotianism to Hillsborovianism. On the other hand there are the others to whom I have given the right to expect that I shall not abandon Hillsborovianism to Pigiebotianism. Whether I was right or wrong, wise or foolish, to have done so originally, is now only an historical question: once having created expectations, one naturally fulfills them. All this I am sure you see: I am sure you did not entertain the idea that you and I could set up a purely Pigiebotian household with the others simple as 'staff' or 'chorus'. One hopes of course that we should live in a 'blend': but pure, unadulterated, orthodox, high flying Pigiebotianism would naturally appear only from time to time when we were off on our own. But then again, it wouldn't be fair on the others if I allowed the 'blend' to become merely the background and our neat Pigiebotian moments to become definitely *my life*. (Of course really *my life* is my own, just as your's is your own, but I'm looking at it as it would appear to the others.) All this is very disagreeable stuff: also, once it gets on paper, it sounds terrible poetical and forbidding. I don't think really that the problems are specially difficult – quite stupid people solve them every day – but I think they had to be set out. I don't want you either to buy or sell a pig in a poke.

Of course I'm not forgetting that for you the question turns on the larger question of retirement: but that seems to be one on which I can say nothing. Not that I can't think of a great many PRO's and CON'S, but after all its your show. Anyway it clearly can't be decided at once. It all comes back to the old tragedy of our civilization: that no one has the decency to give us a good sinecure apiece. (*One sinecure per pigiebudda* would be a good party slogan)! As for spending your leaves here, that of course goes without saying.

And now it is really time to make some immediate arrangements. Will you please reply *instanter* to the next question – do you know the exact date and port of your arrival? If not, will you be able to inform me of same, say by posting at Marseilles? If not, by cable from some port on the way? The present idea is that Minto and Maureen should go to Rostrevor or Cushendall at Easter. If Leeboro is still there, you and I will of course go there. In these circumstances it is highly desirable that we should meet you at Liverpool, if that is your port, so as to save you from travelling to Oxford and back. I also suggest that if the others are still at Rostrevor when we have finished at Leeboro we might go on foot and thus get in our long contemplated walking tour. The chief reason for their going there is to look for some suitable place as a summer resort for us all.

Minto is quite in love with Ulster since her visit (she got on famously with the Witch of Endor). Maureen is dying to see the sea, qua sea, and you and I of course need no persuasion to revisit these counties. One suggestion was that we should permanently rent a house from the Hamiltons at Cloghy. It is next door to the Hamiltons own. However the rent is £15 per annum – i.e. from our point of view £15 for a few weeks every year. True they will 'do it up', but I have my own idea about that. Also I rather doubt whether the younger generation of Hamiltons (and their friends) as next door neighbours, and Uncle Hamilton as a landlord would be a great success. On the other hand there are great attractions: a solitary place, and the elder Hamiltons as neighbours, both of whom we like. I said I would write and consult you about it. One of the things Minto hopes to find out is whether cottages on the Down coast for the summer months can be got at better cheap. Don't forget to reply at once to the questions in the past paragraph.

yours,

J.

TO ARTHUR GREEVES (W):

[Hillsboro]
Jan 26th Sunday [1930]

My dear Arthur,

Thanks very much for sending on the lists: but I was genuinely disappointed not to find a letter inside. Now that term is upon us I shall not be able to keep up letters of my vacation size, but I had certainly hoped that we might manage a short weekly letter as we did in the Bookham days and I think we both had a good deal of pleasure from them.

Of course there is one possibility that must be frankly taken into account – i.e. that my present letters, dealing necessarily so much with a life you don't share and only rarely touching on common reading – may be, if not tedious to you, (note the vanity of the 'if not'), at any rate too little interesting to repay you for the labour of keeping up your side. I shan't be in the least offended if this is so: tho' even then I would like a line occasionally. However, one good result of growing up is that one learns how small accidents everyone's conduct depends on. I do not assume that you have foresworn my acquaintance forever, nor will I 'fly into a passion'.

This you will notice is a very dignified, magnanimous letter on my part: it will look very well to posterity! (As a matter of fact, to write private letters with an eye on posterity is a lovable fault, springing from honest vanity: to try to forestall criticism by parodying ones own mood, as I did in the last sentence, is a beastly modern sophisticated kind of vanity)

And now, for my first week of term. All private reading has ceased, except for 20 minutes before bed (if alone) when I drink a cup of cocoa and try to wash the day off with Macdonalds Diary of an Old Soul. I shall soon have finished it and must look round for another book. Luckily the world is full of books of that general type: that is another of the beauties of coming, I won't say, to religion but to an attempt at religion – one finds oneself on the main road with all humanity, and can compare notes with an endless succession of previous travellers. It is emphatically coming home: as Chaucer says 'Returneth *home* from worldly vanitee.'[20]

I am called at 7.30 (as you remember to your cost) and rise about 8. Monday morning I have no pupils and can devote to my own work or to preparation. Out home at 12, lunch, dig the hen run, walk (on Mondays with Foord-Kelsie) back to home for tea, then into college for a pupil at 5.30. After dinner a meeting of a society. Tuesday, pupils from 10 to 1 then again at 5: and similarly on Wednesday. Thursday differs by pupils beginning at 9, and by an Anglo Saxon class after dinner, which usually develops into informal talk till midnight. Friday and Saturday are like the other days except that there is no pupil after tea. So far, until things close in on me as they presently will, I have five evenings free a week after dinner. For the first week they have mostly been occupied in correcting what we call 'Collection papers' – i.e. exams one sets the young men on what they have done or neglected to do in the Vac.

On Friday Christie came in from about 11 till 12.45: mostly stood on the fender eating biscuits, and talked on a variety of subjects. I never can make up my mind whether I most like or dislike this man. Perhaps his hard, insistant voice is really what prevents him from being nicer. He is genuinely religious: he has a real love of poetry and nature, – real enthusiasm, quite different from the usual blasé, côterie, critical, twaddle wh. is in fashion here: he even likes Macdonald – a bit. But then suddenly a whiff of the schoolmaster comes reeking out of him: you know he is not thinking whether your view is *true*, but what it signifies in relation to your character: he's not thinking what will be true for him to reply, but what will be best for you, what will rouse least opposition and yet do you most good. All this, damn him!, *very* charitably & making full allowances, internally, for all your antecedents and previous history. It is a habit schoolmasters have got from 'understanding' boys. In fact you might say Christie is so taken up with 'understanding' me, that he has no time to understand what I say. 'Yes' he will say 'I quite understand how you can come to think that, and I quite sympathise: but – ' and all the time he hasn't really taken in what I said. But on the whole I think his good points out-number his bad: and as you are always rightly telling me one mustn't demand to[o] much. (So is he, by the way. He is particularly strong on charity. Now what follows isn't a sneer, for I am really

20 Chaucer, *Troilus and Criseyde*, V, 1837.

trying to become more charitable, and I think I can at least admire charity in another. But I don't think Christie's is of the right brand. He always seems to select the really evil people to defend: and the next moment you find him being extraordinarily hard on some harmless old man because he is a bore. I suppose there is such a thing as imagining you have got beyond the stage of hating bad men, when in reality you haven't got *as far* as hating them. Divine charity must be very different from human *truckling* to bullies, or human indulgence for rotters because they are amusing: I doubt if Christie knows this difference.)

Just before term began I had to go and call on Farquharson[21] in Univ. He is the senior tutor there, and of course I have known him since my undergraduate days. On the strength of having done some office work at Whitehall during the war, and having been in the Territorials before, he has called himself Lieutenant Colonel ever since. He lives in a tall, narrow house, cheek by jowl with Univ. Library which itself is like a mortuary chapel. The space between them is about six feet across; into the Fark's house daylight never comes. I have never been beyond the ground floor: here in broad low rooms, lined with books, he works by artificial light most of the day. Somewhere upstairs, is a wife one never meets. He came gliding towards me in the dusk, about five feet four inches high, his face exactly like an egg in shape, with sandy-hair fringing a bald patch, a little military moustache, and eyebrows so far up his forehead that it gives him a perpetual air of astonishment. On this occasion, as on every other on which I have met him, he came towards me with an air (not a gesture, an air) that would have suggested an embrace rather than a handshake: then, laying one hand on my shoulder, he wrung my hand with the other, cooing in refined military voice 'My *dear* fellow, this is very good of you.' (He knew perfectly well that I had come on business and hadn't any choice but to come.) No underlining can convey the emphasis on the word *dear*: it was as if he had said 'darling'. At the same time, however, the eyebrows moved a good deal higher up the forehead and while his voice gave the *darling* effect, his face gave the effect of 'Well what a pair of fools we are, to be sure.'

Waiving the matter in hand, he began to consult me on an incredibly obscure point of Greek – he is one of the people producing the new Lexicon. He knows perfectly well that he knows twenty times more Greek

21 See note 15 to the letter of 11 May 1924.

than I do, but every word and tone suggested that I was the one man in Oxford, if not in Europe, who could help him out of his scrape: but every *look* said just as plainly, 'Isn't this fun? Or course you don't know anything about it, and nobody really knows much about this question, and it doesn't really matter anyway, but you won't mind my pulling your leg a bit, will you?' And I didn't. Then every now and then, his manner would become if possible a little more serious, and a little more insanely deferential, and out would come some extremely indecent story: without a tremor of his gravity: but perhaps a minute later the egg would suddenly crack and he would go off into great solid chunks of laughter – the sort of 'Ha – Ha – Ha' with long intervals between which one imagines Johnson laughing. When I left he told me how much I'd helped him. I said I hadn't known anything at all about the points he'd raised. He said 'It was the stimulus of my presence' (same contradictory effect of voice & face) and left me wondering whether he went back to chuckle at me, or to forget the whole visit as instantly and irrevocably as we sometimes forget a dream. Either seems equally probable. It is an old subject of controversy just how mad the Fark is. (He has put himself down on the list as lecturing on Heraclitus every summer term for years. I am the only person who ever volunteered to go, and he said it was off *that* year: also the surviving fragments of Heraclitus occupy about two pages!)

Well, I have made a big hole in my Sunday time for reading, and I'm glad I have. Tho' you don't reply, I have a friendly feeling from writing and a sort of homeliness: and I enjoy and like the Fark better for having tried to describe him. Try this recipe yourself, and after writing the letter you will go to bed happier.

Minto sends her love to all, & thanks for your mother's letter. A dead still night.

Yours
Jack

TO ARTHUR GREEVES (W):

[Magdalen College]
Jan 30th 1930

My dear Arthur,

Yesterday I was not out to home at all, since morning tutoring ended at one only to be succeeded by a College meeting at 2, which lasted till 5: then evening pupil from 5.30 to 6.30, and a dinner engagement at 7.

Consequently I did not get your letter till to-day. Not even to-day did I read it at once, as I had orange cutting for marmalade with Minto to do after lunch – (this sounds a nice homely job, but is as a matter of fact rather unpleasant as the bitter juice always find little cracks in ones skin and smarts like the devil) which lasted till 3 when I sallied forth taking your unopened letter with me.

I cannot remember that I ever took your letters to read on a walk at Bookham – indeed, funnily enough, I can't remember at what time of day they used to arrive and be read. I wonder did they come at breakfast – and did I read them on my little after breakfast walk? Anyhow, whatever the cause, taking it out to read as I walked like that gave me a remeniscent feeling. I'm afraid (almost) to say much for fear after all we can't keep it up – but at the moment I feel like asking 'Why have we missed this pleasure all these years?' I enjoyed your letter extremely: specially your sight of the

> *Hebrid isles*
> *Set far amid the melancholy main*[22]

or at least of their light. I quite agree about the value of the word Hebrides. What you can hardly feel as I do is the value of such words as 'Causeway' and (even) 'Portrush'. Not that I care or know about the places: but they are places to which people in my Irish life have always 'gone' – they call up the feeling of antedeluvian holiday arrangements and put me back for the moment in a world where Castlerock & Newcastle seemed as far away as Edinburgh and Paris do now.

It was in the Italian that we read Dante and I have been wondering rather hard whether it would be a good thing for you to try in Cary. If you do, I think the great point is to *give up any idea* of reading it in long stretches (with one's feet on the fender) for the general atmosphere and conduct of the story, and, instead, read a small daily portion, in rather a liturgical manner, letting the *images* and the purely intellectual conceptions sink well into the mind. i.e. I think what is important (or most important) here is to remember say 'The figures stand in these positions, coloured thus, and he is explaining about free will' – rather as if one was remembering a philosophical ceremony. It is not really like any of the things we know.

---

22 Thomson, *The Castle of Indolence*, XXX, 1–2.

I quite agree that the new Everyman backs are a great improvement. There, by the way, is the plague of these letters. *That*, in conversation would be a perfectly natural thing not only for me to say to you, but for any booky man to say to another: but in a letter I can't help feeling 'How like our old letters', and thus it has the air of a *revival*. The cure, clearly, is to go boldly on. Let us look forward to the time when instead of feeling 'We have started the old letters again', we shall feel 'Ah yes' – and remember before this long period of correspondence there was that early two years at Bookham that one always forgets. Yet that can never be, perhaps. *Two years* at that age was so enormous. And one can't regret it, for it means that I cannot think of you without thinking of all that so that you have the aroma of the magical past.

Now I come to a more serious problem. What I feel like saying, if I am to give you my news, is 'Things are going very, very well with me (spiritually).' On the other hand, one knows from bitter experience that he who standeth should take heed lest he fall, and that anything remotely like pride is certain to bring an awful crash. The old doctrine is quite true you know – that one must attribute everything to the grace of God, and nothing to oneself. Yet as long as one *is* a conceited ass, there is no good pretending not to be. My self satisfaction cannot be hidden from God, whether I express it to you or not: rather the little bit of self-satisfaction which I (probably wrongly) beleive myself to be fighting against, is probably merely a drop in the bottomless ocean of vanity and self-approval which the Great Eye (or Great I) sees in me. So I will say it after all: that I seem to have been supported in respect to chastity and anger more continuously, and with less struggle, for the last ten days or so than I often remember to have been: and have had the most delicious moments of *It*. Indeed to day – another of those days which I seem to have described so often lately, the same winter sunshine, the same gilt and grey skies shining thro bare shock-headed bushes, the same restful pale ploughland and grass, and more than usual of the birds darting out their sudden, almost cruelly poignant songs – to-day I got such a sudden intense feeling of delight that it sort of stopped me in my walk and spun me round. Indeed the sweetness was so great, & seemed so to affect the whole body as well as the mind, that it gave me pause – it was so very like sex.

One knows what a psychoanalyst would say – it is sublimated lust, a kind of defeated masturbation which fancy gives one to compensate for external chastity. Yet after all, why should that be the right way of looking at it? If he can say that It is sublimated sex, why is it not open to me to say that sex is undeveloped *It*? – as Plato would have said.[23] And if as Plato thought, the material world is a copy or mirror of the spiritual, then the central feature of the material life (=sex), must be a copy of something in the Spirit: and when you get a faint glimpse of the latter, of course you find it like the former: an Original *is* like its copy: a man *is* like his portrait. It occurs to me one might have a myth about the psychoanalyst – the story of a man who was always insisting that real people were only fanciful substitutions for the *real* things (as he thought them) in the mirror. However, one cannot be too careful: one must try to hold fast to ones duties (I wish I did) which are the prose of the spiritual life and not learn to depend too much on these delightful moments.

What worrys me much more is *Pride* – my besetting sin, as yours is *indolence*. During my afternoon 'meditations', – which I at least *attempt* quite regularly now – I have found out ludicrous and terrible things about my own character. Sitting by, watching the rising thoughts to break their necks as they pop up, one learns to know the sort of thoughts that do come. And, will you believe it, one out of every three is a thought of self-admiration: when everything else fails, having had its neck broken, up comes the thought 'What an admirable fellow I am to have broken their necks!' I catch myself posturing before the mirror, so to speak, all day long. I pretend I am carefully thinking out what to say to the next pupil (for *his* good, of course) and then suddenly realise I am really thinking how frightfully clever I'm going to be and how he will admire me. I pretend I am remembering an evening of good fellowship in a really friendly and charitable spirit – and all the time I'm really remembering how good a fellow I am and how well I talked. And then when you force yourself to stop it, you admire yourself for doing *that*. Its like fighting the hydra (you remember, when you cut off one head another grew). There seems to be no end to it. Depth under depth of self-love and self admiration. Closely connected with this is the difficulty

23 Speaking of friendship, Plato said in the *Symposium*, 192c: 'They may be hard put to it to say what they really want with one another, and indeed, the purely sexual pleasures of their friendship could hardly account for the huge delight they take in one another's company. The fact is that both their souls are longing for a something else – a something to which they can neither of them put a name, and which they can only give an inkling of in cryptic sayings and prophetic riddles.' (Translation by Michael Joyce.)

I find in making even the faintest approach to giving up my own will: which as everyone has told us is the only thing to do.

As to my outer news for the past week or so, let me see. On Monday last but one I had to read a paper before the *Junior Linguistic* Society, which led me into strange haunts very typical of one side of Oxford: for the *Junior Linguistic* has hired the rooms belonging to the *Oxford Broadsheet Club*. These are situated in a very small alley on whose right stands the door into the cheap seats at a Cinema, and on whose left – with its lights gleaming out on to the wet cobbles – stood the sinister public house in which the notorious *Shove Halfpenny* Club meets, or used to meet until it was broken up by the interference of the Proctors.[24]

Beyond this after three flights of narrow stairs I found myself at my destination, in a crowd of about thirty young men packed into a tiny room whose furniture seemed all to have been specially made for it by people with 'stunt' ideas of furniture. As soon as my eyes had grown accustomed to the sea of tobacco smoke so as to allow me to take in the decorations etc I discovered that the *Broadside* Club might with much more propriety have been called the Oxford Pornographical Society. The walls were adorned with drawings of singularly powerfully-built female nudes whose bellies and genital organs showed a remarkable degree of development, while, in compensation they usually lacked both head and feet. I speculated on the artistic pretext of this omission, until one of the Junior Linguists suggested to me the very obvious consideration that feet and faces are hard to draw: and the bad execution of the hands led to the conclusion that this was the real reason. On the table were several brochures advertising the work of various private presses, of which they themselves were specimens. I must confess that the printing was in most really beautiful: the works advertised were largely translations of the more indecent classical authors. It really does seem a pity that the cause of good printing should have got itself thus intangled with the cause of obscenity – specially as the catalogue betrayed their real ignorance of the classics. One specimen page offered a translation from Catullus – the poem beginning *Vivamus mea Lesbia*[25] – Come, my Lesbia, let us love.

---

24 Lewis read a paper entitled 'Some Problems of Metaphor' to the Oxford University Junior Linguistic Society on Monday 27 January. The meeting was held in the rooms of the Broadside (not 'Broadsheet') Club at No. 19 Friars Entry. The house was destroyed some years ago and is replaced by a pub named the Fuggle & Firkin which stands across the alley from the Gloucester Arms public house.

25 Catullus, *Poems*, no. 5.

Lesbia, of course, is simply the girl's name, or rather pseudonym. The blockheads, however, with the idea of Lesbianism snivelling round their muddy little minds, had jumped to the wrong conclusion and decorated the poem with a woodcut representing two more of the same beefy female nudes sprawling on a bed.

But what really completed the piquancy of the whole scene was the contrast between the Junior Linguists themselves and the surroundings which they had borrowed: for the Junior Linguists is a society consisting entirely of undergraduates of just the Opposite type – hardworking eccentrics of all ages and social classes as far removed from the conventional games playing mob in one direction as the Broadsheet decadents are in the opposite direction. It gave me a pleasant sense of the real variety of the society in which I live. Later on at about ten, when my paper had been read I got into a long philosophical discussion with a total stranger who appeared to be a lunatic.

By the way, one of the results of my having left my keys at home is that I can't let myself into College and therefore always have to be back by 12 which didn't matter on Monday but did matter at the Icelandic Society (the Kolbítar) (pronounced Coal-béet-are) when I had to leave Tolkien, Bryson, Dawkins[26] just as we were getting comfortable. However, I hope to reap the benefits of the earlier hours I am thus forced to keep. Bryson you know: Tolkien is the man I spoke of when we were last together – the author of the voluminous unpublished metrical romances and of the maps, companions to them, showing the mountains of Dread and Nargothrond the city of the Orcs.[27] In fact he *is*, in one part of him, what we were.

Monday 10th [February]

I had intended to give you a sketch of Dawkins, the fourth Kólbíti (and very well worth describing) but am carried away once more to nature by the heavenly walk I had yesterday. I had gone out to home

26 Richard MacGillivray Dawkins (1871–1955) was educated at Emmanuel College, Cambridge, where he read Classics. He was Director of the British School of Archaeology, Athens, 1906–14, and Bywater and Southby Professor of Byzantine and Modern Greek Language and Literature at Oxford University 1922–39.

27 He is referring to Professor Tolkien's vast, invented world of Middle-earth which we can now read about in *The Hobbit* (1937), *The Lord of the Rings* (1954–5) and *The Silmarillion* (1977).

after breakfast and had to spend the whole day till tea time working on textual criticism – a beastly job involving no interest & continual minute attention, & abominably tiring to the eyes. After tea I went out, thro' old Headington and over the fields towards Forest Hill – i.e. to that spot where (on your last visit to Oxford) you and I saw the low blue bit of distance framed between the two trees which you always say you remember. The evening was wildly cold. Mark what I say: not *intensely* cold, but wildly: i.e. tho there was little movement in the air the cold gave the feeling of *wildness* to the world – a raging silence. I walked out over the big fields and behind me there was the flaming orange colour that you often get at frosty sunset, but only a thin strip, and above that – green: then above that silver: above my head – at the zenith – stars: before me the moon, at present dead & lightless tho' white, a little above the horizon. I walked faster and faster as one does in sympathy with such 'wildness' until – when I had come out of the big fields and was going up among the pines to where you and I sat, rather a funny experience happened. I had not noticed any change in the light: moon rising and sun setting had so evenly divided the sky that there was no break, and I still attributed the light in which I walked to the sunset behind me. Imagine then what it was like when with a quiet shock I saw my shadow *following* me over the turf and thus *in the shadow* first perceived how bright the moonlight must be. I'm afraid I can hardly express it in [a] letter. At any rate the whole walk was wonderful, and that bit in particular ghostly – ghostly in the good sense, not in the spookikal.

Barfield came and had a walk with me on Saturday with tea en route in a pub at Stanton St. John. Splendid talk and splendid evening. I also had Griffiths to stay with me for a night last week. Griffiths was a pupil of mine. He was all mucked up with naturalism, D. H. Lawrence, and so on, but has come right and is I do believe really one of 'us' now: and is even tending on the rebound to a high degree of asceticism. Tobacco and meat he never used <more than he could help>: he now half humorously suggests that hot baths must go the same way, as voluptuous, enervating, and leading to an effeminate love of the clean. He is a magnificent looking creature – a dark Celt, but very big.

I think this is enough now.

Yrs

Jack

P.S. When I said that your besetting sin was Indolence and mine Pride I was thinking of the old classification of the seven deadly sins: They are *Gula* (Gluttony), *Luxuria* (Unchastity), *Accidia* (Indolence), *Ira* (Anger), *Superbia* (Pride), *Invidia* (Envy), *Avaricia* (Avarice). *Accidia*, which is sometimes called *Tristicia* (despondence) is the kind of indolence which comes from indifference to the good – the mood in which though it tries to play on us we have no string to respond. *Pride*, on the other hand, is the mother of *all* sins, and the original sin of Lucifer – so you are rather better off than I am. You at your worst are an instrument unstrung: I am an instrument strung but preferring to play itself because it thinks it knows the tune better than the Musician.

GULA J.A.G.
LUXURIA J.A.G., C.S.L.
ACCIDIA J.A.G.
IRA C.S.L.
SUPERBIA C.S.L.
INVIDIA C.S.L.
AVARICIA (neither, I hope)

TO OWEN BARFIELD (W):

[Magdalen College
3? February 1930]

My dear Barfield,

Domestic strain is, I hope, now over. On Wednesday, however, we have College meeting in the afternoon.

There, an hour from noon,
Men work by lamplight in the month of June.[28]

Either Saturday, or (better still) next Monday wd. be my best day.

I have been up in that balloon or one of similar pattern – what a pity we never met. But the sky is pretty large.

Terrible things are happening to me. The 'Spirit' or 'Real I' is showing an alarming tendency to become much more personal and is taking the

28 'Here, an hour from noon, / Men work by lamplight in the month of June.' The lines are from Lewis's 'The Queen of Drum', V, 3–4, found in his *Narrative Poems* (1969).

offensive, and behaving just like God. You'd better come on Monday at the latest or I may have entered a monastery.[29]

– Interrupted by Wyld!![30]

yrs,

C. S. Lewis

TO ARTHUR GREEVES (W):

Magdalen College,
Oxford.
Feb 24th 1930.

My dear Arthur,

I also have been ill but, more fortunate than you, have contrived to enjoy my illness on the whole – re-reading among other things *Middlemarch*, & reading Pascal (who seems to me pretty poor stuff). I hope to start another real letter to you soon.

In the meantime can you please let us have the following information. (1) Was it Cushendall or Cushendun[31] that we lunched at on the day of our last drive together? (2) What was the name of the hotel? (3) Do you know anything of De Largy's Hotel either at Cushendall or Cushendun?

Lucky devil to come on a deposit of Geo. Macdonalds. I will buy any you don't like – at any rate don't let any go till I've seen them.

Yrs.

C. S. Lewis

---

29 Lewis appeared to be having the very experience he later described in *SBJ* XIV: 'As the dry bones shook and came together in that dreadful valley of Ezekiel's [Ezekiel 37:7], so now a philosophical theorem, cerebrally entertained, began to stir and heave and throw off its gravecloths, and stood upright and became a living presence. I was to be allowed to play at philosophy no longer. It might, as I say, still be true that my "Spirit" differed in some way from "the God of popular religion". My Adversary waived the point. It sank into utter unimportance. He would not argue about it. He only said, "I am the Lord"; "I am that I am"; "I am".'

30 Henry Cecil Kennedy Wyld (1870–1945), English philologist and lexicographer, was a Fellow of Merton College and Merton Professor of English Literature from 1920 to 1945. One of the books used at this time for the study of English was Wyld's *A Short History of English* (1921). Lewis found it a muddled piece of writing, and he may here mean that he was trying to unravel some part of it for use in teaching Anglo-Saxon.

31 Both are in Co. Antrim.

TO ARTHUR GREEVES (W):

Magdalen College,
Oxford.
[26 February 1930]

My dear A

In great haste – the ending up C. S. Lewis must have been due to the fact that I had just written *nine* letters all ending in that way. Other things, reply later

Yours
Jack

TO ARTHUR GREEVES (W):

[Magdalen College]
Feb. 27th [1930]

My dear Arthur,

I am sorry for my mistake about the signature of my last letter but one, but I hope this has now been set right by my note – was it legible? – yesterday. The overwhelming majority of the letters I write (and I seldom get through a day in term without writing a letter) are naturally signed with my surname and initials, so that to add these at the end is almost as mechanical as to turn the envelope over and lick the flap. On this particular occasion, as I said, your letter was the last of nine which I had had to write, and so I inadvertently followed on – or so I now learn, for, of course, until I heard from you I was quite unaware of what I had done. It is the sort of slip [of] the pen that must, I imagine, be not very uncommon with writers in haste – so be prepared for it happening again!

Now as to our plans. My request to you for information was not so much the result of any decision as an attempt to get data for deciding on. I thought you knew that I, at any rate, would be at home in the Easter Vac? For the rest we are in a state of great indecision. The *basic facts* (as the Newspapers say: and by the way, isn't this new party 'The prosperity Party' a portent and a sign: commercialism more *naked* that it has yet dared to show itself in politics. Just imagine the sort of people who are joining it!) the basic facts are as follows. My term ends on March 15th. Maureen's term ends on March 29th. Warnie is expected to be home about April 10th. The idea was that we should all go to stay somewhere in Northern Ireland for about four weeks beginning from March 29th:

but that after W's return he and I should spend a week or so together at Leeboro' for the last time and 'break it up'. I was surprised to hear of your proposed trip as I don't think you had mentioned it. I need hardly say that I had looked forward to seeing you both while W. and I were at home, & also I thought you might run down & see us occasionally while we were at the other place – whether Rostrevor, Cushendall, or elsewhere finally proves best (By the way can you recommend *cheap rooms* at any nice place where you are catered for? If you cd., you wd. do us a *very great service.*) But if you are coming to England, *do* try & arrange it so that you can come & spend a few nights with me in College before I leave it on the 15th. The week 9th–15th March is free: next week is pretty full. Do consider this: I have the pleasantest memories of our joint collegiate life on your last visit.

I am sorry if I failed to make clear to you when we last met that I shd. be in Ireland at Easter – I certainly thought I had done so, but I may not, & confess I am in the habit of forgetting what I have said & what I have merely thought. As to the other matter – the signature (not *Of All Things*, but of my last letter) I hope you now realise that it was quite unintentional and also see how the accident happened.

I can't possibly manage a letter for some days. By the way I said that I couldn't understand Boehme in my first letter on the subject. As for Macdonalds, no need to urge me to read any I can get hold of. The faults are obvious but somehow they don't seem to matter. I hope you are better, now.

Yours
Jack (I v. nearly did it again!!)

TO ARTHUR GREEVES (W):

Magdalen College,
Oxford.
March 5th [1930]

My dear Arthur,

Just a line to tell you that the stay (*en famille*) at Rostrevor or elsewhere is off. This of course does not affect W's and my visit to Leeborough – still less the proposal of your coming to Magdalen next week, which I do hope can be managed.

yrs
Jack

TO ARTHUR GREEVES (W):

Magdalen College,
Oxford.
March 15th 1930

My dear Arthur

(1) Our plans are now fairly settled. We shall be at Oxford till about the 4th of April when the others will go to Southbourne (Hampshire) and I for a four days walking tour after which I shall rejoin them where they are. Any time between the 10th & the 14th I expect to hear of W's arrival upon which he and I will instantly go to Ireland. I leave College to day.

(2) It is a great bore your not being able to come and see me before, as now that Maureen has a separate room instead of the little annex off Mintos we have no spare bedroom when I am at Headington & I therefore can't offer to put you up. If in spite of this inhospitality you still care to come & put up elsewhere I needn't say what a delight it would be. I always lay in a store of real tranquil receptivity for the country when I'm with you, and it is now beginning to wear thin again & needs reviving.

(3) When you leave Bernagh please leave the keys with Mrs Greeves so that I can get 'em when I come home

(4) Now that term is over I hope to begin a proper letter to you again & finish it in the course of a week. Till then good bye

Yours
Jack

P.S. I am very sorry to hear that you have to think of seeing a specialist & hope the result will be good. After that do try to stick to one doctor's advice – don't you think you have been rather blown about between different doctors' views. Yet what is one to do. Best of luck!

TO A.K. HAMILTON JENKIN (B):

Hillsboro,
Western Rd.,
Headington.
March 21st 1930

My dear Jenkin,

How extremely disappointing! Almost as disappointing as when I was in Cornwall a few summers ago and you were in Herts. All the more so, as I don't see my way to sparing a day for a visit to London. And now, what is to be done about it all? I can't become a regular correspondent: and I can't take trips to St Ives.

Is there no chance of your ever being able to do as I suggested and coming to spend a couple of nights with me in College in term? Come and hear the click-click of the antlers of fencing deer in the park: come and dine at Univ. again and see the Fark: come and see the Alpine glow on St. Mary's spire of a fine June evening. You have a place in my mental world – you are a gap in my inner bookshelf – a drawn tooth in my psychic jaw – a *hiatus valde deflendusi*[32] in the manuscript of my mind – a broken lace in my spiritual boots – which no one else supplies. It seems hard that we should never meet. I honestly can't go to you, so you must come to me. Could you run down from London for a day now & visit me (Hillsboro, Western Rd., Headington?): or better still come for a couple of nights next term so that we can really have our feet on the fender together.

There will be many changes to take stock of. I can hardly imagine you as a married man of several years standing. Please lay my compliments at the feet of the family.

On my side there are changes perhaps bigger: you will be surprised to hear that my outlook is now definitely religious. It is not precisely Christianity, tho' it may turn out that way in the end. I can't express the change better than by saying that whereas once I would have said 'Shall I adopt Christianity', I now wait to see whether it will adopt me: i.e. I now know there is another Party in the affair – that I'm playing poker, not Patience, as I once supposed. Let me have a line,

yours
C. S. Lewis
Love from all here.

TO ARTHUR GREEVES (W):

Hillsboro.
April 3rd [1930]

My dear Arthur,

I am very sorry that our correspondence has languished so of late. My plans now are as follows. (1) Leave to morrow for a walking tour

32 'a yawning gap, very much to be lamented'.

on Exmoor, with Barfield and Co. (2) Rejoin the others at The Rest, Hengestbury Rd., Southbourne, Hants on the 8th. (3) Cross to Ireland with W. on the 12th or 14th. (4) Return to Oxford on the 25th. There's glory for you.

As for a visit from you at Southbourne, I hope you will believe me when I say that there are no times or places at which I should not like a walk and talk with you. But there are other factors in the case. Minto has very generously invited W. to make his home with us henceforward when he is on leave. They like one another and I hope, as W. gets broken in to domestic life, they may come to do so still more – but in the interval there is a ticklish time ahead and in any case it is a big sacrifice of our

[Greeves, in a pencilled note at the top of this letter, states that it is 'very private' and 'to be burnt'. What he did, however, before passing the letters on was to destroy half the first page and the whole of pages 2 and 3. What follows is page 4.]

...have fallen so far below – MYSELF!!! Which is rather like a man repenting of being drunk because it was unworthy of his career as a forger.

I hadn't meant to give you such a dose of myself – but there is hardly any of it that I can say to any one but you and it is a relief to let it out. Don't imagine that I'm always like this. I was, on the whole, glad to hear that all your disorders have been traced to the bowels (what a glorious sentence!) Does that mean that the heart is now judged to be alright? As you know, I think there is a great danger of your being buffeted to & fro between the opinions of varying doctors: but heaven knows it is easier to say that than to see how you can avoid it. Does your silence about Harrogate mean that the surrounding country and the people are unworthy of notice or only that you weren't in the mood for a long letter?

I have been nailed down ever since term ended to a very hard, tho' quite interesting, task: a study of the different versions of *Comus*.[33] You know that Milton's MS is extant & we can trace all his corrections. I am sure you, as an author, will be interested to learn that he often crossed out a phrase, put something else, crossed that out, & then returned to the original phrase. Just like ourselves in fact! Or like our

33 The result of this study was his essay, 'A Note on Comus', in *The Review of English Studies*, vol. VIII, no. 30 (1932), reprinted in Lewis's *Studies in Medieval and Renaissance Literature*, ed. Walter Hooper (1966).

brother in law Mr Suckling.[34] (By the way I read her unfinished novel 'The Watsons'[35] the other night & wished there was more of it – a splendid beginning.)

I have had v. little time for general reading. I began *Moby Dick*[36] on the week end when term ended, and thought, despite its obvious defects of rhetoric & un-dramatic dialogue, that I liked it: but somehow I feel no inclination to go on. Have you ever tried it? I have had a few notable walks. Shall I be seeing you in Ireland. At any rate write.

You are my only real Father Confessor so you owe me a line

Yours

Jack

TO ARTHUR GREEVES (W):

[The Rest,
Hengestbury Road,
Southbourne
13? April 1930]

My dear Arthur,

Many thanks for both your letters. You mustn't think of mucking up your arrangements on my account. Of course it would make my impending time in Ireland v. much nicer if you were there, but it would be quite monstrous to expect you to come back from London – especially as the latest news is that W. will not reach Liverpool until Wednesday, so that I shall have only a week at home. ('At home' – an awful feeling comes over me at those words. It is impossible to get accustomed to change.) So don't think of altering your arrangements on my account: accept instead my hearty thanks for your second letter, which was one of the nicest I have ever had, and set out on your trip with a clear conscience. You are doing perfectly right and I should be a most exacting & selfish person to demand for a moment that you should do otherwise. I hope you will do yourself and your Pole good.

Beware of holidays, though. The old puritans were wrong but they had something real at the back of their minds when they denied pleasures

34 A character in Jane Austen's *Emma*.

35 A fragment of a novel by Jane Austen, written about 1805 and appended by J.E. Austen-Leigh to his *Memoir of Jane Austen* (1871).

36 Herman Melville, *Moby Dick* (1851).

because 'it would only unsettle the boy'. I speak feelingly, for, having felt it my duty to drop work here and devote myself entirely to holidaying with the others (heavens knows I did it for the best) I am at present suffering from all the spiritual consequences of idleness.

I am reading Virginia Wolfe's Orlando[37] to Minto at present. Have you read it? And if so what do you make of it? I think there is a quite astonishing power of rendering the feel both of landscapes and moods, rising sometimes to real loveliness, and a total absence of any matter on which to use the power. Also the usual stale cynicism – the nineteenth century guyed as usual – in fact all the tricks of the clevers. I note what you say about your George Macdonalds and will certainly borrow one for my stay. Think of me at your bookcase a few days hence. Ah Arthur – aren't things odd? Many thanks & good bye

Yours
Jack

Warnie arrived in Liverpool on 16 April after being away, as he recorded in his diary, 'three years and five days, and after a journey of fifty days from Shanghai' (LP X: 309). He met Jack in London and after a night in Oxford they joined Mrs Moore and Maureen in Southbourne. Jack and Warnie left for Belfast on 22 April, arriving there on the 23rd. That evening Warnie wrote in his diary:

> *The sight of P's grave with its fresh turned earth, and a handful of withered daffodils at its head, alongside Mammy's, was perfectly beastly...And so out through the dingy familiarity of Ballymacarret and a much altered Strandtown to Little Lea. There was a chill about the rank untended garden, but inside, at first, the house seemed much less strange than I had expected it to be, in spite of J's labours – superficially it was as if a spring cleaning was in progress: but soon I noticed the intense stillness, and as I went from room to room, its utter lifelessness: silent it has of course been for many years during most of the day, but this was something new and horrible. It brought home to me as nothing else could have done, the tremendous personality of the Pudaitabird – the whole*

37 Virginia Woolf, *Orlando* (1928).

> *place is as blank as a frame from which a picture has been stripped...We took turn about in digging a hole in the vegetable garden in which we put our toys...and then carried the old attic trunk down and buried them: what struck us most was the scantiness of the material out of which that remarkable imaginary world was constructed: by tacit mutual consent the boxes of characters were buried unopened.* (LP XI: 5)

They returned to Oxford the next day, where Warnie stayed at Hillsboro until he was posted to Bulford, Wiltshire, as assistant to the officer in charge of supplies.

TO ARTHUR GREEVES (W):

[Magdalen College]
April 29th [1930]

My dear Arthur,

I will write to Mary about the commode. Meanwhile I am tearing my hair and dancing with rage so that the books are rattling on my table and the eyes of the undergraduate in the room beneath have dropped out, and all because in the collection of your letters which I have looked over I cannot find the one in which you went to the door on the evening when you were first read[ing] *Phantastes*. It will be maddening if any are lost. Have you got any of them? Did you bring them all back at the end of that time? Be sure to reply to this.

And by the way how that time has already become a remote memory. During my recent flying visit I saw the summer seat out in the middle of the lawn and had such a vivid recollection of sitting there with you and watching that strange illusion of shadowy people creeping up to the hall door and always vanishing just as we set eyes on them – and avoiding Chevasse. I met him for a moment, with W., just outside our back gate, showing his teeth as ever.

The two days and one night were very queer. I found that even with W. there the memory of *our* Ireland was stronger than the memory of his and mine. At least I don't know that 'stronger' is the right word: 'larger' wd. be better. The Ireland I shared with him seemed to be a strictly limited and rather thirsty land: yours was like dewy hills and woods fading into a mist where I felt that one could wander forever. This is not flattery, nor contempt of him. If I have so lived with him as to call forth mainly the sensual, the trivial, & the conspiratorial part of my nature in his society, then *I* have done *him* as great an injury as one man can do to another, but he has done me none, poor chap. I also feel very strongly – as I fancy you do with John – that so many things are innocent in him when the very same things are wrong in me.

Mary was an old dear as ever. I spent the night, no doubt my last in that house, appropriately enough, lying awake with a stomach ache. About three o'clock, getting up to drink water & eat aspirin, I looked out of the window. A thick white mist gleaming from the lamps in the road, and a dripping from the leaves. How many miserable nights have I looked from that window – terror of rows, terror of ghosts, worrey about Minto, toothache, quarrels with W. away back in early boyhood when he was my only home so to speak. V. odd that at such a moment it was entirely that side of Leeborough that came back to me: pain, fear, loneliness. I suppose it is steeped in my father's long years of loneliness – and pain & fear too, for all I know. Shall we add to the advertisement (boards are ordered to be put up) 'This house has been well suffered in'? Really I think Leeboro' looks best to me seen from Bernagh.

As to what you say in your letter about introspection & scruples, I think you are right in general: but you must remember how much bigger than itself a thing becomes by being put in writing. A very small dose of self-examination, so small as to be quite wholesome, looks a positive jorum in a letter. You must not imagine that I spend all or most of my time thinking the sort of things I have lately written to you: but in the act of writing to you those things naturally come uppermost which I can only imperfectly share with anyone else.

I wish you could have been with me on my walking tour.[38] We motored from Oxford to Dunster, three of us leaving the car about five miles before it & the fourth driving on. It was about six when we did so and we therefore had a delightful evening 'prologue' to the whole walk over moors with a ragged sunset ahead of us lighting up the pools: very like an illustration to Scott: then down into a steep valley, over a swift stream as broad as Connswater but only an inch or so deep above its rattling pebbles and so into the broad, empty, practically dark street of Dunster wh. stretches up to the castle.

---

38 His companions on the walking tour, from 4 to 8 April, were Owen Barfield, Cecil Harwood and Walter Field. These are the same three friends who had taken a walking tour in April 1927 and are mentioned in note 24 to the letter of 26 April 1927.

Next morning there was a thick fog. Some of the others were inclined to swear at it, but I (and I soon converted Barfield) rejoiced to meet the moor at its grimmest. Imagine a wonderful morning following a narrow path along the side of a steep hill with gaunt fir trees looming up suddenly out of the greyness: and sometimes a thinning of the mist that revealed perhaps a corner of a field with drystone wall unexpectedly far beneath us or a rushing brook, or a horse grazing. Then down into greener country and hedges for lunch at the village of Luccombe. In the afternoon the fog thickened but we continued in spite of it to ascend Dunkery Beacon as we had originally intended. There was of course not a particle of view to be seen, and we knew when we had reached the top only by the fact that we could find nothing higher and by the cairn of stones over which the wind was hurrying the fog like smoke from a chimney on a stormy day. The descent, largely guided by compass, was even more exciting: specially the suddenness with which a valley broke upon us – one moment nothing but moor and fog: then ghosts of trees all round us: then a roaring of invisible water beneath, and next moment the sight of the stream itself, the blackness of its pools and the whiteness of its rapids seeming to tear holes (as it were) in the neutral grey of the mist. We drank tea at the tiny hamlet of Stoke Pero where there is a little grey church without a tower that holds only about twenty people. Here, according to an excellent custom of our walks, one of the party read us a chapter of Scripture from the lectern while the rest of us sat heavily in the pews and spread out our mackintoshes to let the linings steam off. Then after a leisurely walk through woods we reached Wilmersham Farm where we found our car parked in the farmyard and Field looking out of a window to assure us that there were beds and suppers for all. We had a little parlour with a wood stove to ourselves, an excellent hot meal, and the bedrooms, – two in a room – were beautifully clean. We had only made about 16 miles but were tired enough as it had been v. rough country.

Next morning when I woke I was delighted to find the sun streaming through the window. Looking out I found a blue sky: the farmyard, with hens scratching and a cat padding stealthily among them, was bright with sunlight: beyond the long blue-grey horizons of the moor rolled up to the sky in every direction. This day we made about ten miles by paths across the open moor to a place where we met a road & there Field met us in the car with lunch. A cold wind was blowing by that time so we had our meal (as you and I have often done) in the closed car with all windows up and had the sensation of snugness. About $2^1/2$ hours after lunch, having done a very tricky walk across heather by pure map reading (no paths) we were relieved to strike the valley of a river called Badgworthy Water (pronounced Badgerry). A glorious comb[e], deepening of course as it proceeds, steep sided, with many rocks in it, and soon with dotted trees that thicken later into woods: not of fir but of stunted oaks, so gnarled that they give the impression of being in a subterranean forest of sea weed, & the branches often coated with moss to the top. We had to ford the Badgworthy: not v. easy as (like all mountain streams) it will be 6 inches deep in one place and 5 feet the next: ice cold and the bottom slippery.

Barfield created great amusement by putting his socks in his boots and trying to throw them across a narrow place so that he shd. not have that encumbrance while wading: instead they lit in the middle and, after sailing a few yards like high-pooped galleons, lit on the top of a fall where they stuck, rocking with the current and threatening every second to go sailing down into a whirlpool beneath. I, who was already safe on the farther shore, ran down in my bare feet and hoiked them to land with a stick. We sat down for about half an hour with our backs against a little cliff of rock, in the sun and out of the wind, to eat chocolate and dry & warm our numbed legs. The first bumble bee buzzed by us. The colours of the stream, broken by a series of falls above us, and floored with green, brown, golden, & red stones, were indescribable. When we were dry we worked our way down the valley to Cloud Farm where billets had been secured by Field. Minto, Maureen and I had stayed here about five years before, so I had a great welcome from the farm people. This evening all four of us had a kind of formal philosophical discussion on The Good. I shared a room with Barfield. Lay awake a little while, listening to the noise of the stream which is only about twenty feet from the farm house: and under that noise a profound silence. These Exmoor farms are the loveliest habitations you can imagine.

Next day we walked down the valley of the Lynn and lunched at Lynmouth. The valley is very deep – about 800 ft. – and the woods on the sides almost deserve to be called forest. The river – which again we had to wade – is much bigger than the Badgworthy and so agonisingly cold that at the first shock it is almost the same feeling as stepping into a bath much too hot for you. Lynmouth you know. After lunch our route lay along the cliffs and through the Valley of Rocks which I had not greatly admired: a place of enormous crags *without water* is a little bit horrible: one needs a stream to give these huge carcases a soul, don't you think? Best of all was after tea when we struck inland again over the moor in one of those golden evening lights that pours a dreamlike *mildness* over the world: light seemed to be a liquid that you could drink, and the surrounding peace was, if anything, deepened by the noise and bustle of a fussy little narrow gauge railway, the only living thing, which had a train puffing slowly along it, all its windows turned to gold in the light of the sunset. We saw several herons this day. That night we slept at Challacombe and composed ex-tempore poetry: telling the story of the Fall between us in the metre of Hiawatha.[39] We had done well over twenty miles and felt immortal.

The next day was grey with occasional rain. We got badly lost on some rather forbidding hills & failed to meet Field for lunch: got a lift along a dull stretch of road in a lorry: had tea at South Molton and motored to Exeter. Here, seeing the cathedral all lit up and notices outside it about a performance of the Messiah, we had supper in great haste and rushed off only to find that the Messiah was next week and that the lights were on for an ordinary evening service. It was horrid to be in a city again. As Field said 'After training ourselves for the last few days to notice *everything* we have now to train ourselves to notice nothing.' Next morning the party broke up, Barfield & Harwood motoring back North, while Field and I trained to Bournemouth where I rejoined Minto & Maureen at Southbourne. I will describe Field, whom you don't yet know, in another letter. I shall post this as soon as I hear your address, when I hope also to hear your news. You must have plenty to write of. I enclose my latest: I think you understand the experience – when we fall not because That is so attractive but because it makes everything else seem so drab.

Yours
J.

When Lilith means to draw me
Within her hungry bower
She does not overawe me
With beauty's pomp and power,

---

39 Henry Wadsworth Longfellow, *The Song of Hiawatha* (1858).

Nor with angelic grace
Of courtesy and the pace
Of gliding ship comes veil'd at evening hour.

Eager, unmasked, she lingers,
Heart shaken and heartsore: –
With hot, dry, jewelled fingers
Outstretched, beside her door,
Offers, with gnawing haste,
Her cup, whereof who taste
(She promises no better) thirst far more.

What moves, you ask, to drink it?
Her charms, that all around
So change the world, we think it
A great waste, where a sound
Of wind like tales twice-told
Blusters, and cloud is rolled
Always above, yet no rain falls to ground.

Across drab iteration
Of gaunt hills line on line
The dull road's sinuation
Creeps: and the witche's wine
Tho' promising nothing, seems,
In that land of no streams,
To promise best – the unrelish'd anodyne.[40]

During his stay at Hillsboro Warnie was considering his brother's and Mrs Moore's invitation to make his home with them when he retired. Meanwhile, he recorded in his diary of 10 May his plan for 'drawing up a scheme for the editing and arrangement of our family papers' (BF, *pp. 45–6). On 15 May he took up his post at the army base at Bulford, on Salisbury Plain. On 25 May he arrived at a decision about the invitation to make his home with Jack and Mrs Moore:*

40 The poem, considerably revised, was later to appear in Lewis's *The Pilgrim's Regress* (1933), and it has subsequently been included in his *Poems* (1964) and *Collected Poems* (1994).

> *The answer seems to be that just as the discomforts of my 'lone wolf' existence are inseparable from its luxuries, so that one cannot expect to have the good of domesticity without the bad. Finally there is the consideration of the assets of Hillsboro life to which the army can show not only no corresponding assets but actual debits – a closer intimacy with J., and a correspondingly fuller intellectual life: a healthier life too, by the cutting out of those hours spent in social and ceremonial drinking...I came home more than ever convinced that I have made a wise decision and should throw in my fortunes with Hillsboro as soon as it becomes economically possible.* (*BF*, p. 52)

On 31 May Warnie went to Belfast to go through Little Lea one last time before it was sold. He stayed in Little Lea for the last time during 1 to 4 June. Little Lea was sold in January 1931 for £2300.

TO ARTHUR GREEVES (W):

[Magdalen College]
June 1st 1930

My dear Arthur,

I have decided to return to the old regulation four page letter once a week as in Bookham days. The long screeds I have been sending you lately will certainly languish some time or other and then there will be an end of the correspondence: but this I think I shall be able to keep up. I hope to get your first letter on Tuesday at latest.

And now let me see (it already seems so long ago since you were here). On the day you left I went our usual walk, through Old Headington, past that little isolated house wh. you admired, across the brook, and then over two fields to our soaking machine. It was just such another glorious summer day with a kind of mist that made the grass and buttercups look watery. I felt that sort of melancholy (you probably know it) wh. comes from going through the same scenes through which you walked with a friend a few hours ago, when he has gone. Now that I come to think of it, you must have had this experience much more often than I: so often in your old letters do I find you describing how you went this or that old walk just after my return to Bookham. Mixed with this melancholy, however, (you will not be offended) there was the freshness of solitude which itself, on such occasions, feels like a friend revisited, and what between the two I fell into an extremely receptive state of mind – a sort of impersonal tenderness, which is the reason why I am mentioning this walk, as one of my good ones wh. was valuable in itself and will, I hope, become even more so in memory.

Just to give you the other side of the picture (I shall not often tell you these things) – I have 'fallen' <twice> since you left after a long period of quite untroubled peace in that respect. Serves me right, for I was beginning to pat myself on the back and even (idiotically) beginning to fancy that I had really escaped, if not for good, at any rate for an indefinite time. The interesting thing was that on both occasions the temptation arose <when I was almost asleep,> quite suddenly, and carried me by storm <before I really had my waking mind fully about me.> I don't mean to disclaim responsibility on this account: but I feel grateful that the enemy has been driven to resort to *stratagems* (not by me, but by God) whereas he used to walk boldly up to me for a frontal attack in the face of all my guns. I hope I don't delude myself in thinking that this is an improvement.

My rooms are quite settled down now and having worked in them for a week I find the novelty falling into the background. The slow business of transferring Headington books to Headington[41] – a little brief-bag full a day – is going regularly forward. Last night I began the business of going through the records, and sorting out those which are such rotten things or so badly worn that I will give them away. I lay on the sofa and played through *The People that Walked,*[42] *Overture & Intermezzo from Carmen,*[43] *Fire Music from the Valkyrie,*[44] *The Laughing Song from the Starlight Express.*[45]

Lying on the study sofa and hearing these old favourites I had sensations which you can imagine. And at once (here is the advantage of growing older) I knew that the enemy would take advantage of the vague longings and tendernesses to try & make me believe later on that *he* had the fulfilment which I really wanted: so I baulked him by letting the longings go even deeper and turning my mind to the One, the real object

---

41 He was unpacking the books and phonograph records from Little Lea, keeping some in his Magdalen College rooms and transferring others to Hillsboro.

42 'The People that Walked in Darkness' from Handel's *Messiah*.

43 Georges Bizet's *Carmen*.

44 From Richard Wagner's *Valkyrie*. See note 38 to letter of 4 May 1915.

45 Edward Elgar, *The Starlight Express*. See note 47 to letter of 16 May 1916.

of all desire, which (you know my view) is what we are *really* wanting in all wants.

At this point it occurred to me that the noise might be disturbing J.A.[46] above and went up to ask him: rather to my disappointment he was so far from being disturbed that he volunteered to come down with me and listen. Still there was something nice and even homely about having the old man there. We went through the *March of the Dwarfs*[47] & *Danse Macabre*[48] (which I thought rubbish) & Delibes *Cortège de Bacchus* from the *Aprez-midi d'un Faune.*[49] How on earth can we ever have liked this latter? It seemed to me the merest music hall patriotic song rhetoric on the brass pretending to be something better. Then, as I had anticipated, J.A. became talkative and we drank together and drifted into philosophical conversation.

In reading I have of course little to record, and never shall have much in term time. I read in two evenings a little book that came from Leeborough called *The Practice of the Presence of God*[50] which I picked up & put in the study when I was there last because it seemed to me a promising title. It is by a Seventeenth century monk. It is full of truth but somehow I didn't like it: it seemed to me a little unctuous. That sort of stuff, when it is not splendid beyond words, is terribly repulsive, or can be, can't it? No doubt it depends v. largely on ones mood. I had just finished the fourth Gospel in Greek (as I think you know) before you came, and after that most other things are a come down. Not that I liked *that* in all respects either. I have also read an essay on Death, in typescript, which Barfield sent me, which is to my mind one of the finest things there is. He handles death as you would expect it to be handled by a pupil & lover of *Lilith & Phantastes.*

Talking of which, I hope you will not be disagreeably surprised to find with this letter the first instalment of a new romance.[51] I don't know

---

46 John Alexander Smith, whose rooms were on the floor above.

47 From Edvard Grieg's *Lyriske Stykker* (1898).

48 By Camille Saint-Saëns (1875).

49 The *Cortège de Bacchus* is from Léo Délibes' *Sylvia* (1875). The *Prélude à l'après-midi d'un Faune* is the work of Debussy.

50 Brother Lawrence (c. 1614–91), *The Practice of the Presence of God.*

51 Nothing is known about this 'romance' Lewis was writing nor about the instalments he sent Arthur. In his letter of 22 June Lewis calls the story 'The Moving Image' and describes it as 'almost a Platonic dialogue in a fantastic setting wth story intermixed. If you take *The Symposium, Phantastes, Tristram Shandy* and stir them up all together you will about have the recipe.' The only unpublished writing which Lewis may have shown Arthur about this time is the fragment of his 'Ulster Novel' found in LP IX: 291–300, but it does not seem possible that 'The Moving Image' and the 'Ulster Novel' can be the same.

how long I shall keep it up, but it occurred to me that I could fit in four pages most weeks and that if I persevered I should thus get quite a lot written. Please criticize freely as it goes on. Of course if I get no answers I shall drop it: on the ground that if you are so changed that you can't write to me, you may also be so changed that you can't be trusted not to use my story for spills. When it is done (if ever) I shall ask you to get it typed in Belfast & sent to me. Is it possible that when you get the novel off your chest you might think of doing *your* next work in instalments? I think there are distinct advantages in that method of writing. But, whatever you do, let me have your weekly letter.

Yours
Jack

TO ARTHUR GREEVES (W):

[Magdalen College]
June 7th 1930

My dear Arthur,

I was delighted to get your prompt letter. Don't you enjoy the feeling of getting back into our old rhythm again? To me there is another pleasure which you, without a regular routine of work to distinguish the days from one another, will hardly feel: I mean the pleasure of adding another *pivotal* point to my week – so that in addition to Wednesday (interesting pupil) Thursday (Times Literary Supplement) etc I shall now have your letter. I enjoyed the description of your walk through our woods with Gribbon, and wish I could see them again.

As to what you say about instalments & the difficulty of seeing the story as a whole: (1) If you mean the *author's* difficulty, then I reply that I have so little time for writing that this is the only way to get a story done: and that benefit compensates for the disadvantages (Benefit to whom, you may ask!) (2) If you mean the *reader's* difficulty, then you may easily remedy that by *not* reading them until you have about ten (or better still, not reading them at all! As I wrote this I had such a vivid imagination of your voice as you might have said that). As regards your criticism, I was conscious of the fault you refer to while I was writing: specially in the sentence ending 'anxiety for the future'. It is not that I am trying to be complex, but a habit that sticks to my pen from years of writing on subjects that almost inevitably lure one into a rather unsimple style. I am glad you noticed it and will try to simplify: though I should say from the outset that the matters this story deals with *can't* beyond a certain point be put into the absolutely plain narrative style.

I have managed to get a few evenings free this week and have read two new books. The first was Kingsley's *Water Babies.*[52] It was one of the books belonging to my mother which my father had locked up at her death and I only recovered at the recent clearance. It was strange – after the first few pages the most incredibly faint memories began to come about me: she must have read it, or started to read it, to me when I was very small indeed. I had even a curious sense of bringing my mother to life – as if she were reading it through me. The feeling was impressive, but not entirely pleasant. (I don't mean that it was at all unpleasant in the commonplace ghostie sense.) The book itself seems to me not very good. There is some fancy, and I don't object to the preaching: but after Macdonald it is tasteless. Put the two side by side and see how imagination differs from mere fancy, and holiness from mere morality. Have you ever read it? As I say it is not *very* good: but well worth reading.

The other was Coventry Patmore's *Angel in the House*. As you know, it is a long poem in a very strict & even monotonous metre, describing a very simple story of love & marriage, interspersed with half philosophic, half religious odes on the author's theory of marriage as a mystical image of & approach to divine love. The story parts are deliberately prosaic & hum-drum, & would be very easy to parody: e.g. such lines as the following (put in the mouth of the housemaid)

> *'The Dean*
> *Is out, Sir, but Miss Honor's in'*[53]

though it is surprising how one feels less and less inclined to sneer as you go on. But the bits in between are really often sublime. Isn't this good, of Love (=God on his view)

> *To praise the thing whose praise it is*
> *That all which can be praised is it.*[54]

---

52 Charles Kingsley, *The Water-Babies* (1863).

53 Coventry Patmore, *The Angel in the House* (1863), book II, canto I, 'Accepted', stanza 2, ll. 12–14.

54 ibid., book I, canto VIII, 'The Praise of Love', stanza 5, ll. 3–4.

He is extremely down on people who take the ascetic view. These will be shut without the fold as 'too good' for God. The whole poem has raised a lot of difficulties in my mind. Even if it were true that marriage is what he says, what help does this give as regards the sexual problem for the innumerable people who can't marry? Surely for them asceticism remains the only path? And if, as he suggests, marriage & romantic love is the real ascent to Spirit, how are we to account for a world in which it is inaccessible to so many, and are we to regard the old saints as simply deluded in thinking it specially denied to them? As a matter of fact he does seem to suggest in one passage that romantic love is *one* ascent, and imagination the other – At all events the book has left me with an extraordinary renewal of my appetite for poetry.

I had an interesting & humiliating experience to-day (Saturday). I had to go out to tea on Boars' Hill and a man I had been lunching with, Lawson,[55] offered to drive me. I used to know him at Univ. and I lunch wth him & Keir[56] once a week for old sakes sake, though Lawson is a most terrible bore. As soon as he got me in the car he decided that we had a good deal of spare time & said he wd. drive me first to see his old father, recently widowed, whom he has just set up in a little house at the neighbouring village of Holton. On the way I bitterly regretted having been let in for this. Lawson is a tiny little man with puffed out cheeks, a pursed in mouth, and a bristly moustache: v. bright staring eyes: and rolls the eyes, jerking his head this way & that, like a ventriloquists dummy, while he talks, talks, talks, all about himself: or else talks big of university politics, retailing opinions which I know not to be his own and wh. in any case I despise. I thought 'Now he is going to show me over this house and tell me how he arranged this and why he did that – reams of it.'

When we arrived we found a lovely wild garden with a little red cottage in it. We met an old man speaking wth a broad Yorkshire accent &

55 Frederick Henry Lawson (1897–1983), academic lawyer, was Lecturer in Law at University College 1924–5, at Christ Church 1925–6, Junior Research Fellow of Merton College 1925–30 and official Fellow and Tutor in Law 1930–48. He was Professor of Comparative Law and a Fellow of Brasenose College from 1948 until his retirement in 1964. See *Essays in Memory of Professor F.H. Lawson*, ed. P. Wallington and R.M. Merkin (1986).

56 David Lindsay Keir (1895–1973) was a Fellow of New College 1921–39, President and Vice-Chancellor of Queen's College, Belfast 1939–49, and Master of Balliol College from 1949 until his retirement in 1965.

plainly in the technical sense 'not a gentleman'. Point No. 1 in favour of Lawson – he is not ashamed of his origins: he rose enormously in my eyes. Then Lawson shut up completely and let the old man talk, which he did, describing all he was doing in the garden. He was just like Lawson, only in an old man it was different: and the courage of him setting to work to build up a new life here in his old age was impressive. When we had been round the whole place and into the house, & when I saw so many things out of Lawson's rooms in Merton brought out here, and saw the affection between them, and realised how Lawson had busied himself about the whole – and then remembered how abominably I had treated *my* father – and worst of all how I had dared to despise Lawson, I was, as I said, humiliated. Yet I wouldn't have missed it for anything. It does one good to see the fine side of people we've always seen the worst of. It reminded me v. much of the clerk in *Bleak Ho*. (or is it *Great Expectations*) who takes the hero out to see his father & has a cannon on the roof.[57] Do you remember?

I am glad to hear that Gribbon was really appreciative on your walk: I always feel he may become much nicer yet in time – at present, for me, he is spoiled by that cynical & coarse-grained side to his character.

Yrs

J.

TO OWEN BARFIELD (W):

Magdalen College,
Oxford.
June 19th 1930

(1) Write short critical notes on the following:

They tell me, Sir, that when I seem
To be in talk with you,
Since you make no replies, it is but dream
– One talker aping two.

And so it is, but not as they
Interpret it. For I
Seek in myself the things I thought to say,
And lo, the wells are dry.

57 It is in Dickens' *Great Expectations* that Wemmick takes Pip to meet 'the aged P'.

Then seeing me empty, you forsake
Your listening part, and through
My dumb lips breathe and into utterance shake
The thoughts I never knew.

Therefore you neither need reply
Nor can; thus, where we seem
Two talking, thou art One forever, and I
No dreamer, but the dream.[58]

(2) I have just finished the *Angel in the House*. Amazing poet! How all of a piece it is – how the rivetted metre both expresses and illustrates his almost fanatical love of incarnation. What particularly impressed me was his taking – what one expects to find mentioned only in anti-feminists – the Lilithian desire to be admired and making it his chief point – the lover as primarily the mechanism by wh. the woman's beauty apprehends itself.[59]

I see now why Janet saw female breasts on the dog collars, and have at last brought into consciousness the important truth: Venus is a female deity, *not* 'because men invented the mythology' but because she is. The idea of female beauty is the erotic stimulus for women as well as men. (You are v. good on this, in Margaret in the novel)[60] i.e. a lascivious man thinks about women's bodies, a lascivious woman thinks about her own. *What* a world we live in! By the way the poem beginning 'When'er I come where ladies are' is delicious.

(3) I hope my walking stick continues to give satisfaction. Do not hesitate to bring it back if you find it disappointing.

---

58 This is perhaps the first version of a poem Lewis was to publish 'anonymously' and in a slightly different version in *Letters to Malcolm: Chiefly on Prayer* (1964), ch. 13, where he says, 'I've just found in an old note book a poem, with no author's name attached, which is rather relevant to something we were talking about a few weeks ago – I mean, the haunting fear that there is no-one listening, and that what we call prayer is soliloquy: someone talking to himself. This writer takes the bull by the horns and says in effect: "Very well, suppose it is", and gets a surprising result.' It is reprinted in Lewis's *Collected Poems* (1994).

59 In Hebrew folklore Lilith is the first wife of Adam, and she stands in contrast to Eve. Lewis was later to point up the difference between them in *That Hideous Strength* (1945), ch. III, pt iii: 'To desire the desiring of her own beauty is the vanity of Lilith, but to desire the enjoying of her own beauty is the obedience of Eve.'

60 Barfield's novel, 'English People'.

(4) When shall I next see you?
Yours,
C.S.L.

TO ARTHUR GREEVES (W):

[Magdalen College]
June 15th 1930

My dear Arthur,

I spoke too soon about the pleasures of adding Tuesday to my list of regular bright spots in the week! My disappointment was aggravated by the fact that for the rest of the week whenever the post came in and I thought 'Ah! This will be it' I actually got (on five several occasions) a beastly business letter from Condlin involving hours of tedious work. I had already mentally resolved (a) Not to write again (b) To write a letter full of such cutting sarcasms as wd make you die of mortification (c) To write a letter in such a strain of solemn, manly pathos that you would expire in an ecstasy of repentance (d) To show my magnanimity by writing as if I hadn't noticed the omission – when on getting back to college at 10 o'clock last night I was delighted to find your letter.

I fully appreciate what you say about the Clandeboye woods and think that I too notice smaller things much more than I did: which is a great advantage since, in what we ordinarily call dull country, a flower or the turn of a stream can now make up for the lack of mountains and woods. As for your other point – any comparison between Spring & Autumn – as between youth & age or man and woman – is, I think, hopeless. One becomes less & less inclined to pick & choose, or to pit one part of reality against another. It is all the one thing working itself out in orderly rhythms & branchings which could not be better or other than they are.

'Sentimental stodge' is exactly what one would think of Coventry Patmore, or certain parts of him, if you read them in the wrong mood – though even then, I think, there is a kind of scholarly keenness and cleanness in language and metre which makes stodge hardly the right word. (I don't know if you get my meaning. Can you imagine a picture in which the subject is extremely sentimental, and even the colouring rather bad, but in wh. the *fine firm* lines reveal that it is a master after all?)

I envy you your shelf of Macdonalds and long to look over them wth your guidance. I have read both *The Princess the Goblins* & *The Princess*

& Curdie.[61] In fact I read the former (the other is a sequel to it) for about the third time when I was ill this spring. Read it at once if you have it, it is the better of the two. There is the fine part about the princess discovering her godmother in the attic spinning. (This reminds me at once of Mrs McNeill, wh. reminds me I recently discovered a letter written by her to my mother at the time of old McNeill's death in wh. she said 'He always said you were his best pupil and when you came to call I always sent to tell him because I knew he loved to see you' – a fact wh. she has told me a hundred times, with solemn shake of the head, and wh. I can hear her saying at this moment.[62] Never omit to say that I have asked for them, when you meet, and that I send my love: and plead my cause when you can. I don't want it to be by any fault of mine if that old link is broken). Another fine thing in *The Pr. & the Goblin* is where Curdie, in a dream, keeps on dreaming that he has waked up and then finding that he is still in bed. This means the same as the passage where Adam says to Lilith 'Unless you unclose your hand you will never die & therefore never wake. *You may think you have died and even that you have risen again*: but both will be a dream.'[63]

This has a terrible meaning, specially for imaginative people. We read of spiritual efforts, and our imagination makes us believe that, because we enjoy the idea of doing them, we have done them. I am appalled to see how much of the change wh. I thought I had undergone lately was only imaginary. The real work seems still to be done. It is so fatally easy to confuse an aesthetic appreciation of the spiritual life with the life itself – to dream that you have waked, washed, and dressed, & then to find yourself still in bed.

I was glad to hear that you had had a long talk with Reid, because I argue from this that the anger wh. Bryson attributed to him has turned out to be all a mare's nest, or at least has blown over. Give him my compliments. As I write I have a vivid memory of that day with you and him in the woods beyond Hannah's Town[64] – what wd. I not give to see them this minute. Tho' I believe that longing for them is as good, for if I were there what could they (or any other beautiful object) give me but more longing.

61 George MacDonald, *The Princess and the Goblin* (1871); *The Princess and Curdie* (1882).

62 Mrs Margaret McNeill's husband, James Adam McNeill (1853–1907) had been the mathematics master at the Methodist College, Belfast, when Flora Lewis was a pupil there at various sessions between 1881 and 1885. Mrs McNeill's letter to Flora of 3 October 1907, quoted above, is found in LP III: 84–5.

63 George MacDonald, *Lilith* (1895), ch. XL, p. 302.

64 i.e. Hannahstown, Co. Antrim.

The period of bright green meadows golden wth buttercups is over here and they are mowing the hay. One hardly *walks*, it is too hot – in spite of a temporary cooling yesterday after a magnificent thunderstorm the night before; but I have had some delightful 'soaks' amid the smell (almost *maddeningly* remeniscent) of the mowing and the sound of the mowers.

This afternoon I have lounged in the garden & began Mary Webb's *Precious Bane.*[65] I can't remember whether you recommended it to me or not. If it goes on as well as it has begun I shall put it very high indeed. In fact I hardly know a book which has given me such a delicious feeling of *country* – homely yet full of eeriness, as in real life. I have it in the *Travellers' Library* edition. The language – tho some people will call it 'pastiche' – seems to me delicious. Why after all should one always write the speech of ones own time & class?

Isn't it an exciting moment when the whole of a work is typed? Be sure to report further progress.

Yrs
Jack

TO ARTHUR GREEVES (W):

Hillsboro,
Western Rd.,
Headington,
Oxford
June 22nd 1930

My dear Arthur,

Your last letter is mysterious. What is the meaning of the cryptic word 'Pharoh' (sic) added to the sentence 'I think I told you this before'? After cudgelling my brains I can make neither head nor tail of it. Again, why should my leaving a margin shorten your weekly allowance? I'm afraid I must be getting very dense. Then why the last page of your letter should be called 'the Jacobean MS of 1930' I cannot remotely conjecture. If your jokes continue to be [as] profound as this you will probably find me in an asylum when you next visit England.

By the way, please note that I moved out to Headington last night and am now to be addressed there. It is delightful to have term over and I can feel it so though to-day has been a most exasperating one. It is terrible to

---

65 Mary Webb, *Precious Bane* (1924; Travellers' Library, 1928).

find how little progress ones philosophy and charity have made when they are brought to the test of domestic life. However I think I got over most of my fusses fairly quickly and (I hope) without letting them hurt anyone else.

Did I tell you in my last that a former pupil of mine, Griffiths, had been to spend a night with me? I mention him now because his name deserves to be honoured. I happened to tell him that Barfield (he has only met him once but then he has read *Poetic Diction* so often that he knows him well) was hoping to edit the unpublished works of Coleridge if an American university, which was at present toying with the idea, made up its mind to finance him: but that if they did not he would go into his father's business. A few days later a letter came from Griffiths to say that he and the two friends he lived with had £800 a year between the three of them: that it was impossible morally to spend this on themselves, and that the surplus, on any right view, was not justly their own: did I therefore think that Barfield could be prevailed on to accept £100 a year for the next few years. This is the sort of thing that really makes one feel fit. Of course I hope he will not accept it, but that doesn't alter the merit of the proposers – specially the other two who don't even know him. They must be a remarkable trio.

They have pooled their money – Griffiths by the way had none – and live together in a Cotswold cottage doing their own work and pursuing their studies.[66] Their aim is, as far as possible, to use nothing which is a product of the factory system or of modern industry in general: for they think these things so iniquitous that every one is more or less party to a crime in using them. I can't help wondering where their own income comes from, and suspect an inconsistency here. Indeed whether the whole thing is folly or not I haven't made up my mind. What do you think? There is certainly something attractive about the idea of living as far as may be on the produce of the land about you: to see in every walk the pastures where your mutton grazed when it was sheep, the gardens where your vegetables grew, the mill where your flour was ground, and the workshop where your chairs were sawn – and to feel that bit of country actually and literally in your veins.

---

66 The two friends, with whom Alan Griffiths (later Dom Bede Griffiths) lived in a commune, were his friends from Magdalen College, Hugh Waterman and Martyn Skinner. The story of the commune and Griffiths' story afterwards is told in Griffiths' *The Golden String*, ch. 4. The correspondence between the three men is found in the Bodleian Library.

Tolkien once remarked to me that the feeling about home must have been quite different in the days when a family had fed on the produce of the same few miles of country for six generations, and that perhaps this was why they saw nymphs in the fountains and dryads in the wood – they were not mistaken for there was in a sense a *real* (not metaphorical) connection between them and the countryside. What had been earth and air & later corn, and later still bread, really was in them. We of course who live on a standardised international diet (you may have had Canadian flour, English meat, Scotch oatmeal, African oranges, & Australian wine to day) are really artificial beings and have no connection (save in sentiment) with any place on earth. We are synthetic men, uprooted. The strength of the hills is not ours.[67] My pen has run away with me on this subject.

I am delighted to hear that you have taken to Johnson. Yes, isn't it a magnificent style – the very essence of manliness and condensation – I find Johnson very *bracing* when I am in my slack, self pitying mood. The amazing thing is his power of stating platitudes – or what in anyone else wd. be platitudes – so that we really believe them at last and realise their importance. Doesn't it remind you a bit of Handel? As to his critical judgement I think he is always sensible and nearly always wrong. He has no ear for metre and little imagination. I personally get more pleasure from the *Rambler* than from anything else of his & at one time I used to read a Rambler every evening as a nightcap. They are so *quieting* in their brave, sensible dignity.

I know the feeling you describe – of talking far into the night wth one friend while the rest of the house sleeps. (I notice it is a feeling you have never given me occasion to indulge in *your* society) By the way, about the 'Moving Image' I should warn you that there is going to be a great deal of conversation: in fact it is to be almost a Platonic dialogue in a fantastic setting wth story intermixed. If you take *The Symposium*, *Phantastes*, *Tristram Shandy* and stir them up all together you will about have the recipe. So now you are prepared for the worst!

I am reading the *Politics* of Aristotle[68] which contains one of the few reasoned defences of slavery in ancient literature – most of th. ancients

67 Psalm 95:4: 'In his hand are all the corners of the earth: and the strength of the hills is his also.'

68 *The Politics of Aristotle*, from the text of Immanel Bekker, with English notes by J.R.T. Eaton (1885).

taking it for granted and therefore feeling no need to defend it. Very subtle, but I think I see his weak point. I have finished *Precious Bane* and think I have enjoyed it more than any novel since the Brontë's. Why do women write such good novels. Men's novels, except Scott, seem to me on the same level as womens' poetry.

Yours
J.

TO ARTHUR GREEVES (W):

[Long Crendon,
Bucks.]
June 31st 1930
[1 July 1930]

My dear Arthur,

As your letter did not reach me till yesterday (that is Monday) – and I had before then passed through all the stages of disappointment, you can hardly complain if this comes late. My excuse is that Warnie came up on Saturday and was with me the whole of Sunday, and on Monday I journeyed to Long Crendon to stay wth Barfield where I now am – amid thatched roofs and the crooning of hens, with a pony & a donkey in the orchard and honeysuckle over the door.

The great event of the last week, in one sense, has been in my library. I have effected the exchange of my Bombay Kipling[69] for the big Morris,[70] with the pleasant surprise that they allowed me £50 for the Kipling and charged only 18 guineas for the Morris so that I have a credit balance of £30 odd at Blackwells. Oh what a feast this would have been in the old days! Have you any advice as to the best way of using it? In the meantime I am delighted with the Morris, tho it seems to be rather carelessly printed – i.e. I have already found readings in it wh. must be mistakes. However this is only a trifle.

The real point is that it has made me read *Love is Enough*[71] wh. I never did before, and I most strongly advise you to do so at the first opportunity. You know that it is a play – you will find a very illuminating account of it in Mackail's life. The story is *in one way* a typical Morris

69 The Bombay Edition of the Works of Rudyard Kipling, 31 vols. (1913–38).
70 *The Collected Works of William Morris*, ed. Mary Morris, 24 vols. (1910–15).
71 William Morris, *Love is Enough* (1872).

story, that of a King who dreams of a fair woman in a distant land and finally abandons his kingdom to go and find her. He does so. Returns and finds his kingdom taken by another, but departs again without bitterness because 'love is enough'. But although this sounds so typical it is extremely different from the usual Morris.

In the first place, his long wanderings, such as you found too long drawn out in the *Well at the Worlds End*, instead of being given in full, are just hinted at in the dialogue, and for this reason gain enormously in suggestiveness. In the second place – I hardly know how to put it. You know I always thought Morris the most essentially *pagan* of all poets. The beauty of the actual world, the vague longings wh. it excites, the inevitable failure to satisfy these longings, and over all the haunting sense of time & change making the world heart breakingly beautiful just because it slips away ('Oh death that makest life so sweet' as he says) all this, I thought, he gave to perfection: but of what this longing really pointed to, of the reason why beauty made us homesick, of the reality *behind*, I thought he had no inkling. And for that reason his poetry always seemed to me dangerous and apt to lead to sensuality – for it is the frustrated longing that drives us to the *pis aller*, and as we lose hope of our real immortal mistress we turn to harlots.

Now in *Love is Enough* he raises himself right out of his own world. He suddenly shows that he is at bottom aware of the real symbolical import of all the longing and even of earthly love itself. In the speeches of Love (who is the most important character) there is clear statement of eternal values (coupled with a refusal to offer you crudely personal immortality) and also, best of all, a full understanding that there is something beyond pleasure & pain. For the first (and last?) time the light of *holiness* shines through Morris' romanticism, not destroying but perfecting it. Reading this has been a great experience to me: and coming on top of the *Angel in the House* has shown me that in my fear of the sensual cheat wh. lurked at the back of my old romantic days (see Dymer VII) I have aimed at too much austerity and even dishonoured love altogether. I have become a dry prig. I do hope I am not being mocked – that this is not merely the masked vanguard of a new sensuality. But I verily believe not. In this light I shall come back to Morris and all that world. I have the key now and perhaps can stand the sweetness safely. For this too is a feature of life that becomes gradually clearer: namely that the road is always turning round and going back to places we seemed to have left –

but they are different (yet in a way the same) when you come to them the second time.

I don't remember your *Lives of the Poets*[72] – what is the new Johnson like?

As to the business about being 'rooted' or 'at home everywhere', I wonder are they really the opposite, or are they the same thing. I mean, don't you enjoy the Alps more precisely because you began by first learning to love in an intimate and homely way our own hills and woods? While the mere globe-trotter, starting not from a home feeling but from guide books & aesthetic chatter, feels *equally* at home everywhere only in the sense that he is really at home nowhere? It is just like the difference between vague general philanthropy (wh. is all balls) and learning first to love your own friends and neighbours wh. makes you *more*, not less, able to love the next stranger who comes along. If a man loveth not his brother whom he hath seen – etc.[73] In other words doesn't one get to the universal (either in people or in inanimate nature) *thro'* the individual – not by going off into a mere generalised mash. I don't know if I make myself clear.

Your description of the empty rooms at home gave me a terrible thought – supposing my father had died when I was sixteen and all that had been lost before I found anything else – and you and I wd. probably never have met again. This week's instalment has been written alright but I forgot to bring it here with me, so you will probably have two next week.

The Barfields have been making wine from the vine that grows on their cottage and next year when it is ready to drink we think of having a Bacchic festival.[74] The adopted baby is to be the infant Bacchus. Harwood with his fat shiny face, on the donkey, will be Silenus. B. and I

---

72 On Johnson's *Lives of the English Poets* see note 56 to letter of 2 August 1928.

73 1 John 4:20: 'If a man say, I love God, and hateth his brother, he is a liar: for he that loveth not his brother whom he hath seen, how can he love God whom he hath not seen?'

74 In Greek mythology Bacchus or Dionysus is the god of wine and merriment whose rites are celebrated with music and dancing. In his entourage are the tipsy satyr, Silenus, and frenzied women followers called maenads. The sedate Corybantes are priests. Of course the real Greek cult of Bacchus was very serious and sometimes frightening, but Lewis had in mind something as lighthearted as he was later to make the Bacchic festival in chapter 11 of the Narnian story, *Prince Caspian* (1951): 'The crowd and dance round Aslan...grew so thick and rapid that Lucy was confused...One was a youth, dressed only in a fawn-skin, with vine-leaves wreathed in his curly hair.

Corybantes. Mrs B. a Maenad. B. and I will write the poetry & she will compose a dance. You ought to come.

Yrs

J.

TO ARTHUR GREEVES (W):

[Hillsboro]
July 8th 1930

My dear Arthur,

Your letters get later and later every week. If you write on Monday the first week, on Tuesday the second week, and so on, then in seven weeks you will be writing on Monday again: but you will have written one letter less than you should. In a year you will have written eight letters less, that is thirty six pages. Assuming that we both live thirty years more you will in that time have cheated me out of one thousand and eighty pages. *Why*, oh why, do you do these things?

My examining begins on the 17th and for about ten days I shall be at it from morning till night, so that you must look for no instalments or letters during that time: but I hope you will continue to write to me – as your letters, if they arrive, will be about the only pleasure that remains.

I am interested to hear that you have a new friend. Is he really one of us? – not that I don't think dozens of people v. well worth having as friends without their sharing the things we specially like – indeed in *some* ways better worth having on that account.

You have I think misunderstood what I said about the return from austerity. I never meant for a moment that I was beginning to doubt whether absolute chastity was the true goal – of that I am certain. What I meant was that I began to think that I was mistaken in aiming at this goal by the means of a stern repression and even a contemptuous distrust of all that emotional & imaginative experience wh. seems to border on the voluptuous: whether it was well to see in certain romances and

---

His face would have been almost too pretty for a boy's, if it had not looked so extremely wild...There were a lot of girls with him, as wild as he. There was even, unexpectedly, someone on a donkey. The man on the donkey, who was old and enormously fat, began calling out at once, "Refreshments! Time for refreshments," and falling off his donkey and being bundled on to it again by the others, while the donkey was under the impression that the whole thing was a circus and tried to give a display of walking on its hind legs.'

certain music nothing but one more wile of the enemy: whether perhaps the right way was not to keep always alive in ones soul a certain tenderness & luxuriousness always reaching out to *that of which* (on my view) sex must be the copy. In other words, whether, while I was right in seeing that a copy must be different from an original, I ought not to have remembered that it must also be *like* it – else how wd. it be a copy? In the second place, what I feared was *not* lest this mood should be temporary but lest it should turn out to be another wile. What I also ought to have said in my last letter but didn't is that the whole thing has made me feel that I have never given half enough importance to love in the sense of the *affections*.

One passage in your letter – in which you corrected *bare* to *bear* amused me v. much, as the original wd. have read 'I find it more difficult to *bare* myself lovingly towards my neighbours & my relations.' The picture of you *baring* yourself 'lovingly' to a long row of neighbours (the O'Mulligan etc) & relations – so remeniscent of a notorious passage in Rousseau – is not easily surpassed!

Almost ever since the Vac. began I have been reading a little every evening in Traherne's *Centuries of Meditations* (Dobell. About 7/-. Lovely paper). I forget whether we have talked of it or not. I think he suffers by making out everything much too easy and really shirking the problem of evil in all its forms: at least, as far as I have got, for it is unfair to say this of a book not yet finished. But apart from this he has extraordinary merits. What do you think of the following; – 'The world...is the beautiful frontispiece to Eternity'[75] – 'You never enjoy the world aright till the sea itself floweth in your veins, till you are clothed with the heavens and crowned with the stars...till you can sing and rejoice and delight in God as misers do in gold'[76] – 'I must lead you out of this into another world to *learn your wants*. For till you find them you will never be happy'[77] – 'They (i.e. Souls) were made to love and are dark and vain and comfortless till they do it. Till they love they are idle or misemployed. Till they love they are desolate.'[78] But I could go on quoting from this book forever.

A complete Coventry Patmore[79] wh. I ordered shortly after reading

75 Thomas Traherne, *Centuries of Meditations*, ed. Bertram Dobell (1927), 'The First Century', no. 20, p. 13.

76 ibid., no. 29, p. 19.

77 ibid., no. 43, p. 28.

78 ibid., 'The Second Century', no. 48, p. 112.

79 *Poems by Coventry Patmore*, with an Introduction by Basil Champneys (G. Bell & Sons, 1906).

the *Angel in the House* has arrived – Bell & Sons, 7/6, quite a pleasant volume – and I have just dipped into it. I don't remember for many years to have felt so disposed for new reading as I do now, and specially poetry. Everything seems – you know the feeling – to be beginning again and one has the sense of immortality.

Barfield and I finished the *Paradiso* when I was with him. I think it reaches heights of poetry which you get nowhere else: an ether almost too fine to breathe. It is a pity that I can give you no notion what it is like. Can you imagine Shelley at his most ecstatic combined with Milton at his most solemn & rigid? It sounds impossible I know, but that is what Dante has done.

We also read some Beowulf with a very remarkable young woman. She was a farmer's daughter who got a county scholarship and went up to London getting a good degree in English. Then – and here's the marvel – she settled down at home again and divides her time between milking the cows & taking occasional pupils, apparently contented in both. Thats what we want, isn't it? *Emigration* from the uneducated class into ours only swells the intellectual unemployed: but to have education transforming people & yet leaving them wth their roots in the earth (which *then* they will be able to appreciate) is the way to make class disappear altogether. She is 'remarkable' only in this: otherwise the adjective does her gross injustice for she is exquisitely ordinary – and not at all pretty except with the bonny open air plumpness of her age & class.

I also had some lovely bathes wth Barfield in a reach of the little river Thame. Picture us lounging naked under the pollards on a flat field: mowers in the next field: and tiny young dragon flies – too small to be frightful yet – darting among the lilies. Here I learned to dive wh. is a great change in my life & has important (religious) connections. I'll explain that later. They are still v. ungraceful dives but I do get in head first.[80]

This is the last letter you'll get till the infernal (but profitable) examining is over – but like a good chap (!) (old man!) do keep on writing to me. So glad you approve of precious bane. Isn't Wizard Beguildy a lovely character: also the scene of Prue Sarn alone in the attic.

Yrs

J.

---

80 C.S. Lewis, *The Pilgrim's Regress* (1933), bk. ix, ch. 4: ' "Alas," said [John], "I have never learned to dive." "There is nothing to learn," said [Mother Kirk]. "The art of diving is not to do anything new but simply to cease doing something. You have only to let yourself go." '

TO ARTHUR GREEVES (W):

[Hillsboro]
July 29th 1930

My dear Arthur,

Harrah! Examining is over. As to your question why I dislike it, it is not the jaunt to Cambridge (by the bye I am not going this year) wh. I dislike but the fortnight or so of actually marking the papers that precedes it. I had fewer than usual this time, but even so it means working absolutely solidly from after breakfast till supper: often it means going on after supper as well. As the work has no interest whatever & yet demands unsleeping attention, one gets very tired.

Thank you for writing – I enjoyed your two letters enormously. Do stop apologising for them and wondering archly (à la Tchanie!) how I can read them. Surely it needs no great imagination for you to realise that every mention of things at home now comes to me with the sweetness that belongs only to what is irrevocable. Secondly, there are a great many subjects on which you are the only person whom I can write to or be written to by with full understanding. Thirdly our common ground represents what is really (I think) the deepest stratum in my life, the thing in me that, if there should be another personal life, is most likely to survive the dissolution of my brain. Certainly when I come to die I am more likely to remember certain things that you and I have explored or suffered or enjoyed together than anything else.

It is an interesting and rather grim enquiry – how much of our present selves we cd. hope to take with us if there were another life. I take it that whatever is *merely* intellectual, *mere* theory, must go, since we probably hold it only by memory habit, wh. may depend on the matter of the brain. Only what has gone far deeper, what has been incorporated into the unconscious depths, can hope to survive. This often comes over me when I think of religion: and it is a shock to realise that the mere *thinking* it may be nothing, and that only the tiny bit which we really practice is likely to be ours in any sense of which death can not make hay.

I think you must be mistaken about having shown me Traherne. Surely it is much more likely that *you* are talking balls. Anyway I am glad you like him. Your question about the difference of writing between my instalments and my letters I don't understand. If you mean handwriting, of course the answer is that in the letters I just scribble as hard as I can lick, while in the instalments[81] I stop to think. If you mean language, the answer is (I shd. have thought) obvious.

Oh you can't imagine the poignancy with wh. your account of the sunny windy day near the dry tree fell across a dreary, dusty afternoon of those sordid papers, when my head was aching and the boys' horrid handwriting seemed to jump on the page.

I don't know quite what I feel about your assistance at the accouchement of our sister the cow. I know what I ought to feel – simply the same thrill that I feel at the first coming up of a flower. Physical disgust is a sensation wh. I have very often and of which I am always ashamed. If one lets it grow upon one it will in the end cut one out from all delighted participation in the life of nature. For God is gross and never heard of decency and cares nothing for refinement: nor do children, nor most women, nor any of the beasts, nor men either except in certain sophisticated classes. And yet its hard to feel that the faculty of disgust is a sheer evil from beginning to end. I don't know what to make of it. (Perhaps in one way it is, in another, it isn't!) At any rate there can be no two opinions about the delightfulness of seeing the other cows coming round to inspect the infant. Did they show any signs of congratulating the mother? for I notice that when one of our hens lays an egg, *all* join in the noise – whether that is congratulation or simply that they regard themselves as a single individual and announce '*We* have laid an egg.'

Talking about hens, have you read the Nonne Prestes Tale in Chaucer – its *delicious*: homely & ridiculous in the best possible way. Which reminds me, did you ever in your 'pink book' stage read any version of Reynard the Fox? It is one of the great medieval creations, and I want someday to get it: the English version is by Caxton,[82] I am afraid from a rather late French version, but probably quite good.

Since writing the last sentence I have come into College to entertain two people to dinner & spend the night. As they did not leave till 3 o'clock (it is now 10) I am feeling rather morning-after-ish! One of them is a man called Dyson[83] who teaches English at Reading. He is only in

81 This was to be his last reference to 'The Moving Image'.

82 *Reynart the Foxe* (Caxton, 1481).

83 Henry Victor Dyson 'Hugo' Dyson (1896–1975) was an undergraduate at Exeter College, Oxford, taking his BA in 1921. He was a lecturer and tutor in the University of Reading 1921–45, and Fellow and Tutor in English Literature at Merton College 1945–63. For details of their friendship, and the part he played in the Inklings, see *SBJ*, *CG* and Humphrey Carpenter's *The Inklings* (1978). See **Henry Victor Dyson 'Hugo' Dyson** in the Biographical Appendix.

Oxford for a few weeks and having met him once I liked him so well that I determined to get to know him better. My feeling was apparently reciprocated and I think we sat up so late with the feeling that heaven knew when we might meet again and the new friendship had to be freed past its youth and into maturity in a single evening. Although my head aches this morning I do not regret it. Such things come rarely and are worth a higher price than this. He is a man who really loves truth: a philosopher and a religious man: who makes his critical & literary activities depend on the former – none of your damned dilettante. In appearance he is like a plumper edition of Uncle Gussie & has something the same vivacity & quickness of speech, but a much more honestly merry laugh. Have you observed that it is the most serious conversations which produce in their course the best laughter? How we roared and fooled at times in the silence of last night – but always in a few minutes buckled to again with renewed seriousness. Then, as always here, the close of the whole thing is the journey through pitch black cloisters to let them out by the little gate with my key, where after the dark one suddenly sees the tower far above, in the light cast up from the street lamps. How I shall remember all this some day!

The other man was Coghill of Exeter, a friend of Chevasse, who talks v. like Chevasse (in voice I mean) but is a far better fellow. I am looking forward to reading *Desert Islands*[84] & am glad to have your judgment of it. Oh, by the way, I forgot to thank you for your offer of the Macdonalds. *Pro tanto quid retribuamus*? as the tramcars say – what can I give you in return? About Johnson & Milton – wasn't it M's politics that made J. so unfair?[85] The old die-hard Tory could never forgive the puritan, republican & regicide.

Yrs.
Jack

84 Walter de la Mare, *Desert Islands* (1930).

85 Johnson, *Lives of the English Poets*, op. cit., vol. I, p. 157: 'Milton's republicanism was, I am afraid, founded in an envious hatred of greatness, and a sullen desire of independence; in petulance impatient of controul, and pride disdainful of superiority. He hated monarchs in the state and prelates in the church; for he hated all whom he was required to obey. It is to be suspected that his predominant desire was to destroy rather than establish, and that he felt not so much the love of liberty as repugnance to authority.'

TO ARTHUR GREEVES (W):

[Hillsboro]
Aug. 3rd 1930

My dear Arthur,

Your account of your novel is certainly v. obscure. I thought the whole was already typed – or was that only a draught? I am sorry that I cannot be present at the accouchement, however 'painful and disgusting'.

I have been wondering why these days of rain & wind in the summer have such a charm for me. Is it simply an offshoot of my general love of winter, and these days please me as a foretaste of winter – as if the wind shook Summer and he buttoned his coat and said 'Dear me. I'm beginning to get old.' I walked in the fields beyond Barton after tea to day and sat under a hedge – the sort of hedge that is nearly all trees. The wind tossed it and tumbled it: and from the field – which was full of stacks of corn – straws kept on blowing up to me. Endless rain clouds went overhead. Somehow I was very happy in it – snug, you know. And yet one ought to feel snugger in a warm ditch in winter. Or is it that such days fall outside ones conventional categories of the seasons, being neither typical summer days nor typical autumn days, nor typical anything, and therefore, thwarting ones *derivative* reactions and all that has been already stereotyped by literature and painting, they force one to wake up and see the thing as it really is? Or is it part of the same general law which makes the landscape look more exciting upside down? However a fool can ask more questions in an hour than a wise man can answer in a life time.

The other thing I was thinking on my walk was this: I had just begun M. Arnold's *Studies In Celtic Literature*[86] and looking on to the end I saw that he said that German Romanticism (he particularly mentioned Novalis[87]) was a kind of clumsy attempt at the 'natural magic' of the Celts. Now I was perfectly certain that whatever else was true, that was not: but this set me puzzling as to what the real difference between the two was. I found that when I tried to get the spirit of German romance I got the idea of smiths, gold, dwarfs, forests, mountains, cottages and castles: while the other gave me the idea of water and rushes and clouds.

86 Matthew Arnold, *On the Study of Celtic Literature* (1867).

87 Novalis was the pseudonym of the German romantic poet and novelist, Friedrich Leopold von Hardenberg (1772–1801).

Then I noted that the Celtic was much more sensuous; also less *homely*: also, entirely lacking in *reverence*, of which the Germanic was full. Then again that the Germanic *glowed* in a sense with rich sombre colours, while the Celtic was all transparent and full of nuances – evanescent – but very bright. One sees that Celtic is essentially Pagan, not merely in the sense of being heathen (not-Christian), as the Germanic may be, but in the sense of being irredeemably Pagan, frivolous under all its melancholy, incapable of growing into religion, and – I think – a little heartless. In fact, add Roman civilisation to it and you get – France. I'm not running it down: before it gets Romanised it is delicious and refreshing. I don't want to give up either: they are almost ones male and female soul. Do you feel at all in sympathy with what I have been saying? And do you agree that the Germanic – gold & smiths – runs peculiarly to mineral images, i.e. the Earth – while Celtic runs to the elements. I think in the *Tempest* Caliban Is – almost a picture of the Germanic at its lowest, and Ariel the Celtic: but look at the lovely earthy poetry put into Caliban's mouth on two occasions.

To be frank I was rather prepared for *Desert Islands* turning out a disappointment, tho' my hopes had been temporarily resurrected by what you said of it. De La Mare has fallen infinitely below himself. I was looking at the *Connoisseur*[88] again not long ago. Of course it is good – he can't write anything that isn't that. But isn't there just a touch of the dilettante about it? – certainly a lack of the real spirituality one finds in the *Veil*? My idea is that he really bade good bye to the best part of himself in the lovely poem 'Be not too wildly amorous of the far'.[89] The peculiar kind of vision he had was of a strangely piercing quality and probably almost unbearable to the possessor: only a man of great solidity, of real character, sound at the bases of his mind & braced with philosophy, could have carried it safely. But De La Mare was not such a man. It was quite likely really leading him to madness, & he knew it. Hardly knowing what he did, and yet just knowing, he *sent* it away. I am told he lives in the midst of the silly London literary sets. His real day is over. Do you think this a possible theory?

Yes. The Witch is gone. Do you ever go into Leeborough garden? How strange it would be for you to sit on that summer seat now: it almost

88 Walter de la Mare, *The Connoisseur* (1926).

89 The opening line of 'The Imagination's Pride' from de la Mare's *The Veil and Other Poems* (1921).

makes me shudder. Do you know it sometimes comes to me as a shock to realise that all the *rest* of Strandtown is going on just the same.

As to when we shall meet: we are moving house in September (I'm going to tell you nothing about this so that it will be a surprise when you see it) so I am afraid I shall not be able to come to Ireland this summer. As to your coming here, it wd. be obviously a bad time to choose the move! (I hear[d] your views on this after your last experience!) I think October would be the best, and will keep you informed. Of course if you *are* in England at the end of August let me know. How I long for one of our walks & talks together: and how I would like to see you peering into the pages of my Ellis' *Metrical Romances*[90] wh. at last I have got: not to mention the Morris. A propos of which (& this is what my whole letter *should* have been about) what with Morris & other things I really seem to have had youth given back to me lately. But I must try to describe this another time, as I am spoiling the margin wh. you demand!

Yrs

J.

TO ARTHUR GREEVES (W):

[Hillsboro]
Aug 13. 1930

My dear Arthur,

I wonder what has happened. Are you ill – or away – or simply lazy? However, as you wrote to me so perseveringly during *my* silence (tho' you must allow that mine was foretold and unavoidable) I will continue to write during yours: and also to prevent a bad habit of silence setting in on both sides.

It is a curious thing that as I look back I can remember no breaks in the regular course of letters during the Bookham period. Breaks I suppose there must have been and my failure to recollect them is part of the same delusion (but not all delusion either) of memory, wh. makes the past summers always fine and the past winters always frosty. Yet on the whole I do really think that we were very regular, and am very anxious to keep it up now without a break – at least until the habit is so fully formed that it is sure to survive a short intermission. This is becoming rather prosy!

---

90 George Ellis, *Specimens of Early English Metrical Romances* (1805).

Talking about the breaking of resolutions – you see how skilfully I glide away from my prosing to something really gay and brilliant and witty and novel – in fact 'much more rational but much less like a ball'[91] – talking then of resolutions (but we weren't talking. Yes, but we are now!) – talking of resolutions, one of the worst things about a moral relapse – to me – is that it throws such a shadow back on the time before during which you thought you were getting on quite well. Having found oneself – for the hundredth time – back where one started, it seems so obvious that one has never really moved at all: and that what seemed progress was only [a] dream, or even the irrelevant result of circumstances or physical condition.

I have again begun my German and do half an hour every morning before beginning my other work. I am still at Novalis – you will wonder how I have not finished it long ago, and even to myself I seem to have been reading it almost all my life. As I go at about the pace of a schoolboy translating Caesar I expect it will last me for the rest of my days. (I am like the man in the story. 'Why not buy a book?' 'Oh I have one already.') This certainly leads to economy. It has better results too. As you know, 'Heinrich Von Ofterdingen'[92] wh. I am reading is a very Macdonaldy book – indeed Novalis is perhaps the greatest single influence on Macdonald – full of 'holiness', gloriously German-romantic (i.e. a delicious mingling of earthy homeliness and magic, also of a sort of spiritual voluptuousness with innocence) and to be compelled to spell out such stuff word by word instead of galloping greedily thro' it as I certainly should if I could find a translation really forces me to get the most out of it. There is *no* translation either into French or English: so you will have to rely on what I tell you. However I have probably said all this before.

Last night I slept very little owing to a pain I sometimes have wh. Joey says is the kidneys: so I have gone a walk longer than usual to day in the hope of tiring myself out. In spite of the heavy green August foliage it really might be October: the wailing wind and the clouds are sheer Autumn. How unfortunate it is that you cannot follow my walks as I can yours. It would convey nothing to you if I said that I went thro' the Eatons (Wood Eaton and Water Eaton). The first half of the walk is all in

91 Austen, *Pride and Prejudice*, ch. 11.
92 Friedrich Leopold von Hardenberg (or Novalis), *Heinrich von Ofterdingen* (1802).

a road, absolutely flat, with a clear stream behind it: through every break in the high hedges you get specimens of that sort of beauty that flat country has: i.e. that you never see further than across the first field, and beyond its further hedge the big elms – tho really scattered – look like a continuous forest. Nearer, of course, are the wild flowers and the cows whisking their tails. Wood Eaton itself is an almost ideal village. There is a great house (Georgian),[93] severe in outline, but mellowed with yellow moss, in a park where there are some fine cedars: about sixteen cottages round a pond and green, all of grey stone and nearly all thatched: a church: and in every direction very high walls of flat stones without mortar, and inside them the invariable rows of huge elms – greatly improved this afternoon by the wind.

Thence my walk led out into open fields, where the flatness made the sky enormous and the cows seemed to go on forever and ever. Do you know the strange sort of contrast there is in such a place on such a day between the utter placidity of the landscape and the hurry and scurry of the clouds – at least of the clouds immediately overhead, far away on the horizon, with the absent sun shining on *them*, one always sees remote, clear, shining clouds that look almost calmer than anything else in the world. The only adventure on the ground was the sudden discovery of a field almost black with crows, which, of course dashed up cawing into the air as I approached them and then were blown about. 'The untidy crows' as Sackville West says in *The Land*[94] (a poem you should read) speaking of their flight on a windy day.

Did I tell you I have been reading a lot of Matthew Arnold's prose (I've got to for tutorial purposes). Oh, I remember, I talked about him in my last letter. I don't know that I recommend him. How do you get on with your Johnson? And how does your accouchement proceed. Perhaps it is that which has hindered you from writing.

I had a most horrible dream the other night, which I retail in case you would like to make use of it. Mrs Lovell was a poor old woman whom Minto used to give odd jobs to: she has now disappeared. I dreamed that I went to a cupboard in the kitchen to look for something. A heavy thing in brown paper dropped out at my feet. Picking it up and unwinding it I found – Mrs Lovel's HEAD! (I think it might be worked in along with

93 Wood Eaton Hall.

94 Vita Sackville-West, *The Land* (1926): 'Autumn', l. 94.

the hairy gums, 'Your grandmother etc etc' into the super-shocker that so often flits about our minds.)

There will, I think, be no shortage of hedgehogs in our new garden.

Do write

Yours

Jack

TO ARTHUR GREEVES (W):

[Hillsboro]
Aug. 18, 1930

My dear Arthur,

The first thing, when one is being worried as to whether one will have to have an operation or whether one is a literary failure, is *to assume absolutely mercilessly that the worst is true*, and to ask *What Then?* If it turns out in the end that the worst is not true, so much the better: but for the meantime the question must be resolutely put out of mind. Otherwise your thoughts merely go round and round a wearisome circle, now hopeful, now despondent, then hopeful again – that way madness lies. Having settled then that the worst is true, one can proceed to consider the situation: and I will talk to you as one in that situation.

Now the worst of all the things we usually say to a man who is suffering is that they inevitably provoke him to retort, in feeling, if not in words, 'Yes. It's all very well for *you*. It isn't *your* tooth that is aching.' So as soon as I read your letter I bethought me of myself on the evening when the MS of *Dymer* came back from Heinemanns rejected without a word of criticism or encouragement: and I remembered that after a very miserable night I sat down to assume the worst, as I advise you to do, and *on that basis* to come to terms with the situation. Only I did it in writing. I have been in to College this morning and found the document wh. I enclose. It is perfectly genuine and unaltered except for the marginal notes wh. I have now added in explanation of one or two expressions you might not have come across. I don't know whether it will be any help to you: it was of the greatest to me. You will be tempted to say that my situation was quite different from yours: for I succeeded in the end. To this I answer (1) That when I wrote this document I did not know I should succeed in publishing. (2) That when I did finally publish, the book was a complete failure.

To you, no doubt, at the moment it seems that to read your own book in print and to have it liked by a few friends would be ample bliss, whether any one bought it or not. Believe me, Arthur, this is an *absolute delusion*. It might satisfy you for a moment: but very soon, if it didn't sell, you would find yourself just as disappointed as you are now. So that in this sense I am *still* as disappointed an author as you. From the age of sixteen onwards I had one single ambition, from which I never wavered, in the prosecution of which I spent every ounce I could, on wh. I really & deliberately staked my whole contentment: and I recognise myself as having unmistakably failed in it. So that not only in my enclosed document, but now, in this letter, I feel that I have some right to talk to you as a man in the same boat.

Suffering of the sort that you are now feeling is my special subject, my profession, my long suit, the thing I claim to be an expert in: and if I were not writing to a man still smarting under the novelty of the blow I should point out at length how absurd it is to dignify such disappointment with the name of suffering in a world like this. (There is a woman lives in our road who is sinking into creeping paralysis and going blind: and for the last three nights she has been awake, and crying, all night, with neuritis. She says 'I feel as if my blood was boiling in my arms.') This side of the question you cannot yet be ready to feel: it wd. be more than human if you did. I only mention it because otherwise I wd. be ashamed, in speaking of myself, to use the noble word 'suffering'. However, whether you call it 'suffering' or not, I claim to be a dab at it.

The worst of it is that all the mental habits contracted during the work, go on after hope is dead. You see a tree waving in the wind and you think 'I'll put that in.' You notice some psychological fact in yourself and think 'By Jove! I'll use that in such a scene.' You read in some review a statement about contemporary literature and think 'I wonder if his opinion will be modified when he reads—, and then *bang*! it comes back again: ALL THAT IS OVER. And yet one has to go through with it: and little by little the real consolations come. Read what Bunyan says about the valley of humiliation.[95] Read about Anodos at the low island where the old woman lived.

95 Bunyan, *The Pilgrim's Progress*, op. cit., pt. II, p. 252: 'When we went...down the Hill, into the Valley of Humiliation, [Mr Fearing] went down as well as ever I saw man in my Life, for he cared not how mean he was, so he might be happy at last. Yes, I think there was a kind of Sympathy betwixt that Valley and him. For I never saw him better in all his Pilgrimage, than when he was in that Valley.'

For its quite true what my document says. The side of me which longs, not to write, for no one can stop us doing that, but to be approved as a writer, is not the side of us that is really worth much. And depend upon it, unless God has abandoned us, he will find means to cauterise that side somehow or other. If we can take the pain well and truly now and by it *forever* get over the wish to be distinguished beyond our fellows, well: if not we shall get it again in some other form. And honestly, the being cured, with all the pain, has pleasure too: one creeps home, tired and bruised, into a state of mind that is really restful, when all ones ambitions have been given up. Then one can really for the first time say 'Thy Kingdom come': for in that Kingdom there will be no pre-eminences and a man must have reached the stage of not caring two straws about his own status before he can enter it.

Think how difficult that would be if one *succeeded* as a writer: how bitter this necessary purgation at the age of sixty, when literary success had made your whole life and you had *then* got to begin to go through the stage of seeing it all as dust and ashes. Perhaps God has been specially kind to us in forcing us to get over it at the beginning. At all events, whether we like it or not, we have got to take the shock. As you know so well, we have got to *die*. Cry, kick, swear, we may: only like Lilith to come in the end and die far more painfully and later. Does it sound like priggery if I say 'I implore you'? Heaven knows I do it as a friend not as a preacher: do it only because you stand very high among the half-dozen people whom I love. I implore you, then, seriously, to regard your present trouble as an opportunity for carrying the dying process a stage further. If necessary, go back to the Puritan language you were brought up in and think of your literary ambitions as an 'idol' you have to give up, as a sacrifice demanded. I 'implore' because such disappointments, if *accepted* as death, and therefore the beginning of new life, are infinitely valuable: but if not, are terrible dangers. Once let self-pity come uppermost and you know where you are sure to turn for consolation. In other words they are bound to leave a man (permanently perhaps) very much better or very much worse than they found him.

So far I have said nothing about Reid's judgement, nor about your going on with the attempt. I am afraid, human nature being what it is, you must have glanced eagerly thro' this letter for some word on those very subjects: even have wondered dismally when I wd. have done moralising and get to business. Perhaps even when you so strongly urged me to write, you had always the hope that my letter would restore your confidence in yourself as a literary man. Perhaps all this time what you are asking yourself is 'Does this letter mean that Jack thinks Reid is probably right and doesn't like to say so?' Poor Arthur! You must – it is only nature – be simply starving for some word of *literary* encouragement instead of all this moral encouragement. But don't you also see that I mustn't give it? For as long as you are still thinking about *that*, still wondering whether Reid is right, you haven't taken the *first step*. Whether you are going to be a writer or not, *in either case*, you must so far die as to get over putting that question first. The other thing is so very much more important. For be sure, until we learn better, we shall get this kind of suffering again and again. Better take it now: better learn the trick that makes you free for the future. It sounds merely brutal I expect: but do remember I'm in the same boat. I would have given almost *anything* – I shudder to think what I would have given if I had been allowed – to be a successful writer. So don't think I am writing this in order to avoid giving my own opinion about your possibilities of success. I couldn't give an opinion in any case without seeing the book: but I am writing as I do simply & solely because I think the only thing for you to do is absolutely to *kill* the part of you that wants success. It's like in Phantastes where the voice said 'Ride at him or be a slave *forever*.'[96]

At present (1) Maureen is away (2) Minto is bad with indigestion (3) We are going to move on Sept. 25th (4) There is a possible visitor in the next three weeks.* In these distressing conditions I can neither go to you nor ask you to come to me. But I could (I am pretty sure) get you quite nice rooms in Old Headington and we cd. meet every day. I am *dying* to show you the new place & to have a walk & talk with you. Wd. you think of this while your mother is away. Do. It wd. honestly give me more pleasure than any (possible) thing at the moment. I am sorry to seem so inhospitable – and I would *love* to come to you for a week if I could.

Write soon. If you eat this you will grow into a unicorn. I hope you won't loathe this letter

Yours
Jack

*which unspecified!

96 MacDonald, *Phantastes*, ch. 22.

[The 'document' referred to in the letter above, with notes added 18 August 1930]

Saturday March 6th 1926

Last night Heinemann's returned the MS. of Dymer on which I have been at work for several years. Though I intend to try all the publishers, it seems good, in the event of a complete failure, to find out by the analysis of my present disappointment what exactly it is I hope to gain by poetical success: and what the abandonment of the hope would mean. To understand is the safest resource.

1. A certain part of my disappointment is clearly special to the present case. Heinemann's had treated me well before. I had allowed myself to think of them as οικειουσ (1) and flattered myself on being admitted to the rank of the number of good poets whose work they publish. I had also hoped that rejection, if it came, wd. come signed by Evans with some personal expression of regret or kindness. This is an element in my feelings at the moment wh. cannot occur when another house returns it. It may therefore be eliminated.

2. I may clearly also eliminate the desire for money, as I never seriously hoped that Dymer would pay. Or if, in more sanguine moods, I sometimes dreamed of having a few pounds of extra pocket money by it, this is something that counts for a negligible quantity in my disappointment.

3. I can also rule out, tho' not entirely, the desire for Fame, if this means the desire to be known as the author of an approved poem, the *monstrari digito*. (2) It is true that I should like and like greatly to be known (and praised) by one or two friends and good judges: but I hold this as a refinement of pleasure easily foregone. If it went by another's name, so long as it was read and liked, I should be quite content.

4. But I cannot say simply that I desire not my fame but that of the poem. In the impossible case of an exactly similar poem written by someone else and winning success I should be very far from content. Though no one else need know that the approved poem is mine, I at least must know it. The feeling is not, therefore, a disinterested love for Dymer simply as a poem I happen to like.

5. It is then a desire that something which I recognize as my own should be publicly found good: whether it is known by others to be mine is of comparatively little importance. Is it then what Aristotle says? I

desire public praise as a proof that it really is good: i.e. I wish to be able to think that I am a good poet and desire applause (tho not paid to my name) as a means to that end.

6. This is the most probable account yet suggested. One objection occurs. If an archangel or a mystical intuition admitting of no doubt, assured me that Dymer was the greatest poem ever written by man, but added that it would never be read, I should be hardly more contented than I am now. The supposition, however, raises many difficulties. (a) Is the reason of my dissatisfaction that a poem unread is not a poem at all, and that there is therefore no sense in calling it great? (b) Does the disinterested wish that, if it were great, humanity should enjoy it, count for anything? (c) Is my acquiescence in not being known (or thought) great by others, not quite what it seemed to be in Para. 3?

7. (b) is very attractive but I cannot find that it is what I feel. No poem is indispensible. In my worst moods I never supposed that the 'spirit of man' would be the worse for not having Dymer. Let it be as good as you like: they will get the same thing out of other books sooner or later. For in a larger sense and in the long run we do get the same thing out of different books.

8. (a) certainly seems to be true. The greatness of a poem can mean only the good that particular readers do actually get from it. And it is certain that no acknowledgement, however public, of my claims as a poet would make up for Dymer's not being read and enjoyed. If my archangel promised that the human race wd. go about ever after lamenting a great lost work of mine, and pay me the highest honours: no doubt this wd. give me some kind of pleasure, but not the kind I am really concerned about at present.

9. (c) This seems to have some truth in it. I shall be forced to admit that tho I do not want public praise for 'someone called Lewis' I do want it for 'the author of Dymer'. In fact the suggestion in Para. 5 is not true. I do not desire the praise *simply* as a proof. I desire that my value as a poet should be acknowledged by others as well as myself, even if they do not know where to find 'this great poet' or what he looks like etc. Perhaps some dream of being sooner or later discovered mixes still with my acquiescence in such anonymous success. I honestly don't know: tho' I might know if I cd. be perfectly honest. *That* problem I leave open for the present.

10. My desire then contains two elements. (a) The desire for some proof to myself that I am a poet. (b) The desire that my poet-hood

should be acknowledged even if no one knows that it is mine. (b) is a means to (a) but it is not valued only as a means.

11. As far as I can see both these are manifestations of the single desire for what may be called mental or spiritual rank. I have flattered myself with the idea of being among my own people when I was reading the poets and it is unpleasing to have to stand down and take my place in the crowd. Such a desire is contrary to my own settled principles: the very principles which I expressed in Dymer. It is fair to say that I had already gone some way towards repressing it – the writing of Dymer was a purgation – when the completion of the poem, Coghill's praise of it, and the sending off to a publishers (after so many years) threw me back into a tumult of self-love that I thought I had escaped. This must be recognised as pure retrogression. The desire will not bear examination. To stand above ὁ τυχῶν (3) is a wish that cannot be universalised. (4) Worst of all I have used the belief in such secret pre-eminence as a compensation for things that wearied or humiliated me in real life: Thomas Browne's insidious nonsense about 'they that look upon my outside etc.'(5).

12. The cure of this disease is not easy to find – except the sort of violent, surgical cure which Reality itself may be preparing for me. I was free from it at times when writing Dymer. Then I was interested in the object, not in my own privileged position of seer of the object. But whenever I stopped writing or thought of publication or showed the MS. to friends I contemplated not that of which I had been writing, but my writing about it: I passed from looking at the macrocosm (6) to looking at a little historical event inside the 'Me'.

The only healthy or happy or eternal life is to look so steadily on the World that the representation 'Me' fades away. Its appearance at all in the field of consciousness is a mark of inferiority in the state where it appears. Its claiming a central position is disease.

13. Is self-consciousness, the possibility of contemplating the object Me, a pure mistake? It may be, rather, that this power of objectifying myself has its value as a necessary preliminary to being rid of it.

(1) 'My ain folk'.

(2) Being pointed at with the finger (i.e. pointed out as the 'great man' in the streets).

(3) The ordinary man.

(4) Kant says that you should desire nothing wh. you can't 'universalise', i.e. desire for every one else as well as for yourself. Now clearly I can't desire that every one shd. be pre-eminent above the ordinary run of people, for there wd. then be no ordinary run, & therefore no pre-eminence.

(5) i.e. used it to console myself by saying 'Ah! I mayn't cut a great figure externally: but if only you knew what a poet I was!'

(6) The great world.

TO ARTHUR GREEVES (W):

[Hillsboro]
Aug 28th 1930

My dear Arthur,

I was delighted to get your cheering letter. Do not thank me, much less admire me. The splendid *talking* has, as usual, fallen to my share: what had to be done and lived fell to yours. All men can give excellent advice!

I quite agree by the bye with your rejection of Forrest's consolatory remark that you may write as a hobby. It reminds me of that romantic saying of R. L. Stevenson's 'It is better to travel hopefully than to arrive':[97] against whose abuse Barfield is always protesting. For as he says, how can you travel hopefully except in the hope of arriving? And if a person, having taken away your hope of arriving, still tells you to travel hopefully, he is talking nonsense. (It's like saying 'What a bore. I see we shant be able to go to the opera after all. However we can still enjoy *looking forward* to going!' or 'It's true that I am going to get nothing to eat. But then what a splendid appetite I have!') If this sort of thing is consolatory, certainly no human evil can lack consolation.

As for the real motives for writing after one has 'got over' the desire for acknowledgement: – in the first place, I found and find, that precisely at the moment when you have really put all that out of your mind and decided not to write again – or if you do, to do it with the clear consciousness that you are only playing yourself – precisely then the ideas –

97 Robert Louis Stevenson, *Virginibus Puerisque* (1881), 'El Dorado': 'O toiling hands of mortals! O unwearied feet, travelling ye know not whither! Soon, soon, it seems to you, you must come forth on some conspicuous hill-top, and but a little way farther, against the setting sun, descry the spires of El Dorado. Little do ye know your own blessedness; for to travel hopefully is a better thing than to arrive, and the true success is to labour.'

which came so rarely in the days when you regarded yourself officially as an author – begin to bubble and simmer, and sooner or later you will *have* to write: and the question *why* won't really enter your mind. In my own case it is a very remarkable thing that in the few religious lyrics which I have written during the last year, in which I had no idea of publication & at first very little idea even of showing them to friends, I have found myself impelled to take infinitely more pains, less ready to be contented with the fairly good and more determined to reach the best attainable, than ever I was in the days when I never wrote without the ardent hope of successful publication.[98]

The truth is, I think, that 'our deeds are ours: their ends none of our own'. Who knows – why should we know? – what will in the end reach the ear of humanity? The successes of our own age may be speedily forgotten: some poem scribbled in pencil on the fly leaf of a schoolbook may survive and be read and be an influence when English is a dead language. Who knows, even, whether to reach the ears of other men is the purpose for which this impulse is really implanted in us? Perhaps in the eyes of the gods the true use of a book lies in its effects upon the author. You remember what Ibsen said, that every play he wrote had been written for the purgation of his own heart. And in my own humbler way I feel quite certain that I could not have certain good things now if I had not gone through the writing of Dymer. Or if a book has an audience of one – surely we must not assume that this may not be, from some superhuman point of view, as much justification as an audience of thousands. I am sure that some are born to write as trees are born to bear leaves: for these, writing is a necessary mode of their own development. If the impulse to write survives the hope of success, then one is among these. If not, then the impulse was at best only pardonable vanity, and it will certainly disappear when the hope is withdrawn. So that whether the necessity and duty of writing is laid on a man or not can soon be discovered by his own feelings. With remote consequences we have no concern. We never know enough.

I think the thing is to obey the ordinary rules of morality: subject to them, to be guided by those impulses which *feel* the most serious and innocent as opposed to those that *feel* trivial and shamefaced: but for

98 Those religious lyrics were later to appear in Lewis's *The Pilgrim's Regress* (1933), and they have subsequently been included in his *Poems* (1964) and *Collected Poems* (1994).

ultimate justifications & results to trust to God. The bee builds its cell and the bird its nest, probably with no knowledge of what purpose they will serve: another sees to that. Nobody knows what the result of your writing, or mine, (or Masefield's) will be. But I think we may depend upon it that endless and devoted work on an object to which a man feels seriously impelled will *tell* somewhere or other: himself or others, in this world or others, will reap a harvest exactly proportional to the output. The accounts of this universe are probably very well kept: everything finds its place in the long run. As Von Hügel (an author you shd. read – remind me about him some other time) says 'No effort will ever be as if it had not been'. The situation may be just the reverse of the nightingale in *Endymion*, who

> '*Sings but to her mate, nor e'er conceives*
> *How tiptoe night holds back her dark grey hood.*'[99]

Unsuccessful writers like us thought that night would stand tiptoe to hear us: perhaps we really are singing to some mysterious mate within. Remember too what Traherne says that our appreciation of this world – and *this* becomes fully conscious only as we express it in art – is a real link in the universal chain. Beauty descends from God into nature: but there it would perish and does except when a Man appreciates it with worship and thus as it were *sends it back* to God: so that through his consciousness what descended ascends again and the perfect circle is made.

Dear oh dear! I never meant to fill this whole letter with the subject: and my pen has been running away with me. I suppose it is natural on a subject that touches both of us so near. In fact my experience at this moment is not a bad example in little of my whole argument. For I started aiming at you and thinking that the value of my words lay in the effect they might have on *you*: but now I have drawn out of my own letter so much unexpected matter for my own needs that if it should be lost in the post, I at least will remain a gainer.

Unfortunately it has crowded out a lot of other things. I wanted to tell you about De Quincey's *Autobiography*[100] which I have just finished the first volume of. Not the *Opium Eater*[101] – tho it covers some of the same

---

99 Keats, *Endymion*, I, 830–1.

100 Thomas De Quincey, *Autobiographical Sketches*, 2 vols. (1853–4).

101 See note 30 to letter of 21? March 1915.

ground. It is really splendid reading, but I'm too tired to try and explain why. I wanted to tell you all about the bonfire I spent most of yesterday in stoking – and so on. By next week perhaps I shall be finding room for other things. It has been a most terribly hot day here to day and I am *dripping*! I'm glad to hear that *Desert Islands* has bucked up again & shall certainly try it at the first opportunity. Good night

Yours

Jack

TO ARTHUR GREEVES (W):

[Hillsboro]
Aug 31st 1930

My dear Arthur,

I have had two delightful moments since I last wrote. The first was the arrival of the Macdonalds. Thank you over and over again! Perhaps the best way I can thank you at the moment is by trying to give you a share in my delight.

Imagine me, then, seated in a shady, but even so sweltering, corner of the garden with a shade temperature of 88°, in the middle of the afternoon. Imagine the sound of Mr Papworth barking and my rising wearily, as at the 100th interruption, to investigate. I took in the bulky parcel carelessly enough and looked at it without hope of interest, till suddenly your handwriting transformed the whole situation and in a minute I had it opened. Three distinguishable waves of pleasure went over me. The first was a welling up of all that Macdonald himself stands for: the second an added delight as this present, coming so appropriately from you, linked itself up with all our joint life and old times (I begin to see that it is not all rot – tho' it often is – when people say they will value a gift more for the sake of the giver): the third a pleased surprise at finding three, at least, of the books respectably bound, and clean pages of decent type and paper within – for I had always taken it for granted that they would be hideous.

If I followed my inclinations I would have read them all by now: but fortunately work forbids me such a dangerous orgy. I have however finished *Wilfrid Cumbermede*[102] – I took it down with me after tea that same afternoon to Parson's Pleasure and read naked under the willows. I shall

102 George MacDonald, *Wilfrid Cumbermede* (1872).

not venture on my next Macdonald, tho' tempted, for some time, for fear of spoiling my own delights.

As you said in one of your letters, his novels have great and almost intolerable faults. His only real form is the symbolical fantasy like *Phantastes* or *Lilith*. This is what he always writes: but unfortunately for financial reasons, he sometimes has to *disguise* it as ordinary Victorian fiction. Hence what you get is a certain amount of the real Macdonald linked (as Mezentius linked live men to corpses)[103] – linked onto a mass of quite worthless plot: and as his *real* parts have to involve strange happenings, the plot is usually improbable, obscure, and melodramatic. Thus Wilfrid's dream of Athanasia, his waking to find Mary (transfigured) by his side, and the sword between them, is pure vision. It is in fact closely connected in *that* world with the sword-divided sleep of Sigurd and Brynhild, and also with Dymer's adventure (For we don't individually invent these things, perhaps. Look how the 'empty castle' theme is present in *Phantastes*, *Wilfrid*, & *Dymer*. No doubt it passed into *Dymer* from *Phantastes*: but then, from it, in Dymer, I passed on to the mysterious bedfellow without any guidance from Macdonald – and only *now* find that he has got that bit of the story too, only in another book. Don't you get the feeling of something waiting there and slowly being recovered in fragments by different human minds according to their abilities, and partially spoiled in each writer by the admixture of his own mere individual invention?) This is pure vision, as I say: unfortunately, in order to keep up the pretence that he is writing a novel, he has to explain it all away – hence all the impossible rigmarole about Clara's putting the sword there and Mary's getting into the wrong bed. Yet the gold is so good that it carries off the dross and I hope to read this book many times again. Things that particularly affected me were the grass plain round the old farm (I don't know why this gives such a magical air), the storm raised by the pendulum and the sudden appearance of the horseman, the chapter called '*On the Leads*', the scene of Wilfrid lost on the Alps, and the dream of Charley (*what* a name!) and Wilfrid dead, and perching on the bushes. I don't think as a whole it is so good as *Sir Gibbie* which seems of all G.M.'s novels so far as I've read to avoid best the mere deadweight of 'plot' that I have complained of. Thanks, Arthur,

103 Mezentius was a mythical Etruscan king who bound living men to corpses and left them to die of starvation. See Virgil, *Aeneid*, VIII, 485–8.

again and again. I know nothing that gives me such a feeling of spiritual healing, of being washed, as to read G. Macdonald.

My second delightful moment was of a different kind, and takes a little arrangement to describe. Imagine first a pure rosy pink sunset: in the extreme distance a sky covered with thin 'mackerel' as delicate as the veins in a shell, & all pink: in the foreground, blackly outlined against this, huge crags and castles and Valkyrie-shapes of cloud. Got that? Now; – imagine that all this existed only for a fraction of [a] second, the pink light being in fact no sunset but a vast flood of summer lightening: so that all those beetling cliffs and tottering cities of the gods, together with the rosy flush behind which made them visible, had leaped out of pure star-set darkness an instant before, and vanished into it instantaneously again – and so times without number. Later in the night it developed into a real thunderstorm: but for a long while it was very distant and I heard thunder at a greater distance (it seemed) than I had ever heard it before. It was *tinkly* – like the crushing of very delicate tumblers by a giant millions of miles away. The comparison is not very good: at any rate it had the most extreme beauty, and the most unlike the grandeur of ordinary thunder, that you can imagine.

I have also had some splendid bathes in the last few days and have suffered, along with the exhaustion of extreme heat, something of a trance-like condition that exhaustion sometimes brings.

We have an old maid, Miss Walsh, staying with us, who, on a very small income, seems to have travelled nearly everywhere. She talks too much of her travels, but there is an old-maidish torrent of details about trunks and trains and an American I met in Corsica (quite *un*like Kelsie – no attempt at humour) which somehow I rather like. A little pinched face with pince-nez. She surprised me by having read the *Crock of Gold* and saying she loved fairy tales: so I have lent her *Phantastes* and await results.

I am now in the second volume of de Quincy's *Autobiography* which continues excellent. We expect to move on Sept. 29th. I suppose I shd. end up 'again thanking you v. much' as we used to do in replying to Christmas boxes! –

Yrs
Jack

TO ARTHUR GREEVES (W):

[Hillsboro]
Sept. 15th 1930

P.S. This is a very mortuary letter, be prepared for the worst!

My dear Arthur,

Apologies for delay! I was feeling rather seedy on Sunday besides having a weary right arm, whether this was neuritis or writer's cramp from making notes all day long: as I am v. busy making notes for an extremely dull subject wh. I have to take next term.

I was glad to get your letter from Cushendun. Did you visit our old friend at the Post-Office? And how did the new friend turn out on closer acquaintance?

Miss Walsh, by the way, did *not* get through *Phantastes* and I now strongly suspect that her alleged love of fantasy was merely a bye-product of her fanatical love of everything Irish. This, wh. in any case cd. only be a respectable weakness took in her case the degraded form of endless chit-chat about all the famous Irish literary people she had met. She referred to Yeats as 'W.B.' – 'for short' – until I asked her how four syllables could be a shortened form of one. The last five minutes of her, while I was seeing her off at the bus, led to the horrible discovery that I was learning Icelandic, and not learning Irish: for which I was soundly scolded. In fact she behaved about Ireland as Americans behave about America, and finally went off with her head in the air as who shd. say Hoity-Toity!

The most interesting thing since I last wrote is a dream I had about my father. As a rule dreams about the dead fall into two distinct classes. (a) Those in wh. one simply forgets that the person has died (b) Those in which the dead appears as a bogey. My dream belonged to neither. I was in the dining room in Little Lea, with all the gasses lit and talking to my father. I knew perfectly well that he had died, and presently put out my hand and touched him. He felt warm and solid. I said 'But of course this body must be only an appearance. You can't really have a body now.' He explained that it *was* only an appearance, and our conversation which was cheerful and friendly, but not solemn or emotional, drifted off onto other topics. I then went over to fetch you and we came across together in a closed car. As we drove I told you of his return in order to prepare you for meeting him: and I think (tho' this may be a waking invention) that at that point I was looking forward to seeing him come to the door and say 'Well, Arthur' and offer you your drink. We were exactly at that place where an increased crushing under the wheels tells you that you have passed off the cinders onto the gravel at the study corner: when you, in a voice of suppressed anxiety, said 'Oh no, Jack. Its just that you've been thinking about him and you've *imagined* he's there.' Till that moment everything had been pleasant and homely: but suddenly, as your words made me see the whole adventure *from outside*, as I realised how it would sound if repeated that I had been TALKING TO A DEAD MAN, the thing wh. had been SO normal in the experiencing it, rose up with such retrospective horror that the nightmare feeling flared up and I woke in terror. The dream seems to me a good idea of what might v. probably happen if one really met a ghost. At least I sometimes hope so.

Have I propounded before to you my theory that the *corpse* and the *ghost* each owe all their terrors to the other? The corpse, tho so horribly different, is yet so like a man that you can't help thinking it has a life of its own – i.e. you put a ghost in it. But for the idea that this un-man may still live, it wd. not be horrible. Conversely, when you think of the spirit, tho you know it to be unpicturable, you can't help picturing it, and yet you feel you must make it different from the man as he was: then in comes the horrible association of the corpse. In each case you are trying to think of a thing as living and dead at the same time, and from the impossible conception comes the horror.

Certainly ones own death wd. be a much pleasanter idea if one cd. be quite rid of the lingering idea that the corpse is alive. I thought I had got over this years ago: but every now and then some old stain of savage materialism starts up and tries to make me believe that it is *me* they will nail in a box and bury. The same sort of confusion explains why the idea of being buried alive, with a hearse & a coffin etc, is so much worse than the idea of being smothered, say, in a landslip, or by getting on your face in sleep, – wh. latter of course are just the same mode of death really. The secret is that what one fears is *not* smothering – wh, tho' bad enough, is probably much nicer than the 'natural' deaths which most of us are going to die.* It is that the funeral accompaniments give you the idea of entering alive into the normal and regular *status* of a corpse – i.e. of being alive and dead at the same time. It can't really be worse than drowning. So the next time you're buried alive, Arthur, be sure and remember that its no worse than drowning. Trust an old hand, my boy.

It pays! Heigh-ho! If we were talking instead of writing letters I shd. begin to fool now ('Beshrew me, the knight's in excellent fooling')

What put you onto the Priestly novel? It may be excellent, but it somehow never occurred to me to try. Perhaps I will after your recommendation.

I think you must have misunderstood me about the Macdonald. I never meant the novels wd. be better without a *story*, nor that the good parts consisted of anything other than story. All I meant was that a really valuable story of the Phantastes kind was constantly being interrupted by a story of a quite inferior kind, and even an inferior specimen of that kind. Also, I agree that the first few chapters of *S. Gibbie* are nothing like as good as the first few chapters of *W. Cumbermede*. But by now you will have got to the good parts. Don't you love 'sleep was scattered all over the world'[104] – and the lovely homeliness of the farm kitchen – and the apparition of Sir Gibbie when the old woman mistakes him for Christ. I hope for your views on it on Saturday – also for a final account of your time at Cushendun.

Yours

Jack

*One might almost leave directions in ones will that one was to be buried alive.

TO ARTHUR GREEVES (W):

[Hillsboro]
Oct. 6th 1930

My dear Arthur,

I had hoped to get off not a letter (that was out of the question) but a line of apology on Sunday: but Sunday when it came was wholly occupied with packing jam. You will excuse my silence when you hear that I am (all at the same time) (a) Having a perfectly stupifying cold, almost 'flu. (b) Packing for a move on Saturday. (c) Preparing for term on Saturday. (d) Finishing a course of lectures. (e) Setting papers for next summers Exams.

Oh Arthur – do you know how lucky you are to be able to say any evening 'I may take a day in bed to-morrow' – the luck of one in a million.

104 MacDonald, *Sir Gibbie*, vol. I, ch. ix, p. 138.

This is just to explain my silence.
Yours
Jack

Lewis had at last acquired the house he had been hinting at. This was The Kilns, at Headington Quarry, which lies about two miles further from the centre of Oxford than Hillsboro. On Sunday 6 July Jack and Warnie saw it for the first time, and the next day Warnie wrote an enthusiastic account in his diary:

> *We did not go inside, but the eight acre garden is such stuff as dreams are made of. I never imagined that for us any such garden would ever come within the sphere of discussion. The house... stands at the entrance to its own grounds at the northern foot of Shotover at the end of a narrow lane, which in turns opens off a very bad and little used road, giving as great privacy as can reasonably be looked for near a large town: to the left of the house are the two brick kilns from which it takes its name – in front, a lawn and hard tennis court – then a large bathing pool, beautifully wooded, and with a delightful circular brick seat overlooking it: after that a steep wilderness broken with ravines and nooks of all kinds runs up to a little cliff topped by a thistly meadow, and then the property ends in a thick belt of fir trees, almost a wood: the view from the cliff over the dim blue distance of the plain is simply glorious.* (*BF*, p. 58)

Jack, Mrs Moore and Warnie bought the house together for £3300 and they moved in on 10 October.

TO ARTHUR GREEVES (W):

Magdalen College,
Oxford.
Oct. 29th 1930

My dear Arthur,

Things are no better and I don't know when I shall have time to write to you properly again. I really am at it from morning till night at present, Sundays included. Thanks so much for your letter. Try to give me another as soon as may be and don't abandon me to my fate. You mustn't think that I am having a specially *nasty* time – in some ways quite a good one, in every respect except leisure. My days are filled with pupils in college and settling in in the new house at Headington: and I am enjoying both. I have made a vow not to tell you anything about our new residence, because if I do you will certainly be disappointed when you actually see it. But oh – ! I never hoped for the like.

About Geo. Macdonald, I am afraid we must agree to a real difference. The exciting story in Wilfrid Cumbermede seems to me a pure drag and Sir Gibbie seems to me much better because the excitement in it is of the *real* sort and not interrupted by the mere machinery of the old melodramatic 3-vol novel. I bought two others in London, *Adela Cathcart* & *What's Mine's Mine*[105] just before term began (By the way the bookseller told me that there was a small but steady demand for Macdonalds – wh. is interesting and encouraging) *Adela* I'm afraid I think definitely bad, tho it begins well: and *The Seaboard Parish*[106] the same. The real holiness is, in them both, degenerating into mere flat moralising and sometimes it is hard to feel that you're reading the author of *Phantastes*.

Have you been having lovely autumn? We have. Woods all speckled with yellow, drifts of leaves at the roadside, and the most exquisite pale skies. The other morning on some gorse bushes I saw a wonderful display of cobwebs – like a thick bridal veil, unbroken, extending for many yards. The smells are delicious. I also had the experience lately of walking under an avenue of trees after a shower, and saw that tho all the rest was still, a kind of wave-motion was passing over the branches on one side, followed by a patter of drops. Coming nearer I found it was a squirrel leaping from branch to branch and sending a wake of tiny showers to earth as they bent under him.

Had tea the other day with the Provost of Worcester[107] who is a wonderful old man and has a huge garden which he has converted into a real country farm in the middle of Oxford. He introduced me to two

105 George MacDonald, *Adela Cathcart* (1864); *What's Mine's Mine* (1886).

106 George MacDonald, *The Seaboard Parish* (1868).

107 The Rev. Francis John Lys (1863–1947) took his degree from Worcester College, Oxford, in 1886, and was an assistant master at Radley College from 1887 to 1888. He returned to Oxford as a lecturer at Worcester in 1889, and was Fellow, Tutor, Senior Tutor, Bursar and Provost of Worcester from 1919 to 1946.

alderneys – lovely creatures, as delicately made as deer: you wd. hardly believe that cows cd. be so dainty – and their sweet breath.

I have started going to morning Chapel at 8, wh. means going to bed earlier: and indeed I live such vigorous days that I am usually glad to go. My moral history of late has been deplorable. More and more clearly one sees how much of one's philosophy & religion is mere talk: the boldest hope is that concealed somewhere within it there is some seed however small of the real thing

Yrs

J.

TO ARTHUR GREEVES (W):

This is the only paper I can find!

[The Kilns,
Kiln Lane,
Headington Quarry,
Oxford]
Dec 24th 1930

My dear Arthur,

I take no blame for the long silence. In the latter half of term writing became quite impossible and then when term was over I had to waste the first fortnight of my Vac. examining – which, as you know, means work from morning till night. I am now free at last – hungry to get back to my *real* work, and ordinary life: in which I include the resumption of my correspondence with you.

By this time you should have a book which I sent you[108] (a) Because I have been asked to help the author by drawing peoples attention to it – he is a friend of mine. (b) Because he is the same man who wrote *Harvest in Poland*,[109] that v. dubious book lent me by the sinister Chevasse. (c) Because I have myself enjoyed it and think – tho' with some doubts – that you will enjoy it too. The get-up is rather what we should once have liked than what we like now: but the Dürer on the wrapper is worth having for its own sake.

I envy you your stay at Ballycastle: even the name gives me a faint pleasant twinge. But there is one odd thing I have been noticing since we

108 Geoffrey Dennis, *The End of the World* (1930).

109 Geoffrey Dennis, *Harvest in Poland* [1925].

came to our new house, which is much more in the country, and it is this. Hitherto there has always been something not so much in the landscape as in every single visual impression (say a cloud, a robbin, or a ditch) in Ireland, which I lacked in England: something for which homeliness is an inadequate word. This something I find I am now getting in England – the feeling of connectedness, of being part of it. I suppose I have been growing into the soil here much more since the move.

You would be surprised how few walks I have taken. My afternoon hours of exercise have been almost wholly occupied with sawing and axing for firewood, or cleaning the lines of future paths with shears, with feeding birds, and messing about in an old punt on a small lake or large pond which is a stone's throw from our house. You have no idea what horrid work sawing is for the first week, and how delightful after that when your muscles have got used to it and your hands are hardened. Almost every afternoon as I stand at my sawing block looking as I work at the sun going down beyond a line of bare pollards. Nearly always a red cannon ball sun, for we have had gloriously winter weather. I also love the sound of the saw and the flying of the sawdust. Then after sawing the log into lengths comes the splitting of each of these with an axe.

It is absurd how remote all simple human activities have been from me all my life: so much so that when I heave up my axe I still always see myself as an illustration in Robinson Crusoe. There is something in country work of this sort which you can't get out of walks. Silently clipping (silent except for the noise of the clipping itself) among thick brambles in the depth of winter afternoon – when the day takes on its *Grendel* hue – I am continually watched by bright-eyed robbins which come surprisingly close. More than once I have seen a pair of squirrels among the fir trees, and rabbits in our own garden: and up at the top (for our bit runs up the side of a hill) there is a burrow too big for rabbits which Foord-Kelsie (the old booky carpenting parson – you remember) avers to be that of a badger. Now to meet a badger on your own land, if such chance ever befell me – would be almost the crown of one kind of earthly bliss!

At night owls are very plentiful: and one thing I have noticed since the very first night I slept here, is that this house has a good night atmosphere about it: in the sense that I have never been in a place where one was *less* likely to get the creeps: a place less sinister. Good life must have been lived here before us. If it is haunted, it is haunted by good spirits.

Perhaps such things are the result of fantasy: yet the feelings are real. Even if they signify nothing more than the state of ones organs, yet are not ones organs real, and is not their state also a fact of spiritual significance? For if anything is spiritual, everything is.

I have of course read very little apart from work. One more Macdonald 'Annals of a Quiet Neighbourhood',[110] which went far to restore my faith in him: badly shaken by an unsuccessful attempt to read the *Seaboard Parish*. Yesterday I picked up for 4/6 *Alec Forbes*[111] in three half leather volumes. Do you know it? One reason I enjoyed the Quiet Neighbourhood so much was that I read it immediately after Trollope's *Belton Estate*:[112] quite a good book, but all the time one was making excuses for the author on the moral side: saying that this bit of uncharitableness and that bit of unconscious cynicism, and, throughout, the bottomless *worldliness* (not knowing itself for such) belonged to the period. Then you turned to Macdonald, also a Victorian, and after a few pages were ashamed to have spent even an hour in a world so inferior as that of Trollope's.

Have you had glorious fogs – frost-fogs? We have had some of the finest I have ever seen. In fact we have had all sorts of beauty – outside. Inside myself the situation has been quite the reverse. I seem to go steadily downhill and backwards. I am certainly further from self control and charity and light than I was last spring. Now that W. is with us I don't get enough solitude: or so I say to myself in excuse, knowing all the time that what God demands is our solution of the problem set, not of some other problem which we think he ought to have set: and that what we call *hindrances* are really the raw material of spiritual life. As if the fire should call the coal a hindrance! (One can imagine a little young fire, which had been getting on nicely with the sticks and paper, regarding it as a mere cruelty when the big lumps were put on: never dreaming what a huge steady glow, how far surpassing its present crackling infancy, the Tender of the Fire designed when he stoked it).

I think the trouble with me is *lack of faith*. I have no *rational* ground for going back on the arguments that convinced me of God's existence: but the irrational deadweight of my old sceptical habits, and the spirit of this age, and the cares of the day, steal away all my lively feeling of the

110 George MacDonald, *Annals of a Quiet Neighbourhood* (1867).

111 George MacDonald, *Alec Forbes of Howglen* (1865).

112 Anthony Trollope, *The Belton Estate* (1865–6).

truth, and often when I pray I wonder if I am not posting letters to a non-existent address. Mind you I don't *think* so – the whole of my reasonable mind is convinced: but I often *feel* so. However, there is nothing to do but to peg away. One falls so often that it hardly seems worth while picking oneself up and going through the farce of starting over again as if you could ever hope to walk. Still, this seeming absurdity is the only sensible thing I do, so I must continue it. And all the time, on the other side, the imaginative side, (the fairy angel) I get such glimpses and vanishing memories as often take my breath away: as if they said 'Look what you're losing' – as if they were there just to deprive one of all excuse.

How well I *talk* about it: how little else I do. I wonder would it be better not to speak to one another of these things at all? Is the talking a substitute for the doing?

Yrs
Jack

1931

TO ARTHUR GREEVES (W):

The Kilns,
Headington Quarry,
Oxford
Jan 10th 1931

My dear Arthur,

I am writing this in the principle sitting room of the new house, which we call the common room, at my Mother's desk which you remember in the drawing room at Little Lea. I wonder when last it was written at? The others are all out: I have come in from my walk – a beautiful pearl grey winter sky – and it is now half past three.

I was delighted to get your letter. Next term, which begins next week, promises to be not quite so hectic as last, so I will do my very level best to get back to our weekly interchange: but you know what my difficulties are in term time and you will not be surprised if I have to give up.

As regards my giving all the reasons but the right one for sending a book – I suppose the right one is friendship. But that can only be a reason for gifts in general: what I was explaining was my reasons for sending *this particular* book at *this particular* time. As regards the latter, I gave special reasons because I did not want it to be a Christmas present since you and I don't give them. Your complaint therefore, my dear Sir, is as if a man said 'We'd better lunch here, because it will be too late when we get to London, and they give you an excellent meal here for 2/6' and you had replied 'Ah but those are not the right reasons for eating lunch. The right reason is that the vital processes are attended by a wastage of the tissues and certain organic substances if introduced into the stomach have the power of repairing this wastage.' In other words, for any action there is usually *a*. A general reason for doing it *at all*. *b*. A particular reason for selecting to do it at such and such a time and place and in such and such a way. We usually take *a*. for granted, and explain *b*. You are the sort of man who would try to persuade a girl to marry you by reading her all the general reasons for marriage out of the prayer book ('procreation of children & prevention of sin' etc) Again, the actual presence of a W.-C. cd. never to you be a reason for emptying your bladder: for you deal only in generalities: and as the general reason for this operation (i.e. the fact that the bladder is finite in size) always holds good, you on your principles, I suppose, think it a matter of indifference where and when it is performed. But come – my pen runs away with me (I am afraid I can never resist a ludicrous piece of logic) and I shall have wasted my whole letter on foolery.

The most important thing since I last wrote is a three days walking tour wh. Warnie and I took.[1] We trained to Chepstow, breaking our journey at Gloucester for a couple of hours to see the cathedral. Got to Chepstow that evening & went out for a stroll after dinner. It was brilliant moonlight and freezing hard. Having reached a bridge over the Wye – the cliffs of the far bank shining in front of us and the little huddled town behind – we looked back and saw on our left, rising above a grassy sweep of hill, the ruins of a big castle.[2] We came back with only a very faint hope of getting near it, when as if by magic a lane led us out of the main street into fields and up without hindrance to the great gate of the castle itself. The doors were shut, but through the chinks and under them a bright light seemed to be streaming 'What is this?' said I. 'A witches' Sabbath' said he. We looked through the key hole and saw nothing but moonlight. The whole thing was an optical delusion: we had been in the shadow of the castle as we came up and the moonlight within, thro the cracks had somehow looked exactly like artificial light. We then walked all round it. The space is empty for a long way from the walls – just grass and a few seats – and you can walk in the bottom of the former moat wh. is very deep. I never saw so huge a castle. The circuit is not much smaller than the town hall at home: tower after tower, and battlements with ivy falling over them like a cascade, and even little wild bushes growing out of crannies, and above them all the roofless gables of what must have been the great hall, not much smaller than a cathedral. Imagine all this under a cloudless moon and the grass, stiff with frost, crunching under our feet.

---

1 The walking tour began on New Year's Day, Lewis and his brother returning home on 4 January.

2 The ruins of this 11th century castle are washed by the River Wye.

Next day we walked to Monmouth, passing Tintern about eleven A.M. Have you seen it? It is an abbey practically intact except that the roof is gone, and the glass out of the windows, and the floor, instead of a pavement is a trim green lawn. Anything like the *sweetness* & peace of the long shafts of sunlight falling through the windows on this grass cannot be imagined. All churches should be roofless. A holier place I never saw.[3] We lunched at St Briavels where there is another castle inhabited by the Aunt of a pupil of mine who is 'worreyed' by 'the ghosts', but won't 'do anything' about them because she doesnt like 'to be unkind'[4] (This is the pupils account. A *very* queer fellow indeed: it was he who put me onto the *End of the World*). That night to Monmouth, after a lovely walk: not on *roads* more than half an hour all day. Next day to Ross, and then next to Hereford I can't describe it all. We had two days of pure winter sunlight, and one of mist: the latter luckily was spent almost entirely in woods whose delicious feeling of confusion it served only to increase.

This was W's first experience of a walking tour. I had been a little nervous as to whether he would really care for it, & whether his selfish habits wd. really accomodate themselves to the inevitable occasional difficulties. My fears however were quite unfounded. He has been with us all the month here and everyone says how greatly he is improved. He and I even went together to Church twice: and – will you believe it – he said to me in conversation that he was beginning to think the religious view of things was after all true. Mind you (like me, at first) he didn't *want* it to be, nor like it: but his intellect is beginning to revolt from the semi-scientific assumptions we all grew up in, and the other explanation of the world seems to him daily more probable. Of course I have not had and probably never shall have any *real* talks on the heart of the subject with him. But it is delightful to feel the whole lot of us gradually beginning to move in that direction. It has done me good to be with him: because while his idea of the good is much lower than mine, he is in so many ways better than I

3 This is the ruined abbey immortalized in William Wordsworth's *Lines Composed a Few Miles Above Tintern Abbey* (1798) in which he reflects that 'we are laid asleep / In body, and become a living soul: / While with an eye made quiet by the power / Of harmony, and the deep power of joy, / We see into the life of things' (ll. 45–9).

4 St Briavels Castle, which was built during the reign of Henry I (1100–35), was inhabited at this time by the Hon. Mrs Ronald Campbell. Her nephew, Lewis's pupil, was John Colquhoun Campbell (1907–) who received his BA from Magdalen in 1930. He worked with the Anglo-Iranian Oil Co. Ltd 1930–52, after which he was in HM Diplomatic Service 1952–67.

am. I keep on crawling up to the heights & slipping back to the depths: he seems to do neither. There always have been these two types.

About Dennis:[5] I doubt whether the kind of effects he aims at could be attained by a simpler style, tho' an effect you and I prefer probably could be. Still, one mustn't be dogmatic about simplicity. It may be our favourite style – but the pomps and sonorities are good in their different way none the less.

I have read Alec Forbes – good things in it, but not by any means a good book. The more I read his novels the more I rage at the tragedy of his being forced to write for money and thus diverted from his true sphere, so that we get only as much of the real Macdonald as he can smuggle in *by the way*. It is, I really think, a loss as irreparable as the early death of Keats.

Glad to hear you are at *Tristram Shandy*. What good company! Isn't Uncle Toby, seriously and morally, one of the loveliest characters ever created.

Must stop now. When are you coming to see me? I have no chance of visiting you till the summer at earliest.

Yours
Jack

At present reading the Autobiography of Keat's friend the painter Haydon[6] – quite good. W. has finished Lockhart's *Scott*[7] & pronounces it excellent.

TO ARTHUR GREEVES (W):

[The Kilns]
Jan 17, 1931

My dear Arthur,

I am much divided in my mind as to whether I should devote this after tea hour – the first free one of the day – to starting a new book or to writing you a letter. The fact that you are in my debt is strong for the first alternative: on the other hand when I hear from you during the week (as I

---

5 i.e. Geoffrey Dennis.

6 *The Life of Benjamin Robert Haydon from his Autobiography and Journals*, ed. Tom Taylor (1853).

7 John Gibson Lockhart's *Memoirs of the Life of Sir Walter Scott*. See note 174 to letter of 25 October 1916.

hope I shall) I shall probably be too busy to reply. Then again I have been in a bad temper to day over trifles: and it is too much to face bedtime with the added knowledge of having neglected you as well – so here goes. Perhaps this sounds unflattering, and you may retort that you wd. rather not have a letter on these terms. However, I am sure you understand how a momentary disinclination to begin is quite compatible with a real interest in going on.

I have read a new Macdonald since I last wrote, which I think the very best of the novels. I would put it immediately below Phantastes, Lilith, the Fairy Tales, & the Diary of an Old Soul. It is called *What's Mine's Mine.*[8] It has very little of the bad plot interest, and quite frankly subordinates story to doctrine. But such doctrine. Some of the conversations in this book I hope to re-read many times. The scene and the characters are Highland Celtic, as opposed to the Lowland Scots of most of the novels: highly idealised. Yet somehow they convince me. Or if they don't quite convince me as real people, they differ from most ideal characters in this, that I wish they *were* real. A young chief of a decaying clan is the hero: and the chief contrast is between the clansmen and a vulgar rich Glasgow family who have come to live in the neighbourhood. These are, like most of Macdonald's worshippers of Mammon, over-drawn. I venture to think that there was some *moral*, as well as some literary, weakness in this. I mean in characters like the baronet in *Sir Gibbie* etc. I observe that M. is constantly praying against anger

Keep me from wrath, let it seem never so right.

I wonder did he indulge (day-dreamily) an otherwise repressed fund of indignation by putting up in his novels bogeys to whom his heroes could make the stunning retorts and deliver the stunning blows which he himself neither could nor would deliver in real life. I am certain that this is morally as well as artistically dangerous and I'll tell you why. The *pleasure* of anger – the gnawing attraction which makes one return again and again to its theme – lies, I believe, in the fact that one feels entirely righteous oneself only when one is angry. *Then* the other person is pure black, and you are pure white. But in real life sanity always returns to break the dream. In fiction you can put absolutely *all* the right, with no

8 See note 104 to letter of 29 October 1930.

snags or reservations, on the side of the hero (with whom you identify yourself) and all the wrong on the side of the villain. You thus revel in unearned self-righteousness, which wd. be vicious even if it were earned.

Haven't you noticed how people with a fixed hatred, say, of Germans or Bolshevists, *resent* anything wh. is pleaded in extenuation, however small, of their supposed crimes. The enemy must be unredeemed black. While all the time one *does* nothing and enjoys the feeling of perfect superiority over the faults one is never tempted to commit:

> '*Compound for sins we are inclined to*
> *By damning those we have no mind to.*'[9]

I suppose that when one hears a tale of hideous cruelty anger is quite the wrong reaction, and merely wastes the energy that ought to go in a different direction: perhaps merely dulls the conscience wh., if it were awake, would ask us 'Well? What are you *doing* about it? How much of your life have you spent in really combatting this? In helping to produce social conditions in which these sort of things will not occur!?

Term began yesterday. Yesterday afternoon & evening and this morning I spent in correcting papers: not only a hard but a depressing job, for ones pupils always seem to do worse than you expect. That, by the way, is the angle from which to understand (instead of being self-righteous about) the cruelty of schoolmasters. One can't gauge the temptation to cruelty for a man who is trying to keep his wife and family on the profits of a decaying private school, and who sees the boys getting fewer & fewer scholarships each year and can never, even if honest, be quite sure that it is not the boys fault. 'God help everyone' as you say.

The night before last (my last night of Vac) we had the most glorious storm: trees plunging like terrified but tethered horses, leaves eddying, chimneys howling, and under all the lesser and lighter noises a great solid roar above the house. I lay in bed and revelled in it – tho' it is partly spoiled for me by the fact that Minto hates it and hears in it only a sound of death and desolation. Odd, what different notes we different souls draw from the organ of nature. Some people hate the cry of an owl at night: I love it.

9 Samuel Butler, *Hudibras* (1663–78), part I, canto I, i, 213.

Oh, by the bye, our new maid says she has been kept awake at night this week by the squirrels! Asked what kind of noise they make she replied 'I don't know' – wh. I think is her way of saying 'I can't describe it.' But what a lovely idea. And what a lovely sentence for the Witch of Endor – 'Please, Mr Lewis, the squirrels – '

You say Reid is reading his new book[10] to 'some of us'. Who are the others? Give him my kind regards.

I find this cold weather desperately trying to the bladder.

Yrs

Jack

TO ARTHUR GREEVES (W):

[The Kilns]
Feb 1st 1931

My dear Arthur,

This will probably be a short, and certainly a dull letter, for I am tired. Minto has been in bed all week with flu' which means a good deal of bustle and extra work: I am recovering from a baddish cold myself and have had a pretty tough week. I was glad to get your letter.

I haven't read Jeans' book[11] and it is unlikely I will – there are so many things I want to read more. One of the blessings of your life is that you ought to be able to read fairly well nearly everything that interests you. As a matter of fact – apart from time – I am not now greatly attracted to that kind of book: though you will remember that astronomy, fed on H. G. Wells' romances, was almost my earliest love. I don't know why it has not lasted, nor why it now interests me much less than I should expect. Partly I think, because one knows that all the really interesting things about other planets and systems can't be found out: partly, too, I suspect that philosophy and religion (in a person of my limited range) rather take the shine out of curiosity about the material universe. It seems like having new bits of a curtain described to one, when one is all agog for hints of what lies behind the curtain. Now that I come to think of it, it is not quite true to say that I don't feel any interest in these things now: rather they rouse a very intense, impatient interest for a very short time, which quite suddenly leaves one at once sated & dissatisfied. Mind I am not *recomending* this state of mind – only recording it.

10 Probably Forrest Reid's *Uncle Stephen* which was published in October 1931.

11 Sir James Jeans, *The Mysterious Universe* (1930).

I liked very much your account of the party who meet to hear Reid's novel. It reminded me of Tristram Shandy – just such an ideally inappropriate conjunction of minds as he delights to bring together. Don't you think the great beauty of that book is its picture of affection existing across unbridgeable gulfs of intellect? My Father & Uncle Toby never understand one another at all, and always love one another. It is the true picture of home life: far better than the modern nonsense in wh. affection (friendship is a different thing) is made to depend on mental affinities.

I am almost shocked to find from more than one passage that Geo. Macdonald hated Sterne. The coarseness apparently revolted him: but I cannot understand how he was not attracted by the overflowing goodness at the heart of the book. One must remember that the wayward Highland temperament, with its reserve and delicacy, may find coarseness a greater trial than our rougher Saxon grain.

I had a lovely ten minutes the afternoon before last in a wood of fir trees in the snow. The wood comes down to within a few yards of the top of a small cliff, from which direction the snow was coming. Just as the flakes got near this edge, some current of air caught them and whirled them upwards so that in the wood they were flying skywards as if the earth was snowing. I am often in this bit of wood, and have seen a great many fine winter sunsets – very pale, you know – through (first) the tall straight firs and then some twisted beechtrees which form the border of the wood. I have also had some fine hours of storm in it when all the trees were groaning and swaying.

I hope you won't be disappointed by What's Mine's Mine. Of course it has not the fantastic charm of Phantastes: nor the plot excitement of Wilfrid Cumbermede. It is just the spiritual quality with some beautiful landscape – nothing more.

I wonder how your tea with the McNeils went off. Give them my love when next you meet.

The O.U.D.S.[12] are doing *Hassan*[13] this term and I think I shall go to it.

---

12 Oxford University Dramatic Society.

13 James Elroy Flecker, *Hassan: The Story of Hassan of Bagdad and How he Came to Make the Golden Journey to Samarkand: A Play in Five Acts* (1922). James Elroy Flecker (1884–1915) was educated at Trinity College, Oxford. He spent some time in the East with the Consular service and wrote several volumes of lyric verse. He is best remembered for this poetic Eastern drama which he wrote in 1914. Following his death it was adapted for the stage by Basil Dean, with music by Frederick Delius, and first performed in 1923.

I can't remember whether we have talked of this play or not, but I imagine you know it. However badly the O.U.D.S. do it, at least they will not turn it into a Chu Chin Chow[14] as (I am told) the London actors did. Which reminds me of Kismet[15] (one of my early thrills) which reminds me of lying on the beech at Donaghadee reading to each other out of the Arabian Nights.

Do or die for it – I *must* manage to get over to Ireland in the summer and revisit some of the old haunts with you. Once more to spend one of our delightful banjo evenings with Jimmy Thompson – to have another of our old rousing evenings at the Hippodrome – once more to dance the Black Bottom at midnight with Sir Robert Ewart & the Witch of Endor – whether-her-mother-will-let-her-or-no – I'm too tired for anything but foolery. Bryson is to marry the Princess Elizabeth: poor chap, it is a pity he was castrated by the Vice Chancellor and Proctors last week for riding a bicycle in St Mary's. I suppose you have heard about Warnie's peerage – for gallantry during the recent manoeuvres. I have grown a beard – Good night

Yrs
Jack

P.S. In that fir wood I suddenly got a terrific return the other day of my earliest Wagner mood – the purely Nibelung, Mime, mood before the Valkyries rose on my horizon. You know – very earthy, and smith-y, and Teutonic. How *inexhaustible* these things are. You think you have done with a thing and – whoop! – it's all back again, strong as ever.

TO ARTHUR GREEVES (W):

[The Kilns]
Feb 23rd 1931

My dear Arthur,

I was glad to hear from you again, despite the fact that your letter, specially towards the end, appears to have been written in a state of intoxication.

14 *Chu Chin Chow: A Musical Tale of the East* (1931) was an enormously popular musical play by Oscar Ashe, with music by Frederick Norton. It was first performed in 1916, and created a record with its 2,238 performances. See *Oscar Asche, by Himself* (1924).

15 Edward Knoblock's *Kismet: An 'Arabian Night' in Three Acts* (1912) was an 'oriental spectacular' first performed in 1911 and which was very popular.

I was almost relieved to hear that you shared my views of *What's Mine's Mine*. Yes, you are right in saying that it is good not despite, but because of, its preaching – or rather (preaching is a bad word) its spiritual knowledge. So many cleverer writers strike one as quite *childish* after Macdonald: they seem not even to have begun to understand so many things.

On Saturday I went to the matinee of Flecker's *Hassan* done by the O.U.D.S. I can't remember whether you saw it in London, but I suppose you read it. It was not very well done, but well enough for me: indeed to see it really well acted would be too much for me. In reading it the cruelty is just about balanced by the extreme beauty of the lyrics and much of the dialogue, so that the total effect, tho' sinister, like a too-bright dream which is sure to turn into nightmare before the end, yet is bearable. On the stage, where one has less time to dwell on the cadence or suggestion of the individual words, the cruelty is unendurable. Warnie went out half way through. I felt quite sick but thought it almost a duty <for one afflicted in my way to remain, saying to myself 'Oh you like cruelty do you? Well now stew in it!'> – the same principle on which one trains a puppy to be clean – 'rub their noses in it'. It has haunted me ever since.

On its merits as a work of art I am very undecided. The intense effect which it produces is not, in itself, proof of greatness, for it is easy to produce an effect by the suggestion of physical pain: and such an effect, reaching the spectator through his nerves rather than his imagination, is perhaps as much outside art in one direction, as pornography is in another. On the other hand, the whole of the ending seems to me almost great. You remember how Ishak finds Hassan fainting after being compelled to witness the torture of the lovers, and how, when Hassan begins to stammer out some of the horrible details, Ishak says 'You are still full of devils. Wake up! STOP DREAMING!!'[16] – and that, flashing ones mind back to what Pervaneh says in the Diwan scene about this world's being an illusion,[17] and leading straight on to the caravan for Samarkand – the broad moonlit desert stretching away and swallowing up the nightmare city in its clean solitude – all that does give one the true tragic

16 Flecker, *Hassan,* V, i: 'Be silent. You are full of devils. I tell you, it is not true. Stop dreaming: look into my eyes: listen!'

17 ibid., III, iii: 'We have heard the Trumpets of Reality that drown the vain din of the Thing that Seems.'

feeling of having been brought, thro horrors, right out of the ordinary illusion of life into some higher world. Another thing that is good is the scene in which all the adventures begin – where they are taken up in the basket into the house with no doors whence they heard the sounds of dancing. This is the only place which strikes the note of the real Arabian nights – the midnight possibilities of an Eastern city full of magicians. It is a pity he didn't work it out on those lines. As it stands it is too morbid: and one sees Flecker in places not feeling it as tragic at all but licking his lips (you remember his horrible face – it is the frontispiece of the *Poems*)[18] and gloating. Still, his powers were extraordinary and one is sorry that he didn't live to grow out of consumption and Parnassianism and decadence: he would have been a great writer in the end I believe.

As a contrast to my nightmare afternoon at the theatre I spent most of Sunday with W. and Dorothea Vaughan[19] (did you meet her?) digging holes for planting trees for what W. calls 'the Kilns Afforestation Scheme'. A lovely afternoon of early spring sunlight – the distance very pale blue, primroses out, and birds trilling and chuckling in abundance. All the better for the contrast with Hassan.

Did I tell you I was reading Ruskin's *Praeterita*[20] i.e. his autobiography? Contains an account of his boyhood which wd. particularly interest you, R's mother having had a great deal in common with your father. The good thing about it is that while not disguising the narrowness & pride at all, the final impression he leaves with you is one of peace & homeliness: the dateless, timeless peace of childhood in a really regular household. Later on there is some of the best description of travel wh. I have ever read.

I have had a baddish cold but am otherwise well. Any sign of the new people moving into Little Lea? How strange it will be to you. Try to reply in less time than last!

Yours
Jack
I was just going to put
C. S. Lewis again

18 James Elroy Flecker, *Forty-Two Poems* (1911).
19 Dorothea Vaughan, who had been a day pupil at Headington School with Maureen, was a frequent visitor at Hillsboro and The Kilns.
20 John Ruskin, *Praeterita*, 28 parts (1885–9).

TO ARTHUR GREEVES (W):

The Kilns,
Kiln Road,
Headington Quarry,
Headington, Oxford
Sunday, March 29th 1931

My dear Arthur,

I am afraid I am badly behind hand with this letter. I am afraid I cannot honestly plead that I have been too busy to write. The trouble is rather that when once the end of term has set me free from my compulsory work, I am so hungry for my real, private work,[21] that I grudge every moment from my books. This is a bad, selfish reason for not writing and I only give it because it happens to be true.

By the bye – I spoke some time ago about coming to visit you for a week in the summer, and you suggested fixing a date. If you still want to have me, how would the second or third week in August do? I should like it because I shall have finished my examining then wh. usually leaves me rather knocked up, and a holiday with you would be just the right tonic. Let me know how it would suit you. If this won't do, I should then – as a second choice – take my week with you as a *preparation* for examining instead of a cure, and come about the second week of July. But of course it is nicer to take the medicine first and the sweet after, than vice-versa. I try not to spoil this visit by thinking too much about it, but every now and then it comes over me with a delicious whiff of anticipation.

The most interesting thing that has happened to me since I last wrote is reading *War and Peace*[22] – at least I am now in the middle of the 4th and last volume so I think, bar accidents, I am pretty sure to finish it. It has completely changed my view of novels.

Hitherto I had always looked on them as rather a *dangerous* form – I mean dangerous to the health of literature as a whole. I thought that the strong 'narrative lust' – the passionate itch to 'see what happened in the end' – which novels aroused, necessarily injured the taste for other, better, but less irresistible, forms of literary pleasure: and that the growth of novel reading largely explained the deplorable division of readers into

21 i.e. the writing of *The Allegory of Love*.
22 Leo Tolstoy, *War and Peace* (1865–72).

low-brow and high-brow – the low being simply those who had learned to expect from books this 'narrative lust', from the time they began to read, and who had thus destroyed in advance their possible taste for better things. I also thought that the intense desire which novels rouse in us for the 'happiness' of the chief characters (no one feels that way about Hamlet or Othello) and the selfishness with which this happiness is concerned, were thoroughly bad (I mean, if the hero and heroine marry, that is felt to be a happy ending, tho every one else in the story is left miserable: if they don't that is an unhappy ending, tho it may mean a much greater good in some other way). Of course I knew there were tragic novels like Hardy's – but somehow they were quite on a different plane from real tragedies.

Tolstoy, in this book, has changed all that. I have felt everywhere – in a sense – you will know what I mean – that sublime *indifference* to the life or death, success or failure, of the chief characters, which is not a *blank* indifference at all, but almost like submission to the will of God. Then the variety of it. The war parts are just the best descriptions of war ever written: all the modern war books are milk and water to this: then the rural parts – lovely pictures of village life and of religious festivals in wh. the relations between the peasants and the nobles almost make you forgive feudalism: the society parts, in which I was astonished to find so much humour – there is a great hostess who always separates two guests when she sees them getting really interested in conversation, who is almost a Jane Austen character. There are love-passages that have the same sort of intoxicating quality you get in Meredith: and passages about soldiers chatting over fires which remind one of Patsy Macan: and a drive in a sledge by moonlight which is better than Hans Andersen. And behind all these, and uniting them, is the profound, religious conception of life and history wh. is beyond J. Stephens and Andersen, and beside which Meredith's worldly wisdom – well just *stinks*, there's no other word.

I go on writing all this because my pen runs away with me: meanwhile perhaps you have read the book long ago and even advised *me* to read it! If you have not, I strongly advise you to try it. Its length, which deters some people, will not frighten you: you will only rejoice, when the right time comes, – say after tea some day next autumn when fires are still a novelty – at that old, delicious feeling of *embarkation* on a long voyage, which one seldom gets now. For it takes a book nearly as long as *War and Peace* to *seem* as long now as a Scott did in boyhood.

And talking of boyhood – I recently re-read (being out-of-sorts) both *She* and the sequel *Ayesha*,[23] and found the story good in both: what troubles one is the v. silly talk put into She's mouth, which is meant to be profound. You feel that she has made very ill use of her opportunities. In re-reading them I re-visited one of the very few parts of my past which is not associated with you – tho' if I remember rightly we once discussed together the pictures in my editn. of Ayesha.

About Flecker's face – I don't think it is just sensuality that's the trouble. There is a sort of slyness and knowingness, tipping-the-wink-ness with it. Some sensuality one pities: other kinds one admires – full, Pagan magnificence. But there is a kind at once furtive and self-satisfied, at once secret and defiant that seems peculiar to very highly educated people in very big cities, which makes me shudder. You know – the atmosphere of the whispered confidence and the leer – one eye always watching to see how you take it and the whole face ready, at a moment's notice, *either* to take you into full conspiratorial confidence (if the man sees you like it) *or else* to turn up his nose and sneer at you (if you don't). In Barfield's long poem it is well described: the man who tells stories

> *Purring with female, strutting in the puddle*
> *Of his great naughtiness.*[24]

We had a fine burst of spring last week and I have sat and worked in the garden: one morning I saw a rabbit come out and wash its face not fifteen yards away from me. To-day I was only just warm enough while sawing wood in the shed in a gale that sent the sawdust whirling round me and covered Mr Papworth like snow.

You wd. have been so amused if you'd been here last week end. Mrs Armitage is a sort of blend of Kelsie and Tchanie and often comes to call. I had had a pupil to tea and took him out for a walk after. Coming back at 7 I found Mrs A. *still there*, seated on the same sofa with Warnie, and

---

23 Sir Henry Rider Haggard, *She* (1887); *Ayesha, or the Return of She* (1905).

24 Owen Barfield, 'The Tower', stanza II, ll. 36–7. This 'long poem' of Owen Barfield's, written between 1922 and 1928, has never been published. Writing about it in his diary of 21 June 1922, Lewis said: 'The "Tower" is full of magnificent material and never a dead phrase...The story is (to me) as hard to follow as *Sordello*. But what genius! The metre *too* eccentric for me, but on that subject Barfield has probably forgotten more than I ever knew' (*AMR*, p. 53). *Sordello* (1840) is by Robert Browning.

conducting a feverish conversation with him about married life, women, and kindred subjects, and under the impression (she is a widow) that she was making great headway. I wish she cd. have seen W., a few minutes later when she had left (for of course my return broke up the party), coming out of the front door into the twilit garden, drawing his hand across his brow, and remarking with great solemnity 'I'm going down to "the Checkers" to have a LARGE whisky and soda.'

Perhaps this doesn't sound funny as I tell it: at the time it reminded me so of the lady and the man (both of whose names I've forgotten) in your '*Trees*'. Let me hear soon. How delightful our old hills will be in a week or two now.

Yrs
Jack

TO ARTHUR GREEVES (W):

The Kilns,
Kiln Rd.,
Headington Quarry,
Oxford. [26? April 1931]

My dear Arthur,

No time for a proper letter. Minto is laid up with pleurisy. She is past the worst and I hope all is now on the right path: but tho' our anxiety is less, of course we are still very busy and tired. I had hoped to be giving you an account of my usual spring walking tour, but of course that's off.

I don't think I shall be able to come for more than a week in the summer – and in a way, wouldn't it be rather a waste to spend any time of our precious holiday except in the old haunts? You can hardly imagine how I pine for our wood, and our new wood, and the shepherds hut, and Divis. I can hardly look forward to it without dancing.

I don't think Barton[25] is insincere – at any rate as far as you are concerned. Maureen met him last summer while staying with her uncle[26] in Cavan and said 'He seemed to think a great deal of Arthur.' The worst of

25 Arthur William Barton, rector of St Mark's, Dundela, 1914–25. See note 47 to letter of 13 May 1915.

26 Mrs Moore's brother, the Very Rev. William James Askins (1879–1955), was Dean of Kilmore Cathedral.

a Parson's life is that the duty of being pleasant to people is bound to give a certain taint of insincerity to the *manner*.

I see this is too late for your address.[27] If they don't forward it, let me know at once.

Yrs
Jack

P.S. I *do* hope you will come and see us on your way back. I'm dying to show you some of my new haunts.

TO ARTHUR GREEVES (W):

The Kilns,
Kiln Rd.,
Headington Quarry,
Oxford.
May 18th (Monday) [1931]

My dear A,

Come on the day you suggest rather than not coming at all – a thousand times rather, but this week is a bad one. I am staying out here recovering from flu: therefore I can't have you in College. We are threatened with two week end visitors: therefore I can't have you here. So there is hardly any week when I should miss so much of your society – specially those odd evening hours which are good for talking. What I should like would be for you to come on *Monday* next – if you can amuse yourself in London till then. In that case we could be in college together.

I shall not book the room without hearing from you again.

I am longing to see you. Reply at once.

Yours
Jack

P.S. Yes I have read Wm. Law[28] – a v. severe but wholesome draught! It may save *trouble* if you bring a dinner jacket, but not absolutely essential. (But a razor and clean handkerchief you *must* bring)

---

27 Arthur had just left for a holiday in London.

28 He is referring to William Law's *A Serious Call to a Devout and Holy Life* (1728).

TO ARTHUR GREEVES (W):

The Kilns,
Kiln Rd.,
Headington Quarry,
Oxford.
Wednesday. [20 May 1931]

My dear Arthur,

I have just got your letter and am rather disappointed. Do you mean that you may possibly not come *at all*? I should be very sorry if that were so. At the same time I am acutely conscious that I have not much to offer in my busy life and chaotic days to such a lover of tranquility as you: and I certainly don't wish to press a visit on you as a duty. All the same – (I don't think this is making a duty of it) I would remind you that there is a good case for coming to see me even at the cost of some discomfort; because it is important to the continuance of a friendship that each should have some experience of the other's life. I have always specially prized those few pleasant walks we had last time you were here, on that ground. Our sitting in the little thicket by that stream is an important addition to our stock of memories shared. And now that I am in quite new surroundings I shall never feel at ease till you have shared them with me. How can I write to you about places you have never seen?

As to your doubt whether you can stay in London till Monday – I quite realise that it is a bore to you just to mark time there for my convenience, when your mind is beginning to turn pleasantly towards books and home. You will admit that I (on whom your letter fell without warning very late in the day) could hardly have made plans to avoid this. And then, is there not perhaps a special reasonableness in asking *you* to do this? I mean being one of the very, very few who can live without a profession and having therefore so few demands on your time, ought you not to yield the more readily to such rare demands as do turn up?

As to staying in College, I take it the real objection is the early rising. I can offer you breakfast at 8.45; not later, for I have a pupil at 9 most mornings. But you will remember that last time, after trying it, you became a complete convert and swore always to be an early bird in future – so little terrible did it prove in actual practice. Of course you must please yourself: but I feel v. strongly that to spend our evenings hanging about in public rooms or in a bedroom at a hotel will be as it always has been, a miserable makeshift. Surely last time was much the most successful time we've had? Surely our snug evenings together (you can go to bed as early as you like) are worth having. The other arrangement is not only inconvenient, but (I find) rather depressing. Conversation does not flow in those conditions, and neither of us is himself.

Well, I have trotted out all my arguments. I wish I could believe they wd. all seem as strong to you as to me: but, as I say, I haven't much to offer. I can only moralise and plead the claims of friendship: but perhaps these will weigh as heavily with you as the more solid claims of comfort and convenience wd. weigh with a more selfish man. I await your reply eagerly

Yrs
Jack

TO ARTHUR GREEVES (W):

[Swiss Cottage,
16 Buckland Crescent,
London]
26th(?) June 1931

My dear Arthur,

My conscience accuses me of laziness. I have done *nothing* since term ended but sit in deck chairs in the shade, bathe twice a day in the pond, and talk. A little pottering about with Donne and Beowulf which I have done hardly deserves the name of work. The truth is that I am not only lazy but tired. I still can't walk a mile without aching legs. Whether I can write a page without aching hand is an experiment now to be tried. I am writing this in London where I am spending a day or two with Barfield – splendid talks and reading of Dante, but of course our nights tend to be late so that perhaps it is not a very judicious kind of holiday. However, it is short.

During this spell of hot weather the Kilns has been delightful. I know the pond looks dirty, but as a matter of fact one comes out perfectly clean. I wish you could join me as I board the punt in the before-breakfast solitude and push out from under the dark shadow of the trees onto the full glare of the open water, usually sending the moor hens and their chicks scudding away into the reeds, half flying and half swimming, with a delicious flurry of silver drops. Then I tie up to the projecting stump in the middle and dive off the stern of the punt. There is one thing in which fresh water bathing surpasses the sea – the beauty of broken ground and trees and flowers seen from an unfamiliar angle as you swim.

Thanks for your account of the fox. I don't see why a fox shouldn't be as happy as a dog in captivity if he is properly treated – but I certainly shudder for one whose owners contemplate such drastic dental treatment!

No – I didn't feel the earthquake and am rather sorry to have missed what must have been (and what we hope will *remain*) so rare a sensation.

You cannot have enjoyed your time in Oxford more than I did – it seemed to me quite one of the best times we have ever had together. Our stroll on the roof, our window seat at the bonfire, our good long talks on one or two evenings, are still in my mind – though of course memory has not yet done its real work in transfiguring them.

It is a long time since I read Peacock:[29] I remember him as having something of the whimsical charm of Lewis Carroll's minor works, and have always meant to go back to him.

Warton's *History of Poetry*[30] marks the beginning of our modern interest in mediaeval literature. Being pioneer work, it is quite unreliable and some of the theories he develops are grotesque: but what it lacks in accuracy it amply makes up in enthusiasm. He is discovering all the charm of the old writers for the first time, and infects you with his feeling, and sends you back to the feelings you had yourself as a boy. In fact, though not a great authority, it is a great book: and its very plentiful quotations will supply you with thousands of lines of old poetry which you will probably never meet elsewhere. If it is a nice edition it would make a really sound purchase for your library: and, besides being a great, it is an eminently 'dippable' book.

I am reading Inge's 'Personal Religion and the Life of Devotion'[31] (Longmans) – one of the best books of the kind I have yet struck.

I am at Hampstead which gives me quite a new idea of the suburbs of London. There is a little quiet court of Georgian houses here which might come out of any beautiful English country town – besides immense views from the Heath. Distant '*town*scapes' have a peculiar *dreamy* beauty of their own which makes one feel it ungrateful to blame them for not being landscapes.

---

29 Thomas Love Peacock (1785–1866). See note 112 to letter of 11 November 1915.

30 Thomas Warton, *The History of English Poetry from the Eleventh to the Eighteenth Century*, 3 vols. (1774–81).

31 William Ralph Inge, *Personal Religion and the Life of Devotion* (1924).

Forgive me for a short letter – even this much has been done with some effort. I hope I shall wake up properly in a week or so.

Yours
Jack

TO ARTHUR GREEVES (W):

The Kilns,
Headington Quarry,
Oxford.
26th [July 1931]

My dear Arthur,

I am in the midst of the annual examining. I propose to cross to Ireland on Saturday night August the 8th and stay with you till Saturday morning August 15th when I will join W. for breakfast on the Liverpool boat. If I can possibly get away from Cambridge on the Friday I will do so, but it is not likely. If any of these arrangements don't suit please let me have a line *at once*. I am looking forward to it almost *unbearably*!

Yours
Jack

P.S. In the event of a hitch about W's times can I come the following week instead? i.e. *from* the 15th.

TO ARTHUR GREEVES (W):

[The Kilns
30? July 1931]

My dear Arthur,

Why do you do (or rather leave undone) these things? Owing to a variety of circumstances I now choose the *second* of the two periods you offer in your wire – i.e. from the 18th. That will be Tuesday and I shall come to you in the evening at about 9. The advantage of the second period is that I can give you a full week (Perhaps this may not seem advantageous to you?)

I shall turn up (D.V) on that evening unless I hear to the contrary – unless you'd like to come in and fetch me from the Liverpool boat where I shall be seeing W. off.

Yours
Jack

TO ARTHUR GREEVES (W):

Queen's College,
Cambridge.
Aug 6th [1931]

My dear Arthur,

I have your letter of the second August. I don't quite understand, as in my wire I said the 2nd period – 19th–26th was preferred (or didn't I?) At any rate I now intend to come to Bernagh on the evening of the 20th (Thursday) and stay till the 27 (following Thursday). If you cared to come in and meet me at the Liverpool boat (where I shall be seeing W. off) at about 8 and bring me out, that would be admirable. Have you and I ever brought off a scheme without these intense complications. However I have some excuse. I now *shall* arrive on the 20th *whatever* you say, so there's no good trying to prevent me!

I am here examining but having quite a good time – a lot of nice people, and I think this College the most beautiful in either University

Yours
C.S.L.

TO ARTHUR GREEVES (W):

Golf Hotel,
Castlerock,
Co. Derry.[32]
Aug. 19th [1931]

My dear Arthur,

Thanks for letter. W. says he would love to come and dine on Thursday night. We want, for sentimental reasons, to make the railway journey from town to Sydenham, so if you wd. meet us at Sydenham that would be capital. As I don't know the exact times of the rail motors I will ring you up from the Co. Down Ry. station at about 6.45 to 7. Isn't this going to be great! I still feel a great fear of something happening to prevent it: perhaps the world will end before to-morrow night!

Yours
Jack

---

32 i.e., Co. Londonderry. Jack and Warnie had spent a few days in Belfast with their relatives before going to Castlerock on 17 August. Castlerock was particularly precious to them because their mother had taken them there for a holiday in 1901.

TO ARTHUR GREEVES (W):

[The Kilns]
Sept 5th 1931

My dear Arthur,

How long ago it seems since I left you. I had a delightful evening, though tinged with melancholy, on the Liverpool boat, watching first the gantries and then the Down coast slipping past and picking out, more by imagination than sight, our favourite woods. I did not go to bed till we were off the Copelands. I felt and still feel that I was returning from one of the very best holidays I have ever had. Please thank your Mother (who was in one sense my hostess) and tell her how I enjoyed myself. I probably enjoyed the time more than you did, for the hills cannot have quite the same feeling for you who have never left them. What sticks in my mind most of all is the walk on which we visited Mrs McNeil. We were both in exactly the right mood. In another kind I have very fine memories of Croob and our session on top of it: as also of our homely and familiar evenings.

Meanwhile, as tangible mementoes of your almost excessive hospitality I have Hooker[33] and Taylor.[34] I did not thank you nearly enough for them at the time. The Taylor has been to the binders and returned very neatly mended yesterday. I started him after church this morning. He is severe and has little of the joyous side of religion in him: and some of his incentives (e.g. where he reminds you that there will be different degrees of glory in Heaven and would have you aim at getting as high a degree as possible) seem to me unspiritual or at least highly dangerous. But his painstaking, practical attitude has the charm of an old family doctor: beautifully homely and sincere. I have dipped into Hooker again and reread some of my favourite passages.

On Thursday W. motored me over to Bulford (his station) on Salisbury plain, where he wanted to get some of his things, and we visited the village of Boscombe where Hooker was vicar and saw (from without) the parsonage in which he wrote most of his book. The church is the smallest one I have ever been in and contains some of the old square pews. It is very primitive and lit by oil lamps and candles. It has not

---

33 Richard Hooker, the theologian mentioned in note 4 to the letter of 3 February 1929.

34 Jeremy Taylor (1613–67), Anglican bishop best known for his *Rule and Exercise of Holy Living* (1650) and *Rule and Exercise of Holy Dying* (1651), which Greeves had given Lewis in one volume.

much real architectural beauty, but being honestly and unaffectedly built and now having the charm of antiquity it is very pleasant. I love these little old parish churches more and more: even the stuffiness delights me, and a sort of cosiness and friendliness in which the dead under their brasses seem to share. It all speaks of a life in which everyone knew every one else, and of real neighbourliness. What a nice word neighbour is – don't you like 'Well, neighbour So-and-So' in Bunyan.[35] I forget whether you know Salisbury plain or not? I love it – all chalky downs and little beech woods and fir woods: a most excellent air.

As for reading – in the train I bought and read Yeats-Brown's 'Bengal Lancer'.[36] Unless you remember the reviews of it (which were what made me buy it) you will wonder at my opening a book with such a title. It is the autobiography of a man who began as an ordinary Cavalry officer in the Indian army and ended up by becoming a Yogi – a mystic on the Hindu pattern. A strange story and in its latter stages told with real beauty. One can't help feeling that if he had been more educated he could have found what he wanted in traditions more hereditary to him than that of the Yogis – but judge not.

I have also been studying the Winters Tale. You remember the last scene – where Hermione is introduced as a statue and then comes to life.[37] Hitherto I had thought it rather silly: this time, seeing that the absurdity of the plot doesn't matter, and is merely the scaffolding whereby Shakespeare (probably unconsciously) is able to give us an image of the whole idea of resurrection, I was simply overwhelmed. You will say that I am here doing to Shakespeare just what I did to Macdonald over Wilfrid Cumbermede. Perhaps I am. I must confess that more and more the value of plays and novels becomes for me dependent on the moments when, by whatever artifice, they succeed in expressing the great *myths*.

This afternoon W. and I have been at work in the wood clipping the undergrowth, he with shears and I with a sickle. I hope you can see the whole scene – the light slanting through the fir trees, the long elder branches swaying and then swooping down with a rustle of leaves, the click-click of the shears, and the heavy odour of crushed vegetation.

---

35 John Bunyan, *The Pilgrim's Progress*, op. cit., part I, pp. 12–13: 'Come Neighbour Pliable, how do you do?...Well Neighbour Obstinate...Come Neighbour Christian.'

36 Francis Yeats-Brown, *Bengal Lancer* (1930).

37 Shakespeare, *The Winter's Tale*, V, iii.

What pleasures there are in the world. I seem to have more than anyone could deserve – a fortnight ago with you on our own hills, and now woodcutting on a fine autumn day in this delightful place.

Minto is well and sends her love. I met Baxter, the professor of English at Belfast,[38] last night. The only common acquaintance we discovered was – Dr Leslie!!

Yours
Jack

*Jack had given the smaller of his rooms at Magdalen to Warnie, who had now turned it into a kind of new 'little end room'. The family papers were there, and Warnie was putting them in order, and typing them out, with editorial notes, on his little Royal typewriter. 'It is one of the most engrossing tasks I have ever undertaken,' he wrote in his diary of 9 January 1931, 'and I look forward with more eagerness than ever to my days of retirement in order to finish it' (*BF*, p. 75). This massive task, undertaken over a number of years, would result in the 11 volumes of 'Lewis Papers: Memoirs of the Lewis Family 1850–1930'. About the middle of the year Warnie re-enlisted for a second tour of duty in China so he could retire earlier than originally planned. He went on embarkation leave on 26 August, and sailed for China on 9 October, not to return home until 14 December 1932.*

TO ARTHUR GREEVES (W):

[The Kilns]
Sept 22nd /31

My dear Arthur,

Thanks for your letter of the 11th. I couldn't write to you last Sunday because I had a week end guest – a man called Dyson[39] who teaches English at Reading University. I meet him I suppose about four or five times a year and am beginning to regard him as one of my friends of the 2nd class – i.e. not in the same rank as yourself or Barfield, but on a level with Tolkien or Macfarlane.

38 Frederick William Baxter (1897–1980) was Professor of English Literature at the Queen's University, Belfast, 1930–49, and Professor of English Language and Literature at the same university 1949–58.

39 See **Henry Victor Dyson 'Hugo' Dyson** in the Biographical Appendix.

He stayed the night with me in College – I sleeping in in order to be able to talk far into the night as one cd. hardly do out here. Tolkien came too, and did not leave till 3 in the morning: and after seeing him out by the little postern on Magdalen bridge Dyson and I found still more to say to one another, strolling up and down the cloister of New Building, so that we did not get to bed till 4. It was really a memorable talk. We began (in Addison's walk just after dinner) on metaphor and myth – interrupted by a rush of wind which came so suddenly on the still, warm evening and sent so many leaves pattering down that we thought it was raining. We all held our breath, the other two appreciating the ecstasy of such a thing almost as you would. We continued (in my room) on Christianity: a good long satisfying talk in which I learned a lot: then discussed the difference between love and friendship – then finally drifted back to poetry and books.[40]

On Sunday he came out here for lunch and Maureen and Minto and I (and Tykes) all motored him to Reading – a very delightful drive with some lovely villages, and the autumn colours are here now.

I am so glad you have really enjoyed a Morris again. I had the same feeling about it as you, in a way, with this proviso – that I don't think Morris was conscious of the meaning either here or in any of his works, except *Love is Enough* where the flame actually breaks through the smoke so to speak. I feel more and more that Morris has taught me things he did not understand himself. These hauntingly beautiful lands which somehow never satisfy, – this passion to escape from death plus the certainty that life owes all its charm to mortality – these push you on to the real thing because they fill you with desire and yet prove absolutely clearly that in Morris's world that desire cannot be satisfied.

The Macdonald conception of death[41] – or, to speak more correctly, St Paul's[42] – is really the answer to Morris: but I don't think I should have understood it without going through Morris. He is an unwilling witness to the truth. He shows you just *how far* you can go without knowing God, and that is far enough to force you (tho' not poor Morris himself) to go further. If ever you feel inclined to relapse into the mundane point

40 Further important details of this 'memorable talk' with Dyson and Tolkien on Saturday 19 September are found in the next two letters to Greeves.

41 There are many good examples in Lewis's *George MacDonald: An Anthology* (1946). Extract number 146 reads: 'All that is not God is death.'

42 e.g. Romans 5:12–21, 6:5–23; 1 Corinthians 15:12–58.

of view – to feel that your book and pipe and chair are enough for happiness – it only needs a page or two of Morris to sting you wide awake into uncontrollable longing and to make you feel that everything is worthless except the hope of finding one of his countries. But if you read any of his romances through you will find the country dull before the end. All he has done is to rouse the desire: but so strongly that you *must* find the real satisfaction. And then you realise that *death* is at the root of the whole matter, and why he chose the subject of the Earthly Paradise, and how the true solution is one he never saw.

I have finished the Taylor, and enjoyed it much from the purely literary point of view. As a religious writer I put him low and still think as I did when I last wrote.

I have been studying Hamlet very intensively, and never enjoyed it more. I have been reading all the innumerable theories about him, and don't despise that sort of thing in the least: but each time I turn back to the play itself I am more delighted than ever with the mere atmosphere of it – an atmosphere hard to describe and made up equally of the prevalent sense of death, solitude, & horror and of the extraordinary graciousness and lovableness of H. himself.[43] Have you read it at all lately? If not, do: and just surrender yourself to the magic, regarding it as a poem or a romance.

I don't *think* I left any pyjamas at Bernagh, but I'm afraid I want you to send me something else, W. is editing (i.e. arranging and typing) all the letters we brought from home (*don't* mention this to any one) so as to give a continuous history of the family.[44] We have just got to 1915 and it is maddening to have all my Bookham letters to my father (wh. tell nothing) and to know that all my Bookham letters to you are eating their heads off at Bernagh. Also, once I had them in type, I could renew those glorious years whenever I read them. Would it be a great bother to you to let me have the lot. If you want, you can have them back when they have been edited: and I promise faithfully that he will see nothing wh. gives you away in any respect, for I will go through them all first by myself. If you wd. let me have them *as soon as possible* and tell me what I owe you for registered postage, I shd. be very much obliged.

43 These are some of the ideas that went into Lewis's essay, 'Hamlet: The Prince or the Poem?' found in *Selected Literary Essays*.

44 The result of which was the Lewis Papers.

It is perfect autumn here – splashes of yellow on every other tree and delicious smells. We have been up in the wood clipping all afternoon.

I think I know the walk at the back of Stormont and may have done it oftener than you. This is a bad business about the rum. Give my love to your Mother. Tell Forrest I ask every one I meet about the human tendency to represent oneself as a daring sinner (untruly) and have met no one yet who doesn't regard it as being too obvious to be worth talking about

Yrs
Jack

About a week after the above letter was written, Monday 28 September, Warnie took Jack to Whipsnade Zoo in the sidecar of his motorbike, and it was during this outing that Jack took the final step in his conversion. 'As I drew near the conclusion,' he wrote in the last chapter of SBJ,

> *I felt a resistance almost as strong as my previous resistance to Theism. As strong, but short-lived, for I understood it better. Every step I had taken, from the Absolute to 'Spirit' to 'God', had been a step towards the more concrete, the more imminent, the more compulsive...I know very well when, but hardly how, the final step was taken. I was driven to Whipsnade one sunny morning. When we set out I did not believe that Jesus Christ is the Son of God, and when we reached the zoo I did. Yet I had not exactly spent the journey in thought. Nor in great emotion. 'Emotional' is perhaps the last word we can apply to some of the most important events. It was more like when a man, after long sleep, still lying motionless in bed, becomes aware that he is now awake.*

TO ARTHUR GREEVES (W):

[The Kilns]
Oct. 1st /31

My dear Arthur,

Very many thanks for the letter and enclosure that arrived this morning. Now, as to their return. I confess that I had not supposed you often read them, and had in view merely an *ultimate* return when W. had finished his editing, that is, in about 4 years' time. If however you want them at once, they are of course your property and will be returned by registered post whenever you wish. I shall follow absolutely your directions. In the meantime you can feel quite confident about their safe keeping. I have spent this morning on them and established a pretty good order for all except about eight. (How maddening my habit of not dating them now becomes! And how ridiculous the arguments by wh. I defended it!)

All the ones that deal with what we used to call 'It' I am suppressing and will return to you in a day or two. I am surprised to find what a very large percentage of the whole they are. I am now inclined to agree with you in *not* regretting that we confided in each other even on this subject, because it has done no harm in the long run – and how could young adolescents really be friends without it? At the same time, the letters give away some of your secrets as well as mine: and I do not wish to recall things of that sort to W's mind, so that in every way they had better be kept out of the final collection. I am also sending back some others in which my replies to you imply that you have said foolish things – you will see what I mean when I return them. Finally, I am suppressing (i.e. sending back at once and keeping from W. – that is what the word 'suppressing' means throughout) all letters that refer to my pretended assignation with the Belgian.[45] I am not at all sure that if J. Taylor were at my elbow he would not tell me that my repentance for that folly was incomplete if I did not submit to the 'mortification' of having them typed and laid open to posterity. I hope, however, this is not really necessary in the case of a sin so old and (I hope) so fully abandoned.

Thanks for all you say about the letters in general. You see mine with too friendly eyes. To me, as I re-read them, the most striking thing is their egotism: sometimes in the form of priggery, intellectual and even social: often in the form of downright affectation (I seem to be posturing and showing off in every letter): and always in the form of complete absorption in ourselves. I have you to thank that it was at least 'ourselves' and not wholly 'myself'. I can now honestly say that I envy you the much more artless letters you were writing me in those days: they all had at least the grace of humility and of affection. How ironical that the very things wh. I was proud of in my letters then should make the reading of them a humiliation to me now!

---

45 See the letter of 2 February 1915 *et seq.*

Don't suppose from this that I have not enjoyed the other aspect of them – the glorious memories they call up. I think I have got over *wishing* for the past back again. I look at it this way. The delights of those days were given to lure us into the world of the Spirit, as sexual rapture is there to lead to offspring and family life. They were nuptial ardours. To ask that they should return, or should remain is like wishing to prolong the honeymoon at an age when a man should rather be interested in the careers of his growing sons. They have done their work, those days and led on to better things. All the 'homeliness' (wh. was your chief lesson to me) was the introduction to the Christian virtue of charity or love. I sometimes manage now to get into a state in wh. I think of all my enemies and can honestly say that I find something lovable (even if it is only an oddity) in them all: and your conception of 'homeliness' is largely the route by wh. I have reached this. On the other hand, all the 'strangeness' (wh. was my lesson to you) has turned out to be only the first step in far deeper mysteries.

How deep I am just now beginning to see: for I have just passed on from believing in God to definitely believing in Christ – in Christianity. I will try to explain this another time. My long night talk with Dyson and Tolkien had a good deal to do with it.

I am so glad you liked the *Seasons*.[46] I agree with you that some parts are frankly boring, and some (e.g. the bathing episode in *Summer*) are in a false taste. I don't myself think that any of it is as good as the opening of *The Castle of Indolence*: the second canto everyone gives up as hopeless. It is delightful to hear of your thinking of having another try at Spenser. I have read nothing that would interest you since my last letter and am engaged on the Poetical Works of Skelton[47] (XVIth century) – a very bad poet except for the half dozen good things I knew already.

W. and I are busy still clearing the undergrowth in the top wood. This place gets more beautiful every day at present, with yellow leaves and crimson leaves and a more and more autumnal smell. I do hope you will some time make an opportunity of visiting it in winter.

---

46 James Thomson, *The Seasons* (1730).

47 John Skelton, *Poetical Works*, ed. Alexander Dyce, 2 vols. (1843). Lewis's fullest treatment of Skelton is found in *English Literature in the Sixteenth Century*, bk. I, ch. 2, pp. 133–43.

Did it strike you in reading those letters how completely *both* of us were wrong in most of our controversies, or rather in the great standing controversy about 'sentiment' wh. was the root of most of our quarrels? If anyone had said 'There is good feeling and bad: you can't have too much of the first, and you can't have too little of the second' it wd. have blown the gaff on the whole argument. But we blundered along – my indiscriminate hardness only provoking you into a more profound self pity (wh. is the root of all bad sentiment) and that bad sentiment in return making me harder and more willing to hurt.

Term begins next Friday.

Yours

Jack

P.S. I have just finished *The Epistle to the Romans*, the first Pauline epistle I have ever seriously read through. It contains many difficult and some horrible things, but the essential idea of Death (the Macdonald idea) is there alright. What I meant about the Earthly Paradise was simply that the whole story turns on a number of people setting out to look for a country where you don't die.

TO ARTHUR GREEVES (W):

[The Kilns]
Oct. 18th 1931

My dear Arthur,

I must have expressed myself rather confusedly about the letters. When I asked you for them I did not think that you would want them back except 'ultimately' – that is, the question of *time* was not seriously in my mind at all. Besides this, as people usually do in such circumstances, I was half consciously fooling myself about the length of time W. had still here. You know how 'He's not going just yet' leads one to plan and feel as if there was a month more when there is really 10 days. Then came your letter, showing your wish (a very flattering one to me) to have the letters back quite soon: and on top of that the *fact* (now unconcealable) that W. was actually packing and wd. be off in a day to two. It was therefore impossible that he should finish his editing of the family letters and get them all typed before he went: if I had known that you wanted them back soon, and if I had faced the real date of his departure, I would not have raised the question of the letters with you till after his return, 3 years hence. That indeed is what I ought to have done.

As things are, the four years I mentioned consist of 1 year's editing preceded by 3 years during wh. W. will be in China and the letters will be lying neatly in a drawer – safe, but idle. You see what a fool I have made of myself! The matter is now entirely in your hands, for of course they are your property not mine. If you want them seriously I will send them back: if you don't, they will be perfectly safe where they are, and safer indeed without the risk of a second postal journey. Still, the next move is to you and I will obey any orders you give.

This has filled up nearly a page so that I don't know whether I should now start to try and explain what I meant about Christianity. For one thing, reading your reply, I began to feel that perhaps I had said too much in my previous letter, that perhaps I was not nearly as clear on the subject as I had led you to think. But I certainly have moved *a bit*, even if it turns out to be a less bit than I thought.

What has been holding me back (at any rate for the last year or so) has not been so much a difficulty in believing as a difficulty in knowing what the doctrine *meant*: you can't believe a thing while you are ignorant *what* the thing is. My puzzle was the whole doctrine of Redemption: in what sense the life and death of Christ 'saved' or 'opened salvation to' the world. I could see how miraculous salvation might be necessary: one could see from ordinary experience how sin (e.g. the case of a drunkard) could get a man to such a point that he was bound to reach Hell (i.e. complete degradation and misery) in this life unless something quite beyond mere natural help or effort stepped in. And I could well imagine a whole world being in the same state and similarly in need of miracle. What I couldn't see was how the life and death of Someone Else (whoever he was) 2000 years ago could help us here and now – except in so far as his *example* helped us. And the example business, tho' true and important, is not Christianity: right in the centre of Christianity, in the Gospels and St Paul, you keep on getting something quite different and very mysterious expressed in those phrases I have so often ridiculed ('propitiation' – 'sacrifice' – 'the blood of the Lamb') – expressions wh. I cd. only interpret in senses that seemed to me either silly or shocking.

Now what Dyson and Tolkien showed me was this: that if I met the idea of sacrifice in a Pagan story I didn't mind it at all: again, that if I met the idea of a god sacrificing himself to himself (cf. the quotation opposite the title page of *Dymer*)[48] I liked it very much and was mysteriously moved by it: again, that the idea of the dying and reviving god (Balder, Adonis, Bacchus) similarly moved me provided I met it anywhere *except* in the Gospels. The reason was that in Pagan stories I was prepared to feel the myth as profound and suggestive of meanings beyond my grasp even tho' I could not say in cold prose 'what it meant'.

Now the story of Christ is simply a true myth: a myth working on us in the same way as the others, but with this tremendous difference that *it really happened*: and one must be content to accept it in the same way, remembering that it is God's myth where the others are men's myths: i.e. the Pagan stories are God expressing Himself through the minds of poets, using such images as He found there, while Christianity is God expressing Himself through what we call 'real things'. Therefore it is *true*, not in the sense of being a 'description' of God (that no finite mind could take in) but in the sense of being the way in which God chooses to (or can) appear to our faculties. The 'doctrines' we get *out* of the true myth are of course *less* true: they are translations into our *concepts* and *ideas* of that wh. God has already expressed in a language more adequate, namely the actual incarnation, crucifixion, and resurrection. Does this amount to a belief in Christianity? At any rate I am now certain (a) That this Christian story is to be approached, in a sense, as I approach the other myths. (b) That it is the most important and full of meaning. I am also *nearly* certain that it really happened.

No time for more now. I hope to have some literary chat in my next letter.

Yours
Jack

48 *The Hávamál*, no. 138: 'Nine nights I hung upon the Tree, wounded with the spear as an offering to Odin, myself sacrificed to myself'. *The Hávamál*, which means 'Sayings of the High One' (i.e. Odin, the chief god of Norse mythology), is a ninth century composite poem of 164 maxims or strophes in Old Norse. It is one of the poems collectively known as the Elder Edda.

BIOGRAPHICAL APPENDIX

* means there is a separate entry

BAKER, Leo Kingsley (1898–1986), was born in London on 14 August 1898, the son of Laura Jane Baker and James Leopold Hawes. He was educated at St George's School, Harpenden, from 1909 to 1917 where he was a school prefect, captain of rugby and of cricket. After matriculating at Wadham College, Oxford, in June 1917 he enlisted in the Royal Flying Corps. He was commissioned a 2nd lieutenant in November 1917, and a 1st lieutenant in April 1918. In May 1918 he went to France as a pilot with the 80th Squadron of the Royal Air Force. After being severely wounded in August 1918, he was awarded the Distinguished Flying Cross.

Baker returned to Oxford in 1919 and read Modern History. He and Lewis, who met soon after Baker arrived in Oxford, were drawn together by a love of poetry, and Lewis's letters to Baker contain some of his most interesting observations on poetry. He was a frequent visitor at Lewis's and Mrs Janie Moore's* home, and there are many references to him in *AMR*. It was Leo Baker who introduced Owen Barfield*, also of Wadham, to Lewis.

After taking his BA in 1922, he was from 1922 to 1925 an actor with the Old Vic Company under Lilian Baylis. His experience included parts in 30 Shakespeare plays, some old comedy, and two years of stage management. In 1925 he married Eileen Brookes and they had three daughters, Susan Mary (b. 1930), Elizabeth Margaret (b. 1933), and Rachel Mary Rosalind (b. 1939). Baker gave up the theatre owing to troubles resulting from his war wounds, and he and his wife set up a handloom weaving business in Chipping Campden, known as the Kingsley Weavers. It was dissolved on the outbreak of the Second World War. He was an Anthroposophist, and in 1933 he became a priest with the Anthroposophical 'Christian Community'. After the war broke out he took the family out of London to Gloucester, where he taught at a Rudolf Steiner school. He left the school in 1942 to become drama adviser for Gloucestershire, and in 1946 he became national drama adviser for the Carnegie United Kingdom Trust.

Upon his retirement at 65 he became head of acting for the Rose Bruford College of Speech and Drama in Sidcup, having been the chairman of governors when it was founded. His final retirement was at the age of 72. His wife suffered a severe stroke in 1976 and for five and a half years he devotedly visited her in hospital every day. She was paralysed and unable to speak. Leo Baker died on 5 September 1986 at the age of 88, his intellectual faculties as bright as ever.

BARFIELD, Owen (1898–1997) was born in Muswell Hill, North London on 9 November 1898, the youngest of four children, two sons and two daughters, born to Arthur Edward Barfield and Elizabeth (Shoults) Barfield. His father was a solicitor and his mother an ardent feminist. Both of his parents had been born Congregationalists, but the family observed no religion. When he was eight, Owen Barfield joined his brother Harry at Highgate School, and it was there he met one of his greatest friends, Cecil Harwood.* During the First World War he served mainly in Belgium as a wireless officer in the signal service of the Royal Engineers – now the Royal Corps of Signals. The wireless (or radio) was at that time in its infancy, and still using the Morse code.

In October 1919 he went up to Wadham College, Oxford, on a Classical scholarship. However, because of his growing interest in English literature, it was not Greats he read, but English Literature. During his first term he met Lewis and they were friends from then on. 'Barfield towers above us all', Lewis wrote in his diary of 9 July 1922. Lewis's diary (*AMR*), which covers the years 1922 to 1927, contains much about their shared interests.

After taking his BA with first class honours in 1921, Barfield began writing a B.Litt. thesis on 'Poetic Diction'. In 1923 he became a follower of Anthroposophy, the religious system evolved by Rudolf Steiner whom Barfield heard lecture on 24 August 1924. He was to be involved with the Anthroposophical Society for the rest of his life. Barfield's beliefs about poetic diction had led him to the Romantic poets and their doctrines of imagination, and then to the conclusion that Romanticism had never fulfilled itself, never been philosophically 'justified'. Now, on reading Steiner, he found that Steiner had understood all this before him. In the Introduction to *Romanticism Comes of Age* (1944), which contains his debt to Steiner, he said: 'Anthroposophy included and transcended not only my own poor stammering theory of poetry as knowledge, but the whole Romantic philosophy. It was nothing less than Romanticism grown up.' Lewis was not in sympathy with Anthroposophy and he and Barfield engaged in a 'Great War' argument through the post. It is recounted in Lionel Adey's *C. S. Lewis's 'Great War' with Owen Barfield* (1978).

During their second year at Oxford, Barfield and Cecil Harwood joined the English Folk Dancing Society, and it was through this society that Barfield met Matilda ('Maud') Douie, a professional dancer and producer who had worked with Gordon Craig. They married on 11 April 1923, and lived for a while in Long Crendon, where Lewis often visited them. In 1925 they moved to London to help with Barfield's literary career. He worked for the magazine *Truth*, and during this time he wrote a fairy tale of the Hans Andersen kind, *The Silver Trumpet* (1925). This was followed by *History in English Words* (1926) which is not merely about the changes in the meanings of words over time but what he called 'evolution of consciousness'. In 1928 he published a revised version of his B. Litt. thesis, *Poetic Diction: A Study in Meaning*, which contains many of his leading philosophic ideas.

Unfortunately, Barfield was forced to abandon his literary career. His father lost the services of a brother in their London firm of Barfield and Barfield, and in 1929 Owen joined the firm in order to help. He received a BCL from Oxford in 1930, and spent the next 28 years as a solicitor in London. One of the most pleasant things to come out of what he called these 'colourless' years was a charming *jeu d'esprit* called *This Ever Diverse Pair* (1950), published under the name G.A.L. Burgeon. In the story 'Burgeon' is the idealistic alter ego or 'sleeping partner' of the practical-minded solicitor named 'Burden'. They represent the tension between the demands of the legal profession and the need to live in the larger world of thought and letters. 'Burden is eating me up,' complains Burgeon in Chapter I,

> *my time, my wit, my memory, my 'shaping spirit of imagination', my whole* me. *Take poetry, for instance. The other evening he was so exhausted and spiritless and devoid of hope that he asked me to write a poem about* his *feelings. That's the sort of thing he does – calls on me to exert the very abilities he is destroying. I produced the following quatrain for him: –*
>
> *'How I hate this bloody business,*
> *Peddling property and strife*
> *While the pulse of Europe falters –*
> *How I hate this bloody life!'*

In the 1940s Lewis asked Barfield to set up a charitable trust into which he could direct most of his royalties, which trust was administered by Barfield. Chapter VI of *This Ever Diverse Pair* is about a client named 'Ramsden' who is based on Lewis, and it deals in a humorous way with the charitable trust which Lewis and Barfield referred to as the 'Agapargyry' (love + money).

But there was colour in his private life. Over the years the Barfields adopted three children, Alexander (b. 30 January 1928), Lucy (b. 2 November 1935) who is Lewis's godchild and to whom he dedicated *The Lion, the Witch and the Wardrobe*, and Jeffrey (b. 6 June 1940) to whom Lewis dedicated *The Voyage of the 'Dawn Treader'*. Barfield was baptized in the Church of England in 1949. Meanwhile, the friendship between Barfield and Lewis afforded them many happy times, and of Lewis's numerous tributes to Barfield the most memorable comes from *SBJ* XIII:

> *There is a sense in which Arthur [Greeves*] and Barfield are the types of every man's First Friend and Second Friend. The First is the* alter ego, *the man who first reveals to you that you are not alone in the world by turning out (beyond hope) to share all your most secret delights. There is nothing to be overcome in making him your friend; he and you join like raindrops on a window. But the Second Friend is the man who disagrees with you about everything. He is not so much the* alter ego *as the antiself. Of course he shares your interests; otherwise he would not become your friend at all. But he has approached them all at a different angle. He has read all the right books but has got the wrong thing out of every one. It is as if he spoke your language but mispronounced it. How can he be so nearly right and yet, invariably, just not right? He is as fascinating (and infuriating) as a woman. When you set out to correct his heresies, you find he forsooth has decided to correct yours! And then you go at it, hammer and tongs, far into the night, night after night, or walking through fine country that neither gives a glance to, each learning the weight of the other's punches, and often more like mutually respectful enemies than friends. Actually (though it never seems so at the time) you modify one another's thought; out of this perpetual dogfight a community of mind and a deep affection emerge. But I think he changed me a good deal more than I him. Much of the thought which he afterward put into* Poetic Diction *had already become mine before that important little book appeared. It would be strange if it had not. He was of course not so learned then as he has since become; but the genius was already there.*

A revolution in his life came about when he was 60. About the time of his retirement in 1959 he at last found time to write many of his best books. They include his own favourite – *Saving the Appearances* (1957) – as well as *Worlds Apart* (1963), *Unancestral Voice* (1965), *Speaker's Meaning* (1967), *What Coleridge Thought* (1971), *The Rediscovery of Meaning, and Other Essays* (1977), and *History, Guilt, and Habit* (1979). Chapter VI of *This Ever Diverse Pair* is reprinted in a work containing nearly everything Barfield has written about Lewis, *Owen Barfield on C. S. Lewis*, ed. G.B. Tennyson (1990).

For the first two decades of this second part of his life he was a visiting scholar in many American colleges and universities. There was always a welcome for his numerous American friends at his home 'Orchard View' in Dartford, Kent. His wife died there on 13 February 1980. In 1986 Barfield moved to Forest Row, Sussex, and he died there on 14 December 1997, a month into his centenary.

For information about him, see *Evolution of Consciousness: Studies in Polarity*, ed. Shirley Sugerman (1976), a volume of essays offered to him. A very good biography is G.B. Tennyson's 'Owen Barfield: A Life in Thought' in *A Barfield Reader: Selections from the Writings of Owen Barfield*, ed. G.B. Tennyson (1999). Another good work of biography is the introduction to *A Barfield Sampler: Poetry and Fiction by Owen Barfield* (1993) by the editors, Jeanne Clayton Hunter and Thomas Kranidas. Of the many studies of his writings the one he thought best is Gareth Knight's *The Magical World of the Inklings: J.R.R. Tolkien, C. S. Lewis, Charles Williams, Owen Barfield* (1990).

CAPRON, Robert ('Oldy' or 'Oldie') (1851–1911), headmaster of Wynyard School, called 'Belsen' in *SBJ* II. Capron was born in Brampton, Devon, on 29 October 1851 and received a BA and a BSc from the University of London in 1873 and 1875 respectively. From 1873 to 1878 he was a teacher at Bowdon College in Altrincham, Cheshire. He was ordained an Anglican clergyman in 1878, and was curate of Wordsley, Staffordshire. In 1881 he moved to 99 Langley Road, Watford, where he founded Wynyard School.

The school was just beginning when, in 1882, he married Ellen Barnes (1849–1909). They had three daughters, Norah, Dorothy and Eva, and a son, John Wynyard (1883–1959) who was educated at King's College, Cambridge. The entire family helped with the school which, for a while, was successful. At its height it could accommodate 30 boarders and as many day-boys. During those early days Robert Capron was considered very successful for his teaching of the classics, and some of his boys gained scholarships to Charterhouse, Malvern, Uppingham and Rugby.

In 1896 a local boy, Ernest Benskin, enrolled at Wynyard. In an unpublished autobiography he revealed that he was there when Capron, who had already shown evidence of cruelty, went into an extreme rage, battering a pupil named 'Punch' Hickmott so unmercifully that the boy's parents took legal proceedings against him in the High Court. The school began to decline from this point.

Albert Lewis* knew nothing about all this when he enrolled his elder son at Wynyard. 'It is difficult to understand how this came about,' wrote Warnie Lewis,* 'having in view the careful and exhaustive enquiries which had culminated in the narrowing of the choice to three or four schools, of which Wynyard was not one' (LP III: 33). In any event, Warnie arrived there with Mrs Lewis on 11 May 1905. In his reminiscences of his years there (LP III: 33–41) Warnie describes Capron:

> *A fine forehead surmounted a pair of piercing eyes of the shade of brown which is nearly black. He wore a short grey beard and moustaches, and his hair, which was plentiful, was of the same colour; his complexion was ruddy, healthy, and weather beaten. The face was marred by the nose, which was small, had the appearance of being varnished, and from which the lobe of the right nostril had at some time been removed. He was, I imagine, above middle height, and was a well built and extremely powerful man physically; I have seen him lift a boy of twelve or so from the floor by the back of his collar, and, holding him at arms length as one might a dog, proceed to refresh the unfortunate youth's memory by applying his cane to his calves.*

By the time C. S. Lewis entered Wynyard on 18 September 1908, Capron had been examined in 1906 by a brain specialist who found him mad. By this time the school had dwindled to eight boarders and about as many day-boys. Capron's only assistants at this time were his daughters and John Wynyard Capron who was ordained in 1909. It was not long before Jack was as appalled by Capron's cruelty as Warnie, and he wrote of this in *SBJ* II.

When a blast of Capron's temper fell upon Warnie on 19 September 1908 both boys wrote to their father. Warnie said: 'I have stood this sort of thing for three years and I cannot stand it any longer. Please let us leave at once' (LP III: 147). Jack, in his letter of 29 September, urged his father to allow them to come home: 'We simply *cannot* wait in this hole till the end of term.' Mr Lewis, trying to be helpful, replied on 20 September 1908: 'All schools – whether for boys or the larger school of life for men – press hardly and sorely at times. Otherwise they would not be schools. But I am sure you will face the good and the bad like a brave Christian boy, for dear, dear Mammy's sake' (LP III: 140).

They did not have to hold on much longer. Mrs Capron died on 1 March 1909, and Warren left to go to Malvern in July 1909. Reduced to a handful of pupils, the school began to sink. Capron wrote to Albert Lewis on 27 April 1910 to say he was 'giving up school work' (LP III: 206). The school closed in July 1910, Capron having been inducted into the living at Radwell on 13 June of that year. There he began flogging the choirboys and, when they tried to stop it, the churchwardens as well. He was put under restraint, certified insane, and he resigned his living in June 1911. He died of pneumonia in Camberwell House Asylum, Peckham, Kent, on 18 November 1911. His body lies with that of his wife in Watford Cemetery.

COGHILL, Nevill (1899–1980). This friend and colleague was born on 19 April 1899 at Castle Townshend, Skibbereen, County Cork, the son of Anglo-Irish Protestant gentry. Nevill's parents were Sir Egerton Bushe Coghill, 5th Baronet, a noted amateur landscape painter, and Elizabeth Hildegarde Augusta Somerville – sister of the writer Edith Anna Oenone Somerville. He was educated at Bilton Grange and Haileybury College, after which he was commissioned a 2nd lieutenant in the trench mortar division of the Royal Artillery. He served as a gunner on the Salonika front in 1918. He went up to Exeter College, Oxford, in 1919 and read History and then English. He gained a First in English in 1923.

Coghill and Lewis began reading English together in 1922 and the first mention of Coghill occurs in Lewis's diary (*AMR*) of 2 February 1923 after they had attended George Gordon's 'Discussion Class': 'He seems an enthusiastic sensible man, without nonsense, and a gentleman, much more attractive than the majority.' It was the practice of the discussion class to keep the minutes of the meetings in verse. After Lewis read a paper about Spenser on 9 February 1923 Coghill wrote the minutes in some of the same Chaucerian verse for which he was to become famous. Describing Lewis's paper on Spenser, he said:

> Sir Lewis *was ther; a good philosópher*
> *He hade a noblé paper for to offer.*

Well couthe he speken in the Greeké tongue;
And yet, his countenance was swythé yong.

Lewis was an unbeliever when he met Coghill and in *SBJ* XIV he explained the 'disturbing factors in Coghill' which threatened his atheism:

> *I soon had the shock of discovering that he – clearly the most intelligent and best-informed man in that class – was a Christian and a thoroughgoing supernaturalist. There were other traits that I liked but found...oddly archaic; chivalry, honour, courtesy, 'freedom', and 'gentilesse'. One could imagine him fighting a duel. He spoke much 'ribaldry' but never 'villeinye'.*

After teaching for a while in the Royal Naval College at Dartmouth, Coghill was elected a research fellow at Exeter in 1924. He became an official fellow and librarian in 1925. In 1927 he married Elspeth Nora Harley and they had a daughter, Carol. The marriage was dissolved in 1933. Over the years he developed his very considerable talents as a dramatic producer. After his production of *Samson Agonistes* at Exeter College in 1930, he went on to produce plays for the OUDS (Oxford University Dramatic Society). When he was casting *Measure for Measure* in 1944 he chose a talented young man from his own college to play the part of Angelo. Although baptized Richard Jenkins, he later took the name Richard Burton. He and Coghill became and remained good friends. A detailed account of Coghill's contributions to OUDS, with a photo of him rehearsing *Dr Faustus* with Richard Burton, is found in Humphrey Carpenter's *O.U.D.S.: A Centenary History of the Oxford University Dramatic Society* (1985).

John Wain left a delightful portrait of the Nevill Coghill in *Dear Shadows* (1986):

> *He was a big man, with a tallness that would not be remarkable now that so many people are tall, but also built on generous lines, broad-shouldered and deep-chested. His head was large, and brown hair, greying in middle life, curled and clustered on it as wiry as heather. He smiled easily, revealing somewhat battered teeth, and indeed his whole face had a slightly rough, knocked-about quality, like a chipped statue. I had one friend who used to say that he looked like one of the emperors' heads outside the Sheldonian...But if his head was*

statue-like, it was a noble statue, generous in expression and bearing. His voice was deep and strong, his speech soft and gentle; and this contrast was carried through everything. He was totally courteous, a gentleman by instinct as well as by tradition...In fact, he was more endowed with grace of manner and of mind than anyone I ever met. (p. 13)

In 1957 Coghill was elected Merton Professor of English Literature. He was a scholar of Middle English literature and his translation into contemporary English of Chaucer's *The Canterbury Tales* (1951) has enjoyed a wide audience. Lewis thought highly of it and he was pleased that Coghill had succeeded in making Chaucer understandable to many who would have never been able to read him. Coghill's translation of Langland's *Piers Plowman* was published as *Visions from Piers Plowman* in 1949, and his translation of Chaucer's *Troilus and Criseyde* in 1971.

Lewis and Coghill saw one another often, and Coghill attended a good many meetings of the Inklings, through which he got to know Warnie Lewis. In his essay 'Approach to English', in *Light on C. S. Lewis*, ed. Jocelyn Gibb (1965), Coghill wrote of those years when he and Lewis were reading English together as undergraduates.

In 1966, the year of his retirement, Coghill directed his former pupil Richard Burton and Elizabeth Taylor in *Dr Faustus* at the Oxford Playhouse. The following year the film, with almost the same cast, was shot in Rome, with Coghill and Burton co-directing. In 1968 he mounted a very successful musical version of *The Canterbury Tales* which ran for five years at the Phoenix Theatre in London. In the late 1960s Coghill went to live with his brother Sir Jocelyn Coghill at Aylburton, Gloucester. He died in Cheltenham on 6 November 1980. See *To Nevill Coghill from Friends*, Collected by John Lawlor and W.H. Auden (1966), John Carey's biography in the *Dictionary of National Biography*, and the biography in *CG*.

DUNBAR OF HEMPRIGGS, Dame Maureen Daisy Helen, Baronetess (1906–97). She was born Maureen Moore in Delgany, County Wicklow, Ireland, on 19 August 1906, the daughter of Courtenay Edward Moore and Jane King Askins Moore,* and the sister of Edward Francis Courtenay 'Paddy' Moore*. Following her parents' separation, her mother moved with Maureen and Paddy to Bristol in 1908. In June 1917 she and her mother took rooms in Wellington Square, Oxford, so they could be near Paddy while he was training with the Officers' Training Corps in Keble College. She met Lewis soon after his arrival there on 7 June. He was sharing a room in Keble with her brother, and over the next few months she and her mother came to know him well. He visited their home in Bristol several times. On one of these visits she heard Lewis and Paddy promise that if one of them survived the war he would look after Lewis's father and Paddy's mother. They went to France soon after this. Paddy was killed in action in March 1918 and was awarded the Military Cross. Lewis wished to keep his side of the bargain, and after he came home from France and returned to Oxford they moved there to be near him.

Maureen was educated at Headington School, with Lewis providing tutorials in Greek and Latin to help her get her School Certificate. Lewis's diary, *All My Road Before Me*, contains much about his life with the Moores, and the various places they lived. Maureen loved music, and had taken lessons in Bristol. After moving to Oxford, her mother did much to encourage her. On leaving Headington School she went to the Royal College of Music where she obtained her Licentiate of the Royal Academy of Music in 1928. She taught music at Monmouth School for Girls from 1930 to 1933; Oxford High School from 1935 to 1940; and at Malvern College from 1957 to 1968. It was appropriate that she should marry someone as musical as she was, and on 27 August 1940 she married Leonard Blake (b. 7 October 1907) who had been Director of Music at Worksop College since 1935, and who in 1945 became Director of Music at Malvern College. They had two children, Richard Francis Blake, Lewis's godson, born on 8 January 1945; and Eleanor Margaret Blake born on 16 November 1949.

Even after she married she did all she could to help her mother. She and her family would often change houses with Jack and Warnie Lewis, so she could look after Mrs Moore and they could have a holiday in Malvern. When Joy Lewis was very ill and in hospital during 1957, Maureen invited her two sons to spend their school holidays in Malvern.

On 4 February 1963 a distant relative, Sir George Cospatrick Duff-Sutherland-Dunbar, died. He was unmarried and Maureen Blake discovered that she was next in line, through her father's side of the family, to a baronetcy and an estate in Caithness, Scotland. She became the 8th Baronet. She had not seen Lewis since this happened when, in July 1963, she visited him in hospital. He had not recognized others that day, and she said: 'Jack, it is Maureen.' 'No,' he replied, 'It's Lady Dunbar of Hempriggs.' 'Oh, Jack,' she said, 'how could you remember that?' 'On the contrary,' he replied, 'How could *I* forget a fairy tale?'

Her inheritance of a baronetcy was more complicated than it first looked, because no one was sure a woman could inherit one. However, it came right in the end. In August 1965 Maureen was proved to be the rightful successor by the Lord Lyon, Chief of Heralds in Edinburgh. The Hempriggs Baronetcy, a 'Nova Scotia' one, was created in 1706 'to heirs whomsoever, whether male or female'. On 6 August 1965 *The Times* carried an article headlined 'Woman Wins Claim to Title – Baronetess of Scotland Recognized'. 'The court, in a judgement issued today,' it said, 'granted a petition brought by Mrs Maureen Daisy Helen Moore or Blake, of The Lees, Malvern, Worcestershire, and recognized her as Dame Maureen Daisy Helen Dunbar of Hempriggs, Baronetess.'

Lady Dunbar and her family spent a month each summer at Ackergill Tower, near Wick, Caithness – in the far north of Scotland. The inheritance did not bring her wealth. Indeed, it brought many responsibilities which she handled with skill and feeling. Her Scottish home also furnished her and her husband with a great deal of interest and they managed to go up north every summer. When they retired from teaching at Malvern, they moved to the small village of Winchcombe in Gloucestershire. Leonard Blake died on 1 August 1989 and Lady Dunbar died on 15 February 1997. At her death, her son became the 9th Baronet, Sir Richard Dunbar of Hempriggs.

DYSON, Henry Victor Dyson, 'Hugo' (1896–1975), was born on 7 April 1896 in Hove, Sussex, the son of Philip Dyson and his wife Henrietta. He was educated at Brighton College. On leaving there in 1911 he went to the Royal Military College at Sandhurst. In December 1915 he was commissioned a 1st lieutenant in the Queen's Own Royal West Kent Regiment and sent to France where he took part in the Battle of the Somme during July–August 1916, and the Battle of Arras during April 1917. It was in the Battle of Passchendaele at Ypres during October–November 1918 that Dyson was seriously wounded.

He came up to Exeter College, Oxford, in October 1919 and read English, taking a BA in 1921. He remained to write a thesis on John Ford and took a B.Litt. degree in 1924, and his MA in 1925. On completing his thesis, Dyson was offered a post as Lecturer and Tutor in English at Reading University where he taught from 1914 until 1945. During this time he was an Oxford Extension Lecturer and an Oxford examiner for St Andrew's and Durham University. In 1925 he married Margaret Mary Bosworth Robinson (b. 26 December 1903) of Wantage. The next year Reading University achieved independence from the University of London and became the University of Reading.

Dyson was introduced to Lewis in 1930 through their mutual friend Nevill Coghill.* Lewis described their second meeting in a letter to Arthur Greeves* of 29–30 July 1930. Dyson and Coghill had dined with Lewis in Magdalen College on 29 July and remained until three o'clock in the morning: 'Having met him once I liked him so well that I determined to get to know him better...He is a man who really loves truth: a philosopher and a religious man: who makes his critical & literary activities depend on the former – none of your damned dilettante.'

When Lewis next wrote to Greeves about Dyson it was about an even more important evening at Magdalen – 19 September 1931 – this time with J.R.R. Tolkien.* The 'memorable talk' between the three of them went on until four in the morning, and when Lewis wrote to Greeves on 1 October 1931 he said: 'I have just passed on from believing in God to definitely believing in Christ – in Christianity...Dyson and Tolkien had a good deal to do with it.' The final letter in this book, that of 18 October 1931, describes in detail what happened to Lewis as a result of the long and important conversation with Dyson and Tolkien. From this time on Dyson was a valued member of the Inklings.

Lewis and the others were to see much more of this charming man when Dyson became a Fellow and Tutor of Merton College in 1945 and moved to Oxford. Warnie Lewis* had met him in 1933 and his diary provides the best description of Dyson's wit and vivacious spirits. He is, he wrote on 18 February 1933, 'a man who gives the impression of being made of quick silver: he pours himself into a room on a cataract of words and gestures, and you are caught up in the stream – but after the first plunge, it is exhilarating' (*BF*). There is much evidence of this 'cataract of words' in the book he wrote with J.E. Butt, *Augustans and Romantics 1689–1830* (1940). Jack wrote to Warnie on 3 March 1940 about reading the book in proof. 'It is, as one would expect,' he said, 'almost too bright, but some of the sparks are admirable.'

Dyson shared Warnie's disappointment in Jack's choice of Mrs Janie Moore* as his companion. On 8 August 1946 Warnie dined with Hugo Dyson in Merton, and that night he wrote in his diary: 'He was in high spirits when I met him, and his spirits rose steadily for the rest of the evening. I was more than ever struck with his amazing knowing of Shakespeare; I don't suppose there is a man in Oxford – with the possible exception of [C.T.] Onions – who can quote so happily, e.g. tonight, apropos of J[ack]: "O cursed spite that gave thee to the Moor": poor [Jack's] whole catastrophe epitomised in nine words!'

Dyson retired from Merton in 1963 and he and his wife moved to a house in Sandfield Road, Headington. His works include *Pope* (1933), '"The Old Cumberland Beggar" and the Wordsworthian Unities' in *Essays on the Eighteenth Century Presented to David Nichol Smith* (1945), and *The Emergence of Shakespeare's Tragedy* (1950). Patrick Garland, the producer, had been one of his pupils, and at his instigation Dyson gave several television talks on Shakespeare for the BBC as well as introducing Garland's television series *Famous Gossips*. In 1965 he made an appearance in John Schlesinger's film *Darling*, which starred Julie Christie and Dirk Bogarde. He died on 6 June 1975, and his beloved Margaret died 27 May 1993. They are buried in a single grave in the cemetery of St Cross Church, Oxford. See Humphrey Carpenter's *The Inklings* (1978).

The Ewart Family. The head of this Belfast family was Sir William Quartus Ewart (1844–1919) who was born on 14 June 1844, the eldest son of Sir William Ewart, MP, the 1st Baronet. After taking a degree from Trinity College, Dublin, he went to work in the family firm of Wm. Ewart & Son Ltd., Flax Spinners and Linen Manufacturers. In 1876 he married Mary Heard (1849–1929), the eldest daughter of Robert Heard JP of Pallastown, Kinsdale, Co. Cork. Mary Heard was the niece of C. S. Lewis's maternal grandmother, Mrs Mary Warren Hamilton (see The Hamilton Family*). Sir William and Lady Ewart were the first cousins of Flora Lewis,* and they are the relatives Lewis refers to as 'Cousin Quartus' and 'Cousin Mary' in *SBJ* III.

The Ewart family lived in Strandtown, very near the Lewises, in a house called 'Glenmachan' – it is referred to in *Surprised by Joy* as 'Mountbracken'. Lewis wrote in *SBJ* III:

> *Lady E. was my mother's first cousin and perhaps my mother's dearest friend, and it was no doubt for my mother's sake that she took upon herself the heroic work of civilizing my brother and me...Sir W. ('Cousin Quartus') was...gracious, childlike, deeply and religiously humble, and abounding in charity. No man could feel more fully his responsibility to descendants. He had a good deal of boyish gaiety about him; at the same time I always felt that the conception of duty dominated his life. His stately figure, his grey beard, and his strikingly handsome profile make up one of the most venerable images of my memory.*

Warnie Lewis also wrote of the Ewarts, and in LP III: 252 he said of Sir William:

> *My father once summed up his character in four words – 'A great Christian Gentleman'. He had the Christian ideal that wealth is a trust, and his disbursements were never the mere largess of a rich man who chooses to avoid the momentary discomfort which the refusal of alms entails...Children loved him, and he was at his best in their company. His love of children knew no restriction of race, class or creed...He found his chief conversation in simple tales of his own town and countryside, and in stories of other lands gathered from the accounts of various missionaries; he had a keen relish for any story illustrative of the shrewd pawky humour of Ulster.*

Of Lady Ewart he wrote (LP III: 253):

> *Tranquillity was her outstanding characteristic, and this quality, engrafted on the easy gracious good breeding of the old fashioned southern Irish aristocrat, made her in her middle and later years a perfect mistress of her table and drawing room, and a very loveable old lady. Her mere presence in a room diffused something of the quiet charm of a still day in autumn.*

The Ewarts had five children: (1) Robert Heard Ewart (1879–1939), who succeeded to the baronetcy after his father; (2) Charles Gordon Ewart (1885–1936), who married Lily Greeves, the sister of Arthur Greeves;* (3) Hope Ewart (1882–1934) who in 1911 married George Harding and moved to Dublin; (4) Kelso 'Kelsie' Ewart (1886–1966), who lived near Glenmachan all her life; (5) Gundreda 'Gunny' Ewart (1888–1978) who married John Forrest in 1927.

Describing the Ewart sisters in *SBJ* III, Lewis said:

> *It was the three daughters whom we knew best. All three were 'grown-up' but in fact much nearer to us in age than any other grown-ups we knew, and all three were strikingly handsome. H., the eldest and the gravest, was a Juno, a dark queen who at certain moments looked like a Jewess. K. was more like a Valkyrie (though all, I think, were good horsewomen) with her father's profile. There was in her face something of the delicate fierceness of a thoroughbred horse, an indignant fineness of nostril, the possibility of an excellent disdain. She had what*

the vanity of my own sex calls a 'masculine' honesty; no man ever was a truer friend. As for the youngest, G., I can only say that she was the most beautiful woman I have ever seen, perfect in shape and colour and voice and every movement – but who can describe beauty?

Warnie added to their portraits as well. Of Hope he said:

She was a handsome woman of a dark, almost Italian type, with an air of dignity which she acquired early in life...She was very near to the Edwardian ideal of the beautiful woman...It was she who gave to Glenmachan an infusion of the larger world which lay outside Belfast and Ireland. She inherited and combined in herself that thoughtfulness and charm which she found in each of her parents...She was the best of good company, even tempered and radiating a cheerful common sense serenity in whatever company she found herself. Her marriage began the break-up of Glenmachan which was never quite the same house again after she left it. (LP III: 256)

Of Kelsie he wrote:

Kelsie was the least intelligent and most energetic member of the household...She had less pretensions to beauty than her sisters, but there was an open air freshness about her which supplied its place. The war was the great event of her life: at the first opportunity she joined the corps of women car drivers known as the 'Fannys', and went to Aldershot where she so enjoyed her experiences that for ever afterwards her conversation was liberally sprinkled with anecdotes of her army days. (LP III: 256–7)

And of Gundreda he said:

Gundreda was the most beautiful woman I ever saw: she had masses of red gold hair, and the glinting brown eyes and perfect complexion which so often goes with such a colouring...She had a radiant and infectious almost childlike gaiety which was always bubbling over into delighted and delightful laughter. She possessed in a supreme degree the Ulster capacity for extracting amusement from the dialect and idiom of her own countryside, and to hear her frequent imitations of the broad Co. Down accent was a joy. (LP III: 257)

GREEVES, Joseph Arthur (1895–1966), was born in Belfast on 27 August 1895, the youngest of five children born to Joseph Malcomson Greeves (1858–1925) and Mary Margretta Gribbon (1861–1949) of Brooklyn, New York. Their home, 'Bernagh', was directly across the road from 'Little Lea', where the Lewis family lived. Arthur's father was the director of J. & T.M. Greeves, Ltd., flax spinners. The family had traditionally been members of the Society of Friends, but had converted to the Plymouth Brethren in 1830. Arthur's only formal education came from his years at Campbell College, Belfast, between 1906 and 1912. He enrolled at the Slade School of Fine Art in London in 1921 and left with a Certificate in 1923. For years he had tried to get to know Jack and Warnie Lewis, but without success. Then came their first real meeting in April 1914. 'I had been so far from thinking such a friend possible,' Lewis wrote in *SBJ* VIII, 'that I had never even longed for one; no more than I longed to be King of England.'

Their correspondence, which began in 1914, lasted half a century. There seems to be almost nothing that Lewis felt unable to mention to Arthur. When Albert Lewis* died in 1929 Jack found a home at 'Bernagh' or wherever Arthur was living. It was during a summer holiday at 'Bernagh' in 1932 that he wrote *The Pilgrim's Regress*. Lewis seems not to have preserved many of Arthur's letters; but Arthur saved nearly all of Lewis's and they were published as *They Stand Together* (1979). During the compilation of the Lewis Papers in 1933–5 Warnie Lewis contributed a portrait of Arthur (IV: 181–2) in which he said:

> *His circumstances have been such that he has never been compelled to face the issues of life, to know it as it is, to gauge the degree of toleration which the community owes to the individual and the individual to the community. I do not here refer to the fact that he has never had to earn his living, but mean that with a child's liking for being liked he has the child's distress at the obtuseness of the grown ups who cannot see that if only everyone would always do as he wants them to do, the world would be a very delightful place to live in.*

Jack 'felt obliged to supplement' this portrait with something from his own pen (LP X: 218–20), and he said of his friend:

> *Arthur was the youngest son of a doting mother and a harsh father, two evils whereof each increased the other. The mother soothed him the more, to compensate for the father's harshness, and the father became harsher to counteract the ill effects of the mother's indulgence.*

Both thus conspired to aggravate a tendency...towards self pity...It can easily be imagined how such a child grew up: but who could have foretold that he would be neither a liar nor a tale bearer, neither a coward nor a misanthrope?

He was the frankest of men. Many of the most ludicrous episodes which could be told against him, turn on his failure to acquire that 'visor to the human face' which such a training usually teaches a man to wear. He was the most faithful of friends, and carried the innumerable secrets of my own furtive and ignoble adolescence locked in a silence which is not commonly thought effeminate. Under illness or inconvenience he was impatient – a loud and violent, but not a lengthy grumbler: but danger left him unmoved...

Until I met him, and during my frequent absences, his position was much the same as that of an imaginative boy in one of our public schools. Yet he never showed any inclination to revenge himself after the fashion so familiar among our modern intelligentsia. *He continued to feel – indeed he taught me to endeavour to feel with him – at once a human affection and a rich aesthetic relish for his antediluvian aunts, his mill-owning uncles, his mother's servants, the postman on our roads, and the cottagers whom we met in our walks. What he called the 'Homely' was the natural food both of his heart and his imagination. A bright hearth seen through an open door as we passed, a train of ducks following a brawny farmer's wife, a drill of cabbages in a suburban garden – these were things that never failed to move him, even to an ecstasy, and he never found them incompatible with his admiration for Proust, or Wyndham Lewis, or Picasso. He was completely unworldly. He never in his life read an 'advanced' book or imitated a 'modern' painter because he felt that he could thus become a superior being. The motive was always either his genuine pleasure in them, or else the advice of ill-chosen friends. For Arthur was both humble and unstable. He could be persuaded to read, or at least begin, any book: to adopt (for a time) any canons of taste. The last speaker was always right to him. But all these fluctuations went on over a fundamental constancy: to the charm of the 'homely' he was never untrue, and if he was easily drawn into the follies of any and every coterie, he could not, by any process, be infected with its pride.*

During the earlier years of our acquaintance he was (as always) a Christian, and I was an atheist. But though (God forgive me) I bombarded him with all the thin artillery of a seventeen year old rationalist, I never made any impression on his faith – a faith both vague and

> *confused, and in some ways too indulgent to our common weaknesses, but inexpugnable. He remains victor in that debate. It is I who have come round. The thing is symbolical of much in our joint history. He was not a clever boy, he was even a dull boy; I was a scholar. He had no 'ideas.' I bubbled over with them. It might seem that I had much to give him, and that he had nothing to give me. But this is not the truth. I could give concepts, logic, facts, arguments, but he had feelings to offer, feelings which most mysteriously – for he was always very inarticulate – he taught me to share. Hence, in our commerce, I dealt in superficies, but he in solids. I learned charity from him and failed, for all my efforts, to teach him arrogance in return...If I had to write his epitaph, I should say of him what I could say of no one else known to me – 'He* despised *nothing'. Contempt – if not the worst, surely the most ludicrously inappropriate of the sins that men commit – was, I believe, unknown to him. He fulfilled the Gospel precept: he 'judged not'.*

Arthur was deemed unable to work because of a bad heart and he lived on an income from the family business. He nevertheless won some recognition as a landscape painter, and was exhibited in 1936. He was a member of the Royal Hibernian Academy. His painting of his friend, Forrest Reid, the novelist, is in the possession of the Royal Academical Institution, Belfast. Much of his time was spent painting in and around his beloved County Down where he spent the whole of his life. After his mother's death in 1949 he moved to a cottage, 'Silver Hill', in Crawfordsburn, Co. Down, where Lewis often stayed. It was here that Arthur entertained Jack and his wife, Joy, during the summers of 1958 and 1959.

It is ironic that, while Lewis's acceptance of thoroughgoing supernatural Christianity was due in part to Arthur's influence, Arthur himself vacillated between religious beliefs. The original damage may have been caused by his Plymouth Brethren parents, but other forces were soon at work. He vacillated between the Church of Ireland and the Baha'i faith. Near the end of his life he settled down to what had always suited him best, Quaker services with about five elderly friends in a small meeting house in Bangor, close to 'Silver Hill'. There he seems to have found the peace he was looking for all his life.

The last time Jack and Arthur were together was a weekend spent at The Kilns in June 1961. Jack was making plans to visit Arthur in Ireland during the summer of 1963, but a heart attack prevented this. 'It looks as if you and I shall never meet again in this life,' he wrote on 11 September 1963, 'Oh, Arthur, never to see you again!' (*TST*).

Among Arthur's closest friends was Lisbeth Greeves, wife of his cousin, Ronald. A fortnight before he died he asked her to lunch with him, after which she recalls that he sensed that he would die soon. He asked her to pray with him that when his time came he would die in his sleep. On 27 August 1966 he celebrated his 71st birthday. Two days later, his cousin Lisbeth recalled, 'he died in his sleep – just like a happy child sleeping peacefully – with a linen handkerchief over his eyes, to shade them from the early morning sun.'

The Hamilton Family. C. S. Lewis's mother's family can be traced back many generations. The Irish branch of her family was descended from (A) Sir James Hamilton of Finnart (d. 1540),[1] who married Helen Cunningham. Their son (B) Hugh Hamilton (d. 1671) settled at Lisbane, Co. Down, in the time of King James I. His second son was (C) Alexander Hamilton (d. 1676) of Killyleath, Co. Down, who married Jean Hamilton of Belfast. Their son was (D) Alexander Hamilton (d. 1768), MP of Knock in the County of Dublin and Newtown Hamilton in the County of Armagh. He married Isabella Maxwell (b. 1729). Their eldest son was (E) the Right Reverend Hugh Hamilton (1729–1805), who was successively a Fellow of Trinity College, Dublin, Dean of Armagh, Bishop of Clonfert, and finally, Bishop of Ossory, which see he occupied from the time of his translation in 1799 until his death on 1 December 1805. He is buried in St Canice's (or St Kenny's) Cathedral in Kilkenny. He married Isabella Wood, and they had two daughters and five sons.[2] (F) Their son, the Reverend Hugh Hamilton (1790–1865) of Inishmacsaint, Co. Fermanagh, married Elizabeth Staples, daughter of the Right Honourable John Staples M.P. of Lissan, Co. Tyrone.[3] (The other daughter, Grace Louise Staples, married the 2nd Marquis of Ormonde.)

1 There is an entry for him in the *Dictionary of National Biography*.

2 Lewis may have inherited some of the talents of his great-great-grandfather, Bishop Hugh Hamilton (1729–1805) who wrote a number of books: *De Sectionibus Conicis Tractatus (A Geometrical Treatise of the Conic Sections)* (1758); *Philosophical Essays* (1766); *On the Duty of Obedience to the Laws and of Submission to Magistrates* (1772); *An Attempt to Probe the Existence and Absolute Perfection of the Supreme Unoriginal Being, in a Demonstrative Manner* (1784). See *The Works of the Right Rev. Hugh Hamilton, D.D., Late Bishop of Ossory*, Collected and Published, With some Alterations and Additions from his Manuscripts, by Alexander Hamilton, Esq., his Eldest Son, 2 vols. (1809). There is an entry on him in the *Dictionary of National Biography*.

3 Clive Staples Lewis derived his second Christian name from this grandfather.

Hugh Hamilton's son was (G) the Rev. Thomas Robert Hamilton (1826–1905) who was born on 28 June 1826. He took his BA degree from Trinity College, Dublin, in 1848, and in 1849 he was ordained a deacon in the Church of Ireland. In October 1850 he set off with his father and mother on the Grand Tour of Europe. Thomas kept his first diary during this tour, and it was reproduced by Warnie Lewis in LP I: 5–30. Because of ill health he undertook a voyage to India between 9 November 1852 and 6 April 1853 (this diary is reproduced in LP I: 32–64). He was ordained a priest in 1853 and during the years 1854–70 he was a chaplain in the Royal Navy, serving with the Baltic squadron of the fleet throughout the Crimean War. Mr Hamilton kept a very detailed diary during much of his period as a chaplain. It covers the periods 21 January to 20 December 1854; 19 February to 10 December 1855; 20 January to 26 June 1856; and about a month between 28 May and the end of June 1868, and it is all reproduced in LP I: 66–207.

In 1859 Thomas married Mary Warren[4] (1826–1916), who was the fifth child and second daughter of Sir John Borlase Warren (1800–63). Mary's sister, Charlotte Warren, married Robert Heard, and their daughter, Mary, married Sir William Ewart (see The Ewart Family*). Thomas and Mary Hamilton had four children: (1) Lilian Hamilton (1860–1934) who married William Suffern (d. 1913) but who never had any children. She was very fond of her nephew, Clive, and there are a number of references to her in *All My Road Before Me*.[5] (2) Florence Augusta 'Flora' Hamilton (1862–1908)* who married Albert James Lewis.* (3) Hugh Cecil Waldegrave Hamilton (1864–1900) was born on 17 November 1864. After an unsuccessful attempt to obtain a regular commission in the Royal Artillery, he emigrated to Australia where he became a sheep farmer in Queensland. He became a captain in the Queensland Artillery and saw active service in the South African war. He died on 12 July 1900, and is buried at Marandellas, South Africa. Finally, there is (4) Augustus Warren Hamilton (1866–1945) who was Albert Lewis's best friend. He was found to have an extraordinary genius for mathematics, but unfortunately his mother would not allow him to go to the university. So after leaving school he went to sea, but returned to Belfast and founded the firm of Hamilton & McMaster, marine boiler makers and engineers. In 1897 he married Anne Sargent Harley (1866–1930). They had four children,

4 It is from this grandmother that Warren Hamilton Lewis takes his name.
5 See the letter to Mrs Lilian Suffern dated [November? 1926].

Molly (d. 1904); Ruth (b. 1900) who married Desmond Parker; Harley; and John Borlase Hamilton (b. 1905).

HARWOOD, Alfred Cecil (1898–1975) was born on 5 January 1898 in Eckington, Derbyshire, where his father, the Rev. William Hardy Harwood, was a Nonconformist minister. He was educated at Highgate School, London, and it was there he met Owen Barfield* in 1910. On leaving school Harwood joined the Royal Warwickshires and served with the infantry as a 2nd lieutenant. He saw some active service in France. He went up to Christ Church, Oxford in Hilary Term 1919, and Barfield followed him there shortly afterwards. Harwood met Lewis through Barfield and thus began a lifelong friendship.

After taking his BA in 1921 Harwood returned with Barfield to Oxford for postgraduate studies. They lived for a time in 'Bee Cottage' in Beckley, where Lewis was a frequent visitor. Their great mutual interest was poetry, and Lewis valued Harwood's criticism highly. Many of the poems Harwood wrote during these years, and which Lewis found 'original, quaint and catchy', are found in *The Voice of Cecil Harwood*, ed. Owen Barfield (1979). Another of their shared interests was the walking tour, and such was his enthusiasm for these that Lewis dubbed him 'Lord of the Walks'.

After leaving Oxford he had a temporary job with the British Empire Exhibition in London, after which he went into publishing. Writing about this period in his life in the Anthroposophical Society's *Supplement to Members' News Sheet* (Feb. 1976), Barfield said: 'He was at that time making a rather half-hearted attempt to turn himself into what used to be called a "young man about town," and even the Bloomsbury set were not wholly outside his orbit. I don't think the experiment could ever have succeeded. But there was another reason why it did not last long.'

The other 'reason' is related to his future wife. During his second year in Oxford, Harwood followed Owen Barfield into the English Folk Dance Society. In the summer of 1922 they joined an amateur concert party touring some Cornish towns and villages. A friend of the organizers, the Honourable Daphne Olivier, was invited and this was Harwood's first meeting with the woman he was to marry. Daphne Olivier was the daughter of Sydney Haldane Olivier (Lord Olivier), Governor of Jamaica from 1907 to 1913. She read the Medieval and Modern Languages Tripos at Newnham College, Cambridge, and after taking her BA in 1913, she became a teacher. In August 1922 she attended a conference on 'Spiritual Values in Education and Social Life' held at Manchester College, Oxford, and it was here that she first heard Rudolf Steiner lecture. She became a convinced and devoted follower, and went to hear him lecture on other occasions. It was during a conference at Ilkley that a group of teachers, including Daphne Olivier, expressed their desire to found a co-educational day school in England on the basis of Dr Steiner's educational principles and along the lines of the Waldorf school in Germany. Steiner approved the formation of a Founders' Committee, whose job it was to find a way of bringing about such a school.

It was through Daphne Olivier that Harwood heard of Anthroposophy. He accompanied Miss Olivier to the second International Summer School held at Torquay from 9 to 23 August 1924 where Rudolf Steiner gave a course of lectures. During this conference Steiner met with the four women who wanted to found a Steiner school in London, and recommended that they would do well to have some male assistance. Pointing to Harwood, he said, 'What about him?'

From that point Harwood was committed to Anthroposophy for the rest of his life, and he was to have a very large part to play in its dissemination in England. 'The New School', as it was called, was founded in January 1925 at 40 Leigham Court Road, Streatham, London, with Harwood and Miss Olivier as two of its original five teachers. On 14 August 1925 Harwood and Daphne married, and moved into a house at 51 Angles Road. Very little was known about Steiner in the country as a whole, and Harwood, who had a talent for lecturing, did much during the early years to spread the knowledge of Anthroposophy throughout the English-speaking world.

The Harwoods' first child, John (who had Lewis as his tutor at Magdalen College), was born 31 May 1926. They were to have four more children: Lois (b. 1929); Laurence (b. 1933) who was Lewis's godson; Mark (b. 1934); and Sylvia (b. 1937). Lewis was often a visitor to their house, and in 1947 he dedicated *Miracles* to Cecil and Daphne. One of the highlights of Lewis's life was the annual walking tour with Harwood and Barfield. The best known of his tributes to Harwood is found in *SBJ* XIII:

> *Closely linked with Barfield of Wadham was his friend (and soon mine) A.C. Harwood of The House, later a pillar of Michael Hall, the Steinerite school at Kidbrooke. He was different from either of us; a wholly imperturbable man. Though poor (like most of us) and wholly without 'prospects', he wore the expression of a nineteenth-century gentleman with something in the funds. On a walking tour when the last light of a wet evening had just revealed some ghastly error in*

> *map-reading (probably his own) and the best hope was 'five miles to Mudham (if we could find it) and we* might *get beds there', he still wore that expression. In the heat of argument he wore it still. You would think that he, if anyone, would have been told to 'take that look off his face'. But I don't believe he ever was. It was no mask and came from no stupidity. He has been tried since by all the usual sorrows and anxieties. He is the sole Horatio known to me in this age of Hamlets; no 'stop for Fortune's finger.'*[6]

Harwood was grieved when his beloved Daphne died in 1950. He nevertheless continued his teaching, lecturing and writing. On 1 November 1954 he married Marguerite Lundgren, the founder of the London School of Eurythmy. After his retirement Harwood remained in Forest Row, Sussex. Even during his last years, when he was afflicted with diabetes, he did not lose that remarkable imperturbability Lewis admired so much. He died on 22 December 1975. Many of his poems, stories and essays are collected in *The Voice of Cecil Harwood.* His other works include *The Way of a Child, an Introduction to the Work of Rudolf Steiner for Children* (1940), *The Recovery of Man in Childhood* (1958), and *Shakespeare's Prophetic Mind* (1964).

JENKIN, Alfred Kenneth Hamilton (1900–80), friend from undergraduate days. He was born on 29 October 1900 at 378 Green Lane, Redruth, Cornwall, the son of Alfred Hamilton Jenkin and Amy Louisa (Keep) Jenkin. His family had lived in Redruth since the 18th century. Jenkin matriculated at University College, Oxford, in 1919 where he began reading English. This was to be an unhappy year for him. While out on a bicycle ride with his father, the latter suffered a heart attack, and Kenneth had to leave him dying at the roadside while he sought help. He nevertheless took his BA in 1922, and then stayed on to write a thesis for a B.Litt. on Richard Carew.

Lewis and Jenkin met soon after each arrived at University College in 1919. Both were members of the Martlets Society, a literary society of University College, and Lewis's diary (*AMR*) is filled with details of their walks, their bicycle rides and their talk. Jenkin became a frequent visitor at the house Lewis shared with Mrs Moore, and in his diary of 25 June 1922, Lewis observed that he and Mrs Moore 'were amused to notice again how in his conversation all roads lead to Cornwall'.

---

6 Shakespeare, *Hamlet*, III, ii, 75–6: 'They are not a pipe for fortune's finger / To sound what stop she please.'

There was no keeping Jenkin from his native county. After leaving Oxford and returning to Cornwall, where he lived at St Ives, he worked as a journalist and broadcaster. Then came his many books. His first major work was *The Cornish Miner: An account of his life above and underground from early times* (1927), the standard work on the subject and one which established him as a historian. This was followed in the next decade by *Cornish Seafarers* (1932), *Cornwall and the Cornish* (1933), *Cornish Homes and Customs* (1934), and *The Story of Cornwall* (1934). In the 1960s he brought out his vast 16-part series on *Mines and Miners of Cornwall* (1961–78), running to nearly a thousand pages and embodying the results of 16 years' research involving visits to some 2,000 Cornish mines.

Lewis met Jenkin infrequently after Cornwall had reclaimed him, but he remained indebted to Jenkin for teaching him to enjoy 'the very quiddity of each thing'. 'The first lifelong friend I made at Oxford,' Lewis wrote in *SBJ* XIII, 'was A.K. Hamilton Jenkin, since known for his books on Cornwall':

> *He continued (what Arthur [Greeves*] had begun) my education as a seeing, listening, smelling, receptive creature. Arthur had had his preference for the Homely. But Jenkin seemed to be able to enjoy everything; even ugliness. I learned from him that we should attempt a total surrender to whatever atmosphere was offering itself at the moment; in a squalid town to seek out those very places where its squalor rose to grimness and almost grandeur, on a dismal day to find the most dismal and dripping wood, on a windy day to seek the windiest ridge. There was no Betjemannic irony about it; only a serious, yet gleeful, determination to rub one's nose in the very quiddity of each thing, to rejoice in its being (so magnificently) what it was.*

In 1926 Jenkin married Luned Jacobs, the daughter of the novelist W.W. Jacobs. They had two daughters, Jennifer Hamilton Heseltine (b. 1929) and Honor Bronwen Goldsmid (b. 1930). The marriage was dissolved about 1934. During the Second World War Jenkin met Elizabeth Lenton (née Le Sueur) at Mullion Cove Hotel, where she was managing director. They married in 1948, and together managed the Poldu Hotel, Mullion, whilst Jenkin also continued his research into *News from Cornwall* (1951). In 1954 they went to live in the family home in Redruth, 'Trewirgie House', where his family had been since 1770. One of the early occupants of this house had been his great-great-grandfather, William Jenkin, who became in later life steward to the Lanhydrock family estates. Elizabeth died in 1977.

Jenkin assisted in the formation of Old Cornwall societies, and he was elected President of the Federation of Old Cornwall Societies in 1959–60. In 1962 he became the Federation's first Life Vice-President. At the Gorsedd of Cornwall in 1978 he was presented with a medal, most appropriately struck in tin, which commemorated the fact that he was one of only two living Bards who had been initiated by Henry Jenner at the first Gorsedd in 1928. He took the bardic name of Lef Stenoryon – 'Voice of the Tinners'. That same year he was awarded a D.Litt. by Exeter University.

Jenkin was largely responsible for setting up the Cornwall County Record Office in Truro, one of the finest in the country. When he died on 20 August 1980 he left his printed books and pamphlets to the Redruth public library and his historical notes, documents, photos, maps and MSS to the County Record Office in Truro.

KIRKPATRICK, William Thompson 'The Great Knock' (1848–1921), was headmaster of Lurgan College, County Armagh, Northern Ireland, 1876–99. Albert Lewis* had been his pupil at Lurgan between 1877 and 1879, and W. H. Lewis* and C. S. Lewis were tutored by him. Chapter IX of *SBJ* is devoted to this extraordinary man, and he is the model for MacPhee in *The Dark Tower* and *That Hideous Strength*. He was born in the little townland of Carrickmaddyroe, Boardmills, Co. Down, on 10 January 1848, the second child of James Kirkpatrick and his wife Sarah Thompson. He was baptized in Boardmills' First Presbyterian Church on 24 February 1848. His sister, Anne Mussen Kirkpatrick, was born on 8 December 1845. Carrickmaddyroe is located approximately 20 miles south of Belfast, between Carryduff and Dromara. William Thompson Kirkpatrick was named after his grandfather, William Kirkpatrick (1766–1848) who is buried with his wife Mary Blackley (1766–1849) in Boardmills First Presbyterian Graveyard.

The family was living at 21 Eliza Street, Belfast, when Kirkpatrick matriculated at the Royal Belfast Academical Institute, a liberal Presbyterian boys' school, in 1862. From there he went to Queen's College, Belfast (now Queen's University) where he graduated in July 1868 with first class honours in English, History and Metaphysics. He wrote the English Prize essay under the nom-de-plume 'Tamberlaine'. That same year he was awarded a Double Gold Medal by the Royal University of Ireland. He took his MA from Queen's College in 1870.

Kirkpatrick became assistant master in the English department of the Royal Belfast Academical Institution in 1868, and he remained there for eight years. The same year, 1868, Kirkpatrick entered the Assembly's College (the Presbyterian seminary in Belfast) and spent the normal three years in theological studies for ordination in the Irish Presbyterian Church. He took classes in Christian Ethics, Oriental Languages, Biblical Criticism, Ecclesiastical History and Rhetoric. Mr Kirkpatrick became a licentiate – i.e. he fulfilled the Church's academic and other demands for ordinands. But he was never ordained and appears in the records of the General Assembly as a licentiate under the care of the Belfast Presbytery for ten years from 1871 to 1880.

Mr Kirkpatrick excelled as a teacher. The Lewises were not the only ones to be impressed by him. Robert Millar Jones, who was Mr Kirkpatrick's student from 1876–9, wrote:

> *No boy and no man could be in his company for even a very short time without being impressed by the fact that he was in the presence of a man of unusual mental power and grasp, of an overmastering influence on the mind, and of an intellectual honesty and vigour before which pretence and make-believe were dissipated like smoke before a strong wind. None who knew him could be surprised that it was he who subsequently made Lurgan College for many years one of the most remarkable and successful schools in Ireland. He became an almost incomparable teacher, and under him the boys swept on to victory over their work and to mastery of their subjects and of themselves. His pistol never missed fire; but he gave you the impression that, if it did, as Goldsmith said of Johnson, you would be knocked down by the butt-end.*[7]

In 1876 Kirkpatrick became headmaster of Lurgan College, Co. Armagh, where he remained until his retirement in 1899. Lurgan College was founded in 1873 on the endowment of Samuel Watts who had extensive interests in brewing and tobacco. When he died in 1850 he left almost £10,000 to endow an 'English, Classical and Agricultural School of boys' in Lurgan. Watts's will is remarkable in that it laid down that no clergyman, or person in holy orders, could have any part in the teaching or the management of the school. Besides this, it prohibited any religious

7 Quoted in Robert M. Jones, *Royal Belfast Academical Institution: Centenary Volume 1810–1910* (Belfast, 1913), pp. 122–3.

instruction during the hours normally laid down for school lessons. These provisions have always been seen as controversial. It is suggested, however, that it was Watts's intention to establish a school for older boys that would be on the same foundation as those National Schools envisaged by the Government in the 1830s, and which combined secular and separate religious instruction. Mr Kirkpatrick had applied for the position as headmaster of Lurgan College in 1873, but the position was given to Edward Vaughan Boulger. When Boulger left Lurgan in December 1875, Mr Kirkpatrick succeeded him. Whatever Mr Kirkpatrick's beliefs were by this time, and he seems to have become an agnostic, this second time he applied he took pains to prove that he was *not* 'in holy orders'. Believer or not, Mr Kirkpatrick insisted that religious instruction be given to the boarders at Lurgan College, and he attended the local Presbyterian church every Sunday with the Presbyterian boarders. Mr Kirkpatrick had brought his sister Anne with him to Lurgan and she helped with the management of the boarders.

Mr Kirkpatrick was a very successful headmaster of Lurgan College. There were 16 pupils when he arrived in 1876, and when Albert Lewis was there he would have witnessed a considerable expansion because in only four years Mr Kirkpatrick had built it up to over 60. Besides expanding the college, high academic records also marked Mr Kirkpatrick's tenure of office. By the late 1880s Lurgan College was one of the top schools in Ireland.

On 15 July 1881 Mr Kirkpatrick married Louisa Ashmore Smyth of 81 Pembroke Road, Dublin, in St Bartholomew's Church, Dublin. Louisa was the daughter of George Smyth, a stockbroker. Two days earlier, on 13 July, Anne Kirkpatrick had married a former assistant at Lurgan, Alexander Stewart Mitchell, in St Anne's Church, Belfast. W.T. Kirkpatrick's only child, George Louis, was born on 23 May 1882 and educated at Charterhouse from 1896 to 1899.

Lewis said of Mr Kirkpatrick in *SBJ* IX: 'He had been a Presbyterian and was now an Atheist...I hasten to add that he was a "Rationalist" of the old, high and dry nineteenth-century type. For Atheism has come down in the world since those days, and mixed itself with politics and learned to dabble in dirt.' As a licentiate of the Presbyterian Church, who preached on a number of occasions, Mr Kirkpatrick almost certainly entertained the ambition of becoming a minister. What led to his loss of faith? The Royal Belfast Academical Institution was a haven of liberalism when he was there, and it may be that caught, as it were, between the liberalism of the Institution and the dogmatism of the Presbyterian Church as a whole, he lost his faith.

Following his retirement in 1899 Mr and Mrs Kirkpatrick went to live in 'Sharston House', Northenden, so they could be near their son Louis who was articled to the electrical engineers Browett, Lindley & Co., Engine Makers of Patricroft, Manchester. Later, while Louis was in Berlin gaining experience with electric tramways, the Kirkpatricks moved to 'Gastons', Great Bookham, Surrey, where Mr Kirkpatrick took private pupils and where they spent the rest of their lives.

Albert Lewis had been acting as Mr Kirkpatrick's solicitor since he qualified, and it was natural that he ask him to tutor Warnie and Jack. This turned out to be yet another great success for Mr Kirkpatrick because, not only did he like them very much, but they benefited greatly from being taught by him. A few weeks after Jack arrived at Bookham, Mr Kirkpatrick wrote to Albert on 2 October 1914 saying:

> *First, I should say, he has the literary temperament in a very marked degree. I look upon this as in the main an inherited quality, and I am the more convinced of this view from the very obvious fact of his physical resemblance to you. When I first saw him at the station I had no hesitation in addressing him. It was as though I was looking at yourself once more in the old days at Lurgan. He has also your good temper and vivacity. These are valuable qualities, and they mean much, both intellectually and morally.* (LP IV: 223)

A little later (25 November 1914) he said:

> *Clive is altogether an exceptional boy. The maturity of his literary judgements is remarkable, he follows his own instinct and is not to be imposed upon by the mere weight of authority. In literary power he is outside the range of ordinary schoolboys altogether, and it would be unfair to herd him with 'Narrow foreheads vacant of his glorious gains'.* (LP IV: 250).

Mr Kirkpatrick had imagined that his best years were behind him when he retired from Lurgan. From another point of view, and in terms of all the good that came from it, one could say his best years began in 1913 with the arrival of Warnie, and then Jack. Besides learning from this wonderful old man, the whole family loved him dearly, and they were grieved when they learned of his death on 22 March 1921.

Mrs Kirkpatrick lived until 1933. Louis, who was married but had no children, was general manager of Bruce Peebles & Co. (Engineers) in

Edinburgh from 1932 until his death in 1943. On Mr Kirkpatrick's years at Lurgan College, see 'A History of Lurgan College, Part II – Consolidation 1876–1899' by J.I. Wilson in *Ulula* (*Lurgan College School Magazine*) (1977), pp. 67–74.

LEWIS, Albert James (1863–1929), father of C. S. Lewis and W. H. Lewis*, was born on 23 August 1863 in Cork. He was one of six children born to Richard Lewis (see The Lewis Family*) and his wife Martha Gee who had emigrated to Ireland from Wales. In 1868 the family moved to Belfast, where his father became a partner in MacIlwaine and Lewis, Boiler Makers, Engineers, and Iron Ship Builders.

Albert attended the District Model National School, after which he spent the years 1877 to 1879 at Lurgan College, in Lurgan, County Armagh. The headmaster was W.T. Kirkpatrick,* who was to become a lifelong friend. On 9 August 1880 Albert was articled to the law firm of Maclean, Boyle and Maclean in Dublin. His first love was always the law, but he was devoted as well to English literature and the liturgy of the Church of Ireland. In 1881 he was elected a member of the Belmont Literary Society.

After qualifying as a solicitor on 10 June 1885 he set up a practice of his own at 83 Royal Avenue, Belfast. Over the years he held a number of important legal appointments in connection with various companies and public bodies, the most important of which was the position of police court prosecuting solicitor for the Belfast Corporation. He was as well solicitor for the Belfast City Council, the Belfast and County Down Railway, the Belfast Harbour Commissioners, the Post Office, the Ministry of Labour, and the National Society for Prevention of Cruelty to Children. Albert was a political speaker of considerable importance for the Conservative Party.

The battle which seemed hardest for him was that of winning the love of Florence Augusta 'Flora' Hamilton,* daughter of the Rev. Thomas Robert Hamilton (1826–1905), rector of his parish church. The Lewis family had been parishioners of St Mark's, Dundela, since Thomas Hamilton arrived there and assisted with its founding in 1874. Albert tried to get to know Flora in 1885, but she was cool towards him. He nevertheless persisted and proposed in September 1886. She replied that she 'had nothing but friendship to give' (LP II: 152). Albert turned to corresponding about literary subjects, and in the end they became engaged in 1893 and were married in St Mark's on 29 August 1894.

It was an exceptionally happy marriage, Flora's cheerful and tranquil affection being exactly the right complement to Albert's sentimental, passionate and rhetorical nature. Their first home was one of two semi-detached houses named Dundela Villas, now covered by Dundela Flats, 47 Dundela Avenue, Belfast. Their first son, Warren Hamilton 'Warnie' Lewis* was born at Dundela Villas in 1895, and Clive Staples 'Jack' Lewis on 29 November 1898. As he became more prosperous Albert had a new house built for his family, 'Little Lea', 76 Circular Road, where they moved in 1905. Theirs was a very happy home until the winter of 1907–8 when Flora was discovered to have cancer. Albert never recovered from her death on 23 August 1908.

With the loss of their mother, Warnie and Jack felt smothered by Albert's love, and Little Lea was never a very happy home to them thereafter. Albert nevertheless did the best he knew, and he never stopped trying. Not having Flora to protect him from excess, he spent most of his time in his law office. When he did relax it was usually with Flora's brother, Augustus ('Gussie'), who was his best friend. He read widely and he was three times churchwarden at St Mark's as well as the church's legal adviser.

In his portrait of his father, Warnie said:

> *He preserved throughout his life a high and scrupulous standard of honour. I have heard his managing clerk relate that not once, but many times, he has seen Albert throw open the door of the inner office and hustle out a would be client with the words, 'In fact, you want to make use of my legal knowledge to help you to commit a swindle! Get out of this!' And I speak from personal knowledge of the man when I say that the latter sentence, delivered with all the force of his formidable personality, had the effect of a kick from a heavy boot...In appearance he was of middle height, well built, and of a commanding presence: his hair, which was black and naturally lustrous, he wore parted at the side: a fine forehead and heavy brows covered a pair of penetrating dark brown eyes: the mouth was concealed by a strong moustache; the chin was firm. In his whole bearing there was an air of authority, heightened by the timbre of his voice, which was strong and resonant. Both women and men considered him good looking. As the years mellowed him, his appearance was improved by the elimination of a sullen, almost sulky air which he had in middle life. He was proud of his appearance, and as sensitive on the score of his age, which he would never disclose, as any fading spinster. Amongst his idiosyncrasies was an almost childish resentment of bodily pain: a corn loomed larger in his horizon than bankruptcy, and a headache was a*

family disaster: but when the end came, he died bravely and without murmuring. (LP II: 66–7)

Albert was not a wealthy man, but he nevertheless provided for all his younger son's undergraduate years at Oxford and until he had a job of his own. His interest in his parish church never flagged, but his greatest natural consolation came from his work as a solicitor. He continued at his practice until his death on 25 September 1929.

There is a short contemporary biography (and photograph) of him in Robert M. Young's *Belfast and the Province of Ulster in the 20th Century* (Brighton, 1909), p. 520. His vast correspondence with his sons and Mr Kirkpatrick is found in the Lewis Papers. Over the years Lewis and Warren preserved 100 of their father's dicta which they copied into a notebook entitled 'Pudaita Pie' after Albert's 'low' Irish pronunciation of 'potato'. Many of the sayings later went into *Surprised by Joy*. The manuscript of 'Pudaita Pie' is in Wheaton College. A photograph of the portrait of Albert painted by A.R. Baker in 1917 is found in Walter Hooper's 'The Lewis That Stayed Behind', in the *Magdalen College Record* (1995). A longer biography is found in *CG*.

LEWIS, Florence Augusta 'Flora' (1862–1908), mother of Warren Hamilton Lewis* and C. S. Lewis, was one of two daughters and two sons born to the Rev. Thomas Robert Hamilton and Mary Warren Hamilton. At the time of her birth on 18 May 1862 in Queenstown, County Cork, her father was a chaplain with the Royal Navy. During 1870 to 1874 the family lived in Rome where Thomas Hamilton was chaplain of Holy Trinity Church.

From Rome the Hamiltons moved to Belfast where Flora's father was rector of St Mark's, Dundela, from 1874 until 1900. Flora attended classes at the Methodist College, Belfast, in the sessions 1881–2, 1883–4 and 1884–5. At the same time that she was going to the Methodist College she was attending Queen's University, Belfast (then the Royal University of Ireland), where she performed brilliantly. She took a first degree in 1880, and in her second examinations in 1881 she passed with first class honours in Geometry and Algebra. In 1885 she passed the second university examination with first class honours in Logic and second class honours in Mathematics, and took a BA in 1886.

Flora had known Albert Lewis* and his family since the Hamiltons arrived in Belfast, but it was years before anything approaching intimacy came about. Albert may have thought it best to save serious matters until he had qualified as a solicitor in 1885. When he proposed to her in 1886 she had already turned down his brother, William, and he seems to have understood this as increasing his own chance. However, in her reply of 21 September 1886 Flora said 'I always thought you knew that I had nothing but friendship to give you' (LP II: 152). She really did want Albert as a friend, and, indeed, seemed to value all friendships highly.

Their first shared interest was literature. Flora had a story, 'The Princess Rosetta', published in *The Household Journal* of London. Albert said at once that he hoped that 'to the collegiate honours' Strandtown had already gained through Flora, 'will be added the higher distinction of producing a great novelist'. Flora presented him with the manuscript of the story, but for whatever reason it has not survived, and no copies of *The Household Journal* containing Flora's story, nor any of the other stories she wrote, can be traced. Flora and Albert exchanged many letters, but only Flora's have survived.

What has, however, survived in the Lewis Papers is a burlesque sermon she wrote sometime before she was married. Her father had a curate, Mr Palmer, in 1892, and this cheerful piece may be a parody of his style of preaching – or that of her father! Flora's 'Modern Sermon' as she called it, begins:

> *Brethren, the words of the text are:*
>
> *'Old Mother Hubbard, she went to the cupboard*
> *To get her poor dog a bone.*
> *But when she got there, the cupboard was bare,*
> *And so the poor dog got none.'*
>
> *Mother Hubbard, you see, was old; there being no mention of others, we may presume she was lone, a widow – a friendless, old, solitary widow. Yet did she despair? Did she sit down and weep, or read a novel, or wring her hands? No. She went to the cupboard, and here observe, she WENT to the cupboard, she did not hop or skip or run or jump, or use any other peripatetic artifice; she solely and merely WENT to the cupboard.*
>
> *We have seen that she was old and lonely, and we now see that she was poor. For, mark, the words, THE cupboard; not 'one of the cupboards', or the 'right hand cupboard' or the 'left hand cupboard' or the one above or the one below, but just THE cupboard. The one humble little cupboard the poor widow possessed. And why did she go to the*

> *cupboard? Was it to bring forth golden goblets or glittering precious stones, or costly apparel, or feast on any other attributes of wealth? IT WAS TO GET HER POOR DOG A BONE. Not only was the widow poor, but the dog, the sole prop of her age, was poor too. We can imagine the scene. The poor dog, crouching in the corner, looking wistfully at the solitary cupboard, and the widow going to the cupboard in hope, in expectation...* (LP II: 213)

Comparing the Lewises and the Hamiltons, C. S. Lewis described his father's people as 'sentimental, passionate, and rhetorical', while the Hamiltons were 'cooler', with minds 'critical and ironic' (*SBJ* I). The 30 letters Flora wrote to Albert before they were married and the 48 she wrote afterwards (preserved in the Lewis Papers) provide evidence of this. They supply as well a clue as to where Lewis got his own clarity of thought. 'I am not quite sure that I would like it if you *only* talk to me on "sensible subjects",' Flora wrote to Albert on 5 July 1893:

> *Why should it bore me to hear about your love for me? You know it does not. I like you to love me, and if your love bored me, your society would, still more, so there would be no use in your talking to me on any subject at all...Gussie [her brother] is right about our not being a demonstrative family. I don't think we are, but do you know I really think it is better than being too demonstrative; men soon get tired of that sort of thing.* (LP II: 251–2)

Albert and Flora became engaged in June 1893, and were married in St Mark's on 29 August 1894. Following a honeymoon in North Wales, they moved into Dundela Villas, Dundela, Belfast. Warren Hamilton 'Warnie' Lewis* was born in 1895 and named after the two sides of Flora's family; Clive Staples 'Jack' Lewis was born in 1898. Because Albert loathed going on holiday, the responsibility of taking the boys on holidays thus fell on Flora, and Warnie and Jack often recalled what happy occasions these holidays were. But Albert was not forgotten. No matter how short the distance from home, Flora wrote to him daily. In the holiday at Castlerock in 1901 she learned that he was fussing over life insurance. 'I wish I could make you feel more satisfied about things of this sort,' she wrote, 'but I am afraid it is your nature to take a gloomy view of life' (LP II: 316).

In 1905 the family moved into 'Little Lea' on the outskirts of Belfast, which Albert had specially built for Flora. Warnie went to Wynyard School in England soon afterwards, while Jack's education began at home, with Flora teaching him French and Latin, and Annie Harper, his governess, teaching him everything else. Flora's last holiday with the boys was in Berneval in the summer of 1907. In the little diary Jack wrote the following Christmas – 'My life During the Exmas Holadys of 1907' – we glimpse the contentment of the happy Lewis family. He described his father as 'very sensible' and 'nice when not in a temper' while his mother is 'like most middle-aged ladys, stout, brown hair, spectaciles, kniting her chief industry'. As Christmas draws near we learn how Warnie comes home from school, of the various Lewis and Hamilton relations who drop in, how 'Mamy stoned raisins for the Xmas pudding', of how Jack and Warnie take to 'rushing about the house' and of the play which Jack is writing to perform for the family on Christmas Day. The diary ends: 'The old year out and the new year in' (LP III: 88–92).

Not long afterwards Flora became ill. On 7 February 1908 she was operated on at home. The doctor found cancer. She rallied for a while, but a few months later she had another operation. The trouble had returned, and Flora was confined to bed. Her faithful husband attended her with touching devotion, rarely leaving her bedside. She died on 23 August 1908, deeply lamented by a devoted family. For a longer biography see *CG*.

LEWIS, Warren Hamilton ('Warnie') (1895–1973): brother of C. S. Lewis. He was born at Dundela Villas, Dundela, Belfast on 16 June 1895, the son of Albert James Lewis* and Florence Hamilton Lewis*. The family was still in Dundela Villas when his brother, Clive Staples 'Jack', was born in 1898. They were to be the best of friends all their lives. The family had only just moved to Little Lea when in May 1905 he was sent to Wynyard School in Watford, Hertfordshire, where he passed four miserable years. His recollections of the school and Robert Capron*, the headmaster, are found in LP III: 33–42.

Warnie entered Malvern College at Malvern, Worcestershire, in September 1909 and here he was very happy. He was made a prefect in May 1913 when he also began considering a career in the Army Service Corps (ASC). He left Malvern in July 1913 and on 10 September 1913 he presented himself to Albert Lewis's old headmaster, W.T. Kirkpatrick* in Great Bookham, Surrey, to be prepared for the Sandhurst entrance examination. It was a very successful move. Reflecting on his time with Mr Kirkpatrick afterwards, Warnie said:

> *When I went to Bookham I had what would now be called 'an inferiority complex,' partly the result of Wynyard, partly of my own idleness, and partly of the laissez faire methods of Malvern. A few weeks of Kirk's generous but sparing praise of my efforts, and of his pungent criticisms of the Malvern masters restored my long lost self confidence: I saw that whilst I was not brilliant or even clever, I had in the past been unsuccessful because I was lazy, and not lazy because I was unsuccessful.* (LP IV: 62)

In 1914 Warnie won a Price Cadetship to Sandhurst after being placed 21st out of 201 successful candidates.

Due to wartime needs his officer's training was accelerated to nine months instead of two years, and on 4 November 1914 he went to France with the 4th Company 7th Divisional Train, British Expeditionary Force. During the First World War he was an officer with the Army Service Corps, and he served in France. It was there he met his first love – the *Grand Siècle*, the splendid century dominated by Louis XIV. 'One day in 1919 in St Omer,' he said, 'I saw in a shop window an abridgement of St Simon's Memoirs, bought it as a change from French novels, and became a life-addict to the period.' Following the Armistice in 1919 he was reassigned to service in England. On 9 March 1921 he left to serve in Sierra Leone, West Africa, where he remained for over a year, arriving home on 7 April 1922. After six months' leave he reported to his new assignment in Colchester. On 11 April 1927 he sailed for China where he was in command of the supply depot at Shanghai for much of the time he was there. He learned of his father's death in October 1929.

On 4 March 1930 when he was standing before the Great Buddha of Kamakura he became convinced of the truth of Christianity. He said in his diary of 13 May 1931: 'I started to say my prayers again after having discontinued doing so for more years than I care to remember: this was no sudden impulse but the result of a conviction of the truth of Christianity which has been growing on me for a considerable time...I intend to go to Communion once again...The wheel has now made the full revolution – indifference, scepticism, atheism, agnosticism, and back again to Christianity' (*BF*, pp. 79–80). He returned home in April 1930 and was assigned to Bulford. During Christmas 1931 at The Kilns he began the mammoth task of editing the Lewis Papers. On 9 October 1931 he left for his second tour of duty in China, and was in Shanghai when the Japanese attacked on 29 January 1932.

He returned home on 14 December 1932, retired from the ASC, and moved into The Kilns with his brother. During 1933 to 1935 he completed his editing of the Lewis Papers, 11 volumes of family papers. On 4 September 1939 he was recalled to active service and was sent to Le Havre. Following his evacuation in May 1940 he was transferred to the Reserve of Officers and sent to Oxford where he served as a private soldier with the 6th Oxford City Home Guard Battalion.

In 1943 he began acting as his brother's secretary, typing many letters for him. He became as well an active member of the Inklings. Warnie was a remarkable diarist, and that portion of it which has been published as *Brothers and Friends* (1982) is a chief source of information about the Inklings. He later regretted that he did not write more about his brother. 'Oh if only I could have known in time that he was to die first,' he wrote on 8 April 1966, 'how I would have Boswellised him!' (*BF*, p. 256). He inspired love in nearly everyone who knew him. John Wain, describing his presence at the Inklings' meetings, said of him in *Sprightly Running: Part of an Autobiography* (1962), ch. V:

> *There was no fixed etiquette, but the rudimentary honours would be done partly by Lewis and partly by his brother, W.H. Lewis, a man who stays in my memory as the most courteous I have ever met – not with mere politeness, but with a genial, self-forgetful considerateness that was as instinctive to him as breathing.*

Over the years he published: *The Splendid Century: Some Aspects of French Life in the Reign of Louis XIV* (1953); *The Sunset of the Splendid Century: The Life and Times of Louis Auguste de Bourbon, Duc de Maine, 1670–1736* (1955); *Assault on Olympus: The Rise of the House of Gramont between 1604 and 1678* (1958); *Louis XIV: An Informal Portrait* (1959); *The Scandalous Regent: A Life of Philippe, Duc d'Orleans, 1674–1723* (1961), and *Levantine Adventurer: The Travels and Missions of the Chevalier d'Arvieux, 1653–1697* (1962). He also published an edition of the *Memoirs of the Duc de Saint-Simon* (1964). Like his brother, he preferred his enjoyment of places to come through books. When asked if he would like to visit Versailles he said 'Oh no! That would ruin it!'

He had a problem with drink that became serious in the 1940s. During a holiday in Ireland in June 1947 he collapsed and was hospitalized in Our Lady of Lourdes Hospital, Drogheda, run by the Medical Missionaries of Mary. With their help he struggled to overcome the problem. Although the reasons for his alcoholism were numerous and complex, one of them was his shyness. In their youth he had been gregarious and Jack something of a recluse. As time went on they seemed to exchange positions. While Jack's fame as a Christian apologist drove him to mingle with all sorts of people, most of whom he came to like, Warnie withdrew more and more into the company of books and fewer friends. With alcohol he regained, briefly, the gregariousness he had known as a young man.

He was devastated by his brother's death. For the first few years he retreated more and more to Ireland. Eventually Our Lady of Lourdes Hospital was unable to accommodate him, and this forced him to remain in Oxford. It was, however, during these lonely years that he edited the *Letters of C. S. Lewis* (1966), to which he attached a touching 'Memoir'. During the summer of 1972 he became seriously ill while on holiday in Drogheda. The Medical Missionaries of Mary took him in and nursed him for the next nine months. He left the hospital at the beginning of April 1973, and died at The Kilns on 9 April 1973. He is buried in the same grave as his brother at Holy Trinity Church, Headington Quarry.

The Lewis Family. C. S. Lewis's family can be traced back four generations to (A) Richard Lewis (c. 1775–1845), a farmer who lived in the small village of Caergwrle situated between the borders of Flint and Denbigh in Wales. Almost nothing is known of him except that he had six sons and one daughter. His fourth son, (B) Joseph Lewis (1803?–90) was also a farmer who moved first to Saltney, Cheshire, and later to Sandycroft, Flint. Although Joseph was brought up in the Church of England, this simple, pious, uneducated man did not feel he was given the prominence he deserved, and he seceded and became a Primitive Methodist minister. In about 1825 he married Jane Ellis and they had five sons and three daughters: Frances, Thomas, Mary, (C) Richard, Jane, John, Joseph, and Samuel.

It was Joseph's and Jane's second son, (C) Richard Lewis (1832–1908) who was the father of Albert James Lewis* and the grandfather of C. S. Lewis. In 1853 he married Martha Gee (1831–1903) of Liverpool. He and his brothers John and Joseph emigrated to Cork in Ireland where they were employed by the Cork Steamship Company. Richard was a master boiler maker, and there is evidence that he was part of the working-class intelligentsia in the forefront of that artisan renaissance which gave birth to the trades union and Co-operative movements. Richard returned to the Church of England, and those interested in tracing C. S. Lewis's theological and writing gifts may wish to look at the two theological essays he read to the Cork Steamship Company's Workmen's Library and Reading Room, an 'Essay on a Special Providence' and an 'Essay on Jonah's Mission to Ninevah', preserved in the Lewis Papers (LP I: 236–46). The Lewis Papers contain as well two papers delivered to the Library and Reading Room dated 18 January 1860 (LP I: 248–72), and an essay, 'Self Denial', which Richard Lewis read to the Cork Steamship Company's Workmen's Library and Reading Room on 15 October 1860 (LP I: 276–84). It was while he was working with the Cork Steamship Company that Richard's children were born.

In July 1864 Richard Lewis left the Cork Steamship Company and went to Dublin where he hoped to better himself as a boiler maker and iron ship builder. This does not seem to have benefited him, and in 1865 he moved to Belfast where he worked with the Abercorn Iron Works. On 1 January 1868 he and John H. MacIlwaine, a draughtsman in the Dublin shipyard, entered into a business which they called 'MacIlwaine and Lewis, Boiler Makers, Engineers, and Iron Ship Builders'. The family settled at 'Ty-isa' in Strandtown. John MacIlwaine was seduced into signing a contract which all but obliterated the firm of MacIlwaine and Lewis. The business was dissolved in August 1887, and Richard went to work for the Belfast Harbour Commission. Martha Lewis died on 19 January 1903, and on 1 April 1907 Richard moved to Little Lea to live with Albert and Flora. However, because of Flora Lewis's illness, he moved out, and he died on 2 April 1908.

The children of Richard and Martha Lewis were: (D) (1) Martha Lewis (1854–60) and (2) Sarah Jane 'Jeannie' Lewis (1856?–1901) who in 1883 married Thomas Heron Keown (1860–1935) and was for most of her life estranged from the rest of the family (see letter of 30 August 1929).

(3) Joseph Lewis (1856–1908) who settled in Belfast at 'Sandycroft', Bloomfield. He was a marine consulting engineer with an office at 19 Donegal Quay and whose work involved a good deal of travelling around the seaports of Great Britain. In his sketch of this uncle, Warnie Lewis said:

> *Though not an educated man, he had a natural shrewdness, and was an interested spectator of men and manners. In spite of, or perhaps on account of his peripatetic mode of life, he always struck me as being the most domesticated of the four brothers; he had married and founded a branch of his own before the middle classes had felt the first stirrings of that disruptive tendency which, coming to full maturity in*

our own times, has practically obliterated the collective family – the clan – as the unity of national life; this fact, coupled with a complete absence of any element of snobbery in his character, made him preeminently the champion of the family in the larger sense of the term...With his Celtic blood he inherited little of the national tendency to violent oscillation between the heights of optimism and the extremes of depression, which had been a marked feature of his father's character, and in consequence, lacking the spasmodic generosity of Albert, the irascibility and prodigality of Richard, and William's morose ostentation, he was the most balanced and most uniformly kindly of the four brothers. He was not without wit; he was not a well read man, though he greatly enjoyed the works of Dickens which formed his ordinary, and indeed his sole reading. His favourite recreations were gardening and the collection of pictures and china, on which he spent money lavishly, but unfortunately neither with knowledge or taste...In appearance he was below middle height, and sturdily built; had blue eyes which generally held a twinkle, and was the only one of the brothers to wear a beard. (LP II: 57–8)

In 1882 Joseph married Mary Tegart (b. 1868) and they had five children, Martha (b. 1884), May (b. 1887), Sarah Elizabeth, Richard (b. 1890), and Joseph Tegart (1898–1969).

(4) William Lewis 'Limpopo' (1859–1946), the second son of Richard Lewis, obtained a certificate from the National School in 1871. He served an apprenticeship of five years to James Moore the printer and stationer. He lost his job as secretary of the Belfast Ropeworks in 1882 and in 1883 he and his brother Richard went to Glasgow where they entered into a partnership called 'W. & R. Lewis, Rope and Twine Manufacturers'. In 1890 he married Wilhelmina Duncanson and they had three children, Norman (b. 1891), Claire (b. 1895) and William Desmond (b. 1897). In 1903 they moved into a new home, 'Moorgate' near Glasgow. In his sketch of him, Warnie said:

He was distinguished from the rest of the family by a nattiness in his dress, which he retained all his life...He was the least amiable of the brothers – the most easily depressed and the most rarely elated. He had less of the boisterous joviality, sometimes rising to wit, less of the inquisitive interest in the pageant of provincial life, than had the others. His mind was heavy, common place, and self centred. With him, sententiousness took the place of sentiment. Albert's children,

> *with the acuteness of childhood, bestowed on him the nick-name of 'Limpopo', and if the word be pronounced in three heavy, distinct syllables, it is itself a felicitous character sketch. Neither family tradition nor papers record of him a single witty saying or amusing tale...In person he was a small man, who became fat in later life. His eyes were deep sunk in fleshy cheeks. His hair, which was scanty, was brushed diagonally across his head in the manner which had come into fashion in the English Public Schools about 1912. He wore a small moustache. Even in old age, his appearance was noticeably soigné; in his tie, he often wore a pearl pin. He enjoyed the pleasures of the table, and, though not intemperate, was fond of the bottle. Albert was the brother who most nearly resembled him.* (LP II: 59)

(5) Richard Lewis (b. 1861), third son of Richard Lewis, obtained a Certificate of Merit from the National School in 1871. He began his working life as a traveller for the tea firm, Richard Twining & Co. of Belfast. On leaving this firm in 1882, he went with his brother William to Glasgow where in 1883 they became partners in the firm W. & R. Lewis, Rope and Twine Manufacturers. In 1890 he married Agnes Young and they had two children, Eileen (b. 1892) and Leonard (b. 1896). 'He was the most transparent of the brothers,' wrote Warnie,

> *at once the simplest and the most zestful. He shared their mercurial temperament, with the difference that in his case short lived irascibility was substituted for sulkiness. He possessed such a fund of animal spirits, such a gusto in observing and narrating the most homely incidents of life's comedy, such an infectious enjoyment of life that, though neither clever nor genuinely witty, there was something of a tonic effect about his company...He was the perfect 'man in the street', the ideal 'stroller'. To him a crowd was an unfailing lure, to know what 'the stir was about' an imperious necessity. It may safely be premised that the appeal on a blank hoarding, 'Watch this space', was never made to him in vain. He keenly enjoyed comic stories and jokes; the simpler the story, the more he enjoyed it...In his domestic life he was, I think, happy. Children loved him. At the annual family reunions which were held until his father's death, he was the axis round which young and old revolved...In appearance, he was of middle height, stoutly built, with large eyes, extraordinarily sensitive in expressing the mood of the moment: a curved sharp bridge nose surmounted a drooping moustache, which gave a faint but unmistakable suggestion of a seal.* (LP II: 60–1)

(6) Albert James Lewis* (1863–1929) who was the father of C. S. Lewis.

MOORE, Edward Francis Courtenay 'Paddy' (1898–1918), was born at 8 Windsor Terrace, Kingstown, County Dublin, Ireland on 17 November 1898, the son of Courtenay Edward Moore and Janie King (Askins) Moore.* When his parents separated, he moved with his mother and his sister Maureen (see Dunbar of Hempriggs, Dame Maureen*), to Bristol where his mother's brother, Dr Robert Askins, was a government medical officer. Paddy was a pupil at Clifton College, Bristol, from 1908 to 1917.

After joining the Officers' Training Corps, he was sent to Keble College, Oxford, for training. Wishing to be with him as long as they could, Mrs Moore and Maureen came to Oxford with him and found rooms in Wellington Square. On reporting to Keble College on 7 June 1917 Paddy found himself sharing a room with C. S. Lewis. They liked one another from the beginning, and Paddy soon introduced Lewis to his mother and sister. In a letter to his father of 10 June 1917 Lewis said, 'Moore of Clifton, my room companion, is a little too childish for real companionship, but I will forgive him much for his appreciation of Newbolt.'

As time went on he began writing about the whole Moore family to his father. 'Moore, my room mate, comes from Clifton and is a very decent sort of man,' he said on 18 June, 'His mother, an Irish lady,' mentioning her for the first time, 'is staying up here and I have met her once or twice.' On 27 August 1917 he wrote to his father about a week of manoeuvres in Warwick. 'The following week,' he said, 'I spent with Moore at the digs of his mother who, as I mentioned, is staying at Oxford. I like her very much and thoroughly enjoyed myself.' From Paddy's point of view, he too had found a friend he liked very much. Lewis invited Paddy to his room in University College (Staircase XII, Room 5). Two photographs of this period, probably taken with Paddy's camera, and reproduced in *All My Road Before Me* show Lewis and Paddy with other OTC cadets on bivouac, and punting on the Cherwell. When all is said, those months of preparing for France were very happy.

On 26 September 1917 they were commissioned 2nd lieutenants and given a month's leave. Rather than go directly home, Lewis went to the Moores' home at 56 Ravenswood Road, Redland, Bristol, where he spent the first three weeks of his leave. Besides his love of the poetry of Sir Henry Newbolt – like himself, an Old Cliftonian – Paddy loved Clifton College, and on Sunday 30 September he took Lewis to see it. It was during these weeks that the young men made a solemn promise to one another. So many officers were being killed at the front – most Oxford colleges lost a quarter of their members in the war – that it was natural for Jack and Paddy to want to make some provision against this. Maureen remembered them promise that if one survived the war he would look after Paddy's mother and Lewis's father.

Jack arrived home on 12 October. On 16 October he was gazetted into the Somerset Light Infantry, and he had to leave his father on 18 October to join his regiment at Crownhill, South Devon. Paddy, meanwhile, had been placed in the 5th Battalion of the Rifle Brigade and he crossed to France in October. Jack was on training in Devon when he wrote to his father on 5 November 1917 saying: 'I have really been very lucky in getting here...Paddy Moore, in the Rifle Brigade, seems to have got in with a most terrible lot of outsiders, so after all our separation was a blessing in disguise. He also seems to be much harder worked than I.'

Paddy, who had been transferred to the 2nd Battalion of the Rifle Brigade, took part in the great German attack which began in the early hours of the morning of 21 March 1918 when General Ludendorff launched the offensive that was intended to bring victory to the German forces on the Western Front. By the end of that day 21,000 British soldiers were taken prisoner, and whole villages had been destroyed. It became worse every minute, and on 24 March the Germans crossed the Somme. The May 1918 issue of *The Cliftonian*, the magazine of Clifton College, contains a letter from the adjutant of Paddy's battalion to Mrs Moore in which he said:

> *Your very gallant son was reported missing on the 24th of last month. He was last seen on the morning of that day with a few men defending a position on a river bank against infinitely superior numbers of the enemy. All the other officers and most of the men of his company have become casualties, and I fear it is impossible to obtain more definite information. He did really fine work on the previous night in beating off a party of Germans who had succeeded in rushing a bridgehead in our lines. We all feel his loss very deeply, and I cannot express too strongly our sympathy with you.*

It was extremely painful for Paddy's family because he was missing for over a month. Then they learned that he had died in battle at Pargny. 'Of all my own particular set at Keble he has been the first to go,' Lewis wrote to his father on 14 May 1918, 'and it is pathetic to remember that he at least was always certain that he would come through.'

William W. Seymour's *History of the Rifle Brigade in the War of 1914–1918*, vol. II (1936) gives a full account of the 2nd Battalion of the Rifle Brigade during the battle in which Paddy played an heroic part and was reported missing.

On 2 December 1918 Paddy was awarded the Military Cross for 'conspicuous gallantry and initiative'. In the *List of Officers and Other Ranks of The Rifle Brigade Awarded Decorations, or Mentioned in Despatches, for Services During the Great War*, compiled by T.R. Eastwood and H.G. Parkyn (1936), the citation (pp. 64–5) reads:

> *Moore, 2nd Lieut. E.F.C. (2nd Bn.) M.C. 2.12.18. For conspicuous gallantry and initiative. When a party of the enemy succeeded in rushing a bridgehead in the dark, their officer, whose company was in support, immediately led forward, under heavy machine-gun fire, a small party to get in touch with the enemy. He did so, and having killed two or three of them returned with information which led to the destruction of them all and the recapture of the bridge. He rendered excellent service.*

Paddy Moore's name is one of the 600 inscribed on the Memorial Gateway of Clifton College, and boys are urged to offer gratitude to these brave men as they pass through. It would have pleased Paddy to see over their names the following lines by Sir Henry Newbolt:

> *From the great Marshal to the last recruit,*
> *These, Clifton, were thy Self, thy Spirit in Deed,*
> *Thy flower of Chivalry, thy fallen fruit,*
> *And thine immortal seed.*

MOORE, Janie King 'Minto' (1872–1951) was born in Pomeroy, County Tyrone, Northern Ireland, on 28 March 1872. She was the eldest of three daughters and two sons of the Rev. William James Askins (1842–95) and Jane King Askins (1846–90) daughter of the Ven. Francis King. The family moved to Dunany, County Louth, Ireland, in 1872 when Mr Askins was Vicar of Dunany and Dunleer from 1872 to 1895. It was at Dunany that Janie grew up. Her brothers and sisters were: Edith 'Edie' Askins (1873–1936), John Hawkins Askins (1877–1923), William James Askins (1879–1955), Robert Askins (1880–1935), and Sarah Askins. Following the death of her mother in 1890 Janie, the eldest of the children, found herself with the task of bringing up the others. Her parents are buried at Dunleer.

On 1 August 1897 she married Courtenay Edward Moore (b. 26 June 1870). He, too, was from a clerical family, his father being Canon Courtenay Moore (1840–1922), rector of Michaelstown in County Cork. Courtenay Edward Moore had taken a BA from Trinity College, Dublin in 1893 and at the time of their marriage he was a civil engineer in Dublin. They had two children, Edward Francis Courtenay 'Paddy'* (b. 1898) and Maureen* (b. 1906). It was an unhappy marriage, and Janie left her husband and moved with the children to Bristol in 1907. Her brother, Robert Askins, a doctor, had his practice there and Paddy became a pupil at Clifton College. Mrs Moore and her husband were never divorced.

In the spring of 1917 Paddy joined the Officers' Training Corps, and in June of that year he was sent to Keble College, Oxford, for training. Mrs Moore and Maureen, wishing to be near him, moved to Oxford and took rooms in Wellington Square. It was probably during the second week of June 1917 that she and Lewis first met. 'I like her immensely,' Lewis wrote to his father on 27 August 1917. It was not long before Lewis came to prefer the company of the Moores to that of his father. After Lewis and Paddy were given a month's leave before embarking overseas, Lewis spent three weeks of it with the Moores at their home in Bristol, and only a week in Belfast with his father. It was during this visit to Bristol that Paddy and Lewis promised that if one or other were spared, the survivor would look after Paddy's mother and Lewis's father.

The young men did not see one another again. In October Paddy was sent to France with the Rifle Brigade, and Lewis followed him over in November with the Somerset Light Infantry. Paddy took part in the great German attack around Pargny which began on 21 March 1918. He fought gallantly and was reported missing on 24 March. His death was confirmed in April, and in December 1918 he was awarded the Military Cross. 'I just lived all my life for my son,' Mrs Moore wrote to Albert Lewis on 1 October 1918, 'and it is hard to go on now. I had built such hopes on my only son, and they are buried with so many others in that wretched Somme...Jack has been so good to me. My poor son asked him to look after me if he did not come back' (LP VI: 44–5).

Before going to France, Lewis had told Arthur Greeves* of his feelings for Mrs Moore, and he later said to him in the letter of 2 February 1918, 'There is room for other things besides love in a man's life.' After Lewis came back from the war and returned to Oxford in January 1919 Mrs Moore took a place there to be near him. From this time onwards they shared a house for the rest of her life. We learn much about their day-today life from Lewis's diary, *All My Road Before Me*, which covers the years 1922–7.

It is not improbable that there was a sexual element to the relationship between Lewis and Mrs Moore before he became a Christian. Be that as it may, what is absolutely certain is that Lewis spent the next 20 years devotedly caring for this ageing and ailing woman.

In her declining years Mrs Moore was often in much pain, and in April 1950 she went into a nursing home in Oxford. She died on 12 January 1951 and is buried in the churchyard of Holy Trinity Church, Headington Quarry. Mr Moore, with whom she was never reconciled, died in Dublin on 9 June 1951.

TOLKIEN, John Ronald Reuel CBE (1892–1973) was born in Bloemfontein, South Africa, to English parents on 3 January 1892. His father, Arthur Reuel Tolkien, who had married Mabel Suffield in 1891, was the manager of the Bank of Africa in Bloemfontein. His brother Hilary Arthur Reuel Tolkien was born on 17 February 1894. Because the intense heat was harming Ronald, Mrs Tolkien returned to England with the boys in 1895 and moved into 5 Gracewell, Sarehole, near Birmingham. Before they could rejoin him in South Africa, Arthur Tolkien died in 1896.

In 1900 Mabel Tolkien, despite family opposition, became a Roman Catholic and began to instruct her sons in the Catholic faith. That same year Ronald went to King Edward's School, Birmingham, where his love of languages blossomed. In 1902 the family moved to 26 Oliver Road, Edgbaston, so that Ronald and his brother could be educated by the priests of Birmingham Oratory at St Philip's School. However, after winning a scholarship, Ronald returned to King Edward's School in 1903.

After her long struggles, Mabel Tolkien died on 14 November 1904. The sacrifice she made to raise her children as Catholics was not lost on Ronald, who later wrote: 'My own mother was a martyr indeed, and it is not to everybody that God grants so easy a way to his great gifts as he did to Hilary and myself, giving us a mother who killed herself with labour and trouble to ensure us keeping the faith.' The boys went to live with their aunt, Beatrice Suffield, in Birmingham.

Tolkien came up to Exeter College, Oxford, in 1911 and read Honour Moderations. For his special subject he chose Comparative Philology and was taught by Joseph Wright. He then read English Language and Literature, taking a First in 1915. It was during these undergraduate years that he developed his interest in painting and drawing. Tolkien was a lieutenant with the Lancashire Fusiliers from 1915 to 1918 and took part in the

Battle of the Somme. While convalescing from an illness he began writing *The Silmarillion*, the myths and legends of what later became known as 'the First Age of the World'.

On 22 March 1916 he married Edith Mary Bratt (1889–1971) and they had four children: John (b. 16 November 1917), Michael (b. 22 October 1920), Christopher (b. 21 November 1924), and Priscilla (b. 18 June 1929). After demobilization from the army in November 1918 Tolkien moved to Oxford where he worked for a while on the Oxford Dictionary. He became a Reader in English Language at the University of Leeds in 1920, and Professor of English Language at Leeds in 1924. In 1925 he returned to Oxford as Rawlinson and Bosworth Professor of Anglo-Saxon. He was elected Merton Professor of English Language and Literature in 1945.

They may have seen one another before, but the first time he and Lewis spoke was at a faculty meeting on 11 May 1926 (*AMR*). The next year Tolkien enrolled Lewis in his Kolbítar or Coalbiters, a society he founded in 1926 for the purposes of reading the Icelandic sagas and myths in the original Old Icelandic or Old Norse. Soon they were meeting regularly, usually on Monday mornings, and this could be taken as the beginnings of The Inklings.

Lewis was converted to Christianity in 1931, and in a letter to Dom Bede Griffiths of 21 December 1941, he spoke of Hugo Dyson* and Tolkien as 'the immediate human carriers' of his conversion. The part these men played in this is explained in detail in the letter to Arthur Greeves* of 18 October 1931, the last letter in this book. Further light is shed on Lewis's conversion and Tolkien's understanding of myth by Tolkien's poem, *Mythopoeia*, found in his *Tree and Leaf*, ed. Christopher Tolkien, (2nd edition: 1988).

Although *The Silmarillion* was in draft form during the 1920s, Tolkien turned from it to *The Hobbit* (1937) which he began in about 1930 to amuse his children. The next work to emerge from the huge mythological world of *The Silmarillion* was *The Lord of the Rings* which he began in 1937. Much of what the Inklings called 'the new Hobbit' was read aloud to them while it was being written. This most famous of all Tolkien's works appeared in three volumes. The first, *The Fellowship of the Ring* came out in 1954, and the other two volumes, *The Two Towers* and *The Return of the King* in 1955. Few works of literature had ever meant so much to Lewis, and Tolkien often mentioned the help he received from Lewis's encouragement.

Tolkien retired in 1959. Mrs Tolkien was by now quite lame from arthritis, and increasingly Tolkien withdrew from the active life of the university to spend more time with her. While the publication of *The*

Lord of the Rings brought fame and wealth, it also brought visitors and an enormous number of fan letters. Still he continued work on *The Silmarillion*, and his publications over the next few years included *The Adventures of Tom Bombadil and other verses from The Red Book* (1962), *Tree and Leaf* (1963), and *Smith of Wootton Major* (1967).

When Lewis died suddenly in November 1963 no one could have been more generous with praise. In a letter to his daughter, Priscilla, of 26 November 1963, he compared the death of Lewis to 'an axe-blow near the roots. Very sad that we should have been so separated in the last years; but our time of close communion endured in memory for both of us. I had a mass said this morning, and was there, and served'.[8] In the letter he wrote to his son Michael, he said: 'We owed a great debt to the other, and that tie with the deep affection that it begot, remains. He was a great man of whom the cold-blooded official obituaries only scraped the surface.'[9]

In 1965 Tolkien learned that an American publisher planned on issuing an unauthorized paperback edition of *The Lord of the Rings*. To remedy the situation Tolkien had to make a number of textual changes in his book so that it would be reprinted as the 'authorized' paperback. In the end he revised both *The Hobbit* and *The Lord of the Rings* and the new editions were published in 1966. In 1968 Tolkien and his wife moved into a bungalow at 19 Lakeside Road, Branksome Park, Poole, which was only a short taxi-ride from the Catholic church and the Miramar, a residential hotel where they often stayed. They were thus able to divide their time between their home and the hotel.

Mrs Tolkien died on 29 November 1971. Following her burial in Oxford, Merton College invited Tolkien to become a resident honorary Fellow, and they gave him a set of rooms in 21 Merton Street. In June 1972 he went to Buckingham Palace to be presented with a CBE by the Queen. Amongst the many honorary degrees conferred on him was an honorary Doctorate of Letters from his own university on 4 June 1972. While in Bournemouth in August 1973 he became ill and he died on 2 September 1973. He and his wife are buried in the Wolvercote Cemetery. For information and photos see Humphrey Carpenter's *J.R.R. Tolkien: A Biography* (1977), and *The Inklings* (1978); *The Tolkien Family Album* (1992) by John and Priscilla Tolkien, and the entry on Christopher Tolkien in *CG* which contains a list of the many works of Tolkien edited by his son.

---

8 *The Letters of J.R.R. Tolkien*, ed. Humphrey Carpenter (1981), p. 341.
9 ibid.

INDEX

Abbott, Evelyn: *Skeleton Outline of Greek History*, 516
Abercorn Iron Works (Belfast): 1015
Abercrombie, Lascelles: 'End of the World', 398
Abraham: 747
Académie Française: 544–5
Acheron: 256
Achilles: 504n
Ackergill Tower (Wick): 988
Acton, Harry Burrows: 836
Acton, John Emerich Edward Dalberg, Lord: 840n
Acts of the Apostles: 425, 447
Adam: 220, 733, 799, 904n, 906
Adams, Fanny: 703
Aden (Yemen): 693
Adey, Lionel: *C. S. Lewis's 'Great War' with Owen Barfield*, 979
Addison, Joseph: 49, 178, 651, 683n; *Vision of Mirzah*, 630
Addison's Walk (Magdalen College): 651, 832, 970
Admiralty (British): 88
Adonis: 419, 977
Aeronautics: 43
Aeschylus: 158; *Agamemnon*, 141, 764; *Prometheus Vinctus*, 764
Aeson: 653
Affection: 820, 914, 953, 973
Africa: 98n, 558, 586
Agapargyry Fund: 981
Agricola, Julius: 102, 788n
Agrippa, Henricus Cornelius: 320
Ainsworth, William Harrison: *Old St Paul's*, 92
Air Balloons: 613
Alaska: 688
Alberich: 293, 405–6
Aldbourne (Wiltshire): 688–9
Aldershot Army Camp: 73, 85, 491n, 507, 517n, 540–1, 542, 562, 992
Aldershot Training College (Army Service Corps): 696n, 735
Alexander the Great: 235
Alexander, Professor: 796–7
Alfred the Great, King: 331, 602, 740, 741
Allah: 501, 589
Allegory: 84, 176, 219, 247, 659n, 680
Allen, Arthur Clement 'Tubbs': 15, 16, 21, 22, 35, 50
Alleyn's School (Dulwich): 432n
Allingham, William: *Diary*, 626
All Souls College (Oxford): 494n, 554n, 624, 686n, 771n
Alphonsus the Wise, King: 700
Alps: 912
Altrincham (Cheshire): 982
Amazon, River: 831
America/Americans: 259, 266, 275, 361, 405, 517, 608–9, 727, 742–3, 937, 982
Amiens (France): 36n
Andersen, Hans Christian: 249, 958, 980; *Mermaid*, 119
Anderson, Edward: 29, 35
Angels: 151, 160
Anglican: see Church of England
Anglo-Catholicism, 7, 8, 425, 485
Anglo-Saxon (Old English): 189n, 244–5, 592, 600, 601–2, 701n, 732, 735, 816, 817, 837, 873, 883n, 1023
Ann Arbor (Michigan): 627
Anne, Queen: 756
'Annie Laurie': 191
Anstey, F.: *Talking Horse and Other Tales*, 272
Anthroposophical Society of Great Britain: 979; *Supplement to Members' News Sheet*, 998
Anthroposophy: 670–1, 978, 979, 998–1000
Antioch: 447
Antrim (Co. Antrim): 853
Antrim, County: 1, 5, 32n, 148n, 369n, 478, 581, 726, 739, 814, 847, 883
Antwerp (Belgium): 79n
Aphrodite (Venus): 282, 308, 355, 447, 521, 904
Apollonius Rhodius: 278; *Argonautica*, 209, 221
Apuleius: *Golden Ass*, 268n, 304–5
Arabian Nights: 268, 437, 954, 956
Arcadia: 386
Ardagh: 120n
Ards (Co. Donegal): 848
Argonauts: 209
Ariosto, Ludovico: *Orlando Furioso*, 312–13
Aristophanes: *Frogs*, 408n
Aristotle: 545, 685, 928; *De Anima*, 658n; *Ethics*, 518, 581, 857; *Politics*, 909–10
Armada, Spanish: 726
Armfield, Maxwell: 119n
Armistice (11 November 1918): 402, 416
Armitage, Mrs: 959–60
Armour, Margaret: 40n
Armstrong, John: *Art of Preserving Health*, 729; *Poetical Works*, 728–9
Army Service Corps: 23–4, 73, 332, 602n, 696n, 720, 735, 891, 1011, 1012, 1013
Arnold, Matthew: 784n, 923; *Balder Dead*, 220, 323; *Scholar-Gipsy*, 558, 559; *Sohrab and Rustum*, 323; *Study of Celtic Literature*, 919; *Thyrsis*, 559; *Tristram and Iseult*, 220
Arnold, Thomas Kerchever: 71n
Arras, Battle of: 364–5, 402n, 414, 988
Arthur, King: 94, 103, 104, 115n, 118, 162, 176n, 234–5, 239, 249, 439–440, 468, 478, 506, 580–1, 861
Articles of War: 602n
Artillery: 316, 322, 328, 347, 351

Arvieux, Laurent, Chevalier d': 1013
Ascham, Roger: 783, 816n; *Scholemaster*, 783n; *Toxophilus*, 783n
Asclepiades: 282n
Asgard: 75, 81, 838
Ashe, Oscar: *Chu Chin Chow*, 954; *Oscar Ashe*, 954n
Ashford, Daisy: *Young Visiters*, 501
Ashmolean Museum: 733n
Ashton Court (Bristol): letters from, 387–402; men. 406n, 413, 414, 442
Asia: 284
Ask: 419
Askins, Edith: 1020
Askins, Jane King: 1020
Askins, Dr John Hawkins: 529n, 530, 547n, 596, 604, 605–6, 611, 831, 1020
Askins, Mary Goldsborough: 529n, 530, 597n
Askins, Peony: 597n
Askins, Dr Robert: 1018, 1020, 1021
Askins, Sarah: 1020
Askins, Rev. William James: 1020
Askins, Very Rev. William James: 960, 1020
Asquith, Hon. Anthony: 432
Asquith, Emma Alice Margaret ('Margot'), Countess of Oxford and Asquith: 592–3, 641; *Autobiography*, 592, 641
Assembly's College (Belfast): 1003
Assisi: 627
Assyrians: 154
Astor, Nancy Witcher, Viscountess: 703
Astronomy: 952
Athens: 145n, 880n
Auber, Daniel: *Fra Diavolo*, 97
Aucassin and Nicolette: 755
Auden, W.H.: see John Lawlor
Augustine, St: *Contra Epistolam Parmeniani*, 670n
Austen, Jane: 74, 146, 174, 235, 245, 256, 458, 559, 660, 772, 958; *Emma*, 182, 197, 889; *Mansfield Park*, 129, 182, 281; *Northanger Abbey*, 181, 257–8; *Persuasion*, 181–2, 186; *Pride and Prejudice*, 260, 772, 922; *Sense and Sensibility*, 71, 223, 762, 792, 794; *Watsons*, 889
Austen-Leigh, J.E.: 889n
Australia: 296n, 695, 997
Austria: 73, 88n, 166n, 404
Avalon: 440
Avebury (Wiltshire): 690
Axbridge (Somerset): 574
Aylburton (Gloucestershire): 986

Baal: 743n
Bablock Hythe (Oxfordshire): 558, 853
Babu: 817
Babylon: 284, 486, 498, 503
Bacchus: 408, 426, 433, 473, 899, 912–13, 977
Bach, Johann Sebastian: 342
Backhurst, Miss: 48n
Bacon, Francis, Baron of Verulam: 150, 238, 493; *Advancement of Learning*, 783n, 854; *Essays*, 121, 147, 783n
Badcock, General Sir Alexander Robert: 696n
Badcock, Colonel Gerald Eliot: 695–6, 719–20, 721, 735, 742; *History of the Transport Services of the Egyptian Expeditionary Force*, 696n; *Two Gentlemen*, 696n
Badgworthy Water (Devon): 894
Baha'i: 995
Bailey, Cyril: 426
Bain, Francis William: *Descent of the Sun*, 274; *Heifer of the Dawn*, 274, 278
Bain's Bookshop (London): 384, 385–6
Baker, Alfred Rawlings: 243–4, 826n, 841, 864, 1008
Baker, Mrs Alfred Rawlings: 243n
Baker, Eileen: 978–9
Baker, Elizabeth Margaret: 978
Baker, G.P.: 777
Baker, Laura Jane: 978
Baker, Leo: biography, 978–9; letters to, 471–2, 503–6, 507–10, 520–4, 567–9; men. 473, 487, 488, 490, 495, 497, 543, 555, 596–7
Baker, Rachel Mary Rosalind: 978
Baker, Susan Mary: 978
Balbec: 743
Balder: 220, 323, 977
Baldwin, Stanley: 667n
Balestier, Wolcott: 149n, 237n
Balfour, Lord: 107
Balin, Sir: 103
Ballads: 170, 173, 191
Balliol College (Oxford): 37n, 198, 203, 229, 296n, 328–9, 426, 430, 446, 453, 485n, 609, 644, 647n, 655, 658n, 732n, 902n
Ballycastle (Co. Antrim): 942
Ballymacarret (Belfast): 890
Ballynahinch (Co. Down): 792
Ballyshannon (Co. Donegal): 626
Balzac, Honoré de: *Père Goriot*, 349
Banagher (Co. Londonderry): 618, 651
Banbridge (Co. Down): 73n
Bangor (Co. Down): 120n, 995
Barbury Castle: 689
Barfield, Alexander: 856, 912, 981
Barfield, Arthur Edward: 979, 980
Barfield, Elizabeth Shoults: 979
Barfield, Harry: 979
Barfield, Jeffrey: 981
Barfield, Lucy: 981
Barfield, Maud: 761n, 764, 836, 856, 912–13, 980, 982
Barfield, Owen: biography, 979–82; letters to, 761–5, 819–21, 882–3, 903–5; men. 505, 509, 522–3, 648, 653, 670, 672, 686, 687–93, 737, 831, 836, 850, 855, 856–7, 881, 888, 892–5, 899, 908, 910–13, 915, 931, 963–5, 969, 978, 998, 999; (ed. G.B. Tennyson) *Barfield Reader*, 982; (ed. Jeanne Clayton Hunter and Thomas Kranidis) *Barfield Sampler*, 982; 'English People', 833, 838, 904; *History, Guilt, and Habit*, 982; *History in*

INDEX

English Words, 980; (ed. G.B. Tennyson) *Owen Barfield on C.S. Lewis*, 982; *Poetic Diction*, 761–2, 908, 979, 980, 981; *Rediscovery of Meaning*, 982; *Romanticism Comes of Age*, 979; *Saving the Appearances*, 982; *Silver Trumpet*, 980; *Speaker's Meaning*, 982; *This Ever Diverse Pair*, 980–1, 982; 'The Tower', 522–3, 959; *What Coleridge Thought*, 982; *Worlds Apart*, 982

Barkworth, John Edmund: *Romeo and Juliet*, 164

Barnstaple Grammar School: 432n

Barrett, William Fletcher: *Psychical Research*, 313

Barrie, Sir James Matthew: 501n; *Dear Brutus*, 482

Barton, Bishop Arthur William: 120n, 585, 960–1

Bates, H.N.: 'Frank Edward Brightman', 658n

Bath (Somerset): 573, 667

Bath, Marquis of: 693

Bathurst, Lord: 756

Battifol, Mgr. Pierre: 554, 557

Bax, Clifford: 858n

Baxter, Frederick William: 969

Baylis, Lilian: 978

BBC: 990

Beacon: 593

Beardsley, Aubrey Vincent: 211, 340, 384, 386, 403

Beath, Dr Robert Maitland: 804

Beatrice: 767

Beaufort, Lady Jane: 796n

Beaumont, Francis: see Fletcher, John

Beauty: 371, 373, 377, 567–8, 933, 944

Beckett, (Sir) Eric: 686

Beckley (Oxfordshire): 523n, 998

Bédier, Joseph: (trans.) *Roman de Tristan et Iseut*, 183

Beecham, Sir Thomas: 381n

Beer and Beowulf Evenings: 732n, 735

Beerbohm, Max: 531; *Zuleika Dobson*, 752–3

Beethoven, Ludwig van: 196, 793; 'Pathétique' Sonata, 87; Piano Sonata No. 14, 81

Behan, John Clifford Valentine: 296, 298, 302–3, 324, 326

Behucourt (France): 366

Bekker, Immanuel: 909n

Bel: 743n

Belfast: 1, 27, 51n, 55, 71, 88, 92, 96–100, 115, 120n, 139n, 141, 166, 177, 210, 212, 256, 263, 266, 334, 352n, 391, 423, 427, 431, 437, 442, 446n, 464, 466, 480, 491n, 500, 511n, 513n, 516n, 552n, 561, 586, 587, 603, 629n, 631n, 644n, 676, 742, 806, 808, 822, 830n, 841n, 864n, 890–1, 900, 906n, 966, 990, 992, 993, 995, 996, 997, 1002–3, 1006–11, 1021

Belfast and County Down Railway Co.: 823n, 1006

Belfast City Council: 1006

Belfast Corporation: 823n, 1006

Belfast Harbour Commission: 823n, 1006, 1015

Belfast Infirmary: 713n

Belfast Lough: 1, 183

Belfast Natural History and Philosophical Society: 631n

Belfast News-Letter: 98n, 822, 823n

Belfast Opera House: 96–7

Belfast Ropeworks: 1016

Belfast Steamship Co. Ltd.: 730

Belfast Telegraph: 822

Belfast Water Commission: 823n

Belgian refugees: 79, 83, 105n, 108

Belgium: 73, 79, 176n, 528, 627n

Belgrade: 73

Belial: 388

Belloc, Hilaire: *Four Men*, 394–5

Benecke, Paul Victor Mendelssohn: 516–17, 677, 781

Benedick, Julius: (with John Oxenford and Dion Boucicault) *Lily of Killarney*, 248

Benedictines: 834n

Benians, Ernest Alfred: 840n

Bennett, Arnold: *Literary Taste*, 240, 246; (with Edward Knoblauch) *Milestones*, 179

Benskin, Ernest: 983

Benson, Arthur Christopher: 65, 330, 354; *From a College Window*, 323; *Upton Letters*, 61, 160, 323, 659

Benson, Edward Francis: *Angel of Pain*, 335

Benson, Sir Frank Robert: 18, 21

Benson, Robert Hugh: 531n

Beowulf: 189, 195, 244–5, 440, 732n, 741–2, 835, 915, 942, 963

Bergerac, Bernice de: *Glorious England*, 596n

Bergson, Henri: 464, 494; *Essai*, 432n; *Évolution Créatrice* 432n

Berkeley, George (1685–1753): 377, 534, 565, 635n; *Principles of Human Knowledge*, 326–7, 330–1; *Three Dialogues*, 331

Berkeley, George (1733–95): 327n

Berkshire Downs: 687–93

Berlin: 1005

Bermuda: 327n

Bernagh (Arthur Greeves's home): 59, 82, 84, 125, 128, 173, 249, 465, 480, 481, 566, 702n, 779, 809, 829, 838, 840, 856, 886, 892, 967, 971, 993–4

Bernardus Silvestris: 519n

Bernetto-Desmond: 759, 776

Berneval (France): 5, 1011

Betws-y-Coed (Wales): 570

Bickerstaffe, Isaac: *Expostulation*, 177

Bickley, Francis: 457n

Bilton Grange: 984

Bircham, Arthur Christopher Halsey: 746

Birchwood (Hertfordshire): 64

Bird, Rev. George Shepheard: 74n

Birkenhead (Cheshire): 583n

Birkenhead, Lord (F.E. Smith): 734

Birmingham: 108, 242, 576, 581, 600n, 1022

Birmingham Oratory: 1022

Bizet, Georges: *Carmen*, 160, 161, 248, 898
Blackwell, Basil: 472, 488, 495, 505, 507, 513
Blackwell's Bookshop (Oxford): 434, 488, 549, 794, 910
Blackwood, Algernon: 495; *Education of Uncle Paul*, 161–2; *Jimbo*, 222, 224–5; *John Silence*, 189, 192, 201, 214–15, 219, 270; *Prisoner in Fairyland*, 179n, 312; *Promise of Air*, 371, 375; *Starlight Express*, 179, 898
Bladud: 468
Blake, Eleanor Margaret: 987
Blake, Leonard: 987, 988
Blake, Richard: see Dunbar of Hempriggs, Sir Richard
Blake, William: 329, 343, 530, 564, 740
Blakiston, Rev. Herbert Edward Douglas: 629
Blank Verse: 220
Bleakley, Rt. Hon. David: 619n; *C. S. Lewis – At Home in Ireland*, 812n
Blenheim Palace: 693
Blore, Eric: *Burlington Arcadian*, 87n
Blunt, Henry Pyot: 432, 594
Blunt, Herbert William: 432
Boardmills First Presbyterian Church (Co. Down): 1002
Boas, Frederick Samuel: 243; *Marlowe and His Circle*, 835; *Shakespeare and his Predecessors*, 237–8; 'Ulster on the Somme', 237n
Boccaccio, Giovanni: *Decameron*, 810
Bodleian Library: 232n, 306, 430n, 431, 435n, 441n, 448n, 481, 749–51, 764, 800, 857, 908n
Boehme, Jacob: *Signature of All Things*, 858–9, 863, 885
Boethius: 740
Bogarde, Dirk: 990
Boiardo, Matteomaria: *Orlando Innamorato*, 660
Bois de Pacaut (France): 364
Bolshevism/Bolshevists: 436–7, 444, 445, 446, 500, 540–1, 550, 704, 951
Bombay: 18n
Bonaparte, Napoleon: 815n
Bookham: see Great Bookham
Bookman: 20, 419, 457, 459
Book of Common Prayer: 16, 379, 512n, 521, 586, 658n, 712n, 791, 947
Book of Common Prayer with the Additions and Deviations Proposed in 1928: 712, 791n
Bootham School (York): 166n
Borrow, George: *Lavengro*, 236, 324, 353, 354–5, 395, 475–6
Boscombe (Wiltshire): 967–8
Boswell, James: 353, 362, 530, 563, 582, 583, 626, 657, 860; *Account of Corsica*, 529; *Journal of a Tour to the Hebrides*, 355, 584; *Life of Samuel Johnson*, 228, 234, 241, 262, 327, 349, 354, 492, 524, 633, 827n
Bottomley, Gordon: 'King Lear's Wife', 398
Boucicault, Dion: *Colleen Bawn*, 248n
Boulger, Edward Vaughan: 1004
Bourbon, Louis Auguste, Duc de: 1013
Bourchier, John: 287n
Bourne, John Arthur Watson: 32
Bournemouth (Dorset): 895
Bowdon College (Cheshire): 982
Boxhill (Surrey): 75
Bradley, Francis Herbert: 634
Bradley, Mary: 118, 176
Bradshaw's Railway Guide: 248
Brasenose College (Oxford): 319n, 902n
Brazil: 831n
Bridges, Robert: 58, 314, 315, 426; 'Ode on the Tercentenary Commemoration of Shakespeare', 213; *Spirit of Man*, 163, 166–7
Brightman, Rev. Frank Edward: 658, 704–5, 715, 782–3; *English Rite*, 658n
Brighton (Sussex): 484
Brighton College: 988
Bristol: 123, 125, 315, 316, 336–7, 339, 345, 346, 350, 387, 415, 444, 576, 604, 667, 684, 693, 986–7, 1018, 1021
British Academy: 658n
British Ballads: see Burrell, Arthur
British Expeditionary Force: 91n, 165n, 1012
British Red Cross Hospital, No. 10: 352–63
British School of Archaeology (Athens): 880n
Broadway (Somerset): 578
Broglie, Louis-Victor, Duc de: 557
Brontë, Anne: 102, 192, 236, 290, 433; *Tenant of Wildfell Hall*, 284–5, 290
Brontë, Charlotte: 58, 192, 201, 236, 260, 281, 285, 289, 290, 291–2, 329, 433, 748; *Jane Eyre*, 117, 161, 189, 202; *Professor*, 134, 245–6; *Shirley*, 117, 143, 145, 146, 174, 180, 189, 211; *Villette*, 102, 103, 117, 245
Brontë, Emily: 102, 192, 236, 290, 433, 460; *Wuthering Heights*, 58, 202, 258, 447
Brooke, Rupert: 342, 407, 522; *Collected Poems*, 342n; *1914 and Other Poems*, 342n
Brooklyn (New York): 993
Brother Lawrence: *Practice of the Presence of God*, 899
Browett, Lindley & Co. (Manchester): 69n, 1005
Browne, Sir Thomas: 700, 930; *Religio Medici*, 743
Browning, D.C.: 418n
Browning, Robert: 368, 418, 626; *Paracelsus*, 418; *Pippa Passes*, 509; *Ring and the Book*, 776, 830; *Sordello*, 959n
Browning, Stanley Forrester: 32, 51, 56, 58, 66–7
Bruce Peebles & Co. (Edinburgh): 69n, 1005–6
Brundrit, Daniel Fernley: 550
Brünhilde: 92, 381–2, 405–6, 935
Brussels: 134, 619
Bryson, John Norman: 644, 738, 841n, 880, 906, 954
Buchman, Frank: 751
Buckingham Palace: 1024
Buckle, H.T.: *History of Civilization in England*, 78
Budd, Kenneth G.: *Story of Donald Hankey*, 243n

Buddha: 234, 567, 1012
Buddhism: 307, 666
Bulford (Wiltshire): 891, 896, 967, 1012
Bull, Charles Edward Bristow: 33
Bunyan, John: 862; *Grace Abounding*, 850, 851; *Mr Badman*, 850; *Pilgrim's Progress*, 247, 254, 331, 400, 492, 925, 968
Burbage, Geoffrey: 357n, 445n
Burdekin, Katharine: *Rebel Passion*, 801
Burke, Edmund: 324; *Reflections on the Revolution*, 767
Burlingham, Russell: *Forrest Reid*, 841n
Burne-Jones, Sir Edward Coley: 254, 306
Burnet, Gilbert: 657
Burnett, John: 10, 744
Burney, Frances: *Evelina*, 233, 706
Burns, Robert: 602, 788–9; 'Auld Lang Syne', 789; 'To a Mouse', 177
Burrell, Arthur: (ed.) *British Ballads*, 170, 173
Burton, Richard: 985, 986
Burton, Robert: *Anatomy of Melancholy*, 343, 358, 385–6, 388, 392–3, 740
Bury, J.B.: 425n
Butcher, Samuel Henry: (trans. with A. Lang) *Odyssey of Homer*, 238, 343, 435
Butler, Samuel: *Hudibras*, 951; *Way of All Flesh*, 758
Butler, Theobald Richard Fitzwalter: 303–4, 306, 307–8, 310, 311, 313, 318, 319–20, 322, 326, 330
Butt, J.E.: (with H.V.D. Dyson) *Augustans and Romantics*, 989
Byrd, William: 851
Byron, George Gordon, Lord: 150; *Destruction of Sennacherib*, 154

Caergwrle (Flintshire): 1014
Caerleon (Monmouthshire): 713
Caesar, Julius: 22; *Commentaries*, 487, 497
Cair Paravel: 468
Caithness (Scotland): 987–8
Calcott, Lady: *Little Arthur's England*, 122n
Calcutta: 817
Caldwell, Jackie: 3
Calestrius Tiro: 717n
Calvin, John: 783
Calvinism: 163, 800
Camberley (Surrey): 47, 48, 583
Camberwell House Asylum (London): 15, 984
Cambridge Modern History: 840
Cambridge University: 18n, 32n, 56n, 317, 318n, 319, 497n, 511–12, 623n, 629n, 646–7, 696n, 703, 714, 716–17, 722, 751n, 783n, 799, 803, 806, 807, 880, 916, 965, 966, 998
Campbell, John Colquhoun: 948n
Campbell, John Edward: 294, 299, 302, 305, 309
Campbell, Mrs Ronald: 948n
Campbell College (Belfast): 15, 16, 53, 73n, 117n, 141n, 142, 150, 238, 319, 352n, 362, 378, 449, 494, 497n, 713n, 993
Campion Hall (Oxford): 531n
Canada: 324, 746, 808n
Capel Curig (Wales): 583n
Capron, Dorothy: 6, 982–3
Capron, Ellen Barnes: 6, 848, 982, 984
Capron, Eva: 6, 982–3
Capron, Norah: 6, 982–3
Capron, Rev. Robert ('Oldie'): biography, 982–4; men. 1, 6–10, 12, 15, 29n, 208, 484, 848, 1011
Capron, Wynyard: 6n, 8, 10, 13, 982–3
Captain: 9
Caraman SJ, Fr Philip: *C.C. Martindale*, 531n
Card playing: 361–2
Carew, Richard: 604n, 1000; *Survey of Cornwall*, 525
Carey, John: 986
Carlisle (Cumbria): 290, 468
Carlyle, Rev. Alexander James: 438, 497, 517, 519, 543–4; (with R.W. Carlyle) *History of Medieval Political Thought*, 438n
Carlyle, Mrs Alexander James: 438, 519, 543–4
Carlyle, Sir R.W.: (with A.J. Carlyle) *History of Medieval Political Thought*, 438n
Carlyle, Thomas: 284, 626; *History of the French Revolution*, 704; *On Heroes*, 483
Carnegie United Kingdom Trust: 978
Carnmoney (Co. Antrim): 34n
Carpenter, Edward: *Intermediate Sex*, 342, 372
Carpenter, Humphrey: *Inklings*, 917n, 990, 1024; (ed.) *Letters of J.R.R. Tolkien*, 658n, 1024; *O.U.D.S.*, 985; *Tolkien: A Biography*, 1024
Carr, William ('Willie'): 131, 140
Carrickmaddyroe (Co. Down): 1002
Carritt, Edgar Frederick: 485–6, 618, 627–8, 742, 747; *Ethical and Political Thinking*, 486n; *Philosophies of Beauty*, 486n; *Theory of Beauty*, 486n
Carroll, Lewis: 964; *Alice's Adventures in Wonderland*, 186, 227, 272, 276, 358, 439, 440, 570; *Hunting of the Snark*, 794; *Through the Looking-Glass*, 628, 693
Carryduff (Co. Down): 1002
Carson, Sir Edward: 51n, 178
Carter, Arthur Norwood: 324
Carter, Harry: *Autobiography*, 525
Cartesianism: 685
Carus, Paul: *Gospel of Buddha*, 567
Caruso, Enrico: 162
Cary, Henry Francis: (trans.) *Vision or Hell, Purgatory and Paradise of Dante Alighieri*, 408, 520, 559–60, 876
Castlerock (Co. Londonderry): letter from, 966; men. 49, 143, 188, 876;
Cathay: 486, 550, 588, 1010
Catholic Church/Catholicism: 7, 8, 277n, 285, 307, 315, 322, 353, 359, 464, 475–6,

500n, 529n, 531, 561, 671n, 783, 834n, 835, 857, 1022, 1024
Cato: 762n
Catullus, Gaius Valerius: 146, 288; *Poems*, 879
Caxton, William: 94n; (trans.) *Reynart the Foxe*, 917
Cecil, Lord Hugh: 791
Cecilia, St: 862
Cellini, Benvenuto: *Memoirs*, 343, 355, 356, 359–60
Central Grammar School (Birmingham): 432n
Chaine, James: 5n
Chaine's Memorial: 5
Chaliapin: see Shalyalpin, Fyodor Ivanovich
Challacombe (Devon): 895
Chamberlain, Neville: 620
Chamisso, Adelbert von: *Peter Schlemihls Wunderbare Geschichte*, 276, 286, 289
Champneys, Basil: 298n, 914n
Chancellor's Prize for an English Essay (Oxford University): 512, 515, 523, 549–50, 564, 595, 642
Chanson de Roland: 189, 207, 212, 597
Characters: 747
Charing Cross Road (London): 380
Charity: 873–4, 901, 908, 974
Charlemagne: 597
Charles I, King: 553, 750
Charles II, King: 453n, 618, 787n
Charles V, Emperor: 783n
Charterhouse School: 69n, 317, 318n, 453, 778, 983, 1004
Chartres Cathedral: 15
Chateaubriand, François-René, Vicomte de: 533
Chatterton, Thomas: 777; *Poems*, 787n
Chaucer, Geoffrey: 157, 384, 386, 435, 519, 605, 851, 855; *Canterbury Tales*, 183, 185, 187, 189, 192, 239, 442, 483, 492, 810, 861, 917, 986; *House of Fame*, 250; *Legend of Good Women*, 157, 763n; *Romaunt of the Rose*, 755n; *Troilus and Criseyde*, 156, 157–8, 239, 873, 986
Chavasse, Rev. Claude Lionel: 861, 891, 918, 942
Checkers (Headington Quarry): 960
Chelmsford, Frederick John Napier Thesiger, Viscount: 771, 781
Chelsea Hospital: 741
Cheltenham (Gloucestershire): 758, 986
Chénier, André: *Elégies*, 488; *Poésies*, 219
Chepstow (Monmouthshire): 947
Cherbourg School (Malvern): letters from, 16–28; men. 15, 35, 39, 44, 50, 357n, 869
Cherbourg School Magazine: 20, 35
Chéruel, Pierre Adolph: 516n
Cherwell, River: 302, 304n, 315, 453, 1018
Cheshire: 574
Chesterfield, Philip Dormer Stanhope, Earl of: 772; *Letters to his Friends*, 445; *Letters to his Son*, 445
Chesterton, G.K.: 342, 513, 836; *Everlasting Man*, 342n; *Orthodoxy*, 342n
Chewton Mendip (Somerset): 573
Chicago: 751n
Chigwell School: 303n
Childe, Wilfred Rowland: 453–4
Childrey (Berkshire): 547n
Chilon: 204n
China/Chinese: 686–7, 695–6, 698–9, 710–12, 716, 719–20, 809, 822, 969, 976, 1012
Chipping Campden (Gloucestershire): 978
Chipping Norton (Oxfordshire): 756
Chivalry: 197, 767n, 816
Chopin, Frédéric: 117, 143, 342; *Marche Funêbre*, 81–2; Mazurkas, 87, 117n, 130; Polonaises, 117n, 119, 138; Preludes, 81, 117n, 174, 216
Christ Church (Cambridge): 623n
Christ Church (Oxford): 30n, 194, 198, 199, 208, 263n, 306, 345, 426, 430, 432, 435, 487, 523n, 546n, 596n, 681, 998
Christian Century: 466n
Christian Social Union: 438n
Christie, John Traill: 835, 850, 873–4
Christie, Julie: 990
Church Missionary Society: 298n
Church of England: 7, 8, 14, 298n, 425, 438n, 512, 528n, 529n, 547, 550n, 638n, 644n, 658n, 750, 981, 982, 1014
Church of Ireland: 995, 996–7, 1006
Churchill, Winston: 73, 88n
Cicero: 137, 434, 682; *Letters to Atticus*, 762n
Cirencester (Gloucestershire): 756
Civil Service: 591
Clandeboye (Co. Down): 905
Clarendon Hotel (Oxford): 571, 769
Clarendon Press: 784, 837n
Clark, Charles Heber: *Out of the Hurly-Burly*, 866
Clarke, Charles Cowden: *Tales from Chaucer*, 442
Classical Honour Moderations ('Mods'): 263n, 296n, 312, 423, 428, 438, 448n, 456–7, 477, 483–4, 497, 498, 518, 531n, 642, 644n, 1022
Clemenceau, Georges: 553–4, 557
Clevedon (Somerset): 597n
Clifford, William Kingdom: 680
Clifton College (Bristol): 150n, 315–16, 317, 318n, 319, 322, 337, 644n, 696n, 1018, 1019, 1020, 1021
Cliftonian: 369–70, 1019
Clodd, Edward: *Memoirs*, 251
Cloghy (Co. Down): 848, 871
Clonfert (Co. Cork): 996
Cloud Farm (Oare, Exmoor): 894
Clough, Francis F.: (with G.J. Cuming) *World's Encyclopedia of Recorded Music*, 116n
Clouston, Joseph Storer: *Lunatic at Large*, 98n
Clouzot, Henri: 810n
Clovelly (Devon): 578–9
Clutterbuck, Jack Ernest: 18
Clutton-Brock, Arthur: 513;

Essays on Art, 701; *Ultimate Belief*, 342; *William Morris*, 117, 342–3
Clyde, River: 431
'Cod' ('codatta', 'kod', 'kodotta'): 32, 48, 57, 70, 79, 94, 110, 111, 115, 141, 148, 160, 222n, 247, 524
Coghill, Carol: 985
Coghill, Sir Egerton Bushe: 984
Coghill, Lady Elizabeth: 984
Coghill, Elspeth: 985
Coghill, Sir Jocelyn: 986
Coghill, Nevill Henry Kendall: biography, 984–6; letters to, 662–4; men. 643, 861n, 918, 930, 989; 'Approach to English', 662n, 986; (trans.) *Canterbury Tales*, 986; (trans.) *Troilus and Criseyde*, 986; (trans.) *Visions from Piers Plowman*, 986
Colchester (Essex): 602n, 617n, 632, 647, 1012
Coleridge, Samuel Taylor: 532; *Biographia Literaria*, 508, 685–6; *Christabel*, 138, 466, 508, 538; *Kubla Khan*, 460; *Rime of the Ancient Mariner*, 138, 484, 852
Coliseum (London): 85, 87
Collections: 526, 873
Collins, Dr Horace Stratford: 462, 463
Collins, Wilkie: *Woman in White*, 715–16
Collins, William: 659; *Odes*, 659n; *Works*, 269
Cologne (Germany): 436–7
Compton (Surrey): 122n, 124
Comte, Auguste: 790n
Condlin, J.W.A.: 808, 811, 824, 825, 828, 832, 836, 838, 842, 845, 855, 867, 905
Congregationalists: 979
Congreve, William: *Mourning Bride*, 758
Conscientious Objectors: 495
Conscription: 125, 131, 159, 163, 171, 178–9, 208, 250, 315
Constantinople: 484
Cooper, Harry Richard Lucas: 30, 64, 255, 292, 430, 437
Copeland Islands (Co. Down): 967
Corelli, Marie: *Sorrows of Satan*, 98n
Cork (Co. Cork): 1014
Cork Steamship Co.: 1014, 1015
Corneille, Pierre: *Works*, 403, 406
Cornish, John B.: 525n
Cornwall: 509, 525–6, 546, 577, 580–2, 718–30, 886, 1000–2
Corpus Christi College (Oxford): 150n, 194, 703, 732n, 783n
Corrigan, Felicitas: *Helen Waddell*, 519n
Corsica: 529, 936
Corybantes: 912n, 913
County Down Railway Station: 966
Courtly Love: 755n, 767, 779n
'Coventry Carol': 851
Coverdale, Miles: 503n
Coverley, Sir Roger de: 683
Cowie, G.E.: 19
Cowper, William: 654, 747–8; *Letters and Prose Writings*, 747–8
Cox, Harold Henry: 641n
Craig, Edwin Stewart: 781
Craig, Gordon: 980
Craigavon, James Craig, Viscount: 51, 347
Craigantlet (Co. Down): 738
Cranmer, Thomas: 512
Crawford, Edward Hugh Martin: 297
Crawford, Francis Marion: *Arethusa*, 272, 274
Crawfordsburn (Co. Down): 995
Crete: 230
Crewe (Cheshire): 6, 268, 512
Crimea: 105n, 536n, 997
Croce, Benedetto: 425
Cromwell, Oliver: 239, 311, 581, 788
Crownhill (Devon): letters from, 338–45; men. 346, 1019
Crucifixion, The: 977
Cruelty: 1, 107, 127, 166, 226, 235, 289, 567, 955
Crusaders: 460
Crusius, Gottlieb Christian: *Complete Greek and English Lexicon for the Poems of Homer and the Homeridae*, 71n, 420
Crusoe, Robinson: see Defoe, Daniel
Crutwell, Mrs: 99–100
Cuckold's Green (Wiltshire): 691–2
Cuckoo Song: 218
Cuddesdon College: 528n
Cullen, Mary ('Witch of Endor'): 339n, 439n, 450, 474, 710, 737, 748, 804, 824, 825, 826, 842, 856, 864, 865, 871, 892, 920, 952, 954
Cuming, G.J.: see Clough, Francis F.
Cumnor (Oxfordshire): 519, 558, 559, 852, 853–4
Cupid and Psyche: 268, 304
Curragh (Dublin): 634n
Curragh Incident: 634
Cushendall (Co. Antrim): 871, 883, 885
Cushendun (Co. Antrim): 739, 883, 937, 939
Cyprus: 282, 733n
Czechoslovakia: 529

Daedalus: 468
Daily Mail: 125, 446, 596
Daily Mirror: 703
Dalhousie University: 297n
Dante Alighieri: 303, 476, 586, 766, 963; *Divine Comedy*, 275, 279n, 407–8; *Inferno*, 560, 857; *Paradiso*, 407–8, 857, 915; *Purgatorio*, 403, 406, 407–8, 560; *Vision or Hell, Purgatory and Paradise* (trans. H.F. Cary), 520, 559–60, 876
Darius: 498
Dartmoor (Devon): 582
Darwin, Charles Robert: 649
Daudet, Alphonse: *Immortel*, 544–5
David, King: 442
David, William Ross: 625n
Davidman, Joy: see Joy Gresham
Davis, Robert Furley: 497
Davy, Thomas Kerrison: 317, 318n, 402n
Dawkins, Richard MacGillivray: 880
Dean, Basil: 953n
Death: 13, 31, 71, 91, 126, 149, 187, 191, 231, 235, 239, 242, 270, 274, 352, 388, 400, 407,

426, 437, 469, 496, 500, 510, 523, 539, 545, 546, 566, 586, 590, 606, 629, 641, 654, 672, 674, 706, 707, 716, 717, 723, 745, 748, 763, 820, 825, 827, 832, 842, 899, 901, 906, 911, 916, 926, 938, 949, 951, 958, 970, 971, 975, 976
Debussy, Claude: 191, 271, 342, 427; 'Fille aux cheveux de lin', 196; *Prélude à l'après-midi d'un Faune*, 899
Defoe, Daniel: *Robinson Crusoe*, 864, 943
De la Mare, Walter: 522, 663, 700; *Connoisseur*, 920; *Desert Islands*, 918, 934; *Peacock Pie*, 390; *Veil*, 920
Delangues, Maurice: 684
Delgany (Co. Wicklow): 986
Délibes, Léo: *Cortège de Bacchus*, 899
Delius, Frederick: 953n
Democracy: 493, 746, 771
De Morgan, William: *Alice-for-Short*, 185–6
Demosthenes: 137, 434; *Corona*, 141
Denbigh (Denbighshire): 1014
Deneke, Margaret: *P.V.M. Benecke*, 517n
Denmark: 11
Dennis, Geoffrey: 949; *End of the World*, 942, 948; *Harvest in Poland*, 942
Dent, J.M., Publishers: 670
De Pass, Denis Howard: 317, 318n
De Quincey, Thomas: *Autobiographical Sketches*, 933–4, 936; *Confessions of an English Opium Eater*, 113, 181, 182, 187, 192, 199, 207, 285, 305, 314, 933
Derbyshire: 862
Derbyshire, HMS: 683n
Descartes, René: 331, 635n
Desponia: 457n
Deuteronomy: 311n
Devizes (Wiltshire): 691
Devon: 56n, 484, 577, 694, 724, 1019
Devoteau, Daisy: 703
Dickens, Charles: 195, 442, 519, 787; *Bleak House*, 903; *David Copperfield*, 154, 343, 630–1; *Great Expectations*, 903; *Martin Chuzzlewit*, 395, 398, 727; *Old Curiosity Shop*, 855; *Pickwick Papers*, 754, 792–3, 795, 860
Dickinson, Lowes: *Meaning of Good*, 478
Dictionary of National Biography: 752, 986, 996n
Dictionnaire de la Bibliographie Nationale: 320
Dido: 157
Dieppe (France): 5, 356
Dionysus: see Bacchus
Disraeli, Benjamin: 179, 184, 699, 747; *Coningsby*, 179n, 739–40; *Sybil*, 179n; *Tancred*, 179n; *Vivian Grey*, 179n
Distinguished Conduct Medal: 204n
District Model National School (Belfast): 1006, 1016, 1017
Divis, Mount (Co. Antrim): 478, 737, 738, 760
Dobson, Henry Austin: *Eighteenth-Century Essays*, 342
Dodds, Eric Robertson: 73, 99, 198, 208, 306, 311–12, 314, 318, 319, 326, 595, 598; *Missing Persons*, 73n
Dolores: 522
Domesday Book: 74n
Donaghadee (Co. Down): 954
Donegal, County: 313, 330, 455, 456, 682
Donne, John: 963
Dorchester (Oxfordshire): 696n
Dorking (Surrey): 160, 794
Dostoevsky, Fyodor: 219
Doughty, Charles Montagu: *Mansoul*, 476, 733
Doullens (France): 366
Dover: 129, 500
Dowden, Edward: *Robert Browning*, 418
Dowding, C.S.: 365
Down, County: 32n, 60, 73n, 95, 115, 120n, 148n, 183, 310–11, 330, 347, 496n, 724, 725, 726, 814, 871, 967, 995
Down, Oliphant: *Dream-Child*, 482; *Three One-Act Plays*, 482n
Doyle, Arthur Conan: 531n; *Adventures of Sherlock Holmes*, 9n, 48
Dragons: 658n, 679n, 835
Dreams: 146, 662n, 678, 937–8
Drinkwater, John: 528; *Abraham Lincoln*, 498
Drogheda (Co. Louth): 1013, 1014
Droitwich (Worcestershire): 697
Dromara (Co. Down): 1002
Druids: 467
Drumshambo (Co. Leitrim): 590
Dryads: 206, 374, 909
Dryden, John: 185, 700, 773; *Absalom and Achitophel*, 618
Drysdale, Capt. J.E.: 695, 704, 720n
Dublin: 34n, 86n, 120n, 263n, 316, 325, 394, 412, 449, 462, 463, 547n, 587, 599, 634, 991, 1015, 1022
Dudeney, Alice: *Gossips Green*, 98n
Duff-Sutherland-Dunbar, Sir George: 987
Duke of Cornwall's Light Infantry: 29n
Duke of Lancaster's Own Yeomanry: 29n
Dulwich College: 779
Dumas, Alexandre: 293, 359, 826, 840; *Three Musketeers*, 98n
Dunany (Co. Louth): 1020
Dunbar of Hempriggs, Dame Maureen: biography, 986–8; men. 316, 336–7, 411, 418, 419, 423, 425, 433, 454n, 459, 473, 474n, 477–9, 537, 595n, 596, 598, 600, 650, 674, 684, 718–19, 722, 774, 777, 794, 829, 851–2, 855, 870, 871, 884–5, 886, 888, 890, 894, 895, 927, 946, 956n, 960, 970, 1018–19, 1021
Dunbar of Hempriggs, Sir Richard: 987, 988
Dundela Villas (Belfast): 1, 28, 812n, 1007, 1010, 1011
Dunkery Beacon (Exmoor): 893
Dunleer (Co. Louth): 1020
Dunluce Castle: 143, 188
Dunsany, Edward: *Tales of Wonder*, 309
Dunster (Somerset): 574, 575–7, 892

Dunster, Castle of (Somerset): 481, 576
Dürer, Albrecht: 307, 434, 441, 447, 942
Dwarfs: 95, 98, 919
Dyce, Alexander: 974n
Dyer, John: *Fleece*, 728; *Poetical Works*, 728–9
Dynasties: 447
Dyson, Henrietta: 988
Dyson, Henry Victor Dyson ('Hugo'): biography, 988–90; men. 917–18, 969–70, 974, 976–7, 1023; (with J.E. Butt) *Augustans and Romantics*, 989; *Emergence of Shakespeare's Tragedy*, 990; '"Old Cumberland Beggar" and the Wordsworthian Unities', 990; *Pope*, 990
Dyson, Margaret: 988, 990
Dyson, Philip: 988

Eadie, Dennis: 179
Earp, T.W.: 454
Eastbourne (Officers' Command Depot): letters from, 416–23
Eastgate Hotel (Oxford): 683, 798
East Ilsley (Berkshire): 686, 688
Eastwood, T.R.: (with H.G. Parkyn) *List of Officers and Other Ranks of the Rifle Brigade*, 1029
Eaton, J.R.T.: 909n
Ecclesiastes: 167
Eckington (Derbyshire): 998
Eddas: 53n, 701, 707, 835, 977n
Eden: 307, 504
Edgell, Lawrence Fayrer Arnold: 298, 301, 303, 304, 310
Edinburgh: 69n, 368n, 555, 876, 988
Edward VII, King: 501, 726, 727
Edwards, John Robert: 303, 307, 308, 315, 322, 427, 428, 430
Egypt: 284, 318n, 402n, 548, 733n, 743n
Egyptian Expeditionary Force: 696n
Elaine the Fair: 115n
Elephantine River: 486
Elgar, Sir Edward: 64–5; *Dream of Gerontius*, 66n; *Starlight Express*, 179n, 898
Eliot, George: 138, 356, 433; *Adam Bede*, 340, 348–9, 352; *Middlemarch*, 362, 433, 883; *Mill on the Floss*, 352; *Romola*, 478; *Scenes of Clerical Life*, 228
Eliot, T.S.: 529n
Elizabeth II, Queen: 954, 1024
Ellis, George: *Specimens of Early English Metrical Romances*, 921
Elphin (Co. Roscommon): 120n
Elyot, Sir Thomas: 783; *Boke of the Governour*, 783n; *Castel of Helth*, 783n; *Image of Governance*, 783n
Emerson, Ralph Waldo: 368, 398, 533
Emmanuel College (Cambridge): 880n
Emmet, Rev. Cyril William: 548
Encaenia (Oxford University): 553–4
Encyclopedia Britannica: 434
Endicott, Lizzie: 265n
Endsleigh Palace Hospital (London): letters from, 373–87
English Folk Dancing Society: 980, 998
English Language and Literature, School of (Oxford): 591–2, 600, 603, 608, 611, 642, 979, 984, 1022
Enock, Charles Reginald: *Mexico*, 474
Entomology: 12–13
Entrance Examinations (Oxford): see Responsions
Envy: 882
Ephesians: 362
Epic Literature: 94, 189, 199, 228, 244, 440, 597, 615, 661n, 679–80, 869
Erasmus, Desiderius: 512, 699, 749, 767
Eros: 127, 143, 146, 174, 820, 902, 958, 970
Essays on the Eighteenth Century Presented to David Nichol Smith, 990
Essex Yeomanry: 47n
Étaples (France): 365–73
Eton College: 317, 319, 778
Euphrates, River: 304n
Euridyce: 122, 124
Euripides: 146, 158, 230; *Alcestis*, 419, 615; *Bacchae*, 408, 426, 433, 473; *Helena*, 107, 166; *Hippolytus*, 408; *Medea*, 467–8
Euston (London): 6, 111
Evans, Charles Sheldon: 397, 409n, 410, 412, 415–16, 440, 928
Evans, Sebastian: 249n, 441n
Eve: 220, 799, 904n
Evelyn, John: *Diary*, 657
Evesham (Worcestershire): 16n
Evolution: 680
Ewart, Charles Gordon: 98n, 129, 143, 148, 165n, 195, 223–4, 238, 257, 528, 991
Ewart, G. Herbert ('Pumblechook'): 303n, 517, 531n, 532
Ewart, Gundreda: see Forrest, Gundreda
Ewart, Hope: see Harding, Hope
Ewart, Kelso ('Kelsie'): 98, 129–30, 143, 174, 184, 195, 223, 226, 260, 387, 453, 552, 560–1, 566, 724, 936, 959, 991–2
Ewart, Mary Elizabeth 'Lily' (Arthur Greeves's sister): 98, 130, 134, 143, 146, 148, 165n, 176, 197, 253, 257, 271, 274, 518, 661, 991
Ewart, Mary Heard, Lady: 98n, 310n, 469, 552, 560–1, 566, 990–1, 997
Ewart, Sir Robert Heard: 99, 107, 130, 204, 453, 588, 843–4, 954, 991
Ewart, Sir William: 990
Ewart, Sir William Quartus: 98n, 129n, 130n, 199, 303n, 469, 990–1, 997
Ewart and Son, William: 303n
Ewart Family ('Glenmachonians'): 79, 97, 990–2, 997
Ewing, Alfred Cecil: 629
Excalibur: 340
Exemption (from Military Service): 159, 178–9, 204–5, 261

Exeter (Devon): 895
Exeter College (Oxford): 19n, 29n, 319, 345, 453, 607–8, 609, 640, 643, 861n, 917n, 984, 985, 988, 1022
Exhibition of the Royal Academy of Art: 183n
Exmoor: 506, 575, 576, 686, 792, 888
Exodus, Book of: 380
Eynsham (Oxfordshire): 854
Ezekiel: 883n

Fablel dou Dieu d'Amours: 754
Fafner: 835
Fairies/Fairy tales: 86, 103, 170, 182, 206, 215, 218, 229, 236, 238, 241, 246, 257, 372–3, 457n, 476, 493, 504, 522, 660, 936, 987
Faith: 944
Fall of Man: 895
Famous Gossips: 990
Fancy (vs. imagination): 685, 901
Farnol, Geoffrey: 405
Faroe Islands: 274
Farquharson, Arthur Spencer Loat: 627–8, 641, 643, 655, 747, 874–5, 887
Farrington Gurney (Somerset): 573
Fasold: 75–7, 81
Fausset, Hugh l'Anson: 675n, 679n
Fawkes, Guy: 426
Featherstone, Miss: 423, 425
Federation of Old Cornwall Societies: 1002
Feminism: 703–4, 904, 979
Ferguson, Mrs Howard: 141–2
Fichte, Johann Gottlieb: 685
Field, Walter Ogilvie ('Wof'): 687–93, 892–5
Fielding, Henry: *Tom Jones*, 324, 687, 706
Figaro, Le: 545n
Fiji Isles: 250
Finland: 222n
Finnart (Scotland): 996
Finnsburg: 837
Firdausi, Abul Kasim Mansur: 581
Firth, A.E.: 277n
Fisher, St John: 512n
Flecker, James Elroy: 959; *Forty-Two Poems*, 956; *Hassan*, 522, 953–4, 955–6
Fleetwood (Lancashire): 104n, 113, 177, 217, 268, 292, 295, 329, 676
Fletcher, John: *Faithful Shepherdess*, 290, 777, 787; (with Francis Beaumont) *Select Plays*, 777
Flint (Flintshire): 1014
Florence: 359, 529n
Flying Corps: see Royal Flying Corps
Foch, Marshal Ferdinand: 364
Foligno, Cesare Carolo: 681–2, 851: *Latin Thought in the Middle Ages*, 832
Foord-Kelcey, Rev. Edward: 836, 860, 873, 943
Ford, Edward Onslow: 298n
Forde, Terence Francis: 141–2, 143, 150, 161, 164–5, 172, 177, 178, 217, 218, 287, 385
Foreign Office: 264, 275, 686n
Forest, Florence de: 683–4, 722, 724
Forest Hill (Oxfordshire): 881
Forest of Dean (Gloucestershire): 690, 774
Forest Row (Sussex): 982, 1000
Forrest, Gundreda (Ewart): 130, 310, 311, 346, 357, 445, 491, 702, 991–2
Forrest, Colonel John: 702n, 991
Fouqué, Frederich, Baron de la Motte: *Magic Ring*, 277; *Sintram*, 289; *Thiodolf the Icelander*, 277; *Undine*, 276–7, 289
Fowler's Modern English Usage: 752
Foy, Tom: 97
France: letters from, 346–52, 363; men. 5, 15, 36n, 73, 99, 140, 165n, 171, 334, 344, 353–73, 391, 394, 395, 414, 436, 445n, 463, 465, 484, 551, 589, 590, 626, 627n, 640, 687n, 815, 920, 987, 988, 998, 1012–13
Francis of Assisi, St: 627
Franz Ferdinand, Archduke: 73
Franz Joseph, Emperor: 68
Fraser, George Gordon ('Old Boy'): 29, 37, 48, 50, 51
Frazer, Sir James George: *Golden Bough*, 657, 763n
Freemasons: 543, 555
Free Thinkers: 312
Freetown (Sierra Leone): 524n
French Language and Literature: 1, 21, 22, 49, 83, 145, 169, 176, 198, 239–40, 273, 275, 285, 300, 323, 1011
French Revolution: 704
Frévent (France): 366
Freya: 75–7, 81
Friday Street (Surrey): 226–7, 231–2
Friends, Society of: see Society of Friends (Quakers)
Friends' Ambulance Corps: 123, 125, 332
Friends' School (Lisburn): 166n
Friendship: 53–4, 143, 146, 161, 174, 252, 253, 355, 496, 820, 878n, 918, 926, 946, 953, 962, 963, 970, 981, 1009
Froissart, Jean: *Chronicles*, 287
Fuggle & Firkin (Oxford): 879
Fyfield (Berkshire): 559

Gadney, H.G.: 426n
Galahad, Sir: 115n, 118, 122
Galsworthy, John: 410, 412, 416, 420; *Man of Property*, 760–1, 841
Garland, Patrick: 990
Garrick, David: 223n, 241, 303, 554n
Garsington (Oxfordshire): 533, 546
Gaskell, Elizabeth Cleghorn: *Cranford*, 235, 239; *Life of Charlotte Brontë*, 285, 289, 290, 291–2, 654, 748
Gastons: see Great Bookham
Gautier, Léon: (ed.) *Chanson de Roland*, 597n
Gautier, Théophile: *Avatar*, 323, 330; *Trio de Romans*, 300, 303
Geddes, Sir Eric: 590, 591
General Strike: 667–8, 852
Genesis, Book of: 749, 801
Genius: 669
Gentleman's Magazine: 748n
Geoffrey of Monmouth: *Historia Regum Britanniae*, 441, 468, 506n, 581

George V, King: 159, 163n, 555, 644n
George VI, King: 644n
Georgian Poetry 1913–1915: 398, 472, 528n
Georgian Poetry 1916–1917: 404, 472, 528n
German Language and Literature: 101, 106, 110, 145, 198, 223, 247, 264, 275, 279, 287, 323–4, 922
Germany/Germans: 73, 79n, 83, 85n, 88n, 92, 104n, 105–6, 110, 140, 146, 151, 326, 328, 357n, 362, 364–5, 369–70, 379–80, 402, 404–5, 449, 500, 590, 631, 671n, 951, 1019–20
Gervais du Bus: *Roman de Fauvel*, 763n
Gesler: 166
Gesta Romanorum: 268
Ghosts: 146, 428, 473, 892, 938, 948
Giant's Causeway (Co. Antrim): 876
Gibb, Jocelyn: (ed.) *Light on C.S. Lewis*, 662n, 986
Gibbon, Edward: *Decline and Fall of the Roman Empire*, 425, 433, 434, 440, 447, 448, 454, 607, 658, 741
Gibraltar: 686, 693
Gidding, Margaret: 494
Gilbert, Martin: *First World War*, 73, 151n
Gilbert, W.S.: *Bab Ballads*, 866; (with Arthur Sullivan) *Mikado*, 97, 163, 203, 570; *Patience*, 212; *Pirates of Penzance*, 97, 155; *Yeomen of the Guard*, 97
Gilfillan, Rev. George: *Gallery of Literary Portraits*, 728n; (ed.) *Poetical Works of Armstrong, Dyer and Green*, 728–9
Gillespie, Mr (taxi driver): 677
Giotto: 'Legend of St Francis', 627n
Gissing, George Robert: *Private Papers of Henry Ryecroft*, 377–8, 440
Gladstone, William Ewart: 534, 541
Glasgow (Scotland): 431n, 485, 950, 1016, 1017
Glenmachan: 79, 98–9, 107, 118, 223, 246, 448, 469, 484, 501, 552, 556
Glenmachonians: see Ewart Family
Gloucester (Gloucestershire): 947, 978
Gloucester Arms (Oxford): 879
Gloucestershire: 978
Gluttony: 882
God the Father: 66n, 91, 206, 231, 233, 252n, 253, 289, 310, 333, 334, 373, 379, 386, 397, 443, 492n, 509, 521, 533, 538n, 545, 546, 555, 557, 561, 562, 623n, 642, 757–8, 797, 805, 862, 877, 882–3, 898, 901–2, 903–4, 912n, 914, 917, 926, 933, 944, 951, 958, 970, 972, 974, 977, 989, 990–2, 994, 1022
Goethe, Johann Wolfgang von: 230, 263n, 671n; *Faust*, 97
Gokuldas, Madhavji Dharamsi Moraji: 319
Golden Fleece: 209
Goldsmith, Oliver: 174, 554n, 1003; *Deserted Village*, 658; *Vicar of Wakefield*, 69, 70
Gollancz, Israel: 424n, 843n
Goodwin, Gordon: 445n
Gordon, E.V.: (ed. with J.R.R. Tolkien) *Sir Gawain and the Green Knight*, 701
Gordon, George Stuart: 642–3, 780, 781, 783, 984
Goring (Oxfordshire): 686, 687–8, 689, 693
Gosse, Edmund: 513
Gough, Sir Hubert: 634n
Gounod, Charles: *Bright Star of Eve*, 98; *Faust*, 97, 98, 143, 248, 390; *New Part Songs*, 98
Goût, Villie: 683
Gower, John: *Confessio Amantis*, 763n
Graham, Samuel: 552, 561
Graham of Claverhouse, John: 787
Grainger, James: *Sugar-Cane*, 728
Gramont, Comte de: *Mémoirs*, 445
Gramophone Records: 25, 59, 66, 116, 118, 119, 127, 134, 143, 145, 164, 176, 183, 188, 216, 323, 843
Grand Guignol: 571; (English theatre company), 571n, 590
Grand Siècle: 445n, 1012
Grant-Murray, Mrs: 110
Graphic: 843
Gray, Thomas: *Elegy Written in a Country Church-Yard*, 615; *Works*, 269
Great Bookham (Surrey): letters from, 67–72, 74–96, 101–58, 159–221, 223–61, 267–94; men. 28, 38, 262, 266, 357, 359, 370, 378, 380–1, 384–5, 459, 461, 513n, 534, 626, 794, 876, 877, 897, 971, 1005, 1011–12
Great Buddha of Kamakura: 1012
Great Kimble (Buckinghamshire): 836n
Great Northern Railway: 823n
Greats: see *Literae Humaniores*
Greece: 284, 486, 816n
Greek Anthology: 282
Greek Language: 21, 22, 39, 49, 58, 61, 71, 134, 238, 248, 286, 481, 487, 492, 816n, 874–5, 880n, 985
Greek Literature: 22, 34, 49, 71, 102, 105, 107, 137, 145, 150, 152, 158, 247, 282, 296n, 320, 420–1, 434, 467, 486, 764, 875, 880n
Green, John Richard: *Short History of the English People*, 245, 341, 356, 359
Green, Matthew: *Poetical Works*, 728–9; *Spleen*, 729
Greeves, Alfred: 352n
Greeves, Arthur:
biography, 993–6
letters to, 58–60, 70–1, 75–8, 80–2, 83–4, 86–7, 89–90, 91–2, 94–5, 102–5, 108–9, 114–19, 121–3, 126–30, 137–40, 142–7, 152–3, 161–2, 164–5, 167–71, 173–7, 179–84, 185–97, 200–2, 205–7, 209–12, 213–17, 218–23, 224–9, 230–3, 234–7, 238–41, 244–6, 248–50, 252–4, 256–8, 258–60, 268–75, 276–8, 280–6, 287–91, 293–4, 296–99, 300–1, 303–5, 306–11, 312–14, 318–21, 323–5, 330–4,

339–43, 348–50, 352–3, 354–6, 358–60, 370–3, 373–5, 376–9, 381–4, 389–91, 392–5, 397–8, 403–4, 405–8, 411–13, 418–19, 424–7, 431–5, 439–42, 446–8, 452–4, 458–61, 463, 464–9, 472–4, 475–9, 480–3, 487–9, 489–91, 493–6, 497–9, 564–6, 596–8, 605–6, 674–5, 700–2, 718–19, 785, 793–4, 798, 801, 803–5, 828–38, 849–64, 872–82, 883–6, 887–90, 891–903, 905–77; men. 4, 53–4, 57, 66, 72, 83, 97, 98, 124, 125, 136, 151, 154–5, 160, 172, 335, 367, 380, 385, 443, 454n, 455, 456, 492–3, 497, 519, 522n, 595–6, 611n, 612, 619n, 644, 648, 651, 653n, 661, 691n, 713, 730, 733n, 737, 738, 779, 791–2, 810n, 821, 841, 842, 843, 847, 981, 989, 991, 993–6, 1001, 1021, 1023
unpublished writings, 'Alice', 185–6, 190, 193, 194–5; 'Dennis'/'Water Sprite', 200, 202, 205, 207, 210, 215–17, 218–19, 223, 225, 227, 232; 'Papillon', 228–9, 232, 236, 257, 277, 287, 308, 794; 'Trees', 674, 701, 718, 960

Greeves, Florence: 260
Greeves, John: 661, 746, 849–50, 892
Greeves, Joseph Malcomson (Arthur's father): 125, 166n, 271, 455, 481, 611, 805n, 956, 993–5
Greeves, Lisbeth: 996
Greeves, Marion Janet Cadbury: 375n
Greeves, Mary Margretta Gribbon (Arthur's mother): 83, 166n, 271, 293, 455, 542, 611, 830, 838, 875, 886, 927, 972, 993–5
Greeves, Ronald: 996
Greeves, Thomas (Arthur's brother): 4, 82n, 83, 226
Greeves, Thomas Malcomson ('Malcolm'): 352n
Greeves, William Edward (Arthur's brother): 98, 375
Greeves, Winifred: 82n, 83
Gresham, David: 987
Gresham, Douglas: 987
Gresham, Joy Davidman: 834, 987, 995
Gribbon, Charles Edward: 166n, 378, 900, 903
Gribbon, Robin W.: 166, 674
Grieg, Edvard: *Lyriske Smaastykker*, 130n; *Lyriske Stykker*, 98n, 899; 'March of the Dwarfs', 98, 138, 899; *Peer Gynt Suite*, 82; 'Watchman's Song', 130
Griffiths, Alan Richard (Dom Bede Griffiths): 834, 858, 881, 908; *Golden String*, 834n, 908n, 1023
Grove Park Grammar School (Wrexham): 303n
Groves, Rev. Sidney John Selby: 546
Grundy Library (Malvern): 57, 59
Gryphons: 284
Guerber, H.M.A.: *Myths of the Norsemen*, 53–4, 76
Guildford (Surrey): 92, 124, 148, 153, 225, 261
Guillaume de Lorris (and Jean de Meun): *Roman de la Rose*, 754–6, 764
Guinevere, Queen: 767
Gunners (Army): see Artillery

Habberton, John: *Other People's Children*, 362
Haggard, H. Rider: *Ayesha*, 959; *King Solomon's Mines*, 506; *Pearl Maiden*, 165; *She*, 959; (with Andrew Lang) *World's Desire*, 309, 435
Haggis, Cyril ('Joe'): 296–7
Haig, Field Marshal Douglas: 364
Haileybury College: 861n, 984
Hakluyt, Richard: 243
Hall, Harry Reginald: *Ancient History of the Near East*, 498, 733
Hamber, Mr: 542–3
Hamber, Mrs: 542–3
Hamburg (Germany): 631n
Hamilton, Alexander (d. 1676): 996
Hamilton, Alexander (d. 1768): 996
Hamilton, Alexander: (ed.) *Works of the Right Rev. Hugh Hamilton*, 996n
Hamilton, Annie Sargent Harley: 7, 9, 11, 41, 107, 136, 137, 223, 335, 501, 562, 566, 570–84, 621, 673n, 824, 842, 846, 847, 848, 855, 871, 997–8
Hamilton, Anthony: *Mémoirs de la Vie du Comte de Gramont*, 445
Hamilton, Augustus ('Gussie'): 7n, 107, 155, 223, 501n, 563, 566, 569, 570–84, 586, 587, 621, 639, 665, 673n, 676, 746, 817, 824, 847, 848, 871, 918, 997–8, 1007, 1010
Hamilton, C. Henry: 670n
Hamilton, Elizabeth Staples: 996, 997
Hamilton, Harley: 673, 998
Hamilton, Henry: see Raleigh, Cecil
Hamilton, Hugh (d. 1671): 996
Hamilton, Rt. Rev. Hugh (1729–1805): 996; *Attempt to Probe the Existence and Absolute Perfection of the Supreme Unoriginal Being*, 996n; *Geometrical Treatise of the Conic Sections*, 996n; *Philosophical Essays*, 996n; *Works*, 996n
Hamilton, Rev. Hugh (1790–1865): 996–7
Hamilton, Hugh Cecil Waldegrave: 997
Hamilton, Isabella Maxwell: 996
Hamilton, Isabella Wood: 996
Hamilton, Sir James: 996
Hamilton, Jean: 996
Hamilton, John Borlase: 998
Hamilton, Mary Warren (CSL's grandmother): 133, 172, 474n, 990, 997, 1008
Hamilton, Molly: 998
Hamilton, Ruth: see Parker, Ruth
Hamilton, Rev. Thomas Robert (CSL's grandfather): 44, 243n, 536, 802, 816, 826n, 864, 997; 'Diary', 841, 997, 1006, 1008
Hamilton, William Gerard: 827n

Hamilton & McMaster: 501n, 997
Hamilton Family: 840, 995–8, 1010
Hamley, Cedric Edwin: 67
Handel, George Frideric: 909; *Messiah*, 17, 99, 851, 895, 898; *Saul*, 573
Hankey, Donald ('Student in Arms'): 'Don't Worry', 242–3; *Student in Arms*, 242; 'Romance', 252
Hannahstown (Co. Antrim): 738, 906
Hardenburg, Friedrich Leopold von ('Novalis'): 919; *Heinrich von Ofterdingen*, 922
Hardie, William Francis Ross: 732
Harding, Major George: 86, 99, 165n, 167, 415, 991
Harding, Hope (Ewart): 86, 99, 139, 165, 167, 415, 991, 992
Harding, Peter: *Corner of Harley Street*, 440
Hardman, (Sir) Donald Innes: 29, 31, 33n, 47, 208–9, 234, 302
Hardman, Wallace George: 33
Hardy, Thomas: 206, 958; *Dynasts*, 498, 505; *Return of the Native*, 605; *Under the Greenwood Tree*, 211
Harpenden (Hertfordshire): 507
Harper, Annie: 1, 503n, 1011
Harris, Percy Gerald Kelsal ('Pogo'): 19, 357
Harrison, Brian: (ed.) *Twentieth Century*, 703n
Harrison, G.M.: 850n
Harrison, John: 107
Harrowgate (Durham): 888
Harrow School: 262
Harte, Bret: 154
Hartmann, Cyril Hughes: 453–4, 465, 471; *Belle Stuart*, 453; *Cavalier Spirit*, 453; *Charles II*, 453; *Cudleigh*, 453
Hartmann, George: 453n
Hartmann, Mrs George: 454, 465
Harvard University: 711n
Harwood, Cecil: biography, 998–1000; letters to, 670–72; men. 523, 653, 687–93, 744, 853, 859–60, 888, 892–5, 912, 979, 980; *Recovery of Man in Childhood*, 1000; *Shakespeare's Prophetic Mind*, 1000; (ed. Owen Barfield) *Voice of Cecil Harwood*, 998, 1000; *Way of a Child*, 1000
Harwood, Daphne: 672, 859, 998–1000
Harwood, John: 999
Harwood, Laurence: 999
Harwood, Lois: 999
Harwood, Marguerite Lundgren: 1000
Harwood, Mark: 999
Harwood, Sylvia: 999
Harwood, Rev. William Hardy: 998
Hastings, John Maurice: 594
Hatfield House: 632n
Hatton, W.K.: 782
Hávamál: 977n
Hawes, James Leopold: 978
Haworth: 285
Hawthorne, Nathaniel: 742–3; *House of the Seven Gables*, 256–7, 258, 261, 340, 742; *Scarlet Letter*, 340, 742; *Transformation* or *The Marble Faun*, 340, 742
Haydon, Benjamin Robert: *Life*, 949
Hayes, Mr: 823–4
Hazlitt, William: 150, 278; *Plain Speaker*, 789
Headington School (Oxford): 537, 956n, 987
Heard, Charlotte Warren: 561n, 997
Heard, Robert: 990
Heaven: 121, 254, 507, 509, 520, 859, 914, 918, 926, 967
Hebrides: 355, 584, 876
Hechle, Hilda: 197n
Heinemann, William: 396, 397, 399, 403, 406, 408–9, 410–11, 412, 413, 415–16, 420, 422, 439, 440, 444, 510, 560
Heinemann, William (Publishers): 396, 397, 549, 924, 928
Helen of Troy: 435, 447, 454
Helensburgh (Scotland): 768, 802, 847
Helen's Tower (Co. Down): 738, 774
Helicopters: 613
Hell (or Inferno): 90, 93, 215, 219, 220, 225, 232, 236, 256, 307, 445, 520, 605, 758, 846
Hemans, Mrs Felicia Dorothea: *Poems*, 172
Hémard, Joseph: 810n
Henesy, E.G.: 496
Henley (Oxfordshire): 688
Henry I, King: 948n
Henry VIII, King: 512n
Henry, M.: 224
Henry, Molly: 503
Henry, Robin: 503
Henty, George: 105; *Out in the Pampas*, 105n
Heracles (Hercules): 231
Heraclitus: 875
Herbert, George: 834; 'Flower', 830
Hereford (Herefordshire): 948
Herodotus: 263n, 486, 498; *Histories*, 284
Heroic Poetry: 440
Herrick, Robert: 238
Hertford College (Oxford): 29n, 294, 296n, 302, 305, 309
Hertfordshire: 886
Hesdin (France): 366
Hesketh, Lady: 748
Hesperides: 209
Hewlett, Maurice: 257, 405, 457n; *Forest Lovers*, 134; *Lore of Proserpine*, 134, 162, 168, 478; *Pan and the Young Shepherd*, 134
Hibbert Journal: 456n, 479
Hichens, Fitzgerald Charles Cecil Baron: 29, 31, 50, 51
Hickes, George: 837
Hickmott, 'Punch': 983
Hicks, Sir William Joynson: 712
Highgate School (London): 979, 998
High History of the Holy Grail: 249–50, 254, 334
Hill, George Birkbeck: (ed.) *Boswell's Life of Johnson*, 262n, 524n, 633
Hill, J.R.: 365
Hillsboro (Western Avenue, Headington): letters from, 683–95, 613–16, 683–95, 702–12, 751–64, 761–4, 768–77, 786–93, 804–5, 823–8, 830–4, 838–75, 886–9, 907–10, 913–40;

men. 725, 828n, 867–71, 891, 896–7, 898, 956n
Hindenberg, General Paul von: 112n, 458
Hinduism: 649, 968
Hinkley, Veronica FitzGerald: 596
Hippodrome (Belfast): 25, 38, 85, 541, 822, 954
Hippolytus: 408, 466
History: 741–4, 787–8
History of the University of Oxford: 703n
Hitchens, Robert: *Spirit in Prison*, 399, 409, 412n
Hobbes, Thomas: 623n, 763
Hogarth, David George: 733, 744, 781; *Wandering Scholar in the Levant*, 733
Hogg, Thomas Jefferson: (with P.B. Shelley) *Necessity of Atheism*, 277n
Holiness: 901, 922, 941
Holland, Lady: 815
Holland House (Manchester): 815
Holton (Oxfordshire): 902–3
Holy Grail: 115n, 118, 227, 239, 401
Holy Spirit: 308, 878, 902, 974
Holy Trinity Church (Headington Quarry): 1014, 1022
Holy Trinity Church (Rome): 1008
Holywood (Co. Down): 34n, 673, 774
Homely, The/Homeliness: 40, 186, 191, 222, 269, 276, 281, 289, 290, 295, 298, 348, 359, 377, 395, 428, 467, 471, 478, 538, 726, 787, 833, 836, 849, 853, 854, 857, 858, 859, 875, 876, 899, 907, 912, 917, 920, 922, 938, 939, 943, 956, 967, 974, 994, 1001
Homer: 105, 128, 137n, 145, 158, 167, 213, 320, 428, 480, 504, 615; *Iliad*, 71, 72, 102, 343n, 401, 434, 443–4; *Odyssey*, 71n, 102, 152, 238, 343, 435
Home Rule (Ireland): 51n, 52, 306, 310, 322, 634n
Hong Kong: 695, 710, 720, 735, 790n
Honorius III, Pope: 627
Hooker, Richard: 783, 967–8; *Laws of Ecclesiastical Polity*, 783, 967
Hooper, Walter: (ed.) *Boxen*, 3n; *C. S. Lewis: A Companion and Guide*, 117n, 466n, 986, 1008, 1011, 1024; 'Lewis That Stayed Behind', 243n, 1008; *Through Joy and Beyond*, 18n, 513n; 'To the Martlets', 430n, 511n
Hopwood, Ronald Arthur: *Old Way*, 327
Horace: 32, 33–5, 49, 145, 200, 437; *Epistles*, 152; *Odes*, 703
Horgan, Frances: 755n
Household Journal: 1009
House of Commons: 712n, 791n
House of Lords: 771
Housman, A.E.: *Shropshire Lad*, 832
Hove (Sussex): 988
Howth (Dublin): 120n
Hügel, Friedrich von, Baron: 933
Hughes, Thomas: *Tom Brown at Oxford*, 230; *Tom Brown's Schooldays*, 230, 450
Hugo, Victor: *Han d'Islande*, 290, 293–4; *Homme Qui Rit*, 98n; *Misérables*, 270; *Notre Dame de Paris*, 278
Humanism: 810
Hume, David: 331, 635n, 787; *Treatise of Human Nature*, 380
Humility: 925–6, 994
Hunter, Jeanne Clayton: (ed. with Thomas Kranidas) *Barfield Sampler*, 982
Huntley, G.P.: 87
Huxley, A.L.: 454
Huxley, Thomas Henry: 680
Hydra: 878
Hylas: 201, 221
Hyperboreans: 284
Hypnotism: 473
Hyslop, James Hervey: *Problems of Philosophy*, 333

Ibsen, Henrik: 78, 773, 932
Iceland: 92, 128n, 290
Icelandic/Icelandic Sagas: 127–8, 168, 937
Idealism: see Subjective Idealism
Iffley (Oxfordshire): 597n, 831
Imagination: 20, 179, 210, 234, 257, 277, 280, 387, 468, 481, 498, 507, 524, 662n, 685–6, 752, 757, 786, 788, 816n, 818, 860, 900, 901, 902, 906, 909, 913, 955, 994
Immaculate Conception, The: 862
Incarnation, The: 977
India: 626, 665, 771n, 816, 817, 834n, 997
Indolence: 878, 882
In Dulci Jubilo: 851
Infantry: 322n, 328, 332, 338, 347–8, 351
Inferno: see Hell
Inge, William Ralph: *Personal Religion*, 964
Inishmacsaint (Co. Fermanagh): 996
Inklings, The: 172n, 917n, 986, 989, 1013, 1023
Inner Temple: 303n
Irish Republican Army (IRA): 590
Irish Sea: 6, 104n, 105, 113, 115, 252, 587, 636
Irving, Washington: *Lives of Mahomet*, 478
Isaiah, Book of: 608, 665
Isis, River: 302
Islam: 711
Isoud, Lady: 103
Israel: 862
'It': see Joy; referring to teenage sexual fantasies, 973
Italian Language and Literature: 264, 275, 279, 287, 294, 312
Italy: 165n, 627n, 687n
Jacks, Lawrence Pearsall: 37n, 455–6
Jacks, Stopford Brooke Ludlow: 37, 455
Jackson, Herbert: 519–20
Jacob, W.W.: 668n, 669, 1001
Jaffé, Arthur: 631n
Jaffé, Sir Otto: 139n, 631
Jaffé, Paula, Lady: 631n
Jaffé, William: 98n, 139, 164, 561, 589, 631n
Jamaica: 998
James I of Scotland, King: 796n, 996
James II, King: 787n
James, Henry: 778

James, Rev. Sydney Rhodes: 21, 25, 32, 33, 37, 48, 51, 56, 147, 208; *Seventy Years*, 21n
James, William: 440, 711; *Varieties of Religious Experience*, 711n
J. and T.M. Greeves, Ltd.: 993
Järnefelt, Armas: *Praeludium*, 38
Jason: 192, 201, 209, 249, 269, 277, 282, 293
Jean de Meun: see Guillaume de Lorris
Jeans, Sir James: *Mysterious Universe*, 952
Jeffrey, John: 474n, 477, 483
Jeffrey, Mrs John: 474n, 476, 477, 483
Jekyll, W.: 406n
Jenkin, Alfred Hamilton: 1000
Jenkin, Alfred Kenneth Hamilton: biography, 1000–2; letters to, 604–5, 613, 652–4, 668–9, 886–7; men. 525–6, 545–6; *Cornish Homes and Customs*, 101; *Cornish Miner*, 1001; *Cornish Seafarers*, 1001; *Mines and Miners of Cornwall* 1001; *News from Cornwall*, 1001; *Story of Cornwall*, 1000
Jenkin, Amy Louisa: 1000
Jenkin, Elizabeth Lenton: 1001–2
Jenkin, Honor Bronwen Goldsmid: 1001
Jenkin, Jennifer Hamilton Heseltine: 1001
Jenkin, Luned Jacob: 668–9, 887, 1001
Jenkin, William: 1001–2
Jenner, Henry: 1002
Jerome, St: 434
Jervis, Edwin Cyril: 32–3
Jesperson, Otto: *Language*, 711
Jesus Christ: 8, 17, 231, 234–5, 242, 271, 309, 397n, 548, 666, 796, 862, 939, 972, 974, 976–7, 989
Jesus College (Cambridge): 512n
Jesus College (Oxford): 32n, 835n
Job, Book of: 333
Joel, Book of: 60
John, St: First Epistle of, 912; Gospel of, 899; Revelation of, 121
Johnson, Laurence Bertrand: 341, 365, 388
Johnson, Sergeant-Major R.: 357n
Johnson, Dr Samuel: 185, 262, 320, 327, 353, 454, 464–5, 467, 492, 524, 532, 565, 583, 626, 633, 661n, 666, 687, 706, 730, 827, 875, 909, 923, 1003; *Dictionary*, 772; *Lives of the English Poets*, 223n, 659n, 721, 772, 773, 912, 918; *Rambler*, 772–3, 909
Jones, Robert Millar: *Royal Belfast Academical Institution*, 1003
Jonson, Ben: *Works*, 837n
Jordan (the postman): 27–8
Jormungander: 835
Joseph, Horace William Brindley: *Introduction to Logic*, 518
Jowett, Benjamin: 329, 430, 641, 644; 'Interpretation of Scripture', 329n
Joy ('It'): 821n, 832, 877, 906, 911–12, 971
Joyce, Michael: 878n
Jubinal, Achille: 754

Kalevala: 222, 228, 232, 235, 476
Kant, Immanuel: 625n, 634, 685, 931
Keats, John: 98, 171, 288, 290, 303, 310, 628, 949; *Endymion*, 220, 499, 933; *Eve of St Agnes*, 220, 466; *Fall of Hyperion*, 544; 'To one who has been long', 385
Keble College (Oxford): letters from, 316–22, 325–7, 329–30, 334–6; men. 315, 369, 416, 436, 986, 1018, 1021
Keefe, Carolyn: (ed.) *C. S. Lewis: Speaker and Teacher*, 430n, 511n
Keir, David Lindsay: 902
Kelmscott (Oxfordshire): 559
Kelmscott Press: 287, 384, 386, 559
Keown, Henry: 812n
Keown, Richard: 812n
Keown, Sarah: 812n
Keown, Sarah Jane Lewis ('Jeannie'): 812–13, 1015
Keown, Thomas: 812n
Keown, Thomas Heron: 812–13, 1015
Ker, Neil Ripley: 837; *Catalogue of Manuscripts containing Anglo-Saxon*, 837n; *Medieval Manuscripts*, 837n
Ker, William Paton: 554, 556–7
Keyes, Sir Roger: 553–4
Kidlington (Oxfordshire): 861n
Kildare (Co. Kildare): 34n
Kilkenny (Co. Kilkenny): 996
Killyleath (Co. Down): 996
Kilmore (Co. Cavan): 120n
Kilmore Cathedral (Co. Cavan): 960n
Kilns, The: letters from, 942–63, 965, 967–77; men. 921, 927, 936, 940, 941, 963–4, 995, 1012–14
King, Ven. Francis: 1020
King, James: 747n
King Arthur Hotel (Tintagel): 581–2
King Edward VI School (Birmingham): 1022
King Edward VII School (Sheffield): 448n
Kinglake, Alexander William: *Eóthen*, 630, 631, 733–4
King's College (Cambridge): 317, 318n, 319, 512, 722
Kingsley, Charles: *Water-Babies*, 901; *Westward Ho!*, 184
Kings 2, Book of: 214, 498
Kingsmill, Hugh: *Matthew Arnold*, 784n
King's Own Scottish Borderers: 328
King's School (Taunton): 19n
Kingstown (Co. Dublin): 1018
Kinsdale (Co. Cork): 990
Kinver (Staffordshire): 19n
Kipling, Rudyard: 26, 149–50, 413, 414, 432, 639; *Barrack-Room Ballads*, 149, 233, 237; 'British Roman Song', 130; 'Brushwood Boy', 149; *Day's Work*, 149; Dedication Poem to Wolcott Balestier, 233, 237; 'First Chantey', 149; 'For All We Have and Are', 149;

'If–', 684; *Jungle Book*, 106, 149, 848; *Kim*, 106, 490; 'Last Chantey', 149; 'Last Rhyme of True Thomas', 149; 'McAndrew's Hymn', 790n; *Puck of Pook's Hill*, 106, 130, 149, 419; *Rewards and Fairies*, 236; *Second Jungle Book*, 106, 848; *Seven Seas*, 106, 149; 'Story of Ung', 106; *Works*, 910
Kirkpatrick, Anne Mussen: see Mitchell, Anne Mussen
Kirkpatrick, George Louis: 69, 83, 102, 123–4, 125, 1004–6
Kirkpatrick, James: 1002
Kirkpatrick, Louisa: 28, 52, 69, 72, 79, 81–2, 83, 84, 88, 102, 105n, 119, 123–4, 125, 145, 153, 163, 169, 174, 177, 180, 182, 185, 191, 208, 211, 224, 233, 257–8, 261, 287, 292, 385, 513n, 535, 626, 1004–5
Kirkpatrick, Sarah Thompson: 1002
Kirkpatrick, William: 1002
Kirkpatrick, William Thompson: biography, 1002–6; men. 28, 31, 36, 38, 46–7, 52–3, 55, 67–9, 71, 72–3, 74, 78, 79, 83, 85, 87–8, 95, 99, 101, 102, 105, 107, 110, 111–12, 114, 123–4, 132, 135–6, 137, 140, 141–2, 145, 147, 150, 151, 155–6, 157, 177, 178–9, 183, 190, 193, 194, 198, 199, 202–4, 208, 217, 218, 223, 224, 229, 237, 238, 247, 251–2, 255, 261, 263–4, 266, 267, 275, 287, 291, 292, 294, 311, 361, 376, 380–1, 384–5, 406, 427, 429, 444, 461, 513, 534–5, 539, 541, 545, 550, 557, 563, 602, 620, 626, 1003–6, 1011–12
Kirtland, E.J.B.: 180n
Kitchener, Lord: 110, 204
Knight, Gareth: *Magical World of the Inklings*, 982
Knoblauch, Edward: *Kismet*, 954; (with Arnold Bennett) *Milestones*, 179–80
Knock (Co. Dublin): 996
Knossos: 733n
'Kod'/'Kodotta': see 'Cod'
Kolbítar Society: 701, 732, 838, 880, 1023
Kölle, Charlotte: 834n
Kowloon (China): 695–6, 719
Kranidas, Thomas: see Hunter, Jeanne Clayton
Kubla Khan: 460

Labour Club (Oxford): 493
Labour Party: 670n
Lady Margaret Hall (Oxford): 519n, 596n, 600n, 667n
Lamb, Charles: 150, 269, 278, 292, 525, 694, 704, 762, 794; *Essays of Elia*, 226, 242, 272, 538; 'Old Familiar Faces', 262; *Rosamund Gray*, 278
Lambourn (Berkshire): 688
Lancashire Fusiliers: 1023
Landor, Walter Savage: 178; *Pericles and Aspasia*, 110
Land's End (Cornwall): 577, 582
Lang, Andrew: 273, 312, 326, 532, 534, 536; *Almae Matres*, 313; *History of English Literature*, 157, 283, 284; (trans. with W. Leaf and E. Myers) *Iliad*, 343n; *Myth, Ritual and Religion*, 800–1; (trans. with S.H. Butcher) *Odyssey of Homer*, 238, 343, 435; (with Rider Haggard) *World's Desire*, 309, 434–5
Langland, William: *Piers Plowman*, 763n, 986
Langlois, Ernest: 754–5
Langton, Stephen (Inn): 227, 232
Langton, Archbishop Stephen: 227
Larger Temple Shakespeare: 843n
Larne (Co. Antrim): 5, 100, 113, 126, 128, 132, 177, 217, 223, 561, 739
La Rochefoucauld, François, Duc de: *Réflexions*, 560
Latin Language: 1, 2, 49, 238, 422, 487, 489–90, 494, 554, 557, 596n, 816n, 817, 1011
Latin Literature: 22, 79, 112, 113, 157, 177, 247, 268, 490
Launcelot, Sir: 103, 115n, 176n, 767
Law, William: *Serious Call*, 961
Lawlor, John: (with W.H. Auden) *Nevill Coghill from Friends*, 861n, 986
Lawrence, D.H.: 881
Lawson, Frederick Henry: 902–3
Laxdaela Saga: 128, 129, 701
Layamon: *Brut*, 162, 439–40, 440, 581
Laybourne, Helen: 722
Leaf, Walter: (with A. Lang and E. Myers) *Iliad*, 343
Lear, King: 468
Leatherhead (Surrey): 72, 143, 150, 172, 188, 192, 261
Leathes, Sir Stanley: 840n
Lebanon: 743n
Leblanc, Georgette: 190n
Lecoy, Félix: 755n
Ledbury (Herefordshire): 637
Lee, Sidney: 787n
Leeborough: see Little Lea
Le Havre: 91n, 93, 1013
Leoncavallo, Ruggiero: *Pagliacci*, 164, 248
Lesbianism: 879–80
Lesbos: 146n
Leslie, Dr Richard Whytock ('Squeaky Dick'): 417, 543, 677, 714, 804, 807, 819, 969
Le Tréport (France): letters from, 352–63; men. 367
Letterkenny (Co. Donegal): 221
Letters from: see Ashton Court (Bristol); Castlerock (Co. Londonderry); Crownhill (Devon); Eastbourne (Officers' Command Depot); Endsleigh Palace Hospital (London); France; Keble College (Oxford); The Kilns; Le Tréport (France); Little Lea; Liverpool Merchants Mobile Hospital; Long Crendon (Bucks.); Magdalen College (Oxford); Mansfield Road (Oxford); Oxford Union Society; *Patriotic*, S.S.; Perham Downs Camp (Ludgershall); Perranporth (Cornwall); Queen's College (Cambridge); Ravenswood Road (Bristol); Southbourne (Hants.); Swiss Cottage (London); University College (Oxford); Warneford Road (Oxford);

Windmill Road (Oxford)
Lewis, Agnes (aunt of CSL): 765–6, 768–71, 1017
Lewis, Albert James (father of CSL):
biography, 1006–8
letters to, 5, 6–14, 16–20, 21–4, 26–31, 33–6, 39–45, 47–52, 54–8, 60–7, 69–70, 72–3, 74–5, 79–80, 82–3, 84–6, 87–8, 90–1, 93–4, 96, 101–2, 105–8, 110–14, 120–1, 123–6, 130–2, 135–7, 140–2, 147–52, 154–8, 159–60, 162–3, 166–7, 171–2, 177–8, 184–5, 198–9, 202–4, 208–9, 212–13, 217–18, 223–4, 229–30, 233–4, 237–8, 242–4, 246–7, 250–2, 255, 258, 261, 267, 275, 279–80, 286–7, 291–2, 295–6, 299–300, 302–3, 305–6, 311–12, 314–15, 321–2, 325–30, 334–9, 344–8, 351–2, 354, 356–8, 361–3, 367–9, 373, 376, 379–81, 384–9, 391–2, 395–6, 398–402, 404–5, 408–11, 413–18, 420–3, 427–31, 436–9, 442–5, 448–51, 456–8, 464, 469–70, 474–5, 479–80, 483–6, 489, 491–3, 496–7, 500–1, 502–3, 510–13, 515–20, 524–5, 534–6, 539–41, 549–55, 569–70, 584–96, 598–602, 606–11, 613–16, 617–36, 637–41, 642–9, 650–2, 654–6, 657–62, 664–8, 676–82, 697–700, 713–18, 732–5, 745–51, 765–8, 777–81, 782–5, 794–7, 798–801, 802–3, 805–6;
men. 1, 2n, 6, 15, 24–5, 28, 33, 38, 46–7, 52–3, 60, 67–8, 96, 98n, 104, 134, 178–9, 204–5, 236, 263–4, 416, 423, 425, 454, 451–2, 455, 460, 461–2, 463, 465, 467, 468, 469, 472, 479, 498, 507, 525, 527, 532–3, 534, 542–3, 545, 556, 557, 560, 563, 566, 570, 571–80, 582–3, 599, 603, 605, 611, 612, 636, 642, 649–50, 670, 676, 693, 695, 696, 700, 702, 705, 710, 712, 718–19, 721, 722, 730–1, 736–8, 739, 742, 744, 751–3, 768–71, 772, 780, 786–7, 791, 794, 803, 804, 805, 806–9, 811–13, 814, 817, 818–19, 820–4, 826n, 827, 839, 840–7, 848, 856, 864n, 867, 890–1, 892, 901, 912, 937–8, 952, 971, 983–4, 987, 991, 993, 997, 1002, 1004, 1005, 1006–11, 1014, 1015, 1016, 1017, 1018, 1019, 1021
Lewis, Claire (cousin of CSL): 212, 217n, 1016
Lewis, Clive Staples 'Jack':
Allegory of Love, writing of, 754–6, 766–7, 779–80, 796, 799, 800, 855, 957; ambition to be poet, 925, 927, 928–31; on anti-Catholicism, 353, 354–5, 475–6; 'APB' (Warnie) and 'SPB' (Jack), meaning of, 265n; Army, joins, 315; Army, demobilized from, 423; and art, 84, 92, 122; Arthur Greeves, his 'father confessor', 889; Arthur Greeves, a portrait, 993–5; at Ashton Court (convalescent home): 387–402; his atheism, 205, 216, 219, 230–1, 234–5, 240, 271, 379, 397, 443, 520, 557; book reviews, first, 784; Boxen toys, burial of, 866–7, 891; cadet battalion, joins, 315, 316, 322, 327; Cambridge, first visit, 511–12; his centenary stone: 651n; Chancellor's Prize for English Essay, 549–50; his character, 89–90, 95, 104, 126, 131–2, 132–3, 136–7, 143, 145, 168, 173, 181, 205, 210, 301, 370; Classical Honour Moderations at Oxford, reads, 423, 428, 438, 456–7, 477, 483–4, 498; College chapel, begins attending, 942; confirmation, 87, 93, 96; conscription, 125, 131, 159, 163, 171, 179, 250, 261; convalesces at Officers' Command Depot (Eastbourne), 416–23; convalesces at Perham Downs Camp, 403–16; conversion to Christianity, 972, 974; conversion to theism, 797; and dancing, 41, 43, 44, 513; on dating of letters, 213–14, 498, 973; and drawing, 84, 138, 145, 211, 216; English Language and Literature, reads, 591–2, 600–11; examinations for Malvern College, 20, 21, 22; examinations for Oxford University, 223, 232, 233–4, 246, 247, 251, 253, 255, 258, 261, 262, 263, 267, 291, 292, 294–5, 302; examining for Lower Certificates, 799–800, 803–4, 806, 807, 816, 913, 916, 917, 942, 957, 965; on experiments on insects, 12–13; fails Responsions for Oxford, 294–5; family characteristics, 126, 130, 848; family tradition, 846–7; father, compared to his brothers, 768–71; father, belittling of, 454, 455, 460, 461–2, 463, 465, 467, 468, 469, 472; father, lies to, 479; father nicknamed 'P'daytabird', 525; father, nurses, 806–22; father, his personality, 827, 848; father, quarrels with, 461–2; father, shame over, 903; father, travels with, 570–84; father, tries to take on holiday, 676–8, 697–8, 712, 713, 716, 717–18, 722, 730–1, 736, 799, 802, 803, 805; father, urges to visit Oxford, 664–5; father, visits to, 461–2, 507, 603, 636, 649–50, 670, 676, 730–1, 736–9, 751–3, 781, 798, 802; father, worries about, 804–6; feelings, 117, 146, 227, 271, 540, 932–3, 945, 964; first class degree in Classical Honour Moderations, 477, 483–4, 497, 498; first class degree in English Language and Literature, 611; first class degree in *Literae Humaniores* ('Greats'), 599; France, serves in, 346–73; happiness, his ideal, 661n; Pope Honorius III, resembles, 627; hospitalized in British Red Cross Hospital, France,

352–63; hospitalized in Liverpool Merchants Mobile Hospital, 365–72; illness, mild, pleasure of, 293, 660–1, 795; illnesses, 22–4, 39, 40–4, 47, 49–50, 88, 267, 352–63, 637, 655, 745, 749, 794–5, 835; Joy and sex, relation between, 877–8, 914; Keble College, Oxford, billeted in, 315–36; Kilns, moves into, 940; W.T. Kirkpatrick, tribute to, 534–5; lectures in English literature, 661–2, 783; first lectures in Oxford, 635–6, 638; letters of the dead, on publishing, 665–6; on letter-writing, 8–9, 61, 89, 91, 103, 104, 126, 130, 131, 137, 152, 173, 175, 181, 188, 213–14, 221, 306, 330, 607, 682, 860–1, 872, 883–4, 885, 897, 916–17, 921, 949–50; literary failure, acceptance of, 924–31; Little End Room, on building of new, 867–8; Little Lea, clearing out of, 823–6, 865–7; Little Lea, last night in, 890–1; Little Lea sold, 897; his looks, 74, 318; defines the Loves, 820; Magdalen College, elected Fellow, 642–6; Magdalen College, his rooms in, 650–1; Magdalen College, moves into, 650; Magdalen College colleagues, disillusioned with, 762–3, 767–8; Magdalen College undergraduates, disillusioned with, 778–9; Malvern College, hatred of, 35, 50–2, 54–5, 59, 61–2, 66–7, 111; matriculates at Oxford, 203, 295; memorial window for parents, 845; and memory, 585; and modern novels, 202, 957–8; and modern poetry, 403, 407, 432–3, 450, 453–4, 490, 492, 522; and morals, 343, 661; nature, love of, 64, 66, 70, 74–5, 79, 83, 88, 89, 95, 101, 105, 108, 109, 114–15, 116, 121, 124, 151, 153, 154, 167–8, 180–1, 184, 188, 199, 222, 225–7, 250, 251–2, 260, 272–3, 275, 276, 283, 310–11, 413, 478, 831–2, 863, 906–7, 936, 944, 951; Northernness, love of, 20; novels, danger of, 957–8; Oxford seen for first time, 262; Oxford, love of, 301, 304, 330, 334, 427; Oxford, return to after the War, 423; 'P'daytabird Spirit' defined, 775–6, 777; pension, not given one by Army, 435–6; pets, 2, 5, 24; Philomastix, 268, 269, 270, 271, 272, 274, 276, 278, 281, 282, 283–4, 287–8, 313, 320, 973; philosophy to English, change from, 84, 92, 122; poetry, definition of, 508–9; poetry, on the end of English, 776–7; pride his besetting sin, 878–9, 882; research degree considered, 610, 623–4; religion, attempt at, 872–3, 887, 906; his religious poems, 895–6, 903–4, 932; romantic strangeness, 122, 138, 169–70, 176–7, 186, 206–7, 227, 230, 974; schedule, his weekly, 732–3, 735–6, 785, 873; scholarship to Malvern College, 20–3, 24, 26, 27; scholarship to University College, 263, 285, 326; correcting School Certificates, 611–12, 613, 630–1, 714–5, 722; his self-examination, 862, 877–9, 888, 892; and sentiments, 117, 118, 122–3, 975; sixteenth century, planning book on, 749, 767; Somerset Light Infantry, joins, 338; and Spanish, 264, 279; and sports, 44, 59, 62, 66–7, 301, 314–15; sub-creator, man as, 933; super-shocker novel, ideas for, 923–4; swimming, 188, 304, 305, 310, 450–1, 453, 563, 723, 963–4; tobacco, enjoyment of, 272, 286, 352, 399, 404, 587; on typing letters to friends, 445; University College, teaches at, 627–8; walking tours, 687–93, 756–9, 792, 793–4, 795–6, 871, 887–8, 892–5, 947–8, 999–1000; his walks, 24, 42, 60, 72, 153, 160, 167–8, 192, 272–3, 405, 467, 488, 521, 558–9, 725, 774, 791–2, 831–2, 833, 851, 852–4, 858, 862, 880–1, 889, 897–8, 922–3, 941, 962; Warnie, his last stay at Little Lea, 897; Warnie, offered home with Jack, 828, 867–71, 888; Warnie's character, 891–2; Warnie's religious views, 948; winter, love of, 191, 234, 272–3, 275, 279, 290, 293, 426, 468, 881, 919, 953; women, on teaching, 667; women in the University, 703–4; wounded in Battle of Arras, 364–5, 366, 367, 414, 417–18; on writing, 89, 185–6, 187, 190, 193, 205, 210, 218–19, 225, 227, 260, 395, 458–9, 523, 900–1; W.B. Yeats, meets, 524–5, 530–2, 533–4, 564–5; writings (published), *Allegory of Love*, 519n, 661n, 754–5, 766–7, 779–80, 796, 799, 800, 855, 957; 'Alliterative Metre', 658n; *All My Road Before Me*, 547n, 595n, 597n, 599, 603, 604n, 612, 625n, 626n, 632n, 643n, 667n, 668n, 684n, 701n, 763n, 781n, 831n, 836n, 851n, 959n, 978, 979, 984, 987, 997, 1000, 1018, 1022, 1023; *Boxen*, 3, 4, 24n, 556, 731–2, 753, 771, 775, 793, 840, 866–7, 891; 'Christianity and Culture', 486n; *Christian Reflections*, 486n; Chronicles of Narnia, 228, 468n; *Collected Poems*, 115, 141, 373n, 593, 651n, 896n, 904n, 932n; *Dark Tower*, 1002; *Dymer*, 269, 277, 282, 285, 289, 294, 419, 662–4, 670, 672, 673, 675, 679–80, 682, 699, 701, 715, 758, 794, 861, 911, 924–30, 932, 935, 977; *English Literature in the Sixteenth Century*, 600n, 783n, 974n; *Four Loves*, 820n; *George MacDonald: An Anthology*, 970n; *God in the Dock: Essays on Theology and*

Ethics, 854n; 'Hamlet: The Prince or the Poem?', 971n; 'Joy', 593; 'Kingis Quair', 796n; *Letters to Malcolm*, 669n, 904n; *Lion, the Witch and the Wardrobe*, 981; *Miracles*, 999; *Narrative Poems*, 467n, 882; 'Note on Comus', 888; *Pilgrim's Regress*, 896n, 915n, 932n, 993; *Poems*, 651n, 896n, 932n; 'Prayer', 903–4; *Prince Caspian*, 912n; 'Queen of Drum', 467n, 882; review of Hugh Kingsmill's *Matthew Arnold*, 784n; review of Evelyn Waugh's *Rossetti*, 784n; *Selected Literary Essays*, 658n, 971n; 'Song', 372–3; *Spirits in Bondage*, 115, 222n, 346n, 373n, 378, 389–90, 392, 396, 397, 399–401, 403, 406, 408–9, 410–11, 412–13, 414, 415–16, 419, 422, 433, 439, 440, 443, 444, 446, 448, 453, 456, 457n, 459, 463, 465, 480–1, 551, 670; 'Star Bath', 222; *Studies in Medieval and Renaissance Literature*, 888n; *Surprised by Joy*, 1, 2, 7n, 8, 15, 19n, 20, 29n, 41, 53–4, 57n, 67–9, 71n, 96, 137n, 262, 263, 341n, 547n, 556n, 606n, 763n, 797, 820, 834n, 883n, 972, 981, 982, 983, 984, 990, 991–2, 993, 999–1000, 1001, 1002, 1004, 1008; *That Hideous Strength*, 117n, 904n, 1002; *They Stand Together*, 993, 995; *Till We Have Faces*, 268n; *Voyage of the 'Dawn Treader'*, 981; 'What the Bird Said Early in the Year', 651n; writings (unpublished), 'Childhood of Medea', 277–8, 282, 286, 460, 465–6; 'Easley Fragment', 260n; 'Foster', 568; 'Hegemony of Moral Values', 623n, 625n; 'Helen', 454; 'Hippolytus', 466, 466–7n; 'King of Drum', 467n; 'Loki Bound', 20, 59, 75–8, 80–1, 87, 214, 249, 323; 'Metrical Meditations of a Cod', 32n, 115, 141, 222, 340, 350; 'Moving Image', 899–901, 909, 912, 916–17; 'My life During the Exmas Holadys of 1907', 1011; 'Narrative Poetry', 511; 'Nimue', 454, 466, 468, 482–3, 505; 'Optimism', 512, 515, 517, 523, 525, 535–6, 540, 541, 549–50, 551–2, 553–4, 556–7, 564, 588, 591, 595; 'Pudaita Pie', 791n, 1008; 'Quest of Bleheris', 181, 183, 184, 186, 188, 190, 193–4, 197, 200, 205, 211, 212, 216, 218–19, 223, 225, 227, 232, 257, 794; 'Some Problems of Metaphor', 879; 'Tristram and King Mark', 419; 'Ulster Novel', 899n; (with Leo Baker) 'Way's the Way', 472, 488, 492, 494–5, 499, 505, 507, 513; 'Wild Hunt', 467n, 490, 494, 505, 506, 513, 523

Lewis, Eileen (cousin of CSL): 731, 1017

Lewis, Florence Augusta 'Flora' (mother of CSL): biography, 1008–11; men. 1, 5, 6, 7n, 98n, 117n, 310n, 356n, 368n, 496, 570, 802n, 812n, 822, 825, 840, 841, 842, 843, 845, 846, 890, 901, 906, 946, 966n, 983, 984, 990, 996–7, 1006–7; 'Modern Sermon', 1009–10; 'Princess Rosetta', 1009

Lewis, Frances (great-aunt of CSL): 1014

Lewis, Jane (great-grandmother of CSL): 1014

Lewis, Jane (great-aunt of CSL): 1014

Lewis, John (great-uncle of CSL): 1014

Lewis, Joseph (1803–90; great-grandfather of CSL): 731n, 826, 1014

Lewis, Joseph (great-uncle of CSL): 1014

Lewis, Joseph (1856–1908; uncle of CSL): 10n, 104n, 204n, 217n, 260n, 449n, 713n, 846, 867, 1015–16

Lewis, Dr Joseph Tegart 'Joey'(1898–1969; cousin of CSL): 10, 142, 260n, 713–14, 730, 736, 804, 806–7, 819, 823, 826, 922, 1016

Lewis, Leonard (cousin of CSL): 1017

Lewis, Martha (cousin of CSL): 260n, 1016

Lewis, Martha (aunt of CSL): 1015

Lewis, Martha Gee (grandmother of CSL): 677, 812n, 840, 1006, 1014–15

Lewis, Mary (great-aunt of CSL): 1014

Lewis, Mary Tegart (aunt of CSL): 10n, 260n, 867, 1016

Lewis, May (cousin of CSL): 260n, 449, 450, 1016

Lewis, Minnie: see Lewis, Wilhelmina

Lewis, Norman (cousin of CSL): 34, 1016

Lewis, Richard (c. 1775–1845; great-great-grandfather of CSL): 1014

Lewis, Richard (1832–1908; grandfather of CSL): 2, 6, 243n, 344, 677, 812, 826, 840, 841, 846, 864, 1006, 1014–16

Lewis, Richard (uncle of CSL): 27, 624, 731, 765–6, 768–71, 779, 791, 799, 802n, 804, 805, 806, 812, 840, 846–7, 855, 1016–17

Lewis, Richard (cousin of CSL): 204, 217–18n, 260n, 1016

Lewis, Samuel (great-uncle of CSL): 1014

Lewis, Sarah Elizabeth (cousin of CSL): 260n, 1016

Lewis, Thomas (great-uncle of CSL): 840, 1014

Lewis, W. & R., Rope and Twine Manufacturers: 1016, 1017

Lewis, Warren Hamilton 'Warnie' (brother of CSL): biography, 1011–14; letters to, 2–4, 5, 24–5, 31–3, 36–8, 96–100, 265–6, 445–6, 454–6, 461, 525–34, 536–8, 542–8, 555–63, 570–84, 683–95, 702–12, 720–32, 735–44, 751–61, 768–77, 786–93, 806–19, 823–8, 838–48, 865–72; men. 1, 6–7, 9, 11, 12, 13, 15, 18, 21, 23–4, 25, 26, 27, 28, 30, 31, 35, 36–7, 40, 41n, 42,

44, 46–7, 48, 49, 52, 55, 73, 74, 79, 85, 88, 91, 93, 96, 108, 111, 120n, 124, 130, 131, 135–6, 137, 142, 155–6, 163, 177, 184, 188, 230, 236, 243n, 246–7, 250–1, 255, 258, 264, 279, 300, 322, 327, 334, 335, 344, 349, 361, 366, 367, 368, 379–80, 396, 418, 421–2, 423, 429, 438, 443n, 449, 451–2, 457, 460, 461–2, 463, 474, 484, 491, 492, 500, 501n, 503, 507, 513, 515, 516, 517, 518, 519, 524, 536, 539n, 540, 541, 550, 552, 569, 585, 586, 587, 588, 589, 590, 593, 599–600, 602, 603, 607, 611, 617n, 618, 619n, 621, 624, 631, 632–3, 634, 636, 637, 638–40, 646, 647, 656, 657, 664, 665, 667, 676, 677, 682, 695–6, 697, 698–9, 716, 719–20, 734, 735, 746, 749, 765, 798, 802n, 803, 805, 822, 828, 829, 851, 864, 884–5, 886, 888, 889, 890–1, 891–2, 896–7, 910, 940, 944, 947–9, 954, 955, 956, 959–60, 965, 966, 967, 968, 969, 971, 972, 973, 974, 975–6, 983–4, 986, 987, 989, 991, 992, 993, 997, 1002, 1005, 1006, 1007–8, 1010–14, 1015–16, 1017
writings, *Assault on Olympus*, 1013; *Brothers and Friends*, 896–7, 940, 969, 989, 1012, 1013; (ed.) *Letters of C. S. Lewis*, 1014; *Levantine Adventurer*, 1013; *Louis XIV*, 1013; (ed.) *Memoirs of the Duc de Saint-Simon*, 1013; *Splendid Century*, 1013; *Sunset of the Splendid Century*, 1013
Lewis, Wilhelmina 'Minnie' (aunt of CSL): 34, 212, 217n, 847, 1016
Lewis, William 'Limpopo' (uncle of CSL): 27, 34n, 212, 217n, 237, 766, 768–71, 799, 804, 805, 812, 813, 824, 825, 840, 846–7, 855, 1009, 1016–17
Lewis, William Desmond (cousin of CSL): 1016
Lewis, Wyndham: 994
Lewis Family: 1014–18
Lewis Papers: 5n, 6, 8, 9n, 20, 23n, 24n, 25, 27n, 30n, 32n, 41n, 44n, 46–7, 52–3, 67n, 81n, 85n, 120n, 156n, 178–9, 243n, 250n, 260n, 263–4, 279n, 294n, 347, 366, 406n, 409n, 417n, 436, 439n, 443n, 451–2, 455n, 462, 474n, 536n, 539n, 549n, 561n, 571n, 583n, 611–12, 613n, 619n, 642, 649–50, 661n, 675n, 676, 695–6, 699n, 710n, 719, 720n, 732n, 733n, 744n, 780, 786n, 802n, 808n, 812n, 828n, 836n, 864n, 896, 899n, 906n, 969, 971, 983–4, 991–2, 993–5, 997, 1005, 1006–12, 1015–17, 1021
Liberal Club (Oxford): 493
Liberalism: 816
Lichfield (Staffordshire): 583
Ligoniel (Co. Antrim): 738
Lilith: 895–6, 899, 904, 906
Lillers (France): 424
Lincoln, Abraham: 498
Lincoln College (Oxford): 591, 600n, 641n
Lindsay, Alexander Dunlop: 331n, 655
Linguistic Society: 838
Lisbane (Co. Down): 996
Lisburn (Co. Antrim): 166
Lissan (Co. Tyrone): 996
Liszt, Franz: 'Auf' den Bergen', 153; *Folkelivsbillender*, 153; 'Hungarian Rhapsody', 129
Literae Humaniores ('Greats'): 73n, 194, 263n, 296n, 303n, 318, 428, 438, 448n, 518, 528n, 531n, 591, 592, 593, 594, 599, 627n, 628, 629n, 641n, 644n, 658n, 733n
Literary Epic: 615
Little, Philip Francis: *Thermopylae*, 172
Little Bookham (Surrey): 68
Little End Room (of Little Lea): 107, 160, 176, 209, 224, 295, 297, 420, 462, 463, 732, 743, 753, 807, 811, 814, 822, 827, 841, 843, 867, 868, 869, 969
Little Lea ('Leeborough'): letters from, 2–4, 96–100, 221–3, 265–6, 424, 471–2, 806–21; men. 1, 6, 24, 26, 28, 31, 51, 55, 57–8, 82, 84, 116, 120, 124, 128, 132, 136, 147, 158–9, 160, 178, 199, 209, 217, 279, 324, 339n, 369n, 423, 439, 450n, 457, 461–2, 471, 509, 513, 543, 569, 571, 584, 587n, 589, 599, 603, 613n, 617n, 636, 657, 670, 682, 702n, 721, 722, 729, 730–2, 734, 736–8, 743, 744, 751–3, 773n, 782, 785, 792, 798, 799, 804, 822, 823, 824–30, 838, 839–48, 849, 856, 861, 864, 865–9, 871, 885, 890–1, 892, 897, 898n, 899, 920–1, 937–8, 946, 956, 993, 1007, 1010–11, 1015
Liverpool (Lancashire): 13, 177, 217, 225, 292, 329, 500, 515, 529n, 555, 657, 665, 736, 807, 813, 865, 889, 890, 965, 966, 967, 1014
Liverpool Cathedral: 678, 807
Liverpool Institute High School: 303n
Liverpool Merchants Mobile Hospital: letters from, 365–72
Liverpool Regiment: 528n
Lloyd George, David: 112, 364, 484
Locke, John: 440, 635n
Lockhart, John Gibson: *Memoirs of Sir Walter Scott*, 239, 240, 356, 949
Lodge, Kenneth Ernest: 29, 31
Logau, Friedrich von: *Sinnegedichte*, 148n
Logic: 90, 434
Logres: 230
Loki: 59, 75–8, 80–1, 82, 87, 214, 231, 323
London: 6, 73, 97, 111, 157, 192, 199, 218, 224, 225, 292, 356, 373–87, 410–11, 444, 449, 456, 469, 493, 548, 564n, 588, 597, 626, 631n, 665, 667, 803, 887, 889, 890, 915, 946, 954, 955, 961, 962, 963–4, 978, 979, 980, 998, 999
London, Jack: *Jacket*, 147
London and North Western Railway: 23–4, 850
London and South Western Railway: 69
London Library: 157
London Rifle Brigade: 67n
London School of Eurythmy: 1000

London University: see University of London
Long Crendon (Buckinghamshire): letter from, 910–13; men. 761
Longfellow, Henry Wadsworth: 148n, 149, 408, 743; *Song of Hiawatha*, 895; *Village Blacksmith*, 154; *Wreck of the Hesperus*, 154
Longleat House (home of Marquis of Bath): 693
Lough Neagh (Ulster): 739
Louis XIV, King: 445n, 593n, 792, 1012, 1013
Louth, County: 596n
Louvre, The: 122, 124
Lovel, Mrs: 923–4
Lovelace, Richard: 453n
Lowe, William Walter: 32
Lowell, James Russell: 742–3; *Writings*, 742
Lubbock, Sir Percy: 581
Lucan: 199
Lucas, Mrs Edgar: 119n
Lucas, E.V.: *Open Road*, 134
Luccombe (Somerset): 893
Lucifer: see Satan
Lucretius: 238, 426
Ludendorff, General Erich: 1019
Ludgershall (Buckinghamshire): 403–16, 442
Ludlow (Shropshire): 637–8
Ludwig, Emil: *Kaiser Wilhelm II*, 866
Luke, St: Gospel of, 208, 277, 797, 862n
Lunghi, Elvio: *Basilica of St Francis of Assisi*, 627n
Lunn, Sir Arnold: *Harrovians*, 48, 55
Lurgan College (Co. Armagh): 28, 69n, 79, 142, 1002–4, 1006
Lyme Regis (Dorset): 793, 794, 795
Lyndhurst (Hampshire): 583
Lynmouth (Devon): 577, 578–9, 894
Lys, Rev. Francis John: 941–2

Macan, Reginald Walter: 263, 264, 266, 267, 268, 302, 417, 428, 444, 453, 457–8, 526, 549, 694; *Goethe in Rome*, 263n; *Herodotus and Thucydides*, 263n
Macan, Mrs Reginald Walter: 267, 268
Macaulay, Hannah More: 815n
Macaulay, Rose: 712; *Crewe Train*, 774–5; *Lee Shore*, 775; *Orphan Island*, 775; *Potterism*, 775
Macaulay, Thomas Babington: 178, 247, 269, 430, 459, 611, 657, 787; *Essays*, 815; *History of England*, 271, 272, 274, 277, 281, 290, 294, 553; *Lays of Ancient Rome*, 43; *Life and Letters*, 814–17; 'Sir William Temple', 238
McConnell, Dr Robert John: 807
McCrea, John: 339n, 584
McCreddy, Hugh: 98n
MacDonald, George: 215, 252, 468, 836, 873, 883, 885, 890, 901, 918, 922, 934–6, 953, 970, 975; *Adela Cathcart*, 941; *Alec Forbes*, 944, 949; *Annals of a Quiet Neighbourhood*, 944; *At the Back of the North Wind*, 175, 180, 209; *Diary of an Old Soul*, 834, 835, 872, 950; 'Giant's Heart', 254n; 'Golden Key', 252, 254, 257; 'Light Princess', 254n; *Lilith*, 899, 906, 926, 935; *Phantastes*, 169–70, 173, 175, 176, 189, 206, 219, 236, 258, 281, 293, 300, 313, 320, 323, 330, 447, 794, 859, 891, 899, 909, 925, 927, 935, 936, 937, 939, 941, 950, 953; Preface to V.A. Thisted's *Letters from Hell*, 215n, 219, 236; *Princess and Curdie*, 905–6, 950; *Princess and the Goblin*, 393, 905–6, 950; *Seaboard Parish*, 941, 944; *Short Stories*, 254n; *Sir Gibbie*, 175, 939, 941, 950; *What's Mine's Mine*, 941, 950, 953, 955; *Wilfrid Cumbermede*, 934–5, 939, 941, 953, 968
MacDonald, James Ramsay: 632
MacDonald, Louisa: 834n
Macdonell, Anne: 355n
McFarlane, Kenneth Bruce: 778n, 836, 837, 852–5, 969
McGrigor's Bank: 602
MacIlwaine, John H.: 1015
MacIlwaine and Lewis, Boiler Makers, Engineers, and Iron Ship Builders: 501n, 1006, 1015
Mackail, John William: 711; *Lectures on Poetry*, 499; *Life of William Morris*, 157, 268, 270, 280, 325, 910; *Springs of Helicon*, 157
Maclean, Boyle and Maclean (Dublin): 1006
McMullen, Miss: 79, 83, 95, 140
McNeill, James Adams: 117n, 906
McNeill, Jane ('Janie'): 117, 127, 219, 253, 309, 334, 349, 403, 476, 490, 495, 496, 499, 518–19, 702, 809, 814, 864, 916, 953, 959
McNeill, Margaret Cunningham: 117n, 219n, 496, 499, 519, 814, 864, 906, 953, 967
McNeill, William Martin: 499
MacNicholl, Douglas: 308n
MacNicholl, John Milne: 308
Macran, Rev. Frederick Walker ('Cranny'): 547–8
Maenads: 912n, 913
Maeterlinck, Maurice: 301, 380, 432; *Alladine et Palomides*, 320, 323; *Bourgmestre de Stilmonde*, 440; *Intérieur*, 320; *Mort*, 270, 274, 320, 323; *Oiseau Bleu* (*Blue Bird*), 176n, 239–40, 320; *Morceaux Choisis*, 190; *Pelléas et Mélisande*, 320
Maeve: 81
Magdalen College (Oxford): letters from, 650–82, 697–702, 713–18, 732–51, 764–8, 777–85, 793–804, 828–30, 834–8, 875–86, 891–907, 940–2; men. 172n, 243n, 304n, 468, 516–17, 585, 591, 594, 595, 599, 600n, 610, 629, 640, 642–6, 683–4, 704–5, 762–3, 769, 824, 826n, 827–8, 833, 834, 839, 850, 851–2, 855, 867, 868, 887, 908, 917, 924, 948n, 961, 962, 969, 970, 989

Magdalen College Record: 243n, 1008
Magdalen College School (Oxford): 596n
Magdalen College Tower: 651, 658, 683–4, 765, 918
Magic: 234, 531, 534, 543, 565
Magnússon, Eiríkr: 165n
Maidenhead (Berkshire): 583
Mais, Stuart Petre Brodie: 432–3, 435, 441, 694; *Schoolmaster's Diary*, 393, 432–3, 694
Majendie, Vivian Henry Bruce: 348; *History of the 1st Battalion The Somerset Light Infantry*, 348n, 357n
Malapropisms: 694
Malory, Sir Thomas: *Morte D'Arthur*, 94, 103, 104, 115n, 128, 169, 192, 196, 207, 211, 227, 229, 230, 232, 239, 245, 249, 268, 274, 278, 320, 331, 340, 384, 403, 440, 460, 506, 581, 857
Malvern (Worcestershire): 11, 15, 16, 17, 18, 23, 35, 47, 64–5, 500, 538, 637, 987, 988
Malvern College: letters from, 29–67; men. 11, 15, 16, 18, 20–2, 23, 25, 26, 28, 72, 82, 86, 87, 89, 91, 111, 114, 131, 132, 143, 147, 198, 208, 234, 255, 292, 299, 300, 301, 302, 345, 363, 374, 409n, 430n, 437, 438, 443n, 624, 642, 779, 802–3, 822, 841, 869, 983, 984, 987, 1011, 1012
Malvernian: 31
Malvernian Society: 32n
Malvern Register: 32n
Mammon: 950
Manchester (Lancashire): 37n, 69n, 141n, 150, 184, 198, 303n, 739, 815
Manchester College (Oxford): 456n, 625n, 998–9
Manchester College of Technology: 647n
Manchester Grammar School: 303n
Manchester Regiment: 33n
Mandeville, Sir John: *Travels*, 214, 243
Manning, Ann: *Household of Sir Thomas More*, 393n
Mansfield Road (Oxford): letter from, 262
Manzoni, Alessandro: *I Promessi Sponsi*, 279n
Marandellas (South Africa): 997
Marcus Aurelius: 627n
Mark, King: 419, 581
Mark, St: Gospel of, 101
Marlborough (Wiltshire): 686, 690
Marlborough College: 56n, 687n, 690
Marlowe, Christopher: 835; *Dr Faustus*, 985, 986
Marriage: 668–9, 902
Mars: 240
Marseilles (France): 871
Marsh, Sir Edward: 398n, 404, 472n
Marshall, Mrs: 488n
Marston (Oxfordshire): 855
Martha, St: 208
Martindale SJ, Fr Cyril Charlie: 531–2, 533, 564–5
Martlets, The (Cambridge University): 511–12
Martlets, The (Oxford University): 430, 431, 435, 438, 441, 443, 448, 453, 468, 507, 511–12, 517, 525n, 556, 602, 655, 1000
Mary, Blessed Virgin: 8, 308
Mary, Queen (wife of William III): 700
Mary Queen of Scots: 835
Mary Tudor, Queen: 783n
Mascagni, Pietro: *Cavalleria Rusticana*, 164, 248
Masefield, John: 342, 430, 431–2, 448, 460, 522, 663, 680, 933; *Dauber*, 679n; *Poem and two Plays*, 432; *Right Royal*, 515
Mason, Eugene: *Arthurian Chronicles*, 162
Materialism: 938
Mathematics: 264, 305, 316, 322, 906n, 997, 1008
Matriculation (Oxford University): 163
Matthew, St: Gospel of, 83, 204, 363, 848
Mecca: 488
Mechanical Transport School of Instruction (St Omer): 349, 366
Medea: 209, 277–8, 282, 460, 465–6, 467, 653
Medical Missionaries of Mary: 1013–14
Meditation: 832–3, 858, 862, 897–8
Melville, Herman: *Moby Dick*, 889
Mendelssohn, Felix: 516; *Elijah*, 207
Meredith, George: 284, 397, 958; *Egoist*, 98n, 395, 770
Merkin, R.M.: see Wallington, P.
Merlin: 118, 259, 340, 466, 468, 482–3
Mermaid Club: 735
Merriman, Henry Seton: 102; *Grey Lady*, 103; *Sowers*, 138, 578; *With Edged Tools*, 98n, 103
Merritt, Percival: *True Story of...Love Letters of Mrs Piozzi*, 687n
Merry, W.W.: 102
Merton College (Oxford): 600n, 643, 644n, 665n, 667, 746, 883n, 902n, 917n, 989, 990, 1024
Mesopotamia: 304n, 498, 831
Methodist Church: 1014
Methodist College (Belfast): 906n, 1008
Metre: 49, 62–3, 89, 149, 150, 151, 170, 210, 220, 232, 492, 508, 904, 909
Mexico: 474
Meyerbeer, Giacomo: *Robert le Diable*, 139
Meynell, Alice: *Colour of Life*, 743n
Mezentius: 935
Michael Hall School (Kidbrooke): 999
Michaelmas Club: 778, 836, 838
Microscope: 12–13, 224, 843
Middle English: 755n, 780n
Military Cross: 33n, 37n, 324n, 357n, 528n, 987, 1020, 1021
Military Service Act: 125n, 159, 163, 171, 178–9, 199, 204–5, 261, 315
Mill, John Stuart: 703; *Subjection of Women*, 368
Milne, Miss: 110
Milton, John: 157, 182, 222, 223, 232–3, 349, 394, 437, 446n, 476, 477, 538, 540, 546, 556, 562–3, 659, 680, 793, 832, 915, 918;

'L'Allegro', 546, 787; *Comus*, 225, 227, 232, 332, 333–4, 546, 562, 638, 790, 888; 'Il Penseroso', 546, 787; *Lycidas*, 523, 545; 'On Being Arrived at Twenty-Three', 600; *Paradise Lost*, 94, 183, 199, 214, 215, 220, 269, 274, 278, 290, 298, 306–7, 400, 412n, 477, 493–4, 504, 521, 546–7, 562, 564, 579–80, 615, 638, 693, 776, 799; *Paradise Regained*, 225, 562, 584; *Reason of Church-Government*, 562; *Samson Agonistes*, 985
Milton, Mary Powell: 546
Mime: 240, 954
Minehead (Somerset): 505, 575, 576–7
Mines (of Cornwall): 725–6
Minicius Fundanus: 542n
Miracles: 666n
Miramar Hotel (Bournemouth): 1024
Mitchell, Anne Mussen: 1002, 1004
Mitchell, Stewart: 1004
Mitford, Mary Russell: *Our Village*, 181, 228, 239
Mitre (Inn): 426n, 452, 457, 532, 561–2, 566
Moberly, Captain: 318
Modernism: 548
Molière, Jean Baptiste Poquelin: *Fourberies de Scapin*, 519; *George Dandin*, 581–2
Monasticism: 810
Monchy-Le-Preux (France): 346n
Monmouth (Monmouthshire): 948
Monmouth School for Girls: 987
Monro, D.B.: 102
Mons Angels: 151
Mons, Battle of: 151
Montague, Charles Edward: *Rough Justice*, 678
Montaigne, Michel Eyquem de: *Essais*, 740
Montgolfier, Jacques: 613
Montgolfier, Joseph Michael: 613
Montmartre (France): 571
Montpensier, Anne Marie Louise de Bourbon, Duchesse de: *Mémoires*, 516n
Montreuil (France): 366
Monypenny, William Flavelle: *Life of Benjamin Disraeli*, 184
Moore, Canon Courtney: 1021
Moore, Courtenay Edward: 316, 317, 318n, 451, 986–7, 1018, 1021, 1022
Moore, Edward Francis Courtenay ('Paddy'): biography, 1018–20; men. 315–16, 319, 322, 334, 336, 344, 361, 369–70, 387, 400, 402n, 986–7, 1021
Moore, George Augustus: 560; *Esther Waters*, 560n; *Heloïse and Abelard*, 545
Moore, James: 1016
Moore, Janie King Askins ('Minto'): biography, 1020–2; men. 316, 322, 334, 336, 339, 345, 348, 352, 367, 369, 372, 374, 386–7, 391, 400, 402, 403, 404, 408, 418, 421, 423, 433, 444, 451–2, 454n, 460–1, 462, 463, 465, 469, 473–4, 474n, 476, 477–9, 481, 488, 491, 495, 529, 530, 538, 547, 558–9, 566, 595n, 596n, 597, 600, 604n, 605–6, 650, 652, 654, 669, 674, 683, 684, 700–1, 702, 707–10, 718–19, 722, 724, 774, 794, 805, 828n, 829–30, 831, 832, 833, 835, 836, 838, 840, 842, 849, 851–2, 856, 864, 870, 871, 875, 876, 884–5, 886, 888, 890, 892, 894, 895, 896–7, 923, 927, 940, 946, 951, 952, 960, 969, 970, 978, 986–7, 989, 1000, 1018–19
Moore, Maureen: see Dunbar of Hempriggs, Dame Maureen
Moore, Tom: 793
Moorgate (Glasgow): 799, 1016
Moral Re-Armament: 751n
Morals/Morality: 623n, 625n, 901, 932–3
More, Henry: 623; *Antidote Against Atheism*, 623n; *Explanation of the Grand Mystery of Godliness*, 623n; *Immortality of the Soul*, 623n
More, St Thomas: 393, 699, 816n
Morgan le Fay, Queen: 103
Morris, Albert: 462, 463
Morris, Mrs Albert: 462, 463
Morris, May: (ed.) *Collected Works of William Morris*, 168n, 910
Morris, William: 104, 117, 118, 121, 124, 157, 169, 195n, 207, 218, 270, 272, 274, 281, 287, 288, 290, 303, 306, 342–3, 384, 432, 435, 443, 453, 460, 524, 559, 566, 727, 921, 970–1; *Collected Works*, 168, 910; *Earthly Paradise*, 220, 227, 278, 300, 308, 776, 971, 975; *Grettir the Strong*, 165; *Life and Death of Jason*, 192, 201, 209, 221, 249, 269, 278, 282, 293, 325; *Love is Enough*, 910–11, 970; (trans.) *Odyssey*, 446; *Roots of the Mountains*, 119, 122, 126, 128; *Sigurd the Volsung*, 92, 278; *Völsunga Saga*, 165, 168; *Water of the Wondrous Isles*, 453; *Well at the World's End*, 92, 94–5, 122, 128, 153, 186, 209, 245, 270, 453, 478, 911
Morrow, George: 501
Morse Code: 979
Moscow: 138
Mother Goose's Nursery Rhymes: 864, 866
Mount Airy Seminary (Philadelphia): 751n
Mountbatten, Louis Alexander, Marquess of Milford Haven: 88
Mount Graupius, Battle of: 788n
Mourne Mountains (Co. Down): 738, 848
Moville: 49
Moynihan, Martin: 'C. S. Lewis and T.D. Weldon', 764n
Mozart, Wolfgang Amadeus: 394, 793; *Magic Flute*, 211–12, 248, 253, 256
Mulligan, Lizzie: 702, 914
Mullion (Cornwall): 1001
Munro, H.E.: 472
Murray, Gilbert: 304, 408, 426, 429, 444, 447;

Hippolytus and the Bacchae of Euripides, and the Frogs of Aristophanes, 408, 433; *History of Ancient Greek Literature*, 158, 457–8
Murray, Miss: 98n
Museum of the History of Science (Oxford): 320n
Muslims: 711, 816
Musset, Alfred de: 356n
Mussolini, Benito: 681–2
Myers, W.: (trans. with A. Lang and W. Leaf) *Iliad*, 343n
Mysticism: 472, 473, 530n, 860
Mythology (Celtic): 59, 81, 84, 86, 87, 89, 92, 103, 132, 330, 521n
Mythology (Classical): 206, 912n
Mythology (General): 79, 230–1, 234–5, 249, 534, 615, 662n, 664, 680, 765, 800–1, 904, 968, 970, 976–7, 1023
Mythology (Norse): 20, 53–4, 59, 82, 92, 321, 476, 483, 701n, 976–7
Mythology (Teutonic): 86
Mythopoeics: 765

Nasir Al-Din (Shah of Persia): *Diary*, 500–1
National Graphic: 843n
Nationalism (Irish): 326
National Society for the Prevention of Cruelty to Children: 823n, 1006
Natural Epic: 615
Nature: 371, 374, 375, 379, 382, 504, 547n, 832, 912, 927
Negroes: 538
Neo-Platonists: 685
Nero: 242, 284
Nesbit, E.: 680; *Five Children and It*, 680n
Newbolt, Sir Henry John: 150, 317, 441, 1018, 1020; *Admirals All*, 150n
New Brunswick (Canada): 324n
Newbury (Berkshire): 834
Newcastle (Co. Down): 792, 804, 876
New College (Oxford): 16n, 194, 198, 199, 208, 213, 247, 261, 263, 600n, 902n
New Forest (Hampshire): 583
New Leader: 670
Newman, John Henry, Cardinal: 315; *Apologia pro Vita Sua*, 243, 670n; *Dream of Gerontius*, 65–6; *Loss and Gain*, 550; *Verses on Various Occasions*, 65–6
Newnham College (Cambridge): 998
Newquay (Cornwall): 729–30
Newtownards (Co. Down): 726
Newtown Hamilton (Co. Armagh): 996
Niamh: 521n
Nichols, Robert: 420, 490; *Ardours and Endurances*, 404, 407, 490; *Assault*, 404
Nietzsche, Friedrich: 74
Nightingale, Florence: 641
Nightingale, Rev. Frank: 638n
Nightmares: 417–18, 503, 678–9, 699, 938, 955, 956
Nile, River: 486
Nimue (Lady of the Lake): 454, 466, 468, 482–3, 505
Nineveh: 498
Nirvana: 516, 567
Noah: 668
Nobel Prize: 525n, 557n
Nodier, Jean Charles: *Contes Fantastiques*, 273
Norfolk: 777n
Norman French: 816, 817
Northenden (Lancashire): 1005
Norton, Frederick: 954n
Norway: 293
Notes and Queries: 756–7
Notre-Dame (Paris): 554, 557
Nottingham: 529n
Novalis: see Hardenburg, Friedrich Leopold von
Nova Scotia: 297n
Novel Magazine: 221
Noyes, Alfred: *William Morris*, 325
Nymphs: 207, 221, 832, 909

O'Brien, Conor Cruise: 767n
O'Brien, Frederick Lucius: 166
Occultism: 19n, 20
Odds & Ends Magazine: 466, 466–7n, 469, 475, 494
Odin: 75–8, 80–1, 231, 235, 323, 977n
Oelsner, H.: 403n
Offenbach, Jacques: *Tales of Hoffman*, 248
Officer Cadet Unit: 294
Officers' Command Depot: see Eastbourne
Officers' Training Corps (Oxford): 30n, 33n, 267, 291, 292, 296, 298, 299, 300, 305, 311, 312, 315–16, 322, 326, 327, 424, 986, 1018, 1021
O'Henry, Muriedach: 619n
Oisin: 521
Okey, Thomas: 403n
Old Cleeve (Somerset): letters from, 477–85, 503–6; men. 574
Old English: see Anglo-Saxon
Old French: 754–6, 779–80
Old Icelandic: 701n, 1023
Old Malvernians: 446
Old Mother Hubbard: 1009–10
Old Norse: 675, 977n, 1023
Old Vic Company: 978
Olivier, Sydney Haldane, Lord: 998
Oman, Carola: 494
Oman, Sir Charles: 494n; *Dark Ages*, 740–1
Omar Khayyám: *Rubáiyat*, 333–4
Onions, Charles Talbut: 780, 989
Opera: 40, 75–8, 80–1, 96–8, 99, 107, 116, 117, 129n, 139, 143, 145, 155, 160, 161, 162, 163, 164, 166, 179, 180, 188, 191, 210, 211–12, 248, 253, 256, 259, 277, 280, 433, 775, 898, 954
Orange Order: 330, 480
Orchard View (Dartford, Kent): 982
Oreads: 221
Orgoglio: 861
Oriel College (Oxford): 194, 198, 208, 262, 625n, 717
Originality: 504, 935
Orléans, Philippe de France, Duc d': 1013
Ormond, Duke of: 553n
Ormond, Grace, Marquess of: 996
Ormond, 2nd Marquis of: 996
Orpheus: 122, 124
Osborne, Dorothy: 241;

Letters to Sir William Temple, 238, 239, 250, 254, 256
Osborne, T.E.: 160, 169, 171, 177, 207, 794
Our Lady of Lourdes Hospital (Drogheda): 1013–14
Outler, Albert C.: 168n
Ovid: 154; *Metamorphoses*, 368; *Pars Estis Pauci*, 62–3; *Tristia*, 510
Owen, George Vale: 531; *How Spirits Communicate*, 531n; *Life Beyond the Vale*, 531n; *Outlands of Heaven*, 531n; *Problems which Perplex*, 531n; *What Happens after Death*, 531n
Oxenford, John: 248n
Oxford and Asquith, 1st Earl of: 432n, 592–3
Oxford Broadside Club: 879–80
Oxford City Home Guard Battalion: 1013
Oxford English Dictionary: 780n, 1023
Oxford Group: 751n
Oxford High School: 987
Oxford History of English Literature: 600n
Oxford Magazine: 784
Oxford Playhouse: 986
Oxford Poetry 1916: 454
Oxford Poetry 1917: 454
Oxford Terms: 767n
Oxford Times: 595n
Oxford Union Society: letters from, 515–25, 584–5, 587–8; men. 301, 304, 306, 310, 312, 548, 584, 587, 734
Oxford University Dramatic Society (OUDS): 953–4, 955, 985
Oxford University Junior Linguistic Society: 879–80
Oxford University Philosophical Society: 625n
Oxford University Socialist Society: 441
Oxford University Socratic Club: 600n

Paganism: 20, 920, 959, 976–7
Palestine: 308n, 318n, 402n
Paley, William: 440; *View of the Evidences of Christianity*, 728
Palmes, Guy Nicholas: 91, 93
Palomides, Sir: 320, 323
Pan: 787
Papacy: 484, 512n, 810
Papworth, Baron (CSL's dog): 683, 695, 722, 724, 726, 774, 830, 832, 833, 835, 837, 852, 855, 934, 959, 970
Paradise: 90, 93, 220, 236, 280
Pargny (France): 369, 402n, 1019, 1021
Paris: 266, 364, 416, 445, 516n, 674n, 876
Paris, Gaston: 183n; *Littérature Française du Moyen Age*, 269, 274, 278, 282, 301
Parker, Desmond: 998
Parker, Gerard: 56
Parker, Henry Michael Denne: 851
Parker, Louis Napoleon: *Disraeli*, 179–80, 184
Parker, Ruth: 998
Parkyn, H.G.: see Eastwood, T.R.
Parry, E.A.: 238n
'Parson's Pleasure': 304n, 305, 310, 453, 563, 934
Parthenon: 743n
Pascal, Blaise: 740, 883
Pasley, Aldyth Werge Hamber ('Johnnie'): 542–3, 668n
Pasley, Sir Rodney Marshall: 432–3, 435, 441, 448, 471, 473, 495, 505, 507–8, 521, 524, 528, 529, 542–3, 544, 563, 568, 570, 668n
Passchendaele, Battle of: 988
Paston Letters: 777
Pater, Walter: 375; *Renaissance*, 219, 331
Patmore, Coventry: *Angel in the House*, 901–2, 904, 905, 911, 915; *Poems*, 914–15
Paton, Lucy Allen: 162n
Patrick, James: *Magdalen Metaphysicals*, 658n
Patriotic, SS: 730–2
Patsy Macan: 330
Patterson, William Hugh: 362; *Glossary of Words*, 32n, 148n
Patterson, William H.F.: 148, 213, 233, 241, 511; *Songs of a Port*, 148n, 511n
Paul, St: 425, 976–7; 1 Corinthians, 312, 444, 776, 970; Ephesians, 362; Romans, 970, 975
Peacock, Thomas Love: 964; *Headlong Hall*, 150
Peacocke, Rev. Gerald: 34, 44, 120n
Peacocke, Most Rev. Joseph Ferguson: 34n
Pearson's Magazine: 9
Pegasus: 172
Pelleas, Sir: 240
Pellinore, King: 103
Peloponnesian War: 145n
Pembroke, Countess of: 193
Pembroke College (Cambridge): 32n, 56n, 511–12, 696n
Pembroke College (Oxford): 836n
Pennsylvania State College: 751n
Pentheus: 473
Pepys, Samuel: 539, 657, 700
Perceval le Gallois: 249n
Perham Downs Camp (Ludgershall): letters from, 403–16; men. 436
Pericles: 145n
Perranporth (Cornwall): letters from, 718–30
Perrault, Charles: *Histoires et Contes*, 248–9, 273
Perrett, Frank Winter: 345, 363, 387
Persia: 284, 298n, 500–1, 581
Peter, St: First Epistle of, 397
Peter (pet canary): 2
Peterborough: 303n
Pewsey (Wiltshire): 690
Pharoahs: 498
Phelps, Lancelot Ridley: 717
Philippians, Letter to: 677
Philips, John: *Cyder*, 728
Philistines: 143, 145, 152, 174, 242, 253, 353, 381, 412, 816
Phillipps, Sir John: 168n
Philosophy: 177, 263n, 312, 330–1, 333, 341, 342, 375, 394, 478, 482, 485–6, 497, 509, 562, 591, 593, 598, 618, 624, 625, 627, 641, 643, 645, 648, 649, 658n, 666, 711n, 718, 732n, 775, 777, 790–1, 836, 858, 883n, 899, 908, 942, 952, 980
Phoenix Theatre (London): 986
Picasso, Pablo: 994
Pindar: 199; *Odes*, 193
Piozzi, Hester Lynch Thrale: 697n

Platitudes: 281, 909
Plato: 140, 145, 533, 594, 783n, 861; *Phaedo*, 141; *Phaedrus*, 130; *Republic*, 644n; *Symposium*, 878, 899n, 909
Platonists: 671
Pliny the Younger: *Letters*, 542, 717
Plowman, Mary: 458–9, 491, 495, 537; *Get out of Your Cage*, 458n; *Letters of Paul Durrant*, 458n; *Monologues and Duologues*, 458n; *Vicar*, 458n
Plunkett, Joseph Mary: 303n
Plutarch: 303, 740
Plymouth (Devon): 338, 340, 575
Plymouth Brethren: 125n, 711, 993, 995
Poe, Edgar Allen: 290; *Raven*, 199
Poland: 458
Pollard, A.W.: 214n
Polo, Marco: *Travels*, 460, 486
Polytheism: 704
Pomeroy, Mrs: 466, 468, 475
Pomeroy (Co. Tyrone): 1020
Poole (Dorset): 1024
Poole, Austin Lane: 269n
Poole, Robert: 835
Pope, Alexander: 49, 773, 990; *Epistle from Mr Pope to Dr Arbuthnot*, 742; *Iliad*, 559, 854
Porch, Robert Bagehot: 87
Porlock (Somerset): 506, 577
Pornography: 879–80, 955
Portrush (Co. Antrim): 83, 143, 876
Portsalon (Co. Donegal): 146, 220, 221n, 224, 249, 274, 307, 455, 476, 719
Potvin, C.: 249n
Powell, G.H.: 560n
Poynton, Arthur Blackburne: 296, 428, 429–30, 431, 432, 438, 444, 447, 450, 456, 486, 497, 544, 614, 615, 635, 641, 747
Poynton, Mrs Arthur Blackburne: 430
Prayer: 20, 33
Presbyterians: 464, 1002–4
Preseau (France): 357n
Press, M.A.C.: 128n
Preston, Frank Sansome: 56, 61, 66
Price, Henry Habberly: 600n, 629
Pride: 878, 882, 994
Priestley, J.B.: 939
Pritchard, Harold Arthur: 625–6, 635; *Kant's Theory of Knowledge*, 625n
Proceedings of the British Academy: 658n
Prodigal Son: 434, 797
Prometheus: 172
Proserpine: 134, 151
Protestantism: 8, 285, 476, 500n
Prothero, George Walter: 840n
Proust, Marcel: 994
Proverbs: 611n
Psalms: 342, 503, 795
Psyche: 268, 304–5
Psychical Research: 313–14
Psychoanalysis: 523, 597n, 612, 877–8
Public Record Office (London): 436
Public Schools: 23, 48, 52–3, 55, 61–2, 114, 147–8, 321, 443n, 778–9, 802–3, 847, 1017
Puccini, Giacomo: 793; *Bohème*, 271; *Madame Butterfly*, 145; *Tosca*, 162, 188, 390
Pufendorf, Samuel: 626
Punch: 110, 140, 148, 179, 184, 501, 681, 752, 818
Purdysburn (Co. Down): 121
Purgatory: 66n, 669n
Puritanism: 281, 353, 379, 512, 561, 692, 889–90, 918
Pusey House (Oxford): 658
Pygmies: 486
Pyrexia (Trench Fever): 354, 356

Quakers: see Society of Friends
Queen's College (Cambridge): letter from, 966; men. 646–7, 803
Queen's College (Oxford): 300, 341, 388, 529n
Queensland (Australia): 997
Queen's Own Royal West Kent Regiment: 988
Queenstown (Co. Cork): 1008
Queen's University (Belfast): 519n, 629n, 644n, 902n, 969, 1002, 1008
Quennel, William Eyre: 47, 48
Quiddity: 1001

Rabelais, François: 386: *Gargantua & Pantagruel*, 809–11
Rackham, Arthur: 20, 40n, 214, 248–9, 273, 293, 320, 324, 325, 405, 434, 447, 452
Radcliffe, Mrs Ann: *Mysteries of Udolpho*, 460
Radley College: 147–8, 941n
Radwell (Hertfordshire): 15, 984
Rajkuman College (India): 432n
Raleigh, Cecil: (with Henry Hamilton) *Whip*, 131
Raleigh, Lady: (ed.) *Letters of Sir Walter Raleigh*, 665n
Raleigh, Sir Walter: 643n, 694; *Letters*, 665–7, 817; *Wordsworth*, 667
Rangoon: 432n
Ravenswood Road (Bristol): letters from, 337, 345–6; men. 1018
Rawlence, A.G.: 365
Reading (Berkshire): 595, 598, 917n, 969
Reading University: see University of Reading
Recorded Music: see Gramophone Records
Redhouse, J.W.: 501n
Redruth (Cornwall): 582, 1000, 1001, 1002
Red Sea: 693, 699
Reid, Forrest: 841, 842, 906, 926–7, 931, 972, 995; *Apostate*, 841; *Private Road*, 841; *Uncle Stephen*, 952, 953
Remarque, Erich Maria: *All Quiet on the Western Front*, 848
Renaissance: 666, 810, 816
Renan, Joseph Ernest: *Vie de Jésus*, 309, 312, 315
Repton School: 16n, 44, 66–7, 317, 318n, 835n
Republicanism: 918
Respectability: 789
Responsions (entrance examinations to Oxford University): 194, 264, 266,

267, 275, 282, 285, 286–7, 291, 292, 295, 299, 302, 316, 322, 336, 337, 428, 487, 489, 493, 612
Rest, The (Southbourne): 888, 889–90
Resurrection, The: 234, 977
Reveille: 410, 412, 413, 414, 416, 420, 422, 443n, 444
Revelation of St John: 121n
Review of English Studies: 888n
Reynart the Foxe: 917
Rhetoric: 61, 137, 205, 682, 713–14, 899
Rhodes Scholars: 296n, 297n, 324n
Rhossilli (Wales): 759–60
Rhyme: 232, 457n, 796
Rhys, Ernest: 94n
Richard Twining & Co. (Belfast): 1017
Richmond (Surrey): 605
Riez du Vinage (France): 364–5
Rifle Brigade: 318n, 336, 344, 369–70, 402n, 1019–20, 1021
Rimmon: 214
Ring of the Nibelung: see Wagner, Richard
Robbins, Cherry: 310, 311, 313, 316, 320–1, 325
Robbins, Herbert E.: 310n
Robbins, Kittie: 310, 311, 313, 588
Roberts, Frederick Sleigh, 1st Earl: 534
Robertson, Thomas William: *David Garrick*, 241, 303
Robertson, William: *History of Scotland*, 787
Robey, (Sir) George: 266
Robinson, William Heath: 214, 293, 390, 434, 447
Robson-Scott, William Douglas: 694
Roebuck Hotel (Oxford): 599
Rogers, Edgar: 629–70
Roland: see *Chanson de Roland*
Rolleston, T.W.: *Myths and Legends of the Celtic Race*, 81
Roman de la Rose: see Guillaume de Lorris and Jean de Meun
Roman Emperors: 584, 985
Romantic/Romanticism: 138, 181, 192, 195, 202, 206, 220, 269, 270, 290, 307, 333, 377, 382, 440, 453, 459, 493, 530n, 563, 606n, 654, 659, 661n, 763, 816, 902, 911, 919, 922, 931, 971
Rome: 102n, 140, 171, 263n, 280, 298n, 542, 832, 1008
Romulus: 762
Roper, William: *Life of Sir Thomas More*, 393
Ros, Amanda McKittrick: *Irene Iddesleigh*, 172; *Poems of Puncture*, 172
Ros, Sir Richard: *Belle Dame*, 763n
Rose Bruford College of Speech and Drama (Sidcup): 978–9
Rosicrucianism: 19n, 394
Rossetti, Christina: 197, 201, 207, 211, 220; *Goblin Market*, 182
Rossetti, Dante Gabriel: 197, 306, 784n
Rossi, Luigi: *Orfeo*, 191
Rossini, Gioacchino: *Guillaume Tell*, 166n
Rostand, Edmond: *Cyrano de Bergerac*, 460
Rostrevor (Co. Down): 792, 871, 885
Round Table: 581
Rousseau, Jean-Jacques: *Confessions*, 282, 285, 914
Routh, Douglas James Lionel: 345
Royal Academy Illustrated: 182–3, 187
Royal Academy of Art: 182–3, 185, 197
Royal Academy of Music: 987
Royal Air Force: 29n, 32n, 67n, 978
Royal Army Medical Corps: 597n, 702n
Royal Army Service Corps: see Army Service Corps
Royal Artillery: 984, 997
Royal Belfast Academical Institution: 629n, 841n, 995, 1002–3, 1004
Royal Canadian Air Force: 297n
Royal College of Arts: 37n
Royal College of Music: 164n
Royal Corps of Signals: 32n, 979
Royal Engineers: 979
Royal Field Artillery: 432n
Royal Flying Corps: 32n, 299, 302, 978
Royal Hibernian Academy: 995
Royal Horse Artillery: 308n
Royal Irish Constabulary: 548
Royal Military Academy (Woolwich): 18n, 198
Royal Military College (Sandhurst): 25, 28, 29n, 33n, 36n, 38, 46–7, 56n, 73, 85n, 91n, 203, 348n, 988, 1012
Royal Naval College (Dartmouth): 985
Royal Navy: 88n, 352n, 536n, 1008
Royal Society: 302
Royal University of Ireland: 631n, 1002
Royal Victoria Hospital (Belfast): 702n
Royal Warwickshires: 998
Royal West Kent Regiment: 42
Rudolf Steiner Schools: 687n, 978
Rugby School: 164n, 614n, 983
Ruskin, John: 65, 247, 331, 626, 657; *A Joy for Ever*, 165; *Praeterita*, 956
Russia: 52, 73, 79, 84–5, 364, 458, 631
Russian Ballet: 87
Russian Expeditionary Force: 445
Rutherford, John: *Bread of the Treshams*, 115
Ryskam, Charles: 747n

Sackville-West, Vita: *Land*, 923
Sade, Donatien Alphonse, Marquis de: 313, 320
Sadism: 313, 320
Sadler, Sir Michael Ernest: 614, 627, 628
Sagas: 53, 127–8, 129, 137, 168, 701n, 837
St Agnes (Cornwall): 723
St Albans (Hertfordshire): 13
St Andrews (Fife, Scotland): 313n
St Anne's Church (Belfast): 1004
St Anne's College (Oxford): 596n
St Bartholomew's Church

(Dublin): 1004
St Bartholomew's Hospital (London): 47n
St Briavels (Gloucestershire): 958
St Briavels Castle: 948
St Canice's Cathedral: 996
St Cross Church (Oxford): 990
St Dubricius' Church (Porlock): 506
St Francis of Assisi Basilica (Assisi): 627n
St George's Church (Dublin): 120n
St George's School (Harpenden): 978
St Hugh's College (Oxford): 600
St Ives (Cornwall): 887, 1001
St John's Church (Watford): 8, 14
St John's College (Cambridge): 497n, 783n
St John's College (Oxford): 29n, 617
St John's School (Leatherhead): 172
St Margaret's Church (Oxford): 485n
St Mark's Anglican Church (Florence): 529n
St Mark's Church (Dundela): 34n, 44n, 87, 96, 120, 123, 124, 155, 166, 228n, 243n, 702, 774, 822, 845n, 861n, 960n, 1006, 1007, 1008, 1010
St Mary the Virgin (Oxford): 305–6, 431, 562, 887, 954
St Nicolas Church (Great Bookham): 74, 123, 163
St Omer (France): 349, 445n, 1012
St Paul's Cathedral (London): 92
St Philip's School (Birmingham): 1022
St Stephen's House (Oxford): 528n
Saint-Saëns, Camille: *Danse Macabre*, 98, 130, 138, 899; *Samson et Dalila*, 97
Saintsbury, George Edward Bateman: *Short History of English Literature*, 332
Saint-Simon, Louis de Rouvoy, Duc de: *Mémoirs*, 445, 1012, 1013
Saladin: 460
Salisbury, Lord: 632n
Salisbury: 449, 577, 639, 686, 793, 794, 795
Salisbury Cathedral: 639–40, 795–6, 797
Salisbury Plain: 403, 647, 686, 691, 896, 968
Salmon, Harry Geoffrey Curwen: 32
Salonika (Greece): 984
Saltney (Wales): 731n, 1014
Salvation Army: 130, 573, 635
Samarkand: 953n, 955
Sampson, John: 666n
Samuel 1, Book of: 108
Samuel 2, Book of: 442
Sand, George: 274, 356n
Sandeman, Austin: 615, 620
Sandeman, Mrs: 620
Sandycroft (Belfast): 10, 1015
Sandycroft (Wales): 731, 1014
Sandys, John Edwin: 193n
Sanskrit: 274, 313, 816, 817
Sappho: 146
Sarajevo: 73
Sassoon, Siegfried: *Counterattack*, 403
Satan: 101, 220, 289, 371, 379, 420, 457n, 584, 720n, 882
Satyrs: 446n
Saul, King: 108
Savage, Richard: 773
Savernake Forest (Wiltshire): 405, 413, 686, 690
Sayers, Dorothy L.: 454n
Schelling, Friedrich Wilhelm Joseph von: 685
Schiller, Friedrich von: *William Tell*, 166n
Schleiermacher, Friedrich Daniel Ernst: 626
Schlesinger, John: *Darling*, 990
Schomberg (Strandtown): 165
School Certificates: 611–12, 613, 646, 722, 987
Schopenhauer, Arthur: 407; *Wisdom of Schopenhauer*, 406n; *World as Will and Idea*, 151
Schubert, Franz: 196; *Rosamund*, 116
Scotland: 82, 305, 655, 757–8, 787–8, 790, 799n, 804, 987–8
Scots, The: 788–9, 790–1
Scotsman: 368–9
Scott, Sir Walter: 92, 168, 192, 214, 225, 239, 240, 245, 293, 394, 787–8, 892, 949, 958; *Antiquary*, 232, 235–6, 249, 254, 257, 788, 792, 794, 795; *Fair Maid of Perth*, 240; *Guy Mannering*, 240, 257, 260, 714, 722, 788; *Heart of Midlothian*, 787n; *Ivanhoe*, 211, 240; *Kenilworth*, 111; *Lay of the Last Minstrel*, 171; *Old Mortality*, 369, 787n, 788; *Pirate*, 307; *Quentin Durward*, 240, 660; *Rob Roy*, 180, 183, 184, 185, 186, 190–1, 293, 787n, 788; *Tales of a Grandfather*, 259; *Talisman*, 459–60; *Waverley*, 478, 479, 481, 483, 788
Scrabo Hill (Co. Down): 855
Scripture, Sacred: 60, 83, 101, 108, 121, 136, 167, 204, 214, 253, 277, 312, 331, 333, 397, 442, 444, 447, 498, 503, 538n, 540, 608, 611, 626, 665, 668, 677, 749, 776, 795, 796, 801, 848, 862, 883n, 893, 899, 912, 970, 975, 976–7, 995
Sculpture: 230
Selwyn College (Cambridge): 837n
Seneca: *Four Tragedies and Octavia*, 448n
Sentimentalism: 281, 975
Serbia: 73, 306
Service Act Proclamation: 159
Seven: 764n
Sex: 877–8, 902, 914, 973–4
Seymour, William W.: *History of the Rifle Brigade*: 1020
Shaftesbury Theatre: 160, 211–12
Shakespeare, William: 31, 107–8, 146, 213, 237–8, 424–5, 659n, 860, 978, 990, 1000; *Antony and Cleopatra*, 539; *As You Like It*, 69, 652; *Hamlet*, 132, 568, 585, 645, 746, 749, 802, 958, 971, 1000; *Henry IV*, 668, 676, 795, 855, 864; *Henry V*, 171; *Julius Caesar*, 21–2, 747; *King John*, 426, 433, 495; *King Lear*, 132, 208, 620, 630; *Love's Labour's Lost*, 832; *Macbeth*, 132, 537, 581, 645, 714–15; *Measure for*

Measure, 418–19, 985; *Merchant of Venice*, 18; *Midsummer Night's Dream*, 241, 246, 280; *Othello*, 132, 137, 958, 989; *Richard II*, 14; *Romeo and Juliet*, 34, 44, 164n, 637; *Sonnets*, 151, 246; *Taming of the Shrew*, 116; *Tempest*, 246, 775, 920; *Titus Andronicus*, 18n; *Troilus and Cressida*, 18n, 433; *Twelfth Night*, 214, 220, 447, 644; *Venus and Adonis*, 419; *Winter's Tale*, 246, 968
Shalyalpin, Fyodor Ivanovich: 139
Shanghai: 683, 719, 735, 742, 786n, 808n, 890, 1012
Sharrock, Roger: 492n
Shaw, George Bernard: 242, 570, 860; *Love Among the Artists*, 190
Shee: 84, 87, 132
Sheffield: 448n
Sheldon, Edward Brewster: *Romance*, 490–1
Sheldonian Theatre: 553–4, 985
Shelley, Lady: 298n
Shelley, Mary Wollstonecraft: *Frankenstein*, 181, 183, 187, 189, 375
Shelley, Percy Bysshe: 98, 150, 187, 298, 303, 793, 915; *Adonais*, 110; *Alastor*, 285; (with T.J. Hogg) *Necessity of Atheism*, 277; 'Ode to the West Wind', 290; *Prometheus Unbound*, 232, 478, 521, 568; 'Song', 171; 'To—: One word is too often profaned', 198
Shenstone, William: *Pastoral Ballad*, 721n
Shepton Mallet (Somerset): 693
Sherborne School: 432n
Sherlock Holmes: 9n
Shetland Islands (Scotland): 307
Shillington, Mrs: 513
Shorter, Clement: 285
Shorthouse, Joseph Henry: *John Inglesant*, 285
Shotover Hill (Oxfordshire): 546, 835, 940
Shove Halfpenny Club: 879
Shrewsbury (Shropshire): 18, 583n
Sicily: 165n
Sidgwick, Arthur: 112n
Sidney, Sir Philip: *Arcadia*, 192–3, 196–7, 199, 201–2, 205, 207, 209, 211, 214
Siegfried: 92, 405
Sienkiewicz, Henryk: *Quo Vadis?*, 284
Sierra Leone: 516n, 517n, 518, 536n, 538, 589, 773, 1012
Sigurd: 240, 935
Silenus: 912
Simon, John Allsebrook, Viscount: 734
Simon Magus: 447
Simpson, Evelyn M.: 837n
Simpson, Percy: 837
Simpson, Philip Overend: 594
Singapore: 695
Sinn Fein: 317–18, 340, 344, 486, 500, 548, 561
Sinn Fein Poets: 303
Sir Gawain and the Green Knight: 180, 187, 192, 195, 701
Skeat, Walter W.: 250n
Skelton, John: *Poetical Works*, 974
Sketch: 246, 581
Skinner, Martyn: 908
Slade School of Fine Art (London): 481, 487, 564n, 566, 612, 993
Slavery: 909–10
Smeaton, Oliphant: 418n
Smiles, Alan: 519
Smith, David Nichol: 746, 817, 990
Smith, Edmund: 223n
Smith, Harry Wakelyn ('Smugy'): 29, 31, 32, 33–4, 37, 39, 47–8, 49, 54, 57n, 62–3, 64–5, 198, 255, 265, 430, 437, 442, 444, 446, 629
Smith, Henry: 71n
Smith, John Alexander: 658–9, 762, 784, 899
Smollett, Tobias George: *Adventures of Roderick Random*, 705–6
Smyth, George: 1004
Smythe, Gerald: 85, 88, 101, 111–12, 198
Smythe, Oswald: 72, 85, 101, 177, 218
'Soaking Machines': 116, 119, 123, 405, 452, 691, 897
Socialism: 280–1, 450, 486n, 544
Society for Promoting Christian Knowledge (S.P.C.K.): 727–8
Society of Friends (Quakers): 125n, 166n, 378n, 993, 995
Somerset Light Infantry: 338, 341n, 357n, 364–5, 366, 367, 387, 391–2, 409n, 1019
Somerville, Edith Anna Oenone: 984
Somerville, Martin Ashworth: 317–18, 319, 402, 424
Somerville College (Oxford): 519n
Somme, Battle of the: 242n, 988, 1019, 1023
Sophocles: 49, 140, 615; *Oedipus Tyrannus*, 420–1; *Theban Plays*, 448n
South Africa: 997
Southampton: 345, 346
Southbourne (Hampshire): letter from, 889–90; men. 886, 888, 890, 895
Southey, Robert: 199, 815; 'Battle of Blenheim', 686
South Molton (Devon): 895
Spain: 454
S.P.C.K.: see Society for Promoting Christian Knowledge
Spectator: 237, 242n, 243n, 251–2n, 651n, 683n, 757
Spencer, Herbert: 440, 649, 790n; *Principles of Biology*, 649n; *Principles of Ethics*, 649n
Spenser, Edmund: 146, 181, 196, 220, 246, 312, 320, 476, 659n, 680, 984; *Faerie Queene*, 106, 144, 146–7, 151, 152, 153, 157, 161, 169, 170, 175, 223, 225, 240, 313, 325, 378, 407, 434, 504, 776, 974; 'Mutabilitie Cantos', 170
Spinoza, Baruch Benedict: 685
Spirit of the Age: 704
Spiritualism: 19n, 20, 605
Sports Battalion: 204n
Staël, Anne-Louise-Germaine, Madame de: *Corinne*, 475n
Stafford, Earl of: 750
Staffordshire: 617–18
Stallybrass, William Teulon Swan: 319n
Stanhope, G.: 560n
Stanley, Sir Henry Morton:

Through the Dark Continent, 98n
Stanning, Colonel: 315
Stanton Harcourt (Oxfordshire): 853, 854
Stanton St John (Oxfordshire): 881
Staples, Rt. Hon. John: 996
Staples, Robert Ponsonby: 619
Starlight Express: see Blackwood, Algernon
Statius: *Silvae*, 497n
Stead, Frances Goldsborough: 529n, 530, 533, 597n
Stead, William Force: 529–32, 533–4, 548, 597n; *Festival in Tuscany*, 529n; *Sweet Miracle*, 529n; *Verd Antique*, 529n
Steele, Sir Richard: 683n
Steeven's Hospital, Doctor (Dublin): 462, 463
Steiner, Rudolf: 670n, 671, 687n, 979, 999; *Anthroposophy and the Social Question*, 671n; *Bible and Wisdom*, 671n; *Cosmic Christianity*, 671n; *Philosophy of Spiritual Activity*, 762n
Stephens, James: 236; *Crock of Gold*, 196, 281–2, 293, 330, 395, 598, 859, 936, 958
Sterne, Laurence: 953; *Tristram Shandy*, 241, 324, 332, 669, 810, 860, 899n, 909, 949, 953
Stevenson, George Hope: 485n, 516, 614, 747; *Roman History*, 485n; *Roman Provincial Administration*, 485n
Stevenson, Robert Louis: 437; *Virginibus Puerisque*, 931
Stoke Pero (Somerset): 893
Stokes, Henry: 109, 145, 176
Stokes, Sal: 118
Stone, Noel Herbert: 36
Stonehenge: 259, 468, 640
Stonyhurst College: 531n
Stopes, Marie: 557
Stormont (Co. Down): 972
Stowe School: 694–5
Strabane (Co. Donegal): 221
Stracher, John St Loe: 242n
Strachey, Lytton: 614; *Eminent Victorians*, 641; *Queen Victoria*, 606
Strahan, Annie: 59, 60, 224, 339n, 439, 584
Strandlake (Oxfordshire): 558–9
Strand Magazine: 9
Strandtown: 1, 2, 3, 4, 41, 117n, 166n, 228, 349, 397, 429, 518–19, 589, 811, 890, 921, 990, 1009
Strandtown School: 501n
Stranraer (Scotland): 113
Stuart, Francis Teresa: 453n
Studer, Madame: 706–10
Studer, Paul: 706n, 707
Styx, River: 757
Subjective Idealism: 327n, 377
Submarines: 104n, 105, 113, 115, 291
Suez: 522, 733, 808
Suffern, Lilian Hamilton: letter to, 672–3; men. 98, 243n, 368–9, 380, 427, 438–9, 445, 452, 474, 479n, 515, 518, 534, 587, 626–7, 682, 997
Suffern, William: 368n, 997
Suffield, Beatrice: 1022
Suffolk: 647
Sugarman, Shirley: (ed.) *Evolution of Consciousness*, 982
Sullivan, Arthur: 401; see also Gilbert, W.S.
Superstition: 231
Surrey: 115, 122n, 143, 154, 164
Sussex: 794
Sutter, Julie: 215n
Sutton, Alexander Gordon: 317, 318n, 402n, 417
Sutton, Mr: 417
Swansea (Wales): 759
Swedenborg, Emanuel: 671
Sweet, Henry: *Anglo-Saxon Reader*, 601–2
Swift, Jonathan: 463; *Gulliver's Travels*, 755
Swinburne, Algernon Charles: 126, 146, 153, 174, 238, 242, 310, 380, 443, 448, 454, 488, 793; *Atalanta in Calydon*, 63, 151; *Charlotte Brontë*, 329; *Erechtheus*, 151; *Forsaken Garden*, 161; *Poems and Ballads*, 112, 144; *Study of Shakespeare*, 107–8; *William Blake*, 329
Swiss Cottage (London): letter from, 963–5
Switzerland: 798
Sydenham (Belfast): 966
Symons, Arthur William: 525; *Days and Nights*, 525n; *London Nights*, 525n
Synge, John Millington: 448
Syracuse: 570
Syrett, Netta: *Victorians*, 312

Tacitus, Cornelius: 145, 541; *Agricola*, 102, 284, 788n; *Annals*, 141, 234, 284; *Germania*, 284; *Histories*, 284
Tadmor: 743
Tagore, Rabindranath: 525; *Gitanjali*, 525n
Talleyrand, Charles Maurice de: 443
Tannhäuser: 116, 129, 281, 521
Tassell, Douglas Spencer Montague: 30, 35
Tasso, Torquato: *Gerusalemme Liberata*, 312–13, 421, 460
Tate Gallery: 122, 124
Tatler: 581
Taunt, Henry W.: (ed.) *Oxford Poems of Matthew Arnold*, 559
Taylor, Elizabeth: 986
Taylor, Jeremy: 610, 973; *Holy Dying*, 967n, 971; *Holy Living*, 967n, 971
Taylor, Tom: 949n
Tchaikovsky, Pyotr Il'yich: *Chanson Triste*, 81
Telescope: 843
Tell, William: 166n
Temple, Sir William: 238, 239, 250, 254, 699–700; *Essays*, 699–700
Temple Guiting (Gloucestershire): 759
Temple Shakespeare: 843n, 861
Temple Shakespeare for Schools: 843n
Tennyson, Alfred, Lord: 43, 309, 534, 626, 644n; *Break, Break, Break*, 172; *Foresters*, 401; *In Memoriam A.H.H.*, 42, 400; *Locksley Hall*, 34, 42, 49; *Swallows*, 401; *Window*, 401
Tennyson, G.B.: (ed.) *Barfield Reader*, 982; (ed.) *Owen*

Barfield on C. S. Lewis, 982
Tennyson, Miss: 425
Textual Criticism: 837, 881, 888
Thackeray, William Makepeace: 657, 772, 773, 787; *Henry Esmond*, 104–5; *Newcomes*, 98n, 223, 225; *Pendennis*, 210, 213, 217, 220; *Vanity Fair*, 281, 618–19, 624, 739
Thame (Oxfordshire): 37n, 673
Thame, River: 915
Thames, River: 559, 831, 853
Théâtre du Grand Grignol (Montmartre): 571n
Theosophy: 19n, 450, 530n, 671
Thirty-Nine Articles: 550n, 644
Thisted, Valdemar Adolph: *Letters from Hell*, 215, 219, 225, 232, 236, 256
Thomas Aquinas, St: 548
Thompson, Bill: 751
Thompson, James A.: 228, 253, 254, 260, 354, 954
Thompson, Miss: 127
Thomson, James: 654; *Castle of Indolence*, 309, 312, 774, 876, 974; *Seasons*, 974
Thorndike, Sybil: 703
Thucydides: 145, 263n
Tigris, River: 304n
Tilly, Arthur: *Decline of the Age of Louis XIV*, 792
Tim (CSL's dog): 2, 25, 124, 204, 569
Times, The: 61, 85n, 112n, 147n, 149, 159, 164, 179, 248, 263, 381n, 390n, 469, 477n, 483–4, 500, 519n, 541n, 600, 609, 632, 647n, 658, 733n, 780, 988
Times Literary Supplement: 74, 110, 172, 199, 211, 213, 233, 243, 309n, 371, 432, 440, 446, 476, 538, 560, 675, 679n, 761–2, 765, 796, 900
Times Recruiting Supplement: 149
Tintagel (Cornwall): 580–2
Tintern Abbey: 948
Titian: 293
Tolkien, Arthur Reuel: 1022
Tolkien, Christopher: 1023
Tolkien, Edith: 1023–4
Tolkien, Hilary Arthur Reuel: 1022
Tolkien, John: 1023; (with Priscilla Tolkien) *Tolkien Family Album*, 1024
Tolkien, John Ronald Reuel: biography, 1022–4; men. 701n, 838, 880, 909, 969, 970, 974, 976–7, 982, 989; *Fellowship of the Ring*, 1023; *Hobbit*, 880n, 1023; *Letters*, 658n, 1024; *Lord of the Rings*, 880, 1023, 1024; *Mythopoeia*, 1023; *Return of the King*, 1023; *Silmarillion*, 880n, 1023, 1024; (ed. with E.V. Gordon) *Sir Gawain and the Green Knight*, 701; *Tom Bombadil*, 1024; *Tree and Leaf*, 1023; *Two Towers*, 1023
Tolkien, Mabel: 1022
Tolkien, Michael: 1023
Tolkien, Priscilla: 1023; (with John Tolkien) *Tolkien Family Album*, 1024
Tolstoy, Leo: *War and Peace*, 957–8
Tom Thumb: 687
Tonbridge (Kent): 588
Toronto: 432n, 647n
Torquay (Devon): 999
Tower of London: 277n, 512, 656
Trades Union Congress (TUC): 667n
Trade Unions: 486, 667n
Traherne, Thomas: *Centuries of Meditation*, 914, 916, 933
Trevelyan, Sir George Otto: *Life and Letters of Lord Macaulay*, 814–17
Trinity College (Dublin): 34n, 120n, 547n, 596n, 990, 996, 997, 1021
Trinity College (Oxford): 194, 198, 223, 229, 328–9, 614n, 621, 625–6, 627–8, 629, 635n, 687n, 953n
Trinity Hall (Cambridge): 18n
Tristan et Iseut, Roman de: 183, 186–7, 188–9, 192, 195, 196, 207
Tristram, Sir: 103, 340, 419, 581
Trollope, Anthony: 174, 374–5; *Barchester Towers*, 369, 370, 371, 640, 657; *Belton Estate*, 944; *Dr Thorne*, 374, 380, 771–2; *Small House at Allington*, 422, 490; *Warden*, 374, 380
Troly-Curtin, Marthe: *Phrynette and London*, 222–3; *Phrynette Married*, 222–3
Troy: 504n
Truro (Cornwall): 726–8, 1002
Truth: 980
Tubb, Carrie: 99
Twain, Mark: 154
Ty-isa (Strandtown): 811–12, 1015

Ulster Hall (Belfast): 92
Ulster Monarch: 813, 849
Ulster Protestantism: 8
Ulster Steamship Company: 501n
Ulster Unionist Council: 634n
Ulster Volunteer Force: 212, 391, 634n
Ulula (Lurgan College School Magazine): 1006
Unchastity: 882
Unicorns: 927
United States: see America
University College (Oxford): letters from, 295–315, 323–5, 327–9, 330–4, 424–61, 464–70, 472–6, 485–503, 507–14, 525–55, 564–6, 569–70, 585–7, 589–96, 598–602, 606–11, 617–49; men. 73n, 263, 264, 266, 267, 268, 278, 285, 294, 316, 317, 318, 319, 320, 322, 326, 336, 356, 361, 423, 651, 655, 658n, 694, 747, 874–5, 887, 902n, 1000, 1018
University College (Reading): see University of Reading
University College Record: 277n, 296n, 304n, 430n, 448n, 486n
University College (Swansea): 836n
University of Birmingham: 73n
University of California: 450
University of Durham: 988
University of Edinburgh: 658n
University of Exeter: 1002

University of Glasgow: 485n
University of Leeds: 600n, 614n, 643n, 796, 1023
University of London: 37n, 554n, 676, 694n
University of Manchester: 614n
University of Naples: 681n
University of Reading: 595, 598, 917n, 969, 988
University of St Andrews: 988
University Training Course: 417, 420
Unwin, William: 748n
Upper Canada College (Toronto): 432n
Uppingham School: 23, 983
Usk, River: 478

Vachell, Horace Annesley: *Paladin*, 228
Valley of Rocks (Devon): 895
Vancouver: 431n
Venice: 132n, 460n
Venus: see Aphrodite
Verchain (France): 357n
Verdi, Giuseppe: 793; *Aida*, 182, 248, 253, 256, 259; *Rigoletto*, 164; *Trovatore*, 9
Versailles: 449, 787, 1013
Vers Libre: 441, 450, 453, 492, 507
Victoria, Queen: 606, 641, 699, 747, 800, 810: *Leaves from a Journal*, 699n
Victoria College (Belfast): 519n
Vienna University: 671n
Villon, François: 303; *Grand Testament*, 353
Vinaver, Eugène: *Malory*, 857
Vinter, Geoffrey Odell: 441n
Virgil: 20, 128, 362, 386, 419, 434, 504, 510, 644n; *Aeneid*, 112, 113, 157, 177, 490, 935; *Georgics*, 79
Virgin Birth, The: 234
Völsunga Saga: 165, 168, 701
Voltaire, François Marie: 545; *Contes*, 274, 569; *Sottisier*, 533n
Voluntary Aid Detachment: 310
Vorticist Poetry: 492
Vortigern: 468
Vulgate (Latin version of the Bible): 797, 848
Wace: *Arthurian Chronicles*, 162n, 439–40
Waddell, Helen: 518–19, 697, 702; *Medieval Latin Lyrics*, 519n; *Peter Abelard*, 519n; *Wandering Scholars*, 519n
Wade Center (Wheaton College): 867n, 1008
Wadham College (Oxford): 194, 198, 199, 471n, 487, 499, 505n, 543, 550, 686n, 734, 864, 978, 979
Wagner, Richard: 210, 290, 325, 342, 433, 478; *Flying Dutchman*, 164, 324; *Götterdämmerung* (*Twilight of the Gods*), 20, 40, 99n, 139n; *Lohengrin*, 116, 119, 126, 139, 514; *Meistersinger*, 117; *Parsifal*, 139; *Rhinegold*, 40, 139n; *Ring of the Nibelung*, 20, 40, 116n, 139, 320–1, 324, 401, 405–6, 433, 954; *Siegfried*, 20, 40, 139n, 323, 405; *Tannhäuser*, 116, 129, 281; *Tristan and Isolde*, 212; *Valkyrie*, 40, 116n, 129–30, 143, 164, 320–1, 381–2, 386, 390, 701, 898, 954
Wain, John: *Dead Shadows*, 985–6; *Sprightly Running*, 1013
Waldorf School: 999
Wales: 17, 478, 484, 505–6, 563, 569, 717–18, 730n, 1010
Waley, Reginald Philip Simon: 42–3
Walker, Lawrence: 144, 174
Walker, Obadiah: 277
Wallington, P.: (with R.M. Merkin) *Essays in Memory of Professor F.H. Lawson*, 902n
Walpole, Horace: 563; *Castle of Otranto*, 459
Walsh, Miss: 936, 937
Walton, Izaak: *Compleat Angler*, 254
Wantage (Berkshire): 988
Ward, Alphonsus William: 840n
Ward, Mrs Humphrey: 475; *Lady Connie*, 230, 234, 251; *Lady Rose's Daughter*, 619
Ward, Richard: *Life of the Learned and Pious Dr Henry More*, 623n
Wardale, Edith Elizabeth: 600, 602, 610; *Introduction to Middle English*, 600n; *Old English Grammar*, 600n
Warminster (Wiltshire): 692–3
Warneford Asylum: 599, 707, 708
Warneford Road (Oxford): letters from, 555–63, 567–9, 570–84, 596–8, 604–6
War Office: 212n, 327, 354n, 364, 367, 386, 413, 423–4, 435–6, 437n, 449, 469, 513, 517n, 696n
Warren, Bessie Geraldina Gundred: 561
Warren, Rear Admiral John Borlase: 561n
Warren, Sir John Borlase (1800–1863): 997
Warren, Mary St Ledger: 561n
Warren, Sir Thomas Herbert ('Sambo'): 644–5, 651, 677, 678, 699, 715; *By Severn Seas*, 644n; *Death of Virgil*, 644n
Warton, Joseph: 659; *Essay on the Writings and Genius of Pope*, 659n
Warton, Thomas: 659; *History of English Poetry*, 659n, 964
Warwick (Warwickshire): 334, 583, 658, 1018
Warwickshire Regiment: 600n
Warwickshire Rifle Regiment: 687n
Washford (Somerset): 477–85
Washington, D.C.: 597n
Watchet (Somerset): 484
Water Eaton (Oxfordshire): 922–3
Waterloo: 619, 624
Waterman, Hugh: 908n
Watford (Hertfordshire): 1, 6–14, 632–3, 982–4, 1011
Watling, Edward Fairchild: 448
Watts, George Frederic: 122, 124, 306
Watts, Samuel: 1003–4
Waugh, Alec: 433, 435; *Loom of Youth*, 433
Waugh, Evelyn: *Rossetti*, 784n

Webb, Mary: *Precious Bane*, 907, 910, 915
Weber, Max: 626
Webster, John: *Duchess of Malfi*, 311
Wei-Hei-Wei (China): 719–20, 735, 773
Weldon, Thomas Dewar: 763, 777, 781, 801
Wellington, Arthur Wellesley, Duke of: 505
Wellington College: 696n
Wells (Somerset): 573–4, 693
Wells Cathedral: 639, 650
Wells, H.G.: 475, 773, 952; *Country of the Blind, and Other Stories*, 70–1, 246; *First Men in the Moon*, 11; *God the Invisible King*, 329; *Marriage*, 472; *Meanwhile*, 852, 854; *Modern Utopia*, 335; *Mr Britling Sees it Through*, 306; *Soul of a Bishop*, 306, 315
Werewolves: 219
Wesley, John: 168
Westminster Abbey: 380
Westminster Confession: 224
Westminster School: 835n
Westmorland: 569
Wharey, James Blanton: 492n
Wheatley (Oxfordshire): 546
Wheen, Arthur Wesley: 848n
Whig: 69
Whipsnade Zoo: 972
Whistler, James Abbott McNeill: 454
Whitehall: 553n, 874
Whitman, Walt: *Leaves of Grass*, 742
Whitty, Kathleen: 684
Wibelin, Vida Mary: 596, 598
Wilbraham, Mrs: 707–10
Wilde, Oscar: 266, 288, 303, 454, 569; *Ballad of Reading Gaol*, 465; *De Profundis*, 465; *Ideal Husband*, 465; *Importance of Being Earnest*, 439
Wilhelm II, Emperor (Kaiser): 98n, 866
Wilkinson, Donald Frederick: 528
William III, King: 700
Williams, Charles: 982
Williton (Somerset): 575
Wilmersham Farm (Somerset): 893
Wilson, Frank Percy: 600, 640, 642–3, 654
Wilson, J.I.: 1006
Wilson, John: 815n
Wilson, Woodrow: 266, 402, 404, 405
Winchcombe (Gloucestershire): 988
Winchester Cathedral: 639
Winchester College: 348n, 432, 659n, 771n, 779, 781
Windmill Road (Oxford): letter from, 463
Wisley (Surrey): 273
Witch of Endor: see Cullen, Mary
Wm. Ewart & Son Ltd., Flax Spinners: 990
Wodehouse, P.G.: *Psmith, Journalist*, 734
Wolvercote Cemetery (Oxford): 1024
Wood Eaton (Oxfordshire): 922–3
Wood Eaton Hall (Oxfordshire): 923
Woolf, Virginia: *Orlando*, 890
Woodnorton (Worcestershire): 16n
Woolwich: see Royal Military Academy
Wordsley (Staffordshire): 982
Wordsworth, Dorothy: 484
Wordsworth, William: 154, 484, 508, 614, 723; *Prelude*, 466, 468, 776; *Tintern Abbey*, 948
Worksop College: 987
World War I: 18n, 29n, 32n, 47n, 56n, 67n, 69, 73, 79, 83, 85, 88, 99, 101–2, 104, 111–12, 113–14, 125, 129, 131, 140, 151, 156n, 163, 191, 208, 212, 224, 252, 291, 297, 310, 315, 318, 322n, 337, 346–416, 627n, 631n, 848n, 978, 979, 1012
World War II: 32n, 47n, 297n, 402n, 529n, 978
Worcester College (Oxford): 529n, 941–2
Worcestershire Regiment: 36n
Wotan: 382
Wright, Joseph: 1022
Wrong, Edward Murray: 647–8, 745–6; *British Empire*, 647n; *Charles Butler*, 647n; *History of England*, 647n
Wyatt, A.J.: 195n
Wycliffe Hall (Oxford): 298n
Wye, River: 774, 947n
Wyld, Henry Cecil Kennedy: 883; *Short History of English*, 883n
Wyllie, Basil Platel: 441
Wynyard School: letters from, 6–14; men. 1, 15, 16, 29n, 120n, 624, 632, 731, 739, 742, 744n, 792, 848, 982–4, 1010, 1011, 1012
Wyrall, Everard: *History of the Somerset Light Infantry*, 357n, 364–5
Wytham (Berkshire): 335

Yeats, Georgia: 530n, 531–2, 565
Yeats, Michael: 530n
Yeats, W.B.: 57, 59, 150, 260, 304, 330, 342, 384, 385, 386, 398, 430, 435, 464, 522, 524–5, 530–2, 533–4, 536, 564–6, 663, 700, 937; *Collected Works*, 385; *Countess Cathleen*, 350; *On Baile's Strand*, 432; *Per Amica Silentia Lunae*, 565; *Plays for an Irish Theatre*, 90; *Wanderings of Oisin*, 521n
Yeats-Brown, Francis: *Bengal Lancer*, 968
Yogi: 968
York: 166n
Yorkshire Light Infantry: 91n
Young, Robert M.: *Belfast and the Province of Ulster*, 1008
Ypres (France): 91n, 988
Ysaÿe, Eugène: 144–5, 153n
Ysaÿe, Théo: 153

Zée, Monsieur: 684
Zeebrugge: 553, 554n
Zeppelins: 105–6, 148, 517
Zeus: 447
Zodiac: 861–2